Occupational

2019–2029 Edition

Outlook
Handbook

U.S. Department of Labor
Eugene Scalia, Secretary of Labor

U.S. Bureau of Labor Statistics
William W. Beach, Commissioner

Suggested citation: Bureau of Labor Statistics, U.S. Department of Labor, *Occupational Outlook Handbook*, 2019–2029 Edition.

Published by Bernan Press
An imprint of The Rowman & Littlefield Publishing Group, Inc.
4501 Forbes Boulevard, Suite 200, Lanham, Maryland 20706
www.rowman.com
800-865-3457

6 Tinworth Street, London SE11 5AL, United Kingdom

ISBN hardback: **978-1-64143-483-6**
ISBN paperback: **978-1-64143-484-3**

Acknowledgments

The U.S. Bureau of Labor Statistics (BLS) produces the *Occupational Outlook Handbook* (*OOH*) under the general guidance and direction of Rebecca Rust, Assistant Commissioner for Occupational Statistics and Employment Projections, and Michael Wolf, Division Chief of Occupational Employment Projections. Kathleen T. Green, Branch Chief of Outreach and Publications, and Teresa L. Morisi and Francisco Velez, Jr., Branch Chiefs of Projections Research and Analysis, provided planning and day-to-day direction.

Staff responsible for research and preparation of material of the OOH included Domingo Angeles, Jennifer Chi, Ryan Farrell, Christopher Harper, Sara Hylton, Lindsey Ice, Stanislava Ilic-Godfrey, Alan Lacey, William Lawhorn, Christine Machovec, Steven Marcroft, Michael J. Rieley, Emily Rolen, Patricia Tate, Elka Torpey, Richard Works, and Alan Zilberman.

Editorial work was provided by staff in the Office of Publications: Richard Hernandez, Maureen S. Hicks, Lisa Huynh, John C. Roach, and Johnathon Yoe, under the supervision of Leslie Brown Joyner, Branch Chief of Special Publications, Terry L. Schau, Monthly Labor Review Branch Chief, and Emily Liddel, Division Chief of Publishing. Data-processing and technical support were provided by Alan Lacey, Curtisjames O. Miller, Andrew G. O'Bar, and Rick Penn, under the supervision of Dave Terkanian, Branch Chief of Methods, Systems, and Support Branch. Technical and computer-programming support was provided by Harry Chauhan, Thao Le-Do, Robbin Galloway, Jerie Refugia, Roopa Sengupta, Connie Sielaff, and Reginald Simmons, all of the Office of Technology and Survey Processing, under the supervision of Jo-Ann Yu, Branch Chief, and Amrit Kohli, Division Chief of Enterprise Web Systems.

Most of the photographs used in the *OOH* are stock photographs; however, BLS wishes to express its appreciation to the organizations that contributed photographs. Situations portrayed in the photographs may not be free of every possible safety or health hazard. The depiction of a company or trade name in no way constitutes endorsement by the U.S. Department of Labor.

Contents

Projections Data

Fastest Growing Occupations, 2019–2029
(Twenty occupations with the highest percent change of employment between 2019–2029.)

Occupation	Growth Rate 2019–2029	2019 Median Pay
Wind turbine service technicians	61%	$52,910
Nurse practitioners	52%	$109,820
Solar photovoltaic installers	51%	$44,890
Occupational therapy assistants	35%	$61,510
Statisticians	35%	$91,160
Home health and personal care aides	34%	$25,280
Physical therapist assistants	33%	$58,790
Medical and health services managers	32%	$100,980
Physician assistants	31%	$112,260
Information security analysts	31%	$99,730

Occupation	Growth Rate 2019–2029	2019 Median Pay
Data scientists and mathematical science occupations, all other	31%	$94,280
Derrick operators, oil and gas	31%	$46,990
Rotary drill operators, oil and gas	27%	$54,980
Roustabouts, oil and gas	25%	$38,910
Speech-language pathologists	25%	$79,120
Operations research analysts	25%	$84,810
Substance abuse, behavioral disorder, and mental health counselors	25%	$46,240
Forest fire inspectors and prevention specialists	24%	$45,270
Cooks, restaurant	23%	$27,790
Animal caretakers	23%	$24,780

Number of New Jobs, Projected, 2019–2029
(Twenty occupations with the highest projected numeric change in employment.)

Occupation	Number of new jobs 2019–2029	2019 Median Pay
Home health and personal care aides	1,159,500	$25,280
Fast food and counter workers	460,900	$22,740
Cooks, restaurant	327,300	$27,790
Software developers and software quality assurance analysts and testers	316,000	$107,510
Registered nurses	221,900	$73,300
General and operations managers	143,800	$100,780
Medical assistants	139,200	$34,800
Medical and health services managers	133,200	$100,980
Market research analysts and marketing specialists	130,300	$63,790
Laborers and freight, stock, and material movers, hand	125,700	$29,510

Occupation	Number of new jobs 2019–2029	2019 Median Pay
Landscaping and groundskeeping workers	119,900	$30,440
Nursing assistants	116,900	$29,660
Nurse practitioners	110,700	$109,820
Financial managers	108,100	$129,890
Janitors and cleaners, except maids and housekeeping cleaners	105,600	$27,430
Waiters and waitresses	97,600	$22,890
Passenger vehicle drivers, except bus drivers, transit and intercity	94,400	$31,340
Management analysts	93,800	$85,260
Project management specialists and business operations specialists, all other	79,800	$73,570
Substance abuse, behavioral disorder, and mental health counselors	79,000	$46,240

Highest Paying Occupations, 2019
(Twenty occupations with the highest median annual pay.)

Occupation	2019 Median Pay
Psychiatrists	This wage is equal to or greater than $208,000 per year
Obstetricians and gynecologists	This wage is equal to or greater than $208,000 per year
Surgeons, except ophthalmologists	This wage is equal to or greater than $208,000 per year
Prosthodontists	This wage is equal to or greater than $208,000 per year
Oral and maxillofacial surgeons	This wage is equal to or greater than $208,000 per year
Orthodontists	This wage is equal to or greater than $208,000 per year
Anesthesiologists	This wage is equal to or greater than $208,000 per year
Physicians, all other; and ophthalmologists, except pediatric	$206,500 per year

Occupation	2019 Median Pay
Family medicine physicians	$205,590 per year
General internal medicine physicians	$201,590 per year
Chief executives	$184,460 per year
Pediatricians, general	$175,310 per year
Nurse anesthetists	$174,790 per year
Dentists, general	$155,600 per year
Airline pilots, copilots, and flight engineers	$147,220 per year
Dentists, all other specialists	$147,220 per year
Computer and information systems managers	$146,360 per year
Architectural and engineering managers	$144,830 per year
Petroleum engineers	$137,720 per year
Judges, magistrate judges, and magistrates	$136,910 per year

Occupational Information Included in the OOH

The *Occupational Outlook Handbook (OOH)* is a career resource offering information on the hundreds of occupations that provide the majority of jobs in the United States. Each occupational profile describes the typical duties performed by the occupation, the work environment of that occupation, the typical education and training needed to enter the occupation, the median pay for workers in the occupation, and the job outlook over the coming decade for that occupation. Each profile is in a standard format that makes it easy to compare occupations, such as by projected employment change.

Sections of Occupational Profiles
- Summary
- What They Do
- Work Environment
- How to Become One
- Pay
- Job Outlook
- State and Area Data
- Similar Occupations
- More Information

Summary
All profiles have a "Quick Facts" table that gives information on the following topics:

Median Pay: The wage at which half of the workers in the occupation earned more than that amount and half earned less. Median wage data are from the Bureau of Labor Statistics (BLS) Occupational Employment Statistics (OES) survey.

Typical Entry-Level Education: The level of education that most workers need to enter an occupation.

Work Experience in a Related Occupation: The skills and know-how that a worker receives in another occupation which is usually considered necessary by employers or is a commonly accepted substitute for more formal types of training or education.

On-the-job Training: Postemployment training necessary to attain competency in the skills needed in the occupation. The training is occupation specific rather than job specific; the skills learned can be transferred to another job in the same occupation.

Number of Jobs: The employment, or size, of the occupation in the base year of the employment projections.

Job Outlook: The projected percent change in employment over the projections decade.

Employment Change: The projected numeric change in employment over the projections decade.

The summary section briefly describes all of the sections included in each occupational profile.

What They Do
This section describes the main work of people in the occupation.

All occupations have a list of duties or typical tasks performed by these workers. The list includes daily responsibilities, such as answering phone calls or taking a patient's medical history.

This section also may describe the equipment, tools, software, or other items that people in the occupation typically use. For example, medical records and health information technicians frequently use electronic health records to document a patient's medical information. The section also may describe those with whom workers in the occupation interact, such as clients, patients, and coworkers.

Some profiles discuss specialties, alternate job titles, or types of occupations within a given occupation. This subsection includes a brief explanation of each specialty's job duties and how specialties differ from one another. For example, the profile on dentists includes several specialties, such as orthodontists, oral and maxillofacial surgeons, and pediatric dentists.

Work Environment
Jobseekers and career planners should learn an occupation's working conditions, including the typical workplace, the expected level of physical activity, and typical working hours.

The section typically begins by noting the employment size of the occupation in the base year and includes a table of the industries which employed the most workers in the occupation that year. The section also notes whether employees sometimes need to travel, and if so, how frequently. The section describes the workplace and discusses whether employees work in a safe work environment (such as an office) or a potentially hazardous one (such as a commercial fishing boat). If the workplace is hazardous, the section typically lists the type of equipment an employee must wear, such as a hardhat or protective goggles, to guard against accidents or exposure to harmful conditions. A subsection on Injuries and Illnesses may appear if this information is notable.

Work Schedules
Information on the typical schedule for workers in an occupation is included in this section, noting whether the majority of

workers are employed full time or part time. Full-time workers typically work 35 or more hours in a week, whereas part-time employees work less than 35 hours. For some occupations, the profile also may include the time of day an employee is expected to begin work and for how long. Registered nurses, for example, may work all hours of the day and on weekends because medical facilities are open 24 hours. A discussion of work schedules for occupations in which work may be seasonal, such as agricultural workers, also is in this section.

How to Become One

Knowing how to prepare to enter an occupation gives jobseekers and students an idea of how to become a doctor, flight attendant, or wind turbine technician, for example. All profiles have subsections on education and important qualities of workers in the occupation. Optional subsections include information on work experience; training; other experience, such as volunteering or internships; licenses, certifications, and registrations; and advancement.

Education

This subsection describes the education that most workers typically need to enter an occupation. Some occupations require no formal education, whereas others may require, for example, a doctoral or professional degree. In some occupations, such as computer support specialists, workers can enter with different educational backgrounds. In these cases, the profile discusses all of the typical paths for entry into the occupation.

This subsection also may include information on the college majors and subjects that people usually study in preparation for the occupation, as well as a list of typical courses that may aid a high school student in preparing for an occupation. For example, high school students interested in applying to respiratory therapy programs should take courses in health, biology, math, chemistry, and physics.

Work Experience in a Related Occupation

This subsection describes whether employers require work experience in a related occupation. Many managerial occupations rely on work experience in a related occupation. For example, architectural and engineering managers typically have previous work experience as an architect or engineer.

Training

This subsection describes the typical on-the-job training necessary to attain competency in an occupation, including both practical and classroom training that workers receive after being hired. For example, firefighters must complete training at a fire academy or at an institution with a similar program before they are considered prepared to combat fires.

Apprenticeships, internships, and residency programs also are discussed in this subsection. For example, the profile on physicians and surgeons includes information on residency programs and the profile for brickmasons, blockmasons, and stonemasons has information on the apprenticeships that they typically complete as part of a training program.

Other Experience

Other types of experience may be helpful or essential in getting a job in the occupation, such as experience gained through volunteering or student internships completed while one is in school. Students and jobseekers may find this section helpful as it may provide additional content for their résumés.

Licenses, Certifications, and Registrations

This subsection describes whether credentials such as licenses, certifications, and registrations typically are needed for an occupation and, if so, how workers can earn the credentials.

States issue licenses to workers to signify that they have met specific legal requirements to practice in certain occupations. To become licensed, workers usually need to pass an exam and comply with eligibility requirements, such as possessing a minimum level of education, work experience, or training; or completing an internship, a residency, or an apprenticeship. States have their own regulatory boards that set standards for practicing a licensed occupation, so rules and eligibility criteria, including recertification requirements, may vary by state, even for the same occupation.

Some occupations have certifications available that typically are voluntary. For example, fitness trainers and instructors may obtain certification on their own before entering the occupation. Certification requires demonstrated competency in a skill or a set of skills and commonly requires passing an exam or having a certain amount and type of work experience or training. For some certification programs, the candidate must have a certain level of education before becoming eligible for certification.

This subsection explains any prerequisites for certification, licensure, or registration, as well as how a person would complete them—such as by passing an exam, performing a certain type of work, or receiving certain training or education. If states require workers to be certified before they can be licensed, this section also notes that information.

Certification should not be confused with certificates from an educational institution. A certificate awarded by a postsecondary educational institution is a postsecondary nondegree award and is discussed in the subsection on education.

Registrations typically are required and issued by state or local governments. Workers seeking registration may need to be licensed or certified. In most cases, workers must pay fees to receive or maintain their registration.

Important Qualities

What does it take to be an engineer or teacher? This subsection describes important characteristics of workers in the occupation and includes an explanation of why those characteristics are useful.

The qualities may include skills, aptitudes, and personal characteristics. For example, an emergency medical technician (EMT) must be physically fit, and a web developer needs creativity and customer-service skills.

Advancement

This subsection explains the requirements for advancement, such as certification or additional formal education.

Opportunities for advancement can come from within the occupation, such as a promotion to a supervisory or managerial level; from advancement into another occupation, such as moving from a computer support specialist to a network and computer systems administrator; or by becoming self-employed, such as a dentist opening up his or her own practice.

Pay

Almost all occupational profiles in the *OOH* show median wage data for wage and salary workers in the occupation. The median wage is the wage at which half of the workers in an occupation earned more and half earned less. The data are from the Bureau of Labor Statistics (BLS) Occupational Employment Statistics (OES) program. A chart that compares the median wage of workers in the occupation to the median wage of workers across all occupations accompanies the wage data.

Profiles typically include median wages and the wages earned by the top 10 percent and bottom 10 percent of workers in the occupation. Profiles also may include wages earned by workers in selected industries—those in which most of an occupation's workers are employed. The wage data by industry also are from the OES survey.

Some occupational profiles may cite wage data from sources other than the BLS. For example, the Medical Group Management Association provides wage data for physicians and surgeons. Unless otherwise noted, the source of pay data for occupations in the *OOH* is the OES survey.

The Pay section provides work schedule information, also found in the Work Environment section. When noteworthy, the section may include information about union membership.

Job Outlook

Is employment projected to grow or decline over the projections decade? This section has a chart that compares the rate of growth or decline for the occupation(s) covered in the profile to the rate for all occupations. The section also discusses the major factors expected to affect the outlook for employment in the occupation. Some of the factors are changes in technology, in business practices, and in demographics.

The outlook section sometimes includes a Job Prospects subsection, which provides a qualitative discussion of the relative ease or difficulty experienced by those who seek to enter the occupation.

State and Area Data

This section has information on sources for employment, wages, and projections data by state and area.

Similar Occupations

Some occupations have similar job duties or similar required skills. This section provides links to those occupations.

More Information

This section includes external links to associations, organizations, and other institutions that provide readers with additional information.

Changing employment between 2019 and 2029

If the statement reads—	Employment is projected to—
Grow much faster than average	increase 8 percent or more
Grow faster than average	increase 5 percent to 7 percent
Grow about as fast as average	increase 3 percent to 4 percent
Grow slower than average	increase 1 percent to 2 percent
Little or no change	Remain largely unchanged
Decline	decrease 1 percent or more

Architecture and Engineering

Aerospace Engineering and Operations Technicians

Summary

Quick Facts: Aerospace Engineering and Operations Technicians	
2019 Median Pay	$66,020 per year $31.74 per hour
Typical Entry-Level Education	Associate's degree
Work Experience in a Related Occupation	None
On-the-job Training	None
Number of Jobs, 2019	11,900
Job Outlook, 2019-29	7% (Faster than average)
Employment Change, 2019-29	800

What Aerospace Engineering and Operations Technicians Do

Aerospace engineering and operations technicians operate and maintain equipment used in developing, testing, producing, and sustaining new aircraft and spacecraft.

Work Environment

Aerospace engineering and operations technicians usually work in manufacturing or industrial plants, laboratories, and offices. Some of these workers may be exposed to hazards from equipment or from toxic materials, but incidents are rare as long as proper procedures are followed.

How to Become an Aerospace Engineering and Operations Technician

Many employers prefer to hire aerospace engineering and operations technicians who have earned an associate's degree in engineering technology or who have completed vocational-technical education in computer programming or robotics and machining. Prospective technicians also may earn certificates or diplomas offered by vocational or technical schools. Some aerospace engineering and operations technicians must have security clearances to work on projects related to national defense.

Pay

The median annual wage for aerospace engineering and operations technicians was $66,020 in May 2019.

Job Outlook

Employment of aerospace engineering and operations technicians is projected to grow 7 percent from 2019 to 2029, faster than the average for all occupations. Most employment growth for these workers will be in the professional, scientific, and technical services industry.

State & Area Data

Explore resources for employment and wages by state and area for aerospace engineering and operations technicians.

Aerospace engineering and operations technicians work to make sure that testing goes smoothly.

Aerospace engineering and operations technicians operate and calibrate computer systems so that they comply with test requirements.

What Aerospace Engineering and Operations Technicians Do

Aerospace engineering and operations technicians operate and maintain equipment used in developing, testing, producing, and sustaining new aircraft and spacecraft. Increasingly, these workers are being required to program and run computer simulations tools and processes in their work, as well as advanced automation and robotics. Their work is critical in preventing the failure of key parts of new aircraft, spacecraft, and missiles. They also help in the quality assurance, testing, and operation of advanced technology equipment used in producing aircraft and the systems that go into the aircraft.

Duties

Aerospace engineering and operations technicians typically do the following:

- Meet with aerospace engineers to discuss details and implications of test procedures
- Build and maintain test facilities for aircraft systems
- Make and install parts and systems to be tested in test equipment
- Operate and calibrate computer systems so that they comply with test and manufacturing requirements
- Ensure that test procedures are performed smoothly and safely
- Record data from test parts and assemblies
- Install instruments in aircraft and spacecraft
- Monitor and ensure quality in producing systems that go into the aircraft

New aircraft designs undergo years of testing before they are put into service, because the failure of key parts during flight can be fatal. As part of the job, technicians often calibrate test equipment, such as wind tunnels, and determine the causes of equipment malfunctions. They also may program and run computer simulations that test the new designs.

Some aerospace engineering and operations technicians are beginning to specialize in three-dimensional printing, or additive manufacturing, as this technology becomes more common in the work they do.

Work Environment

Aerospace engineering and operations technicians held about 11,900 jobs in 2019. The largest employers of aerospace engineering and operations technicians were as follows:

Aerospace product and parts manufacturing	36%
Engineering services	18
Computer and electronic product manufacturing	11
Scientific research and development services	11

Aerospace engineering and operations technicians work in manufacturing or industrial plants, laboratories, and offices.

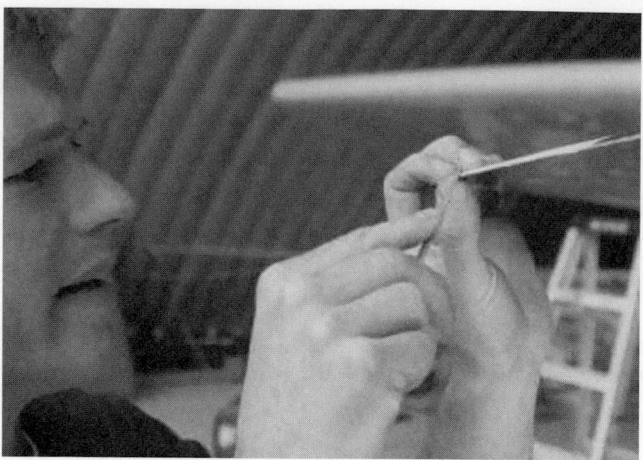

Aerospace engineering and operations technicians install instruments in aircraft and spacecraft.

Those who work in manufacturing or industrial plants are frequently directly involved in assembling aircraft, missiles, and spacecraft. Many are exposed to hazards from equipment or from toxic materials, but incidents are rare as long as proper procedures are followed.

Work Schedules

Aerospace engineering and operations technicians are employed throughout the private sector, with large and small manufacturing organizations, as well as with engineering services firms. Schedules worked tend to parallel those of the other engineering and operations staff members, and most work full time.

How to Become an Aerospace Engineering and Operations Technician

Many employers prefer to hire aerospace engineering and operations technicians who have earned an associate's degree in engineering technology or who have completed vocational-technical education in computer programming or robotics, and machining. Prospective technicians also may earn certificates or diplomas offered by vocational or technical schools. Some aerospace engineering and operations technicians must have security clearances to work on projects related to national defense. U.S. citizenship may be required for certain types and levels of clearances.

Education

High school students interested in becoming aerospace engineering and operations technicians should take classes in math, science, and, if available, drafting and computer skills. Courses that help students develop skills collaboratively with machines also are valuable, because these technicians build what aerospace engineers design. In addition, technicians should have a basic understanding of computers and software in order to model or simulate products.

Aerospace engineering and operations technicians typically need to earn an associate's degree or a certificate from a

Aerospace engineering and operations technicians work to prevent the failure of key parts of new aircraft, spacecraft, or missiles.

community college or vocational–technical school. Community colleges offer programs similar to those in technical institutes but include more theory-based and liberal arts coursework and programs. Community colleges typically award an associate's degree, but some offer a certificate. Vocational–technical schools include postsecondary institutions that emphasize training needed by local employers. Students who complete these programs typically receive a diploma or certificate, but some vocational–technical schools offer an associate's degree as well.

Some vocational schools and community colleges offer cooperative programs with work experience built into the curriculum.

Important Qualities

Communication skills. Aerospace engineering and operations technicians receive instructions from aerospace engineers. Therefore, they must be able to understand and follow those instructions, as well as communicate any problems to their supervisors.

Critical-thinking skills. Aerospace engineering and operations technicians must be able to help aerospace engineers troubleshoot particular design issues. They must be able to help evaluate system capabilities, identify problems, formulate the right question, and then find the right answer.

Detail oriented. Aerospace engineering and operations technicians make and keep precise measurements needed by aerospace engineers. In addition, they keep accurate records of these measurements.

Interpersonal skills. Aerospace engineering and operations technicians must be able to take instructions and offer advice. The ability to work well with supervising engineers, other technicians, and mechanics is essential because technicians interact with people from other divisions, businesses, and governments.

Math skills. Aerospace engineering and operations technicians use the principles of mathematics for measurement, analysis, design, and troubleshooting tasks in their work.

Mechanical skills. Aerospace engineering and operations technicians must be able to assist aerospace engineers by building what the engineers design. Mechanical skills are needed to help with the processes and directions required to move from design to production.

Licenses, Certifications, and Registrations

Although not required for the job, certification is offered by the Federal Aviation Administration (FAA). Certification may be beneficial because it shows employers that a technician can carry out the theoretical designs of aerospace engineers.

Private companies and the FAA both seek to ensure the highest standards for the safety of aircraft. SpaceTEC, the National Science Foundation's Center for Aerospace Technical Education, coordinates a nationwide program through community and technical colleges to help students prepare for certification.

Pay

The median annual wage for aerospace engineering and operations technicians was $66,020 in May 2019. The median wage is the wage at which half the workers in an occupation earned more than that amount and half earned less. The lowest 10 percent earned less than $41,680, and the highest 10 percent earned more than $99,970.

In May 2019, the median annual wages for aerospace engineering and operations technicians in the top industries in which they worked were as follows:

Computer and electronic product manufacturing ..	$69,270
Aerospace product and parts manufacturing	67,850
Engineering services	65,490
Scientific research and development services	59,320

Aerospace engineering and operations technicians are employed throughout the private sector, with large and small manufacturing organizations, as well as with engineering services firms. Schedules worked tend to parallel those of the other engineering and operations staff members, and most work full time.

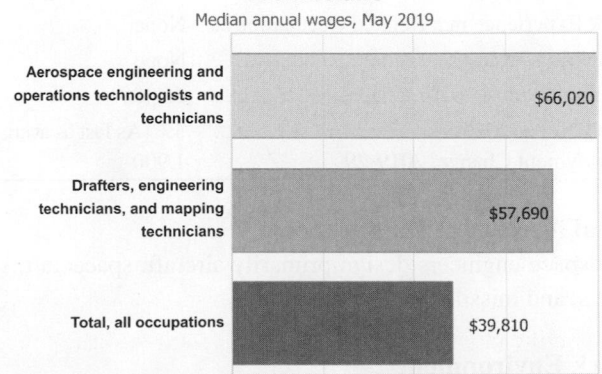

Aerospace Engineering and Operations Technicians

Median annual wages, May 2019

Aerospace engineering and operations technologists and technicians	$66,020
Drafters, engineering technicians, and mapping technicians	$57,690
Total, all occupations	$39,810

Note: All Occupations includes all occupations in the U.S. Economy.
Source: U.S. Bureau of Labor Statistics, Occupational Employment Statistics.

Job Outlook

Employment of aerospace engineering and operations technicians is projected to grow 7 percent from 2019 to 2029, faster than the average for all occupations. Most employment growth for these workers will be in the professional, scientific, and technical services industry. Aircraft may be redesigned to cut down on noise pollution and to raise fuel efficiency, spurring demand for technicians to work on these projects.

Successful research and development projects, ranging from more efficient propulsion systems to new air transport concepts, also will result in new product lines and create demand for these workers. In addition, aerospace engineering and operations technicians will be needed to meet rising demand for manufacturing small satellites known as cubesats or smallsats, which are used for communications, gathering data, and other purposes.

Aerospace Engineering and Operations Technicians

Percent change in employment, projected 2019-29

Note: All Occupations includes all occupations in the U.S. Economy.
Source: U.S. Bureau of Labor Statistics, Employment Projections program.

Employment projections data for aerospace engineering and operations technicians, 2019-29					
Occupational Title	SOC Code	Employment, 2019	Projected Employment, 2029	Change, 2019-29	
				Percent	Numeric
SOURCE: U.S. Bureau of Labor Statistics, Employment Projections program					
Aerospace engineering and operations technologists and technicians	17-3021	11,900	12,700	7	800

State & Area Data

Occupational Employment Statistics (OES)

The Occupational Employment Statistics (OES) program produces employment and wage estimates annually for over 800 occupations. These estimates are available for the nation as a whole, for individual states, and for metropolitan and nonmetropolitan areas.

Contacts for More Information

For more information about careers in engineering, visit
➤ Technology Student Association

For more information about certification, visit
➤ Federal Aviation Administration
➤ SpaceTEC

Aerospace Engineers

Summary

Quick Facts: Aerospace Engineers

2019 Median Pay	$116,500 per year $56.01 per hour
Typical Entry-Level Education	Bachelor's degree
Work Experience in a Related Occupation	None
On-the-job Training	None
Number of Jobs, 2019	66,400
Job Outlook, 2019-29	3% (As fast as average)
Employment Change, 2019-29	1,900

What Aerospace Engineers Do

Aerospace engineers design primarily aircraft, spacecraft, satellites, and missiles.

Work Environment

Aerospace engineers are employed in industries whose workers design or build aircraft, missiles, systems for national defense, or spacecraft. Aerospace engineers are employed primarily in manufacturing, analysis and design, research and development, and the federal government.

How to Become an Aerospace Engineer

Aerospace engineers must have a bachelor's degree in aerospace engineering or another field of engineering or science related to aerospace systems. Aerospace engineers who work on projects that are related to national defense may need a security clearance.

Pay

The median annual wage for aerospace engineers was $116,500 in May 2019.

Job Outlook

Employment of aerospace engineers is projected to grow 3 percent from 2019 to 2029, about as fast as the average for all occupations.

State & Area Data

Explore resources for employment and wages by state and area for aerospace engineers.

Aerospace engineers design aircraft and propulsion systems, and study the aerodynamic performance of aircraft.

Aerospace engineers evaluate designs to see that the products meet engineering principles.

What Aerospace Engineers Do

Aerospace engineers design primarily aircraft, spacecraft, satellites, and missiles. In addition, they create and test prototypes to make sure that they function according to design.

Duties

Aerospace engineers typically do the following:

- Direct and coordinate the design, manufacture, and testing of aircraft and aerospace products
- Assess proposals for projects to determine if they are technically and financially feasible
- Determine if proposed projects will result in safe operations that meet the defined goals
- Evaluate designs to see that the products meet engineering principles, customer requirements, and environmental regulations
- Develop acceptance criteria for design methods, quality standards, sustainment after delivery, and completion dates
- Ensure that projects meet quality standards
- Inspect malfunctioning or damaged products to identify sources of problems and possible solutions

Aerospace engineers may develop new technologies for use in aviation, defense systems, and spacecraft. They often specialize in areas such as aerodynamic fluid flow; structural design; guidance, navigation, and control; instrumentation and communication; robotics; and propulsion and combustion.

Aerospace engineers can specialize in designing different types of aerospace products, such as commercial and military airplanes and helicopters; remotely piloted aircraft and rotorcraft; spacecraft, including launch vehicles and satellites; and military missiles and rockets.

Aerospace engineers often become experts in one or more related fields: aerodynamics, thermodynamics, materials, celestial mechanics, flight mechanics, propulsion, acoustics, and guidance and control systems.

Aerospace engineers typically specialize in one of two types of engineering: aeronautical or astronautical.

Aeronautical engineers work with aircraft. They are involved primarily in designing aircraft and propulsion systems and in studying the aerodynamic performance of aircraft and construction materials. They work with the theory, technology, and practice of flight within the Earth's atmosphere.

Astronautical engineers work with the science and technology of spacecraft and how they perform inside and outside the Earth's atmosphere. This includes work on small satellites such as cubesats, and traditional large satellites.

Aeronautical and astronautical engineers face different environmental and operational issues in designing aircraft and spacecraft. However, the two fields overlap a great deal because they both depend on the basic principles of physics.

Work Environment

Aerospace engineers held about 66,400 jobs in 2019. The largest employers of aerospace engineers were as follows:

Aerospace product and parts manufacturing	36%
Federal government, excluding postal service	16
Engineering services	15
Navigational, measuring, electromedical, and control instruments manufacturing	10
Research and development in the physical, engineering, and life sciences	8

Aerospace engineers are employed in industries in which workers design or build aircraft, missiles, systems for national defense, or spacecraft. They work primarily for firms that engage in manufacturing, analysis and design, research and development, and for the federal government.

Aerospace engineers now spend more of their time in an office environment than they have in the past, because modern aircraft design requires the use of sophisticated computer equipment and software design tools, modeling, and simulations for tests, evaluation, and training.

Aerospace engineers work with other professionals involved in designing and building aircraft, spacecraft, and their components. Therefore, they must be able to communicate well,

Aerospace engineers work in industries that build aircraft and often help oversee construction.

divide work into manageable tasks, and work with others toward a common goal.

Work Schedules

Aerospace engineers typically work full time. Engineers who direct projects must often work extra hours to monitor progress, to ensure that designs meet requirements, to determine how to measure aircraft performance, to see that production meets design standards, to participate in test flights and first flights, and to ensure that deadlines are met.

How to Become an Aerospace Engineer

Aerospace engineers must have a bachelor's degree in aerospace engineering or another field of engineering or science related to aerospace systems. Aerospace engineers who work on projects that are related to national defense may need a security clearance. U.S. citizenship may be required for certain types and levels of clearances.

Education

Entry-level aerospace engineers usually need a bachelor's degree. High school students interested in studying aerospace engineering should take courses in chemistry, physics, advanced math, and computer programming and computer languages.

Bachelor's degree programs include classroom, laboratory, and field studies in subjects such as general engineering principles, propulsion, stability and control, structures, mechanics, and aerodynamics, which is the study of how air interacts with moving objects.

Some colleges and universities offer cooperative programs in partnership with regional businesses, which give students practical experience while they complete their education. Cooperative programs and internships enable students to gain valuable experience and to finance part of their education.

At some universities, a student can enroll in a 5-year program that leads to both a bachelor's degree and a master's degree

Aerospace engineers use the principles of calculus, trigonometry, and other advanced topics in mathematics for analysis, design, and troubleshooting in their work.

upon completion. A graduate degree will allow an engineer to work as an instructor at a university or to do research and development. Programs in aerospace engineering are accredited by ABET.

Important Qualities

Analytical skills. Aerospace engineers must be able to identify design elements that may not meet requirements and then must formulate alternatives to improve the performance of those elements.

Business skills. Much of the work done by aerospace engineers involves meeting federal government standards. Meeting these standards often requires knowledge of standard business practices, as well as knowledge of commercial law. Additionally, project management or systems engineering skills can be useful.

Critical-thinking skills. Aerospace engineers must be able to produce designs that meet governmental standards, and to figure out why a particular design does not work. They must be able to ask the right question, then find an acceptable answer.

Math skills. Aerospace engineers use the principles of calculus, trigonometry, and other advanced topics in math for analysis, design, and troubleshooting in their work.

Problem-solving skills. Aerospace engineers use their education and experience to upgrade designs and troubleshoot problems when meeting new demands for aircraft, such as increased fuel efficiency or improved safety.

Writing skills. Aerospace engineers must be able both to write papers that explain their designs clearly and to create documentation for future reference.

Licenses, Certifications, and Registrations

Licensure for aerospace engineers is not as common as it is for other engineering occupations, nor it is required for entry-level positions. A Professional Engineering (PE) license, which allows for higher levels of leadership and independence, can be acquired later in one's career. Licensed engineers are called professional engineers (PEs). A PE can oversee the work of other engineers, sign off on projects, and provide services directly to the public. State licensure generally requires

- A degree from an ABET-accredited engineering program
- A passing score on the Fundamentals of Engineering (FE) exam
- Relevant work experience, typically at least 4 years
- A passing score on the Professional Engineering (PE) exam.

The initial FE exam can be taken after earning a bachelor's degree. Engineers who pass this exam are commonly called engineers in training (EITs) or engineer interns (EIs). After meeting work experience requirements, EITs and EIs can take the second exam, called the Principles and Practice of Engineering.

Each state issues its own licenses. Most states recognize licensure from other states, as long as the licensing state's requirements meet or exceed their own licensure requirements. Several states require continuing education for engineers to keep their licenses.

Other Experience

During high school, students can attend engineering summer camps to see what these and other engineers do. Attending these camps can help students plan their coursework for the remainder of their time in high school.

Advancement

Eventually, aerospace engineers may advance to become technical specialists or to supervise a team of engineers and technicians. Some may even become engineering managers or move into executive positions, such as program managers.

Pay

The median annual wage for aerospace engineers was $116,500 in May 2019. The median wage is the wage at which half the workers in an occupation earned more than that amount and half earned less. The lowest 10 percent earned less than $72,450, and the highest 10 percent earned more than $166,620.

In May 2019, the median annual wages for aerospace engineers in the top industries in which they worked were as follows:

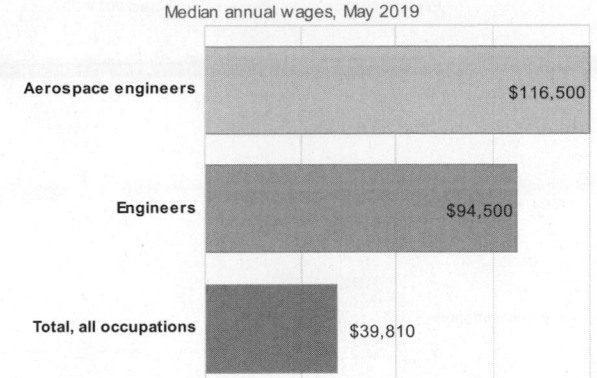

Aerospace Engineers
Median annual wages, May 2019

Aerospace engineers	$116,500
Engineers	$94,500
Total, all occupations	$39,810

Note: All Occupations includes all occupations in the U.S. Economy.
Source: U.S. Bureau of Labor Statistics, Occupational Employment Statistics.

Research and development in the physical, engineering, and life sciences	$123,600
Navigational, measuring, electromedical, and control instruments manufacturing	121,750
Federal government, excluding postal service	118,050
Aerospace product and parts manufacturing	116,620
Engineering services	114,030

Aerospace engineers typically work full time. Engineers who direct projects must often work extra hours to monitor progress, to ensure that designs meet requirements, to determine how to measure aircraft performance, to see that production meets design standards, and to ensure that deadlines are met.

Job Outlook

Employment of aerospace engineers is projected to grow 3 percent from 2019 to 2029, about as fast as the average for all occupations. Aircraft are being redesigned to cause less noise pollution and have better fuel efficiency, which will help sustain demand for research and development. Also, new developments in small satellites have greater commercial viability. Growing interest in unmanned aerial systems will also help drive growth of the occupation.

Job Prospects

Employment opportunities should be favorable for those trained in software, such as C++, or with education and experience in stress and structural engineering.

Employment projections data for aerospace engineers, 2019-29					
Occupational Title	SOC Code	Employment, 2019	Projected Employment, 2029	Change, 2019-29	
				Percent	Numeric
SOURCE: U.S. Bureau of Labor Statistics, Employment Projections program					
Aerospace engineers	17-2011	66,400	68,200	3	1,900

Aerospace Engineers
Percent change in employment, projected 2019-29

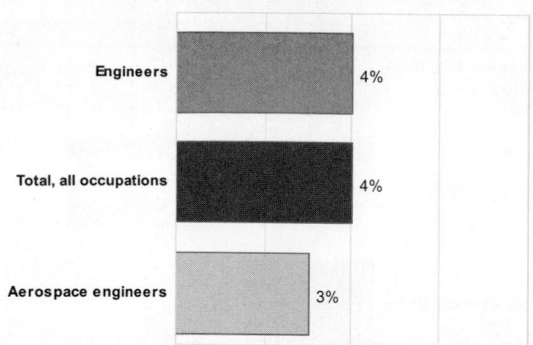

Engineers	4%
Total, all occupations	4%
Aerospace engineers	3%

Note: All Occupations includes all occupations in the U.S. Economy.
Source: U.S. Bureau of Labor Statistics, Employment Projections program.

State & Area Data
Occupational Employment Statistics (OES)
The Occupational Employment Statistics (OES) program produces employment and wage estimates annually for over 800 occupations. These estimates are available for the nation as a whole, for individual states, and for metropolitan and nonmetropolitan areas.

Contacts for More Information
For more information about general engineering education and career resources, visit
➤ American Society for Engineering Education
➤ Technology Student Association
➤ National Council of Examiners for Engineering and Surveying
➤ National Society of Professional Engineers
➤ ABET
➤ The American Institute of Aeronautics and Astronautics
➤ Engineering Education Service Center

Agricultural Engineers

Summary

Quick Facts: Agricultural Engineers

2019 Median Pay	$80,720 per year $38.81 per hour
Typical Entry-Level Education	Bachelor's degree
Work Experience in a Related Occupation	None
On-the-job Training	None
Number of Jobs, 2019	1,700
Job Outlook, 2019-29	2% (Slower than average)
Employment Change, 2019-29	0

What Agricultural Engineers Do
Agricultural engineers solve problems concerning power supplies, machine efficiency, the use of structures and facilities, pollution and environmental issues, and the storage and processing of agricultural products.

Work Environment
Agricultural engineers work mostly in offices, but may spend time traveling to agricultural settings. Agricultural engineers typically work full time.

How to Become an Agricultural Engineer
Agricultural engineers must have a bachelor's degree, preferably in agricultural engineering or biological engineering.

Agricultural engineers sometimes travel to farms to oversee the installation of new systems.

Pay
The median annual wage for agricultural engineers was $80,720 in May 2019.

Job Outlook
Employment of agricultural engineers is projected to grow 2 percent from 2019 to 2029, slower than the average for all occupations. The need to increase the efficiency of agricultural production systems and to reduce environmental damage should maintain demand for these workers.

State & Area Data
Explore resources for employment and wages by state and area for agricultural engineers.

Agricultural engineers often have to observe the results of their work where the crops are actually grown.

What Agricultural Engineers Do

Agricultural engineers attempt to solve agricultural problems concerning power supplies, the efficiency of machinery, the use of structures and facilities, pollution and environmental issues, and the storage and processing of agricultural products.

Duties

Agricultural engineers typically do the following:

- Use computer software to design equipment, systems, or structures
- Modify environmental factors that affect animal or crop production, such as airflow in a barn or runoff patterns on a field
- Test equipment to ensure its safety and reliability
- Oversee construction and production operations
- Plan and work together with clients, contractors, consultants, and other engineers to ensure effective and desirable outcomes

Agricultural engineers work in farming, including aquaculture (farming of seafood), forestry, and food processing. They work on a wide variety of projects. For example, some agricultural engineers work to develop climate control systems that increase the comfort and productivity of livestock whereas others work to increase the storage capacity and efficiency of refrigeration. Many agricultural engineers attempt to develop better solutions for animal waste disposal. Those with computer programming skills work to integrate artificial intelligence and geospatial systems into agriculture. For example, they work to improve efficiency in fertilizer application or to automate harvesting systems.

Work Environment

Agricultural engineers held about 1,700 jobs in 2019. The largest employers of agricultural engineers were as follows:

Federal government, excluding postal service	20%
Colleges, universities, and professional schools; state...	12
Management, scientific, and technical consulting services	9
Engineering services	6

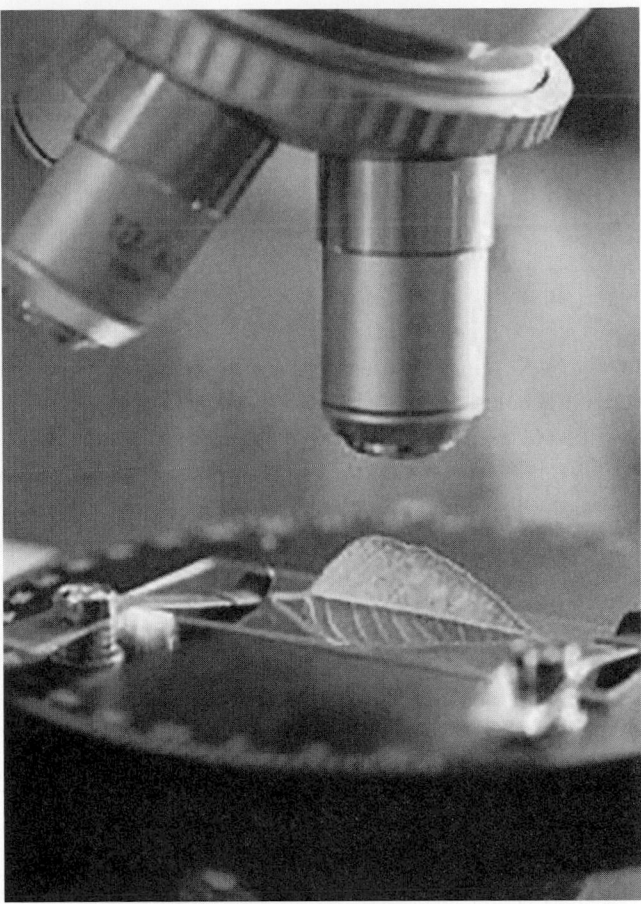

Agricultural engineers may test the effects that specific growing conditions have on plants, in a laboratory setting.

Agricultural engineers typically work in offices, but may spend time at a variety of worksites, both indoors and outdoors. They may travel to agricultural settings to see that equipment and machinery are functioning according to both the manufacturers' specifications and federal and state regulations. Some agricultural engineers occasionally work in laboratories to test the quality of processing equipment. They may work onsite when they supervise livestock facility upgrades or water resource management projects.

Agricultural engineers work with others in designing solutions to problems or applying technological advances. They work with people from a variety of backgrounds, such as business, agronomy, animal sciences, and public policy.

Work Schedules

Agricultural engineers typically work full time. Schedules may vary because of weather conditions or other complications. When working on outdoor projects, agricultural engineers may work more hours to take advantage of good weather or fewer hours in case of bad weather.

In addition, agricultural engineers may need to be available outside of normal work hours to address unexpected problems that come up in manufacturing operations or rural construction projects.

How to Become an Agricultural Engineer

Agricultural engineers must have a bachelor's degree, preferably in agricultural engineering or biological engineering.

Education

Students who are interested in studying agricultural engineering will benefit from taking high school courses in math and science. University students take courses in advanced calculus, physics, biology, and chemistry. They also may take courses in business, public policy, and economics.

Entry-level jobs in agricultural engineering require a bachelor's degree. Bachelor's degree programs in agricultural engineering or biological engineering typically include significant hands-on components in areas such as science, math, and engineering principles. Most colleges and universities encourage students to gain practical experience through projects such as participating in engineering competitions in which teams of students design equipment and attempt to solve real problems.

ABET accredits programs in agricultural engineering.

Bachelor's degree programs in biological and agricultural engineering typically include significant hands-on components in areas such as science.

Important Qualities

Analytical skills. Agricultural engineers must analyze the needs of complex systems that involve workers, crops, animals, machinery and equipment, and the environment.

Communication skills. Agricultural engineers must understand the needs of clients, workers, and others working on a project. Furthermore, they must communicate their thoughts about systems and about solutions to any problems they have been working on.

Math skills. Agricultural engineers use calculus, trigonometry, and other advanced mathematical disciplines for analysis, design, and troubleshooting.

Problem-solving skills. Agricultural engineers' main role is to solve problems found in agricultural production. Goals may include designing safer equipment for food processing or reducing erosion. To solve these problems, agricultural engineers must creatively apply the principles of engineering.

Licenses, Certifications, and Registrations

Licensure is not required for entry-level positions as an agricultural engineer. A Professional Engineering (PE) license, which allows for higher levels of leadership and independence, can be acquired later in one's career. Licensed engineers are called professional engineers (PEs). A PE can oversee the work of other engineers, sign off on projects, and provide services directly to the public. State licensure generally requires

- A degree from an ABET-accredited engineering program
- A passing score on the Fundamentals of Engineering (FE) exam
- Relevant work experience, typically at least 4 years
- A passing score on the Professional Engineering (PE) exam

The initial FE exam can be taken after one earns a bachelor's degree. Engineers who pass this exam are commonly called engineers in training (EITs) or engineer interns (EIs). After meeting work experience requirements, EITs and EIs can take the second exam, called the Principles and Practice of Engineering (PE).

Each state issues its own licenses. Most states recognize licensure from other states, as long as the licensing state's requirements meet or exceed their own licensure requirements. Several states require engineers to take continuing education to keep their licenses. For licensing requirements, check with your state's licensing board.

Advancement

New engineers usually work under the supervision of experienced engineers. As they gain knowledge and experience, beginning engineers move to more difficult projects and increase their independence in developing designs, solving problems, and making decisions.

With experience, agricultural engineers may advance to supervise a team of engineers and technicians. Some advance to become engineering managers. Agricultural engineers who become sales engineers use their engineering background to discuss a product's technical aspects with potential buyers and to help in product planning, installation, and use.

Engineers who have a master's degree or a Ph.D. are more likely to be involved in research and development activities, and may become postsecondary teachers.

Pay

The median annual wage for agricultural engineers was $80,720 in May 2019. The median wage is the wage at which half the workers in an occupation earned more than that amount and half earned less. The lowest 10 percent earned less than $47,330, and the highest 10 percent earned more than $160,950.

In May 2019, the median annual wages for agricultural engineers in the top industries in which they worked were as follows:

Federal government, excluding postal service	$88,050
Engineering services	85,040
Management, scientific, and technical consulting services..	77,190
Colleges, universities, and professional schools; state	59,550

Agricultural engineers typically work full time. Schedules may vary because of weather conditions or other complications. When working on outdoor projects, agricultural engineers may work more hours to take advantage of good weather or fewer hours in case of bad weather.

In addition, agricultural engineers may need to be available outside of normal work hours to address unexpected problems that come up in manufacturing operations or rural construction projects.

Agricultural Engineers
Median annual wages, May 2019

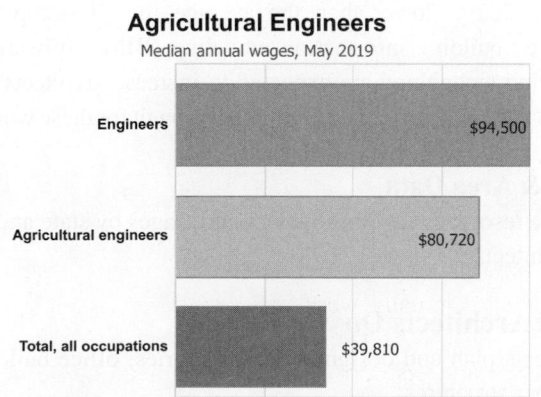

Engineers — $94,500
Agricultural engineers — $80,720
Total, all occupations — $39,810

Note: All Occupations includes all occupations in the U.S. Economy.
Source: U.S. Bureau of Labor Statistics, Occupational Employment Statistics.

Agricultural Engineers
Percent change in employment, projected 2019-29

Engineers — 4%
Total, all occupations — 4%
Agricultural engineers — 2%

Note: All Occupations includes all occupations in the U.S. Economy.
Source: U.S. Bureau of Labor Statistics, Employment Projections program.

Job Outlook

Employment of agricultural engineers is projected to grow 2 percent from 2019 to 2029, slower than the average for all occupations.

Farming establishments will continue to require more machinery, equipment, and buildings to increase the efficiency of agricultural production systems and to reduce environmental damage, which should maintain demand for these workers.

Agricultural engineers are expected to continue working on projects such as alternative energies and biofuels; precision and automated farming technologies for irrigation, spraying, and harvesting; and growing food in space to support future exploration.

More efficient designs for traditional agricultural engineering projects such as irrigation, storage, and worker safety systems will also maintain demand for these workers. Growing populations and stronger global competition will result in the industry needing more efficient means of production, which will increase demand for agricultural engineers.

Job Prospects

Typically, graduates of engineering programs have good job prospects and can often enter related engineering fields in addition to the field in which they have earned their degree. Agricultural engineering offers good opportunities, but it is a small occupation, and engineers trained in other fields, such as civil or mechanical engineering, also may compete for these jobs. Graduates of biological and agricultural engineering programs may have some advantage when applying for agricultural engineering jobs, but some may also find good prospects outside of the agricultural sector.

Employment projections data for agricultural engineers, 2019-29					
Occupational Title	SOC Code	Employment, 2019	Projected Employment, 2029	Change, 2019-29	
				Percent	Numeric
SOURCE: U.S. Bureau of Labor Statistics, Employment Projections program					
Agricultural engineers	17-2021	1,700	1,700	2	0

State & Area Data
Occupational Employment Statistics (OES)
The Occupational Employment Statistics (OES) program produces employment and wage estimates annually for over 800 occupations. These estimates are available for the nation as a whole, for individual states, and for metropolitan and nonmetropolitan areas.

Contacts for More Information
For more information about agricultural engineers, visit
➤ American Society of Agricultural and Biological Engineers

For information about general engineering education and career resources, visit
➤ American Society for Engineering Education
➤ Technology Student Association

For more information about licensure for agricultural engineers, visit
➤ National Council of Examiners for Engineering and Surveying
➤ National Society of Professional Engineers
➤ National Institute for Certification in Engineering Technologies

For information about accredited engineering programs, visit
➤ ABET

For a variety of information concerning agriculture, grants, and government initiatives, visit
➤ Future Farmers of America
➤ National Institute of Food and Agriculture, U.S. Department of Agriculture
➤ U.S. Food and Drug Administration

Architects

Summary

Quick Facts: Architects

2019 Median Pay	$80,750 per year $38.82 per hour
Typical Entry-Level Education	Bachelor's degree
Work Experience in a Related Occupation	None
On-the-job Training	Internship/residency
Number of Jobs, 2019	129,900
Job Outlook, 2019-29	1% (Slower than average)
Employment Change, 2019-29	1,100

What Architects Do
Architects plan and design houses, factories, office buildings, and other structures.

Work Environment
Architects spend much of their time in offices, where they develop plans, meet with clients, and consult with engineers and other architects. They also visit construction sites to prepare initial drawings and review the progress of projects to ensure that clients' objectives are met.

How to Become an Architect
There are typically three main steps to becoming a licensed architect: completing a bachelor's degree in architecture, gaining relevant experience through a paid internship, and passing the Architect Registration Examination.

Pay
The median annual wage for architects was $80,750 in May 2019.

Architects plan and design many different structures.

Job Outlook
Employment of architects is projected to grow 1 percent from 2019 to 2029, slower than the average for all occupations. Improved building information modeling (BIM) software and measuring technology are expected to increase architects' productivity, thereby limiting employment growth for these workers.

State & Area Data
Explore resources for employment and wages by state and area for architects.

What Architects Do
Architects plan and design houses, factories, office buildings, and other structures.

Duties
Architects typically do the following:

- Meet with clients to determine objectives and requirements for structures
- Give preliminary estimates on cost and construction time
- Prepare structure specifications
- Direct workers who prepare drawings and documents
- Prepare scaled drawings, either with computer software or by hand
- Prepare contract documents for building contractors
- Manage construction contracts
- Visit worksites to ensure that construction adheres to architectural plans
- Seek new work by marketing and giving presentations

People need places to live, work, play, learn, shop, and eat. Architects are responsible for designing these places. They work on public or private projects and design both indoor and outdoor spaces. Architects can be commissioned to design anything from a single room to an entire complex of buildings.

Architects discuss with clients the objectives, requirements, and budget of a project. In some cases, architects provide pre-design services, such as feasibility and environmental impact studies, site selection, cost analyses, and design requirements.

Architects develop final construction plans on the initial proposal after discussing with clients. The architects' plans show the building's appearance and details of its construction. These plans include drawings of the structural system;

air-conditioning, heating, and ventilating systems; electrical systems; communications systems; and plumbing. Sometimes, landscape plans are included as well. In developing designs, architects must follow state and local building codes, zoning laws, fire regulations, and other ordinances, such as those requiring reasonable access for people with disabilities.

Architects use computer-aided design and drafting (CADD) and building information modeling (BIM) for creating designs and construction drawings. However, hand-drawing skills are still required, especially during the conceptual stages of a project and when an architect is at a construction site.

As construction continues, architects may visit building sites to ensure that contractors follow the design, adhere to the schedule, use the specified materials, and meet work-quality standards. The job is not complete until all construction is finished, required tests are conducted, and construction costs are paid.

Architects may also help clients get construction bids, select contractors, and negotiate construction contracts.

Architects often collaborate with workers in related occupations, such as civil engineers, urban and regional planners, drafters, interior designers, and landscape architects.

Work Environment

Architects held about 129,900 jobs in 2019. The largest employers of architects were as follows:

Architectural, engineering, and related services	71%
Self-employed workers	17
Government	3
Construction	3

Architects spend much of their time in offices, where they meet with clients, develop reports and drawings, and work with other architects and engineers. They also visit construction sites to ensure that clients' objectives are met and to review the progress of projects. Some architects work from home offices.

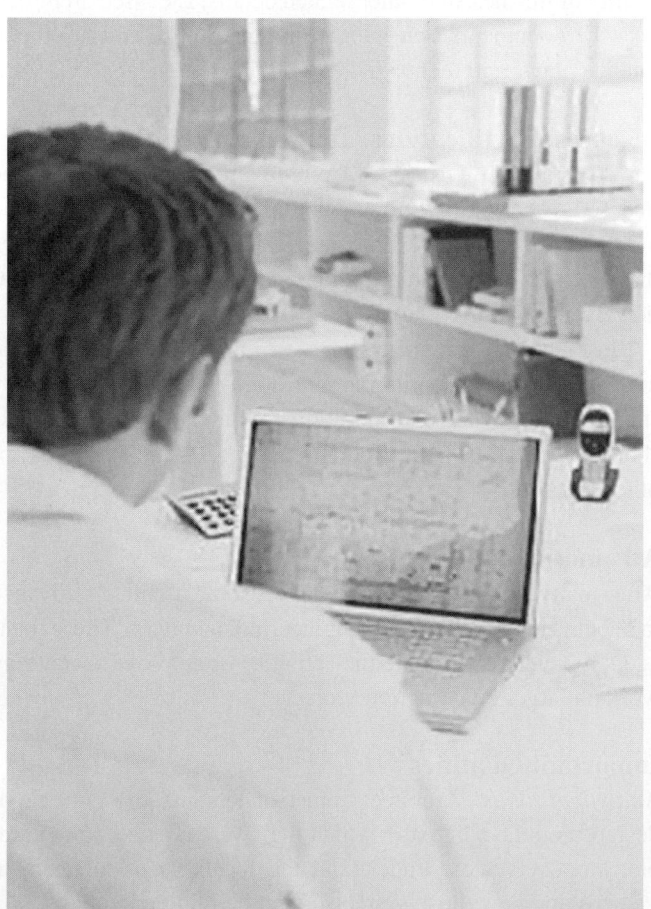

Architects use CADD during the design process.

Although architects usually work in an office, they must also travel to construction sites.

Work Schedules

Most architects work full time and many work additional hours, especially when facing deadlines. Self-employed architects may have more flexible work schedules.

How to Become an Architect

There are typically three main steps to becoming a licensed architect: completing a bachelor's degree in architecture, gaining relevant experience through a paid internship, and passing the Architect Registration Examination.

Education

In all states, earning a bachelor's degree in architecture is typically the first step to becoming an architect. Most architects earn their degree through a 5-year Bachelor of Architecture degree program. Many earn a master's degree in architecture, which can take 1 to 5 additional years. The time required depends on the extent of the student's previous education and training in architecture.

A typical bachelor's degree program includes courses in architectural history and theory, building design with an emphasis on computer-aided design and drafting (CADD), structures, construction methods, professional practices, math, physical sciences, and liberal arts.

Architects need internships to gain practical experience.

About two-thirds of states require that architects hold a degree in architecture from one of more than 120 schools of architecture accredited by the National Architectural Accrediting Board (NAAB). State licensing requirements can be found at the National Council of Architectural Registration Boards (NCARB).

Training

All state architectural registration boards require architecture graduates to complete a lengthy paid internship—generally lasting 3 years—before they may sit for the Architect Registration Examination. Most new graduates complete their training period by working at architectural firms through the Architectural Experience Program (AXP), a program run by NCARB that guides students through the internship process. Some states allow a portion of the training to occur in the offices of employers in related careers, such as engineers and general contractors. Architecture students who complete internships while still in school can count some of that time toward the 3-year training period.

Interns in architectural firms may help design part of a project. They may help prepare architectural documents and drawings, build models, and prepare construction drawings on CADD. Interns may also research building codes and write specifications for building materials, installation criteria, the quality of finishes, and other related details. Licensed architects take the documents that interns produce, make edits to them, finalize plans, and then sign and seal the documents.

Licenses, Certifications, and Registrations

All states and the District of Columbia require architects to be licensed. Licensing requirements typically include completing a degree program in architecture, gaining relevant experience through a paid internship, and passing the Architect Registration Examination.

Most states also require some form of continuing education to keep a license. Continuing education requirements vary by state but usually involve additional education through workshops, university classes, conferences, self-study courses, or other sources.

Advancement

After many years of work experience, some architects advance to become architectural and engineering managers. These managers typically coordinate the activities of employees and may work on larger construction projects.

Important Qualities

Analytical skills. Architects must understand the content of designs and the context in which they were created. For example, architects must understand the locations of mechanical systems and how those systems affect building operations.

Communication skills. Architects share their ideas, both in oral presentations and in writing, with clients, other architects, and workers who help prepare drawings. Many also give presentations to explain their ideas and designs.

Creativity. Architects design the overall look of houses, buildings, and other structures. They must ensure that the final product is both attractive and functional.

Organizational skills. Architects often manage contracts. Therefore, they must keep records related to the details of a project, including total cost, materials used, and progress.

Technical skills. Architects need to use CADD technology to create plans as part of building information modeling (BIM).

Visualization skills. Architects must be able to envision how the parts of a structure relate to each other. They also must be able to visualize how the overall building will look once completed.

Pay

The median annual wage for architects was $80,750 in May 2019. The median wage is the wage at which half the workers in an occupation earned more than that amount and half earned less. The lowest 10 percent earned less than $48,700, and the highest 10 percent earned more than $137,620.

In May 2019, the median annual wages for architects in the top industries in which they worked were as follows:

Government	$93,970
Construction	80,040
Architectural, engineering, and related services	79,830

Most architects work full time and many work additional hours, especially when facing deadlines. Self-employed architects may have more flexible work hours.

Job Outlook

Employment of architects is projected to grow 1 percent from 2019 to 2029, slower than the average for all occupations.

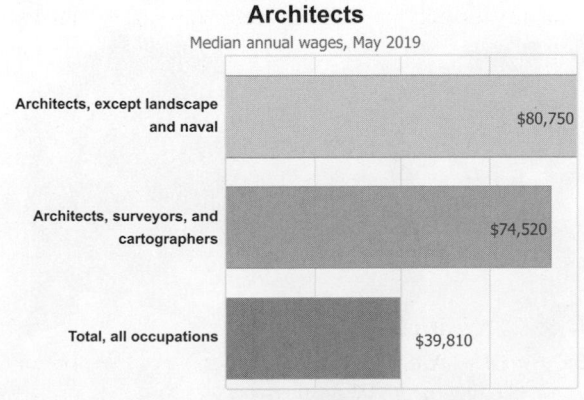

Architects
Median annual wages, May 2019

Architects, except landscape and naval — $80,750
Architects, surveyors, and cartographers — $74,520
Total, all occupations — $39,810

Note: All Occupations includes all occupations in the U.S. Economy.
Source: U.S. Bureau of Labor Statistics, Occupational Employment Statistics.

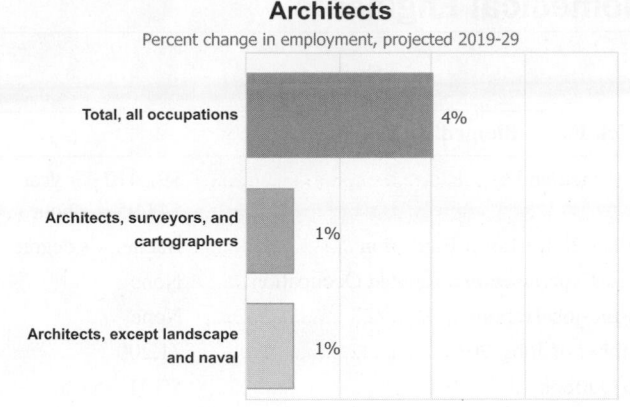

Architects
Percent change in employment, projected 2019-29

Total, all occupations — 4%
Architects, surveyors, and cartographers — 1%
Architects, except landscape and naval — 1%

Note: All Occupations includes all occupations in the U.S. Economy.
Source: U.S. Bureau of Labor Statistics, Employment Projections program.

Architects are expected to be needed to make plans and designs for the construction and renovation of homes, schools, healthcare facilities, and other structures, particularly in the area of sustainable design. However, improved building information modeling (BIM) software and measuring technology are expected to increase architects' productivity, thereby limiting employment growth for these workers.

Job Prospects

With a high number of students graduating with degrees in architecture, strong competition for internships and jobs is expected.

Employment of architects is strongly tied to the activity of the construction industry. Therefore, these workers may experience periods of unemployment when there is a slowdown in requests for new projects or when the overall level of construction falls.

Employment projections data for architects, 2019-29					
Occupational Title	SOC Code	Employment, 2019	Projected Employment, 2029	Change, 2019-29	
				Percent	Numeric
SOURCE: U.S. Bureau of Labor Statistics, Employment Projections program					
Architects, except landscape and naval	17-1011	129,900	130,900	1	1,100

State & Area Data
Occupational Employment Statistics (OES)

The Occupational Employment Statistics (OES) program produces employment and wage estimates annually for over 800 occupations. These estimates are available for the nation as a whole, for individual states, and for metropolitan and nonmetropolitan areas.

Contacts for More Information

For information about careers in architecture, visit
➤ American Institute of Architects
➤ National Architectural Accrediting Board
➤ National Council of Architectural Registration Boards

Biomedical Engineers

Summary

Quick Facts: Biomedical Engineers

2019 Median Pay	$91,410 per year
	$43.95 per hour
Typical Entry-Level Education	Bachelor's degree
Work Experience in a Related Occupation	None
On-the-job Training	None
Number of Jobs, 2019	21,200
Job Outlook, 2019-29	5% (Faster than average)
Employment Change, 2019-29	1,000

What Biomedical Engineers Do

Biomedical engineers combine engineering principles with medical sciences to design and create equipment, devices, computer systems, and software.

Work Environment

Most biomedical engineers work in manufacturing, universities, hospitals, and research facilities of companies and educational and medical institutions. They usually work full time.

How to Become a Biomedical Engineer

Biomedical engineers typically need a bachelor's degree in biomedical engineering or bioengineering, or in a related engineering field. Some positions may require a graduate degree.

Pay

The median annual wage for biomedical engineers was $91,410 in May 2019.

Job Outlook

Employment of biomedical engineers is projected to grow 5 percent from 2019 to 2029, faster than the average for all occupations. Increasing numbers of technologies and applications to medical equipment and devices, along with the medical needs of a growing and aging population, will require the services of biomedical engineers.

State & Area Data

Explore resources for employment and wages by state and area for biomedical engineers.

What Biomedical Engineers Do

Biomedical engineers combine engineering principles with medical and biological sciences to design and create equipment, devices, computer systems, and software used in healthcare.

Duties

Biomedical engineers typically do the following:

- Design biomedical equipment and devices, such as artificial internal organs, replacements for body parts, and machines for diagnosing medical problems
- Install, adjust, maintain, repair, or provide technical support for biomedical equipment
- Evaluate the safety, efficiency, and effectiveness of biomedical equipment
- Train clinicians and other personnel on the proper use of biomedical equipment
- Research the engineering aspects of the biological systems of humans and animals with life scientists, chemists, and medical scientists
- Prepare procedures, write technical reports, publish research papers, and make recommendations based on their research findings
- Present research findings to scientists, nonscientist executives, clinicians, hospital management, engineers, other colleagues, and the public

Biomedical engineers design instruments, devices, and software used in healthcare; develop new procedures using

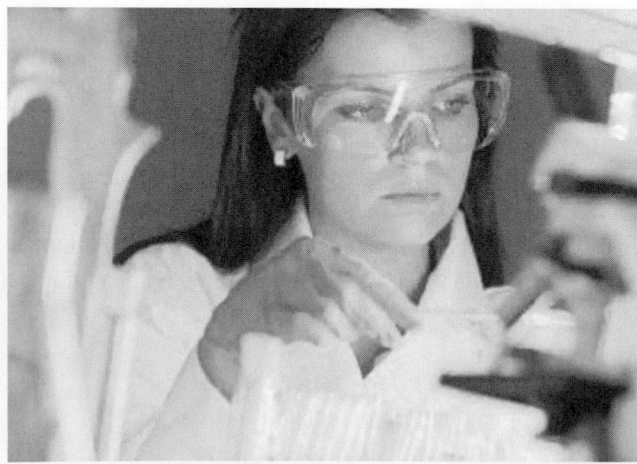

Biomedical engineers design and create equipment and devices used in healthcare.

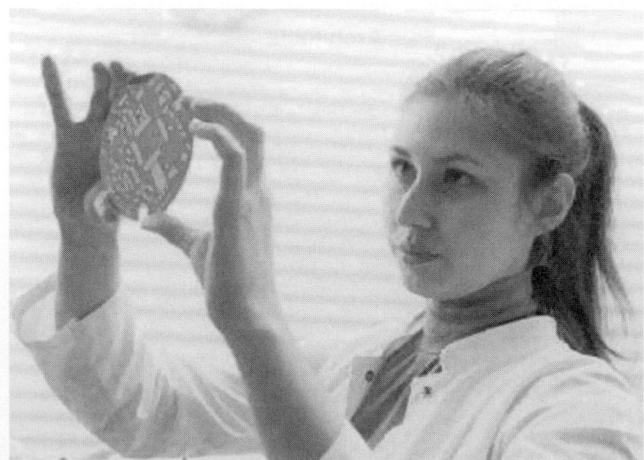

Biomedical engineers install, maintain, or provide technical support for biomedical equipment.

knowledge from many technical sources; or conduct research needed to solve clinical problems. They frequently work in research and development or quality assurance.

Biomedical engineers design electrical circuits, software to run medical equipment, or computer simulations to test new drug therapies. In addition, they design and build artificial body parts, such as hip and knee joints. In some cases, they develop the materials needed to make the replacement body parts. They also design rehabilitative exercise equipment.

The work of these engineers spans many professional fields. For example, although their expertise is based in engineering and biology, they often design computer software to run complicated instruments, such as three-dimensional x-ray machines. Alternatively, many of these engineers use their knowledge of chemistry and biology to develop new drug therapies. Others draw heavily on math and statistics to build models to understand the signals transmitted by the brain or heart. Some may be involved in sales.

The following are examples of specialty areas within the field of biomedical engineering:

Bioinstrumentation uses electronics, computer science, and measurement principles to develop instruments used in the diagnosis and treatment of medical problems.

Biomaterials is the study of naturally occurring or laboratory-designed materials that are used in medical devices or as implantation materials.

Biomechanics involves the study of mechanics, such as thermodynamics, to solve biological or medical problems.

Clinical engineering applies medical technology to optimize healthcare delivery.

Rehabilitation engineering is the study of engineering and computer science to develop devices that assist individuals recovering from or adapting to physical and cognitive impairments.

Systems physiology uses engineering tools to understand how systems within living organisms, from bacteria to humans, function and respond to changes in their environment.

Some people with training in biomedical engineering become postsecondary teachers.

Work Environment

Biomedical engineers held about 21,200 jobs in 2019. The largest employers of biomedical engineers were as follows:

Medical equipment and supplies manufacturing	17%
Research and development in the physical, engineering, and life sciences	14
Navigational, measuring, electromedical, and control instruments manufacturing	9
Colleges, universities, and professional schools; state, local, and private	8
Healthcare and social assistance	8

Biomedical engineers work in laboratory and clinical settings.

Biomedical engineers work in teams with scientists, healthcare workers, or other engineers. Where and how they work depends on the project. For example, a biomedical engineer who has developed a new device designed to help a person with a disability to walk again might have to spend hours in a hospital to determine whether the device works as planned. If the engineer finds a way to improve the device, he or she might have to return to the manufacturer to help alter the manufacturing process to improve the design.

Work Schedules

Biomedical engineers usually work full time on a normal schedule. However, as with employees in almost any engineering occupation, biomedical engineers occasionally may have to work additional hours to meet the needs of patients, managers, colleagues, and clients. Some biomedical engineers work more than 40 hours per week.

How to Become a Biomedical Engineer

Biomedical engineers typically need a bachelor's degree in biomedical engineering or bioengineering, or in a related engineering field. Some positions may require a graduate degree.

Education

Biomedical engineering and traditional engineering programs, such as mechanical and electrical, are typically good preparation for entering biomedical engineering jobs. Students who pursue traditional engineering programs at the bachelor's level may benefit from taking biological science courses.

Students interested in becoming biomedical engineers should take high school science courses, such as chemistry, physics, and biology. They should also take math courses, including algebra, geometry, trigonometry, and calculus. Courses in drafting or mechanical drawing and in computer programming are also useful.

Bachelor's degree programs in biomedical engineering and bioengineering focus on engineering and biological sciences.

Biomedical engineers frequently work in research and development or in quality assurance.

Programs include laboratory- and classroom-based courses, in subjects such as fluid and solid mechanics, computer programming, circuit design, and biomaterials. Other required courses may include biological sciences, such as physiology.

Accredited programs also include substantial training in engineering design. Many programs include co-ops or internships, often with hospitals and medical device and pharmaceutical manufacturing companies, to provide students with practical applications as part of their study. Biomedical engineering and bioengineering programs are accredited by ABET.

Important Qualities

Analytical skills. Biomedical engineers must analyze the needs of patients and customers to design appropriate solutions.

Communication skills. Because biomedical engineers sometimes work with patients and frequently work on teams, they must express themselves clearly. They must seek others' ideas and incorporate those ideas into the problem-solving process.

Creativity. Biomedical engineers must be creative to come up with innovative and integrative advances in healthcare equipment and devices.

Math skills. Biomedical engineers use the principles of calculus and other advanced topics in math and statistics, for analysis, design, and troubleshooting in their work.

Problem-solving skills. Biomedical engineers typically deal with and solve problems in complex biological systems.

Advancement

Biomedical engineers typically receive greater responsibility through experience and more education. To lead a research team, a biomedical engineer generally needs a graduate degree. Biomedical engineers who are interested in basic research may become medical scientists.

Some biomedical engineers attend medical or dental school to specialize in various techniques or topical areas, such as using electric impulses in new ways to get muscles moving again. Some earn law degrees and work as patent attorneys.

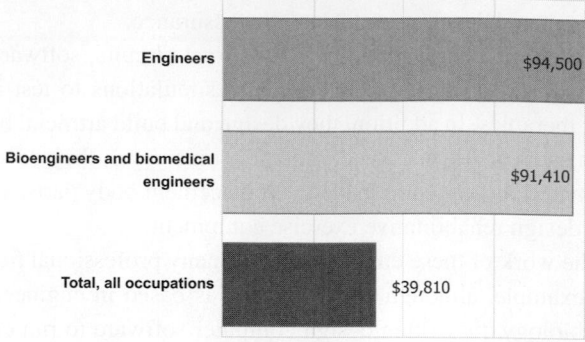

Biomedical Engineers
Median annual wages, May 2019

Engineers	$94,500
Bioengineers and biomedical engineers	$91,410
Total, all occupations	$39,810

Note: All Occupations includes all occupations in the U.S. Economy.
Source: U.S. Bureau of Labor Statistics, Occupational Employment Statistics.

Others pursue a master's degree in business administration (MBA) and move into managerial positions. For more information, see the profiles on lawyers and architectural and engineering managers.

Pay

The median annual wage for biomedical engineers was $91,410 in May 2019. The median wage is the wage at which half the workers in an occupation earned more than that amount and half earned less. The lowest 10 percent earned less than $55,280, and the highest 10 percent earned more than $148,210.

In May 2019, the median annual wages for biomedical engineers in the top industries in which they worked were as follows:

Navigational, measuring, electromedical, and control instruments manufacturing	$105,720
Research and development in the physical, engineering, and life sciences	92,230
Medical equipment and supplies manufacturing	89,400
Healthcare and social assistance	77,520
Colleges, universities, and professional schools; state, local, and private	73,300

Biomedical engineers usually work full time on a normal schedule. However, as with employees in almost any engineering occupation, biomedical engineers occasionally may have to work additional hours to meet the needs of patients, managers, colleagues, and clients. Some biomedical engineers work more than 40 hours per week.

Job Outlook

Employment of biomedical engineers is projected to grow 5 percent from 2019 to 2029, faster than the average for all occupations.

Biomedical engineers likely will see employment growth because of increasing possibilities brought by new technologies and increasing applications to medical equipment and devices.

Biomedical Engineers
Percent change in employment, projected 2019-29

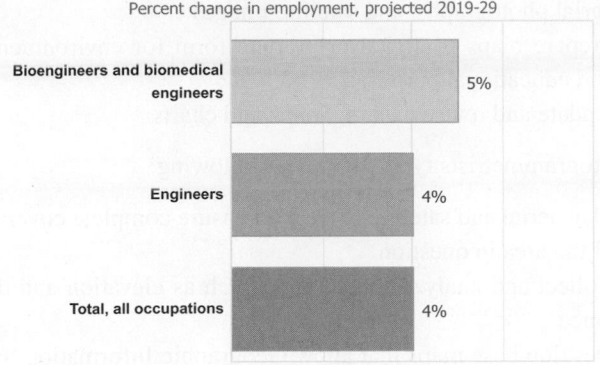

Bioengineers and biomedical engineers — 5%

Engineers — 4%

Total, all occupations — 4%

Note: All Occupations includes all occupations in the U.S. Economy.
Source: U.S. Bureau of Labor Statistics, Employment Projections program.

Smartphone technology and three-dimensional printing are examples of technology being applied to biomedical advances.

As the aging baby-boom generation lives longer and stays active, the demand for biomedical devices and procedures, such as hip and knee replacements, is expected to increase. In addition, as the public continues to become more aware of medical advances, increasing numbers of people will seek biomedical solutions to their health problems from their physicians.

Biomedical engineers work with scientists, other medical researchers, and manufacturers to address a wide range of injuries and physical disabilities. Their ability to work in different activities with workers from other fields is enlarging the range of applications for biomedical engineering products and services.

Employment projections data for biomedical engineers, 2019-29					
Occupational Title	SOC Code	Employment, 2019	Projected Employment, 2029	Change, 2019-29 Percent	Numeric
SOURCE: U.S. Bureau of Labor Statistics, Employment Projections program					
Bioengineers and biomedical engineers	17-2031	21,200	22,200	5	1,000

State & Area Data
Occupational Employment Statistics (OES)
The Occupational Employment Statistics (OES) program produces employment and wage estimates annually for over 800 occupations. These estimates are available for the nation as a whole, for individual states, and for metropolitan and nonmetropolitan areas.

Contacts for More Information
For information about general engineering education and biomedical engineering career resources, visit
➤ American Institute for Medical and Biological Engineering
➤ American Society for Engineering Education
➤ Biomedical Engineering Society
➤ IEEE Engineering in Medicine and Biology Society
➤ Technology Student Association

For information about accredited engineering programs, visit
➤ ABET

Cartographers and Photogrammetrists

Summary

Quick Facts: Cartographers and Photogrammetrists

2019 Median Pay	$65,470 per year $31.47 per hour
Typical Entry-Level Education	Bachelor's degree
Work Experience in a Related Occupation	None
On-the-job Training	None
Number of Jobs, 2019	12,000
Job Outlook, 2019-29	4% (As fast as average)
Employment Change, 2019-29	500

What Cartographers and Photogrammetrists Do
Cartographers and photogrammetrists collect, measure, and interpret geographic information in order to create and update maps and charts for regional planning, education, and other purposes.

Work Environment
Although cartographers and photogrammetrists spend much of their time in offices, certain jobs require extensive travel to locations that are being mapped.

How to Become a Cartographer or Photogrammetrist
Most cartographers and photogrammetrists need a bachelor's degree in cartography, geography, geomatics, or surveying.

Pay
The median annual wage for cartographers and photogrammetrists was $65,470 in May 2019.

Cartographers and photogrammetrists measure, map, and chart the earth's surface.

Job Outlook

Employment of cartographers and photogrammetrists is projected to grow 4 percent from 2019 to 2029, about as fast as the average for all occupations. Job prospects are likely to be excellent due to the increasing use of maps in government planning.

State & Area Data

Explore resources for employment and wages by state and area for cartographers and photogrammetrists.

What Cartographers and Photogrammetrists Do

Cartographers and photogrammetrists collect, measure, and interpret geographic information in order to create and update maps and charts for regional planning, education, and other purposes.

Duties

Cartographers typically do the following:

- Collect geographic data
- Create visual representations of data, such as annual precipitation patterns

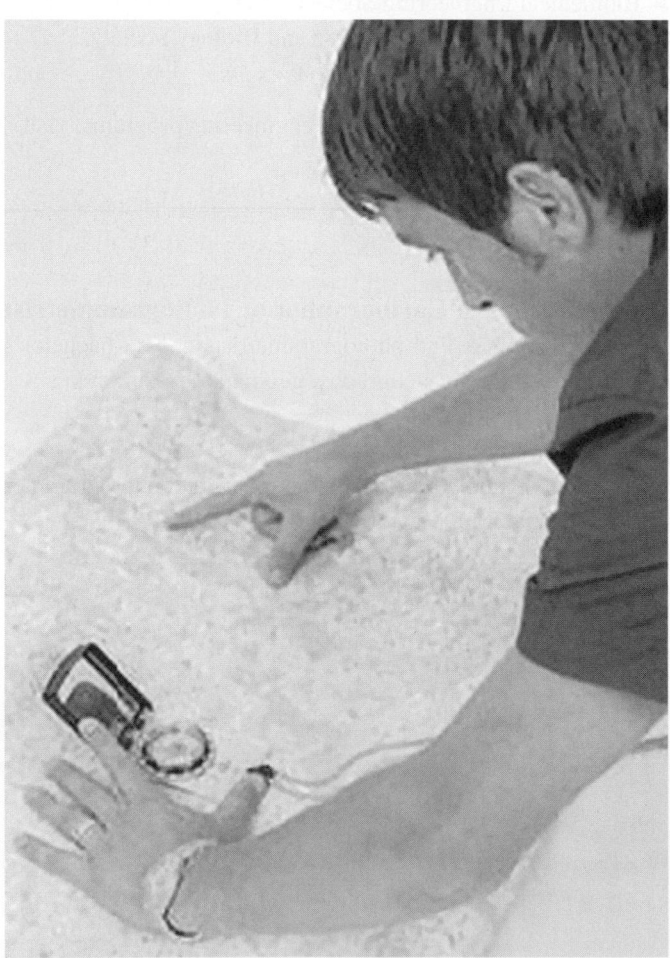

Cartographers and photogrammetrists typically collect and verify data used in creating maps.

- Examine and compile data from ground surveys, reports, aerial photographs, and satellite images
- Prepare maps in digital or graphic form for environmental and educational purposes
- Update and revise existing maps and charts

Photogrammetrists typically do the following:

- Plan aerial and satellite surveys to ensure complete coverage of the area in question
- Collect and analyze spatial data, such as elevation and distance
- Develop base maps that allow Geographic Information System (GIS) data to be layered on top

Cartographers are mapmakers who design user-friendly maps. Photogrammetrists are specialized mapmakers who use various technologies to build models of the Earth's surface and its features for the purpose of creating maps.

Cartographers and photogrammetrists use information from geodetic surveys (land surveys that account for the curvature of the Earth's surface) and remote-sensing systems, including aerial cameras and satellites. Some also use light-imaging detection and ranging (LIDAR) technology. LIDAR systems use lasers attached to planes or cars to digitally map the topography of the Earth. Because LIDAR is often more accurate than traditional surveying methods, it can also be used to collect other forms of data, such as the location and density of forests.

Cartographers and photogrammetrists often develop online and mobile maps. Interactive maps are popular, and cartographers and photogrammetrists collect data and design these maps for mobile phones and navigation systems.

Cartographers and photogrammetrists also create maps and perform aerial surveys for governments, to aid in urban and regional planning. Such maps may include information on population density and demographic characteristics. Some cartographers and photogrammetrists help build maps for government agencies for work involving national security and public safety. Accurate maps help emergency responders provide assistance as quickly as possible.

Cartographers and photogrammetrists who use GIS technology to create maps are often known as *geographic information specialists.* GIS technology is typically used to assemble, integrate, analyze, and present spatial information in a digital format. Maps created with GIS technology combine spatial graphic features with data. These maps are used to provide support for decisions involving environmental studies, geology, engineering, land-use planning, and business marketing.

Work Environment

Cartographers and photogrammetrists held about 12,000 jobs in 2019. The largest employers of cartographers and photogrammetrists were as follows:

Cartographers may travel to the physical locations that they are mapping to better understand the topography of the region.

Local government, excluding education and hospitals......	34%
Architectural, engineering, and related services	24
State government, excluding education and hospitals...	6
Federal government..	5
Management, scientific, and technical consulting services	4

Although cartographers and photogrammetrists spend much of their time in offices, certain jobs require extensive fieldwork to collect data and verify results. For example, cartographers may travel to the physical locations they are mapping to better understand the topography of the region. Similarly, photogrammetrists may conduct fieldwork to plan for aerial surveys and to validate interpretations.

Work Schedules

Most cartographers and photogrammetrists work full time. They may have longer workdays during fieldwork.

How to Become a Cartographer or Photogrammetrist

Most cartographers and photogrammetrists need a bachelor's degree in cartography, geography, geomatics, or surveying. Some states require cartographers and photogrammetrists to be licensed as surveyors, and some states have specific licenses for photogrammetrists.

Education

Cartographers and photogrammetrists usually have a bachelor's degree in cartography, geography, geomatics, or surveying. (Geomatics combines the science, engineering, math, and art of collecting and managing geographically referenced information.) Although it is not as common, some have a bachelor's degree in engineering, forestry, or computer science.

The growing use of Geographic Information System (GIS) technology has resulted in cartographers and photogrammetrists requiring more courses in computer programming, engineering, math, GIS technology, surveying, and geography.

Cartographers must also be familiar with Web-based mapping technologies, including newer modes of compiling data that incorporate the positioning capabilities of mobile phones and in-car navigation systems.

Photogrammetrists must be familiar with remote sensing, image processing, and light-imaging detection and ranging (LIDAR) technology, and they must be knowledgeable about using the software that is necessary with these tools.

Many aspiring cartographers and photogrammetrists benefit from internships while in school.

Cartographers and photogrammetrists usually learn to create maps through degrees in cartography, geography, geomatics, or surveying.

Licenses, Certifications, and Registrations

Licensing requirements for cartographers and photogramme-trists vary by state. Some states require cartographers and photogrammetrists to be licensed as surveyors, and some states have specific licenses for photogrammetry and remote sensing. Although licensing requirements vary by state, candidates must meet educational requirements and pass a test.

Cartographers and photogrammetrists may also receive cer-tification from the American Society for Photogrammetry and Remote Sensing (ASPRS). The United States Geospatial Intel-ligence Foundation offers certifications for GIS professionals. Candidates must meet experience and education requirements and must pass an exam. Although certifications are not required, they can demonstrate competence and may help candidates get a job.

Important Qualities

Computer skills. Both cartographers and photogrammetrists must have experience working with computer data and coding. Maps are created digitally, so knowing how to edit them on a computer is essential.

Critical-thinking skills. Cartographers may work from exist-ing maps, surveys, and other records, and they must be able to determine the accuracy of each feature being mapped.

Decisionmaking skills. Both cartographers and photogram-metrists must make decisions about the accuracy and readabil-ity of a map. They must decide what information they require in order to meet the client's needs.

Detail oriented. Cartographers must focus on details when conceiving a map and deciding what features to include. Photo-grammetrists must pay close attention to detail when interpret-ing aerial photographs and remotely sensed data.

Problem-solving skills. Cartographers and photogramme-trists must be able to reconcile differences between aerial pho-tographs, land surveys, and satellite images.

Pay

The median annual wage for cartographers and photogrammetrists was $65,470 in May 2019. The median wage is the wage at which half the workers in an occupation earned more than that amount and half earned less. The lowest 10 percent earned less than $41,670, and the highest 10 percent earned more than $103,380.

In May 2019, the median annual wages for cartographers and photogrammetrists in the top industries in which they worked were as follows:

Federal government	$90,800
Management, scientific, and technical consulting services	64,910
Local government, excluding education and hospitals	64,780
Architectural, engineering, and related services	62,280
State government, excluding education and hospitals	58,680

Most cartographers and photogrammetrists work full time. They may have longer workdays during fieldwork.

Job Outlook

Employment of cartographers and photogrammetrists is pro-jected to grow 4 percent from 2019 to 2029, about as fast as the average for all occupations.

The use of maps for government planning should lead to some employment growth. Cartographers and photogrammetrists also will be needed to map and locate areas that require help during nat-ural disasters, often using Geographic Information Systems (GIS). However, GIS-related technology increases these workers' produc-tivity, which may reduce employment growth in this occupation.

Job Prospects

Job prospects are likely to be excellent due to the increasing use of maps in government planning.

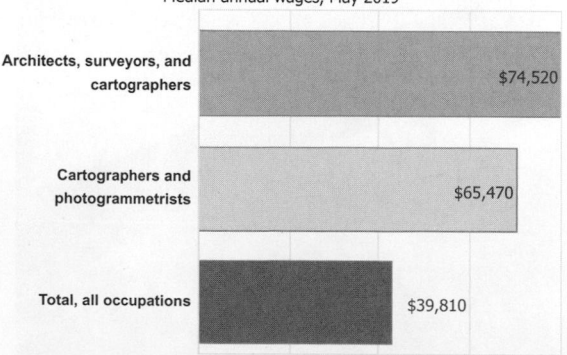

Cartographers and Photogrammetrists
Median annual wages, May 2019

- Architects, surveyors, and cartographers — $74,520
- Cartographers and photogrammetrists — $65,470
- Total, all occupations — $39,810

Note: All Occupations includes all occupations in the U.S. Economy.
Source: U.S. Bureau of Labor Statistics, Occupational Employment Statistics.

Cartographers and Photogrammetrists
Percent change in employment, projected 2019-29

- Cartographers and photogrammetrists — 4%
- Total, all occupations — 4%
- Architects, surveyors, and cartographers — 1%

Note: All Occupations includes all occupations in the U.S. Economy.
Source: U.S. Bureau of Labor Statistics, Employment Projections program.

Employment projections data for cartographers and photogrammetrists, 2019-29					
Occupational Title	SOC Code	Employment, 2019	Projected Employment, 2029	Change, 2019-29	
				Percent	Numeric
SOURCE: U.S. Bureau of Labor Statistics, Employment Projections program					
Cartographers and photogrammetrists	17-1021	12,000	12,500	4	500

State & Area Data
Occupational Employment Statistics (OES)
The Occupational Employment Statistics (OES) program produces employment and wage estimates annually for over 800 occupations. These estimates are available for the nation as a whole, for individual states, and for metropolitan and nonmetropolitan areas.

Contacts for More Information
For more information about cartographers and photogrammetrists, visit

➤ Cartography and Geographic Information Society

For more information about photogrammetrists, photogrammetric technicians, remote-sensing scientists, image-based cartographers, or GIS specialists' careers, visit
➤ American Society for Photogrammetry and Remote Sensing

For information about careers in remote sensing, photogrammetry, surveying, GIS analysis, and other geography-related disciplines, visit
➤ Association of American Geographers

For information related to GIS certification, visit
➤ United States Geospatial Intelligence Foundation

Chemical Engineers

Summary

Quick Facts: Chemical Engineers

2019 Median Pay	$108,770 per year $52.30 per hour
Typical Entry-Level Education	Bachelor's degree
Work Experience in a Related Occupation	None
On-the-job Training	None
Number of Jobs, 2019	32,600
Job Outlook, 2019-29	4% (As fast as average)
Employment Change, 2019-29	1,400

Chemical engineers apply the principles of chemistry, biology, physics, and math to solve problems involving the production of chemicals, fuel, drugs, food, and many other products.

What Chemical Engineers Do
Chemical engineers apply the principles of chemistry, biology, physics, and math to solve problems that involve the use of fuel, drugs, food, and many other products.

Work Environment
Chemical engineers work mostly in offices or laboratories. They may spend time at industrial plants, refineries, and other locations, where they monitor or direct operations or solve onsite problems. Nearly all chemical engineers work full time.

How to Become a Chemical Engineer
Chemical engineers must have a bachelor's degree in chemical engineering or a related field. Employers also value practical experience. Therefore, internships and cooperative engineering programs can be helpful.

Pay
The median annual wage for chemical engineers was $108,770 in May 2019.

Job Outlook
Employment of chemical engineers is projected to grow 4 percent from 2019 to 2029, about as fast as the average for all occupations. Demand for chemical engineers' services depends largely on demand for the products of various manufacturing industries.

State & Area Data
Explore resources for employment and wages by state and area for chemical engineers.

What Chemical Engineers Do
Chemical engineers apply the principles of chemistry, biology, physics, and math to solve problems that involve the production or use of chemicals, fuel, drugs, food, and many other products. They design processes and equipment for large-scale manufacturing, plan and test production methods and byproducts treatment, and direct facility operations.

Chemical engineers develop and design chemical manufacturing processes.

Chemical engineers generally work in offices or laboratory settings, although sometimes they must work in an industrial setting to oversee production.

Duties

Chemical engineers typically do the following:

- Conduct research to develop new and improved manufacturing processes
- Establish safety procedures for those working with dangerous chemicals
- Develop processes for separating components of liquids and gases, or for generating electrical currents, by using controlled chemical processes
- Design and plan the layout of equipment
- Conduct tests and monitor the performance of processes throughout production
- Troubleshoot problems with manufacturing processes
- Evaluate equipment and processes to ensure compliance with safety and environmental regulations
- Estimate production costs for management

Some chemical engineers, known as *process engineers*, specialize in a particular process, such as oxidation (a reaction of oxygen with chemicals to make other chemicals) or polymerization (making plastics and resins).

Others specialize in a particular field, such as nanomaterials (extremely small substances) or biological engineering. Still others specialize in developing specific products.

In addition, chemical engineers work in the production of energy, electronics, food, clothing, and paper. They must understand how the manufacturing process affects the environment and the safety of workers and consumers.

Chemical engineers also conduct research in the life sciences, biotechnology, and business services.

Work Environment

Chemical engineers held about 32,600 jobs in 2019. The largest employers of chemical engineers were as follows:

Research and development in the physical,
  engineering, and life sciences 10%

Engineering services 9
Petroleum and coal products manufacturing 5
Wholesale trade 4
Pharmaceutical and medicine manufacturing 3

Chemical engineers work mostly in offices or laboratories. They may spend time at industrial plants, refineries, and other locations, where they monitor or direct operations or solve onsite problems. Chemical engineers must be able to work with those who design other systems and with the technicians and mechanics who put the designs into practice.

Some engineers travel extensively to plants or worksites, both domestically and abroad.

Injuries and Illnesses

Chemical engineers can be exposed to health or safety hazards when handling certain chemicals and plant equipment, but such exposure can be avoided if proper procedures are followed.

Work Schedules

Nearly all chemical engineers work full time. Occasionally, they may have to work additional hours to meet production targets and design standards or to troubleshoot problems with manufacturing processes. Some chemical engineers work more than 40 hours per week.

How to Become a Chemical Engineer

Chemical engineers must have a bachelor's degree in chemical engineering or a related field. Employers also value practical experience, so internships and cooperative engineering programs, in which students earn college credit and experience, can be helpful.

Education

Chemical engineers must have a bachelor's degree in chemical engineering or a related field. Programs in chemical engineering

Becoming a chemical engineer requires a bachelor's degree in chemical engineering or a related field.

usually take 4 years to complete and include classroom, laboratory, and field studies. High school students interested in studying chemical engineering will benefit from taking science courses, such as chemistry, physics, and biology. They also should take math courses, including algebra, trigonometry, and calculus.

At some universities, students can opt to enroll in 5-year engineering programs that lead to both a bachelor's degree and a master's degree. A graduate degree, which may include a degree up to the Ph.D. level, allows an engineer to work in research and development or as a postsecondary teacher.

Some colleges and universities offer internships and/or cooperative programs in partnership with industry. In these programs, students gain practical experience while completing their education.

ABET accredits engineering programs. ABET-accredited programs in chemical engineering include courses in chemistry, physics, and biology. These programs also include applying the sciences to the design, analysis, and control of chemical, physical, and biological processes.

Important Qualities

Analytical skills. Chemical engineers must troubleshoot designs that do not work as planned. They must ask the right questions and then find answers that work.

Creativity. Chemical engineers must explore new ways of applying engineering principles. They work to invent new materials, advanced manufacturing techniques, and new applications in chemical and biomedical engineering.

Ingenuity. Chemical engineers learn the broad concepts of chemical engineering, but their work requires them to apply those concepts to specific production problems.

Interpersonal skills. Because their role is to put scientific principles into practice in manufacturing industries, chemical engineers must develop good working relationships with other workers involved in production processes.

Math skills. Chemical engineers use the principles of advanced math topics such as calculus for analysis, design, and troubleshooting in their work.

Problem-solving skills. In designing equipment and processes for manufacturing, these engineers must be able to anticipate and identify problems, including such issues as workers' safety and problems related to manufacturing and environmental protection.

Licenses, Certifications, and Registrations

Licensure for chemical engineers is not as common as it is for other engineering occupations, nor is it required for entry-level positions. A Professional Engineering (PE) license, which allows for higher levels of leadership and independence, can be acquired later in one's career. Licensed engineers are called professional engineers (PEs). A PE can oversee the work of other engineers, sign off on projects, and provide services directly to the public. State licensure generally requires

- A degree from an ABET-accredited engineering program
- A passing score on the Fundamentals of Engineering (FE) exam
- Relevant work experience, typically at least 4 years
- A passing score on the Professional Engineering (PE) exam

The initial FE exam can be taken after one earns a bachelor's degree. Engineers who pass this exam are commonly called engineers in training (EITs) or engineer interns (EIs). After meeting work experience requirements, EITs and EIs can take the second exam, called the Principles and Practice of Engineering (PE).

Each state issues its own licenses. Most states recognize licensure from other states, as long as the licensing state's requirements meet or exceed their own licensure requirements. Several states require engineers to take continuing education to keep their licenses.

Other Experience

During high school, students can attend engineering summer camps to see what these and other engineers do. Attending these camps can help students plan their coursework for the remainder of their time in high school.

Advancement

Entry-level engineers usually work under the supervision of experienced engineers. In large companies, new engineers also may receive formal training in classrooms or seminars. As junior engineers gain knowledge and experience, they move to more difficult projects with greater independence to develop designs, solve problems, and make decisions.

Eventually, chemical engineers may advance to supervise a team of engineers and technicians. Some may become architectural and engineering managers. Preparing for management positions usually requires working under the guidance of a more experienced chemical engineer.

An engineering background enables chemical engineers to discuss a product's technical aspects and assist in product planning and use. For more information, see the profile on sales engineers.

Pay

The median annual wage for chemical engineers was $108,770 in May 2019. The median wage is the wage at which half the workers in an occupation earned more than that amount and half earned less. The lowest 10 percent earned less than $66,810, and the highest 10 percent earned more than $176,090.

In May 2019, the median annual wages for chemical engineers in the top industries in which they worked were as follows:

Petroleum and coal products manufacturing	$119,010
Research and development in the physical, engineering, and life sciences	116,250
Engineering services	112,990
Wholesale trade	100,510
Pharmaceutical and medicine manufacturing	98,160

A 2015 survey report by the American Institute of Chemical Engineers indicated that the median yearly salary of those with no supervisory responsibility was $106,300.

Nearly all chemical engineers work full time. Occasionally, they may have to work additional hours to meet production targets and design standards or to troubleshoot problems with manufacturing processes. Some chemical engineers work more than 40 hours per week.

Job Outlook

Employment of chemical engineers is projected to grow 4 percent from 2019 to 2029, about as fast as the average for all occupations. Demand for chemical engineers' services depends

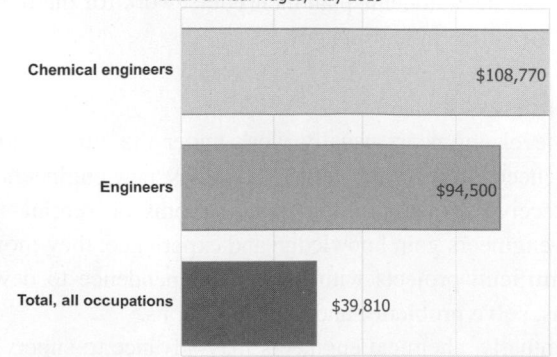

Chemical Engineers
Median annual wages, May 2019

Chemical engineers $108,770
Engineers $94,500
Total, all occupations $39,810

Note: All Occupations includes all occupations in the U.S. Economy. Source: U.S. Bureau of Labor Statistics, Occupational Employment Statistics.

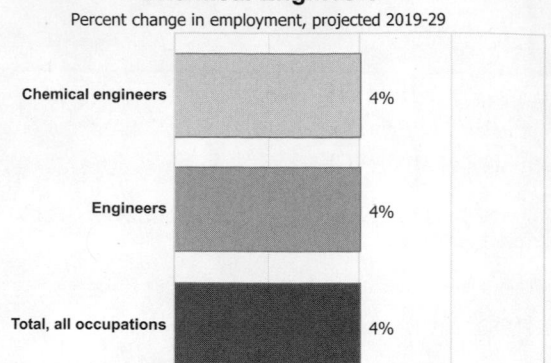

Chemical Engineers
Percent change in employment, projected 2019-29

Chemical engineers   4%
Engineers   4%
Total, all occupations   4%

Note: All Occupations includes all occupations in the U.S. Economy. Source: U.S. Bureau of Labor Statistics, Employment Projections program.

largely on demand for the products of various manufacturing industries. The ability of these engineers to stay on the forefront of new emerging technologies will sustain employment growth.

Many chemical engineers work in industries whose products are sought by many manufacturing firms. For instance, they work for firms that manufacture plastic resins, which are used to increase fuel efficiency in automobiles. Increased availability of domestically produced natural gas should increase manufacturing potential in the industries employing these engineers.

In addition, chemical engineering will continue to migrate into dynamic fields, such as nanotechnology, alternative energies, and biotechnology, and thereby help to sustain demand for engineering services in many manufacturing industries.

However, overall growth of employment will be tempered by declines in employment in some manufacturing sectors.

Job Prospects

The need to find alternative fuels to meet increasing energy demand while maintaining environmental sustainability will continue to require the expertise of chemical engineers in oil- and gas-related industries. In addition, the integration of chemical and biological sciences and rapid advances in innovation will create new areas in biotechnology and in medical and pharmaceutical fields for them to work in. Thus, those with a background in biology will have better chances to gain employment.

Employment projections data for chemical engineers, 2019-29					
Occupational Title	SOC Code	Employment, 2019	Projected Employment, 2029	Change, 2019-29	
				Percent	Numeric
SOURCE: U.S. Bureau of Labor Statistics, Employment Projections program					
Chemical engineers	17-2041	32,600	34,000	4	1,400

State & Area Data
Occupational Employment Statistics (OES)

The Occupational Employment Statistics (OES) program produces employment and wage estimates annually for over 800 occupations. These estimates are available for the nation as a whole, for individual states, and for metropolitan and nonmetropolitan areas.

Contacts for More Information

For more information on becoming a chemical engineer, visit
➤ American Institute of Chemical Engineers

For information about general engineering education and career resources, visit
➤ American Society for Engineering Education
➤ Technology Student Association

For information about accredited engineering programs, visit
➤ ABET

For information on internships opportunities, visit
➤ American Institute of Chemical Engineers Career Center

For more information about licensure as a professional engineer, visit
➤ National Council of Examiners for Engineering and Surveying
➤ National Society of Professional Engineers

Civil Engineering Technicians

Summary

Quick Facts: Civil Engineering Technicians

2019 Median Pay	$53,410 per year $25.68 per hour
Typical Entry-Level Education	Associate's degree
Work Experience in a Related Occupation	None
On-the-job Training	None
Number of Jobs, 2019	70,900
Job Outlook, 2019-29	3% (As fast as average)
Employment Change, 2019-29	1,800

What Civil Engineering Technicians Do

Civil engineering technicians help civil engineers to plan, design, and build highways, bridges, and other infrastructure projects for commercial, industrial, residential, and land development projects.

Work Environment

Civil engineering technicians work in offices, where they help civil engineers plan and design projects. Civil engineering technicians also visit jobsites where a construction project is taking place, to collect or test materials or observe the project and act as a project inspector.

How to Become a Civil Engineering Technician

Although not always required, an associate's degree in civil engineering technology is preferred for employment as a civil engineering technician.

Pay

The median annual wage for civil engineering technicians was $53,410 in May 2019.

Job Outlook

Employment of civil engineering technicians is projected to grow 3 percent from 2019 to 2029, about as fast as the average

Civil engineering technicians help with residential development, and work under civil engineers.

for all occupations. The need to preserve, repair, upgrade, and enhance an aging infrastructure will sustain demand for these workers.

State & Area Data

Explore resources for employment and wages by state and area for civil engineering technicians.

What Civil Engineering Technicians Do

Civil engineering technicians help civil engineers to plan, design, and build highways, bridges, utilities, and other infrastructure projects. They also help to plan, design, and build commercial, industrial, residential, and land development projects.

Duties

Civil engineering technicians typically do the following:

- Read and review project drawings and plans to determine the sizes of structures
- Confer with engineers about preparing plans
- Use computer aided design software under the charge of engineers
- Evaluate preconstruction field conditions

Civil engineering technicians confer with project supervisors to determine details of a project.

- Observe project sites and evaluate contractors' work to detect problems with a design
- Test construction materials and soil samples in laboratories
- Help to ensure that project construction conforms to design specifications and applicable codes
- Develop plans and estimate costs for constructing systems and operating facilities
- Prepare reports and document project activities and data
- Set up and help maintain project files and records

Civil engineering technicians typically work under the charge of licensed civil engineers. These technicians generally help civil engineers by observing progress on a jobsite, collecting data, and completing routine reports to document project activities. Because they are not licensed, civil engineering technicians cannot approve designs or supervise the overall project.

Civil engineering technicians assume varied duties on the job. They sometimes estimate construction costs and develop specifications. Other times, they prepare drawings or survey land. They also may set up and monitor various instruments for traffic studies. These technicians' duties often require familiarity with and use of various computer programs to design projects, collect and analyze data, prepare correspondence and reports, and manage file systems.

Civil engineering technicians work on-site to help civil engineers in implementing project plans correctly.

Work Environment

Civil engineering technicians held about 70,900 jobs in 2019. The largest employers of civil engineering technicians were as follows:

Engineering services 44%
State government, excluding education and hospitals 26
Local government, excluding education and hospitals ... 17
Construction 3

Civil engineering technicians work in offices, where they help civil engineers plan and design projects. Civil engineering technicians also visit jobsites where a construction project is taking place, to collect or test materials or observe the project and act as a project inspector.

When civil engineering technicians visit the jobsite where a construction project is taking place, they may test materials, assist in surveying, or perform field observations in order to help ensure that the designs approved by licensed civil engineers are being built correctly and in a timely manner. Civil engineering technicians may work at several sites, using cars or trucks as a mobile office.

Civil engineering technicians frequently work in teams with civil engineers, surveyors and surveying technicians, construction workers, and others involved with projects.

Work Schedules

Civil engineering technicians usually work full time. When civil engineering technicians work at construction sites, their schedules may be subject to factors that affect construction, such as bad weather. In addition, their schedules vary with the length and completion of construction projects. Those who work mostly in laboratories to test construction materials have more stable work schedules, but may still experience schedule variations related to construction.

How to Become a Civil Engineering Technician

Although not always required, an associate's degree in civil engineering technology is preferred for employment as a civil engineering technician.

Education

To prepare for programs in engineering technology after high school, prospective civil engineering technicians should take science and math courses, such as chemistry, physics, geometry, and trigonometry. They should also have basic knowledge of the use of computers.

Employers generally prefer engineering technicians to have an associate's degree from a program accredited by ABET, although a degree is not always required. Engineering technology programs are also available at technical or vocational schools that award a postgraduate certificate or diploma.

Courses at technical or vocational schools may include engineering, design, and computer software. To complete an associate's degree in civil engineering technology, students also usually need to take other courses in liberal arts and the sciences.

Important Qualities

Critical-thinking skills. As assistants to civil engineers, civil engineering technicians must be able to help the engineers

Civil engineering technicians prepare reports and document project activities and data.

identify and solve problems; to develop infrastructure plans; and to help agencies avoid wasting time, effort, and funds.

Decisionmaking skills. Pressure from deadlines means that technicians must be able to quickly discern which types of information are most important for the work at hand, and which plan of action will help keep the project on schedule.

Math skills. Civil engineering technicians use math for analysis, design, and troubleshooting in their work. For this reason, they need to be familiar with algebra, geometry, and trigonometry.

Observational skills. Civil engineering technicians sometimes have to go to jobsites and assess a project for the engineer. Therefore, they must know what to look for and how best to report back to the engineer who is overseeing the project.

Problem-solving skills. Like civil engineers, civil engineering technicians help design projects to solve a particular problem. Technicians must be able to understand and work with all the related systems involved in building a project.

Reading skills. Civil engineering technicians carry out plans and designs for projects that a civil engineer has approved. Thus, they must be able to understand all the reports, plans, and documents describing these designs.

Writing skills. Civil engineering technicians often are asked to relay their findings in writing. They must be able to write reports that are well organized and clearly written.

Other Experience

Another path for prospective civil engineering technicians is to enter the occupation after gaining work experience in a related occupation, particularly as a drafter or a computer aided design (CAD) operator. A worker who begins as a drafter or CAD operator for an engineering firm may advance to a civil engineering technician position as his or her knowledge of design and construction increases.

Licenses, Certifications, and Registrations

Certification is not needed to enter this occupation, but it can help technicians advance their careers. The National Institute for Certification in Engineering Technologies (NICET) is one of the primary organizations overseeing certification for civil engineering technicians.

Certification as a technician requires passing an exam and providing documentation, including a work history, recommendations, and for most programs, supervisor confirmation of specific experience. NICET requires technicians to update their skills and knowledge through a recertification process that encourages continuing professional development.

Advancement

Civil engineering technicians can advance in their careers by learning to design systems for a variety of projects, such as storm sewers and sanitary systems, or traffic signal systems. It is also useful for civil engineering technicians to become skilled at reading plans and profiles—the graphical depiction of proposed projects.

Civil engineering technicians can also benefit from increasing their knowledge of computer systems and applications; in particular, familiarity with word processing and spreadsheet programs, as well as geographic information systems (GIS) and global positioning systems (GPS).

Pay

The median annual wage for civil engineering technicians was $53,410 in May 2019. The median wage is the wage at which half the workers in an occupation earned more than that amount and half earned less. The lowest 10 percent earned less than $33,880, and the highest 10 percent earned more than $80,650.

In May 2019, the median annual wages for civil engineering technicians in the top industries in which they worked were as follows:

Local government, excluding education and hospitals	$60,510
Construction	55,420
Engineering services	54,430
State government, excluding education and hospitals	45,440

Civil engineering technicians usually work full time. When civil engineering technicians work at construction sites, their schedules may be subject to factors that affect construction, such as bad weather. In addition, schedules vary with the length and completion of construction projects. Those who work mostly in laboratories to test construction materials have more stable work schedules.

Job Outlook

Employment of civil engineering technicians is projected to grow 3 percent from 2019 to 2029, about as fast as the average for all occupations.

The need to preserve, repair, upgrade, and enhance the country's infrastructure continues to increase. Bridges, roads, levees, airports, and dams will need to be rebuilt, maintained, and upgraded. Also, a growing population means that water systems must be maintained in order to reduce or eliminate loss of drinkable water. In addition, more waste treatment plants will be needed to help clean the nation's waterways. Civil engineers must plan, design, and oversee this work, and civil engineering technicians will be needed to assist the engineers in these projects.

Civil engineering technicians also will find work assisting civil engineers with renewable-energy projects. For wind energy projects, these engineering technicians may assist in the development of a wind farm by helping engineers devise solutions to minimize project costs while accommodating for the unique dimensions and weight of wind turbines. For installation of solar power infrastructure, these engineering technicians make sure that civil engineers' designs for foundations to hold up solar arrays are implemented correctly.

Job Prospects

Prospective civil engineering technicians may face strong competition for job openings. Civil engineering technicians learn to use design software that civil engineers might not have learned in their college curriculum. Thus, those civil engineering technicians who master that software, keep their skills current, and stay abreast of new software will improve their chances of finding employment.

Employment projections data for civil engineering technicians, 2019-29					
Occupational Title	SOC Code	Employment, 2019	Projected Employment, 2029	Change, 2019-29	
				Percent	Numeric
SOURCE: U.S. Bureau of Labor Statistics, Employment Projections program					
Civil engineering technologists and technicians	17-3022	70,900	72,700	3	1,800

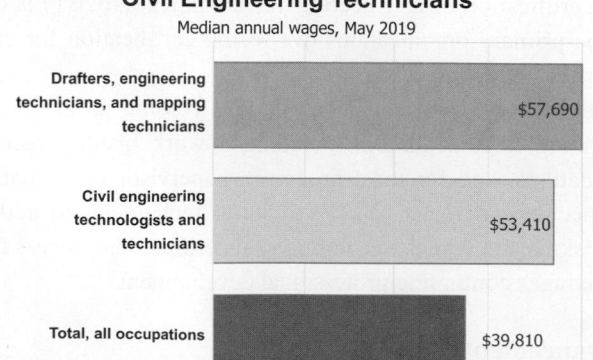

Civil Engineering Technicians

Median annual wages, May 2019

- Drafters, engineering technicians, and mapping technicians — $57,690
- Civil engineering technologists and technicians — $53,410
- Total, all occupations — $39,810

Note: All Occupations includes all occupations in the U.S. Economy.
Source: U.S. Bureau of Labor Statistics, Occupational Employment Statistics.

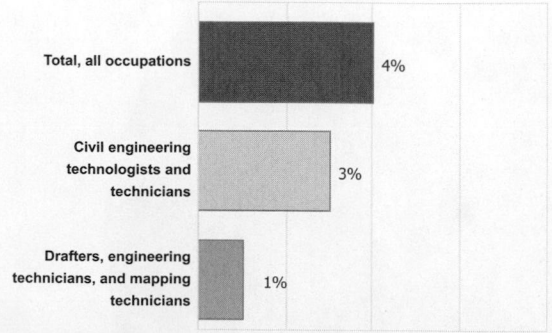

Civil Engineering Technicians

Percent change in employment, projected 2019-29

- Total, all occupations — 4%
- Civil engineering technologists and technicians — 3%
- Drafters, engineering technicians, and mapping technicians — 1%

Note: All Occupations includes all occupations in the U.S. Economy.
Source: U.S. Bureau of Labor Statistics, Employment Projections program.

State & Area Data
Occupational Employment Statistics (OES)

The Occupational Employment Statistics (OES) program produces employment and wage estimates annually for over 800 occupations. These estimates are available for the nation as a whole, for individual states, and for metropolitan and nonmetropolitan areas.

Contacts for More Information

For more information about summer apprenticeships in civil engineering, visit

➤ Pathways to Science

For more information about accredited programs, visit
➤ ABET

For more information about certification, visit
➤ American Society of Certified Engineering Technicians
➤ National Institute for Certification in Engineering Technologies (NICET)

Civil Engineers

Summary

Quick Facts: Civil Engineers

2019 Median Pay	$87,060 per year $41.86 per hour
Typical Entry-Level Education	Bachelor's degree
Work Experience in a Related Occupation	None
On-the-job Training	None
Number of Jobs, 2019	329,200
Job Outlook, 2019-29	2% (Slower than average)
Employment Change, 2019-29	5,500

What Civil Engineers Do

Civil engineers design, build, and supervise infrastructure projects and systems.

Work Environment

Civil engineers generally work in a variety of locations and conditions. It is common for them to split their time between working in an office and working outdoors at construction sites so that they can monitor operations or solve problems onsite. Most work full time.

Civil engineers provide cost estimates for materials and labor to determine a project's economic feasibility.

How to Become a Civil Engineer

Civil engineers need a bachelor's degree in civil engineering, in one of its specialties, or in civil engineering technology. They typically need a graduate degree and licensure for promotion to senior positions. Although licensure requirements vary by state, civil engineers usually must be licensed if they provide services directly to the public.

Pay

The median annual wage for civil engineers was $87,060 in May 2019.

Job Outlook

Employment of civil engineers is projected to grow 2 percent from 2019 to 2029, slower than the average for all occupations. As infrastructure continues to age, civil engineers will be needed to manage projects to rebuild, repair, and upgrade bridges, roads, levees, dams, airports, buildings, and structures of all types.

State & Area Data

Explore resources for employment and wages by state and area for civil engineers.

What Civil Engineers Do

Civil engineers conceive, design, build, supervise, operate, construct and maintain infrastructure projects and systems in the public and private sector, including roads, buildings, airports, tunnels, dams, bridges, and systems for water supply and sewage treatment. Many civil engineers work in planning, design, construction, research, and education.

Duties

Civil engineers typically do the following:

• Analyze long range plans, survey reports, maps, and other data to plan and design projects
• Consider construction costs, government regulations, potential environmental hazards, and other factors during the planning and risk-analysis stages of a project

Civil engineers design major transportation projects.

- Compile and submit permit applications to local, state, and federal agencies, verifying that projects comply with various regulations
- Oversee and analyze the results of soil testing to determine the adequacy and strength of foundations
- Analyze the results of tests on building materials, such as concrete, wood, asphalt, or steel, for use in particular projects
- Prepare cost estimates for materials, equipment, or labor to determine a project's economic feasibility
- Use design software to plan and design transportation systems, hydraulic systems, and structures in line with industry and government standards
- Perform or oversee surveying operations to establish building locations, site layouts, reference points, grades, and elevations to guide construction
- Manage the repair, maintenance, and replacement of public and private infrastructure

Civil engineers also must present their findings to the public on topics such as bid proposals, environmental impact statements, or property descriptions.

Many civil engineers hold supervisory or administrative positions ranging from supervisor of a construction site to city engineer, public works director, and city manager. As supervisors, they are tasked with ensuring that safe work practices are followed at construction sites.

Other civil engineers work in design, construction, research, and teaching. Civil engineers work with others on projects and may be assisted by civil engineering technicians.

Civil engineers prepare permit documents for work on projects in renewable energy. They verify that the projects will comply with federal, state, and local requirements. These engineers conduct structural analyses for large-scale photovoltaic, or solar energy, projects. They also evaluate the ability of solar array support structures and buildings to tolerate stresses from wind, seismic activity, and other sources. For large-scale wind projects, civil engineers often prepare roadbeds to handle large trucks that haul in the turbines.

Civil engineers work on complex projects, and they can achieve job satisfaction in seeing the project reach completion. They usually specialize in one of several areas.

Construction engineers manage construction projects, ensuring that they are scheduled and built in accordance with plans and specifications. These engineers typically are responsible for the design and safety of temporary structures used during construction. They may also oversee budgetary, time-management, and communications aspects of a project.

Geotechnical engineers work to make sure that foundations for built objects ranging from streets and buildings to runways and dams, are solid. They focus on how structures built by civil engineers, such as buildings and tunnels, interact with the earth (including soil and rock). In addition, they design and plan for slopes, retaining walls, and tunnels.

Structural engineers design and assess major projects, such as buildings, bridges, or dams, to ensure their strength and durability.

Transportation engineers plan, design, operate, and maintain everyday systems, such as streets and highways, but they also plan larger projects, such as airports, ship ports, mass transit systems, and harbors.

The work of civil engineers is closely related to the work of environmental engineers.

Work Environment

Civil engineers held about 329,200 jobs in 2019. The largest employers of civil engineers were as follows:

Engineering services	49%
State government, excluding education and hospitals	12
Local government, excluding education and hospitals	10
Nonresidential building construction	6
Federal government, excluding postal service	3

Civil engineers work in a variety of locations and conditions. When working on designs, civil engineers may spend most of their time indoors in offices. However, construction engineers

Though civil engineers must work in an office setting to produce their plans, they must also spend much time on site to oversee construction.

Civil engineers need a bachelor's degree in civil engineering, one of its specialties, or civil engineering technology.

may spend much of their time outdoors at construction sites monitoring operations or solving onsite problems. Some jobs may require frequent relocation to different areas and offices in jobsite trailers.

Civil engineers who function as project managers may work from cars or trucks as they move from site to site. Many civil engineers work for government agencies in government office buildings or facilities. Occasionally, civil engineers travel abroad to work on large engineering projects in other countries.

Work Schedules

Civil engineers typically work full time and some work more than 40 hours per week. Engineers who direct projects may need to work extra hours to monitor progress on the projects, to ensure that designs meet requirements, and to guarantee that deadlines are met.

How to Become a Civil Engineer

Civil engineers need a bachelor's degree. They typically need a graduate degree and a license for promotion to senior positions. Although licensure requirements vary from state to state, civil engineers usually must be licensed if they provide services directly to the public.

Education

Civil engineers need a bachelor's degree in civil engineering, in one of its specialties, or in civil engineering technology. Programs in civil engineering and civil engineering technology include coursework in math, statistics, engineering mechanics and systems, and fluid dynamics, depending on the specialty. Courses include a mix of traditional classroom learning, work in laboratories, and fieldwork. Programs may include cooperative programs, also known as co-ops, in which students gain work experience while pursuing a degree.

A degree from a program accredited by ABET is needed to earn the professional engineer (PE) license. In many states, a bachelor's degree in civil engineering technology also meets the academic requirement for obtaining a license.

Further education after the bachelor's degree, along with the PE license and previous experience, is helpful in getting a job as a manager. For more information on engineering managers, see the profile on architectural and engineering managers.

Important Qualities

Decisionmaking skills. Civil engineers often balance multiple and frequently conflicting objectives, such as determining the feasibility of plans with regard to financial costs and safety concerns. Urban and regional planners often look to civil engineers for advice on these issues. Civil engineers must be able to make good decisions based on best practices, their own technical knowledge, and their own experience.

Leadership skills. Civil engineers take ultimate responsibility for the projects that they manage or research that they perform. Therefore, they must be able to lead planners, surveyors, construction managers, civil engineering technicians, civil engineering technologists, and others in implementing their project plan.

Math skills. Civil engineers use the principles of calculus, trigonometry, and other advanced topics in mathematics for analysis, design, and troubleshooting in their work.

Organizational skills. Only licensed civil engineers can sign the design documents for infrastructure projects. This requirement makes it imperative that civil engineers be able to monitor and evaluate the work at the jobsite as a project progresses. That way, they can ensure compliance with the design documents. Civil engineers also often manage several projects at the same time, and thus must be able to balance time needs and to effectively allocate resources.

Problem-solving skills. Civil engineers work at the highest level of the planning, design, construction, and operation of multifaceted projects or research. The many variables involved require that they possess the ability to identify and evaluate complex problems. They must be able to then use their skill and training to develop cost-effective, safe, and efficient solutions.

Speaking skills. Civil engineers must present reports and plans to audiences of people with a wide range of backgrounds and technical knowledge. This requires the ability to speak clearly and to converse with people in various settings, and to translate engineering and scientific information into easy-to-understand concepts.

Writing skills. Civil engineers must be able to communicate with others, such as architects, landscape architects, urban and regional planners. They also must be able to explain projects to elected officials and citizens. Civil engineers must be able to write reports that are clear, concise, and understandable to those with little or no technical or scientific background.

Licenses, Certifications, and Registrations

Licensure is not required for entry-level positions as a civil engineer. A Professional Engineering (PE) license, which allows for higher levels of leadership and independence, can be acquired later in one's career. Licensed engineers are called professional engineers (PEs). A PE can oversee the work of other engineers, approve design plans, sign off on projects, and provide services directly to the public. State licensure generally requires

- A degree from an ABET-accredited engineering program
- A passing score on the Fundamentals of Engineering (FE) exam
- Relevant work experience, typically at least 4 years working under a licensed engineer
- A passing score on the Professional Engineering (PE) exam

The initial FE exam can be taken after earning a bachelor's degree. Engineers who pass this exam commonly are called engineers in training (EITs) or engineer interns (EIs). After meeting work experience requirements, EITs and EIs can take the second exam, called the Principles and Practice of Engineering.

Each state issues its own licenses. Most states recognize licensure from other states, as long as the licensing state's requirements meet or exceed their own licensure requirements.

Several states require continuing education for engineers to keep their licenses.

The American Society of Civil Engineers offers certifications in coastal engineering, geotechnical engineering, ports engineering, water resources engineering, and other fields. Additionally, civil engineers can become certified in building security and in sustainability.

Other Experience

During high school, students can attend engineering summer camps to see what these and other engineers do. Attending these camps can help students plan their coursework for the remainder of their time in high school.

Advancement

Civil engineers with ample experience may move into senior positions, such as project managers or functional managers of design, construction, operation, or maintenance. However, they would first need to obtain the Professional Engineering (PE) license, because only licensed engineers can assume responsibilities for public projects.

After gaining licensure, a professional engineer may seek credentialing that demonstrates his or her expertise in a civil engineering specialty. Such a credential may be helpful for advancement to senior technical or even managerial positions.

Pay

The median annual wage for civil engineers was $87,060 in May 2019. The median wage is the wage at which half the workers in an occupation earned more than that amount and half earned less. The lowest 10 percent earned less than $55,380, and the highest 10 percent earned more than $144,560.

In May 2019, the median annual wages for civil engineers in the top industries in which they worked were as follows:

Federal government, excluding postal service $95,380

Local government, excluding education and hospitals 93,380

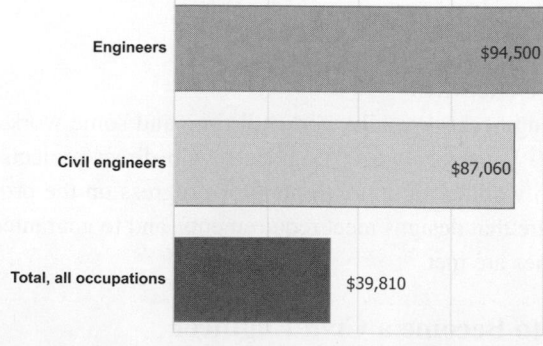

Civil Engineers
Median annual wages, May 2019

Engineers	$94,500
Civil engineers	$87,060
Total, all occupations	$39,810

Note: All Occupations includes all occupations in the U.S. Economy.
Source: U.S. Bureau of Labor Statistics, Occupational Employment Statistics.

Engineering services 87,710

State government, excluding education and
hospitals 82,030

Nonresidential building construction 76,340

Civil engineers typically work full time and some work more than 40 hours per week. Engineers who direct projects may need to work extra hours in order to monitor progress on projects, to ensure that designs meet requirements, and to guarantee that deadlines are met.

Job Outlook

Employment of civil engineers is projected to grow 2 percent from 2019 to 2029, slower than the average for all occupations. As current U.S. infrastructure experiences growing obsolescence, civil engineers will be needed to manage projects to rebuild, repair, and upgrade bridges, roads, levees, dams, airports, buildings, and other structures.

A growing population likely means that new water systems will be required while, at the same time, aging, existing water systems must be maintained to reduce or eliminate leaks. In addition, more waste treatment plants will be needed to help clean the nation's waterways. Civil engineers will continue to play a key part in all of this work.

The work of civil engineers will be needed for renewable-energy projects. Thus, as these new projects gain approval, civil engineers will be further involved in overseeing the construction of structures such as wind farms and solar arrays.

Although state and local governments continue to face financial challenges and may have difficulty funding all projects, some delayed projects will have to be completed to build and maintain critical infrastructure, as well as to protect the public and the environment.

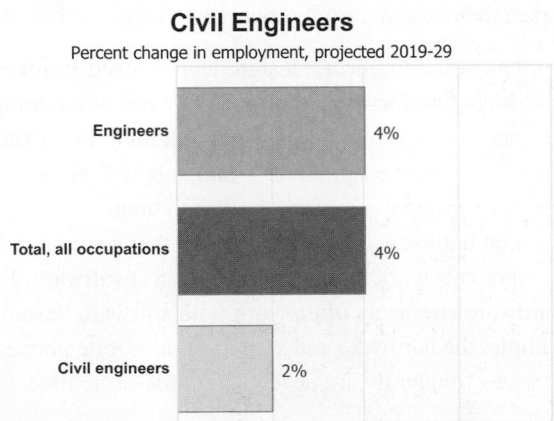

Civil Engineers
Percent change in employment, projected 2019-29

- Engineers: 4%
- Total, all occupations: 4%
- Civil engineers: 2%

Note: All Occupations includes all occupations in the U.S. Economy.
Source: U.S. Bureau of Labor Statistics, Employment Projections program.

Job Prospects

Applicants who gain experience by participating in a co-op program while in college will have the best opportunities. In addition, new standards known collectively as the Body of Knowledge are growing in importance within civil engineering, and this development is likely to result in a heightened need for a graduate education. Therefore, those who enter the occupation with a graduate degree will likely have better prospects.

Employment projections data for civil engineers, 2019-29					
Occupational Title	SOC Code	Employment, 2019	Projected Employment, 2029	Change, 2019-29	
				Percent	Numeric
SOURCE: U.S. Bureau of Labor Statistics, Employment Projections program					
Civil engineers	17-2051	329,200	334,700	2	5,500

State & Area Data
Occupational Employment Statistics (OES)

The Occupational Employment Statistics (OES) program produces employment and wage estimates annually for over 800 occupations. These estimates are available for the nation as a whole, for individual states, and for metropolitan and nonmetropolitan areas.

Similar Occupations

This table shows a list of occupations with job duties that are similar to those of civil engineers.

Contacts for More Information

For information about general engineering education and career resources, visit
➤ American Society for Engineering Education
➤ Technology Student Association

For information about engineering summer camps, visit
➤ Engineering Education Service Center

For more information about licensure, visit
➤ National Council of Examiners for Engineering and Surveying

➤ National Society of Professional Engineers

For information about accredited programs in civil engineering and civil engineering technology, visit
➤ ABET

For more information about civil engineers, visit
➤ American Society of Civil Engineers

Computer Hardware Engineers

Summary

Quick Facts: Computer Hardware Engineers

2019 Median Pay	$117,220 per year $56.36 per hour
Typical Entry-Level Education	Bachelor's degree
Work Experience in a Related Occupation	None
On-the-job Training	None
Number of Jobs, 2019	71,100
Job Outlook, 2019-29	2% (Slower than average)
Employment Change, 2019-29	1,100

What Computer Hardware Engineers Do

Computer hardware engineers research, design, develop, and test computer systems and components.

Work Environment

Computer hardware engineers usually work in research laboratories that build and test various types of computer models. Most work in computer systems design services and in manufacturing.

How to Become a Computer Hardware Engineer

Most computer hardware engineers need a bachelor's degree from an accredited program.

Pay

The median annual wage for computer hardware engineers was $117,220 in May 2019.

Job Outlook

Employment of computer hardware engineers is projected to grow 2 percent from 2019 to 2029, slower than the average for all occupations.

Computer hardware engineers solve problems that arise in computer hardware.

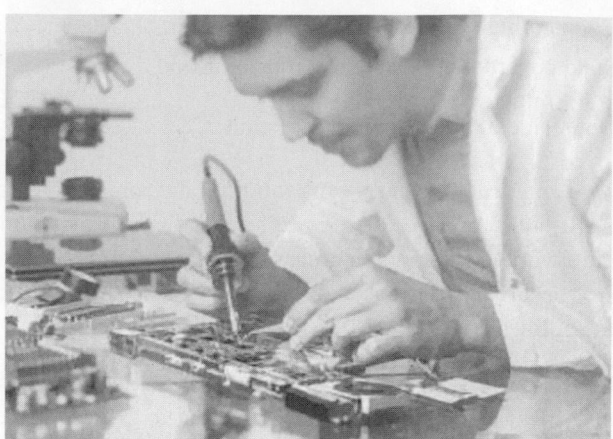

Computer hardware engineers research, design, develop, and test computer systems and components such as circuit boards.

State & Area Data

Explore resources for employment and wages by state and area for computer hardware engineers.

What Computer Hardware Engineers Do

Computer hardware engineers research, design, develop, and test computer systems and components such as processors, circuit boards, memory devices, networks, and routers.

Duties

Computer hardware engineers typically do the following:

- Design new computer hardware, creating schematics of computer equipment to be built
- Test the computer hardware they design
- Analyze the test results and modify the design as needed
- Update existing computer equipment so that it will work with new software
- Oversee the manufacturing process for computer hardware

Many hardware engineers design devices used in manufactured products that incorporate processors and other computer components and that connect to the Internet. For example, many new cars, home appliances, and medical devices have Internet-ready computer systems built into them.

Computer hardware engineers ensure that computer hardware components work together with the latest software. Therefore, hardware engineers often work with software developers. For example, the hardware and software for mobile phones and other devices frequently are developed at the same time.

Work Environment

Computer hardware engineers held about 71,100 jobs in 2019. The largest employers of computer hardware engineers were as follows:

Computer systems design and related services	22%
Semiconductor and other electronic component manufacturing	12

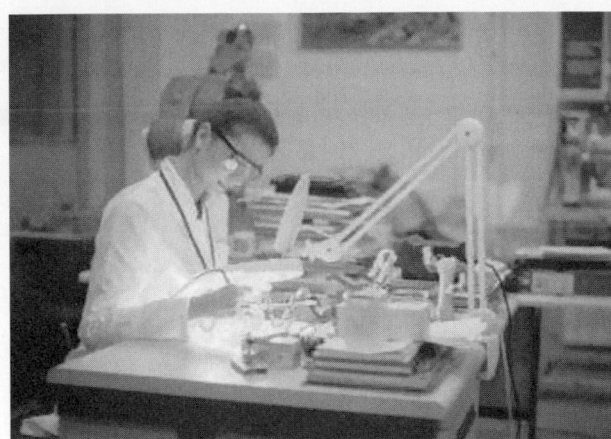

Most hardware engineers work in labs where they test different types of computer models.

Research and development in the physical,
   engineering, and life sciences 11
Federal government 7
Computer and peripheral equipment manufacturing ... 7

Work Schedules

Most computer hardware engineers work full time.

How to Become a Computer Hardware Engineer

Most computer hardware engineers need a bachelor's degree from an accredited computer engineering program.

Education

Most entry-level computer hardware engineers have a bachelor's degree in computer engineering, although a degree in electrical engineering or computer science also is generally acceptable. A computer engineering major is similar to a major in electrical engineering but with a heavy emphasis on computer science.

Many engineering programs are accredited by ABET. Employers may prefer candidates who have graduated from an accredited program. To prepare for a major in computer or electrical engineering, students should have a solid background in math and science.

Because hardware engineers commonly work with computer software systems, a familiarity with computer programming is usually expected. This background may be obtained through computer science courses.

Some large firms or specialized jobs may require a master's degree in computer engineering. Some experienced engineers obtain a master's degree in business administration (MBA). All engineers must continue their learning over the course of their careers in order to keep up with rapid advances in technology.

Most entry-level computer hardware engineers have a bachelor's degree in computer engineering, although a degree in electrical engineering generally is acceptable.

Other Experience

Some students participate in internships while in school so that they can gain practical experience.

Advancement

Some computer hardware engineers can advance to become computer and information systems managers.

Important Qualities

Analytical skills. Computer hardware engineers use computer programming tools to analyze the digital circuits in hardware to determine the best design.

Critical-thinking skills. These engineers use logic and reasoning to clarify goals, examine assumptions, and identify the strengths and weaknesses of alternative solutions.

Problem-solving skills. Computer hardware engineers identify complex problems in computer hardware, develop and evaluate possible solutions, and figure out the best way to implement them.

Communication skills. Engineers often work on teams and must be able to communicate with other types of engineers, software developers and programmers, as well as with nontechnical team members.

Pay

The median annual wage for computer hardware engineers was $117,220 in May 2019. The median wage is the wage at which half the workers in an occupation earned more than that amount and half earned less. The lowest 10 percent earned less than $68,460, and the highest 10 percent earned more than $185,240.

In May 2019, the median annual wages for computer hardware engineers in the top industries in which they worked were as follows:

Computer Hardware Engineers
Median annual wages, May 2019

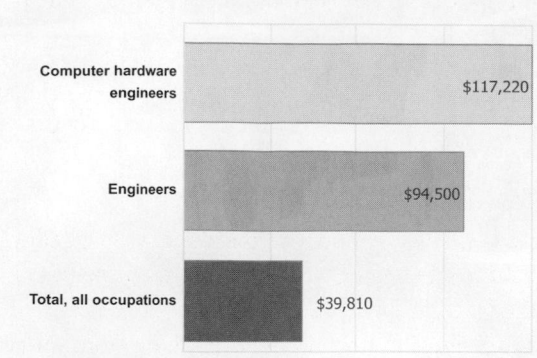

Note: All Occupations includes all occupations in the U.S. Economy.
Source: U.S. Bureau of Labor Statistics, Occupational Employment Statistics.

Computer and peripheral equipment manufacturing..	$140,840
Research and development in the physical, engineering, and life sciences..............................	132,450
Federal government...	113,430
Semiconductor and other electronic component manufacturing...	113,050
Computer systems design and related services.....	111,610

Most computer hardware engineers work full time.

Job Outlook

Employment of computer hardware engineers is projected to grow 2 percent from 2019 to 2029, slower than the average for all occupations.

Demand for these engineers is expected to grow as more industries outside of the computer and electronic product manufacturing industry begin to research and develop their own electronic devices. However, centralized computing and networking services may mean fewer engineers will be needed because these worksites cover large networks and geographic areas.

An increase in hardware startup firms and the ongoing increase in the number of devices with computer chips embedded in them, such as household appliances, medical devices, and automobiles, may also lead to some job growth for these workers.

Computer Hardware Engineers
Percent change in employment, projected 2019-29

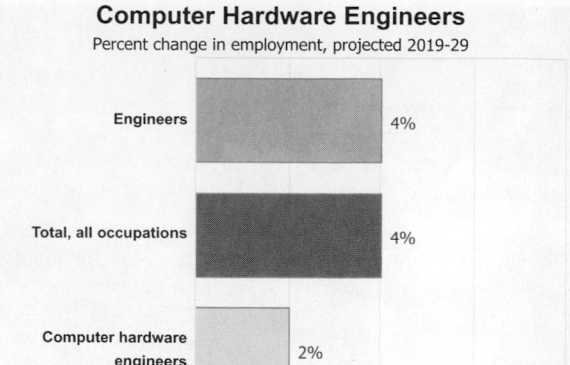

Note: All Occupations includes all occupations in the U.S. Economy.
Source: U.S. Bureau of Labor Statistics, Employment Projections program.

Employment projections data for computer hardware engineers, 2019-29					
Occupational Title	SOC Code	Employment, 2019	Projected Employment, 2029	Change, 2019-29	
				Percent	Numeric
SOURCE: U.S. Bureau of Labor Statistics, Employment Projections program					
Computer hardware engineers	17-2061	71,100	72,200	2	1,100

State & Area Data
Occupational Employment Statistics (OES)

The Occupational Employment Statistics (OES) program produces employment and wage estimates annually for over 800 occupations. These estimates are available for the nation as a whole, for individual states, and for metropolitan and nonmetropolitan areas.

Contacts for More Information

For more information about computer hardware engineers, visit
➤ Association for Computing Machinery
➤ IEEE Computer Society

For more information about ABET-accredited college and university programs in applied science, computing, engineering, and technology, visit
➤ ABET

Drafters

Summary

Quick Facts: Drafters

2019 Median Pay	$56,830 per year $27.32 per hour
Typical Entry-Level Education	Associate's degree
Work Experience in a Related Occupation	None
On-the-job Training	None
Number of Jobs, 2019	200,900
Job Outlook, 2019-29	-4% (Decline)
Employment Change, 2019-29	-7,100

What Drafters Do

Drafters use software to convert the designs of engineers and architects into technical drawings.

Work Environment

Although drafters spend much of their time working on computers in an office, some may visit jobsites in order to collaborate with architects and engineers. Most drafters work full time.

How to Become a Drafter

Drafters typically complete education after high school, often through a program at a community college or technical school. Some programs lead to an associate of applied science in drafting or a related degree. Others result in a certificate or diploma.

Pay

The median annual wage for drafters was $56,830 in May 2019.

Job Outlook

Employment of drafters is projected to decline 4 percent from 2019 to 2029. Employment growth will vary by specialty.

Drafters take designs from engineers and architects and convert them into plans needed for construction.

State & Area Data

Explore resources for employment and wages by state and area for drafters.

Learn more about drafters by visiting additional resources, including O*NET, a source on key characteristics of workers and occupations.

What Drafters Do

Drafters use software to convert the designs of architects and engineers into technical drawings. Most workers specialize in architectural, civil, electrical, or mechanical drafting and use technical drawings to help design everything from microchips to skyscrapers.

Duties

Drafters typically do the following:

- Design plans using computer-aided design (CAD) software
- Work from rough sketches and specifications created by engineers and architects
- Design products with engineering and manufacturing techniques
- Add details to architectural plans from their knowledge of building techniques
- Specify dimensions, materials, and procedures for new products
- Work under the supervision of engineers or architects

Some drafters are referred to as *CAD operators*. Using CAD systems, drafters create and store technical drawings digitally. These drawings contain information on how to build a structure or machine, the dimensions of the project, and what materials are needed to complete the project.

Drafters work with CAD to create schematics that can be viewed, printed, or programmed directly into building information modeling (BIM) systems. These systems allow drafters, architects, construction managers, and engineers to create and collaborate on digital models of physical buildings and

Drafters prepare technical drawings and plans.

machines. Through three-dimensional rendering, BIM software allows designers and engineers to see how different elements in their projects work together.

The following are examples of types of drafters:

Architectural drafters draw structural features and details for buildings and other construction projects. These workers may specialize in a type of building, such as residential or commercial. They may also specialize by the materials used, such as steel, wood, or reinforced concrete.

Civil drafters prepare topographical maps used in construction and civil engineering projects, such as highways, bridges, and dams.

Electrical drafters prepare wiring diagrams that construction workers use to install and repair electrical equipment and wiring in power plants, electrical distribution systems, and residential and commercial buildings.

Electronics drafters produce wiring diagrams, assembly diagrams for circuit boards, and layout drawings used in manufacturing and in installing and repairing electronic devices and components.

Mechanical drafters prepare layouts that show the details for a variety of machinery and mechanical tools and devices, such as medical equipment. These layouts indicate dimensions, fastening methods, and other requirements for assembly. Mechanical drafters sometimes create production molds.

Work Environment

Drafters held about 200,900 jobs in 2019. Employment in the detailed occupations that make up drafters was distributed as follows:

Architectural and civil drafters	102,900
Mechanical drafters	57,500
Electrical and electronics drafters	25,300
Drafters, all other	15,200

The largest employers of drafters were as follows:

Architectural, engineering, and related services	48%
Manufacturing	24
Construction	10
Administrative and support and waste management and remediation services	3
Wholesale trade	2

Although drafters spend much of their time working on computers in an office, some may visit jobsites to collaborate with architects and engineers.

Work Schedules

Most drafters work full time. Some work more than 40 hours a week.

How to Become a Drafter

Drafters typically complete education after high school, often through a program at a community college or technical school. Some programs lead to an associate of applied science in drafting or a related degree. Others result in a certificate or diploma.

Education

Drafters typically need an associate of applied science in drafting or a related degree from a community college or technical school. Some drafters prepare for the occupation by earning a certificate or diploma.

Programs in drafting may include instruction in design fundamentals, sketching, and computer-aided design (CAD) software. It generally takes about 2 years of full-time education to earn an associate's degree. Certificate and diploma programs vary in length but usually may be completed in less time.

Students frequently specialize in a particular type of drafting, such as mechanical or architectural drafting.

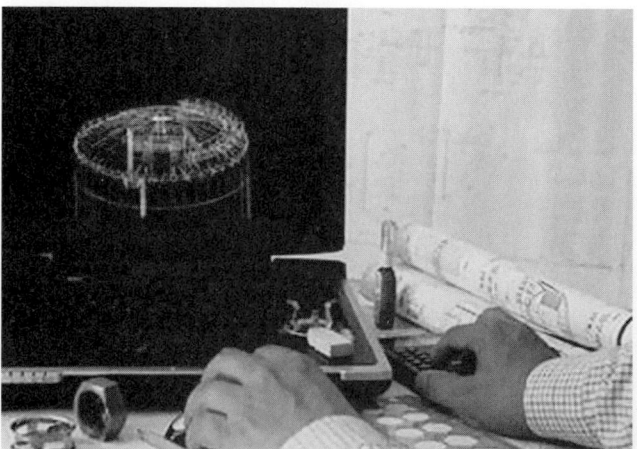

Drafters spend much of their time working on computers using specialized software in an office.

Drafters generally need to complete postsecondary education in drafting.

High school students may begin preparing by taking classes in mathematics, science, computer technology, design, computer graphics, and, where available, drafting.

Licenses, Certifications, and Registrations

The American Design Drafting Association (ADDA) offers certification for drafters. Although not mandatory, certification demonstrates competence and knowledge of nationally recognized practices. Certifications are offered for several specialties, including architectural, civil, and mechanical drafting.

Important Qualities

Creativity. Drafters must be able to turn plans and ideas into technical drawings of buildings, tools, and systems.

Detail oriented. Drafters must take care that the plans they convert are technically accurate according to the outlined specifications.

Interpersonal skills. Drafters work closely with architects, engineers, and other designers to make sure that final plans are accurate. This requires the ability to communicate effectively and work well with others.

Math skills. Drafters work on technical drawings. They may be required to calculate angles, weights, costs, and other values.

Technical skills. Drafters in all specialties must be able to use computer software, such as CAD, and work with database tools, such as building information modeling (BIM).

Time-management skills. Drafters often work under deadline. As a result, they must work efficiently to produce the required output according to set schedules.

Pay

The median annual wage for drafters was $56,830 in May 2019. The median wage is the wage at which half the workers in an occupation earned more than that amount and half earned less. The lowest 10 percent earned less than $35,920, and the highest 10 percent earned more than $87,720.

Median annual wages for drafters in May 2019 were as follows:

Electrical and electronics drafters	$61,530
Mechanical drafters	57,060
Architectural and civil drafters	56,340
Drafters, all other	52,830

In May 2019, the median annual wages for drafters in the top industries in which they worked were as follows:

Construction	$57,860
Administrative and support and waste management and remediation services	57,650
Architectural, engineering, and related services	56,720
Manufacturing	55,670
Wholesale trade	53,970

Most drafters work full time. Some work more than 40 hours a week.

Job Outlook

Overall employment of drafters is projected to decline 4 percent from 2019 to 2029. Employment growth will vary by specialty. (See table below.)

Expected employment decreases in manufacturing and engineering services will more than offset the small increases in construction. These decreases will be driven by the use of computer-aided design (CAD) and building information modeling (BIM) technologies, which allow engineers and architects to perform many tasks that used to be done by drafters.

Job Prospects

Competition for drafting jobs is expected to be strong.

Demand for particular drafting specialties varies across the country because jobs depend on the needs of local industries.

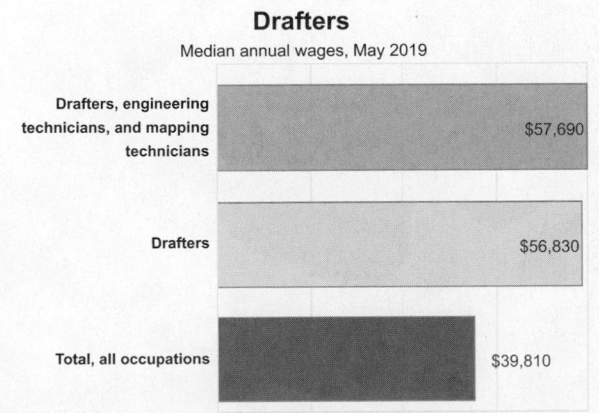

Drafters
Median annual wages, May 2019

Note: All Occupations includes all occupations in the U.S. Economy. Source: U.S. Bureau of Labor Statistics, Occupational Employment Statistics.

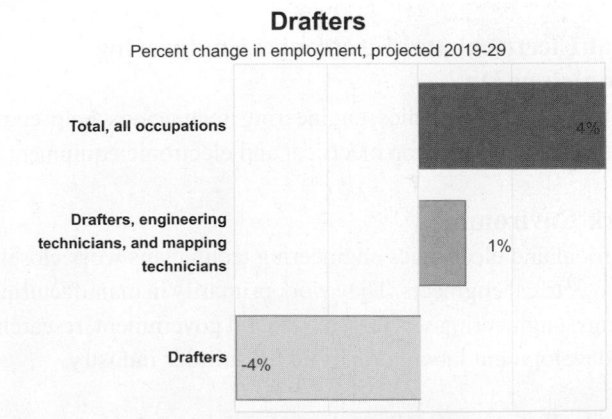

Drafters
Percent change in employment, projected 2019-29

Note: All Occupations includes all occupations in the U.S. Economy. Source: U.S. Bureau of Labor Statistics, Employment Projections program.

For example, job prospects for mechanical drafters should be best in large manufacturing hubs.

Because many drafting jobs are in construction and manufacturing, job opportunities for drafters will be sensitive to fluctuations in the overall economy.

Candidates proficient in CAD and BIM are likely to have better job opportunities.

Employment projections data for drafters, 2019-29					
Occupational Title	SOC Code	Employment, 2019	Projected Employment, 2029	Change, 2019-29	
				Percent	Numeric
SOURCE: U.S. Bureau of Labor Statistics, Employment Projections program					
Drafters	17-3010	200,900	193,700	-4	-7,100
Architectural and civil drafters	17-3011	102,900	100,300	-3	-2,600
Electrical and electronics drafters	17-3012	25,300	25,400	1	100
Mechanical drafters	17-3013	57,500	52,700	-8	-4,700
Drafters, all other	17-3019	15,200	15,300	1	100

State & Area Data
Occupational Employment Statistics (OES)

The Occupational Employment Statistics (OES) program produces employment and wage estimates annually for over 800 occupations. These estimates are available for the nation as a whole, for individual states, and for metropolitan and nonmetropolitan areas.

Contacts for More Information

For more information on schools offering programs in drafting and related fields, visit
➤ Accrediting Commission of Career Schools and Colleges

For more information on certification, visit
➤ American Design Drafting Association

Electrical and Electronics Engineering Technicians

Summary

Quick Facts: Electrical and Electronics Engineering Technicians

2019 Median Pay	$65,260 per year $31.38 per hour
Typical Entry-Level Education	Associate's degree
Work Experience in a Related Occupation	None
On-the-job Training	None
Number of Jobs, 2019	125,800
Job Outlook, 2019-29	2% (Slower than average)
Employment Change, 2019-29	1,900

What Electrical and Electronics Engineering Technicians Do

Electrical and electronics engineering technicians help engineers design and develop electrical and electronic equipment.

Work Environment

Electrical and electronics engineering technicians work closely with electrical engineers. They work primarily in manufacturing settings, engineering services, the federal government, research-and-development laboratories, and the utilities industry.

How to Become an Electrical or Electronics Engineering Technician

Electrical and electronics engineering technicians typically need an associate's degree.

Pay

The median annual wage for electrical and electronics engineering technicians was $65,260 in May 2019.

Job Outlook

Employment of electrical and electronics engineering technicians is projected to grow 2 percent from 2019 to 2029, slower than the average for all occupations.

State & Area Data

Explore resources for employment and wages by state and area for electrical and electronics engineering technicians.

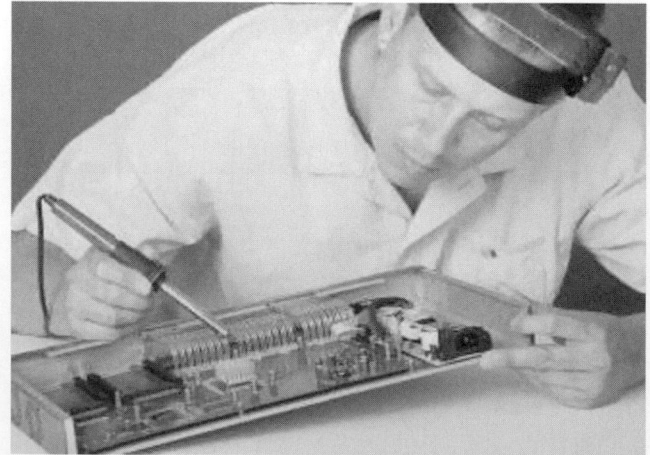

Electrical and electronics engineering technicians use diagnostic devices to adjust, test, and repair equipment.

What Electrical and Electronics Engineering Technicians Do

Electrical and electronics engineering technicians help electrical and electronics engineers design and develop computers, communications equipment, medical monitoring devices, navigational equipment, and other electrical and electronic equipment. They often work in product evaluation and testing, and use measuring and diagnostic devices to adjust, test, and repair equipment. They are also involved in the manufacture and deployment of equipment for automation.

Duties

Electrical engineering technicians typically do the following:

- Put together electrical and electronic systems and prototypes
- Build, calibrate, and repair electrical instruments or testing equipment
- Visit construction sites to observe conditions affecting design
- Identify solutions to technical design problems that arise during the construction of electrical systems
- Inspect designs for quality control, report findings, and make recommendations
- Draw diagrams and write specifications to clarify design details of experimental electronics units

Electrical engineering technicians install and maintain electrical control systems and equipment, and modify electrical prototypes, parts, and assemblies to correct problems. When testing systems, they set up equipment and evaluate the performance of developmental parts, assemblies, or systems under simulated conditions. They then analyze test information to resolve design-related problems.

Electronics engineering technicians typically do the following:

- Design basic circuitry and draft sketches to clarify details of design documentation, under engineers' direction

Electrical and electronics engineering technicians help engineers design and develop computers and other electrical and electronic equipment.

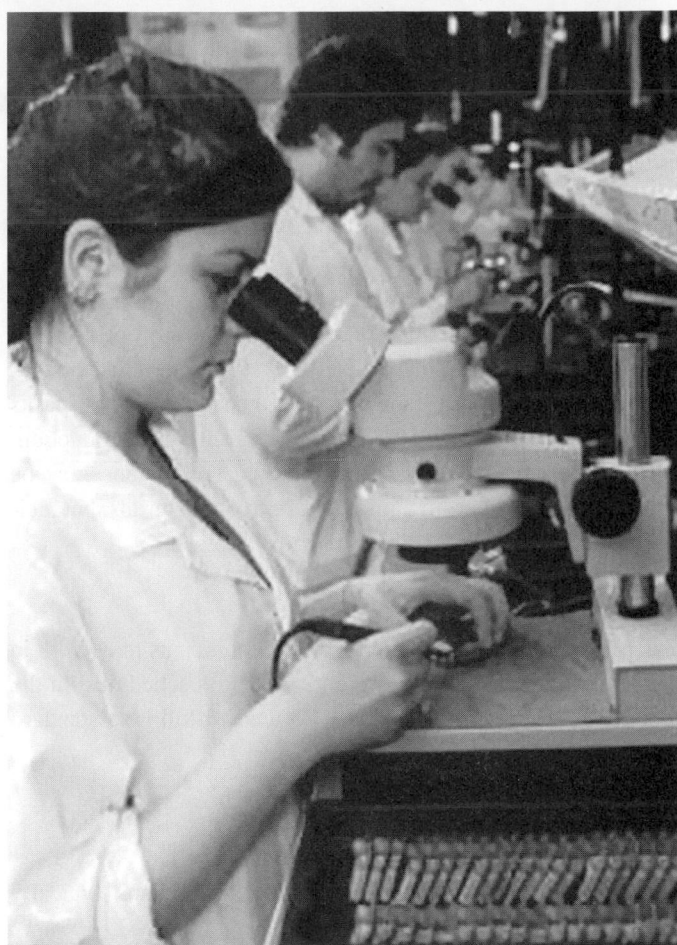

Electrical engineering technicians build, calibrate, and repair electrical instruments or testing equipment.

- Build prototypes from rough sketches or plans
- Assemble, test, and maintain circuitry or electronic components according to engineering instructions, technical manuals, and knowledge of electronics
- Adjust and replace defective circuitry and electronic components
- Make parts, such as coils and terminal boards, by using bench lathes, drills, or other machine tools

Electronics engineering technicians identify and resolve equipment malfunctions and then work with manufacturers to get replacement parts. They also calibrate and perform preventive maintenance on equipment and systems.

These technicians often need to read blueprints, schematic drawings, and engineering instructions for assembling electronic units. They also write reports and record data on testing techniques, laboratory equipment, and specifications.

Work Environment

Electrical and electronics engineering technicians held about 125,800 jobs in 2019. The largest employers of electrical and electronics engineering technicians were as follows:

Engineering services	12%
Semiconductor and other electronic component manufacturing	11
Federal government	10
Navigational, measuring, electromedical, and control instruments manufacturing	7
Merchant wholesalers, durable goods	5

Electrical and electronics engineering technicians work closely with electrical and electronics engineers. For this reason, teamwork is an important part of the job. They work in offices, laboratories, and factories because their job tasks involve both engineering theory and assembly-line production.

Electrical and electronics engineering technicians may be exposed to hazards from equipment or toxic materials, but incidents are rare if proper procedures are followed.

Work Schedules

Electrical and electronics engineering technicians may work in day or night shifts, depending on production schedules. In the federal government, their schedules tend to follow a standard workweek.

How to Become an Electrical or Electronics Engineering Technician

Electrical and electronics engineering technicians typically need an associate's degree.

Education

Programs for electrical and electronics engineering technicians usually lead to an associate's degree in electrical or electronics engineering technology. Vocational–technical schools include postsecondary institutions that serve local students and emphasize training needed by local employers.

Community colleges offer programs similar to those in technical institutes but include more theory-based and liberal arts coursework. Some of these colleges allow students to

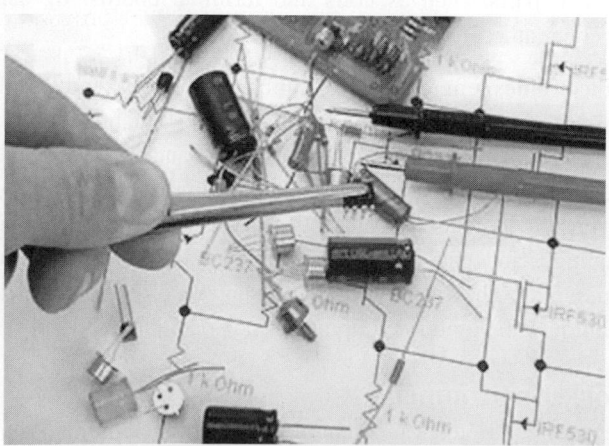

Electrical and electronics engineering technicians typically need an associate's degree.

concentrate in computer electronics, industrial electronics, or communications electronics.

Prospective electrical and electronics engineering technicians usually take courses in programming languages, chemistry, physics, logical processors, and circuitry. Coursework in test equipment is also helpful. The Technology Accreditation Commission of ABET accredits programs that include at least college algebra, trigonometry, and basic science courses.

Important Qualities

Logical-thinking skills. Electrical and electronics engineering technicians must isolate and then identify problems for the engineering staff to work on. They need good reasoning skills to identify and fix problems. Technicians must also follow a logical sequence or specific set of rules to carry out electrical engineers' designs, inspect designs for quality control, and put together prototypes.

Math skills. Electrical and electronics engineering technicians use math for analysis, design, and troubleshooting in their work.

Mechanical skills. Electronics engineering technicians in particular must use hand tools and soldering irons on small circuitry and electronic parts to create detailed electronic components by hand.

Observational skills. Electrical engineering technicians sometimes visit construction sites to make sure that electrical engineers' designs are being carried out correctly. They are responsible for evaluating projects onsite and reporting problems to engineers.

Writing skills. These technicians must write reports about onsite construction, the results of testing, or problems they find when carrying out designs. Their writing must be clear and well organized so that the engineers they work with can understand the reports.

Licenses, Certifications, and Registrations

Technicians may choose to earn certification to show an advanced level of knowledge. Several organizations offer certification.

The National Institute for Certification in Engineering Technologies (NICET) offers certification in electrical power testing. This certification would benefit those technicians working in the electric power generation, transmission, and distribution industry.

ETA International also offers certifications in several fields, including basic electronics, biomedical electronics, and renewable energy.

The International Society of Automation offers certification as a Control Systems Technician. To gain such certification, technicians must demonstrate skills in pneumatic, mechanical, and electronic instrumentation. In addition, they must demonstrate an understanding of process control loops and process control systems.

Electrical and Electronics Engineering Technicians

Median annual wages, May 2019

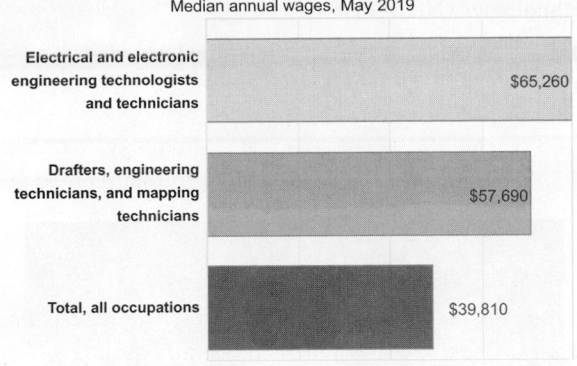

Electrical and electronic engineering technologists and technicians	$65,260
Drafters, engineering technicians, and mapping technicians	$57,690
Total, all occupations	$39,810

Note: All Occupations includes all occupations in the U.S. Economy.
Source: U.S. Bureau of Labor Statistics, Occupational Employment Statistics.

Pay

The median annual wage for electrical and electronics engineering technicians was $65,260 in May 2019. The median wage is the wage at which half the workers in an occupation earned more than that amount and half earned less. The lowest 10 percent earned less than $39,190, and the highest 10 percent earned more than $96,690.

In May 2019, the median annual wages for electrical and electronics engineering technicians in the top industries in which they worked were as follows:

Federal government	$70,510
Merchant wholesalers, durable goods	64,010
Engineering services	62,480
Semiconductor and other electronic component manufacturing	60,710
Navigational, measuring, electromedical, and control instruments manufacturing	60,080

Electrical and electronics engineering technicians may work in day or night shifts, depending on production schedules. In the federal government, their schedules tend to follow a standard workweek.

Job Outlook

Employment of electrical and electronics engineering technicians is projected to grow 2 percent from 2019 to 2029, slower than the average for all occupations.

Employment of these technicians in industries in which many are employed, such as manufacturing and federal government, is expected to decline. However, their employment is expected to grow in professional, scientific, and technical services firms as companies seek to contract out these services as a way to lower costs.

Electrical and electronics engineering technicians also work closely with electrical and electronics engineers and computer hardware engineers in the computer systems design services

Electrical and Electronics Engineering Technicians

Percent change in employment, projected 2019-29

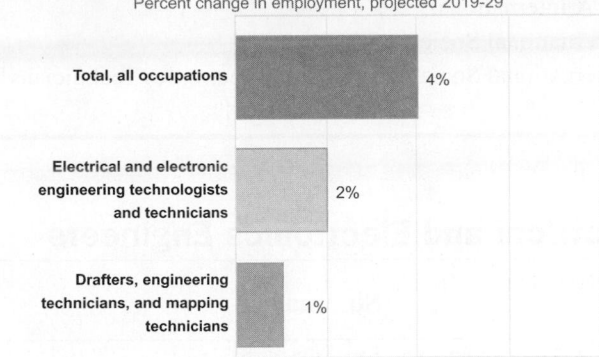

Total, all occupations	4%
Electrical and electronic engineering technologists and technicians	2%
Drafters, engineering technicians, and mapping technicians	1%

Note: All Occupations includes all occupations in the U.S. Economy.
Source: U.S. Bureau of Labor Statistics, Employment Projections program.

industry. Demand for these technicians is expected to be sustained by the continuing integration of computer and electronics systems, especially automation systems. In addition, computer, cellular phone, and Global Positioning System (GPS) technologies are being included in automobiles and various portable and household electronics systems.

Job Prospects

Prospective electrical and electronics engineering technicians may face competition for jobs. Candidates with a certification will likely have the best job opportunities.

Employment projections data for electrical and electronics engineering technicians, 2019-29					
Occupational Title	SOC Code	Employment, 2019	Projected Employment, 2029	Change, 2019-29	
				Percent	Numeric
SOURCE: U.S. Bureau of Labor Statistics, Employment Projections program					
Electrical and electronic engineering technologists and technicians	17-3023	125,800	127,800	2	1,900

State & Area Data
Occupational Employment Statistics (OES)

The Occupational Employment Statistics (OES) program produces employment and wage estimates annually for over 800 occupations. These estimates are available for the nation as a whole, for individual states, and for metropolitan and nonmetropolitan areas.

Contacts for More Information

For more information about general engineering education and career resources, visit
➤ American Society for Engineering Education
➤ Technology Student Association

For more information about accredited programs, visit
➤ ABET

For more information about certification, visit
➤ ETA International
➤ International Society of Automation
➤ International Society of Certified Electronics Technicians

➤ National Institute for Certification in Engineering Technologies (NICET)

For information about working in automation, visit
➤ Automation Federation

Electrical and Electronics Engineers

Summary

Quick Facts: Electrical and Electronics Engineers

2019 Median Pay	$101,250 per year $48.68 per hour
Typical Entry-Level Education	Bachelor's degree
Work Experience in a Related Occupation	None
On-the-job Training	None
Number of Jobs, 2019	328,100
Job Outlook, 2019-29	3% (As fast as average)
Employment Change, 2019-29	10,800

What Electrical and Electronics Engineers Do

Electrical engineers design, develop, test, and supervise the manufacture of electrical equipment.

Work Environment

Electrical and electronics engineers work in industries including research and development, engineering services, manufacturing, telecommunications, and the federal government. Electrical and electronics engineers generally work indoors in offices. However, they may have to visit sites to observe a problem or a piece of complex equipment.

How to Become an Electrical or Electronics Engineer

Electrical and electronics engineers must have a bachelor's degree. Employers also value practical experience, such as internships or participation in cooperative engineering programs.

Pay

The median annual wage for electrical engineers was $98,530 in May 2019.

The median annual wage for electronics engineers, except computer was $105,570 in May 2019.

Job Outlook

Overall employment of electrical and electronics engineers is projected to grow 3 percent from 2019 to 2029, about as fast as the average for all occupations. Employment growth is expected to be tempered by slow growth or decline in some industries, such as manufacturing and utilities.

Electronics engineers design electronic components and systems for commercial, industrial, or scientific applications.

State & Area Data

Explore resources for employment and wages by state and area for electrical and electronics engineers.

What Electrical and Electronics Engineers Do

Electrical engineers design, develop, test, and supervise the manufacture of electrical equipment, such as electric motors, radar and navigation systems, communications systems, or power generation equipment. Electrical engineers also design the electrical systems of automobiles and aircraft.

Electronics engineers design and develop electronic equipment, including broadcast and communications systems, such as portable music players and Global Positioning System (GPS) devices. Many also work in areas closely related to computer hardware.

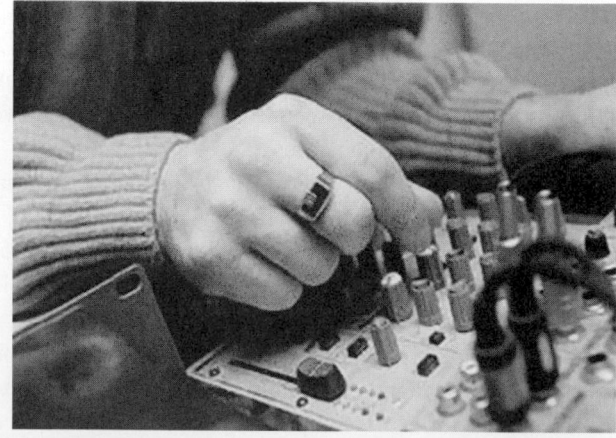

Electronics engineers analyze the requirements and costs of electrical systems.

Duties

Electrical engineers typically do the following:

- Design new ways to use electrical power to develop or improve products
- Perform detailed calculations to develop manufacturing, construction, and installation standards and specifications
- Direct the manufacture, installation, and testing of electrical equipment to ensure that products meet specifications and codes
- Investigate complaints from customers or the public, evaluate problems, and recommend solutions
- Work with project managers on production efforts to ensure that projects are completed satisfactorily, on time, and within budget

Electronics engineers typically do the following:

- Design electronic components, software, products, or systems for commercial, industrial, medical, military, or scientific applications
- Analyze customer needs and determine the requirements, capacity, and cost for developing an electrical system plan
- Develop maintenance and testing procedures for electronic components and equipment
- Evaluate systems and recommend design modifications or equipment repair
- Inspect electronic equipment, instruments, and systems to make sure they meet safety standards and applicable regulations
- Plan and develop applications and modifications for electronic properties used in parts and systems in order to improve technical performance

Electronics engineers who work for the federal government research, develop, and evaluate electronic devices used in a variety of areas, such as aviation, computing, transportation, and manufacturing. They work on federal electronic devices and systems, including satellites, flight systems, radar and sonar systems, and communications systems.

The work of electrical engineers and electronics engineers is often similar. Both use engineering and design software and equipment to do engineering tasks. Both types of engineers also must work with other engineers to discuss existing products and possibilities for engineering projects.

Engineers whose work is related exclusively to computer hardware are considered computer hardware engineers.

Work Environment

Electrical engineers held about 193,100 jobs in 2019. The largest employers of electrical engineers were as follows:

Engineering services	20%
Electric power generation, transmission and distribution	9

Electrical and electronic engineers work in various industries, including engineering services, research and development, and manufacturing.

Navigational, measuring, electromedical, and control instruments manufacturing	7
Research and development in the physical, engineering, and life sciences	5
Semiconductor and other electronic component manufacturing	4

Electronics engineers, except computer held about 134,900 jobs in 2019. The largest employers of electronics engineers, except computer were as follows:

Telecommunications	17%
Semiconductor and other electronic component manufacturing	14
Federal government, excluding postal service	13
Engineering services	7
Navigational, measuring, electromedical, and control instruments manufacturing	5

Electrical and electronics engineers generally work indoors in offices. However, they may visit sites to observe a problem or a piece of complex equipment.

Work Schedules

Most electrical and electronics engineers work full time.

How to Become an Electrical or Electronics Engineer

Electrical and electronics engineers must have a bachelor's degree. Employers also value practical experience, such as internships or participation in cooperative engineering programs, in which students earn academic credit for structured work experience.

Education

High school students interested in studying electrical or electronics engineering benefit from taking courses in physics and math, including algebra, trigonometry, and calculus. Courses in drafting are also helpful, because electrical and electronics engineers often are required to prepare technical drawings.

In order to enter the occupation, prospective electrical and electronics engineers need a bachelor's degree in electrical engineering, electronics engineering, electrical engineering technology, or a related engineering field. Programs include classroom, laboratory, and field studies. Courses include digital systems design, differential equations, and electrical circuit theory. Programs in electrical engineering, electronics engineering, or electrical engineering technology should be accredited by ABET.

Some colleges and universities offer cooperative programs in which students gain practical experience while completing their education. Cooperative programs combine classroom study with practical work. Internships provide similar experience and are growing in number.

At some universities, students can enroll in a 5-year program that leads to both a bachelor's degree and a master's degree. A graduate degree allows an engineer to work as an instructor at some universities, or in research and development.

Important Qualities

Concentration. Electrical and electronics engineers design and develop complex electrical systems and electronic components

Becoming an electrical or electronics engineer involves the study of math and engineering.

and products. They must keep track of multiple design elements and technical characteristics when performing these tasks.

Initiative. Electrical and electronics engineers must apply their knowledge to new tasks in every project they undertake. In addition, they must engage in continuing education to keep up with changes in technology.

Interpersonal skills. Electrical and electronics engineers must work with others during the manufacturing process to ensure that their plans are implemented correctly. This collaboration includes monitoring technicians and devising remedies to problems as they arise.

Math skills. Electrical and electronics engineers must use the principles of calculus and other advanced math in order to analyze, design, and troubleshoot equipment.

Speaking skills. Electrical and electronics engineers work closely with other engineers and technicians. They must be able to explain their designs and reasoning clearly and to relay instructions during product development and production. They also may need to explain complex issues to customers who have little or no technical expertise.

Writing skills. Electrical and electronics engineers develop technical publications related to equipment they develop, including maintenance manuals, operation manuals, parts lists, product proposals, and design methods documents.

Licenses, Certifications, and Registrations

Licensure is not required for entry-level positions as electrical and electronics engineers. A Professional Engineering (PE) license, which allows for higher levels of leadership and independence, can be acquired later in one's career. Licensed engineers are called professional engineers (PEs). A PE can oversee the work of other engineers, sign off on projects, and provide services directly to the public. State licensure generally requires

- A degree from an ABET-accredited engineering program
- A passing score on the Fundamentals of Engineering (FE) exam
- Relevant work experience, typically at least 4 years
- A passing score on the Professional Engineering (PE) exam

The initial FE exam can be taken after earning a bachelor's degree. Engineers who pass this exam commonly are called engineers in training (EITs) or engineer interns (EIs). After meeting work experience requirements, EITs and EIs can take the second exam, called the Principles and Practice of Engineering (PE).

Each state issues its own licenses. Most states recognize licensure from other states, as long as the licensing state's requirements meet or exceed their own licensure requirements. Several states require continuing education for engineers to keep their licenses.

Other Experience

During high school, students can attend engineering summer camps to see what these and other engineers do. Attending these camps can help students plan their coursework for the remainder of their time in high school. The Engineering Education Service Center has a directory of engineering summer camps.

Advancement

Electrical and electronic engineers may advance to supervisory positions in which they lead a team of engineers and technicians. Some may move to management positions, working as engineering or program managers. Preparation for managerial positions usually requires working under the guidance of a more experienced engineer. For more information, see the profile on architectural and engineering managers.

For sales work, an engineering background enables engineers to discuss a product's technical aspects and assist in product planning and use. For more information, see the profile on sales engineers.

Pay

The median annual wage for electrical engineers was $98,530 in May 2019. The median wage is the wage at which half the workers in an occupation earned more than that amount and half earned less. The lowest 10 percent earned less than $63,020, and the highest 10 percent earned more than $155,880.

The median annual wage for electronics engineers, except computer was $105,570 in May 2019. The lowest 10 percent earned less than $66,620, and the highest 10 percent earned more than $164,210.

In May 2019, the median annual wages for electrical engineers in the top industries in which they worked were as follows:

Research and development in the physical,
  engineering, and life sciences $113,050

Semiconductor and other electronic component
  manufacturing 104,170
Navigational, measuring, electromedical, and
  control instruments manufacturing 103,400
Electric power generation, transmission and
  distribution 99,610
Engineering services 96,540

In May 2019, the median annual wages for electronics engineers, except computer in the top industries in which they worked were as follows:

Navigational, measuring, electromedical, and
  control instruments manufacturing $114,260
Federal government, excluding postal service 112,870
Semiconductor and other electronic component
  manufacturing 106,240
Engineering services 101,580
Telecommunications 98,600

Most electrical and electronics engineers work full time.

Job Outlook

Overall employment of electrical and electronics engineers is projected to grow 3 percent from 2019 to 2029, about as fast as the average for all occupations. Employment growth is expected to be tempered by slow growth or decline in some industries, such as manufacturing and utilities.

Job growth for electrical and electronics engineers is projected to occur largely in professional, scientific, and technical services firms, as more companies are expected to tap the expertise of engineers for projects involving electronic devices and systems. These engineers also will be needed to develop sophisticated consumer electronics.

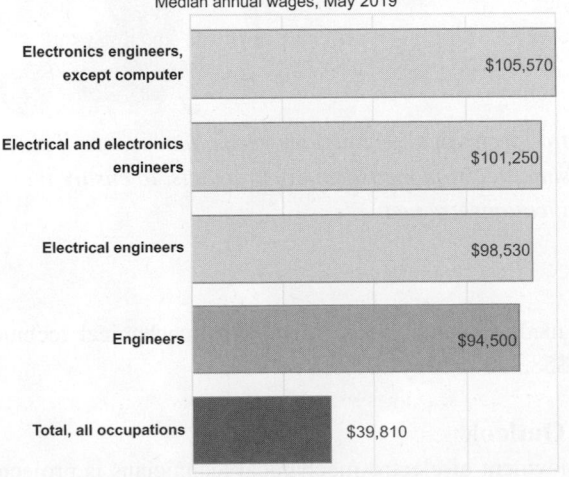

Electrical and Electronics Engineers
Median annual wages, May 2019

Electronics engineers, except computer	$105,570
Electrical and electronics engineers	$101,250
Electrical engineers	$98,530
Engineers	$94,500
Total, all occupations	$39,810

Note: All Occupations includes all occupations in the U.S. Economy.
Source: U.S. Bureau of Labor Statistics, Occupational Employment Statistics.

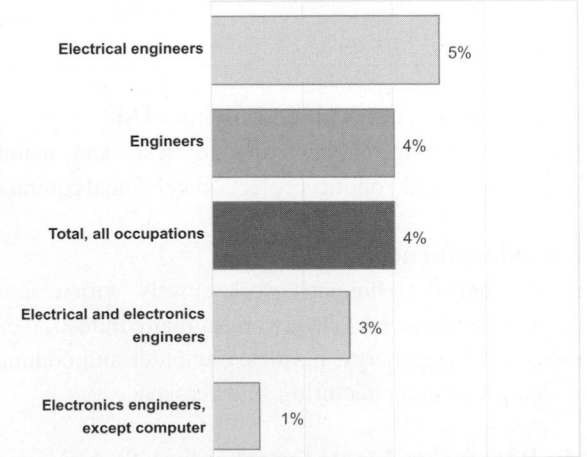

Electrical and Electronics Engineers
Percent change in employment, projected 2019-29

Electrical engineers	5%
Engineers	4%
Total, all occupations	4%
Electrical and electronics engineers	3%
Electronics engineers, except computer	1%

Note: All Occupations includes all occupations in the U.S. Economy.
Source: U.S. Bureau of Labor Statistics, Employment Projections program.

The rapid pace of technological innovation will create some demand for electrical and electronics engineers in research and development, an area in which engineering expertise will be needed to design distribution systems related to new technologies. These engineers will play key roles in new developments with solar arrays, semiconductors, and communications technologies.

Employment projections data for electrical and electronics engineers, 2019-29					
Occupational Title	SOC Code	Employment, 2019	Projected Employment, 2029	Change, 2019-29	
				Percent	Numeric
SOURCE: U.S. Bureau of Labor Statistics, Employment Projections program					
Electrical and electronics engineers	17-2070	328,100	338,900	3	10,800
Electrical engineers	17-2071	193,100	202,100	5	9,000
Electronics engineers, except computer	17-2072	134,900	136,800	1	1,900

State & Area Data
Occupational Employment Statistics (OES)
The Occupational Employment Statistics (OES) program produces employment and wage estimates annually for over 800 occupations. These estimates are available for the nation as a whole, for individual states, and for metropolitan and nonmetropolitan areas.

Contacts for More Information
For more information about general engineering education and career resources, visit
➤ American Society for Engineering Education

➤ Technology Student Association

For more information about licensure as an electrical or electronics engineer, visit
➤ National Council of Examiners for Engineering and Surveying

➤ National Society of Professional Engineers

➤ International Society of Automation

For more information about accredited engineering programs, visit
➤ ABET

For more information about engineering summer camps, visit
➤ Engineering Education Service Center

Electro-mechanical Technicians

Summary

Quick Facts: Electro-mechanical Technicians

2019 Median Pay	$58,350 per year $28.05 per hour
Typical Entry-Level Education	Associate's degree
Work Experience in a Related Occupation	None
On-the-job Training	None
Number of Jobs, 2019	14,600
Job Outlook, 2019-29	3% (As fast as average)
Employment Change, 2019-29	400

What Electro-mechanical Technicians Do
Electro-mechanical technicians operate, test, and maintain unmanned, automated, robotic, or electromechanical equipment.

Work Environment
Electro-mechanical technicians work closely with electrical and mechanical engineers. They work in many industrial environments, including energy, plastics, computer and communications equipment manufacturing, and aerospace.

How to Become an Electro-mechanical Technician
Electro-mechanical technicians typically need either an associate's degree or a postsecondary certificate.

Electro-mechanical technicians verify dimensions of parts, by using precision measuring instruments, to ensure that specifications are met.

Pay
The median annual wage for electro-mechanical technicians was $58,350 in May 2019.

Job Outlook
Employment of electro-mechanical technicians is projected to grow 3 percent from 2019 to 2029, about as fast as the average for all occupations.

State & Area Data

Explore resources for employment and wages by state and area for electro-mechanical technicians.

Similar Occupations

Compare the job duties, education, job growth, and pay of electro-mechanical technicians with similar occupations.

What Electro-mechanical Technicians Do

Electro-mechanical technicians combine knowledge of mechanical technology with knowledge of electrical and electronic circuits. They operate, test, and maintain unmanned, automated, robotic, or electromechanical equipment.

Duties

Electro-mechanical technicians typically do the following:

- Read blueprints, schematics, and diagrams to determine the method and sequence of assembly of a part, machine, or piece of equipment
- Verify dimensions of parts, using precision measuring instruments, to ensure that specifications are met
- Operate metalworking machines to make housings, fittings, and fixtures
- Inspect parts for surface defects
- Repair and calibrate hydraulic and pneumatic assemblies
- Test the performance of electro-mechanical assemblies, using test instruments
- Install electronic parts and hardware, using soldering equipment and hand tools
- Operate, test, or maintain robotic equipment
- Analyze and record test results, and prepare written documentation

Electro-mechanical technicians test and operate machines in factories and other worksites. They also analyze and record test results, and prepare written documentation to describe the tests they performed and what the test results were.

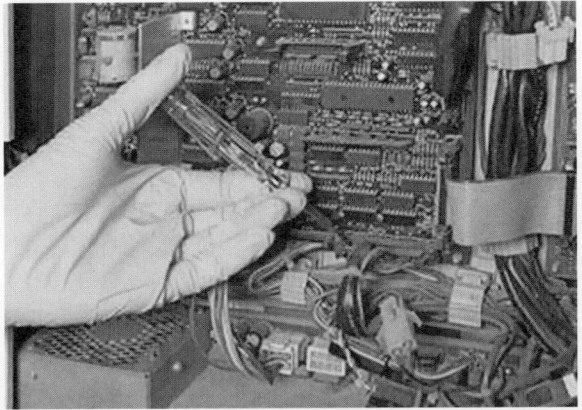

Electro-mechanical technicians install, repair, upgrade, and test electronic and computer-controlled mechanical systems.

Electro-mechanical technicians install, maintain, and repair automated machinery and computer-controlled mechanical systems in industrial settings. This kind of work requires knowledge and training in the application of photonics, the science of light. The technological aspects of the work have to do with the generation, control, and detection of the light waves so that the automated processes can proceed as designed by the engineers.

Electro-mechanical technicians also test, operate, or maintain robotic equipment at worksites. This equipment may include unmanned submarines, aircraft, or similar types of equipment for uses that include oil drilling, deep-ocean exploration, or hazardous-waste removal. These technicians also work on energy projects involving solar power and wind.

Work Environment

Electro-mechanical technicians held about 14,600 jobs in 2019. The largest employers of electro-mechanical technicians were as follows:

Machinery manufacturing	14%
Engineering services	9
Navigational, measuring, electromedical, and control instruments manufacturing	7
Transportation equipment manufacturing	7
Semiconductor and other electronic component manufacturing	7

Electro-mechanical technicians work closely with electrical engineers and mechanical engineers. They work in many industrial environments, including energy, plastics, computer and communications equipment manufacturing, and aerospace. They often work both at production sites and in offices.

Electro-mechanical technicians test the performance of electro-mechanical assemblies, using test instruments.

Because their job involves manual work with many machines and types of equipment, electro-mechanical technicians are sometimes exposed to hazards from equipment or toxic materials. However, incidents are rare as long as they follow proper safety procedures.

Work Schedules

Electro-mechanical technicians often work for large companies in manufacturing or for engineering firms. Like others at these firms, these technicians tend to work regular shifts. However, sometimes they must work additional hours to make repairs so that manufacturing operations can continue.

How to Become an Electro-mechanical Technician

Electro-mechanical technicians typically need either an associate's degree or a postsecondary certificate.

Education

Associate's degree programs and postsecondary certificates for electro-mechanical technicians are offered at vocational–technical schools and community colleges. Vocational–technical schools include postsecondary public institutions that serve local students and emphasize teaching the skills needed by local employers. Community colleges offer programs similar to those in technical institutes, but they may include more theory-based and liberal arts coursework.

ABET accredits associate's and higher degree programs. Most associate's degree programs that are accredited by ABET include at least college algebra and trigonometry, as well as basic science courses.

In community college programs, prospective electro-mechanical technicians can concentrate in fields such as the following:

- Electro-mechanics/mechatronics
- Industrial maintenance
- Process control

Electro-mechanical technicians typically need either an associate's degree or a postsecondary certificate.

Earning an associate's degree in electronic or mechanical technology facilitates entry into bachelor's degree programs in electrical engineering and mechanical engineering. For more information, see the profiles on electrical and electronics engineers and mechanical engineers.

Training in mechatronics provides an understanding of four key systems on which this occupation works: mechanical systems, electronic systems, control systems, and computer systems.

Important Qualities

Detail oriented. Electro-mechanical technicians must make and keep the precise, accurate measurements that mechanical engineers need.

Dexterity. Electro-mechanical technicians must use hand tools and soldering irons on small circuitry and electronic parts to create detailed electronic components by hand.

Interpersonal skills. Electro-mechanical technicians must take instruction and offer advice when needed. In addition, they often need to coordinate their work with that of others.

Logical-thinking skills. To carry out engineers' designs, inspect designs for quality control, and assemble prototypes, electro-mechanical technicians must read instructions and follow a logical sequence or a specific set of rules.

Math skills. Electro-mechanical technicians use math for analysis, design, and troubleshooting in their work.

Mechanical skills. Electro-mechanical technicians apply the theory and instructions of engineers by creating or building new components for industrial machinery or equipment. They must be adept at operating machinery, including drill presses, grinders, and engine lathes.

Writing skills. Electro-mechanical technicians must write reports that cover onsite construction, the results of testing, or problems they find when carrying out designs. Their writing must be clear and well organized so that the engineers they work with can understand the reports.

Licenses, Certifications, and Registrations

Electro-mechanical technicians can gain certification as a way to demonstrate professional competence.

The International Society of Automation offers certification as a Certified Control Systems Technician. This requires, at a minimum, 5 years of experience on the job, or 3 years of work experience if the technician has completed 2 years of postsecondary education.

The National Institute for Certification in Engineering Technologies (NICET) offers certification in electrical power testing, industrial instrumentation, and other specialties.

Pay

The median annual wage for electro-mechanical technicians was $58,350 in May 2019. The median wage is the wage at which half the workers in an occupation earned more than that amount

Electro-mechanical Technicians
Median annual wages, May 2019

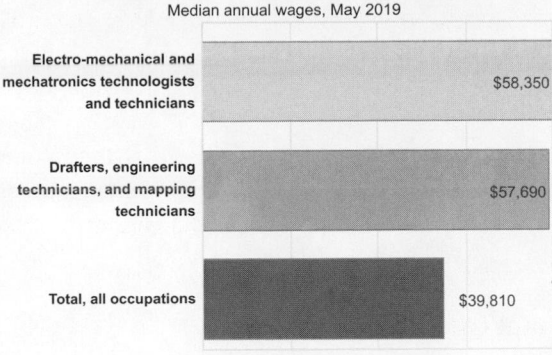

Electro-mechanical Technicians
Percent change in employment, projected 2019-29

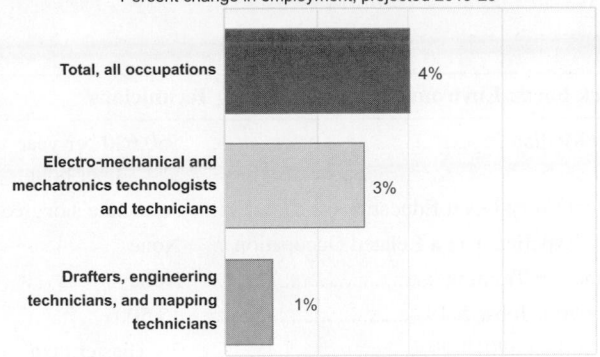

Note: All Occupations includes all occupations in the U.S. Economy.
Source: U.S. Bureau of Labor Statistics, Occupational Employment Statistics.

Note: All Occupations includes all occupations in the U.S. Economy.
Source: U.S. Bureau of Labor Statistics, Employment Projections program.

and half earned less. The lowest 10 percent earned less than $36,520, and the highest 10 percent earned more than $93,450.

In May 2019, the median annual wages for electro-mechanical technicians in the top industries in which they worked were as follows:

Engineering services	$60,360
Navigational, measuring, electromedical, and control instruments manufacturing	57,920
Machinery manufacturing	55,520
Transportation equipment manufacturing	54,930
Semiconductor and other electronic component manufacturing	53,580

Electro-mechanical technicians often work for large companies in manufacturing or for engineering firms. Like others at these firms, these technicians tend to work regular shifts. However, sometimes they must work additional hours to make repairs so that manufacturing operations can continue.

Job Outlook

Employment of electro-mechanical technicians is projected to grow 3 percent from 2019 to 2029, about as fast as the average for all occupations.

Many of these technicians are employed in manufacturing industries, for which employment projections vary. Industries in which new jobs are expected for these workers include machinery manufacturing; motor vehicle parts manufacturing; and navigational, measuring, electro-medical, and control instruments manufacturing.

Employment projections data for electro-mechanical technicians, 2019-29					
Occupational Title	SOC Code	Employment, 2019	Projected Employment, 2029	Change, 2019-29 Percent	Numeric
SOURCE: U.S. Bureau of Labor Statistics, Employment Projections program					
Electro-mechanical and mechatronics technologists and technicians	17-3024	14,600	15,100	3	400

State & Area Data
Occupational Employment Statistics (OES)

The Occupational Employment Statistics (OES) program produces employment and wage estimates annually for over 800 occupations. These estimates are available for the nation as a whole, for individual states, and for metropolitan and nonmetropolitan areas.

Contacts for More Information

For more information about general engineering education and career resources, visit
➤ American Society for Engineering Education
➤ IEEE
➤ Technology Student Association

For more information on accredited programs, visit
➤ ABET

For more information about certification, visit
➤ International Society of Automation
➤ National Institute for Certification in Engineering Technologies (NICET)

For information about working in automation, visit
➤ Automation Federation

Environmental Engineering Technicians

Summary

Quick Facts: Environmental Engineering Technicians

2019 Median Pay	$50,620 per year $24.34 per hour
Typical Entry-Level Education	Associate's degree
Work Experience in a Related Occupation ...	None
On-the-job Training	None
Number of Jobs, 2019	18,500
Job Outlook, 2019-29	7% (Faster than average)
Employment Change, 2019-29	1,400

What Environmental Engineering Technicians Do

Environmental engineering technicians carry out the plans that environmental engineers develop.

Work Environment

Most environmental engineering technicians work full time. They typically work indoors, usually in laboratories, and often have regular working hours. However, they must sometimes work irregular hours in order to monitor operations.

How to Become an Environmental Engineering Technician

Environmental engineering technicians typically need an associate's degree in environmental engineering technology or a related field.

Pay

The median annual wage for environmental engineering technicians was $50,620 in May 2019.

Job Outlook

Employment of environmental engineering technicians is projected to grow 7 percent from 2019 to 2029, faster than the

Environmental engineering technicians conduct pollution surveys, for which they collect and analyze samples such as air and ground water.

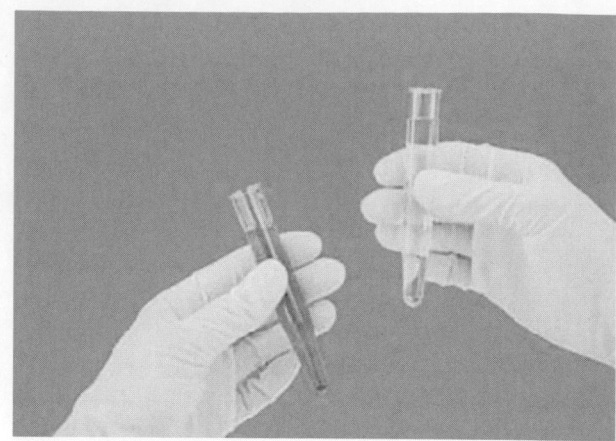

Environmental engineering technicians collect water samples.

average for all occupations. Employment in this occupation typically is tied to projects created by environmental engineers. State and local governments' concerns regarding water availability and quality should lead to efforts to increase the efficiency of water use.

State & Area Data

Explore resources for employment and wages by state and area for environmental engineering technicians.

What Environmental Engineering Technicians Do

Environmental engineering technicians carry out the plans that environmental engineers develop.

Duties

Environmental engineering technicians typically do the following:

- Set up, test, operate, and modify equipment used to prevent or clean up environmental pollution
- Maintain project records and computer program files
- Conduct pollution surveys, for which they collect and analyze samples, such as samples of air and ground water
- Perform indoor and outdoor work on environmental quality
- Work to mitigate sources of environmental pollution
- Review technical documents to ensure their completeness and conformance to requirements
- Review work plans to schedule activities
- Arrange for the disposal of lead, asbestos, and other hazardous materials

In laboratories, environmental engineering technicians record observations, test results, and document photographs. To keep laboratories supplied, they also may gather product information, identify vendors and suppliers, and order materials and equipment.

Environmental engineering technicians help environmental engineers develop devices used to clean up environmental pollution. They also inspect facilities for compliance with the regulations that govern substances such as asbestos, lead, and wastewater.

Work Environment

Environmental engineering technicians held about 18,500 jobs in 2019. The largest employers of environmental engineering technicians were as follows:

Engineering services	25%
Management, scientific, and technical consulting services	19
Government	14
Waste management and remediation services	13
Manufacturing	7

Environmental engineering technicians work under the direction of engineers and as part of a team with other technicians. They must be able to work well with both supervisors and peers.

Environmental engineering technicians typically work indoors, usually in laboratories, and often have regular working hours. They also work outdoors, sometimes in remote locations.

Because environmental engineering technicians help out in environmental cleanup, they can be exposed to hazards from equipment, chemicals, or toxic materials. For this reason, they must follow proper safety procedures, such as wearing hazmat suits and sometimes respirators, even in warm weather. When they work in wet areas, environmental engineering technicians wear heavy rubber boots to keep their legs and feet dry.

Work Schedules

Most environmental engineering technicians work full time and typically have regular hours. However, they must sometimes work irregular hours in order to monitor operations or contain a major environmental threat.

Environmental engineering technicians must wear protective gear when they are working outdoors on environmental remediation.

How to Become an Environmental Engineering Technician

Environmental engineering technicians typically need an associate's degree in environmental engineering technology or a related field.

Education

Environmental engineering technicians typically need an associate's degree in environmental engineering technology or a related field. Programs in environmental engineering technology generally include courses in mathematics, chemistry, hazardous-waste management, and environmental assessment, among others.

Programs can be found in vocational–technical schools and community colleges. Both types of school offer similar programs, but community colleges include more theory-based and liberal arts coursework. Some environmental engineering technicians enter the occupation with a bachelor's degree in a natural science, such as biology or chemistry.

ABET accredits engineering and engineering technology programs at the associate's level and above.

Prospective engineering technicians should take as many high school science and math courses as possible to prepare for programs in engineering technology after high school.

Environmental engineering technicians perform indoor and outdoor environmental quality work.

Important Qualities

Communication skills. When working on teams, environmental engineering technicians must listen well and report back to their group or team leader.

Critical-thinking skills. Environmental engineers rely on environmental engineering technicians to help identify problems and solutions and to implement the engineers' plans. To do these tasks, technicians must be able to think critically and logically.

Observational skills. Environmental engineering technicians are the eyes and ears of environmental engineers and must assume responsibility for properly evaluating situations onsite. These technicians must recognize problems so that the environmental engineers are informed as quickly as possible.

Problem-solving skills. Environmental engineering technicians implement plans designed by engineers. They often operate and maintain complex machinery. They must devise solutions to problems, such as mechanical breakdowns or unexpected findings at a worksite.

Reading skills. Environmental engineering technicians must be able to read and understand legal and technical documents in order to ensure that regulatory requirements are being met.

Training

Some environmental technician positions require training on working with hazardous materials in accordance with Occupational Safety & Health Administration (OSHA) standards.

Advancement

Environmental engineering technicians usually begin work as trainees in entry-level positions supervised by an environmental engineer or a more experienced technician. As they gain experience, technicians take on more responsibility and carry out assignments under general supervision. Some eventually enter positions as senior environmental technicians or lead environmental technicians, who function as supervisors when onsite.

Technicians with a bachelor's degree often are able to advance to become environmental engineers.

Pay

The median annual wage for environmental engineering technicians was $50,620 in May 2019. The median wage is the wage at which half the workers in an occupation earned more than that amount and half earned less. The lowest 10 percent earned less than $32,610, and the highest 10 percent earned more than $82,930.

In May 2019, the median annual wages for environmental engineering technicians in the top industries in which they worked were as follows:

Manufacturing	$56,780
Government	56,520
Management, scientific, and technical consulting services	50,820
Engineering services	49,590
Waste management and remediation services	42,220

Most environmental engineering technicians work full time and typically have regular hours. However, they must sometimes work irregular hours in order to monitor operations or contain a major environmental threat.

Job Outlook

Employment of environmental engineering technicians is projected to grow 7 percent from 2019 to 2029, faster than the average for all occupations.

Employment in this occupation is typically tied to projects created by environmental engineers. State and local governments are expected to focus their efforts and resources on efficient water use, storm water management, and wastewater treatment over the next decade. The demand for more environmental technicians by consulting firms will arise as governments and larger firms look to reduce costs.

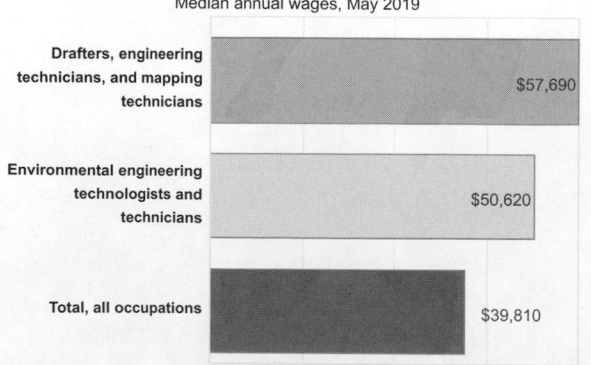

Environmental Engineering Technicians
Median annual wages, May 2019

- Drafters, engineering technicians, and mapping technicians — $57,690
- Environmental engineering technologists and technicians — $50,620
- Total, all occupations — $39,810

Note: All Occupations includes all occupations in the U.S. Economy.
Source: U.S. Bureau of Labor Statistics, Occupational Employment Statistics.

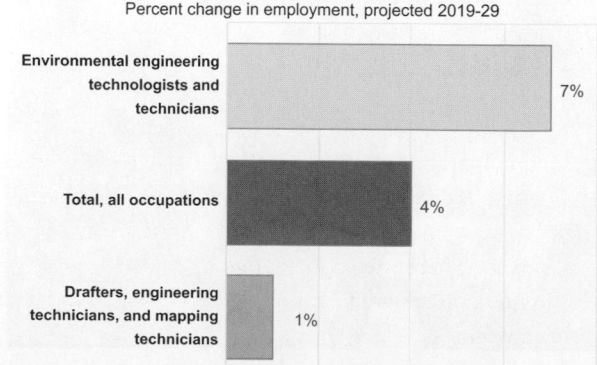

Environmental Engineering Technicians
Percent change in employment, projected 2019-29

- Environmental engineering technologists and technicians — 7%
- Total, all occupations — 4%
- Drafters, engineering technicians, and mapping technicians — 1%

Note: All Occupations includes all occupations in the U.S. Economy.
Source: U.S. Bureau of Labor Statistics, Employment Projections program.

Employment projections data for environmental engineering technicians, 2019-29					
Occupational Title	SOC Code	Employment, 2019	Projected Employment, 2029	Change, 2019-29 Percent	Numeric
SOURCE: U.S. Bureau of Labor Statistics, Employment Projections program					
Environmental engineering technologists and technicians	17-3025	18,500	19,900	7	1,400

State & Area Data
Occupational Employment Statistics (OES)
The Occupational Employment Statistics (OES) program produces employment and wage estimates annually for over 800 occupations. These estimates are available for the nation as a whole, for individual states, and for metropolitan and nonmetropolitan areas.

Contacts for More Information
For more information about accredited programs, visit
➤ ABET

For more information about general engineering education and career resources, visit
➤ Technology Student Association

For information on OSHA certification, visit
➤ U.S. Department of Labor, Occupational Safety & Health Administration

---

Environmental Engineers

Summary

Quick Facts: Environmental Engineers

2019 Median Pay	$88,860 per year $42.72 per hour
Typical Entry-Level Education	Bachelor's degree
Work Experience in a Related Occupation	None
On-the-job Training	None
Number of Jobs, 2019	55,800
Job Outlook, 2019-29	3% (As fast as average)
Employment Change, 2019-29	1,700

Environmental engineers obtain, update, and maintain plans, permits, and standard operating procedures for environmental projects.

What Environmental Engineers Do
Environmental engineers use the principles of engineering, soil science, biology, and chemistry to develop solutions to environmental problems.

Work Environment
Environmental engineers work in a variety of settings because of the nature of the tasks they do. When they are working with other engineers and urban and regional planners, environmental engineers are likely to be in offices. When they are carrying out solutions through construction projects, they are likely to be at construction sites.

How to Become an Environmental Engineer
Environmental engineers must have a bachelor's degree in environmental engineering or a related field, such as civil, chemical, or general engineering. Employers also value practical experience. Therefore, cooperative engineering programs, which provide college credit for structured job experience, are valuable as well.

Pay
The median annual wage for environmental engineers was $88,860 in May 2019.

Job Outlook
Employment of environmental engineers is projected to grow 3 percent from 2019 to 2029, about as fast as the average for all occupations. State and local governments' concerns regarding water availability and quality should lead to efforts to increase the efficiency of water use.

State & Area Data
Explore resources for employment and wages by state and area for environmental engineers.

What Environmental Engineers Do
Environmental engineers use the principles of engineering, soil science, biology, and chemistry to develop solutions to environmental problems. They work to improve recycling, waste disposal, public health, and water and air pollution control. They also address global issues, such as unsafe drinking water, climate change, and environmental sustainability.

Duties
Environmental engineers typically do the following:

Environmental engineers design systems for managing and cleaning municipal water supplies.

Environmental engineers work with other engineers and with urban and regional planners.

- Prepare, review, and update environmental investigation reports
- Design projects that lead to environmental protection, such as water reclamation facilities or air pollution control systems
- Obtain, update, and maintain plans, permits, and standard operating procedures
- Provide technical support for environmental remediation projects and for legal actions
- Analyze scientific data and do quality-control checks
- Monitor the progress of environmental improvement programs
- Inspect industrial and municipal facilities and programs in order to ensure compliance with environmental regulations
- Advise corporations and government agencies about procedures for cleaning up contaminated sites

Environmental engineers conduct hazardous-waste management studies in which they evaluate the significance of a hazard and advise on treating and containing it. They also design systems for municipal and industrial water supplies and industrial wastewater treatment, and research the environmental impact of proposed construction projects. Environmental engineers in government develop regulations to prevent mishaps.

Some environmental engineers study ways to minimize the effects of acid rain, climate change, automobile emissions, and ozone depletion. They also collaborate with environmental scientists, urban and regional planners, hazardous-waste technicians, and other engineers, as well as with specialists such as experts in law and business, to address environmental problems and environmental sustainability. For more information, see the job profiles on environmental scientists and specialists, hazardous materials removal workers, lawyers, and urban and regional planners.

Work Environment

Environmental engineers held about 55,800 jobs in 2019. The largest employers of environmental engineers were as follows:

Engineering services	26%
Management, scientific, and technical consulting services	20
State government, excluding education and hospitals	13
Local government, excluding education and hospitals	7
Federal government, excluding postal service	6

Environmental engineers work in a variety of settings because of the nature of the tasks they do:

- When they are working with other engineers and with urban and regional planners, environmental engineers are likely to be in offices.
- When they are working with businesspeople and lawyers, environmental engineers are likely to be at seminars, presenting information and answering questions.
- When they are working with hazardous materials removal workers and environmental scientists, environmental engineers work at specific sites outdoors.

Work Schedules

Most environmental engineers work full time. Those who manage projects often work more than 40 hours per week to monitor the project's progress, ensure that deadlines are met, and recommend corrective action when needed.

How to Become an Environmental Engineer

Environmental engineers must have a bachelor's degree in environmental engineering or a related field, such as civil, chemical, or general engineering. Employers also value practical experience. Therefore, cooperative engineering programs, in which college credit is awarded for structured job experience, are valuable as well.

Education

Entry-level environmental engineering jobs require a bachelor's degree. Programs include classroom, laboratory, and

A bachelor's degree is needed to become an environmental engineer.

field studies. Some colleges and universities offer cooperative programs in which students gain practical experience while completing their education.

At some colleges and universities, a student can enroll in a 5-year program that leads to both a bachelor's and a master's degree. A graduate degree allows an engineer to work as an instructor at some colleges and universities or to do research and development, and employers may prefer candidates to have a master's degree.

Students interested in becoming an environmental engineer should take high school courses in chemistry, biology, physics, and math, including algebra, trigonometry, and calculus.

Engineering programs are accredited by ABET, and employers may prefer to hire candidates who have graduated from an accredited program. A degree from an ABET-accredited program is usually necessary for a person to become a licensed professional engineer.

Important Qualities

Imagination. Environmental engineers sometimes have to design systems that will be part of larger ones. They must foresee how the proposed designs will interact with components of the larger system, including the workers, machinery, and equipment, as well as with the environment.

Interpersonal skills. Environmental engineers must work with others toward a common goal. They usually work with engineers and scientists who design other systems and with the technicians and mechanics who put the designs into practice.

Problem-solving skills. When designing facilities and processes, environmental engineers strive to solve several issues at once, from workers' safety to environmental protection. They must identify and anticipate problems in order to prevent losses for their employers, safeguard workers' health, and mitigate environmental damage.

Reading skills. Environmental engineers often work with businesspeople, lawyers, and other professionals outside their field. They frequently are required to read and understand documents that deal with topics outside their scope of training.

Writing skills. Environmental engineers must write clearly so that others without their specific training can understand their documents, including plans, proposals, specifications, and findings, among others.

Licenses, Certifications, and Registrations

Licensure is not required for entry-level positions as an environmental engineer. A Professional Engineering (PE) license, which allows for higher levels of leadership and independence, can be acquired later in one's career. Licensed engineers are called professional engineers (PEs). A PE can oversee the work of other engineers, sign off on projects, and provide services directly to the public. State licensure generally requires

- A degree from an ABET-accredited engineering program
- A passing score on the Fundamentals of Engineering (FE) exam
- Relevant work experience, typically at least 4 years
- A passing score on the Professional Engineering (PE) exam

The initial FE exam can be taken after one earns a bachelor's degree. Engineers who pass this exam are commonly called engineers in training (EITs) or engineer interns (EIs). After meeting work experience requirements, EITs and EIs can take the second exam, called the Principles and Practice of Engineering (PE).

Each state issues its own licenses. Most states recognize licensure from other states, as long as the licensing state's requirements meet or exceed their own licensure requirements. Several states require engineers to take continuing education to keep their licenses.

After licensing, environmental engineers can earn board certification from the American Academy of Environmental Engineers and Scientists. This certification shows that an environmental engineer has expertise in one or more areas of specialization.

Other Experience

During high school, students can attend engineering summer camps to see what these and other engineers, do. Attending these camps can help students plan their coursework for the remainder of their time in high school.

Advancement

As beginning engineers gain knowledge and experience, they move on to more difficult projects and they have greater independence to develop designs, solve problems, and make decisions. Eventually, environmental engineers may advance to become technical specialists or to supervise a team of engineers and technicians.

Some may even become engineering managers or move into executive positions, such as program managers. However, before assuming a managerial position, an engineer most often works under the supervision of a more experienced engineer.

Environmental Engineers
Median annual wages, May 2019

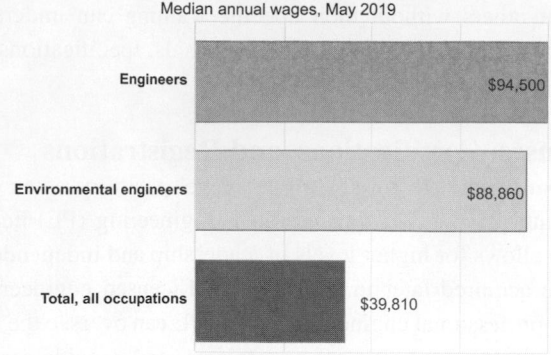

Engineers	$94,500
Environmental engineers	$88,860
Total, all occupations	$39,810

Note: All Occupations includes all occupations in the U.S. Economy.
Source: U.S. Bureau of Labor Statistics, Occupational Employment Statistics.

For more information, see the profile on architectural and engineering managers.

Pay

The median annual wage for environmental engineers was $88,860 in May 2019. The median wage is the wage at which half the workers in an occupation earned more than that amount and half earned less. The lowest 10 percent earned less than $54,330, and the highest 10 percent earned more than $142,070.

In May 2019, the median annual wages for environmental engineers in the top industries in which they worked were as follows:

Federal government, excluding postal service	$105,410
Engineering services	89,050
Local government, excluding education and hospitals	86,540
Management, scientific, and technical consulting services	84,300
State government, excluding education and hospitals	81,290

Most environmental engineers work full time. Those who manage projects often work more than 40 hours per week to monitor the project's progress, ensure that deadlines are met, and recommend corrective action when needed.

Job Outlook

Employment of environmental engineers is projected to grow 3 percent from 2019 to 2029, about as fast as the average for all occupations.

State and local governments' concerns about water are leading to efforts to increase the efficiency of water use. Such a focus differs from that of wastewater treatment, for which this occupation is traditionally known. Most of the projected employment growth for environmental engineers is in professional, scientific, and technical services, as governments at the state and local levels draw on the industry to help address water efficiency concerns.

Environmental Engineers
Percent change in employment, projected 2019-29

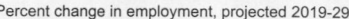

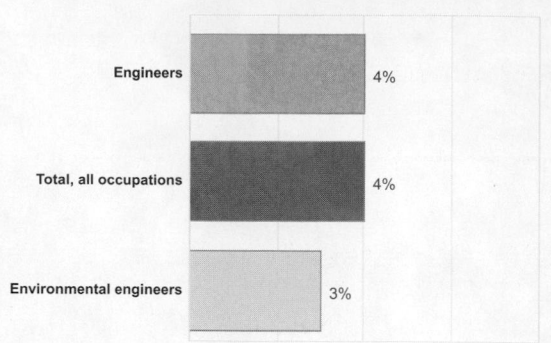

Engineers	4%
Total, all occupations	4%
Environmental engineers	3%

Note: All Occupations includes all occupations in the U.S. Economy.
Source: U.S. Bureau of Labor Statistics, Employment Projections program.

The federal government's requirements to clean up contaminated sites are expected to help sustain demand for these engineers' services. In addition, wastewater treatment is becoming a larger concern in areas of the country where drilling for shale gas requires the use and disposal of massive volumes of water.

Environmental engineers should continue to be needed to help utility companies and water treatment plants comply with federal or state environmental regulations, such as regulations regarding emissions from coal-fired power plants.

Job Prospects

Job prospects should be favorable for candidates who obtain a master's degree in environmental engineering. Opportunities for environmental engineers should be good because of the need to replace workers who will be retiring.

Employment projections data for environmental engineers, 2019-29					
Occupational Title	SOC Code	Employment, 2019	Projected Employment, 2029	Change, 2019-29	
				Percent	Numeric
SOURCE: U.S. Bureau of Labor Statistics, Employment Projections program					
Environmental engineers	17-2081	55,800	57,600	3	1,700

State & Area Data

Occupational Employment Statistics (OES)

The Occupational Employment Statistics (OES) program produces employment and wage estimates annually for over 800 occupations. These estimates are available for the nation as a whole, for individual states, and for metropolitan and nonmetropolitan areas.

Contacts for More Information

For more information about environmental engineers, visit
➤ American Academy of Environmental Engineers and Scientists

For more information about education for engineers, visit
➤ American Society for Engineering Education

For more information about accredited engineering programs, visit

➤ ABET

For more information about becoming licensed as a professional engineer, visit

➤ National Council of Examiners for Engineering and Surveying

➤ National Society of Professional Engineers

For more information about engineering summer camps, visit

➤ Engineering Education Service Center

Health and Safety Engineers

Summary

Quick Facts: Health and Safety Engineers

2019 Median Pay	$91,410 per year $43.95 per hour
Typical Entry-Level Education	Bachelor's degree
Work Experience in a Related Occupation	None
On-the-job Training	None
Number of Jobs, 2019	26,400
Job Outlook, 2019-29	4% (As fast as average)
Employment Change, 2019-29	1,000

What Health and Safety Engineers Do

Health and safety engineers combine knowledge of engineering and of health and safety to develop procedures and design systems to protect people from illness and injury and property from damage.

Work Environment

Health and safety engineers typically work in offices. However, they also must spend time at worksites when necessary, which sometimes requires travel.

How to Become a Health and Safety Engineer

Health and safety engineers must have a bachelor's degree, typically in environmental health and safety or in an engineering

Health and safety engineers identify and correct potential hazards.

discipline. Employers value practical experience, so cooperative-education engineering programs at universities are valuable as well.

Pay

The median annual wage for health and safety engineers was $91,410 in May 2019.

Job Outlook

Employment of health and safety engineers is projected to grow 4 percent from 2019 to 2029, about as fast as the average for all occupations. As buildings, products, and processes continue to become more complex and new regulations are created, these engineers will be needed to reduce costs, save lives, and produce safe consumer products.

State & Area Data

Explore resources for employment and wages by state and area for health and safety engineers.

What Health and Safety Engineers Do

Health and safety engineers develop procedures and design systems to protect people from illness and injury and property from damage. They combine knowledge of engineering and of health and safety to make sure that chemicals, machinery, software, furniture, and other products will not cause harm to people or damage to property.

Duties

Health and safety engineers typically do the following:

- Maintain and apply knowledge of current health and safety policies, regulations, and industrial processes
- Review plans and specifications for new machinery and equipment to make sure that they meet safety requirements
- Identify and correct potential hazards by inspecting facilities, machinery, and safety equipment
- Evaluate the effectiveness of various industrial control mechanisms
- Ensure that buildings or products comply with health and safety regulations, especially after an inspection that required changes
- Install safety devices on machinery or direct the installation of these devices
- Review employee safety programs and recommend improvements

Health and safety in the workplace is a major concern of health and safety engineers.

Health and safety engineers also investigate industrial accidents and injuries to determine their causes and to determine whether the incidents were avoidable or can be prevented in the future. They interview employers and employees to learn about work environments and incidents that lead to accidents or injuries. They also evaluate the corrections that were made to remedy violations found during health inspections.

Health and safety engineering is a broad field covering many activities. The following are examples of types of health and safety engineers:

Fire prevention and protection engineers conduct analyses and make recommendations regarding the potential fire hazards of buildings, materials, and transportation systems. They also design, install, and maintain fire prevention and suppression systems and inspect systems to ensure that they meet government safety regulations. Fire prevention and protection engineers must be licensed and must keep up with changes in fire codes and regulations.

Product safety engineers, sometimes called ***product compliance engineers***, develop and conduct tests to make sure that various products are safe and comply with industry or government safety regulations. These engineers work on a wide range of products, from nuclear submarine reactors and robotics to cell phones and computer systems.

Systems safety engineers identify and analyze risks and hazards associated with system designs in order to make them safe while ensuring that the systems remain operational and effective. They work in many fields, including aerospace, and are moving into new fields, such as software safety, medical safety, and environmental safety.

For information on health and safety engineers who work in mines, see the profile on mining and geological engineers.

Work Environment

Health and safety engineers held about 26,400 jobs in 2019. The largest employers of health and safety engineers were as follows:

Health and safety engineers may need to spend time at worksites.

Manufacturing	27%
Construction	15
Government	13
Engineering services	9
Management, scientific, and technical consulting services	5

Health and safety engineers typically work in offices. However, they also must spend time at worksites when necessary, which sometimes requires travel.

Work Schedules

Most health and safety engineers work full time.

How to Become a Health and Safety Engineer

Health and safety engineers must have a bachelor's degree, typically in environmental health and safety or in an engineering discipline. Employers value practical experience, so cooperative-education engineering programs at universities are valuable as well.

Education

Entry-level jobs for health and safety engineers require a bachelor's degree, typically in environmental health and safety or in an engineering discipline, such as electrical, chemical, mechanical, industrial, or systems engineering. Bachelor's degree programs typically include classroom, laboratory, and field studies in applied engineering. Engineering students interested in becoming health and safety engineers also should take courses in occupational safety and health, industrial hygiene, ergonomics, or environmental safety. ABET accredits programs in engineering.

Many colleges and universities offer cooperative-education programs, which allow students to gain practical experience while completing their education.

A few colleges and universities offer 5-year accelerated programs through which students graduate with both a bachelor's

Health and safety engineers inspect facilities, machinery, and safety equipment to identify and correct potential hazards.

and a master's degree. A master's degree allows engineers to enter the occupation at a higher level, from which they can develop and implement safety systems.

Important Qualities

Communication skills. Health and safety engineers must be able to interpret federal and state regulations and their intent so that they can propose proper designs for specific work environments. Health and safety engineers also prepare and present training materials to workers and must be able to describe new regulations and procedures to a variety of audiences.

Creativity. Health and safety engineers produce designs showing potential problems and remedies for them. They must be creative, in order to deal with situations that are unique to a project.

Critical-thinking skills. Health and safety engineers must be able to identify hazards to humans and property in the workplace or in the home before those hazards cause material damage or become a health threat.

Observational skills. Health and safety engineers must observe and learn how operations function so that they can identify risks to people and property. This requires the ability to think in terms of overall processes within an organization. Health and safety engineers can then recommend systemic changes to minimize risks.

Problem-solving skills. In designing solutions for entire organizational operations, health and safety engineers must take into account processes from more than one system at the same time. In addition, they must try to anticipate a range of human reactions to the changes they recommend.

Licenses, Certifications, and Registrations

Licensure is not required for entry-level positions as a health and safety engineer. A Professional Engineering (PE) license, which allows for higher levels of leadership and independence, can be acquired later in one's career. Licensed engineers are called professional engineers (PEs). A PE can oversee the work of other engineers, sign off on projects, and provide services directly to the public. State licensure generally requires

- A degree from an ABET-accredited engineering program
- A passing score on the Fundamentals of Engineering (FE) exam
- Relevant work experience, typically at least 4 years
- A passing score on the Professional Engineering (PE) exam

The initial FE exam can be taken after one earns a bachelor's degree. Engineers who pass this exam are commonly called engineers in training (EITs) or engineer interns (EIs). After meeting work experience requirements, EITs and EIs can take the second exam, called the Principles and Practice of Engineering (PE).

Each state issues its own licenses. Most states recognize licensure from other states, as long as the licensing state's requirements meet or exceed their own licensure requirements. Several states require continuing education for engineers to keep their licenses.

Health and safety engineers can earn professional certifications, including the following:

- The Board of Certified Safety Professionals offers the Certified Safety Professional (CSP) certification, the Occupational Health and Safety Technologist (OHST) certification, and the new Associate Safety Professional (ASP) certification
- The American Board of Industrial Hygiene awards the Certified Industrial Hygienist (CIH) certification
- The American Society of Safety Professionals offers a Certificate in Safety Management (CSM)
- The International Council on Systems Engineering offers a program leading to designation as a Certified Systems Engineering Professional (CSEP)

Pay

The median annual wage for health and safety engineers was $91,410 in May 2019. The median wage is the wage at which half the workers in an occupation earned more than that amount and half earned less. The lowest 10 percent earned less than $53,650, and the highest 10 percent earned more than $143,880.

In May 2019, the median annual wages for health and safety engineers in the top industries in which they worked were as follows:

Engineering services	$99,410
Management, scientific, and technical consulting services	97,110
Government	89,250
Manufacturing	89,140
Construction	79,570

Most health and safety engineers work full time.

Health and Safety Engineers
Median annual wages, May 2019

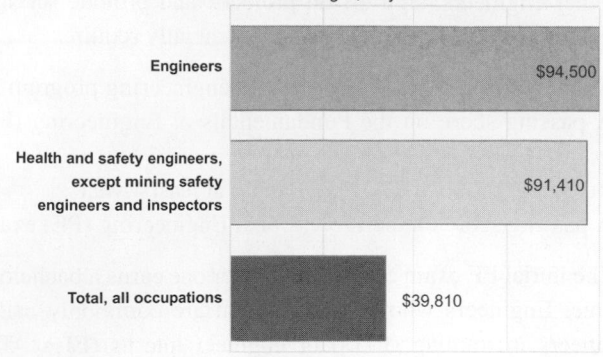

Note: All Occupations includes all occupations in the U.S. Economy.
Source: U.S. Bureau of Labor Statistics, Occupational Employment
Statistics.

Health and Safety Engineers
Percent change in employment, projected 2019-29

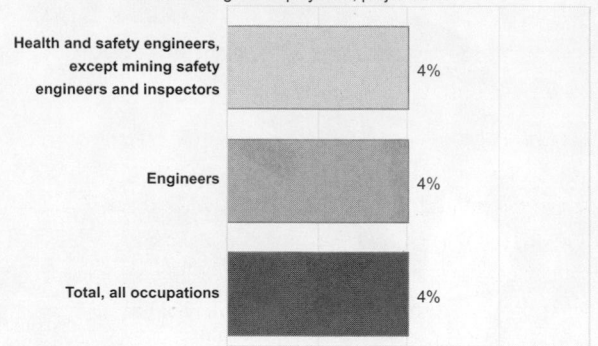

Note: All Occupations includes all occupations in the U.S. Economy.
Source: U.S. Bureau of Labor Statistics, Employment Projections
program.

Job Outlook

Employment of health and safety engineers is projected to grow 4 percent from 2019 to 2029, about as fast as the average for all occupations.

Health and safety engineers are employed mainly in manufacturing, engineering and consulting firms, construction, and state and local government. As buildings, products, and processes continue to become more complex and new regulations are created, these engineers will be needed to reduce costs, save lives, and produce safe consumer products.

Employment projections data for health and safety engineers, 2019-29					
Occupational Title	SOC Code	Employment, 2019	Projected Employment, 2029	Change, 2019-29	
				Percent	Numeric
SOURCE: U.S. Bureau of Labor Statistics, Employment Projections program					
Health and safety engineers, except mining safety engineers and inspectors	17-2111	26,400	27,500	4	1,000

State & Area Data

Occupational Employment Statistics (OES)

The Occupational Employment Statistics (OES) program produces employment and wage estimates annually for over 800 occupations. These estimates are available for the nation as a whole, for individual states, and for metropolitan and nonmetropolitan areas.

Contacts for More Information

For information about general engineering education and career resources, visit
➤ American Society of Safety Professionals
➤ Technology Student Association

For more information about accredited engineering programs, visit
➤ ABET

For more information about the Professional Engineer license, visit
➤ National Council of Examiners for Engineering and Surveying
➤ National Society of Professional Engineers

For information about protecting worker health, visit
➤ American Industrial Hygiene Association

For information about certification, visit
➤ American Board of Industrial Hygiene
➤ American Society of Safety Engineers
➤ Board of Certified Safety Professionals
➤ International Council on Systems Engineering

Industrial Engineering Technicians

Summary

Quick Facts: Industrial Engineering Technicians

2019 Median Pay	$56,550 per year
	$27.19 per hour
Typical Entry-Level Education	Associate's degree
Work Experience in a Related Occupation	None
On-the-job Training	None
Number of Jobs, 2019	68,500
Job Outlook, 2019-29	1% (Slower than average)
Employment Change, 2019-29	1,000

What Industrial Engineering Technicians Do

Industrial engineering technicians assist industrial engineers in creating systems that integrate workers, machines, materials, information, and energy to make a product or provide a service.

Work Environment

Most industrial engineering technicians work in manufacturing industries. Most work full time.

How to Become an Industrial Engineering Technician

Industrial engineering technicians typically need an associate's degree or a postsecondary certificate. Community colleges or technical institutes typically offer associate's degree programs, and vocational–technical schools offer certificate programs.

Pay

The median annual wage for industrial engineering technicians was $56,550 in May 2019.

Job Outlook

Employment of industrial engineering technicians is projected to grow 1 percent from 2019 to 2029, slower than the average for all occupations. Overall employment growth of industrial engineering technicians in manufacturing—the industry in which most of them work—is projected to be slow.

State & Area Data

Explore resources for employment and wages by state and area for industrial engineering technicians.

What Industrial Engineering Technicians Do

Industrial engineering technicians assist industrial engineers in devising efficient systems that integrate workers, machines, materials, information, and energy to make a product or provide a service. They prepare machinery and equipment layouts, plan workflows, conduct statistical production studies, and analyze production costs.

Duties

Industrial engineering technicians typically do the following:

- Suggest revisions to methods of operation, material handling, or equipment layout
- Interpret engineering drawings, schematic diagrams, and formulas
- Confer with management or engineering staff to determine quality and reliability standards
- Help plan work assignments, taking into account workers' performance, the capabilities of machines, and production schedules
- Prepare charts, graphs, and diagrams to illustrate workflow, routing, floor layouts, how materials are handled, and how machines are used
- Collect data to assist in process improvement activities

Industrial engineering technicians study the time and steps workers take to do a task (time and motion studies). To set reasonable production rates, they consider how workers perform operations such as maintenance, production, and service.

Industrial engineering technicians collect data to assist in process improvement activities.

Industrial engineering technicians interpret schematic diagrams and formulas.

The versatility of industrial engineering technicians allows them to be useful in a variety of projects. For example, they work in supply chain management to help businesses minimize inventory costs, in quality assurance to help businesses keep their customers satisfied, and in the growing field of project management to control costs and maximize efficiencies.

Industrial engineering technicians generally work in teams under the supervision of industrial engineers.

Manufacturing engineering technicians are a type of industrial engineering technician whose work improves manufacturing processes to raise product quality and profitability. They plan, test, and custom make industrial products, and thus assist the engineers in implementing improvements in production and output. Specifically, they may assess prototypes, analyze performance of machinery, or try new methods of plant production.

Work Environment

Industrial engineering technicians held about 68,500 jobs in 2019. The largest employers of industrial engineering technicians were as follows:

Computer and electronic product manufacturing 17%
Transportation equipment manufacturing 15
Professional, scientific, and technical services 9
Machinery manufacturing 8
Chemical manufacturing 8

Industrial engineers usually ask industrial engineering technicians to help carry out certain studies and make specific observations. Consequently, these technicians typically work at the location where products are manufactured or where services are delivered.

Work Schedules

Industrial engineering technicians usually work standard schedules. Most work full time.

Industrial engineering technicians help carry out studies and make observations to assist industrial engineers.

How to Become an Industrial Engineering Technician

Industrial engineering technicians typically need an associate's degree or a postsecondary certificate. Community colleges and technical institutes generally offer associate's degree programs, and vocational–technical schools offer certificate programs.

Education

High school students interested in becoming industrial engineering technicians should take courses in math, science, and drafting, where available. Courses that help students develop computer skills are helpful when the students later need to learn computer-aided design/computer-aided manufacturing software, known as CAD/CAM.

Postsecondary programs in industrial engineering are offered at vocational–technical schools, technical institutes, and community colleges. Vocational–technical schools and technical institutes serve local students and emphasize training needed by local employers. These programs generally award a certificate. Community colleges offer programs similar to those in technical institutes, but usually include more theory-based and liberal arts courses. Students who complete these programs earn associate's degrees.

ABET accredits engineering and engineering technology programs.

Generally, prospective industrial engineering technicians should major in applied science, industrial technology, or industrial engineering technology.

Becoming an industrial engineering technician usually requires either an associate's degree or a postsecondary certificate.

Important Qualities

Analytical skills. Industrial engineering technicians must help industrial engineers figure out how systems should work and how changes in conditions, operations, and the environment will affect outcomes.

Communication skills. Industrial engineering technicians receive instructions from industrial engineers. They must clearly understand and follow instructions and communicate problems to their supervisors.

Critical-thinking skills. Industrial engineering technicians must help industrial engineers figure out why certain processes or operations are not working as well as they might. They must ask the right questions to identify and correct weaknesses.

Detail oriented. Industrial engineering technicians must gather and record measurements and observations needed by industrial engineers.

Math skills. Industrial engineering technicians use the principles of mathematics for analysis, design, and troubleshooting in their work.

Observational skills. These technicians spend much of their time evaluating the performance of other people or organizations and then make suggestions for improvements or corrective action. They must gather and record information without interfering with workers in their environments.

Pay

The median annual wage for industrial engineering technicians was $56,550 in May 2019. The median wage is the wage at which half the workers in an occupation earned more than that amount and half earned less. The lowest 10 percent earned less than $35,850, and the highest 10 percent earned more than $87,790.

In May 2019, the median annual wages for industrial engineering technicians in the top industries in which they worked were as follows:

Chemical manufacturing	$59,710
Transportation equipment manufacturing	59,050
Computer and electronic product manufacturing	58,470
Professional, scientific, and technical services	58,210
Machinery manufacturing	54,410

Industrial engineering technicians usually work standard schedules. Most work full time.

Job Outlook

Employment of industrial engineering technicians is projected to grow 1 percent from 2019 to 2029, slower than the average for all occupations.

An emphasis on cost control through increased efficiency, along with industrial engineering technicians' role in assisting with automation, is expected to sustain demand somewhat for these workers.

However, overall employment growth of industrial engineering technicians in manufacturing—the industry in which most of them work—is projected to be slow.

Employment projections data for industrial engineering technicians, 2019-29					
Occupational Title	SOC Code	Employment, 2019	Projected Employment, 2029	Change, 2019-29	
				Percent	Numeric
SOURCE: U.S. Bureau of Labor Statistics, Employment Projections program					
Industrial engineering technologists and technicians	17-3026	68,500	69,500	1	1,000

State & Area Data
Occupational Employment Statistics (OES)

The Occupational Employment Statistics (OES) program produces employment and wage estimates annually for over 800 occupations. These estimates are available for the nation as a whole, for individual states, and for metropolitan and nonmetropolitan areas.

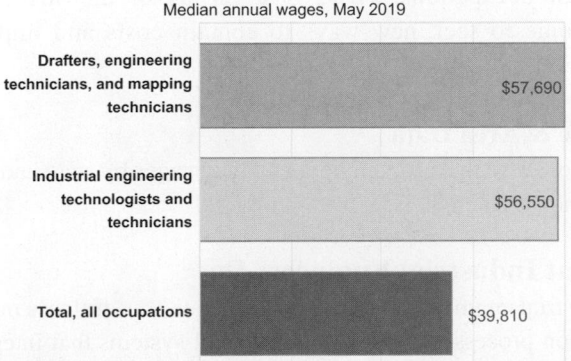

Industrial Engineering Technicians
Median annual wages, May 2019

- Drafters, engineering technicians, and mapping technicians: $57,690
- Industrial engineering technologists and technicians: $56,550
- Total, all occupations: $39,810

Note: All Occupations includes all occupations in the U.S. Economy.
Source: U.S. Bureau of Labor Statistics, Occupational Employment Statistics.

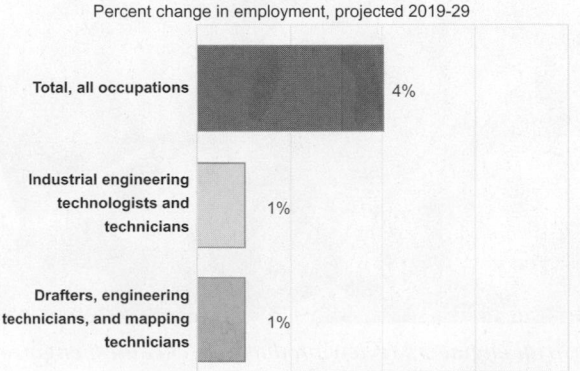

Industrial Engineering Technicians
Percent change in employment, projected 2019-29

- Total, all occupations: 4%
- Industrial engineering technologists and technicians: 1%
- Drafters, engineering technicians, and mapping technicians: 1%

Note: All Occupations includes all occupations in the U.S. Economy.
Source: U.S. Bureau of Labor Statistics, Employment Projections program.

Projections Central

Occupational employment projections are developed for all states by Labor Market Information (LMI) or individual state Employment Projections offices. All state projections data are available at www.projectionscentral.com. Information on this site allows projected employment growth for an occupation to be compared among states or to be compared within one state. In addition, states may produce projections for areas; there are links to each state's websites where these data may be retrieved.

Contacts for More Information

For more information about industrial engineering, visit
➤ Institute of Industrial & Systems Engineers

For more information about manufacturing engineering, visit
➤ Society of Manufacturing Engineers

For information on general engineering education and career resources, visit
➤ American Society for Engineering Education

➤ Technology Student Association

For more information about accredited programs, visit
➤ ABET

Industrial Engineers

Summary

Quick Facts: Industrial Engineers

2019 Median Pay	$88,020 per year / $42.32 per hour
Typical Entry-Level Education	Bachelor's degree
Work Experience in a Related Occupation	None
On-the-job Training	None
Number of Jobs, 2019	295,800
Job Outlook, 2019-29	10% (Much faster than average)
Employment Change, 2019-29	30,000

What Industrial Engineers Do

Industrial engineers devise efficient systems that integrate workers, machines, materials, information, and energy to make a product or provide a service.

Industrial engineers review production schedules, engineering specifications, and process flows to understand activities in manufacturing and services.

Work Environment

Depending on their tasks, industrial engineers work either in offices or in the settings they are trying to improve. For example, when observing problems, they may watch workers assembling parts in a factory. When solving problems, they may be in an office at a computer, looking at data that they or others have collected.

How to Become an Industrial Engineer

Industrial engineers need a bachelor's degree, typically in industrial engineering. However, many industrial engineers have degrees in mechanical engineering, electrical engineering, manufacturing engineering, industrial engineering technology, or general engineering.

Pay

The median annual wage for industrial engineers was $88,020 in May 2019.

Job Outlook

Employment of industrial engineers is projected to grow 10 percent from 2019 to 2029, much faster than the average for all occupations. Firms in a variety of industries will continue to seek new ways to contain costs and improve efficiency.

State & Area Data

Explore resources for employment and wages by state and area for industrial engineers.

What Industrial Engineers Do

Industrial engineers find ways to eliminate wastefulness in production processes. They devise efficient systems that integrate workers, machines, materials, information, and energy to make a product or provide a service.

Industrial engineers develop job evaluation programs, amongst other duties.

Duties

Industrial engineers typically do the following:

- Review production schedules, engineering specifications, process flows, and other information to understand methods that are applied and activities that take place in manufacturing and services
- Figure out how to manufacture parts or products, or deliver services, with maximum efficiency
- Develop management control systems to make financial planning and cost analysis more efficient
- Enact quality control procedures to resolve production problems or minimize costs
- Design control systems to coordinate activities and production planning in order to ensure that products meet quality standards
- Confer with clients about product specifications, vendors about purchases, management personnel about manufacturing capabilities, and staff about the status of projects

Industrial engineers apply their skills to many different situations, from manufacturing to healthcare systems to business administration. For example, they design systems for

- moving heavy parts within manufacturing plants
- delivering goods from a company to customers, including finding the most profitable places to locate manufacturing or processing plants

- evaluating job performance
- paying workers.

Some industrial engineers, called *manufacturing engineers*, focus entirely on the automated aspects of manufacturing processes. They design manufacturing systems to optimize the use of computer networks, robots, and materials.

Industrial engineers focus on how to get the work done most efficiently, balancing many factors, such as time, number of workers needed, available technology, actions workers need to take, achieving the end product with no errors, workers' safety, environmental concerns, and cost.

The versatility of industrial engineers allows them to engage in activities that are useful to a variety of businesses, governments, and nonprofits. For example, industrial engineers engage in supply chain management to help businesses minimize inventory costs, conduct quality assurance activities to help businesses keep their customer bases satisfied, and work in the growing field of project management as industries across the economy seek to control costs and maximize efficiencies.

Work Environment

Industrial engineers held about 295,800 jobs in 2019. The largest employers of industrial engineers were as follows:

Transportation equipment manufacturing	18%
Computer and electronic product manufacturing	13
Professional, scientific, and technical services	12
Machinery manufacturing	8
Fabricated metal product manufacturing	6

Depending on their tasks, industrial engineers work either in offices or in the settings they are trying to improve. For example, when observing problems, they may watch workers assembling parts in a factory. When solving problems, industrial engineers may be in an office at a computer where they analyze data that they or others have collected.

Industrial engineers must work well on teams because they need help from others to collect information about problems and to implement solutions.

Industrial engineers may need to travel to observe processes and make assessments in various work settings.

Work Schedules

Most industrial engineers work full time. Depending upon the projects in which these engineers are engaged, and the industries in which the projects are taking place, hours may vary.

How to Become an Industrial Engineer

Industrial engineers must have a bachelor's degree. Employers also value experience, so cooperative education engineering programs at universities are also beneficial.

Industrial engineers figure out how to manufacture parts or products or deliver services with maximum efficiency.

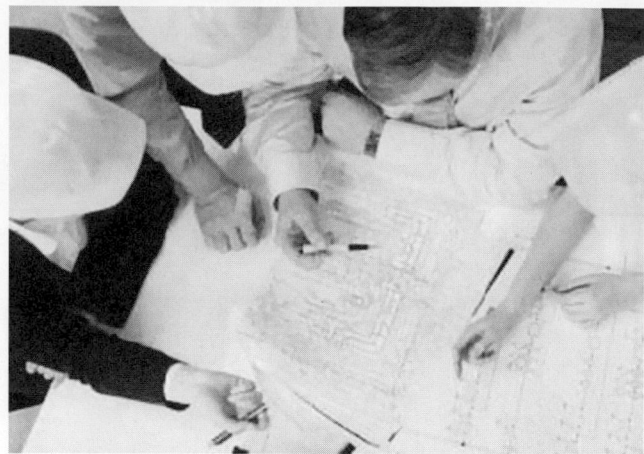

To find ways to reduce waste and improve performance, industrial engineers carefully study product requirements.

Education

Industrial engineers need a bachelor's degree, typically in industrial engineering. However, many industrial engineers have degrees in mechanical engineering, electrical engineering, manufacturing engineering, industrial engineering technology, or general engineering. Students interested in studying industrial engineering should take high school courses in mathematics, such as algebra, trigonometry, and calculus; computer science; and sciences such as chemistry and physics.

Bachelor's degree programs include lectures in classrooms and practice in laboratories. Courses include statistics, production systems planning, and manufacturing systems design, among others. Many colleges and universities offer cooperative education programs in which students gain practical experience while completing their education.

Several colleges and universities offer 5-year degree programs in industrial engineering that lead to a bachelor's and master's degree upon completion, and several more offer similar programs in mechanical engineering. A graduate degree allows an engineer to work as a professor at a college or university or to engage in research and development. Some 5-year or even 6-year cooperative education plans combine classroom study with practical work, permitting students to gain experience and to finance part of their education.

Programs in industrial engineering are accredited by ABET.

Important Qualities

Creativity. Industrial engineers use creativity and ingenuity to design new production processes in many kinds of settings in order to reduce the use of material resources, time, or labor while accomplishing the same goal.

Critical-thinking skills. Industrial engineers create new systems to solve problems related to waste and inefficiency. Solving these problems requires logic and reasoning to identify strengths and weaknesses of alternative solutions, conclusions, or approaches to the problems.

Listening skills. These engineers often operate in teams, but they also must solicit feedback from customers, vendors, and production staff. They must listen to customers and clients in order to fully grasp ideas and problems.

Math skills. Industrial engineers use the principles of calculus, trigonometry, and other advanced topics in mathematics for analysis, design, and troubleshooting in their work.

Problem-solving skills. In designing facilities for manufacturing and processes for providing services, these engineers deal with several issues at once, from workers' safety to quality assurance.

Speaking skills. Industrial engineers sometimes have to explain their instructions to production staff or technicians before they can make written instructions available. Being able to explain concepts clearly and quickly is crucial to preventing costly mistakes and loss of time.

Writing skills. Industrial engineers must prepare documentation for other engineers or scientists, or for future reference. The documentation must be coherent and explain their thinking clearly so that the others can understand the information.

Licenses, Certifications, and Registrations

Licensure is not required for entry-level positions as an industrial engineer. A Professional Engineering (PE) license, which allows for higher levels of leadership and independence, can be acquired later in one's career. Licensed engineers are called professional engineers (PEs). A PE can oversee the work of other engineers, sign off on projects, and provide services directly to the public. State licensure generally requires

- A degree from an ABET-accredited engineering program
- A passing score on the Fundamentals of Engineering (FE) exam
- Relevant work experience, typically at least 4 years
- A passing score on the Professional Engineering (PE) exam.

The initial FE exam can be taken after one earns a bachelor's degree. Engineers who pass this exam are commonly called engineers in training (EITs) or engineer interns (EIs). After meeting work experience requirements, EITs and EIs can take the second exam, called the Principles and Practice of Engineering.

Each state issues its own licenses. Most states recognize licensure from other states, as long as the licensing state's requirements meet or exceed their own licensure requirements. Several states require continuing education for engineers to keep their licenses.

The Society of Manufacturing Engineers offers certification, which requires a minimum of 8 years of a combination of education related to manufacturing and at least 4 years of work experience.

Other Experience

During high school, students can attend engineering summer camps to see what these and other engineers do. Attending these camps can help students plan their coursework for the remainder of their time in high school.

Advancement

Industrial engineers who are just starting out usually work under the supervision of experienced engineers. In large companies, new engineers also may receive formal training in classes or seminars. As beginning engineers gain knowledge and experience, they move on to more difficult projects with greater independence to develop designs, solve problems, and make decisions.

Eventually, industrial engineers may advance to become technical specialists, such as quality engineers or facility planners. In that role, they supervise a team of engineers and technicians. Earning a master's degree facilitates such specialization and thus advancement.

Many industrial engineers move into management positions because the work they do is closely related to the work of managers. For more information, see the profile on architectural and engineering managers.

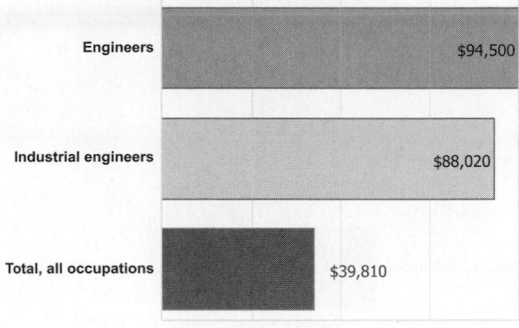

Industrial Engineers
Median annual wages, May 2019

- Engineers: $94,500
- Industrial engineers: $88,020
- Total, all occupations: $39,810

Note: All Occupations includes all occupations in the U.S. Economy.
Source: U.S. Bureau of Labor Statistics, Occupational Employment Statistics.

Pay

The median annual wage for industrial engineers was $88,020 in May 2019. The median wage is the wage at which half the workers in an occupation earned more than that amount and half earned less. The lowest 10 percent earned less than $57,290, and the highest 10 percent earned more than $134,070.

In May 2019, the median annual wages for industrial engineers in the top industries in which they worked were as follows:

Professional, scientific, and technical services......	$96,600
Computer and electronic product manufacturing ...	94,140
Transportation equipment manufacturing	90,250
Machinery manufacturing..	83,720
Fabricated metal product manufacturing................	76,410

Most industrial engineers work full time. Depending upon the projects in which these engineers are engaged, and the industries in which the projects are taking place, hours may vary.

Job Outlook

Employment of industrial engineers is projected to grow 10 percent from 2019 to 2029, faster than the average for all occupations. This occupation is versatile both in the nature of the work it does and in the industries in which its expertise can be put to use.

Because they are not as specialized as other engineers, industrial engineers are employed in a wide range of industries, including major manufacturing industries, consulting and engineering services, and research and development firms. This versatility arises from the fact that these engineers focus on reducing internal costs, making their work valuable for many industries. For example, their work is important for manufacturing industries that are considering relocating from overseas to domestic sites.

Industrial Engineers
Percent change in employment, projected 2019-29

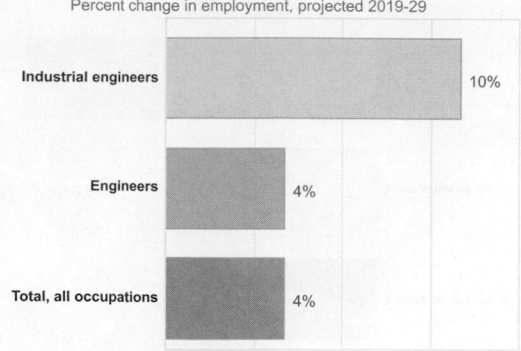

- Industrial engineers: 10%
- Engineers: 4%
- Total, all occupations: 4%

Note: All Occupations includes all occupations in the U.S. Economy.
Source: U.S. Bureau of Labor Statistics, Employment Projections program.

In addition, growth in healthcare and changes in how healthcare is delivered will create demand for industrial engineers in firms in professional, scientific, and consulting services.

Job Prospects

Many companies will be seeking to make use of new technologies to automate production processes in many different kinds of industries, including manufacturing industries. Those with knowledge of manufacturing engineering may have the best prospects for employment.

Employment projections data for industrial engineers, 2019-29					
Occupational Title	SOC Code	Employment, 2019	Projected Employment, 2029	Change, 2019-29	
				Percent	Numeric
SOURCE: U.S. Bureau of Labor Statistics, Employment Projections program					
Industrial engineers	17-2112	295,800	325,800	10	30,000

State & Area Data
Occupational Employment Statistics (OES)

The Occupational Employment Statistics (OES) program produces employment and wage estimates annually for over 800 occupations. These estimates are available for the nation as a whole, for individual states, and for metropolitan and nonmetropolitan areas.

Contacts for More Information

For more information about industrial engineers, visit
➤ Institute of Industrial & Systems Engineers

For more information about general engineering education and career resources, visit
➤ American Society for Engineering Education

➤ Technology Student Association

For more information about engineering summer camps, visit
➤ Engineering Education Service Center

For more information about licensure as an industrial engineer, visit
➤ National Council of Examiners for Engineering and Surveying

➤ National Society of Professional Engineers

For more information about certification as a manufacturing engineer, visit
➤ Society of Manufacturing Engineers

For more information about accredited engineering programs, visit
➤ ABET

Landscape Architects

Summary

Quick Facts: Landscape Architects

2019 Median Pay	$69,360 per year $33.35 per hour
Typical Entry-Level Education	Bachelor's degree
Work Experience in a Related Occupation	None
On-the-job Training	Internship/residency
Number of Jobs, 2019	24,500
Job Outlook, 2019-29	-2% (Decline)
Employment Change, 2019-29	-600

What Landscape Architects Do

Landscape architects design parks and other outdoor spaces.

Landscape architects plan and design land areas for parks, recreational facilities, and other open spaces.

Work Environment

Landscape architects spend much of their time in offices, where they create designs, prepare models, and meet with clients. They spend the rest of their time at jobsites.

How to Become a Landscape Architect

All states require landscape architects to be licensed. Licensing requirements vary by state but usually include at least a bachelor's degree in landscape architecture from an accredited school, internship experience, and passing the Landscape Architect Registration Examination.

Pay

The median annual wage for landscape architects was $69,360 in May 2019.

Job Outlook

Employment of landscape architects is projected to decline 2 percent from 2019 to 2029. Improving technologies are expected to increase landscape architects' productivity, which should reduce overall demand for the occupation over the next 10 years.

State & Area Data

Explore resources for employment and wages by state and area for landscape architects.

Similar Occupations

Compare the job duties, education, job growth, and pay of landscape architects with similar occupations.

What Landscape Architects Do

Landscape architects design parks and the outdoor spaces of campuses, recreational facilities, businesses, private homes, and other open spaces.

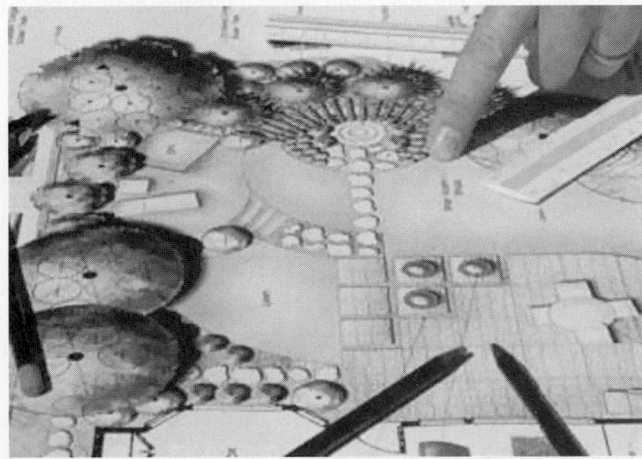

Landscape architects create graphic representations of plans.

Duties

Landscape architects typically do the following:

- Meet with clients, engineers, and building architects to understand the requirements of a project
- Prepare site plans, specifications, and cost estimates
- Coordinate the arrangement of existing and proposed land features and structures
- Prepare graphic representations of plans using computer-aided design and drafting (CADD) software
- Select appropriate landscaping materials
- Analyze environmental reports on land conditions, such as drainage and energy usage
- Inspect landscape project progress to ensure that it adheres to plans
- Seek new work through marketing activities or by giving presentations

Landscape architects design attractive and functional public parks, gardens, playgrounds, residential areas, college campuses, and public spaces. They also plan the locations of buildings, roads, walkways, flowers, shrubs, and trees within these environments. Landscape architects design these areas so that they are not only easy to use but also harmonious with the natural environment.

Landscape architects use various technologies in their work. For example, using CADD software, landscape architects prepare models of their proposed work. They present these models to clients for feedback and then prepare the final look of the project. Many landscape architects also use Geographic Information Systems (GIS) which offer GPS coordinates of different geographical features. This helps landscape architects design different environments by providing clues on where to start planning and how to anticipate future effects of the landscape, such as rainfall running into a valley.

The goals of landscape architects are to enhance the natural beauty of a space and foster environmental benefits. Landscape architects may plan the restoration of natural places that were changed by humans or nature, such as wetlands, streams, and mined areas. They also may design green roofs (roofs that are covered in soil and plants) or rooftop gardens that can retain storm water, absorb air pollution, and cool buildings while also providing pleasant scenery.

Work Environment

Landscape architects held about 24,500 jobs in 2019. The largest employers of landscape architects were as follows:

Architectural, engineering, and related services	53%
Self-employed workers	17
Landscaping services	16
Government	7
Construction	2

Landscape architects may design gardens for resorts.

Landscape architects spend much of their time in offices, where they create plans and designs, prepare models and preliminary cost estimates, and meet with clients and workers involved in designing or planning a project. They spend the rest of their time at jobsites.

How to Become a Landscape Architect

Landscape architects usually need at least a bachelor's degree in landscape architecture and a state-issued license, which typically requires completion of an internship.

Education

A bachelor's or master's degree in landscape architecture is usually necessary for entry into the profession. There are two undergraduate landscape architect degrees: a Bachelor of Landscape Architecture (BLA) and a Bachelor of Science in Landscape Architecture (BSLA). These programs usually require 4 to 5 years of study.

Accredited programs are approved by the Landscape Architectural Accreditation Board (LAAB). Prospective landscape architects whose undergraduate degree is in another field may enroll in a Master of Landscape Architecture (MLA) graduate degree program, which typically takes 3 years of full-time study.

Courses typically include landscape design and construction, landscape ecology, and site design. Other relevant coursework may include history of landscape architecture, plant and soil science, and professional practice.

The design studio is a key component of any curriculum. When possible, students are assigned projects that offer hands-on experience. These projects allow students to work with computer-aided design and drafting (CADD), model building, and other design software.

Training

To become licensed, candidates must meet experience requirements determined by each state. A list of training requirements

Interns are often supervised by more experienced landscape architects.

is available from the Council of Landscape Architectural Registration Boards.

New hires awaiting licensure may be called intern landscape architects. Although duties vary with the type and size of the employing firm, interns typically must work under the supervision of a licensed landscape architect for the experience to count toward licensure. Potential landscape architects may benefit by completing an internship with a landscape architecture firm during educational studies. Interns may improve their technical skills and gain an understanding of the day-to-day operations of the business, including learning how to recruit clients, generate fees, and work within a budget.

Licenses, Certifications, and Registrations

All states require landscape architects to be licensed. Candidates for licensure must pass the Landscape Architect Registration Examination (LARE), which is sponsored by the Council of Landscape Architectural Registration Boards.

Candidates who are interested in taking the exam usually need a degree from an accredited school and experience working under the supervision of a licensed landscape architect, although standards vary by state. For candidates without a degree in landscape architecture, many states offer alternative paths—which usually require more work experience—to qualify to take the LARE.

In addition to the LARE, some states have their own registration exam to test for competency on state-specific issues, such as earthquakes in California or hurricanes in Florida. State-specific exams may focus on laws, environmental regulations, plants, soils, climate, and other characteristics unique to the state.

Licensed landscape architects also may obtain voluntary certification from the Council of Landscape Architectural Registration Boards, which might make it easier to get licensed in another state.

Important Qualities

Analytical skills. Landscape architects must understand how their designs will affect locations. When designing a building's drainage system, for example, landscape architects must understand the interaction between the building and the surrounding land.

Communication skills. Landscape architects share their ideas, both orally and in writing, with clients, other architects, and workers who help prepare drawings. Effective communication is essential to ensuring that the vision for a project gets translated into reality.

Creativity. Landscape architects create the overall look of gardens, parks, and other outdoor areas. Their designs should be both pleasing to the eye and functional.

Problem-solving skills. When designing outdoor spaces, landscape architects must be able to provide solutions to unanticipated challenges. These solutions often involve looking at challenges from different perspectives and providing the best recommendations.

Technical skills. Landscape architects use computer-aided design and drafting (CADD) programs to create representations of their projects. Some also must use Geographic Information Systems (GIS) for their designs.

Visualization skills. Landscape architects must be able to imagine how an overall outdoor space will look once completed.

Pay

The median annual wage for landscape architects was $69,360 in May 2019. The median wage is the wage at which half the workers in an occupation earned more than that amount and half earned less. The lowest 10 percent earned less than $42,320, and the highest 10 percent earned more than $112,290.

In May 2019, the median annual wages for landscape architects in the top industries in which they worked were as follows:

Government	$88,490
Construction	71,270
Architectural, engineering, and related services	70,130
Landscaping services	60,740

Job Outlook

Employment of landscape architects is projected to decline 2 percent from 2019 to 2029.

Improving technologies are expected to increase landscape architects' productivity, which should reduce overall demand for the occupation over the next 10 years.

However, there will continue to be some need for these workers to plan and develop landscapes for commercial, industrial, and residential projects. Environmental concerns and efforts to conserve water and prevent waterway pollution also may create some demand for landscape architects.

Job Prospects

There may be strong competition for the relatively small number of jobs in this occupation. Job opportunities may fluctuate with the overall state of the economy, as the number of landscape architecture projects is often tied to increases or decreases in business and consumer spending.

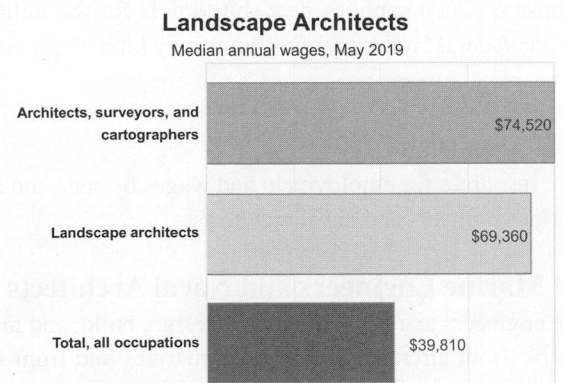

Landscape Architects
Median annual wages, May 2019

Architects, surveyors, and cartographers $74,520

Landscape architects $69,360

Total, all occupations $39,810

Note: All Occupations includes all occupations in the U.S. Economy.
Source: U.S. Bureau of Labor Statistics, Occupational Employment Statistics.

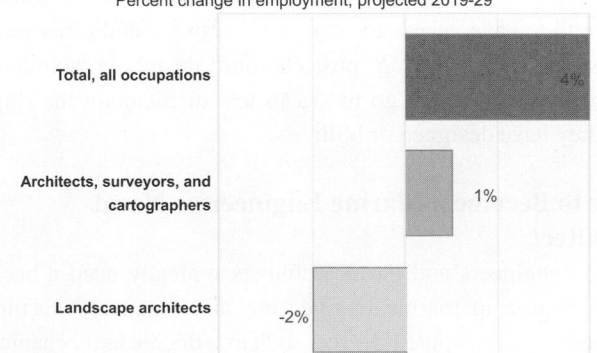

Landscape Architects
Percent change in employment, projected 2019-29

Total, all occupations 4%

Architects, surveyors, and cartographers 1%

Landscape architects -2%

Note: All Occupations includes all occupations in the U.S. Economy.
Source: U.S. Bureau of Labor Statistics, Employment Projections program.

Employment projections data for landscape architects, 2019-29					
Occupational Title	SOC Code	Employment, 2019	Projected Employment, 2029	Change, 2019-29	
				Percent	Numeric
SOURCE: U.S. Bureau of Labor Statistics, Employment Projections program					
Landscape architects	17-1012	24,500	23,900	-2	-600

State & Area Data
Occupational Employment Statistics (OES)

The Occupational Employment Statistics (OES) program produces employment and wage estimates annually for over 800 occupations. These estimates are available for the nation as a whole, for individual states, and for metropolitan and nonmetropolitan areas.

Contacts for More Information

For more information, including a list of colleges and universities offering accredited programs in landscape architecture, visit

➤ American Society of Landscape Architects

For information on registration or licensing requirements, visit

➤ Council of Landscape Architectural Registration Boards

Marine Engineers and Naval Architects

Summary

Quick Facts: Marine Engineers and Naval Architects	
2019 Median Pay	$92,400 per year $44.42 per hour
Typical Entry-Level Education	Bachelor's degree
Work Experience in a Related Occupation	None
On-the-job Training	None
Number of Jobs, 2019	11,800
Job Outlook, 2019-29	1% (Slower than average)
Employment Change, 2019-29	200

What Marine Engineers and Naval Architects Do

Marine engineers and naval architects design, build, and maintain ships, from aircraft carriers to submarines and from sailboats to tankers.

Work Environment

Marine engineers and naval architects typically work in offices, where they have access to computer software and other tools necessary for analyzing projects and designing solutions. Sometimes, they must go to sea to test or maintain the ships that they have designed or built.

How to Become a Marine Engineer or Naval Architect

Marine engineers and naval architects typically need a bachelor's degree in marine engineering and naval architecture, respectively, or a related degree, such as a degree in mechanical or electrical engineering.

Pay

The median annual wage for marine engineers and naval architects was $92,400 in May 2019.

Marine engineers and naval architects design and build ships from sailboats to tankers.

Job Outlook

Employment of marine engineers and naval architects is projected to grow 1 percent from 2019 to 2029, slower than the average for all occupations.

Many jobs for these workers are in the ship and boat building industry, which supplies new ship orders for the military. Therefore, federal budgetary constraints may limit employment growth.

State & Area Data

Explore resources for employment and wages by state and area for marine engineers and naval architects.

What Marine Engineers and Naval Architects Do

Marine engineers and naval architects design, build, and maintain ships, from aircraft carriers to submarines and from sailboats to tankers. Marine engineers are also known as *marine design engineers* or *marine mechanical engineers* and are responsible for the internal systems of a ship, such as the propulsion, electrical, refrigeration, and steering systems. Naval architects are responsible for the ship design, including the form, structure, and stability of hulls.

Marine engineers and naval architects may work directly on ships.

Duties

Marine engineers typically do the following:

- Prepare system layouts and detailed drawings and schematics
- Inspect marine equipment and machinery, and draw up work requests and job specifications
- Conduct environmental, operational, or performance tests on marine machinery and equipment
- Design and oversee the testing, installation, and repair of marine equipment
- Investigate and test machinery and equipment to ensure compliance with standards
- Coordinate activities with regulatory bodies to ensure that repairs and alterations are done safely and at minimal cost
- Prepare technical reports for use by engineers, managers, or sales personnel
- Prepare cost estimates, contract specifications, and design and construction schedules
- Maintain contact with contractors to make sure that the work is being done correctly, on schedule, and within budget

Naval architects typically do the following:

- Study design proposals and specifications to establish basic characteristics of a ship, such as its size, weight, and speed

- Develop sectional and waterline curves of the ship's hull to establish the center of gravity, the ideal hull form, and data on buoyancy and stability
- Design entire ship hulls and superstructures, following safety and regulatory standards
- Design the complete layout of ships' interiors, including spaces for machinery and auxiliary equipment, passenger compartments, cargo space, ladder wells, and elevators
- Confer with marine engineers to design the layout of boiler room equipment, heating and ventilation systems, refrigeration equipment, electrical distribution systems, safety systems, steering systems, and propulsion machinery
- Lead teams from a variety of specialties to oversee building and testing prototypes
- Evaluate how ships perform during trials, both in the dock and at sea, and change designs as needed to make sure that national and international standards are met

Marine engineers and naval architects apply knowledge from a range of engineering fields to the entire water vehicles' design and production processes. Marine engineers also design and maintain offshore oil rigs and may work on alternative energy projects, such as wind turbines located offshore and tidal power.

Marine engineers and naval architects who work for ship and boat building firms design large ships, such as passenger ships and cargo ships, as well as small craft, such as inflatable boats and rowboats. Those who work in the federal government may design or test the designs of ships or systems for the Army, Navy, or Coast Guard.

Marine engineers should not be confused with ship engineers, who operate or supervise the operation of the machinery on a ship. For more information on ship engineers, see the profile on water transportation workers.

Work Environment

Marine engineers and naval architects held about 11,800 jobs in 2019. The largest employers of marine engineers and naval architects were as follows:

Engineering services	22%
Federal government, excluding postal service	10
Other professional, scientific, and technical services	6
Transportation and warehousing	3

Marine engineers and naval architects typically work in offices, where they have access to computer software and other tools necessary for analyzing projects and designing solutions. Sometimes, they must go to sea to test or maintain the ships that they have designed or built.

Marine engineers and naval architects who work on power generation projects, such as offshore wind turbines and tidal power, work along the coast—both offshore and on land. They

Marine engineers and naval architects design and oversee testing, installation, and repair of marine apparatus and equipment.

Marine engineers and naval architects must give clear instructions and explain complex concepts when leading projects.

also sometimes work on oil rigs, where they oversee the repair or maintenance of systems that they may have designed.

Naval architects often lead teams to create feasible designs, and they must effectively use the skills that each person brings to the design process.

Work Schedules

Most marine engineers and naval architects work full time and some work more than 40 hours per week. Marine engineers who work at sea will work a schedule tied to the operations of their particular ship. Those who work onshore will have somewhat more regular work schedules. Naval architects, and marine engineers who are engaged primarily in design, are much more likely to work a regular schedule in an office or at a shipyard.

How to Become a Marine Engineer or Naval Architect

Marine engineers and naval architects typically need a bachelor's degree in marine engineering and naval architecture, respectively, or a related degree, such as a degree in mechanical or electrical engineering. Some marine engineering and naval architecture programs are offered at state maritime academies.

Education

Programs in marine engineering and naval architecture typically include courses in calculus, physics, computer-aided design, fluid mechanics, ship hull strength, and mechanics of materials. Most programs also include time at sea, where students gain hands-on experience on a vessel.

Some marine engineering and naval architecture programs are offered at state maritime academies. Students studying at the maritime academies spend time at sea, usually during the summer, to gain onboard operating experience. For more information about state maritime academies, visit the Maritime Administration of the U.S. Department of Transportation.

Programs in engineering and naval architecture are accredited by ABET.

Students interested in preparing for this occupation benefit from taking high school courses in math, such as algebra, trigonometry, and calculus; and science, such as chemistry and physics. For aspiring naval architects, drafting courses are helpful.

Important Qualities

Communication skills. Marine engineers and naval architects must give clear instructions and explain complex concepts when leading projects.

Ingenuity. Marine engineers and naval architects must use operations analysis to create a design to perform the ship's functions. They then employ critical-thinking skills to anticipate and correct any deficiencies before the ship is built or set to sea.

Interpersonal skills. Marine engineers and naval architects meet with clients to analyze their needs for ship systems. Engineers must discuss progress with clients to keep redesign options open before the project is too far along.

Math skills. Marine engineers and naval architects use the principles of calculus, trigonometry, and other advanced topics in math for analysis, design, and troubleshooting in their work.

Problem-solving skills. Marine engineers must design several systems that work well together in ships. Naval architects and marine engineers are expected to solve problems for their clients. They must draw on their knowledge and experience to make effective decisions.

Licenses, Certifications, and Registrations

Along with earning a bachelor's degree, students at states' maritime academies take exams for licensure from the U.S. Coast Guard.

Another type of engineering license is the Professional Engineering (PE) license, which allows for higher levels of leadership and independence and can be acquired later in one's career. Licensed engineers are called professional engineers (PEs). A PE can oversee the work of other engineers, sign off on projects, and provide services directly to the public. State licensure generally requires

- A degree from an ABET-accredited engineering program
- A passing score on the Fundamentals of Engineering (FE) exam
- Relevant work experience, typically at least 4 years
- A passing score on the Professional Engineering (PE) exam

The initial FE exam can be taken after earning a bachelor's degree. Engineers who pass this exam are commonly called engineers in training (EITs) or engineer interns (EIs). After meeting work experience requirements, EITs and EIs can take the second exam, called the Principles and Practice of Engineering (PE).

Other experience

Employers also value practical experience, so cooperative education programs and internships, which provide college credit or structured job experience, can be helpful in getting a job in this occupation.

Advancement

Beginning marine engineers usually work under the supervision of experienced engineers. In larger companies, new engineers also may receive formal training in classrooms or seminars. As beginning engineers gain knowledge and experience, they move on to more difficult projects, on which they have greater independence to develop designs, solve problems, and make decisions.

Eventually, marine engineers may advance to become technical specialists or to supervise a team of engineers and technicians. Some may even become engineering managers or move into other managerial positions or sales work. In sales, an engineering background enables them to discuss technical aspects of certain kinds of engineering projects. Such knowledge is also useful in assisting clients in project planning, installation, and use. For more information, see the profiles on architectural and engineering managers and sales managers.

Pay

The median annual wage for marine engineers and naval architects was $92,400 in May 2019. The median wage is the wage at which half the workers in an occupation earned more than that amount and half earned less. The lowest 10 percent earned less than $65,440, and the highest 10 percent earned more than $147,710.

In May 2019, the median annual wages for marine engineers and naval architects in the top industries in which they worked were as follows:

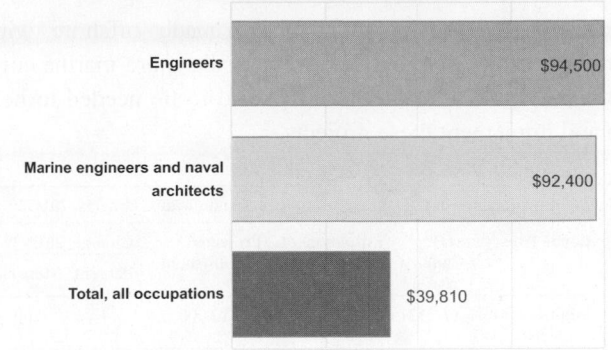

Marine Engineers and Naval Architects
Median annual wages, May 2019

Engineers	$94,500
Marine engineers and naval architects	$92,400
Total, all occupations	$39,810

Note: All Occupations includes all occupations in the U.S. Economy. Source: U.S. Bureau of Labor Statistics, Occupational Employment Statistics.

Transportation and warehousing............................	$101,270
Federal government, excluding postal service ...	100,390
Other professional, scientific, and technical services	90,670
Engineering services...	88,590

Most marine engineers and naval architects work full time and some work more than 40 hours per week. Marine engineers who work at sea will work a schedule tied to the operations of their particular ship. Those who work onshore will have somewhat more regular work schedules. Naval architects, and marine engineers who are engaged primarily in design, are much more likely to work a regular schedule in an office or at a shipyard.

Job Outlook

Employment of marine engineers and naval architects is projected to grow 1 percent from 2019 to 2029, slower than the average for all occupations.

Many jobs for these workers are in the ship and boat building industry, which supplies new ship orders for the military.

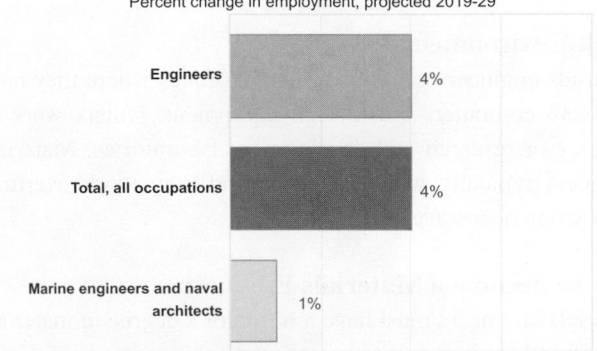

Marine Engineers and Naval Architects
Percent change in employment, projected 2019-29

Engineers	4%
Total, all occupations	4%
Marine engineers and naval architects	1%

Note: All Occupations includes all occupations in the U.S. Economy. Source: U.S. Bureau of Labor Statistics, Employment Projections program.

Therefore, federal budgetary constraints may limit employment growth.

Technological developments have made offshore wind energy projects more feasible. As a result, more marine engineers and naval architects are expected to be needed to help plan and implement these projects.

Employment projections data for marine engineers and naval architects, 2019-29					
Occupational Title	SOC Code	Employment, 2019	Projected Employment, 2029	Change, 2019-29	
				Percent	Numeric
Marine engineers and naval architects	17-2121	11,800	12,000	1	200

State & Area Data
Occupational Employment Statistics (OES)

The Occupational Employment Statistics (OES) program produces employment and wage estimates annually for over 800 occupations. These estimates are available for the nation as a whole, for individual states, and for metropolitan and nonmetropolitan areas.

Contacts for More Information

For more information about marine engineers and naval architects, visit
➤ Marine Engineers' Beneficial Association
➤ American Society of Naval Engineers

For more information about general engineering education and career resources, visit
➤ American Society for Engineering Education
➤ Maritime Administration of the U.S. Department of Transportation
➤ Technology Student Association

For more information about accredited engineering programs, visit
➤ ABET

Materials Engineers

Summary

Quick Facts: Materials Engineers

2019 Median Pay	$93,360 per year $44.88 per hour
Typical Entry-Level Education	Bachelor's degree
Work Experience in a Related Occupation	None
On-the-job Training	None
Number of Jobs, 2019	27,500
Job Outlook, 2019-29	2% (Slower than average)
Employment Change, 2019-29	400

What Materials Engineers Do

Materials engineers develop, process, and test materials used to create a wide range of products.

Work Environment

Materials engineers generally work in offices where they have access to computers and design equipment. Others work in factories or research and development laboratories. Materials engineers typically work full time and may work overtime hours when necessary.

How to Become a Materials Engineer

Materials engineers must have a bachelor's degree in materials science and engineering or in a related engineering field. Completing internships and cooperative engineering programs while in school can be helpful in getting hired as a materials engineer.

Materials engineers develop, process, and test materials to create a wide range of products.

Pay

The median annual wage for materials engineers was $93,360 in May 2019.

Job Outlook

Employment of materials engineers is projected to grow 2 percent from 2019 to 2029, slower than the average for all occupations. About half of all materials engineers work in manufacturing industries, including many that are expected to have slow growth or declines in employment.

State & Area Data

Explore resources for employment and wages by state and area for materials engineers.

Materials engineers work with metals, ceramics, and plastics to create new materials.

What Materials Engineers Do

Materials engineers develop, process, and test materials used to create a range of products, from computer chips and aircraft wings to golf clubs and biomedical devices. They study the properties and structures of metals, ceramics, plastics, composites, nanomaterials (extremely small substances), and other substances in order to create new materials that meet certain mechanical, electrical, and chemical requirements. They also help select materials for specific products and develop new ways to use existing materials.

Duties

Materials engineers typically do the following:

- Plan and evaluate new projects, consulting with other engineers and managers as necessary
- Prepare proposals and budgets, analyze labor costs, write reports, and perform other managerial tasks
- Supervise the work of technologists, technicians, and other engineers and scientists
- Design and direct the testing of processing procedures
- Monitor how materials perform and evaluate how they deteriorate
- Determine causes of product failure and develop ways of overcoming such failure
- Evaluate technical specifications and economic factors relating to the design objectives of processes or products
- Evaluate the impact of materials processing on the environment

Materials engineers create and study materials at the atomic level. They use computers to understand and model the characteristics of materials and their components. They solve problems in several different engineering fields, such as mechanical, chemical, electrical, civil, nuclear, and aerospace.

Materials engineers may specialize in understanding specific types of materials. The following are examples of types of materials engineers:

Ceramic engineers develop ceramic materials and the processes for making them into useful products, from high-temperature rocket nozzles to glass for LCD flat-panel displays.

Composites engineers develop materials with special, engineered properties for applications in aircraft, automobiles, and related products.

Metallurgical engineers specialize in metals, such as steel and aluminum, usually in alloyed form with additions of other elements to provide specific properties.

Plastics engineers develop and test new plastics, known as polymers, for new applications.

Semiconductor processing engineers apply materials science and engineering principles to develop new microelectronic materials for computing, sensing, and related applications.

Work Environment

Materials engineers held about 27,500 jobs in 2019. The largest employers of materials engineers were as follows:

Transportation equipment manufacturing	15%
Engineering services	13
Primary metal manufacturing	9
Computer and electronic product manufacturing	8
Research and development in the physical, engineering, and life sciences	7

Materials engineers often work in offices where they have access to computers and design equipment. Others work in factories or research and development laboratories. Materials engineers may work in teams with scientists and engineers from other backgrounds.

Work Schedules

Materials engineers generally work full time. Some materials engineers work more than 40 hours per week.

Materials engineers may work in laboratories or industrial settings to observe the results of their research and development.

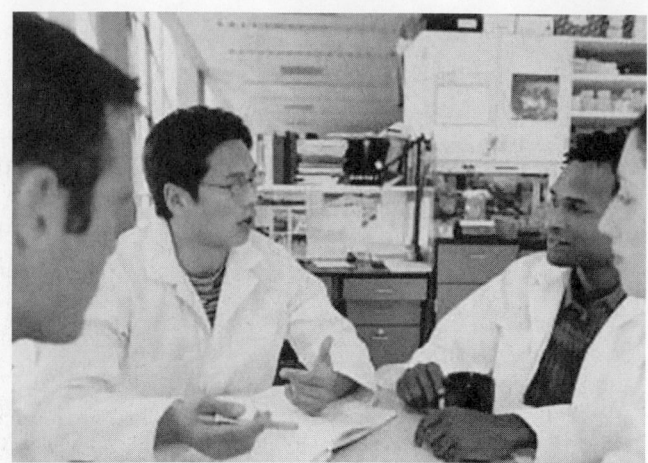

Materials engineers plan and evaluate new projects, consulting with others as necessary.

How to Become a Materials Engineer

Materials engineers must have a bachelor's degree in materials science and engineering or in a related engineering field. Completing internships and cooperative engineering programs while in school can be helpful in getting a position as a materials engineer.

Education

Students interested in studying materials engineering should take high school courses in math, such as algebra, trigonometry, and calculus; in science, such as biology, chemistry, and physics; and in computer programming.

Entry-level jobs as a materials engineer require a bachelor's degree. Bachelor's degree programs include classroom and laboratory work focusing on engineering principles.

Some colleges and universities offer a 5-year program leading to both a bachelor's and master's degree. A graduate degree allows an engineer to work as a postsecondary teacher or to do research and development.

Many colleges and universities offer internships and cooperative programs in partnership with industry. In these programs, students gain practical experience while completing their education.

Many engineering programs are accredited by ABET. Some employers prefer to hire candidates who have graduated from an accredited program. A degree from an ABET-accredited program is usually necessary to become a licensed professional engineer.

Important Qualities

Analytical skills. Materials engineers often work on projects related to other fields of engineering. They must determine how materials will be used and how they must be structured to withstand different conditions.

Math skills. Materials engineers use the principles of calculus and other advanced topics in math for analysis, design, and troubleshooting in their work.

Problem-solving skills. Materials engineers must understand the relationship between materials' structures, their properties, how they are made, and how these factors affect the products they are used to make. They must also figure out why a product might have failed, design a solution, and then conduct tests to make sure that the product does not fail again. These skills involve being able to identify root causes when many factors could be at fault.

Speaking skills. While working with technicians, technologists, and other engineers, materials engineers must state concepts and directions clearly. When speaking with managers, these engineers must also communicate engineering concepts to people who may not have an engineering background.

Writing skills. Materials engineers must write plans and reports clearly so that people without a materials engineering background can understand the concepts.

Licenses, Certifications, and Registrations

Licensure for materials engineers is not as common as it is for other engineering occupations, nor it is required for entry-level positions. A Professional Engineering (PE) license, which allows for higher levels of leadership and independence, can be acquired later in one's career. Licensed engineers are called professional engineers (PEs). A PE can oversee the work of other engineers, sign off on projects, and provide services directly to the public. State licensure generally requires

- A degree from an ABET-accredited engineering program
- A passing score on the Fundamentals of Engineering (FE) exam
- Relevant work experience, typically at least 4 years
- A passing score on the Professional Engineering (PE) exam

The initial FE exam can be taken after earning a bachelor's degree. Engineers who pass this exam are commonly called engineers in training (EITs) or engineer interns (EIs). After meeting work experience requirements, EITs and EIs can take the second exam, called the Principles and Practice of Engineering (PE).

Each state issues its own licenses. Most states recognize licensure from other states, as long as the licensing state's requirements meet or exceed their own licensure requirements. Several states require continuing education for engineers to keep their licenses.

Certification in the field of metallography, the science and art of dealing with the structure of metals and alloys, is available through ASM International and other materials science organizations.

Additional training in fields directly related to metallurgy and materials' properties, such as corrosion or failure analysis, is available through ASM International.

Other Experience

During high school, students can attend engineering summer camps to see what these and other engineers do. Attending these camps can help students plan their coursework for the remainder of their time in high school.

Advancement

Junior materials engineers usually work under the supervision of experienced engineers. In large companies, new engineers may receive formal training in classrooms or seminars. As engineers gain knowledge and experience, they move on to more difficult projects where they have greater independence to develop designs, solve problems, and make decisions.

Eventually, materials engineers may advance to become technical specialists or to supervise a team of engineers and technicians. Many become engineering managers or move into other managerial positions or sales work. An engineering background is useful in sales because it enables sales engineers to discuss a product's technical aspects and assist in product planning, installation, and use. For more information, see the profiles on architectural and engineering managers and sales engineers.

Pay

The median annual wage for materials engineers was $93,360 in May 2019. The median wage is the wage at which half the workers in an occupation earned more than that amount and half earned less. The lowest 10 percent earned less than $57,340, and the highest 10 percent earned more than $148,960.

In May 2019, the median annual wages for materials engineers in the top industries in which they worked were as follows:

Research and development in the physical, engineering, and life sciences	$108,860
Transportation equipment manufacturing	101,120
Computer and electronic product manufacturing	97,030
Engineering services	93,500
Primary metal manufacturing	81,580

Most materials engineers work full time. Some materials engineers work more than 40 hours per week.

Materials Engineers
Median annual wages, May 2019

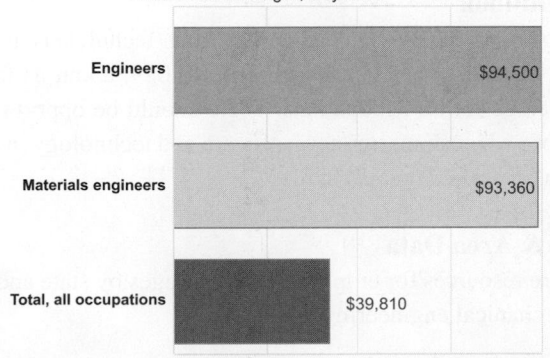

Engineers	$94,500
Materials engineers	$93,360
Total, all occupations	$39,810

Note: All Occupations includes all occupations in the U.S. Economy.
Source: U.S. Bureau of Labor Statistics, Occupational Employment Statistics.

Materials Engineers
Percent change in employment, projected 2019-29

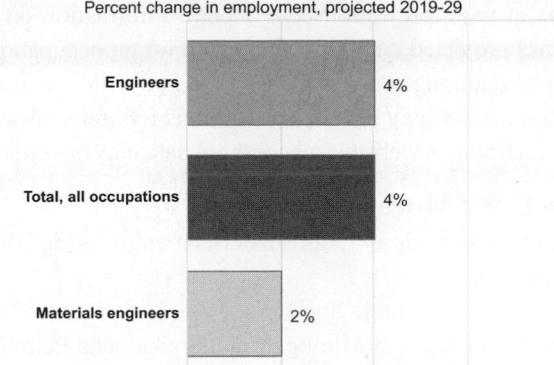

Engineers	4%
Total, all occupations	4%
Materials engineers	2%

Note: All Occupations includes all occupations in the U.S. Economy.
Source: U.S. Bureau of Labor Statistics, Employment Projections program.

Job Outlook

Employment of materials engineers is projected to grow 2 percent from 2019 to 2029, slower than the average for all occupations. About half of all materials engineers work in manufacturing industries, including many that are expected to have slow growth or declines in employment. Modest employment increases are projected for these engineers in professional, scientific, and technical services.

Job Prospects

Prospects should be best for applicants who gained experience by participating in internships or co-op programs while in college.

Computer modeling and simulations, rather than extensive and costly laboratory testing, are increasingly being used to predict the performance of new materials. Thus, those with a background in computer modeling should have the best employment opportunities.

Employment projections data for materials engineers, 2019-29					
Occupational Title	SOC Code	Employment, 2019	Projected Employment, 2029,	Change, 2019-29	
				Percent	Numeric
SOURCE: U.S. Bureau of Labor Statistics, Employment Projections program					
Materials engineers	17-2131	27,500	27,900	2	400

State & Area Data
Occupational Employment Statistics (OES)

The Occupational Employment Statistics (OES) program produces employment and wage estimates annually for over 800 occupations. These estimates are available for the nation as a whole, for individual states, and for metropolitan and nonmetropolitan areas.

Projections Central

Occupational employment projections are developed for all states by Labor Market Information (LMI) or individual state

Employment Projections offices. All state projections data are available at www.projectionscentral.com. Information on this site allows projected employment growth for an occupation to be compared among states or to be compared within one state. In addition, states may produce projections for areas; there are links to each state's websites where these data may be retrieved.

Contacts for More Information

For more information about materials engineering career resources, visit
➤ The American Ceramic Society
➤ American Institute of Mining, Metallurgical, and Petroleum Engineers
➤ Materials Research Society
➤ The Minerals, Metals and Materials Society

For information about general engineering career resources, visit

➤ American Society for Engineering Education
➤ Technology Student Association

For more information about licensure as a professional engineer, visit
➤ National Council of Examiners for Engineering and Surveying
➤ National Society of Professional Engineers

For more information about certification, visit
➤ ASM International

For more information about accredited engineering programs, visit
➤ ABET

For more information about engineering summer camps, visit
➤ Engineering Education Service Center

Mechanical Engineering Technicians

Summary

Quick Facts: Mechanical Engineering Technicians

2019 Median Pay	$56,980 per year $27.40 per hour
Typical Entry-Level Education	Associate's degree
Work Experience in a Related Occupation	None
On-the-job Training	None
Number of Jobs, 2019	43,500
Job Outlook, 2019-29	3% (As fast as average)
Employment Change, 2019-29	1,400

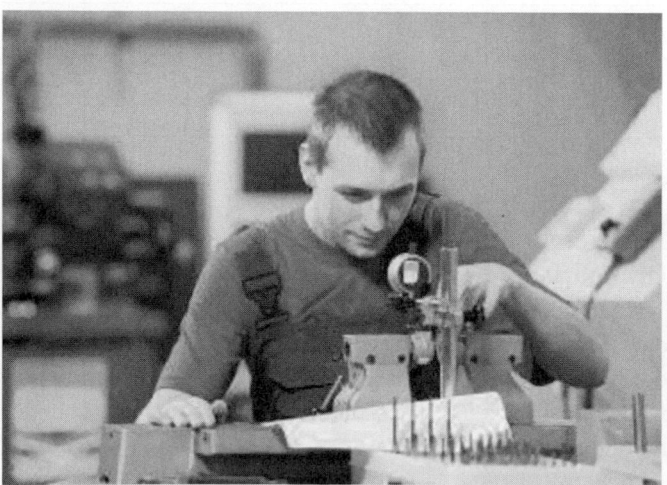

Mechanical engineering technicians plan, produce, and assemble new or changed mechanical parts for products, such as industrial machinery or equipment.

What Mechanical Engineering Technicians Do
Mechanical engineering technicians help mechanical engineers design, develop, test, and manufacture mechanical devices.

Work Environment
Mechanical engineering technicians assist with manufacturing processes in factories or with development phases in research and development labs before manufacturing takes place.

How to Become a Mechanical Engineering Technician
Most employers prefer to hire candidates with an associate's degree or other postsecondary training in mechanical engineering technology. Prospective engineering technicians should take as many science and math courses as possible while in high school.

Pay
The median annual wage for mechanical engineering technicians was $56,980 in May 2019.

Job Outlook
Employment of mechanical engineering technicians is projected to grow 3 percent from 2019 to 2029, about as fast as the average for all occupations. There should be opportunities for those who can master new software and technology in addition to traditional manual skills.

State & Area Data
Explore resources for employment and wages by state and area for mechanical engineering technicians.

What Mechanical Engineering Technicians Do
Mechanical engineering technicians help mechanical engineers design, develop, test, and manufacture mechanical devices,

Mechanical engineering technicians plan the assembly process to be used in industrial settings.

Because mechanical engineering technicians work with machines of all types, they must take safety precautions in their workspace.

including tools, engines, and machines. They may make sketches and rough layouts, record and analyze data, make calculations and estimates, and report their findings.

Duties
Mechanical engineering technicians typically do the following:

- Evaluate design drawings for new or changed tools by measuring dimensions on the drawings and comparing them with the original specifications
- Prepare layouts and drawings of parts to be made and of the process for putting the parts together, often using three-dimensional design software
- Discuss changes with coworkers—for example, in the design of a part and in the way it will be made and assembled
- Review instructions and blueprints for projects in order to ensure that test specifications and procedures are followed and objectives are met
- Plan, produce, and assemble new or changed mechanical parts for products, such as industrial machinery or equipment
- Set up and conduct tests of complete units and their components, and record results
- Compare test results with design specifications and with test objectives and make recommendations for changes in products or in test methods
- Estimate labor costs, equipment life, and plant space

Some mechanical engineering technicians test and inspect machines and equipment or work with engineers to eliminate production problems. For example, they may assist in testing products by setting up instrumentation for vehicle crash tests.

Work Environment
Mechanical engineering technicians held about 43,500 jobs in 2019. The largest employers of mechanical engineering technicians were as follows:

Architectural, engineering, and related services 21%

Machinery manufacturing 15
Transportation equipment manufacturing 12
Scientific research and development services.............. 6
Computer and electronic product manufacturing 6

Some mechanical engineering technicians may be exposed to hazards from equipment, chemicals, or toxic materials, but injuries are rare as long as proper procedures are followed.

Work Schedules
Most mechanical engineering technicians work full time.

How to Become a Mechanical Engineering Technician
Most employers prefer to hire candidates with associate's degrees or other postsecondary training in mechanical engineering technology. Prospective engineering technicians should take as many science and math courses as possible while in high school.

Education
Mechanical engineering technicians typically need an associate's degree or a certificate from a community college or vocational–technical school. Community colleges offer programs similar to those in technical institutes but include more theory-based and liberal arts coursework and programs. Community colleges typically award an associate's degree. Vocational–technical schools include postsecondary public institutions that emphasize training needed by local employers. Students who complete these programs typically receive a diploma or certificate.

ABET accredits associate's degree programs in relevant fields of study, such as mechanical engineering technology.

Completing an associate's degree in mechanical engineering technology is good preparation for studying for a bachelor's degree.

Mechanical engineering technicians help mechanical engineers manufacture industrial machinery and other equipment.

High school students interested in becoming mechanical engineering technicians should take classes in math, science, and computer skills. Courses that help students develop skills working with their hands also are valuable because these technicians build what mechanical engineers design.

Important Qualities

Communication skills. Mechanical engineering technicians must be able to clearly understand and follow instructions or ask their supervisors for clarification if they do not understand. They must be able to clearly explain, both orally and in writing, the need for changes in designs or test procedures.

Creativity. Mechanical engineering technicians help mechanical engineers bring their plans and designs to life. This often requires helping the engineer to overcome problems that might not have been anticipated.

Detail oriented. Mechanical engineering technicians must make precise measurements and keep accurate records for mechanical engineers.

Math skills. Mechanical engineering technicians use mathematics for analysis, design, and troubleshooting in their work.

Mechanical skills. Mechanical engineering technicians must apply theory and instructions from engineers by making new components for industrial machinery or equipment. They may need to be able to operate machinery such as drill presses, grinders, and engine lathes.

Licenses, Certifications, and Registrations

The National Institute for Certification in Engineering Technologies (NICET) offers four levels of certification through its technician certification programs. Mechanical engineering technicians can obtain certification in industrial instrumentation by passing an examination. In addition, an engineering technician's supervisor must verify the competency of the candidate for certification.

Pay

The median annual wage for mechanical engineering technicians was $56,980 in May 2019. The median wage is the wage at which half the workers in an occupation earned more than that amount and half earned less. The lowest 10 percent earned less than $35,140, and the highest 10 percent earned more than $88,640.

In May 2019, the median annual wages for mechanical engineering technicians in the top industries in which they worked were as follows:

Computer and electronic product manufacturing ...	$60,390
Scientific research and development services	60,010
Transportation equipment manufacturing	58,310
Architectural, engineering, and related services	57,300
Machinery manufacturing	56,310

Most mechanical engineering technicians work full time.

Job Outlook

Employment of mechanical engineering technicians is projected to grow 3 percent from 2019 to 2029, about as fast as the average for all occupations. Firms may contract the work of mechanical engineering technicians from industries that provide

Mechanical Engineering Technicians
Median annual wages, May 2019

Drafters, engineering technicians, and mapping technicians	$57,690
Mechanical engineering technologists and technicians	$56,980
Total, all occupations	$39,810

Note: All Occupations includes all occupations in the U.S. Economy.
Source: U.S. Bureau of Labor Statistics, Occupational Employment Statistics.

Mechanical Engineering Technicians
Percent change in employment, projected 2019-29

Category	Percent
Total, all occupations	4%
Mechanical engineering technologists and technicians	3%
Drafters, engineering technicians, and mapping technicians	1%

Note: All Occupations includes all occupations in the U.S. Economy.
Source: U.S. Bureau of Labor Statistics, Employment Projections program.

engineering services, research and development, and consulting services. Contracting for this work allows firms to hire these services at a lower cost than employing in-house technicians.

Mechanical engineering technicians may find work as assistants to mechanical engineers and thus work in emerging fields, such as automation, three-dimensional printing, robotics, and alternative energies.

Job Prospects

Mastering new technology and software will likely become more important for workers in this occupation. Those who gain skills to help deploy the latest technological developments, such as three-dimensional design software, should have the best job prospects.

Employment projections data for mechanical engineering technicians, 2019-29					
Occupational Title	SOC Code	Employment, 2019	Projected Employment, 2029	Change, 2019-29	
				Percent	Numeric
SOURCE: U.S. Bureau of Labor Statistics, Employment Projections program					
Mechanical engineering technologists and technicians	17-3027	43,500	44,900	3	1,400

State & Area Data
Occupational Employment Statistics (OES)

The Occupational Employment Statistics (OES) program produces employment and wage estimates annually for over 800 occupations. These estimates are available for the nation as a whole, for individual states, and for metropolitan and nonmetropolitan areas.

Mechanical Engineers

Summary

Quick Facts: Mechanical Engineers

2019 Median Pay	$88,430 per year / $42.51 per hour
Typical Entry-Level Education	Bachelor's degree
Work Experience in a Related Occupation	None
On-the-job Training	None
Number of Jobs, 2019	316,300
Job Outlook, 2019-29	4% (As fast as average)
Employment Change, 2019-29	12,400

What Mechanical Engineers Do
Mechanical engineers design, develop, build, and test mechanical and thermal sensors and devices.

Work Environment
Mechanical engineers generally work in offices. They may occasionally visit worksites where a problem or piece of equipment needs their personal attention. Mechanical engineers work mostly in engineering services, research and development, and manufacturing.

Many mechanical engineers work in industries that manufacture machinery or automotive parts.

How to Become a Mechanical Engineer
Mechanical engineers typically need a bachelor's degree in mechanical engineering or mechanical engineering technology. All states and the District of Columbia require mechanical engineers who sell services to the public to be licensed.

Pay
The median annual wage for mechanical engineers was $88,430 in May 2019.

Job Outlook

Employment of mechanical engineers is projected to grow 4 percent from 2019 to 2029, about as fast as the average for all occupations. Job prospects may be best for those who stay abreast of the most recent advances in technology.

State & Area Data

Explore resources for employment and wages by state and area for mechanical engineers.

What Mechanical Engineers Do

Mechanical engineers research, design, develop, build, and test mechanical and thermal sensors and devices, including tools, engines, and machines.

Duties

Mechanical engineers typically do the following:

- Analyze problems to see how mechanical and thermal devices might help solve a particular problem
- Design or redesign mechanical and thermal devices or subsystems, using analysis and computer-aided design
- Investigate equipment failures or difficulties to diagnose faulty operation and to recommend remedies
- Develop and test prototypes of devices they design
- Analyze the test results and change the design or system as needed
- Oversee the manufacturing process for the device

Mechanical engineering is one of the broadest engineering fields. Mechanical engineers design and oversee the manufacture of many products ranging from medical devices to new batteries.

Mechanical engineers design power-producing machines, such as electric generators, internal combustion engines, and steam and gas turbines, as well as power-using machines, such as refrigeration and air-conditioning systems.

Computer technology helps mechanical engineers create and analyze designs.

Mechanical engineers design other machines inside buildings, such as elevators and escalators. They also design material-handling systems, such as conveyor systems and automated transfer stations.

Like other engineers, mechanical engineers use computers extensively. Mechanical engineers are routinely responsible for the integration of sensors, controllers, and machinery. Computer technology helps mechanical engineers create and analyze designs, run simulations and test how a machine is likely to work, interact with connected systems, and generate specifications for parts.

The following are examples of types of mechanical engineers:

Auto research engineers seek to improve the performance of cars. These engineers work to improve traditional features of cars such as suspension, and they also work on aerodynamics and new possible fuels.

Heating and cooling systems engineers work to create and maintain environmental systems wherever temperatures and humidity must be kept within certain limits. They develop such systems for airplanes, trains, cars, schools, and even computer rooms.

Robotic engineers plan, build, and maintain robots. These engineers plan how robots will use sensors for detecting things based on light or smell, and they design how these sensors will fit into the designs of the robots.

Work Environment

Mechanical engineers held about 316,300 jobs in 2019. The largest employers of mechanical engineers were as follows:

Architectural, engineering, and related services	20%
Machinery manufacturing	14
Transportation equipment manufacturing	11
Computer and electronic product manufacturing	7
Scientific research and development services	6

Mechanical engineers generally work in offices. They may occasionally visit worksites where a problem or piece of equipment needs their personal attention. In most settings, they work with other engineers, engineering technicians, and other professionals as part of a team.

Work Schedules

Most mechanical engineers work full time and some work more than 40 hours a week.

How to Become a Mechanical Engineer

Mechanical engineers typically need a bachelor's degree in mechanical engineering or mechanical engineering technology. Mechanical engineers who sell services publicly must be licensed in all states and the District of Columbia.

Although they do most of their work in an office setting, mechanical engineers also visit worksites to gain firsthand knowledge of their designs.

Education

Mechanical engineers typically need a bachelor's degree in mechanical engineering or mechanical engineering technology. Mechanical engineering programs usually include courses in mathematics and life and physical sciences, as well as engineering and design. Mechanical engineering technology programs focus less on theory and more on the practical application of engineering principles. They may emphasize internships and co-ops to prepare students for work in industry.

Some colleges and universities offer 5-year programs that allow students to obtain both a bachelor's and a master's degree. Some 5-year or even 6-year cooperative plans combine classroom study with practical work, enabling students to gain valuable experience and earn money to finance part of their education.

ABET accredits programs in engineering and engineering technology. Most employers prefer to hire students from an accredited program. A degree from an ABET-accredited program is usually necessary to become a licensed professional engineer.

Important Qualities

Creativity. Mechanical engineers design and build complex pieces of equipment and machinery. A creative mind is essential for this kind of work.

Listening skills. Mechanical engineers often work on projects with others, such as architects and computer scientists. They must listen to and analyze different approaches made by other experts to complete the task at hand.

Math skills. Mechanical engineers use the principles of calculus, statistics, and other advanced subjects in math for analysis, design, and troubleshooting in their work.

Mechanical skills. Mechanical skills allow engineers to apply basic engineering concepts and mechanical processes to the design of new devices and systems.

Problem-solving skills. Mechanical engineers need good problem-solving skills to take scientific principles and discoveries and use them to design and build useful products.

Licenses, Certifications, and Registrations

Licensure is not required for entry-level positions as a mechanical engineer. A Professional Engineering (PE) license, which allows for higher levels of leadership and independence, can be acquired later in one's career. Licensed engineers are called professional engineers (PEs). A PE can oversee the work of other engineers, sign off on projects, and provide services directly to the public. State licensure generally requires

- A degree from an ABET-accredited engineering program
- A passing score on the Fundamentals of Engineering (FE) exam
- Relevant work experience typically at least 4 years
- A passing score on the Professional Engineering (PE) exam.

The initial FE exam can be taken after one earns a bachelor's degree. Engineers who pass this exam are commonly called engineers in training (EITs) or engineer interns (EIs). After meeting work experience requirements, EITs and EIs can take the second exam, called the Principles and Practice of Engineering.

Mechanical engineers analyze problems to see how a mechanical device might help to solve them.

Several states require engineers to take continuing education to renew their licenses every year. Most states recognize licensure from other states, as long as the other state's licensing requirements meet or exceed their own licensing requirements.

Several professional organizations offer a variety of certification programs for engineers to demonstrate competency in specific fields of mechanical engineering.

Other Experience

During high school students can attend engineering summer camps to see what these and other engineers do. Attending these camps can help students plan their coursework for the remainder of their time in high school.

Advancement

A Ph.D. is essential for engineering faculty positions in higher education, as well as for some research and development programs. Mechanical engineers may earn graduate degrees in engineering or business administration to learn new technology, broaden their education, and enhance their project management skills. Mechanical engineers may become administrators or managers after gaining work experience.

Pay

The median annual wage for mechanical engineers was $88,430 in May 2019. The median wage is the wage at which half the workers in an occupation earned more than that amount and half earned less. The lowest 10 percent earned less than $57,130, and the highest 10 percent earned more than $138,020.

In May 2019, the median annual wages for mechanical engineers in the top industries in which they worked were as follows:

Scientific research and development services.......	$101,780
Computer and electronic product manufacturing ..	95,260
Architectural, engineering, and related services ..	90,560
Transportation equipment manufacturing.............	90,350
Machinery manufacturing.......................................	80,720

Most mechanical engineers work full time and some work more than 40 hours a week.

Job Outlook

Employment of mechanical engineers is projected to grow 4 percent from 2019 to 2029, about as fast as the average for all occupations. Mechanical engineers can work in many industries and on many types of projects. As a result, their growth rate will differ by the industries that employ them.

Mechanical engineers are projected to experience growth in engineering services as companies continue to contract work from these firms. Mechanical engineers will also remain involved in various manufacturing industries, particularly in automotive manufacturing. These engineers will play key roles in improving the range and performance of hybrid and electric cars. However, employment declines in some manufacturing industries will temper overall employment growth of mechanical engineers.

Job Prospects

Prospects for mechanical engineers overall are expected to be good. They will be best for those with training in the latest software tools, particularly for computational design and simulation. Such tools allow engineers and designers to take a project from the conceptual phase directly to a finished product, eliminating the need for prototypes.

Mechanical engineering students who can learn to create virtual simulations before proceeding to the design, build, and test stages might find themselves in high demand by companies because these skills will allow firms to reduce product development cycles.

Engineers who have experience or training in three-dimensional printing also will have better job prospects.

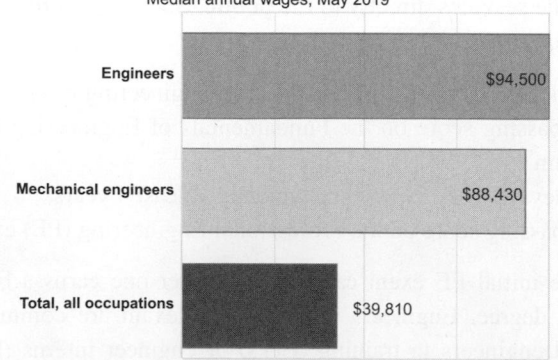

Mechanical Engineers
Median annual wages, May 2019

Engineers $94,500
Mechanical engineers $88,430
Total, all occupations $39,810

Note: All Occupations includes all occupations in the U.S. Economy.
Source: U.S. Bureau of Labor Statistics, Occupational Employment Statistics.

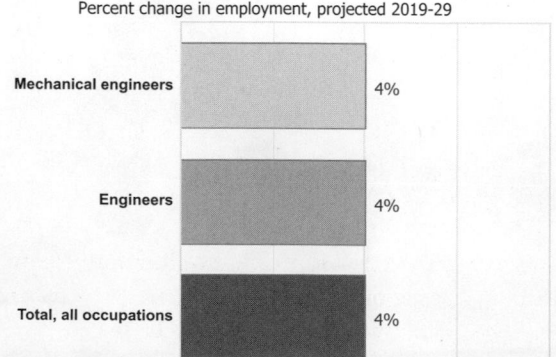

Mechanical Engineers
Percent change in employment, projected 2019-29

Mechanical engineers 4%
Engineers 4%
Total, all occupations 4%

Note: All Occupations includes all occupations in the U.S. Economy.
Source: U.S. Bureau of Labor Statistics, Employment Projections program.

Employment projections data for mechanical engineers, 2019-29					
Occupational Title	SOC Code	Employment, 2019	Projected Employment, 2029	Change, 2019-29	
				Percent	Numeric
SOURCE: U.S. Bureau of Labor Statistics, Employment Projections program					
Mechanical engineers	17-2141	316,300	328,700	4	12,400

State & Area Data
Occupational Employment Statistics (OES)

The Occupational Employment Statistics (OES) program produces employment and wage estimates annually for over 800 occupations. These estimates are available for the nation as a whole, for individual states, and for metropolitan and nonmetropolitan areas.

Contacts for More Information

For more information about general engineering education and mechanical engineering career resources, visit

➤ American Society of Mechanical Engineers
➤ American Society for Engineering Education
➤ Technology Student Association

For information about engineering summer camps, visit
➤ Engineering Education Service Center

For more information about accredited engineering programs, visit
➤ ABET

For more information about licensure as a mechanical engineer, visit
➤ National Council of Examiners for Engineering and Surveying

➤ National Society of Professional Engineers

For information about certification, visit
➤ American Society of Mechanical Engineers

Mining and Geological Engineers

Summary

Quick Facts: Mining and Geological Engineers

2019 Median Pay	$91,160 per year $43.83 per hour
Typical Entry-Level Education	Bachelor's degree
Work Experience in a Related Occupation	None
On-the-job Training	None
Number of Jobs, 2019	6,300
Job Outlook, 2019-29	4% (As fast as average)
Employment Change, 2019-29	300

What Mining and Geological Engineers Do

Mining and geological engineers design mines to safely and efficiently remove minerals for use in manufacturing and utilities.

Work Environment

Many mining and geological engineers work where mining operations are located, such as mineral mines or sand-and-gravel quarries, in remote areas or near cities and towns. Others work in offices or onsite for oil and gas extraction firms or engineering services firms.

How to Become a Mining or Geological Engineer

A bachelor's degree from an accredited engineering program is required to become a mining or geological engineer.

Pay

The median annual wage for mining and geological engineers was $91,160 in May 2019.

Mining engineers and geological engineers ensure that mines are operated in safe and environmentally sound ways.

Job Outlook

Employment of mining and geological engineers is projected to grow 4 percent from 2019 to 2029, about as fast as the average for all occupations. Employment growth for mining and geological engineers will be driven by demand for mining operations. In addition, as companies look for ways to cut costs, they are expected to contract more services with engineering services firms, rather than employ engineers directly.

State & Area Data

Explore resources for employment and wages by state and area for mining and geological engineers.

Similar Occupations

Compare the job duties, education, job growth, and pay of mining and geological engineers with similar occupations.

What Mining and Geological Engineers Do

Mining and geological engineers design mines to safely and efficiently remove minerals such as coal and metals for use in manufacturing and utilities.

Duties

Mining and geological engineers typically do the following:

- Design open-pit and underground mines
- Supervise the construction of mine shafts and tunnels
- Devise methods for transporting minerals to processing plants
- Prepare technical reports for miners, engineers, and managers
- Monitor mine production to assess the effectiveness of operations
- Provide solutions to problems related to land reclamation, water and air pollution, and sustainability
- Ensure that mines are operated in safe and environmentally sound ways

Geological engineers search for mineral deposits and evaluate possible sites. Once a site is identified, they plan how the metals or minerals will be extracted in efficient and environmentally sound ways.

Mining and geological engineers prepare technical reports for miners, engineers, and managers.

Mining engineers often specialize in one particular mineral or metal, such as coal or gold. They typically design and develop mines and determine the best way to extract metal or minerals to get the most out of deposits.

Some mining engineers work with geoscientists and metallurgical engineers to find and evaluate ore deposits. Other mining engineers develop new equipment or direct mineral-processing operations to separate minerals from dirt, rock, and other materials.

Mining safety engineers use best practices and their knowledge of mine design to ensure workers' safety and to maintain compliance with state and federal safety regulations. They inspect the walls and roofs of mines, monitor the air quality, and examine mining equipment for possible hazards.

Engineers who hold a master's or a doctoral degree may teach engineering at colleges and universities. For more information, see the profile on postsecondary teachers.

Work Environment

Mining and geological engineers held about 6,300 jobs in 2019. The largest employers of mining and geological engineers were as follows:

Engineering services	26%
Metal ore mining	17
Coal mining	10
Government	8
Oil and gas extraction	4

Many work where mining operations are located, such as mineral mines or sand-and-gravel quarries, in remote areas or near cities and towns. Others work in offices or onsite for oil and gas extraction firms or engineering services firms.

Work Schedules

Most mining and geological engineers work full time and some work more than 40 hours a week. The remoteness of some mining locations gives rise to variable schedules and weeks during which they work more hours than usual.

How to Become a Mining or Geological Engineer

A bachelor's degree from an accredited engineering program is required to become a mining or geological engineer, including a mining safety engineer. Requirements for licensure vary by state but most states require applicants to pass two exams.

Education

High school students interested in entering mining or geological engineering programs in college should take courses in mathematics and science.

Relatively few schools offer mining engineering or geological engineering programs. Typical bachelor's degree programs

Mining and geological engineers must visit the worksite to keep close watch on the progression of their designs.

in mining engineering include courses in geology, physics, thermodynamics, mine design and safety, and mathematics. Bachelor's degree programs in geological engineering typically include courses in geology, chemistry, fluid mechanics, physics, and mathematics. Both types of programs also include laboratory and field work, as well as traditional classroom study.

A related degree, such as civil or environmental engineering or geoscience, may be acceptable for some positions as a mining or geological engineer.

Programs in mining and geological engineering are accredited by ABET, whose accreditation is based on a program's faculty, curriculum, facilities, and other factors.

Master's degree programs in mining and geological engineering typically are 2-year programs and include coursework in specialized subjects, such as mineral resource development and mining regulations. Some programs require a written thesis for graduation.

Important Qualities

Analytical skills. Mining and geological engineers must take many factors into account when evaluating new mine locations and designing facilities. They must also plan for the restoration of the surrounding environment after operations end.

Decisionmaking skills. These engineers make decisions that influence many critical outcomes—from worker safety to mine

production. The ability to anticipate problems and deal with them immediately is crucial.

Logical-thinking skills. In planning mines' operations, mineral processing, and environmental reclamation, these engineers have to put work plans into a coherent, logical sequence.

Math skills. Mining and geological engineers use the principles of calculus, trigonometry, and other advanced topics in math for analysis, design, and troubleshooting in their work.

Problem-solving skills. Mining and geological engineers must explore for potential mines, plan their operations and mineral processing, and design environmental reclamation projects. These are all complex projects requiring an ability to identify and work toward goals, while solving problems along the way.

Writing skills. Mining and geological engineers must prepare reports and instructions for other workers. Therefore, they must be able to write clearly so that others can easily understand their ideas and plans.

Licenses, Certifications, and Registrations

Licensure is not required for entry-level positions as a mining or geological engineer. A Professional Engineering (PE) license, which allows for higher levels of leadership and independence, can be acquired later in one's career. Licensed engineers are called professional engineers (PEs). A PE can oversee the work of other engineers, sign off on projects, and provide services directly to the public. State licensure generally requires

- A degree from an ABET-accredited engineering program
- A passing score on the Fundamentals of Engineering (FE) exam
- Relevant work experience, typically at least 4 years
- A passing score on the Professional Engineering (PE) exam

The initial FE exam can be taken after one earns a bachelor's degree. Engineers who pass this exam are commonly called engineers in training (EITs) or engineer interns (EIs). After meeting work experience requirements, EITs and EIs

A bachelor's degree from an accredited engineering program is required to become a mining or geological engineer.

can take the second exam, called the Principles and Practice of Engineering.

In several states, engineers must earn continuing education credits to keep their licenses. Most states recognize licenses from other states, provided that licensure requirements in the other states meet or exceed the first state's own requirements.

Advancement

New mining and geological engineers usually work under the supervision of experienced engineers. In large companies, new engineers also may receive formal classroom or seminar-type training. As engineers gain knowledge and experience, they are assigned more difficult projects and they are given greater independence to develop designs, solve problems, and make decisions.

Engineers may advance to become technical specialists or supervise a staff or team of engineers and technicians. Some eventually become engineering managers or enter other managerial or sales jobs. In sales, an engineering background enables them to discuss a product's technical aspects and to assist in product planning, installation, and use. For more information, see the profiles on architectural and engineering managers and sales engineers.

Pay

The median annual wage for mining and geological engineers was $91,160 in May 2019. The median wage is the wage at which half the workers in an occupation earned more than that amount and half earned less. The lowest 10 percent earned less than $52,160, and the highest 10 percent earned more than $151,230.

In May 2019, the median annual wages for mining and geological engineers in the top industries in which they worked were as follows:

Oil and gas extraction $131,850

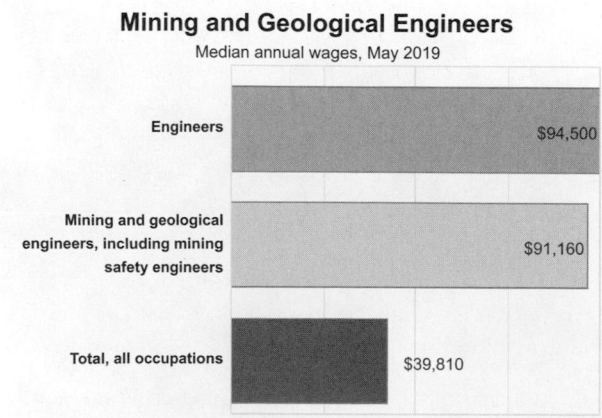

Mining and Geological Engineers
Median annual wages, May 2019

- Engineers — $94,500
- Mining and geological engineers, including mining safety engineers — $91,160
- Total, all occupations — $39,810

Note: All Occupations includes all occupations in the U.S. Economy. Source: U.S. Bureau of Labor Statistics, Occupational Employment Statistics.

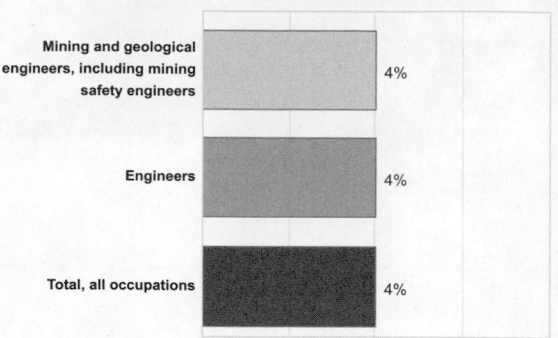

Mining and Geological Engineers
Percent change in employment, projected 2019-29

- Mining and geological engineers, including mining safety engineers — 4%
- Engineers — 4%
- Total, all occupations — 4%

Note: All Occupations includes all occupations in the U.S. Economy. Source: U.S. Bureau of Labor Statistics, Employment Projections program.

Government 110,400
Metal ore mining 88,300
Coal mining 87,990
Engineering services 84,370

Most mining and geological engineers work full time and some work more than 40 hours a week. The remoteness of some mining locations gives rise to variable schedules and weeks during which they work more than usual.

Job Outlook

Employment of mining and geological engineers is projected to grow 4 percent from 2019 to 2029, about as fast as the average for all occupations.

Employment growth for mining and geological engineers will depend upon demand for coal, metals, and minerals. These resources are used in many products, from construction materials and cars to cell phones and computers. As companies look for ways to cut costs, they are expected to contract more services with engineering services firms, rather than employ engineers directly.

Employment projections data for mining and geological engineers, 2019-29					
Occupational Title	SOC Code	Employment, 2019	Projected Employment, 2029	Change, 2019-29	
				Percent	Numeric
SOURCE: U.S. Bureau of Labor Statistics, Employment Projections program					
Mining and geological engineers, including mining safety engineers	17-2151	6,300	6,600	4	300

State & Area Data
Occupational Employment Statistics (OES)

The Occupational Employment Statistics (OES) program produces employment and wage estimates annually for over 800 occupations. These estimates are available for the nation as a whole, for individual states, and for metropolitan and nonmetropolitan areas.

Contacts for More Information

For more information about mining and geological engineers, visit

➤ Society for Mining, Metallurgy, and Exploration

For information about general engineering education and career resources, visit

➤ American Society for Engineering Education
➤ Technology Student Association

For more information about licensure as a mining or geological engineer, visit

➤ National Council of Examiners for Engineering and Surveying

➤ National Society of Professional Engineers

For information about accredited engineering programs, visit

➤ ABET

Nuclear Engineers

Summary

Quick Facts: Nuclear Engineers

2019 Median Pay	$113,460 per year $54.55 per hour
Typical Entry-Level Education	Bachelor's degree
Work Experience in a Related Occupation	None
On-the-job Training	None
Number of Jobs, 2019	16,400
Job Outlook, 2019-29	-13% (Decline)
Employment Change, 2019-29	-2,100

What Nuclear Engineers Do

Nuclear engineers research and develop the processes, instruments, and systems used to derive benefits from nuclear energy and radiation.

Work Environment

Nuclear engineers typically work in offices; however, their work setting varies with the industry in which they are employed. Most nuclear engineers work full time.

Nuclear engineers direct maintenance activities at operational nuclear power plants to ensure that they meet safety standards.

How to Become a Nuclear Engineer

Nuclear engineers must have a bachelor's degree in nuclear engineering. Employers also value experience, which can be gained through cooperative-education engineering programs.

Pay

The median annual wage for nuclear engineers was $113,460 in May 2019.

Job Outlook

Employment of nuclear engineers is projected to decline 13 percent from 2019 to 2029. Traditionally, utilities that own or build nuclear power plants have employed the greatest number of nuclear engineers. However, utilities often are opting for cheaper natural gas in power generation.

State & Area Data

Explore resources for employment and wages by state and area for nuclear engineers.

Similar Occupations

Compare the job duties, education, job growth, and pay of nuclear engineers with similar occupations.

What Nuclear Engineers Do

Nuclear engineers research and develop the processes, instruments, and systems used to derive benefits from nuclear energy and radiation. Many of these engineers find industrial and medical uses for radioactive materials—for example, in equipment used in medical diagnosis and treatment. Many others specialize in the development of nuclear power sources for ships or spacecraft.

Duties

Nuclear engineers typically do the following:

- Design or develop nuclear equipment, such as reactor cores, radiation shielding, and associated instrumentation
- Direct operating or maintenance activities of operational nuclear power plants to ensure that they meet safety standards

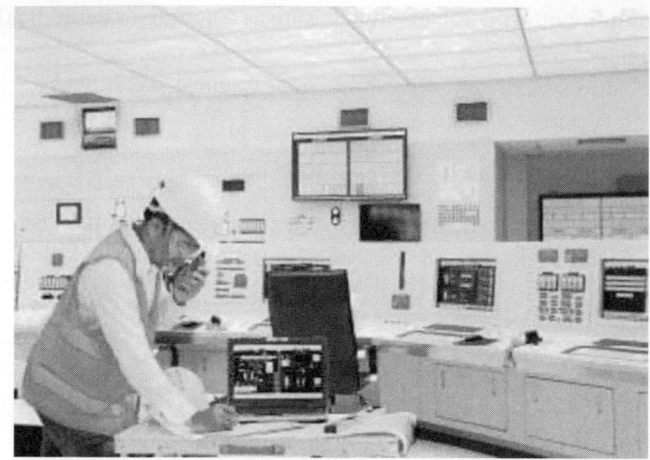

Nuclear engineers monitor nuclear facility operations.

- Write operational instructions to be used in nuclear plant operation or in handling and disposing of nuclear waste
- Monitor nuclear facility operations to identify any design, construction, or operation practices that violate safety regulations and laws
- Perform experiments to test whether methods of using nuclear material, reclaiming nuclear fuel, or disposing of nuclear waste are acceptable
- Take corrective actions or order plant shutdowns in emergencies
- Examine nuclear accidents and gather data that can be used to design preventive measures

In addition, nuclear engineers are at the forefront of developing uses of nuclear material for medical imaging devices, such as positron emission tomography (PET) scanners. They also may develop or design cyclotrons, which produce a high-energy beam that the healthcare industry uses to treat cancerous tumors.

Work Environment

Nuclear engineers held about 16,400 jobs in 2019. The largest employers of nuclear engineers were as follows:

Federal government, excluding postal service	20%
Scientific research and development services..............	14
Manufacturing..	9
Engineering services...	6

Nuclear engineers typically work in offices. However, their work setting varies with the industry in which they are employed. For example, those employed in power generation and supply work in power plants. Many work for the federal government and for consulting firms.

Nuclear engineers work with others, including mechanical engineers and electrical engineers, and they must be able to

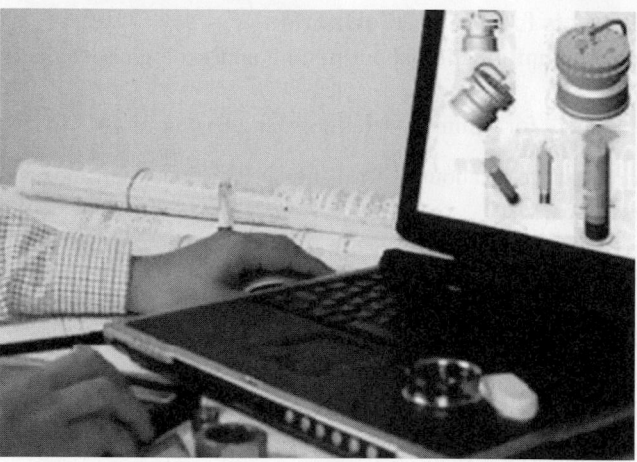

Nuclear engineers design equipment that may be used at nuclear power plants.

incorporate systems designed by these engineers into their own designs.

Work Schedules

The majority of nuclear engineers work full time and some work more than 40 hours per week. Their schedules may vary with the industries in which they work.

How to Become a Nuclear Engineer

Nuclear engineers must have a bachelor's degree in nuclear engineering or a related field of engineering. Employers also value experience, which can be gained through cooperative-education engineering programs.

Education

Entry-level nuclear engineering jobs in private industry require a bachelor's degree. Some entry-level nuclear engineering jobs may require at least a master's degree or even a Ph.D.

Students interested in studying nuclear engineering should take high school courses in mathematics, such as algebra, trigonometry, and calculus; and science, such as biology, chemistry, and physics.

Bachelor's degree programs consist of classroom, laboratory, and field studies in subjects such as mathematics and engineering principles. Most colleges and universities offer cooperative-education programs in which students gain work experience while completing their education.

Some universities offer 5-year programs leading to both a bachelor's and a master's degree. A graduate degree allows an engineer to work as an instructor at a university or engage in research and development. Some 5-year or even 6-year cooperative-education plans combine classroom study with work, permitting students to gain experience and to finance part of their education.

Nuclear engineers write operational instructions to be used in nuclear plant operations or in handling and disposing of nuclear waste.

Master's and Ph.D. programs consist of classroom, laboratory, and research efforts in areas of advanced mathematics and engineering principles. These programs require the successful completion of a research study, usually conducted in conjunction with a professor, on a government or private research grant.

Programs in nuclear engineering are accredited by ABET.

Important Qualities

Analytical skills. Nuclear engineers must identify design elements to help build facilities and equipment that produce material needed by various industries.

Communication skills. Nuclear engineers' work depends heavily on their ability to work with other engineers and technicians. They must communicate effectively, both in writing and in person.

Detail oriented. Nuclear engineers supervise the operation of nuclear facilities. They must pay close attention to what is happening at all times and ensure that operations comply with all regulations and laws pertaining to the safety of workers and the environment.

Logical-thinking skills. Nuclear engineers design complex systems. Therefore, they must order information logically and clearly so that others can follow their written information and instructions.

Math skills. Nuclear engineers use the principles of calculus, trigonometry, and other advanced topics in math for analysis, design, and troubleshooting in their work.

Problem-solving skills. Because of the hazard posed by nuclear materials and by accidents at facilities, nuclear engineers must anticipate problems before they occur and safeguard against them.

Training

A newly hired nuclear engineer at a nuclear power plant usually must complete training onsite, in such areas as safety procedures, practices, and regulations, before being allowed to work independently. Training lasts from 6 weeks to 3 months, depending on the employer. In addition, these engineers must undergo continuous training every year to keep their knowledge, skills, and abilities current with laws, regulations, and safety procedures.

Licenses, Certifications, and Registrations

Licensure is not required for entry-level positions as a nuclear engineer. A Professional Engineering (PE) license, which allows for higher levels of leadership and independence, can be acquired later in one's career. Licensed engineers are called professional engineers (PEs). A PE can oversee the work of other engineers, sign off on projects, and provide services directly to the public. State licensure generally requires

- A degree from an ABET-accredited engineering program
- A passing score on the Fundamentals of Engineering (FE) exam
- Relevant work experience, typically at least 4 years
- A passing score on the Professional Engineering (PE) exam

The initial FE exam can be taken after one earns a bachelor's degree. Engineers who pass this exam are commonly called engineers in training (EITs) or engineer interns (EIs). After meeting work experience requirements, EITs and EIs can take the second exam, called the Principles and Practice of Engineering.

Each state issues its own licenses. Most states recognize licensure from other states, as long as the licensing state's requirements meet or exceed their own licensure requirements. Several states require continuing education for engineers to keep their licenses.

Nuclear engineers can obtain licensing as a Senior Reactor Operator, a designation that is granted after an intensive, 2-year, site-specific program. The credential, granted by the Nuclear Regulatory Commission, asserts that the engineer can operate a nuclear power plant within federal government requirements.

Other Experience
During high school, students can attend engineering summer camps to see what these and other engineers do. Attending these camps can help students plan their coursework for the remainder of their time in high school.

Advancement
New nuclear engineers usually work under the supervision of experienced engineers. In large companies, new engineers may receive formal training in classrooms or seminars. As beginning engineers gain knowledge and experience, they move on to more difficult projects with greater independence to develop designs, solve problems, and make decisions.

Eventually, nuclear engineers may advance to become technical specialists or to supervise a team of engineers and technicians. Some may become engineering managers or move into sales work. For more information, see the profiles on architectural and engineering managers and sales engineers.

Nuclear engineers also can become medical physicists. A master's degree in health physics, radiological sciences, or a related field is necessary for someone to enter this field.

Pay
The median annual wage for nuclear engineers was $113,460 in May 2019. The median wage is the wage at which half the workers in an occupation earned more than that amount and half earned less. The lowest 10 percent earned less than $71,860, and the highest 10 percent earned more than $179,430.

In May 2019, the median annual wages for nuclear engineers in the top industries in which they worked were as follows:

Engineering services	$136,340
Scientific research and development services	134,810
Federal government, excluding postal service	94,610
Manufacturing	89,480

The majority of nuclear engineers work full time and some work more than 40 hours per week. Their schedules may vary with the industries in which they work.

Job Outlook
Employment of nuclear engineers is projected to decline 13 percent from 2019 to 2029. Traditionally, utilities that own or build nuclear power plants have employed the greatest number of nuclear engineers. However, utilities often are opting for cheaper natural gas in power generation. In addition, the increasing viability of renewable energy is putting economic pressure on traditional nuclear power generation.

Job Prospects
Job prospects are expected to be relatively limited. Openings should stem from operating extensions being granted to older nuclear power plants. Those with training in developing fields, such as nuclear medicine, should have better prospects.

Employment projections data for nuclear engineers, 2019-29					
Occupational Title	SOC Code	Employment, 2019	Projected Employment, 2029	Change, 2019-29	
				Percent	Numeric
SOURCE: U.S. Bureau of Labor Statistics, Employment Projections program					
Nuclear engineers	17-2161	16,400	14,300	-13	-2,100

State & Area Data
Occupational Employment Statistics (OES)
The Occupational Employment Statistics (OES) program produces employment and wage estimates annually for over 800 occupations. These estimates are available for the nation as a whole, for individual states, and for metropolitan and nonmetropolitan areas.

Contacts for More Information
For more information about general engineering education and career resources, visit

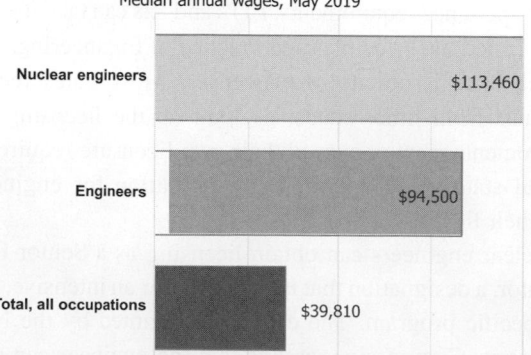

Nuclear Engineers
Median annual wages, May 2019

Nuclear engineers $113,460
Engineers $94,500
Total, all occupations $39,810

Note: All Occupations includes all occupations in the U.S. Economy.
Source: U.S. Bureau of Labor Statistics, Occupational Employment Statistics.

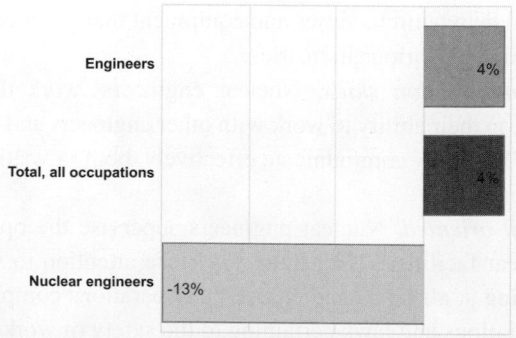

Nuclear Engineers
Percent change in employment, projected 2019-29

Engineers 4%
Total, all occupations 4%
Nuclear engineers -13%

Note: All Occupations includes all occupations in the U.S. Economy.
Source: U.S. Bureau of Labor Statistics, Employment Projections program.

➤ American Nuclear Society
➤ American Society for Engineering Education
➤ Center for Nuclear Science and Technology Information
➤ Health Physics Society
➤ Nuclear Energy Institute
➤ Society of Nuclear Medicine and Molecular Imaging
➤ Technology Student Association

For more information about licensure as a nuclear engineer, visit
➤ National Council of Examiners for Engineering and Surveying

➤ National Society of Professional Engineers

For more information about accredited engineering programs, visit
➤ ABET

For more information about engineering summer camps, visit
➤ Engineering Education Service Center

For more information about federal government education requirements for nuclear engineer positions, visit
➤ U.S. Office of Personnel Management

Petroleum Engineers

Summary

Quick Facts: Petroleum Engineers

2019 Median Pay	$137,720 per year $66.21 per hour
Typical Entry-Level Education	Bachelor's degree
Work Experience in a Related Occupation	None
On-the-job Training	None
Number of Jobs, 2019	33,400
Job Outlook, 2019-29	3% (As fast as average)
Employment Change, 2019-29	1,100

What Petroleum Engineers Do
Petroleum engineers design and develop methods for extracting oil and gas from deposits below the Earth's surface.

Work Environment
Petroleum engineers generally work in offices or at drilling and well sites. Travel is frequently required to visit these sites or to meet with other engineers, oilfield workers, and customers.

How to Become a Petroleum Engineer
Petroleum engineers must have a bachelor's degree in engineering, preferably petroleum engineering. However, a bachelor's degree in mechanical, civil, chemical engineering may meet employer requirements. Employers also value work experience, so cooperative-education programs, in which students earn academic credit and job experience, are valuable as well.

Pay
The median annual wage for petroleum engineers was $137,720 in May 2019.

Job Outlook
Employment of petroleum engineers is projected to grow 3 percent from 2019 to 2029, about as fast as the average for all

Petroleum engineers design equipment to extract oil and gas in the most profitable way.

occupations. Oil prices will be a major determinant of employment growth. Higher prices can cause oil and gas companies to increase capital investment in new facilities and expand existing production operations, along with exploration.

State & Area Data
Explore resources for employment and wages by state and area for petroleum engineers.

Similar Occupations
Compare the job duties, education, job growth, and pay of petroleum engineers with similar occupations.

What Petroleum Engineers Do
Petroleum engineers design and develop methods for extracting oil and gas from deposits below the Earth's surface. Petroleum engineers also find new ways to extract oil and gas from older wells.

Duties
Petroleum engineers typically do the following:

• Design equipment to extract oil and gas from onshore and offshore reserves deep underground

Petroleum engineers help find oil and gas for the country's energy needs.

- Develop plans to drill in oil and gas fields, and then to recover the oil and gas
- Develop ways to inject water, chemicals, gases, or steam into an oil reserve to force out more oil or gas
- Make sure that oilfield equipment is installed, operated, and maintained properly
- Evaluate the production of wells through surveys, testing, and analysis

Oil and gas deposits, or reservoirs, are located deep in rock formations underground. These reservoirs can be accessed only by drilling wells, either on land, or at sea from offshore oil rigs.

Once oil and gas are discovered, petroleum engineers work with geoscientists and other specialists to understand the geologic formation of the rock containing the reservoir. They then determine the drilling methods, design the drilling equipment, implement the drilling plan, and monitor operations.

The best techniques currently being used recover only a portion of the oil and gas in a reservoir, so petroleum engineers also research and develop new ways to recover more of the oil and gas. This additional recovery helps to lower the cost of drilling and production.

The following are examples of types of petroleum engineers:

Completions engineers decide the best way to finish building wells so that oil or gas will flow up from underground. They oversee work to complete the building of wells—a project that might involve the use of tubing, hydraulic fracturing, or pressure-control techniques.

Drilling engineers determine the best way to drill oil or gas wells, taking into account a number of factors, including cost. They also ensure that the drilling process is safe, efficient, and minimally disruptive to the environment.

Production engineers take over wells after drilling is completed. They typically monitor wells' oil and gas production. If wells are not producing as much as expected, production engineers figure out ways to increase the amount being extracted.

Reservoir engineers estimate how much oil or gas can be recovered from underground deposits, known as reservoirs.

They study reservoirs' characteristics and determine which methods will get the most oil or gas out of the reservoirs. They also monitor operations to ensure that optimal levels of these resources are being recovered.

Work Environment

Petroleum engineers held about 33,400 jobs in 2019. The largest employers of petroleum engineers were as follows:

Oil and gas extraction 34%
Management of companies and enterprises 18
Support activities for mining 14
Petroleum and coal products manufacturing 7
Engineering services 7

Petroleum engineers generally work in offices or at drilling and well sites. Travel is frequently required to visit these sites or to meet with other engineers, oilfield workers, and customers.

Large oil and gas companies maintain operations around the world; therefore, petroleum engineers sometimes work in other countries. Petroleum engineers also must be able to work with people from a wide variety of backgrounds, including other types of engineers, scientists, and oil and gas field workers.

Work Schedules

Petroleum engineers typically work full time. Overtime may be necessary when traveling to and from drilling sites to help in their operation or respond to problems when they arise.

How to Become a Petroleum Engineer

Petroleum engineers must have a bachelor's degree in engineering, preferably petroleum engineering. However, a bachelor's degree in mechanical, civil, or chemical engineering may meet employer requirements. Employers also value work experience, so college cooperative-education programs, in which students earn academic credit and job experience, are valuable as well.

Petroleum engineers generally work in an office setting, but must sometimes work on site to monitor operations.

Petroleum engineers must have a bachelor's degree in engineering, preferably in petroleum engineering.

Education

Students interested in studying petroleum engineering will benefit from taking high school courses in math, such as algebra, trigonometry, and calculus; and in science, such as biology, chemistry, and physics.

Entry-level petroleum engineering jobs require a bachelor's degree. Bachelor's degree programs include classes, laboratory work, and field studies in areas such as engineering principles, geology, and thermodynamics. Most colleges and universities offer cooperative programs in which students gain practical experience while completing their education.

Some colleges and universities offer 5-year programs in chemical or mechanical engineering that lead to both a bachelor's degree and a master's degree. Some employers prefer applicants who have earned a graduate degree. A graduate degree also allows an engineer to work as an instructor at some universities or in research and development.

ABET accredits programs in petroleum engineering.

Important Qualities

Analytical skills. Petroleum engineers must be able to compile and make sense of large amounts of technical information and data in order to ensure that facilities operate safely and effectively.

Creativity. Because each new drill site is unique and therefore presents new challenges, petroleum engineers must be able to come up with creative designs to extract oil and gas.

Interpersonal skills. Petroleum engineers must work with others on projects that require highly complex machinery, equipment, and infrastructure. Communicating and working well with other engineers and oil and gas workers is crucial to ensuring that projects meet customer needs and run safely and efficiently.

Math skills. Petroleum engineers use the principles of calculus and other advanced topics in math for analysis, design, and troubleshooting in their work.

Problem-solving skills. Identifying problems in drilling plans is critical for petroleum engineers because these problems can be costly. Petroleum engineers must be careful not to overlook any potential issues and must quickly address those which do occur.

Licenses, Certifications, and Registrations

Licensure is not required for entry-level positions as a petroleum engineer. A Professional Engineering (PE) license, which allows for higher levels of leadership and independence, can be acquired later in one's career. Licensed engineers are called professional engineers (PEs). A PE can oversee the work of other engineers, sign off on projects, and provide services directly to the public. State licensure generally requires

- A degree from an ABET-accredited engineering program
- A passing score on the Fundamentals of Engineering (FE) exam
- Relevant work experience, typically at least 4 years
- A passing score on the Professional Engineering (PE) exam

The initial FE exam can be taken after one earns a bachelor's degree. Engineers who pass this exam are commonly called engineers in training (EITs) or engineer interns (EIs). After meeting work experience requirements, EITs and EIs can take the second exam, called the Principles and Practice of Engineering (PE).

Several states require engineers to take continuing education courses in order to keep their licenses. Most states recognize licensure from other states if the licensing state's requirements meet or exceed their own licensure requirements. The Society of Petroleum Engineers offers certification. To be certified, petroleum engineers must be members of the Society, pass an exam, and meet other qualifications.

Advancement

Entry-level engineers usually work under the supervision of experienced engineers. In large companies, new engineers also may receive formal training. As engineers gain knowledge and experience, they move to more difficult projects on which they have greater independence to develop designs, solve problems, and make decisions.

Petroleum Engineers
Median annual wages, May 2019

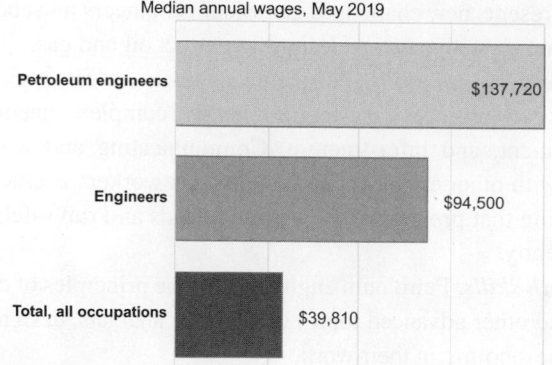

Note: All Occupations includes all occupations in the U.S. Economy.
Source: U.S. Bureau of Labor Statistics, Occupational Employment Statistics.

Petroleum Engineers
Percent change in employment, projected 2019-29

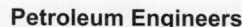
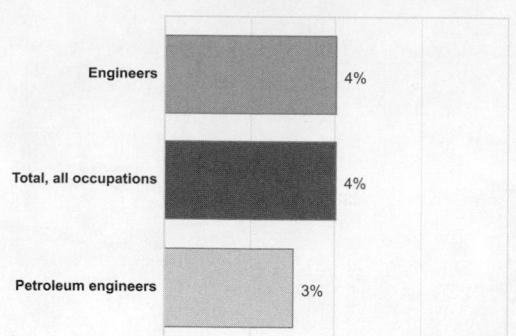

Note: All Occupations includes all occupations in the U.S. Economy.
Source: U.S. Bureau of Labor Statistics, Employment Projections program.

Eventually, petroleum engineers may advance to supervise a team of engineers and technicians. Some become engineering managers or move into other managerial positions. For more information, see the profile on architectural and engineering managers.

Petroleum engineers also may go into sales and use their engineering background to inform the discussion of a product's technical aspects with potential buyers and to help in product planning, installation, and use. For more information, see the profile on sales engineers.

Pay

The median annual wage for petroleum engineers was $137,720 in May 2019. The median wage is the wage at which half the workers in an occupation earned more than that amount and half earned less. The lowest 10 percent earned less than $79,270, and the highest 10 percent earned more than $208,000.

In May 2019, the median annual wages for petroleum engineers in the top industries in which they worked were as follows:

Management of companies and enterprises	$172,000
Oil and gas extraction	137,210
Engineering services	130,790
Petroleum and coal products manufacturing	129,960
Support activities for mining	117,150

Petroleum engineers typically work full time. Overtime may be necessary when traveling to and from drilling and well sites to help in their operation or respond to problems when they arise.

Job Outlook

Employment of petroleum engineers is projected to grow 3 percent from 2019 to 2029, about as fast as the average for all occupations.

Oil prices will be a major determinant of employment growth. Because many petroleum engineers work in oil and gas

extraction, any changes in oil prices will likely affect employment levels. Higher prices can cause oil and gas companies to increase capital investment in new facilities and expand existing production operations. Typically, companies also expand exploration for new reserves of oil and gas when prices are high.

Demand for petroleum engineers in support activities for mining should continue to be strong, as large oil and gas companies find it convenient and cost effective to contract production and drilling work to these firms as needed.

Employment projections data for petroleum engineers, 2019-29					
Occupational Title	SOC Code	Employment, 2019	Projected Employment, 2029	Change, 2019-29	
				Percent	Numeric
SOURCE: U.S. Bureau of Labor Statistics, Employment Projections program					
Petroleum engineers	17-2171	33,400	34,400	3	1,100

State & Area Data
Occupational Employment Statistics (OES)

The Occupational Employment Statistics (OES) program produces employment and wage estimates annually for over 800 occupations. These estimates are available for the nation as a whole, for individual states, and for metropolitan and nonmetropolitan areas.

Contacts for More Information

For information about general engineering education and career resources, visit
➤ American Society for Engineering Education
➤ Technology Student Association

For information about the Professional Engineer license, visit
➤ National Council of Examiners for Engineering and Surveying
➤ National Society of Professional Engineers

For information about accredited engineering programs, visit
➤ ABET

For information about certification, visit
➤ Society of Petroleum Engineers

Surveying and Mapping Technicians

Summary

Quick Facts: Surveying and Mapping Technicians	
2019 Median Pay	$45,010 per year
	$21.64 per hour
Typical Entry-Level Education	High school diploma or equivalent
Work Experience in a Related Occupation	None
On-the-job Training	Moderate-term on-the-job training
Number of Jobs, 2019	58,400
Job Outlook, 2019-29	1% (Slower than average)
Employment Change, 2019-29	400

What Surveying and Mapping Technicians Do

Surveying and mapping technicians collect data and make maps of the Earth's surface.

Work Environment

Surveying technicians work outside extensively and can be exposed to all types of weather. Mapping technicians work primarily indoors on computers. Most surveying and mapping technicians work for firms that provide engineering, surveying, and mapping services on a contract basis. Local governments also employ these workers in highway and planning departments.

How to Become a Surveying or Mapping Technician

Surveying technicians usually need a high school diploma. However, mapping technicians often need formal education after high school to study technology applications, such as Geographic Information Systems (GIS).

Pay

The median annual wage for surveying and mapping technicians was $45,010 in May 2019.

Job Outlook

Employment of surveying and mapping technicians is projected to grow 1 percent from 2019 to 2029, slower than the average for all occupations.

State & Area Data

Explore resources for employment and wages by state and area for surveying and mapping technicians.

Similar Occupations

Compare the job duties, education, job growth, and pay of surveying and mapping technicians with similar occupations.

What Surveying and Mapping Technicians Do

Surveying and mapping technicians collect data and make maps of the Earth's surface. Surveying technicians visit sites to take measurements of the land. Mapping technicians use geographic data to create maps. They both assist surveyors, and cartographers and photogrammetrists.

Duties

Surveying technicians typically do the following:

- Visit sites to record survey measurements and other descriptive data
- Operate surveying instruments, such as electronic distance-measuring equipment (robotic total stations), to collect data on a location
- Set out stakes and marks to conduct a survey
- Search for previous survey points, such as old stone markers
- Enter the data from surveying instruments into computers, either in the field or in an office

Surveying and mapping technicians collect data and make maps of the Earth's surface.

Surveying technicians operate surveying instruments, such as electronic distance-measuring equipment.

Surveying technicians help surveyors in the field on teams known as survey parties. A typical survey party has a party chief and one or more surveying technicians. The party chief, either a surveyor or a senior surveying technician, leads day-to-day work activities. After data is collected by the survey party, surveying technicians help process the data by entering the data into computers.

Mapping technicians typically do the following:

- Select needed information from databases to create maps
- Edit and process images that have been collected in the field
- Produce maps showing boundaries, water locations, elevation, and other features of the terrain
- Update maps to ensure accuracy
- Assist photogrammetrists by laying out aerial photographs in sequence to identify areas not captured by aerial photography

Mapping technicians help cartographers and photogrammetrists produce and update maps. They do this work on computers, combining data from different sources. Mapping technicians may use drones to take photos and collect other information required to complete maps or surveys.

Geographic Information System (GIS) technicians use GIS technology to assemble, integrate, and display data about a particular location in a digital format. GIS technicians also maintain and update databases for GIS devices.

Work Environment

Surveying and mapping technicians held about 58,400 jobs in 2019. The largest employers of surveying and mapping technicians were as follows:

Architectural, engineering, and related services	59%
Local government, excluding education and hospitals	11
Self-employed workers	8
Utilities	4
Mining, quarrying, and oil and gas extraction	1

Most surveying and mapping technicians work for firms that provide engineering, surveying, and mapping services on a contractual basis. Local governments also employ these workers in highway and planning departments.

Surveying technicians work outside extensively and can be exposed to all types of weather. They often stand for long periods, walk considerable distances, and may have to climb hills with heavy packs of surveying instruments. Traveling is sometimes part of the job, and surveying technicians may commute long distances, stay away from home overnight, or temporarily relocate near a survey site.

Mapping technicians work primarily on computers in office environments. However, mapping technicians must sometimes conduct research by using resources such as survey maps and legal documents to verify property lines and to obtain information needed for mapping. This task may require traveling to storage sites, such as county courthouses or lawyers' offices, that house these legal documents.

Work Schedules

Surveying and mapping technicians typically work full time but may work additional hours during the summer, when weather and light conditions are most suitable for fieldwork. Construction-related work may be limited during times of harsh weather.

Mapping technicians who develop and maintain Geographic Information System (GIS) databases generally work normal business hours.

How to Become a Surveying or Mapping Technician

Surveying technicians usually need a high school diploma. However, mapping technicians often need formal education after high school to study technology applications, such as Geographic Information Systems (GIS).

Surveying technicians visit sites to take measurements of the land.

Learning to master the equipment is a big part of the training for surveying and mapping technicians.

Education

Surveying technicians generally need a high school diploma, but some have postsecondary training in survey technology. Postsecondary training is more common among mapping technicians where an associate's degree or bachelor's degree in a relevant field, such as geomatics, is beneficial.

High school students interested in working as a surveying or mapping technician should take courses in algebra, geometry, trigonometry, drafting, mechanical drawing, and computer science. Knowledge of these subjects may help in finding a job and in advancing.

Training

Surveying technicians learn their job duties under the supervision of a surveyor or a surveying party chief. Initially, surveying technicians handle simple tasks, such as placing markers on land and entering data into computers. With experience, they help decide where and how to measure the land.

Mapping technicians receive on-the-job training under the supervision of a lead mapper. During training, technicians learn how maps are created and stored in databases.

Licenses, Certifications, and Registrations

The growing need to make sure that data are useful to other professionals has caused certification to become more common. The American Society for Photogrammetry and Remote Sensing (ASPRS) offers certification for photogrammetry, remote-sensing, and Geographic Information/Land Information Systems (GIS/LIS). The National Society of Professional Surveyors offers the Certified Survey Technician credential, and the GIS Certification Institute offers a GIS Professional certification.

Advancement

Depending on state licensing requirements, surveying technicians with many years of experience and formal training in surveying may be able to become licensed surveyors.

Important Qualities

Decisionmaking skills. Surveying technicians must be able to exercise some independent judgment in the field because they may not always be able to communicate with team members.

Detail oriented. Surveying and mapping technicians must be precise and accurate in their work. Their results are often entered into legal records.

Listening skills. Surveying technicians work outdoors and must communicate with party chiefs and other team members across distances. Following spoken instructions from the party chief is crucial for saving time and preventing errors.

Physical stamina. Surveying technicians usually work outdoors, often in rugged terrain. Physical fitness is necessary to carry equipment and to stand most of the day.

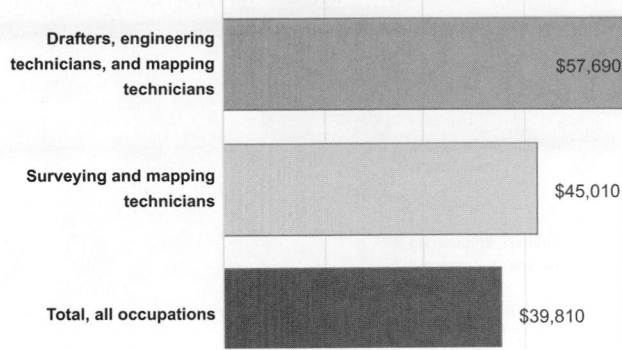

Surveying and Mapping Technicians
Median annual wages, May 2019

Drafters, engineering technicians, and mapping technicians	$57,690
Surveying and mapping technicians	$45,010
Total, all occupations	$39,810

Note: All Occupations includes all occupations in the U.S. Economy.
Source: U.S. Bureau of Labor Statistics, Occupational Employment Statistics.

Problem-solving skills. Surveying and mapping technicians must be able to identify and fix problems with their equipment. They must also note potential problems with the day's work plan.

Pay

The median annual wage for surveying and mapping technicians was $45,010 in May 2019. The median wage is the wage at which half the workers in an occupation earned more than that amount and half earned less. The lowest 10 percent earned less than $28,410, and the highest 10 percent earned more than $75,190.

In May 2019, the median annual wages for surveying and mapping technicians in the top industries in which they worked were as follows:

Utilities	$62,490
Mining, quarrying, and oil and gas extraction	57,900
Local government, excluding education and hospitals	51,550
Architectural, engineering, and related services	42,130

Surveying and mapping technicians typically work regular schedules but may work additional hours during the summer, when weather and light are most suitable for fieldwork. Construction-related work may be limited during times of harsh weather.

Mapping technicians who develop and maintain Geographic Information System (GIS) databases generally work normal business hours.

Job Outlook

Employment of surveying and mapping technicians is projected to grow 1 percent from 2019 to 2029, slower than the average for all occupations.

Increased demand for mapping technology is expected to require technicians to gather and prepare the data, even as

Surveying and Mapping Technicians
Percent change in employment, projected 2019-29

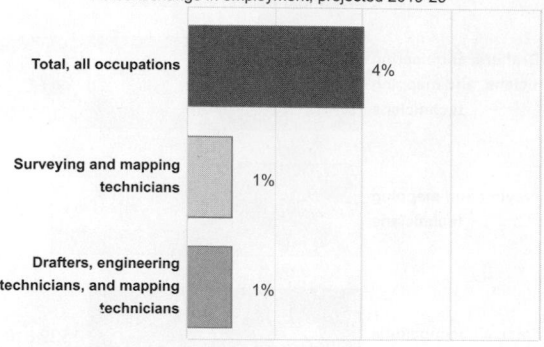

Total, all occupations	4%
Surveying and mapping technicians	1%
Drafters, engineering technicians, and mapping technicians	1%

Note: All Occupations includes all occupations in the U.S. Economy. Source: U.S. Bureau of Labor Statistics, Employment Projections program.

drones and other advancements make workers more efficient and limit projected employment growth.

Job Prospects

Demand for surveying services is closely tied to construction activity, and job opportunities will vary by geographic region, often depending on local economic conditions. When real estate sales and construction activity slow down, surveying technicians may face greater competition for jobs. However, because surveying technicians can work on many different types of projects, they may have steadier work than others when construction slows.

Employment projections data for surveying and mapping technicians, 2019-29					
Occupational Title	SOC Code	Employment, 2019	Projected Employment, 2029	Change, 2019-29	
				Percent	Numeric
SOURCE: U.S. Bureau of Labor Statistics, Employment Projections program					
Surveying and mapping technicians	17-3031	58,400	58,800	1	400

State & Area Data
Occupational Employment Statistics (OES)

The Occupational Employment Statistics (OES) program produces employment and wage estimates annually for over 800 occupations. These estimates are available for the nation as a whole, for individual states, and for metropolitan and nonmetropolitan areas.

Contacts for More Information

For more information on certification in GIS, visit
➤ GIS Certification Institute

For more information about career opportunities and the surveying technician certification program, visit
➤ National Society of Professional Surveyors

For more information about photogrammetric technicians and Geographic Information System specialists, visit
➤ American Society for Photogrammetry and Remote Sensing

Surveyors

Summary

Quick Facts: Surveyors

2019 Median Pay	$63,420 per year $30.49 per hour
Typical Entry-Level Education	Bachelor's degree
Work Experience in a Related Occupation	None
On-the-job Training	Internship/residency
Number of Jobs, 2019	48,000
Job Outlook, 2019-29	2% (Slower than average)
Employment Change, 2019-29	800

What Surveyors Do

Surveyors make precise measurements to determine property boundaries.

Work Environment

Surveying involves both fieldwork and office work. When working outside, surveyors may stand for long periods and

Surveyors map out boundaries for construction.

often walk long distances, sometimes in bad weather. Most work full time.

How to Become a Surveyor

Surveyors typically need a bachelor's degree. They must be licensed before they can certify legal documents and provide surveying services to the public.

Pay
The median annual wage for surveyors was $63,420 in May 2019.

Job Outlook
Employment of surveyors is projected to grow 2 percent from 2019 to 2029, slower than the average for all occupations. Surveyors will continue to be needed to certify boundary lines, work on resource extraction projects, and review sites for construction.

State & Area Data
Explore resources for employment and wages by state and area for surveyors.

What Surveyors Do
Surveyors make precise measurements to determine property boundaries. They provide data relevant to the shape and contour of the Earth's surface for engineering, mapmaking, and construction projects.

Duties
Surveyors typically do the following:

Surveyors update boundary lines and prepare sites for construction so that legal disputes are prevented.

- Measure distances and angles between points on, above, and below the Earth's surface
- Travel to locations and use known reference points to determine the exact location of important features
- Research land records, survey records, and land titles
- Look for evidence of previous boundaries to determine where boundary lines are located
- Record the results of surveying and verify the accuracy of data
- Prepare plots, maps, and reports
- Present findings to clients and government agencies
- Establish official land and water boundaries for deeds, leases, and other legal documents and testify in court regarding survey work

Surveyors mark and document the location of legal property lines. For example, when a house or commercial building is bought or sold, surveyors may mark property boundaries to prevent or resolve disputes. They use a variety of measuring equipment depending upon the type of survey.

When taking measurements in the field, surveyors make use of the Global Positioning System (GPS), a system of satellites that locates reference points with a high degree of precision. Surveyors use handheld GPS units and automated systems known as robotic total stations to collect relevant information about the terrain they are surveying. Surveyors then interpret and verify the results on a computer.

Surveyors also use Geographic Information Systems (GIS)—technology that allows surveyors to present spatial information visually as maps, reports, and charts. For example, a surveyor can overlay aerial or satellite images with GIS data, such as tree density in a given region, and create digital maps. They then use the results to advise governments and businesses on where to plan homes, roads, and landfills.

Although advances in surveying technology now allow many jobs to be performed by just one surveyor, other jobs may be performed by a crew, consisting of a licensed surveyor and trained surveying technicians. The person in charge of the crew, known as the *party chief*, may be either a surveyor or a senior surveying technician. The party chief leads day-to-day work activities.

Surveyors also work with civil engineers, landscape architects, cartographers and photogrammetrists, and urban and regional planners to develop comprehensive design documents.

The following are examples of types of surveyors:

Boundary or land surveyors determine the legal property lines and help determine the exact locations of real estate and construction projects.

Engineering or construction surveyors determine the precise location of roads or buildings and proper depths for building foundations. They show changes to the property line and indicate potential restrictions on the property, such as what can be built on it and how large the structure can be. They also may survey the grade and topography of roads.

Forensic surveyors survey and record accident scenes for potential landscape effects.

Geodetic surveyors use high-accuracy technology, including aerial and satellite observations, to measure large areas of the Earth's surface.

Marine or hydrographic surveyors survey harbors, rivers, and other bodies of water to determine shorelines, the topography of the floor, water depth, and other features.

Mine surveyors survey and map the tunnels in an underground mine. They survey surface mines to determine the volume of materials mined.

Work Environment

Surveyors held about 48,000 jobs in 2019. The largest employers of surveyors were as follows:

Architectural, engineering, and related services	69%
Government	10
Construction	7
Self-employed workers	5
Mining, quarrying, and oil and gas extraction	2

Depending on the specific job duties, surveying involves both fieldwork and office work. Fieldwork involves working outdoors in all types of weather, walking long distances, and standing for extended periods while taking measurements. Surveyors sometimes climb hills with heavy packs of surveying instruments. When working near hazards such as traffic, surveyors generally wear brightly colored or reflective vests so they may be seen more easily. When working in underground mines, surveyors work in enclosed spaces.

Traveling is often part of the job, and surveyors may commute long distances or stay at a project location for an extended period of time. Those who work on resource extraction projects may work in remote areas and spend long periods away from home.

Work Schedules

Surveyors usually work full time. When construction activity is high, they may work more hours than usual.

How to Become a Surveyor

Surveyors typically need a bachelor's degree. They must be licensed before they can certify legal documents and provide surveying services to the public.

Education

Surveyors typically need a bachelor's degree because they work with sophisticated technology and math. Some colleges and universities offer bachelor's degree programs specifically designed to prepare students to become licensed surveyors. Many states require individuals who want to become licensed surveyors to have a bachelor's degree from a school accredited by ABET. A bachelor's degree in a closely related field, such as civil engineering or forestry, is sometimes acceptable as well. An associate's degree may be sufficient in some cases with additional training.

Training

In order to become licensed, most states require approximately 4 years of work experience and training under a licensed surveyor after obtaining a bachelor's degree. Other states may allow substituting more years of work experience and supervised training under a licensed surveyor in place of education.

Work Experience in a Related Occupation

In some states, surveying technicians can become licensed surveyors after working for as many as 10 years under a licensed surveyor. The amount of work experience required varies by state. Check with your state for more information.

Surveyors collect data outdoors.

Surveyors typically need a bachelor's degree, but they also typically work under a licensed surveyor for 4 years.

Licenses, Certifications, and Registrations

All 50 states and the District of Columbia require surveyors to be licensed before they can certify legal documents that show property lines or determine proper markings on construction projects. Candidates with a bachelor's degree usually must work for several years under the direction of a licensed surveyor in order to qualify for licensure.

Although the process of obtaining a license varies by state, the National Council of Examiners for Engineering and Surveying has a generalized process of four steps:

1. Complete the level of education required in your state
2. Pass the Fundamentals of Surveying (FS) exam
3. Gain sufficient work experience under a licensed surveyor
4. Pass the Principles and Practice of Surveying (PS) exam

Most states also have continuing education requirements for surveyors to maintain their license.

Important Qualities

Communication skills. Surveyors must provide clear instructions to team members, clients, and government officials. They also must be able to follow instructions from architects and construction managers, and explain the job's progress to developers, lawyers, financiers, and government authorities.

Detail oriented. Surveyors must work with precision and accuracy because they produce legally binding documents.

Physical stamina. Surveyors traditionally work outdoors, often in rugged terrain. They must be able to walk long distances and for long periods.

Problem-solving skills. Surveyors must figure out discrepancies between documents showing property lines and current conditions on the land. If there were changes in previous years, they must discover the reason behind them and reestablish property lines.

Time-management skills. Surveyors must be able to effectively plan their time and their team members' time on the job. This is critical when pressing deadlines exist or while working outside during winter months when daylight hours are short.

Visualization skills. Surveyors must be able to envision new buildings and altered terrain.

Pay

The median annual wage for surveyors was $63,420 in May 2019. The median wage is the wage at which half the workers in an occupation earned more than that amount and half earned less. The lowest 10 percent earned less than $36,110, and the highest 10 percent earned more than $104,850.

In May 2019, the median annual wages for surveyors in the top industries in which they worked were as follows:

Government	$73,220
Mining, quarrying, and oil and gas extraction	65,640
Construction	65,060

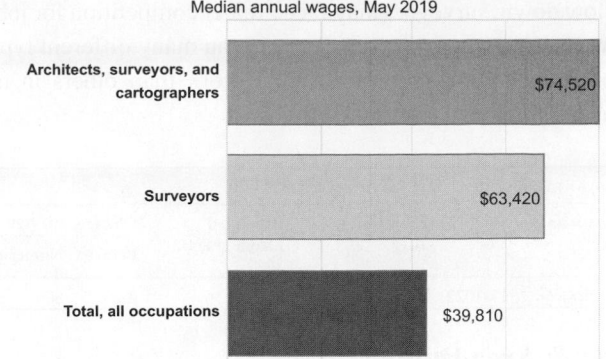

Surveyors
Median annual wages, May 2019

Architects, surveyors, and cartographers — $74,520
Surveyors — $63,420
Total, all occupations — $39,810

Note: All Occupations includes all occupations in the U.S. Economy. Source: U.S. Bureau of Labor Statistics, Occupational Employment Statistics.

Architectural, engineering, and related services	61,640

Surveyors usually work full time. When construction activity is high, they may work more hours than usual.

Job Outlook

Employment of surveyors is projected to grow 2 percent from 2019 to 2029, slower than the average for all occupations.

Surveyors will continue to be needed to certify boundary lines, work on resource extraction projects, and review sites for construction. However, the use of drones and other technologies is expected to increase worker productivity and may therefore limit employment growth.

Job Prospects

Those with knowledge of a variety of surveying specializations and a bachelor's degree from an ABET-accredited school will have the best job opportunities.

Demand for traditional surveying services is closely tied to construction activity; therefore, job opportunities will vary by geographic region and often depend on local economic

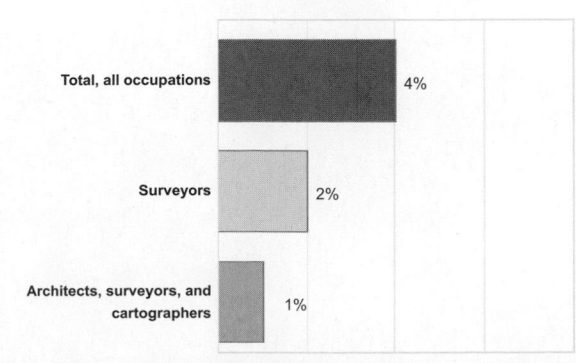

Surveyors
Percent change in employment, projected 2019-29

Total, all occupations — 4%
Surveyors — 2%
Architects, surveyors, and cartographers — 1%

Note: All Occupations includes all occupations in the U.S. Economy. Source: U.S. Bureau of Labor Statistics, Employment Projections program.

conditions. When real estate sales and other construction activity slow down, surveyors may face greater competition for jobs. However, because surveyors can work on many different types of projects, they may have steadier work than others in the industry when construction slows.

Employment projections data for surveyors, 2019-29					
Occupational Title	SOC Code	Employment, 2019	Projected Employment, 2029	Change, 2019-29	
				Percent	Numeric
Surveyors	17-1022	48,000	48,700	2	800

State & Area Data
Occupational Employment Statistics (OES)

The Occupational Employment Statistics (OES) program produces employment and wage estimates annually for over 800 occupations. These estimates are available for the nation as a whole, for individual states, and for metropolitan and nonmetropolitan areas.

Contacts for More Information

For information about surveying, career opportunities, and licensure requirements, visit
➤ National Council of Examiners for Engineering and Surveying
➤ National Society of Professional Surveyors

For information about a career as a geodetic surveyor, visit
➤ American Association for Geodetic Surveying

For a list of schools offering accredited programs, visit
➤ ABET

Arts and Design

Art Directors

Summary

Quick Facts: Art Directors

2019 Median Pay	$94,220 per year
	$45.30 per hour
Typical Entry-Level Education	Bachelor's degree
Work Experience in a Related Occupation	5 years or more
On-the-job Training	None
Number of Jobs, 2019	99,100
Job Outlook, 2019-29	-2% (Decline)
Employment Change, 2019-29	-1,800

What Art Directors Do

Art directors are responsible for the visual style and images in magazines, newspapers, product packaging, and movie and television productions.

Work Environment

Most art directors are self-employed. Others work for advertising and public relations firms, newspaper and magazine publishers, motion picture and video industries, and specialized design services firms.

How to Become an Art Director

Art directors need at least a bachelor's degree in an art or design subject and previous work experience. Depending on the industry, art directors may have previously worked as graphic designers, illustrators, copy editors, or photographers, or in another art or design occupation.

Pay

The median annual wage for art directors was $94,220 in May 2019.

Job Outlook

Employment of art directors is projected to decline 2 percent from 2019 to 2029. As traditional print publications lose ground to other media forms, employment of art directors is projected to decrease in the newspaper, periodical, book, and directory publishers industry.

State & Area Data

Explore resources for employment and wages by state and area for art directors.

Art directors oversee the work of other designers and artists who produce images for television, film, advertisements, or video games.

Art directors determine which photographs, art, or other design elements to use.

What Art Directors Do

Art directors are responsible for the visual style and images in magazines, newspapers, product packaging, and movie and television productions. They create the overall design and direct others who develop artwork or layouts.

Duties

Art directors typically do the following:

- Determine how best to represent a concept visually
- Determine which photographs, art, or other design elements to use
- Develop the overall look or style of a publication, an advertising campaign, or a theater, television, or film set
- Manage graphic designers, set and exhibit designers, or other design staff
- Review and approve designs, artwork, photography, and graphics developed by other staff members
- Talk to clients to develop an artistic approach and style
- Coordinate activities with other artistic and creative departments
- Develop detailed budgets and timelines
- Present designs to clients for approval

Art directors typically oversee the work of other designers and artists who produce images for television, film, live performances, advertisements, or video games. They determine the overall style in which a message is communicated visually to its audience. For each project, they articulate their vision to artists. The artists then create images, such as illustrations, graphics, photographs, or charts and graphs, or design stage and movie sets, according to the art director's vision.

Art directors work with art and design staffs in advertising agencies, public relations firms, or book, magazine, or newspaper publishing to create designs and layouts. They also work with producers and directors of theater, television, or movie productions to oversee set designs. Their work requires them to understand the design elements of projects, inspire other creative workers, and keep projects on budget and on time. Sometimes they are responsible for developing budgets and timelines.

The following are some specifics of what art directors do in different industries:

In advertising and public relations, art directors ensure that their clients' desired message and image are conveyed to consumers. Art directors are responsible for the overall visual aspects of an advertising or media campaign and coordinate the work of other artistic or design staff, such as graphic designers.

In publishing, art directors typically oversee the page layout of catalogs, newspapers, or magazines. They also choose the cover art for books and periodicals. Often, this work includes publications for the Internet, so art directors oversee production of the websites used for publication.

Art directors determine how best to represent a concept visually.

In movie production, art directors collaborate with directors to determine what sets will be needed for the film and what style or look the sets should have. They hire and supervise a staff of assistant art directors or set designers to complete designs.

Work Environment

Art directors held about 99,100 jobs in 2019. The largest employers of art directors were as follows:

Self-employed workers	56%
Advertising, public relations, and related services	13
Motion picture and video industries	4
Newspaper, periodical, book, and directory publishers	3
Specialized design services	3

Even though most art directors are self-employed, they must still collaborate with designers or other staff on visual effects or marketing teams. Art directors usually work in a fast-paced office environment, and they often work under pressure to meet strict deadlines.

How to Become an Art Director

Art directors need at least a bachelor's degree in an art or design subject and previous work experience. Depending on the industry, they may have worked as graphic designers, fine artists, editors, or photographers, or in another art or design occupation before becoming art directors.

Education

Many art directors start out in another art-related occupation, such as fine artists or photographers. Work experience in art or design occupations develops an art director's ability to visually communicate to a specific audience creatively and effectively. Workers gain the appropriate education for that occupation, usually by earning a bachelor of arts or bachelor of fine arts degree.

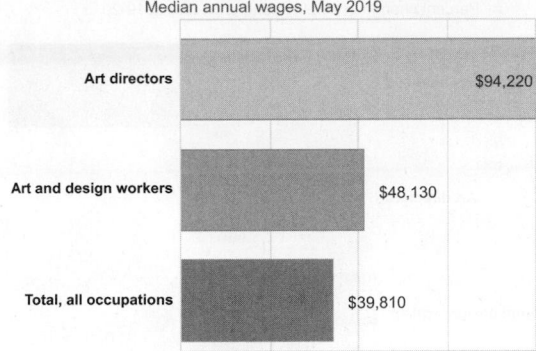

Art Directors

Median annual wages, May 2019

Art directors	$94,220
Art and design workers	$48,130
Total, all occupations	$39,810

Note: All Occupations includes all occupations in the U.S. Economy. Source: U.S. Bureau of Labor Statistics, Occupational Employment Statistics.

Leadership skills. Art directors must be able to organize, direct, and motivate other artists. They need to articulate their visions to artists and oversee the work as it progresses.

Resourcefulness. Art directors must be able to adapt their latest designs to the changing technology used in their industry.

Time-management skills. Balancing competing priorities and multiple projects while meeting strict deadlines is critical for art directors.

Pay

The median annual wage for art directors was $94,220 in May 2019. The median wage is the wage at which half the workers in an occupation earned more than that amount and half earned less. The lowest 10 percent earned less than $53,240, and the highest 10 percent earned more than $188,750.

In May 2019, the median annual wages for art directors in the top industries in which they worked were as follows:

Motion picture and video industries	$121,830
Advertising, public relations, and related services	97,470
Specialized design services	93,780
Newspaper, periodical, book, and directory publishers	82,270

Job Outlook

Employment of art directors is projected to decline 2 percent from 2019 to 2029.

As traditional print publications lose ground to other media forms, employment of art directors is projected to decrease in the newspaper, periodical, book, and directory publishers industry. Rather than focusing on the print layout of images and text, art directors for newspapers and magazines will increasingly design for websites and mobile platforms.

Job Prospects

Strong competition for jobs is expected as many talented designers and artists seek to move into art director positions. Prospective

Many art directors start out as graphic designers or in another art occupation, such as fine artists or photographers.

Some art directors earn a master of fine arts (MFA) degree to supplement their work experience and show their creative or managerial ability.

Work Experience in a Related Occupation

Most art directors have 5 or more years of work experience in another occupation before becoming art directors. Depending on the industry in which they previously worked, art directors may have had jobs as graphic designers, fine artists, editors, photographers, or in another art or design occupation.

For many artists, including art directors, developing a portfolio—a collection of an artist's work that demonstrates his or her styles and abilities—is essential. Managers, clients, and others look at artists' portfolios when they are deciding whether to hire an employee or contract for an art project.

Important Qualities

Communication skills. Art directors must be able to listen to and speak with staff and clients to ensure that they understand employees' ideas and clients' desires for advertisements, publications, or movie sets.

Creativity. Art directors must be able to come up with interesting and innovative ideas to develop advertising campaigns, set designs, or layout options.

Art Directors
Percent change in employment, projected 2019-29

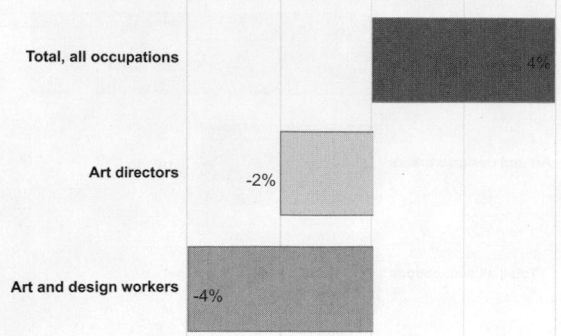

Total, all occupations	4%
Art directors	-2%
Art and design workers	-4%

Note: All Occupations includes all occupations in the U.S. Economy. Source: U.S. Bureau of Labor Statistics, Employment Projections program.

art directors with a strong understanding of how to create intuitive, user-friendly designs will have better prospects working with interactive digital platforms. Workers with a good portfolio, one that demonstrates strong visual design and conceptual work across all multimedia platforms, will have the best prospects.

Employment projections data for art directors, 2019-29					
Occupational Title	SOC Code	Employment, 2019	Projected Employment, 2029	Change, 2019-29	
				Percent	Numeric
SOURCE: U.S. Bureau of Labor Statistics, Employment Projections program					
Art directors	27-1011	99,100	97,300	-2	-1,800

State & Area Data
Occupational Employment Statistics (OES)
The Occupational Employment Statistics (OES) program produces employment and wage estimates annually for over 800 occupations. These estimates are available for the nation as a whole, for individual states, and for metropolitan and nonmetropolitan areas.

Contacts for More Information
For more information about art directors in advertising, public relations, or publishing, visit:
➤ Art Directors Club
For more information about art directors in film and television, visit:
➤ Art Directors Guild

Craft and Fine Artists

Summary

Quick Facts: Craft and Fine Artists

2019 Median Pay	$48,760 per year $23.44 per hour
Typical Entry-Level Education	See below
Work Experience in a Related Occupation	None
On-the-job Training	Long-term on-the-job training
Number of Jobs, 2019	51,900
Job Outlook, 2019-29	0% (Little or no change)
Employment Change, 2019-29	100

What Craft and Fine Artists Do
Craft and fine artists use a variety of materials and techniques to create art for sale and exhibition.

Work Environment
Many artists work in fine- or commercial-art studios located in office buildings, warehouses, or lofts. Others work in private studios in their homes. Some artists share studio space, where they also may exhibit their work.

How to Become a Craft or Fine Artist
Craft and fine artists improve their skills through practice and repetition. A bachelor's degree is common for these artists.

Pay
The median annual wage for craft and fine artists was $48,760 in May 2019.

Job Outlook
Overall employment of craft and fine artists is projected to show little or no change from 2019 to 2029. Employment growth for artists depends largely on the overall state of the economy and whether people are willing to spend money on art, because people usually buy art when they can afford to do so.

Fine art painters paint landscapes, portraits, and other subjects in a variety of styles, ranging from realistic to abstract.

State & Area Data

Explore resources for employment and wages by state and area for craft and fine artists.

What Craft and Fine Artists Do

Craft and fine artists use a variety of materials and techniques to create original works of art for sale and exhibition. Craft artists create objects, such as pottery, glassware, and textiles, that are designed to be functional. Fine artists, including painters, sculptors, and illustrators, create pieces of art more for aesthetics than for function.

Duties

Craft and fine artists typically do the following:

- Use techniques such as knitting, weaving, glassblowing, painting, drawing, and sculpting
- Develop creative ideas or new methods for making art
- Create sketches, templates, or models to guide their work
- Select which materials to use on the basis of color, texture, strength, and other criteria
- Shape, join, or cut materials for a final product
- Use visual techniques, such as composition, color, space, and perspective, to produce desired artistic effects
- Develop portfolios highlighting their artistic styles and abilities to show to gallery owners and others interested in their work
- Display their work at auctions, craft fairs, galleries, museums, and online marketplaces
- Complete grant proposals and applications to obtain financial support for projects

Artists create objects that are beautiful, thought provoking, and sometimes shocking. They often strive to communicate ideas or feelings through their art.

Craft artists work with many different materials, including ceramics, glass, textiles, wood, metal, and paper. They use

Craft and fine artists use a variety of materials and techniques to create art for sale and exhibition.

these materials to create unique pieces of art, such as pottery, quilts, stained glass, furniture, jewelry, and clothing. Many craft artists also use fine-art techniques—for example, painting, sketching, and printing—to add finishing touches to their products.

Fine artists typically display their work in museums, in commercial or nonprofit art galleries, at craft fairs, in corporate collections, on the Internet, and in private homes. Some of their artwork may be commissioned (requested by a client), but most is sold by the artist or through private art galleries or dealers. The artist, gallery, and dealer together decide in advance how much of the proceeds from the sale each will keep.

Most craft and fine artists spend their time and effort selling their artwork to potential customers and building a reputation. In addition to selling their artwork, many artists have at least one other job to support their craft or art careers.

Some artists work in museums or art galleries as art directors or as archivists, curators, or museum workers, planning and setting up exhibits. Others teach craft or art classes or conduct workshops in schools or in their own studios. For more information on workers who teach art classes, see the profiles on kindergarten and elementary school teachers, middle school teachers, high school teachers, career and technical education teachers, and postsecondary teachers.

Craft and fine artists specialize in one or more types of art. The following are examples of types of craft and fine artists:

Cartoonists create simplified or exaggerated drawings to visually convey political, advertising, comic, or sports concepts. Some cartoonists work with others who create the idea or story and write captions. Others create plots and write captions themselves. Most cartoonists have humorous, critical, or dramatic talent, in addition to drawing skills.

Ceramic artists shape, form, and mold artworks out of clay, often using a potter's wheel and other tools. They glaze and fire pieces in kilns, which are large, special furnaces that dry and harden the clay.

Digital artists use design and production software to create interactive art online. The digital imagery may then be transferred to paper or some other form of printmaking or made available directly on web-accessible devices.

Fiber artists use fabric, yarn, or other natural and synthetic materials to weave, knit, crochet, or sew textile art. They may use a loom to weave fabric, needles to knit or crochet yarn, or a sewing machine to join pieces of fabric for quilts or other handicrafts.

Fine-art painters paint landscapes, portraits, and other subjects in a variety of styles, ranging from realistic to abstract. They may work in a variety of media, such as watercolors, oil paints, and acrylics.

Furniture makers cut, sand, join, and finish wood and other materials to make handcrafted furnishings. For information about other workers who assemble wood furniture, see the profile on woodworkers.

Glass artists process glass in a variety of ways—such as by blowing, shaping, staining, or joining it—to create artistic pieces. Some processes require the use of kilns, ovens, and other equipment and tools that bend glass at high temperatures. These workers also decorate glass objects, such as by etching or painting.

Illustrators create pictures for books, magazines, and other publications and for commercial products, such as textiles, wrapping paper, stationery, greeting cards, and calendars. Illustrators increasingly use computers in their work. They might draw in pen or pencil and then scan the image, using software to add color, or they might use a special pen to draw images directly onto the computer.

Jewelry artists use metals, stones, beads, and other materials to make objects for personal adornment, such as earrings or necklaces. For more information about other workers who create jewelry, see the profile on jewelers and precious stone and metal workers.

Medical and scientific illustrators combine drawing skills with knowledge of biology or other sciences. Medical illustrators work with computers or with pen and paper to create images, three-dimensional models, and animations of human anatomy and surgical procedures. Scientific illustrators draw animal and plant life, atomic and molecular structures, and geologic and planetary formations. These illustrations are used in medical and scientific publications and in audiovisual presentations for teaching purposes. Some medical and scientific illustrators work for lawyers, producing exhibits for court cases.

Public artists create large paintings, sculptures, and displays called "installations" that are meant to be seen in open spaces. These works are typically displayed in parks, museum grounds, train stations, and other public areas.

Printmakers create images on a silk screen, woodblock, lithography stone, metal etching plate, or other types of matrices. A printing hand press then creates the final work of art, inking and transferring the matrix to a piece of paper.

Sculptors design and shape three-dimensional works of art, either by molding and joining materials such as clay, glass, plastic, and metal or by cutting and carving forms from a block of plaster, wood, or stone. Some sculptors combine various materials to create mixed-media installations, such as by incorporating light, sound, and motion into their work.

Sketch artists are a type of illustrator who often use pencil, charcoal, or pastels to create likenesses of subjects. Their sketches are used by law enforcement agencies to help identify suspects, by the news media to show courtroom scenes, and by individual customers for their own enjoyment.

Tattoo artists use stencils and draw by hand to create original images and text on skin. With specialized needles, these artists use a variety of styles and colors based on their clients' preferences.

Video artists record avant-garde, moving imagery that is typically shown in a loop in art galleries, museums, or performance spaces. These artists sometimes use multiple monitors or create unusual spaces for the video to be shown.

Many artists work in fine art or commercial art studios located in office buildings, warehouses, or lofts.

Work Environment

Craft and fine artists held about 51,900 jobs in 2019. Employment in the detailed occupations that make up craft and fine artists was distributed as follows:

Fine artists, including painters, sculptors, and illustrators	28,300
Artists and related workers, all other	13,100
Craft artists	10,600

The largest employers of craft and fine artists were as follows:

Self-employed workers	51%
Independent artists, writers, and performers	9
Federal government, excluding postal service	7
Motion picture and sound recording industries	4
Personal care services	3

Many artists work in fine- or commercial-art studios located in office buildings, warehouses, or lofts. Others work in private studios in their homes. Some artists share studio space, where they also may exhibit their work.

Studios are usually well lit and ventilated. However, artists may be exposed to fumes from glue, paint, ink, and other materials. They may also have to deal with dust or other residue from filings, splattered paint, or spilled cleaning and other fluids. Artists often wear protective gear, such as breathing masks and goggles, in order to remain safe from exposure to harmful materials. Ceramic and glass artists must use caution in working with materials that may break into sharp pieces and in using equipment that can get very hot, such as kilns.

Injuries and Illnesses

Artists and related workers, all other have one of the highest rates of injuries and illnesses of all occupations. ("All other" titles represent occupations with a wide range of characteristics that do not fit into any of the other detailed occupations.)

Work Schedules

Most craft and fine artists work full time, although part-time and variable schedules are also common. Many hold another job in addition to their work as an artist. During busy periods, artists may work additional hours to meet deadlines. Those who are self-employed usually determine their own schedules.

How to Become a Craft or Fine Artist

Craft and fine artists improve their skills through practice and repetition. A bachelor's degree is the common for these artists.

Education

Most fine artists pursue postsecondary education to improve their skills and job prospects. A formal educational credential is typically not needed to be a craft artist. However, it is difficult to gain adequate artistic skills without some formal education. For example, high school art classes can teach prospective craft artists the basic drawing skills they need.

A number of colleges and universities offer bachelor's and master's degrees in subjects related to fine arts. In addition to studio art and art history, postsecondary programs may include core subjects, such as English, marketing, social science, and natural science. Independent schools of art and design also

Education gives artists an opportunity to develop their portfolio, which is a collection of an artist's work that demonstrates his or her styles and abilities.

offer postsecondary education programs, which can lead to a certificate in an art-related specialty or to an associate's, bachelor's, or master's degree in fine arts.

The National Association of Schools of Art and Design (NASAD) accredits more than 360 postsecondary institutions with programs in art and design. Most of these schools award a degree in art.

Medical illustrators must have artistic ability and a detailed knowledge of human or animal anatomy, living organisms, and surgical and medical procedures. They usually need a bachelor's degree that combines art and premedical courses. Medical illustrators may choose to get a master's degree in medical illustration. Four accredited schools offer this degree in the United States.

Education gives artists an opportunity to develop their portfolio, which is a collection of an artist's work that demonstrates his or her styles and abilities. Portfolios are essential, because art directors, clients, and others look at them when deciding whether to hire an artist or to buy the artist's work. In addition to compiling a physical portfolio, many artists choose to create a portfolio online.

Those who want to teach fine arts at public elementary or secondary schools usually must have a teaching certificate in addition to a bachelor's degree. For more information on workers who teach art classes, see the profiles on kindergarten and elementary school teachers, middle school teachers, high school teachers, career and technical education teachers, and postsecondary teachers.

Training

Craft and fine artists improve their skills through practice and repetition. They can train in several ways other than, or in addition to, formal schooling. Craft and fine artists may train with simpler projects before attempting something more ambitious.

Some artists learn on the job from more experienced artists. Others attend noncredit classes or workshops or take private lessons, which may be offered in artists' studios or at community colleges, art centers, galleries, museums, or other art-related institutions.

Important Qualities

Artistic ability. Craft and fine artists create artwork and other objects that are visually appealing or thought provoking. This endeavor usually requires significant skill and attention to detail in one or more art forms.

Business skills. Craft and fine artists must promote themselves and their art to build a reputation and to sell their art. They often study the market for their crafts or artwork to increase their understanding of what prospective customers might want. Craft and fine artists also may sell their work on the internet, so developing an online presence is often an important part of their art sales.

Creativity. Artists must have active imaginations to develop new and original ideas for their work.

Customer-service skills. Craft and fine artists, especially those who sell their work themselves, must be good at dealing with customers and prospective buyers.

Dexterity. Artists must be good at manipulating tools and materials to create their art.

Interpersonal skills. Artists should be comfortable interacting with people, including customers, gallery owners, and the public.

Advancement

Craft and fine artists advance professionally as their work circulates and as they establish a reputation for their particular style. Successful artists continually develop new ideas, and their work often evolves over time.

Until they become established as professional artists, many artists create artwork while continuing to hold a full-time job. Others work as an artist part time while still in school to develop experience and to build a portfolio.

Self-employed and freelance artists try to establish a set of clients who regularly contract for work. Some of these artists are recognized for their skill in a specialty, such as cartooning or illustrating children's books. They may earn enough to choose the types of projects they undertake.

Pay

The median annual wage for craft and fine artists was $48,760 in May 2019. The median wage is the wage at which half the workers in an occupation earned more than that amount and half earned less. The lowest 10 percent earned less than $22,290, and the highest 10 percent earned more than $106,000.

Median annual wages for craft and fine artists in May 2019 were as follows:

Artists and related workers, all other	$64,490
Fine artists, including painters, sculptors, and illustrators	50,550
Craft artists	34,710

In May 2019, the median annual wages for craft and fine artists in the top industries in which they worked were as follows:

Federal government, excluding postal service	$88,460
Motion picture and sound recording industries	75,350
Personal care services	50,730
Independent artists, writers, and performers	39,350

Earnings for self-employed artists vary widely. Some charge only a nominal fee while they gain experience and build a reputation for their work. Artists who are well established may earn more than salaried artists.

Most craft and fine artists work full time, although part-time and variable schedules are also common. In addition to pursuing their work as an artist, many hold another job because it may be difficult to rely solely on income earned from selling paintings or other works of art. During busy periods, artists may have long workdays to meet deadlines.

Job Outlook

Overall employment of craft and fine artists is projected to show little or no change from 2019 to 2029.

Employment growth for artists depends largely on the overall state of the economy and whether people are willing to spend money on art, because people usually buy art when they can afford to do so. During good economic times, people and businesses are interested in buying more artwork; during economic downturns, they generally buy less. However, there is always some demand for art by private collectors and museums.

Job growth for craft and fine artists may be limited by the sale of inexpensive, machine-produced items designed to look like handmade crafts. A continued interest in locally made products and crafted goods will likely offset some of these employment losses.

Illustrators and cartoonists who work in publishing may see their job opportunities decline as traditional print publications lose ground to other media forms. However, new opportunities are expected to arise as the number of electronic magazines and other Internet-based publications continues to grow.

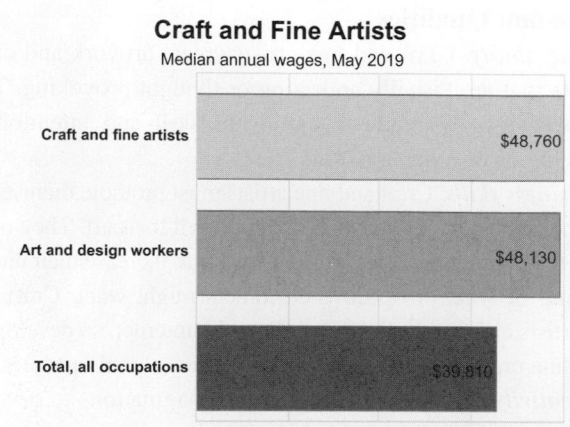

Craft and Fine Artists
Median annual wages, May 2019

Craft and fine artists — $48,760
Art and design workers — $48,130
Total, all occupations — $39,810

Note: All Occupations includes all occupations in the U.S. Economy.
Source: U.S. Bureau of Labor Statistics, Occupational Employment Statistics.

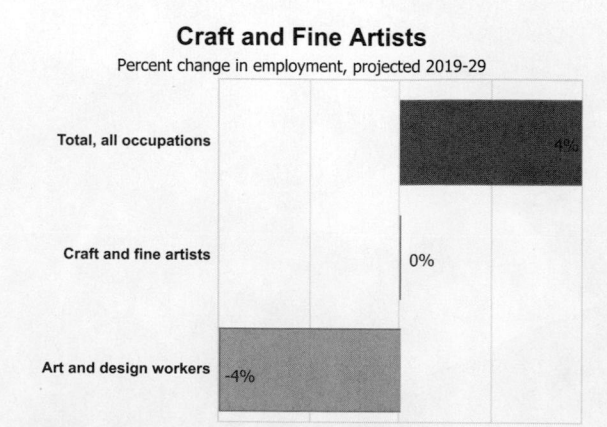

Craft and Fine Artists
Percent change in employment, projected 2019-29

Total, all occupations — 4%
Craft and fine artists — 0%
Art and design workers — -4%

Note: All Occupations includes all occupations in the U.S. Economy.
Source: U.S. Bureau of Labor Statistics, Employment Projections program.

Job Prospects

Competition for jobs as craft and fine artists is expected to be strong because there are more qualified candidates than available jobs. Competition is likely to grow among independent or self-employed artists, given that many of them sell their work in the same online marketplaces. In addition, competition among artists for the privilege of having their work shown in galleries is expected to remain intense.

Because the demand for artwork depends on consumers having extra income to spend, many of these artists will find that their income changes alongside changes in the overall economy. Only the most successful craft and fine artists receive major commissions for their work.

Despite the competition, studios, galleries, and individual clients are always on the lookout for artists who display outstanding talent, creativity, and style. Talented individuals who have developed a mastery of artistic techniques and marketing skills are likely to have the best job prospects.

Employment projections data for craft and fine artists, 2019-29					
Occupational Title	SOC Code	Employment, 2019	Projected Employment, 2029	Change, 2019-29	
				Percent	Numeric
SOURCE: U.S. Bureau of Labor Statistics, Employment Projections program					
Craft and fine artists	—	51,900	52,100	0	100
Craft artists	27-1012	10,600	10,500	-1	-100
Fine artists, including painters, sculptors, and illustrators	27-1013	28,300	28,600	1	300
Artists and related workers, all other	27-1019	13,100	13,000	0	0

State & Area Data
Occupational Employment Statistics (OES)

The Occupational Employment Statistics (OES) program produces employment and wage estimates annually for over 800 occupations. These estimates are available for the nation as a whole, for individual states, and for metropolitan and nonmetropolitan areas.

Contacts for More Information

For more information about art and design and a list of accredited college-level programs, visit
➤ National Association of Schools of Art and Design

For more information about careers in the craft arts and for a list of schools and workshops, visit
➤ American Craft Council

For more information about careers in the arts, visit
➤ New York Foundation for the Arts
For more information about careers in medical illustration, visit
➤ Association of Medical Illustrators

For information about grant-funding programs and other local resources for artists, contact your state arts agency. A list of these agencies is available from the National Assembly of State Arts Agencies.
For more information about how the federal government awards grants for art, visit
➤ National Endowment for the Arts

Fashion Designers

Summary

Quick Facts: Fashion Designers

2019 Median Pay	$73,790 per year $35.48 per hour
Typical Entry-Level Education	Bachelor's degree
Work Experience in a Related Occupation	None
On-the-job Training	None
Number of Jobs, 2019	28,300
Job Outlook, 2019-29	-4% (Decline)
Employment Change, 2019-29	-1,300

What Fashion Designers Do

Fashion designers create clothing, accessories, and footwear.

Work Environment

Fashion designers work in wholesale or manufacturing establishments, apparel companies, retailers, theater or dance companies, and design firms. Most fashion designers work in New York and California.

How to Become a Fashion Designer

Most fashion designers have a bachelor's degree in a related field, such as fashion design or fashion merchandising.

Fashion designers decide on a theme for a collection.

Employers usually seek applicants who are creative and who have technical knowledge of the production processes for clothing, accessories, or footwear.

Pay

The median annual wage for fashion designers was $73,790 in May 2019.

Job Outlook

Employment of fashion designers is projected to decline 4 percent from 2019 to 2029.

State & Area Data

Explore resources for employment and wages by state and area for fashion designers.

Similar Occupations

Compare the job duties, education, job growth, and pay of fashion designers with similar occupations.

What Fashion Designers Do

Fashion designers create original clothing, accessories, and footwear. They sketch designs, select fabrics and patterns, and give instructions on how to make the products they design.

Fashion designers sketch designs of clothing, footwear, and accessories.

Duties

Fashion designers typically do the following:

- Study fashion trends and anticipate designs that will appeal to consumers
- Decide on a theme for a collection
- Use computer-aided design (CAD) programs to create designs
- Visit manufacturers or trade shows to get samples of fabric
- Select fabrics, embellishments, colors, or a style for each garment or accessory
- Work with other designers or team members to create prototype designs
- Present design ideas to creative directors or showcase their ideas in fashion or trade shows
- Market designs to clothing retailers or to consumers
- Oversee the final production of their designs

Larger apparel companies typically employ a team of designers headed by a creative director. Some fashion designers specialize in clothing, footwear, or accessory design; others create designs in all three fashion categories.

For some fashion designers, the first step in creating a new design is researching current fashion and making predictions about future trends, such as by reading reports published by fashion industry trade groups. Other fashion designers create collections using a variety of inspirations, including art media, their surroundings, or cultures they have experienced and places they have visited.

After they have an initial idea, fashion designers try out various fabrics and produce a prototype, often with less expensive material than will be used in the final product. They work with models to see how the design will look and adjust the designs as needed.

Although most designers first sketch their designs by hand, many now also sketch their ideas digitally with computer-aided design (CAD) programs. CAD allows designers to see their work on virtual models. They can try different colors, designs, and shapes while making adjustments more easily than they can when working with real fabric on real people.

Designers produce samples with the actual materials that will be used in manufacturing. Samples that get good responses from fashion editors or trade and fashion shows are then manufactured and sold to consumers.

The design process may vary by specialty, but it generally takes 6 months, from initial design concept to final production, to release either the spring or fall collection. In addition to releasing designs during the spring and fall, some companies release new designs every month.

The Internet and e-commerce allow fashion designers to offer their products outside of traditional brick-and-mortar stores. These designers ship directly to the consumer, without having to invest in a physical shop to showcase their product lines of collections.

The following are examples of types of fashion designers:

Accessory designers design and produce items such as handbags, suitcases, belts, scarves, hats, hosiery, and eyewear.

Costume designers design costumes for the performing arts and for motion picture and television productions. They research the styles worn during the period in which the performance is set, or they work with directors to select and create appropriate attire. They also must stay within the production's costume budget.

Clothing designers create and help produce men's, women's, and children's apparel, including casual wear, suits, sportswear, evening wear, outerwear, maternity clothing, and intimate apparel.

Footwear designers create and help produce different styles of shoes and boots. As new materials, such as lightweight synthetic materials used in shoe soles, become available, footwear designers produce new designs that combine comfort, form, and function.

Work Environment

Fashion designers held about 28,300 jobs in 2019. The largest employers of fashion designers were as follows:

Apparel, piece goods, and notions merchant
  wholesalers.. 29%

Fashion designers select fabrics, colors, or styles for each garment or accessory.

Self-employed workers... 22
Management of companies and enterprises.................. 13
Motion picture and video industries............................. 11
Apparel manufacturing.. 7

Many fashion designers work in-house for wholesalers or manufacturers. These wholesalers and manufacturers sell apparel and accessories to retailers or other marketers for distribution to individual stores, catalog companies, or online retailers.

Self-employed fashion designers typically create high-fashion garments and one-of-a-kind (custom) apparel. In some cases, a self-employed fashion designer may have a clothing line that bears his or her name.

Most designers travel several times a year to trade and fashion shows to learn about the latest trends. Designers also sometimes travel to other countries to meet suppliers of materials and manufacturers who make the final products.

Most fashion designers work in New York and California.

Work Schedules

Fashion designers occasionally work many hours to meet production deadlines or prepare for fashion shows. Generally, designers who freelance are under contract; these designers often have long workdays that require them to adjust to their clients' schedules and deadlines.

How to Become a Fashion Designer

Many fashion designers have a bachelor's degree in a related field, such as fashion design or fashion merchandising. Employers usually seek applicants who are creative and who have technical knowledge of the production processes for clothing, accessories, or footwear.

Education

Many fashion designers have a bachelor's degree in fashion design or fashion merchandising. In these programs, students learn about textiles and fabrics and how to use computer-aided design (CAD) technology. They also work on projects they can add to their portfolio, which showcases their designs.

For many artists, including fashion designers, developing a portfolio—a collection of design ideas that demonstrates their styles and abilities—is essential. Students studying fashion design often have opportunities to develop their portfolios further by entering their designs in student or amateur contests. When making hiring decisions, employers rely on these portfolios to gauge talent and creativity.

The National Association of Schools of Art and Design accredits more than 360 postsecondary institutions with programs in art and design, and many of them award degrees in fashion design. These schools often require students to have completed basic art and design courses before entering a

Fashion designers occasionally work long hours to meet production deadlines or prepare for fashion shows.

program. Applicants usually must submit sketches and other examples of their artistic ability.

Other Experience

Fashion designers often gain experience in the fashion industry through internships or by working as an assistant designer. Internships introduce aspiring fashion designers to the design process, building their knowledge of textiles and colors and of how the industry works.

Important Qualities

Artistic ability. Fashion designers sketch their initial design ideas, which are used to create prototypes. Designers must be able to express their vision for the design through illustration.

Communication skills. Throughout the design process, fashion designers must be able to communicate effectively. For example, they may need to instruct sewers about garment construction.

Computer skills. Fashion designers must be able to use computer-aided design (CAD) programs and be familiar with graphics editing software.

Creativity. Fashion designers work with a variety of fabrics, shapes, and colors. Their ideas must be unique, functional, and stylish.

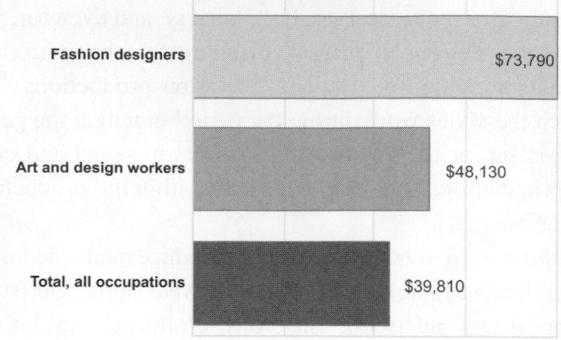

Fashion Designers
Median annual wages, May 2019

Fashion designers	$73,790
Art and design workers	$48,130
Total, all occupations	$39,810

Note: All Occupations includes all occupations in the U.S. Economy. Source: U.S. Bureau of Labor Statistics, Occupational Employment Statistics.

Decisionmaking skills. When working on teams, fashion designers are exposed to many ideas. They must be able to decide which ideas to incorporate into their designs.

Detail oriented. Fashion designers must have a good eye for small differences in color and other details that can make a design successful.

Pay

The median annual wage for fashion designers was $73,790 in May 2019. The median wage is the wage at which half the workers in an occupation earned more than that amount and half earned less. The lowest 10 percent earned less than $37,260, and the highest 10 percent earned more than $149,010.

In May 2019, the median annual wages for fashion designers in the top industries in which they worked were as follows:

Motion picture and video industries.........................	$80,140
Management of companies and enterprises...........	79,420
Apparel manufacturing...	73,600
Apparel, piece goods, and notions merchant wholesalers..	73,060

Fashion designers occasionally work many hours to meet production deadlines or prepare for fashion shows. Generally, designers who freelance are under contract; these designers often have long workdays that require them to adjust to their clients' schedules and deadlines.

Job Outlook

Employment of fashion designers is projected to decline 4 percent from 2019 to 2029.

Most apparel continues to be produced internationally. As a result, employment of fashion designers in the apparel manufacturing industry is expected to decline over the projections decade.

Fashion Designers
Percent change in employment, projected 2019-29

Category	Percent
Total, all occupations	4%
Art and design workers	-4%
Fashion designers	-4%

Note: All Occupations includes all occupations in the U.S. Economy.
Source: U.S. Bureau of Labor Statistics, Employment Projections program.

Job Prospects
Applicants who have formal education in fashion design; are proficient in technologies such as CAD; have excellent portfolios; and have industry experience will have the best job prospects. However, strong competition for jobs is expected because of the large number of people who seek employment as fashion designers and the relatively few positions available.

In addition, it may be necessary for some fashion designers to relocate, because employment opportunities for fashion designers are concentrated in New York and California.

Employment projections data for fashion designers, 2019-29					
Occupational Title	SOC Code	Employment, 2019	Projected Employment, 2029	Change, 2019-29 Percent	Numeric
SOURCE: U.S. Bureau of Labor Statistics, Employment Projections program					
Fashion designers	27-1022	28,300	27,000	-4	-1,300

State & Area Data
Occupational Employment Statistics (OES)
The Occupational Employment Statistics (OES) program produces employment and wage estimates annually for over 800 occupations. These estimates are available for the nation as a whole, for individual states, and for metropolitan and nonmetropolitan areas.

Contacts for More Information
For more information about careers in fashion design, visit
➤ Council of Fashion Designers of America
For more information about educational programs in fashion design, visit
➤ National Association of Schools of Art and Design

Floral Designers

Summary

Quick Facts: Floral Designers

2019 Median Pay	$28,040 per year / $13.48 per hour
Typical Entry-Level Education	High school diploma or equivalent
Work Experience in a Related Occupation	None
On-the-job Training	Moderate-term on-the-job training
Number of Jobs, 2019	51,800
Job Outlook, 2019-29	-20% (Decline)
Employment Change, 2019-29	-10,400

What Floral Designers Do
Floral designers arrange live, dried, and silk flowers and greenery to make decorative displays.

Work Environment
Most floral designers work in retail businesses, usually flower shops and grocery stores.

How to Become a Floral Designer
Most floral designers have a high school diploma or the equivalent and learn their skills on the job in a few months.

Floral designers use their sense of artistry and knowledge of different types of flowers to choose the appropriate flowers for each occasion.

Pay
The median annual wage for floral designers was $28,040 in May 2019.

Job Outlook
Employment of floral designers is projected to decline 20 percent from 2019 to 2029. Many floral designers work in the florist industry, in which overall employment is projected to decline.

State & Area Data

Explore resources for employment and wages by state and area for floral designers.

What Floral Designers Do

Floral designers, also called florists, arrange live, dried, and silk flowers and greenery to make decorative displays. They also help customers select flowers and containers, ribbons, and other accessories.

Duties

Floral designers typically do the following:

- Buy flowers and other products from wholesalers and suppliers to ensure that an adequate supply meets customers' needs
- Determine the type of arrangement desired, the occasion, and the date, time, and location for delivery
- Recommend plants or flowers and greenery for each arrangement in accordance with the customer's budget
- Design floral displays that evoke a particular sentiment or style
- Answer telephones, take orders, and wrap arrangements

Floral designers may create a single arrangement for a specific purpose or multiple displays for special occasions, such as weddings or funerals. They use artistry and their knowledge of different types of blooms to choose appropriate flowers or

Floral designers order flowers from wholesalers and suppliers to ensure an adequate supply to meet customer needs.

plants for each occasion. Floral designers need to know when flowers and plants are in season and available.

Floral designers also need to know the properties of flowers and other plants. Some flowers, such as carnations, can last for many hours outside of water. Other flowers are delicate and wilt more quickly. Some plants are poisonous to certain types of animals. For example, lilies are toxic to cats.

Floral designers must know the color varieties and average size of each flower and plant they sell. They may need to calculate the number of flowers that will fit into a particular vase or how many rose petals cover a space, such as the length of a walkway for a wedding procession.

Floral designers use their knowledge to recommend plants or flowers, greenery, and designs to customers. If the customer selects flowers, the designer uses that type of flower to arrange a visually appealing display. The designer may include items, such as stuffed animals or balloons, or use a decorative basket or vase when creating an arrangement.

Plants typically are showcased in attractive containers and are available for immediate sale. Although more complex floral displays must be ordered in advance, floral designers often create small bouquets or arrangements while customers wait. When they are responsible for multiple arrangements for a special occasion, such as a wedding or funeral, floral designers usually create and set up these decorations just before the event, then remove them afterward. Some floral designers work with event planners on a contract basis when creating arrangements for these types of occasions.

Floral designers also give customers instructions on how to care for flowers and plants, including what the ideal temperature is and how often the water should be changed. For plants or cut flowers, floral designers often provide plant or flower food as part of the sale.

Floral designers also order new flowers, greenery, and plants from suppliers. They process newly arrived shipments by stripping leaves that would be below the water line. Floral designers cut new flowers, transplant plants, mix plant or flower food solutions, fill containers with the food solutions, and sanitize workspaces. They keep most flowers and plants in cool display cases so that the products stay fresh and live longer.

Some floral designers have formal agreements with the managers of hotels and restaurants or the owners of office buildings and private homes to replace old flowers or plants with new ones on a recurring schedule—usually daily, weekly, or monthly—to keep areas looking fresh and appealing. They may work with interior designers in creating displays.

Floral designers who are self-employed or have their own shop also must do business tasks, such as advertising, pricing, inventory, and taxes. Some designers hire and supervise staff to help with these tasks.

Work Environment

Floral designers held about 51,800 jobs in 2019. The largest employers of floral designers were as follows:

Florists	51%
Self-employed workers	23
Food and beverage stores	11
Wholesale trade	5

Floral designers in retail businesses serve walk-in customers as well as customers placing orders over the telephone, on the Internet, or through other florists. Some floral designers who work on a contract basis when creating arrangements for events, such as weddings, have to travel to event locations.

Work Schedules

Many floral designers work full time, although their hours may vary with the work setting.

Independent shops are typically open during regular business hours. Floral departments inside grocery stores or other stores may stay open longer.

Floral designers are busier at certain times of the year, such as holidays, than at other times. Because freshly cut flowers are perishable, most orders cannot be completed too far in advance. Therefore, designers often work additional hours just before and during holidays. In addition, many part-time and seasonal opportunities are available around certain holidays, such as Christmas, Valentine's Day, and Mother's Day.

How to Become a Floral Designer

Most floral designers have a high school diploma or the equivalent and learn their skills on the job in a few months.

Education

Most floral designers have a high school diploma or the equivalent. Postsecondary programs may be useful for florists who want to start their own business. Programs in floral design and caring techniques for flowers and plants are available through private floral schools, vocational schools, and community colleges. Most of these programs offer a certificate or diploma. Classes in flower and plant identification, floral design concepts,

Floral designers perform customer-service duties, such as answering telephones and taking orders.

Most floral designers learn their skills on the job over the course of a few months.

and advertising and other business courses, as well as experience working in a greenhouse, are part of many certificate and diploma programs. Some community colleges and universities offer certificates or associate's degrees in floriculture/floristry operations and management.

Training

New floral designers typically get hands-on experience working with an experienced floral designer. They may start by preparing simple flower arrangements and practicing the basics of tying bows and ribbons, cutting stems to appropriate lengths, and learning about the proper handling and care of flowers and plants. Floral designers also learn about the different types and growth properties of flowers and plants, how to use flowers in complex floral designs, and which flowers and plants complement each other.

Licenses, Certifications, and Registrations

The American Institute of Floral Designers offers the Certified Floral Designer credential. Although certification is voluntary, it indicates a measure of floral design knowledge and expertise gained through work experience or education.

Advancement

Formal training in floral design may be helpful for people who are interested in opening their own business or in becoming a chief floral designer or supervisor.

Important Qualities

Artistic ability. Floral designers use their sense of style to develop aesthetically pleasing designs.

Creativity. Floral designers must develop appropriate designs for different occasions. They must also be open to new ideas because trends in floral design change quickly.

Customer-service skills. Floral designers spend much of their day interacting with customers and suppliers. They must be able to understand what a customer is looking for, explain options, and provide high-quality products and service.

Floral Designers
Median annual wages, May 2019

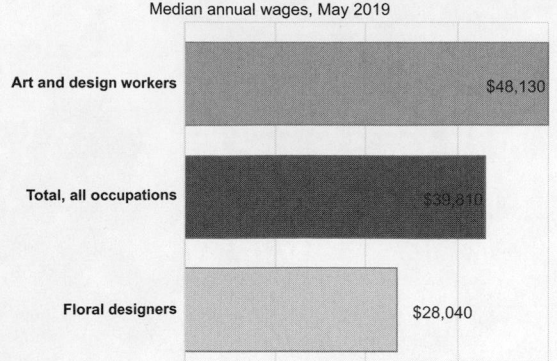

Note: All Occupations includes all occupations in the U.S. Economy.
Source: U.S. Bureau of Labor Statistics, Occupational Employment Statistics.

Organizational skills. Floral designers need to be well organized to keep the business operating smoothly and to ensure that orders are completed on time.

Pay

The median annual wage for floral designers was $28,040 in May 2019. The median wage is the wage at which half the workers in an occupation earned more than that amount and half earned less. The lowest 10 percent earned less than $19,710, and the highest 10 percent earned more than $41,400.

In May 2019, the median annual wages for floral designers in the top industries in which they worked were as follows:

Food and beverage stores	$29,670
Florists	27,770
Wholesale trade	26,940

Many floral designers work full time, although their hours may vary with the work setting.

Independent floral shops are typically open during regular business hours. Floral departments inside grocery stores or other stores may stay open longer.

Floral designers are busier at certain times of the year, such as holidays, than at other times. Because freshly cut flowers are perishable, most orders cannot be completed too far in advance. Therefore, designers often work additional hours just before and during holidays. In addition, many part-time and seasonal opportunities are available around holidays for which flowers or plants are popular gifts, such as Christmas, Valentine's Day, and Mother's Day.

Job Outlook

Employment of floral designers is projected to decline 20 percent from 2019 to 2029. Many floral designers are employed in the florist industry, in which overall industry employment is projected to decline over the decade.

Although demand will continue for floral arrangements at events such as weddings and funerals, the need for floral

Floral Designers
Percent change in employment, projected 2019-29

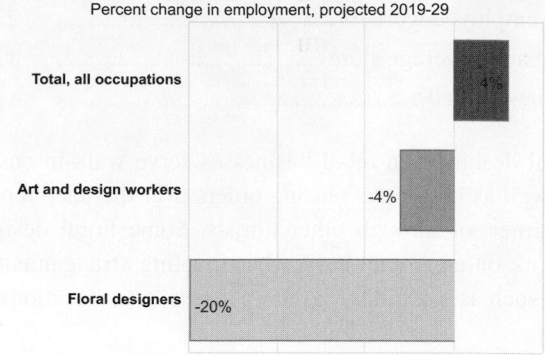

Note: All Occupations includes all occupations in the U.S. Economy.
Source: U.S. Bureau of Labor Statistics, Employment Projections program.

designers is projected to decline along with the number of florist shops in the industry. Local florist shops often fulfill online orders from flower delivery services. This practice may increase the number of orders florist shops receive, but it may also dampen the demand for additional shops as each existing shop widens its customer service area.

In addition, grocery stores offer floral decorations, cut flowers, and plants. Customers may find it more convenient to buy flowers or plants at these stores than to travel to florist shops. As a result, employment of floral designers is projected to grow in grocery stores and decline in florist shops.

Job Prospects

Those with formal education in floral design will have the best prospects.

Employment projections data for floral designers, 2019-29					
Occupational Title	SOC Code	Employment, 2019	Projected Employment, 2029	Change, 2019-29	
				Percent	Numeric
SOURCE: U.S. Bureau of Labor Statistics, Employment Projections program					
Floral designers	27-1023	51,800	41,400	-20	-10,400

State & Area Data
Occupational Employment Statistics (OES)

The Occupational Employment Statistics (OES) program produces employment and wage estimates annually for over 800 occupations. These estimates are available for the nation as a whole, for individual states, and for metropolitan and nonmetropolitan areas.

Contacts for More Information

For more information about becoming a Certified Floral Designer, visit
➤ American Institute of Floral Designers

For more information about careers in floral design, visit
➤ Society of American Florists

Graphic Designers

Summary

Quick Facts: Graphic Designers

2019 Median Pay	$52,110 per year
	$25.05 per hour
Typical Entry-Level Education	Bachelor's degree
Work Experience in a Related Occupation	None
On-the-job Training	None
Number of Jobs, 2019	281,500
Job Outlook, 2019-29	-4% (Decline)
Employment Change, 2019-29	-10,700

What Graphic Designers Do

Graphic designers create visual concepts, using computer software or by hand, to communicate ideas that inspire, inform, and captivate consumers.

Work Environment

Many of these workers are employed in specialized design services, publishing, or advertising, public relations, and related services industries.

How to Become a Graphic Designer

Graphic designers usually need a bachelor's degree in graphic design or a related field. Candidates for graphic design positions should have a portfolio that demonstrates their creativity and originality.

Pay

The median annual wage for graphic designers was $52,110 in May 2019.

Job Outlook

Employment of graphic designers is projected to decline 4 percent from 2019 to 2029. Graphic designers are expected to face strong competition for available positions.

State & Area Data

Explore resources for employment and wages by state and area for graphic designers.

What Graphic Designers Do

Graphic designers create visual concepts, using computer software or by hand, to communicate ideas that inspire, inform, and captivate consumers. They develop the overall layout and production design for applications such as advertisements, brochures, magazines, and reports.

Duties

Graphic designers typically do the following:

- Meet with clients or the art director to determine the scope of a project
- Use digital illustration, photo editing software, and layout software to create designs
- Create visual elements such as logos, original images, and illustrations to help deliver a message
- Design layouts, including selection of colors, images, and typefaces
- Present design concepts to clients or art directors
- Incorporate changes recommended by clients or art directors into final designs
- Review designs for errors before printing or publishing them

Graphic designers, also referred to as graphic artists or communication designers, combine art and technology to communicate ideas through images and the layout of websites and printed pages. They may use a variety of design elements to achieve artistic or decorative effects.

Graphic designers work with both text and images. They often select the type, font, size, color, and line length of headlines, headings, and text. Graphic designers also decide how images and text will go together in print or on a webpage, including how much space each will have. When using text in layouts, graphic designers collaborate with writers, who choose

Graphic designers combine art and technology to develop graphics for product illustrations, logos, and websites.

Graphic designers create designs either by hand or using computer software packages.

the words and decide whether the words will be put into paragraphs, lists, or tables. Through the use of images, text, and color, graphic designers may transform data into visual graphics and diagrams to make complex ideas more accessible.

Graphic design is important to market and sell products, and it is a critical component of brochures and logos. Therefore, graphic designers often work closely with people in advertising and promotions, public relations, and marketing.

Frequently, designers specialize in a particular category or type of client. For example, some designers create the graphics used on product packaging, and others may work on the visual designs used on book jackets.

Graphic designers need to keep up to date with software and computer technologies in order to remain competitive.

Some individuals with a background in graphic design become postsecondary teachers and teach in design schools, colleges, and universities.

Some graphic designers specialize in experiential graphic design. These designers work with architects, industrial designers, landscape architects, and interior designers to create interactive design environments, such as museum exhibitions, public arts exhibits, and retail spaces.

Work Environment

Graphic designers held about 281,500 jobs in 2019. The largest employers of graphic designers were as follows:

Self-employed workers	21%
Specialized design services	10
Advertising, public relations, and related services	8
Printing and related support activities	7
Newspaper, periodical, book, and directory publishers	5

Graphic designers generally work in studios, where they have access to equipment such as drafting tables, computers, and software. Although many graphic designers work

independently, those who work for specialized graphic design firms are often part of a design team. Many graphic designers collaborate with colleagues or work with clients on projects.

Work Schedules

Graphic designers' schedules vary depending on workloads and deadlines.

Those who are self-employed may need to adjust their workday to meet with clients in the evenings or on weekends. In addition, they may spend some of their time looking for new projects or competing with other designers for contracts.

How to Become a Graphic Designer

Graphic designers usually need a bachelor's degree in graphic design or a related field. Candidates for graphic design positions should have a portfolio that demonstrates their creativity and originality.

Education

A bachelor's degree in graphic design or a related field is usually required. However, people who have a bachelor's degree in another field may complete technical training in graphic design to meet most hiring qualifications.

The National Association of Schools of Art and Design accredits more than 360 postsecondary colleges, universities, and independent institutes with programs in art and design. Most programs include courses in studio art, principles of design, computerized design, commercial graphics production, printing techniques, and website design. In addition, students

Graphic designers generally work in a studio where they have access to drafting tables and computers.

Graphic designers should demonstrate their creativity and originality through a professional portfolio.

should consider courses in writing, marketing, and business, all of which are useful in helping designers work effectively on project teams.

High school students interested in graphic design should take basic art and design courses, if available. Many bachelor's degree programs require students to complete a year of basic art and design courses before being admitted to a formal degree program. Some schools require applicants to submit sketches and other examples of their artistic ability.

Many programs provide students with the opportunity to build a portfolio—a collection of completed works that demonstrates an artist's styles and abilities. For many artists, including graphic designers, developing a portfolio is essential because employers rely on portfolios in making hiring decisions.

Graphic designers must keep up with new and updated computer graphics and design software, either on their own or through formal software training programs. Professional associations that specialize in graphic design, such as AIGA, offer courses intended to keep the skills of their members up to date.

Other Experience

Graphic designers often gain experience through internships, which they may undertake while enrolled in a design program. Internships allow aspiring graphic designers to work with designers and to experience the design process from concept to completion.

Licenses, Certifications, and Registrations

Certification programs are generally available through software product vendors. Certification in graphic design software demonstrates competence and may provide jobseekers with a competitive advantage.

Advancement

Experienced graphic designers may advance to chief designer, art director, or other supervisory positions.

Important Qualities

Analytical skills. Graphic designers must be able to perceive their work from their consumers' point of view to ensure that the designs convey the client's message.

Artistic ability. Graphic designers must be able to create designs that are artistically interesting and appealing to clients and consumers. They produce rough illustrations of design ideas, either by hand sketching or by using computer programs.

Communication skills. Graphic designers must communicate with clients, customers, and other designers to ensure that their designs accurately and effectively convey information.

Computer skills. Most graphic designers use specialized graphic design software to prepare their designs.

Creativity. Graphic designers must be able to think of new approaches to communicating ideas to consumers. They develop unique designs that convey their client's message.

Graphic Designers
Median annual wages, May 2019

Graphic designers	$52,110
Art and design workers	$48,130
Total, all occupations	$39,810

Note: All Occupations includes all occupations in the U.S. Economy.
Source: U.S. Bureau of Labor Statistics, Occupational Employment Statistics.

Time-management skills. Graphic designers often work simultaneously on multiple projects, each with a different deadline.

Pay

The median annual wage for graphic designers was $52,110 in May 2019. The median wage is the wage at which half the workers in an occupation earned more than that amount and half earned less. The lowest 10 percent earned less than $30,810, and the highest 10 percent earned more than $89,210.

In May 2019, the median annual wages for graphic designers in the top industries in which they worked were as follows:

Advertising, public relations, and related services....	$54,320
Specialized design services	54,150
Newspaper, periodical, book, and directory publishers	43,950
Printing and related support activities....................	41,290

Graphic designers' schedules vary depending on workload and deadlines.

Those who are self-employed may need to adjust their workday to meet with clients in the evenings or on weekends. In addition, they may spend some of their time looking for new projects or competing with other designers for contracts.

Job Outlook

Employment of graphic designers is projected to decline 4 percent from 2019 to 2029.

While overall employment in this occupation is expected to go down, specific projections vary by industry. For example, employment of graphic designers in newspaper, periodical, book, and directory publishers is projected to decline significantly. In contrast, employment of graphic designers in computer systems design and related services is projected to grow. Companies are continuing to increase their digital presence, which sometimes requires graphic designers to help create visually appealing and effective layouts of websites.

Graphic Designers
Percent change in employment, projected 2019-29

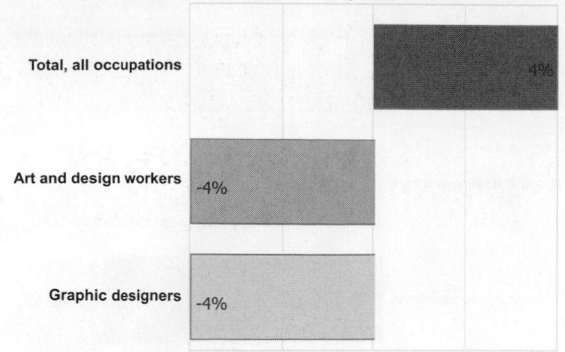

Total, all occupations	4%
Art and design workers	-4%
Graphic designers	-4%

Note: All Occupations includes all occupations in the U.S. Economy. Source: U.S. Bureau of Labor Statistics, Employment Projections program.

Job Prospects

Graphic designers are expected to face strong competition for available positions. Many talented individuals are attracted to careers as graphic designers. Prospects will be best for applicants who keep up with the latest design trends, technologies, and techniques.

Employment projections data for graphic designers, 2019-29					
Occupational Title	SOC Code	Employment, 2019	Projected Employment, 2029	Change, 2019-29	
				Percent	Numeric
SOURCE: U.S. Bureau of Labor Statistics, Employment Projections program					
Graphic designers	27-1024	281,500	270,800	-4	-10,700

State & Area Data
Occupational Employment Statistics (OES)

The Occupational Employment Statistics (OES) program produces employment and wage estimates annually for over 800 occupations. These estimates are available for the nation as a whole, for individual states, and for metropolitan and nonmetropolitan areas.

Contacts for More Information

For more information about graphic design, visit
➤ AIGA
➤ Graphic Artists Guild
➤ Society for Experiential Graphic Design
For more information about art and design and a list of accredited college-level programs, visit
➤ National Association of Schools of Art and Design

Industrial Designers

Summary

Quick Facts: Industrial Designers

2019 Median Pay	$68,890 per year $33.12 per hour
Typical Entry-Level Education	Bachelor's degree
Work Experience in a Related Occupation	None
On-the-job Training	None
Number of Jobs, 2019	42,200
Job Outlook, 2019-29	-4% (Decline)
Employment Change, 2019-29	-1,500

What Industrial Designers Do

Industrial designers combine art, business, and engineering to develop the concepts for manufactured products.

Work Environment

Industrial designers work in a variety of industries. Although industrial designers work primarily in offices, they may travel to testing facilities, design centers, clients' exhibit sites, users' homes or workplaces, and places where the product is manufactured.

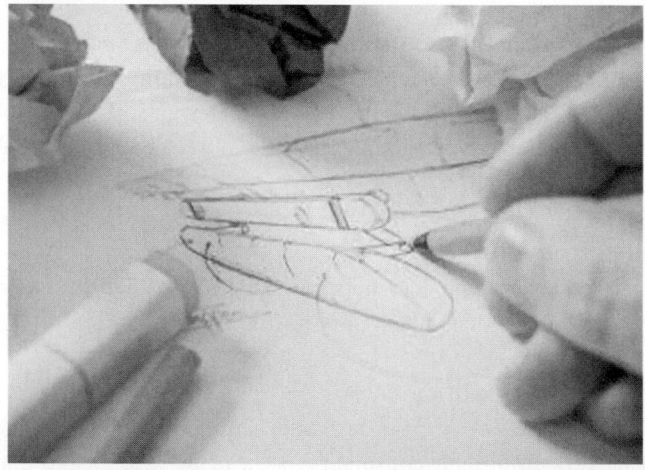

Industrial designers imagine how consumers might use a product when they create and test designs.

How to Become an Industrial Designer

A bachelor's degree is usually required for entry-level industrial design jobs. It is also important for industrial designers to have an electronic portfolio with examples of their design projects.

Pay

The median annual wage for industrial designers was $68,890 in May 2019.

Job Outlook
Employment of industrial designers is projected to decline 4 percent from 2019 to 2029.

State & Area Data
Explore resources for employment and wages by state and area for industrial designers.

What Industrial Designers Do
Industrial designers develop the concepts for manufactured products, such as cars, home appliances, and toys. They combine art, business, and engineering to make products that people use every day. Industrial designers consider the function, aesthetics, production costs, and usability of products when developing new product concepts.

Duties
Industrial designers typically do the following:

- Consult with clients to determine requirements for designs
- Research the various ways a particular product might be used, and who will use it
- Sketch ideas or create renderings, which are images on paper or on a computer that provide a visual of design ideas
- Use computer software to develop virtual models of different designs
- Create physical prototypes of their designs
- Examine materials and manufacturing requirements to determine production costs
- Work with other specialists, such as mechanical engineers and manufacturers, to evaluate whether their design concepts will fill needs at a reasonable cost
- Evaluate product safety, appearance, and function to determine if a design is practical
- Present designs and demonstrate prototypes to clients for approval

Some industrial designers focus on a particular product category. For example, they may design medical equipment or work on consumer electronics products, such as computers and smart phones. Other designers develop ideas for products such as new bicycles, furniture, housewares, and snowboards.

Other designers, sometimes called *user interface designers* or *interaction designers*, focus on the usability of a product, such as an electronic device, and ensure that the product is both simple and enjoyable to use.

Industrial designers imagine how consumers might use a product and test different designs with consumers to see how each design looks and works. Industrial designers often work with engineers, production experts, and market research analysts to find out if their designs are feasible. They apply the input from their colleagues' professional expertise to further develop their designs. For example, industrial designers may work with market research analysts to develop plans to market new product designs to consumers.

Computers are a major tool for industrial designers. Industrial designers use two-dimensional computer-aided design and drafting (CADD) software to sketch ideas, because computers make it easy to make changes and show alternatives. Three-dimensional CAD software is increasingly being used by industrial designers as a tool to transform their two-dimensional designs into models with the help of three-dimensional printers. If they work for manufacturers, they also may use computer-aided industrial design (CAID) software to create specific machine-readable instructions that tell other machines exactly how to build the product.

Work Environment
Industrial designers held about 42,200 jobs in 2019. The largest employers of industrial designers were as follows:

Manufacturing... 33%
Self-employed workers.. 22

Industrial designers work primarily in offices, but they may travel to the places where the products are manufactured.

Work spaces for industrial designers often include drafting tables and meeting rooms for brainstorming with colleagues.

Work spaces for industrial designers often include work tables for sketching designs, meeting rooms with whiteboards for brainstorming with colleagues, and computers and other office equipment for preparing designs and communicating with clients. Although industrial designers work primarily in offices, they may travel to testing facilities, design centers, clients' exhibit sites, users' homes or workplaces, and places where the product is manufactured.

Work Schedules

Industrial designers who are self-employed or work for firms that hire them out to other organizations may need to adjust their workdays frequently in order to meet with clients in the evenings or on weekends. In addition, they may spend some of their time looking for new projects or competing with other designers for contracts.

How to Become an Industrial Designer

A bachelor's degree is usually required for entry-level indus-trial design jobs. It is also important for industrial designers to have an electronic portfolio with examples of their design projects.

Education

A bachelor's degree in industrial design, architecture, or engi-neering is usually required for entry-level industrial design jobs. Most industrial design programs include courses in draw-ing, computer-aided design and drafting (CADD), and three-dimensional modeling, as well as courses in business, industrial materials and processes, and manufacturing methods.

The National Association of Schools of Art and Design accredits more than 360 postsecondary colleges, universities,

A bachelor's degree in industrial design, architecture, or engineering is usually required for entry-level industrial design jobs.

and independent institutes with programs in art and design. Many schools require successful completion of some basic art and design courses before granting entry into a bachelor's degree program. Applicants also may need to submit sketches and other examples of their artistic ability.

Many programs provide students with the opportunity to build a professional portfolio of their designs from classroom projects, internships, or other experiences. Students can use these examples of their work to demonstrate their design skills when applying for jobs and bidding on contracts for work.

Important Qualities

Analytical skills. Industrial designers use logic or reason-ing skills to study consumers and recognize the need for new products.

Artistic ability. Industrial designers sketch their initial design ideas, which are used later to create prototypes. As such, design-ers must be able to express their design through illustration.

Computer skills. Industrial designers use computer-aided design software to develop their designs and create prototypes.

Creativity. Industrial designers must be innovative in their designs and the ways in which they integrate existing technolo-gies into their new product.

Interpersonal skills. Industrial designers must develop cooperative working relationships with clients and colleagues who specialize in related disciplines.

Mechanical skills. Industrial designers must understand how products are engineered, at least for the types of products that they design.

Problem-solving skills. Industrial designers determine the need, size, and cost of a product; anticipate production issues; develop alternatives; evaluate options; and implement solutions.

Advancement

Experienced designers in large firms may advance to chief designer, design department head, or other supervisory posi-tions. Some designers become teachers in design schools or in colleges and universities. Many teachers continue to consult privately or operate small design studios in addition to teach-ing. Some experienced designers open their own design firms.

Pay

The median annual wage for industrial designers was $68,890 in May 2019. The median wage is the wage at which half the workers in an occupation earned more than that amount and half earned less. The lowest 10 percent earned less than $39,860, and the highest 10 percent earned more than $114,950.

In May 2019, the median annual wages for industrial design-ers in the top industries in which they worked were as follows:

Architectural, engineering, and related services ... $84,060

Wholesale trade 68,810

Industrial Designers

Median annual wages, May 2019

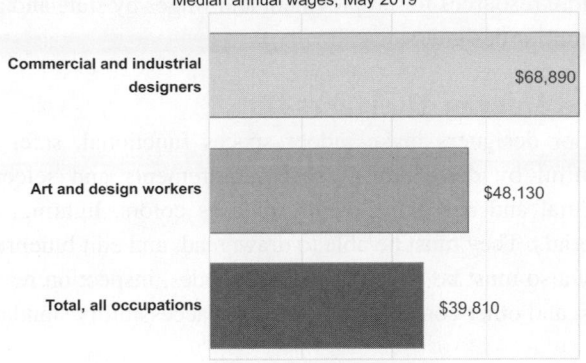

Commercial and industrial designers	$68,890
Art and design workers	$48,130
Total, all occupations	$39,810

Note: All Occupations includes all occupations in the U.S. Economy.
Source: U.S. Bureau of Labor Statistics, Occupational Employment Statistics.

Manufacturing... 65,720

Specialized design services 64,240

Industrial designers who are self-employed or work for firms that hire them out to other organizations may need to adjust their workdays frequently in order to meet with clients in the evenings or on weekends. In addition, they may spend some of their time looking for new projects or competing with other designers for contracts.

Job Outlook

Employment of industrial designers is projected to decline 4 percent from 2019 to 2029.

As fewer products are made in the United States, employment of industrial designers is expected to decline in some manufacturing industries. Although many modern products require detailed specifications as part of the design process, there is less demand for designers as these products become increasingly similar.

Job Prospects

Prospects should be best for job applicants who have a strong background in two- and three-dimensional computer-aided design and drafting (CADD) and computer-aided industrial design (CAID). The increasing trend toward the use of sustainable resources is likely to improve prospects for applicants who know how to work with sustainable resources.

Industrial Designers

Percent change in employment, projected 2019-29

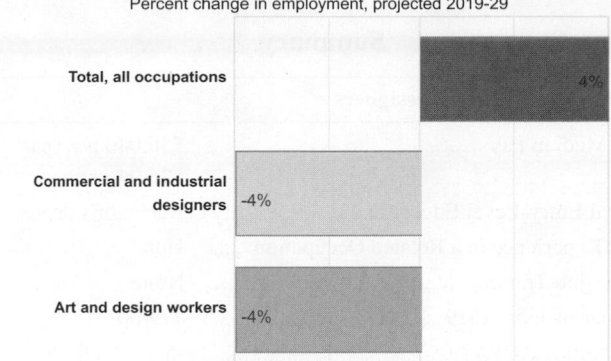

Total, all occupations	4%
Commercial and industrial designers	-4%
Art and design workers	-4%

Note: All Occupations includes all occupations in the U.S. Economy.
Source: U.S. Bureau of Labor Statistics, Employment Projections program.

In addition, as more products become digitized and Internet-capable, applicants with experience in user interface (UI), user experience (UX), and interactive design (IxD) may have better job prospects.

Employment projections data for industrial designers, 2019-29					
Occupational Title	SOC Code	Employment, 2019	Projected Employment, 2029	Change, 2019-29	
				Percent	Numeric
SOURCE: U.S. Bureau of Labor Statistics, Employment Projections program					
Commercial and industrial designers	27-1021	42,200	40,700	-4	-1,500

State & Area Data
Occupational Employment Statistics (OES)

The Occupational Employment Statistics (OES) program produces employment and wage estimates annually for over 800 occupations. These estimates are available for the nation as a whole, for individual states, and for metropolitan and nonmetropolitan areas.

Contacts for More Information

For more information about industrial designers, visit
➤ Industrial Designers Society of America
For more information about accredited college-level programs in art and design, visit
➤ National Association of Schools of Art and Design

Interior Designers

Summary

Quick Facts: Interior Designers

2019 Median Pay	$56,040 per year
	$26.94 per hour
Typical Entry-Level Education	Bachelor's degree
Work Experience in a Related Occupation	None
On-the-job Training	None
Number of Jobs, 2019	77,900
Job Outlook, 2019-29	-5% (Decline)
Employment Change, 2019-29	-3,800

What Interior Designers Do

Interior designers make indoor spaces functional, safe, and beautiful by determining space requirements and selecting essential and decorative items.

Work Environment

Many interior designers work in specialized design services or in architectural, engineering, and related services.

How to Become an Interior Designer

Interior designers usually need a bachelor's degree with a focus on interior design.

Pay

The median annual wage for interior designers was $56,040 in May 2019.

Job Outlook

Employment of interior designers is projected to decline 5 percent from 2019 to 2029.

State & Area Data

Explore resources for employment and wages by state and area for interior designers.

What Interior Designers Do

Interior designers make indoor spaces functional, safe, and beautiful by determining space requirements and selecting essential and decorative items, such as colors, lighting, and materials. They must be able to draw, read, and edit blueprints. They also must be aware of building codes, inspection regulations, and other considerations, such as accessibility standards.

Duties

Interior designers typically do the following:

- Search for and bid on new projects
- Determine the client's goals and requirements for the project
- Consider how the space will be used and how people will move through the space
- Sketch preliminary design plans, including electrical and partition layouts
- Specify materials and furnishings, such as lighting, furniture, wall finishes, flooring, and plumbing fixtures
- Create a timeline for the interior design project and estimate project costs
- Place orders for materials and oversee the installation of the design elements
- Oversee construction and coordinate with general building contractors to implement the plans and specifications for the project
- Visit the site after the project is complete, to ensure that the client is satisfied

Interior designers work closely with architects, civil engineers, mechanical engineers, and construction laborers and helpers to determine how interior spaces will function, look,

Interior designers select and specify colors, furniture, and other materials to create useful and stylish interiors for buildings.

Interior designers make interior spaces functional, safe, and beautiful for almost every type of building.

and be furnished. Interior designers read blueprints and must be aware of building codes and inspection regulations.

Although some sketches may be freehand, most interior designers use computer-aided design (CAD) software for most of their drawings. Throughout the design process, interior designers often use building information modeling (BIM) software to create three-dimensional visualizations that include construction elements such as walls or roofs.

Many designers specialize in particular types of buildings, such as homes, hospitals, or hotels; specific rooms, such as bathrooms or kitchens; or a specific style. Some designers work for home-furnishings stores, providing design services to help customers choose materials and furnishings.

Some interior designers produce designs, plans, and drawings for construction and installation. These products may include information for construction and demolition, electrical layouts, and building permits. Interior designers may draft the preliminary design into documents ranging from simple sketches to construction schedules and attachments.

The following are examples of types of interior designers:

Corporate designers create interior designs for professional workplaces in a variety of settings, from small offices to large buildings. They focus on creating spaces that are efficient, functional, and safe for employees. In their designs, they may incorporate elements of a company's brand.

Healthcare designers plan and renovate healthcare centers, clinics, doctors' offices, hospitals, and residential care facilities. They specialize in evidence-based design, which uses data and research in design decisionmaking to achieve positive results for patients, residents, and facilities.

Kitchen and bath designers specialize in kitchens and bathrooms and have expert knowledge of cabinet, fixture, appliance, plumbing, and electrical solutions for these rooms.

Sustainable designers suggest strategies to improve energy and water efficiencies and indoor air quality as well as environmentally sustainable products, such as bamboo and cork for floors. They may obtain certification in Leadership in Energy and Environmental Design (LEED) from the U.S. Green Building Council. Such certification indicates expertise in designing buildings and spaces with sustainable practices in mind.

Universal designers renovate spaces in order to make them more accessible. Often, these designs are used to renovate spaces for elderly people and people with special needs; however, universal designs benefit everyone. For example, an entryway without steps may be necessary for someone in a wheelchair, but it is also helpful for someone pushing a baby stroller.

Work Environment
Interior designers held about 77,900 jobs in 2019. The largest employers of interior designers were as follows:

Interior designers travel to the clients' design sites.

Specialized design services	27%
Self-employed workers	22
Architectural, engineering, and related services	20
Wholesale trade	6
Furniture stores	5

Most interior designers work in offices, but technology has changed the way many designers work. For example, interior designers now use software rather than drafting tables to create two- or three-dimensional images.

Interior designers also travel to clients' design sites.

Work Schedules
Interior designers may need to adjust their workday to suit their clients' schedules and deadlines, including meeting with clients in the evening and on weekends.

How to Become an Interior Designer
Interior designers usually need a bachelor's degree with a focus in interior design or interior architecture.

Education
Interior designers entering the occupation usually need a bachelor's degree in any field. Coursework should include classes in interior design, drawing, and computer-aided design (CAD).

Programs in interior design are available at the associate's, bachelor's, and master's degree levels. Applicants to these programs may need to submit sketches and other examples of their artistic ability.

The National Association of Schools of Art and Design accredits more than 360 postsecondary colleges, universities, and independent institutes that have programs in art and design. The Council for Interior Design Accreditation accredits about 180 professional-level (bachelor's or master's degree) interior design programs.

Interior designers must be able to work closely with architects and builders to determine the design of the interior space.

The National Kitchen & Bath Association accredits kitchen and bath design specialty programs (certificate, associate's degree, and bachelor's degree levels) in nearly 100 colleges and universities.

Licenses, Certifications, and Registrations

Licensure requirements vary by state. In some states, only licensed designers may do interior design work. In other states, both licensed and unlicensed designers may do such work; however, only licensed designers may use the title "interior designer." In still other states, both licensed and unlicensed designers may call themselves interior designers and do interior design work.

In states with laws restricting the use of the title "interior designer," only candidates who pass their state-approved exam, most commonly the National Council for Interior Design Qualification (NCIDQ) exam, may call themselves registered interior designers. Candidate eligibility for taking the NCIDQ exam includes having at least a bachelor's degree in interior design and 2 years of full-time work experience.

California requires a different exam, administered by the California Council for Interior Design Certification (CCIDC). To take this exam, eligible candidates must have a combination of education and experience.

Voluntary certification in an interior design specialty, such as environmental design, allows designers to demonstrate expertise in a particular area of the occupation. Interior designers often specialize to distinguish the type of design work they do and to promote their expertise. Certifications usually are available through professional and trade associations and are independent of the NCIDQ licensing examination.

Important Qualities

Artistic ability. Interior designers use their sense of style to develop aesthetically pleasing designs.

Creativity. Interior designers need to be imaginative in selecting furnishings and fabrics and in creating functional spaces that serve the client's needs and fit the client's lifestyle.

Detail oriented. Interior designers need to be precise in measuring interior spaces and creating drawings, so that their drawings can be used by workers such as engineers or other designers.

Interpersonal skills. Interior designers need to be able to communicate effectively with clients and others. They spend much of their time soliciting new clients and new work and collaborating with other designers, engineers, and general building contractors on ongoing projects.

Problem-solving skills. Interior designers must address challenges, such as construction delays or unavailability of certain materials, while keeping the project on time and within budget.

Visualization. Interior designers need a strong sense of proportion and visual awareness in order to understand how the pieces of a design will fit together to create the intended environment.

Pay

The median annual wage for interior designers was $56,040 in May 2019. The median wage is the wage at which half the workers in an occupation earned more than that amount and half earned less. The lowest 10 percent earned less than $31,970, and the highest 10 percent earned more than $96,470.

In May 2019, the median annual wages for interior designers in the top industries in which they worked were as follows:

Architectural, engineering, and related services ...	$60,910
Specialized design services	54,710
Wholesale trade	53,870
Furniture stores	47,340

Interior designers may need to adjust their workday to suit their clients' schedules and deadlines, including meeting with clients in the evening and on weekends.

Interior Designers
Median annual wages, May 2019

Interior designers	$56,040
Art and design workers	$48,130
Total, all occupations	$39,810

Note: All Occupations includes all occupations in the U.S. Economy.
Source: U.S. Bureau of Labor Statistics, Occupational Employment Statistics.

Interior Designers
Percent change in employment, projected 2019-29

Note: All Occupations includes all occupations in the U.S. Economy.
Source: U.S. Bureau of Labor Statistics, Employment Projections program.

Job Outlook

Employment of interior designers is projected to decline 5 percent from 2019 to 2029.

There may be some demand created by new construction, but opportunities for self-employed interior designers to renovate existing homes, commercial buildings, and other facilities should be limited. Relatively few interior designers are directly employed in the construction industry, but many of these workers depend heavily on that industry to generate new projects.

Job Prospects

Job prospects should be best in high-income areas, because wealthy clients are more likely than others to engage in remodeling and renovating their spaces. Keeping up to date with the newest design tools, such as three-dimensional computer-aided design (CAD) software, also will improve job prospects.

Employment projections data for interior designers, 2019-29					
Occupational Title	SOC Code	Employment, 2019	Projected Employment, 2029	Change, 2019-29	
				Percent	Numeric
SOURCE: U.S. Bureau of Labor Statistics, Employment Projections program					
Interior designers	27-1025	77,900	74,100	-5	-3,800

State & Area Data
Occupational Employment Statistics (OES)

The Occupational Employment Statistics (OES) program produces employment and wage estimates annually for over 800 occupations. These estimates are available for the nation as a whole, for individual states, and for metropolitan and nonmetropolitan areas.

Contacts for More Information

For more information about interior designers, visit
➤ American Society of Interior Designers
➤ International Interior Design Association

For more information on accredited college degree programs in interior design, visit
➤ National Association of Schools of Art and Design
➤ Council for Interior Design Accreditation

For more information on licensing, visit
➤ National Council for Interior Design Qualification
➤ California Council for Interior Design Certification

For more information on accredited kitchen and bath specialty programs in colleges and universities and on voluntary certification programs in residential kitchen and bath design, visit
➤ National Kitchen & Bath Association

Multimedia Artists and Animators

Summary

Quick Facts: Multimedia Artists and Animators

2019 Median Pay	$75,270 per year
	$36.19 per hour
Typical Entry-Level Education	Bachelor's degree
Work Experience in a Related Occupation	None
On-the-job Training	None
Number of Jobs, 2019	67,500
Job Outlook, 2019-29	4% (As fast as average)
Employment Change, 2019-29	2,800

What Multimedia Artists and Animators Do

Multimedia artists and animators create images that appear to move and visual effects for various forms of media and entertainment.

Work Environment

Many artists and animators work in offices; others work from home.

How to Become a Multimedia Artist or Animator

Most multimedia artists and animators need a bachelor's degree in computer graphics, art, or a related field to develop both an impressive portfolio of work and the strong technical skills that many employers prefer.

Multimedia artists and animators create animation and visual effects for television, movies, video games, and other media.

Multimedia artists and animators create two- and three-dimensional models and animation.

Pay

The median annual wage for multimedia artists and animators was $75,270 in May 2019.

Job Outlook

Employment of multimedia artists and animators is projected to grow 4 percent from 2019 to 2029, about as fast as the average for all occupations. Projected growth will be due to increased demand for animation and visual effects in video games, movies, and television.

State & Area Data

Explore resources for employment and wages by state and area for multimedia artists and animators.

Similar Occupations

Compare the job duties, education, job growth, and pay of multimedia artists and animators with similar occupations.

What Multimedia Artists and Animators Do

Multimedia artists and animators create two- and three-dimensional models, images that appear to move, and visual effects for television, movies, video games, and other forms of media.

Duties

Multimedia artists and animators typically do the following:

- Use computer programs and illustrations to create graphics and animation (images that appear to move)
- Work with a team of animators and artists to create a movie, game, or visual effect
- Research upcoming projects to help create realistic designs or animation
- Edit animation and effects on the basis of feedback from directors, other animators, game designers, or clients
- Meet with clients, other animators, games designers, directors, and other staff (which may include actors) to review deadlines and development timelines

Multimedia artists and animators often work in a specific medium. Some focus on creating animated movies or video games. Others create visual effects for movies and television shows. Creating computer-generated images (known as CGI) may include taking images of an actor's movements and then animating them into three-dimensional characters. Other animators design scenery or backgrounds for locations.

Artists and animators can further specialize within these fields. Within animated movies and video games, artists often specialize in characters or in scenery and background design. Video game artists may focus on level design: creating the look, feel, and layout for the levels of a video game.

Animators work in teams to develop a movie, a visual effect, or an electronic game. Each animator works on a portion of the project, and then the pieces are put together to create one cohesive animation.

Some multimedia artists and animators create their work primarily by using computer software or by writing their own computer code. Many animation companies have their own computer animation software that artists must learn to use. Video game designers also work in a variety of platforms, including mobile gaming and online social networks.

Other artists and animators prefer to work by drawing and painting by hand and then translating the resulting images into computer programs. Some multimedia artists use storyboards or "animatics," which look like a comic strip, to help visualize the final product during the design process.

Many multimedia artists and animators put their creative work on the Internet. If the images become popular, these artists can gain more recognition, which may lead to future employment or freelance work.

Work Environment

Multimedia artists and animators held about 67,500 jobs in 2019. The largest employers of multimedia artists and animators were as follows:

Multimedia artists and animators frequently work in offices.

Self-employed workers	56%
Motion picture and video industries	14
Software publishers	7
Computer systems design and related services	5
Advertising, public relations, and related services	3

Many artists and animators work in offices; others work from home.

Work Schedules

Most multimedia artists and animators work a regular schedule; however, when deadlines are approaching, they may need to work nights and weekends.

How to Become a Multimedia Artist or Animator

Most multimedia artists and animators need a bachelor's degree in computer graphics, art, or a related field to develop both an impressive portfolio of work and the strong technical skills that many employers prefer.

Education

Employers typically require a bachelor's degree, and they look for workers who have a good portfolio and strong technical skills. Multimedia artists and animators typically have a bachelor's degree in fine arts, computer graphics, animation, or a related field. Programs in computer graphics often include courses in computer science in addition to art courses.

Bachelor's degree programs in art include courses in painting, drawing, and sculpture. Degrees in animation often require classes in drawing, animation, and film. Many schools have specialized degrees in topics such as interactive media or game design.

Advancement

Multimedia artists and animators who show strong teamwork and time-management skills can advance to supervisory positions, where they are responsible for one aspect of a visual

Employers look for workers who have a good portfolio of work and strong computer programming skills.

effects team. Some artists might advance to leadership or directorial positions, such as an art director or producer or director.

Other Experience

Skills in graphics and animation can be honed through self-study. Multimedia artists and animators can develop these skills to enhance their portfolios, which may make it easier to find job opportunities.

Important Qualities

Artistic talent. Animators and artists should have artistic ability and a good understanding of color, texture, and light. However, they may be able to compensate for artistic shortcomings with better technical skills.

Communication skills. Multimedia artists and animators need to work as part of a team and respond well to criticism and feedback.

Computer skills. Many multimedia artists and animators use computer programs or write programming code to do most of their work.

Creativity. Artists and animators must be able to think creatively to develop original ideas and make them come to life.

Time-management skills. The workdays required by most studio and game design companies can be long, particularly

Multimedia Artists and Animators
Median annual wages, May 2019

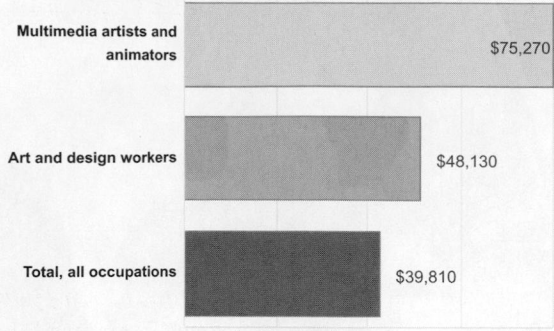

Note: All Occupations includes all occupations in the U.S. Economy.
Source: U.S. Bureau of Labor Statistics, Occupational Employment Statistics.

Pay

The median annual wage for multimedia artists and animators was $75,270 in May 2019. The median wage is the wage at which half the workers in an occupation earned more than that amount and half earned less. The lowest 10 percent earned less than $40,250, and the highest 10 percent earned more than $139,940.

In May 2019, the median annual wages for multimedia artists and animators in the top industries in which they worked were as follows:

Motion picture and video industries...........................	$86,270
Software publishers...	80,290
Computer systems design and related services	71,980
Advertising, public relations, and related services.....	70,510

Most multimedia artists and animators work a regular full-time schedule; however, when deadlines are approaching, they may need to work nights and weekends.

Job Outlook

Employment of multimedia artists and animators is projected to grow 4 percent from 2019 to 2029, about as fast as the average for all occupations. Projected growth will be due to increased demand for animation and visual effects in video games, movies, and television. Job growth may be slowed, however, by companies hiring animators and artists who work overseas. Studios may save money on animation by using lower paid workers outside of the United States.

Consumers will continue to demand more realistic video games, movie and television special effects, and three-dimensional movies. This will create demand for newer computer

Multimedia Artists and Animators
Percent change in employment, projected 2019-29

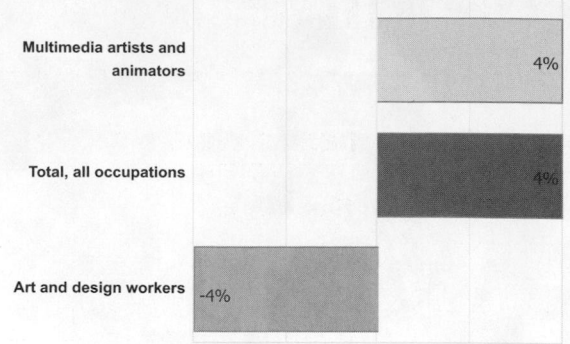

Note: All Occupations includes all occupations in the U.S. Economy.
Source: U.S. Bureau of Labor Statistics, Employment Projections program.

hardware, which will enhance the complexity of animation and visual effects. Additional multimedia artists and animators will be required to meet this increased demand.

Further, an increased demand for computer graphics for mobile devices, such as smart phones, will lead to more job opportunities. Multimedia artists will be needed to create animation for games and applications for mobile devices.

Job Prospects

Despite positive job growth, there will be competition for job openings because many recent graduates will be interested in entering the occupation. In addition to having a robust portfolio, those who specialize in a specific type of animation or in a specific skill, such as drawing or computer programming, should have the best opportunities.

Employment projections data for multimedia artists and animators, 2019-29					
Occupational Title	SOC Code	Employment, 2019	Projected Employment, 2029	Change, 2019-29	
				Percent	Numeric
SOURCE: U.S. Bureau of Labor Statistics, Employment Projections program					
Special effects artists and animators	27-1014	67,500	70,300	4	2,800

State & Area Data
Occupational Employment Statistics (OES)

The Occupational Employment Statistics (OES) program produces employment and wage estimates annually for over 800 occupations. These estimates are available for the nation as a whole, for individual states, and for metropolitan and nonmetropolitan areas.

Contacts for More Information

For information about accredited schools of art and design, visit
➤ National Association of Schools of Art and Design

For more information about careers in video game design, visit
➤ Game Career Guide

Building and Grounds Cleaning

Grounds Maintenance Workers

Summary

Quick Facts: Grounds Maintenance Workers	
2019 Median Pay	$30,890 per year $14.85 per hour
Typical Entry-Level Education	See below
Work Experience in a Related Occupation	None
On-the-job Training	See below
Number of Jobs, 2019	1,305,300
Job Outlook, 2019-29	10% (Much faster than average)
Employment Change, 2019-29	130,800

What Grounds Maintenance Workers Do

Grounds maintenance workers ensure that the grounds of houses, businesses, and parks are attractive, orderly, and healthy.

Work Environment

Some grounds maintenance jobs are seasonal, available mainly in the spring, summer, and fall. Most of the work is done outdoors in all weather conditions. The work can be repetitive and physically demanding, requiring frequent bending, kneeling, lifting, and shoveling.

How to Become a Grounds Maintenance Worker

Most grounds maintenance workers need no formal education and are trained on the job. Most states require licensing for workers who apply pesticides or fertilizers.

Pay

The median hourly wage for grounds maintenance workers was $14.85 in May 2019.

Job Outlook

Employment of grounds maintenance workers is projected to grow 10 percent from 2019 to 2029, much faster than the average for all occupations. More workers will be needed to keep up with increasing demand for lawn care and landscaping services from large institutions and individual homeowners. Job prospects should be very good.

State & Area Data

Explore resources for employment and wages by state and area for grounds maintenance workers.

What Grounds Maintenance Workers Do

Grounds maintenance workers ensure that the grounds of houses, businesses, parks, and urban infrastructure are attractive, orderly, and healthy in order to provide a pleasant outdoor environment.

Duties

Grounds maintenance workers typically do the following:

- Mow, edge, and fertilize lawns
- Weed and mulch landscape beds
- Trim hedges, shrubs, and small trees
- Remove dead, damaged, or unwanted trees
- Plant flowers, trees, and shrubs
- Water lawns, landscapes, and gardens
- Monitor and maintain plant health

Grounds maintenance workers work outdoors in all kinds of weather.

Grounds maintenance workers mow, edge, and fertilize lawns.

Grounds maintenance workers are generally under the direction of a professional grounds manager and perform a variety of tasks to achieve a pleasant and functional outdoor environment. They also care for indoor gardens and plants in commercial and public facilities, such as malls, hotels, and botanical gardens.

The following are examples of types of grounds maintenance workers:

Landscaping workers plant trees, flowers, and shrubs to create new outdoor spaces or upgrade existing ones. They also trim, fertilize, mulch, and water plants. Some grade and install lawns or construct hardscapes such as walkways, patios, and decks. Others help install lighting or sprinkler systems. Landscaping workers are employed in a variety of residential and commercial settings, such as homes, apartment buildings, office buildings, shopping malls, and hotels and motels.

Groundskeeping workers, also called *groundskeepers*, maintain grounds. They care for plants and trees, rake and mulch leaves, and clear snow from walkways. They work on athletic fields, golf courses, cemeteries, university campuses, and parks, as well as in many of the same settings that landscaping workers work. They also see to the proper upkeep of sidewalks, parking lots, fountains, fences, planters, and benches, as well as groundskeeping equipment.

Groundskeeping workers who care for athletic fields keep natural and artificial turf in top condition, mark out boundaries, and paint turf with team logos and names before events. They mow, water, fertilize, and aerate the fields regularly. They must ensure that the underlying soil on fields with natural turf has the composition required to allow proper drainage and to support the grass used on the field. In sports venues, they vacuum and disinfect synthetic turf to prevent the growth of harmful bacteria and they remove the turf and replace the cushioning pad periodically.

Groundskeepers in parks and recreation facilities care for lawns, trees, and shrubs; maintain playgrounds; clean buildings; and keep parking lots, picnic areas, and other public spaces free of litter. They also may erect and dismantle snow fences and maintain swimming pools. These workers inspect buildings and equipment, make needed repairs, and keep everything freshly painted.

Some groundskeepers specialize in caring for cemeteries and memorial gardens. They dig graves to specified depths, generally using a backhoe. They mow grass regularly, apply fertilizers and other chemicals, prune shrubs and trees, plant flowers, and remove debris from graves.

Greenskeepers maintain golf courses. Their work is similar to that of groundskeepers, but they also periodically relocate holes on putting greens and maintain benches and tee markers along the course and provide more intense turf maintenance. In addition, greenskeepers keep canopies, benches, and tee markers repaired and freshly painted.

Pesticide handlers, sprayers, and applicators apply herbicides, fungicides, and insecticides on plants or the soil to prevent or control weeds, insects, and diseases. Those who work for chemical lawn or tree service firms are more specialized, inspecting lawns for problems and applying fertilizers, pesticides, and other chemicals to stimulate growth and prevent or control weeds, diseases, or insect infestations.

Tree trimmers and pruners, also called *arborists,* cut away dead or excess branches from trees or shrubs to clear utility lines, roads, and sidewalks. Many of these workers strive to improve the appearance and health of trees and plants, and some specialize in diagnosing and treating tree diseases. Others specialize in pruning, trimming, and shaping ornamental trees and shrubs. Tree trimmers and pruners use chain saws, chippers, and stump grinders while on the job. When trimming near power lines, they usually work on truck-mounted lifts and use power pruners.

Work Environment

Grounds maintenance workers held about 1.3 million jobs in 2019. Employment in the detailed occupations that make up grounds maintenance workers was distributed as follows:

Landscaping and groundskeeping workers 1,188,000

Tree trimmers and pruners 62,000

Tree trimmers and pruners use chainsaws, chippers, and stump grinders while on the job.

Pesticide handlers, sprayers, and applicators,
vegetation 38,100
Grounds maintenance workers, all other............. 17,400

The largest employers of grounds maintenance workers were as follows:

Services to buildings and dwellings.............................. 46%

Self-employed workers 22

Government.. 8

Amusement, gambling, and recreation industries......... 7

Educational services; state, local, and private.............. 3

Grounds maintenance work is done outdoors in all kinds of weather. The work can be repetitive and physically demanding, requiring frequent bending, lifting, and shoveling.

Injuries and Illnesses

Grounds maintenance work can be dangerous. Workers who use equipment such as lawnmowers and chain saws must wear protective clothing, eyewear, and earplugs. Those who apply chemicals such as pesticides or fertilizers must wear protective gear, including appropriate clothing, gloves, goggles, and sometimes respirators.

Tree trimmers and pruners and "grounds maintenance workers, all other" have some of the highest rates of injuries and illnesses of all occupations.

And although fatalities are uncommon, tree trimmers and pruners experience one of the highest rates of occupational fatalities of all occupations. These workers, who often work at great heights, must always use fall protection gear in addition to wearing hardhats and eye protection for most activities.

Work Schedules

Many grounds maintenance jobs are seasonal. Jobs are most common in the spring, summer, and fall, when planting, mowing, and trimming are most frequent. However, many also provide other seasonal services, such as snow removal and installation and removal of holiday décor.

How to Become a Grounds Maintenance Worker

Most grounds maintenance workers need no formal education and are trained on the job. Most states require licensing for workers who apply pesticides and fertilizers.

Education

Although most grounds maintenance jobs have no education requirements, some employers may require formal education or certification in areas such as landscape design, horticulture, or arboriculture.

Licenses, Certifications, and Registrations

Most states require workers who apply pesticides and fertilizers to be licensed. Obtaining a license usually involves passing a

Some workers obtain a degree in landscape design or horticulture.

test on the proper use and disposal of insecticides, herbicides, and fungicides.

Although professional certification is not required, it can demonstrate competency and reliability for prospective clients and employers.

The National Association of Landscape Professionals offers seven certifications in landscaping and grounds maintenance for workers at various experience levels.

The Tree Care Industry Association offers certification for tree care safety professionals.

The International Society of Arboriculture offers six certifications for workers at various experience levels.

The Professional Grounds Management Society offers certification for workers at various experience levels.

Training

A short period of on-the-job training is usually enough to teach new hires the skills they need, which often include how to plant and maintain areas and how to use mowers, trimmers, leaf blowers, small tractors, and other equipment. Large institutional employers such as golf courses, university campuses, or municipalities may supplement on-the-job training with coursework in horticulture, arboriculture, urban forestry, insect and disease diagnosis, tree climbing, or small-engine repair.

Advancement

Grounds maintenance workers who have good communication skills may become crew leaders or advance into other supervisory positions. Becoming a manager or a landscape contractor may require some formal education and several years of related work experience. Some workers use their experience to start their own landscaping companies.

Important Qualities

Physical stamina. Grounds maintenance workers must be capable of doing physically strenuous labor for long hours, occasionally in extreme heat or cold.

Grounds Maintenance Workers

Median hourly wages, May 2019

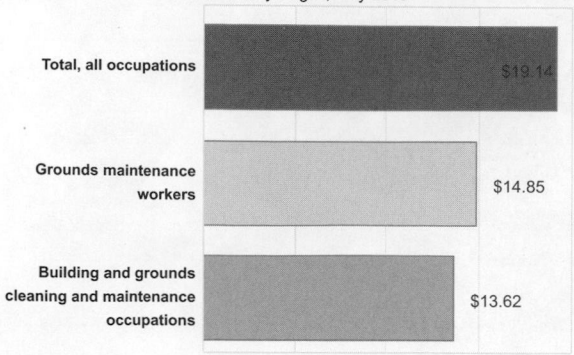

Total, all occupations	$19.14
Grounds maintenance workers	$14.85
Building and grounds cleaning and maintenance occupations	$13.62

Note: All Occupations includes all occupations in the U.S. Economy. Source: U.S. Bureau of Labor Statistics, Occupational Employment Statistics.

Self-motivated. Because they often work with little supervision, grounds maintenance workers must be able to do their job independently.

Visualization. Grounds maintenance workers must have the ability to imagine how plants, trees, shrubs, and other landscaping will look before planting or trimming.

Pay

The median hourly wage for grounds maintenance workers was $14.85 in May 2019. The median wage is the wage at which half the workers in an occupation earned more than that amount and half earned less. The lowest 10 percent earned less than $10.53, and the highest 10 percent earned more than $23.18.

Median hourly wages for grounds maintenance workers in May 2019 were as follows:

Tree trimmers and pruners.. $19.22

Pesticide handlers, sprayers, and applicators,
  vegetation.. 17.23
Grounds maintenance workers, all other..................... 15.43
Landscaping and groundskeeping workers................ 14.63

In May 2019, the median hourly wages for grounds maintenance workers in the top industries in which they worked were as follows:

Educational services; state, local, and private $16.39
Government... 15.10
Services to buildings and dwellings........................... 15.09
Amusement, gambling, and recreation industries..... 12.84

Many grounds maintenance jobs are seasonal. Jobs are most common in the spring, summer, and fall, when planting, mowing, and trimming are most frequent. However, many also provide other seasonal services, such as snow removal and installation and removal of holiday décor.

Grounds Maintenance Workers

Percent change in employment, projected 2019-29

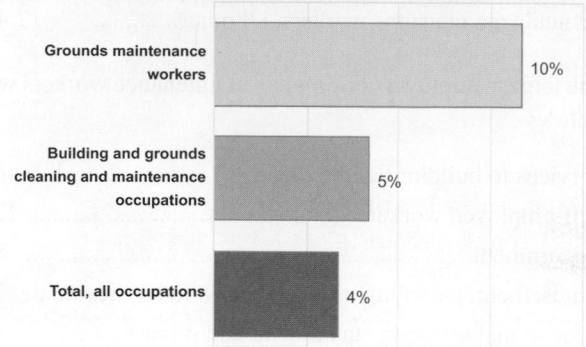

Grounds maintenance workers	10%
Building and grounds cleaning and maintenance occupations	5%
Total, all occupations	4%

Note: All Occupations includes all occupations in the U.S. Economy. Source: U.S. Bureau of Labor Statistics, Employment Projections program.

Job Outlook

Overall employment of grounds maintenance workers is projected to grow 10 percent from 2019 to 2029, much faster than the average for all occupations. Employment growth will vary by specialty (see table below).

Landscaping and groundskeeping workers—the largest specialty—will be needed to keep up with increasing demand for lawn care and landscaping services from aging or busy homeowners and large institutions, such as universities and corporate campuses.

Additionally, many municipalities are planting more trees in urban areas, likely increasing the demand for tree trimmers and pruners among other grounds maintenance workers.

Job Prospects

Overall job opportunities are expected to be very good. Job opportunities will stem from employment growth and from the need to replace workers who leave the occupation each year.

Job opportunities should be best in areas with temperate climates, where more landscaping services are required year round.

Employment projections data for grounds maintenance workers, 2019-29					
Occupational Title	SOC Code	Employment, 2019	Projected Employment, 2029	Change, 2019-29	
				Percent	Numeric
SOURCE: U.S. Bureau of Labor Statistics, Employment Projections program					
Grounds maintenance workers	37-3000	1,305,300	1,436,100	10	130,800
Landscaping and groundskeeping workers	37-3011	1,188,000	1,307,900	10	119,900
Pesticide handlers, sprayers, and applicators, vegetation	37-3012	38,100	41,200	8	3,200
Tree trimmers and pruners	37-3013	62,000	68,600	11	6,600
Grounds maintenance workers, all other	37-3019	17,400	18,500	7	1,100

State & Area Data
Occupational Employment Statistics (OES)

The Occupational Employment Statistics (OES) program produces employment and wage estimates annually for over 800 occupations. These estimates are available for the nation as a whole, for individual states, and for metropolitan and nonmetropolitan areas.

Contacts for More Information

For more information about tree trimmers and pruners, including certification, visit

➤ International Society of Arboriculture

➤ Tree Care Industry Association

For information about landscaping and groundskeeping workers, visit

➤ National Association of Landscape Professionals

➤ Professional Grounds Management Society

For information about becoming a licensed pesticide applicator, contact your state's licensing official.

Janitors and Building Cleaners

Summary

Quick Facts: Janitors and Building Cleaners

2019 Median Pay	$27,430 per year $13.19 per hour
Typical Entry-Level Education	No formal educational credential
Work Experience in a Related Occupation.....	None
On-the-job Training	Short-term on-the-job training
Number of Jobs, 2019................................	2,374,200
Job Outlook, 2019-29................................	4% (As fast as average)
Employment Change, 2019-29	105,600

What Janitors and Building Cleaners Do

Janitors and building cleaners keep many types of buildings clean, orderly, and in good condition.

Work Environment

Most janitors and building cleaners work indoors. However, some work outdoors part of the time, sweeping walkways, mowing lawns, and removing snow. Because office buildings often are cleaned while they are empty, many cleaners work evening hours. The work can be physically demanding and sometimes dirty and unpleasant.

Janitors need physical stamina because they spend much of their time on their feet.

How to Become a Janitor or Building Cleaner

Most janitors and building cleaners learn on the job. Formal education is not required.

Pay

The median hourly wage for janitors and building cleaners was $13.19 in May 2019.

Job Outlook

Employment of janitors and building cleaners is projected to grow 4 percent from 2019 to 2029, about as fast as the average for all occupations. Many new jobs are expected in industries such as administrative and support services, educational services, and healthcare.

State & Area Data

Explore resources for employment and wages by state and area for janitors and building cleaners.

What Janitors and Building Cleaners Do

Janitors and building cleaners keep many types of buildings clean, orderly, and in good condition.

Duties

Janitors and building cleaners typically do the following:

- Gather and empty trash
- Sweep, mop, or vacuum building floors
- Clean restrooms and stock them with supplies
- Lock doors to secure buildings
- Clean spills and other hazards with appropriate equipment
- Wash windows, walls, and glass
- Order cleaning supplies
- Make minor building repairs
- Notify managers when a building needs major repairs

Janitors and building cleaners wash windows and glass.

Janitors and building cleaners keep office buildings, schools, hospitals, retail stores, hotels, and other places clean, sanitary, and in good condition. Some only clean, while others have a wide range of duties.

In addition to keeping the inside of buildings clean and orderly, some janitors and building cleaners work outdoors, mowing lawns, sweeping walkways, and removing snow. Some workers also monitor the building's heating and cooling system, ensuring that it functions properly.

Janitors and building cleaners use many tools and equipment. Simple cleaning tools may include mops, brooms, rakes, and shovels. Other tools may include snowblowers, floor buffers, and carpet extraction equipment.

Some janitors are responsible for repairing minor electrical or plumbing problems, such as leaky faucets.

The following are examples of types of janitors and building cleaners:

Building superintendents are responsible for maintaining residential buildings, such as apartments and condominiums. Although their duties are similar to those of other janitors, some building superintendents also help collect rent and show vacancies to potential tenants.

Custodians are janitors or cleaning workers who typically maintain institutional facilities, such as public schools and hospitals.

Most janitors and building cleaners work indoors, but some may work outdoors.

Work Environment

Janitors and building cleaners held about 2.4 million jobs in 2019. The largest employers of janitors and building cleaners were as follows:

Services to buildings and dwellings	37%
Elementary and secondary schools; state, local, and private	13
Healthcare and social assistance	7
Government	5
Religious, grantmaking, civic, professional, and similar organizations	5

Most janitors and building cleaners work indoors, but some work outdoors part of the time, sweeping walkways, mowing lawns, and shoveling snow. They spend most of the day walking, standing, or bending while cleaning. Sometimes they must move or lift heavy supplies and equipment. As a result, the work may be strenuous on the back, arms, and legs. Some tasks, such as cleaning restrooms and trash areas, can be dirty and unpleasant.

Injuries and Illnesses

Janitors and building cleaners sometimes get injured on the job. For example, they may suffer minor cuts, bruises, and burns from machines, tools, and chemicals. As a result, workers increasingly receive safety and ergonomics training.

How to Become a Janitor or Building Cleaner

Most janitors and building cleaners learn on the job. Formal education is not required.

Education

Janitors and building cleaners do not need any formal educational credential. However, high school courses in shop can be helpful for jobs involving repair work.

Most janitors and building cleaners learn on the job. They use many types of tools and equipment, including snowblowers.

Training
Most janitors and building cleaners learn on the job. Beginners typically work with a more experienced janitor, learning how to use and maintain equipment such as vacuums, floor buffers, and other tools. On the job, they also learn how to repair minor electrical and plumbing problems.

Licenses, Certifications, and Registrations
Although not required, certification is available through the Building Service Contractors Association International, the IEHA (formerly International Executive Housekeepers Association), and ISSA—The International Sanitary Supply Association. Certification can demonstrate competence and may make applicants more appealing to employers.

Important Qualities
Interpersonal skills. Janitors and building cleaners should get along well with their supervisors, other cleaners, and the people who live or work in the buildings they clean.

Mechanical skills. Janitors and building cleaners should understand general building operations. They should be able to make routine repairs, such as repairing leaky faucets.

Physical stamina. Janitors and building cleaners spend most of their workday on their feet, operating cleaning equipment and lifting and moving supplies or tools. As a result, they should have good physical stamina.

Physical strength. Janitors and building cleaners often must lift and move cleaning materials and heavy equipment. Cases of liquid cleaner and trash receptacles, for example, can be very heavy, so workers should be strong enough to lift them without injuring their back.

Time-management skills. Janitors and building cleaners should be able to plan and complete tasks in a timely manner.

Pay
The median hourly wage for janitors and building cleaners was $13.19 in May 2019. The median wage is the wage at

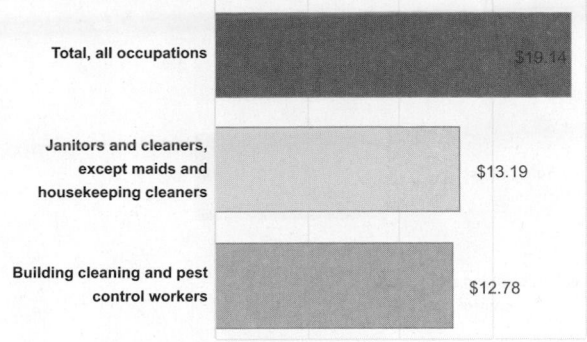

Janitors and Building Cleaners
Median hourly wages, May 2019

Total, all occupations	$19.14
Janitors and cleaners, except maids and housekeeping cleaners	$13.19
Building cleaning and pest control workers	$12.78

Note: All Occupations includes all occupations in the U.S. Economy. Source: U.S. Bureau of Labor Statistics, Occupational Employment Statistics.

which half the workers in an occupation earned more than that amount and half earned less. The lowest 10 percent earned less than $9.43, and the highest 10 percent earned more than $21.58.

In May 2019, the median hourly wages for janitors and building cleaners in the top industries in which they worked were as follows:

Government	$16.52
Elementary and secondary schools; state, local, and private	15.02
Healthcare and social assistance	13.18
Religious, grantmaking, civic, professional, and similar organizations	13.02
Services to buildings and dwellings	12.34

Most janitors and building cleaners work full time. Because office buildings are often cleaned while they are empty, many cleaners work evening hours. When there is a need for 24-hour maintenance, as there often is in hospitals and hotels, cleaners work in shifts.

Job Outlook
Employment of janitors and building cleaners is projected to grow 4 percent from 2019 to 2029, about as fast as the average for all occupations.

These workers are essential to the upkeep of building interiors. Their services will be needed to meet the continued demand for clean spaces.

Many new jobs are expected in industries such as administrative and support services, educational services, and healthcare.

Job Prospects
Overall job prospects are expected to be favorable. Many job openings will come from the need to replace workers who leave or retire from this very large occupation.

Janitors and Building Cleaners
Percent change in employment, projected 2019-29

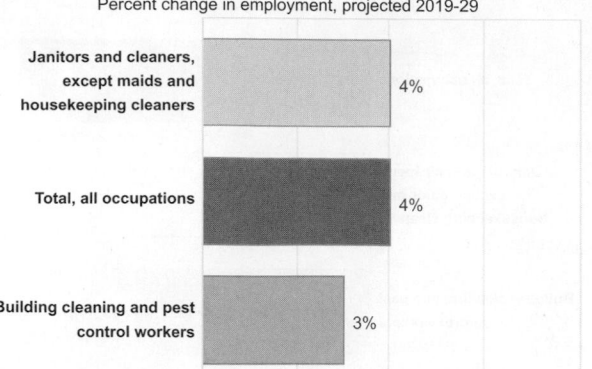

Janitors and cleaners, except maids and housekeeping cleaners — 4%

Total, all occupations — 4%

Building cleaning and pest control workers — 3%

Note: All Occupations includes all occupations in the U.S. Economy.
Source: U.S. Bureau of Labor Statistics, Employment Projections program.

Employment projections data for janitors and building cleaners, 2019-29

Occupational Title	SOC Code	Employment, 2019	Projected Employment, 2029	Change, 2019-29 Percent	Numeric
Janitors and cleaners, except maids and housekeeping cleaners	37-2011	2,374,200	2,479,800	4	105,600

SOURCE: U.S. Bureau of Labor Statistics, Employment Projections program

State & Area Data
Occupational Employment Statistics (OES)
The Occupational Employment Statistics (OES) program produces employment and wage estimates annually for over 800 occupations. These estimates are available for the nation as a whole, for individual states, and for metropolitan and nonmetropolitan areas.

Contacts for More Information
For more information about janitors and building cleaners, visit
➤ Association of Residential Cleaning Services International
➤ Building Service Contractors Association International
➤ IEHA (formerly International Executive Housekeepers Association)
➤ ISSA-The Worldwide Cleaning Industry Association
➤ Information about janitorial and building cleaning jobs is available from state employment service offices.

Pest Control Workers

Summary

Quick Facts: Pest Control Workers

2019 Median Pay	$37,330 per year / $17.95 per hour
Typical Entry-Level Education	High school diploma or equivalent
Work Experience in a Related Occupation	None
On-the-job Training	Moderate-term on-the-job training
Number of Jobs, 2019	87,600
Job Outlook, 2019-29	9% (Much faster than average)
Employment Change, 2019-29	7,500

What Pest Control Workers Do
Pest control workers remove unwanted pests that infest buildings and surrounding areas.

Work Environment
Pest control workers must travel to a client's home or business. Workers often kneel, bend, and crawl into tight spaces to inspect sites. Because there are health risks associated with pesticide use, workers are trained in pesticide safety and, if required by the product label, sometimes wear protective gear, including respirators, gloves, and goggles. Working evenings and weekends is common.

How to Become a Pest Control Worker
State laws require pest control workers to be licensed. Most workers need a high school diploma and receive moderate on-the-job training.

Pay
The median annual wage for pest control workers was $37,330 in May 2019.

Pest control workers determine the type of treatment needed to eliminate pests.

Job Outlook

Employment of pest control workers is projected to grow 9 percent from 2019 to 2029, much faster than the average for all occupations. Job opportunities should be good because of the limited number of people seeking work in pest control and the need to replace workers who leave this occupation.

State & Area Data

Explore resources for employment and wages by state and area for pest control workers.

What Pest Control Workers Do

Pest control workers remove unwanted pests, such as roaches, rats, ants, bedbugs, mosquitoes, ticks, and termites that infest buildings and surrounding areas.

Duties

Pest control workers typically do the following:

- Inspect buildings and premises for signs of pests or infestation
- Determine the type of treatment needed to eliminate pests
- Measure the dimensions of the area needing treatment
- Estimate the cost of their services
- Use baits and set traps to remove, control, or eliminate pests
- Apply pesticides in and around buildings and other structures
- Design and carry out pest management plans
- Drive trucks equipped with power spraying equipment
- Create barriers to prevent pests from entering a building

Unwanted pests that infest buildings and surrounding areas can pose serious risks to the health and safety of occupants. Pest control workers control, manage, and remove these creatures from homes, apartments, offices, and other structures to protect people and to maintain the structural integrity of buildings.

To design and carry out integrated pest management plans, pest control workers must know the identity and biology of a wide range of pests. They must also know the best ways to control and remove the pests.

Although roaches, rats, ants, bedbugs, ticks, and termites are the most common pests, some pest control workers also remove birds, squirrels, and other wildlife from homes and buildings.

Pest control workers' position titles and job duties often vary by state.

The following are examples of types of pest control workers:

Pest control technicians identify potential and actual pest problems, conduct inspections, and design control strategies. They work directly with customers and, as entry-level workers, use only a limited range of pesticides.

Applicators use a wide range of pesticides and may specialize in a particular area of pest control:

- Termite control technicians may use chemicals or baiting techniques and modify structures to eliminate termites and prevent future infestations. Some also repair structural damage caused by termites and build barriers to separate pests from their food source.
- Fumigators use gases, called fumigants, to treat specific kinds of pests or large-scale infestations. Fumigators seal infested buildings before using hoses to fill the structure with fumigants. They post warning signs to keep people from going into fumigated buildings and monitor buildings closely to detect and stop leaks.

Pest control workers inspect a building and its premises for signs of pests.

Pest control workers must travel to a client's home or business.

Work Environment

Pest control workers held about 87,600 jobs in 2019. The largest employers of pest control workers were as follows:

Exterminating and pest control services 87%
Self-employed workers 6

Pest control workers must travel to a client's home or business. They work both indoors and outdoors, in all types of weather. To inspect and treat sites, workers must often kneel, bend, and crawl into tight spaces.

When working with pesticides, pest control workers must wear protective gear, including gloves, goggles, and, when required, respirators.

Injuries and Illnesses

All pesticide products are reviewed and approved by the Environmental Protection Agency (EPA) and workers must follow label directions. Some pest control chemicals are toxic and can be harmful to humans, so care should be taken when using such chemicals. Workers are trained and licensed for pesticide usage and wear protective equipment as necessary based on label requirements.

However, some injuries and illnesses from pesticide exposure may still occur. Pest control workers have one of the highest rates of injuries and illnesses of all occupations. Pest control workers are also susceptible to strains and sprains because workers must often kneel, bend, and crawl into tight spaces.

Work Schedules

Most pest control workers are employed full time. Working evenings and weekends is common. Some work more than 40 hours per week.

How to Become a Pest Control Worker

State laws require pest control workers to be licensed. Most workers need a high school diploma and receive moderate on-the-job training.

State laws require pest control workers to be licensed.

Many pest control companies require that employees have good driving records.

Education

A high school diploma or equivalent is typically the minimum qualification for most pest control jobs.

Training

Most pest control workers begin as technicians, receiving both formal technical instruction and moderate-term on-the-job training from employers. They often study specialties such as rodent control, termite control, and fumigation. Technicians also must complete general training in pesticide use and safety. Pest control training can usually be completed in less than 3 months.

After completing the required training, workers are qualified to provide pest control services. Because pest control methods change, workers often attend continuing education classes.

Licenses, Certifications, and Registrations

Most states require pest control workers to be licensed. Licensure requirements vary by state, but workers usually must complete training and pass an exam. Some states have additional requirements, such as having a high school diploma or equivalent, completing an apprenticeship, and passing a background check. States may have additional requirements for applicators.

Advancement

Pest control workers typically advance as they gain experience. Applicators with several years of experience often become supervisors. Some experienced workers start their own pest management company.

Important Qualities

Bookkeeping skills. Pest control workers must keep accurate records of the hours they work, chemicals they use, and payments they collect. Self-employed workers, in particular, need these skills in order to run their business.

Customer-service skills. Pest control workers should be friendly and polite when they interact with customers at their homes or businesses.

Detail oriented. Because pest control workers apply pesticides, they need to be able to follow instructions carefully in order to prevent harm to residents, pets, the environment, and themselves.

Physical stamina. Pest control workers may spend hours on their feet, often crouching, kneeling, and crawling. They also must be able to withstand uncomfortable conditions, such as heat when they climb into attics in the summertime and cold when they enter crawl spaces during winter.

Pay

The median annual wage for pest control workers was $37,330 in May 2019. The median wage is the wage at which

Pest Control Workers

Median annual wages, May 2019

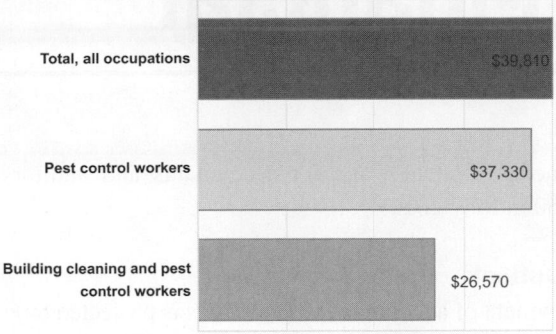

Total, all occupations	$39,810
Pest control workers	$37,330
Building cleaning and pest control workers	$26,570

Note: All Occupations includes all occupations in the U.S. Economy.
Source: U.S. Bureau of Labor Statistics, Occupational Employment Statistics.

half the workers in an occupation earned more than that amount and half earned less. The lowest 10 percent earned less than $24,920, and the highest 10 percent earned more than $60,320.

In May 2019, the median annual wages for pest control workers in the top industries in which they worked were as follows:

Exterminating and pest control services $37,210

Most pest control workers are employed full time. Working evenings and weekends is common. Some work more than 40 hours per week.

Job Outlook

Employment of pest control workers is projected to grow 9 percent from 2019 to 2029, much faster than the average for all occupations.

The growing number of invasive insect species, such as stink bugs, is expected to further increase demand for pest control services. Although some people may choose to control pests themselves, most customers prefer to hire professional pest control services.

Job Prospects

Job opportunities are expected to be good. The limited number of people seeking work in pest control and the need to replace

Pest Control Workers

Percent change in employment, projected 2019-29

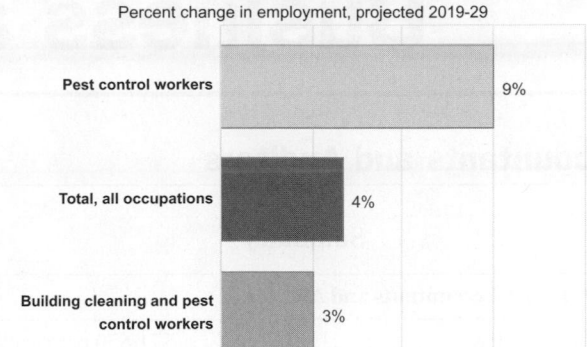

Pest control workers	9%
Total, all occupations	4%
Building cleaning and pest control workers	3%

Note: All Occupations includes all occupations in the U.S. Economy.
Source: U.S. Bureau of Labor Statistics, Employment Projections program.

workers who leave this occupation should result in many job openings.

Employment projections data for pest control workers, 2019-29					
Occupational Title	SOC Code	Employment, 2019	Projected Employment, 2029	Change, 2019-29	
				Percent	Numeric
SOURCE: U.S. Bureau of Labor Statistics, Employment Projections program					
Pest control workers	37-2021	87,600	95,000	9	7,500

State & Area Data
Occupational Employment Statistics (OES)

The Occupational Employment Statistics (OES) program produces employment and wage estimates annually for over 800 occupations. These estimates are available for the nation as a whole, for individual states, and for metropolitan and nonmetropolitan areas.

Contacts for More Information

For information about state licensing requirements, contact state licensing officials.
For information on pest control officials, visit
➤ Association of Structural Pest Control Regulatory Officials

For information on the pest management industry, visit
➤ National Pest Management Association

Business and Financial

Accountants and Auditors

Summary

Quick Facts: Accountants and Auditors	
2019 Median Pay	$71,550 per year $34.40 per hour
Typical Entry-Level Education	Bachelor's degree
Work Experience in a Related Occupation	None
On-the-job Training	None
Number of Jobs, 2019	1,436,100
Job Outlook, 2019-29	4% (As fast as average)
Employment Change, 2019-29	61,700

What Accountants and Auditors Do

Accountants and auditors prepare and examine financial records.

Work Environment

Most accountants and auditors work full time. Some work more than 40 hours per week. Overtime hours are typical at certain times of the year, such as at the end of the budget year or during tax season.

How to Become an Accountant or Auditor

Most employers require a candidate to have a bachelor's degree in accounting or a related field. Certification within a specific field of accounting improves job prospects. For example, many accountants become Certified Public Accountants (CPAs).

Pay

The median annual wage for accountants and auditors was $71,550 in May 2019.

Job Outlook

Employment of accountants and auditors is projected to grow 4 percent from 2019 to 2029, about as fast as the average for all occupations. In general, employment growth of accountants and auditors is expected to be closely tied to the health of the overall economy. As the economy grows, more workers should be needed to prepare and examine financial records.

State & Area Data

Explore resources for employment and wages by state and area for accountants and auditors.

What Accountants and Auditors Do

Accountants and auditors prepare and examine financial records. They ensure that financial records are accurate and that taxes are paid properly and on time. Accountants and auditors assess financial operations and work to help ensure that organizations run efficiently.

Duties

Accountants and auditors typically do the following:

- Examine financial statements to ensure that they are accurate and comply with laws and regulations
- Compute taxes owed, prepare tax returns, and ensure that taxes are paid properly and on time
- Inspect account books and accounting systems for efficiency and use of accepted accounting procedures

Accountants and auditors ensure that financial records are accurate and taxes are paid properly and on time.

Accountants and auditors examine financial statements for accuracy and conformance with laws.

- Organize and maintain financial records
- Assess financial operations and make best-practices recommendations to management
- Suggest ways to reduce costs, enhance revenues, and improve profits

In addition to examining and preparing financial documentation, accountants and auditors must explain their findings. This includes preparing written reports and meeting face-to-face with organization managers and individual clients.

Many accountants and auditors specialize, depending on the particular organization that they work for. Some work for organizations that specialize in assurance services (improving the quality or context of information for decisionmakers) or risk management (determining the probability of a misstatement on financial documentation). Other organizations specialize in specific industries, such as healthcare.

The following are examples of types of accountants and auditors:

Public accountants perform a broad range of accounting, auditing, tax, and consulting tasks. Their clients include corporations, governments, and individuals.

Public accountants work with financial documents that clients are required by law to disclose. These include tax forms and balance sheet statements that corporations must provide to potential investors. For example, some public accountants concentrate on tax matters, advising corporations about the tax advantages of certain business decisions or preparing individual income tax returns.

Public accountants, many of whom are Certified Public Accountants (CPAs), generally have their own businesses or work for public accounting firms. Publicly traded companies are required to have CPAs sign documents they submit to the Securities and Exchange Commission (SEC), including annual and quarterly reports.

Some public accountants specialize in forensic accounting, investigating financial crimes such as securities fraud and embezzlement, bankruptcies and contract disputes, and other complex and potentially criminal financial transactions. Forensic accountants combine their knowledge of accounting and finance with law and investigative techniques to determine if an activity is illegal. Many forensic accountants work closely with law enforcement personnel and lawyers during investigations and often appear as expert witnesses during trials.

Management accountants, also called *cost, managerial, industrial, corporate,* or *private accountants*, record and analyze the financial information of the organizations for which they work. The information that management accountants prepare is intended for internal use by business managers, not by the general public.

Management accountants often work on budgeting and performance evaluation. They also may help organizations plan the cost of doing business. Some may work with financial managers on asset management, which involves planning and selecting financial investments such as stocks, bonds, and real estate.

Government accountants maintain and examine the records of government agencies and audit private businesses and individuals whose activities are subject to government regulations or taxation. Accountants employed by federal, state, and local governments ensure that revenues are received and spent in accordance with laws and regulations.

Internal auditors check for mismanagement of an organization's funds. They identify ways to improve the processes for finding and eliminating waste and fraud. The practice of internal auditing is not regulated, but The Institute of Internal Auditors (IIA) provides generally accepted standards.

External auditors perform similar duties to internal auditors, but are employed by an outside organization, rather than the one they are auditing. They review clients' financial statements and inform investors and authorities that the statements have been correctly prepared and reported.

Information technology auditors are internal auditors who review controls for their organization's computer systems to ensure that the financial data comes from a reliable source.

Work Environment

Accountants and auditors held about 1.4 million jobs in 2019. The largest employers of accountants and auditors were as follows:

Accounting, tax preparation, bookkeeping, and payroll services	24%
Finance and insurance	9
Government	8
Management of companies and enterprises	7
Self-employed workers	6

Most accountants and auditors work in offices, but some work from home. Although they complete much of their work alone, they sometimes work in teams with other accountants

Most accountants and auditors work full time.

and auditors. Accountants and auditors may travel to their clients' places of business.

Work Schedules

Most accountants and auditors work full time. Some work more than 40 hours per week. Longer periods of work are typical at certain times of the year, such as at the end of the budget year or during tax season.

How to Become an Accountant or Auditor

Most accountants and auditors need at least a bachelor's degree in accounting or a related field. Certification, including the Certified Public Accountant (CPA) credential, can improve job prospects.

Education

Most accountant and auditor positions require at least a bachelor's degree in accounting or a related field. Some employers prefer to hire applicants who have a master's degree, either in accounting or in business administration with a concentration in accounting.

A few universities and colleges offer specialized programs, such as a bachelor's degree in internal auditing. In some cases, those with associate's degrees, as well as bookkeepers and accounting clerks who meet the education and experience requirements set by their employers, get junior accounting positions and advance to accountant positions by showing their accounting skills on the job.

Many colleges help students gain practical experience through summer or part-time internships with public accounting or business firms.

Licenses, Certifications, and Registrations

Every accountant filing a report with the Securities and Exchange Commission (SEC) is required by law to be a Certified Public Accountant (CPA). Many other accountants

Most accountants and auditors need at least a bachelor's degree in accounting or a related field.

choose to become a CPA to enhance their job prospects or to gain clients. Many employers will pay the costs associated with the CPA exam.

CPAs are licensed by their state's Board of Accountancy. Becoming a CPA requires passing a national exam and meeting other state requirements. Almost all states require CPA candidates to complete 150 semester hours of college coursework to be licensed, which is 30 hours more than the usual 4-year bachelor's degree. Many schools offer a 5-year combined bachelor's and master's degree to meet the 150-hour requirement, but a master's degree is not required.

A few states allow a number of years of public accounting experience to substitute for a college degree.

All states use the four-part Uniform CPA Examination from the American Institute of Certified Public Accountants (AICPA). Candidates do not have to pass all four parts at once, but most states require that candidates pass all four parts within 18 months of passing their first part.

Almost all states require CPAs to take continuing education to keep their license.

Certification provides an advantage in the job market because it shows professional competence in a specialized field of accounting and auditing. Accountants and auditors seek certifications from a variety of professional societies. Some of the most common certifications are listed below:

The Institute of Management Accountants offers the Certified Management Accountant (CMA) to applicants who complete a bachelor's degree. Applicants must have worked at least 2 years in management accounting, pass a two-part exam, agree to meet continuing education requirements, and comply with standards of professional conduct. The exam covers areas such as financial statement analysis, working-capital policy, capital structure, valuation issues, and risk management.

The Institute of Internal Auditors (IIA) offers the Certified Internal Auditor (CIA) to graduates from accredited colleges and universities who have worked for 2 years as internal auditors and have passed a four-part exam. The IIA also offers the Certified in Control Self-Assessment (CCSA), Certified Government Auditing Professional (CGAP), Certified Financial Services Auditor (CFSA), and Certification in Risk Management Assurance (CRMA) to those who pass the exams and meet educational and experience requirements.

ISACA offers the Certified Information Systems Auditor (CISA) to candidates who pass an exam and have 5 years of experience auditing information systems. Information systems experience, financial or operational auditing experience, or related college credit hours can be substituted for up to 3 years of experience in information systems auditing, control, or security.

For accountants with a CPA, the AICPA offers the option to receive any or all of the Accredited in Business Valuation (ABV), Certified Information Technology Professional (CITP), or Personal Financial Specialist (PFS) certifications. The ABV requires passing a written exam, completion of at least six business valuation projects, and 75 hours of continuing education. The CITP requires 1,000 hours of business technology experience and 75 hours of continuing education. Candidates for the PFS also must complete a certain amount of work experience and continuing education, and pass a written exam.

Advancement

Some top executives and financial managers have a background in accounting, internal auditing, or finance.

Entry-level public accountants can advance to senior positions with more responsibility. Those who excel may become supervisors, managers, or partners; open their own public accounting firm; or transfer to executive positions in management accounting or internal auditing in private firms.

Management accountants often start as cost accountants, junior internal auditors, or trainees for other accounting positions. As they rise through the organization, they may advance to accounting manager, chief cost accountant, budget director, or manager of internal auditing. Some become controllers, treasurers, financial vice presidents, chief financial officers, or corporation presidents.

Public accountants, management accountants, and internal auditors can move from one aspect of accounting and auditing to another. Public accountants often move into management accounting or internal auditing. Management accountants may become internal auditors, and internal auditors may become management accountants. However, it is less common for management accountants or internal auditors to move into public accounting.

Important Qualities

Analytical skills. Accountants and auditors must be able to identify issues in documentation and suggest solutions. For example, public accountants use analytical skills in their work to minimize tax liability, and internal auditors use these skills to detect fraudulent use of funds.

Communication skills. Accountants and auditors must be able to listen carefully to facts and concerns from clients, managers, and others. They must also be able to discuss the results of their work in both meetings and written reports.

Detail oriented. Accountants and auditors must pay attention to detail when compiling and examining documentation.

Math skills. Accountants and auditors must be able to analyze, compare, and interpret facts and figures, although complex math skills are not necessary.

Organizational skills. Strong organizational skills are important for accountants and auditors, who often work with a range of financial documents for a variety of clients.

Pay

The median annual wage for accountants and auditors was $71,550 in May 2019. The median wage is the wage at which

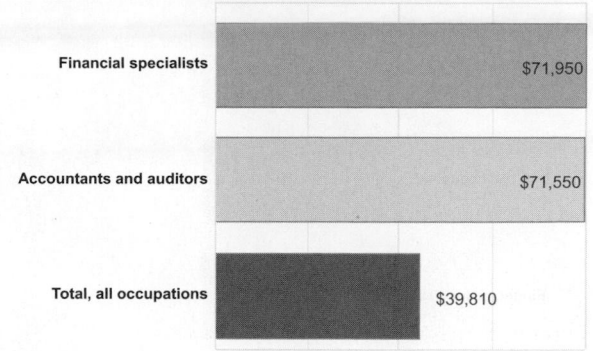

Accountants and Auditors
Median annual wages, May 2019

Financial specialists $71,950
Accountants and auditors $71,550
Total, all occupations $39,810

Note: All Occupations includes all occupations in the U.S. Economy. Source: U.S. Bureau of Labor Statistics, Occupational Employment Statistics.

half the workers in an occupation earned more than that amount and half earned less. The lowest 10 percent earned less than $44,480, and the highest 10 percent earned more than $124,450.

In May 2019, the median annual wages for accountants and auditors in the top industries in which they worked were as follows:

Finance and insurance	$76,440
Management of companies and enterprises	74,060
Accounting, tax preparation, bookkeeping, and payroll services	71,390
Government	70,180

Most accountants and auditors work full time. Some work more than 40 hours per week. Longer hours are typical at certain times of the year, such as at the end of the budget year or during tax season.

Job Outlook

Employment of accountants and auditors is projected to grow 4 percent from 2019 to 2029, about as fast as the average for all occupations. Globalization, a growing economy, and a complex tax and regulatory environment are expected to continue to lead to strong demand for accountants and auditors.

In general, employment growth of accountants and auditors is expected to be closely tied to the health of the overall economy. As the economy grows, these workers will continue to be needed to prepare and examine financial records. In addition, as more companies go public, there will be greater need for public accountants to handle the legally required financial documentation.

The continued globalization of business may lead to increased demand for accounting expertise and services related to international trade and international mergers and acquisitions.

Technological change is expected to affect the role of accountants over the next 10 years. As platforms such as cloud computing become more widespread, some routine accounting tasks may become automated. Although this will allow accountants to become more efficient, this change is not expected to reduce the overall demand for accountants. Instead, with the

Accountants and Auditors
Percent change in employment, projected 2019-29

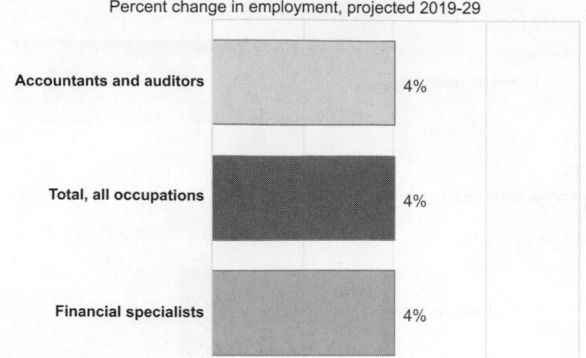

Accountants and auditors	4%
Total, all occupations	4%
Financial specialists	4%

Note: All Occupations includes all occupations in the U.S. Economy.
Source: U.S. Bureau of Labor Statistics, Employment Projections program.

automation of routine tasks, such as data entry, the advisory and analytical duties of accountants will become more prominent.

Job Prospects

Demand for accountants may lead to good prospects for entry-level positions. However, competition will be stronger for jobs with the most prestigious accounting and business firms.

Accountants and auditors who have earned professional recognition, especially as Certified Public Accountants (CPAs), should have the best prospects. Job applicants who have a master's degree in accounting or a master's degree in business administration (MBA) with a concentration in accounting also may have an advantage.

Employment projections data for accountants and auditors, 2019-29					
Occupational Title	SOC Code	Employment, 2019	Projected Employment, 2029	Change, 2019-29 Percent	Numeric
SOURCE: U.S. Bureau of Labor Statistics, Employment Projections program					
Accountants and auditors	13-2011	1,436,100	1,497,900	4	61,700

State & Area Data
Occupational Employment Statistics (OES)

The Occupational Employment Statistics (OES) program produces employment and wage estimates annually for over 800 occupations. These estimates are available for the nation as a whole, for individual states, and for metropolitan and nonmetropolitan areas.

Contacts for More Information

For more information about accredited accounting programs, visit
➤ AACSB International—The Association to Advance Collegiate Schools of Business

For more information about the Certified Public Accountant (CPA) designation, visit
➤ American Institute of Certified Public Accountants (AICPA)

For more information about management accounting and the Certified Management Accountant (CMA) designation, visit
➤ Institute of Management Accountants

For more information about internal auditing and the Certified Internal Auditor (CIA) designation, visit
➤ The Institute of Internal Auditors

For more information about information systems auditing and the Certified Information Systems Auditor (CISA) designation, visit
➤ ISACA

For more information about certifications in accounting, visit
➤ Global Academy of Finance and Management

Appraisers and Assessors of Real Estate

Summary

Quick Facts: Appraisers and Assessors of Real Estate

2019 Median Pay	$57,010 per year $27.41 per hour
Typical Entry-Level Education	Bachelor's degree
Work Experience in a Related Occupation	None
On-the-job Training	Long-term on-the-job training
Number of Jobs, 2019	75,100
Job Outlook, 2019-29	3% (As fast as average)
Employment Change, 2019-29	2,200

What Appraisers and Assessors of Real Estate Do

Appraisers and assessors of real estate provide a value estimate on land and buildings.

Work Environment

Although appraisers and assessors of real estate work in offices, they often spend a large part of their day visiting properties. Most work full time during regular business hours.

How to Become an Appraiser or Assessor of Real Estate

Most appraisers and assessors must be licensed or certified, but requirements vary widely. To obtain a certification, appraisers of residential or commercial property usually need to have at least a bachelor's degree. For assessors, most states set education and experience requirements that they must meet in order to practice.

Appraisers and assessors prepare current data before visiting properties.

Pay

The median annual wage for appraisers and assessors of real estate was $57,010 in May 2019.

Job Outlook

Employment of appraisers and assessors of real estate is projected to grow 3 percent from 2019 to 2029, about as fast as the average for all occupations. Employment opportunities should be best in areas with active real estate markets.

State & Area Data

Explore resources for employment and wages by state and area for appraisers and assessors of real estate.

What Appraisers and Assessors of Real Estate Do

Appraisers and assessors of real estate provide a value estimate on land and buildings usually before they are sold, mortgaged, taxed, insured, or developed.

Appraisers and assessors of real estate inspect new and existing properties.

Duties

Appraisers and assessors of real estate typically do the following:

- Verify legal descriptions of real estate properties in public records
- Inspect new and existing properties, noting the characteristics
- Photograph the interior and exterior of properties
- Analyze "comparables," or similar nearby properties, to help provide values
- Prepare written reports on the property values
- Prepare and maintain current data on each real estate property

Appraisers and assessors work in localities that they are familiar with so that they know any environmental or other concerns that may affect the property's value.

Appraisers typically value one property at a time, and they often specialize in a certain type of real estate:

- Commercial appraisers specialize in income-producing properties, such as office buildings, stores, and hotels.
- Residential appraisers focus on appraising properties in which people live, such as single unit homes and condominiums. They only appraise properties that house one to four units.

When evaluating a property's value, appraisers note the characteristics of the property and surrounding area, such as a view or noisy highway nearby. They also consider the overall condition of a building, including its foundation and roof or any renovations that may have been done. Appraisers photograph the outside of the building and some of the interior features to document its condition. After visiting the property, the appraiser analyzes the property relative to comparable home sales, including lease records, location, view, previous appraisals, and income potential. During the entire process, appraisers record their research, observations, and methods used in providing an estimate of the property's value.

Assessors value properties for property tax assessments. Most work for local governments. Unlike appraisers, who generally focus on one property at a time, assessors often value an entire neighborhood of homes at once by using mass appraisal techniques and computer-assisted appraisal systems.

Assessors must be up to date on tax assessment procedures. Taxpayers sometimes challenge the assessed value because they feel they are being charged too much for property tax. Assessors must be able to defend the accuracy of their property assessments, either to the owner directly or at a public hearing.

Assessors also keep a database of every property in their jurisdiction, identifying the property owner, assessment history, and characteristics of the property, as well as property maps detailing the property distribution of the jurisdiction.

Work Environment

Appraisers and assessors of real estate held about 75,100 jobs in 2019. The largest employers of appraisers and assessors of real estate were as follows:

Appraisers and assessors of real estate research data on properties and write reports.

Local government, excluding education and hospitals	32%
Real estate	28
Self-employed workers	23
Finance and insurance	7

Although appraisers and assessors of real estate work in offices, they may spend a large part of their time conducting site visits to assess properties. Time spent away from the office depends on the specialty. For example, residential appraisers tend to spend less time on office work than commercial appraisers, who might spend up to several weeks analyzing information and writing reports on one property. Appraisers who work for banks and mortgage companies generally spend most of their time inside the office, making site visits only when necessary.

Work Schedules

Appraisers and assessors of real estate typically work full time during regular business hours. However, self-employed appraisers, often called *independent fee appraisers*, usually work more than a standard 40-hour workweek, because they must often write reports during evenings and on weekends.

How to Become an Appraiser or Assessor of Real Estate

The requirements to become a fully qualified appraiser or assessor of real estate are complex and vary by state and, sometimes, by the value or type of property. Most appraisers and assessors of residential or commercial property must have at least a bachelor's degree to obtain certification. The entry-level state license category typically does not require a bachelor's degree. Check with your state's licensing board for specific requirements for both assessors and appraisers.

Education

Although requirements may vary by state, certified appraisers and assessors of residential or commercial property usually need at least a bachelor's degree.

College courses in subjects such as economics, finance, mathematics, computer science, English, and business or real estate law can be useful for prospective appraisers and assessors.

Most states set education and experience requirements that assessors must meet in order to practice. A few states have no statewide requirements; instead, each locality sets the standards. In some localities, candidates may qualify with a high school diploma.

Assessors and appraisers tend to take the same courses for certification.

Training

Employers generally require candidates to take basic appraisal courses, complete long-term on-the-job training, and work enough hours to meet the requirements for licenses or certificates.

Licenses, Certifications, and Registrations

Federal law requires appraisers to have a state license or certification when working on federally related transactions, such as appraisals for loans made by federally insured banks and financial institutions. The Appraisal Foundation (TAF) offers information on appraisal licensing. There is no such federal requirement for assessors, although some states require certification. For state-specific requirements, applicants should contact their state board.

Real property appraisers usually value one property at a time, while assessors value many at once. However, both occupations use similar methods and techniques. As a result, assessors and appraisers tend to take the same courses for certification. In addition to passing a statewide examination, candidates must usually complete a set number of on-the-job hours.

The credential level determines what type of property a person may appraise. The four federal appraiser classifications are as follows:

- Licensed Trainee Appraiser
- Licensed Residential Appraiser
- Certified Residential Appraiser
- Certified General Appraiser

Many states offer a Licensed Trainee Appraiser credential to candidates working toward licensure or certification. Training programs vary by state, but they usually require candidates to take at least 75 hours of specified appraiser education before applying for a job as a trainee.

Many states offer the Licensed Residential Appraiser. With this license, a qualified person may appraise noncomplex one-to-four unit residences with a value of less than $1 million and complex one-to-four unit residences with a value of less than $250,000. A candidate must have the following qualifications to get this license:

- 30 semester hours of college-level education
- 150 hours of appraiser-qualifying education
- 2,000 hours of on-the-job training completed over at least 1 year

Being a Certified Residential Appraiser is the minimum requirement to appraise a one to four unit residential property with a loan amount over $250,000. A candidate must have the following qualifications to get this certificate:

- Bachelor's degree
- 200 hours of appraiser-specific qualifying education
- 2,500 hours of work experience completed over at least 2 years

Being a Certified General Appraiser permits a person to appraise real property of any type and any value. A candidate must have the following qualifications to get this certificate:

- Bachelor's degree
- 300 hours of appraiser-specific qualifying education
- 3,000 hours of work experience completed over at least 2½ years (1,500 hours must be in nonresidential appraisal work)

For all of these credentials, except the Trainee License credential, candidates must have the following qualifications:

- Have 15 hours of instruction on the Uniform Standards of Professional Appraisal Practice
- Pass an exam

Unlike appraisers, assessors have no federal requirement for certification. In states that mandate certification for assessors, the requirements are usually similar to those for appraisers. For example, the International Association of Assessing Officers (IAAO) offers the Certified Assessment Evaluator (CAE). This designation covers topics that include property valuation for tax purposes, property tax administration, and property tax policy. Applicants are required to have a bachelor's degree prior to obtaining the designation.

For those states that do not require certification for assessors, individual companies often require the candidate to take basic appraisal courses, complete on-the-job training, and meet the work-hours requirements for appraisal licenses or certificates. Many assessors also have a state appraiser license or credential.

Assessors tend to start working in an assessor's office that provides on-the-job training; smaller municipalities are often unable to provide this work experience. An alternate source of experience for aspiring assessors is working for a revaluation firm.

Both appraisers and assessors must take continuing education courses to keep the license or certification. Exact requirements vary by state and certification.

Important Qualities

Analytical skills. Appraisers and assessors of real estate use many sources of data when valuing a property. As a result, they must carefully research and analyze all factors before estimating a value and producing a final written report.

Customer-service skills. Because appraisers must regularly interact with clients, being polite and friendly is important. In addition, these characteristics may help expand future business opportunities.

Math skills. Accurately analyzing real estate data includes such steps as calculating square footage of land and building space, so workers must have good math skills.

Organizational skills. To successfully accomplish all the tasks related to appraising and assessing a property, appraisers and assessors of real estate need good organizational skills.

Problem-solving skills. Appraising or assessing a property's value may involve unexpected problems. The ability to develop

Appraisers and Assessors of Real Estate
Median annual wages, May 2019

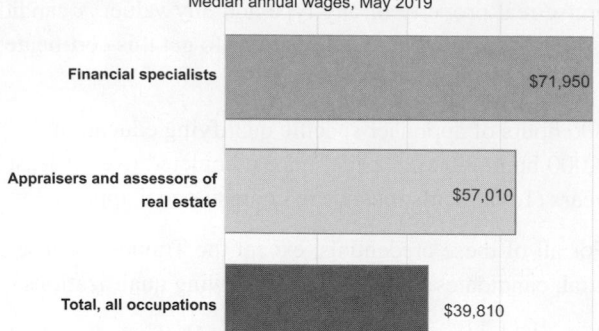

Financial specialists	$71,950
Appraisers and assessors of real estate	$57,010
Total, all occupations	$39,810

Note: All Occupations includes all occupations in the U.S. Economy.
Source: U.S. Bureau of Labor Statistics, Occupational Employment Statistics.

and apply an alternative solution is crucial to successfully completing the appraisal and report on time.

Time-management skills. Appraisers and assessors of real estate often work under time constraints, sometimes appraising many properties in a single day. As a result, managing time and meeting deadlines are important.

Pay

The median annual wage for appraisers and assessors of real estate was $57,010 in May 2019. The median wage is the wage at which half the workers in an occupation earned more than that amount and half earned less. The lowest 10 percent earned less than $31,160, and the highest 10 percent earned more than $104,540.

In May 2019, the median annual wages for appraisers and assessors of real estate in the top industries in which they worked were as follows:

Finance and insurance	$66,430
Real estate	57,290
Local government, excluding education and hospitals	53,540

Earnings for independent fee appraisers can vary significantly because they are paid fees on the basis of each appraisal.

Appraisers and assessors of real estate typically work full time during regular business hours. However, self-employed appraisers, often called *independent fee appraisers*, usually work more than 40 hours per week, because they often write reports during evenings and on weekends.

Job Outlook

Employment of appraisers and assessors of real estate is projected to grow 3 percent from 2019 to 2029, about as fast as the average for all occupations.

Demand for appraisal services is linked to the real estate market, which can fluctuate in the short term. Over the long term, employment growth will be driven by economic expansion and population increases—factors that generate demand for property.

Appraisers and Assessors of Real Estate
Percent change in employment, projected 2019-29

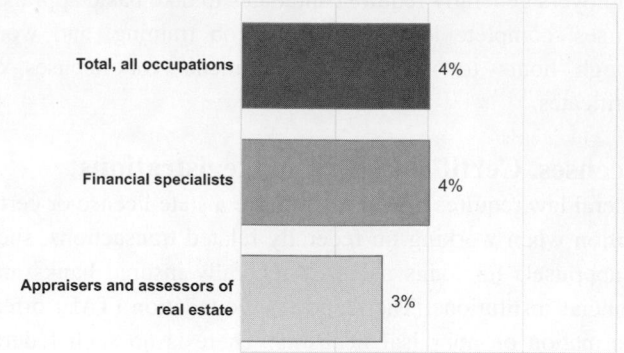

Total, all occupations	4%
Financial specialists	4%
Appraisers and assessors of real estate	3%

Note: All Occupations includes all occupations in the U.S. Economy.
Source: U.S. Bureau of Labor Statistics, Employment Projections program.

Greater use of mobile technology, which enables workers to appraise and assess properties more efficiently, will increase productivity. In addition, the increased use of automated valuation models to aid in the appraisal of property for mortgages might also increase productivity.

Job Prospects

Overall job opportunities are expected to be good. Employment opportunities should be best in areas with active real estate markets. Job prospects should be best for those who are able to switch specialties and appraise different types of properties.

Employment projections data for appraisers and assessors of real estate, 2019-29					
Occupational Title	SOC Code	Employment, 2019	Projected Employment, 2029	Change, 2019-29	
				Percent	Numeric
SOURCE: U.S. Bureau of Labor Statistics, Employment Projections program					
Property appraisers and assessors	13-2020	75,100	77,300	3	2,200

State & Area Data
Occupational Employment Statistics (OES)

The Occupational Employment Statistics (OES) program produces employment and wage estimates annually for over 800 occupations. These estimates are available for the nation as a whole, for individual states, and for metropolitan and nonmetropolitan areas.

Contacts for More Information

For more information about appraisers of real estate, visit
➤ American Society of Appraisers
➤ Appraisal Institute

For more information about assessors of real estate, visit
➤ International Association of Assessing Officers

For more information about licensure requirements for appraisers and assessors of real estate, visit
➤ The Appraisal Foundation

Budget Analysts

Summary

Quick Facts: Budget Analysts

2019 Median Pay	$76,540 per year
	$36.80 per hour
Typical Entry-Level Education	Bachelor's degree
Work Experience in a Related Occupation	None
On-the-job Training	None
Number of Jobs, 2019	55,400
Job Outlook, 2019-29..	3% (As fast as average)
Employment Change, 2019-29	1,900

What Budget Analysts Do

Budget analysts help public and private institutions organize their finances.

Work Environment

Budget analysts work in government agencies, universities, and private companies. Most work full time.

How to Become a Budget Analyst

A bachelor's degree is typically required to become a budget analyst. Courses in accounting, economics, and statistics are helpful.

Pay

The median annual wage for budget analysts was $76,540 in May 2019.

Job Outlook

Employment of budget analysts is projected to grow 3 percent from 2019 to 2029, about as fast as the average for all occupations. The demand for budget analysts should continue because

of the importance of their role in managing the allocation of funds in both governments and businesses.

State & Area Data

Explore resources for employment and wages by state and area for budget analysts.

What Budget Analysts Do

Budget analysts help public and private institutions organize their finances. They prepare budget reports and monitor institutional spending.

Duties

Budget analysts typically do the following:

- Work with program and project managers to develop the organization's budget
- Review managers' budget proposals for completeness, accuracy, and compliance with laws and other regulations
- Combine all the program and department budgets together into a consolidated organizational budget and review all funding requests for merit
- Explain their recommendations for funding requests to others in the organization, to legislators, and to the public
- Help the chief operations officer, agency head, or other top managers analyze proposed plans and find alternatives if the projected results are unsatisfactory
- Monitor organizational spending to ensure that it is within budget
- Inform program managers of the status and availability of funds
- Estimate future financial needs

Budget analysts advise various institutions—including governments, universities, and businesses—on how to organize their finances. They prepare annual and special reports and evaluate budget proposals. They analyze data to determine the costs and benefits of various programs, and they recommend

Budget analysts help public and private institutions organize their finances.

Budget analysts prepare budget reports and monitor spending.

funding levels based on their findings. Although government officials or top executives in a private company usually make the final decision on an organization's budget, they rely on the work of budget analysts to prepare the information for that decision.

Sometimes, budget analysts use cost–benefit analyses to review financial requests, assess program tradeoffs, and explore alternative funding methods. Budget analysts also may examine past budgets and research economic and financial developments that affect the organization's income and expenditures. Budget analysts may recommend cutting spending on particular programs or redistributing extra funds.

Throughout the year, budget analysts oversee spending to ensure compliance with the budget and determine whether changes to funding levels are needed for certain programs. Analysts also evaluate programs to determine whether they are producing the desired results.

In addition to providing technical analysis, budget analysts must communicate their recommendations effectively to officials within the organization. For example, if there is a difference between the approved budget and actual spending, budget analysts may write a report explaining the variations and recommend changes to reconcile the differences.

Budget analysts working in government may attend committee hearings to explain their recommendations to legislators. Occasionally, budget analysts may evaluate how well a program is doing, provide policy analysis, and draft budget-related legislation.

Work Environment

Budget analysts held about 55,400 jobs in 2019. The largest employers of budget analysts were as follows:

Federal government	22%
Educational services; state, local, and private	13
Professional, scientific, and technical services	11

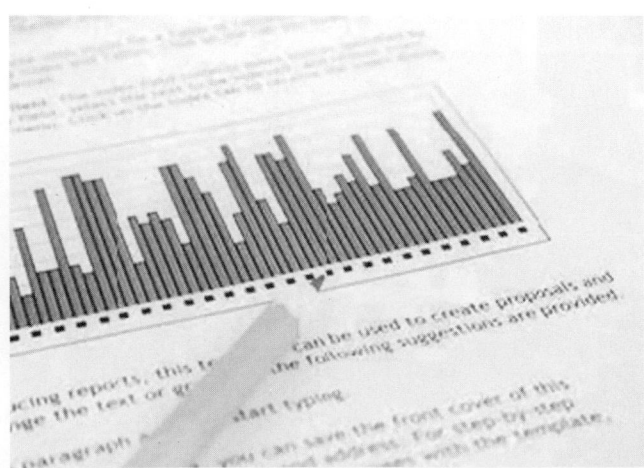

Budget analysts work in a variety of settings including government agencies, universities, and companies.

State government, excluding education and hospitals	11
Local government, excluding education and hospitals	11

Although budget analysts usually work in offices, some may travel to get budget details firsthand or to verify funding allocations.

Work Schedules

Most budget analysts work full time, and overtime is sometimes required during final reviews of budgets. The pressures of deadlines and tight work schedules can be stressful.

How to Become a Budget Analyst

A bachelor's degree is typically required to become a budget analyst. Courses in accounting, economics, and statistics are helpful.

Education

Employers generally require budget analysts to have at least a bachelor's degree. Because developing a budget requires strong numerical and analytical skills, courses in accounting, economics, and statistics are helpful. Federal, state, and local governments have varying requirements, but usually require a

Budget analysts must present technical information in writing that is understandable for the intended audience.

bachelor's degree in one of many areas, such as accounting, finance, business, public administration, economics, statistics, political science, or sociology.

Sometimes, budget-related or finance-related work experience can be substituted for formal education.

Licenses, Certifications, and Registrations

Government budget analysts may earn the Certified Government Financial Manager credential from the Association of Government Accountants. To earn this certification, candidates must have a minimum of a bachelor's degree, 24 credit hours of study in financial management, and 2 years of professional-level experience in governmental financial management. They must also pass a series of exams. To keep the certification, budget analysts must take 80 hours of continuing education every 2 years.

Important Qualities

Analytical skills. Budget analysts must be able to process a variety of information, evaluate costs and benefits, and solve complex problems.

Communication skills. Budget analysts need strong communication skills because they often have to explain and defend their analyses and recommendations in meetings and legislative committee hearings.

Detail oriented. Creating an efficient budget requires careful analysis of each budget item.

Math skills. Most budget analysts need math skills and should be able to use certain software, including spreadsheets, database functions, and financial analysis programs.

Writing skills. Budget analysts must present technical information in writing that is understandable to the intended audience.

The median annual wage for budget analysts was $76,540 in May 2019. The median wage is the wage at which half the workers in an occupation earned more than that amount and half earned less. The lowest 10 percent earned less than $50,230, and the highest 10 percent earned more than $116,510.

In May 2019, the median annual wages for budget analysts in the top industries in which they worked were as follows:

Federal government	$83,070
Professional, scientific, and technical services	82,830
Local government, excluding education and hospitals	72,880
Educational services; state, local, and private	67,760
State government, excluding education and hospitals	67,230

Most budget analysts work full time, and overtime is sometimes required during final reviews of budgets. The pressures of deadlines and tight work schedules can be stressful.

Job Outlook

Employment of budget analysts is projected to grow 3 percent from 2019 to 2029, about as fast as the average for all occupations.

Demand for efficient use of public funds at the state and local levels will lead to continued demand for budget analysts. Although many states are facing budget shortfalls, employment of these workers should remain steady. Because budget analysts are responsible for managing the allocation of resources, the need for these workers remains even during times of tight budgets.

Job Prospects

Since this occupation has relatively few job openings due to separations, jobseekers are likely to face competition for the limited number of budget analyst positions.

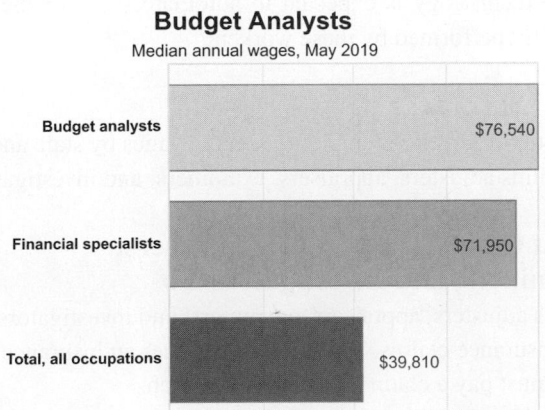

Budget Analysts
Median annual wages, May 2019

- Budget analysts: $76,540
- Financial specialists: $71,950
- Total, all occupations: $39,810

Note: All Occupations includes all occupations in the U.S. Economy.
Source: U.S. Bureau of Labor Statistics, Occupational Employment Statistics.

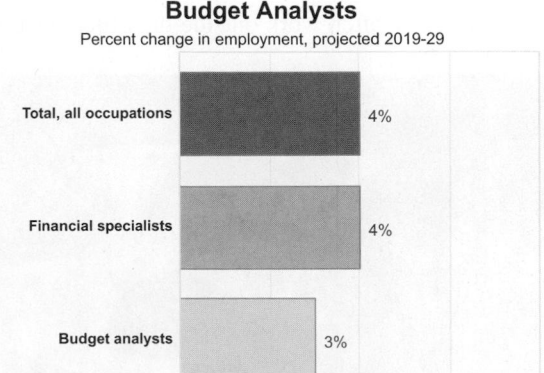

Budget Analysts
Percent change in employment, projected 2019-29

- Total, all occupations: 4%
- Financial specialists: 4%
- Budget analysts: 3%

Note: All Occupations includes all occupations in the U.S. Economy.
Source: U.S. Bureau of Labor Statistics, Employment Projections program.

Employment projections data for budget analysts, 2019-29					
Occupational Title	SOC Code	Employment, 2019	Projected Employment, 2029	Change, 2019-29	
				Percent	Numeric
SOURCE: U.S. Bureau of Labor Statistics, Employment Projections program					
Budget analysts	13-2031	55,400	57,300	3	1,900

State & Area Data
Occupational Employment Statistics (OES)

The Occupational Employment Statistics (OES) program produces employment and wage estimates annually for over 800 occupations.

These estimates are available for the nation as a whole, for individual states, and for metropolitan and nonmetropolitan areas.

Contacts for More Information

For information about the Government Financial Manager certification, visit
➤ Association of Government Accountants

Claims Adjusters, Appraisers, Examiners, and Investigators

Summary

Quick Facts: Claims Adjusters, Appraisers, Examiners, and Investigators

2019 Median Pay	$66,540 per year $31.99 per hour
Typical Entry-Level Education	See below
Work Experience in a Related Occupation	None
On-the-job Training	See below
Number of Jobs, 2019	348,800
Job Outlook, 2019-29	-6% (Decline)
Employment Change, 2019-29	-22,000

What Claims Adjusters, Appraisers, Examiners, and Investigators Do

Claims adjusters, appraisers, examiners, and investigators evaluate insurance claims.

Work Environment

Most claims adjusters, appraisers, examiners, and investigators work full time. They often work outside the office, inspecting

Claims adjusters, appraisers, examiners, and investigators evaluate insurance claims.

properties on which insurance claims have been made, such as damaged buildings and automobiles.

How to Become a Claims Adjuster, Appraiser, Examiner, or Investigator

A high school diploma or equivalent is typically required for a person to work as an entry-level claims adjuster, examiner, or investigator, although some positions may require a bachelor's degree or insurance-related work experience. Auto damage appraisers typically have either a postsecondary nondegree award or previous work experience in identifying and estimating the cost of automotive repair.

Pay

The median annual wage for claims adjusters, examiners, and investigators was $66,790 in May 2019.

The median annual wage for insurance appraisers, auto damage was $63,270 in May 2019.

Job Outlook

Employment of claims adjusters, appraisers, examiners, and investigators is projected to decline 6 percent from 2019 to 2029. Technology is expected to automate some of the tasks currently performed by these workers.

State & Area Data

Explore resources for employment and wages by state and area for claims adjusters, appraisers, examiners, and investigators.

What Claims Adjusters, Appraisers, Examiners, and Investigators Do

Claims adjusters, appraisers, examiners, and investigators evaluate insurance claims. They decide whether an insurance company must pay a claim and if so, how much.

Duties

Claims adjusters, appraisers, examiners, and investigators typically do the following:

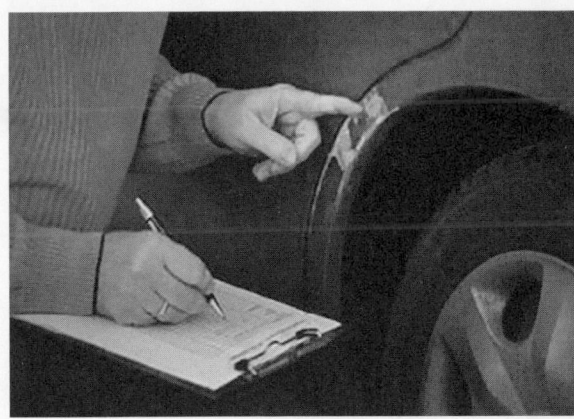

Claims adjusters inspect property damage to determine how much the company should pay for the loss.

- Investigate, evaluate, and settle insurance claims
- Determine whether the insurance policy covers the loss claimed
- Decide the appropriate amount the insurance company should pay
- Ensure that claims are not fraudulent
- Contact claimants' doctors or employers to get additional information on questionable claims
- Confer with legal counsel on claims when needed
- Negotiate settlements
- Authorize payments

Claims adjusters, appraisers, examiners, and investigators have varying duties, depending on the type of insurance company they work for. They must know a lot about what their company insures. For example, workers in property and casualty insurance must know housing and construction costs in order to properly evaluate damage from floods or fires. Workers in health insurance must be able to determine which types of treatments are medically necessary and which are questionable.

Adjusters inspect property damage or personal injury claims to determine how much the insurance company should pay for the loss. They might inspect a home, a business, or an automobile.

Adjusters interview the claimant and witnesses, inspect the property, and do additional research, such as look at police reports. They may consult with other workers, such as accountants, architects, construction workers, engineers, lawyers, and physicians, who can offer a more expert evaluation of a claim.

Adjusters gather information—including photographs and statements, either written or recorded on audio or video—and put together a report for claims examiners to evaluate. When the examiner approves the claim, the adjuster negotiates with the policyholder and settles the claim.

If the claimant contests the outcome of the claim or the settlement, adjusters work with attorneys and expert witnesses to defend the insurer's position.

Some claims adjusters work as *public adjusters*. Often, they are hired by claimants who prefer not to rely on the insurance company's adjuster. The goal of adjusters working for insurance companies is to save as much money for the company as possible. The goal of a public adjuster working for a claimant is to get the highest possible amount paid to the claimant. They are paid a percentage of the settled claim.

Appraisers estimate the cost or value of an insured item. Most appraisers who work for insurance companies and independent adjusting firms are *auto damage appraisers*. They inspect damaged vehicles after an accident and estimate the cost of repairs. This information then goes to the adjuster, who puts the estimated cost of repairs into the settlement.

Claims examiners review claims after they are submitted to ensure claimants and adjusters followed proper guidelines. They may assist adjusters with complicated claims or when, for example, a natural disaster occurs and the volume of claims increases.

Examiners who work for health insurance companies review health-related claims to see whether the costs are reasonable, given the diagnosis. After they review the claim, they authorize appropriate payment, deny the claim, or refer the claim to an investigator.

Examiners who work for life insurance companies review the causes of death and pay particular attention to accidents, because most life insurance companies pay additional benefits if a death is accidental. Examiners also may review new applications for life insurance policies to make sure that the applicants have no serious illnesses that would make them a high risk to insure.

Insurance investigators handle claims in which the company suspects fraudulent or criminal activity such as arson, staged accidents, or unnecessary medical treatments. The severity of insurance fraud cases varies, from overstated claims of damage to vehicles to complicated fraud rings. Investigators often do surveillance work. For example, in the case of a fraudulent workers' compensation claim, an investigator may covertly watch the claimant to see if he or she does anything that would be suspicious based on injuries stated in the claim.

Work Environment

Claims adjusters, examiners, and investigators held about 332,900 jobs in 2019. The largest employers of claims adjusters, examiners, and investigators were as follows:

Direct insurance (except life, health, and medical) carriers	30%
Agencies, brokerages, and other insurance related activities	27
Government	18
Direct health and medical insurance carriers	9
Administrative and support services	2

Workers who inspect damaged buildings must be wary of potential hazards, such as collapsed roofs and floors, as well as weakened structures.

Insurance appraisers, auto damage held about 15,900 jobs in 2019. The largest employers of insurance appraisers, auto damage were as follows:

Agencies, brokerages, and other insurance related activities	28%
Self-employed workers	3
Management of companies and enterprises	1
Professional, scientific, and technical services	0

Claims adjusters and examiners spend time in offices reviewing documents and conducting research. They work outside when examining damaged property. Appraisers and investigators work outside more often, inspecting damaged buildings and automobiles and conducting surveillance. Auto damage appraisers spend much of their time at automotive body shops estimating vehicle damage costs.

Workers who inspect damaged buildings must be wary of potential hazards, such as collapsed roofs and floors, as well as weakened structures.

Work Schedules

Most claims adjusters, appraisers, examiners, and investigators work full time. However, their work schedules vary.

Adjusters often arrange their work schedules to accommodate evening and weekend appointments with clients. This requirement sometimes results in adjusters working irregular schedules, especially when they have a lot of claims to review.

Insurance investigators often work irregular schedules because of the need to conduct surveillance and contact people who are not available during normal business hours. Early morning, evening, and weekend work is common.

In contrast, auto damage appraisers typically work regular hours and rarely work on weekends.

At the beginning of their careers, claims adjusters, appraisers, examiners, and investigators work on small claims, under the supervision of an experienced worker.

How to Become a Claims Adjuster, Appraiser, Examiner, or Investigator

A high school diploma or equivalent is typically required for a person to work as an entry-level claims adjuster, examiner, or investigator, although some positions may require a bachelor's degree or insurance-related work experience. Auto damage appraisers typically have either a postsecondary nondegree award or previous work experience in identifying and estimating the cost of automotive repair.

Education

A high school diploma or equivalent is typically required for a person to work as an entry-level claims adjuster or examiner. However, employers sometimes prefer to hire applicants who have a bachelor's degree or some insurance-related work experience.

For investigator jobs, a high school diploma or equivalent is the typical education requirement. Some insurance companies prefer to hire people trained as law enforcement officers or private investigators, because these workers have good interviewing and interrogation skills.

Auto damage appraisers typically have either a postsecondary nondegree award or experience working in an auto repair shop, identifying and estimating the cost of automotive repair. Many vocational schools and some community colleges offer programs in auto body repair and teach students how to estimate the cost of repairing damaged vehicles.

Training

At the beginning of their careers, claims adjusters, examiners, and investigators work on small claims under the supervision of an experienced worker. As they learn more about claims investigation and settlement, they are assigned larger, more complex claims.

Auto damage appraisers typically get on-the-job training, which may last several months. This training usually involves working under the supervision of a more experienced appraiser while estimating damage costs, until the employer decides that the trainee is ready to do estimates on his or her own.

Licenses, Certifications, and Registrations

Licensing requirements for claims adjusters, appraisers, examiners, and investigators vary by state. Some states have few requirements; others require either completing prelicensing education or receiving a satisfactory score on a licensing exam (or both).

In some states, claims adjusters employed by insurance companies do not have to become licensed themselves because they can work under the company license.

Public adjusters may need to meet separate or additional requirements.

Some states that require licensing also require a certain number of continuing education credits per year to renew the license. Federal and state laws and court decisions affect how claims must be handled and what insurance policies can and must cover. Examiners working on life and health claims must stay up to date on new medical procedures and the latest prescription drugs. Examiners working on auto claims must be familiar with new car models and the most recent repair techniques. In order to fulfill their continuing education requirements, workers can attend classes or workshops, write articles for claims publications, or give lectures and presentations.

Important Qualities

Analytical skills. Adjusters and examiners must each evaluate whether the insurance company is obligated to pay a claim and determine the amount to pay. Adjusters must carefully consider various pieces of information to reach a decision.

Communication skills. Claims adjusters and investigators must get information from a wide range of people, including claimants, witnesses, and medical experts. They must know the right questions to ask in order to gather the information they need.

Detail oriented. Adjusters, appraisers, examiners, and investigators must carefully review documents and damaged property, because small details can have large financial consequences.

Interpersonal skills. Adjusters, examiners, and investigators often meet with claimants and others who may be upset by the situation that requires a claim or by the settlement the company is offering. These workers must be understanding, yet firm with their company's policies.

Math skills. Appraisers must be able to calculate property damage.

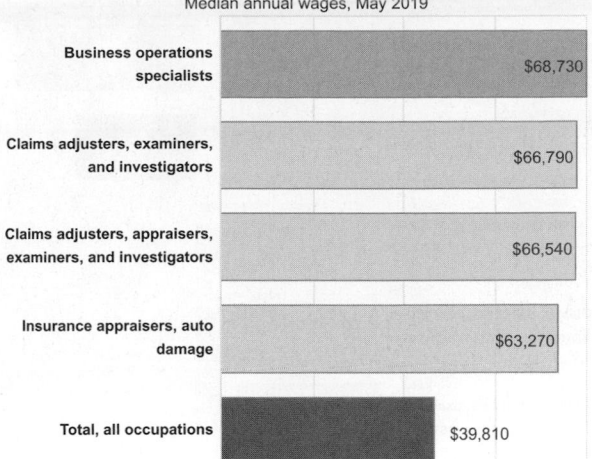

Claims Adjusters, Appraisers, Examiners, and Investigators

Median annual wages, May 2019

Business operations specialists	$68,730
Claims adjusters, examiners, and investigators	$66,790
Claims adjusters, appraisers, examiners, and investigators	$66,540
Insurance appraisers, auto damage	$63,270
Total, all occupations	$39,810

Note: All Occupations includes all occupations in the U.S. Economy.
Source: U.S. Bureau of Labor Statistics, Occupational Employment Statistics.

Pay

The median annual wage for claims adjusters, examiners, and investigators was $66,790 in May 2019. The median wage is the wage at which half the workers in an occupation earned more than that amount and half earned less. The lowest 10 percent earned less than $41,100, and the highest 10 percent earned more than $100,400.

The median annual wage for insurance appraisers, auto damage was $63,270 in May 2019. The lowest 10 percent earned less than $44,430, and the highest 10 percent earned more than $93,720.

In May 2019, the median annual wages for claims adjusters, examiners, and investigators in the top industries in which they worked were as follows:

Government	$73,470
Direct insurance (except life, health, and medical) carriers	66,690
Agencies, brokerages, and other insurance related activities	64,890
Administrative and support services	60,450
Direct health and medical insurance carriers	58,560

In May 2019, the median annual wages for insurance appraisers, auto damage in the top industries in which they worked were as follows:

Management of companies and enterprises	$63,690
Professional, scientific, and technical services	61,440
Agencies, brokerages, and other insurance related activities	61,060

Claims Adjusters, Appraisers, Examiners, and Investigators

Percent change in employment, projected 2019-29

Note: All Occupations includes all occupations in the U.S. Economy.
Source: U.S. Bureau of Labor Statistics, Employment Projections program.

Most claims adjusters, appraisers, examiners, and investigators work full time. However, their work schedules vary.

Adjusters often arrange their work schedules to accommodate evening and weekend appointments with clients. This requirement sometimes results in adjusters working irregular schedules, especially when they have a lot of claims to review.

Insurance investigators often work irregular schedules because of the need to conduct surveillance and contact people who are not available during normal business hours. Early morning, evening, and weekend work is common.

In contrast, auto damage appraisers typically work regular hours and rarely work on weekends.

Job Outlook

Overall employment of claims adjusters, appraisers, examiners, and investigators is projected to decline 6 percent from 2019 to 2029.

Technology is expected to automate some of the tasks currently performed by these workers. For example, computer software can evaluate photographs of damaged property and calculate an estimated claim amount. In addition, data collection and processing speed will increase, which will improve efficiency and make workers more productive.

Demand for these workers should stem primarily from the growth of the health insurance industry. Rising medical costs may result in a greater need for claims examiners to carefully review a growing number of medical claims. An increase in the number of claims being made by a growing elderly population also should spur demand for health insurance claims adjusters and examiners.

The number of natural disasters, such as floods and fires, influences demand for claims adjusters in property and casualty insurance. Future increases in the number of natural disasters could result in some employment growth for claims adjusters in the field.

Job Prospects

Job opportunities for claims adjusters and examiners should be best in firms providing services related to insurance, such as insurance claims adjusting companies. In addition, prospects for claims adjusters in property and casualty insurance will likely be best in areas susceptible to natural disasters. These areas include the Gulf Coast, which can have a large number of hurricanes, and the West Coast, which is vulnerable to wildfires.

As technology continues to affect this work, those who are familiar and comfortable with computers and information technology should also have better prospects.

Employment projections data for claims adjusters, appraisers, examiners, and investigators, 2019-29

Occupational Title	SOC Code	Employment, 2019	Projected Employment, 2029	Change, 2019-29	
				Percent	Numeric
SOURCE: U.S. Bureau of Labor Statistics, Employment Projections program					
Claims adjusters, appraisers, examiners, and investigators	13-1030	348,800	326,800	-6	-22,000
Claims adjusters, examiners, and investigators	13-1031	332,900	311,500	-6	-21,400
Insurance appraisers, auto damage	13-1032	15,900	15,300	-4	-600

State & Area Data
Occupational Employment Statistics (OES)

The Occupational Employment Statistics (OES) program produces employment and wage estimates annually for over 800 occupations. These estimates are available for the nation as a whole, for individual states, and for metropolitan and nonmetropolitan areas.

Contacts for More Information

For more information about insurance, visit
➤ The Institutes
➤ International Claim Association
➤ National Association of Public Insurance Adjusters

Compensation, Benefits, and Job Analysis Specialists

Summary

Quick Facts: Compensation, Benefits, and Job Analysis Specialists

2019 Median Pay	$64,560 per year $31.04 per hour
Typical Entry-Level Education	Bachelor's degree
Work Experience in a Related Occupation	Less than 5 years
On-the-job Training	None
Number of Jobs, 2019	94,400
Job Outlook, 2019-29	8% (Much faster than average)
Employment Change, 2019-29	7,500

What Compensation, Benefits, and Job Analysis Specialists Do

Compensation, benefits, and job analysis specialists conduct an organization's compensation and benefits programs.

Work Environment

Compensation, benefits, and job analysis specialists work in nearly every industry. They typically work in offices, and most work full time during regular business hours.

How to Become a Compensation, Benefits, and Job Analysis Specialist

Compensation, benefits, and job analysis specialists need a combination of a bachelor's degree and related work experience.

Pay

The median annual wage for compensation, benefits, and job analysis specialists was $64,560 in May 2019.

Job Outlook

Employment of compensation, benefits, and job analysis specialists is projected to grow 8 percent from 2019 to 2029, much faster than the average for all occupations. Job prospects should be best for candidates with a bachelor's degree, work experience performing compensation analysis or benefits administration, and related human resources work.

State & Area Data

Explore resources for employment and wages by state and area for compensation, benefits, and job analysis specialists.

What Compensation, Benefits, and Job Analysis Specialists Do

Compensation, benefits, and job analysis specialists conduct an organization's compensation and benefits programs. They also evaluate position descriptions to determine details such as classification and salary.

Duties

Compensation, benefits, and job analysis specialists typically do the following:

- Research compensation and benefits policies and plans
- Use data and cost analyses to compare compensation and benefits plans
- Evaluate position descriptions to determine classification and salary
- Ensure that the company complies with federal and state laws
- Design and prepare reports summarizing research and analysis
- Present recommendations to other human resources managers

Some specialists perform tasks within all areas of compensation, benefits, and job analysis. Others specialize in a specific area.

Specialists may present their analysis and recommendations to management.

Specialists research compensation and benefits policies and plans.

Compensation specialists assess the organization's pay structure. They research compensation trends and review surveys to determine how their organization's pay compares with that of other organizations in a particular industry and region. They often perform complex data or cost analyses to evaluate compensation policies. They also ensure that the organization's pay practices comply with federal and state laws and regulations, such as workers' compensation, minimum wage, overtime, and equal pay laws.

Benefits specialists administer the organization's benefits programs, which include retirement plans, leave policies, wellness programs, and insurance policies, such as health, life, and disability insurance. They research and analyze benefits plans, policies, and programs, and make recommendations based on their analysis. They frequently monitor government regulations, legislation, and benefits trends to ensure that their programs are current, legal, and competitive. They also work closely with insurance brokers and benefits carriers and manage the enrollment, renewal, and delivery of benefits to the organization's employees.

Job analysis specialists, also known as *position classifiers*, evaluate positions by writing or assigning job descriptions, determining position classifications, and preparing salary scales. When an organization introduces a new job or reviews existing jobs, specialists must research and make recommendations to managers on the status, description, classification, and salary of those jobs.

Work Environment

Compensation, benefits, and job analysis specialists held about 94,400 jobs in 2019. The largest employers of compensation, benefits, and job analysis specialists were as follows:

Professional, scientific, and technical services 17%
Insurance carriers and related activities 15
Management of companies and enterprises 12
Local government, excluding education and
   hospitals 8
Healthcare and social assistance 7

Compensation, benefits, and job analysis specialists work in nearly every industry.

They typically work in offices.

Work Schedules

Nearly all compensation, benefits, and job analysis specialists work full time during regular business hours.

How to Become a Compensation, Benefits, and Job Analysis Specialist

Compensation, benefits, and job analysis specialists need a combination of a bachelor's degree and related work experience.

Education

Employers typically require that compensation, benefits, and job analysis specialists have a bachelor's degree. Many specialists have a degree in human resources, business administration, finance, communication, or a related field. Some employers

Specialists typically work in offices, briefing workers about benefits and overseeing the enrollment process.

Specialists typically need previous work experience in human resources occupations.

may accept additional related work experience in lieu of a degree.

Not all colleges and universities offer an undergraduate degree in human resources, but many offer courses in human resources management, compensation analysis, and benefits administration. Students with a background in other disciplines may benefit from taking courses in business, management, finance, and accounting.

Work Experience in a Related Occupation

Compensation, benefits, and job analysis specialists must have related work experience. Employers commonly require that the experience includes performing compensation analysis, benefits administration, or general human resources work. Experience in related fields such as finance, insurance, or business administration, also may be beneficial. Some workers may gain this experience through internships. However, most gain experience from working in human resources occupations, such as human resources specialists.

Licenses, Certifications, and Registrations

Although certification is not required, it can demonstrate professional expertise. Some employers prefer to hire certified candidates, but many employers will have their employees become certified after they are already working. Certification programs often require several years of related work experience in order to qualify for the credential.

Many associations for human resources workers offer classes to enhance the skills of their members. Some associations, including the International Foundation of Employee Benefit Plans and WorldatWork, offer certification programs that specialize in compensation and benefits. Others, including the HR Certification Institute and the Society for Human Resource Management, offer general human resources credentials.

Advancement

Compensation, benefits, and job analysis specialists may advance to a compensation and benefits manager or a human resources manager position. Specialists typically need several years of work experience to advance.

Important Qualities

Analytical skills. Compensation, benefits, and job analysis specialists perform data or cost analyses to form logical conclusions related to wages and benefits. They also need to pay attention to the details of contracts and laws.

Business skills. Specialists must understand basic finance and accounting. They help set initial wages and benefits packages for new employees.

Communication skills. Specialists often work with employees throughout their organization to provide information on compensation and benefits. They may give presentations or

Compensation, Benefits, and Job Analysis Specialists
Median annual wages, May 2019

Note: All Occupations includes all occupations in the U.S. Economy.
Source: U.S. Bureau of Labor Statistics, Occupational Employment Statistics.

advise managers or employees about compensation policies or benefit plans.

Critical-thinking skills. Specialists evaluate job positions, salary scales, promotion practices, and other compensation and benefits policies.

Pay

The median annual wage for compensation, benefits, and job analysis specialists was $64,560 in May 2019. The median wage is the wage at which half the workers in an occupation earned more than that amount and half earned less. The lowest 10 percent earned less than $40,140, and the highest 10 percent earned more than $105,600.

In May 2019, the median annual wages for compensation, benefits, and job analysis specialists in the top industries in which they worked were as follows:

Professional, scientific, and technical services	$69,090
Local government, excluding education and hospitals	68,550
Management of companies and enterprises	67,340
Insurance carriers and related activities	63,060
Healthcare and social assistance	59,020

Nearly all compensation, benefits, and job analysis specialists work full time during regular business hours.

Job Outlook

Employment of compensation, benefits, and job analysis specialists is projected to grow 8 percent from 2019 to 2029, much faster than the average for all occupations.

Organizations will continue to hire benefits specialists to analyze, select, and update their benefits policies. Employee wellness programs are a popular way to reduce healthcare costs. Organizations will need benefits specialists to design, evaluate, and administer these programs.

Compensation, Benefits, and Job Analysis Specialists

Percent change in employment, projected 2019-29

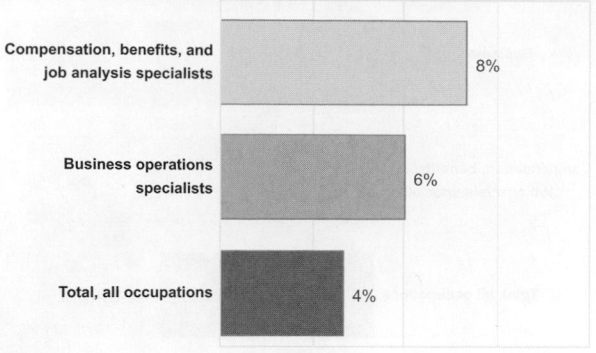

Compensation, benefits, and job analysis specialists — 8%

Business operations specialists — 6%

Total, all occupations — 4%

Note: All Occupations includes all occupations in the U.S. Economy.
Source: U.S. Bureau of Labor Statistics, Employment Projections program.

In addition, organizations must offer competitive compensation packages to attract and keep highly qualified workers. To allocate their compensation funds effectively, many organizations are using strategies such as pay-for-performance plans, which may include bonuses, paid leave, or other incentives as part of the compensation package. Organizations will need specialists to analyze these compensation policies and plans and to ensure that they are both competitive and cost effective.

Job Prospects

Job prospects should be best for candidates with a bachelor's degree, work experience performing compensation analysis or benefits administration, and related human resources work.

Employment projections data for compensation, benefits, and job analysis specialists, 2019-29					
Occupational Title	SOC Code	Employment, 2019	Projected Employment, 2029	Change, 2019-29	
				Percent	Numeric
Compensation, benefits, and job analysis specialists	13-1141	94,400	101,800	8	7,500

State & Area Data

Occupational Employment Statistics (OES)

The Occupational Employment Statistics (OES) program produces employment and wage estimates annually for over 800 occupations. These estimates are available for the nation as a whole, for individual states, and for metropolitan and nonmetropolitan areas.

Contacts for More Information

For more information about compensation, benefits, and job analysis specialists, including certification, visit
➤ International Foundation of Employee Benefit Plans
➤ WorldatWork

For information about human resources careers, visit
➤ Society for Human Resource Management

For more information about human resources certifications, visit
➤ HR Certification Institute

Cost Estimators

Summary

Quick Facts: Cost Estimators

2019 Median Pay	$65,250 per year $31.37 per hour
Typical Entry-Level Education	Bachelor's degree
Work Experience in a Related Occupation	None
On-the-job Training	Moderate-term on-the-job training
Number of Jobs, 2019	214,200
Job Outlook, 2019-29	-1% (Decline)
Employment Change, 2019-29	-3,200

What Cost Estimators Do

Cost estimators collect and analyze data in order to estimate the time, money, materials, and labor required to make a product or provide a service.

Work Environment

Cost estimators work mostly in offices, and some estimators also visit construction sites and factory assembly lines. Most work full time.

How to Become a Cost Estimator

Most cost estimators need a bachelor's degree, although some workers with several years of experience in construction may qualify without a bachelor's degree.

Pay

The median annual wage for cost estimators was $65,250 in May 2019.

Job Outlook

Employment of cost estimators is projected to decline 1 percent from 2019 to 2029. Cost estimation software is improving the productivity of these workers, requiring fewer estimators to perform the same amount of work.

Cost estimators prepare estimates for the time, money, materials, and labor required to manufacture a product.

State & Area Data

Explore resources for employment and wages by state and area for cost estimators.

What Cost Estimators Do

Cost estimators collect and analyze data in order to estimate the time, money, materials, and labor required to manufacture a product, construct a building, or provide a service. They generally specialize in a particular product or industry.

Duties

Cost estimators typically do the following:

- Identify factors affecting costs, such as production time, materials, and labor
- Read blueprints and technical documents in order to prepare estimates
- Collaborate with engineers, architects, clients, and contractors
- Calculate, analyze, and adjust estimates
- Recommend ways to reduce costs

Cost estimators often collaborate with engineers.

- Work with sales teams to prepare estimates and bids for clients
- Maintain records of estimated and actual costs

Accurately estimating the costs of construction and manufacturing projects is vital to the survival of businesses. Cost estimators provide managers with the information they need in order to submit competitive contract bids or price products appropriately.

Estimators analyze production processes to determine how much time, money, and labor a project needs. Their estimates account for many factors, including allowances for wasted material, bad weather, shipping delays, and other variables that can increase costs and lower profits.

In building construction, cost estimators use software to simulate the construction process and evaluate the costs of design choices. They often consult databases and their own records to compare the costs of similar projects.

The following are examples of types of cost estimators:

Construction cost estimators prepare estimates for buildings, roads, and other construction projects. They may calculate the total cost of building a bridge or commercial shopping center, or they may calculate the cost of just one component, such as the foundation. They identify costs of elements such as raw materials and labor, and they may set a timeline for how long they expect the project to take. Although many work directly for construction firms, some work for contractors and engineering firms.

Manufacturing cost estimators calculate the costs of developing, producing, or redesigning a company's goods or services. For example, a cost estimator working for a home appliance manufacturer may determine a new dishwasher's production costs, allowing managers to make production decisions.

Other workers, such as operations research analysts and construction managers, may also estimate costs in the course of their usual duties.

Work Environment

Cost estimators held about 214,200 jobs in 2019. The largest employers of cost estimators were as follows:

Specialty trade contractors	36%
Construction of buildings	17
Manufacturing	13
Automotive repair and maintenance	7
Heavy and civil engineering construction	6

Cost estimators work mostly in offices, and some estimators visit construction sites and factory assembly lines during the course of their work.

Work Schedules

Most cost estimators work full time and some work more than 40 hours per week.

Cost estimators may visit construction sites to gather information.

How to Become a Cost Estimator

Most cost estimators need a bachelor's degree, although some workers with several years of experience in construction may qualify without a bachelor's degree.

Education

Employers generally prefer candidates who have a bachelor's degree.

Construction cost estimators typically need a bachelor's degree in an industry-related field, such as construction management or engineering. Manufacturing cost estimators typically need a bachelor's degree in engineering, business, or finance.

Training

Most cost estimators receive on-the-job training, which may include instruction in cost estimation techniques and software, as well as industry-specific software, such as building information modeling (BIM) and computer-aided design (CAD) software.

Work Experience in a Related Occupation

Some employers prefer that construction cost estimators, particularly those without a bachelor's degree, have previous work

Cost estimators learn to use specialized cost estimating software.

experience in the construction industry. Some construction cost estimators become qualified solely through extensive work experience.

Important Qualities

Analytical skills. Cost estimators consider and evaluate different construction and manufacturing methods and options to determine the most cost-effective solution that meets the required specifications.

Communication skills. Cost estimators write comprehensive reports, which often help managers make production decisions.

Detail oriented. Cost estimators must pay attention to details because minor changes can greatly affect the overall cost of a project or product.

Math skills. Cost estimators calculate labor, material, and equipment cost estimates for construction projects. They use software, such as spreadsheets and databases, and they need excellent math skills to calculate these estimates accurately.

Time-management skills. Cost estimators often work on fixed deadlines, so they must plan in advance and work efficiently.

Pay

The median annual wage for cost estimators was $65,250 in May 2019. The median wage is the wage at which half the workers in an occupation earned more than that amount and half earned less. The lowest 10 percent earned less than $39,380, and the highest 10 percent earned more than $111,350.

In May 2019, the median annual wages for cost estimators in the top industries in which they worked were as follows:

Heavy and civil engineering construction...........	$75,890
Construction of buildings....................................	69,240
Specialty trade contractors.................................	65,650
Manufacturing..	62,630
Automotive repair and maintenance	57,780

Cost Estimators

Median annual wages, May 2019

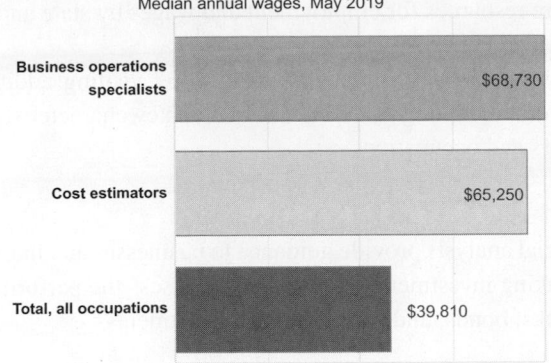

Note: All Occupations includes all occupations in the U.S. Economy.
Source: U.S. Bureau of Labor Statistics, Occupational Employment Statistics.

Most cost estimators work full time and some work more than 40 hours per week.

Job Outlook

Employment of cost estimators is projected to decline 1 percent from 2019 to 2029.

Cost estimation software is improving the productivity of these workers, requiring fewer estimators to perform the same amount of work. This will reduce employment demand and lead to job losses for these workers.

However, technology will not eliminate this work entirely, and there will continue to be some demand for cost estimators because companies need accurate cost projections to ensure that their products and services are profitable.

Job Prospects

Despite a projected employment decline, about 17,500 openings for cost estimators are projected each year, on average, over the decade.

These openings are expected to result from the need to replace workers who transfer to different occupations or exit the labor force, such as to retire.

Knowledge of building information modeling (BIM) and computer-aided design (CAD) software may improve job prospects, especially for those seeking employment in construction.

Cost Estimators

Percent change in employment, projected 2019-29

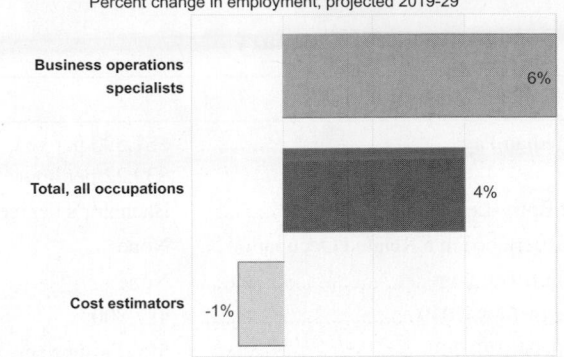

Note: All Occupations includes all occupations in the U.S. Economy.
Source: U.S. Bureau of Labor Statistics, Employment Projections program.

Jobs of cost estimators working in construction, like those of workers in many other trades in the construction industry, are sensitive to changing economic conditions.

Employment projections data for cost estimators, 2019-29					
Occupational Title	SOC Code	Employment, 2019	Projected Employment, 2029	Change, 2019-29	
				Percent	Numeric
SOURCE: U.S. Bureau of Labor Statistics, Employment Projections program					
Cost estimators	13-1051	214,200	211,000	-1	-3,200

State & Area Data
Occupational Employment Statistics (OES)

The Occupational Employment Statistics (OES) program produces employment and wage estimates annually for over 800 occupations. These estimates are available for the nation as a whole, for individual states, and for metropolitan and nonmetropolitan areas.

Contacts for More Information

For more information about cost estimators, visit
➤ American Society of Professional Estimators
➤ Association for the Advancement of Cost Engineering International (AACE International)
➤ International Cost Estimating and Analysis Association

Financial Analysts

Summary

Quick Facts: Financial Analysts

2019 Median Pay	$81,590 per year
	$39.22 per hour
Typical Entry-Level Education	Bachelor's degree
Work Experience in a Related Occupation	None
On-the-job Training	None
Number of Jobs, 2019....................................	487,800
Job Outlook, 2019-29....................................	5% (Faster than average)
Employment Change, 2019-29	26,800

What Financial Analysts Do

Financial analysts provide guidance to businesses and individuals making investment decisions.

Work Environment

Financial analysts work in offices. Most work full time and some work more than 40 hours per week.

How to Become a Financial Analyst

Financial analysts typically must have a bachelor's degree.

Pay

The median annual wage for financial analysts was $81,590 in May 2019.

Job Outlook

Employment of financial analysts is projected to grow 5 percent from 2019 to 2029, faster than the average for all occupations. A growing range of financial products and the need for in-depth knowledge of geographic regions are expected to lead to strong employment growth.

State & Area Data

Explore resources for employment and wages by state and area for financial analysts.

Learn more about financial analysts by visiting additional resources, including O*NET, a source on key characteristics of workers and occupations.

What Financial Analysts Do

Financial analysts provide guidance to businesses and individuals making investment decisions. They assess the performance of stocks, bonds, and other types of investments.

Duties

Financial analysts typically do the following:

- Recommend individual investments and collections of investments, which are known as portfolios
- Evaluate current and historical financial data
- Study economic and business trends
- Examine a company's financial statements to determine its value
- Meet with company officials to gain better insight into the company's prospects
- Assess the strength of the management team
- Prepare written reports

Financial analysts evaluate investment opportunities. They work in banks, pension funds, mutual funds, securities firms, insurance companies, and other businesses. Financial analysts are also called *securities analysts* and *investment analysts*.

Financial analysts can be divided into two categories: buy-side analysts and sell-side analysts.

- Buy-side analysts develop investment strategies for companies that have a lot of money to invest. These companies, called institutional investors, include hedge funds, insurance companies, independent money managers, and

Financial analysts recommend individual investments and collections of investments, which are known as portfolios.

Financial analysts work in banks, pension funds, insurance companies, and other businesses.

nonprofit organizations with large endowments, such as some universities.

- Sell-side analysts advise financial services sales agents who sell stocks, bonds, and other investments.

Some analysts work for the business media or other research houses, which are independent from the buy and sell side.

Financial analysts generally focus on trends affecting a specific industry, geographical region, or type of product. For example, an analyst may focus on a subject area such as the energy industry, a world region such as Eastern Europe, or the foreign exchange market. They must understand how new regulations, policies, political situations, and economic trends may affect investments.

Investing is becoming more global, and some financial analysts specialize in a particular country or region. Companies want those financial analysts to understand the language, culture, business environment, and political conditions in the country or region that they cover.

The following are examples of types of financial analysts:

Portfolio managers select the mix of products, industries, and regions for their company's investment portfolio. These managers are responsible for the overall performance of the portfolio. They are also expected to explain investment decisions and strategies in meetings with stakeholders.

Fund managers work exclusively with hedge funds or mutual funds. Both fund and portfolio managers frequently make buy or sell decisions in reaction to quickly changing market conditions.

Ratings analysts evaluate the ability of companies or governments to pay their debts, including bonds. On the basis of their evaluation, a management team rates the risk of a company or government not being able to repay its bonds.

Risk analysts evaluate the risk in investment decisions and determine how to manage unpredictability and limit potential losses. This job is carried out by making investment decisions such as selecting dissimilar stocks or having a combination of stocks, bonds, and mutual funds in a portfolio.

Work Environment

Financial analysts held about 487,800 jobs in 2019. The largest employers of financial analysts were as follows:

Securities, commodity contracts, and other financial investments and related activities	18%
Credit intermediation and related activities	15
Professional, scientific, and technical services	12
Management of companies and enterprises	11
Insurance carriers and related activities	6

Financial analysts work primarily in offices but travel frequently to visit companies or clients.

Many financial analysts work at large financial institutions based in New York City or other major financial centers.

Many financial analysts work at large financial institutions based in New York City or other major financial centers.

Work Schedules

Most financial analysts work full time and some work more than 40 hours per week. Much of their research must be done after office hours because their days are filled with telephone calls and meetings.

How to Become a Financial Analyst

Financial analysts typically must have a bachelor's degree.

Education

Most positions require a bachelor's degree. A number of fields of study provide appropriate preparation, including accounting, economics, finance, statistics, and mathematics.

Licenses, Certifications, and Registrations

The Financial Industry Regulatory Authority (FINRA) is the main licensing organization for the securities industry. A license is generally required to sell financial products, which may apply to some financial analyst positions. Because most of the licenses require sponsorship by an employer, companies do not expect individuals to have these licenses before starting a job.

Financial analysts must process a range of information in finding profitable investments.

Employers often recommend certification, which can improve the chances for advancement. An example is the Chartered Financial Analyst (CFA) certification from the CFA Institute. Financial analysts can become CFA certified if they have a bachelor's degree, 4 years of qualified work experience, and pass three exams. Financial analysts can also become certified in their field of specialty.

Advancement
Financial analysts typically start by specializing in a specific investment field. As they gain experience, they can become portfolio managers and select the mix of investments for a company's portfolio. They can also become fund managers and manage large investment portfolios for individual investors. A master's degree in finance or business administration can improve an analyst's chances of advancing to one of these positions.

Important Qualities
Analytical skills. Financial analysts must process a range of information in finding profitable investments.

Communication skills. Financial analysts must explain their recommendations to clients in clear language that clients can easily understand.

Computer skills. Financial analysts must be adept at using software packages to analyze financial data, see trends, create portfolios, and make forecasts.

Decisionmaking skills. Financial analysts must provide a recommendation to buy, hold, or sell a security.

Detail oriented. Financial analysts must pay attention to details when reviewing possible investments, as small issues may have large implications for the health of an investment.

Math skills. Financial analysts use mathematical skills when estimating the value of financial securities.

Pay
The median annual wage for financial analysts was $81,590 in May 2019. The median wage is the wage at which half the

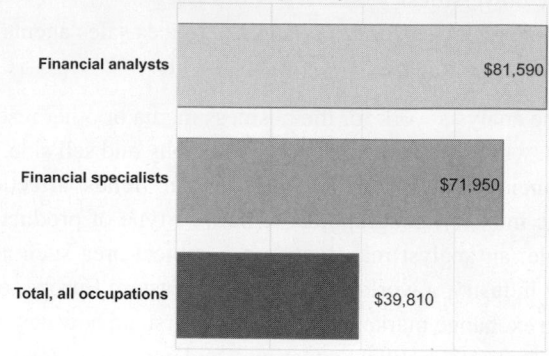

Financial Analysts
Median annual wages, May 2019

Financial analysts	$81,590
Financial specialists	$71,950
Total, all occupations	$39,810

Note: All Occupations includes all occupations in the U.S. Economy.
Source: U.S. Bureau of Labor Statistics, Occupational Employment Statistics.

workers in an occupation earned more than that amount and half earned less. The lowest 10 percent earned less than $47,230, and the highest 10 percent earned more than $156,150.

In May 2019, the median annual wages for financial analysts in the top industries in which they worked were as follows:

Securities, commodity contracts, and other financial investments and related activities	$98,690
Professional, scientific, and technical services	84,190
Management of companies and enterprises	82,870
Insurance carriers and related activities	78,850
Credit intermediation and related activities	77,450

Fund managers are typically compensated by fees, usually structured as a percentage of assets under management and a percentage of the fund's annual return.

Most financial analysts work full time and some work more than 40 hours per week. Much of their research must be done after office hours because their days are filled with telephone calls and meetings.

Job Outlook
Employment of financial analysts is projected to grow 5 percent from 2019 to 2029, faster than the average for all occupations. A growing range of financial products and the need for in-depth knowledge of geographic regions are expected to lead to strong employment growth.

Demand for financial analysts tends to grow with overall economic activity. Financial analysts will be needed to evaluate investment opportunities when new businesses are established or existing businesses expand. In addition, emerging markets throughout the world are providing new investment opportunities, which require expertise in geographic regions where those markets are located.

Demand is also projected to increase as the growth of "big data" and technological improvements allow financial analysts to access a wide range of data and conduct high-quality analysis. This analysis will help businesses manage their finances,

Financial Analysts
Percent change in employment, projected 2019-29

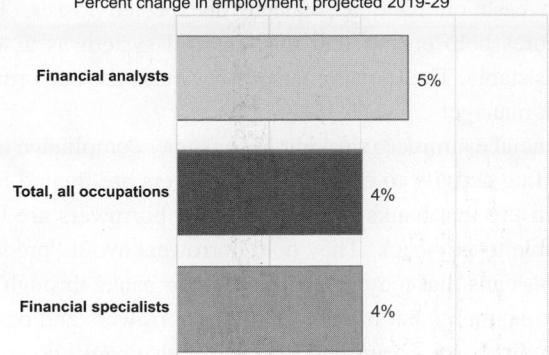

Financial analysts 5%

Total, all occupations 4%

Financial specialists 4%

Note: All Occupations includes all occupations in the U.S. Economy.
Source: U.S. Bureau of Labor Statistics, Employment Projections program.

identify investment trends, and deliver new products or services to clients.

Job Prospects

Despite employment growth, competition is expected for financial analyst positions. Growth in financial services is projected to create new positions, but there are still far more people who would like to enter the occupation than there are jobs in the occupation. Having certifications and a graduate degree can significantly improve an applicant's prospects.

Employment projections data for financial analysts, 2019-29					
Occupational Title	SOC Code	Employment, 2019	Projected Employment, 2029	Change, 2019-29	
				Percent	Numeric
SOURCE: U.S. Bureau of Labor Statistics, Employment Projections program					
Financial and investment analysts, financial risk specialists, and financial specialists, all other	13-2098	487,800	514,600	5	26,800

State & Area Data
Occupational Employment Statistics (OES)

The Occupational Employment Statistics (OES) program produces employment and wage estimates annually for over 800 occupations. These estimates are available for the nation as a whole, for individual states, and for metropolitan and nonmetropolitan areas.

Contacts for More Information

For more information about licensure for financial analysts, visit
➤ Financial Industry Regulatory Authority (FINRA)

For more information about training and certification, visit
➤ CFA Institute

For more information about certifications in financial analysis, visit
➤ Global Academy of Finance and Management

Financial Examiners

Summary

Quick Facts: Financial Examiners

2019 Median Pay	$81,090 per year $38.99 per hour
Typical Entry-Level Education	Bachelor's degree
Work Experience in a Related Occupation	None
On-the-job Training	Long-term on-the-job training
Number of Jobs, 2019	66,900
Job Outlook, 2019-29	7% (Faster than average)
Employment Change, 2019-29	4,900

What Financial Examiners Do
Financial examiners ensure compliance with laws governing financial institutions and transactions.

Work Environment
Most financial examiners work for the finance and insurance industry, the federal government, or state governments. Most financial examiners work full time.

Financial examiners ensure compliance with laws governing financial institutions and transactions.

How to Become a Financial Examiner
Financial examiners typically need a bachelor's degree that includes some coursework in accounting. Entry-level examiners are trained on the job by senior examiners.

Pay
The median annual wage for financial examiners was $81,090 in May 2019.

Job Outlook

Employment of financial examiners is projected to grow 7 percent from 2019 to 2029, faster than the average for all occupations. Financial examiners will be in demand as financial institutions seek help with federal regulatory compliance.

State & Area Data

Explore resources for employment and wages by state and area for financial examiners.

What Financial Examiners Do

Financial examiners ensure compliance with laws governing financial institutions and transactions. They review balance sheets, evaluate the risk level of loans, and assess bank management.

Duties

Financial examiners typically do the following:

- Monitor the financial condition of banks and other financial institutions
- Review balance sheets, operating income and expense accounts, and loan documentation to confirm institution assets and liabilities
- Prepare reports that detail an institution's safety and soundness
- Examine the minutes of meetings of managers and directors
- Train other examiners in the financial examination process
- Review and analyze new regulations and policies to determine their impact on the organization
- Establish guidelines for procedures and policies that comply with new and revised regulations

Financial examiners typically work in one of two main areas: risk assessment or consumer compliance.

Those working in risk assessment evaluate the health of financial institutions. Their role is to ensure that banks and other financial institutions offer safe loans and that they have enough cash on hand to manage unexpected losses. These procedures help ensure that the financial system as a whole remains stable. These examiners also evaluate the performance of bank managers.

Financial examiners working in consumer compliance monitor lending activity to ensure that borrowers are treated fairly. They ensure that banks extend loans that borrowers are likely to be able to pay back. They help borrowers avoid "predatory loans"—loans that may generate profit for banks through high interest payments but may be costly to borrowers and damage their credit scores. Examiners also ensure that banks do not discriminate against borrowers based on race, ethnicity, or other characteristics.

Work Environment

Financial examiners held about 66,900 jobs in 2019. The largest employers of financial examiners were as follows:

Credit intermediation and related activities	41%
Securities, commodity contracts, and other financial investments and related activities	16
Federal government	11
Management of companies and enterprises	9
State government, excluding education and hospitals	7

Financial examiners typically work in offices. They frequently have to travel to inspect a bank onsite.

Work Schedules

Most financial examiners work full time.

How to Become a Financial Examiner

Financial examiners typically need a bachelor's degree that includes some coursework in accounting. Entry-level examiners are trained on the job by senior examiners.

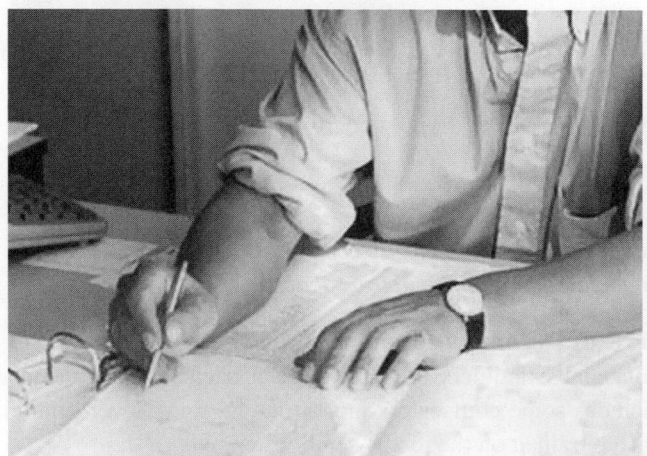

Financial examiners working in consumer compliance monitor lending activity to ensure that borrowers are treated fairly.

Financial examiners typically work in offices. They frequently have to travel to inspect a bank onsite.

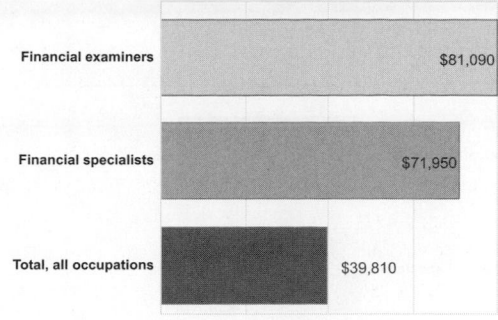

Financial Examiners
Median annual wages, May 2019

Financial examiners	$81,090
Financial specialists	$71,950
Total, all occupations	$39,810

Note: All Occupations includes all occupations in the U.S. Economy.
Source: U.S. Bureau of Labor Statistics, Occupational Employment Statistics.

Examiners working for the Federal Deposit Insurance Corporation (FDIC) must have at least six semester hours in accounting.

Education

Financial examiners typically need a bachelor's degree. Although a specific major is usually not required, examiners generally need some coursework in accounting, finance, economics, or a related field. Examiners working for the Federal Deposit Insurance Corporation (FDIC) typically must have at least 6 semester hours in accounting.

Training

Once hired, financial examiners receive on-the-job training. Entry-level workers begin under the supervision of senior examiners, as they learn their job duties. The length of this training varies, but typically lasts over 1 year.

Advancement

After a few years of experience, financial examiners can advance to a senior examiner position. Senior examiners handle more complex cases, and can lead and direct examination teams. Requirements for these positions vary by employer but often a master's degree in either accounting or business administration, or becoming a Certified Public Accountant (CPA), makes jobseekers more competitive.

Important Qualities

Analytical skills. Financial examiners need strong analytical skills to evaluate how well the managers of financial institutions are handling risk and whether the individual loans the institution makes are safe.

Detail oriented. Financial examiners must pay close attention to details when reviewing balance sheets in order to identify risky assets.

Math skills. Financial examiners need good math skills to monitor balance sheets and see if the bank's or other financial institution's available cash is dangerously low.

Writing skills. Financial examiners regularly write reports on the safety and soundness of financial institutions. They must be able to explain technical information clearly.

Pay

The median annual wage for financial examiners was $81,090 in May 2019. The median wage is the wage at which half the workers in an occupation earned more than that amount and half earned less. The lowest 10 percent earned less than $43,500, and the highest 10 percent earned more than $158,200.

In May 2019, the median annual wages for financial examiners in the top industries in which they worked were as follows:

Federal government	$121,060
Securities, commodity contracts, and other financial investments and related activities	90,120
Management of companies and enterprises	85,550
Credit intermediation and related activities	73,830
State government, excluding education and hospitals	73,040

Most financial examiners work full time.

Job Outlook

Employment of financial examiners is projected to grow 7 percent from 2019 to 2029, faster than the average for all occupations. Employment growth for financial examiners will vary by industry group. Financial examiners will be in demand as financial institutions seek help with federal regulatory compliance.

Demand for these workers has risen in the financial industry because of the need for financial institutions to effectively comply with federal regulation. More financial institutions are hiring financial examiners to help navigate the regulatory environment and reduce the cost of compliance. Financial examiners' employment is projected to grow 8 percent from 2019 to 2029 in the finance and insurance industry.

At the federal level, the creation of the Consumer Financial Protection Bureau (CFPB) has increased employment of financial examiners in recent years. However, changes to this agency and overall budget constraints in the federal government may limit employment growth. Employment of financial examiners

Financial Examiners
Percent change in employment, projected 2019-29

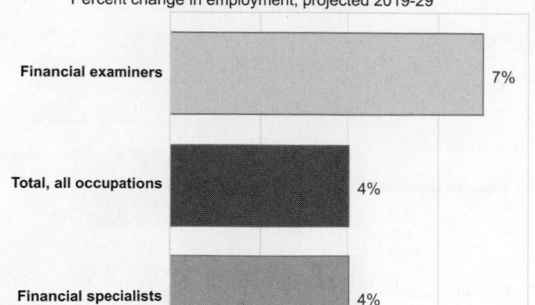

- Financial examiners — 7%
- Total, all occupations — 4%
- Financial specialists — 4%

Note: All Occupations includes all occupations in the U.S. Economy.
Source: U.S. Bureau of Labor Statistics, Employment Projections program.

in the federal government is projected to decline 4 percent from 2019 to 2029.

Job Prospects

Financial examiners should face competition for jobs. Those with previous work experience in banking, insurance, or accounting, for example having worked as accountants and auditors or financial analysts, should have the best prospects.

Employment projections data for financial examiners, 2019-29					
Occupational Title	SOC Code	Employment, 2019	Projected Employment, 2029	Change, 2019-29	
				Percent	Numeric
SOURCE: U.S. Bureau of Labor Statistics, Employment Projections program					
Financial examiners	13-2061	66,900	71,800	7	4,900

State & Area Data
Occupational Employment Statistics (OES)

The Occupational Employment Statistics (OES) program produces employment and wage estimates annually for over 800 occupations. These estimates are available for the nation as a whole, for individual states, and for metropolitan and nonmetropolitan areas.

Contacts for More Information

For more information about financial examiners, visit

➤ Federal Deposit Insurance Corporation
➤ Consumer Financial Protection Bureau

Fundraisers

Summary

Quick Facts: Fundraisers

2019 Median Pay	$57,970 per year $27.87 per hour
Typical Entry-Level Education	Bachelor's degree
Work Experience in a Related Occupation	None
On-the-job Training	None
Number of Jobs, 2019	100,600
Job Outlook, 2019-29	14% (Much faster than average)
Employment Change, 2019-29	14,400

What Fundraisers Do

Fundraisers organize events and campaigns to raise money and other kinds of donations for an organization.

Work Environment

Fundraisers work primarily for nonprofit organizations, including educational institutions, religious organizations, health research foundations, social services organizations, and political campaigns. Most work full time.

How to Become a Fundraiser

Fundraisers typically need a bachelor's degree and strong communication and organizational skills. Employers generally

Fundraisers plan and oversee campaigns and events to raise money and other donations for an organization.

prefer candidates who have studied public relations, journalism, communications, English, or business.

Pay

The median annual wage for fundraisers was $57,970 in May 2019.

Job Outlook

Employment of fundraisers is projected to grow 14 percent from 2019 to 2029, much faster than the average for all occupations. Employment growth is expected to be driven by the continued need of various types of organizations to raise money.

State & Area Data

Explore resources for employment and wages by state and area for fundraisers.

What Fundraisers Do

Fundraisers organize events and campaigns to raise money and other kinds of donations for an organization. They also may design promotional materials and increase awareness of an organization's work, goals, and financial needs.

Duties

Fundraisers typically do the following:

- Research prospective donors
- Create a strong fundraising message that appeals to potential donors
- Identify and contact potential donors
- Use online platforms to raise donations
- Organize campaigns or events to solicit donations
- Maintain records of donor information
- Evaluate the success of previous fundraising events
- Train volunteers in fundraising procedures and practices
- Ensure that all legal reporting requirements are satisfied

Fundraisers plan and oversee campaigns and events to raise money and other kinds of donations for an organization. They ensure that campaigns are effective by researching potential donors and examining records of those who have given in the past.

Fundraisers who work for political campaigns must be knowledgeable about campaign finance laws, such as the contribution limits of an individual giving to a specific candidate.

The following are examples of types of fundraisers:

Annual campaign fundraisers solicit donations once a year for their organization. Many nonprofit organizations have annual giving campaigns.

Capital campaign fundraisers raise money for a specific project, such as the construction of a new building at a university. Capital campaigns also raise money for renovations and the creation or expansion of an endowment.

Major-gifts fundraisers specialize in face-to-face interaction with donors who can give large amounts.

Planned-giving fundraisers solicit donations from those who are looking to pledge money at a future date or in installments over time. These fundraisers must have specialized training in taxes regarding gifts of stocks, bonds, charitable annuities, and real estate bequests in a will.

Work Environment

Fundraisers held about 100,600 jobs in 2019. The largest employers of fundraisers were as follows:

Religious, grantmaking, civic, professional, and similar organizations	41%
Educational services; state, local, and private	23
Healthcare and social assistance	17
Arts, entertainment, and recreation	5
Administrative and support services	3

Fundraisers must create a strong fundraising message that appeals to potential donors.

Fundraisers spend much of their time communicating with potential donors.

Most fundraisers raise funds for an organization which employs them directly, although some fundraisers work for consulting firms that have many clients.

Fundraisers spend much of their time communicating with other employees and potential donors, either in person, on the phone, or through email.

Some fundraisers may need to travel to locations where fundraising events are held. Events may include charity runs, walks, galas, and dinners.

Work Schedules

Most fundraisers work full time. Some attend fundraising events on nights and weekends, possibly requiring additional hours.

How to Become a Fundraiser

Fundraisers typically need a bachelor's degree and strong communication and organizational skills. Employers generally prefer candidates who have studied public relations, journalism, communications, English, or business.

Education

Although fundraisers have a variety of academic backgrounds, employers typically prefer a candidate with a bachelor's degree in public relations, journalism, communications, English, or business. Degrees in other subjects also may be acceptable.

Other Experience

Internships and previous work experience are important in obtaining a paid position as a fundraiser. Many fundraising campaigns rely on volunteers having face-to-face or over-the-phone interaction with potential donors. It is important for the fundraiser who organizes the campaign to have experience with this type of work.

Licenses, Certifications, and Registrations

Laws vary by state, but many states require some types of fundraisers to register with a state authority. Check with your state for more information.

Advancement

Fundraisers can advance to fundraising manager positions. However, some manager positions may also require a master's degree, in addition to years of work experience as a fundraiser.

Important Qualities

Communication skills. Fundraisers need strong communication skills to clearly explain the message and goals of their organization so that people will make donations.

Detail oriented. Fundraisers must be detail oriented because they deal with large volumes of data, including lists of people's names and phone numbers, and must comply with state and federal regulations. Failing to do so may result in penalties.

Interpersonal skills. Fundraisers need strong interpersonal skills to develop and maintain relationships with donors.

Organizational skills. Fundraisers manage large campaigns and events. They must have strong planning and organizational skills in order to succeed.

Pay

The median annual wage for fundraisers was $57,970 in May 2019. The median wage is the wage at which half the workers in an occupation earned more than that amount and half earned less. The lowest 10 percent earned less than $33,530, and the highest 10 percent earned more than $100,410.

In May 2019, the median annual wages for fundraisers in the top industries in which they worked were as follows:

Educational services; state, local, and private....　$63,090

Religious, grantmaking, civic, professional, and
　similar organizations......................................　57,750
Administrative and support services.................　54,970

Fundraisers typically need a bachelor's degree and strong communication skills.

Fundraisers
Median annual wages, May 2019

Business operations specialists	$68,730
Fundraisers	$57,970
Total, all occupations	$39,810

Note: All Occupations includes all occupations in the U.S. Economy.
Source: U.S. Bureau of Labor Statistics, Occupational Employment Statistics.

Fundraisers
Percent change in employment, projected 2019-29

- Fundraisers — 14%
- Business operations specialists — 6%
- Total, all occupations — 4%

Note: All Occupations includes all occupations in the U.S. Economy.
Source: U.S. Bureau of Labor Statistics, Employment Projections program.

Arts, entertainment, and recreation	54,600
Healthcare and social assistance	53,440

Most fundraisers work full time. Some attend fundraising events on nights and weekends, possibly requiring additional hours.

Job Outlook

Employment of fundraisers is projected to grow 14 percent from 2019 to 2029, much faster than the average for all occupations. Employment growth will be driven by the continued need of nonprofit organizations to collect donations in order to run their operations.

Many nonprofit organizations are focusing on cultivating an online presence and are increasingly using social media for fundraising activities. As a result, social media platforms have created new avenues for fundraisers to connect with potential donors and to spread their organization's message.

Job Prospects

Job prospects for fundraisers are expected to be good because organizations are always looking to raise more donations. Candidates with internship or volunteer experience in nonprofit and grantmaking organizations should have better job opportunities.

Employment projections data for fundraisers, 2019-29					
Occupational Title	SOC Code	Employment, 2019	Projected Employment, 2029	Change, 2019-29	
				Percent	Numeric
SOURCE: U.S. Bureau of Labor Statistics, Employment Projections program					
Fundraisers	13-1131	100,600	115,000	14	14,400

State & Area Data
Occupational Employment Statistics (OES)

The Occupational Employment Statistics (OES) program produces employment and wage estimates annually for over 800 occupations. These estimates are available for the nation as a whole, for individual states, and for metropolitan and nonmetropolitan areas.

Human Resources Specialists

Summary

Quick Facts: Human Resources Specialists

2019 Median Pay	$61,920 per year $29.77 per hour
Typical Entry-Level Education	Bachelor's degree
Work Experience in a Related Occupation	None
On-the-job Training	None
Number of Jobs, 2019	666,500
Job Outlook, 2019-29	7% (Faster than average)
Employment Change, 2019-29	46,900

What Human Resources Specialists Do

Human resources specialists recruit, screen, interview, and place workers. They also handle employee relations, compensation and benefits, and training.

Work Environment

Human resources specialists generally work in offices. Some, particularly recruitment specialists, travel extensively to attend job fairs, visit college campuses, and meet with applicants. Most human resources specialists work full time during regular business hours.

How to Become a Human Resources Specialist

Applicants must usually have a bachelor's degree in human resources, business, or a related field. However, the level of

Many human resources specialists interview applicants and help place workers.

education and experience required varies by position and employer.

Pay

The median annual wage for human resources specialists was $61,920 in May 2019.

Job Outlook

Employment of human resources specialists is projected to grow 7 percent from 2019 to 2029, faster than the average for all occupations. Human resources specialists will be needed to handle increasingly complex employment laws and healthcare coverage options. Most growth is projected to be in the professional, scientific, and technical services industry.

State & Area Data

Explore resources for employment and wages by state and area for human resources specialists.

What Human Resources Specialists Do

Human resources specialists recruit, screen, interview, and place workers. They often handle tasks related to employee relations, compensation and benefits, and training.

Duties

Human resources specialists typically do the following:

- Consult with employers to identify employment needs
- Interview applicants about their experience, education, and skills
- Contact references and perform background checks on job applicants
- Inform applicants about job details, such as duties, benefits, and working conditions
- Hire or refer qualified candidates for employers
- Conduct or help with new employee orientation
- Keep employment records and process paperwork

Human resources specialists are often trained in all human resources disciplines and perform tasks throughout all areas of the department. In addition to recruiting and placing workers, human resources specialists help guide employees through all human resources procedures and answer questions about policies. They sometimes administer benefits, process payroll, and handle any associated questions or problems, although many specialists may focus more on strategic planning and hiring instead of administrative duties. They also ensure that all human resources functions comply with federal, state, and local regulations.

The following are examples of types of human resources specialists:

Human resources generalists handle all aspects of human resources work. They may have duties in all areas of human resources including recruitment, employee relations, compensation, benefits, training, as well as the administration of human resources policies, procedures, and programs.

Recruitment specialists, sometimes known as *personnel recruiters* or "*head hunters*," find, screen, and interview applicants for job openings in an organization. They search for applicants by posting listings, attending job fairs, and visiting college campuses. They also may test applicants, contact references, and extend job offers.

Work Environment

Human resources specialists held about 666,500 jobs in 2019. The largest employers of human resources specialists were as follows:

Employment services 15%
Professional, scientific, and technical services 13
Government... 11
Healthcare and social assistance 11
Manufacturing.. 8

Recruitment specialists may distribute information at job fairs or online.

Employment interviewers speak with applicants and ask them questions before referring them to appropriate jobs.

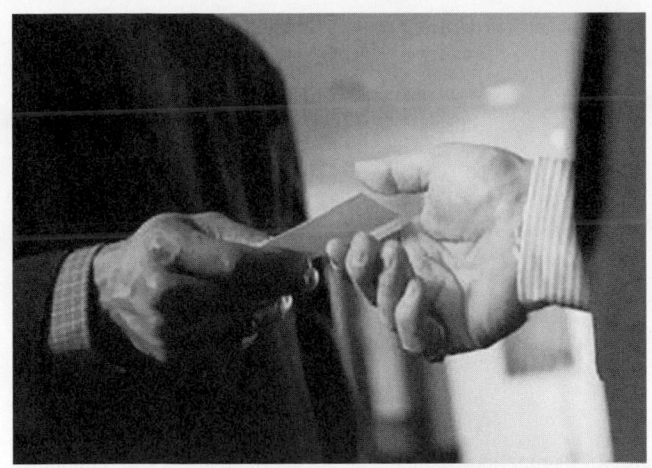

Human resources specialists must usually have a bachelor's degree in human resources, business, or a related field.

Some organizations contract recruitment and placement work to outside firms, such as those in the employment services industry or consulting firms in the professional, scientific, and technical industry.

Work Schedules

Human resources specialists generally work in offices. Some, particularly recruitment specialists, travel extensively to attend job fairs, visit college campuses, and meet with applicants.

Most specialists work full time during regular business hours.

How to Become a Human Resources Specialist

Human resources specialists usually must have a bachelor's degree.

Education

Applicants seeking positions as a human resources specialist usually must have a bachelor's degree in human resources, business, or a related field.

Coursework typically includes business, industrial relations, psychology, professional writing, human resource management, and accounting.

Work Experience in a Related Occupation

Some positions, particularly human resources generalists, may require previous work experience. Candidates can gain experience as human resources assistants, in customer service positions, or in other related jobs.

Licenses, Certifications, and Registrations

Many professional associations that specialize in human resources offer courses intended to enhance the skills of their members, and some offer certification programs. For example, the Society for Human Resource Management (SHRM) offers the SHRM Certified Professional (SHRM-CP) and SHRM Senior Certified Professional (SHRM-SCP). In addition, the HR Certification Institute (HRCI) offers a range of certifications for varying levels of expertise.

Certification usually requires passing an exam, and candidates typically need to meet minimum education and experience requirements. Exams check for human resources knowledge and how candidates apply their knowledge and judgment to different situations.

Although certification is usually voluntary, some employers may prefer or require it. Human resources generalists, in particular, can benefit from certification because it shows knowledge and professional competence across all human resources areas.

Advancement

Human resources specialists who possess a thorough knowledge of their organization, as well as an understanding of regulatory compliance needs, can advance to become human resources managers. Specialists can increase their chance of advancement by completing voluntary certification programs.

Important Qualities

Communication skills. Listening and speaking skills are essential for human resources specialists. They must convey information effectively, and pay careful attention to questions and concerns from job applicants and employees.

Decisionmaking skills. Human resources specialists use decisionmaking skills when reviewing candidates' qualifications or when working to resolve disputes.

Detail oriented. Specialists must be detail oriented when evaluating applicants' qualifications, performing background checks, maintaining records of an employee grievance, and ensuring that a workplace is in compliance with labor standards.

Interpersonal skills. Specialists continually interact with new people and must be able to converse and connect with people from different backgrounds.

Pay

The median annual wage for human resources specialists was $61,920 in May 2019. The median wage is the wage at which half the workers in an occupation earned more than that

Human Resources Specialists
Median annual wages, May 2019

Business operations specialists	$68,730
Human resources specialists	$61,920
Total, all occupations	$39,810

Note: All Occupations includes all occupations in the U.S. Economy.
Source: U.S. Bureau of Labor Statistics, Occupational Employment Statistics.

amount and half earned less. The lowest 10 percent earned less than $37,180, and the highest 10 percent earned more than $105,930.

In May 2019, the median annual wages for human resources specialists in the top industries in which they worked were as follows:

Professional, scientific, and technical services....	$70,180
Government...	67,590
Manufacturing...	64,900
Employment services	54,660
Healthcare and social assistance	53,190

Many human resources specialists, particularly recruitment specialists, travel extensively to attend job fairs, visit college campuses, and meet with applicants.

Most specialists work full time during regular business hours.

Job Outlook

Employment of human resources specialists is projected to grow 7 percent from 2019 to 2029, faster than the average for all occupations.

Companies are likely to continue to outsource human resources functions to organizations that provide these services, rather than directly employing human resources specialists. In addition, the services of human resources generalists will likely be needed to handle increasingly complex employment laws and benefit options.

Job Prospects

Job prospects for human resources specialists are expected to be favorable, with 64,500 openings projected annually, on average, over the decade.

Many of these openings are expected to result from the need to replace workers who transfer to different occupations or exit the labor force, such as to retire.

Overall, candidates with a bachelor's degree and professional certification should have the best job prospects.

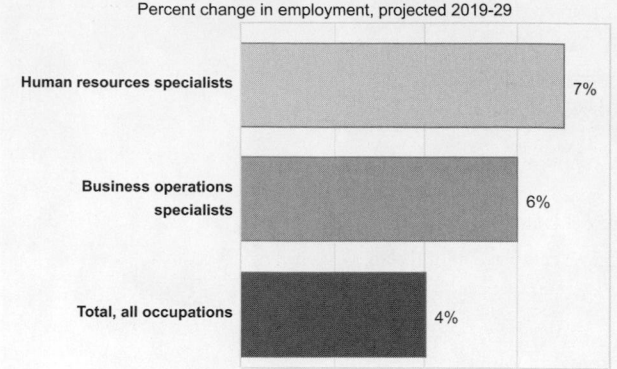

Human Resources Specialists
Percent change in employment, projected 2019-29

Human resources specialists 7%
Business operations specialists 6%
Total, all occupations 4%

Note: All Occupations includes all occupations in the U.S. Economy.
Source: U.S. Bureau of Labor Statistics, Employment Projections program.

Employment projections data for human resources specialists, 2019-29					
Occupational Title	SOC Code	Employment, 2019	Projected Employment, 2029	Change, 2019-29	
				Percent	Numeric
SOURCE: U.S. Bureau of Labor Statistics, Employment Projections program					
Human resources specialists	13-1071	666,500	713,500	7	46,900

State & Area Data
Occupational Employment Statistics (OES)

The Occupational Employment Statistics (OES) program produces employment and wage estimates annually for over 800 occupations. These estimates are available for the nation as a whole, for individual states, and for metropolitan and nonmetropolitan areas.

Contacts for More Information

For more information about human resources careers and certification, visit
➤ Society for Human Resource Management
➤ HR Certification Institute
➤ WorldatWork
➤ International Public Management Association for Human Resources

Insurance Underwriters

Summary

Quick Facts: Insurance Underwriters

2019 Median Pay	$70,020 per year $33.67 per hour
Typical Entry-Level Education	Bachelor's degree
Work Experience in a Related Occupation	None
On-the-job Training	Moderate-term on-the-job training
Number of Jobs, 2019	114,700
Job Outlook, 2019-29	-6% (Decline)
Employment Change, 2019-29	-7,100

What Insurance Underwriters Do

Insurance underwriters evaluate insurance applications and decide whether to provide insurance, and under what terms.

Work Environment

Insurance underwriters work indoors in offices. Most work full time.

How to Become an Insurance Underwriter

Employers prefer to hire candidates who have a bachelor's degree. However, insurance-related work experience and strong computer skills may be enough for some positions. Certification is generally necessary for advancement to senior underwriter and underwriter manager positions.

Pay

The median annual wage for insurance underwriters was $70,020 in May 2019.

Job Outlook

Employment of insurance underwriters is projected to decline 6 percent from 2019 to 2029. Automated underwriting software allows workers to process applications more quickly than before, reducing the need for as many underwriters.

Insurance underwriters determine the risk of insuring a client.

State & Area Data

Explore resources for employment and wages by state and area for insurance underwriters.

What Insurance Underwriters Do

Insurance underwriters decide whether to provide insurance, and under what terms. They evaluate insurance applications and determine coverage amounts and premiums.

Duties

Insurance underwriters typically do the following:

- Analyze information stated on insurance applications
- Determine the risk involved in insuring a client
- Screen applicants on the basis of set criteria
- Evaluate recommendations from underwriting software
- Contact field representatives, medical personnel, and others to obtain further information
- Decide whether to offer insurance
- Determine appropriate premiums and amounts of coverage
- Review and update the rules that govern automation software

Underwriters are the main link between an insurance company and an insurance agent. Insurance underwriters use computer software programs to determine whether to approve an applicant. They take specific information about a client and enter it into a program. The program then provides recommendations on coverage and premiums. Underwriters evaluate these recommendations and decide whether to approve or reject the application. If a decision is difficult, they may consult additional sources, such as medical documents and credit scores.

For simple and common types of insurance, such as automobile insurance, underwriters can typically rely on automated recommendations. For more specific and complex insurance types, such as workers' compensation, underwriters need to rely more on their own analytical insight.

Underwriters analyze the risk factors appearing on an application. For instance, if an applicant reports a previous bankruptcy, the underwriter must determine whether that information is

Insurance underwriters use computer software programs to determine whether an applicant should be approved.

relevant to the policy being applied for. The underwriter would likely consider how far in the past the bankruptcy occurred and how the applicant's financial situation has changed since the applicant filed for bankruptcy.

Insurance underwriters must achieve a balance between risky and cautious decisions. If underwriters allow too much risk, the insurance company will pay out too many claims. But if they don't approve enough applications, the company will not make enough money from premiums.

Most insurance underwriters specialize in one of three broad fields: life, health, and property and casualty. Although the job duties in each field are similar, the criteria that underwriters use vary. For example, for someone seeking life insurance, underwriters consider the person's age and financial history. For someone applying for car insurance (a form of property and casualty insurance), underwriters consider the person's driving record.

Within the broad field of property and casualty, underwriters may specialize even further into commercial (business) insurance or personal insurance. They may also specialize by the type of policy, such as for automobiles, boats (marine insurance), or homes (homeowners' insurance).

Work Environment

Insurance underwriters held about 114,700 jobs in 2019. The largest employers of insurance underwriters were as follows:

Direct insurance (except life, health, and medical)
carriers.. 44%
Insurance agencies and brokerages........................... 20
Other insurance related activities............................. 6
Direct health and medical insurance carriers............ 5
Credit intermediation and related activities.............. 4

Most underwriters work full time.

Underwriters work indoors in offices. Although underwriters spend most of their time working alone on applications at a computer, they sometimes must handle customer inquiries.

Some property and casualty underwriters may travel to assess properties in person.

Work Schedules

Most underwriters work full time.

How to Become an Insurance Underwriter

Employers prefer to hire candidates who have a bachelor's degree. However, insurance-related work experience and strong computer skills may be enough for some positions. Certification is generally necessary for advancement to senior underwriter and underwriter manager positions.

Education

Most employers prefer to hire applicants who have a bachelor's degree. Although a specific major is not required, some coursework in business, finance, economics, and mathematics is helpful.

Training

Beginning underwriters usually work as trainees under the supervision of senior underwriters. Trainees work on basic applications and learn the most common risk factors. Some companies offer training programs that include classroom instruction on the basics of underwriting.

As new underwriters gain experience, they work independently and handle more complex applications.

Licenses, Certifications, and Registrations

Employers often expect underwriters to become certified through coursework. These courses are important for keeping current with new insurance policies and for adjusting to new technology and changes in state and federal regulations. Certification is often necessary for advancement to senior

Most firms prefer to hire applicants with a bachelor's degree.

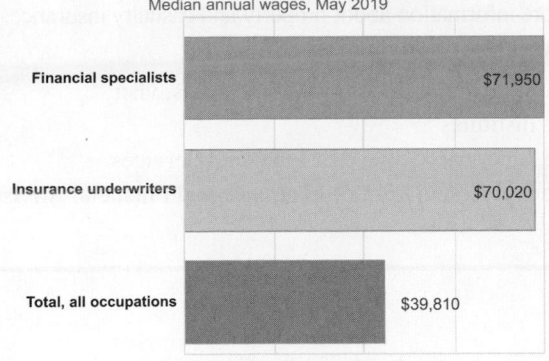

Insurance Underwriters
Median annual wages, May 2019

Financial specialists $71,950

Insurance underwriters $70,020

Total, all occupations $39,810

Note: All Occupations includes all occupations in the U.S. Economy.
Source: U.S. Bureau of Labor Statistics, Occupational Employment Statistics.

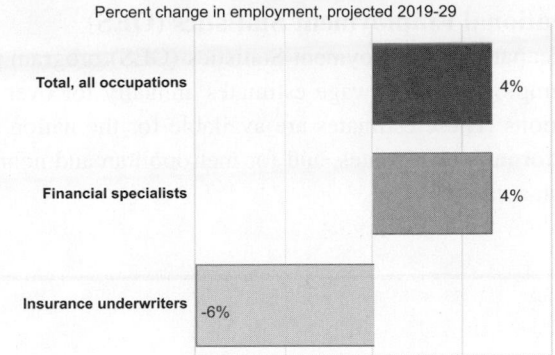

Insurance Underwriters
Percent change in employment, projected 2019-29

Total, all occupations   4%

Financial specialists   4%

Insurance underwriters   -6%

Note: All Occupations includes all occupations in the U.S. Economy.
Source: U.S. Bureau of Labor Statistics, Employment Projections program.

underwriter and underwriter management positions. Many certification options are available.

For underwriters with at least 2 years of insurance experience, The Institutes offer the Chartered Property and Casualty Underwriter (CPCU) designation. For beginning underwriters, The Institutes offer a training program.

The Institutes also offer several other designations in insurance specialties, including the Associate in Commercial Underwriting (AU) and Associate in Personal Insurance (API). To earn these designations, underwriters complete a series of courses and exams that generally takes 1 to 2 years.

The National Association of Insurance and Financial Advisors offers the Life Underwriter Training Council Fellow (LUTCF) designation, which consists of a three-part curriculum in basic insurance concepts.

The American College of Financial Services offers the Chartered Life Underwriter (CLU) certification. This certification consists of five core courses and three electives, and candidates must have 3 years of related work experience.

Important Qualities

Analytical skills. Underwriters must be able to evaluate information from a variety of sources and solve complex problems.

Decisionmaking skills. The core function of an underwriter is making decisions, such as whether to offer insurance coverage and at what level to set premiums.

Detail oriented. Underwriters must pay attention to detail, because each individual item on an insurance application can affect the coverage decision.

Interpersonal skills. Underwriters need good communication and interpersonal skills because much of their work involves dealing with other people, such as insurance agents.

Math skills. Determining the probability of losses on an insurance policy and calculating appropriate premiums require mathematical ability.

Pay

The median annual wage for insurance underwriters was $70,020 in May 2019. The median wage is the wage at which

half the workers in an occupation earned more than that amount and half earned less. The lowest 10 percent earned less than $42,360, and the highest 10 percent earned more than $124,320.

In May 2019, the median annual wages for insurance underwriters in the top industries in which they worked were as follows:

Credit intermediation and related activities	$75,390
Other insurance related activities	70,110
Direct insurance (except life, health, and medical) carriers	69,760
Direct health and medical insurance carriers	68,700
Insurance agencies and brokerages	68,430

Most underwriters work full time.

Job Outlook

Employment of insurance underwriters is projected to decline 6 percent from 2019 to 2029. Automated underwriting software allows workers to process applications more quickly than before, reducing the need for as many underwriters. As this technology improves and becomes more widely adopted in the insurance industry, more underwriting decisions will likely be made automatically.

However, there still will be a need for underwriters to review and update the criteria that run the automation. In addition, their analytical insight will still be needed in complex or specific insurance fields, such as workers' compensation, marine insurance, or health insurance.

Job Prospects

Job opportunities should be best for those with a background in finance and strong computer and analytical skills.

Employment projections data for insurance underwriters, 2019-29				Change, 2019-29	
Occupational Title	SOC Code	Employment, 2019	Projected Employment, 2029	Percent	Numeric
SOURCE: U.S. Bureau of Labor Statistics, Employment Projections program					
Insurance underwriters	13-2053	114,700	107,600	-6	-7,100

State & Area Data
Occupational Employment Statistics (OES)

The Occupational Employment Statistics (OES) program produces employment and wage estimates annually for over 800 occupations. These estimates are available for the nation as a whole, for individual states, and for metropolitan and nonmetropolitan areas.

Contacts for More Information

For more information about property and casualty insurance, visit
➤ Insurance Information Institute

For more information about certifications, visit
➤ The Institutes
➤ The American College of Financial Services
➤ National Association of Insurance and Financial Advisors

Labor Relations Specialists

Summary

Quick Facts: Labor Relations Specialists

2019 Median Pay	$69,020 per year
	$33.18 per hour
Typical Entry-Level Education	Bachelor's degree
Work Experience in a Related Occupation	Less than 5 years
On-the-job Training	None
Number of Jobs, 2019	78,900
Job Outlook, 2019-29.....................................	-7% (Decline)
Employment Change, 2019-29	-5,400

What Labor Relations Specialists Do

Labor relations specialists interpret and administer labor contracts.

Work Environment

Labor relations specialists generally work in offices. Most work full time during regular business hours.

How to Become a Labor Relations Specialist

Applicants usually have a bachelor's degree in labor relations, human resources, industrial relations, business, or a related field. However, the level of education and experience required varies by position and employer.

Pay

The median annual wage for labor relations specialists was $69,020 in May 2019.

Job Outlook

Employment of labor relations specialists is projected to decline 7 percent from 2019 to 2029. Union membership has declined, resulting in less demand for the services of labor relations specialists.

State & Area Data

Explore resources for employment and wages by state and area for labor relations specialists.

What Labor Relations Specialists Do

Labor relations specialists interpret and administer labor contracts regarding issues such as wages and salaries, healthcare, pensions, and union and management practices.

Duties

Labor relations specialists typically do the following:

Labor relations specialists interpret and administer labor contracts regarding issues such as employee welfare, healthcare, and pensions.

Labor relations specialists draft proposals and rules or regulations in order to help facilitate collective bargaining.

- Advise management on contracts, worker grievances, and disciplinary procedures
- Lead meetings between management and labor
- Meet with union representatives
- Draft proposals and rules or regulations
- Ensure that human resources policies are consistent with union agreements
- Interpret formal communications between management and labor
- Investigate validity of labor grievances
- Train management on labor relations

Labor relations specialists work with representatives from a labor union and a company's management. In addition to leading meetings between the two groups, these specialists draft formal language as part of the collective bargaining process. These contracts are called collective bargaining agreements (CBAs), and they serve as a legal and procedural guide for employee/management relations.

Labor relations specialists also address specific grievances workers might have, and ensure that all labor and management solutions comply within the relevant CBA.

Work Environment
Labor relations specialists held about 78,900 jobs in 2019. The largest employers of labor relations specialists were as follows:

Labor unions and similar labor organizations	76%
Government	4
Management of companies and enterprises	2

Labor relations specialists generally work in offices. Some may travel for arbitration meetings or to discuss contracts with employees or management. The work of labor relations specialists can be stressful because negotiating contracts and resolving labor grievances can be tense.

Work Schedules
Most labor relations specialists work full time during regular business hours. Some specialists work longer periods when preparing for meetings or settling disputes.

How to Become a Labor Relations Specialist
Applicants usually have a bachelor's degree in labor relations, human resources, industrial relations, business, or a related field. However, the level of education and experience required to become a labor relations specialist varies by position and employer.

Education
Labor relations specialists usually have a bachelor's degree. Some schools offer a bachelor's degree in labor or employment relations. These programs focus on labor-specific topics such as employment law and contract negotiation.

Candidates also may qualify for labor relations specialist positions with a bachelor's degree in human resources, industrial relations, business, or a related field. Coursework typically includes business, professional writing, human resource management, and accounting.

Work Experience in a Related Occupation
Many positions require previous work experience. Candidates can gain experience as human resources specialists, compensation, benefits, and job analysis specialists, or human resources generalists before specializing in labor relations.

Licenses, Certifications, and Registrations
Some colleges and universities offer labor relations certificates to specialists who prefer greater specialization in certain topics, such as mediation. Earning these certificates give participants a better understanding of labor law, the collective bargaining process, and worker grievance procedures.

Labor relations specialists generally work in offices.

Labor relations specialists usually have a bachelor's degree in labor relations, human resources, industrial relations, business, or a related field.

Labor Relations Specialists
Median annual wages, May 2019

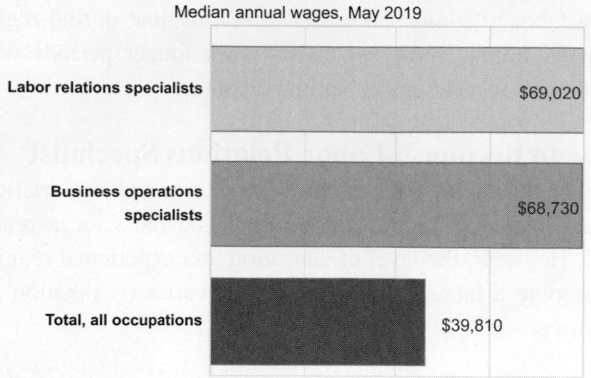

Labor relations specialists — $69,020
Business operations specialists — $68,730
Total, all occupations — $39,810

Note: All Occupations includes all occupations in the U.S. Economy.
Source: U.S. Bureau of Labor Statistics, Occupational Employment Statistics.

Advancement

Labor relations specialists who seek further expertise in contract negotiation, labor law, and similar topics may become lawyers. They will need to earn a law degree and pass their state's bar exam.

Important Qualities

Decisionmaking skills. Labor relations specialists use decisionmaking skills to help management and labor agree on decisions when resolving grievances or other disputes.

Detail oriented. Specialists must be detail oriented when evaluating labor laws and maintaining records of an employee grievance.

Interpersonal skills. Interpersonal skills are essential for labor relations specialists. When mediating between labor and management, specialists must be able to converse and connect with people from different backgrounds.

Listening skills. Listening skills are essential for labor relations specialists. When evaluating grievances, for example, they must pay careful attention to workers' responses, understand the points they are making, and ask relevant follow-up questions.

Writing skills. All labor relations specialists need strong writing skills to be effective at their job. They often draft proposals, and these proposals must be able to convey complex information to both workers and management.

Pay

The median annual wage for labor relations specialists was $69,020 in May 2019. The median wage is the wage at which half the workers in an occupation earned more than that amount and half earned less. The lowest 10 percent earned less than $19,230, and the highest 10 percent earned more than $124,380.

In May 2019, the median annual wages for labor relations specialists in the top industries in which they worked were as follows:

Labor Relations Specialists
Percent change in employment, projected 2019-29

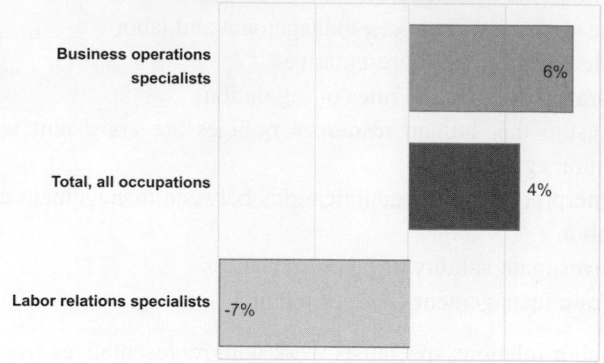

Business operations specialists — 6%
Total, all occupations — 4%
Labor relations specialists — -7%

Note: All Occupations includes all occupations in the U.S. Economy.
Source: U.S. Bureau of Labor Statistics, Employment Projections program.

Management of companies and enterprises	$87,130
Government	72,980
Labor unions and similar labor organizations	65,870

Most labor relations specialists work full time during regular business hours. Some specialists work longer periods when preparing for meetings or settling disputes.

Job Outlook

Employment of labor relations specialists is projected to decline 7 percent from 2019 to 2029.

The rate of union membership in 1983 was 20.1 percent; the current rate is about half that. The number of wage and salary workers who are union members is likely to continue declining. Although this will result in less overall demand for the services of labor relations specialists, their expertise and unique skills will maintain some demand for these workers as union negotiations and contract disputes continue.

Job Prospects

Job prospects for labor relations specialists are expected to be less than favorable because there will be less demand for their work. Overall, candidates with a bachelor's degree, related work experience, and professional certificates should have the best job prospects.

Employment projections data for labor relations specialists, 2019-29					
Occupational Title	SOC Code	Employment, 2019	Projected Employment, 2029	Change, 2019-29	
				Percent	Numeric
SOURCE: U.S. Bureau of Labor Statistics, Employment Projections program					
Labor relations specialists	13-1075	78,900	73,500	-7	-5,400

State & Area Data
Occupational Employment Statistics (OES)

The Occupational Employment Statistics (OES) program produces employment and wage estimates annually for over 800 occupations. These estimates are available for the nation as a whole, for individual states, and for metropolitan and nonmetropolitan areas.

Contacts for More Information

For more information about labor relations careers and certification, visit
➤ Society for Human Resource Management
➤ Federal Labor Relations Authority

Loan Officers

Summary

Quick Facts: Loan Officers

2019 Median Pay	$63,270 per year $30.42 per hour
Typical Entry-Level Education	Bachelor's degree
Work Experience in a Related Occupation	None
On-the-job Training	Moderate-term on-the-job training
Number of Jobs, 2019	316,900
Job Outlook, 2019-29	3% (As fast as average)
Employment Change, 2019-29	10,100

What Loan Officers Do

Loan officers evaluate, authorize, or recommend approval of loan applications for people and businesses.

Work Environment

Most loan officers are employed by commercial banks, credit unions, mortgage companies, and related financial institutions. Most loan officers work full time and some work extensive hours. Except for consumer loan officers, traveling to visit clients is common.

Loan officers meet with potential borrowers and approve loans.

How to Become a Loan Officer

Most loan officers need a bachelor's degree and receive on-the-job training. Mortgage loan officers must be licensed.

Pay

The median annual wage for loan officers was $63,270 in May 2019.

Job Outlook

Employment of loan officers is projected to grow 3 percent from 2019 to 2029, about as fast as the average for all occupations. Although the demand for loan officers will increase as the overall economy grows, the decline of bank branches may moderate employment growth.

State & Area Data

Explore resources for employment and wages by state and area for loan officers.

What Loan Officers Do

Loan officers evaluate, authorize, or recommend approval of loan applications for people and businesses.

Duties

Loan officers typically do the following:

- Contact companies or people to ask if they need a loan
- Meet with loan applicants to gather personal information and answer questions
- Explain different types of loans and the terms of each type to applicants
- Obtain, verify, and analyze the applicant's financial information, such as the credit rating and income level
- Review loan agreements to ensure that they comply with federal and state regulations
- Approve loan applications or refer them to management for a decision

Loan officers use a process called underwriting to assess whether applicants qualify for loans. After collecting and verifying all the required financial documents, the loan officer evaluates the information they obtain to determine the applicant's need for a loan and ability to pay back the loan. Most firms

Consumer loan officers specialize in loans to people, such as loans for buying cars or paying for college tuition.

use underwriting software, which produces a recommendation for the loan based on the applicant's financial status. After the underwriting software produces a recommendation, loan officers review the output of the software and consider any additional information to make a final decision.

The work of loan officers has sizable customer-service and sales components. Loan officers often answer questions and guide customers through the application process. In addition, many loan officers must market the products and services of their lending institution and actively solicit new business.

The following are common types of loan officers:

Commercial loan officers specialize in loans to businesses, which often use the loans to buy supplies and upgrade or expand operations. Commercial loans frequently are larger and more complicated than other types of loans. Because companies have such complex financial situations and statements, commercial loans usually require human judgment in addition to the analysis by underwriting software. Furthermore, some commercial loans are so large that no single bank will provide the entire amount requested. In such cases, loan officers may have to work with multiple banks to put together a package of loans.

Consumer loan officers specialize in loans to people. Consumers take out loans for many reasons, such as buying a car or paying college tuition. For some simple consumer loans,

the underwriting process is fully automated. However, the loan officer is still needed to guide applicants through the process and to handle cases with unusual circumstances. Some institutions—usually small banks and credit unions—do not use underwriting software and instead rely on loan officers to complete the underwriting process manually.

Mortgage loan officers specialize in loans used to buy real estate (property and buildings), which are called mortgage loans. Mortgage loan officers work on loans for both residential and commercial properties. Often, mortgage loan officers must seek out clients, which requires developing relationships with real estate companies and other sources that can refer prospective applicants.

Within these three fields, some loan officers specialize in a particular part of the loan process:

Loan collection officers contact borrowers who fail to make their loan payments on time. They work with borrowers to help them find a way to keep paying off the loan. If the borrower continues to miss payments, loan officers start the process of taking away what the borrower used to secure the loan (called "collateral")—often a home or car—and selling it to repay the loan.

Loan underwriters specialize in evaluating whether a client is creditworthy. They collect, verify, and evaluate the client's financial information provided on their loan applications and then use loan underwriting software to produce recommendations.

Work Environment

Loan officers held about 316,900 jobs in 2019. The largest employers of loan officers were as follows:

Credit intermediation and related activities	83%
Management of companies and enterprises	5
Automobile dealers	4

Most loan officers work full time.

Loan officers must pay attention to detail, as each piece of information on an application can have a major effect on the profitability of a loan.

The depository credit intermediation industry includes commercial banks and savings institutions, and nondepository credit intermediation includes mortgage companies.

Loan officers who specialize in consumer loans usually work in offices. Mortgage and commercial loan officers often work outside the office and meet with clients at their homes or businesses.

Work Schedules

Most loan officers work full time and some work extensive hours.

How to Become a Loan Officer

Most loan officers need a bachelor's degree and receive on-the-job training. Mortgage loan officers must be licensed.

Education

Loan officers typically need a bachelor's degree, usually in a field such as business or finance. Because commercial loan officers analyze the finances of businesses applying for credit, they need to understand general business accounting, including how to read financial statements.

Some jobseekers may be able to enter the occupation without a bachelor's degree if they have related work experience, such as experience in sales, customer service, or banking.

Training

Once hired, loan officers usually receive some on-the-job training. This may be a combination of formal, company-sponsored training and informal training during the first few months on the job.

Licenses, Certifications, and Registrations

Mortgage loan officers must have a Mortgage Loan Originator (MLO) license. To become licensed, they must complete at least 20 hours of coursework, pass an exam, and submit to background and credit checks. Licenses must be renewed annually, and individual states may have additional requirements.

Several banking associations, including the American Bankers Association and the Mortgage Bankers Association, as well as a number of schools, offer courses, training programs, or certifications for loan officers. Although not required, certification shows dedication and expertise and thus may enhance a candidate's employment opportunities.

Important Qualities

Decisionmaking skills. Loan officers must assess an applicant's financial information and decide whether to award the applicant a loan.

Detail oriented. Each piece of information on an application can have a major effect on the profitability of a loan, so loan officers must pay attention to detail.

Initiative. Loan officers need to seek out new clients. They often act as salespeople, promoting their lending institution and contacting people and firms to determine their need for a loan.

Interpersonal skills. Because loan officers work with people, they must be able to guide customers through the application process and answer their questions.

Pay

The median annual wage for loan officers was $63,270 in May 2019. The median wage is the wage at which half the workers in an occupation earned more than that amount and half earned less. The lowest 10 percent earned less than $32,560, and the highest 10 percent earned more than $132,680.

In May 2019, the median annual wages for loan officers in the top industries in which they worked were as follows:

Automobile dealers	$82,380
Management of companies and enterprises	65,910
Credit intermediation and related activities	62,210

The form of compensation varies widely by employer. Some loan officers are paid a flat salary; others are paid on commission. Those on commission usually are paid a base salary plus a commission for the loans they originate. Loan officers also may receive extra commission or bonuses based on the number of loans they originate or how well the loans perform.

Most loan officers work full time and some work extensive hours.

Job Outlook

Employment of loan officers is projected to grow 3 percent from 2019 to 2029, about as fast as the average for all occupations.

Increased demand for loan officers is expected as both businesses and individuals seek credit to finance commercial investments and personal spending. Loan officers will be needed to

Loan Officers
Median annual wages, May 2019

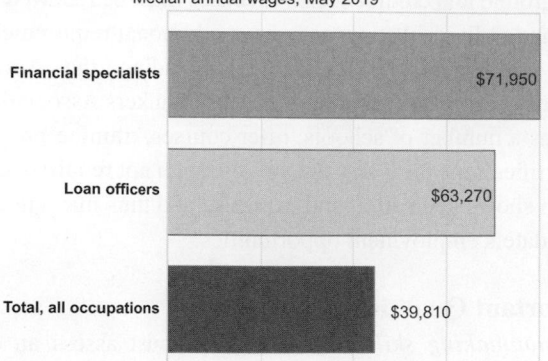

Note: All Occupations includes all occupations in the U.S. Economy.
Source: U.S. Bureau of Labor Statistics, Occupational Employment Statistics.

evaluate the creditworthiness of applicants and to determine the likelihood that loans will be paid back in full and on time.

However, the decline of bank branches and the increased use of productivity-enhancing technology in loan processing are expected to slow employment growth.

Job Prospects

Job opportunities should be good for people with lending, banking, or sales experience. In addition, some firms require loan officers to find their own clients, so candidates with established contacts and a referral network should have the best job opportunities.

Employment projections data for loan officers, 2019-29					
Occupational Title	SOC Code	Employment, 2019	Projected Employment, 2029	Change, 2019-29	
				Percent	Numeric
SOURCE: U.S. Bureau of Labor Statistics, Employment Projections program					
Loan officers	13-2072	316,900	327,000	3	10,100

State & Area Data
Occupational Employment Statistics (OES)

The Occupational Employment Statistics (OES) program produces employment and wage estimates annually for over 800

Loan Officers
Percent change in employment, projected 2019-29

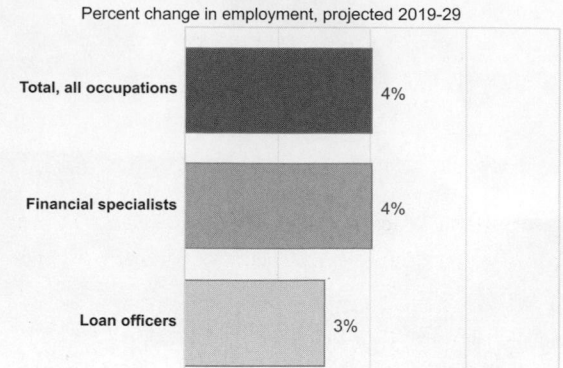

Note: All Occupations includes all occupations in the U.S. Economy.
Source: U.S. Bureau of Labor Statistics, Employment Projections program.

occupations. These estimates are available for the nation as a whole, for individual states, and for metropolitan and nonmetropolitan areas.

Contacts for More Information

For more information about certification and training for loan officers, visit
➤ American Bankers Association

For more information about a career as a mortgage loan officer, visit
➤ Mortgage Bankers Association

For more information about licensing for mortgage loan officers, visit
➤ Nationwide Mortgage Licensing System & Registry Resource Center

State bankers associations have specific information about job opportunities in their state. Also, individual banks can supply information about job openings and the activities, responsibilities, and preferred qualifications of their loan officers.

Logisticians

Summary

Quick Facts: Logisticians

2019 Median Pay	$74,750 per year $35.94 per hour
Typical Entry-Level Education	Bachelor's degree
Work Experience in a Related Occupation	None
On-the-job Training	None
Number of Jobs, 2019	188,200
Job Outlook, 2019-29	4% (As fast as average)
Employment Change, 2019-29	8,200

What Logisticians Do

Logisticians analyze and coordinate an organization's supply chain.

Work Environment

Logisticians work in nearly every industry. The job can be stressful because logistical work is fast-paced. Most logisticians work full time during regular business hours.

How to Become a Logistician

A bachelor's degree is typically required to enter the occupation, although an associate's degree may be sufficient for some logistician jobs.

Pay

The median annual wage for logisticians was $74,750 in May 2019.

Job Outlook

Employment of logisticians is projected to grow 4 percent from 2019 to 2029, about as fast as the average for all occupations.

Logisticians work to understand customers' needs and how to meet them.

Job prospects should be best for candidates who have experience using logistical software or doing logistical work for the military.

State & Area Data

Explore resources for employment and wages by state and area for logisticians.

What Logisticians Do

Logisticians analyze and coordinate an organization's supply chain—the system that moves a product from supplier to consumer. They manage the entire life cycle of a product, which includes how a product is acquired, allocated, and delivered.

Duties

Logisticians typically do the following:

- Manage a product's life cycle from design to disposal
- Direct the allocation of materials, supplies, and products
- Develop business relationships with suppliers and clients
- Understand clients' needs and how to meet them
- Review logistical functions and identify areas for improvement
- Propose strategies to minimize the cost or time required to transport goods

Logisticians oversee activities that include purchasing, transportation, inventory, and warehousing. They may direct the movement of a range of goods, people, or supplies, from common consumer goods to military supplies and personnel.

Logisticians use software systems to plan and track the movement of products. They operate software programs designed specifically to manage logistical functions, such as procurement, inventory management, and other supply chain planning and management systems.

Work Environment

Logisticians held about 188,200 jobs in 2019. The largest employers of logisticians were as follows:

Manufacturing	24%
Federal government	18
Professional, scientific, and technical services	16
Management of companies and enterprises	10
Wholesale trade	9

Logisticians work in almost every industry. Some logisticians work in the logistical department of a company, and others work for firms that specialize in logistical work, such as freight-shipping companies.

The job can be stressful because logistical work is fast-paced. Logisticians must ensure that operations stay on schedule, and they must work quickly to solve any problems that arise. Some logisticians travel to manufacturing plants or distribution centers.

Work Schedules
The majority of logisticians work full time and they sometimes work overtime to ensure that operations stay on schedule.

How to Become a Logistician
A bachelor's degree is typically required for most positions, although an associate's degree may be sufficient for some logistician jobs. In some cases, related work experience may substitute for education. Industry certification is helpful for jobseekers.

Education
Logisticians may qualify for some positions with an associate's degree. However, due to complex logistics and supply chains, companies prefer to hire workers who have at least a bachelor's degree. Many logisticians have a bachelor's degree in business, systems engineering, or supply chain management.

Bachelor's degree programs often include coursework in operations and database management, and system dynamics. In addition, most programs offer courses that train students on software and technologies commonly used by logisticians, such as radio-frequency identification (RFID).

Licenses, Certifications, and Registrations
Although not required, certification can demonstrate professional competence and a broad knowledge of logistics. Logisticians can obtain certification through APICS or the International Society of Logistics (SOLE). To become certified, a logistician typically needs to meet education and work experience requirements and pass an exam.

There are several certifications available from the Defense Acquisition University (DAU). These certifications are required for Department of Defense acquisitions.

When problems arise, logisticians must respond quickly and devise solutions.

Work Experience in a Related Occupation
Some employers allow applicants to substitute work experience in place of a specific degree. Previous work experience in a field related to logistics, supply chains, or business can be beneficial. Some gain work experience while working in a logistical support role, such as dispatchers and clerks or while serving in

Logisticians manage the life cycle of a product, which includes how a product is distributed and delivered.

A bachelor's degree is typically required for most positions, although an associate's degree may be sufficient for some logistician jobs.

the military. Experience allows a worker to learn about production and supply chain processes.

Important Qualities

Communication skills. Logisticians need strong communication skills to collaborate with colleagues and do business with suppliers and customers.

Critical-thinking skills. Logisticians must develop, adjust, and carry out logistical plans. They often must find ways to reduce costs and improve efficiency.

Customer service skills. Logisticians must know the needs of their customers in order to coordinate the movement of materials between suppliers and customers. They gain this knowledge through listening to the customer and applying their knowledge of the products and systems to provide what is required.

Organizational skills. Logisticians must be able to keep detailed records and simultaneously manage several projects in a fast-paced environment.

Problem-solving skills. Logisticians must handle unforeseen issues, such as delivery problems, and adjust plans as needed to resolve the issues.

Pay

The median annual wage for logisticians was $74,750 in May 2019. The median wage is the wage at which half the workers in an occupation earned more than that amount and half earned less. The lowest 10 percent earned less than $44,020, and the highest 10 percent earned more than $120,400.

In May 2019, the median annual wages for logisticians in the top industries in which they worked were as follows:

Federal government.. $85,450
Manufacturing.. 76,480

Management of companies and enterprises 75,010
Professional, scientific, and technical services 72,340
Wholesale trade... 65,820

The majority of logisticians work full time and they sometimes work overtime to ensure that operations stay on schedule.

Job Outlook

Employment of logisticians is projected to grow 4 percent from 2019 to 2029, about as fast as the average for all occupations.

The performance of the logistical and supply chain process is an important factor in a company's profitability. Companies rely on logisticians to manage the movement of their products and supplies. Supply and distribution systems have become increasingly complex as they continue to try to gain more efficiencies at minimal cost. Employment is expected to grow as companies need more logisticians to move products more efficiently, solve problems, and identify areas for improvement. However, this growth may be limited by mergers of third-party logistics companies.

Job Prospects

Overall job opportunities should be good because of employment growth and the need to replace logisticians who transfer to other occupations or leave the labor force, such as to retire. Prospects should be best for candidates who have experience using logistical software or doing logistical work for the military.

Employment projections data for logisticians, 2019-29					
Occupational Title	SOC Code	Employment, 2019	Projected Employment, 2029	Change, 2019-29	
				Percent	Numeric
SOURCE: U.S. Bureau of Labor Statistics, Employment Projections program					
Logisticians	13-1081	188,200	196,400	4	8,200

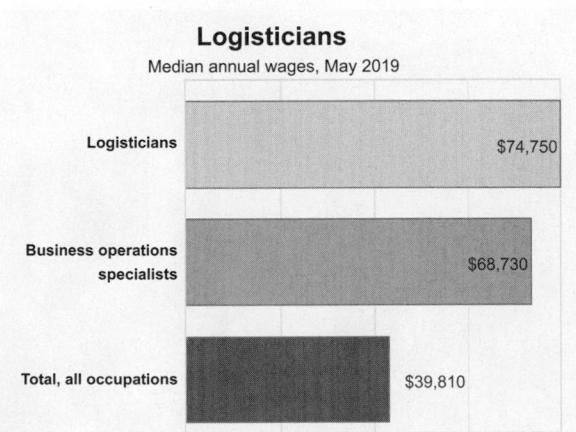

Logisticians
Median annual wages, May 2019

Logisticians $74,750
Business operations specialists $68,730
Total, all occupations $39,810

Note: All Occupations includes all occupations in the U.S. Economy.
Source: U.S. Bureau of Labor Statistics, Occupational Employment Statistics.

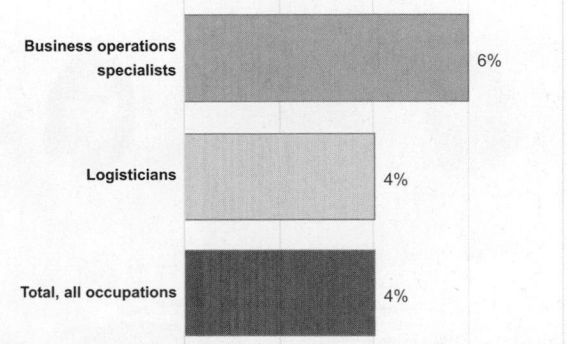

Logisticians
Percent change in employment, projected 2019-29

Business operations specialists 6%
Logisticians 4%
Total, all occupations 4%

Note: All Occupations includes all occupations in the U.S. Economy.
Source: U.S. Bureau of Labor Statistics, Employment Projections program.

State & Area Data
Occupational Employment Statistics (OES)
The Occupational Employment Statistics (OES) program produces employment and wage estimates annually for over 800 occupations. These estimates are available for the nation as a whole, for individual states, and for metropolitan and nonmetropolitan areas.

Contacts for More Information
For more information about logisticians, including certification, visit
➤ APICS
➤ Defense Acquisition University
➤ International Society of Logistics

Management Analysts

Summary

Quick Facts: Management Analysts

2019 Median Pay	$85,260 per year $40.99 per hour
Typical Entry-Level Education	Bachelor's degree
Work Experience in a Related Occupation	Less than 5 years
On-the-job Training	None
Number of Jobs, 2019	876,300
Job Outlook, 2019-29	11% (Much faster than average)
Employment Change, 2019-29	93,800

What Management Analysts Do
Management analysts recommend ways to improve an organization's efficiency.

Work Environment
Management analysts may travel frequently to meet with clients. Some work more than 40 hours per week.

How to Become a Management Analyst
Management analysts typically need at least a bachelor's degree and several years of related work experience.

Pay
The median annual wage for management analysts was $85,260 in May 2019.

Job Outlook
Employment of management analysts is projected to grow 11 percent from 2019 to 2029, much faster than the average for all occupations. Demand for the services of these workers is expected to increase as organizations continue to seek ways to improve efficiency and control costs.

State & Area Data
Explore resources for employment and wages by state and area for management analysts.

What Management Analysts Do
Management analysts, often called *management consultants*, recommend ways to improve an organization's efficiency. They advise managers on how to make organizations more profitable through reduced costs and increased revenues.

Duties
Management analysts typically do the following:

- Gather and organize information about the problems to be solved or the procedures to be improved

Management analysts propose ways to improve an organization's efficiency.

Although some management analysts work for the company that they are analyzing, most work as consultants on a contractual basis.

- Interview personnel and conduct onsite observations to determine the methods, equipment, and personnel that will be needed
- Analyze financial and other data, including revenue, expenditure, and employment reports
- Develop solutions or alternative practices
- Recommend new systems, procedures, or organizational changes
- Make recommendations to management through presentations or written reports
- Confer with managers to ensure changes are working

Although some management analysts work for the organization that they analyze, many work as consultants on a contractual basis.

The work of management analysts may vary from project to project. Some projects require a team of analysts, each specializing in one area. On other projects, analysts work independently with the client organization's managers.

Management analysts often specialize in certain areas, such as inventory control or reorganizing corporate structures for efficiency. Some focus on a specific industry, such as healthcare or telecommunications. In government, management analysts usually specialize by type of agency.

Organizations hire management analysts to develop strategies for entering and remaining competitive in the market.

Management analysts who work on contract may write proposals and bid for jobs. Typically, an organization that needs the help of a management analyst requests proposals from a number of consultants and consulting companies that specialize in the needed work. Interested companies then submit a proposal that explains details such as how the work will be completed, what the schedule will be, and how much it will cost. The organization selects the proposal that best meets its needs and budget.

Work Environment

Management analysts held about 876,300 jobs in 2019. The largest employers of management analysts were as follows:

Professional, scientific, and technical services	32%
Government	17
Self-employed workers	15
Finance and insurance	12
Management of companies and enterprises	5

Management analysts usually divide their time between their offices and the client's site. Because they must spend a significant amount of time with clients, analysts travel frequently. Analysts may experience stress, especially when trying to meet a client's demands on a tight schedule.

Because they must spend a significant portion of their time with clients, analysts travel frequently.

Work Schedules

Analysts often work many hours under tight deadlines. Some work more than 40 hours per week.

How to Become a Management Analyst

Management analysts typically need at least a bachelor's degree and several years of related work experience.

Education

A bachelor's degree is the typical entry-level requirement for management analysts. However, some employers prefer to hire candidates who have a master's degree in business administration (MBA).

Management analysts address a range of topics, and many fields of study provide a suitable educational background. Common fields of study include business, economics, finance, marketing, and psychology.

Licenses, Certifications, and Registrations

The Institute of Management Consultants USA (IMC USA) offers the Certified Management Consultant (CMC) designation to those who meet minimum levels of education and experience and who complete other requirements. Management

A bachelor's degree is the typical entry-level requirement for obtaining a management analyst position.

Management Analysts

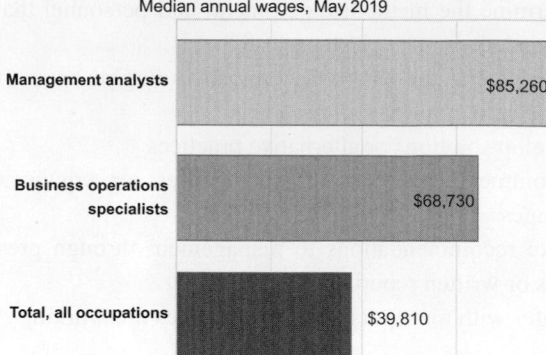

Median annual wages, May 2019

Management analysts	$85,260
Business operations specialists	$68,730
Total, all occupations	$39,810

Note: All Occupations includes all occupations in the U.S. Economy.
Source: U.S. Bureau of Labor Statistics, Occupational Employment Statistics.

analysts are not required to get certification, but having the credential may give jobseekers a competitive advantage.

Work Experience in a Related Occupation

Many analysts enter the occupation with several years of work experience. Organizations that specialize in certain fields typically try to hire candidates who have experience in those areas. For example, tax preparation firms may prefer candidates who have worked as an accountant or auditor, and software companies might seek those with experience as a computer systems analyst.

Advancement

As management analysts gain experience, they often take on more responsibility. Senior-level analysts may supervise teams working on complex projects and may become involved in seeking out new business. Those with exceptional skills may eventually become partners in their organization and focus on attracting new clients and bringing in revenue. Senior analysts may leave consulting and move to management positions at non-consulting organizations.

Important Qualities

Analytical skills. Management analysts must be able to interpret information and use their findings to make proposals.

Communication skills. Management analysts must be able to convey information clearly in both writing and speaking. Analysts also need good listening skills to understand an organization's problems and recommend appropriate solutions.

Interpersonal skills. Management analysts work with managers and other employees of the organizations for which they provide consulting services. They should be able to work as a team toward achieving the organization's goals.

Problem-solving skills. Management analysts must be able to think creatively to solve clients' problems. Although some aspects of clients' problems may be similar, each situation is likely to present unique challenges for the analyst to solve.

Time-management skills. Management analysts often work under tight deadlines and must use their time efficiently to complete projects on schedule.

Pay

The median annual wage for management analysts was $85,260 in May 2019. The median wage is the wage at which half the workers in an occupation earned more than that amount and half earned less. The lowest 10 percent earned less than $49,700, and the highest 10 percent earned more than $154,310.

In May 2019, the median annual wages for management analysts in the top industries in which they worked were as follows:

Professional, scientific, and technical services	$91,160
Finance and insurance	84,940
Management of companies and enterprises	84,390
Government	79,720

Management analysts working for consulting firms are usually paid a base salary in addition to a year-end bonus. Self-employed analysts are paid directly by their clients, typically by either the hour or the project.

Analysts often work many hours under tight deadlines. Some work more than 40 hours per week.

Job Outlook

Employment of management analysts is projected to grow 11 percent from 2019 to 2029, much faster than the average for all occupations. Demand for consulting services is expected to increase as organizations seek ways to improve efficiency and control costs. As markets become more competitive, firms will need to use resources more efficiently.

Demand for management analysts is expected to be strong in healthcare. This industry segment is experiencing higher costs in part because of an aging population. In addition, more management analysts may be needed to help navigate the regulatory environment within health insurance.

Management Analysts
Percent change in employment, projected 2019-29

Note: All Occupations includes all occupations in the U.S. Economy.
Source: U.S. Bureau of Labor Statistics, Employment Projections program.

Information technology (IT) consultants are also expected to see high demand. Businesses will seek out consulting firms to help them attain a high level of cybersecurity and make sure their IT systems are efficient and up to date.

Growth is expected to be particularly strong in smaller consulting companies that specialize in specific industries or types of business function, such as information technology or human resources. Government agencies also are expected to seek the services of management analysts as they look for ways to reduce spending and improve efficiency.

Job Prospects
About 87,100 openings for management analysts are projected each year, on average, over the decade. Many of those openings are expected to result from the need to replace workers who transfer to different occupations or exit the labor force, such as to retire.

Job opportunities are expected to be best for those who have a graduate degree or a certification, specialized expertise, fluency in a foreign language, or a talent for sales and public relations.

Employment projections data for management analysts, 2019-29					
Occupational Title	SOC Code	Employment, 2019	Projected Employment, 2029	Change, 2019-29	
				Percent	Numeric
SOURCE: U.S. Bureau of Labor Statistics, Employment Projections program					
Management analysts	13-1111	876,300	970,200	11	93,800

State & Area Data
Occupational Employment Statistics (OES)
The Occupational Employment Statistics (OES) program produces employment and wage estimates annually for over 800 occupations. These estimates are available for the nation as a whole, for individual states, and for metropolitan and nonmetropolitan areas.

Contacts for More Information
For more information about the Certified Management Consultant designation, visit
➤ Institute of Management Consultants USA

For more information about other certifications in management consulting, visit
➤ Global Academy of Finance and Management

Market Research Analysts

Summary

Quick Facts: Market Research Analysts

2019 Median Pay	$63,790 per year $30.67 per hour
Typical Entry-Level Education	Bachelor's degree
Work Experience in a Related Occupation	None
On-the-job Training	None
Number of Jobs, 2019	738,100
Job Outlook, 2019-29	18% (Much faster than average)
Employment Change, 2019-29	130,300

What Market Research Analysts Do
Market research analysts study market conditions to examine potential sales of a product or service.

Work Environment
Because most industries use market research, these analysts are employed throughout the economy. Most analysts work full time during regular business hours. Some work under pressure of deadlines and tight schedules.

How to Become a Market Research Analyst
Most market research analysts need at least a bachelor's degree. Some research positions may require a master's degree. Strong math and analytical skills are essential.

Pay
The median annual wage for market research analysts was $63,790 in May 2019.

Job Outlook
Employment of market research analysts is projected to grow 18 percent from 2019 to 2029, much faster than the

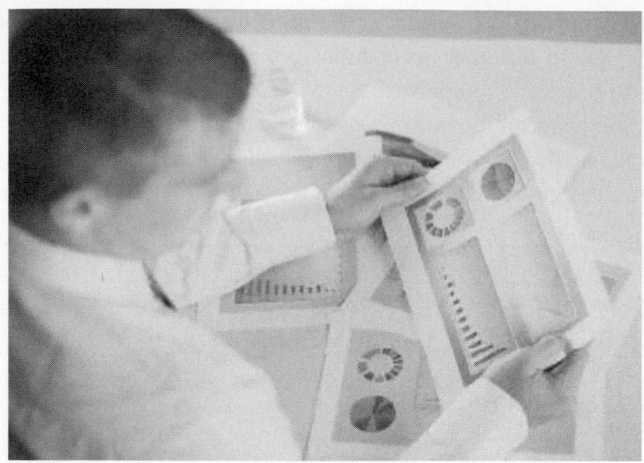

Market research analysts perform research and gather data to help a company market its products or services.

average for all occupations. Employment growth will be driven by an increased use of data and market research across many industries.

State & Area Data

Explore resources for employment and wages by state and area for market research analysts.

What Market Research Analysts Do

Market research analysts study market conditions to examine potential sales of a product or service. They help companies understand what products people want, who will buy them, and at what price.

Duties

Market research analysts typically do the following:

- Monitor and forecast marketing and sales trends
- Measure the effectiveness of marketing programs and strategies

Market research analysts gather and analyze data on consumers and competitors.

- Devise and evaluate methods for collecting data, such as surveys, questionnaires, and opinion polls
- Gather data on consumers, competitors, and market conditions
- Analyze data using statistical software
- Convert complex data and findings into understandable tables, graphs, and written reports
- Prepare reports and present results to clients and management

Market research analysts research and gather data to help a company market its products or services. They gather data on consumer demographics, preferences, needs, and buying habits. They collect data and information using a variety of methods, such as interviews, questionnaires, focus groups, market analysis surveys, public opinion polls, and literature reviews.

Analysts help determine a company's position in the marketplace by researching their competitors and analyzing their prices, sales, and marketing methods. Using this information, they may determine potential markets, product demand, and pricing. Their knowledge of the targeted consumer enables them to develop advertising brochures and commercials, sales plans, and product promotions.

Market research analysts evaluate data using statistical techniques and software. They must interpret what the data mean for their client, and they may forecast future trends. They often make charts, graphs, infographics, and other visual aids to present the results of their research.

Workers who design and conduct surveys are known as survey researchers.

Work Environment

Market research analysts held about 738,100 jobs in 2019. The largest employers of market research analysts were as follows:

Management, scientific, and technical consulting services	11%
Finance and insurance	10
Management of companies and enterprises	8
Wholesale trade	8
Publishing industries (except Internet)	4

Because most industries use market research, these analysts are employed throughout the economy.

Market research analysts can work individually or as part of a team, collecting, analyzing, and presenting data. For example, some analysts may work with graphic designers and artists to create charts, graphs, and infographics summarizing the research and findings.

Work Schedules

Most market research analysts work full time during regular business hours. Some, however, work under pressure of deadlines and tight schedules, which may require additional hours of work.

Market research analysts may give presentations to clients.

How to Become a Market Research Analyst

Most market research analysts need at least a bachelor's degree. Some research positions may require a master's degree. Strong math and analytical skills are essential.

Education

Market research analysts typically need a bachelor's degree in market research or a related field. Many have degrees in fields such as statistics, math, or computer science. Others have backgrounds in business administration, the social sciences, or communications.

Courses in statistics, research methods, and marketing are essential for these workers. Courses in communications and social sciences, such as economics or consumer behavior, are also important.

Some market research analyst jobs require a master's degree. Several schools offer graduate programs in marketing research, but many analysts complete degrees in other fields, such as statistics and marketing, and/or earn a master's degree in business administration (MBA). A master's degree is often required for leadership positions or positions that perform more technical research.

Licenses, Certifications, and Registrations

Certification is voluntary, but analysts may pursue certification to demonstrate a level of professional competency. The Marketing Research Association offers the Professional

Market research analysts measure the effectiveness of marketing strategies.

Researcher Certification (PRC) for market research analysts. Candidates qualify on the basis of experience and knowledge; they must pass an exam, have at least 3 years working in opinion and marketing research, and complete 12 hours of industry-related education courses. Individuals must complete 20 hours of industry-related continuing education courses every 2 years to renew their certification.

Important Qualities

Analytical skills. Market research analysts must be able to understand large amounts of data and information.

Communication skills. Market research analysts need strong communication skills when gathering information, interpreting data, and presenting results to clients.

Critical-thinking skills. To determine what marketing strategy would work best for a company, market research analysts must assess all available information.

Detail oriented. Market research analysts must be detail oriented because they often do precise data analysis.

Pay

The median annual wage for market research analysts was $63,790 in May 2019. The median wage is the wage at which half the workers in an occupation earned more than that amount and half earned less. The lowest 10 percent earned less than $34,350, and the highest 10 percent earned more than $122,630.

In May 2019, the median annual wages for market research analysts in the top industries in which they worked were as follows:

Publishing industries (except Internet)	$75,720
Management of companies and enterprises	74,510
Finance and insurance..	71,500
Wholesale trade...	61,780
Management, scientific, and technical consulting services	61,520

Market Research Analysts
Median annual wages, May 2019

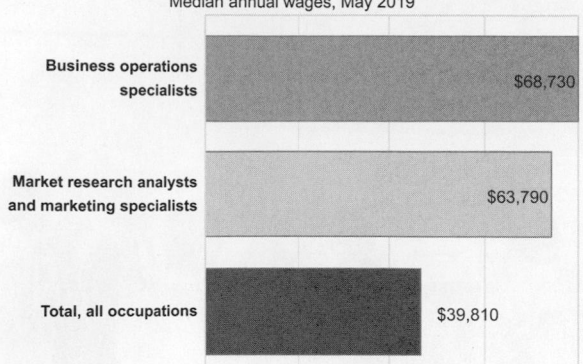

Note: All Occupations includes all occupations in the U.S. Economy.
Source: U.S. Bureau of Labor Statistics, Occupational Employment Statistics.

Most market research analysts work full time during regular business hours. Some, however, work under pressure of deadlines and tight schedules, which may require additional hours of work.

Job Outlook

Employment of market research analysts is projected to grow 18 percent from 2019 to 2029, much faster than the average for all occupations.

Employment growth will be driven by an increasing use of data and market research across many industries. They will be needed to help understand the needs and wants of customers, measure the effectiveness of marketing and business strategies, and identify the factors affecting product demand.

The increase in the collection and analyses of "big data"—extremely large sets of information, such as social media comments or online product reviews—can provide insight on consumer behaviors and preferences. Businesses will need market research analysts to conduct analyses of the data and information.

Job Prospects

Job prospects should be best for those with a master's degree in market research, marketing, statistics, or business administration.

Market Research Analysts
Percent change in employment, projected 2019-29

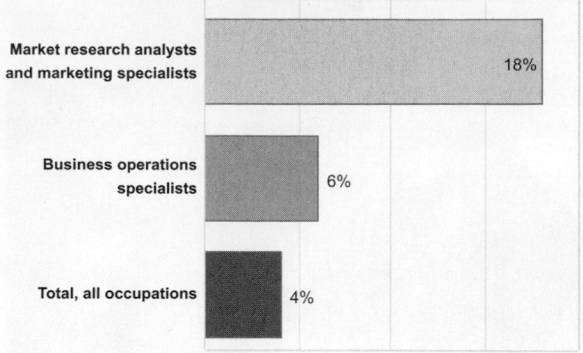

Note: All Occupations includes all occupations in the U.S. Economy.
Source: U.S. Bureau of Labor Statistics, Employment Projections program.

Those with a strong quantitative background in statistical and data analysis or related work experience will have better job opportunities than those without it.

Employment projections data for market research analysts, 2019-29					
Occupational Title	SOC Code	Employment, 2019	Projected Employment, 2029	Change, 2019-29	
				Percent	Numeric
SOURCE: U.S. Bureau of Labor Statistics, Employment Projections program					
Market research analysts and marketing specialists	13-1161	738,100	868,400	18	130,300

State & Area Data
Occupational Employment Statistics (OES)

The Occupational Employment Statistics (OES) program produces employment and wage estimates annually for over 800 occupations. These estimates are available for the nation as a whole, for individual states, and for metropolitan and nonmetropolitan areas.

Contacts for More Information

For more information about market research analysts, visit
➤ Insights Association

Meeting, Convention, and Event Planners

Summary

Quick Facts: Meeting, Convention, and Event Planners	
2019 Median Pay	$50,600 per year $24.33 per hour
Typical Entry-Level Education	Bachelor's degree
Work Experience in a Related Occupation	None
On-the-job Training	None
Number of Jobs, 2019	138,600
Job Outlook, 2019-29	8% (Much faster than average)
Employment Change, 2019-29	10,800

What Meeting, Convention, and Event Planners Do

Meeting, convention, and event planners arrange all aspects of events and professional gatherings.

Work Environment

Meeting, convention, and event planners work in their offices and onsite at hotels or conference centers. They often travel to attend events and visit meeting sites. During meetings or conventions, planners may work many more hours than usual.

How to Become a Meeting, Convention, or Event Planner

Meeting, convention, and event planners typically need a bachelor's degree. Some experience related to event planning may be helpful.

Pay

The median annual wage for meeting, convention, and event planners was $50,600 in May 2019.

Meeting, convention, and event planners coordinate all aspects of events and professional meetings. They arrange meeting locations, transportation, and other details.

Job Outlook

Employment of meeting, convention, and event planners is projected to grow 8 percent from 2019 to 2029, much faster than the average for all occupations. Job opportunities should be best for candidates who have experience and a bachelor's degree in meeting and event management, hospitality, or tourism management.

State & Area Data

Explore resources for employment and wages by state and area for meeting, convention, and event planners.

What Meeting, Convention, and Event Planners Do

Meeting, convention, and event planners arrange all aspects of events and professional gatherings. They arrange meeting locations, transportation, and other details.

Duties

Meeting, convention, and event planners typically do the following:

- Meet with clients to understand the purpose of the event
- Plan the scope of the event, including its time, location, and cost

Meeting, convention, and event planners meet with clients to understand the purpose of their meeting or event.

- Solicit bids from venues and service providers
- Inspect venues to ensure that they meet the client's requirements
- Coordinate event services such as rooms, transportation, and food
- Monitor event activities to ensure that the client and the attendees are satisfied
- Review event bills and approve payments

Meeting, convention, and event planners organize a variety of social and professional events, including weddings, educational conferences, and business conventions. They coordinate every detail of these events, including finances. Before planning a meeting, for example, planners meet with clients to estimate attendance and determine the meeting's purpose. During the event, they handle logistics, such as registering guests and organizing audiovisual equipment. After the meeting, they make sure that all vendors are paid, and they may survey attendees to obtain feedback on the event.

Meeting, convention, and event planners search for potential meeting sites, such as hotels and convention centers. They consider the lodging and services that the facility can provide, how easy it will be for people to get there, and the attractions that the surrounding area has to offer.

Once a location is selected, planners arrange the meeting space and support services, such as catering and interpreters. They negotiate contracts with suppliers and coordinate plans with the venue's staff. They may also organize speakers, entertainment, and activities.

The following are examples of types of meeting, convention, and event planners:

Meeting planners plan large meetings for organizations. *Healthcare meeting planners* specialize in organizing meetings and conferences for healthcare professionals. *Corporate planners* organize internal business meetings and meetings between businesses. These events may be in person or online and held either within corporate facilities or offsite to include more people.

Convention planners plan conventions and conferences for organizations. *Association planners* organize annual conferences and trade shows for professional associations. *Convention service managers* work for hotels and convention centers. They act as liaisons between the meeting facility and the planners who work for associations, businesses, and governments. They present food service options to outside planners, coordinate special requests, and suggest hotel services that work within a planner's budget.

Event planners arrange the details of a variety of events. *Wedding planners* are the most well known, but event planners also coordinate celebrations such as anniversaries, reunions, and other large social events, as well as corporate events, including product launches, galas, and award ceremonies. *Nonprofit event planners* plan large events with the goal of raising donations for

Meeting, convention, and event planners regularly collaborate with clients, hospitality workers, and meeting attendees.

a charity or advocacy organization. Events may include banquets, charity races, and food drives.

Exhibition organizers are responsible for all aspects of planning, promoting, and producing a display. They are also called exhibit managers, show managers, or show organizer.

Work Environment

Meeting, convention, and event planners held about 138,600 jobs in 2019. The largest employers of meeting, convention, and event planners were as follows:

Religious, grantmaking, civic, professional, and similar organizations	19%
Accommodation and food services	11
Administrative and support services	10
Arts, entertainment, and recreation	10
Self-employed workers	5

Meeting, convention, and event planners spend time in their offices and at event locations, such as hotels and convention centers. They may travel regularly to attend the events they organize and to visit meeting sites.

The work of meeting, convention, and event planners can be fast paced and demanding. Planners oversee many aspects of an event at the same time and face numerous deadlines, and they may coordinate multiple meetings or events at the same time.

Work Schedules

Most meeting, convention, and event planners work full time, and many work more than 40 hours per week. They often work additional hours to finalize preparations as major events approach. During meetings or conventions, planners may work on weekends.

How to Become a Meeting, Convention, or Event Planner

Meeting, convention, and event planners typically need a bachelor's degree. Some experience related to event planning may be helpful.

Education

Meeting, convention, and event planners typically need a bachelor's degree. Although some colleges offer degree programs in meeting and event management, other common fields of study include communications, business management, marketing, and business administration.

Planners who have studied meeting and event management or hospitality management may start out with greater responsibilities than do those from other academic disciplines. Some colleges offer continuing education courses in meeting and event planning.

Licenses, Certifications, and Registrations

A number of voluntary certifications are available for meeting and convention planners. Although not required, these certifications demonstrate specific knowledge or professional expertise.

The Events Industry Council offers the Certified Meeting Professional (CMP) credential, which is widely recognized in the industry and may help in career advancement. To qualify for the CMP, candidates' applications must include proof of experience and education. Those who qualify must then pass an exam that covers topics such as strategic planning, financial and risk management, facility operations and services, and logistics.

The Society of Government Meeting Professionals offers the Certified Government Meeting Professional (CGMP) designation for meeting planners who work for, or contract with, federal, state, or local government. This certification is helpful for candidates who want to show that they know government purchasing policies and travel regulations. To qualify, candidates must have worked as a meeting planner for at least 1 year and have been a member of SGMP for 6 months. To become a certified planner, members must take a 3-day course and pass an exam.

The International Association of Exhibitions and Events offers the Certified in Exhibition Management (CEM) designation, which demonstrates meeting professional standards for exhibitions and events management. Candidates obtain this credential by completing nine courses.

Some organizations, including the American Association of Certified Wedding Planners and the Association of Certified Professional Wedding Consultants, offer certifications in wedding planning that may be helpful for attracting clients.

Other Experience

Meeting, convention, and event planners may benefit from having some experience in meeting and event planning. Working in a variety of positions at hotels, convention centers, and convention bureaus provides knowledge of how the hospitality industry operates. Other beneficial work experiences include coordinating university or volunteer events and shadowing professionals.

Important Qualities

Communication skills. Meeting, convention, and event planners exchange information with clients, suppliers, and event staff. They must have excellent written and oral communication skills to express the needs of their clients.

Interpersonal skills. Meeting, convention, and event planners must establish and maintain positive relationships with clients and suppliers.

Negotiation skills. Meeting, convention, and event planners must be able to secure quality products and services at reasonable prices for their clients.

Organizational skills. Meeting, convention, and event planners must multitask, pay attention to details, and meet tight deadlines.

Problem-solving skills. Meeting, convention, and event planners must be able to anticipate potential issues and prepare creative solutions that satisfy clients.

Pay

The median annual wage for meeting, convention, and event planners was $50,600 in May 2019. The median wage is the wage at which half the workers in an occupation earned more than that amount and half earned less. The lowest 10 percent earned less than $28,590, and the highest 10 percent earned more than $86,390.

In May 2019, the median annual wages for meeting, convention, and event planners in the top industries in which they worked were as follows:

Administrative and support services	$53,460
Religious, grantmaking, civic, professional, and similar organizations	51,970
Accommodation and food services	44,590
Arts, entertainment, and recreation	43,380

Most meeting, convention, and event planners work full time, and many work more than 40 hours per week. They often work additional hours to finalize preparations as major events

Meeting, convention, and event planners typically need a bachelor's degree.

Meeting, Convention, and Event Planners

Median annual wages, May 2019

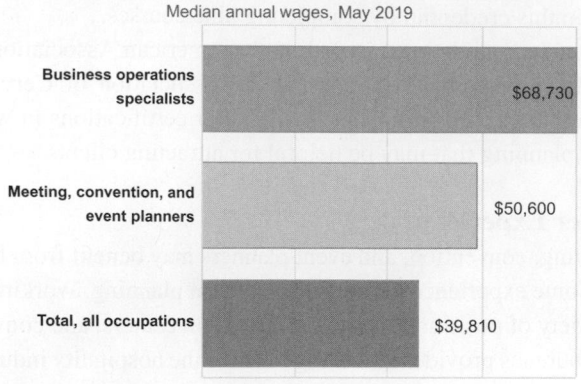

Note: All Occupations includes all occupations in the U.S. Economy.
Source: U.S. Bureau of Labor Statistics, Occupational Employment Statistics.

approach. During meetings or conventions, planners may work on weekends.

Job Outlook

Employment of meeting, convention, and event planners is projected to grow 8 percent from 2019 to 2029, much faster than the average for all occupations.

Demand for professionally planned meetings and events is expected to remain steady as businesses and organizations continue to host events regularly.

Job Prospects

About 15,200 openings for meeting, convention, and event planners are projected each year, on average, over the decade.

Many of those openings are expected to result from the need to replace workers who transfer to different occupations or exit the labor force, such as to retire.

Candidates with a bachelor's degree in meeting and event management, hospitality, or tourism management should have the best job opportunities. Those who have experience in the hospitality industry or with virtual meeting software and social media outlets should also have an advantage.

Employment projections data for meeting, convention, and event planners, 2019-29					
Occupational Title	SOC Code	Employment, 2019	Projected Employment, 2029	Change, 2019-29	
				Percent	Numeric
SOURCE: U.S. Bureau of Labor Statistics, Employment Projections program					

Meeting, Convention, and Event Planners

Percent change in employment, projected 2019-29

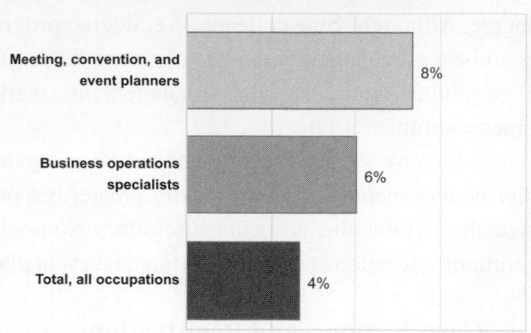

Note: All Occupations includes all occupations in the U.S. Economy.
Source: U.S. Bureau of Labor Statistics, Employment Projections program.

Employment projections data for meeting, convention, and event planners, 2019-29					
Occupational Title	SOC Code	Employment, 2019	Projected Employment, 2029	Change, 2019-29	
				Percent	Numeric
Meeting, convention, and event planners	13-1121	138,600	149,500	8	10,800

State & Area Data
Occupational Employment Statistics (OES)

The Occupational Employment Statistics (OES) program produces employment and wage estimates annually for over 800 occupations. These estimates are available for the nation as a whole, for individual states, and for metropolitan and nonmetropolitan areas.

Contacts for More Information

For more information about professional planning for meetings, conventions, exhibitions, and events, including information about certification and industry trends, visit

➤ Events Industry Council
➤ International Association of Exhibitions and Events
➤ Society of Government Meeting Professionals

For more information about wedding planners, including information about certification, visit

➤ American Association of Certified Wedding Planners
➤ Association of Bridal Consultants
➤ Association of Certified Professional Wedding Consultants

Personal Financial Advisors

Summary

Quick Facts: Personal Financial Advisors

2019 Median Pay	$87,850 per year $42.24 per hour
Typical Entry-Level Education	Bachelor's degree
Work Experience in a Related Occupation	None
On-the-job Training	Long-term on-the-job training
Number of Jobs, 2019	263,000
Job Outlook, 2019-29	4% (As fast as average)
Employment Change, 2019-29	11,600

What Personal Financial Advisors Do

Personal financial advisors provide advice to help individuals manage their finances and plan for their financial future.

Work Environment

Most personal financial advisors work in the finance and insurance industry or are self-employed. They typically work full time and may meet with clients in the evenings or on weekends.

How to Become a Personal Financial Advisor

Personal financial advisors typically need a bachelor's degree. A master's degree and certification can improve one's chances for advancement in the occupation.

Pay

The median annual wage for personal financial advisors was $87,850 in May 2019.

Job Outlook

Employment of personal financial advisors is projected to grow 4 percent from 2019 to 2029, about as fast as the average for all occupations. As the population ages and life expectancies rise, demand for financial planning services should increase.

State & Area Data

Explore resources for employment and wages by state and area for personal financial advisors.

What Personal Financial Advisors Do

Personal financial advisors provide advice on investments, insurance, mortgages, college savings, estate planning, taxes, and retirement to help individuals manage their finances.

Duties

Personal financial advisors typically do the following:

- Meet with clients in person to discuss their financial goals
- Explain the types of financial services they provide to potential clients
- Educate clients and answer questions about investment options and potential risks
- Recommend investments to clients or select investments on their behalf
- Help clients plan for specific circumstances, such as education expenses or retirement
- Monitor clients' accounts and determine if changes are needed to improve financial performance or to accommodate life changes, such as getting married or having children
- Research investment opportunities

Personal financial advisors assess the financial needs of individuals and help them with decisions on investments (such as stocks and bonds), tax laws, and insurance. Advisors help clients plan for short- and long-term goals, such as meeting education expenses and saving for retirement through investments. They invest clients' money based on the clients' decisions. Many advisors also provide tax advice or sell insurance.

Although most planners offer advice on a wide range of topics, some specialize in areas such as retirement or risk

Personal financial advisors help people with investments, taxes, and insurance decisions.

Personal financial advisors meet with clients to discuss their financial goals.

management (evaluating how willing the investor is to take chances and adjusting investments accordingly).

Many personal financial advisors spend a lot of time marketing their services, and they meet potential clients by giving seminars or participating in business and social networking. Networking is the process of meeting and exchanging information with people, or groups of people, who have similar interests.

After financial advisors have invested funds for a client, they and the client receive regular investment reports. Advisors monitor the client's investments and usually meet with each client at least once a year to update the client on potential investments and to adjust the financial plan based on the client's circumstances or because investment options may have changed.

Many personal financial advisors are licensed to directly buy and sell financial products, such as stocks, bonds, annuities, and insurance. Depending on the agreement they have with their clients, personal financial advisors may have the client's permission to make decisions about buying and selling stocks and bonds.

Private bankers or *wealth managers* are personal financial advisors who work for people who have a lot of money to invest. These clients are similar to institutional investors (commonly, companies or organizations), and they approach investing differently than the general public does. Private bankers manage a collection of investments, called a portfolio, for these clients by using the resources of the bank, including teams of financial analysts, accountants, and other professionals.

Work Environment

Personal financial advisors held about 263,000 jobs in 2019. The largest employers of personal financial advisors were as follows:

Securities, commodity contracts, and other financial investments and related activities............................	58%
Self-employed workers	19
Credit intermediation and related activities	13
Insurance carriers and related activities	4
Management of companies and enterprises	2

Personal financial advisors typically work in offices. Some also travel to attend conferences, teach finance seminars in the evening, and attend networking events to bring in more clients.

Work Schedules

Most personal financial advisors work full time and some work more than 40 hours per week. They often go to meetings on evenings and weekends to meet with prospective or existing clients.

How to Become a Personal Financial Advisor

Personal financial advisors typically need a bachelor's degree. A master's degree and certification can improve one's chances for advancement in the occupation.

Education

Personal financial advisors typically need a bachelor's degree. Although employers usually do not require personal financial advisors to have completed a specific course of study, a degree in finance, economics, accounting, business, mathematics, or law is good preparation for this occupation. Courses in investments, taxes, estate planning, and risk management are also helpful. Programs in financial planning are becoming more available in colleges and universities.

Training

Once they are hired, personal financial advisors often enter an on-the-job training period. During this time, new advisors work under the supervision of senior advisors and learn how to perform their duties, including building a client network and developing investment portfolios. This training usually lasts for more than a year.

Many personal financial advisors travel to attend conferences or teach finance classes in the evening to bring in more clients.

Personal financial advisors must establish trust with clients and respond to their questions and concerns.

Licenses, Certifications, and Registrations

Personal financial advisors who directly buy or sell stocks, bonds, or insurance policies, or who provide specific investment advice, need a combination of licenses that varies with the products they sell. In addition to being required to have those licenses, advisors in smaller firms that manage clients' investments must be registered with state regulators and those in larger firms must be registered with the Securities and Exchange Commission. Personal financial advisors who choose to sell insurance need licenses issued by state boards. Information on state licensing board requirements for registered investment advisors is available from the North American Securities Administrators Association.

Certifications can enhance a personal financial advisor's reputation and can help bring in new clients. The Certified Financial Planner Board of Standards offers the Certified Financial Planner (CFP) certification. For this certification, advisors must have a bachelor's degree, complete at least 3 years of relevant work experience, pass an exam, and agree to adhere to a code of ethics. The CFP exam covers the general principles of financial planning, insurance planning, risk management, employee benefits planning, income taxes and retirement planning, investment and real estate planning, debt management, planning liability, emergency fund reserves, and statistical modeling.

Advancement

A master's degree in an area such as finance or business administration can improve a personal financial advisor's chances of moving into a management position and attracting new clients.

Important Qualities

Analytical skills. In determining an investment portfolio for a client, personal financial advisors must be able to take into account a range of information, including economic trends, regulatory changes, and the client's comfort with risky decisions.

Interpersonal skills. A major part of a personal financial advisor's job is making clients feel comfortable. Advisors must establish trust with clients and respond well to their questions and concerns.

Math skills. Personal financial advisors should be good at mathematics because they constantly work with numbers. They determine the amount invested, how that amount has grown or decreased over time, and how a portfolio is distributed among different investments.

Sales skills. To expand their base of clients, personal financial advisors must be convincing and persistent in selling their services.

Speaking skills. Personal financial advisors interact with clients every day. They must explain complex financial concepts in understandable language.

Pay

The median annual wage for personal financial advisors was $87,850 in May 2019. The median wage is the wage at which

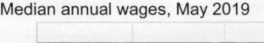

Personal Financial Advisors

Median annual wages, May 2019

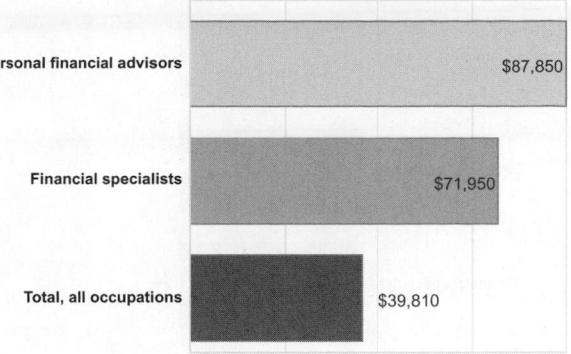

Personal financial advisors	$87,850
Financial specialists	$71,950
Total, all occupations	$39,810

Note: All Occupations includes all occupations in the U.S. Economy. Source: U.S. Bureau of Labor Statistics, Occupational Employment Statistics.

half the workers in an occupation earned more than that amount and half earned less. The lowest 10 percent earned less than $42,950, and the highest 10 percent earned more than $208,000.

In May 2019, the median annual wages for personal financial advisors in the top industries in which they worked were as follows:

Securities, commodity contracts, and other financial investments and related activities	$95,540
Management of companies and enterprises	85,150
Credit intermediation and related activities	76,590
Insurance carriers and related activities	71,280

Personal financial advisors who work for financial services firms are often paid a salary plus bonuses. Bonuses are not included in the wage data here.

Advisors who work for financial investment firms or financial planning firms, or who are self-employed, typically earn their money by charging a percentage of the clients' assets that they manage. They also may earn money by charging an hourly fee or by getting fees on stock and insurance purchases. In addition to their fees, advisors generally get commissions for financial products that they sell.

Most personal financial advisors work full time and some work more than 40 hours per week. They often go to meetings on evenings and weekends to meet with existing clients or to try to bring in new ones.

Job Outlook

Employment of personal financial advisors is projected to grow 4 percent from 2019 to 2029, about as fast as the average for all occupations.

The primary driver of employment growth will be the aging population. As large numbers of baby boomers approach retirement, more are likely to seek planning advice from personal financial advisors. Also, longer lifespans will lead to longer retirement periods, further increasing demand for financial planning services.

Personal Financial Advisors

Percent change in employment, projected 2019-29

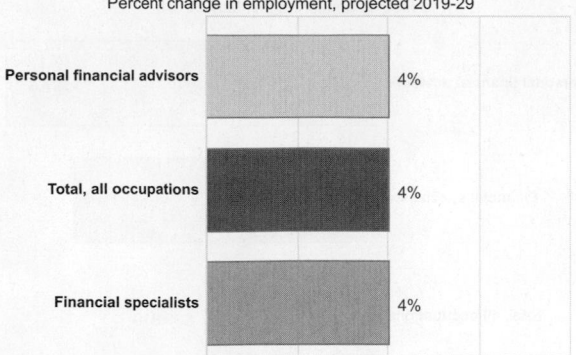

Personal financial advisors	4%
Total, all occupations	4%
Financial specialists	4%

Note: All Occupations includes all occupations in the U.S. Economy.
Source: U.S. Bureau of Labor Statistics, Employment Projections
program.

In addition, the replacement of traditional pension plans with individual retirement accounts is expected to continue. Many people used to receive defined pension payments in retirement, but most companies no longer offer these plans. Therefore, individuals must save and invest for their own retirement, increasing the demand for personal financial advisors.

The emergence of "robo-advisors," computer programs that provide automated investment advice based on user inputs, will partially temper demand for personal financial advisors. However, the impact of this technology should be limited as consumers continue turning to human advisors for more complex and specialized investment advice over the next 10 years.

Job Prospects

About 19,200 openings for personal financial advisors are projected each year, on average, over the decade.

Many of those openings are expected to result from the need to replace workers who transfer to different occupations or exit the labor force, such as to retire.

Those who obtain certification will likely have the best prospects.

Employment projections data for personal financial advisors, 2019-29					
Occupational Title	SOC Code	Employment, 2019	Projected Employment, 2029	Change, 2019-29	
				Percent	Numeric
SOURCE: U.S. Bureau of Labor Statistics, Employment Projections program					
Personal financial advisors	13-2052	263,000	274,600	4	11,600

State & Area Data
Occupational Employment Statistics (OES)

The Occupational Employment Statistics (OES) program produces employment and wage estimates annually for over 800 occupations. These estimates are available for the nation as a whole, for individual states, and for metropolitan and nonmetropolitan areas.

Contacts for More Information

For more information about personal financial advisors, visit
➤ Financial Industry Regulatory Authority (FINRA)
➤ North American Securities Administrators Association
➤ U.S. Securities and Exchange Commission (SEC)
➤ Certified Financial Planner Board of Standards
➤ Global Academy of Finance and Management

Purchasing Managers, Buyers, and Purchasing Agents

Summary

Quick Facts: Purchasing Managers, Buyers, and Purchasing Agents

2019 Median Pay	$69,600 per year $33.46 per hour
Typical Entry-Level Education	Bachelor's degree
Work Experience in a Related Occupation	See below
On-the-job Training	See below
Number of Jobs, 2019	526,200
Job Outlook, 2019-29	-7% (Decline)
Employment Change, 2019-29	-37,600

What Purchasing Managers, Buyers, and Purchasing Agents Do

Buyers and purchasing agents buy products and services for organizations. Purchasing managers oversee the work of buyers and purchasing agents.

Work Environment

Most purchasing managers and buyers and purchasing agents work full time. Some work more than 40 hours per week.

How to Become a Purchasing Manager, Buyer, or Purchasing Agent

Buyers and purchasing agents typically have a bachelor's degree. Purchasing managers must also have a few years of work experience.

Pay

The median annual wage for buyers and purchasing agents was $64,380 in May 2019.

The median annual wage for purchasing managers was $121,110 in May 2019.

Job Outlook

Overall employment of purchasing managers and buyers and purchasing agents is projected to decline 7 percent from 2019 to 2029. However, many openings are expected each year because of the need to replace workers who leave the occupation.

Purchasing managers, buyers, and purchasing agents evaluate suppliers, negotiate contracts, and review product quality.

State & Area Data

Explore resources for employment and wages by state and area for purchasing managers, buyers, and purchasing agents.

What Purchasing Managers, Buyers, and Purchasing Agents Do

Buyers and purchasing agents buy products and services for organizations to use or resell. They evaluate suppliers, negotiate contracts, and review the quality of products. Purchasing managers oversee the work of buyers and purchasing agents and typically handle more complex procurement tasks.

Duties

Purchasing managers and buyers and purchasing agents typically do the following:

- Evaluate suppliers on the basis of the price, quality, and speed of delivery of their products and services
- Interview vendors and visit suppliers' plants and distribution centers to examine and learn about products, services, and prices
- Attend meetings, trade shows, and conferences to learn about new industry trends and make contacts with suppliers
- Analyze price proposals, financial reports, and other information to determine reasonable prices
- Negotiate contracts on behalf of their organization
- Work out agreements with suppliers, such as when products will be delivered
- Meet with staff and vendors to discuss defective or unacceptable goods or services and determine corrective action
- Evaluate and monitor contracts to be sure that vendors and suppliers comply with the terms and conditions of the contract and to determine the need for changes
- Maintain and review records of items bought, costs, deliveries, product performance, and inventories

In addition to these tasks, purchasing managers also plan and coordinate the work of buyers and purchasing agents and hire and train new staff.

Purchasing agents and buyers consider price, quality, availability, reliability, and technical support when choosing suppliers and merchandise.

Purchasing managers are also responsible for developing their organization's procurement policies and procedures. These policies help ensure that procurement professionals are meeting ethical standards to avoid potential conflicts of interest or inappropriate supplier and customer relations.

Buyers and purchasing agents buy farm products, durable and nondurable goods, and services for organizations and institutions. They try to get the best deal for their organization: the highest quality goods and services at the lowest cost. They do this by studying sales records and inventory levels of current stock, identifying foreign and domestic suppliers, and keeping up to date with changes affecting both the supply of, and demand for, products and materials.

Purchasing agents and buyers consider price, quality, availability, reliability, and technical support when choosing suppliers and merchandise. To be effective, purchasing agents and buyers must have a working technical knowledge of the goods or services they are purchasing.

Evaluating suppliers is one of the most critical functions of a buyer or purchasing agent. They ensure the supplies are ordered in time so that any delays in the supply chain does not shut down production and cause the organization to lose customers.

Buyers and purchasing agents use many resources to find out all they can about potential suppliers. They attend meetings, trade shows, and conferences to learn about new industry trends and make contacts with suppliers.

They often interview prospective suppliers and visit their plants and distribution centers to assess their capabilities. For example, they may discuss the design of products with design engineers, quality concerns with production supervisors, or shipping issues with managers in the receiving department.

Buyers and purchasing agents must make certain that the supplier can deliver the desired goods or services on time, in the correct quantities, and without sacrificing quality. Once they have gathered information on suppliers, they sign contracts with suppliers who meet the organization's needs and they place orders.

Buyers who purchase items to resell to customers may determine which products their organization will sell. They need to be able to predict what will appeal to their customers. If they are wrong, they could jeopardize the profits and reputation of their organization.

Buyers who work for large organizations often specialize in purchasing one or two categories of products or services. Buyers who work for smaller businesses or government agencies may be responsible for making a greater variety of purchases.

The following are examples of types of buyers and purchasing agents:

Purchasing agents and buyers of farm products buy agricultural products for further processing or resale. Examples of these products are grain, cotton, and tobacco.

Purchasing agents, except wholesale, retail, and farm products buy items for the operation of an organization. Examples of these items are chemicals and industrial equipment needed for a manufacturing establishment, and office supplies.

Wholesale and retail buyers purchase goods for resale to consumers. Examples of these goods are clothing and electronics. Purchasing specialists who buy finished goods for resale are commonly known as *buyers* or *merchandise managers*.

Work Environment

Buyers and purchasing agents held about 449,300 jobs in 2019. The largest employers of buyers and purchasing agents were as follows:

Manufacturing	23%
Wholesale trade	14
Government	13
Management of companies and enterprises	10
Retail trade	8

Purchasing managers held about 76,900 jobs in 2019. The largest employers of purchasing managers were as follows:

Purchasing managers plan and coordinate the work of buyers and purchasing agents.

Manufacturing	26%
Management of companies and enterprises	16
Government	12
Wholesale trade	11

Most purchasing managers and buyers and purchasing agents work in offices. Travel is sometimes necessary to visit suppliers or review products.

Work Schedules

Most purchasing managers and buyers and purchasing agents work full time. Overtime is common in these occupations.

How to Become a Purchasing Manager, Buyer, or Purchasing Agent

Buyers and purchasing agents typically have a bachelor's degree. A bachelor's degree and a few years of work experience in procurement is required for purchasing manager positions.

Education

Purchasing managers usually have at least a bachelor's degree and some work experience in procurement.

Educational requirements for buyers and purchasing agents usually vary with the size of the organization. Although a high school diploma may be enough at some organizations, many businesses require applicants to have a bachelor's degree. For many positions, a degree in business, finance, or supply management is sufficient.

For those interested in a career as a buyer or purchasing agent of farm products, a degree in agriculture, agriculture production, or animal science is often beneficial.

Training

Buyers and purchasing agents typically get on-the-job training for a few months. During this time, they learn how to perform their basic duties, including monitoring inventory levels and negotiating with suppliers.

Licenses, Certifications, and Registrations

There are several certifications available for buyers and purchasing agents. Although some employers may require certification, many do not.

Most of these certifications involve oral or written exams and have education and work experience requirements.

The American Purchasing Society offers the Certified Purchasing Professional (CPP) certification. The CPP certification is valid for 5 years. Candidates must earn a certain number of professional development "points" to renew their certification. Candidates initially become eligible and can renew their certification through a combination of purchasing-related experience, education, and professional contributions (such as published articles or delivered speeches).

Buyers and purchasing agents typically receive on-the-job training which lasts for more than 1 year.

APICS offers the Certified Supply Chain Professional (CSCP) credential. Applicants must have 3 years of relevant business experience or a bachelor's degree in order to be eligible for the CSCP credential. The credential is valid for 5 years. Candidates must also earn a certain number of professional development points to renew their certification.

The Next Level Purchasing Association offers the Senior Professional in Supply Management (SPSM) certification. Although there are no education or work experience requirements, applicants must complete six online courses and pass an SPSM exam. Certification is valid for 4 years. Candidates must complete 32 continuing education hours in procurement-related topics to recertify for an additional 4-year period.

The Universal Public Procurement Certification Council (UPPCC) offers two certifications for workers in federal, state, and local government. The Certified Professional Public Buyer (CPPB) credential requires applicants to have earned at least an associate's degree, possess at least 3 years of public procurement experience, and complete relevant training courses. The Certified Public Purchasing Officer (CPPO) requires applicants to have earned a bachelor's degree, possess

at least 5 years of public procurement experience, and complete additional training courses.

Those with the CPPB or the CPPO designation must renew their certification every 5 years by completing continuing education courses or attending procurement-related conferences or events.

The National Institute of Government Purchasing (NIGP) and the National Association of State Procurement Officials (NASPO) offer preparation courses for the UPPCC certification exams.

Work Experience in a Related Occupation

Purchasing managers typically must have at least 5 years of experience as a buyer or purchasing agent. At the top levels, purchasing manager duties may overlap with other management functions, such as production, planning, logistics, and marketing.

Advancement

An experienced purchasing agent or buyer may become an assistant purchasing manager before advancing to purchasing manager, supply manager, or director of materials management.

Purchasing managers and buyers and purchasing agents with extensive work experience can also advance to become the Chief Procurement Officer (CPO) for an organization.

Important Qualities

Analytical skills. When evaluating suppliers, purchasing managers and buyers and purchasing agents must analyze their options and choose a supplier with the best combination of price, quality, delivery, or service.

Decisionmaking skills. Purchasing managers and buyers and purchasing agents must have the ability to make informed and timely decisions, choosing products that they think will sell.

Math skills. Purchasing managers and buyers and purchasing agents must possess math skills. They must be able to compare prices from different suppliers to ensure that their organization is getting the best deal.

Negotiating skills. Purchasing managers and buyers and purchasing agents often must negotiate the terms of a contract with a supplier. Interpersonal skills and self-confidence, in addition to knowledge of the product, can help lead to successful negotiations.

Pay

The median annual wage for buyers and purchasing agents was $64,380 in May 2019. The median wage is the wage at which half the workers in an occupation earned more than that amount and half earned less. The lowest 10 percent earned less than $38,230, and the highest 10 percent earned more than $107,510.

The median annual wage for purchasing managers was $121,110 in May 2019. The lowest 10 percent earned less than $71,450, and the highest 10 percent earned more than $193,400.

Purchasing Managers, Buyers, and Purchasing Agents

Median annual wages, May 2019

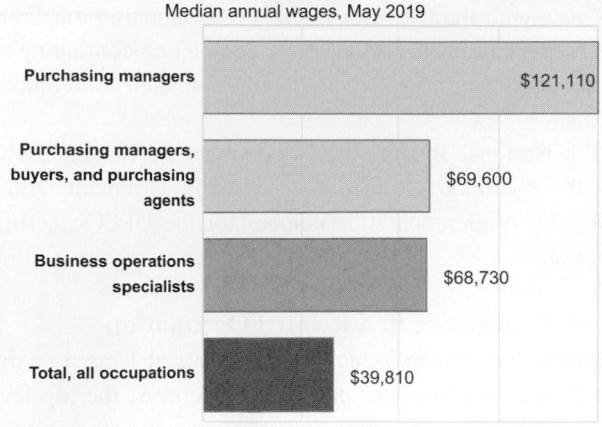

Note: All Occupations includes all occupations in the U.S. Economy.
Source: U.S. Bureau of Labor Statistics, Occupational Employment Statistics.

In May 2019, the median annual wages for buyers and purchasing agents in the top industries in which they worked were as follows:

Government	$78,030
Management of companies and enterprises	71,870
Manufacturing	64,340
Wholesale trade	59,010
Retail trade	50,990

In May 2019, the median annual wages for purchasing managers in the top industries in which they worked were as follows:

Management of companies and enterprises	$134,080
Government	126,050
Manufacturing	115,820
Wholesale trade	113,520

Most purchasing managers and buyers and purchasing agents work full time. Overtime is common in these occupations.

Job Outlook

Overall employment of purchasing managers and buyers and purchasing agents is projected to decline 7 percent from 2019 to 2029. Employment growth will vary by occupation.

Projected employment declines of buyers and purchasing agents are expected due to increased automation and outsourcing of some procurement tasks. As procurement technology continues to improve, less complex procurement functions, such as finding suppliers or processing purchase orders, will likely be automated. In addition, some organizations may rely on third parties to handle other tasks, such as market research or supplier risk assessments. Organizations may outsource

Purchasing Managers, Buyers, and Purchasing Agents

Percent change in employment, projected 2019-29

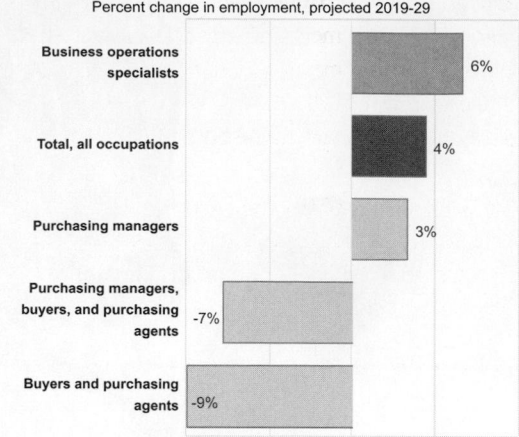

Note: All Occupations includes all occupations in the U.S. Economy.
Source: U.S. Bureau of Labor Statistics, Employment Projections program.

these functions in order to focus on more complex or strategic procurement tasks and to reduce costs.

In the public sector, employment demand may be negatively affected by the increasing use of cooperative purchasing agreements. These agreements allow state and local governments to share resources in order to buy supplies and make other general purchases. Because the same standard contracts can be used multiple times by multiple government agencies, the rise of purchasing cooperatives may limit the need to hire additional procurement officers.

Employment for purchasing managers is projected to increase because they will continue to be needed to help procure goods and services for business operations or for resale to customers.

Job Prospects

About 5,600 openings for purchasing managers are projected each year, on average, over the decade. Despite declining employment, about 36,000 openings for buyers and purchasing agents are projected annually over the decade in this relatively large occupation.

Most of those openings for purchasing managers and all of the openings for buyers and purchasing agents are expected to result from the need to replace workers who transfer to other occupations or exit the labor force, such as to retire.

Employment projections data for purchasing managers, buyers, and purchasing agents, 2019-29					
Occupational Title	SOC Code	Employment, 2019	Projected Employment, 2029	Change, 2019-29	
				Percent	Numeric
SOURCE: U.S. Bureau of Labor Statistics, Employment Projections program					
Purchasing managers, buyers, and purchasing agents	—	526,200	488,600	-7	-37,600
Purchasing managers	11-3061	76,900	78,900	3	2,000
Buyers and purchasing agents	13-1020	449,300	409,700	-9	-39,700

State & Area Data
Occupational Employment Statistics (OES)
The Occupational Employment Statistics (OES) program produces employment and wage estimates annually for over 800 occupations. These estimates are available for the nation as a whole, for individual states, and for metropolitan and nonmetropolitan areas.

Contacts for More Information
For more information about buyers and purchasing agents, including information on education, training, employment, and certification, visit

➤ American Purchasing Society
➤ APICS
➤ Next Level Purchasing Association

The National Institute of Government Purchasing (NIGP), Institute for Public Procurement

➤ Universal Public Procurement Certification Council
➤ National Association of State Procurement Officials

Tax Examiners and Collectors, and Revenue Agents

Summary

Quick Facts: Tax Examiners and Collectors, and Revenue Agents

2019 Median Pay	$54,890 per year $26.39 per hour
Typical Entry-Level Education	Bachelor's degree
Work Experience in a Related Occupation	None
On-the-job Training	Moderate-term on-the-job training
Number of Jobs, 2019	57,600
Job Outlook, 2019-29	-4% (Decline)
Employment Change, 2019-29	-2,400

Tax examiners and collectors, and revenue agents review tax returns, conduct audits, identify taxes owed, and collect overdue tax payments.

What Tax Examiners and Collectors, and Revenue Agents Do
Tax examiners and collectors, and revenue agents determine how much is owed in taxes and collect tax from individuals and businesses on behalf of the government.

Work Environment
Tax examiners and collectors, and revenue agents work for federal, state, and local governments. Many work primarily in an office environment; others spend most of their time doing field audits in taxpayers' homes or places of business.

How to Become a Tax Examiner or Collector, or Revenue Agent
Most tax examiners and collectors, and revenue agents need a bachelor's degree in accounting or a related field. However, the level of education and experience required varies with the position and employer.

Pay
The median annual wage for tax examiners and collectors, and revenue agents was $54,890 in May 2019.

Job Outlook
Employment of tax examiners and collectors, and revenue agents is projected to decline 4 percent from 2019 to 2029. Employment of these workers will depend primarily on future changes to federal, state, and local government budgets.

State & Area Data
Explore resources for employment and wages by state and area for tax examiners and collectors, and revenue agents.

What Tax Examiners and Collectors, and Revenue Agents Do
Tax examiners and collectors, and revenue agents determine how much is owed in taxes and collect tax from individuals and businesses on behalf of federal, state, and local governments.

They review tax returns, conduct audits, identify taxes owed, and collect overdue tax payments.

Duties

Tax examiners and collectors, and revenue agents typically do the following:

- Review filed tax returns to determine whether credits and deductions claimed are allowed by law
- Contact taxpayers to address problems and to request supporting documentation
- Conduct field audits and investigations of income tax returns to verify information or to update tax liabilities
- Evaluate financial information, using their familiarity with accounting procedures and knowledge of changes to tax laws and regulations
- Keep records on each case they deal with, including contacts, telephone numbers, and actions taken
- Notify taxpayers of any overpayment or underpayment and either issue a refund or request additional payment

Tax examiners and collectors, and revenue agents are responsible for ensuring that individuals and businesses pay the appropriate amount of taxes they owe, as prescribed by laws and regulations. In addition to verifying that tax returns are filed properly, they follow up with taxpayers whose returns are questionable or who owe more money.

Different levels of government collect different types of taxes. The federal government deals primarily with personal and business income taxes. State governments collect income and sales taxes. Local governments collect sales and property taxes.

Because many states assess individual income taxes on the basis of the taxpayer's reported federal income, tax examiners working for the federal government report to the states any adjustments or corrections they make. State tax examiners then

Tax examiners and collectors, and revenue agents are responsible for ensuring that individuals and businesses pay the taxes they owe.

determine whether the adjustments affect the state taxpayer liability.

Tax examiners and collectors, and revenue agents have different duties and responsibilities:

Tax examiners usually deal with the simplest tax returns: those filed by individual taxpayers who claim few deductions and those filed by small businesses. Tax examiners also may contact individual taxpayers in order to resolve any outstanding problems with their returns.

Much of a tax examiner's job involves making sure that tax credits and deductions claimed by taxpayers are lawful. If a taxpayer owes additional taxes, tax examiners adjust the total amount by assessing fees, interest, and penalties and then notify the taxpayer of the total amount owed.

Revenue agents specialize in tax-related accounting for the U.S. Internal Revenue Service (IRS) and for equivalent agencies in state and local governments. Like tax examiners, they review returns for accuracy. However, revenue agents handle complicated tax returns of large businesses and corporations.

Many experienced revenue agents specialize in a particular area. For example, they may focus exclusively on multinational businesses. Regardless of their specialty, revenue agents must keep up to date with changes in the lengthy and complex tax laws and regulations.

Collectors, also called *revenue officers* in the IRS, deal with overdue accounts. The process of collecting an overdue payment starts with the revenue agent or tax examiner sending a report to the taxpayer. If the taxpayer makes no effort to pay, the case is assigned to a collector.

When a collector takes a case, he or she first sends a notice to the taxpayer. The collector then works with the taxpayer to settle the debt. Settlement may involve setting up a plan in which the amount owed is paid back in small amounts over time.

When delinquent taxpayers claim that they cannot pay their taxes, collectors investigate and verify the claims. Collectors research information on taxpayer mortgages or financial statements and locate taxpayer-owned items of value through third parties, such as neighbors or local departments of motor vehicles. Ultimately, collectors must decide whether the IRS should take a lien—a claim on an asset such as a bank account, real estate, or an automobile—to settle a debt. Collectors also have the authority to garnish wages—that is, take a portion of earned wages—to collect taxes owed.

Work Environment

Tax examiners and collectors, and revenue agents held about 57,600 jobs in 2019. The largest employers of tax examiners and collectors, and revenue agents were as follows:

Federal government	42%
State government, excluding education and hospitals	39
Local government, excluding education and hospitals	19

Tax examiners and collectors, and revenue agents work for federal, state, and local governments.

Tax examiners and collectors, and revenue agents work primarily in an office environment; others spend most of their time conducting field audits in taxpayers' homes or places of business.

Work Schedules
Most tax examiners and collectors, and revenue agents work full time.

How to Become a Tax Examiner or Collector, or Revenue Agent
Most tax examiners and collectors, and revenue agents need a bachelor's degree in accounting or a related field. However, the required level of education and experience varies with the position and employer.

Education
Tax examiners need a bachelor's degree in accounting or a related field, or a combination of relevant education and specialized experience in accounting, auditing, or tax compliance work. Candidates for tax examiner positions at the Internal

Most tax examiners and collectors, and revenue agents need a bachelor's degree in accounting or a related field.

Revenue Service (IRS) must have a bachelor's degree or 1 year of full-time specialized experience.

Revenue agents need a bachelor's degree in accounting, business administration, economics, or a related discipline. A combination of relevant education and full-time experience in business administration, accounting, or auditing is also qualifying. Revenue agents with the IRS must have either a bachelor's degree or 30 semester hours of accounting coursework, along with specialized experience. Specialized experience includes work in accounting, bookkeeping, or tax analysis.

Collectors usually must have some combination of relevant college education and specialized experience. Specialized experience may include previous work as a loan officer or credit manager, or a background in collections, management, customer service, or tax compliance. A bachelor's degree is needed for employment as a collector with the IRS; no additional experience is required, and experience may not be substituted for the degree. Employers desire degrees in business, finance, accounting, and criminal justice.

Although a bachelor's degree is not always required at the state and local levels, related work experience is desired.

Training
Newly hired tax examiners get some formal training, which typically lasts between 1 month and 1 year. All tax examiners must keep current with changes in the tax code and in enforcement procedures.

Entry-level collectors get both formal training and on-the-job training under an instructor's guidance before working independently. Collectors also are encouraged to continue their professional education by attending meetings to exchange information about how modifications to tax laws affect collection methods.

Work Experience in a Related Occupation
Some state and local governments accept work experience as a substitute for education. In these cases, employers may hire tax examiners and revenue agents who have work experience as accountants or bookkeepers. Employers may also hire tax collectors who have work experience in related occupations, such as bill and account collectors, customer service representatives, and credit checkers.

Advancement
Tax examiners, revenue agents, and collectors have different opportunities for career advancement. Tax examiners who review individual tax returns may advance to revenue agent positions, working on more complex business returns. Those with experience in supervisory or managerial roles may move to jobs that involve supervision of other examiners and revenue agents. Collectors who demonstrate leadership skills and a thorough knowledge of tax collection activities may advance to supervisory or managerial collector positions.

Important Qualities

Analytical skills. Tax examiners and revenue agents must be able to identify questionable claims for credits and deductions. Ultimately, on further review of financial documentation, they must be able to determine if the credits or deductions are lawful.

Computer skills. Tax examiners and revenue agents must be comfortable using a variety of computer programs. These programs include tax preparation and bookkeeping software used by individuals and businesses.

Detail oriented. Tax examiners and revenue agents verify the accuracy of each entry on the tax returns they review. Therefore, it is important that they pay attention to detail.

Interpersonal skills. Collectors must be comfortable dealing with people, including speaking with them during confrontational situations. When pursuing overdue accounts, collectors should be firm and composed.

Organizational skills. Tax examiners and revenue agents often work with multiple returns and a variety of financial documents. Keeping the various pieces of information organized is essential.

Pay

The median annual wage for tax examiners and collectors, and revenue agents was $54,890 in May 2019. The median wage is the wage at which half the workers in an occupation earned more than that amount and half earned less. The lowest 10 percent earned less than $33,090, and the highest 10 percent earned more than $101,780.

In May 2019, the median annual wages for tax examiners and collectors, and revenue agents in the top industries in which they worked were as follows:

Federal government... $61,590

State government, excluding education and
   hospitals 53,760

Local government, excluding education and
   hospitals 45,410

Most tax examiners and collectors, and revenue agents work full time.

Job Outlook

Employment of tax examiners and collectors, and revenue agents is projected to decline 4 percent from 2019 to 2029. Employment of these workers will depend primarily on future changes to federal, state, and local government budgets. Budget reductions in recent years have resulted in decreased hiring for the agencies that employ these workers.

Within the federal government, the primary employer of tax examiners and collectors, and revenue agents is the Internal Revenue Service (IRS), which has experienced more severe budget cuts than many other federal agencies. Further employment declines for these workers in the federal government may occur if the IRS continues to operate with decreased budgets. Employment of these workers in the federal government is projected to decline 14 percent.

At the state and local levels, funding for the departments in which tax examiners and collectors, and revenue agents work has been more stable. Therefore, employment of these workers in state and local government is expected to grow in line with overall state and local government employment.

Job Prospects

Because tax examiners and collectors, and revenue agents is projected to be a slightly declining occupation, jobseekers are likely to face competition for these positions. Still, although projections indicate that there will be fewer of these jobs in the next 10 years, some openings will arise through retirements and separations.

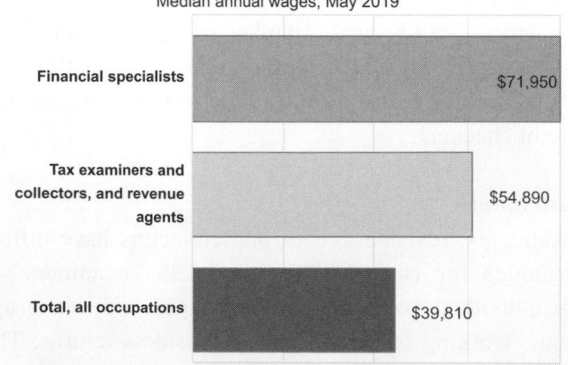

Tax Examiners and Collectors, and Revenue Agents
Median annual wages, May 2019

Financial specialists — $71,950
Tax examiners and collectors, and revenue agents — $54,890
Total, all occupations — $39,810

Note: All Occupations includes all occupations in the U.S. Economy.
Source: U.S. Bureau of Labor Statistics, Occupational Employment Statistics.

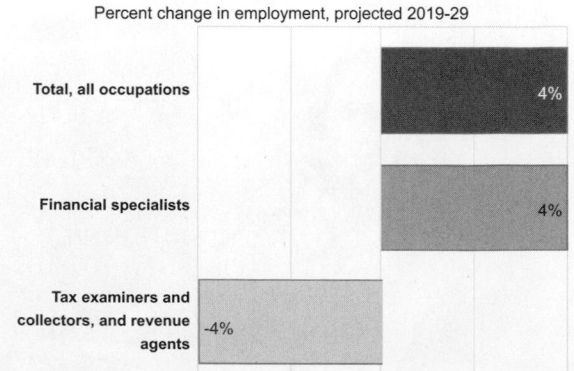

Tax Examiners and Collectors, and Revenue Agents
Percent change in employment, projected 2019-29

Total, all occupations — 4%
Financial specialists — 4%
Tax examiners and collectors, and revenue agents — -4%

Note: All Occupations includes all occupations in the U.S. Economy.
Source: U.S. Bureau of Labor Statistics, Employment Projections program.

Employment projections data for tax examiners and collectors, and revenue agents, 2019-29					
Occupational Title	SOC Code	Employment, 2019	Projected Employment, 2029	Change, 2019-29	
				Percent	Numeric
SOURCE: U.S. Bureau of Labor Statistics, Employment Projections program					
Tax examiners and collectors, and revenue agents	13-2081	57,600	55,300	-4	-2,400

State & Area Data
Occupational Employment Statistics (OES)
The Occupational Employment Statistics (OES) program produces employment and wage estimates annually for over 800 occupations. These estimates are available for the nation as a whole, for individual states, and for metropolitan and nonmetropolitan areas.

Contacts for More Information
For more information about careers as tax examiners and collectors, and revenue agents at the Internal Revenue Service (IRS), visit
➤ Internal Revenue Service

For more information about requirements for federal government positions as an internal revenue officer or an internal revenue agent, visit
➤ U.S. Office of Personnel Management

Training and Development Specialists

Summary

Quick Facts: Training and Development Specialists

2019 Median Pay	$61,210 per year $29.43 per hour
Typical Entry-Level Education	Bachelor's degree
Work Experience in a Related Occupation	Less than 5 years
On-the-job Training	None
Number of Jobs, 2019	327,900
Job Outlook, 2019-29	9% (Much faster than average)
Employment Change, 2019-29	28,200

What Training and Development Specialists Do
Training and development specialists plan and administer programs that improve the skills and knowledge of their employees.

Training and development specialists often lead educational sessions.

Work Environment
Training and development specialists work in nearly every industry. They spend much of their time working with people, giving presentations, and leading training activities.

How to Become a Training and Development Specialist
In addition to a bachelor's degree, training and development specialists also need work experience and strong communication skills.

Pay
The median annual wage for training and development specialists was $61,210 in May 2019.

Job Outlook
Employment of training and development specialists is projected to grow 9 percent from 2019 to 2029, much faster than the average for all occupations. Job prospects should be best for those with experience developing online and mobile training programs.

State & Area Data
Explore resources for employment and wages by state and area for training and development specialists.

What Training and Development Specialists Do
Training and development specialists help plan, conduct, and administer programs that train employees and improve their skills and knowledge.

Duties
Training and development specialists typically do the following:

• Assess training needs through surveys, interviews with employees, or consultations with managers or instructors

Training and development specialists guide employees through exercises.

- Design and create training manuals, online learning modules, and course materials
- Review training materials from a variety of sources and choose appropriate materials
- Deliver training to employees using a variety of instructional techniques
- Assist in the evaluation of training programs
- Perform administrative tasks such as monitoring costs, scheduling classes, setting up systems and equipment, and coordinating enrollment

Training and development specialists help create, administer, and deliver training programs for businesses and organizations. To do this, they must first assess the needs of an organization, and then develop custom training programs that take place in classrooms or training facilities. Training programs are increasingly delivered through computers, tablets, or other hand-held devices.

Training and development specialists organize or deliver training sessions using lectures, group discussions, team exercises, hands-on examples, and other formats. Training can also be in the form of a video, self-guided instructional manual, or online application. Training may be collaborative, which allows employees to connect informally with experts, mentors, and colleagues, often through the use of technology.

Training and development specialists may monitor instructors, guide employees through media-based programs, or facilitate informal or collaborative learning programs.

Work Environment

Training and development specialists held about 327,900 jobs in 2019. The largest employers of training and development specialists were as follows:

Professional, scientific, and technical services 13%
Healthcare and social assistance 12

They spend much of their time working with people, giving presentations, and leading training activities.

Educational services; state, local, and private............ 11
Finance and insurance.. 10
Administrative and support services 7

Training and development specialists spend much of their time working with people, giving presentations, and leading training activities. They may need to travel to training sites.

Work Schedules

Most training and development specialists work full time during regular business hours. Some work more than 40 hours per week.

How to Become a Training and Development Specialist

Training and development specialists need a bachelor's degree, and most need related work experience.

Education

Training and development specialists need a bachelor's degree. Specialists may have a variety of education backgrounds, but most have a bachelor's degree in training and development, human resources, education, or instructional design. Others may have a degree in business administration or a social science, such as educational or organizational psychology.

Work Experience in a Related Occupation

Related work experience is important for most training and development specialists. Many positions require work experience in areas such as training and development or instructional design, or in related occupations, such as human resources specialists or teachers.

Employers may prefer to hire candidates with previous work experience in the industry in which the company operates, or with experience in e-learning, mobile training, and technology-based tools. However, some employers may hire candidates with a master's degree in lieu of work experience.

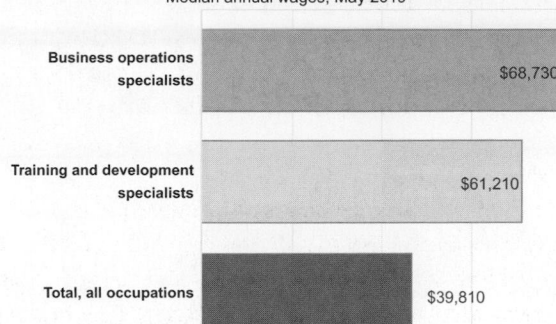

Training and Development Specialists
Median annual wages, May 2019

Business operations specialists	$68,730
Training and development specialists	$61,210
Total, all occupations	$39,810

Note: All Occupations includes all occupations in the U.S. Economy.
Source: U.S. Bureau of Labor Statistics, Occupational Employment Statistics.

Training and development specialists need strong interpersonal and speaking skills to effectively present training programs.

Licenses, Certifications, and Registrations

Many human resources associations offer classes to enhance the skills of their members. Some associations, including the Association for Talent Development and International Society for Performance Improvement, specialize in training and development and offer certification programs. Although not required, certification can show professional expertise and credibility. Some employers prefer to hire certified candidates, and some positions may require certification.

Advancement

Training and development specialists may advance to training and development manager or human resources manager positions. Workers typically need several years of experience to advance. Some employers require managers to have a master's degree in a related area.

Important Qualities

Analytical skills. Training and development specialists must evaluate training programs, methods, and materials, and choose those that best fit each situation.

Communication skills. Specialists need strong interpersonal skills because delivering training programs requires collaboration with instructors, trainees, and subject-matter experts. They accomplish much of their work through teams. Specialists must communicate information clearly and facilitate learning by diverse audiences.

Creativity. Specialists should be creative when developing training materials. They may need to think of and implement new approaches, such as new technology, when evaluating existing training methods.

Instructional skills. Training and development specialists often deliver training programs to employees. They use a variety of teaching techniques and sometimes must adapt their methods to meet the needs of particular groups.

Pay

The median annual wage for training and development specialists was $61,210 in May 2019. The median wage is the wage at which half the workers in an occupation earned more than that amount and half earned less. The lowest 10 percent earned less than $32,680, and the highest 10 percent earned more than $104,200.

In May 2019, the median annual wages for training and development specialists in the top industries in which they worked were as follows:

Professional, scientific, and technical services	$71,460
Finance and insurance	64,530
Educational services; state, local, and private	62,720
Healthcare and social assistance	55,910
Administrative and support services	54,160

Most training and development specialists work full time during regular business hours. Some work more than 40 hours per week.

Job Outlook

Employment of training and development specialists is projected to grow 9 percent from 2019 to 2029, much faster than the average for all occupations. Employees in many occupations are required to take continuing education and skill

Training and Development Specialists
Percent change in employment, projected 2019-29

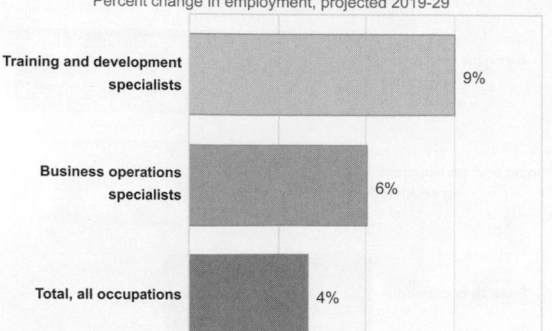

Note: All Occupations includes all occupations in the U.S. Economy.
Source: U.S. Bureau of Labor Statistics, Employment Projections program.

development courses throughout their careers, creating demand for workers who lead training activities.

Employment of training and development specialists is projected to grow in many industries as companies develop and introduce new media and technology into their training programs. Innovations in training methods and learning technology should continue throughout the next decade. For example, organizations increasingly use social media, visual simulations, and mobile learning in their training programs. Training and development specialists will need to modify their programs in order to fit a new generation of workers for whom technology is a part of daily life and work.

Because training and development contracting firms may have greater access to technical expertise in order to produce new training initiatives, some organizations outsource specific training efforts when internal staff or resources are not able to meet the training needs of the organization.

Job Prospects
Overall, job opportunities should be good. Job prospects should be best for those with experience developing online and mobile training programs.

Occupational Title	SOC Code	Employment, 2019	Projected Employment, 2029	Change, 2019-29	
				Percent	Numeric
SOURCE: U.S. Bureau of Labor Statistics, Employment Projections program					
Training and development specialists	13-1151	327,900	356,100	9	28,200

Employment projections data for training and development specialists, 2019-29

State & Area Data
Occupational Employment Statistics (OES)
The Occupational Employment Statistics (OES) program produces employment and wage estimates annually for over 800 occupations. These estimates are available for the nation as a whole, for individual states, and for metropolitan and nonmetropolitan areas.

Contacts for More Information
For more information about training and development specialists, visit
➤ Association for Talent Development
➤ International Society for Performance Improvement

Community and Social Service

Health Educators and Community Health Workers

Summary

Quick Facts: Health Educators and Community Health Workers	
2019 Median Pay	$46,910 per year $22.55 per hour
Typical Entry-Level Education	See below
Work Experience in a Related Occupation	None
On-the-job Training	See below
Number of Jobs, 2019	127,100
Job Outlook, 2019-29	13% (Much faster than average)
Employment Change, 2019-29	17,000

What Health Educators and Community Health Workers Do

Health educators teach people about behaviors that promote wellness. Community health workers collect data and discuss health concerns with members of specific populations or communities.

Work Environment

Health educators and community health workers work in a variety of settings, including hospitals, nonprofit organizations, government, doctors' offices, private businesses, and colleges. They generally work full time.

How to Become a Health Educator or Community Health Worker

Health educators need at least bachelor's degree. Many employers require the Certified Health Education Specialist (CHES) credential. Community health workers typically need to have at least a high school diploma and must complete a brief period of on-the-job training. Some states have certification programs for community health workers.

Pay

The median annual wage for community health workers was $40,360 in May 2019.

The median annual wage for health education specialists was $55,220 in May 2019.

Job Outlook

Overall employment of health educators and community health workers is projected to grow 13 percent from 2019 to 2029, much faster than the average for all occupations. Growth will be driven by efforts to improve health outcomes and to reduce healthcare costs by teaching people healthy behaviors and explaining how to use available healthcare services.

State & Area Data

Explore resources for employment and wages by state and area for health educators and community health workers.

What Health Educators and Community Health Workers Do

Health educators teach people about behaviors that promote wellness. They develop and implement strategies to improve the health of individuals and communities. Community health workers provide a link between the community and healthcare professionals. They develop and implement strategies to improve the health of individuals and communities. They

Health educators and community health workers teach people about behaviors that promote wellness.

Health educators and community health workers educate people about the availability of healthcare services.

collect data and discuss health concerns with members of specific populations or communities. Although the two occupations often work together, responsibilities of health educators and community health workers are distinct.

Duties

Health educators typically do the following:

- Assess the health needs of the people and communities they serve
- Develop programs, materials, and events to teach people about health topics
- Teach people how to manage existing health conditions
- Evaluate the effectiveness of programs and educational materials
- Help people find health services or information
- Provide training programs for community health workers or other health professionals
- Supervise staff who implement health education programs
- Collect and analyze data to learn about a particular community and improve programs and services
- Advocate for improved health resources and policies that promote health
  Community health workers typically do the following:
- Discuss health concerns with community members
- Educate people about the importance and availability of healthcare services, such as cancer screenings
- Collect data
- Report findings to health educators and other healthcare providers
- Provide informal counseling and social support
- Conduct outreach programs
- Facilitate access to the healthcare services
- Advocate for individual and community needs

Health educators, also known as *health education specialists*, have different duties depending on their work setting. Most work in healthcare facilities, colleges, public health departments, nonprofits, and private businesses. People who teach health classes in middle and high schools are considered teachers. For more information, see the profiles on middle school teachers and high school teachers.

The following are descriptions of duties for health educators, by work setting:

- In *healthcare facilities*, health educators may work one-on-one with patients or with their families. They may be called *patient navigators* because they help consumers understand their health insurance options and direct people to outside resources, such as support groups or home health agencies. They teach patients about their diagnoses and about any necessary treatments or procedures. They lead hospital efforts in developing and administering surveys to identify major health issues and concerns of the surrounding communities

and developing programs to meet those needs. Health educators also help organize health screenings, such as blood pressure checks, and classes on topics such as installing a car seat correctly. They also create programs to train medical staff to interact more effectively with patients.

- In *colleges*, health educators create programs and materials on topics that affect young adults, such as smoking and alcohol use. They may train students to be peer educators and supervise the students' delivery of health information in person or through social media. Health educators also advocate for campus wide policies to promote health.
- In *public health departments,* health educators administer public health campaigns on topics such as emergency preparedness, immunizations, proper nutrition, or stress management. They develop materials to be used by other public health officials. During emergencies, they may provide safety information to the public and the media. Some health educators work with other professionals to create public policies that support healthy behaviors and environments. They may also oversee grants and grant-funded programs to improve the health of the public. Some participate in statewide and local committees dealing with topics such as aging.
- In *nonprofits*, health educators create programs and materials about health issues faced by the community that they serve. They help organizations obtain funding and other resources. They educate policymakers about ways to improve public health and work on securing grant funding for programs to promote health and disease awareness. Many nonprofits focus on a particular disease or audience, so health educators in these organizations limit programs to that specific topic or audience.
- In *private businesses,* health educators identify common health problems among employees and create programs to improve health. They work to develop incentives for employees to adopt healthy behaviors, such as losing weight or controlling cholesterol. Health educators recommend changes in the workplace to improve employee health, such as creating smoke-free areas.

Community health workers have an in-depth knowledge of the communities they serve. Within their community, they identify health-related issues, collect data, and discuss health concerns with the people they serve. For example, they may help eligible residents of a neighborhood enroll in programs such as Medicaid or Medicare and explain the benefits that these programs offer. Community health workers address any barriers to care and provide referrals for such needs as food, housing, education, and mental health services

Community health workers share information with health educators and healthcare providers so that health educators can create new programs or adjust existing programs or events to better suit the needs of the community. Community health workers also advocate for the health needs of community

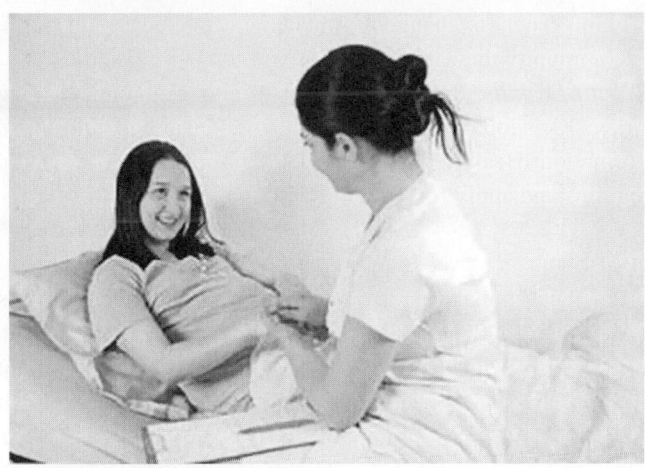

Health educators often work in hospitals, where they help patients understand and adjust to their diagnosis.

members. In addition, they conduct outreach to engage community residents, assist residents with health system navigation, and to improve care coordination.

Work Environment

Community health workers held about 64,900 jobs in 2019. The largest employers of community health workers were as follows:

Government	18%
Individual and family services	17
Religious, grantmaking, civic, professional, and similar organizations	14
Hospitals; state, local, and private	8
Outpatient care centers	8

Health education specialists held about 62,200 jobs in 2019. The largest employers of health education specialists were as follows:

Government	24%
Hospitals; state, local, and private	22
Individual and family services	8
Religious, grantmaking, civic, professional, and similar organizations	7
Outpatient care centers	7

Although most health educators work in offices, they may spend a lot of time away from the office to carry out programs or attend meetings.

Community health workers may spend much of their time in the field, communicating with community members, holding events, and collecting data.

Work Schedules

Most health educators and community health workers work full time. They may need to work nights and weekends to attend programs or meetings.

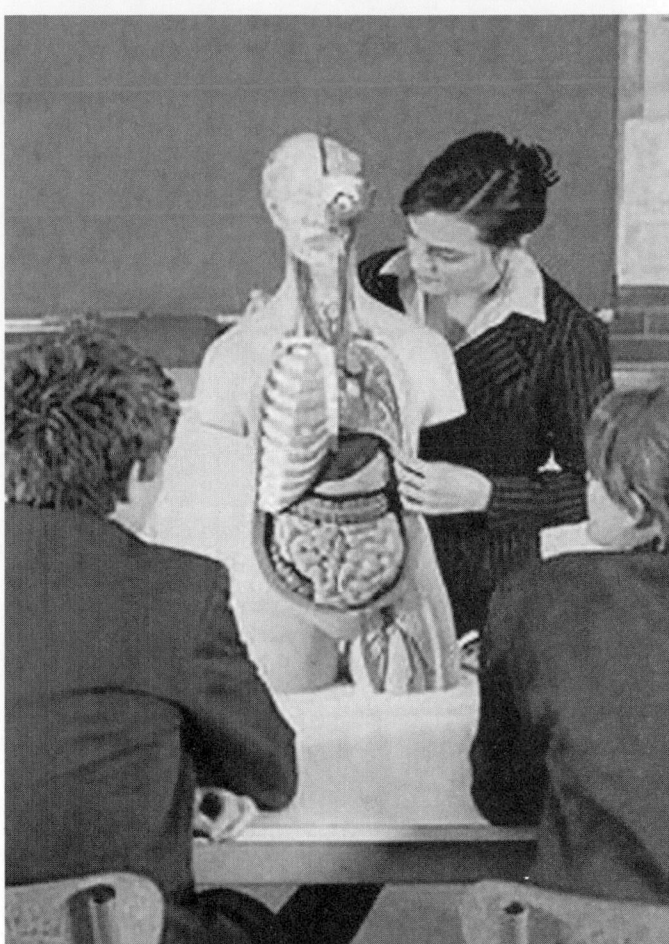

Health educators need at least a bachelor's degree.

How to Become a Health Educator or Community Health Worker

Health educators need at least bachelor's degree. Some employers require the Certified Health Education Specialist (CHES) credential.

Community health workers need at least a high school diploma and must complete a brief period of on-the-job training. Some states have certification programs for community health workers.

Education

Health educators need at least a bachelor's degree in health education or health promotion. Students learn theories and methods of health behavior and health education and gain the knowledge and skills they will need to develop health education materials and programs. Most programs include an internship.

Some health educator positions require candidates to have a master's or doctoral degree. Graduate programs are commonly in community health education, school health education, public health education, or health promotion. A variety of undergraduate majors may be acceptable for entry to a master's degree program.

Community health workers need at least a high school diploma, although some jobs may require some postsecondary education. Education programs may lead to a 1-year certificate or a 2-year associate's degree and cover topics such as wellness, ethics, and cultural awareness.

Training

Community health workers typically complete a brief period of on-the-job training. Training often covers core competencies, such as communication or outreach skills, and information about the specific health topics that they will be focusing on. For example, community health workers who work with Alzheimer's patients may learn about how to communicate effectively with patients dealing with dementia.

Other Experience

Community health workers usually have some knowledge of a specific community, culture, medical condition, or disability. The ability to speak a foreign language may be helpful.

Licenses, Certifications, and Registrations

Some employers require health educators to obtain the Certified Health Education Specialist (CHES) credential, which is offered by the National Commission for Health Education Credentialing, Inc.

Candidates must pass an exam that is aimed at entry-level health educators who have completed at least a bachelor's degree. To maintain their certification, they must complete 75 hours of continuing education every 5 years. There is also the Master Certified Health Education Specialist (MCHES) credential for health educators with advanced education and experience.

Most states do not require community health workers to obtain certification, however, voluntary certification exists or is being considered or developed in a number of states. Requirements vary but may include completing an approved training program. For more information, contact your state's board of health, nursing, or human services.

Important Qualities

Analytical skills. Health educators collect and analyze data in order to evaluate programs and to determine the needs of the people they serve.

Instructional skills. Health educators and community health workers should be comfortable with public speaking so that they can lead programs, teach classes, and facilitate discussion with clients and families.

Interpersonal skills. Health educators and community health workers interact with many people from a variety of backgrounds. They must be good listeners and be culturally sensitive to respond to the needs of the people they serve.

Problem-solving skills. Health educators and community health workers must think creatively about how to improve the health of the community through health education programs. In addition, they may need to solve problems that arise in planning

programs, such as changes to their budget or resistance from the community they are serving.

Writing skills. Health educators and community health workers develop written materials to convey health-related information. Health educators also write proposals to develop programs and apply for funding.

Pay

The median annual wage for community health workers was $40,360 in May 2019. The median wage is the wage at which half the workers in an occupation earned more than that amount and half earned less. The lowest 10 percent earned less than $26,660, and the highest 10 percent earned more than $68,350.

The median annual wage for health education specialists was $55,220 in May 2019. The lowest 10 percent earned less than $32,890, and the highest 10 percent earned more than $98,680.

In May 2019, the median annual wages for community health workers in the top industries in which they worked were as follows:

Hospitals; state, local, and private	$47,250
Government	44,240
Religious, grantmaking, civic, professional, and similar organizations	42,290
Outpatient care centers	38,800
Individual and family services	37,110

In May 2019, the median annual wages for health education specialists in the top industries in which they worked were as follows:

Hospitals; state, local, and private	$64,680
Government	57,410
Outpatient care centers	52,360

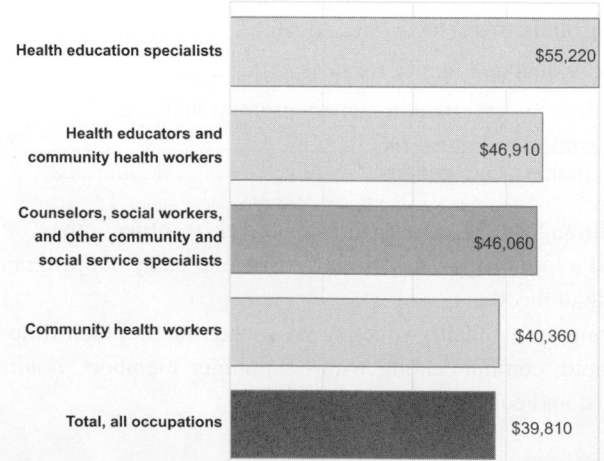

Health Educators and Community Health Workers
Median annual wages, May 2019

Health education specialists	$55,220
Health educators and community health workers	$46,910
Counselors, social workers, and other community and social service specialists	$46,060
Community health workers	$40,360
Total, all occupations	$39,810

Note: All Occupations includes all occupations in the U.S. Economy.
Source: U.S. Bureau of Labor Statistics, Occupational Employment Statistics.

Health Educators and Community Health Workers
Percent change in employment, projected 2019-29

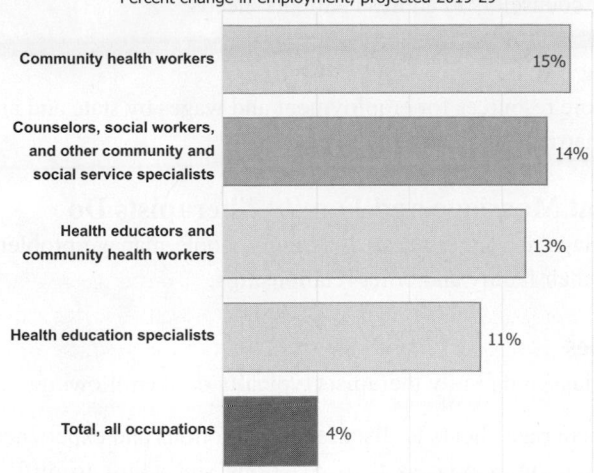

Note: All Occupations includes all occupations in the U.S. Economy.
Source: U.S. Bureau of Labor Statistics, Employment Projections program.

Religious, grantmaking, civic, professional, and	
similar organizations	49,340
Individual and family services	42,710

Most health educators and community health workers work full time. They may need to work nights and weekends to attend programs or meetings.

Job Outlook
Overall employment of health educators and community health workers is projected to grow 13 percent from 2019 to 2029, much faster than the average for all occupations. Growth will be driven by efforts to improve health outcomes and to reduce healthcare costs by teaching people healthy behaviors and explaining how to use available healthcare services.

Governments, healthcare providers, and social services providers want to find ways to improve the quality of care and health outcomes while reducing costs. This should increase demand for health educators and community health workers, who teach people how to live healthy lives and how to avoid costly diseases and medical procedures.

Job Prospects
Community health workers who have completed a formal education program and have experience working with a specific population should have the best job prospects. In addition, opportunities may be better for candidates who speak a foreign language and understand the culture of the community that they intend to serve.

Health educators may improve their job prospects by obtaining a certification.

Employment projections data for health educators and community health workers, 2019-29					
Occupational Title	SOC Code	Employment, 2019	Projected Employment, 2029	Change, 2019-29	
				Percent	Numeric
SOURCE: U.S. Bureau of Labor Statistics, Employment Projections program					
Health educators and community health workers	—	127,100	144,100	13	17,000
Health education specialists	21-1091	62,200	69,300	11	7,100
Community health workers	21-1094	64,900	74,800	15	9,900

State & Area Data
Occupational Employment Statistics (OES)
The Occupational Employment Statistics (OES) program produces employment and wage estimates annually for over 800 occupations. These estimates are available for the nation as a whole, for individual states, and for metropolitan and nonmetropolitan areas.

Contacts for More Information
For more information about health educators and community health workers, visit
➤ Society for Public Health Education
➤ American Public Health Association

For more information about the Certified Health Education Specialist (CHES) credential, visit
➤ National Commission for Health Education Credentialing, Inc.

Marriage and Family Therapists

Summary

Quick Facts: Marriage and Family Therapists

2019 Median Pay	$49,610 per year $23.85 per hour
Typical Entry-Level Education	Master's degree
Work Experience in a Related Occupation	None
On-the-job Training	Internship/residency
Number of Jobs, 2019	66,200
Job Outlook, 2019-29	22% (Much faster than average)
Employment Change, 2019-29	14,800

What Marriage and Family Therapists Do

Marriage and family therapists help people manage and overcome problems with family and other relationships.

Work Environment

Marriage and family therapists work in a variety of settings, such as private practice and mental health centers. Most work full time.

How to Become a Marriage and Family Therapist

Marriage and family therapists are required to have a master's degree and a license to practice.

Pay

The median annual wage for marriage and family therapists was $49,610 in May 2019.

Job Outlook

Employment of marriage and family therapists is projected to grow 22 percent from 2019 to 2029, much faster than the average for all occupations. Growth is expected due to an increasing use of teams for treatment, in which these therapists work with other counselors to address patients' needs.

State & Area Data

Explore resources for employment and wages by state and area for marriage and family therapists.

What Marriage and Family Therapists Do

Marriage and family therapists help people manage problems with their family and other relationships.

Duties

Marriage and family therapists typically do the following:

- Encourage clients to discuss their emotions and experiences
- Help clients process their reactions and adjust to difficult changes in their life, such as divorce and layoffs
- Guide clients through the process of making decisions about their future
- Help clients develop strategies and skills to change their behavior and to cope with difficult situations
- Refer clients to other resources or services in the community, such as support groups or inpatient treatment facilities
- Complete and maintain confidential files and mandated records

Marriage and family therapists use a variety of techniques and tools to help their clients. Many apply cognitive behavioral therapy, a goal-oriented approach that helps clients understand harmful thoughts, feelings, and beliefs and teaches how to replace them with positive, life-enhancing ones.

Many marriage and family therapists work in private practice. They must market their practice to prospective clients and work with insurance companies and clients to get payment for their services.

Marriage and family therapists work with individuals, couples, and families. They bring a family-centered perspective to treatment, even when treating individuals. They evaluate family

Marriage and family therapists help people manage problems with their family and relationships.

Marriage and family therapists encourage clients to discuss their emotions and experiences.

Many marriage and family therapists work in private practice.

Master's programs in marriage and family therapy prepare students to provide counseling to couples, individuals, and groups.

roles and development, to understand how clients' families affect their mental health. They treat the clients' relationships, not just the clients themselves. They address issues, such as low self-esteem, stress, addiction, and substance abuse.

Marriage and family therapists coordinate patient treatment with other professionals, such as psychologists and social workers.

Work Environment

Marriage and family therapists held about 66,200 jobs in 2019. The largest employers of marriage and family therapists were as follows:

Individual and family services	31%
Offices of other health practitioners	21
Outpatient care centers	12
Self-employed workers	8
State government, excluding education and hospitals	8

Marriage and family therapists work in a variety of settings, such as mental health centers, substance abuse treatment centers, and hospitals. They also work in private practice and in Employee Assistance Programs (EAPs), which are mental health programs that some employers provide to help employees deal with personal problems.

Work Schedules

Marriage and family therapists generally work full time. Some therapists work evenings and weekends to accommodate their clients' schedules.

How to Become a Marriage and Family Therapist

Marriage and family therapists are required to have a master's degree and a license to practice.

Education

To become a marriage and family therapist, applicants need a master's degree in psychology, marriage and family therapy, or a related mental health field. A bachelor's degree in most fields is acceptable to enter one of these master's degree programs.

Marriage and family therapy programs teach students about how marriages, families, and relationships function and how these relationships can affect mental and emotional disorders.

There are several organizations that accredit counseling programs, including the Council for Accreditation of Counseling & Related Educational Programs (CACREP), the Commission on Accreditation for Marriage and Family Therapy Education (COAMFTE), and the Masters in Psychology and Counseling Accreditation Council (MPCAC).

Training

Candidates gain hands-on experience through postdegree supervised clinical work, sometimes referred to as an internship or residency. In training, they learn to provide family therapy, group therapy, psychotherapy, and other therapeutic interventions, under the supervision of a licensed counselor.

Licenses, Certifications, and Registrations

All states require marriage and family therapists to be licensed. Licensure requires a master's degree and 2,000 to 4,000 hours of postdegree supervised clinical experience, sometimes referred to as an internship or residency. In addition, therapists must pass a state-recognized exam and complete annual continuing education classes.

Contact and licensing information for marriage and family therapists is available through the Association of Marital and Family Therapy Regulatory Boards.

Important Qualities

Compassion. Marriage and family therapists often work with people who are dealing with stressful and difficult situations, so they must be compassionate and empathize with their clients.

Interpersonal skills. Marriage and family therapists work with different types of people. They spend most of their time working directly with clients and other professionals and must be able to encourage good relationships.

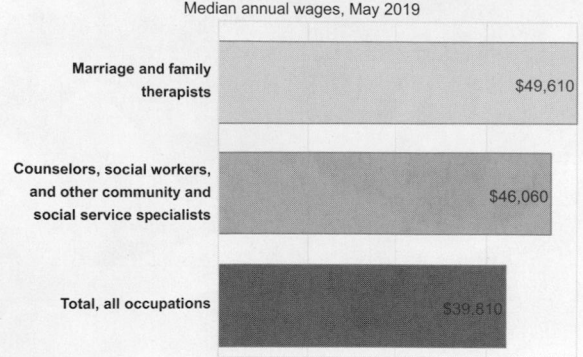

Marriage and Family Therapists
Median annual wages, May 2019

Marriage and family therapists — $49,610

Counselors, social workers, and other community and social service specialists — $46,060

Total, all occupations — $39,810

Note: All Occupations includes all occupations in the U.S. Economy.
Source: U.S. Bureau of Labor Statistics, Occupational Employment Statistics.

Listening skills. Marriage and family therapists need to give their full attention to their clients to understand their problems, values, and goals.

Organizational skills. Marriage and family therapists in private practice must keep track of payments and work with insurance companies.

Speaking skills. Marriage and family therapists need to be able to communicate with clients effectively. They must express information in a way that clients can understand easily.

Pay

The median annual wage for marriage and family therapists was $49,610 in May 2019. The median wage is the wage at which half the workers in an occupation earned more than that amount and half earned less. The lowest 10 percent earned less than $32,070, and the highest 10 percent earned more than $87,700.

In May 2019, the median annual wages for marriage and family therapists in the top industries in which they worked were as follows:

State government, excluding education and hospitals	$72,230
Outpatient care centers	52,140
Individual and family services	45,660
Offices of other health practitioners	45,150

Marriage and family therapists generally work full time. Some therapists work evenings and weekends to accommodate their clients' schedules.

Job Outlook

Employment of marriage and family therapists is projected to grow 22 percent from 2019 to 2029, much faster than the average for all occupations. Growth is expected due to the increasing use of integrated care, which is a treatment of multiple problems at one time by a group of specialists. In providing integrated care, marriage and family therapists are working with counselors such as substance abuse, behavior

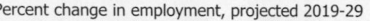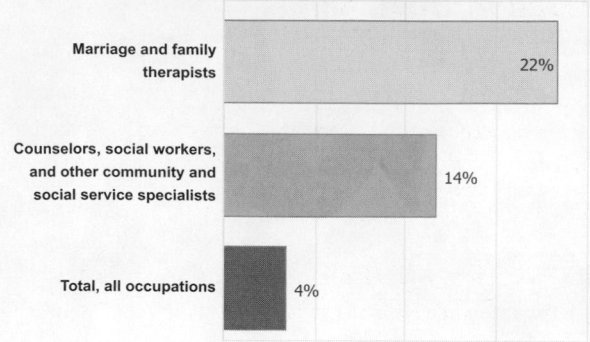

Marriage and Family Therapists
Percent change in employment, projected 2019-29

Marriage and family therapists — 22%

Counselors, social workers, and other community and social service specialists — 14%

Total, all occupations — 4%

Note: All Occupations includes all occupations in the U.S. Economy.
Source: U.S. Bureau of Labor Statistics, Employment Projections program.

disorder, or mental health counselors to address patients' issues as a team.

Employment projections data for marriage and family therapists, 2019-29					
Occupational Title	SOC Code	Employment, 2019	Projected Employment, 2029	Change, 2019-29 Percent	Numeric
SOURCE: U.S. Bureau of Labor Statistics, Employment Projections program					
Marriage and family therapists	21-1013	66,200	80,900	22	14,800

State & Area Data
Occupational Employment Statistics (OES)

The Occupational Employment Statistics (OES) program produces employment and wage estimates annually for over 800 occupations. These estimates are available for the nation as a whole, for individual states, and for metropolitan and nonmetropolitan areas.

Contacts for More Information

For more information about accredited programs, visit
➤ Commission on Accreditation for Marriage and Family Therapy Education
➤ Council for Accreditation of Counseling & Related Educational Programs
➤ Masters in Psychology and Counseling Accreditation Council

For more information about marriage and family therapists, visit
➤ American Association for Marriage and Family Therapy
➤ Association of Marital and Family Therapy Regulatory Boards

For general information about counseling and for information about counseling specialties, visit
➤ American Counseling Association

For information about contacting state regulating boards, visit
➤ National Board for Certified Counselors

Probation Officers and Correctional Treatment Specialists

Summary

Quick Facts: Probation Officers and Correctional Treatment Specialists

2019 Median Pay	$54,290 per year $26.10 per hour
Typical Entry-Level Education	Bachelor's degree
Work Experience in a Related Occupation	None
On-the-job Training	Short-term on-the-job training
Number of Jobs, 2019	91,800
Job Outlook, 2019-29	4% (As fast as average)
Employment Change, 2019-29	3,400

What Probation Officers and Correctional Treatment Specialists Do

Probation officers and correctional treatment specialists assist in rehabilitation of law offenders in custody or on probation or parole.

Work Environment

Probation officers and correctional treatment specialists work with probationers and parolees. Workers may be assigned to fieldwork in high-crime areas or in institutions. As a result, the work can be stressful and dangerous.

How to Become a Probation Officer or Correctional Treatment Specialist

Probation officers and correctional treatment specialists usually need a bachelor's degree. In addition, most employers require candidates to pass oral, written, and psychological exams.

Pay

The median annual wage for probation officers and correctional treatment specialists was $54,290 in May 2019.

Job Outlook

Employment of probation officers and correctional treatment specialists is projected to grow 4 percent from 2019 to 2029, about as fast as the average for all occupations. Job openings should remain plentiful because many people leave the occupation each year.

State & Area Data

Explore resources for employment and wages by state and area for probation officers and correctional treatment specialists.

What Probation Officers and Correctional Treatment Specialists Do

Probation officers and correctional treatment specialists provide social services to assist in rehabilitation of law offenders in custody or on probation or parole.

Duties

Probation officers and correctional treatment specialists typically do the following:

- Interview with probationers and parolees, their friends, and their relatives in an office or at a residence to assess progress
- Evaluate probationers and parolees to determine the best course of rehabilitation
- Provide probationers and parolees with resources, such as job training
- Test offenders for drugs and offer substance abuse counseling
- Complete prehearing investigations and testify in court regarding offender's backgrounds

- Write reports and maintain case files on offenders

Probation officers and correctional treatment specialists work with and monitor law offenders to prevent them from committing new crimes.

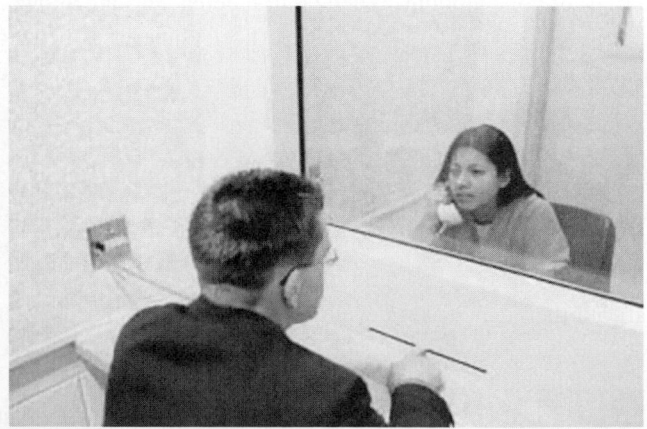

Correctional treatment specialists counsel law offenders and create rehabilitation plans for them to follow when they are no longer in prison.

The following are examples of types of probation officers and correctional treatment specialists:

Probation officers, who are sometimes referred to as *community supervision officers*, supervise people who have been placed on probation instead of sent to prison. They work to ensure that the probationer is not a danger to the community and to help in their rehabilitation through frequent visits with the probationer. Probation officers write reports that detail each probationer's treatment plan and their progress since being put on probation. Most work exclusively with either adults or juveniles.

Parole officers work with people who have been released from prison and are serving parole, helping them re-enter society. Parole officers monitor post-release parolees and provide them with information on various resources, such as substance abuse counseling or job training, to aid in their rehabilitation. By doing so, the officers try to change the parolee's behavior and thus reduce the risk of that person committing another crime and having to return to prison.

Both probation and parole officers supervise probationers and parolees through personal contact with them and their families (also known as community supervision). Probation and parole officers require regularly scheduled contact with parolees and probationers by telephone or through office visits, and they also check on them at their homes or places of work. When making home visits, probation and parole officers take into account the safety of the neighborhood in which the probationers and parolees live and any mental health considerations that may be pertinent. Probation and parole officers also oversee drug testing and electronic monitoring of those under supervision. In some states, workers perform the duties of both probation and parole officers.

Pretrial services officers investigate a pretrial defendant's background to determine if the defendant can be safely allowed back into the community before his or her trial date. Officers must assess the risk and make a recommendation to a judge, who decides on the appropriate sentencing (in settled cases with no trial) or bond amount. When pretrial defendants are allowed back into the community, pretrial officers supervise them to make sure that they stay within the terms of their release and appear at their trials.

Correctional treatment specialists, also known as *case managers* or *correctional counselors*, advise probationers and parolees and develop rehabilitation plans for them to follow. They may evaluate inmates using questionnaires and psychological tests. They also work with inmates, parole officers, and staff of other agencies to develop parole and release plans. For example, they may plan education and training programs to improve probationers' job skills.

Correctional treatment specialists write case reports that cover the inmate's history and the likelihood that he or she will commit another crime. When inmates are eligible for release, the case reports are given to the appropriate parole board. The specialist may help set up counseling for the parolees and their families, find substance abuse or mental health treatment options, aid in job placement, and find housing. Correctional treatment specialists also explain the terms and conditions of the prisoner's release and keep detailed written accounts of each parolee's progress.

The number of cases a probation officer or correctional treatment specialist handles at one time depends on the needs of individuals under supervision and the risks associated with each individual. Higher risk probationers usually command more of an officer's time and resources. Caseload size also varies by agency.

Improved tests for drug screening and electronic devices to monitor clients help probation officers and correctional treatment specialists supervise and counsel probationers.

Work Environment

Probation officers and correctional treatment specialists held about 91,800 jobs in 2019. The largest employers of probation officers and correctional treatment specialists were as follows:

State government, excluding education and hospitals 52%
Local government, excluding education and hospitals ... 45
Social assistance... 1

Probation officers and correctional treatment specialists work with probationers and parolees. While supervising individuals, they may interact with others, such as family members and friends of their clients, who may be upset or difficult to work with. Workers may be assigned to fieldwork in high-crime areas or in institutions where there is a risk of violence.

Probation officers and correctional treatment specialists may have court deadlines imposed by the statute of limitations. In addition, many officers travel to perform home and employment checks and property searches. Because of the hostile environments they may encounter, some may carry a firearm or pepper spray for protection.

Extensive travel and paperwork can also contribute to more hours of work.

All of these factors, in addition to the challenge some officers experience in dealing with probationers and parolees who violate the terms of their release, can contribute to a stressful work environment. Although the high stress levels can make the job difficult at times, this work can also be rewarding. Many officers and specialists receive personal satisfaction from counseling members of their community and helping them become productive citizens.

Work Schedules

Although many officers and specialists work full time, the demands of the job sometimes lead to working overtime and variable hours. For example, many agencies rotate an on-call officer position. When these workers are on-call, they must respond to any issues with probationers, parolees, or law enforcement 24 hours a day.

Extensive travel and paperwork can also contribute to more hours of work.

How to Become a Probation Officer or Correctional Treatment Specialist

Probation officers and correctional treatment specialists usually need a bachelor's degree. In addition, most employers require candidates to pass competency exams, drug testing, and a criminal background check.

A valid driver's license is often required, and most agencies require applicants to be at least 21 years old.

Education

A bachelor's degree in social work, criminal justice, behavioral sciences, or a related field is usually required. Requirements vary by jurisdiction.

Training

Most probation officers and correctional treatment specialists must complete a training program sponsored by their

Probation officers may go on to specialize in a certain type of casework, such as working with juvenile law offenders.

state government or the federal government, after which they may have to pass a certification test. In addition, they may be required to work as trainees for up to 1 year before being offered a permanent position.

Some probation officers and correctional treatment specialists specialize in a certain type of casework. For example, an officer may work only with domestic violence probationers or deal only with substance abuse cases. Some may work only cases involving juvenile offenders. Officers receive the appropriate specific training so that they are better prepared to help that type of probationer.

Other Experience

Although job requirements vary, work experience obtained by way of internships in courthouses or with probationers in the criminal justice field can be helpful for some positions.

Advancement

Advancement to supervisory positions is primarily based on experience and performance. A master's degree in criminal justice, social work, or psychology may be required for advancement.

Important Qualities

Communication skills. Probation officers and correctional treatment specialists must be able to effectively interact with probationers, probationers' family members, lawyers, judges, treatment providers, and law enforcement.

Critical-thinking skills. Probation officers and correctional treatment specialists must be able to assess the needs of individual probationers before determining the best resources for helping them.

Decisionmaking skills. Probation officers and correctional treatment specialists must consider the best rehabilitation plan for offenders.

Emotional stability. Probation officers and correctional treatment specialists cope with hostile individuals or otherwise upsetting circumstances on the job.

Organizational skills. Probation officers and correctional treatment specialists manage multiple cases at the same time.

Pay

The median annual wage for probation officers and correctional treatment specialists was $54,290 in May 2019. The median wage is the wage at which half the workers in an occupation earned more than that amount and half earned less. The lowest 10 percent earned less than $36,370, and the highest 10 percent earned more than $94,860.

In May 2019, the median annual wages for probation officers and correctional treatment specialists in the top industries in which they worked were as follows:

Local government, excluding education and $57,920
   hospitals ....

Probation Officers and Correctional Treatment Specialists

Median annual wages, May 2019

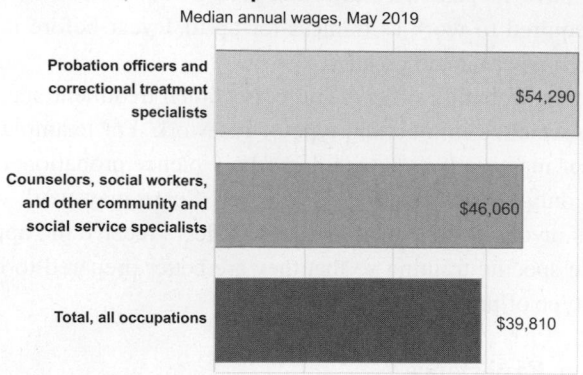

Probation officers and correctional treatment specialists	$54,290
Counselors, social workers, and other community and social service specialists	$46,060
Total, all occupations	$39,810

Note: All Occupations includes all occupations in the U.S. Economy.
Source: U.S. Bureau of Labor Statistics, Occupational Employment Statistics.

Probation Officers and Correctional Treatment Specialists

Percent change in employment, projected 2019-29

Counselors, social workers, and other community and social service specialists	14%
Total, all occupations	4%
Probation officers and correctional treatment specialists	4%

Note: All Occupations includes all occupations in the U.S. Economy.
Source: U.S. Bureau of Labor Statistics, Employment Projections program.

State government, excluding education and
    hospitals 52,500
Social assistance.. 35,730

Although many officers and specialists work full time, the demands of the job sometimes lead to working overtime and variable hours. For example, many agencies rotate an on-call officer position. When these workers are on-call, they must respond to any issues with probationers or law enforcement 24 hours a day.

Extensive travel and paperwork can also contribute to more hours of work.

Job Outlook

Employment of probation officers and correctional treatment specialists is projected to grow 4 percent from 2019 to 2029, about as fast as the average for all occupations.

Employment growth depends primarily on the amount of state and local government funding for corrections, especially the amount allocated to probation and parole systems.

Because community corrections is viewed as an economically viable alternative to incarceration in some cases, demand for probation officers and correctional treatment specialists should continue. Parole officers will continue to be needed to supervise individuals who will be released from prison in the future.

Job Prospects

Many job openings will result from the need to replace those who leave the occupation each year due to the heavy workloads

and high job-related stress. Job opportunities should be plentiful for those who qualify. The ability to speak Spanish is also desirable in this occupation and may present better job prospects.

Employment projections data for probation officers and correctional treatment specialists, 2019-29					
Occupational Title	SOC Code	Employment, 2019	Projected Employment, 2029	Change, 2019-29	
				Percent	Numeric
SOURCE: U.S. Bureau of Labor Statistics, Employment Projections program					
Probation officers and correctional treatment specialists	21-1092	91,800	95,300	4	3,400

State & Area Data
Occupational Employment Statistics (OES)

The Occupational Employment Statistics (OES) program produces employment and wage estimates annually for over 800 occupations. These estimates are available for the nation as a whole, for individual states, and for metropolitan and nonmetropolitan areas.

Contacts for More Information

For more information about probation officers and correctional treatment specialists, visit
➤ American Probation and Parole Association
➤ Discover Corrections

For more information about criminal justice job opportunities in your area, contact the departments of corrections, criminal justice, or probation for individual states.

Rehabilitation Counselors

Summary

Quick Facts: Rehabilitation Counselors

2019 Median Pay	$35,950 per year $17.28 per hour
Typical Entry-Level Education	Master's degree
Work Experience in a Related Occupation	None
On-the-job Training	None
Number of Jobs, 2019	120,200
Job Outlook, 2019-29	10% (Much faster than average)
Employment Change, 2019-29	12,300

What Rehabilitation Counselors Do

Rehabilitation counselors help people with physical, mental, developmental, or emotional disabilities live independently.

Work Environment

Rehabilitation counselors work in a variety of settings, such as community rehabilitation centers, senior citizen centers, and youth guidance organizations.

How to Become a Rehabilitation Counselor

Rehabilitation counselors typically need a master's degree in rehabilitation counseling or a related field. Some positions require certification or a license.

Pay

The median annual wage for rehabilitation counselors was $35,950 in May 2019.

Job Outlook

Employment of rehabilitation counselors is projected to grow 10 percent from 2019 to 2029, much faster than the average for all occupations. Demand for rehabilitation counselors is

Rehabilitation counselors help people with physical, mental, developmental, and emotional disabilities live independently.

Rehabilitation counselors help people with disabilities develop strategies to live with their disability and transition to employment.

expected to grow with the increase in the elderly population and with the continued rehabilitation needs of other groups, such as veterans and people with disabilities.

State & Area Data

Explore resources for employment and wages by state and area for rehabilitation counselors.

What Rehabilitation Counselors Do

Rehabilitation counselors help people with physical, mental, developmental, or emotional disabilities live independently. They work with clients to overcome or manage the personal, social, or psychological effects of disabilities on employment or independent living.

Duties

Rehabilitation counselors typically do the following:

- Provide individual and group counseling to help clients adjust to their disability
- Evaluate clients' abilities, interests, experiences, skills, health, and education
- Develop a treatment plan for clients, in consultation with other professionals, such as doctors, therapists, and psychologists
- Arrange for clients to obtain services, such as medical care or career training
- Help employers understand the needs and abilities of people with disabilities, as well as laws and resources that affect people with disabilities
- Help clients develop their strengths and adjust to their limitations
- Locate resources, such as wheelchairs or computer programs, that help clients live and work more independently
- Maintain client records and monitor clients' progress, adjusting the rehabilitation or treatment plan as necessary

• Advocate for the rights of people with disabilities to live in a community and work in the job of their choice

Rehabilitation counselors help people with disabilities at various stages in their lives. Some work with students, to develop strategies to live with their disability and transition from school to work. Others help veterans cope with the mental or physical effects of their military service. Still others help elderly people adapt to disabilities developed later in life from illness or injury. Some may provide expert testimony or assessments during personal-injury or workers' compensation cases.

Some rehabilitation counselors deal specifically with employment issues. These counselors, sometimes called *vocational rehabilitation counselors*, typically work with older students and adults.

Work Environment

Rehabilitation counselors held about 120,200 jobs in 2019. The largest employers of rehabilitation counselors were as follows:

Community and vocational rehabilitation services...... 30%
Individual and family services 17
State government, excluding education and hospitals ... 14
Nursing and residential care facilities......................... 13
Self-employed workers 7

Rehabilitation counselors work in a variety of settings, such as community rehabilitation centers, senior citizen centers, and youth guidance organizations.

Work Schedules

Depending on where they work, some rehabilitation counselors may work evenings or weekends.

How to Become a Rehabilitation Counselor

Rehabilitation counselors typically need a master's degree in rehabilitation counseling or a related field. Some positions require certification or a license.

Education

Most employers require a master's degree in rehabilitation counseling or a related field. Master's degree programs teach students to evaluate clients' needs, formulate and implement job placement strategies, and understand the medical and psychological aspects of disabilities. These programs typically include a period of supervised clinical experience, such as an internship.

Although some employers hire workers with a bachelor's degree in rehabilitation and disability studies, these workers

Rehabilitation counselors work in a variety of settings, such as community rehabilitation centers, senior citizen centers, and youth guidance organizations.

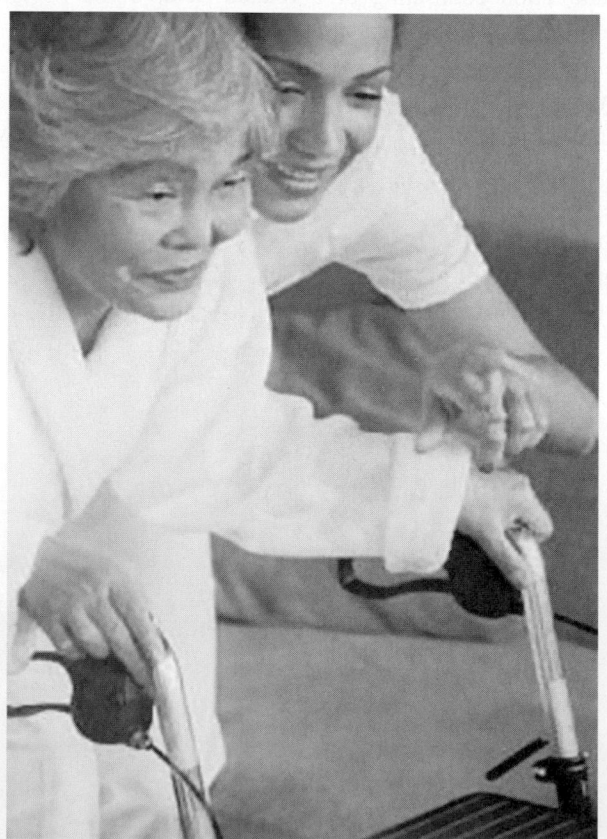

Rehabilitation counselors may need to complete a period of supervised clinical experience as part of a master's degree.

typically cannot offer the full range of services that a rehabilitation counselor with a master's degree can provide. Students in bachelor's degree programs learn about issues faced by people with disabilities and about the process of providing rehabilitation services. Some universities offer dual-degree programs in rehabilitation counseling, in which students can earn a bachelor's and master's degree in 5 years.

Licenses, Certifications, and Registrations

Licensing requirements for rehabilitation counselors differ by state and by type of services provided. Rehabilitation counselors who provide counseling services to clients and patients must attain a counselor license through their state licensing board. Rehabilitation counselors who provide other services, however, may be exempt from state licensing requirements. For example, rehabilitation counselors who provide only vocational rehabilitation services or job placement assistance may not need a license.

Licensure typically requires a master's degree and 2,000 to 4,000 hours of supervised clinical experience. In addition, counselors must pass a state-recognized exam. To maintain their license, counselors must complete annual continuing education credits.

Applicants should contact their state licensing board for information on which services or counseling positions require licensure. Contact information for these state licensing boards can be found through the Commission on Rehabilitation Counselor Certification.

Some employers prefer or require rehabilitation counselors to be certified. The Commission on Rehabilitation Counselor Certification offers the Certified Rehabilitation Counselor (CRC) certification. Applicants must meet advanced education, work experience, and clinical supervision requirements and pass a test. Certification must be renewed every 5 years. Counselors must complete continuing education requirements or pass a reexamination to renew their certification.

Important Qualities

Communication skills. Rehabilitation counselors need to be able to communicate effectively with clients. They must express ideas and information in a way that is easy to understand.

Compassion. Rehabilitation counselors often work with people who are dealing with stressful and difficult situations. They must be compassionate and empathize with their clients.

Critical-thinking skills. Rehabilitation counselors must be able to develop a treatment plan to help clients reach their goals by considering each client's abilities and interests.

Interpersonal skills. Rehabilitation counselors must be able to work with different types of people. They spend most of their time working directly with clients, families, employers, or

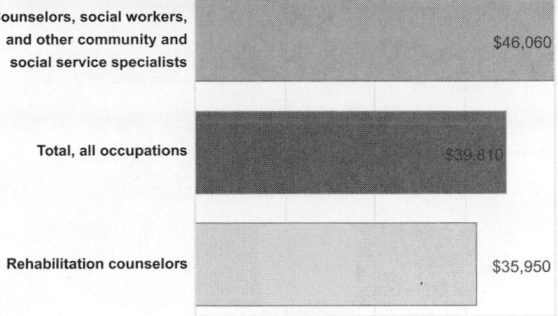

Rehabilitation Counselors

Median annual wages, May 2019

Counselors, social workers, and other community and social service specialists	$46,060
Total, all occupations	$39,810
Rehabilitation counselors	$35,950

Note: All Occupations includes all occupations in the U.S. Economy.
Source: U.S. Bureau of Labor Statistics, Occupational Employment Statistics.

other professionals. They must be able to develop and maintain good working relationships.

Listening skills. Good listening skills are essential for rehabilitation counselors. They need to give their full attention in sessions in order to understand clients' problems, concerns, and values.

Patience. Rehabilitation counselors must have patience to help clients learn new skills and strategies to address their disabilities.

Pay

The median annual wage for rehabilitation counselors was $35,950 in May 2019. The median wage is the wage at which half the workers in an occupation earned more than that amount and half earned less. The lowest 10 percent earned less than $23,820, and the highest 10 percent earned more than $63,790.

In May 2019, the median annual wages for rehabilitation counselors in the top industries in which they worked were as follows:

State government, excluding education and hospitals	$51,260
Individual and family services	33,590
Community and vocational rehabilitation services..	32,310
Nursing and residential care facilities	31,070

Depending on where they work, some rehabilitation counselors may work evenings or weekends.

Job Outlook

Employment of rehabilitation counselors is projected to grow 10 percent from 2019 to 2029, much faster than the average for all occupations. Demand for rehabilitation counselors is expected to grow with the increase in the elderly population and with the continued rehabilitation needs of other groups, such as veterans and people with disabilities.

Rehabilitation Counselors
Percent change in employment, projected 2019-29

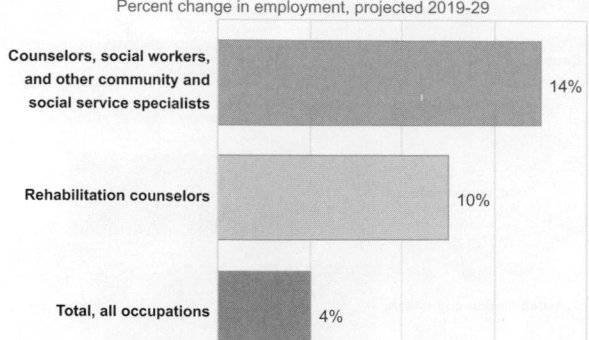

Counselors, social workers, and other community and social service specialists — 14%

Rehabilitation counselors — 10%

Total, all occupations — 4%

Note: All Occupations includes all occupations in the U.S. Economy.
Source: U.S. Bureau of Labor Statistics, Employment Projections program.

Older adults are more likely than other age groups to become disabled or injured. Rehabilitation counselors will be needed to help the elderly learn to adapt to any new limitations and learn strategies to live independently.

In addition, there will be a continued need for rehabilitation counselors to work with veterans who were disabled during their military service. They will also be needed to work with other groups, such as people who have learning disabilities, autism spectrum disorders, or substance abuse problems.

Job Prospects

Job prospects are expected to be good because of job growth and the need to replace workers.

Employment projections data for rehabilitation counselors, 2019-29					
Occupational Title	SOC Code	Employment, 2019	Projected Employment, 2029	Change, 2019-29	
				Percent	Numeric
SOURCE: U.S. Bureau of Labor Statistics, Employment Projections program					
Rehabilitation counselors	21-1015	120,200	132,500	10	12,300

State & Area Data
Occupational Employment Statistics (OES)

The Occupational Employment Statistics (OES) program produces employment and wage estimates annually for over 800 occupations. These estimates are available for the nation as a whole, for individual states, and for metropolitan and nonmetropolitan areas.

Contacts for More Information

For more information about counseling and information about counseling specialties, visit
➤ American Counseling Association
➤ American Rehabilitation Counseling Association

For more information about accredited degree programs in rehabilitation counseling, visit
➤ Council for Accreditation of Counseling & Related Educational Programs

For more information about the Certified Rehabilitation Counselors certification and state licensing boards, visit
➤ Commission on Rehabilitation Counselor Certification

School and Career Counselors

Summary

Quick Facts: School and Career Counselors

2019 Median Pay	$57,040 per year $27.42 per hour
Typical Entry-Level Education	Master's degree
Work Experience in a Related Occupation	None
On-the-job Training	None
Number of Jobs, 2019	333,500
Job Outlook, 2019-29	8% (Much faster than average)
Employment Change, 2019-29	26,800

What School and Career Counselors Do

School counselors help students develop the academic and social skills needed to succeed. Career counselors help people choose a path to employment.

School counselors help students develop social skills and succeed in school.

Work Environment

School counselors work in public and private schools. Career counselors work in colleges, career centers, and private practices. Both types of counselors generally work full time.

How to Become a School or Career Counselor

Most school counselors need a master's degree in school counseling or a related field and have a state-issued credential. Some states require licensure for career counselors.

Pay

The median annual wage for school and career counselors was $57,040 in May 2019.

Job Outlook

Employment of school and career counselors is projected to grow 8 percent from 2019 to 2029, much faster than the average for all occupations. Increasing school enrollment is expected to lead to employment growth of these workers.

State & Area Data

Explore resources for employment and wages by state and area for school and career counselors.

What School and Career Counselors Do

School counselors help students develop the academic and social skills that lead to success in school. Career counselors help people develop skills, explore a career, or choose an educational program that will lead to a career.

Duties

School counselors typically do the following:

- Evaluate students' abilities and interests through aptitude assessments, interviews, and individual planning
- Identify issues that affect school performance, such as poor classroom attendance rates
- Help students understand and overcome social or behavioral problems through classroom guidance lessons and counseling

Career counselors assist people with the process of making career decisions.

- Counsel individuals and small groups on the basis of student and school needs
- Work with students to develop skills, such as organizational and time management abilities and effective study habits
- Help students create a plan to achieve academic and career goals
- Collaborate with teachers, administrators, and parents to help students succeed
- Teach students and school staff about specific topics, such as bullying, drug abuse, and planning for college or careers after graduation
- Maintain records as required
- Report possible cases of neglect or abuse and refer students and parents to resources outside the school for additional support

The specific duties of school counselors vary with the ages of their students.

Elementary school counselors focus on helping students develop certain skills, such as those used in decisionmaking and studying, that they need in order to be successful in their social and academic lives. School counselors meet with parents or guardians to discuss their child's strengths and weaknesses, and any special needs and behavioral issues that the child might have. School counselors also work with teachers and administrators to ensure that the curriculum addresses both the developmental and academic needs of students.

Middle school counselors work with school staff, parents, and the community to create a caring, supportive environment for students to achieve academic success. They help the students develop the skills and strategies necessary to succeed academically and socially.

High school counselors advise students in making academic and career plans. Many help students overcome personal issues that interfere with their academic development. They help students choose classes and plan for their lives after graduation. Counselors provide information about choosing and applying for colleges, training programs, financial aid, and internships and apprenticeships. They may present career workshops to help students search and apply for jobs, write résumés, and improve their interviewing skills.

Career counselors typically do the following:

- Use aptitude and achievement assessments to help clients evaluate their interests, skills, and abilities
- Evaluate clients' background, education, and training, to help them develop realistic goals
- Guide clients through making decisions about their careers, such as choosing a new profession and the type of degree to pursue
- Help clients learn job search skills, such as interviewing and networking
- Assist clients in locating and applying for jobs, by teaching them strategies that will be helpful in finding openings and writing a résumé

- Advise clients on how to resolve problems in the workplace, such as conflicts with bosses or coworkers
- Help clients select and apply for educational programs, to obtain the necessary degrees, credentials, and skills

Career counselors work with clients at various stages of their careers. Some work in colleges, helping students choose a major or determine the jobs they are qualified for with their degrees. Career counselors also help people find and get jobs by teaching them job search, résumé writing, and interviewing techniques.

Career counselors also work with people who have already entered the workforce. These counselors develop plans to improve their clients' current careers. They also provide advice about entering a new profession or helping to resolve workplace issues.

Some career counselors work in outplacement firms and assist laid-off workers with transitioning into new jobs or careers.

Work Environment

School and career counselors held about 333,500 jobs in 2019. The largest employers of school and career counselors were as follows:

Elementary and secondary schools; state, local, and private	44%
Junior colleges, colleges, universities, and professional schools; state, local, and private	35
Healthcare and social assistance	7
Other educational services; state, local, and private	4
Self-employed workers	3

School counselors often have private offices so that they can have confidential conversations with students.

Work Schedules

Most school and career counselors work full time. Some school counselors do not work during the summer when school is not in session.

School counselors work in private and public schools where they have private offices.

How to Become a School or Career Counselor

Most school counselors must have a master's degree in school counseling or a related field and have a state-issued credential. Some states require licensure for career counselors.

Education

Nearly all states and the District of Columbia require school counselors to have a master's degree in school counseling or a related field. Degree programs teach counselors the essential skills of the job, such as how to foster academic development; conduct group and individual counseling; work with parents, school staff, and community organizations; and use data to develop, implement, and evaluate comprehensive school counseling programs for all students. These programs often require counselors to complete an internship.

Some employers prefer that career counselors have a master's degree in counseling with a focus on career development. Career counseling programs prepare students to assess clients' skills and interests and to teach career development techniques.

Many master's degree programs in counseling require students to have a period of supervised experience, such as an internship.

Career counselors who work in private practices may also need a license.

Licenses, Certifications, and Registrations

Public school counselors must have a state-issued credential to practice. This credential can be called a certification, a license, or an endorsement, depending on the state. Licensure or certification typically requires a master's degree in school counseling, an internship or practicum completed under the supervision of a licensed professional school counselor, and successful completion of a test.

Some states require applicants to have classroom teaching experience, or to hold a teaching license, prior to being certified. Most states require a criminal background check as part of the credentialing process. Information about requirements for each state is available from the American School Counselor Association.

Some states require licensure for career counselors; check with your state for more information. Contact information for state regulating boards is available from the National Board for Certified Counselors.

Work Experience in a Related Occupation

Some states require school counselors to have 1 to 2 years of experience as a teacher, or to hold a teaching license, prior to being certified.

Important Qualities

Analytical skills. School and career counselors interpret assessments to match interests and abilities with potential careers.

Compassion. School and career counselors often work with people who are dealing with stressful and difficult situations, so they must be compassionate and empathize with their clients and students.

Interpersonal skills. School and career counselors must be able to work with people of all backgrounds and personalities. They spend most of their time working directly with clients, students, or other professionals and need to form and maintain good working relationships with them.

Listening skills. School and career counselors need good listening skills. They need to give their full attention to students and clients in order to understand their problems.

Speaking skills. School and career counselors must communicate effectively with clients and students. They should express ideas and information in a way that their clients and students understand easily.

Pay

The median annual wage for school and career counselors was $57,040 in May 2019. The median wage is the wage at which half the workers in an occupation earned more than that amount and half earned less. The lowest 10 percent earned less than $34,380, and the highest 10 percent earned more than $96,090.

In May 2019, the median annual wages for school and career counselors in the top industries in which they worked were as follows:

Elementary and secondary schools; state, local, and private	$64,060
Other educational services; state, local, and private	51,880
Junior colleges, colleges, universities, and professional schools; state, local, and private	51,120
Healthcare and social assistance	40,620

Most school and career counselors work full time. Some school counselors do not work during the summer when school is not in session.

Job Outlook

Employment of school and career counselors is projected to grow 8 percent from 2019 to 2029, much faster than the average for all occupations.

Rising student enrollment in elementary, middle, and high schools is expected to increase demand for school counselors. As enrollments grow, schools will require more counselors to respond to the developmental and academic needs of their students. Colleges will need to hire additional counselors to meet the demand for career counseling services from their students.

School and Career Counselors
Median annual wages, May 2019

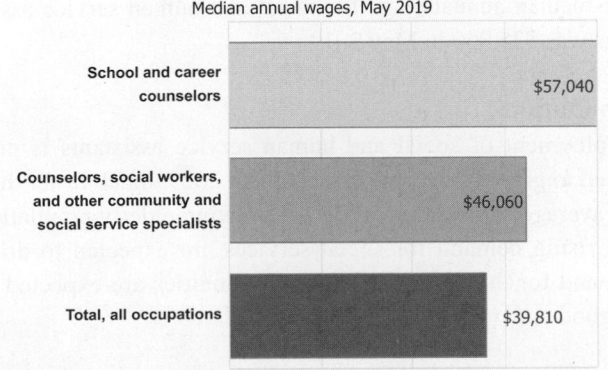

School and career counselors	$57,040
Counselors, social workers, and other community and social service specialists	$46,060
Total, all occupations	$39,810

Note: All Occupations includes all occupations in the U.S. Economy.
Source: U.S. Bureau of Labor Statistics, Occupational Employment Statistics.

School and Career Counselors
Percent change in employment, projected 2019-29

Counselors, social workers, and other community and social service specialists	14%
School and career counselors	8%
Total, all occupations	4%

Note: All Occupations includes all occupations in the U.S. Economy.
Source: U.S. Bureau of Labor Statistics, Employment Projections program.

Demand for career counseling is projected to increase in universities as an increasing number of campuses open onsite career centers to help students develop skills and prepare for transition to the workforce.

Career counselors also will be needed to assist those who change careers, to help laid-off workers find employment, and to help military personnel transition into the civilian job market.

Job Prospects

Job prospects are expected to be good for those with counseling degrees, especially in schools and colleges, because of the need to replace the workers who leave the occupation each year.

Employment projections data for school and career counselors, 2019-29					
Occupational Title	SOC Code	Employment, 2019	Projected Employment, 2029	Change, 2019-29	
				Percent	Numeric
SOURCE: U.S. Bureau of Labor Statistics, Employment Projections program					
Educational, guidance, and career counselors and advisors	21-1012	333,500	360,400	8	26,800

State & Area Data

Occupational Employment Statistics (OES)

The Occupational Employment Statistics (OES) program produces employment and wage estimates annually for over 800 occupations. These estimates are available for the nation as a whole, for individual states, and for metropolitan and nonmetropolitan areas.

Contacts for More Information

For more information about counseling and information about counseling specialties, visit
➤ American Counseling Association

For more information about school counselors, visit
➤ American School Counselor Association

For more information about career counselors, visit
➤ National Career Development Association

For more information about state credentialing, visit
➤ National Board for Certified Counselors

Social and Human Service Assistants

Summary

Quick Facts: Social and Human Service Assistants

2019 Median Pay	$35,060 per year $16.85 per hour
Typical Entry-Level Education	High school diploma or equivalent
Work Experience in a Related Occupation	None
On-the-job Training	Short-term on-the-job training
Number of Jobs, 2019	425,600
Job Outlook, 2019-29	17% (Much faster than average)
Employment Change, 2019-29	71,500

What Social and Human Service Assistants Do

Social and human service assistants provide client services in a variety of fields, such as psychology, rehabilitation, and social work.

Work Environment

Many social and human service assistants work for nonprofit organizations, for-profit social service agencies, and state and local governments. They generally work full time, and some work nights and weekends.

How to Become a Social and Human Service Assistant

Requirements for social and human service assistants vary, although they typically have at least a high school diploma and must complete a brief period of on-the-job training.

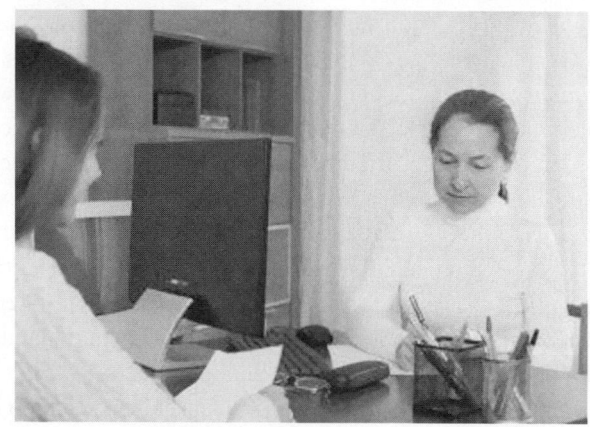

Social and human service assistants help clients identify and obtain benefits and services.

Pay

The median annual wage for social and human service assistants was $35,060 in May 2019.

Job Outlook

Employment of social and human service assistants is projected to grow 17 percent from 2019 to 2029, much faster than the average for all occupations. A growing elderly population and rising demand for social services are expected to drive demand for these workers. Job opportunities are expected to be good.

State & Area Data

Explore resources for employment and wages by state and area for social and human service assistants.

Social and human service assistants help the elderly stay in their own homes and live under their own care whenever possible.

What Social and Human Service Assistants Do

Social and human service assistants provide client services, including support for families, in a wide variety of fields, such as psychology, rehabilitation, and social work. They assist other workers, such as social workers, and they help clients find benefits or community services.

Duties

Social and human service assistants typically do the following:

- Help determine what type of aid their clients need
- Work with clients and other professionals, such as social workers, to develop a treatment plan
- Help clients find assistance with daily activities, such as eating and bathing
- Research services, such as food stamps and Medicaid, that are available to clients
- Coordinate services provided to clients
- Help clients complete paperwork to apply for assistance programs
- Check in with clients to ensure that services are provided appropriately

Social and human service assistants have many job titles, including *case work aide*, *clinical social work aide*, *family service assistant*, *social work assistant*, *addictions counselor assistant*, and *human service worker*.

Social and human service assistants help clients identify and obtain benefits and services. In addition to initially connecting clients with benefits or services, social and human service assistants may follow up with clients to ensure that they are receiving the intended services and that the services are meeting their needs. They work under the direction of social workers, psychologists, or other community and social service workers.

With *children and families*, social and human service assistants ensure that the children live in safe homes. They help parents get needed resources for their children, such as food stamps or childcare.

With the *elderly*, these workers help clients stay in their own homes and live under their own care whenever possible. Social and human service assistants may coordinate meal deliveries or find personal care aides to help with the clients' day-to-day needs, such as running errands and bathing. In some cases, human service assistants help look for residential care facilities, such as nursing homes.

For *people with disabilities*, social and human service assistants help find rehabilitation services that aid their clients. They may work with employers to make a job more accessible to people with disabilities. Some workers find personal care services to help clients with daily living activities, such as bathing and making meals.

For *people with addictions*, human service assistants find rehabilitation centers that meet their clients' needs. They also may find support groups for people who are dependent on alcohol, drugs, gambling, or other substances or behaviors.

With *veterans*, assistants help people who have been discharged from the military adjust to civilian life. They help with practical needs, such as locating housing and finding ways to apply skills gained in the military to civilian jobs. They may also help their clients navigate the services available to veterans.

For *people with mental illnesses*, social and human service assistants help clients find the appropriate resources to help them cope with their illness. They find self-help and support groups to provide their clients with an assistance network. In addition, they may find personal care services or group housing to help those with more severe mental illnesses care for themselves.

With *immigrants*, workers help clients adjust to living in a new country. They help the clients locate jobs and housing. They may also help them find programs that teach English, or they may find legal assistance to help immigrants get administrative paperwork in order.

With *former prison inmates*, human service assistants find job training or placement programs to help clients reenter society. Human service assistants help former inmates find housing and connect with programs that help them start a new life for themselves.

With *homeless people*, assistants help clients meet their basic needs. They find temporary or permanent housing for their clients and locate places, such as soup kitchens, that provide

Social and human service assistants sometimes travel around their community to see clients.

meals. Human service assistants also help homeless people find resources to address other problems they may have, such as joblessness.

Work Environment

Social and human service assistants held about 425,600 jobs in 2019. The largest employers of social and human service assistants were as follows:

Individual and family services	30%
Nursing and residential care facilities...........................	12
Local government, excluding education and hospitals....	11
Community and vocational rehabilitation services.......	10
State government, excluding education and hospitals ..	9

Social and human service assistants work in offices, clinics, hospitals, group homes, and shelters. Some travel around their communities to see clients.

Work Schedules

Most social and human service assistants work full time. Some work nights and weekends.

How to Become a Social and Human Service Assistant

Requirements for social and human service assistants vary, although they typically have at least a high school diploma and must complete a brief period of on-the-job training.

Some employers require a criminal background check. Social and human service assistants also may need a valid driver's license.

Education

Although a high school diploma is typically required, some employers prefer to hire workers who have relevant work experience or education beyond high school. A certificate or an associate's degree in a subject such as human services,

The duties of social and human service assistants are often determined by their level of education.

gerontology (working with older adults), or social or behavioral science is becoming more common for workers entering this occupation.

Human service degree programs train students to observe and interview patients, carry out treatment plans, and handle people who are undergoing a crisis. Many programs include fieldwork to give students hands-on experience.

The level of education that social and human service assistants have completed often determines the responsibilities they are given. Those with a high school diploma are likely to do lower level work, such as helping clients fill out paperwork. Assistants with some college education may coordinate program activities or manage a group home.

Training

Many social and human service assistants, particularly those without any postsecondary education, undergo a short period of on-the-job training. Because such workers often are dealing with multiple clients from a wide variety of backgrounds, on-the-job training in case management helps prepare them to respond appropriately to the different needs and situations of their clients.

Advancement

For social and human service assistants, additional education is almost always necessary for advancement. In general, advancement to case management or social work jobs requires a bachelor's or master's degree in human services, counseling, rehabilitation, social work, or a related field.

Important Qualities

Communication skills. Social and human service assistants talk with clients about the challenges in their lives and assist them in getting help. These workers must be able to listen to their clients and to communicate the clients' needs to organizations that can help them.

Social and Human Service Assistants
Median annual wages, May 2019

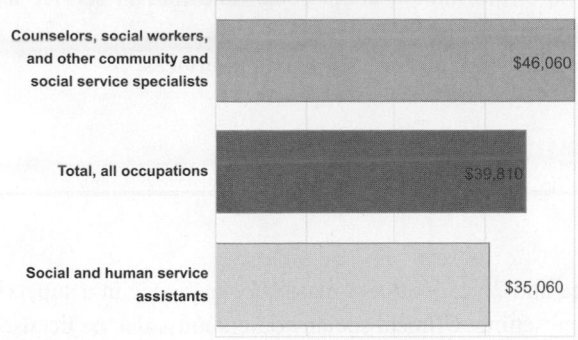

Counselors, social workers, and other community and social service specialists	$46,060
Total, all occupations	$39,810
Social and human service assistants	$35,060

Social and Human Service Assistants
Percent change in employment, projected 2019-29

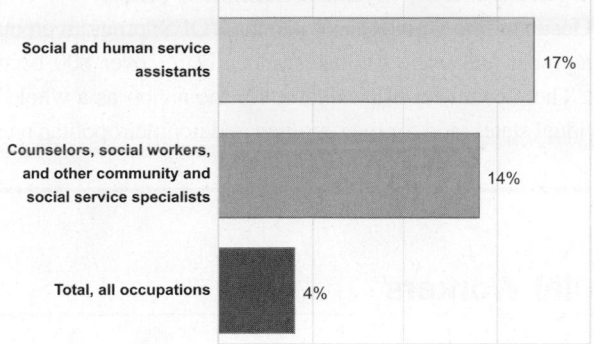

Social and human service assistants	17%
Counselors, social workers, and other community and social service specialists	14%
Total, all occupations	4%

Note: All Occupations includes all occupations in the U.S. Economy. Source: U.S. Bureau of Labor Statistics, Occupational Employment Statistics.

Note: All Occupations includes all occupations in the U.S. Economy. Source: U.S. Bureau of Labor Statistics, Employment Projections program.

Compassion. Social and human service assistants often work with people who are in stressful and difficult situations. To develop strong relationships, they must have compassion and empathy for their clients.

Interpersonal skills. Social and human service assistants must make their clients feel comfortable discussing sensitive issues. Assistants also build relationships with other service providers to become familiar with all of the resources that are available in their communities.

Organizational skills. Social and human service assistants must often complete lots of paperwork and work with many different clients. They must be organized in order to ensure that the paperwork is filed properly and that clients are getting the help they need.

Problem-solving skills. Social and human service assistants help clients find solutions to their problems. They must be able to listen carefully to their clients' needs and offer practical solutions.

Time-management skills. Social and human service assistants often work with many clients. They must manage their time effectively to ensure that their clients are getting the attention they need.

Pay

The median annual wage for social and human service assistants was $35,060 in May 2019. The median wage is the wage at which half the workers in an occupation earned more than that amount and half earned less. The lowest 10 percent earned less than $23,750, and the highest 10 percent earned more than $54,230.

In May 2019, the median annual wages for social and human service assistants in the top industries in which they worked were as follows:

Local government, excluding education and hospitals	$41,030
State government, excluding education and hospitals	38,760

Individual and family services	34,450
Community and vocational rehabilitation services	31,370
Nursing and residential care facilities	31,020

Most social and human service assistants work full time. Some work nights and weekends.

Job Outlook

Employment of social and human service assistants is projected to grow 17 percent from 2019 to 2029, much faster than the average for all occupations. A growing elderly population and rising demand for social services are expected to drive demand for these workers.

An increase in the number of older adults is expected to result in growing demand for social services such as delivery of meals and adult daycare. Because social and human service assistants often arrange for these services, there will need to be more of them to meet this increased demand.

In addition, growth is expected as more people seek treatment for their addictions and more drug offenders are sent to treatment programs rather than to jail. As a result, demand should increase for social and human service assistants who work in treatment programs or work with people with addictions.

Job Prospects

Job prospects are expected to be good, but should be best for those with a related social or human service postsecondary degree.

Employment projections data for social and human service assistants, 2019-29					
Occupational Title	SOC Code	Employment, 2019	Projected Employment, 2029	Change, 2019-29	
				Percent	Numeric
SOURCE: U.S. Bureau of Labor Statistics, Employment Projections program					
Social and human service assistants	21-1093	425,600	497,100	17	71,500

State & Area Data
Occupational Employment Statistics (OES)

The Occupational Employment Statistics (OES) program produces employment and wage estimates annually for over 800 occupations. These estimates are available for the nation as a whole, for individual states, and for metropolitan and nonmetropolitan areas.

Contacts for More Information

For more information about social and human service assistants, visit

➤ National Organization for Human Services

Social Workers

Summary

Quick Facts: Social Workers

2019 Median Pay	$50,470 per year
	$24.26 per hour
Typical Entry-Level Education	See below
Work Experience in a Related Occupation	None
On-the-job Training	See below
Number of Jobs, 2019	713,200
Job Outlook, 2019-29	13% (Much faster than average)
Employment Change, 2019-29	90,700

What Social Workers Do

Social workers help people solve and cope with problems in their everyday lives.

Work Environment

Social workers work in a variety of settings, including mental health clinics, schools, child welfare and human service agencies, hospitals, settlement houses, community development corporations, and private practices. They generally work full time and may need to work evenings, weekends, and holidays.

How to Become a Social Worker

Although some social workers only need a bachelor's degree in social work, clinical social workers must have a master's degree and 2 years of post-master's experience in a supervised clinical setting. Clinical social workers must also be licensed in the state in which they practice.

Pay

The median annual wage for social workers was $50,470 in May 2019.

Job Outlook

Overall employment of social workers is projected to grow 13 percent from 2019 to 2029, much faster than the average for all occupations. Employment growth will vary by specialization.

State & Area Data

Explore resources for employment and wages by state and area for social workers.

What Social Workers Do

Social workers help people solve and cope with problems in their everyday lives. Clinical social workers also diagnose and treat mental, behavioral, and emotional issues.

Duties

Social workers typically do the following:

- Identify people and communities in need of help
- Assess clients' needs, situations, strengths, and support networks to determine their goals

Social workers help people solve and cope with problems.

Child and family social workers protect vulnerable children and support families in need of assistance.

- Help clients adjust to changes and challenges in their lives, such as illness, divorce, or unemployment
- Research, refer, and advocate for community resources, such as food stamps, childcare, and healthcare to assist and improve a client's well-being
- Respond to crisis situations such as child abuse and mental health emergencies
- Follow up with clients to ensure that their situations have improved
- Maintain case files and records
- Develop and evaluate programs and services to ensure that basic client needs are met
- Provide psychotherapy services

Social workers help people cope with challenges in their lives. They help with a wide range of situations, such as adopting a child or being diagnosed with a terminal illness.

Advocacy is an important aspect of social work. Social workers advocate or raise awareness with and on behalf of their clients and the social work profession on local, state, and national levels.

Some social workers—referred to as *bachelor's social workers* (BSW)—work with groups, community organizations, and policymakers to develop or improve programs, services, policies, and social conditions. This focus of work is referred to as macro social work.

Social workers who are licensed to diagnose and treat mental, behavioral, and emotional disorders are called *clinical social workers* (CSW) or *licensed clinical social workers* (LCSW). They provide individual, group, family, and couples therapy; they work with clients to develop strategies to change behavior or cope with difficult situations; and they refer clients to other resources or services, such as support groups or other mental health professionals. Clinical social workers can develop treatment plans with the client, doctors, and other healthcare professionals and may adjust the treatment plan if necessary based on their client's progress. They may work in a variety of specialties. Clinical social workers who have not completed two years of supervised work are often called *master's social workers* (MSW).

The following are examples of types of social workers:

Child and family social workers protect vulnerable children and help families in need of assistance. They help families find housing or services, such as childcare, or apply for benefits, such as food stamps. They intervene when children are in danger of neglect or abuse. Some help arrange adoptions, locate foster families, or work to reunite families.

School social workers work with teachers, parents, and school administrators to develop plans and strategies to improve students' academic performance and social development. Students and their families are often referred to social workers to deal with problems such as aggressive behavior, bullying, or frequent absences from school.

Although most social workers work in an office, they may spend a lot of time away from the office visiting clients.

Healthcare social workers help patients understand their diagnosis and make the necessary adjustments to their lifestyle, housing, or healthcare. For example, they may help people make the transition from the hospital back to their homes and communities. In addition, they may provide information on services, such as home healthcare or support groups, to help patients manage their illness or disease. Social workers help doctors and other healthcare professionals understand the effects that diseases and illnesses have on patients' mental and emotional health. Some healthcare social workers specialize in geriatric social work, hospice and palliative care, or medical social work.

Mental health and substance abuse social workers help clients with mental illnesses or addictions. They provide information on services, such as support groups and 12-step programs, to help clients cope with their illness. Many clinical social workers function in these roles as well.

Work Environment

Social workers held about 713,200 jobs in 2019. Employment in the detailed occupations that make up social workers was distributed as follows:

Child, family, and school social workers	342,500
Healthcare social workers	185,000
Mental health and substance abuse social workers	123,200
Social workers, all other	62,500

The largest employers of social workers were as follows:

Individual and family services	18%
Local government, excluding education and hospitals	14
Ambulatory healthcare services	14
State government, excluding education and hospitals	13

Although most social workers work in an office, they may spend time visiting clients. School social workers may be assigned to multiple schools and travel around the school district to see students. Understaffing and large caseloads may cause the work to be stressful.

Social workers may work remotely through distance counseling, using videoconferencing or mobile technology to meet with clients and organize support and advocacy groups.

Injuries and Illnesses

Social workers, all other have one of the highest rates of injuries and illnesses of all occupations. ("All other" titles represent occupations with a wide range of characteristics that do not fit into any of the other detailed occupations.)

Work Schedules

The majority of social workers work full time. They sometimes work evenings, weekends, and holidays to see clients or attend meetings, and they may be on call.

How to Become a Social Worker

Although some social workers only need a bachelor's degree in social work, clinical social workers must have a master's degree and 2 years of experience in a supervised clinical setting after they've completed their degree. Clinical social workers must also be licensed by their state.

Education and Training

There are multiple educational pathways to becoming a social worker, depending on the specialty.

A bachelor's degree in social work (BSW) is the most common requirement for entry-level administrative positions. However, some employers may hire workers who have a bachelor's degree in a related field, such as psychology or sociology.

A BSW prepares students for direct-service positions such as caseworker or mental health assistant. These programs teach students about diverse populations, human behavior, social

Clinical social workers need a master's degree, supervised experience, and a license to provide mental health or counseling services.

welfare policy, and ethics in social work. All programs require students to complete supervised fieldwork or an internship.

Clinical positions require a master's degree in social work (MSW), which generally takes 2 years to complete. MSW programs prepare students for work in their chosen specialty by developing clinical assessment and management skills. All programs require students to complete a supervised practicum or an internship.

A bachelor's degree in social work is not required in order to enter a master's degree program in social work. Although a bachelor's degree in almost any major is acceptable, courses in psychology, sociology, economics, and political science are recommended. Some programs allow graduates with a bachelor's degree in social work to earn their master's degree in 1 year.

In 2017, there were more than 500 bachelor's degree programs and more than 200 master's degree programs accredited by the Council on Social Work Education.

Two years of supervised training and experience after obtaining an MA degree is typically required for clinical social workers.

Licenses, Certifications, and Registrations

All states require clinical social workers to be licensed, and most states require licensure or certification for nonclinical social workers. Becoming a licensed clinical social worker requires a master's degree in social work and a minimum of 2 years of supervised clinical experience after graduation. After completing their supervised experience, clinical social workers must pass a clinical exam to be licensed.

Because licensing requirements vary by state, those interested should contact their state licensure board. For more information about regulatory licensure boards by state, visit the Association of Social Work Boards.

Important Qualities

Communication skills. Clients talk to social workers about challenges in their lives. To provide effective help, social workers must be able to listen to and understand their clients' needs.

Emotional skills. Social workers often work with people who are in stressful and difficult situations. To develop strong relationships, they must have patience, compassion, and empathy for their clients.

Interpersonal skills. Social workers need to be able to work with different groups of people. They need strong interpersonal skills to foster healthy and productive relationships with their clients and colleagues.

Organizational skills. Social workers must help and manage multiple clients, often assisting with their paperwork or documenting their treatment.

Problem-solving skills. Social workers need to develop practical and innovative solutions to their clients' problems.

Social Workers
Median annual wages, May 2019

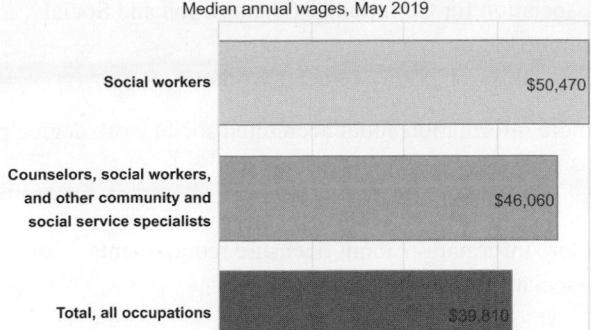

Social workers	$50,470
Counselors, social workers, and other community and social service specialists	$46,060
Total, all occupations	$39,810

Note: All Occupations includes all occupations in the U.S. Economy.
Source: U.S. Bureau of Labor Statistics, Occupational Employment Statistics.

Social Workers
Percent change in employment, projected 2019-29

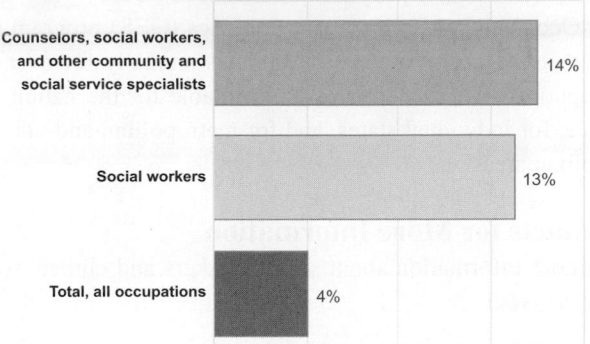

Counselors, social workers, and other community and social service specialists	14%
Social workers	13%
Total, all occupations	4%

Note: All Occupations includes all occupations in the U.S. Economy.
Source: U.S. Bureau of Labor Statistics, Employment Projections program.

Pay

The median annual wage for social workers was $50,470 in May 2019. The median wage is the wage at which half the workers in an occupation earned more than that amount and half earned less. The lowest 10 percent earned less than $31,790, and the highest 10 percent earned more than $82,540.

Median annual wages for social workers in May 2019 were as follows:

Social workers, all other	$61,230
Healthcare social workers	56,750
Child, family, and school social workers	47,390
Mental health and substance abuse social workers	46,650

In May 2019, the median annual wages for social workers in the top industries in which they worked were as follows:

Local government, excluding education and hospitals	$55,500
Ambulatory healthcare services	51,290
State government, excluding education and hospitals	49,100
Individual and family services	43,030

The majority of social workers work full time. They sometimes work evenings, weekends, and holidays to see clients or attend meetings, and they may be on call.

Job Outlook

Overall employment of social workers is projected to grow 13 percent from 2019 to 2029, much faster than the average for all occupations. Employment growth will vary by specialization.

Employment of child, family, and school social workers is projected to grow 12 percent from 2019 to 2029, much faster than the average for all occupations. Child and family social workers will be needed to work with families to strengthen parenting skills, prevent child abuse, and identify alternative homes for children who are unable to live with their biological

families. In schools, more social workers will be needed as student enrollments rise. However, employment growth of child, family, and school social workers may be limited by federal, state, and local budget constraints.

Employment of healthcare social workers is projected to grow 14 percent from 2019 to 2029, much faster than the average for all occupations. Healthcare social workers will continue to be needed to help aging populations and their families adjust to new treatments, medications, and lifestyles.

Employment of mental health and substance abuse social workers is projected to grow 17 percent from 2019 to 2029, much faster than the average for all occupations. Employment will grow as more people seek treatment for mental illness and substance abuse. In addition, drug offenders are increasingly being sent to treatment programs, which are staffed by these social workers, rather than being sent to jail.

Job Prospects

Overall, job prospects should be very good, particularly for clinical social workers. The continuing growth of healthcare spending and treatment increases the opportunities for clinical social workers as compared to social workers who do not offer treatment services.

Employment projections data for social workers, 2019-29					
Occupational Title	SOC Code	Employment, 2019	Projected Employment, 2029	Change, 2019-29	
				Percent	Numeric
SOURCE: U.S. Bureau of Labor Statistics, Employment Projections program					
Social workers	21-1020	713,200	803,800	13	90,700
Child, family, and school social workers	21-1021	342,500	382,600	12	40,100
Healthcare social workers	21-1022	185,000	211,700	14	26,700
Mental health and substance abuse social workers	21-1023	123,200	143,800	17	20,700
Social workers, all other	21-1029	62,500	65,600	5	3,200

State & Area Data
Occupational Employment Statistics (OES)

The Occupational Employment Statistics (OES) program produces employment and wage estimates annually for over 800 occupations. These estimates are available for the nation as a whole, for individual states, and for metropolitan and nonmetropolitan areas.

Contacts for More Information

For more information about social workers and clinical social workers, visit

➤ American Board of Examiners in Clinical Social Work
➤ Association for Community Organization and Social Administration
➤ National Association of Social Workers

For more information about accredited social work degree programs, visit
➤ Council on Social Work Education

For more information about licensure requirements, visit
➤ Association of Social Work Boards

Substance Abuse, Behavioral Disorder, and Mental Health Counselors

Summary

Quick Facts: Substance Abuse, Behavioral Disorder, and Mental Health Counselors

2019 Median Pay	$46,240 per year $22.23 per hour
Typical Entry-Level Education	Bachelor's degree
Work Experience in a Related Occupation	None
On-the-job Training	None
Number of Jobs, 2019	319,400
Job Outlook, 2019-29	25% (Much faster than average)
Employment Change, 2019-29	79,000

What Substance Abuse, Behavioral Disorder, and Mental Health Counselors Do

Substance abuse, behavioral disorder, and mental health counselors provide treatment and advise people who suffer from

Substance abuse, behavioral disorder, and mental health counselors help clients recover from addiction or mental health issues, or modify problem behaviors.

alcoholism, drug addiction, or other mental or behavioral problems.

Work Environment

Substance abuse, behavioral disorder, and mental health counselors work in a wide variety of settings, such as mental health centers, community health centers, prisons, and private practice. Most work full time.

How to Become a Substance Abuse, Behavioral Disorder, or Mental Health Counselor

Most positions require at least a bachelor's degree. Although educational requirements can vary from a high school diploma and certification to a master's degree for substance abuse and behavioral disorder counselors, a master's degree and an internship is typically required to become a mental health counselor.

Pay

The median annual wage for substance abuse, behavioral disorder, and mental health counselors was $46,240 in May 2019.

Job Outlook

Employment of substance abuse, behavioral disorder, and mental health counselors is projected to grow 25 percent from 2019 to 2029, much faster than the average for all occupations. Employment growth is expected as people continue to seek addiction and mental health counseling.

State & Area Data

Explore resources for employment and wages by state and area for substance abuse, behavioral disorder, and mental health counselors.

What Substance Abuse, Behavioral Disorder, and Mental Health Counselors Do

Substance abuse, behavioral disorder, and mental health counselors advise people who suffer from alcoholism, drug addiction, eating disorders, mental health issues, or other mental

Substance abuse, behavioral disorder, and mental health counselors provide treatment and support.

or behavioral problems. They provide treatment and support to help clients recover from addiction or modify problem behaviors.

Duties

Substance abuse, behavioral disorder, and mental health counselors typically do the following:

- Evaluate clients' mental and physical health, addiction, or problematic behavior and assess their readiness for treatment
- Develop, recommend, and review treatment goals and plans with clients and their families
- Assist clients in developing skills and behaviors necessary to recover from their addiction or modify their behavior
- Work with clients to identify behaviors or situations that interfere with their recovery
- Teach clients' family members about addiction or behavior disorders and help them develop strategies to cope with those problems
- Refer clients to other resources and services, such as job placement services and support groups
- Conduct outreach programs to help people identify the signs of addiction and other destructive behavior, as well as steps to take to avoid such behavior

Substance abuse counselors and *behavioral disorder counselors*, also called *addiction counselors*, work with clients individually and in group sessions. Many incorporate the principles of 12-step programs, such as Alcoholics Anonymous (AA), to guide their practice. They teach clients how to cope with stress and life's problems in ways that help them recover. Furthermore, they help clients rebuild professional relationships and, if necessary, reestablish their career. They also help clients improve their personal relationships and find ways to discuss their addiction or other problems with family and friends.

Some addiction counselors work in facilities that employ many types of healthcare and mental health professionals. Addiction counselors may work with psychologists, psychiatrists, social workers, physicians, and registered nurses to develop treatment plans and coordinate care for patients.

Some counselors work with clients who have been ordered by a judge to receive treatment for addiction. Others work with specific populations, such as teenagers, veterans, or people with disabilities. Some specialize in crisis intervention; these counselors step in when someone is endangering his or her own life or the lives of others. Other counselors specialize in noncrisis interventions, which encourage a person with addictions or other issues, such as difficulty managing anger, to get help. Noncrisis interventions often are performed at the request of friends and family.

Mental health counselors provide treatment to individuals, families, couples, and groups. Some work with specific populations, such as the elderly, college students, or children. Mental health counselors treat clients with a variety of conditions, including anxiety, depression, grief, low self-esteem, stress, and suicidal impulses. They also help with mental and emotional health issues and relationship problems.

Work Environment

Substance abuse, behavioral disorder, and mental health counselors held about 319,400 jobs in 2019. The largest employers of substance abuse, behavioral disorder, and mental health counselors were as follows:

Outpatient mental health and substance abuse centers.. 19%
Individual and family services 16
Hospitals; state, local, and private.............................. 10
Residential mental health and substance abuse
    facilities... 10
Government.. 8

Substance abuse, behavioral disorder, and mental health counselors work in a wide variety of settings, including mental health centers, prisons, probation or parole agencies, and juvenile detention facilities. They also work in halfway houses, detox centers, or in employee assistance programs (EAPs). EAPs are mental health programs provided by some employers to help employees deal with personal problems.

Substance abuse, behavioral disorder, and mental health counselors work in a wide variety of settings, including mental health centers, prisons, probation or parole agencies, and juvenile detention facilities.

Some addiction counselors work in residential treatment centers, where clients live in the facility for a fixed period of time. Others work with clients in outpatient treatment centers. Some counselors work in private practice, where they may work alone or with a group of counselors or other professionals.

Although rewarding, the work of substance abuse, behavioral disorder, and mental health counselors is often stressful. Many counselors have to deal with large workloads. They do not always have enough resources to meet the demand for their services. Also, they may have to intervene in crisis situations or work with agitated clients, which can be difficult.

Work Schedules

Most substance abuse, behavioral disorder, and mental health counselors work full time. In some settings, such as inpatient facilities, they may need to work evenings, nights, or weekends.

How to Become a Substance Abuse, Behavioral Disorder, or Mental Health Counselor

Most positions require at least a bachelor's degree. Although educational requirements can vary from a high school diploma and certification to a master's degree for substance abuse and behavioral disorder counselors, a master's degree and an internship is typically required to become a mental health counselor.

Education

Most substance abuse, behavioral disorder, and mental health counselor positions require at least a bachelor's degree. However, depending on the state and employer, educational requirements for substance abuse, behavioral disorder, and mental health counselors can vary from a high school diploma and certification to a master's degree. Workers with psychology, clinical social work, mental health counseling, and similar master's degrees can provide more services to their clients, such as private one-on-one counseling sessions, and they require less

Substance abuse, behavioral disorder, and mental health counselors need a license in private practice.

supervision than those with less education. Those interested should research their state's educational requirements.

Licenses, Certifications, and Registrations

Substance abuse and behavioral disorder counselors in private practice must be licensed. Licensing requirements vary by state, but all states require these counselors to have a master's degree and 2,000 to 4,000 hours of supervised clinical experience. In addition, counselors must pass a state-issued exam and complete continuing education every year. Contact information for your state's regulating board can be found through the National Board for Certified Counselors.

The licensure criteria for substance abuse and behavioral disorder counselors outside of private practice vary from state to state. For example, not all states require applicants to have a specific degree, but many require them to pass an exam. Contact information for individual states' licensing boards can be found through the Addiction Technology Transfer Center Network.

All states require mental health counselors to be licensed, after completing a period of postdegree supervised clinical work under the supervision of a licensed counselor.

Other Experience

There is a long tradition of people who have overcome their own addictions to be involved in counseling others to overcome their addictions. Counselors with personal experience overcoming alcohol or drug addictions are sometimes viewed as especially helpful and insightful to those seeking treatment.

Important Qualities

Compassion. Substance abuse, behavioral disorder, and mental health counselors often work with people who are dealing with stressful and difficult situations, so they must be compassionate and empathize with their clients.

Interpersonal skills. Substance abuse, behavioral disorder, and mental health counselors must be able to work with different types of people. They spend most of their time working directly with clients or other professionals and must be able to develop and nurture good relationships.

Listening skills. Substance abuse, behavioral disorder, and mental health counselors need good listening skills. They must give their full attention to a client to be able to understand that client's problems and values.

Patience. Substance abuse, behavioral disorder, and mental health counselors must be able to remain calm when working with all types of clients, including those who may be distressed or angry.

Speaking skills. Substance abuse, behavioral disorder, and mental health counselors need to be able to effectively communicate with clients. They must express ideas and information in a way that their clients easily understand.

Pay

The median annual wage for substance abuse, behavioral disorder, and mental health counselors was $46,240 in May 2019. The median wage is the wage at which half the workers in an occupation earned more than that amount and half earned less. The lowest 10 percent earned less than $29,520, and the highest 10 percent earned more than $76,080.

In May 2019, the median annual wages for substance abuse, behavioral disorder, and mental health counselors in the top industries in which they worked were as follows:

Government	$52,720
Hospitals; state, local, and private	49,100
Individual and family services	46,090
Outpatient mental health and substance abuse centers	44,750
Residential mental health and substance abuse facilities	39,690

Most substance abuse, behavioral disorder, and mental health counselors work full time. In some settings, such as inpatient facilities, they may need to work evenings, nights, or weekends.

Job Outlook

Employment of substance abuse, behavioral disorder, and mental health counselors is projected to grow 25 percent from 2019 to 2029, much faster than the average for all occupations. Employment growth is expected as people continue to seek addiction and mental health counseling services.

Demand for substance abuse, behavioral disorder, and mental health counselors is also expected to increase as states seek treatment and counseling services for drug offenders rather than jail time. In recent years, the criminal justice system has recognized that drug and other substance abuse addicts are less likely to offend again if they get treatment for their addiction. As a result, sentences often require drug offenders to attend treatment and counseling programs. In addition, some research suggests that these programs are more cost effective than incarceration and states may use them as a method to reduce recidivism rates.

In addition, there will be a continued need for counselors to work with military veterans to provide them the appropriate mental health or substance abuse counseling care.

Job Prospects

Job prospects are expected to be very good for substance abuse and behavioral disorder counselors, particularly for those with a bachelor's or master's degree. In addition, many workers leave the field after a few years and need to be replaced. As a result, those interested in entering this field should find favorable prospects.

Job prospects are also expected to be very good for mental health counselors, particularly in rural areas or other communities that are underserved by mental health practitioners.

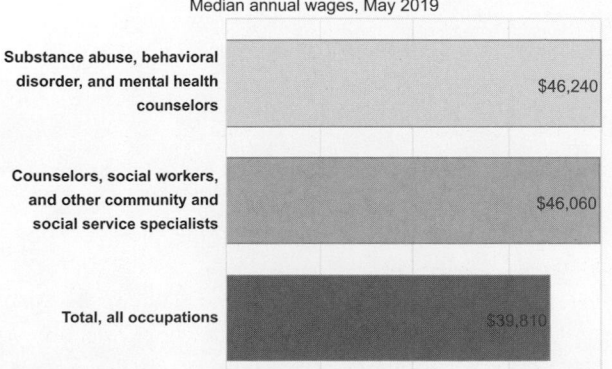

Substance Abuse, Behavioral Disorder, and Mental Health Counselors

Median annual wages, May 2019

- Substance abuse, behavioral disorder, and mental health counselors: $46,240
- Counselors, social workers, and other community and social service specialists: $46,060
- Total, all occupations: $39,810

Note: All Occupations includes all occupations in the U.S. Economy.
Source: U.S. Bureau of Labor Statistics, Occupational Employment Statistics.

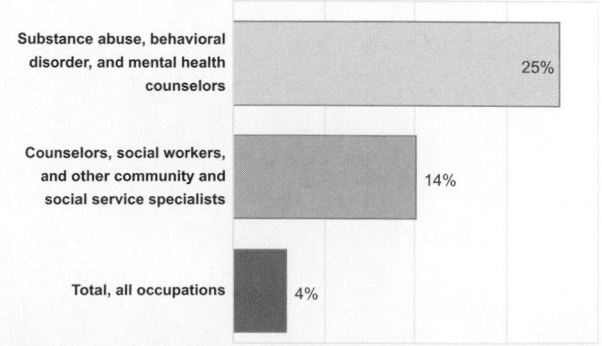

Substance Abuse, Behavioral Disorder, and Mental Health Counselors

Percent change in employment, projected 2019-29

- Substance abuse, behavioral disorder, and mental health counselors: 25%
- Counselors, social workers, and other community and social service specialists: 14%
- Total, all occupations: 4%

Note: All Occupations includes all occupations in the U.S. Economy.
Source: U.S. Bureau of Labor Statistics, Employment Projections program.

Employment projections data for substance abuse, behavioral disorder, and mental health counselors, 2019-29					
Occupational Title	SOC Code	Employment, 2019	Projected Employment, 2029	Change, 2019-29 Percent	Numeric
SOURCE: U.S. Bureau of Labor Statistics, Employment Projections program					
Substance abuse, behavioral disorder, and mental health counselors	21-1018	319,400	398,400	25	79,000

State & Area Data
Occupational Employment Statistics (OES)
The Occupational Employment Statistics (OES) program produces employment and wage estimates annually for over 800 occupations. These estimates are available for the nation as a whole, for individual states, and for metropolitan and nonmetropolitan areas.

Contacts for More Information
For more information about addiction counselors, visit
➤ Addiction Technology Transfer Center Network
➤ NAADAC, The Association for Addiction Professionals

For more information about counseling and counseling specialties, visit
➤ American Counseling Association
For contact information for state regulating boards, visit
➤ National Board for Certified Counselors

Computer and Information Technology

Computer and Information Research Scientists

Summary

Quick Facts: Computer and Information Research Scientists

2019 Median Pay	$122,840 per year $59.06 per hour
Typical Entry-Level Education	Master's degree
Work Experience in a Related Occupation	None
On-the-job Training	None
Number of Jobs, 2019	32,700
Job Outlook, 2019-29	15% (Much faster than average)
Employment Change, 2019-29	5,000

What Computer and Information Research Scientists Do

Computer and information research scientists invent and design new approaches to computing technology and find innovative uses for existing technology.

Work Environment

Most computer and information research scientists work full time. Some work more than 40 hours per week.

Computer and information research scientists study and solve complex problems in computing.

How to Become a Computer and Information Research Scientist

Most jobs for computer and information research scientists require a master's degree in computer science or a related field. In the federal government, a bachelor's degree may be sufficient for some jobs.

Pay

The median annual wage for computer and information research scientists was $122,840 in May 2019.

Job Outlook

Employment of computer and information research scientists is projected to grow 15 percent from 2019 to 2029, much faster than the average for all occupations. Job prospects are expected to be excellent.

State & Area Data

Explore resources for employment and wages by state and area for computer and information research scientists.

What Computer and Information Research Scientists Do

Computer and information research scientists invent and design new approaches to computing technology and find innovative uses for existing technology. They study and solve complex problems in computing for business, science, medicine, and other fields.

Duties

Computer and information research scientists typically do the following:

- Explore fundamental issues in computing and develop theories and models to address those issues
- Help scientists and engineers solve complex computing problems
- Invent new computing languages, tools, and methods to improve the way in which people work with computers
- Develop and improve the software systems that form the basis of the modern computing experience
- Design experiments to test the operation of these software systems
- Analyze the results of their experiments

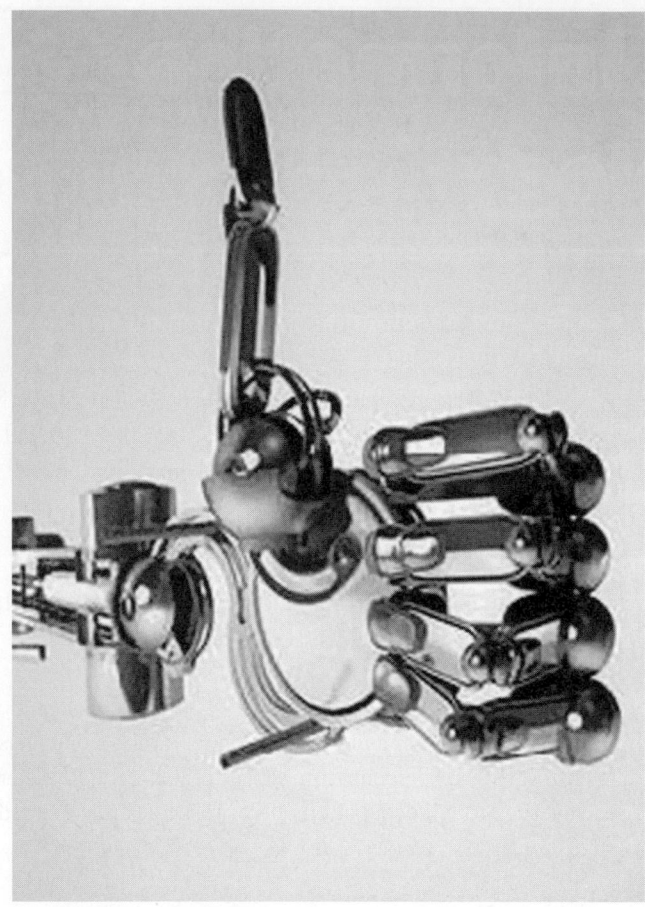

Some computer scientists create programs to control robots.

- Publish their findings in academic journals and present their findings at conferences

Computer and information research scientists create and improve computer software and hardware.

Creating and improving software involves working with algorithms, which are sets of instructions that tell a computer what to do. Some computing tasks are very difficult and require complex algorithms. Computer and information research scientists try to simplify these algorithms to make computer systems as efficient as possible. The algorithms allow advancements in many types of technology, such as machine learning systems and cloud computing.

Computer and information research scientists design new computer architecture that improves the performance and efficiency of computer hardware. Their work often leads to technological advancements and efficiencies, such as better networking technology, faster computing speeds, and improved information security. In general, computer and information research scientists work at a more theoretical level than do other computer professionals.

Some computer scientists work with electrical engineers, computer hardware engineers, and other specialists on multidisciplinary projects. The following are examples of types of specialties for computer and information research scientists:

Robotics. Some computer and information research scientists study how to improve robots. Robotics explores how a machine can interact with the physical world. Computer and information research scientists create the programs that control the robots. They work closely with engineers who focus on the hardware design of robots. Together, these workers test how well the robots do the tasks they were created to do, such as assemble cars or collect data on other planets.

Programming. Computer and information research scientists design new programming languages that are used to write software. The new languages make software writing more efficient by improving an existing language, such as Java, or by making a specific aspect of programming, such as image processing, easier.

Work Environment

Computer and information research scientists held about 32,700 jobs in 2019. The largest employers of computer and information research scientists were as follows:

Federal government, excluding postal service	28%
Computer systems design and related services	19
Research and development in the physical, engineering, and life sciences	16
Software publishers	8
Colleges, universities, and professional schools; state, local, and private	6

Some computer scientists may work on teams with electrical engineers, computer hardware engineers, and other specialists on multidisciplinary projects.

Work Schedules

Most computer and information research scientists work full time. Some work more than 40 hours per week.

Computer and information research scientists improve ways to sort, manage, and display data.

Some computer scientists specialize in computer languages.

How to Become a Computer and Information Research Scientist

Most jobs for computer and information research scientists require a master's degree in computer science or a related field. In the federal government, a bachelor's degree may be sufficient for some jobs.

Education

Most computer and information research scientists need a master's degree in computer science or a related field, such as computer engineering. A master's degree usually requires 2 to 3 years of study after earning a bachelor's degree in a computer-related field, such as computer science or information systems.

Computer scientists who work in a specialized field may need knowledge of that field. For example, those working on biomedical applications may need to have taken some biology classes.

Advancement

Some computer scientists may become computer and information systems managers.

Important Qualities

Analytical skills. Computer and information research scientists must be organized in their thinking and analyze the results of their research to formulate conclusions.

Communication skills. Computer and information research scientists must communicate well with programmers and managers and be able to clearly explain their conclusions to people with no technical background. They often present their research at conferences.

Critical-thinking skills. Computer and information research scientists work on many complex problems.

Detail oriented. Computer and information research scientists must pay close attention to their work, because a small programming error can cause an entire project to fail.

Ingenuity. Computer and information research scientists must continually come up with innovative ways to solve problems, particularly when their ideas do not initially work as intended.

Logical thinking. Computer algorithms rely on logic. Computer and information research scientists must have a talent for reasoning.

Math skills. Computer and information research scientists must have knowledge of advanced math and other technical topics that are critical in computing.

Pay

The median annual wage for computer and information research scientists was $122,840 in May 2019. The median wage is the wage at which half the workers in an occupation earned more than that amount and half earned less. The lowest 10 percent earned less than $69,990, and the highest 10 percent earned more than $189,780.

In May 2019, the median annual wages for computer and information research scientists in the top industries in which they worked were as follows:

Software publishers	$141,820
Research and development in the physical, engineering, and life sciences	134,490
Computer systems design and related services	129,290
Federal government, excluding postal service	109,370
Colleges, universities, and professional schools; state, local, and private	81,910

Most computer and information research scientists work full time. Some work more than 40 hours per week.

Job Outlook

Employment of computer and information research scientists is projected to grow 15 percent from 2019 to 2029, much faster than the average for all occupations.

The research and development work of computer and information research scientists turns ideas into industry-leading

Computer and Information Research Scientists

Median annual wages, May 2019

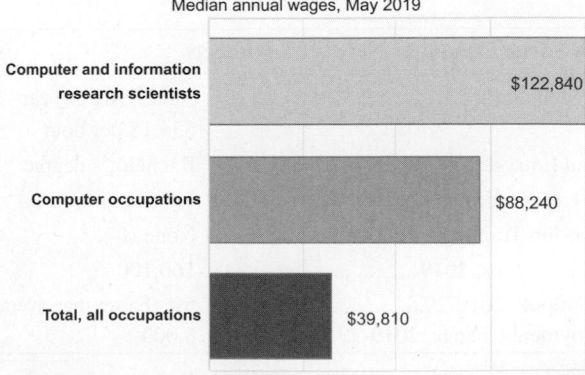

Computer and information research scientists	$122,840
Computer occupations	$88,240
Total, all occupations	$39,810

Note: All Occupations includes all occupations in the U.S. Economy.
Source: U.S. Bureau of Labor Statistics, Occupational Employment Statistics.

Computer and Information Research Scientists

Percent change in employment, projected 2019-29

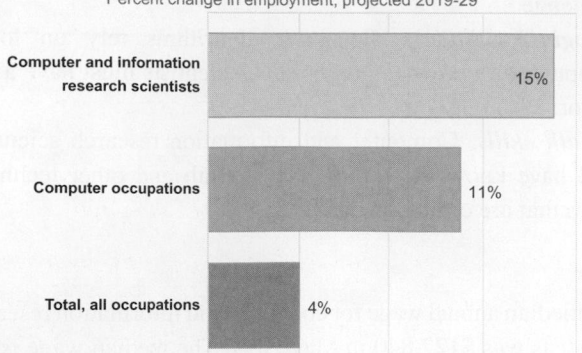

Computer and information
research scientists — 15%

Computer occupations — 11%

Total, all occupations — 4%

Note: All Occupations includes all occupations in the U.S. Economy.
Source: U.S. Bureau of Labor Statistics, Employment Projections program.

technology. As demand for new and better technology grows, demand for computer scientists will grow as well.

Rapid growth in data collection by businesses will lead to an increased need for data-mining services. Computer scientists will be needed to write algorithms that help businesses make sense of very large amounts of data. With this information, businesses understand their consumers better, making the work of computer and information research scientists increasingly vital.

A growing emphasis on cybersecurity also should lead to new jobs, because computer scientists will be needed to find innovative ways to prevent cyberattacks.

In addition, an increase in demand for software may increase the need for computer scientists who create new programming languages to make software writing more efficient.

Job Prospects

Computer and information research scientists are likely to have excellent job prospects.

For applicants seeking employment in a specialized field, such as finance or biology, knowledge of that field, along with a computer science degree, may be helpful in getting a job.

Employment projections data for computer and information research scientists, 2019-29					
Occupational Title	SOC Code	Employment, 2019	Projected Employment, 2029	Change, 2019-29	
				Percent	Numeric
SOURCE: U.S. Bureau of Labor Statistics, Employment Projections program					
Computer and information research scientists	15-1221	32,700	37,700	15	5,000

State & Area Data
Occupational Employment Statistics (OES)

The Occupational Employment Statistics (OES) program produces employment and wage estimates annually for over 800 occupations. These estimates are available for the nation as a whole, for individual states, and for metropolitan and nonmetropolitan areas.

Contacts for More Information

For more information about computer and information research scientists, visit

➤ Association for Computing Machinery
➤ IEEE Computer Society

For information about opportunities for women pursuing information technology careers, visit

➤ National Center for Women & Information Technology

To find job openings for computer and information research scientists in the federal government, visit

➤ USAJOBS

Computer Network Architects

Summary

Quick Facts: Computer Network Architects

2019 Median Pay	$112,690 per year $54.18 per hour
Typical Entry-Level Education	Bachelor's degree
Work Experience in a Related Occupation	5 years or more
On-the-job Training	None
Number of Jobs, 2019	160,100
Job Outlook, 2019-29	5% (Faster than average)
Employment Change, 2019-29	8,000

What Computer Network Architects Do

Computer network architects design and build data communication networks, including local area networks (LANs), wide area networks (WANs), and Intranets.

Work Environment

Most computer network architects work full time. Some work more than 40 hours per week.

How to Become a Computer Network Architect

Most computer network architects have a bachelor's degree in a computer-related field and experience in a related occupation, such as network and computer systems administrators.

Pay

The median annual wage for computer network architects was $112,690 in May 2019.

Job Outlook

Employment of computer network architects is projected to grow 5 percent from 2019 to 2029, faster than the average for all occupations. Demand for computer network architects will

Computer network architects plan and lay out the internal computer networks used by workers in an organization.

increase as firms continue to expand their information technology (IT) networks.

State & Area Data

Explore resources for employment and wages by state and area for computer network architects.

What Computer Network Architects Do

Computer network architects design and build data communication networks, including local area networks (LANs), wide area networks (WANs), and Intranets. These networks range from small connections between two offices to next-generation networking capabilities such as a cloud infrastructure that serves multiple customers. Network architects must have extensive knowledge of an organization's business plan to design a network that can help the organization achieve its goals.

Duties

Computer network architects typically do the following:

- Create plans and layouts for data communication networks

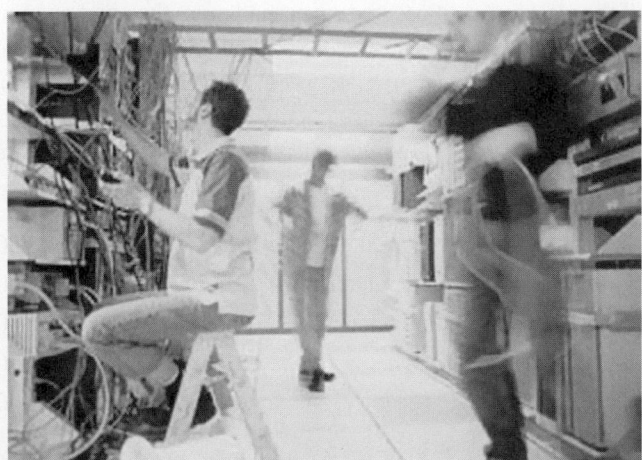

Network architects design LANs, WANs, and intranets.

- Present plans to management and explain why they are in the organization's best interest to pursue them
- Consider information security when designing networks
- Upgrade hardware, such as routers or adaptors, and software, such as network drivers, as needed to support computer networks
- Research new networking technologies to determine what would best support their organization in the future

Computer network architects, or *network engineers*, design and deploy computer and information networks. After deployment, they also may manage the networks and troubleshoot any issues as they arise. Network architects also predict future network needs by analyzing current data traffic and estimating how growth will affect the network.

Some computer network architects work with other IT workers, such as network and computer system administrators and computer and information systems managers to ensure workers' and clients' networking needs are being met. They also must work with equipment and software vendors to manage upgrades and support the networks.

Work Environment

Computer network architects held about 160,100 jobs in 2019. The largest employers of computer network architects were as follows:

Computer systems design and related services	27%
Telecommunications	10
Management of companies and enterprises	8
Insurance carriers and related activities	5
Educational services; state, local, and private	4

Computer network architects spend most of their time in offices, but occasionally work in server rooms where they have access to the hardware that make up an organization's computer and information network.

Work Schedules

Most computer network architects work full time. Some work more than 40 hours per week.

How to Become a Computer Network Architect

Most computer network architects have a bachelor's degree in a computer-related field and experience in a related occupation, such as network and computer systems administrators.

Education

Computer network architects usually need at least a bachelor's degree in computer science, information systems, engineering, or a related field. Degree programs in a computer-related field give prospective network architects hands-on experience in classes such as network security or database design. These

Most network architects work full time.

programs prepare network architects to be able to work with the wide array of technologies used in networks.

Employers of network architects sometimes prefer applicants to have a master's of business administration (MBA) in information systems. MBA programs generally require 2 years of study beyond the undergraduate level and include both business and computer-related courses.

Network architects often have several years of experience in a related occupation, such as a network administrator.

Work Experience in a Related Occupation

Network architects generally need to have at least 5 to 10 years of experience working with information technology (IT) systems. They often have experience as a network and computer system administrator but also may come from other computer-related occupations such as database administrator or computer systems analyst.

Licenses, Certifications, and Registrations

Certification programs are generally offered by product vendors or software firms. Vendor-specific certification verifies a set of skills to ensure network architects are able to work in specific networking environments. Companies may require their network architects to be certified in the products they use.

Advancement

Some network architects advance to become computer and information systems managers.

Important Qualities

Analytical skills. Computer network architects have to examine data networks and decide how to best connect the networks based on the needs and resources of the organization.

Detail oriented. Computer network architects create comprehensive plans of the networks they are creating with precise information describing how the network parts will work together.

Interpersonal skills. These workers must work with different types of employees to successfully design and implement computer and information networks.

Leadership skills. Many computer network architects direct teams of engineers, such as computer hardware engineers, who build the networks they have designed.

Organizational skills. Computer network architects who work for large firms must coordinate many different types of communication networks and make sure they work well together.

Pay

The median annual wage for computer network architects was $112,690 in May 2019. The median wage is the wage at which half the workers in an occupation earned more than that amount and half earned less. The lowest 10 percent earned less than $64,770, and the highest 10 percent earned more than $168,390.

In May 2019, the median annual wages for computer network architects in the top industries in which they worked were as follows:

Insurance carriers and related activities	$117,720
Computer systems design and related services	115,430
Management of companies and enterprises	114,330
Telecommunications	112,660
Educational services; state, local, and private	81,400

Most computer network architects work full time. Some work more than 40 hours per week.

Computer Network Architects
Median annual wages, May 2019

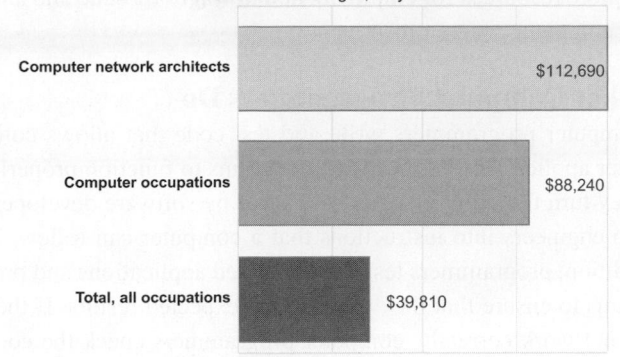

Computer Network Architects
Percent change in employment, projected 2019-29

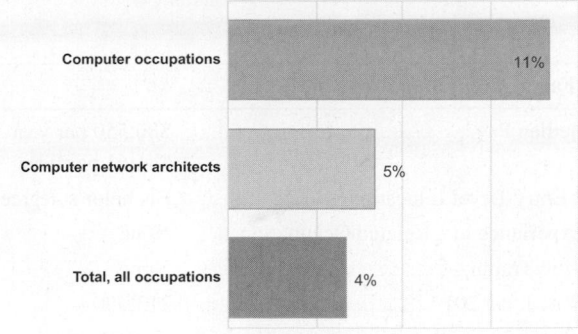

Note: All Occupations includes all occupations in the U.S. Economy.
Source: U.S. Bureau of Labor Statistics, Occupational Employment Statistics.

Note: All Occupations includes all occupations in the U.S. Economy.
Source: U.S. Bureau of Labor Statistics, Employment Projections program.

Job Outlook

Employment of computer network architects is projected to grow 5 percent from 2019 to 2029, faster than the average for all occupations.

Demand for computer network architects will increase as firms continue to expand their information technology (IT) networks. Designing and building these new networks, as well as upgrading existing ones, will create opportunities for computer network architects. The expansion of healthcare information technology will also contribute to employment growth.

Adoption of cloud computing, which allows users to access storage, software, and other computer services over the Internet, is likely to dampen the demand for computer network architects. Organizations will no longer have to design and build networks in-house; instead, firms that provide cloud services will do this. Smaller firms with minimal IT requirements will find it more cost effective to contract services from cloud service providers. However, because architects at cloud providers can work on more than one organization's network, these providers will not have to employ as many architects as individual organizations do for the same amount of work.

Job Prospects

Applicants with relevant certification should have better prospects for positions in which specific hardware or software knowledge and expertise is preferred.

Employment projections data for computer network architects, 2019-29

Occupational Title	SOC Code	Employment, 2019	Projected Employment, 2029	Change, 2019-29	
				Percent	Numeric
SOURCE: U.S. Bureau of Labor Statistics, Employment Projections program					
Computer network architects	15-1241	160,100	168,100	5	8,000

State & Area Data
Occupational Employment Statistics (OES)

The Occupational Employment Statistics (OES) program produces employment and wage estimates annually for over 800 occupations. These estimates are available for the nation as a whole, for individual states, and for metropolitan and nonmetropolitan areas.

Contacts for More Information

For more information about computer careers, visit
➤ Association for Computing Machinery
➤ IEEE Computer Society
➤ Computing Research Association
➤ CompTIA

For information about opportunities for women pursuing information technology careers, visit
➤ National Center for Women & Information Technology

Computer Programmers

Summary

Quick Facts: Computer Programmers

2019 Median Pay	$86,550 per year
	$41.61 per hour
Typical Entry-Level Education	Bachelor's degree
Work Experience in a Related Occupation	None
On-the-job Training	None
Number of Jobs, 2019	213,900
Job Outlook, 2019-29	-9% (Decline)
Employment Change, 2019-29	-20,100

What Computer Programmers Do

Computer programmers write and test code that allows computer applications and software programs to function properly.

Work Environment

Programmers usually work in offices, most commonly in the computer systems design and related services industry.

How to Become a Computer Programmer

Most computer programmers have a bachelor's degree; however, some employers hire workers with an associate's degree. Most programmers specialize in a few programming languages.

Pay

The median annual wage for computer programmers was $86,550 in May 2019.

Job Outlook

Employment of computer programmers is projected to decline 9 percent from 2019 to 2029. Computer programming can be done from anywhere in the world, so companies sometimes hire programmers in countries where wages are lower.

State & Area Data

Explore resources for employment and wages by state and area for computer programmers.

What Computer Programmers Do

Computer programmers write and test code that allows computer applications and software programs to function properly. They turn the program designs created by software developers and engineers into instructions that a computer can follow. In addition, programmers test newly created applications and programs to ensure that they produce the expected results. If they do not work correctly, computer programmers check the code for mistakes and fix them.

Duties

Computer programmers typically do the following:

- Write programs in a variety of computer languages, such as C++ and Java
- Update and expand existing programs
- Test programs for errors and fix the faulty lines of computer code
- Create and test code in an integrated development environment (IDE)
- Use code libraries, which are collections of independent lines of code, to simplify the writing

Programmers work closely with software developers, and in some businesses their duties overlap. When such overlap occurs, programmers can do work that is typical of developers, such as designing programs. Program design entails planning the software initially, creating models and flowcharts detailing how the code is to be written, writing and debugging code, and designing an application or systems interface.

A program's purpose determines the complexity of its computer code. For example, a weather application for a mobile device will require less programming than a social-networking

Programmers spend most of their time writing and testing computer code.

Computer programmers write programs in a variety of computer languages, such as C++ and Java.

application. Simpler programs can be written in less time. Complex programs, such as computer operating systems, can take a year or more to complete.

Software-as-a-service (SaaS), which consists of applications provided through the Internet, is a growing field. Although programmers typically need to rewrite their programs to work on different system platforms, such as Windows or OS X, applications created with SaaS work on all platforms. Accordingly, programmers writing SaaS applications may not have to rewrite as much code as other programmers do and can instead spend more time writing new programs.

Work Environment

Computer programmers held about 213,900 jobs in 2019. The largest employers of computer programmers were as follows:

Computer systems design and related services	38%
Finance and insurance	8
Manufacturing	6
Software publishers	5
Self-employed workers	3

Programmers normally work alone, but sometimes work with other computer specialists on large projects. Because writing code can be done anywhere, many programmers work from their homes.

Work Schedules

Most computer programmers work full time.

How to Become a Computer Programmer

Most computer programmers have a bachelor's degree in computer science or a related subject; however, some employers hire workers with an associate's degree. Most programmers specialize in a few programming languages.

Most programmers work independently in offices.

Most programmers have a degree in computer science or a related field.

Education

Most computer programmers have a bachelor's degree; however, some employers hire workers who have other degrees or experience in specific programming languages. Most programmers get a degree in computer science or a related subject. Programmers who work in specific fields, such as healthcare or accounting, may take classes in that field to supplement their degree in computer programming. In addition, employers value experience, which many students gain through internships.

Most programmers learn a few computer languages while in school. However, a computer science degree gives students the skills needed to learn new computer languages easily. Students get hands-on experience writing code, testing programs, fixing errors, and doing many other tasks that they will perform on the job.

To keep up with changing technology, computer programmers may take continuing education classes and attend professional development seminars to learn new programming languages or about upgrades to programming languages they already know.

Licenses, Certifications, and Registrations

Programmers can become certified in specific programming languages or for vendor-specific programming products. Some companies require their computer programmers to be certified in the products they use.

Advancement

Programmers who have general business experience may become computer systems analysts. With experience, some programmers may become software developers. They may also be promoted to managerial positions. For more information, see the profiles on computer systems analysts, software developers, and computer and information systems managers.

Important Qualities

Analytical skills. Computer programmers must understand complex instructions in order to create computer code.

Computer Programmers
Median annual wages, May 2019

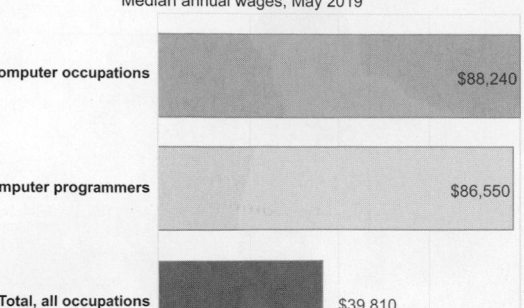

Computer occupations — $88,240

Computer programmers — $86,550

Total, all occupations — $39,810

Note: All Occupations includes all occupations in the U.S. Economy.
Source: U.S. Bureau of Labor Statistics, Occupational Employment
Statistics.

Computer Programmers
Percent change in employment, projected 2019-29

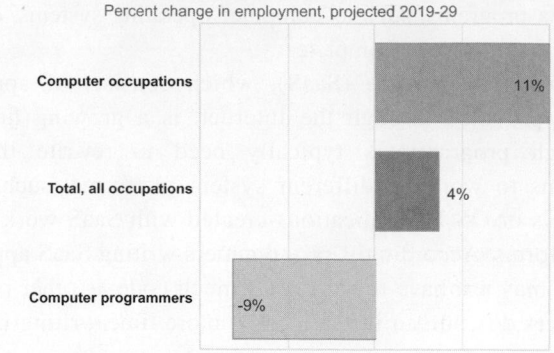

Computer occupations — 11%

Total, all occupations — 4%

Computer programmers — -9%

Note: All Occupations includes all occupations in the U.S. Economy.
Source: U.S. Bureau of Labor Statistics, Employment Projections
program.

Concentration. Programmers must focus their attention on their work as they write code or check existing code for errors.

Detail oriented. Computer programmers must closely examine the code they write because a small mistake can affect the entire computer program.

Troubleshooting skills. An important part of a programmer's job is to check the code for errors and fix any they find.

Pay

The median annual wage for computer programmers was $86,550 in May 2019. The median wage is the wage at which half the workers in an occupation earned more than that amount and half earned less. The lowest 10 percent earned less than $50,150, and the highest 10 percent earned more than $140,250.

In May 2019, the median annual wages for computer programmers in the top industries in which they worked were as follows:

Software publishers	$98,230
Finance and insurance	89,920
Manufacturing	86,620
Computer systems design and related services	85,640

Most computer programmers work full time.

Job Outlook

Employment of computer programmers is projected to decline 9 percent from 2019 to 2029. Computer programming can be done from anywhere in the world, so companies sometimes hire programmers in countries where wages are lower. This ongoing trend is projected to limit employment growth for computer programmers in the United States. However, the high costs associated with managing projects given to overseas

programmers sometimes offsets the savings from the lower wages, causing some companies to bring back or keep programming jobs in the United States.

Job Prospects

Job prospects will be best for programmers who have a bachelor's degree or higher and knowledge of a variety of programming languages. Keeping up to date with the newest programming tools will also improve job prospects.

Employment projections data for computer programmers, 2019-29					
Occupational Title	SOC Code	Employment, 2019	Projected Employment, 2029	Change, 2019-29	
				Percent	Numeric
SOURCE: U.S. Bureau of Labor Statistics, Employment Projections program					
Computer programmers	15-1251	213,900	193,800	-9	-20,100

State & Area Data
Occupational Employment Statistics (OES)

The Occupational Employment Statistics (OES) program produces employment and wage estimates annually for over 800 occupations. These estimates are available for the nation as a whole, for individual states, and for metropolitan and nonmetropolitan areas.

Contacts for More Information

For more information about computer programmers, visit
➤ Association for Computing Machinery
➤ CompTIA
➤ IEEE Computer Society

For information about opportunities for women pursuing information technology careers, visit
➤ National Center for Women & Information Technology

Computer Support Specialists

Summary

Quick Facts: Computer Support Specialists

2019 Median Pay	$54,760 per year $26.33 per hour
Typical Entry-Level Education	See below
Work Experience in a Related Occupation	None
On-the-job Training	None
Number of Jobs, 2019	882,300
Job Outlook, 2019-29	8% (Much faster than average)
Employment Change, 2019-29	67,300

What Computer Support Specialists Do

Computer support specialists provide help and advice to computer users and organizations.

Work Environment

Most computer support specialists have full-time work schedules; however, many do not work typical 9-to-5 jobs. Because computer support is important for businesses, support services may need to be available 24 hours a day. As a result, many support specialists must work nights or weekends.

How to Become a Computer Support Specialist

Because of the wide range of skills used in different computer support jobs, there are many paths into the occupation. A bachelor's degree is required for some computer support specialist positions, but an associate's degree or postsecondary classes may be enough for others.

Pay

The median annual wage for computer network support specialists was $63,460 in May 2019.

The median annual wage for computer user support specialists was $52,270 in May 2019.

Job Outlook

Employment of computer support specialists is projected to grow 8 percent from 2019 to 2029, much faster than the average for all occupations. More support services will be needed as organizations upgrade their computer equipment and software.

State & Area Data

Explore resources for employment and wages by state and area for computer support specialists.

What Computer Support Specialists Do

Computer support specialists provide help and advice to computer users and organizations. These specialists either support computer networks or they provide technical assistance directly to computer users.

Duties

Computer network support specialists typically do the following:

- Test and evaluate existing network systems
- Perform regular maintenance to ensure that networks operate correctly
- Troubleshoot local area networks (LANs), wide area networks (WANs), and Internet systems

Computer network support specialists, also called *technical support specialists*, analyze, troubleshoot, and evaluate computer network problems. They play an important role in the routine maintenance of their organization's networks, such as performing file backups on the network. Maintenance can be performed daily, weekly, or monthly and is important to an organization's disaster recovery efforts. Solving an information technology (IT) problem promptly is important because

Some computer support specialists, called help-desk technicians, assist non-IT users who are having computer problems.

Network support specialists analyze, troubleshoot, and evaluate computer network problems.

organizations depend on their network systems. Network support specialists may assist computer users through phone, email, or in-person visits. They often work under network and computer systems administrators, who handle more complex tasks.

Computer user support specialists typically do the following:

- Pay attention to customers' descriptions of their computer problems
- Ask customers questions to properly diagnose the problem
- Walk customers through the recommended problem-solving steps
- Set up or repair computer equipment and related devices
- Train users to work with new computer hardware or software, such as printers, word-processing software, and email
- Provide other team members and managers in the organization with information about what gives customers the most trouble and about other concerns customers have

Computer user support specialists, also called *help-desk technicians*, usually provide technical help to non-IT computer users. They respond to phone and email requests for help. They can usually help users remotely, but they also may make site visits so that they can solve a problem in person.

Help-desk technicians may solve a range of problems that vary with the industry and the particular firm. Some technicians work for large software companies or for support service firms and must give instructions to business customers on how to use business-specific programs such as an electronic health records program used in hospitals or physicians' offices. Sometimes they work with other technicians to resolve problems.

Other help-desk technicians work in call centers, answering simpler questions from nonbusiness customers. They may walk customers through basic steps in reestablishing an Internet connection or troubleshooting household IT products such as Wi-Fi routers.

Work Environment

Computer network support specialists held about 195,100 jobs in 2019. The largest employers of computer network support specialists were as follows:

Computer systems design and related services	19%
Telecommunications	11
Finance and insurance	7
Management of companies and enterprises	6
Data processing, hosting, and related services	4

Computer user support specialists held about 687,200 jobs in 2019. The largest employers of computer user support specialists were as follows:

Computer systems design and related services	22%
Educational services; state, local, and private	12

Computer support specialists work for a variety of industries.

Management of companies and enterprises	5
Software publishers	4
Temporary help services	4

Faster computer networks are making it possible for some support specialists, particularly help-desk technicians, to telework, or work from their home. However, a few specialized help-desk technicians may have to travel to a client's location to solve a problem.

Work Schedules

Most computer support specialists have full-time work schedules; however, many do not work typical 9-to-5 jobs. Because computer support is important for businesses, support services may need to be available 24 hours a day. As a result, many support specialists must work nights or weekends.

How to Become a Computer Support Specialist

Because of the wide range of skills used in different computer support jobs, there are many paths into the occupation. A bachelor's degree is required for some applicants applying to

Speaking skills are important for computer support specialists.

computer support specialist positions, but an associate's degree or postsecondary classes may be enough for others.

Education

Education requirements for computer support specialists vary. Computer user support specialist jobs require some computer knowledge, but not necessarily a postsecondary degree. Applicants who have taken some computer-related classes may be qualified for these jobs. For computer network support specialists, many employers accept applicants with an associate's degree, although some prefer applicants to have a bachelor's degree.

Large software companies that provide support to business users who buy their products or services often require applicants to have a bachelor's degree. Positions that are more technical are likely to require a degree in a field such as computer science, engineering, or information science, but for others, the applicant's field of study is less important.

To keep up with changes in technology, many computer support specialists continue their education throughout their careers.

Licenses, Certifications, and Registrations

Certification programs are generally offered by vendors or from vendor-neutral certification providers. Certification validates the knowledge of and best practices required by computer support specialists. Companies may require their computer support specialists to hold certifications in the products the companies use.

Advancement

Many computer support specialists advance to other information technology positions, such as network and computer systems administrators and software developers. Some become managers in the computer support services department. Some organizations provide paths for support specialists to move into other parts of the organization, such as sales. For more information, see the profiles on network and computer systems administrators and software developers.

Important Qualities

Customer-service skills. Computer support specialists must be patient and sympathetic. They often help people who are frustrated with the software or hardware they are trying to use.

Listening skills. Support workers must be able to understand the problems that their customers are describing and know when to ask questions to clarify the situation.

Problem-solving skills. Support workers must identify both simple and complex computer problems, analyze them, and solve them.

Speaking skills. Support workers must describe the solutions to computer problems in a way that a nontechnical person can understand.

Writing skills. Strong writing skills are useful for preparing instructions and email responses for employees and customers, as well as for real-time web chat interactions.

Pay

The median annual wage for computer network support specialists was $63,460 in May 2019. The median wage is the wage at which half the workers in an occupation earned more than that amount and half earned less. The lowest 10 percent earned less than $38,990, and the highest 10 percent earned more than $106,420.

The median annual wage for computer user support specialists was $52,270 in May 2019. The lowest 10 percent earned less than $32,330, and the highest 10 percent earned more than $88,470.

In May 2019, the median annual wages for computer network support specialists in the top industries in which they worked were as follows:

Telecommunications	$72,160
Data processing, hosting, and related services	65,680
Computer systems design and related services	64,930
Finance and insurance	64,450
Management of companies and enterprises	61,990

In May 2019, the median annual wages for computer user support specialists in the top industries in which they worked were as follows:

Software publishers	$57,230
Management of companies and enterprises	52,980
Computer systems design and related services	52,100
Educational services; state, local, and private	48,870
Temporary help services	47,560

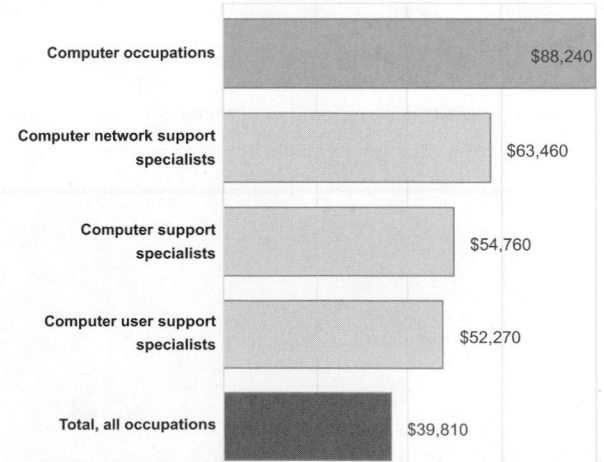

Computer Support Specialists
Median annual wages, May 2019

Computer occupations	$88,240
Computer network support specialists	$63,460
Computer support specialists	$54,760
Computer user support specialists	$52,270
Total, all occupations	$39,810

Note: All Occupations includes all occupations in the U.S. Economy.
Source: U.S. Bureau of Labor Statistics, Occupational Employment Statistics.

Most computer support specialists have full-time work schedules; however, many do not work typical 9-to-5 jobs. Because computer support is important for businesses, support services may need to be available 24 hours a day. As a result, many support specialists must work nights or weekends.

Job Outlook

Employment of computer support specialists is projected to grow 8 percent from 2019 to 2029, much faster than the average for all occupations. More support services will be needed as organizations upgrade their computer equipment and software. Computer support staff will be needed to respond to the installation and repair requirements of increasingly complex computer equipment and software. However, a rise in cloud computing could increase the productivity of computer support specialists, slowing their growth at many firms. Smaller businesses that do not have information technology (IT) departments will contract services from IT consulting firms and increase the demand for computer support specialists in those firms.

Employment growth also may come from increasing demand for IT support services from healthcare industries. This field is expected to greatly increase its use of IT, and support services will be crucial to keep everything running properly.

Job Prospects

Job prospects should be favorable. There are usually clear advancement possibilities for computer support specialists, creating new job openings. Applicants with a bachelor's degree and a strong technical background should have the best job opportunities.

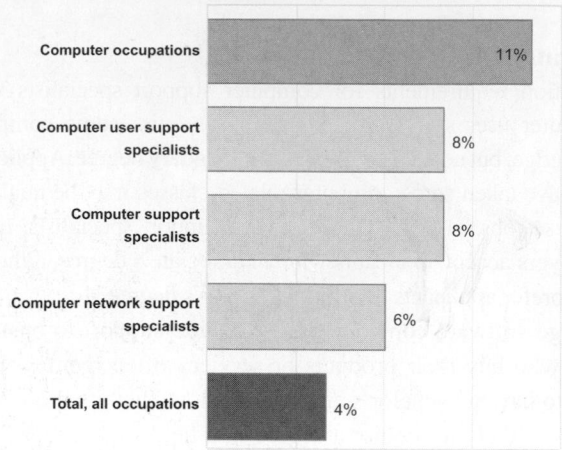

Computer Support Specialists
Percent change in employment, projected 2019-29

- Computer occupations: 11%
- Computer user support specialists: 8%
- Computer support specialists: 8%
- Computer network support specialists: 6%
- Total, all occupations: 4%

Note: All Occupations includes all occupations in the U.S. Economy.
Source: U.S. Bureau of Labor Statistics, Employment Projections program.

State & Area Data
Occupational Employment Statistics (OES)

The Occupational Employment Statistics (OES) program produces employment and wage estimates annually for over 800 occupations. These estimates are available for the nation as a whole, for individual states, and for metropolitan and nonmetropolitan areas.

Contacts for More Information

For more information about computer support specialists, visit
- ➤ Association of Support Professionals
- ➤ Help Desk Institute (HDI)
- ➤ Technology Services Industry Association

For more information about computer careers, visit
- ➤ Association for Computing Machinery
- ➤ Computing Research Association
- ➤ IEEE Computer Society

For information about opportunities for women pursuing information technology careers, visit
- ➤ National Center for Women & Information Technology

Employment projections data for computer support specialists, 2019-29					
Occupational Title	SOC Code	Employment, 2019	Projected Employment, 2029	Change, 2019-29	
				Percent	Numeric
SOURCE: U.S. Bureau of Labor Statistics, Employment Projections program					
Computer support specialists	15-1230	882,300	949,600	8	67,300
Computer network support specialists	15-1231	195,100	207,700	6	12,600
Computer user support specialists	15-1232	687,200	741,900	8	54,800

Computer Systems Analysts

Summary

Quick Facts: Computer Systems Analysts

2019 Median Pay	$90,920 per year $43.71 per hour
Typical Entry-Level Education	Bachelor's degree
Work Experience in a Related Occupation	None
On-the-job Training	None
Number of Jobs, 2019	632,400
Job Outlook, 2019-29	7% (Faster than average)
Employment Change, 2019-29	46,600

What Computer Systems Analysts Do

Computer systems analysts study an organization's current computer systems and find a solution that is more efficient and effective.

Work Environment

Most computer systems analysts work full time. Some work more than 40 hours per week.

How to Become a Computer Systems Analyst

A bachelor's degree in a computer or information science field is common, although not always a requirement. Some firms hire analysts with business or liberal arts degrees who have skills in information technology or computer programming.

Pay

The median annual wage for computer systems analysts was $90,920 in May 2019.

Job Outlook

Employment of computer systems analysts is projected to grow 7 percent from 2019 to 2029, faster than the average for all occupations. The further adoption of cloud computing by both large and small businesses and an increasing use of IT services in healthcare settings is expected to increase demand for these workers.

State & Area Data

Explore resources for employment and wages by state and area for computer systems analysts.

What Computer Systems Analysts Do

Computer systems analysts, sometimes called *systems architects*, study an organization's current computer systems and procedures, and design solutions to help the organization operate more efficiently and effectively. They bring business and information technology (IT) together by understanding the needs and limitations of both.

Duties

Computer systems analysts typically do the following:

- Consult with managers to determine the role of IT systems in an organization
- Research emerging technologies to decide if installing them can increase the organization's efficiency and effectiveness

Computer systems analysts help organizations evaluate their computer system needs.

Analysts create diagrams to help programmers and architects build computer systems.

- Prepare an analysis of costs and benefits so that management can decide if IT systems and computing infrastructure upgrades are financially worthwhile
- Devise ways to add new functionality to existing computer systems
- Design and implement new systems by choosing and configuring hardware and software
- Oversee the installation and configuration of new systems to customize them for the organization
- Conduct testing to ensure that the systems work as expected
- Train the systems' end users and write instruction manuals

Most computer systems analysts specialize in computer systems that are specific to the organization they work with. For example, an analyst might work predominantly with financial computer systems or with engineering computer systems. Computer systems analysts help other IT team members understand how computer systems can best serve an organization by working closely with the organization's business leaders.

Computer systems analysts use a variety of techniques, such as data modeling, to design computer systems. Data modeling allows analysts to view processes and data flows. Analysts conduct indepth tests and analyze information and trends in the data to increase a system's performance and efficiency.

Analysts calculate requirements for how much memory, storage, and computing power the computer system needs. They prepare flowcharts or other kinds of diagrams for programmers or engineers to use when building the system. Analysts also work with these people to solve problems that arise after the initial system is set up. Most analysts do some programming in the course of their work.

In some cases, analysts who supervise the initial installation or upgrade of IT systems from start to finish may be called IT project managers. They monitor a project's progress to ensure that deadlines, standards, and cost targets are met. IT project managers who also plan and direct an organization's IT department or IT policies are included in the profile on computer and information systems managers.

Many computer systems analysts are general-purpose analysts who develop new systems or fine-tune existing ones; however, there are some specialized systems analysts. The following are examples of types of computer systems analysts:

Software quality assurance (QA) analysts do indepth testing and diagnose problems of the systems they design. Testing and diagnosis are done in order to make sure that critical requirements are met. QA analysts also write reports to management recommending ways to improve the systems.

Programmer analysts design and update their system's software and create applications tailored to their organization's needs. They do more coding and debugging than other types of analysts, although they still work extensively with management and business analysts to determine the business needs that the applications are meant to address. Other occupations that do programming are computer programmers and software developers.

Work Environment

Computer systems analysts held about 632,400 jobs in 2019. The largest employers of computer systems analysts were as follows:

Computer systems design and related services	28%
Finance and insurance	14
Management of companies and enterprises	9
Information	7
Government	6

Computer systems analysts can work directly for an organization or as contractors, often working for an information technology firm. The projects that computer systems analysts work on usually require them to collaborate and coordinate with others.

Analysts who work on contracts in the computer systems design and related services industry may move from one project to the next as they complete work for clients.

Some systems analysts work as consultants.

Work Schedules

Most systems analysts work full time. Some work more than 40 hours per week.

How to Become a Computer Systems Analyst

A bachelor's degree in a computer or information science field is common, although not always a requirement. Some firms hire analysts with business or liberal arts degrees who have skills in information technology or computer programming.

Education

Most computer systems analysts have a bachelor's degree in a computer-related field. Because these analysts also are heavily involved in the business side of a company, it may be helpful to take business courses or major in management information systems.

Some employers prefer applicants who have a master's degree in business administration (MBA) with a concentration in information systems. For more technically complex jobs, a master's degree in computer science may be more appropriate.

Although many computer systems analysts have technical degrees, such a degree is not always a requirement. Many analysts have liberal arts degrees and have gained programming or technical expertise elsewhere.

Many systems analysts continue to take classes throughout their careers so that they can learn about new and innovative technologies. Technological advances come so rapidly in the computer field that continual study is necessary to remain competitive.

Systems analysts must understand the business field they are working in. For example, a hospital may want an analyst with a thorough understanding of health plans and programs such as Medicare and Medicaid, and an analyst working for a bank may need to understand finance. Having knowledge of their industry helps systems analysts communicate with managers to determine the role of the information technology (IT) systems in an organization.

Advancement

With experience, systems analysts can advance to project manager and lead a team of analysts. Some can eventually become IT directors or chief technology officers. For more information, see the profile on computer and information systems managers.

Important Qualities

Analytical skills. Analysts must interpret complex information from various sources and decide the best way to move forward on a project. They must also figure out how changes may affect the project.

Communication skills. Analysts work as a go-between with management and the IT department and must explain complex issues in a way that both will understand.

Creativity. Because analysts are tasked with finding innovative solutions to computer problems, an ability to "think outside the box" is important.

Pay

The median annual wage for computer systems analysts was $90,920 in May 2019. The median wage is the wage at which half the workers in an occupation earned more than that amount and half earned less. The lowest 10 percent earned less than $55,180, and the highest 10 percent earned more than $147,670.

In May 2019, the median annual wages for computer systems analysts in the top industries in which they worked were as follows:

Information	$93,710
Computer systems design and related services	93,280
Management of companies and enterprises	93,220
Finance and insurance	92,000
Government	80,570

Most computer systems analysts have a bachelor's degree in a computer-related field.

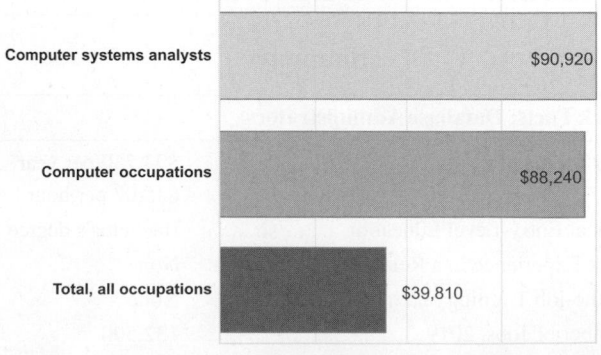

Computer Systems Analysts
Median annual wages, May 2019

Computer systems analysts	$90,920
Computer occupations	$88,240
Total, all occupations	$39,810

Note: All Occupations includes all occupations in the U.S. Economy.
Source: U.S. Bureau of Labor Statistics, Occupational Employment Statistics.

Computer Systems Analysts
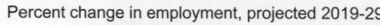
Percent change in employment, projected 2019-29

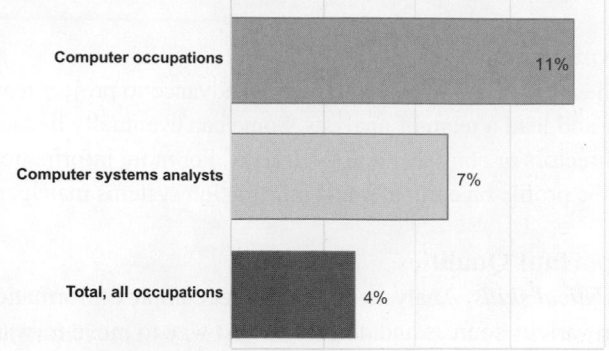

Computer occupations — 11%

Computer systems analysts — 7%

Total, all occupations — 4%

Note: All Occupations includes all occupations in the U.S. Economy.
Source: U.S. Bureau of Labor Statistics, Employment Projections program.

Most systems analysts work full time. Some work more than 40 hours per week.

Job Outlook

Employment of computer systems analysts is projected to grow 7 percent from 2019 to 2029, faster than the average for all occupations.

As organizations across the economy increase their reliance on information technology (IT), analysts will be hired to design and install new computer systems. Smaller firms with minimal IT requirements will find it more cost effective to contract with cloud service providers, or to industries that employ expert IT service providers, for these workers. This contracting should lead to job growth in both the data processing, hosting, and related services industry and the computer systems design and related services industry.

Additional job growth is expected in healthcare fields. Computer systems analysts will be needed to accommodate the anticipated increase in the use and implementation of electronic health records, e-prescribing, and other forms of healthcare IT.

Job Prospects

An understanding of the specific field an analyst is working in is helpful in getting a position. For example, a hospital may desire an analyst with a background or coursework in health management. Overall, candidates with a background in business may have better prospects because jobs for computer systems analysts often require knowledge of an organization's business needs.

Employment projections data for computer systems analysts, 2019-29					
Occupational Title	SOC Code	Employment, 2019	Projected Employment, 2029	Change, 2019-29	
				Percent	Numeric
SOURCE: U.S. Bureau of Labor Statistics, Employment Projections program					
Computer systems analysts	15-1211	632,400	679,000	7	46,600

State & Area Data
Occupational Employment Statistics (OES)

The Occupational Employment Statistics (OES) program produces employment and wage estimates annually for over 800 occupations. These estimates are available for the nation as a whole, for individual states, and for metropolitan and nonmetropolitan areas. Computer systems analysts

Contacts for More Information

For more information about computer systems analysts, visit
➤ Association for Computing Machinery
➤ Computing Research Association
➤ IEEE Computer Society

For information about opportunities for women pursuing information technology careers, visit
➤ National Center for Women & Information Technology

Database Administrators

Summary

Quick Facts: Database Administrators

2019 Median Pay	$93,750 per year
	$45.07 per hour
Typical Entry-Level Education	Bachelor's degree
Work Experience in a Related Occupation	None
On-the-job Training	None
Number of Jobs, 2019	132,500
Job Outlook, 2019-29	10% (Much faster than average)
Employment Change, 2019-29	12,800

What Database Administrators Do

Database administrators (DBAs) use specialized software to store and organize data.

Work Environment

Many database administrators work in firms that provide computer design services or in industries that have large databases, such educational institutions and insurance companies. Almost all database administrators work full time.

How to Become a Database Administrator

Database administrators usually have a bachelor's degree in an information- or computer- related subject, such as computer science.

Database administrators ensure that data are available to many different users.

Pay

The median annual wage for database administrators was $93,750 in May 2019.

Job Outlook

Employment of database administrators is projected to grow 10 percent from 2019 to 2029, much faster than the average for all occupations. Growth in this occupation will be driven by the increased data needs of companies across the economy.

State & Area Data

Explore resources for employment and wages by state and area for database administrators.

What Database Administrators Do

Database administrators use specialized software to store and organize data, such as financial information and customer shipping records. They make sure that data are available to users and secure from unauthorized access.

Database administrators ensure databases run efficiently.

Duties

Database administrators typically do the following:

- Ensure that organizational data are secure
- Back up and restore data to prevent data loss
- Identify user needs to create and administer databases
- Ensure that databases operate efficiently and without error
- Make and test modifications to database structure when needed
- Maintain databases and update permissions
- Merge old databases into new ones

Database administrators, often called DBAs, make sure that data analysts and other users can easily use databases to find the information they need and that systems perform as they should. Some DBAs oversee the development of new databases. They have to determine the needs of the database and who will be using it. They often monitor database performance and conduct performance-tuning support.

Many databases contain personal or financial information, making security important. Database administrators often plan security measures, making sure that data are secure from unauthorized access.

Many database administrators are general-purpose DBAs and have all of these duties. However, some DBAs specialize in certain tasks that vary with an organization and its needs. Two common specialties are as follows:

System DBAs are responsible for the physical and technical aspects of a database, such as installing upgrades and patches to fix program bugs. They typically have a background in system architecture and ensure that the firm's database management systems work properly.

Application DBAs support a database that has been designed for a specific application or a set of applications, such as customer-service software. Using complex programming languages, they may write or debug programs and must be able to manage the applications that work with the database. They also do all the tasks of a general DBA, but only for their particular application.

Work Environment

Database administrators held about 132,500 jobs in 2019. The largest employers of database administrators were as follows:

Computer systems design and related services	16%
Educational services; state, local, and private	9
Management of companies and enterprises	8
Insurance carriers and related activities	6
Data processing, hosting, and related services	4

Some DBAs administer databases for retail companies that keep track of their buyers' credit card and shipping information;

Database administrators are often referred to as DBAs.

others work in healthcare settings and manage patients' medical records.

Work Schedules

Almost all database administrators work full time.

How to Become a Database Administrator

Database administrators (DBAs) usually have a bachelor's degree in an information- or computer-related subject, such as computer science.

Education

Most database administrators have a bachelor's degree in an information- or computer-related subject such as computer science. Firms with large databases may prefer applicants who have a master's degree focusing on data or database management, typically either in computer science, information systems, or information technology.

Database administrators need an understanding of database languages, the most common of which is Structured Query Language, commonly called SQL. Most database systems use some variation of SQL, and a DBA will need to become familiar with whichever programming language the firm uses.

Licenses, Certifications, and Registrations

Certification is generally offered directly from software vendors or vendor-neutral certification providers. Certification validates the knowledge and best practices required from DBAs. Companies may require their database administrators to be certified in the products they use.

Advancement

Database administrators can advance to become computer and information systems managers.

Important Qualities

Analytical skills. DBAs must monitor a database system's performance to determine when action is needed. They must evaluate complex information that comes from a variety of sources.

Communication skills. Most database administrators work on teams and need to communicate effectively with developers, managers, and other workers.

Detail oriented. Working with databases requires an understanding of complex systems, in which a minor error can cause major problems. For example, mixing up customers' credit card information can cause someone to be charged for a purchase he or she didn't make.

Problem-solving skills. When database problems arise, administrators must troubleshoot and correct the problems.

Pay

The median annual wage for database administrators was $93,750 in May 2019. The median wage is the wage at which half the workers in an occupation earned more than that amount and half earned less. The lowest 10 percent earned less than $51,800, and the highest 10 percent earned more than $148,060.

Database administrators usually have a bachelor's degree in an information- or computer-related subject such as computer science.

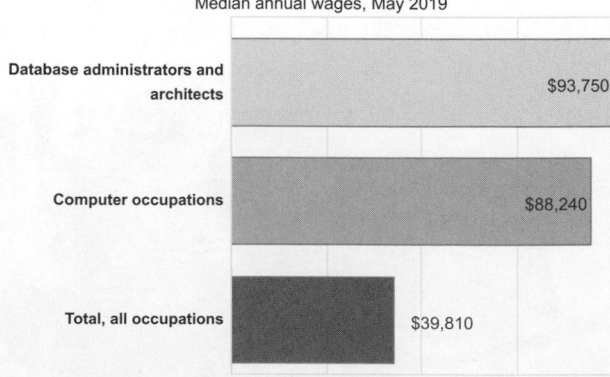

Database Administrators
Median annual wages, May 2019

Database administrators and architects	$93,750
Computer occupations	$88,240
Total, all occupations	$39,810

Note: All Occupations includes all occupations in the U.S. Economy.
Source: U.S. Bureau of Labor Statistics, Occupational Employment Statistics.

Database Administrators

Percent change in employment, projected 2019-29

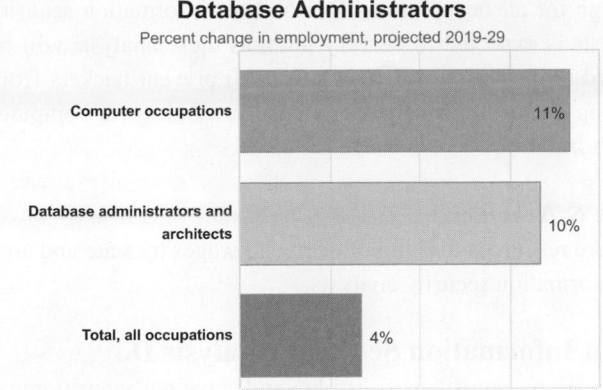

Note: All Occupations includes all occupations in the U.S. Economy.
Source: U.S. Bureau of Labor Statistics, Employment Projections program.

In May 2019, the median annual wages for database administrators in the top industries in which they worked were as follows:

Data processing, hosting, and related services....	$103,930
Insurance carriers and related activities..............	101,650
Computer systems design and related services...	99,310
Management of companies and enterprises........	97,610
Educational services; state, local, and private.....	75,520

Almost all database administrators work full time.

Job Outlook

Employment of database administrators is projected to grow 10 percent from 2019 to 2029, much faster than the average for all occupations.

Employment growth in this occupation will be driven by the increased data needs of companies in nearly all sectors of the economy. Database administrators will be needed to organize data and present them to stakeholders in a user-friendly format.

The increasing popularity of database-as-a-service, which allows third parties to do database administration over the Internet, is expected to increase employment of database administrators at cloud computing firms in the data processing, hosting, and related services industry.

Employment of database administrators in the computer systems design and related services industry is also projected to grow. The continued adoption of cloud services by small and medium-sized businesses that do not have their own dedicated information technology (IT) departments is expected to increase the employment of database administrators in this industry.

Job Prospects

Job prospects should be favorable. Database administrators are in high demand, and firms sometimes have difficulty finding qualified workers. Applicants who have experience with the latest technology should have the best prospects.

Employment projections data for database administrators, 2019-29					
Occupational Title	SOC Code	Employment, 2019	Projected Employment, 2029	Change, 2019-29	
				Percent	Numeric
SOURCE: U.S. Bureau of Labor Statistics, Employment Projections program					
Database administrators and architects	15-1245	132,500	145,300	10	12,800

State & Area Data
Occupational Employment Statistics (OES)

The Occupational Employment Statistics (OES) program produces employment and wage estimates annually for over 800 occupations. These estimates are available for the nation as a whole, for individual states, and for metropolitan and nonmetropolitan areas.

Contacts for More Information

For more information about database administrators, visit
➤ Association for Computing Machinery
➤ Computing Research Association
➤ IEEE Computer Society

For more information about opportunities for women pursuing information technology careers, visit
➤ National Center for Women & Information Technology

Information Security Analysts

Summary

Quick Facts: Information Security Analysts	
2019 Median Pay	$99,730 per year $47.95 per hour
Typical Entry-Level Education	Bachelor's degree
Work Experience in a Related Occupation	Less than 5 years
On-the-job Training	None
Number of Jobs, 2019	131,000
Job Outlook, 2019-29	31% (Much faster than average)
Employment Change, 2019-29	40,900

What Information Security Analysts Do

Information security analysts plan and carry out security measures to protect an organization's computer networks and systems.

Work Environment

Most information security analysts work for computer companies, consulting firms, or business and financial companies.

How to Become an Information Security Analyst

Most information security analyst positions require a bachelor's degree in a computer-related field. Employers usually prefer to hire analysts with experience in a related occupation.

Pay

The median annual wage for information security analysts was $99,730 in May 2019.

Job Outlook

Employment of information security analysts is projected to grow 31 percent from 2019 to 2029, much faster than the average for all occupations. Demand for information security analysts is expected to be very high, as these analysts will be needed to create innovative solutions to prevent hackers from stealing critical information or causing problems for computer networks.

State & Area Data

Explore resources for employment and wages by state and area for information security analysts.

What Information Security Analysts Do

Information security analysts plan and carry out security measures to protect an organization's computer networks and systems. Their responsibilities are continually expanding as the number of cyberattacks increases.

Duties

Information security analysts typically do the following:

- Monitor their organization's networks for security breaches and investigate a violation when one occurs
- Install and use software, such as firewalls and data encryption programs, to protect sensitive information
- Prepare reports that document security breaches and the extent of the damage caused by the breaches
- Conduct penetration testing, which is when analysts simulate attacks to look for vulnerabilities in their systems before they can be exploited
- Research the latest information technology (IT) security trends
- Develop security standards and best practices for their organization
- Recommend security enhancements to management or senior IT staff
- Help computer users when they need to install or learn about new security products and procedures

Information security analysts work to protect a company's computer systems.

Information security analysts install software, such as firewalls, to protect computer networks.

IT security analysts are heavily involved with creating their organization's disaster recovery plan, a procedure that IT employees follow in case of emergency. These plans allow for the continued operation of an organization's IT department. The recovery plan includes preventive measures such as regularly copying and transferring data to an offsite location. It also involves plans to restore proper IT functioning after a disaster. Analysts continually test the steps in their recovery plans.

Information security analysts must stay up to date on IT security and on the latest methods attackers are using to infiltrate computer systems. Analysts need to research new security technology to decide what will most effectively protect their organization.

Work Environment

Information security analysts held about 131,000 jobs in 2019. The largest employers of information security analysts were as follows:

Computer systems design and related services	26%
Finance and insurance	18
Management of companies and enterprises	9
Information	8
Administrative and support services	6

Many information security analysts work with other members of an information technology department, such as network administrators or computer systems analysts.

Work Schedules

Most information security analysts work full time. Information security analysts sometimes have to be on call outside of normal business hours in case of an emergency. Some work more than 40 hours per week.

How to Become an Information Security Analyst

Most information security analyst positions require a bachelor's degree in a computer-related field. Employers usually prefer analysts to have experience in a related occupation.

Many analysts work in IT departments and manage the security of their companies computer networks.

Education

Information security analysts usually need at least a bachelor's degree in computer science, information assurance, programming, or a related field.

Some employers prefer applicants who have a Master of Business Administration (MBA) in information systems. Programs offering the MBA in information systems generally require 2 years of study beyond the undergraduate level and include both business and computer-related courses.

Work Experience in a Related Occupation

Information security analysts generally need to have previous experience in a related occupation. Many analysts have experience in an information technology department, often as a network or computer systems administrator. Some employers look for people who have already worked in fields related to the one in which they are hiring. For example, if the job opening is in database security, they may look for a database administrator. If they are hiring in systems security, a computer systems analyst may be an ideal candidate.

There are a number of information security certifications available, and many employers prefer candidates to have certification.

Licenses, Certifications, and Registrations

There are a number of information security certifications available, and many employers prefer candidates to have certification, which validates the knowledge and best practices required from information security analysts. Some are general information security certificates, such as the Certified Information Systems Security Professional (CISSP), while others have a more narrow focus, such as penetration testing or systems auditing.

Advancement

Information security analysts can advance to become chief security officers or another type of computer and information systems manager.

Important Qualities

Analytical skills. Information security analysts must carefully study computer systems and networks and assess risks to determine how security policies and protocols can be improved.

Detail oriented. Because cyberattacks can be difficult to detect, information security analysts must pay careful attention to computer systems and watch for minor changes in performance.

Ingenuity. Information security analysts must anticipate information security risks and implement new ways to protect their organizations' computer systems and networks.

Problem-solving skills. Information security analysts must respond to security alerts and uncover and fix flaws in computer systems and networks.

Pay

The median annual wage for information security analysts was $99,730 in May 2019. The median wage is the wage at which half the workers in an occupation earned more than that amount and half earned less. The lowest 10 percent earned less than $57,810, and the highest 10 percent earned more than $158,860.

In May 2019, the median annual wages for information security analysts in the top industries in which they worked were as follows:

Finance and insurance	$103,510
Computer systems design and related services	101,980
Information	100,560
Management of companies and enterprises	97,440
Administrative and support services	96,190

Most information security analysts work full time. Information security analysts sometimes have to be on call outside of normal business hours in case of an emergency. Some work more than 40 hours per week.

Job Outlook

Employment of information security analysts is projected to grow 31 percent from 2019 to 2029, much faster than the average for all occupations.

Demand for information security analysts is expected to be very high. Cyberattacks have grown in frequency, and analysts will be needed to come up with innovative solutions to prevent hackers from stealing critical information or creating problems for computer networks.

Banks and financial institutions, as well as other types of corporations, will need to increase their information security capabilities in the face of growing cybersecurity threats. In addition, as the healthcare industry expands its use of electronic medical records, ensuring patients' privacy and protecting personal data are becoming more important. More information security analysts are likely to be needed to create the safeguards that will satisfy patients' concerns.

Employment of information security analysts is projected to grow 56 percent in computer systems design and related services from 2019 to 2029. The increasing adoption of cloud services by small and medium-sized businesses and a rise in

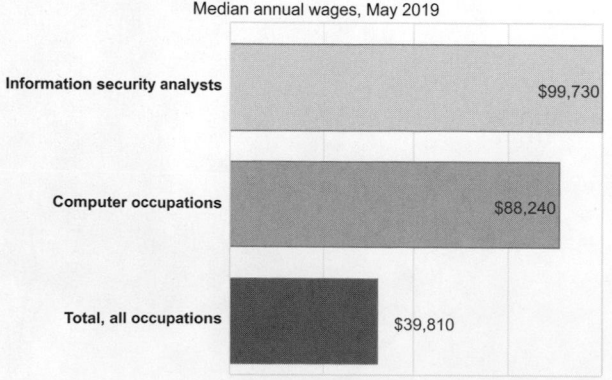

Information Security Analysts

Median annual wages, May 2019

- Information security analysts: $99,730
- Computer occupations: $88,240
- Total, all occupations: $39,810

Note: All Occupations includes all occupations in the U.S. Economy.
Source: U.S. Bureau of Labor Statistics, Occupational Employment Statistics.

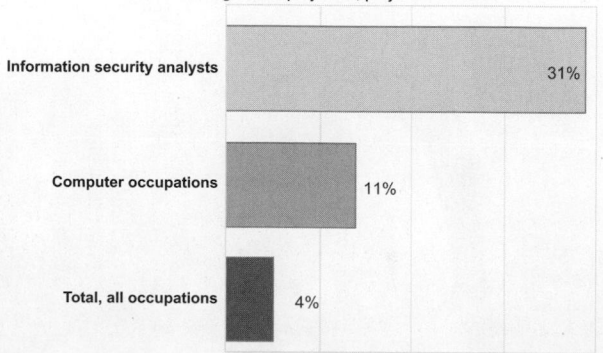

Information Security Analysts

Percent change in employment, projected 2019-29

- Information security analysts: 31%
- Computer occupations: 11%
- Total, all occupations: 4%

Note: All Occupations includes all occupations in the U.S. Economy.
Source: U.S. Bureau of Labor Statistics, Employment Projections program.

cybersecurity threats will create demand for managed security services providers in this industry.

Job Prospects

Job prospects for information security analysts should be good. Information security analysts with related work experience will have the best prospects. For example, an applicant with experience as a database administrator would have better prospects in database security than someone without that experience.

Employment projections data for information security analysts, 2019-29					
Occupational Title	SOC Code	Employment, 2019	Projected Employment, 2029	Change, 2019-29 Percent	Numeric
SOURCE: U.S. Bureau of Labor Statistics, Employment Projections program					
Information security analysts	15-1212	131,000	171,900	31	40,900

State & Area Data
Occupational Employment Statistics (OES)

The Occupational Employment Statistics (OES) program produces employment and wage estimates annually for over 800 occupations. These estimates are available for the nation as a whole, for individual states, and for metropolitan and nonmetropolitan areas.

Contacts for More Information

For more information about computer careers, visit
➤ Association for Computing Machinery
➤ Computing Research Association
➤ IEEE Computer Society

For information about opportunities for women pursuing information technology careers, visit:
➤ National Center for Women & Information Technology

Network and Computer Systems Administrators

Summary

Quick Facts: Network and Computer Systems Administrators

2019 Median Pay	$83,510 per year $40.15 per hour
Typical Entry-Level Education	Bachelor's degree
Work Experience in a Related Occupation	None
On-the-job Training	None
Number of Jobs, 2019	373,900
Job Outlook, 2019-29	4% (As fast as average)
Employment Change, 2019-29	16,000

Administrators maintain network LANs, WANs, and intranets.

What Network and Computer Systems Administrators Do

Network and computer systems administrators are responsible for the day-to-day operation of computer networks.

Work Environment

Network and computer systems administrators work with the physical computer networks of a variety of organizations and therefore are employed in many industries.

How to Become a Network and Computer Systems Administrator

Most employers require network and computer systems administrators to have a bachelor's degree in a field related to computer or information science. Others may require only a postsecondary certificate or an associate's degree.

Pay

The median annual wage for network and computer systems administrators was $83,510 in May 2019.

Job Outlook

Employment of network and computer systems administrators is projected to grow 4 percent from 2019 to 2029, about as fast as the average for all occupations. Demand for information technology (IT) workers is high and should continue to grow as firms invest in newer, faster technology and mobile networks.

State & Area Data

Explore resources for employment and wages by state and area for network and computer systems administrators.

What Network and Computer Systems Administrators Do

Computer networks are critical parts of almost every organization. Network and computer systems administrators are responsible for the day-to-day operation of these networks. They organize, install, and support an organization's computer systems, including local area networks (LANs), wide area networks (WANs), network segments, intranets, and other data communication systems.

Duties

Network and computer systems administrators typically do the following:

- Determine an organization's system needs and install network hardware and software
- Make needed upgrades and repairs to networks and ensure that systems are operating correctly
- Maintain network and computer system security
- Evaluate and optimize network or system performance
- Add users to a network, and assign and update security permissions on the network
- Train users in the proper use of hardware and software
- Interpret and solve problems when a user or an automated monitoring system alerts them that a problem exists

Administrators fix computer server problems.

Network and computer systems administrators work with both IT and non-IT staff.

Administrators manage an organization's servers and desktop and mobile equipment. They ensure that email and data storage networks work properly. They also make sure that employees' workstations are working efficiently and stay connected to the central computer network. Some administrators manage telecommunication networks.

Administrators may help network architects design and analyze network models. They also participate in decisions about buying future hardware or software to upgrade their organization's network. Some administrators provide technical support to computer users, and they also may supervise computer support specialists who help solve users' problems.

Work Environment

Network and computer systems administrators held about 373,900 jobs in 2019. The largest employers of network and computer systems administrators were as follows:

Computer systems design and related services	18%
Educational services; state, local, and private	10
Information	10
Finance and insurance	9
Management of companies and enterprises	7

Although many network and computer systems administrators are employed by firms in the computer systems design and related services industry, they work in a variety of settings. Some might administer systems and networks for financial firms, and others work in hospitals or local government offices.

Network and computer systems administrators work with many types of workers, including other IT workers, such as computer support specialists, database administrators, computer network architects, and computer and information systems managers.

Work Schedules

Most network and computer systems administrators work full time. Organizations depend on their computer networks, so

Administrators evaluate network and system performance and determine how changes in the environment will affect them.

administrators may need to work overtime to ensure that the networks are operating properly around the clock.

How to Become a Network and Computer Systems Administrator

Most employers require network and computer systems administrators to have a bachelor's degree in a field related to computer or information science. Others may require only a postsecondary certificate or an associate's degree.

Education

Although some employers require only a postsecondary certificate or an associate's degree, most require a bachelor's degree in a field related to computer or information science. There are degree programs that focus on computer network and system administration. However, because administrators work with computer hardware and equipment, a degree in computer engineering or electrical engineering usually is acceptable as well. Programs in these fields frequently include classes in computer programming, networking, or systems design.

Because network technology is constantly changing, administrators need to keep up with the latest developments. Many continue to take courses throughout their careers and attend information technology (IT) conferences to keep up with the latest technology. Some businesses require that administrators have a master's degree.

Licenses, Certifications, and Registrations

Companies generally require their network and computer systems administrators to be certified in the products they use. Certification programs usually are offered directly from vendors or from vendor-neutral certification providers. Certification validates the knowledge and the use of best practices that are required of network and computer systems administrators. Microsoft and Cisco offer some of the most common certifications.

Advancement

Network administrators can advance to become computer network architects. They can also advance to managerial jobs in

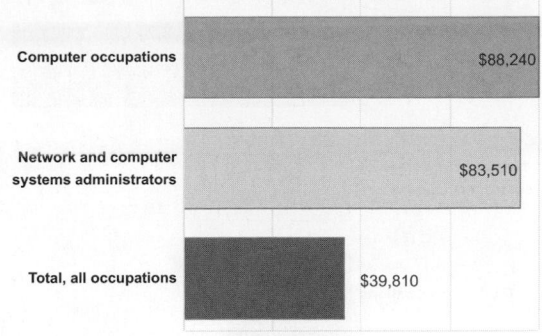

Network and Computer Systems Administrators

Median annual wages, May 2019

Computer occupations	$88,240
Network and computer systems administrators	$83,510
Total, all occupations	$39,810

Note: All Occupations includes all occupations in the U.S. Economy.
Source: U.S. Bureau of Labor Statistics, Occupational Employment Statistics.

information technology (IT) departments, such as computer and information systems managers.

Important Qualities

Analytical skills. Administrators need to evaluate networks and systems to make sure that they perform reliably and to anticipate new requirements as customers' needs change.

Communication skills. Administrators must describe problems and their solutions to non-IT workers.

Multitasking skills. Administrators may have to work on many problems and tasks at the same time.

Problem-solving skills. Administrators must quickly resolve problems that arise with computer networks.

Pay

The median annual wage for network and computer systems administrators was $83,510 in May 2019. The median wage is the wage at which half the workers in an occupation earned more than that amount and half earned less. The lowest 10 percent earned less than $52,370, and the highest 10 percent earned more than $132,520.

In May 2019, the median annual wages for network and computer systems administrators in the top industries in which they worked were as follows:

Finance and insurance	$89,420
Information	89,300
Management of companies and enterprises	87,360
Computer systems design and related services	87,110
Educational services; state, local, and private	73,640

Most network and computer systems administrators work full time. Organizations depend on their computer networks, so administrators may need to work overtime to ensure that the networks are operating properly around the clock.

Job Outlook

Employment of network and computer systems administrators is projected to grow 4 percent from 2019 to 2029, about as fast as the average for all occupations.

Network and Computer Systems Administrators
Percent change in employment, projected 2019-29

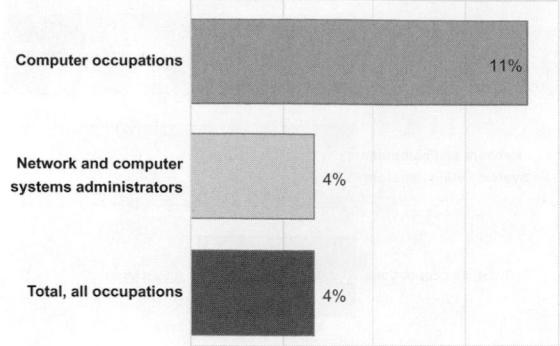

Computer occupations	11%
Network and computer systems administrators	4%
Total, all occupations	4%

Note: All Occupations includes all occupations in the U.S. Economy.
Source: U.S. Bureau of Labor Statistics, Employment Projections program.

Demand for information technology (IT) workers is high and should continue to grow as firms invest in newer, faster technology and mobile networks. Employment growth also is expected as the use of IT in healthcare increases. However, an increase in cloud computing could raise the productivity of network administrators, slowing their employment growth across many industries.

Job Prospects

Job opportunities should be favorable. Prospects should be best for applicants who have a bachelor's degree in computer network and systems administration or computer science and who are up to date on the latest technology, especially cloud computing.

Employment projections data for network and computer systems administrators, 2019-29					
Occupational Title	SOC Code	Employment, 2019	Projected Employment, 2029	Change, 2019-29	
				Percent	Numeric
SOURCE: U.S. Bureau of Labor Statistics, Employment Projections program					
Network and computer systems administrators	15-1244	373,900	389,900	4	16,000

State & Area Data
Occupational Employment Statistics (OES)

The Occupational Employment Statistics (OES) program produces employment and wage estimates annually for over 800 occupations. These estimates are available for the nation as a whole, for individual states, and for metropolitan and nonmetropolitan areas.

Contacts for More Information

For more information about computer careers, visit
➤ Association for Computing Machinery
➤ CompTIA
➤ IEEE Computer Society

For information about opportunities for women pursuing information technology careers, visit
➤ National Center for Women & Information Technology

Software Developers

Summary

Quick Facts: Software Developers

2019 Median Pay	$107,510 per year $51.69 per hour
Typical Entry-Level Education	Bachelor's degree
Work Experience in a Related Occupation	None
On-the-job Training	None
Number of Jobs, 2019	1,469,200
Job Outlook, 2019-29	22% (Much faster than average)
Employment Change, 2019-29	316,000

What Software Developers Do

Software developers create the applications or systems that run on a computer or another device.

Work Environment

Many software developers work for firms that deal in computer systems design and related services, manufacturing, or for software publishers.

How to Become a Software Developer

Software developers usually have a bachelor's degree in computer science and strong computer programming skills.

Pay

The median annual wage for software developers was $107,510 in May 2019.

Software developers design computer programs.

Job Outlook

Employment of software developers is projected to grow 22 percent from 2019 to 2029, much faster than the average for all occupations. Software developers will be needed to respond to an increased demand for computer software.

State & Area Data

Explore resources for employment and wages by state and area for software developers.

What Software Developers Do

Software developers are the creative minds behind computer programs. Some develop the applications that allow people to do specific tasks on a computer or another device. Others develop the underlying systems that run the devices or that control networks.

Duties

Software developers typically do the following:

- Analyze users' needs and then design, test, and develop software to meet those needs
- Recommend software upgrades for customers' existing programs and systems
- Design each piece of an application or system and plan how the pieces will work together
- Create a variety of models and diagrams (such as flowcharts) that show programmers the software code needed for an application
- Ensure that a program continues to function normally through software maintenance and testing
- Document every aspect of an application or system as a reference for future maintenance and upgrades
- Collaborate with other computer specialists to create optimum software

Software developers are in charge of the entire development process for a software program. They may begin by asking how the customer plans to use the software. They must identify the core functionality that users need from software programs. Software developers must also determine user requirements that are unrelated to the functions of the software, such as the level of security and performance needs. They design the program and then give instructions to programmers, who write computer code and test it.

If the program does not work as expected or if testers find it too difficult to use, software developers go back to the design process to fix the problems or improve the program. After the program is released to the customer, a developer may perform upgrades and maintenance.

Developers usually work closely with computer programmers. However, in some companies, developers write code themselves instead of giving instructions to programmers.

Developers who supervise a software project from the planning stages through implementation sometimes are called information technology (IT) project managers. These workers monitor the project's progress to ensure that it meets deadlines, standards, and cost targets. IT project managers who plan and direct an organization's IT department or IT policies are included in the profile on computer and information systems managers.

The following are examples of types of software developers:

Applications software developers design computer applications, such as word processors and games, for consumers. They may create custom software for a specific customer or commercial software to be sold to the general public. Some applications software developers create complex databases for organizations. They also create programs that people use over the Internet and within a company's intranet.

Systems software developers create the systems that keep computers functioning properly. These could be operating systems for computers that the general public buys or systems built specifically for an organization. Often, systems software

Developers create flow charts that help programmers write computer code.

Developers may oversee a team of people during the software development process.

developers also build the system's interface, which is what allows users to interact with the computer. Systems software developers create the operating systems that control most of the consumer electronics in use today, including those used by cell phones and cars.

Work Environment

Software developers held about 1.5 million jobs in 2019. The largest employers of software developers were as follows:

Computer systems design and related services	33%
Manufacturing	11
Software publishers	9
Management of companies and enterprises	5
Insurance carriers and related activities	4

In general, software development is a collaborative process, and developers work on teams with others who also contribute to designing, developing, and programming successful software. However, some developers work at home.

Work Schedules

Most software developers work full time and additional work hours are common.

How to Become a Software Developer

Software developers usually have a bachelor's degree in computer science and strong computer programming skills.

Education

Software developers usually have a bachelor's degree, typically in computer science, software engineering, or a related field. Computer science degree programs are the most common, because they tend to cover a broad range of topics. Students should focus on classes related to building software to better

Software developers usually have a bachelor's degree in computer science and strong computer-programming skills.

prepare themselves for work in the occupation. Many students gain experience in software development by completing an internship at a software company while in college. For some positions, employers may prefer that applicants have a master's degree.

Although writing code is not their first priority, developers must have a strong background in computer programming. They usually gain this experience in school. Throughout their career, developers must keep up to date on new tools and computer languages.

Software developers also need skills related to the industry in which they work. Developers working in a bank, for example, should have knowledge of finance so that they can understand a bank's computing needs.

Advancement

Software developers can advance to become information technology (IT) project managers, also called computer and information systems managers, a position in which they oversee the software development process.

Important Qualities

Analytical skills. Developers must analyze users' needs and then design software to meet those needs.

Communication skills. Developers must be able to give clear instructions to others working on a project. They must also explain to their customers how the software works and answer any questions that arise.

Creativity. Developers are the creative minds behind new computer software.

Detail oriented. Developers often work on many parts of an application or system at the same time and must therefore be able to concentrate and pay attention to detail.

Interpersonal skills. Software developers must be able to work well with others who contribute to designing, developing, and programming successful software.

Problem-solving skills. Because developers are in charge of software from beginning to end, they must be able to solve problems that arise throughout the design process.

Pay

The median annual wage for software developers was $107,510 in May 2019. The median wage is the wage at which half the workers in an occupation earned more than that amount and half earned less. The lowest 10 percent earned less than $64,240, and the highest 10 percent earned more than $164,590.

In May 2019, the median annual wages for software developers in the top industries in which they worked were as follows:

Software publishers	$122,110
Manufacturing	116,080

Software Developers
Median annual wages, May 2019

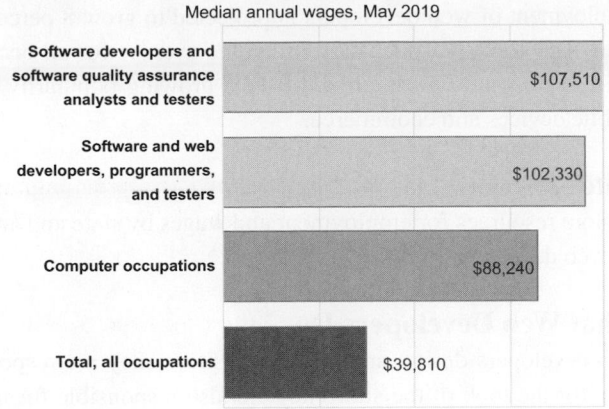

Software developers and software quality assurance analysts and testers — $107,510

Software and web developers, programmers, and testers — $102,330

Computer occupations — $88,240

Total, all occupations — $39,810

Note: All Occupations includes all occupations in the U.S. Economy.
Source: U.S. Bureau of Labor Statistics, Occupational Employment Statistics.

Management of companies and enterprises 107,640

Computer systems design and related services.... 103,670

Insurance carriers and related activities 100,980

Most software developers work full time and additional work hours are common.

Job Outlook

Employment of software developers is projected to grow 22 percent from 2019 to 2029, much faster than the average for all occupations.

The need for new applications on smart phones and tablets will help increase the demand for software developers.

The health and medical insurance and reinsurance carriers industry will need innovative software to manage new healthcare policy enrollments and administer existing policies digitally. As the number of people who use this digital platform increases over time, demand for software developers will grow.

Software developers are likely to see new opportunities because of an increase in the number of products that use software. For example, more computer systems are being built into consumer electronics and other products, such as cell phones and appliances.

Concerns over threats to computer security could result in more investment in security software to protect computer networks and electronic infrastructure. In addition, an increase in software offered over the Internet should lower costs and allow more customization for businesses, also increasing demand for software developers.

Software Developers
Percent change in employment, projected 2019-29

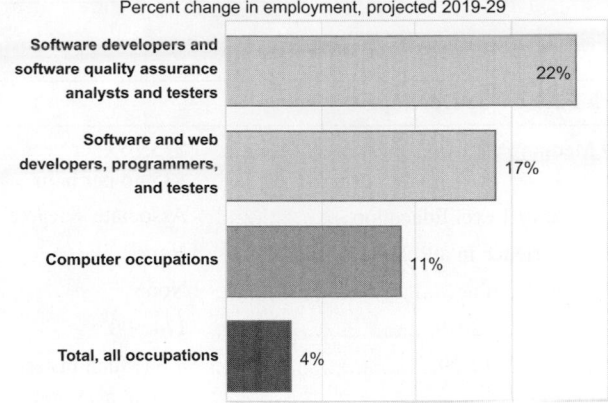

Software developers and software quality assurance analysts and testers — 22%

Software and web developers, programmers, and testers — 17%

Computer occupations — 11%

Total, all occupations — 4%

Note: All Occupations includes all occupations in the U.S. Economy.
Source: U.S. Bureau of Labor Statistics, Employment Projections program.

Job Prospects

Job prospects will be best for applicants with knowledge of the most up-to-date programming tools and for those who are proficient in one or more programming languages.

Employment projections data for software developers, 2019-29					
Occupational Title	SOC Code	Employment, 2019	Projected Employment, 2029	Change, 2019-29	
				Percent	Numeric
SOURCE: U.S. Bureau of Labor Statistics, Employment Projections program					
Software developers and software quality assurance analysts and testers	15-1256	1,469,200	1,785,200	22	316,000

State & Area Data
Occupational Employment Statistics (OES)

The Occupational Employment Statistics (OES) program produces employment and wage estimates annually for over 800 occupations. These estimates are available for the nation as a whole, for individual states, and for metropolitan and nonmetropolitan areas.

Contacts for More Information

For more information about software developers, visit
➤ Association for Computing Machinery
➤ IEEE Computer Society
➤ Computing Research Association
➤ CompTIA

For information about opportunities for women pursuing information technology careers, visit
➤ National Center for Women & Information Technology

Web Developers

Summary

Quick Facts: Web Developers

2019 Median Pay	$73,760 per year $35.46 per hour
Typical Entry-Level Education	Associate's degree
Work Experience in a Related Occupation	None
On-the-job Training	None
Number of Jobs, 2019	174,300
Job Outlook, 2019-29	8% (Much faster than average)
Employment Change, 2019-29	14,000

What Web Developers Do

Web developers design and create websites.

Work Environment

Some web developers work in the computer systems design and related services industry. Others are self-employed. Still others work in industries including publishing, management consulting, and advertising.

How to Become a Web Developer

Educational requirements for web developers vary with the setting they work in and the type of work they do. Requirements range from a high school diploma to a bachelor's degree. Web developers need knowledge of both programming and graphic design.

Pay

The median annual wage for web developers was $73,760 in May 2019.

Web developers are responsible for both the look of a website and its technical aspects.

Job Outlook

Employment of web developers is projected to grow 8 percent from 2019 to 2029, much faster than the average for all occupations. Demand will be driven by the growing popularity of mobile devices and ecommerce.

State & Area Data

Explore resources for employment and wages by state and area for web developers.

What Web Developers Do

Web developers design and create websites. They are responsible for the look of the site. They are also responsible for the site's technical aspects, such as its performance and capacity, which are measures of a website's speed and how much traffic the site can handle. In addition, web developers may create content for the site.

Duties

Web developers typically do the following:

- Meet with clients or management to discuss the needs and design of a website
- Create and test applications for a website
- Write code for the website, using programming languages such as HTML or XML
- Work with other team members to determine what information the site will contain
- Work with graphics and other designers to determine the website's layout
- Integrate graphics, audio, and video into the website
- Monitor website traffic

When creating a website, developers have to make their client's vision a reality. They build particular types of websites, such as ecommerce, news, or gaming sites, to fit clients' needs.

Some developers work with graphics and other designers to determine the website's layout.

Different types of websites require different applications. For example, a gaming site should be able to handle advanced graphics, whereas an ecommerce site would need a payment-processing application. The developer decides which applications and designs will best fit the site.

Some developers handle all aspects of a website's construction, and others specialize in a certain aspect of it. The following are examples of types of specialized web developers:

Back-end web developers are responsible for the overall technical construction of the website. They create the basic framework of the site and ensure that it works as expected. Back-end web developers also establish procedures for allowing others to add new pages to the website and meet with management to discuss major changes to the site.

Front-end web developers are responsible for how a website looks. They create the site's layout and integrate graphics, applications (such as a retail checkout tool), and other content. They also write webdesign programs in a variety of computer languages, such as HTML or JavaScript.

Webmasters maintain websites and keep them updated. They ensure that websites operate correctly, and they test for errors such as broken links. Many webmasters respond to user comments as well.

Work Environment

Web developers held about 174,300 jobs in 2019. The largest employers of web developers were as follows:

Computer systems design and related services	17%
Publishing industries (except Internet)	10
Self-employed workers	10
Management, scientific, and technical consulting services	5
Advertising, public relations, and related services	4

Work Schedules

Most web developers work full time.

How to Become a Web Developer

Educational requirements for web developers vary with the setting they work in and the type of work they do. Web developers need knowledge of both programming and graphic design.

Education

Educational requirements for web developers vary with the setting they work in and the type of work they do. Requirements range from a high school diploma to a bachelor's degree. An associate's degree in web design or related field is the most common requirement.

However, for more specialized developer positions, such as back-end web developers, some employers prefer workers who have at least a bachelor's degree in computer science, programming, or a related field.

Web developers need to have a thorough understanding of HTML programming. Many employers also want developers to understand other programming languages, such as JavaScript or SQL, and have knowledge of multimedia publishing tools, such as Flash. Throughout their career, web developers must keep up to date on new tools and computer languages.

Some employers prefer web developers who have both a computer degree and coursework in graphic design, especially if the developer will be heavily involved in the website's visual appearance.

Developers build websites for all types of businesses.

Developers often have both programming and graphic design knowledge.

Web Developers
Median annual wages, May 2019

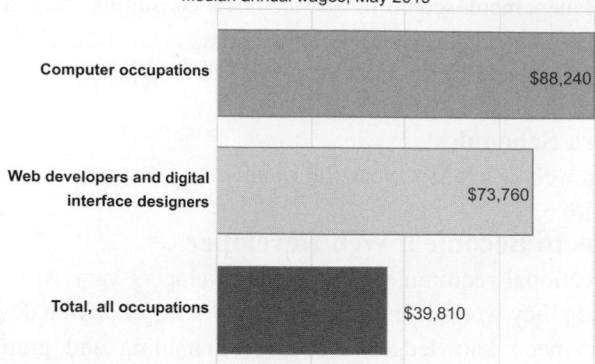

Note: All Occupations includes all occupations in the U.S. Economy.
Source: U.S. Bureau of Labor Statistics, Occupational Employment Statistics.

Advancement

Web developers who have a bachelor's degree can advance to become project managers. For more information, see the profile on computer and information systems managers.

Important Qualities

Concentration. Web developers must sit at a computer and write detailed code for long periods.

Creativity. Web developers often are involved in designing the appearance of a website and must make sure that it is appealing as well as functional.

Customer-service skills. Webmasters have to respond politely and correctly to user questions and requests.

Detail oriented. Web developers need to have an eye for detail, because a minor error in coding could cause an entire webpage to stop working.

Pay

The median annual wage for web developers was $73,760 in May 2019. The median wage is the wage at which half the workers in an occupation earned more than that amount and half earned less. The lowest 10 percent earned less than $39,550, and the highest 10 percent earned more than $142,080.

In May 2019, the median annual wages for web developers in the top industries in which they worked were as follows:

Publishing industries (except Internet)	$121,160
Computer systems design and related services...	72,050
Management, scientific, and technical consulting services...	68,560
Advertising, public relations, and related services..	68,050

Most web developers work full time.

Web Developers
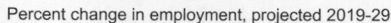
Percent change in employment, projected 2019-29

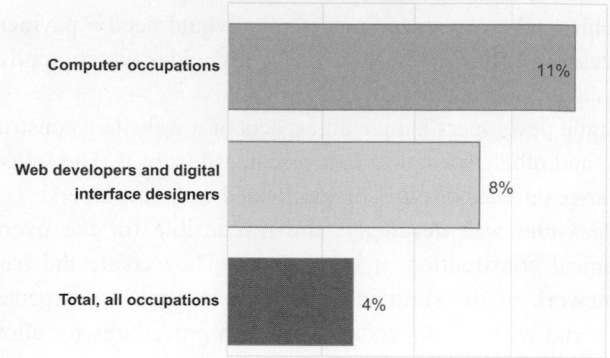

Note: All Occupations includes all occupations in the U.S. Economy.
Source: U.S. Bureau of Labor Statistics, Employment Projections program.

Job Outlook

Employment of web developers is projected to grow 8 percent from 2019 to 2029, much faster than the average for all occupations.

Employment of web developers is projected to grow as ecommerce continues to expand. Online purchasing is expected to grow faster than the overall retail industry. As retail firms expand their online offerings, demand for web developers will grow. In addition, an increase in the use of mobile devices to search the web will lead to increased demand for web developers. Instead of designing a website for a desktop computer, developers will have to create sites that work on mobile devices with many different screen sizes, leading to more work.

Because websites can be built from anywhere in the world, some web developer jobs may be moved to countries with lower wages. However, this practice may decline because the cost of managing web developers in multiple countries can offset the savings to businesses. Furthermore, web developers must understand cultural nuances that allow webpages to communicate effectively with users, and domestic web developers are better equipped for this task, curtailing the work that may be moved to other countries.

Job Prospects

Job opportunities for web developers are expected to be good. Those with knowledge of multiple programming languages and digital multimedia tools, such as Flash and Photoshop, will have the best opportunities.

Employment projections data for web developers, 2019-29					
Occupational Title	SOC Code	Employment, 2019	Projected Employment, 2029	Change, 2019-29	
				Percent	Numeric
SOURCE: U.S. Bureau of Labor Statistics, Employment Projections program					
Web developers and digital interface designers	15-1257	174,300	188,300	8	14,000

State & Area Data
Occupational Employment Statistics (OES)

The Occupational Employment Statistics (OES) program produces employment and wage estimates annually for over 800 occupations. These estimates are available for the nation as a whole, for individual states, and for metropolitan and nonmetropolitan areas.

Contacts for More Information

For more information about web developers, visit

➤ World Organization of Webmasters

For more information about computer careers, visit
➤ Association for Computing Machinery
➤ Computing Research Association
➤ IEEE Computer Society

For information about opportunities for women pursuing information technology careers, visit
➤ National Center for Women & Information Technology

Construction and Extraction

Boilermakers

Summary

Quick Facts: Boilermakers

2019 Median Pay	$63,100 per year $30.34 per hour
Typical Entry-Level Education	High school diploma or equivalent
Work Experience in a Related Occupation...	None
On-the-job Training	Apprenticeship
Number of Jobs, 2019	15,900
Job Outlook, 2019-29	1% (Slower than average)
Employment Change, 2019-29	100

What Boilermakers Do

Boilermakers assemble, install, maintain, and repair boilers, closed vats, and other large vessels or containers that hold liquids and gases.

Work Environment

Boilermakers do physically demanding work. They may travel to worksites and be away from home for extended periods.

How to Become a Boilermaker

Boilermakers typically learn their trade through an apprenticeship program.

Pay

The median annual wage for boilermakers was $63,100 in May 2019.

Boilermakers assemble and install containers that hold liquids and gases.

Job Outlook

Employment of boilermakers is projected to grow 1 percent from 2019 to 2029, slower than the average for all occupations.

State & Area Data

Explore resources for employment and wages by state and area for boilermakers.

What Boilermakers Do

Boilermakers assemble, install, maintain, and repair boilers, closed vats, and other large vessels or containers that hold liquids and gases.

Duties

Boilermakers typically do the following:

- Read blueprints to determine locations, positions, and dimensions of boiler parts
- Install small, premade boilers in buildings and manufacturing facilities
- Lay out prefabricated parts of large boilers before assembling them

Boilermakers install and maintain boiler systems.

- Assemble boiler tanks, often using robotic or automatic welders
- Test and inspect boiler systems for leaks or defects
- Clean vats with scrapers, wire brushes, and cleaning solvents
- Replace or repair broken valves, pipes, or joints, using hand and power tools, gas torches, and welding equipment

Boilers, tanks, and vats are used in many buildings, factories, and ships. Boilers heat water or other fluids under extreme pressure to generate electric power and to provide heat. Large tanks and vats are used to process and store chemicals, oil, beer, and hundreds of other products.

Boilers are made of steel, iron, copper, or stainless steel. Most manufacturers have automated the production of boilers for improved quality. However, boilermakers still assemble and maintain boilers manually. For example, they often use hand and power tools and flame-cutting torches to align, cut, and shape pieces for a boiler. Boilermakers also use plumb bobs, levels, wedges, and turnbuckles to align pieces.

During a boiler installation, boilermakers align boilerplates and boiler parts, using metalworking machinery and other tools to remove irregular edges so that the parts fit together properly. If the plate sections are very large, boilermakers signal crane operators to lift the plates into place. Boilermakers then join the plates and parts by bolting, welding, and riveting them together.

Boilermakers may help erect and repair air pollution abatement equipment, blast furnaces, water treatment plants, storage and process tanks, and smokestacks. Boilermakers also install refractory brick and other heat-resistant materials in fireboxes or pressure vessels. Some install and maintain the huge pipes used in dams to send water to and from hydroelectric power generation turbines.

During regular maintenance, boilermakers inspect systems and their components, including safety and check valves, water and pressure gauges, and boiler controls. They also clean boilers and boiler furnaces and repair and replace parts, as needed.

Work Environment

Boilermakers held about 15,900 jobs in 2019. The largest employers of boilermakers were as follows:

Utility system construction	23%
Nonresidential building construction	16
Plumbing, heating, and air-conditioning contractors	11
Fabricated metal product manufacturing	8
Other building equipment contractors	5

Boilermakers do physically demanding work in cramped spaces inside boilers, vats, or tanks that are often dark, damp, noisy, and poorly ventilated. They frequently work outdoors in all types of weather, including extreme heat and cold.

Because dams, boilers, storage tanks, and pressure vessels are large, boilermakers frequently work at great heights. For

Boilermakers must wear protective gear to reduce injuries.

example, they may be hundreds of feet above the ground when working on a dam.

Injuries and Illnesses

The work that boilermakers do can be dangerous. Workers must follow specific safety procedures to avoid injuries and illnesses and must be mindful of potential dangers to themselves and their coworkers. To reduce the risk of injury, boilermakers wear hardhats, earplugs, safety glasses, and other protective equipment. When working in enclosed spaces, boilermakers often wear a respirator.

Work Schedules

Most boilermakers work full time, and work schedules may vary. Boilermakers may experience extended periods of overtime when equipment is shut down for maintenance or repair, or when necessary to meet construction or production deadlines. In contrast, because most field construction and repair is contract work, there may be periods of unemployment upon completion of a contract.

Boilermakers may travel to worksites and be away from home for extended periods.

How to Become a Boilermaker

Most boilermakers learn their trade through an apprenticeship program.

Education

A high school diploma or equivalent is generally required.

Training

Boilermakers typically learn their trade through an apprenticeship program. During training, workers learn how to use boilermaker tools and equipment on the job. They also learn about metals and installation techniques, blueprint reading and sketching, safety practices, and other topics.

Apprenticeship programs typically last 4 years. When boilermakers finish an apprenticeship, they are considered to be

Candidates have a better chance to be accepted into training programs if they have welding experience.

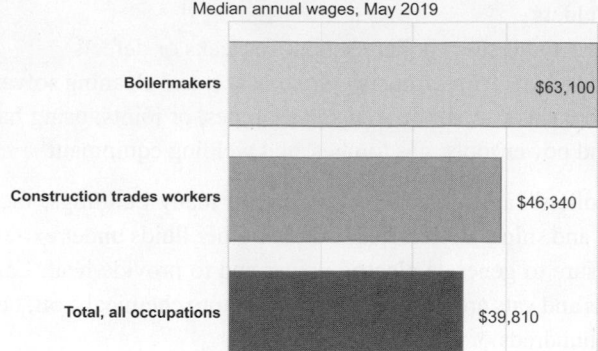

Boilermakers
Median annual wages, May 2019

Boilermakers	$63,100
Construction trades workers	$46,340
Total, all occupations	$39,810

Note: All Occupations includes all occupations in the U.S. Economy.
Source: U.S. Bureau of Labor Statistics, Occupational Employment Statistics.

journey-level workers. A few groups, including unions and contractor associations, sponsor apprenticeship programs.

Apprenticeship applicants who have previous welding or other related experience, such as through the military, may have priority over applicants without experience. In addition, those with experience or education may qualify for a shortened apprenticeship.

Some boilermakers enter apprenticeships after working as pipefitters, millwrights, sheet metal workers, or welders. The core training for these occupations is similar to the training for boilermakers.

Licenses, Certifications, and Registrations

Some states require boilermakers to have a license; check with your state for more information. Licensure requirements typically include work experience and passing an exam.

Employers may require or prefer that boilermakers hold certification from the National Center for Construction Education and Research (NCCER). Welding certifications may also be helpful.

Important Qualities

Mechanical skills. Boilermakers use and maintain a variety of equipment, such as hoists and welding machines.

Physical stamina. Boilermakers spend many hours on their feet while lifting heavy boiler components.

Physical strength. Boilermakers must be able to move heavy vat components into place.

Unafraid of confined spaces. Boilermakers often work inside boilers and vats.

Unafraid of heights. Some boilermakers work at great heights. While installing water storage tanks, for example, workers may need to weld tanks several stories above the ground.

Pay

The median annual wage for boilermakers was $63,100 in May 2019. The median wage is the wage at which half the workers in an occupation earned more than that amount and half earned less. The lowest 10 percent earned less than $39,840, and the highest 10 percent earned more than $94,440.

In May 2019, the median annual wages for boilermakers in the top industries in which they worked were as follows:

Plumbing, heating, and air-conditioning contractors	$80,350
Nonresidential building construction	64,380
Utility system construction	64,310
Other building equipment contractors	63,840
Fabricated metal product manufacturing	58,120

Apprentices receive less pay than fully trained boilermakers. They receive pay increases as they learn more skills.

Most boilermakers work full time, and work schedules may vary. Boilermakers may experience extended periods of overtime when equipment is shut down for maintenance or repair, or when necessary to meet construction or production deadlines. In contrast, because most field construction and repair work is contract work, there may be periods of unemployment upon completion of a contract.

Boilermakers may travel to worksites and be away from home for extended periods.

Boilermakers
Percent change in employment, projected 2019-29

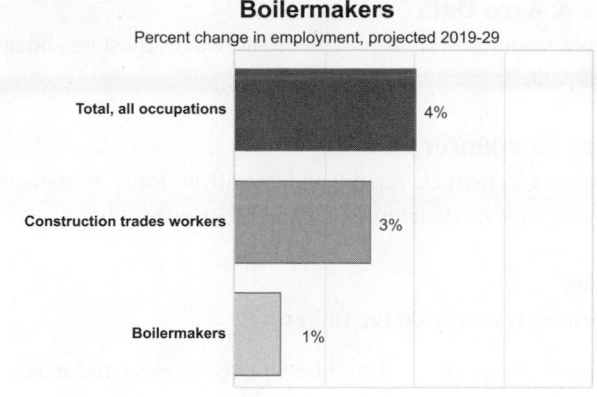

Total, all occupations	4%
Construction trades workers	3%
Boilermakers	1%

Note: All Occupations includes all occupations in the U.S. Economy.
Source: U.S. Bureau of Labor Statistics, Employment Projections program.

Job Outlook

Employment of boilermakers is projected to grow 1 percent from 2019 to 2029, slower than the average for all occupations.

Boilers typically last for decades, but there will be an ongoing need for boilermakers to replace and maintain parts, such as boiler tubes, heating elements, and ductwork. Boilermakers will also continue to be needed to install new equipment, including boilers, pressure vessels, air pollution abatement equipment, and storage and process tanks.

Job Prospects

Despite slow growth, about 1,400 openings for boilermakers are projected each year, on average, over the decade.

Many of those openings are expected to result from the need to replace workers who transfer to different occupations or exit the labor force, such as to retire.

As with other construction occupations, employment of boilermakers is sensitive to fluctuations of the economy. On the one hand, workers may experience periods of unemployment when the overall level of construction falls. On the other hand, additional workers may be needed during peak periods of building activity in some areas.

Employment projections data for boilermakers, 2019-29

Occupational Title	SOC Code	Employment, 2019	Projected Employment, 2029	Change, 2019-29	
				Percent	Numeric
Boilermakers	47-2011	15,900	16,000	1	100

SOURCE: U.S. Bureau of Labor Statistics, Employment Projections program

State & Area Data
Occupational Employment Statistics (OES)

The Occupational Employment Statistics (OES) program produces employment and wage estimates annually for over 800 occupations. These estimates are available for the nation as a whole, for individual states, and for metropolitan and nonmetropolitan areas.

Contacts for More Information

For information about apprenticeships or job opportunities as a boilermaker, contact local boiler construction contractors; a local chapter of the International Brotherhood of Boilermakers, Iron Ship Builders, Blacksmiths, Forgers and Helpers; a local joint union–management apprenticeship committee; or the nearest office of your state employment service or apprenticeship agency. Apprenticeship information is available from the U.S. Department of Labor's Apprenticeship program online, or by phone at 877-872-5627. Visit Apprenticeship.gov to search for apprenticeship opportunities.

For more information about apprenticeship and training, visit
➤ Boilermakers National Apprenticeship Program
➤ International Brotherhood of Boilermakers, Iron Ship Builders, Blacksmiths, Forgers and Helpers

For more information about certification, visit
➤ National Center for Construction Education and Research (NCCER)

For information about welding certification, visit
➤ American Welding Society

For information about opportunities for former military service members, visit:
➤ Helmet to Hard Hats

Carpenters

Summary

Quick Facts: Carpenters

2019 Median Pay	$48,330 per year $23.24 per hour
Typical Entry-Level Education	High school diploma or equivalent
Work Experience in a Related Occupation ..	None
On-the-job Training	Apprenticeship
Number of Jobs, 2019.................................	1,024,100
Job Outlook, 2019-29..................................	0% (Little or no change)
Employment Change, 2019-29	-4,200

What Carpenters Do

Carpenters construct, repair, and install building frameworks and structures made from wood and other materials.

Work Environment

Carpenters work indoors and outdoors on many types of construction projects, from installing kitchen cabinets to building highways and bridges.

How to Become a Carpenter

Carpenters typically learn on the job and through apprenticeships.

Pay

The median annual wage for carpenters was $48,330 in May 2019.

Job Outlook

Employment of carpenters is projected to show little or no change from 2019 to 2029.

Carpenters are involved in many different types of construction.

State & Area Data

Explore resources for employment and wages by state and area for carpenters.

What Carpenters Do

Carpenters construct, repair, and install building frameworks and structures made from wood and other materials.

Duties

Carpenters typically do the following:

- Follow blueprints and building plans to meet the needs of clients
- Install structures and fixtures, such as windows and molding
- Measure, cut, and shape wood, plastic, and other materials
- Construct and install building frameworks, including walls, floors, and doorframes
- Inspect and replace damaged framework or other structures and fixtures
- Instruct and direct laborers and other construction helpers

Carpenters have many different tasks. Some carpenters insulate office buildings; others install drywall or kitchen cabinets in homes. Still others focus on production or commercial work

Carpenters work with different tools.

to help construct tall buildings or bridges, installing wooden concrete forms for cement footings or pillars. These carpenters also erect shoring and scaffolding for buildings.

Carpenters use many different tools to cut and shape wood, plastic, fiberglass, or drywall. They use handtools, including squares, levels, and chisels, as well as many power tools, such as sanders, circular saws, nail guns, and welding machines. On large projects, carpenters may use rigging hardware and cranes as part of the installation process. Carpenters may also use smart phones, tablets, and other personal electronic devices to assist with planning, drafting, or other calculations.

Carpenters fasten materials with nails, screws, staples, and adhesives and check their work to ensure that it is correct. They use tape measures or laser measures on nearly every project to quickly determine distances. Many employers require carpenters to supply their own tools on the job.

The following are examples of types of carpenters:

Construction carpenters construct, install, and repair structures and fixtures of wood, plywood, and wallboard, using carpenters' handtools and power tools.

Rough carpenters build rough wooden structures, such as concrete forms; scaffolds; tunnel, bridge, or sewer supports; and temporary frame shelters, according to sketches, blueprints, or oral instructions.

Wood flooring installers put in a variety of materials, including plank, strip, end-grain, and parquet flooring. These wood products may be nailed in place or glued down. Floor sanders and finishers may smooth the flooring onsite or it may be prefinished prior to installation.

Work Environment

Carpenters held about 1.0 million jobs in 2019. The largest employers of carpenters were as follows:

Self-employed workers	28%
Residential building construction	21
Nonresidential building construction	13
Building finishing contractors	12
Foundation, structure, and building exterior contractors	10

Carpenters work indoors and outdoors on many types of construction projects, from installing kitchen cabinets to building highways and bridges. Carpenters may work in cramped spaces and frequently alternate between lifting, standing, and kneeling. Those who work outdoors are subject to variable weather, which may affect a project's schedule.

Injuries and Illnesses

Carpenters sometimes get injured on the job, such as from strains caused by overexertion due to lifting and moving

Self-employed carpenters often work in residential construction.

materials. Other common injuries result from falls, slips, trips, and contact with objects or equipment. Workers often wear equipment such as boots, hardhats, protective eyewear, and reflective vests as a safeguard against injuries.

Work Schedules

Most carpenters work full time, which may include evenings and weekends to meet clients' deadlines. Extreme temperatures or inclement weather may impact building construction timelines, which in turn may affect carpenters' work hours.

How to Become a Carpenter

Carpenters typically need a high school diploma and learn on the job or through apprenticeships.

Education

A high school diploma or equivalent is typically required to enter the occupation. Certain high school courses, such as mathematics and mechanical drawing, may be useful. Some vocational-technical schools offer associate's degrees in carpentry. The programs vary in length and teach basics and specialties in carpentry.

Apprentice carpenters learn by working with more experienced coworkers.

Training

Carpenters typically learn on the job or through apprenticeships. They often begin doing simple tasks, such as measuring and cutting wood, under the guidance of experienced carpenters or other construction workers. They then progress to more complex tasks, such as reading blueprints and building wooden structures.

Several groups, such as unions and contractor associations, sponsor apprenticeship programs. For each year of a typical program, apprentices must complete a predetermined number of hours of technical training and paid on-the-job training. Apprenticeship program requirements differ based on the type of program and by region. Apprentices learn carpentry basics, blueprint reading, mathematics, building code requirements, and safety and first aid practices. They also may receive specialized training in creating and setting concrete forms, rigging, welding, scaffold building, and working within confined workspaces. All carpenters must pass the Occupational Safety and Health Administration (OSHA) 10-hour safety course.

Work Experience in a Related Occupation

Some carpenters work as construction laborers or helpers before becoming carpenters. Laborers and helpers learn tasks that are similar to those of carpenters.

Licenses, Certifications, and Registrations

Carpenters may need a driver's license to travel to jobsites.

Optional programs offer certification by specialty that may allow carpenters to find additional work opportunities or lead to career advancement. For example, the National Association of the Remodeling Industry offers various levels of certification for remodeling. The National Wood Flooring Association offers certification for installers, craftsman, and master craftsman.

Advancement

Carpenters are involved in many phases of construction and may have opportunities to become first-line supervisors, lead carpenters, independent contractors, or general construction supervisors.

Important Qualities

Business skills. Self-employed carpenters must conduct activities such as bidding on new jobs, tracking inventory, and directing workers.

Detail oriented. Carpenters must be able to precisely cut, measure, and modify the materials they work with.

Dexterity. Carpenters use many tools and need hand-eye coordination to avoid injuring themselves or damaging materials.

Interpersonal skills. Carpenters need to work as a member of a team, cooperating with and assisting others. They also may interact with customers.

Math skills. Carpenters frequently use math skills, including basic trigonometry, to calculate the area, size, and amount of material needed for the job.

Physical strength. Carpenters use heavy tools and materials that weigh up to 100 pounds. They also must be able to stand, climb, or bend for many hours.

Problem-solving skills. Carpenters may work independently with little guidance. They need to be able to modify building materials and make adjustments onsite to complete projects.

Reading comprehension skills. Carpenters need advanced reading ability to understand and follow complex instructions for installing certain products, such as doors.

Pay

The median annual wage for carpenters was $48,330 in May 2019. The median wage is the wage at which half the workers in an occupation earned more than that amount and half earned less. The lowest 10 percent earned less than $30,170, and the highest 10 percent earned more than $84,690.

In May 2019, the median annual wages for carpenters in the top industries in which they worked were as follows:

Nonresidential building construction	$53,040
Building finishing contractors	49,440
Foundation, structure, and building exterior contractors	46,850
Residential building construction	46,290

Carpenters
Median annual wages, May 2019

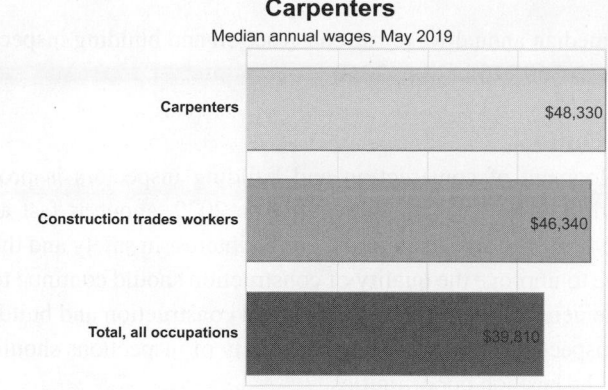

Carpenters	$48,330
Construction trades workers	$46,340
Total, all occupations	$39,810

Note: All Occupations includes all occupations in the U.S. Economy.
Source: U.S. Bureau of Labor Statistics, Occupational Employment Statistics.

The starting pay for apprentices is less than what fully trained carpenters make. As apprentices gain experience, they receive more pay.

Most carpenters work full time, which may include evenings and weekends to meet clients' deadlines. Extreme temperatures or inclement weather may impact building construction timelines, which in turn may affect carpenters' hours.

Job Outlook

Employment of carpenters is projected to show little or no change from 2019 to 2029.

Population growth should result in more new-home construction—one of the largest segments employing carpenters—which will create some jobs for carpenters. Construction of factories and power plants is also expected to result in some new jobs over the decade.

However, the increasing popularity of modular and prefabricated components and homes reduces the need for carpenters to build and install them onsite. Roofs, bathrooms, windows, and buildings can be manufactured in a separate facility and then assembled onsite.

Carpenters
Percent change in employment, projected 2019-29

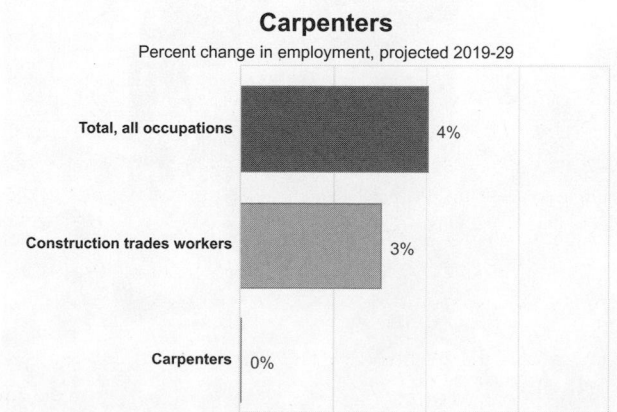

Total, all occupations	4%
Construction trades workers	3%
Carpenters	0%

Note: All Occupations includes all occupations in the U.S. Economy.
Source: U.S. Bureau of Labor Statistics, Employment Projections program.

Job Prospects

About 89,000 openings for carpenters are projected each year, on average, over the decade.

Most of those openings are expected to result from the need to replace workers who transfer to different occupations or exit the labor force, such as to retire.

Overall job prospects for carpenters should be good as construction activity continues to increase. Prospective carpenters with a set of basic carpentry tools will have the best prospects.

Carpenters and other occupations in the construction industry are subject to periods of unemployment as building construction slows during cold months. Additionally, the number of job openings is expected to vary regionally, because different areas of the country are experiencing more development than others.

Employment projections data for carpenters, 2019-29					
Occupational Title	SOC Code	Employment, 2019	Projected Employment, 2029	Change, 2019-29	
				Percent	Numeric
SOURCE: U.S. Bureau of Labor Statistics, Employment Projections program					
Carpenters	47-2031	1,024,100	1,019,900	0	-4,200

State & Area Data
Occupational Employment Statistics (OES)

The Occupational Employment Statistics (OES) program produces employment and wage estimates annually for over 800 occupations. These estimates are available for the nation as a whole, for individual states, and for metropolitan and nonmetropolitan areas.

Contacts for More Information

For details about apprenticeships or other work opportunities in this trade, contact the offices of the state employment service, the state apprenticeship agency, local contractors or firms that employ carpenters, or local union–management carpenter apprenticeship committees. Apprenticeship information is available from the U.S. Department of Labor's Apprenticeship program online or by phone at 877-872-5627. Visit Apprenticeship.gov to search for apprenticeship opportunities.

For more information about carpenters, including training opportunities, visit
➤ Associated Builders and Contractors
➤ Associated General Contractors of America
➤ Home Builders Institute
➤ National Association of the Remodeling Industry
➤ NCCER
➤ National Wood Flooring Association
➤ Occupational Safety and Health Administration
➤ United Brotherhood of Carpenters and Joiners of America, Carpenters Training Fund

For more information about pre-apprenticeship training, visit
➤ Home Builders Institute
➤ National Building Trades Union

For information about opportunities for military veterans, visit:
➤ Helmets to Hard Hats

Construction and Building Inspectors

Summary

Quick Facts: Construction and Building Inspectors

2019 Median Pay	$60,710 per year $29.19 per hour
Typical Entry-Level Education	High school diploma or equivalent
Work Experience in a Related Occupation..	5 years or more
On-the-job Training	Moderate-term on-the-job training
Number of Jobs, 2019	120,800
Job Outlook, 2019-29................................	3% (As fast as average)
Employment Change, 2019-29	3,900

What Construction and Building Inspectors Do

Construction and building inspectors ensure that construction meets building codes and ordinances, zoning regulations, and contract specifications.

Work Environment

Construction and building inspectors spend considerable time inspecting worksites, alone or as part of a team. Some inspectors may have to climb ladders or crawl in tight spaces. Most work full time during regular business hours.

How to Become a Construction or Building Inspector

Most employers require construction and building inspectors to have at least a high school diploma and work experience in construction trades. Inspectors also typically learn on the job. Many states and local jurisdictions require some type of license or certification.

Construction inspectors take detailed notes during inspections.

Pay

The median annual wage for construction and building inspectors was $60,710 in May 2019.

Job Outlook

Employment of construction and building inspectors is projected to grow 3 percent from 2019 to 2029, about as fast as the average for all occupations. Public interest in safety and the desire to improve the quality of construction should continue to create demand for inspectors. Certified construction and building inspectors who can perform a variety of inspections should have the best job opportunities.

State & Area Data

Explore resources for employment and wages by state and area for construction and building inspectors.

What Construction and Building Inspectors Do

Construction and building inspectors ensure that construction meets local and national building codes and ordinances, zoning regulations, and contract specifications.

Duties

Construction and building inspectors typically do the following:

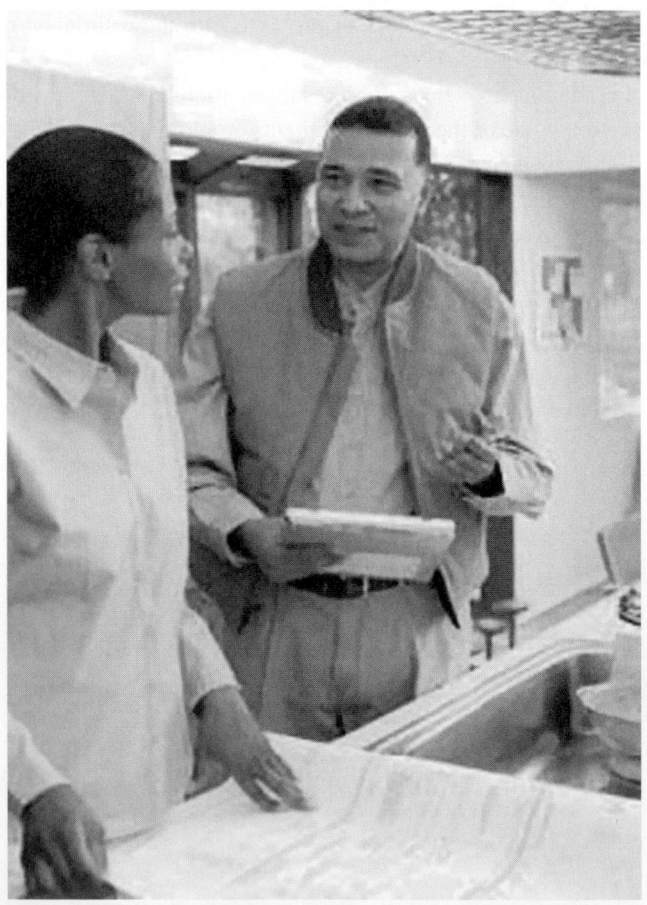

Home inspectors inform potential homebuyers of a home's deficiencies.

- Review plans to ensure they meet building codes, local ordinances, zoning regulations, and contract specifications
- Approve building plans that are satisfactory
- Monitor construction sites periodically to ensure overall compliance
- Use survey instruments, metering devices, and test equipment to perform inspections
- Inspect plumbing, electrical, and other systems to ensure that they meet code
- Verify alignment, level, and elevation of structures to ensure building meets specifications
- Issue violation notices and stop-work orders until building is compliant
- Keep daily logs, including photographs taken during inspections
- Provide written documentation of findings

People want to live and work in safe places, and construction and building inspectors ensure that construction meets codified requirements. Construction and building inspectors examine buildings, highways and streets, sewer and water systems, dams, bridges, and other structures. They also inspect electrical; heating, ventilation, air-conditioning, and refrigeration (HVACR); and plumbing systems. Although no two inspections are alike, inspectors perform an initial check during the first phase of construction and followup inspections throughout the construction project. When the project is finished, they perform a final, comprehensive inspection and provide written and oral feedback related to their findings.

The following are examples of types of construction and building inspectors:

Building inspectors check the structural quality and general safety of buildings. Some specialize further, inspecting only structural steel or reinforced-concrete structures, for example.

Coating inspectors examine the exterior paint and coating on bridges, pipelines, and large holding tanks. Inspectors perform checks at various stages of the painting process to ensure proper coating.

Electrical inspectors examine the installed electrical systems to ensure they function properly and comply with electrical codes and standards. The inspectors visit worksites to inspect new and existing sound and security systems, wiring, lighting, motors, photovoltaic systems, and generating equipment. They also inspect the installed electrical wiring for HVACR systems and appliances.

Elevator inspectors examine lifting and conveying devices, such as elevators, escalators, moving sidewalks, lifts and hoists, inclined railways, ski lifts, and amusement rides. The inspections include both the mechanical and electrical control systems.

Home inspectors typically inspect newly built or previously owned homes, condominiums, townhomes, and other dwellings. Prospective home buyers often hire home inspectors to check and report on a home's structure and overall condition. Sometimes, homeowners hire a home inspector to evaluate their home's condition before placing it on the market.

In addition to examining structural quality, home inspectors examine all home systems and features, including the roof, exterior walls, attached garage or carport, foundation, interior walls, plumbing, electrical, and HVACR systems. They look for violations of building codes, but home inspectors do not have the power to enforce compliance with the codes.

Mechanical inspectors examine the installation of HVACR systems and equipment to ensure that they are installed and function properly. They also may inspect commercial kitchen equipment, gas-fired appliances, and boilers. Mechanical inspectors should not be confused with quality control inspectors, who inspect goods at manufacturing plants.

Plan examiners determine whether the plans for a building or other structure comply with building codes. They also determine whether the structure is suited to the engineering and environmental demands of the building site.

Plumbing inspectors examine the installation of systems that ensure the safety and health of drinking water, the sanitary disposal of waste, and the safety of industrial piping.

Public works inspectors ensure that the construction of federal, state, and local government water and sewer systems, highways, streets, bridges, and dams conforms to detailed contract specifications. Workers inspect excavation and fill operations, the placement of forms for concrete, concrete mixing and pouring, asphalt paving, and grading operations. Public works inspectors may specialize in highways, structural steel, reinforced concrete, or ditches. Others may specialize in dredging operations required for bridges, dams, or harbors.

Specification inspectors ensure that construction work is performed according to design specifications. Specification inspectors represent the owner's interests, not those of the general public. Insurance companies and financial institutions also may use their services.

Some building inspectors are concerned with fire prevention safety. Fire inspectors and investigators ensure that buildings meet fire codes.

Work Environment

Construction and building inspectors held about 120,800 jobs in 2019. The largest employers of construction and building inspectors were as follows:

Local government, excluding education and hospitals	37%
Engineering services	16
Construction	7
Self-employed workers	7
State government, excluding education and hospitals	5

Building inspectors often work outdoors to check the exterior structure of a house.

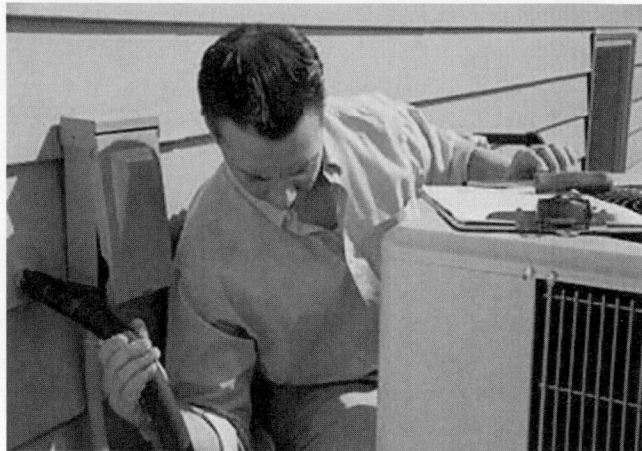

Inspectors often have a combination of certifications and previous experience in various construction and maintenance trades.

Although construction and building inspectors spend most of their time inspecting worksites, they also spend time in a field office reviewing blueprints, writing reports, and scheduling inspections.

Some inspectors may have to climb ladders or crawl in tight spaces to complete their inspections.

Inspectors typically work alone. However, some inspectors may work as part of a team on large, complex projects, particularly because inspectors usually specialize in different areas of construction.

Work Schedules

Most inspectors work full time during regular business hours. However, some may work additional hours during periods of heavy construction activity. Also, if an accident occurs at a construction site, inspectors must respond immediately and may work additional hours to complete their report. Some inspectors—especially those who are self-employed—may have to work evenings and weekends. This is particularly true of home inspectors, who typically inspect homes during the day and write reports in the evening.

How to Become a Construction or Building Inspector

Most employers require construction and building inspectors to have at least a high school diploma and work experience in construction trades. Inspectors also typically learn on the job. Many states and local jurisdictions require some type of license or certification.

Education

Most employers require inspectors to have at least a high school diploma, even for workers who have considerable related work experience.

Some employers may seek candidates who have studied engineering or architecture or who have a certificate or an associate's degree that includes courses in building inspection,

home inspection, construction technology, and drafting. Many community colleges offer programs in building inspection technology. Courses in blueprint reading, vocational subjects, algebra, geometry, and writing are also useful. Courses in business management are helpful for those who plan to run their own inspection business.

Training

Training requirements vary by state, locality, and type of inspector. In general, construction and building inspectors receive much of their training on the job, although they must learn building codes and standards on their own. Working with an experienced inspector, they learn about inspection techniques; codes, ordinances, and regulations; contract specifications; and recordkeeping and reporting duties. Training also may include supervised onsite inspections.

Work Experience in a Related Occupation

Because inspectors must possess the right mix of technical knowledge, work experience, and education, employers prefer applicants who have both training and experience in a construction trade. For example, many inspectors have experience working as carpenters, electricians, or plumbers. Many home inspectors obtain experience in multiple specialties so that they enter the occupation with a combination of certifications and previous experience in various construction trades.

Licenses, Certifications, and Registrations

Most states and local jurisdictions require construction and building inspectors to have a license or certification. Some states have individual licensing programs for construction and building inspectors. Others may require certification by associations such as the International Code Council, the International Association of Plumbing and Mechanical Officials, the International Association of Electrical Inspectors, and the National Fire Protection Association.

Similarly, most states require home inspectors to follow defined trade practices or obtain a state-issued license or certification. Currently, more than a half of states have policies regulating the conduct of home inspectors.

Home inspector license or certification requirements vary by state but may require that inspectors do the following:

- Achieve a specified level of education
- Possess experience with inspections
- Maintain liability insurance
- Pass an exam

Exams are often based on the American Society of Home Inspectors certification exams. Most inspectors must renew their license periodically and take continuing education courses.

Inspectors must have a valid driver's license to travel to inspection sites.

Important Qualities

Communication skills. Inspectors must explain problems they find in order to help people understand what is needed to fix the problems. In addition, they need to provide a written report of their findings.

Craft experience. Inspectors perform checks and inspections throughout the construction project. Experience in a related construction occupation provides inspectors with the necessary background to become certified.

Detail oriented. Inspectors thoroughly examine many different construction activities. Therefore, they must pay close attention to detail so as to not overlook any items that need to be checked.

Mechanical knowledge. Inspectors use a variety of testing equipment as they check complex systems. In order to perform tests properly, they also must have detailed knowledge of how the systems operate.

Physical stamina. Inspectors are constantly on their feet and often climb and crawl through attics and other tight spaces. As a result, they should be somewhat physically fit.

Pay

The median annual wage for construction and building inspectors was $60,710 in May 2019. The median wage is the wage at which half the workers in an occupation earned more than that amount and half earned less. The lowest 10 percent earned less than $36,440, and the highest 10 percent earned more than $98,820.

In May 2019, the median annual wages for construction and building inspectors in the top industries in which they worked were as follows:

Construction	$62,580
Engineering services	61,150
Local government, excluding education and hospitals	60,110
State government, excluding education and hospitals	57,580

Most inspectors work full time during regular business hours. However, some may work additional hours during periods of heavy construction activity. Also, if an accident occurs at a construction site, inspectors must respond immediately and may work additional hours to complete their report. Some inspectors—especially those who are self-employed—may have to work evenings and weekends. This is particularly true of home inspectors, who typically inspect homes during the day and write reports in the evening.

Job Outlook

Employment of construction and building inspectors is projected to grow 3 percent from 2019 to 2029, about as fast as the average for all occupations.

Public interest in safety and the desire to improve the quality of construction are factors that are expected to continue to create demand for inspectors. Employment growth for inspectors is expected to be strongest in local government.

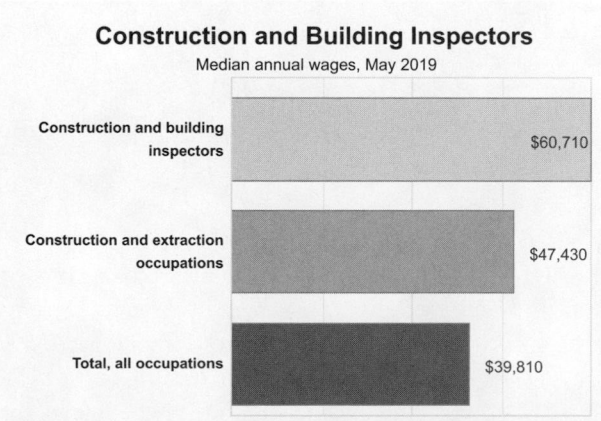

Construction and Building Inspectors

Median annual wages, May 2019

Construction and building inspectors	$60,710
Construction and extraction occupations	$47,430
Total, all occupations	$39,810

Note: All Occupations includes all occupations in the U.S. Economy.
Source: U.S. Bureau of Labor Statistics, Occupational Employment Statistics.

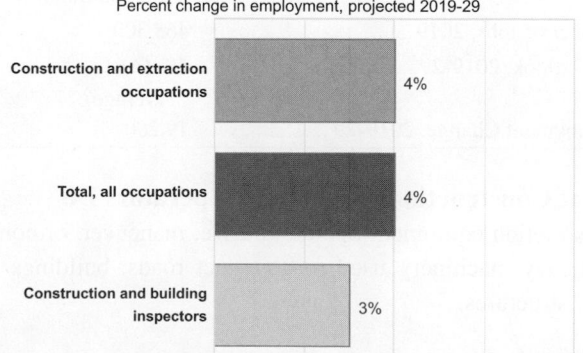

Construction and Building Inspectors

Percent change in employment, projected 2019-29

Construction and extraction occupations	4%
Total, all occupations	4%
Construction and building inspectors	3%

Note: All Occupations includes all occupations in the U.S. Economy.
Source: U.S. Bureau of Labor Statistics, Employment Projections program.

Job Prospects

Certified construction and building inspectors who can perform a variety of inspections should have the best job opportunities. Inspectors with construction-related work experience or training in engineering, architecture, construction technology, or related fields are also likely to have better job prospects.

Those who are self-employed, such as home inspectors, are more likely to be affected by economic downturns or fluctuations in the real estate market.

Employment projections data for construction and building inspectors, 2019-29					
Occupational Title	SOC Code	Employment, 2019	Projected Employment, 2029	Change, 2019-29	
				Percent	Numeric
SOURCE: U.S. Bureau of Labor Statistics, Employment Projections program					
Construction and building inspectors	47-4011	120,800	124,600	3	3,900

State & Area Data

Occupational Employment Statistics (OES)

The Occupational Employment Statistics (OES) program produces employment and wage estimates annually for over 800 occupations. These estimates are available for the nation as a whole, for individual states, and for metropolitan and nonmetropolitan areas.

Contacts for More Information

For more information about building codes, certification, and a career as a construction or building inspector, visit
➤ International Code Council
➤ National Fire Protection Association

For more information about coating inspectors, visit
➤ NACE International

For more information about construction inspectors, visit
➤ Association of Construction Inspectors

For more information about electrical inspectors, visit
➤ International Association of Electrical Inspectors

For more information about elevator inspectors, visit
➤ National Association of Elevator Safety Authorities International

For more information about education and training for mechanical and plumbing inspectors, visit
➤ International Association of Plumbing and Mechanical Officials

For information about becoming a home inspector, visit
➤ American Society of Home Inspectors
➤ International Association of Certified Home Inspectors (InterNACHI)

Construction Equipment Operators

Summary

Quick Facts: Construction Equipment Operators	
2019 Median Pay	$48,160 per year $23.16 per hour
Typical Entry-Level Education	High school diploma or equivalent
Work Experience in a Related Occupation	None
On-the-job Training	Moderate-term on-the-job training
Number of Jobs, 2019	468,300
Job Outlook, 2019-29	4% (As fast as average)
Employment Change, 2019-29	19,200

What Construction Equipment Operators Do

Construction equipment operators drive, maneuver, or control the heavy machinery used to construct roads, buildings and other structures.

Work Environment

Construction equipment operators work in nearly all weather conditions. They often get dirty, greasy, muddy, or dusty. The majority of operators work full time, and some operators have irregular work schedules. Some construction projects, especially road building, are done at night.

How to Become a Construction Equipment Operator

Many workers learn equipment operation on the job after earning a high school diploma or equivalent, and others learn through an apprenticeship or by attending vocational schools.

Construction equipment operators may use excavators to prepare sites.

Pay

The median annual wage for construction equipment operators was $48,160 in May 2019

Job Outlook

Overall employment of construction equipment operators is projected to grow 4 percent from 2019 to 2029, about as fast as the average for all occupations.

State & Area Data

Explore resources for employment and wages by state and area for construction equipment operators.

What Construction Equipment Operators Do

Construction equipment operators drive, maneuver, or control the heavy machinery used to construct roads, bridges, buildings, and other structures.

Duties

Construction equipment operators typically do the following:

- Clean and maintain equipment, making basic repairs as necessary
- Report malfunctioning equipment to supervisors
- Move levers, push pedals, or turn valves to control equipment
- Drive and maneuver equipment
- Coordinate machine actions with crew members using hand or audio signals
- Follow safety standards

Construction equipment operators use machinery to move construction materials, earth, and other heavy materials at construction sites and mines. They operate equipment that clears and grades land to prepare it for the construction of roads, bridges, and buildings, as well as runways, power generation facilities, dams, levees, and other structures.

The following are examples of types of construction equipment operators:

Pile-drivers drive piles to support structures such as piers.

Operating engineers and other construction equipment operators work with one or several types of power construction equipment. They may operate excavation and loading machines equipped with scoops, shovels, or buckets that dig sand, gravel, earth, or similar materials. In addition to operating bulldozers, they operate trench excavators, road graders, and similar equipment. Sometimes, they may drive and control industrial trucks or tractors equipped with forklifts or booms for lifting materials. They may also operate and maintain air compressors, pumps, and other power equipment at construction sites.

Paving and surfacing equipment operators control the machines that spread and level asphalt or spread and smooth concrete for roadways or other structures.

- Asphalt spreader operators turn valves to regulate the temperature and flow of asphalt being applied to the roadbed. They must ensure a constant flow of asphalt into the hopper and that the machine distributes the paving material evenly.
- Concrete paving machine operators control levers and turn handwheels to move attachments that spread, vibrate, and level wet concrete. They must watch the surface of the concrete carefully to identify low spots that need additional concrete.
- Tamping equipment operators use machines that compact earth and other fill materials for roadbeds, railroads, or other construction sites. They also may operate machines with interchangeable hammers to cut or break up old pavement and drive guardrail posts into the ground.

Pile-driver operators use large machines mounted on skids, barges, or cranes to hammer piles into the ground. Piles are long, heavy beams of concrete, wood, or steel driven into the ground to support retaining walls, bridges, piers, or building foundations. Some pile-driver operators work on offshore oil rigs.

Work Environment

Construction equipment operators held about 468,300 jobs in 2019. Employment in the detailed occupations that make up construction equipment operators was distributed as follows:

Operating engineers and other construction equipment operators	418,000
Paving, surfacing, and tamping equipment operators	46,600
Pile driver operators	3,600

The largest employers of construction equipment operators were as follows:

Heavy and civil engineering construction	30%
Specialty trade contractors	28
Local government, excluding education and hospitals	13
Mining, quarrying, and oil and gas extraction	6
Construction of buildings	5

Construction equipment operators work in nearly all weather conditions.

Construction equipment operators work in nearly every weather condition, although rain or extremely cold weather can stop some types of construction. Workers often get dirty, greasy, muddy, or dusty. Some operators work in remote locations on large construction projects, such as highways and dams, or in factories or mines.

Injuries and Illnesses
Construction equipment operators risk injury from hazards such as slips, falls, and transportation incidents. Workers can generally avoid injury by observing proper operating procedures and safety practices. Bulldozers, scrapers, and pile-drivers are noisy and shake or jolt the operator, which may lead to repetitive stress injuries.

Work Schedules
Construction equipment operators may have irregular schedules because work on construction projects must sometimes continue around the clock or be done late at night. The majority of construction equipment operators work full time.

How to Become a Construction Equipment Operator
Many workers learn equipment operation on the job after earning a high school diploma or equivalent, while others learn through an apprenticeship or by attending vocational schools.

Education
A high school diploma or equivalent is required for most jobs. Vocational training and math courses are useful, and a course in auto mechanics can be helpful because workers often perform maintenance on their equipment.

Learning at vocational schools may be beneficial in finding a job. Schools may specialize in a particular brand or type of construction equipment.

Some schools incorporate sophisticated simulator training into their courses, allowing beginners to familiarize themselves

Construction equipment operators should have steady hands and feet to guide and control heavy machinery precisely.

with the equipment in a virtual environment before operating real machines.

Training
Many workers learn their jobs by operating light equipment under the guidance of an experienced operator. Later, they may operate heavier equipment, such as bulldozers. Some construction equipment with computerized controls requires greater skill to operate. Operators of such equipment may need more training and some understanding of electronics.

Other workers learn their trade through a 3- or 4-year apprenticeship. For each year of the program, apprentices must have at least 144 hours of technical instruction and 2,000 hours of paid on-the-job training. On the job, apprentices learn to maintain equipment, operate machinery, and use technology, such as Global Positioning System (GPS) devices. In the classroom, apprentices learn operating procedures for equipment, safety practices, and first aid, as well as how to read grading plans.

A few groups, including unions and contractor associations, sponsor apprenticeship programs. The basic qualifications for entering an apprenticeship program are as follows:

- Minimum age of 18
- High school education or equivalent
- Physically able to do the work
- Valid driver's license

After completing an apprenticeship program, apprentices are considered journey workers and perform tasks with less guidance.

Licenses, Certifications, and Registrations
Construction equipment operators often need a commercial driver's license (CDL) to haul their equipment to various jobsites. State laws governing CDLs vary.

A few states have special licenses for operators of backhoes, loaders, and bulldozers.

Currently, 17 states require pile-driver operators to have a crane license because similar operational concerns apply to both pile-drivers and cranes. In addition, the cities of Chicago, Cincinnati, New Orleans, New York, Omaha, Philadelphia, and Washington, DC require special crane licensure.

Important Qualities

Hand-eye-foot coordination. Construction equipment operators should have steady hands and feet to guide and control heavy machinery precisely, sometimes in tight spaces.

Mechanical skills. Construction equipment operators often perform basic maintenance on the equipment they operate. As a result, they should be familiar with hand and power tools and standard equipment care.

Physical strength. Construction equipment operators may be required to lift more than 50 pounds as part of their duties.

Unafraid of heights. Construction equipment operators may work at great heights. For example, pile-driver operators may need to service the pulleys located at the top of the pile-driver's tower, which may be several stories tall.

Pay

The median annual wage for construction equipment operators was $48,160 in May 2019. The median wage is the wage at which half the workers in an occupation earned more than that amount and half earned less. The lowest 10 percent earned less than $31,780, and the highest 10 percent earned more than $84,650.

Median annual wages for construction equipment operators in May 2019 were as follows:

Pile driver operators	$62,600
Operating engineers and other construction equipment operators	48,980
Paving, surfacing, and tamping equipment operators	40,130

In May 2019, the median annual wages for construction equipment operators in the top industries in which they worked were as follows:

Construction of buildings	$54,180
Heavy and civil engineering construction	52,280
Specialty trade contractors	48,070
Mining, quarrying, and oil and gas extraction	46,950
Local government, excluding education and hospitals	43,080

The starting pay for apprentices is usually between 60 percent and 70 percent of what fully trained operators make. They receive pay increases as they learn to operate more complex equipment.

Construction equipment operators may have irregular schedules because work on construction projects must sometimes continue around the clock or be done late at night. The majority of construction equipment operators work full time.

Job Outlook

Overall employment of construction equipment operators is projected to grow 4 percent from 2019 to 2029, about as fast as the average for all occupations. Employment growth is expected to vary across the construction equipment operator occupations. (See table.)

Spending on infrastructure is expected to increase, resulting in some new jobs over the next 10 years. Across the country, many roads, bridges, and water and sewer systems are in need of repair. In addition, population growth will require new infrastructure projects, such as roads and sewer lines, which is also expected to generate jobs.

Job Prospects

Workers with the ability to operate multiple types of equipment should have the best job opportunities. In addition, employment opportunities should be best in metropolitan areas, where most

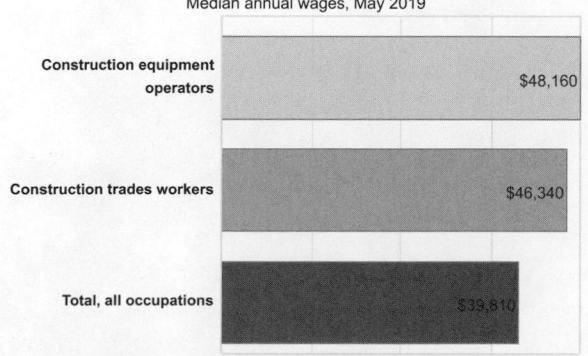

Construction Equipment Operators
Median annual wages, May 2019

Construction equipment operators — $48,160
Construction trades workers — $46,340
Total, all occupations — $39,810

Note: All Occupations includes all occupations in the U.S. Economy.
Source: U.S. Bureau of Labor Statistics, Occupational Employment Statistics.

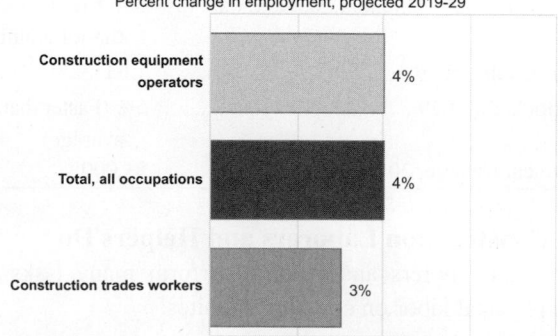

Construction Equipment Operators
Percent change in employment, projected 2019-29

Construction equipment operators — 4%
Total, all occupations — 4%
Construction trades workers — 3%

Note: All Occupations includes all occupations in the U.S. Economy.
Source: U.S. Bureau of Labor Statistics, Employment Projections program.

large commercial and residential buildings are constructed, and in states that undertake large transportation-related projects. Because apprentices learn to operate a wider variety of machines than do other beginners, they usually have better job opportunities.

As with many other types of construction worker jobs, employment of construction equipment operators is sensitive to fluctuations of the economy. On the one hand, workers may experience periods of unemployment when the overall level of construction falls. On the other hand, some areas may need additional workers during peak periods of building activity.

Employment projections data for construction equipment operators, 2019-29					
Occupational Title	SOC Code	Employment, 2019	Projected Employment, 2029	Change, 2019-29	
				Percent	Numeric
SOURCE: U.S. Bureau of Labor Statistics, Employment Projections program					
Construction equipment operators	47-2070	468,300	487,500	4	19,200
Paving, surfacing, and tamping equipment operators	47-2071	46,600	48,800	5	2,200
Pile driver operators	47-2072	3,600	3,800	4	200
Operating engineers and other construction equipment operators	47-2073	418,000	434,900	4	16,900

State & Area Data
Occupational Employment Statistics (OES)
The Occupational Employment Statistics (OES) program produces employment and wage estimates annually for over 800 occupations. These estimates are available for the nation as a whole, for individual states, and for metropolitan and nonmetropolitan areas.

Contacts for More Information
For information about apprenticeships or job opportunities as a construction equipment operator, contact local cement or highway construction contractors, a local joint union-management apprenticeship committee, or the nearest office of your state employment service or apprenticeship agency. Apprenticeship information is available from the U.S. Department of Labor's Apprenticeship program online or by phone at 877-872-5627.

For more information about construction equipment operators, visit
➤ The Associated General Contractors of America
➤ Pile Driving Contractors Association

For more information about training of construction equipment operators, visit
➤ International Union of Operating Engineers
➤ NCCER

For more information about crane certification and licensure, visit
➤ National Commission for the Certification of Crane Operators

Construction Laborers and Helpers

Summary

Quick Facts: Construction Laborers and Helpers

2019 Median Pay	$36,000 per year $17.31 per hour
Typical Entry-Level Education	See below
Work Experience in a Related Occupation	None
On-the-job Training	Short-term on-the-job training
Number of Jobs, 2019	1,643,900
Job Outlook, 2019-29	5% (Faster than average)
Employment Change, 2019-29	81,000

What Construction Laborers and Helpers Do
Construction laborers and helpers perform many tasks that require physical labor on construction sites.

Work Environment
Most construction laborers and helpers typically work full time and do physically demanding work. Some work at great heights or outdoors in all weather conditions. Construction laborers have one of the highest rates of injuries and illnesses of all occupations.

How to Become a Construction Laborer or Helper
Construction laborers and helpers learn their trade through on-the-job training. Formal education is not typically required.

Construction laborers and helpers perform physical labor on construction sites.

Pay

The median annual wage for construction laborers and helpers was $36,000 in May 2019.

Job Outlook

Overall employment of construction laborers and helpers is projected to grow 5 percent from 2019 to 2029, faster than the average for all occupations.

State & Area Data

Explore resources for employment and wages by state and area for construction laborers and helpers.

What Construction Laborers and Helpers Do

Construction laborers and helpers perform many tasks that require physical labor on construction sites.

Duties

Construction laborers and helpers typically do the following:

- Clean and prepare construction sites by removing debris and possible hazards
- Load or unload building materials to be used in construction
- Build or take apart bracing, scaffolding, and temporary structures
- Dig trenches, backfill holes, or compact earth to prepare for construction
- Operate or tend equipment and machines used in construction
- Follow construction plans and instructions from supervisors or more experienced workers
- Assist craftworkers with their duties

Construction laborers and helpers work on almost all construction sites, performing a wide range of tasks varying in complexity from very easy to extremely difficult and hazardous.

Construction laborers, also referred to as *construction craft laborers*, perform a wide variety of construction-related activities during all phases of construction. Many laborers spend

Construction laborers and helpers assist craftworkers.

their time preparing and cleaning up construction sites, using tools such as shovels and brooms. Other workers, such as those on road crews, may specialize and learn to control traffic patterns and operate pavement breakers, jackhammers, earth tampers, or surveying equipment.

With special training, laborers may help transport and use explosives or run hydraulic boring machines to dig out tunnels. They may learn to use lasers to place pipes and to use computers to control robotic pipe cutters. They may become certified to remove asbestos, lead, or chemicals.

Helpers assist construction craftworkers, such as electricians and carpenters, with a variety of tasks. They may carry tools and materials or help set up equipment. For example, many helpers work with cement masons to move and set the forms that determine the shape of poured concrete. Many other helpers assist with taking apart equipment, cleaning up sites, and disposing of waste, as well as helping with any other needs of craftworkers.

Many construction trades have helpers who assist craftworkers. The following trades have associated helpers:

- Brickmasons, blockmasons, and stonemasons, and tile and marble setters
- Carpenters
- Electricians
- Painters, paperhangers, plasterers, and stucco masons
- Pipelayers, plumbers, pipefitters, and steamfitters
- Roofers

Work Environment

Construction laborers and helpers held about 1.6 million jobs in 2019. Employment in the detailed occupations that make up construction laborers and helpers was distributed as follows:

Construction laborers	1,398,000
Helpers--electricians	81,100
Helpers--pipelayers, plumbers, pipefitters, and steamfitters	59,300
Helpers--carpenters	33,200
Helpers, construction trades, all other	28,800
Helpers--brickmasons, blockmasons, stonemasons, and tile and marble setters	23,400
Helpers--painters, paperhangers, plasterers, and stucco masons	11,000
Helpers--roofers	9,100

The largest employers of construction laborers and helpers were as follows:

Specialty trade contractors	34%
Self-employed workers	23
Construction of buildings	17
Heavy and civil engineering construction	15
Temporary help services	3

Construction laborers and helpers wear gloves, safety glasses, and other protective gear.

Most construction laborers and helpers perform physically demanding work. Some work at great heights or outdoors in all weather conditions; others may be required to work in tunnels. They must use earplugs around loud equipment and wear gloves, safety glasses, and other protective gear.

Injuries and Illnesses

Construction laborers and helpers, construction trades, all other have some of the highest rates of injuries and illnesses of all occupations. ("All other" titles represent occupations with a wide range of characteristics that do not fit into any of the other detailed occupations.)

Workers may experience cuts from materials and tools, fatal and nonfatal falls from ladders and scaffolding, and burns from chemicals or equipment. Some jobs expose workers to harmful materials, fumes, or odors, or to dangerous machinery. Workers may also experience muscle fatigue and injuries related to lifting and carrying heavy materials.

Work Schedules

Like many construction workers, most laborers and helpers work full time. Although they must sometimes stop work because of bad weather, they may work overtime to meet deadlines. Laborers and helpers on highway and bridge projects may need to work overnight to avoid causing major traffic disruptions. In some parts of the country, construction laborers and helpers may work only during certain seasons. For example, in northern climates, cold weather frequently disrupts construction activity in the winter.

Some construction laborers are self-employed. In contrast, very few helpers are self-employed.

How to Become a Construction Laborer or Helper

Construction laborers and helpers learn their trade through on-the-job training (OJT). The length of training depends on the employer and the specialization. Formal education is not typically required.

While formal education is not required to enter the occupation, some construction laborers take classes as part of an apprenticeship.

Education

Although formal education is not typically required for most positions, helpers of electricians and helpers of pipelayers, plumbers, pipefitters, and steamfitters typically need a high school diploma. High school classes in mathematics, blueprint reading, welding, and other vocational subjects can be helpful.

Training

Construction laborers and helpers typically learn through OJT after being hired by a construction contractor. Workers usually learn by performing tasks under the guidance of experienced workers.

Although the majority of construction laborers and helpers learn by assisting experienced workers, some construction laborers may opt for apprenticeship programs. These programs generally include 2 to 4 years of technical instruction and OJT. The Laborers' International Union of North America (LIUNA) requires a combination of OJT and related classroom instruction in such areas as signaling, blueprint reading, using proper tools and equipment, and following health and safety procedures. The remainder of the curriculum consists of specialized training in one of these eight areas:

- Building construction
- Demolition and deconstruction
- Environmental remediation
- Road and utility construction
- Tunneling
- Masonry
- Landscaping
- Pipeline construction

Licenses, Certifications, and Registrations

Laborers who remove hazardous materials (hazmat) must meet the federal and state requirements for hazardous materials removal workers.

Depending on the work they do, laborers may need specific certifications, which may be attained through LIUNA. Rigging and scaffold building are commonly attained certifications. Certification can help workers prove that they have the knowledge to perform more complex tasks.

Advancement

Through experience and training, construction laborers and helpers can advance into positions that involve more complex tasks. For example, laborers may earn certifications in welding, erecting scaffolding, or finishing concrete, and then spend more time performing those activities. Similarly, helpers sometimes move into construction craft occupations after gaining experience in the field. For example, experience as an electrician's helper may lead someone to becoming an apprentice electrician.

Important Qualities

Color vision. Construction laborers and helpers may need to be able to distinguish colors to do their job. For example, an electrician's helper must be able to distinguish different colors of wire to help the lead electrician.

Math skills. Construction laborers and some helpers need to perform basic math calculations while measuring on jobsites or assisting a surveying crew.

Mechanical skills. Construction laborers are frequently required to operate and maintain equipment, such as jackhammers.

Physical stamina. Construction laborers and helpers must have the endurance to perform strenuous tasks throughout the day. Highway laborers, for example, spend hours on their feet—often in hot temperatures—with few breaks.

Physical strength. Construction laborers and helpers must often lift heavy materials or equipment. For example, cement mason helpers must move cinder blocks, which typically weigh more than 40 pounds each.

Pay

The median annual wage for construction laborers and helpers was $36,000 in May 2019. The median wage is the wage at which half the workers in an occupation earned more than that amount and half earned less. The lowest 10 percent earned less than $24,420, and the highest 10 percent earned more than $64,100.

Median annual wages for construction laborers and helpers in May 2019 were as follows:

Construction laborers	$36,860
Helpers--brickmasons, blockmasons, stonemasons, and tile and marble setters	35,410
Helpers--carpenters	33,060
Helpers--electricians	32,830
Helpers--roofers	32,110

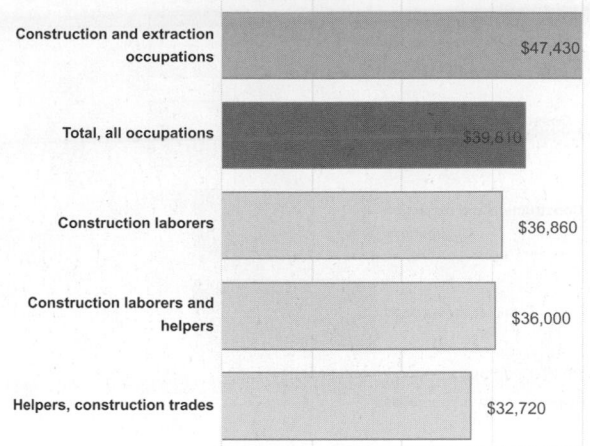

Construction Laborers and Helpers
Median annual wages, May 2019

Construction and extraction occupations	$47,430
Total, all occupations	$39,810
Construction laborers	$36,860
Construction laborers and helpers	$36,000
Helpers, construction trades	$32,720

Note: All Occupations includes all occupations in the U.S. Economy.
Source: U.S. Bureau of Labor Statistics, Occupational Employment Statistics.

Helpers--pipelayers, plumbers, pipefitters, and steamfitters	32,100
Helpers, construction trades, all other	31,910
Helpers--painters, paperhangers, plasterers, and stucco masons	31,340

In May 2019, the median annual wages for construction laborers and helpers in the top industries in which they worked were as follows:

Heavy and civil engineering construction	$37,950
Construction of buildings	37,260
Specialty trade contractors	35,110
Temporary help services	29,710

The starting pay for most apprentices is usually about 60 percent of what fully trained laborers make. Apprentices receive pay increases as they learn more skills.

Like many construction workers, most construction laborers and helpers work full time. Although they sometimes stop work because of bad weather, they may work overtime to meet deadlines. Laborers and helpers on highway and bridge projects may need to work overnight to avoid causing major traffic disruptions. In some parts of the country, construction laborers and helpers may work only during certain seasons. For example, in northern climates, cold weather frequently disrupts construction activity in the winter.

Some construction laborers are self-employed. In contrast, very few helpers are self-employed.

Job Outlook

Overall employment of construction laborers and helpers is projected to grow 5 percent from 2019 to 2029, faster than the average for all occupations.

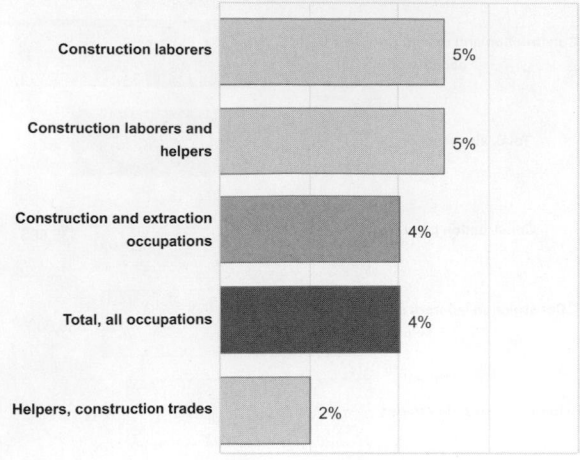

Construction Laborers and Helpers

Percent change in employment, projected 2019-29

Construction laborers	5%
Construction laborers and helpers	5%
Construction and extraction occupations	4%
Total, all occupations	4%
Helpers, construction trades	2%

Note: All Occupations includes all occupations in the U.S. Economy.
Source: U.S. Bureau of Labor Statistics, Employment Projections program.

Employment projections data for construction laborers and helpers, 2019-29

Occupational Title	SOC Code	Employment, 2019	Projected Employment, 2029	Change, 2019-29	
				Percent	Numeric
Construction laborers and helpers	—	1,643,900	1,724,900	5	81,000
Construction laborers	47-2061	1,398,000	1,473,400	5	75,400
Helpers--brickmasons, blockmasons, stonemasons, and tile and marble setters	47-3011	23,400	22,300	-5	-1,100
Helpers--carpenters	47-3012	33,200	33,700	1	400
Helpers--electricians	47-3013	81,100	82,300	2	1,200
Helpers--painters, paperhangers, plasterers, and stucco masons	47-3014	11,000	11,200	2	200
Helpers--pipelayers, plumbers, pipefitters, and steamfitters	47-3015	59,300	62,600	6	3,300
Helpers--roofers	47-3016	9,100	9,500	3	300
Helpers, construction trades, all other	47-3019	28,800	30,000	4	1,200

SOURCE: U.S. Bureau of Labor Statistics, Employment Projections program

Construction laborers work in all fields of construction, and demand for laborers should mirror the level of overall construction activity. Repairing and replacing the nation's infrastructure, such as roads, bridges, and water lines, may result in steady demand for laborers. The increased use of prefabricated components, such as panels and modular rooms that are made offsite, will create a need for laborers in some areas to assemble them onsite.

Although employment growth of specific types of helpers is expected to vary (see table), overall demand is expected to be driven by the construction of homes, schools, office buildings, factories, and power plants. Increased use of prefabrication may result in more employment of helpers to build wall panels and other construction components offsite. However, prefabrication is also projected to result in the need for fewer helpers of brickmasons, blockmasons, stonemasons, and tile and marble setters in the production process and of workers such as construction laborers in onsite installation.

Job Prospects

Because of the large size of these combined occupations and their relatively high turnover, job prospects should be favorable.

Employment of construction laborers and helpers is especially sensitive to the fluctuations of the economy. On the one hand, workers in these trades may experience periods of unemployment when the overall level of construction falls. On the other hand, during peak periods of building activity some areas may require additional number of these workers.

State & Area Data
Occupational Employment Statistics (OES)

The Occupational Employment Statistics (OES) program produces employment and wage estimates annually for over 800 occupations. These estimates are available for the nation as a whole, for individual states, and for metropolitan and nonmetropolitan areas.

- Construction laborers
- Helpers, construction trades, all other
- Helpers--brickmasons, blockmasons, stonemasons, and tile and marble setters
- Helpers--carpenters
- Helpers--electricians
- Helpers--painters, paperhangers, plasterers, and stucco masons
- Helpers--pipelayers, plumbers, pipefitters, and steamfitters
- Helpers--roofers

Contacts for More Information

For details about apprenticeships or other work opportunities for construction laborers and helpers, contact the offices of the state employment service, the state apprenticeship agency, local construction contractors or firms that employ laborers, or local union-management apprenticeship committees. Apprenticeship information is available from the U.S. Department of Labor's Apprenticeship program online or by phone at 877-872-5627.

For more information about education programs for laborers, visit

➤ Laborers' International Union of North America

➤ NCCER

Drywall Installers, Ceiling Tile Installers, and Tapers

Summary

Quick Facts: Drywall Installers, Ceiling Tile Installers, and Tapers

2019 Median Pay	$47,360 per year $22.77 per hour
Typical Entry-Level Education	No formal educational credential
Work Experience in a Related Occupation ...	None
On-the-job Training	Moderate-term on-the-job training
Number of Jobs, 2019	146,900
Job Outlook, 2019-29..................................	0% (Little or no change)
Employment Change, 2019-29	-300

What Drywall Installers, Ceiling Tile Installers, and Tapers Do

Drywall and ceiling tile installers hang wallboard and install ceiling tile inside buildings. Tapers prepare the wallboard for painting.

Work Environment

Drywall installers, ceiling tile installers, and tapers work indoors. Workers spend most of the day standing, bending, or reaching, and they often must lift and maneuver heavy wallboard.

How to Become a Drywall Installer, Ceiling Tile Installer, or Taper

Most drywall installers, ceiling tile installers, and tapers learn their trade on the job. A formal educational credential is typically not required to enter the occupation.

Drywall and ceiling tile installers hang wallboard and install ceiling tile inside buildings.

Pay

The median annual wage for drywall and ceiling tile installers was $45,700 in May 2019.

The median annual wage for tapers was $59,070 in May 2019.

Job Outlook

Employment of drywall installers, ceiling tile installers, and tapers is projected to show little or no change from 2019 to 2029. However, there will be openings each year because of the need to replace workers who leave the occupation.

State & Area Data

Explore resources for employment and wages by state and area for drywall installers, ceiling tile installers, and tapers.

What Drywall Installers, Ceiling Tile Installers, and Tapers Do

Drywall installers and ceiling tile installers hang wallboard and install ceiling tile inside buildings. Tapers prepare the wallboard for painting, using tape and other materials. Many workers both install and tape wallboard.

Drywall installers, ceiling tile installers, and tapers work with many different types of tools.

Duties

Drywall installers, ceiling tile installers, and tapers typically do the following:

- Measure, mark, and cut drywall panels according to design plans
- Fasten panels and tiles to support structures
- Patch, trim, and smooth rough spots and edges
- Apply tape and sealing compound to cover joints between wallboards
- Add coats of sealing compound to create an even surface
- Sand all joints and holes for a smooth, seamless finish

Drywall and ceiling tile installers place panels over the walls and ceilings of interior rooms in buildings. The panels cover insulation, electrical wires, and pipes; dampen sound; and provide fire resistance. Tapers prepare the drywall for finishing.

Workers may use mechanical lifts or stand on stilts, ladders, or scaffolds to hang and prepare ceilings. After hanging wallboards, workers use trowels to spread coats of sealing compound over cracks, indentations, and other imperfections. Some workers use a mechanical applicator, a tool that spreads sealing compound on the wall joint while dispensing and setting tape at the same time.

Drywall installers are also called *drywallers* or *hangers*. They cut and hang the panels of wallboard. The tools they use include tape measures, straightedges, utility knives, and power saws.

Ceiling tile installers hang ceiling tiles and create suspended ceilings. Tiles may be applied directly to the ceiling, attached to furring strips, or suspended on runners that are connected by wire to the ceiling. Workers are sometimes called *acoustical carpenters*, because they also install tiles that block sound.

Tapers, also called *finishers*, prepare the drywall for covering by paint and wallpaper. Tapers apply paper or fiberglass mesh tape to cover drywall seams. They also smooth the tape after affixing it and apply a finishing compound to the tape.

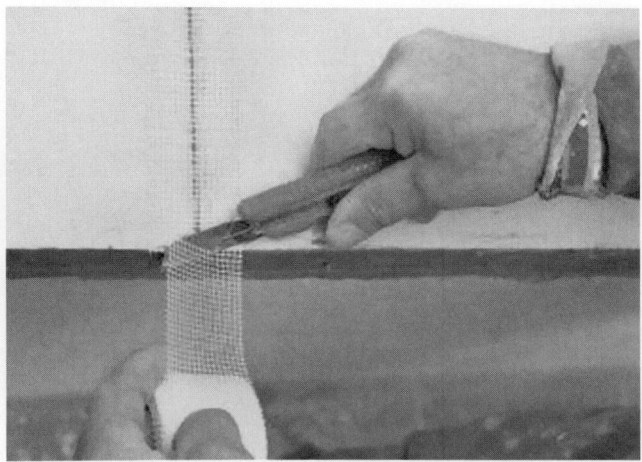

Tapers cover the seams where drywall edges meet.

In addition to performing new installations, many installers and tapers make repairs such as fixing damaged drywall and replacing ceiling tiles. The wall coverings applied to the finished drywall are installed by painters, plasterers, and paperhangers.

Work Environment

Drywall and ceiling tile installers held about 125,100 jobs in 2019. The largest employers of drywall and ceiling tile installers were as follows:

Drywall and insulation contractors	64%
Self-employed workers	18
Nonresidential building construction	5

Tapers held about 21,800 jobs in 2019. The largest employers of tapers were as follows:

Drywall and insulation contractors	69%
Self-employed workers	18
Nonresidential building construction	6
Painting and wall covering contractors	2

Drywall installers, ceiling tile installers, and tapers work indoors. The work is physically demanding. Workers spend most of the day standing, bending, or reaching, and they must often lift and maneuver heavy wallboard.

Work Schedules

Most drywall installers, ceiling tile installers, and tapers work full time.

How to Become a Drywall Installer, Ceiling Tile Installer, or Taper

Most drywall installers, ceiling tile installers, and tapers learn their trade on the job. A formal educational credential is typically not required to enter the occupation.

Education

There are no educational credential requirements for becoming a drywall installer, ceiling tile installer, or taper, although some employers prefer to hire candidates who have a high school diploma or equivalent.

A high school diploma or equivalent is typically required for workers starting an apprenticeship.

Training

Most drywall installers, ceiling tile installers, and tapers learn their trade on the job by helping experienced workers and gradually taking on more duties. They start by carrying materials and cleaning up and then learn to use the tools of the trade. They learn to measure, cut, and install or apply materials. They may start out working on less visible areas, such as closets. Their on-the-job training typically lasts up to 12 months.

New drywall installers, ceiling tile installers, and tapers typically learn their job by working with more experienced workers.

A few groups, including the United Brotherhood of Carpenters, International Union of Painters and Allied Trades, and contractor associations, sponsor apprenticeship programs for drywall installers, ceiling tile installers, and tapers. Apprenticeships combine on-the-job training with technical instruction and typically last 2 to 4 years.

During their apprenticeship training, drywall installers, ceiling tile installers, and tapers learn a number of safety rules, many of which are standardized through the Occupational Safety & Health Administration (OSHA).

Advancement

Drywall installers, ceiling tile installers, and tapers may advance to become supervisors, general superintendents, project managers, or estimators. Workers may also choose to start their own business after gaining experience in the occupation.

Workers who join a union may also find career advancement opportunities within their union, such as becoming the business manager for a local chapter or becoming an instructor for the apprenticeship program.

Important Qualities

Ability to work at heights. Drywall installers, ceiling tile installers, and tapers may be required to work on ladders, scaffolding, lifts, or stilts.

Attention to detail. Drywall installers, ceiling tile installers, and tapers must take precise measurements, follow specific instructions, and be meticulous in their work.

Balance. Drywall installers, ceiling tile installers, and tapers often wear stilts. They must be able to move around and use tools overhead without falling.

Dexterity. Drywall installers, ceiling tile installers, and tapers work with hand tools on every job.

Math skills. Drywall installers, ceiling tile installers, and tapers must be able to estimate the quantity of materials needed when cutting panels.

Physical stamina. Drywall installers, ceiling tile installers, and tapers routinely lift and move heavy materials into place, so workers should be physically fit.

Physical strength. Drywall and ceiling tile installers must often lift heavy panels over their heads to secure onto the ceiling and must carry heavy materials to work areas.

Pay

The median annual wage for drywall and ceiling tile installers was $45,700 in May 2019. The median wage is the wage at which half the workers in an occupation earned more than that amount and half earned less. The lowest 10 percent earned less than $28,490, and the highest 10 percent earned more than $85,090.

The median annual wage for tapers was $59,070 in May 2019. The lowest 10 percent earned less than $34,190, and the highest 10 percent earned more than $95,950.

In May 2019, the median annual wages for drywall and ceiling tile installers in the top industries in which they worked were as follows:

Nonresidential building construction	$49,480
Drywall and insulation contractors	46,190

In May 2019, the median annual wages for tapers in the top industries in which they worked were as follows:

Nonresidential building construction	$68,730
Drywall and insulation contractors	58,280
Painting and wall covering contractors	57,140

Most drywall installers, ceiling tile installers, and tapers work full time.

Drywall Installers, Ceiling Tile Installers, and Tapers

Median annual wages, May 2019

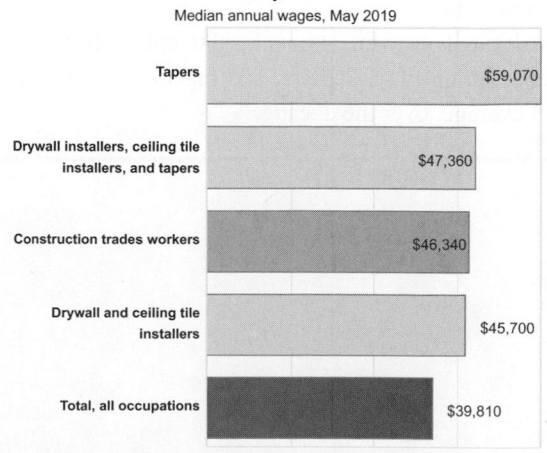

Tapers	$59,070
Drywall installers, ceiling tile installers, and tapers	$47,360
Construction trades workers	$46,340
Drywall and ceiling tile installers	$45,700
Total, all occupations	$39,810

Note: All Occupations includes all occupations in the U.S. Economy.
Source: U.S. Bureau of Labor Statistics, Occupational Employment Statistics.

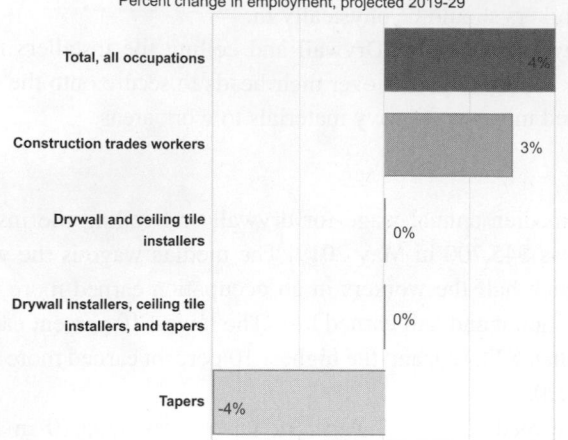

Drywall Installers, Ceiling Tile Installers, and Tapers

Percent change in employment, projected 2019-29

Total, all occupations	4%
Construction trades workers	3%
Drywall and ceiling tile installers	0%
Drywall installers, ceiling tile installers, and tapers	0%
Tapers	-4%

Note: All Occupations includes all occupations in the U.S. Economy.
Source: U.S. Bureau of Labor Statistics, Employment Projections program.

Job Outlook

Employment of drywall installers, ceiling tile installers, and tapers is projected to show little or no change from 2019 to 2029.

Drywall continues to be the most common interior wall covering in buildings, so the demand for these workers is expected to continue to come from the construction of new buildings. Home-remodeling projects are also expected to be a source of job growth as owners of existing homes and other buildings make improvements.

However, overall employment in the drywall and insulation contractors industry—an industry employing about two-thirds of drywall installers, ceiling tile installers, and tapers—is projected to decline over the decade, offsetting employment growth in other industries. In addition, tapers will continue to use new tools that allow workers to do more in less time.

Job Prospects

Despite limited growth, about 11,800 openings for drywall installers, ceiling tile installers, and tapers are projected each year, on average, over the decade.

Nearly all of those openings are expected to result from the need to replace workers who transfer to other occupations or exit the labor force, such as to retire.

Employment projections data for drywall installers, ceiling tile installers, and tapers, 2019-29					
Occupational Title	SOC Code	Employment, 2019	Projected Employment, 2029	Change, 2019-29	
				Percent	Numeric
SOURCE: U.S. Bureau of Labor Statistics, Employment Projections program					
Drywall installers, ceiling tile installers, and tapers	47-2080	146,900	146,600	0	-300
Drywall and ceiling tile installers	47-2081	125,100	125,600	0	500
Tapers	47-2082	21,800	21,000	-4	-900

State & Area Data
Occupational Employment Statistics (OES)

The Occupational Employment Statistics (OES) program produces employment and wage estimates annually for over 800 occupations. These estimates are available for the nation as a whole, for individual states, and for metropolitan and nonmetropolitan areas.

Contacts for More Information

For details about apprenticeships or other work opportunities in this trade, contact the offices of the state employment service; the state apprenticeship agency; local contractors or firms that employ drywall installers, ceiling tile installers, and tapers; or local union–management finishing trade apprenticeship committees. Apprenticeship information is available from the U.S. Department of Labor's Apprenticeship program online or by phone at 877-872-5627. Visit Apprenticeship.gov to search for apprenticeship opportunities.

For more information about drywall installers, ceiling tile installers, and tapers, visit

➤ Associated Builders and Contractors
➤ Association of the Wall and Ceiling Industry
➤ Finishing Trades Institute
➤ National Association of Home Builders
➤ NCCER
➤ United Brotherhood of Carpenters

Electricians

Summary

Quick Facts: Electricians

2019 Median Pay	$56,180 per year $27.01 per hour
Typical Entry-Level Education	High school diploma or equivalent
Work Experience in a Related Occupation	None
On-the-job Training	Apprenticeship
Number of Jobs, 2019	739,200
Job Outlook, 2019-29	8% (Much faster than average)
Employment Change, 2019-29	62,200

What Electricians Do

Electricians install, maintain, and repair electrical power, communications, lighting, and control systems.

Work Environment

Almost all electricians work full time. Work schedules may include evenings and weekends. Overtime is common.

How to Become an Electrician

Most electricians learn through an apprenticeship, but some start out by attending a technical school. Most states require electricians to be licensed.

Pay

The median annual wage for electricians was $56,180 in May 2019.

Job Outlook

Employment of electricians is projected to grow 8 percent from 2019 to 2029, much faster than the average for all occupations.

Electricians connect a variety of fixtures to internal and external electricity sources.

Homes and businesses continue to require wiring, and electricians will be needed to install the necessary components.

State & Area Data

Explore resources for employment and wages by state and area for electricians.

What Electricians Do

Electricians install, maintain, and repair electrical power, communications, lighting, and control systems in homes, businesses, and factories.

Duties

Electricians typically do the following:

- Read blueprints or technical diagrams
- Install and maintain wiring, control, and lighting systems
- Inspect electrical components, such as transformers and circuit breakers
- Identify electrical problems using a variety of testing devices
- Repair or replace wiring, equipment, or fixtures using handtools and power tools
- Follow state and local building regulations based on the National Electrical Code

Electricians often cap wires before installing an outlet.

- Direct and train workers to install, maintain, or repair electrical wiring or equipment

Almost every building has an electrical power, communications, lighting, and control system that is installed during construction and maintained after that. These systems power the lights, appliances, and equipment that make people's lives and jobs easier and more comfortable.

Installing electrical systems in newly constructed buildings is often less complicated than maintaining equipment in existing buildings because electrical wiring is more easily accessible during construction. Maintaining equipment and systems involves identifying problems and repairing broken equipment that is sometimes difficult to reach. Maintenance work may include fixing or replacing parts, light fixtures, control systems, motors, and other types of electrical equipment.

Electricians read blueprints, which include technical diagrams of electrical systems that show the location of circuits, outlets, and other equipment. They use different types of hand-tools and power tools, such as conduit benders, to run and protect wiring. Other commonly used tools include screwdrivers, wire strippers, drills, and saws. While troubleshooting, electricians also may use ammeters, voltmeters, thermal scanners, and cable testers to find problems and ensure that components are working properly.

Many electricians work alone, but sometimes they collaborate with others. For example, experienced electricians may work with building engineers and architects to help design electrical systems for new construction. Some electricians may also consult with other construction specialists, such as elevator installers and heating and air conditioning workers, to help install or maintain electrical or power systems. Electricians employed by large companies are likely to work as part of a crew; they may direct helpers and apprentices to complete jobs.

Lineman electricians install distribution and transmission lines to deliver electricity from its source to customers; this occupation is covered in the line installers and repairers profile.

Work Environment

Electricians held about 739,200 jobs in 2019. The largest employers of electricians were as follows:

Electrical contractors and other wiring installation contractors	67%
Manufacturing	7
Self-employed workers	5
Government	3
Employment services	3

Electricians work indoors and outdoors at homes, businesses, factories, and construction sites. Because electricians must travel to different worksites, local or long-distance commuting is often required.

Electricians wear a variety of safety equipment to reduce their risk of injury.

On the jobsite, they occasionally work in cramped spaces. The long periods of standing and kneeling can be tiring. Electricians may be exposed to dirt, dust, debris, or fumes. Those working outside may be exposed to hot or cold temperatures and inclement weather. Those who work in factories are often subject to noisy machinery.

Electricians may be required to work at great heights, such as when working on construction sites, inside buildings, or on renewable energy projects.

Many electricians work alone, but sometimes they collaborate with others. Electricians employed by large companies are likely to work as part of a crew, directing helpers and apprentices to complete jobs.

Injuries and Illnesses

Working with electricity is dangerous. Electricians must take precautions to avoid getting hurt. Although accidents are potentially fatal, common injuries include electrical shocks, falls, burns, and other minor injuries.

To reduce these risks, workers must wear protective clothing and safety glasses. Electricians who are subject to loud noises, such as those in factories, must wear hearing protection.

Work Schedules

Almost all electricians work full time. Work schedules may include evenings and weekends. Overtime is common.

Self-employed electricians often work in residential construction and may be able to set their own schedule.

How to Become an Electrician

Most electricians learn through an apprenticeship, but some start out by attending a technical school. Most states require electricians to be licensed. For more information, contact your local or state electrical licensing board.

Education

A high school diploma or equivalent is required to become an electrician.

Most electricians learn on the job through an apprenticeship.

Some electricians start out by attending a technical school. Many technical schools offer programs related to circuitry, safety practices, and basic electrical information. Graduates of these programs usually receive credit toward their apprenticeship.

Training

Most electricians learn their trade in a 4- or 5-year apprenticeship program. For each year of the program, apprentices typically receive 2,000 hours of paid on-the-job training as well as some technical instruction.

Workers who gained electrical experience in the military or in the construction industry may qualify for a shortened apprenticeship based on their experience and testing.

Technical instruction for apprentices includes electrical theory, blueprint reading, mathematics, electrical code requirements, and safety and first-aid practices. They may also receive specialized training related to soldering, communications, fire alarm systems, and elevators.

Several groups, including unions and contractor associations, sponsor apprenticeship programs. Apprenticeship requirements vary by state and locality.

Some electrical contractors have their own training programs, which are not recognized apprenticeship programs but include both technical and on-the-job training. Although most workers enter apprenticeships directly, some electricians enter apprenticeship programs after working as a helper. The Home Builders Institute offers a preapprenticeship certificate training (PACT) program for eight construction trades, including electricians.

After completing an apprenticeship program, electricians are considered to be journey workers and may perform duties on their own, subject to local or state licensing requirements.

Licenses, Certifications, and Registrations

Most states require electricians to pass a test and be licensed. Requirements vary by state. For more information, contact your local or state electrical licensing board. Many of the requirements can be found on the National Electrical Contractors Association's website.

The tests have questions related to the National Electrical Code and state and local electrical codes, all of which set standards for the safe installation of electrical wiring and equipment.

Electricians may be required to take continuing education courses in order to maintain their licenses. These courses are usually related to safety practices, changes to the electrical code, and training from manufacturers in specific products.

Electricians may obtain additional certifications, which demonstrate competency in areas such as solar photovoltaic, electrical generating, or lighting systems.

Electricians may be required to have a driver's license.

Advancement

After meeting additional requirements and working as a qualified electrician, journey workers may advance to become master electricians. Electricians may also find opportunities to advance to supervisor or to other roles in project management.

Important Qualities

Color vision. Electricians must identify electrical wires by color.

Critical-thinking skills. Electricians perform tests and use the results to diagnose problems. For example, when an outlet is not working, they may use a multimeter to check the voltage, amperage, or resistance in order to determine the best course of action.

Customer-service skills. Electricians work with people on a regular basis. They should be friendly and be able to address customers' questions.

Physical stamina. Electricians often need to move around all day while running wire and connecting fixtures to the wire.

Physical strength. Electricians need to be strong enough to move heavy components, which may weigh up to 50 pounds.

Troubleshooting skills. Electricians find, diagnose, and repair problems. For example, if a motor stops working, they perform tests to determine the cause of its failure and then, depending on the results, fix or replace the motor.

Electricians
Median annual wages, May 2019

Electricians	$56,180
Construction trades workers	$46,340
Total, all occupations	$39,810

Note: All Occupations includes all occupations in the U.S. Economy.
Source: U.S. Bureau of Labor Statistics, Occupational Employment Statistics.

Pay

The median annual wage for electricians was $56,180 in May 2019. The median wage is the wage at which half the workers in an occupation earned more than that amount and half earned less. The lowest 10 percent earned less than $33,410, and the highest 10 percent earned more than $96,580.

In May 2019, the median annual wages for electricians in the top industries in which they worked were as follows:

Government	$62,940
Manufacturing	60,000
Electrical contractors and other wiring installation contractors	54,630
Employment services	49,140

Apprentices receive less pay than fully trained electricians, but their pay increases as they learn to do more.

Almost all electricians work full time. Work schedules may include evenings and weekends and may vary during times of inclement weather. During scheduled maintenance or on construction sites, electricians should expect to work overtime.

Self-employed electricians often work in residential construction and may be able to set their own schedule.

Job Outlook

Employment of electricians is projected to grow 8 percent from 2019 to 2029, much faster than the average for all occupations. Increases in construction spending and demand for alternative energy sources will drive demand for electricians.

Alternative power generation, such as solar and wind, is an emerging field that should require more electricians for installation. Increasingly, electricians will be needed to link these alternative power sources to homes and power grids over the coming decade. Employment growth stemming from these sources, however, will largely depend on government policy.

Electricians
Percent change in employment, projected 2019-29

Electricians	8%
Total, all occupations	4%
Construction trades workers	3%

Note: All Occupations includes all occupations in the U.S. Economy.
Source: U.S. Bureau of Labor Statistics, Employment Projections program.

Job Prospects

About 82,200 openings for electricians are projected each year, on average, over the decade.

Many of those openings are expected to result from the need to replace workers who transfer to different occupations or exit the labor force, such as to retire.

Electricians who can perform many different tasks, such as electronic systems repair, solar photovoltaic installation, and industrial component wiring, should have the best job opportunities.

Employment of electricians fluctuates with the overall economy. On the one hand, there is greater demand for electricians during peak periods of building construction and maintenance. On the other hand, workers may experience periods of unemployment when the overall level of construction and maintenance falls.

Employment projections data for electricians, 2019-29					
Occupational Title	SOC Code	Employment, 2019	Projected Employment, 2029	Change, 2019-29	
				Percent	Numeric
SOURCE: U.S. Bureau of Labor Statistics, Employment Projections program					
Electricians	47-2111	739,200	801,400	8	62,200

State & Area Data
Occupational Employment Statistics (OES)

The Occupational Employment Statistics (OES) program produces employment and wage estimates annually for over 800 occupations. These estimates are available for the nation as a whole, for individual states, and for metropolitan and nonmetropolitan areas.

Contacts for More Information

For more details about apprenticeships or other work opportunities in this trade, contact the offices of the state employment service, the state apprenticeship agency, local electrical contractors, firms that employ maintenance electricians, or local union-management electrician apprenticeship committees. Apprenticeship information is available from the U.S. Department of Labor's Apprenticeship program online or by phone at 877-872-5627. Visit apprenticeship.gov to search for apprenticeship opportunities.

For more information about apprenticeship and training programs for electricians, visit

➤ Associated Builders and Contractors, Inc.

➤ Explore the Trades
➤ Home Builders Institute
➤ IBEW – NECA Electrical Training Alliance
➤ Independent Electrical Contractors, Inc.
➤ National Association of Home Builders
➤ National Electrical Contractors Association
➤ NCCER

Elevator Installers and Repairers

Summary

Quick Facts: Elevator Installers and Repairers

2019 Median Pay	$84,990 per year $40.86 per hour
Typical Entry-Level Education	High school diploma or equivalent
Work Experience in a Related Occupation...	None
On-the-job Training	Apprenticeship
Number of Jobs, 2019	28,900
Job Outlook, 2019-29	7% (Faster than average)
Employment Change, 2019-29	1,900

What Elevator Installers and Repairers Do

Elevator installers and repairers install, maintain, and fix elevators, escalators, moving walkways, and other lifts.

Work Environment

Elevator installers and repairers often work in cramped areas inside crawl spaces and machine rooms, and they may work at heights in elevator shafts. Most elevator installers and repairers work full time. Repairers may be on call 24 hours a day or may need to work overtime.

Elevator mechanics often work in elevator machine rooms, which are at the top of some elevator hoistways.

How to Become an Elevator Installer and Repairer

Elevator installers and repairers typically need a high school diploma or equivalent. Nearly all learn how to do the work through an apprenticeship. Most states require workers to be licensed.

Pay

The median annual wage for elevator installers and repairers was $84,990 in May 2019.

Job Outlook

Employment of elevator installers and repairers is projected to grow 7 percent from 2019 to 2029, faster than the average for all occupations. New installation and maintenance of elevators and escalators in stores and residential and commercial buildings is expected to spur demand for workers.

State & Area Data

Explore resources for employment and wages by state and area for elevator installers and repairers.

What Elevator Installers and Repairers Do

Elevator installers and repairers install, maintain, and fix elevators, escalators, moving walkways, and other lifts.

Duties

Elevator installers and repairers typically do the following:

Mechanics check many parts, including the rails of an escalator.

- Read and interpret blueprints to determine the layout of system components and to select the equipment needed for installation or repair
- Assemble elevator cars and components for similar systems
- Connect electrical wiring to control panels and motors
- Test newly installed equipment to ensure that it meets specifications
- Troubleshoot malfunctions in brakes, motors, switches, and control systems
- Dismantle elevator, escalator, or similar units to remove and replace defective parts, using hoists, ladders, and handtools or power tools
- Repair or replace faulty components in order to return elevator to fully operational status
- Conduct preventive maintenance and inspections of elevators, escalators, and similar equipment to comply with safety regulations and building codes
- Keep service records of all maintenance and repair tasks

Elevator installers and repairers, also called *elevator constructors* or *elevator mechanics*, assemble, install, maintain, and replace elevators, escalators, chairlifts, moving walkways, and similar equipment.

Elevator installers and repairers usually specialize in installation, maintenance, or repair work. Maintenance and repair workers generally need to know more about electronics, hydraulics, and electricity than do installers. Most elevators and similar mechanisms have computerized control systems, requiring maintenance and repair workers to do complex troubleshooting.

After an elevator, escalator, or other equipment is installed, workers must regularly maintain and repair it. Maintenance includes oiling and greasing moving parts, replacing worn parts, and adjusting equipment for optimal performance. Workers also troubleshoot and may be called for emergency repair.

A service crew usually handles major repairs—for example, replacing cables, doors and other components, or machine bearings. Service crews may need to use cutting torches or rigging equipment and also may need to do major modernization and alteration, such as replacing electric motors, hydraulic pumps, and control panels.

Work Environment

Elevator installers and repairers held about 28,900 jobs in 2019. The largest employers of elevator installers and repairers were as follows:

Building equipment contractors	86%
Government	2
Educational services; state, local, and private	1

Elevator installation and repair work is usually physically demanding. They may sit or stand for extensive periods, lift

Elevator mechanics also work on chair lifts.

items that weigh up to 200 pounds, and work in cramped areas inside crawl spaces and machine rooms. They also may work at heights in elevator shafts, in dusty and dirty places with oily and greasy equipment, and in hot or cold environments.

Injuries and Illnesses

Elevator installers and repairers may suffer injuries from falls, burns from electrical shocks, and muscle strains from lifting and carrying heavy equipment. To reduce their risks and prevent injury, workers must wear protective equipment such as hardhats, harnesses, and safety glasses.

Work Schedules

Most elevator installers and repairers work full time. They may work overtime to make emergency repairs or to meet construction deadlines. They may be on call 24 hours a day.

How to Become an Elevator Installer and Repairer

Elevator installers and repairers typically need a high school diploma or equivalent. Nearly all learn how to do the work through an apprenticeship. Most states require workers to be licensed.

Education

A high school diploma or equivalent is typically required. High school classes in math, mechanical drawing, and physics may be helpful.

Training

A career in elevator installation and repair typically begins with a 4-year apprenticeship program sponsored by a union, industry association, or employer. For each year of a typical program, apprentices must complete a predetermined number of hours of technical instruction and paid on-the-job training. During training, apprentices learn about safety, blueprint

The fine tuning of an elevator is done by an adjustor.

reading, mathematics, applied physics, elevator and escalator parts, electrical and digital theory, and electronics.
When they finish the apprenticeship program, fully trained elevator installers and repairers become mechanics or assistant mechanics. Elevator installers and repairers need ongoing training in order to keep up with technological developments.

Workers with relevant experience who can document it and demonstrate their skill may qualify for a shorter apprenticeship.

Licenses, Certifications, and Registrations

Most states require elevator installers and repairers to be licensed. Check with your state for more information.

Although not required, certification shows competence and proficiency in the field.

Elevator installers and repairers can become Certified Elevator Technicians (CET) or Certified Accessibility and Private Residence Lift Technicians (CAT) through the National Association of Elevator Contractors. They can also be certified as Qualified Elevator Inspectors (QEI) through the National Association of Elevator Safety Authorities International.

Employers may require elevator installers to have a driver's license or reliable transportation to travel to jobsites.

Advancement

Installers may receive additional training to specialize and advance to become a mechanic-in-charge, adjuster, or supervisor.

Important Qualities

Ability to work at heights. Some elevator installers may have to work atop ladders, mechanical lifts, or in elevator shafts.

Detail oriented. Elevator installers must keep accurate records of their service schedules. They need to carefully review complex blueprints and follow blueprint instructions exactly.

Mechanical skills. Elevator installers use a variety of power tools and handtools to install and repair lifts.

Physical stamina. Elevators installers must be able to do strenuous work, including in cramped and confined spaces, for long periods.

Physical strength. Elevator installers often lift heavy equipment and parts, including escalator steps, conduit, and metal tracks. They may be required to lift equipment weighing up to 200 pounds.

Troubleshooting skills. Elevator installers must be able to diagnose problems, especially when making repairs.

Pay

The median annual wage for elevator installers and repairers was $84,990 in May 2019. The median wage is the wage at which half the workers in an occupation earned more than that amount and half earned less. The lowest 10 percent earned less than $44,620, and the highest 10 percent earned more than $124,150.

In May 2019, the median annual wages for elevator installers and repairers in the top industries in which they worked were as follows:

Government	$93,110
Building equipment contractors	84,140
Educational services; state, local, and private	74,820

The starting pay for apprentices is usually about 50 percent of what fully trained elevator installers and repairers make. They earn pay increases as they progress in their apprenticeship.

Elevator and Escalator Installers and Repairers
Median annual wages, May 2019

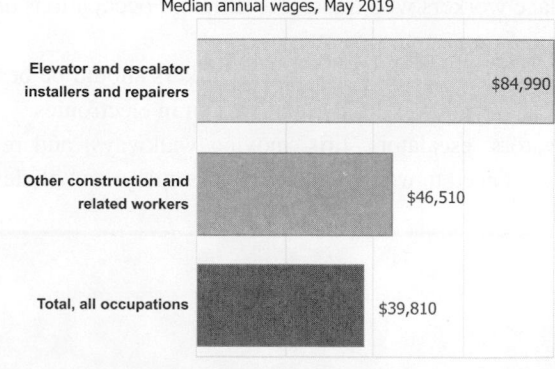

Elevator and escalator installers and repairers	$84,990
Other construction and related workers	$46,510
Total, all occupations	$39,810

Note: All Occupations includes all occupations in the U.S. Economy.
Source: U.S. Bureau of Labor Statistics, Occupational Employment Statistics.

Elevator and Escalator Installers and Repairers

Percent change in employment, projected 2019-29

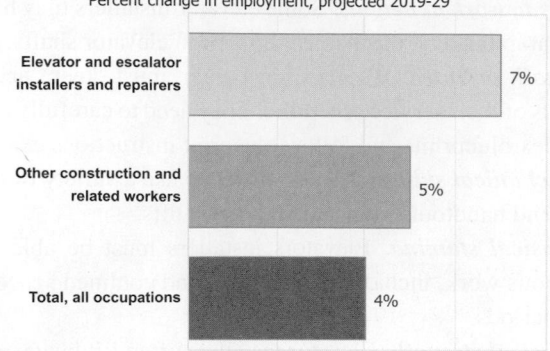

Note: All Occupations includes all occupations in the U.S. Economy.
Source: U.S. Bureau of Labor Statistics, Employment Projections program.

Apprentices who are also certified welders usually receive higher wages while welding.

Most elevator installers and repairers work full time. They may work overtime to make emergency repairs or to meet construction deadlines. Workers may be on call 24 hours a day.

Job Outlook

Employment of elevator installers and repairers is projected to grow 7 percent from 2019 to 2029, faster than the average for all occupations.

Demand for these workers is closely tied to nonresidential construction, such as office buildings and stores that have elevators and escalators, and this type of construction is expected to increase during the next decade.

In addition, the need to regularly maintain, update, and repair old equipment; provide access for the disabled; and install increasingly sophisticated equipment and controls will maintain demand for elevator installers and repairers.

Job Prospects

About 3,000 openings for elevator installers and repairers are projected each year, on average, over the decade.

Many of those openings are expected to result from the need to replace workers who transfer to different occupations or exit the labor force, such as to retire.

Job opportunities for entry-level workers should be best for those who have postsecondary education in electronics.

Elevators, escalators, lifts, moving walkways, and related equipment need to work year round, so employment of elevator

repairers is less affected by economic downturns and seasonality than employment in other construction occupations.

Employment projections data for elevator installers and repairers, 2019-29					
Occupational Title	SOC Code	Employment, 2019	Projected Employment, 2029	Change, 2019-29	
				Percent	Numeric
SOURCE: U.S. Bureau of Labor Statistics, Employment Projections program					
Elevator and escalator installers and repairers	47-4021	28,900	30,800	7	1,900

State & Area Data

Occupational Employment Statistics (OES)

The Occupational Employment Statistics (OES) program produces employment and wage estimates annually for over 800 occupations. These estimates are available for the nation as a whole, for individual states, and for metropolitan and nonmetropolitan areas.

Contacts for More Information

For information about apprenticeships or job opportunities as an elevator installer or repairer, contact local elevator contractors, a local chapter of the International Union of Elevator Constructors, a local joint union–management apprenticeship committee, or the nearest office of your state employment service or apprenticeship agency. Apprenticeship information is available from the U.S. Department of Labor's Apprenticeship program online or by phone at 877-872-5627. Visit Apprenticeship.gov to search for apprenticeship opportunities.

For more information about elevator installers and repairers, visit

➤ International Union of Elevator Constructors

➤ National Elevator Industry Educational Program

For more information about the NAEC Apprenticeship Program, the Certified Elevator Technician program, or the Certified Accessibility and Private Residence Lift Technician program, visit

➤ National Association of Elevator Contractors

For more information about certification as a Qualified Elevator Inspector, visit

➤ National Association of Elevator Safety Authorities International

For information about opportunities for military veterans, visit:

➤ Helmets to Hard Hats

Flooring Installers and Tile and Marble Setters

Summary

Quick Facts: Flooring Installers and Tile and Marble Setters

2019 Median Pay	$42,050 per year $20.22 per hour
Typical Entry-Level Education	No formal educational credential
Work Experience in a Related Occupation ...	None
On-the-job Training	See below
Number of Jobs, 2019	123,400
Job Outlook, 2019-29	3% (As fast as average)
Employment Change, 2019-29	4,100

What Flooring Installers and Tile and Marble Setters Do

Flooring installers and tile and marble setters lay and finish carpet, wood, vinyl, and tile.

Work Environment

Installing flooring, tile, and marble is physically demanding, with workers spending much of their time reaching, bending, and kneeling. In commercial settings, they may need to work evenings and weekends.

How to Become a Flooring Installer or Tile and Marble Setter

Flooring installers and tile and marble setters typically need no formal educational credential. They learn their trade on the job, sometimes starting as a helper.

Pay

The median annual wage for flooring installers and tile and marble setters was $42,050 in May 2019.

Floor sanders and finishers must remove old stain before applying the new coats.

Job Outlook

Employment of flooring installers and tile and marble setters is projected to grow 3 percent from 2019 to 2029, about as fast as the average for all occupations.

State & Area Data

Explore resources for employment and wages by state and area for flooring installers and tile and marble setters.

What Flooring Installers and Tile and Marble Setters Do

Flooring installers and tile and marble setters lay and finish carpet, wood, vinyl, and tile.

Duties

Flooring installers and tile and marble setters typically do the following:

- Remove existing flooring or wall covering
- Clean and level the surface to be covered
- Measure the area and cut flooring material to fit
- Arrange flooring according to design plans
- Place flooring and secure with adhesives, nails, or staples
- Fill joints with filler compound and remove excess compound
- Trim excess carpet or linoleum
- Apply finishes, such as sealants and stains

Flooring installers and tile and marble setters lay the materials that improve the look and feel of homes, offices, restaurants, and other buildings. Although the materials these workers install are primarily for floors, some materials also cover walls, countertops, and showers.

Installing floors and tiles requires a smooth, even base of mortar or plywood. Flooring installers and tile and marble setters or other construction craftworkers lay this base. On remodeling jobs, workers may need to remove old flooring and smooth the surface before laying the base.

Some tile and marble setters create intricate designs.

The following are examples of types of flooring installers and tile and marble setters:

Carpet installers lay carpet on new floors or over existing flooring. They use special tools, including "knee kickers" to position the carpet and power stretchers to pull the carpet snugly against walls. They also join carpet edges and seam edges by sewing or by using tape with glue and a heated carpet iron.

Carpet tile installers lay modular pieces of carpet that may be glued into place. Installing carpet tiles may be an option where standard carpet is impractical, such as in designing a pattern over an area.

Floor sanders and finishers perform the final steps in hardwood floor installation. After carpenters install the hardwood floor, workers use power sanders to smooth it. They apply stains and sealants to preserve the wood.

Floor layers, except carpet, wood, and hard tiles, install a variety of resilient flooring materials. Linoleum installers lay washable flooring material of the same name, cutting the linoleum to size and gluing it into place. *Vinyl installers* lay plastic-based flooring that includes vinyl ester, vinyl sheeting, and vinyl tile. Installers of laminate, manufactured wood, and wood tile floors are included in this category.

Tile and marble setters install modular pieces of flooring made of ceramic, marble, or other material, such as glass. *Tile installers*, sometimes called *tile setters*, cut tiles using wet saws, tile scribes, or handheld tile cutters. They then use trowels of different sizes to spread mortar or a sticky paste, called mastic, evenly on the work surface before placing the tiles. *Tile finishers* apply grout between tiles after the tiles are set by using a rubber trowel, called a float, and then wipe the tiles clean after the grout dries. *Marble setters* cut stone, such as marble, to a specified size with a wet saw. Next, they use thinset, a substance that is less thick than mortar, to fasten the stone to the tiling surface; in remodeling projects, they may first need to smooth the underlying surface after removing old flooring materials. Finally, marble setters polish the stone, using hand or power sanders.

Work Environment

Flooring installers and tile and marble setters held about 123,400 jobs in 2019. Employment in the detailed occupations that make up flooring installers and tile and marble setters was distributed as follows:

Tile and stone setters	57,000
Carpet installers	36,500
Floor layers, except carpet, wood, and hard tiles	22,900
Floor sanders and finishers	7,000

The largest employers of flooring installers and tile and marble setters were as follows:

Self-employed workers	28%
Home furnishings stores	8
Manufacturing	4
Construction of buildings	4

Installing flooring, tile, and marble is physically demanding, requiring workers to spend much of their time reaching, bending, and kneeling. Workers typically wear kneepads while kneeling; safety goggles when using grinders, saws, and sanders; and dust masks or respirator systems to prevent inhaling work-generated dust in enclosed areas with poor ventilation.

Injuries and Illnesses

Both carpet installers and floor sanders and finishers have one of the highest rates of injuries and illnesses of all occupations

Work Schedules

Most flooring installers and tile and marble setters work full time. In commercial settings, they may need to work evenings and weekends to avoid disturbing regular business operations.

How to Become a Flooring Installer or Tile and Marble Setter

Flooring installers and tile and marble setters typically need no formal educational credential. They learn their trade on the

Carpet installers spend a lot of time kneeling when stretching carpet.

Most flooring installers and tile and marble setters learn on the job working with experienced installers.

job, sometimes starting as a helper. Some learn through an apprenticeship.

Education

There are typically no formal education requirements for someone to become a flooring installer or tile and marble setter, although candidates entering an apprenticeship program may need a high school diploma or equivalent.

Certain high school courses, such as art and math, may be helpful for flooring installers and tile and marble setters.

Training

Flooring installers and tile and marble setters typically learn on the job, working with experienced installers or starting as helpers.

New workers usually do simple tasks, such as moving materials. As they gain experience, they take on more complex tasks, such as cutting carpet. Some helpers work as tile finishers before becoming tile installers.

Some flooring installers and tile and marble setters learn their trade through a 2- to 4-year apprenticeship. For each year of a typical program, apprentices must complete a predetermined number of hours of technical instruction and paid on-the-job training. Technical instruction in the apprenticeship may include mathematics, building code requirements, safety and first-aid practices, and blueprint reading. After completing an apprenticeship program, flooring installers and tile and marble setters are considered journey workers and may perform duties on their own.

Certification

Several organizations offer certification for floor and tile installers. Although certification is not required, it demonstrates that a flooring installer and tile and marble setter has a specific mastery of skills to do a job.

The Ceramic Tile Education Foundation (CTEF) offers the Certified Tile Installer (CTI) designation for workers with 2

or more years of experience as a tile installer. Applicants must pass a written test and a hands-on performance evaluation.

Several groups, including the Ceramic Tile Education Foundation, the International Masonry Institute (IMI), the International Union of Bricklayers & Allied Craftworkers (IUBAC), the National Tile Contractors Association (NTCA), the Tile Contractors' Association of America (TCAA), and the Tile Council of North America (TCNA) have created the Advanced Certifications for Tile Installers (ACT) program. To qualify for the program, applicants must have either completed a qualified apprenticeship program or earned the CTI certification. Requirements for certification include passing both an exam and a field test.

The National Wood Flooring Association (NWFA) offers optional certification for floor sanders and finishers. Sanders and finishers must have 2 years of experience and must have completed NWFA-approved training. Applicants are required to complete written and performance tests.

The International Certified Floorcovering Installers Association (CFI) offers certification for flooring and tile installers. Installers need 2 years of experience before they can take the written test and performance evaluation.

The International Standards & Training Alliance (INSTALL) offers a comprehensive flooring certification program for flooring and tile installers. INSTALL certification requires both classroom and hands-on training and covers all major types of flooring.

Important Qualities

Color vision. Flooring installers and tile and marble setters often determine small color variations and must be able to distinguish among colors in patterns for the best looking finish.

Customer-service skills. Flooring installers and tile and marble setters must be courteous with and considerate of customers, especially while completing tasks in customers' homes.

Detail oriented. Flooring installers and tile and marble setters need to be thorough and exacting to ensure that tile, wood, and carpet patterns are properly aligned.

Math skills. Flooring installers and tile and marble setters use math to measure an area to be covered and to calculate the amount of material needed to cover it.

Physical stamina. Flooring installers and tile and marble setters must be able to stand or kneel for many hours in order to spread adhesive quickly and place tiles before the adhesive hardens.

Physical strength. Flooring installers and tile and marble setters must be able to lift, carry, and set heavy pieces of flooring material into position.

Pay

The median annual wage for flooring installers and tile and marble setters was $42,050 in May 2019. The median wage

Flooring Installers and Tile and Marble Setters
Median annual wages, May 2019

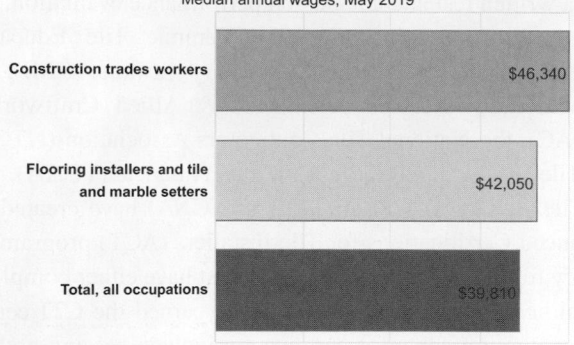

Note: All Occupations includes all occupations in the U.S. Economy.
Source: U.S. Bureau of Labor Statistics, Occupational Employment Statistics.

is the wage at which half the workers in an occupation earned more than that amount and half earned less. The lowest 10 percent earned less than $25,780, and the highest 10 percent earned more than $74,630.

Median annual wages for flooring installers and tile and marble setters in May 2019 were as follows:

Floor layers, except carpet, wood, and hard tiles...	$44,240
Tile and stone setters	43,050
Carpet installers	40,090
Floor sanders and finishers	39,610

In May 2019, the median annual wages for flooring installers and tile and marble setters in the top industries in which they worked were as follows:

Construction of buildings	$44,240
Home furnishings stores	41,050
Manufacturing	36,390

Most flooring installers and tile and marble setters work full time. In commercial settings, they may need to work evenings and weekends to avoid disturbing regular business operations.

Job Outlook

Employment of flooring installers and tile and marble setters is projected to grow 3 percent from 2019 to 2029, about as fast as the average for all occupations.

The construction of new housing units will be the primary source of flooring and tile and marble installation work over the projections decade. More flooring installers and tile and marble setters will be needed for remodeling and replacement projects in existing homes. Although carpet is still the dominant flooring, other products, including resilient flooring such as vinyl, are growing in popularity.

Tile and marble will continue to be commonly installed in bathrooms, shopping malls, and restaurants, as well as in other commercial and government buildings.

Flooring Installers and Tile and Marble Setters
Percent change in employment, projected 2019-29

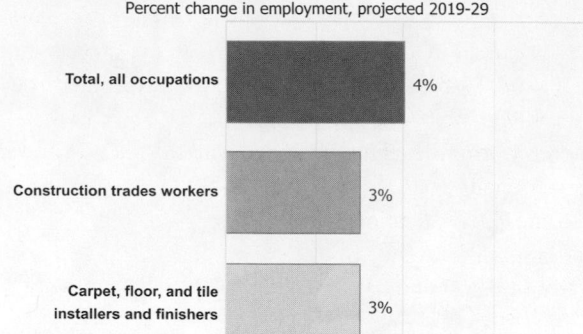

Note: All Occupations includes all occupations in the U.S. Economy.
Source: U.S. Bureau of Labor Statistics, Employment Projections program.

Job Prospects

About 10,700 openings for flooring installers and tile and marble setters are projected each year, on average, over the decade.

Many of those openings are expected to result from the need to replace workers who transfer to different occupations or exit the labor force, such as to retire.

As with many other types of construction occupations, employment of these workers is sensitive to fluctuations of the economy. On the one hand, workers may experience periods of unemployment when the overall level of construction falls. On the other hand, additional workers may be needed in some areas during peak periods of building activity.

Employment projections data for flooring installers and tile and marble setters, 2019-29					
Occupational Title	SOC Code	Employment, 2019	Projected Employment, 2029	Change, 2019-29	
				Percent	Numeric
SOURCE: U.S. Bureau of Labor Statistics, Employment Projections program					
Carpet, floor, and tile installers and finishers	47-2040	123,400	127,500	3	4,100
Carpet installers	47-2041	36,500	33,300	-9	-3,200
Floor layers, except carpet, wood, and hard tiles	47-2042	22,900	25,200	10	2,300
Floor sanders and finishers	47-2043	7,000	7,100	2	200
Tile and stone setters	47-2044	57,000	61,900	9	4,900

State & Area Data
Occupational Employment Statistics (OES)

The Occupational Employment Statistics (OES) program produces employment and wage estimates annually for over 800 occupations. These estimates are available for the nation as a whole, for individual states, and for metropolitan and nonmetropolitan areas.

Contacts for More Information

For details about apprenticeships, training, or other work opportunities in this trade, contact the offices of the state employment service, the state apprenticeship agency, local contractors or firms that employ flooring installers and tile and marble setters, or local union–management apprenticeship committees. Apprenticeship information is available from the U.S. Department of Labor's Apprenticeship program online or by phone at 877-872-5627. Visit Apprenticeship.gov to search for apprenticeship opportunities.

For more information about flooring installers and tile and marble setters, visit
➤ Ceramic Tile Education Foundation
➤ International Masonry Institute
➤ International Union of Bricklayers & Allied Craftworkers

➤ Tile Contractors' Association of America
➤ The Tile Council of North America, Inc.
➤ Home Builders Institute

For more information about training and certification of flooring installers and tile and marble setters, visit
➤ International Certified Floorcovering Installers Association
➤ Finishing Trades Institute International
➤ International Standards & Training Alliance (INSTALL)
➤ National Tile Contractors Association
➤ National Wood Flooring Association

Glaziers

Summary

Quick Facts: Glaziers

2019 Median Pay	$44,630 per year $21.46 per hour
Typical Entry-Level Education	High school diploma or equivalent
Work Experience in a Related Occupation	None
On-the-job Training	Apprenticeship
Number of Jobs, 2019	52,800
Job Outlook, 2019-29	4% (As fast as average)
Employment Change, 2019-29	2,100

What Glaziers Do
Glaziers install glass in windows, skylights, and other fixtures in buildings.

Work Environment
As in many other construction trades, the work of glaziers is physically demanding. They may experience cuts from tools and glass, falls from ladders and scaffolding, and exposure to solvents. Most work full time.

How to Become a Glazier
Glaziers typically enter the occupation with a high school diploma and learn their trade through an apprenticeship or on-the-job training.

Pay
The median annual wage for glaziers was $44,630 in May 2019.

Job Outlook
Employment of glaziers is projected to grow 4 percent from 2019 to 2029, about as fast as the average for all occupations. Job opportunities are expected from growth in the construction industry and from the need to replace glaziers who leave the occupation each year.

State & Area Data
Explore resources for employment and wages by state and area for glaziers.

What Glaziers Do
Glaziers install glass in windows, skylights, and other fixtures in buildings.

Glaziers may use specialized equipment to move windows into place.

Suction handles are used to pick up and maneuver glass.

Duties

Glaziers typically do the following:

- Follow blueprints and specifications
- Remove any existing glass before installing replacement glass
- Cut glass to the specified size and shape
- Use measuring tape, plumb lines, and levels to ensure proper fitting
- Make or install sashes and moldings for installing glass
- Fasten glass into sashes or frames with clips, moldings, or other types of fasteners
- Add weather seal or putty around pane edges to seal joints

Glaziers specialize in installing different glass products, such as insulated glass that retains warm or cool air and tempered glass that is less prone to breaking.

In homes, glaziers install or replace glass items including windows, mirrors, shower doors, and bathtub enclosures. On commercial projects, glaziers install items such as room dividers, display cases, and security windows. For either residential or commercial exterior projects, glaziers may install items such as architectural glass systems (glass used for exterior walls or other building material) or storefront windows in businesses.

For most large construction projects, glass is precut and mounted into frames at a factory or shop. The finished glass arrives at the jobsite ready for glaziers to position and secure into place. Using cranes or hoists with suction cups, workers lift large, heavy pieces of glass for installation. If the glass is not secure inside the frame, glaziers may attach steel and aluminum sashes or frames to the building and then secure the glass with clips, moldings, or other types of fasteners.

Workers who replace and repair glass in motor vehicles are described in the automotive body and glass repairers profile.

Work Environment

Glaziers held about 52,800 jobs in 2019. The largest employers of glaziers were as follows:

Foundation, structure, and building exterior contractors	69%
Building material and garden equipment and supplies dealers	14
Building finishing contractors	5
Manufacturing	5
Self-employed workers	1

As in many other construction trades, the work of glaziers is physically demanding. Glaziers spend most of the day standing, bending, or reaching, and they often must lift and maneuver heavy, cumbersome materials, such as large glass plates. Glaziers are often exposed to the weather while installing glass. They may be required to travel to different jobsites for commercial or residential work.

Injuries and Illnesses

The work of glaziers can be dangerous, and workers risk injury. Injuries may include cuts from tools and glass, falls from ladders and scaffolding, and exposure to solvents. To minimize their risk of harm, workers may wear protective gear, such as safety glasses, harnesses, and gloves.

Work Schedules

Most glaziers work full time.

How to Become a Glazier

Glaziers typically enter the occupation with a high school diploma and learn their trade through an apprenticeship or on-the-job training.

Education

Glaziers typically need a high school diploma or equivalent to enter the occupation.

Training

Glaziers typically learn their trade through a 3- or 4-year apprenticeship or on-the-job training. On the job, they learn to use the tools and equipment of the trade; handle, measure, cut, and install glass and metal framing; cut and fit moldings; and install and balance glass doors. Technical training includes learning different installation techniques, blueprint reading and sketching, general construction techniques, safety practices, and first aid.

A few groups sponsor apprenticeship programs, including several union and contractor associations. Most programs require apprentices to have a high school diploma or equivalent and be at least 18 years old. After completing an apprenticeship program, glaziers are considered to be journey workers who may do tasks on their own.

Licenses, Certifications, and Registrations

Some states may require glaziers to have a license; check with your state for more information. Licensure requirements

Glaziers may need to work at great heights.

Glaziers typically learn their trade through a 4-year apprenticeship or on-the-job training.

typically include passing a test and having a combination of education and work experience.

Glaziers may choose to get optional certification, such the Architectural Glass and Metal Technician (AGMT), to demonstrate competency and to broaden employment opportunities.

Important Qualities

Ability to work at heights. Glaziers must not be afraid to work at great heights while installing glass windows in skyscrapers or other tall buildings.

Communication skills. Glaziers need to be able to convey information to other team members and customers to ensure that the work is done correctly.

Detail oriented. Glaziers must be precise in their measurements, cuts, and modifications to avoid making costly mistakes.

Physical stamina. Glaziers are on their feet most of the day moving heavy pieces of glass. They also need to be able to hold glass in place until it can be fully secured.

Physical strength. Glaziers often must lift heavy pieces of glass for hanging.

Reading comprehension skills. Glaziers must be able to understand and follow complex blueprints and instruction manuals.

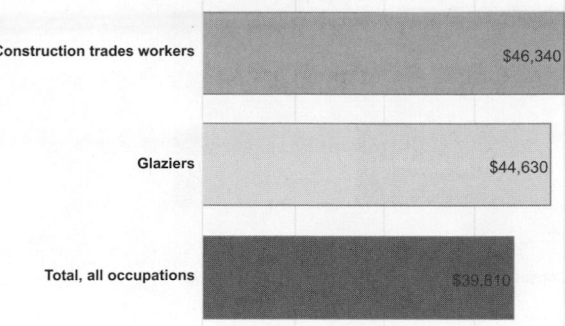

Glaziers
Median annual wages, May 2019

Construction trades workers	$46,340
Glaziers	$44,630
Total, all occupations	$39,810

Note: All Occupations includes all occupations in the U.S. Economy.
Source: U.S. Bureau of Labor Statistics, Occupational Employment Statistics.

Pay

The median annual wage for glaziers was $44,630 in May 2019. The median wage is the wage at which half the workers in an occupation earned more than that amount and half earned less. The lowest 10 percent earned less than $27,860, and the highest 10 percent earned more than $83,780.

In May 2019, the median annual wages for glaziers in the top industries in which they worked were as follows:

Foundation, structure, and building exterior contractors	$46,500
Building finishing contractors	44,030
Building material and garden equipment and supplies dealers	39,270
Manufacturing	33,540

Pay for apprentices is less than what fully trained glaziers make. Apprentices receive more pay as they gain experience. Glaziers who work at heights may be eligible for hazard pay.

Most glaziers work full time.

Job Outlook

Employment of glaziers is projected to 4 percent from 2019 to 2029, about as fast as the average for all occupations.

Demand for glaziers stems both from new construction and from the need to repair and replace windows and other glass in existing buildings. The availability of prefabricated windows that carpenters and construction laborers can install is expected to moderate the employment growth of glaziers.

Job Prospects

About 5,400 openings for glaziers are projected each year, on average, over the decade.

Many of those openings are expected to result from the need to replace workers who transfer to different occupations or exit the labor force, such as to retire.

Glaziers
Percent change in employment, projected 2019-29

Glaziers 4%

Total, all occupations 4%

Construction trades workers 3%

Note: All Occupations includes all occupations in the U.S. Economy.
Source: U.S. Bureau of Labor Statistics, Employment Projections program.

Like many other types of construction worker jobs, employment of glaziers is sensitive to the fluctuations of the economy. On the one hand, glaziers may experience periods of unemployment when the overall level of construction falls. On the other hand, shortages of workers may occur in some areas during peak periods of building activity.

Employment projections data for glaziers, 2019-29					
Occupational Title	SOC Code	Employment, 2019	Projected Employment, 2029	Change, 2019-29	
				Percent	Numeric
SOURCE: U.S. Bureau of Labor Statistics, Employment Projections program					
Glaziers	47-2121	52,800	54,800	4	2,100

State & Area Data
Occupational Employment Statistics (OES)
The Occupational Employment Statistics (OES) program produces employment and wage estimates annually for over 800 occupations. These estimates are available for the nation as a whole, for individual states, and for metropolitan and nonmetropolitan areas.

Contacts for More Information
For more details about apprenticeships or other work opportunities in this trade, contact the offices of the state employment service, the state apprenticeship agency, local contractors or firms that employ glaziers, or local union-management finishing trade apprenticeship committees. Apprenticeship information is available from the U.S. Department of Labor's Apprenticeship program online or by phone at 877-872-5627. Visit Apprenticeship.gov to search for apprenticeship opportunities.

For more information about glaziers, visit
➤ Associated Builders and Contractors, Inc.
➤ Finishing Trades Institute
➤ International Union of Painters and Allied Trades
➤ National Glass Association

For information about opportunities for military veterans, visit:
➤ Helmets to Hard Hats

Hazardous Materials Removal Workers

Summary

Quick Facts: Hazardous Materials Removal Workers

2019 Median Pay	$43,900 per year $21.11 per hour
Typical Entry-Level Education	High school diploma or equivalent
Work Experience in a Related Occupation	None
On-the-job Training	Moderate-term on-the-job training
Number of Jobs, 2019	45,300
Job Outlook, 2019-29	8% (Much faster than average)
Employment Change, 2019-29	3,700

What Hazardous Materials Removal Workers Do
Hazardous materials removal workers identify and dispose of harmful substances such as asbestos, lead, and radioactive waste.

Work Environment
Work environments for hazmat removal workers vary. Completing projects may require night and weekend work.

Overtime is common for some workers, particularly for those who respond to emergencies or disasters.

How to Become a Hazardous Materials Removal Worker
Hazmat removal workers typically need a high school diploma and are trained on the job. Workers may complete training that follows Occupational Safety and Health Administration (OSHA) standards. Some hazmat removal workers need federally or state-mandated training, licensing, or permits, depending on the type of waste remediation.

Pay
The median annual wage for hazardous materials removal workers was $43,900 in May 2019.

Job Outlook
Employment of hazmat removal workers is projected to grow 8 percent from 2019 to 2029, much faster than the average for all occupations.

State & Area Data
Explore resources for employment and wages by state and area for hazardous materials removal workers.

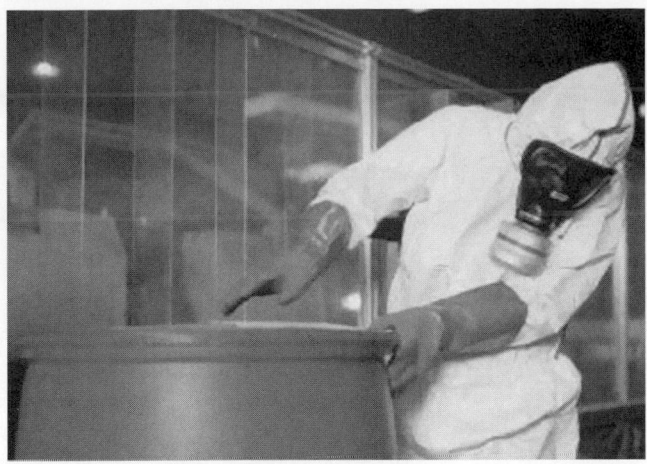

Workers dispose of hazardous materials.

What Hazardous Materials Removal Workers Do

Hazardous materials (hazmat) removal workers identify and dispose of harmful substances, such as asbestos, lead, mold, and radioactive waste. They also neutralize and clean up materials that are flammable, corrosive, or toxic.

Duties

Hazmat removal workers typically do the following:

- Follow safety procedures before, during, and after cleanup
- Comply with state and federal laws regarding waste disposal
- Test hazardous materials to determine the proper way to clean up
- Construct scaffolding or build containment areas before cleaning up
- Remove, neutralize, or clean up hazardous materials that are found or spilled
- Clean contaminated tools and equipment for reuse
- Package, transport, or store hazardous materials
- Keep records of cleanup activities

Hazmat removal workers remove, neutralize, or clean up hazardous materials.

Hazmat removal workers clean up materials that are harmful to people and the environment. They usually work in teams and follow strict instructions and guidelines. The specific duties of hazmat removal workers depend on the substances that are targeted and the location of the cleanup. For example, some workers remove and treat radioactive materials generated by nuclear facilities and power plants. They break down contaminated items such as "glove boxes," which are used to process radioactive materials, and they clean and decontaminate facilities that are closed or decommissioned (taken out of service).

Hazmat removal workers may clean up hazardous materials in response to natural or human-made disasters and accidents, such as those involving trains, trucks, or other vehicles transporting hazardous materials.

Workers dealing with radiation may also measure, record, and report radiation levels; operate high-pressure cleaning equipment for decontamination; and package radioactive materials for removal or storage.

In addition, workers may prepare and transport hazardous materials for treatment, storage, or disposal following U.S. Environmental Protection Agency (EPA) or Occupational Safety and Health Administration (OSHA) regulations. Using equipment such as forklifts, earthmoving machinery, and trucks, workers move materials from contaminated sites to incinerators, landfills, or storage facilities. They also organize and track the locations of items in these facilities.

Asbestos abatement workers and *lead abatement workers* remove asbestos and lead, respectively, from buildings and structures, particularly those being renovated or demolished. Most of this work is in older buildings that were originally built with asbestos insulation and lead-based paints—both of which are now banned.

Asbestos and lead abatement workers apply chemicals to surfaces, such as walls and ceilings, in order to soften asbestos or remove lead-based paint. Once the chemicals are applied, workers remove asbestos from the surfaces or strip the walls. They package the residue or paint chips and place them in approved bags or containers for proper disposal. Asbestos abatement workers use scrapers or vacuums to remove asbestos from buildings. Lead abatement workers operate sandblasters, high-pressure water sprayers, and other tools to remove paint.

Work Environment

Hazardous materials removal workers held about 45,300 jobs in 2019. The largest employers of hazardous materials removal workers were as follows:

Remediation and other waste management services	60%
Waste treatment and disposal	11
Construction	7

Working conditions vary with the hazardous material being removed. For example, workers removing lead or asbestos

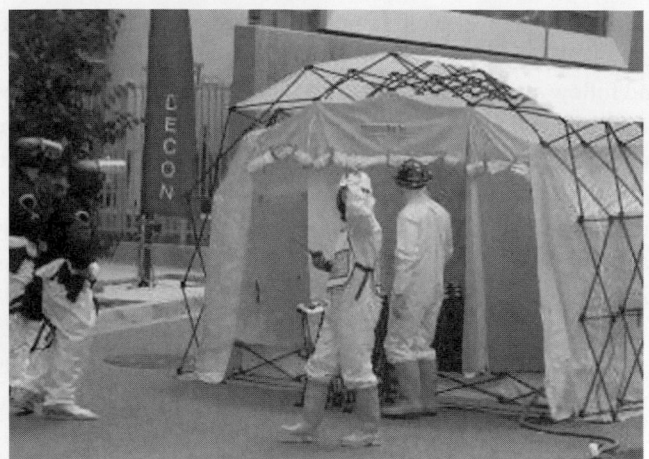

Hazmat removal workers wear protective clothing to reduce exposure to toxic materials.

Hazmat removal workers learn on the job.

often spend time in confined spaces or at great heights and must bend or stoop to remove the material. Workers responding to emergency and disaster scenarios may be outside in all types of weather.

Asbestos and lead abatement workers typically are in buildings being renovated or torn down, or in confined spaces.

Hazmat removal work may be physically demanding and strenuous.

Injuries and Illnesses

Cleaning or removing hazardous materials is dangerous, and workers must follow specific safety procedures to avoid injuries and illnesses. They usually work in teams and follow instructions from a team leader or site supervisor.

Workers wear coveralls, gloves, shoe covers, and safety glasses or goggles to reduce their exposure to harmful materials. Some must wear fully closed protective suits for several hours at a time, which may be hot and uncomfortable. For extremely toxic cleanups, hazmat removal workers also are required to wear respirators to protect themselves from airborne particles or noxious gases. Lead abatement workers wear personal air monitors that measure the amount of lead exposure.

Work Schedules

Most hazmat removal workers are employed full time. Overtime is common for some workers, especially for those who respond to emergency and disaster scenarios.

Some hazmat removal workers travel to areas affected by a disaster. During a cleanup, workers may be away from home for several days or weeks until the project is completed.

How to Become a Hazardous Materials Removal Worker

Hazardous materials (hazmat) removal workers typically need a high school diploma and are trained on the job. They must complete training that follows federal, state, and local standards.

Education

Hazmat removal workers typically need a high school diploma.

Training

Hazmat removal workers receive training on the job. Training generally includes a combination of technical instruction and fieldwork. For technical training, they learn safety procedures and the proper use of personal protective equipment. Onsite, they learn about equipment and chemicals and are supervised by an experienced worker.

The length of training and the information covered in training varies, depending on regulatory requirements and type of hazardous material that a worker is being trained to remove or reduce.

Employers may require workers to have completed OSHA Hazardous Waste Operations and Emergency Response Standard (HAZWOPER) training. The training covers health hazards, personal protective equipment, site safety, recognizing and identifying hazards, and decontamination. Refresher training may be required periodically.

To work with a specific hazardous material, workers must complete training requirements and work requirements set by state or federal agencies on handling that material.

Workers who treat asbestos or lead, the most common contaminants, must complete an employer-sponsored training program that covers technical and safety subjects outlined by OSHA.

Workers at nuclear facilities receive extensive training. In addition to completing HAZWOPER training, workers must take courses on nuclear materials and radiation safety as mandated by the U.S. Nuclear Regulatory Commission.

Organizations and companies provide training through programs that are approved by the U.S. Environmental Protection Agency.

Apprenticeships, such as Construction Craft Laborer through the Laborers' International Union of North America (LIUNA), provide training, hands-on instruction, and certification tests for hazmat workers.

Licenses, Certifications, and Registrations

Some states require workers to have permits or licenses for each type of hazardous waste they remove, particularly asbestos and lead. Workers who transport hazardous materials may need a state or federal permit.

License requirements vary by state, but candidates typically must meet the following criteria:

- Be at least 18 years old
- Complete training mandated by a state or federal agency
- Pass a written exam

To maintain licensure, workers must take continuing education courses each year. For more information, check with the state's licensing agency.

Some certifications, such as for HAZWOPER training, may be required. Others, such as Department of Transportation (DOT) hazmat transportation certification, are optional but may lead to more employment opportunities.

Work Experience in a Related Occupation

Hazmat materials removal workers typically do not need related experience to enter the occupation. However, some employers prefer candidates who have experience in the construction trades—workers such as construction laborers and helpers—or in military careers.

Advancement

Hazmat removal workers may advance to become a supervisor after gaining experience and completing additional training, such as the OSHA HAZWOPER supervisor training. Workers also may advance to different positions within their industry, such as a radiation safety technician later becoming a supervisor in the nuclear power industry. After gaining experience, workers also may choose to start their own hazmat removal business.

Important Qualities

Decision-making skills. Hazmat removal workers identify materials in a spill or leak and choose the proper method for safe cleanup.

Detail oriented. Hazmat removal workers must follow safety procedures, understand laws and regulations, and keep records of their work.

Mechanical skills. Hazmat removal workers may operate heavy equipment to clean up contaminated sites and set up machinery needed for remediation.

Physical stamina. Workers may have to stand and scrub equipment or surfaces for hours at a time to remove toxic materials.

Physical strength. Some hazmat removal workers lift and move heavy pieces of materials they are removing from a site.

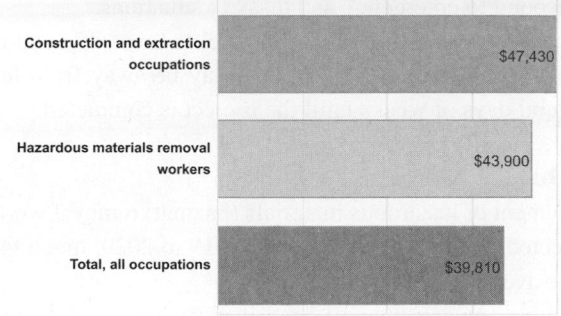

Hazardous Materials Removal Workers
Median annual wages, May 2019

Construction and extraction occupations — $47,430
Hazardous materials removal workers — $43,900
Total, all occupations — $39,810

Note: All Occupations includes all occupations in the U.S. Economy.
Source: U.S. Bureau of Labor Statistics, Occupational Employment Statistics.

Pay

The median annual wage for hazardous materials removal workers was $43,900 in May 2019. The median wage is the wage at which half the workers in an occupation earned more than that amount and half earned less. The lowest 10 percent earned less than $29,100, and the highest 10 percent earned more than $74,650.

In May 2019, the median annual wages for hazardous materials removal workers in the top industries in which they worked were as follows:

Construction	$46,190
Waste treatment and disposal	44,750
Remediation and other waste management services	43,310

Apprentices are paid less than fully trained hazmat removal workers. Apprentices receive pay increases as they advance through the apprenticeship program.

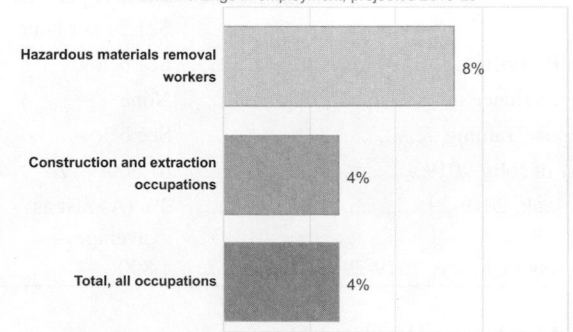

Hazardous Materials Removal Workers
Percent change in employment, projected 2019-29

Hazardous materials removal workers — 8%
Construction and extraction occupations — 4%
Total, all occupations — 4%

Note: All Occupations includes all occupations in the U.S. Economy.
Source: U.S. Bureau of Labor Statistics, Employment Projections program.

Most hazmat removal workers are employed full time. Overtime is common for some workers, especially for those who respond to emergency and disaster situations.

Some hazmat removal workers travel to areas affected by a disaster. During a cleanup, workers may be away from home for several days or weeks until the project is completed.

Job Outlook

Employment of hazardous materials (hazmat) removal workers is projected to grow 8 percent from 2019 to 2029, much faster than the average for all occupations.

Employment growth will be driven by the need to safely remove and clean up hazardous materials at sites recognized by the U.S. Environmental Protection Agency.

In addition, with nuclear plants continuing to be decommissioned in the next decade, hazmat removal workers will be needed to decontaminate equipment, store waste, and clean up these facilities for safe closure.

Job Prospects

About 5,600 openings for hazmat removal workers are projected each year, on average, over the decade.

Many of those openings are expected to result from the need to replace workers who transfer to different occupations or exit the labor force.

Because hazmat removal is often project based, downtime may occur depending on project type. For example, nuclear abatement workers may have downtime after completing a project and before they are assigned to a new nuclear abatement project.

Employment projections data for hazardous materials removal workers, 2019-29

Occupational Title	SOC Code	Employment, 2019	Projected Employment, 2029	Change, 2019-29	
				Percent	Numeric
Hazardous materials removal workers	47-4041	45,300	49,000	8	3,700

SOURCE: U.S. Bureau of Labor Statistics, Employment Projections program

State & Area Data
Occupational Employment Statistics (OES)

The Occupational Employment Statistics (OES) program produces employment and wage estimates annually for over 800 occupations. These estimates are available for the nation as a whole, for individual states, and for metropolitan and nonmetropolitan areas.

Contacts for More Information

For more information about hazardous materials removal workers in the construction industry, including information on training, visit
➤ Laborers' International Union of North America

For more information about working in the nuclear industry, visit
➤ Nuclear Energy Institute

For information about training and regulations mandated by federal agencies, visit
➤ Mine Safety and Health Administration
➤ Occupational Safety & Health Administration
➤ U.S. Department of Energy
➤ U.S. Department of Transportation
➤ U.S. Environmental Protection Agency
➤ U.S. Nuclear Regulatory Commission

Insulation Workers

Summary

Quick Facts: Insulation Workers

2019 Median Pay	$44,180 per year $21.24 per hour
Typical Entry-Level Education	See below
Work Experience in a Related Occupation	None
On-the-job Training	See below
Number of Jobs, 2019	61,300
Job Outlook, 2019-29	3% (As fast as average)
Employment Change, 2019-29	1,800

What Insulation Workers Do

Insulation workers install and replace the materials used to insulate buildings or mechanical systems.

Work Environment

Insulators generally work indoors. Mechanical insulators work both indoors and outdoors, sometimes in extreme temperatures. They spend most of their workday standing, bending, or kneeling, often in confined spaces.

How to Become an Insulation Worker

Floor, ceiling, and wall insulators typically learn their trade on the job. Mechanical insulators may complete an apprenticeship program after earning a high school diploma or equivalent.

Pay

The median annual wage for insulation workers, floor, ceiling, and wall was $40,380 in May 2019.

The median annual wage for insulation workers, mechanical was $48,690 in May 2019.

Job Outlook

Overall employment of insulation workers is projected to grow 3 percent from 2019 to 2029, about as fast as the average for all occupations. However, growth rates will vary by occupation.

State & Area Data

Explore resources for employment and wages by state and area for insulation workers.

Insulators must wear safety gear when working in confined spaces.

What Insulation Workers Do

Insulation workers, also called *insulators*, install and replace the materials used to insulate buildings or mechanical systems.

Duties

Insulators typically do the following:

- Remove and dispose of old insulation
- Review blueprints and specifications to determine the amount and type of insulation needed
- Measure and cut insulation to fit into walls and around pipes
- Secure insulation with staples, tape, or screws
- Use air compressors to spray foam insulation
- Install plastic barriers to protect insulation from moisture

Insulators install and replace the material that saves energy and helps reduce noise in buildings and around vats, vessels, boilers, steam pipes, and water pipes. Insulators also install fire-stopping materials to prevent the spread of a fire and smoke throughout a building.

Insulators often must remove old insulation when renovating buildings. In the past, asbestos—now known to cause cancer—was used extensively to insulate walls, ceilings, pipes, and industrial equipment. Because of the health risks associated with handling asbestos, hazardous materials removal workers or specially trained insulators must remove asbestos before workers begin installing new insulation.

Insulators use common handtools, such as knives, trowels, and scissors. They also may use a variety of power tools, such as welders to secure clamps, staple guns to fasten insulation to walls, and air compressors to spray insulation.

Insulators sometimes wrap a cover of aluminum, sheet metal, or plastic over the insulation. Doing so protects the insulation from contact damage and keeps moisture out.

Floor, ceiling, and wall insulators install insulation in attics, under floors, and behind walls in homes and other buildings. To fill the space between wall studs and ceiling joists, workers either unroll, cut, fit, and staple batts of insulation or spray foam insulation.

Mechanical insulators apply insulation to equipment, pipes, or ductwork in many types of buildings.

Work Environment

Insulation workers, floor, ceiling, and wall held about 34,000 jobs in 2019. The largest employers of insulation workers, floor, ceiling, and wall were as follows:

Drywall and insulation contractors	67%
Building equipment contractors	11
Nonresidential building construction	2
Foundation, structure, and building exterior contractors	1
Self-employed workers	1

Insulation workers, mechanical held about 27,300 jobs in 2019. The largest employers of insulation workers, mechanical were as follows:

Building equipment contractors	62%
Drywall and insulation contractors	18

Mechanical insulators install preformed insulation.

Mechanical insulators often work in large industrial buildings.

Insulators generally work indoors. Mechanical insulators work both indoors and outdoors, sometimes in extreme temperatures. They spend most of their workday standing, bending, or kneeling in confined spaces. Insulators may work at great heights on scaffolding, work platforms, or ladders.

Injuries and Illnesses

Common hazards for insulation workers include falls from ladders and cuts from knives. In addition, small particles from insulation materials can irritate the eyes, skin, and lungs. To protect themselves, insulators must keep the work area well-ventilated and follow product and employer safety recommendations. They also may wear personal protective equipment (PPE), including suits, masks, and respirators, to protect against hazardous fumes or materials.

Mechanical insulators may get burns from insulating pipes that are in service.

Work Schedules

Most insulators work full time, and more than 40 hours a week may be required to meet construction deadlines. Those who insulate outdoors may not be able to work in bad weather, such as during a storm or in extreme heat or cold.

How to Become an Insulation Worker

Most floor, ceiling, and wall insulators learn their trade on the job. Many mechanical insulators complete an apprenticeship program after earning a high school diploma or equivalent.

Education

There are no specific education requirements for floor, ceiling, and wall insulators. Apprenticeships for mechanical insulators typically require a high school diploma or equivalent. High

Many insulators are trained on the job.

school courses in subjects such as math, mechanical drawing, and science are helpful for all types of insulators.

Training

Most floor, ceiling, and wall insulators learn their trade on the job. New workers learn about installation and get mandatory Occupational Safety and Health Administration (OSHA) safety training on insulation handling and asbestos abatement. Beginning insulators work alongside more experienced ones to learn how to use equipment for installing spray insulation.

Many mechanical insulators learn their trade through a 4- to 5-year apprenticeship, which includes both technical instruction and paid on-the-job training.

Unions and individual contractors offer apprenticeships. Although most insulators start out by entering apprenticeships directly, others begin by working as helpers. The International Association of Heat and Frost Insulators and Allied Workers, an affiliate of the North American Building Trades Union, provides contact information on local union chapters.

Licenses, Certifications, and Registrations

Insulation workers who remove and handle asbestos must be trained through programs accredited by the U.S. Environmental Protection Agency. Some states require a license for asbestos abatement. Check with your state for more information. Mechanical insulators who complete an apprenticeship through the International Association of Heat and Frost Insulators and Allied Workers may receive this license as part of their apprenticeship.

The National Insulation Association offers a certification for mechanical insulators who conduct energy appraisals to determine if and how insulation can benefit industrial customers. Mechanical insulators also may receive certification in other job duties, such as fire stopping

Advancement

After completing an apprenticeship, mechanical insulators reach journey-level status. After becoming journey workers, mechanical insulators may advance to supervisor or superintendent positions, or they may choose to start their own business offering mechanical insulation services.

Important Qualities

Ability to work at heights. Insulators may be required to work high on ladders or scaffolds to install or remove insulation.

Dexterity. To install insulation, insulators often must reach overhead, sometimes while confined in spaces where maneuvering is difficult.

Math skills. Insulators need to measure the equipment or areas they are insulating and to calculate the amount and dimensions of insulation needed.

Mechanical skills. Insulators must be adept at using a variety of handtools and power tools to install insulation.

Physical stamina. Insulators spend much of the workday standing, kneeling, and bending in uncomfortable positions.

Physical strength. Insulators may be required to lift or carry up to 50 pounds of tools or materials.

Pay

The median annual wage for insulation workers, floor, ceiling, and wall was $40,380 in May 2019. The median wage is the wage at which half the workers in an occupation earned more than that amount and half earned less. The lowest 10 percent earned less than $25,860, and the highest 10 percent earned more than $68,860.

The median annual wage for insulation workers, mechanical was $48,690 in May 2019. The lowest 10 percent earned less than $31,880, and the highest 10 percent earned more than $89,350.

In May 2019, the median annual wages for insulation workers, floor, ceiling, and wall in the top industries in which they worked were as follows:

Nonresidential building construction	$49,340
Building equipment contractors	44,750
Drywall and insulation contractors	39,350
Foundation, structure, and building exterior contractors	35,220

In May 2019, the median annual wages for insulation workers, mechanical in the top industries in which they worked were as follows:

Other specialty trade contractors	$57,910
Building equipment contractors	47,900
Drywall and insulation contractors	47,040

The starting pay for apprentices is less than that of a fully trained insulator. Apprentices earn more pay as they acquire skills.

Most insulators work full time, and they sometimes need to work more than 40 hours a week to meet construction deadlines. Those who insulate outdoors may not be able to work in bad weather, such as during a storm or in extreme heat or cold.

Job Outlook

Overall employment of insulation workers is projected to grow 3 percent from 2019 to 2029, about as fast as the average for all occupations. However, growth rates will vary by occupation.

The need to make new and existing buildings and systems more energy efficient will drive the demand for mechanical insulation workers.

The amount of home building and retrofitting of insulation is linked to the employment of floor, ceiling, and wall insulation workers over the coming decade.

The precutting and preforming of insulation has made all insulation workers more productive, and therefore may limit the potential for employment growth in this occupation.

Job Prospects

About 6,000 openings for insulation workers are projected each year, on average, over the decade.

Many of those openings are expected to result from the need to replace workers who transfer to different occupations or exit the labor force, such as to retire.

Floor, ceiling, and wall insulators face competition for jobs because of the occupation's relatively few entry requirements.

Mechanical insulation workers who have completed training should have the best opportunities.

Insulation workers in the construction industry may experience periods of unemployment because of the short duration

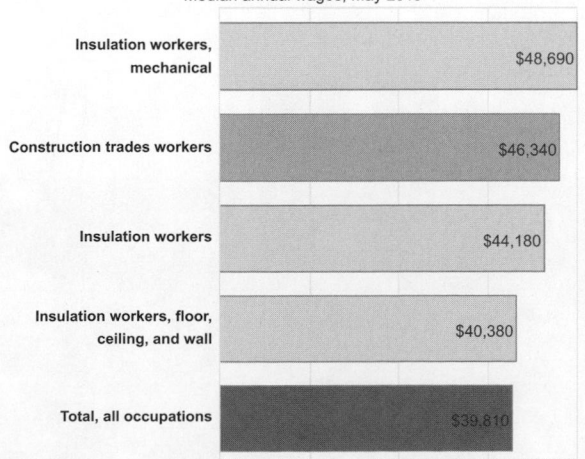

Insulation Workers

Median annual wages, May 2019

Insulation workers, mechanical	$48,690
Construction trades workers	$46,340
Insulation workers	$44,180
Insulation workers, floor, ceiling, and wall	$40,380
Total, all occupations	$39,810

Note: All Occupations includes all occupations in the U.S. Economy.
Source: U.S. Bureau of Labor Statistics, Occupational Employment Statistics.

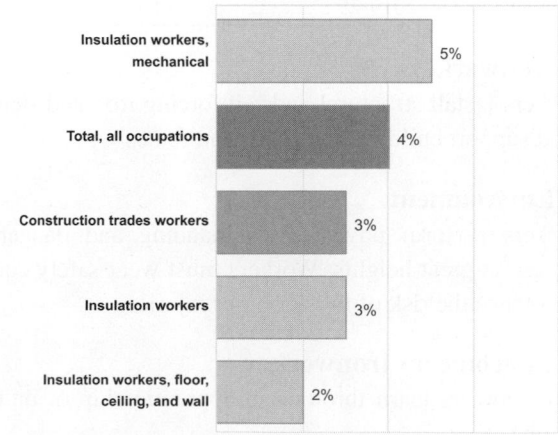

Insulation Workers

Percent change in employment, projected 2019-29

Insulation workers, mechanical	5%
Total, all occupations	4%
Construction trades workers	3%
Insulation workers	3%
Insulation workers, floor, ceiling, and wall	2%

Note: All Occupations includes all occupations in the U.S. Economy.
Source: U.S. Bureau of Labor Statistics, Employment Projections program.

of many construction projects and the cyclical nature of construction activity. Workers employed to perform industrial plant maintenance generally have more stable employment because maintenance and repair must be done regularly.

Employment projections data for insulation workers, 2019-29					
Occupational Title	SOC Code	Employment, 2019	Projected Employment, 2029	Change, 2019-29	
				Percent	Numeric
SOURCE: U.S. Bureau of Labor Statistics, Employment Projections program					
Insulation workers	47-2130	61,300	63,100	3	1,800
Insulation workers, floor, ceiling, and wall	47-2131	34,000	34,500	2	600
Insulation workers, mechanical	47-2132	27,300	28,600	5	1,200

State & Area Data
Occupational Employment Statistics (OES)
The Occupational Employment Statistics (OES) program produces employment and wage estimates annually for over 800 occupations. These estimates are available for the nation as a whole, for individual states, and for metropolitan and nonmetropolitan areas.

Contacts for More Information
For details about apprenticeships or other opportunities for insulators, contact the offices of the state employment service, the state apprenticeship agency, local insulation contractors, or firms that employ insulators. Apprenticeship information is available from the U.S. Department of Labor's Apprenticeship program online or by phone at 877-872-5627. Visit Apprenticeship.gov to search for apprenticeship opportunities.

For more information about apprenticeship or training for insulators, visit
- ➤ National Insulation Association
- ➤ NCCER
- ➤ International Association of Heat and Frost Insulators and Allied Workers
- ➤ North American Building Trades Union
- ➤ U.S. Environmental Protection Agency

Ironworkers

Summary

Quick Facts: Ironworkers

2019 Median Pay	$53,650 per year $25.79 per hour
Typical Entry-Level Education	High school diploma or equivalent
Work Experience in a Related Occupation	None
On-the-job Training	Apprenticeship
Number of Jobs, 2019	95,900
Job Outlook, 2019-29	5% (Faster than average)
Employment Change, 2019-29	4,500

What Ironworkers Do
Ironworkers install structural and reinforcing iron and steel to form and support buildings, bridges, and roads.

Work Environment
Ironworkers perform physically demanding and dangerous work, often at great heights. Workers must wear safety equipment to reduce the risk of falls or other injuries.

How to Become an Ironworker
Most ironworkers learn through an apprenticeship or on-the-job training.

Pay
The median annual wage for reinforcing iron and rebar workers was $49,100 in May 2019.

The median annual wage for structural iron and steel workers was $55,040 in May 2019.

Job Outlook
Overall employment of ironworkers is projected to grow 5 percent from 2019 to 2029, faster than the average for all occupations. The construction of large projects, such as high-rise buildings, is expected to drive employment growth, as will the need to rehabilitate, maintain, and replace an increasing number of older roads and bridges.

State & Area Data
Explore resources for employment and wages by state and area for ironworkers.

Ironworkers connect iron and steel with bolts, wire, or welds.

What Ironworkers Do

Ironworkers install structural and reinforcing iron and steel to form and support bridges, roads, and other structures.

Duties

Ironworkers typically do the following:

- Read and follow blueprints, sketches, and other instructions
- Unload and stack prefabricated iron and steel so that it can be lifted with slings
- Signal crane operators who lift and position structural and reinforcing iron and steel
- Use shears, rod-bending machines, torches, handtools, and welding equipment to cut, bend, and weld the structural and reinforcing iron and steel
- Align structural and reinforcing iron and steel vertically and horizontally, using tag lines, plumb bobs, lasers, and levels
- Connect iron and steel with bolts, wire, or welds
- Install metal decking used in building construction

Structural and reinforcing iron and steel are important components of buildings, bridges, roads, and other structures. Even though the primary metal involved in this work is steel, workers often are known as ironworkers or *erectors*. Most of the work involves erecting new structures, but some ironworkers also help in the demolition, decommissioning, and rehabilitation of older buildings and bridges.

Structural iron and steel workers erect, place, and join steel girders, columns, and other pieces to form structural frameworks. They also may assemble precut metal buildings and the cranes and derricks that move materials and equipment around the construction site. Some ironworkers install precast walls or work with wood or composite materials.

Reinforcing iron and rebar workers position and secure steel bars or mesh in concrete forms for purposes of reinforcement. Those who work with reinforcing steel (rebar) are sometimes called *rod busters*, in reference to rods of rebar.

Structural metal fabricators and fitters manufacture metal products in shops that are usually located away from construction sites.

Work Environment

Reinforcing iron and rebar workers held about 18,800 jobs in 2019. The largest employers of reinforcing iron and rebar workers were as follows:

Foundation, structure, and building exterior contractors	71%
Nonresidential building construction	8
Heavy and civil engineering construction	7
Other specialty trade contractors	5
Manufacturing	4

Structural iron and steel workers held about 77,000 jobs in 2019. The largest employers of structural iron and steel workers were as follows:

Foundation, structure, and building exterior contractors	46%
Nonresidential building construction	23
Building equipment contractors	7
Heavy and civil engineering construction	7
Manufacturing	6

Ironworkers usually work outside in many types of weather. Some work at great heights. Their tasks are physically demanding, as they spend much of their time moving and stooping to carry, bend, cut, and connect iron or steel at a steady pace so projects stay on schedule.

Injuries and Illnesses

The work of ironworkers can be dangerous. Common injuries include cuts, sprains, overexertion, and falls; from great heights, falls can be deadly. To reduce these risks, ironworkers must wear safety equipment such as harnesses, hard hats, boots, gloves, and safety glasses.

Reinforcing ironworkers install rebar to strengthen concrete walls.

Ironworkers wear safety harnesses when they work at heights.

Work Schedules

Most ironworkers work full time. They may have to travel to jobsites.

Structural ironworkers who work at great heights do not work when conditions are wet, icy, or extremely windy. Reinforcing ironworkers may be limited by precipitation.

How to Become an Ironworker

Most ironworkers learn through an apprenticeship or on-the-job training.

Education

A high school diploma or equivalent is generally required to enter an apprenticeship. Workers learning through on-the-job training may not need a high school diploma or equivalent. Courses in math, as well as training in vocational subjects such as blueprint reading and welding, are useful.

Training

Many ironworkers learn their trade through a 3- or 4-year apprenticeship. Sponsors of apprenticeship programs, nearly all of which teach both reinforcing and structural ironworking, include unions and contractor associations. For each year of the program, apprentices must have at least 144 hours of related technical instruction and 2,000 hours of paid on-the-job

Many ironworkers learn their trade through a 3- or 4-year apprenticeship.

training. Ironworkers who complete an apprenticeship program are considered journey-level workers and may perform tasks without direct supervision.

Other ironworkers receive on-the-job training that varies in length and is provided by their employer.

On the job, apprentices and trainees learn to use the tools and equipment of the trade; handle, measure, cut, and lay rebar; and construct metal frameworks. They also learn about topics such as blueprint reading and sketching, general construction techniques, safety practices, and first aid.

Licenses, Certifications, and Registrations

Certifications in welding, rigging, and crane signaling may make ironworkers more attractive to prospective employers. Several organizations provide certifications for different aspects of the work. For example, the American Welding Society offers welding certification, and several organizations offer rigging certifications, including the National Commission for the Certification of Crane Operators, and the National Center for Construction Education and Research.

Advancement

After gaining experience, ironworkers may advance to become a supervisor or a manager, a position in which they have more responsibilities and are tasked with directing other ironworkers.

Important Qualities

Ability to work at heights. Ironworkers must not be afraid to work at great heights. For example, workers connecting girders during skyscraper construction may have to walk on narrow beams that are 50 stories or higher.

Balance. Ironworkers often walk on narrow beams, so a good sense of balance is important to keep them from falling.

Critical thinking. Ironworkers need to identify problems, monitor and assess potential risks, and evaluate the best courses of action. They must use logic and reasoning when finding alternatives so that they safely accomplish their tasks

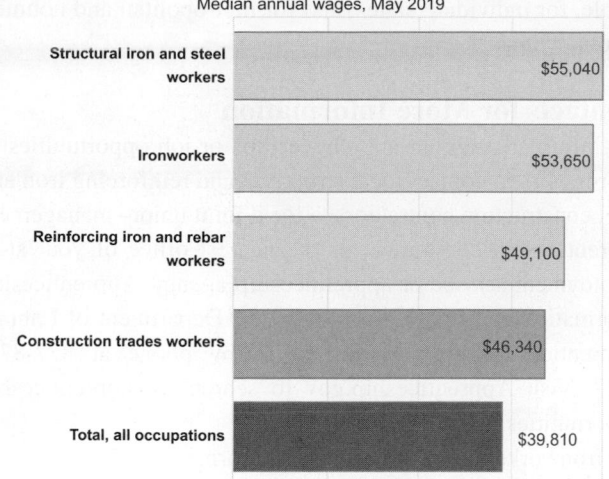

Ironworkers
Median annual wages, May 2019

Structural iron and steel workers	$55,040
Ironworkers	$53,650
Reinforcing iron and rebar workers	$49,100
Construction trades workers	$46,340
Total, all occupations	$39,810

Note: All Occupations includes all occupations in the U.S. Economy.
Source: U.S. Bureau of Labor Statistics, Occupational Employment Statistics.

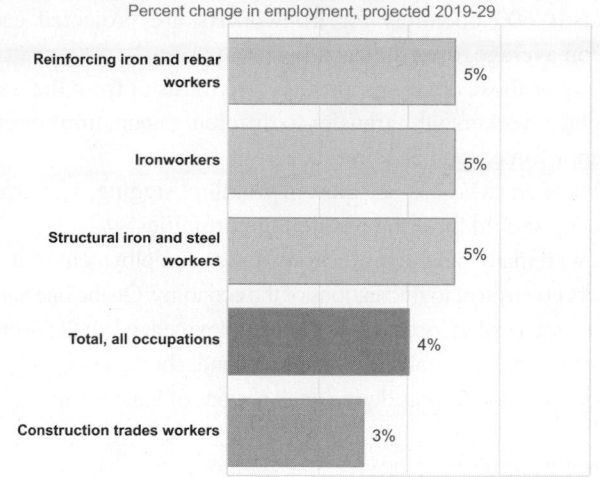

Ironworkers
Percent change in employment, projected 2019-29

Reinforcing iron and rebar workers	5%
Ironworkers	5%
Structural iron and steel workers	5%
Total, all occupations	4%
Construction trades workers	3%

Note: All Occupations includes all occupations in the U.S. Economy.
Source: U.S. Bureau of Labor Statistics, Employment Projections program.

Depth perception. Ironworkers often signal crane operators who move beams and bundles of rebar, so they must be able to judge the distance between objects.

Hand-eye coordination. Ironworkers must be able to tie rebar together quickly and precisely.

Physical stamina. Ironworkers must have physical endurance because they spend many hours each day performing physically demanding tasks, such as moving rebar.

Physical strength. Ironworkers must be strong enough to guide heavy beams into place and tighten bolts.

Pay

The median annual wage for reinforcing iron and rebar workers was $49,100 in May 2019. The median wage is the wage at which half the workers in an occupation earned more than that amount and half earned less. The lowest 10 percent earned less than $32,930, and the highest 10 percent earned more than $89,790.

The median annual wage for structural iron and steel workers was $55,040 in May 2019. The lowest 10 percent earned less than $32,790, and the highest 10 percent earned more than $95,650.

In May 2019, the median annual wages for reinforcing iron and rebar workers in the top industries in which they worked were as follows:

Heavy and civil engineering construction	$60,120
Nonresidential building construction	54,940
Manufacturing	53,180
Other specialty trade contractors	49,830

Foundation, structure, and building exterior contractors	47,550

In May 2019, the median annual wages for structural iron and steel workers in the top industries in which they worked were as follows:

Building equipment contractors	$60,560
Heavy and civil engineering construction	59,430
Foundation, structure, and building exterior contractors	56,760
Nonresidential building construction	52,610
Manufacturing	46,030

The starting pay for apprentices is usually about 50 percent of what journey-level ironworkers make. They receive pay increases as they learn to do more.

Most ironworkers work full time. Structural ironworkers who work at great heights do not work when conditions are wet, icy, or extremely windy. Reinforcing ironworkers may be limited by precipitation.

Job Outlook

Overall employment of ironworkers is projected to grow 5 percent from 2019 to 2029, faster than the average for all occupations.

Steel and reinforced concrete are an important part of commercial and industrial buildings. Future construction of these structures is expected to require ironworkers. The need to rehabilitate, maintain, or replace an increasing number of older highways and bridges is also expected to lead to some employment growth.

Job Prospects

About 10,600 openings for ironworkers are projected each year, on average, over the decade.

Many of those openings are expected to result from the need to replace workers who transfer to different occupations or exit the labor force, such as to retire.

Jobseekers who are certified in welding, rigging, and crane signaling should have the best job opportunities.

As with many other construction workers, employment of ironworkers is sensitive to fluctuations of the economy. On the one hand, workers may experience periods of unemployment when the overall level of construction falls. On the other hand, shortages of workers may occur in some areas during peak periods of building activity.

Employment projections data for ironworkers, 2019-29					
Occupational Title	SOC Code	Employment, 2019	Projected Employment, 2029	Change, 2019-29	
				Percent	Numeric
SOURCE: U.S. Bureau of Labor Statistics, Employment Projections program					
Ironworkers	—	95,900	100,400	5	4,500
Reinforcing iron and rebar workers	47-2171	18,800	19,800	5	900
Structural iron and steel workers	47-2221	77,000	80,600	5	3,600

State & Area Data

Occupational Employment Statistics (OES)

The Occupational Employment Statistics (OES) program produces employment and wage estimates annually for over 800 occupations. These estimates are available for the nation as a whole, for individual states, and for metropolitan and nonmetropolitan areas.

Contacts for More Information

For information about apprenticeships or job opportunities as an ironworker, contact local structural and reinforcing iron and steel construction contractors, a local joint union–management apprenticeship committee, or the nearest office of your state employment service or apprenticeship agency. Apprenticeship information is available from the U.S. Department of Labor's Apprenticeship program online or by phone at 877-872-5627. Visit Apprenticeship.gov to search for apprenticeship opportunities.

For ironworker and apprenticeship information, visit

➤ International Association of Bridge, Structural, Ornamental and Reinforcing Iron Workers

For more information about ironworkers, visit

➤ Associated Builders and Contractors
➤ Associated General Contractors of America
➤ National Center for Construction Education and Research

For more information about certification, visit

➤ National Commission for the Certification of Crane Operators
➤ American Welding Society

Masonry Workers

Summary

Quick Facts: Masonry Workers

2019 Median Pay	$46,500 per year $22.35 per hour
Typical Entry-Level Education	See below
Work Experience in a Related Occupation	None
On-the-job Training	See below
Number of Jobs, 2019	302,100
Job Outlook, 2019-29	-3% (Decline)
Employment Change, 2019-29	-10,000

What Masonry Workers Do

Masonry workers use bricks, concrete and concrete blocks, and natural and manmade stones to build structures.

Work Environment

Masonry work is physically demanding, requiring heavy lifting and long periods of standing, kneeling, and bending. Most masons work full time.

How to Become a Masonry Worker

Masons typically need a high school diploma or equivalent and learn the trade either through an apprenticeship or on the job.

Pay

The median annual wage for masonry workers was $46,500 in May 2019.

Masons construct walls using bricks, blocks, and stones.

Job Outlook

Employment of masonry workers is projected to decline 3 percent from 2019 to 2029.

State & Area Data

Explore resources for employment and wages by state and area for masonry workers.

What Masonry Workers Do

Masonry workers, also known as *masons,* use bricks, concrete and concrete blocks, and natural and manmade stones to build walkways, walls, and other structures.

Duties

Masons typically do the following:

- Read blueprints or drawings to calculate materials needed
- Lay out patterns, forms, or foundations according to plans
- Break or cut materials to required size
- Mix mortar or grout and spread it onto a slab or foundation
- Clean excess mortar with trowels and other handtools
- Construct masonry walls
- Align structures, using levels and plumbs
- Clean and polish surfaces with handtools or power tools

Masons clean excess mortar with trowels and other hand tools.

- Fill expansion joints with caulking materials
- Lay out and install rainscreen water systems

Masons build structures with brick, block, and stone, some of the most common and durable materials used in construction. They also use concrete—a mixture of cement, sand, gravel, and water—as the foundation for everything from patios and floors to dams and roads.

The following are examples of types of masons:

Brickmasons and *blockmasons*—often called *bricklayers*—build and repair walls, fireplaces, and other structures with brick, terra cotta, precast masonry panels, concrete block, and other masonry materials. *Pointing, cleaning, and caulking workers* are brickmasons who repair brickwork, particularly on older structures. *Refractory masons* are brickmasons who specialize in installing heat- and fire-resistant masonry materials in high-temperature areas such as boilers, furnaces, and soaking pits in industrial buildings.

Cement masonsandconcrete finishers place and finish concrete. They may color concrete surfaces, expose small stones in walls and sidewalks, or make concrete beams, columns, and panels. Throughout the process of pouring, leveling, and finishing concrete, cement masons use their knowledge of how conditions may affect concrete and take steps to prevent defects. On small jobs, such as constructing sidewalks, cement masons may use a supportive wire mesh called a lath. On large jobs, such as constructing building foundations, reinforcing iron and rebar workers install the reinforcing mesh.

Stonemasons build stone walls and set stone exteriors and floors. They work with two types of stone: natural-cut stone, such as marble, granite, and limestone; and artificial stone, made from concrete, marble chips, or other masonry materials. Using a special hammer or a diamond-blade saw, workers cut stone into various shapes and sizes. Some stonemasons specialize in setting marble, which is similar to setting large pieces of stone.

Terrazzo workers and finishers, also known as *terrazzo masons*, create decorative walkways, floors, patios, and panels. Much of the preliminary work of pouring, leveling, and finishing concrete for terrazzo is similar to that of cement masons. Terrazzo workers create decorative finishes by blending fine marble chips into the epoxy, resin, or cement, which is often colored. Once the terrazzo is thoroughly set, workers correct imperfections with a grinder. Terrazzo workers also install decorative microtoppings or polishing compounds to new or existing concrete.

Work Environment

Masonry workers held about 302,100 jobs in 2019. Employment in the detailed occupations that make up masonry workers was distributed as follows:

Cement masons and concrete finishers	200,400
Brickmasons and blockmasons	81,900

Masons typically work outdoors.

Stonemasons...	16,800
Terrazzo workers and finishers..............................	3,000

The largest employers of masonry workers were as follows:

Poured concrete foundation and structure contractors....	27%
Masonry contractors	21
Construction of buildings.................................	11
Self-employed workers......................................	10
Heavy and civil engineering construction....................	7

As with many other construction occupations, masonry work is strenuous. Masons often lift heavy materials and stand, kneel, and bend for long periods. The work may be either indoors or outdoors in areas that are dusty, dirty, or muddy. Inclement weather may affect outdoor masonry work.

Injuries and Illnesses

Brickmasons and blockmasons risk injury on the job. Cuts are common, as are injuries occurring from falls and being struck by objects. To avoid injury, workers wear protective gear such as hardhats, safety glasses, high-visibility vests, and harnesses and other apparel to prevent falls.

Work Schedules

Most masons work full time, and some work overtime to meet construction deadlines. Masons work mostly outdoors, so inclement weather may affect their schedules. Terrazzo masons may need to work hours that differ from a regular business schedule, to avoid disrupting normal operations.

How to Become a Masonry Worker

Masons typically need a high school diploma or equivalent and learn the trade either through an apprenticeship or on the job.

Education

A high school diploma or equivalent is typically required to enter the occupation.

Many technical schools offer programs in masonry. These programs operate both independently and in conjunction with apprenticeship training.

Training

Masons typically learn the trade through apprenticeships and on the job, working with experienced masons.

Several groups, including unions and contractor associations, sponsor apprenticeship programs. Apprentices learn construction basics, such as blueprint reading; mathematics for measurement; building code requirements; and safety and first-aid practices. After completing an apprenticeship program, masons are considered journey workers and are able to do tasks on their own.

The Home Builders Institute and the International Masonry Institute offer pre-apprenticeship training programs for eight construction trades, including masonry.

Work Experience in a Related Occupation

Some workers start out as construction laborers and helpers before becoming masons.

Advancement

After becoming a journey worker, masonry workers may find opportunities to advance to supervisor, superintendent, or other construction management positions. Experienced masonry workers may choose to become independent contractors. Masonry workers in a union may also find opportunities for advancement within their union.

Important Qualities

Ability to work at heights. Masonry workers often use scaffolding, so they should be comfortable working at heights.

Color vision. Masonry workers need to be able to distinguish between small variations in color when setting terrazzo patterns in order to produce the best looking finish.

Dexterity. Masonry workers must be able to place bricks, stones, and other materials with precision.

Cement masons and concrete finishers................. 44,810

Stonemasons... 43,280

In May 2019, the median annual wages for masonry workers in the top industries in which they worked were as follows:

Masonry contractors $51,100

Construction of buildings.. 49,840

Poured concrete foundation and structure   44,610
   contractors..

Heavy and civil engineering construction............... 44,590

Most masons work full time, and some work overtime to meet construction deadlines. Masons work mostly outdoors, so inclement weather may affect schedules. Terrazzo masons may need to work hours that differ from a regular business schedule, to avoid disrupting normal operations.

Job Outlook

Overall employment of masonry workers is projected to decline 3 percent from 2019 to 2029.

The employment of masons is linked to the overall demand for new building and road construction. Masonry, such as brick and stone, is still popular in both interior and exterior applications, but changes in products and installation practices are expected to decrease the need for masons. For example, fewer workers are needed to install innovations such as thin bricks, which allow buildings to have the look of brick construction at a lower cost. Additionally, the increased use of prefabricated panels will reduce the demand for most masonry workers. These panels are created offsite by either contractors or manufacturers in climate-protected environments, but fewer masons are needed to install the panels at the construction site.

Employment of terrazzo workers and finishers is expected to decline due to the increased installation of polished concrete, which will shift some work from terrazzo workers to cement masons and concrete finishers.

Apprentices learn by working with experienced masons.

Hand–eye coordination. Masonry workers need to apply smooth, even layers of mortar; set bricks; and remove any excess before the mortar hardens.

Physical stamina. Masonry workers must keep up a steady pace while setting bricks, and the constant lifting can be tiring.

Physical strength. Masonry workers should be able to lift more than 50 pounds. They carry heavy tools, equipment, and other materials, such as bags of mortar and grout.

Pay

The median annual wage for masonry workers was $46,500 in May 2019. The median wage is the wage at which half the workers in an occupation earned more than that amount and half earned less. The lowest 10 percent earned less than $30,250, and the highest 10 percent earned more than $78,250.

Median annual wages for masonry workers in May 2019 were as follows:

Brickmasons and blockmasons............................... $53,100

Terrazzo workers and finishers............................... 52,180

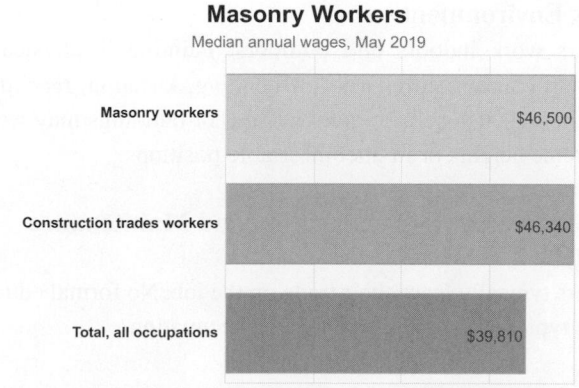

Note: All Occupations includes all occupations in the U.S. Economy.
Source: U.S. Bureau of Labor Statistics, Occupational Employment Statistics.

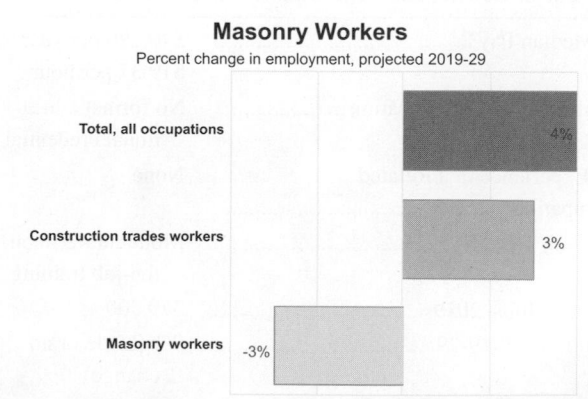

Note: All Occupations includes all occupations in the U.S. Economy.
Source: U.S. Bureau of Labor Statistics, Employment Projections program.

Job Prospects

Despite declining employment, about 24,800 openings for masonry workers are projected each year, on average, over the decade.

Those openings are expected to result from the need to replace workers who transfer to different occupations or exit the labor force, such as to retire.

Overall job prospects should be good as construction activity continues to grow to meet the demand for new buildings and roads. Workers with construction experience should have the best opportunities.

As with many other construction workers, employment of masons is sensitive to the fluctuations of the economy. On the one hand, workers may experience periods of unemployment when the overall level of construction falls. On the other hand, during peak periods of building activity some areas may require additional number of these workers.

Employment projections data for masonry workers, 2019-29					
Occupational Title	SOC Code	Employment, 2019	Projected Employment, 2029	Change, 2019-29	
				Percent	Numeric
SOURCE: U.S. Bureau of Labor Statistics, Employment Projections program					
Masonry workers	—	302,100	292,100	-3	-10,000
brickmasons and blockmasons	47-2021	81,900	76,700	-6	-5,200
Stonemasons	47-2022	16,800	16,300	-3	-500
Cement masons and concrete finishers	47-2051	200,400	196,400	-2	-3,900
Terrazzo workers and finishers	47-2053	3,000	2,700	-10	-300

State & Area Data
Occupational Employment Statistics (OES)

The Occupational Employment Statistics (OES) program produces employment and wage estimates annually for over 800 occupations. These estimates are available for the nation as a whole, for individual states, and for metropolitan and nonmetropolitan areas.

Contacts for More Information

For details about apprenticeships or other work opportunities for masonry workers, contact the offices of the state employment service, the state apprenticeship agency, local contractors or firms that employ masons, or local union–management apprenticeship committees. Apprenticeship information is available from the U.S. Department of Labor's Apprenticeship program online or by phone at 877-872-5627. Visit Apprenticeship.gov to search for apprenticeship opportunities.

For more information about training for masons, visit
➤ Associated Builders and Contractors, Inc.
➤ Bricklayers and Allied Craftworkers International Union
➤ Home Builders Institute
➤ International Masonry Institute
➤ Mason Contractors Association of America
➤ National Association of Home Builders
➤ NCCER
➤ Operative Plasterers' and Cement Masons' International Association
➤ The Associated General Contractors of America
➤ The National Terrazzo and Mosaic Association

Painters, Construction and Maintenance

Summary

Quick Facts: Construction and Maintenance Painters	
2019 Median Pay	$40,280 per year $19.37 per hour
Typical Entry-Level Education	No formal educational credential
Work Experience in a Related Occupation	None
On-the-job Training	Moderate-term on-the-job training
Number of Jobs, 2019	379,500
Job Outlook, 2019-29	0% (Little or no change)
Employment Change, 2019-29	900

What Construction and Maintenance Painters Do

Painters apply paint, stain, and coatings to walls and ceilings, buildings, large machinery and equipment, and bridges and other structures.

Work Environment

Painters work indoors and outdoors. Painting is physically demanding and requires a lot of bending, kneeling, reaching, and climbing. Those who paint bridges or buildings may work at extreme heights or in uncomfortable positions.

How to Become a Construction and Maintenance Painter

Painters typically learn their trade on the job. No formal education is typically required to enter the occupation.

Pay

The median annual wage for painters, construction and maintenance was $40,280 in May 2019.

Painters cover trim and molding before applying paint.

Job Outlook

Employment of painters is projected to show little or no change from 2019 to 2029. Openings are expected to arise from the need to replace workers who leave the occupation each year.

State & Area Data

Explore resources for employment and wages by state and area for painters, construction and maintenance .

What Construction and Maintenance Painters Do

Painters apply paint, stain, and coatings to walls and ceilings, buildings, large machinery and equipment, and bridges and other structures.

Duties

Painters typically do the following:

- Protect floors, furniture, and trim by covering surfaces with drop cloths and tarps and securing with tape
- Install scaffolding and raise ladders
- Fill holes and cracks with putty or plaster
- Prepare surfaces by removing outlet and switch covers and by scraping, wire brushing, or sanding to a smooth finish
- Calculate the size of the area to be painted and the amount of paint needed for the area
- Apply primers or sealers so the paint will stick to the surface
- Apply paint, coatings, or other finishes, using hand brushes, rollers, or sprayers

Painters apply liquid coatings and other sealers that dry into solids to add texture or color to interiors and to protect exterior surfaces from damage caused by weather, sunlight, and pollution.

For each job, painters must choose the correct tool, such as a roller, power sprayer, or brush. There are several ways to apply paint, and deciding on which tool to use typically depends on both the type of surface to be painted and the characteristics

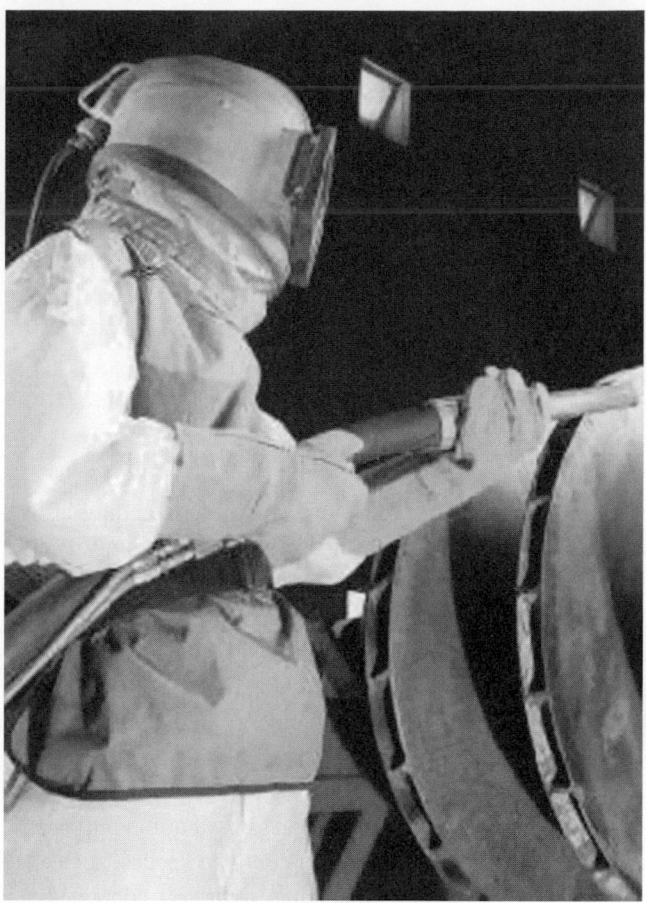

Painters sometimes wear self-contained suits for protection.

of the paint. Some employers require painters to provide their own tools

The following are types of painters:

Commercial painters prepare and paint the interiors and exteriors of offices, businesses, and other nonresidential buildings. Commercial painters may work with and be responsible for large areas due to the size of buildings involved in nonresidential projects.

Industrial painters prepare and paint large machinery, such as industrial or manufacturing equipment; vehicles, such as cars and ships; and structures, such as bridges and water towers. Industrial painters may also apply special coating materials to structure or equipment surfaces to protect them from corrosion or deterioration.

Industrial painters must contain the area in which they are working to prevent hazardous materials from contaminating the environment and exposing the public to risks. Industrial and commercial painters also must perform quality control and quality assurance to ensure that they find mistakes, meet technical specifications, and use materials appropriately.

Residential painters prepare and paint the interiors and exteriors of homes and multifamily residential buildings. Residential painters may interact with customers living in the home while painting is in progress. As a result, residential painters may need to adjust their hours or work plans to accommodate customer needs or schedules.

Work Environment

Painters, construction and maintenance held about 379,500 jobs in 2019. The largest employers of painters, construction and maintenance were as follows:

Painting and wall covering contractors	39%
Self-employed workers	38
Residential building construction	4
Government	2
Nonresidential building construction	2

Painters work on a variety of structures, including bridges, machinery, and the interiors and exteriors of buildings. Painting requires a lot of bending, kneeling, reaching, and climbing. Those who paint bridges or buildings may work at extreme heights or in uncomfortable positions; some painters are suspended by ropes or cables as they work.

Painters typically work both indoors and outdoors. When working outside or in confined spaces, painters may be exposed to extreme temperatures.

Painters may need to wear special safety equipment for a job. For example, painters working in confined spaces, such as the inside of a large storage tank, must wear self-contained suits to avoid inhaling toxic fumes. Some painters wear additional clothing and protective eyewear when operating abrasive blasters to remove old coatings. When painting bridges, ships, tall buildings, or oil rigs, painters may work from scaffolding or harnesses.

Injuries and Illnesses

Painters risk injury on the job. Common hazards include falls from ladders, muscle strains from lifting, and exposure to drywall dust and other irritants.

Work Schedules

Most painters work full time. Self-employed painters may be able to set their own schedules. Industrial painters may be required to travel for work. Painting jobs that are outdoors may be seasonal.

How to Become a Construction and Maintenance Painter

Painters typically learn their trade on the job. No formal education is typically required to enter the occupation.

Education

There are no formal education requirements to become a painter. Some technical schools offer optional certificates in painting.

Training

Painters typically learn on the job: how to prepare surfaces, apply coating, hang wall covering, and match colors. Painters may have to complete additional safety training in order to work with scaffolding and harnesses.

Although less common, painting apprenticeships lasting 3 or 4 years may be available for candidates who have a high school diploma or equivalent and who are at least 18 years old. For example, the International Union of Painters and Allied Trades, in conjunction with the Finishing Trades Institute, offers a 3-year apprenticeship for painters. For each year of a typical program, apprentices must complete a predetermined number of hours of technical training and paid on-the-job training before becoming journey workers. Apprenticeship program requirements differ based on the type of program and by region.

Although most painters learn their trade on the job or through an apprenticeship, some new workers enter training programs offered by the hiring contractor.

Licenses, Certifications, and Registrations

Those interested in industrial painting can earn several certifications from NACE International Institute or from the Society

Many painters work outdoors.

Some specialty painters may need certification.

for Protective Coatings. Courses range from 1 day to several weeks, depending on the certification program and specialty. Applicants also must meet work experience requirements.

The U.S. Environmental Protection Agency provides certification for lead paint abatement.

Some states require licensing for lead paint removal. Contact your state's licensing board for more information.

Employers may require workers to have a driver's license to commute to jobsites.

Advancement

After gaining experience, painters may advance to supervisors, superintendents, or managers, directing other painters and the jobsite. Painters may also work as estimators or start their own business.

Painters who work in a union may have advancement opportunities within the organization as a union official, training instructor, or business manager.

Important Qualities

Ability to work at heights. Painters must be able to work at heights on scaffolding, lifts, and ladders.

Communication skills. Painters interact with clients and must be able to convey information in order to ensure accuracy of color selection and application techniques. Painters must also communicate with coworkers.

Detail oriented. Painters must be precise when creating or painting edges for overall quality of appearance.

Physical stamina. Painters should be able to stay physically active for many hours and spend much of the workday standing or climbing ladders.

Physical strength. Painters must be able to lift at least 50 pounds and move heavy items during the course of a job.

Pay

The median annual wage for painters, construction and maintenance was $40,280 in May 2019. The median wage is the wage at which half the workers in an occupation earned more than that amount and half earned less. The lowest 10 percent earned less than $27,130, and the highest 10 percent earned more than $67,560.

In May 2019, the median annual wages for painters, construction and maintenance in the top industries in which they worked were as follows:

Government	$56,090
Nonresidential building construction	44,130
Residential building construction	39,780
Painting and wall covering contractors	39,150

Apprentices make less than fully trained painters, but they receive increases as they learn to do more.

Most painters work full time. Self-employed workers may be able to set their own schedule.

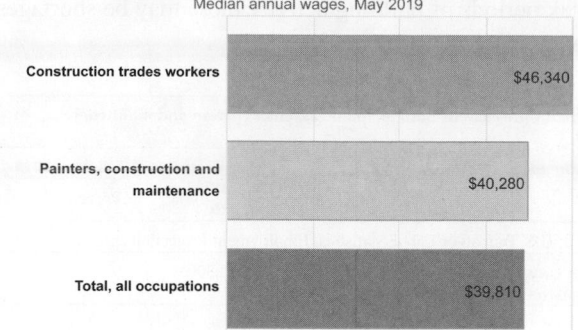

Construction and Maintenance Painters
Median annual wages, May 2019

Construction trades workers $46,340
Painters, construction and maintenance $40,280
Total, all occupations $39,810

Note: All Occupations includes all occupations in the U.S. Economy.
Source: U.S. Bureau of Labor Statistics, Occupational Employment Statistics.

Job Outlook

Employment of painters is projected to show little or no change from 2019 to 2029.

The expected increase in new construction activity will continue to create a need for painters. Investors who sell or lease properties also will require painters' services. However, many homeowners choose to paint themselves, which will temper employment growth for painters.

Job Prospects

About 32,300 openings for painters are projected each year, on average, over the decade.

Most of those openings are expected to result from the need to replace workers who transfer to different occupations or exit the labor force, such as to retire.

Because there are no formal education requirements for entry into this occupation, many people work as painters for a relatively short time and then move on to other occupations that have higher pay or better working conditions.

Employment of painters, like that of many other construction workers, is sensitive to fluctuations in the economy. On the one hand, painters may experience periods of unemployment when

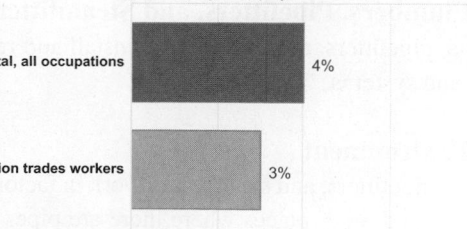

Construction and Maintenance Painters
Percent change in employment, projected 2019-29

Total, all occupations   4%
Construction trades workers   3%
Painters, construction and maintenance   0%

Note: All Occupations includes all occupations in the U.S. Economy.
Source: U.S. Bureau of Labor Statistics, Employment Projections program.

the overall level of construction falls. On the other hand, during peak periods of building activity there may be shortages of painters.

Employment projections data for painters, construction and maintenance , 2019-29					
Occupational Title	SOC Code	Employment, 2019	Projected Employment, 2029	Change, 2019-29	
				Percent	Numeric
SOURCE: U.S. Bureau of Labor Statistics, Employment Projections program					
Painters, construction and maintenance	47-2141	379,500	380,300	0	900

State & Area Data
Occupational Employment Statistics (OES)
The Occupational Employment Statistics (OES) program produces employment and wage estimates annually for over 800 occupations. These estimates are available for the nation as a whole, for individual states, and for metropolitan and nonmetropolitan areas.

Contacts for More Information
Apprenticeship information is available from the U.S. Department of Labor's Apprenticeship program online or by phone at 877-872-5627. For details about apprenticeships or other work opportunities for painters, contact the offices of the state employment service, the state apprenticeship agency, local contractors, or firms that employ painters. Visit Apprenticeship.gov to search for apprenticeship opportunities.

For more information about painters and training opportunities, visit
➤ Associated Builders and Contractors
➤ International Union of Painters and Allied Trades
➤ Home Builders Institute
➤ NCCER
➤ Painting and Decorating Contractors of America

For more information about pre-apprenticeship training, visit
➤ Home Builders Institute

For more information about the work of industrial painters and about opportunities for training and certification as a protective coating specialist, visit
➤ NACE International Institute
➤ Society of Protective Coatings

For information about opportunities for military veterans, visit:
➤ Helmets to Hard Hats

Plumbers, Pipefitters, and Steamfitters

Summary

Quick Facts: Plumbers, Pipefitters, and Steamfitters	
2019 Median Pay	$55,160 per year $26.52 per hour
Typical Entry-Level Education	High school diploma or equivalent
Work Experience in a Related Occupation	None
On-the-job Training	Apprenticeship
Number of Jobs, 2019	490,200
Job Outlook, 2019-29	4% (As fast as average)
Employment Change, 2019-29	20,900

What Plumbers, Pipefitters, and Steamfitters Do
Plumbers, pipefitters, and steamfitters install and repair piping fixtures and systems.

Work Environment
Plumbers, pipefitters, and steamfitters work in factories, homes, businesses, and other places where there are pipes and related systems. Plumbers are often on call for emergencies, so evening and weekend work is common.

How to Become a Plumber, Pipefitter, or Steamfitter
Most plumbers, pipefitters, and steamfitters learn on the job through an apprenticeship. Some attend a vocational-technical school before receiving on-the-job training. Most states require plumbers to be licensed.

Pay
The median annual wage for plumbers, pipefitters, and steamfitters was $55,160 in May 2019.

Job Outlook
Employment of plumbers, pipefitters, and steamfitters is projected to grow 4 percent from 2019 to 2029, about as fast as the average for all occupations. Building construction, maintenance, and repair should drive demand for these workers, and overall job opportunities are expected to be good.

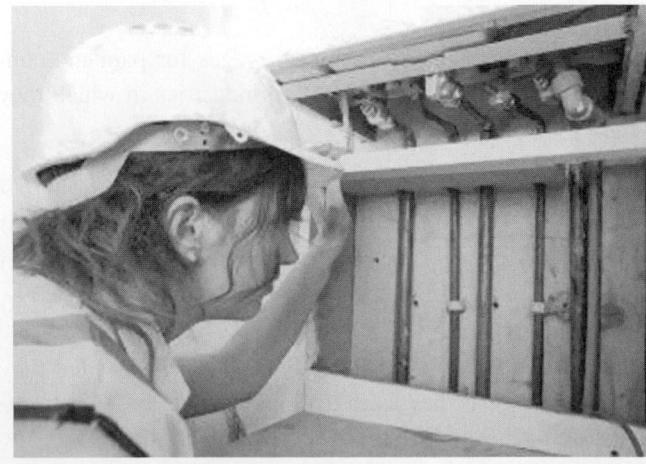

Plumbers inspect pipes for damage.

State & Area Data

Explore resources for employment and wages by state and area for plumbers, pipefitters, and steamfitters.

What Plumbers, Pipefitters, and Steamfitters Do

Plumbers, pipefitters, and steamfitters install and repair piping fixtures and systems.

Duties

Plumbers, pipefitters, and steamfitters typically do the following:

- Prepare cost estimates for clients
- Read blueprints and follow state and local building codes
- Determine the materials and equipment needed for a job
- Install pipes and fixtures
- Inspect and test installed pipe systems and pipelines
- Troubleshoot malfunctioning systems
- Maintain and repair plumbing sysems

Although plumbers, pipefitters, and steamfitters have distinct responsibilities, they often have similar duties. For example, they all install pipes and fittings that carry water, gas, and other fluids and substances. They determine the necessary materials for a job, connect pipes, and test pressure to ensure that a

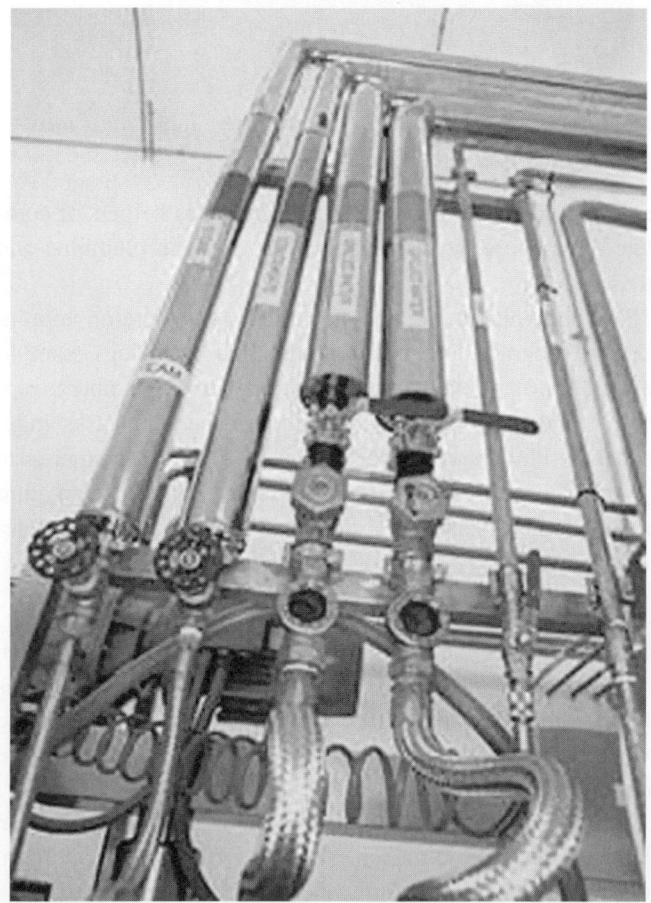

Pipefitters install a variety of pipes to move liquids and gasses.

pipe system is airtight and watertight. Their tools include drills, saws, welding torches, press fitting tools, and drain cleaning tools.

Plumbers, pipefitters, and steamfitters may use different materials and construction techniques, depending on the project. For example, residential water systems use copper, steel, and plastic pipe that one or two plumbers install. Industrial plant water systems, in contrast, are made of large steel pipes that usually take a crew of pipefitters to install.

Journey- and master-level plumbers, pipefitters, and steamfitters frequently direct apprentices and helpers.

Master plumbers on construction jobs may help develop blueprints that show the placement of pipes and fixtures. Their input ensures that a structure's plumbing meets building codes, stays within budget, and works well with the location of other features, such as electric wires. Many diagrams are created digitally with Building Information Modeling (BIM), which allows workers in several occupations to collaborate in planning a building's physical systems.

Some of the specific tasks performed by these workers are as follows:

Plumbers install and repair water, gas, and other piping systems in homes, businesses, and factories. They install plumbing fixtures, such as bathtubs and toilets, and appliances, such as dishwashers and water heaters. They clean drains, remove obstructions, and repair or replace broken pipes and fixtures. Plumbers also help maintain septic systems—large, underground holding tanks that collect waste from houses that are not connected to a sewer system.

Pipefitters and steamfitters, sometimes simply called *fitters*, install and maintain pipes that may carry chemicals, acids, and gases. These pipes are mostly in manufacturing, commercial, and industrial settings. Fitters install and repair pipe systems in power plants, as well as heating and cooling systems in large office buildings. *Steamfitters* specialize in systems that are designed for the flow of liquids or gases at high pressure. Other fitters may specialize as gasfitters or sprinklerfitters.

Work Environment

Plumbers, pipefitters, and steamfitters held about 490,200 jobs in 2019. The largest employers of plumbers, pipefitters, and steamfitters were as follows:

Plumbing, heating, and air-conditioning contractors ...	65%
Self-employed workers	8
Heavy and civil engineering construction	4
Manufacturing	4
Government	3

Plumbers, pipefitters, and steamfitters work in factories, homes, businesses, and other places where there are pipes and related systems. Plumbers and fitters lift heavy materials, climb ladders, and work in tight spaces. Some plumbers travel

Plumbers risk getting burned as they solder pipes.

to worksites every day. Outdoor work, in all types of weather, may be required.

Injuries and Illnesses
Plumbers, pipefitters, and steamfitters sometimes get injured on the job. Common injuries include cuts from sharp tools, burns from hot pipes and soldering equipment, and falls from ladders.

Work Schedules
Most plumbers, pipefitters, and steamfitters work full time, including nights and weekends. They are often on call to handle emergencies. Self-employed plumbers may be able to set their own schedules.

How to Become a Plumber, Pipefitter, or Steamfitter
Most plumbers, pipefitters, and steamfitters learn on the job through an apprenticeship. Some also attend vocational-technical school. Most states and some localities require plumbers to be licensed.

Education
A high school diploma or equivalent is typically required to become a plumber, pipefitter, or steamfitter. Vocational-technical schools offer courses in pipe system design, safety, and tool use. They also offer welding courses that are required by some pipefitter and steamfitter apprenticeship training programs.

Training
Most plumbers, pipefitters, and steamfitters learn their trade through a 4- or 5-year apprenticeship. Apprentices typically receive 2,000 hours of paid on-the-job training, as well as some technical instruction, each year. Technical instruction includes safety, local plumbing codes and regulations, and blueprint reading. Apprentices also study mathematics, applied physics, and chemistry. Apprenticeship programs are sponsored by unions, trade associations, and businesses. Most apprentices

Most plumbers, pipefitters, and steamfitters learn their jobs through an apprenticeship.

enter a program directly, but some start out as helpers or complete a pre-apprenticeship training programs in plumbing and other trades.

Plumbers, pipefitters, and steamfitters complete an apprenticeship program and pass the required licensing exam to become journey-level workers. Journey-level plumbers, pipefitters, and steamfitters are qualified to perform tasks independently. Plumbers with several years of plumbing experience who pass another exam earn master status. Some states require master plumber status in order to obtain a plumbing contractor's license.

Licenses, Certifications, and Registrations
Most states and some localities require plumbers to be licensed. Although licensing requirements vary, states and localities often require workers to have 2 to 5 years of experience and to pass an exam that shows their knowledge of the trade before allowing plumbers to work independently.

Plumbers may also obtain optional certification, such as in plumbing design, to broaden career opportunities. In addition, most employers require plumbers to have a driver's license.

Some states require pipefitters and steamfitters to be licensed; they may also require a special license to work on gas lines.

Licensing typically requires an exam or work experience or both. Contact your state's licensing board for more information.

Advancement

After completing an apprenticeship and becoming licensed at the journey level, plumbers may advance to become a master plumber, supervisor, or project manager. Some plumbers choose to start their own business as an independent contractor, which may require additional licensing.

Important Qualities

Communication skills. Plumbers must be able to direct workers, bid on jobs, and plan work schedules. Plumbers also talk to customers regularly.

Dexterity. Plumbers must be able to maneuver parts and tools precisely, often in tight spaces.

Mechanical skills. Plumbers, pipefitters, and steamfitters choose from a variety of tools to assemble, maintain, and repair pipe systems.

Physical strength. Plumbers, pipefitters, and steamfitters must be able to lift and move heavy tools and materials.

Troubleshooting skills. Plumbers, pipefitters, and steamfitters find, diagnose, and repair problems. They also help with setting up and testing new plumbing and piping systems.

Pay

The median annual wage for plumbers, pipefitters, and steamfitters was $55,160 in May 2019. The median wage is the wage at which half the workers in an occupation earned more than that amount and half earned less. The lowest 10 percent earned less than $32,690, and the highest 10 percent earned more than $97,170.

In May 2019, the median annual wages for plumbers, pipefitters, and steamfitters in the top industries in which they worked were as follows:

Manufacturing	$57,150
Government	56,790
Plumbing, heating, and air-conditioning contractors	54,760
Heavy and civil engineering construction	52,820

Apprentices earn less than fully trained plumbers, pipefitters, and steamfitters. However, their pay increases as they learn to do more.

Most plumbers, pipefitters, and steamfitters work full time, including nights and weekends. Plumbers are often on call to handle emergencies. Self-employed plumbers may be able to set their own schedules.

Job Outlook

Employment of plumbers, pipefitters, and steamfitters is projected to grow 4 percent from 2019 to 2029, about as fast as the average for all occupations.

Most demand for plumbers will stem from new construction and the need to maintain and repair plumbing systems in existing residences and other buildings. Employment of sprinklerfitters is expected to increase as states continue to adopt changes to building codes that require the use of fire suppression systems.

Job Prospects

About 49,800 openings for plumbers, pipefitters, and steamfitters are projected each year, on average, over the decade.

Many of those openings are expected to result from the need to replace workers who transfer to different occupations or exit the labor force, such as to retire.

Workers with knowledge of Building Information Modeling (BIM) software should have the best opportunities.

As with other construction workers, employment of plumbers, pipefitters, and steamfitters is sensitive to fluctuations in the economy. On the one hand, workers may experience periods of unemployment when the overall level of construction falls. On the other hand, shortages of workers may occur in some areas during peak periods of building activity.

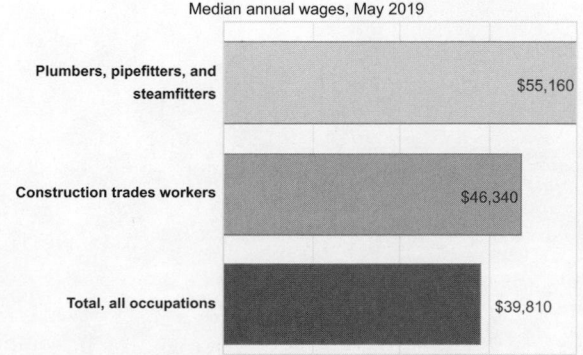

Plumbers, Pipefitters, and Steamfitters
Median annual wages, May 2019

Plumbers, pipefitters, and steamfitters: $55,160
Construction trades workers: $46,340
Total, all occupations: $39,810

Note: All Occupations includes all occupations in the U.S. Economy.
Source: U.S. Bureau of Labor Statistics, Occupational Employment Statistics.

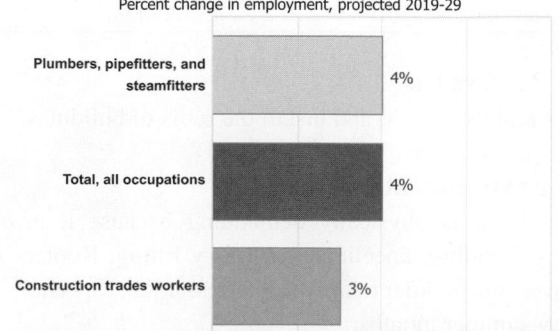

Plumbers, Pipefitters, and Steamfitters
Percent change in employment, projected 2019-29

Plumbers, pipefitters, and steamfitters: 4%
Total, all occupations: 4%
Construction trades workers: 3%

Note: All Occupations includes all occupations in the U.S. Economy.
Source: U.S. Bureau of Labor Statistics, Employment Projections program.

However, maintenance and repair of plumbing and pipe systems must continue even during economic downturns, so plumbers and fitters outside of construction often have more stable employment.

Employment projections data for plumbers, pipefitters, and steamfitters, 2019-29					
Occupational Title	SOC Code	Employment, 2019	Projected Employment, 2029	Change, 2019-29	
				Percent	Numeric
SOURCE: U.S. Bureau of Labor Statistics, Employment Projections program					
Plumbers, pipefitters, and steamfitters	47-2152	490,200	511,100	4	20,900

State & Area Data
Occupational Employment Statistics (OES)
The Occupational Employment Statistics (OES) program produces employment and wage estimates annually for over 800 occupations. These estimates are available for the nation as a whole, for individual states, and for metropolitan and nonmetropolitan areas.

Contacts for More Information
For more information about plumbers, pipefitters, and steamfitters, including apprenticeship opportunities, visit

- Mechanical Contractors Association of America
- NCCER
- Plumbing-Heating-Cooling Contractors Association
- American Fire Sprinkler Association
- National Fire Sprinkler Association
- United Association: Union of Plumbers, Fitters, Welders, and Service Techs

For apprenticeship information from the U.S. Department of Labor, visit the Apprenticeship program online or call 877-872-5627. To search for opportunities, visit apprenticeship.gov.

For more information about apprenticeship or other opportunities, contact the offices of the state employment service; the state apprenticeship agency; local plumbing, heating, and cooling contractors or firms that employ fitters; or local union–management apprenticeship committees.

For more information about pre-apprenticeship training, visit
- Home Builders Institute
- Plumbing Heating Cooling Contractors Association
- National Building Trades Union

Roofers

Summary

Quick Facts: Roofers

2019 Median Pay	$42,100 per year $20.24 per hour
Typical Entry-Level Education	No formal educational credential
Work Experience in a Related Occupation ..	None
On-the-job Training	Moderate-term on-the-job training
Number of Jobs, 2019	161,600
Job Outlook, 2019-29	2% (Slower than average)
Employment Change, 2019-29	3,800

What Roofers Do
Roofers replace, repair, and install the roofs of buildings.

Work Environment
Roofing work is physically demanding because it involves climbing, bending, kneeling, and heavy lifting. Roofers may work overtime in order to finish a particular job, especially during busy summer months.

How to Become a Roofer
There are typically no formal education requirements for roofers. Although most roofers learn on the job, some enter the occupation through an apprenticeship.

Pay
The median annual wage for roofers was $42,100 in May 2019.

Job Outlook
Employment of roofers is projected to grow 2 percent from 2019 to 2029, slower than the average for all occupations. In addition, openings are projected to arise from the need to replace workers who retire or leave the occupation for other reasons.

State & Area Data
Explore resources for employment and wages by state and area for roofers.

Roofers use a variety of tools when working on roofs depending on the type of roof being installed.

What Roofers Do

Roofers replace, repair, and install the roofs of buildings, using a variety of materials, including shingles, bitumen, and metal.

Duties

Roofers typically do the following:

- Inspect problem roofs to determine the best way to repair them
- Measure roofs to calculate the quantities of materials needed
- Replace damaged or rotting joists or plywood
- Remove existing roof systems
- Install vapor barriers or layers of insulation
- Install roof ventilation
- Install shingles, asphalt, metal, or other materials to make the roof weatherproof
- Align roofing materials with edges of the roof
- Cut roofing materials to fit around walls or vents
- Cover exposed nail or screw heads with roofing cement or caulk to prevent leakage

Properly installing and repairing roofs keeps water from leaking into buildings and damaging the interior, including equipment and furnishings. Roofers install or repair two basic types of roofs: low slope and steep slope.

Roofers install shingles, asphalt, metal, or other materials to make the roof weatherproof.

Low-slope roofs are the most common, as they are typical on commercial, industrial, and apartment buildings. The complexity of installing low-slope roofs varies with the type of building. Roofers may install these roofs in layers, building up piles of felt set in hot bitumen over insulation boards to form a waterproof membrane. They also may install a single-ply membrane of waterproof rubber or thermoplastic compound over roof insulation boards.

Steep-slope roofs are typical on single-family homes. Roofers commonly install asphalt shingles, although they may also lay tile, solar shingles, metal shingles, slate, or shakes (rough wooden shingles) on steep-slope roofs.

Roofers also install green technology rooftop applications. These include vegetative roofs, rainwater harvesting systems, and photovoltaic products, such as solar shingles and solar tiles; however, solar photovoltaic (PV) installers typically install PV panels. Plumbers and heating, air conditioning, and refrigeration mechanics also may install solar thermal systems.

Roofers use a variety of tools when installing or repairing roofs. Their tools include roofing shovels, roof cutters, and pry bars to remove old roofing systems and hammers, nail guns, and framing squares to install new ones.

Work Environment

Roofers held about 161,600 jobs in 2019. The largest employers of roofers were as follows:

Roofing contractors	73%
Self-employed workers	19
Construction of buildings	3

Roofing work is physically demanding because it involves climbing, bending, kneeling, and heavy lifting. Roofers work outdoors in extreme temperatures, but they usually do not work during inclement weather.

Although some roofers work alone, many work as part of a crew.

Injuries and Illnesses

Roofers have one of the highest rates of injuries and illnesses of all occupations, as well as one of the highest rates of occupational fatalities.

Workers may slip or fall from scaffolds, ladders, or roofs. They may also be burned by hot bitumen. Roofs can become extremely hot during the summer, causing heat-related illnesses. Roofers must wear proper safety equipment to reduce the risk of injuries.

Work Schedules

Most roofers work full time. In northern states, roofing work may be limited during the winter months. During the busy summer months, roofers may work overtime to complete jobs.

Roofing work can be physically demanding since it involves heavy lifting, climbing, bending, and kneeling.

How to Become a Roofer

There are no specific education requirements for roofers. Although most learn on the job, some roofers enter the occupation through an apprenticeship.

Education

No formal educational credential is typically required for roofers.

Training

Roofers typically receive on-the-job training to become competent in the occupation. In most on-the-job training programs, experienced roofers teach new workers how to use roofing tools, equipment, machines, and materials. Trainees begin with tasks such as carrying equipment and material and erecting scaffolds and hoists. Within a few months, they learn to measure, cut, and fit roofing materials. Later, they lay asphalt or fiberglass shingles. Because some roofing materials, such as solar tiles, are used infrequently, it may take several years to gain experience for all types of roofing.

A few groups, including the United Union of Roofers, Waterproofers & Allied Workers and some contractor associations, sponsor apprenticeship programs for roofers. Apprenticeships

combine on-the-job training with technical instruction, usually requiring a predetermined number of hours for both.

Licenses, Certifications, and Registrations

Roofers may obtain specific certification to qualify for additional work opportunities or greater pay.

The National Roofing Contractors Association offers certification for experienced roofers. Experienced roofers may become certified in various roofing systems, such as thermoplastic systems or asphalt shingles. Certification as a roofing foreman is also available for experienced roofers.

Most employers require that roofers complete safety certification that meets Occupational Safety and Health Administration (OSHA) guidelines, either before or after being hired.

Some employers require roofers to have a driver's license to enable commuting to different jobsites.

Advancement

After gaining experience in the occupation, roofers may have opportunities to advance to become a supervisor, job superintendent, or estimator or to start their own business. Roofers working in a union may advance within their local union to become a business manager or apprenticeship instructor or to other positions of union leadership.

Important Qualities

Ability to work at heights. Roofers must be comfortable working at great heights.

Attention to detail. Roofing materials must be installed to precisely match design patterns and to ensure that the roof is waterproof.

Balance. Roofers should have excellent balance to avoid falling, because they often work on steep slopes at great heights.

Manual dexterity. Roofers need to be precise in handling and installing roofing materials in order to prevent damage to the roof and building.

Most roofers learn their trade on the job working with experienced coworkers.

Math skills. Roofers use math to measure and calculate roofing areas.

Physical stamina. Roofers must be able to endure spending hours on their feet or bending and stooping, often in hot weather.

Physical strength. Roofers often lift and carry heavy materials, such as bundles of shingles that weigh 60 pounds or more.

Pay

The median annual wage for roofers was $42,100 in May 2019. The median wage is the wage at which half the workers in an occupation earned more than that amount and half earned less. The lowest 10 percent earned less than $26,540, and the highest 10 percent earned more than $70,920.

In May 2019, the median annual wages for roofers in the top industries in which they worked were as follows:

Roofing contractors	$42,320
Construction of buildings	39,160

Most roofers work full time. In northern states, roofing work may be limited during the winter months. During the busy summer months, roofers may work overtime to complete jobs.

The starting pay for apprentices is usually 50 percent of what journey workers receive. Apprentices get pay increases as they advance through the apprenticeship program.

Job Outlook

Employment of roofers is projected to grow 2 percent from 2019 to 2029, slower than the average for all occupations. Replacement and repair of roofs, as well as the installation of new roofs, will create demand for roofers.

Roofs deteriorate more quickly than most other parts of buildings, and as a result, they need to be replaced or repaired more often. Demand for roofers will be driven by the need to repair and replace roofs on existing buildings. In addition to replacement and repair work, the need to install roofs on new

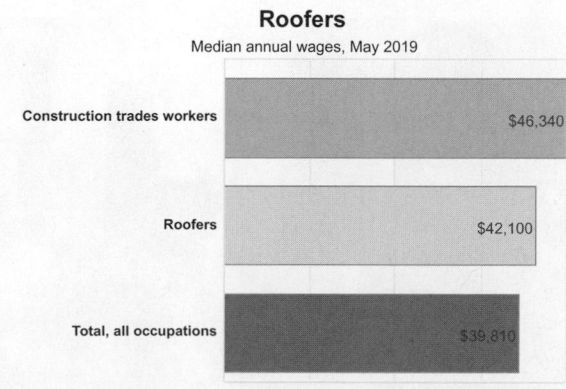

Roofers
Median annual wages, May 2019

- Construction trades workers $46,340
- Roofers $42,100
- Total, all occupations $39,810

Note: All Occupations includes all occupations in the U.S. Economy.
Source: U.S. Bureau of Labor Statistics, Occupational Employment Statistics.

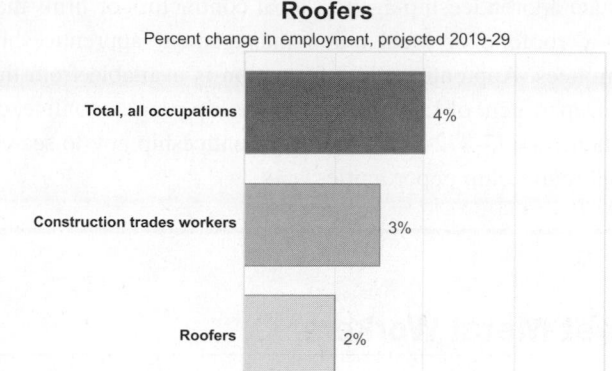

Roofers
Percent change in employment, projected 2019-29

- Total, all occupations 4%
- Construction trades workers 3%
- Roofers 2%

Note: All Occupations includes all occupations in the U.S. Economy.
Source: U.S. Bureau of Labor Statistics, Employment Projections program.

buildings is expected to result in job growth. Some demand for roofers may come from the installation of solar photovoltaic panels on building rooftops.

Job Prospects

Despite slow growth, about 14,700 openings for roofers are projected each year, on average, over the decade.

Many of those openings are expected to result from the need to replace workers who transfer to different occupations (especially in other construction trades) or exit the labor force, such as to retire. Jobs for roofers are generally easier to find during spring and summer.

Demand for roofers is less vulnerable to downturns than demand for other construction workers, because much roofing work consists of repair and reroofing, in addition to new construction. Still, workers may experience periods of unemployment when the overall level of new construction falls, and shortages of workers may occur in some areas during peak periods of building activity.

Employment projections data for roofers, 2019-29					
Occupational Title	SOC Code	Employment, 2019	Projected Employment, 2029	Change, 2019-29	
				Percent	Numeric
SOURCE: U.S. Bureau of Labor Statistics, Employment Projections program					
Roofers	47-2181	161,600	165,400	2	3,800

State & Area Data
Occupational Employment Statistics (OES)

The Occupational Employment Statistics (OES) program produces employment and wage estimates annually for over 800 occupations. These estimates are available for the nation as a whole, for individual states, and for metropolitan and nonmetropolitan areas.

Contacts for More Information

For details about apprenticeships or other work opportunities for roofers, contact the offices of the state employment service, the state apprenticeship agency, local contractors or firms that employ roofers, or local union–management apprenticeship committees. Apprenticeship information is available from the U.S. Department of Labor's Apprenticeship program online, or by phone at 877-872-5627. Visit Apprenticeship.gov to search for apprenticeship opportunities.

For more information about the work of roofers, visit
➤ National Roofing Contractors Association
➤ United Union of Roofers, Waterproofers & Allied Workers

For more information about OSHA training, visit
➤ Occupational Safety and Health Administration

Sheet Metal Workers

Summary

Quick Facts: Sheet Metal Workers

2019 Median Pay	$50,400 per year $24.23 per hour
Typical Entry-Level Education	High school diploma or equivalent
Work Experience in a Related Occupation	None
On-the-job Training	Apprenticeship
Number of Jobs, 2019	137,700
Job Outlook, 2019-29	1% (Slower than average)
Employment Change, 2019-29	1,800

What Sheet Metal Workers Do
Sheet metal workers fabricate or install products that are made from thin metal sheets.

Work Environment
Sheet metal workers often lift heavy materials and stand for long periods of time. Those who install sheet metal must often bend, climb, and squat. Most work full time.

How to Become a Sheet Metal Worker
Sheet metal workers employed in construction typically learn their trade through an apprenticeship. Those employed in manufacturing typically learn on the job or at a technical school.

Pay
The median annual wage for sheet metal workers was $50,400 in May 2019.

Job Outlook
Employment of sheet metal workers is projected to grow 1 percent from 2019 to 2029, slower than the average for all occupations. Employment growth reflects an expected increase in the number of industrial, commercial, and residential structures that will be built over the decade.

State & Area Data
Explore resources for employment and wages by state and area for sheet metal workers.

What Sheet Metal Workers Do
Sheet metal workers fabricate or install products that are made from thin metal sheets, such as ducts used in heating and air conditioning systems.

Duties
Sheet metal workers typically do the following:

• Select types of sheet metal according to building or design plans

Sheet metal workers carefully place sheet metal so that it can be bent evenly.

Sheet metal workers mark metal before drilling holes.

- Measure and mark dimensions and reference lines on metal sheets
- Drill holes in metal for screws, bolts, and rivets
- Install metal sheets with supportive frameworks
- Fabricate or alter parts at construction sites
- Maneuver and anchor large sheet metal parts
- Fasten seams or joints by welding, bolting, riveting, or soldering

Sheet metal workers use pieces of thin steel, aluminum, or other alloyed metal in both manufacturing and construction. Sheet metal products include heating and air conditioning ducts, rain gutters, outdoor signs, and siding.

The following are examples of types of sheet metal workers:

Fabrication sheet metal workers, sometimes called *precision sheet metal workers*, make precision sheet metal parts for a variety of industries, including power generation and medical device manufacturing. They often work in shops and factories, operating tools and equipment. In large-scale manufacturing, their tasks may be highly automated and repetitive. Some fabrication shops have automated machinery, such as computer-controlled saws, lasers, shears, and presses, which measure, cut, bend, and fasten pieces of sheet metal. Workers may use computer-aided drafting and design (CADD) systems to make products. Some of these workers are responsible for limited programming of the computers controlling their equipment. Workers who primarily program computerized equipment are called metal and plastic machine workers.

Installation sheet metal workers put in heating, ventilation, and air conditioning (HVAC) ducts. They also install other sheet metal products, such as metal roofs, siding, and gutters. They typically work on new construction and on renovation projects. In addition to installing sheet metal, some workers install nonmetallic materials such as fiberglass and plastic board. Information about workers who install or repair roofing systems is in the profile on roofers.

Maintenance sheet metal workers repair and clean ventilation systems so the systems use less energy. Workers remove dust and moisture and fix leaks or breaks in the sheet metal that makes up the ductwork.

Testing and balancing sheet metal specialists ensure that HVAC systems heat and cool rooms properly by adjusting sheet metal ducts to achieve proper airflow. Information on workers who install or repair HVAC systems is in the profile on heating, air conditioning, and refrigeration mechanics and installers.

Work Environment

Sheet metal workers held about 137,700 jobs in 2019. The largest employers of sheet metal workers were as follows:

Specialty trade contractors	60%
Manufacturing	21
Government	6

Some sheet metal workers install sheet metal at construction sites, which requires climbing and working at great heights.

Construction of buildings	3
Employment services	3

Sheet metal fabricators usually work in manufacturing plants and small shops, where they often lift heavy materials and stand for long periods of time.

Workers who install sheet metal at construction sites must bend, climb, and squat, sometimes in close quarters, in awkward positions, or at great heights. Sheet metal installers who work outdoors are exposed to all types of weather. The work environment may be noisy or dusty, and job tasks may create vibrations.

Injuries and Illnesses

Sheet metal workers risk injury on the job. Common injuries include cuts from sharp metal, burns from soldering or welding, and falls from ladders or scaffolding.

Some sheet metal fabricators work around high-speed machines, which may be dangerous and also may carry risks of loud noise, dust particles, and vibrations. To reduce injuries resulting from these hazards, workers often must wear safety glasses, ear protection, and dust masks and must not wear jewelry or loose-fitting clothing that could easily get caught in a machine. To avoid repetitive strain injuries, sheet metal workers may rotate through different production stations.

Work Schedules

Most sheet metal workers work full time.

How to Become a Sheet Metal Worker

Sheet metal workers who work in construction typically learn their trade through an apprenticeship. Those who work in manufacturing often learn on the job or at a technical school.

Education

Sheet metal workers typically need a high school diploma or equivalent. Those interested in becoming a sheet metal

Sheet metal workers learn their trade through an apprenticeship or on-the- job training, or at a technical school.

worker should take high school classes in algebra and geometry. Vocational-education courses such as blueprint reading, mechanical drawing, and welding are also helpful.

Technical schools may have programs that teach welding and metalworking. These programs help provide the basic welding and sheet metal fabrication knowledge that sheet metal workers need to do their job.

Some manufacturers have partnerships with local technical schools to develop training programs specific to their factories.

Training

Most construction sheet metal workers learn their trade through 4- or 5-year apprenticeships, which include both paid on-the-job training and related technical instruction. Apprentices learn construction basics such as blueprint reading, math, building code requirements, and safety and first aid practices. Welding may be included as part of the training.

Some workers start out as helpers before entering apprenticeships.

Apprenticeship programs are sponsored by unions and businesses. The basic qualifications for entering an apprenticeship program are being 18 years old and having a high school diploma or the equivalent.

After completing an apprenticeship program, sheet metal workers are considered journey workers who are qualified to perform tasks on their own.

Licenses, Certifications, and Registrations

Some states require licenses for sheet metal workers. Check with your state for more information.

Although not required, sheet metal workers may earn certifications for several tasks that they perform. For example, some sheet metal workers become certified in welding from the American Welding Society. In addition, the International Certification Board offers certification in testing and balancing, HVAC fire life safety, and other related activities for eligible sheet metal workers. The Fabricators & Manufacturers Association, International, offers a certification in precision sheet metal work.

Important Qualities

Detail oriented. Sheet metal workers must precisely measure and cut, follow detailed directions, and monitor their surroundings for safety risks.

Dexterity. Sheet metal workers need good hand–eye coordination and motor control to make precise cuts and bends in metal pieces.

Math skills. Sheet metal workers must calculate the proper sizes and angles of fabricated sheet metal to ensure the alignment and fit of ductwork.

Mechanical skills. Sheet metal workers use saws, lasers, shears, and presses. They should have good mechanical skills in order to operate and maintain equipment.

Physical stamina. Sheet metal workers in factories may spend many hours standing at their workstation.

Physical strength. Sheet metal workers must be able to lift and move ductwork that is heavy and cumbersome. Some jobs require workers to push, pull, or lift 50 pounds or more.

Pay

The median annual wage for sheet metal workers was $50,400 in May 2019. The median wage is the wage at which half the workers in an occupation earned more than that amount and half earned less. The lowest 10 percent earned less than $29,260, and the highest 10 percent earned more than $88,070.

In May 2019, the median annual wages for sheet metal workers in the top industries in which they worked were as follows:

Government	$58,420
Specialty trade contractors	51,910
Construction of buildings	46,070
Manufacturing	43,590
Employment services	41,230

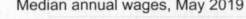
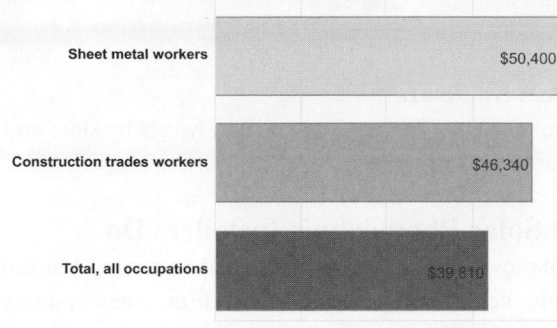

Sheet Metal Workers
Median annual wages, May 2019

Sheet metal workers — $50,400
Construction trades workers — $46,340
Total, all occupations — $39,810

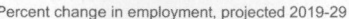
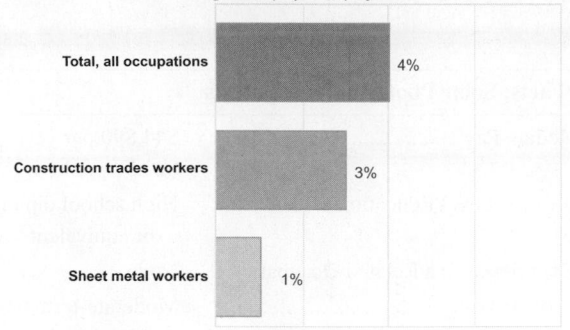

Sheet Metal Workers
Percent change in employment, projected 2019-29

Total, all occupations — 4%
Construction trades workers — 3%
Sheet metal workers — 1%

Note: All Occupations includes all occupations in the U.S. Economy. Source: U.S. Bureau of Labor Statistics, Occupational Employment Statistics.

Note: All Occupations includes all occupations in the U.S. Economy. Source: U.S. Bureau of Labor Statistics, Employment Projections program.

The starting pay for apprentices is usually less than what fully trained sheet metal workers make. As apprentices learn more skills, their pay increases.

Most sheet metal workers work full time.

Job Outlook

Employment of sheet metal workers is projected to grow 1 percent from 2019 to 2029, slower than the average for all occupations.

Employment growth reflects an expected increase in the number of industrial, commercial, and residential structures that will be built over the coming decade. It also reflects the continuing need to install and maintain energy-efficient air conditioning, heating, and ventilation systems in existing buildings.

Job Prospects

Despite limited employment growth, about 12,700 openings for sheet metal workers are projected each year, on average, over the decade.

Many of those openings are expected to result from the need to replace workers who transfer to different occupations or exit the labor force, such as to retire.

Employment of construction sheet metal workers, like that of many other construction workers, is sensitive to fluctuations in the economy. On the one hand, workers in these trades may experience periods of unemployment when the overall level of construction falls. On the other hand, peak periods of building activity may produce shortages of sheet metal workers.

Employment projections data for sheet metal workers, 2019-29					
Occupational Title	SOC Code	Employment, 2019	Projected Employment, 2029	Change, 2019-29 Percent	Numeric
SOURCE: U.S. Bureau of Labor Statistics, Employment Projections program					
Sheet metal workers	47-2211	137,700	139,500	1	1,800

State & Area Data
Occupational Employment Statistics (OES)

The Occupational Employment Statistics (OES) program produces employment and wage estimates annually for over 800 occupations. These estimates are available for the nation as a whole, for individual states, and for metropolitan and nonmetropolitan areas.

Contacts for More Information

For more information about apprenticeships or other work opportunities, contact local sheet metal contractors or heating, refrigeration, and air conditioning contractors; a local of the Sheet Metal Workers International Association; a local of the Sheet Metal and Air Conditioning Contractors' National Association; a local joint union–management apprenticeship committee; or the nearest office of your state employment service or apprenticeship agency. Apprenticeship information is available from the U.S. Department of Labor's Apprenticeship program online or by phone at 877-872-5627. Visit Apprenticeship.gov to search for apprenticeship opportunities.

For more information about sheet metal workers, visit
➤ International Association of Sheet Metal, Air, Rail and Transportation Workers (SMART)
➤ International Training Institute for the Sheet Metal and Air Conditioning Industry
➤ NCCER
➤ Sheet Metal and Air Conditioning Contractors' National Association

For more information about certification for sheet metal workers, visit
➤ American Welding Society
➤ Fabricators & Manufacturers Association, International
➤ International Certification Board

For information about opportunities for military veterans, visit:
➤ Helmet to Hard Hats

Solar Photovoltaic Installers

Summary

Quick Facts: Solar Photovoltaic Installers

2019 Median Pay	$44,890 per year $21.58 per hour
Typical Entry-Level Education	High school diploma or equivalent
Work Experience in a Related Occupation ..	None
On-the-job Training	Moderate-term on- the-job training
Number of Jobs, 2019	12,000
Job Outlook, 2019-29...................................	51% (Much faster than average)
Employment Change, 2019-29	6,100

What Solar Photovoltaic Installers Do

Solar photovoltaic (PV) installers assemble, set up, and maintain rooftop or other systems that convert sunlight into energy.

Work Environment

Most solar panel installations are done outdoors, but PV installers sometimes work in attics and crawl spaces to connect panels to the electrical grid. Installers also must travel to jobsites.

How to Become a Solar Photovoltaic Installer

Although installers typically need a high school diploma, some take courses at a technical school or community college. Installers typically receive on-the-job training lasting up to 1 year.

Pay

The median annual wage for solar photovoltaic installers was $44,890 in May 2019.

Job Outlook

Employment of solar photovoltaic (PV) installers is projected to grow 51 percent from 2019 to 2029, much faster than the average for all occupations. The continued expansion and adoption of solar PV systems will result in excellent job opportunities, particularly for those who complete training courses on solar panel installation.

State & Area Data

Explore resources for employment and wages by state and area for solar photovoltaic installers.

What Solar Photovoltaic Installers Do

Solar photovoltaic (PV) installers, also known as *PV installers*, assemble, set up, and maintain rooftop or other systems that convert sunlight into energy.

Duties

PV installers typically do the following:

- Plan PV system configurations based on customer needs and site conditions
- Measure, cut, and assemble the support structure for solar PV panels
- Install solar modules, panels, and support structures according to building codes and standards
- Connect PV panels to the electrical system
- Apply weather sealant to equipment being installed
- Activate and test PV systems
- Perform routine PV system maintenance

At the jobsite, PV installers verify the measurements and design of the structure on which the PV system is being set up. For PV systems on flat roofs, PV installers must first add a structure that allows the PV system to be mounted at an angle. PV installers set up new systems on support structures and place PV panels or PV shingles on top of them. Once the panels are in place, they sometimes connect the panels to electrical components. After the system is in place, PV installers must test the system and its components.

PV installers use a variety of handtools and power tools, including drills, wrenches, saws, and screwdrivers, to set up PV panels and connect them to frames, wires, and support structures.

Depending on the job and state laws, PV installers may connect the solar panels to the electrical grid, although electricians

PV panels are placed on specially built framework.

Solar photovoltaic installers usually work as part of a team.

sometimes do this task. Once the panels are set up, workers check the electrical systems for proper wiring, polarity, and grounding, and they also perform maintenance as needed.

Work Environment

Solar photovoltaic installers held about 12,000 jobs in 2019. The largest employers of solar photovoltaic installers were as follows:

Electrical contractors and other wiring installation contractors..	35%
Plumbing, heating, and air-conditioning contractors..	33
Self-employed workers...	6
Utilities...	5

Because photovoltaic (PV) panels convert sunlight into electricity, most PV installation is done outdoors. Residential installers work on rooftops but also sometimes work in attics and crawl spaces to connect panels to the electrical grid. PV installers who build solar farms work at ground level.

PV installers may work alone or as part of a team. Installation of solar panels may require the help of roofers and electricians.

Injuries and Illnesses

Solar photovoltaic installers risk falls from ladders and roofs, shocks from electricity, and burns from hot equipment and materials while installing and maintaining PV systems. To reduce the risk of injury, PV installers must wear safety equipment, such as harnesses, gloves, and hard hats.

How to Become a Solar Photovoltaic Installer

There are multiple paths to becoming a solar photovoltaic (PV) installer, or *PV installer*. These workers typically need a high school diploma, but some take courses at a technical school or community college; they also receive on-the-job training lasting up to 1 year. Some PV installers learn to install panels as part of an apprenticeship.

Some photovoltaic installers place thin solar film on rooftops.

Education

PV installers typically need a high school diploma. Some PV installers take courses at local community colleges or technical schools to learn about solar panel installation. Courses range from basic safety and PV knowledge to system design. Although course length varies, most usually last a few days to several months.

Some candidates, especially those with construction experience, enter the field by taking online training courses.

Training

Some PV installers learn their trade on the job by working with experienced installers. On-the-job training usually lasts between 1 month and 1 year. During training, PV installers learn about safety, tools, and PV system installation techniques.

Electrician and roofing apprentices and journey workers may complete photovoltaic-specific training modules through apprenticeships.

Solar PV system manufacturers may also provide training on specific products. Such training usually includes a system overview and proper installation techniques for the manufacturer's products.

Military veterans may benefit from the Solar Ready Vets program, which is funded by the U.S Department of Energy and

Most photovoltaic installers learn on the job working with experienced installers.

prepares veterans to connect with training and jobs in the solar industry.

Work Experience in a Related Occupation

Experience in construction may shorten a new employee's training time. For example, workers with experience as an electrician, roofer, carpenter, or laborer typically already understand and can perform basic construction duties.

Licenses, Certifications, and Registrations

Some states require a license for PV installers. Contact your state's licensing board for more information.

PV installers must travel to jobsites, so employers may require them to have a driver's license.

Although not required for employment, certification demonstrates competency in solar panel installation. The Electronics Technicians Association, International (ETA) and the North American Board of Certified Energy Practitioners offer certification for PV installers. Some states require that for projects to qualify for solar-related subsidies, all PV installers working on the projects must have certification.

Advancement

PV installers may advance to become a project supervisor or project manager after gaining experience in the trade. PV installers may also transition to sales roles within the industry, given their knowledge of and experience with PV installation. They also may choose to start their own PV installation business.

Important Qualities

Ability to work at heights. PV installers often must work on roofs, ladders, or lifts that are far above the ground.

Communication skills. PV installers need to convey information effectively to clients, team members, and other workers.

Detail oriented. PV installers must carefully follow instructions to ensure that the system works properly.

Math skills. PV installers use algebra, geometry, and trigonometry to calculate angles, measurements, and areas.

Mechanical skills. PV installers work with complex electrical and mechanical equipment in order to build support structures for solar panels, connect the panels to the electrical system, and troubleshoot problems.

Physical stamina. PV installers are often on their feet carrying panels and other heavy equipment. Especially when installing rooftop panels, workers may need to climb ladders many times throughout the day.

Physical strength. PV installers must lift heavy equipment and materials weighing up to 60 pounds.

Pay

The median annual wage for solar photovoltaic installers was $44,890 in May 2019. The median wage is the wage at which

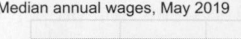

Solar Photovoltaic Installers
Median annual wages, May 2019

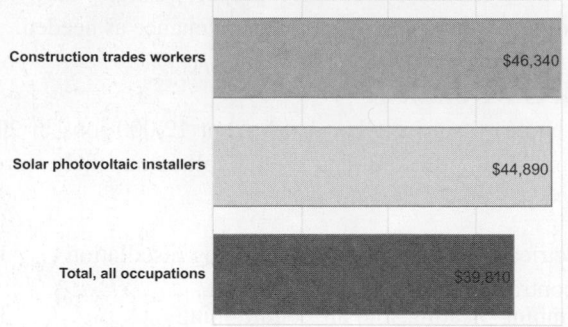

Construction trades workers	$46,340
Solar photovoltaic installers	$44,890
Total, all occupations	$39,810

Note: All Occupations includes all occupations in the U.S. Economy.
Source: U.S. Bureau of Labor Statistics, Occupational Employment Statistics.

half the workers in an occupation earned more than that amount and half earned less. The lowest 10 percent earned less than $31,600, and the highest 10 percent earned more than $63,880.

In May 2019, the median annual wages for solar photovoltaic installers in the top industries in which they worked were as follows:

Electrical contractors and other wiring installation contractors	$46,630
Plumbing, heating, and air-conditioning contractors	44,870
Utilities	42,280

Job Outlook

Employment of solar photovoltaic (PV) installers, often called *PV installers*, is projected to grow 51 percent from 2019 to 2029, much faster than the average for all occupations.

The continued expansion and adoption of solar PV systems is expected to create jobs for their installation and upkeep. As the cost of PV panels and shingles continues to decrease, more households are expected to take advantage of these systems, resulting in greater demand for the workers who install and maintain them. The increasing popularity of solar leasing plans—in which homeowners lease, rather than purchase, systems—should create additional demand, because homeowners no longer bear the upfront costs of installation.

Demand may be greatest in states and localities that provide incentives to reduce the cost of PV systems.

Job Prospects

About 2,300 openings for solar photovoltaic installers are projected each year, on average, over the decade.

Many of those openings are expected to result from the need to replace workers who transfer to different occupations or exit the labor force, such as to retire.

Despite fast growth, this occupation is small and has limited employment; therefore, strong competition for jobs is expected.

Solar Photovoltaic Installers
Percent change in employment, projected 2019-29

Solar photovoltaic installers	51%
Total, all occupations	4%
Construction trades workers	3%

Note: All Occupations includes all occupations in the U.S. Economy.
Source: U.S. Bureau of Labor Statistics, Employment Projections program.

Job candidates who complete a course in photovoltaic systems at a community college or technical school should have the best opportunities. Those who enter apprenticeships also are expected to have very good job opportunities. Candidates with experience in construction occupations, such as laborers, roofers, and carpenters, should have better job opportunities than those without construction experience.

Employment projections data for solar photovoltaic installers, 2019-29

Occupational Title	SOC Code	Employment, 2019	Projected Employment, 2029	Change, 2019-29 Percent	Numeric
SOURCE: U.S. Bureau of Labor Statistics, Employment Projections program					
Solar photovoltaic installers	47-2231	12,000	18,100	51	6,100

State & Area Data
Occupational Employment Statistics (OES)
The Occupational Employment Statistics (OES) program produces employment and wage estimates annually for over 800 occupations. These estimates are available for the nation as a whole, for individual states, and for metropolitan and nonmetropolitan areas.

Contacts for More Information
For more information about accredited training programs, visit
➤ American Solar Workforce
➤ Electronics Technicians Association, International (ETA)
➤ Interstate Renewable Energy Council, Inc.
➤ North American Board of Certified Energy Practitioners
➤ NCCER

For details about apprenticeships or other training opportunities in this trade, contact the offices of the state employment service, technical colleges, the state apprenticeship agency, local photovoltaic contractors, firms that employ PV installers, or local union–management apprenticeship committees. Apprenticeship information is available from the U.S. Department of Labor's Apprenticeship program online or by phone at 877-872-5627. Visit Apprenticeship.gov to search for apprenticeship opportunities.
For more information about apprenticeships for solar photovoltaic installers, visit
➤ IBEW–NECA Electrical Training Alliance
➤ For career and industry resources, visit
➤ The Solar Foundation

Education, Training, and Library

Adult Literacy and High School Equivalency Diploma Teachers

Summary

Quick Facts: Adult Literacy and High School Equivalency Diploma Teachers

2019 Median Pay	$54,350 per year $26.13 per hour
Typical Entry-Level Education	Bachelor's degree
Work Experience in a Related Occupation	None
On-the-job Training	None
Number of Jobs, 2019	59,300
Job Outlook, 2019-29	-10% (Decline)
Employment Change, 2019-29	-6,200

What Adult Literacy and High School Equivalency Diploma Teachers Do

Adult literacy and high school equivalency diploma teachers instruct adults in basic skills, such as reading and speaking English. They also help students earn their high school equivalent diploma.

Work Environment

Adult literacy and high school equivalency diploma teachers are often employed by community colleges, community-based organizations, and public schools. They typically work part time.

Adult literacy and high school equivalency diploma teachers instruct adults in basic skills.

How to Become an Adult Literacy or High School Equivalency Diploma Teacher

Adult literacy and high school equivalency diploma teachers who work in public schools must have at least a bachelor's degree and a license or certification.

Pay

The median annual wage for adult literacy and high school equivalency diploma teachers was $54,350 in May 2019.

Job Outlook

Employment of adult literacy and high school equivalency diploma teachers is projected to decline 10 percent from 2019 to 2029. Declining enrollment in adult education and ESL programs and an increase in the high school graduation rate may lower demand for these types of teachers.

State & Area Data

Explore resources for employment and wages by state and area for adult literacy and high school equivalency diploma teachers.

What Adult Literacy and High School Equivalency Diploma Teachers Do

Adult literacy and high school equivalency diploma teachers instruct adults in basic skills, such as reading, writing, and speaking English. They also help students earn their high school equivalent diploma.

Duties

Adult literacy and high school equivalency diploma teachers typically do the following:

- Plan and teach lessons to help students gain the knowledge and skills needed to earn their high school equivalent diploma
- Adapt teaching methods based on students' strengths and weaknesses
- Emphasize skills that will help students find jobs, such as learning English words and common phrases used in the workplace
- Assess students for learning disabilities
- Monitor students' progress
- Help students develop study skills
- Connect students to other resources in their community, such as job placement services

Students' educational level and skills are assessed before they enter these programs. Teachers may conduct the assessments;

Adult literacy and high school equivalency diploma teachers need to use different teaching strategies to meet their students' needs.

however, sometimes another staff member assesses students. Based on the results of the assessment and the student's goals, teachers develop an education plan.

Teachers must formally evaluate their students periodically to determine their progress and potential to go on to the next level of classes. However, teachers may informally evaluate their students' progress continually.

Adult literacy and high school equivalency diploma teachers often have students of various education levels in their classes. As a result, these teachers need to use different strategies to meet the needs of all of their students. They may work with students in classes or teach them one-on-one.

There are three types of education that adult literacy and high school equivalency diploma teachers provide:

Adult basic education (ABE) classes teach students the basics of reading, writing, and math. The students generally are age 16 or older and need to gain proficiency in these skills to improve their job situation. Teachers prepare students for further education and help them to develop skills that they will need in the workplace. For example, they may teach students how to write a resume.

English as a Second Language (ESL), also called *English for Speakers of Other Languages (ESOL)*, classes teach students to read, write, and speak English. Students in these classes are immigrants to the United States or those whose native language is not English. ESL teachers may have students from many different countries and cultures in their classroom. Because the ESL teacher and the students may not share a common native language, ESL teachers must be creative with their communication in the classroom.

ESL teachers often focus on helping their students with practical vocabulary for jobs and daily living. They also may focus on preparing their students to take the citizenship exam.

High school equivalency and adult secondary education classes prepare students to take the test to earn a high school equivalent diploma. Some programs are combined with career preparation programs so that students can earn a high school equivalent diploma and a career-related credential at the same time.

The high school equivalency exam is composed of four subjects: language arts, math, science, and social studies. In addition to teaching these subjects, teachers also help their students improve their skills in communicating, critical thinking, and problem solving—skills they will need in preparing for further education and successful careers.

Work Environment

Adult literacy and high school equivalency diploma teachers held about 59,300 jobs in 2019. The largest employers of adult literacy and high school equivalency diploma teachers were as follows:

Elementary and secondary schools; state, local, and
  private.. 35%
Junior colleges; state, local, and private 24

Adult literacy and high school equivalency diploma teachers often work in community colleges, community-based organizations, and public schools.

Other schools and instruction; state, local, and
private.. 9
Self-employed workers... 7
Colleges, universities, and professional schools;
state, local, and private.. 5

Students in adult literacy and high school equivalency programs attend classes by choice. As a result, they are often highly motivated, which may make teaching them rewarding and satisfying.

Work Schedules

Teachers often work in the mornings and evenings, because classes are held at times when students are not at work. They typically work part time.

How to Become an Adult Literacy or High School Equivalency Diploma Teacher

Adult literacy and high school equivalency diploma teachers who work in public schools must have at least a bachelor's degree and a license or certification.

Education

Adult literacy and high school equivalency diploma teachers in public schools must have at least a bachelor's degree. Some community colleges may prefer to hire those with a master's degree or graduate coursework in adult education or English as a Second Language (ESL).

Programs in adult education prepare prospective teachers to use effective strategies for adult learners, work with students from a variety of cultures and backgrounds, and teach adults with learning disabilities. Some programs allow these prospective teachers to specialize in adult basic education, secondary education, or ESL.

Working with students of different abilities and backgrounds can be difficult and teachers must respond with patience when students struggle with material.

Prospective ESL teachers should take courses or training in linguistics and theories of how people learn second languages. Knowledge of a second language is not necessary to teach ESL, but it can be helpful.

Teacher education programs instruct prospective teachers in how to present information to students and how to work with students of varying abilities and backgrounds. Programs typically include an opportunity for student-teachers to work with a mentor and get experience in a classroom. For information about teacher preparation programs in your state, visit Teach. org.

Adult literacy and high school equivalency diploma teachers may take professional development classes to improve their teaching skills and ensure that they keep up with research about teaching adults.

Licenses, Certifications, and Registrations

Adult literacy and high school equivalency diploma teachers who work in public schools must have a teaching certificate. Some states have certificates specifically for adult education. Other states require teachers to have a certificate in elementary or secondary education.

To obtain a license, adult literacy and high school equivalency diploma teachers typically need a bachelor's degree and must complete a student-teaching program. For more information, contact the director of adult education for your state. Contact information is available from the U.S. Department of Education.

Important Qualities

Communication skills. Adult literacy and high school equivalency teachers must collaborate with other teachers and program administrators. In addition, they must explain concepts in terms that students can understand.

Cultural sensitivity. Teachers work with students from a variety of cultural, educational, and economic backgrounds. They must be respectful of their students' backgrounds and be understanding of their concerns.

Patience. Working with students of different abilities and backgrounds can be difficult. Teachers must be patient when students struggle to understand the material.

Resourcefulness. Teachers must be able to think on their feet and find ways to keep students engaged in learning. They may have to change their methods of instruction to address the different needs of their students.

Pay

The median annual wage for adult literacy and high school equivalency diploma teachers was $54,350 in May 2019. The median wage is the wage at which half the workers in an occupation earned more than that amount and half earned less. The lowest 10 percent earned less than $32,580, and the highest 10 percent earned more than $93,760.

**Adult Literacy and High School Equivalency
Diploma Teachers**

Median annual wages, May 2019

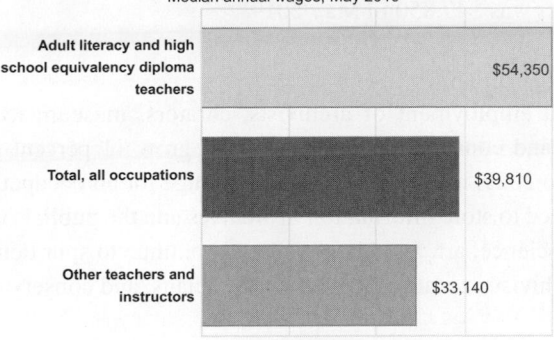

Note: All Occupations includes all occupations in the U.S. Economy.
Source: U.S. Bureau of Labor Statistics, Occupational Employment
Statistics.

In May 2019, the median annual wages for adult literacy and high school equivalency diploma teachers in the top industries in which they worked were as follows:

Elementary and secondary schools; state, local, and private	$61,630
Junior colleges; state, local, and private	52,500
Other schools and instruction; state, local, and private	48,770
Colleges, universities, and professional schools; state, local, and private	47,580

Teachers often work in the mornings and evenings, because classes are held at times when students are not at work. They typically work part time.

Job Outlook

Employment of adult literacy and high school equivalency diploma teachers is projected to decline 10 percent from 2019 to 2029.

Enrollment in adult education and ESL programs has declined in recent years. At the same time, high school graduation rates have increased, reducing the number of adults seeking to obtain high school equivalent diplomas. As these trends continue, the demand for adult literacy and high school equivalency diploma teachers may decline.

Changes in government funding for adult education and ESL programs may impact the demand for adult literacy and high school equivalency diploma teachers.

**Adult Literacy and High School Equivalency
Diploma Teachers**

Percent change in employment, projected 2019-29

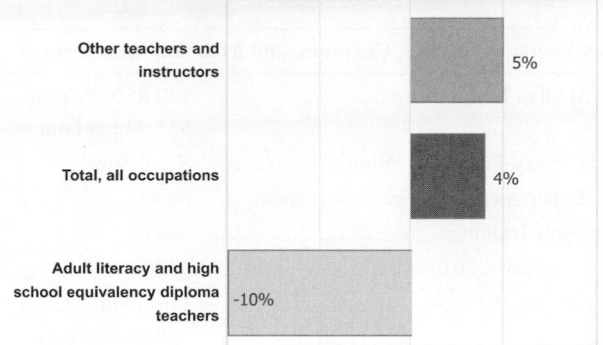

Note: All Occupations includes all occupations in the U.S. Economy.
Source: U.S. Bureau of Labor Statistics, Employment Projections
program.

Job Prospects

Many adult literacy and high school equivalency diploma teacher positions are part time. As a result, prospects will be best for workers who are willing and able to take a part-time position. In addition, those with experience teaching will have better opportunities than those without experience.

Employment projections data for adult literacy and high school equivalency diploma teachers, 2019-29					
Occupational Title	SOC Code	Employment, 2019	Projected Employment, 2029	Change, 2019-29	
				Percent	Numeric
SOURCE: U.S. Bureau of Labor Statistics, Employment Projections program					
Adult basic education, adult secondary education, and English as a Second Language instructors	25-3011	59,300	53,100	-10	-6,200

State & Area Data
Occupational Employment Statistics (OES)

The Occupational Employment Statistics (OES) program produces employment and wage estimates annually for over 800 occupations. These estimates are available for the nation as a whole, for individual states, and for metropolitan and nonmetropolitan areas.

Contacts for More Information

For more information about adult education in your state, visit
➤ U.S. Department of Education

For more information about teaching and becoming a teacher, visit
➤ Teach.org

Archivists, Curators, and Museum Workers

Summary

Quick Facts: Archivists, Curators, and Museum Workers

2019 Median Pay	$49,850 per year
	$23.97 per hour
Typical Entry-Level Education	See below
Work Experience in a Related Occupation	None
On-the-job Training	None
Number of Jobs, 2019	37,500
Job Outlook, 2019-29	11% (Much faster than average)
Employment Change, 2019-29	4,200

What Archivists, Curators, and Museum Workers Do

Archivists and curators oversee institutions' collections, such as of historical items or of artwork. Museum technicians and conservators prepare and restore items in those collections.

Work Environment

Archivists, curators, museum technicians, and conservators work in museums, historical sites, governments, colleges and universities, corporations, and other institutions. Most work full time.

How to Become an Archivist, Curator, or Museum Worker

Archivists, curators, and conservators typically need a master's degree in a field related to their position. Museum technicians typically have a bachelor's degree. Experience gained through an internship or by volunteering in archives or museums is helpful.

Pay

The median annual wage for archivists, curators, and museum workers was $49,850 in May 2019.

Job Outlook

Overall employment of archivists, curators, museum technicians, and conservators is projected to grow 11 percent from 2019 to 2029, much faster than the average for all occupations. The need to store information in archives and the public's interest in science, art, and history should continue to spur demand for archivists, curators, museum technicians, and conservators.

State & Area Data

Explore resources for employment and wages by state and area for archivists, curators, and museum workers.

What Archivists, Curators, and Museum Workers Do

Archivists appraise, process, catalog, and preserve permanent records and historically valuable documents. Curators oversee collections of artwork and historical items and may conduct public service activities for an institution. Museum technicians and conservators prepare and restore objects and documents in museum collections and exhibits.

Duties

Archivists typically do the following:

- Authenticate and appraise historical documents and archival materials
- Preserve and maintain documents and objects
- Create and manage a system to maintain and preserve electronic records
- Organize and classify archival materials
- Safeguard records by creating film and digital copies
- Direct workers to help arrange, exhibit, and maintain collections

Archivists, curators, and museum workers maintain and display art.

Museum technicians often prepare materials for display.

- Set and administer policy guidelines concerning public access to materials
- Find and acquire new materials for their archives

Curators, museum technicians, and conservators typically do the following:

- Acquire, store, and exhibit collections
- Select the theme and design of exhibits
- Design, organize, and conduct tours and workshops for the public
- Attend meetings and civic events to promote their institution
- Clean objects such as ancient tools, coins, and statues
- Direct and supervise curatorial, technical, and student staff
- Plan and conduct special research projects

Archivists preserve important or historically significant documents and records. They coordinate educational and public outreach programs, such as tours, lectures, and classes. They also may work with researchers on topics and items relevant to their collections.

Some archivists specialize in a particular era of history so that they can have a better understanding of the records from that period. Archivists typically work with specific forms of documentation, such as manuscripts, electronic records, websites, photographs, maps, motion pictures, or sound recordings.

Curators, who also may be *museum directors,* lead the acquisition, storage, and exhibition of collections. They negotiate and authorize the purchase, sale, exchange, and loan of collections. They also may research, authenticate, evaluate, and categorize the items in a collection.

Curators often perform administrative tasks and help manage their institution's research projects and related educational programs. They may represent their institution in the media, at public events, and at professional conferences.

In large institutions, some curators may specialize in a particular field, such as botany, art, or history. For example, a large natural history museum might employ separate curators for its collections of birds, fish, and mammals.

In small institutions, one curator may be responsible for many tasks, from taking care of collections to directing the affairs of the museum.

Museum technicians, who may be known as *preparators, registrars,* or *collections specialists,* care for and safeguard objects in museum collections and exhibitions.

Preparators focus on readying items in museum collections for display or storage. For example, they might make frames and mats for artwork or fit mounts to support objects. They also help to create exhibits, such as by building exhibit cases, installing items, and ensuring proper lighting. And they transport items and prepare them for shipping.

Registrars and collections specialists oversee the logistics of acquisitions, insurance policies, risk management, and loaning of objects to and from the museum for exhibition or research.

They keep detailed records of the conditions and locations of the objects that are on display, in storage, or being transported to another museum. They also maintain and store any documentation associated with the objects.

These workers also may answer questions from the public and help curators and outside scholars use the museum's collections.

Conservators handle, preserve, treat, and keep records of artifacts, specimens, and works of art. They may perform substantial historical, scientific, and archeological research. They document their findings and treat items in order to minimize deterioration or restore them to their original state. Conservators usually specialize in a particular material or group of objects, such as documents and books, paintings, or textiles.

Some conservators use x rays, chemical testing, microscopes, special lights, and other laboratory equipment and techniques to examine objects, determine their condition, and decide on the best way to preserve them. They also may participate in outreach programs, research topics in their specialty, and write articles for scholarly journals.

Work Environment

Archivists, curators, and museum workers held about 37,500 jobs in 2019. Employment in the detailed occupations that make up archivists, curators, and museum workers was distributed as follows:

Museum technicians and conservators	14,800
Curators	14,500
Archivists	8,100

The largest employers of archivists, curators, and museum workers were as follows:

Museums, historical sites, and similar institutions	40%
Government	22
Educational services; state, local, and private	17

Depending on the size of the institution and the position archivists, curators, and museum workers hold, these workers may spend time either at a desk or with the public, providing reference assistance and educational services. Museum workers who restore and set up exhibits or work with bulky, heavy record containers may have to lift objects, climb ladders and scaffolding, and stretch to reach items.

Work Schedules

Most archivists, curators, museum technicians, and conservators work full time.

Archivists in government agencies and corporations generally work during regular business hours. Curators in large institutions may travel extensively to evaluate potential additions to the collection, organize exhibits, and conduct research.

Some archivists coordinate educational and public outreach programs.

Prior experience through an internship or by volunteering in archives and museums is helpful in getting a position as an archivist, curator, museum technician, or conservator.

For curators in small institutions, however, travel may be rare. Museum technicians may need to work evenings and weekends if their institutions are open to the public during those times.

How to Become an Archivist, Curator, or Museum Worker

Archivists, curators, and conservators typically need a master's degree in a field related to their position. Museum technicians typically have a bachelor's degree. Experience gained through an internship or by volunteering in archives or museums is helpful.

Education

Archivists. Archivists typically need a master's degree in history, library science, archival studies, political science, or public administration. Students may gain valuable archiving experience through volunteer or internship opportunities.

Curators. Curators typically need a master's degree in art history, history, archaeology, or museum studies. In small museums, curator positions may be available to applicants with a bachelor's degree. Because curators have administrative and managerial responsibilities, courses in business administration, public relations, marketing, and fundraising are recommended.

Museum technicians. Museum technicians typically need a bachelor's degree in museum studies or a related field, such as archaeology, art history, or history. Some jobs require candidates to have a master's degree in museum studies. In addition, museum employers may prefer candidates who have knowledge of the museum's specialty or have experience working in museums.

Conservators. Conservators typically need a master's degree in conservation or a related field. Graduate programs last 2 to 4 years, the latter part of which includes an internship. To qualify for entry into these programs, a student must have a background in archaeology, art history, chemistry, or studio art. Completing a conservation internship as an undergraduate may enhance an applicant's prospects into a graduate program.

Licenses, Certifications, and Registrations

Although most employers do not require certification, some archivists may choose to earn voluntary certification because it allows them to demonstrate expertise in a particular area.

The Academy of Certified Archivists offers the Certified Archivist credential. To earn certification, candidates usually must have a master's degree, have professional archival experience, and pass an exam. They must renew their certification periodically by retaking the exam or fulfilling continuing education credits.

Other Experience

To gain experience, candidates may have to work part time, as an intern or as a volunteer, during or after completing their education. Substantial experience in collection management, research, exhibit design, or restoration, as well as database management skills, is necessary for full-time positions.

Advancement

Continuing education is available through meetings, conferences, and workshops sponsored by archival, historical, and museum associations. Some large organizations, such as the U.S. National Archives and Records Administration in Washington, DC, offer in-house training.

Top museum positions are highly sought after. Performing unique research and producing published work are important for advancement in large institutions. In addition, a doctoral degree may be needed for some advanced positions.

Museum workers employed in small institutions may have limited opportunities for promotion. They typically advance by transferring to a larger institution that has supervisory positions.

Important Qualities

Analytical skills. Archivists, curators, museum technicians, and conservators must explore minutiae to determine the origin, history, and importance of the objects they work with.

Customer-service skills. Archivists, curators, museum technicians, and conservators work regularly with the general public. They must be courteous, friendly, and able to help users find materials.

Detail oriented. Archivists and museum technicians must be able to focus on specifics because they use and develop complex databases related to the materials they store and access.

Organizational skills. Archivists, curators, museum technicians, and conservators store and easily retrieve records and documents. They must also develop logical systems of storage for the public to use.

Pay

The median annual wage for archivists, curators, and museum workers was $49,850 in May 2019. The median wage is the wage at which half the workers in an occupation earned more than that amount and half earned less. The lowest 10 percent earned less than $28,330, and the highest 10 percent earned more than $87,760.

Median annual wages for archivists, curators, and museum workers in May 2019 were as follows:

Curators	$54,570
Archivists	53,950
Museum technicians and conservators	44,430

In May 2019, the median annual wages for archivists, curators, and museum workers in the top industries in which they worked were as follows:

Educational services; state, local, and private	$55,460
Government	50,840
Museums, historical sites, and similar institutions	46,550

Most archivists, curators, museum technicians, and conservators work full time.

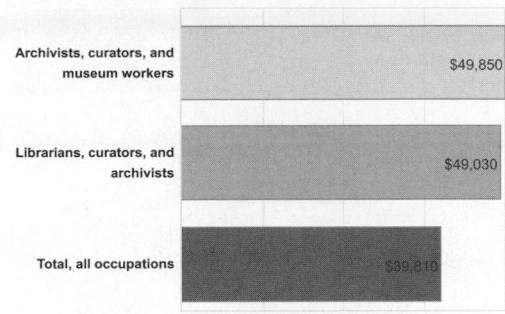

Archivists, Curators, and Museum Workers
Median annual wages, May 2019

Archivists, curators, and museum workers	$49,850
Librarians, curators, and archivists	$49,030
Total, all occupations	$39,810

Note: All Occupations includes all occupations in the U.S. Economy.
Source: U.S. Bureau of Labor Statistics, Occupational Employment Statistics.

Archivists in government agencies and corporations generally work during regular business hours. Curators in large institutions may travel extensively to evaluate potential additions to the collection, organize exhibits, and conduct research. However, for curators in small institutions, travel may be rare. Museum technicians may need to work evenings and weekends if their institutions are open to the public during those times.

Job Outlook

Overall employment of archivists, curators, museum technicians, and conservators is projected to grow 11 percent from 2019 to 2029, much faster than the average for all occupations.

Employment of archivists is projected to grow 8 percent from 2019 to 2029, much faster than the average for all occupations. However, because it is a small occupation, the fast growth will result in only about 600 new jobs over the 10-year period. Demand for archivists is expected to increase, as public and private organizations require that more volumes of records and information be organized and made accessible. The growing use of electronic records may cause an increase in demand for archivists who specialize in electronic records and records management.

Employment of curators is projected to grow 13 percent from 2019 to 2029, much faster than the average for all occupations. However, because it is a small occupation, the fast growth will result in only about 1,800 new jobs over the 10-year period. Continued public interest in museums and other cultural centers should lead to increased demand for curators and for the collections they manage.

Employment of museum technicians and conservators is projected to grow 12 percent from 2019 to 2029, faster than the average for all occupations. However, because it is a small occupation, the fast growth will result in only about 1,700 new jobs over the 10-year period. Public interest in science, art, history, and technology is expected to spur some demand for museum technicians and conservators.

Archivists, Curators, and Museum Workers

Percent change in employment, projected 2019-29

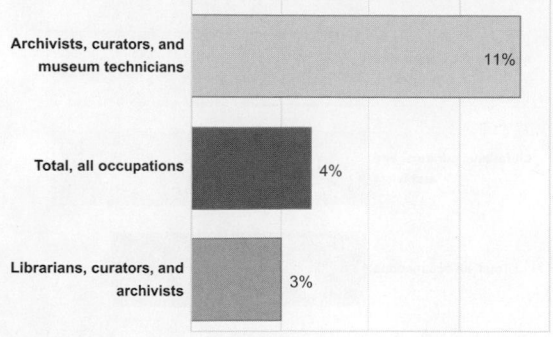

Archivists, curators, and museum technicians	11%
Total, all occupations	4%
Librarians, curators, and archivists	3%

Note: All Occupations includes all occupations in the U.S. Economy.
Source: U.S. Bureau of Labor Statistics, Employment Projections program.

Archives and museums that receive federal funds can be affected by changes to the federal budget. When funding is cut, there may be a reduction in the demand for these workers. However, budget surpluses may lead to more job openings.

Job Prospects

About 4,500 openings for archivists, curators, and museum workers are projected each year, on average, over the decade.

Many of those openings are expected to result from the need to replace workers who transfer to different occupations or exit the labor force, such as to retire.

Candidates seeking archivist, curator, museum technician, or conservator jobs should expect competition because of the high number of qualified applicants per job opening. Jobseekers with highly specialized training, a master's degree, and internship or volunteer experience should have the best job prospects.

Employment projections data for archivists, curators, and museum workers, 2019-29

Occupational Title	SOC Code	Employment, 2019	Projected Employment, 2029	Change, 2019-29	
				Percent	Numeric
SOURCE: U.S. Bureau of Labor Statistics, Employment Projections program					
Archivists, curators, and museum technicians	—	37,500	41,700	11	4,200
Archivists	25-4011	8,100	8,800	8	600

Employment projections data for archivists, curators, and museum workers, 2019-29

Occupational Title	SOC Code	Employment, 2019	Projected Employment, 2029	Change, 2019-29	
				Percent	Numeric
Curators	25-4012	14,500	16,400	13	1,800
Museum technicians and conservators	25-4013	14,800	16,500	12	1,700

State & Area Data

Occupational Employment Statistics (OES)

The Occupational Employment Statistics (OES) program produces employment and wage estimates annually for over 800 occupations. These estimates are available for the nation as a whole, for individual states, and for metropolitan and nonmetropolitan areas.

Contacts for More Information

For information about archivists and about schools offering courses in archival studies, visit
➤ Society of American Archivists

For more information about archivists and archivist certification, visit
➤ Academy of Certified Archivists
➤ For information about government archivists, visit
➤ Council of State Archivists
➤ U.S. National Archives and Records Administration

For information about museum technicians, registrars, or collections specialists, visit
➤ Association of Registrars and Collections Specialists

For more information about museum careers, including schools offering museum studies and related programs, visit
➤ American Alliance of Museums

For more information about careers and education programs in conservation and preservation for conservators, visit
➤ American Institute for Conservation

For information about job openings as curators, museum technicians, and conservators with the federal government, visit
➤ USAJobs

Career and Technical Education Teachers

Summary

Quick Facts: Career and Technical Education Teachers

2019 Median Pay	$58,110 per year
Typical Entry-Level Education	Bachelor's degree
Work Experience in a Related Occupation	Less than 5 years
On-the-job Training	None
Number of Jobs, 2019	209,700
Job Outlook, 2019-29	2% (Slower than average)
Employment Change, 2019-29	3,400

What Career and Technical Education Teachers Do

Career and technical education teachers instruct students in various technical and vocational subjects, such as auto repair, healthcare, and culinary arts.

Work Environment

Most career and technical education teachers work in middle, high, and postsecondary schools, such as 2-year colleges. Others work in technical, trade, and business schools. Although they generally work during school hours, some teach evening or weekend classes.

How to Become a Career or Technical Education Teacher

Career and technical education teachers typically must have at least a bachelor's degree. They also need work experience in the subject that they teach. Public school teachers may be required to have a state-issued teaching certification or license.

Pay

The median annual wage for career and technical education teachers was $58,110 in May 2019.

Career and technical education teachers teach academic and technical content to provide students with the skills and knowledge necessary to enter an occupation.

Job Outlook

Overall employment of career and technical education teachers is projected to grow 2 percent from 2019 to 2029, slower than the average for all occupations.

State & Area Data

Explore resources for employment and wages by state and area for career and technical education teachers.

What Career and Technical Education Teachers Do

Career and technical education (CTE) teachers provide training in subjects such as auto repair, cosmetology, and culinary arts. They teach vocational and technical content to give students the skills and knowledge necessary to enter an occupation.

Duties

Career and technical education teachers typically do the following:

- Create lesson plans and assignments
- Instruct students on how to develop certain skills
- Show students how to apply classroom knowledge through hands-on activities
- Demonstrate and supervise safe and proper use of tools and equipment
- Monitor students' progress, assign tasks, and grade assignments
- Discuss students' progress with parents, students, and counselors
- Develop and enforce classroom rules and safety procedures

CTE teachers help students explore and prepare to enter a career or technical occupation. They use a variety of teaching methods to help students learn and develop skills related to a specific occupation or career field. They demonstrate tasks, techniques, and tools used in an occupation. They may assign

Technical education teachers often work in classrooms and help students.

hands-on tasks, such as replacing brakes on cars, taking blood pressure, or applying makeup. Teachers typically oversee these activities in workshops and laboratories in the school.

Some teachers work with local businesses and nonprofit organizations to provide practical work experience for students. They also serve as advisers to students participating in career and technical student organizations.

The specific duties of CTE teachers vary by the grade and subject they teach. In middle schools and high schools, they teach general concepts in a classroom and practical exercises in workshops and laboratories.

In postsecondary schools, they teach specific career skills that help students earn a certificate, a diploma, or an associate's degree and prepare them for a specific job. For example, welding instructors teach students welding techniques and safety practices. They also monitor the use of tools and equipment and have students practice procedures until they meet the standards required by the trade.

In most states, teachers in middle and high schools teach one subject within major career fields. CTE teachers combine academic instruction with experiential learning in their subject of expertise.

For example, teachers of courses in **agricultural, food, and natural resources** teach topics such as agricultural production; agriculture-related business; veterinary science; and plant, animal, and food systems. They may have students plant and care for crops and animals to apply what they have learned in the classroom.

For information about the programs for major career fields, visit Advance CTE.

Work Environment

Career and technical education teachers held about 209,700 jobs in 2019. Employment in the detailed occupations that make up career and technical education teachers was distributed as follows:

Career/technical education teachers, postsecondary	124,100
Career/technical education teachers, secondary school	73,800
Career/technical education teachers, middle school	11,800

The largest employers of career and technical education teachers were as follows:

Junior colleges; state, local, and private	24%
Technical and trade schools; state, local, and private	22
Colleges, universities, and professional schools; state, local, and private	6

Career and technical education teachers typically work in middle, high, and postsecondary schools, such as 2-year colleges. Others work in technical, trade, and business schools.

Work Schedules

Career and technical education teachers in middle and high schools generally work during school hours. They may meet with parents, students, and school staff before and after classes.

Some career and technical education teachers, especially those in postsecondary schools, teach courses and develop lesson plans during evening hours and on weekends.

Teachers usually work the traditional 10-month school year and have a 2-month break during the summer. They also have a short midwinter break. Some teachers work for summer programs.

Teachers in districts with a year-round schedule typically work 9 weeks in a row and then have a break for 3 weeks before starting a new school session.

How to Become a Career or Technical Education Teacher

Career and technical education teachers typically must have at least a bachelor's degree. They also need work experience

Technical education teachers demonstrate the theories and techniques of their field.

Teachers need years of experience in their field of expertise.

in the subject they teach. Public schools may require a state-issued teaching certification or license.

Education

Career and technical education teachers generally need a bachelor's degree in the field they teach, such as agriculture, engineering, or computer science.

All states require prospective career and technical education teachers in public schools to complete a period of fieldwork, called a student-teaching program, in which they work with a mentor teacher and get experience teaching students in a classroom. For information about teacher preparation programs in your state, visit Teach.org.

Work Experience in a Related Occupation

Many career and technical education teachers need work experience in the field they teach. For example, automotive mechanics, chefs, and nurses typically spend years in their career before moving into teaching.

Licenses, Certifications, and Registrations

States may require career and technical education teachers in public schools to be licensed or certified. Requirements for certification or licensure vary by state, but generally involve the following:

- A bachelor's degree with a minimum grade point average
- Completion of a student-teaching program
- Passing a background check
- Passing a general teaching certification test, as well as a test that demonstrates their knowledge of the subject they will teach.

For information on certification requirements in your state, visit Teach.org.

Career and technical education teachers who prepare students for an occupation that requires a license or certification may need to have and maintain the same credential. For example, career and technical education teachers who teach welding may need to have certification in welding. In addition, teachers may be required to complete annual professional development courses to maintain their license or certification.

Some states offer an alternative route to certification or licensure for prospective teachers who have a bachelor's degree or work experience in their field but lack the education courses required for certification. Alternative programs typically cover teaching methods, development of lesson plans, and classroom management.

Advancement

Experienced teachers may advance to become mentors or lead teachers, helping less experienced teachers to improve their teaching skills.

Teachers may become school counselors, instructional coordinators, or principals. These positions generally require additional education, an advanced degree, or certification. An advanced degree in education administration or leadership may be helpful.

Important Qualities

Communication skills. Career and technical education teachers must explain concepts in terms that students can understand.

Organizational skills. Career and technical education teachers must coordinate their time and teaching materials.

Patience. Working with students of different abilities and backgrounds can be difficult. Teachers must be even-tempered with students to develop a positive learning environment.

Resourcefulness. Teachers need to create different ways of presenting information and demonstrating tasks so that all students learn the material.

Pay

The median annual wage for career and technical education teachers was $58,110 in May 2019. The median wage is the wage at which half the workers in an occupation earned more than that amount and half earned less. The lowest 10 percent earned less than $35,830, and the highest 10 percent earned more than $96,730.

Median annual wages for career and technical education teachers in May 2019 were as follows:

Career/technical education teachers, secondary school	$61,710
Career/technical education teachers, middle school	60,800
Career/technical education teachers, postsecondary	54,620

In May 2019, the median annual wages for career and technical education teachers in the top industries in which they worked were as follows:

Colleges, universities, and professional schools; state, local, and private	$58,580

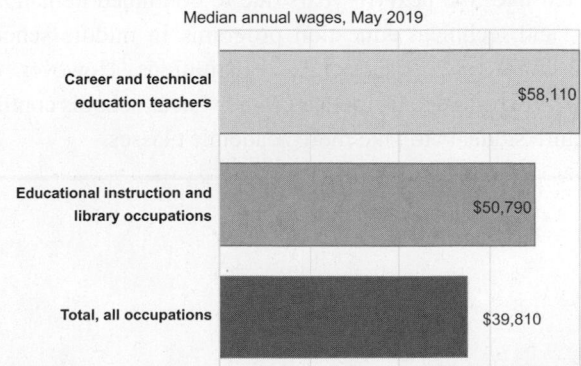

Career and Technical Education Teachers
Median annual wages, May 2019

Career and technical education teachers — $58,110
Educational instruction and library occupations — $50,790
Total, all occupations — $39,810

Note: All Occupations includes all occupations in the U.S. Economy.
Source: U.S. Bureau of Labor Statistics, Occupational Employment Statistics.

Career and Technical Education Teachers
Percent change in employment, projected 2019-29

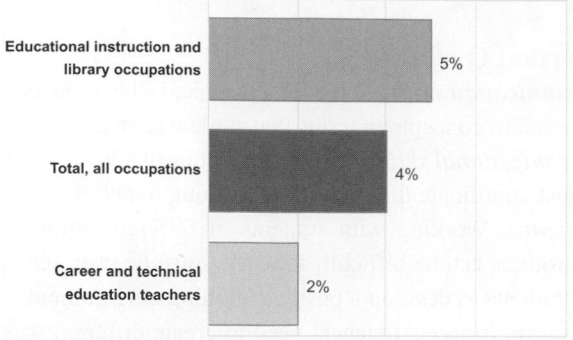

Note: All Occupations includes all occupations in the U.S. Economy.
Source: U.S. Bureau of Labor Statistics, Employment Projections program.

Junior colleges; state, local, and private 56,950

Technical and trade schools; state, local, and private 51,750

Career and technical education teachers in middle and high schools generally work during school hours. They may meet with parents, students, and school staff before and after classes.

Some career and technical education teachers, especially those in postsecondary schools, teach courses and develop lesson plans during evening hours and on weekends.

Teachers usually work the traditional 10-month school year and have a 2-month break during the summer. They also have a short midwinter break. Some teachers work for summer programs.

Teachers in districts with a year-round schedule typically work 9 weeks in a row and then have a break for 3 weeks before starting a new school session.

Job Outlook

Overall employment of career and technical education teachers is projected to grow 2 percent from 2019 to 2029, slower than the average for all occupations.

Some employment growth across all types of institutions is expected over the next 10 years due to continued demand for career and technical education programs in middle schools, high schools, and postsecondary institutions. However, this growth is expected to be reduced somewhat as schools continue to require students to take more academic classes.

In addition, public schools often depend on government funding for career and technical education programs. When budgets for these programs are reduced, employment growth for career and technical education teachers may be limited.

Job Prospects

Teachers with work experience and certifications in the subject they teach should have the best job prospects.

Job opportunities also may be better in some specialties, particularly at the postsecondary level, than in others. For example, job opportunities are expected to be good for those with experience in healthcare support occupations who can teach skills for work as medical or dental assistants.

Employment projections data for career and technical education teachers, 2019-29					
Occupational Title	SOC Code	Employment, 2019	Projected Employment, 2029	Change, 2019-29	
				Percent	Numeric
SOURCE: U.S. Bureau of Labor Statistics, Employment Projections program					
Career and technical education teachers	—	209,700	213,100	2	3,400
Career/technical education teachers, postsecondary	25-1194	124,100	125,500	1	1,300
Career/technical education teachers, middle school	25-2023	11,800	12,100	3	400
Career/technical education teachers, secondary school	25-2032	73,800	75,500	2	1,700

State & Area Data
Occupational Employment Statistics (OES)

The Occupational Employment Statistics (OES) program produces employment and wage estimates annually for over 800 occupations. These estimates are available for the nation as a whole, for individual states, and for metropolitan and nonmetropolitan areas.

Contacts for More Information

For more information about career and technical education teachers, visit
➤ Association for Career and Technical Education
➤ Advance CTE

For more information about teaching and becoming a teacher, visit
➤ Teach.org

High School Teachers

Summary

Quick Facts: High School Teachers

2019 Median Pay	$61,660 per year
Typical Entry-Level Education	Bachelor's degree
Work Experience in a Related Occupation	None
On-the-job Training	None
Number of Jobs, 2019	1,050,800
Job Outlook, 2019-29	4% (As fast as average)
Employment Change, 2019-29	40,200

What High School Teachers Do

High school teachers teach academic lessons and various skills that students will need to attend college and to enter the job market.

Work Environment

High school teachers work in schools. They work during school hours but may also work evenings and weekends to prepare lessons and grade papers. Most do not teach during the summer.

How to Become a High School Teacher

High school teachers typically have at least a bachelor's degree. In addition, public school teachers must have a state-issued certification or license, which may require an academic background in the subject(s) they will be certified to teach.

Pay

The median annual wage for high school teachers was $61,660 in May 2019.

Job Outlook

Employment of high school teachers is projected to grow 4 percent from 2019 to 2029, about as fast as the average for all occupations. Rising student enrollment should increase demand for high school teachers.

State & Area Data

Explore resources for employment and wages by state and area for high school teachers.

What High School Teachers Do

High school teachers help prepare students for life after graduation. They teach academic lessons and various skills that students will need to attend college or to enter the job market.

Duties

High school teachers typically do the following:

- Plan lessons and instruct their students in the subject they teach
- Assess students' abilities, strengths, and weaknesses
- Adapt lessons to changes in class size
- Grade students' assignments and exams
- Communicate with parents about students' progress
- Work with individual students to challenge them and to improve their abilities
- Prepare students for standardized tests required by the state
- Develop and enforce classroom rules and administrative policies
- Supervise students outside of the classroom—for example, during lunchtime or detention

High school teachers generally teach students from the 9th through 12th grades. They usually specialize in one area. Some teach core subjects, such as math, science, or history. Others specialize in elective courses, such as art, music, or physical education. They may teach several different classes within their subject area. For example, a high school math teacher may teach algebra, calculus, and/or geometry.

High school teachers may instruct students from different grades throughout the day. For example, one class may have mostly students from the 9th grade, and another may have

High school teachers prepare students for life after graduation by teaching lessons and skills students will need to attend college or enter the job market.

High school teachers generally specialize in a subject, such as English, math, or science.

12th-grade students. In many schools, students are divided into classes on the basis of their abilities, so teachers need to adapt their lessons based on students' skills.

Outside of their instructional time, teachers plan lessons, grade assignments, and meet with other teachers and staff.

Teachers of English as a second language (ESL) or English for speakers of other languages (ESOL) work exclusively with students who are learning the English language. These teachers work with students individually or in groups to help them improve their English language skills and help them with assignments for other classes.

Students with learning disabilities and emotional or behavioral disorders are often taught in traditional classes. High school teachers work with special education teachers to adapt lessons to these students' needs and to monitor the students' progress.

Teachers must be comfortable with using and learning new technology. With parents, they may use text-messaging applications to communicate about students' assignments and upcoming events. With students, teachers may create websites or discussion boards to present information and to expand a lesson taught in class.

Some high school teachers take on additional responsibilities, such as coaching sports or advising academic clubs, activities that frequently take place before or after school.

Work Environment

High school teachers held about 1.1 million jobs in 2019. The largest employers of high school teachers were as follows:

Elementary and secondary schools; local..................... 83%
Elementary and secondary schools; private................. 15

Most states have tenure laws, which provide job security after a certain number of years of satisfactory classroom teaching.

Teachers may find it rewarding to watch students develop new skills and gain an appreciation for knowledge.

However, teaching may be stressful. Some schools have large classes and lack important teaching tools, such as current technology and up-to-date textbooks. Occasionally, teachers must cope with unmotivated or disrespectful students. Some states are developing teacher mentoring programs and teacher development courses to help with the challenges of being a teacher.

Work Schedules

High school teachers generally work during school hours when students are present. They may meet with parents, students, and other teachers before and after school. They often spend time in the evenings and on weekends grading papers and preparing lessons. Teachers who coach sports or advise clubs generally do so before or after school.

Many teachers work a traditional 10-month school year and have a 2-month break during the summer. They also have a short midwinter break. Some teachers work during the summer.

Teachers in districts with a year-round schedule typically work 9 weeks in a row and then have a break for 3 weeks before starting a new school session.

How to Become a High School Teacher

High school teachers typically must have at least a bachelor's degree. In addition, public school teachers must have a state-issued certification or license.

Education

All states require public high school teachers to have at least a bachelor's degree. Many states require high school teachers to have majored in a subject area, such as science or history.

High school teachers typically enroll in their college's teacher education program, which instructs them on presenting information to students of different abilities and background. Programs typically include a student-teaching program, in which prospective teachers work with a mentor teacher and get experience instructing students in a classroom. For information

High school teachers who specialize in science class may spend some of their day working in a lab.

High school teachers need to explain difficult concepts in terms students can understand.

about teacher preparation programs in your state, visit Teach. org.

Some states require high school teachers to earn a master's degree after earning their teaching certification and obtaining a job.

Teachers in private schools do not need to meet state requirements. However, private schools typically seek high school teachers who have a bachelor's degree and a major in a subject area.

Licenses, Certifications, and Registrations

All states require teachers in public schools to be licensed or certified in the specific grade level they will teach. Those who teach in private schools typically are not required to be licensed. High school teachers typically are awarded a secondary or high school certification, which allows them to teach the 7th through the 12th grades.

Requirements for certification or licensure vary by state but generally involve the following:

- A bachelor's degree with a minimum grade point average
- Completion of a student-teaching program
- Passing a background check
- Passing a general teaching certification test, as well as a test that demonstrates their knowledge in the subject they will teach.

For information on certification requirements in your state, visit Teach.org.

Teachers often are required to complete professional development classes to keep their license or certification. Some states require teachers to complete a master's degree after receiving their certification and obtaining a job.

All states offer an alternative route to certification or licensure for people who already have a bachelor's degree but lack the education courses required for certification. Some alternative certification programs allow candidates to begin teaching immediately with supervision by an experienced teacher. These programs cover teaching methods and other topics, such as resource management. After they complete the program, candidates are awarded full certification. Other programs require students to take classes in education before they can teach.

Important Qualities

Communication skills. Teachers must share ideas with their students, other teachers, and school administrators and staff. In addition, they need to discuss students' progress with parents.

Patience. High school teachers must stay calm in difficult situations, such as when students struggle with material.

Resourcefulness. High school teachers need to engage students in learning and adapt lessons to each student's needs.

Advancement

Experienced teachers may advance to serve as mentors to new teachers; they may also become a lead teacher. In these positions, they help less experienced teachers improve their teaching skills.

With additional education or certification, teachers may become school counselors, school librarians, or instructional coordinators. Some become assistant principals or principals. Becoming a principal usually requires additional instruction in education administration or leadership. For more information, see the profiles on school and career counselors, librarians, instructional coordinators, and elementary, middle, and high school principals.

Pay

The median annual wage for high school teachers was $61,660 in May 2019. The median wage is the wage at which half the workers in an occupation earned more than that amount and half earned less. The lowest 10 percent earned less than $40,540, and the highest 10 percent earned more than $99,660.

In May 2019, the median annual wages for high school teachers in the top industries in which they worked were as follows:

Elementary and secondary schools; local	$62,310
Elementary and secondary schools; private	56,270

High school teachers generally work during school hours when students are present. They may meet with parents, students, and other teachers before and after school. They often spend time in the evenings and on weekends grading papers and preparing lessons. Teachers who coach sports or advise clubs generally do so before or after school.

Many teachers work a traditional 10-month school year and have a 2-month break during the summer. They also have a short midwinter break. Although most do not teach during the summer, some teach in summer school programs for which they are paid.

Teachers in districts with a year-round schedule typically work 9 weeks in a row and then have a break for 3 weeks before starting a new school session.

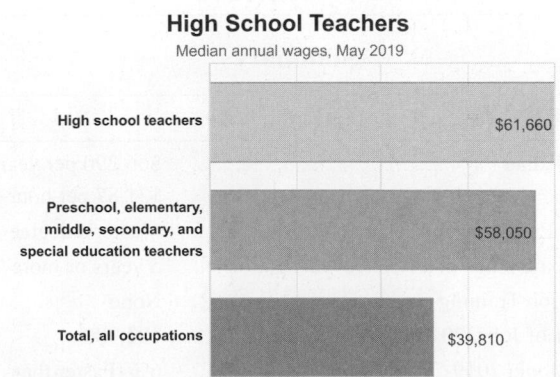

High School Teachers
Median annual wages, May 2019

High school teachers	$61,660
Preschool, elementary, middle, secondary, and special education teachers	$58,050
Total, all occupations	$39,810

Note: All Occupations includes all occupations in the U.S. Economy.
Source: U.S. Bureau of Labor Statistics, Occupational Employment Statistics.

High School Teachers
Percent change in employment, projected 2019-29

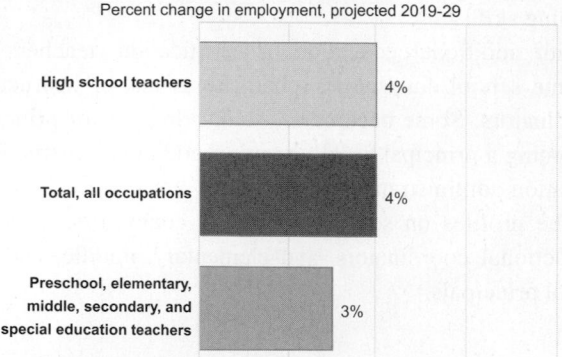

Note: All Occupations includes all occupations in the U.S. Economy.
Source: U.S. Bureau of Labor Statistics, Employment Projections program.

Job Outlook

Employment of high school teachers is projected to grow 4 percent from 2019 to 2029, about as fast as the average for all occupations. Rising student enrollment should increase demand for high school teachers, but employment growth will vary by region.

Employment growth for public high school teachers may depend on state and local government budgets. If state and local governments experience budget deficits, school boards may lay off employees, including teachers. As a result, employment growth of high school teachers may be reduced by state and local government budget deficits. Conversely, budget surpluses at the state and local level could lead to additional employment growth for high school teachers.

Job Prospects

Many teachers will be needed to replace those who retire or who leave the occupation for other reasons.

Many schools report that they have difficulty filling teaching positions for certain subjects, including math, science, English as a second language, and special education. As a result, teachers who specialize in these subjects should have the best job prospects. For more information about high school special education teachers, see the profile on special education teachers.

Employment projections data for high school teachers, 2019-29					
Occupational Title	SOC Code	Employment, 2019	Projected Employment, 2029	Change, 2019-29	
				Percent	Numeric
SOURCE: U.S. Bureau of Labor Statistics, Employment Projections program					
Secondary school teachers, except special and career/technical education	25-2031	1,050,800	1,090,900	4	40,200

State & Area Data
Occupational Employment Statistics (OES)

The Occupational Employment Statistics (OES) program produces employment and wage estimates annually for over 800 occupations. These estimates are available for the nation as a whole, for individual states, and for metropolitan and nonmetropolitan areas.

Contacts for More Information

For more information about teaching and becoming a teacher, visit
➤ Teach.org
➤ American Federation of Teachers
➤ National Education Association

For more information about teacher preparation programs, visit
➤ Council for the Accreditation of Educator Preparation

Instructional Coordinators

Summary

Quick Facts: Instructional Coordinators

2019 Median Pay	$66,290 per year $31.87 per hour
Typical Entry-Level Education	Master's degree
Work Experience in a Related Occupation	5 years or more
On-the-job Training	None
Number of Jobs, 2019	192,900
Job Outlook, 2019-29	6% (Faster than average)
Employment Change, 2019-29	11,400

What Instructional Coordinators Do

Instructional coordinators oversee school curriculums and teaching standards. They develop instructional material, implement it, and assess its effectiveness.

Work Environment

Most instructional coordinators work in elementary and secondary schools, colleges, professional schools, or educational support services or for state and local governments. They typically work year round.

How to Become an Instructional Coordinator

Instructional coordinators need a master's degree and related work experience, such as teaching or school administration.

Instructional coordinators work with teachers and school administrators to implement curriculums.

Coordinators in public schools may be required to have a state-issued license.

Pay

The median annual wage for instructional coordinators was $66,290 in May 2019.

Job Outlook

Employment of instructional coordinators is projected to grow 6 percent from 2019 to 2029, faster than the average for all occupations. As states and school districts put greater emphasis on student achievement data, schools may increasingly turn to instructional coordinators to develop better curriculums and improve teachers' effectiveness.

State & Area Data

Explore resources for employment and wages by state and area for instructional coordinators.

What Instructional Coordinators Do

Instructional coordinators oversee school curriculums and teaching standards. They develop educational material, implement it with teachers and principals, and assess its effectiveness.

Duties

Instructional coordinators typically do the following:

- Develop and implement the curriculums
- Plan, organize, and conduct teacher training, conferences, or workshops
- Analyze students' test data
- Assess and discuss the curriculum standards with school staff
- Review and suggest textbooks and other educational materials
- Recommend teaching techniques and the use of different or new technologies
- Develop procedures for teachers to implement a curriculum

Instructional coordinators need a master's degree and related work experience.

- Train teachers and other instructional staff in new content or programs
- Mentor or coach teachers to improve their skills

Instructional coordinators, also known as *curriculum specialists*, evaluate the effectiveness of curriculums and teaching techniques established by school boards, states, or federal regulations. They observe teachers in the classroom, review student test data, and discuss the curriculum with the school staff. Based on their research, they may recommend changes in curriculums to the school board.

Instructional coordinators may conduct training for teachers related to teaching or technology. For example, instructional coordinators explain new learning standards to teachers and demonstrate effective teaching methods to achieve them.

Instructional coordinators may specialize in particular grade levels or specific subjects. Those in elementary and secondary schools may focus on programs such as special education or English as a second language.

Work Environment

Instructional coordinators held about 192,900 jobs in 2019. The largest employers of instructional coordinators were as follows:

Most instructional coordinators work in an office but they may also spend time traveling to schools within their school district.

Elementary and secondary schools; state, local, and private...	44%
Colleges, universities, and professional schools; state, local, and private..	19
Government..	7
Educational support services; state, local, and private...	6

Most instructional coordinators work in elementary and secondary schools, colleges, professional schools, or educational support services or for state and local governments. They typically work year round.

Work Schedules

Instructional coordinators generally work full time. They typically work year round and do not have summer breaks. Coordinators may meet with teachers and other administrators outside of classroom hours.

How to Become an Instructional Coordinator

Instructional coordinators need a master's degree and related work experience, such as teaching or in school administration. Coordinators in public schools may be required to have a state-issued license.

Education

Instructional coordinators in public schools are required to have a master's degree in education or curriculum and instruction. Some instructional coordinators need a degree in a specialized field, such as math or history.

Master's degree programs in curriculum and instruction teach about curriculum design, instructional theory, and collecting and analyzing data. To enter these programs, candidates usually need a bachelor's degree in education.

Licenses, Certifications, and Registrations

Instructional coordinators in public schools may be required to have a license, such as a teaching license or an education

Instructional coordinators need to be able to train teachers on the newest teaching techniques and tools.

administrator license. For information about teaching licenses, see the profiles on kindergarten and elementary school teachers, middle school teachers, and high school teachers. For information about education administrator licenses, see the profile on elementary, middle, and high school principals. Check with your state's Board of Education for specific license requirements.

Work Experience in a Related Occupation

Most instructional coordinators need several years of related work experience as a teacher or an instructional leader. For some positions, experience teaching a specific subject or grade level is required.

Advancement

With enough experience and more education, instructional coordinators may become superintendents.

Important Qualities

Analytical skills. Instructional coordinators evaluate student test data and teaching strategies. Based on their analysis, they recommend improvements in curriculums and teaching.

Communication skills. Instructional coordinators need to clearly explain changes in the curriculum and teaching standards to school staff.

Decision-making skills. Instructional coordinators must be decisive when recommending changes to curriculums, teaching methods, and textbooks.

Interpersonal skills. Instructional coordinators need to be able to establish and maintain positive working relationships with teachers, principals, and other administrators.

Leadership skills. Instructional coordinators serve as mentors to teachers. They train teachers in developing useful and effective teaching techniques.

Pay

The median annual wage for instructional coordinators was $66,290 in May 2019. The median wage is the wage at which

Instructional Coordinators

Median annual wages, May 2019

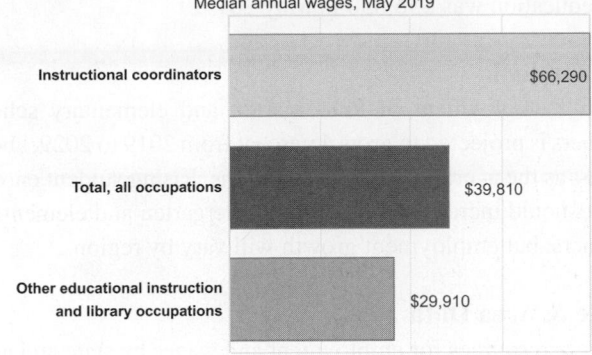

Instructional Coordinators

Percent change in employment, projected 2019-29

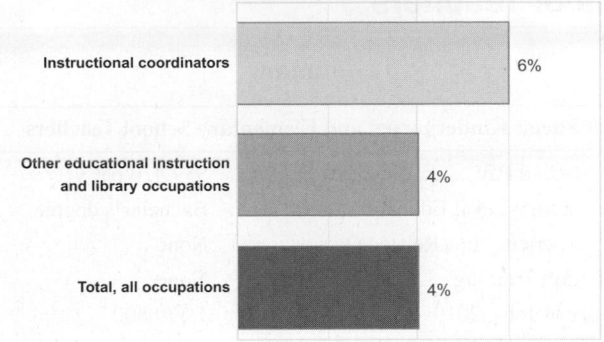

Note: All Occupations includes all occupations in the U.S. Economy.
Source: U.S. Bureau of Labor Statistics, Occupational Employment
Statistics.

Note: All Occupations includes all occupations in the U.S. Economy.
Source: U.S. Bureau of Labor Statistics, Employment Projections
program.

half the workers in an occupation earned more than that amount and half earned less. The lowest 10 percent earned less than $38,260, and the highest 10 percent earned more than $103,790.

In May 2019, the median annual wages for instructional coordinators in the top industries in which they worked were as follows:

Government	$76,270
Elementary and secondary schools; state, local, and private	70,690
Educational support services; state, local, and private	67,580
Colleges, universities, and professional schools; state, local, and private	60,910

Instructional coordinators generally work full time. They typically work year round and do not have summer breaks. Coordinators may meet with teachers and other administrators outside of classroom hours.

Job Outlook

Employment of instructional coordinators is projected to grow 6 percent from 2019 to 2029, faster than the average for all occupations.

States and school districts will continue to be held accountable for test scores and graduation rates, putting more of an emphasis on student achievement data. Schools may increasingly turn to instructional coordinators to develop better curriculums and improve teachers' effectiveness. The training that instructional coordinators provide for teachers in curriculum changes and teaching techniques should help schools meet their

standards in student achievement. As schools seek additional training for teachers, demand for instructional coordinators is projected to grow.

However, many instructional coordinators are employed by state and local governments. Therefore, employment growth will depend largely on state and local government budgets.

Job Prospects

Instructional coordinators with a solid teaching background and leadership experience should have the best job prospects.

Employment projections data for instructional coordinators, 2019-29

Occupational Title	SOC Code	Employment, 2019	Projected Employment, 2029	Change, 2019-29	
				Percent	Numeric
SOURCE: U.S. Bureau of Labor Statistics, Employment Projections program					
Instructional coordinators	25-9031	192,900	204,300	6	11,400

State & Area Data
Occupational Employment Statistics (OES)

The Occupational Employment Statistics (OES) program produces employment and wage estimates annually for over 800 occupations. These estimates are available for the nation as a whole, for individual states, and for metropolitan and nonmetropolitan areas.

Contacts for More Information

For more information about instructional coordinators, visit
➤ Learning Forward
➤ ASCD (formerly the Association for Supervision and Curriculum Development)

Kindergarten and Elementary School Teachers

Summary

Quick Facts: Kindergarten and Elementary School Teachers

2019 Median Pay	$59,420 per year
Typical Entry-Level Education	Bachelor's degree
Work Experience in a Related Occupation ..	None
On-the-job Training	None
Number of Jobs, 2019	1,579,800
Job Outlook, 2019-29................................	4% (As fast as average)
Employment Change, 2019-29	56,100

What Kindergarten and Elementary School Teachers Do

Kindergarten and elementary school teachers instruct young students in basic subjects in order to prepare them for future schooling.

Work Environment

Kindergarten and elementary school teachers work in public and private schools. They generally work during school hours when students are present and use nights and weekends to prepare lessons and grade papers. Most kindergarten and elementary school teachers do not work during the summer.

How to Become a Kindergarten or Elementary School Teacher

Kindergarten and elementary school teachers usually must have at least a bachelor's degree. In addition, public school teachers must have a state-issued certification or license.

Pay

The median annual wage for elementary school teachers, except special education was $59,670 in May 2019.

The median annual wage for kindergarten teachers, except special education was $56,850 in May 2019.

Job Outlook

Overall employment of kindergarten and elementary school teachers is projected to grow 4 percent from 2019 to 2029, about as fast as the average for all occupations. Rising student enrollment should increase demand for kindergarten and elementary teachers, but employment growth will vary by region.

State & Area Data

Explore resources for employment and wages by state and area for kindergarten and elementary school teachers.

What Kindergarten and Elementary School Teachers Do

Kindergarten and elementary school teachers instruct young students in basic subjects, such as math and reading, in order to prepare them for middle school.

Duties

Kindergarten and elementary school teachers typically do the following:

- Create lesson plans to teach students subjects, such as reading, science, and math
- Teach students how to interact with others
- Observe students to evaluate their abilities, strengths, and weaknesses
- Instruct an entire class or smaller groups of students
- Grade students' assignments
- Communicate with parents or guardian about their child's progress
- Work with students individually to help them overcome specific learning challenges
- Prepare students for standardized tests required by the state

Kindergarten and elementary school teachers teach basic subjects.

Kindergarten and elementary school teachers use a variety of tools, such as computers, to present information to students.

- Develop and enforce classroom rules to teach children proper behavior
- Supervise children outside of the classroom—for example, during lunchtime or recess

Kindergarten and elementary school teachers help students learn and apply important concepts. Many teachers use a hands-on approach to help students understand abstract concepts, solve problems, and develop critical-thinking skills. For example, they may demonstrate how to do a science experiment and then have the students conduct the experiment themselves. They may have students work together to solve problems.

Elementary school typically goes from first through fifth or sixth grades. However, in some schools, elementary school continues through eighth grade.

Kindergarten and elementary school teachers typically instruct students in several subjects throughout the day. Teachers may escort students to assemblies, recess, or classes taught by other teachers, such as art or music. While students are away from the classroom, teachers plan lessons, grade assignments, or meet with other teachers and staff.

In some schools, teachers may work on subject specialization teams in which they teach one or two specific subjects, typically either English and social studies or math and science. Generally, students spend half their time with one teacher and half their time with the other.

There are kindergarten and elementary school teachers who specialize in subjects such as art, music, or physical education.

Some schools employ *English as a second language (ESL)* or *English for speakers of other languages (ESOL) teachers* who work exclusively with students learning the English language. These teachers work with students individually or in groups to help them improve their English language skills and to help them with class assignments.

Students with learning disabilities or emotional or behavioral disorders are often taught in traditional classes. Kindergarten and elementary teachers work with special education teachers to adapt lesson plans to these students' needs and monitor the students' progress. In some cases, kindergarten and elementary school teachers may co-teach lessons with special education teachers.

Some teachers use technology in their classroom as a teaching aide. They must be comfortable with using and learning new technology. Teachers also may maintain websites to communicate with parents about students' assignments, upcoming events, and grades. For students in higher grades, teachers may create websites or discussion boards to present information or to expand on a lesson taught in class.

Work Environment

Elementary school teachers, except special education held about 1.5 million jobs in 2019. The largest employers of

Kindergarten and elementary school teachers may meet with parents, students, and other teachers before and after school.

elementary school teachers, except special education were as follows:

Elementary and secondary schools; local	85%
Elementary and secondary schools; private	13

Kindergarten teachers, except special education held about 127,700 jobs in 2019. The largest employers of kindergarten teachers, except special education were as follows:

Elementary and secondary schools; local	81%
Elementary and secondary schools; private	14
Child day care services	3

Most states have tenure laws, which provide job security after a certain number of years of satisfactory teaching.

Kindergarten and elementary school teachers may find it rewarding to watch students develop new skills and learn information. However, teaching may be stressful. Some schools have large classes and lack important teaching tools, such as computers and up-to-date textbooks. Some states are developing teacher mentoring programs and teacher development courses to help with the challenges of being a teacher.

Work Schedules

Kindergarten and elementary school teachers generally work during school hours when students are present. They may meet with parents, students, and other teachers before and after school. They often spend time in the evenings and on weekends grading papers and preparing lessons.

Many kindergarten and elementary school teachers work the traditional 10-month school year and have a 2-month break during the summer. They also have a short midwinter break. Some teachers work during the summer.

Teachers in districts with a year-round schedule typically work 9 weeks in a row, and then have a break for 3 weeks before starting a new schooling session.

Kindergarten and elementary school teachers need to be able to explain concepts in terms young students can understand.

How to Become a Kindergarten or Elementary School Teacher

Kindergarten and elementary school teachers usually must have a bachelor's degree. In addition, public school teachers must have a state-issued certification or license.

Education

Public kindergarten and elementary school teachers typically need at least a bachelor's degree in elementary education. Private schools typically have the same requirement. Some states also require public kindergarten and elementary school teachers to major in a content area, such as math or science.

Those with a bachelor's degree in another subject can still become elementary education teachers. They must complete a teacher education program to obtain certification to teach. Requirements vary by state.

In teacher education programs, future teachers learn how to present information to young students and how to work with young students of varying abilities and backgrounds. Programs typically include a student-teaching program, in which they work with a mentor teacher and get experience teaching students in a classroom setting. For information about teacher preparation programs in your state, visit Teach.org.

Some states require teachers to earn a master's degree after receiving their teaching certification and obtaining a job.

Licenses, Certifications, and Registrations

All states require teachers in public schools to be licensed or certified in the specific grade level that they will teach. Those who teach in private schools typically do not need a license. Requirements for certification or licensure vary by state but generally involve the following:

- A bachelor's degree with a minimum grade point average
- Completion of a student teaching program
- Passing a background check
- Passing a general teaching certification test, as well as a test that demonstrates their knowledge of the subject they will teach.

For information on certification requirements in your state, visit Teach.org.

Teachers are frequently required to complete professional development classes to keep their license or certification. Some states require teachers to complete a master's degree after receiving their certification and obtaining a job.

All states offer an alternative route to certification or licensure for people who already have a bachelor's degree but lack the education courses required for certification. Some alternative certification programs allow candidates to begin teaching immediately after graduation, under the supervision of an experienced teacher. These programs cover teaching methods and child development. After they complete the program, candidates are awarded full certification. Other programs require students to take classes in education before they can teach.

Important Qualities

Communication skills. Teachers need to discuss students' needs with parents and administrators. They also need to be able to communicate the subject content to students in a manner in which they will understand.

Patience. Kindergarten and elementary school teachers must respond with patience when students struggle with material. Working with students of different abilities and backgrounds can be difficult.

Physical stamina. Working with kindergarten- and elementary-age students can be tiring. Teachers need to be able to physically, mentally, and emotionally keep up with the students.

Resourcefulness. Kindergarten and elementary school teachers must be able to get students engaged in learning. They also should be prepared to adapt their lessons to meet students' needs.

Advancement

Experienced teachers may advance to serve as mentors to new teachers or become lead teachers. In these roles, they help less-experienced teachers to improve their teaching skills.

With additional education or certification, teachers may become school counselors, school librarians, or instructional coordinators. Some become assistant principals or principals, both of which generally require additional schooling in education administration or leadership.

Kindergarten and Elementary School Teachers

Median annual wages, May 2019

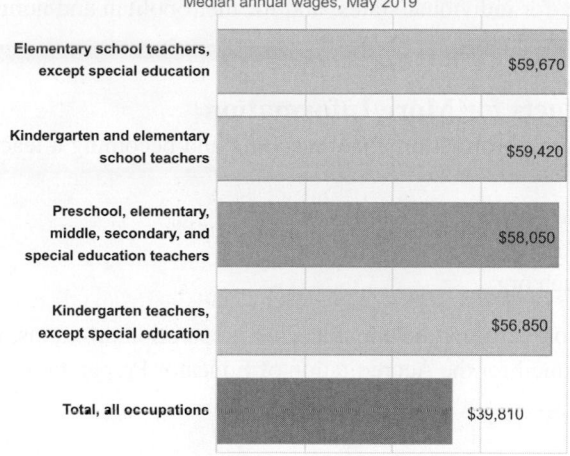

Kindergarten and Elementary School Teachers

Percent change in employment, projected 2019-29

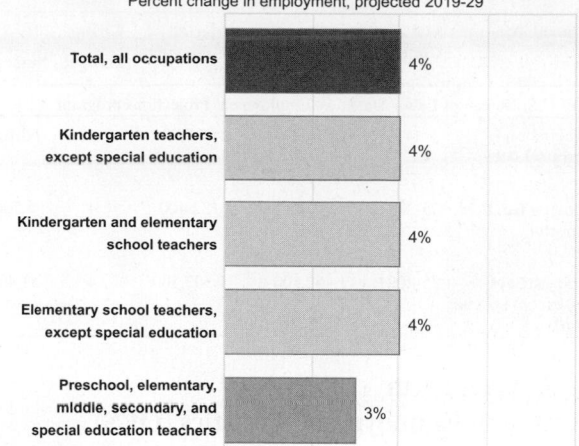

Note: All Occupations includes all occupations in the U.S. Economy.
Source: U.S. Bureau of Labor Statistics, Occupational Employment
Statistics.

Note: All Occupations includes all occupations in the U.S. Economy.
Source: U.S. Bureau of Labor Statistics, Employment Projections
program.

Pay

The median annual wage for elementary school teachers, except special education was $59,670 in May 2019. The median wage is the wage at which half the workers in an occupation earned more than that amount and half earned less. The lowest 10 percent earned less than $39,020, and the highest 10 percent earned more than $97,900.

The median annual wage for kindergarten teachers, except special education was $56,850 in May 2019. The lowest 10 percent earned less than $37,420, and the highest 10 percent earned more than $90,180.

In May 2019, the median annual wages for elementary school teachers, except special education in the top industries in which they worked were as follows:

Elementary and secondary schools; local	$60,870
Elementary and secondary schools; private	48,100

In May 2019, the median annual wages for kindergarten teachers, except special education in the top industries in which they worked were as follows:

Elementary and secondary schools; local	$58,380
Elementary and secondary schools; private	46,470
Child day care services	34,190

Kindergarten and elementary school teachers generally work during school hours when students are present. They may meet with parents, students, and other teachers before and after school. They often spend time in the evenings and on weekends grading papers and preparing lessons.

Many kindergarten and elementary school teachers work the traditional 10-month school year and have a 2-month break during the summer. They also have a short midwinter break. Some teachers work during the summer.

Teachers in districts with a year-round schedule typically work 9 weeks in a row and then have a break for 3 weeks before starting a new school session.

Job Outlook

Overall employment of kindergarten and elementary school teachers is projected to grow 4 percent from 2019 to 2029, about as fast as the average for all occupations. Rising student enrollment should increase demand for kindergarten and elementary teachers, but employment growth will vary by region.

The number of students enrolling in public kindergarten and elementary schools is expected to increase over the coming decade, and the number of classes needed to accommodate these students should rise. As a result, more teachers will be needed to teach public kindergarten and elementary school students.

Despite expected increases in enrollment in public schools, employment growth for kindergarten and elementary school teachers will depend on state and local government budgets. If state and local governments experience budget deficits, they may lay off employees, including teachers. As a result, employment growth of public kindergarten and elementary school teachers may be somewhat reduced.

Job Prospects

Some teachers are expected to reach retirement age over the coming decade. Their retirements may increase the need to replace workers who leave the occupation.

Opportunities will vary by region and school setting. There will be better opportunities in urban and rural school districts than in suburban school districts. Flexibility in job location may increase prospects.

Employment projections data for kindergarten and elementary school teachers, 2019-29					
Occupational Title	SOC Code	Employment, 2019	Projected Employment, 2029	Change, 2019-29	
				Percent	Numeric
SOURCE: U.S. Bureau of Labor Statistics, Employment Projections program					
Kindergarten and elementary school teachers	—	1,579,800	1,635,900	4	56,100
Kindergarten teachers, except special education	25-2012	127,700	132,400	4	4,700
Elementary school teachers, except special education	25-2021	1,452,100	1,503,500	4	51,400

State & Area Data
Occupational Employment Statistics (OES)
The Occupational Employment Statistics (OES) program produces employment and wage estimates annually for over 800 occupations. These estimates are available for the nation as a whole, for individual states, and for metropolitan and nonmetropolitan areas.

Contacts for More Information
For more information about teaching and becoming a teacher, visit
➤ American Federation of Teachers
➤ National Education Association
➤ Teach.org

For more information about teacher preparation programs, visit
➤ Council for the Accreditation of Educator Preparation

Librarians

Summary

Quick Facts: Librarians

2019 Median Pay	$59,500 per year $28.61 per hour
Typical Entry-Level Education	Bachelor's degree
Work Experience in a Related Occupation	None
On-the-job Training	None
Number of Jobs, 2019	146,500
Job Outlook, 2019-29	5% (Faster than average)
Employment Change, 2019-29	7,300

What Librarians Do
Librarians help people find information and conduct research for personal and professional use.

Work Environment
Librarians work for local governments, companies, and elementary, secondary and postsecondary schools. Most work full time.

How to Become a Librarian
Librarians typically need a master's degree in library science. Some positions have additional requirements, such as a teaching certificate or a degree in another field.

Pay
The median annual wage for librarians was $59,500 in May 2019.

Job Outlook
Employment of librarians is projected to grow 5 percent from 2019 to 2029, faster than the average for all occupations. Communities are increasingly turning to libraries for a variety of services and activities. Therefore, there will be a need for librarians to manage libraries and help patrons find information.

State & Area Data
Explore resources for employment and wages by state and area for librarians.

What Librarians Do
Librarians help people find information and conduct research for personal and professional use. Their job duties may change based on the type of library they work in, such as public, academic, or medical libraries.

Librarians help people find information and conduct research for personal and professional use.

Librarian's job duties vary based on the type of library they work in, such as a public, school, or medical library.

Duties

Librarians typically do the following:

- Create and use databases of library materials
- Organize library materials so they are easy to find
- Help library patrons to conduct research to evaluate search results and reference materials
- Research new books and materials by reading book reviews, publishers' announcements, and catalogs
- Maintain existing collections and choose new books, videos, and other materials for purchase
- Plan programs for different audiences, such as story time for children
- Teach classes about information resources
- Research computers and other equipment for purchase, as needed
- Train and supervise library technicians, assistants, other support staff, and volunteers
- Prepare library budgets

In small libraries, librarians are often responsible for many or all aspects of library operations. In large libraries, they usually focus on one aspect of the library, such as user services, technical services, or administrative services.

The following are examples of types of librarians:

Academic librarians assist students, faculty, and staff in postsecondary institutions. They help students research topics related to their coursework and teach students how to access

information. They also assist faculty and staff in locating resources related to their research projects or studies. Some campuses have multiple libraries, and librarians may specialize in a particular subject.

Administrative services librarians manage libraries, prepare budgets, and negotiate contracts for library materials and equipment. Some conduct public relations or fundraising activities for the library.

Public librarians work in their communities to serve all members of the public. They help patrons find books to read for pleasure; conduct research for schoolwork, business, or personal interest; and learn how to access the library's resources. Many public librarians plan programs for patrons, such as story time for children, book clubs, or educational activities.

School librarians, sometimes called *school media specialists*, work in elementary, middle, and high school libraries and teach students how to use library resources. They also help teachers develop lesson plans and find materials for classroom instruction.

Special librarians work in settings other than school or public libraries. They are sometimes called *information professionals*. Businesses, museums, government agencies, and many other groups have their own libraries that use special librarians. The main purpose of these libraries and information centers is to serve the information needs of the organization that houses the library. Therefore, special librarians collect and organize materials focused on those subjects. Special librarians may need an additional degree in the subject that they specialize in. The following are examples of special librarians:

- *Corporate librarians* assist employees of private businesses in conducting research and finding information. They work for a wide range of organizations, including insurance companies, consulting firms, and publishers.
- *Law librarians* conduct research or help lawyers, judges, law clerks, and law students locate and analyze legal resources. They often work in law firms and law school libraries.
- *Medical librarians*, also called *health science librarians*, help health professionals, patients, and researchers find health and science information. They may provide information about new clinical trials and medical treatments and procedures, teach medical students how to locate medical information, or answer consumers' health questions.

Technical services librarians obtain, prepare, and organize print and electronic library materials. They arrange materials for patrons' ease in finding information. They are also responsible for ordering new library materials and archiving to preserve older items.

User services librarians help patrons conduct research using both electronic and print resources. They teach patrons how to use library resources to find information on their own. This may include familiarizing patrons with catalogs of print materials, helping them access and search digital libraries, or educating them on Internet search techniques. Some user services librarians work with a particular audience, such as children or young adults.

Work Environment

Librarians held about 146,500 jobs in 2019. The largest employers of librarians were as follows:

Elementary and secondary schools; state, local, and private..	34%
Local government, excluding education and hospitals....	29
Colleges, universities, and professional schools; state, local, and private	17
Information...	7

Most librarians typically work on the floor with patrons, behind the circulation desk, or in offices. Some librarians have private offices, but those in small libraries usually share work space with others.

Work Schedules

Most librarians work full time. Public and academic librarians often work on weekends and evenings and may work holidays. School librarians usually have the same work and vacation schedules as teachers, including summers off. Special librarians, such as corporate librarians, typically work normal business hours but may need to work more than 40 hours per week to help meet deadlines.

How to Become a Librarian

Librarians typically need a master's degree in library science. Some positions have additional requirements, such as a teaching certificate or a degree in another field.

Education

Librarians typically need a master's degree in library science (MLS). Some colleges and universities have other names for their library science programs, such as Master of Information Studies or Master of Library and Information Studies. Students need a bachelor's degree in any major to enter MLS programs.

MLS programs usually take 1 to 2 years to complete. Coursework typically covers information such as learning different research methods and strategies, online reference systems, and Internet search techniques.

The American Library Association accredits master's degree programs in library and information studies.

Special librarians, such as those in a corporate, law, or medical library, usually supplement a master's degree in library science with knowledge of their specialized field. Some employers require special librarians to have a master's degree, a professional degree, or a Ph.D. in that subject. For example, a law librarian may be required to have a law degree.

Licenses, Certifications, and Registrations

Public school librarians typically need a teacher's certification. Some states require school librarians to pass a standardized test, such as the PRAXIS II Library Media Specialist test. Contact your state department of education for details about requirements in your state.

Some states also require certification for librarians in public libraries. Contact your state's licensing board for specific requirements.

Important Qualities

Communication skills. Librarians need to be able to explain ideas and information in ways that patrons understand.

Initiative. New information, technology, and resources constantly change librarians' duties. Librarians must be able and willing to continually update their knowledge of these changes to be effective at their jobs.

Interpersonal skills. Librarians must be able to work both as part of a team and with the public or with researchers.

Librarians plan outreach programs targeted toward different groups, such as story time for children.

Some librarians assist patrons with research.

Organizational skills. Librarians help patrons research topics efficiently. They should be able to direct the logical use of resources, databases, and other materials.

Problem-solving skills. Librarians need to be able to identify a problem, figure out where to find information to solve the problem, and draw conclusions based on the information found.

Reading skills. Librarians must be excellent readers. Those working in special libraries are expected to read the latest literature in their field of specialization.

Pay

The median annual wage for librarians was $59,500 in May 2019. The median wage is the wage at which half the workers in an occupation earned more than that amount and half earned less. The lowest 10 percent earned less than $33,820, and the highest 10 percent earned more than $94,520.

In May 2019, the median annual wages for librarians in the top industries in which they worked were as follows:

Colleges, universities, and professional schools; state, local, and private	$64,750
Elementary and secondary schools; state, local, and private	60,940
Information	58,140
Local government, excluding education and hospitals	53,950

Most librarians work full time. Public and academic librarians often work on weekends and evenings, and may work holidays. School librarians usually have the same work and vacation schedules as teachers, including summers off. Special librarians, such as corporate librarians, typically work normal business hours but may need to work more than 40 hours per week to help meet deadlines.

Job Outlook

Employment of librarians is projected to grow 5 percent from 2019 to 2029, faster than the average for all occupations.

Communities are increasingly turning to libraries for a variety of services and activities. Therefore, there will be a need for librarians to manage libraries and help patrons find information. Parents value the learning opportunities that libraries present for children because libraries have information and learning materials that children often cannot access from home. In addition, the availability of electronic information and media materials is expected to increase the demand for librarians and media collections specialists in research and special libraries, where patrons may need help sorting through the large amount of digital information and collections materials.

Job Prospects

About 13,800 openings for librarians are projected each year, on average, over the decade.

Many of those openings are expected to result from the need to replace workers who transfer to different occupations or exit the labor force, such as to retire.

A degree from an American Library Association accredited program and work experience may lead to job opportunities. Candidates who are able to adapt with the rapidly changing technology will have the best prospects.

Employment projections data for librarians, 2019-29					
Occupational Title	SOC Code	Employment, 2019	Projected Employment, 2029	Change, 2019-29	
				Percent	Numeric
SOURCE: U.S. Bureau of Labor Statistics, Employment Projections program					
Librarians and media collections specialists	25-4022	146,500	153,800	5	7,300

State & Area Data
Occupational Employment Statistics (OES)

The Occupational Employment Statistics (OES) program produces employment and wage estimates annually for over 800

Librarians
Median annual wages, May 2019

Librarians — $59,500
Librarians, curators, and archivists — $49,030
Total, all occupations — $39,810

Note: All Occupations includes all occupations in the U.S. Economy.
Source: U.S. Bureau of Labor Statistics, Occupational Employment Statistics.

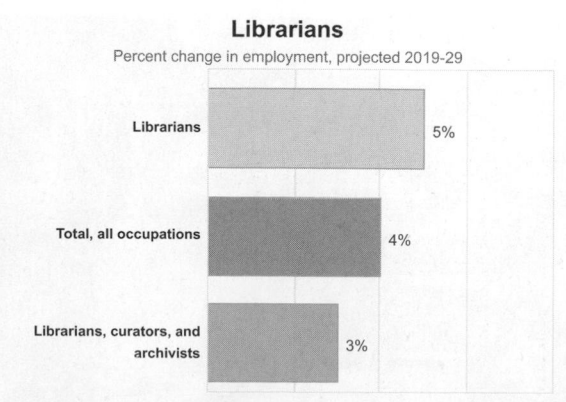

Librarians
Percent change in employment, projected 2019-29

Librarians — 5%
Total, all occupations — 4%
Librarians, curators, and archivists — 3%

Note: All Occupations includes all occupations in the U.S. Economy.
Source: U.S. Bureau of Labor Statistics, Employment Projections program.

occupations. These estimates are available for the nation as a whole, for individual states, and for metropolitan and nonmetropolitan areas.

Contacts for More Information

For more information about librarians, including accredited library education programs, visit
➤ American Library Association

For information about medical librarians, visit
➤ Medical Library Association

For information about law librarians, visit
➤ American Association of Law Libraries

For information about many different types of special librarians, visit
➤ Special Libraries Association

Library Technicians and Assistants

Summary

Quick Facts: Library Technicians and Assistants

2019 Median Pay	$30,560 per year $14.69 per hour
Typical Entry-Level Education	See below
Work Experience in a Related Occupation	None
On-the-job Training	See below
Number of Jobs, 2019	184,600
Job Outlook, 2019-29..	-4% (Decline)
Employment Change, 2019-29	-7,100

What Library Technicians and Assistants Do

Library technicians and assistants help librarians with all aspects of running a library.

Work Environment

Library technicians and assistants work in local public libraries, corporate and specialty libraries, and school and university libraries.

How to Become a Library Technician or Assistant

Library technicians typically need a postsecondary certificate. Library assistants typically need a high school diploma or its equivalent, combined with short-term on-the-job training.

Library technicians and assistants help patrons find library resources.

Pay

The median hourly wage for library assistants, clerical was $13.22 in May 2019.

The median hourly wage for library technicians was $16.78 in May 2019.

Job Outlook

Overall employment of library technicians and assistants is projected to decline 4 percent from 2019 to 2029. Although communities have tried to rebrand libraries for a variety of services and activities, library use has decreased.

State & Area Data

Explore resources for employment and wages by state and area for library technicians and assistants.

What Library Technicians and Assistants Do

Library technicians and assistants help librarians with all aspects of running a library. They assist patrons, organize library materials and information, and do clerical and administrative tasks.

Duties

Library technicians and assistants typically do the following:

- Loan library materials to patrons and collect returned materials
- Sort and reshelve returned books, periodicals, and other materials
- Catalogue and maintain library materials
- Handle interlibrary loans
- Register new patrons and issue library cards
- Answer routine reference questions from patrons
- Teach patrons how to use library resources
- Maintain computer databases used to locate library materials
- Perform routine clerical tasks such as answering phones and organizing files
- Help plan and participate in special programs, such as used-book sales, story times, or outreach programs

A librarian usually supervises library technicians and assistants. Both technicians and assistants help patrons find information and

Library technicians and assistants help shelve and organize materials.

organize library materials. However, library technicians typically have more responsibilities than library assistants.

Library technicians and assistants in small libraries have a broad range of duties. In large libraries, they tend to specialize in a particular area, such as user services or technical services. Those specializing in user services assist library patrons with locating resources and information. Those specializing in technical services research, acquire, catalog, and process materials to be added to the library's collections.

The following are examples of types of library technicians and assistants:

Academic library technicians and assistants help students, faculties, and staff in colleges and universities access resources and information related to coursework or research projects. Some teach students how to access and use library resources. They may work at service desks for reserve materials, special collections, or computer labs.

Public library technicians and assistants work in community libraries to serve members of the public. They help patrons find books to read for pleasure, assist patrons with their research, or teach patrons how to access the library's resources. Some technicians in public libraries may help plan programs for users, such as story time for children or book clubs for teens or adults.

School library technicians and assistants show students how to find and use library resources, maintain textbook collections, and help teachers develop curriculum materials.

Special library technicians and assistants work in settings other than school or public libraries, including government agencies, corporations, museums, law firms, and medical centers. They assist users, search library resources, compile bibliographies, and provide information on subjects of interest to the organization.

Work Environment

Library assistants, clerical held about 90,500 jobs in 2019. The largest employers of library assistants, clerical were as follows:

Local government, excluding education and hospitals...	61%
Colleges, universities, and professional schools; state, local, and private................................	14
Elementary and secondary schools; local......................	11
Other information services	9

Library technicians held about 94,100 jobs in 2019. The largest employers of library technicians were as follows:

Local government, excluding education and hospitals...	52%
Colleges, universities, and professional schools; state, local, and private................................	17
Elementary and secondary schools; state, local, and private...	14
Other information services	10

Library technicians and assistants generally work indoors. They spend much of their time at public service desks or at computer terminals. They may spend time in the library stacks reshelving books, a task that may require bending or stretching to reach the shelves.

Cataloguing or reshelving books may require bending or stretching to reach shelves.

Work Schedules

Many library technicians and assistants work part time. Library technicians and assistants in school libraries work during school hours. Those in public or college libraries may work weekends, evenings, and some holidays. In special libraries, technicians and assistants typically work during normal business hours but may have to work evenings and weekends.

How to Become a Library Technician or Assistant

Library technicians typically need a postsecondary certificate. Library assistants typically need a high school diploma or its equivalent, combined with short-term on-the-job training.

Education

Library technicians typically need a postsecondary certificate in library technology, which may include coursework in acquisitions, cataloguing, circulation, reference, and automated library systems. The American Library Association has information about certificate programs available by state.

Most library assistants typically need a high school diploma or equivalent.

Library technicians and assistants provide customer service to library patrons.

Training

Library assistants usually receive short-term on-the-job training to learn about libraries and library resources.

Important Qualities

Communication skills. Library technicians and assistants must be able to answer patrons' questions clearly and explain use of library resources.

Detail oriented. Library technicians and assistants must pay close attention to ensure that library materials and information are organized correctly and according to the library's organizational system.

Interpersonal skills. Library technicians and assistants need to work with library patrons, librarians, teachers, or researchers.

Listening skills. Library technicians and assistants need to listen to patrons to help them with research topics or with finding materials.

Advancement

Library technicians and assistants may advance to become supervisors and oversee daily library operations. To become a librarian, technicians and assistants need to earn a master's degree in library science.

Pay

The median hourly wage for library assistants, clerical was $13.22 in May 2019. The median wage is the wage at which half the workers in an occupation earned more than that amount and half earned less. The lowest 10 percent earned less than $9.15, and the highest 10 percent earned more than $21.62.

The median hourly wage for library technicians was $16.78 in May 2019. The lowest 10 percent earned less than $10.58, and the highest 10 percent earned more than $27.00.

In May 2019, the median hourly wages for library assistants, clerical in the top industries in which they worked were as follows:

Colleges, universities, and professional schools; state, local, and private	$15.48
Elementary and secondary schools; local	14.01
Local government, excluding education and hospitals	12.73
Other information services	12.16

In May 2019, the median hourly wages for library technicians in the top industries in which they worked were as follows:

Colleges, universities, and professional schools; state, local, and private	$19.81
Elementary and secondary schools; state, local, and private	17.14
Other information services	17.05
Local government, excluding education and hospitals	15.44

Library Technicians and Assistants
Median hourly wages, May 2019

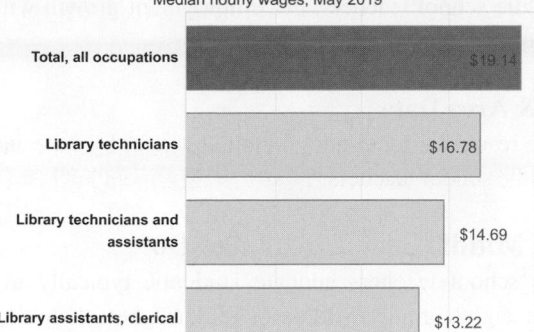

Total, all occupations	$19.14
Library technicians	$16.78
Library technicians and assistants	$14.69
Library assistants, clerical	$13.22

Note: All Occupations includes all occupations in the U.S. Economy.
Source: U.S. Bureau of Labor Statistics, Occupational Employment Statistics.

Many library technicians and assistants work part time. Library technicians and assistants in school libraries work during regular school hours. Those in public or college libraries may work weekends, evenings, and some holidays. In corporate libraries, library technicians and assistants work normal business hours but may have to work evenings and weekends.

Job Outlook

Overall employment of library technicians and assistants is projected to decline 4 percent from 2019 to 2029.

Although communities have tried to rebrand libraries for a variety of services and activities, library use has decreased. This reduces the need for library workers to help patrons find information and operate the libraries on a day-to-day basis. Additionally, budget constraints may limit the number of library technicians and assistants in local government and education services.

Job Prospects

Despite projected employment declines, about 24,900 openings for library technicians and assistants are projected each year, on average, over the decade.

All of those openings are expected to result from the need to replace workers who transfer to different occupations or exit the labor force, such as to retire.

Candidates who have an associate's or bachelor's degree may have the best prospects.

Library Technicians and Assistants
Percent change in employment, projected 2019-29

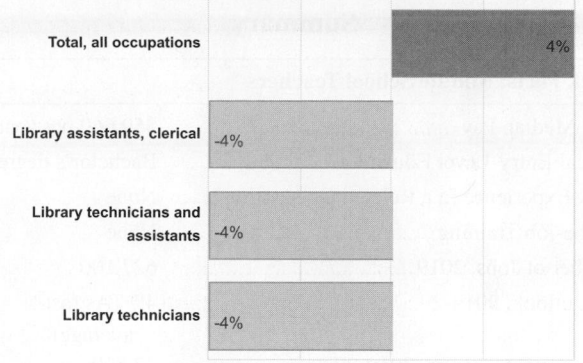

Total, all occupations	4%
Library assistants, clerical	-4%
Library technicians and assistants	-4%
Library technicians	-4%

Note: All Occupations includes all occupations in the U.S. Economy.
Source: U.S. Bureau of Labor Statistics, Employment Projections program.

Employment projections data for library technicians and assistants, 2019-29					
Occupational Title	SOC Code	Employment, 2019	Projected Employment, 2029	Change, 2019-29	
				Percent	Numeric
SOURCE: U.S. Bureau of Labor Statistics, Employment Projections program					
Library technicians and assistants	—	184,600	177,500	-4	-7,100
Library technicians	25-4031	94,100	90,500	-4	-3,600
Library assistants, clerical	43-4121	90,500	87,000	-4	-3,500

State & Area Data
Occupational Employment Statistics (OES)

The Occupational Employment Statistics (OES) program produces employment and wage estimates annually for over 800 occupations.

Contacts for More Information

For more information about library technicians and assistants careers, visit
➤ American Library Association

For information about medical libraries, visit
➤ Medical Library Association

For information about law libraries, visit
➤ American Association of Law Libraries

For information about many different types of special libraries, visit
➤ Special Libraries Association

Middle School Teachers

Summary

Quick Facts: Middle School Teachers

2019 Median Pay	$59,660 per year
Typical Entry-Level Education	Bachelor's degree
Work Experience in a Related Occupation	None
On-the-job Training	None
Number of Jobs, 2019	627,100
Job Outlook, 2019-29	4% (As fast as average)
Employment Change, 2019-29	22,500

What Middle School Teachers Do

Middle school teachers educate students, typically in sixth through eighth grades.

Work Environment

Middle school teachers work in public and private schools. They generally work during school hours when students are present and use nights and weekends to prepare lessons and grade papers. Most do not work during the summer.

How to Become a Middle School Teacher

Middle school teachers typically must have at least a bachelor's degree. In addition, public school teachers must have a state-issued certification or license.

Pay

The median annual wage for middle school teachers was $59,660 in May 2019.

Job Outlook

Employment of middle school teachers is projected to grow 4 percent from 2019 to 2029, about as fast as the average for all occupations. Rising student enrollment should increase demand for middle school teachers, but employment growth will vary by region.

State & Area Data

Explore resources for employment and wages by state and area for middle school teachers.

What Middle School Teachers Do

Middle school teachers educate students, typically in sixth through eighth grade. Middle school teachers help students build on the fundamentals taught in elementary school and prepare students for high school.

Duties

Middle school teachers typically do the following:

- Create lesson plans to teach students a subject
- Assess students to evaluate their abilities, strengths, and weaknesses
- Teach lessons they have planned to an entire class or to smaller groups
- Grade students' assignments and exams
- Communicate with parents or guardians about their child's progress
- Work with students individually to help them overcome specific learning challenges
- Prepare students for standardized tests required by the state
- Develop and enforce classroom rules
- Supervise students outside of the classroom—for example, during lunchtime or detention

Middle school typically goes from sixth to eighth grades. However, in some school districts, middle school may begin in fourth grade or extend through ninth grade.

In many schools, middle school teachers are responsible for certain subjects. For example, one teacher may teach math

Middle school teachers help students build on the fundamentals they learned in elementary schools to prepare them for the more difficult subjects and lessons in high school.

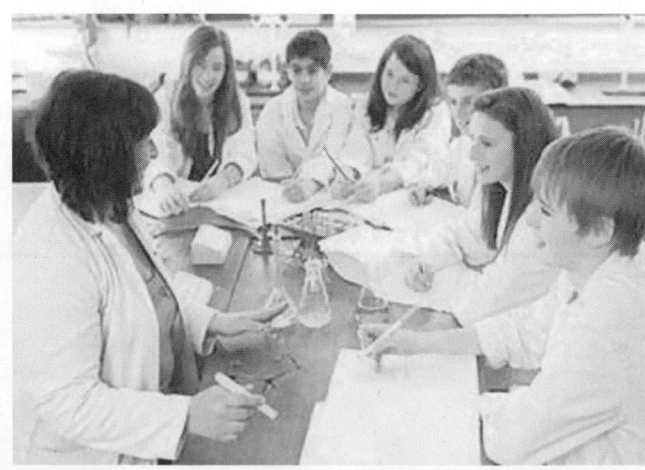

Some middle school teachers specialize in teaching a particular subject, such as science or math.

to several different classes of students throughout the day. However, other middle school teachers instruct on every subject to a single class.

Teachers use time during the day when they do not have classes to plan lessons, grade assignments, or meet with other teachers and staff.

Some middle schools have *English as a second language (ESL)* or *English for speakers of other languages (ESOL)* teachers who work with students learning the English language. ESL and ESOL teachers work with students individually or in groups to help them improve their English language skills and to help the students with assignments for their classes.

Middle school teachers may also work with special education teachers to adapt lessons. In some cases, middle school teachers may co-teach lessons with special education teachers.

Teachers must be comfortable using and learning new technology. With parents, teachers may use text-messaging applications to communicate about students' assignments and upcoming events. With their students, teachers may create websites or discussion boards to present information or to expand on a lesson taught in class.

Some middle school teachers coach sports teams and advise student clubs and groups, whose practices and meetings frequently take place before or after school.

Work Environment

Middle school teachers held about 627,100 jobs in 2019. The largest employers of middle school teachers were as follows:

Elementary and secondary schools; local...................... 86%

Most states have tenure laws, which provide job security after a certain number of years of satisfactory teaching.

Middle school teachers may find it rewarding to watch students develop new skills and gain an appreciation for knowledge and learning. However, teaching may be stressful. Schools may have large classes and lack important teaching tools, such

as current technology and textbooks. Some states are developing teacher mentoring programs and teacher development courses to help with the challenges of being a teacher.

Working with middle school students as they become adolescents also can be challenging. Teachers need to be aware of and understand what their students are going through outside of the classroom.

Work Schedules

Middle school teachers generally work during school hours when students are present. They may meet with parents, students, and other teachers before and after school. Teachers who coach sports or advise clubs generally do so before or after school. They often spend time in the evenings and on weekends grading papers and preparing lessons.

Many teachers work a traditional 10-month school year and have a 2-month break during the summer. They also have a short midwinter break. Some teachers work during the summer.

Teachers in districts with a year-round schedule typically work 9 weeks in a row and then have a break for 3 weeks before starting a new school session.

How to Become a Middle School Teacher

Middle school teachers typically must have a bachelor's degree. In addition, public school teachers must have a state-issued certification or license.

Middle school teachers need good communications skills in order to discuss students' needs with parents and administrators.

Middle school teachers may advise clubs or meet with students and parents before or after school.

Education

All states require public middle school teachers to have at least a bachelor's degree. Many states require middle school teachers to major in a content area, such as math or science. Other states require middle school teachers to major in elementary education.

Middle school teachers typically enroll in their college's teacher education program, which instructs them on presenting information to students of different abilities and backgrounds. Programs typically include a student-teaching program, in which they work with a mentor teacher and get experience teaching students in a classroom setting. For information about teacher preparation programs in your state, visit Teach.org.

Some states require middle school teachers to earn a master's degree after receiving their teaching certification and obtaining a job.

Teachers in private schools do not need to meet state requirements. However, private schools typically seek middle school teachers who have a bachelor's degree and a major in elementary education or a content area.

Licenses, Certifications, and Registrations

All states require teachers in public schools to be licensed or certified in the specific grade level that they will teach. Those who teach in private schools typically do not need a license. Requirements for certification or licensure vary by state but generally involve the following:

- A bachelor's degree with a minimum grade point average
- Completion of a student-teaching program
- Passing a background check
- Passing a general teaching certification test, as well as a test that demonstrates their knowledge of the subject they will teach.

For information about certification requirements in your state, visit Teach.org. Teachers are often required to complete professional development classes to keep their license or certification. Some states require teachers to complete a master's degree after receiving their certification and obtaining a job.

All states offer an alternative route to certification or licensure for people who already have a bachelor's degree but lack the education courses required for certification. Some alternative certification programs allow candidates to begin teaching immediately under the supervision of an experienced teacher. These programs cover teaching methods and child development. After they complete the program, candidates are awarded full certification. Other programs require students to take classes in education before they can teach.

Important Qualities

Communication skills. Teachers must share ideas with their students, other teachers, and school administrators and staff. In addition, they need to discuss student progress with parents.

Patience. Middle school teachers must stay calm in challenging situations, such as when students struggle with material or create disturbances in class.

Physical stamina. Working with middle school students can be tiring. Teachers need to keep up with the students physically, mentally, and emotionally.

Resourcefulness. Middle school teachers need to get students engaged in learning and adapt lessons to each student's needs.

Advancement

Experienced teachers may advance to serve as mentors to new teachers; they may also become lead teachers. In these positions, they help less experienced teachers to improve teaching skills.

With additional education or certification, teachers may become school counselors, school librarians, or instructional coordinators. Some become assistant principals or principals, both of which generally require additional education in education administration or leadership. For more information, see the profiles on school and career counselors, librarians, instructional coordinators, and elementary, middle, and high school principals.

Pay

The median annual wage for middle school teachers was $59,660 in May 2019. The median wage is the wage at which half the workers in an occupation earned more than that amount and half earned less. The lowest 10 percent earned less than $39,990, and the highest 10 percent earned more than $96,280.

In May 2019, the median annual wages for middle school teachers in the top industries in which they worked were as follows:

Elementary and secondary schools; local.............. $60,580

Middle school teachers generally work school hours when students are present. They may meet with parents, students,

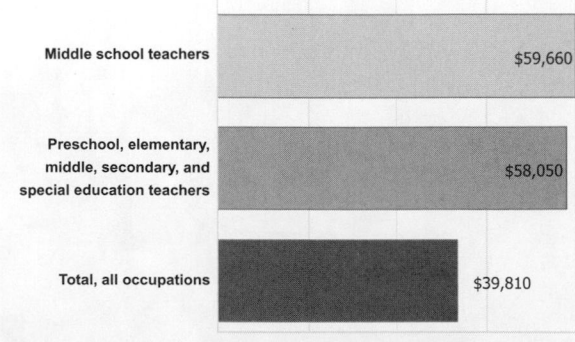

Middle School Teachers
Median annual wages, May 2019

Middle school teachers	$59,660
Preschool, elementary, middle, secondary, and special education teachers	$58,050
Total, all occupations	$39,810

Note: All Occupations includes all occupations in the U.S. Economy.
Source: U.S. Bureau of Labor Statistics, Occupational Employment Statistics.

Middle School Teachers

Percent change in employment, projected 2019-29

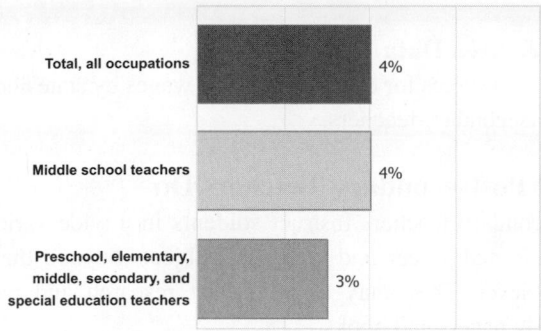

Total, all occupations	4%
Middle school teachers	4%
Preschool, elementary, middle, secondary, and special education teachers	3%

Note: All Occupations includes all occupations in the U.S. Economy.
Source: U.S. Bureau of Labor Statistics, Employment Projections program.

and other teachers before and after school. Teachers who coach sports or advise clubs generally do so before or after school. Teachers often spend time in the evenings and on weekends grading papers and preparing lessons.

Many teachers work the traditional 10-month school year and have a 2-month break during the summer. They also have a short midwinter break. Some teachers work during the summer.

Teachers in districts with a year-round schedule typically work 9 weeks in a row and then have a break for 3 weeks before starting a new school session.

Job Outlook

Employment of middle school teachers is projected to grow 4 percent from 2019 to 2029, about as fast as the average for all occupations. Rising student enrollment should increase demand for middle school teachers, but employment growth will vary by region.

The number of students in public middle schools is expected to increase over the coming decade, and the number of classes needed to accommodate these students is projected to rise. Despite expected increases in enrollment in public schools, employment

growth for middle school teachers often depends on state and local government budgets. If state and local governments experience budget deficits, they may increase class size while maintaining or reducing teaching staff levels. Conversely, budget surpluses at the state and local level could lead to additional employment growth for middle school teachers.

Job Prospects

Opportunities will vary by region and school setting. There may be better opportunities in urban and rural school districts than in suburban school districts. Flexibility in job location may increase job prospects.

Employment projections data for middle school teachers, 2019-29					
Occupational Title	SOC Code	Employment, 2019	Projected Employment, 2029	Change, 2019-29	
				Percent	Numeric
SOURCE: U.S. Bureau of Labor Statistics, Employment Projections program					
Middle school teachers, except special and career/technical education	25-2022	627,100	649,600	4	22,500

State & Area Data
Occupational Employment Statistics (OES)

The Occupational Employment Statistics (OES) program produces employment and wage estimates annually for over 800 occupations. These estimates are available for the nation as a whole, for individual states, and for metropolitan and nonmetropolitan areas.

Contacts for More Information

For more information about teaching and becoming a teacher, visit
➤ Teach.org
➤ American Federation of Teachers
➤ National Education Association

For more information about teacher preparation programs, visit
➤ Council for the Accreditation of Educator Preparation

Postsecondary Teachers

Summary

Quick Facts: Postsecondary Teachers

2019 Median Pay	$79,540 per year
Typical Entry-Level Education	See below
Work Experience in a Related Occupation	See below
On-the-job Training	None
Number of Jobs, 2019	1,329,900
Job Outlook, 2019-29...	9% (Much faster than average)
Employment Change, 2019-29	121,500

What Postsecondary Teachers Do

Postsecondary teachers instruct students in a wide variety of academic and technical subjects beyond the high school level.

Work Environment

Most postsecondary teachers work in public and private colleges and universities, professional schools, and junior or community colleges. Outside of class time, their schedules are generally flexible, and they may spend that time in administrative duties, advising students, and conducting research.

How to Become a Postsecondary Teacher

Educational requirements vary by subject and the type of educational institution. Typically, postsecondary teachers must have a Ph.D. However, a master's degree may be enough for some postsecondary teachers at community colleges, and others may need work experience in their field of expertise.

Pay

The median annual wage for postsecondary teachers was $79,540 in May 2019.

Job Outlook

Overall employment of postsecondary teachers is projected to grow 9 percent from 2019 to 2029, much faster than the average for all occupations. Projected employment growth varies by academic field.

State & Area Data

Explore resources for employment and wages by state and area for postsecondary teachers.

What Postsecondary Teachers Do

Postsecondary teachers instruct students in a wide variety of academic and career and technical subjects beyond the high school level. They may also conduct research and publish scholarly papers and books.

Duties

Postsecondary teachers typically do the following:

- Teach courses in their subject area
- Work with students who are taking classes to improve their knowledge or career skills
- Develop an instructional plan (known as a course outline or syllabus) for the course(s) they teach and ensure that it meets college and department standards

- Plan lessons and assignments
- Work with colleagues to develop or modify the curriculum for a degree or certificate program involving a series of courses
- Assess students' progress by grading assignments, papers, exams, and other work
- Advise students about which classes to take and how to achieve their goals
- Stay informed about changes and innovations in their field

Postsecondary teachers, often referred to as *professors* or *faculty*, specialize in a variety of subjects and fields. At colleges and universities, professors are organized into departments that specialize in a degree field, such as history, science, business, or music. A professor may teach one or more courses within

Postsecondary teachers instruct students in a wide variety of academic and technical subjects beyond the high school level.

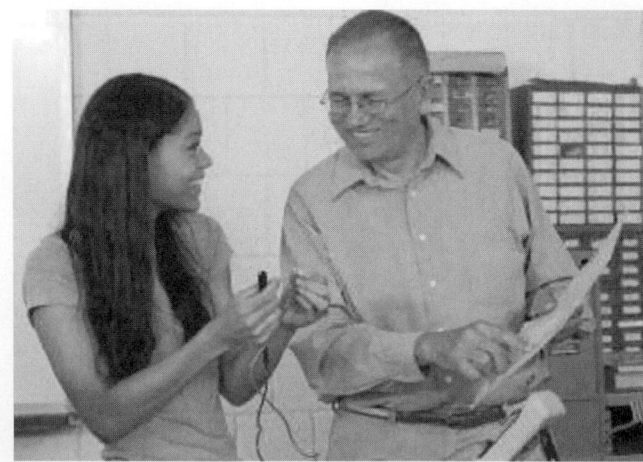

Professors may teach a wide variety of subjects, such as history, science, business, or music.

that department. For example, a mathematics professor may teach calculus, statistics, and a graduate seminar in a very specific area of mathematics.

Postsecondary teachers' duties vary with their positions in a university or college. In large colleges or universities, they may spend their time teaching, conducting research or experiments, publishing original research, applying for grants to fund their research, or supervising graduate teaching assistants who are teaching classes.

Postsecondary teachers who work in small colleges and universities or in community colleges often spend more time teaching classes and working with students. They may spend some time conducting research, but they do not have as much time to devote to it.

Full-time professors, particularly those who have tenure (a professor who cannot be fired without just cause), often are expected to spend more time on their research. They also may be expected to serve on more college and university committees.

Part-time professors, often known as *adjunct professors*, spend most of their time teaching students.

Professors may teach large classes of several hundred students (often with the help of graduate teaching assistants), smaller classes of about 40 to 50 students, seminars with just a few students, or laboratories where students practice the subject matter. They work with an increasingly varied student population as more part-time, older, and culturally diverse students are going to postsecondary schools.

Professors read scholarly articles, talk with colleagues, and participate in professional conferences to keep up with developments in their field. A tenured professor must do original research, document their analyses or critical reviews, and publish their findings.

Some postsecondary teachers work for online universities or teach online classes. They use the Internet to present lessons and information, to assign and accept students' work, and to participate in course discussions. Online professors use email, phone, and video chat apps to communicate with students, and might never meet their students in person.

Work Environment

Postsecondary teachers held about 1.3 million jobs in 2019. Employment in the detailed occupations that make up postsecondary teachers was distributed as follows:

Health specialties teachers, postsecondary	254,000
Art, drama, and music teachers, postsecondary	116,300
Business teachers, postsecondary	105,100
English language and literature teachers, postsecondary	81,300
Education teachers, postsecondary	77,300
Nursing instructors and teachers, postsecondary	72,900
Biological science teachers, postsecondary	64,700
Mathematical science teachers, postsecondary	60,100
Psychology teachers, postsecondary	46,800
Engineering teachers, postsecondary	44,600
Computer science teachers, postsecondary	38,500
Communications teachers, postsecondary	35,600
Philosophy and religion teachers, postsecondary	30,900
Foreign language and literature teachers, postsecondary	30,600
Chemistry teachers, postsecondary	26,400
History teachers, postsecondary	26,000
Law teachers, postsecondary	21,300
Political science teachers, postsecondary	19,800
Social sciences teachers, postsecondary, all other	19,300
Social work teachers, postsecondary	17,300
Physics teachers, postsecondary	17,100
Sociology teachers, postsecondary	17,000
Criminal justice and law enforcement teachers, postsecondary	16,800
Economics teachers, postsecondary	16,800
Area, ethnic, and cultural studies teachers, postsecondary	13,400
Atmospheric, earth, marine, and space sciences teachers, postsecondary	13,100
Agricultural sciences teachers, postsecondary	11,400
Architecture teachers, postsecondary	8,500
Environmental science teachers, postsecondary	7,600
Anthropology and archeology teachers, postsecondary	7,200
Library science teachers, postsecondary	5,400
Geography teachers, postsecondary	4,800
Forestry and conservation science teachers, postsecondary	2,100

Most classes are held during the day, but some are held on nights and weekends.

The largest employers of postsecondary teachers were as follows:

Colleges, universities, and professional schools;   40%
    private..
Colleges, universities, and professional schools; state...   37
Junior colleges; local   11
Junior colleges; state..   6

Many postsecondary teachers find their jobs rewarding because they are surrounded by others who enjoy the subject they teach. The opportunity to share their expertise with others is appealing to many.

However, some postsecondary teachers must find a balance between teaching students and doing research and publishing their findings. This can be stressful, especially for beginning teachers seeking advancement in 4-year research universities. At the community college level, professors focus mainly on teaching students and administrative duties.

Classes are generally held during the day, although some are offered in the evenings and weekends to accommodate students who have jobs or family obligations.

Although some postsecondary teachers teach summer courses, many use that time to conduct research, involve themselves in professional development, or to travel.

Work Schedules

Many postsecondary teachers teach part time, and may teach courses at several colleges or universities. Some may have a full-time job in their field of expertise in addition to a part-time teaching position. For example, an active lawyer or judge might teach a law school class during the evening.

Postsecondary teachers' schedules generally are flexible. Full-time teachers need to be on campus to teach classes and have office hours. Otherwise, they are free to set their schedule to prepare for classes and grade assignments. They may also spend time carrying out administrative responsibilities, such as serving on committees.

How to Become a Postsecondary Teacher

Educational requirements vary with the subject taught and the type of educational institution. Typically postsecondary teachers must have a Ph.D. However, a master's degree may be enough for some postsecondary teachers at community colleges. Other postsecondary teachers may need work experience in their field of expertise.

Education

Postsecondary teachers who work for 4-year colleges and universities typically need a doctoral degree in their field. Some schools may hire those with a master's degree or those who are doctoral degree candidates for some specialties, such as fine arts, or for some part-time positions.

Some institutions prefer to hire professors who have teaching experience, which can be gained by working as a graduate teaching assistant.

Doctoral programs generally take multiple years to complete, and students must already possess a bachelor's or master's degree before enrolling in a doctoral program. Doctoral students spend time writing a doctoral dissertation, which is a paper presenting original research in the student's field of study. Candidates usually specialize in a subfield, such as organic chemistry or European history.

Community colleges or career and technical schools also may hire those with a master's degree. However, some fields have more applicants than available positions. In these situations, institutions can be more selective, and they frequently choose applicants who have a Ph.D. over those with a master's degree.

Work Experience in a Related Occupation

Some institutions may prefer to hire those with teaching or other work experience, but this is not a requirement for all fields or for all employers.

In health specialties, art, law, or education fields, hands-on work experience in the industry can be important. Postsecondary teachers in these fields often gain experience by working in an occupation related to their field of expertise.

In fields such as biological science, physics, and chemistry, some postsecondary teachers have postdoctoral research experience. These short-term jobs, sometimes called "post-docs," usually involve working for 2 to 3 years as a research associate or in a similar position, often at a college or university.

Some postsecondary teachers gain teaching experience by working as graduate teaching assistants—students who are enrolled in a graduate program and teach classes in the institution in which they are enrolled.

Licenses, Certifications, and Registrations

Postsecondary teachers who prepare students for an occupation that requires a license, certification, or registration, may need to have—or they may benefit from having—the same credential. For example, a postsecondary nursing teacher might need a nursing license or a postsecondary education teacher might need a teaching license.

Advancement

A major goal for postsecondary teachers with a doctoral degree is attaining a tenure—a guarantee that a professor cannot be fired without just cause. It can take up to 7 years of moving up the ranks in tenure-track positions. The ranks are assistant professor, associate professor, and professor. Tenure is granted through a review of the candidate's research, contribution to the institution, and teaching.

Tenure and tenure-track positions are declining as institutions are relying more heavily on part-time professors.

Some tenured professors advance to administrative positions, such as dean or president. For information on deans and other administrative positions, see the profile on postsecondary education administrators. For more information about college and university presidents, see the profile on top executives.

Important Qualities

Critical-thinking skills. To challenge established theories and beliefs, conduct original research, and design experiments, postsecondary teachers need to apply analyses and logic to arrive at sound conclusions.

Interpersonal skills. Most postsecondary teachers need to be able to work well with others and must have good communication skills to serve on committees and give lectures.

Resourcefulness. Postsecondary teachers need to be able to present information in a way that students will understand. They need to adapt to the different learning styles of their students and teach students who have little or no experience with the subject.

Speaking skills. Postsecondary teachers need good verbal skills to give lectures.

Writing skills. Postsecondary teachers need to be skilled writers to publish original research and analysis.

Pay

The median annual wage for postsecondary teachers was $79,540 in May 2019. The median wage is the wage at which half the workers in an occupation earned more than that amount

and half earned less. The lowest 10 percent earned less than $40,480, and the highest 10 percent earned more than $174,960.

Median annual wages for postsecondary teachers in May 2019 were as follows:

Law teachers, postsecondary	$113,530
Economics teachers, postsecondary	104,370
Engineering teachers, postsecondary	101,010
Health specialties teachers, postsecondary	97,320
Atmospheric, earth, marine, and space sciences teachers, postsecondary	92,040
Physics teachers, postsecondary	89,590
Architecture teachers, postsecondary	87,900
Business teachers, postsecondary	87,200
Anthropology and archeology teachers, postsecondary	86,220
Political science teachers, postsecondary	85,930
Forestry and conservation science teachers, postsecondary	85,450
Computer science teachers, postsecondary	85,180
Biological science teachers, postsecondary	83,300
Agricultural sciences teachers, postsecondary	83,260
Environmental science teachers, postsecondary	82,430
Geography teachers, postsecondary	80,520
Chemistry teachers, postsecondary	79,550
Area, ethnic, and cultural studies teachers, postsecondary	77,070
Psychology teachers, postsecondary	76,620
Sociology teachers, postsecondary	75,290
Philosophy and religion teachers, postsecondary	75,240
History teachers, postsecondary	75,170
Nursing instructors and teachers, postsecondary	74,600
Mathematical science teachers, postsecondary	73,690
Social work teachers, postsecondary	72,070
Social sciences teachers, postsecondary, all other	71,530

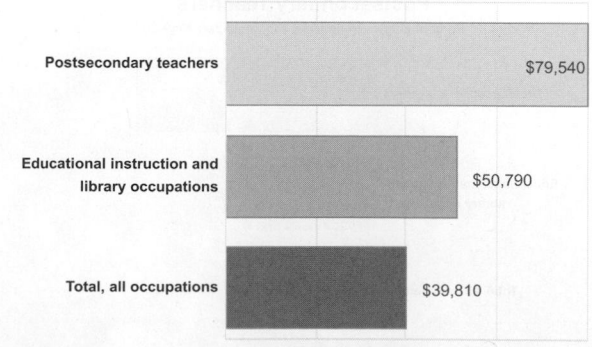

Postsecondary Teachers
Median annual wages, May 2019

Postsecondary teachers $79,540

Educational instruction and library occupations $50,790

Total, all occupations $39,810

Note: All Occupations includes all occupations in the U.S. Economy.
Source: U.S. Bureau of Labor Statistics, Occupational Employment Statistics.

Library science teachers, postsecondary 71,410

Communications teachers, postsecondary 70,630

Foreign language and literature teachers,
    postsecondary 69,990
Art, drama, and music teachers, postsecondary ... 69,530

English language and literature teachers,
    postsecondary 68,490
Education teachers, postsecondary......................... 65,510

Criminal justice and law enforcement teachers,
    postsecondary 62,860

In May 2019, the median annual wages for postsecondary teachers in the top industries in which they worked were as follows:

Junior colleges; local $82,850

Colleges, universities, and professional schools;   80,960
    state...

Colleges, universities, and professional schools;   80,760
    private...
Junior colleges; state.. 61,430

Wages can vary by institution type. Postsecondary teachers typically have higher wages in colleges, universities, and professional schools than they do in community colleges or other types of schools.

Many postsecondary teachers work part time. They may work part time at several colleges or universities, or have a full-time job in their field of expertise in addition to a part-time teaching position.

Postsecondary teachers' schedules generally are flexible. Full-time teachers need to be on campus to teach classes and have office hours. Otherwise, they are free to set their schedule to prepare for classes and grade assignments. They may also spend time carrying out administrative responsibilities, such as serving on committees.

Job Outlook

Overall employment of postsecondary teachers is projected to grow 9 percent from 2019 to 2029, much faster than the average

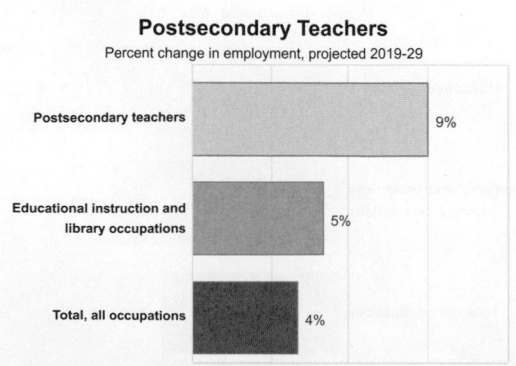

About this section

Postsecondary Teachers
Percent change in employment, projected 2019-29

Postsecondary teachers — 9%

Educational instruction and library occupations — 5%

Total, all occupations — 4%

Note: All Occupations includes all occupations in the U.S. Economy.
Source: U.S. Bureau of Labor Statistics, Employment Projections program.

for all occupations. Both part-time and full-time postsecondary teachers are included in this projection.

The number of people attending postsecondary institutions is expected to grow in the next decade. Students will continue to seek higher education to gain the additional education and skills necessary to meet their career goals. As more people enter colleges and universities, more postsecondary teachers will be needed to serve these additional students. Colleges and universities are likely to hire more part-time teachers to meet this demand. In all disciplines, there is expected to be a limited number of full-time nontenure and full-time tenure positions.

However, despite expected increases in enrollment, employment growth in public colleges and universities will depend on state and local government budgets. If budgets for higher education are reduced, employment growth may be limited.

Overall employment of postsecondary teachers is projected to increase, but it will vary by field. For example, employment of health specialties teachers is projected to grow 21 percent from 2019 to 2029, much faster than the average for all occupations. As an aging population increasingly demands healthcare services, additional postsecondary teachers are expected to be needed to help educate the workers who will provide these services.

Job Prospects

There are expected to be more job opportunities for part-time postsecondary teachers since many institutions are filling vacancies with part-time rather than full-time teachers. There will be a limited number of full-time tenure-track positions and competition is expected to be high.

Some fields, such as health specialties and nursing, will likely experience better job prospects than others, such as those in the humanities.

Occupational Title	SOC Code	Employment, 2019	Projected Employment, 2029	Change, 2019-29 Percent	Change, 2019-29 Numeric
Postsecondary teachers	—	1,329,900	1,451,400	9	121,500
Business teachers, postsecondary	25-1011	105,100	117,700	12	12,700
Computer science teachers, postsecondary	25-1021	38,500	39,500	3	1,000
Mathematical science teachers, postsecondary	25-1022	60,100	60,800	1	800
Architecture teachers, postsecondary	25-1031	8,500	9,000	5	400
Engineering teachers, postsecondary	25-1032	44,600	48,400	9	3,800
Agricultural sciences teachers, postsecondary	25-1041	11,400	11,700	2	200
Biological science teachers, postsecondary	25-1042	64,700	70,700	9	6,000
Forestry and conservation science teachers, postsecondary	25-1043	2,100	2,200	2	0

Employment projections data for postsecondary teachers, 2019-29

SOURCE: U.S. Bureau of Labor Statistics, Employment Projections program

Employment projections data for postsecondary teachers, 2019-29					
Occupational Title	SOC Code	Employment, 2019	Projected Employment, 2029	Change, 2019-29	
				Percent	Numeric
Atmospheric, earth, marine, and space sciences teachers, postsecondary	25-1051	13,100	13,400	2	200
Chemistry teachers, postsecondary	25-1052	26,400	27,500	4	1,100
Environmental science teachers, postsecondary	25-1053	7,600	7,800	4	300
Physics teachers, postsecondary	25-1054	17,100	17,800	4	800
Anthropology and archeology teachers, postsecondary	25-1061	7,200	7,500	4	300
Area, ethnic, and cultural studies teachers, postsecondary	25-1062	13,400	14,000	5	700
Economics teachers, postsecondary	25-1063	16,800	17,600	5	900
Geography teachers, postsecondary	25-1064	4,800	5,000	3	100
Political science teachers, postsecondary	25-1065	19,800	20,800	5	1,000
Psychology teachers, postsecondary	25-1066	46,800	51,000	9	4,100
Sociology teachers, postsecondary	25-1067	17,000	17,600	4	600
Social sciences teachers, postsecondary, all other	25-1069	19,300	19,200	0	-100
Health specialties teachers, postsecondary	25-1071	254,000	306,100	21	52,100
Nursing instructors and teachers, postsecondary	25-1072	72,900	85,700	18	12,800
Education teachers, postsecondary	25-1081	77,300	81,000	5	3,700
Library science teachers, postsecondary	25-1082	5,400	5,500	3	200

Employment projections data for postsecondary teachers, 2019-29					
Occupational Title	SOC Code	Employment, 2019	Projected Employment, 2029	Change, 2019-29	
				Percent	Numeric
Criminal justice and law enforcement teachers, postsecondary	25-1111	16,800	17,900	7	1,100
Law teachers, postsecondary	25-1112	21,300	22,800	7	1,500
Social work teachers, postsecondary	25-1113	17,300	18,300	6	1,000
Art, drama, and music teachers, postsecondary	25-1121	116,300	122,800	6	6,500
Communications teachers, postsecondary	25-1122	35,600	36,700	3	1,100
English language and literature teachers, postsecondary	25-1123	81,300	82,900	2	1,700
Foreign language and literature teachers, postsecondary	25-1124	30,600	32,300	6	1,700
History teachers, postsecondary	25-1125	26,000	27,000	4	900
Philosophy and religion teachers, postsecondary	25-1126	30,900	32,900	7	2,100

State & Area Data
Occupational Employment Statistics (OES)
The Occupational Employment Statistics (OES) program produces employment and wage estimates annually for over 800 occupations. These estimates are available for the nation as a whole, for individual states, and for metropolitan and nonmetropolitan areas.

Contacts for More Information
For more information about postsecondary teachers, visit
➤ Council of Graduate Schools

Preschool Teachers

Summary

Quick Facts: Preschool Teachers

2019 Median Pay	$30,520 per year $14.67 per hour
Typical Entry-Level Education	Associate's degree
Work Experience in a Related Occupation	None
On-the-job Training	None
Number of Jobs, 2019	540,400
Job Outlook, 2019-29	2% (Slower than average)
Employment Change, 2019-29	13,500

What Preschool Teachers Do
Preschool teachers educate and care for children younger than age 5 who have not yet entered kindergarten.

Work Environment
Preschool teachers typically work in public and private schools or childcare centers. Many work the traditional 10-month school year, but some work year-round.

How to Become a Preschool Teacher
Education and training requirements vary based on settings and state regulations. Preschool teachers typically need at least an associate's degree.

Preschool teachers educate and care for children, younger than the age of 5, who have not yet entered kindergarten.

Pay

The median annual wage for preschool teachers was $30,520 in May 2019.

Job Outlook

Employment of preschool teachers is projected to grow 2 percent from 2019 to 2029, slower than the average for all occupations.

State & Area Data

Explore resources for employment and wages by state and area for preschool teachers.

What Preschool Teachers Do

Preschool teachers educate and care for children younger than age 5 who have not yet entered kindergarten. They teach language, motor, and social skills to young children.

Duties

Preschool teachers typically do the following:

- Teach children basic skills such as identifying colors, shapes, numbers, and letters
- Work with children in groups or one on one, depending on the needs of children and on the subject matter
- Plan and carry out a curriculum that focuses on different areas of child development
- Organize activities so children can learn about the world, explore interests, and develop skills
- Develop schedules and routines to ensure children have enough physical activity and rest
- Watch for signs of emotional or developmental problems in each child and bring them to the attention of the child's parents
- Keep records of the children's progress, routines, and interests, and inform parents about their child's development

Preschool teachers use play to teach children about the world.

Young children learn from playing, problem solving, and experimenting. Preschool teachers use play and other instructional techniques to teach children. For example, they use storytelling and rhyming games to teach language and vocabulary. They may help improve children's social skills by having them work together to build a neighborhood in a sandbox or teach math by having children count when building with blocks.

Preschool teachers work with children from different ethnic, racial, and religious backgrounds. Teachers include topics in their lessons that teach children how to respect people of different backgrounds and cultures.

Work Environment

Preschool teachers held about 540,400 jobs in 2019. The largest employers of preschool teachers were as follows:

Child day care services	62%
Religious, grantmaking, civic, professional, and similar organizations	16
Elementary and secondary schools; state, local, and private	14
Individual and family services	2

Preschool teachers usually work in public schools, private schools, and childcare centers that have preschool programs.

It may be rewarding to see children develop new skills and gain an appreciation of knowledge and learning. However, it can also be tiring to work with young, active children all day.

Work Schedules

Preschool teachers in public schools generally work during school hours. Many work the traditional 10-month school year and have a 2-month break during the summer. Some preschool teachers may teach in summer programs.

Teachers in districts with a year-round schedule typically work 9 weeks in a row and then have a break for 3 weeks before starting a new school session.

Those working in daycare settings may work year-round with longer hours.

How to Become a Preschool Teacher

Education and training requirements vary based on settings and state regulations. Preschool teachers typically need at least an associate's degree.

Education

Preschool teachers typically need at least an associate's degree.

Preschool teachers in center-based Head Start programs are required to have at least an associate's degree. However, at least 50 percent of all preschool teachers in Head Start programs nationwide must have a bachelor's degree in early childhood education or a related field. Those with a degree in a related field must have experience teaching preschool-age children.

In public schools, preschool teachers are generally required to have at least a bachelor's degree in early childhood education or a related field. Bachelor's degree programs include instruction on children's development, teaching young children, and observing and documenting children's progress.

Licenses, Certifications, and Registrations

Some states require preschool teachers to obtain the Child Development Associate (CDA) credential offered by the

Preschool teachers must plan lessons that engage young students and must also adapt their lessons to suit different learning styles.

Council for Professional Recognition. Obtaining the CDA credential requires coursework, experience in the field, a written exam, and observation of the candidate working with children. The CDA credential must be renewed every 3 years.

In public schools, preschool teachers must be licensed to teach early childhood education, which covers preschool through third grade. Requirements vary by state, but they generally require a bachelor's degree and passing an exam to demonstrate competency. Most states require teachers to complete continuing education credits in order to maintain their license.

Other Experience

A few states require preschool teachers to have some work experience in a childcare setting. In these states, preschool teachers often start out as childcare workers or teacher assistants. The amount of experience needed varies by state.

Important Qualities

Communication skills. Preschool teachers need good writing and speaking skills to talk to parents and colleagues about children's progress. They must also be able to communicate well with small children.

Creativity. Preschool teachers must plan lessons that engage young children. In addition, they need to adapt their lessons to suit different learning styles.

Interpersonal skills. Preschool teachers must understand children's emotional needs and be able to develop relationships with parents, children, and coworkers.

Organizational skills. Teachers need to be organized to plan lessons and keep records of the children.

Patience. Working with children may be stressful. Preschool teachers should be able to respond calmly to overwhelming and difficult situations.

Physical stamina. Preschool teachers should have a lot of energy, because working with children can be physically demanding.

Preschool Teachers
Median annual wages, May 2019

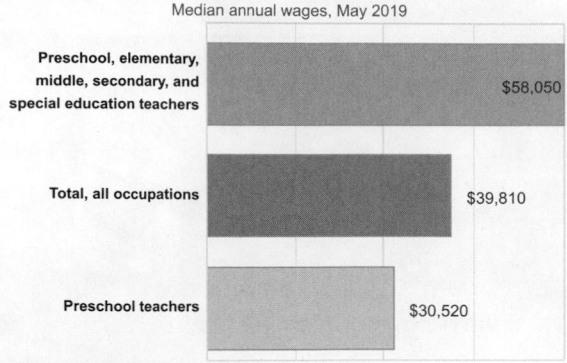

Note: All Occupations includes all occupations in the U.S. Economy.
Source: U.S. Bureau of Labor Statistics, Occupational Employment
Statistics.

Preschool Teachers
Percent change in employment, projected 2019-29

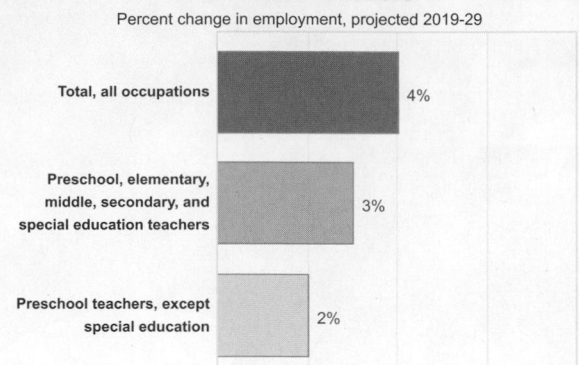

Note: All Occupations includes all occupations in the U.S. Economy.
Source: U.S. Bureau of Labor Statistics, Employment Projections
program.

Advancement

Experienced preschool teachers may advance to become the director of a preschool or childcare center or a lead teacher. Those with a bachelor's degree in early childhood education frequently are qualified to teach kindergarten through grade 3, in addition to preschool. Teaching positions at these higher grades typically pay more. For more information, see the profiles on preschool and childcare center directors and kindergarten and elementary school teachers.

Pay

The median annual wage for preschool teachers was $30,520 in May 2019. The median wage is the wage at which half the workers in an occupation earned more than that amount and half earned less. The lowest 10 percent earned less than $21,140, and the highest 10 percent earned more than $55,050.

In May 2019, the median annual wages for preschool teachers in the top industries in which they worked were as follows:

Elementary and secondary schools; state, local, and private...	$46,710
Individual and family services	32,510
Religious, grantmaking, civic, professional, and similar organizations	31,660
Child day care services...	28,700

Preschool teachers in public schools generally work during school hours. Many work the traditional 10-month school year and a 2-month break during the summer. Some preschool teachers may teach in summer programs.

Teachers in districts with a year-round schedule typically work 8 weeks in a row and then have a break for 1 week before starting a new school session. They also have a 5-week midwinter break.

Those working in daycare settings may work year-round and have longer hours.

Job Outlook

Employment of preschool teachers is projected to grow 2 percent from 2019 to 2029, slower than the average for all occupations.

Early childhood education is important for a child's intellectual and social development. Preschool teachers should be needed to meet the slowly increasing demand for early childhood education.

Job Prospects

Teachers who have experience working with preschool-aged children may have better opportunities finding a job than those without experience.

Employment projections data for preschool teachers, 2019-29				Change, 2019-29	
Occupational Title	SOC Code	Employment, 2019	Projected Employment, 2029	Percent	Numeric
SOURCE: U.S. Bureau of Labor Statistics, Employment Projections program					
Preschool teachers, except special education	25-2011	540,400	553,900	2	13,500

State & Area Data
Occupational Employment Statistics (OES)

The Occupational Employment Statistics (OES) program produces employment and wage estimates annually for over 800 occupations. These estimates are available for the nation as a whole, for individual states, and for metropolitan and nonmetropolitan areas.

Contacts for More Information

For more information about early childhood education, visit
➤ National Association for the Education of Young Children

For more information about professional credentials, visit
➤ Council for Professional Recognition

Special Education Teachers

Summary

Quick Facts: Special Education Teachers

2019 Median Pay	$61,030 per year
Typical Entry-Level Education	Bachelor's degree
Work Experience in a Related Occupation	None
On-the-job Training	None
Number of Jobs, 2019	443,700
Job Outlook, 2019-29	3% (As fast as average)
Employment Change, 2019-29	14,300

What Special Education Teachers Do

Special education teachers work with students who have a wide range of learning, mental, emotional, and physical disabilities.

Work Environment

Most special education teachers work in public schools, teaching students from preschool to high school. Many work the traditional 10-month school year, but some work year round.

How to Become a Special Education Teacher

Special education teachers in public schools are required to have a bachelor's degree and a state-issued certification or license. Teachers in private schools typically need a bachelor's degree but may not be required to have a state license or certification.

Pay

The median annual wage for special education teachers was $61,030 in May 2019.

Job Outlook

Overall employment of special education teachers is projected to grow 3 percent from 2019 to 2029, about as fast as the average for all occupations. Demand for special education services and teachers should rise as disabilities are being identified earlier and as children with disabilities are enrolled into special education programs.

State & Area Data

Explore resources for employment and wages by state and area for special education teachers.

What Special Education Teachers Do

Special education teachers work with students who have learning, mental, emotional, or physical disabilities. They adapt general education lessons and teach various subjects to students with mild to moderate disabilities. They also teach basic skills to students with severe disabilities.

Duties

Special education teachers typically do the following:

- Assess students' skills and determine their educational needs
- Adapt general lessons to meet students' needs
- Develop Individualized Education Programs (IEPs) for each student
- Plan activities that are specific to each student's abilities
- Teach and mentor students as a class, in small groups, and one-on-one
- Implement IEPs, assess students' performance, and track their progress
- Update IEPs throughout the school year to reflect students' progress and goals
- Discuss students' progress with parents, other teachers, counselors, and administrators
- Supervise and mentor teacher assistants who work with students with disabilities
- Prepare and help students transition from grade to grade and from school to life outside of school

Special education teachers work with students who have a wide range of learning disabilities.

Special education teachers may teach students in small groups or on a one-on-one basis.

Special education teachers work with students from pre-school to high school. They instruct students who have mental, emotional, physical, or learning disabilities. For example, some help students develop study skills, such as highlighting text and using flashcards. Others work with students who have physical disabilities and may use a wheelchair or other adaptive devices. Still others work with students who have sensory disabilities, such as visual or hearing impairments. They also may work with those who have autism spectrum disorders or emotional disorders, such as anxiety and depression.

Special education teachers work with general education teachers, specialists, administrators, and parents to develop IEPs. Students' IEPs outline their goals, including academic or behavioral milestones, and services they are to receive, such as speech therapy. Educators and parents also meet to discuss updates and changes to IEPs.

Special education teachers must be comfortable using and learning new technology. Most use computers to keep records of their students' performance, prepare lesson plans, and update IEPs. Some teachers also use assistive technology aids, such as Braille writers and computer software, that help them communicate with their students.

Special education teachers' duties vary by their work setting, students' disabilities, and specialties.

Some special education teachers work in classrooms or resource centers that include only students with disabilities. In these settings, teachers plan, adapt, and present lessons to meet each student's needs. They teach students individually or in small groups.

In inclusive classrooms, special education teachers instruct students with disabilities who are in general education classrooms. They work with general education teachers to adapt lessons so that students with disabilities can more easily understand them.

Some special education teachers work with students who have moderate to severe disabilities. These teachers help students, who may be eligible for services until age 21, develop basic life skills. Some teach the skills necessary for students with moderate disabilities to live independently, find a job, and manage money and their time. For more information about other workers who help individuals with disabilities develop skills necessary to live independently, see the profiles on occupational therapists and occupational therapy assistants and aides.

Work Environment

Special education teachers held about 443,700 jobs in 2019. Employment in the detailed occupations that make up special education teachers was distributed as follows:

Special education teachers, kindergarten and elementary school	193,000
Special education teachers, secondary school	143,000
Special education teachers, middle school	84,700
Special education teachers, preschool	23,000

Special education teachers work with students from preschool to high school.

The largest employers of special education teachers were as follows:

Elementary and secondary schools; local	86%
Elementary and secondary schools; private	7

A small number of special education teachers work with students in residential facilities, hospitals, and the students' homes. They may travel to these locations. Some teachers work with infants and toddlers at the child's home. They teach the child's parents ways to help the child develop skills.

Helping students with disabilities may be rewarding. It also can be stressful, emotionally demanding, and physically draining.

Work Schedules

Special education teachers typically work during school hours. In addition to providing instruction during this time, they grade papers, update students' records, and prepare lessons. They may meet with parents, students, and other teachers or specialists before and after classes.

Many work the traditional 10-month school year and have a 2-month break during the summer. They also have a short mid-winter break. Some teachers work in summer programs.

Teachers in districts with a year-round schedule typically work 9 weeks in a row and then are on break for 3 weeks.

How to Become a Special Education Teacher

Special education teachers in public schools are required to have at least a bachelor's degree and a state-issued certification or license. Private schools typically require teachers to have a bachelor's degree, but the teachers are not required to be licensed or certified.

Education

All states require special education teachers in public schools to have at least a bachelor's degree. Some require teachers to

Special education teachers need to be able to explain concepts in terms students with learning disabilities can understand.

earn a degree specifically in special education. Others allow them to major in elementary education or a content area, such as math or science, and pursue a minor in special education.

In a program leading to a bachelor's degree in special education, prospective teachers learn about the different types of disabilities and how to present information so that students will understand. Programs typically include a student-teaching program, in which prospective teachers work with a mentor and get experience instructing students in a classroom setting. To become fully certified, states may require special education teachers to complete a master's degree in special education after obtaining a job.

Private schools typically require teachers to have at least a bachelor's degree in special education.

Licenses, Certifications, and Registrations

All states require teachers in public schools to be licensed in the specific grade level that they teach. A license frequently is referred to as a certification. Those who teach in private schools typically do not need to be licensed.

Requirements for certification or licensure can vary by state but generally involve the following:

- A bachelor's degree with a minimum grade point average
- Completion of a student-teaching program
- Passing a background check
- Passing a general teaching certification test, as well as a test that demonstrates knowledge of the subject the candidate will teach

For information about teacher preparation programs and certification requirements, visit Teach.org or contact your state's board of education.

All states offer an alternative route to certification or licensure for people who already have a bachelor's degree. These alternative programs cover teaching methods and child development. Candidates are awarded full certification after they complete the program. Other alternative programs require prospective teachers to take classes in education before they can start to teach. Teachers may be awarded a master's degree after completing either type of program.

Advancement

Experienced teachers may advance to become mentors who help less experienced teachers improve their instructional skills. They also may become lead teachers.

Teachers may become school counselors, instructional coordinators, and elementary, middle, and high school principals. These positions generally require additional education, an advanced degree, or certification. An advanced degree in education administration or leadership may be helpful.

Important Qualities

Communication skills. Special education teachers need to explain concepts in terms that students with learning disabilities can understand. They also must write Individualized Education Programs (IEPs) and share students' progress with general education teachers, counselors and other specialists, administrators, and parents.

Critical-thinking skills. Special education teachers must be able to assess students' progress and use the information to adapt lessons.

Interpersonal skills. Special education teachers work regularly with a team of educators and the student's parents to develop IEPs. As a result, they need to be able to build positive working relationships.

Patience. Special education teachers must be able to stay calm instructing students with disabilities, who may lack basic skills, present behavioral or other challenges, or require repeated efforts to understand material.

Resourcefulness. Special education teachers must develop different ways to present information that meet their students' needs. They also help general education teachers adapt their lessons to the needs of students with disabilities.

Pay

The median annual wage for special education teachers was $61,030 in May 2019. The median wage is the wage at which half the workers in an occupation earned more than that amount and half earned less. The lowest 10 percent earned less than $40,730, and the highest 10 percent earned more than $98,530.

Median annual wages for special education teachers in May 2019 were as follows:

Special education teachers, secondary school	$61,710
Special education teachers, middle school	61,440
Special education teachers, kindergarten and elementary school	60,460
Special education teachers, preschool	60,000

Special Education Teachers
Median annual wages, May 2019

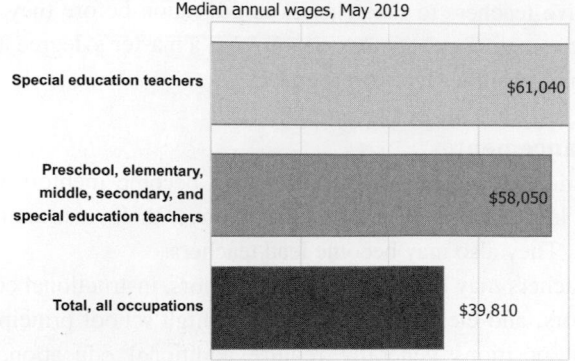

Special Education Teachers
Percent change in employment, projected 2019-29

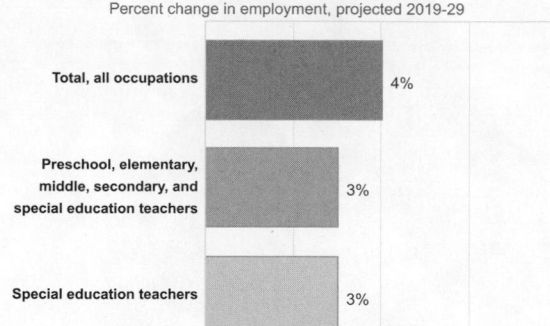

Note: All Occupations includes all occupations in the U.S. Economy.
Source: U.S. Bureau of Labor Statistics, Occupational Employment
Statistics.

Note: All Occupations includes all occupations in the U.S. Economy.
Source: U.S. Bureau of Labor Statistics, Employment Projections
program.

In May 2019, the median annual wages for special education teachers in the top industries in which they worked were as follows:

Elementary and secondary schools; local............... $61,620

Elementary and secondary schools; private............ 53,560

Special education teachers typically work during school hours. In addition to providing instruction during this time, they grade papers, update students' records, and prepare lessons. They may meet with parents, students, and other teachers or specialists before and after classes.

Many work the traditional 10-month school year and have a 2-month break during the summer. They also have a short midwinter break. Some teachers work in summer programs.

Teachers in districts with a year-round schedule typically work 9 weeks in a row and then are on break for 3 weeks.

Job Outlook

Overall employment of special education teachers is projected to grow 3 percent from 2019 to 2029, about as fast as the average for all occupations. Employment of preschool education teachers is projected to grow 8 percent from 2019 to 2029, much faster than the average for all occupations. However, because it is a small occupation, the fast growth will result in only about 1,900 new jobs over the 10-year period. Demand will be driven by school enrollments and the need for special education services.

Demand for special education services and teachers should rise as disabilities are being identified earlier and as children with disabilities are enrolled into special education programs.

Federal laws require that every state must maintain the same level of financial support for special education every year. This reduces the threat of employment layoffs due to state or federal budget constraints. However, employment growth may depend on increases in funding.

Employment projections data for special education teachers, 2019-29					
Occupational Title	SOC Code	Employment, 2019	Projected Employment, 2029	Change, 2019-29	
				Percent	Numeric
SOURCE: U.S. Bureau of Labor Statistics, Employment Projections program					
Special education teachers	—	443,700	458,000	3	14,300
Special education teachers, preschool	25-2051	23,000	24,900	8	1,900
Special education teachers, kindergarten and elementary school	25-2052	193,000	198,600	3	5,600
Special education teachers, middle school	25-2057	84,700	86,900	3	2,200
Special education teachers, secondary school	25-2058	143,000	147,600	3	4,600

State & Area Data
Occupational Employment Statistics (OES)

The Occupational Employment Statistics (OES) program produces employment and wage estimates annually for over 800 occupations. These estimates are available for the nation as a whole, for individual states, and for metropolitan and nonmetropolitan areas.

Contacts for More Information

For more information about special education teachers, visit
➤ Council for Exceptional Children
➤ Personnel Improvement Center
➤ National Association of Special Education Teachers

For more information about teaching and becoming a teacher, visit
➤ Teach.org
➤ American Federation of Teachers
➤ National Education Association

Teacher Assistants

Summary

Quick Facts: Teacher Assistants

2019 Median Pay	$27,920 per year
Typical Entry-Level Education	Some college, no degree
Work Experience in a Related Occupation	None
On-the-job Training	None
Number of Jobs, 2019	1,395,900
Job Outlook, 2019-29	4% (As fast as average)
Employment Change, 2019-29	50,500

What Teacher Assistants Do

Teacher assistants work with a licensed teacher to give students additional attention and instruction.

Work Environment

Teacher assistants typically work in schools, at childcare centers, and for religious organizations. Some teacher assistants work part time. Most do not work during the summer.

How to Become a Teacher Assistant

Teacher assistants typically need to have completed at least 2 years of college coursework.

Pay

The median annual wage for teacher assistants was $27,920 in May 2019.

Job Outlook

Employment of teacher assistants is projected to grow 4 percent from 2019 to 2029, about as fast as the average for all occupations. Rising student enrollment along with state and federal funding for education programs should affect growth.

State & Area Data

Explore resources for employment and wages by state and area for teacher assistants.

What Teacher Assistants Do

Teacher assistants work with a licensed teacher to give students additional attention and instruction.

Duties

Teacher assistants typically do the following:

- Reinforce lessons by reviewing material with students one-on-one or in small groups
- Follow school and class rules to teach students proper behavior
- Help teachers with recordkeeping, such as taking attendance and calculating grades
- Get equipment or materials ready to help teachers prepare for lessons
- Supervise students outside of the classroom, such as between classes, during lunch and recess, and on field trips

Teacher assistants also are called *teacher aides*, *instructional aides*, *paraprofessionals*, *education assistants*, and *paraeducators*.

Teacher assistants work with or under the guidance of a licensed teacher. Reviewing with students individually or in small groups, teacher assistants help reinforce the lessons that teachers introduce.

Teacher assistants may provide feedback to teachers for monitoring student progress. Some teacher assistants meet regularly with teachers to discuss lesson plans and students' development.

Some teacher assistants work only with special education students. When special education students attend regular classes, these teacher assistants help them understand the material and adapt the information to their learning style. Teacher assistants may also work with students who have severe disabilities in

Teacher assistants work under the supervision of a teacher and provide additional attention and instruction to students.

Some teacher assistants work exclusively with special education students who attend traditional classes.

separate classrooms. They help these students with basic needs, such as eating or personal hygiene. Teacher assistants may help young adults with disabilities to learn skills necessary for finding a job or living independently after graduation.

Some teacher assistants help in specific areas. For example, they may work in a computer laboratory, helping students use programs or software. Others may work as cafeteria attendants, supervising students during lunchtime.

Teacher assistants in childcare centers work with a lead teacher to provide individualized attention that young children need. They help with educational activities, supervise the children at play, and help with feeding and other basic care.

Work Environment

Teacher assistants held about 1.4 million jobs in 2019. The largest employers of teacher assistants were as follows:

Elementary and secondary schools; local	70%
Child day care services	11
Elementary and secondary schools; private	8

Teacher assistants may spend some time outside, when students are at recess or getting on and off the bus. They may need to lift the students at certain times.

Some teacher assistants work in specific locations within schools, such as libraries.

Injuries and Illnesses

Teacher assistants sometimes get injured on the job. They actively work with students, including lifting and otherwise assisting special education students, which can place them at risk for injuries such as strains.

Work schedules

Some teacher assistants work part time. Some monitor students on school buses before and after school. Although many do not work during the summer, some work in year-round schools or assist teachers in summer school.

How to Become a Teacher Assistant

Teacher assistants typically need to have completed at least 2 years of college coursework.

Education

Teacher assistants in public schools need at least 2 years of college coursework or an associate's degree. Those who work in schools with a Title 1 program (a federal program for schools that have a large proportion of students from low-income households) must have at least a 2-year degree, 2 years of college, or pass a state or local assessment.

Associate's degree programs for teacher assistants prepare participants to develop educational materials, observe students, and understand the role of teaching assistants in working with classroom teachers.

Most states require teacher assistants who work with special-needs students to pass a skills test.

Licenses, Certifications, and Registrations

Some jobs may require staff to have certifications in cardiopulmonary resuscitation (CPR) and first aid.

Important Qualities

Communication skills. Teacher assistants need to be clear and concise in discussing student progress with teachers and parents.

Teacher assistants reinforce lessons presented in class by reviewing material with students one-on-one or in small groups.

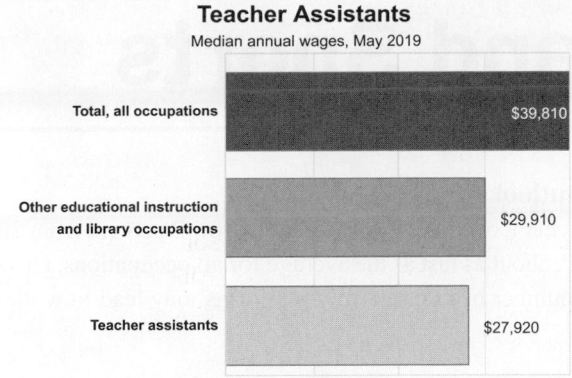

Teacher Assistants
Median annual wages, May 2019

Total, all occupations	$39,810
Other educational instruction and library occupations	$29,910
Teacher assistants	$27,920

Note: All Occupations includes all occupations in the U.S. Economy.
Source: U.S. Bureau of Labor Statistics, Occupational Employment Statistics.

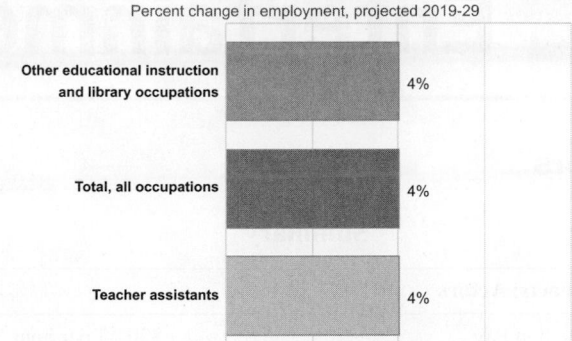

Teacher Assistants
Percent change in employment, projected 2019-29

Other educational instruction and library occupations	4%
Total, all occupations	4%
Teacher assistants	4%

Note: All Occupations includes all occupations in the U.S. Economy.
Source: U.S. Bureau of Labor Statistics, Employment Projections program.

Interpersonal skills. Teacher assistants must be able to develop relationships with a variety of people, including teachers, students, parents, and administrators.

Patience. Working with students of different abilities and backgrounds may be difficult. Teacher assistants must be understanding with students.

Resourcefulness. Teacher assistants must find ways to explain information to students who have different learning styles.

Advancement

Teacher assistants may become a kindergarten and elementary school teacher, middle school teacher, high school teacher, or special education teacher upon obtaining additional education, training, and a license or certification.

Pay

The median annual wage for teacher assistants was $27,920 in May 2019. The median wage is the wage at which half the workers in an occupation earned more than that amount and half earned less. The lowest 10 percent earned less than $18,940, and the highest 10 percent earned more than $43,040.

In May 2019, the median annual wages for teacher assistants in the top industries in which they worked were as follows:

Elementary and secondary schools; local	$28,520
Elementary and secondary schools; private	27,700
Child day care services	24,680

Some teacher assistants work part time. Some monitor students on school buses before and after school. Although many do not work during the summer, some work in year-round schools or assist teachers in summer school.

Job Outlook

Employment of teacher assistants is projected to grow 4 percent from 2019 to 2029, about as fast as the average for all

occupations. Rising student enrollment along with state and federal funding for education programs should affect growth.

Teacher assistants are more of a supplementary position, as opposed to teachers, who hold a primary position. Therefore, teacher assistants' employment opportunities may depend on school districts' budgets. Schools are more likely to eliminate teacher assistant positions rather than teacher positions when there is a budget shortfall and more likely to hire teacher assistants when there is a budget surplus.

Job Prospects

In addition to job openings due to employment growth, numerous openings will arise as teacher assistants leave the occupation and must be replaced. Because of the education requirements and low pay, many workers transfer to other occupations or leave the labor force.

Employment projections data for teacher assistants, 2019-29					
Occupational Title	SOC Code	Employment, 2019	Projected Employment, 2029	Change, 2019-29	
				Percent	Numeric
SOURCE: U.S. Bureau of Labor Statistics, Employment Projections program					
Teaching assistants, except postsecondary	25-9045	1,395,900	1,446,400	4	50,500

State & Area Data
Occupational Employment Statistics (OES)

The Occupational Employment Statistics (OES) program produces employment and wage estimates annually for over 800 occupations. These estimates are available for the nation as a whole, for individual states, and for metropolitan and nonmetropolitan areas.

Contacts for More Information

For more information about teacher assistants, visit
➤ National Education Association
➤ American Federation of Teachers
➤ National Resource Center for Paraeducators

Entertainment and Sports

Actors

Summary

Quick Facts: Actors

2019 Median Pay	$20.43 per hour
Typical Entry-Level Education	Some college, no degree
Work Experience in a Related Occupation	None
On-the-job Training	Long-term on-the-job training
Number of Jobs, 2019	70,100
Job Outlook, 2019-29	3% (As fast as average)
Employment Change, 2019-29	2,100

What Actors Do

Actors express ideas and portray characters in theater, film, television, and other performing arts media.

Work Environment

Actors work in various settings, including production studios, theaters, and theme parks, or on location. Work assignments are usually short, ranging from 1 day to a few months.

How to Become an Actor

Many actors enhance their skills through formal dramatic education, and long-term training is common.

Pay

The median hourly wage for actors was $20.43 in May 2019.

Actors interpret a writer's script to entertain or inform an audience.

Job Outlook

Employment of actors is projected to grow 3 percent from 2019 to 2029, about as fast as the average for all occupations. Growth in the number of Internet-only platforms may lead to work for actors.

State & Area Data

Explore resources for employment and wages by state and area for actors.

What Actors Do

Actors express ideas and portray characters in theater, film, television, and other performing arts media. They interpret a writer's script to entertain or inform an audience.

Duties

Actors typically do the following:

- Read scripts and meet with agents and other professionals before accepting a role
- Audition in front of directors, producers, and casting directors

Actors must memorize and rehearse their lines.

- Research their character's personal traits and circumstances to portray the characters more authentically to an audience
- Memorize their lines
- Rehearse their lines and performance, including on stage or in front of the camera, with other actors
- Discuss their role with the director, producer, and other actors to improve the overall performance of the show
- Perform the role, following the director's directions

Most actors struggle to find steady work, and few achieve recognition as stars. Some work as "extras"—actors who have no lines to deliver but are included in scenes to give a more realistic setting. Some actors do voiceover or narration work for animated features, audiobooks, or other electronic media.

In some stage or film productions, actors sing, dance, or play a musical instrument. For some roles, an actor must learn a new skill, such as horseback riding or stage fighting.

Most actors have long periods of unemployment between roles and often hold other jobs in order to make a living. Some actors teach acting classes as a second job.

Work Environment

Actors held about 70,100 jobs in 2019. The largest employers of actors were as follows:

Self-employed workers	24%
Theater companies and dinner theaters	13
Colleges, universities, and professional schools; state, local, and private	5
Professional, scientific, and technical services	5

Work assignments are usually short, ranging from 1 day to a few months, and actors often hold another job in order to make a living. They are frequently under the stress of having to find their next job. Some actors in touring companies may be employed for several years.

Actors may perform in unpleasant conditions, such as outdoors in bad weather, under hot stage lights, or while wearing an uncomfortable costume or makeup.

Some actors wear elaborate makeup and costumes.

Work Schedules

Work hours for actors are extensive and irregular. Early morning, evening, weekend, and holiday work is common. Some actors work part time. Few actors work full time, and many have variable schedules. Those who work in theater may travel with a touring show across the country. Film and television actors may also travel to work on location.

How to Become an Actor

Many actors enhance their skills through formal dramatic education, and long-term training is common.

Education

Many actors enhance their skills through formal dramatic education. Many who specialize in theater have bachelor's degrees, but a degree is not required.

Although some people succeed in acting without getting a formal education, most actors acquire some formal preparation through a theater company's acting conservatory or a university drama or theater arts program. Students can take college classes in drama or filmmaking to prepare for a career as an actor. Classes in dance or music may help as well.

Actors who do not have a college degree may take acting or film classes to learn their craft. Community colleges, acting

Actors may audition for many roles before getting a job.

conservatories, and private film schools typically offer these classes. Many theater companies also have education programs.

Important Qualities

Creativity. Actors interpret their characters' feelings and motives in order to portray the characters in the most compelling way.

Memorization skills. Actors memorize many lines before filming begins or a show opens. Television actors often appear on camera with little time to memorize scripts, and scripts frequently may be revised or even written just moments before filming.

Persistence. Actors may audition for many roles before getting a job. They must be able to accept rejection and keep going.

Physical stamina. Actors should be in good enough physical condition to endure the heat from stage or studio lights and the weight of heavy costumes or makeup. They may work many hours, including acting in more than one performance a day, and they must do so without getting overly tired.

Reading skills. Actors must read scripts and be able to interpret how a writer has developed their character.

Speaking skills. Actors—particularly stage actors—must say their lines clearly, project their voice, and pronounce words so that audiences understand them.

In addition to these qualities, actors usually must be physically coordinated to perform predetermined, sometimes complex movements with other actors, such as dancing or stage fighting, in order to complete a scene.

Training

It takes many years of practice to develop the skills needed to be a successful actor, and actors never truly finish training. They work to improve their acting skills throughout their career. Many actors continue to train through workshops, rehearsals, or mentoring by a drama coach.

Every role is different, and an actor may need to learn something new for each one. For example, a role may require learning how to sing or dance, or an actor may have to learn to speak with an accent or to play a musical instrument or sport.

Many aspiring actors begin by participating in school plays or local theater productions. In television and film, actors usually start out in smaller roles or independent movies and work their way up to bigger productions.

Advancement

As an actor's reputation grows, he or she may work on bigger projects or in more prestigious venues. Some actors become producers and directors.

Pay

The median hourly wage for actors was $20.43 in May 2019. The median wage is the wage at which half the workers in an occupation earned more than that amount and half earned less.

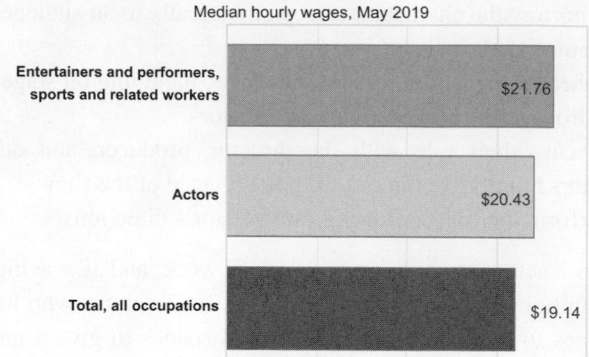

Actors

Median hourly wages, May 2019

- Entertainers and performers, sports and related workers: $21.76
- Actors: $20.43
- Total, all occupations: $19.14

Note: All Occupations includes all occupations in the U.S. Economy. Source: U.S. Bureau of Labor Statistics, Occupational Employment Statistics.

The lowest 10 percent earned less than $9.52, and the highest 10 percent earned more than $60.41.

In May 2019, the median hourly wages for actors in the top industries in which they worked were as follows:

Colleges, universities, and professional schools;
state, local, and private $21.11
Professional, scientific, and technical services.......... 19.27
Theater companies and dinner theaters 17.72

Work hours for actors are extensive and irregular. Early morning, evening, weekend, and holiday work is common. Some actors work part time. Few actors work full time, and many have variable schedules. Those who work in theater may travel with a touring show across the country. Actors in movies may also travel to work on location.

Job Outlook

Employment of actors is projected to grow 3 percent from 2019 to 2029, about as fast as the average for all occupations. The number of Internet-only platforms, such as streaming services, is likely to increase, along with the number of shows produced for these platforms. This growth may lead to more work for actors.

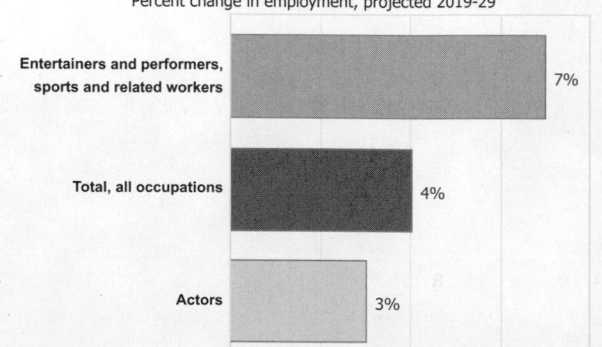

Actors

Percent change in employment, projected 2019-29

- Entertainers and performers, sports and related workers: 7%
- Total, all occupations: 4%
- Actors: 3%

Note: All Occupations includes all occupations in the U.S. Economy. Source: U.S. Bureau of Labor Statistics, Employment Projections program.

Many small and medium-sized theaters have difficulty getting funding. As a result, the number of performances is expected to decline. Large theaters, with their more stable sources of funding and more well-known plays and musicals, should provide more opportunities for actors.

Job Prospects

Actors face intense competition for jobs. Most roles, no matter how minor, have many actors auditioning for them. For stage roles, actors with a bachelor's degree in theater may have a better chance of landing a part than those without one.

Employment projections data for actors, 2019-29					
Occupational Title	SOC Code	Employment, 2019	Projected Employment, 2029	Change, 2019-29 Percent	Numeric
SOURCE: U.S. Bureau of Labor Statistics, Employment Projections program					
Actors	27-2011	70,100	72,200	3	2,100

State & Area Data

Occupational Employment Statistics (OES)

The Occupational Employment Statistics (OES) program produces employment and wage estimates annually for over 800 occupations. These estimates are available for the nation as a whole, for individual states, and for metropolitan and nonmetropolitan areas.

Contacts for More Information

For more information about actors, visit
➤ Actors' Equity Association
➤ National Endowment for the Arts
➤ SAG-AFTRA

Athletes and Sports Competitors

Summary

Quick Facts: Athletes and Sports Competitors

2019 Median Pay	$51,370 per year
Typical Entry-Level Education	No formal educational credential
Work Experience in a Related Occupation ...	None
On-the-job Training	Long-term on-the-job training
Number of Jobs, 2019.................................	13,600
Job Outlook, 2019-29..................................	10% (Much faster than average)
Employment Change, 2019-29	1,400

What Athletes and Sports Competitors Do

Athletes and sports competitors participate in organized, officiated sporting events to entertain spectators.

Work Environment

Athletes and sports competitors often work irregular hours, including evenings, weekends, and holidays. They usually work more than 40 hours a week for several months during their particular sports season. They frequently work outside, so they may be exposed to all weather conditions.

How to Become an Athlete or Sports Competitor

No formal educational credential is required for anyone to become an athlete or sports competitor. Athletes must have superior athletic talent and an extensive knowledge of their sport. They usually get such knowledge through years of practice and experience at lower levels of competition.

Pay

The median annual wage for athletes and sports competitors was $51,370 in May 2019.

Job Outlook

Employment of athletes and sports competitors is projected to grow 10 percent from 2019 to 2029, much faster than the average for all occupations. Competition for most professional athlete jobs will remain very strong.

State & Area Data

Explore resources for employment and wages by state and area for athletes and sports competitors.

What Athletes and Sports Competitors Do

Athletes and sports competitors participate in organized, officiated sporting events to entertain spectators.

Athletes and sports competitors participate in officiated sports events to entertain spectators.

Athletes and sports competitors practice under the direction of coaches, sports instructors, or athletic trainers.

Duties

Athletes and sports competitors typically do the following:

- Practice to develop and improve their skills
- Maintain their sports equipment in good condition
- Train, exercise, and follow special diets to stay in the best physical condition
- Take instructions regarding strategy and tactics from coaches and other sports staff during games
- Follow the rules of the sport during competitions and games
- Assess their individual and team performance after each event and identify their strengths and weaknesses

Many people dream of becoming a paid professional athlete. Few people, however, beat the odds and make a full-time living from professional athletics—and when they do, professional athletes often have short careers with little job security.

When playing a game, athletes and sports competitors must understand the strategies involved while following the rules and regulations of the sport. The events in which athletes compete include team sports, such as baseball, softball, hockey, and soccer, and individual sports, such as golf, tennis, swimming, and skiing. The level of play varies greatly. Some athletes may compete in regional competitions, while other athletes compete in national or international events.

Being an athlete involves more than competing in athletic events. Athletes spend most days practicing their skills and improving teamwork under the guidance of a coach or a sports instructor. They review videotapes to critique and improve their own performance and technique. Athletes also must study their opponents' tendencies and weaknesses so as to gain a competitive advantage.

Some athletes work regularly with fitness trainers and instructors to gain muscle and stamina and to prevent injury. Because of the physical demands required by many sports, career-ending injuries are always a risk. Even minor injuries may put a player at risk of replacement.

Because competition at all levels is extremely intense and job security is always in question, many athletes train throughout the year to maintain or improve their form and technique and remain in peak physical condition. Very little downtime from the sport exists at the professional level.

Work Environment

Athletes and sports competitors held about 13,600 jobs in 2019. The largest employers of athletes and sports competitors were as follows:

Spectator sports	58%
Self-employed workers	14
Fitness and recreational sports centers	5

Athletes and sports competitors who participate in outdoor competitions may be exposed to all weather conditions of the season in which they play their sport. In addition, many athletes must travel to sporting events. Such travel may include long bus rides or plane trips, and, in some cases, international travel.

Injuries and Illnesses

Athletes and sports competitors have one of the highest rates of injuries and illnesses of all occupations. Many of these workers wear pads, gloves, goggles, helmets, and other protective gear to protect against injury. And although fatalities are uncommon, athletes and sports competitors experience one of the highest rates of occupational fatalities of all occupations.

Work Schedules

Athletes and sports competitors often work irregular hours, including evenings, weekends, and holidays. During the sports season, they usually work more than 40 hours a week for several months as they practice, train, travel, and compete.

How to Become an Athlete or Sports Competitor

No formal educational credential is required for anyone to become an athlete or sports competitor. Athletes must have superior athletic talent and extensive knowledge of their sport.

Athletes and sports competitors are often exposed to all types of weather conditions.

Athletes and sports competitors gain experience by competing in high school, college, or club teams.

They usually get such knowledge through years of experience at lower levels of competition.

Education

Although athletes and sports competitors typically have at least a high school diploma or equivalent, no formal educational credential is required for them to enter the occupation. They must have extensive knowledge of the way the sport is played—especially its rules, regulations, and strategies.

Other Experience

Athletes typically learn the rules of the game and develop their skills by playing the sport at lower levels of competition. For most sports, athletes compete in high school and collegiate athletics or on club teams. In addition, athletes may improve their skills by taking private or group lessons or attending sports camps.

Training

It typically takes many years of practice and experience to become an athlete or sports competitor.

Licenses, Certifications, and Registrations

Some sports and localities require athletes and sports competitors to be licensed or certified to practice. For example, race car drivers need to be licensed to compete in the various races. The governing body of the sport may revoke licenses and suspend participants who do not meet the required performance or training. In addition, athletes may have their licenses or certification suspended for inappropriate activity.

Advancement

Turning professional is often the biggest advancement that aspiring athletes can make in their careers. They often begin to compete immediately, although some may spend more time on the bench (as a reserve) to gain experience. In some sports, such as baseball, athletes may begin their professional career on a minor league team before moving up to the major leagues. Professional athletes generally advance in their sport by displaying superior performance and receiving accolades; in turn, they earn a higher salary. Others may receive endorsements from companies and brands.

Important Qualities

Athleticism. Nearly all athletes and sports competitors must possess superior athletic ability to be able to compete successfully against opponents.

Concentration. Athletes and sports competitors must be extremely focused when competing and must block out distractions from fans and opponents. The difference between winning and losing can sometimes be a result of a momentary lapse in concentration.

Decisionmaking skills. Athletes and sports competitors often must make split-second decisions. Quarterbacks, for example, usually have only seconds to decide whether to pass the football or not.

Dedication. Athletes and sports competitors must practice regularly to develop their skills and improve or maintain their physical conditioning. It often takes years to become successful, so athletes must be dedicated to their sport.

Hand–eye coordination. In many sports, including tennis and baseball, the need to gauge and strike a fast-moving ball is highly dependent on the athlete's hand–eye coordination.

Stamina. Endurance can benefit athletes and sports competitors, particularly those who participate in long-lasting sports competitions, such as marathons.

Teamwork. Because many athletes compete in a team sport, such as hockey or soccer, the ability to work with teammates as a cohesive unit is important for success.

Many professional athletes are also required to pass drug tests.

Pay

The median annual wage for athletes and sports competitors was $51,370 in May 2019. The median wage is the wage at which half the workers in an occupation earned more than that amount and half earned less. The lowest 10 percent earned less than $19,280, and the highest 10 percent earned more than $208,000.

In May 2019, the median annual wages for athletes and sports competitors in the top industries in which they worked were as follows:

Spectator sports	$61,040
Fitness and recreational sports centers	48,550

Athletes and sports competitors often work irregular schedules, including evenings, weekends, and holidays. During the sports season, they usually work more than 40 hours a week for several months as they practice, train, travel, and compete.

Athletes and Sports Competitors
Median annual wages, May 2019

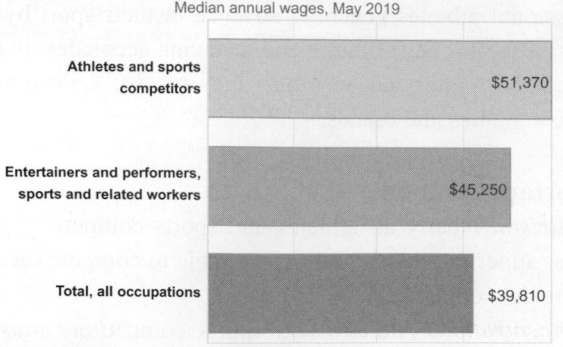

Note: All Occupations includes all occupations in the U.S. Economy.
Source: U.S. Bureau of Labor Statistics, Occupational Employment Statistics.

Job Outlook

Employment of athletes and sports competitors is projected to grow 10 percent from 2019 to 2029, much faster than the average for all occupations. However, because it is a small occupation, the fast growth will result in only about 1,400 new jobs over the 10-year period. Employment growth will be primarily due to population growth and increasing public interest in professional sports.

Growth and geographic shifts in population may lead to an increase in the number of professional sports teams. Some professional sports leagues may expand to new cities in the United States, creating new teams and new job opportunities for individuals looking to become professional athletes.

However, expansion is rare in professional sports leagues. Creating new teams is very costly and risky, requiring strong support from fans and both local and state government. When leagues do expand, they typically create only one or two teams at a time. Conversely, some teams and sports leagues may disband altogether because of a lack of interest in the sport.

Instead of disbanding, some teams simply relocate to another city that has a greater interest in the sport and a larger fan base. In this case, no new jobs for athletes would be created.

Job Prospects

Competition for professional athlete jobs will continue to be extremely intense. A very small number of high school or college athletes become professional athletes.

Most professional athletes can deliver peak performances for only a short time. Careers last just a few years because of

Athletes and Sports Competitors
Percent change in employment, projected 2019-29

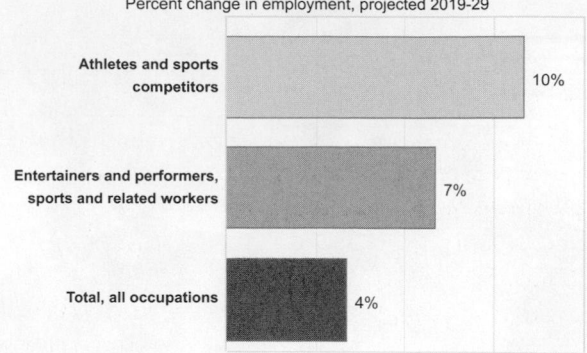

Note: All Occupations includes all occupations in the U.S. Economy.
Source: U.S. Bureau of Labor Statistics, Employment Projections program.

debilitating injuries or retirements. Yearly replacement needs for these jobs is high and may create some job opportunities.

However, the talented young men and women who dream of becoming sports superstars greatly outnumber the number of openings.

Employment projections data for athletes and sports competitors, 2019-29					
Occupational Title	SOC Code	Employment, 2019	Projected Employment, 2029	Change, 2019-29	
				Percent	Numeric
SOURCE: U.S. Bureau of Labor Statistics, Employment Projections program					
Athletes and sports competitors	27-2021	13,600	15,000	10	1,400

State & Area Data

Occupational Employment Statistics (OES)

The Occupational Employment Statistics (OES) program produces employment and wage estimates annually for over 800 occupations. These estimates are available for the nation as a whole, for individual states, and for metropolitan and nonmetropolitan areas.

Contacts for More Information

For more information about team and individual sports, visit
➤ National Collegiate Athletic Association
➤ National Council of Youth Sports
➤ National Federation of State High School Associations

For more information related to individual sports, refer to the organization that represents the sport.

Coaches and Scouts

Summary

Quick Facts: Coaches and Scouts

2019 Median Pay	$34,840 per year
Typical Entry-Level Education	Bachelor's degree
Work Experience in a Related Occupation	None
On-the-job Training	None
Number of Jobs, 2019	292,000
Job Outlook, 2019-29	12% (Much faster than average)
Employment Change, 2019-29	34,300

What Coaches and Scouts Do

Coaches teach amateur or professional athletes the skills they need to succeed at their sport.

Work Environment

Coaches and scouts often work irregular hours, including evenings, weekends, and holidays. Full-time coaches usually work more than 40 hours a week for several months during the sports season. Coaches travel frequently to sporting events. Scouts may be required to travel more extensively when searching for talented athletes.

How to Become a Coach or Scout

Coaches and scouts typically need a bachelor's degree. They also must have extensive knowledge of the game. Coaches typically gain this knowledge through their own experiences playing the sport at some level. Although previous playing experience may be beneficial, it is typically not required for most scouting jobs.

Pay

The median annual wage for coaches and scouts was $34,840 in May 2019.

Coaches instruct amateur and professional athletes, teaching them the fundamental skills of sports.

Job Outlook

Employment of coaches and scouts is projected to grow 12 percent from 2019 to 2029, much faster than the average for all occupations. Increasing participation in high school and college sports may boost demand for coaches and scouts.

State & Area Data

Explore resources for employment and wages by state and area for coaches and scouts.

What Coaches and Scouts Do

Coaches teach amateur and professional athletes the skills they need to succeed at their sport. Scouts look for new players, evaluating their skills and likelihood for success at the college, amateur, or professional level. Many coaches also are involved in scouting potential athletes.

Duties

Coaches typically do the following:

- Plan, organize, and conduct practice sessions
- Analyze the strengths and weaknesses of individual athletes and opposing teams
- Plan strategies and choose team members for each game

Coaches and scouts analyze the strengths and weaknesses of individual athletes and opposing teams.

- Provide direction, encouragement, and motivation to prepare athletes for games
- Call plays and make decisions about strategy and player substitutions during games
- Plan and direct physical conditioning programs that enable athletes to achieve maximum performance
- Instruct athletes on proper techniques, game strategies, sportsmanship, and the rules of the sport
- Keep records of athletes' and opponents' performances
- Identify and recruit potential athletes
- Arrange for and offer incentives to prospective players

Coaches teach professional and amateur athletes the fundamental skills of individual and team sports. They hold training and practice sessions to improve the athletes' form, technique, skills, and stamina. Along with refining athletes' individual skills, coaches are responsible for instilling in their players the importance of good sportsmanship, a competitive spirit, and teamwork.

Many coaches evaluate their opponents to determine game strategies and to establish particular plays to practice. During competition, coaches call specific plays intended to surprise or overpower the opponent, and they may substitute players to achieve optimum team chemistry and success.

Many high school coaches are primarily academic teachers or other school administrators who supplement their income by coaching part time.

Coaches may assign specific drills and correct athletes' techniques. They may also spend their time working one-on-one with athletes, designing customized training programs for each individual. Coaches may specialize in teaching the skills of an individual sport, such as tennis, golf, or ice skating. Some coaches, such as baseball coaches, may teach individual athletes involved in team sports.

Scouts typically do the following:

- Read newspapers and other news sources to find athletes to consider
- Attend games, view videotapes of the athletes' performances, and study statistics about the athletes to determine their talent and potential
- Talk to the athlete and the coaches to see if the athlete has what it takes to succeed
- Report to the coach, manager, or owner of the team for which he or she is scouting
- Arrange for and offer incentives to prospective players

Scouts evaluate the skills of both amateur and professional athletes. Scouts seek out top athletic candidates for colleges or professional teams and evaluate their likelihood of success at a higher competitive level.

Work Environment

Coaches and scouts held about 292,000 jobs in 2019. The largest employers of coaches and scouts were as follows:

Coaches provide direction, encouragement, and motivation to athletes.

Arts, entertainment, and recreation	20%
Colleges, universities, and professional schools; state, local, and private	20
Elementary and secondary schools; state, local, and private	18
Self-employed workers	10

Some scouts work for organizations that deal directly with high school athletes. These scouts collect information on the athlete and help sell his or her talents to potential colleges.

At the college level, scouts typically work for scouting organizations or are self-employed. In either case, they help colleges recruit the best high school athletes.

Scouts who work at the professional level are typically employed by the team or organization directly.

Those people who coach and scout for outdoor sports may be exposed to all weather conditions of the season. In addition, they must travel often to attend sporting events. This is particularly true for those in professional sports.

Work Schedules

Work hours can vary for coaches and scouts and may include evenings, weekends, and holidays. Professional or college coaches may work additional hours during the sport's season.

How to Become a Coach or Scout

Coaches and scouts typically need a bachelor's degree. They also must have extensive knowledge of the sport. Coaches typically gain this knowledge through their own experiences playing the sport at some level. Although previous playing experience may be beneficial, it is not required for most scouting jobs.

Education

College and professional coaches usually must have a bachelor's degree, typically in any subject. However, some coaches may decide to study exercise and sports science, physiology, kinesiology, nutrition and fitness, physical education, or sports medicine.

High schools typically hire teachers or administrators at the school for most coaching jobs. If no suitable teacher is found, schools hire a qualified candidate from outside the school. For more information on education requirements for teachers, see the profile on high school teachers.

Like coaches, scouts must typically have a bachelor's degree. Some scouts decide to get a degree in business, marketing, sales, or sports management.

Other Experience

College and professional coaching jobs typically require experience playing the sport at some level.

Scouting jobs typically do not require experience playing a sport at the college or professional level, but doing so can be beneficial. Employers look for applicants with a passion for sports and an ability to spot young players who have exceptional athletic ability and skills.

Licenses, Certifications, and Registrations

Most state high school athletic associations require coaches to be certified or at least complete mandatory education courses.

Certification often requires coaches to be a minimum age (at least 18 years old) and be trained in cardiopulmonary

Coaches and scouts must have overall knowledge of the game or sport.

resuscitation (CPR) and first aid. Some states also require coaches to attend classes related to sports safety and coaching fundamentals prior to becoming certified. For information about specific state coaching requirements, contact the state's high school athletic association or visit the National Association of State Boards of Education.

Although most public high school coaches need to meet these state requirements in order to become a coach, certification may not be required for coaching jobs in private schools.

Some schools may require coaches to have a teaching license and complete a background check.

Certification requirements for college coaching positions also vary.

Additional certification may be highly desirable or even required for someone to coach individual sports such as tennis or golf. There are many certifying organizations specific to the various sports, and their requirements vary.

Part-time workers and those in smaller facilities or youth leagues are less likely to need formal education or training and may not need certification.

Advancement

To reach the rank of a professional coach, a candidate usually needs years of coaching experience and a winning record at a college. Some coaches may not have previous coaching experience but are nevertheless hired at the professional level because of their success as an athlete in their sport.

Some college coaches begin their careers as graduate assistants or assistant coaches in order to gain the knowledge and experience needed to become a head coach. Large schools and colleges that compete at the highest levels require a head coach who has had substantial experience at another school or as an assistant coach.

Other college coaches may start out as high school coaches before moving up to the collegiate level.

Scouts may begin working as talent spotters in a particular area or region. They typically advance to become supervising scouts responsible for a whole territory or region.

Important Qualities

Communication skills. Because coaches instruct, organize, and motivate athletes, they must have excellent communication skills. They must communicate proper techniques, strategies, and rules of the sport effectively enough that every player on the team understands what he or she has been told.

Decisionmaking skills. Coaches must choose the appropriate players to use at a given position at a given time during a game and must know the proper time to utilize game-managing tools such as timeouts. Coaches and scouts must also be very selective when recruiting players.

Dedication. Coaches must attend daily practices and assist their team and individual athletes in improving their skills and physical conditioning. Coaches must be dedicated to their sport, as it often takes years to become successful.

Coaches and Scouts
Median annual wages, May 2019

Entertainers and performers, sports and related workers	$45,250
Total, all occupations	$39,810
Coaches and scouts	$34,840

Note: All Occupations includes all occupations in the U.S. Economy.
Source: U.S. Bureau of Labor Statistics, Occupational Employment Statistics.

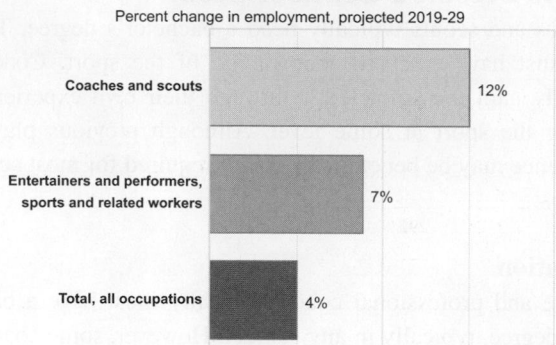

Coaches and Scouts
Percent change in employment, projected 2019-29

Coaches and scouts	12%
Entertainers and performers, sports and related workers	7%
Total, all occupations	4%

Note: All Occupations includes all occupations in the U.S. Economy.
Source: U.S. Bureau of Labor Statistics, Employment Projections program.

Interpersonal skills. Being able to relate to athletes helps coaches and scouts foster positive relationships with their current players and recruit potential players.

Leadership skills. Coaches must demonstrate good leadership skills to get the most out of athletes. They must be able to motivate, develop, and direct young athletes.

Resourcefulness. Coaches must find and develop a game plan and strategy that yields the best chances for winning. Coaches often need to create original plays or formations that provide a competitive advantage and confuse opponents.

Pay

The median annual wage for coaches and scouts was $34,840 in May 2019. The median wage is the wage at which half the workers in an occupation earned more than that amount and half earned less. The lowest 10 percent earned less than $19,040, and the highest 10 percent earned more than $78,890.

In May 2019, the median annual wages for coaches and scouts in the top industries in which they worked were as follows:

Colleges, universities, and professional schools; state, local, and private	$46,180
Arts, entertainment, and recreation	37,320
Elementary and secondary schools; state, local, and private	29,960

Coaches and scouts often work irregular hours, including evenings, weekends, and holidays. Professional or college coaches usually work more than 40 hours a week for several months during the sport's season, if not most of the year. Many high school coaches work part time and may have other jobs aside from coaching.

Job Outlook

Employment of coaches and scouts is projected to grow 12 percent from 2019 to 2029, much faster than the average for all occupations. Rising participation in high school and college sports should increase demand for coaches and scouts.

High school enrollment is projected to increase over the next decade, resulting in a rise in the number of student athletes. As schools offer more athletic programs and as more students participate in sports, the demand for coaches may increase.

Participation in college sports also is projected to increase over the next decade, particularly at smaller colleges and in women's sports. Many small, Division III colleges are expanding their sports programs and adding new teams as a way to help promote the school and recruit potential students.

The growing interest in college and professional sports also will increase demand for scouts. Colleges must attract the best athletes to remain competitive. Successful teams help colleges enhance their reputation, recruit future students, and raise donations from alumni. Colleges, therefore, will increasingly rely on scouts to recruit the best possible high school athletes. In addition, as college tuition increases and scholarships become more competitive, high school athletes will hire scouts directly in an effort to increase the athletes' chances of receiving a college scholarship.

However, funding for athletic programs at schools often is cut when budgets become tight. For example, some high schools within the same school district may combine their sports programs in an effort to reduce costs. Still, the popularity of team sports often enables shortfalls to be offset with help from fundraisers, booster clubs, and parents.

Job Prospects

Strong competition is expected for higher paying jobs at the college level, and competition will be even greater for jobs in professional sports.

Job prospects at the high school level should be good, but coaching jobs typically go to those teaching in the school. Candidates who have a degree or are state certified to teach academic subjects, therefore, should have the best prospects for getting coaching jobs at high schools. The need to replace the number of high school coaches who change occupations or leave the labor force also will provide some jobs.

Coaches in girls' and women's sports may have better job opportunities because of a growing number of participants and leagues.

Competition is also likely to be strong for jobs as scouts, particularly for professional teams.

Employment projections data for coaches and scouts, 2019-29					
Occupational Title	SOC Code	Employment, 2019	Projected Employment, 2029	Change, 2019-29	
				Percent	Numeric
SOURCE: U.S. Bureau of Labor Statistics, Employment Projections program					
Coaches and scouts	27-2022	292,000	326,400	12	34,300

Dancers and Choreographers

Summary

Quick Facts: Dancers and Choreographers

2019 Median Pay	$18.68 per hour
Typical Entry-Level Education	See below
Work Experience in a Related Occupation	See below
On-the-job Training	Long-term on-the-job training
Number of Jobs, 2019	16,900
Job Outlook, 2019-29	6% (Faster than average)
Employment Change, 2019-29	1,000

What Dancers and Choreographers Do

Dancers and choreographers use dance performances to express ideas and stories.

Work Environment

Some dancers work in performing arts companies, or are self-employed. Choreographers may work in dance schools, and others may work as self-employed choreographers.

There are many different types of dance, such as ballet, tango, modern dance, tap, and jazz.

How to Become a Dancer or Choreographer

Education and training requirements vary with the type of dancer; however, all dancers need many years of formal training. Nearly all choreographers began their careers as dancers.

Pay

The median hourly wage for choreographers was $22.27 in May 2019.

The median hourly wage for dancers was $17.49 in May 2019.

Job Outlook

Overall employment of dancers and choreographers is projected to grow 6 percent from 2019 to 2029, faster than the average for all occupations. However, projected employment growth varies by occupation.

State & Area Data

Explore resources for employment and wages by state and area for dancers and choreographers.

What Dancers and Choreographers Do

Dancers and choreographers use dance performances to express ideas and stories. There are many types of dance, such as ballet, tango, modern dance, tap, and jazz.

Duties

Dancers typically do the following:

- Audition for a part in a show or for a job within a dance company
- Learn complex dance movements that entertain an audience
- Rehearse several hours each day to prepare for their performance
- Study new and emerging types of dance
- Work closely with instructors, choreographers, or other dancers to interpret or modify their routines
- Attend promotional events, such as photography sessions, for the production in which they are appearing

Dancers spend years learning dances and perfecting their skills. They usually perform as part of a group and know a

Some dancers perform in theater productions.

variety of dance styles, including ballet, tap, and modern dance. In addition to traditional performances in front of a live audience, many perform on TV, in videos on the Internet, and in music videos, in which they also may sing or act. Many dancers perform in shows at casinos, in theme parks, and on cruise ships.

Choreographers typically do the following:

- Put together moves in a sequence to create new dances or interpretations of existing dances
- Choose the music that will accompany a dance routine
- Audition dancers for a role in a show or within a dance company
- Assist with costume design, lighting, and other artistic aspects of a show
- Teach complex dance movements
- Study new and emerging types of dance to design more creative dance routines
- Help with the administrative duties of a dance company, such as budgeting

Choreographers create original dances and develop new interpretations of existing dances. They work in dance schools, theaters, dance companies, and movie studios. During rehearsals, they typically demonstrate dance moves, to instruct dancers in the proper technique. Many choreographers also perform

the dance routines they create. Some choreographers work with performers who are not trained dancers. For example, the complex martial arts scenes performed by actors in movies are arranged by choreographers who specialize in martial arts.

Some dancers and choreographers hold other jobs between roles to make a living.

Work Environment

Choreographers held about 5,500 jobs in 2019. The largest employers of choreographers were as follows:

Educational services; state, local, and private	54%
Performing arts companies	22
Self-employed workers	15

Dancers held about 11,400 jobs in 2019. The largest employers of dancers were as follows:

Performing arts companies	30%
Self-employed workers	15
Educational services; state, local, and private	10
Spectator sports	7

Dancers may rehearse several hours each day to prepare for their performance.

Injuries and Illnesses

Dance takes a toll on a person's body, so on-the-job injuries are common in dancers. In fact, dancers have one of the highest rates of injuries and illnesses of all occupations.

Many dancers stop performing by the time they reach their late thirties because of the physical demands of their work. Nonperforming dancers may continue to work as choreographers, directors, or dance teachers.

Work Schedules

Schedules for dancers and choreographers vary with where they work. During tours, dancers and choreographers have long workdays, rehearsing most of the day and performing at night. Choreographers who work in dance schools may have a standard workweek when they are instructing students. They also spend hours working independently to create new dance routines.

How to Become a Dancer or Choreographer

Education and training requirements vary with the type of dancer; however, all dancers need many years of formal training. Nearly all choreographers began their careers as dancers.

Education and Training

Many dancers begin training when they are young and continue to learn throughout their careers. Ballet dancers begin training the earliest, usually between the ages of 5 and 8 for girls and a few years later for boys. Their training becomes more serious as they enter their teens, and most ballet dancers begin their professional careers by the time they are 18.

Leading professional dance companies sometimes have intensive summer training programs from which they might select candidates for admission to their regular full-time training programs.

Modern dancers normally begin formal training while they are in high school. They attend afterschool dance programs and summer training programs to prepare for their career or for a college dance program.

Most dancers begin training at a young age.

Some dancers and choreographers pursue postsecondary education. Many colleges and universities offer bachelor's and/or master's degrees in dance, typically through departments of theater or fine arts. As of March 2016, there were about 75 dance programs accredited by the National Association of Schools of Dance. Most programs include coursework in a variety of dance styles, including modern dance, jazz, ballet, and hip-hop. Most entrants into college dance programs have previous formal training.

Some choreographers work as dance teachers. Teaching dance in a college, high school, or elementary school requires a college degree. Some dance studios and conservatories prefer instructors who have a degree; however, they may accept previous work in lieu of a degree.

Work Experience in a Related Occupation

Nearly all choreographers begin their careers as dancers. While working as dancers, they study different types of dance and learn how to choreograph routines.

Advancement

Some dancers take on more responsibility if they are promoted to dance captain in musical theater companies. They lead rehearsals or work with less experienced dancers when the choreographer is not present.

Some dancers become choreographers. Dancers and choreographers also may become theater, film, or television producers and directors.

Important Qualities

Athleticism. Successful dancers must have excellent balance, physical strength, and physical dexterity so that they can move their bodies without falling or losing their sense of rhythm.

Creativity. Dancers need artistic ability and creativity to express ideas through movement. Choreographers also must have artistic ability and innovative ideas, to create new and interesting dance routines.

Leadership skills. Choreographers must be able to direct a group of dancers to perform the routines that they have created.

Persistence. Dancers must commit to years of intense practice. They need to be able to accept rejection after auditions and to continue to practice for future performances. Choreographers must keep studying and creating new routines.

Physical stamina. Dancers are often physically active for long periods, so they must be able to rehearse for many hours without getting tired.

Teamwork. Most dance routines involve a group or pairs, so dancers must be able to work together to be successful.

Pay

The median hourly wage for choreographers was $22.27 in May 2019. The median wage is the wage at which half the workers in an occupation earned more than that amount and

Dancers and Choreographers
Median hourly wages, May 2019

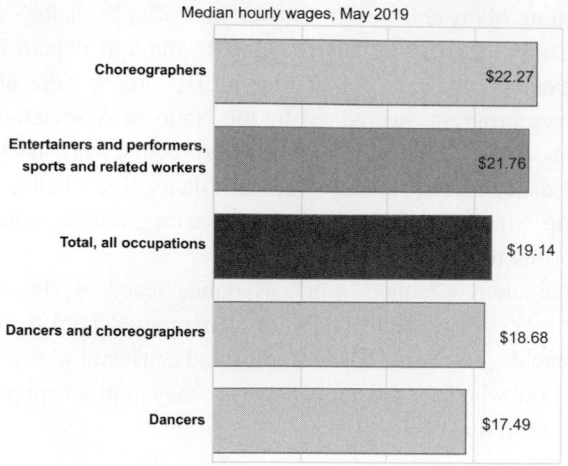

Note: All Occupations includes all occupations in the U.S. Economy.
Source: U.S. Bureau of Labor Statistics, Occupational Employment Statistics.

Dancers and Choreographers
Percent change in employment, projected 2019-29

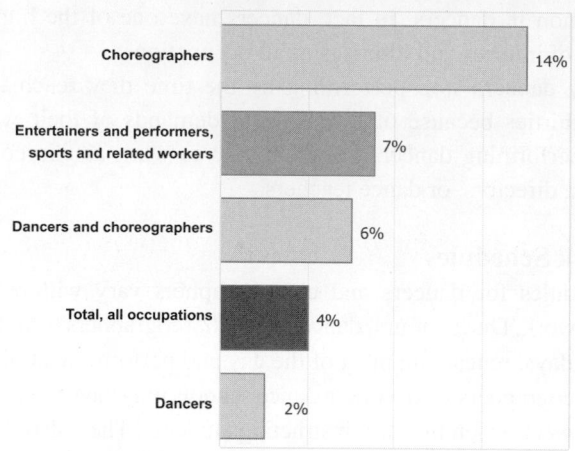

Note: All Occupations includes all occupations in the U.S. Economy.
Source: U.S. Bureau of Labor Statistics, Employment Projections program.

half earned less. The lowest 10 percent earned less than $10.48, and the highest 10 percent earned more than $48.90.

The median hourly wage for dancers was $17.49 in May 2019. The lowest 10 percent earned less than $10.10, and the highest 10 percent earned more than $43.41.

In May 2019, the median hourly wages for choreographers in the top industries in which they worked were as follows:

Educational services; state, local, and private $22.58
Performing arts companies 21.77

In May 2019, the median hourly wages for dancers in the top industries in which they worked were as follows:

Educational services; state, local, and private $24.40
Performing arts companies 18.20
Spectator sports... 15.52

Schedules for dancers and choreographers vary with where they work. During tours, dancers and choreographers have long workdays, rehearsing most of the day and performing at night.

Choreographers who work in dance schools may have a standard workweek when they are instructing students. They also spend hours working independently to create new dance routines.

Job Outlook

Overall employment of dancers and choreographers is projected to grow 6 percent from 2019 to 2029, faster than the average for all occupations. However, projected employment growth varies by occupation.

Employment of dancers is projected to grow 2 percent from 2019 to 2029, slower than the average for all occupations. Many of the new jobs for these workers are expected to be in private dance schools. Employment in performing arts

companies, the largest industry employer of dancers, is projected to go down.

Employment of choreographers is projected to grow 14 percent from 2019 to 2029, much faster than the average for all occupations. However, because it is a small occupation, the fast growth will result in only about 800 new jobs over the decade. Most of these new jobs are expected to be in private dance schools, the largest industry employer of choreographers.

A continued interest in dance and in pop culture also should provide new opportunities in venues outside of dance companies, such as TV or movies, casinos, and theme parks. Demand for dancers and choreographers is expected to be greatest in large cities, such as New York and Las Vegas.

Job Prospects

Dancers and choreographers face intense competition, and the number of applicants is expected to vastly exceed the number of job openings.

Dancers who attend schools or conservatories associated with a dance company may have a better chance of finding work at that company than other dancers have.

Employment projections data for dancers and choreographers, 2019-29					
Occupational Title	SOC Code	Employment, 2019	Projected Employment, 2029	Change, 2019-29	
				Percent	Numeric
SOURCE: U.S. Bureau of Labor Statistics, Employment Projections program					
Dancers and choreographers	27-2030	16,900	18,000	6	1,000
Dancers	27-2031	11,400	11,700	2	300
Choreographers	27-2032	5,500	6,300	14	800

State & Area Data
Occupational Employment Statistics (OES)

The Occupational Employment Statistics (OES) program produces employment and wage estimates annually for over 800 occupations.

These estimates are available for the nation as a whole, for individual states, and for metropolitan and nonmetropolitan areas.

Contacts for More Information

For more information about dancers and choreographers, visit

➤ Dance/USA
➤ National Endowment for the Arts
➤ National Association of Schools of Dance
➤ USA Dance

Music Directors and Composers

Summary

Quick Facts: Music Directors and Composers

2019 Median Pay	$51,670 per year $24.84 per hour
Typical Entry-Level Education	Bachelor's degree
Work Experience in a Related Occupation	Less than 5 years
On-the-job Training	None
Number of Jobs, 2019	58,000
Job Outlook, 2019-29	2% (Slower than average)
Employment Change, 2019-29	1,000

What Music Directors and Composers Do

Music directors lead musical groups during performances and recording sessions. Composers write and arrange original music in a variety of musical styles.

Work Environment

Most music directors work for religious organizations and schools, or are self-employed. Music directors may spend a lot of time traveling to different performances. Composers can work in offices, recording studios, or their own homes.

How to Become a Music Director or Composer

Educational and training requirements for music directors and composers vary, although most positions require related work

Music directors lead choirs and other musical groups during performance sessions.

experience. A music director or conductor for a symphony orchestra typically needs a master's degree; a choir director may need a bachelor's degree. There are no formal educational requirements for those interested in writing popular music.

Pay

The median annual wage for music directors and composers was $51,670 in May 2019.

Job Outlook

Employment of music directors and composers is projected to grow 2 percent from 2019 to 2029, slower than the average for all occupations. The number of people attending musical performances, such as symphonies and concerts, and theatrical performances, such as ballets and musical theater, is expected to remain steady. Tough competition for jobs is anticipated because of the large number of people interested in entering this field.

State & Area Data

Explore resources for employment and wages by state and area for music directors and composers.

What Music Directors and Composers Do

Music directors, also called *conductors*, lead orchestras and other musical groups during performances and recording sessions. Composers write and arrange original music in a variety of musical styles.

Duties

Music directors typically do the following:

- Select musical arrangements and compositions to be performed for live audiences or recordings
- Prepare for performances by reviewing and interpreting musical scores
- Direct rehearsals to prepare for performances and recordings
- Choose guest performers and soloists
- Audition new performers or assist section leaders with auditions
- Practice conducting to improve their technique
- Meet with potential donors and attend fundraisers

Music directors lead orchestras, choirs, and other musical groups. They ensure that musicians play with one coherent

Composers write and arrange original music in a variety of musical styles.

Music directors ensure that musicians play with one coherent sound, balancing the melody, timing, rhythm, and volume.

sound, balancing the melody, timing, rhythm, and volume. They also give feedback to musicians and section leaders on sound and style.

Music directors may work with a variety of musical groups, including church choirs, youth orchestras, and high school or college bands, choirs, or orchestras. Some work with orchestras that accompany dance and opera companies.

Composers typically do the following:

- Write original music that orchestras, bands, and other musical groups perform
- Arrange existing music into new compositions
- Write lyrics for music or work with a lyricist
- Meet with orchestras, musical groups, and others who are interested in commissioning a piece of music
- Study and listen to music of various styles for inspiration
- Work with musicians to record their music

Composers write music for a variety of types of musical groups and users. Some work in a particular style of music, such as classical or jazz. They also may write for musicals, operas, or other types of theatrical productions.

Some composers write scores for movies or television; others write jingles for commercials. Many songwriters focus on composing music for audiences of popular music.

Some composers use instruments to help them as they write music. Others use software that allows them to hear a piece without musicians.

Some music directors and composers give private music lessons to children and adults. Others teach music in elementary, middle, or high schools. For more information, see the profiles on kindergarten and elementary school teachers, middle school teachers, and high school teachers.

For more information about careers in music, see the profile on musicians and singers.

Work Environment

Music directors and composers held about 58,000 jobs in 2019. The largest employers of music directors and composers were as follows:

Religious, grantmaking, civic, professional, and similar organizations	61%
Self-employed workers	28
Performing arts companies	5
Elementary and secondary schools; state, local, and private	3

Music directors commonly work in concert halls and recording studios, and they may spend a lot of time traveling to different performances. Composers can work in offices, recording studios, or their own homes.

Jobs for music directors and composers are found all over the country. However, many jobs are located in cities in which entertainment activities are concentrated, such as New York, Los Angeles, Nashville, and Chicago.

Work Schedules

Rehearsals and recording sessions are commonly held during business hours, but performances take place most often on nights and weekends. Because music writing is done primarily independently, composers may be able to set their own schedules.

How to Become a Music Director or Composer

Educational and training requirements for music directors and composers vary, although most positions require related work experience. A conductor for a symphony orchestra typically needs a master's degree; a choir director may need a bachelor's degree. There are no formal educational requirements for those interested in writing popular music.

Education

Employers generally prefer candidates with a master's degree in music theory, music composition, or conducting for positions as a conductor or classical composer.

Applicants to postsecondary programs in music typically are required to submit recordings, audition in person, or both. These programs teach students about music history and styles, and educate them in composing and conducting techniques.

In order to become a music director or composer, one must have the talent to play, write, and conduct music.

Information on degree programs is available from the National Association of Schools of Music.

A bachelor's degree typically is required for those who want to work as a choir director. Those who work in public schools may need a teaching license or certification. For more information, see the profiles on teachers.

There are no specific educational requirements for those interested in writing popular music. These composers usually find employment by submitting recordings of their compositions to bands, singers, record companies, and movie studios. Composers may promote themselves through personal websites, social media, or online video or audio of their musical work.

Important Qualities

Discipline. Talent is not enough for most music directors and composers to find employment in this field. They must constantly practice and seek to improve their technique and style.

Interpersonal skills. Music directors and composers need to work with agents, musicians, and recording studio personnel. Being friendly, respectful, and open to criticism as well as praise, while enjoying being with others, can help music directors and composers work well with a variety of people.

Leadership. Music directors and composers must guide musicians and singers by preparing musical arrangements and helping them achieve the best possible sound.

Musical talent. To become a music director or composer, one must have musical talent.

Perseverance. Music directors and composers need determination to continue submitting their compositions after receiving rejections. Also, reviewing auditions can be frustrating because it may take many different auditions to find the best musicians.

Promotional skills. Music directors and composers need to promote their performances through local communities, word of mouth, and social media platforms. Good self-promotional skills are helpful in building a fan base and getting more work opportunities.

Training

Music directors and composers typically begin their musical training at a young age by learning to play an instrument or singing, and perhaps performing as a musician or singer. Music directors and composers who are interested in classical music may seek additional training through music camps and fellowships. These programs provide participants with classes, lessons, and performance opportunities.

Work Experience in a Related Occupation

Music directors and composers often work as musicians or singers in a group, a choir, or an orchestra before they take on a leadership role. They use this time to master their instrument and gain an understanding of how the group functions. For more information, see the profile on musicians and singers.

Pay

The median annual wage for music directors and composers was $51,670 in May 2019. The median wage is the wage at which half the workers in an occupation earned more than that amount and half earned less. The lowest 10 percent earned less than $23,100, and the highest 10 percent earned more than $125,200.

In May 2019, the median annual wages for music directors and composers in the top industries in which they worked were as follows:

Performing arts companies	$55,280
Elementary and secondary schools; state, local, and private	55,170
Religious, grantmaking, civic, professional, and similar organizations	41,910

Rehearsals and recording sessions are commonly held during business hours, but performances take place most often on nights and weekends. Because music writing is done primarily independently, composers may be able to set their own schedules.

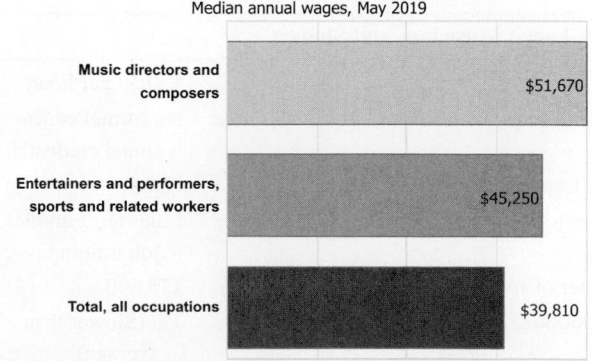

Note: All Occupations includes all occupations in the U.S. Economy.
Source: U.S. Bureau of Labor Statistics, Occupational Employment Statistics.

Music Directors and Composers
Percent change in employment, projected 2019-29

Note: All Occupations includes all occupations in the U.S. Economy.
Source: U.S. Bureau of Labor Statistics, Employment Projections program.

Job Outlook

Employment of music directors and composers is projected to grow 2 percent from 2019 to 2029, slower than the average for all occupations.

Music directors will be needed to lead orchestras for concerts and musical theater performances. They also will conduct the music that accompanies ballet troupes and opera companies.

In addition, there will likely be a need for composers to write original music and arrange known works for performances. Composers will be needed as well to write film scores and music for television and commercials.

However, orchestras, opera companies, and other musical groups can have difficulty getting funds. Some music groups are nonprofit organizations that rely on donations and corporate sponsorships, in addition to ticket sales, to fund their work. These organizations often have difficulty finding enough money to cover their expenses. In addition, growth may be limited for music directors in schools due to struggles with school funding, and music programs may be cut.

Job Prospects

Tough competition for jobs is anticipated because of the large number of people interested in entering this field. In particular, there will be considerable competition for full-time music director and composer positions. Candidates with exceptional musical talent and dedication should have the best opportunities.

Music directors and composers may experience periods without work. During these times, they may work in other occupations, give music lessons, attend auditions, or write music.

Employment projections data for music directors and composers, 2019-29					
Occupational Title	SOC Code	Employment, 2019	Projected Employment, 2029	Change, 2019-29 Percent	Numeric
SOURCE: U.S. Bureau of Labor Statistics, Employment Projections program					
Music directors and composers	27-2041	58,000	59,000	2	1,000

State & Area Data
Occupational Employment Statistics (OES)

The Occupational Employment Statistics (OES) program produces employment and wage estimates annually for over 800 occupations. These estimates are available for the nation as a whole, for individual states, and for metropolitan and nonmetropolitan areas.

Contacts for More Information

For more information about music degree programs, visit
➤ National Association of Schools of Music

For more information about careers in music, visit
➤ Future of Music Coalition

Musicians and Singers

Summary

Quick Facts: Musicians and Singers

2019 Median Pay	$30.39 per hour
Typical Entry-Level Education	No formal educational credential
Work Experience in a Related Occupation	None
On-the-job Training	Long-term on-the-job training
Number of Jobs, 2019	175,600
Job Outlook, 2019-29	1% (Slower than average)
Employment Change, 2019-29	1,600

What Musicians and Singers Do

Musicians and singers play instruments or sing for live audiences and in recording studios.

Work Environment

Musicians and singers often perform in settings such as concert halls, arenas, and clubs.

How to Become a Musician or Singer

There are no postsecondary education requirements for musicians or singers interested in performing popular music. However, many performers of classical music and opera have at least a bachelor's degree. Musicians and singers need extensive training and regular practice to acquire the skills and knowledge necessary to interpret music at a professional level.

Pay

The median hourly wage for musicians and singers was $30.39 in May 2019.

Job Outlook

Employment of musicians and singers is projected to grow 1 percent from 2019 to 2029, slower than the average for all occupations.

Musicians must practice playing instruments to improve their technique.

State & Area Data

Explore resources for employment and wages by state and area for musicians and singers.

What Musicians and Singers Do

Musicians and singers play instruments or sing for live audiences and in recording studios. They perform in a variety of styles, such as classical, jazz, opera, hip-hop, and rock.

Duties

Musicians and singers typically do the following:

- Perform music for live audiences and recordings
- Audition for positions in orchestras, choruses, bands, and other types of music groups
- Practice playing instruments or singing to improve their technique
- Rehearse to prepare for performances
- Find and book locations for performances or concerts
- Travel, sometimes great distances, to performance venues
- Promote their careers by maintaining a website or social media presence or by doing photo shoots and interviews

Musicians play one or more instruments. To make themselves more marketable, many musicians become proficient in multiple musical instruments or styles.

Musicians play solo or in bands, orchestras, or small groups. Those in bands may play at weddings, private parties, clubs, or bars while they try to build enough fans to get a recording contract or representation by an agent. Some musicians work as part of a large group of musicians, such as an orchestra, whose members must work and practice together. A few musicians become section leaders, who may be responsible for assigning parts to other musicians or for leading rehearsals.

Others musicians are session musicians, specializing in playing backup for a singer or band leader during recording sessions and live performances.

Singers perform vocal music in a variety of styles. Some specialize in a particular vocal style, such as opera or jazz; others perform in a variety of musical genres. Singers, particularly

Musicians in bands may play clubs and bars while they try to build enough fans to get a recording contract or representation by an agent.

those who specialize in opera or classical music, may perform in different languages, such as French or Italian. Opera and musical theater singers act out a story by singing instead of speaking the dialogue. Some singers become background singers, providing vocals to harmonize with or support a lead singer.

In some cases, musicians and singers write their own music to record and perform. For more information about careers in songwriting, see the profile on music directors and composers.

Some musicians and singers give private music lessons to children and adults. Others with a background in music may teach music in public and private schools, but they typically need a bachelor's degree and a teaching license. For more information, see the profiles on kindergarten and elementary school teachers, middle school teachers, and high school teachers.

Work Environment

Musicians and singers held about 175,600 jobs in 2019. The largest employers of musicians and singers were as follows:

Religious, grantmaking, civic, professional, and
    similar organizations 43%
Self-employed workers... 38

Performing arts, spectator sports, and related
    industries 13
Educational services; state, local, and private 4

Some musicians and singers spend time in recording studios.

Musicians and singers perform in settings such as concert halls, arenas, and clubs. Musicians and singers who give recitals or perform in nightclubs travel frequently and may tour nationally or internationally. Some spend time in recording studios. There are many jobs in cities that have a high concentration of entertainment activities, such as New York, Los Angeles, Chicago, and Nashville.

Work Schedules

Rehearsals and recording sessions are commonly held during business hours, but live performances are most often at night and on weekends.

Many musicians and singers find only part-time or intermittent work and may have long periods of unemployment between jobs. The stress of constantly looking for work leads many to accept permanent full-time jobs in other occupations while working part time as a musician or singer.

How to Become a Musician or Singer

There are no postsecondary education requirements for musicians or singers interested in performing popular music. However, many performers of classical music and opera have at least a bachelor's degree.

Education

There are no postsecondary education requirements for those interested in performing popular music. Many musicians and singers of classical music and opera have a bachelor's degree in music theory or performance. To be accepted into one of these programs, applicants are typically required to submit recordings or to audition in person and sometimes must do both.

Undergraduate music programs teach students about music history and styles. In addition, they teach methods for improving instrumental and vocal techniques and musical expression. Undergraduate voice programs also teach courses in diction. Such courses help students perform opera in foreign languages.

To work as a classical musician or singer, a bachelor's degree in music theory or music performance is generally required.

Some musicians and singers choose to continue their education by pursuing a master's degree in fine arts or music.

Training

Musicians and singers need extensive training and regular practice to acquire the skills and knowledge necessary to interpret music at a professional level. They typically begin singing or learning to play an instrument by taking lessons and classes when they are at a young age. In addition, they must practice often to develop their talent and technique.

Musicians and singers interested in performing classical music may seek further training through music camps and fellowships. These programs provide participants with classes, lessons, and performance opportunities.

Important Qualities

Dedication. Auditioning for jobs can be a frustrating process because it may take many different auditions to get hired. Musicians and singers need determination and dedication to continue to audition after receiving many rejections.

Discipline. Talent is not enough for most musicians and singers to find employment in this field. They must constantly practice and rehearse to improve their technique, style, and performance.

Interpersonal skills. Musicians and singers need to work well with a variety of people, such as agents, music producers, conductors, and other musicians. Good people skills are helpful in building good working relationships.

Musical talent. Professional musicians or singers must have superior musical abilities.

Physical stamina. Musicians and singers who play in concerts or in nightclubs, and those who tour, must be able to endure frequent travel and irregular performance schedules.

Promotional skills. Musicians and singers need to promote their performances through local communities, word of mouth, and social media. Good self-promotional skills are helpful in building a fan base.

Advancement

As with other occupations in which people perform, advancement for musicians and singers means becoming better known, finding work more easily, and earning more money for each performance. Successful musicians and singers often rely on agents or managers to find them jobs, negotiate contracts, and develop their careers. Some musicians and singers advance to leading musical groups or to writing complex music such as symphonies. For more information, see the profile on music directors and composers.

Pay

The median hourly wage for musicians and singers was $30.39 in May 2019. The median wage is the wage at which half the workers in an occupation earned more than that amount and half earned less. The lowest 10 percent earned less than $11.11, and the highest 10 percent earned more than $80.70.

In May 2019, the median hourly wages for musicians and singers in the top industries in which they worked were as follows:

Performing arts, spectator sports, and related industries	$36.49
Educational services; state, local, and private	24.09
Religious, grantmaking, civic, professional, and similar organizations	23.90

Rehearsals and recording sessions are commonly held during business hours, but live performances are most often at night and on weekends.

Many musicians and singers find only part-time or intermittent work and may have long periods of unemployment between jobs. The stress of constantly looking for work leads many to accept permanent full-time jobs in other occupations while working part time as a musician or singer.

Job Outlook

Employment of musicians and singers is projected to grow 1 percent from 2019 to 2029, slower than the average for all occupations.

Decreased demand for musicians and singers in performing arts companies, which are expected to have reduced attendance and difficulty getting funding, is expected to limit employment growth.

Digital downloads and streaming platforms make it easy for music fans to listen to recordings and view performances. Easier access to recordings gives musicians more publicity and grows interest in their work, and concertgoers may become interested in seeing them perform live. Moreover, some musicians and singers license their music for use in advertisements or for other commercial purposes, creating more exposure and revenue opportunities.

There may be some additional demand for musicians to serve as session musicians and backup artists for recordings and to go on tour. Singers may be needed to sing backup and to make recordings for commercials, films, and television.

Job Prospects

There will be tough competition for jobs because of the large number of people who are interested in becoming musicians and singers. Many musicians and singers experience periods of unemployment, and there will likely be considerable competition for full-time positions.

Musicians and singers with exceptional musical talent and dedication should have the best opportunities.

Employment projections data for musicians and singers, 2019-29					
Occupational Title	SOC Code	Employment, 2019	Projected Employment, 2029	Change, 2019-29	
				Percent	Numeric
SOURCE: U.S. Bureau of Labor Statistics, Employment Projections program					
Musicians and singers	27-2042	175,600	177,200	1	1,600

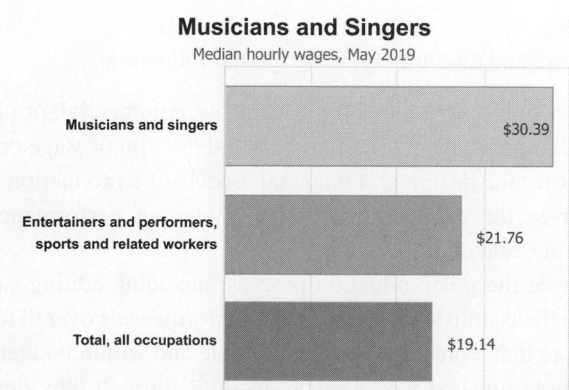

Musicians and Singers
Median hourly wages, May 2019

Musicians and singers — $30.39
Entertainers and performers, sports and related workers — $21.76
Total, all occupations — $19.14

Note: All Occupations includes all occupations in the U.S. Economy.
Source: U.S. Bureau of Labor Statistics, Occupational Employment Statistics.

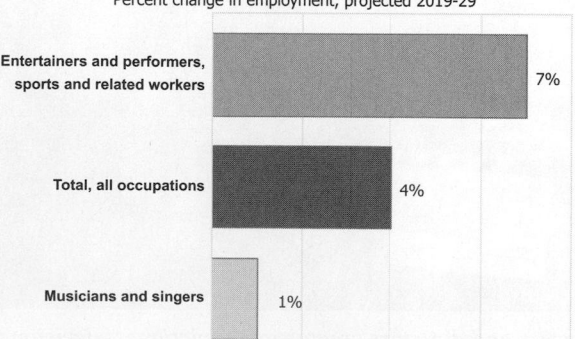

Musicians and Singers
Percent change in employment, projected 2019-29

Entertainers and performers, sports and related workers — 7%
Total, all occupations — 4%
Musicians and singers — 1%

Note: All Occupations includes all occupations in the U.S. Economy.
Source: U.S. Bureau of Labor Statistics, Employment Projections program.

State & Area Data
Occupational Employment Statistics (OES)

The Occupational Employment Statistics (OES) program produces employment and wage estimates annually for over 800 occupations. These estimates are available for the nation as a whole, for individual states, and for metropolitan and nonmetropolitan areas.

Contacts for More Information

For more information about music careers and compensation, visit
➤ Future of Music Coalition

For more information about music degree programs, visit
➤ National Association of Schools of Music

Producers and Directors

Summary

Quick Facts: Producers and Directors

2019 Median Pay	$74,420 per year $35.78 per hour
Typical Entry-Level Education	Bachelor's degree
Work Experience in a Related Occupation	Less than 5 years
On-the-job Training	None
Number of Jobs, 2019	159,500
Job Outlook, 2019-29	10% (Much faster than average)
Employment Change, 2019-29	16,000

What Producers and Directors Do

Producers and directors create motion pictures, television shows, live theater, commercials, and other performing arts productions.

Work Environment

Producers and directors work under a lot of pressure, and many are under stress to finish their work on time. Work hours for producers and directors can be long and irregular.

Producers and directors create motion pictures, television shows, live theater, and other performing arts productions.

How to Become a Producer or Director

Most producers and directors have a bachelor's degree and several years of experience in motion picture, TV, or theater production, working as an actor, a film and video editor, or a cinematographer, or in another, related occupation.

Pay

The median annual wage for producers and directors was $74,420 in May 2019.

Job Outlook

Employment of producers and directors is projected to grow 10 percent from 2019 to 2029, much faster than the average for all occupations. Job growth in the motion picture and video industry is expected to stem from strong demand from the public for more movies and television shows, as well as an increased demand from foreign audiences for U.S.-produced films.

State & Area Data

Explore resources for employment and wages by state and area for producers and directors.

What Producers and Directors Do

Producers and directors create motion pictures, television shows, live theater, commercials, and other performing arts productions. They interpret a writer's script to entertain or inform an audience.

Duties

Producers and directors typically do the following:

- Select scripts or topics for a film, show, commercial, or play
- Audition and select cast members and the film or stage crew
- Approve the design and financial aspects of a production
- Oversee the production process, including performances, lighting, and choreography
- Oversee the postproduction process, including editing, special effects, music selection, and a performance's overall tone
- Ensure that a project stays on schedule and within budget
- Promote finished works or productions through interviews, advertisements, and film festivals

Stage directors make sure the cast and crew give a consistently strong live performance.

Producers make the business and financial decisions for a motion picture, TV show, commercial, or stage production. They raise money for the project and hire the director and crew. The crew may include set and costume designers, film and video editors, a musical director, a choreographer, and other workers. Some producers may assist in the selection of cast members. Producers set the budget and approve any major changes to the project. They make sure that the production is completed on time, and they are ultimately responsible for the final product.

Directors are responsible for the creative decisions of a production. They select cast members, conduct rehearsals, and direct the work of the cast and crew. During rehearsals, they work with the actors to help them portray their characters more accurately. For nonfiction video, such as documentaries or live broadcasts, directors choose topics or subjects to film. They investigate the topic and may interview relevant participants or experts on camera. Directors also work with cinematographers and other crew members to ensure that the final product matches the overall vision.

Directors work with set designers, costume designers, location scouts, and art directors to build a project's set. During a film's postproduction phase, they work closely with film editors and music supervisors to make sure that the final product comes out the way the producer and director envisioned. *Stage directors*, unlike *television or film directors*, who document their product with cameras, make sure that the cast and crew give a consistently strong live performance. For more information, see the profiles on actors, writers and authors, film and video editors and camera operators, dancers and choreographers, and multimedia artists and animators.

Large productions often have various producers who share responsibilities. For example, on a large movie set, an *executive producer* is in charge of the entire production and a *line producer* runs the day-to-day operations. A TV show may employ several *assistant producers* to whom the head or executive producer gives certain duties, such as supervising the costume and makeup teams.

Similarly, large productions usually employ several *assistant directors*, who help the director with smaller production tasks such as making set changes or notifying the performers when it is their time to go onstage. The specific responsibilities of assistant producers or directors vary with the size and type of production they work on.

Although directors are in charge of the creative aspects of a show, they ultimately answer to producers. Some directors also share producing duties for their own films.

Work Environment

Producers and directors held about 159,500 jobs in 2019. The largest employers of producers and directors were as follows:

Motion picture and video industries	28%
Radio and television broadcasting	20
Self-employed workers	17
Performing arts, spectator sports, and related industries	8
Advertising, public relations, and related services	5

Producers and directors work under a lot of pressure, and many are under constant stress to finish their work on time. Work assignments may be short, ranging from 1 day to a few months. They sometimes must work in unpleasant conditions, such as bad weather.

Producers and directors audition and select cast members.

Theater directors and producers may travel with a touring show across the country, while those in film and television may work on location (a site away from the studio and where all or part of the filming occurs).

Work Schedules

Work hours for producers and directors can be long and irregular. Evening, weekend, and holiday work is common. Some work more than 40 hours per week. Many producers and directors do not work a standard workweek, because their schedules may change with each assignment or project.

How to Become a Producer or Director

Most producers and directors have a bachelor's degree and several years of work experience in an occupation related to motion picture, TV, or theater production, such as experience as an actor, a film and video editor, or a cinematographer.

Education

Producers and directors usually have a bachelor's degree. Many students study film or cinema in programs at colleges and universities. In these programs, students learn about film history, editing, screenwriting, cinematography, and the filmmaking process. As of 2017, the National Association of Schools of

Producers and directors ensure that a project stays on schedule and within budget.

Theatre provided accreditation to more than 180 postsecondary institutions for their programs in theater arts.

Others producers and directors have degrees in writing, acting, journalism, or communications. Some producers earn a degree in business, arts management, or nonprofit management.

Many stage directors complete a degree in theater, and some go on to earn a Master of Fine Arts (MFA) degree. Classes may include directing, playwriting, set design, and acting.

Work Experience in a Related Occupation

Producers and directors might start out working in theatrical management offices as business or company managers. In television or film, they might start out as assistants or in other low-profile studio jobs. For more information, see the profiles on film and video editors and camera operators.

Advancement

As a producer's or director's reputation grows, he or she may work on larger, more expensive projects that attract more attention or publicity.

Important Qualities

Communication skills. Producers and directors must coordinate the work of many different people to finish a production on time and within budget.

Creativity. Because a script can be interpreted in different ways, directors must decide how they want to interpret it and then how to represent the script's ideas on the screen or stage.

Leadership skills. Directors instruct actors and help them portray their characters in a believable manner. They also supervise the crew, which is responsible for behind-the-scenes work.

Time-management skills. Producers must find and hire the best director and crew for the production. They make sure that all involved do their jobs effectively, keeping within a production schedule and a budget.

Pay

The median annual wage for producers and directors was $74,420 in May 2019. The median wage is the wage at which half the workers in an occupation earned more than that amount and half earned less. The lowest 10 percent earned less than $35,480, and the highest 10 percent earned more than $173,680.

In May 2019, the median annual wages for producers and directors in the top industries in which they worked were as follows:

Advertising, public relations, and related services	$93,100
Motion picture and video industries	87,790
Radio and television broadcasting	64,030
Performing arts, spectator sports, and related industries	61,340

Producers and Directors
Median annual wages, May 2019

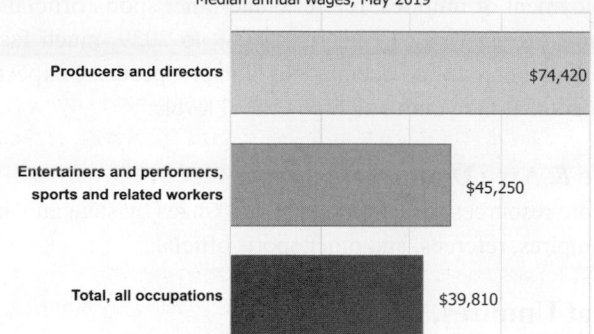

Producers and directors — $74,420
Entertainers and performers, sports and related workers — $45,250
Total, all occupations — $39,810

Producers and Directors
Percent change in employment, projected 2019-29

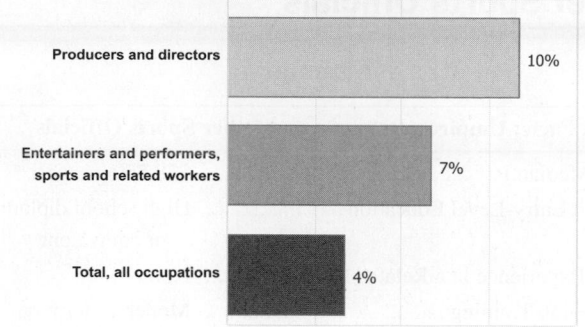

Producers and directors — 10%
Entertainers and performers, sports and related workers — 7%
Total, all occupations — 4%

Note: All Occupations includes all occupations in the U.S. Economy.
Source: U.S. Bureau of Labor Statistics, Occupational Employment Statistics.

Some producers and directors earn a percentage of ticket sales. A few of the most successful producers and directors have extraordinarily high earnings, but most do not.

Work hours for producers and directors can be long and irregular. Evening, weekend, and holiday work is common. Some work more than 40 hours per week. Many producers and directors do not work a standard workweek, because their schedules may change with each assignment or project.

Job Outlook

Employment of producers and directors is projected to grow 10 percent from 2019 to 2029, much faster than the average for all occupations. Some job growth in the motion picture and video industry is expected to stem from strong demand from the public for movies and television shows, as well as an increased demand from foreign audiences for U.S.-produced films.

Consumer demand for reality shows on television is likely to increase, so more producers and directors will be needed to create and oversee editing of these programs. In addition, the volume of TV shows is expected to grow as the number of Internet-only platforms, such as streaming services, increases along with the number of shows produced for these platforms. This growth should lead to more work opportunities for producers and directors.

Theater producers and directors who work in small- and medium-sized theaters may see slower job growth because many of those theaters have difficulty finding funding as fewer tickets are sold. Large theaters in big cities, such as New York and Los Angeles, which usually have more stable sources of funding, should provide more opportunities.

Note: All Occupations includes all occupations in the U.S. Economy.
Source: U.S. Bureau of Labor Statistics, Employment Projections program.

Job Prospects

Producers and directors face intense competition for jobs because there are more people who want to work in this field than there are jobs available. In film, directors who have experience on film sets should have the best job prospects. Producers who have good business skills will likely have the best prospects.

Employment projections data for producers and directors, 2019-29					
Occupational Title	SOC Code	Employment, 2019	Projected Employment, 2029	Percent	Numeric
SOURCE: U.S. Bureau of Labor Statistics, Employment Projections program					
Producers and directors	27-2012	159,500	175,500	10	16,000

State & Area Data
Occupational Employment Statistics (OES)

The Occupational Employment Statistics (OES) program produces employment and wage estimates annually for over 800 occupations. These estimates are available for the nation as a whole, for individual states, and for metropolitan and nonmetropolitan areas.

Contacts for More Information

For more information about producers and directors, visit
➤ Directors Guild of America
➤ Producers Guild of America
➤ National Association of Schools of Theatre
➤ National Endowment for the Arts

Umpires, Referees, and Other Sports Officials

Summary

Quick Facts: Umpires, Referees, and Other Sports Officials

2019 Median Pay	$28,550 per year
Typical Entry-Level Education	High school diploma or equivalent
Work Experience in a Related Occupation	None
On-the-job Training	Moderate-term on-the-job training
Number of Jobs, 2019	22,800
Job Outlook, 2019-29	8% (Much faster than average)
Employment Change, 2019-29	1,800

What Umpires, Referees, and Other Sports Officials Do

Umpires, referees, and other sports officials preside over competitive athletic or sporting events to help maintain standards of play.

Work Environment

Umpires, referees, and other sports officials work indoors and outdoors. They often work irregular hours, including evenings, weekends, and holidays. Officials working outdoors are exposed to all types of weather conditions.

How to Become an Umpire, Referee, or Other Sports Official

Educational requirements vary by state and local sports association. Although some states have no formal education requirements, other states require umpires, referees, and other sports officials to have a high school diploma.

Pay

The median annual wage for umpires, referees, and other sports officials was $28,550 in May 2019.

Job Outlook

Employment of umpires, referees, and other sports officials is projected to grow 8 percent from 2019 to 2029, much faster than the average for all occupations. Job prospects are expected to be good at the youth and high school levels.

State & Area Data

Explore resources for employment and wages by state and area for umpires, referees, and other sports officials.

What Umpires, Referees, and Other Sports Officials Do

Umpires, referees, and other sports officials preside over competitive athletic or sporting events to help maintain standards of play. They detect infractions and decide penalties according to the rules of the game.

Duties

Umpires, referees, and other sports officials typically do the following:

- Officiate sporting events, games, and competitions
- Judge performances in sporting competitions to determine a winner
- Inspect sports equipment and examine all participants to ensure safety
- Keep track of event times, starting or stopping play when necessary
- Signal participants and other officials when infractions occur or to regulate play or competition
- Settle claims of infractions or complaints by participants
- Enforce the rules of the game and assess penalties when necessary

While officiating at sporting events, umpires, referees, and other sports officials must anticipate play and position themselves where they can best see the action, assess the situation, and identify any violations of the rules.

Umpires, referees, and other sports officials preside over competitive athletic or sporting events.

Umpires, referees, and other sports officials regulate play by signaling participants and other officials.

Sports officials typically rely on their judgment to rule on infractions and penalties. Officials in some sports may use video replay to help make the correct call.

Some sports officials, such as boxing referees, may work independently. Others, such as baseball or softball umpires, work in groups. Each official working in a group may have different responsibilities. For example, in baseball, one umpire is responsible for signaling balls and strikes while others are responsible for signaling fair and foul balls out in the field.

Regardless of the sport, the job is highly stressful because officials often must make split-second rulings. These rulings sometimes result in strong disagreement expressed by players, coaches, and spectators.

Many umpires, referees, and other sports officials are employed primarily in other occupations and supplement their income by officiating part time.

Work Environment

Umpires, referees, and other sports officials held about 22,800 jobs in 2019. The largest employers of umpires, referees, and other sports officials were as follows:

Amusement, gambling, and recreation industries	19%
Performing arts, spectator sports, and related industries	13
Civic, social, professional, and similar organizations	11
Educational services; state, local, and private	9
Self-employed workers	8

Umpires, referees, and other sports officials work indoors and outdoors. Those working outdoors will be exposed to all types of weather conditions. Some officials must travel on long bus rides to sporting events. Others, especially officials in professional sports, travel by air.

Some sports require officials to run, sprint, or jog for an extended period of time.

Because sports officials must observe play and often make split-second rulings, the work can be filled with pressure. Strong disagreements and criticism from athletes, coaches, and fans can result in additional stress.

Work Schedules

Umpires, referees, and other sports officials often work irregular hours, including evenings, weekends, and holidays. Many work part time.

How to Become an Umpire, Referee, or Other Sports Official

Educational requirements vary by state and are sometimes determined by the local sports association. Although some states have no formal education requirements, other states require umpires, referees, and other sports officials to have a high school diploma. Training requirements also vary by state and the level and type of sport. Officiating sports requires extensive knowledge of the rules of the game.

Education and Training

Each state and sport association has its own education requirements for umpires, referees, and other sports officials. Some states do not require formal education, while others require sports officials to have a high school diploma.

For more information on educational requirements by state, refer to the specific state athletic or activity association.

Umpires, referees, and other sports officials may be required to attend training sessions and seminars before, during, and after the season. These sessions allow officials to learn about rule changes, review and evaluate their own performances, and improve their officiating.

Licenses, Certifications, and Registrations

To officiate at high school athletic events, umpires, referees, and other officials must typically register with the state or local agency that oversees high school athletics. They also typically need to pass an exam on the rules of the particular game. Some states and associations may require applicants to attend umpiring or refereeing classes before taking the exam or joining an association. Other associations require officials to attend

Umpires, referees and other sports officials work indoors and out, in all types of weather.

Education and training requirements for umpires, referees, and other sports officials vary by the level and type of sport.

annual training workshops before renewing their officiating license.

For more information on licensing and certification requirements, visit your state's high school athletic association website or the National Association of Sports Officials.

Advancement

Most new umpires, referees, and other sports officials begin by officiating youth or freshmen high school sports. After a few years, they may advance to the junior varsity or varsity level. Those who wish to advance to the collegiate level must typically officiate at the varsity high school level for many years.

Some umpires, referees, and other officials may advance through the high school and collegiate levels to reach the professional level. Some sports, such as baseball, have their own professional training schools that prepare aspiring umpires and officials for a career at the minor and major league levels. Baseball umpires begin their professional careers officiating in the minor leagues and typically need 7 to 10 years of experience there before moving on to the major leagues.

Standards for umpires and other officials become more stringent as the level of competition increases.

Other Experience

Umpires, referees, and other sports officials must have an extensive knowledge of the rules of the game they are officiating. Many officials gain the knowledge of the game by attending training sessions or camps that teach the important rules and regulations of the sport.

Some officials may have gained much of their knowledge through years of playing the sport at some level. However, previous playing experience is not a requirement for becoming an umpire, referee, or other sports official.

Important Qualities

Communication skills. Umpires, referees, and other sports officials must have good communication skills because they inform athletes on the rules of the game, discuss infractions, and settle disputes.

Decisionmaking skills. Umpires, referees, and other sports officials must observe play, assess various situations, and often make split-second decisions.

Good vision. Umpires, referees, and other sports officials must have good vision to view infractions and identify any violations during play. In some sports, such as diving or gymnastics, sports officials must also be able to observe an athlete's form for imperfections.

Physical stamina. Many umpires, referees, and other sports officials are required to stand, walk, run, or squat for long periods during games and events.

Teamwork. Because many umpires, referees, and other sports officials work in groups to officiate a game, the ability to cooperate and come to a mutual decision is essential.

Pay

The median annual wage for umpires, referees, and other sports officials was $28,550 in May 2019. The median wage is the wage at which half the workers in an occupation earned more than that amount and half earned less. The lowest 10 percent earned less than $18,310, and the highest 10 percent earned more than $62,490.

In May 2019, the median annual wages for umpires, referees, and other sports officials in the top industries in which they worked were as follows:

Performing arts, spectator sports, and related industries	$37,400
Civic, social, professional, and similar organizations	31,260
Amusement, gambling, and recreation industries...	27,150
Educational services; state, local, and private	24,680

Most umpires, referees, and other sports officials are paid on a per-game basis. Pay typically rises as the level of competition increases.

Umpires, referees, and other sports officials often work irregular hours, including evenings, weekends, and holidays. Many work part time.

Umpires, Referees, and Other Sports Officials
Median annual wages, May 2019

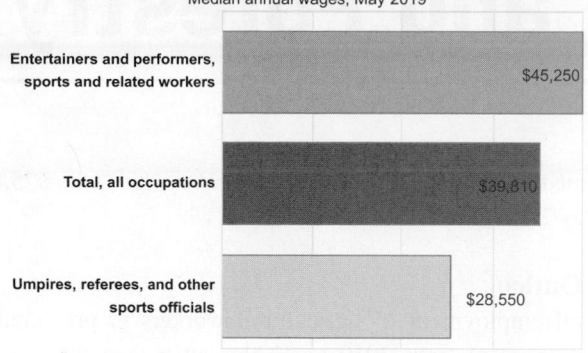

Entertainers and performers, sports and related workers $45,250

Total, all occupations $39,810

Umpires, referees, and other sports officials $28,550

Note: All Occupations includes all occupations in the U.S. Economy.
Source: U.S. Bureau of Labor Statistics, Occupational Employment Statistics.

Umpires, Referees, and Other Sports Officials
Percent change in employment, projected 2019-29

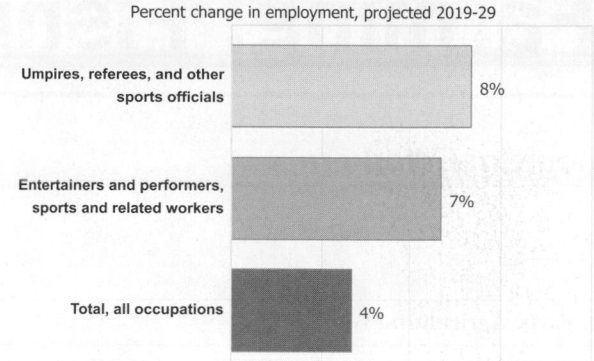

Umpires, referees, and other sports officials   8%

Entertainers and performers, sports and related workers   7%

Total, all occupations   4%

Note: All Occupations includes all occupations in the U.S. Economy.
Source: U.S. Bureau of Labor Statistics, Employment Projections program.

Job Outlook

Employment of umpires, referees, and other sports officials is projected to grow 8 percent from 2019 to 2029, much faster than the average for all occupations. However, because it is a small occupation, the fast growth will result in only about 1,800 new jobs over the 10-year period. As the population grows, so will the overall number of people participating in organized sports.

High school enrollment is projected to increase over the next decade, which could result in a rise in the number of student athletes. As schools offer more athletic programs and as more students participate in sports, the demand for umpires, referees, and other sports officials may increase.

However, funding for athletic programs often is the first thing to be cut when budgets become tight. Still, the popularity of interscholastic sports sometimes enables shortfalls to be off-set with assistance from fundraisers, booster clubs, and parents.

Participation in college sports also is projected to increase over the next decade, particularly at smaller colleges and in women's sports. Many small, Division III colleges are expanding their sports programs and adding new teams to help promote the school and recruit students.

However, new rules allowing an increase in scholarship payments to student athletes may result in funding cuts to smaller collegiate sports programs. The latter cuts could curtail the employment of umpires, referees, and officials if enough programs are eliminated.

Job Prospects

Overall job prospects for umpires, referees, and other sports officials are expected to be good at the youth and high school levels. Those with prior officiating experience will have the best job opportunities.

However, competition is expected to be very strong for the collegiate and professional levels. Many people are attracted to working in sports, and the collegiate and professional levels typically have few job openings and low turnover.

Employment projections data for umpires, referees, and other sports officials, 2019-29					
Occupational Title	SOC Code	Employment, 2019	Projected Employment, 2029	Change, 2019-29	
				Percent	Numeric
SOURCE: U.S. Bureau of Labor Statistics, Employment Projections program					
Umpires, referees, and other sports officials	27-2023	22,800	24,600	8	1,800

State & Area Data

Occupational Employment Statistics (OES)

The Occupational Employment Statistics (OES) program produces employment and wage estimates annually for over 800 occupations. These estimates are available for the nation as a whole, for individual states, and for metropolitan and nonmetropolitan areas.

Contacts for More Information

For more information about umpires, referees, and other sports officials, visit
➤ National Association of Sports Officials

For more information on umpires, referees, and other sports officials, refer to the organization that represents the sport and the locality.

Farming, Fishing, and Forestry

Agricultural Workers

Summary

Quick Facts: Agricultural Workers	
2019 Median Pay	$25,840 per year $12.42 per hour
Typical Entry-Level Education	See below
Work Experience in a Related Occupation	None
On-the-job Training	See below
Number of Jobs, 2019	902,900
Job Outlook, 2019-29	1% (Slower than average)
Employment Change, 2019-29	9,200

What Agricultural Workers Do

Agricultural workers maintain crops and tend to livestock.

Work Environment

Agricultural workers usually perform their duties outdoors in all kinds of weather.

How to Become an Agricultural Worker

Agricultural workers typically receive on-the-job training. A high school diploma is not needed for most jobs as an agricultural worker; however, a high school diploma typically is needed for animal breeders.

Pay

The median annual wage for agricultural workers was $25,840 in May 2019.

Job Outlook

Overall employment of agricultural workers is projected to grow 1 percent from 2019 to 2029, slower than the average for all occupations. Despite increased demand for crops and other agricultural products, employment growth is expected to be tempered as agricultural establishments continue to use technologies that increase output per farmworker.

State & Area Data

Explore resources for employment and wages by state and area for agricultural workers.

What Agricultural Workers Do

Agricultural workers maintain crops and tend to livestock. They perform physical labor and operate machinery under the supervision of farmers, ranchers, and other agricultural managers.

Duties

Agricultural workers typically do the following:

- Harvest and inspect crops by hand
- Irrigate farm soil and maintain ditches or pipes and pumps
- Operate and service farm machinery and tools
- Spray fertilizer or pesticide solutions to control insects, fungi, and weeds
- Move shrubs, plants, and trees with wheelbarrows or tractors
- Feed livestock and clean and disinfect their pens, cages, yards, and hutches

Agricultural workers maintain crops and tend to livestock.

Agricultural workers operate farm machinery.

- Examine animals to detect symptoms of illnesses or injuries and administer vaccines to protect animals from diseases
- Use brands, tags, or tattoos to mark livestock in order to identify ownership and grade
- Herd livestock to pastures for grazing or to scales, trucks, or other enclosures

The following are examples of types of agricultural workers:

Agricultural equipment operators use a variety of farm equipment to plow and sow seeds, as well as maintain and harvest crops. They may use tractors, fertilizer spreaders, balers, combines, threshers, and trucks. These workers also operate machines such as conveyor belts, loading machines, separators, cleaners, and dryers. Workers may make adjustments and minor repairs to equipment.

Animal breeders use their knowledge of genetics and animal science to select and breed animals that will produce offspring with desired traits and characteristics. For example, they breed chickens that lay more eggs, pigs that produce leaner meat, and sheep with more desirable wool. Others breed and raise cats, dogs, and other household pets.

To know which animals to breed and when to breed them, animal breeders keep detailed records. Breeders note animals' health, size, and weight, as well as the amount and quality of the product they produce. Animal breeders also track the traits of animals' offspring.

Some animal breeders may consult with farmers, ranchers, and other agricultural managers about their livestock.

Crop, nursery, and greenhouse farmworkers and laborers perform numerous tasks related to growing and harvesting grains, fruits, vegetables, nuts, and other crops. They plant, seed, prune, irrigate, and harvest crops, and pack and load them for shipment.

Farmworkers also apply pesticides, herbicides, and fertilizers to crops. They repair fences and some farm equipment.

Nursery and greenhouse workers prepare land or greenhouse beds for growing horticultural products such as trees, plants, flowers, and sod. They also plant, water, prune, weed, and spray the plants. They may cut, roll, and stack sod; stake trees; tie, wrap, and pack plants to fill orders; and dig up or move field-grown shrubs and trees.

Farm and ranch animal farmworkers care for live animals, including cattle, sheep, pigs, goats, horses, poultry, finfish, shellfish, and bees. These animals usually are raised to supply meat, fur, skins, feathers, eggs, milk, or honey.

These farmworkers may feed, herd, brand, weigh, and load animals. They also keep records on animals; examine animals to detect diseases and injuries; and administer medications, vaccinations, or insecticides.

Many workers clean and maintain animal housing areas every day. On dairy farms, animal farmworkers operate milking machines.

Many agricultural workers have seasonal work schedules.

Work Environment

Agricultural workers held about 902,900 jobs in 2019. Employment in the detailed occupations that make up agricultural workers was distributed as follows:

Farmworkers and laborers, crop, nursery, and greenhouse	566,500
Farmworkers, farm, ranch, and aquacultural animals	245,400
Agricultural equipment operators	70,300
Agricultural workers, all other	12,300
Animal breeders	8,400

The largest employers of agricultural workers were as follows:

Crop production	55%
Animal production and aquaculture	27
Support activities for agriculture and forestry	6
Wholesale trade	4

Agricultural workers usually perform their duties outdoors in all kinds of weather.

Agricultural workers' jobs can be difficult. To harvest fruits and vegetables by hand, workers frequently bend and crouch. They also lift and carry crops and tools that may be heavy.

Injuries and Illnesses

Agricultural work can be dangerous. Although agricultural workers risk exposure to pesticides sprayed on crops or plants, improper exposure can be controlled if workers follow appropriate safety procedures. Tractors and other farm machinery can cause serious injuries, so workers must be constantly alert. Additionally, agricultural workers who work directly with animals risk being bitten or kicked.

Work Schedules

Many agricultural workers have seasonal work schedules. Seasonal workers typically work longer periods during planting or harvesting times or when animals must be sheltered and fed.

Some agricultural workers, called *migrant farmworkers*, move from location to location as crops ripen. Their unsettled lifestyles and periods of unemployment between jobs can cause stress.

How to Become an Agricultural Worker

Agricultural workers typically receive on-the-job training. A high school diploma is not needed for most jobs as an agricultural worker; however, a high school diploma typically is needed for animal breeders.

Education and Training

Most agricultural workers do not need a high school diploma; however, a high school diploma typically is needed for animal breeders. Some jobs as an animal breeder may require obtaining postsecondary education.

Many agricultural workers receive short-term on-the-job training lasting up to a month. Employers instruct them on how to use simple farming tools and more complex machinery while following appropriate safety procedures. Agricultural equipment operators, however, may need more extensive training before being allowed to operate expensive farming equipment.

Agricultural workers typically receive on-the-job training once they are hired.

Licenses, Certifications, and Registrations

Some agricultural workers, especially those who operate equipment, need a valid driver's license. Agricultural workers who handle pesticides might need a pesticide applicator license. And in a few states, certain types of animal breeders must be licensed.

Important Qualities

Dexterity. Agricultural workers need excellent hand-eye coordination to harvest crops and operate farm machinery.

Listening skills. Agricultural workers need to work well with others. Because they take instructions from farmers and other agricultural managers, effective listening is critical.

Physical stamina. Agricultural workers need to be able to perform laborious tasks repeatedly.

Physical strength. Agricultural workers must be strong enough to lift heavy objects, including tools and crops.

Mechanical skills. Agricultural workers must be able to operate complex farm machinery. They also occasionally do routine maintenance on the machinery.

Other Experience

Animal breeders sometimes need previous work experience interacting with livestock. Ranch workers may transition into animal breeding after they become more familiar with animals and learn how to handle them.

Some agricultural equipment operators might need previous work experience on a farm or operating heavy equipment.

Advancement

Agricultural workers may advance to crew leader or other supervisory positions. The ability to speak both English and Spanish is helpful for agricultural supervisors.

Some agricultural workers aspire to become farmers, ranchers, or agricultural managers or to own their own farms and ranches. Knowledge of produce and livestock may provide an excellent background for becoming buyers or purchasing agents of farm products. Those who earn a college degree in agricultural science could become agricultural or food scientists.

Pay

The median annual wage for agricultural workers was $25,840 in May 2019. The median wage is the wage at which half the workers in an occupation earned more than that amount and half earned less. The lowest 10 percent earned less than $22,850, and the highest 10 percent earned more than $38,990.

Median annual wages for agricultural workers in May 2019 were as follows:

Animal breeders	$42,920
Agricultural equipment operators	31,950
Agricultural workers, all other	29,590

Agricultural Workers

Median annual wages, May 2019

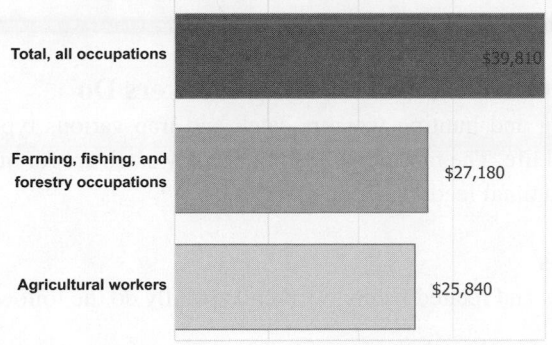

Total, all occupations	$39,810
Farming, fishing, and forestry occupations	$27,180
Agricultural workers	$25,840

Note: All Occupations includes all occupations in the U.S. Economy.
Source: U.S. Bureau of Labor Statistics, Occupational Employment Statistics.

Farmworkers, farm, ranch, and aquacultural
animals 27,830
Farmworkers and laborers, crop, nursery, and
greenhouse 25,440

In May 2019, the median annual wages for agricultural workers in the top industries in which they worked were as follows:

Wholesale trade... $28,070

Many agricultural workers have seasonal work schedules. Seasonal workers typically work longer hours during planting or harvesting times or when animals must be sheltered and fed.

Some agricultural workers, called *migrant farmworkers*, move from location to location as crops ripen. Their unsettled lifestyles and periods of unemployment between jobs can cause stress.

Job Outlook

Overall employment of agricultural workers is projected to grow 1 percent from 2019 to 2029, slower than the average for all occupations.

Despite increased demand for crops and other agricultural products, employment growth is expected to be tempered as agricultural establishments continue to use technologies that increase output per farmworker.

Employment of agricultural equipment operators is projected to increase 11 percent from 2019 to 2029, much faster than the average for all occupations, and faster than any other type of agricultural worker. Increased use of mechanization on farms is expected to lead to more jobs for agricultural equipment operators relative to farmworkers and laborers.

Smaller farms that sell their products directly to consumers through venues such as farmer's markets might create some new opportunities for agricultural workers. These direct-to-consumer farms have grown in popularity, and farmers at these operations may hire agricultural workers as an alternative to expensive machinery.

Agricultural Workers

Percent change in employment, projected 2019-29

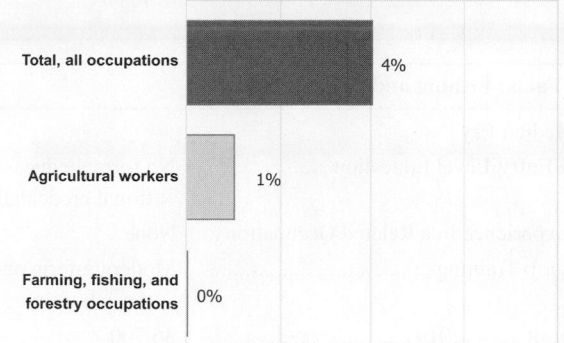

Total, all occupations	4%
Agricultural workers	1%
Farming, fishing, and forestry occupations	0%

Note: All Occupations includes all occupations in the U.S. Economy.
Source: U.S. Bureau of Labor Statistics, Employment Projections program.

Job Prospects

Job prospects for agricultural workers—especially farmworkers and laborers and agricultural equipment operators—should be very good because workers frequently leave the occupation due to the intense physical nature of the work.

Prospects are expected to be best for those who can speak both English and Spanish.

Employment projections data for agricultural workers, 2019-29					
Occupational Title	SOC Code	Employment, 2019	Projected Employment, 2029	Change, 2019-29	
				Percent	Numeric
SOURCE: U.S. Bureau of Labor Statistics, Employment Projections program					
Agricultural workers	—	902,900	912,100	1	9,200
Animal breeders	45-2021	8,400	8,100	-3	-300
Agricultural equipment operators	45-2091	70,300	78,300	11	8,000
Farmworkers and laborers, crop, nursery, and greenhouse	45-2092	566,500	587,900	4	21,400
Farmworkers, farm, ranch, and aquacultural animals	45-2093	245,400	225,100	-8	-20,300
Agricultural workers, all other	45-2099	12,300	12,700	3	400

State & Area Data
Occupational Employment Statistics (OES)

The Occupational Employment Statistics (OES) program produces employment and wage estimates annually for over 800 occupations. These estimates are available for the nation as a whole, for individual states, and for metropolitan and nonmetropolitan areas.

Contacts for More Information

For more information about agricultural workers, visit
➤ Association of Farmworker Opportunity Programs

For more information about careers in agriculture, visit
➤ AgExplorer, National FFA Organization
➤ New Farmers, U.S. Department of Agriculture

Fishing and Hunting Workers

Summary

Quick Facts: Fishing and Hunting Workers

2019 Median Pay	
Typical Entry-Level Education	No formal educational credential
Work Experience in a Related Occupation	None
On-the-job Training	Moderate-term on-the-job training
Number of Jobs, 2019	36,700
Job Outlook, 2019-29	-8% (Decline)
Employment Change, 2019-29	-2,800

What Fishing and Hunting Workers Do

Fishing and hunting workers catch and trap various types of animal life.

Work Environment

The work environment for fishing and hunting operations varies with the region, body of water or land, and kinds of animals sought. Fishing and hunting workers often work under hazardous conditions that can lead to injuries or fatalities.

How to Become a Fishing or Hunting Worker

Fishing and hunting workers usually learn on the job. No formal education is required.

Pay

Wage data reported for this occupation were updated most recently in May 2017.

The median annual wage for fishing and hunting workers was $28,530 in May 2017.

Job Outlook

Employment of fishing and hunting workers is projected to decline 8 percent from 2019 to 2029.

Fishers use nets to catch fish.

State & Area Data

Explore resources for employment and wages by state and area for fishing and hunting workers.

What Fishing and Hunting Workers Do

Fishing and hunting workers catch and trap various types of animal life. The fish and wild animals they catch are for human food, animal feed, bait, and other uses.

Duties

Fishers and related fishing workers typically do the following:

- Locate fish with the use of fish-finding equipment
- Steer vessels and operate navigational instruments
- Maintain engines, fishing gear, and other onboard equipment by making minor repairs
- Sort, pack, and store the catch in holds with ice and other freezing methods
- Measure fish to ensure that they are of legal size
- Return undesirable or illegal catches to the water
- Guide nets, traps, and lines onto vessels by hand or with hoisting equipment
- Signal other workers to move, hoist, and position loads of the catch

Hunters and trappers typically do the following:

- Locate wild animals with the use of animal-finding equipment
- Catch wild animals with weapons, such as rifles or bows, or with traps, such as snares
- Sort, pack, and store the catch with ice and other freezing methods
- Follow hunting regulations, which vary by state and always include a safety component
- Sell what they catch for food and decorative purposes

Fishers and related fishing workers work in deep or shallow water. In deep water, they typically perform their duties on

The fish and wild animals that fishers and hunting workers catch and trap are used for food, bait, and other purposes.

large fishing boats that are equipped for long stays at sea. Some process the catch on board and prepare the fish for sale.

Other fishers work in shallow water on small boats that often have a crew of only one or two. They might put nets across the mouths of rivers or inlets; use pots and traps to catch fish or shellfish, such as lobsters and crabs; or use dredges to gather other shellfish, such as oysters and scallops.

Some fishers harvest marine vegetation rather than fish. They use rakes and hoes to gather Irish moss and kelp.

The following are types of fishers and related fishing workers:

- *Fishing boat captains* plan and oversee the fishing operation including the species of fish to be caught, the location of the best fishing grounds, the method of capture, trip length, and sale of the catch. They also supervise the crew and record daily activities in the ship's log. To plot a ship's course, fishing boat captains use electronic navigational equipment, including Global Positioning System (GPS) instruments. They also use radar and sonar to avoid obstacles above and below the water and to find fish.
- *Fishing deckhands* perform the everyday tasks of baiting; setting lines or traps; hauling in and sorting the catch; and maintaining the boat and fishing gear. Deckhands also secure and remove mooring lines when docking or undocking the boat.

Fishers work in commercial fishing, which does not include recreational fishing. For more information on workers on boats that handle fishing charters, see the profile on water transportation workers.

Aquaculture—raising and harvesting fish and other aquatic life under controlled conditions in ponds or confined bodies of water—is a different field. For more information, see the profile on farmers, ranchers, and other agricultural managers.

Hunters and trappers locate wild animals with GPS instruments, compasses, charts, and whistles. They then catch or kill them with traps or weapons. Hunters and trappers sell the wild animals they catch, for either food, fur, or decorative purposes.

Work Environment

Fishing and hunting workers held about 36,700 jobs in 2019. The largest employers of fishing and hunting workers were as follows:

Fishing, hunting and trapping	54%
Self-employed workers	34

Fishing and hunting operations are conducted under various environmental conditions, depending on the geographic region, body of water or land, and kinds of animals sought. Storms, fog, and wind may hamper fishing vessels or cause them to suspend fishing operations and return to port.

Although fishing gear has improved and operations have become more mechanized, netting and processing fish are

Fishing and hunting workers work under various environmental conditions, depending on the region, body of water, and the kind of species sought.

nonetheless strenuous activities. Newer vessels have improved living quarters and amenities, but crews still experience the aggravations of confined quarters and the absence of family.

Injuries and Illnesses

Commercial fishing and hunting can be dangerous and can lead to workplace injuries or fatalities. Fishing and hunting workers often work under hazardous conditions. Transportation to a hospital or doctor is often not readily available for these workers because they can be out at sea or in a remote area.

And although fatalities are uncommon, fishing and hunting workers experience one of the highest rates of occupational fatalities of all occupations.

Most fatalities that happen to fishers and related fishing workers are from drowning. The crew must guard against the danger of injury from malfunctioning fishing gear, entanglement in fishing nets and gear, slippery decks, ice formation, or large waves washing over the deck. Malfunctioning navigation and communication equipment and other factors may lead to collisions, shipwrecks, or other dangerous situations, such as vessels becoming caught in storms. For more information on injuries and fatalities of fishers and fishing related works, read the *Beyond the Numbers* article "Facts of the catch:

occupational injuries, illnesses, and fatalities to fishing workers, 2003–2009."

Hunting accidents can occur because of the weapons and traps these workers use. Hunters and trappers minimize injury by wearing the appropriate gear and following detailed safety procedures. Specific safety guidelines vary by state.

Work Schedules

Fishing and hunting workers often endure long shifts and irregular work schedules. Commercial fishing trips may require workers to be away from their home port for several weeks or months.

Many fishers are seasonal workers, and those jobs are usually filled by students and by people from other occupations who are available for seasonal work, such as teachers. For example, employment of fishers in Alaska increases significantly during the summer months, which constitute the salmon season. During these times, fishers can expect to work long hours. Additionally, states may only allow hunters and trappers to hunt or trap during certain times of the year depending on the type of wild animals sought.

How to Become a Fishing or Hunting Worker

Fishing and hunting workers usually learn on the job. A formal educational credential is not required.

Education

A formal educational credential is not required for one to become fishing or hunting worker. However, fishers may improve their chances of getting a job by enrolling in a 2-year vocational–technical program. Some community colleges and universities offer fishery technology and related programs that include courses in seamanship, vessel operations, marine safety, navigation, vessel repair, and fishing gear technology. These programs are typically located near coastal areas and include hands-on experience.

Fishers and hunting workers usually acquire their occupational skills on the job.

Training

Most fishing and hunting workers learn on the job. They first learn how to sort and clean the animals they catch. Fishers would go on to learn how to operate the boat and fishing equipment.

Other Experience

Many prospective fishers start by finding work through family or friends, or simply by walking around the docks and asking for employment. Aspiring fishers also can look online for employment. Some larger trawlers and processing ships are run by big fishing companies with human resources departments to which new workers can apply. Operators of large commercial fishing vessels must complete a training course approved by the U.S. Coast Guard.

Most hunters and trappers have previous recreational hunting experience.

Licenses, Certifications, and Registrations

Captains of fishing boats and hunters and trappers must be licensed.

Crewmembers on certain fish-processing vessels may need a merchant mariner's document. The U.S. Coast Guard issues these documents, as well as licenses, to people who meet specific health, physical, and academic requirements.

States set licensing requirements for boats operating in state waters, defined as inland waters and waters within 3 miles of the coast.

Fishers need a permit to fish in almost any water. Permits are distributed by states for state waters and by regional fishing councils for federal waters. The permits specify the fishing season, the type and amount of fish that may be caught, and, sometimes, the type of permissible fishing gear.

Hunters and trappers need a state license to hunt in any land or forest. Licenses specify the hunting season, the type and amount of wild animals that may be caught, and the type of weapons or traps that can be used.

Advancement

Experienced, reliable fishing boat deckhands can become boatswains, then second mates, first mates, and, finally, captains. Those who are interested in ship engineering may gain experience with maintaining and repairing ship engines to become licensed chief engineers on large commercial boats. In doing so, they must meet the Coast Guard's licensing requirements as well. For more information, see the profile on water transportation workers.

Almost all captains are self-employed, and most eventually own, or partially own, one or more fishing boats.

Important Qualities

Critical-thinking skills. Fishing and hunting workers must reach conclusions through sound reasoning and judgment.

They determine how to improve their catch and must react appropriately to weather conditions.

Detail oriented. Fishing and hunting workers must be precise and accurate when measuring the quality of their catch or prey. They must also pay attention to detail when working with various fishing and hunting gear to guard against injury.

Listening skills. Because they take instructions from captains and other crewmembers or hunters, fishing and hunting workers need to communicate well and listen effectively.

Machine operation skills. Fishing and hunting workers must be able to operate and perform routine maintenance on complex fishing and navigation machinery, as well as weapons and traps.

Physical stamina. Fishing and hunting workers need endurance. They must be able to work long hours, often under strenuous conditions.

Physical strength. Fishing and hunting workers must use physical strength, along with hand dexterity and coordination, to perform difficult tasks repeatedly.

Pay

Wage data reported for this occupation were updated most recently in May 2017.

The median annual wage for fishing and hunting workers was $28,530 in May 2017. The median wage is the wage at which half the workers in an occupation earned more than that amount and half earned less. The lowest 10 percent earned less than $18,710, and the highest 10 percent earned more than $48,170.

Fishers are typically paid a percentage of the boat's overall catch, commonly referred to as a crew share. The more fish that are caught, the greater the crew share becomes. This can lead to unpredictable swings in pay from one season to another, as the overall catch can vary. More experienced crewmembers often receive a greater share compared to entry-level workers.

Trappers are typically paid per pelt, and the amount received can vary depending on the species and the quality of the fur. For example, trappers typically receive more for coyote pelts than for smaller species, such as muskrats.

Fishing and hunting workers endure strenuous outdoor work and long hours. Commercial fishing trips may require workers to be away from their home port for several weeks or months.

Many fishers are seasonal workers, and those jobs are usually filled by students and by people from other occupations who are available for seasonal work, such as teachers. For example, employment of fishers in Alaska increases significantly during the summer months, which constitute the salmon season. During these times, fishers can expect to work long hours. Additionally, states may only allow hunters and trappers to hunt or trap during certain times of the year.

Job Outlook

Employment of fishing and hunting workers is projected to decline 8 percent from 2019 to 2029. Fishing and hunting workers depend on the ability of fish stocks and wild animals to reproduce and grow.

Governmental efforts to replenish fish stocks have led to some species being regulated under fishing quotas or catch shares. These quotas dictate how many fish each fisher may catch and keep. Additional quotas or catch shares can typically be purchased, but they are often very expensive. The implementation of additional catch share programs may reduce demand for fishers. However, new programs must undergo several years of research and public review before being approved.

Animal pelts will continue be used to manufacture fur coats, hats, and gloves, which may increase demand for trappers. However, the majority of fur used in clothing comes from ranches or farms that breed, maintain, and harvest desirable species, such as mink.

Job Prospects

Job openings will result from the need to replace fishing and hunting workers who leave the occupation. Many workers leave because of the strenuous and hazardous nature of the job and the lack of a steady year-round income. The best prospects should be with large fishing operations and for seasonal employment.

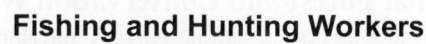

Fishing and Hunting Workers
Median annual wages, May 2019

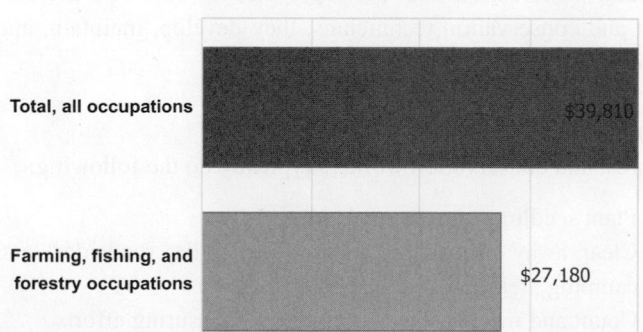

Total, all occupations	$39,810
Farming, fishing, and forestry occupations	$27,180

Note: All Occupations includes all occupations in the U.S. Economy.
Source: U.S. Bureau of Labor Statistics, Occupational Employment Statistics.

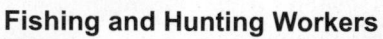

Fishing and Hunting Workers
Percent change in employment, projected 2019-29

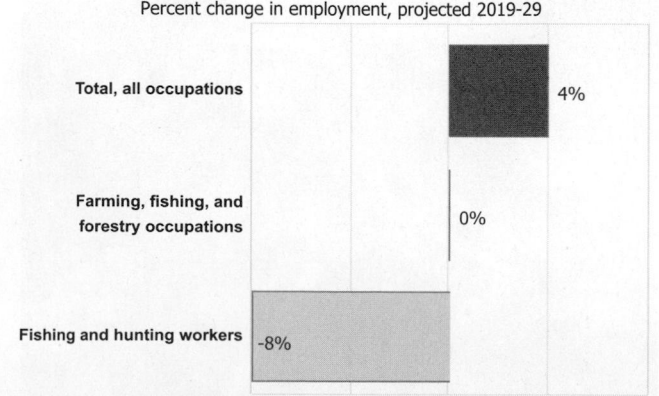

Total, all occupations	4%
Farming, fishing, and forestry occupations	0%
Fishing and hunting workers	-8%

Note: All Occupations includes all occupations in the U.S. Economy.
Source: U.S. Bureau of Labor Statistics, Employment Projections program.

Employment projections data for fishing and hunting workers, 2019-29					
Occupational Title	SOC Code	Employment, 2019	Projected Employment, 2029	Change, 2019-29	
				Percent	Numeric
SOURCE: U.S. Bureau of Labor Statistics, Employment Projections program					
Fishing and hunting workers	45-3031	36,700	33,900	-8	-2,800

State & Area Data
Occupational Employment Statistics (OES)

The Occupational Employment Statistics (OES) program produces employment and wage estimates annually for over 800 occupations. These estimates are available for the nation as a whole, for individual states, and for metropolitan and nonmetropolitan areas.

Contacts for More Information

For more information about licensing of fishing boat captains and about requirements for merchant mariner documentation, visit
➤ National Maritime Center, U.S. Coast Guard Headquarters

For more information about hunting licenses, visit
➤ Where to Hunt

Forest and Conservation Workers

Summary

Quick Facts: Forest and Conservation Workers	
2019 Median Pay	$31,770 per year $15.27 per hour
Typical Entry-Level Education	High school diploma or equivalent
Work Experience in a Related Occupation	None
On-the-job Training	Moderate-term on-the-job training
Number of Jobs, 2019	13,200
Job Outlook, 2019-29	0% (Little or no change)
Employment Change, 2019-29	-100

What Forest and Conservation Workers Do

Forest and conservation workers measure and improve the quality of forests.

Work Environment

Forest and conservation workers typically work for state and local governments or on privately owned forest lands or nurseries. Governments also employ forest and conservation workers on a contract basis.

How to Become a Forest and Conservation Worker

Forest and conservation workers typically need a high school diploma before they begin working. Most workers receive training on the job.

Pay

The median annual wage for forest and conservation workers was $31,770 in May 2019.

Job Outlook

Employment of forest and conservation workers is projected to show little or no change from 2019 to 2029. Although heightened international demand for U.S. timber and wood pellets will continue to demand forest and conservation workers, improved technology will also lessen the need for workers to perform certain tasks.

State & Area Data

Explore resources for employment and wages by state and area for forest and conservation workers.

What Forest and Conservation Workers Do

Forest and conservation workers measure and improve the quality of forests. Under the supervision of foresters and forest and conservation technicians, they develop, maintain, and protect forests.

Duties

Forest and conservation workers typically do the following:

- Plant seedlings to reforest land
- Clear away brush and debris from trails, roadsides, and camping areas
- Count and measure trees during tree-measuring efforts
- Select or cut trees according to markings, sizes, types, or grades

Forest and conservation workers measure and improve the quality of forests.

Forest and conservation workers count trees during tree-measuring efforts.

- Spray trees with insecticides and fungicides to kill insects and fungi and to protect the trees from disease
- Identify and remove diseased or undesirable trees
- Inject vegetation with insecticides and herbicides
- Help prevent and suppress forest fires
- Check equipment to ensure that it is operating properly

Forest and conservation workers are supervised by foresters and forest and conservation technicians, who direct their work and evaluate their progress.

Forest and conservation workers perform basic tasks to maintain and improve the quality of the forest. They use digging and planting tools to plant seedlings and power saws to cut down diseased trees.

Some work on tree farms or orchards, where they plant, cultivate, and harvest many different kinds of trees. Their duties vary with the type of farm and may include planting seedlings or spraying to control weed growth and insects.

Some forest and conservation workers work in forest nurseries, where they sort through tree seedlings, discarding the ones that do not meet standards. Others use handtools or their hands to gather woodland products, such as decorative greenery, tree cones, bark, moss, and other wild plantlife. Some may tap trees to make syrup or chemicals.

Forest and conservation workers who are employed by or are under contract with state and local governments may clear brush and debris from trails, roads, roadsides, and camping areas. They may clean kitchens and restrooms at recreational facilities and campgrounds.

Workers with a fire protection background help to suppress forest fires. For example, they may construct firebreaks, which are gaps in vegetation that can help slow down or stop the progress of a fire. In addition, they may work with technicians to determine how quickly fires spread and how successful fire suppression activities were. For example, workers help count how many trees will be affected by a fire. They also sometimes respond to forest emergencies.

Work Environment

Forest and conservation workers held about 13,200 jobs in 2019. The largest employers of forest and conservation workers were as follows:

State government, excluding education and hospitals	27%
Self-employed workers	20
Support activities for agriculture and forestry	13
Local government, excluding education and hospitals	11
Forestry	10

Forest and conservation workers work outdoors, sometimes in remote locations and in all types of weather.

Forest and conservation workers work mainly in the western and southeastern areas of the United States, where there are many national and state forests, and on private forests and parks.

Forest and conservation workers work outdoors, sometimes in remote locations and in all types of weather. Workers use proper safety measures and equipment, such as hardhats, protective eyewear, and safety clothing.

Most of these jobs are physically demanding. Forest and conservation workers may have to walk long distances through densely wooded areas and carry their equipment with them.

Injuries and Illnesses

Forest and conservation workers have one of the highest rates of injuries and illnesses of all occupations. The work may be especially dangerous for those whose primary duties involve fire suppression. To protect against injury, forest and conservation workers must wear special gear and follow prescribed safety procedures.

Work Schedules

Many forest and conservation workers are employed full time and work regular hours. Responding to an emergency may require workers to work additional hours and at any time of day.

How to Become a Forest and Conservation Worker

Forest and conservation workers typically need a high school diploma before they begin working. Most workers receive training on the job.

Education

Forest and conservation workers typically need a high school diploma and a valid driver's license before they begin working. Some vocational and technical schools and community colleges offer courses leading to a 2-year technical degree in forestry. The programs typically offer courses in forest management

Forest and conservation workers typically need a high school diploma before they begin working.

technology, wildlife management, conservation, or timber harvesting. Programs that include field trips to watch and participate in forestry activities provide particularly good background knowledge.

Training

Entry-level forest and conservation workers generally get on-the-job training as they help more experienced workers. They do routine labor-intensive tasks, such as planting or thinning trees. When the opportunity arises, they learn from experienced technicians and foresters who do more complex tasks, such as gathering data. Workers also learn safety procedures, including how to operate equipment safely and how to maintain safety gear.

In addition, some states require that crews and individuals receive training, and sometimes a license, in the use of commercial pesticides. For more information, consult states' Departments of Agriculture.

Important Qualities

Communication skills. Forest and conservation workers must convey information effectively to technicians and other workers.

Decisionmaking skills. Forest and conservation workers must make quick, intelligent decisions, especially when they face dangerous conditions.

Detail oriented. Forest and conservation workers must watch gauges, dials, or other indicators to determine whether equipment and tools are working properly. Workers must follow safety procedures with precision.

Listening skills. Forest and conservation workers must give full attention to what their superiors are saying. They must understand the instructions they are given before performing tasks.

Physical stamina. Forest and conservation workers plant trees and repeatedly perform a variety of physical tasks. They also must be able to walk long distances through densely wooded areas and carry heavy equipment with them.

Advancement

To advance their careers and become forest and conservation technicians or foresters, forest and conservation workers usually need an associate's or bachelor's degree in forestry or a related field.

Pay

The median annual wage for forest and conservation workers was $31,770 in May 2019. The median wage is the wage at which half the workers in an occupation earned more than that amount and half earned less. The lowest 10 percent earned less than $22,770, and the highest 10 percent earned more than $46,870.

In May 2019, the median annual wages for forest and conservation workers in the top industries in which they worked were as follows:

Forest and Conservation Workers
Median annual wages, May 2019

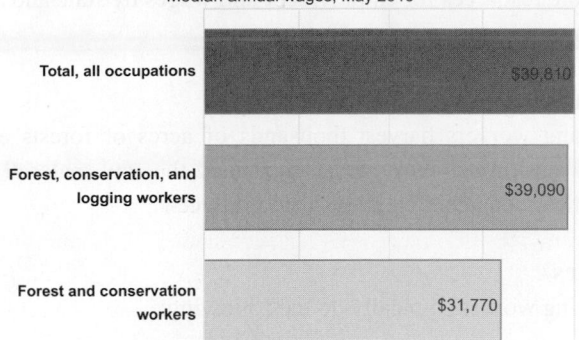

Forest and Conservation Workers
Percent change in employment, projected 2019-29

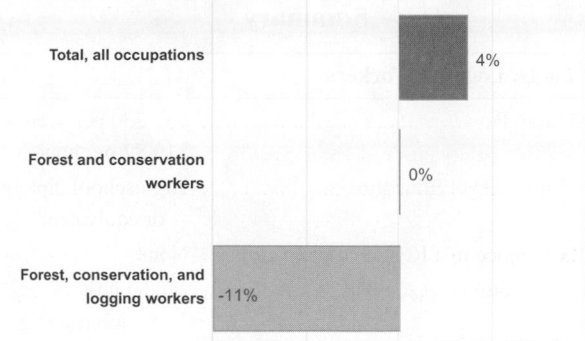

Note: All Occupations includes all occupations in the U.S. Economy.
Source: U.S. Bureau of Labor Statistics, Occupational Employment Statistics.

Note: All Occupations includes all occupations in the U.S. Economy.
Source: U.S. Bureau of Labor Statistics, Employment Projections program.

Local government, excluding education and
hospitals... $33,360
State government, excluding education and
hospitals... 31,770

Many forest and conservation workers are employed full time and work regular hours. Responding to an emergency may require workers to work additional hours and at any time of day.

Job Outlook

Employment of forest and conservation workers is projected to show little or no change from 2019 to 2029. Although demand for forestry products and services will likely be steady, it is expected to be counteracted by the automation of much of the work that these workers do.

New technologies, such as remote sensing, allow fewer workers to perform certain tasks, such as tree counts and tree identifications. As the automation of manual forest tasks continues, fewer of these workers will be needed to perform the same amount of work.

Despite heightened international demand for U.S. timber and wood pellets that will continue to demand forest and conservation workers, improved technology will also lessen the need for workers to perform certain tasks.

There is likely to be an increase in wildfires caused by unpredictable climate conditions and overgrown vegetation on forest lands. This rise in the number of wildfires would in turn increase demand for the fire suppression activities of forest and conservation workers. Most employment activities for forest and conservation workers is likely to be in state-owned forest lands. As more people continue to build homes in western

forests, there will be need for workers to protect those areas from fires.

Job Prospects

Workers who follow standard safety procedures, remain physically fit, and work well on teams will have the best job opportunities.

Employment projections data for forest and conservation workers, 2019-29					
Occupational Title	SOC Code	Employment, 2019	Projected Employment, 2029	Change, 2019-29	
				Percent	Numeric
SOURCE: U.S. Bureau of Labor Statistics, Employment Projections program					
Forest and conservation workers	45-4011	13,200	13,100	0	-100

State & Area Data
Occupational Employment Statistics (OES)

The Occupational Employment Statistics (OES) program produces employment and wage estimates annually for over 800 occupations. These estimates are available for the nation as a whole, for individual states, and for metropolitan and nonmetropolitan areas.

Contacts for More Information

For information about forestry careers and about schools offering education in forestry, visit
➤ Society of American Foresters

For information about careers in forestry, particularly conservation forestry and land management, visit
➤ Forest Stewards Guild
➤ National Association of State Departments of Agriculture
➤ U.S. Forest Service

Logging Workers

Summary

Quick Facts: Logging Workers

2019 Median Pay	$41,230 per year $19.82 per hour
Typical Entry-Level Education	High school diploma or equivalent
Work Experience in a Related Occupation	None
On-the-job Training	Moderate-term on-the-job training
Number of Jobs, 2019	56,900
Job Outlook, 2019-29	-13% (Decline)
Employment Change, 2019-29	-7,500

What Logging Workers Do

Logging workers harvest forests to provide the raw material for many consumer goods and industrial products.

Work Environment

Logging is physically demanding and can be dangerous. Workers spend all their time outdoors, sometimes in poor weather and often in isolated areas.

How to Become a Logging Worker

Most logging workers have a high school diploma. They get on-the-job training to become familiar with forest environments and to learn how to operate logging machinery.

Pay

The median annual wage for logging workers was $41,230 in May 2019.

Job Outlook

Overall employment of logging workers is projected to decline 13 percent from 2019 to 2029. However, there will be a need to replace workers who retire or leave the occupation permanently.

Logging workers harvest thousands of acres of forests each year.

State & Area Data

Explore resources for employment and wages by state and area for logging workers.

What Logging Workers Do

Logging workers harvest thousands of acres of forests each year. The timber they harvest provides the raw material for countless consumer and industrial products.

Duties

Logging workers typically do the following:

- Cut down trees
- Fasten cables around logs to be dragged by tractors
- Operate machinery that drag logs to the landing or deck area
- Separate logs by species and type of wood and load them onto trucks
- Drive and maneuver feller–buncher tree harvesters to shear trees and cut logs into desired lengths
- Grade logs according to characteristics such as knot size and straightness
- Inspect equipment for safety, and perform necessary basic maintenance tasks, before using the equipment

The cutting and logging of timber is done by a logging crew. The following are examples of types of logging workers:

Fallers cut down trees with hand-held power chain saws.

Buckers work alongside fallers, trimming the tops and branches of felled trees and bucking (cutting) the logs into specific lengths.

Tree climbers use special equipment to scale tall trees and remove their limbs. They carry heavy tools and safety gear as they climb the trees, and are kept safe by a harness attached to a rope.

Choke setters fasten steel cables or chains, known as chokers, around logs to be skidded (dragged) by tractors or forwarded by the cable-yarding system to the landing or deck area, where the logs are separated by species and type of product.

Loggers cut trees with hand-held power chain saws or mobile felling machines.

Rigging slingers and chasers set up and dismantle the cables and guy wires of the yarding system.

Log sorters, markers, movers, and chippers sort, mark, and move logs on the basis of their species, size, and ownership. They also tend machines that chip up logs.

Logging equipment operators use tree harvesters to fell trees, shear off tree limbs, and cut trees into desired lengths. They drive tractors and operate self-propelled machines called skidders or forwarders, which drag or otherwise transport logs to a loading area.

Log graders and scalers inspect logs for defects and measure the logs to determine their volume. They estimate the value of logs or pulpwood. These workers often use hand-held data collection devices into which they enter data about trees.

A logging crew might consist of the following members:

- one or two tree fallers or one or two logging equipment operators with a tree harvester to cut down trees
- one bucker to cut logs
- two choke setters with tractors to drag felled trees to the loading deck
- one logging equipment operator to delimb, cut logs to length, and load the logs onto trucks

Work Environment

Logging workers held about 56,900 jobs in 2019. Employment in the detailed occupations that make up logging workers was distributed as follows:

Logging equipment operators	39,200
Fallers	7,200
Logging workers, all other	5,700
Log graders and scalers	4,800

The largest employers of logging workers were as follows:

Self-employed workers	27%
Sawmills and wood preservation	9
Crop production	2
Support activities for agriculture and forestry	1

Logging is physically demanding and can be dangerous. Workers spend all their time outdoors, sometimes in poor weather and often in isolated areas. The increased use of enclosed machines has decreased some of the discomforts caused by bad weather and has generally made logging much safer.

Most logging work involves lifting, climbing, and other strenuous activities, although machinery has eliminated some heavy labor. Falling branches, vines, and rough terrain are constant hazards, as are dangers associated with felling trees and handling logs.

Chain saws and other power equipment can be dangerous; therefore, workers must be careful and must use proper safety measures and equipment, such as hardhats, safety clothing, hearing protection devices, and boots.

Injuries and Illnesses

Despite the industry's strong emphasis on safety, logging workers sometimes get injured on the job. And although fatalities are uncommon, fallers experience one of the highest rates of occupational fatalities of all occupations. Most fatalities occur through contact with a machine or an object, such as a log.

Work Schedules

Workers sometimes commute long distances between their homes and logging sites. In more densely populated states, commuting distances are shorter. Logging work is often seasonal, and workers can find more employment opportunities during the warmer months because snow and cold weather adversely affect working conditions.

How to Become a Logging Worker

Most logging workers have a high school diploma. They get on-the-job training to become familiar with forest environments and to learn how to operate logging machinery.

Workers spend their time outdoors, sometimes in poor weather and often in isolated areas.

Most logging workers have a high school diploma.

Education

A high school diploma is enough for most logging worker jobs. Some vocational or technical schools and community colleges offer associate's degrees or certificates in forest technology. This additional education may help workers get a job. Programs may include field trips to observe or participate in logging activities.

A few community colleges offer education programs for logging equipment operators.

Training

Many states have training programs for loggers. Although specific coursework may vary by state, programs usually include technical instruction or field training in a number of areas, including best management practices, environmental compliance, and reforestation.

Safety training is a vital part of logging workers' instruction. Many state forestry or logging associations provide training sessions for logging equipment operators, whose jobs require more technical skill than other logging positions. Sessions take place in the field, where trainees have the opportunity to practice various logging techniques and use particular equipment.

Logging companies and trade associations offer training programs for workers who operate large, expensive machinery and equipment. These programs often culminate in a state-recognized safety certification from the logging company.

Important Qualities

Communication skills. Logging workers must communicate with other crew members so that they can cut and delimb trees efficiently and safely.

Decisionmaking skills. Logging workers must make quick, intelligent decisions when hazards arise.

Detail oriented. Logging workers must watch gauges, dials, and other indicators to determine whether their equipment and tools are working properly.

Physical stamina. Logging workers need to be able to perform laborious tasks repeatedly.

Physical strength. Logging workers must be able to handle heavy equipment.

Pay

The median annual wage for logging workers was $41,230 in May 2019. The median wage is the wage at which half the workers in an occupation earned more than that amount and half earned less. The lowest 10 percent earned less than $25,720, and the highest 10 percent earned more than $61,920.

Median annual wages for logging workers in May 2019 were as follows:

Fallers... $44,650
Logging equipment operators 41,440

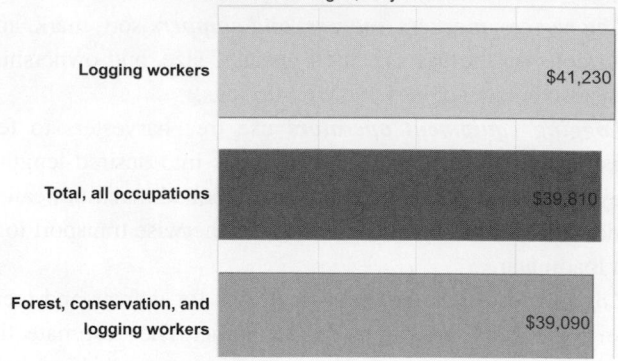

Logging Workers
Median annual wages, May 2019

Logging workers $41,230
Total, all occupations $39,810
Forest, conservation, and logging workers $39,090

Note: All Occupations includes all occupations in the U.S. Economy. Source: U.S. Bureau of Labor Statistics, Occupational Employment Statistics.

Logging workers, all other 39,780
Log graders and scalers.. 37,280

In May 2019, the median annual wages for logging workers in the top industries in which they worked were as follows:

Sawmills and wood preservation $35,670

Workers sometimes commute long distances between their homes and logging sites. In more densely populated states, commuting distances are shorter. Logging work is often seasonal, and workers can find more employment opportunities during the warmer months because snow and cold weather adversely affect working conditions.

Job Outlook

Overall employment of logging workers is projected to decline 13 percent from 2019 to 2029. Much of the employment decline for these workers stems from declining employment in the logging industry.

Mechanization of logging operations and improvements in logging equipment have increased productivity, resulting in less

Logging Workers
Percent change in employment, projected 2019-29

Total, all occupations 4%
Forest, conservation, and logging workers -11%
Logging workers -13%

Note: All Occupations includes all occupations in the U.S. Economy. Source: U.S. Bureau of Labor Statistics, Employment Projections program.

demand for logging workers, especially those who work by hand. Despite the projected employment declines, some fallers will continue to be needed to fell trees on slopes that cannot be accessed by large machinery. Additionally, the need to prevent destructive wildfires by thinning susceptible forests may result in some new jobs.

Job Prospects

Despite projected employment declines, job opportunities should be good because of the need to replace workers who leave the occupation for retirement or for other jobs that are less physically demanding.

Employment of logging workers can be unsteady because changes in the level of construction, particularly residential construction, can cause short-term slowdowns in logging activities.

Employment projections data for logging workers, 2019-29					
Occupational Title	SOC Code	Employment, 2019	Projected Employment, 2029	Change, 2019-29	
				Percent	Numeric
SOURCE: U.S. Bureau of Labor Statistics, Employment Projections program					
Logging workers	45-4020	56,900	49,400	-13	-7,500

Employment projections data for logging workers, 2019-29					
Occupational Title	SOC Code	Employment, 2019	Projected Employment, 2029	Change, 2019-29	
				Percent	Numeric
Fallers	45-4021	7,200	6,000	-17	-1,200
Logging equipment operators	45-4022	39,200	34,300	-13	-4,900
Log graders and scalers	45-4023	4,800	4,300	-11	-600
Logging workers, all other	45-4029	5,700	4,900	-15	-800

State & Area Data
Occupational Employment Statistics (OES)

The Occupational Employment Statistics (OES) program produces employment and wage estimates annually for over 800 occupations. These estimates are available for the nation as a whole, for individual states, and for metropolitan and nonmetropolitan areas.

Contacts for More Information

For information about timber-cutting and logging careers, visit
➤ Forest Resources Association

Food Preparation and Serving

Bartenders

Summary

Quick Facts: Bartenders

2019 Median Pay	$23,680 per year $11.39 per hour
Typical Entry-Level Education	No formal educational credential
Work Experience in a Related Occupation	None
On-the-job Training	Short-term on-the-job training
Number of Jobs, 2019	654,700
Job Outlook, 2019-29	6% (Faster than average)
Employment Change, 2019-29	38,400

What Bartenders Do

Bartenders mix drinks and serve them directly to customers or through wait staff.

Work Environment

Bartenders work at restaurants, bars, clubs, hotels, and other food service and drinking establishments. During busy hours, they are under pressure to serve customers quickly and efficiently. They often work late evenings, on weekends, and on holidays. Some work part time.

How to Become a Bartender

Most bartenders learn their skills on the job. No formal education is required. Most states require workers who serve alcoholic beverages to be at least 18 years old.

Pay

The median hourly wage for bartenders was $11.39 in May 2019.

Job Outlook

Employment of bartenders is projected to grow 6 percent from 2019 to 2029, faster than the average for all occupations. Overall job prospects are expected to be very good because of the need to replace workers who leave the occupation.

State & Area Data

Explore resources for employment and wages by state and area for bartenders.

What Bartenders Do

Bartenders mix drinks and serve them directly to customers or through wait staff.

Duties

Bartenders typically do the following:

- Greet customers, give them menus, and inform them about daily specials
- Take drink orders from customers
- Pour and serve wine, beer, and other drinks and beverages
- Mix drinks according to recipes
- Check the identification of customers to ensure that they are of legal drinking age
- Clean bars, tables, and work areas
- Collect payments from customers and return change
- Manage the operation of the bar, and order and maintain liquor and bar supplies
- Monitor the level of intoxication of customers

Bartenders mix drinks and serve them to customers.

Bartenders mix drinks according to recipes.

Bartenders fill drink orders either directly from customers at the bar or through waiters and waitresses who place drink orders for dining room customers. Bartenders must know a wide range of drink recipes and be able to mix drinks correctly and quickly. When measuring and pouring beverages, they must avoid spillage or overpouring. They also must work well with waiters and waitresses and other kitchen staff to ensure that customers receive prompt service.

Some establishments, especially busy establishments with many customers, use equipment that automatically measures and pours drinks at the push of a button. Bartenders who use this equipment, however, still must become familiar with the ingredients for special drink requests and be able to work quickly to handle numerous drink orders.

In addition to mixing and serving drinks, bartenders stock and prepare garnishes for drinks and maintain an adequate supply of ice, glasses, and other bar supplies. They also wash glassware and utensils and serve food to customers who eat at the bar. Bartenders are usually responsible for ordering and maintaining an inventory of liquor, mixers, and other bar supplies.

Work Environment

Bartenders held about 654,700 jobs in 2019. The largest employers of bartenders were as follows:

Restaurants and other eating places	46%
Drinking places (alcoholic beverages)	26
Traveler accommodation	7
Civic and social organizations	6
Amusement, gambling, and recreation industries	5

Bartenders typically work indoors, some work outdoors at pool or beach bars or at catered events.

During busy hours, bartenders are under pressure to serve customers quickly and efficiently while ensuring that no alcohol is served to minors or overly intoxicated customers.

Bartenders perform repetitive tasks, and sometimes they lift heavy kegs of beer and cases of liquor. In addition, the work can be stressful, particularly when they deal with intoxicated customers to whom they must deny service.

Because bartenders often are on the front lines of customer service in bars and restaurants, a neat appearance may be important. This is especially true in upscale restaurants and bars, where they may be required to wear uniforms.

Work Schedules

Bartenders often work late evenings, on weekends, and on holidays. Some work part time.

How to Become a Bartender

Most bartenders learn their skills through short-term on-the-job training usually lasting a few weeks. No formal education is required.

Many bartenders are promoted from other jobs at the establishments in which they work. Bartenders at upscale establishments usually have attended bartending classes or have previous work experience.

Most states require workers who serve alcoholic beverages to be at least 18 years old. Bartenders must be familiar with state and local laws concerning the sale of alcoholic beverages.

Education

No formal education is required for anyone to become a bartender. However, some aspiring bartenders acquire their skills by attending a school for bartending or by attending bartending classes at a vocational or technical school. Programs in these schools often include instruction on state and local laws and regulations concerning the sale of alcohol, cocktail recipes, proper attire and conduct, and stocking a bar. The length of each program varies, but most courses last a few weeks. Some schools help their graduates find jobs.

Bartenders usually work evenings and weekends.

Bartenders should be friendly, tactful, and attentive when dealing with customers.

Training

Most bartenders receive on-the-job training, usually lasting a few weeks, under the guidance of an experienced bartender. Training focuses on cocktail recipes, bar-setup procedures, and customer service, including how to handle unruly customers and other challenging situations. In establishments where bartenders serve food, the training may cover teamwork and proper food-handling procedures.

Some employers teach bartending skills to new workers by providing self-study programs, online programs, videos, and instructional booklets that explain service skills. Such programs communicate the philosophy of the establishment, help new bartenders build rapport with other staff, and instill a desire to work as part of a team.

Many states and localities require bartenders to complete a responsible-server course. The course is related to state and local alcohol laws, responsible serving practices, and conflict management. Courses may be available both in person and online. Depending on the state and locality, the server, owner, manager, or business may maintain a license to sell alcohol.

Work Experience in a Related Occupation

Some bartenders qualify through related work experience. They may start as bartender helpers and progress into full-fledged bartenders as they learn basic mixing procedures and recipes. Some bartenders may start as waiters and waitresses or food and beverage serving and related workers.

Important Qualities

Communication skills. Bartenders must listen carefully to their customers' orders, explain drink and food items, and make menu recommendations. They also should be able to converse with customers on a variety of subjects and create a friendly and welcoming environment.

Customer-service skills. Bartenders must have good customer-service skills to ensure repeat business.

Decisionmaking skills. Bartenders must be able to make good decisions. For example, they should be able to detect intoxicated and underage customers and deny service to those individuals.

Physical stamina. Bartenders spend hours on their feet walking and standing while preparing drinks and serving customers.

Physical strength. Bartenders should be able to lift and carry heavy cases of liquor, beer, and other bar supplies—cases that often weigh up to 50 pounds.

Pay

The median hourly wage for bartenders was $11.39 in May 2019. The median wage is the wage at which half the workers in an occupation earned more than that amount and half earned less. The lowest 10 percent earned less than $8.55, and the highest 10 percent earned more than $22.18.

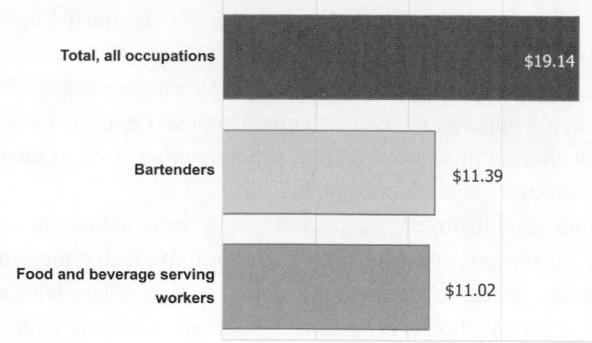

Bartenders
Median hourly wages, May 2019

- Total, all occupations — $19.14
- Bartenders — $11.39
- Food and beverage serving workers — $11.02

Note: All Occupations includes all occupations in the U.S. Economy. Source: U.S. Bureau of Labor Statistics, Occupational Employment Statistics.

In May 2019, the median hourly wages for bartenders in the top industries in which they worked were as follows:

Traveler accommodation... $12.12
Restaurants and other eating places 11.74
Amusement, gambling, and recreation industries..... 11.22
Drinking places (alcoholic beverages)...................... 11.00
Civic and social organizations 10.08

Bartenders' earnings often come from a combination of hourly wages and customers' tips. Earnings vary greatly with the type of establishment. For example, in some upscale, popular, or busy restaurants, bars, and casinos, bartenders make more in tips than in wages.

Tipped employees earn at least the federal minimum wage ($7.25 per hour, as of July 24, 2009), which may be paid as a combination of direct wages and tips, depending on the state. Direct wages may be as low as $2.13 per hour, according to the Fair Labor Standards Act (FLSA).

Also according to the FLSA, tipped employees are employees who regularly receive more than $30 a month in tips. The Wage and Hour Division of the U.S. Department of Labor maintains a website listing minimum wages for tipped employees, by state, although some localities have enacted minimum wages higher than their state requires.

Bartenders often work late evenings, on weekends, and on holidays. Some work part time.

Job Outlook

Employment of bartenders is projected to grow 6 percent from 2019 to 2029, faster than the average for all occupations.

Population and income growth are expected to result in increased demand for food, drinks, and entertainment. More bartenders will be needed to meet this demand, especially in full-service restaurants and drinking places. Grocery stores and movie theaters are also adding bar services, which will create demand for bartenders in these businesses.

Bartenders

Percent change in employment, projected 2019-29

Food and beverage serving workers	8%
Bartenders	6%
Total, all occupations	4%

Note: All Occupations includes all occupations in the U.S. Economy.
Source: U.S. Bureau of Labor Statistics, Employment Projections program.

Job Prospects

Job prospects are expected to be very good because of the need to replace the many workers who leave the occupation each year.

Competition is expected for bartending jobs in popular restaurants and fine-dining establishments, in both of which tips are highest. Those who have graduated from bartending schools or those with previous work experience and excellent customer-service skills should have the best job prospects.

Employment projections data for bartenders, 2019-29					
Occupational Title	SOC Code	Employment, 2019	Projected Employment, 2029	Change, 2019-29	
				Percent	Numeric
SOURCE: U.S. Bureau of Labor Statistics, Employment Projections program					
Bartenders	35-3011	654,700	693,100	6	38,400

State & Area Data
Occupational Employment Statistics (OES)

The Occupational Employment Statistics (OES) program produces employment and wage estimates annually for over 800 occupations. These estimates are available for the nation as a whole, for individual states, and for metropolitan and nonmetropolitan areas.

Contacts for More Information

For more information about bartenders, visit
➤ National Restaurant Association

Chefs and Head Cooks

Summary

Quick Facts: Chefs and Head Cooks

2019 Median Pay	$51,530 per year $24.78 per hour
Typical Entry-Level Education	High school diploma or equivalent
Work Experience in a Related Occupation	5 years or more
On-the-job Training	None
Number of Jobs, 2019	148,700
Job Outlook, 2019-29	6% (Faster than average)
Employment Change, 2019-29	9,500

What Chefs and Head Cooks Do

Chefs and head cooks oversee the daily food preparation at restaurants and other places where food is served.

Work Environment

Chefs and head cooks work in restaurants, private households, and other establishments where food is served. They often work early mornings, late evenings, weekends, and holidays. The work can be hectic and fast-paced. Most chefs and head cooks work full time.

How to Become a Chef or Head Cook

Most chefs and head cooks learn their skills through work experience. Others receive training at a community college, technical school, culinary arts school, or 4-year college. Some learn through apprenticeship programs.

Pay

The median annual wage for chefs and head cooks was $51,530 in May 2019.

Job Outlook

Employment of chefs and head cooks is projected to grow 6 percent from 2019 to 2029, faster than the average for all occupations. Most job opportunities for chefs and head cooks are expected to be in food services, including restaurants. Job opportunities will result from growth and from the need to replace workers who leave the occupation.

Chefs direct kitchen staff in restaurants.

State & Area Data

Explore resources for employment and wages by state and area for chefs and head cooks.

What Chefs and Head Cooks Do

Chefs and head cooks oversee the daily food preparation at restaurants and other places where food is served. They direct kitchen staff and handle any food-related concerns.

Duties

Chefs and head cooks typically do the following:

- Check the freshness of food and ingredients
- Supervise and coordinate activities of cooks and other food preparation workers
- Develop recipes and determine how to present dishes
- Plan menus and ensure the quality of meals
- Inspect supplies, equipment, and work areas for cleanliness and functionality
- Hire, train, and supervise cooks and other food preparation workers
- Order and maintain an inventory of food and supplies
- Monitor sanitation practices and follow kitchen safety standards

Chefs and head cooks use a variety of kitchen and cooking equipment, including step-in coolers, high-quality knives, meat slicers, and grinders. They also have access to large quantities of meats, spices, and produce. Some chefs use scheduling and purchasing software to help them in their administrative tasks.

Chefs who run their own restaurant or catering business are often busy with kitchen and office work. Some chefs use social media to promote their business by advertising new menu items or addressing customer reviews.

The following are examples of types of chefs and head cooks:

Executive chefs, head cooks, and chefs de cuisine are responsible primarily for overseeing the operation of a kitchen. They coordinate the work of sous chefs and other cooks, who prepare most of the meals. Executive chefs also have many duties beyond the kitchen. They design the menu, review food and beverage purchases, and often train cooks and other food preparation workers. Some executive chefs primarily handle administrative tasks and may spend less time in the kitchen.

Sous chefs are a kitchen's second-in-command. They supervise the restaurant's cooks, prepare meals, and report results to the head chefs. In the absence of the head chef, sous chefs run the kitchen.

Private household chefs typically work full time for one client, such as a corporate executive, university president, or diplomat, who regularly entertains as part of his or her official duties.

Work Environment

Chefs and head cooks held about 148,700 jobs in 2019. The largest employers of chefs and head cooks were as follows:

Restaurants and other eating places	45%
Special food services	10
Self-employed workers	10
Traveler accommodation	10
Amusement, gambling, and recreation industries	6

Chefs plan menus and order supplies.

Chefs and head cooks must stand for long periods.

Chefs and head cooks work in restaurants, hotels, private households, and other food service establishments. All of the cooking and food preparation areas in these facilities must be kept clean and sanitary. Chefs and head cooks usually stand for long periods and work in a fast-paced environment.

Some self-employed chefs run their own restaurants or catering businesses and their work can be more stressful. For example, outside the kitchen, they often spend many hours managing all aspects of the business to ensure that bills and salaries are paid and that the business is profitable.

Injuries and Illnesses

Chefs and head cooks risk injury in kitchens, which are usually crowded and potentially dangerous. Common hazards include burns from hot ovens, falls on slippery floors, and cuts from knives and other sharp objects, but these injuries are seldom serious. To reduce the risk of harm, workers often wear long-sleeve shirts and nonslip shoes.

Work Schedules

Most chefs and head cooks work full time, including early mornings, late evenings, weekends, and holidays. Many chefs and head cooks work more than 40 hours a week.

How to Become a Chef or Head Cook

Most chefs and head cooks learn their skills through work experience. Others receive training at a community college, technical school, culinary arts school, or 4-year college. A small number learn through apprenticeship programs or in the Armed Forces.

Education

Although postsecondary education is not required for chefs and head cooks, many attend programs at community colleges, technical schools, culinary arts schools, and 4-year colleges. Candidates are typically required to have a high school diploma or equivalent to enter these programs.

Students in culinary programs spend most of their time in kitchens, practicing their cooking skills. Programs cover all aspects of kitchen work, including menu planning, food sanitation procedures, and purchasing and inventory methods. Most training programs also require students to gain experience in a commercial kitchen through an internship or apprenticeship program.

Work Experience in a Related Occupation

Most chefs and head cooks start by working in other positions, such as line cooks, learning cooking skills from the chefs they work for. Many spend years working in kitchens before gaining enough experience to be promoted to chef or head cook positions.

Most chefs and head cooks learn their skills through work experience.

Training

Some chefs and head cooks train on the job, where they learn the same skills as in a formal education program. Some train in mentorship programs, where they work under the direction of an experienced chef. Executive chefs, head cooks, and sous chefs who work in upscale restaurants often have many years of training and experience.

Chefs and head cooks also may learn through apprenticeship programs sponsored by professional culinary institutes, industry associations, or trade unions. Some of these apprenticeship programs are registered with the U.S. Department of Labor. Apprenticeship programs generally last 2 years and combine instruction and on-the-job training. Apprentices typically receive about 2,000 hours of both instruction and paid on-the-job training per year. Courses typically cover food sanitation and safety, basic knife skills, and equipment operation. Apprentices spend the rest of their training learning practical skills in a commercial kitchen under a chef's supervision.

The American Culinary Federation accredits more than 200 academic training programs at postsecondary schools and sponsors apprenticeships around the country. The basic qualifications required for entering an apprenticeship program are as follows:

- Minimum age of 17
- High school education or equivalent

Licenses, Certifications, and Registrations

Although not required, certification can show competence and lead to advancement and higher pay. The American Culinary Federation certifies personal chefs, in addition to various levels of chefs, such as certified sous chefs or certified executive chefs. Certification standards are based primarily on work-related experience and formal training. Minimum work experience for certification can range from about 6 months to 5 years, depending on the level of certification.

Important Qualities

Business skills. Executive chefs and chefs who run their own restaurant need to understand the restaurant business. They should know how to budget for supplies, set prices, and manage workers so that the restaurant is profitable.

Communication skills. Chefs must communicate their instructions clearly and effectively to staff so that customers' orders are prepared correctly.

Creativity. Chefs and head cooks need to be creative in order to develop and prepare interesting and innovative recipes. They should be able to use various ingredients to create appealing meals for their customers.

Dexterity. Chefs and head cooks need excellent dexterity, including proper knife techniques for cutting, chopping, and dicing.

Leadership skills. Chefs and head cooks must have the ability to motivate kitchen staff and develop constructive and cooperative working relationships with them.

Physical stamina. Chefs and head cooks often work long shifts and sometimes spend entire evenings on their feet, overseeing the preparation and serving of meals.

Sense of taste and smell. Chefs and head cooks must have a keen sense of taste and smell in order to inspect food quality and to design meals that their customers will enjoy.

Time-management skills. Chefs and head cooks must efficiently manage their time and the time of their staff. They ensure that meals are prepared correctly and that customers are served on time, especially during busy hours.

Pay

The median annual wage for chefs and head cooks was $51,530 in May 2019. The median wage is the wage at which half the workers in an occupation earned more than that amount and half earned less. The lowest 10 percent earned less than $28,370, and the highest 10 percent earned more than $86,990.

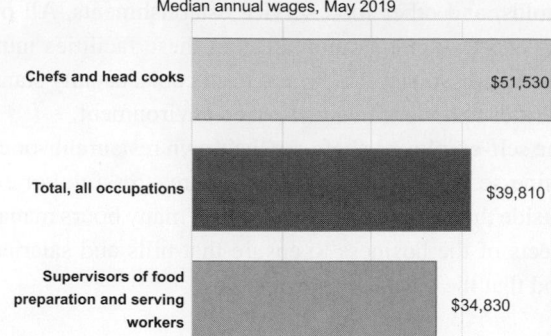

Chefs and Head Cooks
Median annual wages, May 2019

Note: All Occupations includes all occupations in the U.S. Economy.
Source: U.S. Bureau of Labor Statistics, Occupational Employment Statistics.

In May 2019, the median annual wages for chefs and head cooks in the top industries in which they worked were as follows:

Traveler accommodation	$58,250
Special food services	56,800
Amusement, gambling, and recreation industries	56,310
Restaurants and other eating places	47,980

The level of pay for chefs and head cooks varies greatly by region and employer. Pay is usually highest in upscale restaurants and hotels, where many executive chefs work, as well as in major metropolitan and resort areas.

Most chefs and head cooks work full time and often work early mornings, late evenings, weekends, and holidays. Many chefs and head cooks work more than 40 hours a week.

Job Outlook

Employment of chefs and head cooks is projected to grow 6 percent from 2019 to 2029, faster than the average for all occupations.

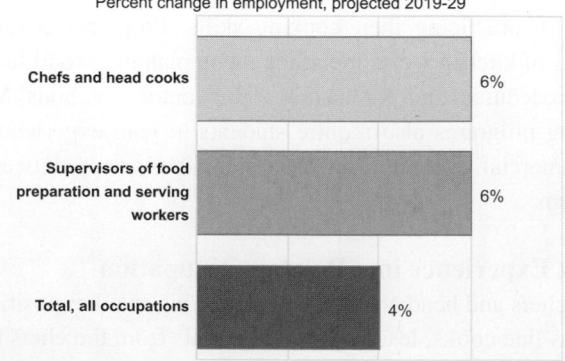

Chefs and Head Cooks
Percent change in employment, projected 2019-29

Note: All Occupations includes all occupations in the U.S. Economy.
Source: U.S. Bureau of Labor Statistics, Employment Projections program.

Income growth will result in greater demand for high-quality dishes at a variety of dining venues. As a result, more restaurants and other dining places are expected to open to satisfy consumer desire for dining out.

Consumers are continuing to demand healthier meals made from scratch in restaurants, in cafeterias, in grocery stores, and by catering services. To ensure high-quality dishes, these establishments are increasingly hiring experienced chefs to oversee food preparation.

Job Prospects

Job opportunities should be best for chefs and head cooks with several years of work experience in a kitchen. Many job openings will result from the need to replace workers who leave the occupation. The fast pace, time demands, and high energy levels required for these jobs often lead to a high rate of turnover.

There will be strong competition for jobs at upscale restaurants, hotels, and casinos, where the pay is typically highest. Workers with a combination of business skills, previous work experience, and culinary creativity should have the best job prospects.

Employment projections data for chefs and head cooks, 2019-29					
Occupational Title	SOC Code	Employment, 2019	Projected Employment, 2029	Change, 2019-29	
				Percent	Numeric
SOURCE: U.S. Bureau of Labor Statistics, Employment Projections program					
Chefs and head cooks	35-1011	148,700	158,100	6	9,500

State & Area Data
Occupational Employment Statistics (OES)

The Occupational Employment Statistics (OES) program produces employment and wage estimates annually for over 800 occupations. These estimates are available for the nation as a whole, for individual states, and for metropolitan and nonmetropolitan areas.

Contacts for More Information

For more information about chefs, including a directory of 2-year and 4-year colleges that offer courses or training programs, visit
➤ American Culinary Federation
➤ National Restaurant Association

For information about becoming a private chef, visit
➤ American Personal & Private Chef Association

Cooks

Summary

Quick Facts: Cooks

2019 Median Pay	$26,360 per year $12.67 per hour
Typical Entry-Level Education	See below
Work Experience in a Related Occupation	See below
On-the-job Training	See below
Number of Jobs, 2019	2,571,700
Job Outlook, 2019-29	10% (Much faster than average)
Employment Change, 2019-29	256,600

What Cooks Do

Cooks prepare, season, and cook a wide range of foods.

Work Environment

Cooks work in restaurants, schools, hospitals, private households, and other places where food is prepared and served. They often work early mornings, late evenings, holidays, and weekends.

How to Become a Cook

Most cooks learn their skills through on-the-job training and related work experience. Although no formal education is required, some restaurant cooks attend culinary school.

Pay

The median hourly wage for cooks was $12.67 in May 2019.

Job Outlook

Overall employment of cooks is projected to grow 10 percent from 2019 to 2029, much faster than the average for all occupations. Individual growth rates will vary by specialty.

State & Area Data

Explore resources for employment and wages by state and area for cooks.

Cooks prepare a wide range of dishes.

What Cooks Do

Cooks prepare, season, and cook a wide range of foods, which may include soups, salads, entrees, and desserts.

Duties

Cooks typically do the following:

- Ensure the freshness of food and ingredients
- Weigh, measure, and mix ingredients according to recipes
- Bake, grill, or fry meats, fish, vegetables, and other foods
- Boil and steam meats, fish, vegetables, and other foods
- Arrange, garnish, and sometimes serve food
- Clean work areas, equipment, utensils, and dishes
- Cook, handle, and store food or ingredients

Cooks usually work under the direction of chefs, head cooks, or food service managers. Large restaurants and food service establishments often have multiple menus and large kitchen staffs. Teams of restaurant cooks, sometimes called *assistant cooks* or *line cooks*, work at assigned stations equipped with the necessary types of stoves, grills, pans, and ingredients.

Job titles often reflect the principal ingredient cooks prepare or the type of cooking they do—*vegetable cook, fry cook,* or *grill cook,* for example.

Cooks use a variety of kitchen equipment, including broilers, grills, slicers, grinders, and blenders.

The responsibilities of cooks vary depending on the type of food service establishment, the size of the facility, and the level of service offered. However, in all establishments, they follow sanitation procedures when handling food. For example, they store food and ingredients at the correct temperatures to prevent bacterial growth.

The following are examples of types of cooks:

Restaurant cooks prepare a wide selection of dishes and cook most orders individually. Some restaurant cooks may order supplies and help maintain the stock room.

Fast-food cooks prepare a limited selection of menu items in fast-food restaurants. They cook and package food, such as hamburgers and fried chicken, to be kept warm until served. For more information on workers who prepare and serve items in fast-food restaurants, see the profiles on food preparation workers and food and beverage serving and related workers.

Institution and cafeteria cooks work in the kitchens of schools, cafeterias, businesses, hospitals, and other institutions. Although they typically prepare a large quantity of a limited number of entrees, vegetables, and desserts, according to preset menus, they do sometimes customize meals according to diners' dietary considerations.

Short-order cooks prepare foods in restaurants and coffee shops that emphasize fast service and quick food preparation. They usually prepare sandwiches, fry eggs, and cook french fries, often working on several orders at the same time.

Private household cooks, sometimes called *personal chefs,* plan and prepare meals in private homes, according to the client's tastes and dietary needs. They order groceries and supplies, clean the kitchen, and wash dishes and utensils. They also may cater parties, holiday meals, luncheons, and other social events. Private household cooks typically work full-time for one client, although many are self-employed or employed by an agency, regularly making meals for multiple clients.

Work Environment

Cooks held about 2.6 million jobs in 2019. Employment in the detailed occupations that make up cooks was distributed as follows:

Cooks, restaurant	1,417,300
Cooks, fast food	534,000
Cooks, institution and cafeteria	420,200
Cooks, short order	154,700
Cooks, private household	23,800
Cooks, all other	21,800

The largest employers of cooks were as follows:

Restaurants and other eating places	71%

Cooks prepare fresh vegetables.

Cooks usually work in restaurants.

Cooks work in restaurants, schools, hospitals, hotels, and other establishments where food is prepared and served. They often prepare only part of a dish and coordinate with other cooks and kitchen workers to complete meals on time. Some work in private homes.

Cooks stand for long periods and work under pressure in a fast-paced environment. Although most cooks work indoors in kitchens, some may work outdoors at food stands, at catered events, or in mobile food trucks.

Injuries and Illnesses

Kitchens are usually crowded and filled with potential dangers, such as hot ovens or slippery floors. Cooks, all other, in particular, have one of the highest rates of injuries and illnesses of all occupations. ("All other" titles represent occupations with a wide range of characteristics that do not fit into any of the other detailed occupations.)

The most common hazards are slips, falls, cuts, and burns, although injuries are seldom serious. To reduce the risks, cooks wear long-sleeve shirts, gloves, aprons, and nonslip shoes.

Work Schedules

Most cooks work full time. Work shifts can include early mornings, late evenings, weekends, and holidays. Schedules for cooks in school cafeterias and some institutional cafeterias are usually more regular. Cooks working in schools may work just during the school year, typically for 9 or 10 months. Similarly, some resort establishments offer seasonal employment only.

How to Become a Cook

Most cooks learn their skills through on-the-job training and work-related experience. Although no formal education is required, some restaurant cooks and private household cooks attend culinary schools. Others attend vocational or apprenticeship programs.

Education

Vocational cooking schools, professional culinary institutes, and some colleges offer culinary programs for aspiring cooks. These programs generally last from a few months to 2 years and may offer courses in advanced cooking techniques, international cuisines, and various cooking styles. To enter these programs, candidates may be required to have a high school diploma or equivalent. Depending on the type and length of the program, graduates generally qualify for entry-level positions as a restaurant cook.

Training

Most cooks learn their skills through on-the-job training, usually lasting a few weeks. Trainees generally first learn kitchen

Cooks typically learn their skills on the job from an experienced chef.

basics and workplace safety and then learn how to handle and cook food.

Some cooks learn through an apprenticeship program. Professional culinary institutes, industry associations, and trade unions may sponsor such programs for cooks. Typical apprenticeships last 1 year and combine technical training and work experience. Apprentices complete courses in food sanitation and safety, basic knife skills, and equipment operation. They also learn practical cooking skills under the supervision of an experienced chef.

The American Culinary Federation accredits many academic training programs and sponsors apprenticeships through these programs around the country. The basic qualifications for entering an apprenticeship program are as follows:

• Minimum age of 17
• High school education or equivalent

Some hotels and a number of restaurants offer their own training programs.

Work Experience in a Related Occupation

Many cooks learn their skills through work-related experience. They typically start as a kitchen helper or food preparation worker, learning basic cooking skills before they advance to assistant cook or line cook positions. Some learn by working under the guidance of a more experienced cook.

Advancement

The American Culinary Federation certifies chefs, personal chefs, pastry chefs, and culinary administrators, among others. For cooks seeking advancement to higher level chef positions, certification can show accomplishment and lead to higher paying positions.

Advancement opportunities for cooks often depend on training, work experience, and the ability to prepare more complex dishes. Those who learn new cooking skills and who handle greater responsibility, such as supervising kitchen staff in the absence of a chef, often advance. Some cooks may train or supervise kitchen staff, and some may become head cooks, chefs, or food service managers.

Important Qualities

Comprehension. Cooks need to understand orders and follow recipes to prepare dishes correctly.

Dexterity. Cooks should have excellent hand–eye coordination. For example, they need to use proper knife techniques for cutting, chopping, and dicing.

Physical stamina. Cooks spend a lot of time standing in one place, cooking food over hot stoves, and cleaning work areas.

Sense of taste and smell. Cooks must have a keen sense of taste and smell to prepare meals that customers enjoy.

Pay

The median hourly wage for cooks was $12.67 in May 2019. The median wage is the wage at which half the workers in an occupation earned more than that amount and half earned less. The lowest 10 percent earned less than $9.06, and the highest 10 percent earned more than $18.27.

Median hourly wages for cooks in May 2019 were as follows:

Cooks, private household $18.21

Cooks, all other 14.79

Cooks, restaurant... 13.36

Cooks, institution and cafeteria.............................. 13.34

Cooks, short order... 12.09

Cooks, fast food 11.30

In May 2019, the median hourly wages for cooks in the top industries in which they worked were as follows:

Healthcare and social assistance $13.55

Educational services; state, local, and private.......... 12.52

Restaurants and other eating places 12.40

Pay for cooks varies greatly by region and type of employer. Pay is usually highest in hotels, many of which are located in major metropolitan and resort areas.

Most cooks work full time. Work shifts can include early mornings, late evenings, weekends, and holidays. Schedules for cooks in school cafeterias and some institutional cafeterias are usually more regular. Cooks working in schools may work just during the school year, typically for 9 or 10 months. Similarly, some resort establishments offer seasonal employment only.

Job Outlook

Overall employment of cooks is projected to grow 10 percent from 2019 to 2029, much faster than the average for all occupations. Individual growth rates will vary by specialty.

Population and income growth are expected to result in greater consumer demand for food at a variety of dining places. People will continue to eat out, buy takeout meals, or have food delivered. In response to increased consumer demand, more restaurants, cafeterias, and catering services will open and serve more meals. These establishments will require more cooks to prepare meals for customers.

In addition, consumers continue to prefer healthier foods and faster service in restaurants, grocery stores, and other dining venues. To prepare high quality meals at these places, many

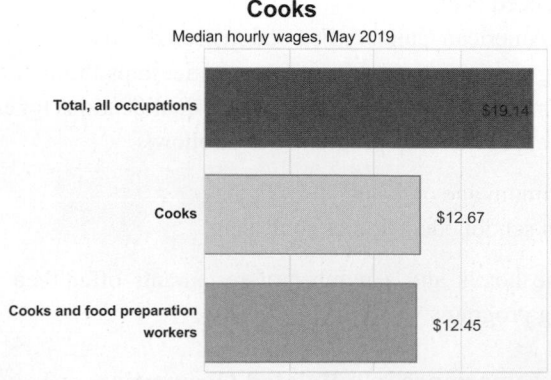

Cooks
Median hourly wages, May 2019

Total, all occupations — $19.14
Cooks — $12.67
Cooks and food preparation workers — $12.45

Note: All Occupations includes all occupations in the U.S. Economy.
Source: U.S. Bureau of Labor Statistics, Occupational Employment Statistics.

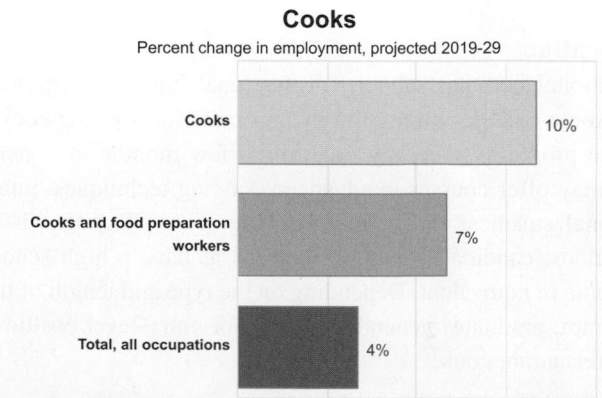

Cooks
Percent change in employment, projected 2019-29

Cooks — 10%
Cooks and food preparation workers — 7%
Total, all occupations — 4%

Note: All Occupations includes all occupations in the U.S. Economy.
Source: U.S. Bureau of Labor Statistics, Employment Projections program.

managers and chefs will require experienced cooks, such as restaurant cooks.

Employment of fast food cooks is projected to decline as many establishments attempt to streamline operations by hiring other workers, such as fast food and counter workers, who both prepare and serve food to customers. Employment of short order cooks also is projected to decline as other workers take on the duties of these cooks in full-service restaurants. Cooks in private households face competition from the many food delivery service options that are expected to reduce the need for these workers, who are often self-employed.

Job Prospects

Overall job opportunities are expected to be very good as a result of employment growth and the need to replace workers who leave the occupation. Cooks with previous training and related work experience will have the best job prospects.

Those who can prepare more complex dishes will have the best job opportunities at restaurant chains, upscale restaurants, and hotels.

Employment projections data for cooks, 2019-29

Occupational Title	SOC Code	Employment, 2019	Projected Employment, 2029	Change, 2019-29 Percent	Numeric
SOURCE: U.S. Bureau of Labor Statistics, Employment Projections program					
Cooks	35-2010	2,571,700	2,828,400	10	256,600
Cooks, fast food	35-2011	534,000	462,300	-13	-71,600
Cooks, institution and cafeteria	35-2012	420,200	428,700	2	8,500

Employment projections data for cooks, 2019-29

Occupational Title	SOC Code	Employment, 2019	Projected Employment, 2029	Change, 2019-29 Percent	Numeric
Cooks, private household	35-2013	23,800	22,300	-6	-1,500
Cooks, restaurant	35-2014	1,417,300	1,744,600	23	327,300
Cooks, short order	35-2015	154,700	147,900	-4	-6,800
Cooks, all other	35-2019	21,800	22,500	3	800

State & Area Data
Occupational Employment Statistics (OES)

The Occupational Employment Statistics (OES) program produces employment and wage estimates annually for over 800 occupations. These estimates are available for the nation as a whole, for individual states, and for metropolitan and nonmetropolitan areas.

Contacts for More Information

For information about culinary apprenticeship programs registered with the U.S. Department of Labor, contact the local office of your state employment service agency, or check the U.S. Department of Labor's Apprenticeship program online or by phone at 877-872-5627.

For more information about cooking careers, visit

➤ American Culinary Federation

➤ National Restaurant Association

For information about becoming a personal chef, visit

➤ American Personal & Private Chef Association

Food and Beverage Serving and Related Workers

Summary

Quick Facts: Food and Beverage Serving and Related Workers

2019 Median Pay	$23,000 per year $11.06 per hour
Typical Entry-Level Education	No formal educational credential
Work Experience in a Related Occupation	None
On-the-job Training	Short-term on-the-job training
Number of Jobs, 2019	5,324,100
Job Outlook, 2019-29	10% (Much faster than average)
Employment Change, 2019-29	552,400

What Food and Beverage Serving and Related Workers Do

Food and beverage serving and related workers perform a variety of customer service, food preparation, and cleaning duties in eating and drinking establishments.

Work Environment

Food and beverage serving and related workers are employed in restaurants, schools, hospitals, cafeterias, and other dining places. Work shifts often include early mornings, late evenings, weekends, and holidays. Many food and beverage serving and related workers work part time.

Food and beverage serving workers serve coffee, soda, and other beverages.

How to Become a Food and Beverage Serving or Related Worker

Most food and beverage serving and related workers learn their skills on the job. No formal education or previous work experience is required.

Pay

The median hourly wage for food and beverage serving and related workers was $11.06 in May 2019.

Job Outlook

Employment of food and beverage serving and related workers is projected to grow 10 percent from 2019 to 2029, much faster than the average for all occupations. Job prospects in most dining establishments will be excellent because many workers leave the occupation each year, resulting in numerous job openings.

State & Area Data

Explore resources for employment and wages by state and area for food and beverage serving and related workers.

What Food and Beverage Serving and Related Workers Do

Food and beverage serving and related workers perform a variety of customer service, food preparation, and cleaning duties in restaurants, cafeterias, and other eating and drinking establishments.

Duties

Food and beverage serving and related workers typically do the following:

- Greet customers and answer their questions about menu items and specials
- Take food or drink orders from customers
- Relay customers' orders to other kitchen staff

Food and beverage workers may work directly with customers.

- Prepare food and drink orders, such as sandwiches, salads, and coffee
- Accept payments and balance receipts
- Serve food and drinks to customers at a counter, at a stand, or in a hotel room
- Clean assigned work areas, dining tables, or serving counters
- Replenish and stock service stations, cabinets, and tables
- Set tables or prepare food trays for new customers

Food and beverage serving and related workers are the front line of customer service in restaurants, cafeterias, and other food service establishments. Depending on the establishment, they take customers' food and drink orders and serve food and beverages.

Most work as part of a team, helping coworkers to improve workflow and customer service. The job titles of food and beverage serving and related workers vary with where they work and what they do.

The following are examples of types of food and beverage serving and related workers:

Combined food preparation and serving workers, including fast food, are employed primarily by fast-food and fast-casual restaurants. They take food and beverage orders, prepare or retrieve items when ready, fill cups with beverages, and accept customers' payments. They also heat food items and make salads and sandwiches.

Counter attendants take orders and serve food over a counter in snack bars, cafeterias, movie theaters, and coffee shops. They fill cups with coffee, soda, and other beverages, and may prepare fountain specialties, such as milkshakes and ice cream sundaes. Counter attendants take carryout orders from diners and wrap or place items in containers. They clean counters, prepare itemized bills, and accept customers' payments.

Dining room and cafeteria attendants and bartender helpers—sometimes collectively referred to as bus staff—help waiters, waitresses, and bartenders by cleaning and setting tables, removing dirty dishes, and keeping serving areas stocked with supplies. They also may help waiters and waitresses by bringing meals out of the kitchen, distributing dishes to diners, filling water glasses, and delivering condiments. ***Cafeteria attendants*** stock serving tables with food trays, dishes, and silverware. They sometimes carry trays to dining tables for customers. ***Bartender helpers*** keep bar equipment clean and glasses washed.

Food servers, nonrestaurant, serve food to customers outside of a restaurant environment. Many deliver room service meals in hotels or meals to hospital rooms. Some act as carhops, bringing orders to customers in parked cars.

Hosts and hostesses greet customers and manage reservations and waiting lists. They may direct customers to coatrooms, restrooms, or a waiting area until their table is ready. Hosts and hostesses provide menus after seating guests.

Work Environment

Food and beverage serving and related workers held about 5.3 million jobs in 2019. Employment in the detailed occupations

Food servers bring meals to customers outside a restaurant.

that make up food and beverage serving and related workers was distributed as follows:

Fast food and counter workers	4,047,700
Dining room and cafeteria attendants and bartender helpers	488,000
Hosts and hostesses, restaurant, lounge, and coffee shop	429,700
Food servers, nonrestaurant	284,600
Food preparation and serving related workers, all other	74,100

The largest employers of food and beverage serving and related workers were as follows:

Restaurants and other eating places	74%
Special food services	5
Healthcare and social assistance	5
Retail trade	4
Educational services; state, local, and private	4

Food and beverage serving and related workers spend most of the time on their feet and often carry heavy trays of food, dishes, and glassware. During busy dining periods, they are under pressure to serve customers quickly and efficiently.

Injuries and Illnesses

Food preparation and serving areas in restaurants often have potential safety hazards, such as hot ovens and slippery floors. Food preparation and serving related workers, all other, in particular, have one of the highest rates of injuries and illnesses of all occupations. («All other» titles represent occupations with a wide range of characteristics that do not fit into any of the other detailed occupations.)

Common hazards include slips, cuts, and burns, but the injuries are seldom serious. To reduce these risks, workers often wear gloves, aprons, or nonslip shoes.

Work Schedules

Many food and beverage serving and related workers are employed part time. Because food service and drinking establishments typically have extended dining hours, early morning, late evening, weekend, and holidays work is common. Those who work in school cafeterias have more regular hours and may work only during the school year, usually 9 to 10 months.

In addition, business hours in restaurants allow for flexible schedules that appeal to many teenagers, who can gain work experience. Compared with all other occupations, a much larger proportion of food and beverage serving and related workers are 16 to 19 years old.

How to Become a Food and Beverage Serving or Related Worker

Most food and beverage service workers receive short-term on-the-job training. There are no formal educational requirements.

Most states require workers, such as nonrestaurant servers, who serve alcoholic beverages to be 18 years of age or older.

Education

There are no formal education requirements for becoming a food and beverage serving worker.

Training

Most workers learn through on-the-job training, usually lasting several weeks. Training includes basic customer service,

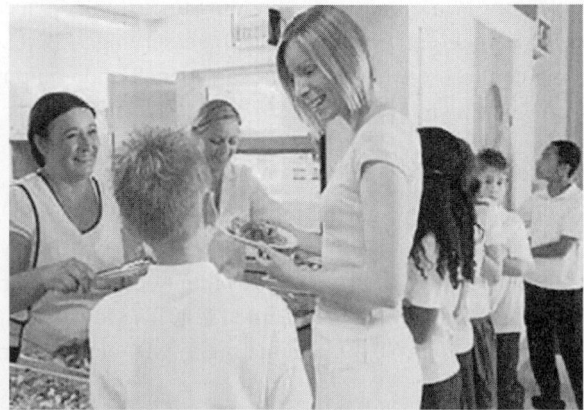

Food and beverage and related workers need customer service skills.

kitchen safety, safe food-handling procedures, and good sanitation habits.

Some employers, particularly those in fast-food restaurants, teach new workers with the use of self-study programs, online programs, audiovisual presentations, or instructional booklets that explain food preparation and service procedures. However, most food and beverage serving and related workers learn duties by watching and working with more experienced workers.

Some full-service restaurants provide new dining room employees with classroom training sessions that alternate with periods of on-the-job work experience. The training communicates the operating philosophy of the restaurant, helps new employees establish a personal rapport with other staff, teaches employees formal serving techniques, and instills a desire in the staff to work as a team.

Some nonrestaurant servers and bartender helpers who work in establishments where alcohol is served may need training on state and local laws concerning the sale of alcoholic beverages. Some states, counties, and cities mandate such training, which typically lasts a few hours and can be taken online or in-person.

Advancement

Advancement opportunities are limited to those who remain on the job for a long time. However, some dining room and cafeteria attendants and bartender helpers may advance to waiter, waitress, or bartender positions as they learn the basics of serving food or preparing drinks.

Important Qualities

Communication skills. Food and beverage serving and related workers must listen carefully to their customers' orders and relay them correctly to the kitchen staff so that the orders are prepared to the customers' request.

Customer-service skills. Food service establishments rely on good food and customer service to keep customers and succeed in a competitive industry. As a result, workers should be courteous and be able to attend to customers' requests.

Physical stamina. Food and beverage serving and related workers spend most of their work time standing, carrying heavy trays, cleaning work areas, and attending to customers' needs.

Physical strength. Food and beverage serving and related workers need to be able to lift and carry stock and equipment that can weigh up to 50 pounds.

Pay

The median hourly wage for food and beverage serving and related workers was $11.06 in May 2019. The median wage is the wage at which half the workers in an occupation earned more than that amount and half earned less. The lowest 10 percent earned less than $8.49, and the highest 10 percent earned more than $14.92.

Median hourly wages for food and beverage serving and related workers in May 2019 were as follows:

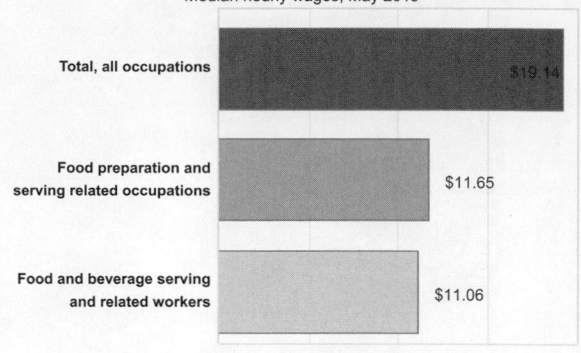

Food and Beverage Serving and Related Workers
Median hourly wages, May 2019

Total, all occupations	$19.14
Food preparation and serving related occupations	$11.65
Food and beverage serving and related workers	$11.06

Note: All Occupations includes all occupations in the U.S. Economy.
Source: U.S. Bureau of Labor Statistics, Occupational Employment Statistics.

Food preparation and serving related workers, all other	$12.01
Food servers, nonrestaurant	11.74
Dining room and cafeteria attendants and bartender helpers	11.28
Hosts and hostesses, restaurant, lounge, and coffee shop	11.10
Fast food and counter workers	10.93

In May 2019, the median hourly wages for food and beverage serving and related workers in the top industries in which they worked were as follows:

Healthcare and social assistance	$11.93
Retail trade	11.85
Educational services; state, local, and private	11.80
Special food services	11.53
Restaurants and other eating places	10.73

Although some workers in these occupations earn tips, most get their earnings from hourly wages alone. Many beginning or inexperienced workers earn the federal minimum wage ($7.25 per hour as of July 24, 2009), although many states set minimum wages higher than the federal minimum.

Tipped employees earn at least the federal minimum wage ($7.25 per hour, as of July 24, 2009), which may be paid as a combination of direct wages and tips, depending on the state. Direct wages may be as low as $2.13 per hour, according to the Fair Labor Standards Act (FLSA).

Also according to the FLSA, tipped employees are employees who regularly receive more than $30 a month in tips. The Wage and Hour Division of the U.S. Department of Labor maintains a website listing minimum wages for tipped employees, by state, although some localities have enacted minimum wages higher than their state requires.

In some restaurants, workers may contribute all or a portion of their tips to a tip pool, which is distributed among qualifying workers. Tip pools allow workers who do not usually receive

Food and Beverage Serving and Related Workers

Percent change in employment, projected 2019-29

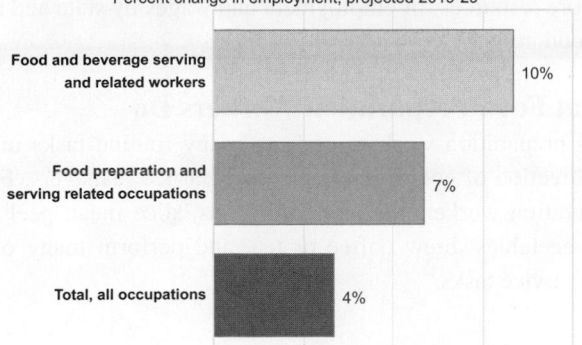

Food and beverage serving and related workers 10%

Food preparation and serving related occupations 7%

Total, all occupations 4%

Note: All Occupations includes all occupations in the U.S. Economy.
Source: U.S. Bureau of Labor Statistics, Employment Projections program.

tips directly from customers, such as dining room attendants, to be part of a team and to share in the rewards for good service.

Employers may provide meals and uniforms, but may deduct the costs from the worker's wages.

Many food and beverage serving and related workers are employed part time. Because of dining hours in food service and drinking establishments, early morning, late evening, weekend, and holidays work is common. Those who work in school cafeterias have more regular hours and may work only during the school year, usually 9 to 10 months.

In addition, business hours in restaurants allow for flexible schedules that appeal to many teenagers, who can gain work experience. Compared with all other occupations, a much larger proportion of food and beverage serving and related workers are 16 to 19 years old.

Job Outlook

Overall employment of food and beverage serving and related workers is projected to grow 10 percent from 2019 to 2029, much faster than the average for all occupations.

As a growing population continues to dine out, purchase take-out meals, or have food delivered, more restaurants, particularly fast-food and casual dining restaurants, are expected to open. In response, more food and beverage serving workers will be required to serve customers. Employment of fast food and counter workers is expected to show the fastest growth, as these workers have a variety of tasks in restaurants.

In addition, nontraditional food service operations, such as those inside grocery stores and cafeterias in hospitals and residential care facilities, will serve more prepared meals. Because these workers are essential to the operation of a food-serving establishment, they will continue to be in demand.

Job Prospects

Job prospects for food and beverage serving and related workers will be excellent because many workers leave the occupation each year, resulting in a large number of job openings.

Workers with related work experience and excellent customer-service skills should have the best job prospects at higher paying restaurants. Still, those seeking positions at these establishments will face strong competition because the prospect of higher earnings attracts many applicants.

Employment projections data for food and beverage serving and related workers, 2019-29					
Occupational Title	SOC Code	Employment, 2019	Projected Employment, 2029	Change, 2019-29	
				Percent	Numeric
SOURCE: U.S. Bureau of Labor Statistics, Employment Projections program					
Food and beverage serving and related workers	—	5,324,100	5,876,500	10	552,400
Fast food and counter workers	35-3023	4,047,700	4,508,600	11	460,900
Food servers, nonrestaurant	35-3041	284,600	303,900	7	19,300
Dining room and cafeteria attendants and bartender helpers	35-9011	488,000	519,900	7	31,900
Hosts and hostesses, restaurant, lounge, and coffee shop	35-9031	429,700	464,900	8	35,200
Food preparation and serving related workers, all other	35-9099	74,100	79,200	7	5,100

State & Area Data
Occupational Employment Statistics (OES)

The Occupational Employment Statistics (OES) program produces employment and wage estimates annually for over 800 occupations. These estimates are available for the nation as a whole, for individual states, and for metropolitan and nonmetropolitan areas.

Contacts for More Information

For more information on food and beverage serving careers, visit
➤ National Restaurant Association

Food Preparation Workers

Summary

Quick Facts: Food Preparation Workers

2019 Median Pay	$24,800 per year $11.92 per hour
Typical Entry-Level Education	No formal educational credential
Work Experience in a Related Occupation ...	None
On-the-job Training	Short-term on-the-job training
Number of Jobs, 2019	886,700
Job Outlook, 2019-29	-1% (Decline)
Employment Change, 2019-29	-9,500

What Food Preparation Workers Do

Food preparation workers perform many routine tasks under the direction of cooks, chefs, or food service managers.

Work Environment

Food preparation workers are employed in restaurants, hotels, and other places where food is served, such as cafeterias, grocery stores, hospitals, and schools. They often work early mornings, late evenings, weekends, or holidays. Many food preparation workers work part time.

How to Become a Food Preparation Worker

Food preparation workers learn through short-term on-the-job training, usually lasting several weeks. No formal education or previous work experience is required.

Pay

The median hourly wage for food preparation workers was $11.92 in May 2019.

Job Outlook

Employment of food preparation workers is projected to decline 1 percent from 2019 to 2029.

Food preparation workers prepare ingredients for dishes.

State & Area Data

Explore resources for employment and wages by state and area for food preparation workers.

What Food Preparation Workers Do

Food preparation workers perform many routine tasks under the direction of cooks, chefs, or food service managers. Food preparation workers prepare cold foods, slice meat, peel and cut vegetables, brew coffee or tea, and perform many other food service tasks.

Duties

Food preparation workers typically do the following:

- Clean and sanitize work areas, equipment, utensils, and dishes
- Weigh or measure ingredients, such as meats and liquids
- Prepare fruit and vegetables for cooking
- Cut meats, poultry, and seafood and prepare them for cooking
- Mix ingredients for salads
- Store food in designated containers and storage areas to prevent spoilage
- Take and record the temperature of food and food storage areas
- Place food trays over food warmers for immediate service

Food preparation workers perform routine, repetitive tasks under the direction of cooks, chefs, or food service managers. To help cooks and other kitchen staff, they prepare ingredients for dishes by slicing and dicing vegetables and by making salads and cold food items. Other common duties include keeping salad bars and buffet tables stocked and clean.

Food preparation workers retrieve pots and pans, clean and store kitchen equipment, and unload and store food supplies. When needed, they retrieve food and equipment for cooks and chefs. In some kitchens, food preparation workers use a variety of commercial kitchen equipment, such as commercial dishwashers, blenders, slicers, or grinders.

Food preparation workers clean and sanitize work areas.

In restaurants, workers stock and use soda machines, coffeemakers, and espresso machines to prepare beverages for customers.

Work Environment

Food preparation workers held about 886,700 jobs in 2019. The largest employers of food preparation workers were as follows:

Restaurants and other eating places	50%
Food and beverage stores	21
Healthcare and social assistance	6
Special food services	6

The work is often strenuous. Food preparation workers may stand for hours at a time while cleaning or preparing ingredients. Some may be required to lift and carry heavy pots or unload heavy food supplies.

The fast-paced environment in kitchens can be hectic and stressful, especially during peak dining hours. Therefore, food preparation workers must work well with cooks and other kitchen staff so that dishes are prepared properly and on time.

Injuries and Illnesses

Food preparation areas in kitchens often have potential safety hazards, such as hot ovens and slippery floors. As a result, food preparation workers have one of the highest rates of injuries and illnesses of all occupations. The most common hazards include slips, falls, cuts, and burns, but these injuries are seldom serious. To reduce risks, workers often wear gloves, aprons, and nonslip shoes.

Work Schedules

Many food preparation workers work part time. Because many restaurants are open extended hours, working early mornings, late evenings, weekends, or holidays is common. Those who work in school cafeterias may have hours that are more regular and may work only during the school year, usually for 9 or 10 months. Some resorts offer seasonal employment.

How to Become a Food Preparation Worker

Food preparation workers typically learn through on-the-job training. No formal education or previous work experience is required.

Education

There are no formal education requirements for becoming a food preparation worker.

Training

Most food preparation workers learn through short-term on-the-job training, usually lasting several weeks. Trainees typically start by working under the supervision of an experienced worker, who teaches them basic kitchen duties. Training also may include basic sanitation and workplace safety regulations, as well as instructions on how to handle and prepare food.

Important Qualities

Dexterity. Food preparation workers chop vegetables, cut meat, and perform many other tasks with sharp knives. They must have the ability to work quickly and safely with sharp objects.

Listening skills. Food preparation workers must understand customers' orders and follow directions from cooks, chefs, or food service managers.

Physical stamina. Food preparation workers stand on their feet for long periods while they prepare food, clean work areas, or lift heavy pots from the stove.

Food preparation workers wear gloves for safe food handling.

Food preparation workers typically learn their skills on the job from an experienced worker.

Food Preparation Workers
Median hourly wages, May 2019

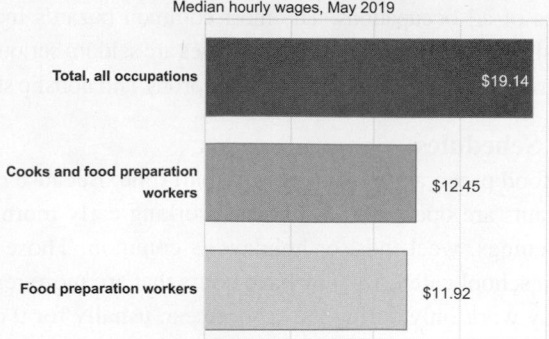

Total, all occupations $19.14

Cooks and food preparation workers $12.45

Food preparation workers $11.92

Food Preparation Workers
Percent change in employment, projected 2019-29

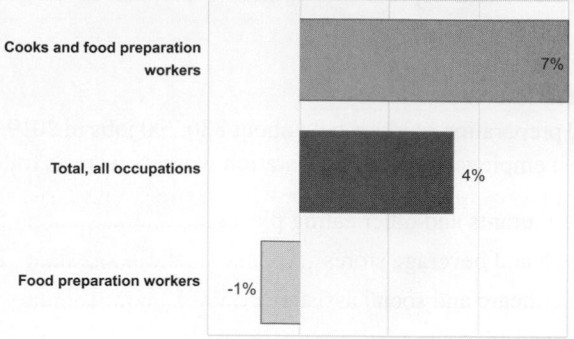

Cooks and food preparation workers 7%

Total, all occupations 4%

Food preparation workers -1%

Note: All Occupations includes all occupations in the U.S. Economy.
Source: U.S. Bureau of Labor Statistics, Occupational Employment Statistics.

Note: All Occupations includes all occupations in the U.S. Economy.
Source: U.S. Bureau of Labor Statistics, Employment Projections program.

Physical strength. Food preparation workers should be strong enough to lift and carry heavy food supply boxes, which often can weigh up to 50 pounds.

Advancement

Advancement opportunities for food preparation workers depend on their training and work experience. Many food preparation workers advance to assistant or line cook positions as they learn basic cooking skills.

Pay

The median hourly wage for food preparation workers was $11.92 in May 2019. The median wage is the wage at which half the workers in an occupation earned more than that amount and half earned less. The lowest 10 percent earned less than $8.76, and the highest 10 percent earned more than $17.07.

In May 2019, the median hourly wages for food preparation workers in the top industries in which they worked were as follows:

Special food services	$12.46
Food and beverage stores	12.19
Healthcare and social assistance	12.09
Restaurants and other eating places	11.55

Many food preparation workers work part time. Because many restaurants are open extended hours, working early mornings, late evenings, weekends, or holidays is common. Those who work in school cafeterias may have hours that are more regular and may work only during the school year, usually for 9 or 10 months. Some resorts offer seasonal employment.

Job Outlook

Employment of food preparation workers is projected to decline 1 percent from 2019 to 2029.

Some restaurants and cafeterias customize their food orders from wholesalers and distributors in an effort to lower costs. For example, they may order prewashed, precut, or preseasoned ingredients, such as meat or vegetables. Additionally, some establishments prefer to employ fast food and counter workers, who both prepare and serve food to customers. These options will lead to the need for fewer food preparation workers.

However, population and income growth are still expected to result in some consumer demand for food at a variety of dining places, including restaurants and grocery stores.

Job Prospects

Job prospects for food preparation workers should be very good because of the need to replace workers who leave the occupation each year.

Jobseekers with related work experience should find opportunities at upscale restaurants. However, individuals seeking full-time positions at these restaurants may face strong competition because the number of job applicants often exceeds the number of job openings.

Employment projections data for food preparation workers, 2019-29					
Occupational Title	SOC Code	Employment, 2019	Projected Employment, 2029	Change, 2019-29	
				Percent	Numeric
SOURCE: U.S. Bureau of Labor Statistics, Employment Projections program					
Food preparation workers	35-2021	886,700	877,200	-1	-9,500

State & Area Data
Occupational Employment Statistics (OES)

The Occupational Employment Statistics (OES) program produces employment and wage estimates annually for over 800 occupations. These estimates are available for the nation as a whole, for individual states, and for metropolitan and nonmetropolitan areas.

Contacts for More Information

For more information about job opportunities, contact local employers and local offices of the state employment service.
For more information about food preparation workers, visit
➤ National Restaurant Association

Waiters and Waitresses

Summary

Quick Facts: Waiters and Waitresses

2019 Median Pay	$22,890 per year $11.00 per hour
Typical Entry-Level Education	No formal educational credential
Work Experience in a Related Occupation	None
On-the-job Training	Short-term on-the-job training
Number of Jobs, 2019	2,613,800
Job Outlook, 2019-29	4% (As fast as average)
Employment Change, 2019-29	97,600

What Waiters and Waitresses Do

Waiters and waitresses take orders and serve food and beverages to customers in dining establishments.

Work Environment

Waiters and waitresses work in restaurants, bars, hotels, and other food-serving and drinking establishments. Work schedules include early mornings, late evenings, weekends, and holidays. Many work part time. During busy hours, they may be under pressure to serve customers quickly and efficiently.

How to Become a Waiter or Waitress

Most waiters and waitresses learn on the job. No formal education is required.

Pay

The median hourly wage for waiters and waitresses was $11.00 in May 2019.

Waiters and waitresses serve food and beverages to customers.

Job Outlook

Employment of waiters and waitresses is projected to grow 4 percent from 2019 to 2029, about as fast as the average for all occupations. Job prospects are expected to be very good because of the many workers who leave their jobs each year. Candidates seeking employment at upscale restaurants may face strong competition for jobs.

State & Area Data

Explore resources for employment and wages by state and area for waiters and waitresses.

What Waiters and Waitresses Do

Waiters and waitresses take orders and serve food and beverages to customers in dining establishments.

Duties

Waiters and waitresses typically do the following:

- Greet customers, present menus, and explain daily specials to customers
- Answer questions related to the menu and offer item suggestions
- Take food and beverage orders from customers
- Relay food and beverage orders to the kitchen staff
- Prepare drinks and food garnishes
- Carry trays of food or drinks from the kitchen to the dining tables
- Remove dirty dishes and glasses, and clean tables after customers finish meals
- Prepare itemized checks and take payments from customers
- Set up dining areas, refill condiments, and stock service areas

Waiters and waitresses, also called *servers*, are responsible for ensuring that customers have a satisfying dining experience. The specific duties of servers vary with the establishment in which they work.

In casual-dining restaurants that offer simple menu items, such as salads, soups, and sandwiches, servers provide fast, efficient, and courteous service. In fine-dining restaurants, where more complicated meals are typically prepared and served over several courses, waiters and waitresses emphasize personal, attentive treatment at a more leisurely pace. For example, they may offer a wine recommendation with certain foods.

Servers may meet with managers and chefs before each shift to discuss the menu or specials, review ingredients for potential food allergies, or talk about any food safety concerns. They also discuss coordination between the kitchen and the dining room and review any customer service issues from the previous day or shift.

In establishments where alcohol is served, waiters and waitresses verify the age of customers and ensure that they meet legal requirements for the purchase of alcohol.

Waiters and waitresses may make wine recommendations.

Work Environment

Waiters and waitresses held about 2.6 million jobs in 2019. The largest employers of waiters and waitresses were as follows:

Restaurants and other eating places 81%

Traveler accommodation 6

Arts, entertainment, and recreation 4

Waiters and waitresses are on their feet most of the time and often carry heavy trays of food, dishes, and drinks. The work can be hectic and fast-paced. During busy dining periods, they may be under pressure to serve customers quickly and efficiently. They must be able to work well as a team with kitchen staff to ensure that customers receive prompt service.

Because waiters and waitresses are the front line of customer service in food-service and drinking establishments, appearance is important. Those who work in fine-dining and upscale restaurants may be required to wear uniforms.

Work Schedules

Many waiters and waitresses work part time. Many work early mornings, late evenings, weekends, and holidays. This is especially true for those who work in full-service restaurants, which employ the vast majority of waiters and waitresses.

Waiters and waitresses mostly work in full-service restaurants.

In establishments that offer seasonal employment, waiters and waitresses may be employed for only a few months each year.

How to Become a Waiter or Waitress

Most waiters and waitresses learn through short-term on-the-job training. No formal education or previous work experience is required to enter the occupation.

Most states require workers who serve alcoholic beverages to be at least 18 years of age, but some states require servers to be older. Waiters and waitresses who serve alcohol must be familiar with state and local laws concerning the sale of alcoholic beverages.

Education

No formal education is required to become a waiter or waitress.

Training

Most waiters and waitresses learn through short-term on-the-job-training, usually lasting a few weeks. Trainees typically work with an experienced waiter or waitress, who teaches them basic serving techniques.

Waiters and waitresses typically learn on the job.

Some full-service restaurants provide new employees with some form of classroom training in combination with periods of on-the-job work experience. These training programs communicate the operating philosophy of the restaurant, help new servers establish a rapport with other staff, teach serving techniques, and instill a desire to work as a team. They also discuss customer service situations and the proper ways to handle unpleasant circumstances or unruly customers.

Training for waiters and waitresses in establishments that serve alcohol typically involves learning state and local laws concerning the sale of alcoholic beverages. Some states, counties, and cities mandate the training, which typically lasts a few hours and can be taken online or in-house.

Some states may require that any staff who handle food need to take training related to the safe handling of food.

Important Qualities

Communication skills. Waiters and waitresses must listen carefully to customers' specific requests, ask questions, and relay the information to the kitchen staff, so that orders are prepared to the customers' satisfaction.

Customer-service skills. Waiters and waitresses spend most of their work time serving customers. They should be friendly and polite and be able to develop a rapport with customers.

Detail oriented. Waiters and waitresses must record customers' orders accurately. They need to be able to recall the details of each order and match the food or drink orders to the correct customers.

Physical stamina. Waiters and waitresses spend hours on their feet carrying trays, dishes, and drinks.

Physical strength. Waiters and waitresses need to be able to lift and carry trays or materials that can weigh up to 50 pounds.

Pay

The median hourly wage for waiters and waitresses was $11.00 in May 2019. The median wage is the wage at which half the workers in an occupation earned more than that amount and half earned less. The lowest 10 percent earned less than $8.37, and the highest 10 percent earned more than $20.65.

In May 2019, the median hourly wages for waiters and waitresses in the top industries in which they worked were as follows:

Traveler accommodation.. $11.72

Arts, entertainment, and recreation....................... 11.20

Restaurants and other eating places...................... 10.73

Many waiters and waitresses get their earnings from a combination of hourly wages and customer tips. Earnings vary greatly with the type of establishment and locality. For example, tips are generally much higher in upscale restaurants in major metropolitan areas and resorts.

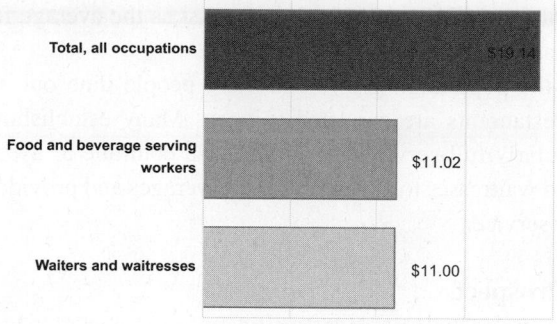

Waiters and Waitresses
Median hourly wages, May 2019

Note: All Occupations includes all occupations in the U.S. Economy.
Source: U.S. Bureau of Labor Statistics, Occupational Employment Statistics.

Tipped employees earn at least the federal minimum wage ($7.25 per hour, as of July 24, 2009), which may be paid as a combination of direct wages and tips, depending on the state. Direct wages may be as low as $2.13 per hour according to the Fair Labor Standards Act (FLSA).

According to the FLSA, tipped employees are those who regularly receive more than $30 a month in tips. The Wage and Hour Division of the U.S. Department of Labor maintains a website with a list of minimum wages for tipped employees, by state, although some localities have enacted minimum wages higher than their state requires.

Some employers may provide meals and furnish uniforms, but other employers may deduct the cost from wages.

Many waiters and waitresses work part time. Many work early mornings, late evenings, weekends, and holidays. This is especially true for those who work in full-service restaurants, which employ the vast majority of waiters and waitresses.

In establishments that offer seasonal employment, waiters and waitresses may be employed for only a few months each year.

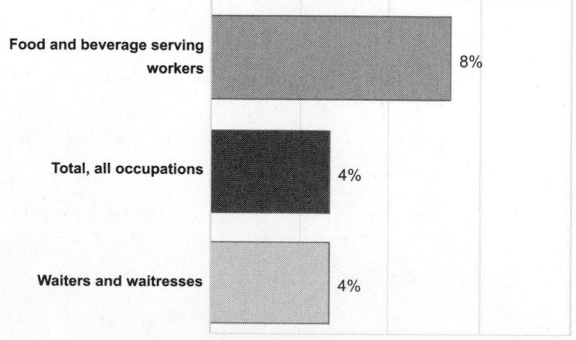

Waiters and Waitresses
Percent change in employment, projected 2019-29

Note: All Occupations includes all occupations in the U.S. Economy.
Source: U.S. Bureau of Labor Statistics, Employment Projections program.

Job Outlook

Employment of waiters and waitresses is projected to grow 4 percent from 2019 to 2029, about as fast as the average for all occupations.

As the population grows and more people dine out, many new restaurants are expected to open. Many establishments, particularly full-service restaurants, will continue to use waiters and waitresses to serve food and beverages and provide customer service.

Job Prospects

Job prospects for waiters and waitresses are expected to be very good, primarily because of the large number of workers who leave the occupation each year. There should be competition for jobs at upscale establishments, however, as potential earnings from tips are greater than at other restaurants and the number of job applicants usually exceeds the number of job openings.

Employment projections data for waiters and waitresses, 2019-29					
Occupational Title	SOC Code	Employment, 2019	Projected Employment, 2029	Change, 2019-29	
				Percent	Numeric
Waiters and waitresses	35-3031	2,613,800	2,711,400	4	97,600

SOURCE: U.S. Bureau of Labor Statistics, Employment Projections program

State & Area Data
Occupational Employment Statistics (OES)

The Occupational Employment Statistics (OES) program produces employment and wage estimates annually for over 800 occupations. These estimates are available for the nation as a whole, for individual states, and for metropolitan and nonmetropolitan areas.

Contacts for More Information

For more information on careers as a waiter or waitress, visit
➤ National Restaurant Association

Healthcare

Athletic Trainers

Summary

Quick Facts: Athletic Trainers

2019 Median Pay	$48,440 per year
Typical Entry-Level Education	Bachelor's degree
Work Experience in a Related Occupation	None
On-the-job Training	None
Number of Jobs, 2019	32,100
Job Outlook, 2019-29	16% (Much faster than average)
Employment Change, 2019-29	5,200

What Athletic Trainers Do

Athletic trainers specialize in preventing, diagnosing, and treating muscle and bone injuries and illnesses.

Work Environment

Many athletic trainers work in educational settings, such as colleges, universities, elementary schools, and secondary schools. Others work in hospitals, fitness centers, or physicians' offices, or for professional sports teams.

How to Become an Athletic Trainer

Athletic trainers need at least a bachelor's degree. Nearly all states require athletic trainers to have a license or certification; requirements vary by state.

Pay

The median annual wage for athletic trainers was $48,440 in May 2019.

Job Outlook

Employment of athletic trainers is projected to grow 16 percent from 2019 to 2029, much faster than the average for all occupations. Demand for athletic trainers is expected to increase as people become more aware of the effects of sports-related injuries, and as the middle-aged and older population remains active.

State & Area Data

Explore resources for employment and wages by state and area for athletic trainers.

What Athletic Trainers Do

Athletic trainers specialize in preventing, diagnosing, and treating muscle and bone injuries and illnesses.

Duties

Athletic trainers typically do the following:

- Apply protective or injury-preventive devices, such as tape, bandages, and braces
- Recognize and evaluate injuries
- Provide first aid or emergency care
- Develop and carry out rehabilitation programs for injured athletes
- Plan and implement comprehensive programs to prevent injury and illness among athletes
- Perform administrative tasks, such as keeping records and writing reports on injuries and treatment programs

Athletic trainers work with people of all ages and all skill levels, from young children to soldiers and professional athletes.

Athletic trainers specialize in preventing, diagnosing, and treating muscle and bone injuries and illnesses.

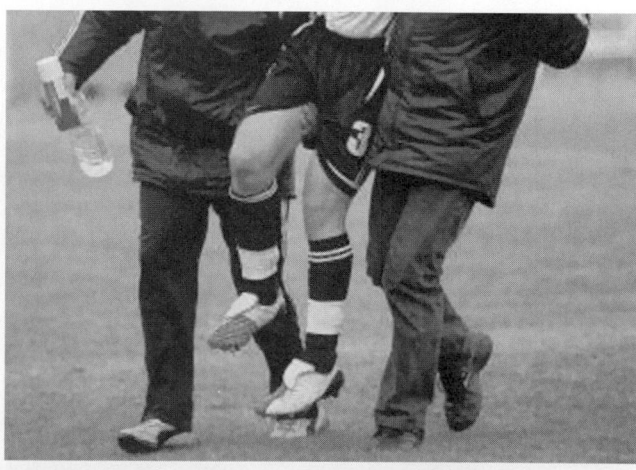

Athletic trainers carry out rehabilitation programs for injured athletes.

Athletic trainers are usually one of the first healthcare providers on the scene when injuries occur on the field. They work under the direction of a licensed physician and with other healthcare providers, often discussing specific injuries and treatment options or evaluating and treating patients, as directed by a physician. Some athletic trainers meet with a team physician or consulting physician regularly.

An athletic trainer's administrative responsibilities may include regular meetings with an athletic director or another administrative officer to deal with budgets, purchasing, policy implementation, and other business-related issues. Athletic trainers plan athletic programs that are compliant with federal and state regulations; for example, they may ensure a football program adheres to laws related to athlete concussions.

Athletic trainers should not be confused with fitness trainers and instructors, which include *personal trainers*.

Work Environment

Athletic trainers held about 32,100 jobs in 2019. The largest employers of athletic trainers were as follows:

Educational services; state, local, and private.............	36%
Hospitals; state, local, and private...............................	19
Offices of physical, occupational and speech therapists, and audiologists......................................	14
Fitness and recreational sports centers.........................	6
Self-employed workers	4

Athletic trainers also may work with military, with law enforcement, with professional sports teams, or with performing artists.

Athletic trainers may spend their time working outdoors on sports fields in all types of weather.

Work Schedules

Most athletic trainers work full time. Athletic trainers who work with teams during sporting events may work evenings or weekends and travel often.

How to Become an Athletic Trainer

Athletic trainers need at least a bachelor's degree. Nearly all states require athletic trainers to have a license or certification; requirements vary by state.

Education

Athletic trainers need at least a bachelor's degree from an accredited college or university. Master's degree programs are also common, and may be preferred by some employers. Degree programs have classroom and clinical components, including science and health-related courses, such as biology, anatomy, physiology, and nutrition.

The Commission on Accreditation of Athletic Training Education (CAATE) accredits hundreds of athletic trainer programs, including postprofessional and residency athletic trainer programs.

High school students interested in postsecondary athletic training programs should take courses in anatomy, physiology, and physics.

Licenses, Certifications, and Registrations

Nearly all states require athletic trainers to be licensed or certified; requirements vary by state. For specific requirements, contact the particular state's licensing or credentialing board or athletic trainer association.

The Board of Certification for the Athletic Trainer (BOC) offers the standard certification examination that most states use for licensing athletic trainers. Certification requires graduating from a CAATE-accredited program and passing the BOC exam. To maintain certification, athletic trainers must adhere to the BOC Standards of Professional Practice and take continuing education courses.

Important Qualities

Compassion. Athletic trainers work with athletes and patients who may be in considerable pain or discomfort. The trainers must be sympathetic while providing treatments.

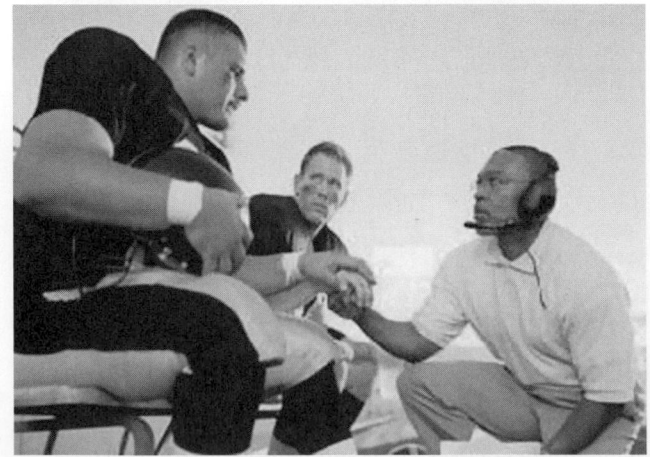

Athletic trainers may travel to games with athletes.

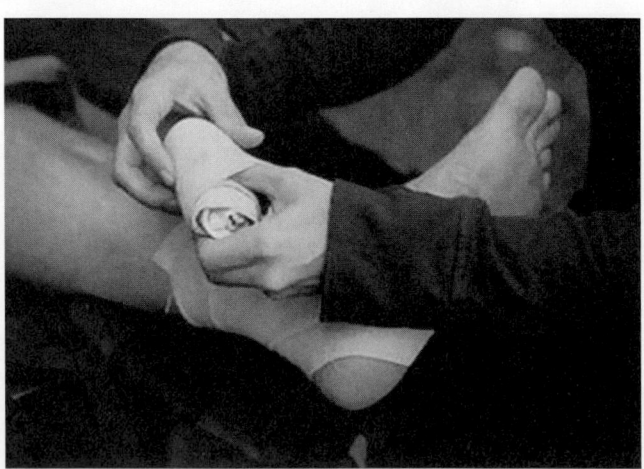

Athletic trainers must be licensed or certified in nearly all states.

Decisionmaking skills. Athletic trainers must make informed clinical decisions that could affect the health or livelihood of patients.

Detail oriented. Athletic trainers must record patients' progress accurately and ensure that they are receiving the appropriate treatments or practicing the correct fitness regimen.

Interpersonal skills. Athletic trainers must have strong interpersonal skills in order to manage difficult situations. They must communicate well with others, including physicians, patients, athletes, coaches, and parents.

Advancement

Assistant athletic trainers may become head athletic trainers, athletic directors, or physician, hospital, or clinic practice administrators. In any of these positions, they will assume a management role. Athletic trainers working in colleges and universities may pursue an advanced degree to increase their advancement opportunities.

Pay

The median annual wage for athletic trainers was $48,440 in May 2019. The median wage is the wage at which half the workers in an occupation earned more than that amount and half earned less. The lowest 10 percent earned less than $31,300, and the highest 10 percent earned more than $73,470.

In May 2019, the median annual wages for athletic trainers in the top industries in which they worked were as follows:

Educational services; state, local, and private........	$52,660
Hospitals; state, local, and private..........................	47,880
Fitness and recreational sports centers...................	46,890
Offices of physical, occupational and speech therapists, and audiologists................................	45,240

Most athletic trainers work full time. Athletic trainers who work with teams during sporting events may work evenings or weekends and travel often.

Job Outlook

Employment of athletic trainers is projected to grow 16 percent from 2019 to 2029, much faster than the average for all occupations.

Demand for athletic trainers is expected to increase as people become more aware of the effects of sports-related injuries, and as the middle-aged and older population remains active. The effects of concussions are particularly severe and long lasting for child athletes. Although concussions are dangerous at any age, children's brains are still developing and are at risk for permanent complications. Some states require public secondary schools to employ athletic trainers as part of their sports programs. Because athletic trainers are usually onsite with athletes and are often the first responders when injuries occur, the demand for trainers in schools should continue to increase.

Sophisticated treatments in injury prevention and detection are projected to increase the demand for athletic trainers. Growth in an increasingly active middle-aged and older population will likely lead to an increased incidence of athletic-related injuries, such as sprains. Sports programs at all ages and for all experience levels will continue to create demand for athletic trainers.

Insurance and workers' compensation costs have become a concern for many employers and insurance companies, especially in areas where employees are often injured on the job. For example, military bases hire athletic trainers to help train and rehabilitate injured military personnel. These trainers also create programs aimed at keeping injury rates down. Depending on the state, some insurance companies recognize athletic trainers as healthcare providers and reimburse the cost of an athletic trainer's services.

Job Prospects

Job prospects will be best for candidates with a bachelor's or master's degree from a program that is accredited by the Commission on Accreditation of Athletic Training Education

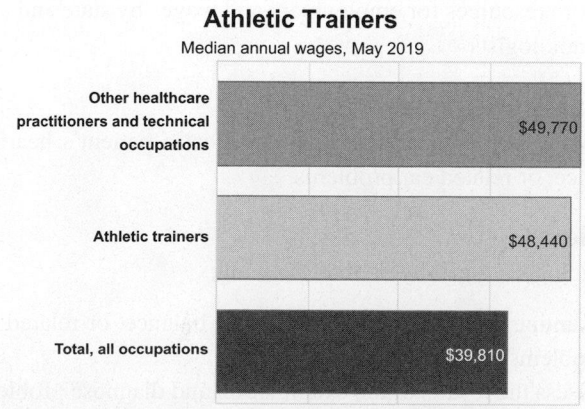

Athletic Trainers
Median annual wages, May 2019

Other healthcare practitioners and technical occupations: $49,770
Athletic trainers: $48,440
Total, all occupations: $39,810

Note: All Occupations includes all occupations in the U.S. Economy.
Source: U.S. Bureau of Labor Statistics, Occupational Employment Statistics.

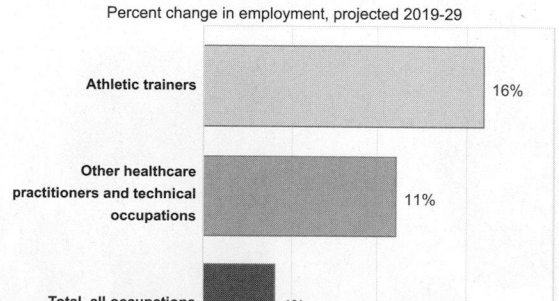

Athletic Trainers
Percent change in employment, projected 2019-29

Athletic trainers: 16%
Other healthcare practitioners and technical occupations: 11%
Total, all occupations: 4%

Note: All Occupations includes all occupations in the U.S. Economy.
Source: U.S. Bureau of Labor Statistics, Employment Projections program.

(CAATE) and for those who have certification from the Board of Certification for the Athletic Trainer (BOC).

State & Area Data
Occupational Employment Statistics (OES)

The Occupational Employment Statistics (OES) program produces employment and wage estimates annually for over 800 occupations. These estimates are available for the nation as a whole, for individual states, and for metropolitan and nonmetropolitan areas.

Contacts for More Information

For more information about athletic trainers, visit
➤ National Athletic Trainers' Association

For more information about accredited athletic training programs, visit
➤ Commission on Accreditation of Athletic Training Education

For more information about certification and state regulatory requirements for athletic trainers, visit
➤ Board of Certification for the Athletic Trainer

Audiologists

Summary

Quick Facts: Audiologists

2019 Median Pay	$77,600 per year $37.31 per hour
Typical Entry-Level Education	Doctoral or professional degree
Work Experience in a Related Occupation	None
On-the-job Training	None
Number of Jobs, 2019	13,800
Job Outlook, 2019-29	13% (Much faster than average)
Employment Change, 2019-29	1,800

What Audiologists Do

Audiologists diagnose, manage, and treat a patient's hearing, balance, or ear problems.

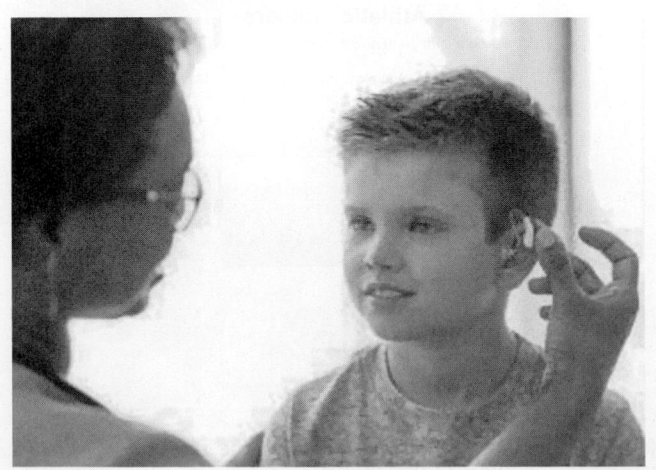

Audiologists fit and dispense hearing aids.

Work Environment

Most audiologists work in healthcare facilities, such as physicians' offices, audiology clinics, and hospitals. Some work in schools or for school districts, and travel between facilities. Others work in health and personal care stores.

How to Become an Audiologist

Audiologists need a doctoral degree and must be licensed in all states. Requirements for licensure vary by state.

Pay

The median annual wage for audiologists was $77,600 in May 2019.

Job Outlook

Employment of audiologists is projected to grow 13 percent from 2019 to 2029, much faster than the average for all occupations. Hearing loss increases as people age, so the aging population is likely to increase demand for audiologists.

State & Area Data

Explore resources for employment and wages by state and area for audiologists.

What Audiologists Do

Audiologists diagnose, manage, and treat a patient's hearing, balance, or related ear problems.

Duties

Audiologists typically do the following:

- Examine patients who have hearing, balance, or related ear problems
- Assess the results of the examination and diagnose problems
- Determine and administer treatment to meet patients' goals
- Provide treatment for tinnitus, a condition that causes ringing in the ear

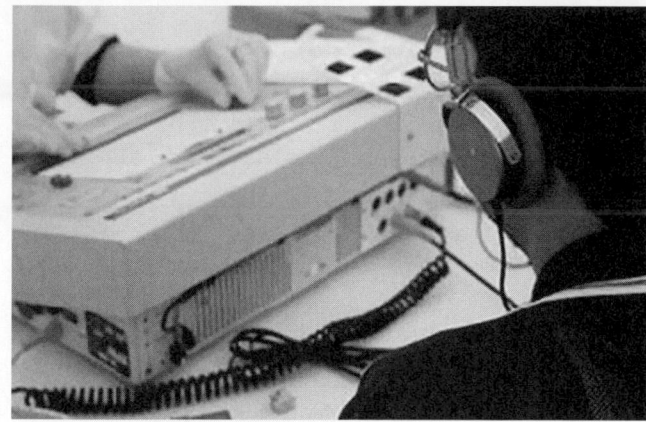

Audiologists diagnose and treat a patient's hearing, balance, or related ear problems.

- Fit and dispense hearing aids
- Counsel patients and their families on ways to listen and communicate, such as lip reading or through technology
- Evaluate patients regularly to check on hearing and balance and to continue or change treatment plans
- Record patient progress
- Research the causes and treatment of hearing and balance disorders
- Educate patients on ways to prevent hearing loss

Audiologists use audiometers, computers, and other devices to test patients' hearing ability and balance. They work to determine the extent of hearing damage and identify the underlying cause. Audiologists measure the loudness at which a person begins to hear sounds and the person's ability to distinguish between sounds and understand speech.

Before determining treatment options, audiologists evaluate psychological information to measure the impact of hearing loss on a patient. Treatment may include cleaning wax out of ear canals, fitting and checking hearing aids, or working with physicians to fit the patient with cochlear implants to improve hearing. Cochlear implants are tiny devices that are placed under the skin near the ear and deliver electrical impulses directly to the auditory nerve in the brain. This allows a person with certain types of deafness to be able to hear.

Audiologists also counsel patients on other ways to cope with profound hearing loss, such as lip reading or using technology.

Audiologists can help a patient suffering from vertigo or other balance problems. They work with patients and provide them with exercises involving head movement or positioning that might relieve some of their symptoms.

Some audiologists specialize in working with the elderly or with children. Others educate the public on hearing loss prevention. Audiologists may design products to help protect the hearing of workers on the job. Audiologists who are self-employed hire employees, keep records, order equipment and supplies, and complete other tasks related to running a business.

Work Environment

Audiologists held about 13,800 jobs in 2019. The largest employers of audiologists were as follows:

Offices of physicians	27%
Offices of physical, occupational and speech therapists, and audiologists	24
Hospitals; state, local, and private	16
Educational services; state, local, and private	10

Some audiologists travel between multiple facilities. Audiologists work closely with registered nurses, audiology assistants (a type of medical assistant), and other healthcare workers.

Work Schedules

Most audiologists work full time and some work more than 40 hours per week. Some work weekends and evenings to meet patients' needs. Those who work on a contract basis may spend time traveling between facilities. For example, an audiologist who is contracted by a school system may have to travel between different schools to provide services.

How to Become an Audiologist

Audiologists need a doctoral degree and must be licensed in all states. Requirements for licensure vary by state.

Education

The doctoral degree in audiology (Au.D.) is a graduate program that typically takes 4 years to complete. A bachelor's degree in any field is needed to enter one of these programs.

Graduate coursework includes anatomy, physiology, physics, genetics, normal and abnormal communication development, diagnosis and treatment, pharmacology, and ethics. Programs also include supervised clinical practice. Graduation from a program accredited by the Council on Academic Accreditation is required to get a license in most states.

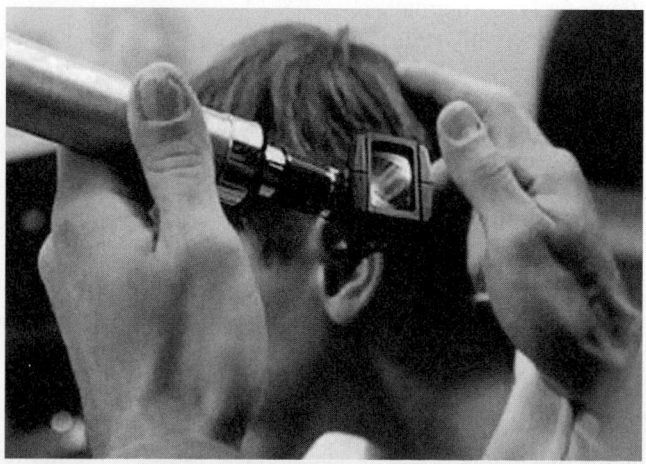

Audiologists identify symptoms of hearing loss and other auditory, balance, and related sensory and neural disorders.

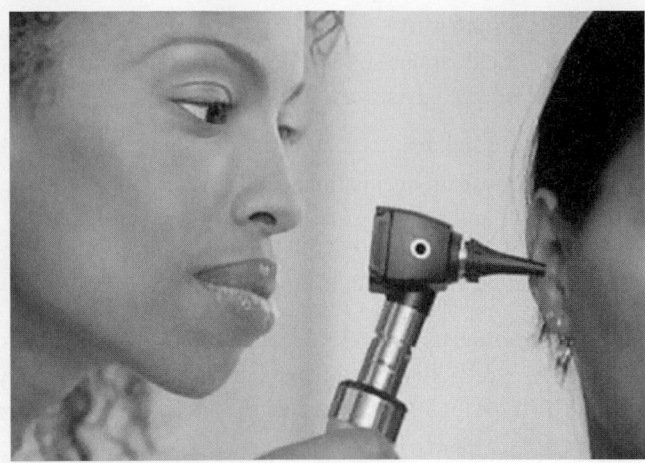

Audiologists must be licensed in all states.

Licenses, Certifications, and Registrations

Audiologists must be licensed in all states. Requirements vary by state. For specific requirements, contact your state's licensing board for audiologists.

Audiologists can earn the Certificate of Clinical Competence in Audiology (CCC-A), offered by the American Speech-Language-Hearing Association. They also may be credentialed through the American Board of Audiology. Certification can be earned by graduating from an accredited doctoral program and passing a standardized exam. Certification may be required by some states or employers. Some states may allow certification in place of some education or training requirements needed for licensure.

Important Qualities

Communication skills. Audiologists need to communicate test results, diagnoses, and proposed treatments, so patients clearly understand the situation and options. They also may need to work on teams with other healthcare providers and education specialists regarding patient care.

Compassion. Audiologists work with patients who may be frustrated or emotional because of their hearing or balance problems. They should be empathetic and supportive of patients and their families.

Critical-thinking skills. Audiologists must concentrate when testing a patient's hearing and be able to analyze each patient's situation, in order to offer the best treatment. They must also be able to provide alternative plans when patients do not respond to initial treatment.

Patience. Audiologists must work with patients who may need a lot of time and special attention.

Problem-solving skills. Audiologists must figure out the causes of problems with hearing and balance and determine the appropriate treatment or treatments to address them.

Pay

The median annual wage for audiologists was $77,600 in May 2019. The median wage is the wage at which half the workers in an occupation earned more than that amount and half earned

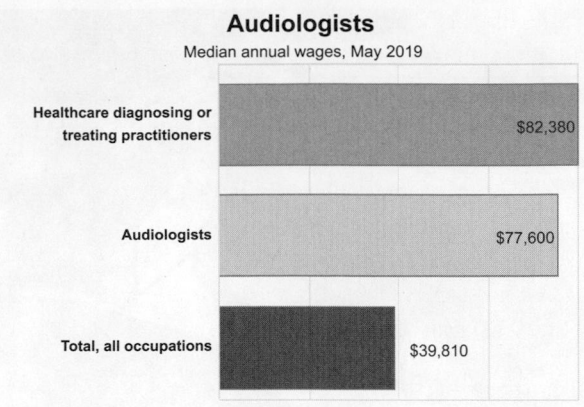

Audiologists
Median annual wages, May 2019

Healthcare diagnosing or treating practitioners — $82,380

Audiologists — $77,600

Total, all occupations — $39,810

Note: All Occupations includes all occupations in the U.S. Economy. Source: U.S. Bureau of Labor Statistics, Occupational Employment Statistics.

less. The lowest 10 percent earned less than $54,010, and the highest 10 percent earned more than $120,750.

In May 2019, the median annual wages for audiologists in the top industries in which they worked were as follows:

Hospitals; state, local, and private	$83,820
Educational services; state, local, and private	81,190
Offices of physical, occupational and speech therapists, and audiologists	75,520
Offices of physicians	75,490

Most audiologists work full time and some work more than 40 hours per week. Some may work weekends and evenings to meet patients' needs. Those who work on a contract basis may spend time traveling between facilities.

Job Outlook

Employment of audiologists is projected to grow 13 percent from 2019 to 2029, much faster than the average for all occupations. However, because it is a small occupation, the fast growth will result in only about 1,800 new jobs over the 10-year period.

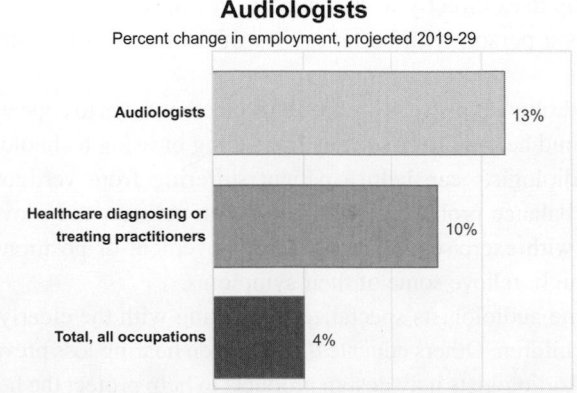

Audiologists
Percent change in employment, projected 2019-29

Audiologists — 13%

Healthcare diagnosing or treating practitioners — 10%

Total, all occupations — 4%

Note: All Occupations includes all occupations in the U.S. Economy. Source: U.S. Bureau of Labor Statistics, Employment Projections program.

An aging baby-boom population and growing life expectancies will continue to increase the demand for most healthcare services. Hearing loss and balance disorders become more prevalent as people age, so the aging population is likely to increase demand for audiologists.

The early identification and diagnosis of hearing disorders in infants also may spur employment growth. Advances in hearing aid design, such as smaller size and the reduction of feedback, may make such devices more appealing as a means to minimize the effects of hearing loss. This may lead to more demand for audiologists.

Job Prospects

Demand may be greater in areas with large numbers of retirees, so audiologists who are willing to relocate may have the best job prospects.

Occupational Title	SOC Code	Employment, 2019	Projected Employment, 2029	Change, 2019-29 Percent	Change, 2019-29 Numeric
Employment projections data for audiologists, 2019-29					
SOURCE: U.S. Bureau of Labor Statistics, Employment Projections program					
Audiologists	29-1181	13,800	15,600	13	1,800

State & Area Data
Occupational Employment Statistics (OES)
The Occupational Employment Statistics (OES) program produces employment and wage estimates annually for over 800 occupations. These estimates are available for the nation as a whole, for individual states, and for metropolitan and nonmetropolitan areas.

Contacts for More Information
For more information on state-specific licensing requirements, contact the state's licensing board.

For more information about audiologists, including requirements for certification and state licensure, visit
➤ American Speech-Language-Hearing Association (ASHA)
➤ American Board of Audiology
➤ American Academy of Audiology

Chiropractors

Summary

Quick Facts: Chiropractors

2019 Median Pay	$70,340 per year $33.82 per hour
Typical Entry-Level Education	Doctoral or professional degree
Work Experience in a Related Occupation	None
On-the-job Training	None
Number of Jobs, 2019	51,100
Job Outlook, 2019-29	4% (As fast as average)
Employment Change, 2019-29	2,300

What Chiropractors Do
Chiropractors treat patients with health problems of the neuromusculoskeletal system, which includes nerves, bones, muscles, ligaments, and tendons.

Work Environment
Most chiropractors work in a solo or group chiropractic practice. A large number are self-employed.

How to Become a Chiropractor
Chiropractors must earn a Doctor of Chiropractic (D.C.) degree and get a state license. Doctor of Chiropractic programs typically take 4 years to complete and require at least 3 years of undergraduate college education for admission.

Pay
The median annual wage for chiropractors was $70,340 in May 2019.

Job Outlook
Employment of chiropractors is projected to grow 4 percent from 2019 to 2029, about as fast as the average for all occupations. People across all age groups are increasingly becoming interested in integrative or complementary healthcare as a way to treat pain and to improve overall wellness. Chiropractic care is appealing to patients because chiropractors use nonsurgical methods of treatment and do not prescribe drugs.

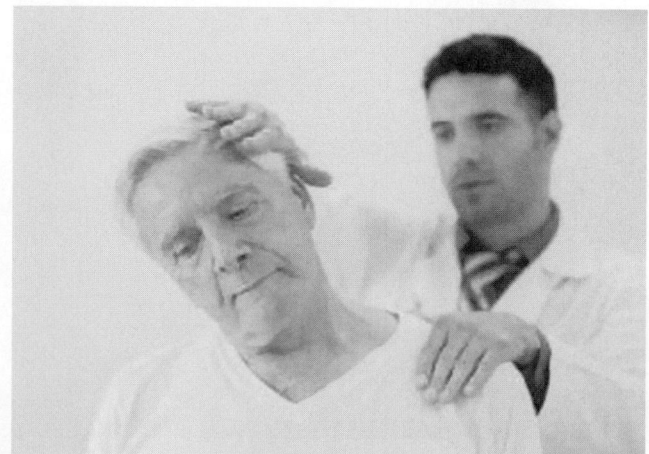

Chiropractors treat patients with health problems of the neuromusculoskeletal system.

State & Area Data

Explore resources for employment and wages by state and area for chiropractors.

What Chiropractors Do

Chiropractors care for patients with health problems of the neuromusculoskeletal system, which includes nerves, bones, muscles, ligaments, and tendons. They use spinal adjustments and manipulation, as well as other clinical interventions, to manage patients' health concerns, such as back and neck pain.

Duties

Chiropractors typically do the following:

- Assess a patient's medical condition by reviewing the patient's medical history and concerns, and by performing a physical examination
- Analyze the patient's posture, spine, and reflexes
- Conduct tests, including evaluating a patient's posture and taking x rays
- Provide neuromusculoskeletal therapy, which often involves adjusting a patient's spinal column and other joints
- Give additional treatments, such as applying heat or cold to a patient's injured areas

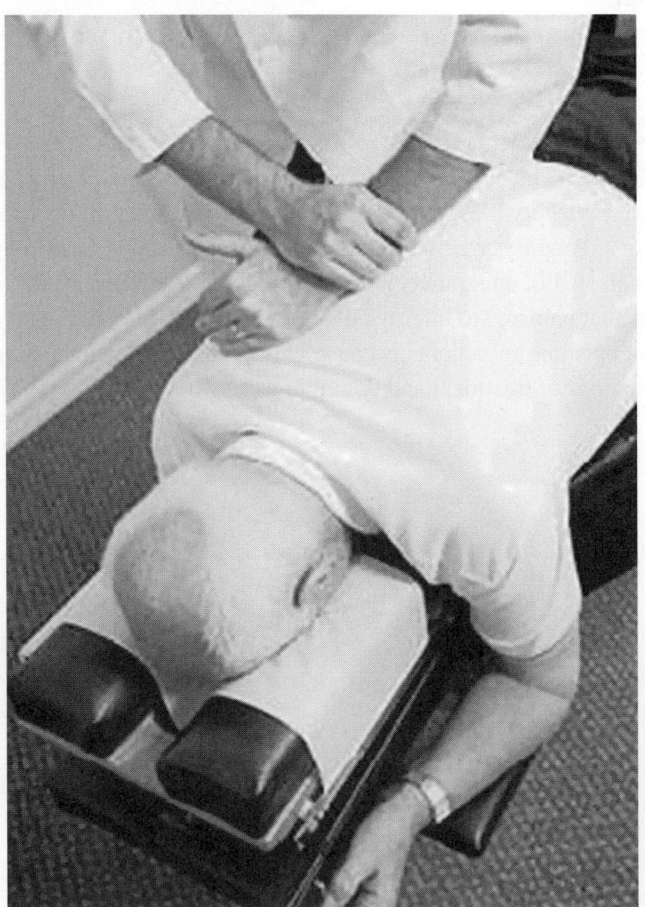

Chiropractors perform manual therapy to help patients with back and neck pain.

- Advise patients on health and lifestyle issues, such as exercise, nutrition, and sleep habits
- Refer patients to other healthcare professionals if needed

Chiropractors focus on patients' overall health. Chiropractors believe that malfunctioning spinal joints and other somatic tissues interfere with a person's neuromuscular system and can result in poor health.

Some chiropractors use procedures such as massage therapy, rehabilitative exercise, and ultrasound in addition to spinal adjustments and manipulation. They also may apply supports, such as braces or shoe inserts, to treat patients and relieve pain.

In addition to operating a general chiropractic practice, some chiropractors specialize in areas such as sports, neurology, orthopedics, pediatrics, or nutrition, among others. Chiropractors in private practice are responsible for marketing their businesses, hiring staff, and keeping records.

Work Environment

Chiropractors held about 51,100 jobs in 2019. The largest employers of chiropractors were as follows:

Offices of chiropractors	63%
Self-employed workers	31
Offices of physicians	3

Chiropractors typically work in office settings. They may be on their feet for long periods when examining and treating patients.

Work Schedules

Most chiropractors work full time. Chiropractors may work in the evenings or on weekends to accommodate patients. Some chiropractors travel to patients' homes to give treatment. Self-employed chiropractors set their own hours.

How to Become a Chiropractor

Chiropractors must earn a Doctor of Chiropractic (D.C.) degree and a state license. Doctor of Chiropractic programs typically

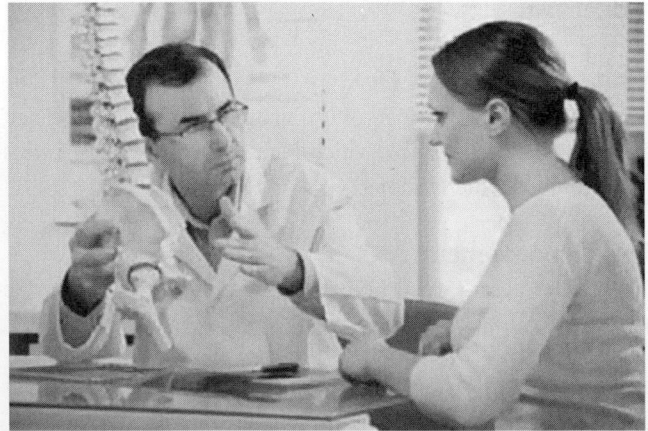

Chiropractors assess a patient's medical condition and explain treatment options.

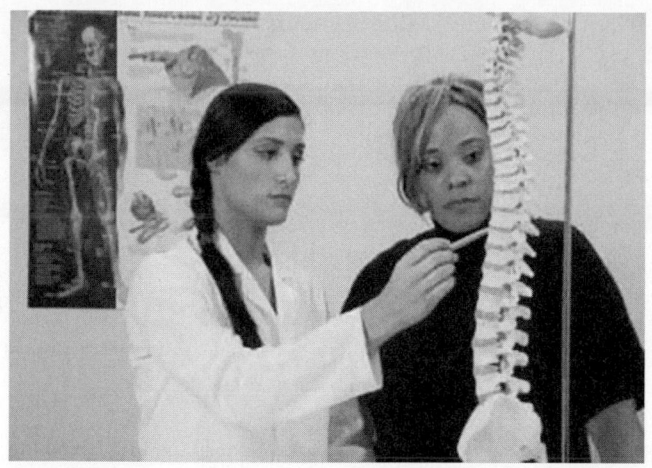

Chiropractors must earn a Doctor of Chiropractic (D.C.) degree and get a state license.

take 4 years to complete and require at least 3 years of undergraduate college education for admission.

Education

Prospective chiropractors are required to have a Doctor of Chiropractic (D.C.) degree—a postgraduate professional degree that typically takes 4 years to complete. In 2017, there were 15 Doctor of Chiropractic programs on 18 campuses accredited by The Council on Chiropractic Education.

Admission to D.C. programs requires at least 90 semester hours of undergraduate education, and some D.C. programs require a bachelor's degree for entry. Most students typically earn a bachelor's degree before applying to a chiropractic program. Schools have specific requirements for their chiropractic programs, but they generally require coursework in the liberal arts and in sciences such as physics, chemistry, and biology. Candidates should check with individual schools regarding their specific requirements.

A D.C. program includes classwork in anatomy, physiology, biology, and similar subjects. Chiropractic students also get supervised clinical experience in which they train in spinal assessment, adjustment techniques, and making diagnoses. D.C. programs also may include classwork in business management and in billing and finance. Most D.C. programs offer a dual-degree option, in which students may earn either a bachelor's or a master's degree in another field while completing their D.C.

Some chiropractors complete postgraduate programs that lead to diplomate credentials. These programs provide additional training in specialty areas, such as orthopedics and pediatrics. Classes are taken at chiropractic colleges.

Licenses, Certifications, and Registrations

All states and the District of Columbia require chiropractors to be licensed. Although specific requirements vary by state, all require the completion of an accredited Doctor of Chiropractic (D.C.) degree program and passing all four parts of the National Board of Chiropractic Examiners (NBCE) exam.

Many states also require applicants to pass a background check and state-specific law exams, called jurisprudence exams. All states require a practicing chiropractor to take continuing education classes to maintain his or her chiropractic license. Check with your state's board of chiropractic examiners or health department for more specific information on licensure.

Important Qualities

Decisionmaking skills. Chiropractors must determine the best course of action when treating a patient. They must also decide when to refer patients to other healthcare professionals.

Detail oriented. Chiropractors must be observant and pay attention to details so that they can make proper diagnoses and avoid mistakes that could harm patients.

Dexterity. Because they use their hands to perform manual adjustments to the spine and other joints, chiropractors should have good coordination to perform therapy effectively.

Empathy. Chiropractors often care for people who are in pain. They must be understanding and sympathetic to their patients' problems and needs.

Interpersonal skills. Chiropractors must be personable in order to keep clients coming to their practice. Also, because chiropractors frequently touch patients in performing therapy, they should be able to put their patients at ease.

Organizational skills. Self-employed chiropractors may need to schedule appointments, manage employees, bill insurance companies, and maintain patients' files. Good record-keeping and other organizational skills are critical in running a successful business.

Pay

The median annual wage for chiropractors was $70,340 in May 2019. The median wage is the wage at which half the workers in an occupation earned more than that amount and half earned less. The lowest 10 percent earned less than $35,290, and the highest 10 percent earned more than $147,480.

In May 2019, the median annual wages for chiropractors in the top industries in which they worked were as follows:

Offices of physicians	$88,020
Offices of chiropractors	69,460

Earnings vary with the chiropractor's number of years in practice, geographic region of practice, and hours worked. Chiropractors tend to earn more as they build a client base and become owners of, or partners in, a practice.

Most chiropractors work full time. Chiropractors may work in the evenings or on weekends to accommodate patients. Some chiropractors travel to patients' homes to give treatment. Self-employed chiropractors set their own hours.

Job Outlook

Employment of chiropractors is projected to grow 4 percent from 2019 to 2029, about as fast as the average for all occupations. People across all age groups are increasingly becoming

Chiropractors
Median annual wages, May 2019

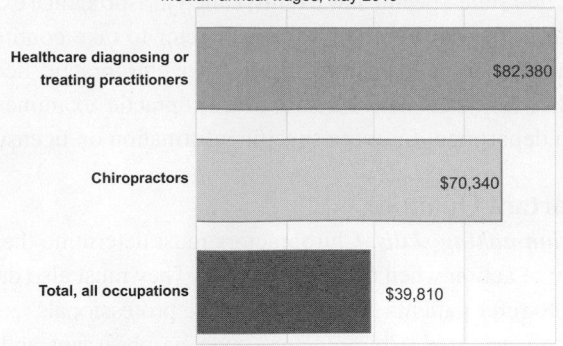

Note: All Occupations includes all occupations in the U.S. Economy.
Source: U.S. Bureau of Labor Statistics, Occupational Employment
Statistics.

Chiropractors
Percent change in employment, projected 2019-29

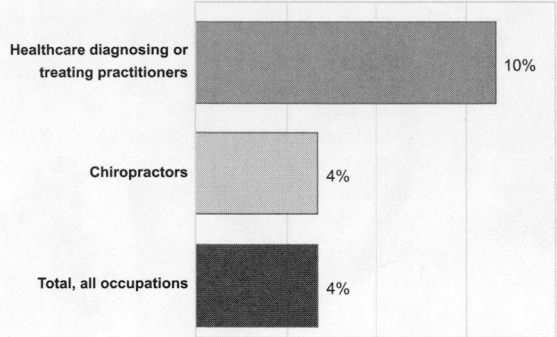

Note: All Occupations includes all occupations in the U.S. Economy.
Source: U.S. Bureau of Labor Statistics, Employment Projections
program.

interested in integrative or complementary healthcare as a way to treat pain and improve overall wellness. Chiropractic care is appealing to patients because chiropractors use nonsurgical methods of treatment and do not prescribe drugs.

Chiropractic treatment of the back, neck, limbs, and involved joints has become more accepted as a result of research and changing attitudes about additional approaches to healthcare. As a result, chiropractors are increasingly working with other healthcare workers, such as physicians and physical therapists, through referrals and complementary care.

The aging of the large baby-boom generation will lead to new opportunities for chiropractors because older adults are more likely than younger people to have neuromusculoskeletal and joint problems. Members of the aging population will likely continue to seek treatment for these conditions as they lead longer, more active lives.

Demand for chiropractic treatment is related to the ability of patients to pay, either directly or through health insurance. Although most insurance plans now cover chiropractic services, the extent of such coverage varies among plans.

State & Area Data
Occupational Employment Statistics (OES)

The Occupational Employment Statistics (OES) program produces employment and wage estimates annually for over 800 occupations. These estimates are available for the nation as a whole, for individual states, and for metropolitan and nonmetropolitan areas.

Contacts for More Information

For more information on a career as a chiropractor, visit
➤ American Chiropractic Association
➤ International Chiropractors Association
➤ Discover Chiropractic

For a list of chiropractic programs and institutions, as well as for general information on chiropractic education, visit
➤ Association of Chiropractic Colleges
➤ The Council on Chiropractic Education

For information on state education and licensure requirements, visit
➤ Federation of Chiropractic Licensing Boards

For information about licensing exams, visit
➤ National Board of Chiropractic Examiners

Employment projections data for chiropractors, 2019-29					
Occupational Title	SOC Code	Employment, 2019	Projected Employment, 2029	Change, 2019-29	
				Percent	Numeric
SOURCE: U.S. Bureau of Labor Statistics, Employment Projections program					
Chiropractors	29-1011	51,100	53,400	4	2,300

Clinical Laboratory Technologists and Technicians

Summary

Quick Facts: Clinical Laboratory Technologists and Technicians

2019 Median Pay	$53,120 per year $25.54 per hour
Typical Entry-Level Education	Bachelor's degree
Work Experience in a Related Occupation	None
On-the-job Training	None
Number of Jobs, 2019	337,800
Job Outlook, 2019-29	7% (Faster than average)
Employment Change, 2019-29	24,700

What Clinical Laboratory Technologists and Technicians Do

Clinical laboratory technologists and technicians collect samples and perform tests to analyze body fluids, tissue, and other substances.

Work Environment

Many clinical laboratory technologists and technicians work in hospitals. Others work in medical and diagnostic laboratories or doctors' offices.

How to Become a Clinical Laboratory Technologist or Technician

Clinical laboratory technologists typically need a bachelor's degree. Technicians usually need an associate's degree or a postsecondary certificate. Some states require technologists and technicians to be licensed.

Pay

The median annual wage for clinical laboratory technologists and technicians was $53,120 in May 2019.

Job Outlook

Overall employment of clinical laboratory technologists and technicians is projected to grow 7 percent from 2019 to 2029, faster than the average for all occupations. An increase in the aging population is expected to lead to a greater need to diagnose medical conditions, such as cancer or type 2 diabetes, through laboratory procedures.

State & Area Data

Explore resources for employment and wages by state and area for clinical laboratory technologists and technicians.

What Clinical Laboratory Technologists and Technicians Do

Clinical laboratory technologists (commonly known as *medical laboratory scientists*) and clinical laboratory technicians collect samples and perform tests to analyze body fluids, tissue, and other substances.

Duties

Clinical laboratory technologists and technicians typically do the following:

- Analyze body fluids, such as blood, urine, and tissue samples, and record normal or abnormal findings
- Study blood samples for use in transfusions by identifying the number of cells, the cell morphology or the blood group, blood type, and compatibility with other blood types
- Operate sophisticated laboratory equipment, such as microscopes and cell counters
- Use automated equipment and computerized instruments capable of performing a number of tests at the same time
- Log data from medical tests and enter results into a patient's medical record
- Discuss results and findings of laboratory tests and procedures with physicians

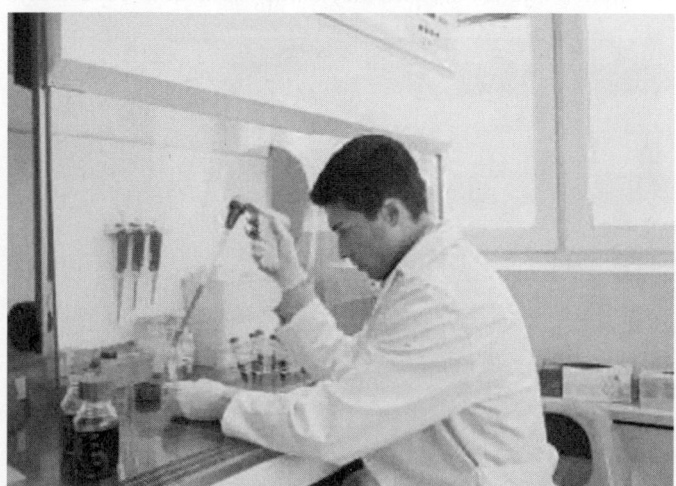

Clinical laboratory personnel examine and test body fluids and cells.

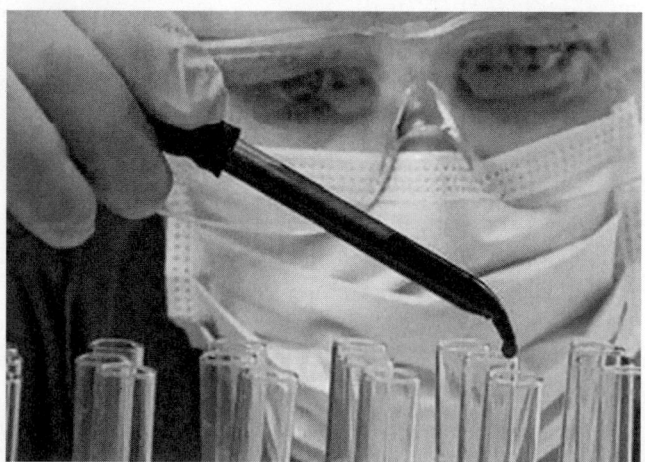

Laboratory personnel wear protective masks, gloves, and goggles to ensure their safety.

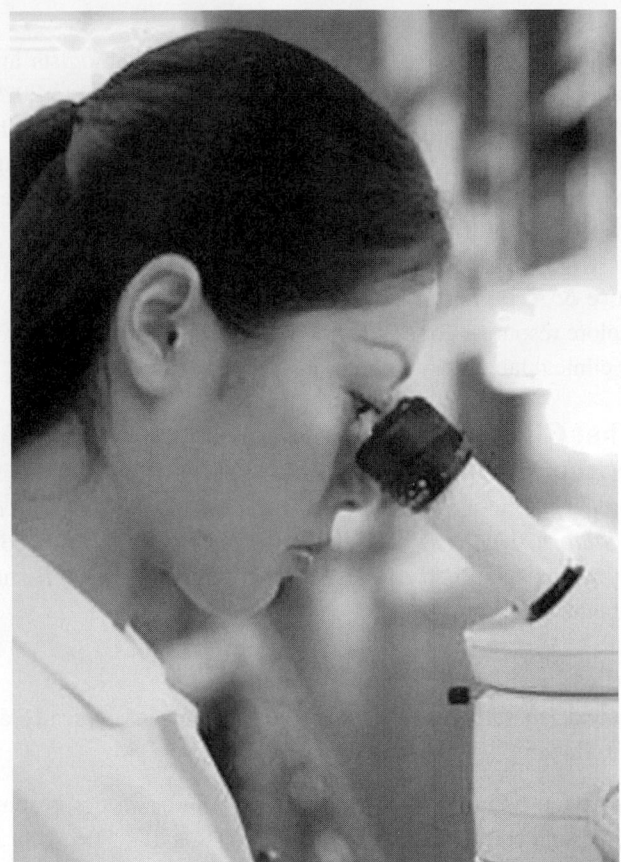

Clinical laboratory technologists operate sophisticated laboratory equipment, such as microscopes and cell counters.

Both technicians and technologists perform tests and procedures that physicians and surgeons or other healthcare personnel order. However, technologists perform more complex tests and laboratory procedures than technicians do. For example, technologists may prepare specimens and perform detailed manual tests, whereas technicians perform routine tests that may be more automated. Clinical laboratory technicians usually work under the general supervision of clinical laboratory technologists or laboratory managers.

Technologists in small laboratories perform many types of tests; in large laboratories, they sometimes specialize. The following are examples of types of specialized clinical laboratory technologists:

Blood bank technologists, or *immunohematology technologists*, collect blood, classify it by type, and prepare blood and its components for transfusions.

Clinical chemistry technologists prepare specimens and analyze the chemical and hormonal contents of body fluids.

Cytotechnologists prepare slides of body cells and examine these cells under a microscope for abnormalities that may signal the beginning of a cancerous growth.

Immunology technologists examine elements of the human immune system and its response to foreign bodies.

Microbiology technologists examine and identify bacteria and other microorganisms.

Molecular biology technologists perform complex protein and nucleic acid tests on cell samples.

Like technologists, clinical laboratory technicians may work in several areas of the laboratory or specialize in one area. For example, *histotechnicians* are a type of clinical laboratory technician who cut and stain tissue specimens for pathologists—doctors who study the cause and development of diseases at a microscopic level.

Technologists and technicians often specialize after they have worked in a particular area for a long time or have received advanced education or training in that area.

Work Environment

Clinical laboratory technologists and technicians held about 337,800 jobs in 2019. The largest employers of clinical laboratory technologists and technicians were as follows:

General medical and surgical hospitals; state, local, and private	47%
Medical and diagnostic laboratories	20
Offices of physicians	9
Junior colleges, colleges, universities, and professional schools; state, local, and private	6
Outpatient care centers	3

Clinical laboratory personnel are trained to work with infectious specimens or with materials that are caustic or produce fumes. When they follow proper methods to control infection and sterilize equipment, the risk decreases. They wear protective masks, gloves, and goggles for their safety.

Technologists and technicians can be on their feet for long periods, and they may need to lift or turn disabled patients to collect samples.

Injuries and Illnesses

Clinical laboratory technologists and technicians risk injury or illness on the job. For example, they may be subject to repetitive motion injuries because they do the same tasks repeatedly.

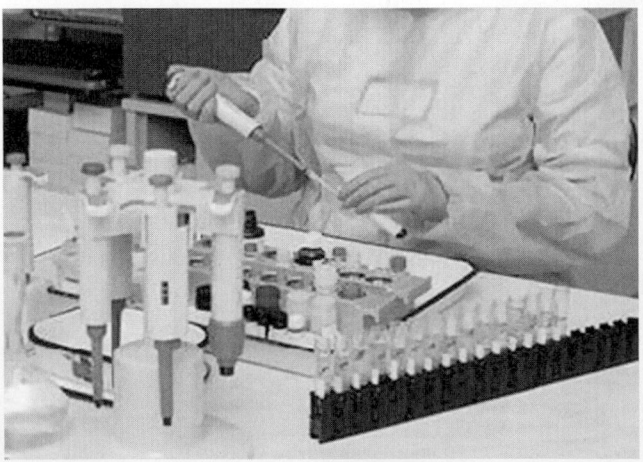

Clinical laboratory technologists typically need a bachelor's degree.

Work Schedules

Most clinical laboratory technologists and technicians work full time. Technologists and technicians who work in facilities that operate around the clock, such as hospitals and some independent laboratories, may work evening, weekend, or overnight hours.

How to Become a Clinical Laboratory Technologist or Technician

Clinical laboratory technologists typically need a bachelor's degree. Technicians usually need an associate's degree or a postsecondary certificate. Some states require technologists and technicians to be licensed.

Education

An entry-level job for technologists usually requires a bachelor's degree in medical technology or life sciences.

A bachelor's degree program in medical laboratory technology, also known as a medical laboratory scientist degree, includes courses in chemistry, biology, microbiology, math, and statistics. Students typically complete college coursework and then apply to the clinical portion of the program. Coursework emphasizes laboratory skills, including safety procedures and lab management, while the clinical portion includes hands-on training in a typical work setting like a hospital. Some laboratory science programs can be completed in 2 years or less and require prior college coursework or a bachelor's degree.

Clinical laboratory technicians often complete an associate's degree program in clinical laboratory science. The Armed Forces and vocational or technical schools also may offer certificate programs for medical laboratory technicians. Technician coursework addresses the theoretical and practical aspects of each of the major laboratory disciplines.

High school students who are interested in pursuing a career in the medical laboratory sciences should take classes in chemistry, biology, and math.

Licenses, Certifications, and Registrations

Some states require laboratory personnel to be licensed. Requirements vary by state and specialty. For specific requirements, contact state departments of health, state boards of occupational licensing, or visit The American Society for Clinical Laboratory Science.

Certification of clinical laboratory technologists and technicians is required for licensure in some states. Although certification is not required to enter the occupation in all cases, employers typically prefer to hire certified technologists and technicians.

Clinical laboratory technologists and technicians can obtain a general certification as a medical laboratory technologist or technician, respectively, or a certification in a specialty, such as cytotechnology or medical biology. Most credentialing institutions require that technologists complete an accredited education program in order to qualify to sit for an exam. For more credentialing information, visit the National Accrediting Agency for Clinical Laboratory Sciences, American Medical Technologists, and the American Society for Clinical Pathology.

Important Qualities

Ability to use technology. Clinical laboratory technologists and technicians must understand how to operate computerized lab equipment.

Detail oriented. Clinical laboratory technologists and technicians must follow exact instructions in order to perform tests or procedures correctly.

Dexterity. Clinical laboratory technologists and technicians need to be skilled with their hands. They work closely with needles and precision laboratory instruments and must handle these tools effectively.

Physical stamina. Clinical laboratory technologists and technicians may work on their feet for long periods while collecting samples. They may need to lift or turn disabled patients to collect samples for testing.

Advancement

After additional education, work experience, or certification, technologists and technicians may specialize in one of many areas of laboratory science, such as immunology, histotechnology, or clinical chemistry. Some clinical laboratory technicians advance to technologist positions after gaining experience and additional education. Some colleges have bachelor's degree programs for medical laboratory technicians to become technologists (often referred to as MLT to MLS programs).

Pay

The median annual wage for clinical laboratory technologists and technicians was $53,120 in May 2019. The median wage is the wage at which half the workers in an occupation earned more than that amount and half earned less. The lowest 10 percent earned less than $30,920, and the highest 10 percent earned more than $81,530.

In May 2019, the median annual wages for clinical laboratory technologists and technicians in the top industries in which they worked were as follows:

General medical and surgical hospitals; state, local, and private	$55,780
Outpatient care centers	54,810
Medical and diagnostic laboratories	50,760
Junior colleges, colleges, universities, and professional schools; state, local, and private	49,600
Offices of physicians	47,990

Most clinical laboratory technologists and technicians work full time. Technologists and technicians who work in facilities that are always open, such as hospitals and some independent laboratories, may work evening, weekend, or overnight hours.

Clinical Laboratory Technologists and Technicians

Median annual wages, May 2019

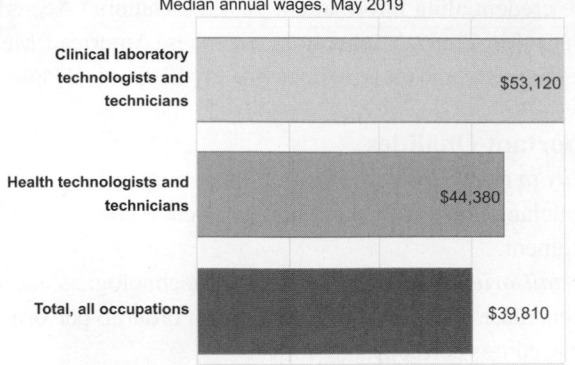

Note: All Occupations includes all occupations in the U.S. Economy.
Source: U.S. Bureau of Labor Statistics, Occupational Employment
Statistics.

Clinical Laboratory Technologists and Technicians

Percent change in employment, projected 2019-29

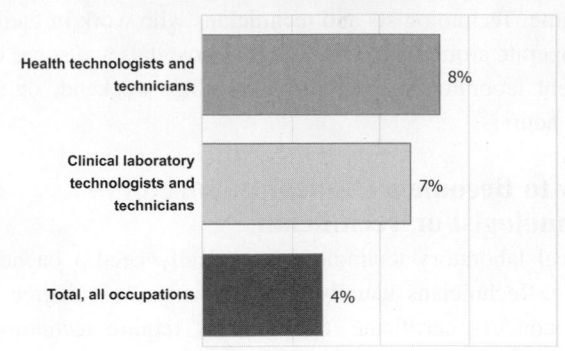

Note: All Occupations includes all occupations in the U.S. Economy.
Source: U.S. Bureau of Labor Statistics, Employment Projections
program.

Job Outlook

Employment of clinical laboratory technologists and technicians is projected to grow 7 percent from 2019 to 2029, faster
than the average for all occupations.

An increase in the aging population is expected to lead to a greater
need to diagnose medical conditions, such as cancer or type 2 diabetes, through laboratory procedures. Prenatal testing for various
types of genetic conditions also is increasingly common. Clinical
laboratory technologists and technicians will be in demand to use
and maintain the equipment needed for diagnosis and treatment.

Job Prospects

Job prospects will be best for clinical laboratory technologists
and technicians who complete an accredited education program
and earn professional certification.

Employment projections data for clinical laboratory technologists and technicians, 2019-29					
Occupational Title	SOC Code	Employment, 2019	Projected Employment, 2029	Change, 2019-29 Percent	Numeric
SOURCE: U.S. Bureau of Labor Statistics, Employment Projections program					
Clinical laboratory technologists and technicians	29-2010	337,800	362,500	7	24,700

State & Area Data
Occupational Employment Statistics (OES)

The Occupational Employment Statistics (OES) program produces employment and wage estimates annually for over 800
occupations. These estimates are available for the nation as a
whole, for individual states, and for metropolitan and nonmetropolitan areas.

Contacts for More Information

For more information about clinical laboratory technologists
and technicians, visit
➤ The American Society for Clinical Laboratory Science
➤ American Society of Cytopathology

For a list of accredited and approved educational programs for
medical laboratory personnel, visit
➤ National Accrediting Agency for Clinical Laboratory
  Sciences

For information on certification, visit
➤ American Association of Bioanalysts
➤ American Medical Technologists
➤ American Society for Clinical Pathology

Dental Assistants

Summary

Quick Facts: Dental Assistants

2019 Median Pay	$40,080 per year $19.27 per hour
Typical Entry-Level Education	Postsecondary non-degree award
Work Experience in a Related Occupation ...	None
On-the-job Training	None
Number of Jobs, 2019	354,600
Job Outlook, 2019-29..................................	7% (Faster than average)
Employment Change, 2019-29	23,400

What Dental Assistants Do

Dental assistants provide patient care, take x rays, keep records, and schedule appointments.

Work Environment

Almost all dental assistants work in dentists' offices. Most work full time.

How to Become a Dental Assistant

There are several possible paths to becoming a dental assistant. Some states require assistants to graduate from an accredited program and pass an exam. In other states, there are no formal educational requirements, and dental assistants learn through on-the-job training.

Pay

The median annual wage for dental assistants was $40,080 in May 2019.

Job Outlook

Employment of dental assistants is projected to grow 7 percent from 2019 to 2029, faster than the average for all occupations. The aging population and ongoing research linking oral health and general health will lead to continued increases in the demand for preventive dental services.

State & Area Data

Explore resources for employment and wages by state and area for dental assistants.

What Dental Assistants Do

Dental assistants have many tasks, including patient care, recordkeeping, and appointment scheduling. Their duties vary by state and by the dentists' offices in which they work.

Duties

Dental assistants typically do the following:

- Ensure that patients are comfortable in the dental chair
- Prepare patients and the work area for treatments and procedures
- Sterilize dental instruments
- Hand instruments to dentists during procedures
- Dry patients' mouths using suction hoses and other equipment

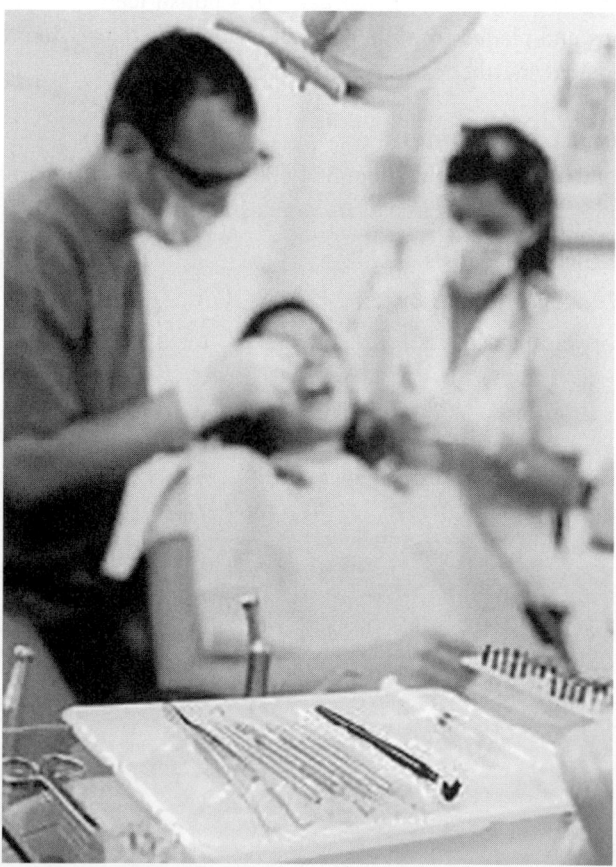

Assistants prepare and organize tools needed by dentists to work on a patient.

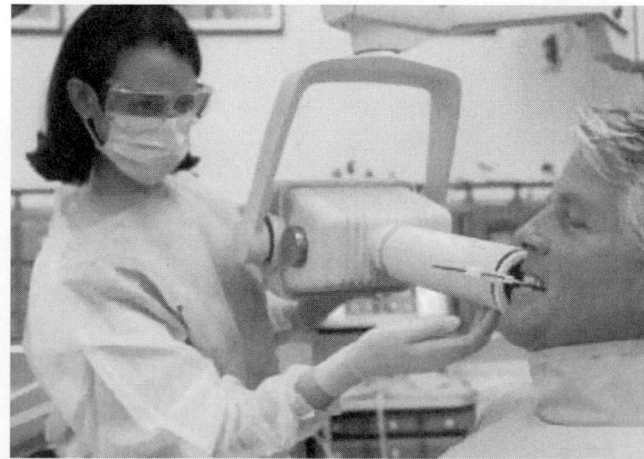

Dental assistants perform many tasks, ranging from providing patient care and taking x rays to recordkeeping and scheduling appointments.

- Instruct patients in proper oral hygiene
- Process x rays and complete lab tasks, under the direction of a dentist
- Keep records of dental treatments
- Schedule patient appointments
- Work with patients on billing and payment

Dental assistants often spend much of their day working closely with patients and dentists. For example, dental assistants might take a patient's medical history, blood pressure, and pulse before a procedure; explain what will be done; and talk to patients about oral care. They help dentists during a procedure by passing instruments and holding equipment such as suction hoses, matrix bands, and dental curing lights. Other tasks include preparing the treatment room and making sure that instruments and equipment are sterile. Dental assistants also may document the procedure that is done and schedule followup appointments.

Some dental assistants are specially trained to take x rays of teeth and the surrounding areas. They place a protective apron over patients' chest and lap, position the x-ray machine, place the x-ray sensor or film in patients' mouths, and take the x rays. Afterward, dental assistants ensure that the images are clear.

Assistants who perform lab tasks, such as taking impressions of a patient's teeth, work under the direction of a dentist. They may prepare materials for dental impressions or temporary crowns.

Each state regulates the scope of practice for dental assistants. Some states let dental assistants polish teeth to remove stains and plaque from the enamel or apply sealants, fluoride, or topical anesthetic.

Work Environment

Dental assistants held about 354,600 jobs in 2019. The largest employers of dental assistants were as follows:

Offices of dentists	90%
Offices of physicians	2
Government	2

Dental assistants work under the supervision of dentists and work closely with dental hygienists in their day-to-day activities.

Dental assistants wear safety glasses, surgical masks, protective clothing, and gloves to protect themselves and patients from infectious diseases. They also must follow safety procedures to minimize risks associated with x-ray machines.

Work Schedules

Most dental assistants work full time. Some work evenings or weekends.

How to Become a Dental Assistant

There are several possible paths to becoming a dental assistant. Some states require assistants to graduate from an accredited program and pass an exam. In other states, there are no formal educational requirements, and dental assistants learn through on-the-job training.

Education

Some states require dental assistants to graduate from an accredited program and pass an exam. Most programs are offered by community colleges, although they also may be offered by vocational or technical schools.

Many dental assisting programs take about 1 year to complete and lead to a certificate or diploma. Programs that last 2 years are less common and lead to an associate's degree. The Commission on Dental Accreditation (CODA), part of the American Dental Association, accredits about 250 dental assisting training programs.

Accredited programs include classroom and laboratory work. Students learn about teeth, gums, jaws, and other areas that dentists work on and the instruments that dentists use. These programs also include supervised practical experience.

High school students interested in a career as a dental assistant should take courses in anatomy, biology, and chemistry.

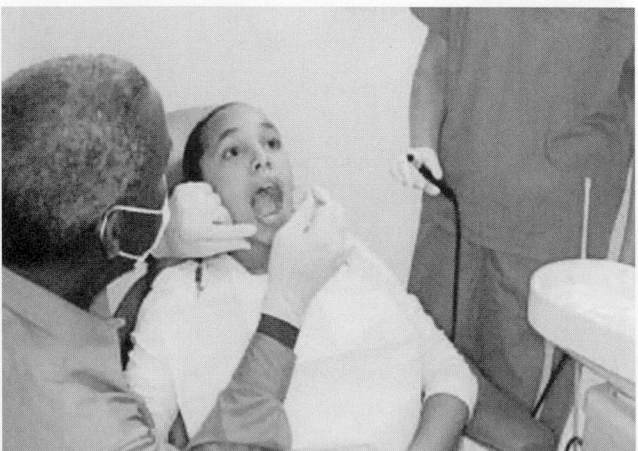

Dental assistants provide support to dentists as they work on patients.

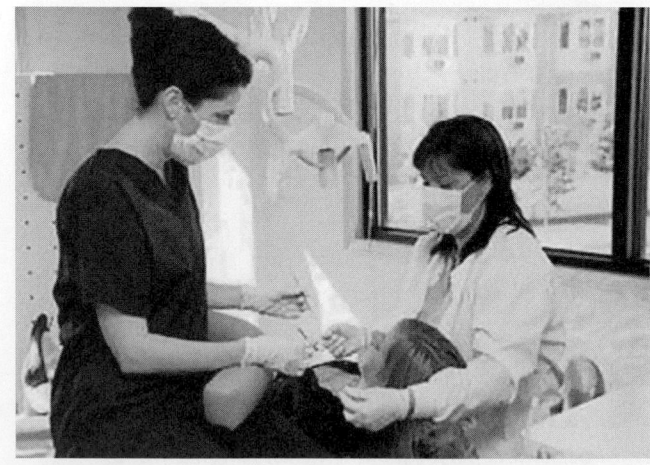

Sometimes, patients are in extreme pain and/or mental distress, so the assistant should be sensitive to their emotions.

Training

Dental assistants who do not have formal education in dental assisting may learn their duties through on-the-job training. In the office, a dental hygienist, dentist, or experienced dental assistant teaches the new assistant dental terminology, the names of the instruments, how to complete daily tasks, how to interact with patients, and other activities necessary to help keep the dental office running smoothly.

Important Qualities

Detail oriented. Dental assistants must follow specific rules and protocols, such as infection control procedures, when helping dentists treat patients.

Dexterity. Dental assistants must be good at working with their hands. They generally work in tight spaces on a small part of the body, using precise tools and instruments.

Interpersonal skills. Dental assistants work closely with dentists. They also must be considerate in working with patients who are sensitive to pain or have a fear of undergoing dental treatment.

Listening skills. Dental assistants must pay attention to patients and other healthcare workers. They need to follow directions from a dentist or dental hygienist so they can help treat patients and do tasks, such as taking x rays.

Organizational skills. Dental assistants should have excellent organizational skills. They need to have the correct tools in place for a dentist or dental hygienist to use when treating a patient, and they need to maintain patient schedules and office records.

Licenses, Certifications, and Registrations

States typically do not require licenses for entry-level dental assistants. Some states require dental assistants to be licensed, registered, or certified for entry or advancement. For example, states may require assistants to meet specific licensing requirements in order to work in radiography (x ray), infection control, or other specialties. For specific requirements, contact your state's Board of Dental Examiners.

States that allow assistants to perform expanded duties, such as coronal polishing, require that they be licensed, registered, or hold certifications from the Dental Assisting National Board (DANB). To earn certification from DANB, applicants must pass an exam. The educational requirements for DANB certification are that dental assistants must either have graduated from an accredited program or have a high school diploma and complete the required amount of work experience. Applicants also must have current certification in CPR (cardiopulmonary resuscitation).

Pay

The median annual wage for dental assistants was $40,080 in May 2019. The median wage is the wage at which half the workers in an occupation earned more than that amount and half earned less. The lowest 10 percent earned less than $27,980, and the highest 10 percent earned more than $56,930.

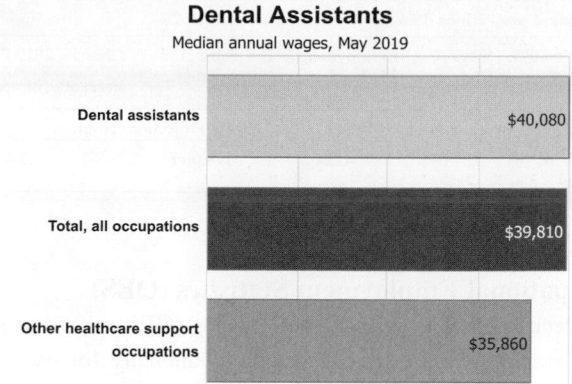

Dental Assistants
Median annual wages, May 2019

Note: All Occupations includes all occupations in the U.S. Economy.
Source: U.S. Bureau of Labor Statistics, Occupational Employment Statistics.

In May 2019, the median annual wages for dental assistants in the top industries in which they worked were as follows:

Government $42,960
Offices of dentists 40,120
Offices of physicians 37,570

Most dental assistants work full time. Some work evenings or weekends.

Job Outlook

Employment of dental assistants is projected to grow 7 percent from 2019 to 2029, faster than the average for all occupations. Ongoing research linking oral health and general health will continue to increase the demand for preventive dental services. Dentists will continue to hire dental assistants to complete routine tasks, allowing dentists to work more efficiently. As dental practices grow, more dental assistants will be needed.

As the large baby-boom population ages and as people keep more of their original teeth than did previous generations, the need to maintain and treat teeth will lead to continued increases in the need for dental care.

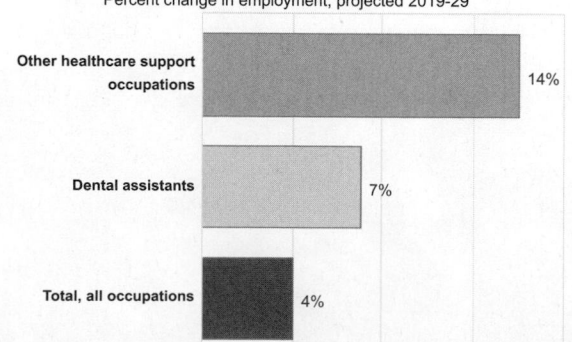

Dental Assistants
Percent change in employment, projected 2019-29

Note: All Occupations includes all occupations in the U.S. Economy.
Source: U.S. Bureau of Labor Statistics, Employment Projections program.

Employment projections data for dental assistants, 2019-29					
Occupational Title	SOC Code	Employment, 2019	Projected Employment, 2029	Change, 2019-29	
				Percent	Numeric
SOURCE: U.S. Bureau of Labor Statistics, Employment Projections program					
Dental assistants	31-9091	354,600	378,000	7	23,400

State & Area Data
Occupational Employment Statistics (OES)
The Occupational Employment Statistics (OES) program produces employment and wage estimates annually for over 800 occupations. These estimates are available for the nation as a whole, for individual states, and for metropolitan and nonmetropolitan areas.

Contacts for More Information
For more information about becoming a dental assistant and for a list of accredited dental assistant programs, visit
➤ American Dental Assistants Association
➤ Commission on Dental Accreditation, American Dental Association

For more information about becoming a Certified Dental Assistant and for a list of state boards of dentistry, visit
➤ Dental Assisting National Board, Inc.

Dental Hygienists

Summary

Quick Facts: Dental Hygienists

2019 Median Pay	$76,220 per year $36.65 per hour
Typical Entry-Level Education	Associate's degree
Work Experience in a Related Occupation	None
On-the-job Training	None
Number of Jobs, 2019	226,400
Job Outlook, 2019-29	6% (Faster than average)
Employment Change, 2019-29	13,300

What Dental Hygienists Do
Dental hygienists examine patients for signs of oral diseases, such as gingivitis, and provide preventive care, including oral hygiene.

Work Environment
Nearly all dental hygienists work in dentists' offices, and many work part time.

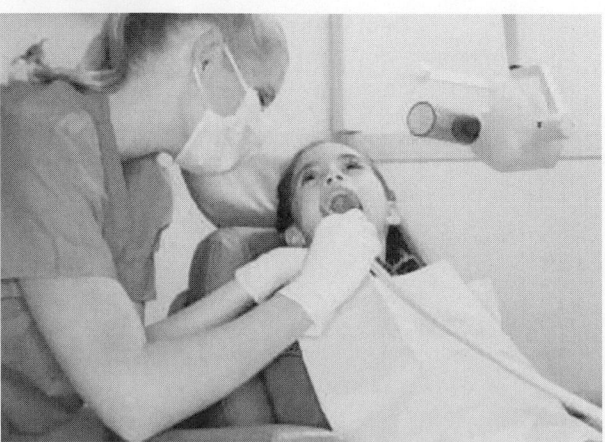

Dental hygienists examine patients' teeth and gums for signs of oral diseases or abnormalities.

How to Become a Dental Hygienist
Dental hygienists typically need an associate's degree in dental hygiene. Programs usually take 3 years to complete. All states require dental hygienists to be licensed; requirements vary by state.

Pay
The median annual wage for dental hygienists was $76,220 in May 2019.

Job Outlook
Employment of dental hygienists is projected to grow 6 percent from 2019 to 2029, faster than the average for all occupations. The demand for dental services will increase as the population ages and as research continues to link oral health to overall health.

State & Area Data
Explore resources for employment and wages by state and area for dental hygienists.

What Dental Hygienists Do
Dental hygienists examine patients for signs of oral diseases, such as gingivitis, and provide preventive care, including oral hygiene. They also educate patients about oral health.

Duties
Dental hygienists typically do the following:

• Remove tartar, stains, and plaque from teeth
• Apply sealants and fluorides to help protect teeth
• Take and develop dental x rays
• Assess patients' oral health and report findings to dentists
• Document patient care and treatment plans
• Educate patients about oral hygiene techniques, such as how to brush and floss correctly

Dental hygienists use many types of tools—including hand, power, and ultrasonic tools—in their work. In some cases, they use lasers. Hygienists remove stains with an air-polishing device, which sprays a combination of air, water, and baking soda. They polish teeth with a power tool that works like an automatic toothbrush. Hygienists also use x-ray machines to take pictures to check for tooth or jaw problems.

Dental hygienists talk to patients about ways to keep their teeth and gums healthy. For example, they may explain the relationship between diet and oral health. They may also advise patients on how to select toothbrushes and other oral care devices.

The tasks hygienists may perform, and the extent to which they must be supervised by a dentist, vary by state and by the setting in which the dental hygienist works. A few states allow hygienists with additional training, sometimes called *dental therapists*, to provide some restorative services, such as extracting primary teeth and placing temporary crowns.

Work Environment

Dental hygienists held about 226,400 jobs in 2019. The largest employers of dental hygienists were as follows:

Offices of dentists	93%
Offices of physicians	1
Government	1

Dental hygienists wear safety glasses, surgical masks, and gloves to protect themselves and patients from infectious diseases. When taking x rays, they follow procedures to protect themselves and patients from radiation.

Work Schedules

Many dental hygienists work part time. Dentists may hire hygienists to work only a few days a week, so some hygienists work for more than one dentist.

How to Become a Dental Hygienist

Dental hygienists typically need an associate's degree in dental hygiene. Programs usually take 3 years to complete. All states require dental hygienists to be licensed; requirements vary by state.

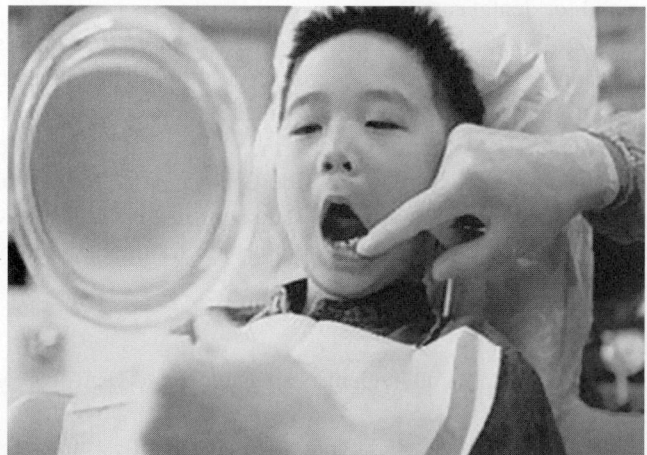

Dental hygienists wear safety glasses, surgical masks, and gloves to protect themselves and their patients from diseases.

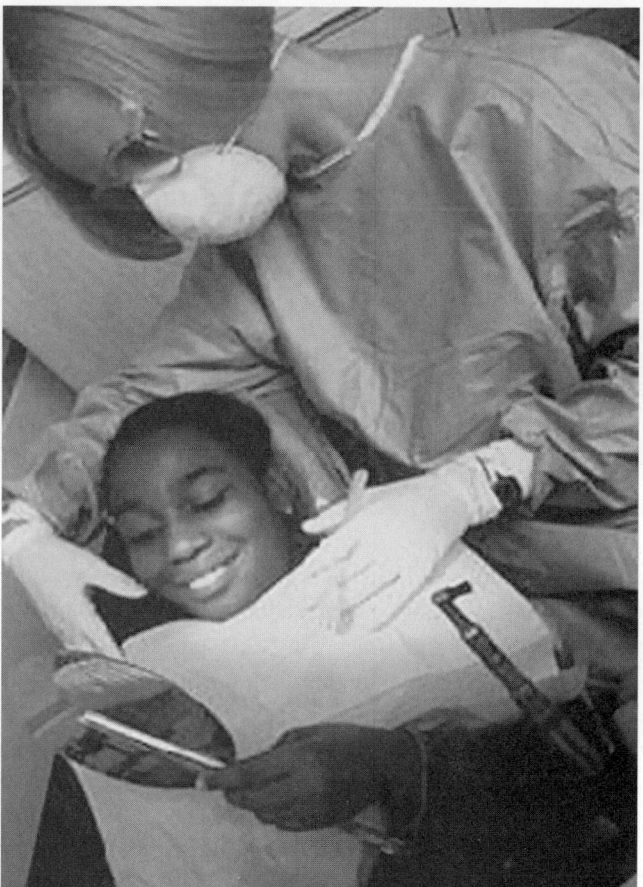

Dental hygienists discuss diet and other topics that affect a patient's dental health.

Education

Dental hygienists typically need an associate's degree in dental hygiene; they may also get a bachelor's degree. Master's degree programs in dental hygiene are available but are relatively uncommon. A bachelor's or master's degree usually is required for research, teaching, or clinical practice in public or school health programs.

Dental hygiene programs are often found in community colleges, technical schools, and universities. The Commission on Dental Accreditation, part of the American Dental Association, accredits more than 300 dental hygiene programs.

Programs typically take 3 years to complete and offer laboratory, clinical, and classroom instruction. Areas of study include anatomy, medical ethics, and periodontics, which is the study of gum disease.

High school students interested in becoming dental hygienists should take courses in biology, chemistry, and math. Most dental hygiene programs also require applicants to complete prerequisites, which often include college-level courses. Specific requirements vary by school.

Important Qualities

Critical thinking. Dental hygienists must be able to assess and evaluate patients and to develop oral hygiene care plans.

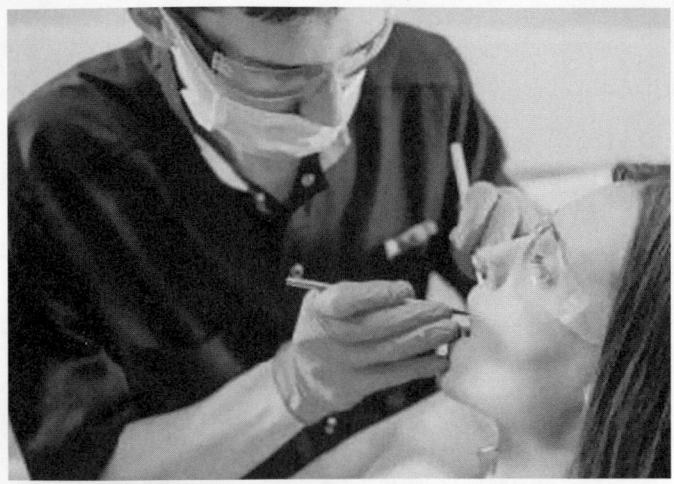

Dental hygienists remove tartar and plaque from teeth.

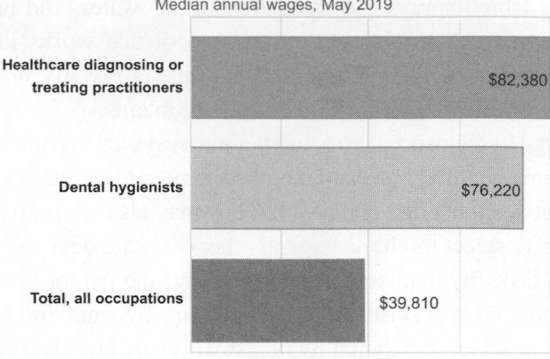

Dental Hygienists
Median annual wages, May 2019

Healthcare diagnosing or treating practitioners	$82,380
Dental hygienists	$76,220
Total, all occupations	$39,810

Note: All Occupations includes all occupations in the U.S. Economy.
Source: U.S. Bureau of Labor Statistics, Occupational Employment Statistics.

Communication skills. Dental hygienists must share information with dentists and patients about oral health status, oral hygiene care plans, and, if necessary, lifestyle counseling.

Detail oriented. Dental hygienists must follow specific rules and protocols to help dentists diagnose and treat a patient. Depending on the state in which they work and/or the treatment provided, dental hygienists may work without the direct supervision of a dentist.

Dexterity. Dental hygienists must be good at working with their hands. They generally work in tight spaces on a small part of the body, which requires fine motor skills using precise tools and instruments.

Interpersonal skills. Dental hygienists work closely with dentists. They also must be considerate in working with patients, especially with those who are sensitive to pain or who have fears about undergoing dental treatment.

Problem-solving skills. Dental hygienists develop and implement oral hygiene care plans to maintain or improve patients' oral health.

Licenses, Certifications, and Registrations

Every state requires dental hygienists to be licensed; requirements vary by state. In most states, a degree from an accredited dental hygiene program and passing written and clinical examinations are required for licensure. To maintain licensure, hygienists must complete continuing education requirements. For specific requirements, contact your state's Board of Dental Examiners.

Many jobs also require cardiopulmonary resuscitation (CPR) certification.

Pay

The median annual wage for dental hygienists was $76,220 in May 2019. The median wage is the wage at which half the workers in an occupation earned more than that amount and half earned less. The lowest 10 percent earned less than $53,130, and the highest 10 percent earned more than $103,340.

In May 2019, the median annual wages for dental hygienists in the top industries in which they worked were as follows:

Offices of dentists	$76,510
Offices of physicians	72,690
Government	60,390

Benefits, such as vacation, sick leave, and retirement contributions, vary by employer and may be available only to full-time workers.

Many dental hygienists work part time. Dentists may hire hygienists to work only a few days a week, so some hygienists work for more than one dentist.

Job Outlook

Employment of dental hygienists is projected to grow 6 percent from 2019 to 2029, faster than the average for all occupations.

The demand for dental services will increase as the population ages. As the large baby-boom population ages and people keep more of their original teeth than did previous generations, the need to maintain and treat teeth will continue to drive demand for dental care.

Studies linking oral health and general health, and efforts to expand access to oral hygiene services, will continue to drive the demand for preventive dental services. As a result, the demand for all dental services, including those performed by hygienists, will increase. In addition, demand for dental hygienists is expected to grow as state laws increasingly allow dental hygienists to work at the top of their training, and they effectively become more productive.

Job Prospects

Job prospects for dental hygienists are expected to vary by geographic location.

Entry into dental hygiene programs is often competitive, with the number of applicants to accredited dental hygiene programs exceeding the number of students accepted. In addition,

Dental Hygienists
Percent change in employment, projected 2019-29

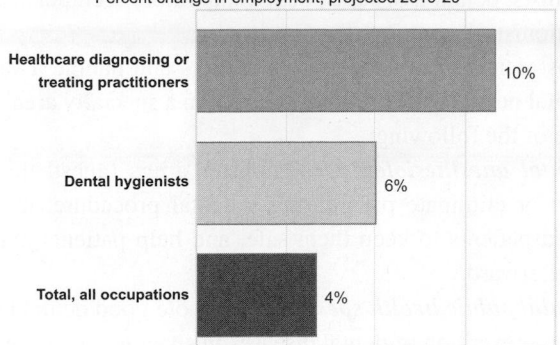

Healthcare diagnosing or treating practitioners	10%
Dental hygienists	6%
Total, all occupations	4%

Note: All Occupations includes all occupations in the U.S. Economy.
Source: U.S. Bureau of Labor Statistics, Employment Projections program.

Employment projections data for dental hygienists, 2019-29					
Occupational Title	SOC Code	Employment, 2019	Projected Employment, 2029	Change, 2019-29	
				Percent	Numeric
SOURCE: U.S. Bureau of Labor Statistics, Employment Projections program					
Dental hygienists	29-1292	226,400	239,700	6	13,300

dental hygienists are less likely to leave their occupation than are workers in other occupations. But overall job prospects are expected to be relatively good as the number of openings in this occupation is projected to exceed the number of graduates from dental hygiene programs.

Opportunities are expected to be best for dental hygienists who are willing to work in underserved areas and for those who are open to working less than 40 hours a week.

State & Area Data
Occupational Employment Statistics (OES)

The Occupational Employment Statistics (OES) program produces employment and wage estimates annually for over 800 occupations. These estimates are available for the nation as a whole, for individual states, and for metropolitan and nonmetropolitan areas.

Contacts for More Information

For information about educational requirements and available accredited programs for dental hygienists, visit
➤ American Dental Hygienists' Association

For information about accredited programs and educational requirements, visit
➤ Commission on Dental Accreditation, American Dental Association
➤ The State Board of Dental Examiners in each state can provide information on licensing requirements.

Dentists

Summary

Quick Facts: Dentists

2019 Median Pay	$159,200 per year $76.54 per hour
Typical Entry-Level Education	Doctoral or professional degree
Work Experience in a Related Occupation	None
On-the-job Training	See below
Number of Jobs, 2019	151,600
Job Outlook, 2019-29	3% (As fast as average)
Employment Change, 2019-29	4,000

What Dentists Do

Dentists diagnose and treat problems with patients' teeth, gums, and related parts of the mouth.

Work Environment

Some dentists have their own business and work alone or with a small staff. Other dentists have partners in their practice. Still others work as associate dentists for established dental practices.

How to Become a Dentist

Dentists must be licensed in the state in which they work. Licensure requirements vary by state, although candidates usually must graduate from an accredited dental program and pass written and clinical exams.

Pay

The median annual wage for dentists was $159,200 in May 2019.

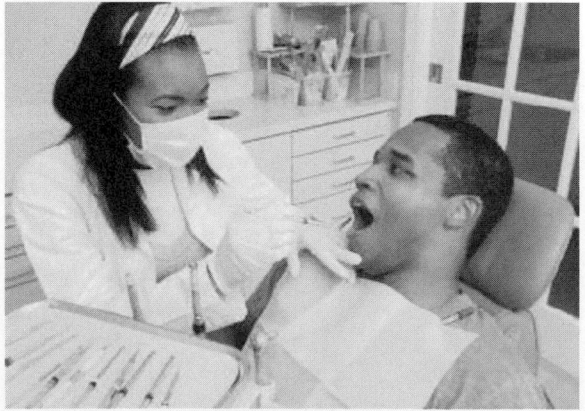

Dentists diagnose and treat problems with a patient's teeth, gums, and related parts of the mouth.

Job Outlook

Overall employment of dentists is projected to grow 3 percent from 2019 to 2029, about as fast as the average for all occupations. The demand for dental services will increase as the population ages and as research continues to link oral health to overall health.

State & Area Data

Explore resources for employment and wages by state and area for dentists.

What Dentists Do

Dentists diagnose and treat problems with patients' teeth, gums, and related parts of the mouth. They provide advice and instruction on taking care of the teeth and gums and on diet choices that affect oral health.

Duties

Dentists typically do the following:

- Remove decay from teeth and fill cavities
- Repair or remove damaged teeth
- Place sealants or whitening agents on teeth
- Administer anesthetics to keep patients from feeling pain during procedures
- Prescribe antibiotics or other medications
- Examine x rays of teeth, gums, the jaw, and nearby areas in order to diagnose problems
- Make models and measurements for dental appliances, such as dentures
- Teach patients about diets, flossing, the use of fluoride, and other aspects of dental care

Dentists use a variety of equipment, including x-ray machines, drills, mouth mirrors, probes, forceps, brushes, and scalpels. They also use lasers, digital scanners, and other technologies.

In addition, dentists in private practice oversee a variety of administrative tasks, including bookkeeping and buying equipment and supplies. They employ and supervise dental hygienists, dental assistants, dental laboratory technicians, and receptionists.

Most dentists are general practitioners and handle a variety of dental needs. Other dentists practice in a specialty area, such as one of the following:

Dental anesthesiologists administer drugs (anesthetics) to reduce or eliminate pain during a dental procedure, monitor sedated patients to keep them safe, and help patients manage pain afterward.

Dental public health specialists promote good dental health and the prevention of dental diseases in specific communities.

Endodontists perform root canal therapy, removing the nerves and blood supply from injured or infected teeth.

Oral and maxillofacial radiologists diagnose diseases in the head and neck through the use of imaging technologies.

Oral and maxillofacial surgeons operate on the mouth, jaws, teeth, gums, neck, and head, performing procedures such as surgically repairing a cleft lip and palate or removing impacted teeth.

Oral pathologists diagnose conditions in the mouth, such as bumps or ulcers, and oral diseases, such as cancer.

Orthodontists straighten teeth by applying pressure to the teeth with braces or other appliances.

Pediatric dentists focus on dentistry for children and special-needs patients.

Periodontists treat the gums and bones supporting the teeth.

Dentists also may do research. Or, they may teach part time, including supervising students in dental school clinics. For more information, see the profiles on medical scientists and postsecondary teachers.

Work Environment

Dentists held about 151,600 jobs in 2019. Employment in the detailed occupations that make up dentists was distributed as follows:

Dentists, general	132,100
Orthodontists	7,200
Dentists, all other specialists	6,200
Oral and maxillofacial surgeons	5,600
Prosthodontists	600

The largest employers of dentists were as follows:

Offices of dentists	74%
Self-employed workers	15
Government	3
Offices of physicians	2
Outpatient care centers	2

Some dentists have their own business and work alone or with a small staff. Other dentists have partners in their practice. Still others work as associate dentists for established dental practices.

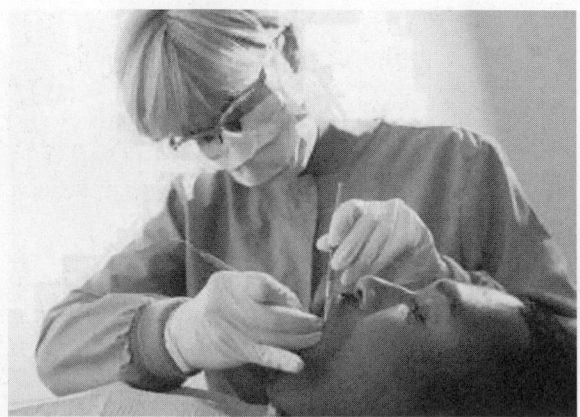

Dentists remove tooth decay, fill cavities, and repair fractured teeth.

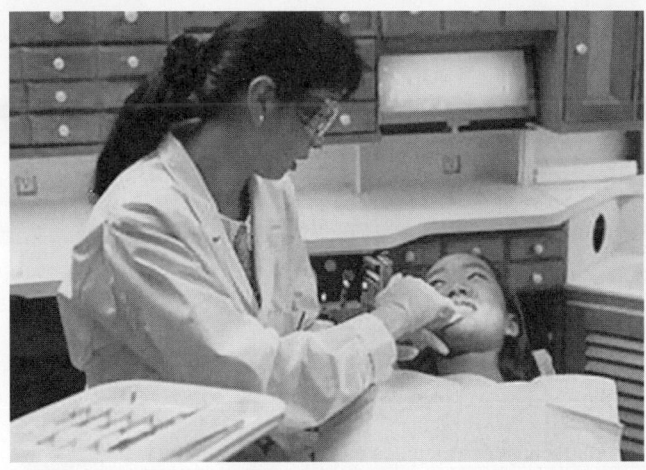

Dentists provide instruction on diet, brushing, flossing, the use of fluorides, and other areas of dental care.

Dentists wear masks, gloves, and safety glasses to protect themselves and their patients from infectious diseases.

Work Schedules

Dentists' work schedules vary. Some work evenings and weekends to meet their patients' needs. Many dentists work less than 40 hours a week, although some work considerably more.

How to Become a Dentist

Dentists must be licensed in the state in which they work. Licensure requirements vary by state, although candidates usually must have a Doctor of Dental Surgery (DDS) or Doctor of Medicine in Dentistry/Doctor of Dental Medicine (DMD) degree from an accredited dental program and pass written and clinical exams. Dentists who practice in a specialty area must complete postdoctoral training.

Education

Dentists typically need a DDS or DMD degree from a dental program that has been accredited by the Commission on Dental Accreditation (CODA). Most programs require that applicants have at least a bachelor's degree and have completed certain science courses, such as biology or chemistry. Although no specific undergraduate major is required, programs may prefer applicants who major in a science, such as biology.

Applicants to dental schools usually take the Dental Admission Test (DAT). Dental schools use this test along with other factors, such as grade point average, interviews, and recommendations, to admit students into their programs.

Dental school programs typically include coursework in subjects such as local anesthesia, anatomy, periodontics (the study of oral disease and health), and radiology. All programs at dental schools include clinical experience in which students work directly with patients under the supervision of a licensed dentist.

As early as high school, students interested in becoming dentists can take courses in subjects such as biology, chemistry, and math.

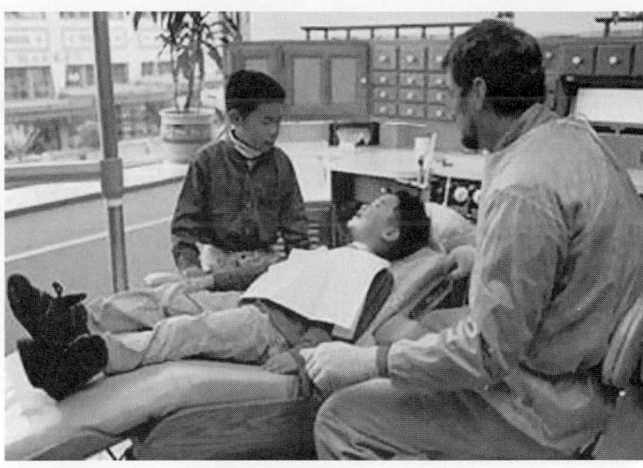

Dentists must be licensed in all states; requirements vary by state.

Training

All dental specialties require dentists to complete additional training before practicing that specialty. This training is usually a 2- to 4-year residency in a CODA-accredited program related to the specialty, which often culminates in a postdoctoral certificate or master's degree. Oral and maxillofacial surgery programs typically take 4 to 6 years and may result in candidates earning a joint Medical Doctor (M.D.) degree.

General dentists do not need additional training after dental school.

Dentists who want to teach or do research full time may need advanced dental training, such as in a postdoctoral program in general dentistry.

Licenses, Certifications, and Registrations

Dentists must be licensed in the state in which they work. All states require dentists to be licensed; requirements vary by state. Most states require a dentist to have a DDS or DMD degree from an accredited dental program, pass the written National Board Dental Examinations, and pass a state or regional clinical examination.

In addition, a dentist who wants to practice in a dental specialty must have a license in that specialty. Licensure requires the completion of a residency after dental school and, in some cases, the completion of a special state exam.

Important Qualities

Communication skills. Dentists must communicate effectively with patients, dental hygienists, dental assistants, and receptionists.

Detail oriented. Dentists must pay attention to the shape and color of teeth and to the space between them. For example, they may need to closely match a false tooth with a patient's other teeth.

Dexterity. Dentists must be good with their hands. They must work carefully with tools in small spaces to ensure the safety of their patients.

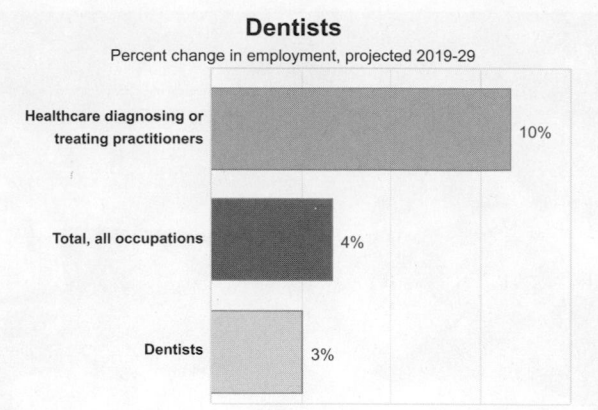

Dentists
Median annual wages, May 2019

Dentists	$159,200
Healthcare diagnosing or treating practitioners	$82,380
Total, all occupations	$39,810

Note: All Occupations includes all occupations in the U.S. Economy.
Source: U.S. Bureau of Labor Statistics, Occupational Employment Statistics.

Dentists
Percent change in employment, projected 2019-29

Healthcare diagnosing or treating practitioners	10%
Total, all occupations	4%
Dentists	3%

Note: All Occupations includes all occupations in the U.S. Economy.
Source: U.S. Bureau of Labor Statistics, Employment Projections program.

Leadership skills. Dentists, especially those with their own practices, may need to manage staff or mentor other dentists.

Organizational skills. Keeping accurate records of patient care is critical in both medical and business settings.

Patience. Dentists may work for long periods with patients who need special attention, including children and those with a fear of dental work.

Problem-solving skills. Dentists must evaluate patients' symptoms and choose the appropriate treatment.

Pay

The median annual wage for dentists was $159,200 in May 2019. The median wage is the wage at which half the workers in an occupation earned more than that amount and half earned less. The lowest 10 percent earned less than $79,670, and the highest 10 percent earned more than $208,000.

Median annual wages for dentists in May 2019 were as follows:

Orthodontists	$208,000 or more
Prosthodontists	208,000 or more
Oral and maxillofacial surgeons	208,000 or more
Dentists, general	155,600
Dentists, all other specialists	147,220

In May 2019, the median annual wages for dentists in the top industries in which they worked were as follows:

Offices of dentists	$163,470
Outpatient care centers	149,830
Offices of physicians	149,310
Government	132,320

Wages vary with the dentist's location, number of hours worked, specialty, and number of years in practice.

Dentists' work schedules vary. Some work evenings and weekends to meet their patients' needs. Many dentists work less than 40 hours a week, although some may work considerably more.

Job Outlook

Overall employment of dentists is projected to grow 3 percent from 2019 to 2029, about as fast as the average for all occupations.

Demand for dental services will increase as the population ages. Many members of the aging baby-boom generation will need dental work. Because those in each generation are more likely to keep their teeth than those in past generations, more dental care will be needed in the years to come. In addition, there will be increased demand for complicated dental work, including dental implants and bridges. The risk of oral cancer increases significantly with age, and complications can require both cosmetic and functional dental reconstruction.

Demand for dentists' services will increase as studies continue to link oral health to overall health. They will need to provide care and instruction aimed at promoting good oral hygiene, rather than just providing treatments such as fillings.

Job Prospects

Job prospects for dentists are expected to be relatively good, especially for dentists who are willing to work in underserved areas. However, the number of graduates from dental programs has increased in recent years. And the rate at which these workers leave the occupation is expected to be lower than that for other occupations. Therefore, there may be competition for jobs, particularly in areas where there are already sufficient numbers of dentists.

Employment projections data for dentists, 2019-29					
Occupational Title	SOC Code	Employment, 2019	Projected Employment, 2029	Change, 2019-29	
				Percent	Numeric
SOURCE: U.S. Bureau of Labor Statistics, Employment Projections program					
Dentists	29-1020	151,600	155,500	3	4,000
Dentists, general	29-1021	132,100	135,700	3	3,700
Oral and maxillofacial surgeons	29-1022	5,600	5,700	2	100

Employment projections data for dentists, 2019-29					
Occupational Title	SOC Code	Employment, 2019	Projected Employment, 2029	Change, 2019-29	
				Percent	Numeric
Orthodontists	29-1023	7,200	7,300	2	200
Prosthodontists	29-1024	600	600	2	0
Dentists, all other specialists	29-1029	6,200	6,200	0	0

State & Area Data
Occupational Employment Statistics (OES)
The Occupational Employment Statistics (OES) program produces employment and wage estimates annually for over 800 occupations. These estimates are available for the nation as a whole, for individual states, and for metropolitan and nonmetropolitan areas.

Contacts for More Information
For more information about dentists, including information on accredited dental schools and state boards of dental examiners, visit
➤ American Dental Association, Commission on Dental Accreditation

For information about admission to dental schools, visit
➤ American Dental Education Association

For more information about general dentistry or on a specific dental specialty, visit
➤ Academy of General Dentistry
➤ American Academy of Oral and Maxillofacial Pathology
➤ American Academy of Oral and Maxillofacial Radiology
➤ American Association of Oral and Maxillofacial Surgeons
➤ American Academy of Pediatric Dentistry
➤ American Academy of Periodontology
➤ American Association of Endodontists
➤ American Association of Orthodontists
➤ American Association of Public Health Dentistry
➤ American College of Prosthodontists
➤ American Society of Dentist Anesthesiologists

Diagnostic Medical Sonographers and Cardiovascular Technologists and Technicians, Including Vascular Technologists

Summary

Quick Facts: Diagnostic Medical Sonographers and Cardiovascular Technologists and Technicians, Including Vascular Technologists

2019 Median Pay	$68,750 per year $33.05 per hour
Typical Entry-Level Education	Associate's degree
Work Experience in a Related Occupation	None
On-the-job Training	None
Number of Jobs, 2019	131,700
Job Outlook, 2019-29	12% (Much faster than average)
Employment Change, 2019-29	15,600

What Diagnostic Medical Sonographers and Cardiovascular Technologists and Technicians, Including Vascular Technologists Do
Diagnostic medical sonographers and cardiovascular technologists and technicians, including vascular technologists operate special imaging equipment to create images or to conduct tests.

Work Environment
Most diagnostic medical sonographers and cardiovascular technologists and technicians, including vascular technologists, work full time. Most diagnostic imaging workers are employed in hospitals, while most of the rest worked in physicians' offices or medical and diagnostic laboratories.

How to Become a Diagnostic Medical Sonographer or Cardiovascular Technologist or Technician, Including Vascular Technologist
Diagnostic medical sonographers and cardiovascular technologists and technicians, including vascular technologists, need formal education, such as an associate's degree or a postsecondary certificate. Many employers also require professional certification.

Pay
The median annual wage for cardiovascular technologists and technicians was $57,720 in May 2019.

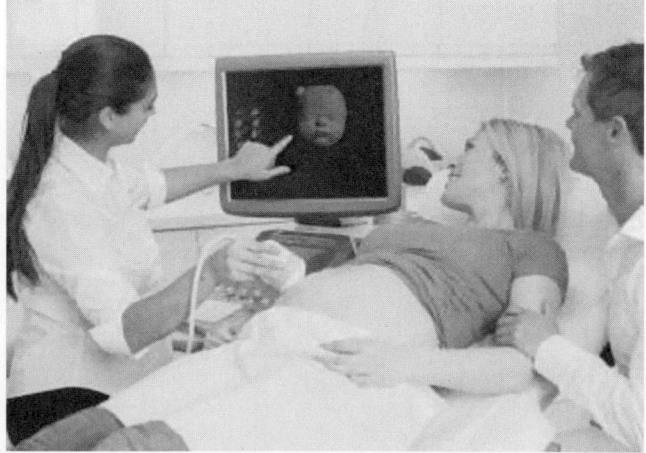

Diagnostic medical sonographers operate special equipment to create images.

The median annual wage for diagnostic medical sonographers was $74,320 in May 2019.

Job Outlook

Overall employment of diagnostic medical sonographers and cardiovascular technologists and technicians is projected to grow 12 percent from 2019 to 2029, much faster than the average for all occupations. As the large baby-boom population ages, the need to diagnose medical conditions—such as blood clots and heart disease—will likely increase. Imaging technology is a tool used in making these diagnoses.

State & Area Data

Explore resources for employment and wages by state and area for diagnostic medical sonographers and cardiovascular technologists and technicians, including vascular technologists.

What Diagnostic Medical Sonographers and Cardiovascular Technologists and Technicians, Including Vascular Technologists Do

Diagnostic medical sonographers and cardiovascular technologists and technicians, including vascular technologists, also called *diagnostic imaging workers*, operate special imaging equipment to create images or conduct tests. The images and test results help physicians assess and diagnose medical conditions. Sonographers and technologists may work closely with physicians and surgeons before, during, and after procedures.

Duties

Diagnostic medical sonographers and cardiovascular technologists and technicians, including vascular technologists, typically do the following:

- Prepare patients for procedures by taking their medical history and answering any questions about the procedure
- Prepare and maintain diagnostic imaging equipment

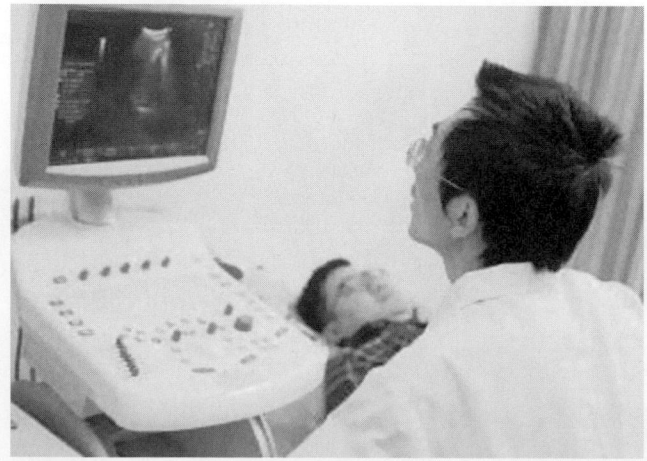

Diagnostic sonographers use high-frequency sound waves to produce images of the inside of the body.

- Operate equipment to obtain diagnostic images or to conduct tests
- Review images or test results to check for quality and adequate coverage of the areas needed for diagnoses
- Recognize the difference between normal and abnormal images, and identify other diagnostic information
- Analyze diagnostic information to provide a summary of findings for physicians
- Record findings and keep track of patients' records

Diagnostic medical sonographers specialize in creating images of the body's organs and tissues. The images are known as sonograms or ultrasounds. Sonograms are often the first imaging tests performed when disease is suspected.

Diagnostic sonography uses high-frequency sound waves to produce images of the inside of the body. The sonographer uses an instrument called an ultrasound transducer to scan parts of the patient's body that are being examined. The transducer emits pulses of sound that bounce back, causing echoes. The echoes are then sent to an ultrasound machine, which processes them and displays them as images used by physicians for diagnosis.

The following are examples of types of diagnostic medical sonographers:

- *Abdominal sonographers* specialize in imaging a patient's abdominal cavity and nearby organs, such as the kidney, liver, gallbladder, pancreas, or spleen. Abdominal sonographers may assist with biopsies or other examinations requiring ultrasound guidance.
- *Breast sonographers* specialize in imaging a patient's breast tissues. Sonography can confirm the presence of cysts and tumors that may have been detected by the patient, the physician, or a mammogram. Breast sonographers work closely with physicians and assist with procedures that track tumors and help to provide information that will aid doctors in making decisions about the best treatment options for breast cancer patients.
- *Cardiac sonographers* (*echocardiographers*) specialize in imaging a patient's heart. They use ultrasound equipment to examine the heart's chambers, valves, and vessels. The images obtained are known as echocardiograms. An echocardiogram may be performed either while the patient is resting or after the patient has been physically active. Cardiac sonographers also may take echocardiograms of fetal hearts so that physicians can diagnose cardiac conditions during pregnancy. Cardiac sonographers work closely with physicians or surgeons before, during, and after procedures.
- *Musculoskeletal sonographers* specialize in imaging muscles, ligaments, tendons, and joints. These sonographers may assist with ultrasound guidance for injections, or during surgical procedures, that deliver medication or treatment directly to affected tissues.
- *Pediatric sonographers* specialize in imaging children and infants. Many of the medical conditions they image are

associated with premature births or birth defects. Pediatric sonographers may work closely with pediatricians and other caregivers.

- *Obstetric and gynecologic sonographers* specialize in imaging the female reproductive system. Many pregnant women receive sonograms to track the baby's growth and health. Obstetrical sonographers work closely with physicians in detecting congenital birth defects.

- *Vascular technologists* (*vascular sonographers*) create images of blood vessels and collect data that help physicians diagnose disorders affecting blood flow. Vascular technologists often measure a patient's blood pressure and the volume of blood in their arms, legs, fingers, and toes in order to evaluate blood flow and identify blocked arteries or blood clots in the body.

Cardiovascular technologists and technicians create images and conduct tests involving the heart and lungs. The following are examples of types of cardiovascular technologists and technicians:

- *Cardiovascular invasive specialists*, also known as *cardiac catheterization technologists* or *cardiovascular technologists*, monitor patients' heart rates and help physicians in diagnosing and treating problems with patients' hearts. They assist with cardiac catheterization, which involves threading a catheter through a patient's artery to the heart. They also prepare and monitor patients during open-heart surgery and during the insertion of pacemakers and stents. Technologists prepare patients for procedures by shaving and cleansing the area into which the catheter will be inserted and by administering topical anesthesia. During the procedure, they monitor the patient's blood pressure and heart rate.

- *Cardiographic or electrocardiogram (EKG) technicians* specialize in EKG testing. EKG machines monitor the heart's performance through electrodes attached to a patient's chest, arms, and legs. The tests can be done while the patient is at rest or while the patient is physically active. For a stress test, the patient walks on a treadmill and the technician gradually increases the speed to observe the effect on the heart of increased exertion.

- *Pulmonary function technologists*, also known as *cardiopulmonary technologists*, monitor and test patients' lungs and breathing. For example, they use spirometry to measure the amount of air that a patient can inhale or exhale. These technologists help physicians in diagnosing and treating problems of the pulmonary system.

Work Environment

Cardiovascular technologists and technicians held about 57,400 jobs in 2019. The largest employers of cardiovascular technologists and technicians were as follows:

Hospitals; state, local, and private 79%

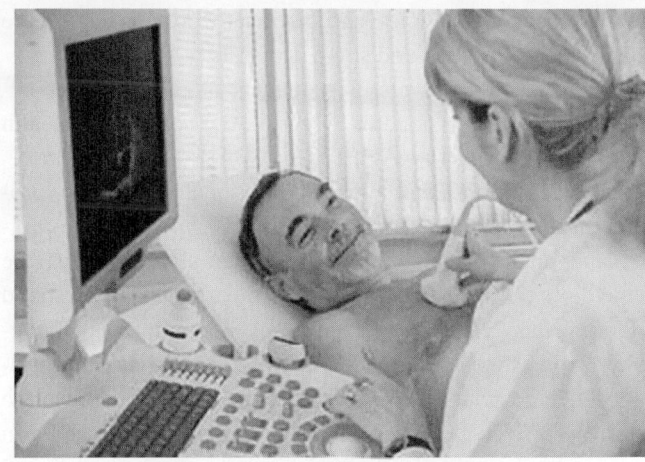

Diagnostic imaging workers may perform procedures at patients' bedsides.

Offices of physicians 12
Outpatient care centers 3
Medical and diagnostic laboratories 2

Diagnostic medical sonographers held about 74,300 jobs in 2019. The largest employers of diagnostic medical sonographers were as follows:

Hospitals; state, local, and private 61%
Offices of physicians 21
Medical and diagnostic laboratories 11
Outpatient care centers 4

Diagnostic medical sonographers and cardiovascular technologists and technicians, including vascular technologists, complete most of their work at diagnostic imaging machines in dimly lit rooms. They may perform procedures at patients' bedsides. Diagnostic imaging workers may be on their feet for long periods and may need to lift or turn patients who are ill or disabled.

Work Schedules

Most diagnostic imaging workers work full time. Some may work evenings, weekends, or overnight because they work in facilities that are always open.

How to Become a Diagnostic Medical Sonographer or Cardiovascular Technologist or Technician, Including Vascular Technologist

Diagnostic medical sonographers and cardiovascular technologists and technicians, including vascular technologists, need formal education, such as an associate's degree or a postsecondary certificate. Many employers also require professional certification.

Education

Colleges and universities offer both associate's and bachelor's degree programs in sonography and in cardiovascular and vascular technology. One-year certificate programs also are available from colleges and some hospitals.

Employers typically prefer graduates of programs accredited by the Commission on Accreditation of Allied Health Education Programs (CAAHEP).

Sonography, cardiovascular, and vascular education programs usually include courses in anatomy, medical terminology, and applied sciences. Most sonography programs are divided into the specialized fields listed earlier that correspond to the relevant certification exams, such as abdominal sonography or breast sonography. Cardiovascular and vascular programs include coursework in either invasive or noninvasive cardiovascular or vascular technology procedures. In addition to requiring classroom study, most programs include a clinical component in which students earn credit while working under a more experienced technologist in a hospital, a physician's office, or an imaging laboratory.

High school students who are interested in diagnostic medical sonography, cardiovascular technology, or vascular technology should take courses in anatomy, physiology, physics, and math.

Licenses, Certifications, and Registrations

Most employers prefer to hire diagnostic imaging workers with professional certification, or they may expect applicants to earn certification shortly after being hired. Many insurance providers and Medicare pay for procedures only if a certified sonographer, technologist, or technician performed the work. Certification is available from the American Registry for Diagnostic Medical Sonographers, Cardiovascular Credentialing International, and American Registry of Radiologic Technologists.

Diagnostic imaging workers can earn certification by graduating from an accredited program, although candidates also may qualify through alternative combinations of education and experience. All candidates must pass an exam. Most of

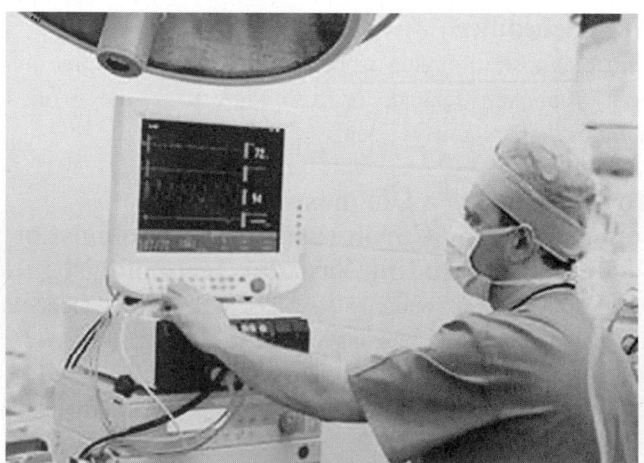

Cardiovascular technologists monitor patients' heart rates and perform and assist in the diagnosis and treatment of problems having to do with the patient's heart.

the certifications are for specialties in diagnostic imaging; for example, a sonographer can earn a certification in abdominal sonography. Most diagnostic imaging workers have at least one certification, but many earn multiple certifications.

In addition, many employers prefer to hire candidates who have a basic life support (BLS) certification, which affirms that they are trained to provide CPR.

Few states require diagnostic medical sonographers to be licensed. Typically, professional certification is required for licensure; other requirements vary by state. Contact state medical boards for more information.

Important Qualities

Detail oriented. Diagnostic imaging workers must follow precise instructions to obtain the images needed to diagnose and treat patients. They must also pay attention to the screen while scanning a patient's body, because the cues that contrast healthy areas with unhealthy ones may be subtle.

Hand–eye coordination. To get quality images, diagnostic imaging workers must accurately move equipment on the patient's body in response to what they see on the screen.

Interpersonal skills. Diagnostic imaging workers must work closely with patients. Sometimes patients are in extreme pain or mental stress, and these workers must get cooperation from the patients in order to create usable images. Diagnostic imaging workers must also communicate clearly when discussing images with physicians and other members of the healthcare team.

Physical stamina. Diagnostic imaging workers are on their feet for long periods and must be able to lift and move patients who need assistance.

Technical skills. Diagnostic imaging workers must understand how to operate complex machinery and computerized instruments.

Pay

The median annual wage for cardiovascular technologists and technicians was $57,720 in May 2019. The median wage is the wage at which half the workers in an occupation earned more than that amount and half earned less. The lowest 10 percent earned less than $29,710, and the highest 10 percent earned more than $94,370.

The median annual wage for diagnostic medical sonographers was $74,320 in May 2019. The lowest 10 percent earned less than $52,770, and the highest 10 percent earned more than $102,060.

In May 2019, the median annual wages for cardiovascular technologists and technicians in the top industries in which they worked were as follows:

Outpatient care centers	$71,480
Offices of physicians	61,700
Hospitals; state, local, and private	56,720
Medical and diagnostic laboratories	54,990

Diagnostic Medical Sonographers and Cardiovascular Technologists and Technicians, Including Vascular Technologists

Median annual wages, May 2019

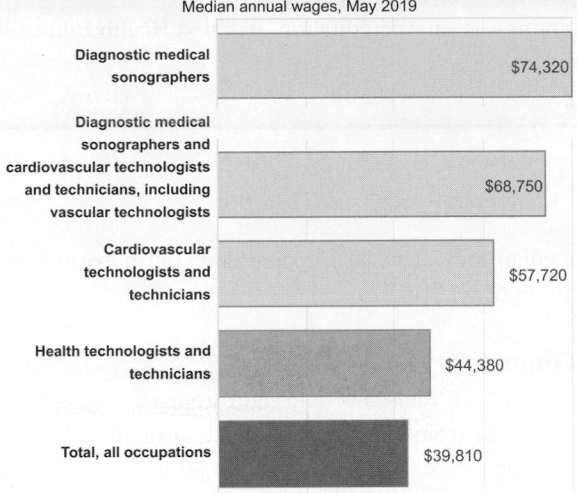

Note: All Occupations includes all occupations in the U.S. Economy.
Source: U.S. Bureau of Labor Statistics, Occupational Employment Statistics.

In May 2019, the median annual wages for diagnostic medical sonographers in the top industries in which they worked were as follows:

Outpatient care centers	$89,880
Hospitals; state, local, and private	74,440
Offices of physicians	73,810
Medical and diagnostic laboratories	70,100

Most diagnostic imaging workers work full time. Some may work evenings, weekends, or overnight because they work in facilities that are always open.

Job Outlook

Employment of diagnostic medical sonographers is projected to grow 17 percent from 2019 to 2029, much faster than the average for all occupations. Employment of cardiovascular technologists and technicians, including vascular technologists, is projected to grow 5 percent from 2019 to 2029, faster than the average for all occupations.

As the large baby-boom population ages, the need to diagnose medical conditions—such as blood clots and heart disease—will likely increase. Imaging technology is a tool used in making these diagnoses. Moreover, diagnostic medical sonographers, cardiovascular technologists and technicians, and vascular technologists will continue to be needed in healthcare settings to provide an alternative to imaging techniques that involve radiation.

Job Prospects

Diagnostic imaging personnel who are certified are expected to have the best job opportunities. Those certified in more than one specialty are expected to find even greater job opportunities.

Diagnostic Medical Sonographers and Cardiovascular Technologists and Technicians, Including Vascular Technologists

Percent change in employment, projected 2019-29

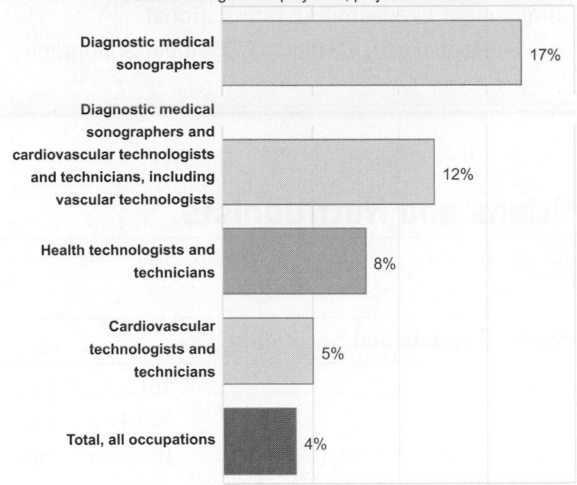

Note: All Occupations includes all occupations in the U.S. Economy.
Source: U.S. Bureau of Labor Statistics, Employment Projections program.

Employment projections data for diagnostic medical sonographers and cardiovascular technologists and technicians, including vascular technologists, 2019-29					
Occupational Title	SOC Code	Employment, 2019	Projected Employment, 2029	Change, 2019-29	
				Percent	Numeric
SOURCE: U.S. Bureau of Labor Statistics, Employment Projections program					
Diagnostic medical sonographers and cardiovascular technologists and technicians, including vascular technologists	—	131,700	147,300	12	15,600
Cardiovascular technologists and technicians	29-2031	57,400	60,500	5	3,100
Diagnostic medical sonographers	29-2032	74,300	86,800	17	12,500

State & Area Data
Occupational Employment Statistics (OES)

The Occupational Employment Statistics (OES) program produces employment and wage estimates annually for over 800 occupations. These estimates are available for the nation as a whole, for individual states, and for metropolitan and nonmetropolitan areas.

Contacts for More Information

For more information about diagnostic medical sonographers, visit
➤ Society of Diagnostic Medical Sonography
For more information about cardiovascular technologists and technicians, including vascular technologists, visit
➤ Alliance of Cardiovascular Professionals
➤ American Society of Echocardiography
➤ Society for Vascular Ultrasound

For more information about registration and certification, visit

➤ American Registry of Radiologic Technologists
➤ Cardiovascular Credentialing International
➤ American Registry for Diagnostic Medical Sonography

For a current list of accredited education programs in diagnostic medical sonography and cardiovascular technology, including vascular technology, visit

➤ Commission on Accreditation of Allied Health Education Programs

Dietitians and Nutritionists

Summary

Quick Facts: Dietitians and Nutritionists

2019 Median Pay	$61,270 per year $29.46 per hour
Typical Entry-Level Education	Bachelor's degree
Work Experience in a Related Occupation	None
On-the-job Training	Internship/residency
Number of Jobs, 2019	74,200
Job Outlook, 2019-29	8% (Much faster than average)
Employment Change, 2019-29	5,900

What Dietitians and Nutritionists Do

Dietitians and nutritionists advise people on what to eat in order to lead a healthy lifestyle or achieve a specific health-related goal.

Work Environment

Dietitians and nutritionists work in many settings, including hospitals, nursing homes, clinics, cafeterias, and for state and local governments.

How to Become a Dietitian or Nutritionist

Dietitians and nutritionists typically need a bachelor's degree, along with supervised training through an internship. Many states require dietitians and nutritionists to be licensed.

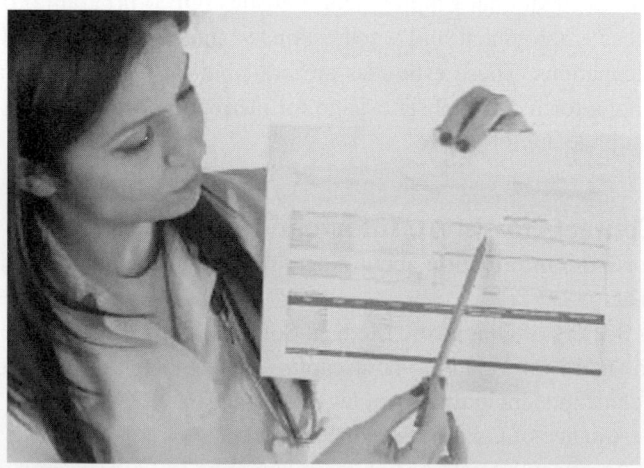

Dietitians and nutritionists may help clients maintain a healthy weight.

Pay

The median annual wage for dietitians and nutritionists was $61,270 in May 2019.

Job Outlook

Employment of dietitians and nutritionists is projected to grow 8 percent from 2019 to 2029, much faster than the average for all occupations. The role of food in preventing and treating diseases, such as diabetes, is now well known. More dietitians and nutritionists will be needed to provide care for patients with various medical conditions and to advise people who want to improve their overall health.

State & Area Data

Explore resources for employment and wages by state and area for dietitians and nutritionists.

What Dietitians and Nutritionists Do

Dietitians and nutritionists are experts in the use of food and nutrition to promote health and manage disease. They advise people on what to eat in order to lead a healthy lifestyle or achieve a specific health-related goal.

Duties

Dietitians and nutritionists typically do the following:

• Assess patients' and clients' nutritional and health needs
• Counsel patients on nutrition issues and healthy eating habits

Dietitians and nutritionists counsel patients on nutrition issues.

- Develop meal and nutrition plans, taking both clients' preferences and budgets into account
- Evaluate the effects of meal plans and change the plans as needed
- Promote better health by speaking to groups about diet, nutrition, and the relationship between good eating habits and preventing or managing specific diseases
- Create educational materials about healthy food choices
- Keep up with or contribute to the latest food and nutritional science research
- Document patients' progress

Dietitians and nutritionists evaluate the health of their clients. Based on their findings, dietitians and nutritionists advise clients on which foods to eat—and which to avoid—to improve their health.

Many dietitians and nutritionists provide customized information for specific individuals. For example, a dietitian or nutritionist might teach a client with diabetes how to plan meals to balance the client's blood sugar. Others work with groups of people who have similar needs. For example, a dietitian or nutritionist might plan a diet with healthy fat and limited sugar to help clients who are at risk for heart disease. They may work with other healthcare professionals to coordinate patient care.

Dietitians and nutritionists who are self-employed may meet with patients, or they may work as consultants for a variety of organizations. They may need to spend time on marketing and other business-related tasks, such as scheduling appointments, keeping records, and preparing educational programs or informational materials for clients.

Although many dietitians and nutritionists do similar tasks, there are several specialties within the occupations. The following are examples of types of dietitians and nutritionists:

Clinical dietitians and clinical nutritionists provide medical nutrition therapy. They work in hospitals, long-term care facilities, clinics, private practice, and other institutions. They create customized nutritional programs based on the health needs of patients or residents and counsel patients on how to improve their health through nutrition. Clinical dietitians and clinical nutritionists may further specialize, such as by working only with patients with specific conditions such as kidney disease, diabetes, or digestive disorders.

Community dietitians and community nutritionists develop programs and counsel the public on topics related to food, health, and nutrition. They often work with specific groups of people, such as adolescents or the elderly. They work in public health clinics, government and nonprofit agencies, health maintenance organizations (HMOs), and other settings.

Management dietitians plan food programs. They work in food service settings such as cafeterias, hospitals, prisons, and schools. They may be responsible for buying food and for carrying out other business-related tasks, such as budgeting. Management dietitians may oversee kitchen staff or other dietitians.

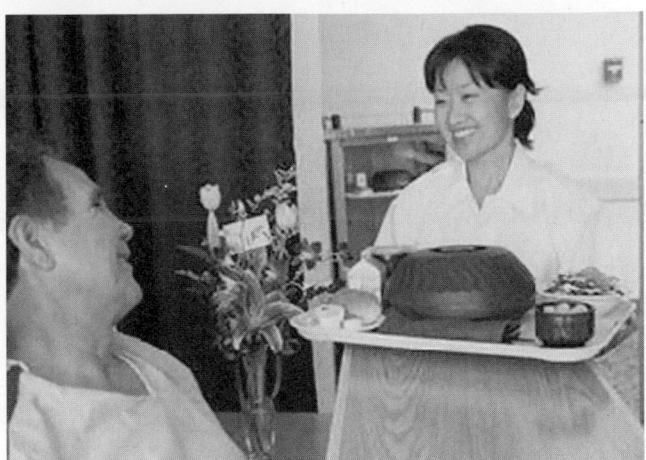

Dietitians and nutritionists tailor meal plans to meet the health needs of patients.

Work Environment

Dietitians and nutritionists held about 74,200 jobs in 2019. The largest employers of dietitians and nutritionists were as follows:

Hospitals; state, local, and private	30%
Government	13
Nursing and residential care facilities	10
Outpatient care centers	9
Self-employed workers	4

Work Schedules

Most dietitians and nutritionists work full time. They may work evenings and weekends to meet with clients who are unavailable at other times.

How to Become a Dietitian or Nutritionist

Dietitians and nutritionists typically need a bachelor's degree, along with supervised training through an internship. Many states require dietitians and nutritionists to be licensed.

Education

Dietitians and nutritionists typically need a bachelor's degree in dietetics, foods and nutrition, clinical nutrition, public health nutrition, or a related area. Dietitians also may study food service systems management. Programs include courses in nutrition, psychology, chemistry, and biology.

Many dietitians and nutritionists have advanced degrees.

Training

Dietitians and nutritionists typically receive several hundred hours of supervised training, usually in the form of an internship following graduation from college. Some schools offer coordinated programs in dietetics that allow students to complete supervised training as part of their undergraduate or graduate-level coursework.

Dietitians and nutritionists must clearly explain eating plans to other healthcare professionals.

Licenses, Certifications, and Registrations

Many states require dietitians and nutritionists to be licensed in order to practice. Other states require only state registration or certification to use certain titles, and a few states have no regulations for this occupation.

The requirements for state licensure and state certification vary by state, but most include having a bachelor's degree in food and nutrition or a related area, completing supervised practice, and passing an exam.

Many dietitians choose to earn the Registered Dietitian Nutritionist (RDN) credential. Although the RDN is not always required, the qualifications are often the same as those necessary for becoming a licensed dietitian in states that require a license. Many employers prefer or require the RDN, which is administered by the Commission on Dietetic Registration, the credentialing agency for the Academy of Nutrition and Dietetics.

The RDN requires dietitian nutritionists to complete a minimum of a bachelor's degree and a Dietetic Internship (DI), which consists of at least 1,200 hours of supervised experience. Students may complete both criteria at once through a coordinated program, or they may finish their required coursework and degree before applying for an internship. These programs are accredited by the Accreditation Council for Education in Nutrition and Dietetics (ACEND), part of the Academy of Nutrition and Dietetics. In order to maintain the RDN credential, dietitians and nutritionists who have earned it must complete 75 continuing professional education credits every 5 years.

Nutritionists may earn the Certified Nutrition Specialist (CNS) credential to show an advanced level of knowledge. The CNS credential or exam is accepted in several states for licensure purposes. To qualify for the credential, applicants must have a master's or doctoral degree, complete 1,000 hours of supervised experience, and pass an exam. The credential is administered by the Board for Certification of Nutrition Specialists. To maintain the CNS credential, nutritionists must complete 75 continuing education credits every 5 years.

Dietitians and nutritionists may seek additional certifications in an area of specialty. The Commission on Dietetic Registration offers several specialty certifications in topics such as oncology nutrition, pediatric nutrition, renal nutrition, and sports dietetics, among others.

Important Qualities

Analytical skills. Dietitians and nutritionists must keep up to date with the latest food and nutrition research. They should interpret scientific studies and translate nutrition science into practical eating advice.

Compassion. Dietitians and nutritionists must be caring and empathetic when helping clients address health and dietary issues and any related emotions.

Listening skills. Dietitians and nutritionists must listen carefully to understand clients' goals and concerns. They may work with other healthcare workers as part of a team to improve the health of a patient, and they need to listen to team members when constructing eating plans.

Organizational skills. Because there are many aspects to the work of dietitians and nutritionists, they should stay organized. Management dietitians, for example, must consider the nutritional needs of their clients, the costs of meals, and access to food. Self-employed dietitians and nutritionists may need to schedule appointments, manage employees, bill insurance companies, and maintain patient files.

Problem-solving skills. Dietitians and nutritionists must evaluate the health status of patients and determine the most appropriate food choices for a client to improve his or her overall health or manage a disease.

Speaking skills. Dietitians and nutritionists must explain complicated topics in a way that people with less technical knowledge can understand. They must clearly explain eating plans to clients and to other healthcare professionals involved in a patient's care.

Pay

The median annual wage for dietitians and nutritionists was $61,270 in May 2019. The median wage is the wage at which half the workers in an occupation earned more than that amount and half earned less. The lowest 10 percent earned less than $38,890, and the highest 10 percent earned more than $87,360.

In May 2019, the median annual wages for dietitians and nutritionists in the top industries in which they worked were as follows:

Outpatient care centers	$68,000
Hospitals; state, local, and private	62,110
Government	60,670
Nursing and residential care facilities	59,320

Most dietitians and nutritionists work full time. They may work evenings and weekends to meet with clients who are unavailable at other times.

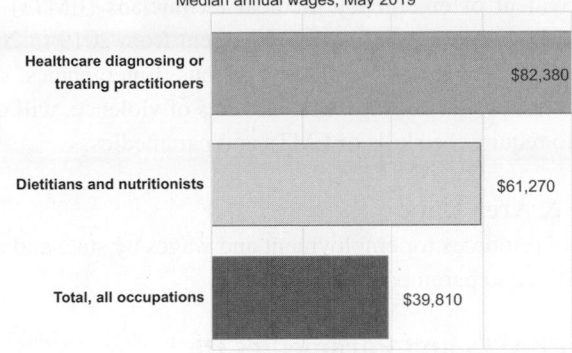

Dietitians and Nutritionists
Median annual wages, May 2019

Healthcare diagnosing or treating practitioners — $82,380

Dietitians and nutritionists — $61,270

Total, all occupations — $39,810

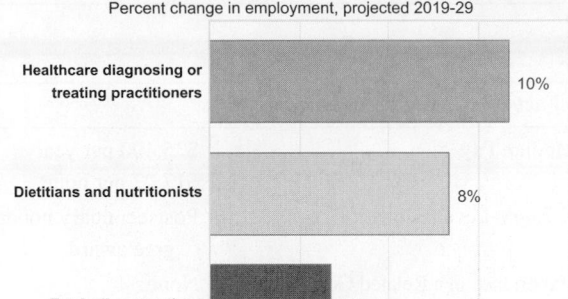

Dietitians and Nutritionists
Percent change in employment, projected 2019-29

Healthcare diagnosing or treating practitioners — 10%

Dietitians and nutritionists — 8%

Total, all occupations — 4%

Note: All Occupations includes all occupations in the U.S. Economy. Source: U.S. Bureau of Labor Statistics, Occupational Employment Statistics.

Note: All Occupations includes all occupations in the U.S. Economy. Source: U.S. Bureau of Labor Statistics, Employment Projections program.

Job Outlook

Employment of dietitians and nutritionists is projected to grow 8 percent from 2019 to 2029, much faster than the average for all occupations. In recent years, interest in the role of food and nutrition in promoting health and wellness has increased, particularly as a part of preventative healthcare in medical settings.

According to the Centers for Disease Control, more than one-third of U.S. adults are obese. Many diseases, such as diabetes and heart disease, are associated with obesity. The importance of diet in preventing and treating illnesses is now well known. More dietitians and nutritionists will be needed to provide care for people with these conditions.

Moreover, as the baby-boom generation grows older and looks for ways to stay healthy, there will be more demand for dietetic and nutrition services. In addition, there will be demand for dietitians and nutritionists in grocery stores to help consumers make healthy food choices.

Job Prospects

Dietitians and nutritionists who have earned advanced degrees or certification in a specialty area may enjoy better job prospects.

State & Area Data
Occupational Employment Statistics (OES)

The Occupational Employment Statistics (OES) program produces employment and wage estimates annually for over 800 occupations. These estimates are available for the nation as a whole, for individual states, and for metropolitan and nonmetropolitan areas.

Contacts for More Information

For more information about dietitians and nutritionists, visit
➤ Academy of Nutrition and Dietetics

For a list of academic programs, visit
➤ Accreditation Council for Education in Nutrition and Dietetics

For information on the Registered Dietitian Nutritionist (RDN) exam and other specialty credentials, visit
➤ Commission on Dietetic Registration

For information on the Certified Nutrition Specialist (CNS) exam and credential, visit
➤ Board for Certification of Nutrition Specialists

Occupational Title	SOC Code	Employment, 2019	Projected Employment, 2029	Change, 2019-29	
				Percent	Numeric
Employment projections data for dietitians and nutritionists, 2019-29					
SOURCE: U.S. Bureau of Labor Statistics, Employment Projections program					
Dietitians and nutritionists	29-1031	74,200	80,100	8	5,900

EMTs and Paramedics

Summary

Quick Facts: EMTs and Paramedics

2019 Median Pay	$35,400 per year
	$17.02 per hour
Typical Entry-Level Education	Postsecondary nonde-gree award
Work Experience in a Related Occupation ...	None
On-the-job Training	None
Number of Jobs, 2019	265,200
Job Outlook, 2019-29	6% (Faster than average)
Employment Change, 2019-29	17,000

What EMTs and Paramedics Do

Emergency medical technicians (EMTs) and paramedics respond to emergency calls, performing medical services and transporting patients to medical facilities.

Work Environment

Most EMTs and paramedics work full time. Their work can be physically strenuous and stressful, sometimes involving life-or-death situations.

How to Become an EMT or Paramedic

Emergency medical technicians (EMTs) and paramedics typically complete a postsecondary educational program. All states require EMTs and paramedics to be licensed; requirements vary by state.

Pay

The median annual wage for EMTs and paramedics was $35,400 in May 2019.

Job Outlook

Employment of emergency medical technicians (EMTs) and paramedics is projected to grow 6 percent from 2019 to 2029, faster than the average for all occupations. Emergencies, such as car crashes, natural disasters, and acts of violence, will continue to require the skills of EMTs and paramedics.

State & Area Data

Explore resources for employment and wages by state and area for EMTs and paramedics.

What EMTs and Paramedics Do

Emergency medical technicians (EMTs) and paramedics care for the sick or injured in emergency medical settings. People's lives often depend on the quick reaction and competent care provided by these workers. EMTs and paramedics respond to emergency calls, performing medical services and transporting patients to medical facilities.

A 911 operator sends EMTs and paramedics to the scene of an emergency, where they often work with police and firefighters.

Duties

EMTs and paramedics typically do the following:

- Respond to 911 calls for emergency medical assistance, such as cardiopulmonary resuscitation (CPR) or bandaging a wound
- Assess a patient's condition and determine a course of treatment
- Provide first-aid treatment or life support care to sick or injured patients
- Transport patients safely in an ambulance
- Transfer patients to the emergency department of a hospital or other healthcare facility
- Report their observations and treatment to physicians, nurses, or other healthcare facility staff
- Document medical care given to patients

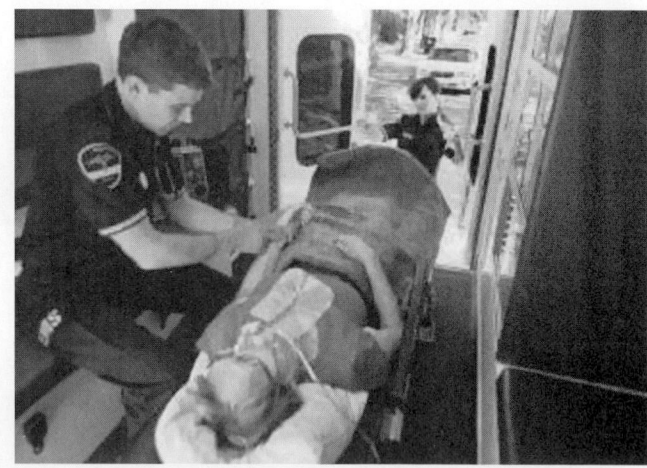

EMTs and paramedics transport patients to medical facilities.

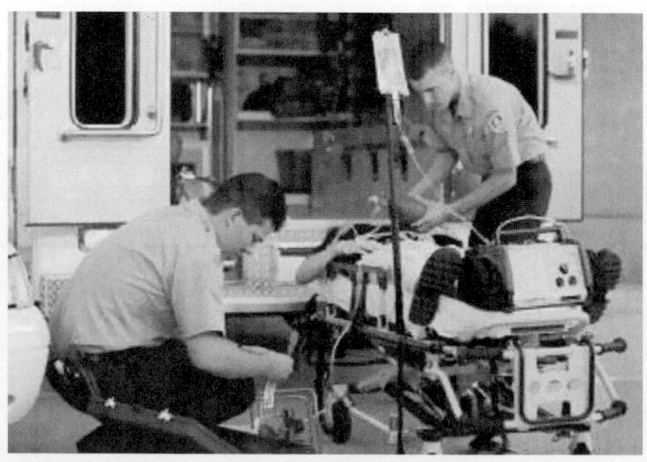

EMTs and paramedics assess a patient's condition and administer emergency medical care.

- Inventory, replace, and clean supplies and equipment after use

When transporting a patient in an ambulance, one EMT or paramedic may drive the ambulance while another monitors the patient's vital signs and gives additional care. Some paramedics work as part of a helicopter's or an airplane's flight crew to transport critically ill or injured patients to a hospital.

EMTs and paramedics also transport patients from one medical facility to another. Some patients may need to be transferred to a hospital that specializes in treating their particular injury or illness or to a facility that provides long-term care, such as a nursing home.

If a patient has a contagious disease, EMTs and paramedics decontaminate the interior of the ambulance and may need to report the case to the proper authorities.

The specific responsibilities of EMTs and paramedics depend on their level of certification and the state they work in. The National Registry of Emergency Medical Technicians (NREMT) provides national certification of EMTs and paramedics at four levels: EMR, EMT, Advanced EMT, and Paramedic. Some states, however, have their own certification programs and use similar titles.

Emergency Medical Responders, or EMRs, are trained to provide basic medical care with minimal equipment. These workers may provide immediate lifesaving interventions while waiting for other emergency medical services (EMS) resources to arrive. Jobs in this category may also go by a variety of titles including Emergency Care Attendants, Certified First Responders, or similar.

An *EMT*, also known as an *EMT-Basic*, cares for patients at the scene of an incident and while taking patients by ambulance to a hospital. An EMT has the skills to assess a patient's condition and to manage respiratory, cardiac, and trauma emergencies.

An *Advanced EMT*, also known as an *EMT-Intermediate*, has completed the requirements for the EMT level, as well as instruction in more advanced medical procedures, such as administering intravenous fluids and some medications.

Paramedics provide more extensive prehospital care than do EMTs. In addition to doing the tasks of EMTs, paramedics can give medications orally and intravenously, interpret electrocardiograms (EKGs)—which monitor heart function—and use other monitors and complex equipment.

The specific tasks or procedures EMTs and paramedics are allowed to perform vary by state.

Work Environment

EMTs and paramedics held about 265,200 jobs in 2019. The largest employers of EMTs and paramedics were as follows:

Ambulance services	46%
Local government, excluding education and hospitals	28
Hospitals; state, local, and private	19

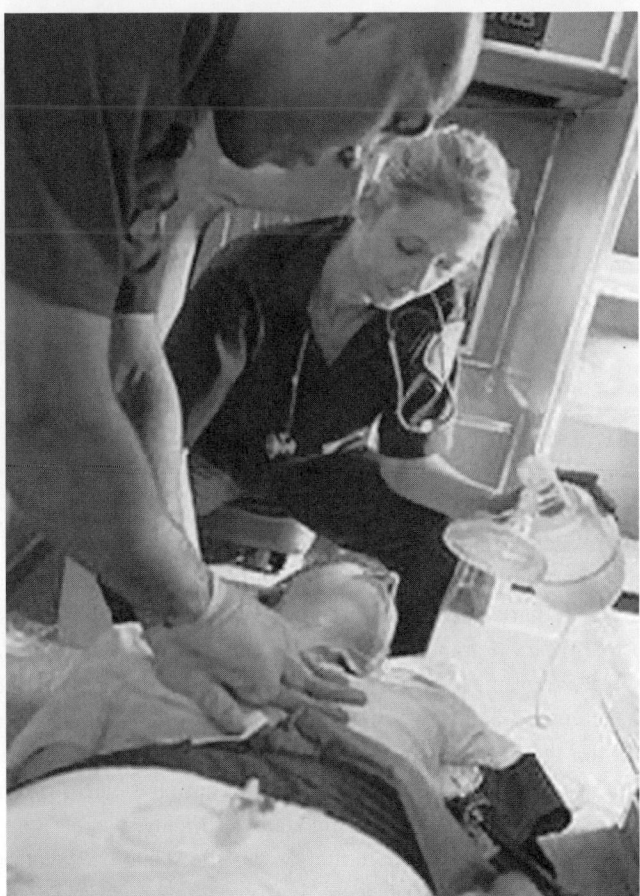

EMTs and paramedics care for sick or injured patients in a prehospital setting.

The above percentages exclude volunteer EMTs and paramedics who do not receive pay.

EMTs and paramedics work both indoors and outdoors, in all types of weather. Their work is physically strenuous and can be stressful, sometimes involving life-or-death situations.

Volunteer EMTs and paramedics share many of the same duties as paid EMTs and paramedics. They volunteer for fire departments, providers of emergency medical services, or hospitals. They may respond to only a few calls per month.

Injuries and Illnesses

EMTs and paramedics have one of the highest rates of injuries and illnesses of all occupations. They are required to do considerable kneeling, bending, and lifting while caring for and moving patients. They may be exposed to contagious diseases and viruses, such as hepatitis B and HIV. Sometimes they can be injured by combative patients. These risks can be reduced by following proper safety procedures, such as waiting for police to clear an area in violent situations or wearing gloves while working with a patient.

Work Schedules

Most paid EMTs and paramedics work full time. Some work more than 40 hours per week. Because EMTs and paramedics must be available to work in emergencies, they may work overnight and on weekends. Some EMTs and paramedics work shifts in 12- or 24-hour increments. Volunteer EMTs and paramedics have variable work schedules. For example, they may work only a few days per week.

How to Become an EMT or Paramedic

Emergency medical technicians (EMTs) and paramedics typically complete a postsecondary educational program. All states require EMTs and paramedics to be licensed; requirements vary by state.

Education

Both a high school diploma or equivalent and cardiopulmonary resuscitation (CPR) certification typically are required for entry into postsecondary educational programs in emergency medical technology. Most of these programs are nondegree award programs that can be completed in less than 1 year; others last up to 2 years. Paramedics, however, may need an associate's degree. Programs in emergency medical technology are offered by technical institutes, community colleges, universities, and facilities that specialize in emergency care training. Some states have EMR positions that do not require national certification. These positions typically require state certification.

The Commission on Accreditation of Allied Health Education Programs offers a list of accredited programs for EMTs and paramedics, by state.

Programs at the EMT level include instruction in assessing patients' conditions, dealing with trauma and cardiac emergencies, clearing obstructed airways, using field equipment, and handling emergencies. Formal courses include about 150 hours of specialized instruction, and some instruction may take place in a hospital or ambulance setting.

Programs at the Advanced EMT level typically require about 400 hours of instruction. At this level, candidates learn EMT-level skills as well as more advanced ones, such as

EMTs and paramedics need to be physically fit as their job requires bending, lifting, and kneeling.

using complex airway devices, intravenous fluids, and some medications.

Paramedics have the most advanced level of education. To enter specific paramedical training programs, they must already be EMT certified. Community colleges and universities may offer these programs, which require about 1,200 hours of instruction and may lead to an associate's or bachelor's degree. Paramedics' broader scope of practice may include stitching wounds or administering intravenous medications.

High school students interested in becoming EMTs or paramedics should take courses in anatomy and physiology and consider becoming certified in CPR.

Licenses, Certifications, and Registrations

The National Registry of Emergency Medical Technicians (NREMT) certifies EMTs and paramedics at the national level. All levels of NREMT certification require completing a certified education program and passing the national exam. The national exam has both written and practical parts. Some states have first-level state certifications that do not require national certification.

All states require EMTs and paramedics to be licensed; requirements vary by state. In most states, an individual who has NREMT certification qualifies for licensure; in others, passing an equivalent state exam is required. Usually, an applicant must be over the age of 18. Many states require background checks and may not give a license to an applicant who has a criminal history.

Although some emergency medical services hire separate drivers, most EMTs and paramedics take a course requiring about 8 hours of instruction before they can drive an ambulance.

Important Qualities

Compassion. EMTs and paramedics must be able to provide emotional support to patients in an emergency, especially patients who are in life-threatening situations or extreme mental distress.

Interpersonal skills. EMTs and paramedics usually work on teams and must be able to coordinate their activities closely with others in stressful situations.

Listening skills. EMTs and paramedics need to listen to patients to determine the extent of their injuries or illnesses.

Physical strength. EMTs and paramedics need to be physically fit. Their job requires a lot of bending, lifting, and kneeling.

Problem-solving skills. EMTs and paramedics must evaluate patients' symptoms and administer appropriate treatments.

Speaking skills. EMTs and paramedics need to clearly explain procedures to patients, give orders, and relay information to others.

Advancement

EMTs and paramedics may advance into other related health-care occupations, such as physician assistants and medical

EMTs and Paramedics
Median annual wages, May 2019

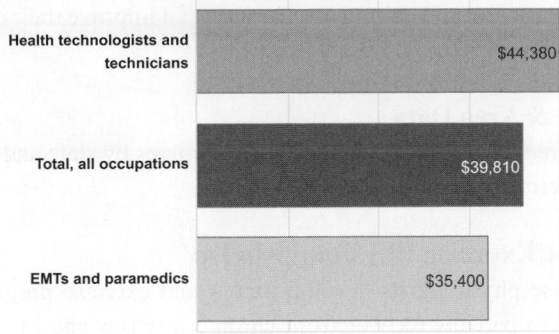

Health technologists and technicians $44,380
Total, all occupations $39,810
EMTs and paramedics $35,400

EMTs and Paramedics
Percent change in employment, projected 2019-29

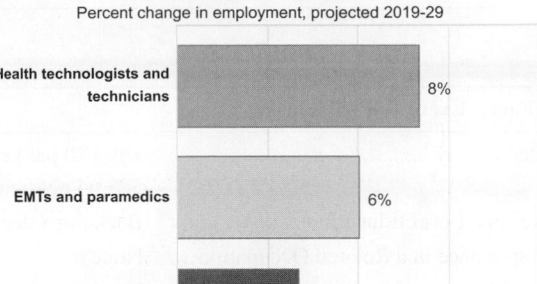

Health technologists and technicians 8%
EMTs and paramedics 6%
Total, all occupations 4%

Note: All Occupations includes all occupations in the U.S. Economy.
Source: U.S. Bureau of Labor Statistics, Occupational Employment Statistics.

Note: All Occupations includes all occupations in the U.S. Economy.
Source: U.S. Bureau of Labor Statistics, Employment Projections program.

assistants, as well as administrative positions in various healthcare settings, such as ambulatory care companies or hospitals.

Pay

The median annual wage for EMTs and paramedics was $35,400 in May 2019. The median wage is the wage at which half the workers in an occupation earned more than that amount and half earned less. The lowest 10 percent earned less than $23,490, and the highest 10 percent earned more than $59,860.

In May 2019, the median annual wages for EMTs and paramedics in the top industries in which they worked were as follows:

Local government, excluding education and hospitals.................................... $37,570
Hospitals; state, local, and private........................... 37,570
Ambulance services.. 32,730

Most paid EMTs and paramedics work full time. Some work more than 40 hours per week. Because EMTs and paramedics must be available to work in emergencies, they may work overnight and on weekends. Some EMTs and paramedics work shifts in 12- or 24-hour increments. Volunteer EMTs and paramedics have variable work schedules. For example, they may work only a few days per week.

Job Outlook

Employment of emergency medical technicians (EMTs) and paramedics is projected to grow 6 percent from 2019 to 2029, faster than the average for all occupations. Emergencies, such as car crashes, natural disasters, and acts of violence, will continue to require the skills of EMTs and paramedics. The need for volunteer EMTs and paramedics in rural areas and smaller metropolitan areas will also continue.

Growth in the middle-aged and older population will lead to an increase in age-related health emergencies, such as heart attacks and strokes. This increase, in turn, will create greater demand for EMT and paramedic services. An increase in the

number of specialized medical facilities will require more EMTs and paramedics to transfer patients with specific conditions to these facilities for treatment.

Job Prospects

Job opportunities should be good because the growing population will require more emergency services generally. There will also be a need to replace workers who leave the occupation due to the high stress nature of the job or to seek job opportunities in other healthcare occupations.

Employment projections data for EMTs and paramedics, 2019-29					
Occupational Title	SOC Code	Employment, 2019	Projected Employment, 2029	Change, 2019-29	
				Percent	Numeric
Emergency medical technicians and paramedics	29-2040	265,200	282,200	6	17,000

State & Area Data
Occupational Employment Statistics (OES)

The Occupational Employment Statistics (OES) program produces employment and wage estimates annually for over 800 occupations. These estimates are available for the nation as a whole, for individual states, and for metropolitan and nonmetropolitan areas.

Contacts for More Information

For more information about emergency medical technicians and paramedics, visit
➤ National Association of Emergency Medical Technicians
➤ National Association of State EMS Officials
➤ National Highway Traffic Safety Administration, Office of Emergency Medical Services
➤ National Registry of Emergency Medical Technicians

For information about educational programs, visit
➤ Commission on Accreditation of Allied Health Education Programs

Exercise Physiologists

Summary

Quick Facts: Exercise Physiologists

2019 Median Pay	$49,170 per year $23.64 per hour
Typical Entry-Level Education	Bachelor's degree
Work Experience in a Related Occupation	None
On-the-job Training	None
Number of Jobs, 2019....................................	19,800
Job Outlook, 2019-29....................................	11% (Much faster than average)
Employment Change, 2019-29	2,200

What Exercise Physiologists Do

Exercise physiologists develop fitness and exercise programs that help injured or sick patients recover.

Work Environment

About half of exercise physiologists are self-employed. Most others work for hospitals and other healthcare providers. Most exercise physiologists work full time.

How to Become an Exercise Physiologist

Exercise physiologists typically need at least a bachelor's degree. Degree programs include science and health-related courses, such as biology, anatomy, kinesiology, and nutrition, as well as clinical work.

Pay

The median annual wage for exercise physiologists was $49,170 in May 2019.

Job Outlook

Employment of exercise physiologists is projected to grow 11 percent from 2019 to 2029, much faster than the average for all occupations. Demand may rise as healthcare providers emphasize exercise and preventive care to help patients recover from cardiovascular and pulmonary diseases and improve their overall health.

State & Area Data

Explore resources for employment and wages by state and area for exercise physiologists.

What Exercise Physiologists Do

Exercise physiologists develop fitness and exercise programs that help patients recover from chronic diseases and improve cardiovascular function, body composition, and flexibility.

Duties

Exercise physiologists typically do the following:

- Analyze a patient's medical history to assess their risk during exercise and to determine the best possible exercise and fitness regimen for the patient
- Perform fitness and stress tests with medical equipment and analyze the resulting patient data
- Measure blood pressure, oxygen usage, heart rhythm, and other key patient health indicators
- Develop exercise programs to improve patients' health

Exercise physiologists work to improve overall patient health. Many of their patients suffer from health problems such as cardiovascular disease or pulmonary (lung) disease. Exercise physiologists provide health education and exercise plans to improve key health indicators.

Some physiologists work closely with primary care physicians, who may prescribe exercise regimens for their patients and refer them to exercise physiologists. The physiologists then work with patients to develop individualized treatment plans that will help the patients meet their health and fitness goals.

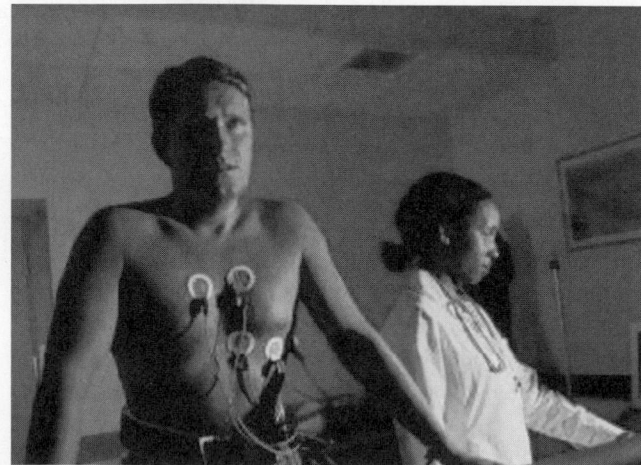

Exercise physiologists develop fitness and exercise programs that help patients recover from chronic diseases.

Exercise physiologists analyze a patient's medical history to determine the best possible exercise and fitness regimen.

Exercise physiologists should not be confused with fitness trainers and instructors (including personal trainers) or athletic trainers.

Work Environment

Exercise physiologists held about 19,800 jobs in 2019. The largest employers of exercise physiologists were as follows:

Self-employed workers	62%
Hospitals; state, local, and private	22
Offices of physical, occupational and speech therapists, and audiologists	4
Offices of physicians	2
Government	2

Work Schedules

Most exercise physiologists work full time.

How to Become an Exercise Physiologist

Exercise physiologists typically need at least a bachelor's degree. Degree programs include science and health-related courses, such as biology, anatomy, kinesiology, and nutrition, as well as clinical work.

Education

Exercise physiologists typically need at least a bachelor's degree in exercise physiology, exercise science, kinesiology, or a related field. Master's degree programs also are available. Programs include courses in science and health-related subjects, such as biology, anatomy, statistics, kinesiology, and nutrition, as well as clinical work. In 2017, there were about 60 programs in exercise physiology, exercise science, and kinesiology accredited by the Commission on Accreditation of Allied Health Education Programs (CAAHEP).

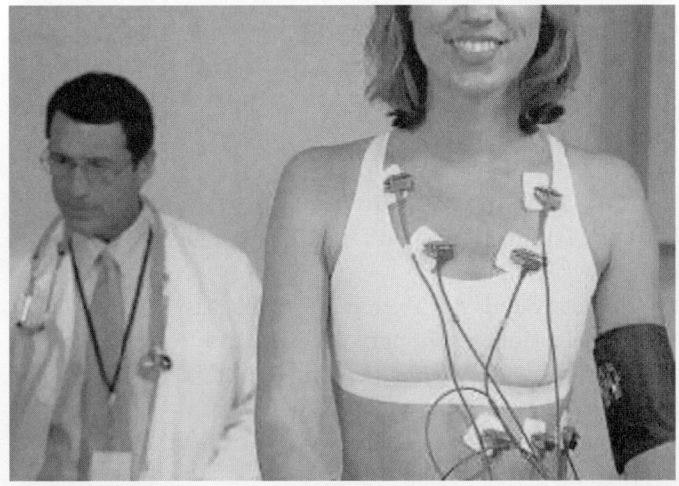

Exercise physiologists perform fitness and stress tests with medical equipment and analyze the subsequent patient data.

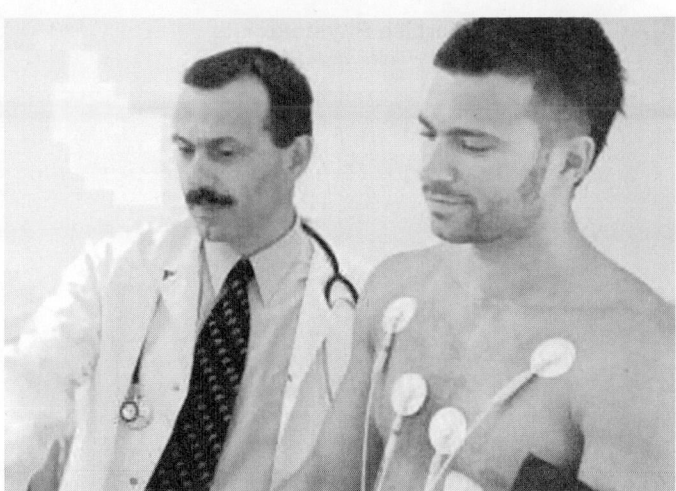

Exercise physiologists typically need at least a bachelor's degree.

Licenses, Certifications, and Registrations

Louisiana is the only state that requires exercise physiologists to be licensed, although some states have pending legislation to create licensure requirements.

Employers typically require exercise physiologists to have Basic Life Support (BLS) certification or Advanced Life Support (ACLS) certification, both of which include training in cardiopulmonary resuscitation (CPR).

The American Society of Exercise Physiologists (ASEP) offers the Exercise Physiologist Certified (EPC) certification, which physiologists can use to demonstrate their qualifications. To be eligible for certification, candidates must pass the ASEP exam and hold ASEP membership. In addition, candidates must have either a bachelor's degree in exercise physiology or a bachelor's degree in a related field, and they must have completed specific coursework requirements. To maintain certification, candidates must complete continuing education courses every 5 years.

The American College of Sports Medicine (ACSM) also offers certifications for exercise physiologists: the Certified Exercise Physiologist (EP-C) and the Certified Clinical Exercise Physiologist (CEP) credentials for candidates with a bachelor's degree, as well as the Registered Clinical Exercise Physiologist (RCEP) for candidates with a master's or higher degree. All three ACSM credentials require CPR certification and passing an exam. Candidates for the CEP and the RCEP also must have at least 400 and 600 hours of supervised clinical experience, respectively. All three ACSM certifications require candidates to complete continuing education courses every 3 years, and keep their CPR certification up to date.

Important Qualities

Compassion. Because exercise physiologists work with patients who may be in considerable pain or discomfort, they must be sympathetic while working with patients.

Exercise Physiologists
Median annual wages, May 2019

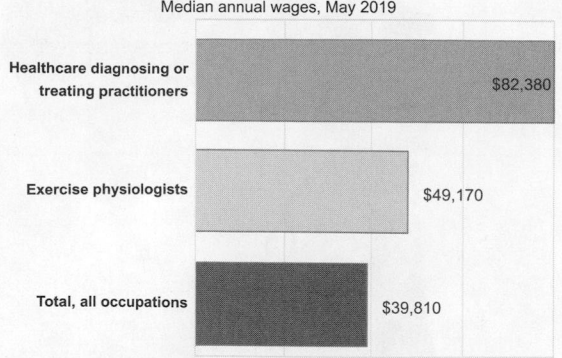

Healthcare diagnosing or treating practitioners — $82,380

Exercise physiologists — $49,170

Total, all occupations — $39,810

Note: All Occupations includes all occupations in the U.S. Economy.
Source: U.S. Bureau of Labor Statistics, Occupational Employment Statistics.

Exercise Physiologists
Percent change in employment, projected 2019-29

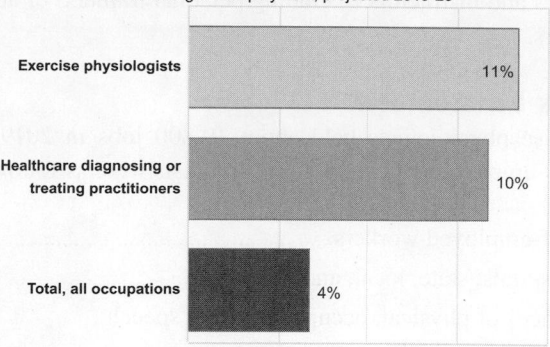

Exercise physiologists — 11%

Healthcare diagnosing or treating practitioners — 10%

Total, all occupations — 4%

Note: All Occupations includes all occupations in the U.S. Economy.
Source: U.S. Bureau of Labor Statistics, Employment Projections program.

Decisionmaking skills. Exercise physiologists must make informed clinical decisions because those decisions could affect the health or livelihood of patients.

Detail oriented. Exercise physiologists must record detailed, accurate information about their patients' conditions and about any progress the patients make. For example, they must ensure that patients are completing the appropriate stress tests or practicing the correct fitness regimen.

Interpersonal skills. Exercise physiologists must have strong interpersonal skills and manage difficult situations. They must communicate clearly with others, including physicians, patients, and patients' families.

Pay

The median annual wage for exercise physiologists was $49,170 in May 2019. The median wage is the wage at which half the workers in an occupation earned more than that amount and half earned less. The lowest 10 percent earned less than $34,990, and the highest 10 percent earned more than $78,310.

In May 2019, the median annual wages for exercise physiologists in the top industries in which they worked were as follows:

Government $72,440
Hospitals; state, local, and private 49,390
Offices of physicians 48,200
Offices of physical, occupational and speech
therapists, and audiologists 45,190

Most exercise physiologists work full time.

Job Outlook

Employment of exercise physiologists is projected to grow 11 percent from 2019 to 2029, much faster than the average for all occupations. However, because it is a small occupation, the fast growth will result in only about 2,200 new jobs over the decade. Demand may rise as healthcare providers emphasize

exercise and preventive care to help patients recover from cardiovascular and pulmonary diseases and improve their overall health.

Job Prospects

About 1,400 openings for exercise physiologists are projected each year, on average, over the decade.

In addition to openings arising from employment growth, other openings are expected to result from the need to replace workers who transfer to other occupations or exit the labor force, such as to retire.

Employment projections data for exercise physiologists, 2019-29				Change, 2019-29	
Occupational Title	SOC Code	Employment, 2019	Projected Employment, 2029	Percent	Numeric
SOURCE: U.S. Bureau of Labor Statistics, Employment Projections program					
Exercise physiologists	29-1128	19,800	22,100	11	2,200

State & Area Data
Occupational Employment Statistics (OES)

The Occupational Employment Statistics (OES) program produces employment and wage estimates annually for over 800 occupations. These estimates are available for the nation as a whole, for individual states, and for metropolitan and nonmetropolitan areas.

Contacts for More Information

For more information about exercise physiologists and certifications, visit
➤ American Society of Exercise Physiologists
➤ American College of Sports Medicine
➤ Committee on Accreditation for the Exercise Sciences
➤ Clinical Exercise Physiology Association
➤ Commission on Accreditation of Allied Health Education Programs

Genetic Counselors

Summary

Quick Facts: Genetic Counselors

2019 Median Pay	$81,880 per year $39.36 per hour
Typical Entry-Level Education	Master's degree
Work Experience in a Related Occupation	None
On-the-job Training	None
Number of Jobs, 2019	2,600
Job Outlook, 2019-29	21% (Much faster than average)
Employment Change, 2019-29	600

What Genetic Counselors Do

Genetic counselors assess individual or family risk for a variety of inherited conditions, such as genetic disorders and birth defects.

Work Environment

Genetic counselors work in university medical centers, private and public hospitals, diagnostic laboratories, and physicians' offices. They work with families, patients, and other medical professionals. Most genetic counselors work full time.

How to Become a Genetic Counselor

Genetic counselors typically need a master's degree in genetic counseling or genetics, and board certification.

Pay

The median annual wage for genetic counselors was $81,880 in May 2019.

Genetic counselors assess individual or family risk for a variety of inherited conditions, such as genetic disorders and birth defects.

Job Outlook

Employment of genetic counselors is projected to grow 21 percent from 2019 to 2029, much faster than the average for all occupations. Ongoing technological innovations, including improvements in lab tests and developments in genomics, which is the study of the whole genome, are giving counselors opportunities to conduct more types of analyses.

State & Area Data

Explore resources for employment and wages by state and area for genetic counselors.

What Genetic Counselors Do

Genetic counselors assess individual or family risk for a variety of inherited conditions, such as genetic disorders and birth defects. They provide information and support to other healthcare providers, or to individuals and families concerned with the risk of inherited conditions.

Duties

Genetic counselors typically do the following:

- Interview patients to get comprehensive individual family and medical histories
- Evaluate genetic information to identify patients or families at risk for specific genetic disorders
- Write detailed consultation reports to provide information on complex genetic concepts for patients or referring physicians
- Discuss testing options and the associated risks, benefits, and limitations with patients, families, and other healthcare providers
- Counsel patients and family members by providing information, education, or reassurance regarding genetic risks and inherited conditions
- Participate in professional organizations or conferences to keep abreast of developments in genetics and genomics

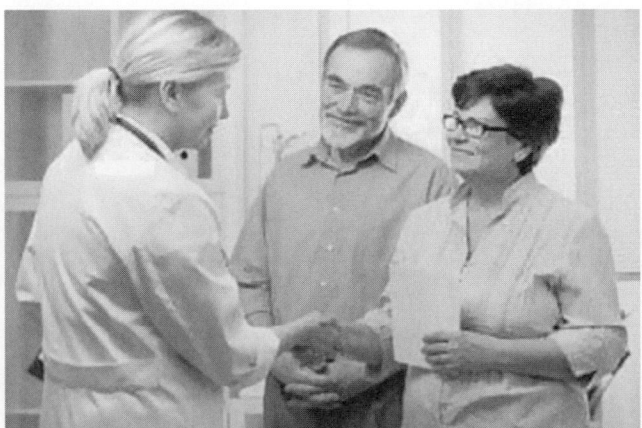

Genetic counselors provide information and advice to other healthcare providers, or to individuals and families concerned with the risk of inherited conditions.

Genetic counselors identify specific genetic disorders or risks through the study of genetics. A genetic disorder or syndrome is inherited. For parents who are expecting children, counselors use genetics to predict whether a baby is likely to have hereditary disorders, such as Down syndrome and cystic fibrosis, among others. Genetic counselors also assess the risk for an adult to develop diseases with a genetic component, such as certain forms of cancer.

Counselors identify these conditions by studying patients' genes through DNA testing. Medical laboratory technologists perform lab tests, which genetic counselors then evaluate and use for counseling patients and their families. They share this information with other health professionals, such as physicians and medical and clinical laboratory technologists and technicians.

According to a 2016 survey from the National Society of Genetic Counselors, most genetic counselors specialize in traditional areas of genetic counseling: prenatal, cancer, and pediatric. The survey noted that genetic counselors also may work in one or more specialty fields such as cardiovascular health, genomic medicine, neurogenetics, and psychiatry.

Work Environment

Genetic counselors held about 2,600 jobs in 2019. The largest employers of genetic counselors were as follows:

Hospitals; state, local, and private	43%
Offices of physicians	13
Colleges, universities, and professional schools; state, local, and private	12
Medical and diagnostic laboratories	11
Self-employed workers	5

Genetic counselors work with families, patients, and other medical professionals.

Work Schedules

Most genetic counselors work full time and have a standard work schedule.

Genetic counselors work in university medical centers, private and public hospitals, and physicians' offices.

How to Become a Genetic Counselor

Genetic counselors typically need a master's degree in genetic counseling or genetics, and board certification.

Education

Genetic counselors typically need a master's degree in genetic counseling or genetics.

Coursework in genetic counseling includes public health, epidemiology, psychology, and developmental biology. Classes emphasize genetics, public health, and patient empathy. Students also must complete clinical rotations, during which they work directly with patients and clients. Clinical rotations provide supervised experience for students, allowing them to work in different work environments, such as prenatal diagnostic centers, pediatric hospitals, or cancer centers.

The Accreditation Council for Genetic Counseling accredits master›s degree programs.

Licenses, Certifications, and Registrations

The American Board of Genetic Counseling provides certification for genetic counselors. To become certified, a student must complete an accredited master's degree program and pass an exam. Counselors must complete continuing education courses to maintain their board certification.

Genetic counselors must be sensitive and compassionate when communicating their findings.

About half of the states require genetic counselors to be licensed and other states have pending legislation for licensure. Certification is typically needed to get a license. For specific licensing requirements, contact the state's medical board.

Employers typically require or prefer prospective genetic counselors to be certified, even if the state does not require it.

Important Qualities

Communication skills. Genetic counselors must be able to simplify complex findings so that their patients understand them.

Compassion. Patients may seek advice on family care or serious illnesses. Genetic counselors must be sensitive and compassionate when communicating their findings.

Critical-thinking skills. Genetic counselors analyze laboratory findings to determine how best to advise a patient or family. They use their applied knowledge of genetics to assess inherited risks properly.

Decisionmaking skills. Genetic counselors must use their expertise and experience to determine how to share their findings properly with patients.

Pay

The median annual wage for genetic counselors was $81,880 in May 2019. The median wage is the wage at which half the workers in an occupation earned more than that amount and half earned less. The lowest 10 percent earned less than $61,310, and the highest 10 percent earned more than $114,750.

In May 2019, the median annual wages for genetic counselors in the top industries in which they worked were as follows:

Medical and diagnostic laboratories......................... $94,290

Offices of physicians.. 81,400

Hospitals; state, local, and private........................... 81,230

Colleges, universities, and professional schools;
state, local, and private.. 76,440

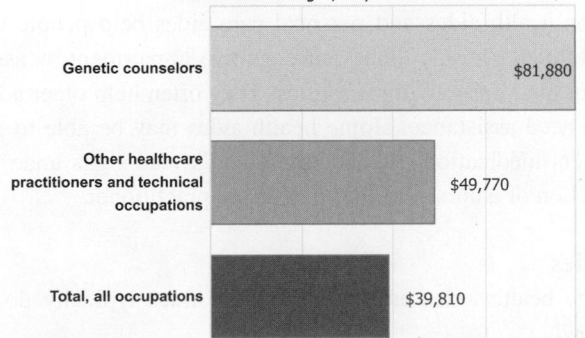

Genetic Counselors
Median annual wages, May 2019

Genetic counselors — $81,880

Other healthcare practitioners and technical occupations — $49,770

Total, all occupations — $39,810

Note: All Occupations includes all occupations in the U.S. Economy.
Source: U.S. Bureau of Labor Statistics, Occupational Employment Statistics.

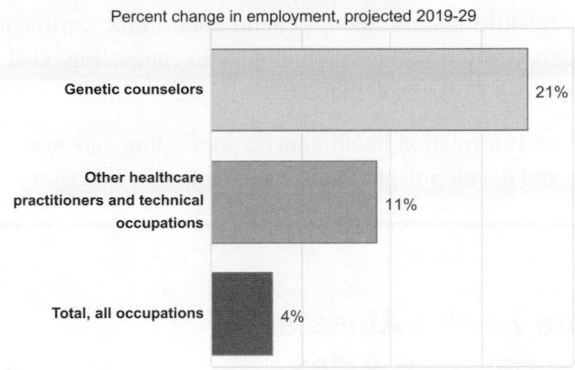

Genetic Counselors
Percent change in employment, projected 2019-29

Genetic counselors — 21%

Other healthcare practitioners and technical occupations — 11%

Total, all occupations — 4%

Note: All Occupations includes all occupations in the U.S. Economy.
Source: U.S. Bureau of Labor Statistics, Employment Projections program.

Most genetic counselors work full time and have a standard work schedule.

Job Outlook

Employment of genetic counselors is projected to grow 21 percent from 2019 to 2029, much faster than the average for all occupations. However, because it is a small occupation, the fast growth will result in only about 600 new jobs over the 10-year period.

Ongoing technological innovations, including lab tests and developments in genomics, are giving counselors opportunities to conduct more types of analyses. Cancer genomics, for example, can determine a patient's risk for specific types of cancer. The number and types of tests that genetic counselors can administer and evaluate have increased over the past few years. Many types of genetic tests are covered by health insurance providers.

Job Prospects

Genetic counselors who graduate from an accredited program and pass the board certification exam can generally expect the most favorable job prospects.

Occupational Title	SOC Code	Employment, 2019	Projected Employment, 2029	Change, 2019-29	
				Percent	Numeric
SOURCE: U.S. Bureau of Labor Statistics, Employment Projections program					
Genetic counselors	29-9092	2,600	3,200	21	600

Employment projections data for genetic counselors, 2019-29

State & Area Data
Occupational Employment Statistics (OES)

The Occupational Employment Statistics (OES) program produces employment and wage estimates annually for over 800 occupations. These estimates are available for the nation as a whole, for individual states, and for metropolitan and nonmetropolitan areas.

Contacts for More Information

For more information about genetic counselors, certification, and schools offering education in genetic counseling, visit

➤ American Board of Genetic Counseling

For more information about genetic counseling career requirements and developments in genetics, including licensure, visit

➤ National Society of Genetic Counselors

For more information about accreditation and schools offering education in genetic counseling, visit

➤ Accreditation Council for Genetic Counseling

Home Health Aides and Personal Care Aides

Summary

Quick Facts: Home Health Aides and Personal Care Aides

2019 Median Pay	$25,280 per year $12.15 per hour
Typical Entry-Level Education	High school diploma or equivalent
Work Experience in a Related Occupation	None
On-the-job Training	Short-term on-the-job training
Number of Jobs, 2019	3,439,700
Job Outlook, 2019-29	34% (Much faster than average)
Employment Change, 2019-29	1,159,500

What Home Health Aides and Personal Care Aides Do

Home health aides and personal care aides help people with disabilities, chronic illnesses, or cognitive impairment by assisting in their daily living activities.

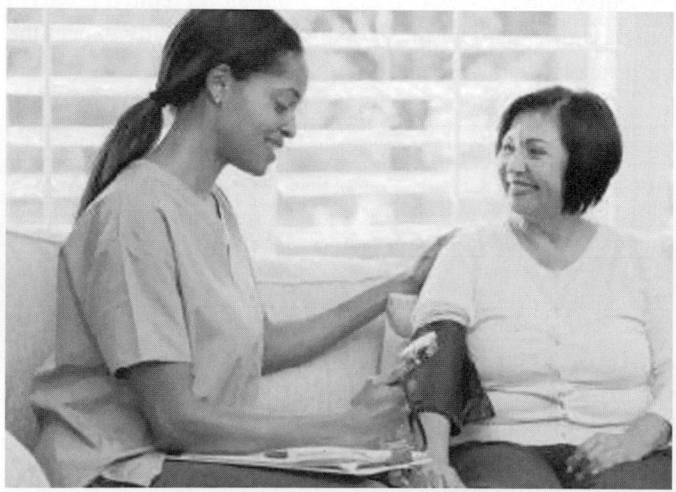

Home health aides may provide some basic health-related services, such as checking a client's blood pressure.

Work Environment

Home health aides and personal care aides work in a variety of settings, including clients' homes, group homes, and day services programs.

How to Become a Home Health Aide or Personal Care Aide

Home health aides and personal care aides typically need a high school diploma or equivalent, though some positions do not require it. Those working in certified home health or hospice agencies must complete formal training and pass a standardized test.

Pay

The median annual wage for home health aides and personal care aides was $25,280 in May 2019.

Job Outlook

Overall employment of home health aides and personal care aides is projected to grow 34 percent from 2019 to 2029, much faster than the average for all occupations. As the baby-boom generation ages and the elderly population grows, the demand for the services of home health aides and personal care aides will continue to increase.

State & Area Data

Explore resources for employment and wages by state and area for home health aides and personal care aides.

What Home Health Aides and Personal Care Aides Do

Home health aides and personal care aides help people with disabilities, chronic illness, or cognitive impairment by assisting in their daily living activities. They often help older adults who need assistance. Home health aides may be able to give a client medication or check the client's vital signs under the direction of a nurse or other healthcare practitioner.

Duties

Home health aides and personal care aides typically do the following:

• Assist clients in their daily personal tasks, such as bathing or dressing

Personal care aides assist clients in everyday tasks.

- Housekeeping, such as laundry, washing dishes, and vacuuming
- Help to organize a client's schedule and plan appointments
- Arrange transportation to doctors' offices or other outings
- Shop for groceries and prepare meals to meet a client's dietary specifications
- Keep clients engaged in their social networks and communities

Home health aides may provide some basic health-related services (depending on the state they work in), such as checking a client's pulse, temperature, and respiration rate. They may also help with simple prescribed exercises and or with giving medications. Occasionally, they change bandages or dressings, give massages, care for skin, or help with braces and artificial limbs. With special training, experienced home health aides also may help with medical equipment such as ventilators, which help clients breathe.

Personal care aides—sometimes called caregivers or personal attendants—are generally limited to providing non-medical services, including companionship, cleaning, cooking, and driving.

Direct support professionals work with people who have developmental or intellectual disabilities. They may help create a behavior plan and teach self-care skills, such as doing laundry or cooking meals.

Certified home health or hospice agencies often receive payments from government programs and therefore must comply with regulations regarding aides' employment. Aides work under the direct supervision of medical professionals, usually nurses. These aides keep records of services performed and of clients' conditions and progress. They report changes in clients' conditions to supervisors or case managers, and work with therapists and other medical staff.

Work Environment

Home health aides and personal care aides held about 3.4 million jobs in 2019. The largest employers of home health aides and personal care aides were as follows:

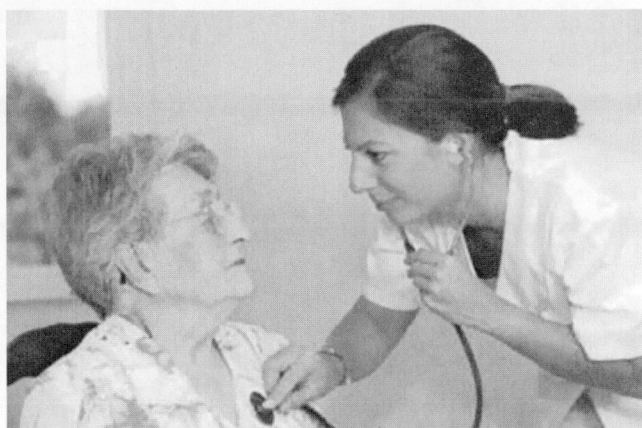

Most aides work in a client's home; others work in small group homes or larger care communities.

Individual and family services	44%
Home healthcare services	25
Residential intellectual and developmental disability facilities	7
Continuing care retirement communities and assisted living facilities for the elderly....................................	7

Most home health aides and personal care aides work in clients' homes; others work in small group homes or larger care communities. Some visit four or five clients in the same day, and others only work with one client all day—in some cases staying with one client on a long-term basis. They may work with other aides in shifts so that the client always has an aide. They help people in hospices and day services programs, and may travel as they also help people with disabilities go to work and stay engaged in their communities.

Injuries and Illnesses

Work as a home health or personal care aide can be physically and emotionally demanding. Because they often move clients into and out of bed or help with standing or walking, aides must use proper lifting techniques to guard against back injury.

In addition, aides frequently work with clients who have cognitive impairments or mental health issues and who may display difficult or violent behaviors. Aides also face hazards from minor infections and exposure to communicable diseases but can lessen their chance of infection by following proper procedures.

Work Schedules

Most aides work full-time. They may work evening and weekend hours, depending on their clients' needs.

How to Become a Home Health Aide or Personal Care Aide

Home health aides and personal care aides typically need a high school diploma or equivalent, though some positions do not require it. Those working in certified home health or hospice

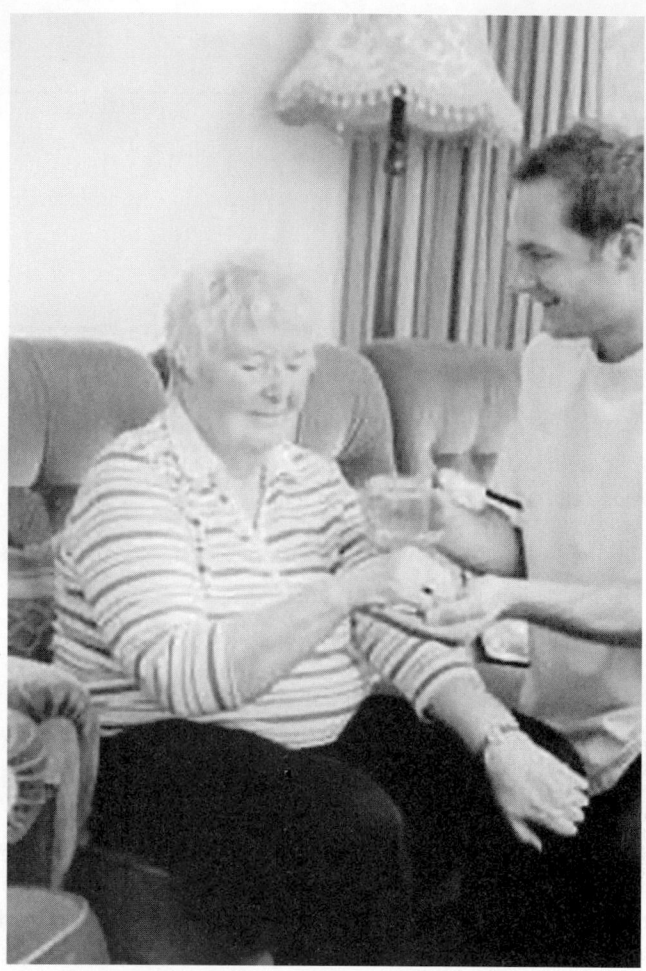

Some home health aides may work under the direction of other health professionals to administer medications to clients.

agencies must complete formal training and pass a standardized test.

Education

Home health aides and personal care aides typically need a high school diploma or equivalent, though some positions do not require it. There are also postsecondary nondegree award programs at community colleges and vocational schools.

Training

Home health aides and personal care aides may be trained in housekeeping tasks, such as cooking for clients who have special dietary needs. Aides may learn basic safety techniques, including how to respond in an emergency. Specific training may be needed for certification if state certification is required.

Training may be done on the job or through specialized programs. Training typically includes learning about personal hygiene, reading and recording vital signs, infection control, and basic nutrition.

In addition, clients have their own preferences, and aides may need time to become comfortable working with them.

Licenses, Certifications, and Registrations

Aides who work for agencies that receive reimbursement from Medicare or Medicaid must get a minimum level of training and pass a competency evaluation to be certified. Some states allow aides to take a competency exam in order to become certified without taking any training.

Additional requirements for certification vary by state. In some states, the only requirement for employment is on-the-job training, which employers generally provide. Other states require formal training, which is available from community colleges, vocational schools, elder care programs, and home healthcare agencies. In addition, states may conduct background checks on prospective aides. For specific state requirements, contact the state's health board.

Aides also may be required to obtain CPR certification.

Important Qualities

Detail oriented. Home health aides and personal care aides must adhere to specific rules and protocols and carefully follow instructions to help take care of clients. Aides must carefully follow instructions from healthcare professionals, such as how to care for wounds or how to identify changes in a client's condition.

Integrity. Home health aides and personal care aides should make clients feel comfortable when they tend to personal activities, such as helping a client bathe. In addition, aides must be dependable and trustworthy so that clients and their families can rely on them.

Interpersonal skills. Home health aides and personal care aides must work closely with clients. Sometimes, clients are in extreme pain or distress, and aides must be sensitive to their emotions. Aides must be compassionate, and they must enjoy helping people.

Physical stamina. Home health aides and personal care aides should be comfortable performing physical tasks. They might need to lift or turn clients.

Pay

The median annual wage for home health aides and personal care aides was $25,280 in May 2019. The median wage is the wage at which half the workers in an occupation earned more than that amount and half earned less. The lowest 10 percent earned less than $19,430, and the highest 10 percent earned more than $34,180.

In May 2019, the median annual wages for home health aides and personal care aides in the top industries in which they worked were as follows:

Residential intellectual and developmental disability facilities...	$25,680
Continuing care retirement communities and assisted living facilities for the elderly...............	25,660
Individual and family services	25,330
Home healthcare services	24,670

Home Health Aides and Personal Care Aides
Median annual wages, May 2019

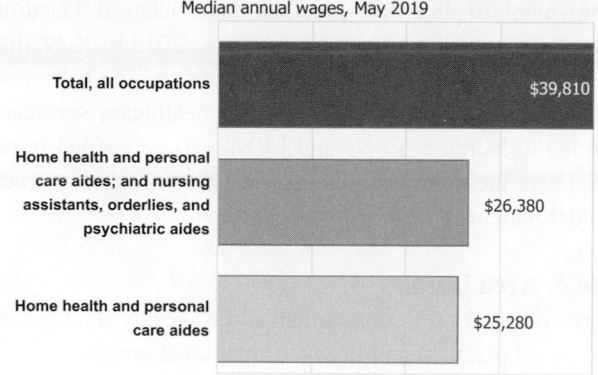

Total, all occupations	$39,810
Home health and personal care aides; and nursing assistants, orderlies, and psychiatric aides	$26,380
Home health and personal care aides	$25,280

Note: All Occupations includes all occupations in the U.S. Economy.
Source: U.S. Bureau of Labor Statistics, Occupational Employment Statistics.

Most aides work full-time. They may work evening and weekend hours, depending on their clients' needs.

Job Outlook
Overall employment of home health aides and personal care aides is projected to grow 34 percent from 2019 to 2029, much faster than the average for all occupations. As the baby-boom generation ages and the elderly population grows, the demand for the services of home health aides and personal care aides will continue to increase.

Elderly clients and people with disabilities are increasingly relying on home care as an alternative to nursing homes or hospitals. Families may prefer to keep aging family members in their homes rather than in nursing homes or hospitals. Clients who need help with everyday tasks and household chores, rather than medical care, may be able to reduce their medical expenses by staying in or returning to their homes.

Job Prospects
Job prospects for home health aides and personal care aides are excellent. These occupations are large and are projected to add many jobs. In addition, the low pay and high emotional demands may cause many workers to leave this occupation, and they will have to be replaced.

Home Health Aides and Personal Care Aides
Percent change in employment, projected 2019-29

Home health and personal care aides	34%
Home health and personal care aides; and nursing assistants, orderlies, and psychiatric aides	25%
Total, all occupations	4%

Note: All Occupations includes all occupations in the U.S. Economy.
Source: U.S. Bureau of Labor Statistics, Employment Projections program.

Employment projections data for home health aides and personal care aides, 2019-29					
Occupational Title	SOC Code	Employment, 2019	Projected Employment, 2029	Change, 2019-29	
				Percent	Numeric
SOURCE: U.S. Bureau of Labor Statistics, Employment Projections program					
Home health and personal care aides	31-1120	3,439,700	4,599,200	34	1,159,500

State & Area Data
Occupational Employment Statistics (OES)
The Occupational Employment Statistics (OES) program produces employment and wage estimates annually for over 800 occupations. These estimates are available for the nation as a whole, for individual states, and for metropolitan and nonmetropolitan areas.

Contacts for More Information
For more information about home health aides and personal care aides, including voluntary credentials for aides, visit
➤ American Society on Aging
➤ National Association for Home Care & Hospice
➤ Paraprofessional Healthcare Institute

Licensed Practical and Licensed Vocational Nurses

Summary

Quick Facts: Licensed Practical and Licensed Vocational Nurses

2019 Median Pay	$47,480 per year $22.83 per hour
Typical Entry-Level Education	Postsecondary non-degree award
Work Experience in a Related Occupation	None
On-the-job Training	None
Number of Jobs, 2019	721,700
Job Outlook, 2019-29	9% (Much faster than average)
Employment Change, 2019-29	65,700

What Licensed Practical and Licensed Vocational Nurses Do

Licensed practical nurses (LPNs) and licensed vocational nurses (LVNs) provide basic nursing care.

Work Environment

Licensed practical and licensed vocational nurses work in many settings, including nursing homes and extended care facilities, hospitals, physicians' offices, and private homes. Most work full time.

How to Become a Licensed Practical or Licensed Vocational Nurse

Licensed practical and licensed vocational nurses must complete a state-approved educational program, which typically takes about 1 year to complete. They must be licensed.

Pay

The median annual wage for licensed practical and licensed vocational nurses was $47,480 in May 2019.

Job Outlook

Employment of licensed practical and licensed vocational nurses is projected to grow 9 percent from 2019 to 2029, much faster than the average for all occupations. As the baby-boom population ages, the overall need for healthcare services is expected to increase. LPNs and LVNs will be needed in residential care facilities and in home health environments to care for older patients.

State & Area Data

Explore resources for employment and wages by state and area for licensed practical and licensed vocational nurses.

What Licensed Practical and Licensed Vocational Nurses Do

Licensed practical nurses (LPNs) and licensed vocational nurses (LVNs) provide basic medical care. They work under the direction of registered nurses and doctors.

Duties

Licensed practical and licensed vocational nurses typically do the following:

- Monitor patients' health—for example, by checking their blood pressure
- Administer basic patient care, including changing bandages and inserting catheters
- Provide for the basic comfort of patients, such as helping them bathe or dress
- Discuss the care they are providing with patients and listen to their concerns
- Report patients' status and concerns to registered nurses and doctors
- Keep records on patients' health

Duties of LPNs and LVNs vary, depending on their work setting and the state in which they work. For example, they may reinforce teaching done by registered nurses regarding how

Licensed practical and licensed vocational nurses discuss the care they are providing with patients.

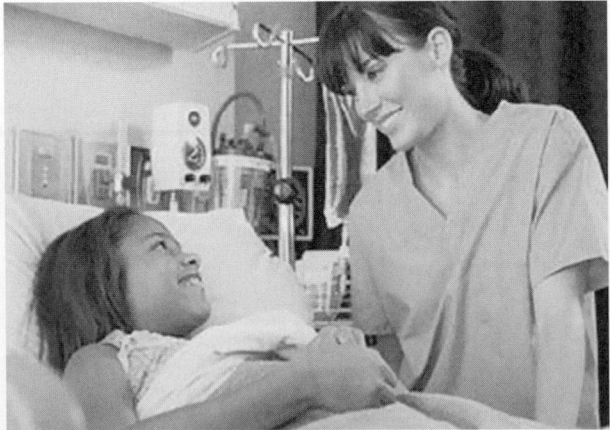

Licensed practical and vocational nurses must be empathetic and caring toward the people they serve.

family members should care for a relative; help to deliver, care for, and feed infants; collect samples for testing and do routine laboratory tests; or feed patients who need help eating.

LPNs and LVNs may be limited to doing certain tasks, depending on the state where they work. For example, in some states, LPNs with proper training can give medication or start intravenous (IV) drips, but in other states LPNs cannot perform these tasks. State regulations also govern the extent to which LPNs and LVNs must be directly supervised. For example, an LPN may provide certain forms of care only with instructions from a registered nurse.

In some states, experienced licensed practical and licensed vocational nurses supervise and direct other LPNs or LVNs and unlicensed medical staff.

Work Environment

Licensed practical and licensed vocational nurses held about 721,700 jobs in 2019. The largest employers of licensed practical and licensed vocational nurses were as follows:

Nursing and residential care facilities	38%
Hospitals; state, local, and private	15
Offices of physicians	13
Home healthcare services	13
Government	6

Nurses must often be on their feet for much of the day. They are vulnerable to back injuries, because they may have to lift patients who have trouble moving in bed, standing, or walking. These duties can be stressful, as can dealing with ill and injured people.

Work Schedules

Most licensed practical and licensed vocational nurses (LPNs and LVNs) work full time. Many work nights, weekends, and holidays, because medical care takes place at all hours. They may be required to work shifts of longer than 8 hours.

How to Become a Licensed Practical or Licensed Vocational Nurse

Becoming a licensed practical or licensed vocational nurse (LPN or LVN) requires completing an approved educational program. LPNs and LVNs must have a license.

Education

LPNs and LVNs must complete an approved educational program. These programs award a certificate or diploma and typically take about 1 year to complete, but may take longer. They are commonly found in technical schools and community colleges, although some programs may be available in high schools or hospitals.

Practical nursing programs combine classroom learning in subjects such as nursing, biology, and pharmacology. All programs also include supervised clinical experience.

Contact state boards of nursing for lists of approved programs.

Licenses, Certifications, and Registrations

After completing a state-approved educational program, prospective LPNs and LVNs can take the National Council

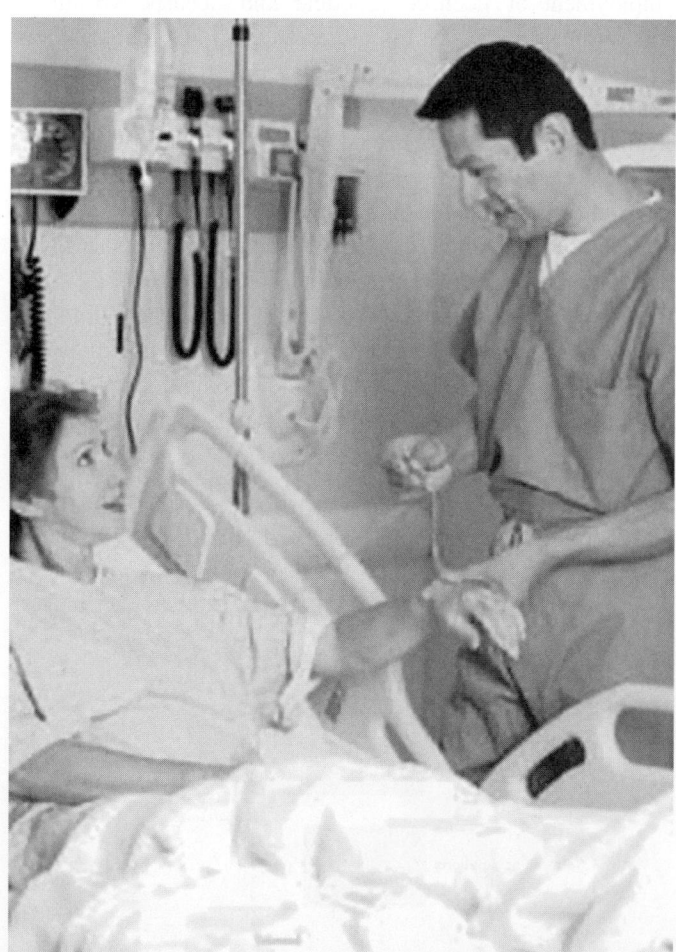

In some states, licensed practical and vocational nurses can give medication or start intravenous (IV) drips.

Licensed practical and vocational nurses provide basic medical care, such as checking a patient's blood pressure.

Licensure Examination (NCLEX-PN). In all states, they must pass the exam to get a license and work as an LPN or LVN. For more information on the NCLEX-PN examination and a list of state boards of nursing, visit the National Council of State Boards of Nursing.

LPNs and LVNs may choose to become certified through professional associations in areas such as gerontology and intravenous (IV) therapy. Certifications show that an LPN or LVN has an advanced level of knowledge about a specific subject.

In addition, employers may prefer to hire candidates who are trained to provide cardiopulmonary resuscitation (CPR).

Advancement

With experience, licensed practical and licensed vocational nurses may advance to supervisory positions. Some LPNs and LVNs advance to other healthcare occupations. For example, an LPN may complete a LPN to RN education program to become a registered nurse.

Important Qualities

Compassion. Licensed practical and licensed vocational nurses must be empathetic and caring toward the people they serve.

Detail oriented. LPNs and LVNs need to be responsible and detail oriented, because they must make sure that patients get the correct care at the right time.

Interpersonal skills. Interacting with patients and other healthcare providers is a big part of their jobs, so LPNs and LVNs need good interpersonal skills.

Patience. Dealing with sick and injured people may be stressful. LPNs and LVNs should be patient, so they can cope with any stress that stems from providing care to these patients.

Physical stamina. LPNs and LVNs should be comfortable performing physical tasks, such as bending over patients for a long time.

Speaking skills. It is important that LPNs and LVNs communicate effectively. For example, they may need to relay information about a patient's current condition to a registered nurse.

Pay

The median annual wage for licensed practical and licensed vocational nurses was $47,480 in May 2019. The median wage is the wage at which half the workers in an occupation earned more than that amount and half earned less. The lowest 10 percent earned less than $34,560, and the highest 10 percent earned more than $63,360.

In May 2019, the median annual wages for licensed practical and licensed vocational nurses in the top industries in which they worked were as follows:

Nursing and residential care facilities..................	$48,840
Government..	48,400
Home healthcare services	48,130
Hospitals; state, local, and private........................	45,550
Offices of physicians...	43,620

Most licensed practical and licensed vocational nurses (LPNs and LVNs) work full time. Many work nights, weekends, and holidays, because medical care takes place at all hours. They may be required to work shifts of longer than 8 hours.

Job Outlook

Employment of licensed practical and licensed vocational nurses (LPNs and LVNs) is projected to grow 9 percent from 2019 to 2029, much faster than the average for all occupations.

As the baby-boom population ages, the overall need for healthcare services is expected to increase. LPNs and LVNs will be needed in residential care facilities and in home health environments to care for older patients.

A number of chronic conditions, such as diabetes and obesity, have become more prevalent in recent years. LPNs and LVNs will be needed to assist and care for patients with these and other conditions. In addition, many procedures that once could be done only in hospitals are now being done outside of hospitals, creating demand in other settings, such as outpatient care centers.

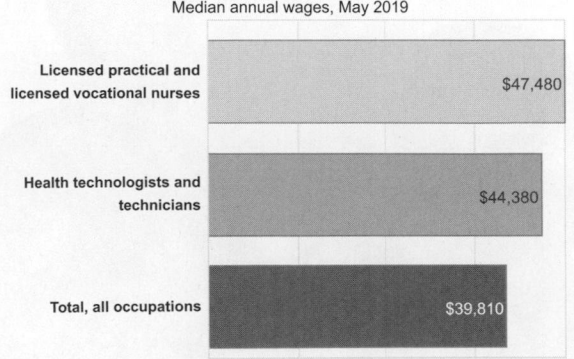

Licensed Practical and Licensed Vocational Nurses

Median annual wages, May 2019

Licensed practical and licensed vocational nurses — $47,480

Health technologists and technicians — $44,380

Total, all occupations — $39,810

Note: All Occupations includes all occupations in the U.S. Economy.
Source: U.S. Bureau of Labor Statistics, Occupational Employment Statistics.

Licensed Practical and Licensed Vocational Nurses

Percent change in employment, projected 2019-29

Licensed practical and licensed vocational nurses — 9%

Health technologists and technicians — 8%

Total, all occupations — 4%

Note: All Occupations includes all occupations in the U.S. Economy.
Source: U.S. Bureau of Labor Statistics, Employment Projections program.

Job Prospects

Job prospects should be favorable for LPNs and LVNs who are willing to work in rural and medically underserved areas. Employers also may prefer candidates who have certification in a specialty area such as gerontology or intravenous (IV) therapy.

Employment projections data for licensed practical and licensed vocational nurses, 2019-29					
Occupational Title	SOC Code	Employment, 2019	Projected Employment, 2029	Change, 2019-29	
				Percent	Numeric
SOURCE: U.S. Bureau of Labor Statistics, Employment Projections program					
Licensed practical and licensed vocational nurses	29-2061	721,700	787,400	9	65,700

State & Area Data

Occupational Employment Statistics (OES)

The Occupational Employment Statistics (OES) program produces employment and wage estimates annually for over 800 occupations. These estimates are available for the nation as a whole, for individual states, and for metropolitan and nonmetropolitan areas.

Contacts for More Information

For more information about licensed practical or licensed vocational nurses, visit
➤ National Association of Licensed Practical Nurses

For more information about the National Council Licensure Examination (NCLEX-PN) and a list of individual state boards of nursing, visit
➤ National Council of State Boards of Nursing

Massage Therapists

Summary

Quick Facts: Massage Therapists

2019 Median Pay	$42,820 per year $20.59 per hour
Typical Entry-Level Education	Postsecondary non-degree award
Work Experience in a Related Occupation	None
On-the-job Training	None
Number of Jobs, 2019	166,700
Job Outlook, 2019-29	21% (Much faster than average)
Employment Change, 2019-29	34,400

What Massage Therapists Do

Massage therapists treat clients by using touch to manipulate the muscles and other soft tissues of the body.

Work Environment

Massage therapists work in an array of settings, such as spas, franchised clinics, physicians' offices, hotels, and fitness centers. Some massage therapists also travel to clients' homes or offices to give a massage.

How to Become a Massage Therapist

Massage therapists typically complete a postsecondary education program of 500 or more hours of study and experience, although standards and requirements vary by state or other jurisdictions. Most states regulate massage therapy and require massage therapists to have a license or certification.

Pay

The median annual wage for massage therapists was $42,820 in May 2019.

Job Outlook

Employment of massage therapists is projected to grow 21 percent from 2019 to 2029, much faster than the average for all occupations. Demand will likely increase as more healthcare providers understand the benefits of massage and these services become part of treatment plans.

State & Area Data

Explore resources for employment and wages by state and area for massage therapists.

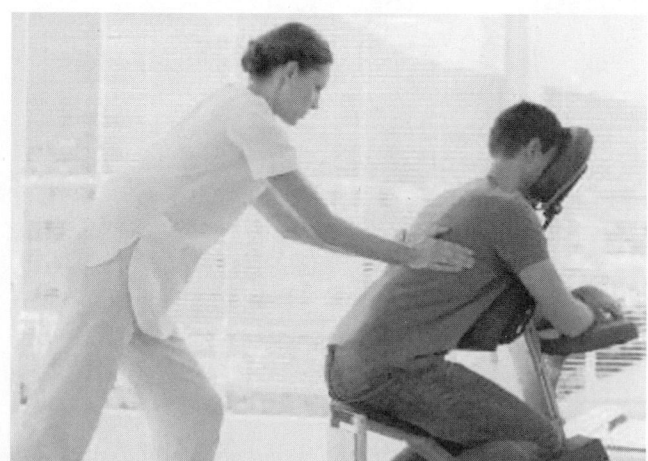

Massage therapists use touch to manipulate a client's muscles and other soft tissues.

What Massage Therapists Do

Massage therapists treat clients by using touch to manipulate the muscles and other soft tissues of the body. With their touch, therapists relieve pain, help heal injuries, improve circulation, relieve stress, increase relaxation, and aid in the general wellness of clients.

Duties

Massage therapists typically do the following:

- Talk with clients about their symptoms, medical history, and desired results
- Evaluate clients to locate painful or tense areas of the body
- Manipulate muscles and other soft tissues of the body
- Provide clients with guidance on stretching, strengthening, overall relaxation, and how to improve their posture
- Document clients' conditions and progress

Massage therapists use touch to treat clients' injuries and to promote the clients' general wellness. They use their hands, fingers, forearms, elbows, and sometimes feet to knead muscles and soft tissues of the body.

Massage therapists may use lotions and oils, and massage tables or chairs, when treating a client. A massage can be as short as 5–10 minutes or could last more than an hour.

Massage therapists talk with clients about what they hope to achieve through massage. They may suggest personalized treatment plans for their clients, including information about additional relaxation techniques to practice between sessions.

Massage therapists can specialize in many different types of massage or modalities. Swedish massage, deep-tissue massage, and sports massage are just a few of the many modalities of massage therapy. Most massage therapists specialize in several modalities, which require different techniques.

The type of massage given typically depends on the client's needs and physical condition. For example, massage therapists

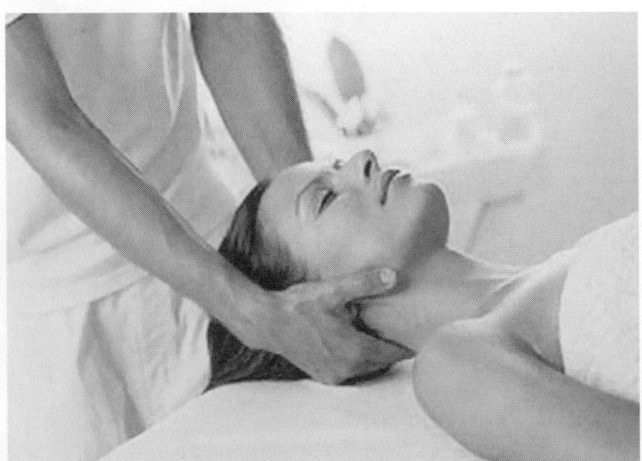

Massage therapists knead muscles and other soft tissues of the body to provide treatment for injuries and to promote general wellness.

may use a special technique for elderly clients that they would not use for athletes. Some forms of massage are given solely to one type of client; for example, prenatal massage is given only to pregnant women.

Work Environment

Massage therapists held about 166,700 jobs in 2019. The largest employers of massage therapists were as follows:

Self-employed workers	35%
Personal care services	33
Offices of all other health practitioners	11
Offices of chiropractors	8
Accommodation	6

Some massage therapists travel to clients' homes or offices to give a massage. Others work out of their own homes. Many massage therapists, especially those who are self-employed, provide their own table or chair, sheets, pillows, and body lotions or oils.

A massage therapist's working conditions depend heavily on the venue in which the massage is performed and on what the client wants. For example, when giving a massage to help clients relax, massage therapists generally work in dimly lit settings and use candles, incense, and calm, soothing music. In

Massage therapists create an environment intended to make clients feel relaxed.

contrast, a massage meant to help rehabilitate a client with an injury may be conducted in a well-lit setting with several other people receiving treatment in the same room.

Injuries and Illnesses

Because giving a massage is physically demanding, massage therapists can injure themselves if they do not use the proper techniques. Repetitive-motion problems and fatigue from standing for extended periods are most common.

Therapists can limit these risks by using good body mechanics, spacing sessions properly, exercising, and, in many cases, receiving a massage themselves regularly.

Work Schedules

Many massage therapists work part time. Because therapists work by appointment in most cases, their schedules and the number of hours worked each week vary considerably. Moreover, because of the strength and endurance needed to give a massage, many therapists cannot perform massage services 8 hours per day, 5 days per week.

In addition to giving massages, therapists, especially those who are self-employed, may spend time recording clients' notes, marketing, booking clients, washing linens, and conducting other general business tasks.

How to Become a Massage Therapist

Massage therapists typically complete a postsecondary education program of 500 or more hours of study and experience, although standards and requirements vary greatly by state or other jurisdiction. Most states regulate massage therapy and require massage therapists to have a license or certification.

Education

Education requirements for massage therapists vary greatly by state or locality. Education programs are typically found in private or public postsecondary institutions. Most programs require at least 500 hours of study for their completion; some programs require 1,000 or more hours.

A high school diploma or equivalent is usually required for admission to a massage therapy program. Programs generally include both classroom study and hands-on practice of massage techniques. Programs cover subjects such as anatomy; physiology, which is the study of organs and tissues; kinesiology, which is the study of motion and body mechanics; pathology, which is the study of disease; business management; and ethics.

Programs may concentrate on certain modalities, or specialties, of massage. Several programs also offer job placement services and continuing education. Both full-time and part-time programs are available.

Licenses, Certifications, and Registrations

In 2016, 45 states and the District of Columbia regulated massage therapy. Although not all states license massage therapy, they may have regulations at the local level.

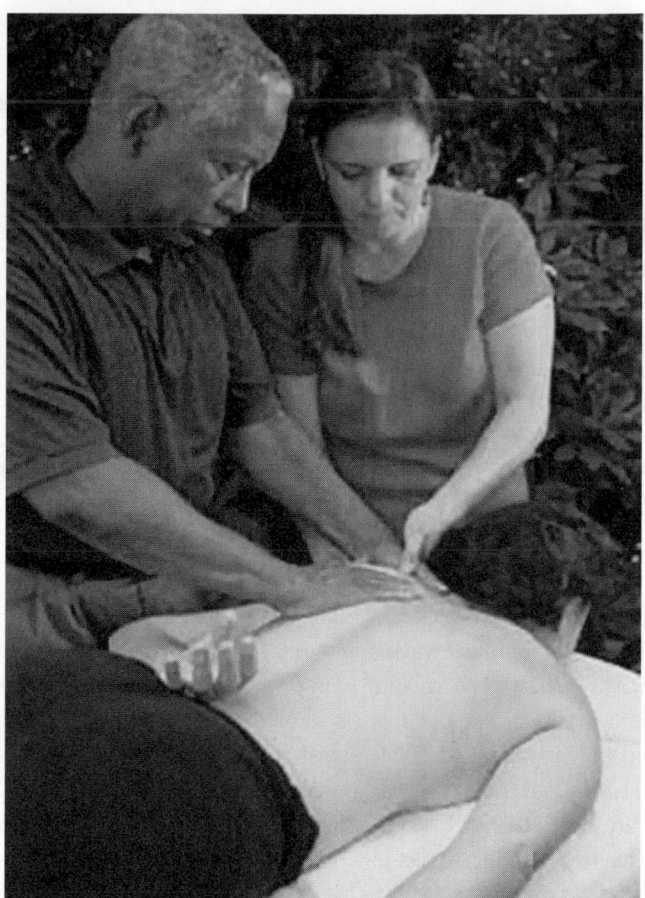

Massage therapists typically complete a postsecondary education program of 500 or more hours of study and experience.

In states with massage therapy regulations, workers must get a license or certification before practicing massage therapy. State regulations typically require graduation from an approved massage therapy program and passing an exam.

The exam may be a state-specific exam or the Massage and Bodywork Licensing Examination (MBLEx) licensure exam, offered by the Federation of State Massage Therapy Boards.

Massage therapists also may need to pass a background check, have liability insurance, and be certified in cardiopulmonary resuscitation (CPR). Many states require massage therapists to complete continuing education credits and to renew their license periodically. Those wishing to practice massage therapy should look into legal requirements for the state and locality in which they intend to practice.

Important Qualities

Communication skills. Massage therapists need to listen carefully to clients in order to understand what they want to achieve through massage sessions.

Decisionmaking skills. Massage therapists must evaluate each client's needs and recommend the best treatment on the basis of that person's needs.

Empathy. Massage therapists must give clients a positive experience, which requires building trust between therapist and client. Making clients feel comfortable is necessary for therapists to expand their client base.

Integrity. Massage therapists often have access to client information such as medical histories. Therefore, they must be trustworthy and protect the privacy of their clients.

Physical stamina. Massage therapists may give several treatments during a workday and have to stay on their feet throughout massage appointments.

Physical strength and dexterity. Massage therapists must be strong and able to exert pressure through a variety of movements of the arms and hands when manipulating a client's muscles.

Time-management skills. Massage therapists must tailor an appointment to a client's specific needs. They must use their appointment time wisely to help each client accomplish his or her goals.

Pay

The median annual wage for massage therapists was $42,820 in May 2019. The median wage is the wage at which half the workers in an occupation earned more than that amount and half earned less. The lowest 10 percent earned less than $21,810, and the highest 10 percent earned more than $80,630.

In May 2019, the median annual wages for massage therapists in the top industries in which they worked were as follows:

Offices of chiropractors	$52,230
Offices of all other health practitioners	46,670
Personal care services	40,380
Accommodation	30,160

Most massage therapists earn a combination of wages and tips and may receive free or discounted massages as a benefit.

Many massage therapists work part time. Because therapists work by appointment in most cases, their schedules and the number of hours worked each week vary considerably. In addition to giving massages, therapists, especially those who are self-employed, may spend time recording clients' notes, marketing, booking clients, washing linens, and conducting other general business tasks.

Job Outlook

Employment of massage therapists is projected to grow 21 percent from 2019 to 2029, much faster than the average for all occupations. Continued growth in the demand for massage services will lead to new openings for massage therapists.

As more states adopt licensing requirements and standards for massage therapists, the practice of massage is likely to be respected and accepted by more people as a way to treat pain and to improve overall wellness.

Similarly, demand will likely increase as more healthcare providers understand the benefits of massage and these services become part of treatment plans. However, demand in some healthcare settings will be tempered by limited insurance coverage for massage services.

Massage also offers specific benefits to particular groups of people whose continued demand for massage services will lead to overall growth for the occupation. For example, many sports teams hire massage therapists to help their athletes rehabilitate from injuries and to relieve or manage pain.

The number of massage clinic franchises has increased in recent years. Many franchised clinics offer more affordable massages than those provided at spas and resorts, making massage services available to a wider range of customers.

Job Prospects

In states that regulate massage therapy, opportunities should be available to those who complete formal programs and pass a professionally recognized exam. However, new massage therapists should expect that it can take time to build a client base.

Because referrals are an important source of work for massage therapists, marketing and networking may help increase the number of job opportunities. Joining a professional association also can help build strong contacts and further increase

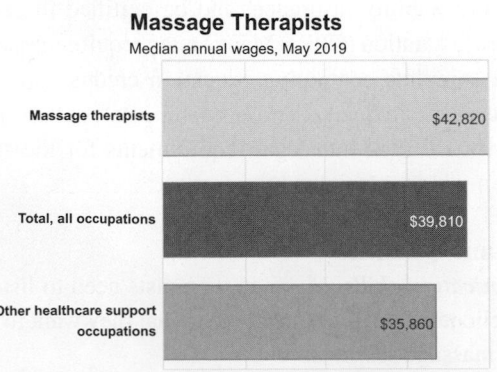

Note: All Occupations includes all occupations in the U.S. Economy.
Source: U.S. Bureau of Labor Statistics, Occupational Employment Statistics.

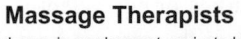
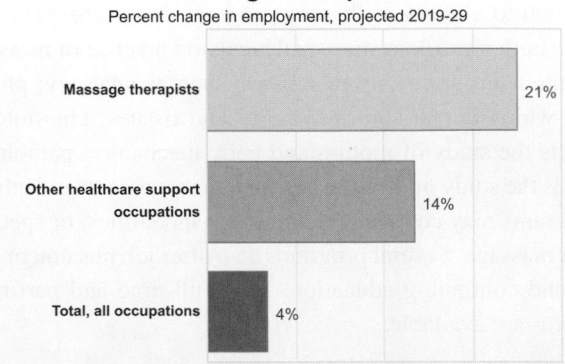

Note: All Occupations includes all occupations in the U.S. Economy.
Source: U.S. Bureau of Labor Statistics, Employment Projections program.

the likelihood of steady work. In addition, massage therapists may be able to attract a wider variety of clients by completing education programs in multiple modalities.

Employment projections data for massage therapists, 2019-29					
Occupational Title	SOC Code	Employment, 2019	Projected Employment, 2029	Change, 2019-29	
				Percent	Numeric
SOURCE: U.S. Bureau of Labor Statistics, Employment Projections program					
Massage therapists	31-9011	166,700	201,100	21	34,400

State & Area Data
Occupational Employment Statistics (OES)

The Occupational Employment Statistics (OES) program produces employment and wage estimates annually for over 800 occupations. These estimates are available for the nation as a whole, for individual states, and for metropolitan and nonmetropolitan areas.

Contacts for More Information

For more information about careers in massage therapy, visit
➤ Associated Bodywork & Massage Professionals
➤ American Massage Therapy Association
➤ National Certification Board for Therapeutic Massage & Bodywork

For more information about national testing and national certification, visit
➤ Federation of State Massage Therapy Boards

For more information about accredited massage therapy programs, visit
➤ Commission on Massage Therapy Accreditation

Medical Assistants

Summary

Quick Facts: Medical Assistants

2019 Median Pay	$34,800 per year $16.73 per hour
Typical Entry-Level Education	Postsecondary nondegree award
Work Experience in a Related Occupation	None
On-the-job Training	None
Number of Jobs, 2019	725,200
Job Outlook, 2019-29	19% (Much faster than average)
Employment Change, 2019-29	139,200

What Medical Assistants Do

Medical assistants complete administrative and clinical tasks in hospitals, offices of physicians, and other healthcare facilities.

Work Environment

Most medical assistants work in physicians' offices, hospitals, outpatient clinics, and other healthcare facilities.

How to Become a Medical Assistant

Most medical assistants have postsecondary education such as a certificate. Others enter the occupation with a high school diploma and learn through on-the-job training.

Pay

The median annual wage for medical assistants was $34,800 in May 2019.

Job Outlook

Employment of medical assistants is projected to grow 19 percent from 2019 to 2029, much faster than the average for all occupations. The growth of the aging baby-boom population will continue to increase demand for preventive medical services, which are often provided by physicians. As a result, physicians will hire more assistants to perform routine administrative and clinical duties, allowing the physicians to see more patients.

State & Area Data

Explore resources for employment and wages by state and area for medical assistants.

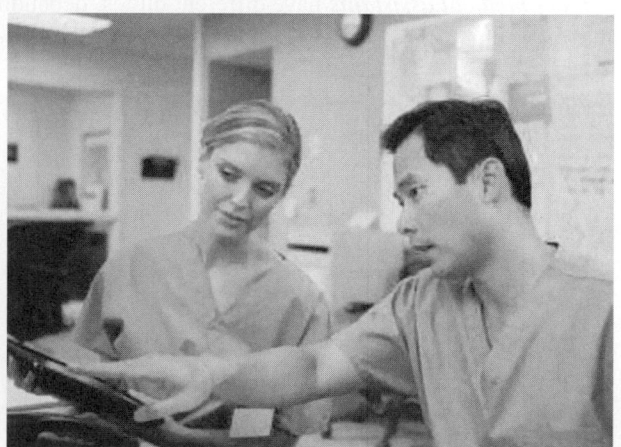

Medical assistants complete administrative and clinical tasks in the offices of physicians, hospitals, and other healthcare facilities.

What Medical Assistants Do

Medical assistants complete administrative and clinical tasks in the offices of physicians, hospitals, and other healthcare facilities. Their duties vary with the location, specialty, and size of the practice.

Duties

Medical assistants typically do the following:

- Record patient history and personal information
- Measure vital signs, such as blood pressure
- Help physicians with patient examinations
- Give patients injections or medications as directed by physicians and as permitted by state law
- Schedule patient appointments
- Prepare blood samples for laboratory tests
- Enter patient information into medical records

Medical assistants take and record patients' personal information. They must be able to keep that information confidential and discuss it only with other medical personnel who are involved in treating the patient.

Electronic health records (EHRs) are changing some medical assistants' jobs. More and more physicians are adopting EHRs, moving all their patient information from paper to electronic records. Assistants need to learn the EHR software that their office uses.

Medical assistants should not be confused with physician assistants, who examine, diagnose, and treat patients under a physician's supervision.

In larger practices or hospitals, medical assistants may specialize in either administrative or clinical work.

Administrative medical assistants often fill out insurance forms or code patients' medical information. They often answer telephones and schedule patient appointments.

Clinical medical assistants have different duties, depending on the state where they work. They may do basic laboratory tests, dispose of contaminated supplies, and sterilize medical instruments. They may have additional responsibilities, such as instructing patients about medication or special diets, preparing patients for x rays, removing stitches, drawing blood, or changing dressings.

Some medical assistants specialize according to the type of medical office where they work. The following are examples of *specialized medical assistants*:

Ophthalmic medical assistants and optometric assistants help ophthalmologists and optometrists provide eye care. They show patients how to insert, remove, and care for contact lenses. Ophthalmic medical assistants also may help an ophthalmologist in surgery.

Podiatric medical assistants work closely with podiatrists (foot doctors). They may make castings of feet, expose and develop x rays, and help podiatrists in surgery.

Work Environment

Medical assistants held about 725,200 jobs in 2019. The largest employers of medical assistants were as follows:

Offices of physicians	57%
Hospitals; state, local, and private	15
Outpatient care centers	8
Offices of chiropractors	4

Work Schedules

Most medical assistants work full time. Some work evenings, weekends, or holidays to cover shifts in medical facilities that are always open.

How to Become a Medical Assistant

Most medical assistants have a postsecondary education award such as a certificate. Others enter the occupation with a high school diploma and learn through on-the-job training.

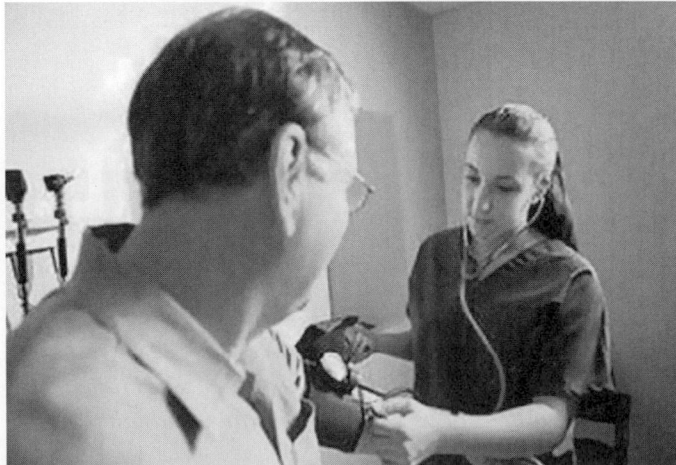

Medical assistants often take medical histories and record vital signs of patients.

Medical assistants perform administrative and clinical tasks to keep the offices of health practitioners running smoothly.

Assistants may update a patient's medical file, fill out insurance forms, and answer telephone calls in a practitioner's office.

Education

Medical assistants typically graduate from postsecondary education programs. Although there are no formal educational requirements for becoming a medical assistant in most states, employers may prefer to hire assistants who have completed these programs.

Programs for medical assisting are available from community colleges, vocational schools, technical schools, and universities and take about 1 year to complete. These programs usually lead to a certificate or diploma. Some community colleges offer 2-year programs that lead to an associate's degree. All programs have classroom and laboratory portions that include lessons in anatomy and medical terminology.

Some medical assistants have a high school diploma or equivalent and learn their duties on the job. High school students interested in a career as a medical assistant should take courses in biology, chemistry, and anatomy, and possibly business and computers.

Important Qualities

Analytical skills. Medical assistants must be able to understand and follow medical charts and diagnoses. They may be required to code a patient's medical records for billing purposes.

Detail oriented. Medical assistants need to be precise when taking vital signs or recording patient information. Physicians and insurance companies rely on accurate records.

Interpersonal skills. Medical assistants need to be able to discuss patient information with other medical personnel, such as physicians. They often interact with patients who may be in pain or in distress, so they need to be able to act in a calm and professional manner.

Technical skills. Medical assistants should be able to use basic clinical instruments so they can take a patient's vital signs, such as heart rate and blood pressure.

Training

Medical assistants who do not have postsecondary education certificates learn their skills through on-the-job training. Physicians or other medical assistants may teach a new assistant medical terminology, the names of the instruments, how to do daily tasks, how to interact with patients, and other tasks that help keep an office running smoothly. Medical assistants also learn how to code both paper and electronic health records (EHRs) and how to record patient information. It can take several months for an assistant to complete training, depending on the facility.

Licenses, Certifications, and Registrations

Medical assistants are not required to be certified in most states. However, employers may prefer to hire certified assistants.

Several organizations offer certification. An applicant must pass an exam and have taken one of several routes to be eligible for each certification. These routes include graduation from an accredited program and work experience, among others. In most cases, an applicant must be at least 18 years old before applying for certification.

The National Commission for Certifying Agencies, part of the Institute for Credentialing Excellence, accredits five certifications for medical assistants:

- Certified Medical Assistant (CMA) from the American Association of Medical Assistants
- Registered Medical Assistant (RMA) from American Medical Technologists
- National Certified Medical Assistant (NCMA) from the National Center for Competency Testing
- Certified Clinical Medical Assistant (CCMA) from the National Healthcareer Association
- Certified Medical Administrative Assistant (CMAA) from the National Healthcareer Association

Some states may require assistants to graduate from an accredited program, pass an exam, or both, in order to practice. Contact the state board of medicine for more information.

Advancement

With experience, medical assistants can specialize and move into leadership roles. With more education they may advance into other healthcare occupations such as registered nurse, physician assistant, or nurse practitioner.

Pay

The median annual wage for medical assistants was $34,800 in May 2019. The median wage is the wage at which half the workers in an occupation earned more than that amount and half earned less. The lowest 10 percent earned less than $25,820, and the highest 10 percent earned more than $48,720.

In May 2019, the median annual wages for medical assistants in the top industries in which they worked were as follows:

Outpatient care centers	$36,810
Hospitals; state, local, and private	36,080
Offices of physicians	34,870

Medical Assistants

Median annual wages, May 2019

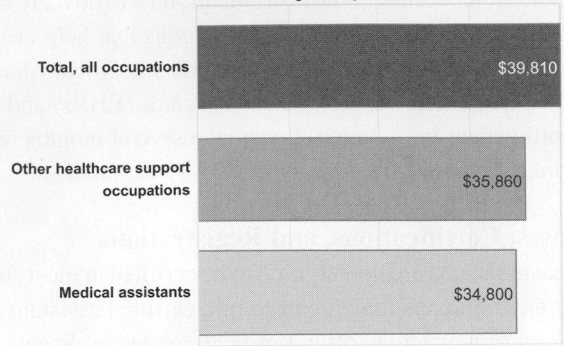

Note: All Occupations includes all occupations in the U.S. Economy.
Source: U.S. Bureau of Labor Statistics, Occupational Employment
Statistics.

Offices of chiropractors.. 30,870

Most medical assistants work full time. Some work evenings, weekends, or holidays to cover shifts in medical facilities that are always open.

Job Outlook

Employment of medical assistants is projected to grow 19 percent from 2019 to 2029, much faster than the average for all occupations. The growth of the aging baby-boom population will continue to increase demand for preventive medical services, which are often provided by physicians. As a result, physicians will hire more assistants to perform routine administrative and clinical duties, allowing the physicians to see more patients.

An increasing number of group practices, clinics, and other healthcare facilities will also need support workers, particularly medical assistants, to complete both administrative and clinical duties. Medical assistants work mostly in primary care, a steadily growing sector of the healthcare industry.

Job Prospects

Medical assistants are expected to have good job prospects; however, those who earn certification and have familiarity with electronic health records (EHRs) may have better job prospects.

Employment projections data for medical assistants, 2019-29

Occupational Title	SOC Code	Employment, 2019	Projected Employment, 2029	Change, 2019-29	
				Percent	Numeric
SOURCE: U.S. Bureau of Labor Statistics, Employment Projections program					
Medical assistants	31-9092	725,200	864,400	19	139,200

Medical Assistants

Percent change in employment, projected 2019-29

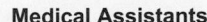
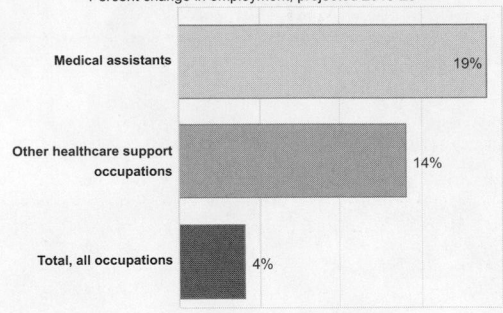

Note: All Occupations includes all occupations in the U.S. Economy.
Source: U.S. Bureau of Labor Statistics, Employment Projections program.

State & Area Data
Occupational Employment Statistics (OES)

The Occupational Employment Statistics (OES) program produces employment and wage estimates annually for over 800 occupations. These estimates are available for the nation as a whole, for individual states, and for metropolitan and nonmetropolitan areas.

Contacts for More Information

For more information about becoming a medical assistant, including information on certification, visit
- American Association of Medical Assistants
- American Medical Technologists
- National Center for Competency Testing
- National Healthcareer Association
- Institute for Credentialing Excellence
- American Optometric Association
- American Society of Podiatric Medical Assistants
- Joint Commission on Allied Health Personnel in Ophthalmology
- American Medical Certification Association

For lists of accredited educational programs in medical assisting, visit
- Commission on Accreditation of Allied Health Education Programs
- Accrediting Bureau of Health Education Schools
- Medical Assistant Schools Directory

Medical Records and Health Information Technicians

Summary

Quick Facts: Medical Records and Health Information Technicians

2019 Median Pay	$42,630 per year $20.50 per hour
Typical Entry-Level Education	Postsecondary non-degree award
Work Experience in a Related Occupation	None
On-the-job Training	None
Number of Jobs, 2019	341,600
Job Outlook, 2019-29	8% (Much faster than average)
Employment Change, 2019-29	29,000

What Medical Records and Health Information Technicians Do

Medical records and health information technicians organize and manage health information data.

Work Environment

Medical records and health information technicians typically work in offices and may spend many hours in front of computer monitors. Some technicians may work from home.

How to Become a Medical Records or Health Information Technician

Health information technicians typically need a postsecondary certificate to enter the occupation, although some may need an associate's degree. Certification is often required.

Pay

The median annual wage for medical records and health information technicians was $42,630 in May 2019.

Job Outlook

Employment of medical records and health information technicians is projected to grow 8 percent from 2019 to 2029, much faster than the average for all occupations. The demand for health services is expected to increase as the population ages.

State & Area Data

Explore resources for employment and wages by state and area for medical records and health information technicians.

What Medical Records and Health Information Technicians Do

Medical records and health information technicians, commonly referred to as *health information technicians*, organize and manage health information data by ensuring that it maintains its quality, accuracy, accessibility, and security in both paper files and electronic systems. They use various classification systems to code and categorize patient information for insurance reimbursement purposes, for databases and registries, and to maintain patients' medical and treatment histories.

Duties

Health information technicians typically do the following:

- Review patients' records for timeliness, completeness, accuracy, and appropriateness of data
- Organize and maintain data for clinical databases and registries
- Track patient outcomes for quality assessment
- Use classification software to assign clinical codes for insurance reimbursement and data analysis

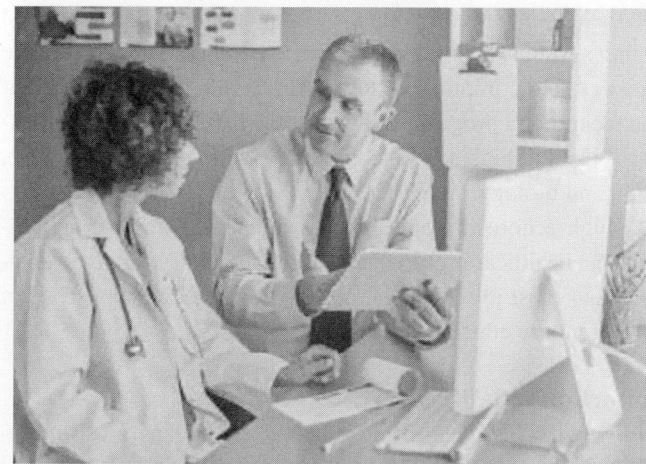

Medical records and health information technicians meet with other healthcare workers to clarify diagnoses or to get additional information to make sure that records are complete and accurate.

Health information technicians assemble patients' health information including medical history, symptoms, examination results, tests, and treatments.

- Electronically record data for collection, storage, analysis, retrieval, and reporting
- Maintain confidentiality of patients' records

Health information technicians document patients' health information, including their medical history, symptoms, examination and test results, treatments, and other information about healthcare services that are provided to patients. Their duties vary by employer and by the size of the facility in which they work.

Although health information technicians do not provide direct patient care, they work regularly with registered nurses and other healthcare professionals. They meet with these workers to clarify diagnoses or to get additional information to make sure that records are complete and accurate.

The increasing adaptation and use of electronic health records (EHRs) will continue to change the job responsibilities of health information technicians. Technicians will need to be familiar with, or be able to learn, EHR computer software, follow EHR security and privacy practices, and analyze electronic data to improve healthcare information.

Health information technicians can specialize in many aspects of health information. Some work as *medical coders*, sometimes called *coding specialists*, or as *cancer registrars*.

Medical coders typically do the following:

- Review patient information for preexisting conditions, such as diabetes, so patient data can be coded properly
- Assign appropriate diagnoses and procedure codes for patient care, population health statistics, and billing purposes
- Work as a liaison between the healthcare providers and billing offices

Cancer registrars typically do the following:

- Review patients' records and pathology reports to verify completeness and accuracy
- Assign classification codes to represent the diagnosis and treatment of cancers and benign tumors
- Conduct annual followups to track treatment, survival, and recovery
- Compile and analyze cancer patient information for research purposes
- Maintain facility, regional, and national databases of cancer patients

Work Environment

Medical records and health information technicians held about 341,600 jobs in 2019. The largest employers of medical records and health information technicians were as follows:

Hospitals; state, local, and private	37%
Offices of physicians	15
Administrative and support services	5
Professional, scientific, and technical services	5
Nursing care facilities (skilled nursing facilities)	3

This is one of the few health-related occupations in which there is no direct hands-on patient care.

Medical records and health information technicians typically work in offices and may spend many hours in front of computer monitors. Some technicians may work from home.

Work Schedules

Most health information technicians work full time. In healthcare facilities that are always open, such as hospitals, technicians may work evening or overnight shifts.

How to Become a Medical Records or Health Information Technician

Health information technicians typically need a postsecondary certificate to enter the occupation, although some may need an associate's degree. Certification is often required.

Education

Postsecondary certificate and associate's degree programs in health information technology typically include courses in medical terminology, anatomy and physiology, communication, health data requirements and standards, classification and coding systems, healthcare reimbursement methods, healthcare statistics, and computer systems. Applicants to health information technology programs may increase their chances of admission by taking high school courses in health, computer science, math, and biology.

A high school diploma or equivalent and previous experience in a healthcare setting are enough to qualify for some positions, but most jobs for health information technicians require postsecondary education.

Important Qualities

Analytical skills. Health information technicians must understand and follow medical records and diagnoses, and then decide how best to code them in a patient's medical records.

Detail oriented. Health information technicians must be accurate when recording and coding patient information.

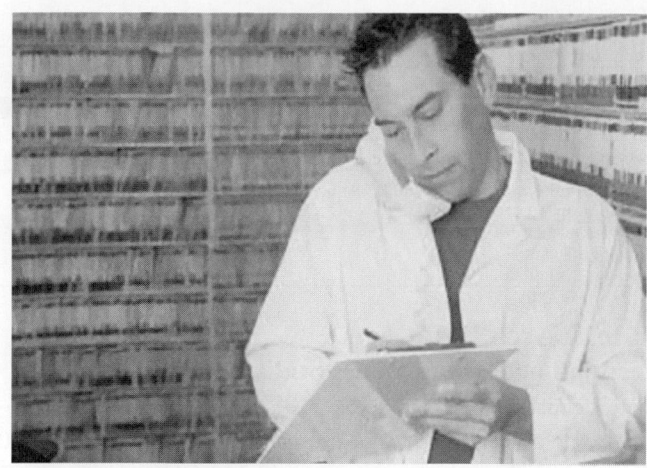

Health information technicians organize and maintain data for clinical databases and registries.

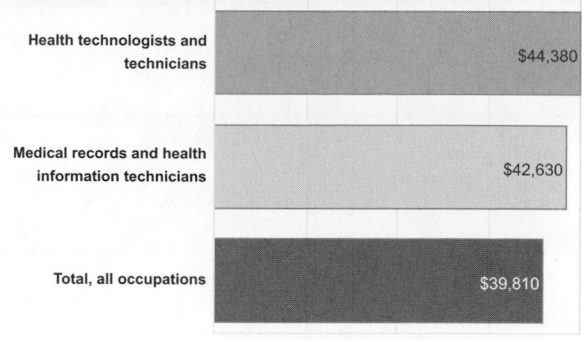

Medical Records and Health Information Technicians

Median annual wages, May 2019

Health technologists and technicians	$44,380
Medical records and health information technicians	$42,630
Total, all occupations	$39,810

Note: All Occupations includes all occupations in the U.S. Economy.
Source: U.S. Bureau of Labor Statistics, Occupational Employment Statistics.

Integrity. Health information technicians work with patient data that are required, by law, to be kept confidential. They must exercise discretion and a strong sense of ethics when working with this information in order to protect patient confidentiality.

Interpersonal skills. Health information technicians need to be able to discuss patient information, discrepancies, and data requirements with other professionals such as physicians and finance personnel.

Technical skills. Health information technicians must use coding and classification software and the electronic health record (EHR) system that their healthcare organization or physician practice has adopted.

Licenses, Certifications, and Registrations

Most employers prefer to hire health information technicians who have certification, or they may expect applicants to earn certification shortly after being hired. A health information technician can earn certification from several organizations. Certifications include the Registered Health Information Technician (RHIT) and the Certified Tumor Registrar (CTR), among others.

Some organizations base certification on passing an exam. Others require graduation from an accredited program. Many coding certifications also require coding experience in a work setting. Once certified, technicians typically must renew their certification regularly and take continuing education courses.

A few states and facilities require cancer registrars to be certified. Certification as a Certified Tumor Registrar (CTR) requires completion of a formal education program and experience, along with passing an exam.

Advancement

Technicians may advance to a position as a medical or health services manager after completing a bachelor's or master's degree program and taking the required certification courses. Requirements vary by facility.

Pay

The median annual wage for medical records and health information technicians was $42,630 in May 2019. The median wage is the wage at which half the workers in an occupation earned more than that amount and half earned less. The lowest 10 percent earned less than $27,820, and the highest 10 percent earned more than $71,150.

In May 2019, the median annual wages for medical records and health information technicians in the top industries in which they worked were as follows:

Hospitals; state, local, and private	$45,710
Administrative and support services	43,200
Professional, scientific, and technical services	43,050
Nursing care facilities (skilled nursing facilities)	38,270
Offices of physicians	38,040

Most health information technicians work full time. In healthcare facilities that are always open, such as hospitals, technicians may work evening or overnight shifts.

Job Outlook

Employment of medical records and health information technicians is projected to grow 8 percent from 2019 to 2029, much faster than the average for all occupations.

An aging population will require more medical services, and health information technicians will be needed to organize and manage the older generations' health information data. This will mean more claims for reimbursement from insurance companies.

Medical Records and Health Information Technicians

Percent change in employment, projected 2019-29

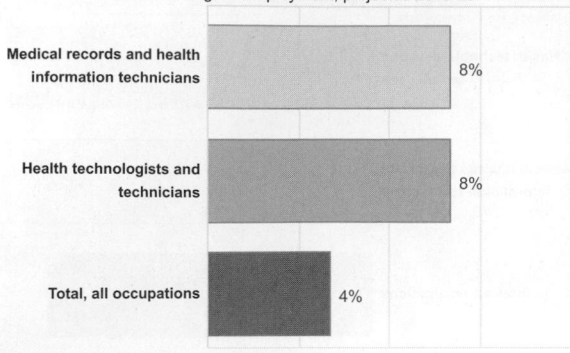

Medical records and health information technicians	8%
Health technologists and technicians	8%
Total, all occupations	4%

Note: All Occupations includes all occupations in the U.S. Economy.
Source: U.S. Bureau of Labor Statistics, Employment Projections program.

Additional records, coupled with widespread use of electronic health records (EHRs) by all types of healthcare providers, will lead to an increased need for technicians to organize and manage the associated information in all areas of the healthcare industry.

Cancer registrars are expected to continue to be in high demand. As the population ages, there will likely be more types of special purpose registries because many illnesses are detected and treated later in life.

Job Prospects

Prospects will be best for those with a certification in health information, such as the Registered Health Information Technician (RHIT) or the Certified Tumor Registrar (CTR). As EHR systems continue to become more common, health information technicians with computer skills will be needed to use them.

Employment projections data for medical records and health information technicians, 2019-29					
Occupational Title	SOC Code	Employment, 2019	Projected Employment, 2029	Change, 2019-29	
				Percent	Numeric
SOURCE: U.S. Bureau of Labor Statistics, Employment Projections program					
Medical dosimetrists, medical records specialists, and health technologists and technicians, all other	29-2098	341,600	370,600	8	29,000

State & Area Data

Occupational Employment Statistics (OES)

The Occupational Employment Statistics (OES) program produces employment and wage estimates annually for over 800 occupations. These estimates are available for the nation as a whole, for individual states, and for metropolitan and nonmetropolitan areas.

Contacts for More Information

For more information about health information technicians, including details about certification, visit
➤ American Health Information Management Association
➤ American Academy of Professional Coders
➤ Professional Association of Healthcare Coding Specialists
➤ National Healthcareer Association
➤ For more information about medical coding and billing, visit
➤ MB&CC (formerly known as Medical Billing & Coding)
➤ For more information about cancer registrars, visit
➤ National Cancer Registrars Association

For a list of accredited training programs, visit
➤ Commission on Accreditation for Health Informatics and Information Management Education

Medical Transcriptionists

Summary

Quick Facts: Medical Transcriptionists

2019 Median Pay	$33,380 per year $16.05 per hour
Typical Entry-Level Education	Postsecondary non-degree award
Work Experience in a Related Occupation	None
On-the-job Training	None
Number of Jobs, 2019	58,500
Job Outlook, 2019-29	-2% (Decline)
Employment Change, 2019-29	-1,300

What Medical Transcriptionists Do

Medical transcriptionists listen to voice recordings that physicians and other healthcare workers make and convert them into written reports.

Work Environment

Most medical transcriptionists work for hospitals, physicians' offices, and third-party transcription service companies that provide transcription services to healthcare establishments. Others are self-employed.

How to Become a Medical Transcriptionist

Medical transcriptionists typically need postsecondary education. Prospective medical transcriptionists must have an

Medical transcriptionists listen to recorded dictation from a physician.

understanding of medical terminology, anatomy and physiology, grammar, and word-processing software.

Pay

The median annual wage for medical transcriptionists was $33,380 in May 2019.

Job Outlook

Employment of medical transcriptionists is projected to decline 2 percent from 2019 to 2029. The growing volume of healthcare services is expected to continue to increase demand for transcription services. However, employment is projected to decline because of increased productivity stemming from technological advances and outsourcing.

State & Area Data

Explore resources for employment and wages by state and area for medical transcriptionists.

What Medical Transcriptionists Do

Medical transcriptionists, sometimes referred to as *healthcare documentation specialists*, listen to voice recordings that physicians and other healthcare workers make and convert them into written reports. They also may review and edit medical documents created using speech recognition technology. Transcriptionists interpret medical terminology and abbreviations in preparing patients' medical histories, discharge summaries, and other documents.

Duties

Medical transcriptionists typically do the following:

- Listen to the recorded dictation of a doctor or other healthcare worker
- Interpret and transcribe the dictation into patient history, exam notes, operative reports, referral letters, discharge summaries, and other documents

Medical transcriptionists review medical reports for accuracy.

- Review and edit drafts prepared by speech recognition software, making sure that the transcription is correct, complete, and consistent in style
- Translate medical abbreviations and jargon into the appropriate long form
- Identify inconsistencies, errors, and missing information within a report that could compromise patient care
- Follow up with the healthcare provider to ensure that reports are accurate
- Submit health records for physicians to approve
- Follow patient confidentiality guidelines and legal documentation requirements
- Enter medical reports into electronic health records (EHR) systems
- Perform quality improvement audits

Traditionally, medical transcriptionists used audio playback equipment to listen to an entire dictation in order to produce a transcribed report, and some transcription is still done this way. It has become more common for medical documents to be prepared using speech recognition technology, in which specialized software automatically prepares an initial draft of a report. The transcriptionist then listens to the voice file and reviews the draft for accuracy, identifying any errors and editing the report, when necessary. Transcriptionists use word-processing and other specialized software to prepare the transcripts, as well as medical reference materials when needed.

Medical transcriptionists must be familiar with medical terminology, anatomy and physiology, diagnostic procedures, pharmacology, and treatment assessments. Their ability to understand what the healthcare worker has recorded, correctly transcribe that information, and identify any inaccuracies in the transcript is critical to reducing the chance that patients will get ineffective or even harmful treatments. Medical transcriptionists also may need to be familiar with EHR systems.

Medical transcriptionists who work in doctors' offices may have other duties, such as answering phones and greeting patients.

Medical transcriptions must understand what the healthcare worker has recorded and correctly transcribe that information.

Work Environment

Medical transcriptionists held about 58,500 jobs in 2019. The largest employers of medical transcriptionists were as follows:

Administrative and support services	37%
Offices of physicians	26
Hospitals; state, local, and private	18
Self-employed workers	4
Medical and diagnostic laboratories	2

Administrative and support services includes companies that provide transcription services.

Medical transcriptionists may work from home, receiving dictation and submitting drafts electronically.

Work Schedules

Most medical transcriptionists work full time. Medical transcriptionists who work from home may work outside typical business hours and/or may have some flexibility in determining their schedules. Their work can be stressful because they need to ensure that reports are accurate within a quick turnaround time.

How to Become a Medical Transcriptionist

Medical transcriptionists typically need postsecondary education. Some choose to become certified.

Education

Employers prefer to hire transcriptionists who have completed postsecondary education in medical transcription, which is offered by vocational schools, community colleges, and distance-learning programs. Medical transcription programs are typically 1-year certificate programs, although there are also associate's degree programs.

Programs normally include coursework in anatomy, medical terminology, risk management, legal issues relating to healthcare documentation, and English grammar and punctuation. Many of these programs include supervised on-the-job experience. Some transcriptionists, especially those already familiar with medical terminology from previous experience as a nursing assistant or medical secretary, become proficient through refresher courses and training.

Licenses, Certifications, and Registrations

Although certification is not required, some medical transcriptionists choose to become certified. The Association for Healthcare Documentation Integrity offers the Registered Healthcare Documentation Specialist (RHDS) and the Certified Healthcare Documentation Specialist (CHDS) certifications. Both certifications require passing an exam and periodic retesting or continuing education.

The RHDS certification, formerly known as the Registered Medical Transcriptionist (RMT), is for recent graduates with less than 2 years of experience and who work in a single specialty environment, such as a clinic or a doctor's office.

The CHDS certification, formerly known as the Certified Medical Transcriptionist (CMT), is for transcriptionists who hold the RHDS designation. In addition, CHDS candidates must have at least 2 years of acute care experience, including experience handling dictation in various medical specialties.

Transcriptionists listen to dictated recordings made by physicians and other healthcare professionals and transcribe them into medical reports, correspondence, and other administrative material.

Medical Transcriptionists

Median annual wages, May 2019

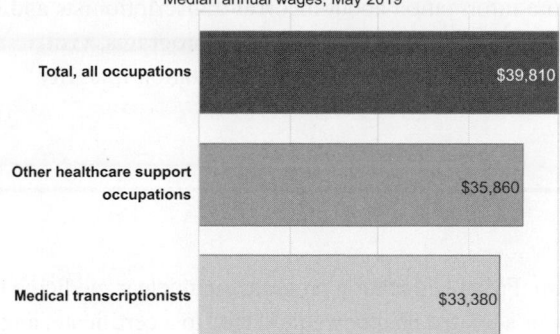

Total, all occupations	$39,810
Other healthcare support occupations	$35,860
Medical transcriptionists	$33,380

Note: All Occupations includes all occupations in the U.S. Economy. Source: U.S. Bureau of Labor Statistics, Occupational Employment Statistics.

Medical Transcriptionists

Percent change in employment, projected 2019-29

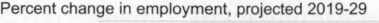
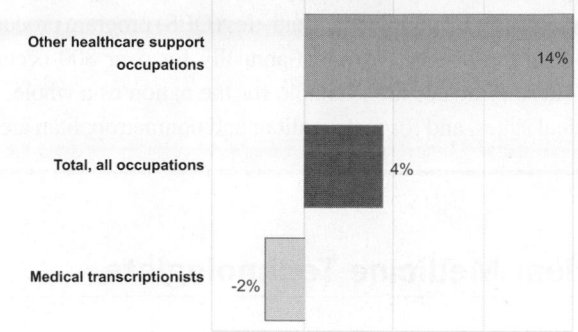

Other healthcare support occupations	14%
Total, all occupations	4%
Medical transcriptionists	-2%

Note: All Occupations includes all occupations in the U.S. Economy. Source: U.S. Bureau of Labor Statistics, Employment Projections program.

To maintain certification, medical transcriptionists must complete continuing education requirements every 3 years.

Important Qualities

Computer skills. Medical transcriptionists must be comfortable using computers and word-processing software, because those tools are an essential part of their jobs. They also may need to know how to operate electronic health records (EHR) systems.

Critical-thinking skills. Medical transcriptionists must assess medical reports and spot any inaccuracies and inconsistencies in finished drafts. They must also think critically when doing research to find the information that they need and to ensure that sources are both accurate and reliable.

Listening skills. Medical transcriptionists must listen carefully to dictation from physicians. They need to hear and interpret the intended meaning of the medical report.

Time-management skills. Because dictation must be done quickly, medical transcriptionists should be comfortable working under short deadlines.

Writing skills. Medical transcriptionists need a good understanding of the English language and grammar.

Pay

The median annual wage for medical transcriptionists was $33,380 in May 2019. The median wage is the wage at which half the workers in an occupation earned more than that amount and half earned less. The lowest 10 percent earned less than $22,160, and the highest 10 percent earned more than $51,260.

In May 2019, the median annual wages for medical transcriptionists in the top industries in which they worked were as follows:

Medical and diagnostic laboratories	$41,660
Hospitals; state, local, and private	39,850
Offices of physicians	35,560
Administrative and support services	26,700

Some medical transcriptionists are paid based on the volume of transcription they produce. Others are paid an hourly rate or an annual salary.

Most medical transcriptionists work full time. Medical transcriptionists who work from home may work outside typical business hours and/or have some flexibility in determining their schedules. Their work can be stressful because they need to ensure that reports are accurate within a quick turnaround time.

Job Outlook

Employment of medical transcriptionists is projected to decline 2 percent from 2019 to 2029. Technological advances have changed the way medical transcription is done. Speech recognition and electronic health records (EHR) software advances often allow physicians to create some of this documentation in the moment, reducing the need for transcriptionists.

The aging population and growing rates of chronic conditions will continue to increase demand for healthcare services. This will result in a growing number of medical tests and procedures, all of which will require transcription. However, technological advances, such as speech recognition software, allow transcriptions to be prepared by fewer medical transcriptionists.

As healthcare providers seek to cut costs, some will contract out transcription services and not do transcription in-house. Some of this work may be outsourced to other countries, which would reduce domestic employment.

Employment projections data for medical transcriptionists, 2019-29					
Occupational Title	SOC Code	Employment, 2019	Projected Employment, 2029	Change, 2019-29	
				Percent	Numeric
SOURCE: U.S. Bureau of Labor Statistics, Employment Projections program					
Medical transcriptionists	31-9094	58,500	57,200	-2	-1,300

State & Area Data
Occupational Employment Statistics (OES)

The Occupational Employment Statistics (OES) program produces employment and wage estimates annually for over 800 occupations. These estimates are available for the nation as a whole, for individual states, and for metropolitan and nonmetropolitan areas.

Contacts for More Information

For more information about medical transcriptionists and for a list of accredited medical transcription programs, visit
➤ Association for Healthcare Documentation Integrity

Nuclear Medicine Technologists

Summary

Quick Facts: Nuclear Medicine Technologists

2019 Median Pay	$77,950 per year $37.48 per hour
Typical Entry-Level Education	Associate's degree
Work Experience in a Related Occupation	None
On-the-job Training	None
Number of Jobs, 2019	18,500
Job Outlook, 2019-29	5% (Faster than average)
Employment Change, 2019-29	1,000

What Nuclear Medicine Technologists Do

Nuclear medicine technologists prepare radioactive drugs and administer them to patients for imaging or therapeutic purposes.

Work Environment

Most nuclear medicine technologists work in hospitals. Some work in physicians' offices, diagnostic laboratories, or imaging clinics. Most nuclear medicine technologists work full time.

How to Become a Nuclear Medicine Technologist

Nuclear medicine technologists typically need an associate's degree from an accredited nuclear medicine technology program. Formal education programs in nuclear medicine technology or a related healthcare field lead to a certificate, an associate's degree, or a bachelor's degree. Most nuclear medicine technologists become certified.

Pay

The median annual wage for nuclear medicine technologists was $77,950 in May 2019.

Job Outlook

Employment of nuclear medicine technologists is projected to grow 5 percent from 2019 to 2029, faster than the average for all occupations. An aging population may lead to the need for nuclear medicine technologists who can provide imaging to patients with certain medical conditions, such as heart disease, or treatments for cancers and other diseases.

State & Area Data

Explore resources for employment and wages by state and area for nuclear medicine technologists.

What Nuclear Medicine Technologists Do

Nuclear medicine technologists prepare radioactive drugs and administer them to patients for imaging or therapeutic purposes. They provide technical support to physicians or other professional nuclear medicine personnel in the diagnosis, care, and treatment of patients and for research and investigation into

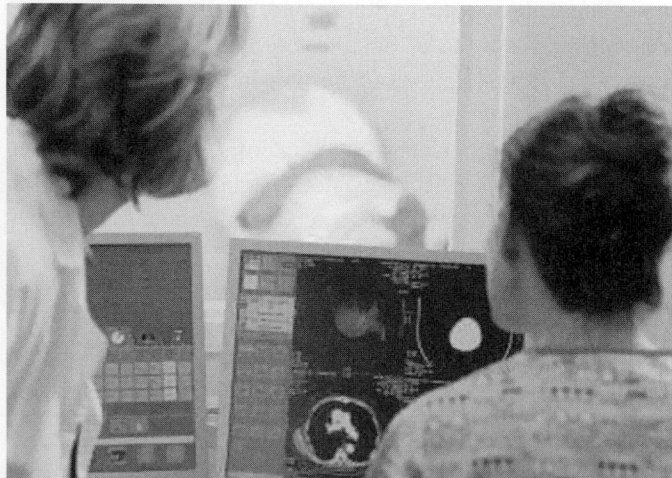

Nuclear medicine technologists operate equipment that creates images of areas of a patient's body.

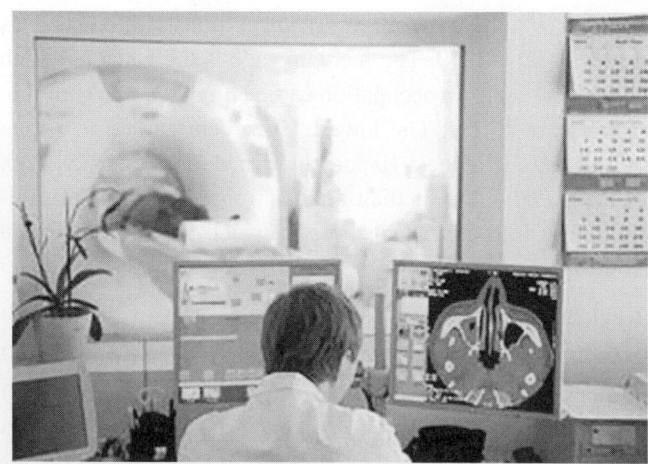

Most nuclear medicine technologists work in hospitals.

the uses of radioactive drugs. They also may act as emergency responders in the event of a nuclear disaster.

Duties

Nuclear medicine technologists typically do the following:

- Explain medical procedures to the patient and answer questions
- Follow safety procedures to protect themselves and the patient from unnecessary radiation exposure
- Prepare radioactive drugs and administer them to the patient
- Monitor the patient to check for unusual reactions to the drugs
- Operate imaging equipment
- Keep detailed records of procedures
- Follow radiation disposal and safety procedures

Radioactive drugs, known as radiopharmaceuticals, give off radiation, allowing special scanners to monitor tissue and organ functions. Abnormal areas show higher-than-expected or lower-than-expected concentrations of radioactivity. Physicians and surgeons then interpret the images to help diagnose the patient's condition. For example, tumors can be seen in organs during a scan because of their concentration of the radioactive drugs.

Radiopharmaceuticals can also be used to deliver concentrated doses of radiation to specific areas, such as tumors, for treatment of conditions that may not allow other forms of treatment. Various forms of internal radiation treatments also may be good alternatives to invasive surgical procedures.

In the event of a radioactive incident or nuclear disaster, some nuclear medicine technologists may be involved in emergency response efforts. These workers' experience with radiation detection and monitoring equipment could be useful during the response to events that involve radiological materials.

After graduation from an accredited program, a technologist can choose to earn a certification in positron emission tomography (PET) or nuclear cardiology. PET uses a machine that creates a three-dimensional image of a part of the body, such as the brain. Nuclear cardiology uses radioactive drugs to obtain images of the heart. Patients may exercise during the imaging process while the technologist creates images of the heart and blood flow.

Some nuclear medicine technologists work in support of researchers in the development of new nuclear medicine applications in imagery or therapy.

Work Environment

Nuclear medicine technologists held about 18,500 jobs in 2019. The largest employers of nuclear medicine technologists were as follows:

Hospitals; state, local, and private	73%
Offices of physicians	16
Medical and diagnostic laboratories	6
Outpatient care centers	3

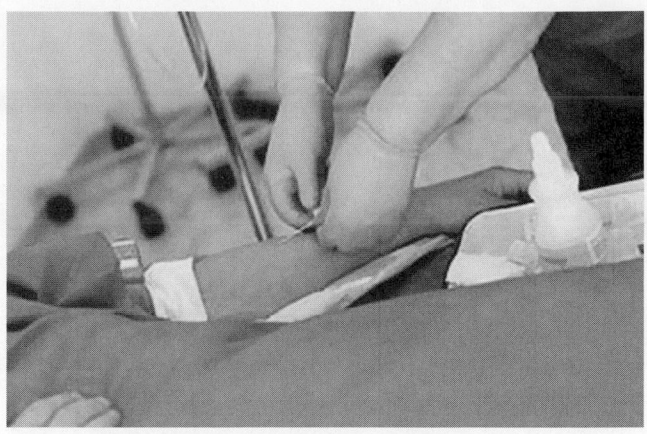

Some radiopharmaceuticals are given intravenously to treat cancers, blood diseases, or other illnesses.

Technologists are on their feet for long periods and may need to lift or turn patients who are disabled.

Injuries and Illnesses

Although radiation hazards exist in this occupation, they are minimized by the use of gloves and other shielding devices. Nuclear medicine technologists wear badges that measure radiation levels in the radiation area. Instruments monitor their radiation exposure and detailed records are kept on how much radiation they get over their lifetime. When preparing radioactive drugs, technologists use safety procedures to minimize radiation exposure to patients, other healthcare workers, and themselves.

Like other healthcare workers, nuclear medicine technologists may be exposed to infectious diseases.

Work Schedules

Most nuclear medicine technologists work full time. Some nuclear medicine technologists work evenings, weekends, or nights.

How to Become a Nuclear Medicine Technologist

Nuclear medicine technologists typically need an associate's degree from an accredited nuclear medicine technology program. Formal education programs in nuclear medicine technology or a related healthcare field lead to a certificate, an associate's degree, or a bachelor's degree. Most nuclear medicine technologists become certified.

Education

Nuclear medicine technologists typically need an associate's degree in nuclear medicine technology. Bachelor's degrees are also common. Some technologists become qualified by completing an associate's or a bachelor's degree program in a related health field, such as radiologic technology or nursing, and then completing a 12-month certificate program in nuclear medicine technology.

Nuclear medicine technology programs often include courses in human anatomy and physiology, physics, chemistry,

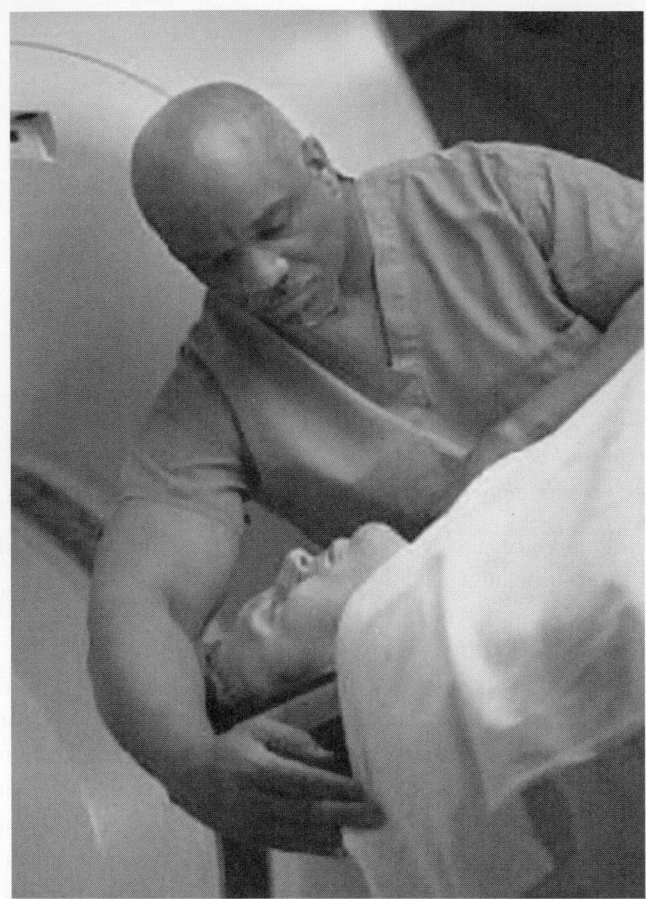

Nuclear medicine technologists can earn specialty certifications that show their proficiency in specific procedures or equipment.

radioactive drugs, and computer science. In addition, these programs include clinical experience—practice under the supervision of a certified nuclear medicine technologist and a physician or surgeon who specializes in nuclear medicine.

The Joint Review Committee on Educational Programs in Nuclear Medicine Technology accredits nuclear medicine programs. Graduating from an accredited program may be required for licensure or by an employer.

High school students who are interested in nuclear medicine technology should take courses in math and science, such as biology, chemistry, anatomy, and physics.

Licenses, Certifications, and Registrations

Most nuclear medicine technologists become certified. Although certification is not required for a license, it fulfills most of the requirements for state licensure. Licensing requirements vary by state. For specific requirements, contact the state's health board.

Some employers require certification, regardless of state regulations. Certification usually involves graduating from an accredited nuclear medicine technology program. Certification is available from the American Registry of Radiologic Technologists (ARRT) and the Nuclear Medicine Technology Certification Board (NMTCB).

In addition to receiving general certification, technologists can earn specialty certifications that show their proficiency in specific procedures or on certain equipment. A technologist can earn certification in positron emission tomography (PET), nuclear cardiology (NCT), or computed tomography (CT). The NMTCB offers NCT, PET, and CT certification exams.

Important Qualities

Ability to use technology. Nuclear medicine technologists work with computers and large pieces of technological equipment and must be comfortable operating them.

Analytical skills. Nuclear medicine technologists must understand anatomy, physiology, and other sciences and be able to calculate accurate dosages.

Compassion. Nuclear medicine technologists must be able to reassure and calm patients who are under physical and emotional stress.

Detail oriented. Nuclear medicine technologists must follow exact instructions to make sure that the correct dosage is given and that the patient is not overexposed to radiation.

Interpersonal skills. Nuclear medicine technologists interact with patients and often work as part of a team. They must be able to follow instructions from a supervising physician.

Physical stamina. Nuclear medicine technologists must stand for long periods and be able to lift and move patients who need help.

Pay

The median annual wage for nuclear medicine technologists was $77,950 in May 2019. The median wage is the wage at which half the workers in an occupation earned more than that amount and half earned less. The lowest 10 percent earned less than $56,560, and the highest 10 percent earned more than $105,690.

In May 2019, the median annual wages for nuclear medicine technologists in the top industries in which they worked were as follows:

Nuclear Medicine Technologists
Median annual wages, May 2019

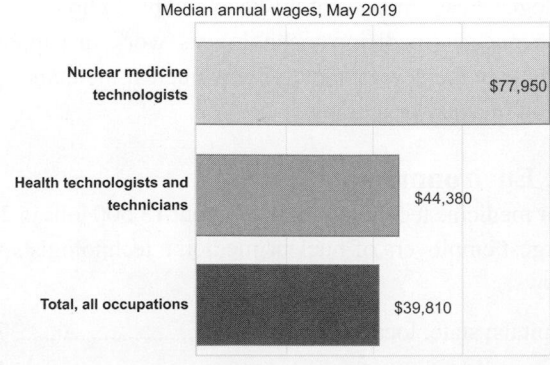

Nuclear medicine technologists	$77,950
Health technologists and technicians	$44,380
Total, all occupations	$39,810

Note: All Occupations includes all occupations in the U.S. Economy.
Source: U.S. Bureau of Labor Statistics, Occupational Employment Statistics.

Nuclear Medicine Technologists

Percent change in employment, projected 2019-29

- Health technologists and technicians — 8%
- Nuclear medicine technologists — 5%
- Total, all occupations — 4%

Note: All Occupations includes all occupations in the U.S. Economy.
Source: U.S. Bureau of Labor Statistics, Employment Projections program.

Outpatient care centers	$107,070
Hospitals; state, local, and private	78,040
Offices of physicians	77,850
Medical and diagnostic laboratories	73,240

Most nuclear medicine technologists work full time. Some nuclear medicine technologists work evenings, weekends, or nights.

Job Outlook

Employment of nuclear medicine technologists is projected to grow 5 percent from 2019 to 2029, faster than the average for all occupations.

An aging population may lead to the need for nuclear medicine technologists who can provide imaging to patients with certain medical conditions, such as heart disease, or treatments for cancers and other diseases. In addition, technological advancements may increase the types of imaging and treatments that nuclear medicine technologists provide, leading to increased demand for their services.

Job Prospects

Nuclear medicine technologists can improve their job prospects by completing a bachelor's degree from an accredited program or earning a specialty certification, such as in positron emission tomography (PET), nuclear cardiology (NCT), or computed tomography (CT). Certification is available from the American Registry of Radiologic Technologists (ARRT) and the Nuclear Medicine Technology Certification Board (NMTCB).

Employment projections data for nuclear medicine technologists, 2019-29

Occupational Title	SOC Code	Employment, 2019	Projected Employment, 2029	Change, 2019-29 Percent	Change, 2019-29 Numeric
Nuclear medicine technologists	29-2033	18,500	19,500	5	1,000

SOURCE: U.S. Bureau of Labor Statistics, Employment Projections program

State & Area Data
Occupational Employment Statistics (OES)

The Occupational Employment Statistics (OES) program produces employment and wage estimates annually for over 800 occupations. These estimates are available for the nation as a whole, for individual states, and for metropolitan and nonmetropolitan areas.

Contacts for More Information

For more information about nuclear and radiologic medicine, visit
➤ American Board of Nuclear Medicine
➤ American Board of Radiology
➤ American College of Nuclear Medicine
➤ Society of Nuclear Medicine and Molecular Imaging

For a list of accredited programs in nuclear medicine technology, visit
➤ Joint Review Committee on Educational Programs in Nuclear Medicine Technology

For more information about certification for nuclear medicine technologists, visit
➤ Nuclear Medicine Technology Certification Board
➤ American Registry of Radiologic Technologists

Nurse Anesthetists, Nurse Midwives, and Nurse Practitioners

Summary

Quick Facts: Nurse Anesthetists, Nurse Midwives, and Nurse Practitioners

2019 Median Pay	$115,800 per year $55.67 per hour
Typical Entry-Level Education	Master's degree
Work Experience in a Related Occupation	None
On-the-job Training	None
Number of Jobs, 2019	263,400
Job Outlook, 2019-29	45% (Much faster than average)
Employment Change, 2019-29	117,700

What Nurse Anesthetists, Nurse Midwives, and Nurse Practitioners Do

Nurse anesthetists, nurse midwives, and nurse practitioners coordinate patient care and may provide primary and specialty healthcare.

Work Environment

Nurse anesthetists, nurse midwives, and nurse practitioners work in a variety of healthcare settings, including hospitals, physicians' offices, and clinics. Most advanced practice registered nurses (APRNs) work full time.

How to Become a Nurse Anesthetist, Nurse Midwife, or Nurse Practitioner

Nurse anesthetists, nurse midwives, and nurse practitioners must earn at least a master's degree in one of the APRN roles. They must also be licensed in their state and pass a national certification exam.

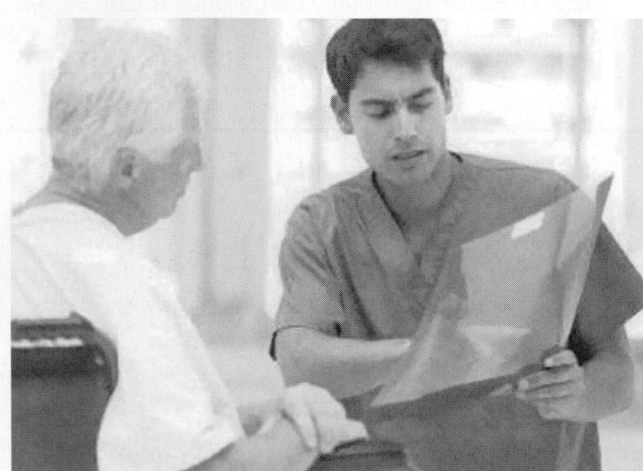

APRNs focus on patient-centered care, which means understanding a patient's concerns and lifestyle before choosing a course of action.

Pay

The median annual wage for nurse anesthetists, nurse midwives, and nurse practitioners was $115,800 in May 2019.

Job Outlook

Overall employment of nurse anesthetists, nurse midwives, and nurse practitioners is projected to grow 45 percent from 2019 to 2029, much faster than the average for all occupations. Growth will occur primarily because of an increased emphasis on preventive care and demand for healthcare services from an aging population.

State & Area Data

Explore resources for employment and wages by state and area for nurse anesthetists, nurse midwives, and nurse practitioners.

What Nurse Anesthetists, Nurse Midwives, and Nurse Practitioners Do

Nurse anesthetists, nurse midwives, and nurse practitioners, also referred to as *advanced practice registered nurses (APRNs)*, coordinate patient care and may provide primary and specialty healthcare. The scope of practice varies from state to state.

Duties

Advanced practice registered nurses typically do the following:

- Take and record patients' medical histories and symptoms
- Perform physical exams and observe patients
- Create patient care plans or contribute to existing plans
- Perform and order diagnostic tests
- Operate and monitor medical equipment
- Diagnose various health problems
- Analyze test results or changes in a patient's condition and alter treatment plans, as needed
- Give patients medicines and treatments
- Evaluate a patient's response to medicines and treatments
- Consult with doctors and other healthcare professionals, as needed

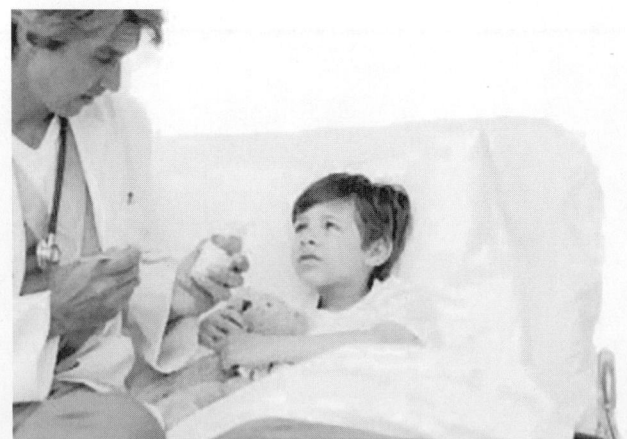

APRNs give patients medicines and treatments.

- Counsel and teach patients and their families how to stay healthy or manage their illnesses or injuries
- Conduct research

APRNs work independently or in collaboration with physicians. In most states, they can prescribe medications, order medical tests, and diagnose health problems. APRNs may provide primary and preventive care and may specialize in care for certain groups of people, such as children, pregnant women, or patients with mental health disorders.

APRNs have some of the same duties as registered nurses, including gathering information about a patient's condition and taking action to treat or manage the patient's health. However, APRNs are trained to do other tasks, including ordering and evaluating test results, referring patients to specialists, and diagnosing and treating ailments. APRNs focus on patient-centered care, which means understanding a patient's concerns and lifestyle before choosing a course of action.

Some APRNs also conduct research or teach staff about new policies or procedures. Others may provide consultation services based on a specific field of knowledge, such as oncology, which is the study of cancer.

The following are types of APRNs:

Nurse anesthetists (CRNAs) administer anesthesia and provide care before, during, and after surgical, therapeutic, diagnostic, and obstetrical procedures. They also provide pain management and some emergency services. Before a procedure begins, nurse anesthetists discuss with a patient any medications the patient is taking as well as any allergies or illnesses the patient may have, so that anesthesia can be safely administered. Nurse anesthetists then give a patient general anesthesia to put the patient to sleep so they feel no pain during surgery or administer a regional or local anesthesia to numb an area of the body. During the procedure, they monitor the patient's vital signs and adjust the anesthesia as necessary.

Nurse midwives (CNMs) provide care to women, including gynecological exams, family planning services, and prenatal care. They deliver babies, manage emergency situations during labor, repair lacerations, and may provide surgical assistance to physicians during cesarean births. Nurse midwives may act as primary maternity care providers for women. They also provide wellness care, educating their patients on how to lead healthy lives by discussing topics such as nutrition and disease prevention. Nurse midwives also provide care to their patients' partners for sexual or reproductive health issues.

Nurse practitioners (NPs) serve as primary and specialty care providers, delivering advanced nursing services to patients and their families. They assess patients, determine how to improve or manage a patient's health, and discuss ways to integrate health promotion strategies into a patient's life. Nurse practitioners typically care for a certain population of people. For instance, NPs may work in adult and geriatric health, pediatric health, or psychiatric and mental health.

Although the scope of their duties varies by state, many nurse practitioners work independently, prescribe medications, and order laboratory tests. Nurse practitioners consult with physicians and other health professionals when needed.

See the profile on registered nurses for more information about *clinical nurse specialists* (**CNSs**), also considered to be a type of APRN.

Work Environment

Nurse anesthetists, nurse midwives, and nurse practitioners held about 263,400 jobs in 2019. Employment in the detailed occupations that make up nurse anesthetists, nurse midwives, and nurse practitioners was distributed as follows:

Nurse practitioners	211,300
Nurse anesthetists	44,900
Nurse midwives	7,200

The largest employers of nurse anesthetists, nurse midwives, and nurse practitioners were as follows:

Offices of physicians	47%
Hospitals; state, local, and private	27
Outpatient care centers	8
Educational services; state, local, and private	4
Offices of other health practitioners	3

Some advanced practice registered nurses (APRNs) provide care in patients' homes. Some nurse midwives work in birthing centers, which are a type of outpatient care center.

APRNs may travel long distances to help care for patients in places where there are not enough healthcare workers.

Injuries and Illnesses

APRN work can be both physically and emotionally demanding. Some APRNs spend much of their day on their feet. They are vulnerable to back injuries because they must lift and move

APRNs work in a variety of healthcare settings, including hospitals.

patients. APRN work can also be stressful because they make critical decisions that affect a patient's health.

Because of the environments in which they work, APRNs may come in close contact with infectious diseases. Therefore, they must follow strict guidelines to guard against diseases and other dangers, such as accidental needle sticks or patient outbursts.

Work Schedules

Most APRNs work full time. In physicians' offices, APRNs typically work during normal business hours. In hospitals and other healthcare facilities, they may work in shifts—including nights, weekends, and holidays—to provide round-the-clock patient care. Some APRNs, especially those who work in critical care or those who deliver babies, also may need to be on call.

How to Become a Nurse Anesthetist, Nurse Midwife, or Nurse Practitioner

Nurse anesthetists, nurse midwives, and nurse practitioners, also referred to as *advanced practice registered nurses (APRNs)*, must have at least a master's degree in their specialty role. APRNs also must be licensed registered nurses in their state, pass a national certification exam, and have a state APRN license.

Education

Nurse anesthetists, nurse midwives, and nurse practitioners must have at least a master's degree from an accredited program. These programs include classroom education and clinical experience. Courses in subjects such as advanced health assessment, pathophysiology, and pharmacology are common as well as coursework specific to the chosen APRN role.

An APRN must have a registered nursing (RN) license before pursuing education in one of the advanced practice roles, and a strong background in science is helpful.

Most APRN programs prefer candidates who have a bachelor's degree in nursing. However, some schools offer bridge programs for registered nurses with an associate's degree or diploma in nursing. Graduate-level programs are also available

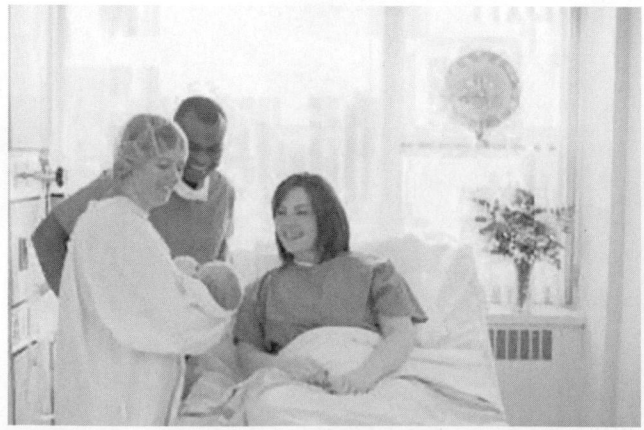

APRNs must earn a master's degree which typically includes clinical experience.

for individuals who did not obtain a bachelor's degree in nursing but in a related health science field. These programs prepare the student for the RN licensure exam in addition to offering the APRN curriculum.

Although a master's degree is the most common form of entry-level education, APRNs may choose to earn a Doctor of Nursing Practice (DNP) or a Ph.D. The specific educational requirements and qualifications for each of the roles are available on professional organizations' websites.

Prospective nurse anesthetists must have 1 year of experience working as registered nurse in a critical care setting as a prerequisite for admission to an accredited nurse anesthetist program.

Licenses, Certifications, and Registrations

States' requirements for APRNs vary. In general, APRNs must have a registered nursing license, complete an accredited graduate-level program, pass a national certification exam, and have an APRN license. Details are available from each state's board of nursing.

To become licensed and use an APRN title, most states require national certification.

The National Board of Certification and Recertification for Nurse Anesthetists (NBCRNA) offers the National Certification Examination (NCE). Certified registered nurse anesthetists (CRNAs) must maintain their certification through the Continued Professional Certification (CPC) Program.

The American Midwifery Certification Board offers the Certified Nurse-Midwife (CNM). Individuals with this designation must recertify via the Certificate Maintenance Program.

There are several different certifications for nurse practitioners, including those available from the American Academy of Nurse Practitioners Certification Board (AANPCB), the American Nurses Credentialing Center (ANCC), and the Pediatric Nursing Certification Board (PNCB). Each of these certifications requires periodic renewal.

In addition, APRN positions may require cardiopulmonary resuscitation (CPR), basic life support (BLS), or advanced cardiac life support (ACLS) certification.

Important Qualities

Communication skills. Advanced practice registered nurses have to be able to communicate with patients and other healthcare professionals to ensure the appropriate course of action.

Critical-thinking skills. APRNs must be able to assess changes in a patient's health, quickly determine the most appropriate course of action, and decide if a consultation with another healthcare professional is needed.

Compassion. APRNs should be caring and sympathetic when treating patients.

Detail oriented. APRNs need to be thorough in providing treatments and medications that affect their patients' health. During an evaluation, they must notice even small changes in a patient's condition.

Interpersonal skills. APRNs must work with patients and families as well as with other healthcare providers and staff. They work as part of a team to determine and execute healthcare options for the patients they treat.

Leadership skills. APRNs often work in positions of seniority. They must effectively direct and sometimes manage other nurses on staff when providing patient care.

Resourcefulness. APRNs should know where to find the answers that they need.

Advancement

Some APRNs take on managerial or administrative roles; others go into academia. APRNs who earn a doctoral degree may conduct independent research or work on an interprofessional research team.

Pay

The median annual wage for nurse anesthetists, nurse midwives, and nurse practitioners was $115,800 in May 2019. The median wage is the wage at which half the workers in an occupation earned more than that amount and half earned less. The lowest 10 percent earned less than $82,460, and the highest 10 percent earned more than $184,180.

Median annual wages for nurse anesthetists, nurse midwives, and nurse practitioners in May 2019 were as follows:

Nurse anesthetists	$174,790
Nurse practitioners	109,820
Nurse midwives	105,030

In May 2019, the median annual wages for nurse anesthetists, nurse midwives, and nurse practitioners in the top industries in which they worked were as follows:

Hospitals; state, local, and private	$122,420
Outpatient care centers	118,530
Offices of physicians	113,190

Offices of other health practitioners	112,590
Educational services; state, local, and private	108,790

Most advanced practice registered nurses (APRNs) work full time. In physicians' offices, APRNs typically work during normal business hours. In hospitals and other healthcare facilities, they may work in shifts—including nights, weekends, and holidays—to provide round-the-clock patient care. Some APRNs, especially those who work in critical care or those who deliver babies, also may need to be on call.

Job Outlook

Overall employment of nurse anesthetists, nurse midwives, and nurse practitioners is projected to grow 45 percent from 2019 to 2029, much faster than the average for all occupations. Employment growth will vary by occupation. Because nurse midwives is a small occupation, however, the fast growth will result in only about 800 new jobs in this occupation over the 10-year period.

Growth will occur because of an increase in the demand for healthcare services. Several factors will contribute to this demand, including an increased emphasis on preventive care and demand for healthcare services from the aging population.

Advanced practice registered nurses (APRNs) perform many of the same services as physicians. APRNs will be increasingly used in team-based models of care, particularly in hospitals, offices of physicians, clinics, and other ambulatory care settings, where they will be needed to provide preventive and primary care.

APRNs will also be needed to care for the large baby-boom population. As baby boomers age, they will experience ailments and complex conditions that require medical care. APRNs will be needed to keep these patients healthy and to treat the growing number of patients with chronic and acute conditions.

As states change their laws governing APRN practice authority, APRNs are being allowed to perform more services.

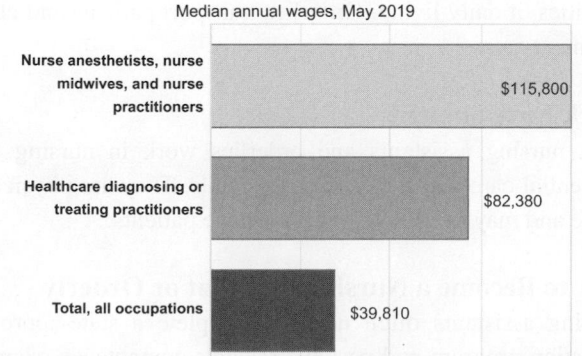

Nurse Anesthetists, Nurse Midwives, and Nurse Practitioners

Median annual wages, May 2019

Note: All Occupations includes all occupations in the U.S. Economy.
Source: U.S. Bureau of Labor Statistics, Occupational Employment Statistics.

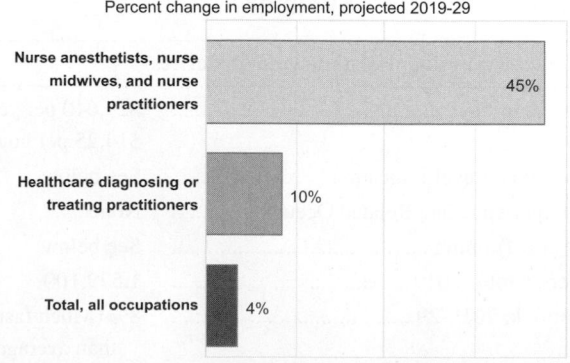

Nurse Anesthetists, Nurse Midwives, and Nurse Practitioners

Percent change in employment, projected 2019-29

Note: All Occupations includes all occupations in the U.S. Economy.
Source: U.S. Bureau of Labor Statistics, Employment Projections program.

APRNs also are being recognized more widely by the public as a source for primary healthcare.

Job Prospects

About 24,200 openings for nurse practitioners, 2,900 openings for nurse anesthetists, and 500 openings for nurse midwives are projected each year, on average, over the decade.

Many of those openings are expected to result from the need to replace workers who transfer to different occupations or exit the labor force, such as to retire.

Overall, job opportunities for advanced practice registered nurses are likely to be excellent. APRNs will be in high demand, particularly in medically underserved areas such as inner cities and rural areas.

Employment projections data for nurse anesthetists, nurse midwives, and nurse practitioners, 2019-29

Occupational Title	SOC Code	Employment, 2019	Projected Employment, 2029	Change, 2019-29	
				Percent	Numeric
SOURCE: U.S. Bureau of Labor Statistics, Employment Projections program					
Nurse anesthetists, nurse midwives, and nurse practitioners	—	263,400	381,100	45	117,700
Nurse anesthetists	29-1151	44,900	51,000	14	6,200
Nurse midwives	29-1161	7,200	8,100	12	800
Nurse practitioners	29-1171	211,300	322,000	52	110,700

State & Area Data
Occupational Employment Statistics (OES)

The Occupational Employment Statistics (OES) program produces employment and wage estimates annually for over 800 occupations. These estimates are available for the nation as a whole, for individual states, and for metropolitan and nonmetropolitan areas.

Contacts for More Information

For more information about nurse anesthetists, including a list of accredited programs, visit
➤ American Association of Nurse Anesthetists

For more information about nurse midwives, including a list of accredited programs, visit
➤ American College of Nurse-Midwives

For more information about nurse practitioners, including a list of accredited programs, visit
➤ American Association of Nurse Practitioners

For more information about registered nurses, including credentialing, visit
➤ American Nurses Association

For more information about nursing education and being a registered nurse, visit
➤ National League for Nursing

For more information about undergraduate and graduate nursing education, nursing career options, and financial aid, visit
➤ American Association of Colleges of Nursing

For more information about states' Boards of Nursing, visit
➤ National Council of State Boards of Nursing

For more information about certification, visit
➤ American Academy of Nurse Practitioners Certification Board
➤ American Association of Critical-Care Nurses
➤ American Midwifery Certification Board
➤ American Nurses Credentialing Center
➤ National Certification Corporation
➤ National Board of Certification and Recertification for Nurse Anesthetists
➤ Pediatric Nursing Certification Board

Nursing Assistants and Orderlies

Summary

Quick Facts: Nursing Assistants and Orderlies

2019 Median Pay	$29,640 per year $14.25 per hour
Typical Entry-Level Education	See below
Work Experience in a Related Occupation	None
On-the-job Training	See below
Number of Jobs, 2019	1,579,100
Job Outlook, 2019-29	8% (Much faster than average)
Employment Change, 2019-29	119,500

What Nursing Assistants and Orderlies Do

Nursing assistants provide basic care and help patients with activities of daily living. Orderlies transport patients and clean treatment areas.

Work Environment

Most nursing assistants and orderlies work in nursing and residential care facilities and in hospitals. They are physically active and may need to help lift or move patients.

How to Become a Nursing Assistant or Orderly

Nursing assistants often need to complete a state-approved education program and pass their state's competency exam to become licensed or certified. Orderlies typically have at least a high school diploma.

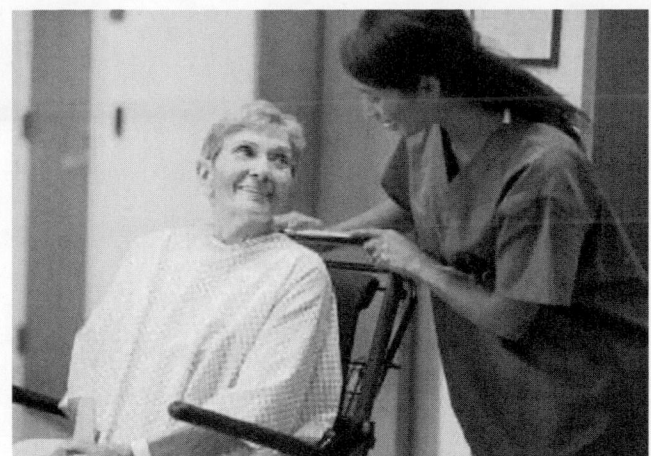

Orderlies help transport patients in hospitals or residents in nursing homes.

Pay

The median annual wage for nursing assistants was $29,660 in May 2019.

The median annual wage for orderlies was $28,980 in May 2019.

Job Outlook

Overall employment of nursing assistants and orderlies is projected to grow 8 percent from 2019 to 2029, much faster than the average for all occupations. As the baby-boom population ages, nursing assistants and orderlies will be needed to help care for an increasing number of older patients.

State & Area Data

Explore resources for employment and wages by state and area for nursing assistants and orderlies.

What Nursing Assistants and Orderlies Do

Nursing assistants, sometimes called *nursing aides*, provide basic care and help patients with activities of daily living. Orderlies transport patients and clean treatment areas.

Duties

Nursing assistants and orderlies work as part of a healthcare team under the supervision of licensed practical or licensed vocational nurses and registered nurses.

Nursing assistants provide basic care and help with activities of daily living. They typically do the following:

 Clean and bathe patients
 Help patients use the toilet and dress
 Turn, reposition, and transfer patients between beds and wheelchairs
 Listen to and record patients' health concerns and report that information to nurses
 Measure patients' vital signs, such as blood pressure and temperature
 Serve meals and help patients eat

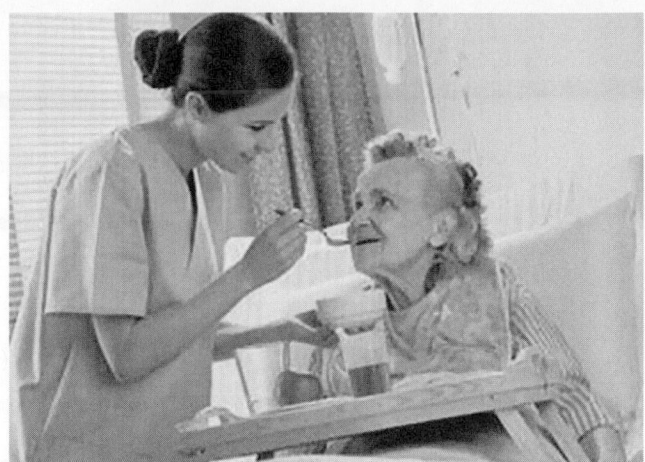

Nursing assistants help patients with activities of daily living like eating and bathing.

Depending on their training level and the state in which they work, nursing assistants also may dispense medication.

Nursing assistants are often the principal caregivers in nursing and residential care facilities. Nursing assistants often develop relationships with their patients because some patients stay in these facilities for months or years.

Orderlies typically do the following:

- Help patients to move around the facility, such as by pushing their wheelchairs
- Clean equipment and facilities
- Change linens
- Stock supplies

Work Environment

Nursing assistants held about 1.5 million jobs in 2019. The largest employers of nursing assistants were as follows:

Nursing care facilities (skilled nursing facilities)	37%
Hospitals; state, local, and private	27
Continuing care retirement communities and assisted living facilities for the elderly	11
Home healthcare services	5
Government	4

Orderlies held about 50,600 jobs in 2019. The largest employers of orderlies were as follows:

Hospitals; state, local, and private	78%
Ambulatory healthcare services	5
Government	2

The work of nursing assistants and orderlies may be strenuous. They spend much of their time on their feet as they care for patients.

Injuries and Illnesses

Nursing assistants and orderlies have one of the highest rates of injuries and illnesses of all occupations. These workers

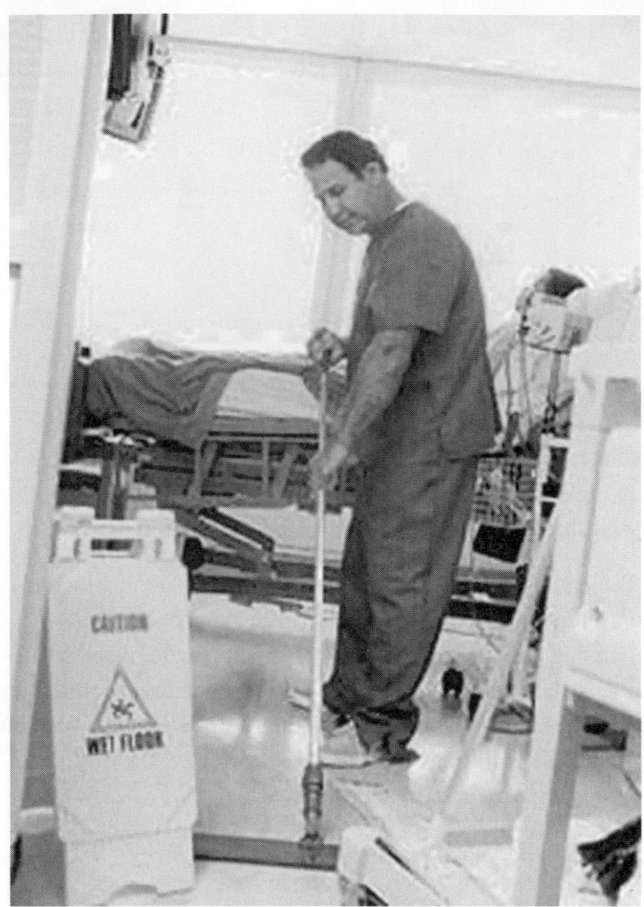

Orderlies are responsible for keeping hospitals and other facilities clean and tidy.

frequently move patients and have other physically demanding tasks. They typically get training in how to properly lift people, which can reduce the risk of injuries.

Work Schedules

Although most nursing assistants and orderlies work full time, some work part time. Because nursing and residential care facilities and hospitals provide care at all hours, nursing assistants and orderlies may need to work nights, weekends, and holidays.

How to Become a Nursing Assistant or Orderly

Nursing assistants typically must complete a state-approved education program and pass their state's competency exam. Orderlies typically have at least a high school diploma or equivalent.

Education and Training

Nursing assistants often need to complete a state-approved education program that includes both instruction on the principles of nursing and supervised clinical work. These programs are available in high schools, community colleges, vocational and technical schools, hospitals, and nursing homes.

In addition, nursing assistants typically complete a brief period of on-the-job training to learn about their specific employer's policies and procedures.

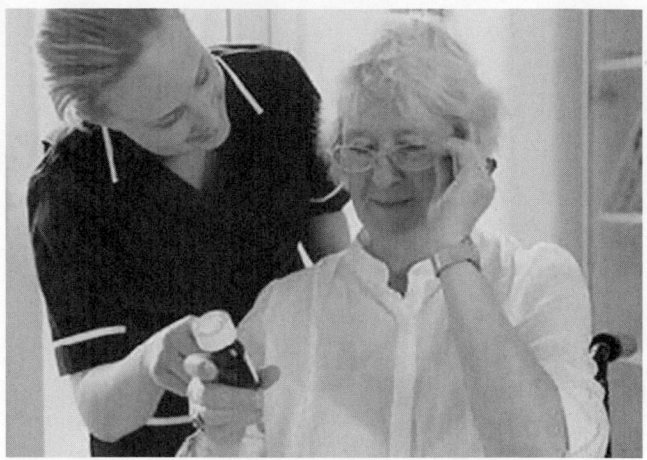

Nursing assistants must be able to communicate effectively to address patients' or residents' concerns.

Orderlies typically have at least a high school diploma or equivalent and receive a short period of on-the-job training.

Licenses, Certifications, and Registrations

Specific requirements for nursing assistants vary by state. Nursing assistants often need a state-issued license or certification. After completing an approved education program, nursing assistants often must pass a competency exam, which allows them to use state-specific titles. In some states, a nursing assistant is called a Certified Nursing Assistant (CNA), but titles vary by state.

Nursing assistants who have passed the competency exam are placed on a state registry. They must be on the state registry to work in a nursing home.

Some states have other requirements as well, such as continuing education and a criminal background check. Check with state boards of nursing or health for more information.

In some states, nursing assistants may earn additional credentials, such as Certified Medication Assistant (CMA). As a CMA, they may dispense medications.

Orderlies do not need a license; however, jobs might require certification in cardiopulmonary resuscitation (CPR) or basic life support (BLS).

Important Qualities

Communication skills. Nursing assistants and orderlies must listen and respond to patients' concerns. They also need to share information with other healthcare workers.

Compassion. Nursing assistants and orderlies help and care for people who are sick, injured, or need aid for other reasons. They need an empathetic attitude to do their work.

Patience. The routine tasks of cleaning, feeding, and bathing patients may be stressful. Nursing assistants and orderlies must be able to complete these tasks with professionalism.

Physical stamina. Nursing assistants and orderlies spend much of their time on their feet. They must be able to perform tasks such as lifting or moving patients.

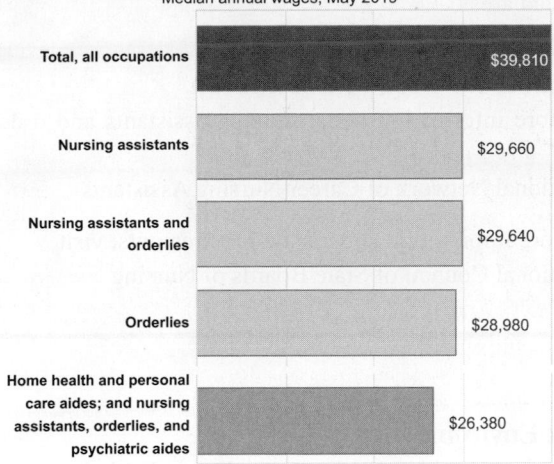

Nursing Assistants and Orderlies
Median annual wages, May 2019

Total, all occupations	$39,810
Nursing assistants	$29,660
Nursing assistants and orderlies	$29,640
Orderlies	$28,980
Home health and personal care aides; and nursing assistants, orderlies, and psychiatric aides	$26,380

Note: All Occupations includes all occupations in the U.S. Economy.
Source: U.S. Bureau of Labor Statistics, Occupational Employment Statistics.

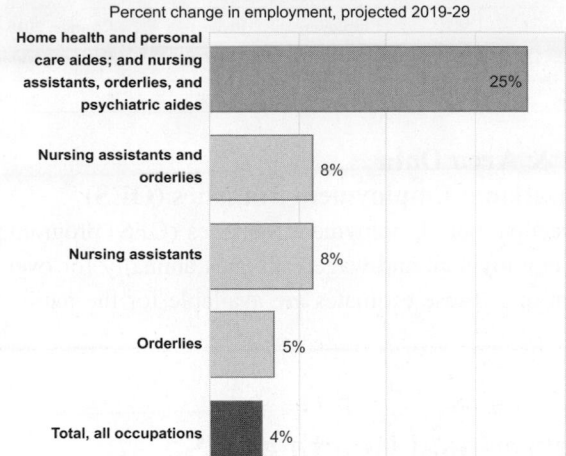

Nursing Assistants and Orderlies
Percent change in employment, projected 2019-29

Home health and personal care aides; and nursing assistants, orderlies, and psychiatric aides	25%
Nursing assistants and orderlies	8%
Nursing assistants	8%
Orderlies	5%
Total, all occupations	4%

Note: All Occupations includes all occupations in the U.S. Economy.
Source: U.S. Bureau of Labor Statistics, Employment Projections program.

Pay

The median annual wage for nursing assistants was $29,660 in May 2019. The median wage is the wage at which half the workers in an occupation earned more than that amount and half earned less. The lowest 10 percent earned less than $21,960, and the highest 10 percent earned more than $40,620.

The median annual wage for orderlies was $28,980 in May 2019. The lowest 10 percent earned less than $21,590, and the highest 10 percent earned more than $42,860.

In May 2019, the median annual wages for nursing assistants in the top industries in which they worked were as follows:

Government	$35,500
Hospitals; state, local, and private	31,120
Nursing care facilities (skilled nursing facilities)	28,910
Home healthcare services	28,600
Continuing care retirement communities and assisted living facilities for the elderly	28,590

In May 2019, the median annual wages for orderlies in the top industries in which they worked were as follows:

Ambulatory healthcare services	$31,950
Government	30,740
Hospitals; state, local, and private	29,050

Although most nursing assistants and orderlies work full time, some work part time. Because nursing and residential care facilities and hospitals provide care at all hours, nursing aides and orderlies may need to work nights, weekends, and holidays.

Job Outlook

Employment of nursing assistants is projected to grow 8 percent from 2019 to 2029, much faster than the average for all occupations. Employment of orderlies is projected to grow 5 percent from 2019 to 2029, faster as the average for all occupations.

As the baby-boom population ages, nursing assistants and orderlies will be needed to help care for an increasing number of older patients in nursing and residential care facilities. Older people are more likely than younger people to have disorders such as dementia, or to live with chronic diseases such as heart disease and diabetes. More nursing assistants will be needed to care for patients with these conditions.

Demand for nursing assistants may be constrained by the fact that many nursing homes rely on government funding. Cuts to programs such as Medicare and Medicaid may affect patients' ability to pay for nursing home care. In addition, patient preferences and shifts in federal and state funding are increasing the demand for home and community-based long-term care, which should lead to increased opportunities for nursing assistants working in home health and community rehabilitation services.

Job Prospects

About 174,000 openings for nursing assistants and 5,600 openings for orderlies are projected each year, on average, over the decade.

Many of those openings are expected to result from the need to replace workers who leave the occupations, often because of their low pay and high emotional and physical demands.

Employment projections data for nursing assistants and orderlies, 2019-29					
Occupational Title	SOC Code	Employment, 2019	Projected Employment, 2029	Change, 2019-29	
				Percent	Numeric
SOURCE: U.S. Bureau of Labor Statistics, Employment Projections program					
Nursing assistants and orderlies	—	1,579,100	1,698,600	8	119,500
Nursing assistants	31-1131	1,528,500	1,645,500	8	116,900

Employment projections data for nursing assistants and orderlies, 2019-29					
Occupational Title	SOC Code	Employment, 2019	Projected Employment, 2029	Change, 2019-29	
				Percent	Numeric
Orderlies	31-1132	50,600	53,100	5	2,500

State & Area Data
Occupational Employment Statistics (OES)

The Occupational Employment Statistics (OES) program produces employment and wage estimates annually for over 800 occupations. These estimates are available for the nation as a whole, for individual states, and for metropolitan and nonmetropolitan areas.

Contacts for More Information

For more information about nursing assistants and orderlies, visit
➤ National Network of Career Nursing Assistants

For more information about state requirements, visit
➤ National Council of State Boards of Nursing

Occupational Health and Safety Specialists and Technicians

Summary

Quick Facts: Occupational Health and Safety Specialists and Technicians

2019 Median Pay	$70,480 per year $33.88 per hour
Typical Entry-Level Education	See below
Work Experience in a Related Occupation	None
On-the-job Training	See below
Number of Jobs, 2019	122,600
Job Outlook, 2019-29	4% (As fast as average)
Employment Change, 2019-29	4,800

What Occupational Health and Safety Specialists and Technicians Do

Occupational health and safety specialists and technicians collect data on and analyze many types of work environments and work procedures.

Occupational health and safety specialists and technicians collect data on and analyze many types of work environments and work procedures.

Work Environment

Occupational health and safety specialists and technicians work in a variety of settings, such as offices or factories. Their jobs often involve considerable fieldwork and travel. Most work full time.

How to Become an Occupational Health and Safety Specialist or Technician

Occupational health and safety specialists typically need a bachelor's degree in occupational health and safety or in a related scientific or technical field. Occupational health and safety technicians typically enter the occupation through one of two paths: on-the-job training or postsecondary education, such as an associate's degree or certificate.

Pay

The median annual wage for occupational health and safety specialists was $74,100 in May 2019.

The median annual wage for occupational health and safety technicians was $51,550 in May 2019.

Job Outlook

Overall employment of occupational health and safety specialists and technicians is projected to grow 4 percent from

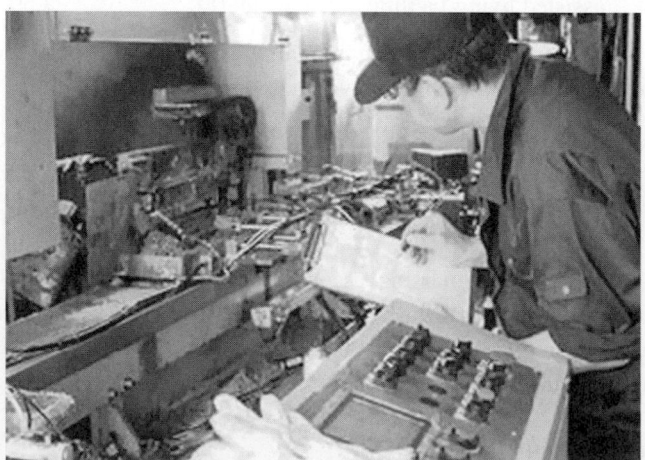

Occupational health and safety specialists inspect workplaces for adherence to regulations on safety, health, and the environment.

2019 to 2029, about as fast as the average for all occupations. Specialists and technicians will be needed in a wide variety of industries to ensure that employers adhere to both existing and new regulations.

State & Area Data

Explore resources for employment and wages by state and area for occupational health and safety specialists and technicians.

What Occupational Health and Safety Specialists and Technicians Do

Occupational health and safety specialists and technicians collect data on and analyze many types of work environments and work procedures. Specialists inspect workplaces for adherence to regulations on safety, health, and the environment. Technicians work with specialists in conducting tests and measuring hazards to help prevent harm to workers, property, the environment, and the general public.

Duties

Occupational health and safety specialists and technicians typically do the following:

- Inspect, test, and evaluate workplace environments, equipment, and practices to ensure that they follow safety standards and government regulations
- Prepare written reports on their findings
- Design and implement workplace processes and procedures that help protect workers from hazardous work conditions
- Evaluate programs on workplace health and safety
- Educate employers and workers about workplace safety by preparing and providing training programs
- Demonstrate the correct use of safety equipment
- Investigate incidents and accidents to identify what caused them and how they might be prevented

Occupational health and safety specialists examine the workplace for environmental or physical factors that could affect

Occupational health and safety technicians often work with complex equipment to test and evaluate workplace environments and equipment.

employee health, safety, comfort, and performance. They may examine factors such as lighting, equipment, materials, and ventilation. Technicians may check to make sure that workers are using required protective gear, such as masks and hardhats.

Some develop and conduct employee safety and training programs. These programs cover a range of topics, such as how to use safety equipment correctly and how to respond in an emergency.

Work Environment

Occupational health and safety specialists held about 100,500 jobs in 2019. The largest employers of occupational health and safety specialists were as follows:

Government	22%
Manufacturing	17
Construction	11
Management, scientific, and technical consulting services	6
Hospitals; state, local, and private	4

Occupational health and safety technicians held about 22,100 jobs in 2019. The largest employers of occupational health and safety technicians were as follows:

Manufacturing	21%
Government	12
Construction	10
Management, scientific, and technical consulting services	9
Hospitals; state, local, and private	4

Occupational health and safety specialists and technicians work in a variety of settings, such as offices or factories. Their jobs often involve considerable fieldwork and travel. They may be exposed to strenuous, dangerous, or stressful conditions. They use gloves, helmets, respirators, and other personal protective and safety equipment to minimize the risk of illness and injury.

Work Schedules

Most occupational health and safety specialists and technicians work full time. Some may work weekends or irregular hours in emergencies.

How to Become an Occupational Health and Safety Specialist or Technician

Occupational health and safety specialists typically need a bachelor's degree in occupational health and safety or in a related scientific or technical field. Occupational health and safety technicians typically enter the occupation through one of two paths: on-the-job training or postsecondary education, such as an associate's degree or certificate.

Education

Occupational health and safety specialists typically need a bachelor's degree in occupational health and safety or a related

Specialists and technicians carry out and evaluate programs on workplace safety and health.

scientific or technical field, such as engineering, biology, or chemistry. For some positions, a master's degree in industrial hygiene, health physics, or a related subject is required. In addition to science courses, typical courses include ergonomics, writing and communications, occupational safety management, and accident prevention.

Employers typically require technicians to have at least a high school diploma. High school students interested in this occupation should complete courses in English, mathematics, chemistry, biology, and physics.

Some employers prefer to hire technicians who have earned an associate's degree or certificate from a community college or vocational school. These programs typically take 2 years or less. They include courses in respiratory protection, hazard communication, and material-handling and storage procedures.

Important Qualities

Ability to use technology. Occupational health and safety specialists and technicians must be able to use advanced technology. They often work with complex testing equipment.

Communication skills. Occupational health and safety specialists and technicians must be able to communicate safety instructions and concerns to employees and managers. They frequently prepare written reports and prepare and deliver safety training to other workers.

Detail oriented. Occupational health and safety specialists and technicians need to understand and follow safety standards and complex government regulations.

Physical stamina. Occupational health and safety specialists and technicians must be able to stand for long periods and be able to travel regularly. Some work in environments that can be uncomfortable, such as tunnels or mines.

Problem-solving skills. Occupational health and safety specialists and technicians must be able to solve problems in order to design and implement workplace processes and procedures that help protect workers from hazardous conditions.

Licenses, Certifications, and Registrations

Although certification is voluntary, many employers encourage it. Certification is available through several organizations, depending on the field in which the specialists work. Specialists must have graduated from an accredited educational program and have work experience to be eligible to take most certification exams. To keep their certification, specialists usually are required to complete periodic continuing education.

Occupational safety and health specialists and technicians can earn professional certifications including the following:

- The Board of Certified Safety Professionals offers the following certifications:
- Certified Safety Professional (CSP) certification
- Associate Safety Professional (ASP)
- Occupational Health and Safety Technologist (OHST)
- Construction Health and Safety Technician (CHST)
- The American Board of Industrial Hygiene awards a certification known as a Certified Industrial Hygienist (CIH)

Training

Occupational health and safety technicians usually receive on-the-job training. They learn about specific laws and inspection procedures, and learn to conduct tests and recognize hazards. The length of training varies with the employee's level of experience, education, and industry in which he or she works.

Some technicians enter the occupation through a combination of related work experience and training. They may take on health and safety tasks at the company where they are employed. For example, an employee may volunteer to complete annual workstation inspections for an office in which he or she already works.

Pay

The median annual wage for occupational health and safety specialists was $74,100 in May 2019. The median wage is the wage at which half the workers in an occupation earned more than that amount and half earned less. The lowest 10 percent earned less than $43,630, and the highest 10 percent earned more than $111,130.

The median annual wage for occupational health and safety technicians was $51,550 in May 2019. The lowest 10 percent earned less than $32,830, and the highest 10 percent earned more than $89,720.

In May 2019, the median annual wages for occupational health and safety specialists in the top industries in which they worked were as follows:

Manufacturing	$74,820
Hospitals; state, local, and private	74,600
Management, scientific, and technical consulting services	73,210
Government	72,870
Construction	72,840

Occupational Health and Safety Specialists and Technicians

Median annual wages, May 2019

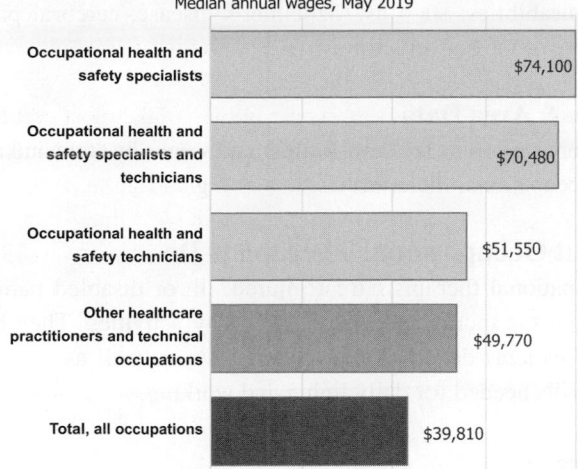

Occupational health and safety specialists	$74,100
Occupational health and safety specialists and technicians	$70,480
Occupational health and safety technicians	$51,550
Other healthcare practitioners and technical occupations	$49,770
Total, all occupations	$39,810

Note: All Occupations includes all occupations in the U.S. Economy.
Source: U.S. Bureau of Labor Statistics, Occupational Employment Statistics.

In May 2019, the median annual wages for occupational health and safety technicians in the top industries in which they worked were as follows:

Construction	$58,340
Government	51,030
Manufacturing	50,080
Management, scientific, and technical consulting services	46,390
Hospitals; state, local, and private	43,350

Most occupational health and safety specialists and technicians work full time. Some may work weekends or irregular hours in emergencies.

Job Outlook

Employment of occupational health and safety specialists is projected to grow 4 percent from 2019 to 2029, about as fast as the average for all occupations. Employment of occupational health and safety technicians is projected to grow 5 percent from 2019 to 2029, faster than the average for all occupations.

Specialists and technicians will be needed to work in a variety of industries and government agencies to ensure that employers are adhering to both existing and new regulations. In addition, specialists will be necessary because insurance costs and workers' compensation costs have become a concern for many employers and insurance companies. An aging population is remaining in the workforce longer than past generations did, and older workers usually have a greater proportion of workers' compensation claims.

Job Prospects

Applicants for jobs as occupational health and safety specialists or technicians with a background in the sciences, experience in more than one area of health and safety, or certification will have the best prospects.

Occupational Health and Safety Specialists and Technicians

Percent change in employment, projected 2019-29

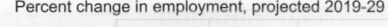
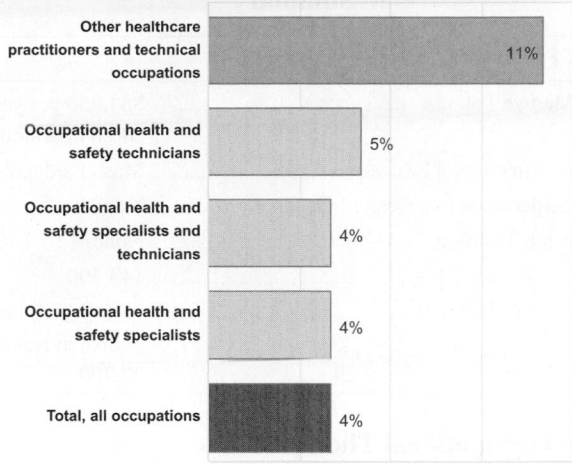

Other healthcare practitioners and technical occupations	11%
Occupational health and safety technicians	5%
Occupational health and safety specialists and technicians	4%
Occupational health and safety specialists	4%
Total, all occupations	4%

Note: All Occupations includes all occupations in the U.S. Economy.
Source: U.S. Bureau of Labor Statistics, Employment Projections program.

Employment projections data for occupational health and safety specialists and technicians, 2019-29

Occupational Title	SOC Code	Employment, 2019	Projected Employment, 2029	Change, 2019-29 Percent	Change, 2019-29 Numeric
Occupational health and safety specialists and technicians	19-5000	122,600	127,400	4	4,800
Occupational health and safety specialists	19-5011	100,500	104,300	4	3,800
Occupational health and safety technicians	19-5012	22,100	23,100	5	1,000

SOURCE: U.S. Bureau of Labor Statistics, Employment Projections program

State & Area Data
Occupational Employment Statistics (OES)

The Occupational Employment Statistics (OES) program produces employment and wage estimates annually for over 800 occupations. These estimates are available for the nation as a whole, for individual states, and for metropolitan and nonmetropolitan areas.

Contacts for More Information

For more information about credentialing in industrial hygiene, visit
➤ American Board of Industrial Hygiene

For more information about occupations in safety, a list of safety and related academic programs, and credentialing, visit
➤ Board of Certified Safety Professionals

For more information about occupational health and safety, visit
➤ U.S. Department of Labor, Occupational Safety and Health Administration (OSHA)

➤ Centers for Disease Control and Prevention, National Institute for Occupational Safety and Health (NIOSH)
➤ To find job openings for occupational health and safety positions in the federal government, visit
➤ USAJOBS

Occupational Therapists

Summary

Quick Facts: Occupational Therapists

2019 Median Pay	$84,950 per year $40.84 per hour
Typical Entry-Level Education	Master's degree
Work Experience in a Related Occupation	None
On-the-job Training	None
Number of Jobs, 2019.......................................	143,300
Job Outlook, 2019-29..	16% (Much faster than average)
Employment Change, 2019-29	22,700

What Occupational Therapists Do

Occupational therapists treat patients who have injuries, illnesses, or disabilities through the therapeutic use of everyday activities.

Work Environment

About half of occupational therapists work in offices of occupational therapy or in hospitals. Others work in schools, nursing homes, and home health services. Therapists may spend a lot of time on their feet while working with patients.

How to Become an Occupational Therapist

Occupational therapists typically have a master's degree in occupational therapy. All states require occupational therapists to be licensed.

Pay

The median annual wage for occupational therapists was $84,950 in May 2019.

Job Outlook

Employment of occupational therapists is projected to grow 16 percent from 2019 to 2029, much faster than the average for

all occupations. Occupational therapy will continue to be an important part of treatment for people with various illnesses and disabilities, such as Alzheimer's disease, cerebral palsy, autism, or the loss of a limb.

State & Area Data

Explore resources for employment and wages by state and area for occupational therapists.

What Occupational Therapists Do

Occupational therapists treat injured, ill, or disabled patients through the therapeutic use of everyday activities. They help these patients develop, recover, improve, as well as maintain the skills needed for daily living and working.

Duties

Occupational therapists typically do the following:

- Review patients' medical history, ask the patients questions, and observe them doing tasks
- Evaluate a patient's condition and needs
- Develop a treatment plan for patients, identifying specific goals and the types of activities that will be used to help the patient work toward those goals

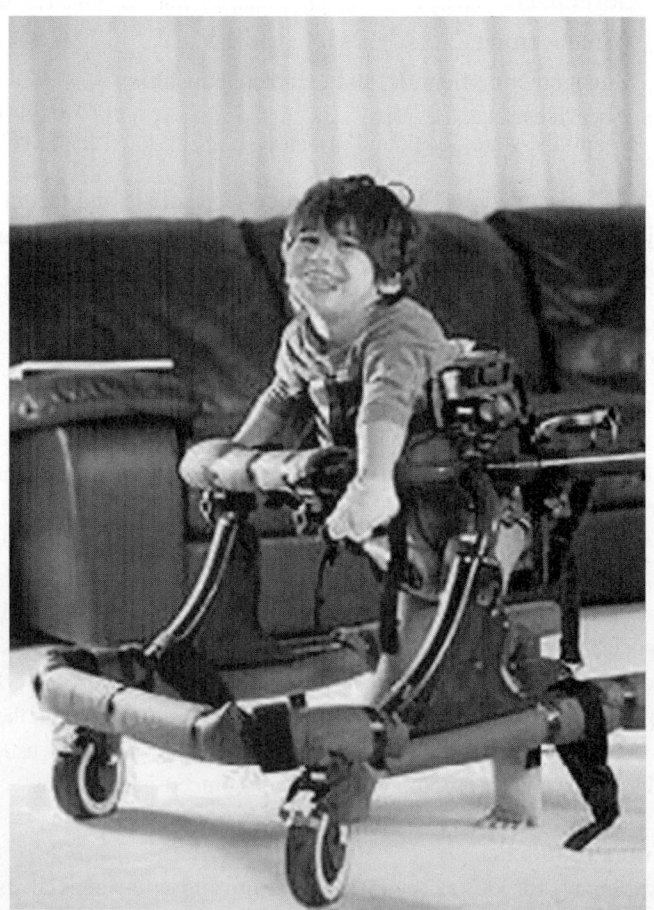

Occupational therapists use special equipment to help children with developmental disabilities.

Occupational therapists develop a treatment plan for patients.

- Help people with various disabilities perform different tasks, such as teaching a stroke victim how to get dressed
- Demonstrate exercises—for example, stretching the joints for arthritis relief—that can help relieve pain in people with chronic conditions
- Evaluate a patient's home or workplace and, on the basis of the patient's health needs, identify potential improvements, such as labeling kitchen cabinets for an older person with poor memory
- Educate a patient's family and employer about how to accommodate and care for the patient
- Recommend special equipment, such as wheelchairs and eating aids, and instruct patients on how to use that equipment
- Assess and record patients' activities and progress for patient evaluations, for billing, and for reporting to physicians and other healthcare providers

Patients with permanent disabilities, such as cerebral palsy, often need help performing daily tasks. Therapists show patients how to use appropriate adaptive equipment, such as leg braces, wheelchairs, and eating aids. These devices help patients perform a number of daily tasks, allowing them to function more independently.

Some occupational therapists work with children in educational settings. They evaluate disabled children's abilities, modify classroom equipment to accommodate children with disabilities, and help children participate in school activities. Therapists also may provide early intervention therapy to infants and toddlers who have, or are at risk of having, developmental delays.

Therapists who work with the elderly help their patients lead more independent and active lives. They assess patients' abilities and environment and make recommendations to improve the patients' everyday lives. For example, therapists may identify potential fall hazards in a patient's home and recommend their removal.

In some cases, occupational therapists help patients create functional work environments. They evaluate the workspace, recommend modifications, and meet with the patient's employer to collaborate on changes to the patient's work environment or schedule.

Occupational therapists also may work in mental health settings, where they help patients who suffer from developmental disabilities, mental illness, or emotional problems. Therapists teach these patients skills such as managing time, budgeting, using public transportation, and doing household chores in order to help them cope with, and engage in, daily life activities. In addition, therapists may work with individuals who have problems with drug abuse, alcoholism, depression, or other disorders. They may also work with people who have been through a traumatic event, such as a car accident.

Some occupational therapists, such as those employed in hospitals, work as part of a healthcare team along with doctors, registered nurses, and other types of therapists. They may work with patients who have chronic conditions, such as diabetes, or help rehabilitate a patient recovering from hip replacement surgery. Occupational therapists also oversee the work of occupational therapy assistants and aides.

Work Environment

Occupational therapists held about 143,300 jobs in 2019. The largest employers of occupational therapists were as follows:

Hospitals; state, local, and private..................................	26%
Offices of physical, occupational and speech therapists, and audiologists	26
Elementary and secondary schools; state, local, and private...	12
Home healthcare services	9
Nursing care facilities (skilled nursing facilities)........	8

Therapists may spend a lot of time on their feet while working with patients. They also may be required to lift and move patients or heavy equipment. Many work in multiple facilities and have to travel from one job to another.

Work Schedules

Most occupational therapists work full time. They may work nights or weekends, as needed, to accommodate patients' schedules.

How to Become an Occupational Therapist

Occupational therapists need at least a master's degree in occupational therapy; some therapists have a doctoral degree. Occupational therapists also must be licensed.

Education

Most occupational therapists enter the occupation with a master's degree in occupational therapy. In 2017, there were about 200 occupational therapy programs accredited by the Accreditation Council for Occupational Therapy

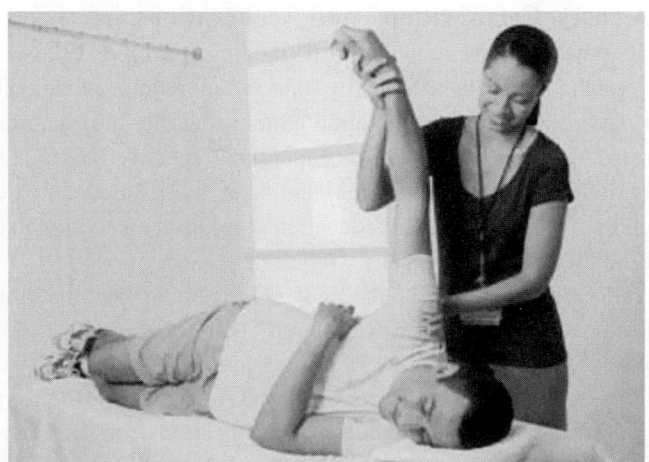

Occupational therapists may spend a lot of time on their feet working with patients.

Occupational therapists can help people cope with arthritis and other ailments.

Education, part of the American Occupational Therapy Association.

Admission to graduate programs in occupational therapy generally requires a bachelor's degree and specific course-work, including biology and physiology. Many programs also require applicants to have volunteered or worked in an occupational therapy setting. Candidates should contact the program that they are interested in attending about specific requirements.

Master's programs usually take 2 to 3 years to complete; doctoral programs take about 3 and a half years. Some schools offer a dual-degree program in which the student earns a bachelor's degree and a master's degree in 5 years. Part-time programs that offer courses on nights and weekends are also available.

Both master's and doctoral programs require at least 24 weeks of supervised fieldwork, in which prospective occupational therapists gain clinical work experience. In addition, doctoral programs require a 16-week capstone experience.

Licenses, Certifications, and Registrations

All states require occupational therapists to be licensed. Licensing requirements vary by state, but all require candidates to pass the national examination administered by the National Board for Certification in Occupational Therapy (NBCOT). To sit for the NBCOT exam, candidates must have earned a degree from an accredited educational program and completed all fieldwork requirements.

Therapists must pass the NBCOT exam to use the title "Occupational Therapist, Registered" (OTR). They must also take continuing education classes to maintain certification.

The American Occupational Therapy Association also offers a number of board and specialty certifications for therapists who want to demonstrate their advanced or specialized knowledge in areas of practice, such as pediatrics, mental health, or low vision.

Important Qualities

Adaptability. Occupational therapists must be flexible when treating patients. Because not every type of therapy will work for each patient, therapists may need to be creative when determining the treatment plans and adaptive devices that best suit each patient's needs.

Communication skills. Occupational therapists must listen attentively to what patients tell them and must explain what they want their patients to do. When communicating with other members of the patient's medical team, therapists must clearly explain the treatment plan for the patient and any progress made by the patient.

Compassion. Occupational therapists are usually drawn to the profession by a desire to help people and improve their daily lives. Therapists must be sensitive to a patient's needs and concerns, especially when assisting the patient with personal activities.

Interpersonal skills. Because occupational therapists spend their time teaching and explaining therapies to patients, they need to earn the trust and respect of those patients and their families.

Patience. Dealing with injuries, illnesses, and disabilities is frustrating for many people. Occupational therapists should exhibit patience in order to provide quality care to the people they serve.

Pay

The median annual wage for occupational therapists was $84,950 in May 2019. The median wage is the wage at which half the workers in an occupation earned more than that amount and half earned less. The lowest 10 percent earned less than $56,800, and the highest 10 percent earned more than $121,490.

In May 2019, the median annual wages for occupational therapists in the top industries in which they worked were as follows:

Nursing care facilities (skilled nursing facilities)... $90,830

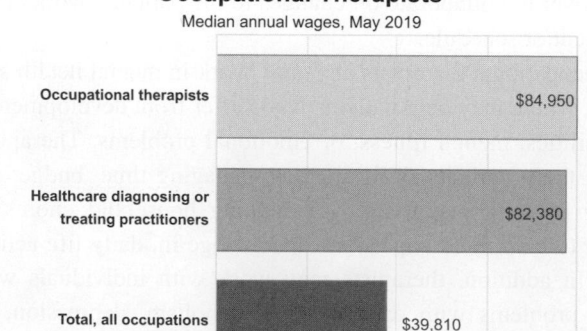

Occupational Therapists
Median annual wages, May 2019

Occupational therapists	$84,950
Healthcare diagnosing or treating practitioners	$82,380
Total, all occupations	$39,810

Note: All Occupations includes all occupations in the U.S. Economy.
Source: U.S. Bureau of Labor Statistics, Occupational Employment Statistics.

Home healthcare services 89,220

Offices of physical, occupational and speech 87,190
therapists, and audiologists ....

Hospitals; state, local, and private 85,510

Elementary and secondary schools; state, local, 74,670
and private ....

Most occupational therapists work full time. They may work nights or weekends, as needed, to accommodate patients' schedules.

Job Outlook

Employment of occupational therapists is projected to grow 16 percent from 2019 to 2029, much faster than the average for all occupations. Occupational therapy will continue to be an important part of treatment for people with various illnesses and disabilities, such as Alzheimer's disease, cerebral palsy, autism, or the loss of a limb. However, demand for occupational therapy services is related to the ability of patients to pay, either directly or through health insurance.

The need for occupational therapists is expected to increase as the large baby-boom generation ages and people remain active later in life. Occupational therapists can help senior citizens maintain their independence by recommending home modifications and strategies that make daily activities easier. Therapists also play a role in the treatment of many conditions and ailments commonly associated with aging, such as arthritis and stroke.

Occupational therapists also will be needed in a variety of healthcare settings to treat patients with chronic conditions, such as diabetes. Patients will continue to seek noninvasive outpatient treatment for long-term disabilities and illnesses, either in their homes or in residential care environments. These patients may need occupational therapy to become more independent and to perform a variety of daily tasks.

Demand for occupational therapy services also will stem from patients with autism spectrum disorder. Therapists will continue to be needed in schools to assist children with autism in improving their social skills and accomplishing a variety of daily tasks.

Job Prospects

Job opportunities should be good for licensed occupational therapists in all settings, particularly acute hospital, rehabilitation, and orthopedic settings where the elderly receive

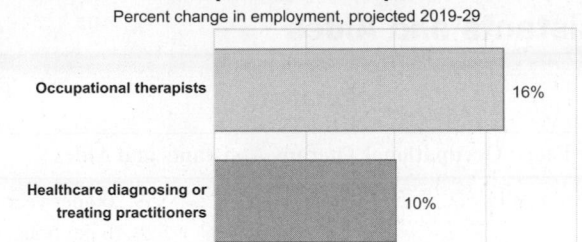

Occupational Therapists
Percent change in employment, projected 2019-29

Occupational therapists — 16%
Healthcare diagnosing or treating practitioners — 10%
Total, all occupations — 4%

Note: All Occupations includes all occupations in the U.S. Economy.
Source: U.S. Bureau of Labor Statistics, Employment Projections program.

treatment. Occupational therapists with specialized knowledge in a treatment area also will have better job prospects.

Occupational Title	SOC Code	Employment, 2019	Projected Employment, 2029	Change, 2019-29	
				Percent	Numeric
SOURCE: U.S. Bureau of Labor Statistics, Employment Projections program					
Occupational therapists	29-1122	143,300	166,000	16	22,700

Employment projections data for occupational therapists, 2019-29

State & Area Data
Occupational Employment Statistics (OES)

The Occupational Employment Statistics (OES) program produces employment and wage estimates annually for over 800 occupations. These estimates are available for the nation as a whole, for individual states, and for metropolitan and nonmetropolitan areas.

Contacts for More Information

For more information about occupational therapists, visit
➤ American Occupational Therapy Association, Inc.

For more information about the certification exam for Occupational Therapist, Registered, visit
➤ National Board for Certification in Occupational Therapy

For information regarding the requirements for practice as an occupational therapist in schools, contact state occupational therapy regulatory agencies.

Occupational Therapy Assistants and Aides

Summary

Quick Facts: Occupational Therapy Assistants and Aides

2019 Median Pay	$59,200 per year
	$28.46 per hour
Typical Entry-Level Education	See below
Work Experience in a Related Occupation	None
On-the-job Training	See below
Number of Jobs, 2019....................................	55,100
Job Outlook, 2019-29....................................	32% (Much faster than average)
Employment Change, 2019-29	17,900

What Occupational Therapy Assistants and Aides Do

Occupational therapy assistants and aides help patients develop, recover, improve, as well as maintain the skills needed for daily living and working.

Work Environment

Occupational therapy assistants and aides work primarily in occupational therapists' offices, in hospitals, and in nursing care facilities. Occupational therapy assistants and aides spend much of their time on their feet while setting up equipment and, in the case of assistants, providing therapy to patients.

How to Become an Occupational Therapy Assistant or Aide

Occupational therapy assistants need an associate's degree from an accredited occupational therapy assistant program. All states regulate the practice of occupational therapy assistants. Occupational therapy aides typically need a high school diploma or equivalent and receive training on the job.

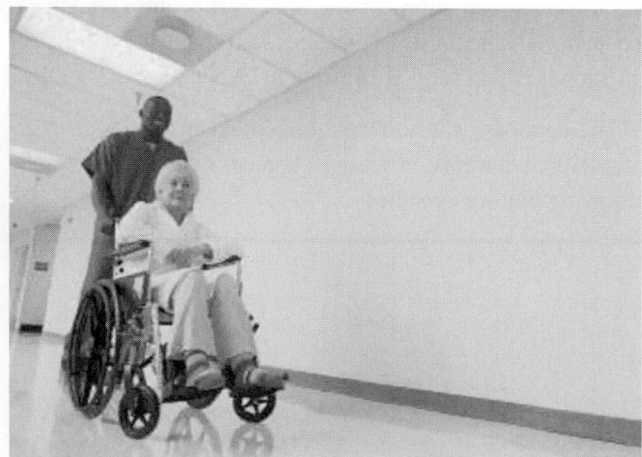

Occupational therapy aides transport patients to and from treatment areas.

Pay

The median annual wage for occupational therapy aides was $29,230 in May 2019.

The median annual wage for occupational therapy assistants was $61,510 in May 2019.

Job Outlook

Overall employment of occupational therapy assistants and aides is projected to grow 32 percent from 2019 to 2029, much faster than the average for all occupations. Occupational therapy will continue to be an important part of treatment for people with various illnesses and disabilities.

State & Area Data

Explore resources for employment and wages by state and area for occupational therapy assistants and aides.

What Occupational Therapy Assistants and Aides Do

Occupational therapy assistants and aides help patients develop, recover, improve, as well as maintain the skills needed for daily living and working. Occupational therapy assistants are directly involved in providing therapy to patients; occupational therapy aides typically perform support activities. Both assistants and aides work under the direction of occupational therapists.

Duties

Occupational therapy assistants typically do the following:

- Help patients do therapeutic activities, such as stretches and other exercises
- Lead children who have developmental disabilities in play activities that promote coordination and socialization
- Encourage patients to complete activities and tasks
- Teach patients how to use special equipment—for example, showing a patient with Parkinson's disease how to use devices that make eating easier

Occupational therapy aides may handle some clerical tasks, like answering calls from patients and scheduling appointments.

- Record patients' progress, report to occupational therapists, and do other administrative tasks

Occupational therapy aides typically do the following:

- Prepare treatment areas, such as setting up therapy equipment
- Transport patients
- Clean treatment areas and equipment
- Help patients with billing and insurance forms
- Perform clerical tasks, including scheduling appointments and answering telephones

Occupational therapy assistants collaborate with occupational therapists to develop and carry out a treatment plan for each patient. Plans include diverse activities such as teaching the proper way for patients to move from a bed into a wheelchair and advising patients on the best way to stretch their muscles. For example, an occupational therapy assistant might work with injured workers to help them get back into the workforce by teaching them how to work around lost motor skills. Occupational therapy assistants also may work with people who have learning disabilities, teaching them skills that allow them to be more independent.

Assistants monitor activities to make sure that patients are doing them correctly. They record the patient's progress and provide feedback to the occupational therapist so that the therapist can change the treatment plan if the patient is not getting the desired results.

Occupational therapy aides typically prepare materials and assemble equipment used during treatment. They may assist patients with moving to and from treatment areas. After a therapy session, aides clean the treatment area, put away equipment, and gather laundry.

Occupational therapy aides fill out insurance forms and other paperwork and are responsible for a range of clerical tasks, such as scheduling appointments, answering the telephone, and monitoring inventory levels.

Work Environment

Occupational therapy aides held about 8,000 jobs in 2019. The largest employers of occupational therapy aides were as follows:

Offices of physical, occupational and speech
    therapists, and audiologists 47%
Hospitals; state, local, and private 23
Nursing care facilities (skilled nursing facilities) 12
Social assistance 1

Occupational therapy assistants held about 47,100 jobs in 2019. The largest employers of occupational therapy assistants were as follows:

Offices of physical, occupational and speech
    therapists, and audiologists 47%
Nursing care facilities (skilled nursing facilities) 16
Hospitals; state, local, and private 15

Occupational therapy assistants may work with children who have developmental disabilities.

Home healthcare services 6
Educational services; state, local, and private 4

Occupational therapy assistants and aides spend much of their time on their feet while setting up equipment and, in the case of assistants, providing therapy to patients. Constant kneeling and stooping are part of the job, as is the occasional need to lift patients.

Injuries and Illnesses

Occupational therapy aides have one of the highest rates of injuries and illnesses of all occupations. Their work may require physically demanding tasks, such as lifting patients, which can cause injuries.

Work Schedules

Most occupational therapy assistants and aides work full time. Occupational therapy assistants and aides may work during evenings or on weekends to accommodate patients' schedules.

How to Become an Occupational Therapy Assistant or Aide

Occupational therapy assistants need an associate's degree from an accredited occupational therapy assistant program. All states regulate the practice of occupational therapy assistants. Occupational therapy aides typically need a high school diploma or equivalent and are trained on the job.

Education and Training

Occupational therapy assistants typically need an associate's degree from an accredited program. Occupational therapy assistant programs are commonly found in community colleges and technical schools. In 2017, there were more than 200 occupational therapy assistant programs accredited by the Accreditation Council for Occupational Therapy Education, a part of the American Occupational Therapy Association.

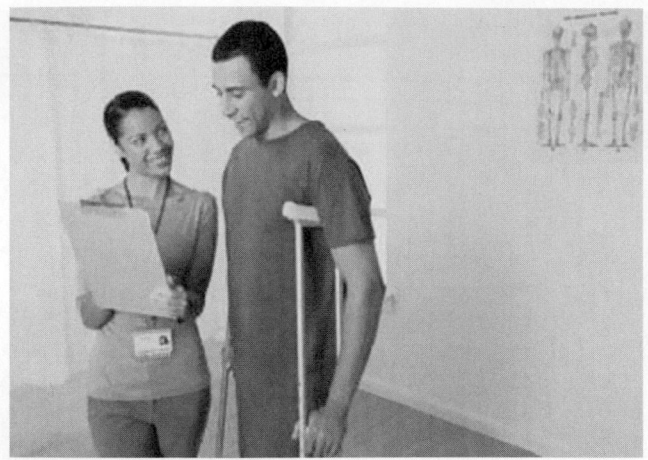

Occupational therapy aides help patients with billing and insurance forms.

These programs generally require 2 years of full-time study and include instruction in subjects such as psychology, biology, and pediatric health. In addition to taking coursework, occupational therapy assistants must complete at least 16 weeks of fieldwork to gain hands-on work experience.

People interested in becoming an occupational therapy assistant should take high school courses in biology and health education. They also can increase their chances of getting into a community college or technical school program by doing volunteer work in a healthcare setting, such as a nursing care facility, an occupational therapist's office, or a physical therapist's office.

Occupational therapy aides typically need a high school diploma or equivalent. They are trained on the job under the supervision of more experienced assistants or aides. Training can last from several days to a few weeks and covers a number of topics, including the setting up of therapy equipment and infection control procedures, among others. Previous work experience in healthcare may be helpful in getting a job.

Both occupational therapy assistants and aides often need certifications in cardiopulmonary resuscitation (CPR) and basic life support (BLS).

Important Qualities

Adaptability. Assistants must be flexible when treating patients. Because not every type of therapy will work for each patient, assistants may need to be creative when working with occupational therapists to determine the best therapy to achieve a patient's goals.

Compassion. Occupational therapy assistants and aides frequently work with patients who struggle with many of life's basic activities. As a result, they should be compassionate and have the ability to encourage others.

Detail oriented. Occupational therapy assistants and aides must quickly and accurately follow the instructions, both written and spoken, of an occupational therapist. In addition, aides must pay attention to detail when performing clerical tasks, such as helping a patient fill out an insurance form.

Interpersonal skills. Occupational therapy assistants and aides spend much of their time interacting with patients and therefore should be friendly and courteous. They also should communicate clearly with patients and with patients' families to the extent of their training.

Physical strength. Assistants and aides need to have a moderate degree of strength because of the physical exertion required to assist patients. Constant kneeling, stooping, and standing for long periods also are part of the job.

Licenses, Certifications, and Registrations

All states regulate the practice of occupational therapy assistants, with most requiring licensure. Licensure typically requires the completion of an accredited occupational therapy assistant education program, completion of all fieldwork requirements, and passing the National Board for Certification in Occupational Therapy (NBCOT) exam. Some states have additional requirements.

Occupational therapy assistants must pass the NBCOT exam to use the title "Certified Occupational Therapy Assistant" (COTA). They must also take continuing education classes to maintain their certification.

The American Occupational Therapy Association also offers a number of specialty certifications for occupational therapy assistants who want to demonstrate their specialized level of knowledge, skills, and abilities in specialized areas of practice such as low vision or feeding, eating, and swallowing.

Occupational therapy aides are not regulated by state law.

Advancement

Some occupational therapy assistants and aides advance by gaining additional education and becoming occupational therapists. A small number of occupational therapist "bridge" education programs are designed to qualify occupational therapy assistants to advance and become therapists.

Pay

The median annual wage for occupational therapy aides was $29,230 in May 2019. The median wage is the wage at which half the workers in an occupation earned more than that amount and half earned less. The lowest 10 percent earned less than $18,960, and the highest 10 percent earned more than $62,120.

The median annual wage for occupational therapy assistants was $61,510 in May 2019. The lowest 10 percent earned less than $41,730, and the highest 10 percent earned more than $82,210.

In May 2019, the median annual wages for occupational therapy aides in the top industries in which they worked were as follows:

Nursing care facilities (skilled nursing facilities)....	$36,140
Social assistance	35,960

Occupational Therapy Assistants and Aides
Median annual wages, May 2019

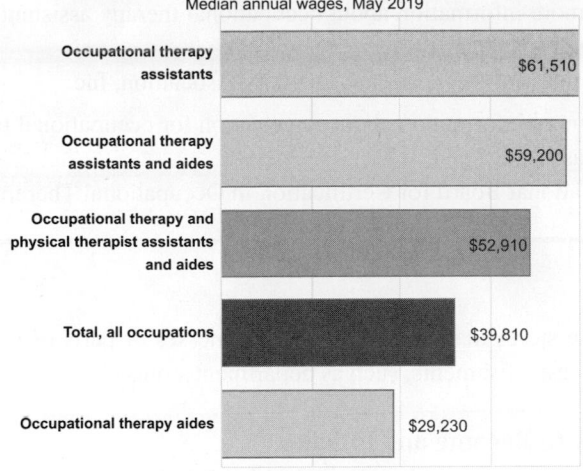

Occupational Therapy Assistants and Aides
Percent change in employment, projected 2019-29

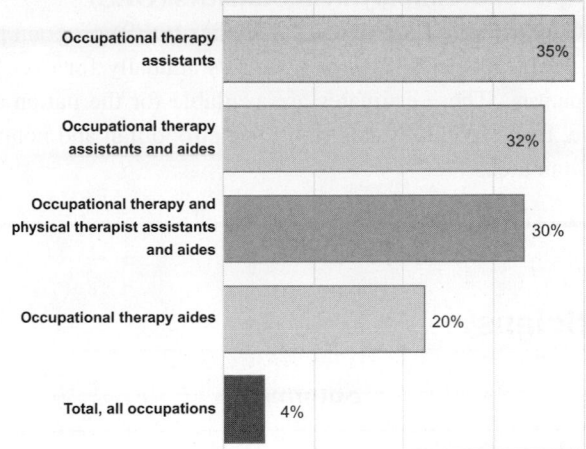

Note: All Occupations includes all occupations in the U.S. Economy. Source: U.S. Bureau of Labor Statistics, Occupational Employment Statistics.

Note: All Occupations includes all occupations in the U.S. Economy. Source: U.S. Bureau of Labor Statistics, Employment Projections program.

Hospitals; state, local, and private 31,630

Offices of physical, occupational and speech
therapists, and audiologists 23,520

In May 2019, the median annual wages for occupational therapy assistants in the top industries in which they worked were as follows:

Nursing care facilities (skilled nursing facilities) ... $66,750

Home healthcare services 65,560

Offices of physical, occupational and speech
therapists, and audiologists 61,860

Hospitals; state, local, and private 57,600

Educational services; state, local, and private 52,460

Most occupational therapy assistants and aides work full time. Occupational therapy assistants and aides may work during evenings or on weekends to accommodate patients' schedules.

Job Outlook

Employment of occupational therapy assistants is projected to grow 35 percent from 2019 to 2029, much faster than the average for all occupations.

Employment of occupational therapy aides is projected to grow 20 percent from 2019 to 2029, much faster than the average for all occupations. However, because it is a small occupation, the fast growth will result in only about 1,600 new jobs over the 10-year period.

Occupational therapy assistants and aides will be needed to help therapists treat additional patients and to ensure that treatment facility operations run smoothly. However, demand for occupational therapy services is related to the ability of patients to pay, either directly or through health insurance.

Demand for occupational therapy is likely to grow over the coming decade in response to the health needs of the aging baby-boom generation and a growing elderly population. Older adults are more prone than younger people to conditions and ailments such as arthritis and stroke. These conditions can affect one's ability to perform a variety of everyday activities. Occupational therapy assistants and aides will be needed to help occupational therapists in caring for these patients. Occupational therapy will also continue to be used to treat children and young adults with developmental disabilities, such as autism.

Healthcare providers, especially those specializing in long-term care such as nursing homes and home healthcare services, will continue to employ assistants to reduce the cost of occupational therapy services. After the therapist has evaluated a patient and designed a treatment plan, the occupational therapy assistant can provide many aspects of the treatment that the therapist prescribed.

Job Prospects

Occupational therapy assistants and aides with experience working in an occupational therapy office or other healthcare setting should have the best job opportunities. However, occupational therapy aides may face strong competition from the large pool of qualified people, because there are relatively few requirements to enter the occupation.

Employment projections data for occupational therapy assistants and aides, 2019-29					
Occupational Title	SOC Code	Employment, 2019	Projected Employment, 2029	Change, 2019-29 Percent	Numeric
SOURCE: U.S. Bureau of Labor Statistics, Employment Projections program					
Occupational therapy assistants and aides	31-2010	55,100	73,000	32	17,900
Occupational therapy assistants	31-2011	47,100	63,500	35	16,300
Occupational therapy aides	31-2012	8,000	9,500	20	1,600

State & Area Data
Occupational Employment Statistics (OES)

The Occupational Employment Statistics (OES) program produces employment and wage estimates annually for over 800 occupations. These estimates are available for the nation as a whole, for individual states, and for metropolitan and nonmetropolitan areas.

Contacts for More Information

For more information about occupational therapy assistants or aides, visit
➤ American Occupational Therapy Association, Inc.

For more information about certification for occupational therapy assistants, visit
➤ National Board for Certification in Occupational Therapy

Opticians

Summary

Quick Facts: Opticians

2019 Median Pay	$37,840 per year $18.19 per hour
Typical Entry-Level Education	High school diploma or equivalent
Work Experience in a Related Occupation	None
On-the-job Training	Long-term on-the-job training
Number of Jobs, 2019	73,800
Job Outlook, 2019-29	4% (As fast as average)
Employment Change, 2019-29	3,000

What Opticians Do

Opticians help fit eyeglasses and contact lenses, following prescriptions from ophthalmologists and optometrists.

Work Environment

About half of opticians work in offices of optometrists or offices of physicians. Other opticians worked in stores that sell eyeglasses, contact lenses, visual aids, and other optical goods. These stores may be stand-alone businesses or parts of larger retail establishments, such as department stores.

How to Become an Optician

Opticians typically have a high school diploma or equivalent and some form of on-the-job training. Some opticians enter the occupation with an associate's degree or a certificate from a community college or technical school. About half of the states require opticians to be licensed.

Pay

The median annual wage for opticians was $37,840 in May 2019.

Job Outlook

Employment of opticians is projected to grow 4 percent from 2019 to 2029, about as fast as the average for all occupations. An aging population and increasing rates of chronic disease are expected to lead to greater demand for corrective eyewear.

State & Area Data

Explore resources for employment and wages by state and area for opticians.

What Opticians Do

Opticians help fit eyeglasses and contact lenses, following prescriptions from ophthalmologists and optometrists. They also

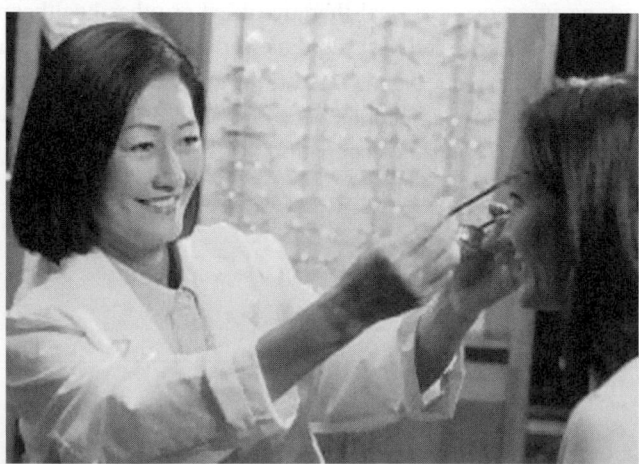

Opticians help customers choose eyeglass frames and lens treatments.

Opticians advise customers on styles of eyewear that suit their needs.

help customers decide which eyeglass frames or contact lenses to buy.

Duties

Opticians typically do the following:

- Receive customers' prescriptions for eyeglasses or contact lenses
- Measure customers' eyes and faces, such as the distance between their pupils
- Help customers choose eyeglass frames and lens treatments, such as eyewear for occupational use or sports, tints, or antireflective coatings, based on their vision needs and style preferences
- Create work orders for ophthalmic laboratory technicians, providing information about the lenses needed
- Adjust eyewear to ensure a good fit
- Repair or replace broken eyeglass frames
- Educate customers about eyewear—for example, show them how to care for their contact lenses
- Perform business tasks, such as maintaining sales records, keeping track of customers' prescriptions, and ordering and maintaining inventory

Opticians who work in small shops or prepare custom orders may cut lenses and insert them into frames—tasks usually performed by ophthalmic laboratory technicians.

Work Environment

Opticians held about 73,800 jobs in 2019. The largest employers of opticians were as follows:

Offices of optometrists	41%
Health and personal care stores.....................................	29
Offices of physicians..	10
Self-employed workers...	3

Opticians who work as part of a group optometry or medical practice work with optometrists and ophthalmologists to provide eye-related medical care to patients.

Opticians may work in retail stores that sell eyeglasses and other optical goods.

Work Schedules

Opticians who work in large retail establishments, such as department stores, may have to work evenings and weekends. Most opticians work full time, although part-time opportunities also are available.

How to Become an Optician

Opticians typically have a high school diploma or equivalent and receive some form of on-the-job training. Some opticians enter the occupation with an associate's degree or a certificate from a community college or technical school. About half of the states require opticians to be licensed.

Education and Training

Opticians typically have a high school diploma or equivalent and learn job skills through on-the-job training. Training includes technical instruction in which, for example, a new optician measures a customer's eyes or adjusts frames under the supervision of an experienced optician. Trainees also learn sales and office management practices. Some opticians complete an apprenticeship, which typically takes at least 2 years. Other opticians complete a postsecondary education program at a community college or technical school. These programs award a 2-year associate's degree or a 1-year certificate. As of 2017, the Commission on Opticianry Accreditation accredited 19 programs in 11 states.

Education programs typically include both classroom instruction and clinical experience. Coursework includes classes in optics, eye physiology, math, and business management, among other topics. Students also do supervised clinical work that gives them hands-on experience working as opticians and learning optical math, optical physics, and the use of precision measuring instruments. Some programs have distance-learning options.

The National Academy of Opticianry offers the Ophthalmic Career Progression Program (OCPP), a program designed for individuals who are already working in the field. The OCPP

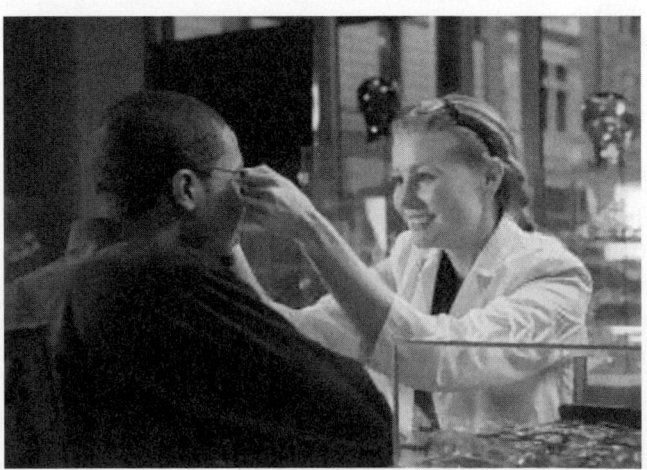

Opticians learn to adjust eyeglass frames during training.

offers opticians another way to prepare for licensure exams or certifications.

Licenses, Certifications, and Registrations

About half of the states require opticians to be licensed. Licensure usually requires completing formal education through an approved program or completing an apprenticeship. In addition, opticians must pass one or more exams to be licensed. The opticianry licensing board in each state can supply information on licensing requirements.

Opticians may choose to become certified in eyeglass dispensing or contact lens dispensing or both. Certification requires passing exams from the American Board of Opticianry (ABO) and National Contact Lens Examiners (NCLE). Nearly all state licensing boards use the ABO and NCLE exams as the basis for state licensing. Some states also require opticians to pass state-specific practical exams.

In most states that require licensure, opticians must renew their license every 1 to 3 years and must complete continuing education requirements.

Important Qualities

Business skills. Opticians are often responsible for the business aspects of running an optical store. They should be comfortable making decisions and have some knowledge of sales and inventory management.

Communication skills. Opticians must listen closely to what customers want. They must clearly explain options and instructions for care in ways that customers understand.

Customer-service skills. Because some opticians work in stores, they must answer questions and know about the products they sell. They interact with customers on a personal level, fitting eyeglasses or contact lenses. To succeed, they must be friendly, courteous, patient, and helpful to customers.

Decisionmaking skills. Opticians must determine what adjustments need to be made to eyeglasses and contact lenses. They must decide which materials and styles are most appropriate for each customer on the basis of their preferences and lifestyle.

Dexterity. Opticians frequently use special tools to make final adjustments and repairs to eyeglasses. They must have good hand-eye coordination to do that work quickly and accurately.

Pay

The median annual wage for opticians was $37,840 in May 2019. The median wage is the wage at which half the workers in an occupation earned more than that amount and half earned less. The lowest 10 percent earned less than $25,640, and the highest 10 percent earned more than $60,840.

In May 2019, the median annual wages for opticians in the top industries in which they worked were as follows:

Offices of physicians... $42,010

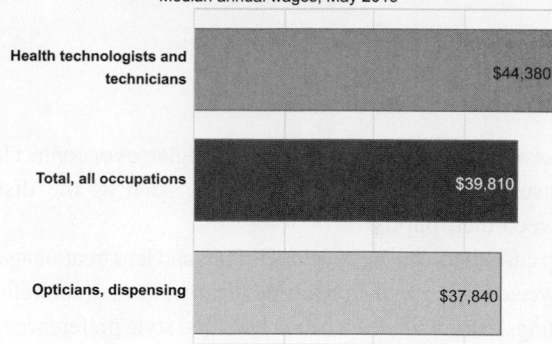

Opticians
Median annual wages, May 2019

Note: All Occupations includes all occupations in the U.S. Economy.
Source: U.S. Bureau of Labor Statistics, Occupational Employment Statistics.

Health and personal care stores................................. 37,760
Offices of optometrists 36,370

Opticians employed in retail settings may work evenings and weekends. Most opticians work full time, although part-time opportunities also are available.

Job Outlook

Employment of opticians is projected to grow 4 percent from 2019 to 2029, about as fast as the average for all occupations.

The growth in the older population is anticipated to lead to greater demand for eye care services. Because people usually have eye problems more frequently as they age, the need for opticians is likely to grow with the increase in the number of older people.

Increasing rates of chronic diseases such as diabetes also may increase demand for opticianry services because some chronic diseases cause vision problems. Additional opticians will be needed to fill prescriptions for corrective eyewear for individuals with conditions that damage their eyesight.

However, employment growth is expected to be constrained by increases in productivity that will allow a given number of opticians to serve more customers.

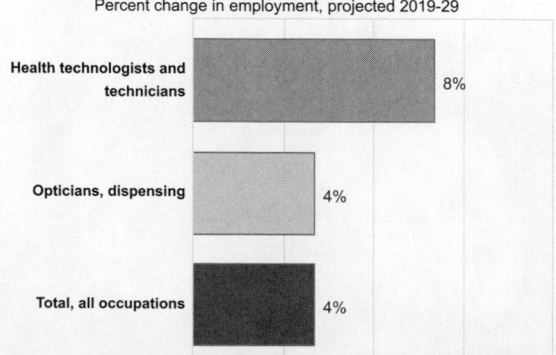

Opticians
Percent change in employment, projected 2019-29

Note: All Occupations includes all occupations in the U.S. Economy.
Source: U.S. Bureau of Labor Statistics, Employment Projections program.

Job Prospects

Having an associate's degree from an accredited program and American Board of Opticianry (ABO) and National Contact Lens Examiners (NCLE) certifications may improve an applicant's job prospects.

Employment projections data for opticians, 2019-29					
Occupational Title	SOC Code	Employment, 2019	Projected Employment, 2029	Change, 2019-29	
				Percent	Numeric
SOURCE: U.S. Bureau of Labor Statistics, Employment Projections program					
Opticians, dispensing	29-2081	73,800	76,800	4	3,000

State & Area Data
Occupational Employment Statistics (OES)

The Occupational Employment Statistics (OES) program produces employment and wage estimates annually for over 800 occupations. These estimates are available for the nation as a whole, for individual states, and for metropolitan and nonmetropolitan areas.

Contacts for More Information

For more information about opticians, including certifications and a list of state licensing boards for opticians, visit
➤ American Board of Opticianry and National Contact Lens Examiners

For a list of accredited programs, visit
➤ Commission on Opticianry Accreditation

For more information about optician education, visit
➤ National Academy of Opticianry
➤ National Federation of Opticianry Schools
➤ Opticians Association of America

Optometrists

Summary

Quick Facts: Optometrists

2019 Median Pay	$115,250 per year $55.41 per hour
Typical Entry-Level Education	Doctoral or professional degree
Work Experience in a Related Occupation	None
On-the-job Training	None
Number of Jobs, 2019	44,400
Job Outlook, 2019-29	4% (As fast as average)
Employment Change, 2019-29	1,900

What Optometrists Do

Optometrists diagnose and treat visual problems and manage diseases, injuries, and other disorders of the eyes.

Work Environment

Most optometrists work in stand-alone offices of optometry. Optometrists may also work in doctors' offices and optical goods stores, and some are self-employed. Most work full time, and some work evenings and weekends to accommodate patients' needs.

How to Become an Optometrist

Optometrists must complete a Doctor of Optometry (O.D.) degree program and obtain a license to practice in a particular state. O.D. programs take 4 years to complete, and most students have a bachelor's degree before entering such a program.

Pay

The median annual wage for optometrists was $115,250 in May 2019.

Job Outlook

Employment of optometrists is projected to grow 4 percent from 2019 to 2029, about as fast as the average for all occupations. Because vision problems tend to occur more frequently later in life, an aging population will lead to demand for more optometrists.

State & Area Data

Explore resources for employment and wages by state and area for optometrists.

What Optometrists Do

Optometrists examine the eyes and other parts of the visual system. They also diagnose and treat visual problems and manage

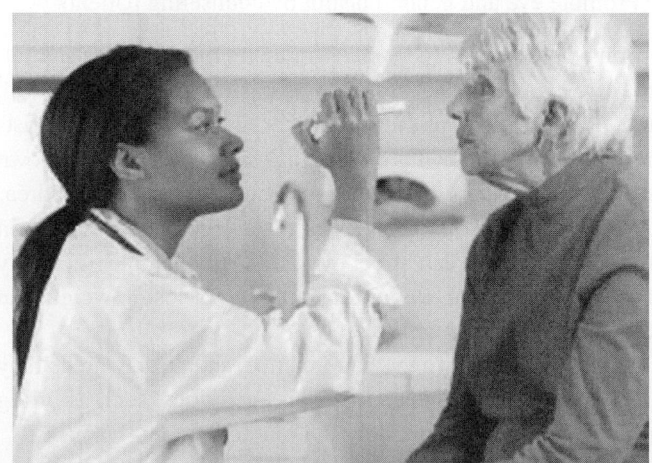

Optometrists diagnose and treat eye problems in children and adults.

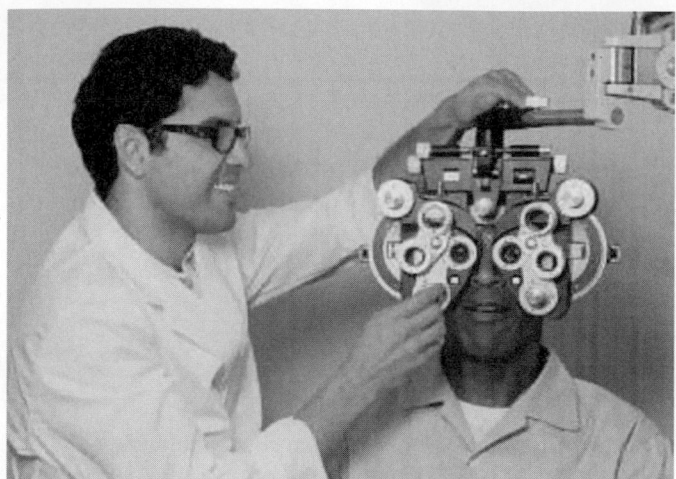

Optometrists work in exam rooms where they use tools to determine patients' prescriptions.

diseases, injuries, and other disorders of the eyes. They prescribe eyeglasses or contact lenses as needed.

Duties

Optometrists typically do the following:

- Perform vision tests and analyze results
- Diagnose sight problems, such as nearsightedness or farsightedness, and eye diseases, such as glaucoma
- Prescribe eyeglasses, contact lenses, and other visual aids, and if state law permits, medications
- Perform minor surgical procedures to correct or treat visual or eye health issues
- Provide treatments such as vision therapy or low-vision rehabilitation
- Provide pre- and postoperative care to patients undergoing eye surgery—for example, examining a patient's eyes the day after surgery
- Evaluate patients for the presence of other diseases and conditions, such as diabetes or hypertension, and refer patients to other healthcare providers as needed
- Promote eye and general health by counseling patients

Some optometrists spend much of their time providing specialized care, particularly if they are working in a group practice with other optometrists or physicians. For example, some optometrists mostly treat patients with only partial sight, a condition known as low vision. Others may focus on treating infants and children.

Optometrists promote eye health and counsel patients on how general health can affect eyesight. For example, they may counsel patients on how quitting smoking or losing weight can reduce vision problems.

Many optometrists own their practice, and those who do may spend more time on general business activities, such as hiring employees, ordering supplies, and marketing their business.

Optometrists also may work as postsecondary teachers, do research in optometry colleges, or work as consultants in the eye care industry.

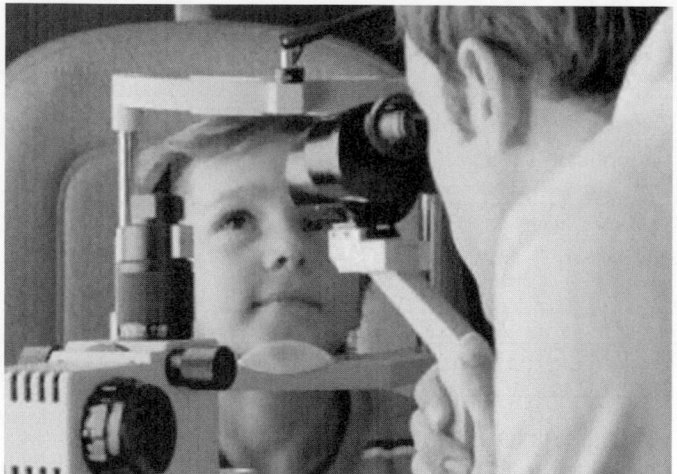

Optometrists check patients for common vision problems, like astigmatism.

Optometrists should not be confused with ophthalmologists or opticians. Ophthalmologists are physicians who perform eye surgery and treat eye diseases in addition to performing eye exams and prescribing eyeglasses and contact lenses. For more information on ophthalmologists, see the physicians and surgeons profile. Opticians fit and adjust eyeglasses and, in some states, fill contact lens prescriptions that an optometrist or ophthalmologist has written.

Work Environment

Optometrists held about 44,400 jobs in 2019. The largest employers of optometrists were as follows:

Offices of optometrists	51%
Offices of physicians	15
Health and personal care stores	14
Self-employed workers	11

Work Schedules

Most optometrists work full time. Some work evenings and weekends to accommodate patients' needs.

How to Become an Optometrist

Optometrists must complete a Doctor of Optometry (O.D.) degree program and obtain a license to practice in a particular state. O.D. programs take 4 years to complete, and most students have a bachelor's degree before entering such a program.

Education

Optometrists need an O.D. degree. In 2016, there were 20 accredited O.D. programs in the United States, one of which was in Puerto Rico.

Applicants to O.D. programs must have completed at least 3 years of postsecondary education. Required courses include those in biology, chemistry, physics, English, and math. Most students have a bachelor's degree with a premedical

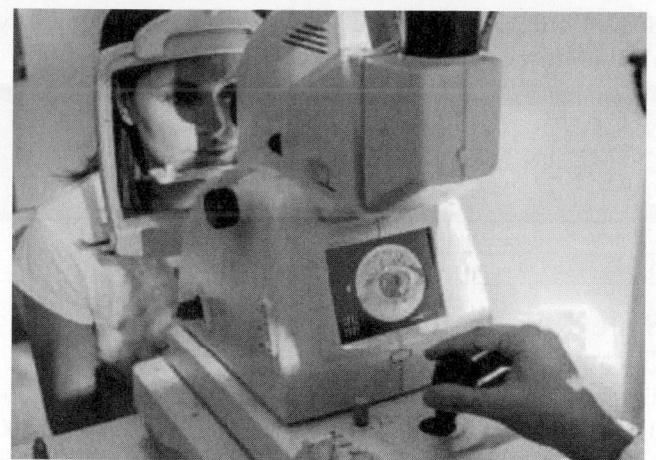

Doctor of Optometry programs combine classroom learning and clinical experience.

or biological sciences emphasis before enrolling in an O.D. program.

Applicants to O.D. programs must also take the Optometry Admission Test (OAT), a computerized exam that tests applicants in four subject areas: science, reading comprehension, physics, and quantitative reasoning.

O.D. programs take 4 years to complete. They combine classroom learning and supervised clinical experience. Coursework includes anatomy, physiology, biochemistry, optics, visual science, and the diagnosis and treatment of diseases and disorders of the visual system.

After finishing an O.D. degree, some optometrists complete a 1-year residency program to get advanced clinical training in the area in which they wish to specialize. Areas of specialization for residency programs include family practice, low vision rehabilitation, pediatric or geriatric optometry, and ocular disease, among others.

Licenses, Certifications, and Registrations

All states require optometrists to be licensed. To get a license, a prospective optometrist must have an O.D. degree from an accredited optometry school and must complete all sections of the National Board of Examiners in Optometry exam.

Some states require individuals to pass an additional clinical exam or an exam on laws relating to optometry. All states require optometrists to take continuing education classes and to renew their license periodically. The board of optometry in each state can provide information on licensing requirements.

Optometrists who wish to demonstrate an advanced level of knowledge may choose to become board certified by the American Board of Optometry.

Important Qualities

Decisionmaking skills. Optometrists must evaluate the results of a variety of diagnostic tests and decide on the best course of treatment for a patient.

Detail oriented. Optometrists must ensure that patients receive appropriate treatment and that medications and prescriptions are accurate. They must also monitor and record various pieces of information related to patient care.

Interpersonal skills. Optometrists spend most of their time examining patients, so they must be at ease interacting with patients and must make them feel comfortable during treatment.

Speaking skills. Optometrists must clearly explain eye care instructions to their patients, as well as answer patients' questions.

Pay

The median annual wage for optometrists was $115,250 in May 2019. The median wage is the wage at which half the workers in an occupation earned more than that amount and half earned less. The lowest 10 percent earned less than $59,200, and the highest 10 percent earned more than $194,100.

In May 2019, the median annual wages for optometrists in the top industries in which they worked were as follows:

Offices of physicians	$122,800
Health and personal care stores	116,370
Offices of optometrists	110,930

Most optometrists work full time. Some work evenings and weekends to accommodate their patients' needs.

Job Outlook

Employment of optometrists is projected to grow 4 percent from 2019 to 2029, about as fast as the average for all occupations.

Because vision problems tend to occur more frequently later in life, an aging population will lead to demand for optometrists. As people age, they become more susceptible to conditions that impair vision, such as cataracts and macular degeneration, and will need vision care.

The number of people with chronic diseases, such as diabetes, has grown in recent years. Diabetes has been linked to increased rates of several eye conditions, including diabetic

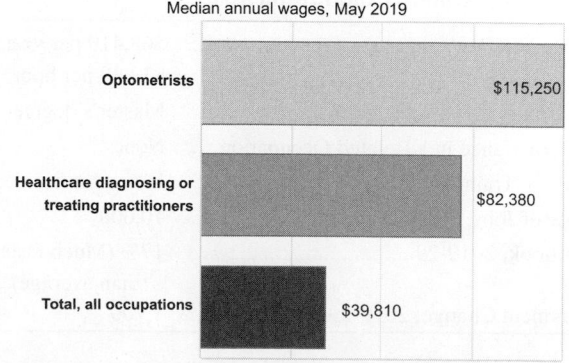

Optometrists
Median annual wages, May 2019

Optometrists	$115,250
Healthcare diagnosing or treating practitioners	$82,380
Total, all occupations	$39,810

Note: All Occupations includes all occupations in the U.S. Economy.
Source: U.S. Bureau of Labor Statistics, Occupational Employment Statistics.

Optometrists

Percent change in employment, projected 2019-29

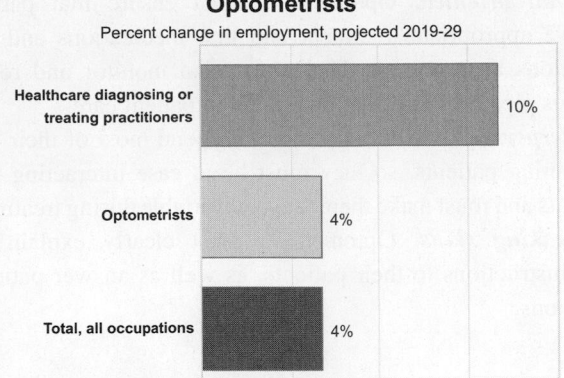

Note: All Occupations includes all occupations in the U.S. Economy.
Source: U.S. Bureau of Labor Statistics, Employment Projections program.

retinopathy, a condition that affects the blood vessels in the eye and may lead to loss of vision. More optometrists will be needed to monitor, treat, and refer individuals with chronic conditions stemming from diabetes.

In addition, nearly all health plans cover medical eye care and many cover preventive eye exams. More optometrists will be needed to provide services to more patients.

Job Prospects

Because the number of optometrists is limited by the number of accredited optometry schools, licensed optometrists should expect good job prospects. Like admission to professional degree programs in other fields, admission to optometry programs is highly competitive.

Students who choose to complete a residency program gain additional experience that may improve their job prospects.

Board certification from the American Board of Optometry also may be viewed favorably by employers.

Employment projections data for optometrists, 2019-29					
Occupational Title	SOC Code	Employment, 2019	Projected Employment, 2029	Change, 2019-29	
				Percent	Numeric
SOURCE: U.S. Bureau of Labor Statistics, Employment Projections program					
Optometrists	29-1041	44,400	46,300	4	1,900

State & Area Data

Occupational Employment Statistics (OES)

The Occupational Employment Statistics (OES) program produces employment and wage estimates annually for over 800 occupations. These estimates are available for the nation as a whole, for individual states, and for metropolitan and nonmetropolitan areas.

Contacts for More Information

For more information about optometry, visit
➤ American Optometric Association

For more information about optometrists, including a list of accredited optometric programs, visit
➤ Association of Schools and Colleges of Optometry

For information on specific admission requirements and sources of financial aid, contact the admissions officers of individual optometry schools.

For more information about the national board exam, visit
➤ National Boards of Examiners in Optometry

For more information about board certification, visit
➤ American Board of Optometry

Orthotists and Prosthetists

Summary

Quick Facts: Orthotists and Prosthetists

2019 Median Pay	$68,410 per year $32.89 per hour
Typical Entry-Level Education	Master's degree
Work Experience in a Related Occupation	None
On-the-job Training	Internship/residency
Number of Jobs, 2019	10,000
Job Outlook, 2019-29	17% (Much faster than average)
Employment Change, 2019-29	1,700

What Orthotists and Prosthetists Do

Orthotists and prosthetists design and fabricate medical supportive devices and measure and fit patients for them.

Work Environment

Orthotists and prosthetists work in various industries, including manufacturing, health and personal care stores, doctors' offices, and hospitals. Most work full time.

How to Become an Orthotist and Prosthetist

Orthotists and prosthetists need a master's degree and certification. Both orthotists and prosthetists must complete a residency before they can be certified.

Pay

The median annual wage for orthotists and prosthetists was $68,410 in May 2019.

Job Outlook

Employment of orthotists and prosthetists is projected to grow 17 percent from 2019 to 2029, much faster than the average for all occupations. The large baby-boom population is

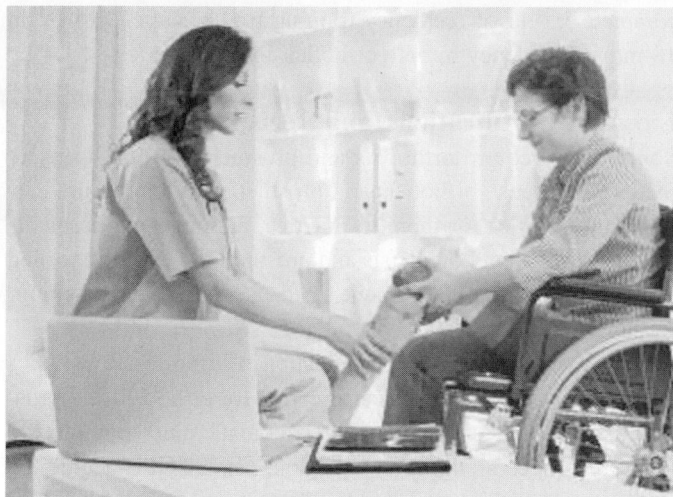

Orthotists and prosthetists fit, test, and adjust orthotic and prosthetic devices.

aging, and orthotists and prosthetists will be needed because both diabetes and cardiovascular disease, the two leading causes of limb loss, are more common among older people.

State & Area Data
Explore resources for employment and wages by state and area for orthotists and prosthetists.

What Orthotists and Prosthetists Do
Orthotists and prosthetists design and fabricate medical supportive devices and measure and fit patients for them. These devices include artificial limbs (arms, hands, legs, and feet), braces, and other medical or surgical devices.

Duties
Orthotists and prosthetists typically do the following:

- Evaluate and interview patients to determine their needs
- Take measurements or impressions of the part of a patient's body that will be fitted with a brace or artificial limb
- Design and fabricate orthopedic and prosthetic devices based on physicians' prescriptions
- Select materials to be used for the orthotic or prosthetic device
- Instruct patients in how to use and care for their devices
- Adjust, repair, or replace prosthetic and orthotic devices
- Document care in patients' records

Orthotists and prosthetists may work in both orthotics and prosthetics, or they may choose to specialize in one area. Orthotists are specifically trained to work with medical supportive devices, such as spinal or knee braces. Prosthetists are specifically trained to work with prostheses, such as artificial limbs and other body parts.

Some orthotists and prosthetists construct devices for their patients. Others supervise the construction of the orthotic or prosthetic devices by medical appliance technicians.

Orthotists and prosthetists create devices that allow patients to regain or improve mobility and functionality.

Work Environment
Orthotists and prosthetists held about 10,000 jobs in 2019. The largest employers of orthotists and prosthetists were as follows:

Ambulatory healthcare services	28%
Medical equipment and supplies manufacturing	26
Health and personal care stores	21
Hospitals; state, local, and private	10
Federal government, excluding postal service	9

Orthotists and prosthetists who fabricate orthotics and prosthetics may be exposed to health or safety hazards when handling certain materials, but there is little risk of injury if workers follow proper procedures, such as wearing goggles, gloves, and masks.

Work Schedules
Most orthotists and prosthetists work full time.

How to Become an Orthotist and Prosthetist
Orthotists and prosthetists need a master's degree and certification. Both orthotists and prosthetists must complete a residency before they can be certified.

Orthotists and prosthetists evaluate and interview patients to determine their needs.

Education

All orthotists and prosthetists must complete a master's degree in orthotics and prosthetics. These programs include courses in upper and lower extremity orthotics and prosthetics, spinal orthotics, and plastics and other materials used for fabrication. In addition, orthotics and prosthetics programs have a clinical component in which the student works under the direction of an orthotist or prosthetist.

Master's programs usually take 2 years to complete. Prospective students seeking a master's degree can have a bachelor's degree in any discipline if they have fulfilled pre-requisite courses in science and math. Requirements vary by program.

In 2016, there were about a dozen orthotics and prosthetics programs accredited by the Commission on Accreditation of Allied Health Education Programs (CAAHEP).

Training

Following graduation from a master's degree program, candidates must complete a residency that has been accredited by the National Commission on Orthotic and Prosthetic Education (NCOPE). Candidates typically complete a 1-year residency program in either orthotics or prosthetics. Individuals who want to become certified in both orthotics and prosthetics need to complete 1 year of residency training for each specialty or an 18-month residency in both orthotics and prosthetics.

Licenses, Certifications, and Registrations

Some states require orthotists and prosthetists to be licensed. States that license orthotists and prosthetists often require certification in order for them to practice, although requirements vary by state. Many orthotists and prosthetists become certified regardless of state requirements, because certification demonstrates competence.

The American Board for Certification in Orthotics, Prosthetics & Pedorthics (ABC) offers certification for orthotists and prosthetists. To earn certification, a candidate must complete a CAAHEP-accredited master's program, an NCOPE-accredited residency program, and pass a series of three exams.

Important Qualities

Communication skills. Orthotists and prosthetists must be able to communicate effectively with the technicians who often fabricate the medical devices. They must also be able to explain to patients how to use and care for the devices.

Detail oriented. Orthotists and prosthetists must be precise when recording measurements to ensure that devices are fabricated and fit properly.

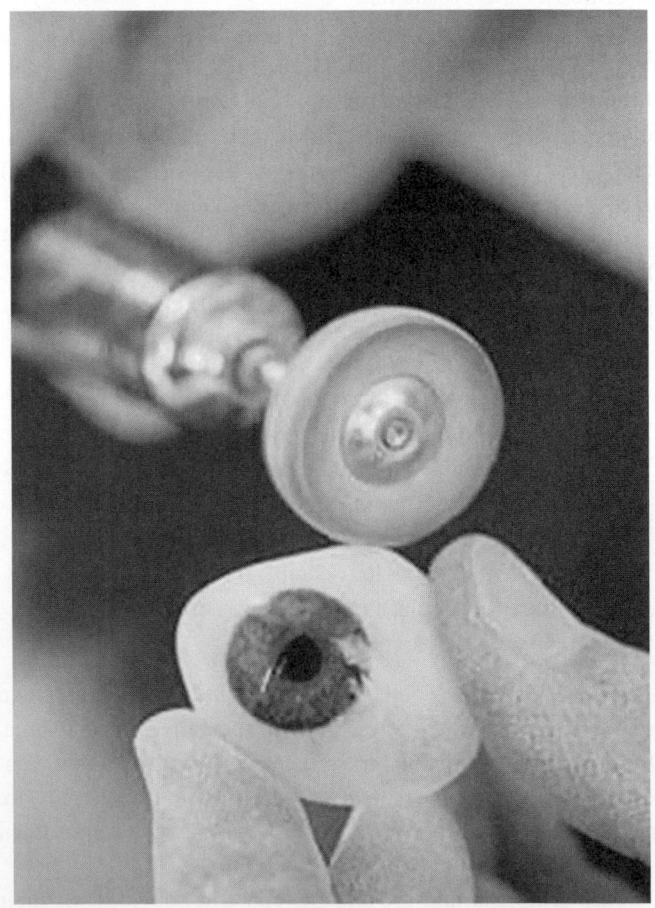

Orthotists and prosthetists must be precise to ensure that devices are fabricated and fit properly.

Patience. Orthotists and prosthetists may work for long periods with patients who need special attention.

Physical dexterity. Orthotists and prosthetists must be good at working with their hands. They may fabricate orthotics or prosthetics with intricate mechanical parts.

Physical stamina. Orthotists and prosthetists should be comfortable performing physical tasks, such as working with shop equipment and hand tools. They may spend a lot of time bending over or crouching to examine or measure patients.

Problem-solving skills. Orthotists and prosthetists must evaluate their patients' situations and often look for creative solutions to their rehabilitation needs.

Pay

The median annual wage for orthotists and prosthetists was $68,410 in May 2019. The median wage is the wage at which half the workers in an occupation earned more than that amount and half earned less. The lowest 10 percent earned less than $41,360, and the highest 10 percent earned more than $108,130.

In May 2019, the median annual wages for orthotists and prosthetists in the top industries in which they worked were as follows:

Medical equipment and supplies manufacturing	$74,400
Federal government, excluding postal service	71,480
Ambulatory healthcare services	69,710
Health and personal care stores	63,600
Hospitals; state, local, and private	63,270

Most orthotists and prosthetists work full time.

Job Outlook

Employment of orthotists and prosthetists is projected to grow 17 percent from 2019 to 2029, much faster than the average for all occupations. However, because it is a small occupation, the fast growth will result in only about 1,700 new jobs over the 10-year period.

The large baby-boom population is aging, and orthotists and prosthetists will be needed because both diabetes and cardiovascular disease, two leading causes of limb loss, are more common among older people. In addition, older people will continue to need other devices designed and fitted by orthotists and prosthetists, such as braces and orthopedic footwear.

Advances in technology are allowing more people to survive traumatic events. Patients with traumatic injuries, such as some veterans, will continue to need orthotists and prosthetists to create devices that allow the patients to regain or improve mobility and functionality.

Job Prospects

Job prospects should be best for orthotists and prosthetists with professional certification. Although it is not required in all states, certification shows a specific level of educational knowledge and training that employers may prefer.

Employment projections data for orthotists and prosthetists, 2019-29					
Occupational Title	SOC Code	Employment, 2019	Projected Employment, 2029	Change, 2019-29	
				Percent	Numeric
SOURCE: U.S. Bureau of Labor Statistics, Employment Projections program					
Orthotists and prosthetists	29-2091	10,000	11,700	17	1,700

State & Area Data
Occupational Employment Statistics (OES)

The Occupational Employment Statistics (OES) program produces employment and wage estimates annually for over 800 occupations. These estimates are available for the nation as a whole, for individual states, and for metropolitan and nonmetropolitan areas.

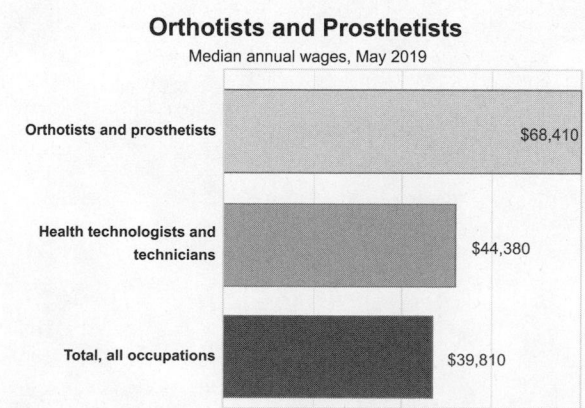

Orthotists and Prosthetists
Median annual wages, May 2019

- Orthotists and prosthetists: $68,410
- Health technologists and technicians: $44,380
- Total, all occupations: $39,810

Note: All Occupations includes all occupations in the U.S. Economy.
Source: U.S. Bureau of Labor Statistics, Occupational Employment Statistics.

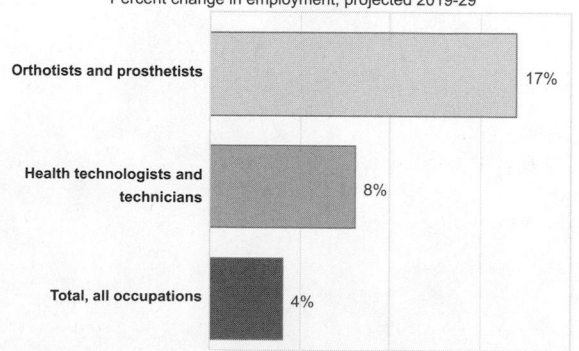

Orthotists and Prosthetists
Percent change in employment, projected 2019-29

- Orthotists and prosthetists: 17%
- Health technologists and technicians: 8%
- Total, all occupations: 4%

Note: All Occupations includes all occupations in the U.S. Economy.
Source: U.S. Bureau of Labor Statistics, Employment Projections program.

Contacts for More Information

For more information about orthotists and prosthetists, visit
➤ American Academy of Orthotists & Prosthetists
➤ Board of Certification/Accreditation

For a list of accredited programs for orthotists and prosthetists, visit
➤ Commission on Accreditation of Allied Health Education Programs

For a list of accredited residency programs for orthotists and prosthetists, visit
➤ National Commission on Orthotic and Prosthetic Education

For more information about certification for orthotists and prosthetists, visit
➤ American Board for Certification in Orthotics, Prosthetics & Pedorthics

Pharmacists

Summary

Quick Facts: Pharmacists

2019 Median Pay	$128,090 per year $61.58 per hour
Typical Entry-Level Education	Doctoral or professional degree
Work Experience in a Related Occupation	None
On-the-job Training	None
Number of Jobs, 2019	321,700
Job Outlook, 2019-29	-3% (Decline)
Employment Change, 2019-29	-10,500

What Pharmacists Do

Pharmacists dispense prescription medications to patients and offer expertise in the safe use of prescriptions.

Work Environment

Pharmacists work in pharmacies, including those in drug, general merchandise, and grocery stores. They also work in hospitals and other healthcare facilities.

How to Become a Pharmacist

Pharmacists must have a Doctor of Pharmacy (Pharm.D.), a 4-year professional degree. They must also be licensed, which requires passing two exams.

Pay

The median annual wage for pharmacists was $128,090 in May 2019.

Job Outlook

Employment of pharmacists is projected to decline 3 percent from 2019 to 2029.

State & Area Data

Explore resources for employment and wages by state and area for pharmacists.

What Pharmacists Do

Pharmacists dispense prescription medications to patients and offer expertise in the safe use of prescriptions. They also may conduct health and wellness screenings, provide immunizations, oversee the medications given to patients, and provide advice on healthy lifestyles.

Pharmacists fill prescriptions and instruct customers on the safe use of medications.

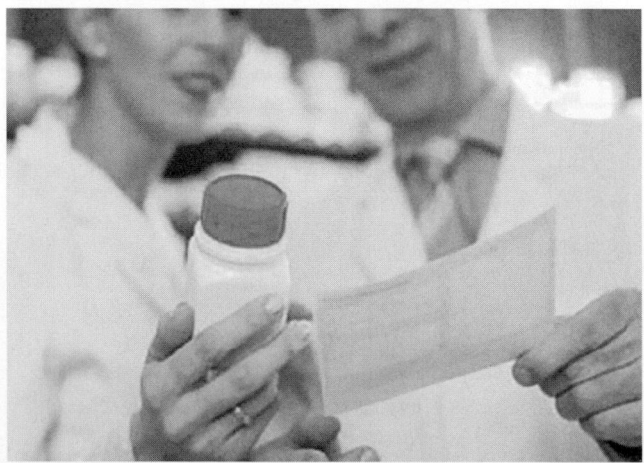

Pharmacists review the accuracy of each filled prescription before it is given to the customer.

Duties

Pharmacists typically do the following:

- Fill prescriptions, verifying instructions from physicians on the proper amounts of medication to give to patients
- Check whether prescriptions will interact negatively with other drugs that a patient is taking or any medical conditions the patient has
- Instruct patients on how and when to take a prescribed medicine and inform them about potential side effects from taking the medicine
- Give flu shots and, in most states, other vaccinations
- Advise patients about general health topics, such as diet, exercise, and managing stress, and on other issues, such as what equipment or supplies would be best to treat a health problem
- Complete insurance forms and work with insurance companies to ensure that patients get the medicines they need
- Oversee the work of pharmacy technicians and pharmacists in training (interns)
- Keep records and do other administrative tasks
- Teach other healthcare practitioners about proper medication therapies for patients

Some pharmacists who own their pharmacy or manage a chain pharmacy spend time on business activities, such as inventory management. With most drugs, pharmacists use standard dosages from pharmaceutical companies. However, some pharmacists create customized medications by mixing ingredients themselves, a process known as compounding.

The following are examples of types of pharmacists:

Community pharmacists work in retail stores such as chain drug stores or independently owned pharmacies. They dispense medications to patients and answer any questions that patients may have about prescriptions, over-the-counter medications, or any health concerns that the patient may have. They also may provide some primary care services such as giving flu shots.

Clinical pharmacists work in hospitals, clinics, and other healthcare settings. They spend little time dispensing prescriptions. Instead, they are involved in direct patient care. Clinical pharmacists may go on rounds in a hospital with a physician or healthcare team. They recommend medications to give to patients and oversee the dosage and timing of the delivery of those medications. They also may conduct some medical tests and offer advice to patients. For example, pharmacists working in a diabetes clinic may counsel patients on how and when to take medications, suggest healthy food choices, and monitor patients' blood sugar.

Consultant pharmacists advise healthcare facilities or insurance providers on patient medication use or improving pharmacy services. They also may give advice directly to patients, such as helping seniors manage their prescriptions.

Pharmaceutical industry pharmacists work in areas such as marketing, sales, or research and development. They may design or conduct clinical drug trials and help to develop new drugs. They may also help to establish safety regulations and ensure quality control for drugs.

Some pharmacists work as college professors. They may teach pharmacy students or conduct research. For more information, see the profile on postsecondary teachers.

Work Environment

Pharmacists held about 321,700 jobs in 2019. The largest employers of pharmacists were as follows:

Pharmacies and drug stores	42%
Hospitals; state, local, and private	26
Food and beverage stores	8
General merchandise stores	5

Some pharmacists work for the government and the military. In most settings, they spend much of the workday on their feet.

Work Schedules

Most pharmacists work full time. Because many pharmacies are open at all hours, some pharmacists work nights and weekends.

How to Become a Pharmacist

Pharmacists must have a Doctor of Pharmacy (Pharm.D.) degree from an accredited pharmacy program. They must also be licensed, which requires passing licensure and law exams.

Pharmacists may consult with physicians if they have questions concerning a patient's prescription.

Pharmacists must pay attention to detail, ensuring the accuracy of the prescriptions they fill.

Education

Prospective pharmacists are required to have a Doctor of Pharmacy (Pharm.D.) degree, a postgraduate professional degree. In August 2017, there were 128 Doctor of Pharmacy programs fully accredited by the Accreditation Council for Pharmacy Education (ACPE).

Admissions requirements vary by program, however, all Pharm.D. programs require applicants to take postsecondary courses such as chemistry, biology, and physics. Most programs require at least 2 years of undergraduate study, although some require a bachelor's degree. Most programs also require applicants to take the Pharmacy College Admissions Test (PCAT).

Pharm.D. programs usually take 4 years to finish, although some programs offer a 3-year option. Some schools admit high school graduates into a 6-year program. A Pharm.D. program includes courses in chemistry, pharmacology, and medical ethics. Students also complete supervised work experiences, sometimes referred to as internships, in different settings such as hospitals and retail pharmacies.

Some pharmacists who own their own pharmacy may choose to get a master's degree in business administration (MBA) in addition to their Pharm.D. degree. Others may get a degree in public health.

Pharmacists also must take continuing education courses throughout their career to keep up with the latest advances in pharmacological science.

Training

Following graduation from a Pharm.D. program, pharmacists seeking an advanced position, such as a clinical pharmacy or research job, may need to complete a 1- to 2-year residency. Pharmacists who choose to complete the 2-year residency option receive additional training in a specialty area such as internal medicine or geriatric care.

Licenses, Certifications, and Registrations

All states license pharmacists. After they finish the Pharm.D. program, prospective pharmacists must pass two exams to get a license. The North American Pharmacist Licensure Exam (NAPLEX) tests pharmacy skills and knowledge. The Multistate Pharmacy Jurisprudence Exam (MPJE) or a state-specific test on pharmacy law is also required. Applicants also must complete a number of hours as an intern, which varies by state.

Pharmacists who administer vaccinations and immunizations need to be certified in most states. States typically use the American Pharmacists Association's Pharmacy-Based Immunization Delivery program as a qualification for certification.

Pharmacists also may choose to earn a certification to show their advanced level of knowledge in a certain area. For instance, a pharmacist may become a Certified Diabetes Educator, a qualification offered by the National Certification Board for Diabetes Educators, or earn certification in a specialty area, such as nutrition or oncology, from the Board of Pharmacy Specialties. Certifications from both organizations require pharmacists to have varying degrees of work experience, to pass an exam, and pay a fee.

Important Qualities

Analytical skills. Pharmacists must provide safe medications efficiently. To do this, they must be able to evaluate a patient's needs and the prescriber's orders, and have extensive knowledge of the effects and appropriate circumstances for giving out a specific medication.

Communication skills. Pharmacists frequently offer advice to patients. They might need to explain how to take medicine, for example, and what its side effects are. They also need to offer clear direction to pharmacy technicians and interns.

Computer skills. Pharmacists need computer skills in order to use any electronic health record (EHR) systems that their organization has adopted.

Detail oriented. Pharmacists are responsible for ensuring the accuracy of the prescriptions they fill. They must be able to find the information that they need to make decisions about what medications are appropriate for each patient, because improper use of medication can pose serious health risks.

Managerial skills. Pharmacists—particularly those who run a retail pharmacy—must have good managerial skills, including the ability to manage inventory and oversee a staff.

Pay

The median annual wage for pharmacists was $128,090 in May 2019. The median wage is the wage at which half the workers in an occupation earned more than that amount and half earned less. The lowest 10 percent earned less than $88,400, and the highest 10 percent earned more than $162,900.

In May 2019, the median annual wages for pharmacists in the top industries in which they worked were as follows:

General merchandise stores	$136,320
Food and beverage stores	132,750
Hospitals; state, local, and private	129,740
Pharmacies and drug stores	125,910

Pharmacists
Median annual wages, May 2019

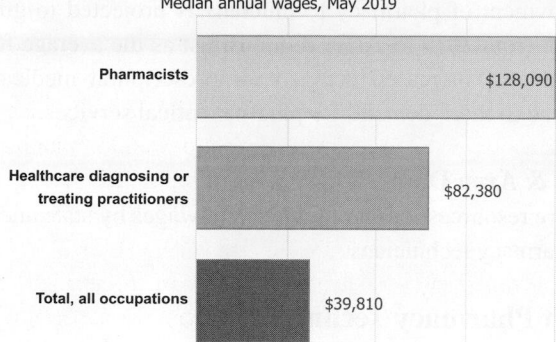

Pharmacists	$128,090
Healthcare diagnosing or treating practitioners	$82,380
Total, all occupations	$39,810

Pharmacists
Percent change in employment, projected 2019-29

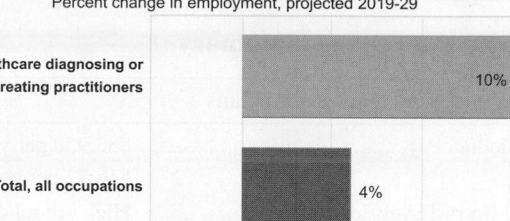

Healthcare diagnosing or treating practitioners	10%
Total, all occupations	4%
Pharmacists	-3%

Note: All Occupations includes all occupations in the U.S. Economy.
Source: U.S. Bureau of Labor Statistics, Occupational Employment Statistics.

Note: All Occupations includes all occupations in the U.S. Economy.
Source: U.S. Bureau of Labor Statistics, Employment Projections program.

Most pharmacists work full time. Because many pharmacies are open at all hours, some pharmacists work nights and weekends.

Job Outlook

Employment of pharmacists is projected to decline 3 percent from 2019 to 2029.

Many pharmacists work in in retail pharmacies and drug stores, which are expected to lose jobs as more people fill their prescriptions via mail order and online. In addition, fewer of these workers are expected to be needed as pharmacy technicians increasingly perform tasks previously done by pharmacists, such as collecting patient information, preparing some types of medications, and verifying the work of other technicians.

However, demand is projected to increase for pharmacists in some healthcare settings, including hospitals and clinics. These facilities will need more pharmacists to oversee the medications given to patients and to provide patient care, doing tasks such as testing blood sugar or cholesterol.

Employment projections data for pharmacists, 2019-29					
Occupational Title	SOC Code	Employment, 2019	Projected Employment, 2029	Change, 2019-29	
				Percent	Numeric
SOURCE: U.S. Bureau of Labor Statistics, Employment Projections program					
Pharmacists	29-1051	321,700	311,200	-3	-10,500

State & Area Data
Occupational Employment Statistics (OES)

The Occupational Employment Statistics (OES) program produces employment and wage estimates annually for over 800 occupations. These estimates are available for the nation as a whole, for individual states, and for metropolitan and nonmetropolitan areas.

Contacts for More Information

For more information about pharmacists, visit
➤ American Society of Health-System Pharmacists
➤ National Association of Chain Drug Stores
➤ American Pharmacists Association
➤ American College of Clinical Pharmacy

For information on pharmacy as a career, preprofessional and professional requirements, programs offered by colleges of pharmacy, and student financial aid, visit
➤ American Association of Colleges of Pharmacy

For more information about accredited Doctor of Pharmacy programs, visit
➤ Accreditation Council for Pharmacy Education

For more information about certification options, visit
➤ Board of Pharmacy Specialties
➤ National Certification Board for Diabetes Educators

Pharmacy Technicians

Summary

Quick Facts: Pharmacy Technicians

2019 Median Pay	$33,950 per year $16.32 per hour
Typical Entry-Level Education	High school diploma or equivalent
Work Experience in a Related Occupation	None
On-the-job Training	Moderate-term on-the-job training
Number of Jobs, 2019	422,300
Job Outlook, 2019-29	4% (As fast as average)
Employment Change, 2019-29	15,200

What Pharmacy Technicians Do

Pharmacy technicians help pharmacists dispense prescription medication to customers or health professionals.

Work Environment

Pharmacy technicians work in pharmacies, including those found in drug, general merchandise, and grocery stores, and in hospitals. Most work full time, but many work part time.

How to Become a Pharmacy Technician

Pharmacy technicians usually need a high school diploma or equivalent and learn their duties through on-the-job training, or they may complete a postsecondary education program in pharmacy technology. Most states regulate pharmacy technicians, which is a process that may require passing an exam or completing a formal education or training program.

Pay

The median annual wage for pharmacy technicians was $33,950 in May 2019.

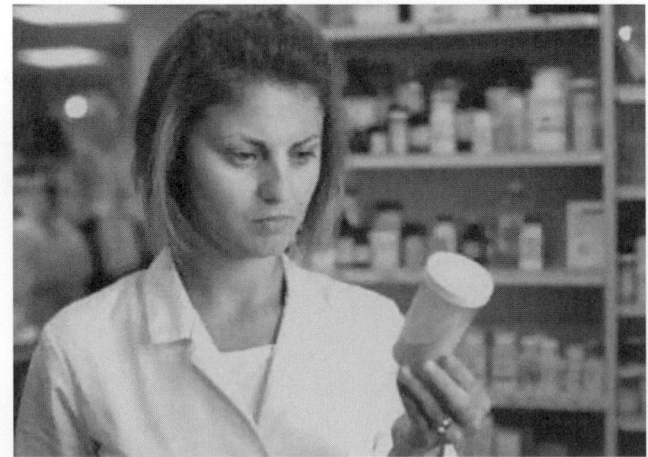

Pharmacy technicians measure amounts of medication for prescriptions.

Job Outlook

Employment of pharmacy technicians is projected to grow 4 percent from 2019 to 2029, about as fast as the average for all occupations. Increased demand for prescription medications will lead to more demand for pharmaceutical services.

State & Area Data

Explore resources for employment and wages by state and area for pharmacy technicians.

What Pharmacy Technicians Do

Pharmacy technicians help pharmacists dispense prescription medication to customers or health professionals. They mainly work in retail pharmacies and hospitals.

Duties

Pharmacy technicians typically do the following:

- Collect information needed to fill a prescription from customers or health professionals
- Measure amounts of medication for prescriptions
- Package and label prescriptions
- Organize inventory and alert pharmacists to any shortages of medications or supplies
- Accept payment for prescriptions and process insurance claims
- Enter customer or patient information, including any prescriptions taken, into a computer system
- Answer phone calls from customers
- Arrange for customers to speak with pharmacists if customers have questions about medications or health matters

Pharmacy technicians work under the supervision of pharmacists, who must review prescriptions before they are given to patients. In most states, technicians can compound or mix some medications and call physicians for prescription refill authorizations. Technicians also may need to operate automated dispensing equipment when filling prescription orders.

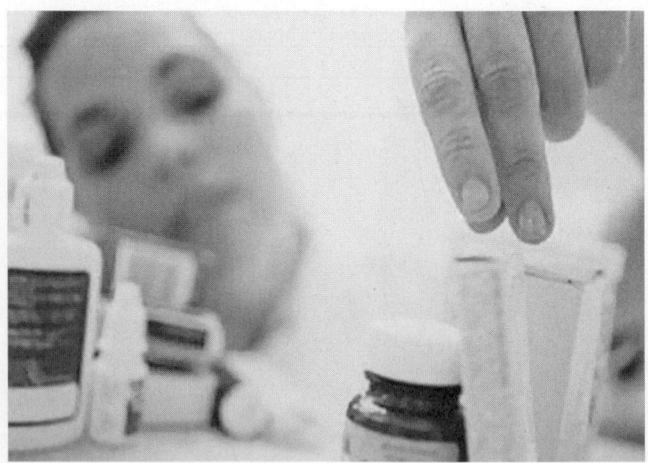

Pharmacy technicians fill prescriptions and check inventory.

Pharmacy technicians working in hospitals and other medical facilities prepare a greater variety of medications, such as intravenous medications. They may make rounds in the hospital, giving medications to patients.

Work Environment

Pharmacy technicians held about 422,300 jobs in 2019. The largest employers of pharmacy technicians were as follows:

Pharmacies and drug stores	51%
Hospitals; state, local, and private	17
Food and beverage stores	9

Pharmacy technicians spend most of the workday on their feet.

Work Schedules

Most pharmacy technicians work full time. Pharmacies may be open at all hours. Therefore, pharmacy technicians may have to work nights or weekends.

How to Become a Pharmacy Technician

Pharmacy technicians usually need a high school diploma or equivalent and learn their duties through on-the-job training, or they may complete a postsecondary education program in pharmacy technology. Most states regulate pharmacy technicians,

Pharmacy technicians work primarily in pharmacies, including those found in grocery and drug stores, and in hospitals.

Pharmacy technicians spend much of their time interacting with customers.

which is a process that may require passing an exam or completing a formal education or training program.

Education and Training

Pharmacy technicians usually need a high school diploma or equivalent and typically learn their duties through on-the-job training. The training periods vary in length and subject matter according to the employer's requirements.

Other pharmacy technicians enter the occupation after completing postsecondary education programs in pharmacy technology. These programs are usually offered by vocational schools or community colleges. Most programs award a certificate after 1 year or less, although some programs last longer and lead to an associate's degree. They cover a variety of subjects, such as arithmetic used in pharmacies, recordkeeping, ways of dispensing medications, and pharmacy law and ethics. Technicians also learn the names, uses, and doses of medications. Most programs also include clinical experience opportunities, in which students gain hands-on experience in a pharmacy.

The American Society of Health-System Pharmacists (ASHP) accredits pharmacy technician programs that include at least 600 hours of instruction over a minimum of 15 weeks. In 2017, there were 309 fully accredited programs, including a few in retail drugstore chains.

Licenses, Certifications, and Registrations

Most states regulate pharmacy technicians in some way. Consult state Boards of Pharmacy for particular regulations. Requirements for pharmacy technicians in the states that regulate them typically include some or all of the following:

- High school diploma or GED
- Formal education or training program
- Exam
- Fees
- Continuing education
- Criminal background check

Some states and employers require pharmacy technicians to be certified. Even where it is not required, certification may make it easier to get a job. Many employers of pharmacy technicians will pay for employees to take the certification exam.

Two organizations offer certification. The Pharmacy Technician Certification Board (PTCB) certification requires a high school diploma and the passing of an exam. Applicants for the National Healthcareer Association (NHA) certification must be at least 18 years old, have a high school diploma, and have completed a training program or have 1 year of work experience. Technicians must recertify every 2 years by completing 20 hours of continuing education courses.

Important Qualities

Customer-service skills. Pharmacy technicians spend much of their time interacting with customers, so being helpful and polite is required of pharmacy technicians in a retail setting.

Detail oriented. Serious health problems can result from mistakes in filling prescriptions. Although the pharmacist is responsible for ensuring the safety of all medications dispensed, pharmacy technicians should pay attention to detail so that complications are avoided.

Listening skills. Pharmacy technicians must communicate clearly with pharmacists and doctors when taking prescription orders. When speaking with customers, technicians must listen carefully to understand customers' needs and determine if they need to speak with a pharmacist.

Math skills. Pharmacy technicians need to have an understanding of the math concepts used in pharmacies when counting pills and compounding medications.

Organizational skills. Working as a pharmacy technician involves balancing a variety of responsibilities. Pharmacy technicians need good organizational skills to complete the work delegated by pharmacists while at the same time providing service to customers or patients.

Pay

The median annual wage for pharmacy technicians was $33,950 in May 2019. The median wage is the wage at which half the workers in an occupation earned more than that amount and half earned less. The lowest 10 percent earned less than $24,120, and the highest 10 percent earned more than $49,130.

In May 2019, the median annual wages for pharmacy technicians in the top industries in which they worked were as follows:

Hospitals; state, local, and private	$38,310
Pharmacies and drug stores	31,840
Food and beverage stores	31,610

Most pharmacy technicians work full time. Pharmacies may be open at all hours. Therefore, pharmacy technicians may have to work nights or weekends.

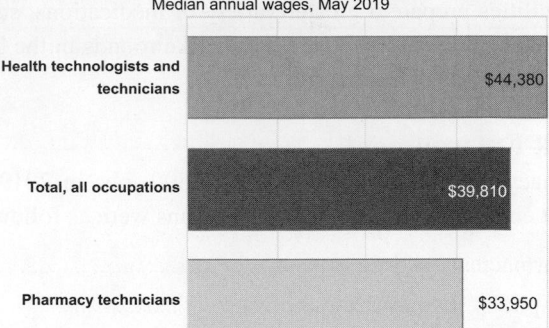

Pharmacy Technicians
Median annual wages, May 2019

- Health technologists and technicians: $44,380
- Total, all occupations: $39,810
- Pharmacy technicians: $33,950

Note: All Occupations includes all occupations in the U.S. Economy.
Source: U.S. Bureau of Labor Statistics, Occupational Employment Statistics.

Job Outlook

Employment of pharmacy technicians is projected to grow 4 percent from 2019 to 2029, about as fast as the average for all occupations.

The population is aging, and older people typically use more prescription medicines than younger people. Higher rates of chronic diseases, such as diabetes, among all age groups also will lead to increased demand for prescription medications. Advances in pharmaceutical research will allow for more prescription medications to be used to fight diseases.

In addition, pharmacy technicians will be needed to take on a greater role in pharmacy operations because pharmacists are increasingly performing more patient care activities, such as giving flu shots. Technicians will need to perform tasks—such as collecting patient information, preparing more types of medications, and verifying the work of other technicians—that were previously done by pharmacists.

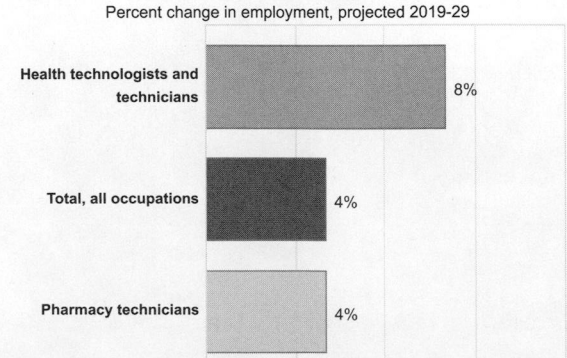

Pharmacy Technicians
Percent change in employment, projected 2019-29

- Health technologists and technicians: 8%
- Total, all occupations: 4%
- Pharmacy technicians: 4%

Note: All Occupations includes all occupations in the U.S. Economy.
Source: U.S. Bureau of Labor Statistics, Employment Projections program.

Employment projections data for pharmacy technicians, 2019-29					
Occupational Title	SOC Code	Employment, 2019	Projected Employment, 2029	Change, 2019-29	
				Percent	Numeric
SOURCE: U.S. Bureau of Labor Statistics, Employment Projections program					
Pharmacy technicians	29-2052	422,300	437,600	4	15,200

State & Area Data
Occupational Employment Statistics (OES)

The Occupational Employment Statistics (OES) program produces employment and wage estimates annually for over 800 occupations. These estimates are available for the nation as a whole, for individual states, and for metropolitan and nonmetropolitan areas.

Contacts for More Information

For more information about accredited pharmacy technician programs, visit
➤ American Society of Health-System Pharmacists

For more information about state licensure laws, contact individual state Boards of Pharmacy, or visit
➤ National Association of Boards of Pharmacy

For more information about certification, visit
➤ Pharmacy Technician Certification Board
➤ National Healthcareer Association

Phlebotomists

Summary

Quick Facts: Phlebotomists

2019 Median Pay	$35,510 per year $17.07 per hour
Typical Entry-Level Education	Postsecondary nondegree award
Work Experience in a Related Occupation	None
On-the-job Training	None
Number of Jobs, 2019	132,600
Job Outlook, 2019-29	17% (Much faster than average)
Employment Change, 2019-29	22,800

What Phlebotomists Do

Phlebotomists draw blood for tests, transfusions, research, or blood donations.

Work Environment

Phlebotomists work mainly in hospitals, medical and diagnostic laboratories, blood donor centers, and doctors' offices.

How to Become a Phlebotomist

Phlebotomists typically enter the occupation with a postsecondary nondegree award from a phlebotomy program. Almost all employers look for phlebotomists who have earned professional certification.

Pay

The median annual wage for phlebotomists was $35,510 in May 2019.

Job Outlook

Employment of phlebotomists is projected to grow 17 percent from 2019 to 2029, much faster than the average for all

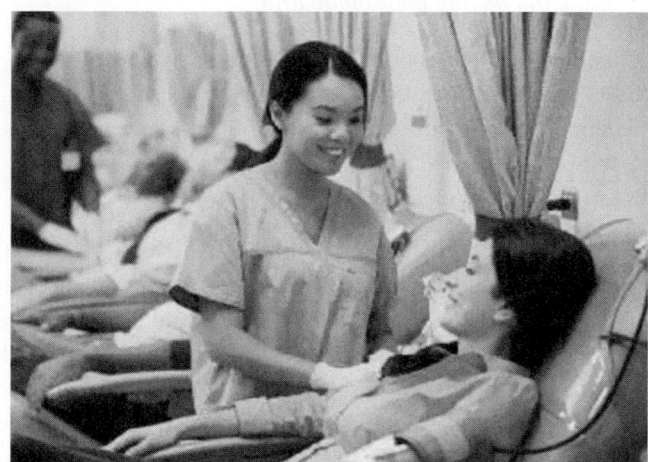

Phlebotomists draw blood for tests, transfusions, research, or blood donations.

occupations. Hospitals, diagnostic laboratories, blood donor centers, and other locations will need phlebotomists to perform bloodwork.

State & Area Data

Explore resources for employment and wages by state and area for phlebotomists.

What Phlebotomists Do

Phlebotomists draw blood for tests, transfusions, research, or blood donations. Some of them explain their work to patients and provide assistance if patients have adverse reactions after their blood is drawn.

Duties

Phlebotomists typically do the following:

- Draw blood from patients and blood donors
- Talk with patients and donors to help them feel less nervous about having their blood drawn
- Verify a patient's or donor's identity to ensure proper labeling of the blood

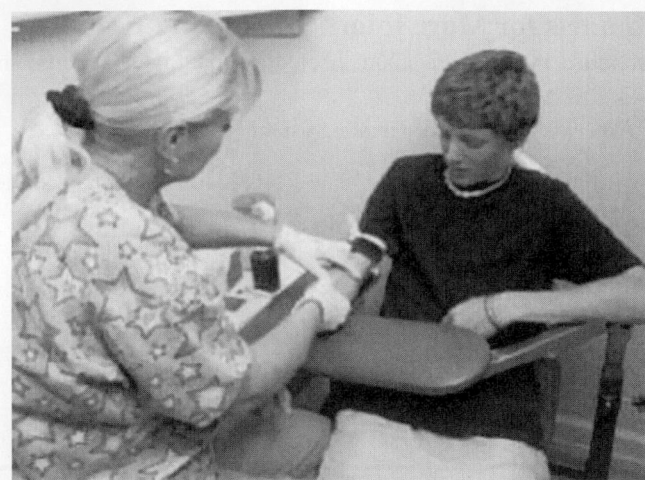

Phlebotomists talk with patients and donors so they are less nervous about having their blood drawn.

- Label the drawn blood for testing or processing
- Enter patient information into a database
- Assemble and maintain medical instruments such as needles, test tubes, and blood vials
- Keep work areas clean and sanitary

Phlebotomists primarily draw blood, which is then used for different kinds of medical laboratory testing. In medical and diagnostic laboratories, patient interaction is sometimes only with the phlebotomist. Because all blood samples look the same, phlebotomists must carefully identify and label the sample they have drawn and enter it into a database. Some phlebotomists draw blood for other purposes, such as at blood drives where people donate blood. In order to avoid causing infection or other complications, phlebotomists must keep their work area and instruments clean and sanitary.

Work Environment

Phlebotomists held about 132,600 jobs in 2019. The largest employers of phlebotomists were as follows:

Hospitals; state, local, and private	38%
Medical and diagnostic laboratories	32
All other ambulatory healthcare services	15
Offices of physicians	7
Outpatient care centers	2

Phlebotomists who collect blood donations sometimes travel to different offices and sites in order to set up mobile donation centers. They also sometimes travel to long-term care centers or patients' homes.

Injuries and Illnesses

Phlebotomists often stand for long periods, and must be careful when handling blood, needles, and other medical supplies. Injuries may occur if they are not careful with medical equipment.

Phlebotomists work mainly in hospitals, medical and diagnostic laboratories, and doctor's offices.

Work Schedules

Most phlebotomists work full time. Phlebotomists who work in hospitals and labs may need to work nights, weekends, and holidays.

How to Become a Phlebotomist

Phlebotomists typically enter the occupation with a postsecondary nondegree award from a phlebotomy program. Almost all employers look for phlebotomists who have earned professional certification.

Education and Training

Phlebotomists typically enter the occupation with a postsecondary nondegree award from a phlebotomy program. Programs are available from community colleges, vocational schools, or technical schools. These programs usually take less than 1 year to complete and lead to a certificate. Certification programs involve classroom sessions and laboratory work, and they include instruction in anatomy, physiology, and medical terminology.

Some phlebotomists enter the occupation with a high school diploma and are trained to be a phlebotomist on the job. No matter their education level, phlebotomists also receive specific instructions on how to identify, label, and track blood samples.

Licenses, Certifications, and Registrations

Almost all employers prefer to hire phlebotomists who have earned professional certification.

Several organizations offer certifications for phlebotomists. The National Center for Competency Testing (NCCT), National Healthcareer Association (NHA), American Society for Clinical Pathology (ASCP), National Phlebotomy Association, and American Medical Technologists (AMT) offer Phlebotomy Technician certifications.

Candidates for certification typically need some classroom education, as well as some clinical experience. Certification testing usually includes a written exam and may include

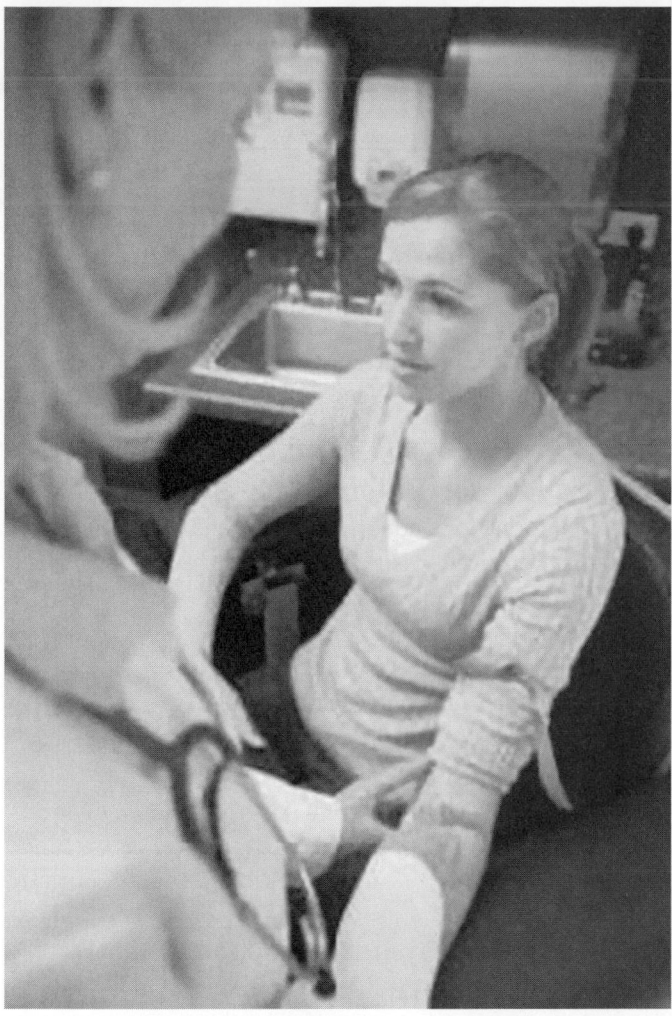

Many employers look for phlebotomists who have completed some kind of professional certification.

practical components, such as drawing blood. Requirements vary by certifying organization. California, Louisiana, Nevada, and Washington require their phlebotomists to be certified.

Important Qualities

Compassion. Some patients or clients are afraid of having their blood drawn, so phlebotomists should be caring in performing their duties.

Detail oriented. Phlebotomists must draw the correct vials of blood for the tests ordered, track vials of blood, and enter data into a database. Attention to detail is necessary; otherwise, the specimens may be misplaced or lost, or a patient may be injured.

Dexterity. Phlebotomists work with their hands, and they must be able to use their equipment efficiently and properly.

Hand–eye coordination. Phlebotomists draw blood from many patients, and they must perform their duties successfully on the first attempt, or their patients will experience discomfort.

Physical stamina. Phlebotomists are on their feet for long periods, and must continue to take accurate blood samples throughout their workday.

Pay

The median annual wage for phlebotomists was $35,510 in May 2019. The median wage is the wage at which half the workers in an occupation earned more than that amount and half earned less. The lowest 10 percent earned less than $26,000, and the highest 10 percent earned more than $49,750.

In May 2019, the median annual wages for phlebotomists in the top industries in which they worked were as follows:

Outpatient care centers	$41,620
Medical and diagnostic laboratories	37,220
All other ambulatory healthcare services	34,460
Offices of physicians	34,400
Hospitals; state, local, and private	33,720

Most phlebotomists work full time. Phlebotomists who work in hospitals and labs may need to work nights, weekends, and holidays.

Job Outlook

Employment of phlebotomists is projected to grow 17 percent from 2019 to 2029, much faster than the average for all occupations. Hospitals, diagnostic laboratories, blood donor centers, and other locations will need phlebotomists to perform bloodwork.

Blood analysis remains an essential function in medical laboratories and hospitals. Demand for phlebotomists will remain high as doctors and other healthcare professionals require bloodwork for analysis and diagnosis.

In addition to blood analysis, phlebotomists are necessary for blood collection, either at mobile blood centers or dedicated donation centers. These phlebotomists may be especially busy during a health emergency, which can correspond with heightened interest in blood donations.

Phlebotomists
Median annual wages, May 2019

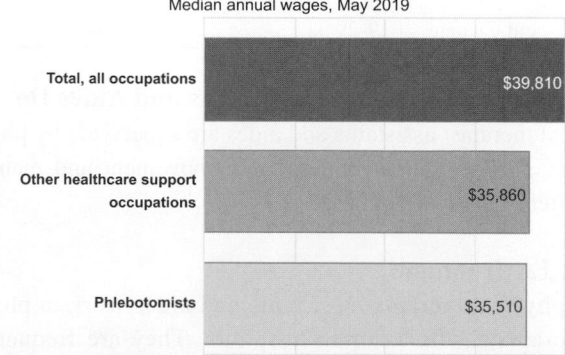

Note: All Occupations includes all occupations in the U.S. Economy.
Source: U.S. Bureau of Labor Statistics, Occupational Employment Statistics.

Phlebotomists
Percent change in employment, projected 2019-29

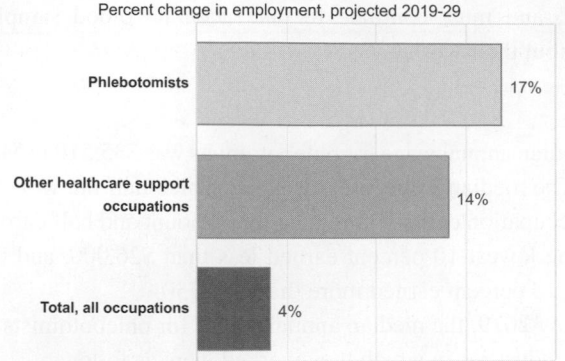

Phlebotomists	17%
Other healthcare support occupations	14%
Total, all occupations	4%

Note: All Occupations includes all occupations in the U.S. Economy.
Source: U.S. Bureau of Labor Statistics, Employment Projections program.

Job Prospects

Job prospects are greatest for phlebotomists who receive certification from one of several reputable organizations, such as the National Center for Competency Testing (NCCT), National Healthcareer Association (NHA), the American Society for Clinical Pathology (ASCP), the National Phlebotomy Association, and the American Medical Technologists (AMT).

Employment projections data for phlebotomists, 2019-29					
Occupational Title	SOC Code	Employment, 2019	Projected Employment, 2029	Change, 2019-29	
				Percent	Numeric
SOURCE: U.S. Bureau of Labor Statistics, Employment Projections program					
Phlebotomists	31-9097	132,600	155,500	17	22,800

State & Area Data
Occupational Employment Statistics (OES)

The Occupational Employment Statistics (OES) program produces employment and wage estimates annually for over 800 occupations. These estimates are available for the nation as a whole, for individual states, and for metropolitan and nonmetropolitan areas.

Contacts for More Information

For more information about phlebotomy and how to receive a phlebotomy certificate, visit
➤ Center for Phlebotomy Education
➤ American Medical Technologists (AMT)
➤ National Healthcareer Association
➤ National Center for Competency Testing
➤ American Society for Clinical Pathology
➤ National Phlebotomy Association
➤ American Medical Certification Association

Physical Therapist Assistants and Aides

Summary

Quick Facts: Physical Therapist Assistants and Aides

2019 Median Pay	$48,990 per year $23.55 per hour
Typical Entry-Level Education	See below
Work Experience in a Related Occupation	None
On-the-job Training	See below
Number of Jobs, 2019	149,300
Job Outlook, 2019-29	29% (Much faster than average)
Employment Change, 2019-29	43,000

What Physical Therapist Assistants and Aides Do

Physical therapist assistants and aides are supervised by physical therapists to help patients regain movement and manage pain after injuries and illnesses.

Work Environment

Most physical therapist assistants and aides work in physical therapists' offices or in hospitals. They are frequently on their feet as they set up equipment and help care for patients.

How to Become a Physical Therapist Assistant or Aide

Physical therapist assistants entering the occupation typically need an associate's degree from an accredited program and a license or certification. Physical therapist aides usually need a high school diploma or equivalent and on-the-job training.

Physical therapist aides do a variety of clerical tasks, such as scheduling patients and recording insurance information.

Pay

The median annual wage for physical therapist aides was $27,000 in May 2019.

The median annual wage for physical therapist assistants was $58,790 in May 2019.

Job Outlook

Overall employment of physical therapist assistants and aides is projected to grow 29 percent from 2019 to 2029, much faster than the average for all occupations. Demand for physical therapy is expected to increase in response to the healthcare needs of an aging population and individuals with chronic conditions, such as diabetes and obesity.

State & Area Data

Explore resources for employment and wages by state and area for physical therapist assistants and aides.

What Physical Therapist Assistants and Aides Do

Physical therapist assistants, sometimes called *PTAs*, and physical therapist aides work under the direction and supervision of physical therapists. They help patients who are recovering from injuries and illnesses to regain movement and manage pain.

Physical therapist assistants are involved in the direct care of patients.

Physical therapist aides often have tasks that are indirectly related to patient care, such as cleaning and setting up the treatment area, moving patients, and doing clerical duties.

Duties

Physical therapist assistants typically do the following:

- Observe patients before, during, and after therapy, noting the patient's status and reporting it to a physical therapist
- Help patients do specific exercises as part of the plan of care
- Treat patients using a variety of techniques, such as massage and stretching
- Use devices and equipment, such as walkers, to help patients
- Educate patients and family members about what to do after treatment

Under the direction and supervision of physical therapists, physical therapist assistants treat patients through exercise, massage, gait and balance training, and other therapeutic interventions. They record patients' progress and report the results of each treatment to the physical therapist.

Physical therapist aides typically do the following:

- Clean treatment areas and set up therapy equipment
- Wash linens
- Help patients move to or from a therapy area
- Do clerical tasks, such as answering phones and scheduling patients

Physical therapist aides are supervised by physical therapists or physical therapist assistants. The tasks that physical therapist aides are allowed to do vary by state. They usually are responsible for keeping the treatment area clean and organized, preparing for each patient's therapy, and helping patients as needed in moving to or from a treatment area. In addition, aides do a variety of clerical tasks, such as ordering supplies, scheduling treatment sessions, and completing insurance forms.

Work Environment

Physical therapist aides held about 50,600 jobs in 2019. The largest employers of physical therapist aides were as follows:

Offices of physical, occupational and speech therapists, and audiologists	60%
Hospitals; state, local, and private	22
Offices of physicians	7
Nursing care facilities (skilled nursing facilities)	4
Government	2

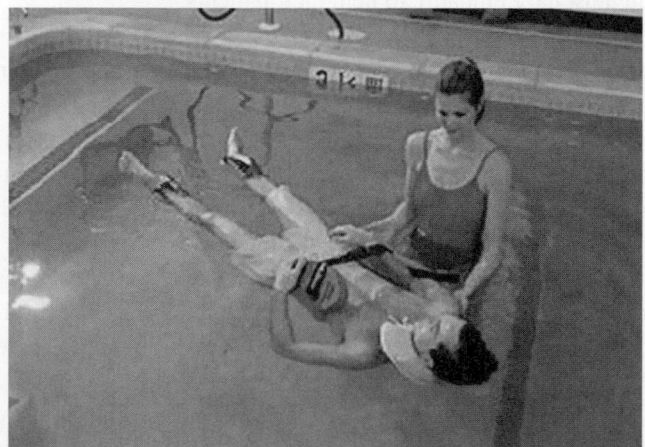

Physical therapist assistants help patients do specific exercises as part of the plan of care.

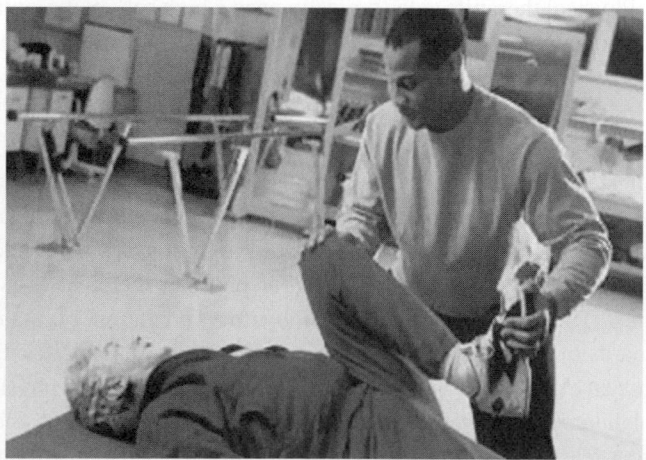

Physical therapist assistants give therapy through exercise, stretching, and other interventions.

Physical therapist assistants held about 98,700 jobs in 2019. The largest employers of physical therapist assistants were as follows:

Offices of physical, occupational and speech therapists, and audiologists	46%
Hospitals; state, local, and private..............................	23
Nursing care facilities (skilled nursing facilities)	10
Home healthcare services	9
Offices of physicians...	5

Physical therapist assistants and aides are frequently on their feet and moving as they set up equipment and help and treat patients. Because they must often lift and move patients, they are vulnerable to back injuries. Assistants and aides can limit these risks by using proper techniques when they work with patients.

Work Schedules

Most physical therapist assistants and aides work full time, although part time work is common. Some work nights and weekends because many physical therapy offices and clinics have extended hours to accommodate patients' schedules.

How to Become a Physical Therapist Assistant or Aide

Physical therapist assistants entering the occupation typically need an associate's degree from an accredited program and a license or certification. Physical therapist aides usually need a high school diploma or equivalent and on-the-job training.

Education and Training

All states require physical therapist assistants to have an associate's degree from a program accredited by the Commission on Accreditation in Physical Therapy Education. Programs typically last about 2 years and include coursework in subjects such as anatomy, physiology, and kinesiology. Assistants also gain hands-on experience during supervised clinical work.

Physical therapist aides typically need a high school diploma or equivalent. They also usually need on-the-job training that can last from about one week to one month.

Licenses, Certifications, and Registrations

All states require physical therapist assistants to be licensed or certified. Licensure typically requires graduation from an accredited physical therapist assistant program and passing the National Physical Therapy Exam for physical therapist assistants. The exam is administered by the Federation of State Boards of Physical Therapy. Some states require that applicants pass an exam on the state's laws regulating the practice of physical therapy assistants, undergo a criminal background check, and be at least 18 years old. Physical therapist assistants also may need to take continuing education courses to keep their license. Check with your state board for specific licensing requirements.

Physical therapist assistants gain hands-on experience during supervised clinical work.

Additionally, physical therapy assistants may earn certifications in cardiopulmonary resuscitation (CPR), basic life support (BLS), or other first-aid skills.

States do not require physical therapist aides to be licensed.

Important Qualities

Compassion. Physical therapist assistants and aides should enjoy helping people. They work with people who are in pain and must have empathy to help their patients.

Detail oriented. Physical therapist assistants and aides should be organized, keep accurate records, and follow written and verbal instructions carefully to ensure quality care.

Dexterity. Physical therapist assistants should be comfortable using their hands to provide manual therapy and therapeutic exercises. Aides should also be comfortable working with their hands to set up equipment and prepare treatment areas.

Interpersonal skills. Physical therapist assistants and aides spend much of their time interacting with patients, their families, and other healthcare practitioners; therefore, they should be courteous and friendly.

Physical stamina. Physical therapist assistants and aides are frequently on their feet and moving as they work with their patients. They must often kneel, stoop, bend, and stand for long periods.

Physical Therapist Assistants and Aides
Median annual wages, May 2019

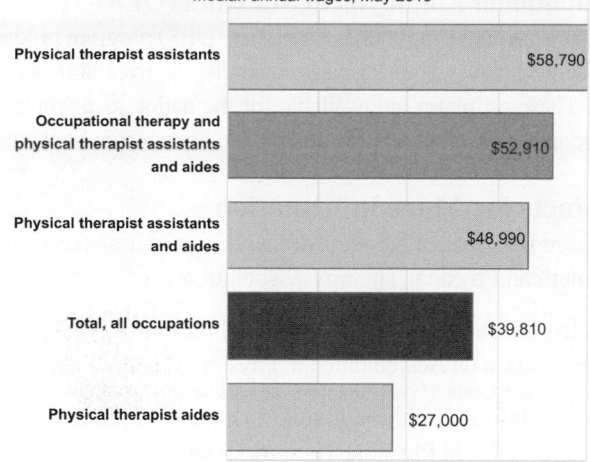

Note: All Occupations includes all occupations in the U.S. Economy.
Source: U.S. Bureau of Labor Statistics, Occupational Employment Statistics.

Pay

The median annual wage for physical therapist aides was $27,000 in May 2019. The median wage is the wage at which half the workers in an occupation earned more than that amount and half earned less. The lowest 10 percent earned less than $20,310, and the highest 10 percent earned more than $39,740.

The median annual wage for physical therapist assistants was $58,790 in May 2019. The lowest 10 percent earned less than $33,450, and the highest 10 percent earned more than $80,840.

In May 2019, the median annual wages for physical therapist aides in the top industries in which they worked were as follows:

Nursing care facilities (skilled nursing facilities)...	$34,490
Hospitals; state, local, and private	29,570
Offices of physicians	28,430
Government	28,090
Offices of physical, occupational and speech therapists, and audiologists	25,600

In May 2019, the median annual wages for physical therapist assistants in the top industries in which they worked were as follows:

Nursing care facilities (skilled nursing facilities)...	$66,840
Home healthcare services	63,200
Offices of physical, occupational and speech therapists, and audiologists	57,520
Hospitals; state, local, and private	57,140
Offices of physicians	55,490

Most physical therapist assistants and aides work full time, although part time work is common. Some work nights and weekends because many physical therapy offices and clinics have extended hours to accommodate patients' schedules.

Physical Therapist Assistants and Aides
Percent change in employment, projected 2019-29

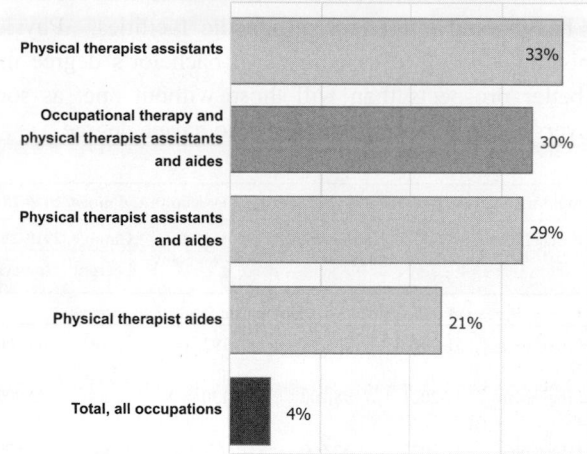

Note: All Occupations includes all occupations in the U.S. Economy.
Source: U.S. Bureau of Labor Statistics, Employment Projections program.

Job Outlook

Employment of physical therapist assistants is projected to grow 33 percent from 2019 to 2029, much faster than the average for all occupations. Employment of physical therapist aides is projected to grow 21 percent from 2019 to 2029, much faster than the average for all occupations.

Demand for physical therapy is expected to increase in response to the health needs of an aging population, particularly the large baby-boom generation. This group is staying more active later in life than previous generations did. However, many baby boomers also are entering the prime age for heart attacks, strokes, and mobility-related injuries, increasing the demand for physical therapy needed for rehabilitation.

In addition, more physical therapist assistants and aides will be needed to help patients maintain their mobility and manage the effects of chronic conditions, such as diabetes and obesity. Moreover, medical and technological developments should permit an increased number of trauma victims and newborns with birth defects to survive, creating added demand for therapy and rehabilitative services.

Physical therapists are expected to rely on physical therapist assistants, particularly in long-term care environments, in order to reduce the cost of physical therapy services. After the physical therapist has evaluated a patient and designed a plan of care, the assistant provides many parts of the treatment, as directed by the therapist.

Job Prospects

About 15,100 openings for physical therapist assistants and 6,900 openings for physical therapist aides are projected each year, on average, over the decade.

Many of those openings are expected to result from the need to replace workers who transfer to different occupations or exit the labor force, such as to retire.

Job opportunities should be good in settings where the aging population is most often treated, such as skilled-nursing homes, home health, and outpatient orthopedic facilities. Physical therapist aides with an associate's or bachelor's degree may have better prospects than will those without one, as some employers prefer to hire candidates who have a degree.

Employment projections data for physical therapist assistants and aides, 2019-29					
Occupational Title	SOC Code	Employment, 2019	Projected Employment, 2029	Change, 2019-29	
				Percent	Numeric
SOURCE: U.S. Bureau of Labor Statistics, Employment Projections program					
Physical therapist assistants and aides	31-2020	149,300	192,300	29	43,000
Physical therapist assistants	31-2021	98,700	130,900	33	32,200
Physical therapist aides	31-2022	50,600	61,300	21	10,800

State & Area Data
Occupational Employment Statistics (OES)
The Occupational Employment Statistics (OES) program produces employment and wage estimates annually for over 800 occupations. These estimates are available for the nation as a whole, for individual states, and for metropolitan and nonmetropolitan areas.

Contacts for More Information
For more information about physical therapist assistants, visit
➤ American Physical Therapy Association

For a list of schools offering accredited programs, visit
➤ Commission on Accreditation in Physical Therapy Education

For more information about state licensing requirements and about the National Physical Therapy Exam, visit
➤ Federation of State Boards of Physical Therapy

Physical Therapists

Summary

Quick Facts: Physical Therapists

2019 Median Pay	$89,440 per year $43.00 per hour
Typical Entry-Level Education	Doctoral or professional degree
Work Experience in a Related Occupation	None
On-the-job Training	None
Number of Jobs, 2019	258,200
Job Outlook, 2019-29	18% (Much faster than average)
Employment Change, 2019-29	47,000

What Physical Therapists Do
Physical therapists help injured or ill people improve movement and manage pain.

Work Environment
Physical therapists typically work in private offices and clinics, hospitals, patients' homes, and nursing homes. They spend much of their time on their feet, actively working with patients.

How to Become a Physical Therapist
Physical therapists entering the occupation need a Doctor of Physical Therapy (DPT) degree. All states require physical therapists to be licensed.

Pay
The median annual wage for physical therapists was $89,440 in May 2019.

Job Outlook
Employment of physical therapists is projected to grow 18 percent from 2019 to 2029, much faster than the average for all occupations. Demand for physical therapy is expected to come from aging baby boomers, who are not only staying active later in life but are susceptible to health conditions, such as strokes, that may require physical therapy. In addition, physical therapists will be needed to treat people with mobility issues stemming from chronic conditions, such as diabetes or obesity.

State & Area Data
Explore resources for employment and wages by state and area for physical therapists.

What Physical Therapists Do
Physical therapists help injured or ill people improve movement and manage pain. They are often an important part of

Physical therapists develop individualized plans of care for patients.

Physical therapists evaluate and record a patient's progress.

preventive care, rehabilitation, and treatment for patients with chronic conditions, illnesses, or injuries.

Duties

Physical therapists typically do the following:

- Review patients' medical history and referrals or notes from doctors, surgeons, or other healthcare workers
- Diagnose patients' functions and movements by observing them stand or walk and by listening to their concerns
- Develop individualized plans of care for patients, outlining the patients' goals and the expected outcomes of the plans
- Use exercises, stretching maneuvers, hands-on therapy, and equipment to ease patients' pain, help them increase their mobility, prevent further pain or injury, and facilitate health and wellness
- Evaluate and record a patients' progress, modifying the plan of care and trying new treatments as needed
- Educate patients and their families about what to expect from the recovery process and how to cope with challenges throughout the process

Physical therapists, sometimes called *PTs*, care for people of all ages who have functional problems resulting from back and neck injuries; sprains, strains, and fractures; arthritis; amputations; neurological disorders, such as stroke or cerebral palsy; injuries related to work and sports; and other conditions.

Physical therapists use a variety of techniques to care for their patients. These techniques include exercises; training in functional movement, which may include the use of equipment such as canes, crutches, wheelchairs, and walkers; and special movements of joints, muscles, and other soft tissue to improve mobility and decrease pain.

The work of physical therapists varies by type of patient. For example, a patient working to recover mobility lost after a stroke needs care different from that of a patient recovering from a sports injury. Some physical therapists specialize in one type of care, such as orthopedics or geriatrics. Many physical therapists also help patients maintain or improve mobility

by developing fitness and wellness programs that encourage healthy, active lifestyles.

Physical therapists work as part of a healthcare team, overseeing the work of physical therapist assistants and aides and consulting with physicians and surgeons and other specialists.

Work Environment

Physical therapists held about 258,200 jobs in 2019. The largest employers of physical therapists were as follows:

Offices of physical, occupational and speech therapists, and audiologists	33%
Hospitals; state, local, and private	26
Home healthcare services	11
Self-employed workers..	8
Nursing and residential care facilities............................	6

Physical therapists spend much of their time on their feet, working with patients. Because they must often lift and move patients, they are vulnerable to back injuries. Physical therapists can limit these risks by using proper body mechanics and lifting techniques when assisting patients.

Work Schedules

Most physical therapists work full time, although part time work is common. They usually work during normal business hours, but some work evenings or weekends.

How to Become a Physical Therapist

Physical therapists entering the occupation need a Doctor of Physical Therapy (DPT) degree. All states require physical therapists to be licensed.

Education

Physical therapists need a Doctor of Physical Therapy (DPT) degree from a program accredited by the Commission on Accreditation in Physical Therapy Education (CAPTE).

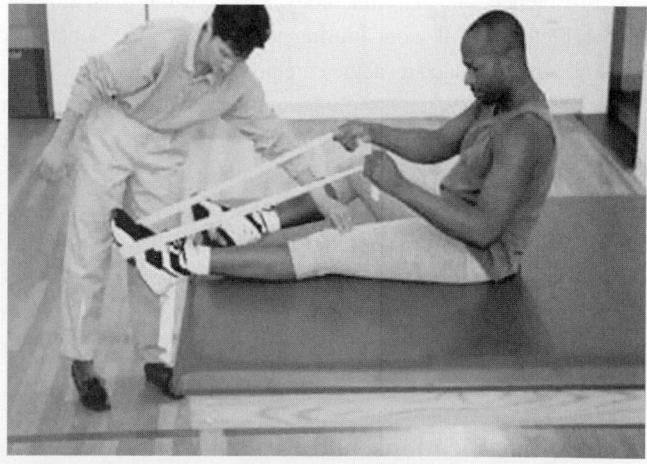

Physical therapists use exercises and stretching maneuvers to ease patients' pain.

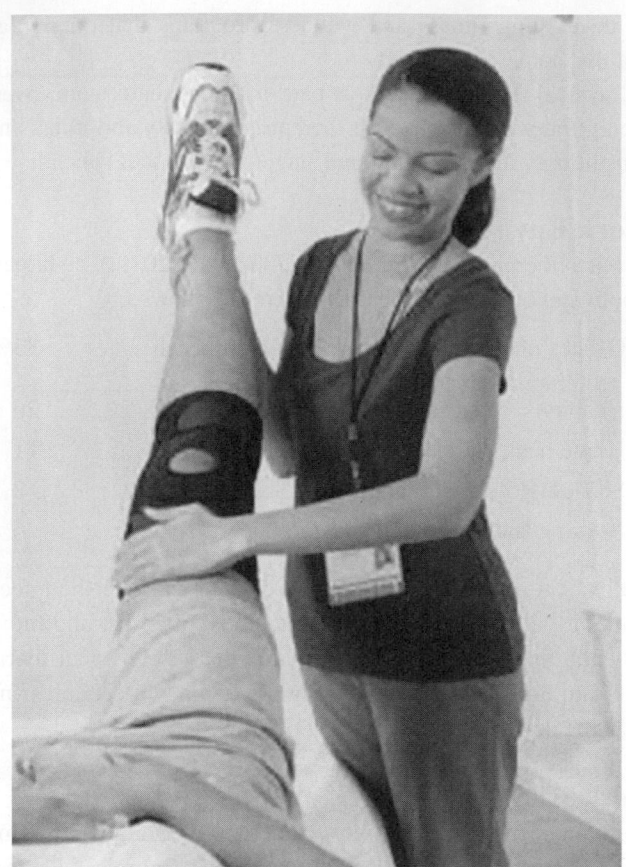

Physical therapists use a variety of techniques, such as massage and stretching, to treat patients.

DPT programs typically last 3 years. Many programs require a bachelor's degree for admission as well as prerequisite courses, such as anatomy, biology, chemistry, physics, and physiology. Some programs admit college freshmen into 6- or 7-year programs that allow students to graduate with both a bachelor's degree and a DPT. Most DPT programs require candidates to apply through the Physical Therapist Centralized Application Service (PTCAS).

Physical therapist programs often include courses in biomechanics, neuroscience, and pharmacology. Physical therapist students also complete clinical work, during which they gain supervised experience in areas such as acute care and orthopedic care.

Physical therapists may apply to a clinical residency program after graduation. Residencies typically last about 1 year and provide additional training and experience in specialty areas of care. Physical therapists who have completed a residency program may choose to specialize further by participating in a fellowship in an advanced clinical area. The American Board of Physical Therapy Residency and Fellowship Education has directories of physical therapist residency and fellowship programs.

Licenses, Certifications, and Registrations

All states require physical therapists to be licensed, which includes passing the National Physical Therapy Examination administered by the Federation of State Boards of Physical Therapy. Other requirements vary by state. For example, some states also require a law exam and a criminal background check. Continuing education is typically required for physical therapists to keep their license. Check with your state board for specific licensing requirements.

After gaining work experience, some physical therapists choose to become a board-certified specialist. The American Board of Physical Therapy Specialties offers certification in clinical specialty areas of physical therapy, such as orthopedics, sports, and geriatrics. Board specialist certification requires passing an exam and completing clinical work in the specialty area.

Important Qualities

Communication skills. Physical therapists must clearly explain treatment programs, motivate patients, and listen to patients' concerns in order to provide effective therapy.

Compassion. Physical therapists spend a lot of time interacting with patients, so they should have a desire to help people. They work with people who are in pain and must have empathy for their patients.

Detail oriented. Like other healthcare providers, physical therapists should have strong analytic and observational skills to diagnose a patient's problem, evaluate treatments, and provide safe, effective care.

Dexterity. Physical therapists must use their hands to provide manual therapy and therapeutic exercises. They should feel comfortable massaging and otherwise physically assisting patients.

Physical stamina. Physical therapists spend much of their time on their feet, moving to demonstrate proper techniques and to help patients perform exercises. They should enjoy physical activity.

Resourcefulness. Physical therapists customize treatment plans for patients. They must be flexible and adapt plans of care to meet the needs of each patient.

Time-management skills. Physical therapists typically treat several patients each day. They must be able to provide appropriate care to patients as well as complete administrative tasks, such as documenting patient progress.

Pay

The median annual wage for physical therapists was $89,440 in May 2019. The median wage is the wage at which half the workers in an occupation earned more than that amount and half earned less. The lowest 10 percent earned less than $62,120, and the highest 10 percent earned more than $124,740.

In May 2019, the median annual wages for physical therapists in the top industries in which they worked were as follows:

Nursing and residential care facilities	$95,540
Home healthcare services	94,080

Physical Therapists
Median annual wages, May 2019

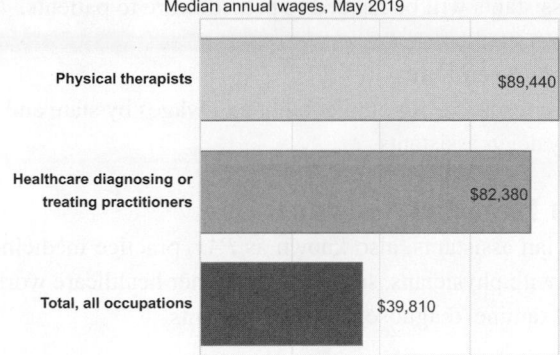

Physical therapists	$89,440
Healthcare diagnosing or treating practitioners	$82,380
Total, all occupations	$39,810

Note: All Occupations includes all occupations in the U.S. Economy.
Source: U.S. Bureau of Labor Statistics, Occupational Employment Statistics.

Hospitals; state, local, and private 91,260

Offices of physical, occupational and speech
therapists, and audiologists 85,130

Most physical therapists work full time. Although most therapists work during normal business hours, some work evenings or weekends.

Job Outlook

Employment of physical therapists is projected to grow 18 percent from 2019 to 2029, much faster than the average for all occupations.

Demand for physical therapy will come in part from the large number of aging baby boomers, who are staying more active later in life than their counterparts of previous generations. Older people are more likely to experience heart attacks, strokes, and mobility-related injuries that require physical therapy for rehabilitation.

In addition, a number of chronic conditions, such as diabetes and obesity, have become more prevalent in recent years. More physical therapists will be needed to help these patients maintain their mobility and manage the effects of chronic conditions.

Advances in medical technology have increased the use of outpatient surgery to treat a variety of injuries and illnesses. Medical and technological developments also are expected to permit survival of a greater number of trauma victims and newborns with birth defects, creating additional demand for rehabilitative care. Physical therapists will continue to help these patients recover from surgery.

Job Prospects

About 15,200 openings for physical therapists are projected each year, on average, over the decade.

Many of those openings are expected to result from the need to replace workers who transfer to different occupations or exit the labor force, such as to retire.

Job prospects should be especially favorable in rural areas, where physical therapy services are less prevalent than in urban and suburban areas.

Physical Therapists
Percent change in employment, projected 2019-29

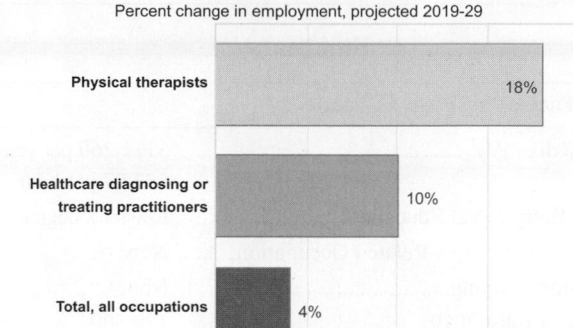

Physical therapists	18%
Healthcare diagnosing or treating practitioners	10%
Total, all occupations	4%

Note: All Occupations includes all occupations in the U.S. Economy.
Source: U.S. Bureau of Labor Statistics, Employment Projections program.

Employment projections data for physical therapists, 2019-29					
Occupational Title	SOC Code	Employment, 2019	Projected Employment, 2029	Change, 2019-29	
				Percent	Numeric
SOURCE: U.S. Bureau of Labor Statistics, Employment Projections program					
Physical therapists	29-1123	258,200	305,200	18	47,000

State & Area Data
Occupational Employment Statistics (OES)

The Occupational Employment Statistics (OES) program produces employment and wage estimates annually for over 800 occupations. These estimates are available for the nation as a whole, for individual states, and for metropolitan and nonmetropolitan areas.

Contacts for More Information

For more information about physical therapists, visit
➤ American Physical Therapy Association

For more information about accredited physical therapy programs, visit
➤ Commission on Accreditation in Physical Therapy Education

For more information about state licensing requirements and about the National Physical Therapy Exam, visit
➤ Federation of State Boards of Physical Therapy

For more information about certification, visit
➤ American Board of Physical Therapy Specialties

For more information about residency and fellowship opportunities, visit
➤ American Board of Physical Therapy Residency and Fellowship Education

For more information about how to apply to DPT programs, visit
➤ Physical Therapist Centralized Application Service (PTCAS)

Physician Assistants

Summary

Quick Facts: Physician Assistants

2019 Median Pay	$112,260 per year $53.97 per hour
Typical Entry-Level Education	Master's degree
Work Experience in a Related Occupation	None
On-the-job Training	None
Number of Jobs, 2019......................................	125,500
Job Outlook, 2019-29.......................................	31% (Much faster than average)
Employment Change, 2019-29	39,300

What Physician Assistants Do

Physician assistants practice medicine on teams with physicians, surgeons, and other healthcare workers.

Work Environment

Physician assistants work in physicians' offices, hospitals, outpatient clinics, and other healthcare settings. Most work full time.

How to Become a Physician Assistant

Physician assistants typically need a master's degree from an accredited educational program. All states require physician assistants to be licensed.

Pay

The median annual wage for physician assistants was $112,260 in May 2019.

Job Outlook

Employment of physician assistants is projected to grow 31 percent from 2019 to 2029, much faster than the average for all occupations. As demand for healthcare services grows, physician assistants will be needed to provide care to patients.

State & Area Data

Explore resources for employment and wages by state and area for physician assistants.

What Physician Assistants Do

Physician assistants, also known as *PAs*, practice medicine on teams with physicians, surgeons, and other healthcare workers. They examine, diagnose, and treat patients.

Duties

Physician assistants typically do the following:

- Take or review patients' medical histories
- Examine patients
- Order and interpret diagnostic tests, such as x rays or blood tests
- Diagnose a patient's injury or illness
- Give treatment, such as setting broken bones and immunizing patients
- Educate and counsel patients and their families—for example, answering questions about how to care for a child with asthma
- Prescribe medicine
- Assess and record a patient's progress
- Research the latest treatments to ensure the quality of patient care
- Conduct or participate in outreach programs, talking to groups about managing diseases and promoting wellness

Physician assistants work on teams with physicians or surgeons and other healthcare workers. Their specific duties and the extent to which they must be supervised by physicians or surgeons differ from state to state.

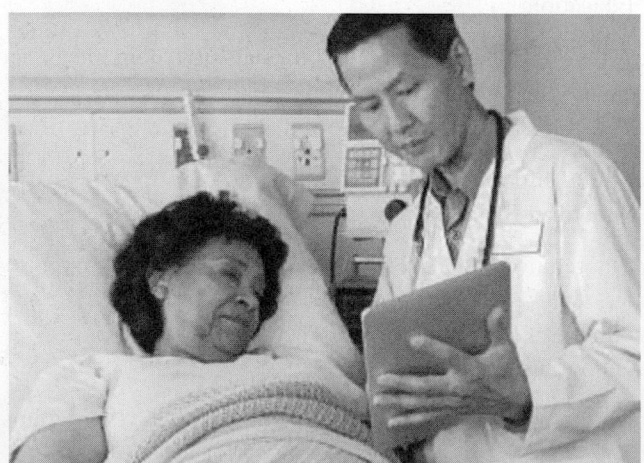

Physician assistants practice medicine on a team with physicians and surgeons and other healthcare workers.

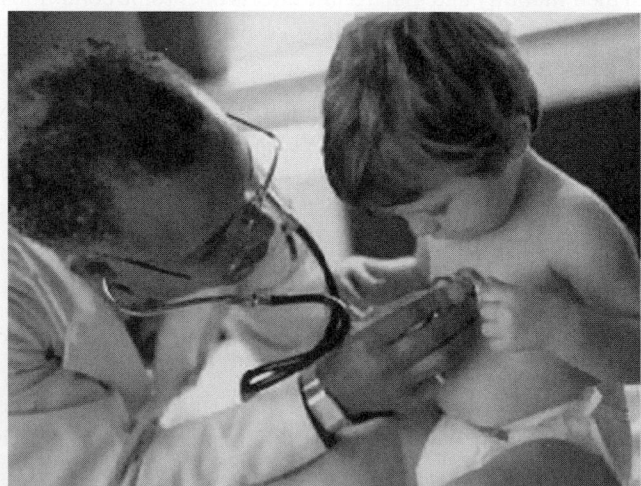

Physician assistants work in all areas of medicine, including primary care and family medicine, emergency medicine, and psychiatry.

Physician assistants work in all areas of medicine, including primary care and family medicine, emergency medicine, surgery, and psychiatry. The work of physician assistants depends in large part on their specialty or the type of medical practice where they work. For example, a physician assistant working in surgery may close incisions and provide care before, during, and after the operation. A physician assistant working in pediatrics may examine a child and give routine vaccinations.

In some areas, especially rural and medically underserved communities, physician assistants may be the primary care providers at clinics where a physician is present only 1 or 2 days per week. In these locations, physician assistants collaborate with the physician as needed and as required by law.

Some physician assistants make house calls or visit nursing homes to treat patients.

Physician assistants are different from medical assistants. Medical assistants do routine clinical and clerical tasks and do not practice medicine.

Work Environment

Physician assistants held about 125,500 jobs in 2019. The largest employers of physician assistants were as follows:

Offices of physicians	54%
Hospitals; state, local, and private	26
Outpatient care centers	8
Educational services; state, local, and private	4
Employment services	1

Working with patients can be both physically and emotionally demanding. Physician assistants spend much of their time on their feet, making rounds and evaluating patients. Physician assistants who work in operating rooms often stand for extended periods.

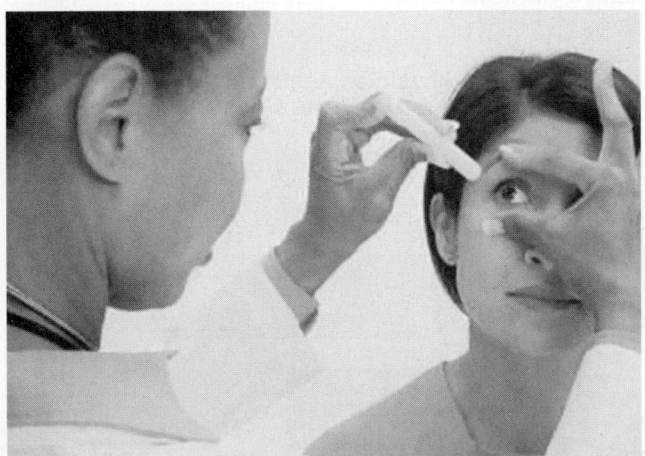

Many physician assistants work in primary care specialties, such as general internal medicine, pediatrics, and family medicine.

Work Schedules

Most physician assistants work full time. Some work more than 40 hours per week. Physician assistants may work nights, weekends, or holidays. They may also be on call, meaning that they must be ready to respond to a work request with little notice.

How to Become a Physician Assistant

Physician assistants typically need a master's degree from an accredited educational program. Earning that degree usually takes at least 2 years of full-time postgraduate study. All states require physician assistants to be licensed. Physician assistant graduate school applicants typically have experience caring directly for patients.

Education

Most applicants to physician assistant education programs already have a bachelor's degree and some patient care work experience. Although admissions requirements vary from program to program, most programs require 2 to 4 years of undergraduate coursework with a focus in science. Many applicants already have experience as registered nurses or as EMTs or paramedics before they apply to a physician assistant program.

Physician assistant education programs usually take at least 2 years of full-time study. More than 200 education programs

Physician assistants often treat minor injuries, instruct and counsel patients, and order or carry out therapy.

were accredited by the Accreditation Review Commission on Education for the Physician Assistant, Inc. (ARC-PA) in 2017. Almost all of these accredited programs offer a master's degree.

Physician assistant education includes classroom and laboratory instruction in subjects such as pathology, human anatomy, physiology, clinical medicine, pharmacology, physical diagnosis, and medical ethics. The programs also include supervised clinical training in several areas, including family medicine, internal medicine, emergency medicine, and pediatrics.

Sometimes students serve in one or more clinical rotations in these areas under the supervision of a physician who is looking to hire a physician assistant. In this way, clinical rotations may lead to permanent employment.

Work Experience in a Related Occupation

Applicants to physician assistant graduate programs typically need patient care experience for admission or to be competitive in entering the programs. Work as an EMT or paramedic, registered nurse, nursing assistant, or similar care position typically fulfills patient care experience requirements for admission to academic programs. Some applicants gain healthcare experience through volunteer opportunities at hospitals or clinics, or working with special-needs or at-risk groups, such as orphaned youth or homeless populations. For specific requirements, contact the program in which you are interested.

Licenses, Certifications, and Registrations

All states and the District of Columbia require physician assistants to be licensed. To become licensed, candidates must pass the Physician Assistant National Certifying Examination (PANCE) from the National Commission on Certification of Physician Assistants (NCCPA). A physician assistant who passes the exam may use the credential "Physician Assistant-Certified (PA-C)."

To keep their certification, physician assistants must complete 100 hours of continuing education every 2 years. The recertification exam is required every 10 years.

In addition, state licensure laws require physician assistants to hold an agreement with a supervising physician. Although the physician does not need to be onsite at all times, collaboration between physicians and physician assistants is required for practice.

Important Qualities

Communication skills. Physician assistants must explain complex medical issues in a way that patients can understand. They must also effectively communicate with doctors and other healthcare workers to ensure that they provide the best possible patient care.

Compassion. Physician assistants deal with patients who are sick or injured and may be in extreme pain or distress. They must treat patients and their families with compassion and understanding.

Detail oriented. Physician assistants should be observant and have a strong ability to focus when evaluating and treating patients.

Emotional stability. Physician assistants, particularly those working in surgery or emergency medicine, should work well under pressure. They must remain calm in stressful situations in order to provide quality care.

Problem-solving skills. Physician assistants need to evaluate patients' symptoms and administer the appropriate treatments. They must be diligent when investigating complicated medical issues so they can determine the best course of treatment for each patient.

Advancement

Some physician assistants pursue additional education in a specialty. Postgraduate educational programs are available in areas such as emergency medicine and psychiatry. To enter one of these programs, a physician assistant must be a graduate of an accredited program and be certified by the NCCPA.

As they gain greater clinical knowledge and experience, physician assistants can earn new responsibilities and higher wages. For example, experienced physician assistants may supervise other staff and physician assistant students, or they may become an executive leader of a healthcare organization.

Pay

The median annual wage for physician assistants was $112,260 in May 2019. The median wage is the wage at which half the workers in an occupation earned more than that amount and half earned less. The lowest 10 percent earned less than $72,720, and the highest 10 percent earned more than $157,120.

In May 2019, the median annual wages for physician assistants in the top industries in which they worked were as follows:

Outpatient care centers	$119,090
Hospitals; state, local, and private	115,190
Employment services	114,220

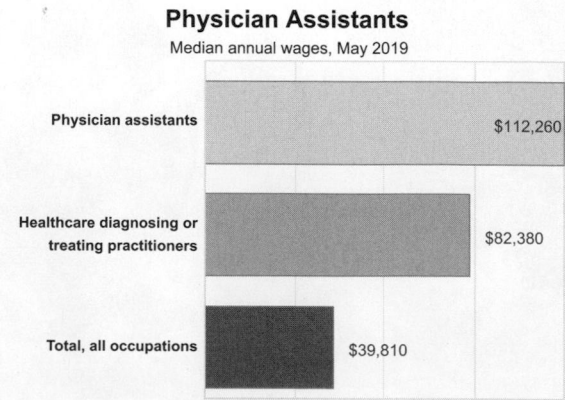

Physician Assistants
Median annual wages, May 2019

Physician assistants	$112,260
Healthcare diagnosing or treating practitioners	$82,380
Total, all occupations	$39,810

Note: All Occupations includes all occupations in the U.S. Economy.
Source: U.S. Bureau of Labor Statistics, Occupational Employment Statistics.

Physician Assistants
Percent change in employment, projected 2019-29

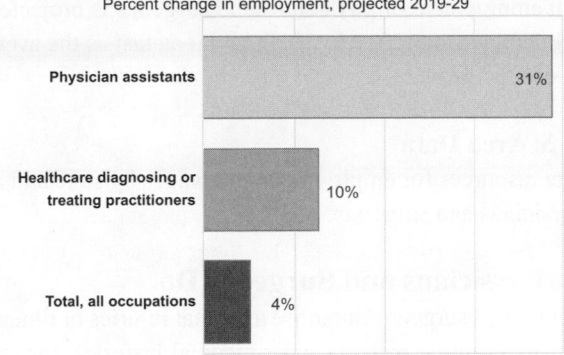

Physician assistants — 31%

Healthcare diagnosing or treating practitioners — 10%

Total, all occupations — 4%

Note: All Occupations includes all occupations in the U.S. Economy.
Source: U.S. Bureau of Labor Statistics, Employment Projections program.

Offices of physicians.. 110,670

Educational services; state, local, and private 109,080

Most physician assistants work full time. Some work more than 40 hours per week. Physician assistants may work nights, weekends, or holidays. They may also be on call, meaning that they must be ready to respond to a work request with little notice.

Job Outlook

Employment of physician assistants is projected to grow 31 percent from 2019 to 2029, much faster than the average for all occupations.

Demand for healthcare services will increase because of the growing and aging population. Growth of the population means more need for healthcare services generally, and members of the large baby boom generation will require more medical care as they age. An increase in the number of patients with chronic diseases, such as diabetes, will also increase healthcare demand and, in turn, drive the need for healthcare providers including physician assistants who often provide preventive care and treat the sick. Furthermore, increases in incomes may improve access to healthcare services, and advances in medical technology will continue to increase the number and types of treatments available.

Physician assistants can provide many of the same services as physicians. PAs are expected to continue to have a growing role in providing healthcare services because they can be trained more quickly than physicians. Team-based healthcare provision models will continue to evolve and become more commonly used. Physician assistants will have growing roles in all areas of medicine as states expand allowable procedures and autonomy, and as insurance companies expand their coverage of physician assistant services.

Job Prospects

Good job prospects are expected in primary care and across all specialties, particularly for physician assistants working in rural and medically underserved areas.

Employment projections data for physician assistants, 2019-29					
Occupational Title	SOC Code	Employment, 2019	Projected Employment, 2029	Change, 2019-29	
				Percent	Numeric
SOURCE: U.S. Bureau of Labor Statistics, Employment Projections program					
Physician assistants	29-1071	125,500	164,800	31	39,300

State & Area Data
Occupational Employment Statistics (OES)

The Occupational Employment Statistics (OES) program produces employment and wage estimates annually for over 800 occupations. These estimates are available for the nation as a whole, for individual states, and for metropolitan and nonmetropolitan areas.

Contacts for More Information

For more information about physician assistants, visit
➤ American Academy of PAs

For a list of accredited physician assistant programs, visit
➤ Physician Assistant Education Association
➤ Accreditation Review Commission on Education for the Physician Assistant, Inc. (ARC-PA)
➤ Association of Postgraduate Physician Assistant Programs

For information about certification requirements, visit
➤ National Commission on Certification of Physician Assistants

Physicians and Surgeons

Summary

Quick Facts: Physicians and Surgeons

2019 Median Pay	This wage is equal to or greater than $208,000 per year or $100.00 per hour.
Typical Entry-Level Education	Doctoral or professional degree
Work Experience in a Related Occupation ...	None
On-the-job Training	Internship/residency
Number of Jobs, 2019	752,400
Job Outlook, 2019-29	4% (As fast as average)
Employment Change, 2019-29	27,300

What Physicians and Surgeons Do

Physicians and surgeons diagnose and treat injuries or illnesses.

Work Environment

Many physicians and surgeons worked in physicians' offices. Others worked in hospitals, in academia, or for the government.

How to Become a Physician or Surgeon

Physicians and surgeons have demanding education and training requirements. Physicians typically need a bachelor's degree, a degree from a medical school, which takes 4 years to complete, and, depending on their specialty, 3 to 7 years in internship and residency programs.

Pay

Wages for physicians and surgeons are among the highest of all occupations, with a median wage equal to or greater than $208,000 per year.

Job Outlook

Overall employment of physicians and surgeons is projected to grow 4 percent from 2019 to 2029, about as fast as the average for all occupations.

State & Area Data

Explore resources for employment and wages by state and area for physicians and surgeons.

What Physicians and Surgeons Do

Physicians and surgeons diagnose and treat injuries or illnesses. Physicians examine patients; take medical histories; prescribe medications; and order, perform, and interpret diagnostic tests. They often counsel patients on diet, hygiene, and preventive healthcare. Surgeons operate on patients to treat injuries, such as broken bones; diseases, such as cancerous tumors; and deformities, such as cleft palates.

There are two types of physicians, with similar degrees: M.D. (Medical Doctor) and D.O. (Doctor of Osteopathic Medicine). Both use the same methods of treatment, including drugs and surgery, but D.O.s place additional emphasis on the body's musculoskeletal system, preventive medicine, and holistic (whole-person) patient care. D.O.s are most likely to be primary care physicians, although they can be found in all specialties.

Duties

Physicians and surgeons typically do the following:

- Take a patient's medical history
- Update charts and patient information to show current findings and treatments
- Order tests for nurses or other healthcare staff to perform
- Review test results to identify any abnormal findings
- Recommend and design a plan of treatment

Physicians examine patients; obtain medical histories; and order, perform, and interpret diagnostic tests.

Physicians often work closely with other healthcare staff including physician assistants, registered nurses, and medical records and health information technicians.

- Address concerns or answer questions that patients have about their health and well-being
- Help patients take care of their health by discussing topics such as proper nutrition and hygiene

Physicians and surgeons work in one or more specialties. The following are examples of types of physicians and surgeons:

Anesthesiologists focus on the care of surgical patients and pain relief. They administer drugs (anesthetics) that reduce or eliminate the sensation of pain during an operation or another medical procedure. During surgery, they are responsible for adjusting the amount of anesthetic as needed, and monitoring the patient's heart rate, body temperature, blood pressure, and breathing. They also work outside of the operating room, providing pain relief for patients in the intensive care unit, for women in labor and delivery of babies, and for patients who suffer from chronic pain. Anesthesiologists work with other physicians and surgeons to decide on treatments and procedures before, during, and after surgery.

Family and general physicians assess and treat a range of conditions that occur in everyday life. These conditions include sinus and respiratory infections to broken bones. Family and general physicians typically have regular, long-term patients.

General internists diagnose and provide nonsurgical treatment for a range of problems that affect internal organ systems such as the stomach, kidneys, liver, and digestive tract. Internists use a variety of diagnostic techniques to treat patients through medication or hospitalization. They work mostly with adult patients.

General pediatricians provide care for infants, children, teenagers, and young adults. They specialize in diagnosing and treating problems specific to younger people. Most pediatricians treat common illnesses, minor injuries, and infectious diseases, and administer vaccinations. Some pediatricians specialize in pediatric surgery or serious medical conditions that commonly affect younger patients, such as autoimmune disorders or chronic ailments.

Obstetricians and gynecologists (OB/GYNs) provide care related to pregnancy, childbirth, and the female reproductive system. They treat and counsel women throughout their pregnancy and deliver babies. They also diagnose and treat health issues specific to women, such as breast cancer, cervical cancer, hormonal disorders, and symptoms related to menopause.

Psychiatrists are primary mental health physicians. They diagnose and treat mental illnesses through a combination of personal counseling (psychotherapy), psychoanalysis, hospitalization, and medication. Psychotherapy involves regular discussions with patients about their problems. The psychiatrist helps them find solutions through changes in their behavioral patterns, explorations of their past experiences, or group and family therapy sessions. Psychoanalysis involves long-term psychotherapy and counseling for patients. Psychiatrists may prescribe medications to correct chemical imbalances that cause some mental illnesses.

Surgeons treat injuries, diseases, and deformities through operations. Using a variety of instruments, a surgeon corrects physical deformities, repairs bone and tissue after injuries, or performs preventive or elective surgeries on patients. Although a large number perform general surgery, many surgeons choose to specialize in a specific area. Specialties include orthopedic surgery (the treatment of the musculoskeletal system), neurological surgery (treatment of the brain and nervous system), cardiovascular surgery, and plastic or reconstructive surgery. Like other physicians, surgeons examine patients, perform and interpret diagnostic tests, and counsel patients on preventive healthcare. Some specialist physicians also perform surgery.

Physicians and surgeons may work in a number of other medical and surgical specialties and subspecialties. The following specialists are some of the most common examples:

- Allergists (specialists in diagnosing and treating hay fever or other allergies)
- Cardiologists (heart specialists)
- Dermatologists (skin specialists)
- Gastroenterologists (digestive system specialists)
- Ophthalmologists (eye specialists)
- Pathologists (specialists who study body tissue to see if it is normal or abnormal)
- Radiologists (specialists who review and interpret x rays and other images and deliver radiation treatments for cancer and other illnesses)

Physicians in healthcare establishments work daily with other healthcare staff, such as registered nurses, other physicians, medical assistants, and medical records and health information technicians.

Some physicians may choose to work in fields that do not involve patient care, such as medical research or public policy.

Work Environment

Physicians and surgeons held about 752,400 jobs in 2019. Employment in the detailed occupations that make up physicians and surgeons was distributed as follows:

Physicians, all other; and ophthalmologists, except pediatric	429,500
Family medicine physicians	119,300
General internal medicine physicians	49,500
Surgeons, except ophthalmologists	39,600
Anesthesiologists	33,800
Pediatricians, general	32,500
Psychiatrists	27,900
Obstetricians and gynecologists	20,300

Many physicians and surgeons work in physicians' offices. Others worked in hospitals, in academia, or for the government.

Increasingly, physicians are working in group practices, healthcare organizations, or hospitals, where they share a large number of patients with other doctors. The group setting allows

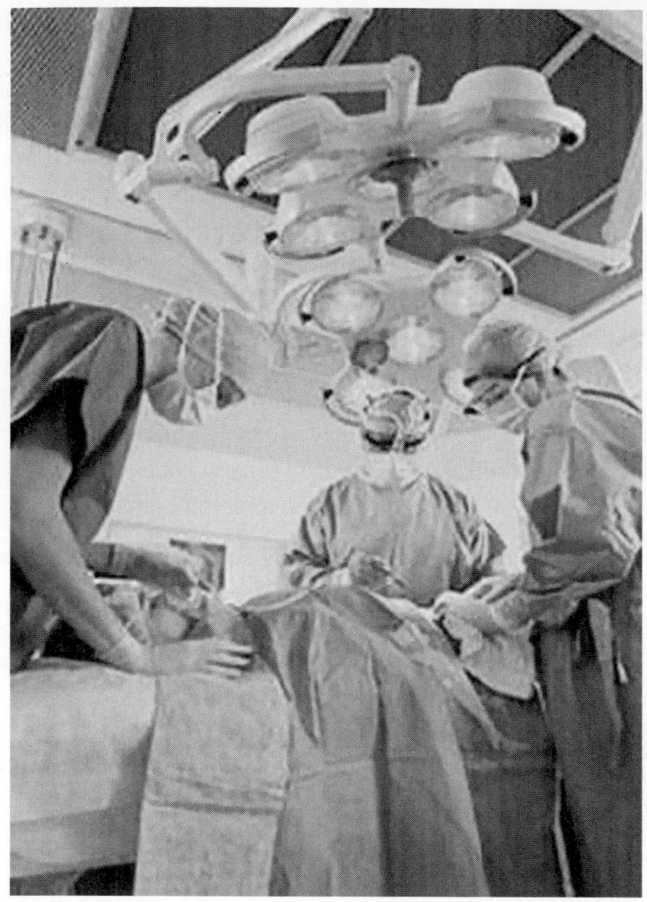

Surgeons and anesthesiologists usually work in well-lighted, sterile environments, and often stand for long periods.

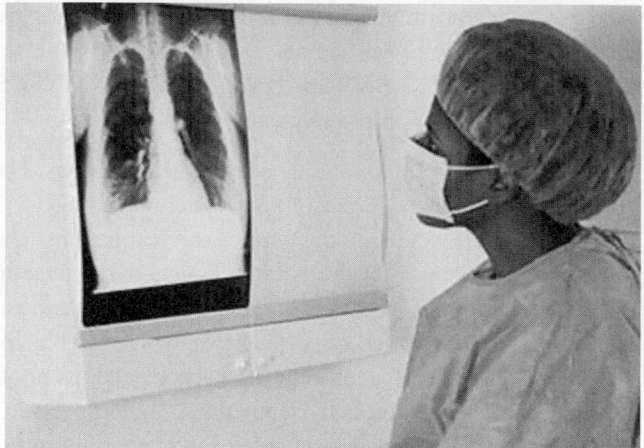

Physicians and surgeons may work in a medical specialty, such as cardiology, dermatology, pathology, or radiology.

them more time off and lets them coordinate care for their patients, but it gives them less independence than solo practitioners have.

Surgeons and anesthesiologists usually work in sterile environments while performing surgery and may stand for long periods.

Work Schedules

Most physicians and surgeons work full time. Many physicians and surgeons work long, irregular, and overnight hours. Physicians and surgeons may travel between their offices and hospitals to care for their patients. While on call, a physician may need to address a patient's concerns over the phone or make an emergency visit to a hospital or nursing home.

How to Become a Physician or Surgeon

Physicians and surgeons have demanding education and training requirements. Physicians typically need a bachelor's degree, a degree from a medical school, which takes 4 years to complete, and, depending on their specialty, 3 to 7 years in internship and residency programs.

Education

Most applicants to medical school have at least a bachelor's degree, and many have advanced degrees. Although no specific major is required, students usually complete undergraduate work in biology, chemistry, physics, math, and English. Students also may take courses in the humanities and social sciences. In addition, some students volunteer at local hospitals or clinics to gain experience in a healthcare setting.

Medical schools are highly competitive. Most applicants must submit transcripts, scores from the Medical College Admission Test (MCAT), and letters of recommendation. Schools also consider an applicant's personality, leadership qualities, and participation in extracurricular activities. Most schools require applicants to interview with members of the admissions committee.

A few medical schools offer combined undergraduate and medical school programs that last 6 to 8 years.

Students spend most of the first 2 years of medical school in laboratories and classrooms, taking courses such as anatomy, biochemistry, pharmacology, psychology, medical ethics, and in the laws governing medicine. They also gain practical skills; learning to take medical histories, examine patients, and diagnose illnesses.

During their last 2 years, medical students work with patients under the supervision of experienced physicians in hospitals and clinics. Through rotations in internal medicine, family practice, obstetrics and gynecology, pediatrics, psychiatry, and surgery, they gain experience in diagnosing and treating illnesses in a variety of areas.

Training

After medical school, almost all graduates enter a residency program in their specialty of interest. A residency usually takes place in a hospital and varies in duration, generally lasting from 3 to 7 years, depending on the specialty.

Licenses, Certifications, and Registrations

All states require physicians and surgeons to be licensed; requirements vary by state. To qualify for a license, candidates must graduate from an accredited medical school and complete residency training in their specialty.

All physicians and surgeons also must pass a standardized national licensure exam. M.D.s take the U.S. Medical Licensing Examination (USMLE). D.O.s take the Comprehensive Osteopathic Medical Licensing Examination (COMLEX-USA). For specific state information about licensing, contact your state's medical board.

Certification is not required for physicians and surgeons; however, it may increase their employment opportunities. M.D.s and D.O.s seeking board certification in a specialty may spend up to 7 years in residency training; the length of time varies with the specialty. To become board certified, candidates must complete a residency program and pass a specialty certification exam from a certifying board including the American Board of Medical Specialties (ABMS), the American Osteopathic Association (AOA), or the American Board of Physician Specialties (ABPS).

Important Qualities

Communication skills. Physicians and surgeons need to be excellent communicators. They must communicate effectively with their patients and other healthcare support staff.

Compassion. Patients who are sick or injured may be in extreme pain or distress. Physicians and surgeons must treat patients and their families with compassion and understanding.

Detail oriented. Patients must receive appropriate treatment and medications. Physicians and surgeons must accurately monitor and record various pieces of information related to patient care.

Dexterity. Physicians and surgeons may work with very precise and sometimes sharp tools, and mistakes can have serious consequences.

Leadership skills. Physicians who work in their own practice must manage a staff of other professionals.

Organizational skills. Good recordkeeping and other organizational skills are critical in both medical and business settings.

Patience. Physicians and surgeons may work for long periods with patients who need special attention. Persons who fear medical treatment may require more patience.

Physical stamina. Physicians and surgeons should be comfortable lifting or turning disabled patients, or performing other physical tasks. Surgeons may spend a great deal of time bending over patients during surgery.

Problem-solving skills. Physicians and surgeons need to evaluate patients' symptoms and administer the appropriate treatments. They need to do this quickly if a patient's life is threatened.

Pay

Wages for physicians and surgeons are among the highest of all occupations, with a median wage equal to or greater than $208,000 per year. Median wages showing the differences in pay between types of physicians and surgeons are not available,

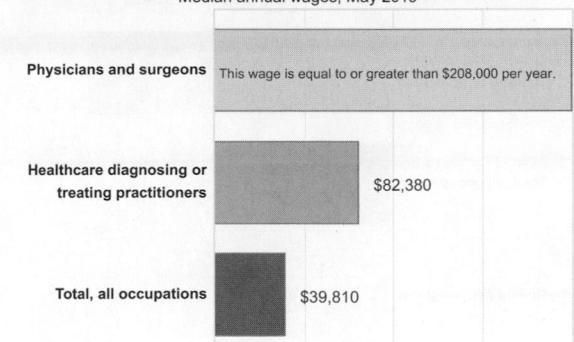

Physicians and Surgeons
Median annual wages, May 2019

Physicians and surgeons	This wage is equal to or greater than $208,000 per year.
Healthcare diagnosing or treating practitioners	$82,380
Total, all occupations	$39,810

Note: All Occupations includes all occupations in the U.S. Economy.
Source: U.S. Bureau of Labor Statistics, Occupational Employment Statistics.

but mean (average) annual wages for physicians and surgeons in May 2019 were as follows:

Anesthesiologists	$261,730
Surgeons	252,040
Obstetricians and gynecologists	233,610
Psychiatrists	220,430
Family and general practitioners	213,270
Physicians and surgeons, all other	203,450
Internists, general	201,440
Pediatricians, general	184,410

Many physicians and surgeons work long, irregular, and overnight hours. Physicians and surgeons may travel between their offices and hospitals to care for their patients. While on call, a physician may need to address a patient's concerns over the phone or make an emergency visit to a hospital or nursing home.

Job Outlook

Overall employment of physicians and surgeons is projected to grow 4 percent from 2019 to 2029, about as fast as the average for all occupations.

The growing and aging population is expected to drive overall growth in the demand for physician services. As the older population grows and rates of chronic illnesses increase, consumers will seek high levels of care that use the latest technologies, diagnostic tests, and therapies.

Demand for most types of physicians and surgeons is expected to increase despite factors that can temper growth. New technologies, such as improved information technologies or remote monitoring, are expected to allow physicians to treat more patients in the same amount of time. If adopted, new technologies can reduce the number of physicians who would be needed to complete the same tasks. In addition, physician assistants and nurse practitioners can do many of the routine duties of physicians and may be used to reduce costs at hospitals and doctor's offices.

Physicians and Surgeons
Percent change in employment, projected 2019-29

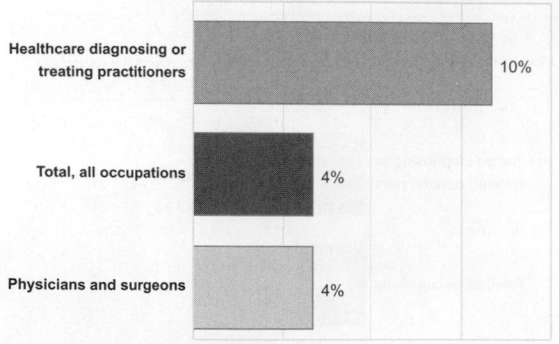

Note: All Occupations includes all occupations in the U.S. Economy.
Source: U.S. Bureau of Labor Statistics, Employment Projections program.

Demand for physicians' services is sensitive to changes in healthcare reimbursement policies. Consumers may seek fewer physician services if changes to health coverage result in higher out-of-pocket costs for them.

Employment projections data for physicians and surgeons, 2019-29

Occupational Title	SOC Code	Employment, 2019	Projected Employment, 2029	Change, 2019-29 Percent	Change, 2019-29 Numeric
SOURCE: U.S. Bureau of Labor Statistics, Employment Projections program					
Physicians and surgeons	—	752,400	779,700	4	27,300
Anesthesiologists	29-1211	33,800	34,000	0	200
Family medicine physicians	29-1215	119,300	126,600	6	7,300
General internal medicine physicians	29-1216	49,500	49,200	-1	-300
Obstetricians and gynecologists	29-1218	20,300	20,100	-1	-300
Pediatricians, general	29-1221	32,500	32,000	-2	-500
Psychiatrists	29-1223	27,900	31,300	12	3,300

Employment projections data for physicians and surgeons, 2019-29

Occupational Title	SOC Code	Employment, 2019	Projected Employment, 2029	Change, 2019-29 Percent	Change, 2019-29 Numeric
Physicians, all other; and ophthalmologists, except pediatric	29-1228	429,500	447,900	4	18,500
Surgeons, except ophthalmologists	29-1248	39,600	38,800	-2	-900

State & Area Data
Occupational Employment Statistics (OES)
The Occupational Employment Statistics (OES) program produces employment and wage estimates annually for over 800 occupations. These estimates are available for the nation as a whole, for individual states, and for metropolitan and nonmetropolitan areas.

Contacts for More Information
For more information about physicians and surgeons, visit
➤ American Medical Association
➤ American Osteopathic Association

For more information about various medical specialties, visit
➤ American Academy of Family Physicians
➤ American Board of Medical Specialties
➤ American Board of Physician Specialties
➤ American Congress of Obstetricians and Gynecologists
➤ American College of Surgeons

For a list of medical schools and residency programs, as well as for general information on premedical education, financial aid, and medicine as a career, visit
➤ Association of American Medical Colleges
➤ American Association of Colleges of Osteopathic Medicine

For information about licensing, visit
➤ Federation of State Medical Boards

Podiatrists

Summary

Quick Facts: Podiatrists

2019 Median Pay	$126,240 per year $60.69 per hour
Typical Entry-Level Education	Doctoral or professional degree
Work Experience in a Related Occupation	None
On-the-job Training	Internship/residency
Number of Jobs, 2019	10,500
Job Outlook, 2019-29	0% (Little or no change)
Employment Change, 2019-29	0

What Podiatrists Do
Podiatrists provide medical and surgical care for people with foot, ankle, and lower leg problems.

Work Environment
Most podiatrists work in offices of podiatry, either on their own or with other podiatrists. Some work in group practices with other physicians or specialists. Others work in private and public hospitals, in outpatient care centers, or for the government.

How to Become a Podiatrist
Podiatrists must earn a Doctor of Podiatric Medicine (DPM) degree and complete a 3-year residency program. Every state requires podiatrists to be licensed.

Podiatrists may diagnose foot, ankle, and lower leg problems through x rays.

Pay

The median annual wage for podiatrists was $126,240 in May 2019.

Job Outlook

Employment of podiatrists is projected to show little or no change from 2019 to 2029. Despite limited employment growth, some podiatrists will be needed to replace those who leave the occupation.

State & Area Data

Explore resources for employment and wages by state and area for podiatrists.

What Podiatrists Do

Podiatrists provide medical and surgical care for people with foot, ankle, and lower leg problems. They diagnose illnesses, treat injuries, and perform surgery involving the lower extremities.

Duties

Podiatrists typically do the following:

- Assess the condition of a patient's feet, ankles, or lower legs by reviewing the patient's medical history, listening to his or her concerns, and performing a physical examination
- Diagnose foot, ankle, and lower leg problems through physical exams, x rays, medical laboratory tests, and other methods
- Provide treatment for foot, ankle, and lower leg ailments, such as prescribing special shoe inserts (orthotics) to improve a patient's mobility
- Perform foot and ankle surgeries, such as removing bone spurs, fracture repairs, and correcting other foot and ankle deformities
- Advise and instruct patients on foot and ankle care and on general wellness techniques

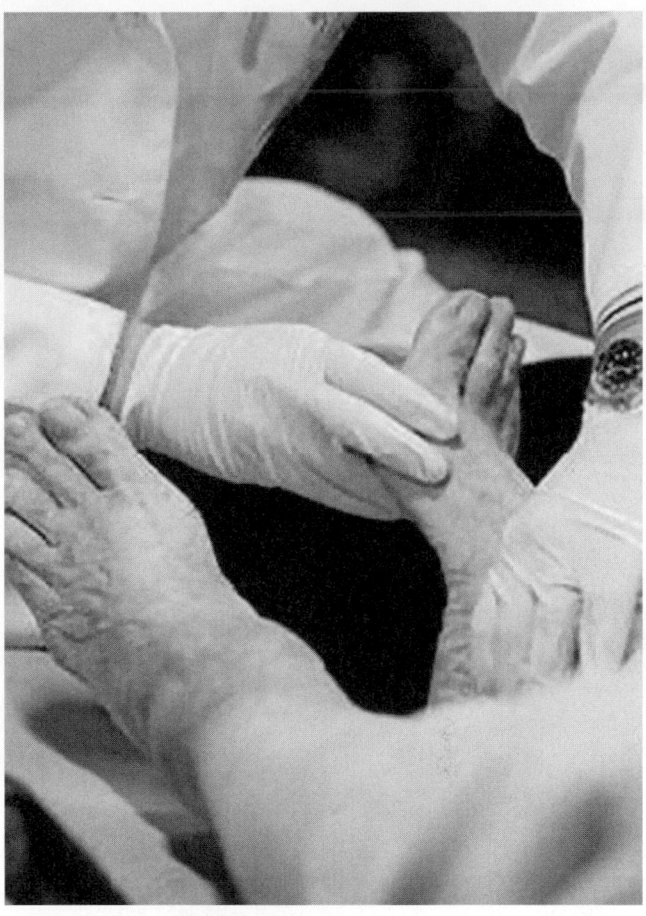

Podiatrists treat injuries involving the lower extremities.

- Prescribe medications
- Coordinate patient care with other physicians
- Refer patients to other physicians or specialists if they detect larger health problems, such as diabetes or vascular disease
- Conduct research, read journals, and attend conferences to keep up with advances in podiatric medicine and surgery

Podiatrists treat a variety of foot and ankle ailments, including calluses, ingrown toenails, heel spurs, arthritis, congenital foot and ankle deformities, and arch problems. They also treat foot and leg problems associated with diabetes and other diseases. Some podiatrists spend most of their time performing surgery, such as foot and ankle reconstruction. Others may choose a specialty such as sports medicine, pediatrics, or diabetic foot care.

Podiatrists who own their practice may spend time on business-related activities, such as hiring employees and managing inventory.

Work Environment

Podiatrists held about 10,500 jobs in 2019. The largest employers of podiatrists were as follows:

Offices of other health practitioners 62%
Offices of physicians 14

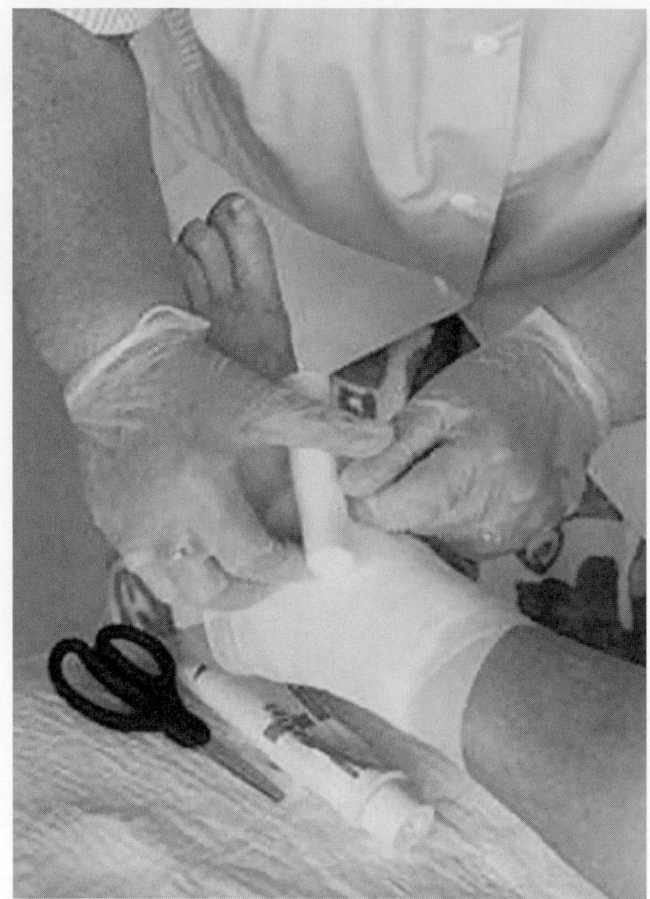

Patients with diabetes may develop foot problems that require the care of a podiatrist.

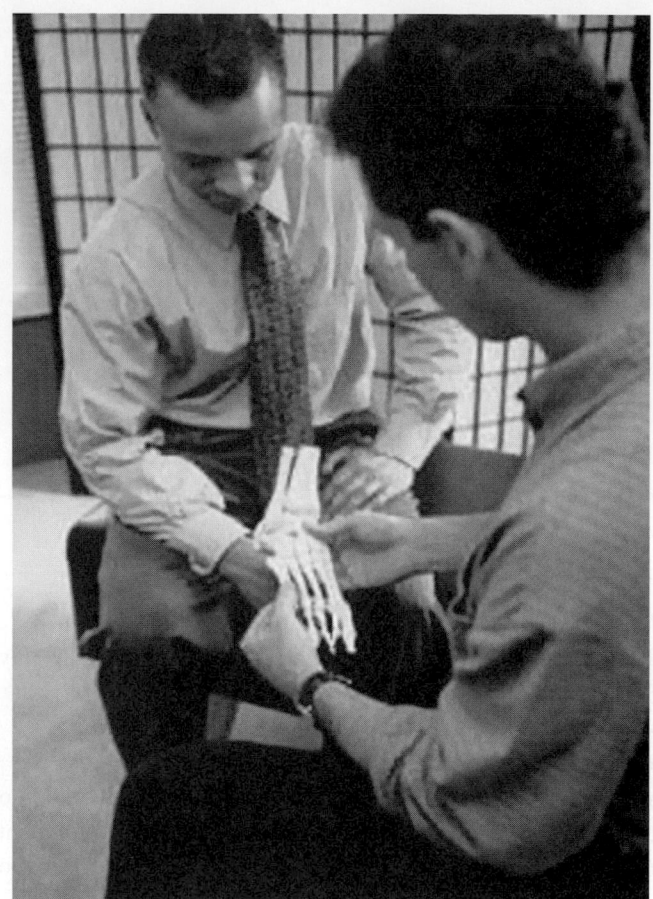

Podiatrists listen to patients' concerns about their feet, ankles, or lower legs.

Federal government, excluding postal service 9

Hospitals; state, local, and private 7

Self-employed workers.. 5

Podiatrists' offices are included in offices of other healthcare practitioners.

Some podiatrists work in group practices with other physicians or specialists. Podiatrists may work closely with physicians and surgeons, physician assistants, nurse practitioners, registered nurses, and medical assistants.

Work Schedules

Most podiatrists work full time. Podiatrists' offices may be open in the evenings or on weekends to accommodate patients. Self-employed podiatrists or those who own their practice may set their own hours. In hospitals, podiatrists may have to work occasional nights or weekends, or may be on call.

How to Become a Podiatrist

Podiatrists must earn a Doctor of Podiatric Medicine (DPM) degree and complete a 3-year residency program. Every state requires podiatrists to be licensed.

Education

Podiatrists must have a Doctor of Podiatric Medicine (DPM) degree from an accredited college of podiatric medicine. A DPM degree program takes 4 years to complete. In 2017, there were 9 colleges of podiatric medicine accredited by the Council on Podiatric Medical Education.

Admission to podiatric medicine programs requires at least 3 years of undergraduate education, including specific courses in laboratory sciences such as biology, chemistry, and physics, as well as general coursework in subjects such as English. In practice, nearly all prospective podiatrists earn a bachelor's degree before attending a college of podiatric medicine. Admission to DPM programs requires taking the Medical College Admission Test (MCAT).

Courses for a DPM degree are similar to those for other medical degrees. They include anatomy, physiology, pharmacology, and pathology, among other subjects. During their last 2 years, podiatric medical students gain supervised experience by completing clinical rotations.

Training

After earning a DPM, podiatrists must apply to and complete a 3-year podiatric medicine and surgery residency (PMSR) program. Residency programs take place in hospitals and provide both medical and surgical experience.

Podiatrists may complete additional training in specific fellowship areas, such as podiatric wound care or diabetic foot care, among others.

Licenses, Certifications, and Registrations

Podiatrists in every state must be licensed. Podiatrists must pay a fee and pass all parts of the American Podiatric Medical Licensing Exam (APMLE), offered by the National Board of Podiatric Medical Examiners. Some states also require podiatrists to take a state-specific exam.

Many podiatrists choose to become board certified. Certification generally requires a combination of work experience and passing an exam. Board certification is offered by the American Board of Foot and Ankle Surgery, the American Board of Podiatric Medicine, and the American Board of Multiple Specialties in Podiatry.

Important Qualities

Compassion. Since podiatrists provide care for patients who may be in pain, they must treat patients with compassion and understanding.

Critical-thinking skills. Podiatrists must have a sharp, analytical mind to correctly diagnose a patient and determine the best course of treatment.

Detail oriented. To provide safe, effective healthcare, a podiatrist should be detail oriented. For example, a podiatrist must pay attention to a patient's medical history as well as current conditions when diagnosing a problem.

Interpersonal skills. Because podiatrists spend much of their time interacting with patients, they should listen well and communicate effectively. For example, they should be able to tell a patient who is slated to undergo surgery what to expect and calm his or her fears.

Pay

The median annual wage for podiatrists was $126,240 in May 2019. The median wage is the wage at which half the workers in an occupation earned more than that amount and half earned less. The lowest 10 percent earned less than $54,150, and the highest 10 percent earned more than $208,000.

In May 2019, the median annual wages for podiatrists in the top industries in which they worked were as follows:

Offices of physicians	$141,920
Offices of other health practitioners	125,330
Hospitals; state, local, and private	124,200
Federal government, excluding postal service	116,900

Most podiatrists work full time. Podiatrists' offices may be open in the evenings or on weekends to accommodate patients. Self-employed podiatrists or those who own their practice may set their own hours. In hospitals, podiatrists may have to work occasional nights or weekends, or may be on call.

Job Outlook

Employment of podiatrists is projected to show little or no change from 2019 to 2029.

The U.S. population continues to age and to see an associated increase in its rates of chronic diseases, such as diabetes and obesity. As a result, people will continue to have mobility and foot-related problems, and podiatrists will be needed to treat many of these conditions. However, demand for podiatrists is expected to be limited because many patients may acquire services from a non-podiatrist physician or other appropriate caregiver.

Job Prospects

Despite limited employment growth, about 500 openings for podiatrists are projected each year, on average, over the decade.

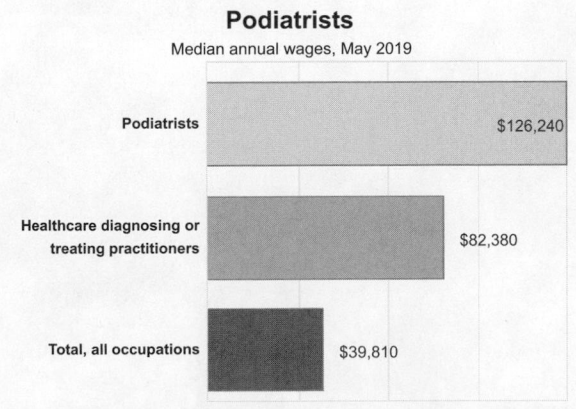

Podiatrists
Median annual wages, May 2019

Podiatrists $126,240
Healthcare diagnosing or treating practitioners $82,380
Total, all occupations $39,810

Note: All Occupations includes all occupations in the U.S. Economy.
Source: U.S. Bureau of Labor Statistics, Occupational Employment Statistics.

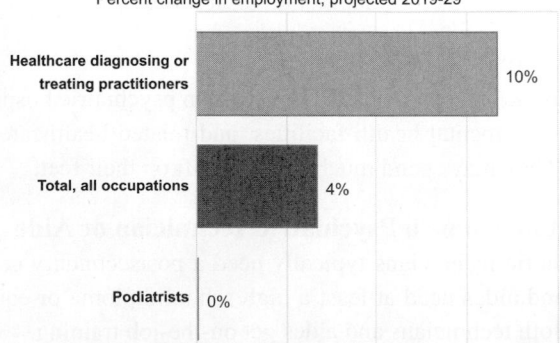

Podiatrists
Percent change in employment, projected 2019-29

Healthcare diagnosing or treating practitioners 10%
Total, all occupations 4%
Podiatrists 0%

Note: All Occupations includes all occupations in the U.S. Economy.
Source: U.S. Bureau of Labor Statistics, Employment Projections program.

Nearly all of those openings are expected to result from the need to replace workers who transfer to different occupations or exit the labor force, such as to retire.

Employment projections data for podiatrists, 2019-29					
Occupational Title	SOC Code	Employment, 2019	Projected Employment, 2029	Change, 2019-29	
				Percent	Numeric
SOURCE: U.S. Bureau of Labor Statistics, Employment Projections program					
Podiatrists	29-1081	10,500	10,600	0	0

State & Area Data
Occupational Employment Statistics (OES)
The Occupational Employment Statistics (OES) program produces employment and wage estimates annually for over 800 occupations. These estimates are available for the nation as a whole, for individual states, and for metropolitan and nonmetropolitan areas.

Contacts for More Information
For more information about podiatrists, visit
➤ American Podiatric Medical Association

For information on colleges of podiatric medicine and their entrance requirements, curricula, and student financial aid, visit
➤ American Association of Colleges of Podiatric Medicine

For a list of accredited podiatric programs and residency programs, visit
➤ Council on Podiatric Medical Education

For more information about the podiatric licensing exam, visit
➤ National Board of Podiatric Medical Examiners

For more information about board certification, visit
➤ American Board of Foot and Ankle Surgery
➤ American Board of Podiatric Medicine
➤ American Board of Multiple Specialties in Podiatry

Psychiatric Technicians and Aides

Summary

Quick Facts: Psychiatric Technicians and Aides

2019 Median Pay	$32,020 per year $15.40 per hour
Typical Entry-Level Education	See below
Work Experience in a Related Occupation	See below
On-the-job Training	Short-term on-the-job training
Number of Jobs, 2019	142,300
Job Outlook, 2019-29	12% (Much faster than average)
Employment Change, 2019-29	17,500

What Psychiatric Technicians and Aides Do
Psychiatric technicians and aides care for people who have mental illness and developmental disabilities.

Work Environment
Psychiatric technicians and aides work in psychiatric hospitals, residential mental health facilities, and related healthcare settings. They may spend much of their shift on their feet.

How to Become a Psychiatric Technician or Aide
Psychiatric technicians typically need a postsecondary certificate, and aides need at least a high school diploma or equivalent. Both technicians and aides get on-the-job training.

Pay
The median annual wage for psychiatric aides was $31,110 in May 2019.

The median annual wage for psychiatric technicians was $33,780 in May 2019.

Job Outlook
Overall employment of psychiatric technicians and aides is projected to grow 12 percent from 2019 to 2029, much faster than the average for all occupations. Demand for this occupation will be affected by the growth of the older population. Older people typically experience higher rates of cognitive illnesses than younger people do.

State & Area Data
Explore resources for employment and wages by state and area for psychiatric technicians and aides.

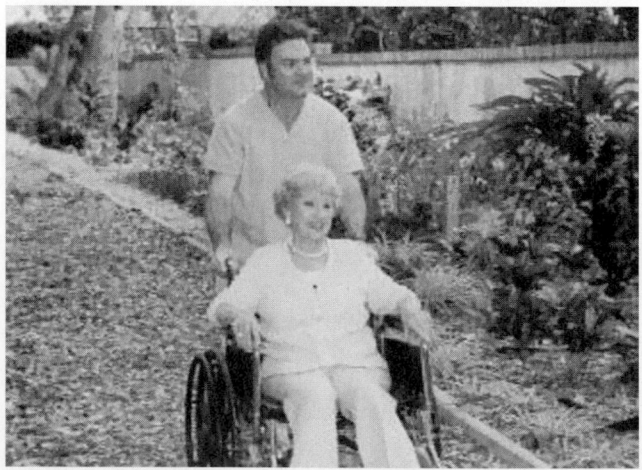

Psychiatric technicians and aides care for people who have mental illness and developmental disabilities.

What Psychiatric Technicians and Aides Do

Psychiatric technicians and aides care for people who have mental illness and developmental disabilities. Technicians typically provide therapeutic care and monitor their patients' conditions. Aides help patients in their daily activities and ensure a safe and clean environment.

Duties

Psychiatric technicians, sometimes called mental health technicians, typically do the following:

- Observe patients' behavior, listen to their concerns, and record their condition
- Lead patients in therapeutic and recreational activities
- Give medications and other treatments to patients, following instructions from doctors and other medical professionals
- Help with admitting and discharging patients
- Monitor patients' vital signs, such as their blood pressure
- Help patients with activities of daily living, including eating and bathing
- Restrain patients who may become physically violent

Psychiatric aides typically do the following:

- Monitor patients' behavior and location in a mental health-care facility
- Help patients with their daily living activities, such as bathing and dressing
- Serve meals and help patients eat
- Keep facilities clean by doing tasks such as changing bed linens
- Participate in group activities, such as playing sports and going on field trips
- Help transport patients within a hospital or residential care facility
- Restrain patients who may become physically violent

Many psychiatric technicians and aides work with patients who are severely developmentally disabled and need intensive care. Others work with patients undergoing rehabilitation for drug and alcohol addiction. The work of psychiatric technicians and aides varies with the types of patients they work with.

Psychiatric technicians and aides work as part of a medical team under the direction of physicians and with other team members, who may include psychiatrists, psychologists, psychiatric nurses, social workers, counselors, and therapists. For more information on the counselors and therapists they may work with, see the profiles on substance abuse, behavioral disorder, and mental health counselors, rehabilitation counselors, and marriage and family therapists.

Because they have such close contact with patients, psychiatric technicians and aides can have a great deal of influence on patients' outlook and treatment.

Work Environment

Psychiatric aides held about 59,500 jobs in 2019. The largest employers of psychiatric aides were as follows:

Psychiatric and substance abuse hospitals; state, local, and private 39%
State government, excluding education and hospitals 23

Psychiatric aides and technicians work as part of a medical team, under the direction of physicians.

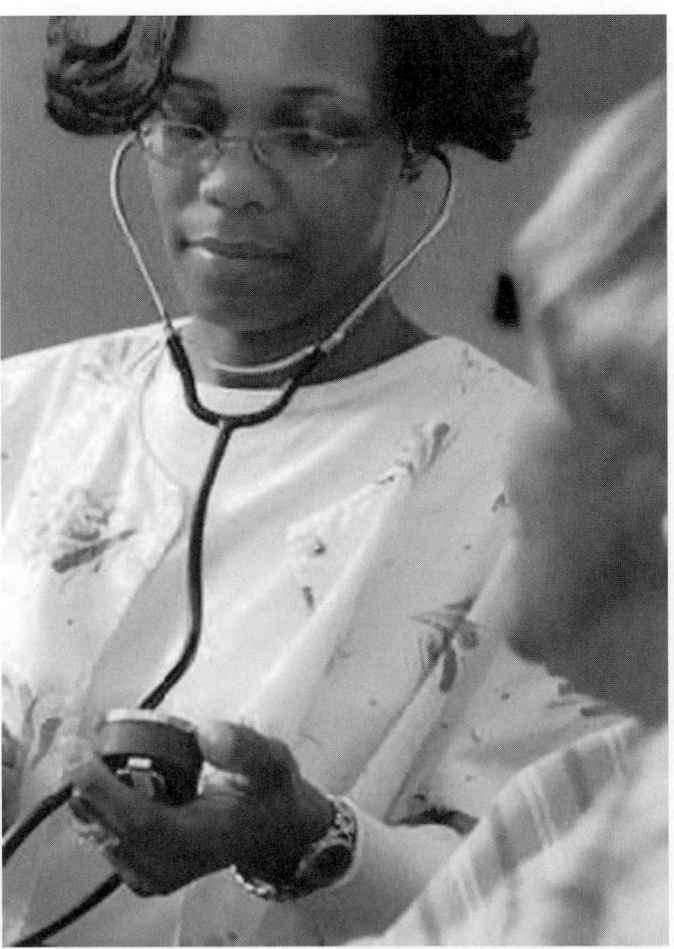

Psychiatric technicians may monitor patients' vital signs, such as taking their blood pressure.

Residential mental health and substance abuse
facilities 7

Psychiatric technicians held about 82,800 jobs in 2019. The largest employers of psychiatric technicians were as follows:

Psychiatric and substance abuse hospitals; state,
local, and private 40%
General medical and surgical hospitals; private........... 13
State government, excluding education and hospitals 8
Residential mental health and substance abuse
facilities 7
Outpatient mental health and substance abuse centers.. 5

Psychiatric technicians and aides may spend much of their shift on their feet. Some of the work that psychiatric aides do may be unpleasant. They may care for patients whose illnesses make them disoriented, uncooperative, or violent.

Injuries and Illnesses

Psychiatric technicians and aides have some of the highest rates of injuries and illnesses of all occupations. Their work requires many physically demanding tasks, such as lifting patients. They also work with patients who may be physically uncooperative, which can cause injuries.

Work Schedule

Psychiatric technicians and aides may work full time or part time. Because hospitals and residential facilities operate 24 hours a day, many psychiatric technicians and aides work nights, weekends, and holidays

How to Become a Psychiatric Technician or Aide

Psychiatric technicians typically need a postsecondary certificate, and aides need at least a high school diploma or equivalent. Both technicians and aides get on-the-job training.

Education

Psychiatric technicians typically have a postsecondary certificate. Often, they have experience as a nursing assistant or

Psychiatric technicians observe patients' behavior and listen to their concerns.

a licensed practical nurse and have completed postsecondary education in nursing.

Other psychiatric technicians may have a postsecondary certificate or associate's degree in psychiatric or mental health technology. These programs are offered by community colleges and technical schools and include courses in biology, psychology, and counseling. Psychiatric technician programs may include supervised work experience or cooperative programs, in which students gain academic credit for structured work experience.

Psychiatric aides typically need a high school diploma or equivalent.

Training

Psychiatric technicians and aides usually have a short period of on-the-job training before they can work without direct supervision.

Training may include working with patients while under the close supervision of an experienced technician or aide. Technicians and aides may also attend workshops, lectures, or in-service training.

Work Experience in a Related Occupation

Psychiatric technicians typically need clinical experience, which can be gained by working in occupations such as nursing assistant or licensed practical nurse.

Important Qualities

Compassion. Because psychiatric technicians and aides spend much of their time interacting with patients, they should be caring and want to help people.

Interpersonal skills. Psychiatric technicians and aides often provide ongoing care for patients, so they should develop a rapport with them. Gaining such rapport makes psychiatric technicians and aides better able to treat their patients and evaluate their condition.

Observational skills. Technicians must watch patients closely and be sensitive to any changes in behavior. For their safety and that of their patients, they must recognize signs of discomfort or trouble among patients.

Patience. Working with the mentally ill can be emotionally challenging. Psychiatric technicians and aides must stay calm in stressful situations.

Physical stamina. Psychiatric technicians and aides must lift, move, and sometimes restrain patients. They must also spend much of their time on their feet.

Licenses, Certifications, and Registrations

Most states do not require psychiatric technicians to have a license. California is one of the larger states that requires a license. In those states which license them, technicians usually are required to complete an accredited education program, pass an exam, and pay a fee to be licensed.

Psychiatric Technicians and Aides
Median annual wages, May 2019

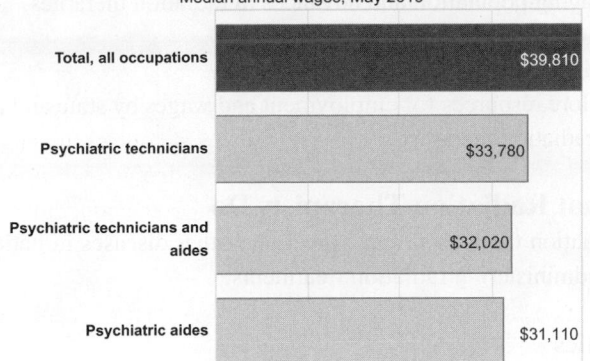

Total, all occupations	$39,810
Psychiatric technicians	$33,780
Psychiatric technicians and aides	$32,020
Psychiatric aides	$31,110

Psychiatric Technicians and Aides
Percent change in employment, projected 2019-29

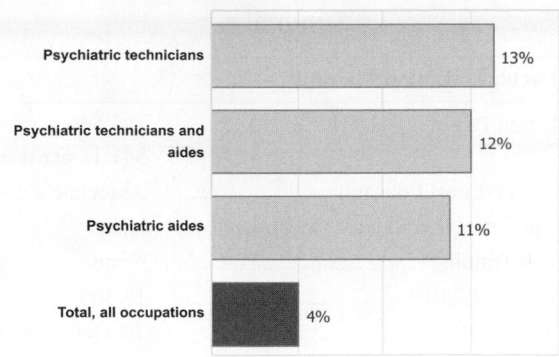

Psychiatric technicians	13%
Psychiatric technicians and aides	12%
Psychiatric aides	11%
Total, all occupations	4%

Note: All Occupations includes all occupations in the U.S. Economy.
Source: U.S. Bureau of Labor Statistics, Occupational Employment Statistics.

Note: All Occupations includes all occupations in the U.S. Economy.
Source: U.S. Bureau of Labor Statistics, Employment Projections program.

The American Association of Psychiatric Technicians offers four levels of certification for psychiatric technicians. The certifications allow technicians to show a high level of professional competency. Requirements vary by certification.

Psychiatric aides are not required to be licensed.

Pay

The median annual wage for psychiatric aides was $31,110 in May 2019. The median wage is the wage at which half the workers in an occupation earned more than that amount and half earned less. The lowest 10 percent earned less than $21,440, and the highest 10 percent earned more than $47,690.

The median annual wage for psychiatric technicians was $33,780 in May 2019. The lowest 10 percent earned less than $23,440, and the highest 10 percent earned more than $62,120.

In May 2019, the median annual wages for psychiatric aides in the top industries in which they worked were as follows:

Psychiatric and substance abuse hospitals; state, local, and private $33,680
State government, excluding education and hospitals 31,950
Residential mental health and substance abuse facilities 28,060

In May 2019, the median annual wages for psychiatric technicians in the top industries in which they worked were as follows:

State government, excluding education and hospitals $45,280
Psychiatric and substance abuse hospitals; state, local, and private 34,340
General medical and surgical hospitals; private..... 33,550
Residential mental health and substance abuse facilities 30,360
Outpatient mental health and substance abuse centers 29,240

Psychiatric technicians and aides may work full time or part time. Because hospitals and residential facilities operate

24 hours a day, many psychiatric technicians and aides work nights, weekends, and holidays.

Job Outlook

Overall employment of psychiatric technicians and aides is projected to grow 12 percent from 2019 to 2029, much faster than the average for all occupations.

Cognitive mental disorders, such as Alzheimer's disease and dementia, are more likely to occur among older persons. As the nation's population ages and people live longer, demand for psychiatric technicians and aides is expected to increase because these workers will be needed to care for patients affected by such disorders.

Psychiatric technicians and aides also will be needed in correctional facilities, to care for the aging prisoner population and for those with mental health issues.

Employment projections data for psychiatric technicians and aides, 2019-29					
Occupational Title	SOC Code	Employment, 2019	Projected Employment, 2029	Change, 2019-29	
				Percent	Numeric
SOURCE: U.S. Bureau of Labor Statistics, Employment Projections program					
Psychiatric technicians and aides	—	142,300	159,800	12	17,500
Psychiatric technicians	29-2053	82,800	93,800	13	11,000
Psychiatric aides	31-1133	59,500	66,000	11	6,500

State & Area Data
Occupational Employment Statistics (OES)

The Occupational Employment Statistics (OES) program produces employment and wage estimates annually for over 800 occupations. These estimates are available for the nation as a whole, for individual states, and for metropolitan and nonmetropolitan areas.

Contacts for More Information

For more information about psychiatric technicians and aides, visit
➤ American Association of Psychiatric Technicians

Radiation Therapists

Summary

Quick Facts: Radiation Therapists

2019 Median Pay	$85,560 per year $41.14 per hour
Typical Entry-Level Education	Associate's degree
Work Experience in a Related Occupation	None
On-the-job Training	None
Number of Jobs, 2019	18,500
Job Outlook, 2019-29	7% (Faster than average)
Employment Change, 2019-29	1,300

What Radiation Therapists Do

Radiation therapists treat cancer and other diseases in patients by administering radiation treatments.

Work Environment

Radiation therapists work in hospitals, offices of physicians, and outpatient centers. Most radiation therapists work full time.

How to Become a Radiation Therapist

Most radiation therapists complete programs that lead to an associate's degree or a bachelor's degree in radiation therapy. Radiation therapists must be licensed or certified in most states. Requirements vary by state, but often include passing a national certification exam.

Pay

The median annual wage for radiation therapists was $85,560 in May 2019.

Job Outlook

Employment of radiation therapists is projected to grow 7 percent from 2019 to 2029, faster than the average for all occupations. Demand for radiation therapists may stem from the aging population and advances in radiation therapies.

State & Area Data

Explore resources for employment and wages by state and area for radiation therapists.

What Radiation Therapists Do

Radiation therapists treat cancer and other diseases in patients by administering radiation treatments.

Duties

Radiation therapists typically do the following:

- Explain treatment plans to the patient and answer questions about treatment
- Protect the patients and themselves from improper exposure to radiation
- Determine the exact location of the area requiring treatment
- Calibrate and operate the machine to treat the patient with radiation
- Monitor the patient to check for unusual reactions to the treatment
- Keep detailed records of treatment

Radiation therapists operate machines, such as linear accelerators, to deliver concentrated radiation therapy to the region of a patient's tumor. Radiation treatment can shrink or remove cancers and tumors.

Radiation therapists are part of the oncology teams that treat patients with cancer. They often work with the following specialists:

- Radiation oncologists are physicians who specialize in radiation therapy
- Oncology nurses specialize in caring for patients with cancer
- Medical physicists help in planning of radiation treatments, develop better and safer radiation therapies, and check that radiation output is accurate

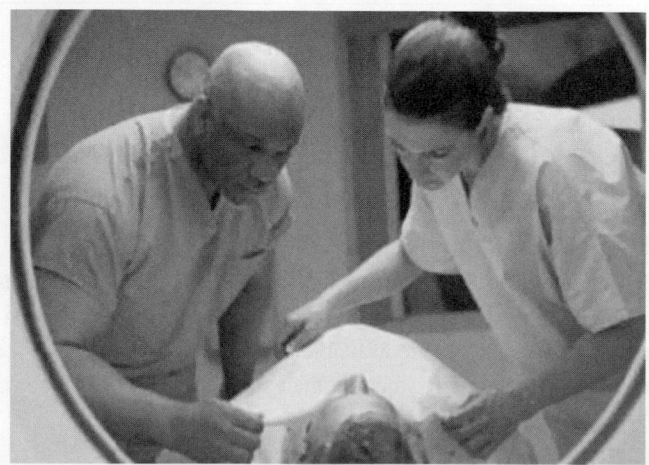

Radiation therapists treat cancer and other diseases in patients by administering radiation treatments.

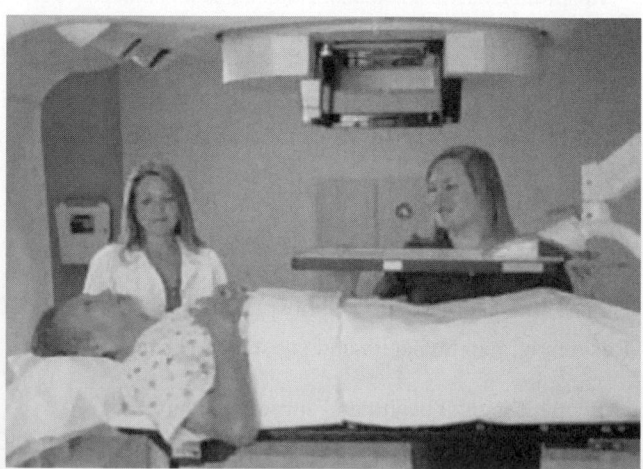

Radiation therapists are part of the oncology teams that treat patients with cancer.

Work Environment

Radiation therapists held about 18,500 jobs in 2019. The largest employers of radiation therapists were as follows:

Hospitals; state, local, and private 63%

Offices of physicians 24

Outpatient care centers 6

Radiation therapists are on their feet for long periods and may need to lift or turn disabled patients. Because they work with radiation and radioactive material, radiation therapists must follow safety procedures to make sure that they are not exposed to a potentially harmful amount of radiation. These procedures usually require therapists to stand in a different room while the patient undergoes radiation procedures.

Injuries and illnesses

Since radiation therapists administer radiation treatments over many years they should take precautions to limit exposure and be aware of the risks involved.

Work Schedules

Most radiation therapists work full time. Radiation therapists keep a regular work schedule because radiation therapy procedures are usually planned in advance.

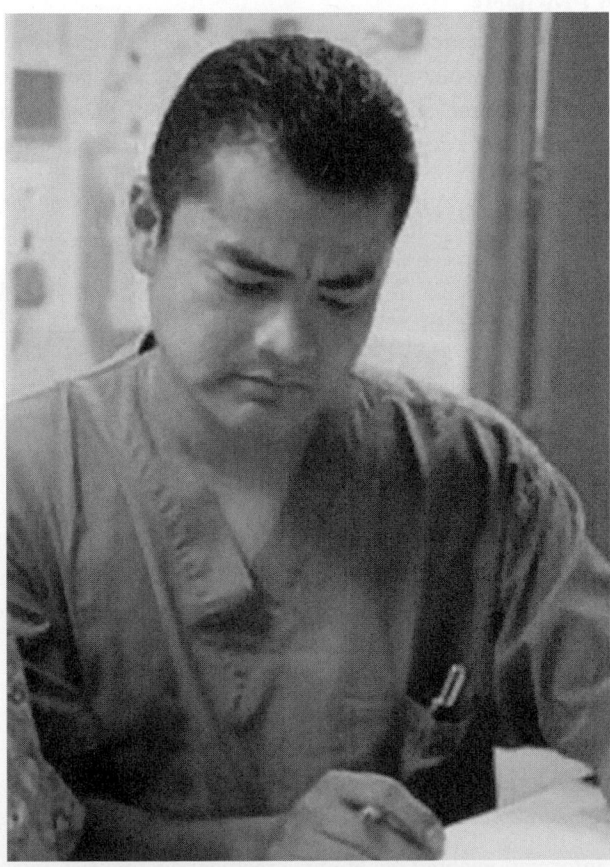

Radiation therapists work in hospitals, offices of physicians, and outpatient centers.

How to Become a Radiation Therapist

Most radiation therapists complete programs that lead to an associate's degree or bachelor's degree in radiation therapy. Radiation therapists must be licensed or certified in most states. Requirements vary by state, but often include passing a national certification exam.

Education

Employers usually prefer to hire applicants who have an associate's degree or a bachelor's degree in radiation therapy. However, candidates may qualify for some positions by completing a certificate program.

Radiation therapy programs include courses in radiation therapy procedures and the scientific theories behind them. These programs often include experience in a clinical setting and courses in human anatomy and physiology, physics, algebra, computer science, and research methodology. In 2016, there were about 110 accredited educational programs recognized by the American Registry of Radiologic Technologists (ARRT).

Important Qualities

Detail oriented. Radiation therapists must follow exact instructions and input exact measurements to make sure the patient is exposed to the correct amount of radiation.

Interpersonal skills. Radiation therapists work closely with patients. It is important that therapists be comfortable interacting with people who may be going through physical and emotional stress.

Physical stamina. Radiation therapists must be able to be on their feet for long periods and be able to lift and move patients who need assistance.

Technical skills. Radiation therapists work with computers and large pieces of technological equipment, so they must be comfortable operating those devices.

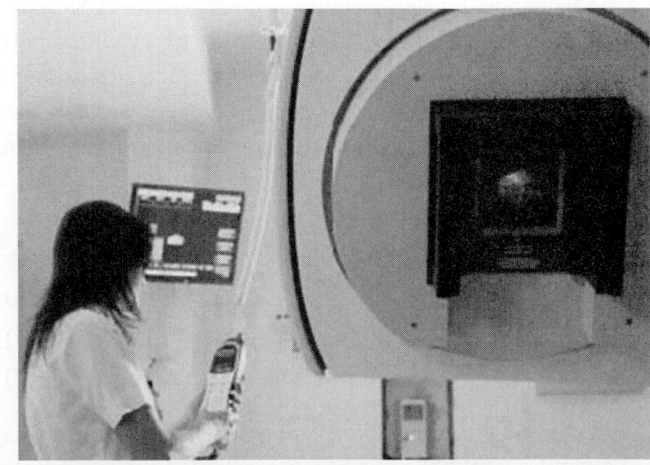

Radiation therapists must be licensed or certified in most states.

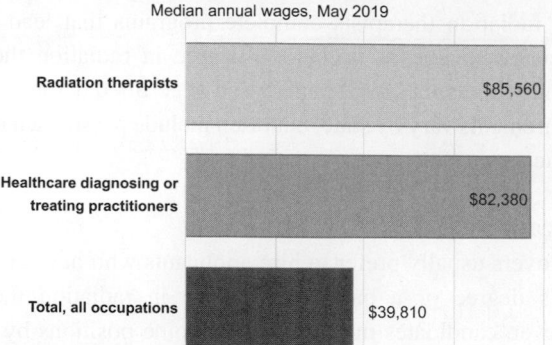

Radiation Therapists
Median annual wages, May 2019

- Radiation therapists — $85,560
- Healthcare diagnosing or treating practitioners — $82,380
- Total, all occupations — $39,810

Note: All Occupations includes all occupations in the U.S. Economy.
Source: U.S. Bureau of Labor Statistics, Occupational Employment Statistics.

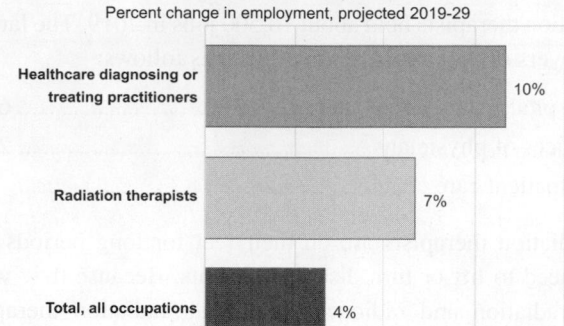

Radiation Therapists
Percent change in employment, projected 2019-29

- Healthcare diagnosing or treating practitioners — 10%
- Radiation therapists — 7%
- Total, all occupations — 4%

Note: All Occupations includes all occupations in the U.S. Economy.
Source: U.S. Bureau of Labor Statistics, Employment Projections program.

Licenses, Certifications, and Registrations

In most states, radiation therapists must be licensed or certified. Requirements vary by state, but typically include graduation from an accredited radiation therapy program and ARRT certification.

To become ARRT certified, an applicant must complete an accredited radiation therapy program, adhere to ARRT ethical standards, and pass the certification exam. The exam covers radiation protection and quality assurance, clinical concepts in radiation oncology, treatment planning, treatment delivery, and patient care and education. A list of accredited programs is available from ARRT.

Many jobs also require cardiopulmonary resuscitation (CPR) or basic life support (BLS) certification.

Advancement

With additional education and certification, therapists can become *medical dosimetrists*. Dosimetrists are responsible for calculating the correct dose of radiation that is used in the treatment of cancer patients.

Pay

The median annual wage for radiation therapists was $85,560 in May 2019. The median wage is the wage at which half the workers in an occupation earned more than that amount and half earned less. The lowest 10 percent earned less than $59,280, and the highest 10 percent earned more than $128,630.

In May 2019, the median annual wages for radiation therapists in the top industries in which they worked were as follows:

Outpatient care centers	$97,150
Offices of physicians	87,620
Hospitals; state, local, and private	83,900

Most radiation therapists work full time. Radiation therapists keep a regular work schedule because radiation therapy procedures are usually planned in advance.

Job Outlook

Employment of radiation therapists is projected to grow 7 percent from 2019 to 2029, faster than the average for all occupations.

The incidence of cancer increases as people age, so an aging population may increase demand for radiation therapists. Continued advancements in the detection of cancer and the development of more sophisticated treatment techniques may also lead to greater demand for radiation therapy.

Job Prospects

Candidates can expect competition for most radiation therapist positions. Jobseekers with prior work experience in patient care positions and more education, such as related allied health certifications or a relevant bachelor's degree, should have the best job opportunities.

Employment projections data for radiation therapists, 2019-29					
Occupational Title	SOC Code	Employment, 2019	Projected Employment, 2029	Change, 2019-29	
				Percent	Numeric
SOURCE: U.S. Bureau of Labor Statistics, Employment Projections program					
Radiation therapists	29-1124	18,500	19,900	7	1,300

State & Area Data
Occupational Employment Statistics (OES)

The Occupational Employment Statistics (OES) program produces employment and wage estimates annually for over 800 occupations. These estimates are available for the nation as a whole, for individual states, and for metropolitan and nonmetropolitan areas.

Contacts for More Information

For more information about radiation therapists, visit
➤ American Society of Radiologic Technologists
➤ The American Registry of Radiologic Technologists

For information about becoming a medical dosimetrist, visit
➤ American Association of Medical Dosimetrists

Radiologic and MRI Technologists

Summary

Quick Facts: Radiologic and MRI Technologists

2019 Median Pay	$62,280 per year
	$29.94 per hour
Typical Entry-Level Education	Associate's degree
Work Experience in a Related Occupation	See below
On-the-job Training	None
Number of Jobs, 2019	250,700
Job Outlook, 2019-29	7% (Faster than average)
Employment Change, 2019-29	16,800

What Radiologic and MRI Technologists Do

Radiologic technologists perform diagnostic imaging examinations on patients. MRI technologists operate magnetic resonance imaging (MRI) scanners to create diagnostic images.

Work Environment

Radiologic and MRI technologists work in healthcare facilities, and more than half work in hospitals.

How to Become a Radiologic or MRI Technologist

Radiologic technologists and MRI technologists typically need an associate's degree. Many MRI technologists start out as radiologic technologists and specialize later in their career. Radiologic technologists must be licensed or certified in most states. Few states license MRI technologists. Employers typically require or prefer prospective technologists to be certified even if the state does not require it.

Pay

The median annual wage for magnetic resonance imaging technologists was $73,410 in May 2019.

The median annual wage for radiologic technologists and technicians was $60,510 in May 2019.

Job Outlook

Overall employment of radiologic and MRI technologists is projected to grow 7 percent from 2019 to 2029, faster than the average for all occupations. As the population grows older, there will be an increase in medical conditions that require imaging as a tool for making diagnoses.

State & Area Data

Explore resources for employment and wages by state and area for radiologic and MRI technologists.

What Radiologic and MRI Technologists Do

Radiologic technologists, also known as *radiographers*, perform diagnostic imaging examinations, such as x rays, on patients. MRI technologists operate magnetic resonance imaging (MRI) scanners to create diagnostic images.

Duties

Radiologic and MRI technologists typically do the following:

- Adjust and maintain imaging equipment
- Precisely follow orders from physicians on what areas of the body to image
- Prepare patients for procedures, including taking a medical history and answering questions about the procedure
- Protect the patient by shielding exposed areas that do not need to be imaged
- Position the patient and the equipment in order to get the correct image
- Operate the computerized equipment to take the images
- Work with physicians to evaluate the images and to determine whether additional images need to be taken
- Keep detailed patient records

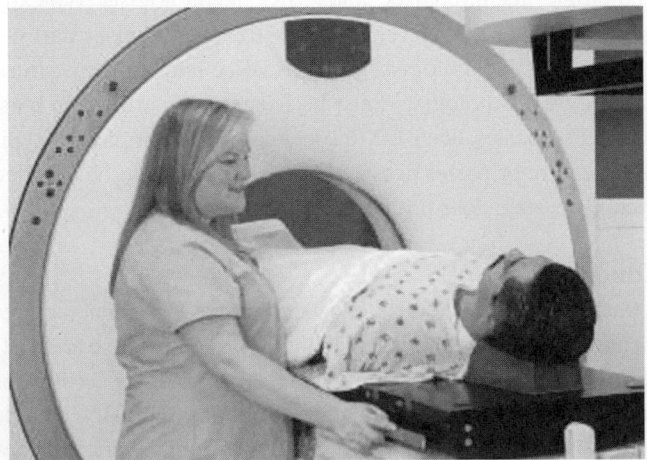

Radiologic and MRI technologists perform diagnostic imaging examinations, such as magnetic resonance, on patients.

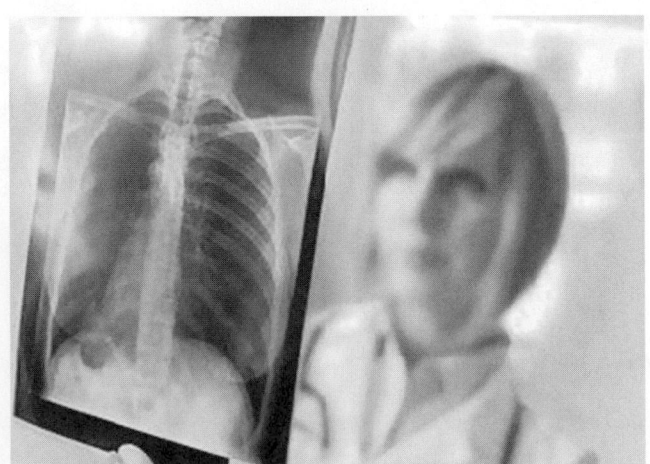

Radiologic technologists specialize in x-ray and computed tomography (CT) imaging.

Healthcare professionals use many types of equipment to diagnose patients. Radiologic technologists specialize in x-ray and computed tomography (CT) imaging. Some radiologic technologists prepare a mixture for the patient to drink that allows soft tissue to be viewed on the images that the radiologist reviews.

Radiologic technologists might also specialize in mammography. **Mammographers** use low-dose x-ray systems to produce images of the breast. Technologists may be certified in multiple specialties.

MRI technologists specialize in magnetic resonance imaging scanners. They inject patients with contrast dyes so that the images will show up on the scanner. The scanners use magnetic fields in combination with the contrast agent to produce images that a physician can use to diagnose medical problems.

Healthcare professionals who specialize in other diagnostic equipment include nuclear medicine technologists and diagnostic medical sonographers, and cardiovascular technologists and technicians, including vascular technologists.

Work Environment

Magnetic resonance imaging technologists held about 38,700 jobs in 2019. The largest employers of magnetic resonance imaging technologists were as follows:

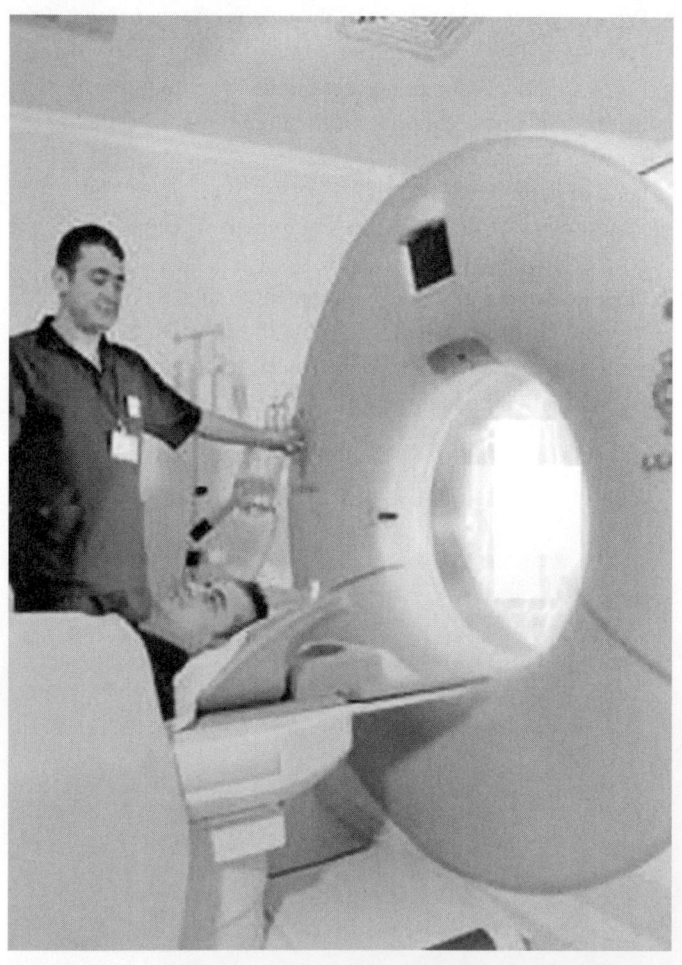

Radiologic and MRI technologists work in hospitals and other healthcare facilities.

Hospitals; state, local, and private	61%
Medical and diagnostic laboratories	18
Offices of physicians	14
Outpatient care centers	3

Radiologic technologists and technicians held about 212,000 jobs in 2019. The largest employers of radiologic technologists and technicians were as follows:

Hospitals; state, local, and private	60%
Offices of physicians	20
Outpatient care centers	7
Medical and diagnostic laboratories	7
Federal government, excluding postal service	3

Radiologic and MRI technologists are often on their feet for long periods and may need to lift or turn patients who are disabled.

Injuries and Illnesses

Like other healthcare workers, radiologic and MRI technologists may be exposed to infectious diseases. In addition, because radiologic technologists work with imaging equipment that uses radiation, they must wear badges that measure radiation levels in the radiation area. Detailed records are kept on their cumulative lifetime dose. Although radiation hazards exist in this occupation, they are minimized by the use of protective lead aprons, gloves, and other shielding devices, and by badges that monitor exposure to radiation.

Work Schedules

Most radiologic and MRI technologists work full time. Because imaging is sometimes needed in emergency situations, some technologists work evenings, weekends, or overnight.

How to Become a Radiologic or MRI Technologist

Radiologic technologists and MRI technologists typically need an associate's degree. Many MRI technologists start out as radiologic technologists and specialize later in their career. Radiologic technologists must be licensed or certified in most states. Few states license MRI technologists. Employers typically require or prefer prospective technologists to be certified even if the state does not require it.

Education

An associate's degree is the most common educational requirement for radiologic and MRI technologists. There also are post-secondary education programs that lead to graduate certificates or bachelor's degrees. Education programs typically include both classroom study and clinical work. Coursework includes anatomy, pathology, patient care, radiation physics and protection, and image evaluation.

Radiologic technologists must follow exact instructions to get the images needed to diagnose and treat the patient.

The Joint Review Committee on Education in Radiologic Technology (JRCERT) accredits programs in radiography and the American Registry of Magnetic Resonance Imaging Technologists (ARMRIT) accredits MRI programs. Completing an accredited program is required for licensure in some states.

High school students who are interested in radiologic or MRI technology should take courses that focus on math and science, such as anatomy, biology, chemistry, physiology, and physics.

Work Experience in a Related Occupation

MRI technologists typically have less than 5 years of work experience as radiologic technologists.

Licenses, Certifications, and Registrations

Radiologic technologists must be licensed or certified in most states. Few states license MRI technologists. Requirements vary by state.

To become licensed, technologists must usually graduate from an accredited program, and pass a certification exam from the state or obtain a certification from a certifying body. Certifications for radiologic technologists are available from the American Registry of Radiologic Technologists (ARRT). Certifications for MRI technologists are available from the ARRT and from the American Registry of Magnetic Resonance Imaging Technologists (ARMRIT). For specific licensure requirements for radiologic technologists and MRI technologists, contact the state's health board.

Employers typically require or prefer prospective technologists to be certified even if the state does not require it.

Important Qualities

Detail oriented. Radiologic and MRI technologists must follow exact instructions to get the images needed for diagnoses.

Interpersonal skills. Radiologic and MRI technologists work closely with patients who may be in extreme pain or mentally stressed. They must put the patient at ease to get usable images.

Math skills. Radiologic and MRI technologists may need to calculate and mix the right doses of chemicals used in imaging procedures.

Physical stamina. Radiologic and MRI technologists often work on their feet for long periods during their shift and they must lift and move patients who need assistance.

Technical skills. Radiologic and MRI technologists must understand how to operate complex machinery.

Pay

The median annual wage for magnetic resonance imaging technologists was $73,410 in May 2019. The median wage is the wage at which half the workers in an occupation earned more than that amount and half earned less. The lowest 10 percent earned less than $51,150, and the highest 10 percent earned more than $101,580.

The median annual wage for radiologic technologists and technicians was $60,510 in May 2019. The lowest 10 percent earned less than $41,480, and the highest 10 percent earned more than $89,760.

In May 2019, the median annual wages for magnetic resonance imaging technologists in the top industries in which they worked were as follows:

Outpatient care centers	$90,820
Medical and diagnostic laboratories	74,560
Hospitals; state, local, and private	72,750
Offices of physicians	72,400

In May 2019, the median annual wages for radiologic technologists and technicians in the top industries in which they worked were as follows:

Federal government, excluding postal service	$65,780

Radiologic and MRI Technologists
Median annual wages, May 2019

Occupation	Median annual wage
Magnetic resonance imaging technologists	$73,410
Radiologic and MRI technologists	$62,280
Radiologic technologists and technicians	$60,510
Health technologists and technicians	$44,380
Total, all occupations	$39,810

Note: All Occupations includes all occupations in the U.S. Economy.
Source: U.S. Bureau of Labor Statistics, Occupational Employment Statistics.

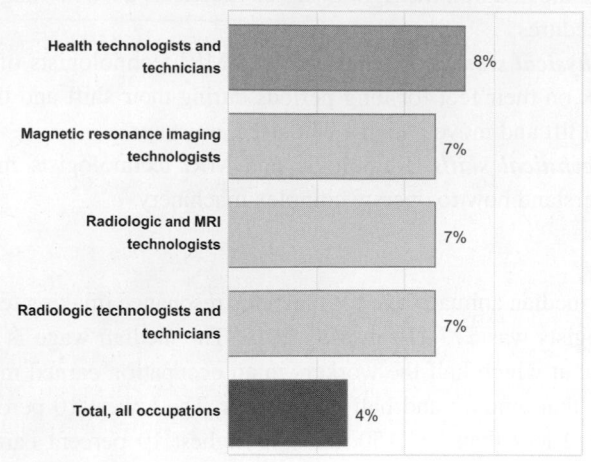

Radiologic and MRI Technologists
Percent change in employment, projected 2019-29

Health technologists and technicians	8%
Magnetic resonance imaging technologists	7%
Radiologic and MRI technologists	7%
Radiologic technologists and technicians	7%
Total, all occupations	4%

Note: All Occupations includes all occupations in the U.S. Economy.
Source: U.S. Bureau of Labor Statistics, Employment Projections program.

Outpatient care centers	63,000
Hospitals; state, local, and private	61,670
Medical and diagnostic laboratories	61,270
Offices of physicians	55,170

Most radiologic and MRI technologists work full time. Because imaging is sometimes needed in emergency situations, some technologists work evenings, weekends, or overnight.

Job Outlook

Employment of radiologic technologists is projected to grow 7 percent from 2019 to 2029, faster than the average for all occupations. Employment of MRI technologists is projected to grow 7 percent from 2019 to 2029, faster than the average for all occupations.

As the baby-boom population grows older, there may be an increase in medical conditions, such as cancer and Alzheimer's disease, which require imaging as a tool for making diagnoses. Radiologic and MRI technologists will be needed to take the images.

Job Prospects

Technologists who graduate from accredited programs and those with multiple certifications will have the best job prospects.

Employment projections data for radiologic and MRI technologists, 2019-29					
Occupational Title	SOC Code	Employment, 2019	Projected Employment, 2029	Change, 2019-29	
				Percent	Numeric
Radiologic and MRI technologists	—	250,700	267,600	7	16,800
Radiologic technologists and technicians	29-2034	212,000	226,100	7	14,100
Magnetic resonance imaging technologists	29-2035	38,700	41,400	7	2,700

SOURCE: U.S. Bureau of Labor Statistics, Employment Projections program

State & Area Data
Occupational Employment Statistics (OES)

The Occupational Employment Statistics (OES) program produces employment and wage estimates annually for over 800 occupations. These estimates are available for the nation as a whole, for individual states, and for metropolitan and nonmetropolitan areas.

Contacts for More Information

For more information about radiologic and MRI technology, visit
➤ American Society of Radiologic Technologists
➤ Joint Review Committee on Education in Radiologic Technology
➤ American Registry of Radiologic Technologists
➤ American Registry of Magnetic Resonance Imaging Technologists

Recreational Therapists

Summary

Quick Facts: Recreational Therapists

2019 Median Pay	$48,220 per year $23.18 per hour
Typical Entry-Level Education	Bachelor's degree
Work Experience in a Related Occupation	None
On-the-job Training	None
Number of Jobs, 2019	19,900
Job Outlook, 2019-29	8% (Much faster than average)
Employment Change, 2019-29	1,700

What Recreational Therapists Do

Recreational therapists plan, direct, and coordinate recreation-based treatment programs for people with disabilities, injuries, or illnesses.

Work Environment

Recreational therapists work in a variety of settings, including hospitals, nursing homes, and government parks and recreation departments. Most therapists work full time.

How to Become a Recreational Therapist

Recreational therapists typically need a bachelor's degree. Many employers require therapists to be certified.

Recreational therapists use a variety of modalities, including arts and crafts, to help maintain or improve a patient's physical, social, and emotional well-being.

Pay
The median annual wage for recreational therapists was $48,220 in May 2019.

Job Outlook
Employment of recreational therapists is projected to grow 8 percent from 2019 to 2029, much faster than the average for all occupations. However, because it is a small occupation, the fast growth will result in only about 1,700 new jobs over the 10-year period.

State & Area Data
Explore resources for employment and wages by state and area for recreational therapists.

What Recreational Therapists Do
Recreational therapists plan, direct, and coordinate recreation-based treatment programs for people with disabilities, injuries, or illnesses. These therapists use a variety of modalities, including arts and crafts; drama, music, and dance; sports and games; aquatics; and community outings to help maintain or improve a patient's physical, social, and emotional well-being.

Duties
Recreational therapists typically do the following:

- Assess patients' needs using observation, medical records, tests, and discussions with other healthcare professionals, patients' families, and patients
- Develop treatment plans and programs that meet patients' needs and interests
- Plan and implement interventions to support the client in meeting his or her goals
- Engage patients in therapeutic activities, such as exercise, games, and community outings
- Help patients learn social skills needed to become or remain independent
- Teach patients about ways to cope with stress, anxiety, or depression
- Document and analyze a patient's progress
- Evaluate interventions for effectiveness

Recreational therapists help people reduce depression, stress, and anxiety; recover basic physical and mental abilities; build confidence; and socialize effectively.

They use interventions, such as arts and crafts, dance, or sports, to help their patients. For example, a recreational therapist can help a patient who is paralyzed on one side of his or her body by teaching patients to adapt activities, such as casting a fishing rod or swinging a golf club, by using his or her functional side.

Therapists often treat specific groups of patients, such as children with cancer. Therapists may use activities such as kayaking or a ropes course to teach patients to stay active and to form social relationships.

Recreational therapists help people with disabilities integrate into the community by teaching them how to use community resources and recreational activities. For example, therapists may teach a patient who uses a wheelchair how to use public transportation.

Therapists may also provide interventions for patients who need help developing social and coping skills. For example, a therapist may use a therapy dog to help patients manage their depression or anxiety.

Therapists may work with physicians or surgeons, registered nurses, psychologists, social workers, physical therapists, teachers, or occupational therapists. Recreational therapists are different from recreation workers, who organize recreational activities primarily for enjoyment.

Work Environment
Recreational therapists held about 19,900 jobs in 2019. The largest employers of recreational therapists were as follows:

Hospitals; state, local, and private 38%
Government 17

Recreational therapists engage patients in therapeutic activities, such as swimming.

Therapy may be provided in a clinical setting or out in a community.

Nursing care facilities (skilled nursing facilities)	13
Ambulatory healthcare services	9
Social assistance	7

They use offices for planning or other administrative activities, such as patient assessment, but may travel when working with patients. Therapy may be provided in a clinical setting or out in a community. For example, therapists may take their patients to community recreation centers or parks for sports and other outdoor activities.

Some therapists may spend a lot of time on their feet actively working with patients. They may also need to physically assist patients or lift heavy objects such as wheelchairs.

Work Schedules

Most recreational therapists work full time. Some recreational therapists work evenings and weekends to meet the needs of their patients.

How to Become a Recreational Therapist

Recreational therapists typically need a bachelor's degree. Many employers require therapists to be certified by the National Council for Therapeutic Recreation Certification (NCTRC).

Education

Recreational therapists typically need a bachelor's degree, usually in recreational therapy or a related field such as recreation and leisure studies.

Recreational therapy programs include courses in assessment, human anatomy, medical and psychiatric terminology, characteristics of illnesses and disabilities, and the use of assistive devices and technology. Bachelor's degree programs usually include an internship.

Licenses, Certifications, and Registrations

Most employers prefer to hire certified recreational therapists. The NCTRC offers the Certified Therapeutic Recreation

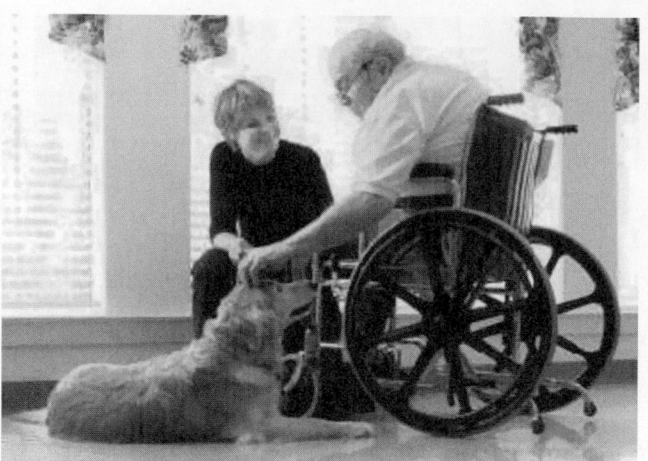

Most recreational therapists need a bachelor's degree in recreational therapy or a related field.

Specialist (CTRS) credential. Candidates may qualify for certification through one of three pathways. The first option requires a bachelor's degree in recreational therapy, completion of a supervised internship of at least 560 hours, and passing an exam. The other options also require passing an exam, but allow candidates with a bachelor's degree in an unrelated subject to qualify with various combinations of education and work experience. In order to maintain certification, therapists must either pass an exam or complete work experience and continuing education requirements every 5 years.

The NCTRC also offers specialty certification in five areas of practice: behavioral health, community inclusion services, developmental disabilities, geriatrics, and physical medicine/rehabilitation. Therapists also may earn certificates from other organizations to show proficiency in specific therapy techniques, such as aquatic therapy or aromatherapy.

As of 2017, only a small number of states require licensure or otherwise regulate the work of recreational therapists. For specific requirements, contact the state's medical board.

Important Qualities

Compassion. Recreational therapists should be kind and empathetic when providing support to patients and their families. They may deal with patients who are in pain or under emotional stress.

Leadership skills. Recreational therapists must plan, develop, and implement intervention programs in an effective manner. They must be engaging and able to motivate patients to participate in a variety of therapeutic activities.

Listening skills. Recreational therapists must listen carefully to a patient's problems and concerns. They can then determine an appropriate course of treatment for that patient.

Patience. Recreational therapists may work with some patients who require more time and special attention than others.

Resourcefulness. Recreational therapists customize treatment plans for patients. They must be both creative and flexible when adapting activities or programs to each patient's needs.

Speaking skills. Recreational therapists need to communicate well with their patients. They must give clear directions during activities or instructions on healthy coping techniques.

Pay

The median annual wage for recreational therapists was $48,220 in May 2019. The median wage is the wage at which half the workers in an occupation earned more than that amount and half earned less. The lowest 10 percent earned less than $30,880, and the highest 10 percent earned more than $77,970.

In May 2019, the median annual wages for recreational therapists in the top industries in which they worked were as follows:

Government	$60,140
Hospitals; state, local, and private	50,840
Ambulatory healthcare services	48,040
Nursing care facilities (skilled nursing facilities)	42,110
Social assistance	42,000

Most recreational therapists work full time. Some recreational therapists work evenings and weekends to meet the needs of their patients.

Job Outlook

Employment of recreational therapists is projected to grow 8 percent from 2019 to 2029, much faster than the average for all occupations. However, because it is a small occupation, the fast growth will result in only about 1,700 new jobs over the 10-year period.

As the U.S. population ages, more people will need recreational therapists to help treat age-related injuries and illnesses. Older people are more likely to experience a stroke, Alzheimer's disease, and mobility-related injuries that may benefit from recreational therapy. Therapists will also be needed to help healthy seniors remain social and active in their communities. Recreational therapy services can help the aging population to maintain their independence later in life. For example, recreational therapists can help older people prevent falls by teaching them modified yoga exercises that improve balance and strength.

In addition, the number of people with chronic conditions, such as diabetes and obesity, is growing. Recreational therapists will be needed to help patients maintain their mobility, to teach patients about managing their conditions, and to help patients adjust recreational activities to accommodate any physical limitations. Therapists will be needed also to plan and lead programs designed to maintain overall wellness through participation in activities such as camps, day trips, and sports.

Recreational therapists will increasingly be utilized in helping veterans manage service-related conditions such as posttraumatic stress disorder (PTSD) or injuries such as the loss of a limb. Recreational therapists can lead activities that help veterans to reintegrate into their communities and help them to adjust to any physical, social, or cognitive limitations.

Job Prospects

Job prospects will be best for recreational therapists with both a bachelor's degree and certification. Therapists who specialize in working with older adults may have particularly good job opportunities. In addition, demand may be greater in highly populated areas, so recreational therapists who are willing to relocate may have favorable job prospects.

Employment projections data for recreational therapists, 2019-29					
Occupational Title	SOC Code	Employment, 2019	Projected Employment, 2029	Change, 2019-29	
				Percent	Numeric
SOURCE: U.S. Bureau of Labor Statistics, Employment Projections program					
Recreational therapists	29-1125	19,900	21,600	8	1,700

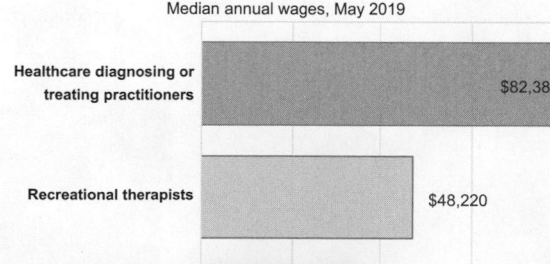

Recreational Therapists
Median annual wages, May 2019

Healthcare diagnosing or treating practitioners $82,380

Recreational therapists $48,220

Total, all occupations $39,810

Note: All Occupations includes all occupations in the U.S. Economy.
Source: U.S. Bureau of Labor Statistics, Occupational Employment Statistics.

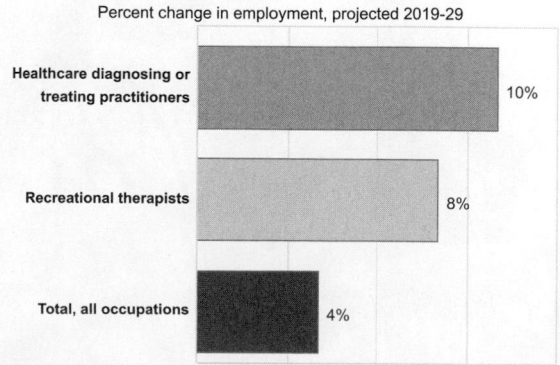

Recreational Therapists
Percent change in employment, projected 2019-29

Healthcare diagnosing or treating practitioners 10%

Recreational therapists 8%

Total, all occupations 4%

Note: All Occupations includes all occupations in the U.S. Economy.
Source: U.S. Bureau of Labor Statistics, Employment Projections program.

State & Area Data
Occupational Employment Statistics (OES)
The Occupational Employment Statistics (OES) program produces employment and wage estimates annually for over 800 occupations. These estimates are available for the nation as a whole, for individual states, and for metropolitan and nonmetropolitan areas.

Contacts for More Information
For more information and materials on careers and academic programs in recreational therapy, visit
➤ American Therapeutic Recreation Association

For more information about certification, visit
➤ National Council for Therapeutic Recreation Certification

Registered Nurses

Summary

Quick Facts: Registered Nurses

2019 Median Pay	$73,300 per year
	$35.24 per hour
Typical Entry-Level Education	Bachelor's degree
Work Experience in a Related Occupation	None
On-the-job Training	None
Number of Jobs, 2019	3,096,700
Job Outlook, 2019-29	7% (Faster than average)
Employment Change, 2019-29	221,900

What Registered Nurses Do
Registered nurses (RNs) provide and coordinate patient care and educate patients and the public about various health conditions.

Work Environment
Registered nurses work in hospitals, physicians' offices, home healthcare services, and nursing care facilities. Others work in outpatient clinics and schools.

How to Become a Registered Nurse
Registered nurses usually take one of three education paths: a bachelor's degree in nursing, an associate's degree in nursing, or a diploma from an approved nursing program. Registered nurses must be licensed.

Pay
The median annual wage for registered nurses was $73,300 in May 2019.

Job Outlook
Employment of registered nurses is projected to grow 7 percent from 2019 to 2029, faster than the average for all occupations. Growth will occur for a number of reasons, including an increased emphasis on preventive care; increasing rates of chronic conditions, such as diabetes and obesity; and demand for healthcare services from the baby-boom population, as this group leads longer and more active lives.

State & Area Data
Explore resources for employment and wages by state and area for registered nurses.

What Registered Nurses Do
Registered nurses (RNs) provide and coordinate patient care, educate patients and the public about various health conditions,

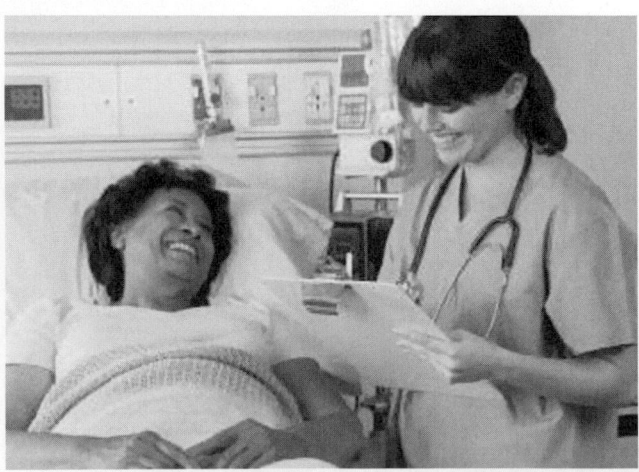

Registered nurses teach patients how to manage their illnesses or injuries.

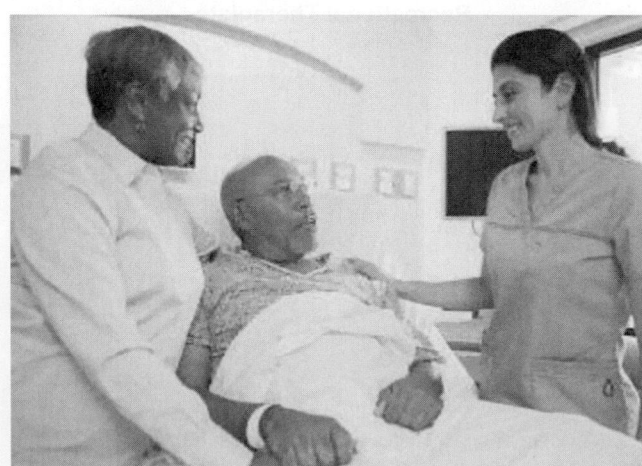

Registered nurses set up plans for patient care.

and provide advice and emotional support to patients and their families.

Duties

Registered nurses typically do the following:

- Assess patients' conditions
- Record patients' medical histories and symptoms
- Observe patients and record the observations
- Administer patients' medicines and treatments
- Set up plans for patients' care or contribute information to existing plans
- Consult and collaborate with doctors and other healthcare professionals
- Operate and monitor medical equipment
- Help perform diagnostic tests and analyze the results
- Teach patients and their families how to manage illnesses or injuries
- Explain what to do at home after treatment

Most registered nurses work as part of a team with physicians and other healthcare specialists. Some registered nurses oversee licensed practical nurses, nursing assistants, and home health aides.

Registered nurses' duties and titles often depend on where they work and the patients they work with. For example, an oncology nurse works with cancer patients and a geriatric nurse works with elderly patients. Some registered nurses combine one or more areas of practice. For example, a pediatric oncology nurse works with children and teens who have cancer.

Many possibilities exist for working with specific patient groups. The following list includes some examples:

Addiction nurses care for patients who need help to overcome addictions to alcohol, drugs, and other substances.

Cardiovascular nurses care for patients who have heart disease or heart conditions and people who have had heart surgery.

Critical care nurses work in intensive-care units in hospitals, providing care to patients with serious, complex, and acute illnesses and injuries that need close monitoring and treatment.

Genetics nurses provide screening, counseling, and treatment for patients with genetic disorders, such as cystic fibrosis.

Neonatal nurses take care of newborn babies who have health issues.

Nephrology nurses care for patients who have kidney-related health issues stemming from diabetes, high blood pressure, substance abuse, or other causes.

Public health nurses promote public health by educating people on warning signs and symptoms of disease or managing chronic health conditions. They may also run health screenings, immunization clinics, blood drives, or other community outreach programs.

Rehabilitation nurses care for patients who have temporary or permanent disabilities or have chronic illnesses.

Some nurses do not work directly with patients, but they must still have an active registered nurse license. For example, they may work as nurse educators, healthcare consultants, or hospital administrators.

Clinical nurse specialists (**CNSs**) are a type of advanced practice registered nurse (APRN). They provide direct patient care in one of many nursing specialties, such as psychiatric-mental health or pediatrics. CNSs also provide indirect care by working with other nurses and medical staff to improve the quality of care that patients receive. They often serve in leadership roles and may educate and advise other nursing staff. CNSs also may conduct research and may advocate for certain policies.

Work Environment

Registered nurses held about 3.1 million jobs in 2019. The largest employers of registered nurses were as follows:

Hospitals; state, local, and private	60%
Ambulatory healthcare services	18
Nursing and residential care facilities	7
Government	5
Educational services; state, local, and private	3

Registered nurses work in many settings, from schools to doctors' offices.

Ambulatory healthcare services includes industries such as physicians' offices, home healthcare, and outpatient care centers. Nurses who work in home health travel to patients' homes; public health nurses may travel to community centers, schools, and other sites.

Some nurses travel frequently in the United States and throughout the world to help care for patients in places where there are not enough healthcare workers.

Injuries and Illnesses

Registered nurses may spend a lot of time walking, bending, stretching, and standing. They are vulnerable to back injuries because they often must lift and move patients.

The work of registered nurses may put them in close contact with people who have infectious diseases, and they frequently come into contact with potentially harmful and hazardous drugs and other substances. Therefore, registered nurses must follow strict guidelines to guard against diseases and other dangers, such as accidental needle sticks and exposure to radiation or to chemicals used in creating a sterile environment.

Work Schedules

Nurses who work in hospitals and nursing care facilities usually work in shifts to provide round-the-clock coverage. They may work nights, weekends, and holidays. They may be on call, which means that they are on duty and must be available to work on short notice.

Nurses who work in offices, schools, and other places that do not provide 24-hour care are more likely to work regular business hours.

How to Become a Registered Nurse

Registered nurses usually take one of three education paths: a bachelor's degree in nursing, an associate's degree in nursing, or a diploma from an approved nursing program. Registered nurses must be licensed.

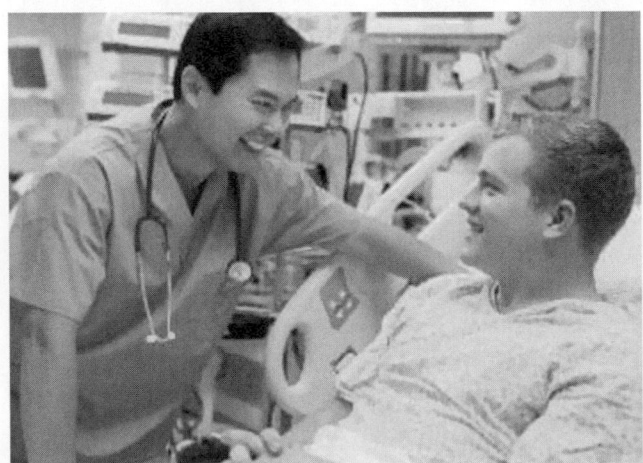

Registered nurses must be able to effectively communicate with patients to understand their concerns and assess their health conditions.

Education

Nursing education programs usually include courses in anatomy, physiology, microbiology psychology, and other social and behavioral sciences, as well as in liberal arts. Bachelor of science in nursing (BSN) degree programs typically take 4 years to complete; associate's degree in nursing (ADN), associate of science in nursing (ASN) degree, and diploma programs usually take 2 to 3 years to complete. Diploma programs are typically offered by hospitals or medical centers, and there are far fewer diploma programs than there are BSN, ADN, and ASN programs. All programs include supervised clinical experience.

Bachelor's degree programs usually include additional education in physical and social sciences, communication, leadership, and critical thinking. A bachelor's or higher degree is often necessary for administrative positions, research, consulting, and teaching.

Generally, licensed graduates of any of the three types of education programs (bachelor's, associate's, or diploma) qualify for entry-level positions as a staff nurse. However, employers—particularly those in hospitals—may require a bachelor's degree.

Registered nurses with an ADN, ASN, or diploma may go back to school to earn a bachelor's degree through an RN-to-BSN program. There are also master's degree programs in nursing, combined bachelor's and master's programs, and accelerated programs for those who wish to enter the field of nursing and already hold a bachelor's degree in another field. Some employers offer tuition reimbursement.

Clinical nurse specialists (CNSs) must earn a master's degree in nursing and typically already have 1 year or more of work experience as an RN or in a related field. CNSs who conduct research typically need a doctoral degree.

Licenses, Certifications, and Registrations

Registered nurses must have a nursing license issued by the state in which they work. To become licensed, nurses must graduate from an approved nursing program and pass the National Council Licensure Examination (NCLEX-RN).

Other requirements for licensing, such as passing a criminal background check, vary by state. Each state's board of nursing provides specific requirements. For more information on the NCLEX-RN and a list of state boards of nursing, visit the National Council of State Boards of Nursing.

Nurses may become certified through professional associations in specific areas, such as ambulatory care, gerontology, or pediatrics. Although certification is usually voluntary, it demonstrates adherence to a specific level of competency, and some employers require it.

In addition, registered nursing positions may require cardiopulmonary resuscitation (CPR), basic life support (BLS), or advanced cardiac life support (ACLS) certification.

CNSs must satisfy additional state licensing requirements, such as earning specialty certifications. Contact state boards of nursing for specific requirements.

Important Qualities

Critical-thinking skills. Registered nurses must assess changes in the health status of patients, such as determining when to take corrective action.

Communication skills. Registered nurses must be able to communicate effectively with patients in order to understand their concerns and evaluate their health conditions. Nurses need to clearly explain instructions, such as how to take medication. They must work in teams with other health professionals and communicate patients' needs.

Compassion. Registered nurses should be caring and empathetic when working with patients.

Detail oriented. Registered nurses must be precise because they must ensure that patients get the correct treatments and medicines at the right time.

Emotional stability. Registered nurses need emotional resilience and the ability to cope with human suffering, emergencies, and other stressors.

Organizational skills. Nurses often work with multiple patients who have a variety of health needs. The ability to coordinate numerous treatment plans and records is critical to ensure that each patient receives appropriate care.

Physical stamina. Nurses should be comfortable performing physical tasks, such as lifting patients. They may be on their feet for most of their shift.

Advancement

Most registered nurses begin as staff nurses in hospitals or community health settings. With experience, good performance, and continuing education, they can move to other settings or be promoted to positions with more responsibility.

In management, nurses may advance from assistant clinical nurse manager, charge nurse, or head nurse to more senior-level administrative roles, such as assistant director or director of nursing, vice president of nursing, or chief nursing officer. Increasingly, management-level nursing positions require a graduate degree in nursing or health services administration. Administrative positions require leadership skills, communication ability, negotiation skills, and good judgment.

Some nurses move into the business side of healthcare. Their nursing expertise and experience on a healthcare team equip them to manage ambulatory, acute, home-based, and chronic care businesses. Employers—including hospitals, insurance companies, pharmaceutical manufacturers, and managed care organizations—need registered nurses for jobs in health planning and development, marketing, consulting, policy development, and quality assurance.

Some RNs may become nurse anesthetists, nurse midwives, or nurse practitioners, which, along with clinical nurse specialists, are types of advanced practice registered nurses (APRNs). APRNs need a master's degree but many have a doctoral degree. APRNs may provide primary and specialty care, and in many states they may prescribe medications.

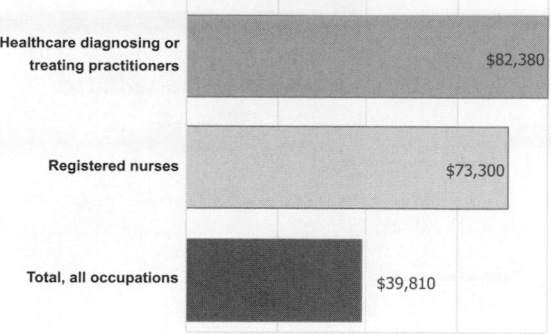

Registered Nurses
Median annual wages, May 2019

Healthcare diagnosing or treating practitioners: $82,380

Registered nurses: $73,300

Total, all occupations: $39,810

Note: All Occupations includes all occupations in the U.S. Economy.
Source: U.S. Bureau of Labor Statistics, Occupational Employment Statistics.

Other nurses work as postsecondary teachers or researchers in colleges and universities, which typically requires a Ph.D.

Pay

The median annual wage for registered nurses was $73,300 in May 2019. The median wage is the wage at which half the workers in an occupation earned more than that amount and half earned less. The lowest 10 percent earned less than $52,080, and the highest 10 percent earned more than $111,220.

In May 2019, the median annual wages for registered nurses in the top industries in which they worked were as follows:

Government	$79,790
Hospitals; state, local, and private	75,030
Ambulatory healthcare services	70,330
Nursing and residential care facilities	66,250
Educational services; state, local, and private	63,690

Nurses who work in hospitals and nursing care facilities usually work in shifts to provide round-the-clock coverage. They may work nights, weekends, and holidays. They may be on call, which means that they are on duty and must be available to work on short notice. Nurses who work in offices, schools, and other places that do not provide 24-hour care are more likely to have regular business hours.

Job Outlook

Employment of registered nurses is projected to grow 7 percent from 2019 to 2029, faster than the average for all occupations. Growth will occur for a number of reasons.

Demand for healthcare services will increase because of the aging population, given that older people typically have more medical problems than younger people. Nurses also will be needed to educate and care for patients with chronic conditions, such as arthritis, dementia, diabetes, and obesity.

The financial pressure on hospitals to discharge patients as soon as possible may result in more people being admitted to long-term care facilities and outpatient care centers and in

Registered Nurses

Percent change in employment, projected 2019-29

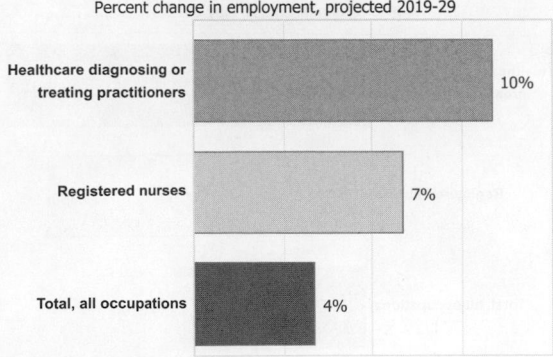

Healthcare diagnosing or
treating practitioners   10%

Registered nurses   7%

Total, all occupations   4%

Note: All Occupations includes all occupations in the U.S. Economy.
Source: U.S. Bureau of Labor Statistics, Employment Projections program.

greater need for healthcare at home. Job growth is expected in facilities that provide long-term rehabilitation for stroke and head injury patients and in facilities that treat people with Alzheimer's disease. In addition, because many older people prefer to be treated at home or in residential care facilities, registered nurses will be in demand in those settings.

Growth is also expected to be faster than average in outpatient care centers, where patients do not stay overnight, such as those that provide same-day chemotherapy, rehabilitation, and surgery. In addition, a large number of procedures, including sophisticated procedures previously done only in hospitals, are now done in ambulatory care settings and physicians' offices.

Job Prospects

About 175,900 openings for registered nurses are projected each year, on average, over the decade.

Many of those openings are expected to result from the need to replace workers who transfer to different occupations or exit the labor force, such as to retire.

Overall, job opportunities for registered nurses are expected to be good. However, there may be competition for jobs in some areas of the country. Generally, registered nurses who have a bachelor of science degree in nursing (BSN) will have better job prospects than those without one. Employers also

may prefer candidates who have some related work experience or certification in a specialty area, such as gerontology.

Employment projections data for registered nurses, 2019-29					
Occupational Title	SOC Code	Employment, 2019	Projected Employment, 2029	Change, 2019-29	
				Percent	Numeric
SOURCE: U.S. Bureau of Labor Statistics, Employment Projections program					
Registered nurses	29-1141	3,096,700	3,318,700	7	221,900

State & Area Data
Occupational Employment Statistics (OES)

The Occupational Employment Statistics (OES) program produces employment and wage estimates annually for over 800 occupations. These estimates are available for the nation as a whole, for individual states, and for metropolitan and nonmetropolitan areas.

Contacts for More Information

For more information about registered nurses, including credentialing, visit
➤ American Nurses Association

For more information about nursing education and being a registered nurse, visit
➤ American Society of Registered Nurses
➤ Johnson & Johnson, Discover Nursing
➤ National League for Nursing
➤ National Student Nurses' Association

For more information about undergraduate and graduate nursing education, nursing career options, and financial aid, visit
➤ American Association of Colleges of Nursing

For more information about the National Council Licensure Examination (NCLEX-RN) and a list of individual state boards of nursing, visit
➤ National Council of State Boards of Nursing

For more information about clinical nurse specialists, including a list of accredited programs, visit
➤ National Association of Clinical Nurse Specialists

Respiratory Therapists

Summary

Quick Facts: Respiratory Therapists

2019 Median Pay	$61,330 per year $29.48 per hour
Typical Entry-Level Education	Associate's degree
Work Experience in a Related Occupation	None
On-the-job Training	None
Number of Jobs, 2019	135,800
Job Outlook, 2019-29	19% (Much faster than average)
Employment Change, 2019-29	26,300

What Respiratory Therapists Do

Respiratory therapists care for patients who have trouble breathing—for example, from a chronic respiratory disease, such as asthma or emphysema.

Work Environment

Most respiratory therapists work full time. Because they may work in medical facilities, such as hospitals that are always open, some may work evening, night, or weekend hours.

How to Become a Respiratory Therapist

Respiratory therapists typically need an associate's degree, but some have bachelor's degrees. Respiratory therapists are licensed in all states except Alaska; requirements vary by state.

Pay

The median annual wage for respiratory therapists was $61,330 in May 2019.

Job Outlook

Employment of respiratory therapists is projected to grow 19 percent from 2019 to 2029, much faster than the average for all occupations. Growth in the middle-aged and elderly population will lead to an increased incidence of respiratory conditions such as chronic obstructive pulmonary disease (COPD) and pneumonia. These respiratory disorders can permanently damage the lungs or restrict lung function.

State & Area Data

Explore resources for employment and wages by state and area for respiratory therapists.

What Respiratory Therapists Do

Respiratory therapists care for patients who have trouble breathing—for example, from a chronic respiratory disease, such as asthma or emphysema. Their patients range from premature infants with undeveloped lungs to elderly patients who have diseased lungs. They also provide emergency care to patients suffering from heart attacks, drowning, or shock.

Duties

Respiratory therapists typically do the following:

- Interview and examine patients with breathing or cardiopulmonary disorders
- Consult with physicians to develop patient treatment plans
- Perform diagnostic tests, such as measuring lung capacity
- Treat patients by using a variety of methods, including chest physiotherapy and aerosol medications
- Monitor and record patients' progress
- Teach patients how to take medications and use equipment, such as ventilators

Respiratory therapists use various tests to evaluate patients. For example, therapists test lung capacity by having patients breathe into an instrument that measures the volume and flow of oxygen when they inhale and exhale. Respiratory therapists also may take blood samples and use a blood gas analyzer to test oxygen and carbon dioxide levels.

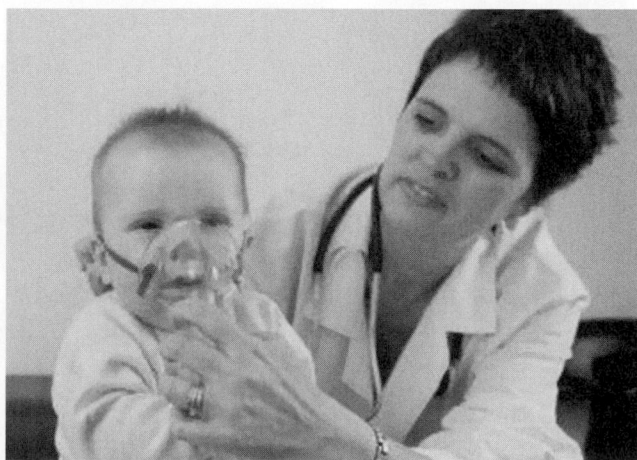

Respiratory therapists work with patients who have breathing problems, such as asthma.

Respiratory therapists interview and examine patients with breathing or cardiopulmonary disorders.

Respiratory therapists perform chest physiotherapy on patients to remove mucus from their lungs and make it easier for them to breathe. Removing mucus is necessary for patients suffering from lung diseases, such as cystic fibrosis, and involves the therapist vibrating the patient's rib cage, often by tapping the patient's chest and encouraging him or her to cough.

Respiratory therapists may connect patients who cannot breathe on their own to ventilators that deliver oxygen to the lungs. Therapists insert a tube in the patient's windpipe (trachea) and connect the tube to ventilator equipment. They set up and monitor the equipment to ensure that the patient is receiving the correct amount of oxygen at the correct rate.

Respiratory therapists who work in home care teach patients and their families to use ventilators and other life-support systems in their homes. During these visits, they may inspect and clean equipment, check the home for environmental hazards, and ensure that patients know how to use their medications. Therapists also make emergency home visits when necessary.

In some hospitals, respiratory therapists are involved in related areas, such as diagnosing breathing problems for people with sleep apnea and counseling people on how to stop smoking.

Work Environment

Respiratory therapists held about 135,800 jobs in 2019. The largest employers of respiratory therapists were as follows:

Hospitals; state, local, and private	82%
Nursing care facilities (skilled nursing facilities)	4
Offices of physicians	2

Respiratory therapists are on their feet for long periods and may need to lift or turn disabled patients. Therapists work closely with registered nurses, physicians and surgeons, and medical assistants.

Work Schedules

Most respiratory therapists work full time. Because they may work in medical facilities, such as hospitals that are always open, some may work evening, night, or weekend hours.

How to Become a Respiratory Therapist

Respiratory therapists typically need an associate's degree, but some have bachelor's degrees in respiratory therapy. Respiratory therapists are licensed in all states except Alaska; requirements vary by state.

Education

Respiratory therapists need at least an associate's degree, but employers may prefer applicants who have a bachelor's degree. Educational programs are offered by colleges and universities, vocational–technical institutes, and the Armed Forces. Completion of a program that is accredited by the Commission on Accreditation for Respiratory Care may be required for licensure.

Respiratory therapy programs typically include courses in human anatomy and physiology, chemistry, physics, microbiology, pharmacology, and math. Other courses deal with therapeutic and diagnostic procedures and tests, equipment, patient assessment, and cardiopulmonary resuscitation (CPR). In addition to coursework, programs have clinical components that allow students to gain supervised, practical experience in treating patients.

High school students interested in applying to respiratory therapy programs should take courses in health, biology, math, chemistry, and physics.

Licenses, Certifications, and Registrations

Respiratory therapists are licensed in all states except Alaska, where national certification is recommended, although not required. Licensure requirements vary by state; for most states they include passing a state or professional certification exam. For specific state requirements, contact the state's health board.

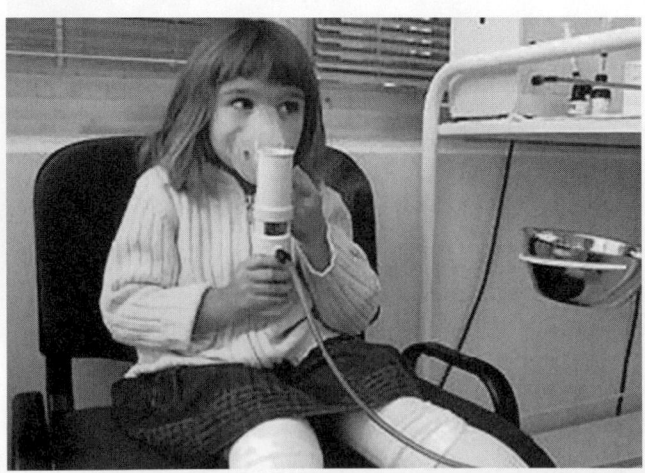

Respiratory therapists treat patients in every age group.

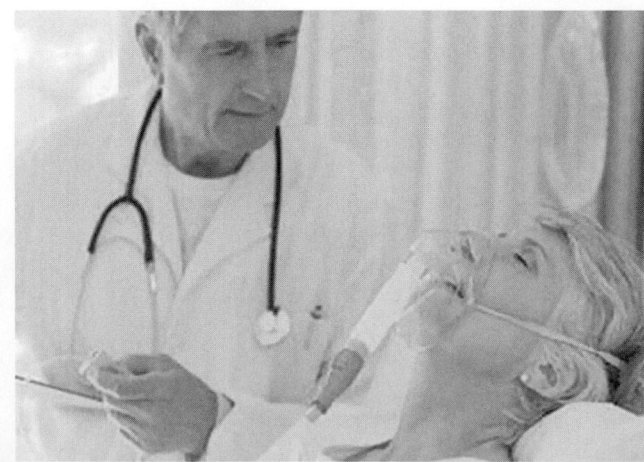

Respiratory therapists typically need an associate's degree, but some have bachelor's degrees.

The National Board for Respiratory Care (NBRC) is the main certifying body for respiratory therapists. The Board offers two levels of certification: Certified Respiratory Therapist (CRT) and Registered Respiratory Therapist (RRT).

Important Qualities

Compassion. Respiratory therapists should be able to provide emotional support to patients undergoing treatment and be sympathetic to their needs.

Detail oriented. Respiratory therapists must be detail oriented to ensure that patients are receiving the appropriate treatments and medications in a timely manner. They must also monitor and record various pieces of information related to patient care.

Interpersonal skills. Respiratory therapists interact with patients and often work as part of a team. They must be able to follow instructions from a supervising physician.

Patience. Respiratory therapists may work for long periods with patients who need special attention.

Problem-solving skills. Respiratory therapists need strong problem-solving skills. They must evaluate patients' symptoms, consult with other healthcare professionals, and recommend and administer the appropriate treatments.

Science and math skills. Respiratory therapists must understand anatomy, physiology, and other sciences and be able to calculate the right dose of a patient's medicine.

Pay

The median annual wage for respiratory therapists was $61,330 in May 2019. The median wage is the wage at which half the workers in an occupation earned more than that amount and half earned less. The lowest 10 percent earned less than $44,850, and the highest 10 percent earned more than $86,980.

In May 2019, the median annual wages for respiratory therapists in the top industries in which they worked were as follows:

Hospitals; state, local, and private $61,670

Offices of physicians.. 61,120

Nursing care facilities (skilled nursing facilities)... 59,260

Most respiratory therapists work full time. Because they may work in medical facilities, such as hospitals that are always open, some therapists work evening, night, or weekend hours.

Job Outlook

Employment of respiratory therapists is projected to grow 19 percent from 2019 to 2029, much faster than the average for all occupations. Growth in the middle-aged and older population will lead to an increased incidence of respiratory conditions such as pneumonia, chronic obstructive pulmonary disease (COPD), and other disorders that can permanently damage the lungs or restrict lung function. The aging population will in turn lead to an increased demand for respiratory therapy services and treatments, mostly in hospitals.

In addition, a growing emphasis on reducing readmissions in hospitals may result in more demand for respiratory therapists in nursing homes and in doctors' offices.

Advances in preventing and detecting disease, improved medications, and more sophisticated treatments will also increase the demand for respiratory therapists. Other conditions affecting the general population, such as respiratory problems due to smoking and air pollution, along with respiratory emergencies, will continue to create demand for respiratory therapists.

Job Prospects

Job prospects will be best for therapists willing to travel to look for job opportunities. Some areas will be saturated with workers, and other areas (more often, rural areas) will be in need of respiratory therapists' services. Certification is generally recommended, as it may increase an applicant's competitiveness in the job market.

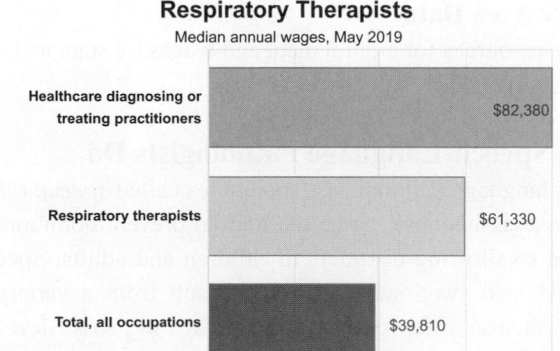

Respiratory Therapists
Median annual wages, May 2019

Healthcare diagnosing or treating practitioners — $82,380
Respiratory therapists — $61,330
Total, all occupations — $39,810

Note: All Occupations includes all occupations in the U.S. Economy.
Source: U.S. Bureau of Labor Statistics, Occupational Employment Statistics.

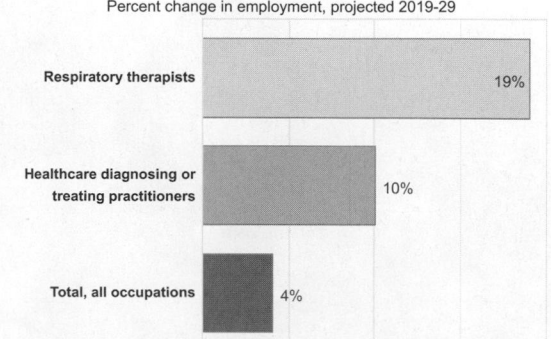

Respiratory Therapists
Percent change in employment, projected 2019-29

Respiratory therapists — 19%
Healthcare diagnosing or treating practitioners — 10%
Total, all occupations — 4%

Note: All Occupations includes all occupations in the U.S. Economy.
Source: U.S. Bureau of Labor Statistics, Employment Projections program.

Employment projections data for respiratory therapists, 2019-29					
Occupational Title	SOC Code	Employment, 2019	Projected Employment, 2029	Change, 2019-29	
				Percent	Numeric
SOURCE: U.S. Bureau of Labor Statistics, Employment Projections program					
Respiratory therapists	29-1126	135,800	162,000	19	26,300

State & Area Data
Occupational Employment Statistics (OES)
The Occupational Employment Statistics (OES) program produces employment and wage estimates annually for over 800 occupations. These estimates are available for the nation as a whole, for individual states, and for metropolitan and nonmetropolitan areas.

Contacts for More Information
For more information about respiratory therapists, visit
➤ American Association for Respiratory Care

For a list of accredited educational programs for respiratory care practitioners, visit
➤ Commission on Accreditation for Respiratory Care

For a list of state licensing agencies, as well as information on gaining credentials in respiratory care, visit
➤ The National Board for Respiratory Care, Inc.

Speech-Language Pathologists

Summary

Quick Facts: Speech-Language Pathologists

2019 Median Pay	$79,120 per year $38.04 per hour
Typical Entry-Level Education	Master's degree
Work Experience in a Related Occupation	None
On-the-job Training	Internship/residency
Number of Jobs, 2019	162,600
Job Outlook, 2019-29	25% (Much faster than average)
Employment Change, 2019-29	40,500

What Speech-Language Pathologists Do
Speech-language pathologists assess, diagnose, treat, and help to prevent communication and swallowing disorders in children and adults.

Speech-language pathologists working in schools may meet regularly with individual students or groups of students.

Work Environment
Some speech-language pathologists work in schools. Most others worked in healthcare facilities, such as hospitals.

How to Become a Speech-Language Pathologist
Speech-language pathologists typically need at least a master's degree. Most states require that speech-language pathologists be licensed. Requirements vary by state.

Pay
The median annual wage for speech-language pathologists was $79,120 in May 2019.

Job Outlook
Employment of speech-language pathologists is projected to grow 25 percent from 2019 to 2029, much faster than the average for all occupations. As the large baby-boom population grows older, there will be more instances of health conditions that can cause speech or language impairments, such as strokes or dementia.

State & Area Data
Explore resources for employment and wages by state and area for speech-language pathologists.

What Speech-Language Pathologists Do
Speech-language pathologists (sometimes called *speech therapists*) assess, diagnose, treat, and help to prevent communication and swallowing disorders in children and adults. Speech, language, and swallowing disorders result from a variety of causes, such as a stroke, brain injury, hearing loss, developmental delay, Parkinson's disease, a cleft palate, or autism.

Duties
Speech-language pathologists typically do the following:

• Evaluate levels of speech, language, or swallowing difficulty

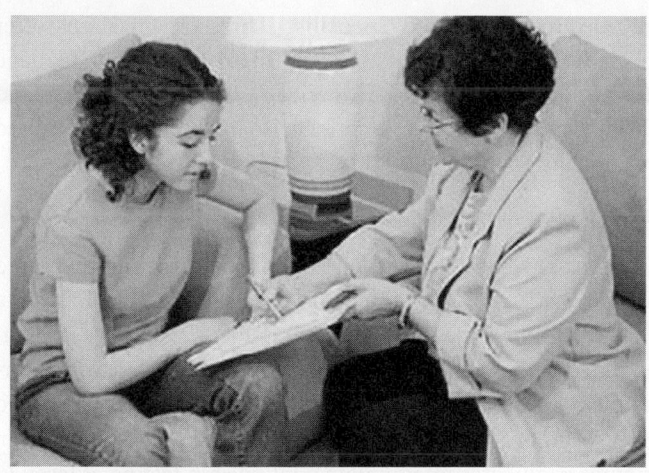

Speech-language pathologists must be able to listen to and communicate with their patient in order to determine the right course of treatment.

- Identify treatment options
- Create and carry out an individualized treatment plan that addresses specific functional needs
- Teach children and adults how to make sounds and improve their voices and maintain fluency
- Help individuals improve vocabulary and sentence structure used in oral and written language
- Work with children and adults to develop and strengthen the muscles used to swallow
- Counsel individuals and families on how to cope with communication and swallowing disorders

Speech-language pathologists work with children and adults who have problems with speech and language, including related cognitive or social communication problems. They may be unable to speak at all, or they may speak with difficulty or have rhythm and fluency problems, such as stuttering. Speech-language pathologists may work with people who are unable to understand language or with those who have voice disorders, such as inappropriate pitch or a harsh voice.

Speech-language pathologists also must complete administrative tasks, including keeping accurate records and documenting billing information. They record their initial evaluations and diagnoses, track treatment progress, and note any changes in a individual's condition or treatment plan.

Some speech-language pathologists specialize in working with specific age groups, such as children or the elderly. Others focus on treatment programs for specific communication or swallowing problems, such as those resulting from strokes, trauma, or a cleft palate.

In medical facilities, speech-language pathologists work with physicians and surgeons, social workers, psychologists, occupational therapists, physical therapists, and other healthcare workers. In schools, they evaluate students for speech and language disorders and work with teachers, other school personnel, and parents to develop and carry out individual or group programs, provide counseling, and support classroom activities. For more information on teachers, see the profiles on preschool teachers, kindergarten and elementary school teachers, middle school teachers, high school teachers, and special education teachers.

Work Environment

Speech-language pathologists held about 162,600 jobs in 2019. The largest employers of speech-language pathologists were as follows:

Educational services; state, local, and private	38%
Offices of physical, occupational and speech therapists, and audiologists	23
Hospitals; state, local, and private	14
Nursing and residential care facilities...........................	5
Self-employed workers..	4

Work Schedules

Most speech-language pathologists work full time. Some speech-language pathologists, such as those working for schools, may need to travel between different schools or facilities.

How to Become a Speech-Language Pathologist

Speech-language pathologists typically need at least a master's degree. Most states require that speech-language pathologists be licensed. Requirements vary by state.

Education

Speech-language pathologists typically need at least a master's degree. Although master's programs do not require a particular undergraduate degree for admission, certain courses must be taken before entering a program. Required courses vary by institution.

Most speech-language pathologists work in schools or healthcare facilities.

Some speech-language pathologists specialize in working with specific age groups, such as children.

Graduate programs often include courses in speech and language development, age-specific speech disorders, alternative communication methods, and swallowing disorders. These programs also include supervised clinical experience.

The Council on Academic Accreditation (CAA), part of the American Speech-Language-Hearing Association, accredits education programs in speech-language pathology. Graduation from an accredited program is required for certification and, often, for state licensure.

Licenses, Certifications, and Registrations

All states regulate speech-language pathologists. Most states require speech-language pathologists to be licensed; other states require registration. Licensure typically requires at least a master's degree from an accredited program, supervised clinical experience, and passing an exam. For specific requirements, contact your state's medical or health licensure board.

Speech-language pathologists can earn the Certificate of Clinical Competence in Speech-Language Pathology (CCC-SLP), offered by the American Speech-Language-Hearing Association. Certification typically satisfies some or all of the requirements for state licensure and may be required by some employers. To earn CCC-SLP certification, candidates must graduate from an accredited program, pass an exam, and complete a fellowship under the supervision of a certified speech-language pathologist. To maintain the CCC-SLP credential, speech-language pathologists must complete 30 hours of continuing education every 3 years.

Speech-language pathologists who work in schools may need a specific teaching certification. For specific requirements, contact your state's department of education or the private institution in which you are interested.

Speech language pathologists may choose to earn specialty certifications in child language, fluency, or swallowing. Candidates who hold the CCC-SLP, meet work experience requirements, and pass a specialty certification exam may use the title Board Certified Specialist. Three organizations offer specialty certifications: American Board of Child Language and Language Disorders, American Board of Fluency and Fluency Disorders, and American Board of Swallowing and Swallowing Disorders.

Training

Candidates can gain hands-on experience through supervised clinical work, which is typically referred to as a fellowship. This training is a type of internship in that prospective speech-language pathologists apply and refine the skills learned during their academic program under the supervision of a certified speech-language pathologist. The CCC-SLP certification requires candidates to complete a fellowship lasting at least 36 weeks.

Important Qualities

Analytical skills. Speech-language pathologists must select the most appropriate diagnostic tools and analyze results to arrive at an accurate diagnosis and develop an appropriate treatment plan.

Communication skills. Speech-language pathologists need to communicate test results, diagnoses, and proposed treatments in a way that individuals and their families can understand.

Compassion. Speech-language pathologists work with people who are often frustrated by their difficulties. Speech-language pathologists must support emotionally demanding individuals and their families.

Critical-thinking skills. Speech-language pathologists must adjust their treatment plans as needed, finding alternative ways to help.

Detail oriented. Speech-language pathologists must take detailed notes on progress and treatment.

Listening skills. Speech-language pathologists must listen to symptoms and concerns to decide on the appropriate course of treatment.

Pay

The median annual wage for speech-language pathologists was $79,120 in May 2019. The median wage is the wage at which half the workers in an occupation earned more than that amount and half earned less. The lowest 10 percent earned less than $49,840, and the highest 10 percent earned more than $121,260.

In May 2019, the median annual wages for speech-language pathologists in the top industries in which they worked were as follows:

Nursing and residential care facilities	$95,250
Hospitals; state, local, and private	85,420
Offices of physical, occupational and speech therapists, and audiologists	83,550
Educational services; state, local, and private	70,290

Speech-Language Pathologists
Median annual wages, May 2019

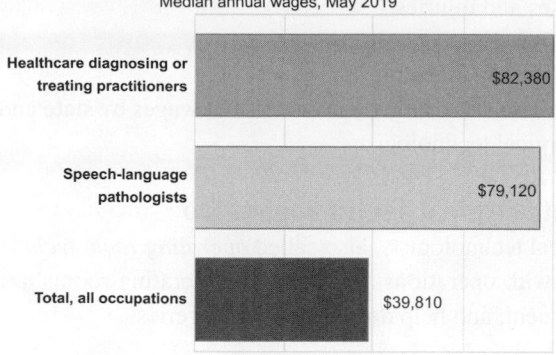

Healthcare diagnosing or treating practitioners	$82,380
Speech-language pathologists	$79,120
Total, all occupations	$39,810

Note: All Occupations includes all occupations in the U.S. Economy.
Source: U.S. Bureau of Labor Statistics, Occupational Employment Statistics.

Most speech-language pathologists work full time. Some speech language pathologists, such as those working for schools, may need to travel between different schools or facilities.

Job Outlook
Employment of speech-language pathologists is projected to grow 25 percent from 2019 to 2029, much faster than the average for all occupations.

As the large baby-boom population grows older, there will be more instances of health conditions such as strokes or dementia, which can cause speech or language impairments. Speech-language pathologists will be needed to treat the increased number of speech and language disorders in the older population.

Increased awareness of speech and language disorders, such as stuttering, in younger children should lead to a need for more speech-language pathologists who specialize in treating that age group. Also, an increasing number of speech-language pathologists will be needed to work with children with autism to improve their ability to communicate and socialize effectively.

In addition, medical advances are improving the survival rate of premature infants and victims of trauma and strokes, many of whom need help from speech-language pathologists.

Job Prospects
Overall job opportunities for speech-language pathologists are expected to be good. Generally, speech-language pathologists who are willing to relocate will have the best job opportunities.

Speech-Language Pathologists
Percent change in employment, projected 2019-29

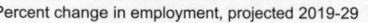
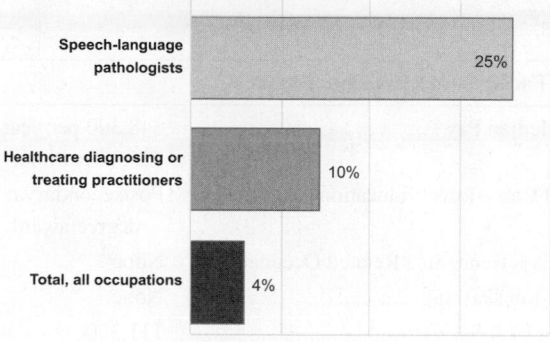

Speech-language pathologists	25%
Healthcare diagnosing or treating practitioners	10%
Total, all occupations	4%

Note: All Occupations includes all occupations in the U.S. Economy.
Source: U.S. Bureau of Labor Statistics, Employment Projections program.

Employment projections data for speech-language pathologists, 2019-29					
Occupational Title	SOC Code	Employment, 2019	Projected Employment, 2029	Change, 2019-29	
				Percent	Numeric
SOURCE: U.S. Bureau of Labor Statistics, Employment Projections program					
Speech-language pathologists	29-1127	162,600	203,100	25	40,500

State & Area Data
Occupational Employment Statistics (OES)
The Occupational Employment Statistics (OES) program produces employment and wage estimates annually for over 800 occupations. These estimates are available for the nation as a whole, for individual states, and for metropolitan and nonmetropolitan areas.

Contacts for More Information
For more information about speech-language pathologists, a description of the Certificate of Clinical Competence in Speech-Language Pathology (CCC-SLP) credential, and a list of accredited graduate programs in speech-language pathology, visit
➤ American Speech-Language-Hearing Association

For more information about specialty certifications, visit
American Board of Child Language and Language Disorders
American Board of Fluency and Fluency Disorders
➤ American Board of Swallowing and Swallowing Disorders

State licensing boards have information about licensure requirements. State departments of education can provide information about certification requirements for those who want to work in public schools.

Surgical Technologists

Summary

Quick Facts: Surgical Technologists

2019 Median Pay	$48,300 per year $23.22 per hour
Typical Entry-Level Education	Postsecondary non-degree award
Work Experience in a Related Occupation ..	None
On-the-job Training	None
Number of Jobs, 2019	111,300
Job Outlook, 2019-29	7% (Faster than average)
Employment Change, 2019-29	7,600

What Surgical Technologists Do

Surgical technologists assist in surgical operations.

Work Environment

Most surgical technologists work in hospitals. They spend much of their time on their feet.

How to Become a Surgical Technologist

Surgical technologists typically need a postsecondary nondegree award or an associate's degree. Certification can be beneficial in finding a job. A small number of states regulate surgical technologists.

Pay

The median annual wage for surgical technologists was $48,300 in May 2019.

Job Outlook

Employment of surgical technologists is projected to grow 7 percent from 2019 to 2029, faster than the average for all occupations. Advances in medical technology have made surgery

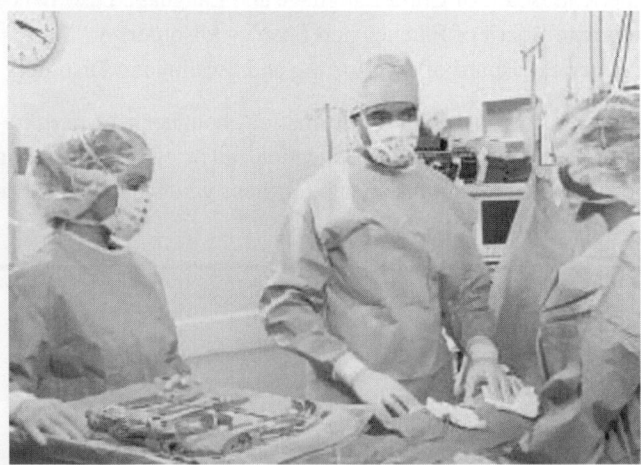

Surgical technologists hand instruments and supplies to surgeons during an operation.

safer, and more operations are being done to treat a variety of illnesses and injuries.

State & Area Data

Explore resources for employment and wages by state and area for surgical technologists.

What Surgical Technologists Do

Surgical technologists, also called *operating room technicians*, assist with operations. They prepare operating rooms, arrange equipment, and help doctors during surgeries.

Duties

Surgical technologists typically do the following:

- Prepare operating rooms for surgery
- Sterilize equipment and make sure that there are adequate supplies for surgery
- Ready patients for surgery, such as by washing and disinfecting incision sites
- Help surgeons during surgery by passing them instruments and other sterile supplies
- Count supplies, such as surgical instruments, to ensure that no foreign objects are retained in patients
- Maintain a sterile environment to prevent patient infection

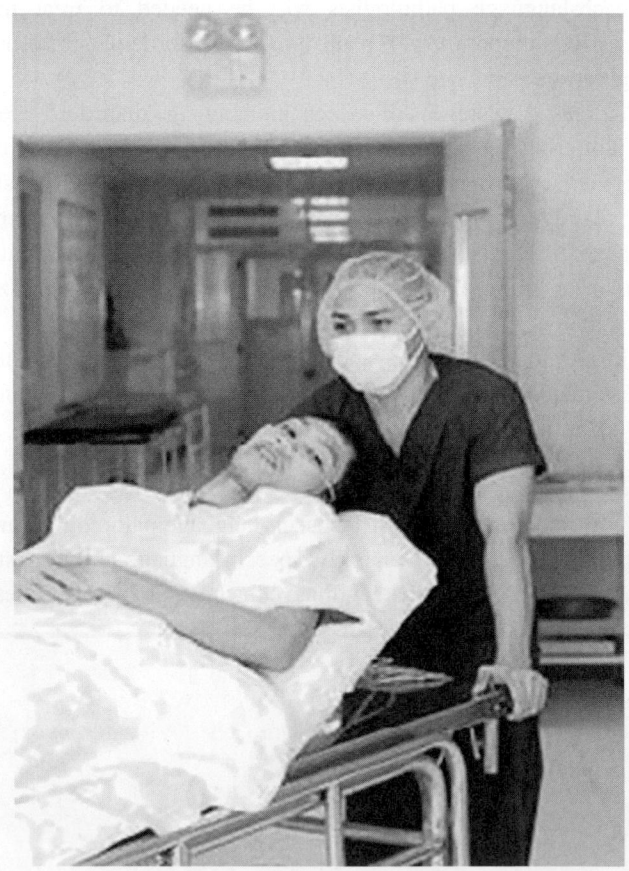

Surgical technologists may transport patients to surgery.

Surgical technologists work as members of a healthcare team alongside physicians and surgeons, registered nurses, and other healthcare workers.

Before an operation, surgical technologists prepare the operating room by setting up surgical instruments and equipment. They prepare sterile solutions and medications used in surgery and check that all surgical equipment is working properly. Surgical technologists also bring patients to the operating room and get them ready for surgery by positioning them on the table, covering them with sterile drapes, and washing and disinfecting incision sites. And they help the surgical team put on sterile gowns.

During an operation, surgical technologists pass the sterile instruments and supplies to surgeons and first assistants. They might hold retractors, hold internal organs in place during the procedure, or set up robotic surgical equipment. Technologists also may handle specimens taken for laboratory analysis.

After the operation is complete, surgical technologists may apply bandages and other dressings to the incision site. They may also transfer patients to recovery rooms and restock operating rooms after a procedure.

Surgical first assistants have a hands-on role, directly assisting surgeons during a procedure. For example, they may help to suction the incision site or suture a wound.

Work Environment

Surgical technologists held about 111,300 jobs in 2019. The largest employers of surgical technologists were as follows:

Hospitals; state, local, and private	73%
Outpatient care centers	10
Offices of physicians	10
Offices of dentists	3

Ambulatory surgical centers are included in outpatient care centers.

Surgical technologists wear scrubs and sterile gowns, gloves, caps, and masks while they are in the operating room. Their work may be physically demanding, requiring them to be on their feet for long periods. Surgical technologists also may need to help move patients or lift heavy trays of medical supplies. At times, they may be exposed to communicable diseases and unpleasant sights, odors, and materials.

Work Schedules

Most surgical technologists work full time. Surgical technologists employed in hospitals may work or be on call during nights, weekends, and holidays. They may also be required to work shifts lasting longer than 8 hours.

How to Become a Surgical Technologist

Surgical technologists typically need a postsecondary nondegree award or an associate's degree. Certification can be beneficial in finding a job. A small number of states regulate surgical technologists.

Education

Surgical technologists typically need a diploma, certificate, or associate's degree from an accredited surgical technology program. Many community colleges and vocational schools, as well as some universities and hospitals, offer accredited programs that range in length from several months to 2 years.

Surgical technology education includes courses such as anatomy, microbiology, and physiology. They also learn about the care and safety of patients, sterilization techniques, how to set up technical or robotic equipment, and preventing and controlling infections. In addition to classroom study, students gain hands-on experience in supervised clinical settings.

Surgical first assistants may complete a formal education program in surgical assisting. Others may work as surgical

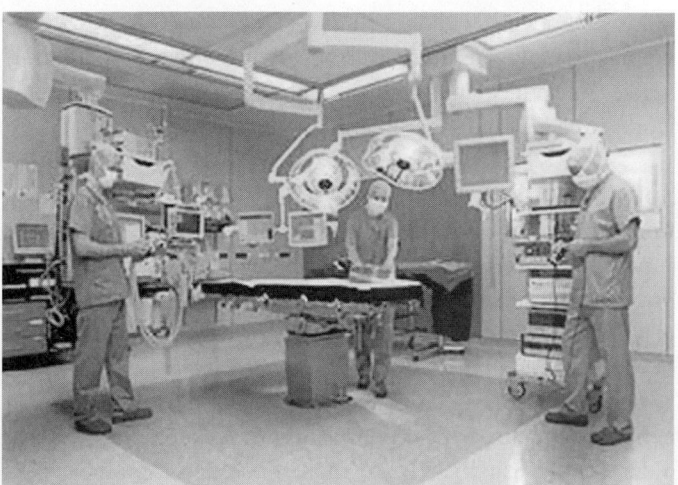

Surgical technologists are trained to maintain the sterile field, preventing the risk of infection during surgery.

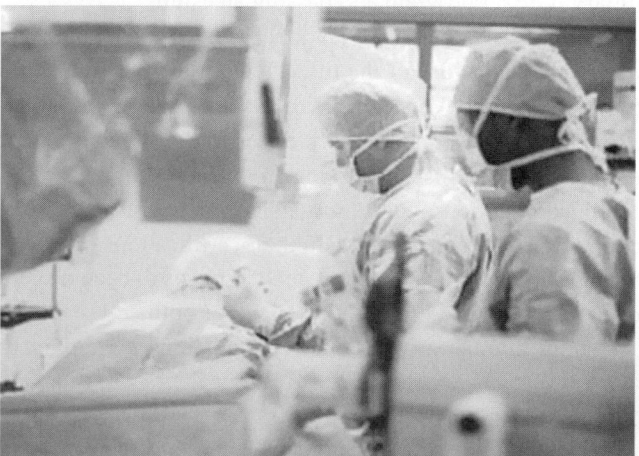

Surgical technologists work as members of a healthcare team alongside physicians and surgeons, registered nurses, and other healthcare workers.

technologists and receive additional on-the-job training to become first assistants.

There are about 500 surgical technologist programs accredited by the Commission on Accreditation of Allied Health Education Programs (CAAHEP).

Important Qualities

Communication. To prevent infections or other complications, surgical technologists must relay any issues that arise during surgery to the other members of the healthcare team.

Detail oriented. Surgical technologists must pay close attention to their work. For example, they need to provide the correct sterile equipment for surgeons during an operation.

Dexterity. Surgical technologists should be comfortable working with their hands. They must provide needed equipment quickly.

Integrity. Because they are trusted to provide sterile supplies and care for patients during surgical procedures, surgical technologists must be ethical and honest.

Listening skills. Responding to requests from surgeons and others on the surgical team requires the ability to listen to and understand spoken directions.

Physical stamina. Surgical technologists should be comfortable standing for extended periods.

Stress-management skills. Working in an operating room can be stressful. Surgical technologists should work well under pressure.

Licenses, Certifications, and Registrations

Certification may be beneficial for finding a job. Surgical technologists may earn certification through credentialing organizations.

Certification through the National Board of Surgical Technology and Surgical Assisting allows the use of the title "Certified Surgical Technologist (CST)." Certification typically requires completing an accredited formal education program or military training program and passing an exam.

Certification through the National Center for Competency Testing allows the use of the title "Tech in Surgery – Certified or TS-C (NCCT)." Applicants may qualify through formal education, military training, or work experience. All require documenting critical skills and passing an exam.

Both certifications require surgical technologists to complete continuing education to maintain their certification.

In addition, many jobs require technologists to become certified in CPR or basic life support (BLS), or both.

A small number of states have regulations governing the work of surgical technologists or surgical first assistants, or both.

The National Board of Surgical Technology and Surgical Assisting, the National Commission for the Certification of Surgical Assistants, and the American Board of Surgical Assistants offer certification for surgical first assistants.

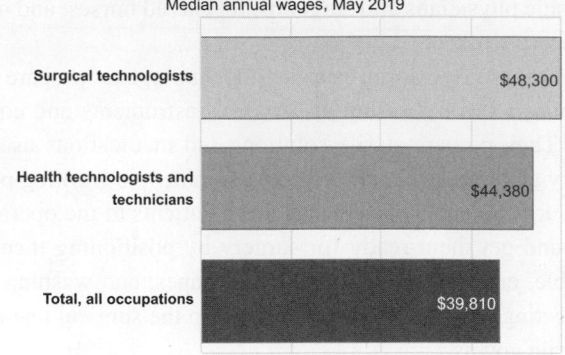

Surgical Technologists
Median annual wages, May 2019

Surgical technologists	$48,300
Health technologists and technicians	$44,380
Total, all occupations	$39,810

Note: All Occupations includes all occupations in the U.S. Economy.
Source: U.S. Bureau of Labor Statistics, Occupational Employment Statistics.

Advancement

Surgical technologists may choose to advance to other healthcare occupations, such as registered nurse. Advancement to other healthcare occupations usually requires additional education, training, and/or certifications or licenses. A technologist may also choose to become a postsecondary teacher of health specialties.

Pay

The median annual wage for surgical technologists was $48,300 in May 2019. The median wage is the wage at which half the workers in an occupation earned more than that amount and half earned less. The lowest 10 percent earned less than $33,420, and the highest 10 percent earned more than $71,400.

In May 2019, the median annual wages for surgical technologists in the top industries in which they worked were as follows:

Outpatient care centers	$51,840
Hospitals; state, local, and private	48,010
Offices of physicians	47,640
Offices of dentists	46,090

Most surgical technologists work full time. Surgical technologists employed in hospitals may work or be on call during nights, weekends, and holidays. They may also be required to work shifts lasting longer than 8 hours.

Job Outlook

Employment of surgical technologists is projected to grow 7 percent from 2019 to 2029, faster than the average for all occupations. Advances in medical technology have made surgery safer, and more operations are being done to treat a variety of illnesses and injuries.

In addition, the aging of the large baby-boom generation is expected to increase the need for surgical technologists because older people usually require more operations. Moreover, as these individuals age, they may be more willing than those in previous generations to seek medical treatment to improve their

Surgical Technologists
Percent change in employment, projected 2019-29

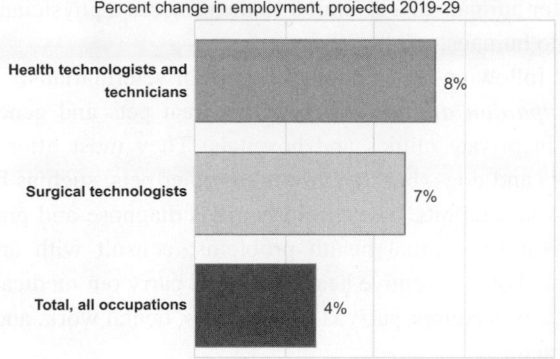

- Health technologists and technicians: 8%
- Surgical technologists: 7%
- Total, all occupations: 4%

Note: All Occupations includes all occupations in the U.S. Economy.
Source: U.S. Bureau of Labor Statistics, Employment Projections program.

quality of life. For example, an individual may decide to have a knee replacement operation in order to maintain an active lifestyle or to have cataracts removed to improve vision.

Job Prospects

Job prospects should be best for surgical technologists who have completed an accredited education program and hold a certification.

Employment projections data for surgical technologists, 2019-29					
Occupational Title	SOC Code	Employment, 2019	Projected Employment, 2029	Change, 2019-29	
				Percent	Numeric
SOURCE: U.S. Bureau of Labor Statistics, Employment Projections program					
Surgical technologists	29-2055	111,300	118,900	7	7,600

State & Area Data
Occupational Employment Statistics (OES)

The Occupational Employment Statistics (OES) program produces employment and wage estimates annually for over 800 occupations. These estimates are available for the nation as a whole, for individual states, and for metropolitan and nonmetropolitan areas.

Contacts for More Information

For more information about surgical technologists, visit
➤ Association of Surgical Technologists

For a list of accredited programs for surgical technologists, visit
➤ Commission on Accreditation of Allied Health Education Programs

For information about certification, visit
➤ The National Board of Surgical Technology and Surgical Assisting
➤ National Center for Competency Testing
➤ National Commission for the Certification of Surgical Assistants
➤ American Board of Surgical Assistants

Veterinarians

Summary

Quick Facts: Veterinarians

2019 Median Pay	$95,460 per year $45.90 per hour
Typical Entry-Level Education	Doctoral or professional degree
Work Experience in a Related Occupation	None
On-the-job Training	None
Number of Jobs, 2019	89,200
Job Outlook, 2019-29	16% (Much faster than average)
Employment Change, 2019-29	14,200

What Veterinarians Do

Veterinarians care for the health of animals and work to protect public health.

Work Environment

Most veterinarians work in private clinics and hospitals. Others travel to farms or work in settings such as laboratories, classrooms, or zoos.

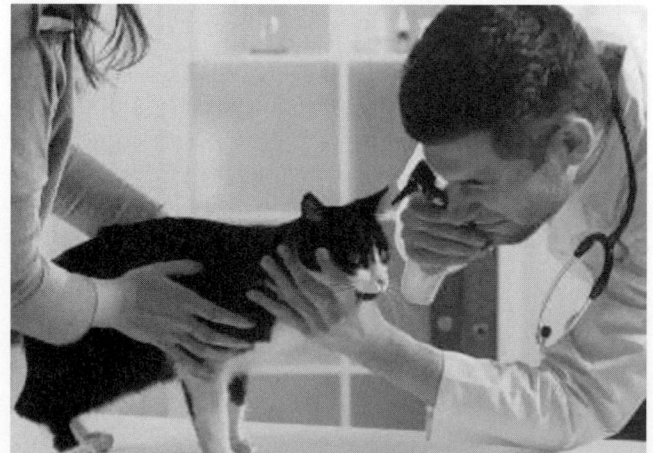

Veterinarians check for symptoms of illnesses in pets.

How to Become a Veterinarian

Veterinarians must have a Doctor of Veterinary Medicine degree from an accredited veterinary college, as well as a state license.

Pay

The median annual wage for veterinarians was $95,460 in May 2019.

Job Outlook

Employment of veterinarians is projected to grow 16 percent from 2019 to 2029, much faster than the average for all occupations. Overall job prospects are expected to be very good.

State & Area Data

Explore resources for employment and wages by state and area for veterinarians.

What Veterinarians Do

Veterinarians care for the health of animals and work to protect public health. They diagnose, treat, and research medical conditions and diseases of pets, livestock, and other animals.

Duties

Veterinarians typically do the following:

- Examine animals to assess their health and diagnose problems
- Treat and dress wounds
- Perform surgery on animals
- Test for and vaccinate against diseases
- Operate medical equipment, such as x-ray machines
- Advise animal owners about general care, medical conditions, and treatments
- Prescribe medication
- Euthanize animals

Veterinarians treat the injuries and illnesses of pets and other animals with a variety of medical equipment, including surgical tools and x-ray and ultrasound machines. They provide treatment for animals that is similar to the services a physician provides to humans.

The following are examples of types of veterinarians:

Companion animal veterinarians treat pets and generally work in private clinics and hospitals. They most often care for cats and dogs, but they also treat other pets, such as birds, ferrets, and rabbits. These veterinarians diagnose and provide treatment for animal health problems; consult with animal owners about preventive healthcare; and carry out medical and surgical procedures, such as vaccinations, dental work, and setting fractures.

Food animal veterinarians work with farm animals such as pigs, cattle, and sheep, which are raised to be food sources. They spend their time visiting farms and ranches to treat ill and injured animals and to test for and vaccinate against disease. They may advise farm owners or managers about feeding, housing, and general health practices.

Food safety and inspection veterinarians inspect and test livestock and animal products for major animal diseases. They also provide vaccines to treat animals, enhance animal welfare, conduct research to improve animal health, and enforce government food safety regulations. They design and administer animal and public health programs to prevent and control diseases transmissible among animals and between animals and people.

Work Environment

Veterinarians held about 89,200 jobs in 2019. The largest employers of veterinarians were as follows:

Veterinary services	76%
Self-employed workers	14
Government	3
Educational services; state, local, and private	1
Social advocacy organizations	1

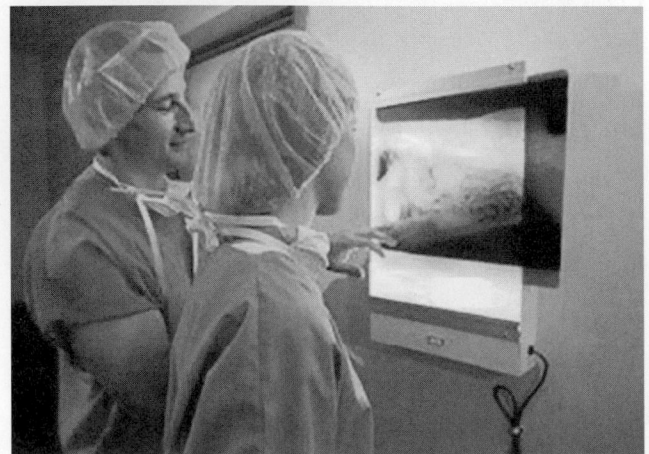

Veterinarians use x rays to diagnose animals.

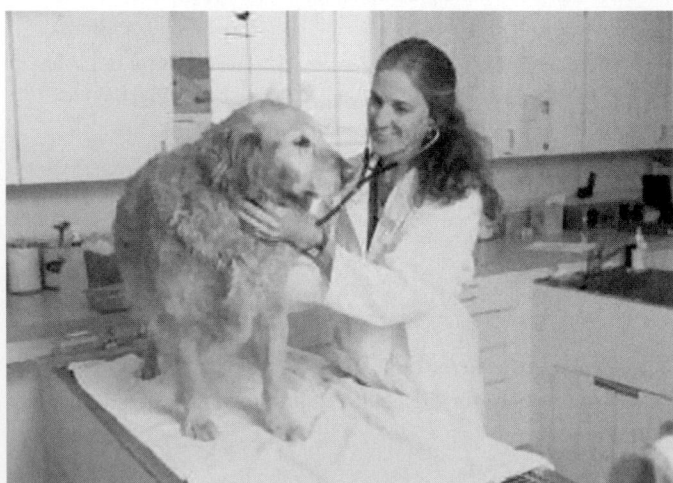

Most veterinarians work in veterinary clinics.

Most veterinarians work in private clinics and hospitals. Others travel to farms or work in settings such as laboratories, classrooms, or zoos.

Veterinarians who treat horses or food animals travel between their offices and farms and ranches. They work outdoors in all kinds of weather and may have to perform surgery, often in remote locations.

Veterinarians who work in food safety and inspection travel to farms, slaughterhouses, and food-processing plants to inspect the health of animals and to ensure that the facility follows safety protocols.

The work can be emotionally stressful, as veterinarians care for abused animals, euthanize sick ones, and offer support to the animals' anxious owners. Working on farms and ranches, in slaughterhouses, or with wildlife can also be physically demanding.

Injuries and Illnesses

When working with animals that are frightened or in pain, veterinarians risk being bitten, kicked, and scratched. In addition, veterinarians working with diseased animals risk being infected by the disease.

Work Schedules

Most veterinarians work full time, often working more than 40 hours per week. Some work nights or weekends, and they may have to respond to emergencies outside of scheduled work hours.

How to Become a Veterinarian

Veterinarians must have a Doctor of Veterinary Medicine degree from an accredited veterinary college, as well as a state license.

Education

Veterinarians must complete a Doctor of Veterinary Medicine (DVM or VMD) degree at an accredited college of veterinary

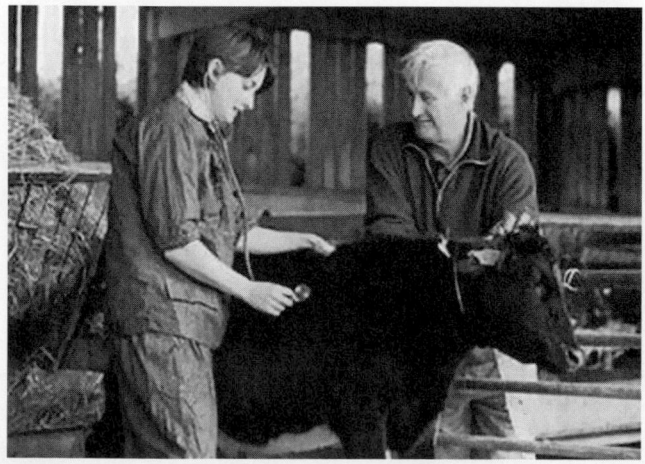

A veterinary medicine program generally takes 4 years to complete and includes classroom, laboratory, and clinical components.

medicine. A veterinary medicine program generally takes 4 years to complete and includes classroom, laboratory, and clinical components.

Admission to veterinary programs is competitive. Most applicants to veterinary school have a bachelor's degree. Veterinary medical colleges typically require applicants to have taken many science classes, including biology, chemistry, and animal science. Most programs also require math, humanities, and social science courses.

Some veterinary medical colleges prefer candidates to have experience such as previous work with veterinarians in clinics, or working with animals on a farm, at a stable, or in an animal shelter.

In veterinary medicine programs, students take courses on animal anatomy and physiology, as well as disease prevention, diagnosis, and treatment. Most programs include 3 years of classroom, laboratory, and clinical work. Students typically spend the final year of the 4-year program doing clinical rotations in a veterinary medical center or hospital.

Licenses, Certifications, and Registrations

Veterinarians must be licensed in order to practice in the United States. Licensing requirements vary by state, but prospective veterinarians in all states must complete an accredited veterinary program and pass the North American Veterinary Licensing Examination.

In addition to passing the national exam, most states require that veterinarians pass a state licensing exam. However, veterinarians employed by state or federal government may not need a state license, because government agencies differ in what they require.

Each state's exam covers its laws and regulations. Few states accept licenses from other states, so veterinarians usually must take exams for the states in which they want to be licensed.

The American Veterinary Medical Association has an Educational Commission for Foreign Veterinary Graduates (ECFVG) certification program, which allows foreign graduates to fulfill the educational prerequisites for licensure.

Important Qualities

Communication skills. Strong communication skills are essential for veterinarians, who must be able to discuss their recommendations and explain treatment options to animal owners and give instructions to their staff.

Compassion. Veterinarians must be compassionate when working with animals and their owners. They must treat animals with kindness and respect, and they must be sensitive when dealing with the animal owners.

Decision-making skills. Veterinarians must decide the correct method for treating the injuries and illnesses of animals.

Manual dexterity. Veterinarians must control their hand movements and be precise when treating injuries and performing surgery.

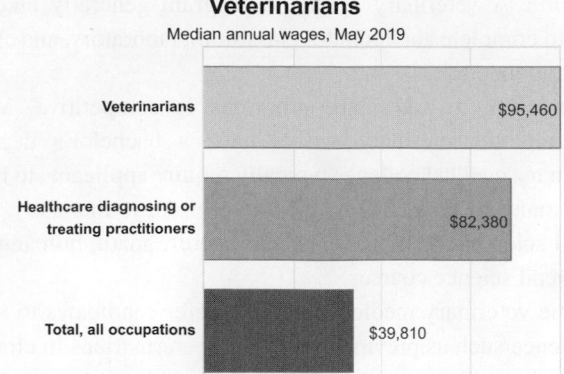

Veterinarians
Median annual wages, May 2019

Veterinarians	$95,460
Healthcare diagnosing or treating practitioners	$82,380
Total, all occupations	$39,810

Note: All Occupations includes all occupations in the U.S. Economy.
Source: U.S. Bureau of Labor Statistics, Occupational Employment Statistics.

Problem-solving skills. Veterinarians need strong problem-solving skills because they must figure out what is ailing animals. Those who test animals to determine the effects of drug therapies also need excellent diagnostic skills.

Pay

The median annual wage for veterinarians was $95,460 in May 2019. The median wage is the wage at which half the workers in an occupation earned more than that amount and half earned less. The lowest 10 percent earned less than $58,080, and the highest 10 percent earned more than $160,780.

In May 2019, the median annual wages for veterinarians in the top industries in which they worked were as follows:

Social advocacy organizations	$97,010
Veterinary services	95,500
Government	90,500
Educational services; state, local, and private	80,800

Most veterinarians work full time, often working more than 40 hours per week. Some work nights or weekends, and they may have to respond to emergencies outside of scheduled work hours.

Job Outlook

Employment of veterinarians is projected to grow 16 percent from 2019 to 2029, much faster than the average for all occupations. Increases in consumers' pet-related spending are expected to drive employment in the veterinary services industry, which employs most veterinarians.

Veterinary medicine has advanced considerably. Today's veterinarians are able to offer many services that are

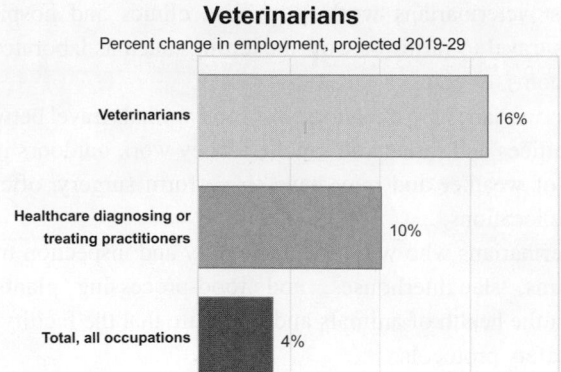

Veterinarians
Percent change in employment, projected 2019-29

Veterinarians	16%
Healthcare diagnosing or treating practitioners	10%
Total, all occupations	4%

Note: All Occupations includes all occupations in the U.S. Economy.
Source: U.S. Bureau of Labor Statistics, Employment Projections program.

comparable to healthcare for humans, including more complicated procedures such as cancer treatments and kidney transplants.

Job Prospects

Overall job prospects are expected to be very good.

Employment projections data for veterinarians, 2019-29					
Occupational Title	SOC Code	Employment, 2019	Projected Employment, 2029	Change, 2019-29	
				Percent	Numeric
SOURCE: U.S. Bureau of Labor Statistics, Employment Projections program					
Veterinarians	29-1131	89,200	103,400	16	14,200

State & Area Data
Occupational Employment Statistics (OES)

The Occupational Employment Statistics (OES) program produces employment and wage estimates annually for over 800 occupations. These estimates are available for the nation as a whole, for individual states, and for metropolitan and nonmetropolitan areas.

Contacts for More Information

For more information about careers in veterinary medicine, a list of U.S. schools and colleges of veterinary medicine, and information on accreditation policies, visit
➤ American Veterinary Medical Association

For more information about veterinary education, visit
➤ Association of American Veterinary Medical Colleges

For information about the licensing exam, visit
➤ International Council for Veterinary Assessment

Veterinary Assistants and Laboratory Animal Caretakers

Summary

Quick Facts: Veterinary Assistants and Laboratory Animal Caretakers	
2019 Median Pay	$28,590 per year $13.75 per hour
Typical Entry-Level Education	High school diploma or equivalent
Work Experience in a Related Occupation ...	None
On-the-job Training	Short-term on-the-job training
Number of Jobs, 2019	99,500
Job Outlook, 2019-29	16% (Much faster than average)
Employment Change, 2019-29	15,700

What Veterinary Assistants and Laboratory Animal Caretakers Do

Veterinary assistants and laboratory animal caretakers handle routine animal care and help scientists, veterinarians, and others with their daily tasks.

Work Environment

Veterinary assistants and laboratory animal caretakers work mainly in clinics, animal hospitals, and research laboratories. Their work may be physically and emotionally demanding.

How to Become a Veterinary Assistant or Laboratory Animal Caretaker

Most veterinary assistants and laboratory animal caretakers have a high school diploma or equivalent and learn the occupation on the job.

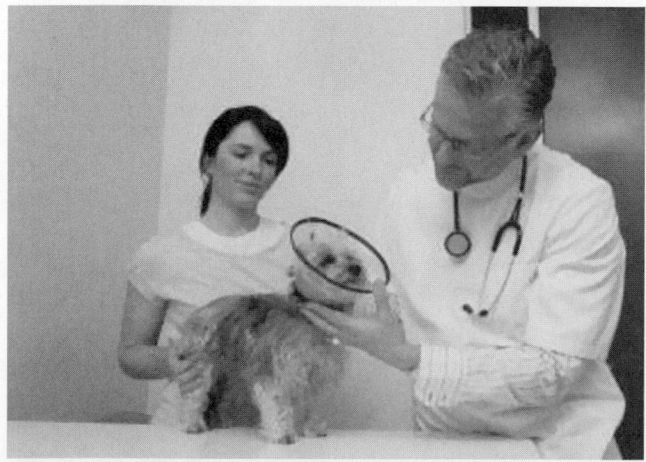

Veterinary assistants care for animals under the supervision of veterinarians and veterinary technicians.

Pay

The median annual wage for veterinary assistants and laboratory animal caretakers was $28,590 in May 2019.

Job Outlook

Employment of veterinary assistants and laboratory animal caretakers is projected to grow 16 percent from 2019 to 2029, much faster than the average for all occupations. High turnover should result in good job opportunities.

State & Area Data

Explore resources for employment and wages by state and area for veterinary assistants and laboratory animal caretakers.

What Veterinary Assistants and Laboratory Animal Caretakers Do

Veterinary assistants and laboratory animal caretakers handle routine animal care and help scientists, veterinarians, and veterinary technologists and technicians with their daily tasks.

Duties

Veterinary assistants and laboratory animal caretakers typically do the following:

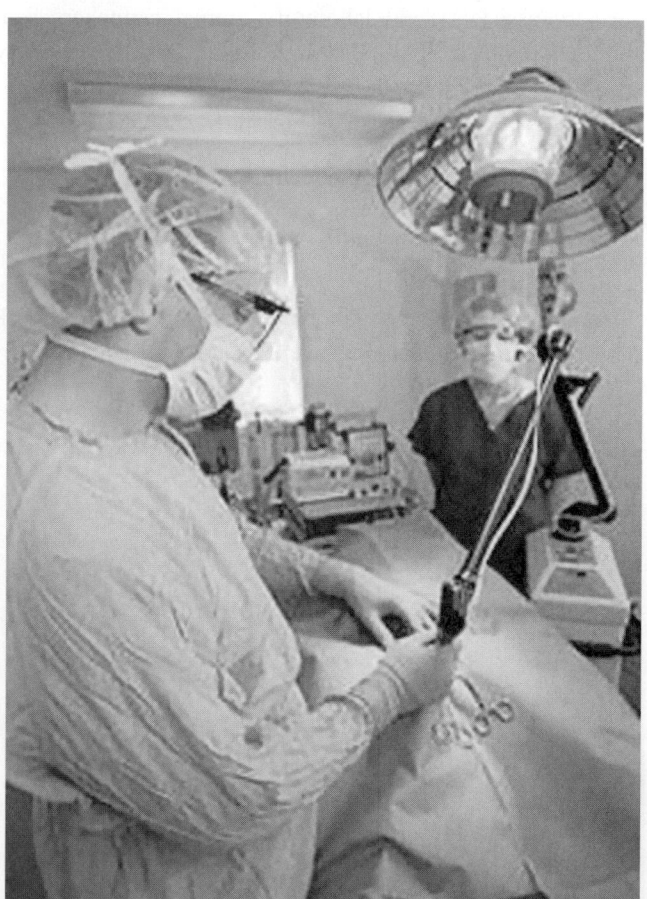

Veterinary assistants may maintain and sterilize surgical instruments and equipment.

- Feed, bathe, and exercise animals
- Clean and disinfect cages, kennels, and examination and operating rooms
- Restrain animals during examination and laboratory procedures
- Maintain and sterilize surgical instruments and equipment
- Monitor and care for animals after surgery
- Help provide emergency first aid to sick and injured animals
- Give medication or immunizations that veterinarians prescribe
- Assist in collecting blood, urine, and tissue samples

Veterinary assistants and laboratory animal caretakers also provide nursing care before surgery and other medical procedures.

They may prepare equipment and pass surgical instruments and materials to veterinarians during surgery. They also move animals during testing and other procedures.

Veterinary assistants typically help veterinarians and veterinary technologists and technicians treat injuries and illnesses of animals.

Laboratory animal caretakers' daily tasks include feeding animals, cleaning kennels, and monitoring animals.

Work Environment

Veterinary assistants and laboratory animal caretakers held about 99,500 jobs in 2019. The largest employers of veterinary assistants and laboratory animal caretakers were as follows:

Veterinary services	87%
Junior colleges, colleges, universities, and professional schools; state, local, and private	5
Research and development in the physical, engineering, and life sciences	3

Veterinary assistants and laboratory animal caretakers work primarily in clinics and animal hospitals, colleges and universities, and research laboratories.

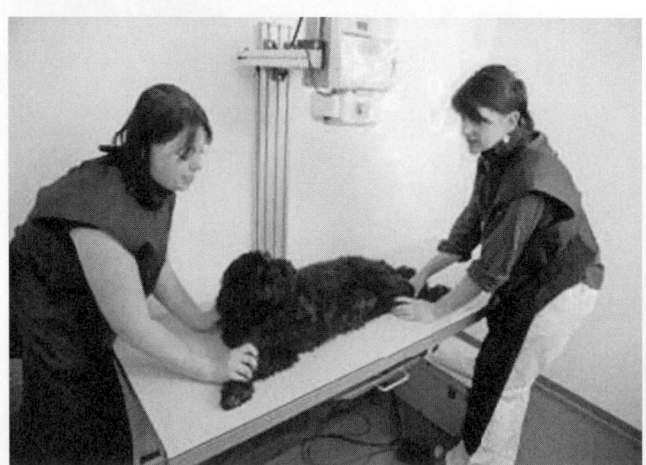

Veterinary assistants move animals and prepare equipment before procedures.

The work of veterinary assistants and laboratory animal caretakers may be physically and emotionally demanding. Workers may handle sick or abused animals and may assist in euthanizing animals.

Injuries and Illnesses

Veterinary assistants and laboratory animal caretakers have one of the highest rates of injuries and illnesses of all occupations. When working with scared and aggressive animals, workers may be bitten, scratched, or kicked. Workers may also be injured while holding, bathing, or restraining an animal.

Work Schedules

Some veterinary assistants and laboratory animal caretakers work part time. Veterinary assistants and laboratory animal caretakers may work nights, weekends, or holidays.

How to Become a Veterinary Assistant or Laboratory Animal Caretaker

Most veterinary assistants and laboratory animal caretakers have a high school diploma or equivalent and learn the occupation on the job. Experience working with or being around animals may be helpful for jobseekers.

Education

Most workers entering the occupation have a high school diploma or equivalent.

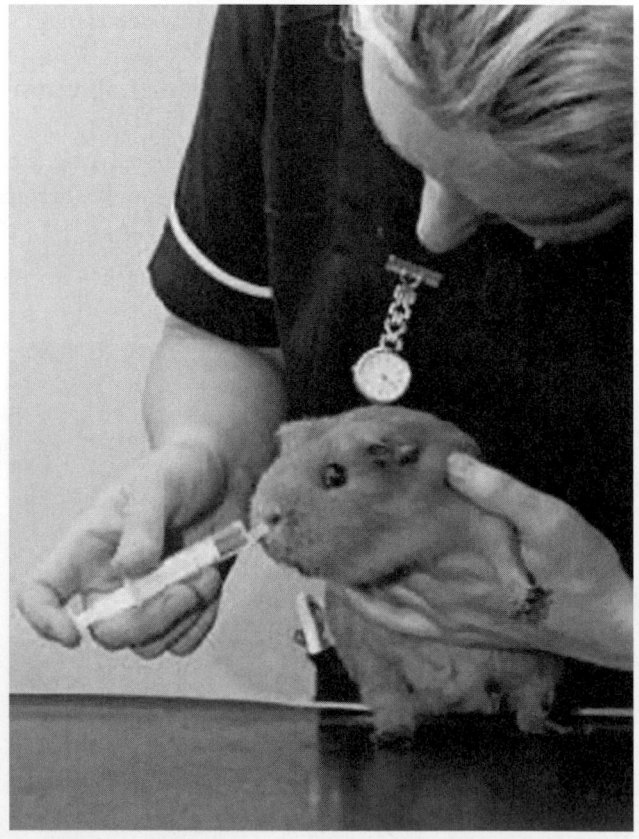

Veterinary assistants learn through on-the-job training.

Training
Most veterinary assistants and laboratory animal caretakers receive short-term on-the-job training.

Licenses, Certifications, and Registrations
Although certification is not mandatory, it allows workers to demonstrate competency in animal husbandry, health and welfare, and facility administration.

The National Association of Veterinary Technicians in America (NAVTA) offers the Approved Veterinary Assistant (AVA) designation for veterinary assistants. To qualify for the designation, candidates must graduate from a NAVTA-approved program and pass an exam.

Laboratory animal caretakers become certified through the American Association for Laboratory Animal Science (AALAS). AALAS offers three levels of certification: Assistant Laboratory Animal Technician (ALAT), Laboratory Animal Technician (LAT), and Laboratory Animal Technologist (LATG). For AALAS certification, candidates must have experience working in a laboratory animal facility and pass an exam.

Important Qualities
Communication skills. Veterinary assistants and laboratory animal caretakers communicate with pet owners, veterinarians, veterinary technologists and technicians, and other assistants. They need to be able to explain instructions, procedures, and other information clearly and effectively.

Compassion. Veterinary assistants and laboratory animal caretakers must treat animals with kindness and show compassion to both the animals and their owners.

Detail oriented. Veterinary assistants and laboratory animal caretakers must follow instructions exactly as directed. For example, they must be precise when sterilizing surgical equipment, monitoring animals, and giving medication.

Manual dexterity. Veterinary assistants and laboratory animal caretakers must be adept in both handling animals and using medical instruments and laboratory equipment.

Physical strength. Veterinary assistants and laboratory animal caretakers must be strong enough to handle, move, and restrain animals.

Pay
The median annual wage for veterinary assistants and laboratory animal caretakers was $28,590 in May 2019. The median wage is the wage at which half the workers in an occupation earned more than that amount and half earned less. The lowest 10 percent earned less than $20,790, and the highest 10 percent earned more than $39,800.

In May 2019, the median annual wages for veterinary assistants and laboratory animal caretakers in the top industries in which they worked were as follows:

Junior colleges, colleges, universities, and professional schools; state, local, and private....	$37,910
Research and development in the physical, engineering, and life sciences............................	32,950
Veterinary services..	28,150

Some veterinary assistants and laboratory animal caretakers work part time. Veterinary assistants and laboratory animal caretakers may work nights, weekends, or holidays.

Job Outlook
Employment of veterinary assistants and laboratory animal caretakers is projected to grow 16 percent from 2019 to 2029, much faster than the average for all occupations. These workers are expected to be needed to assist veterinarians and other veterinary care staff.

Increases in consumers' pet-related spending are expected to drive employment in the veterinary services industry, which

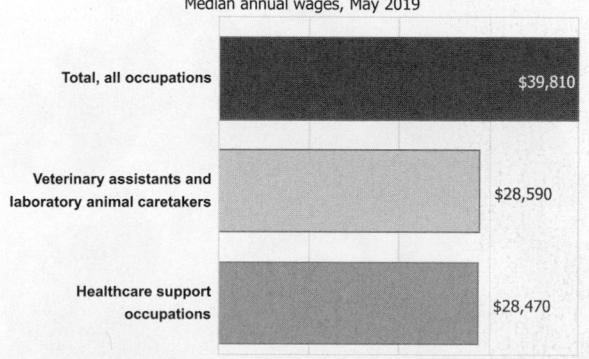

Note: All Occupations includes all occupations in the U.S. Economy.
Source: U.S. Bureau of Labor Statistics, Occupational Employment Statistics.

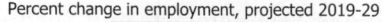
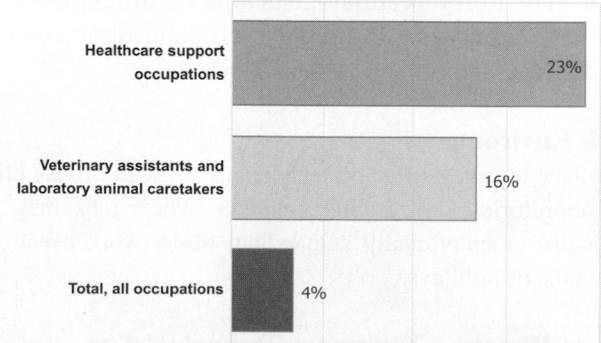

Note: All Occupations includes all occupations in the U.S. Economy.
Source: U.S. Bureau of Labor Statistics, Employment Projections program.

employs most veterinary assistants and laboratory animal caretakers. In clinics and other veterinary service establishments, assistants help veterinarians and veterinary technicians and technologists with various procedures. Demand for veterinary assistants will continue as the demand for these procedures increases.

Job Prospects

Overall job opportunities for veterinary assistants and laboratory animal caretakers are expected to be good. These assistants and caretakers experience a high rate of job turnover, so many positions will become available when workers leave the occupation each year.

Employment projections data for veterinary assistants and laboratory animal caretakers, 2019-29					
Occupational Title	SOC Code	Employment, 2019	Projected Employment, 2029	Change, 2019-29	
				Percent	Numeric
SOURCE: U.S. Bureau of Labor Statistics, Employment Projections program					
Veterinary assistants and laboratory animal caretakers	31-9096	99,500	115,200	16	15,700

State & Area Data
Occupational Employment Statistics (OES)

The Occupational Employment Statistics (OES) program produces employment and wage estimates annually for over 800 occupations. These estimates are available for the nation as a whole, for individual states, and for metropolitan and nonmetropolitan areas.

Contacts for More Information

For more information about certification as a laboratory animal caretaker, visit

➤ American Association for Laboratory Animal Science

For more information about certification as a veterinary assistant, visit

➤ National Association of Veterinary Technicians in America

For more information about becoming a veterinary assistant, including career opportunities, visit

➤ American Animal Hospital Association

Veterinary Technologists and Technicians

Summary

Quick Facts: Veterinary Technologists and Technicians

2019 Median Pay	$35,320 per year $16.98 per hour
Typical Entry-Level Education	Associate's degree
Work Experience in a Related Occupation	None
On-the-job Training	None
Number of Jobs, 2019	112,900
Job Outlook, 2019-29	16% (Much faster than average)
Employment Change, 2019-29	18,300

What Veterinary Technologists and Technicians Do

Veterinary technologists and technicians do medical tests that help diagnose animals' injuries and illnesses.

Work Environment

Veterinary technologists and technicians work in private clinics, laboratories, and animal hospitals. Their jobs may be physically or emotionally demanding. Many work evenings, weekends, or holidays.

How to Become a Veterinary Technologist or Technician

Veterinary technologists and technicians must complete a postsecondary program in veterinary technology. Technologists usually need a 4-year bachelor's degree, and technicians need a 2-year associate's degree. Typically, both technologists and technicians must take a credentialing exam and become registered, licensed, or certified, depending on the requirements of the state in which they work.

Pay

The median annual wage for veterinary technologists and technicians was $35,320 in May 2019.

Job Outlook

Employment of veterinary technologists and technicians is projected to grow 16 percent from 2019 to 2029, much faster than

Veterinary technologists and technicians perform medical tests under the supervision of a licensed veterinarian to assist in diagnosing the injuries and illnesses of animals.

the average for all occupations. Employment is expected to grow as veterinarians continue to use technicians and technologists to do general care and lab work on household pets.

State & Area Data

Explore resources for employment and wages by state and area for veterinary technologists and technicians.

What Veterinary Technologists and Technicians Do

Veterinary technologists and technicians, supervised by licensed veterinarians, do medical tests that help diagnose animals' injuries and illnesses.

Duties

Veterinary technologists and technicians typically do the following:

- Observe the behavior and condition of animals
- Provide nursing care or emergency first aid to recovering or injured animals
- Bathe animals, clip nails or claws, and brush or cut animals' hair
- Restrain animals during exams or procedures
- Administer anesthesia to animals and monitor their responses
- Take x rays and collect and perform laboratory tests, such as urinalyses and blood counts
- Prepare animals and instruments for surgery
- Administer medications, vaccines, and treatments prescribed by a veterinarian
- Collect and record animals' case histories

In addition to helping veterinarians during animal exams, veterinary technologists and technicians do a variety of clinical, care, and laboratory tasks.

Veterinary technologists and technicians who work in research-related jobs ensure that animals are handled carefully and are treated humanely. They may help veterinarians or scientists on research projects in areas such as biomedical research, disaster preparedness, and food safety.

Typically working with small-animal practitioners who care for cats and dogs, veterinary technologists and technicians also may have tasks that involve mice, cattle, or other animals.

Veterinary technologists and technicians may specialize in a particular discipline, such as dentistry, anesthesia, emergency and critical care, and zoological medicine.

Veterinary technologists typically work in more advanced research-related jobs, usually under the guidance of a scientist or veterinarian. Some technologists work in private clinical practices. Working primarily in a laboratory setting, they may administer medications; prepare tissue samples for examination; or record an animal's genealogy, weight, diet, and signs of pain.

Veterinary technicians generally work in private clinical practices under the guidance of a licensed veterinarian. Technicians may do laboratory tests, such as a urinalysis, and help veterinarians conduct a variety of other diagnostic tests. Although they do some of their work in a laboratory, technicians also talk with animal owners. For example, they explain a pet's condition or how to administer medication prescribed by a veterinarian.

Work Environment

Veterinary technologists and technicians held about 112,900 jobs in 2019. The largest employers of veterinary technologists and technicians were as follows:

Veterinary services	90%
Junior colleges, colleges, universities, and professional schools; state, local, and private	4
Social advocacy organizations	2

Veterinary technologists and technicians typically work in private clinics and animal hospitals. They also may work in laboratories, colleges and universities, and humane societies.

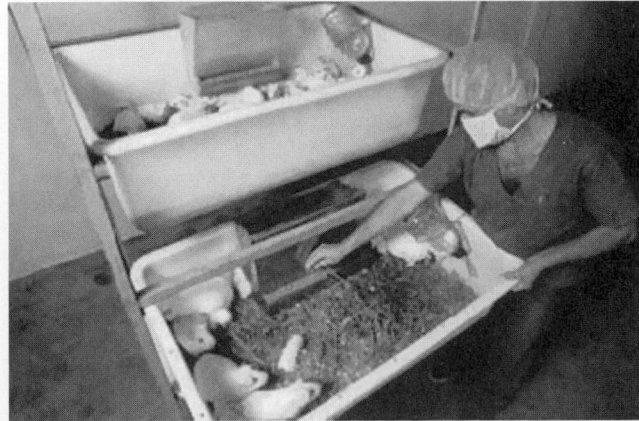

Veterinary technologists and technicians are responsible for the careful and humane handling of laboratory animals.

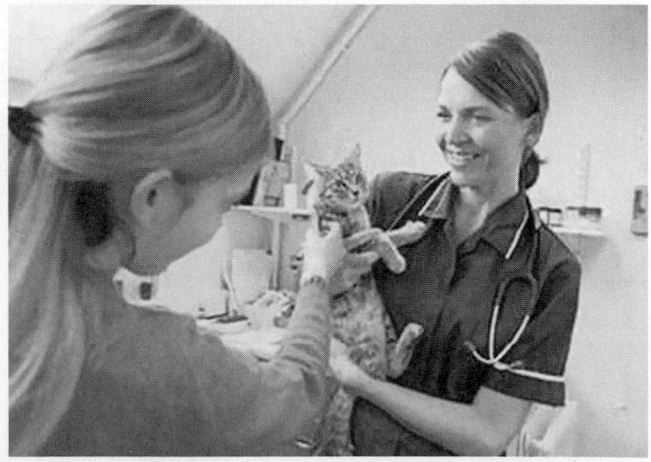

Veterinary technologists and technicians typically work in private clinics and animal hospitals.

Their jobs may be physically or emotionally demanding. For example, they may witness abused animals or may need to help euthanize sick, injured, or unwanted animals.

Injuries and Illnesses

Veterinary technologists and technicians risk injury on the job. They may be bitten, scratched, or kicked while working with scared or aggressive animals. Injuries may happen while the technologist or technician is holding, cleaning, or restraining an animal.

Work Schedules

Veterinary technologists and technicians may have to work evenings, weekends, or holidays.

How to Become a Veterinary Technologist or Technician

Veterinary technologists and technicians must complete a post-secondary program in veterinary technology. Technologists usually need a 4-year bachelor's degree, and technicians need a 2-year associate's degree. Typically, both technologists and technicians must pass a credentialing exam to become registered, licensed, or certified, depending on the requirements of the state in which they work.

Education

Veterinary technologists usually have a 4-year bachelor's degree in veterinary technology. Veterinary technicians usually have a 2-year associate's degree in a veterinary technology program. The American Veterinary Medical Association (AVMA) accredits veterinary technology programs. Most of these programs offer a 2-year associate's degree for veterinary technicians; others offer a 4-year bachelor's degree for veterinary technologists

People interested in becoming a veterinary technologist or technician can prepare by taking biology and other science courses in high school.

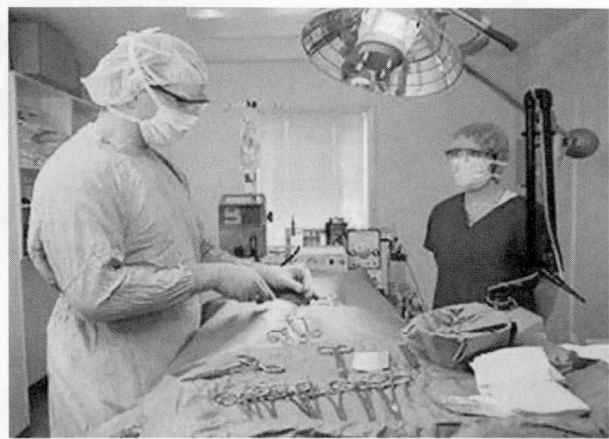

Typically, both technologists and technicians must pass a credentialing exam and must become registered, licensed, or certified, depending on the state in which they work.

Licenses, Certifications, and Registrations

Although each state regulates veterinary technologists and technicians differently, most candidates must pass a credentialing exam. Most states require technologists and technicians to pass the Veterinary Technician National Examination (VTNE), offered by the American Association of Veterinary State Boards.

Important Qualities

Communication skills. Veterinary technologists and technicians communicate with supervisors, other staff, and animal owners. A growing number of technicians counsel pet owners on animal behavior and nutrition.

Compassion. Veterinary technologists and technicians must treat animals with kindness and must be sensitive when dealing with the owners of sick pets.

Detail oriented. Veterinary technologists and technicians must pay attention to detail. They must be precise when recording information, performing diagnostic tests, and administering medication.

Manual dexterity. Veterinary technologists and technicians must handle animals, medical instruments, and laboratory equipment with care. They need a steady hand for intricate tasks such as doing dental work, giving anesthesia, and taking x rays.

Physical strength. Veterinary technologists and technicians need to be able to manage and lift animals.

Pay

The median annual wage for veterinary technologists and technicians was $35,320 in May 2019. The median wage is the wage at which half the workers in an occupation earned more than that amount and half earned less. The lowest 10 percent earned less than $24,530, and the highest 10 percent earned more than $51,230.

In May 2019, the median annual wages for veterinary technologists and technicians in the top industries in which they worked were as follows:

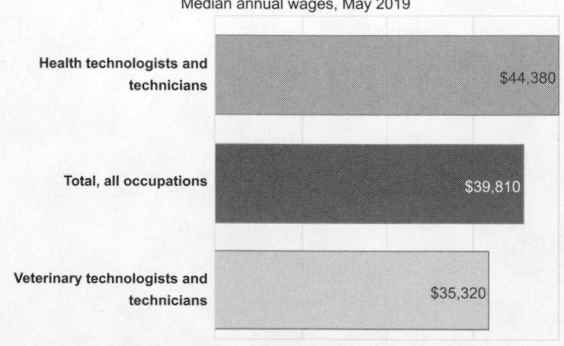

Veterinary Technologists and Technicians
Median annual wages, May 2019

Health technologists and technicians	$44,380
Total, all occupations	$39,810
Veterinary technologists and technicians	$35,320

Note: All Occupations includes all occupations in the U.S. Economy.
Source: U.S. Bureau of Labor Statistics, Occupational Employment Statistics.

Junior colleges, colleges, universities, and professional schools; state, local, and private	$40,990
Veterinary services	34,990
Social advocacy organizations	34,980

Veterinary technologists and technicians working in research positions often earn more than those in other fields.

Veterinary technologists and technicians may have to work evenings, weekends, or holidays.

Job Outlook

Employment of veterinary technologists and technicians is projected to grow 16 percent from 2019 to 2029, much faster than the average for all occupations.

As the number of households with pets and spending on pets continue to rise, demand is expected to increase for veterinary technologists and technicians to do laboratory work and imaging services on household pets.

Job Prospects

Overall job opportunities for veterinary technologists and technicians are expected to be good due to the projected growth in the number of jobs, as well as the commitment required to enter the occupation (obtaining a degree and passing a credentialing exam).

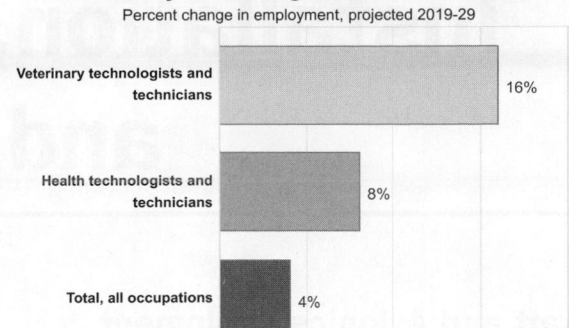

Veterinary Technologists and Technicians
Percent change in employment, projected 2019-29

Note: All Occupations includes all occupations in the U.S. Economy.
Source: U.S. Bureau of Labor Statistics, Employment Projections program.

occupations. These estimates are available for the nation as a whole, for individual states, and for metropolitan and nonmetropolitan areas.

Contacts for More Information

For information about careers in veterinary medicine and a listing of AVMA-accredited veterinary technology programs, visit
➤ American Veterinary Medical Association

For more information about becoming a veterinary technician or technologist, visit
➤ National Association of Veterinary Technicians in America

For information about certification as a laboratory animal technician or technologist, visit
➤ American Association for Laboratory Animal Science

For information about the Veterinary Technician National Examination (VTNE), visit
➤ American Association of Veterinary State Boards

Employment projections data for veterinary technologists and technicians, 2019-29

Occupational Title	SOC Code	Employment, 2019	Projected Employment, 2029	Change, 2019-29 Percent	Change, 2019-29 Numeric
SOURCE: U.S. Bureau of Labor Statistics, Employment Projections program					
Veterinary technologists and technicians	29-2056	112,900	131,200	16	18,300

State & Area Data
Occupational Employment Statistics (OES)

The Occupational Employment Statistics (OES) program produces employment and wage estimates annually for over 800

Installation, Maintenance, and Repair

Aircraft and Avionics Equipment Mechanics and Technicians

Summary

Quick Facts: Aircraft and Avionics Equipment Mechanics and Technicians

2019 Median Pay	$64,310 per year
	$30.92 per hour
Typical Entry-Level Education	See below
Work Experience in a Related Occupation	None
On-the-job Training	None
Number of Jobs, 2019	160,000
Job Outlook, 2019-29	5% (Faster than average)
Employment Change, 2019-29	7,300

What Aircraft and Avionics Equipment Mechanics and Technicians Do

Aircraft and avionics equipment mechanics and technicians repair and perform scheduled maintenance on aircraft.

Work Environment

Aircraft and avionics equipment mechanics and technicians work in hangars, in repair stations, or on airfields. The environment can be loud because of aircraft engines and equipment.

How to Become an Aircraft and Avionics Equipment Mechanic or Technician

Most aircraft and avionics equipment mechanics and technicians learn their trade at an Federal Aviation Administration (FAA)-approved aviation maintenance technician school or on the job. Some learn through training received in the military.

Pay

The median annual wage for aircraft mechanics and service technicians was $64,090 in May 2019.

The median annual wage for avionics technicians was $65,700 in May 2019.

Job Outlook

Overall employment of aircraft and avionics equipment mechanics and technicians is projected to grow 5 percent from 2019 to 2029, faster than the average for all occupations. Job opportunities are expected to be good because there will be a need to replace those workers leaving the occupation.

State & Area Data

Explore resources for employment and wages by state and area for aircraft and avionics equipment mechanics and technicians.

What Aircraft and Avionics Equipment Mechanics and Technicians Do

Aircraft and avionics equipment mechanics and technicians repair and perform scheduled maintenance on aircraft.

Aircraft and avionics equipment mechanics and technicians perform scheduled maintenance, make repairs, and complete inspections.

Aircraft mechanics diagnose mechanical or electrical problems.

Duties

Aircraft mechanics typically do the following:

- Diagnose mechanical or electrical problems
- Repair wings, brakes, electrical systems, and other aircraft components
- Replace defective parts, using hand tools or power tools
- Examine replacement aircraft parts for defects
- Read maintenance manuals to identify repair procedures
- Test aircraft parts with gauges and other diagnostic equipment
- Inspect completed work to ensure that it meets performance standards
- Keep records of maintenance and repair work

Avionics technicians typically do the following:

- Test electronic instruments, using circuit testers, oscilloscopes, and voltmeters
- Interpret flight test data to diagnose malfunctions and performance problems
- Assemble components, such as electrical controls and junction boxes, and install software
- Install instrument panels, using hand tools, power tools, and soldering irons
- Repair or replace malfunctioning components
- Keep records of maintenance and repair work

Airplanes require reliable parts and maintenance in order to fly safely. To keep an airplane in operating condition, aircraft and avionics equipment mechanics and technicians perform scheduled maintenance, make repairs, and complete inspections. They must follow detailed regulations set by the Federal Aviation Administration (FAA) that dictate maintenance schedules for different operations.

Many mechanics are generalists and work on many different types of aircraft, such as jets, piston-driven airplanes, and helicopters. Others specialize in one section, such as the engine, hydraulic system, or electrical system, of a particular type of aircraft. In independent repair shops, mechanics usually inspect and repair many types of aircraft.

The following are examples of types of aircraft and avionics equipment mechanics and technicians:

Airframe and Powerplant (A&P) mechanics are certified generalist mechanics who can independently perform many maintenance and alteration tasks on aircraft. A&P mechanics repair and maintain most parts of an aircraft, including the engines, landing gear, brakes, and air-conditioning system. Some specialized activities require additional experience and certification.

Maintenance schedules for aircraft may be based on hours flown, days since the last inspection, trips flown, or a combination of these factors. Maintenance also may need to be done at other times to address specific issues recognized by mechanics or manufacturers.

Mechanics use precision instruments to measure wear and identify defects. They may use x rays or magnetic or ultrasonic inspection equipment to discover cracks that cannot be seen on a plane's exterior. They check for corrosion, distortion, and cracks in the aircraft's main body, wings, and tail. They then repair the metal, fabric, wood, or composite materials that make up the airframe and skin.

After completing all repairs, mechanics test the equipment to ensure that it works properly and record all maintenance completed on an aircraft.

Avionics technicians are specialists who repair and maintain a plane's electronic instruments, such as radio communication devices and equipment, radar systems, and navigation aids. As the use of digital technology increases, more time is spent maintaining computer systems. The ability to repair and maintain many avionics and flight instrument systems is granted through the Airframe rating, but other licenses or certifications may be needed as well.

Designated airworthiness representatives (DARs) examine, inspect, and test aircraft for airworthiness. They issue airworthiness certificates, which aircraft must have to fly. There are two types of DARs: manufacturing DARs and maintenance DARs.

Inspection authorized (IA) mechanics are mechanics who have both Airframe and Powerplant certification and may perform inspections on aircraft and return them to service. IA mechanics are able to do a wider variety of maintenance activities and alterations than any other type of maintenance personnel. They can do comprehensive annual inspections or return aircraft to service after a major repair.

Repairmen certificate holders may or may not have the A&P certificate or other certificates. Repairmen certificates are issued by certified repair stations to aviation maintenance personnel, and the certificates allow them to do specific duties. Repairmen certificates are valid only while the mechanic works at the issuing repair center and are not transferable to other employers.

Work Environment

Aircraft mechanics and service technicians held about 137,200 jobs in 2019. The largest employers of aircraft mechanics and service technicians were as follows:

Support activities for air transportation	29%
Scheduled air transportation	23
Aerospace product and parts manufacturing	14
Federal government, excluding postal service	13
Nonscheduled air transportation	5

Avionics technicians held about 22,800 jobs in 2019. The largest employers of avionics technicians were as follows:

Aerospace product and parts manufacturing	38%

Aircraft mechanics climb, reach, and balance on a plane's exterior.

Aircraft and avionics equipment mechanics and technicians work in hangars, in repair stations, or on airfields. They must meet strict deadlines while following safety standards.

Most of these mechanics and technicians work near major airports. They may work outside on the airfield, or in climate-controlled shops and hangars. Civilian aircraft and avionics equipment mechanics and technicians employed by the U.S. Armed Forces work on military installations.

Injuries and Illnesses

Aircraft and avionics equipment mechanics and technicians often lift heavy objects, handle dangerous chemicals, or operate large power tools. They may work on scaffolds or ladders, and noise and vibrations are common, especially when engines are being tested. Workers must take precautions against injuries, such as wearing ear protection and brightly colored vests to ensure that they are seen when working around large aircraft.

Work Schedules

Aircraft and avionics equipment mechanics and technicians usually work full time on rotating 8-hour shifts. Overtime and weekend work are common.

How to Become an Aircraft and Avionics Equipment Mechanic or Technician

Some aircraft and avionics equipment mechanics and technicians learn their trade at an Federal Aviation Administration (FAA)-approved aviation maintenance technician school. Others are trained on the job or learn through training in the military. Aircraft mechanics and avionics technicians typically are certified by the FAA. (See Title 14 of the Code of Federal Regulations (14 CFR), part 65, subparts D and E, for the most current requirements for becoming a certified mechanic.)

Some aircraft and avionics equipment mechanics and technicians learn their trade on the job.

Education

Aircraft mechanics and service technicians typically enter the occupation after attending a Part 147 FAA-approved aviation maintenance technician school. These schools award a certificate of completion that the FAA recognizes as an alternative to the experience requirements stated in regulations. The schools also grant holders the right to take the relevant FAA exams.

Avionics technicians typically earn an associate's degree before entering the occupation. Aircraft controls, systems, and flight instruments have become increasingly digital and computerized. Workers who have the proper background in aviation flight instruments or computer repair are needed to maintain these complex systems

Training

Some aircraft mechanics and service technicians enter the occupation with a high school diploma or equivalent and receive on-the-job training to learn their skills and to be able to pass the FAA exams. Aviation maintenance personnel who are not certified by the FAA work under supervision until they have enough experience and knowledge and become certified.

Licenses, Certifications, and Registrations

The FAA requires that aircraft maintenance be done either by a certified mechanic with the appropriate ratings or authorizations or under the supervision of such a mechanic.

The FAA offers separate certifications for bodywork (Airframe mechanics, or "A") and engine work (Powerplant mechanics, or "P"), but employers may prefer to hire mechanics who have both Airframe and Powerplant (A&P) ratings. The A&P ratings generally certify that aviation mechanics meet basic knowledge and ability standards.

Mechanics must be at least 18 years of age, be fluent in English, and have 30 months of experience to qualify for either the A or the P rating or both (the A&P rating). Completion of a program at a Part 147 FAA-approved aviation maintenance technician school can substitute for the experience requirement and shorten the time requirements for becoming eligible to take the FAA exams.

Applicants must pass written, oral, and practical exams that demonstrate the required skills within a timeframe of 2 years.

To keep their certification, mechanics must have completed relevant repair or maintenance work within the previous 24 months. To fulfill this requirement, mechanics may take classes from their employer, a school, or an aircraft manufacturer.

The Inspection Authorization (IA) is available to mechanics who have had their A&P ratings for at least 3 years and meet other requirements. These mechanics are able to review and approve many major repairs and alterations.

Avionics technicians typically are certified through a repair station for the specific work they perform on aircraft, or they hold the Airframe rating to work on an aircraft's electronic and flight instrument systems. An Aircraft Electronics Technician (AET) certification is available through the National Center for Aerospace & Transportation Technologies (NCATT). It certifies that aviation mechanics have a basic level of knowledge in the subject area, but it is not required by the FAA for any specific tasks. Avionics technicians who work on communications equipment may need to have the proper radiotelephone operator certification issued by the Federal Communications Commission (FCC).

Work Experience in a Related Occupation

Some avionics technicians begin their careers as aircraft mechanics and service technicians. As aircraft mechanics and service technicians gain experience, they may attend classes or otherwise choose to pursue additional certifications that grant privileges to work on specialized flight instruments. Eventually, they may become avionics technicians who work exclusively on flight instruments.

Advancement

As aircraft mechanics gain experience, they may advance to lead mechanic, lead inspector, or shop supervisor. Opportunities to advance may be best for those who have an inspection authorization (IA). Mechanics with broad experience in maintenance and repair may become inspectors or examiners for the FAA.

Important Qualities

Detail oriented. Mechanics and technicians need to adjust airplane parts to exact specifications. For example, they often use precision tools to tighten wheel bolts to a specified tension.

Dexterity. Mechanics and technicians need to coordinate the movement of their fingers and hands in order to grasp, manipulate, or assemble parts.

Observational skills. Mechanics and technicians must recognize engine noises, read gauges, and collect other information to determine whether an aircraft's systems are working properly.

Strength. Mechanics and technicians may carry or move heavy equipment or aircraft parts, climb on airplanes, balance, and reach without falling.

Pay

The median annual wage for aircraft mechanics and service technicians was $64,090 in May 2019. The median wage is the wage at which half the workers in an occupation earned more than that amount and half earned less. The lowest 10 percent earned less than $37,890, and the highest 10 percent earned more than $101,070.

The median annual wage for avionics technicians was $65,700 in May 2019. The lowest 10 percent earned less than $40,350, and the highest 10 percent earned more than $97,150.

In May 2019, the median annual wages for aircraft mechanics and service technicians in the top industries in which they worked were as follows:

Scheduled air transportation	$89,820
Aerospace product and parts manufacturing	67,180
Nonscheduled air transportation	60,350
Federal government, excluding postal service	60,070
Support activities for air transportation	54,920

In May 2019, the median annual wages for avionics technicians in the top industries in which they worked were as follows:

Aerospace product and parts manufacturing	$74,860
Professional, scientific, and technical services	72,810
Federal government	58,530
Support activities for air transportation	56,020

Mechanics and technicians usually work full time on rotating 8-hour shifts. Overtime and weekend work are common.

Aircraft and Avionics Equipment Mechanics and Technicians

Median annual wages, May 2019

Avionics technicians	$65,700
Aircraft and avionics equipment mechanics and technicians	$64,310
Aircraft mechanics and service technicians	$64,090
Installation, maintenance, and repair occupations	$46,630
Total, all occupations	$39,810

Note: All Occupations includes all occupations in the U.S. Economy.
Source: U.S. Bureau of Labor Statistics, Occupational Employment Statistics.

Aircraft and Avionics Equipment Mechanics and Technicians

Percent change in employment, projected 2019-29

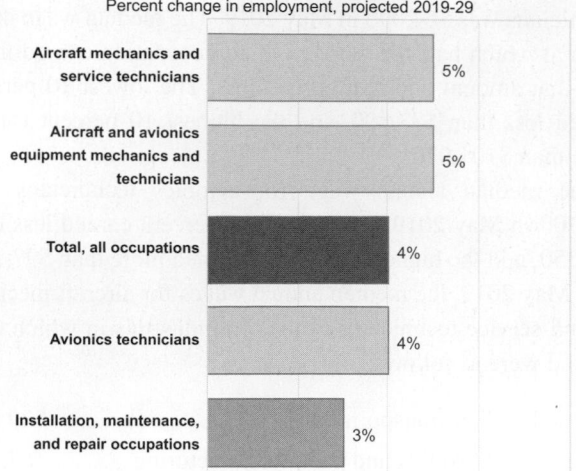

Note: All Occupations includes all occupations in the U.S. Economy.
Source: U.S. Bureau of Labor Statistics, Employment Projections program.

Job Outlook

Overall employment of aircraft and avionics equipment mechanics and technicians is projected to grow 5 percent from 2019 to 2029, faster than the average for all occupations. Employment growth will vary by occupation (see table below).

Air traffic is expected to increase gradually over the coming decade, and will require additional aircraft maintenance, including that performed on new aircraft.

Job Prospects

Job opportunities are expected to be good because there will be a need to replace those workers leaving the occupation.

Occupational Title	SOC Code	Employment, 2019	Projected Employment, 2029	Change, 2019-29	
				Percent	Numeric
SOURCE: U.S. Bureau of Labor Statistics, Employment Projections program					
Aircraft and avionics equipment mechanics and technicians	—	160,000	167,300	5	7,300
Avionics technicians	49-2091	22,800	23,800	4	1,000
Aircraft mechanics and service technicians	49-3011	137,200	143,500	5	6,300

Employment projections data for aircraft and avionics equipment mechanics and technicians, 2019-29

State & Area Data
Occupational Employment Statistics (OES)

The Occupational Employment Statistics (OES) program produces employment and wage estimates annually for over 800 occupations. These estimates are available for the nation as a whole, for individual states, and for metropolitan and nonmetropolitan areas.

Contacts for More Information

For more information about aircraft and avionics equipment mechanics and technicians, visit

- ➤ Aircraft Mechanics Fraternal Association
- ➤ Aviation Maintenance Magazine
- ➤ Federal Aviation Administration
- ➤ National Business Aviation Association
- ➤ National Center for Aerospace & Transportation Technologies
- ➤ Professional Aviation Maintenance Association

Automotive Body and Glass Repairers

Summary

Quick Facts: Automotive Body and Glass Repairers

2019 Median Pay	$42,350 per year $20.36 per hour
Typical Entry-Level Education	High school diploma or equivalent
Work Experience in a Related Occupation	None
On-the-job Training	See below
Number of Jobs, 2019	179,700
Job Outlook, 2019-29	2% (Slower than average)
Employment Change, 2019-29	4,300

What Automotive Body and Glass Repairers Do

Automotive body and glass repairers restore, refinish, and replace vehicle bodies and frames, windshields, and window glass.

Work Environment

Automotive body repairers work indoors in body shops, which are often noisy. Shops are typically well ventilated, so that dust and paint fumes can be dispersed. Repairers sometimes work in awkward and cramped positions, and their work can be physically demanding.

Automotive glass installers and repairers often travel to the customer's location to repair damaged windshields and window glass.

How to Become an Automotive Body or Glass Repairer

Most employers prefer to hire automotive body and glass repairers who have completed a training program in automotive body or glass repair. Still, many new automotive body and glass repairers begin work without previous training. Industry certification is becoming increasingly important.

Pay

The median annual wage for automotive body and related repairers was $43,580 in May 2019.

Automotive body repairers restore automobile frames to factory specifications.

The median annual wage for automotive glass installers and repairers was $35,790 in May 2019.

Job Outlook

Overall employment of automotive body and glass repairers is projected to grow 2 percent from 2019 to 2029, slower than the average for all occupations. However, many openings will arise from the need to replace workers who leave the occupation.

State & Area Data

Explore resources for employment and wages by state and area for automotive body and glass repairers.

What Automotive Body and Glass Repairers Do

Automotive body and glass repairers restore, refinish, and replace vehicle bodies and frames, windshields, and window glass.

Duties

Automotive body repairers typically do the following:

- Review damage reports, prepare cost estimates, and plan work
- Inspect cars for structural damage
- Remove damaged body parts, including bumpers, fenders, hoods, grilles, and trim
- Realign car frames and chassis to repair structural damage
- Hammer out or patch dents, dimples, and other minor body damage
- Fit, attach, and weld replacement parts into place
- Sand, buff, and prime refurbished and repaired surfaces
- Apply new finish to restored body parts

Automotive glass installers and repairers typically do the following:

- Examine damaged glass or windshields and assess repairability

Automotive body and glass repairers inspect car frames for structural damage.

- Clean damaged areas and prepare the surfaces for repair
- Stabilize chips and cracks with clear resin
- Remove glass that cannot be repaired
- Check windshield frames for rust
- Clean windshield frames and prepare them for installation
- Apply urethane sealant to the windshield frames
- Install replacement glass
- Replace any parts removed prior to repairs

Automotive body and glass repairers can repair most damage from vehicle collisions and make vehicles look and drive like new. Repairs may be minor, such as replacing a cracked windshield, or major, such as replacing an entire door panel. After a major collision, the underlying frame of a car can become weakened or compromised. Body repairers restore the structural integrity of car frames to manufacturer specifications.

Body repairers use pneumatic tools and plasma cutters to remove damaged parts, such as bumpers and door panels. They also often use heavy-duty hydraulic jacks and hammers for major structural repairs, such as aligning the body. For some work, they use common hand tools, such as metal files, pliers, wrenches, hammers, and screwdrivers.

In some cases, body repairers complete an entire job by themselves. In other cases, especially in large shops, they use an assembly line approach in which they work as a team with each individual performing a specialized task.

Although body repairers sometimes prime and paint repaired parts, painting and coating workers generally perform these tasks.

Glass installers and repairers often travel to the customer's location and perform their work in the field. They commonly use specialized tools such as vacuum pumps to fill windshield cracks and chips with a stabilizing resin. When windshields are badly damaged, they use knives to remove the damaged windshield, and then they secure the new windshield using a special urethane adhesive.

Work Environment

Automotive body and related repairers held about 155,500 jobs in 2019. The largest employers of automotive body and related repairers were as follows:

Automotive body, paint, interior, and glass repair	61%
Automobile dealers	17
Self-employed workers	6
Automotive mechanical and electrical repair and maintenance	5

Automotive glass installers and repairers held about 24,300 jobs in 2019. The largest employers of automotive glass installers and repairers were as follows:

Automotive body, paint, interior, and glass repair	73%
Self-employed workers	19
Construction	2

Body repairers typically work indoors in body shops, which are often noisy. Most shops are well ventilated, so that dust and paint fumes can be dispersed. Glass installers and repairers often travel to the customer's location to repair damaged windshields and window glass.

Automotive body and glass repairers sometimes work in awkward and cramped positions, and their work can be physically demanding.

Injuries and Illnesses

Automotive glass installers and repairers have one of the highest rates of injuries and illnesses of all occupations. These workers may suffer minor injuries, such as cuts, burns, and scrapes. Following safety procedures helps to avoid serious accidents.

Work Schedules

Most automotive body and glass repairers work full time. When shops have to complete a backlog of work, overtime is common. This often includes working evenings and weekends.

How to Become an Automotive Body or Glass Repairer

Most employers prefer to hire automotive body and glass repairers who have completed a training program in automotive body or glass repair. Still, many new body and glass repairers begin work without previous training. Industry certification is increasingly important.

Education

High school, trade and technical school, and community college programs in collision repair combine hands-on practice and technical instruction. Topics usually include electronics, repair cost estimation, and welding, all of which provide a strong educational foundation for a career as a body repairer.

Trade and technical school programs typically award certificates after 6 months to 1 year of study. Some community colleges offer 2-year programs in collision repair. Many of these schools also offer certificates for individual courses, so students can take classes part time or as needed.

Training

New workers typically begin their on-the-job training by helping an experienced body repairer with basic tasks, such as fixing minor dents. As they gain experience, they move on to more complex work, such as aligning car frames. Some body repairers may become trained in as little as 1 year, but they generally need 2 or 3 years of hands-on training to become fully independent body repairers.

Basic automotive glass installation and repair can be learned in as little as 6 months, but becoming fully independent can take up to a year of training.

Workers who complete programs in collision repair often require significantly less on-the-job training. They typically advance to independent work more quickly than those who do not have the same level of education.

Throughout their careers, body repairers need to continue their training to keep up with rapidly changing automotive

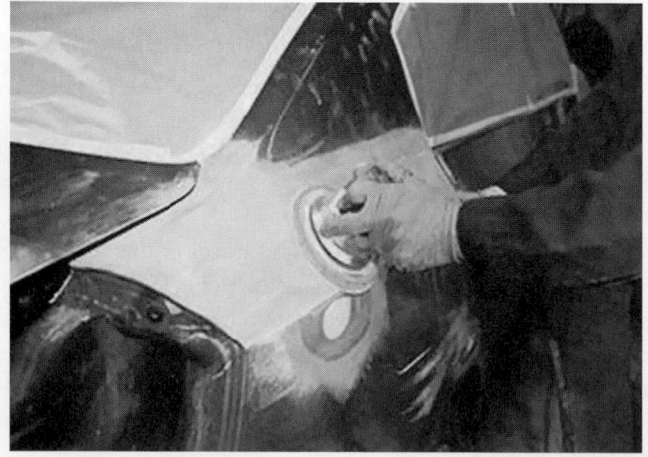

Automotive body repairers typically work indoors in body shops.

Automotive glass repairers receive hands-on practice while attending programs in collision repair.

technology and materials. Body repairers are expected to develop their skills by reading technical manuals and by attending classes and seminars. Many employers regularly send workers to advanced training programs, such as those offered by the Inter-Industry Conference on Auto Collision Repair (I-CAR).

Licenses, Certifications, and Registrations

Although not required, certification is recommended because it shows competence and usually brings higher pay. In some instances it is required for advancement beyond entry-level work.

Certification from the National Institute for Automotive Service Excellence (ASE) is a standard credential for body repairers. In addition, many vehicle and paint manufacturers have product certification programs that are used to train body repairers in specific technologies and repair methods.

A few states require a license to perform automotive glass installation and repair. Check with your state for more information.

Advancement

Automotive body and glass repairers earn more money as they gain experience, and some may advance into management positions within body shops, especially those workers with 2- or 4-year degrees.

Important Qualities

Critical-thinking skills. Automotive body and glass repairers evaluate vehicle damage and determine necessary repair strategies. In some cases, they must decide if a vehicle is "totaled," or too damaged to justify the cost of repair.

Customer-service skills. Automotive body and glass repairers discuss auto body and glass problems, along with options to fix them, with customers. Workers must be courteous, good listeners, and ready to answer customers' questions.

Detail oriented. Automotive body and glass repairers must pay close attention to detail. Restoring a damaged auto body or windshield requires workers to have a keen eye for even the smallest imperfection.

Dexterity. Automotive body repairers' tasks, such as removing door panels, hammering out dents, and using hand tools to install parts, require a steady hand and good hand–eye coordination.

Mechanical skills. Automotive body repairers must know which diagnostic, hydraulic, pneumatic, and other power equipment and tools are appropriate for certain procedures and repairs. They must know how to apply the correct techniques and methods necessary to repair automobiles.

Physical strength. Automotive body and glass repairers must sometimes lift heavy parts, such as door panels and windshields.

Time-management skills. Automotive body and glass repairers must be timely in their repairs. For many people, their automobile is their primary mode of transportation.

Pay

The median annual wage for automotive body and related repairers was $43,580 in May 2019. The median wage is the wage at which half the workers in an occupation earned more than that amount and half earned less. The lowest 10 percent earned less than $26,710, and the highest 10 percent earned more than $73,470.

The median annual wage for automotive glass installers and repairers was $35,790 in May 2019. The lowest 10 percent earned less than $24,660, and the highest 10 percent earned more than $52,710.

In May 2019, the median annual wages for automotive body and related repairers in the top industries in which they worked were as follows:

Automotive body, paint, interior, and glass repair ..	$44,100
Automotive mechanical and electrical repair and maintenance	41,810
Automobile dealers	40,930

In May 2019, the median annual wages for automotive glass installers and repairers in the top industries in which they worked were as follows:

Construction	$36,840
Automotive body, paint, interior, and glass repair ...	35,530

The majority of repair shops and auto dealers pay automotive body and glass repairers on an incentive basis. In addition to receiving a guaranteed base salary, employers pay workers a set amount for completing various tasks. Their earnings depend on both the amount of work assigned and how fast they complete it.

Automotive Body and Glass Repairers
Median annual wages, May 2019

Vehicle and mobile equipment mechanics, installers, and repairers	$44,590
Automotive body and related repairers	$43,580
Automotive body and glass repairers	$42,350
Total, all occupations	$39,810
Automotive glass installers and repairers	$35,790

Note: All Occupations includes all occupations in the U.S. Economy.
Source: U.S. Bureau of Labor Statistics, Occupational Employment Statistics.

Most automotive body and glass repairers work full time. When shops have to complete a backlog of work, overtime is common. This often includes working evenings and weekends.

Job Outlook

Overall employment of automotive body and glass repairers is projected to grow 2 percent from 2019 to 2029, slower than the average for all occupations.

Job Prospects

Despite limited employment growth, about 15,700 openings for automotive body and glass repairers are projected each year, on average, over the decade.

Most of those openings are expected to result from the need to replace workers who transfer to different occupations or exit the labor force, such as to retire.

The best opportunities in automotive body repair will be available for those with industry certification and training in automotive body repair and refinishing, and in collision repair.

Employment projections data for automotive body and glass repairers, 2019-29					
Occupational Title	SOC Code	Employment, 2019	Projected Employment, 2029	Change, 2019-29	
				Percent	Numeric
SOURCE: U.S. Bureau of Labor Statistics, Employment Projections program					
Automotive body and glass repairers	—	179,700	184,000	2	4,300
Automotive body and related repairers	49-3021	155,500	159,900	3	4,400
Automotive glass installers and repairers	49-3022	24,300	24,200	0	-100

State & Area Data

Occupational Employment Statistics (OES)

The Occupational Employment Statistics (OES) program produces employment and wage estimates annually for over 800

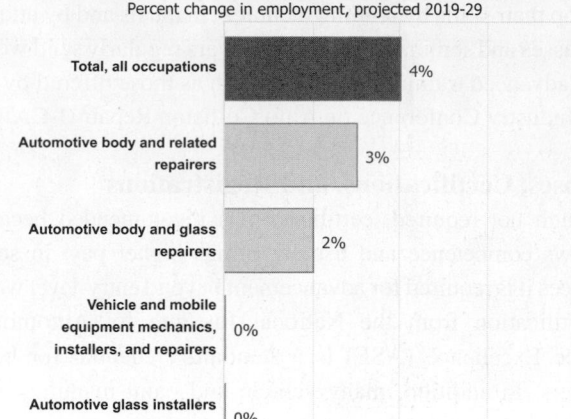

Automotive Body and Glass Repairers
Percent change in employment, projected 2019-29

- Total, all occupations: 4%
- Automotive body and related repairers: 3%
- Automotive body and glass repairers: 2%
- Vehicle and mobile equipment mechanics, installers, and repairers: 0%
- Automotive glass installers and repairers: 0%

Note: All Occupations includes all occupations in the U.S. Economy.
Source: U.S. Bureau of Labor Statistics, Employment Projections program.

occupations. These estimates are available for the nation as a whole, for individual states, and for metropolitan and nonmetropolitan areas.

Contacts for More Information

For more information about careers in automotive body and glass repair, visit

➤ Accrediting Commission of Career Schools and Colleges
➤ Inter-Industry Conference on Auto Collision Repair
➤ National Automotive Technicians Education Foundation
➤ National Glass Association
➤ National Institute for Automotive Service Excellence
➤ Society of Collision Repair Specialists

Automotive Service Technicians and Mechanics

Summary

Quick Facts: Automotive Service Technicians and Mechanics	
2019 Median Pay	$42,090 per year $20.24 per hour
Typical Entry-Level Education	Postsecondary non-degree award
Work Experience in a Related Occupation	None
On-the-job Training	Short-term on-the-job training
Number of Jobs, 2019	756,600
Job Outlook, 2019-29	-4% (Decline)
Employment Change, 2019-29	-27,800

What Automotive Service Technicians and Mechanics Do

Automotive service technicians and mechanics inspect, maintain, and repair cars and light trucks.

Work Environment

Most automotive service technicians and mechanics work in well-ventilated and well-lit repair shops. Although technicians often identify and fix automotive problems with computers, they commonly work with greasy parts and tools, sometimes in uncomfortable positions.

How to Become an Automotive Service Technician or Mechanic

Employers prefer that automotive service technicians and mechanics complete a program at a postsecondary institution.

Automotive service technicians and mechanics use a variety of tools throughout their day.

Industry certification is usually required once the person is employed.

Pay
The median annual wage for automotive service technicians and mechanics was $42,090 in May 2019.

Job Outlook
Employment of automotive service technicians and mechanics is projected to decline 4 percent from 2019 to 2029.

State & Area Data
Explore resources for employment and wages by state and area for automotive service technicians and mechanics.

What Automotive Service Technicians and Mechanics Do
Automotive service technicians and mechanics, often called *service technicians* or *service techs*, inspect, maintain, and repair cars and light trucks.

Automotive service technicians and mechanics perform oil changes on vehicles.

Duties
Automotive service technicians and mechanics typically do the following:

- Identify problems, often by using computerized diagnostic equipment
- Plan work procedures, using charts, technical manuals, and experience
- Test parts and systems to ensure that they work properly
- Follow checklists to ensure that all critical parts are examined
- Perform basic care and maintenance, including changing oil, checking fluid levels, and rotating tires
- Repair or replace worn parts, such as brake pads, wheel bearings, and sensors
- Perform repairs to manufacturer and customer specifications
- Explain automotive problems and repairs to clients

Although service technicians work on traditional mechanical systems, such as engines, transmissions, and drivebelts, they also must be familiar with a growing number of electronic systems. Braking, transmission, and steering systems, for example, are controlled primarily by computers and electronic components.

Other integrated electronic systems, such as accident-avoidance sensors, are becoming common as well. In addition, a growing number of technicians are required to work on vehicles that use electricity or alternative fuels, such as ethanol.

Service technicians use many different tools, including computerized diagnostic tools and power tools such as pneumatic wrenches, lathes, welding torches, and jacks and hoists. These tools usually are owned by their employers.

Service technicians also use many common hand tools, such as wrenches, pliers, and sockets and ratchets. Service technicians generally own these tools themselves. In fact, experienced workers often have thousands of dollars invested in their personal tool collection. For example, some invest in their own set of pneumatic tools—such as impact wrenches—powered by compressed air.

The following are examples of types of service technicians:

Automotive air-conditioning technicians install and repair air-conditioners and parts, such as compressors, condensers, and controls. These workers must be trained and certified in handling refrigerants.

Brake technicians diagnose brake system problems, adjust brakes, replace brake rotors and pads, and make other repairs on brake systems. Some technicians specialize in both brake and front-end work. (See "Front-end technicians.")

Drivability technicians, also known as *diagnostic technicians,* use their extensive knowledge of engine management and fuel, electrical, ignition, and emissions systems to diagnose issues that prevent engines from performing efficiently. They often use the onboard diagnostic system of a car and electronic testing equipment such as scan tools and multimeters to find the malfunction.

Front-end technicians diagnose ride, handling, and tire wear problems. To correct these problems, they frequently use special alignment equipment and wheel-balancing machines.

Transmission technicians and rebuilders work on gear trains, couplings, hydraulic pumps, and other parts of transmissions. An extensive knowledge of computer controls and the ability to diagnose electrical and hydraulic problems are needed to work on these complex components.

Technicians who work on large trucks and buses are described in the diesel service technicians and mechanics profile.

Technicians who work on farm equipment, construction vehicles, and railcars are described in the heavy vehicle and mobile equipment service technicians profile.

Technicians who repair and service motorcycles, motorboats, and small all-terrain vehicles are described in the profile on small engine mechanics.

Work Environment

Automotive service technicians and mechanics held about 756,600 jobs in 2019. The largest employers of automotive service technicians and mechanics were as follows:

Automobile dealers	33%
Automotive mechanical and electrical repair and maintenance	27
Self-employed workers	13
Automotive parts, accessories, and tire stores	8

Service technicians stand for most of the day, and they typically work in well-ventilated and well-lit repair shops. Although technicians often identify and fix automotive problems with computers, they commonly work with greasy parts and tools, sometimes in uncomfortable positions.

Work Schedules

Most service technicians work full time, and many work evenings or weekends. Overtime is common.

Automotive service technicians and mechanics keep records of diagnostic tests and repairs.

Injuries and Illnesses

Automotive service technicians and mechanics frequently work with heavy parts and tools. As a result, workplace injuries, such as small cuts, sprains, and bruises, are common.

How to Become an Automotive Service Technician or Mechanic

Employers prefer that automotive service technicians and mechanics complete a program at a postsecondary institution. Industry certification is usually required once the person is employed.

Education

High school courses in automotive repair, electronics, computers, and mathematics provide a good background for prospective service technicians. However, high school graduates typically need further training to become fully qualified.

Completing a vocational or other postsecondary education program in automotive service technology is considered the best preparation for entry-level positions. Programs usually last 6 months to a year and provide intensive career preparation through classroom instruction and hands-on practice. Short-term certificate programs in a particular subject, such as brake maintenance or engine performance, are also available.

Some service technicians get an associate's degree. Courses usually include mathematics, electronics, and automotive repair. Some programs add classes in customer service and other necessary skills.

Various automobile manufacturers and dealers sponsor associate's degree programs. Students in these programs typically spend alternating periods attending classes full time and working full time in service shops under the guidance of an experienced technician.

Training

Service technicians who have graduated from postsecondary programs in automotive service technology generally require little on-the-job training.

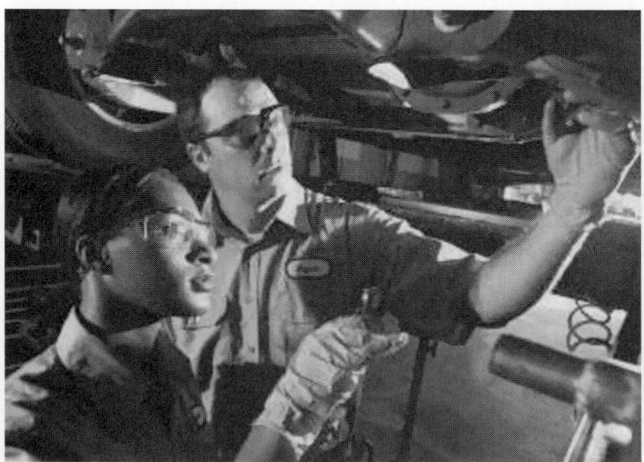

Automotive service technicians and mechanics learn from more experienced workers.

Those who have not completed postsecondary education, however, generally start as trainee technicians, technicians' helpers, or lubrication workers. They gradually acquire more knowledge and experience by working with experienced mechanics and technicians.

Licenses, Certifications, and Registrations

The U.S. Environmental Protection Agency (EPA) requires all technicians who buy or work with refrigerants to be certified in proper refrigerant handling. No formal test preparation is required, but many trade schools, unions, and employer associations offer training programs designed for the EPA exam.

Certification from the National Institute for Automotive Service Excellence (ASE) is the standard credential for service technicians. Certification demonstrates competence and usually brings higher pay. Many employers require their service technicians to become certified.

ASE certification is available in nine different automobile specialty areas: automatic transmission/transaxle, brakes, light vehicle diesel engines, electrical/electronic systems, engine performance, engine repair, heating and air-conditioning, manual drive train and axles, and suspension and steering.

To become certified, technicians must have at least 2 years of experience (or relevant schooling and 1 year of experience) and pass an exam. Technicians who achieve certification in all of the foregoing areas (light vehicle diesel engine certification is not required) may earn ASE Master Technician status.

Important Qualities

Customer-service skills. Service technicians discuss automotive problems—along with options to fix them—with their customers. Because workers may depend on repeat clients for business, they must be courteous, good listeners, and ready to answer customers' questions.

Detail oriented. Service technicians must be aware of small details when inspecting or repairing vehicle systems, because mechanical and electronic malfunctions are often due to misalignments or other easy-to-miss causes.

Dexterity. Service technicians perform many tasks that require steady hands and good hand–eye coordination, such as assembling or attaching components and subassemblies.

Mechanical skills. Service technicians must be familiar with engine components and systems and know how they interact with each other. They often must take apart major parts for repairs and be able to put them back together properly.

Organizational skills. Service technicians must keep workspaces clean and organized in order to maintain safety and ensure accountability of parts.

Physical strength. Service technicians must sometimes lift and maneuver heavy parts such as engines and body panels.

Troubleshooting skills. Service technicians use diagnostic equipment on engine systems and components in order to identify and fix problems in increasingly complicated mechanical and electronic systems. They must be familiar with electronic control systems and the appropriate tools needed to fix and maintain them.

Pay

The median annual wage for automotive service technicians and mechanics was $42,090 in May 2019. The median wage is the wage at which half the workers in an occupation earned more than that amount and half earned less. The lowest 10 percent earned less than $24,400, and the highest 10 percent earned more than $68,880.

In May 2019, the median annual wages for automotive service technicians and mechanics in the top industries in which they worked were as follows:

Automobile dealers	$45,710
Automotive mechanical and electrical repair and maintenance	39,820
Automotive parts, accessories, and tire stores	36,180

Many experienced technicians working for automobile dealers and independent repair shops receive a commission related to the labor cost charged to the customer. Under this system, which is commonly known as "flat rate" or "flag rate," weekly earnings depend on the amount of work completed. Some repair shops pay technicians on an hourly basis instead.

Most service technicians work full time, and many work evenings or weekends. Overtime is common.

Job Outlook

Employment of automotive service technicians and mechanics is projected to decline 4 percent from 2019 to 2029.

The number of vehicles already in use is expected to continue to rise, and some service technicians will still be needed to perform basic maintenance and repair tasks, such as replacing brake pads and changing oil. Increasingly, however, new vehicles are being built with interconnected sensors, cameras, and instruments that allow for predictive maintenance and remote diagnosis, thus reducing maintenance workhours.

Automotive Service Technicians and Mechanics
Median annual wages, May 2019

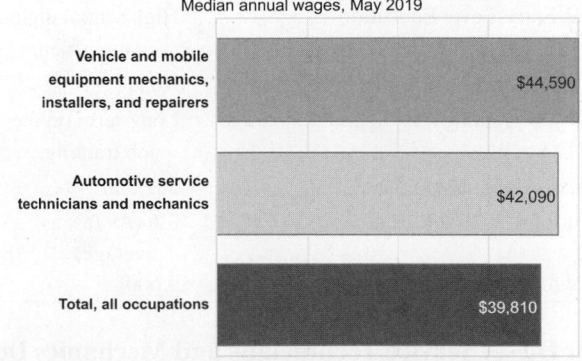

Vehicle and mobile equipment mechanics, installers, and repairers	$44,590
Automotive service technicians and mechanics	$42,090
Total, all occupations	$39,810

Note: All Occupations includes all occupations in the U.S. Economy.
Source: U.S. Bureau of Labor Statistics, Occupational Employment Statistics.

Automotive Service Technicians and Mechanics
Percent change in employment, projected 2019-29

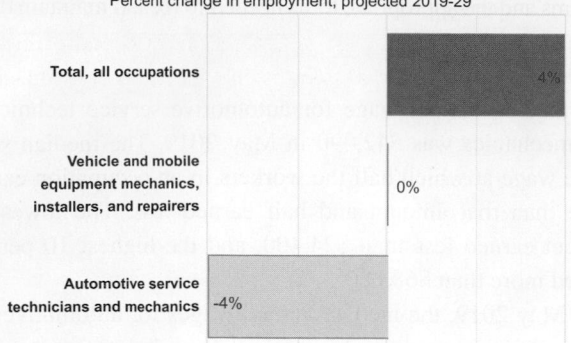

Total, all occupations	4%
Vehicle and mobile equipment mechanics, installers, and repairers	0%
Automotive service technicians and mechanics	-4%

Note: All Occupations includes all occupations in the U.S. Economy.
Source: U.S. Bureau of Labor Statistics, Employment Projections program.

Additionally, the increasing prevalence of electric vehicles in the marketplace may limit future demand for automotive service technicians and mechanics, because these vehicles require less maintenance and repair.

Job Prospects
Job opportunities for qualified applicants should be very good, whether they obtained their knowledge through education or experience.

Many job openings will be in automobile dealerships and independent repair shops, where most service technicians currently work.

Employment projections data for automotive service technicians and mechanics, 2019-29					
Occupational Title	SOC Code	Employment, 2019	Projected Employment, 2029	Change, 2019-29	
				Percent	Numeric
SOURCE: U.S. Bureau of Labor Statistics, Employment Projections program					
Automotive service technicians and mechanics	49-3023	756,600	728,800	-4	-27,800

State & Area Data
Occupational Employment Statistics (OES)
The Occupational Employment Statistics (OES) program produces employment and wage estimates annually for over 800 occupations. These estimates are available for the nation as a whole, for individual states, and for metropolitan and nonmetropolitan areas.

Contacts for More Information
For more details about work opportunities, contact local automobile dealers and repair shops or local offices of the state employment service. The state employment service also may have information about training programs.

For information about careers, education, and training programs, visit
➤ Automotive Youth Educational Systems
➤ National Automotive Technicians Education Foundation

For information about certification, visit
➤ National Institute for Automotive Service Excellence

Diesel Service Technicians and Mechanics

Summary

Quick Facts: Diesel Service Technicians and Mechanics

2019 Median Pay	$48,500 per year / $23.32 per hour
Typical Entry-Level Education	High school diploma or equivalent
Work Experience in a Related Occupation	None
On-the-job Training	Long-term on-the-job training
Number of Jobs, 2019	281,300
Job Outlook, 2019-29	3% (As fast as average)
Employment Change, 2019-29	9,600

What Diesel Service Technicians and Mechanics Do
Diesel service technicians and mechanics inspect, repair, and overhaul buses, trucks, or any vehicle with a diesel engine.

Work Environment
Diesel service technicians and mechanics usually work in well-ventilated and sometimes noisy repair shops. They occasionally repair vehicles on roadsides or at worksites. Most diesel

Diesel service technicians and mechanics repair diesel engine vehicles, such as buses and trucks.

technicians work full time, and overtime and evening shifts are common.

How to Become a Diesel Service Technician or Mechanic

Although most diesel service technicians and mechanics learn on the job after a high school education, employers are increasingly preferring applicants who have completed postsecondary training programs in diesel engine repair. In addition, industry certification may be important.

Pay

The median annual wage for diesel service technicians and mechanics was $48,500 in May 2019.

Job Outlook

Employment of diesel service technicians and mechanics is projected to grow 3 percent from 2019 to 2029, about as fast as the average for all occupations. Job prospects should be best for those who have completed postsecondary training in diesel engine repair.

State & Area Data

Explore resources for employment and wages by state and area for diesel service technicians and mechanics.

What Diesel Service Technicians and Mechanics Do

Diesel service technicians and mechanics (also known as *diesel technicians*) inspect, repair, or overhaul buses and trucks, or maintain and repair any type of diesel engine.

Duties

Diesel service technicians and mechanics typically do the following:

Diesel service technicians and mechanics may work on a vehicle's electrical system, make major engine repairs, or retrofit engines with emission control systems to comply with pollution regulations.

- Consult with customers, read work orders, and determine work required
- Plan work procedures, using technical charts and manuals
- Inspect brake systems, steering mechanisms, transmissions, engines, and other parts of vehicles
- Follow checklists to ensure that all critical parts are examined
- Read and interpret diagnostic test results to identify mechanical problems
- Repair or replace malfunctioning components, parts, and other mechanical or electrical equipment
- Perform basic care and maintenance, including changing oil, checking fluid levels, and rotating tires
- Test-drive vehicles to ensure that they run smoothly

Because of their efficiency and durability, diesel engines have become the standard in powering trucks and buses. Other heavy vehicles and mobile equipment, including bulldozers and cranes, also are powered by diesel engines, as are many commercial boats and some passenger vehicles and pickups.

Diesel technicians make major and minor engine repairs, and work on a vehicle's electrical and exhaust systems to comply with pollution regulations.

Diesel engine maintenance and repair is becoming more complex as engines and other components use more electronic systems to control their operation. For example, fuel injection and engine timing systems rely on microprocessors to maximize fuel efficiency and minimize harmful emissions. In most shops, workers often use hand-held or laptop computers to diagnose problems and adjust engine functions.

Diesel technicians also use a variety of power and machine tools, such as pneumatic wrenches, lathes, grinding machines, and welding equipment. Hand tools, including pliers, sockets and ratchets, and screwdrivers, are commonly used.

Employers typically provide expensive power tools and computerized equipment, but workers generally acquire their own hand tools over time.

Technicians and mechanics who work primarily on automobiles are described in the profile on automotive service technicians and mechanics.

Technicians and mechanics who work primarily on farm equipment, construction vehicles, and railcars, are described in the profile on heavy vehicle and mobile equipment service technicians.

Technicians and mechanics who work primarily on motorboats, motorcycles, and small all-terrain vehicles are described in the small engine mechanics profile.

Work Environment

Diesel service technicians and mechanics held about 281,300 jobs in 2019. The largest employers of diesel service technicians and mechanics were as follows:

Truck transportation.. 20%

Diesel technicians usually work in well-ventilated and sometimes noisy repair shops.

Wholesale trade	14
Automotive repair and maintenance	9
Local government, excluding education and hospitals	9
Self-employed workers	4

Diesel technicians usually work in well-ventilated and sometimes noisy repair shops. They occasionally repair vehicles on roadsides or at worksites.

Injuries and Illnesses

Diesel service technicians and mechanics often lift heavy parts and tools, handle greasy or dirty equipment, and work in uncomfortable positions. Sprains and cuts are common among these workers. Diesel technicians need to follow some safety precautions when in the workplace.

Work Schedules

Most diesel technicians work full time. Overtime is common, as many repair shops extend their service hours during evenings and weekends. In addition, some truck and bus repair shops provide 24-hour maintenance and repair services.

How to Become a Diesel Service Technician or Mechanic

Although most diesel technicians learn on the job after a high school education, employers are increasingly preferring applicants who have completed postsecondary training programs in diesel engine repair. In addition, obtaining industry certification may be helpful because certification demonstrates a diesel technician's competence and experience.

Education

Most employers require a high school diploma or equivalent. High school or postsecondary courses in automotive repair, electronics, and mathematics provide a strong educational background for a career as a diesel technician.

Some employers prefer to hire workers with postsecondary education in diesel engine repair. Many community colleges and trade and vocational schools offer certificate or degree programs in diesel engine repair.

These degree programs mix classroom instruction with hands-on training and include learning the basics of diesel technology, repair techniques and equipment, and practical exercises. Students also learn how to interpret technical manuals and electronic diagnostic reports.

Training

Diesel technicians who begin working without any postsecondary education are trained extensively on the job. Trainees are assigned basic tasks, such as cleaning parts, checking fuel and oil levels, and driving vehicles in and out of the shop.

After they learn routine maintenance and repair tasks and demonstrate competence, trainees move on to more complicated subjects, such as vehicle diagnostics. This process can take from 3 to 4 years, at which point a trainee is usually considered a journey-level diesel technician.

Over the course of their careers, diesel technicians must learn to use new techniques and equipment. Employers often

Diesel technicians initially learn to perform routine maintenance and repair tasks.

send experienced technicians to special training classes conducted by manufacturers and vendors to learn about the latest diesel technology.

Licenses, Certifications, and Registrations

Certification from the National Institute for Automotive Service Excellence (ASE) is the standard credential for diesel and other automotive service technicians and mechanics. Although not required, this certification demonstrates a diesel technician's competence and experience to potential employers and clients, and often brings higher pay.

Diesel technicians may be certified in specific repair areas, such as drivetrains, electronic systems, and preventative maintenance and inspection. To earn certification, technicians must have 2 years of work experience and pass one or more ASE exams. To remain certified, diesel technicians must pass a recertification exam every 5 years.

Many diesel technicians are required to have a commercial driver's license so that they may test-drive buses and large trucks.

Important Qualities

Customer-service skills. Diesel technicians frequently discuss automotive problems and necessary repairs with their customers. They must be courteous, good listeners, and ready to answer customers' questions.

Detail oriented. Diesel technicians must be aware of small details when inspecting or repairing engines and components, because mechanical and electronic malfunctions are often due to misalignments and other easy-to-miss causes.

Dexterity. Mechanics need a steady hand and good hand–eye coordination for many tasks, such as disassembling engine parts, connecting or attaching components, and using hand tools.

Mechanical skills. Diesel technicians must be familiar with engine components and systems and know how they interact with each other. They often disassemble major parts for repairs, and they must be able to put them back together properly.

Organizational skills. Diesel technicians must keep workspaces clean and organized in order to maintain safety and accountability for parts.

Physical strength. Diesel technicians often lift heavy parts and tools, such as exhaust system components and pneumatic wrenches.

Troubleshooting skills. Diesel technicians use diagnostic equipment on engine systems and components in order to identify and fix problems in mechanical and electronic systems. They must be familiar with electronic control systems and the appropriate tools needed to fix and maintain them.

Pay

The median annual wage for diesel service technicians and mechanics was $48,500 in May 2019. The median wage is the wage at which half the workers in an occupation earned more than that amount and half earned less. The lowest 10 percent

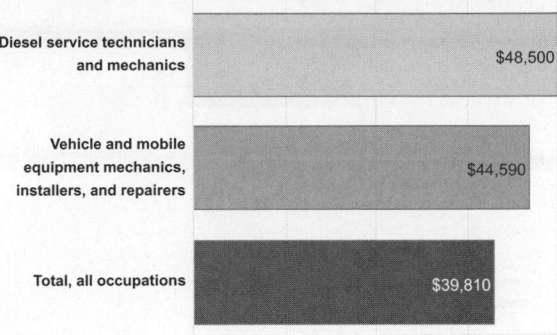

Diesel Service Technicians and Mechanics
Median annual wages, May 2019

Diesel service technicians and mechanics	$48,500
Vehicle and mobile equipment mechanics, installers, and repairers	$44,590
Total, all occupations	$39,810

Note: All Occupations includes all occupations in the U.S. Economy.
Source: U.S. Bureau of Labor Statistics, Occupational Employment Statistics.

earned less than $31,990, and the highest 10 percent earned more than $74,090.

In May 2019, the median annual wages for diesel service technicians and mechanics in the top industries in which they worked were as follows:

Local government, excluding education and hospitals	$57,940
Wholesale trade	49,940
Automotive repair and maintenance	46,320
Truck transportation	44,970

Many diesel technicians, especially those employed by truck fleet dealers and repair shops, receive a commission in addition to their base salary.

Most diesel technicians work full time. Overtime is common, as many repair shops extend their service hours during evenings and weekends. In addition, some truck and bus repair shops provide 24-hour maintenance and repair services.

Job Outlook

Employment of diesel service technicians and mechanics is projected to grow 3 percent from 2019 to 2029, about as fast as the average for all occupations.

As more freight is shipped across the country, additional diesel-powered trucks will be needed to carry freight wherever trains and pipelines are not available or economical. In addition, diesel cars and light trucks are becoming more popular, and more diesel technicians will be needed to maintain and repair these vehicles.

Job Prospects

Workers who have completed postsecondary education should have the best job opportunities, followed by graduates of accredited high school automotive programs.

Workers without postsecondary education often require more supervision and on-the-job instruction than others. These untrained

Diesel Service Technicians and Mechanics
Percent change in employment, projected 2019-29

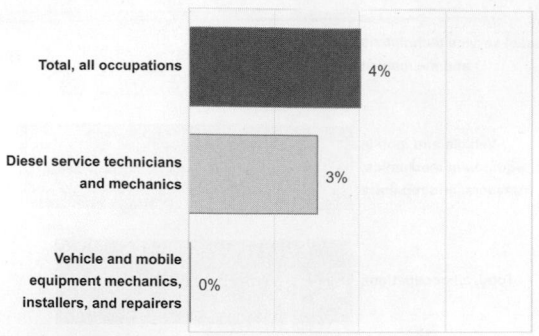

Total, all occupations	4%
Diesel service technicians and mechanics	3%
Vehicle and mobile equipment mechanics, installers, and repairers	0%

Note: All Occupations includes all occupations in the U.S. Economy.
Source: U.S. Bureau of Labor Statistics, Employment Projections program.

workers will face stronger competition for jobs because training is an expensive and time-consuming process for employers.

Employment projections data for diesel service technicians and mechanics, 2019-29

Occupational Title	SOC Code	Employment, 2019	Projected Employment, 2029	Change, 2019-29	
				Percent	Numeric
SOURCE: U.S. Bureau of Labor Statistics, Employment Projections program					
Bus and truck mechanics and diesel engine specialists	49-3031	281,300	290,800	3	9,600

State & Area Data
Occupational Employment Statistics (OES)
The Occupational Employment Statistics (OES) program produces employment and wage estimates annually for over 800 occupations. These estimates are available for the nation as a whole, for individual states, and for metropolitan and nonmetropolitan areas.

Contacts for More Information
For more information about careers and education for diesel service technicians and mechanics, visit
➤ Association of Diesel Specialists
➤ National Automotive Technicians Education Foundation

For more information about certification, visit
➤ National Institute for Automotive Service Excellence

Electrical and Electronics Installers and Repairers

Summary

Quick Facts: Electrical and Electronics Installers and Repairers

2019 Median Pay	$59,080 per year $28.40 per hour
Typical Entry-Level Education	See below
Work Experience in a Related Occupation	See below
On-the-job Training	See below
Number of Jobs, 2019	121,700
Job Outlook, 2019-29	-1% (Decline)
Employment Change, 2019-29	-1,000

What Electrical and Electronics Installers and Repairers Do
Electrical and electronics installers and repairers install or repair a variety of electrical equipment.

Work Environment
Many electrical and electronics installers and repairers work in repair shops or in factories. Installers and repairers may have to lift heavy equipment and work in awkward positions. The majority work full time.

How to Become an Electrical or Electronics Installer and Repairer
Electrical and electronics installers and repairers need at least a high school education, but most specializations require further

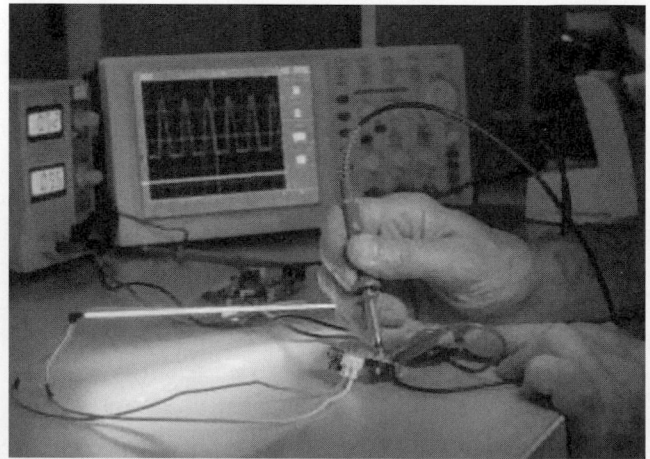

Electrical and electronics installers and repairers use special testing equipment to determine problems.

preparation through advanced education, apprenticeship training, or work experience.

Pay

The median annual wage for electrical and electronics installers and repairers was $59,080 in May 2019.

Job Outlook

Overall employment of electrical and electronics installers and repairers is projected to decline 1 percent from 2019 to 2029.

State & Area Data

Explore resources for employment and wages by state and area for electrical and electronics installers and repairers.

What Electrical and Electronics Installers and Repairers Do

Electrical and electronics installers and repairers install or repair a variety of electrical equipment in telecommunications, transportation, utilities, and other industries.

Duties

Electrical and electronics installers and repairers typically do the following:

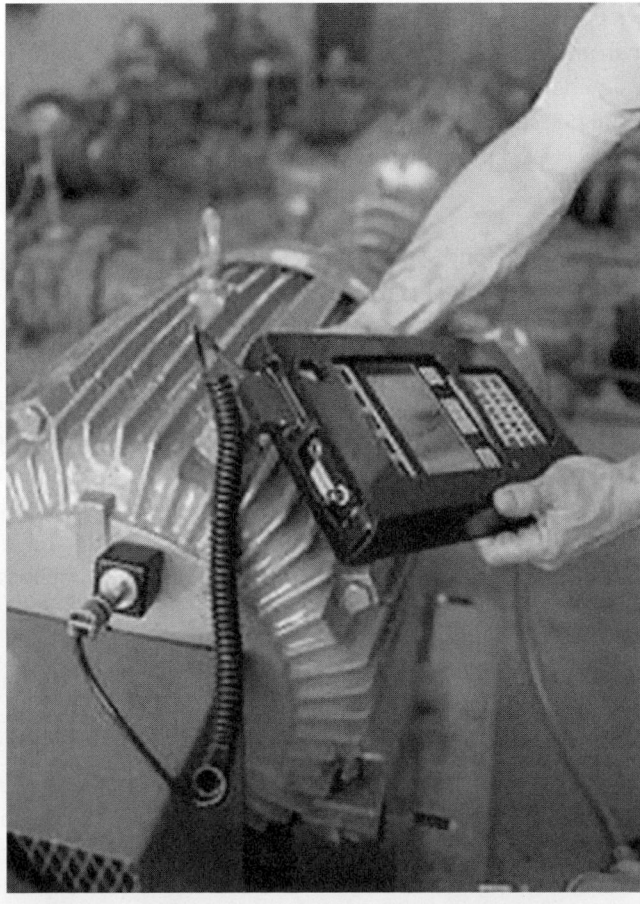

Electrical and electronics installers and repairers use diagnostic equipment to troubleshoot electric motors.

- Discuss problems and requirements with customers
- Inspect and test equipment
- Reproduce, isolate, and diagnose problems
- Disassemble equipment as necessary to access problematic components
- Clean, repair, and replace components
- Reassemble and test equipment after repairs
- Keep records of repairs, tests, parts, and labor hours

Modern manufacturing plants and transportation systems use a large amount of electrical and electronics equipment, from assembly line motors to sonar systems. Electrical and electronics installers and repairers fix and maintain these complex pieces of equipment.

Because automated electronic control systems are becoming more complex, repairers use software programs and testing equipment to diagnose malfunctions. Among their diagnostic tools are multimeters—which measure voltage, current, and resistance—and advanced multimeters, which measure the capacitance, inductance, and current gain of transistors.

Repairers also use signal generators, which provide test signals, and oscilloscopes, which display signals graphically. In addition, repairers often use hand tools such as pliers, screwdrivers, and wrenches to replace faulty parts and adjust equipment.

The following are examples of types of electrical and electronics installers and repairers:

Commercial and industrial electrical and electronics equipment repairers adjust, test, repair, or install electronic equipment, such as industrial controls, transmitters, and antennas.

Electric motor, power tool, and related repairers—such as *armature winders, generator mechanics,* and *electric golf cart repairers*—specialize in installing, maintaining, and repairing electric motors, wiring, or switches.

Electrical and electronics installers and repairers of transportation equipment install, adjust, or maintain mobile communication equipment, including sound, sonar, security, navigation, and surveillance systems on trains, watercraft, or other vehicles.

Electronic equipment installers and repairers of motor vehicles install, diagnose, and repair sound, security, and navigation equipment in motor vehicles. These installers and repairers work with a range of complex electronic equipment, including digital audio and video players, navigation systems, and passive and active security systems.

Powerhouse, substation, and relay electrical and electronics repairers inspect, test, maintain, or repair electrical equipment used in generating stations, substations, and in-service relays. These workers also may be known as *powerhouse electricians, relay technicians,* or *power transformer repairers.*

Work Environment

Electrical and electronics installers and repairers held about 121,700 jobs in 2019. Employment in the detailed occupations

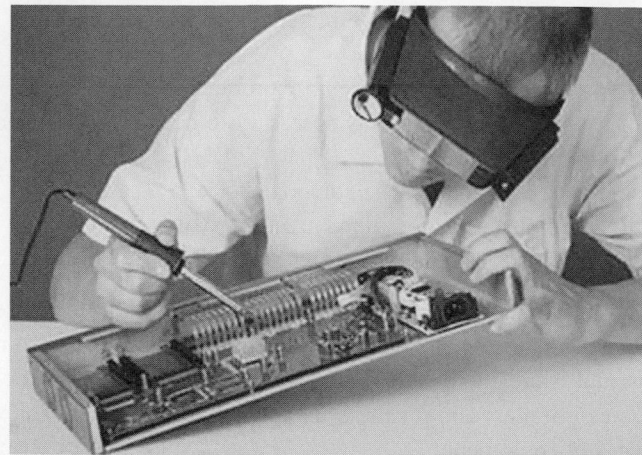

Electrical and electronics installers and repairers usually work in a clean shop.

Many technical colleges have basic electronics programs that include practical experience labs.

that make up electrical and electronics installers and repairers was distributed as follows:

Electrical and electronics repairers, commercial and industrial equipment	61,200
Electrical and electronics repairers, powerhouse, substation, and relay	23,000
Electric motor, power tool, and related repairers	17,900
Electronic equipment installers and repairers, motor vehicles	10,400
Electrical and electronics installers and repairers, transportation equipment	9,200

The largest employers of electrical and electronics installers and repairers were as follows:

Manufacturing	19%
Utilities	13
Repair and maintenance	11
Wholesale trade	10
Federal government, excluding postal service	9

Many electrical and electronics installers and repairers work in repair shops or in factories, and some may work outside when they travel to job sites.

Installers and repairers may have to lift heavy equipment and work in awkward positions. They spend most of their day walking, standing, or kneeling.

Work Schedules

The majority of electrical and electronics installers and repairers work full time.

How to Become an Electrical or Electronics Installer and Repairer

Electrical and electronics installers and repairers need at least a high school education, but most specializations require further preparation through advanced education, work experience, or both.

Education

Electrical and electronics installers and repairers must understand electrical equipment and electronics. As a result, employers often prefer applicants who have taken courses in electronics at a community college or technical school. Courses usually cover AC and DC electronics, electronic devices, and microcontrollers. It is important for prospects to choose schools that include hands-on training in order to gain practical experience.

Training

In addition to technical education, workers usually receive training on specific types of equipment. This may involve manufacturer-specific training for repairers who will perform warranty work.

Before working independently, entry-level repairers usually develop their skills while working with experienced technicians who provide technical guidance.

Work Experience in a Related Occupation

Some electrical and electronics installers and repairers need prior work experience. Electric motor, power tool, and related repairers typically begin by helping in machine or electrical workshops, where they gain experience with tools and motors.

Powerhouse, substation, and relay electrical and electronics repairers often gain experience by first working as electricians.

Licenses, Certifications, and Registrations

While certification is not required, a number of organizations offer it, and it can be useful in getting a job. For example, the Electronics Technicians Association International (ETA International) offers more than 50 certification programs in numerous electronics specialties for various levels of competency. The International Society of Certified Electronics Technicians (ISCET) also offers certification for several levels of competence. The ISCET focuses on a broad range of topics, including basic electronics, electronic systems, and appliance service. To become certified, applicants must meet prerequisites and pass a comprehensive exam.

Important Qualities

Color vision. Electrical and electronics installers and repairers must be able to identify the color-coded components that are often used in electronic equipment.

Communication skills. Electrical and electronics installers and repairers work closely with customers, so they must listen to and understand customers' descriptions of problems and explain solutions in a simple, clear manner.

Physical stamina. Some electrical and electronics installers and repairers must stand at their station for their full shift, which can be tiring.

Physical strength. Electrical and electronics installers and repairers may need to lift heavy parts during the repair process. Some components weigh over 50 pounds.

Technical skills. Electrical and electronics installers and repairers use a variety of mechanical and diagnostic tools to install or repair equipment.

Troubleshooting skills. Electrical and electronics installers and repairers must be able to identify problems with equipment and systems and make the necessary repairs.

Pay

The median annual wage for electrical and electronics installers and repairers was $59,080 in May 2019. The median wage is the wage at which half the workers in an occupation earned more than that amount and half earned less. The lowest 10 percent earned less than $33,730, and the highest 10 percent earned more than $93,650.

Median annual wages for electrical and electronics installers and repairers in May 2019 were as follows:

Electrical and electronics repairers, powerhouse, substation, and relay	$82,780
Electrical and electronics installers and repairers, transportation equipment	62,530
Electrical and electronics repairers, commercial and industrial equipment	59,300
Electric motor, power tool, and related repairers	44,070
Electronic equipment installers and repairers, motor vehicles	37,380

In May 2019, the median annual wages for electrical and electronics installers and repairers in the top industries in which they worked were as follows:

Utilities	$85,170
Federal government, excluding postal service	61,990
Manufacturing	59,820
Wholesale trade	48,420
Repair and maintenance	46,760

The majority of electrical and electronics installers and repairers work full time.

Job Outlook

Overall employment of electrical and electronics installers and repairers is projected to decline 1 percent from 2019 to 2029. Growth will vary by occupation (see table below).

Improvements in electrical and electronic equipment design, as well as the increased use of disposable tool parts, are expected to reduce the need for more electrical and electronic equipment installers and repairers.

Motor vehicle manufacturers continue to install more and higher quality sound, security, entertainment, and navigation systems in new vehicles. These electronic systems require less maintenance and will limit installation of aftermarket products, reducing demand for electrical and electronics installers and repairers.

Job Prospects

Overall job opportunities should be good for qualified workers who are familiar with electronics, especially those with an associate's degree in electronics.

Electrical and Electronics Installers and Repairers

Median annual wages, May 2019

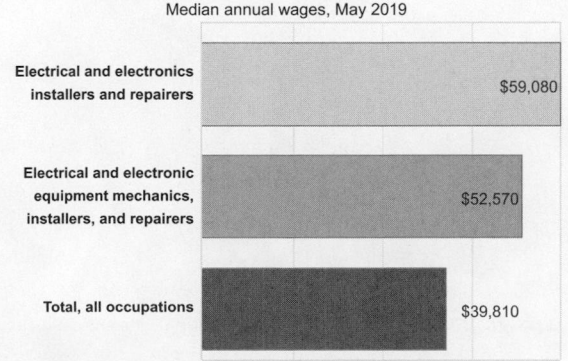

- Electrical and electronics installers and repairers: $59,080
- Electrical and electronic equipment mechanics, installers, and repairers: $52,570
- Total, all occupations: $39,810

Note: All Occupations includes all occupations in the U.S. Economy.
Source: U.S. Bureau of Labor Statistics, Occupational Employment Statistics.

Electrical and Electronics Installers and Repairers

Percent change in employment, projected 2019-29

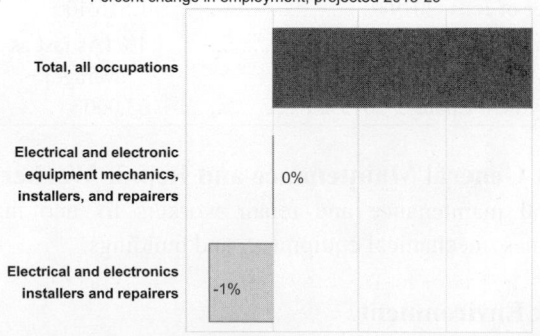

- Total, all occupations: 4%
- Electrical and electronic equipment mechanics, installers, and repairers: 0%
- Electrical and electronics installers and repairers: -1%

Note: All Occupations includes all occupations in the U.S. Economy.
Source: U.S. Bureau of Labor Statistics, Employment Projections program.

The best job opportunities should be for commercial and industrial equipment installers and repairers, as the need to replace those who leave the occupation permanently should result in some openings for these workers. Conversely, few opportunities will be available for motor vehicle equipment installers and repairers as the amount of aftermarket installations continues to decline.

Occupational Title	SOC Code	Employment, 2019	Projected Employment, 2029	Change, 2019-29	
				Percent	Numeric
SOURCE: U.S. Bureau of Labor Statistics, Employment Projections program					
Electrical and electronics installers and repairers	—	121,700	120,600	-1	-1,000
Electric motor, power tool, and related repairers	49-2092	17,900	18,600	4	700
Electrical and electronics installers and repairers, transportation equipment	49-2093	9,200	9,400	2	200
Electrical and electronics repairers, commercial and industrial equipment	49-2094	61,200	62,400	2	1,200

Employment projections data for electrical and electronics installers and repairers, 2019-29

Occupational Title	SOC Code	Employment, 2019	Projected Employment, 2029	Change, 2019-29	
				Percent	Numeric
Electrical and electronics repairers, powerhouse, substation, and relay	49-2095	23,000	22,200	-3	-700
Electronic equipment installers and repairers, motor vehicles	49-2096	10,400	8,000	-23	-2,400

State & Area Data
Occupational Employment Statistics (OES)
The Occupational Employment Statistics (OES) program produces employment and wage estimates annually for over 800 occupations. These estimates are available for the nation as a whole, for individual states, and for metropolitan and nonmetropolitan areas.

Contacts for More Information
For more information about electrical and electronics installers and repairers, including careers and certification, visit

➤ Electronics Technicians Association International
➤ International Society of Certified Electronics Technicians

General Maintenance and Repair Workers

Summary

Quick Facts: General Maintenance and Repair Workers

2019 Median Pay	$39,080 per year $18.79 per hour
Typical Entry-Level Education	High school diploma or equivalent
Work Experience in a Related Occupation	None
On-the-job Training	Moderate-term on-the-job training
Number of Jobs, 2019	1,516,400
Job Outlook, 2019-29	4% (As fast as average)
Employment Change, 2019-29	63,000

What General Maintenance and Repair Workers Do
General maintenance and repair workers fix and maintain machines, mechanical equipment, and buildings.

Work Environment
General maintenance and repair workers often carry out many different tasks in a single day. They could work at any number of indoor or outdoor locations. They may work inside a single building, such as a hotel or hospital, or be responsible for the maintenance of many buildings, such as those in an apartment complex or on a college campus.

How to Become a General Maintenance and Repair Worker
Jobs in this occupation typically require a high school diploma or equivalent. General maintenance and repair workers often learn their skills on the job for several years. They start out

Workers use hand tools and power tools to fix appliances and equipment.

performing simple tasks while watching and learning from skilled maintenance workers.

Pay

The median annual wage for general maintenance and repair workers was $39,080 in May 2019.

Job Outlook

Employment of general maintenance and repair workers is projected to grow 4 percent from 2019 to 2029, about as fast as the average for all occupations. Employment may rise as increasing home prices and sales drive demand for remodeling and maintenance work.

State & Area Data

Explore resources for employment and wages by state and area for general maintenance and repair workers.

What General Maintenance and Repair Workers Do

General maintenance and repair workers fix and maintain machines, mechanical equipment, and buildings. They paint, repair flooring, and work on plumbing, electrical, and air-conditioning and heating systems.

Workers are responsible for the upkeep of many homes and apartment buildings.

Duties

General maintenance and repair workers typically do the following:

- Maintain and repair machines, mechanical equipment, and buildings
- Fix or replace faulty electrical switches, outlets, and circuit breakers
- Inspect and diagnose problems and figure out the best way to correct them
- Perform routine preventive maintenance to ensure that machines continue to run smoothly
- Assemble and set up machinery or equipment
- Plan repair work using blueprints or diagrams
- Do general cleaning and upkeep of buildings and properties
- Order supplies from catalogs and storerooms
- Meet with clients to estimate repairs and costs
- Keep detailed records of their work

General maintenance and repair workers are hired for maintenance and repair tasks that are not complex enough to need the specialized training of a licensed tradesperson, such as a plumber or electrician.

These workers are also responsible for recognizing when a job is above their skill level and requires the expertise of an electrician; a carpenter; a heating, air-conditioning, and refrigeration mechanic or installer; or a plumber, pipefitter, or steamfitter.

General maintenance and repair workers may fix or paint roofs, windows, doors, floors, woodwork, walls, and other parts of buildings.

They also maintain and repair specialized equipment and machinery in cafeterias, laundries, hospitals, stores, offices, and factories.

General maintenance and repair workers get supplies and parts from distributors or storerooms to fix problems. They use common hand and power tools, such as screwdrivers, saws, drills, wrenches, and hammers to fix, replace, or repair equipment and parts of buildings.

Work Environment

General maintenance and repair workers held about 1.5 million jobs in 2019. The largest employers of general maintenance and repair workers were as follows:

Real estate and rental and leasing	22%
Manufacturing	13
Government	12
Educational services; state, local, and private	8
Healthcare and social assistance	8

General maintenance and repair workers often carry out many different tasks in a single day at any number of locations. They may work inside a single building, such as a hotel or

Many workers need safety gear when working with certain tools and equipment.

Beginners often work under the supervision of more experienced workers.

hospital, or be responsible for the maintenance of many buildings, such as those in an apartment complex or on a college campus.

General maintenance and repair workers may have to stand for long periods or lift heavy objects. These workers may work in uncomfortably hot or cold environments, in uncomfortable or cramped positions, or on ladders. The work involves a lot of walking, climbing, and reaching.

Injuries and Illnesses

General maintenance and repair work can be dangerous. Common injuries include electrical shocks, falls, cuts, and bruises.

Work Schedules

Most general maintenance and repair workers work full time, including evenings or weekends. Some are on call for emergency repairs.

How to Become a General Maintenance and Repair Worker

Jobs in this field typically do not require any formal education beyond high school. General maintenance and repair workers often learn their skills on the job. They start by doing simple tasks and watching and learning from skilled maintenance workers.

Education

Many maintenance and repair workers learn some basic skills in high school shop or technical education classes, postsecondary trade or vocational schools, or community colleges.

Courses in mechanical drawing, electricity, woodworking, blueprint reading, mathematics, and computers are useful. Maintenance and repair workers often do work that involves electrical, plumbing, heating, and air-conditioning systems or painting and roofing tasks. Workers need a good working knowledge of many repair and maintenance tasks.

Practical training, available at many adult education centers and community colleges, is another option for workers to learn tasks such as drywall repair and basic plumbing.

Training

General maintenance and repair workers usually start by watching and learning from skilled maintenance workers. They begin by doing simple tasks, such as fixing leaky faucets and replacing lightbulbs. After gaining experience, general maintenance and repair workers move on to more difficult tasks, such as overhauling machinery or building walls.

Some general maintenance and repair workers learn their skills by assisting other types of repair or construction workers, including machinery repairers, carpenters, or electricians.

Licenses, Certifications, and Registrations

Licensing requirements vary by state and locality. For more complex tasks, workers may need to be licensed in a particular specialty, such as electrical or plumbing work.

Advancement

Some maintenance and repair workers decide to train in one specific craft and become craftworkers, such as electricians, heating and air-conditioning mechanics, or plumbers.

Other maintenance workers eventually open their own repair or contracting business. However, those who want to become a project manager or own their own business may need some postsecondary education or a degree in construction management. For more information, see the profile on construction managers.

Within small organizations, promotion opportunities may be limited.

Important Qualities

Customer-service skills. These workers interact with customers on a regular basis. They need to be friendly and able to address customers' questions.

Dexterity. Many repair and maintenance tasks, such as repairing small devices, connecting or attaching components, and using hand tools, require a steady hand and good hand–eye coordination.

Troubleshooting skills. Workers find, diagnose, and repair problems. They perform tests to figure out the cause of problems before fixing equipment.

Pay

The median annual wage for general maintenance and repair workers was $39,080 in May 2019. The median wage is the wage at which half the workers in an occupation earned more than that amount and half earned less. The lowest 10 percent earned less than $24,600, and the highest 10 percent earned more than $63,140.

In May 2019, the median annual wages for general maintenance and repair workers in the top industries in which they worked were as follows:

Manufacturing	$46,070
Government	42,330
Educational services; state, local, and private	41,880
Healthcare and social assistance	37,880
Real estate and rental and leasing	37,200

Most general maintenance and repair workers work full time, including evenings or weekends. Some are on call for emergency repairs.

Job Outlook

Employment of general maintenance and repair workers is projected to grow 4 percent from 2019 to 2029, about as fast as the average for all occupations.

Employment may rise as increasing home prices and sales drive demand for remodeling and maintenance work. In addition, maintenance and repair workers will continue to be needed to upgrade and renovate older homes.

Demographic changes also may affect the demand for general maintenance and repair workers. Because homeowners typically prefer to remain in their homes as they age, demand may increase for workers as the large baby-boom generation nears retirement. These older homeowners will invest in projects and renovations to accommodate their future living needs and allow them to remain in their homes after retirement.

The large millennial generation will also be entering the prime working-age and household-forming age cohort over the next decade. Although this generation has delayed home ownership because of financial and debt obligations, it is projected that many will enter the housing market over the next 10 years. These first-time homebuyers may favor existing older homes, which are often smaller and cheaper than new houses. This should help boost demand for maintenance and repair work to help keep these older homes in good condition.

In addition to single-family homes, maintenance and repair work is also needed for other types of properties. Due to the aging of many types of buildings, maintenance and repair workers will be needed to work on rental units and commercial and public buildings.

Many general maintenance and repair workers are employed in industries related to real estate, so employment opportunities may be sensitive to fluctuations in the economy. Some workers may experience periods of unemployment when the overall level of construction and real estate development falls. However, maintenance and repairs continue during economic downturns as people opt to repair, rather than replace, equipment.

Job Prospects

Employment growth and the need to replace workers who leave the occupation each year will likely result in good job prospects. Many job openings are expected as experienced workers retire.

Those with experience in repair- or maintenance-related fields should continue to have the best job prospects.

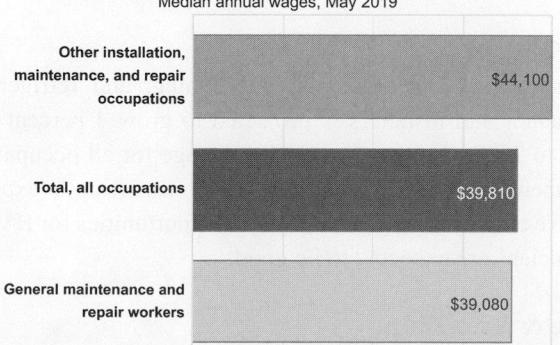

General Maintenance and Repair Workers
Median annual wages, May 2019

Other installation, maintenance, and repair occupations — $44,100
Total, all occupations — $39,810
General maintenance and repair workers — $39,080

Note: All Occupations includes all occupations in the U.S. Economy.
Source: U.S. Bureau of Labor Statistics, Occupational Employment Statistics.

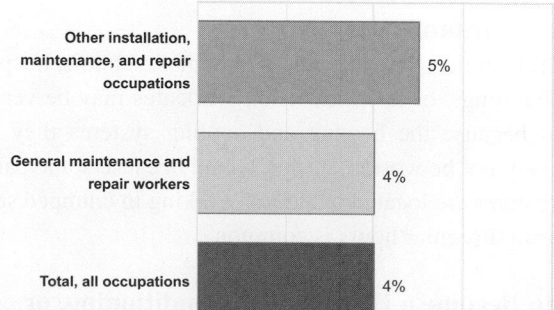

General Maintenance and Repair Workers
Percent change in employment, projected 2019-29

Other installation, maintenance, and repair occupations — 5%
General maintenance and repair workers — 4%
Total, all occupations — 4%

Note: All Occupations includes all occupations in the U.S. Economy.
Source: U.S. Bureau of Labor Statistics, Employment Projections program.

Employment projections data for general maintenance and repair workers, 2019-29					
Occupational Title	SOC Code	Employment, 2019	Projected Employment, 2029	Change, 2019-29	
				Percent	Numeric
SOURCE: U.S. Bureau of Labor Statistics, Employment Projections program					
Maintenance and repair workers, general	49-9071	1,516,400	1,579,400	4	63,000

State & Area Data
Occupational Employment Statistics (OES)

The Occupational Employment Statistics (OES) program produces employment and wage estimates annually for over 800 occupations. These estimates are available for the nation as a whole, for individual states, and for metropolitan and nonmetropolitan areas.

Contacts for More Information

For more information, visit

➤ United Handyman Association

Heating, Air Conditioning, and Refrigeration Mechanics and Installers

Summary

Quick Facts: Heating, Air Conditioning, and Refrigeration Mechanics and Installers

2019 Median Pay	$48,730 per year $23.43 per hour
Typical Entry-Level Education	Postsecondary non-degree award
Work Experience in a Related Occupation	None
On-the-job Training	Long-term on-the-job training
Number of Jobs, 2019	376,800
Job Outlook, 2019-29	4% (As fast as average)
Employment Change, 2019-29	15,100

What Heating, Air Conditioning, and Refrigeration Mechanics and Installers Do

Heating, air conditioning, and refrigeration mechanics and installers work on heating, ventilation, cooling, and refrigeration systems.

Work Environment

HVACR technicians work mostly in homes, schools, hospitals, office buildings, or factories. Their worksites may be very hot or cold because the heating and cooling systems they must repair may not be working properly and because some parts of these systems are located outdoors. Working in cramped spaces and during irregular hours is common.

How to Become a Heating, Air Conditioning, or Refrigeration Mechanic and Installer

Because HVACR systems have become increasingly complex, employers generally prefer applicants with postsecondary

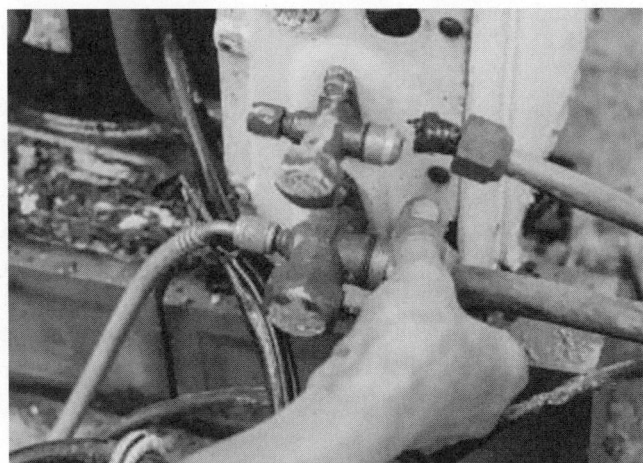

HVACR technicians must follow EPA rules when they work with gases and refrigerants.

education or those who have completed an apprenticeship. Some states and localities may require technicians to be licensed.

Pay

The median annual wage for heating, air conditioning, and refrigeration mechanics and installers was $48,730 in May 2019.

Job Outlook

Employment of heating, air conditioning, and refrigeration mechanics and installers is projected to grow 4 percent from 2019 to 2029, about as fast as the average for all occupations. Commercial and residential building construction is expected to drive employment growth, and job opportunities for HVACR technicians are expected to be good.

State & Area Data

Explore resources for employment and wages by state and area for heating, air conditioning, and refrigeration mechanics and installers.

What Heating, Air Conditioning, and Refrigeration Mechanics and Installers Do

Heating, air conditioning, and refrigeration mechanics and installers—often called *HVACR technicians*—work on heating, ventilation, cooling, and refrigeration systems that control the temperature and air quality in buildings.

Duties

Heating, air conditioning, and refrigeration mechanics and installers typically do the following:

- Install, clean, and maintain HVACR systems
- Install electrical components and wiring
- Inspect and test HVACR systems and components
- Discuss system malfunctions with customers
- Repair or replace worn or defective parts
- Recommend maintenance to improve system performance
- Keep records of work performed

Heating and air conditioning systems control the temperature, humidity, and overall air quality in homes, businesses, and other buildings. By providing a climate-controlled environment, refrigeration systems make it possible to store and transport food, medicine, and other perishable items.

Some HVACR technicians specialize in one or more specific aspects of HVACR, such as radiant heating systems, solar panels, testing and balancing, or commercial refrigeration.

When installing or repairing air conditioning and refrigeration systems, technicians must follow government regulations regarding the conservation, recovery, and recycling of refrigerants. The regulations include those concerning the proper handling and disposal of fluids and pressurized gases.

Some HVACR technicians sell service contracts to their clients, providing periodic maintenance of heating and cooling systems. The service usually includes inspecting the system, cleaning ducts, replacing filters, and checking refrigerant levels.

HVACR technicians install, maintain, and repair heating, cooling, and refrigeration systems.

Other workers sometimes help HVACR technicians install or repair cooling and heating systems. For example, on a large air conditioning installation job, especially one in which workers are covered by union contracts, ductwork may be installed by sheet metal workers, electrical work by electricians, and pipework by plumbers, pipefitters, and steamfitters. Boiler systems are sometimes installed by a boilermaker.

Home appliance repairers usually service window air conditioners and household refrigerators.

Work Environment

Heating, air conditioning, and refrigeration mechanics and installers held about 376,800 jobs in 2019. The largest employers of heating, air conditioning, and refrigeration mechanics and installers were as follows:

Plumbing, heating, and air-conditioning contractors ..	66%
Self-employed workers..	7
Wholesale trade	4
Educational services; state, local, and private	3
Retail trade	3

HVACR technicians work mostly in homes, schools, stores, hospitals, office buildings, or factories. Some technicians are

HVACR technicians work indoors and outdoors.

assigned to specific jobsites at the beginning of each day. Others travel to several different locations, making service calls.

Although most technicians work indoors, some may have to work on outdoor heat exchangers, even in bad weather. Technicians often work in awkward or cramped spaces, and some work in buildings that are uncomfortable because the air conditioning or heating system is not working properly.

Injuries and Illnesses

HVACR technicians have one of the highest rates of injuries and illnesses of all occupations. Potential hazards include electrical shock, burns, muscle strains, and injuries from handling heavy equipment.

Appropriate safety equipment is necessary in handling refrigerants, because they are hazardous and contact can cause skin damage, frostbite, or blindness. When working in tight spaces, inhalation of refrigerants is also a potential hazard. Several refrigerants are highly flammable and require additional care.

Work Schedules

The majority of HVACR technicians work full time. Evening or weekend shifts may be required, and HVACR technicians often work overtime or irregular hours during peak heating and cooling seasons.

How to Become a Heating, Air Conditioning, or Refrigeration Mechanic and Installer

Because HVACR systems have become increasingly complex, employers generally prefer applicants with postsecondary education or those who have completed an apprenticeship. Some states and localities may require technicians to be licensed. Workers may need to pass a background check prior to being hired.

Education

Many HVACR technicians receive postsecondary instruction from technical and trade schools or community colleges that offer programs in heating, air conditioning, and refrigeration. These programs generally last from 6 months to 2 years and lead to a certificate or an associate's degree.

High school students interested in becoming an HVACR technician should take courses in vocational education, math, and physics. Knowledge of plumbing or electrical work and a basic understanding of electronics is also helpful.

Training

New HVACR technicians typically begin by working alongside experienced technicians. At first, they perform basic tasks such as insulating refrigerant lines or cleaning furnaces. In time, they move on to more difficult tasks, including cutting and soldering pipes or checking electrical circuits.

Some technicians receive their training through an apprenticeship. Apprenticeship programs usually last 3 to 5 years.

New HVACR technicians typically begin by working alongside experienced technicians.

Over the course of the apprenticeship, technicians learn safety practices, blueprint reading, and how to use tools. They also learn about the numerous systems that heat and cool buildings.

Several groups, including unions and contractor associations, sponsor apprenticeship programs. Apprenticeship requirements vary by state and locality.

Licenses, Certifications, and Registrations

The U.S. Environmental Protection Agency (EPA) requires all technicians who buy, handle, or work with refrigerants to be certified in proper refrigerant handling. Many trade schools, unions, and employer associations offer training programs designed to prepare students for the EPA certification exam.

In addition, some states and localities require HVACR technicians to be licensed; check with your state and locality for more information.

Important Qualities

Customer-service skills. HVACR technicians often work in customers' homes or business offices, so it is important that they be friendly, polite, and punctual. Repair technicians sometimes deal with unhappy customers whose heating or air conditioning is not working.

Detail oriented. HVACR technicians must carefully maintain records of all work performed. The records must include the nature of the work performed and the time it took, as well as a list of specific parts and equipment that were used.

Math skills. HVACR technicians need to calculate the correct load requirements to ensure that the HVACR equipment properly heats or cools the space required.

Mechanical skills. HVACR technicians install and work on complicated climate-control systems, so they must understand the HVAC components and be able to properly assemble, disassemble, and, if needed, program them.

Physical stamina. HVACR technicians may spend many hours walking and standing. The constant physical activity can be tiring.

Physical strength. HVACR technicians may have to lift and support heavy equipment and components, often without help.

Time-management skills. HVACR technicians frequently have a set number of daily maintenance calls. They should be able to keep a schedule and complete all necessary repairs or tasks.

Troubleshooting skills. HVACR technicians must be able to identify problems on malfunctioning heating, air conditioning, and refrigeration systems and then determine the best way to repair them.

Pay

The median annual wage for heating, air conditioning, and refrigeration mechanics and installers was $48,730 in May 2019. The median wage is the wage at which half the workers in an occupation earned more than that amount and half earned less. The lowest 10 percent earned less than $30,610, and the highest 10 percent earned more than $77,920.

In May 2019, the median annual wages for heating, air conditioning, and refrigeration mechanics and installers in the top industries in which they worked were as follows:

Wholesale trade	$52,430
Educational services; state, local, and private	52,260
Retail trade	48,620
Plumbing, heating, and air-conditioning contractors	47,380

Apprentices usually earn about half of the wage paid to experienced workers. As they learn to do more, their pay increases.

The majority of HVACR technicians work full time. Evening or weekend shifts may be required, and HVACR technicians often work overtime or irregular hours during peak heating and cooling seasons.

Job Outlook

Employment of heating, air conditioning, and refrigeration mechanics and installers is projected to grow 4 percent from 2019 to 2029, about as fast as the average for all occupations.

Commercial and residential building construction is expected to drive employment growth. The growing number of sophisticated climate-control systems is also expected to increase demand for qualified HVACR technicians.

Repair and replacement of HVACR systems is a large part of what technicians do. The growing emphasis on energy efficiency and pollution reduction is likely to increase the demand for HVACR technicians as climate-control systems are retrofitted, upgraded, or replaced entirely.

Job Prospects

Job opportunities for HVACR technicians are expected to be good. Candidates familiar with tablet computers and electronics, as well as those who have developed troubleshooting skills, will have the best job prospects.

Technicians who specialize in new installation work may experience periods of unemployment when the level of new construction activity declines. Maintenance and repair work, however, usually remains relatively stable. Business owners

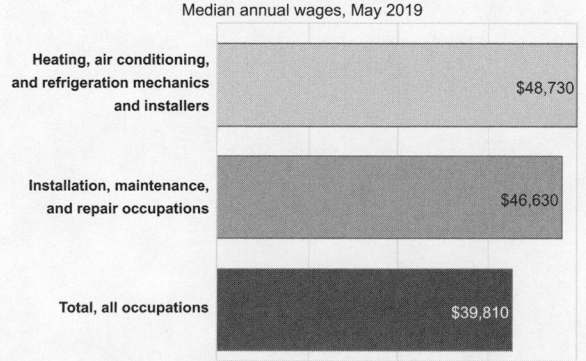

Heating, Air Conditioning, and Refrigeration Mechanics and Installers

Median annual wages, May 2019

Heating, air conditioning, and refrigeration mechanics and installers: $48,730

Installation, maintenance, and repair occupations: $46,630

Total, all occupations: $39,810

Note: All Occupations includes all occupations in the U.S. Economy.
Source: U.S. Bureau of Labor Statistics, Occupational Employment Statistics.

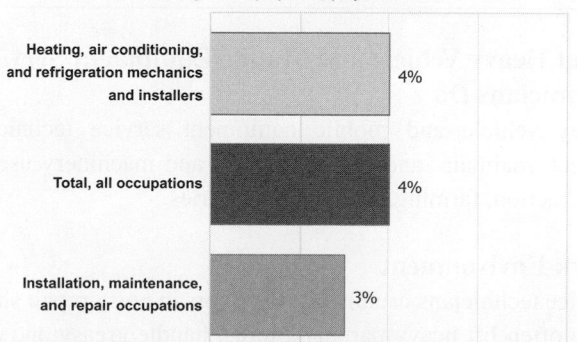

Heating, Air Conditioning, and Refrigeration Mechanics and Installers

Percent change in employment, projected 2019-29

Heating, air conditioning, and refrigeration mechanics and installers: 4%

Total, all occupations: 4%

Installation, maintenance, and repair occupations: 3%

Note: All Occupations includes all occupations in the U.S. Economy.
Source: U.S. Bureau of Labor Statistics, Employment Projections program.

and homeowners depend on their climate-control or refrigeration systems year round and must keep them in good working order, regardless of economic conditions.

Employment projections data for heating, air conditioning, and refrigeration mechanics and installers, 2019-29					
Occupational Title	SOC Code	Employment, 2019	Projected Employment, 2029	Change, 2019-29	
				Percent	Numeric
SOURCE: U.S. Bureau of Labor Statistics, Employment Projections program					
Heating, air conditioning, and refrigeration mechanics and installers	49-9021	376,800	391,900	4	15,100

State & Area Data
Occupational Employment Statistics (OES)

The Occupational Employment Statistics (OES) program produces employment and wage estimates annually for over 800 occupations. These estimates are available for the nation as a whole, for individual states, and for metropolitan and nonmetropolitan areas.

Contacts for More Information

For details about apprenticeships or other work opportunities, contact the offices of the state employment service, the state apprenticeship agency, local contractors, or local union–management HVACR apprenticeship committees. Apprenticeship information is available from the U.S. Department of Labor's Apprenticeship program online or by phone at 877-872-5627.

For more information about career opportunities, training, and certification, visit
➤ Associated Builders and Contractors
➤ North American Technician Excellence
➤ Plumbing-Heating-Cooling Contractors Association
➤ Refrigerating Engineers and Technicians Association
➤ Refrigeration Service Engineers Society (RSES)
➤ United Association Union of Plumbers, Fitters, Welders, and Service Techs

Heavy Vehicle and Mobile Equipment Service Technicians

Summary

Quick Facts: Heavy Vehicle and Mobile Equipment Service Technicians

2019 Median Pay	$51,590 per year $24.80 per hour
Typical Entry-Level Education	High school diploma or equivalent
Work Experience in a Related Occupation	None
On-the-job Training	Long-term on-the-job training
Number of Jobs, 2019	218,100
Job Outlook, 2019-29	0% (Little or no change)
Employment Change, 2019-29	900

What Heavy Vehicle and Mobile Equipment Service Technicians Do

Heavy vehicle and mobile equipment service technicians inspect, maintain, and repair vehicles and machinery used in construction, farming, and other industries.

Work Environment

Service technicians usually work indoors in noisy repair shops. They often lift heavy parts and tools, handle greasy and dirty equipment, and stand or lie in uncomfortable positions. Most service technicians work full time, and many work evenings and weekends.

How to Become a Heavy Vehicle or Mobile Equipment Service Technician

Most heavy vehicle and mobile equipment service technicians have a high school diploma or equivalent. Because vehicle and equipment technology is increasingly sophisticated and computerized, some employers prefer to hire service technicians who have completed a training program at a postsecondary institution.

Pay

The median annual wage for heavy vehicle and mobile equipment service technicians was $51,590 in May 2019.

Job Outlook

Overall employment of heavy vehicle and mobile equipment service technicians is projected to show little or no change from 2019 to 2029.

Heavy vehicle and mobile equipment service technicians repair vehicles such as bulldozers and tractors.

State & Area Data

Explore resources for employment and wages by state and area for heavy vehicle and mobile equipment service technicians.

What Heavy Vehicle and Mobile Equipment Service Technicians Do

Heavy vehicle and mobile equipment service technicians, also called *mechanics*, inspect, maintain, and repair vehicles and machinery used in construction, farming, rail transportation, and other industries.

Duties

Heavy vehicle and mobile equipment service technicians typically do the following:

- Consult equipment operating manuals, blueprints, and drawings
- Perform scheduled maintenance, such as cleaning and lubricating parts
- Diagnose and identify malfunctions, using computerized tools and equipment
- Inspect, repair, and replace defective or worn parts, such as bearings, pistons, and gears
- Overhaul and test major components, such as engines, hydraulic systems, and electrical systems
- Disassemble and reassemble heavy equipment and components
- Travel to worksites to repair large equipment, such as cranes
- Maintain logs of equipment condition and work performed

Heavy vehicles and mobile equipment are critical to many industrial activities, including construction and railroad transportation. Various types of equipment, such as tractors, cranes, and bulldozers, are used to haul materials, till land, lift beams, and dig earth to pave the way for development and construction.

Heavy vehicle and mobile equipment service technicians repair and maintain engines, hydraulic systems, transmissions, and electrical systems of agricultural, industrial, construction, and rail equipment. They ensure the performance and safety of fuel lines, brakes, and other systems.

These service technicians use diagnostic computers and equipment to identify problems and make adjustments or repairs. For example, they may use an oscilloscope to observe the signals produced by electronic components. Service technicians also use many different power and machine tools, including pneumatic wrenches, lathes, and welding equipment. A pneumatic tool, such as an impact wrench, is a tool powered by compressed air.

Service technicians also use many different hand tools, such as screwdrivers, pliers, and wrenches, to work on small parts and in hard-to-reach areas. They generally purchase these tools over the course of their careers, often investing thousands of dollars in their inventory.

After identifying malfunctioning equipment, service technicians repair, replace, and recalibrate components such as hydraulic pumps and spark plugs. Doing this may involve disassembling and reassembling major equipment or making adjustments through an onboard computer program.

The following are examples of types of heavy vehicle and mobile equipment service technicians:

Farm equipment mechanics and service technicians service and repair farm equipment, such as tractors and harvesters. They also work on smaller consumer-grade lawn and garden tractors. Most work for dealer repair shops, where farmers increasingly send their equipment for maintenance.

Mobile heavy equipment mechanics repair and maintain construction and surface mining equipment, such as bulldozers, cranes, graders, and excavators. Most work for governments, equipment rental and leasing shops, and large construction and mining companies.

Rail car repairers specialize in servicing railroad locomotives, subway cars, and other rolling stock. They usually work for railroads, public and private transit companies, and railcar manufacturers.

Mechanics who work primarily on automobiles are described in the profile on automotive service technicians and mechanics.

Mechanics who work primarily on large trucks and buses are described in the profile on diesel service technicians and mechanics.

Mechanics who work primarily on motorboats, motorcycles, and small all-terrain vehicles are described in the profile on small engine mechanics.

Work Environment

Heavy vehicle and mobile equipment service technicians held about 218,100 jobs in 2019. Employment in the detailed occupations that make up heavy vehicle and mobile equipment service technicians was distributed as follows:

Mobile heavy equipment mechanics, except
 engines 152,900

Mechanics inspect, repair, and replace defective or worn parts.

Farm equipment mechanics and service
   technicians.. 40,800
Rail car repairers 24,300

The largest employers of heavy vehicle and mobile equipment service technicians were as follows:

Farm and garden machinery and equipment merchant   12%
   wholesalers...
Government.. 9
Heavy and civil engineering construction..................... 7
Rental and leasing services...................................... 7

Although many service technicians work indoors in repair shops, some service technicians travel to worksites to make repairs because it is often too expensive to transport heavy or mobile equipment to a shop. Generally, more experienced service technicians specialize in field service. These workers drive trucks that are specially equipped with replacement parts and tools, and they spend considerable time outdoors and often drive long distances.

Heavy vehicle and mobile equipment service technicians frequently lift heavy parts and tools, handle greasy and dirty equipment, and stand or lie in awkward positions.

Some service technicians travel to worksites to make repairs.

Work Schedules

Most heavy vehicle and mobile equipment service technicians work full time, and many work evenings or weekends. Overtime is common.

Farm equipment mechanics' work varies by time of the year. During busy planting and harvesting seasons, for example, mechanics often work six or seven 12-hour days per week. In the winter months, however, they may work less than full time.

How to Become a Heavy Vehicle or Mobile Equipment Service Technician

Most heavy vehicle and mobile equipment service technicians have a high school diploma or equivalent. Because vehicle and equipment technology is increasingly sophisticated and computerized, some employers prefer to hire service technicians who have completed a formal training program at a postsecondary institution.

Education

Most heavy vehicle and mobile equipment service technicians have a high school diploma or equivalent. High school courses in automotive repair, electronics, physics, and welding provide a strong foundation for a service technician's career. However, high school graduates often need further training to become fully qualified.

Completing a vocational or other postsecondary training program in diesel technology or heavy equipment mechanics is increasingly considered the best preparation for some entry-level positions. Offered by vocational schools and community colleges, these programs cover the basics of diagnostic techniques, electronics, and other related subjects. Each program may last 1 to 2 years and lead to a certificate of completion. Other programs, which lead to associate's degrees, generally take 2 years to complete.

Training

Entry-level workers with no formal background in heavy vehicle repair often receive a few months of on-the-job training

Heavy vehicle and mobile equipment service technicians must be familiar with engine components and systems.

before they begin performing routine service tasks and making minor repairs. Trainees advance to more complex work as they show competence, and they usually become fully qualified after 3 to 4 years of work.

Service technicians who have completed a postsecondary training program in diesel technology or heavy equipment mechanics typically require less on-the-job training.

Many employers send new service technicians to training sessions conducted by equipment manufacturers. Training sessions may focus on particular components and technologies or particular types of equipment.

Licenses, Certifications, and Registrations

Some manufacturers offer certification in specific repair methods or equipment. Although not required, certification can demonstrate a service technician's competence and usually commands higher pay.

Important Qualities

Dexterity. Heavy vehicle and mobile equipment service technicians must perform many tasks, such as disassembling engine parts, connecting or attaching components, and using hand tools, with a steady hand and good hand-eye coordination.

Mechanical skills. Heavy vehicle and mobile equipment service technicians must be familiar with engine components and systems and know how they interact with each other. They must often disassemble major parts for repairs and be able to reassemble them.

Organizational skills. Heavy vehicle and mobile equipment service technicians must maintain accurate service records and parts inventories.

Physical strength. Heavy vehicle and mobile equipment service technicians must be able to lift and move heavy equipment, tools, and parts without risking injury.

Troubleshooting skills. Heavy vehicle and mobile equipment service technicians must be familiar with diagnostic equipment to find the source of malfunctions.

Pay

The median annual wage for heavy vehicle and mobile equipment service technicians was $51,590 in May 2019. The median wage is the wage at which half the workers in an occupation earned more than that amount and half earned less. The lowest 10 percent earned less than $33,170, and the highest 10 percent earned more than $76,830.

Median annual wages for heavy vehicle and mobile equipment service technicians in May 2019 were as follows:

Rail car repairers $56,390

Mobile heavy equipment mechanics, except
    engines 53,370

Farm equipment mechanics and service
    technicians 42,200

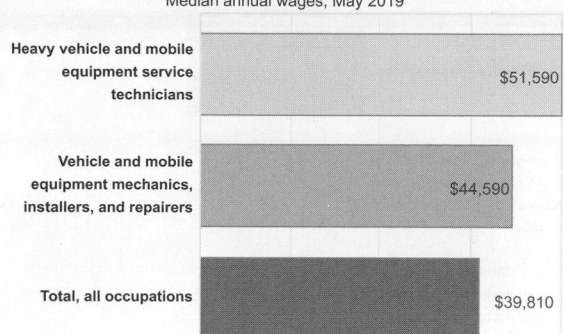

Heavy Vehicle and Mobile Equipment Service Technicians
Median annual wages, May 2019

Heavy vehicle and mobile equipment service technicians	$51,590
Vehicle and mobile equipment mechanics, installers, and repairers	$44,590
Total, all occupations	$39,810

Note: All Occupations includes all occupations in the U.S. Economy.
Source: U.S. Bureau of Labor Statistics, Occupational Employment Statistics.

In May 2019, the median annual wages for heavy vehicle and mobile equipment service technicians in the top industries in which they worked were as follows:

Government $58,270

Heavy and civil engineering construction 52,210

Rental and leasing services 49,410

Farm and garden machinery and equipment
    merchant wholesalers 42,900

Most heavy vehicle and mobile equipment service technicians work full time, and many work evenings or weekends. Overtime is common.

Farm equipment mechanics' work varies by time of the year. During busy planting and harvesting seasons, for example, mechanics often work six or seven 12-hour days per week. In the winter months, however, they may work less than full time.

Job Outlook

Overall employment of heavy vehicle and mobile equipment service technicians is projected to show little or no change from 2019 to 2029. Projected employment change varies by specialty.

Agricultural products used to feed a growing population are produced with the use of increasingly complex farm equipment, which will require farm equipment repairers to make them operational. However, new automated and precision farm equipment is often built with predictive maintenance and software systems that are more reliable, requiring fewer workhours.

Population and business growth will result in the construction of houses, office buildings, roads, bridges, and other structures, which in turn will require mobile heavy equipment mechanics in the construction industry. However, nearly 3 in 10 of these workers are employed in wholesale trade, which is projected to decrease in employment over the next decade.

Heavy Vehicle and Mobile Equipment Service Technicians

Percent change in employment, projected 2019-29

Total, all occupations	4%
Heavy vehicle and mobile equipment service technicians and mechanics	0%
Vehicle and mobile equipment mechanics, installers, and repairers	0%

Note: All Occupations includes all occupations in the U.S. Economy.
Source: U.S. Bureau of Labor Statistics, Employment Projections program.

Some rail car repairers will continue to be needed to repair railcars used for freight shipping and transportation, as well as public transportation. However, reduced employment for these workers is expected to over the next 10 years due to projected employment declines in the rail transportation and support activities for rail transportation industries.

Job Prospects

Most job opportunities will come from the need to replace workers who retire or leave the occupation. Those who have completed postsecondary education programs should enjoy the best job prospects. Those without postsecondary education or certification are likely to face stronger competition for entry-level jobs.

The majority of job openings are expected to be in sectors that sell, rent, or lease heavy vehicles and mobile equipment. These sectors employ a large proportion of service technicians.

The construction and mining industries, which use a large amount of heavy equipment, are sensitive to fluctuations in the economy. As a result, job opportunities for service technicians in these sectors will vary with overall economic conditions.

Job opportunities for farm equipment mechanics are seasonal and are generally best during warmer months.

Employment projections data for heavy vehicle and mobile equipment service technicians, 2019-29

Occupational Title	SOC Code	Employment, 2019	Projected Employment, 2029	Change, 2019-29	
				Percent	Numeric
SOURCE: U.S. Bureau of Labor Statistics, Employment Projections program					
Heavy vehicle and mobile equipment service technicians and mechanics	49-3040	218,100	218,900	0	900
Farm equipment mechanics and service technicians	49-3041	40,800	41,300	1	500
Mobile heavy equipment mechanics, except engines	49-3042	152,900	154,000	1	1,100
Rail car repairers	49-3043	24,300	23,500	-3	-800

State & Area Data
Occupational Employment Statistics (OES)

The Occupational Employment Statistics (OES) program produces employment and wage estimates annually for over 800 occupations. These estimates are available for the nation as a whole, for individual states, and for metropolitan and nonmetropolitan areas.

For more details about job openings for heavy vehicle and mobile equipment service technicians, consult local heavy and mobile equipment dealers and distributors, construction contractors, and government agencies. Local offices of the state employment service also may have information on job openings and training programs.

For more information about careers and training programs, visit
➤ Associated Equipment Distributors
➤ National Automotive Technicians Education Foundation
➤ National Institute for Automotive Service Excellence

Industrial Machinery Mechanics, Machinery Maintenance Workers, and Millwrights

Summary

Quick Facts: Industrial Machinery Mechanics, Machinery Maintenance Workers, and Millwrights	
2019 Median Pay	$52,860 per year $25.41 per hour
Typical Entry-Level Education	High school diploma or equivalent
Work Experience in a Related Occupation	None
On-the-job Training	See below
Number of Jobs, 2019	521,300
Job Outlook, 2019-29	13% (Much faster than average)
Employment Change, 2019-29	70,100

What Industrial Machinery Mechanics, Machinery Maintenance Workers, and Millwrights Do

Industrial machinery mechanics, machinery maintenance workers, and millwrights install, maintain, and repair factory equipment and other industrial machinery.

Work Environment

Workers in this occupation must follow safety precautions and use protective equipment, such as hardhats, safety glasses, and hearing protectors. Most work full time in manufacturing facilities. However, they may be on call and work night or weekend shifts. Overtime is common.

How to Become an Industrial Machinery Mechanic, Machinery Maintenance Worker, or Millwright

Industrial machinery mechanics, machinery maintenance workers, and millwrights typically need a high school diploma.

Industrial machinery mechanics and machinery maintenance workers also usually need at least a year of on-the-job training. Most millwrights go through an apprenticeship program that may last up to 4 years.

Pay

The median annual wage for industrial machinery mechanics, machinery maintenance workers, and millwrights was $52,860 in May 2019.

Job Outlook

Overall employment of industrial machinery mechanics, machinery maintenance workers, and millwrights is projected to grow 13 percent from 2019 to 2029, much faster than the average for all occupations. Employment growth will vary by occupation.

State & Area Data

Explore resources for employment and wages by state and area for industrial machinery mechanics, machinery maintenance workers, and millwrights.

What Industrial Machinery Mechanics, Machinery Maintenance Workers, and Millwrights Do

Industrial machinery mechanics and machinery maintenance workers maintain and repair factory equipment and other industrial machinery, such as conveying systems, production machinery, and packaging equipment. Millwrights install, dismantle, repair, reassemble, and move machinery in factories, power plants, and construction sites.

Duties

Industrial machinery mechanics, machinery maintenance workers, and millwrights typically do the following:

Industrial machinery mechanics, machinery maintenance workers, and millwrights all repair manufacturing equipment.

Industrial machinery mechanics and machinery maintenance workers adjust and calibrate equipment.

- Read technical manuals to understand equipment and controls
- Disassemble machinery and equipment when there is a problem
- Repair or replace broken or malfunctioning components
- Perform tests and run initial batches to make sure that the machine is running smoothly
- Detect minor problems by performing basic diagnostic tests
- Test malfunctioning machinery to determine whether major repairs are needed
- Adjust and calibrate equipment and machinery to optimal specifications
- Clean and lubricate equipment or machinery
- Move machinery and equipment

Industrial machinery mechanics, also called *maintenance machinists*, keep machines in working order by detecting and correcting errors before the machine or the products it produces are damaged. Many of these machines are increasingly run by computers. Industrial machinery mechanics use technical manuals, their understanding of industrial equipment, and observation to determine the cause of a problem. For example, after detecting a vibration from a machine, they must decide whether it is the result of worn belts, weak motor bearings, or some other problem. They may use computerized diagnostic systems and vibration analysis techniques to help figure out the source of problems. Examples of machines they may work with are robotic welding arms, automobile assembly line conveyor belts, and hydraulic lifts.

After diagnosing a problem, the industrial machinery mechanic may take the equipment apart to repair or replace the necessary parts. Once a repair is made, mechanics test a machine to ensure that it is operating correctly.

In addition to working with hand tools, mechanics commonly use lathes, grinders, and drill presses. Many also are required to weld.

Machinery maintenance workers do basic maintenance and repairs on machines. They clean and lubricate machinery, perform basic diagnostic tests, check the performance of the machine, and test damaged machine parts to determine whether major repairs are necessary.

Machinery maintenance workers must follow machine specifications and adhere to maintenance schedules. They perform minor repairs, generally leaving major repairs to industrial machinery mechanics.

Maintenance workers use a variety of tools to do repairs and preventive maintenance. For example, they may use a screwdriver or socket wrenches to adjust a motor's alignment, or they might use a hoist to lift a heavy printing press off the ground.

Millwrights install, maintain, and disassemble industrial machines. Putting together a machine can take a few days or several weeks.

Millwrights perform repairs that include replacing worn or defective parts of machines. They also may be involved in taking apart the entire machine, a common situation when a manufacturing plant needs to clear floor space for new machinery. In taking apart a machine, millwrights carefully disassemble, categorize, and package each part of the machine.

Millwrights use a variety of hand tools, such as hammers and levels, as well as equipment for welding, brazing, and cutting. They also use measuring tools, such as micrometers, measuring tapes, lasers, and other precision-measuring devices. On large projects, they commonly use cranes and trucks. When millwrights and managers determine the best place for a machine, millwrights use forklifts, hoists, winches, cranes, and other equipment to bring the parts to the desired location.

Work Environment

Industrial machinery mechanics, machinery maintenance workers, and millwrights held about 521,300 jobs in 2019. Employment in the detailed occupations that make up industrial machinery mechanics, machinery maintenance workers, and millwrights was distributed as follows:

Industrial machinery mechanics	399,400
Maintenance workers, machinery	73,200
Millwrights	48,700

The largest employers of industrial machinery mechanics, machinery maintenance workers, and millwrights were as follows:

Manufacturing	53%
Wholesale trade	11
Commercial and industrial machinery and equipment (except automotive and electronic) repair and maintenance	10
Construction	6

Industrial machinery mechanics, machinery maintenance workers, and millwrights usually work in manufacturing facilities.

Injuries and Illnesses

Working with industrial machinery can be dangerous. To avoid injury, workers must follow safety precautions and use protective equipment, such as hardhats, safety glasses, steel-toed shoes, gloves, and earplugs.

Work Schedules

Most industrial machinery mechanics and machinery maintenance workers are employed full time during regular business hours. However, mechanics may be on call and work night or weekend shifts. Overtime is common, particularly for mechanics.

How to Become an Industrial Machinery Mechanic, Machinery Maintenance Worker, or Millwright

Industrial machinery mechanics, machinery maintenance workers, and millwrights typically need a high school diploma. Industrial machinery mechanics and machinery maintenance workers also usually need a year or more of training after high school.

Most millwrights go through an apprenticeship program that lasts about 4 years.

Education

Industrial machinery mechanics, machinery maintenance workers, and millwrights generally need at least a high school diploma or equivalent. Some mechanics and millwrights complete a 2-year associate's degree program in industrial maintenance. Industrial maintenance programs may include courses such as welding, mathematics, hydraulics, and pneumatics.

Training

Industrial machinery mechanics and machinery maintenance workers typically receive more than a year of on-the-job

Industrial machinery mechanics may receive more than a year of on-the-job training, while machinery maintenance workers typically receive training that lasts a few months to a year.

training. Industrial machinery mechanics and machinery maintenance workers learn how to perform routine tasks, such as setting up, cleaning, lubricating, and starting machinery. They also may be instructed in subjects such as shop mathematics, blueprint reading, proper hand tool use, welding, electronics, and computer programming. This training may be offered on the job by professional trainers hired by the employer or by representatives of equipment manufacturers.

Most millwrights learn their trade through a 3- or 4-year apprenticeship. For each year of the program, apprentices must have at least 144 hours of relevant technical instruction and up to 2,000 hours of paid on-the-job training. On the job, apprentices learn to set up, clean, lubricate, repair, and start machinery. During technical instruction, they are taught welding, mathematics, how to read blueprints, and machinery troubleshooting. Many also receive computer training.

After completing an apprenticeship program, millwrights are considered fully qualified and can usually perform tasks with less guidance.

Employers, local unions, contractor associations, and the state labor department often sponsor apprenticeship programs. The basic qualifications for entering an apprenticeship program are as follows:

- Minimum age of 18
- High school diploma or equivalent
- Physically able to do the work

Important Qualities

Manual dexterity. Industrial machinery mechanics, machinery maintenance workers, and millwrights must have a steady hand and good hand–eye coordination when handling very small parts.

Mechanical skills. Industrial machinery mechanics, machinery maintenance workers, and millwrights use technical manuals and sophisticated diagnostic equipment to figure out why machines are not working. Workers must be able to reassemble large, complex machines after finishing a repair.

Troubleshooting skills. Industrial machinery mechanics, machinery maintenance workers, and millwrights must observe, diagnose, and fix problems that a machine may be having.

Pay

The median annual wage for industrial machinery mechanics, machinery maintenance workers, and millwrights was $52,860 in May 2019. The median wage is the wage at which half the workers in an occupation earned more than that amount and half earned less. The lowest 10 percent earned less than $33,760, and the highest 10 percent earned more than $79,150.

Median annual wages for industrial machinery mechanics, machinery maintenance workers, and millwrights in May 2019 were as follows:

Millwrights $55,560

Industrial Machinery Mechanics, Machinery Maintenance Workers, and Millwrights

Median annual wages, May 2019

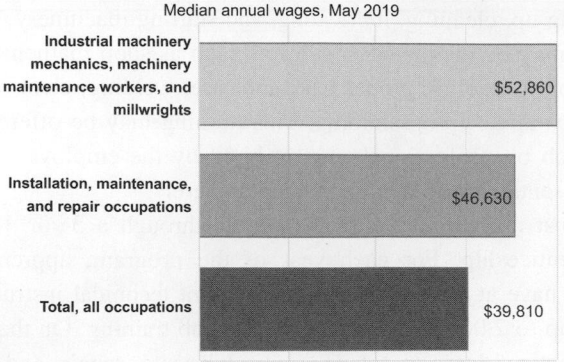

Note: All Occupations includes all occupations in the U.S. Economy.
Source: U.S. Bureau of Labor Statistics, Occupational Employment Statistics.

Industrial machinery mechanics 53,590

Maintenance workers, machinery 47,520

In May 2019, the median annual wages for industrial machinery mechanics, machinery maintenance workers, and millwrights in the top industries in which they worked were as follows:

Manufacturing.. $53,130

Construction 52,860

Wholesale trade 51,410

Commercial and industrial machinery and
equipment (except automotive and electronic)
repair and maintenance 48,350

Most industrial machinery mechanics and machinery maintenance workers are employed full time during regular business hours. However, mechanics may be on call or assigned to work night or weekend shifts. Overtime is common, particularly for mechanics.

Job Outlook

Overall employment of industrial machinery mechanics, machinery maintenance workers, and millwrights is projected to grow 13 percent from 2019 to 2029, much faster than the average for all occupations. Employment growth will vary by occupation.

The continuing adoption of automated manufacturing machinery will require more maintenance workers, mechanics, and millwrights to keep machines in good working order over the next decade. The use of automated conveyors to move products and materials in factories is an area of high demand for these workers, because the conveyor belts, motors, and rollers need regular care and maintenance.

Job Prospects

Job prospects will be good, particularly for applicants with a broad range of skills in machine repair as older workers retire or otherwise leave the occupation.

Industrial Machinery Mechanics, Machinery Maintenance Workers, and Millwrights

Percent change in employment, projected 2019-29

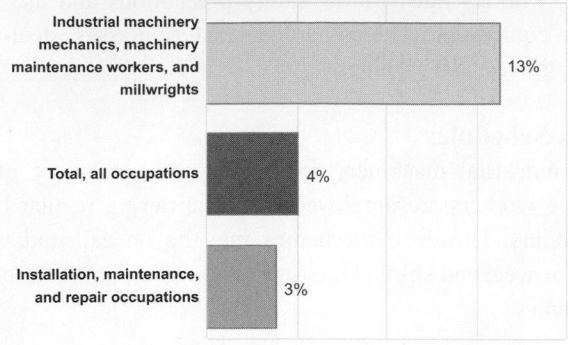

Note: All Occupations includes all occupations in the U.S. Economy.
Source: U.S. Bureau of Labor Statistics, Employment Projections program.

Employment projections data for industrial machinery mechanics, machinery maintenance workers, and millwrights, 2019-29					
Occupational Title	SOC Code	Employment, 2019	Projected Employment, 2029	Change, 2019-29	
				Percent	Numeric
SOURCE: U.S. Bureau of Labor Statistics, Employment Projections program					
Industrial machinery mechanics, machinery maintenance workers, and millwrights	—	521,300	591,400	13	70,100
Industrial machinery mechanics	49-9041	399,400	461,700	16	62,300
Maintenance workers, machinery	49-9043	73,200	77,700	6	4,500
Millwrights	49-9044	48,700	52,100	7	3,400

State & Area Data

Occupational Employment Statistics (OES)

The Occupational Employment Statistics (OES) program produces employment and wage estimates annually for over 800 occupations. These estimates are available for the nation as a whole, for individual states, and for metropolitan and nonmetropolitan areas.

Contacts for More Information

For information about industrial machinery mechanics and machinery maintenance workers, visit
➤ National Association of Manufacturers
➤ Society for Maintenance & Reliability Professionals

For information about millwrights and the precision-machined products industry, training, and apprenticeships, visit
➤ Precision Machined Products Association

For further information on apprenticeship programs, write to the Apprenticeship Council of your state's labor department or to local firms that employ machinery mechanics and repairers. Apprenticeship information is also available from the U.S. Department of Labor's Apprenticeship program online or by phone at 877-872-5627.

Line Installers and Repairers

Summary

Quick Facts: Line Installers and Repairers

2019 Median Pay	$65,700 per year $31.59 per hour
Typical Entry-Level Education	High school diploma or equivalent
Work Experience in a Related Occupation	None
On-the-job Training	Long-term on-the-job training
Number of Jobs, 2019	238,600
Job Outlook, 2019-29	0% (Little or no change)
Employment Change, 2019-29	0

What Line Installers and Repairers Do

Line installers and repairers install or repair electrical power systems and telecommunications cables, including fiber optics.

Work Environment

Line workers encounter serious hazards on the job, including working with high-voltage electricity, often at great heights. The work also can be physically demanding. Although most work full time during regular business hours, some work irregular hours on evenings, nights, weekends, and holidays when needed.

How to Become a Line Installer or Repairer

To become proficient, most line installers and repairers require technical instruction and long-term on-the-job training. Apprenticeships are common.

Pay

The median annual wage for electrical power-line installers and repairers was $72,520 in May 2019.

Line installers and repairers often work in teams to install and fix cables and wires.

The median annual wage for telecommunications line installers and repairers was $56,750 in May 2019.

Job Outlook

Overall employment of line installers and repairers is projected to show little or no change from 2019 to 2029.

State & Area Data

Explore resources for employment and wages by state and area for line installers and repairers.

What Line Installers and Repairers Do

Line installers and repairers, also known as *line workers*, install or repair electrical power systems and telecommunications cables, including fiber optics.

Duties

Electrical power-line installers and repairers typically do the following:

* Install, maintain, or repair the power lines that move electricity
* Identify defective devices, voltage regulators, transformers, and switches
* Inspect and test power lines and auxiliary equipment
* String power lines between poles, towers, and buildings
* Climb poles and transmission towers and use truck-mounted buckets to get to equipment
* Operate power equipment when installing and repairing poles, towers, and lines
* Drive work vehicles to job sites
* Follow safety standards and procedures

Telecommunications line installers and repairers typically do the following:

* Install, maintain, or repair telecommunications equipment
* Inspect or test lines or cables
* Lay underground cable, including fiber optic lines, directly in trenches
* Pull cables in underground conduit
* Install aerial cables, including over lakes or across rivers
* Operate power equipment when installing and repairing poles, towers, and lines
* Drive work vehicles to job sites
* Set up service for customers

A complex network of physical power lines and cables provides consumers with electricity, landline telephone communication, cable television, and Internet access. Line installers and repairers, also known as *line workers*, are responsible for installing and maintaining these networks.

Line installers and repairers can specialize in different areas depending on the type of network and industry in which they work:

Line installers and repairers use a truck-mounted bucket to access equipment.

Electrical power-line installers and repairers install and maintain the power grid—the network of power lines that moves electricity from generating plants to customers. They routinely work with high-voltage electricity, which requires extreme caution. The electrical current can range from hundreds of thousands of volts for long-distance transmission lines that make up the power grid to less than 10,000 volts for distribution lines that supply electricity to homes and businesses.

Line workers who maintain the interstate power grid work in crews that travel to locations throughout a large region to service transmission lines and towers. Workers employed by local utilities work mainly with lower voltage distribution lines, maintaining equipment such as transformers, voltage regulators, and switches. They also may work on traffic lights and street lights.

Telecommunications line installers and repairers install and maintain the lines and cables used by network communications companies. Depending on the service provided—local and long-distance telephone, cable television, or Internet—telecommunications companies use different types of cables, including fiber optic cables. Unlike metallic cables that carry electricity, fiber optic cables are made of glass and transmit signals using light. Working with fiber optics requires special skills, such as the ability to splice and terminate optical cables. In addition, workers use specialized equipment to test and troubleshoot cables and networking equipment.

Because these systems are complicated, many line workers also specialize by duty:

Line installers install new cable. They may work for construction contractors, utilities, or telecommunications companies. Workers generally start a new job by digging underground trenches or erecting utility poles and towers to carry the wires and cables. They use a variety of construction equipment, including digger derricks, which are trucks equipped with augers and cranes used to dig holes and set poles in place. Line installers also use trenchers, cable plows, and directional bore machines, which are used to cut openings in the earth to lay underground cables. Once the poles, towers, tunnels, or trenches are ready, workers install the new cable.

Line repairers are employed by utilities and telecommunications companies that maintain existing power and telecommunications lines. Maintenance needs may be identified in a variety of ways, including remote monitoring, aerial inspections, and by customer reports of service outages. Line repairers often must replace aging or outdated equipment, so many of these workers have installation duties in addition to their repair duties.

When a problem is reported, line repairers must identify the cause and fix it. This usually involves diagnostic testing using specialized equipment and repair work. To work on poles, line installers usually use bucket trucks to raise themselves to the top of the structure, although all line workers must be adept at climbing poles and towers when necessary. Workers use special safety equipment to keep them from falling when climbing utility poles and towers.

Storms and other natural disasters can cause extensive damage to power lines. When power is lost, line repairers must work quickly to restore service to customers.

Work Environment

Electrical power-line installers and repairers held about 115,000 jobs in 2019. The largest employers of electrical power-line installers and repairers were as follows:

Line installers and repairers may be required to work at great heights.

Electric power generation, transmission and distribution 47%

Power and communication line and related structures construction 27

Local government, excluding education and hospitals.. 12

Electrical contractors and other wiring installation contractors 4

Telecommunications line installers and repairers held about 123,600 jobs in 2019. The largest employers of telecommunications line installers and repairers were as follows:

Telecommunications 58%

Utility system construction 16

Building equipment contractors 15

Self-employed workers 2

The work of line installers and repairers can be physically demanding. Line installers must be comfortable working at great heights and in confined spaces. Despite the help of bucket trucks, all line workers must be able to climb utility poles and transmission towers and balance while working on them.

Their work often requires that they drive utility vehicles, travel long distances, and work outdoors.

Line installers and repairers often must work under challenging weather conditions, such as in snow, wind, rain, and extreme heat and cold, in order to keep electricity and telecommunications flowing.

Injuries and Illnesses

Line workers encounter serious hazards on their jobs and must follow safety procedures to minimize danger. For example, workers must wear safety equipment when entering underground manholes and test for the presence of gas before going underground.

Electrical power-line installers and repairers can be electrocuted if they come in contact with a live cable on a high-voltage power line. When workers engage live wires, they use electrically insulated protective devices and tools to minimize their risk.

To prevent injuries, line installers and repairers use fall-protection equipment when working on poles or towers. Safety procedures and training have significantly reduced the danger for line workers. However, telecommunications line installers and repairers still have one of the highest rates of injuries and illnesses of all occupations.

Work Schedules

Although most work full time during regular business hours, some line installers and repairers must work evenings and weekends. In emergencies or after storms and other natural disasters, workers may have to work long hours for several days in a row.

How to Become a Line Installer or Repairer

A high school diploma or equivalent is typically required for entry-level positions, but most line installers and repairers

Most installers and repairers have a high school diploma and receive long-term on-the-job training.

need technical instruction and long-term on-the-job training to become proficient. Apprenticeships are also common.

Education

Most companies require line installers and repairers to have a high school diploma or equivalent. Employers prefer candidates with basic knowledge of algebra and trigonometry. In addition, technical knowledge of electricity or electronics obtained through military service, vocational programs, or community colleges can also be helpful.

Many community colleges offer programs in telecommunications, electronics, or electricity. Some programs work with local companies to offer 1-year certificates that emphasize hands-on fieldwork.

More advanced 2-year associate's degree programs provide students with a broad knowledge of the technology used in telecommunications and electrical utilities. These programs offer courses in electricity, electronics, fiber optics, and microwave transmission.

Training

Electrical line installers and repairers often must complete apprenticeships or other employer training programs. These programs, which can last up to 3 years, combine on-the-job training with technical instruction and are sometimes administered jointly by the employer and the union representing the workers. For example, the Electrical Training Alliance offers apprenticeship programs in four specialty areas. The basic qualifications to enter an apprenticeship program are as follows:

- Minimum age of 18
- High school education or equivalent
- One year of algebra
- Qualifying score on an aptitude test
- Pass substance abuse screening

Line installers and repairers who work for telecommunications companies typically receive several years of on-the-job training. They also may be encouraged to attend training from equipment manufacturers, schools, unions, or industry training organizations.

Licenses, Certifications, and Registrations

Although not mandatory, certification for line installers and repairers is also available from several associations. For example, BICSI offers certification for line installers and repairers, and the Electrical Training ALLIANCE offers certification for line installers and repairers in several specialty areas.

In addition, The Fiber Optic Association (FOA) offers two levels of fiber optic certification for telecommunications line installers and repairers.

Workers who drive heavy company vehicles usually need a commercial driver's license.

Advancement

Entry-level line workers generally begin with an apprenticeship, which includes both classroom training and hands-on work experience. As they learn additional skills from more experienced workers, they may advance to more complex tasks. In time, experienced line workers advance to more sophisticated maintenance and repair positions in which they are responsible for increasingly large portions of the network.

After 3 to 4 years of working, qualified line workers reach the journey level. A journey-level line worker is no longer considered an apprentice and can perform most tasks without supervision. Journey-level line workers also may qualify for positions at other companies. Workers with many years of experience may become first-line supervisors or trainers.

Important Qualities

Color vision. Workers who handle electrical wires and cables must distinguish colors because the wires and cables are often color coded.

Mechanical skills. Line installers and repairers must have the knowledge and skills to repair or replace complex electrical and telecommunications lines and equipment.

Physical stamina. Line installers and repairers often must climb poles and work at great heights with heavy tools and equipment. Therefore, installers and repairers need to work for long periods without tiring easily.

Physical strength. Line installers and repairers must be strong enough to lift heavy tools, cables, and equipment on a regular basis.

Teamwork. Because workers often rely on their fellow crew members for their safety, teamwork is critical.

Technical skills. Line installers use sophisticated diagnostic equipment on circuit breakers, switches, and transformers. They must be familiar with electrical systems and the appropriate tools needed to fix and maintain them.

Troubleshooting skills. Line installers and repairers must diagnose problems in increasingly complex electrical systems and telecommunication lines.

Pay

The median annual wage for electrical power-line installers and repairers was $72,520 in May 2019. The median wage is the wage at which half the workers in an occupation earned more than that amount and half earned less. The lowest 10 percent earned less than $38,810, and the highest 10 percent earned more than $103,500.

The median annual wage for telecommunications line installers and repairers was $56,750 in May 2019. The lowest 10 percent earned less than $32,590, and the highest 10 percent earned more than $94,880.

In May 2019, the median annual wages for electrical power-line installers and repairers in the top industries in which they worked were as follows:

Electric power generation, transmission and distribution	$79,220
Electrical contractors and other wiring installation contractors	67,280
Local government, excluding education and hospitals	66,920
Power and communication line and related structures construction	58,510

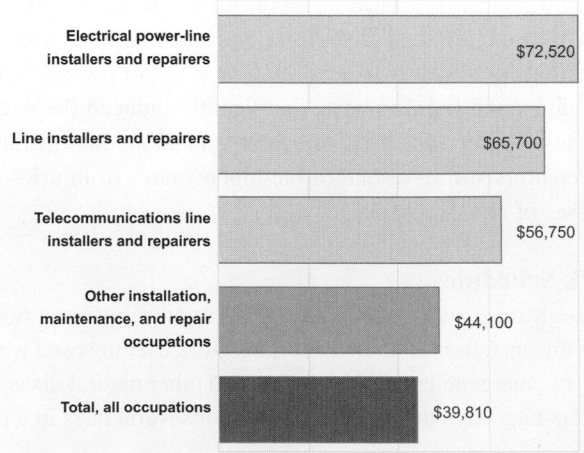

Line Installers and Repairers
Median annual wages, May 2019

Electrical power-line installers and repairers	$72,520
Line installers and repairers	$65,700
Telecommunications line installers and repairers	$56,750
Other installation, maintenance, and repair occupations	$44,100
Total, all occupations	$39,810

Note: All Occupations includes all occupations in the U.S. Economy.
Source: U.S. Bureau of Labor Statistics, Occupational Employment Statistics.

In May 2019, the median annual wages for telecommunications line installers and repairers in the top industries in which they worked were as follows:

Telecommunications	$68,880
Building equipment contractors	44,670
Utility system construction	43,170

Although most work full time during regular business hours, some line installers and repairers may work evenings and weekends. In emergencies or after storms and other natural disasters, they may have to work long hours for several days in a row.

Job Outlook

Overall employment of line installers and repairers is projected to show little or no change from 2019 to 2029.

Employment of telecommunications line installers and repairers is expected to decrease over the decade due to new technological developments in wireless broadband services and the development of the 5G mobile broadband network, reducing the need for hard-wired telecommunication lines. Employment is projected to decline in the telecommunications industry, as consumers increasingly demand wireless and mobile services instead of landline-based services.

Employment of electrical power-line installers and repairers is expected to grow, largely due to growing population and expanding cities. With each new housing development or office park, new electric power lines are installed and will require maintenance. In addition, the interstate power grid will continue to become more complex to ensure reliability.

Job Prospects

Good job opportunities are expected for line installers and repairers overall. Highly skilled workers with apprenticeship training or a 2-year associate's degree in telecommunications, electronics, or electricity should have the best job opportunities.

Line Installers and Repairers
Percent change in employment, projected 2019-29

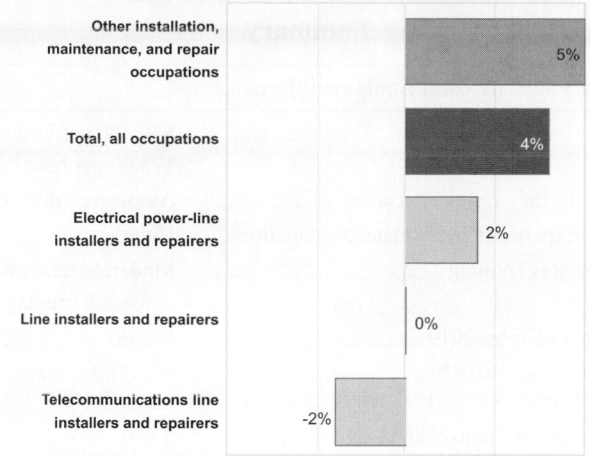

Note: All Occupations includes all occupations in the U.S. Economy.
Source: U.S. Bureau of Labor Statistics, Employment Projections program.

State & Area Data
Occupational Employment Statistics (OES)

The Occupational Employment Statistics (OES) program produces employment and wage estimates annually for over 800 occupations. These estimates are available for the nation as a whole, for individual states, and for metropolitan and nonmetropolitan areas.

Contacts for More Information

For information about apprenticeships or job opportunities for line installers and repairers, contact local electrical contractors, a local chapter of the International Brotherhood of Electrical Workers, a local joint union-management apprenticeship committee, or the nearest office of your state employment service or apprenticeship agency. Apprenticeship information is available from the U.S. Department of Labor's toll-free help line, 1 (877) 872-5627 or the Employment and Training Administration.

For more information about line installers and repairers, visit
➤ American Public Power Association
➤ Center for Energy Workforce Development
➤ Telecommunications Industry Association
➤ For information about certification, visit
➤ BICSI
➤ The Fiber Optic Association
➤ Electrical Training ALLIANCE

Employment projections data for line installers and repairers, 2019-29					
Occupational Title	SOC Code	Employment, 2019	Projected Employment, 2029	Change, 2019-29	
				Percent	Numeric
SOURCE: U.S. Bureau of Labor Statistics, Employment Projections program					
Line installers and repairers	49-9050	238,600	238,600	0	0
Electrical power-line installers and repairers	49-9051	115,000	116,900	2	2,000
Telecommunications line installers and repairers	49-9052	123,600	121,600	-2	-2,000

Medical Equipment Repairers

Summary

Quick Facts: Medical Equipment Repairers

2019 Median Pay	$49,280 per year $23.69 per hour
Typical Entry-Level Education	Associate's degree
Work Experience in a Related Occupation	None
On-the-job Training	Moderate-term on-the-job training
Number of Jobs, 2019	53,900
Job Outlook, 2019-29	5% (Faster than average)
Employment Change, 2019-29	2,800

What Medical Equipment Repairers Do

Medical equipment repairers install, maintain, and repair patient care equipment.

Work Environment

Although medical equipment repairers usually work during the day, they are sometimes expected to be on call, including evenings and weekends. Because repairing vital medical equipment is urgent, the work is sometimes stressful. Those who work in a patient-caring environment are potentially exposed to germs, diseases, and other health risks.

How to Become a Medical Equipment Repairer

Employers generally prefer candidates who have an associate's degree in biomedical technology or engineering. Depending on the area of specialization, repairers may need a bachelor's degree, especially for advancement.

Pay

The median annual wage for medical equipment repairers was $49,280 in May 2019.

Job Outlook

Employment of medical equipment repairers is projected to grow 5 percent from 2019 to 2029, faster than the average for all occupations.

State & Area Data

Explore resources for employment and wages by state and area for medical equipment repairers.

What Medical Equipment Repairers Do

Medical equipment repairers install, maintain, and repair patient care equipment.

Duties

Medical equipment repairers typically do the following:

- Install medical equipment
- Test and calibrate parts and equipment
- Repair and replace parts
- Perform preventive maintenance and service
- Keep records of maintenance and repairs
- Review technical manuals and regularly attend training sessions
- Explain and demonstrate how to operate medical equipment
- Manage replacement of medical equipment

Medical equipment repairers, also known as *biomedical equipment technicians* (BMETs), repair a wide range of electronic, electromechanical, and hydraulic equipment used in hospitals and health practitioners' offices. They may work on patient monitors, defibrillators, ventilators, anesthesia machines, and other life-supporting equipment. They also may work on medical imaging equipment (x rays, CAT scanners, and ultrasound equipment), voice-controlled operating tables, and electric wheelchairs. In addition, they repair medical equipment that dentists and eye doctors use.

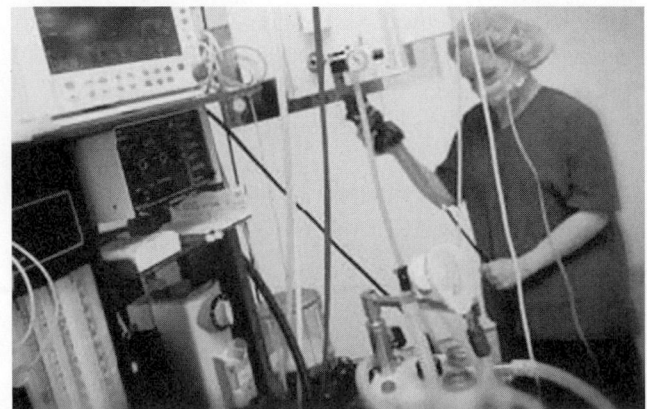

Medical equipment repairers adjust and repair medical equipment.

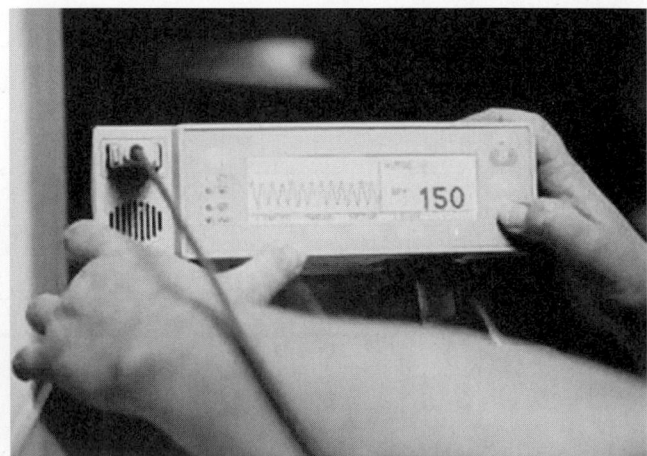

Medical equipment repairers often test and calibrate equipment.

If a machine has problems or is not functioning to its potential, repairers first diagnose the problem. They then adjust the mechanical, electronic, or hydraulic parts or modify the software in order to recalibrate the equipment and fix the issue.

Medical equipment repairers use a variety of tools. Most use hand tools, such as screwdrivers, wrenches, and soldering irons. Others use electronic tools, such as multimeters (an electronic measuring device that combines several measures) and computers. Much of the equipment that they maintain and repair uses specialized test-equipment software. Repairers use this software to calibrate the machines.

Many doctors, particularly specialty practitioners, rely on complex medical devices to run tests and diagnose patients, and they must be confident that the readings are accurate. Therefore, medical equipment repairers sometimes perform routine scheduled maintenance to ensure that sophisticated equipment, such as x-ray machines and CAT scanners, are in good working order. For less complicated equipment, such as electric hospital beds, workers make repairs as needed.

In a hospital setting, medical equipment repairers must be comfortable working around patients because repairs occasionally must take place while equipment is being used. When this is the case, the repairer must take great care to ensure that their work activities do not disturb patients.

Although some medical equipment repairers are trained to fix a variety of equipment, others specialize in repairing one or a small number of machines.

Work Environment

Medical equipment repairers held about 53,900 jobs in 2019. The largest employers of medical equipment repairers were as follows:

Professional and commercial equipment and supplies
merchant wholesalers 26%
Electronic and precision equipment repair and
maintenance 16

Hospitals; state, local, and private 14
Rental and leasing services 9
Ambulatory healthcare services 9

Medical equipment repairers who work as contractors often have to travel—sometimes long distances—to perform needed repairs. Repairers often must work in a patient-caring environment, which has the potential to expose them to germs, diseases and other health risks.

Because repairing vital medical equipment is urgent, the work can be stressful. In addition, installing and repairing medical equipment often involves lifting and carrying heavy objects as well as working in tight spaces.

Work Schedules

Although medical equipment repairers usually work during the day, they are sometimes expected to be on call, including evenings and weekends. Most medical equipment repairers work full time, but some repairers have variable schedules.

How to Become a Medical Equipment Repairer

Employers generally prefer candidates who have an associate's degree in biomedical technology or engineering. Depending on the area of specialization, repairers may need a bachelor's degree, especially for advancement.

Education

Education requirements for medical equipment repairers vary, depending on a worker's experience and area of specialization. However, the most common education is an associate's degree in biomedical equipment technology or engineering. Those who repair less-complicated equipment, such as hospital beds and electric wheelchairs, may learn entirely through on-the-job training, sometimes lasting up to 1 year. Repairers who work on more sophisticated equipment, such as CAT scanners and defibrillators, may need a bachelor's degree.

Medical equipment repairers often must work in a patient-caring environment.

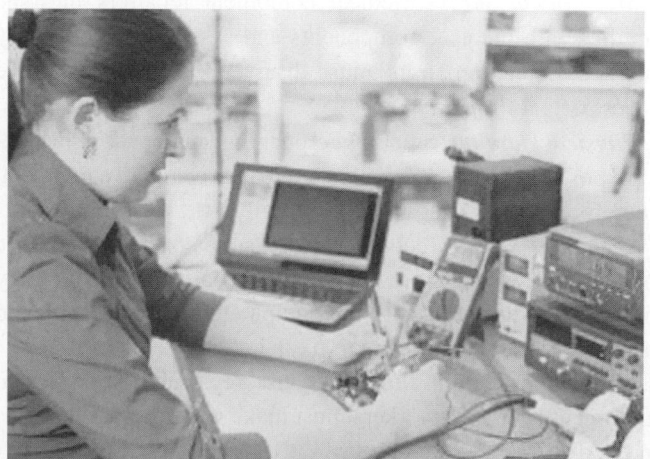

Medical equipment repairers need good technical skills in order to diagnose problems and fix equipment.

Training

New workers generally observe and help experienced repairers for 3 to 6 months to start. As they learn, workers gradually become more independent while still under supervision.

Each piece of equipment is different, so medical equipment repairers must learn each one separately. In some cases, this requires studying a machine's technical specifications and operating manual. Medical device manufacturers also may provide technical training.

Medical equipment technology is rapidly evolving, and new devices are frequently introduced. Repairers must continually update their skills and knowledge of new technologies and equipment through seminars and self-study. The original equipment manufacturers (OEMs) may also offer training.

Licenses, Certifications, and Registrations

Although not mandatory, certification can demonstrate competence and professionalism, making candidates more attractive to employers. It can also increase a repairer's opportunities for advancement. Most manufacturers and employers, particularly those in hospitals, often pay for their in-house medical repairers to become certified.

Some associations offer certifications for medical equipment repairers. For example, the Association for the Advancement of Medical Instrumentation (AAMI) offers certification in three specialty areas—Certified Biomedical Equipment Technician (CBET), Certified Radiology Equipment Specialists (CRES), and Certified Laboratory Equipment Specialist (CLES).

Important Qualities

Communication skills. Medical equipment repairers must effectively communicate technical information by telephone, in writing, and in person when speaking to clients, supervisors, and co-workers.

Dexterity. Many tasks, such as connecting or attaching parts and using hand tools, require a steady hand and good hand-eye coordination.

Mechanical skills. Medical equipment repairers must be familiar with medical components and systems and how they interact. Often, repairers must disassemble and reassemble major parts for repair.

Physical stamina. Standing, crouching, and bending in awkward positions are common when making repairs to equipment. Therefore, workers should be physically fit.

Technical skills. Technicians use sophisticated diagnostic tools when working on complex medical equipment. They must be familiar with both the equipment's internal parts and the appropriate tools needed to fix them.

Time-management skills. Because repairing vital medical equipment is urgent, workers must make good use of their time and perform repairs quickly.

Troubleshooting skills. As medical equipment becomes more intricate, problems become more difficult to identify.

Therefore, repairers must be able to find and solve problems that are not immediately apparent.

Pay

The median annual wage for medical equipment repairers was $49,280 in May 2019. The median wage is the wage at which half the workers in an occupation earned more than that amount and half earned less. The lowest 10 percent earned less than $29,630, and the highest 10 percent earned more than $82,500.

In May 2019, the median annual wages for medical equipment repairers in the top industries in which they worked were as follows:

Hospitals; state, local, and private	$59,500
Electronic and precision equipment repair and maintenance	50,360
Professional and commercial equipment and supplies merchant wholesalers	50,270
Ambulatory healthcare services	46,990
Rental and leasing services	35,320

Although medical equipment repairers usually work during the day, they are sometimes expected to be on call, including evenings and weekends. Most work full time, but some repairers have variable schedules.

Job Outlook

Employment of medical equipment repairers is projected to grow 5 percent from 2019 to 2029, faster than the average for all occupations. These repairers will be needed to repair medical equipment in healthcare settings.

A significant factor in the greater demand for healthcare services is the aging population. As people age, they usually need more medical care. With the expected increase in the number of older adults and with people living longer, health professionals are prescribing more medical tests that use new, complex equipment. In addition, some medical facilities are increasingly purchasing refurbished medical equipment in order to save money. Medical equipment repairers will be needed to provide routine service to ensure the machines work properly.

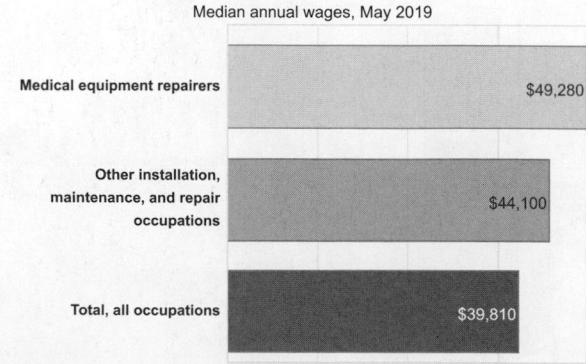

Medical Equipment Repairers
Median annual wages, May 2019

Medical equipment repairers $49,280

Other installation, maintenance, and repair occupations $44,100

Total, all occupations $39,810

Note: All Occupations includes all occupations in the U.S. Economy.
Source: U.S. Bureau of Labor Statistics, Occupational Employment Statistics.

Medical Equipment Repairers
Percent change in employment, projected 2019-29

Medical equipment repairers — 5%

Other installation, maintenance, and repair occupations — 5%

Total, all occupations — 4%

Note: All Occupations includes all occupations in the U.S. Economy.
Source: U.S. Bureau of Labor Statistics, Employment Projections program.

Job Prospects

A combination of industry growth and the need to replace workers who leave the occupation each year should result in good job opportunities over the coming decade.

Candidates who have an associate's degree in biomedical equipment technology or engineering and professional certification should have the best job prospects.

Employment projections data for medical equipment repairers, 2019-29

Occupational Title	SOC Code	Employment, 2019	Projected Employment, 2029	Change, 2019-29	
				Percent	Numeric
Medical equipment repairers	49-9062	53,900	56,700	5	2,800

SOURCE: U.S. Bureau of Labor Statistics, Employment Projections program

State & Area Data
Occupational Employment Statistics (OES)

The Occupational Employment Statistics (OES) program produces employment and wage estimates annually for over 800 occupations. These estimates are available for the nation as a whole, for individual states, and for metropolitan and nonmetropolitan areas.

Contacts for More Information

For more information about medical equipment repairers, including a listing of schools offering related programs of study and information about certification, visit

➤ Association for the Advancement of Medical Instrumentation
➤ Medical Equipment & Technology Association

Small Engine Mechanics

Summary

Quick Facts: Small Engine Mechanics

2019 Median Pay	$37,840 per year $18.19 per hour
Typical Entry-Level Education	See below
Work Experience in a Related Occupation	None
On-the-job Training	See below
Number of Jobs, 2019	78,100
Job Outlook, 2019-29	3% (As fast as average)
Employment Change, 2019-29	2,200

What Small Engine Mechanics Do

Small engine mechanics inspect, service, and repair motorized power equipment.

Work Environment

Small engine mechanics generally work in well-ventilated but noisy repair shops. They sometimes make onsite repair calls, which may require working in poor weather conditions. Although most work full time, seasonal workers often see their hours fluctuate. Workers frequently are busiest during the spring and summer, when equipment use is the highest.

How to Become a Small Engine Mechanic

Small engine mechanics typically enter the occupation with a high school diploma or postsecondary nondegree award and learn their trade through on-the-job training.

Pay

The median annual wage for small engine mechanics was $37,840 in May 2019.

Small engine mechanics test and inspect engines for malfunctioning parts.

Job Outlook

Overall employment of small engine mechanics is projected to grow 3 percent from 2019 to 2029, about as fast as the average for all occupations. Those who have completed postsecondary training programs should have better job prospects.

State & Area Data

Explore resources for employment and wages by state and area for small engine mechanics.

What Small Engine Mechanics Do

Small engine mechanics inspect, service, and repair motorized power equipment. Mechanics often specialize in one type of equipment, such as motorcycles, motorboats, or outdoor power equipment.

Duties

Small engine mechanics typically do the following:

- Discuss equipment issues, maintenance plans, and work performed with customers
- Perform routine engine maintenance, such as lubricating parts and replacing spark plugs
- Test and inspect engines for malfunctioning parts
- Adjust components according to specifications
- Repair or replace worn, defective, or broken parts
- Reassemble and reinstall components and engines following repairs
- Keep records of inspections, test results, work performed, and parts used

Small engine mechanics work on power equipment ranging from snowmobiles to chain saws. When equipment breaks down, mechanics use many strategies to diagnose the source and extent of the problem. Small engine mechanics identify mechanical, electrical, and fuel system problems and make necessary repairs.

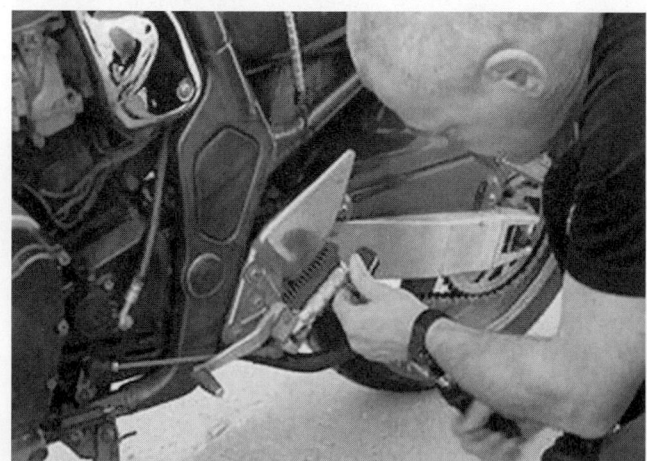

Motorcycle mechanics specialize in working on motorcycles, scooters, mopeds, dirt bikes, and all-terrain vehicles.

Mechanics' tasks vary in complexity and difficulty. Maintenance inspections and repairs, for example, involve minor adjustments or the replacement of a single part. Hand calibration, piston calibration, and spark plug replacement, however, may require taking an engine apart completely. Some mechanics use computerized equipment to tune racing motorcycles and motorboats.

Mechanics use a variety of hand tools, including screwdrivers, wrenches, and pliers, for many common tasks. Some mechanics also may use compression gauges, ammeters, and voltmeters to test engine performance. For more complicated procedures, they commonly use pneumatic tools, which are powered by compressed air, or diagnostic equipment.

Although employers usually provide the more expensive tools and testing equipment, some mechanics may be required to use their own hand tools. Some mechanics have thousands of dollars invested in their tool collections.

The following are examples of types of small engine mechanics:

Motorboat mechanics and service technicians maintain and repair the mechanical and electrical components of boat engines. Most of their work, whether on small outboard engines or large diesel-powered inboard motors, is performed at docks and marinas where the repair shop is located. Motorboat mechanics also may work on propellers, steering mechanisms, marine plumbing, and other boat equipment.

Motorcycle mechanics specialize in working on motorcycles, scooters, mopeds, dirt bikes, and all-terrain vehicles. They service engines, transmissions, brakes, and ignition systems and make minor body repairs, among other tasks. Most work for dealerships, servicing and repairing specific makes and models.

Outdoor power equipment and other small engine mechanics service and repair outdoor power equipment, such as lawnmowers, edge trimmers, garden tractors, and portable generators. Some mechanics may work on snowblowers and snowmobiles, but this work is highly seasonal and regional.

Technicians and mechanics who work primarily on automobiles are described in the profile on automotive service technicians and mechanics.

Technicians who work primarily on large trucks and buses are described in the profile on diesel service technicians and mechanics.

Technicians and mechanics who work primarily on farm equipment, construction vehicles, and rail cars are described in the profile on heavy vehicle and mobile equipment service technicians.

Work Environment

Small engine mechanics held about 78,100 jobs in 2019. Employment in the detailed occupations that make up small engine mechanics was distributed as follows:

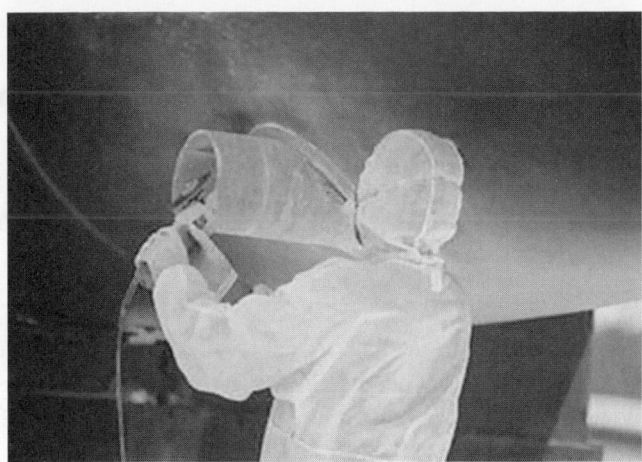

Motorboat mechanics and service technicians maintain and repair the mechanical and electrical components of boat engines.

Outdoor power equipment and other small engine mechanics.. 35,000

Motorboat mechanics and service technicians 25,700

Motorcycle mechanics.. 17,400

The largest employers of small engine mechanics were as follows:

Motor vehicle and parts dealers 34%

Lawn and garden equipment and supplies stores......... 12

Repair and maintenance 11

Amusement, gambling, and recreation industries........ 11

Self-employed workers.. 9

Small engine mechanics generally work in well-ventilated but noisy repair shops. They sometimes make onsite repair calls, which may require working in poor weather conditions. When repairing onboard engines, motorboat mechanics may work in cramped and uncomfortable positions.

Work Schedules

Most small engine mechanics work full time, although seasonal workers often see their work hours fluctuate.

Most mechanics are busiest during the spring and summer, when demand for work on equipment from lawnmowers to motorboats is the highest. During the peak seasons, some mechanics work many overtime hours. In contrast, some may work only part time during the winter, when demand for small engine work is lowest.

Many employers try to keep work more consistent by scheduling major repair work, such as rebuilding engines, during the off-season.

How to Become a Small Engine Mechanic

Small engine mechanics typically enter the occupation with a high school diploma or postsecondary nondegree award and learn their trade through on-the-job training.

Many tasks, such as disassembling engine parts, connecting or attaching components, and using hand tools, require a steady hand and good hand-eye coordination.

Education

Motorboat and outdoor power equipment mechanics typically begin work with a high school diploma and learn on the job, although some of them seek postsecondary education. High school or vocational school courses in small engine repair and automobile mechanics are often beneficial.

Motorcycle mechanics typically complete postsecondary education programs in motorcycle repair, and employers prefer to hire these workers because they usually require less on-the-job training.

Training

Trainees work closely with experienced mechanics while learning basic tasks, such as replacing spark plugs or disassembling engine components. As they gain experience, trainees move on to more difficult tasks, such as advanced computerized diagnosis and engine overhauls. Achieving competency may take anywhere from several months to 3 years, depending on a mechanic's specialization and ability.

Because of the increased complexity of boat and motorcycle engines, motorcycle and motorboat mechanics who do not complete postsecondary education often need more on-the-job training than that needed by outdoor power equipment mechanics.

Employers frequently send mechanics to training courses run by motorcycle, motorboat, and outdoor power equipment manufacturers and dealers. These courses teach mechanics the most up-to-date technology and techniques. Often, such courses are a prerequisite to performing warranty and manufacturer-specific work.

Licenses, Certifications, and Registrations

Many motorboat and motorcycle manufacturers offer certification specific to their own models, and certification from the Equipment & Engine Training Council is the recognized industry credential for outdoor power equipment mechanics.

Although not required, certification can demonstrate a mechanic's competence and usually brings higher pay.

Motorcycle mechanics usually need a driver's license with a motorcycle endorsement.

Important Qualities

Customer-service skills. Small engine mechanics frequently discuss problems and necessary repairs with their customers. They must be courteous, be good listeners, and always remain ready to answer customers' questions.

Detail oriented. Small engine mechanics must be aware of small details when inspecting or repairing engines and components, because mechanical and electronic malfunctions are often due to misalignments and other easy-to-miss causes.

Dexterity. Small engine mechanics need a steady hand and good hand–eye coordination for many tasks, such as disassembling engine parts, connecting or attaching components, and using hand tools.

Mechanical skills. Small engine mechanics must be familiar with engine components and systems and know how they interact with each other. They often disassemble major parts for repairs, and they must be able to put them back together properly.

Organizational skills. Small engine mechanics keep workspaces clean and organized in order to maintain safety and ensure accountability for parts.

Troubleshooting skills. Small engine mechanics use diagnostic equipment on engine systems and components to identify and fix problems. They must be familiar with electronic control systems and the appropriate tools needed to fix and maintain them.

Pay

The median annual wage for small engine mechanics was $37,840 in May 2019. The median wage is the wage at which half the workers in an occupation earned more than that amount and half earned less. The lowest 10 percent earned less than $24,300, and the highest 10 percent earned more than $60,070.

Median annual wages for small engine mechanics in May 2019 were as follows:

Motorboat mechanics and service technicians $41,330
Motorcycle mechanics 37,600
Outdoor power equipment and other small engine
    mechanics 36,100

In May 2019, the median annual wages for small engine mechanics in the top industries in which they worked were as follows:

Amusement, gambling, and recreation industries... $39,120
Repair and maintenance 38,230
Motor vehicle and parts dealers 38,110
Lawn and garden equipment and supplies stores.... 35,470

Most small engine mechanics work full time, although seasonal workers often see their work hours fluctuate.

Most mechanics are busiest during the spring and summer, when demand for work on equipment from lawnmowers to boats is the highest. During the peak seasons, some mechanics work many overtime hours. In contrast, some mechanics may work only part time during the winter, when demand for small engine work is lowest.

Many employers try to keep work more consistent by scheduling major repair work, such as rebuilding engines, during the off-season.

Job Outlook

Overall employment of small engine mechanics is projected to grow 3 percent from 2019 to 2029, about as fast as the average for all occupations. Growth rates will vary by occupation.

Boat engines, as well as engines and parts for outdoor power equipment, have become more efficient—but also more

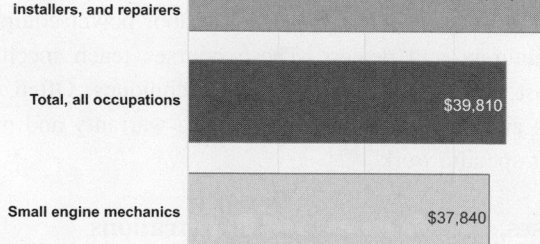

Small Engine Mechanics
Median annual wages, May 2019

Vehicle and mobile equipment mechanics, installers, and repairers	$44,590
Total, all occupations	$39,810
Small engine mechanics	$37,840

Note: All Occupations includes all occupations in the U.S. Economy.
Source: U.S. Bureau of Labor Statistics, Occupational Employment Statistics.

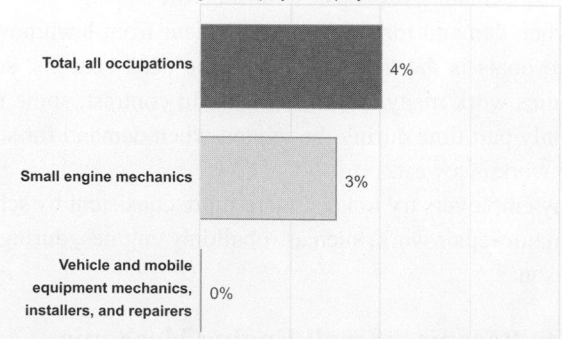

Small Engine Mechanics
Percent change in employment, projected 2019-29

Total, all occupations	4%
Small engine mechanics	3%
Vehicle and mobile equipment mechanics, installers, and repairers	0%

Note: All Occupations includes all occupations in the U.S. Economy.
Source: U.S. Bureau of Labor Statistics, Employment Projections program.

sophisticated. Thus, maintaining and repairing these engines and parts will require more workers.

Motorcycle mechanics adept at repairing electric motorcycles, new to the commercial market, may see increasing opportunities over the decade.

Mechanics who work on outdoor power equipment and other small engines will continue to be in demand because of the widespread use of these engines in gardening, tree work, landscape construction, and similar activities.

Job Prospects

Job prospects are expected to be best for candidates who have completed postsecondary training programs.

Employment projections data for small engine mechanics, 2019-29					
Occupational Title	SOC Code	Employment, 2019	Projected Employment, 2029	Change, 2019-29	
				Percent	Numeric
SOURCE: U.S. Bureau of Labor Statistics, Employment Projections program					
Small engine mechanics	49-3050	78,100	80,300	3	2,200
Motorboat mechanics and service technicians	49-3051	25,700	25,900	1	200
Motorcycle mechanics	49-3052	17,400	18,000	4	600

Employment projections data for small engine mechanics, 2019-29					
Occupational Title	SOC Code	Employment, 2019	Projected Employment, 2029	Change, 2019-29	
				Percent	Numeric
Outdoor power equipment and other small engine mechanics	49-3053	35,000	36,300	4	1,300

State & Area Data
Occupational Employment Statistics (OES)

The Occupational Employment Statistics (OES) program produces employment and wage estimates annually for over 800 occupations. These estimates are available for the nation as a whole, for individual states, and for metropolitan and nonmetropolitan areas.

Contacts for More Information

For more information on outdoor power equipment and other small engine mechanics and training programs, visit
➤ Equipment & Engine Training Council

To learn about job opportunities for small engine mechanics, contact local motorcycle, motorboat, and lawn and garden equipment dealers; boatyards; and marinas. Local offices of the state employment service also may have information about employment and training opportunities.

Telecommunications Equipment Installers and Repairers

Summary

Quick Facts: Telecommunications Equipment Installers and Repairers	
2019 Median Pay	$57,910 per year $27.84 per hour
Typical Entry-Level Education	Postsecondary non-degree award
Work Experience in a Related Occupation	None
On-the-job Training	Moderate-term on-the-job training
Number of Jobs, 2019	215,700
Job Outlook, 2019-29	-3% (Decline)
Employment Change, 2019-29	-5,600

What Telecommunications Equipment Installers and Repairers Do

Telecommunications equipment installers and repairers set up and maintain devices that carry communications signals.

Work Environment

Telecommunications equipment installers and repairers generally work in central offices or electronic service centers. They also work in the homes and offices of customers. Some technicians travel frequently to installation and repair sites.

How to Become a Telecommunications Equipment Installer or Repairer

Telecommunications equipment installers and repairers typically need postsecondary education in electronics, telecommunications, or computer technology. They also receive on-the-job training.

Pay

The median annual wage for telecommunications equipment installers and repairers was $57,910 in May 2019.

Job Outlook

Employment of telecommunications equipment installers and repairers is projected to decline 3 percent from 2019 to 2029.

Telecom technicians install and repair telecommunications equipment.

Consumers increasingly demand wireless and mobile services, which often require less installation. Candidates with a 2-year degree and strong customer-service skills should have the best job prospects.

State & Area Data

Explore resources for employment and wages by state and area for telecommunications equipment installers and repairers.

What Telecommunications Equipment Installers and Repairers Do

Telecommunications equipment installers and repairers, also known as *telecom technicians*, set up and maintain devices or equipment that carry communications signals, such as telephone lines and Internet routers.

Duties

Telecommunicsations equipment installers and repairers typically do the following:

- Install communications equipment in offices, private homes, and buildings that are under construction
- Set up, rearrange, and replace routing and dialing equipment
- Inspect and service equipment, wiring, and phone jacks
- Repair or replace faulty, damaged, and malfunctioning equipment
- Test repaired, newly installed, and updated equipment to ensure that it works properly
- Adjust or calibrate equipment to improve its performance
- Keep records of maintenance, repairs, and installations
- Demonstrate and explain the use of equipment to customers

These workers use many different tools to inspect equipment and diagnose problems. For instance, to locate distortions in signals, they may employ spectrum analyzers and polarity probes. They also commonly use hand tools, including screwdrivers and pliers, to take equipment apart and repair it.

Many telecom technicians work with computers, specialized hardware, and other diagnostic equipment. They follow manufacturers' instructions or technical manuals to install or update software and programs on devices.

Telecommunications equipment installers and repairers who work at a client's location must track hours worked, parts used, and costs incurred. Workers who set up and maintain lines outdoors are classified as line installers and repairers.

The specific tasks of telecom technicians vary with their specialization and where they work.

The following are examples of types of telecommunications equipment installers and repairers:

Central office technicians set up and maintain switches, routers, fiber-optic cables, and other equipment at switching hubs, called central offices. These hubs send, process, and amplify data from thousands of telephone, Internet, and cable connections. Telecom technicians receive alerts about equipment malfunctions from automonitoring switches and are able to correct the problems remotely.

Headend technicians perform work similar to that of central office technicians, but work at distribution centers for cable and television companies, called headends. Headends are control centers in which technicians monitor signals for local cable networks.

Home installers and repairers—sometimes known as *station installers and repairers*—set up and repair telecommunications equipment in customers' homes and businesses. For example, they set up modems to install telephone, Internet, and cable television services.

When customers have problems, home installers and repairers test the customer's lines to determine if the problem is inside the building or outside. If the problem is inside, they try to repair it. If the problem is outside, they refer the problem to line repairers.

Work Environment

Telecommunications equipment installers and repairers held about 215,700 jobs in 2019. The largest employers of

Telecom technicians inspect and service equipment and wiring.

Some telecom technicians provide in-home installation and repair services, while others work in central offices or electronic service centers.

telecommunications equipment installers and repairers were as follows:

Telecommunications	64%
Electrical contractors and other wiring installation contractors	13
Merchant wholesalers, durable goods	3
Professional, scientific, and technical services	3
Cable and other subscription programming	2

Some telecom technicians provide in-home installation and repair services, while others work in central offices or electronic service centers. Equipment installation may require climbing onto rooftops and into attics, and climbing ladders and telephone poles.

Telecom technicians occasionally work in cramped, awkward positions, in which they stoop, crouch, crawl, or reach high to do their work. Sometimes they must lift or move heavy equipment and parts. They also may work on equipment while it is powered, so they need to take necessary precautions.

Injuries and Illnesses

The work of telecom technicians can be dangerous. Telecommunications equipment installers and repairers have one of the highest rates of injuries and illnesses of all occupations.

Common injuries include falls and strains.

To reduce risk of injury, workers wear hardhats and harnesses when working on ladders or on elevated equipment. To prevent electrical shocks, technicians may lock off power to equipment that is under repair.

Work Schedules

Most telecom technicians work full time.

Some businesses offer 24-hour repair services. Telecom technicians in these companies work shifts, including evenings, holidays, and weekends. Some are on call around the clock in case of emergencies.

How to Become a Telecommunications Equipment Installer or Repairer

Telecommunications equipment installers and repairers typically need postsecondary education in electronics, telecommunications, or computer networking. They also receive on-the-job training.

Education

Telecom technicians typically need postsecondary education in electronics, telecommunications, or computer networking. Generally, postsecondary programs include classes such as data transmission systems, data communication, AC/DC electrical circuits, and computer programming.

Most programs lead to a certificate or an associate's degree in telecommunications or related subjects.

Postsecondary education in electronics, telecommunications, or computer networking is typically needed to become a telecom technician.

Some employers prefer to hire candidates with an associate's degree.

Training

Once hired, telecom technicians receive on-the-job training, typically lasting a few weeks to a few months. Training involves a combination of classroom instruction and hands-on work with an experienced technician. In these settings, workers learn the equipment's internal parts and the tools needed for repair. Technicians who have completed postsecondary education often require less on-the-job instruction than those who have not.

Some companies may send new employees to training sessions to learn about equipment, procedures, and technologies offered by equipment manufacturers or industry organizations.

Because technology in this field constantly changes, telecom technicians must continue learning about new equipment over the course of their careers.

Important Qualities

Color vision. Telecom technicians work with color-coded wires, and they need to be able to tell them apart.

Customer-service skills. Telecom technicians who work in customers' homes and offices should be friendly and polite.

They must be able to teach people how to maintain and operate communications equipment.

Dexterity. Telecom technicians' tasks, such as repairing small devices, connecting components, and using hand tools, require a steady hand and good hand–eye coordination.

Mechanical skills. Telecom technicians must be familiar with the devices they install and repair, with their internal parts, and with the appropriate tools needed to use, install, or fix them. They must also be able to understand manufacturers' instructions when installing or repairing equipment.

Troubleshooting skills. Telecom technicians must be able to troubleshoot and devise solutions to problems that are not immediately apparent.

Pay

The median annual wage for telecommunications equipment installers and repairers was $57,910 in May 2019. The median wage is the wage at which half the workers in an occupation earned more than that amount and half earned less. The lowest 10 percent earned less than $33,090, and the highest 10 percent earned more than $85,620.

In May 2019, the median annual wages for telecommunications equipment installers and repairers in the top industries in which they worked were as follows:

Telecommunications	$60,850
Cable and other subscription programming	58,290
Professional, scientific, and technical services	55,400
Merchant wholesalers, durable goods	50,870
Electrical contractors and other wiring installation contractors	47,700

Most telecom technicians work full time.

Some businesses offer 24-hour repair services. Telecom technicians in these companies work shifts, including evenings,

holidays, and weekends. Some are on call around the clock in case of emergencies.

Job Outlook

Employment of telecommunications equipment installers and repairers is projected to decline 3 percent from 2019 to 2029.

Employment is projected to decline in telecommunications, the industry that employs most of these workers. Consumers increasingly demand wireless and mobile services, which often require less installation, instead of landline-based services. This shift in demand means that telecommunications companies are expected to require fewer telecommunications equipment installers.

Job Prospects

Some job opportunities should come from the need to replace workers who leave the occupation. Although job opportunities will vary by specialty, those with an associate's degree and strong customer-service skills should have the best job prospects.

Technologies such as mobile video streaming and broadband Internet require high data transfer rates in telecommunications systems. Central office and headend technicians are likely to be needed to service and upgrade switches and routers to handle increased data usage, resulting in some job opportunities for them.

Employment projections data for telecommunications equipment installers and repairers, 2019-29					
Occupational Title	SOC Code	Employment, 2019	Projected Employment, 2029	Change, 2019-29	
				Percent	Numeric
SOURCE: U.S. Bureau of Labor Statistics, Employment Projections program					
Telecommunications equipment installers and repairers, except line installers	49-2022	215,700	210,100	-3	-5,600

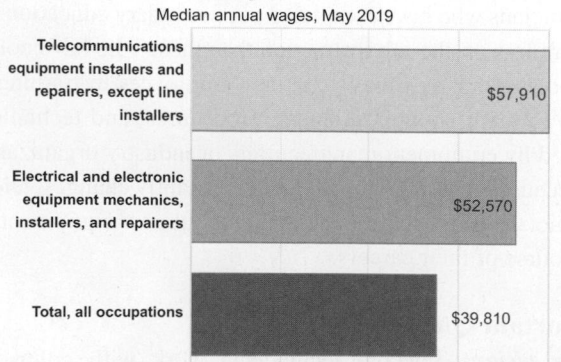

Telecommunications Equipment Installers and Repairers
Median annual wages, May 2019

Note: All Occupations includes all occupations in the U.S. Economy.
Source: U.S. Bureau of Labor Statistics, Occupational Employment Statistics.

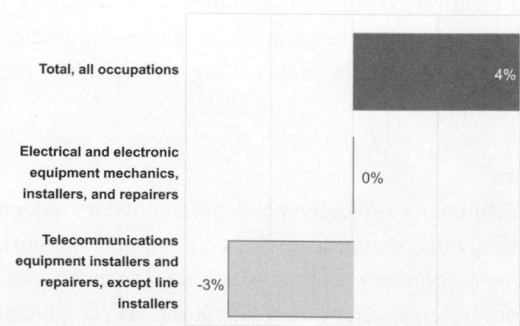

Telecommunications Equipment Installers and Repairers
Percent change in employment, projected 2019-29

Note: All Occupations includes all occupations in the U.S. Economy.
Source: U.S. Bureau of Labor Statistics, Employment Projections program.

State & Area Data
Occupational Employment Statistics (OES)

The Occupational Employment Statistics (OES) program produces employment and wage estimates annually for over 800 occupations. These estimates are available for the nation as a whole, for individual states, and for metropolitan and nonmetropolitan areas.

Contacts for More Information

For information about career, training, and certification opportunities for telecommunications equipment installers and repairers, visit
➤ National Coalition for Telecommunications Education and Learning
➤ Society of Cable Telecommunications Engineers
➤ Telecommunications Industry Association

Wind Turbine Technicians

Summary

Quick Facts: Wind Turbine Technicians

2019 Median Pay	$52,910 per year $25.44 per hour
Typical Entry-Level Education	Postsecondary nondegree award
Work Experience in a Related Occupation	None
On-the-job Training	Long-term on-the-job training
Number of Jobs, 2019	7,000
Job Outlook, 2019-29	61% (Much faster than average)
Employment Change, 2019-29	4,300

What Wind Turbine Technicians Do

Wind turbine service technicians install, maintain, and repair wind turbines.

Work Environment

Wind turbine service technicians generally work outdoors, in confined spaces, and often at great heights. Although the majority of windtechs work full time, they may also be on call to handle emergencies during evenings and weekends.

Wind turbine technicians visually inspect wind turbines for damage

How to Become a Wind Turbine Technician

Most wind turbine service technicians learn their trade by attending a technical school. They also receive on-the-job training.

Pay

The median annual wage for wind turbine technicians was $52,910 in May 2019.

Job Outlook

Employment of wind turbine service technicians is projected to grow 61 percent from 2019 to 2029, much faster than the average for all occupations. Because wind electricity generation is expected to grow rapidly over the coming decade, additional technicians will be needed to install and maintain new turbines. Job prospects are expected to be excellent.

State & Area Data

Explore resources for employment and wages by state and area for wind turbine technicians.

What Wind Turbine Technicians Do

Wind turbine service technicians, also known as *windtechs*, install, maintain, and repair wind turbines.

Duties

Wind turbine service technicians typically do the following:

Wind turbine technicians often monitor turbines from the ground.

- Inspect the exterior and physical integrity of wind turbine towers
- Climb wind turbine towers to inspect or repair wind turbine equipment
- Perform routine maintenance on wind turbines
- Test and troubleshoot electrical, mechanical, and hydraulic components and systems
- Replace worn or malfunctioning components
- Collect turbine data for testing or research and analysis
- Service underground transmission systems, wind field sub-stations, or fiber optic sensing and control systems

Wind turbines are large mechanical devices that convert wind energy into electricity. The turbine is made up of three major components: a tower, three blades, and a nacelle, which is composed of an outer case, generator, gearbox, and brakes. Wind turbine service technicians install and repair the components of these structures.

Although some windtechs are involved in building new wind turbines, most of their work is in maintaining them, particularly the nacelles, which contain the equipment that generates electricity.

Maintenance schedules are largely determined by a turbine's hours in operation, but can also vary by manufacturer. Turbines are monitored electronically from a central office, 24 hours a day. When a problem is detected, windtechs travel to the worksite and make the repairs. Typical maintenance includes inspecting components and lubricating parts. For turbines that operate year round, routine maintenance may occur one to three times a year.

Windtechs use safety harnesses and a variety of hand and power tools to do their work. They also use computers to diagnose electrical malfunctions. Most turbine monitoring equipment is located in the nacelle, which can be accessed both onsite and off.

Work Environment

Wind turbine technicians held about 7,000 jobs in 2019. The largest employers of wind turbine technicians were as follows:

Electric power generation	28%
Repair and maintenance	25
Utility system construction	17
Self-employed workers	14
Professional, scientific, and technical services	6

Wind turbine service technicians, also known as *windtechs*, generally work outdoors, often at great heights and with a partner. For example, when repairing blades, windtechs rappel—or descend by sliding down a rope—from the nacelle to the section of the blade that needs servicing. To reach the mechanical equipment, workers must climb ladders—sometimes more than 260 feet tall—while wearing a fall

Wind turbine technicians often work at great heights.

protection harness and carrying tools. When maintaining mechanical systems, windtechs work in the confined space of the nacelle.

For major service or repairs, additional windtechs and other specialists, such as electricians, may be needed to complete the job quickly.

Work Schedules

Although the majority of windtechs work full time, they may also be on call to handle emergencies during evenings and weekends.

When a wind turbine is not functioning, technicians must find the problem and make the necessary repairs as quickly as possible.

Windtechs often travel to rural areas, where many wind farms are located.

How to Become a Wind Turbine Technician

Most wind turbine service technicians, also known as *windtechs*, learn their trade by attending a technical school. They are also trained by their employer after hiring.

Education

Most windtechs learn their trade by attending technical schools or community colleges, where they typically complete

Wind turbine technicians receive on-the-job training from experienced workers.

certificates in wind energy technology, although some workers choose to earn an associate's degree.

Many technical schools have onsite wind turbines that students can work on as part of their studies. In addition to lab coursework, other areas of focus that reflect the various skill sets needed to do the job include the following:

- Rescue, safety, first aid, and CPR training
- Electrical maintenance
- Hydraulic maintenance
- Braking systems
- Mechanical systems, including blade inspection and maintenance
- Computers and programmable logic control systems

Training

In addition to their coursework, windtechs typically receive more than 12 months of on-the-job training related to the specific wind turbines they will maintain and service. Part of this training is manufacturer training. Other training may include an internship with a wind turbine servicing contractor.

Licenses, Certifications, and Registrations

Although not mandatory, professional certification can demonstrate a basic level of knowledge and competence. Some employers prefer to hire workers who are already certified in subjects such as workplace electrical safety, tower climbing, and self-rescue. There are many organizations who offer certifications in each of these subjects, and some certificate and degree programs include these certifications.

Important Qualities

Communication skills. Windtechs rely on proper communication with their coworkers in order to perform their duties safely and effectively.

Detail oriented. Windtechs must maintain records of all of the services they perform. Turbine maintenance requires precise measurements, a strict order of operations, and numerous safety procedures.

Mechanical skills. Windtechs must understand and be able to maintain and repair all mechanical, hydraulic, braking, and electrical systems of a turbine.

Physical stamina. Windtechs must be able to climb to the tops of turbines, often with tools and equipment. Some tower ladders may be 260 feet high or taller.

Physical strength. Windtechs must lift heavy equipment, parts, and tools, some of which weigh in excess of 50 pounds.

Troubleshooting skills. Windtechs must diagnose and repair problems. When a turbine performs abnormally, technicians must determine the cause and make the necessary repairs.

Pay

The median annual wage for wind turbine technicians was $52,910 in May 2019. The median wage is the wage at which half the workers in an occupation earned more than that amount and half earned less. The lowest 10 percent earned less than $39,820, and the highest 10 percent earned more than $80,150.

In May 2019, the median annual wages for wind turbine technicians in the top industries in which they worked were as follows:

Professional, scientific, and technical services.......	$57,050
Electric power generation	56,600
Utility system construction	50,780
Repair and maintenance	49,750

The majority of wind turbine service technicians, also known as *windtechs*, work full time, and they may also be on call to handle emergencies during evenings and weekends.

When a wind turbine is not functioning, technicians must find the problem and make the necessary repairs as quickly as possible.

Windtechs often travel to rural areas, where many wind farms are located.

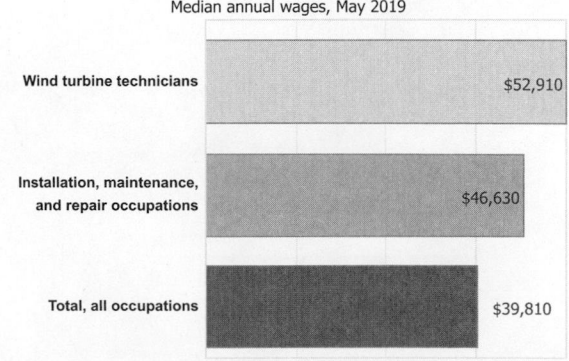

Wind Turbine Technicians
Median annual wages, May 2019

Wind turbine technicians	$52,910
Installation, maintenance, and repair occupations	$46,630
Total, all occupations	$39,810

Note: All Occupations includes all occupations in the U.S. Economy.
Source: U.S. Bureau of Labor Statistics, Occupational Employment Statistics.

Wind Turbine Technicians
Percent change in employment, projected 2019-29

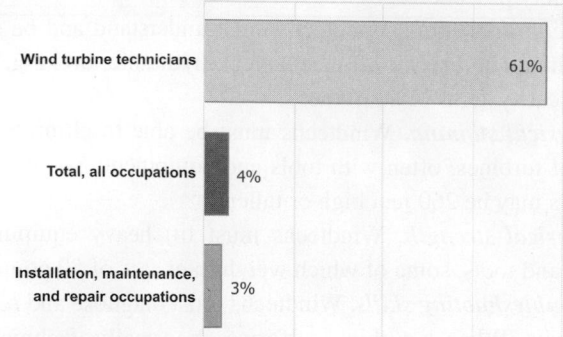

Wind turbine technicians	61%
Total, all occupations	4%
Installation, maintenance, and repair occupations	3%

Note: All Occupations includes all occupations in the U.S. Economy.
Source: U.S. Bureau of Labor Statistics, Employment Projections program.

Job Outlook

Employment of wind turbine service technicians, also known as *windtechs*, is projected to grow 61 percent from 2019 to 2029, much faster than the average for all occupations.

Development of taller towers with larger blades has reduced the cost of wind power generation, making it more competitive with coal, natural gas, and other forms of power generation. As additional wind turbines are erected, more windtechs will be needed to install and maintain turbines.

Job Prospects

Job prospects are expected to be excellent. The number of wind turbines being installed is increasing, which should result in continuing demand for windtechs.

Job opportunities vary by individual state. Wind farms are generally more prevalent in the Great Plains, the Midwest, and along coasts, and windtechs will likely find more job opportunities in these areas.

Employment projections data for wind turbine technicians, 2019-29					
Occupational Title	SOC Code	Employment, 2019	Projected Employment, 2029	Change, 2019-29	
				Percent	Numeric
SOURCE: U.S. Bureau of Labor Statistics, Employment Projections program					
Wind turbine service technicians	49-9081	7,000	11,300	61	4,300

State & Area Data
Occupational Employment Statistics (OES)

The Occupational Employment Statistics (OES) program produces employment and wage estimates annually for over 800 occupations. These estimates are available for the nation as a whole, for individual states, and for metropolitan and nonmetropolitan areas.

Contacts for More Information

For more information about educational opportunities and career paths, visit

➤ U.S. Department of Energy, Office of Energy Efficiency & Renewable Energy

Legal

Arbitrators, Mediators, and Conciliators

Summary

Quick Facts: Arbitrators, Mediators, and Conciliators

2019 Median Pay	$63,930 per year $30.74 per hour
Typical Entry-Level Education	Bachelor's degree
Work Experience in a Related Occupation	Less than 5 years
On-the-job Training	Moderate-term on-the-job training
Number of Jobs, 2019	7,300
Job Outlook, 2019-29.......................................	8% (Much faster than average)
Employment Change, 2019-29	600

What Arbitrators, Mediators, and Conciliators Do

Arbitrators, mediators, and conciliators facilitate negotiation and dialogue between disputing parties to help resolve conflicts outside of the court system.

Work Environment

Many arbitrators, mediators, and conciliators work for state or local governments or in the legal services industry.

How to Become an Arbitrator, Mediator, or Conciliator

Arbitrators, mediators, and conciliators typically learn their skills through a combination of education, training, and work experience.

Pay

The median annual wage for arbitrators, mediators, and conciliators was $63,930 in May 2019.

Job Outlook

Employment of arbitrators, mediators, and conciliators is projected to grow 8 percent from 2019 to 2029, much faster than the average for all occupations. This projected growth is driven by the fact that mediations and arbitrations are typically faster and less costly than litigation and may be required in certain types of legal cases.

State & Area Data

Explore resources for employment and wages by state and area for arbitrators, mediators, and conciliators.

What Arbitrators, Mediators, and Conciliators Do

Arbitrators, mediators, and conciliators facilitate negotiation and dialogue between disputing parties to help resolve conflicts outside of the court system.

Duties

Arbitrators, mediators, and conciliators typically do the following:

- Facilitate communication between disputants to guide parties toward mutual agreement
- Clarify issues, concerns, needs, and interests of all parties involved
- Conduct initial meetings with disputants to outline the arbitration process
- Settle procedural matters such as fees, or determine details such as witness numbers and time requirements
- Set up appointments for parties to meet for mediation or arbitration

Arbitrators, mediators, and conciliators help disputing parties resolve their conflict by facilitating dialogue and negotiations.

Arbitrators, mediators, and conciliators help parties come to mutually acceptable agreements.

- Interview claimants, agents, or witnesses to obtain information about disputed issues
- Prepare settlement agreements for disputants to sign
- Apply relevant laws, regulations, policies, or precedents to reach conclusions
- Evaluate information from documents such as claim applications, birth or death certificates, and physician or employer records

Arbitrators, mediators, and conciliators help opposing parties settle disputes outside of court. They hold private, confidential hearings, which are less formal than a court trial.

Arbitrators are usually attorneys, business professionals, or retired judges with expertise in a particular field. As impartial third parties, they hear and decide disputes between opposing parties. Arbitrators may work alone or in a panel with other arbitrators. In some cases, arbitrators may decide procedural issues, such as what evidence may be submitted and when hearings will be held.

Arbitration may be required by law for some claims and disputes. When it is not required, the parties in dispute sometimes voluntarily agree to arbitration rather than proceed with litigation or a trial. In some cases, parties may appeal the arbitrator's decision.

Mediators are neutral parties who help people resolve their disputes. However, unlike arbitrators, they do not render binding decisions. Rather, mediators help facilitate discussion and guide the parties toward a mutually acceptable agreement. If the opposing sides cannot reach a settlement with the mediator's help, they are free to pursue other options.

Conciliators are similar to mediators. Although their role is to help guide opposing sides to a settlement, they typically meet with the parties separately. The opposing sides must decide in advance if they will be bound by the conciliator's recommendations.

Work Environment

Arbitrators, mediators, and conciliators held about 7,300 jobs in 2019. The largest employers of arbitrators, mediators, and conciliators were as follows:

Local government, excluding education and hospitals...	20%
State government, excluding education and hospitals....	17
Self-employed workers...	12
Legal services...	9
Healthcare and social assistance....................................	8

Arbitrators, mediators, and conciliators usually work in private offices or meeting rooms. They may travel to a neutral site chosen for negotiations.

The work may be stressful because arbitrators, mediators, and conciliators sometimes work with difficult or confrontational individuals or with highly charged and emotional situations, such as injury settlements or family disputes.

Arbitrators, mediators, and conciliators usually work in private offices or meeting rooms.

How to Become an Arbitrator, Mediator, or Conciliator

Arbitrators, mediators, and conciliators learn their skills through a combination of education, training, and work experience.

Education

Education is one part of becoming an arbitrator, mediator, or conciliator.

Few candidates receive a degree specific to the field of arbitration, mediation, or conflict resolution. Rather, many positions require an educational degree appropriate to the applicant's field of expertise, and a bachelor's degree is often sufficient. Many other positions, however, require applicants to have a law degree, a master's in business administration, or some other advanced degree.

Work Experience in a Related Occupation

Arbitrators, mediators, and conciliators are usually lawyers, retired judges, or business professionals with expertise in a particular field, such as construction, finance, or insurance. They need to have knowledge of that industry and be able to relate well to people from different cultures and backgrounds.

Training

Mediators typically work under the supervision of an experienced mediator for a certain number of cases before working independently.

Arbitrators, mediators, and conciliators are usually lawyers or business professionals with expertise in a particular field.

Training for arbitrators, mediators, and conciliators is available through independent mediation programs, national and local mediation membership organizations, and postsecondary schools. Training is also available by volunteering at a community mediation center.

Licenses, Certifications, and Registrations

There is no national license for arbitrators, mediators, and conciliators. However, some states require arbitrators and mediators to become certified to work on certain types of cases. Qualifications, standards, and the number of training hours required vary by state or by court. Most states require mediators to complete 20 to 40 hours of training courses to become certified. Some states require additional hours of training in a specialty area.

Some states require licenses appropriate to the applicant's field of expertise. For example, some courts may require applicants to be licensed attorneys or certified public accountants.

Important Qualities

Critical-thinking skills. Arbitrators, mediators, and conciliators must apply rules of law. They must remain neutral and not let their own personal assumptions interfere with the proceedings.

Decisionmaking skills. Arbitrators, mediators, and conciliators must be able to weigh facts, apply the law or rules, and make a decision relatively quickly.

Interpersonal skills. Arbitrators, mediators, and conciliators deal with disputing parties and must be able to facilitate discussion in a calm and respectful way.

Listening skills. Arbitrators, mediators, and conciliators must pay close attention to what is being said in order for them to evaluate information.

Reading skills. Arbitrators, mediators, and conciliators must be able to evaluate and distinguish important facts from large amounts of complex information.

Writing skills. Arbitrators, mediators, and conciliators write recommendations or decisions relating to appeals or disputes.

They must be able to write their decisions clearly so that all sides understand the decision.

Pay

The median annual wage for arbitrators, mediators, and conciliators was $63,930 in May 2019. The median wage is the wage at which half the workers in an occupation earned more than that amount and half earned less. The lowest 10 percent earned less than $37,420, and the highest 10 percent earned more than $123,730.

In May 2019, the median annual wages for arbitrators, mediators, and conciliators in the top industries in which they worked were as follows:

Legal services..	$73,610
Local government, excluding education and hospitals..	66,410
State government, excluding education and hospitals..	64,080
Healthcare and social assistance.............................	46,300

Job Outlook

Employment of arbitrators, mediators, and conciliators is projected to grow 8 percent from 2019 to 2029, much faster than the average for all occupations. However, because it is a small occupation, the fast growth will result in only about 600 new jobs over the 10-year period.

Arbitration and other alternative dispute resolution methods often are quicker and less expensive than trials and litigation. In addition, many contracts, including employment, customer, and real estate contracts, include clauses requiring complaints and disputes to be decided through mediation or arbitration.

However, many arbitrators, mediators, and conciliators work for state or local governments, and budgetary constraints may limit employment growth. Also, in some cases or industries, litigation is unavoidable or its benefits are preferred over the benefits gained in other types of conflict resolution.

Arbitrators, Mediators, and Conciliators
Median annual wages, May 2019

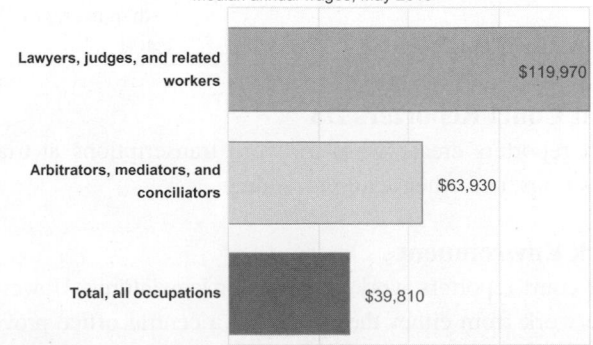

Lawyers, judges, and related workers	$119,970
Arbitrators, mediators, and conciliators	$63,930
Total, all occupations	$39,810

Note: All Occupations includes all occupations in the U.S. Economy.
Source: U.S. Bureau of Labor Statistics, Occupational Employment Statistics.

Arbitrators, Mediators, and Conciliators
Percent change in employment, projected 2019-29

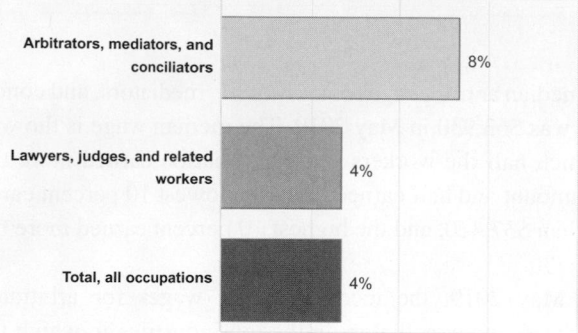

Arbitrators, mediators, and conciliators — 8%

Lawyers, judges, and related workers — 4%

Total, all occupations — 4%

Note: All Occupations includes all occupations in the U.S. Economy.
Source: U.S. Bureau of Labor Statistics, Employment Projections program.

Job Prospects

Because arbitrators, mediators, and conciliators deal extensively with legal issues and disputes, those with a law degree should have better job prospects. In addition, lawyers with expertise or experience in one or more particular legal areas, such as environmental, health, or corporate law, should have the best job prospects.

Employment projections data for arbitrators, mediators, and conciliators, 2019-29

Occupational Title	SOC Code	Employment, 2019	Projected Employment, 2029	Change, 2019-29	
				Percent	Numeric
SOURCE: U.S. Bureau of Labor Statistics, Employment Projections program					
Arbitrators, mediators, and conciliators	23-1022	7,300	7,900	8	600

State & Area Data
Occupational Employment Statistics (OES)

The Occupational Employment Statistics (OES) program produces employment and wage estimates annually for over 800 occupations. These estimates are available for the nation as a whole, for individual states, and for metropolitan and nonmetropolitan areas.

Contacts for More Information

For more information about arbitrators, mediators, and conciliators, visit

➤ American Arbitration Association
➤ Association for Conflict Resolution

Court Reporters

Summary

Quick Facts: Court Reporters

2019 Median Pay	$60,130 per year $28.91 per hour
Typical Entry-Level Education	Postsecondary non-degree award
Work Experience in a Related Occupation	None
On-the-job Training	Short-term on-the-job training
Number of Jobs, 2019	15,700
Job Outlook, 2019-29	9% (Much faster than average)
Employment Change, 2019-29	1,400

What Court Reporters Do

Court reporters create word-for-word transcriptions at trials, depositions, and other legal proceedings.

Work Environment

Most court reporters work in courts or legislatures. However, some work from either their home or a central office providing broadcast captioning for television stations or for hard-of-hearing individuals.

How to Become a Court Reporter

Many community colleges and technical institutes offer postsecondary certificate programs for court reporters. Court reporters typically receive a few weeks of on-the-job training. Many states require court reporters who work in legal settings to have a state license or a certification from a professional association.

Pay

The median annual wage for court reporters was $60,130 in May 2019.

Court reporters attend legal proceedings to create word-for-word transcriptions.

Job Outlook

Employment of court reporters is projected to grow 9 percent from 2019 to 2029, much faster than the average for all occupations. Those with experience and training in techniques for helping deaf or hard-of-hearing people, such as real-time captioning and communication access real-time translation (CART), will have the best job prospects.

State & Area Data

Explore resources for employment and wages by state and area for court reporters.

What Court Reporters Do

Court reporters create word-for-word transcriptions at trials, depositions, administrative hearings, and other legal proceedings. Some court reporters provide captioning for television and real-time translation for deaf or hard-of-hearing people at public events, in business meetings, and in classrooms.

Duties

Court reporters typically do the following:

- Attend depositions, hearings, proceedings, and other events that require written transcripts

Court reporters provide an accurate description of court proceedings.

- Capture spoken dialogue with specialized equipment, including stenography machines, video and audio recording devices, and covered microphones
- Report speakers' identification, gestures, and actions
- Read or play back all or a portion of the proceedings upon request from the judge
- Ask speakers to clarify inaudible or unclear statements or testimony
- Review the notes they have taken, including the names of speakers and any technical terminology
- Provide copies of transcripts and recordings to the courts, counsels, and parties involved
- Transcribe television or movie dialogue to help deaf or hard-of-hearing viewers
- Provide real-time translation in classes and other public forums for the deaf or hard-of-hearing population

Court reporters create word-for-word transcripts of speeches, conversations, legal proceedings, meetings, or other events.

Court reporters play a critical role in legal proceedings, which require an exact record of what was said. They are responsible for producing a complete, accurate, and secure legal transcript of courtroom proceedings, witnesses' testimonies, and depositions.

Court reporters in the legal setting also help judges and lawyers by capturing, organizing, and producing the official record of the proceedings. The official record allows users to efficiently search for important information contained in the transcript. Court reporters also index and catalog exhibits used during court proceedings.

Some court reporters, however, do not work in the legal setting or in courtrooms. These reporters primarily serve people who are deaf or hard-of-hearing by transcribing speech to text as the speech occurs.

The following are examples of types of court reporters who do not work in a legal setting:

Broadcast captioners are court reporters who provide captions for television programs (called closed captions). These reporters transcribe dialogue onto television monitors to help deaf or hard-of-hearing viewers or others viewing television programs in public places. Some broadcast captioners may translate dialogue in real time during broadcasts; others may caption during the postproduction of a program.

Communication access real-time translation (CART) providers are court reporters who work primarily with deaf or hard-of-hearing people in a variety of settings. They assist clients during board meetings, doctors' appointments, and any other events in which real-time translation is needed. For example, CART providers may caption the dialogue of high school and college classes and provide an immediate transcript to students with hearing problems or who are learning English as a second language.

Although some court reporters may accompany their clients to events, many broadcast captioners and CART providers work remotely. An Internet or phone connection allows them to hear and type without having to be in the room.

Court reporters who work with deaf or hard-of-hearing people turn speech into text. For information on workers who help deaf or hard-of-hearing people through sign language, cued speech, or other spoken or gestural means, see the profile on interpreters and translators.

Court reporters may use different methods for recording speech, such as stenotype machine recording, steno mask recording, and electronic recording.

Court reporters use stenotype machines to record dialogue as it is spoken. Stenotype machines work like keyboards, but create words through key combinations rather than single characters, allowing court reporters to keep up with fast-moving dialogue.

Key combinations entered on a stenotype machine are recorded in a computer program. The program uses computer-assisted transcription to translate the key combinations into the words and phrases they represent, creating real-time, readable text. The court reporter then reviews the text for accuracy and corrects spelling and grammatical errors.

Court reporters also may use steno masks to transcribe speech. Court reporters who use steno masks speak directly into a covered microphone, recording dialogue and reporting gestures and actions. Because the microphone is covered, others cannot hear what the reporter is saying. The recording is sometimes converted by computerized voice-recognition software into a transcript that the court reporter reviews for accuracy, spelling, and grammar.

For both stenotype machine recording and steno mask recording, court reporters must create, maintain, and continuously update an online dictionary that the computer software uses to transcribe the key presses or voice recordings into text. For example, court reporters may put in the names of people involved in a court case, or the specific words or technical jargon typically used in that type of legal proceeding.

Court reporters also may use digital recorders in their job. Digital recording creates an audio or video record rather than a written transcript. Court reporters who use digital recorders operate and monitor the recording equipment. They also take notes to identify the speakers and provide context for the recording. In some cases, court reporters use the audio recording to create a written transcript.

Work Environment

Court reporters held about 15,700 jobs in 2019. The largest employers of court reporters were as follows:

Local government, excluding education and
   hospitals.. 33%
Business support services 30

Court reporters may work in courtrooms or office buildings.

State government, excluding education and hospitals... 27
Self-employed workers.. 5

Many court reporters work in courts or legislatures. Many also work as freelance reporters and are hired by law firms or corporations for pretrial depositions and other events on an as-needed basis.

Many court reporters must travel to various courthouses or offices in different locations. However, some broadcast captioners and communication access real-time translation (CART) providers work remotely from either their home or a central office.

Because of the speed and accuracy required to capture a verbatim record and the time-sensitive nature of legal proceedings, court reporting positions may be stressful.

Work Schedules

Court reporters who work in a court setting typically work full time recording events and preparing transcripts. Freelance reporters have more flexibility in setting their work schedules.

How to Become a Court Reporter

Many community colleges and technical institutes offer postsecondary certificate programs for court reporters. Court reporters typically receive a few weeks of on-the-job training. Many states require court reporters who work in legal settings to be licensed by a state or certified by a professional association.

Education

Many court reporters receive formal education at community colleges or technical institutes, which have different programs that lead to either a certificate or an associate's degree in court reporting. Either degree will qualify applicants for many entry-level positions. Certification programs prepare students to pass the licensing exams and typing-speed tests required by most states and employers.

Court reporters must give their full attention to the speaker and capture every word that is said.

Most court reporting programs include courses in English grammar and phonetics, legal procedures, and legal terminology. Students also practice preparing transcripts to improve the speed and accuracy of their work.

Some schools also offer training in the use of different transcription machines, such as stenotype machines or steno masks.

Graduating from a court reporting program can take between 2 and 5 years.

Licenses, Certifications, and Registrations

Many states require court reporters who work in legal settings to be licensed or certified by a professional association. Licensing requirements vary by state and by method of court reporting.

The National Court Reporters Association (NCRA) offers certification for court reporters, broadcast captioners, and communication access real-time translation (CART) providers. Currently, about half of states accept or use the Registered Professional Reporter (RPR) certification in place of a state certification or licensing exam.

Digital and voice reporters may obtain certification through the American Association of Electronic Reporters and Transcribers (AAERT), which offers the Certified Electronic Reporter (CER) and Certified Electronic Transcriber (CET) designations.

Voice reporters also may obtain certification through the National Verbatim Reporters Association (NVRA). As with the RPR designation, some states with certification or licensing requirements will accept the NVRA designation in place of a state license.

Certification through the NCRA, AAERT, and NVRA all require the successful completion of a written test, as well as a skills test in which applicants must type, record, or transcribe a minimum number of words per minute with a high level of accuracy.

In addition, all associations require court reporters to obtain a certain amount of continuing education credits in order to renew their certification.

For more information on certification, exams, and continuing education requirements, visit the specific association's website. State licensing and continuing education requirements can be found by visiting the state association's or state judicial agency's website.

Training

After completing their formal program, court reporters must undergo a few weeks of on-the-job training. This typically includes training on the specific types of equipment and more technical terminology that may be used during complex medical or legal proceedings.

Important Qualities

Concentration. Court reporters must concentrate for long periods. They must remain focused on the dialogue they are recording, even in the presence of auditory distractions.

Detail oriented. Court reporters must produce error-free work because they create transcripts that serve as legal records.

Listening skills. Court reporters must give their full attention to speakers and capture every word that is said.

Writing skills. Court reporters need a good command of grammar, vocabulary, and punctuation.

Pay

The median annual wage for court reporters was $60,130 in May 2019. The median wage is the wage at which half the workers in an occupation earned more than that amount and half earned less. The lowest 10 percent earned less than $31,570, and the highest 10 percent earned more than $106,210.

In May 2019, the median annual wages for court reporters in the top industries in which they worked were as follows:

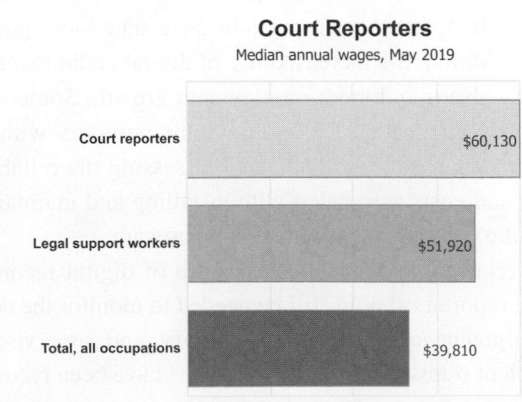

Court Reporters
Median annual wages, May 2019

Court reporters	$60,130
Legal support workers	$51,920
Total, all occupations	$39,810

Note: All Occupations includes all occupations in the U.S. Economy.
Source: U.S. Bureau of Labor Statistics, Occupational Employment Statistics.

State government, excluding education and
 hospitals.. $68,020

Local government, excluding education and
 hospitals..   63,700

Business support services   48,690

Freelance court reporters are paid for their time, but can also sell their transcripts per page for an additional profit.

Court reporters who work in a court setting typically work full time recording events and preparing transcripts. Freelance reporters have more flexibility in setting their work schedules.

Job Outlook

Employment of court reporters is projected to grow 9 percent from 2019 to 2029, much faster than the average for all occupations. However, because it is a small occupation, the fast growth will result in only about 1,400 new jobs over the 10-year period. Demand for court reporters will be influenced by federal regulations requiring an expanded use of captioning for television, the Internet, and other technologies. Employment growth, may be affected, however, by budgetary constraints and the use of technology.

Reporters will increasingly be needed for captioning outside of legal proceedings. All new television programming will continue to need closed captioning. In addition, federal regulations have expanded captioning requirements and set quality and accuracy standards for both live and prerecorded programs. Networks will likely increase their use of broadcast captioners in order to comply with these federal regulations.

Growth of the elderly population also will increase demand for court reporters who are communication access real-time translation (CART) providers or who can accompany their clients to doctor's appointments, town hall meetings, and religious services. In addition, movie theaters and sports stadiums will provide closed captioning for deaf or hard-of-hearing customers.

Employment growth, however, may be somewhat limited because of budgetary constraints in state and local governments. In addition, the increased use of digital audio recording technology also may hinder employment growth. Some states already have replaced stenographic court reporters with this technology; other states are currently assessing the reliability, accuracy, and costs associated with installing and maintaining digital audio and video equipment and software.

However, even with the increased use of digital recorders, electronic reporters should still be needed to monitor the courtroom equipment and to transcribe, verify, and supervise the production of transcripts after proceedings have been recorded.

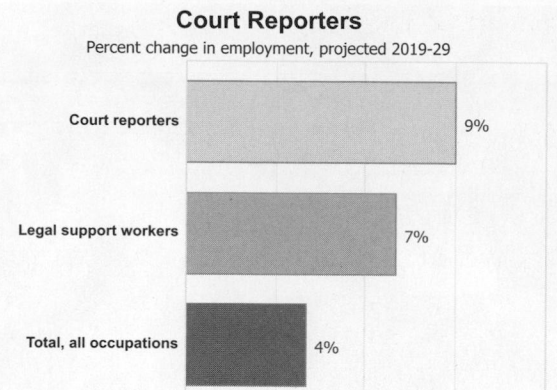

Court Reporters
Percent change in employment, projected 2019-29

Court reporters   9%
Legal support workers   7%
Total, all occupations   4%

Note: All Occupations includes all occupations in the U.S. Economy.
Source: U.S. Bureau of Labor Statistics, Employment Projections program.

Job Prospects

Job prospects will be best for graduates of court reporting programs and for candidates with experience and training in CART and real-time captioning.

Employment projections data for court reporters, 2019-29					
Occupational Title	SOC Code	Employment, 2019	Projected Employment, 2029	Change, 2019-29	
				Percent	Numeric
SOURCE: U.S. Bureau of Labor Statistics, Employment Projections program					
Court reporters and simultaneous captioners	27-3092	15,700	17,000	9	1,400

State & Area Data
Occupational Employment Statistics (OES)

The Occupational Employment Statistics (OES) program produces employment and wage estimates annually for over 800 occupations. These estimates are available for the nation as a whole, for individual states, and for metropolitan and nonmetropolitan areas.

Contacts for More Information

For more information on becoming a court reporter, including information on training programs and certification as a Registered Professional Reporter, visit
➤ National Court Reporters Association

For more information on certification and legal resources, as well as becoming an electronic or digital reporter, visit
➤ American Association of Electronic Reporters and Transcribers

For more information on voice writing and certification, visit
➤ National Verbatim Reporters Association

Judges and Hearing Officers

Summary

Quick Facts: Judges and Hearing Officers

2019 Median Pay	$120,090 per year $57.74 per hour
Typical Entry-Level Education	Doctoral or professional degree
Work Experience in a Related Occupation	5 years or more
On-the-job Training	Short-term on-the-job training
Number of Jobs, 2019	45,300
Job Outlook, 2019-29	2% (Slower than average)
Employment Change, 2019-29	1,100

What Judges and Hearing Officers Do

Judges and hearing officers apply the law by overseeing the legal process in courts.

Work Environment

All judges and hearing officers are employed by the federal government or by local and state governments. Most work in courts.

How to Become a Judge or Hearing Officer

Judges usually have law degrees and work experience as lawyers. However, some administrative law judge, hearing officer, and magistrate positions require only a bachelor's degree.

Pay

The median annual wage for administrative law judges, adjudicators, and hearing officers was $97,870 in May 2019.

The median annual wage for judges, magistrate judges, and magistrates was $136,910 in May 2019.

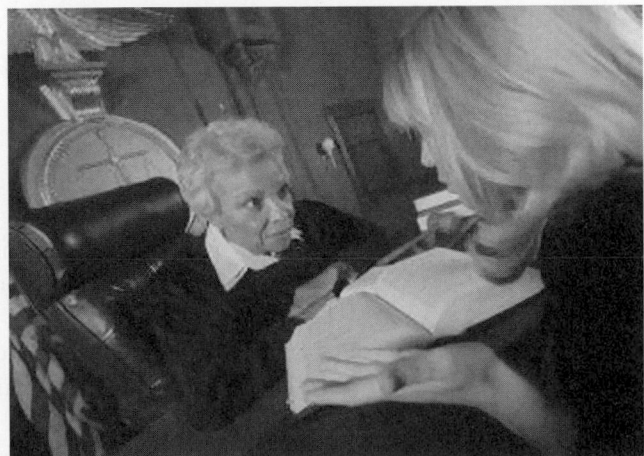

Judges and hearing officers research and apply laws to reach judgments or resolve disputes between parties.

Job Outlook

Employment of judges and hearing officers is projected to grow 2 percent from 2019 to 2029, slower than the average for all occupations. These workers play an essential role in the legal system, and their services will continue to be needed into the future.

State & Area Data

Explore resources for employment and wages by state and area for judges and hearing officers.

What Judges and Hearing Officers Do

Judges and hearing officers apply the law by overseeing the legal process in courts. They also conduct pretrial hearings, resolve administrative disputes, facilitate negotiations between opposing parties, and issue legal decisions.

Duties

Judges and hearing officers typically do the following:

- Research legal issues
- Read and evaluate information from documents, such as motions, claim applications, and records
- Preside over hearings and listen to and read arguments by opposing parties
- Determine if the information presented supports the charge, claim, or dispute

Judges preside over hearings and listen to the arguments of opposing parties.

- Decide if the procedure is being conducted according to the rules and law
- Apply laws or precedents to reach judgments and to resolve disputes between parties
- Write opinions, decisions, and instructions regarding cases, claims, and disputes

Judges commonly preside over trials and hearings of cases regarding nearly every aspect of society, from individual traffic offenses to issues concerning the rights of large corporations. Judges listen to arguments and determine if the evidence presented deserves a trial. In criminal cases, judges may decide that people charged with crimes should be held in jail until the trial, or they may set conditions for their release. They also approve search warrants and arrest warrants.

Judges interpret the law to determine how a trial will proceed, which is particularly important when unusual circumstances arise for which standard procedures have not been established. They ensure that hearings and trials are conducted fairly and that the legal rights of all involved parties are protected.

In trials in which juries are selected to decide the case, judges instruct jurors on applicable laws and direct them to consider the facts from the evidence. For other trials, judges decide the case. A judge who determines guilt in criminal cases may impose a sentence or penalty on the guilty party. In civil cases, the judge may award relief, such as compensation for damages, to the parties who win lawsuits.

Judges use various forms of technology, such as electronic databases and software, to manage cases and to prepare for trials. In some cases, a judge may manage the court's administrative and clerical staff.

The following are examples of types of judges and hearing officers:

Judges, magistrate judges, and magistrates preside over trials and hearings. They typically work in local, state, and federal courts.

In local and state court systems, they have a variety of titles, such as *municipal court judge*, *county court judge*, and *justice of the peace*. Traffic violations, misdemeanors, small-claims cases, and pretrial hearings make up the bulk of these judges' work.

In federal and state court systems, *district court judges* and *general trial court judges* have authority over any case in their system. *Appellate court judges* rule on a small number of cases, by reviewing decisions of the lower courts and lawyers' written and oral arguments.

Administrative law judges, adjudicators, and hearing officers usually work for local, state, and federal government agencies. They decide many issues, such as whether a person is eligible for workers' compensation benefits or whether employment discrimination occurred.

Work Environment

Administrative law judges, adjudicators, and hearing officers held about 15,400 jobs in 2019. The largest employers of

Judges do some of their work in courtrooms.

administrative law judges, adjudicators, and hearing officers were as follows:

State government, excluding education and hospitals..	48%
Federal government..	33
Local government, excluding education and hospitals..	19

Judges, magistrate judges, and magistrates held about 29,900 jobs in 2019. The largest employers of judges, magistrate judges, and magistrates were as follows:

State government, excluding education and hospitals..	55%
Local government, excluding education and hospitals..	45

Judges and hearing officers do most of their work in offices and courtrooms. Their jobs can be demanding, because they must sit in the same position in the court or hearing room for long periods and give undivided attention to the process.

Some judges and hearing officers may be required to travel to different counties and courthouses throughout their state.

The work may be stressful as judges and hearing officers sometimes work with difficult or confrontational individuals.

Work Schedules

Some courthouses have evening and weekend hours. In addition, judges may have to be on call during nights or weekends to issue emergency orders, such as search warrants and restraining orders.

How to Become a Judge or Hearing Officer

Judges and hearing officers typically must have a law degree and work experience as a lawyer.

Education

Although there may be a few positions available for those with a bachelor's degree, a law degree is typically required for most jobs as a local, state, or federal judge or hearing officer.

In addition to earning a law degree, federal administrative law judges must pass a competitive exam from the U.S. Office of Personnel Management.

Earning a law degree usually takes 7 years of full-time study after high school: 4 years of undergraduate study, followed by 3 years of law school. Law degree programs include courses such as constitutional law, contracts, property law, civil procedure, and legal writing.

Most judges and magistrates must be appointed or elected into their positions, a procedure that often requires political support. Many local and state judges are appointed to serve fixed renewable terms, ranging from 4 to 14 years. A few judges, such as appellate court judges, are appointed for life. Judicial nominating commissions screen candidates for judgeships in many states and for some federal judgeships.

For specific state information, including information on the number of judgeships by state, term lengths, and requirements for qualification, visit the National Center for State Courts.

Work Experience in a Related Occupation

Most judges and hearing officers learn their skills through years of experience as practicing lawyers. Some states allow those

Judges must be able to listen well to the facts provided by opposing parties.

who are not lawyers to hold limited-jurisdiction judgeships, but opportunities are better for those with law experience.

Training

All states have some type of orientation and training requirements for newly elected or appointed judges. The Federal Judicial Center, American Bar Association, National Judicial College, and National Center for State Courts provide judicial education and training for judges and other judicial branch personnel.

More than half of all states, as well as Puerto Rico, require judges to take continuing education courses while serving on the bench. General and continuing education courses usually last from a few days to 3 weeks.

Licenses, Certifications, and Registrations

Most judges and hearing officers are required to have a law license. In addition, they typically must maintain their law license and good standing with their state bar association while working as a judge or hearing officer.

Advancement

Advancement for some judicial workers means moving to courts with a broader jurisdiction. Advancement for various hearing officers includes taking on more complex cases, practicing law, and becoming district court judges.

Important Qualities

Critical-thinking skills. Judges and hearing officers must apply rules of law. They cannot let their own personal assumptions interfere with the proceedings. For example, they must base their decisions on specific meanings of the law when evaluating and deciding whether a person is a threat to others and must be sent to jail.

Decisionmaking skills. Judges and hearing officers must be able to weigh the facts, to apply the law and rules, and to make a decision relatively quickly.

Listening skills. Judges and hearing officers evaluate information, so they must pay close attention to what is being said.

Reading skills. Judges and hearing officers must be able to distinguish important facts from large amounts of sometimes complex information and then evaluate the facts objectively.

Writing skills. Judges and hearing officers write recommendations and decisions on appeals and disputes. They must be able to write their decisions clearly so that all sides understand the decision.

Pay

The median annual wage for administrative law judges, adjudicators, and hearing officers was $97,870 in May 2019. The median wage is the wage at which half the workers in an occupation earned more than that amount and half earned less. The

Judges and Hearing Officers
Median annual wages, May 2019

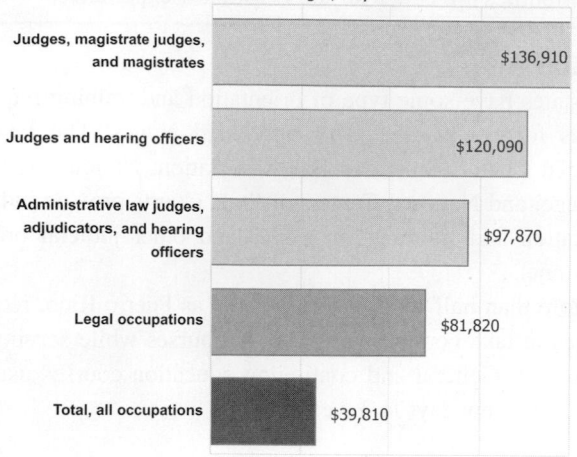

Judges, magistrate judges, and magistrates — $136,910

Judges and hearing officers — $120,090

Administrative law judges, adjudicators, and hearing officers — $97,870

Legal occupations — $81,820

Total, all occupations — $39,810

Note: All Occupations includes all occupations in the U.S. Economy.
Source: U.S. Bureau of Labor Statistics, Occupational Employment Statistics.

Judges and Hearing Officers
Percent change in employment, projected 2019-29

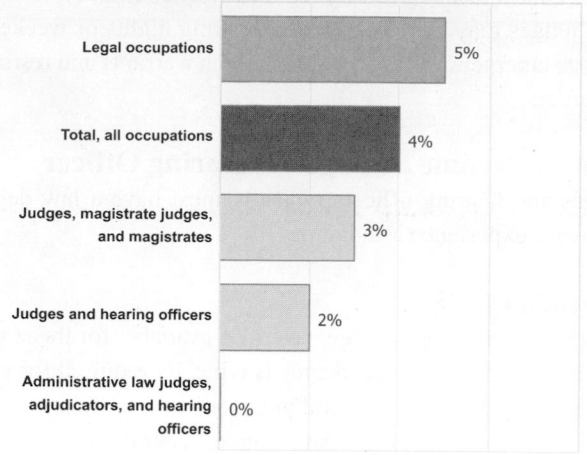

Legal occupations — 5%

Total, all occupations — 4%

Judges, magistrate judges, and magistrates — 3%

Judges and hearing officers — 2%

Administrative law judges, adjudicators, and hearing officers — 0%

Note: All Occupations includes all occupations in the U.S. Economy.
Source: U.S. Bureau of Labor Statistics, Employment Projections program.

lowest 10 percent earned less than $45,970, and the highest 10 percent earned more than $172,010.

The median annual wage for judges, magistrate judges, and magistrates was $136,910 in May 2019. The lowest 10 percent earned less than $39,110, and the highest 10 percent earned more than $204,200.

In May 2019, the median annual wages for administrative law judges, adjudicators, and hearing officers in the top industries in which they worked were as follows:

Federal government	$129,860
State government, excluding education and hospitals	81,510
Local government, excluding education and hospitals	75,270

In May 2019, the median annual wages for judges, magistrate judges, and magistrates in the top industries in which they worked were as follows:

State government, excluding education and hospitals	$151,750
Local government, excluding education and hospitals	92,270

Some courthouses have evening and weekend hours. In addition, judges have to be on call during nights or weekends to issue emergency orders, such as search warrants and restraining orders.

Job Outlook

Employment of judges and hearing officers is projected to grow 2 percent from 2019 to 2029, slower than the average for all occupations.

These workers play an essential role in the legal system, and their services will continue to be needed into the future.

However, budgetary constraints in federal, state, and local governments may limit the ability of these governments to fill vacant judge and hearing officer positions or authorize new ones. If there are governmental budget concerns, this could limit the employment growth opportunities of hearing officers and administrative law judges working for local, state, and federal government agencies, despite the continued need for these workers to settle disputes.

Job Prospects

The prestige associated with becoming a judge, and the fact that many need to be elected or nominated into the position, will ensure continued competition for these positions. Most job openings will arise as a result of judges and hearing officers leaving the occupation because of retirement, to teach, or because their elected term is over.

Employment projections data for judges and hearing officers, 2019-29					
Occupational Title	SOC Code	Employment, 2019	Projected Employment, 2029	Change, 2019-29	
				Percent	Numeric
SOURCE: U.S. Bureau of Labor Statistics, Employment Projections program					
Judges and hearing officers	—	45,300	46,300	2	1,100
Administrative law judges, adjudicators, and hearing officers	23-1021	15,400	15,400	0	0
Judges, magistrate judges, and magistrates	23-1023	29,900	30,900	3	1,000

State & Area Data
Occupational Employment Statistics (OES)

The Occupational Employment Statistics (OES) program produces employment and wage estimates annually for over 800 occupations. These estimates are available for the nation as a whole, for individual states, and for metropolitan and nonmetropolitan areas.

Contacts for More Information

For more information about state courts and judgeships, visit
➤ National Center for State Courts

For more information about federal judges, visit
➤ Administrative Office of the United States Courts
➤ U.S. Office of Personnel Management

For more information about judicial education and training for judges and other judicial branch personnel, visit
➤ American Bar Association
➤ Federal Judicial Center
➤ The National Judicial College

Lawyers

Summary

Quick Facts: Lawyers

2019 Median Pay	$122,960 per year $59.11 per hour
Typical Entry-Level Education	Doctoral or professional degree
Work Experience in a Related Occupation	None
On-the-job Training	None
Number of Jobs, 2019	813,900
Job Outlook, 2019-29	4% (As fast as average)
Employment Change, 2019-29	32,300

What Lawyers Do

Lawyers advise and represent individuals, businesses, and government agencies on legal issues and disputes.

Work Environment

The majority of lawyers work in private and corporate legal offices. Some work for federal, local, and state governments. Most work full time and many work more than 40 hours a week.

How to Become a Lawyer

Lawyers must have a law degree and must also typically pass a state's written bar examination.

Pay

The median annual wage for lawyers was $122,960 in May 2019.

Job Outlook

Employment of lawyers is projected to grow 4 percent from 2019 to 2029, about as fast as the average for all occupations. Competition for jobs over the next 10 years is expected to be strong because more students graduate from law school each year than there are jobs available.

State & Area Data

Explore resources for employment and wages by state and area for lawyers.

What Lawyers Do

Lawyers advise and represent individuals, businesses, and government agencies on legal issues and disputes.

Duties

Lawyers typically do the following:

• Advise and represent clients in courts, before government agencies, and in private legal matters

Lawyers advise and represent individuals, businesses, or government agencies on legal issues or disputes.

Lawyers often specialize in a particular legal field.

- Communicate with their clients, colleagues, judges, and others involved in the case
- Conduct research and analysis of legal problems
- Interpret laws, rulings, and regulations for individuals and businesses
- Present facts in writing and verbally to their clients or others, and argue on behalf of their clients
- Prepare and file legal documents, such as lawsuits, appeals, wills, contracts, and deeds

Lawyers, also called *attorneys*, act as both advocates and advisors.

As advocates, they represent one of the parties in a criminal or civil trial by presenting evidence and arguing in support of their client.

As advisors, lawyers counsel their clients about their legal rights and obligations and suggest courses of action in business and personal matters. All attorneys research the intent of laws and judicial decisions and apply the laws to the specific circumstances that their clients face.

Lawyers often oversee the work of support staff, such as paralegals and legal assistants and legal secretaries.

Lawyers may have different titles and different duties, depending on where they work.

In law firms, lawyers, sometimes called *associates*, perform legal work for individuals or businesses. Those who represent and defend the accused may be called *criminal law attorneys* or *defense attorneys*.

Attorneys also work for federal, state, and local governments. *Prosecutors* typically work for the government to file a lawsuit, or charge, against an individual or corporation accused of violating the law. Some may also work as *public defense attorneys*, representing individuals who could not afford to hire their own private attorney.

Others may work as *government counsels* for administrative bodies and executive or legislative branches of government. They write and interpret laws and regulations and set up procedures to enforce them. Government counsels also write legal reviews of agency decisions. They argue civil and criminal cases on behalf of the government.

Corporate counsels, also called *in-house counsels*, are lawyers who work for corporations. They advise a corporation's executives about legal issues related to the corporation's business activities. These issues may involve patents, government regulations, contracts with other companies, property interests, taxes, or collective-bargaining agreements with unions.

Public-interest lawyers work for private, nonprofit organizations that provide legal services to disadvantaged people or others who otherwise might not be able to afford legal representation. They generally handle civil cases, such as those having to do with leases, job discrimination, and wage disputes, rather than criminal cases.

In addition to working in different industries, lawyers may specialize in particular legal fields. Following are examples of types of lawyers in these fields:

Environmental lawyers deal with issues and regulations that are related to the environment. For example, they may work for advocacy groups, waste disposal companies, or government agencies to help ensure compliance with relevant laws.

Tax lawyers handle a variety of tax-related issues for individuals and corporations. They may help clients navigate complex tax regulations, so that clients pay the appropriate tax on items such as income, profits, and property. For example, tax lawyers may advise a corporation on how much tax it needs to pay from profits made in different states in order to comply with Internal Revenue Service (IRS) rules.

Intellectual property lawyers deal with the laws related to inventions, patents, trademarks, and creative works, such as music, books, and movies. For example, an intellectual property lawyer may advise a client about whether it is okay to use published material in the client's forthcoming book.

Family lawyers handle a variety of legal issues that pertain to the family. They may advise clients regarding divorce, child custody, and adoption proceedings.

Securities lawyers work on legal issues arising from the buying and selling of stocks, ensuring that all disclosure requirements are met. They may advise corporations that are interested in listing in the stock exchange through an initial public offering (IPO) or in buying shares in another corporation.

Work Environment

Lawyers held about 813,900 jobs in 2019. The largest employers of lawyers were as follows:

Legal services	50%
Self-employed workers	17
Local government, excluding education and hospitals	7
State government, excluding education and hospitals	6
Federal government	5

Lawyers work mostly in offices. However, some travel to attend meetings with clients at various locations, such as homes, hospitals, or prisons. Others travel to appear before courts.

Lawyers may face heavy pressure during work—for example, during trials or when trying to meet deadlines.

Work Schedules

The majority of lawyers work full time and many work more than 40 hours per week. Lawyers who are in private practice and those who work in large firms often work additional hours, conducting research and preparing and reviewing documents.

Lawyers typically work in law offices.

How to Become a Lawyer

Lawyers must have a law degree and must also typically pass a state's written bar examination.

Education

Becoming a lawyer usually takes 7 years of full-time study after high school—4 years of undergraduate study, followed by 3 years of law school. Most states and jurisdictions require lawyers to complete a Juris Doctor (J.D.) degree from a law

All lawyers must have a law degree and must also typically pass a state's written bar examination.

school accredited by the American Bar Association (ABA). ABA accreditation signifies that the law school—particularly its curricula and faculty—meets certain standards.

A bachelor's degree is required for entry into most law schools, and courses in English, public speaking, government, history, economics, and mathematics are useful.

Almost all law schools, particularly those approved by the ABA, require applicants to take the Law School Admission Test (LSAT). This test measures applicants' aptitude for the study of law.

A J.D. degree program includes courses such as constitutional law, contracts, property law, civil procedure, and legal writing. Law students may choose specialized courses in areas such as tax, labor, and corporate law.

Licenses, Certifications, and Registrations

Prospective lawyers take licensing exams called "bar exams." Lawyers who receive a license to practice law are "admitted to the bar."

To practice law in any state, a person must be admitted to the state's bar under rules established by the jurisdiction's highest court. The requirements vary by state and jurisdiction. For more details on individual state and jurisdiction requirements, visit the National Conference of Bar Examiners.

Most states require that applicants graduate from an ABA-accredited law school, pass one or more written bar exams, and be found by an admitting board to have the character to represent and advise others. Prior felony convictions, academic misconduct, and a history of substance abuse are just some factors that may disqualify an applicant from being admitted to the bar.

Lawyers who want to practice in more than one state often must take the bar exam in each state.

After graduation, lawyers must keep informed about legal developments that affect their practices. Almost all states require lawyers to participate in continuing legal education either every year or every 3 years.

Many law schools and state and local bar associations provide continuing legal education courses that help lawyers stay current with recent developments. Courses vary by state and generally cover a subject within the practice of law, such as legal ethics, taxes and tax fraud, and healthcare. Some states allow lawyers to take continuing education credits through online courses.

Advancement

Newly hired attorneys usually start as associates and work on teams with more experienced lawyers. After several years, some lawyers may advance to partnership in their firm, meaning that they become partial owners of the firm. Those who do not advance within their firm may be forced to leave, a practice commonly known as "up or out."

After gaining a few years of work experience, some lawyers go into practice for themselves or move to the legal department of a large corporation. Very few in-house attorneys are hired directly out of law school.

Other Experience

Part-time jobs or summer internships in law firms, government agencies, and corporate legal departments provide valuable experience. Some smaller firms, government agencies, and public-interest organizations may hire students as summer associates after they have completed their first year at law school. Many larger firms' summer associate programs are eligible only to law students who have completed their second year. All of these experiences can help law students decide what kind of legal work they want to focus on in their careers and may lead directly to a job after graduation.

Important Qualities

Analytical skills. Lawyers help their clients resolve problems and issues. As a result, they must be able to analyze large amounts of information, determine relevant facts, and propose viable solutions.

Interpersonal skills. Lawyers must win the respect and confidence of their clients by building a trusting relationship so that clients feel comfortable enough to share personal information related to their case.

Problem-solving skills. Lawyers must separate their emotions and prejudice from their clients' problems and objectively evaluate the relevant applicable information. Therefore, good problem-solving skills are important for lawyers, to prepare the best defense and recommendations for their clients.

Research skills. Lawyers need to be able to find those laws and regulations which apply to a specific matter, in order to provide the appropriate legal advice for their clients.

Speaking skills. Lawyers must be able to clearly present and explain their case to arbitrators, mediators, opposing parties, judges, or juries, because they are speaking on behalf of their clients.

Writing skills. Lawyers need to be precise and specific when preparing documents, such as wills, trusts, and powers of attorney.

Pay

The median annual wage for lawyers was $122,960 in May 2019. The median wage is the wage at which half the workers in an occupation earned more than that amount and half earned less. The lowest 10 percent earned less than $59,670, and the highest 10 percent earned more than $208,000.

In May 2019, the median annual wages for lawyers in the top industries in which they worked were as follows:

Federal government	$144,300
Legal services	123,620
Local government, excluding education and hospitals	95,870

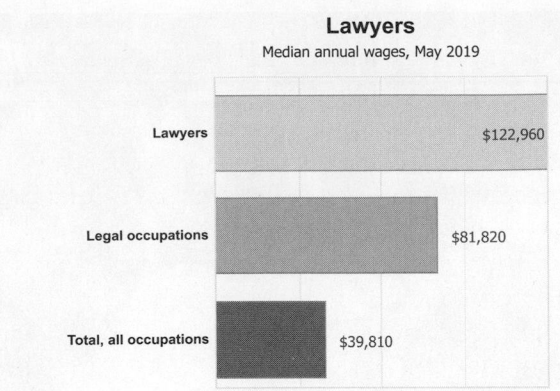

Lawyers
Median annual wages, May 2019

- Lawyers — $122,960
- Legal occupations — $81,820
- Total, all occupations — $39,810

Note: All Occupations includes all occupations in the U.S. Economy. Source: U.S. Bureau of Labor Statistics, Occupational Employment Statistics.

State government, excluding education and hospitals	89,090

Lawyers who own their own practices usually earn less than those who work in law firms or other business establishments. Occupational Employment Statistics (OES) survey wage data only includes lawyers working in business establishments.

The majority of lawyers work full time and many work more than 40 hours per week. Lawyers who are in private practice and those who work in large firms often work additional hours, conducting research and preparing and reviewing documents.

Job Outlook

Employment of lawyers is projected to grow 4 percent from 2019 to 2029, about as fast as the average for all occupations. Demand for legal work is expected to continue as individuals, businesses, and all levels of government require legal services in many areas.

Despite this need for legal services, more price competition over the next decade may lead law firms to rethink their project staffing in order to reduce costs to clients. Clients are expected to cut back on legal expenses by demanding less expensive rates

Lawyers
Percent change in employment, projected 2019-29

- Legal occupations — 5%
- Lawyers — 4%
- Total, all occupations — 4%

Note: All Occupations includes all occupations in the U.S. Economy. Source: U.S. Bureau of Labor Statistics, Employment Projections program.

and scrutinizing invoices. Work that was previously assigned to lawyers, such as document review, may now be given to paralegals and legal assistants. Also, some routine legal work may be outsourced to other, lower cost legal providers located overseas.

Although law firms will continue to be among the largest employers of lawyers, many large corporations are increasing their in-house legal departments in order to cut costs. For many companies, the high cost of hiring outside counsel lawyers and their support staffs makes it more economical to shift work to their in-house legal department. This shift will lead to an increase in the demand for lawyers in a variety of settings, such as financial and insurance firms, consulting firms, and healthcare providers.

The federal government is likely to continue to need lawyers to prosecute or defend civil cases on behalf of the United States, prosecute criminal cases brought by the federal government, and collect money owed to the federal government. However, budgetary constraints at all levels of government, especially the federal level, will likely moderate employment growth.

Job Prospects

Despite the projected growth in new jobs for lawyers, competition for jobs should continue to be strong because more students are graduating from law school each year than there are jobs available. Some law school graduates who have been unable to find permanent positions turn to temporary staffing firms that place attorneys in short-term jobs. These firms allow companies to hire lawyers as needed and permit beginning lawyers to develop practical experience. Many other law school graduates and licensed lawyers end up finding work in other occupations or industries due to the difficulty in finding jobs with traditional legal employers.

Because of the strong competition, a law school graduate's willingness to relocate and his or her practical experiences are becoming more important. However, to be licensed in another state, a lawyer may have to take an additional state bar examination.

While many new lawyers are hired each year by law firms, this does not guarantee stable employment in the profession. Newly hired lawyers, known as associates, must either advance within their firm or may be forced to leave, a practice commonly known as "up or out." Those who leave law firms may find work as in-house counsel with companies, with government agencies, or as self-employed lawyers.

Employment projections data for lawyers, 2019-29					
Occupational Title	SOC Code	Employment, 2019	Projected Employment, 2029	Change, 2019-29	
				Percent	Numeric
SOURCE: U.S. Bureau of Labor Statistics, Employment Projections program					
Lawyers	23-1011	813,900	846,300	4	32,300

State & Area Data
Occupational Employment Statistics (OES)

The Occupational Employment Statistics (OES) program produces employment and wage estimates annually for over 800 occupations. These estimates are available for the nation as a whole, for individual states, and for metropolitan and nonmetropolitan areas.

Contacts for More Information

For more information about law schools and a career in law, visit
➤ American Bar Association
➤ National Association for Law Placement

For more information about the Law School Admission Test (LSAT) and the law school application process, visit
➤ Law School Admission Council

For a list of state and jurisdiction admission bar offices, visit
➤ National Conference of Bar Examiners

The requirements for admission to the bar in a particular state or other jurisdiction may be obtained at the state capital, from the clerk of the state Supreme Court, or from the administrator of the State Board of Bar Examiners.

Paralegals and Legal Assistants

Summary

Quick Facts: Paralegals and Legal Assistants

2019 Median Pay	$51,740 per year
	$24.87 per hour
Typical Entry-Level Education	Associate's degree
Work Experience in a Related Occupation	None
On-the-job Training	None
Number of Jobs, 2019	337,800
Job Outlook, 2019-29	10% (Much faster than average)
Employment Change, 2019-29	35,300

What Paralegals and Legal Assistants Do

Paralegals and legal assistants perform a variety of tasks to support lawyers.

Work Environment

Paralegals and legal assistants are found in all types of organizations, but most work for law firms, corporate legal departments, and government agencies. They usually work full time, and some may have to work more than 40 hours a week to meet deadlines.

How to Become a Paralegal or Legal Assistant

Most paralegals and legal assistants have at least an associate's degree or a certificate in paralegal studies. In some cases, employers may hire college graduates with a bachelor's degree but no legal experience or specialized education and train them on the job.

Pay

The median annual wage for paralegals and legal assistants was $51,740 in May 2019.

Job Outlook

Employment of paralegals and legal assistants is projected to grow 10 percent from 2019 to 2029, much faster than the average for all occupations. Formally trained paralegals with strong computer and database management skills should have the best job prospects.

State & Area Data

Explore resources for employment and wages by state and area for paralegals and legal assistants.

What Paralegals and Legal Assistants Do

Paralegals and legal assistants perform a variety of tasks to support lawyers, including maintaining and organizing files, conducting legal research, and drafting documents.

Duties

Paralegals and legal assistants typically do the following:

- Investigate and gather the facts of a case
- Conduct research on relevant laws, regulations, and legal articles
- Organize and maintain documents in paper or electronic filing systems
- Gather and arrange evidence and other legal documents for attorney review and case preparation
- Write or summarize reports to help lawyers prepare for trials
- Draft correspondence and legal documents, such as contracts and mortgages
- Get affidavits and other formal statements that may be used as evidence in court
- Help lawyers during trials by handling exhibits, taking notes, or reviewing trial transcripts
- File exhibits, briefs, appeals and other legal documents with the court or opposing counsel
- Call clients, witnesses, lawyers, and outside vendors to schedule interviews, meetings, and depositions

Paralegals and legal assistants help lawyers prepare for hearings, trials, and corporate meetings.

Paralegals and legal assistants may conduct legal research.

Paralegals and legal assistants help lawyers prepare for hearings, trials, and corporate meetings.

Paralegals use technology and computer software for managing and organizing the increasing amount of documents and data collected during a case. Many paralegals use computer software to catalog documents, and to review documents for specific keywords or subjects. Because of these responsibilities, paralegals must be familiar with electronic database management and be current on the latest software used for electronic discovery. Electronic discovery refers to all electronic materials obtained by the parties during the litigation or investigation. These materials may be emails, data, documents, accounting databases, and websites.

Paralegals' specific duties often vary depending on the area of law in which they work. The following are examples of types of paralegals and legal assistants:

Corporate paralegals, for example, often help lawyers prepare employee contracts, shareholder agreements, stock-option plans, and companies' annual financial reports. Corporate paralegals may monitor and review government regulations to ensure that the corporation is aware of new legal requirements.

Litigation paralegals maintain documents received from clients, conduct research for lawyers, retrieve and organize evidence for use at depositions and trials, and draft settlement agreements. Some litigation paralegals may also help coordinate the logistics of attending a trial, including reserving office space, transporting exhibits and documents to the courtroom, and setting up computers and other equipment.

Paralegals may also specialize in other legal areas, such as personal injury, criminal law, employee benefits, intellectual property, bankruptcy, immigration, family law, and real estate.

Specific job duties may also vary by the size of the law firm.

In small firms, paralegals' duties tend to vary more. In addition to reviewing and organizing documents, paralegals may prepare written reports that help lawyers determine how to handle their cases. If lawyers decide to file lawsuits on behalf of clients, paralegals may help draft documents to be filed with the court.

In large organizations, paralegals may work on a particular phase of a case, rather than handling a case from beginning to end. For example, paralegals may only review legal material for internal use, maintain reference files, conduct research for lawyers, or collect and organize evidence for hearings. After gaining experience, a paralegal may become responsible for more complicated tasks.

Unlike the work of other administrative and legal support staff employed in a law firm, the paralegal's work is often billed to the client.

Paralegals may have frequent interactions with clients and third-party vendors. In addition, experienced paralegals may assume supervisory responsibilities, such as overseeing team projects or delegating work to other paralegals.

Work Environment

Paralegals and legal assistants held about 337,800 jobs in 2019. The largest employers of paralegals and legal assistants were as follows:

Legal services	76%
Federal government	4
Local government, excluding education and hospitals	4
State government, excluding education and hospitals	3
Finance and insurance	3

Paralegals and legal assistants often work in teams with attorneys, fellow paralegals, and other legal support staff.

Paralegals do most of their work in offices. Occasionally, they may travel to gather information, collect and review documents, accompany attorneys to depositions or trials, and do other tasks.

Some of the work can be fast-paced, and paralegals must be able to work on multiple projects under tight deadlines.

Work Schedules

Most paralegals and legal assistants work full time. Some may work more than 40 hours per week in order to meet deadlines.

Most paralegals and legal assistants work in law offices.

How to Become a Paralegal or Legal Assistant

Most paralegals and legal assistants have an associate's degree in paralegal studies, or a bachelor's degree in another field and a certificate in paralegal studies.

Education

There are several paths a person can take to become a paralegal. A common path is for candidates to earn an associate's degree in paralegal studies from a postsecondary institution.

However, many employers may prefer, or even require, applicants to have a bachelor's degree. Because only a small number of schools offer bachelor's degrees in paralegal studies, applicants will typically have a bachelor's degree in another subject and earn a certificate in paralegal studies from a paralegal education program approved by the American Bar Association.

Associate's and bachelor's degree programs in legal or paralegal studies usually offer paralegal training courses in legal research, legal writing, and the legal applications of computers, along with courses in other academic subjects, such as corporate law and international law. Most certificate programs provide intensive paralegal training for people who already hold college degrees.

Employers sometimes hire college graduates with no legal experience or legal education and train them on the job.

Licenses, Certifications, and Registrations

Although not required, some employers may prefer to hire applicants who have completed a paralegal certification program.

Some national and local paralegal organizations offer voluntary paralegal certifications to students able to pass an exam. Other organizations offer voluntary paralegal certifications for paralegals who meet certain experience and education criteria.

Important Qualities

Communication skills. Paralegals must be able to document and present their research and related information to their supervising attorney.

Computer skills. Paralegals need to be familiar with using computers for legal research and litigation support. They also use computer programs for organizing and maintaining important documents.

Interpersonal skills. Paralegals spend most of their time working with clients and other professionals and must be able to develop good relationships. They must make clients feel comfortable sharing personal information related to their cases.

Organizational skills. Paralegals may be responsible for many cases at one time. They must adapt quickly to changing deadlines.

Research skills. Paralegals gather facts of the case and research information on relevant laws and regulations to prepare drafts of legal documents for attorneys and help them prepare for a case.

Pay

The median annual wage for paralegals and legal assistants was $51,740 in May 2019. The median wage is the wage at which half the workers in an occupation earned more than that amount and half earned less. The lowest 10 percent earned less than $32,160, and the highest 10 percent earned more than $82,500.

In May 2019, the median annual wages for paralegals and legal assistants in the top industries in which they worked were as follows:

Federal government	$67,080
Finance and insurance	64,190
Local government, excluding education and hospitals	51,030
Legal services	49,630
State government, excluding education and hospitals	46,820

Most paralegals and legal assistants work full time. Some may work more than 40 hours per week in order to meet deadlines.

Many paralegals and legal assistants have an associate's degree or a certificate in paralegal studies.

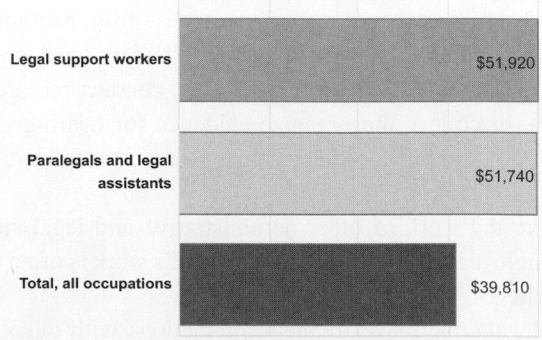

Paralegals and Legal Assistants
Median annual wages, May 2019

Legal support workers	$51,920
Paralegals and legal assistants	$51,740
Total, all occupations	$39,810

Note: All Occupations includes all occupations in the U.S. Economy.
Source: U.S. Bureau of Labor Statistics, Occupational Employment Statistics.

Paralegals and Legal Assistants
Percent change in employment, projected 2019-29

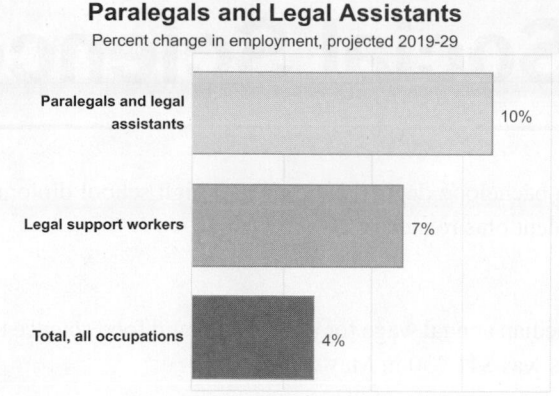

Note: All Occupations includes all occupations in the U.S. Economy.
Source: U.S. Bureau of Labor Statistics, Employment Projections program.

Job Outlook

Employment of paralegals and legal assistants is projected to grow 10 percent from 2019 to 2029, much faster than the average for all occupations.

As law firms try to increase the efficiency of legal services and reduce their costs, they are expected to hire more paralegals and legal assistants. In these cases, paralegals and legal assistants can take on a "hybrid" role within the firm, performing not only traditional paralegal duties but also some of the tasks previously assigned to legal secretaries or other legal support workers.

Law firms also are attempting to reduce billing costs as clients push for less expensive legal services. Due to their lower billing rates to clients, paralegals can be a less costly alternative to lawyers, performing a wide variety of tasks once done by entry-level lawyers. This should cause an increase in demand for paralegals and legal assistants.

Although law firms will continue to be the largest employers of paralegals, many large corporations are increasing their in-house legal departments to cut costs. For many companies, the high cost of outside counsel makes it more economical to have an in-house legal department. This will lead to an increase in the demand for legal workers in a variety of settings, such as finance and insurance firms, consulting firms, and healthcare providers.

Job Prospects

Due to the rise of electronic discovery, formally trained paralegals with strong computer and database management skills should have the best job prospects.

Employment projections data for paralegals and legal assistants, 2019-29					
Occupational Title	SOC Code	Employment, 2019	Projected Employment, 2029	Change, 2019-29	
				Percent	Numeric
SOURCE: U.S. Bureau of Labor Statistics, Employment Projections program					
Paralegals and legal assistants	23-2011	337,800	373,100	10	35,300

State & Area Data
Occupational Employment Statistics (OES)

The Occupational Employment Statistics (OES) program produces employment and wage estimates annually for over 800 occupations. These estimates are available for the nation as a whole, for individual states, and for metropolitan and nonmetropolitan areas.

Contacts for More Information

For more information on the Certified Legal Assistant certification, schools that offer training programs in a specific State, and standards and guidelines for paralegals, visit
➤ NALA – The National Association of Legal Assistants

For more information on the Professional Paralegal certification, visit
➤ NALS – The Association for Legal Professionals

For more information on the Paralegal Advanced Competency Exam, paralegal careers, and paralegal training programs visit
➤ National Federation of Paralegal Associations

For a list of American Bar Association approved paralegal education programs, visit
➤ American Bar Association

Life, Physical, and Social Science

Agricultural and Food Science Technicians

Summary

Quick Facts: Agricultural and Food Science Technicians

2019 Median Pay	$41,230 per year $19.82 per hour
Typical Entry-Level Education	Associate's degree
Work Experience in a Related Occupation	None
On-the-job Training	Moderate-term on-the-job training
Number of Jobs, 2019	24,200
Job Outlook, 2019-29	4% (As fast as average)
Employment Change, 2019-29	1,000

What Agricultural and Food Science Technicians Do

Agricultural and food science technicians assist agricultural and food scientists.

Work Environment

Agricultural and food science technicians work in laboratories, processing plants, farms and ranches, greenhouses, and offices.

How to Become an Agricultural or Food Science Technician

Agricultural and food science technicians typically need an associate's degree in biology, chemistry, crop or animal science, or a related field. Some positions require candidates to have a bachelor's degree, and others a high school diploma or equivalent plus related work experience.

Pay

The median annual wage for agricultural and food science technicians was $41,230 in May 2019.

Job Outlook

Employment of agricultural and food science technicians is projected to grow 4 percent from 2019 to 2029, about as fast as the average for all occupations. Agricultural and food science technicians will be needed to assist scientists as research into agricultural production methods and techniques continues.

State & Area Data

Explore resources for employment and wages by state and area for agricultural and food science technicians.

What Agricultural and Food Science Technicians Do

Agricultural and food science technicians assist agricultural and food scientists by performing duties such as measuring and analyzing the quality of food and agricultural products. Duties range from performing agricultural labor with added record-keeping duties to laboratory testing with significant amounts of office work, depending on the particular field the technician works in.

Duties

Specific duties of these technicians vary with their specialty.

Agricultural and food science technicians may apply new agricultural chemicals to plants and perform tests to verify their effects.

Agricultural and food science technicians may keep detailed records and collect samples for analyses.

Agricultural science technicians typically do the following:

- Follow protocols to collect, prepare, analyze, and properly store crop or animal samples
- Operate farm equipment and maintain agricultural production areas to conform to scientific testing parameters
- Examine animal and crop specimens to determine the presence of diseases or other problems
- Measure ingredients used in animal feed and other inputs
- Prepare and operate laboratory testing equipment
- Compile and analyze test results
- Prepare charts, presentations, and reports describing test results

Food science technicians typically do the following:

- Collect and prepare samples in accordance with established procedures
- Test food, food additives, and food containers to ensure that they comply with established safety standards
- Help food scientists with food research, development, and quality control
- Analyze chemical properties of food to determine ingredients and formulas
- Compile and analyze test results
- Prepare charts, presentations, and reports describing test results
- Prepare and maintain quantities of chemicals needed to perform laboratory tests
- Maintain a safe, sterile laboratory environment

Agricultural and food science technicians often specialize by subject area, which includes animal health, farm machinery, fertilizers, agricultural chemicals, or processing technology. Duties can vary considerably by specialization.

Agricultural science technicians typically study ways to increase the productivity of crops and animals. These workers may keep detailed records, collect samples for analyses, ensure that samples meet proper safety and quality standards, and test crops and animals for disease or to confirm the results of scientific experiments.

Food science technicians who work in manufacturing investigate new production or processing techniques. They also ensure that products will be fit for distribution or are produced as efficiently as expected. Many food science technicians spend time inspecting foodstuffs, chemicals, and additives to determine whether they are safe and have the proper combination of ingredients.

Work Environment

Agricultural and food science technicians held about 24,200 jobs in 2019. The largest employers of agricultural and food science technicians were as follows:

Food manufacturing...32%

Agricultural and food science technicians work on farms and ranches, in greenhouses, offices, laboratories, and processing plants.

Professional, scientific, and technical services...............20
Colleges, universities, and professional schools; state...15
Support activities for agriculture and forestry...............5
Crop production...2

Technicians work in a variety of settings, including laboratories, processing plants, farms and ranches, greenhouses, and offices. Technicians who work in processing plants and agricultural settings may face noise from processing and farming machinery, extreme temperatures, and odors from chemicals or animals. They may need to lift and carry objects, and be physically active for long periods of time.

Work Schedules

Agricultural and food science technicians typically work full time and have standard work schedules. Technicians may need to travel, including international travel.

How to Become an Agricultural or Food Science Technician

Agricultural and food science technicians typically need an associate's degree in biology, chemistry, crop or animal science, or a related field. Some positions require candidates to have a bachelor's degree, and others a high school diploma or equivalent plus related work experience.

Education

Students interested in a career as an agricultural or food science technician should take as many high school science and math classes as possible. A solid background in applied chemistry, biology, physics, math, and statistics is important. Knowledge of how to use spreadsheets and databases also may be necessary.

Agricultural and food science technicians typically need an associate's degree in biology, chemistry, crop or animal

Agricultural and food science technicians conduct a variety of observations and on-site measurements.

science, or a related field from an accredited college or university. Some agricultural and food science technician positions require a bachelor's degree.

Students may take courses in biology, chemistry, plant or animal science, and agricultural engineering as part of their programs. Programs include technical instruction and hands-on experience. Many schools offer internships, cooperative-education, and other programs designed to provide practical experience and enhance employment prospects.

Some agricultural and food science technicians successfully enter the occupation with a high school diploma or equivalent, but they typically need related work experience and on-the-job training that may last a year or more.

Training

Agricultural and food science technicians typically undergo on-the-job training. Various federal government regulations outline the types of training needed for technicians, which varies by work environment and specific job requirements. Training may cover topics such as production techniques, personal hygiene, and sanitation procedures.

Important Qualities

Analytical skills. Agricultural and food science technicians must conduct a variety of observations and on-site measurements, all of which require precision, accuracy, and math skills.

Communication skills. Agricultural and food science technicians must understand and give clear instructions, keep detailed records, and, occasionally, write reports.

Critical-thinking skills. Agricultural and food science technicians reach conclusions through sound reasoning and judgment. They determine how to improve food quality and must test products for a variety of safety standards.

Interpersonal skills. Agricultural and food science technicians need to work well with others. They may supervise agricultural and food processing workers and receive instruction from scientists or specialists, so effective communication is critical.

Physical stamina. Agricultural and food science technicians who work in manufacturing or agricultural settings may need to stand for long periods, lift objects, and generally perform physical labor.

Work Experience in a Related Occupation

Workers who enter the occupation with only a high school diploma or equivalent often must have experience in a related occupation during which they develop their knowledge of agriculture or manufacturing processes. These related occupations include food and tobacco processing workers and agricultural workers.

Pay

The median annual wage for agricultural and food science technicians was $41,230 in May 2019. The median wage is the wage at which half the workers in an occupation earned more than that amount and half earned less. The lowest 10 percent earned less than $28,030, and the highest 10 percent earned more than $64,180.

In May 2019, the median annual wages for agricultural and food science technicians in the top industries in which they worked were as follows:

Agricultural and Food Science Technicians
Median annual wages, May 2019

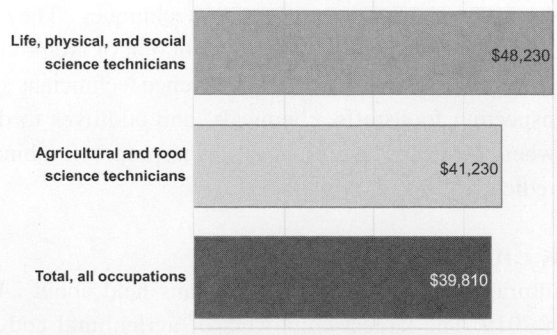

Life, physical, and social science technicians	$48,230
Agricultural and food science technicians	$41,230
Total, all occupations	$39,810

Note: All Occupations includes all occupations in the U.S. Economy.
Source: U.S. Bureau of Labor Statistics, Occupational Employment Statistics.

Agricultural and Food Science Technicians
Percent change in employment, projected 2019-29

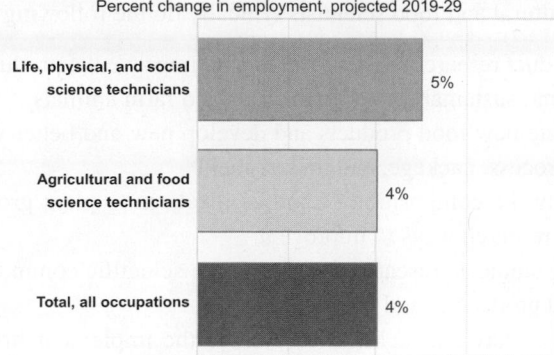

Life, physical, and social science technicians 5%

Agricultural and food science technicians 4%

Total, all occupations 4%

Note: All Occupations includes all occupations in the U.S. Economy.
Source: U.S. Bureau of Labor Statistics, Employment Projections program.

Colleges, universities, and professional schools;
state.. $42,320
Food manufacturing... 41,370
Professional, scientific, and technical services........ 38,300

Agricultural and food science technicians typically work full time and have standard work schedules. Technicians may need to travel, including international travel.

Job Outlook

Employment of agricultural and food science technicians is projected to grow 4 percent from 2019 to 2029, about as fast as the average for all occupations. Demand will continue for agricultural research into areas such as the effects of population growth, increased demand for water resources, harm from pests and pathogens, changes in climate and weather patterns, and demand for agricultural products, such as biofuels.

Agricultural science technicians will be needed to assist agricultural and food scientists in investigating and improving the diets, living conditions, and even genetic makeup of livestock. Food science technicians will assist scientists to improve food-processing techniques, ensuring that products are safe, waste is limited, and food is shipped efficiently. Technicians will also continue to assist in studies that analyze soil composition and soil improvement techniques, find uses for agricultural byproducts, and selectively breed crops to resist pests and disease, or improve taste.

Employment projections data for agricultural and food science technicians, 2019-29					
Occupational Title	SOC Code	Employment, 2019	Projected Employment, 2029	Change, 2019-29	
				Percent	Numeric
SOURCE: U.S. Bureau of Labor Statistics, Employment Projections program					
Agricultural and food science technicians	19-4010	24,200	25,100	4	1,000

State & Area Data
Occupational Employment Statistics (OES)
The Occupational Employment Statistics (OES) program produces employment and wage estimates annually for over 800 occupations. These estimates are available for the nation as a whole, for individual states, and for metropolitan and nonmetropolitan areas.

Contacts for More Information
For more information about agricultural and soil science occupations, visit
➤ American Society of Agronomy
➤ Future Farmers of America
➤ Soil Science Society of America

For more information about food and animal science occupations, visit
➤ American Registry of Professional Animal Scientists
➤ American Society of Animal Science
➤ Institute of Food Technologists

For information from related governmental agencies, visit
➤ U.S. Department of Agriculture
➤ U.S. Food and Drug Administration
➤ Smithsonian Institution

Agricultural and Food Scientists

Summary

Quick Facts: Agricultural and Food Scientists

2019 Median Pay	$65,160 per year $31.33 per hour
Typical Entry-Level Education	Bachelor's degree
Work Experience in a Related Occupation	None
On-the-job Training	None
Number of Jobs, 2019	34,800
Job Outlook, 2019-29	6% (Faster than average)
Employment Change, 2019-29	2,000

What Agricultural and Food Scientists Do
Agricultural and food scientists research ways to improve the efficiency and safety of agricultural establishments and products.

Work Environment
Agricultural and food scientists work in laboratories, in offices, and in the field. Most agricultural and food scientists work full time.

How to Become an Agricultural or Food Scientist
Agricultural and food scientists need at least a bachelor's degree from an accredited postsecondary institution, although many get advanced degrees.

Soil scientists examine the composition of soil and how it affects plant or crop growth.

Pay

The median annual wage for agricultural and food scientists was $65,160 in May 2019.

Job Outlook

Overall employment of agricultural and food scientists is projected to grow 6 percent from 2019 to 2029, faster than the average for all occupations. Employment of agricultural and food scientists is projected to grow as research into agricultural production methods and techniques continues.

State & Area Data

Explore resources for employment and wages by state and area for agricultural and food scientists.

What Agricultural and Food Scientists Do

Agricultural and food scientists research ways to improve the efficiency and safety of agricultural establishments and products.

Agricultural and food scientists may observe the production of field crops and farm animals so that they can research solutions to problems.

Duties

Agricultural and food scientists typically do the following:

- Conduct research and experiments to improve the productivity and sustainability of field crops and farm animals
- Create new food products and develop new and better ways to process, package, and deliver them
- Study the composition of soil as it relates to plant growth, and research ways to improve it
- Communicate research findings to the scientific community, food producers, and the public
- Travel between facilities to oversee the implementation of new projects

Agricultural and food scientists play an important role in maintaining and expanding the nation's food supply. Many work in basic or applied research and development. Basic research seeks to understand the biological and chemical processes by which crops and livestock grow. Applied research seeks to discover ways to improve the quality, quantity, and safety of agricultural products.

Many agricultural and food scientists work with little supervision, forming their own hypotheses and developing their research methods. In addition, they often lead teams of technicians or students who help in their research. Agricultural and food scientists who are employed in private industry may need to travel between different worksites.

The following are types of agricultural and food scientists:

Animal scientists typically conduct research on domestic farm animals. With a focus on food production, they explore animal genetics, nutrition, reproduction, diseases, growth, and development. They work to develop efficient ways to produce and process meat, poultry, eggs, and milk. Animal scientists may crossbreed animals to make them more productive or improve other characteristics. They advise farmers on how to upgrade housing for animals, lower animal death rates, increase growth rates, or otherwise increase the quality and efficiency of livestock.

Food scientists and technologists use chemistry, biology, and other sciences to study the basic elements of food. They analyze the nutritional content of food, discover new food sources, and research ways to make processed foods safe and healthy. Food technologists generally work in product development, applying findings from food science research to develop new or better ways of selecting, preserving, processing, packaging, and distributing food. Some food scientists use problem-solving techniques from nanotechnology—the science of manipulating matter on an atomic scale—to develop sensors that can detect contaminants in food. Other food scientists enforce government regulations, inspecting food-processing areas to ensure that they are sanitary and meet waste management standards.

Plant scientists work to improve crop yields and advise food and crop developers about techniques that could enhance production. They may develop ways to control pests and weeds.

Soil scientists examine the composition of soil, how it affects plant or crop growth, and how alternative soil treatments affect crop productivity. They develop methods of conserving and managing soil that farmers and forestry companies can use. Because soil science is closely related to environmental science, people trained in soil science also work to ensure environmental quality and effective land use.

Agricultural and food scientists in private industry commonly work for food production companies, farms, and processing plants. They may improve inspection standards or overall food quality. They spend their time in a laboratory, where they do tests and experiments, or in the field, where they take samples or assess overall conditions. Other agricultural and food scientists work for pharmaceutical companies, where they use biotechnology processes to develop drugs or other medical products. Some look for ways to process agricultural products into fuels, such as ethanol produced from corn.

At universities, agricultural and food scientists do research and investigate new methods of improving animal or soil health, nutrition, and other facets of food quality. They also write grants to organizations, such as the United States Department of Agriculture (USDA) or the National Institutes of Health (NIH), to get funding for their research. For more information on professors who teach agricultural and food science at universities, see the profile on postsecondary teachers.

In the federal government, agricultural and food scientists conduct research on animal safety and on methods of improving food and crop production. They spend most of their time conducting clinical trials or developing experiments on animal and plant subjects.

Agricultural and food scientists may eventually present their findings in peer-reviewed journals or other publications.

Work Environment

Agricultural and food scientists held about 34,800 jobs in 2019. Employment in the detailed occupations that make up agricultural and food scientists was distributed as follows:

Soil and plant scientists	17,800
Food scientists and technologists	14,200
Animal scientists	2,800

The largest employers of agricultural and food scientists were as follows:

Food manufacturing	21%
Colleges, universities, and professional schools; state, local, and private	17
Government	9
Research and development in the physical, engineering, and life sciences	9
Management, scientific, and technical consulting services	8

Agricultural and food scientists work in laboratories, in offices, and in the field. They spend most of their time studying data and reports in a laboratory or an office. Fieldwork includes visits to farms or processing plants.

When visiting a food or animal production facility, agricultural and food scientists must follow biosecurity measures, wear suitable clothing, and tolerate the environment associated with food production processes. This environment may include noise associated with large production machinery, cold temperatures associated with food production or storage, and close proximity to animal byproducts.

Certain positions may require travel, either domestic, international, or both. The amount of travel can vary widely.

Work Schedules

Agricultural and food scientists typically work full time.

How to Become an Agricultural or Food Scientist

Agricultural and food scientists need at least a bachelor's degree from an accredited postsecondary institution, although

Agricultural and food scientists spend most of their time in laboratories and offices.

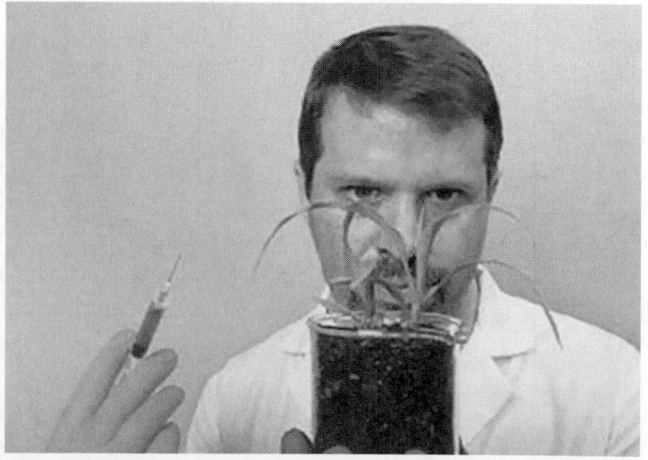

Agricultural and food scientists need at least a bachelor's degree.

many earn advanced degrees. Some animal scientists earn a doctor of veterinary medicine (DVM) degree.

Education

Every state has at least one land-grant college that offers agricultural science degrees. Many other colleges and universities also offer agricultural science degrees or related courses. Degrees in related sciences, such as biology, chemistry, and physics, or in a related engineering specialty also may qualify people for many agricultural science jobs.

Undergraduate coursework for food scientists and technologists and for soil and plant scientists typically includes biology, chemistry, botany, and plant conservation. Students preparing to be food scientists take courses such as food chemistry, food analysis, food microbiology, food engineering, and food-processing operations. Students preparing to be soil and plant scientists take courses in plant pathology, soil chemistry, entomology (the study of insects), plant physiology, and biochemistry.

Undergraduate students in agricultural and food sciences typically gain a strong foundation in their specialty, with an emphasis on teamwork through internships and research opportunities. Students also are encouraged to take humanities courses, which can help them develop good communication skills, and computer courses, which can familiarize them with common programs and databases.

Many people with bachelor's degrees in agricultural sciences find work in related jobs rather than becoming an agricultural or food scientist. For example, a bachelor's degree in agricultural science is a useful background for farming, ranching, agricultural inspection, farm credit institutions, or companies that make or sell feed, fertilizer, seed, or farm equipment. Combined with coursework in business, agricultural and food science could be a good background for managerial jobs in farm-related or ranch-related businesses. For more information, see the profile on farmers, ranchers, and other agricultural managers.

Many students with bachelors' degrees in application-focused food sciences or agricultural sciences earn advanced degrees in applied topics such as toxicology or dietetics. Students who major in a more basic field, such as biology or chemistry, may be better suited for getting their Ph.D. and doing research within the agricultural and food sciences. During graduate school, there is additional emphasis on lab work and original research, in which prospective animal scientists have the opportunity to do experiments and sometimes supervise undergraduates.

Advanced research topics include genetics, animal reproduction, agronomy, and biotechnology, among others. Advanced coursework also emphasizes statistical analysis and experiment design, which are important as Ph.D. candidates begin their research.

Some agricultural and food scientists receive a doctor of veterinary medicine (DVM). Like Ph.D. candidates in animal science, a prospective veterinarian must first have a bachelor's degree before getting into veterinary school.

Important Qualities

Communication skills. Communication skills are critical for agricultural and food scientists. They must explain their studies: what they were trying to learn, the methods they used, what they found, and what they think the implications of their findings are. They must also communicate well when working with others, including technicians and student assistants.

Critical-thinking skills. Agricultural and food scientists must use their expertise to determine the best way to answer a specific research question.

Data-analysis skills. Agricultural and food scientists, like other researchers, collect data using a variety of methods, including quantitative surveys. They must then apply standard data analysis techniques to understand the data and get the answers to the questions they are studying.

Math skills. Agricultural and food scientists, like many other scientists, must have a sound grasp of mathematical concepts.

Observation skills. Agricultural and food scientists conduct experiments that require precise observation of samples and other data. Any mistake could lead to inconclusive or inaccurate results.

Licenses, Certifications, and Registrations

Some states require soil scientists to be licensed to practice. Licensing requirements vary by state, but generally include holding a bachelor's degree with a certain number of credit hours in soil science, working under a licensed scientist for a certain number of years, and passing an exam.

Otherwise, certifications are generally not required for agriculture and food scientists, but they can be useful in advancing one's career. Agricultural and food scientists can get certifications from organizations such as the American Society of Agronomy, the American Registry of Professional Animal Scientists (ARPAS), the Institute of Food Technologists (IFT), or the Soil Science Society of America (SSSA), and others. These certifications recognize expertise in agricultural and food science, and enhance the status of those who are certified.

Qualification for certification is generally based on education, previous professional experience, and passing a comprehensive exam. Scientists may need to take continuing education courses to keep their certification, and they must follow the organization's code of ethics.

Other Experience

Internships are highly recommended for prospective food scientists and technologists. Many entry-level jobs in this occupation are related to food manufacturing, and firsthand experience is often valued in that environment.

Pay

The median annual wage for agricultural and food scientists was $65,160 in May 2019. The median wage is the wage at which half the workers in an occupation earned more than that

Agricultural and Food Scientists

Median annual wages, May 2019

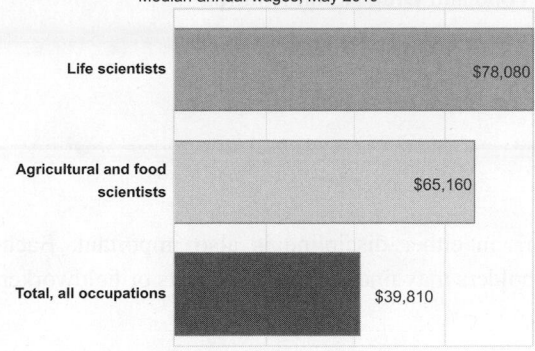

Agricultural and Food Scientists

Percent change in employment, projected 2019-29

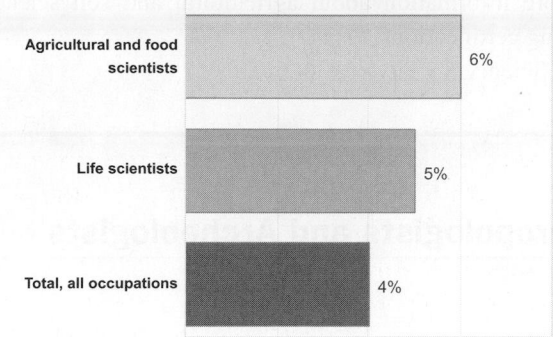

Note: All Occupations includes all occupations in the U.S. Economy.
Source: U.S. Bureau of Labor Statistics, Occupational Employment
Statistics.

Note: All Occupations includes all occupations in the U.S. Economy.
Source: U.S. Bureau of Labor Statistics, Employment Projections
program.

amount and half earned less. The lowest 10 percent earned less than $39,280, and the highest 10 percent earned more than $118,830.

Median annual wages for agricultural and food scientists in May 2019 were as follows:

Food scientists and technologists	$68,970
Soil and plant scientists	63,200
Animal scientists	60,300

In May 2019, the median annual wages for agricultural and food scientists in the top industries in which they worked were as follows:

Research and development in the physical, engineering, and life sciences	$76,220
Government	69,370
Food manufacturing	68,540
Management, scientific, and technical consulting services	60,470
Colleges, universities, and professional schools; state, local, and private	55,180

Agricultural and food scientists typically work full time.

Job Outlook

Overall employment of agricultural and food scientists is projected to grow 6 percent from 2019 to 2029, faster than the average for all occupations.

Employment of agricultural and food scientists is projected to grow as research into agricultural production methods and techniques continues. Challenges such as population growth, increased demand for water resources, combating pests and pathogens, changes in climate and weather patterns, and additional demand for agriculture products, such as biofuels, will continue to create demand for research in agricultural efficiency and sustainability.

Animal scientists will be needed to investigate and improve the diets, living conditions, and even genetic makeup of livestock. Food scientists and technologists will work to improve food-processing techniques, ensuring that products are safe, waste is limited, and food is shipped efficiently and safely. Soil and plant scientists will continue to try to understand and map soil composition. They will investigate ways to improve soils, to find uses for byproducts, and selectively breed crops to resist pests and disease, or improve taste.

Employment projections data for agricultural and food scientists, 2019-29					
Occupational Title	SOC Code	Employment, 2019	Projected Employment, 2029	Change, 2019-29	
				Percent	Numeric
SOURCE: U.S. Bureau of Labor Statistics, Employment Projections program					
Agricultural and food scientists	19-1010	34,800	36,800	6	2,000
Animal scientists	19-1011	2,800	3,000	6	200
Food scientists and technologists	19-1012	14,200	14,900	4	600
Soil and plant scientists	19-1013	17,800	19,000	7	1,200

State & Area Data

Occupational Employment Statistics (OES)

The Occupational Employment Statistics (OES) program produces employment and wage estimates annually for over 800 occupations. These estimates are available for the nation as a whole, for individual states, and for metropolitan and nonmetropolitan areas.

Contacts for More Information

For more information about food and animal scientists, including certifications, visit

➤ American Society of Agronomy
➤ American Society of Animal Science
➤ American Registry of Professional Animal Scientists
➤ Future Farmers of America

➤ Institute of Food Technologists

For more information about agricultural and soil scientists, including certifications, visit
➤ Soil Science Society of America

For information from related governmental agencies, visit
➤ U.S. Food and Drug Administration
➤ Smithsonian Institution
➤ U.S. Department of Agriculture
➤ National Institutes of Health

Anthropologists and Archeologists

Summary

Quick Facts: Anthropologists and Archeologists

2019 Median Pay	$63,670 per year $30.61 per hour
Typical Entry-Level Education	Master's degree
Work Experience in a Related Occupation	None
On-the-job Training	None
Number of Jobs, 2019......................................	8,000
Job Outlook, 2019-29......................................	5% (Faster than average)
Employment Change, 2019-29	400

What Anthropologists and Archeologists Do

Anthropologists and archeologists study the origin, development, and behavior of humans.

Work Environment

Anthropologists and archeologists typically work in research organizations, government, and consulting firms. Although most work in offices, some analyze samples in laboratories or do fieldwork. Fieldwork may require travel for extended periods.

How to Become an Anthropologist or Archeologist

Anthropologists and archeologists need a master's degree or Ph.D. in anthropology or archeology. Experience doing fieldwork in either discipline is also important. Bachelor's degree holders may find work as assistants or fieldworkers.

Pay

The median annual wage for anthropologists and archeologists was $63,670 in May 2019.

Job Outlook

Employment of anthropologists and archeologists is projected to grow 5 percent from 2019 to 2029, faster than the average for all occupations. Prospective anthropologists and archeologists will likely face strong competition for jobs because of the small number of positions relative to applicants.

State & Area Data

Explore resources for employment and wages by state and area for anthropologists and archeologists.

What Anthropologists and Archeologists Do

Anthropologists and archeologists study the origin, development, and behavior of humans. They examine the cultures, languages, archeological remains, and physical characteristics of people in various parts of the world.

Duties

Anthropologists and archeologists typically do the following:

- Plan cultural research
- Customize data collection methods according to a particular region, specialty, or project

Anthropologists and archeologists often do fieldwork.

Some anthropologists and archeologists excavate artifacts.

- Collect information from observations, interviews, and documents
- Record and manage records of observations taken in the field
- Analyze data, laboratory samples, and other sources of information to uncover patterns about human life, culture, and origins
- Prepare reports and present research findings
- Advise organizations on the cultural impact of policies, programs, and products

By drawing and building on knowledge from the humanities and the social, physical, and biological sciences, anthropologists and archeologists examine the ways of life, languages, archeological remains, and physical characteristics of people in various parts of the world. They also examine the customs, values, and social patterns of different cultures.

Although the equipment used by anthropologists and archeologists varies by task and specialty, it often includes excavation and measurement tools, laboratory and recording equipment, statistical and database software, and Geographic Information Systems (GIS).

Archeologists examine, recover, and preserve evidence of human activity from past cultures. They analyze human remains and artifacts, such as tools, pottery, cave paintings, and ruins of buildings. They connect their findings with information about past environments to learn about the history, customs, and living habits of people in earlier eras.

Archeologists also manage and protect archeological sites. Some work in national parks or at historical sites, providing site protection and educating the public. Others assess building sites to ensure that construction plans comply with federal regulations related to site preservation. Archeologists often specialize in a particular geographic area, period, or object of study, such as animal remains or underwater sites.

Anthropology is divided into three primary fields: biological or physical anthropology, cultural or social anthropology, and linguistic anthropology. Biological and physical anthropologists study the changing nature of the biology of humans and closely related primates. Cultural anthropologists study the social and cultural consequences of various human-related issues, such as overpopulation, natural disasters, warfare, and poverty. Linguistic anthropology studies the history and development of languages.

A growing number of anthropologists perform market research for businesses, studying the demand for products by a particular culture or social group. Using their anthropological background and a variety of techniques—including interviews, surveys, and observations—they may collect data on how a product is used by specific demographic groups.

Many people with a Ph.D. in anthropology or archeology become professors or museum curators. For more information, see the profiles on postsecondary teachers, and archivists, curators, and museum technicians.

Work Environment

Anthropologists and archeologists held about 8,000 jobs in 2019. The largest employers of anthropologists and archeologists were as follows:

Management, scientific, and technical consulting services	27%
Federal government, excluding postal service	19
Research and development in the social sciences and humanities	19
Self-employed workers	11
Engineering services	8

The work of anthropologists varies according to the specific job. Although most anthropologists work in offices, some analyze samples in laboratories or work in the field.

Archeologists often work for cultural resource management (CRM) firms. These firms identify, assess, and preserve archeological sites and ensure that developers and builders comply with regulations regarding those sites. Archeologists also work in museums, at historical sites, and for government agencies, such as the U.S. Department of the Interior's National Park Service.

Anthropologists and archeologists often do fieldwork, either in the United States or in foreign countries. Fieldwork may involve learning foreign languages, living in remote areas, and examining and excavating archeological sites. Fieldwork usually requires travel for extended periods—about 4 to 8 weeks per year. Those doing fieldwork often will have to return to the field for several years to complete their research.

During fieldwork, anthropologists and archeologists must live with the people they study to learn about their culture. The work can involve rugged living conditions and strenuous physical exertion. While in the field, anthropologists and archeologists often work many hours to meet research deadlines. They also may work with limited funding for their projects.

Anthropologists often travel to and live with the people they are studying.

Work Schedules

Many anthropologists and archeologists work full time during regular business hours. When doing fieldwork, however, anthropologists and archeologists may be required to travel and to work many and irregular hours, including evenings and weekends.

How to Become an Anthropologist or Archeologist

Anthropologists and archeologists need a master's degree or Ph.D. in anthropology or archeology. Experience doing fieldwork in either discipline is also important. Those with a bachelor's degree may find work as assistants or fieldworkers.

Education

Most anthropologists and archeologists qualify for available positions with a master's degree in anthropology or archeology. The typical master's degree program takes 2 years to complete and includes field or laboratory research.

Anthropology and archeology students typically conduct field research during their graduate programs, often working abroad or doing community-based research. Many students also attend archeological field schools, which teach students how to excavate historical and archeological sites and how to record and interpret their findings and data.

Although a master's degree is enough for many positions, a Ph.D. may be needed for jobs that require leadership skills and advanced technical knowledge. Anthropologists and archeologists typically need a Ph.D. to work internationally in order to comply with the requirements of foreign governments. A Ph.D. takes additional years of study beyond a master's degree. Also, Ph.D. students must complete a doctoral dissertation, which typically includes between 18 and 30 months of field research and knowledge of a foreign language.

Those with a bachelor's degree in anthropology or archeology and work experience gained through an internship or field school can work as field or laboratory technicians or research assistants.

Other Experience

Graduates of anthropology and archeology programs usually need experience in their respective fields and training in quantitative and qualitative research methods. Many students gain this experience through field training or internships with museums, historical societies, or nonprofit organizations while still in school.

Important Qualities

Analytical skills. Anthropologists and archeologists must possess knowledge of scientific methods and data, which are often used in their research.

Critical-thinking skills. Anthropologists and archeologists must be able to draw conclusions from observations, laboratory experiments, and other methods of research. They must be able to combine various sources of information to try to solve problems and to answer research questions.

Communication skills. Anthropologists and archeologists often have to write reports or papers in academic journals and present their research and findings to their peers and to general audiences. These activities require strong writing, speaking, and listening skills.

Physical stamina. Anthropologists and archeologists working in the field may need to hike or walk several miles while carrying equipment to a research site.

Pay

The median annual wage for anthropologists and archeologists was $63,670 in May 2019. The median wage is the wage at which half the workers in an occupation earned more than that amount and half earned less. The lowest 10 percent earned less than $39,460, and the highest 10 percent earned more than $97,950.

Students assist in the surveying of proposed building sites for artifacts.

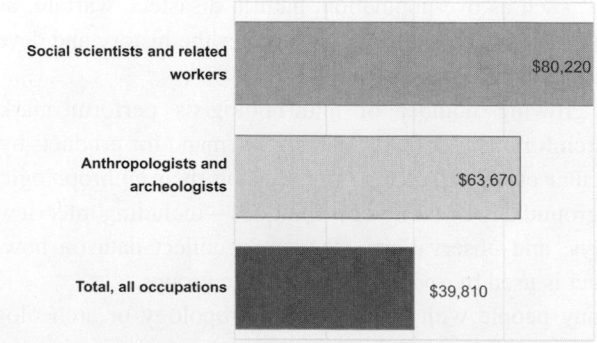

Anthropologists and Archeologists

Median annual wages, May 2019

Social scientists and related workers	$80,220
Anthropologists and archeologists	$63,670
Total, all occupations	$39,810

Note: All Occupations includes all occupations in the U.S. Economy.
Source: U.S. Bureau of Labor Statistics, Occupational Employment Statistics.

Anthropologists and Archeologists

Percent change in employment, projected 2019-29

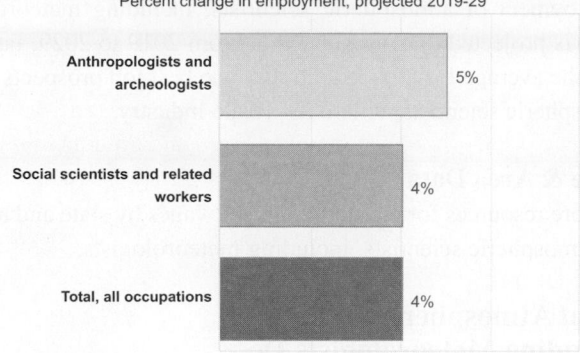

Anthropologists and archeologists: 5%

Social scientists and related workers: 4%

Total, all occupations: 4%

Note: All Occupations includes all occupations in the U.S. Economy.
Source: U.S. Bureau of Labor Statistics, Employment Projections program.

In May 2019, the median annual wages for anthropologists and archeologists in the top industries in which they worked were as follows:

Federal government, excluding postal service $77,560

Engineering services 68,690

Management, scientific, and technical consulting services 61,360

Research and development in the social sciences and humanities.. 55,950

Many anthropologists and archeologists work full time during regular business hours. When doing fieldwork, however, anthropologists and archeologists may be required to travel and to work many and irregular hours, including evenings and weekends.

Job Outlook

Employment of anthropologists and archeologists is projected to grow 5 percent from 2019 to 2029, faster than the average for all occupations.

Corporations will continue to use anthropological research to gain a better understanding of consumer demand within specific cultures or social groups. Anthropologists also will be needed to analyze markets, allowing businesses to serve their clients better or to target new customers or demographic groups.

Archeologists will be needed to monitor construction projects, ensuring that builders comply with federal regulations pertaining to the preservation and handling of archeological and historical artifacts.

Because anthropological and archeological research may depend on research funding, federal budgetary decisions can affect the rate of employment growth in research.

Job Prospects

Overall, prospective anthropologists and archeologists will likely face strong competition for jobs because of the small number of positions relative to applicants. Job prospects will be best for candidates with a Ph.D. or an applied master's degree, extensive anthropological or archeological fieldwork experience, and experience in quantitative and qualitative research methods.

Employment projections data for anthropologists and archeologists, 2019-29					
Occupational Title	SOC Code	Employment, 2019	Projected Employment, 2029	Change, 2019-29	
				Percent	Numeric
SOURCE: U.S. Bureau of Labor Statistics, Employment Projections program					
Anthropologists and archeologists	19-3091	8,000	8,400	5	400

State & Area Data
Occupational Employment Statistics (OES)

The Occupational Employment Statistics (OES) program produces employment and wage estimates annually for over 800 occupations. These estimates are available for the nation as a whole, for individual states, and for metropolitan and nonmetropolitan areas.

Contacts for More Information

For more information about careers in anthropology and archeology, visit
➤ American Anthropological Association

For more information about careers in archeology, visit
➤ Archaeological Institute of America
➤ Society for American Archaeology

For more information about physical anthropologists, visit
➤ American Association of Physical Anthropologists

Atmospheric Scientists, Including Meteorologists

Summary

Quick Facts: Atmospheric Scientists, Including Meteorologists

2019 Median Pay	$95,380 per year
	$45.86 per hour
Typical Entry-Level Education	Bachelor's degree
Work Experience in a Related Occupation	None
On-the-job Training	None
Number of Jobs, 2019....................................	9,900
Job Outlook, 2019-29....................................	6% (Faster than average)
Employment Change, 2019-29	600

What Atmospheric Scientists, Including Meteorologists Do

Atmospheric scientists study the weather and climate.

Work Environment

Most atmospheric scientists work indoors in weather stations, offices, or laboratories. Occasionally, they do fieldwork, which means working outdoors to examine the weather. Some atmospheric scientists may have to work extended hours during weather emergencies.

How to Become an Atmospheric Scientist

Atmospheric scientists need a bachelor's degree in atmospheric science or a closely related field for most positions. Those who work in research usually need a master's degree or a Ph.D.

Pay

The median annual wage for atmospheric scientists, including meteorologists was $95,380 in May 2019.

Job Outlook

Employment of atmospheric scientists, including meteorologists, is projected to grow 6 percent from 2019 to 2029, faster than the average for all occupations. The best job prospects for atmospheric scientists will be in private industry.

State & Area Data

Explore resources for employment and wages by state and area for atmospheric scientists, including meteorologists.

What Atmospheric Scientists, Including Meteorologists Do

Atmospheric scientists study the weather and climate, and examine how those conditions affect human activity and the earth in general. They may develop forecasts, collect and compile data from the field, assist in the development of new data collection instruments, or advise clients on risks or opportunities caused by weather events and climate change.

Duties

Atmospheric scientists typically do the following:

- Measure temperature, atmospheric pressure, humidity, wind speed, dew point, and other properties of the atmosphere
- Use computer models that analyze data about the atmosphere (also called meteorological data)
- Write computer programs to support their modeling efforts
- Conduct research to improve understanding of weather phenomena
- Generate weather graphics for users
- Report current weather conditions
- Prepare long- and short-term weather forecasts by using computers, mathematical models, satellites, radar, and local station data
- Plan, organize, and participate in outreach programs aimed at educating the public about weather

Research meteorologists prepare to test hurricane resiliency of homes and warehouses in their lab.

Research meteorologists study atmospheric phenomena such as lightning.

- Issue warnings to protect life and property when threatened by severe weather, such as hurricanes, tornadoes, and flash floods

Atmospheric scientists use highly developed instruments and computer programs to do their jobs. For example, they use weather balloons, radar systems, and satellites to monitor the weather and collect data. The data they collect and analyze are critical to understanding global warming and other issues. Atmospheric scientists also use graphics software to illustrate their forecasts and reports in order to advise their clients or the public.

Many atmospheric scientists work with other geoscientists or even social scientists to help solve problems in areas such as commerce, energy, transportation, agriculture, and the environment. For example, some atmospheric scientists work closely with hydrologists and government organizations to study the impact climate change may have on water supplies and to manage water resources.

The following are examples of types of atmospheric scientists:

Atmospheric chemists study atmospheric components, reactions, measurement techniques, and processes. They study climates and gases, chemical reactions that occur in clouds, and ultraviolet radiation.

Atmospheric physicists and dynamists study the physical movements and interactions that occur in the atmosphere. They may study how terrain affects weather and causes turbulence, how solar phenomena affect satellite communications and navigation, or they may study the causes and effects of lightning.

Broadcast meteorologists give forecasts to the general public through television, radio, and the Internet. They use graphics software to develop maps and charts that explain their forecasts. Not all weather broadcasters seen on television are meteorologists or atmospheric scientists; reporters, correspondents, and broadcast news analysts present weather conditions and forecasts, but do not have specific training in meteorology.

Climatologists study historical weather patterns to interpret long-term weather patterns or shifts in climate by using primarily statistical methods. Global climate change is the main area of study for climatologists. Paleoclimatology is a specialization within this field. Climatologists who specialize in paleoclimatology may take samples from icebergs and other sources to gather data on the atmosphere that cover very long periods of time.

Climate scientists work on the theoretical foundations and the modeling of climate change. The nature of this work requires the use of complex mathematical models to try to forecast many months, and sometimes longer, into the future. Their studies can be used to design buildings, plan heating and cooling systems, and aid in efficient land use and agricultural production.

Forensic meteorologists use historical weather data to reconstruct the weather conditions for a specific location and time. They investigate what role weather played in unusual events such as traffic accidents and fires. Forensic meteorologists may be called as experts to testify in court.

Research meteorologists develop new methods of data collection, observation, and forecasting. They also conduct studies to improve basic understandings of climate, weather, and other aspects of the atmosphere. For example, some research meteorologists study severe weather patterns that produce hurricanes and tornadoes to understand why cyclones form and to develop better ways of predicting them. Others focus on environmental problems, such as air pollution. Research meteorologists often work with scientists in other fields. For example, they may work with computer scientists to develop new forecasting software or with oceanographers to study interactions between the ocean and the atmosphere. They may also work with engineers to develop new instruments so that they can collect the data they need.

Weather forecasters use computer and mathematical models to produce weather reports and short-term forecasts that can range from a few minutes to more than a week. They develop forecasts for the general public and for specific customers such as airports, water transportation, shippers, farmers, utility companies, insurance companies, and other businesses. For example, they may provide forecasts to power suppliers so that the suppliers can plan for events, such as heat waves, that would cause a change in electricity demand. They also issue advanced warnings for potentially severe weather, such as blizzards and hurricanes. Some forecasters prepare long-range outlooks to predict whether temperatures and precipitation levels will be above or below average in a particular month or season. These workers become familiar with general weather patterns, atmospheric predictability, precipitation, and forecasting techniques.

Some people with an atmospheric science background may become professors or postsecondary teachers.

Work Environment

Atmospheric scientists, including meteorologists held about 9,900 jobs in 2019. The largest employers of atmospheric scientists, including meteorologists were as follows:

Federal government, excluding postal service	32%
Research and development in the physical, engineering, and life sciences	12
Television broadcasting	11
Management, scientific, and technical consulting services	6

In the federal government, most atmospheric scientists work as weather forecasters with the National Weather Service of the National Oceanic and Atmospheric Administration (NOAA) in weather stations throughout the United States—at airports, in

Many atmospheric scientists work at weather stations located throughout the country.

Atmospheric scientists issue warnings for severe weather.

or near cities, and in isolated and remote areas. In smaller stations, they often work alone; in larger ones, they work as part of a team. In addition, hundreds of members of the Armed Forces are involved in atmospheric science.

Atmospheric scientists involved in professional, scientific, and technical services or research often work in offices and laboratories. Some may travel frequently to collect data in the field and to observe weather events, such as tornadoes, up close. They also observe actual weather conditions from the ground or from an aircraft.

Broadcast meteorologists present their reports to the general public from television and radio studios. They also may broadcast from outdoor locations to tell audiences about current weather conditions.

Atmospheric scientists who work in private industry may have to travel to meet with clients or to gather information in the field. For example, forensic meteorologists may need to collect information from the scene of an accident as part of their investigation.

Work Schedules

Most atmospheric scientists work full time. Weather conditions can change quickly, so weather forecasters need to continuously monitor conditions. Many, especially entry-level staff at field stations, work rotating shifts to ensure staff coverage for

all 24 hours in a day. For this reason, they may work nights, weekends, and holidays. In addition, they may work extended hours during severe weather, such as hurricanes. Some work more than 40 hours per week. Other atmospheric scientists have a standard workweek, although researchers may work nights and weekends on particular projects.

How to Become an Atmospheric Scientist

Atmospheric scientists need a bachelor's degree in meteorology or a closely related earth sciences field for most positions. For research positions, atmospheric scientists need a master's degree at minimum, but usually will need a Ph.D.

Education

Atmospheric scientists typically need a bachelor's degree, either in atmospheric science or a related scientific field that specifically studies atmospheric qualities and phenomena. Bachelor's degrees in physics, chemistry, or geology are usually adequate, alternative preparation for those who wish to enter the atmospheric sciences. Prospective meteorologists usually take courses outside of the typical atmospheric sciences field.

Course requirements, in addition to courses in meteorology and atmospheric science, usually include advanced courses in physics and mathematics. Classes in computer programming are important because many atmospheric scientists have to write and edit the computer software programs that produce forecasts. Coursework in remote sensing of the environment, by radar or satellite, may be required.

Atmospheric scientists who work in research must at least have a master's degree, but will usually need a Ph.D. in atmospheric science or a related field. Most graduate programs do not require prospective students to have a bachelor's degree in atmospheric science; a bachelor's degree in mathematics, physics, or engineering is excellent preparation for graduate study in atmospheric science. In addition to advanced meteorological coursework, graduate students take courses in other disciplines, such as oceanography and geophysics.

Atmospheric Scientists, Including Meteorologists
Median annual wages, May 2019

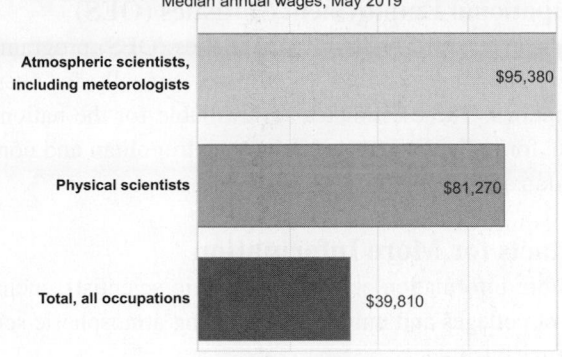

Atmospheric scientists, including meteorologists — $95,380

Physical scientists — $81,270

Total, all occupations — $39,810

Atmospheric Scientists, Including Meteorologists
Percent change in employment, projected 2019-29

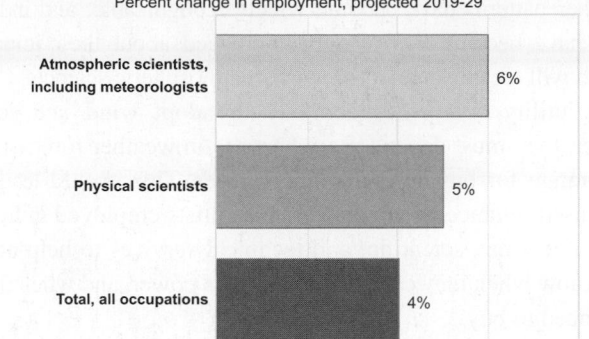

Atmospheric scientists, including meteorologists — 6%

Physical scientists — 5%

Total, all occupations — 4%

Note: All Occupations includes all occupations in the U.S. Economy.
Source: U.S. Bureau of Labor Statistics, Occupational Employment Statistics.

Note: All Occupations includes all occupations in the U.S. Economy.
Source: U.S. Bureau of Labor Statistics, Employment Projections program.

Important Qualities

Analytical skills. Atmospheric scientists must be able to focus for many hours, working with computer models and massive amounts of data to prepare analyses on their findings.

Communication skills. Atmospheric scientists need to be able to write and speak clearly so that their knowledge about the weather can be used effectively by communities and individuals.

Critical-thinking skills. Atmospheric scientists need to be able to analyze the results of their computer models and forecasts to determine the most likely outcome.

Math skills. Atmospheric scientists use calculus, statistics, and other advanced topics in mathematics to develop models used to forecast the weather. They also use mathematical calculations to study the relationship between properties of the atmosphere, such as how changes in air pressure may affect air temperature.

Training

Atmospheric scientists and meteorologists who find employment in the National Weather Service will need to take training when they begin employment to be able to use equipment needed to issue warnings of severe weather.

Other experience

The National Weather Service offers opportunities for students through internship, fellowship, volunteer, and scholarship programs.

Pay

The median annual wage for atmospheric scientists, including meteorologists was $95,380 in May 2019. The median wage is the wage at which half the workers in an occupation earned more than that amount and half earned less. The lowest 10 percent earned less than $49,700, and the highest 10 percent earned more than $147,160.

In May 2019, the median annual wages for atmospheric scientists, including meteorologists in the top industries in which they worked were as follows:

Research and development in the physical, engineering, and life sciences $113,130
Federal government, excluding postal service 103,300
Television broadcasting 91,410
Management, scientific, and technical consulting services 90,810

Most atmospheric scientists work full time. Weather conditions can change quickly, so weather forecasters need to continuously monitor conditions. Many, especially entry-level staff at field stations, work rotating shifts to ensure staff coverage for all 24 hours in a day, and they may work on nights, weekends, and holidays. In addition, they may work extended hours during severe weather, such as hurricanes. Some work more than 40 hours per week. Other atmospheric scientists have a standard workweek, although researchers may work nights and weekends on particular projects.

Job Outlook

Employment of atmospheric scientists, including meteorologists is projected to grow 6 percent from 2019 to 2029, faster than the average for all occupations.

New types of computer models have vastly improved the accuracy of forecasts and allowed atmospheric scientists to tailor forecasts to specific purposes. This should maintain, and perhaps increase, the need for atmospheric scientists working in private industry as businesses demand more specialized weather information.

Businesses increasingly rely on just-in-time delivery to avoid the expenses incurred by traditional inventory management methods. Severe weather can interrupt ground or air transportation and delay inventory delivery. Businesses have begun to maintain forecasting teams around the clock to advise delivery personnel, and this availability helps them stay on schedule. In addition, severe weather patterns have become widely recognizable, and industries have become increasingly concerned about their impact, which will create demand for work in atmospheric science.

As utility companies continue to adopt wind and solar power, they must depend more heavily on weather forecasting to arrange for buying and selling power. This should lead to increased reliance on atmospheric scientists employed in firms in professional, scientific, and technical services to help utilities know when they can sell their excess power, and when they will need to buy.

Job Prospects

Prospective atmospheric scientists should expect continued competition because the number of graduates from meteorology programs is expected to exceed the number of job openings requiring only a bachelor's degree. Workers with a graduate degree should have better prospects than those with a bachelor's degree only. Prospective atmospheric scientists with knowledge of advanced mathematics also will have better job prospects because of the highly quantitative nature of much of this occupation's work.

Competition may be strong for research positions at colleges and universities because of the limited number of positions available. In addition, hiring by federal agencies is subject to budget constraints. The best job prospects for meteorologists are expected to be in private industry.

The National Weather Service and the University Corporation for Atmospheric Research (UCAR) sponsor an online training program called COMET. Completing such coursework may help prospective atmospheric scientists to have better job prospects.

Employment projections data for atmospheric scientists, including meteorologists, 2019-29					
Occupational Title	SOC Code	Employment, 2019	Projected Employment, 2029	Change, 2019-29	
				Percent	Numeric
SOURCE: U.S. Bureau of Labor Statistics, Employment Projections program					
Atmospheric and space scientists	19-2021	9,900	10,600	6	600

State & Area Data
Occupational Employment Statistics (OES)

The Occupational Employment Statistics (OES) program produces employment and wage estimates annually for over 800 occupations. These estimates are available for the nation as a whole, for individual states, and for metropolitan and nonmetropolitan areas.

Contacts for More Information

For more information about atmospheric scientists, including a list of colleges and universities offering atmospheric science programs, visit
➤ American Meteorological Society

For a broad range of information concerning atmospheric scientists within the geosciences perspective, visit
➤ American Geosciences Institute

For more information about atmospheric science careers in research, visit
➤ University Corporation for Atmospheric Research (UCAR)

For more information about federal government education requirements for atmospheric science positions, visit
➤ U.S. Office of Personnel Management

For more information about the COMET training program, visit
➤ MetEd

To find job openings for atmospheric scientists in the federal government, visit
➤ USAJOBS

For more information about federal government atmospheric science careers in the National Weather Service and other agencies within the National Oceanic and Atmospheric Administration, visit
➤ National Oceanic and Atmospheric Administration, National Weather Service

Biochemists and Biophysicists

Summary

Quick Facts: Biochemists and Biophysicists

2019 Median Pay	$94,490 per year $45.43 per hour
Typical Entry-Level Education	Doctoral or professional degree
Work Experience in a Related Occupation	None
On-the-job Training	None
Number of Jobs, 2019	34,600
Job Outlook, 2019-29	4% (As fast as average)
Employment Change, 2019-29	1,400

What Biochemists and Biophysicists Do

Biochemists and biophysicists study the chemical and physical principles of living things and of biological processes.

Work Environment

Biochemists and biophysicists typically work in laboratories and offices to conduct experiments and analyze the results. Most work full time.

How to Become a Biochemist or Biophysicist

Biochemists and biophysicists need a Ph.D. to work in independent research and development. Many Ph.D. holders begin their careers in temporary postdoctoral research positions. Bachelor's and master's degree holders qualify for some entry-level positions in biochemistry and biophysics.

Pay

The median annual wage for biochemists and biophysicists was $94,490 in May 2019.

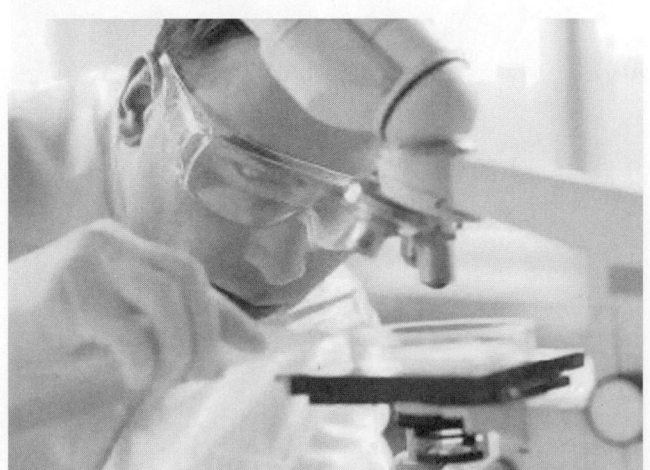

Biochemists and biophysicists study the chemical and physical properties of cells.

Job Outlook

Employment of biochemists and biophysicists is projected to grow 4 percent from 2019 to 2029, about as fast as the average for all occupations. Biochemists and biophysicists will continue to be needed to use the knowledge they have gained from basic research to develop biological products and processes that improve people's lives.

State & Area Data

Explore resources for employment and wages by state and area for biochemists and biophysicists.

What Biochemists and Biophysicists Do

Biochemists and biophysicists study the chemical and physical principles of living things and of biological processes, such as cell development, growth, heredity, and disease.

Duties

Biochemists and biophysicists typically do the following:

- Plan and conduct complex projects in basic and applied research
- Manage laboratory teams and monitor the quality of their work

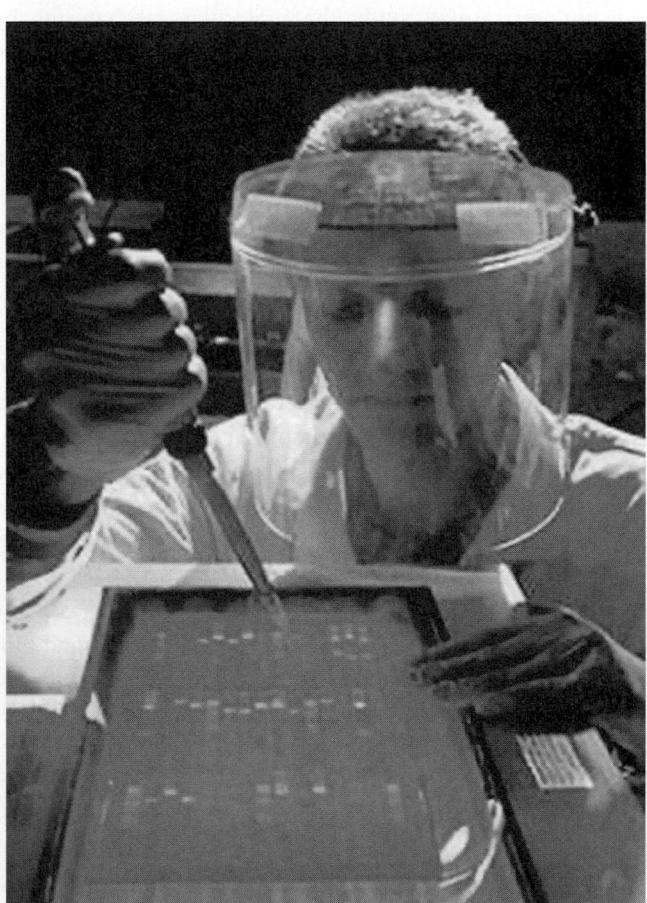

Biochemists and biophysicists play a key role in developing new medicines to fight diseases such as cancer.

- Isolate, analyze, and synthesize proteins, fats, DNA, and other molecules
- Research the effects of substances such as drugs, hormones, and nutrients on tissues and biological processes
- Review literature and the findings of other researchers and attend conferences
- Prepare technical reports, research papers, and recommendations based on their research findings
- Present research findings to scientists, engineers, and other colleagues
- Secure funding and write grant applications

Biochemists and biophysicists use advanced technologies, such as lasers and fluorescent microscopes, to conduct scientific experiments and analyses. They also use x rays and computer modeling software to determine the three-dimensional structures of proteins and other molecules. Biochemists and biophysicists involved in biotechnology research use chemical enzymes to synthesize recombinant DNA.

Biochemists and biophysicists work in basic and applied research. Basic research is conducted without any immediately known application; the goal is to expand human knowledge. Applied research is directed toward solving a particular problem.

Biochemists, sometimes called *molecular biologists* or *cellular biologists*, may study the molecular mechanisms by which cells feed, divide, and grow. Others study the evolution of plants and animals, to understand how genetic traits are carried through successive generations.

Biophysicists may conduct basic research to learn how nerve cells communicate or how proteins work. Biochemists and biophysicists who conduct basic research typically must submit written grant proposals to colleges and universities, private foundations, and the federal government to get the money they need for their research.

Biochemists and biophysicists who conduct applied research attempt to develop products and processes that improve people's lives. For example, in medicine, biochemists and biophysicists develop tests used to detect infections, genetic disorders, and other diseases. They also develop new drugs and medications, such as those used to treat cancer or Alzheimer's disease.

Applied research in biochemistry and biophysics has many uses outside of medicine. In agriculture, biochemists and biophysicists research ways to genetically engineer crops so that they will be resistant to drought, disease, insects, and other afflictions. Biochemists and biophysicists also investigate alternative fuels, such as biofuels—renewable energy sources from plants. In addition, they develop ways to protect the environment and clean up pollution.

Many people with a biochemistry background become professors and teachers. For more information, see the profile on postsecondary teachers.

Work Environment

Biochemists and biophysicists held about 34,600 jobs in 2019. The largest employers of biochemists and biophysicists were as follows:

Pharmaceutical and medicine manufacturing	10%
Colleges, universities, and professional schools; state, local, and private	8
Management, scientific, and technical consulting services	3
Wholesale trade	3

Biochemists and biophysicists typically work in laboratories and offices, to conduct experiments and analyze the results. Those who work with dangerous organisms or toxic substances in the laboratory must follow safety procedures to avoid contamination.

Most biochemists and biophysicists work on teams. Research projects are often interdisciplinary, and biochemists and biophysicists frequently work with experts in other fields, such as physics, chemistry, computer science, and engineering. Those working in biological research generate large amounts of data. They collaborate with specialists called *bioinformaticians*, who use their knowledge of statistics, math, engineering, and

Most biochemists and biophysicists work in laboratories.

computer science to mine datasets for correlations that might explain biological phenomena.

Some biotech companies need researchers to help sell their products. These products often rely on very complex technologies, and having an expert explain them to potential customers might be necessary. This role for researchers may be more common in smaller companies, where workers often fulfill multiple roles, such as working in research and in sales. Working in sales may require a substantial amount of travel. For more information on sales representatives, see the profile on wholesale and manufacturing sales representatives.

Work Schedules

Most biochemists and biophysicists work full time and keep regular hours. They may have to work additional hours to meet project deadlines or to perform time-sensitive laboratory experiments.

How to Become a Biochemist or Biophysicist

Biochemists and biophysicists need a Ph.D. to work in independent research-and-development positions. Most Ph.D. holders begin their careers in temporary postdoctoral research positions. Bachelor's and master's degree holders are qualified for some entry-level positions in biochemistry and biophysics.

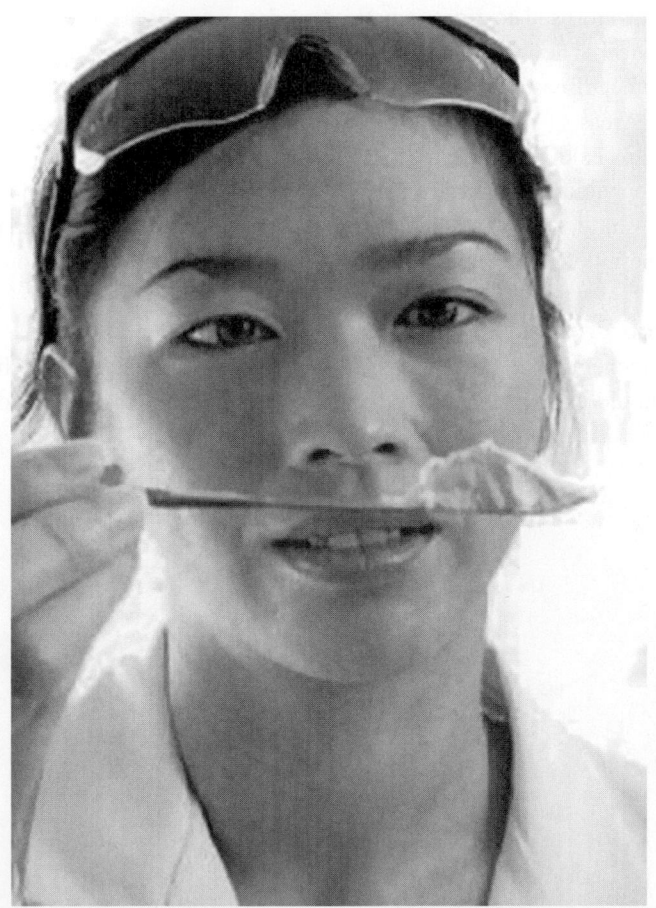

Biochemists and biophysicists need a Ph.D. to work in independent research and development positions.

Education

Most Ph.D. holders in biochemistry and biophysics have bachelor's degrees in biochemistry or a related field, such as biology, chemistry, physics, or engineering. High school students can prepare for college by taking classes related to the natural and physical sciences, as well as math and computer science.

Students in bachelor's degree programs in biochemistry or a related field typically take courses in math, physics, and computer science in addition to courses in the biological and chemical sciences. Courses in math and computer science are important for biochemists and biophysicists, who must be able to do complex data analysis. Most bachelor's degree programs include required laboratory coursework. Additional laboratory coursework is excellent preparation for graduate school or for getting an entry-level position in industry. Students can gain valuable laboratory experience by working for a university's laboratories. Occasionally, they can also gain such experience through internships with prospective employers, such as pharmaceutical and medicine manufacturers.

Ph.D. programs typically include advanced coursework in topics such as toxicology, genetics, and proteomics (the study of proteins). Several graduate programs include courses in bioinformatics, which involves using computers to study and analyze large amounts of biological data. Graduate students also spend a lot of time conducting laboratory research. Study at the master's level is generally considered good preparation for those interested in doing hands-on laboratory work. Ph.D.-level studies provide additional training in the planning and execution of research projects.

Training

Many biochemistry and biophysics Ph.D. holders begin their careers in temporary postdoctoral research positions. During their postdoctoral appointments, they work with experienced scientists as they continue to learn about their specialties or develop a broader understanding of related areas of research.

Postdoctoral positions frequently offer the opportunity to publish research findings. A solid record of published research is essential to getting a permanent college or university faculty position.

Important Qualities

Analytical skills. Biochemists and biophysicists must be able to conduct scientific experiments and analyses with accuracy and precision.

Communication skills. Biochemists and biophysicists have to write and publish reports and research papers, give presentations of their findings, and communicate clearly with team members.

Critical-thinking skills. Biochemists and biophysicists draw conclusions from experimental results through sound reasoning and judgment.

Interpersonal skills. Biochemists and biophysicists typically work on interdisciplinary research teams and need to work well

Biochemists and Biophysicists
Median annual wages, May 2019

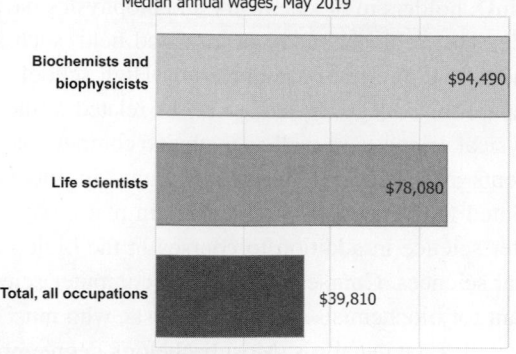

Note: All Occupations includes all occupations in the U.S. Economy.
Source: U.S. Bureau of Labor Statistics, Occupational Employment
Statistics.

with others toward a common goal. Many serve as team leaders and must be able to motivate and direct other team members.

Math skills. Biochemists and biophysicists use complex equations and formulas regularly in their work. They need a broad understanding of math, including calculus and statistics.

Perseverance. Biochemists and biophysicists need to be thorough in their research and in their approach to problems. Scientific research involves substantial trial and error, and biochemists and biophysicists must not become discouraged in their work.

Problem-solving skills. Biochemists and biophysicists use scientific experiments and analysis to find solutions to complex scientific problems.

Time-management skills. Biochemists and biophysicists usually need to meet deadlines when conducting research. They must be able to manage time and prioritize tasks efficiently while maintaining their quality of work.

Advancement

Some biochemists and biophysicists become natural sciences managers. Those who pursue management careers spend much of their time on administrative tasks, such as preparing budgets and schedules.

Pay

The median annual wage for biochemists and biophysicists was $94,490 in May 2019. The median wage is the wage at which half the workers in an occupation earned more than that amount and half earned less. The lowest 10 percent earned less than $50,620, and the highest 10 percent earned more than $182,870.

In May 2019, the median annual wages for biochemists and biophysicists in the top industries in which they worked were as follows:

Wholesale trade	$120,240
Management, scientific, and technical consulting services	94,090

Pharmaceutical and medicine manufacturing	78,820
Colleges, universities, and professional schools; state, local, and private	57,060

Most biochemists and biophysicists work full time and keep regular hours. They may have to work additional hours to meet project deadlines or to perform time-sensitive laboratory experiments.

Job Outlook

Employment of biochemists and biophysicists is projected to grow 4 percent from 2019 to 2029, about as fast as the average for all occupations. Biochemists and biophysicists will continue to be needed to do basic research that increases scientific knowledge and to research and develop biological products and processes that improve people's lives. Techniques, tools, and applications of biochemistry and biophysics are expanding as technology and knowledge progress. However, budgetary concerns may limit researchers' access to funding for basic research.

The aging population will drive demand for new drugs and procedures to cure and to prevent disease. This increased demand is, in turn, likely to drive demand for biochemists and biophysicists involved in biomedical research. For example, biochemists and biophysicists will be needed to conduct genetic research and to develop new medicines and treatments that are used to fight genetic disorders and diseases such as cancer. They will also be needed to develop new tests used to detect diseases and other illnesses.

Areas of research and development in biotechnology other than health also are expected to provide employment growth for biochemists and biophysicists. These researchers will continue to study topics that advance our capabilities related to clean energy, efficient food production, and environmental protection.

Job Prospects

Biochemists and biophysicists involved in basic research should expect strong competition for permanent research and

Biochemists and Biophysicists
Percent change in employment, projected 2019-29

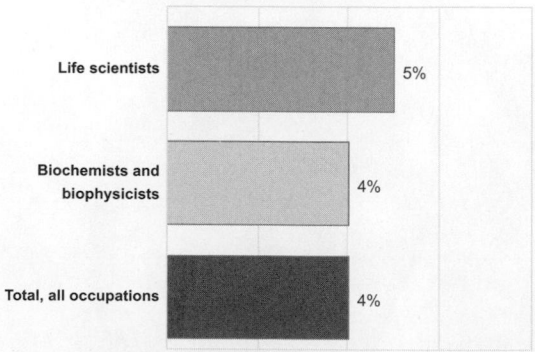

Note: All Occupations includes all occupations in the U.S. Economy.
Source: U.S. Bureau of Labor Statistics, Employment Projections
program.

faculty positions at colleges and universities. Biochemists and biophysicists with postdoctoral experience who have had research articles published in scientific journals should have the best prospects for these positions. Many biochemists and biophysicists work through multiple postdoctoral appointments before getting a permanent position in academia.

A portion of basic research in biochemistry and biophysics is dependent on funding from the federal government through the National Institutes of Health and the National Science Foundation. Therefore, changes in the federal budget will affect job prospects in basic research. Typically, there is strong competition among biochemists and biophysicists for research funding.

Biochemists and biophysicists tend to be interdisciplinary themselves but also require the expertise of scientists in multiple fields, such as microbiology, medicine, and chemistry. Biochemists and biophysicists who have a broad understanding of multiple disciplines, including math and computer science, should have the best job opportunities.

Candidates who gain laboratory experience through coursework or employment during their undergraduate studies will be the best prepared and have the best chances of gaining employment or entering graduate-level programs.

Employment projections data for biochemists and biophysicists, 2019-29					
Occupational Title	SOC Code	Employment, 2019	Projected Employment, 2029	Change, 2019-29	
				Percent	Numeric
SOURCE: U.S. Bureau of Labor Statistics, Employment Projections program					
Biochemists and biophysicists	19-1021	34,600	36,000	4	1,400

State & Area Data
Occupational Employment Statistics (OES)
The Occupational Employment Statistics (OES) program produces employment and wage estimates annually for over 800 occupations. These estimates are available for the nation as a whole, for individual states, and for metropolitan and nonmetropolitan areas.

Contacts for More Information
For more information about biochemists, visit
➤ American Chemical Society
➤ American Chemical Society, Division of Biological Chemistry
➤ American Society for Biochemistry and Molecular Biology
➤ International Union of Biochemistry and Molecular Biology

For more information about biophysicists, visit
➤ Biophysical Society
➤ International Union for Pure and Applied Biophysics

For general information about careers in biological sciences, visit
➤ American Institute of Biological Sciences
➤ Federation of American Societies for Experimental Biology

For information about grants and funding for healthcare-related research, visit
➤ National Institutes of Health

Biological Technicians

Summary

Quick Facts: Biological Technicians

2019 Median Pay	$45,860 per year $22.05 per hour
Typical Entry-Level Education	Bachelor's degree
Work Experience in a Related Occupation	None
On-the-job Training	None
Number of Jobs, 2019	87,500
Job Outlook, 2019-29	5% (Faster than average)
Employment Change, 2019-29	4,300

What Biological Technicians Do
Biological technicians help biological and medical scientists conduct laboratory tests and experiments.

Work Environment
Biological technicians typically work in laboratories. Most biological technicians work full time.

How to Become a Biological Technician
Biological technicians typically need a bachelor's degree in biology or a closely related field. It is important for prospective biological technicians to gain laboratory experience while in school.

Pay
The median annual wage for biological technicians was $45,860 in May 2019.

Job Outlook
Employment of biological technicians is projected to grow 5 percent from 2019 to 2029, faster than the average for all

Biological technicians gather and prepare biological samples for laboratory analysis.

occupations. Continued growth in biotechnology and medical research is expected to increase demand for these workers.

State & Area Data

Explore resources for employment and wages by state and area for biological technicians.

What Biological Technicians Do

Biological technicians help biological and medical scientists conduct laboratory tests and experiments.

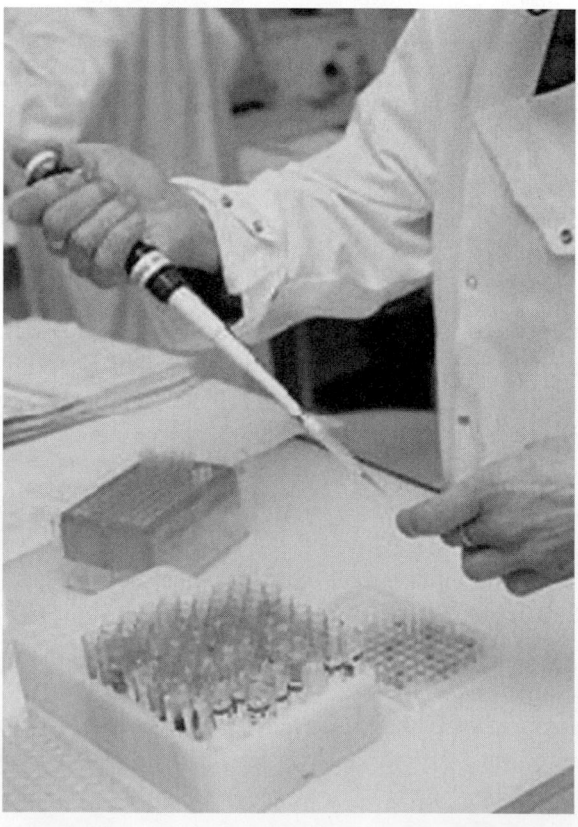

Biological technicians prepare samples for further testing.

Duties

Biological technicians typically do the following:

- Set up, maintain, and clean laboratory instruments and equipment, such as microscopes, scales, pipets, and test tubes
- Gather and prepare biological samples, such as blood, food, and bacteria cultures, for laboratory analysis
- Conduct biological tests and experiments
- Document their work, including procedures, observations, and results
- Analyze experimental data and interpret results
- Write reports that summarize their findings

Biological technicians, sometimes called *laboratory assistants*, typically are responsible for doing scientific tests, experiments, and analyses under the supervision of biologists (such as microbiologists) or medical scientists who direct and evaluate their work. Biological technicians use traditional laboratory instruments, advanced robotics, and automated equipment to conduct experiments. They use specialized computer software to collect, analyze, and model experimental data. Some biological technicians, such as those who assist the work of zoologists and wildlife biologists, may collect samples in the field, so they may need the ability to hike rugged terrain or otherwise travel through wilderness areas.

Biological technicians work in many research areas. They may assist medical researchers by administering new medicines and treatments to laboratory animals. They may separate proteins from other cell material, and analyze data from an experiment.

Biological technicians working in a microbiological context typically study living microbes and perform techniques specific to microbiology, such as staining specimens to aid identification.

Biological technicians also may work in private industry and assist in the study of a wide range of topics concerning industrial production. They may test samples in environmental impact studies, or monitor production processes to help ensure that products are not contaminated.

Work Environment

Biological technicians held about 87,500 jobs in 2019. The largest employers of biological technicians were as follows:

Research and development in the physical, engineering, and life sciences	32%
Colleges, universities, and professional schools; state, local, and private	27
Hospitals; state, local, and private	10
Federal government, excluding postal service	8
Pharmaceutical and medicine manufacturing	5

Biological technicians typically work in laboratories and offices, where they conduct experiments and analyze the results under the supervision of biological scientists and medical scientists. Some biological technicians who do fieldwork may be exposed to weather events and wildlife, such as mosquitoes.

Biological technicians must follow strict procedures to avoid contaminating the experiment, themselves, or the environment. Some experiments may involve dangerous organisms or toxic substances.

Biological technicians work together on teams under the direction of biologists or other scientists.

Work Schedules

Most biological technicians work full time and keep regular hours.

How to Become a Biological Technician

Biological technicians typically need a bachelor's degree in biology or a closely related field. Although it is less common, some positions may be available to those with less than a bachelor's degree. It is important for prospective biological technicians to gain laboratory experience while they are in school.

Education

Biological technicians typically need a bachelor's degree in biology or a closely related field. Most colleges and universities offer bachelor's degree programs in the biological sciences. Some positions may be available to associate's degree holders or those without a degree but who have biological laboratory experience.

Most biological technicians work in laboratories.

Biological science programs usually include courses in general biology, as well as in specific subfields such as ecology, microbiology, and physiology. In addition to taking courses in biology, students must study chemistry, math, and physics. Computer science courses are helpful for learning how to model and simulate biological processes and for learning how to operate some laboratory equipment.

Laboratory experience is important for prospective biological technicians, so students should take biology courses that emphasize laboratory work.

Other Experience

Prospective biological technicians should have laboratory experience. In addition to coursework, students may gain laboratory experience during summer internships with prospective employers, such as pharmaceutical and medicine manufacturers, or in university laboratories.

Advancement

Biological technicians may advance to scientist positions, such as microbiologist or biochemist and biophysicist, after a few years of experience working as a technician or after earning a master's degree or Ph.D. Gaining more experience and higher levels of education often allows biological technicians to move into positions such as natural sciences managers or postsecondary teachers.

Important Qualities

Analytical skills. Biological technicians need to conduct scientific experiments and analyses with accuracy and precision.

Communication skills. Biological technicians must understand and follow the instructions of their managing scientists. They also need to communicate their processes and findings clearly in written reports.

Critical-thinking skills. Biological technicians draw conclusions from experimental results through sound reasoning and judgment.

Most biological technicians gain laboratory experience while in school.

Biological Technicians
Median annual wages, May 2019

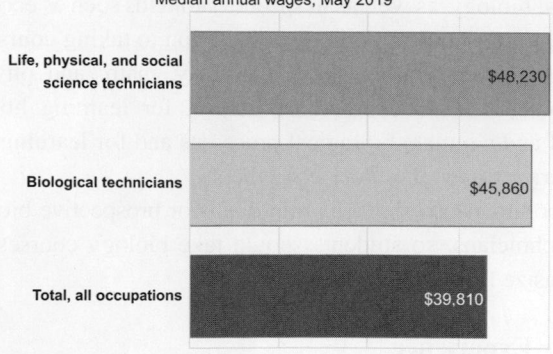

Life, physical, and social science technicians	$48,230
Biological technicians	$45,860
Total, all occupations	$39,810

Note: All Occupations includes all occupations in the U.S. Economy.
Source: U.S. Bureau of Labor Statistics, Occupational Employment Statistics.

Observational skills. Biological technicians must constantly monitor their experiments. They need to keep a complete, accurate record of their work, including the conditions under which the experiment was carried out, the procedures they followed, and the results they obtained.

Technical skills. Biological technicians need to set up and operate sophisticated equipment and instruments. They also may need to adjust equipment to ensure that experiments are conducted properly.

Pay

The median annual wage for biological technicians was $45,860 in May 2019. The median wage is the wage at which half the workers in an occupation earned more than that amount and half earned less. The lowest 10 percent earned less than $29,540, and the highest 10 percent earned more than $73,350.

In May 2019, the median annual wages for biological technicians in the top industries in which they worked were as follows:

Pharmaceutical and medicine manufacturing	$51,100
Research and development in the physical, engineering, and life sciences	48,210
Hospitals; state, local, and private	47,400
Colleges, universities, and professional schools; state, local, and private...	44,480
Federal government, excluding postal service	43,430

Most biological technicians work full time and keep regular hours.

Job Outlook

Employment of biological technicians is projected to grow 5 percent from 2019 to 2029, faster than the average for all occupations. Greater demand for biological and medical research is expected to increase the need for these workers.

Biotechnology research plays a key role in scientific advancements that improve people's quality of life. One new area of biotechnology, synthetic biology, will employ biological

Biological Technicians
Percent change in employment, projected 2019-29

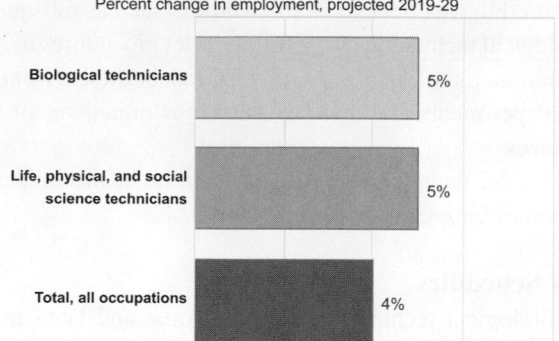

Biological technicians	5%
Life, physical, and social science technicians	5%
Total, all occupations	4%

Note: All Occupations includes all occupations in the U.S. Economy.
Source: U.S. Bureau of Labor Statistics, Employment Projections program.

technicians in attempts to redesign biological systems or living organisms to produce useful things, such as chemicals, in more efficient ways than are currently used. New applications of biotechnology may be the subject of research topics ranging from new ways to produce biofuels to providing new treatments for diseases, such as cancer and Alzheimer's disease.

Job Prospects

Applicants who have laboratory experience, either through coursework or through previous work experience, should have the best opportunities.

Employment projections data for biological technicians, 2019-29					
Occupational Title	SOC Code	Employment, 2019	Projected Employment, 2029	Change, 2019-29	
				Percent	Numeric
SOURCE: U.S. Bureau of Labor Statistics, Employment Projections program					
Biological technicians	19-4021	87,500	91,800	5	4,300

State & Area Data
Occupational Employment Statistics (OES)

The Occupational Employment Statistics (OES) program produces employment and wage estimates annually for over 800 occupations. These estimates are available for the nation as a whole, for individual states, and for metropolitan and nonmetropolitan areas.

Contacts for More Information

For more information about career opportunities in the biological sciences, visit
➤ American Institute of Biological Sciences
➤ American Society for Cell Biology
➤ American Society for Microbiology
➤ DIYbio
➤ Federation of American Societies for Experimental Biology

To find job openings for biological technicians in the federal government, visit
➤ USAJOBS

Chemical Technicians

Summary

Quick Facts: Chemical Technicians

2019 Median Pay	$49,260 per year $23.68 per hour
Typical Entry-Level Education	Associate's degree
Work Experience in a Related Occupation	None
On-the-job Training	Moderate-term on-the-job training
Number of Jobs, 2019..............................	68,100
Job Outlook, 2019-29..............................	3% (As fast as average)
Employment Change, 2019-29	1,900

What Chemical Technicians Do

Chemical technicians use special instruments and techniques to assist chemists and chemical engineers.

Work Environment

Technicians typically work in laboratories, where they conduct experiments, or in manufacturing facilities, such as chemical or pharmaceutical manufacturing plants, where they monitor production processes. Most technicians work full time.

How to Become a Chemical Technician

Chemical technicians need an associate's degree or 2 years of postsecondary education for most jobs. Most chemical technicians receive on-the-job training.

Pay

The median annual wage for chemical technicians was $49,260 in May 2019.

Job Outlook

Employment of chemical technicians is projected to grow 3 percent from 2019 to 2029, about as fast as the average for all occupations. Graduates of applied science technology programs who are trained to use equipment typically found in laboratories or production facilities should have the best opportunities.

State & Area Data

Explore resources for employment and wages by state and area for chemical technicians.

What Chemical Technicians Do

Chemical technicians use laboratory instruments and techniques to help chemists and chemical engineers research, develop, produce, and test chemical products and processes.

Duties

Chemical technicians typically do the following:

- Monitor chemical processes and test the quality of products to make sure that they meet standards and specifications
- Set up and maintain laboratory instruments and equipment
- Troubleshoot production problems or malfunctioning instruments
- Prepare chemical solutions
- Conduct, compile, and interpret results of chemical and physical experiments, tests, and analyses for a variety of purposes, including research and development
- Prepare technical reports, graphs, and charts, and give presentations that summarize their results

Most chemical technicians work on teams. Typically, they are led by chemists or chemical engineers who direct their work and evaluate their results. However, they may serve as mentors to chemists who are new to a lab or to a specialized area of research.

Chemical technicians often use laboratory equipment to help chemists and chemical engineers test chemical products.

Chemical technicians monitor and adjust processing equipment at manufacturing facilities.

Technicians who work in laboratories may help conduct experiments that contribute to research and development. For example, some chemical technicians help chemists and other scientists develop new medicines. In this way, chemical technicians often bridge the gap in knowledge remaining when a chemist moves on to a new assignment.

Other chemical technicians work in manufacturing and assist in developing more efficient production processes.

Work Environment

Chemical technicians held about 68,100 jobs in 2019. The largest employers of chemical technicians were as follows:

Testing laboratories	17%
Pharmaceutical and medicine manufacturing	8
Wholesale trade	4
Colleges, universities, and professional schools; state, local, and private	3

Chemical technicians typically work in laboratories or in industrial facilities such as chemical and pharmaceutical manufacturing plants.

Injuries and Illnesses

Chemical technicians can be exposed to health or safety hazards when handling certain chemicals and plant equipment, but there is little risk if proper procedures are followed.

Work Schedules

Most technicians work full time. Occasionally, they may have to work additional hours to meet project deadlines or troubleshoot problems with manufacturing processes. Some may work irregular hours to monitor laboratory experiments or plant operations.

How to Become a Chemical Technician

Chemical technicians need an associate's degree or 2 years of postsecondary education for most jobs. Most chemical technicians also receive on-the-job training.

Chemical technicians typically work in laboratories or in industrial facilities.

Education

For most jobs, chemical technicians need an associate's degree in applied science or chemical technology or 2 years of postsecondary education.

Many technical and community colleges offer programs in applied sciences or chemical technology. Students typically take classes in math, physics, and biology, in addition to chemistry courses. Coursework in statistics and computer science is also useful because technicians routinely do data analysis and modeling.

One of the most important aspects of any degree program is laboratory time because it provides students with hands-on practice in conducting experiments and using various instruments and techniques properly. Many schools also offer internships and cooperative-education programs that help students gain employment experience while attending school.

Important Qualities

Ability to use technology. Chemical technicians must set up, operate, troubleshoot, and repair sophisticated equipment and instruments. They also may need to adjust the equipment to ensure that experiments and processes are running properly and safely.

Analytical skills. Chemical technicians must conduct scientific experiments with accuracy and precision.

Communication skills. Chemical technicians must explain their work to scientists and engineers, and to workers who may not have a technical background. They often write reports to communicate their results.

Critical-thinking skills. Chemical technicians reach their conclusions through sound reasoning and judgment.

Interpersonal skills. Chemical technicians must work well with others as part of a team because they often work with scientists, engineers, and other technicians.

Observation skills. Chemical technicians must carefully monitor chemical experiments and processes to note any unusual or unexpected results observed during an experiment.

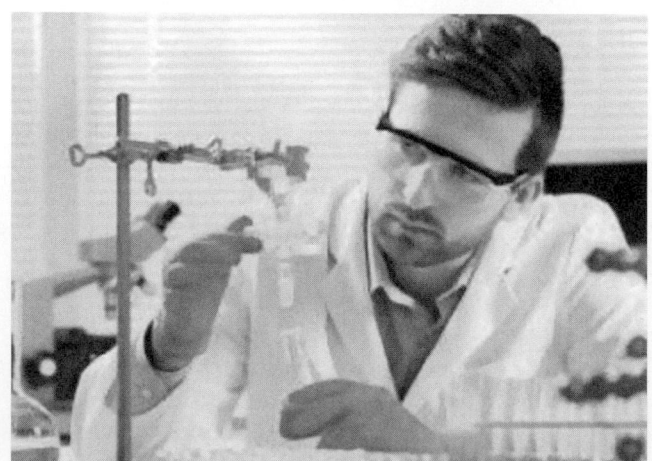

Laboratory experience provides students with hands-on experience in using various instruments and techniques properly.

They must keep complete records of their work, including conditions and procedures.

Time-management skills. Chemical technicians often work on multiple tasks and projects at the same time and must prioritize their assignments.

Training

Most chemical technicians receive on-the-job training. Typically, experienced technicians teach new employees proper methods and procedures for conducting experiments and operating equipment. The length of training varies with the new employee's level of experience and education, and the industry the worker is employed in.

Advancement

Technicians who have a bachelor's degree may advance to positions as chemical engineers or chemists.

Pay

The median annual wage for chemical technicians was $49,260 in May 2019. The median wage is the wage at which half the workers in an occupation earned more than that amount and half earned less. The lowest 10 percent earned less than $31,110, and the highest 10 percent earned more than $80,350.

In May 2019, the median annual wages for chemical technicians in the top industries in which they worked were as follows:

Colleges, universities, and professional schools; state, local, and private	$49,220
Pharmaceutical and medicine manufacturing	48,140
Wholesale trade	47,780
Testing laboratories	39,820

Most technicians work full time. Occasionally, they may have to work additional hours to meet project deadlines or troubleshoot problems with manufacturing processes. Some may work irregular hours to monitor laboratory experiments or plant operations.

Job Outlook

Employment of chemical technicians is projected to grow 3 percent from 2019 to 2029, about as fast as the average for all occupations. Many chemical technicians are employed in manufacturing industries that are projected to decline.

However, chemical technicians will continue to be in demand in testing laboratories to test new materials and products developed by chemists and chemical engineers. They will also be needed in scientific research and development (R&D) and to monitor the quality of chemical products and processes. Greater interest in environmental issues, such as pollution control, clean energy, and sustainability, is expected to increase the demand for chemistry R&D.

Job Prospects

As the instrumentation and techniques used in research, development, and production become more complex, employers will seek candidates with highly developed technical skills. Job opportunities are expected to be best for graduates of applied science technology programs who are well trained in the latest technology and sophisticated equipment used in laboratories or production facilities.

Employment projections data for chemical technicians, 2019-29					
Occupational Title	SOC Code	Employment, 2019	Projected Employment, 2029	Change, 2019-29	
				Percent	Numeric
SOURCE: U.S. Bureau of Labor Statistics, Employment Projections program					
Chemical technicians	19-4031	68,100	70,000	3	1,900

State & Area Data
Occupational Employment Statistics (OES)

The Occupational Employment Statistics (OES) program produces employment and wage estimates annually for over

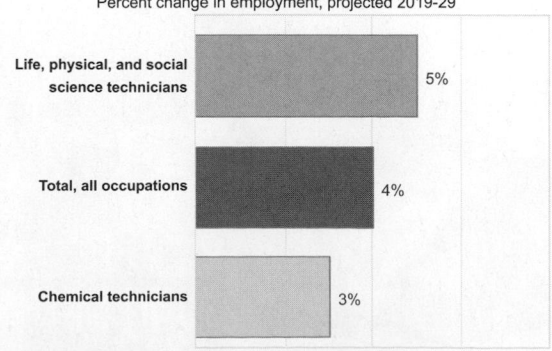

Chemical Technicians
Median annual wages, May 2019

- Chemical technicians: $49,260
- Life, physical, and social science technicians: $48,230
- Total, all occupations: $39,810

Note: All Occupations includes all occupations in the U.S. Economy.
Source: U.S. Bureau of Labor Statistics, Occupational Employment Statistics.

Chemical Technicians
Percent change in employment, projected 2019-29

- Life, physical, and social science technicians: 5%
- Total, all occupations: 4%
- Chemical technicians: 3%

Note: All Occupations includes all occupations in the U.S. Economy.
Source: U.S. Bureau of Labor Statistics, Employment Projections program.

800 occupations. These estimates are available for the nation as a whole, for individual states, and for metropolitan and nonmetropolitan areas.

Contacts for More Information

For more information about chemical technicians, visit

➤ American Chemical Society
➤ American Chemistry Council

Chemists and Materials Scientists

Summary

Quick Facts: Chemists and Materials Scientists

2019 Median Pay	$78,790 per year
	$37.88 per hour
Typical Entry-Level Education	Bachelor's degree
Work Experience in a Related Occupation	None
On-the-job Training	None
Number of Jobs, 2019	93,700
Job Outlook, 2019-29	5% (Faster than average)
Employment Change, 2019-29	4,300

What Chemists and Materials Scientists Do

Chemists and materials scientists study substances at the atomic and molecular levels and analyze the ways in which the substances interact with one another.

Work Environment

Chemists and materials scientists work in laboratories and offices. They typically work full time and keep regular hours.

How to Become a Chemist or Materials Scientist

Chemists and materials scientists need at least a bachelor's degree in chemistry or a related field. However, a master's degree or Ph.D. is needed for many research jobs.

Pay

The median annual wage for chemists was $77,630 in May 2019.

The median annual wage for materials scientists was $96,810 in May 2019.

Job Outlook

Overall employment of chemists and materials scientists is projected to grow 5 percent from 2019 to 2029, faster than the average for all occupations. Chemists and materials scientists who have an advanced degree, particularly a Ph.D., are expected to have the best opportunities.

State & Area Data

Explore resources for employment and wages by state and area for chemists and materials scientists.

What Chemists and Materials Scientists Do

Chemists and materials scientists study substances at the atomic and molecular levels and analyze the ways in which the substances interact with one another. They use their knowledge to develop new and improved products and to test the quality of manufactured goods.

Duties

Chemists and materials scientists typically do the following:

- Plan and carry out complex research projects, such as the development of new products and testing methods

Chemists and materials scientists perform experiments that require creative problem solving and detailed recordkeeping.

Most chemists and materials scientists work as part of a team.

- Instruct scientists and technicians on proper chemical processing and testing procedures, including ingredients, mixing times, and operating temperatures
- Prepare solutions, compounds, and reagents used in laboratory procedures
- Analyze substances to determine their composition and concentration of elements
- Conduct tests on materials and other substances to ensure that safety and quality standards are met
- Write technical reports that detail methods and findings
- Present research findings to scientists, engineers, and other colleagues

Some chemists and materials scientists work in basic research. Others work in applied research. In basic research, chemists investigate the properties, composition, and structure of matter. They also experiment with combinations of elements and the ways in which they interact. In applied research, chemists investigate possible new products and ways to improve existing ones. Chemistry research has led to the discovery and development of new and improved drugs, plastics, fertilizers, flavors, batteries, and cleaners, as well as thousands of other products.

Materials scientists study the structures and chemical properties of various materials to develop new products or enhance existing ones. They determine ways to strengthen or combine existing materials, or develop new materials for use in a variety of products. Applications of materials science include inventing or improving ceramics, plastics/polymers, metallic alloys, and superconducting materials.

Chemists and materials scientists use computers and a wide variety of sophisticated laboratory instrumentation for modeling, simulation, and experimental analysis. For example, some chemists use three-dimensional computer modeling software to study the structure and properties of complex molecules.

If a chemist specializes in green chemistry, he or she will design chemical processes and products that are environmentally sustainable. Green chemistry processes minimize the creation of toxins and waste.

Most chemists and materials scientists work as part of a team. The number of scientific research projects that involve multiple disciplines is increasing, and it is common for chemists and materials scientists to work on teams with other scientists, such as biologists, physicists, computer specialists, and engineers. For example, in pharmaceutical research, chemists may work with biologists to develop new drugs and with engineers to design ways to mass-produce the new drugs. For more information, see the profiles on biochemists and biophysicists, microbiologists, zoologists and wildlife biologists, physicists and astronomers, computer and information technology occupations, and engineering occupations.

Because chemists and materials scientists typically work on research teams, they need to be able to work well with others toward a common goal. Many serve in a leadership capacity and need to be able to motivate and direct other team members.

Chemists often specialize in a particular branch of the field. The following are examples of types of chemists:

Analytical chemists determine the structure, composition, and nature of substances by examining and identifying their various elements or compounds. They also study the relationships and interactions among the parts of compounds. Some analytical chemists specialize in developing new methods of analysis and new techniques for carrying out their work. Their research has a wide range of applications, including food safety, pharmaceuticals, and pollution control.

Forensic chemists analyze evidence for clues to help solve crimes. These chemists aid in criminal investigations by testing evidence, such as DNA, and interpreting their findings. Not only is human DNA evidence tested; DNA evidence can be used to exonerate animals suspected of having killed people or other animals. These chemists work primarily in laboratories, though they sometimes testify in court.

Inorganic chemists study the structure, properties, and reactions of molecules that do not contain carbon, such as metals. They work to understand the behavior and the characteristics of inorganic substances. Inorganic chemists figure out how these materials, such as ceramics and superconductors, can be modified, separated, or used in products.

Medicinal chemists research and develop chemical compounds that can be used as pharmaceutical drugs. They work on teams with other scientists and engineers to create and test new drug products. They also help develop new and improved manufacturing processes to effectively produce new drugs on a large scale.

Organic chemists study the structure, properties, and reactions of molecules that contain carbon. They also design and make new organic substances that have unique properties and applications. These compounds, in turn, have been used to develop many commercial products, such as pharmaceutical drugs and plastics.

Physical chemists study the fundamental characteristics of how matter behaves on a molecular and atomic level and how chemical reactions occur. From their analyses, physical chemists may develop new theories, such as how complex structures are formed. Physical chemists often work closely with materials scientists, to research and develop potential uses for new materials.

Theoretical chemists investigate theoretical methods that can predict the outcomes of chemical experiments. Theoretical chemistry encompasses a variety of specializations, although most specializations incorporate advanced computation and programming. Some examples of *theoretical chemists* are *computational chemists*, *mathematical chemists*, and *chemical informaticians*.

Materials scientists tend to specialize by the material they work with most often. A few examples of materials in which these scientists specialize are ceramics, glasses, metals, nanomaterials (extremely small substances), polymers, and semiconductors.

A growing number of chemists work in interdisciplinary fields, such as biochemistry and geochemistry. For more information, see the profiles on biochemists and biophysicists and geoscientists.

Many people with a chemistry background become postsecondary teachers or high school teachers.

Work Environment

Chemists held about 86,700 jobs in 2019. The largest employers of chemists were as follows:

Chemical manufacturing	33%
Research and development in the physical, engineering, and life sciences	14
Testing laboratories	10
Federal government, excluding postal service	7
Administrative and support and waste management and remediation services	4

Materials scientists held about 7,000 jobs in 2019. The largest employers of materials scientists were as follows:

Research and development in the physical, engineering, and life sciences	23%
Chemical manufacturing	13
Management of companies and enterprises	11
Computer and electronic product manufacturing	9
Architectural, engineering, and related services	8

Chemists and materials scientists typically work in laboratories and offices, where they conduct experiments and analyze their results. In addition to working in laboratories, materials scientists work with engineers and processing specialists in industrial manufacturing facilities. Some chemists also work in these facilities and usually are responsible for monitoring the environmental conditions at the plant.

Chemists and materials scientists who work for manufacturing companies may have to travel occasionally, especially if their company has multiple facilities. Others may work outdoors to collect samples and conduct onsite analysis of air, soil, or water.

Injuries and Illnesses

Chemists and materials scientists may be exposed to health or safety hazards when handling certain chemicals, but there is little risk if they follow proper procedures, such as wearing protective clothing when handling hazardous chemicals.

Work Schedules

Chemists and materials scientists typically work full time and keep regular hours. Occasionally, they may have to work additional hours to meet project deadlines or perform time-sensitive laboratory experiments during off-hours.

How to Become a Chemist or Materials Scientist

Chemists and materials scientists need at least a bachelor's degree in chemistry or a related field. However, a master's degree or Ph.D. is required for many research jobs.

Education

A bachelor's degree in chemistry or a related field is needed for entry-level chemist or materials scientist jobs. Research jobs require a master's degree or a Ph.D. and also may require significant levels of work experience. Chemists and materials scientists with a Ph.D. and postdoctoral experience typically lead basic- or applied-research teams. Combined programs, which offer an accelerated bachelor's and master's degree in chemistry, also are available.

Many colleges and universities offer degree programs in chemistry that are approved by the American Chemical Society.

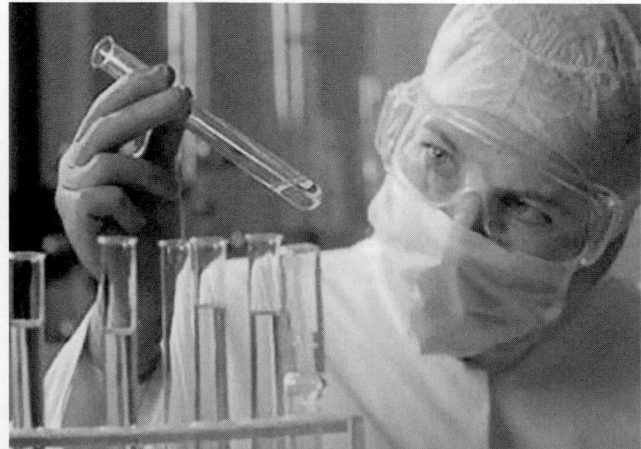

Chemists must wear protective clothing such as gloves and goggles when handling hazardous chemicals.

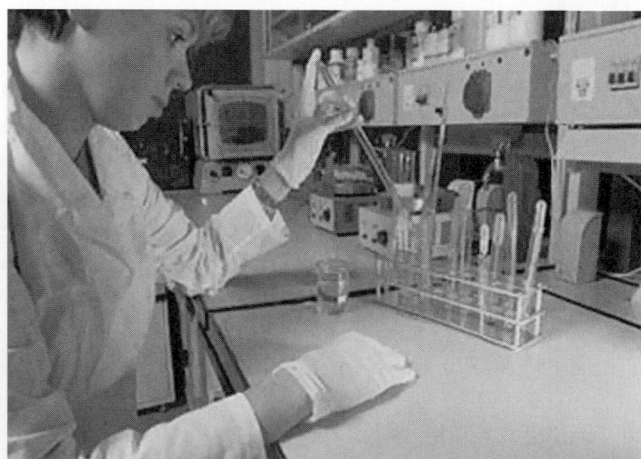

Laboratory experience through internships, fellowships, or work–study programs in industry is useful.

Some colleges offer materials science as a specialization within their chemistry programs, and some engineering schools offer degrees in the joint field of materials science and engineering. High school students can prepare for college coursework by taking chemistry, math, and computer science classes.

Undergraduate chemistry majors typically are required to take courses in analytical, organic, inorganic, and physical chemistry. In addition, they take classes in math, biological sciences, and physics. Computer science courses are essential because chemists and materials scientists need computer skills to perform modeling and simulation tasks, manage and manipulate databases, and operate computerized laboratory equipment.

Laboratory experience through internships, fellowships, or work–study programs in industry is also useful. Some universities offer cooperative programs in which students gain work experience while pursuing a degree.

Graduate students studying chemistry commonly specialize in a subfield, such as analytical chemistry or inorganic chemistry. For example, those interested in doing research in the pharmaceutical industry usually develop a strong background in medicinal or organic chemistry.

Important Qualities

Analytical skills. Chemists and materials scientists carry out scientific experiments and studies. They must be precise and accurate in their analyses because errors could invalidate their research.

Communication skills. Chemists and materials scientists need to communicate clearly with team members and other scientists. They must read and write technical reports and give presentations.

Interpersonal skills. Chemists and materials scientists typically work on interdisciplinary research teams and need to work well with others toward a common goal. Many serve as team leaders and must motivate and direct other team members.

Math skills. Chemists and materials scientists regularly use complex mathematical equations and formulas, and they need a broad understanding of math, including calculus, algebra, and statistics.

Organizational skills. Chemists and materials scientists need to document processes carefully in order to conform to regulations and industry procedures. Disorganization in the workplace can lead to legal problems, damage to equipment, and chemical spills.

Perseverance. Scientific research involves substantial trial and error, and chemists and materials scientists must not become discouraged in their work.

Problem-solving skills. Chemists and materials scientists research and develop new and improved chemical products, processes, and materials. This work requires a great deal of trial and error on the part of chemists and materials scientists before a unique solution is found.

Time-management skills. Chemists and materials scientists usually need to meet deadlines when conducting research. They must be able to manage time and prioritize tasks efficiently while maintaining their quality of work.

Advancement

Chemists typically receive greater responsibility and independence in their work as they gain experience. Greater responsibility also is gained through further education. Ph.D. chemists usually lead research teams and have control over the direction and content of projects, but even Ph.D. holders have room to advance as they gain experience. As chemists become more proficient in managing research projects, they may take on larger, more complicated, and more expensive projects.

Some chemists and materials scientists become natural sciences managers.

Pay

The median annual wage for chemists was $77,630 in May 2019. The median wage is the wage at which half the workers in an occupation earned more than that amount and half earned less. The lowest 10 percent earned less than $44,460, and the highest 10 percent earned more than $133,690.

The median annual wage for materials scientists was $96,810 in May 2019. The lowest 10 percent earned less than $51,950, and the highest 10 percent earned more than $157,780.

In May 2019, the median annual wages for chemists in the top industries in which they worked were as follows:

Federal government, excluding postal service	$111,840
Research and development in the physical, engineering, and life sciences	90,290
Chemical manufacturing	75,510
Administrative and support and waste management and remediation services	67,280
Testing laboratories	59,540

Chemists and Materials Scientists
Median annual wages, May 2019

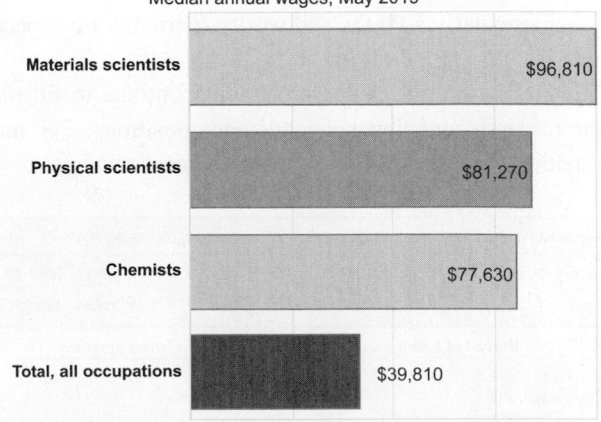

Materials scientists	$96,810
Physical scientists	$81,270
Chemists	$77,630
Total, all occupations	$39,810

Note: All Occupations includes all occupations in the U.S. Economy.
Source: U.S. Bureau of Labor Statistics, Occupational Employment Statistics.

In May 2019, the median annual wages for materials scientists in the top industries in which they worked were as follows:

Management of companies and enterprises	$121,890
Computer and electronic product manufacturing	117,410
Research and development in the physical, engineering, and life sciences	101,310
Chemical manufacturing	89,980
Architectural, engineering, and related services	80,150

Chemists and materials scientists typically work full time and keep regular hours.

Job Outlook

Overall employment of chemists and materials scientists is projected to grow 5 percent from 2019 to 2029, faster than the average for all occupations.

Employment of chemists is projected to grow 5 percent. In pharmaceutical and medicine manufacturing, chemists will be needed to develop nanotechnology for medicinal uses. And in chemical manufacturing, these workers will be needed for improving environmental safety in the workplace and community.

Employment of materials scientists is projected to grow 3 percent. Materials scientists will be needed to develop cheaper, safer, and better quality materials for a variety of purposes, such as electronics, energy, and transportation.

Job Prospects

In addition to job openings resulting from employment growth, some openings are expected to result from the need to replace chemists and materials scientists who transfer to other occupations or leave the labor force, such as to retire.

Chemists who have laboratory experience outside of a classroom environment, such as through a cooperative program or internship, should have better employment prospects than do those without experience.

Chemists and materials scientists who have an advanced degree, particularly a Ph.D., and work experience are expected to have the best opportunities.

Chemists with advanced degrees will continue to fill most senior research and upper-management positions. For more information, see the profile on natural sciences managers.

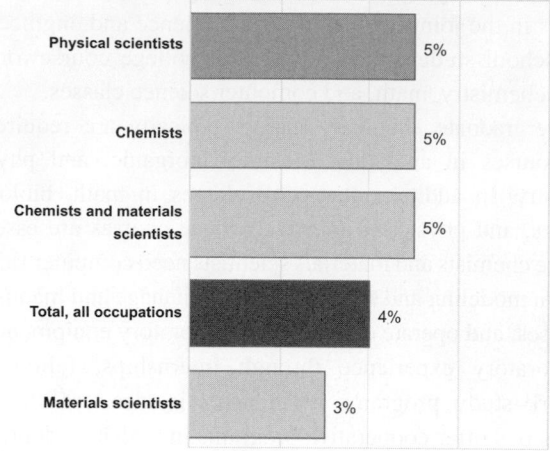

Chemists and Materials Scientists

Percent change in employment, projected 2019-29

- Physical scientists: 5%
- Chemists: 5%
- Chemists and materials scientists: 5%
- Total, all occupations: 4%
- Materials scientists: 3%

Note: All Occupations includes all occupations in the U.S. Economy.
Source: U.S. Bureau of Labor Statistics, Employment Projections program.

State & Area Data

Occupational Employment Statistics (OES)

The Occupational Employment Statistics (OES) program produces employment and wage estimates annually for over 800 occupations. These estimates are available for the nation as a whole, for individual states, and for metropolitan and nonmetropolitan areas.

- Chemists
- Materials scientists

Contacts for More Information

For information on career opportunities, earnings, and education for chemists and materials scientists, visit
➤ American Chemical Society
➤ American Chemistry Council
➤ ASM International
➤ Materials Research Society
➤ National Resource Center for Materials Technology Education

For more information about certified degree programs in chemistry, visit
➤ American Chemical Society Committee on Professional Training

For information about academic programs in green chemistry, visit
➤ American Chemical Society Green Chemistry Academic Programs

To find job openings for chemists and scientists in the federal government, visit
➤ USAJOBS

Employment projections data for chemists and materials scientists, 2019-29					
Occupational Title	SOC Code	Employment, 2019	Projected Employment, 2029	Change, 2019-29	
				Percent	Numeric
SOURCE: U.S. Bureau of Labor Statistics, Employment Projections program					
Chemists and materials scientists	19-2030	93,700	98,000	5	4,300
Materials scientists	19-2032	7,000	7,200	3	200
Chemists	19-2031	86,700	90,800	5	4,100

Conservation Scientists and Foresters

Summary

Quick Facts: Conservation Scientists and Foresters

2019 Median Pay	$62,410 per year
	$30.01 per hour
Typical Entry-Level Education	Bachelor's degree
Work Experience in a Related Occupation	None
On-the-job Training	None
Number of Jobs, 2019	36,100
Job Outlook, 2019-29	5% (Faster than average)
Employment Change, 2019-29	1,700

What Conservation Scientists and Foresters Do

Conservation scientists and foresters manage the overall land quality of forests, parks, rangelands, and other natural resources.

Work Environment

Conservation scientists and foresters work for governments (federal, state, and local), on privately owned lands, or in social advocacy organizations.

How to Become a Conservation Scientist or Forester

Conservation scientists and foresters typically need a bachelor's degree in forestry or a related field.

Pay

The median annual wage for conservation scientists was $62,660 in May 2019.

The median annual wage for foresters was $61,790 in May 2019.

Job Outlook

Employment of conservation scientists and foresters is projected to grow 5 percent from 2019 to 2029, faster than the average for all occupations. The continued need for wildfire prevention and suppression services will help drive demand for conservation scientists and foresters.

State & Area Data

Explore resources for employment and wages by state and area for conservation scientists and foresters.

What Conservation Scientists and Foresters Do

Conservation scientists and foresters manage the overall land quality of forests, parks, rangelands, and other natural resources.

Duties

Conservation scientists typically do the following:

- Oversee forestry and conservation activities to ensure compliance with government regulations and habitat protection
- Negotiate terms and conditions for forest harvesting and for land-use contracts
- Establish plans for managing forest lands and resources
- Monitor forest-cleared lands to ensure that they are suitable for future use
- Work with private landowners, governments, farmers, and others to improve land for forestry purposes, while at the same time protecting the environment

Conservation scientists and foresters study forest and soil quality.

Conservation scientists and foresters manage and monitor overall land quality of forests, parks, rangelands, and other natural resources.

Foresters typically do the following:

- Supervise activities of forest and conservation workers and technicians
- Choose and prepare sites for new trees, using controlled burning, bulldozers, or herbicides to clear land
- Monitor the regeneration of forests
- Direct and participate in forest fire suppression
- Determine ways to remove timber with minimum environmental damage

Conservation scientists manage, improve, and protect the country's natural resources. They work with private landowners and federal, state, and local governments to find ways to use and improve the land while safeguarding the environment. Conservation scientists advise farmers, ranchers, and other agricultural managers on how they can improve their land for agricultural purposes and to control erosion.

Foresters have a wide range of duties, and their responsibilities vary with their employer. Some primary duties of foresters are drawing up plans to regenerate forested lands, monitoring the progress of those lands, and supervising tree harvests. Another duty of a forester is devising plans to keep forests free from disease, harmful insects, and damaging wildfires. Many foresters supervise forest and conservation workers and technicians, directing their work and evaluating their progress.

Conservation scientists and foresters evaluate data on forest and soil quality, assessing damage to trees and forest lands caused by fires and logging activities. In addition, they lead activities such as suppressing fires and planting seedlings. Fire suppression activities include measuring how quickly fires will spread and how successfully the planned suppression activities turn out.

Conservation scientists and foresters use their skills to determine a fire's impact on a region's environment. Communication with firefighters and other forest workers is an important component of fire suppression and controlled burn activities because the information that conservation scientists and foresters provide can determine how firefighters work.

Conservation scientists and foresters use a number of tools to perform their jobs. They use clinometers to measure the heights of trees, diameter tapes to measure a tree's circumference, and increment borers and bark gauges to measure the growth of trees so that timber volumes can be computed and growth rates estimated.

In addition, conservation scientists and foresters often use remote sensing (aerial photographs and other imagery taken from airplanes and satellites) and Geographic Information System (GIS) data to map large forest or range areas and to detect widespread trends of forest and land use. They make extensive use of hand-held computers and Global Positioning System (GPS) receivers to study these maps.

The following are examples of types of conservation scientists:

Conservation land managers work for land trusts or other conservation organizations to protect the wildlife habitat, biodiversity, scenic value, and other unique attributes of preserves and conservation lands.

Range managers, also called *range conservationists*, protect rangelands to maximize their use without damaging the environment. Rangelands contain many natural resources and cover hundreds of millions of acres in the United States, mainly in the western states and Alaska.

Range managers may inventory soils, plants, and animals; develop resource management plans; help to restore degraded ecosystems; or help manage a ranch. They also maintain soil stability and vegetation for uses such as wildlife habitats and outdoor recreation. Like foresters, they work to prevent and reduce wildfires and invasive animal species.

Soil and water conservationists give technical help to people who are concerned with the conservation of soil, water, and related natural resources. For private landowners, they develop programs to make the most productive use of land without damaging it. They also help landowners with issues such as dealing with erosion. They help private landowners and governments by advising on water quality, preserving water supplies, preventing ground-water contamination, and conserving water.

The following are examples of types of foresters:

Procurement foresters buy timber by contacting local forest owners and negotiating a sale. This activity typically involves taking inventory on the type, amount, and location of all standing timber on the property. Procurement foresters then appraise the timber's worth, negotiate its purchase, and draw up a contract. The forester then subcontracts with loggers or pulpwood cutters to remove the trees and to help lay out roads to get to the timber.

Urban foresters live and work in larger cities and manage urban trees. These workers are concerned with quality-of-life issues, including air quality, shade, and storm water runoff.

Conservation education foresters train teachers and students about issues facing forest lands.

Work Environment

Conservation scientists held about 24,500 jobs in 2019. The largest employers of conservation scientists were as follows:

Federal government, excluding postal service	28%
State government, excluding education and hospitals	21
Local government, excluding education and hospitals	21
Social advocacy organizations	13
Professional, scientific, and technical services	4

Foresters held about 11,600 jobs in 2019. The largest employers of foresters were as follows:

Conservation scientists and foresters typically work in offices, in laboratories, and outdoors, sometimes in remote locations performing fieldwork.

State government, excluding education and hospitals..	30%
Forestry and logging	15
Federal government, excluding postal service	12
Local government, excluding education and hospitals.	10
Support activities for agriculture and forestry	3

In the western and southwestern United States, conservation scientists and foresters usually work for the federal government because of the number of national parks in that part of the country. In the eastern United States, they often work for private landowners. Social advocacy organizations employ foresters and conservation scientists in working with lawmakers on behalf of sustainable land use and other issues facing forest land.

Conservation scientists and foresters typically work in offices, in laboratories, and outdoors, sometimes doing fieldwork in remote locations. When visiting or working near logging operations or wood yards, they wear a hardhat and other protective gear.

The work can be physically demanding. Some conservation scientists and foresters work outdoors in all types of weather. They may need to walk long distances through dense woods and underbrush to carry out their work. Insect bites, poisonous plants, and other natural hazards present some risk.

In an isolated location, a forester or conservation scientist may work alone, measuring tree densities and regeneration or performing other outdoor activities. Other foresters work closely with the public, educating them about the forest or the proper use of recreational sites.

Fire suppression activities are an important aspect of the duties of a forester or conservation scientist. Because those activities involve prevention as well as emergency responses, the work of a forester or conservation scientist has occasional risk.

Work Schedules
Most conservation scientists and foresters work full time and have a standard work schedule.

How to Become a Conservation Scientist or Forester
Conservation scientists and foresters typically need a bachelor's degree in forestry or a related field.

Education
Conservation scientists and foresters typically need a bachelor's degree in forestry or a related field, such as agricultural science, rangeland management, or environmental science.

Bachelor's degree programs are designed to prepare conservation scientists and foresters for their career or a graduate degree. Alongside practical skills, theory and education are important parts of these programs.

Bachelor's and advanced degree programs in forestry and related fields typically include courses in ecology, biology, and forest resource measurement. Scientists and foresters also typically have a background in Geographic Information System (GIS) technology, remote sensing, and other forms of computer modeling.

In 2017, more than 50 bachelor's and master's degree programs in forestry, urban forestry, and natural resources

Conservation scientists and foresters typically need a bachelor's degree in forestry or a related field.

and ecosystem management were accredited by the Society of American Foresters.

Important Qualities

Analytical skills. Conservation scientists and foresters must evaluate the results of a variety of field tests and experiments, all of which require precision and accuracy. They use sophisticated computer modeling to prepare their analyses.

Critical-thinking skills. Conservation scientists and foresters reach conclusions through sound reasoning and judgment. They determine how to improve forest conditions, and they must react appropriately to fires.

Decisionmaking skills. Conservation scientists and foresters must use their expertise and experience to determine whether their findings will have an impact on soil, forest lands, and the spread of fires.

Management skills. Conservation scientists and foresters need to work well with the forest and conservation workers and technicians they supervise, so effective communication is critical.

Physical stamina. Conservation scientists and foresters often walk long distances in steep and wooded areas. They work in all kinds of weather, including extreme heat and cold.

Speaking skills. Conservation scientists and foresters must give clear instructions to forest and conservation workers and technicians, who typically do the labor necessary for proper forest maintenance. They also need to communicate clearly with landowners and, in some cases, the general public.

Licenses, Certifications, and Registrations

Several states have some type of credentialing process for foresters. In some of these states, foresters must be licensed; check with your state for more information. Conservation workers do not need a license.

Although certification is not required, conservation scientists and foresters may choose to earn it because it shows a high level of professional competency.

The Society of American Foresters (SAF) offers certification to foresters. Candidates must have at least a bachelor's degree from an SAF-accredited program or from a forestry program that is substantially equivalent. Candidates also must have qualifying professional experience and pass an exam.

The Society for Range Management offers professional certification in rangeland management or as a range management consultant. To be certified, candidates must hold a bachelor's degree in range management or a related field, have 5 years of full-time related work experience, and pass an exam.

Advancement

Many conservation scientists and foresters advance to take on managerial duties. They also may conduct research or work on policy issues, often after getting an advanced degree. Foresters in management usually leave fieldwork behind, spending more of their time in an office, working with teams to develop management plans and supervising others.

Soil conservationists usually begin working within one district and may advance to a state, regional, or national level. Soil conservationists also can transfer to occupations such as farm or ranch management advisor or land appraiser.

Pay

The median annual wage for conservation scientists was $62,660 in May 2019. The median wage is the wage at which half the workers in an occupation earned more than that amount and half earned less. The lowest 10 percent earned less than $39,270, and the highest 10 percent earned more than $98,060.

The median annual wage for foresters was $61,790 in May 2019. The lowest 10 percent earned less than $38,890, and the highest 10 percent earned more than $90,080.

In May 2019, the median annual wages for conservation scientists in the top industries in which they worked were as follows:

Federal government, excluding postal service	$76,230
Social advocacy organizations	61,700
Professional, scientific, and technical services	59,440
State government, excluding education and hospitals	57,200
Local government, excluding education and hospitals	55,460

In May 2019, the median annual wages for foresters in the top industries in which they worked were as follows:

Federal government, excluding postal service	$65,780
Local government, excluding education and hospitals	60,580
State government, excluding education and hospitals	55,330

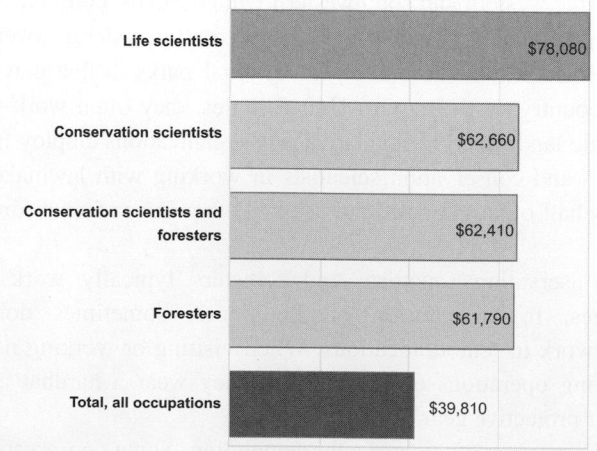

Conservation Scientists and Foresters
Median annual wages, May 2019

Life scientists	$78,080
Conservation scientists	$62,660
Conservation scientists and foresters	$62,410
Foresters	$61,790
Total, all occupations	$39,810

Note: All Occupations includes all occupations in the U.S. Economy.
Source: U.S. Bureau of Labor Statistics, Occupational Employment Statistics.

Most conservation scientists and foresters work full time and have a standard work schedule.

Job Outlook

Employment of conservation scientists and foresters is projected to grow 5 percent from 2019 to 2029, faster than the average for all occupations.

Most employment growth is expected to be in state and local government-owned forest lands, particularly in the western United States. In recent years, the prevention and suppression of wildfires has become the primary concern for government agencies managing forests and rangelands. State and local governments are likely to hire more foresters as the number of forest fires increases and more people live on or near forest lands. Both the development of previously unused lands and changing weather conditions have contributed to increasingly devastating and costly fires.

Job Prospects

Some openings for conservation scientists and foresters are expected to arise from the need to replace workers who transfer to other occupations or exit the labor force, such as to retire. Job prospects will likely be best for conservation scientists and foresters who have a strong understanding of Geographic Information System (GIS) technology, remote sensing, and other software tools.

Conservation Scientists and Foresters

Percent change in employment, projected 2019-29

Note: All Occupations includes all occupations in the U.S. Economy.
Source: U.S. Bureau of Labor Statistics, Employment Projections program.

State & Area Data
Occupational Employment Statistics (OES)

The Occupational Employment Statistics (OES) program produces employment and wage estimates annually for over 800 occupations. These estimates are available for the nation as a whole, for individual states, and for metropolitan and nonmetropolitan areas.

Contacts for More Information

For more information about conservation scientists and foresters, including schools offering education in forestry, visit
➤ Society of American Foresters

For information about careers in forestry, particularly conservation forestry and land management, visit
➤ Forest Stewards Guild
➤ Society for Range Management
➤ U.S. Forest Service

Occupational Title	SOC Code	Employment, 2019	Projected Employment, 2029	Change, 2019-29 Percent	Change, 2019-29 Numeric
Employment projections data for conservation scientists and foresters, 2019-29					
SOURCE: U.S. Bureau of Labor Statistics, Employment Projections program					
Conservation scientists and foresters	19-1030	36,100	37,800	5	1,700
Conservation scientists	19-1031	24,500	25,800	5	1,200
Foresters	19-1032	11,600	12,000	4	400

Economists

Summary

Quick Facts: Economists

2019 Median Pay	$105,020 per year
	$50.49 per hour
Typical Entry-Level Education	Master's degree
Work Experience in a Related Occupation	None
On-the-job Training	None
Number of Jobs, 2019	20,500
Job Outlook, 2019-29	14% (Much faster than average)
Employment Change, 2019-29	2,900

What Economists Do

Economists collect and analyze data, research trends, and evaluate economic issues for resources, goods, and services.

Work Environment

Although the majority of economists work independently in an office, many collaborate with other economists and statisticians. Most economists work full time during regular business hours, but occasionally they work overtime to meet deadlines.

How to Become an Economist

Most economists need a master's degree or Ph.D. However, some entry-level jobs—primarily in the federal government—are available for workers with a bachelor's degree.

Pay

The median annual wage for economists was $105,020 in May 2019.

Job Outlook

Employment of economists is projected to grow 14 percent from 2019 to 2029, much faster than the average for all occupations.

Job prospects should be best for those with a master's degree or Ph.D., strong analytical skills, and experience using statistical analysis software.

State & Area Data

Explore resources for employment and wages by state and area for economists.

What Economists Do

Economists study the production and distribution of resources, goods, and services by collecting and analyzing data, researching trends, and evaluating economic issues.

Duties

Economists typically do the following:

- Research economic issues
- Conduct surveys and collect data
- Analyze data using mathematical models, statistical techniques, and software
- Present research results in reports, tables, and charts
- Interpret and forecast market trends
- Advise businesses, governments, and individuals on economic topics
- Recommend solutions to economic problems
- Write articles for academic journals and other media

Economists apply both qualitative and quantitative economic analysis to topics within a variety of fields, such as education, health, development, and the environment. Some economists study the cost of products, healthcare, or energy, while others examine employment levels, business cycles, exchange rates, taxes, inflation, or interest rates.

Economists often study historical trends and use them to make forecasts. They research and analyze data using a variety of software programs. They sometimes present their research to various audiences.

Economists interpret and forecast market trends.

Economists prepare reports, tables, and charts.

Many economists work in federal, state, and local government. Federal government economists collect and analyze data about the U.S. economy, including employment, prices, productivity, and wages, among other types of data. They also project spending needs and inform policymakers on the economic impact of laws and regulations.

Economists working for corporations help managers and decisionmakers understand how the economy will affect their business. Specifically, economists may analyze issues such as consumer demand and sales to help a company maximize its profits.

Economists also work for international organizations, research firms, and think tanks, where they study and analyze a variety of economic issues. Their analyses and forecasts are frequently published in newspapers and journals.

Many PhD economists become postsecondary teachers.

Work Environment

Economists held about 20,500 jobs in 2019. The largest employers of economists were as follows:

Federal government, excluding postal service	23%
Scientific research and development services	18
Management, scientific, and technical consulting services	17
State government, excluding education and hospitals	9
Finance and insurance	7

Economists typically work independently in an office. However, many economists collaborate with other economists and statisticians, sometimes working on teams. Some economists work from home, and others may be required to travel as part of their job or to attend conferences.

Economists spend much of their time using computers to analyze data, review research, or write findings.

Work Schedules

Most economists work full time. In addition to working full time at a business or university, some economists consult part-time. Some perform work that may require overtime hours.

Economists typically work with computers.

How to Become an Economist

Most economists need a master's degree or Ph.D. However, some entry-level jobs—primarily in government—are available for workers with a bachelor's degree.

Education

A master's degree or Ph.D. is required for most economist jobs. Positions in business, research, or international organizations often require a combination of graduate education and work experience. In addition, courses that introduce students to statistical analysis software are helpful.

Students can pursue an advanced degree in economics with a bachelor's degree in a number of fields, but a strong background in mathematics is essential. A Ph.D. in economics may require several years of study after earning a bachelor's degree, including completion of detailed research in a specialty field.

Candidates with a bachelor's degree may qualify for some entry-level economist positions, including jobs with the federal government. An advanced degree is sometimes required for advancement to higher level positions.

Other Experience

Aspiring economists can gain valuable experience from internships where the work involves gathering and analyzing data, researching economic issues and trends, and writing reports on their findings. In addition, related experience, such as using statistical analysis software, can be advantageous.

Important Qualities

Analytical skills. Economists must be able to review data in detail, observe patterns, perform advanced calculations, and draw logical conclusions. For example, labor economists analyze the effects of labor policies on employment.

Critical-thinking skills. Economists must be able to use logic and reasoning to solve complex problems. For instance, they might identify how economic trends may affect an organization.

Communication skills are important for economists, since they sometimes present research to colleagues.

Economists

Median annual wages, May 2019

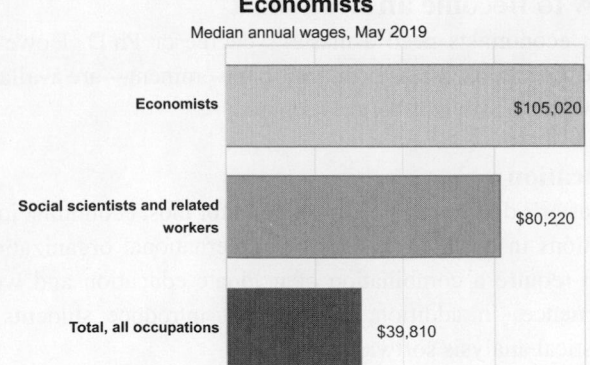

Economists	$105,020
Social scientists and related workers	$80,220
Total, all occupations	$39,810

Note: All Occupations includes all occupations in the U.S. Economy.
Source: U.S. Bureau of Labor Statistics, Occupational Employment Statistics.

Speaking skills. Economists must be able to explain their work to others. They often give presentations and explain reports to clients who may not have a background in economics.

Writing skills. Economists must be able to present their findings clearly. Many economists prepare reports for colleagues or clients; others write for publication in journals or for news media.

Pay

The median annual wage for economists was $105,020 in May 2019. The median wage is the wage at which half the workers in an occupation earned more than that amount and half earned less. The lowest 10 percent earned less than $59,450, and the highest 10 percent earned more than $185,020.

In May 2019, the median annual wages for economists in the top industries in which they worked were as follows:

Finance and insurance	$120,770
Federal government, excluding postal service	119,580
Scientific research and development services	114,140
Management, scientific, and technical consulting services	108,190
State government, excluding education and hospitals	73,400

Most economists work full time. Some perform work that may require overtime hours.

Job Outlook

Employment of economists is projected to grow 14 percent from 2019 to 2029, much faster than the average for all occupations. However, because it is a small occupation, the fast growth will result in only about 2,900 new jobs over the decade. Many of the new jobs for these workers are expected to be in firms that specialize in research and consulting services.

Organizations across many industries use economic analysis and quantitative methods to study and forecast business, sales, and other market trends. Employment demand is expected to be

Economists

Percent change in employment, projected 2019-29

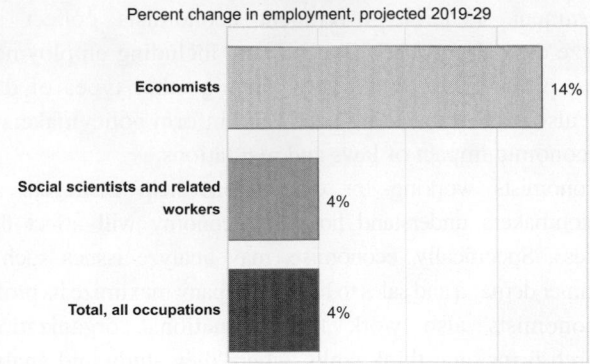

Economists	14%
Social scientists and related workers	4%
Total, all occupations	4%

Note: All Occupations includes all occupations in the U.S. Economy.
Source: U.S. Bureau of Labor Statistics, Employment Projections program.

strong for these workers, as organizations increasingly turn to economists to apply analysis of "big data" to pricing, advertising, and other areas. The increasing complexity of the global economy and a more competitive business environment also are expected to support demand for economists.

Job Prospects

In general, job opportunities should be good. Job prospects should be best for those with a master's degree or Ph.D., strong analytical skills, and experience using statistical analysis software.

Applicants with a bachelor's degree may face strong competition for jobs. As a result, bachelor's degree holders will likely find jobs in other occupations.

Employment projections data for economists, 2019-29					
Occupational Title	SOC Code	Employment, 2019	Projected Employment, 2029	Change, 2019-29	
				Percent	Numeric
SOURCE: U.S. Bureau of Labor Statistics, Employment Projections program					
Economists	19-3011	20,500	23,500	14	2,900

State & Area Data
Occupational Employment Statistics (OES)

The Occupational Employment Statistics (OES) program produces employment and wage estimates annually for over 800 occupations. These estimates are available for the nation as a whole, for individual states, and for metropolitan and nonmetropolitan areas.

Contacts for More Information

For more information about economists, visit
➤ American Economic Association

For information about careers in business economics, visit
➤ National Association for Business Economics

For information on federal government education requirements for economist positions, visit
➤ U.S. Office of Personnel Management

Environmental Science and Protection Technicians

Summary

Quick Facts: Environmental Science and Protection Technicians

2019 Median Pay	$46,540 per year $22.38 per hour
Typical Entry-Level Education	Associate's degree
Work Experience in a Related Occupation ...	None
On-the-job Training	None
Number of Jobs, 2019	34,700
Job Outlook, 2019-29	8% (Much faster than average)
Employment Change, 2019-29	2,900

What Environmental Science and Protection Technicians Do

Environmental science and protection technicians monitor the environment and investigate sources of pollution and contamination.

Work Environment

Environmental science and protection technicians work in offices, laboratories, and the field.

How to Become an Environmental Science and Protection Technician

Environmental science and protection technicians typically need an associate's degree or 2 years of postsecondary education, although some positions require a bachelor's degree.

Pay

The median annual wage for environmental science and protection technicians was $46,540 in May 2019.

Environmental science and protection technicians must carry out a wide range of field tests.

Job Outlook

Employment of environmental science and protection technicians is projected to grow 8 percent from 2019 to 2029, much faster than the average for all occupations. However, because it is a small occupation, the fast growth will result in only about 2,900 new jobs over the 10-year period.

State & Area Data

Explore resources for employment and wages by state and area for environmental science and protection technicians.

What Environmental Science and Protection Technicians Do

Environmental science and protection technicians monitor the environment and investigate sources of pollution and contamination, including those affecting public health.

Duties

Environmental science and protection technicians typically do the following:

- Inspect establishments, including public places and businesses, to ensure that there are no environmental, health, or safety hazards

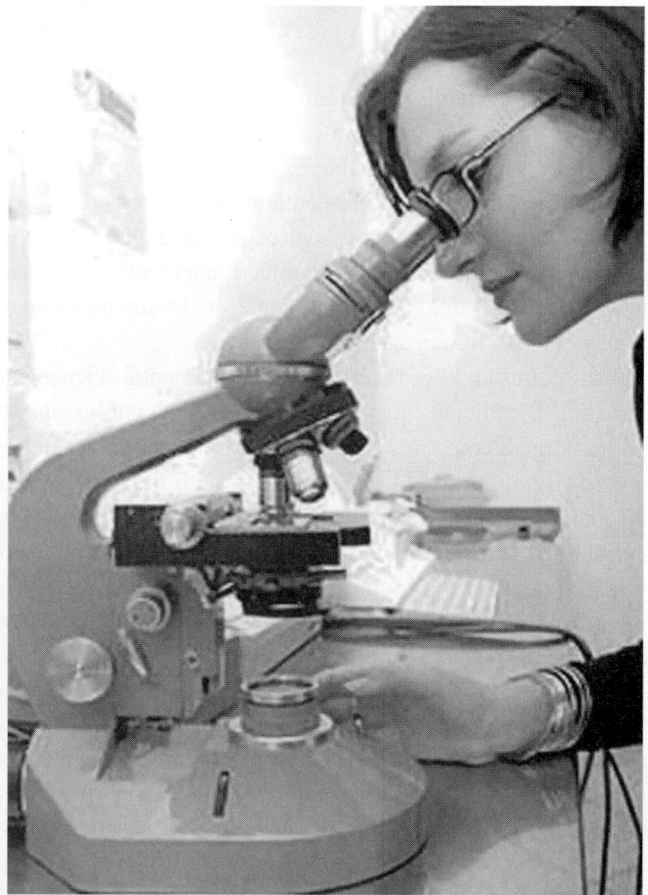

Environmental science and protection technicians use laboratory equipment, such as microscopes, to analyze samples collected in the field.

- Set up and maintain equipment used to monitor pollution levels, such as remote sensors that measure emissions from smokestacks
- Collect samples of air, soil, water, and other materials for laboratory analysis
- Clearly label, track, and ensure the integrity of samples being transported to the laboratory
- Use equipment, such as microscopes, to evaluate and analyze samples for the presence of pollutants or other contaminants
- Prepare charts and reports that summarize test results
- Discuss test results and analyses with clients
- Verify compliance with regulations that help prevent pollution

Many environmental science and protection technicians work under the supervision of environmental scientists and specialists, who direct the technicians' work and evaluate their results. In addition, technicians often work on teams with scientists, engineers, and technicians in other fields to solve complex problems related to environmental degradation and public health. For example, they may work on teams with geoscientists and hydrologists to manage the cleanup of contaminated soils and ground water around an abandoned bomb-manufacturing site.

Most environmental science and protection technicians work for consulting firms, state or local governments, or testing laboratories.

In **consulting firms**, environmental science and protection technicians help clients monitor and manage the environment and comply with regulations. For example, they help businesses develop cleanup plans for contaminated sites, and they recommend ways to reduce, control, or eliminate pollution. Also, environmental science and protection technicians conduct feasibility studies for, and monitor the environmental impact of, new construction projects.

In **state and local governments**, environmental science and protection technicians inspect businesses and public places, and investigate complaints related to air quality, water quality, and food safety. They may be involved with the enforcement of environmental regulations. They also may help protect the environment and people's health by performing environmental impact studies of new construction. Or they may evaluate the environmental health of sites that may contaminate the environment, such as abandoned industrial sites.

In **testing laboratories**, environmental science and protection technicians collect and track samples, and perform tests that are often similar to those carried out by chemical technicians, biological technicians, or microbiologists. However, in contrast to the work done by these science workers, that done by environmental science and protection technicians focuses on topics that are directly related to the environment and how it affects human health.

Environmental science and protection technicians typically specialize either in laboratory testing or in fieldwork and sample collection. However, it is common for laboratory technicians to occasionally collect samples from the field and for fieldworkers to do some work in a laboratory.

Work Environment

Environmental science and protection technicians held about 34,700 jobs in 2019. The largest employers of environmental science and protection technicians were as follows:

Management, scientific, and technical consulting services	24%
Local government, excluding education and hospitals......	19
Testing laboratories..	12
Engineering services...	7
State government, excluding education and hospitals	6

Environmental science and protection technicians work in laboratories, offices, and the field. Fieldwork offers a variety of settings. For example, technicians may investigate an abandoned manufacturing plant, or work outdoors to test the water quality of lakes and rivers. They may work near streams and rivers, monitoring the levels of pollution caused by runoff from cities and landfills, or they may have to use the crawl spaces under a house in order to neutralize natural health risks such as radon. While working outdoors, they may be exposed to adverse weather conditions.

In the field, environmental science and protection technicians spend most of their time on their feet, which can be physically demanding. They also may need to carry and set up testing equipment, which can involve some heavy lifting and frequent bending and crouching. Fieldwork may be seasonal, depending on the location, since low temperatures in the winter could inhibit taking samples from water sources or soil.

Depending on the type of work and fieldwork they do, technicians may need to wear protective gear such as hardhats, masks, and coveralls to protect them from hazards.

Environmental science and protection technicians monitor levels of pollution.

Work Schedules

Environmental science and protection technicians typically work full time. Working in the field exposes them to all types of weather. Also, technicians may need to travel to meet with clients or to perform fieldwork, either of which may require technicians to work additional or irregular hours.

How to Become an Environmental Science and Protection Technician

Environmental science and protection technicians typically need an associate's degree or 2 years of postsecondary education, although some positions require a bachelor's degree.

Education

Environmental science and protection technicians typically need an associate's degree in environmental science, environmental health, or public health, or a related degree. Because of the wide range of tasks, environments, and industries in which these technicians work, there are jobs that do not require postsecondary education and others that require a bachelor's degree.

A background in natural sciences is important for environmental science and protection technicians. Students should take courses in chemistry, biology, geology, and physics. Coursework in math, statistics, and computer science also is useful, because technicians routinely do data analysis and modeling.

Many technical and community colleges offer programs in environmental studies or a related technology, such as remote sensing or geographic information systems (GISs). While in college, students should include coursework that provides laboratory experience.

Associate's degree programs at community colleges often are designed to allow students to easily transfer to bachelor's degree programs at public colleges and universities.

Environmental science and protection technicians need an associate's degree or comparable postsecondary training.

Training

Technicians whose jobs involve handling hazardous waste typically need to complete training in accordance with Occupational Safety & Health Administration (OSHA) standards. The length of training depends on the type of hazardous material that workers handle. The training covers health hazards, personal protective equipment and clothing, site safety, recognizing and identifying hazards, and decontamination.

Important Qualities

Analytical skills. Environmental science and protection technicians must carry out a wide range of laboratory and field tests, and their results must be accurate and precise.

Communication skills. Environmental science and protection technicians must have good listening and writing skills, because they must follow precise directions for sample collection and communicate their results effectively in written reports. They also need to discuss their results with colleagues, clients, and, sometimes, public audiences.

Critical-thinking skills. Environmental science and protection technicians reach their conclusions through sound reasoning and judgment. They have to determine the best way to address environmental hazards.

Interpersonal skills. Environmental science and protection technicians need to work well and collaborate with others, because they often work with scientists and other technicians.

Licenses, Certifications, and Registrations

In some states, environmental science and protection technicians can benefit from obtaining certification to conduct certain types of environmental and health inspections. For example, certification for technicians who test buildings for radon is offered through the National Radon Safety Board (NRSB).

The Registered Environmental Health Specialist/Registered Sanitarian (REHS/RS) credential is offered through the National Environmental Health Association (NEHA).

Pay

The median annual wage for environmental science and protection technicians was $46,540 in May 2019. The median wage is the wage at which half the workers in an occupation earned more than that amount and half earned less. The lowest 10 percent earned less than $29,040, and the highest 10 percent earned more than $80,710.

In May 2019, the median annual wages for environmental science and protection technicians in the top industries in which they worked were as follows:

Local government, excluding education and hospitals	$50,230
Engineering services	46,940
State government, excluding education and hospitals	46,510

Environmental Science and Protection Technicians
Median annual wages, May 2019

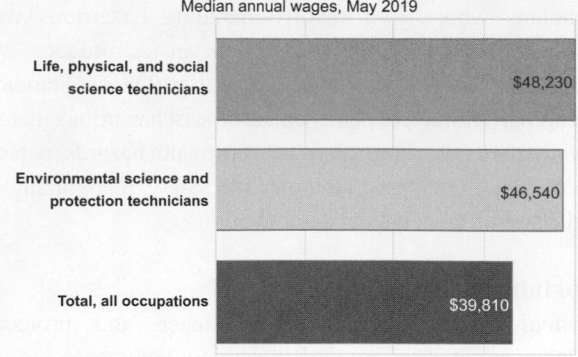

Note: All Occupations includes all occupations in the U.S. Economy.
Source: U.S. Bureau of Labor Statistics, Occupational Employment Statistics.

Management, scientific, and technical consulting
services 44,240
Testing laboratories 39,660

Environmental science and protection technicians typically work full time. Working in the field exposes them to all types of weather. Also, technicians may need to travel to meet with clients or to perform fieldwork, either of which may require technicians to work additional or irregular hours.

Job Outlook

Employment of environmental science and protection technicians is projected to grow 8 percent from 2019 to 2029, much faster than the average for all occupations. However, because it is a small occupation, the fast growth will result in only about 2,900 new jobs over the 10-year period. Heightened public interest in issues involving the environment, such as fracking, as well as the increasing demands placed on the environment by population growth, is expected to spur demand for environmental science and protection technicians.

Most employment growth for environmental science and protection technicians is projected to be in the industry of management, scientific, and technical consulting services. More businesses and governments are expected to use these firms in the future to help them monitor and manage the environment and comply with regulations.

Environmental Science and Protection Technicians
Percent change in employment, projected 2019-29

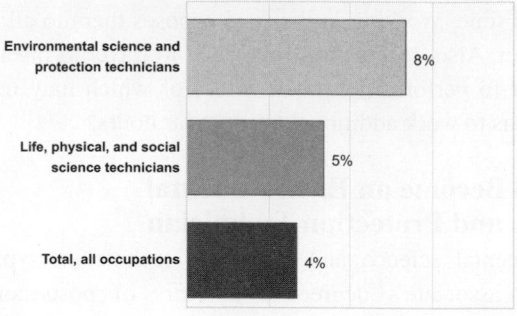

Note: All Occupations includes all occupations in the U.S. Economy.
Source: U.S. Bureau of Labor Statistics, Employment Projections program.

Employment projections data for environmental science and protection technicians, 2019-29					
Occupational Title	SOC Code	Employment, 2019	Projected Employment, 2029	Change, 2019-29	
				Percent	Numeric
SOURCE: U.S. Bureau of Labor Statistics, Employment Projections program					
Environmental science and protection technicians, including health	19-4042	34,700	37,600	8	2,900

State & Area Data
Occupational Employment Statistics (OES)

The Occupational Employment Statistics (OES) program produces employment and wage estimates annually for over 800 occupations. These estimates are available for the nation as a whole, for individual states, and for metropolitan and nonmetropolitan areas.

Contacts for More Information

For more information about environmental health technicians and related occupations, visit
➤ National Environmental Health Association

For more information about training, visit
➤ UCAR
➤ Occupational Safety and Health Administration

For more information specific to radon technicians, visit
➤ National Radon Safety Board

Environmental Scientists and Specialists

Summary

Quick Facts: Environmental Scientists and Specialists

2019 Median Pay	$71,360 per year $34.31 per hour
Typical Entry-Level Education	Bachelor's degree
Work Experience in a Related Occupation....	None
On-the-job Training	None
Number of Jobs, 2019................................	90,900
Job Outlook, 2019-29.................................	8% (Much faster than average)
Employment Change, 2019-29	7,100

What Environmental Scientists and Specialists Do

Environmental scientists and specialists use their knowledge of the natural sciences to protect the environment and human health.

Work Environment

Environmental scientists and specialists work in offices and laboratories. Some may spend time in the field gathering data and monitoring environmental conditions firsthand. Most environmental scientists and specialists work full time.

How to Become an Environmental Scientist or Specialist

Environmental scientists and specialists need at least a bachelor's degree in a natural science or science-related field for most entry-level jobs.

Pay

The median annual wage for environmental scientists and specialists was $71,360 in May 2019.

Environmental scientists and specialists analyze environmental problems and develop solutions.

Job Outlook

Employment of environmental scientists and specialists is projected to grow 8 percent from 2019 to 2029, much faster than the average for all occupations. Heightened public interest in the hazards facing the environment, as well as increasing demands placed on the environment by population growth, are expected to spur demand for environmental scientists and specialists.

State & Area Data

Explore resources for employment and wages by state and area for environmental scientists and specialists.

What Environmental Scientists and Specialists Do

Environmental scientists and specialists use their knowledge of the natural sciences to protect the environment and human health. They may clean up polluted areas, advise policymakers, or work with industry to reduce waste.

Duties

Environmental scientists and specialists typically do the following:

Environmental scientists use their knowledge of the natural sciences to protect the environment.

- Determine data collection methods for research projects, investigations, and surveys
- Collect and compile environmental data from samples of air, soil, water, food, and other materials for scientific analysis
- Analyze samples, surveys, and other information to identify and assess threats to the environment
- Develop plans to prevent, control, or fix environmental problems, such as land or water pollution
- Provide information and guidance to government officials, businesses, and the general public on possible environmental hazards and health risks
- Prepare technical reports and presentations that explain their research and findings

Environmental scientists and specialists analyze environmental problems and develop solutions to them. For example, many environmental scientists and specialists work to reclaim lands and waters that have been contaminated by pollution. Others assess the risks that new construction projects pose to the environment and make recommendations to governments and businesses on how to minimize the environmental impact of these projects. Environmental scientists and specialists may do research and provide advice on manufacturing practices, such as advising against the use of chemicals that are known to harm the environment.

The federal government and many state and local governments have regulations to ensure that there is clean air to breathe and safe water to drink, and that there are no hazardous materials in the soil. The regulations also place limits on development, particularly near sensitive ecosystems, such as wetlands. Environmental scientists and specialists who work for governments ensure that the regulations are followed. Other environmental scientists and specialists work for consulting firms that help companies comply with regulations and policies.

Some environmental scientists and specialists focus on environmental regulations that are designed to protect people's health, while others focus on regulations designed to minimize society's impact on the ecosystem. The following are examples of types of specialists:

Climate change analysts study effects on ecosystems caused by the changing climate. They may do outreach education activities and grant writing typical of scientists.

Environmental health and safety specialists study how environmental factors affect human health. They investigate potential environmental health risks. For example, they may investigate and address issues arising from soil and water contamination caused by nuclear weapons manufacturing. They also educate the public about health risks that may be present in the environment.

Environmental restoration planners assess polluted sites and determine the cost and activities necessary to clean up the area.

Industrial ecologists work with industry to increase the efficiency of their operations and thereby limit the impacts

these activities have on the environment. They analyze costs and benefits of various programs, as well as their impacts on ecosystems.

Other environmental scientists and specialists perform work and receive training similar to that of other physical or life scientists, but they focus on environmental issues. For example, *environmental chemists* study the effects that various chemicals have on ecosystems. To illustrate, they may study how acids affect plants, animals, and people. Some areas in which they work include waste management and the remediation of contaminated soils, water, and air.

Many people with backgrounds in environmental science become postsecondary teachers or high school teachers.

Work Environment

Environmental scientists and specialists held about 90,900 jobs in 2019. The largest employers of environmental scientists and specialists were as follows:

Management, scientific, and technical consulting services	24%
State government, excluding education and hospitals...	23
Local government, excluding education and hospitals...	11
Engineering services...	9
Federal government, excluding postal service	6

Environmental scientists and specialists work in offices and laboratories. Some may spend time in the field gathering data and monitoring environmental conditions firsthand, but this work is much more likely to be done by environmental science and protection technicians. Fieldwork can be physically demanding, and environmental scientists and specialists may work in all types of weather. Environmental scientists and specialists may have to travel to meet with clients or present research at conferences.

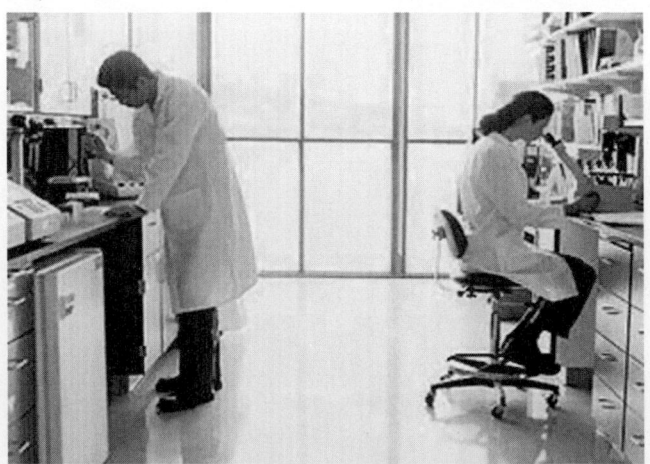

Many environmental scientists and specialists work in laboratories.

Work Schedules

Most environmental scientists and specialists work full time. They may have to work more than 40 hours a week when working in the field.

How to Become an Environmental Scientist or Specialist

For most jobs, environmental scientists and specialists need at least a bachelor's degree in a natural science.

Education and Training

For most entry-level jobs, environmental scientists and specialists must have a bachelor's degree in environmental science or a science-related field, such as biology, chemistry, physics, geosciences, or engineering. However, a master's degree may be needed for advancement. Environmental scientists and specialists who have a doctoral degree make up a small percentage of the occupation, and this level of training typically is needed only for the relatively few postsecondary teaching and basic research positions.

A bachelor's degree in environmental science offers a broad approach to the natural sciences. Students typically take courses

For most jobs, environmental scientists and specialists need at least a bachelor's degree in environmental science or a related field.

in biology, chemistry, geology, and physics. Students often take specialized courses in hydrology or waste management as part of their degree as well. Classes in environmental policy and regulation are also beneficial. Students who want to reach the Ph.D. level may find it advantageous to major in a more specific natural science, such as chemistry, biology, physics, or geology, rather than earn a broader environmental science degree.

Many environmental science programs include an internship, which allows students to gain practical experience. Prospective scientists also may volunteer for or participate in internships after graduation to develop skills needed for the occupation.

Students should look for classes and internships that include work in computer modeling, data analysis, and Geographic Information Systems (GISs). Students with experience in these programs will be the best prepared to enter the job market. The University Corporation for Atmospheric Research (UCAR) offers several programs to help students broaden their understanding of environmental sciences.

Important Qualities

Analytical skills. Environmental scientists and specialists base their conclusions on careful analysis of scientific data. They must consider all possible methods and solutions in their analyses.

Communication skills. Environmental scientists and specialists may need to present and explain their findings to audiences of varying backgrounds and write technical reports.

Interpersonal skills. Environmental scientists and specialists typically work on teams along with scientists, engineers, and technicians. Team members must be able to work together effectively to achieve their goals.

Problem-solving skills. Environmental scientists and specialists try to find the best possible solution to problems that affect the environment and people's health.

Self-discipline. Environmental scientists and specialists may spend a lot of time working alone. They need to stay motivated and get their work done without supervision.

Advancement

As environmental scientists and specialists gain experience, they earn more responsibilities and autonomy, and may supervise the work of technicians or other scientists. Eventually, they may be promoted to project leader, program manager, or some other management or research position.

Other environmental scientists and specialists go on to work as researchers or faculty at colleges and universities. For more information, see the profile on postsecondary teachers.

Licenses, Certifications, and Registrations

Environmental scientists and specialists can become Certified Hazardous Materials Managers through the Institute of Hazardous Materials Management. This certification, which must be renewed every 5 years, shows that an environmental scientist or specialist is staying current with developments relevant to the occupation's work. In addition, the Ecological Society of America offers several levels of certification for environmental scientists who wish to demonstrate their proficiency in ecology.

Work Experience in a Related Occupation

Environmental scientists and specialists often begin their careers as field analysts, research assistants, or environmental science and protection technicians in laboratories and offices.

Some environmental scientists and specialists begin their careers as scientists in related occupations, such as hydrology or engineering, and then move into the more interdisciplinary field of environmental science.

Pay

The median annual wage for environmental scientists and specialists was $71,360 in May 2019. The median wage is the wage at which half the workers in an occupation earned more than that amount and half earned less. The lowest 10 percent earned less than $42,810, and the highest 10 percent earned more than $124,760.

In May 2019, the median annual wages for environmental scientists and specialists in the top industries in which they worked were as follows:

Federal government, excluding postal service	$102,910
Engineering services...	73,410
Management, scientific, and technical consulting services	70,590
Local government, excluding education and hospitals..	68,190
State government, excluding education and hospitals..	65,180

Most environmental scientists and specialists work full time. They may have to work more than 40 hours a week if they work in the field.

Environmental Scientists and Specialists
Median annual wages, May 2019

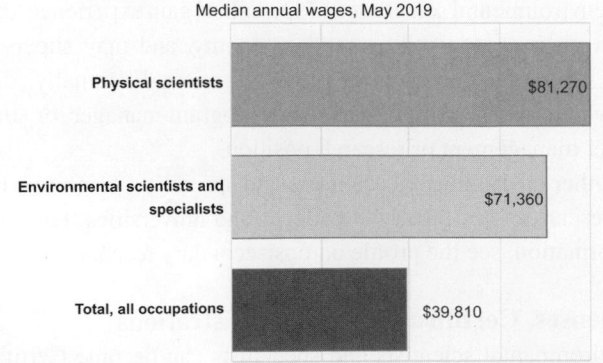

Physical scientists — $81,270

Environmental scientists and specialists — $71,360

Total, all occupations — $39,810

Note: All Occupations includes all occupations in the U.S. Economy.
Source: U.S. Bureau of Labor Statistics, Occupational Employment Statistics.

Environmental Scientists and Specialists
Percent change in employment, projected 2019-29

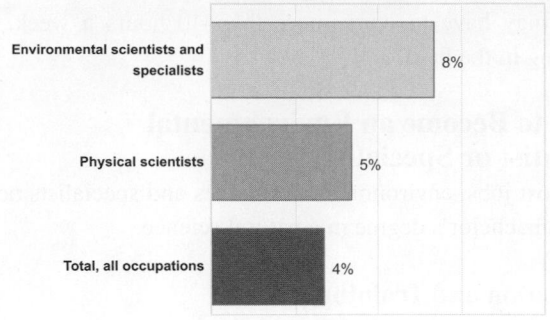

Environmental scientists and specialists — 8%

Physical scientists — 5%

Total, all occupations — 4%

Note: All Occupations includes all occupations in the U.S. Economy.
Source: U.S. Bureau of Labor Statistics, Employment Projections program.

Job Outlook

Employment of environmental scientists and specialists is projected to grow 8 percent from 2019 to 2029, much faster than the average for all occupations.

Heightened public interest in the hazards facing the environment, as well as increasing demands placed on the environment by population growth, are projected to spur demand for environmental scientists and specialists. Many jobs will remain concentrated in state and local governments, and in industries that provide consulting services. Scientists and specialists will continue to be needed in these industries to analyze environmental problems and develop solutions that ensure communities' health.

Businesses are expected to continue to consult with environmental scientists and specialists to help them minimize the impact their operations have on the environment. For example, environmental consultants help businesses to develop practices that minimize waste, prevent pollution, and conserve resources. Other environmental scientists and specialists are expected to be needed to help planners develop and construct buildings, utilities, and transportation systems that protect natural resources and limit damage to the land.

Job Prospects

Environmental scientists and specialists should have good job opportunities. In addition to growth, many job openings will be created by scientists who retire, advance to management positions, or change careers.

Candidates may improve their employment prospects by gaining hands-on experience through an internship.

Employment projections data for environmental scientists and specialists, 2019-29					
Occupational Title	SOC Code	Employment, 2019	Projected Employment, 2029	Change, 2019-29	
				Percent	Numeric
SOURCE: U.S. Bureau of Labor Statistics, Employment Projections program					
Environmental scientists and specialists, including health	19-2041	90,900	98,000	8	7,100

State & Area Data
Occupational Employment Statistics (OES)
The Occupational Employment Statistics (OES) program produces employment and wage estimates annually for over 800 occupations. These estimates are available for the nation as a whole, for individual states, and for metropolitan and nonmetropolitan areas.

Contacts for More Information
For more information about environmental scientists and specialists, including training, visit

➤ American Geosciences Institute
➤ UCAR

For more information about certification as a Certified Hazardous Materials Manager, visit
➤ Institute of Hazardous Materials Management

For more information about certification as an ecologist, visit
➤ Ecological Society of America

For information about environmental health specialists and related occupations, visit
➤ National Environmental Health Association

Epidemiologists

Summary

Quick Facts: Epidemiologists

2019 Median Pay	$70,990 per year $34.13 per hour
Typical Entry-Level Education	Master's degree
Work Experience in a Related Occupation	None
On-the-job Training	None
Number of Jobs, 2019	8,000
Job Outlook, 2019-29	5% (Faster than average)
Employment Change, 2019-29	400

What Epidemiologists Do
Epidemiologists are public health professionals who investigate patterns and causes of disease and injury in humans.

Epidemiologists collect and analyze data, sometimes through interviews, to find the causes of diseases or other health problems.

Work Environment
Epidemiologists work in offices and laboratories, usually at health departments for state and local governments, in hospitals, and at colleges and universities. Epidemiologists are also employed in the federal government by agencies such as the Centers for Disease Control and Prevention (CDC). Some do fieldwork to conduct interviews and collect samples for analyses. Fieldwork may bring epidemiologists into contact with infectious disease, but the risk is minimal because they receive appropriate training and take extensive precautions before interacting with samples or patients.

How to Become an Epidemiologist
Epidemiologists need at least a master's degree from an accredited college or university. Most epidemiologists have a master's degree in public health (MPH) or a related field, and some have completed a doctoral degree in epidemiology or medicine.

Pay
The median annual wage for epidemiologists was $70,990 in May 2019.

Job Outlook
Employment of epidemiologists is projected to grow 5 percent from 2019 to 2029, faster than the average for all occupations. Epidemiologists are likely to have good job prospects overall.

State & Area Data
Explore resources for employment and wages by state and area for epidemiologists.

What Epidemiologists Do
Epidemiologists are public health professionals who investigate patterns and causes of disease and injury in humans. They seek to reduce the risk and occurrence of negative health outcomes through research, community education and health policy.

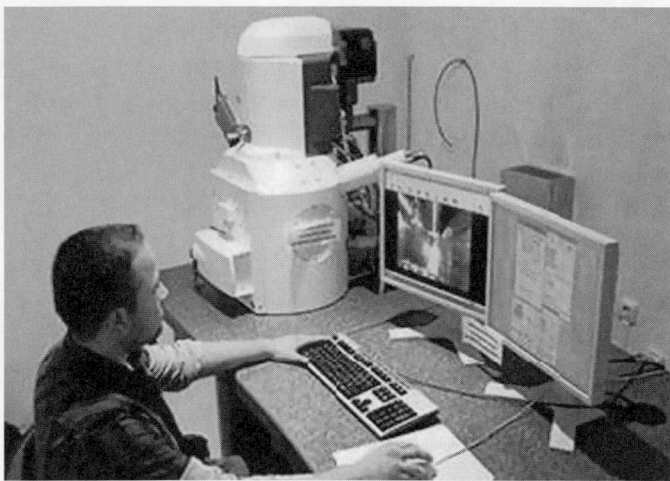

Epidemiologists monitor infectious diseases, bioterrorism threats, and other problem areas for public health agencies.

Duties

Epidemiologists typically do the following:

- Plan and direct studies of public health problems to find ways to prevent and treat them if they arise
- Collect and analyze data—through observations, interviews, and surveys, and by using samples of blood or other bodily fluids—to find the causes of diseases or other health problems
- Communicate their findings to health practitioners, policymakers, and the public
- Manage public health programs by planning programs, monitoring their progress, analyzing data, and seeking ways to improve the programs in order to improve public health outcomes
- Supervise professional, technical, and clerical personnel

Epidemiologists collect and analyze data to investigate health issues. For example, an epidemiologist might collect and analyze demographic data to determine who is at the highest risk for a particular disease. They also may research and investigate the trends in populations of survivors of certain diseases, such as cancer, so that effective treatments can be identified and repeated across the population.

Epidemiologists typically work in applied public health or in research. Applied epidemiologists work for state and local governments, addressing public health problems directly. They often are involved with education outreach and survey efforts in communities. Research epidemiologists typically work for universities or in affiliation with federal agencies, such as the Centers for Disease Control and Prevention (CDC) or the National Institutes of Health (NIH).

Epidemiologists who work in private industry commonly conduct research for health insurance companies or pharmaceutical companies. Those in nonprofit companies often do public health advocacy work. Epidemiologists involved in research are rarely advocates, because scientific research is expected to be unbiased.

Epidemiologists typically specialize in one or more of the following public health areas:

- Infectious diseases
- Chronic diseases
- Maternal and child health
- Public health preparedness and emergency response
- Environmental health
- Injury
- Occupational health
- Oral health
- Substance abuse
- Mental health

For more information on occupations that concentrate on the biological workings of disease or the effects of disease on individuals, see the profiles for biochemists and biophysicists, medical scientists, microbiologists, and physicians and surgeons.

Work Environment

Epidemiologists held about 8,000 jobs in 2019. The largest employers of epidemiologists were as follows:

State government, excluding education and hospitals..	36%
Local government, excluding education and hospitals..	18
Hospitals; state, local, and private..................................	15
Colleges, universities, and professional schools; state, local, and private..	14
Scientific research and development services...............	8

Epidemiologists typically work in offices and laboratories at health departments for state and local governments, in hospitals, and at colleges and universities. Epidemiologists are also employed in the federal government by agencies such as

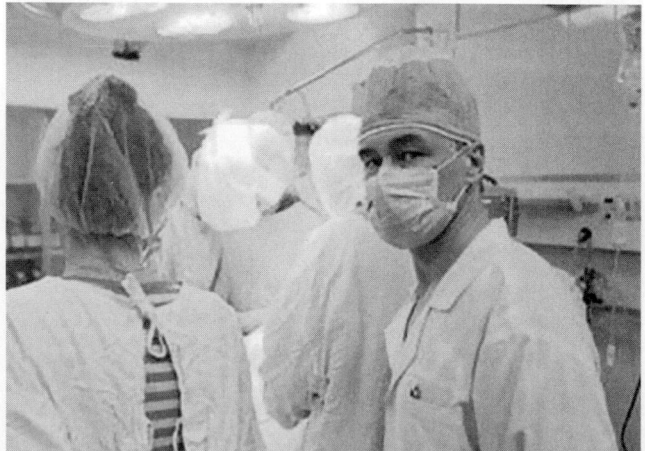

Field work may require interaction with sick patients, yet safety precautions ensure that the likelihood of exposure to disease is minimal.

the Centers for Disease Control and Prevention (CDC). Work environments can vary widely, however, because of the diverse nature of epidemiological specializations. Epidemiologists also may work in clinical settings or in the field, where they support emergency actions.

Most epidemiologists spend their time studying data and reports in an office setting. Work in laboratories and the field tends to be delegated to specialized scientists and other technical staff. In state and local government public health departments, epidemiologists may be more active in the community and may need to travel to support community education efforts or to administer studies and surveys.

Because modern science has greatly reduced the amount of infectious disease in developed countries, infectious disease epidemiologists are more likely to travel to remote areas and developing nations in order to carry out their studies. Epidemiologists encounter minimal risk when they work in laboratories or in the field, because they have received appropriate training and take extensive precautions before interacting with samples or patients.

Work Schedules

Most epidemiologists work full time and have a standard work schedule. Occasionally, epidemiologists may have to work long or irregular hours in order to complete fieldwork or tend to duties during public health emergencies.

How to Become an Epidemiologist

Epidemiologists need at least a master's degree from an accredited college or university. Most epidemiologists have a master's degree in public health (MPH) or a related field, and some have completed a doctoral degree in epidemiology or medicine.

Education

Epidemiologists typically need at least a master's degree from an accredited college or university. A master's degree in public

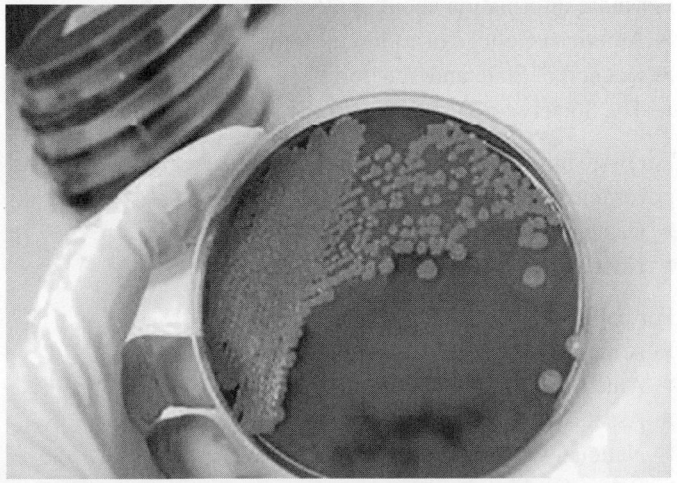

Epidemiologists need at least a master's degree from an accredited postsecondary institution.

health with an emphasis in epidemiology is most common, but epidemiologists can earn degrees in a wide range of related fields and specializations. Epidemiologists who direct research projects—including those who work as postsecondary teachers in colleges and universities—often have a Ph.D. or medical degree in their chosen field.

Coursework in epidemiology includes classes in public health, biological and physical sciences, and math and statistics. Classes emphasize statistical methods, causal analysis, and survey design. Advanced courses emphasize multiple regression, medical informatics, reviews of previous biomedical research, comparisons of healthcare systems, and practical applications of data.

Many master's degree programs in public health, as well as other programs that are specific to epidemiology, require students to complete an internship or practicum that typically ranges in length from a semester to a year.

Some epidemiologists have both a degree in epidemiology and a medical degree. These scientists often work in clinical capacities. In medical school, students spend most of their first 2 years in laboratories and classrooms, taking courses such as anatomy, biochemistry, physiology, pharmacology, psychology, microbiology, and pathology. Medical students also have the option to choose electives such as medical ethics and medical laws. They also learn to take medical histories, examine patients, and diagnose illnesses.

Important Qualities

Communication skills. Epidemiologists must use their speaking and writing skills to inform the public and community leaders about public health risks. Clear communication is required for an epidemiologist to work effectively with other health professionals.

Critical-thinking skills. Epidemiologists analyze data to determine how best to respond to a public health problem or an urgent health-related emergency.

Detail oriented. Epidemiologists must be precise and accurate in moving from observation and interview to conclusions.

Math and statistical skills. Epidemiologists may need advanced math and statistical skills to design and administer studies and surveys. Skill in using large databases and statistical computer programs may also be important.

Teaching skills. Epidemiologists may be involved in community outreach activities that educate the public about health risks and healthy living.

Pay

The median annual wage for epidemiologists was $70,990 in May 2019. The median wage is the wage at which half the workers in an occupation earned more than that amount and half earned less. The lowest 10 percent earned less than $44,000, and the highest 10 percent earned more than $119,290.

Epidemiologists

Median annual wages, May 2019

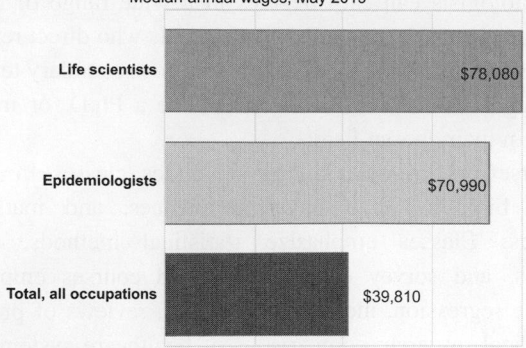

Life scientists	$78,080
Epidemiologists	$70,990
Total, all occupations	$39,810

Note: All Occupations includes all occupations in the U.S. Economy.
Source: U.S. Bureau of Labor Statistics, Occupational Employment
Statistics.

Epidemiologists

Percent change in employment, projected 2019-29

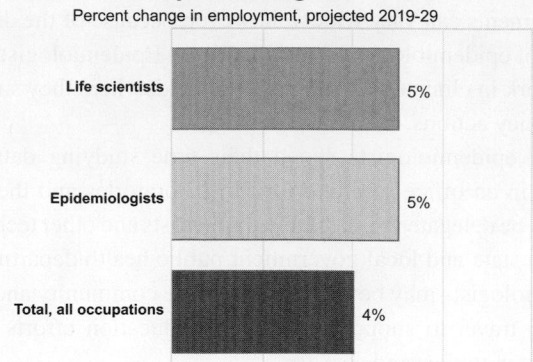

Life scientists	5%
Epidemiologists	5%
Total, all occupations	4%

Note: All Occupations includes all occupations in the U.S. Economy.
Source: U.S. Bureau of Labor Statistics, Employment Projections
program.

In May 2019, the median annual wages for epidemiologists in the top industries in which they worked were as follows:

Scientific research and development services.......... $99,770

Hospitals; state, local, and private............................ 81,810

Local government, excluding education and
hospitals... 68,410

State government, excluding education and
hospitals... 64,380

Colleges, universities, and professional schools;
state, local, and private.. 62,440

Most epidemiologists work full time and have a standard work schedule. Occasionally, epidemiologists may have to work long or irregular hours in order to complete fieldwork or tend to duties during public health emergencies.

Job Outlook

Employment of epidemiologists is projected to grow 5 percent from 2019 to 2029, faster than the average for all occupations.

Many jobs for these workers are in state and local governments, where they are needed to help respond to emergencies and to provide public health services. However, because epidemiological and public health programs are largely dependent on public funding, budgetary conditions may directly impact employment growth.

Demand for epidemiologists in hospitals is expected to increase as more hospitals join programs such as the National Healthcare Safety Network and realize the benefits of strengthened infection control programs.

Job Prospects

Interest in public health and epidemiology has increased over the past decade. The number of master's degree programs in public health specializing in epidemiology, as well as the number of graduates from these programs, has increased. Some entrants are finding strong competition for jobs, but applicants who are willing to work in any of the various specialties found in this occupation, rather than those tied to one specialty, may have less difficulty finding work. Because epidemiology is a diverse field, opportunities can generally be found if one takes a broad view.

Employment projections data for epidemiologists, 2019-29					
Occupational Title	SOC Code	Employment, 2019	Projected Employment, 2029	Change, 2019-29	
				Percent	Numeric
SOURCE: U.S. Bureau of Labor Statistics, Employment Projections program					
Epidemiologists	19-1041	8,000	8,300	5	400

State & Area Data
Occupational Employment Statistics (OES)

The Occupational Employment Statistics (OES) program produces employment and wage estimates annually for over 800 occupations. These estimates are available for the nation as a whole, for individual states, and for metropolitan and nonmetropolitan areas.

Contacts for More Information

For more information about epidemiologists, visit
➤ American College of Epidemiology
➤ Council of State and Territorial Epidemiologists
➤ The Society for Healthcare Epidemiology of America

For more information about epidemiology careers in the federal government, visit
➤ Centers for Disease Control and Prevention
➤ National Institutes of Health

For public health–related information, visit
➤ American Epidemiological Society
➤ American Public Health Association
➤ Association of State and Territorial Health Officials
➤ National Academy for State Health Policy
➤ Public Health Foundation

Forensic Science Technicians

Summary

Quick Facts: Forensic Science Technicians

2019 Median Pay	$59,150 per year $28.44 per hour
Typical Entry-Level Education	Bachelor's degree
Work Experience in a Related Occupation	None
On-the-job Training	Moderate-term on-the-job training
Number of Jobs, 2019	17,200
Job Outlook, 2019-29	14% (Much faster than average)
Employment Change, 2019-29	2,400

What Forensic Science Technicians Do

Forensic science technicians aid criminal investigations by collecting and analyzing evidence.

Work Environment

Most laboratory forensic science technicians work during regular business hours. Crime scene investigators may work extended or unusual hours and travel to crime scenes within their jurisdiction.

How to Become a Forensic Science Technician

Forensic science technicians typically need at least a bachelor's degree in a natural science, such as chemistry or biology, or in forensic science. On-the-job training is generally required for both those who investigate crime scenes and those who work in labs.

Pay

The median annual wage for forensic science technicians was $59,150 in May 2019.

Job Outlook

Employment of forensic science technicians is projected to grow 14 percent from 2019 to 2029, much faster than the average for all occupations. However, because it is a small occupation, the fast growth will result in only about 2,400 new jobs over the 10-year period. Competition for jobs is expected to be strong.

State & Area Data

Explore resources for employment and wages by state and area for forensic science technicians.

What Forensic Science Technicians Do

Forensic science technicians aid criminal investigations by collecting and analyzing evidence. Many technicians specialize in either crime scene investigation or laboratory analysis.

Duties

Forensic science technicians work in laboratories and on crime scenes. At crime scenes, forensic science technicians typically do the following:

- Analyze crime scenes to determine what evidence should be collected and how
- Take photographs of the crime scene and evidence
- Make sketches of the crime scene
- Record observations and findings, such as the location and position of evidence

Forensic science technicians perform chemical, biological, and physical analysis on evidence taken from crime scenes.

Crime scene investigators collect evidence from crime scenes.

- Collect evidence, including weapons, fingerprints, and bodily fluids
- Catalog and preserve evidence for transfer to crime labs
- Reconstruct crime scenes

In laboratories, forensic science technicians typically do the following:

- Perform chemical, biological, and microscopic analyses on evidence taken from crime scenes
- Explore possible links between suspects and criminal activity, using the results of DNA or other scientific analyses
- Consult with experts in specialized fields, such as toxicology (the study of poisons and their effect on the body) and odontology (a branch of forensic medicine that concentrates on teeth)

Forensic science technicians may be generalists who perform many or all of the duties listed above or they may specialize in certain techniques and sciences. Generalist forensic science technicians, sometimes called *criminalists* or *crime scene investigators,* collect evidence at the scene of a crime and perform scientific and technical analysis in laboratories or offices.

Forensic science technicians who work primarily in laboratories may specialize in the natural sciences or engineering. These workers, such as *forensic biologists* and *forensic chemists,* typically use chemicals and laboratory equipment such as microscopes when analyzing evidence. They also may use computers to examine DNA, substances, and other evidence collected at crime scenes. They often work to match evidence to people or other known elements, such as vehicles or weapons. Most forensic science technicians who perform laboratory analysis specialize in a specific type of evidence, such as DNA or ballistics.

Some forensic science technicians, called *forensic computer examiners* or *digital forensics analysts,* specialize in computer-based crimes. They collect and analyze data to uncover and prosecute electronic fraud, scams, and identity theft. The abundance of digital data helps them solve crimes in the physical world as well. Computer forensics technicians must adhere to the same strict standards of evidence gathering found in general forensic science because legal cases depend on the integrity of evidence.

All forensic science technicians prepare written reports that detail their findings and investigative methods. They must be able to explain their reports to lawyers, detectives, and other law enforcement officials. In addition, forensic science technicians may be called to testify in court about their findings and methods.

Work Environment

Forensic science technicians held about 17,200 jobs in 2019. The largest employers of forensic science technicians were as follows:

Forensic science technicians often work in crime labs.

Local government, excluding education and hospitals	58%
State government, excluding education and hospitals	29
Medical and diagnostic laboratories	4
Testing laboratories	2

Forensic science technicians may have to work outside in all types of weather, spend many hours in laboratories and offices, or do some combination of both. They often work with specialists and other law enforcement personnel. Many specialist forensic science technicians work only in laboratories.

Crime scene investigators may travel throughout their jurisdictions, which may be cities, counties, or states.

Work Schedules

Crime scene investigators may work staggered day, evening, or night shifts and may have to work overtime because they must always be available to collect or analyze evidence. Technicians working in laboratories usually work a standard workweek, although they may have to be on call outside of normal business hours if they are needed to work immediately on a case.

How to Become a Forensic Science Technician

Forensic science technicians typically need at least a bachelor's degree in a natural science, such as chemistry or biology, or in forensic science. On-the-job training is usually required both for those who investigate crime scenes and for those who work in labs.

Education

Forensic science technicians typically need at least a bachelor's degree in a natural science, such as chemistry or biology, or in forensic science. Forensic science programs may specialize in a specific area of study, such as toxicology, pathology, or DNA. Students who enroll in general natural science programs should make an effort to take classes related to forensic science. A list of schools that offer degrees in forensic science is available

Forensic science technicians usually have a background in natural sciences.

from the American Academy of Forensic Sciences. Many of those who seek to become forensic science technicians will have an undergraduate degree in the natural sciences and a master's degree in forensic science.

Many crime scene investigators who work for police departments are sworn police officers and have met educational requirements necessary for admittance into a police academy. Applicants for civilian crime scene investigator jobs should have a bachelor's degree in either forensic science, with a strong basic science background, or the natural sciences. For more information on police officers, see the profile on police and detectives.

Training

Forensic science technicians receive on-the-job training before they are ready to work on cases independently.

Newly hired crime scene investigators may work under experienced investigators while they learn proper procedures and methods for collecting and documenting evidence.

Forensic science technicians learn laboratory specialties on the job. The length of this training varies by specialty, but is usually less than a year. Technicians may need to pass a proficiency exam or otherwise be approved by a laboratory or accrediting body before they are allowed to perform independent casework.

Throughout their careers, forensic science technicians need to keep up with advances in technology and science that improve the collection or analysis of evidence.

Licenses, Certifications, and Registrations

A range of licenses and certifications is available to help credential, and aid in the professional development of, many types of forensic science technicians. Certifications and licenses are not typically necessary for entry into the occupation. Credentials can vary widely because standards

and regulations vary considerably from one jurisdiction to another.

Important Qualities

Communication skills. Forensic science technicians write reports and testify in court. They often work with other law enforcement officials and specialists.

Critical-thinking skills. Forensic science technicians use their best judgment when matching physical evidence, such as fingerprints and DNA, to suspects.

Detail oriented. Forensic science technicians must be able to notice small changes in mundane objects to be good at collecting and analyzing evidence.

Math and science skills. Forensic science technicians need a solid understanding of statistics and natural sciences to be able to analyze evidence.

Problem-solving skills. Forensic science technicians use scientific tests and methods to help law enforcement officials solve crimes.

Pay

The median annual wage for forensic science technicians was $59,150 in May 2019. The median wage is the wage at which half the workers in an occupation earned more than that amount and half earned less. The lowest 10 percent earned less than $35,620, and the highest 10 percent earned more than $97,350.

In May 2019, the median annual wages for forensic science technicians in the top industries in which they worked were as follows:

State government, excluding education and hospitals..	$60,830
Local government, excluding education and hospitals..	59,840
Testing laboratories..	55,100
Medical and diagnostic laboratories........................	38,380

Forensic Science Technicians
Median annual wages, May 2019

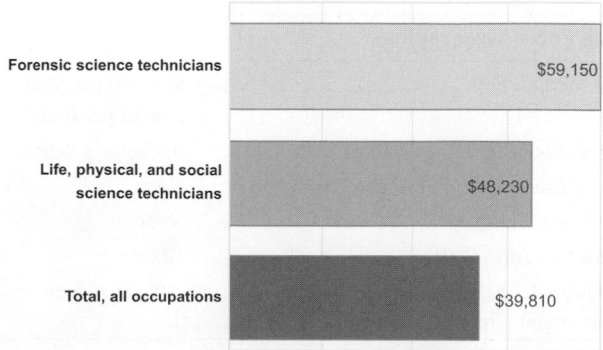

Forensic science technicians	$59,150
Life, physical, and social science technicians	$48,230
Total, all occupations	$39,810

Note: All Occupations includes all occupations in the U.S. Economy.
Source: U.S. Bureau of Labor Statistics, Occupational Employment Statistics.

Forensic Science Technicians
Percent change in employment, projected 2019-29

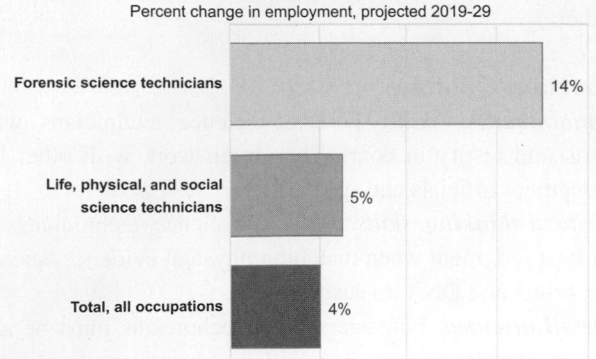

- Forensic science technicians — 14%
- Life, physical, and social science technicians — 5%
- Total, all occupations — 4%

Note: All Occupations includes all occupations in the U.S. Economy.
Source: U.S. Bureau of Labor Statistics, Employment Projections program.

Crime scene investigators may work staggered day, evening, or night shifts and may have to work overtime because they must always be available to collect or analyze evidence. Technicians working in laboratories usually work a standard workweek, although they may have to be on call outside of normal business hours if they are needed to work immediately on a case.

Job Outlook

Employment of forensic science technicians is projected to grow 14 percent from 2019 to 2029, much faster than the average for all occupations. However, because it is a small occupation, the fast growth will result in only about 2,400 new jobs over the 10-year period.

State and local governments are expected to hire additional forensic science technicians to process their high case loads. Additionally, scientific and technological advances are expected to increase the availability, reliability, and usefulness of objective forensic information used as evidence in trials. As a result, forensic science technicians will be able to provide even greater value than before, and more forensic science technicians will be needed to provide timely forensics information to law enforcement agencies and courts.

Job Prospects

Competition for jobs is expected to be strong. Applicants who have a master's degree should have the best opportunities.

Employment projections data for forensic science technicians, 2019-29					
Occupational Title	SOC Code	Employment, 2019	Projected Employment, 2029	Change, 2019-29	
				Percent	Numeric
SOURCE: U.S. Bureau of Labor Statistics, Employment Projections program					
Forensic science technicians	19-4092	17,200	19,600	14	2,400

State & Area Data
Occupational Employment Statistics (OES)

The Occupational Employment Statistics (OES) program produces employment and wage estimates annually for over 800 occupations. These estimates are available for the nation as a whole, for individual states, and for metropolitan and nonmetropolitan areas.

Contacts for More Information

For more information about forensic science technicians and related specialists, visit

➤ American Academy of Forensic Sciences
➤ American Board of Criminalistics
➤ American Board of Medicolegal Death Investigators
➤ Association of Firearm and Tool Mark Examiners
➤ International Crime Scene Investigators Association

Geographers

Summary

Quick Facts: Geographers

2019 Median Pay	$81,540 per year $39.20 per hour
Typical Entry-Level Education	Bachelor's degree
Work Experience in a Related Occupation	None
On-the-job Training	None
Number of Jobs, 2019	1,600
Job Outlook, 2019-29	-1% (Decline)
Employment Change, 2019-29	0

What Geographers Do

Geographers study the Earth and the distribution of its land, features, and inhabitants.

Work Environment

Most geographers work full time during standard business hours. Many geographers do fieldwork, which may include travel to foreign countries or remote locations.

How to Become a Geographer

Geographers need a bachelor's degree for most entry-level positions and for positions within the federal government. Work experience and a master's degree are typically required for more advanced positions.

Pay

The median annual wage for geographers was $81,540 in May 2019.

Job Outlook

Employment of geographers is projected to decline 1 percent from 2019 to 2029.

Geographers use Geographic Information Systems (GIS) equipment to create maps.

State & Area Data

Explore resources for employment and wages by state and area for geographers.

What Geographers Do

Geographers study the Earth and the distribution of its land, features, and inhabitants. They also examine political or cultural structures and study the physical and human geographic characteristics of regions ranging in scale from local to global.

Duties

Geographers typically do the following:

- Gather geographic data through field observations, maps, photographs, satellite imagery, and censuses
- Conduct research via surveys, interviews, and focus groups
- Create and modify maps or other visual representations of geographic data
- Analyze the geographic distribution of physical and cultural characteristics and occurrences
- Collect, analyze, and display geographic data with Geographic Information Systems (GIS)
- Write reports and present research findings
- Assist, advise, or lead others in using GIS and geographic data
- Link geographic data with data pertaining to a particular specialty, such as economics, the environment, health, or politics

Geographers use several technologies in their work, such as GIS, remote sensing, and global positioning systems (GPS). Geographers use GIS to find relationships and trends in geographic data. These systems allow geographers to present data visually as maps, reports, and charts. For example, geographers can overlay aerial or satellite images with GIS data, such as population density in a given region, and create digital maps. They then use the maps to inform governments, businesses, and the general public on a

Geographers use maps and global positioning systems in their work.

variety of issues, such as developing marketing strategies; planning homes, roads, and landfills; and responding to disasters.

The following are examples of types of geographers:

Physical geographers examine the physical aspects of a region and how they relate to humans. They study features of the natural environment, such as landforms, climates, soils, natural hazards, water, and plants. For example, physical geographers may map where a natural resource occurs in a country or study the implications of proposed economic development on the surrounding natural environment.

Human geographers analyze the organization of human activity and its relationships with the physical environment. Human geographers often combine issues from other disciplines into their research, which may include economic, environmental, medical, cultural, social, or political topics. In their research, some human geographers rely primarily on statistical techniques or quantitative methods, and others rely on nonstatistical sources or qualitative methods, such as field observations and interviews.

Geographers often work on projects with people in related fields. For example, geographers may work with urban planners, civil engineers, legislators, or real estate professionals to determine the best location for new public transportation infrastructure.

Some people with a geography degree become postsecondary teachers.

Many people who study geography and who use GIS in their work are employed as surveyors, cartographers and photogrammetrists, surveying and mapping technicians, urban and regional planners, or geoscientists.

Work Environment

Geographers held about 1,600 jobs in 2019. The largest employers of geographers were as follows:

Federal government, excluding postal service 61%

State government, excluding education and hospitals... 7

Architectural, engineering, and related services 6

Many geographers do fieldwork to gather information and data. For example, geographers often make site visits to observe geographic features, such as the landscape and environment. Some geographers travel to the region they are studying, and sometimes that means working in foreign countries and remote locations.

Work Schedules

Most geographers work full time during regular business hours.

How to Become a Geographer

Geographers need a bachelor's degree for most entry-level positions and for positions within the federal government. Work experience and a master's degree are typically required for more advanced positions.

Education

Geographers with a bachelor's degree qualify for most entry-level jobs and for positions with the federal government. Geographers outside of the federal government may need a master's degree in geography or in Geographic Information Systems (GIS). Some positions allow candidates to substitute work experience or GIS proficiency for an advanced degree.

Some geographers travel to do fieldwork.

Geographers may perform fieldwork as part of their education.

Top research positions usually require a Ph.D., or a master's degree and several years of relevant work experience.

Most geography programs include courses in both physical and human geography, statistics or math, remote sensing, and GIS. In addition, courses in specialized areas of expertise are becoming increasingly important because the geography field is broad and interdisciplinary. For example, business, economics, or real estate courses are becoming increasingly important for geographers working in private industry.

Other Experience

Students and new graduates often gain experience through internships. This type of practical experience allows students to develop new skills, explore their interests, and become familiar with geography in practice. Internships can be useful for jobseekers, because some employers prefer workers who have practical experience.

Licenses, Certifications, and Registrations

Although certification is not required, most positions require geographers to be proficient in GIS, and certification can demonstrate a level of professional expertise. The GIS Certification Institute offers the GIS Professional (GISP) certification for geographers. Candidates may qualify for certification through a combination of education, professional experience, and contributions to the profession, such as publications or participation in conferences. The American Society for Photogrammetry and Remote Sensing also offers certification in GIS. Candidates may qualify for certification with 3 years of experience in GIS, four references, and the passing of a written exam.

Important Qualities

Analytical skills. Geographers analyze information and spatial data from a variety of sources, such as maps, photographs, and censuses. They must then be able to draw conclusions from their analyses of different sets of data.

Geographers
Median annual wages, May 2019

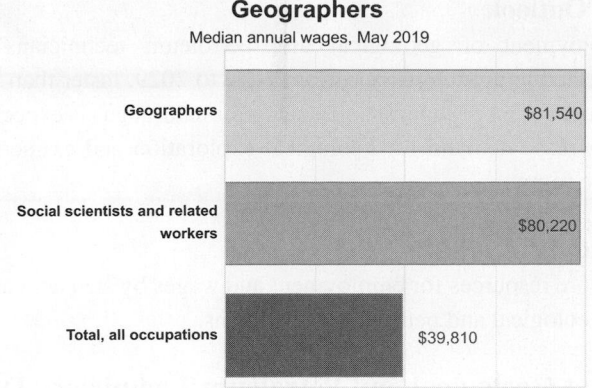

Geographers	$81,540
Social scientists and related workers	$80,220
Total, all occupations	$39,810

Note: All Occupations includes all occupations in the U.S. Economy.
Source: U.S. Bureau of Labor Statistics, Occupational Employment Statistics.

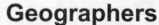

Geographers
Percent change in employment, projected 2019-29

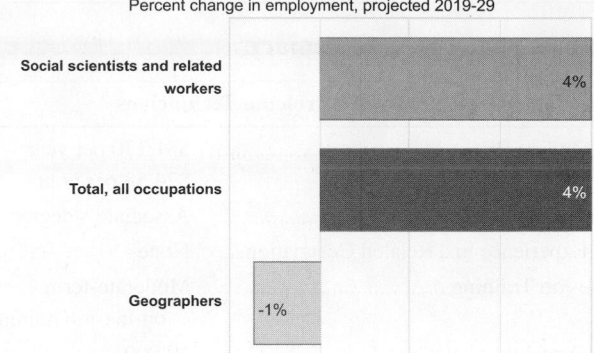

Social scientists and related workers	4%
Total, all occupations	4%
Geographers	-1%

Note: All Occupations includes all occupations in the U.S. Economy.
Source: U.S. Bureau of Labor Statistics, Employment Projections program.

Computer skills. Geographers must be proficient in GIS programming and database management and should be comfortable creating and manipulating digital images with the GIS software.

Critical-thinking skills. Geographers need critical-thinking skills when doing research because they must choose the appropriate data, methods, and scale of analysis for projects. For example, after reviewing a set of population data, they may determine the implications of a particular development plan.

Speaking skills. Geographers must be able to communicate with coworkers; present, explain, and defend their research; and be a contributing member of teams.

Writing skills. Geographers often write reports or articles detailing their research findings. They also may need to write proposals so that they can receive funding for their research or projects.

Pay

The median annual wage for geographers was $81,540 in May 2019. The median wage is the wage at which half the workers in an occupation earned more than that amount and half earned less. The lowest 10 percent earned less than $52,280, and the highest 10 percent earned more than $113,140.

In May 2019, the median annual wages for geographers in the top industries in which they worked were as follows:

Federal government, excluding postal service	$86,850
Architectural, engineering, and related services	76,220
State government, excluding education and hospitals	57,860

Most geographers work full time during regular business hours.

Job Outlook

Employment of geographers is projected to decline 1 percent from 2019 to 2029.

Budget constraints are expected to reduce employment for geographers in federal government. However, governments and businesses will still need geographers to research topics such as natural hazards and the use of resources. For example,

geographers' analyses on population distribution and land use are important for infrastructure planning and development by both governments and businesses.

Job Prospects

Job seekers can expect strong competition for jobs because of the small size of the occupation and large number of potential candidates. Those with master's degrees, specialized subject matter expertise, and experience working with geographic technologies, such as Geographic Information Systems (GIS), should have the best job prospects. Workers who have used geographic technologies to complete projects and solve problems within their specialized subfields should have better job opportunities.

Employment projections data for geographers, 2019-29					
Occupational Title	SOC Code	Employment, 2019	Projected Employment, 2029	Change, 2019-29	
				Percent	Numeric
SOURCE: U.S. Bureau of Labor Statistics, Employment Projections program					
Geographers	19-3092	1,600	1,600	-1	0

State & Area Data
Occupational Employment Statistics (OES)

The Occupational Employment Statistics (OES) program produces employment and wage estimates annually for over 800 occupations. These estimates are available for the nation as a whole, for individual states, and for metropolitan and nonmetropolitan areas.

Contacts for More Information

For more information about geographers, visit
➤ Association of American Geographers

For more information about geographic information systems (GIS) certification, visit
➤ American Society for Photogrammetry and Remote Sensing
➤ GIS Certification Institute

For information about federal government education requirements for geographer positions, visit
➤ U.S. Office of Personnel Management

Geological and Petroleum Technicians

Summary

Quick Facts: Geological and Petroleum Technicians

2019 Median Pay	$51,130 per year $24.58 per hour
Typical Entry-Level Education	Associate's degree
Work Experience in a Related Occupation	None
On-the-job Training	Moderate-term on-the-job training
Number of Jobs, 2019...................................	19,000
Job Outlook, 2019-29...................................	5% (Faster than average)
Employment Change, 2019-29	1,000

What Geological and Petroleum Technicians Do

Geological and petroleum technicians provide support to scientists and engineers in exploring and extracting natural resources.

Work Environment

Geological and petroleum technicians work in offices, laboratories, and the field. Most geological and petroleum technicians work full time.

How to Become a Geological or Petroleum Technician

Geological and petroleum technicians typically need an associate's degree or 2 years of postsecondary training in applied science or a science-related technology. Some jobs may require a bachelor's degree. Geological and petroleum technicians also receive on-the-job training.

Pay

The median annual wage for geological and petroleum technicians was $51,130 in May 2019.

Job Outlook

Employment of geological and petroleum technicians is projected to grow 5 percent from 2019 to 2029, faster than the average for all occupations. Demand for natural gas is expected to increase demand for geological exploration and extraction in the future.

State & Area Data

Explore resources for employment and wages by state and area for geological and petroleum technicians.

What Geological and Petroleum Technicians Do

Geological and petroleum technicians provide support to scientists and engineers in exploring and extracting natural resources, such as oil and natural gas.

Duties

Geological and petroleum technicians typically do the following:

- Install and maintain laboratory and field equipment
- Gather samples such as rock, mud, and soil in the field and prepare samples for laboratory analysis
- Conduct scientific tests on samples to determine their content and characteristics
- Record data from tests and compile information from reports, computer databases, and other sources
- Prepare reports and maps that can be used to identify geological characteristics of areas that may have valuable resources

Geological and petroleum technicians tend to specialize either in fieldwork and laboratory work, or in office work analyzing data. However, many technicians have duties that overlap into multiple areas.

In the field, geological and petroleum technicians use sophisticated equipment, such as seismic instruments, to gather

Geological and petroleum technicians monitor well exploration activities, and record data such as well temperatures and pressures.

Geological and petroleum technicians help identify locations that are suitable for oil and gas wells.

geological data. They also use tools to collect samples for scientific analysis. In laboratories, these technicians analyze the samples for evidence of hydrocarbons, useful metals, or precious gemstones.

Geological and petroleum technicians use computers to analyze data from samples collected in the field and from previous research. The results of their analyses may explain a new site's potential for further exploration and development or may focus on monitoring the current and future productivity of an existing site.

Geological and petroleum technicians work on geological prospecting and surveying teams under the supervision of scientists and engineers, who evaluate the work for accuracy and make final decisions about current and potential production sites. Geologic and petroleum technicians might work with scientists and technicians in other fields as well. For example, geological and petroleum technicians might work with environmental scientists and technicians to monitor the environmental impact of drilling and other activities.

Work Environment

Geological and petroleum technicians held about 19,000 jobs in 2019. The largest employers of geological and petroleum technicians were as follows:

Support activities for mining	17%
Oil and gas extraction	14
Engineering services	13
Management, scientific, and technical consulting services	5
Management of companies and enterprises	2

Geological and petroleum technicians spend their time in the field and in laboratories, or analyzing data in offices. Fieldwork requires technicians to work outdoors, sometimes in remote locations, where they are exposed to all types of weather. In addition, technicians may need to stay on location in the field for days or weeks to collect data and monitor equipment. Geological and petroleum technicians who work in offices spend most of their time working on computers—organizing and analyzing data, writing reports, and producing maps.

Work Schedules

Most geological and petroleum technicians work full time. Technicians generally work a standard schedule in laboratories and offices, but hours spent in the field may be long or irregular.

How to Become a Geological or Petroleum Technician

Geological and petroleum technicians typically need an associate's degree or 2 years of postsecondary training in applied science or science-related technology. Some jobs may require

Fieldwork requires technicians to work outdoors, sometimes in remote locations, where they are exposed to all types of weather.

a bachelor's degree. Geological and petroleum technicians also receive on-the-job training.

Education

Although some entry-level positions require only a high school diploma, most employers prefer applicants who have at least an associate's degree or 2 years of postsecondary training in applied science or a science-related technology. Geological and petroleum technician jobs that are data intensive or otherwise highly technical may require a bachelor's degree.

Many community colleges and technical institutes offer programs in the geosciences, petroleum, mining, or a related technology, such as geographic information systems (GISs). Community colleges offer associate's degree programs designed to provide an easy transition to bachelor's degree programs at colleges and universities; such programs can be useful for future career advancement.

Regardless of the program, most students take classes in geology, mathematics, computer science, chemistry, and physics. Many schools also offer internships and cooperative-education programs that help students gain experience while attending school.

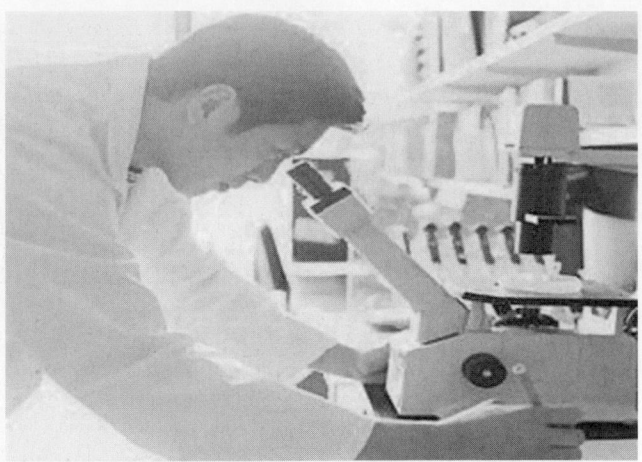

Geological and petroleum technicians use laboratory equipment such as microscopes to analyze samples collected in the field.

Important Qualities

Analytical skills. Geological and petroleum technicians examine data and samples, using a variety of complex techniques, including laboratory experimentation and computer modeling.

Communication skills. Geological and petroleum technicians explain their methods and findings through oral and written reports to scientists, engineers, managers, and other technicians.

Critical-thinking skills. Geological and petroleum technicians must use their best judgment when interpreting scientific data and determining what is relevant to their work.

Interpersonal skills. Geological and petroleum technicians need to be able to work well with others and as part of a team.

Physical stamina. To do fieldwork, geological and petroleum technicians need to be in good physical shape in order to hike to remote locations while carrying testing and sampling equipment.

Training

Most geological and petroleum technicians receive on-the-job training under the supervision of technicians who have more experience. During training, new technicians gain hands-on experience using field and laboratory equipment, as well as computer programs such as modeling and mapping software. The length of training can vary with the technician's previous experience and education and with the specifics of the job.

Pay

The median annual wage for geological and petroleum technicians was $51,130 in May 2019. The median wage is the wage at which half the workers in an occupation earned more than that amount and half earned less. The lowest 10 percent earned less than $28,530, and the highest 10 percent earned more than $104,660.

In May 2019, the median annual wages for geological and petroleum technicians in the top industries in which they worked were as follows:

Management of companies and enterprises............	$94,510
Oil and gas extraction...	72,440
Management, scientific, and technical consulting services	55,040
Engineering services...	45,450
Support activities for mining.....................................	41,050

Most geological and petroleum technicians work full time. Technicians generally work a standard schedule while in laboratories and offices, but hours spent in the field may be long or irregular.

Job Outlook

Employment of geological and petroleum technicians is projected to grow 5 percent from 2019 to 2029, faster than the average for all occupations. However, because it is a small occupation, the fast growth will result in only about 1,000 new

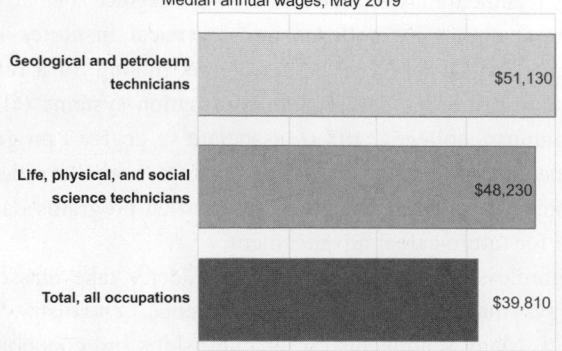

Geological and Petroleum Technicians
Median annual wages, May 2019

Geological and petroleum technicians	$51,130
Life, physical, and social science technicians	$48,230
Total, all occupations	$39,810

Note: All Occupations includes all occupations in the U.S. Economy.
Source: U.S. Bureau of Labor Statistics, Occupational Employment Statistics.

Geological and Petroleum Technicians
Percent change in employment, projected 2019-29

Geological and petroleum technicians	5%
Life, physical, and social science technicians	5%
Total, all occupations	4%

Note: All Occupations includes all occupations in the U.S. Economy.
Source: U.S. Bureau of Labor Statistics, Employment Projections program.

jobs over the decade. Demand for petroleum and natural gas, along with exploration of resources such as metals and minerals, is expected to increase demand for geological exploration and extraction in the future.

Job Prospects

Job opportunities will stem from growth and the need to replace workers who leave the occupation permanently over the projection period. The best job prospects will be for those candidates who have had hands-on training and who have good technical and analytical skills, which can be acquired through internships, co-op programs, and postsecondary education.

Employment projections data for geological and petroleum technicians, 2019-29					
Occupational Title	SOC Code	Employment, 2019	Projected Employment, 2029	Change, 2019-29	
				Percent	Numeric
SOURCE: U.S. Bureau of Labor Statistics, Employment Projections program					
Geological and hydrologic technicians	19-4045	19,000	20,100	5	1,000

State & Area Data
Occupational Employment Statistics (OES)

The Occupational Employment Statistics (OES) program produces employment and wage estimates annually for over 800 occupations. These estimates are available for the nation as a whole, for individual states, and for metropolitan and nonmetropolitan areas.

Contacts for More Information

For more information about careers in geology, visit
➤ American Geosciences Institute

For more information about careers in oil and gas exploration, visit
➤ American Association of Petroleum Geologists
➤ Society of Petroleum Engineers

For more information about careers in coal and mineral extraction, visit
➤ National Mining Association

Geoscientists

Summary

Quick Facts: Geoscientists

2019 Median Pay	$92,040 per year $44.25 per hour
Typical Entry-Level Education	Bachelor's degree
Work Experience in a Related Occupation	None
On-the-job Training	None
Number of Jobs, 2019	31,800
Job Outlook, 2019-29	5% (Faster than average)
Employment Change, 2019-29	1,600

What Geoscientists Do

Geoscientists study the physical aspects of the Earth.

Work Environment

Most geoscientists split their time between working indoors in offices and laboratories, and working outdoors. Doing research and investigations outdoors is commonly called fieldwork and can require irregular working hours and extensive travel to remote locations.

How to Become a Geoscientist

Geoscientists need at least a bachelor's degree for most entry-level positions. However, some workers begin their careers as geoscientists with a master's degree.

Pay

The median annual wage for geoscientists was $92,040 in May 2019.

Job Outlook

Employment of geoscientists is projected to grow 5 percent from 2019 to 2029, faster than the average for all occupations. The need for energy, environmental protection, and responsible land and resource management is projected to spur demand for geoscientists in the future.

State & Area Data

Explore resources for employment and wages by state and area for geoscientists.

Geoscientists often work outdoors, sometimes in remote areas and in both warm and cold climates.

What Geoscientists Do

Geoscientists study the physical aspects of the Earth, such as its composition, structure, and processes, to learn about its past, present, and future.

Duties

Geoscientists typically do the following:

- Plan and carry out field studies, in which they visit locations to collect samples and conduct surveys
- Analyze aerial photographs, well logs (detailed records of geologic formations found during drilling), rock samples, and other data sources to locate deposits of natural resources and estimate their size
- Conduct laboratory tests on samples collected in the field
- Make geologic maps and charts
- Prepare written scientific reports
- Present their findings to clients, colleagues, and other interested parties

Geoscientists use a wide variety of tools, both simple and complex. During a typical day in the field, they may use a hammer and chisel to collect rock samples and then use ground-penetrating radar equipment to search for oil or minerals. In laboratories, they may use x rays and electron microscopes to determine the chemical and physical composition of rock samples. They may also use remote sensing equipment to collect data, as well as geographic information systems (GIS) and modeling software to analyze the data collected.

Geoscientists often supervise the work of technicians and coordinate work with other scientists, both in the field and in the lab.

Many geoscientists are involved in the search for and development of natural resources, such as petroleum. Others work in environmental protection and preservation, and are involved in projects to clean up and reclaim land. Some specialize in a particular aspect of the Earth, such as its oceans.

Petroleum geologists (a type of geoscientist) search for oil and gas deposits that are suitable for commercial extraction.

The following are examples of types of geoscientists:

Geologists study the materials, processes, and history of the Earth. They investigate how rocks were formed and what has happened to them since their formation. There are subgroups of geologists as well, such as *stratigraphers*, who study stratified rock, and mineralogists, who study the structure and composition of minerals.

Geochemists use physical and organic chemistry to study the composition of elements found in ground water, such as water from wells or aquifers, and of earth materials, such as rocks and sediment.

Geophysicists use the principles of physics to learn about the Earth's surface and interior. They also study the properties of Earth's magnetic, electric, and gravitational fields.

Oceanographers study the motion and circulation of ocean waters; the physical and chemical properties of the oceans; and how these properties affect coastal areas, climate, and weather.

Paleontologists study fossils found in geological formations in order to trace the evolution of plant and animal life and the geologic history of the Earth.

Petroleum geologists explore the Earth for oil and gas deposits. They analyze geological information to identify sites that should be explored. They collect rock and sediment samples from sites through drilling and other methods and test the samples for the presence of oil and gas. They also estimate the size of oil and gas deposits and work to develop sites to extract oil and gas.

Seismologists study earthquakes and related phenomena, such as tsunamis. They use seismographs and other instruments to collect data on these events.

For a more extensive list of geoscientist specialties, visit the American Geosciences Institute.

People with a geoscience background may become postsecondary teachers.

Work Environment

Geoscientists held about 31,800 jobs in 2019. The largest employers of geoscientists were as follows:

Architectural, engineering, and related services	26%
Mining, quarrying, and oil and gas extraction	21
Federal government, excluding postal service	7
State government, excluding education and hospitals	7
Colleges, universities, and professional schools; state, local, and private	6

Geoscientists work in states that have a prominence of oil and gas activities. Workers in natural resource extraction fields usually work as part of a team, with other scientists and engineers. For example, they may work closely with petroleum engineers to find and develop new sources of oil and natural gas.

Most geoscientists split their time between working in the field, in laboratories, and in offices. Fieldwork can take

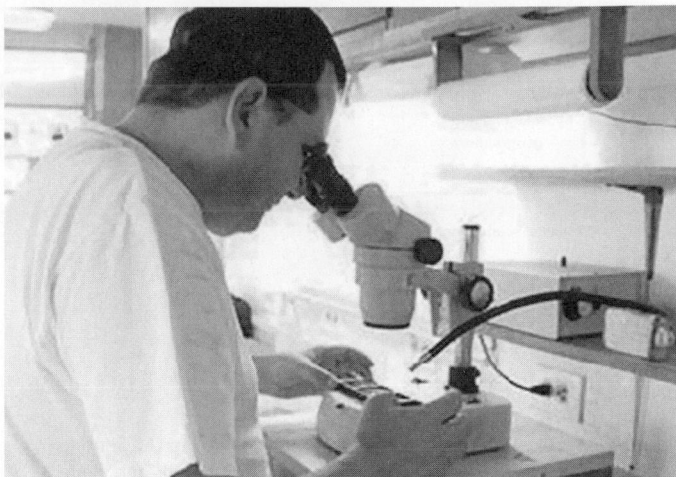

Laboratory experience is important for prospective geoscientists.

Geoscientists frequently work outdoors so they can study geological aspects of the Earth, such as geysers, up close.

geoscientists to remote locations all over the world. For example, oceanographers may spend months at sea on a research ship, and petroleum geologists may spend long periods in remote areas while doing exploration activities. Extensive travel and long periods away from home can be physically and psychologically demanding. Having outdoor skills, such as camping and hiking skills, may be useful.

Work Schedules

Most geoscientists work full time. They may work additional or irregular hours when doing fieldwork. Geoscientists travel frequently to meet with clients and to conduct fieldwork.

How to Become a Geoscientist

Geoscientists need at least a bachelor's degree for most entry-level positions. However, some workers begin their careers as geoscientists with a master's degree.

Education

Geoscientists typically need at least a bachelor's degree for most entry-level positions. A geosciences degree is generally preferred by employers, although some geoscientists begin their

careers with degrees in environmental science or engineering. Some geoscientist jobs require a master's degree.

Most geoscience programs include geology courses in mineralogy, petrology, and structural geology, which are important for all geoscientists. In addition to classes in geology, most programs require students to take courses in other physical sciences, mathematics, engineering, and computer science.

Some programs include training on specific software packages that will be useful to those seeking a career as a geoscientist. In addition to classroom and lab courses, most degree programs also include summer geology field camp courses that provide students with practical experience before graduating.

Important Qualities

Communication skills. Geoscientists write reports and research papers. They must be able to present their findings clearly to other scientists and team members as well as clients or professionals who do not have a background in geoscience.

Critical-thinking skills. Geoscientists base their findings on sound observation and careful evaluation of data.

Outdoor skills. Geoscientists may spend significant time outdoors. Familiarity with camping and hiking and a general sense of comfort being outside for long periods is useful when performing fieldwork.

Physical stamina. Geoscientists may need to hike to remote locations while carrying testing and sampling equipment when they conduct fieldwork.

Problem-solving skills. Geoscientists work on complex projects filled with challenges. Evaluating statistical data and other forms of information in order to make judgments and inform the actions of other workers requires a special ability to perceive and address problems.

Licenses, Certifications, and Registrations

Geologists are licensed in 31 states. Although a license is not required to work as a geologist in many cases, geologists that

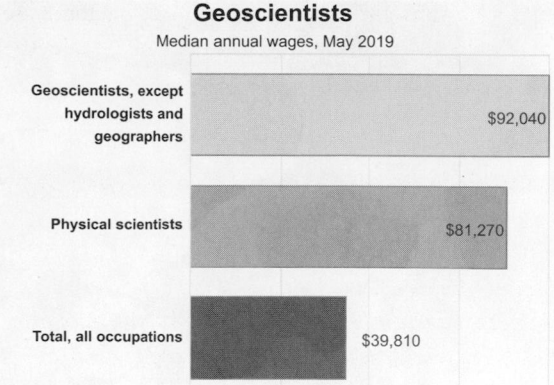

Geoscientists
Median annual wages, May 2019

Geoscientists, except hydrologists and geographers	$92,040
Physical scientists	$81,270
Total, all occupations	$39,810

Note: All Occupations includes all occupations in the U.S. Economy.
Source: U.S. Bureau of Labor Statistics, Occupational Employment Statistics.

offer services to the public in these states must be licensed. Public services include activities such as those associated with civil engineering projects, environmental protection, and regulatory compliance. Applicants must meet minimum education and experience requirements and earn a passing score on an exam. All states that license geologists use the National Association of State Boards of Geology (ASBOG), Fundamentals of Geology Exam (FGE).

Contact your state board of registration of geologists for more information.

Pay

The median annual wage for geoscientists was $92,040 in May 2019. The median wage is the wage at which half the workers in an occupation earned more than that amount and half earned less. The lowest 10 percent earned less than $51,000, and the highest 10 percent earned more than $187,910.

In May 2019, the median annual wages for geoscientists in the top industries in which they worked were as follows:

Mining, quarrying, and oil and gas extraction......	$126,750
Federal government, excluding postal service	100,590
Architectural, engineering, and related services.....	82,190
Colleges, universities, and professional schools; state, local, and private...	76,580
State government, excluding education and hospitals...	74,010

Most geoscientists work full time. They may work additional or irregular hours when doing fieldwork. Geoscientists travel frequently to meet with clients and to conduct fieldwork.

Job Outlook

Employment of geoscientists is projected to grow 5 percent from 2019 to 2029, faster than the average for all occupations. The need for energy, environmental protection, and responsible land and resource management is projected to spur demand for geoscientists.

Employment of geoscientists in the professional, scientific, and technical services industry, where most of them work, is

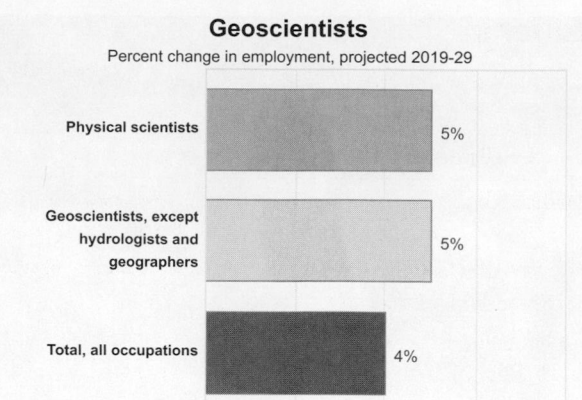

Geoscientists
Percent change in employment, projected 2019-29

Physical scientists	5%
Geoscientists, except hydrologists and geographers	5%
Total, all occupations	4%

Note: All Occupations includes all occupations in the U.S. Economy.
Source: U.S. Bureau of Labor Statistics, Employment Projections program.

projected to rise modestly. This increase will offset slower growth in the mining, quarrying, and oil and gas extraction industry, the second-largest employer of geoscientists.

Geoscientists will be involved in discovering and developing sites for alternative energies, such as geothermal energy and wind energy. For example, geothermal energy plants must be located near sufficient hot ground water, and one task for geoscientists would be evaluating if the site is suitable.

Employment projections data for geoscientists, 2019-29					
Occupational Title	SOC Code	Employment, 2019	Projected Employment, 2029	Change, 2019-29	
				Percent	Numeric
SOURCE: U.S. Bureau of Labor Statistics, Employment Projections program					
Geoscientists, except hydrologists and geographers	19-2042	31,800	33,400	5	1,600

State & Area Data
Occupational Employment Statistics (OES)

The Occupational Employment Statistics (OES) program produces employment and wage estimates annually for over 800 occupations. These estimates are available for the nation as a whole, for individual states, and for metropolitan and nonmetropolitan areas.

Contacts for More Information

For more information about geoscientists, visit
➤ American Geophysical Union
➤ American Geosciences Institute
➤ Geological Society of America
➤ U.S. National Committee for Geological Sciences

For information about petroleum geologists, visit
➤ American Association of Petroleum Geologists

For more information about licensure for geologists, visit
➤ American Institute of Professional Geologists
➤ National Association of State Boards of Geology

To find job openings for geoscientists in the federal government, visit
➤ USAJOBS

Historians

Summary

Quick Facts: Historians

2019 Median Pay	$63,680 per year $30.62 per hour
Typical Entry-Level Education	Master's degree
Work Experience in a Related Occupation	None
On-the-job Training	None
Number of Jobs, 2019	3,500
Job Outlook, 2019-29	3% (As fast as average)
Employment Change, 2019-29	100

What Historians Do

Historians research, analyze, interpret, and write about the past by studying historical documents and sources.

Work Environment

Historians must travel to carry out research. Most work full time.

How to Become a Historian

Although most historian positions require a master's degree, some research positions require a doctoral degree. Candidates with a bachelor's degree may qualify for some entry-level positions, but most will find jobs in different fields.

Pay

The median annual wage for historians was $63,680 in May 2019.

Job Outlook

Employment of historians is projected to grow 3 percent from 2019 to 2029, about as fast as the average for all occupations. Competition for jobs may be very strong because there are few positions available relative to the number of people seeking jobs in the field.

State & Area Data

Explore resources for employment and wages by state and area for historians.

What Historians Do

Historians research, analyze, interpret, and write about the past by studying historical documents and sources.

Duties

Historians typically do the following:

- Gather historical data from various sources, including archives, books, and artifacts
- Analyze and interpret historical information to determine its authenticity and significance
- Trace historical developments in a particular field
- Engage with the public through educational programs and presentations
- Archive or preserve materials and artifacts in museums, visitor centers, and historic sites
- Provide advice or guidance on historical topics and preservation issues
- Write reports, articles, and books on findings and theories

Historians conduct research and analysis for governments, businesses, individuals, nonprofits, historical associations, and other organizations. They use a variety of sources in their work, including government and institutional records, newspapers, photographs, interviews, films, and unpublished manuscripts, such as personal diaries, letters, and other primary source documents. They also may process, catalog, and archive these documents and artifacts.

Historians may engage with the public through educational programs and presentations.

Historians often study and preserve archival materials.

Many historians present and interpret history in order to inform or build upon public knowledge of past events. They often trace and build a historical profile of a particular person, area, idea, organization, or event. Once their research is complete, they present their findings through articles, books, reports, exhibits, websites, and educational programs.

In government, some historians conduct research to provide information on specific events or groups. Many write about the history of a particular government agency, activity, or program, such as a military operation or space missions. For example, they may research the people and events related to Operation Desert Storm.

In historical associations, historians may work with archivists, curators, and museum workers to preserve artifacts and explain the historical significance of a wide variety of subjects, such as historic buildings, religious groups, and battlegrounds. Workers with a background in history also may go into one of these occupations.

Many people with a degree in history also become high school teachers or postsecondary teachers.

Work Environment

Historians held about 3,500 jobs in 2019. The largest employers of historians were as follows:

Federal government, excluding postal service	22%
Local government, excluding education and hospitals	19
Professional, scientific, and technical services	17
State government, excluding education and hospitals	15

Historians work in museums, archives, historical societies, and research organizations. Some work as consultants for these organizations while being employed by consulting firms, and some work as independent consultants.

Historians may spend much of their time researching and writing reports.

Work Schedules

Most historians work full time during regular business hours. Some work independently and are able to set their own schedules. Historians who work in museums or other institutions open to the public may work evenings or weekends. Some historians may travel to collect artifacts, conduct interviews, or visit an area to better understand its culture and environment.

How to Become a Historian

Although most historian positions require a master's degree, some research positions require a doctoral degree. Candidates with a bachelor's degree may qualify for some entry-level positions, but most will not be traditional historian jobs.

Education

Historians need a master's degree or Ph.D. for most positions. Many historians have a master's degree in history or public history. Others complete degrees in related fields, such as museum studies, historical preservation, or archival management.

In addition to coursework, most master's programs in public history and similar fields require an internship as part of the curriculum.

Research positions within the federal government and positions in academia typically require a Ph.D. Students in history Ph.D. programs usually concentrate in a specific area

Historians learn to use primary sources, such as letters and photographs, in their research.

of history. Possible specializations include a particular country or region, period, or field, such as social, political, or cultural history.

Candidates with a bachelor's degree in history may qualify for entry-level positions at museums, historical associations, or other small organizations. However, most bachelor's degree holders usually work outside of traditional historian jobs—for example, jobs in education, communications, law, business, publishing, or journalism.

Other Experience

Many employers recommend that prospective historians complete an internship during their formal educational studies. Internships offer an opportunity for students to learn practical skills, such as handling and preserving artifacts and creating exhibits. They also give students an opportunity to apply their academic knowledge in a hands-on setting.

Important Qualities

Analytical skills. Historians must be able to examine various types of historical resources and draw clear and logical conclusions based on their findings.

Communication skills. Historians must communicate effectively when collecting information, collaborating with colleagues, and presenting their research to the public through written documents and presentations.

Foreign language skills. Historians may need to review primary source materials that are not in English. This makes knowledge of the other language useful during research.

Problem-solving skills. Historians try to answer questions about the past. They may investigate something unknown about a past idea, event, or person; decipher historical information; or identify how the past has affected the present.

Research skills. Historians must be able to examine and process information from a large number of historical resources, including documents, images, and material artifacts.

Pay

The median annual wage for historians was $63,680 in May 2019. The median wage is the wage at which half the workers in an occupation earned more than that amount and half earned less. The lowest 10 percent earned less than $29,760, and the highest 10 percent earned more than $114,810.

In May 2019, the median annual wages for historians in the top industries in which they worked were as follows:

Federal government, excluding postal service	$97,850
Professional, scientific, and technical services	65,060
State government, excluding education and hospitals	52,780
Local government, excluding education and hospitals	31,450

Most historians work full time during standard business hours. Some work independently and are able to set their own schedules. Historians who work in museums or other institutions open to the public may work evenings or weekends. Some historians may travel to collect artifacts, conduct interviews, or visit an area to better understand its culture and environment.

Job Outlook

Employment of historians is projected to grow 3 percent from 2019 to 2029, about as fast as the average for all occupations.

Many organizations that employ historians, such as historical societies and historical consulting firms, depend on donations or public funding. Thus, employment growth will depend largely on the amount of funding available.

Job Prospects

Historians may face very strong competition for most jobs. Because of the popularity of history degree programs, applicants are expected to outnumber positions available. Those with a master's degree or Ph.D. should have the best job opportunities.

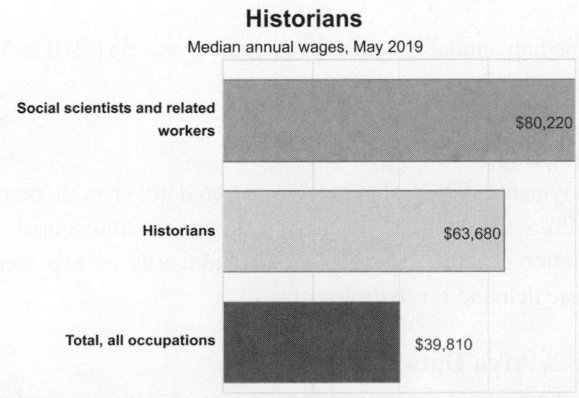

Historians
Median annual wages, May 2019

Social scientists and related workers — $80,220
Historians — $63,680
Total, all occupations — $39,810

Note: All Occupations includes all occupations in the U.S. Economy.
Source: U.S. Bureau of Labor Statistics, Occupational Employment Statistics.

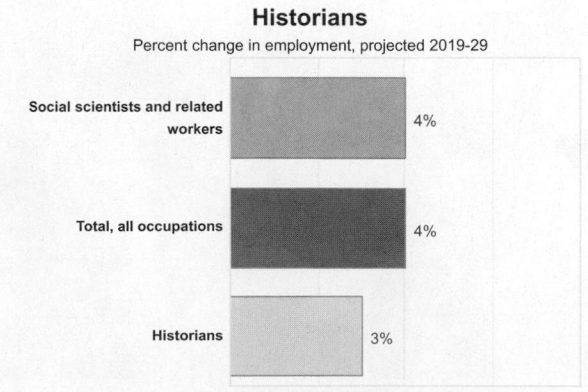

Historians
Percent change in employment, projected 2019-29

Social scientists and related workers — 4%
Total, all occupations — 4%
Historians — 3%

Note: All Occupations includes all occupations in the U.S. Economy.
Source: U.S. Bureau of Labor Statistics, Employment Projections program.

Practical skills or hands-on work experience in a specialized field such as collections, fundraising, or exhibit design also may be beneficial. Jobseekers may gain this experience through internships, related work experience, or volunteering. Positions are often available at local museums, historical societies, government agencies, or nonprofit and other organizations.

Because historians have broad training and education in writing, analytical research, and critical thinking, they can apply their skills to many different occupations. Thus, many people with history degrees do not compete for the limited number of historian positions.

Employment projections data for historians, 2019-29					
Occupational Title	SOC Code	Employment, 2019	Projected Employment, 2029	Change, 2019-29	
				Percent	Numeric
SOURCE: U.S. Bureau of Labor Statistics, Employment Projections program					
Historians	19-3093	3,500	3,600	3	100

State & Area Data
Occupational Employment Statistics (OES)

The Occupational Employment Statistics (OES) program produces employment and wage estimates annually for over 800 occupations. These estimates are available for the nation as a whole, for individual states, and for metropolitan and nonmetropolitan areas.

Contacts for More Information

For more information about historians, visit
➤ American Association for State and Local History
➤ American Historical Association
➤ National Council on Public History
➤ Organization of American Historians

Hydrologists

Summary

Quick Facts: Hydrologists

2019 Median Pay	$81,270 per year $39.07 per hour
Typical Entry-Level Education	Bachelor's degree
Work Experience in a Related Occupation	None
On-the-job Training	None
Number of Jobs, 2019	7,000
Job Outlook, 2019-29	5% (Faster than average)
Employment Change, 2019-29	400

Hydrologists work closely with engineers, scientists, and public officials to study and manage the water supply.

What Hydrologists Do

Hydrologists study how water moves across and through the Earth's crust.

Work Environment

Hydrologists work in offices and in the field. In offices, hydrologists spend much of their time using computers to analyze data and model their findings. In the field, hydrologists may have to wade into lakes and streams to collect samples or to read and inspect monitoring equipment.

How to Become a Hydrologist

Hydrologists need at least a bachelor's degree for entry-level positions; however, some workers begin their careers with a master's degree.

Pay

The median annual wage for hydrologists was $81,270 in May 2019.

Job Outlook

Employment of hydrologists is projected to grow 5 percent from 2019 to 2029, faster than the average for all occupations. Population growth and environmental concerns are expected to increase demand for hydrologists.

State & Area Data

Explore resources for employment and wages by state and area for hydrologists.

What Hydrologists Do

Hydrologists study how water moves across and through the Earth's crust. They study how rain, snow, and other forms of precipitation impact river flows or groundwater levels, and how surface water and groundwater evaporate back into the atmosphere or eventually reach the oceans. Hydrologists analyze how water influences the surrounding environment and how changes to the environment influence the quality and quantity of water. They use their expertise to solve problems concerning water quality and availability.

Duties

Hydrologists typically do the following:

- Measure the properties of bodies of water, such as volume and stream flow
- Collect water and soil samples to test for certain properties, such as the pH or pollution levels
- Analyze data on the environmental impacts of pollution, erosion, drought, and other problems
- Research ways to minimize the negative impacts of erosion, sedimentation, or pollution on the environment
- Use computer models to forecast future water supplies, the spread of pollution, floods, and other events

Hydrologists collect water samples in the field.

- Evaluate the feasibility of water-related projects, such as hydroelectric power plants, irrigation systems, and wastewater treatment facilities
- Prepare written reports and presentations of their findings

Hydrologists may use remote sensing equipment to collect data. They, or technicians whom they supervise, usually install and maintain this equipment. Hydrologists also use sophisticated computer programs to analyze the data collected. Computer models are often developed by hydrologists to help them understand complex datasets.

Hydrologists work closely with engineers, scientists, and public officials to study and manage the water supply. For example, they work with policymakers to develop water conservation plans and with biologists to monitor wildlife in order to allow for their water needs.

Most hydrologists specialize in a particular water source or a certain aspect of the water cycle, such as the evaporation of water from lakes and streams. The following are examples of types of hydrologists:

Groundwater hydrologists study the water below the Earth's surface. Some groundwater hydrologists focus on water supply and decide the best locations for wells and the amount of water available for pumping. Other groundwater hydrologists focus on the cleanup of groundwater contaminated by spilled chemicals at a factory, an airport, or a gas station. These hydrologists often give advice about the best places to build waste disposal sites to ensure that groundwater is not contaminated.

Surface water hydrologists study water from aboveground sources such as streams, lakes, and snowpacks. They may predict future water levels by tracking usage and precipitation data to help reservoir managers decide when to release or store water. They also produce flood forecasts and help develop flood management plans.

Work done by hydrologists can sometimes include topics typically associated with atmospheric scientists, including meteorologists. Scientists with an education in hydrology and a concentration in water quality are environmental scientists and specialists. Some people with a hydrology background become high school teachers or postsecondary teachers.

Work Environment

Hydrologists held about 7,000 jobs in 2019. The largest employers of hydrologists were as follows:

Federal government, excluding postal service	26%
Management, scientific, and technical consulting services	22
State government, excluding education and hospitals	21
Engineering services	11
Local government, excluding education and hospitals	10

Hydrologists solve problems concerning water quality and availability.

Hydrologists work in offices and in the field. In offices, hydrologists spend much their time using computers to analyze data and model their findings. In the field, hydrologists may have to wade into lakes and streams to collect samples or to read and inspect monitoring equipment. Hydrologists also need to write reports detailing the status of surface water and groundwater in specific regions. Many jobs require significant travel. Jobs in the private sector may require international travel.

Work Schedules

Most hydrologists work full time. However, the length of daily shifts may vary when hydrologists work in the field.

How to Become a Hydrologist

Hydrologists need at least a bachelor's degree for entry-level positions; however, some workers begin their careers with a master's degree.

Hydrologists may be involved in ensuring waste water and other waste disposal sites do not leak contaminates into the groundwater.

Education

Hydrologists need at least a bachelor's degree, and some begin their careers with a master's degree. Applicants for advanced research and university faculty positions typically need a Ph.D.

Few universities offer undergraduate degrees in hydrology; instead, most universities offer hydrology concentrations in their geosciences, engineering, or earth science programs. Students interested in becoming hydrologists need to complete coursework in math, statistics, and physical, computer, and life sciences. Hydrologists may find it helpful to have a background in economics, environmental law, and other government policy related topics. Knowledge of these areas may help hydrologists communicate with and understand the goals of policymakers and other government workers.

Important Qualities

Analytical skills. Hydrologists need to analyze data collected in the field and examine the results of laboratory tests.

Communication skills. Hydrologists prepare detailed reports that document their research methods and findings. They may have to present their findings to people who do not have a technical background, such as government officials or the general public.

Critical-thinking skills. Hydrologists develop and use models to assess the potential risks to the water supply by pollution, floods, droughts, and other threats. They develop water management plans to handle these threats.

Interpersonal skills. Most hydrologists work as part of a diverse team with engineers, technicians, and other scientists.

Physical stamina. When they are in the field, hydrologists may need to hike to remote locations while carrying testing and sampling equipment.

Pay

The median annual wage for hydrologists was $81,270 in May 2019. The median wage is the wage at which half the workers in an occupation earned more than that amount and half earned

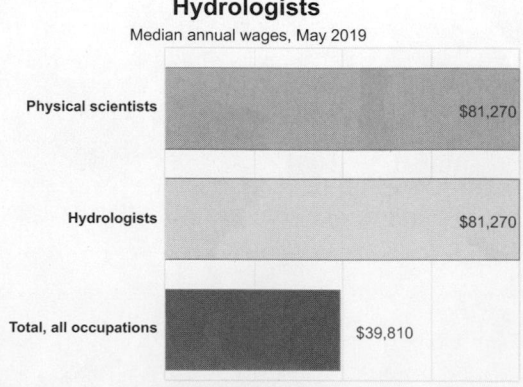

Hydrologists
Median annual wages, May 2019

Physical scientists	$81,270
Hydrologists	$81,270
Total, all occupations	$39,810

Note: All Occupations includes all occupations in the U.S. Economy.
Source: U.S. Bureau of Labor Statistics, Occupational Employment Statistics.

less. The lowest 10 percent earned less than $51,220, and the highest 10 percent earned more than $127,400.

In May 2019, the median annual wages for hydrologists in the top industries in which they worked were as follows:

Management, scientific, and technical consulting services	$93,820
Engineering services	91,810
Federal government, excluding postal service	88,330
Local government, excluding education and hospitals	77,960
State government, excluding education and hospitals	68,690

Most hydrologists work full time. However, the length of daily shifts may vary when hydrologists work in the field.

Job Outlook

Employment of hydrologists is projected to grow 5 percent from 2019 to 2029, faster than the average for all occupations. Demand for the services of hydrologists will stem from increases in human activities such as mining, construction, and hydraulic fracturing. Environmental concerns, especially global climate change and the possibility of sea-level rise in addition to local concerns such as flooding and drought, are likely to increase demand for hydrologists in the future.

Managing the nation's water resources will be critical as the population grows and increased human activity changes the natural water cycle. Population expansion into areas that were previously uninhabited may increase the risk of flooding, and new communities may encounter water availability issues. These issues will all need the understanding and knowledge that hydrologists have to find sustainable solutions. However, as governments are the main consumers of hydrologic information, budget constraints will limit growth.

Hydrologists will be necessary to assess the threats that global climate change poses to local, state, and national water supplies. For example, changes in climate affect the severity and frequency of droughts and floods. Hydrologists are critical to developing comprehensive water management plans that address these and other problems linked to climate change.

Hydrologists
Percent change in employment, projected 2019-29

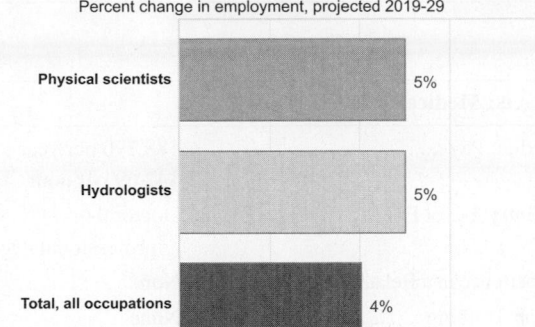

Note: All Occupations includes all occupations in the U.S. Economy.
Source: U.S. Bureau of Labor Statistics, Employment Projections program.

State & Area Data
Occupational Employment Statistics (OES)

The Occupational Employment Statistics (OES) program produces employment and wage estimates annually for over 800 occupations. These estimates are available for the nation as a whole, for individual states, and for metropolitan and nonmetropolitan areas.

Contacts for More Information

For more information about hydrology and the work of hydrologists in the federal government, visit
➤ U.S. Geological Survey

For information on federal government requirements for hydrology positions, visit
➤ U.S. Office of Personnel Management

To find job openings for hydrologists in the federal government, visit
➤ USAJOBS

For more information about careers in hydrology, visit
➤ American Geophysical Union
➤ American Geosciences Institute
➤ American Institute of Hydrology
➤ American Water Resources Association

For information from universities about research in the water sciences, visit
➤ Consortium of Universities for the Advancement of Hydrologic Science, INC. (CUAHSI)

For informal education and training in hydrology and other geoscience topics, visit
➤ MetEd

Employment projections data for hydrologists, 2019-29					
Occupational Title	SOC Code	Employment, 2019	Projected Employment, 2029	Change, 2019-29	
				Percent	Numeric
SOURCE: U.S. Bureau of Labor Statistics, Employment Projections program					
Hydrologists	19-2043	7,000	7,300	5	400

Medical Scientists

Summary

Quick Facts: Medical Scientists

2019 Median Pay	$88,790 per year $42.69 per hour
Typical Entry-Level Education	Doctoral or professional degree
Work Experience in a Related Occupation	None
On-the-job Training	None
Number of Jobs, 2019	138,300
Job Outlook, 2019-29	6% (Faster than average)
Employment Change, 2019-29	8,400

What Medical Scientists Do

Medical scientists conduct research aimed at improving overall human health.

Work Environment

Medical scientists work in offices and laboratories. Most work full time.

How to Become a Medical Scientist

Medical scientists typically have a Ph.D., usually in biology or a related life science. Some medical scientists get a medical degree instead of, or in addition to, a Ph.D.

Pay

The median annual wage for medical scientists was $88,790 in May 2019.

Job Outlook

Employment of medical scientists is projected to grow 6 percent from 2019 to 2029, faster than the average for all occupations. Medical scientists will continue to be needed because they contribute to the development of treatments and medicines that improve human health.

State & Area Data

Explore resources for employment and wages by state and area for medical scientists.

What Medical Scientists Do

Medical scientists conduct research aimed at improving overall human health. They often use clinical trials and other investigative methods to reach their findings.

Duties

Medical scientists typically do the following:

- Design and conduct studies that investigate both human diseases and methods to prevent and treat them
- Prepare and analyze medical samples and data to investigate causes and treatment of toxicity, pathogens, or chronic diseases
- Standardize drug potency, doses, and methods to allow for the mass manufacturing and distribution of drugs and medicinal compounds
- Create and test medical devices
- Develop programs that improve health outcomes, in partnership with health departments, industry personnel, and physicians
- Write research grant proposals and apply for funding from government agencies and private funding sources
- Follow procedures to avoid contamination and maintain safety

Many medical scientists form hypotheses and develop experiments, with little supervision. They often lead teams of technicians and, sometimes, students, who perform support tasks. For example, a medical scientist working in a university laboratory may have undergraduate assistants take measurements and make observations for the scientist's research.

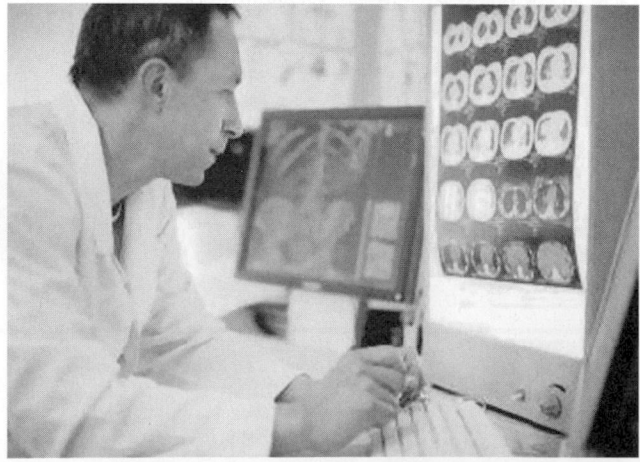

Medical scientists usually specialize in a area of research, such as neuroscience.

Medical scientists design and conduct studies to investigate human diseases, and methods to prevent and treat them.

Medical scientists study the causes of diseases and other health problems. For example, a medical scientist who does cancer research might put together a combination of drugs that could slow the cancer's progress. A clinical trial may be done to test the drugs. A medical scientist may work with licensed physicians to test the new combination on patients who are willing to participate in the study.

In a clinical trial, patients agree to help determine if a particular drug, a combination of drugs, or some other medical intervention works. Without knowing which group they are in, patients in a drug-related clinical trial receive either the trial drug or a placebo—a pill or injection that looks like the trial drug but does not actually contain the drug.

Medical scientists analyze the data from all of the patients in the clinical trial, to see how the trial drug performed. They compare the results with those obtained from the control group that took the placebo, and they analyze the attributes of the participants. After they complete their analysis, medical scientists may write about and publish their findings.

Medical scientists do research both to develop new treatments and to try to prevent health problems. For example, they may study the link between smoking and lung cancer or between diet and diabetes.

Medical scientists who work in private industry usually have to research the topics that benefit their company the most, rather than investigate their own interests. Although they may not have the pressure of writing grant proposals to get money for their research, they may have to explain their research plans to nonscientist managers or executives.

Medical scientists usually specialize in an area of research within the broad area of understanding and improving human health. Medical scientists may engage in basic and translational research that seeks to improve the understanding of, or strategies for, improving health. They may also choose to engage in clinical research that studies specific experimental treatments.

Work Environment

Medical scientists held about 138,300 jobs in 2019. The largest employers of medical scientists were as follows:

Research and development in the physical, engineering, and life sciences	35%
Colleges, universities, and professional schools; state, local, and private	23
Hospitals; state, local, and private	17
Pharmaceutical and medicine manufacturing	7
Offices of physicians	2

Medical scientists usually work in offices and laboratories. They spend most of their time studying data and reports. Medical scientists sometimes work with dangerous biological samples and chemicals, but they take precautions that ensure a safe environment.

Work Schedules

Most medical scientists work full time.

How to Become a Medical Scientist

Medical scientists typically have a Ph.D., usually in biology or a related life science. Some medical scientists get a medical degree instead of, or in addition to, a Ph.D.

Education

Students planning careers as medical scientists generally pursue a bachelor's degree in biology, chemistry, or a related

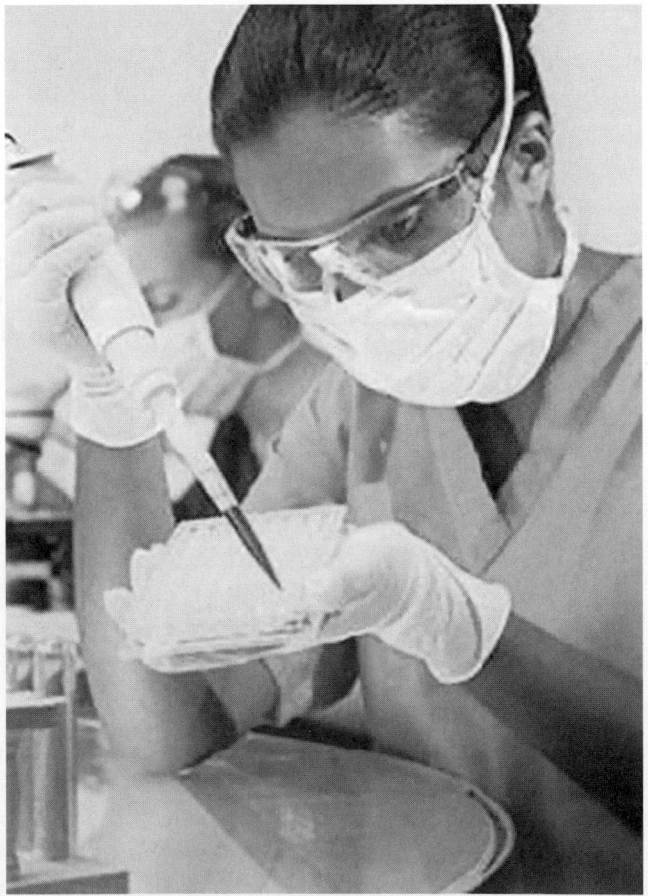

Medical scientists typically have a Ph.D. and sometimes are certified medical doctors as well.

Medical scientists usually work in offices and laboratories.

field. Undergraduate students benefit from taking a broad range of classes, including life sciences, physical sciences, and math. Students also typically take courses that develop communication and writing skills, because they must learn to write grants effectively and publish their research findings.

After students have completed their undergraduate studies, they typically enter Ph.D. programs. Dual-degree programs are available that pair a Ph.D. with a range of specialized medical degrees. A few degree programs that are commonly paired with Ph.D. studies are Medical Doctor (M.D.), Doctor of Dental Surgery (D.D.S.), Doctor of Dental Medicine (D.M.D.), Doctor of Osteopathic Medicine (D.O.), and advanced nursing degrees. Whereas Ph.D. studies focus on research methods, such as project design and data interpretation, students in dual-degree programs learn both the clinical skills needed to be a physician and the research skills needed to be a scientist.

Graduate programs emphasize both laboratory work and original research. These programs offer prospective medical scientists the opportunity to develop their experiments and, sometimes, to supervise undergraduates. Ph.D. programs culminate in a dissertation that the candidate presents before a committee of professors. Students may specialize in a particular field, such as gerontology, neurology, or cancer.

Those who go to medical school spend most of the first 2 years in labs and classrooms, taking courses such as anatomy, biochemistry, physiology, pharmacology, psychology, microbiology, pathology, medical ethics, and medical law. They also learn how to record medical histories, examine patients, and diagnose illnesses. They may be required to participate in residency programs, meeting the same requirements that physicians and surgeons have to fulfill.

Medical scientists often continue their education with postdoctoral work. This provides additional and more independent lab experience, including experience in specific processes and techniques, such as gene splicing. Often, that experience is transferable to other research projects.

Licenses, Certifications, and Registrations

Medical scientists primarily conduct research and typically do not need licenses or certifications. However, those who administer drugs or gene therapy or who otherwise practice medicine on patients in clinical trials or a private practice need a license to practice as a physician.

Training

Medical scientists often begin their careers in temporary postdoctoral research positions or in medical residency. During their postdoctoral appointments, they work with experienced scientists as they continue to learn about their specialties or develop a broader understanding of related areas of research. Graduates of M.D. or D.O. programs may enter a residency program in their specialty of interest. A residency usually takes place in a hospital and varies in duration, generally lasting from

3 to 7 years, depending on the specialty. Some fellowships exist that train medical practitioners in research skills. These may take place before or after residency.

Postdoctoral positions frequently offer the opportunity to publish research findings. A solid record of published research is essential to getting a permanent college or university faculty position.

Work Experience in a Related Occupation

Although it is not a requirement for entry, many medical scientists become interested in research after working as a physician or surgeon, or in another medical profession, such as dentist.

Important Qualities

Communication skills. Communication is critical, because medical scientists must be able to explain their conclusions. In addition, medical scientists write grant proposals, because grants often are required to fund their research.

Critical-thinking skills. Medical scientists must use their expertise to determine the best method for solving a specific research question.

Data-analysis skills. Medical scientists use statistical techniques, so that they can properly quantify and analyze health research questions.

Decisionmaking skills. Medical scientists must determine what research questions to ask, how best to investigate the questions, and what data will best answer the questions.

Observation skills. Medical scientists conduct experiments that require precise observation of samples and other health-related data. Any mistake could lead to inconclusive or misleading results.

Pay

The median annual wage for medical scientists was $88,790 in May 2019. The median wage is the wage at which half the workers in an occupation earned more than that amount and half earned less. The lowest 10 percent earned less

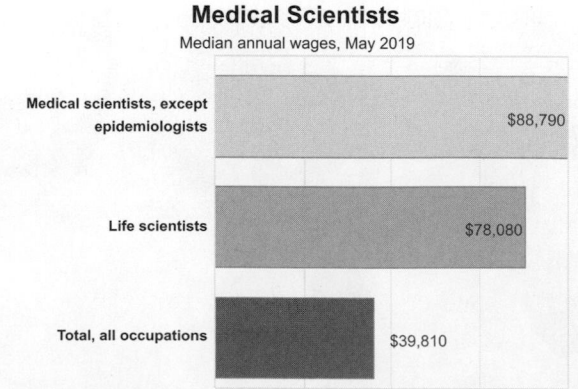

Medical Scientists
Median annual wages, May 2019

Note: All Occupations includes all occupations in the U.S. Economy.
Source: U.S. Bureau of Labor Statistics, Occupational Employment Statistics.

Medical Scientists

Percent change in employment, projected 2019-29

Medical scientists, except epidemiologists — 6%

Life scientists — 5%

Total, all occupations — 4%

Note: All Occupations includes all occupations in the U.S. Economy.
Source: U.S. Bureau of Labor Statistics, Employment Projections program.

than $49,020, and the highest 10 percent earned more than $159,680.

In May 2019, the median annual wages for medical scientists in the top industries in which they worked were as follows:

Pharmaceutical and medicine manufacturing....... $111,630

Research and development in the physical, engineering, and life sciences............................. 95,770

Hospitals; state, local, and private......................... 84,280

Offices of physicians.. 83,710

Colleges, universities, and professional schools; state, local, and private... 64,140

Most medical scientists work full time.

Job Outlook

Employment of medical scientists is projected to grow 6 percent from 2019 to 2029, faster than the average for all occupations. A larger and aging population, increased rates of several chronic conditions, and a growing reliance on pharmaceuticals are all factors that are expected to increase demand for medical scientists. In addition, frontiers in medical research are expected to require the services of medical scientists.

Medical scientists will be needed for research related to treating diseases such as AIDS, Alzheimer's disease, and cancer. Research into treatment problems, such as resistance to antibiotics, also continue to provide opportunities for medical researchers. In addition, a higher population density and the increasing frequency of international travel may facilitate the spread of existing diseases and give rise to new ones. Medical scientists will continue to be needed because they contribute to the development of treatments and medicines that improve human health.

The federal government is a major source of funding for medical research. Going forward, the level of federal funding will continue to affect competition for winning and renewing research grants.

Employment projections data for medical scientists, 2019-29					
Occupational Title	SOC Code	Employment, 2019	Projected Employment, 2029	Change, 2019-29 Percent	Numeric
SOURCE: U.S. Bureau of Labor Statistics, Employment Projections program					
Medical scientists, except epidemiologists	19-1042	138,300	146,700	6	8,400

State & Area Data
Contacts for More Information

For more information about research specialties and opportunities within specialized fields for medical scientists, visit
➤ American Association for Cancer Research
➤ American Society for Biochemistry and Molecular Biology
➤ The American Society for Clinical Laboratory Science
➤ American Society for Clinical Pathology
➤ American Society for Clinical Pharmacology and Therapeutics
➤ The American Society for Pharmacology and Experimental Therapeutics
➤ The Gerontological Society of America
➤ Infectious Diseases Society of America
➤ National Institute of General Medical Sciences
➤ Society for Neuroscience
➤ Society of Toxicology

Microbiologists

Summary

Quick Facts: Microbiologists

2019 Median Pay	$75,650 per year $36.37 per hour
Typical Entry-Level Education	Bachelor's degree
Work Experience in a Related Occupation	None
On-the-job Training	None
Number of Jobs, 2019	20,200
Job Outlook, 2019-29.....................................	3% (As fast as average)
Employment Change, 2019-29	600

What Microbiologists Do

Microbiologists study microorganisms such as bacteria, viruses, algae, fungi, and some types of parasites.

Work Environment

Microbiologists work in laboratories and offices, where they conduct scientific experiments and analyze the results. Most microbiologists work full time and keep regular hours.

How to Become a Microbiologist

A bachelor's degree in microbiology or a closely related field is needed for entry-level microbiologist jobs. A Ph.D. is typically needed to carry out independent research and to work in colleges and universities.

Pay

The median annual wage for microbiologists was $75,650 in May 2019.

Job Outlook

Employment of microbiologists is projected to grow 3 percent from 2019 to 2029, about as fast as the average for all occupations. More microbiologists will be needed to contribute to basic research, solve problems encountered in industrial production processes, and monitor environmental conditions to ensure public health and safety.

State & Area Data

Explore resources for employment and wages by state and area for microbiologists.

What Microbiologists Do

Microbiologists study microorganisms such as bacteria, viruses, algae, fungi, and some types of parasites. They try to understand how these organisms live, grow, and interact with their environments.

Duties

Microbiologists typically do the following:

- Plan and conduct complex research projects, such as improving sterilization procedures or developing new drugs to combat infectious diseases
- Perform laboratory experiments that are used in the diagnosis and treatment of illnesses
- Supervise the work of biological technicians and other workers and evaluate the accuracy of their results
- Isolate and maintain cultures of bacteria or other microorganisms for study
- Identify and classify microorganisms found in specimens collected from humans, plants, animals, or the environment
- Monitor the effect of microorganisms on plants, animals, other microorganisms, or the environment
- Review literature and the findings of other researchers and attend conferences
- Prepare technical reports, publish research papers, and make recommendations based on their research findings
- Present research findings to scientists, nonscientist executives, engineers, other colleagues, and the public

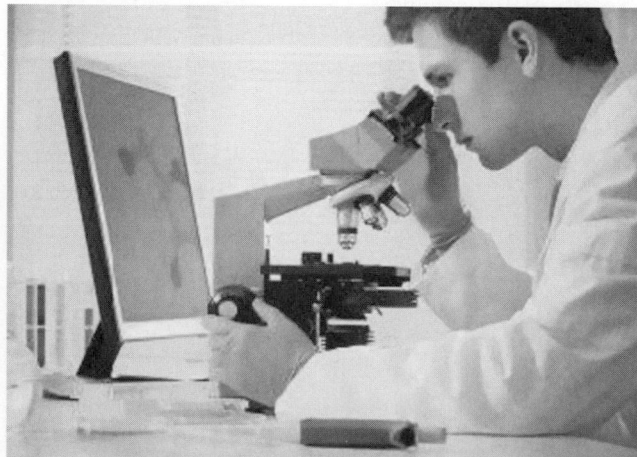

Microbiologists use laboratory equipment such as microscopes to study microorganisms.

Most microbiologists work on research teams with other scientists and technicians.

Many microbiologists work in research and development conducting basic research or applied research. The aim of basic research is to increase scientific knowledge. An example is growing strains of bacteria in various conditions to learn how they react to those conditions. Other microbiologists conduct applied research and develop new products to solve particular problems. For example, microbiologists may aid in the development of genetically engineered crops, better biofuels, or new vaccines.

Microbiologists use computers and a wide variety of sophisticated laboratory instruments to do their experiments. Electron microscopes are used to study bacteria, and advanced computer software is used to analyze the growth of microorganisms found in samples.

It is increasingly common for microbiologists to work on teams with technicians and scientists in other fields, because many scientific research projects involve multiple disciplines. Microbiologists may work with medical scientists or molecular biologists while researching new drugs, or they may work in medical diagnostic laboratories alongside physicians and nurses to help prevent, treat, and cure diseases.

The following are examples of types of microbiologists:

Bacteriologists study the growth, development, and other properties of bacteria, including the positive and negative effects that bacteria have on plants, animals, and humans.

Clinical microbiologists perform a wide range of clinical laboratory tests on specimens collected from plants, humans, and animals to aid in detection of disease. Clinical and medical microbiologists whose work involves directly researching human health may be classified as medical scientists.

Environmental microbiologists study how microorganisms interact with the environment and each other. They may study the use of microbes to clean up areas contaminated by heavy metals or study how microbes could aid crop growth.

Industrial microbiologists study and solve problems related to industrial production processes. They may examine microbial growth found in the pipes of a chemical factory, monitor the impact industrial waste has on the local ecosystem, or oversee the microbial activities used in cheese production to ensure quality.

Mycologists study the properties of fungi such as yeast and mold. They also study the ways fungi can be used to benefit society (for example, in food or the environment) and the risks fungi may pose.

Parasitologists study the life cycle of parasites, the parasite-host relationship, and how parasites adapt to different environments. They may investigate the outbreak and control of parasitic diseases such as malaria.

Public health microbiologists examine specimens to track, control, and prevent communicable diseases and other health hazards. They typically provide laboratory services for local health departments and community health programs.

Virologists study the structure, development, and other properties of viruses and any effects viruses have on infected organisms.

Many people with a microbiology background become high school teachers or postsecondary teachers.

Work Environment

Microbiologists held about 20,200 jobs in 2019. The largest employers of microbiologists were as follows:

Research and development in the physical, engineering, and life sciences	23%
Colleges, universities, and professional schools; state, local, and private	13
Federal government, excluding postal service	12
Pharmaceutical and medicine manufacturing	11
State government, excluding education and hospitals	7

Microbiologists typically work in laboratories, offices, and industrial settings where they conduct experiments and analyze the results. Microbiologists who work with dangerous organisms must follow strict safety procedures to avoid contamination. Some microbiologists may conduct onsite visits or collect samples from the environment or worksites, and, as a result, may travel occasionally and spend some time outside.

Basic researchers who work in academia usually choose the focus of their research and run their own laboratories. Applied researchers who work for companies study the products that the company will sell or suggest modifications to the production process so that the company can become more efficient. Basic researchers often need to fund their research by winning grants. These grants often put pressure on researchers to meet deadlines and other specifications. Research grants are generally awarded through a competitive selection process.

Work Schedules

Most microbiologists work full time and keep regular hours.

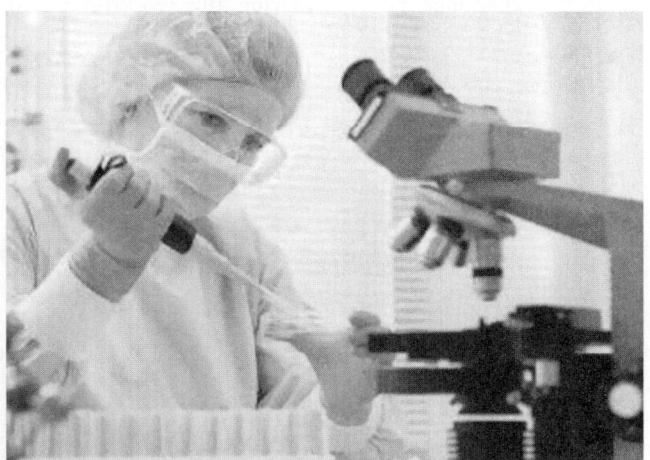

Microbiologists who work with dangerous organisms must follow strict safety procedures to avoid contamination.

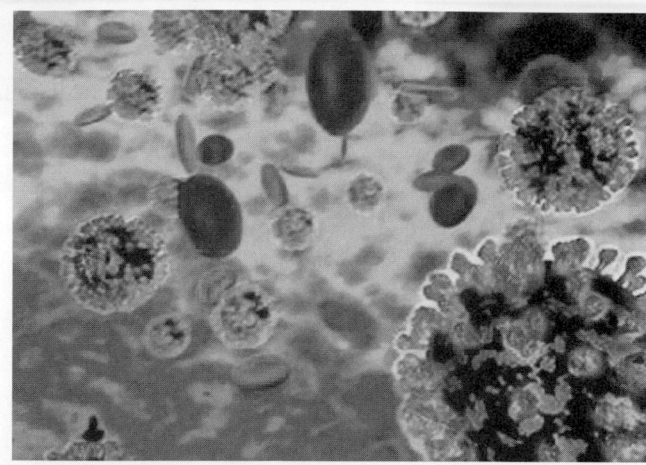

Microbiologists study the growth and characteristics of microscopic organisms such as viruses.

How to Become a Microbiologist

A bachelor's degree in microbiology or a closely related field is needed for entry-level microbiologist jobs. A Ph.D. is needed to carry out independent research and to work in universities.

Education

Microbiologists need at least a bachelor's degree in microbiology or a closely related program that offers substantial coursework in microbiology, such as biochemistry or cell biology. Many colleges and universities offer degree programs in biological sciences, including microbiology.

Most microbiology majors take core courses in microbial genetics and microbial physiology and elective classes such as environmental microbiology and virology. Students also should take classes in other sciences, such as biochemistry, chemistry, and physics, because it is important for microbiologists to have a broad understanding of the sciences. Courses in statistics, math, and computer science are important for microbiologists because they may need to do complex data analysis.

It is important for prospective microbiologists to have laboratory experience before entering the workforce. Most undergraduate microbiology programs include a mandatory laboratory requirement, but additional laboratory coursework is recommended. Students also can gain valuable laboratory experience through internships with prospective employers, such as drug manufacturers.

Microbiologists typically need a Ph.D. to carry out independent research and work in colleges and universities. Graduate students studying microbiology commonly specialize in a subfield such as bacteriology or immunology. Ph.D. programs usually include class work, laboratory research, and completing a thesis or dissertation.

Training

Many microbiology Ph.D. holders begin their careers in temporary postdoctoral research positions. During their postdoctoral appointment, they work with experienced scientists as they continue to learn about their specialties and develop a broader understanding of related areas of research.

Postdoctoral positions typically offer the opportunity to publish research findings. A solid record of published research is essential to getting a permanent college or university faculty position.

Important Qualities

Communication skills. Microbiologists should be able to effectively communicate their research processes and findings so that knowledge may be applied correctly.

Detail oriented. Microbiologists must be able to conduct scientific experiments and analyses with accuracy and precision.

Interpersonal skills. Microbiologists typically work on research teams and thus must work well with others toward a common goal. Many also lead research teams and must be able to motivate and direct other team members.

Logical-thinking skills. Microbiologists draw conclusions from experimental results through sound reasoning and judgment.

Math skills. Microbiologists regularly use complex mathematical equations and formulas in their work. Therefore, they need a broad understanding of math, including calculus and statistics.

Observation skills. Microbiologists must constantly monitor their experiments. They need to keep a complete, accurate record of their work, noting conditions, procedures, and results.

Perseverance. Microbiological research involves substantial trial and error, and microbiologists must not become discouraged in their work.

Problem-solving skills. Microbiologists use scientific experiments and analysis to find solutions to complex scientific problems.

Time-management skills. Microbiologists usually need to meet deadlines when conducting research and laboratory tests. They must be able to manage time and prioritize tasks efficiently while maintaining their quality of work.

Advancement

Microbiologists typically receive greater responsibility and independence in their work as they gain experience. They also gain greater responsibility through certification and higher education. Ph.D. microbiologists usually lead research teams and control the direction and content of projects.

Some microbiologists move into managerial positions, often as natural sciences managers. Those who pursue management careers spend much of their time on administrative tasks, such as preparing budgets and schedules.

Licenses, Certifications, and Registrations

Certifications are not mandatory for the majority of work done by microbiologists. However, certifications are available for

Microbiologists

Median annual wages, May 2019

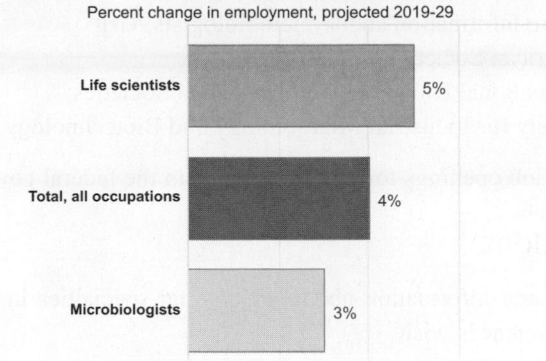

Life scientists $78,080

Microbiologists $75,650

Total, all occupations $39,810

Note: All Occupations includes all occupations in the U.S. Economy.
Source: U.S. Bureau of Labor Statistics, Occupational Employment Statistics.

Microbiologists

Percent change in employment, projected 2019-29

Life scientists 5%

Total, all occupations 4%

Microbiologists 3%

Note: All Occupations includes all occupations in the U.S. Economy.
Source: U.S. Bureau of Labor Statistics, Employment Projections program.

clinical microbiologists and for those who specialize in the fields of food safety and quality and pharmaceuticals and medical devices. Certification may help workers gain employment in the occupation or advance to new positions of responsibility.

Pay

The median annual wage for microbiologists was $75,650 in May 2019. The median wage is the wage at which half the workers in an occupation earned more than that amount and half earned less. The lowest 10 percent earned less than $43,500, and the highest 10 percent earned more than $133,280.

In May 2019, the median annual wages for microbiologists in the top industries in which they worked were as follows:

Federal government, excluding postal service $106,670

Research and development in the physical, engineering, and life sciences 101,100

Pharmaceutical and medicine manufacturing 67,990

State government, excluding education and hospitals 57,770

Colleges, universities, and professional schools; state, local, and private 56,850

Most microbiologists work full time and keep regular hours.

Job Outlook

Employment of microbiologists is projected to grow 3 percent from 2019 to 2029, about as fast as the average for all occupations. More microbiologists will be needed to contribute to basic research and solve problems of industrial production.

Microbiologists will be needed to research and develop new medicines and treatments, such as vaccines and antibiotics. In addition, microbiologists will be needed to help pharmaceutical and biotechnology companies develop drugs that are produced with the aid of microorganisms.

Aside from improving health, other areas of research and development are expected to provide employment growth for microbiologists. Many companies, from food producers to chemical companies, will need microbiologists to ensure

product quality and production efficiency. Efforts to find more clean sources of energy will involve microbiologists, such as mycologists and industrial microbiologists, who research and develop alternative energy sources such as biofuels and biomass. In agriculture, microbiologists will be needed to help develop genetically engineered crops that provide greater yields or require less pesticide and fertilizer. Finally, efforts to discover new and improved ways to preserve the environment and safeguard public health also will make use of microbiologists.

Job Prospects

Microbiology is a thriving field that should provide good prospects for qualified workers. Most of the applied research projects that microbiologists are involved in require the expertise of scientists in multiple fields such as geology, chemistry, and medicine. Microbiologists with some familiarity of other disciplines should have the best opportunities.

Much of basic research depends on funding from the federal government through the National Institutes of Health and the National Science Foundation. Federal budgetary decisions and private capital availability will affect job prospects in basic research from year to year. There is strong competition among microbiologists for research funding. However, many opportunities for microbiologists are likely to be available.

Employment projections data for microbiologists, 2019-29

Occupational Title	SOC Code	Employment, 2019	Projected Employment, 2029	Change, 2019-29	
				Percent	Numeric
SOURCE: U.S. Bureau of Labor Statistics, Employment Projections program					
Microbiologists	19-1022	20,200	20,900	3	600

State & Area Data
Occupational Employment Statistics (OES)

The Occupational Employment Statistics (OES) program produces employment and wage estimates annually for over 800 occupations. These estimates are available for the nation as a whole, for individual states, and for metropolitan and nonmetropolitan areas.

Contacts for More Information

For more information about microbiologists, visit
➤ American Society for Microbiology
➤ International Union of Microbiological Societies
➤ Society for Industrial Microbiology and Biotechnology

To find job openings for microbiologists in the federal government, visit
➤ USAJOBS

For general information about careers and specialties in biological sciences, visit

➤ American Institute of Biological Sciences
➤ The American Society for Cell Biology
➤ American Society for Clinical Pathology
➤ Federation of American Societies for Experimental Biology

For information about microbiologists' tools and activities, visit
➤ Virtual Urchin

For more information about microbiological topics, visit
➤ Microbiological Garden
➤ Tree of Life Web Project

Nuclear Technicians

Summary

Quick Facts: Nuclear Technicians

2019 Median Pay	$82,080 per year $39.46 per hour
Typical Entry-Level Education	Associate's degree
Work Experience in a Related Occupation	None
On-the-job Training	Moderate-term on-the-job training
Number of Jobs, 2019	6,700
Job Outlook, 2019-29	-19% (Decline)
Employment Change, 2019-29	-1,300

What Nuclear Technicians Do

Nuclear technicians assist physicists, engineers, and other professionals in nuclear research and nuclear energy production.

Work Environment

In nuclear power plants, nuclear technicians typically work in offices and control rooms where they use computers and other equipment to monitor and help operate nuclear reactors. Most nuclear technicians work full-time, variable schedules in the nuclear power industry. Their schedules may include working nights, holidays, and weekends. Nuclear technicians must take safety precautions to avoid exposure to radiation.

How to Become a Nuclear Technician

Nuclear technicians typically need an associate's degree in nuclear science or a nuclear-related technology. Nuclear technicians also go through extensive on-the-job training.

Pay

The median annual wage for nuclear technicians was $82,080 in May 2019.

Job Outlook

Employment of nuclear technicians is projected to decline 19 percent from 2019 to 2029. Although technicians will be needed to help maintain and upgrade existing nuclear power plants, traditional forms of power generation will likely come under increasing pressure from alternative forms of energy.

State & Area Data

Explore resources for employment and wages by state and area for nuclear technicians.

What Nuclear Technicians Do

Nuclear technicians typically work in nuclear energy production or assist physicists, engineers, and other professionals in nuclear research. They operate special equipment used in these activities and monitor the levels of radiation that are produced.

Duties

Nuclear technicians typically do the following:

- Monitor the performance of equipment used in nuclear experiments and power generation
- Measure the levels and types of radiation produced by nuclear experiments, power generation, and other activities

Nuclear technicians working for nuclear power plants use computers and other equipment to monitor and help operate nuclear reactors.

Some nuclear technicians work in laboratories. They help nuclear physicists, nuclear engineers, and other scientists conduct research and develop new types of nuclear reactors, fuels, medicines, and other technologies. They use equipment such as radiation detectors, spectrometers (utilized to measure gamma ray and x-ray radiation), and particle accelerators to conduct experiments and gather data. They also may use remote-controlled equipment to manipulate radioactive materials or materials exposed to radiation.

Work Environment

Nuclear technicians held about 6,700 jobs in 2019. The largest employers of nuclear technicians were as follows:

Electric power generation, transmission and distribution	53%
Manufacturing..	13
Employment services..	2
Engineering services..	1

Most nuclear technicians work in nuclear power plants, where they typically work in offices and control rooms. The technicians use computers and other equipment to monitor and help operate nuclear reactors. Nuclear technicians also need to measure radiation levels onsite, requiring them to visit several areas in and

Nuclear technicians use instruments, such as geiger counters, to monitor radiation levels.

- Collect samples of air, water, and soil, and test for radioactive contamination
- Instruct personnel on radiation safety procedures and warn them of hazardous conditions
- Operate and maintain radiation monitoring equipment

Job duties and titles of nuclear technicians often depend on where they work and what purpose the facility serves. Most nuclear technicians work in nuclear power plants, where they ensure that reactors and other equipment are operated safely and efficiently. The following are types of nuclear technicians who work in the power generation industry:

Operating technicians monitor the performance of systems in nuclear power plants. They measure levels of radiation and other contaminants in water systems. The levels they find could indicate a leak or could decrease the efficiency of the turbines in the power plants. They measure efficiency and ensure safety by making calculations based on factors such as temperature, pressure, and radiation intensity. Operating technicians must make adjustments and repairs to maintain or improve the performance of reactors and other equipment.

Radiation protection technicians monitor levels of radiation contamination to protect personnel in nuclear power facilities and the surrounding environment. They use radiation detectors to measure levels in and around facilities, and they use dosimeters to measure the levels present in people and objects. Technicians map radiation levels throughout the plant and the surrounding environment and recommend radioactive decontamination plans and safety procedures for personnel. They also monitor worker activity from a control room and alert personnel who may be entering a dangerous area or working in an unsafe way.

Nuclear technicians also work in waste management and treatment facilities, where they monitor the disposal, recycling, and storage of nuclear waste. They perform duties similar to those of radiation protection technicians at nuclear power plants.

Nuclear technicians may monitor radiation levels at nuclear power plants.

around the plant throughout the workday. This task may some-times require them to work outside, regardless of weather condi-tions. Working around nuclear reactors may involve exposure to high temperatures. Nuclear technicians who conduct scientific tests for scientists and engineers typically work in laboratories.

Nuclear technicians must take precautions when working with or around nuclear materials. They often have to wear pro-tective gear and special badges that indicate whether they have been exposed to radiation. Protective gear may include hard-hats, hearing and eye protection, plastic suits, and respirators.

Work Schedules

Most nuclear technicians work full time. In power plants, which operate 24 hours a day, technicians may work variable schedules that include nights, holidays, and weekends. Occasionally, plants stop operations for maintenance and upgrades. Workers may need to work overtime during these periods. In laboratories, technicians typically work during normal business hours.

How to Become a Nuclear Technician

Nuclear technicians typically need an associate's degree in nuclear science or a nuclear-related technology. Some may

Most employers prefer applicants who have at least an associate's degree in nuclear science or a nuclear-related technology.

have gained equivalent experience from serving in the military. Nuclear technicians also go through extensive on-the-job training. For safety and security reasons, nuclear technicians usually must undergo a background check and receive some type of security clearance after they are hired.

Education

Nuclear technicians typically need an associate's degree, or they may have equivalent experience from serving in the military—specifically, the U.S. Navy. Many community colleges and technical institutes offer associate's degree programs in nuclear science, nuclear technology, or related fields. Students study nuclear energy, radiation, and the equipment and components used in nuclear power plants and laboratories. Other coursework includes mathematics, physics, and chemistry.

Training

In nuclear power plants, nuclear technicians start out as trainees under the supervision of more experienced technicians. During their training, they are taught the proper ways to use operating and monitoring equipment. They are also taught safety procedures, regulations, and plant policies. Workers who do not have the appropriate associate's degree or its equivalent usually have a substantial period of onsite technical training provided by their employer before they begin full duties and a normal training schedule.

Training varies with the technician's previous experience and education. Most training programs last between 6 months and 2 years. Nuclear technicians go through additional training and education throughout their careers to keep up with advances in nuclear science and technology.

Licenses, Certifications, and Registrations

The Nuclear Energy Institute offers a certificate through its Nuclear Uniform Curriculum Program. The American Society for Nondestructive Testing offers Industrial Radiography and Radiation Safety Personnel certification. The National Registry of Radiation Protection Technologists offers certification as a Registered Radiation Protection Technologist.

Important Qualities

Communication skills. Nuclear technicians receive complex instructions from scientists and engineers that they must follow exactly. They have to ask questions to clarify anything they do not understand. Nuclear technicians must explain their work to scientists, engineers, and reactor operators. They must also instruct others on safety procedures and warn them of hazard-ous conditions. Many of the daily procedures and work pro-cesses must be thoroughly documented because of the risky nature of the work.

Computer skills. Nuclear technicians must use computers for plant operations and for normal office work, such as docu-menting their activities.

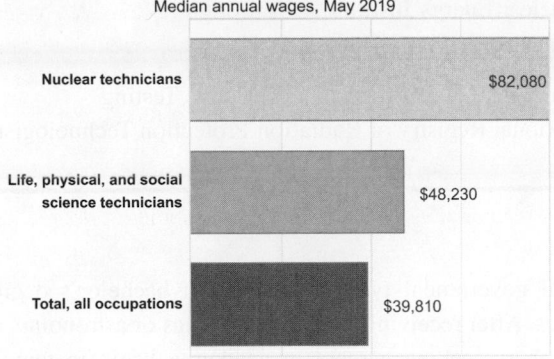

Nuclear Technicians
Median annual wages, May 2019

Nuclear technicians $82,080

Life, physical, and social
science technicians $48,230

Total, all occupations $39,810

Note: All Occupations includes all occupations in the U.S. Economy.
Source: U.S. Bureau of Labor Statistics, Occupational Employment
Statistics.

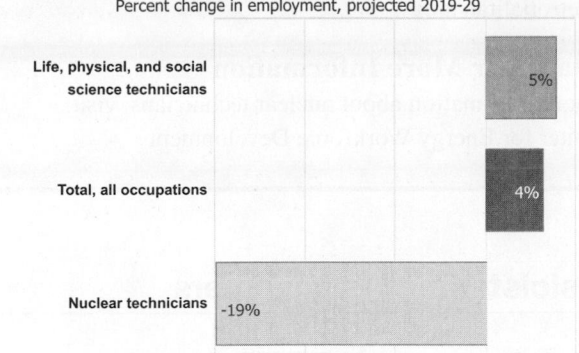

Nuclear Technicians
Percent change in employment, projected 2019-29

Life, physical, and social
science technicians   5%

Total, all occupations   4%

Nuclear technicians   -19%

Note: All Occupations includes all occupations in the U.S. Economy.
Source: U.S. Bureau of Labor Statistics, Employment Projections
program.

Critical-thinking skills. Nuclear technicians must carefully evaluate all available information before deciding on a course of action. For example, radiation protection technicians must evaluate data from radiation detectors to determine if areas are safe and must develop decontamination plans if they are not safe.

Math skills. Nuclear technicians use scientific and mathematical formulas to analyze experimental and production data, such as reaction rates and radiation exposures.

Mechanical skills. Nuclear technicians need to have strong mechanical aptitude. Nuclear power facilities are complex, and workers need to understand how the facilities work in order to make adjustments and repairs to equipment and to maintain a safe working environment. Employers hiring nuclear technicians in nuclear power plants often conduct mechanical aptitude tests as part of the hiring process.

Monitoring skills. Nuclear technicians must assess data from sensors, gauges, and other instruments to make sure that equipment and experiments are functioning properly and that radiation levels are controlled.

Advancement

With additional training and experience, technicians may become nuclear power reactor operators at nuclear power plants. Technicians can become nuclear engineers by earning a bachelor's degree in nuclear engineering. Nuclear physicists need a Ph.D. in physics. For more information, see the profiles on power plant operators, distributors, and dispatchers; nuclear engineers; and physicists and astronomers.

Pay

The median annual wage for nuclear technicians was $82,080 in May 2019. The median wage is the wage at which half the workers in an occupation earned more than that amount and half earned less. The lowest 10 percent earned less than $52,860, and the highest 10 percent earned more than $117,480.

In May 2019, the median annual wages for nuclear technicians in the top industries in which they worked were as follows:

Electric power generation, transmission and distribution	$90,410
Employment services...	81,020
Engineering services...	70,400
Manufacturing..	64,260

Most nuclear technicians work full time. In power plants, which operate 24 hours a day, technicians may work variable schedules that include nights, holidays, and weekends. Occasionally, plants stop operations for maintenance and upgrades. Workers may need to work overtime during these periods. In laboratories, technicians typically work during normal business hours.

Job Outlook

Employment of nuclear technicians is projected to decline 19 percent from 2019 to 2029.

Technicians will be needed to help maintain and upgrade existing nuclear power plants. However, traditional forms of power generation are becoming more productive because of increased automation. In addition, increasing pressure from alternative forms of power generation, such as solar arrays and wind turbines, will impact employment growth in traditional energy production.

Employment projections data for nuclear technicians, 2019-29					
Occupational Title	SOC Code	Employment, 2019	Projected Employment, 2029	Change, 2019-29	
				Percent	Numeric
SOURCE: U.S. Bureau of Labor Statistics, Employment Projections program					
Nuclear technicians	19-4051	6,700	5,400	-19	-1,300

State & Area Data
Occupational Employment Statistics (OES)

The Occupational Employment Statistics (OES) program produces employment and wage estimates annually for over 800 occupations. These estimates are available for the nation as a whole, for individual states, and for metropolitan and nonmetropolitan areas.

Contacts for More Information

For more information about nuclear technicians, visit
➤ Center for Energy Workforce Development

➤ Get Into Energy
➤ Nuclear Energy Institute

For information about certification, visit
➤ American Society for Nondestructive Testing
➤ National Registry of Radiation Protection Technologists

Physicists and Astronomers

Summary

Quick Facts: Physicists and Astronomers

2019 Median Pay	$122,220 per year $58.76 per hour
Typical Entry-Level Education	Doctoral or professional degree
Work Experience in a Related Occupation	None
On-the-job Training	None
Number of Jobs, 2019	20,500
Job Outlook, 2019-29	7% (Faster than average)
Employment Change, 2019-29	1,400

What Physicists and Astronomers Do

Physicists and astronomers study the ways in which various forms of matter and energy interact.

Work Environment

Physicists and astronomers spend much of their time working in offices, but they also conduct research in laboratories and observatories. Most physicists and astronomers work full time.

How to Become a Physicist or Astronomer

Physicists and astronomers typically need a Ph.D. for jobs in research and academia. However, physicist jobs in the federal government typically require a bachelor's degree in physics. After receiving a Ph.D. in physics or astronomy, many researchers seeking careers in academia begin in temporary postdoctoral research positions.

Pay

The median annual wage for astronomers was $114,590 in May 2019.

The median annual wage for physicists was $122,850 in May 2019.

Job Outlook

Overall employment of physicists and astronomers is projected to grow 7 percent from 2019 to 2029, faster than the average for all occupations.

State & Area Data

Explore resources for employment and wages by state and area for physicists and astronomers.

What Physicists and Astronomers Do

Physicists and astronomers study the ways in which various forms of matter and energy interact. Theoretical physicists and astronomers may study the nature of time or the origin of the universe. Some physicists design and perform experiments with sophisticated equipment such as particle accelerators, electron microscopes, and lasers.

Some physicists study theoretical areas while other physicists design and perform experiments.

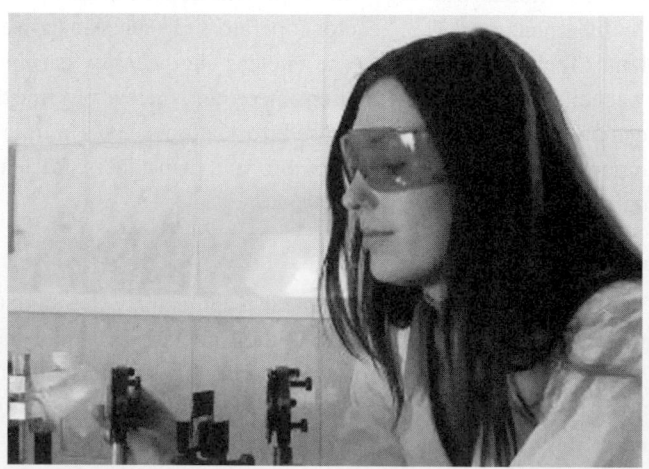

Physicists plan and conduct scientific experiments and studies to test theories and to discover properties of matter and energy.

Duties

Physicists and astronomers typically do the following:

- Develop scientific theories and models that attempt to explain the properties of the natural world, such as the force of gravity or the formation of sub-atomic particles
- Plan and conduct scientific experiments and studies to test theories and discover properties of matter and energy
- Write proposals and apply for funding to conduct research
- Do complex mathematical calculations to analyze physical and astronomical data, such as data that may indicate the existence of planets in distant solar systems or new properties of materials
- Design new scientific equipment, such as telescopes and lasers
- Develop computer software to analyze and model data
- Write scientific papers that may be published in scholarly journals
- Present research findings at scientific conferences and lectures

Physicists explore the fundamental properties and laws that govern space, time, energy, and matter. Some physicists study theoretical areas, such as the fundamental properties of atoms and molecules and the evolution of the universe. Others design and perform experiments with sophisticated equipment such as particle accelerators, electron microscopes, and lasers. Many apply their knowledge of physics to practical objectives, such as developing advanced materials and medical equipment.

Astronomers study planets, stars, galaxies, and other celestial bodies. They use ground-based equipment, such as radio and optical telescopes, and space-based equipment, such as the Hubble Space Telescope. Some astronomers study distant stars, galaxies, and phenomena such as neutron stars and black holes, and others monitor space debris that could interfere with satellite operations.

Many physicists and astronomers work in basic research with the aim of increasing scientific knowledge. These researchers may attempt to develop theories that better explain what gravity is or how the universe works or was formed. Other physicists and astronomers work in applied research. They use the knowledge gained from basic research to effect new developments in areas such as energy storage, electronics, communications, navigation, and medical technology.

Astronomers and physicists typically work on research teams together with engineers, technicians, and other scientists. Some senior astronomers and physicists may be responsible for assigning tasks to other team members and monitoring their progress. They may also be responsible for finding funding for their projects and therefore may need to write applications for research funding.

Experimental physicists develop new equipment or sensors to study properties of matter, create theories, and test them through experiments. *Theoretical and computational physicists* develop new theories that can predict properties of materials, or describe unexplained experimental results. Although all of physics involves the same fundamental principles, physicists generally specialize in one of many subfields. The following are examples of types of physicists:

Astrophysicists study the physics of the universe. "Astrophysics" is a term that is often used interchangeably with "astronomy."

Atomic, molecular, and optical physicists study atoms, simple molecules, electrons, and light, as well as the interactions among them. Some look for ways to control the states of individual atoms, because such control might allow for further miniaturization or might contribute toward the development of new materials or computer technology.

Condensed matter and materials physicists study the physical properties of matter in molecules, nanostructures, or novel compounds. They study a wide range of phenomena, such as superconductivity, liquid crystals, sensors, and nanomachines.

Medical physicists work in healthcare and use their knowledge of physics to develop new medical technologies and radiation-based treatments. For example, some develop better and safer radiation therapies for cancer patients. Others may develop more accurate imaging technologies that use various forms of radiant energy, such as magnetic resonance imaging (MRI) and ultrasound imaging.

Particle and nuclear physicists study the properties of atomic and subatomic particles, such as quarks, electrons, and nuclei, and the forces that cause their interactions.

Plasma physicists study plasmas, which are considered a distinct state of matter and occur naturally in stars and interplanetary space and artificially in neon signs and plasma screen televisions. Many plasma physicists study ways to create fusion reactors that might be a future source of energy.

Unlike physicists, astronomers cannot experiment on their subjects, because they are so far away that they cannot be touched or interacted with. Therefore, astronomers generally make observations or work on theory. *Observational astronomers* observe celestial objects and collect data on them. *Theoretical astronomers* analyze, model, and theorize about systems and how they work and evolve. The following are examples of types of astronomers who specialize by the objects and phenomena they study:

Cosmologists and *extragalactic astronomers* study the entire universe. They study the creation, evolution, and possible futures of the universe and its galaxies. These scientists have recently developed several theories important to the study of physics and astronomy, including string, dark-matter, and dark-energy theories.

Galactic, planetary, solar, and stellar astronomers study phenomena that take place in the universe at the scale of stars, planets, and solar systems. For example, these astronomers study the sun, stellar evolution, planetary formation, and interactions between stars

Optical and radio astronomers use optical or radio telescopes to study motions and evolution of stars, galaxies, and the larger scale structure of the universe.

Growing numbers of physicists work in interdisciplinary fields, such as biophysics, chemical physics, and geophysics. For more information, see the profiles on biochemists and biophysicists and geoscientists.

Many people with a physics or astronomy background become professors or teachers. For more information, see the profiles on high school teachers and postsecondary teachers.

Work Environment

Astronomers held about 2,300 jobs in 2019. The largest employers of astronomers were as follows:

Colleges, universities, and professional schools; state, local, and private...	38%
Federal government, excluding postal service	22

Physicists held about 18,200 jobs in 2019. The largest employers of physicists were as follows:

Scientific research and development services.................	31%
Colleges, universities, and professional schools; state, local, and private	22
Federal government, excluding postal service	19
Ambulatory healthcare services......................................	4

The National Aeronautics and Space Administration (NASA) and agencies within the U.S. Department of Defense have traditionally been two of the largest employers of physicists and astronomers in the federal government. The scientific research-and-development industry includes both private and federally funded national laboratories, such as the Lawrence Livermore Laboratory in California, the Los Alamos National Laboratory in New Mexico, and the Goddard Institute in Maryland.

Physics research is usually done in small- or medium-sized laboratories. However, experiments in some areas of physics, such as nuclear and high-energy physics, may require extremely large and expensive equipment, such as particle accelerators and nuclear reactors. Although physics research may require extensive experimentation in laboratories, physicists still spend much of their time in offices, planning, analyzing, fundraising, and reporting on research.

Most astronomers work in offices and may visit observatories a few times a year. An observatory is a building that houses ground-based telescopes used to gather data and make observations. Some astronomers work full time in observatories.

Some physicists and astronomers work away from home temporarily at national or international facilities that have unique equipment, such as particle accelerators and gamma ray telescopes. They also frequently travel to meetings to present research results, discuss ideas with colleagues, and learn more about new developments in their field.

Work Schedules

Most physicists and astronomers work full time. Astronomers may need to work at night, because radiation from the sun tends to interfere less with observations made during nighttime hours. Astronomers typically visit observatories only a few times per year and therefore keep normal office hours.

How to Become a Physicist or Astronomer

Physicists and astronomers typically need a Ph.D. for jobs in research and academia. However, physicist jobs in the federal government typically require a bachelor's degree in physics. After receiving a Ph.D. in physics or astronomy, many researchers seeking careers in academia begin in temporary postdoctoral research positions.

Education

A Ph.D. in physics, astronomy, or a related field is needed for jobs in research or academia or for independent research positions in industry.

Graduate students usually concentrate in a subfield of physics or astronomy, such as condensed matter physics or cosmology. In

Some astronomers work away from home temporarily at national or international facilities that have unique equipment.

Astronomers study planets, stars, galaxies, and other celestial bodies.

addition to taking courses in physics or astronomy, Ph.D. students need to take courses in math, such as calculus, linear algebra, and statistics. Computer science classes also are essential, because physicists and astronomers often develop specialized computer programs that are used to gather, analyze, and model data.

Those with a master's degree in physics may qualify for jobs in applied research and development for manufacturing and healthcare companies. Many master's degree programs specialize in preparing students for physics-related research-and-development positions that do not require a Ph.D.

Most physics and astronomy graduate students have a bachelor's degree in physics or a related field. A bachelor's degree in physics is often considered good preparation for Ph.D. programs in astronomy, although an undergraduate degree in astronomy may be preferred by some universities. Undergraduate physics programs provide a broad background in the natural sciences and mathematics. Typical courses include classical and quantum mechanics, thermodynamics, optics, and electromagnetism.

Students may choose to complete an internship during their undergraduate curriculum in order to gain additional hands-on experience. The American Astronomical Society has a directory of internships for astronomy students, and the American Physical Society lists internships for students in physics.

Jobseekers with only a bachelor's degree in physics usually are qualified to work as technicians and research assistants in related fields, such as engineering and computer science. Those with a bachelor's degree in astronomy also may qualify to work as an assistant at an observatory. Students who do not want to continue their studies to the doctoral level may want to take courses in instrument building and computer science.

Some master's degree and bachelor's degree holders find work in the federal government. Others may become science teachers in middle schools and high schools.

Training

Many physics and astronomy Ph.D. holders who seek employment as full-time researchers begin their careers in a temporary postdoctoral research position, which typically lasts 2 to 3 years. During their postdoctoral appointment, they work with experienced scientists and continue to learn about their specialties or develop a broader understanding of related areas of research. Senior scientists may carefully supervise their initial work, but as these postdoctoral workers gain experience, they usually do more complex tasks and have greater independence in their work.

Important Qualities

Analytical skills. Physicists and astronomers need to think logically in order to carry out scientific experiments and studies. They must be precise and accurate in their analyses because errors could invalidate their research.

Communication skills. Physicists and astronomers present their research at scientific conferences, to the public, or to government and business leaders. Physicists and astronomers write technical reports that may be published in scientific journals. They also write proposals for research funding.

Critical-thinking skills. Physicists and astronomers must carefully evaluate their own work and the work of others. They must determine whether results and conclusions are accurate and based on sound science.

Curiosity. Physicists and astronomers work in fields that are on the cutting edge of technology. They must be very keen to learn continuously throughout their careers in order to keep up with advances in a wide range of technical subjects.

Interpersonal skills. Physicists and astronomers must collaborate extensively with others in both academic and industrial research contexts. They need to work well with others toward a common goal. Interpersonal skills also should help researchers secure funding for their projects.

Math skills. Physicists and astronomers perform complex calculations involving calculus, geometry, algebra, and other areas of math. They must express their research in mathematical terms.

Problem-solving skills. Physicists and astronomers use scientific observation and analysis, as well as creative thinking, to solve complex scientific problems. Physicists and astronomers may need to redesign their approach and find a solution when an experiment or theory fails to produce the needed information or result.

Self-discipline. Physicists and astronomers need to stay motivated, since they spend a lot of time analyzing large datasets to try to discern patterns that will yield information. This work requires the ability to focus for long periods.

Licenses, Certifications, and Registrations

Some positions with the federal government, such as those involving nuclear energy and other sensitive research areas, may require applicants to be U.S. citizens and hold a security clearance.

Advancement

With experience, physicists and astronomers may gain greater independence in their work, as well as larger research budgets. Those in university positions may also gain tenure with more experience. Some physicists and astronomers move into managerial positions, typically as a natural sciences manager, and spend a large part of their time preparing budgets and schedules. Physicists and astronomers need a Ph.D. for most management positions.

Pay

The median annual wage for astronomers was $114,590 in May 2019. The median wage is the wage at which half the workers in an occupation earned more than that amount and half earned less. The lowest 10 percent earned less than $59,420, and the highest 10 percent earned more than $185,780.

The median annual wage for physicists was $122,850 in May 2019. The lowest 10 percent earned less than $62,470, and the highest 10 percent earned more than $201,990.

In May 2019, the median annual wages for astronomers in the top industries in which they worked were as follows:

Federal government, excluding postal service	$148,110
Colleges, universities, and professional schools; state, local, and private...	86,850

In May 2019, the median annual wages for physicists in the top industries in which they worked were as follows:

Ambulatory healthcare services.............................	$178,690
Scientific research and development services.......	131,870
Federal government, excluding postal service	120,370
Colleges, universities, and professional schools; state, local, and private...	78,800

Most physicists and astronomers work full time. Astronomers may need to work at night, because radiation from the sun tends to interfere less with observations made during nighttime hours. Astronomers typically visit observatories only a few times per year and therefore keep normal office hours.

Job Outlook

Overall employment of physicists and astronomers is projected to grow 7 percent from 2019 to 2029, faster than the average for all occupations.

Physicists are projected to have employment growth in the scientific research and development services, educational services, and healthcare and social assistance industries.

Job Prospects

Competition for permanent research appointments, such as those at colleges and universities, is expected to be strong. Increasingly, those with a Ph.D. may need to work through multiple postdoctoral appointments before finding a permanent position. In addition, the number of research proposals submitted for funding has been growing faster than the amount of funds available, causing more competition for research grants.

Despite competition for traditional research jobs, prospects should be good for physicists in applied research, development, and related technical fields. Graduates with any academic degree in physics or astronomy, from a bachelor's degree to a doctorate, will find their knowledge of science and math useful for entry into many other occupations. Database management skills also are beneficial, because of the large datasets these professionals work with.

A large part of physics and astronomy research depends on federal funds, so federal budgets have a substantial impact on job prospects from year to year.

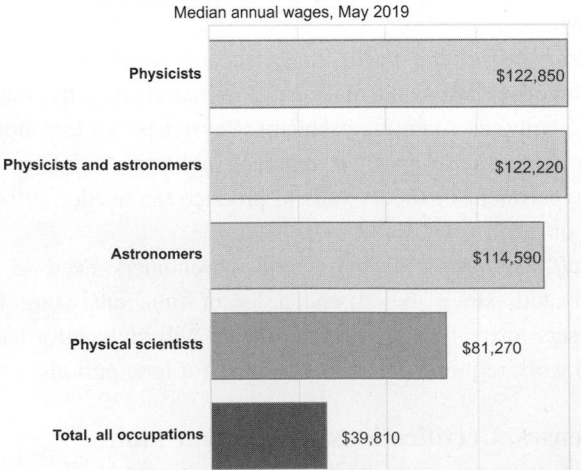

Physicists and Astronomers
Median annual wages, May 2019

Physicists	$122,850
Physicists and astronomers	$122,220
Astronomers	$114,590
Physical scientists	$81,270
Total, all occupations	$39,810

Note: All Occupations includes all occupations in the U.S. Economy.
Source: U.S. Bureau of Labor Statistics, Occupational Employment Statistics.

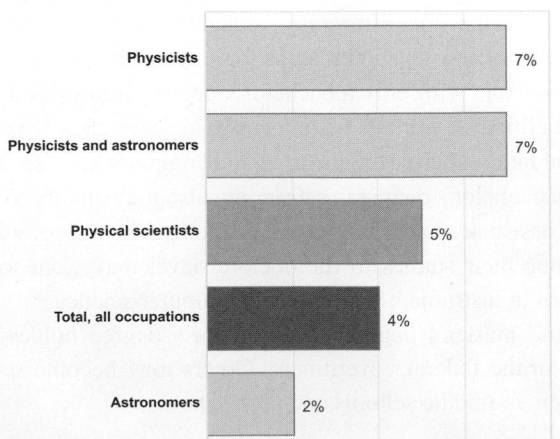

Physicists and Astronomers
Percent change in employment, projected 2019-29

Physicists	7%
Physicists and astronomers	7%
Physical scientists	5%
Total, all occupations	4%
Astronomers	2%

Note: All Occupations includes all occupations in the U.S. Economy.
Source: U.S. Bureau of Labor Statistics, Employment Projections program.

Employment projections data for physicists and astronomers, 2019-29					
Occupational Title	SOC Code	Employment, 2019	Projected Employment, 2029	Change, 2019-29	
				Percent	Numeric
SOURCE: U.S. Bureau of Labor Statistics, Employment Projections program					
Astronomers and physicists	19-2010	20,500	21,900	7	1,400
Physicists	19-2012	18,200	19,500	7	1,300
Astronomers	19-2011	2,300	2,400	2	100

State & Area Data
Occupational Employment Statistics (OES)

The Occupational Employment Statistics (OES) program produces employment and wage estimates annually for over 800 occupations. These estimates are available for the nation as a whole, for individual states, and for metropolitan and nonmetropolitan areas.

Contacts for More Information

For more information about astronomy careers and for a listing of colleges and universities offering astronomy programs, visit
➤ American Astronomical Society

For a listing of colleges and universities offering physics programs, visit
➤ Physics Careers Resource

For more information about physics careers and education, visit
➤ American Institute of Physics
➤ American Physical Society

For information about internship programs, visit
➤ American Astronomical Society
➤ American Physical Society

To find job openings for physicists and astronomers in the federal government, visit
➤ USAJOBS

Political Scientists

Summary

Quick Facts: Political Scientists

2019 Median Pay	$122,220 per year $58.76 per hour
Typical Entry-Level Education	Master's degree
Work Experience in a Related Occupation	None
On-the-job Training	None
Number of Jobs, 2019	7,000
Job Outlook, 2019-29	6% (Faster than average)
Employment Change, 2019-29	400

What Political Scientists Do
Political scientists study the origin, development, and operation of political systems.

Work Environment
Political scientists typically work full time in an office. They sometimes work additional hours to finish reports and meet deadlines.

How to Become a Political Scientist
Political scientists need a master's degree or Ph.D. in political science, public administration, or a related field.

Pay
The median annual wage for political scientists was $122,220 in May 2019.

Job Outlook
Employment of political scientists is projected to grow 6 percent from 2019 to 2029, faster than the average for all occupations. Increased demand for public policy analysis in both government and non-government organizations will support employment growth for these workers.

State & Area Data
Explore resources for employment and wages by state and area for political scientists.

Political scientists research policies, trends, and issues.

What Political Scientists Do

Political scientists study the origin, development, and operation of political systems. They research political ideas and analyze governments, policies, political trends, and related issues.

Duties

Political scientists typically do the following:

- Research political subjects, such as the U.S. political system and foreign relations
- Collect and analyze data from sources such as public opinion surveys
- Develop and test political theories
- Evaluate the effects of policies and laws on government, businesses, and people
- Monitor current events, policy decisions, and other related issues
- Forecast political, economic, and social trends
- Submit research results by giving presentations and publishing articles

Political scientists usually conduct research in one of the following areas: national politics, comparative politics, international relations, or political theory.

Often, political scientists use qualitative methods in their research, gathering information from numerous sources. For example, they may use historical documents to analyze past government structures and policies. Political scientists also rely on quantitative methods to develop and research theories. For example, they may analyze voter registration data to identify voting patterns. Political scientists study a wide range of topics such as U.S. political parties, how political structures differ among countries, globalization, and the history of political thought.

Political scientists also work as *policy analysts* for organizations that have a stake in policy, such as government, labor unions, and political groups. They evaluate current policies and events using public opinion surveys, economic data, and election results. From these sources, they try to anticipate the effects of new policies.

Political scientists often research the effects of government policies on a particular region or population, both domestically and internationally. As a result, they provide information and analysis that help in planning, developing, or carrying out policies.

Many people with a political science background become postsecondary teachers and high school teachers.

Work Environment

Political scientists held about 7,000 jobs in 2019. The largest employers of political scientists were as follows:

Federal government, excluding postal service	48%
Professional, scientific, and technical services	26
Educational services; state, local, and private	7
Self-employed workers	7
Religious, grantmaking, civic, professional, and similar organizations	5

Work Schedules

Political scientists typically work full time in an office. They may work additional hours to finish reports and meet deadlines.

How to Become a Political Scientist

Political scientists need a master's degree or Ph.D. in political science, public administration, or a related field.

Education

Most political scientists need to complete either a master's or Ph.D. program. To be admitted to a graduate program, applicants should complete undergraduate courses in political science, writing, and statistics. Applicants also benefit from having related work or internship experience.

Political scientists often present their findings.

Political scientists work in a variety of organizations that have a stake in policy, such as government, labor, and political organizations.

Political scientists learn to analyze quantitative and qualitative data.

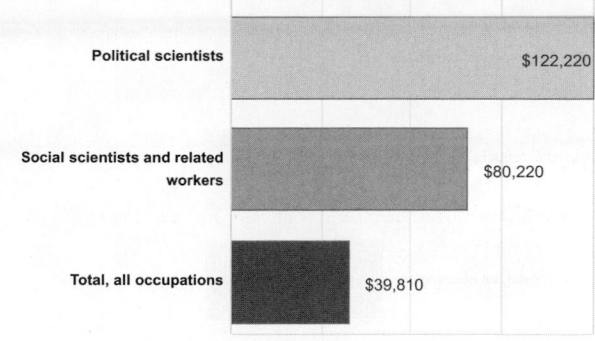

Political Scientists
Median annual wages, May 2019

Political scientists	$122,220
Social scientists and related workers	$80,220
Total, all occupations	$39,810

Note: All Occupations includes all occupations in the U.S. Economy.
Source: U.S. Bureau of Labor Statistics, Occupational Employment Statistics.

Political scientists often complete a master of public administration (MPA), master of public policy (MPP), or master of public affairs degree. These programs usually combine several disciplines, and students can choose to concentrate in a specific area of interest. Most offer core courses in research methods, policy formation, program evaluation, and statistics. Some colleges and universities also offer master's degrees in political science, international relations, or other applied political science specialties.

Some political scientists also complete a Ph.D. program, which requires several years of coursework followed by independent research for a dissertation. Most Ph.D. candidates choose to specialize in one of four primary subfields of political science: national politics, comparative politics, international relations, or political theory.

Jobseekers with a bachelor's degree in political science usually qualify for entry-level positions in a related field, such as assistants or research assistants for research organizations, political campaigns, or nonprofit organization. They may also qualify for some government positions. Others go into fields outside of politics and policymaking, such as business or law.

Other Experience
Entry-level jobseekers can benefit from internships or volunteer work through clubs and political organizations. These activities can give students a chance to apply their academic knowledge in a professional setting and to develop the analytic, research, and writing skills needed for the field.

Important Qualities
Analytical skills. Political scientists often use qualitative and quantitative research methods. They require analytical skills to collect, evaluate, and interpret data.

Communication skills. Political scientists often collaborate with other researchers when writing reports or giving presentations. They must communicate their findings to a wide variety of audiences.

Creativity. Political scientists must continually explore new ideas and information to produce original papers and research. They must stay current on political subjects and come up with new ways to think about and address issues.

Critical-thinking skills. Political scientists must be able to examine and process available information and draw logical conclusions from their findings.

Pay
The median annual wage for political scientists was $122,220 in May 2019. The median wage is the wage at which half the workers in an occupation earned more than that amount and half earned less. The lowest 10 percent earned less than $60,960, and the highest 10 percent earned more than $164,210.

In May 2019, the median annual wages for political scientists in the top industries in which they worked were as follows:

Professional, scientific, and technical services.....	$133,200
Federal government, excluding postal service	126,060
Religious, grantmaking, civic, professional, and similar organizations	80,800
Educational services; state, local, and private	79,640

Political scientists typically work full time in an office. They may work additional hours to finish reports and meet deadlines.

Job Outlook
Employment of political scientists is projected to grow 6 percent from 2019 to 2029, faster than the average for all occupations. Increased demand for public policy analysis in both government and non-government organizations will support employment growth for these workers.

half of all political scientists are employed by the federal government. Political scientists will continue to be needed in government to assess the impact of government policies, such

Political Scientists

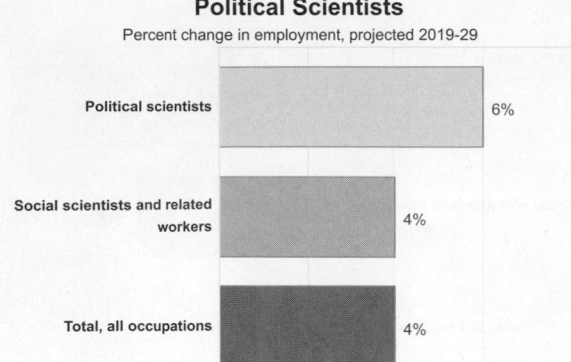

Percent change in employment, projected 2019-29

Political scientists — 6%
Social scientists and related workers — 4%
Total, all occupations — 4%

Note: All Occupations includes all occupations in the U.S. Economy.
Source: U.S. Bureau of Labor Statistics, Employment Projections program.

as the efficiencies of public services, effects of budget changes, and advantages of proposed improvements.

Political organizations, lobbying firms, and labor unions rely on the knowledge of political scientists to manage complicated legal and regulatory issues and policies. Political scientists will be needed at research and policy institutes to focus specifically on politics and political theory. Organizations that research or advocate for specific causes, such as immigration policy, healthcare, or the environment, also need political scientists to analyze policies relating to their field.

Job Prospects

Political scientists should face strong competition for most jobs. The small number of positions, combined with the popularity of political science programs in colleges and universities, means that there will likely be many qualified candidates for relatively few positions.

Candidates with advanced degrees, strong writing and analytical skills, and experience researching or performing policy analysis should have the best job prospects. Candidates who have specialized knowledge or experience in their field of interest will also have better job opportunities. Internships or volunteer work also may be helpful.

Employment projections data for political scientists, 2019-29					
Occupational Title	SOC Code	Employment, 2019	Projected Employment, 2029	Change, 2019-29	
				Percent	Numeric
SOURCE: U.S. Bureau of Labor Statistics, Employment Projections program					
Political scientists	19-3094	7,000	7,400	6	400

State & Area Data
Occupational Employment Statistics (OES)

The Occupational Employment Statistics (OES) program produces employment and wage estimates annually for over 800 occupations. These estimates are available for the nation as a whole, for individual states, and for metropolitan and nonmetropolitan areas.

Contacts for More Information

For more information about political scientists and political science careers, visit
➤ American Political Science Association
➤ American Association of Political Consultants

For more information about college programs in public affairs and administration, visit
➤ Network of Schools of Public Policy, Affairs, and Administration

Psychologists

Summary

Quick Facts: Psychologists

2019 Median Pay	$80,370 per year $38.64 per hour
Typical Entry-Level Education	See below
Work Experience in a Related Occupation	None
On-the-job Training	Internship/residency
Number of Jobs, 2019	192,300
Job Outlook, 2019-29	3% (As fast as average)
Employment Change, 2019-29	5,700

What Psychologists Do

Psychologists study cognitive, emotional, and social processes and behavior by observing, interpreting, and recording how individuals relate to one another and to their environments.

Work Environment

Some psychologists work independently, conducting research, consulting with clients, or working with patients. Others work as part of a healthcare team, collaborating with physicians and social workers, or in school settings, working with students, teachers, parents, and other educators. Those in private practice often work evenings and weekends to accommodate clients.

How to Become a Psychologist

Although psychologists typically need a doctoral degree in psychology, a master's degree is sufficient for some positions. Most psychologists also need a license.

Psychologists study cognitive, emotional, and social processes and behavior.

Industrial-organizational psychologists apply psychological research and methods to workplace issues.

Pay

The median annual wage for psychologists was $80,370 in May 2019.

Job Outlook

Employment of psychologists is projected to grow 3 percent from 2019 to 2029, about as fast as the average for all occupations. Job prospects should be best for those who have a doctoral degree in an applied specialty.

State & Area Data

Explore resources for employment and wages by state and area for psychologists.

What Psychologists Do

Psychologists study cognitive, emotional, and social processes and behavior by observing, interpreting, and recording how people relate to one another and to their environments. They use their findings to help improve processes and behaviors.

Duties

Psychologists typically do the following:

- Conduct scientific studies of behavior and brain function
- Observe, interview, and survey individuals
- Identify psychological, emotional, behavioral, or organizational issues and diagnose disorders
- Research and identify behavioral or emotional patterns
- Test for patterns that will help them better understand and predict behavior
- Discuss the treatment of problems with clients
- Write articles, research papers, and reports to share findings and educate others
- Supervise interns, clinicians, and counseling professionals

Psychologists seek to understand and explain thoughts, emotions, feelings, and behavior. They use techniques such as observation, assessment, and experimentation to develop theories about the beliefs and feelings that influence individuals.

Psychologists often gather information and evaluate behavior through controlled laboratory experiments, psychoanalysis, or psychotherapy. They also may administer personality, performance, aptitude, or intelligence tests. They look for patterns of behavior or relationships between events, and they use this information when testing theories in their research or when treating patients.

The following are examples of types of psychologists:

Clinical psychologists assess, diagnose, and treat mental, emotional, and behavioral disorders. Clinical psychologists help people deal with problems ranging from short-term personal issues to severe, chronic conditions.

Clinical psychologists are trained to use a variety of approaches to help individuals. Although strategies generally differ by specialty, clinical psychologists often interview patients, give diagnostic tests, and provide individual, family, or group psychotherapy. They also design behavior modification programs and help patients implement their particular program. Some clinical psychologists focus on specific populations, such as children or the elderly, or on certain specialties, such as neuropsychology.

Clinical psychologists often consult with other health professionals regarding the best treatment for patients, especially treatment that includes medication. Currently, only Idaho, Illinois, Iowa, Louisiana, and New Mexico allow clinical psychologists to prescribe medication to patients.

Counseling psychologists help patients deal with and understand problems, including issues at home, at the workplace, or in their community. Through counseling, these psychologists work with patients to identify their strengths or resources they can use to manage problems. For information on other counseling occupations, see the profiles on marriage and family therapists, substance abuse, behavioral disorder, and mental health counselors, and social workers.

Developmental psychologists study the psychological progress and development that take place throughout life. Many developmental psychologists focus on children and adolescents, but they also may study aging and problems facing older adults.

Forensic psychologists use psychological principles in the legal and criminal justice system to help judges, attorneys, and other legal specialists understand the psychological aspects of a particular case. They often testify in court as expert witnesses. They typically specialize in family, civil, or criminal casework.

Industrial–organizational psychologists apply psychology to the workplace by using psychological principles and research methods to solve problems and improve the quality of worklife. They study issues such as workplace productivity, management or employee working styles, and employee morale. They also help top executives, training and development managers, and training and development specialists with policy planning, employee screening or training, and organizational development.

Rehabilitation psychologists work with physically or developmentally disabled individuals. They help improve quality of life or help individuals adjust after a major illness or accident. They may work with physical therapists and teachers to improve health and learning outcomes.

School psychologists apply psychological principles and techniques to education disorders and developmental disorders. They may address student learning and behavioral problems; design and implement performance plans, and evaluate performances; and counsel students and families. They also may consult with other school-based professionals to suggest improvements to teaching, learning, and administrative strategies.

Some psychologists become postsecondary teachers or high school teachers.

Work Environment

Psychologists held about 192,300 jobs in 2019. Employment in the detailed occupations that make up psychologists was distributed as follows:

Clinical, counseling, and school psychologists	171,500
Psychologists, all other	19,800
Industrial-organizational psychologists	1,100

The largest employers of psychologists were as follows:

Self-employed workers	31%
Elementary and secondary schools; state, local, and private	24
Ambulatory healthcare services	18
Government	9
Hospitals; state, local, and private	6

Some psychologists work alone, doing independent research, consulting with clients, or counseling patients. Others work as part of a healthcare team, collaborating with physicians, social workers, and others to treat illness and promote overall wellness.

Work Schedules

Psychologists in private practice often set their own hours, and many work part time as independent consultants. They may work evenings or weekends to accommodate clients. Those employed in hospitals or other healthcare facilities may also have evening or weekend shifts. Most psychologists in clinics, government, industry, or schools work full-time schedules during regular business hours.

How to Become a Psychologist

Although psychologists typically need a doctoral degree in psychology, a master's degree may be sufficient for school and industrial organizational positions. Psychologists in clinical practice need a license.

Education

Most clinical, counseling, and research psychologists need a doctoral degree. Students can complete a Ph.D. in psychology

Counseling psychologists often have their own practices.

In most states, practicing psychology or using the title of "psychologist" requires licensure.

or a Doctor of Psychology (Psy.D.) degree. A Ph.D. in psychology is a research degree that is obtained after taking a comprehensive exam and writing a dissertation based on original research. Ph.D. programs typically include courses on statistics and experimental procedures. The Psy.D. is a clinical degree often based on practical work and examinations rather than a dissertation. In clinical, counseling, school, or health service settings, students usually complete a 1-year internship as part of the doctoral program.

School psychologists need an advanced degree and either certification or licensure to work. Common advanced degrees include education specialist degrees (Ed.S.) and doctoral degrees (Ph.D. or Psy.D.). School psychologist programs include coursework in education and psychology because their work addresses both education and mental health components of students' development.

Industrial–organizational psychologists typically need a master's degree, usually including courses in industrial–organizational psychology, statistics, and research design.

When working under the supervision of a doctoral psychologist, other master's degree graduates can also work as psychological assistants in clinical, counseling, or research settings.

Licenses, Certifications, and Registrations

In most states, practicing psychology or using the title "psychologist" requires licensure. In all states and the District of Columbia, psychologists who practice independently must be licensed where they work.

Licensing laws vary by state and by type of position. Most clinical and counseling psychologists need a doctorate in psychology, an internship, and at least 1 to 2 years of supervised professional experience. They also must pass the Examination for Professional Practice in Psychology. Information on specific state requirements can be obtained from the Association of State and Provincial Psychology Boards. In many states, licensed psychologists must complete continuing education courses to keep their licenses.

The American Board of Professional Psychology awards specialty certification in 15 areas of psychology, such as clinical health psychology, couple and family psychology, and rehabilitation psychology. The American Board of Clinical Neuropsychology offers certification in neuropsychology. Board certification can demonstrate professional expertise in a specialty area. Certification is not required for most psychologists, but some hospitals and clinics do require certification. In those cases, candidates must have a doctoral degree in psychology, a state license or certification, and any additional criteria required by the specialty field.

Training

Most prospective psychologists must have pre- or postdoctoral supervised experience, including an internship. Internships allow students to gain experience in an applied setting. Candidates must complete an internship before they can qualify for state licensure. The required number of hours of the internship varies by state.

Important Qualities

Analytical skills. Psychologists must examine the information they collect and draw logical conclusions.

Communication skills. Psychologists must have strong communication skills because they spend much of their time listening to and speaking with patients or describing their research.

Integrity. Psychologists must keep patients' problems in confidence, and patients must be able to trust psychologists' expertise in treating sensitive problems.

Interpersonal skills. Psychologists study and help individuals, so they must be able to work well with clients, patients, and other professionals.

Observational skills. Psychologists study attitude and behavior. They must understand the possible meanings of facial expressions, body positions, actions, and interactions.

Patience. Psychologists must demonstrate patience, because conducting research or treating patients may take a long time.

Problem-solving skills. Psychologists need problem-solving skills to collect information, design research, evaluate programs, and find treatments or solutions to mental and behavioral problems.

Pay

The median annual wage for psychologists was $80,370 in May 2019. The median wage is the wage at which half the workers in an occupation earned more than that amount and half earned less. The lowest 10 percent earned less than $45,380, and the highest 10 percent earned more than $132,070.

Median annual wages for psychologists in May 2019 were as follows:

Psychologists, all other	$101,790
Industrial-organizational psychologists	92,880
Clinical, counseling, and school psychologists	78,200

In May 2019, the median annual wages for psychologists in the top industries in which they worked were as follows:

Government	$96,870
Hospitals; state, local, and private	88,480
Ambulatory healthcare services	82,250
Elementary and secondary schools; state, local, and private	76,960

Psychologists in private practice often set their own hours, and many work part time as independent consultants. They may work evenings or weekends to accommodate clients. Those employed in hospitals or other healthcare facilities also may

Psychologists
Median annual wages, May 2019

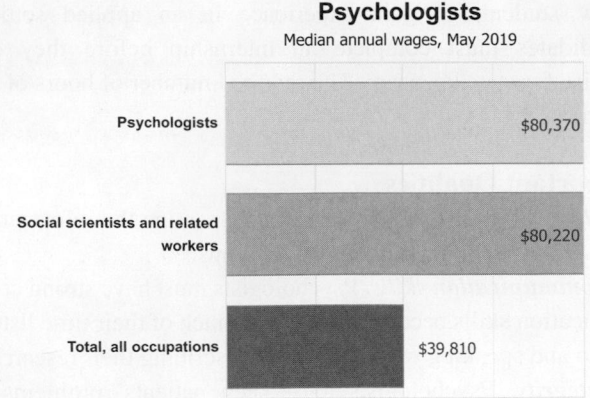

Note: All Occupations includes all occupations in the U.S. Economy.
Source: U.S. Bureau of Labor Statistics, Occupational Employment Statistics.

Psychologists
Percent change in employment, projected 2019-29

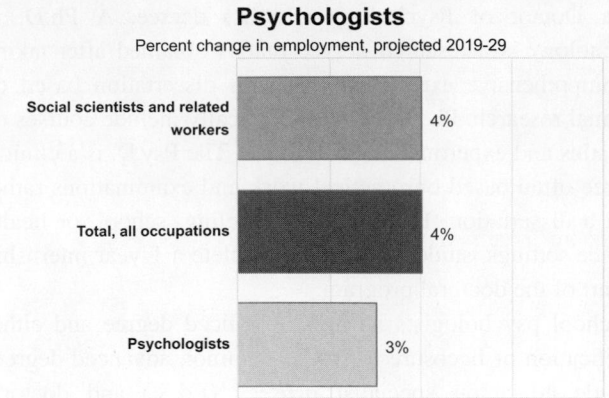

Note: All Occupations includes all occupations in the U.S. Economy.
Source: U.S. Bureau of Labor Statistics, Employment Projections program.

have evening or weekend shifts. Most psychologists in clinics, government, industry, or schools work full-time schedules during regular business hours.

Job Outlook

Overall employment of psychologists is projected to grow 3 percent from 2019 to 2029, about as fast as the average for all occupations. Employment growth will vary by occupation.

Employment of clinical, counseling, and school psychologists is projected to grow because of greater demand for psychological services in schools, hospitals, mental health centers, and social service agencies. Demand for clinical and counseling psychologists will increase as people continue to turn to psychologists for help with their problems. Psychologists also will be needed to provide services to an aging population, helping people deal with the mental and physical changes that happen as they grow older. Psychological services will also be needed for veterans suffering from war trauma, for survivors of other trauma, and for people with developmental disorders, such as autism.

Employment of school psychologists will continue to grow because of the increased awareness of the connection between mental health and learning and because of the need for mental health services in schools. School psychologists will be needed to work with students, particularly those with special needs, learning disabilities, and behavioral issues. Schools rely on school psychologists to assess and counsel students. In addition, school psychologists will be needed to study how factors both in school and outside of school affect learning. Once aware of those factors, teachers and administrators can use them to improve education. Job opportunities may be limited, however, because employment of school psychologists in public schools and universities is contingent on state and local budgets.

Organizations will continue to use industrial–organizational psychologists to help select and retain employees, increase

organizational productivity and efficiency, and improve office morale.

Job Prospects

Competition for jobs for psychologists will vary by specialty and level of education obtained.

Industrial–organizational psychologists are expected to face competition for positions because of the large number of qualified applicants. Industrial–organizational psychologists with extensive training in quantitative research methods may have a competitive edge.

Candidates with a doctoral or education specialist degree and postdoctoral work experience will have the best job opportunities in clinical, counseling, or school psychology positions.

There are expected to be better opportunities for psychologists who specialize in working with the elderly and in rehabilitation psychology.

Employment projections data for psychologists, 2019-29					
Occupational Title	SOC Code	Employment, 2019	Projected Employment, 2029	Change, 2019-29	
				Percent	Numeric
SOURCE: U.S. Bureau of Labor Statistics, Employment Projections program					
Psychologists	19-3030	192,300	198,100	3	5,700
Clinical, counseling, and school psychologists	19-3031	171,500	176,700	3	5,300
Industrial-organizational psychologists	19-3032	1,100	1,100	3	0
Psychologists, all other	19-3039	19,800	20,200	2	400

State & Area Data
Occupational Employment Statistics (OES)

The Occupational Employment Statistics (OES) program produces employment and wage estimates annually for over 800 occupations. These estimates are available for the nation as a whole, for individual states, and for metropolitan and nonmetropolitan areas.

Contacts for More Information

For more information about careers in all fields of psychology, visit
➤ American Psychological Association

For more information about careers for school psychologists, visit
➤ National Association of School Psychologists

For more information about state licensing requirements, visit
➤ Association of State and Provincial Psychology Boards

For more information about psychology specialty certifications, visit
➤ American Board of Professional Psychology

For more information about industrial–organizational psychologists, visit
➤ Society for Industrial and Organizational Psychology

For more information about careers and certification in neuropsychology, visit
➤ American Board of Professional Neuropsychology

Sociologists

Summary

Quick Facts: Sociologists

2019 Median Pay	$83,420 per year $40.10 per hour
Typical Entry-Level Education	Master's degree
Work Experience in a Related Occupation	None
On-the-job Training	None
Number of Jobs, 2019	3,200
Job Outlook, 2019-29	4% (As fast as average)
Employment Change, 2019-29	100

What Sociologists Do

Sociologists study society and social behavior.

Work Environment

Sociologists typically work full time during regular business hours.

Sociologists design research projects to test theories about social issues.

How to Become a Sociologist

Most sociology jobs require a master's degree or Ph.D.

Pay

The median annual wage for sociologists was $83,420 in May 2019.

Job Outlook

Employment of sociologists is projected to grow 4 percent from 2019 to 2029, about as fast as the average for all occupations. Sociologists can expect strong competition because sociology is a popular field of study with a relatively small number of positions.

State & Area Data

Explore resources for employment and wages by state and area for sociologists.

What Sociologists Do

Sociologists study society and social behavior by examining the groups, cultures, organizations, social institutions, and processes that develop when people interact and work together.

Duties

Sociologists typically do the following:

- Design research projects to test theories about social issues
- Collect data through surveys, observations, interviews, and other sources
- Analyze and draw conclusions from data
- Prepare reports, articles, or presentations detailing their research findings
- Collaborate with and advise other social scientists, policymakers, or other groups on research findings and sociological issues

Sociologists study human behavior, interaction, and organization. They observe the activity of social, religious, political, and economic groups, organizations, and institutions. They

Some sociologists conduct interviews for their research.

examine the effect of social influences, including organizations and institutions, on different individuals and groups. They also trace the origin and growth of these groups and interactions. For example, they may research the impact of a new law or policy on a specific demographic.

Sociologists often use both quantitative and qualitative methods when conducting research, and they frequently use statistical analysis programs during the research process.

Their research may help administrators, educators, lawmakers, and social workers to solve social problems and formulate public policy. Sociologists may specialize in a wide range of social topics, including, but not limited to:

- education and health;
- crime and poverty;
- families and population;
- and gender, racial, and ethnic relations.

Sociologists who specialize in crime may be called *criminologists* or *penologists*. These workers apply their sociological knowledge to conduct research and analyze penal systems and populations and to study the causes and effects of crime.

Many people with a sociology background become postsecondary teachers and high school teachers. Most others find work in related jobs outside the sociologist profession such as policy analysts, demographers, survey researchers, and statisticians.

Work Environment

Sociologists held about 3,200 jobs in 2019. The largest employers of sociologists were as follows:

Research and development in the social sciences and humanities	38%
Educational services; state, local, and private	16
State government, excluding education and hospitals	15
Self-employed workers	11

Sociologists typically work in an office. They may work outside of an office setting when conducting research through interviews or observations or presenting research results.

Work Schedules

Most sociologists work full time during regular business hours.

How to Become a Sociologist

Most sociology jobs require a master's degree or Ph.D. Many bachelor's degree holders find positions in related fields, such as social services, education, or public policy.

Education

Sociologists typically need a master's degree or Ph.D. There are two types of sociology master's degree programs: traditional programs and applied, clinical, and professional programs. Traditional programs prepare students to enter a Ph.D. program. Applied, clinical, and professional programs prepare students to enter the workplace, teaching them the necessary analytical skills to perform sociological research in a professional setting.

Courses in research methods and statistics are important for candidates in both master's and Ph.D. programs. Many programs also offer opportunities to gain experience through internships or by preparing reports for clients.

Sociologists may work outside of an office setting when conducting research through interviews or observations or presenting research results.

Many sociology programs offer opportunities to gain experience through internships or by preparing reports.

Other Experience

Candidates with a bachelor's degree may benefit from internships or volunteer work when looking for entry-level positions in sociology or a related field. These types of opportunities give students a chance to apply their academic knowledge in a professional setting and develop skills needed for the field.

Important Qualities

Analytical skills. Sociologists must be able to examine data and other information, often using statistical methods to test their theories.

Communication skills. Sociologists need strong communication skills when they conduct interviews, collaborate with colleagues, and write and present research results.

Critical-thinking skills. Sociologists design research projects and collect, process, and analyze information to draw logical conclusions about society and various groups of people.

Pay

The median annual wage for sociologists was $83,420 in May 2019. The median wage is the wage at which half the workers in an occupation earned more than that amount and half earned less. The lowest 10 percent earned less than $46,920, and the highest 10 percent earned more than $141,770.

In May 2019, the median annual wages for sociologists in the top industries in which they worked were as follows:

State government, excluding education and hospitals	$92,460
Research and development in the social sciences and humanities	91,840
Educational services; state, local, and private	63,310

Most sociologists work full time during regular business hours.

Job Outlook

Employment of sociologists is projected to grow 4 percent from 2019 to 2029, about as fast as the average for all occupations.

Sociologists will continue to be needed to apply sociological research to other disciplines. For example, sociologists may collaborate with researchers in other social sciences, such as economists, psychologists, and survey researchers, to study how social structures or groups influence policy decisions about health, education, politics, criminal justice, business, or economics.

Job Prospects

Candidates with a Ph.D., strong statistical and research skills, and a background in applied sociology will have the best job prospects. However, Ph.D. holders can expect to face strong competition for sociologist positions because sociology is a popular field of study with a relatively small number of positions.

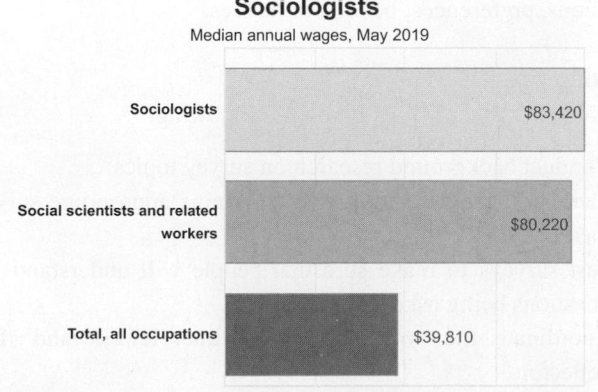

Sociologists
Median annual wages, May 2019

Sociologists	$83,420
Social scientists and related workers	$80,220
Total, all occupations	$39,810

Note: All Occupations includes all occupations in the U.S. Economy.
Source: U.S. Bureau of Labor Statistics, Occupational Employment Statistics.

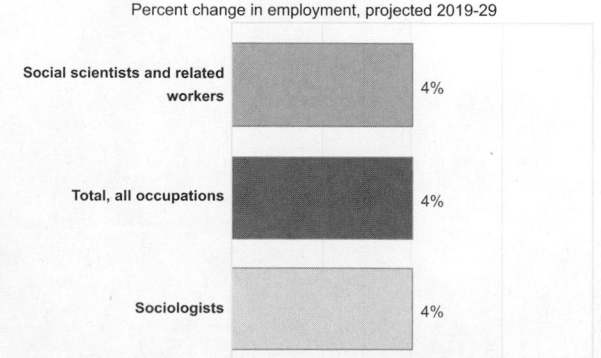

Sociologists
Percent change in employment, projected 2019-29

Social scientists and related workers	4%
Total, all occupations	4%
Sociologists	4%

Note: All Occupations includes all occupations in the U.S. Economy.
Source: U.S. Bureau of Labor Statistics, Employment Projections program.

Employment projections data for sociologists, 2019-29					
Occupational Title	SOC Code	Employment, 2019	Projected Employment, 2029	Change, 2019-29	
				Percent	Numeric
SOURCE: U.S. Bureau of Labor Statistics, Employment Projections program					
Sociologists	19-3041	3,200	3,300	4	100

State & Area Data
Occupational Employment Statistics (OES)

The Occupational Employment Statistics (OES) program produces employment and wage estimates annually for over 800 occupations. These estimates are available for the nation as a whole, for individual states, and for metropolitan and nonmetropolitan areas.

Contacts for More Information

For more information about careers in sociology, visit
➤ American Sociological Association

Survey Researchers

Summary

Quick Facts: Survey Researchers

2019 Median Pay	$59,170 per year $28.45 per hour
Typical Entry-Level Education	Master's degree
Work Experience in a Related Occupation	None
On-the-job Training	None
Number of Jobs, 2019	12,200
Job Outlook, 2019-29	-4% (Decline)
Employment Change, 2019-29	-400

What Survey Researchers Do

Survey researchers design and conduct surveys and analyze data.

Work Environment

Most survey researchers work in research firms, polling organizations, nonprofits, corporations, colleges and universities, and government agencies. The majority work full time during regular business hours.

How to Become a Survey Researcher

Many research positions require a master's degree or Ph.D., although a bachelor's degree may be sufficient for some entry-level positions.

Pay

The median annual wage for survey researchers was $59,170 in May 2019.

Job Outlook

Employment of survey researchers is projected to decline 4 percent from 2019 to 2029.

State & Area Data

Explore resources for employment and wages by state and area for survey researchers.

What Survey Researchers Do

Survey researchers design surveys and analyze data. Surveys are used to collect factual data, such as employment and salary information, or to ask questions in order to understand people's opinions, preferences, beliefs, or desires.

Duties

Survey researchers typically do the following:

- Conduct background research on survey topics
- Plan and design surveys, and determine appropriate survey methods
- Test surveys to make sure that people will understand the questions being asked
- Coordinate the work of survey interviewers and data collectors
- Account for and solve problems caused by nonresponse or other sampling issues
- Analyze data, using statistical software and techniques

Survey researchers meet with clients to determine appropriate survey methods.

Survey researchers often present their findings.

- Summarize survey data, using tables, graphs, and fact sheets
- Evaluate surveys, the methods underlying them, and their performance to improve future surveys

Survey researchers design and conduct surveys for different research purposes. Surveys for scientific research cover various topics, including government, health, social sciences, and education. For example, a survey researcher may try to capture information about the prevalence of drug use or disease.

Some survey researchers design public opinion surveys, which are intended to gather information about the attitudes and opinions of society or of a certain group. Surveys can cover a wide variety of topics, including politics, culture, the economy, or health.

Other survey researchers design marketing surveys which examine products or services that consumers want, need, or prefer. Researchers who collect and analyze market research data are known as market research analysts.

Survey researchers may conduct surveys in many different formats, such as interviews, questionnaires, and focus groups (in-person, small group sessions led by a facilitator). They use different methods to collect data, including the Internet, mail, and telephone and in-person interviews.

Some researchers use surveys to solicit the opinions of an entire population. The decennial census is an example of such a survey. Others use surveys to target a smaller group, such as a specific demographic group, residents of a particular state, or members of a political party.

Researchers survey a sample of the population and use statistics to make sure that the sample accurately represents the target population group. Researchers use a variety of statistical techniques and analytical software to plan surveys, adjust for errors in the data, and analyze the results.

Survey researchers sometimes supervise interviewers who collect survey data through in-person interviews or by telephone.

Work Environment

Survey researchers held about 12,200 jobs in 2019. The largest employers of survey researchers were as follows:

Other professional, scientific, and technical services	38%
Scientific research and development services...............	16
Self-employed workers...	15
Educational services; state, local, and private..............	8
Religious, grantmaking, civic, professional, and similar organizations	6

Survey researchers work in research firms, polling organizations, nonprofits, and corporations.

Survey researchers who conduct interviews have frequent contact with the public. Some may work outside the office, traveling to meet with clients or conducting in-person interviews and focus group sessions. When designing surveys and analyzing data, they usually work alone in an office setting, although some work on teams with other researchers.

How to Become a Survey Researcher

Many research positions require a master's degree or Ph.D., although a bachelor's degree may be sufficient for some entry-level positions.

Survey researchers often work alone, compiling results and analyzing data.

Many research positions require a master's degree or Ph.D., though a bachelor's degree may be sufficient for some entry-level positions.

Education

Many research positions require a master's degree or Ph.D. Survey researchers can have a master's degree in a variety of fields, including marketing or survey research, statistics, and the social sciences. A bachelor's degree is sufficient for some entry-level positions.

To prepare to enter this occupation, students should take courses in research methods, survey methodology, computer science, mathematics, and statistics. Many also may benefit from taking business courses, such as marketing and consumer behavior, and social science courses, such as psychology, sociology, and economics.

Other Experience

Prospective survey researchers can gain experience through internships or fellowships. Many businesses, research and polling firms, and marketing companies offer internships for college students or recent graduates who want to work in market and survey research. These opportunities, which provide valuable experience, can be very helpful toward getting a job.

Licenses, Certifications, and Registrations

Although survey researchers are not required by law to be licensed or certified, certification can show a level of professional competence.

The Insights Association offers the Professional Researcher Certification for survey researchers. To qualify, candidates must have at least 3 years of experience working in opinion and marketing research, pass an exam, and be a member of a professional organization. Researchers must complete continuing education courses and apply for renewal every 2 years to maintain their certification.

Important Qualities

Analytical skills. Survey researchers must be able to apply statistical techniques to large amounts of data and interpret the results correctly. They also should be proficient in the statistical software used to analyze data.

Communication skills. Survey researchers need strong communication skills when conducting surveys and interpreting and presenting results to clients.

Critical-thinking skills. Survey researchers must design or choose a survey and a survey method that together best capture the information needed. They must also be able to look at the data and draw reasonable conclusions from the results of the survey.

Detail oriented. Survey researchers must pay attention to details, because survey results depend on collecting, analyzing, and reporting the data accurately.

Problem-solving skills. Survey researchers need problem-solving skills when identifying survey design issues, adjusting survey questions, and interpreting survey results.

Pay

The median annual wage for survey researchers was $59,170 in May 2019. The median wage is the wage at which half the workers in an occupation earned more than that amount and half earned less. The lowest 10 percent earned less than $32,150, and the highest 10 percent earned more than $108,860.

In May 2019, the median annual wages for survey researchers in the top industries in which they worked were as follows:

Scientific research and development services..........	$71,620
Educational services; state, local, and private.........	61,760
Religious, grantmaking, civic, professional, and similar organizations..	57,740
Other professional, scientific, and technical services	56,120

Job Outlook

Employment of survey researchers is projected to decline 4 percent from 2019 to 2029.

Survey research is an evolving field, with companies regularly adopting new methods and data sources in an effort to increase productivity. For example, data mining—finding trends in large sets of existing data—and collecting information from social media sites are expected to reduce the need for some traditional survey methods, such as telephone and in-person interviews. These changing research methods are expected to allow more survey research work to be done with fewer survey researchers, thus reducing the number of workers needed.

Job Prospects

Job opportunities should be best for those with an advanced degree in market or survey research, statistics, or the social sciences. Because of the relatively small number of survey researcher positions, bachelor's degree holders will likely face strong competition from more qualified candidates.

Survey Researchers
Median annual wages, May 2019

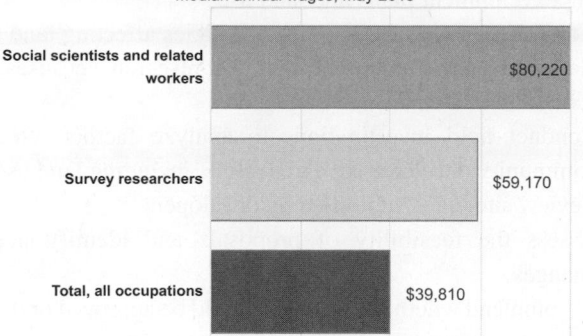

Social scientists and related workers — $80,220

Survey researchers — $59,170

Total, all occupations — $39,810

Note: All Occupations includes all occupations in the U.S. Economy.
Source: U.S. Bureau of Labor Statistics, Occupational Employment Statistics.

Employment projections data for survey researchers, 2019-29

Occupational Title	SOC Code	Employment, 2019	Projected Employment, 2029	Change, 2019-29 Percent	Numeric
SOURCE: U.S. Bureau of Labor Statistics, Employment Projections program					
Survey researchers	19-3022	12,200	11,700	-4	-400

State & Area Data
Occupational Employment Statistics (OES)
The Occupational Employment Statistics (OES) program produces employment and wage estimates annually for over

Survey Researchers
Percent change in employment, projected 2019-29

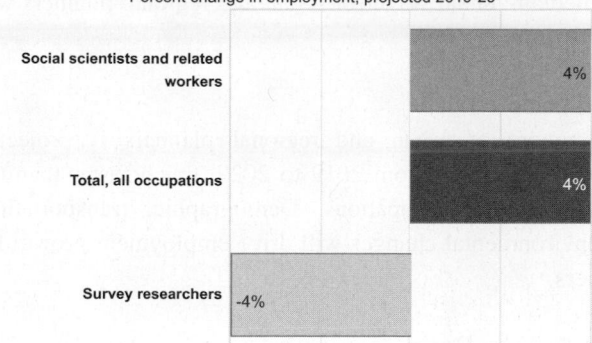

Social scientists and related workers — 4%

Total, all occupations — 4%

Survey researchers — -4%

Note: All Occupations includes all occupations in the U.S. Economy.
Source: U.S. Bureau of Labor Statistics, Employment Projections program.

800 occupations. These estimates are available for the nation as a whole, for individual states, and for metropolitan and nonmetropolitan areas.

Contacts for More Information
For more information about careers in survey research, visit
➤ American Association for Public Opinion Research
➤ Insights Association

Urban and Regional Planners

Summary

Quick Facts: Urban and Regional Planners

2019 Median Pay	$74,350 per year / $35.75 per hour
Typical Entry-Level Education	Master's degree
Work Experience in a Related Occupation	None
On-the-job Training	None
Number of Jobs, 2019	39,700
Job Outlook, 2019-29	11% (Much faster than average)
Employment Change, 2019-29	4,400

What Urban and Regional Planners Do
Urban and regional planners develop land use plans and programs that help create communities, accommodate population growth, and revitalize physical facilities.

Work Environment
Most urban and regional planners work full time during normal business hours, and some may work evenings or weekends

to attend meetings with officials, planning commissions, and neighborhood groups.

How to Become an Urban or Regional Planner
Urban and regional planners need a master's degree from an accredited planning program to qualify for most positions.

Urban and regional planners often present projects to communities and planning officials.

Pay

The median annual wage for urban and regional planners was $74,350 in May 2019.

Job Outlook

Employment of urban and regional planners is projected to grow 11 percent from 2019 to 2029, much faster than the average for all occupations. Demographic, transportation, and environmental changes will drive employment growth for planners.

State & Area Data

Explore resources for employment and wages by state and area for urban and regional planners.

What Urban and Regional Planners Do

Urban and regional planners develop land use plans and programs that help create communities, accommodate population growth, and revitalize physical facilities in towns, cities, counties, and metropolitan areas.

Duties

Urban and regional planners typically do the following:

Urban and regional planners review site plans submitted by developers.

- Meet with public officials, developers, and the public regarding development plans and land use
- Administer government plans or policies affecting land use
- Gather and analyze data from market research, censuses, and economic and environmental studies
- Conduct field investigations to analyze factors affecting community development and decline, including land use
- Review site plans submitted by developers
- Assess the feasibility of proposals and identify needed changes
- Recommend whether proposals should be approved or denied
- Present projects to communities, planning officials, and planning commissions
- Stay current on zoning and building codes, environmental regulations, and other legal issues

Urban and regional planners identify community needs and develop short- and long-term solutions to improve and revitalize communities and areas. As an area grows or changes, planners help communities manage the related economic, social, and environmental issues, such as planning new parks, sheltering the homeless, and making the region more attractive to businesses.

When beginning a project, planners often work with public officials, community members, and other groups to identify community issues and goals. Through research, data analysis, and collaboration with interest groups, they formulate strategies to address issues and to meet goals. Planners may also help carry out community plans by overseeing projects, enforcing zoning regulations, and organizing the work of the groups involved.

Urban and regional planners use a variety of tools and technology in their work. They commonly use statistical software, data visualization and presentation programs, financial spreadsheets, and other database and software programs. Geographic Information System (GIS) software is used to integrate data, such as for population density, with digital maps.

Urban and regional planners may specialize in areas such as transportation planning, community development, historic preservation, or urban design, among other fields of interest.

Planners often collaborate with public officials, civil engineers, environmental engineers, architects, lawyers, and real estate developers.

Work Environment

Urban and regional planners held about 39,700 jobs in 2019. The largest employers of urban and regional planners were as follows:

Local government, excluding education and hospitals 72%

Architectural, engineering, and related services 11

Management, scientific, and technical consulting
   services 3

Federal government.. 2

Urban and regional planners may travel to development sites.

Planners work throughout the country, but most work in large metropolitan areas.

Urban and regional planners may travel to inspect proposed changes and their impacts on land conditions, the environment, and land use.

Work Schedules

Most urban and regional planners work full time during normal business hours, and some may work evenings or weekends to attend meetings with officials, planning commissions, and neighborhood groups. Some planners work more than 40 hours per week.

How to Become an Urban or Regional Planner

Urban and regional planners need a master's degree from an accredited planning program to qualify for most positions.

Education

Most urban and regional planners have a master's degree from an accredited urban or regional planning program. In 2016, there

Urban and regional planners must be effective communicators when they meet with public officials, developers, and the public regarding development plans and land use.

were 71 programs accredited by the Planning Accreditation Board (PAB) that offered a master's degree in planning.

Master's degree programs accept students with a wide range of undergraduate backgrounds. However, many candidates who enter these programs have a bachelor's degree in economics, geography, political science, or environmental design.

Most master's programs have students spending considerable time in seminars, workshops, and laboratory courses, in which they learn to analyze and solve planning problems. Although most master's programs have a similar core curriculum, there is some variability in the courses they offer and the issues they focus on. For example, programs located in agricultural states may focus on rural planning, and programs located in larger cities may focus on urban revitalization.

Bachelor's degree holders can qualify for a small number of jobs as assistant or junior planners. In 2016, there were 15 accredited bachelor's degree programs in planning. Candidates with a bachelor's degree typically need work experience in planning, public policy, or a related field.

Other Experience

Although not necessary for all positions, some entry-level positions require 1 to 2 years of work experience in a related field, such as architecture, public policy, or economic development. Many students gain experience through real planning projects or part-time internships while enrolled in a master's planning program. Others enroll in full-time internships after completing their degree.

Licenses, Certifications, and Registrations

As of 2016, New Jersey was the only state that required urban and regional planners to be licensed. More information is available from the regulatory board of New Jersey.

The American Institute of Certified Planners (AICP) offers the AICP certification for planners. To become certified, candidates must meet certain education and experience requirements and pass an exam.

Important Qualities

Analytical skills. Urban and regional planners analyze information and data from a variety of sources, such as market research studies, censuses, and environmental impact studies. They use statistical techniques and technologies such as Geographic Information Systems (GIS) in their analyses to determine the significance of the data.

Communication skills. Urban and regional planners must be able to communicate clearly and effectively because they interact with colleagues and stakeholders, prepare research reports, give presentations, and meet with a wide variety of audiences, including public officials, interest groups, and community members.

Decisionmaking skills. Urban and regional planners must weigh all possible planning options and combine analysis, creativity, and realism to choose the appropriate action or plan.

Urban and Regional Planners
Median annual wages, May 2019

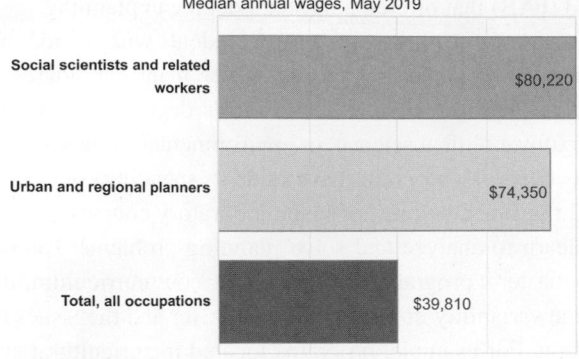

Social scientists and related workers	$80,220
Urban and regional planners	$74,350
Total, all occupations	$39,810

Note: All Occupations includes all occupations in the U.S. Economy.
Source: U.S. Bureau of Labor Statistics, Occupational Employment Statistics.

Urban and Regional Planners
Percent change in employment, projected 2019-29

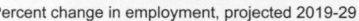
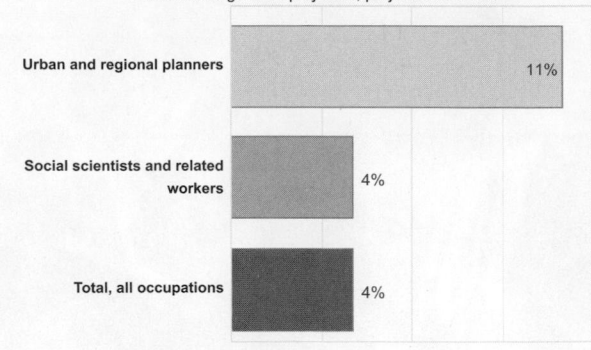

Urban and regional planners	11%
Social scientists and related workers	4%
Total, all occupations	4%

Note: All Occupations includes all occupations in the U.S. Economy.
Source: U.S. Bureau of Labor Statistics, Employment Projections program.

Leadership skills. Urban and regional planners must be able to manage projects, which may include overseeing tasks and planning assignments.

Pay

The median annual wage for urban and regional planners was $74,350 in May 2019. The median wage is the wage at which half the workers in an occupation earned more than that amount and half earned less. The lowest 10 percent earned less than $45,850, and the highest 10 percent earned more than $116,280.

In May 2019, the median annual wages for urban and regional planners in the top industries in which they worked were as follows:

Federal government	$95,990
Architectural, engineering, and related services	80,050
Local government, excluding education and hospitals	72,640
Management, scientific, and technical consulting services	71,120

Most urban and regional planners work full time during normal business hours, and some may work evenings or weekends to attend meetings with officials, planning commissions, and neighborhood groups. Some planners work more than 40 hours per week.

Job Outlook

Employment of urban and regional planners is projected to grow 11 percent from 2019 to 2029, much faster than the average for all occupations. Demographic, transportation, and environmental changes will drive employment growth for planners.

Within cities, urban planners will be needed to develop revitalization projects and address issues associated with population growth, environmental degradation, the movement of people and goods, and resource scarcity. Similarly, suburban

areas and municipalities will need planners to address the challenges associated with population changes, including housing needs and transportation systems covering larger areas with less population density.

Planners will also be needed as new and existing communities require extensive development and improved infrastructure, including housing, roads, sewer systems, parks, and schools.

However, federal, state, and local government budgets may affect the employment of planners in government, because development projects are contingent on available funds.

Job Prospects

Urban and regional planners should expect to face competition for positions. Job opportunities for planners often depend on government budgets and economic conditions. When municipalities and developers have funds for development projects, planners are in higher demand.

Employment projections data for urban and regional planners, 2019-29					
Occupational Title	SOC Code	Employment, 2019	Projected Employment, 2029	Change, 2019-29	
				Percent	Numeric
SOURCE: U.S. Bureau of Labor Statistics, Employment Projections program					
Urban and regional planners	19-3051	39,700	44,100	11	4,400

State & Area Data

Occupational Employment Statistics (OES)

The Occupational Employment Statistics (OES) program produces employment and wage estimates annually for over 800 occupations. These estimates are available for the nation as a whole, for individual states, and for metropolitan and nonmetropolitan areas.

Contacts for More Information

For more information about careers in urban and regional planning, visit

➤ American Planning Association

For more information about certification in urban and regional planning, visit
➤ American Institute of Certified Planners

For more information about New Jersey licensure in planning, visit

➤ New Jersey State Board of Professional Planners

For more information about accredited urban and regional planning programs, visit
➤ Planning Accreditation Board

Zoologists and Wildlife Biologists

Summary

Quick Facts: Zoologists and Wildlife Biologists

2019 Median Pay	$63,270 per year $30.42 per hour
Typical Entry-Level Education	Bachelor's degree
Work Experience in a Related Occupation	None
On-the-job Training	None
Number of Jobs, 2019	21,000
Job Outlook, 2019-29	4% (As fast as average)
Employment Change, 2019-29	800

What Zoologists and Wildlife Biologists Do

Zoologists and wildlife biologists study animals and other wildlife and how they interact with their ecosystems.

Work Environment

Zoologists and wildlife biologists work in offices, laboratories, or outdoors. Depending on their job, they may spend considerable time in the field gathering data and studying animals in their natural habitats.

How to Become a Zoologist or Wildlife Biologist

Zoologists and wildlife biologists need a bachelor's degree for entry-level positions; a master's degree is often needed for higher-level investigative or scientific work. A Ph.D. is necessary to lead independent research and for most university research positions.

Pay

The median annual wage for zoologists and wildlife biologists was $63,270 in May 2019.

Job Outlook

Employment of zoologists and wildlife biologists is projected to grow 4 percent from 2019 to 2029, about as fast as the average for all occupations. Zoologists and wildlife biologists will be needed to study human and wildlife interactions as the human population grows and development impacts wildlife and their natural habitats. However, because most funding comes from governmental agencies, demand for zoologists and wildlife biologists will be limited by budgetary constraints.

State & Area Data

Explore resources for employment and wages by state and area for zoologists and wildlife biologists.

What Zoologists and Wildlife Biologists Do

Zoologists and wildlife biologists study animals and other wildlife and how they interact with their ecosystems. They study the physical characteristics of animals, animal behaviors, and the impacts humans have on wildlife and natural habitats.

Zoologists and wildlife biologists often work outdoors in the field gathering data and studying animals in their natural habitats.

Marine biologists study fish and other wildlife that inhabit the oceans.

Duties

Zoologists and wildlife biologists typically do the following:

- Develop and conduct experimental studies with animals in controlled or natural surroundings
- Collect biological data and specimens for analysis
- Study the characteristics of animals, such as their interactions with other species, reproduction, population dynamics, diseases, and movement patterns
- Analyze the influence that human activity has on wildlife and their natural habitats
- Research, initiate, and maintain ways of improving breeding programs that support healthy game animals, endangered species, or other wild populations of land or aquatic life
- Estimate, monitor, and manage wildlife populations and invasive plants and animals
- Develop and implement programs to reduce risk to human activities from wildlife and invasive species, such as keeping wildlife from impacting airport operations or livestock and crop production
- Write research papers, reports, and scholarly articles that explain their findings
- Give presentations on research findings to academics and the general public
- Develop conservation plans and make recommendations on wildlife conservation and management issues to policymakers and the general public

Zoologists and wildlife biologists perform a variety of scientific tests and experiments. For example, they take blood samples from animals to assess their nutrition levels, check animals for disease and parasites, and tag animals in order to track them. Although the roles and abilities of zoologists and wildlife biologists often overlap, zoologists typically conduct scientific investigations and basic research on particular types of animals, such as birds or amphibians, whereas wildlife biologists are more likely to study specific ecosystems or animal populations, such as a particular at-risk species. Wildlife biologists also do applied work, such as the conservation and management of wildlife populations.

Zoologists and wildlife biologists use geographic information systems (GIS), modeling software, and other computer programs to estimate wildlife populations and track the movements of animals. They also use these computer programs to forecast the spread of invasive species or diseases, project changes in the availability of habitat, and assess other potential threats to wildlife.

Zoologists and wildlife biologists conduct research for a variety of purposes. For example, many zoologists and wildlife biologists work to increase our knowledge and understanding of wildlife species. Traditionally, many wildlife biologists researched ways to encourage abundant game animal populations to support recreational hunting and tourism. Today, many also work with public officials in conservation efforts that protect species from threats and help animal populations return to and remain at sustainable levels.

Most zoologists and wildlife biologists work on research teams with other scientists and technicians. For example, zoologists and wildlife biologists may work with environmental scientists and hydrologists to monitor water pollution and its effects on fish populations.

Zoologists generally specialize first in either vertebrates or invertebrates and then in specific species. Following are some examples of specialization by species:

- Cetologists study marine mammals, such as whales and dolphins.
- Entomologists study insects, such as beetles and butterflies.
- Herpetologists study reptiles and amphibians, such as snakes and frogs.
- Ichthyologists study wild fish, such as sharks and lungfish.
- Malacologists study mollusks, such as snails and clams.
- Mammalogists study mammals, such as monkeys and bears.
- Ornithologists study birds, such as hawks and penguins.
- Teuthologists study cephalopods, such as octopuses and cuttlefish.

Other zoologists and wildlife biologists are identified by the aspects of zoology and wildlife biology they study, such as evolution and animal behavior. Following are some examples:

- Anatomy is the study of structure of organisms and their parts.
- Embryology is the study of the development of embryos and fetuses.
- Ethology, sometimes called behavioral ecology, is the study of animal behaviors as natural or adaptive traits.
- Histology, or microscopic anatomy, is the study of cells and tissues in plants and animals.
- Physiology is the study of the normal function of living systems.
- Soil zoology is the study of animals which live fully or partially in the soil.
- Teratology is the study of abnormal physiological development.
- Zoography is the study of descriptive zoology, and describes plants and animals.

Many people with a zoology and wildlife biology background become high school teachers or college or university professors. For more information, see the profiles on high school teachers and postsecondary teachers.

Work Environment

Zoologists and wildlife biologists held about 21,000 jobs in 2019. The largest employers of zoologists and wildlife biologists were as follows:

Fieldwork can require zoologists and wildlife biologists to travel to remote locations anywhere in the world.

State government, excluding education and hospitals....... 39%

Federal government, excluding postal service 21

Management, scientific, and technical consulting
    services 9

Colleges, universities, and professional schools;
    state, local, and private.............................. 8

Research and development in the physical,
    engineering, and life sciences 4

Zoologists and wildlife biologists work in offices, laboratories, and outdoors. Depending on their job and interests, they may spend considerable time in the field gathering data and studying animals in their natural habitats. Other zoologists and wildlife biologists may spend very little time in the field.

Fieldwork can require zoologists and wildlife biologists to travel to remote locations anywhere in the world. For example, cetologists studying whale populations may spend months at sea on a research ship. Other zoologists and wildlife biologists may spend significant amounts of time in deserts or remote mountainous and woodland regions. The ability to travel and study nature firsthand is often viewed as a benefit of working in these occupations, but few modern amenities may be available to those who travel in remote areas.

Fieldwork can be physically demanding, and zoologists and wildlife biologists work in both warm and cold climates and in all types of weather. For example, ornithologists who study penguins in Antarctica may need to spend significant amounts of time in cold weather and on ships, which may cause seasickness. In all environments, working as a zoologist or wildlife biologist can be emotionally demanding because interpersonal contact may be limited.

Injuries and Illnesses

Some zoologists and wildlife biologists handle wild animals or spend significant amounts of time outdoors in difficult terrain or in inclement weather. To avoid injury, they should use caution when handling wildlife or working in remote areas.

Work Schedules

Most zoologists and wildlife biologists work full time. They may work long or irregular hours, especially when doing fieldwork. Zoologists and wildlife biologists who work with nocturnal animals may need to work at night at least some of the time.

How to Become a Zoologist or Wildlife Biologist

Zoologists and wildlife biologists typically need a bachelor's degree for entry-level positions; a master's degree is often needed for higher level investigative or scientific work. A Ph.D. is necessary to lead independent research and for most university research positions.

Education

Zoologists and wildlife biologists typically need at least a bachelor's degree. Many schools offer bachelor's degree programs in zoology and wildlife biology or in a closely related field, such as ecology. An undergraduate degree in biology with coursework in zoology and wildlife biology also is good preparation for a career as a zoologist or wildlife biologist.

Zoologists and wildlife biologists typically need at least a master's degree for higher level investigative or scientific work. A Ph.D. is necessary for the majority of independent research positions and for university research positions. Most Ph.D.-level researchers need to be familiar with computer programming and statistical software.

Students typically take zoology and wildlife biology courses in ecology, anatomy, wildlife management, and cellular biology. They also take courses that focus on a particular group of animals, such as herpetology (reptiles and amphibians) or ornithology (birds). Courses in botany, chemistry, and physics are important because zoologists and wildlife biologists must have a well-rounded scientific background. Wildlife biology programs may focus on applied techniques in habitat analysis and conservation. Students also should take courses in

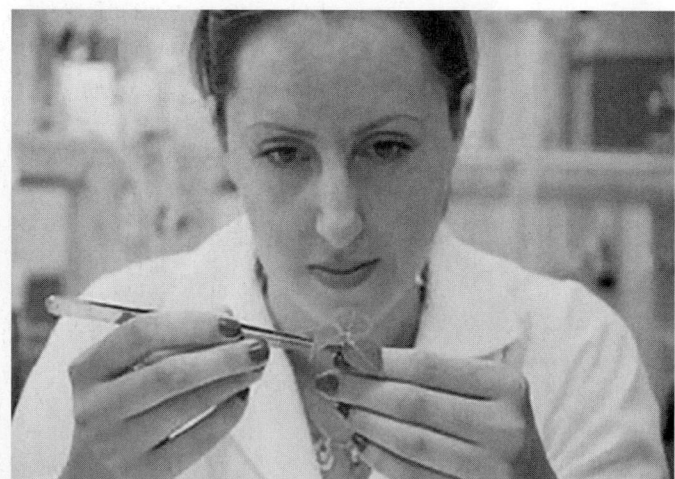

Zoologists and wildlife biologists study specimens collected in the field.

Zoologists and Wildlife Biologists
Median annual wages, May 2019

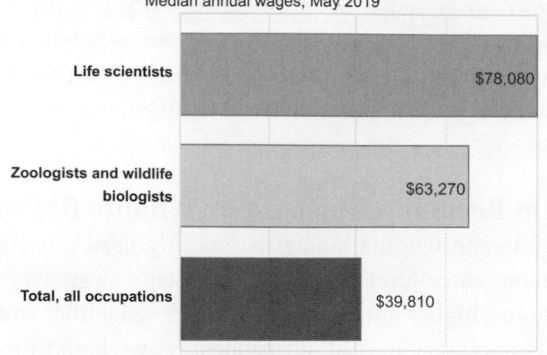

Note: All Occupations includes all occupations in the U.S. Economy.
Source: U.S. Bureau of Labor Statistics, Occupational Employment Statistics.

Zoologists and Wildlife Biologists
Percent change in employment, projected 2019-29

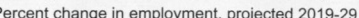
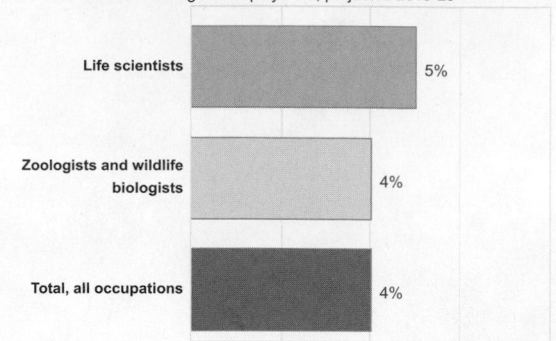

Note: All Occupations includes all occupations in the U.S. Economy.
Source: U.S. Bureau of Labor Statistics, Employment Projections program.

mathematics and statistics, given that zoologists and wildlife biologists must be able to do complex data analysis.

Knowledge of computers is important because zoologists and wildlife biologists frequently use advanced computer software, such as geographic information systems (GIS) and modeling software, to do their work.

Important Qualities

Communication skills. Zoologists and wildlife biologists write scientific papers and give talks to the public, policymakers, and academics.

Critical-thinking skills. Zoologists and wildlife biologists need sound reasoning and judgment to draw conclusions from experimental results and scientific observations.

Emotional stamina and stability. Zoologists and wildlife biologists may need to endure long periods with little human contact. As with other occupations that deal with animals, emotional stability is important in working with injured or sick animals.

Interpersonal skills. Zoologists and wildlife biologists typically work on teams. They must be able to work effectively with others to achieve their goals or to negotiate conflicting goals.

Observation skills. Zoologists and wildlife biologists must be able to notice slight changes in an animal's behavior or appearance.

Outdoor skills. Zoologists and wildlife biologists may need to chop firewood, swim in cold water, navigate rough terrain in poor weather, carry heavy packs or equipment long distances, or perform other activities associated with life in remote areas.

Problem-solving skills. Zoologists and wildlife biologists try to find the best possible solutions to threats that affect wildlife, such as disease and habitat loss.

Other Experience

Some zoologists and wildlife biologists may need to have well-rounded outdoor skills. They may need to be able to drive a tractor, boat, or ATV, use a generator, or provide for themselves in remote locations.

Many zoology and wildlife biology students gain practical experience through internships, volunteer work, or some other type of employment during college or soon after graduation.

Advancement

Zoologists and wildlife biologists typically receive greater responsibility and independence in their work as they gain experience. More education also can lead to greater responsibility. Zoologists and wildlife biologists with a Ph.D. usually lead independent research and control the direction and content of projects. In addition, they may be responsible for finding much of their own funding.

Pay

The median annual wage for zoologists and wildlife biologists was $63,270 in May 2019. The median wage is the wage at which half the workers in an occupation earned more than that amount and half earned less. The lowest 10 percent earned less than $38,880, and the highest 10 percent earned more than $101,780.

In May 2019, the median annual wages for zoologists and wildlife biologists in the top industries in which they worked were as follows:

Federal government, excluding postal service	$78,090
Research and development in the physical, engineering, and life sciences	67,100
Management, scientific, and technical consulting services	66,940
Colleges, universities, and professional schools; state, local, and private..	62,550
State government, excluding education and hospitals..	56,320

Most zoologists and wildlife biologists work full time. They may work long or irregular hours, especially when doing fieldwork.

Job Outlook

Employment of zoologists and wildlife biologists is projected to grow 4 percent from 2019 to 2029, about as fast as the average for all occupations. Zoologists and wildlife biologists will be needed to study human and wildlife interactions as the human population grows and development impacts wildlife and their natural habitats. However, because most funding comes from governmental agencies, demand for zoologists and wildlife biologists will be limited by budgetary constraints.

As the human population grows and expands into new areas, it will create threats that endanger wildlife. Zoologists and wildlife biologists will be needed to study the impact of disease, habitat loss, pollution, and other factors on wildlife. Many states will continue to employ zoologists and wildlife biologists to manage animal populations for tourism purposes, such as hunting game, sightseeing, and conservation. Zoologists and wildlife biologists will be needed to develop and implement conservation plans that combat threats to animals and protect our natural resources.

Job Prospects

Zoologists and wildlife biologists may face strong competition when looking for employment. Job candidates who have practical experience gained through internships, summer jobs, or volunteer work completed before or shortly after graduation should have the best opportunities.

Employment projections data for zoologists and wildlife biologists, 2019-29					
Occupational Title	SOC Code	Employment, 2019	Projected Employment, 2029	Change, 2019-29	
				Percent	Numeric
SOURCE: U.S. Bureau of Labor Statistics, Employment Projections program					
Zoologists and wildlife biologists	19-1023	21,000	21,800	4	800

State & Area Data
Occupational Employment Statistics (OES)

The Occupational Employment Statistics (OES) program produces employment and wage estimates annually for over 800 occupations. These estimates are available for the nation as a whole, for individual states, and for metropolitan and nonmetropolitan areas.

Contacts for More Information

For more information about zoologists and wildlife biologists, visit
➤ The Wildlife Society
➤ Association of Zoos and Aquariums
➤ American Society of Mammalogists
➤ American Society of Ichthyologists and Herpetologists
➤ MarineBio
➤ Ornithological Societies of North America
➤ Zoological Association of America

For more information about issues in zoology and wildlife biology, visit
➤ U.S. Fish and Wildlife Service
➤ U.S. Geographical Survey
➤ National Park Service

For more information about careers in botany, visit
➤ Botanical Society of America

For more information about careers in ecology, visit
➤ Ecological Society of America

For information on federal government education requirements for zoologists and wildlife biologists, visit
➤ U.S. Office of Personnel Management

To find job openings for zoologists and wildlife biologists in the federal government, visit
➤ USAJOBS

Management

Administrative Services Managers

Summary

Quick Facts: Administrative Services Managers

2019 Median Pay	$96,940 per year
	$46.61 per hour
Typical Entry-Level Education	Bachelor's degree
Work Experience in a Related Occupation	Less than 5 years
On-the-job Training	None
Number of Jobs, 2019	325,900
Job Outlook, 2019-29	6% (Faster than average)
Employment Change, 2019-29	21,200

What Administrative Services Managers Do

Administrative services managers plan, direct, and coordinate activities that help an organization run efficiently.

Work Environment

Most administrative services managers work full time. Some work more than 40 hours per week.

How to Become an Administrative Services Manager

Although administrative services managers' educational requirements vary by organization and the work they do, they usually must have a bachelor's degree and related work experience.

Pay

The median annual wage for administrative services managers was $96,940 in May 2019.

Job Outlook

Employment of administrative services managers is projected to grow 6 percent from 2019 to 2029, faster than the average for all occupations. Tasks such as managing facilities and preparing for emergencies will remain important in a range of industries.

State & Area Data

Explore resources for employment and wages by state and area for administrative services managers.

What Administrative Services Managers Do

Administrative services managers plan, direct, and coordinate activities that help an organization run efficiently. The specific responsibilities vary, but these managers typically maintain facilities and supervise activities that include recordkeeping, mail distribution, and office upkeep. In a small organization, they may direct all support services and may be called the *business office manager*. Large organizations may have several layers of administrative managers who specialize in different areas.

Duties

Administrative services managers typically do the following:

- Supervise clerical and administrative staff
- Set goals and deadlines for their department
- Develop, manage, and monitor records
- Recommend changes to policies or procedures in order to improve operations, such as reassessing supplies or recordkeeping
- Monitor facilities to make sure that they remain safe, secure, and well maintained

Administrative services managers keep records, distribute supplies, and maintain facilities.

Administrative services managers plan, coordinate, and direct a broad range of services that allow organizations to operate efficiently.

- Oversee the maintenance and repair of machinery, equipment, and electrical and mechanical systems
- Make sure that facilities meet environmental, health, and security standards and comply with regulations

Administrative services managers plan, coordinate, and direct a broad range of activities that allow organizations to run efficiently. An organization may have several managers who oversee services for multiple departments, such as mail, printing and copying, recordkeeping, security, building maintenance, and recycling.

Specific tasks and responsibilities may vary. For example, an administrative services manager might be responsible for making sure that the organization has the supplies and services it needs. An administrative services manager who coordinates space allocation might consider employee morale and available funds when determining how to arrange a physical space.

Administrative services managers may examine energy consumption patterns, technology use, and office equipment. They also may plan for maintenance and replacement of equipment, such as computers.

The following are examples of types of administrative services managers:

Facilities managers oversee buildings, grounds, equipment, and supplies. Their responsibilities cover several categories, including operations, maintenance, and planning and managing projects.

Facilities managers may oversee renovation projects to improve efficiency or to meet regulations and environmental, health, and security standards. For example, they may recommend energy-saving alternatives or efficiencies that reduce waste. In addition, they continually monitor facilities to ensure that the premises are safe, secure, and well maintained. Facilities managers also direct staff, including grounds maintenance workers, janitors and building cleaners, and general maintenance and repair workers.

Records and information managers develop, monitor, and manage an organization's records. They provide information to chief executives and ensure that employees follow records and information management guidelines. They may direct the operations of onsite or offsite records facilities. These managers also work closely with an organization's attorneys and its technology and business operations staff. Records and information managers do not handle medical records, which are administered by medical and health services managers.

Work Environment

Administrative services managers held about 325,900 jobs in 2019. The largest employers of administrative services managers were as follows:

Healthcare and social assistance	13%
Educational services; state, local, and private	12

Administrative services managers spend much of their day in an office.

Professional, scientific, and technical services	10
Local government, excluding education and hospitals	8
Finance and insurance	7

Administrative services managers spend much of their day in an office. They may observe workers throughout the building, go outdoors to supervise groundskeeping activities, or visit other facilities they direct.

Work Schedules

Most administrative services managers work full time. Some work more than 40 hours per week. Facilities managers often are on call to address problems that arise at all hours.

How to Become an Administrative Services Manager

Although educational requirements for administrative services managers vary by organization and the work they do, they usually must have a bachelor's degree and related work experience.

Education

Administrative services managers typically need a bachelor's degree, usually in business or a related field. However, some people enter the occupation with a high school diploma.

Work Experience

Administrative services managers must have related work experience that reflects managerial and leadership abilities. Facilities managers should have experience in business operations, project management, and building maintenance, such as from jobs as a general maintenance and repair worker or a cost estimator. Records and information managers should have administrative or business operations experience involving recordkeeping. Records and information managers in the legal field often must have experience as a paralegal or legal assistant.

In managing workers and coordinating administrative duties, administrative services managers must show leadership ability.

Licenses, Certifications, and Registrations

Although it is not required, professional certification may give candidates an advantage when applying for jobs.

Several professional associations for administrative services managers offer certifications. Some associations, including the International Facility Management Association (IFMA), offer certification that specializes in facility management. Others offering certification include the Institute of Certified Records Managers (ICRM), for records and information managers, and the ARMA International for those specializing in information governance.

Important Qualities

Analytical skills. Administrative services managers must be able to review an organization's procedures for ways to improve efficiency.

Communication skills. Administrative services managers often work with others. They must be able to convey ideas clearly, both orally and in writing.

Detail oriented. Administrative services managers must pay attention to details across a range of tasks, such as ensuring that the organization complies with building codes and managing the process of buying equipment.

Leadership skills. In directing workers and coordinating organizational duties, administrative services managers must be able to motivate employees and handle problems that arise.

Pay

The median annual wage for administrative services managers was $96,940 in May 2019. The median wage is the wage at which half the workers in an occupation earned more than that amount and half earned less. The lowest 10 percent earned less than $55,210, and the highest 10 percent earned more than $166,330.

In May 2019, the median annual wages for administrative services managers in the top industries in which they worked were as follows:

Finance and insurance	$110,170
Professional, scientific, and technical services	106,760
Local government, excluding education and hospitals	93,770
Educational services; state, local, and private	92,270
Healthcare and social assistance	86,960

Most administrative services managers work full time. Some work more than 40 hours per week. Facilities managers often are on call to address problems that arise at all hours.

Job Outlook

Employment of administrative services managers is projected to grow 6 percent from 2019 to 2029, faster than the average for all occupations. Administrative tasks, including facilities management and records and information management, will remain important in a range of industries.

A continuing focus on the environmental impact and energy efficiency of buildings will keep facilities managers in demand. Improving energy efficiency can reduce costs and often is required by regulation. For example, building codes typically ensure that buildings meet environmental standards. Facilities managers will be needed to oversee these improvements in a wide range of areas, from heating and air-conditioning systems to roofing. In addition, facilities managers will be needed to plan for natural disasters, ensuring that any damage to a

Administrative Services Managers
Median annual wages, May 2019

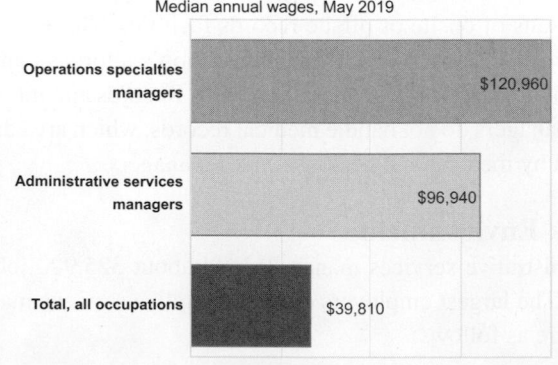

Note: All Occupations includes all occupations in the U.S. Economy.
Source: U.S. Bureau of Labor Statistics, Occupational Employment Statistics.

Administrative Services Managers
Percent change in employment, projected 2019-29

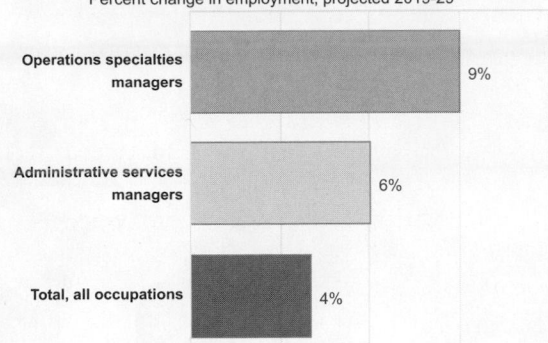

- Operations specialties managers — 9%
- Administrative services managers — 6%
- Total, all occupations — 4%

Note: All Occupations includes all occupations in the U.S. Economy.
Source: U.S. Bureau of Labor Statistics, Employment Projections program.

building will be minimal and that the organization can get back to work quickly.

"Smart building" technology is expected to affect the work of facilities managers over the next decade. This technology will provide facilities managers with timely and detailed information, such as equipment failure alerts and reminders to do maintenance. This information should allow facilities managers to complete their work more efficiently.

Employment of records and information managers also is expected to grow. Demand is expected to be particularly strong for those working in "information governance," which includes the privacy and legal aspects of records management. As cloud computing and mobile devices become more prevalent, records and information managers will have a critical role in helping organizations develop new records and information management practices and in maintaining data security.

Job Prospects
About 26,300 openings for administrative services managers are projected each year, on average, over the decade.

Many of those openings are expected to result from the need to replace workers who transfer to different occupations or exit the labor force, such as to retire.

Employment projections data for administrative services managers, 2019-29					
Occupational Title	SOC Code	Employment, 2019	Projected Employment, 2029	Change, 2019-29	
				Percent	Numeric
SOURCE: U.S. Bureau of Labor Statistics, Employment Projections program					
Administrative services and facilities managers	11-3010	325,900	347,000	6	21,200

State & Area Data
Occupational Employment Statistics (OES)
The Occupational Employment Statistics (OES) program produces employment and wage estimates annually for over 800 occupations. These estimates are available for the nation as a whole, for individual states, and for metropolitan and nonmetropolitan areas.

Contacts for More Information
For more information about facilities management and related certifications, visit
➤ International Facility Management Association

For more information about records and information management and related certifications, visit
➤ ARMA International
➤ Institute of Certified Records Managers

Advertising, Promotions, and Marketing Managers

Summary

Quick Facts: Advertising, Promotions, and Marketing Managers	
2019 Median Pay	$135,900 per year $65.34 per hour
Typical Entry-Level Education	Bachelor's degree
Work Experience in a Related Occupation	See below
On-the-job Training	None
Number of Jobs, 2019	314,900
Job Outlook, 2019-29	6% (Faster than average)
Employment Change, 2019-29	18,800

What Advertising, Promotions, and Marketing Managers Do
Advertising, promotions, and marketing managers plan programs to generate interest in products or services.

Work Environment
Many of these workers are employed in advertising agencies or in corporate or regional managing offices.

How to Become an Advertising, Promotions, or Marketing Manager
A bachelor's degree is required for most advertising, promotions, and marketing management positions. These managers typically have work experience in advertising, marketing, promotions, or sales.

Pay
The median annual wage for advertising and promotions managers was $125,510 in May 2019.

The median annual wage for marketing managers was $136,850 in May 2019.

Job Outlook
Overall employment of advertising, promotions, and marketing managers is projected to grow 6 percent from 2019 to 2029,

Advertising, promotions, and marketing managers inspect layouts, which are sketches or plans for an advertisement.

faster than the average for all occupations. Advertising, promotions, and marketing campaigns will continue to be essential for organizations as they seek to maintain and expand their share of the market.

State & Area Data

Explore resources for employment and wages by state and area for advertising, promotions, and marketing managers.

What Advertising, Promotions, and Marketing Managers Do

Advertising, promotions, and marketing managers plan programs to generate interest in products or services. They work with art directors, advertising sales agents, and financial staff members.

Duties

Advertising, promotions, and marketing managers typically do the following:

- Work with department heads or staff to discuss topics such as budgets and contracts, marketing plans, and the selection of advertising media
- Plan promotional campaigns such as contests, coupons, or giveaways
- Plan advertising campaigns, including which media to advertise in, such as radio, television, print, online media, and billboards
- Negotiate advertising contracts
- Evaluate the look and feel of websites used in campaigns or layouts, which are sketches or plans for an advertisement
- Initiate market research studies and analyze their findings to understand customer and market opportunities for businesses
- Develop pricing strategies for products or services marketed to the target customers
- Meet with clients to provide marketing or related advice

Advertising managers can be found in advertising agencies that put together advertising campaigns for clients, in media firms that sell advertising space or time, and in companies that advertise heavily.

- Direct the hiring of advertising, promotions, and marketing staff and oversee their daily activities

Advertising managers create interest among potential buyers of a product or service. They do this for a department, for an entire organization, or on a project basis (referred to as an account). Advertising managers work in advertising agencies that put together advertising campaigns for clients, in media firms that sell advertising space or time, and in organizations that advertise heavily.

Advertising managers work with sales staff and others to generate ideas for an advertising campaign. They oversee the staff that develops the advertising. They work with the finance department to prepare a budget and cost estimates for the campaign.

Often, advertising managers serve as liaisons between the client and the advertising or promotion agency that develops and places the ads. In larger organizations with extensive advertising departments, different advertising managers may oversee in-house accounts and creative and media services departments.

In addition, some advertising managers specialize in a particular field or type of advertising. For example, *media directors* determine the way in which an advertising campaign reaches customers. They can use any or all of various media, including radio, television, newspapers, magazines, the Internet, and outdoor signs.

Advertising managers known as *account executives* manage clients' accounts, but they are not responsible for developing or supervising the creation or presentation of advertising. That task becomes the work of the creative services department.

Promotions managers direct programs that combine advertising with purchasing incentives to increase sales. Often, the programs use direct mail, inserts in newspapers, Internet advertisements, in-store displays, product endorsements, or special events to target customers. Purchasing incentives may include discounts, samples, gifts, rebates, coupons, sweepstakes, or contests.

Marketing managers estimate the demand for products and services that an organization and its competitors offer. They identify potential markets for the organization's products.

Marketing managers also develop pricing strategies to help organizations maximize their profits and market share while ensuring that the organizations' customers are satisfied. They work with sales, public relations, and product development staff.

For example, a marketing manager may monitor trends that indicate the need for a new product or service. Then he or she may assist in the development of that product or service and to create a marketing plan for it.

Work Environment

Advertising and promotions managers held about 28,600 jobs in 2019. The largest employers of advertising and promotions managers were as follows:

Advertising, public relations, and related services	43%
Self-employed workers	11
Information	10

Management of companies and enterprises	7
Wholesale trade	4

Marketing managers held about 286,300 jobs in 2019. The largest employers of marketing managers were as follows:

Professional, scientific, and technical services	23%
Management of companies and enterprises	14
Finance and insurance	10
Manufacturing	9
Wholesale trade	8

Because the work of advertising, promotions, and marketing managers directly affects a firm's revenue, people in these occupations typically work closely with top executives.

The jobs of advertising, promotions, and marketing managers can often be stressful, particularly near deadlines. Additionally, they may travel to meet with clients or media representatives.

Work Schedules

Most advertising, promotions, and marketing managers work full time. Some advertising and promotions managers work more than 40 hours per week.

How to Become an Advertising, Promotions, or Marketing Manager

A bachelor's degree is required for most advertising, promotions, and marketing management positions. These managers typically have work experience in advertising, marketing, promotions, or sales.

Education

A bachelor's degree is required for most advertising, promotions, and marketing management positions. For advertising management positions, some employers prefer a bachelor's degree in advertising or journalism. A relevant course of study

Advertising, promotions, and marketing managers may travel to meet with clients or representatives of communications media.

These managers typically have previous work experience in advertising, marketing, promotions, or sales.

might include classes in marketing, consumer behavior, market research, sales, communication methods and technology, visual arts, art history, and photography.

Most marketing managers need a bachelor's degree. Courses in business law, management, economics, finance, computer science, mathematics, and statistics are advantageous. For example, courses in computer science are helpful in developing an approach to maximize online traffic, by utilizing online search results, because maximizing such traffic is critical for the success of digital advertisements and promotions. In addition, completing an internship while in school can be useful.

Work Experience in a Related Occupation

Advertising, promotions, and marketing managers typically have work experience in advertising, marketing, promotions, or sales. For example, many managers are former sales representatives; buyers or purchasing agents; or public relations specialists.

Important Qualities

Analytical skills. Advertising, promotions, and marketing managers must be able to analyze industry trends to determine the most promising strategies for their organization.

Communication skills. Managers must be able to communicate effectively with a broad-based team made up of other managers or staff members during the advertising, promotions, and marketing process. They must also be able to communicate persuasively with the public.

Creativity. Advertising, promotions, and marketing managers must be able to generate new and imaginative ideas.

Decisionmaking skills. Managers often must choose between competing advertising and marketing strategies put forward by staff.

Interpersonal skills. Managers must deal with a range of people in different roles, both inside and outside the organization.

Organizational skills. Advertising, promotions, and marketing managers must manage their time and budget efficiently while directing and motivating staff members.

Pay

The median annual wage for advertising and promotions managers was $125,510 in May 2019. The median wage is the wage at which half the workers in an occupation earned more than that amount and half earned less. The lowest 10 percent earned less than $61,930, and the highest 10 percent earned more than $208,000.

The median annual wage for marketing managers was $136,850 in May 2019. The lowest 10 percent earned less than $71,010, and the highest 10 percent earned more than $208,000.

In May 2019, the median annual wages for advertising and promotions managers in the top industries in which they worked were as follows:

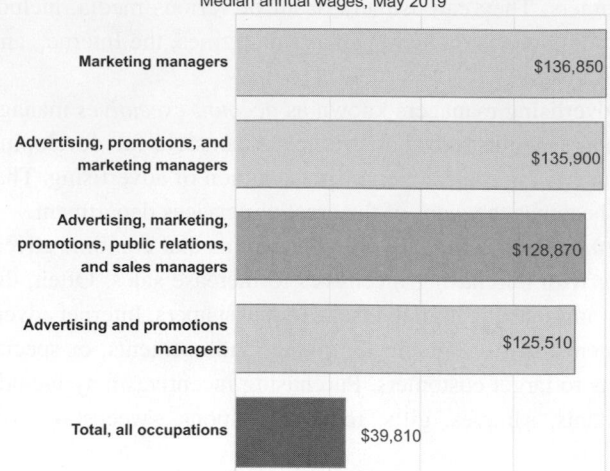

Advertising, Promotions, and Marketing Managers
Median annual wages, May 2019

Marketing managers	$136,850
Advertising, promotions, and marketing managers	$135,900
Advertising, marketing, promotions, public relations, and sales managers	$128,870
Advertising and promotions managers	$125,510
Total, all occupations	$39,810

Note: All Occupations includes all occupations in the U.S. Economy. Source: U.S. Bureau of Labor Statistics, Occupational Employment Statistics.

Advertising, public relations, and related
services $147,100
Management of companies and enterprises 119,250
Information 106,270
Wholesale trade 86,700

In May 2019, the median annual wages for marketing managers in the top industries in which they worked were as follows:

Finance and insurance $145,720
Management of companies and enterprises 145,510
Professional, scientific, and technical services 145,300
Manufacturing 138,950
Wholesale trade 128,680

Most advertising, promotions, and marketing managers work full time. Some advertising and promotions managers work more than 40 hours per week.

Job Outlook

Overall employment of advertising, promotions, and marketing managers is projected to grow 6 percent from 2019 to 2029, faster than the average for all occupations. Employment growth will vary by occupation.

Employment of marketing managers is projected to grow 7 percent from 2019 to 2029, faster than the average for all occupations. Marketing managers will continue to be in demand as organizations use marketing campaigns to maintain and expand their market share. These managers will be sought after for their advice on crafting pricing strategies and finding new ways to reach customers.

Advertising, Promotions, and Marketing Managers

Percent change in employment, projected 2019-29

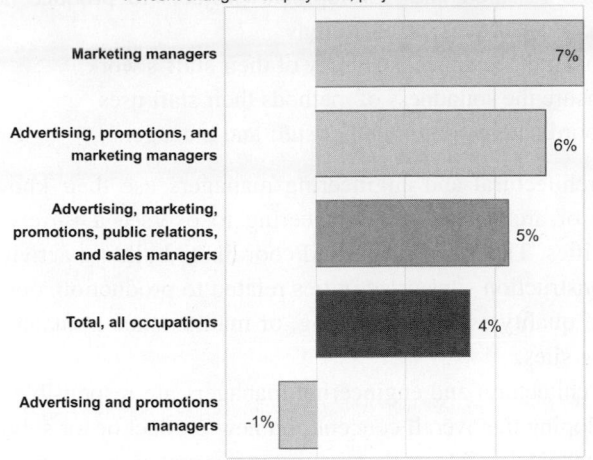

Marketing managers — 7%

Advertising, promotions, and marketing managers — 6%

Advertising, marketing, promotions, public relations, and sales managers — 5%

Total, all occupations — 4%

Advertising and promotions managers — -1%

Note: All Occupations includes all occupations in the U.S. Economy.
Source: U.S. Bureau of Labor Statistics, Employment Projections program.

Employment of advertising and promotions managers is projected to decline 1 percent from 2019 to 2029. The continued rise of electronic media will result in decreasing demand for print advertisements. The newspaper publishing industry, which employs many of these workers, is projected to lose jobs over the next 10 years. Despite overall employment declines for advertising and promotions managers, there may be some growth in industries that rely on these workers to create digital media campaigns that target customers through the use of websites, social media, or live chats.

Job Prospects

Advertising, promotions, and marketing manager positions are highly desirable and are often sought by other managers and experienced professionals. With Internet-based advertising becoming more important, advertising managers who can navigate the digital world should have the best prospects.

Occupational Title	SOC Code	Employment, 2019	Projected Employment, 2029	Change, 2019-29	
				Percent	Numeric
SOURCE: U.S. Bureau of Labor Statistics, Employment Projections program					
Advertising, promotions, and marketing managers	—	314,900	333,700	6	18,800
Advertising and promotions managers	11-2011	28,600	28,300	-1	-300
Marketing managers	11-2021	286,300	305,400	7	19,100

Employment projections data for advertising, promotions, and marketing managers, 2019-29

State & Area Data
Occupational Employment Statistics (OES)

The Occupational Employment Statistics (OES) program produces employment and wage estimates annually for over 800 occupations. These estimates are available for the nation as a whole, for individual states, and for metropolitan and nonmetropolitan areas.

Contacts for More Information

For more information about advertising managers, visit:
➤ American Association of Advertising Agencies

Architectural and Engineering Managers

Summary

Quick Facts: Architectural and Engineering Managers

2019 Median Pay	$144,830 per year $69.63 per hour
Typical Entry-Level Education	Bachelor's degree
Work Experience in a Related Occupation	5 years or more
On-the-job Training	None
Number of Jobs, 2019	198,100
Job Outlook, 2019-29	3% (As fast as average)
Employment Change, 2019-29	5,100

What Architectural and Engineering Managers Do

Architectural and engineering managers plan, direct, and coordinate activities in architectural and engineering companies.

Work Environment

Most architectural and engineering managers work in offices, although some may also work in research laboratories and industrial production plants or at construction sites. Most work full time and some work more than 40 hours a week.

How to Become an Architectural or Engineering Manager

Architectural and engineering managers typically need at least a bachelor's degree and considerable work experience as an architect or engineer.

Pay

The median annual wage for architectural and engineering managers was $144,830 in May 2019.

Job Outlook

Employment of architectural and engineering managers is projected to grow 3 percent from 2019 to 2029, about as fast as the average for all occupations. Many of the new jobs for

Architectural and engineering managers plan activities in architectural and engineering companies.

architectural and engineering managers are expected to be in computer systems design and related services and in consulting firms.

State & Area Data

Explore resources for employment and wages by state and area for architectural and engineering managers.

What Architectural and Engineering Managers Do

Architectural and engineering managers plan, direct, and coordinate activities in architectural and engineering companies.

Duties

Architectural and engineering managers typically do the following:

- Make detailed plans for the development of new products and designs
- Determine staff, training, and equipment needs
- Propose budgets for projects and programs

Architectural and engineering managers assign workers specific parts of a project to carry out.

- Hire and supervise staff
- Lead research and development projects to produce new products, processes, or designs
- Check the technical accuracy of their staff's work
- Ensure the soundness of methods their staff uses
- Coordinate work with other staff and managers

Architectural and engineering managers use their knowledge of architecture or engineering to oversee a variety of activities. They may direct and coordinate building activities at construction sites or activities related to production, operations, quality assurance, testing, or maintenance at manufacturing sites.

Architectural and engineering managers are responsible for developing the overall concept of a new product or for solving the technical problems that prevent the completion of a project. To accomplish this, they must determine technical goals and produce detailed plans.

Architectural and engineering managers spend a great deal of time coordinating the activities of their staff with the activities of other staff or organizations. They often confer with other managers, including those in finance, production, and marketing, as well as with contractors and equipment and materials suppliers.

In addition, architectural and engineering managers must know how to prepare budgets, hire staff, and supervise employees. They propose budgets for projects and programs and determine staff, training, and equipment needs. These managers must also hire people and assign them specific parts of each project to carry out. Architectural and engineering managers supervise the work of their employees, set schedules, and create administrative procedures.

Work Environment

Architectural and engineering managers held about 198,100 jobs in 2019. The largest employers of architectural and engineering managers were as follows:

Manufacturing	35%
Architectural, engineering, and related services	26
Government	9
Scientific research and development services	6
Management of companies and enterprises	6

Most architectural and engineering managers work in offices, although some may also work in research laboratories and industrial production plants or at construction sites.

Work Schedules

Most architectural and engineering managers work full time and some work more than 40 hours a week. These managers are often under considerable pressure to meet deadlines and budgets.

Architectural and engineering managers frequently work in groups.

How to Become an Architectural or Engineering Manager

Architectural and engineering managers typically need at least a bachelor's degree and considerable work experience as an architect or engineer.

Education

Most architectural and engineering managers have at least a bachelor's degree in an engineering specialty or a master's degree in architecture.

Some also obtain business management skills by completing a master's degree in engineering management (MEM or MsEM) or technology management (MSTM) or a master's degree in business administration (MBA). Some workers earn their master's degree before advancing to management positions, and others earn it while they work as a manager. Typically, those who prefer to manage in technical areas pursue an MsEM or MSTM and those interested in more general management skills earn an MBA.

Architectural and engineering managers advance to their positions after years of employment as an architect or engineer.

Engineering management programs usually include classes in accounting, engineering economics, financial management, industrial and human resources management, and quality control.

Technology management programs typically provide instruction in production and operations management, project management, computer applications, quality control, safety and health issues, statistics, and general management principles.

Work Experience in a Related Occupation

Managers advance to their positions after years of employment as an architect or engineer. They usually have experience working on difficult or complex projects, developing designs, solving problems, and making decisions. Before moving up to a management position, they also typically gain experience leading engineering teams.

Important Qualities

Analytical skills. Architectural and engineering managers must evaluate information carefully and solve complex problems.

Communication skills. Architectural and engineering managers oversee staff and work together with other levels of management. They must effectively communicate orders and lead teams to meet goals.

Detail oriented. Architectural and engineering managers must pay attention to detail. Their duties require an understanding of complex systems since a minor error can cause major problems.

Math skills. Architectural and engineering managers use calculus and other advanced mathematics to develop new products and processes.

Organizational skills. Architectural and engineering managers keep track of many workers, schedules, and budgets simultaneously.

Pay

The median annual wage for architectural and engineering managers was $144,830 in May 2019. The median wage is the wage at which half the workers in an occupation earned more than that amount and half earned less. The lowest 10 percent earned less than $92,510, and the highest 10 percent earned more than $208,000.

In May 2019, the median annual wages for architectural and engineering managers in the top industries in which they worked were as follows:

Scientific research and development services	$167,290
Management of companies and enterprises	152,640
Manufacturing	143,550
Architectural, engineering, and related services	143,160
Government	133,320

In addition, some architectural and engineering managers may receive more benefits—such as expense accounts and bonuses—than workers who are not managers.

Architectural and Engineering Managers
Median annual wages, May 2019

Architectural and engineering managers $144,830

Management occupations $105,660

Total, all occupations $39,810

Note: All Occupations includes all occupations in the U.S. Economy.
Source: U.S. Bureau of Labor Statistics, Occupational Employment Statistics.

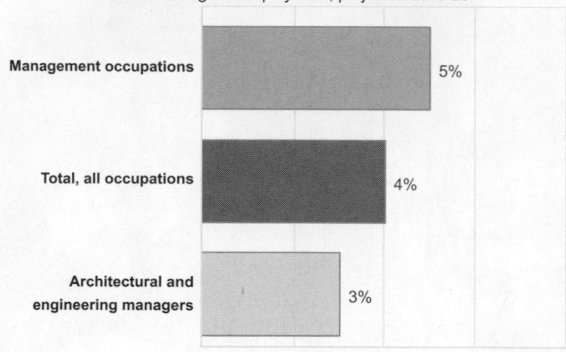

Architectural and Engineering Managers
Percent change in employment, projected 2019-29

Management occupations   5%

Total, all occupations   4%

Architectural and engineering managers   3%

Note: All Occupations includes all occupations in the U.S. Economy.
Source: U.S. Bureau of Labor Statistics, Employment Projections program.

Most architectural and engineering managers work full time and some work more than 40 hours a week. These managers are often under considerable pressure to meet deadlines and budgets.

Job Outlook

Employment of architectural and engineering managers is projected to grow 3 percent from 2019 to 2029, about as fast as the average for all occupations. Many of the new jobs for architectural and engineering managers are expected to be in computer systems design and related services and in consulting firms.

Demand for civil engineering services is expected to continue as the nation's aging infrastructure requires expansion and repair. Mechanical and electrical engineering services also should be needed for projects such as wind turbine farms and other renewable energy construction and design.

Job Prospects

Because these jobs are highly desirable, candidates can expect competition for openings.

Those with technical knowledge, strong communication skills, and years of related work experience, especially working on complex projects, will likely be in the best position to become managers.

In addition, because architectural and engineering managers are involved in the financial, production, and marketing activities of their firm, business management skills can be beneficial for those seeking management positions.

Employment projections data for architectural and engineering managers, 2019-29					
Occupational Title	SOC Code	Employment, 2019	Projected Employment, 2029	Change, 2019-29	
				Percent	Numeric
SOURCE: U.S. Bureau of Labor Statistics, Employment Projections program					
Architectural and engineering managers	11-9041	198,100	203,200	3	5,100

State & Area Data
Occupational Employment Statistics (OES)

The Occupational Employment Statistics (OES) program produces employment and wage estimates annually for over 800 occupations. These estimates are available for the nation as a whole, for individual states, and for metropolitan and nonmetropolitan areas.

Contacts for More Information

For information on architecture and engineering management programs, visit
➤ ABET
➤ American Institute of Architects
➤ Association of Technology, Management, and Applied Engineering

Compensation and Benefits Managers

Summary

Quick Facts: Compensation and Benefits Managers	
2019 Median Pay	$122,270 per year $58.78 per hour
Typical Entry-Level Education	Bachelor's degree
Work Experience in a Related Occupation	5 years or more
On-the-job Training	None
Number of Jobs, 2019	18,000
Job Outlook, 2019-29	3% (As fast as average)
Employment Change, 2019-29	500

What Compensation and Benefits Managers Do

Compensation and benefits managers plan, develop, and oversee programs to pay employees.

Work Environment

Compensation and benefits managers work in nearly every industry. Some work more than 40 hours per week.

How to Become a Compensation or Benefits Manager

Compensation and benefits managers typically need a bachelor's degree and related work experience.

Pay

The median annual wage for compensation and benefits managers was $122,270 in May 2019.

Job Outlook

Employment of compensation and benefits managers is projected to grow 3 percent from 2019 to 2029, about as fast as the average for all occupations.

State & Area Data

Explore resources for employment and wages by state and area for compensation and benefits managers.

What Compensation and Benefits Managers Do

Compensation and benefits managers plan, develop, and oversee programs to pay employees.

Duties

Compensation and benefits managers typically do the following:

- Coordinate and supervise the work activities of staff
- Set the organization's pay and benefits structure
- Monitor competitive wage rates to develop or modify compensation plans
- Choose and manage outside partners, such as benefits vendors, insurance brokers, and investment managers
- Oversee the distribution of pay and benefits information to the organization's employees
- Ensure that pay and benefits plans comply with federal and state regulations
- Prepare a program budget and operate within that budget

Although some managers administer both the compensation and benefits programs in an organization, other managers—particularly at large organizations—specialize and oversee one or the other. However, all compensation and benefits managers routinely meet with senior staff, managers of other human resources departments, and the financial officers of their organization. They use their expertise to recommend compensation and benefits policies, programs, and plans.

Compensation and benefits managers may analyze data to determine the best pay and benefits plans for an organization. They may also monitor trends affecting pay and benefits and assess ways for their organization to improve practices or policies. Using analytical, database, and presentation software,

Compensation and benefits managers work in nearly every industry.

Managers ensure that pay plans comply with federal regulations.

managers draw conclusions, present their findings, and make recommendations to other managers in the organization.

Compensation managers direct an organization's pay structure. They monitor market conditions and government regulations to ensure that their organization's pay rates are current and competitive. They analyze data on wages and salaries, and they evaluate how their organization's pay structure compares with that of other organizations. Compensation managers use this information to maintain or develop pay levels for an organization.

Some also design pay-for-performance plans, which include guidelines for bonuses and incentive pay. They also may help determine commission rates and other incentives for sales staff.

Benefits managers administer an organization's employee benefits program, which may include retirement plans, leave policies, wellness programs, and insurance policies such as health, life, and disability. They select benefits vendors and oversee enrollment, renewal, and delivery of benefits to the organization's employees. They frequently monitor government regulations and market trends to ensure that their programs are current, competitive, and legal.

Work Environment

Compensation and benefits managers held about 18,000 jobs in 2019. The largest employers of compensation and benefits managers were as follows:

Management of companies and enterprises	19%
Professional, scientific, and technical services	17
Insurance carriers and related activities	11
Government	8
Healthcare and social assistance	7

Compensation and benefits managers work in nearly every industry. Most of these managers work in offices.

Compensation and benefits managers coordinate the work activities of specialists in offices.

Work Schedules

Most compensation and benefits managers work full time. Some work more than 40 hours per week. They may work more hours during peak times to meet deadlines, especially during the benefits enrollment period of their organization.

How to Become a Compensation or Benefits Manager

Compensation and benefits managers typically need a combination of education and related work experience.

Education

For most positions, compensation and benefits managers typically need a bachelor's degree in business, human resources, or a related field.

Work Experience in a Related Occupation

Work experience is essential for compensation and benefits managers. Managers often specialize in either compensation or benefits, depending on the experience they gain in previous jobs. Managers often start out as compensation, benefits, and job analysis specialists. Work experience in other human resource fields, in finance, or in management is also helpful.

Compensation and benefits managers often start out as compensation, benefits, and job analysis specialists.

Licenses, Certifications, and Registrations

Although not required, certification gives compensation and benefits managers credibility because it shows that they have expertise. Employers may prefer to hire candidates with certification, and some positions require it.

Certification often requires several years of related work experience and passing an exam. Professional associations, including the Society for Human Resource Management, the International Foundation of Employee Benefit Plans and WorldatWork, offer certification programs that may be helpful for compensation and benefits managers.

Important Qualities

Analytical skills. Compensation and benefits managers analyze data on wages and salaries and the cost of benefits, and they assess and devise programs that best fit an organization and its employees.

Business skills. These managers oversee a budget, build a case for their recommendations, and understand how compensation and benefits plans affect an organization's finances.

Communication skills. Compensation and benefits managers direct staff, give presentations, and work with colleagues. With each of these groups, they must be able to clearly explain concepts and respond to concerns.

Decisionmaking skills. These managers weigh the strengths and weaknesses of different pay structures and benefits plans and choose the best options for an organization.

Leadership skills. Compensation and benefits managers coordinate the activities of their staff and administer compensation and benefits programs, ensuring that the work is completed accurately and on schedule.

Pay

The median annual wage for compensation and benefits managers was $122,270 in May 2019. The median wage is the wage at which half the workers in an occupation earned more than that amount and half earned less. The lowest 10 percent earned less than $69,870, and the highest 10 percent earned more than $208,000.

In May 2019, the median annual wages for compensation and benefits managers in the top industries in which they worked were as follows:

Management of companies and enterprises	$130,640
Insurance carriers and related activities	127,920
Professional, scientific, and technical services	127,910
Healthcare and social assistance	115,040
Government	104,640

Most compensation and benefits managers work full time. Some work more than 40 hours per week. They may work more hours during peak times to meet deadlines, especially during the benefits enrollment period of their organization.

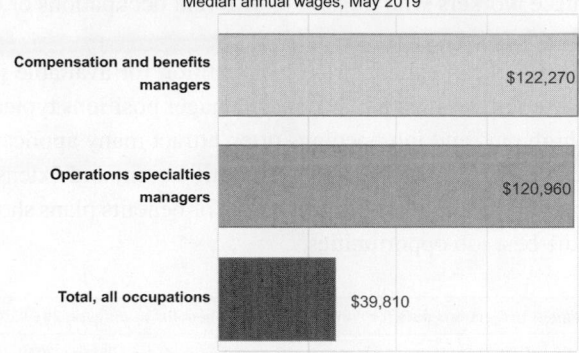

Compensation and Benefits Managers
Median annual wages, May 2019

Compensation and benefits managers $122,270
Operations specialties managers $120,960
Total, all occupations $39,810

Note: All Occupations includes all occupations in the U.S. Economy.
Source: U.S. Bureau of Labor Statistics, Occupational Employment Statistics.

Job Outlook

Employment of compensation and benefits managers is projected to grow 3 percent from 2019 to 2029, about as fast as the average for all occupations.

Organizations continue to focus on reducing compensation and benefits costs, such as by introducing pay-for-performance and health and wellness programs. Organizations will need managers to evaluate and direct these compensation and benefits policies and plans.

However, organizations may contract out a portion of their compensation and benefits functions to human resources consulting firms in order to reduce costs and gain access to technical expertise. For example, to reduce administrative costs, organizations commonly use an outside vendor for processing payroll and insurance claims. These consulting firms automate tasks and operate call centers to handle employee questions, thereby reducing the need for compensation and benefits managers.

Job Prospects

Despite limited employment growth, about 1,300 openings for compensation and benefits managers are projected annually, on average, over the decade.

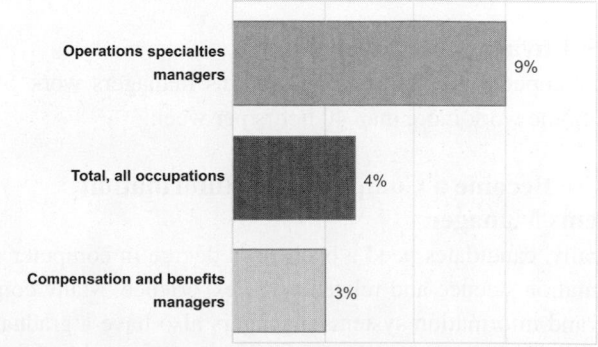

Compensation and Benefits Managers
Percent change in employment, projected 2019-29

Operations specialties managers 9%
Total, all occupations 4%
Compensation and benefits managers 3%

Note: All Occupations includes all occupations in the U.S. Economy.
Source: U.S. Bureau of Labor Statistics, Employment Projections program.

Most of those openings are expected to result from the need to replace workers who transfer to different occupations or exit the labor force, such as to retire.

Jobseekers can expect strong competition for available jobs because compensation and benefits manager positions typically offer high pay, and job openings often attract many applicants. Those who have a master's degree, certification, and extensive experience working with compensation or benefits plans should have the best job opportunities.

Employment projections data for compensation and benefits managers, 2019-29					
Occupational Title	SOC Code	Employment, 2019	Projected Employment, 2029	Change, 2019-29	
				Percent	Numeric
SOURCE: U.S. Bureau of Labor Statistics, Employment Projections program					
Compensation and benefits managers	11-3111	18,000	18,400	3	500

State & Area Data
Occupational Employment Statistics (OES)
The Occupational Employment Statistics (OES) program produces employment and wage estimates annually for over 800 occupations. These estimates are available for the nation as a whole, for individual states, and for metropolitan and nonmetropolitan areas.

Contacts for More Information
For more information about compensation and benefits managers, including certification, visit
➤ International Foundation of Employee Benefit Plans
➤ WorldatWork

For more information about human resources careers and certification, visit
➤ Society for Human Resource Management

Computer and Information Systems Managers

Summary

Quick Facts: Computer and Information Systems Managers

2019 Median Pay	$146,360 per year $70.37 per hour
Typical Entry-Level Education	Bachelor's degree
Work Experience in a Related Occupation	5 years or more
On-the-job Training	None
Number of Jobs, 2019	461,000
Job Outlook, 2019-29	10% (Much faster than average)
Employment Change, 2019-29	48,100

What Computer and Information Systems Managers Do
Computer and information systems managers plan, coordinate, and direct computer-related activities in an organization.

Work Environment
Most computer and information systems managers work full time. Some work more than 40 hours per week.

How to Become a Computer and Information Systems Manager
Typically, candidates need a bachelor's degree in computer or information science and related work experience. Many computer and information systems managers also have a graduate degree.

Pay
The median annual wage for computer and information systems managers was $146,360 in May 2019.

Job Outlook
Employment of computer and information systems managers is projected to grow 10 percent from 2019 to 2029, much faster than the average for all occupations. Demand for computer and information systems managers will grow as firms increasingly expand their business to digital platforms.

State & Area Data
Explore resources for employment and wages by state and area for computer and information systems managers.

Computer and information systems managers learn about new technology and look for ways to upgrade their organization's computer systems.

What Computer and Information Systems Managers Do

Computer and information systems managers, often called information technology (IT) managers or IT project managers, plan, coordinate, and direct computer-related activities in an organization. They help determine the information technology goals of an organization and are responsible for implementing computer systems to meet those goals.

Duties

Computer and information systems managers typically do the following:

- Analyze their organization's computer needs and recommend possible upgrades for top executives to consider
- Plan and direct the installation and maintenance of computer hardware and software
- Ensure the security of an organization's network and electronic documents
- Assess the costs and benefits of new projects and justify funding on projects to top executives
- Learn about new technology and look for ways to upgrade their organization's computer systems
- Determine short- and long-term personnel needs for their department
- Plan and direct the work of other IT professionals, including computer systems analysts, software developers, information security analysts, and computer support specialists
- Negotiate with vendors to get the highest level of service for the organization's technology

Few managers carry out all of these duties. There are various types of computer and information systems managers, and the specific duties of each are determined by the size and structure of the firm. Smaller firms may not employ every type of manager.

IT directors sometimes present new ideas to a firm's top executives.

The following are examples of types of computer and information systems managers:

Chief information officers (CIOs) determine the technology or information goals of an organization and then oversee implementation of technology to meet those goals.

CIOs may focus on a specific area, such as electronic data processing or information systems, but CIOs tend to focus more on long-term or big picture issues. At small organizations a CIO has more direct control over the IT department, and at larger organizations other managers under the CIO may handle the day-to-day activities of the IT department.

CIOs who do not have technical expertise and who focus solely on a company's business aspects are included in top executives.

Chief technology officers (CTOs) evaluate new technology and determine how it can help their organization. When both CIOs and CTOs are present, the CTO usually has more technical expertise.

The CTO usually reports directly to the CIO and is responsible for designing and recommending the appropriate technology solutions to support the CIO's policies and directives. CTOs also work with different departments to implement the organization's technology plans.

When a company does not have a CIO, the CTO determines the overall technology strategy for the firm and presents it to top executives.

IT directors, including management information systems (MIS) directors, are in charge of their organizations' information technology (IT) departments, and they directly supervise other employees. IT directors help to determine the business requirements for IT systems, and they implement the policies that have been chosen by top executives. IT directors often have a direct role in hiring members of the IT department. It is their job to ensure the availability of data and network services by coordinating IT activities. IT directors also oversee the financial aspects of their department, such as budgeting.

IT security managers oversee their organizations' network and data security. They work with top executives to plan security policies and promote a culture of information security throughout the organization. They develop programs to keep employees aware of security threats. These managers must keep up to date on IT security measures. They also supervise investigations if there is a security violation.

Work Environment

Computer and information systems managers held about 461,000 jobs in 2019. The largest employers of computer and information systems managers were as follows:

Computer systems design and related services	22%
Information	11
Finance and insurance	11

Computer and information systems managers plan and direct the work of other information technology (IT) professionals.

Management of companies and enterprises 9

Manufacturing 7

Work Schedules

Most computer and information systems managers work full time. If problems arise, managers may need to work more than 40 hours a week to come up with solutions.

How to Become a Computer and Information Systems Manager

Typically, a bachelor's degree in computer or information science, plus related work experience, is required. Many computer and information systems managers also have a graduate degree.

Education

Computer and information systems managers normally must have a bachelor's degree in a computer- or information science–related field. These degrees include courses in computer programming, software development, and mathematics. Management information systems (MIS) programs usually include business classes as well as computer-related ones.

Many organizations require their computer and information systems managers to have a graduate degree as well. A Master of Business Administration (MBA) is common and takes 2 years beyond the undergraduate level to complete. Many people pursuing an MBA take classes while working, an option that can increase the time required to complete that degree.

Work Experience in a Related Occupation

Most jobs for computer and information systems managers require several years of experience in a related information technology (IT) job. Lower-level management positions may require only a few years of experience. Directors are more likely to need 5 to 10 years of related work experience. A chief technology officer (CTO), who oversees the technology plan for a large organization, may need more than 15 years of experience in the IT field before being considered for a job.

Most jobs for computer and information systems managers require several years of experience in a related information technology (IT) job.

The number of years of experience required varies with the organization. Generally, smaller or newer companies do not require as much experience as larger or more established ones.

Computer systems are used throughout the economy, and IT employees may gain experience in a variety of industries. However, an applicant's work experience should be in the same industry they are applying to work in. For example, an IT security manager should have previously worked in information security. A hospital IT director should have experience in the healthcare field.

Advancement

Most computer and information systems managers start out as lower-level managers and advance to higher positions within the IT department. IT directors or project managers can advance to become CTOs. A CTO or other manager who is especially business-minded can advance to become a chief information officer (CIO), the person in charge of all IT-related decisions in an organization. CIOs can advance to become top executives in an organization.

Important Qualities

Analytical skills. IT managers must analyze problems and consider and select the best ways to solve them.

Computer and Information Systems Managers

Median annual wages, May 2019

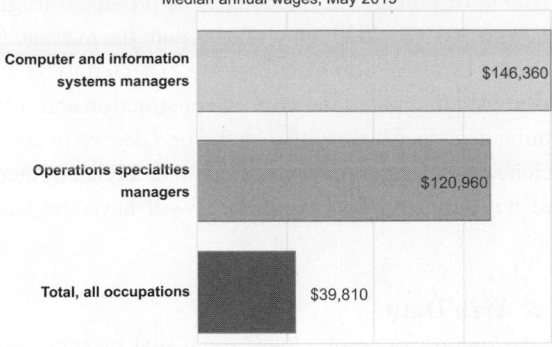

Computer and Information Systems Managers

Percent change in employment, projected 2019-29

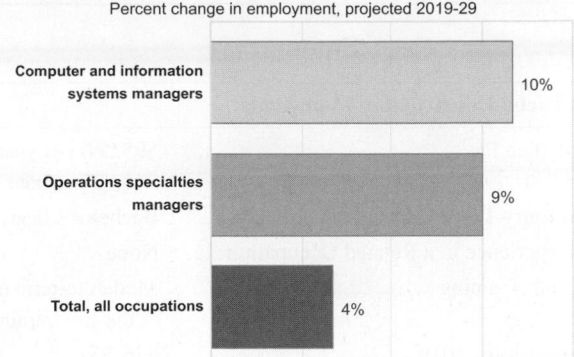

Note: All Occupations includes all occupations in the U.S. Economy.
Source: U.S. Bureau of Labor Statistics, Occupational Employment
Statistics.

Note: All Occupations includes all occupations in the U.S. Economy.
Source: U.S. Bureau of Labor Statistics, Employment Projections
program.

Business skills. IT managers must develop and implement strategic plans to reach the goals of their organizations.

Communication skills. IT managers must explain their work to top executives and give clear instructions to their subordinates.

Decisionmaking skills. Some IT managers must make important decisions about how to allocate resources in order to reach their organizations' goals.

Leadership skills. IT managers must lead and motivate IT teams or departments so that workers are efficient and effective.

Organizational skills. Some IT managers must coordinate the work of several different IT departments to make the organization run efficiently.

Pay

The median annual wage for computer and information systems managers was $146,360 in May 2019. The median wage is the wage at which half the workers in an occupation earned more than that amount and half earned less. The lowest 10 percent earned less than $87,480, and the highest 10 percent earned more than $208,000.

In May 2019, the median annual wages for computer and information systems managers in the top industries in which they worked were as follows:

Information	$161,930
Computer systems design and related services	152,840
Finance and insurance	150,810
Management of companies and enterprises	148,290
Manufacturing	146,720

Most computer and information systems managers work full time. If problems arise, managers may need to work more than 40 hours a week to come up with solutions.

Job Outlook

Employment of computer and information systems managers is projected to grow 10 percent from 2019 to 2029, much faster than the average for all occupations.

Demand for computer and information systems managers will grow as firms increasingly expand their operations to digital platforms. Computer and information systems managers will be responsible for implementing these goals.

Employment growth will result from the need to bolster cybersecurity in computer and information systems used by businesses. Industries such as retail trade will need to implement more robust security policies as cyber threats increase.

An increase in the popularity of cloud computing may result in firms outsourcing services from in-house IT departments to cloud-computing companies. This will shift IT services from IT departments in noncomputer industries, such as financial firms or schools, to firms engaged in computer systems design and related services and those in data processing, hosting, and related services.

Employment projections data for computer and information systems managers, 2019-29					
Occupational Title	SOC Code	Employment, 2019	Projected Employment, 2029	Change, 2019-29	
				Percent	Numeric
SOURCE: U.S. Bureau of Labor Statistics, Employment Projections program					
Computer and information systems managers	11-3021	461,000	509,200	10	48,100

State & Area Data
Occupational Employment Statistics (OES)

The Occupational Employment Statistics (OES) program produces employment and wage estimates annually for over 800 occupations. These estimates are available for the nation as a whole, for individual states, and for metropolitan and nonmetropolitan areas.

Contacts for More Information

For more information about computer careers, visit:
➤ Association for Computing Machinery
➤ CompTIA
➤ Computing Research Association
➤ IEEE Computer Society

For more information about opportunities for women pursuing information technology careers, visit:
➤ National Center for Women & Information Technology

Construction Managers

Summary

Quick Facts: Construction Managers

2019 Median Pay	$95,260 per year $45.80 per hour
Typical Entry-Level Education	Bachelor's degree
Work Experience in a Related Occupation	None
On-the-job Training	Moderate-term on-the-job training
Number of Jobs, 2019	476,700
Job Outlook, 2019-29	8% (Much faster than average)
Employment Change, 2019-29	40,400

What Construction Managers Do

Construction managers plan, coordinate, budget, and supervise construction projects from start to finish.

Work Environment

Many construction managers have a main office, but spend most of their time working out of a field office at a construction site, where they monitor the project and make daily decisions about construction activities. The need to meet deadlines and respond to emergencies often requires construction managers to work many hours.

How to Become a Construction Manager

Construction managers typically must have a bachelor's degree, and learn management techniques through on-the-job training. Large construction firms increasingly prefer candidates with both construction experience and a bachelor's degree in a construction-related field.

Pay

The median annual wage for construction managers was $95,260 in May 2019.

Job Outlook

Employment of construction managers is projected to grow 8 percent from 2019 to 2029, much faster than the average for all occupations. Construction managers are expected to be needed to oversee the anticipated increase in construction activity over the coming decade. Those with a bachelor's degree in construction science, construction management, or civil engineering, coupled with construction experience, will have the best job prospects.

State & Area Data

Explore resources for employment and wages by state and area for construction managers.

What Construction Managers Do

Construction managers plan, coordinate, budget, and supervise construction projects from start to finish.

Duties

Construction managers typically do the following:

- Prepare cost estimates, budgets, and work timetables
- Interpret and explain contracts and technical information to other professionals
- Report work progress and budget matters to clients
- Collaborate with architects, engineers, and other construction specialists
- Select subcontractors and schedule and coordinate their activities
- Respond to work delays, emergencies, and other problems
- Comply with legal requirements, building and safety codes, and other regulations

Construction managers, often called *general contractors* or *project managers*, coordinate and supervise a wide variety of projects, including the building of all types of public, residential, commercial, and industrial structures, as well as roads, memorials, and bridges. Either a general contractor or

Construction managers need to coordinate activities on large projects.

Construction managers often collaborate with engineers and architects.

a construction manager oversees the construction phase of a project, but a construction manager may also consult with the client during the design phase to help refine construction plans and control costs.

Construction managers oversee specialized contractors and other personnel. They schedule and coordinate all construction processes so that projects meet design specifications. They ensure that projects are completed on time and within budget. Some construction managers may be responsible for several projects at once—for example, the construction of multiple apartment buildings.

Construction managers work closely with other building specialists, such as architects, civil engineers, and a variety of trade workers, including stonemasons, electricians, and carpenters. Projects may require specialists in everything from structural steel and painting to landscaping, paving roads, and excavating sites. Depending on the project, construction managers may interact with lawyers and local government officials. For example, when working on city-owned property or municipal buildings, construction managers sometimes confer with city inspectors to ensure that all regulations are met.

For projects too large to be managed by one person, such as office buildings and industrial complexes, a top-level construction manager hires other construction managers to be in charge of different aspects of the project. For example, each construction manager would oversee a specific phase of the project, such as structural foundation, plumbing, or electrical work, and choose subcontractors to complete it. The top-level construction manager would then collaborate and coordinate with the other construction managers.

To maximize efficiency and productivity, construction managers often perform the tasks of a cost estimator. They use specialized cost-estimating and planning software to show how to allocate time and money in order to complete their projects. Many construction managers also use software to plan the best way to get materials to the building site.

Work Environment

Construction managers held about 476,700 jobs in 2019. The largest employers of construction managers were as follows:

Self-employed workers	38%
Specialty trade contractors	17
Nonresidential building construction	16
Residential building construction	10
Heavy and civil engineering construction	8

Many construction managers have a main office, but they spend most of their time working out of a field office at the construction site, where they monitor the project and make daily decisions about construction activities. For those managing multiple projects, frequent travel between sites is required.

Construction managers supervise on-site activity.

Work Schedules

Most construction managers work full time. However, the need to meet deadlines and to respond to delays and emergencies often requires construction managers to work many additional hours. Many construction managers may also be on call 24 hours a day. Some construction managers work more than 40 hours per week.

How to Become a Construction Manager

Construction managers typically must have a bachelor's degree, and learn management techniques through on-the-job training. Large construction firms increasingly prefer candidates with both construction experience and a bachelor's degree in a construction-related field. Although some individuals with a high school diploma and many years of experience in a construction trade may be hired as construction managers, these individuals are typically qualified to become self-employed general contractors.

Education

Although there are various ways to enter this occupation, it is becoming increasingly important for construction managers to have a bachelor's degree in construction science, construction

New construction managers are typically hired as assistants and work under the guidance of an experienced manager.

management, architecture, or engineering. As construction processes become more complex, employers are placing greater importance on specialized education.

More than 100 colleges and universities offer accredited bachelor's degree programs in construction science, building science, or construction engineering. These programs include courses in project control and management, design, construction methods and materials, cost estimation, building codes and standards, and contract administration. Courses in mathematics and statistics are also relevant.

More than fifty 2-year colleges offer construction management or construction technology programs. An associate's degree combined with work experience is typical for managers who supervise smaller projects.

A few universities offer master's degree programs in construction management.

Jobseekers with a high school diploma and several years of relevant work experience may qualify to become a construction manager, although most are qualified to become self-employed general contractors.

Training

New construction managers are typically hired as assistants and work under the guidance of an experienced manager. This training period may last several months to several years, depending on the firm.

Work Experience in a Related Occupation

If the typical education is not obtained, practical construction experience is important for jobseekers, because it reduces the need for initial on-the-job training. Internships, cooperative education programs, and previous work in the construction industry can provide that experience. Some construction managers become qualified solely through extensive construction experience, spending many years in carpentry, masonry, or other construction specialties.

Licenses, Certifications, and Registrations

Although not required, certification is valuable because it can demonstrate that a person has gained knowledge and experience.

The Construction Management Association of America awards the Certified Construction Manager (CCM) designation to workers who have the required experience and who pass a technical exam. It is recommended that applicants for this certification complete a self-study course that covers the professional role of a construction manager, legal issues, the allocation of risk, and other topics related to construction management.

The American Institute of Constructors awards the Associate Constructor (AC) and Certified Professional Constructor (CPC) designations to candidates who meet its requirements and pass the appropriate construction exams.

Some states require licensure for construction managers. For more information, contact your state licensing board.

Important Qualities

Analytical skills. Construction managers plan project strategies, handle unexpected issues and delays, and solve problems that arise over the course of the project. In addition, many managers use cost-estimating and planning software to determine costs and the materials and time required to complete projects.

Business skills. Construction managers address budget matters and coordinate and supervise workers. Choosing competent staff and establishing good working relationships with them is critical.

Customer-service skills. Construction managers are in constant contact with owners, inspectors, and the public. They must form good working relationships with these people and ensure their needs are met.

Decisionmaking skills. Construction managers choose personnel and subcontractors for specific tasks and jobs. Often, these choices must be made quickly to meet deadlines and budgets.

Initiative. Self-employed construction managers generate their own business opportunities and must be proactive in finding new clients. They often market their services and bid on jobs, and they must also learn to perform special home improvement projects, such as installing mosaic glass tiles, sanding wood floors, and insulating homes.

Leadership skills. Construction managers must effectively delegate tasks to construction workers, subcontractors, and other lower level managers.

Speaking skills. Construction managers must give clear orders, explain complex information to construction workers and clients, and discuss technical details with other building specialists, such as architects. Self-employed construction managers must get their own projects, so the need to sell their services to potential clients is critical.

Technical skills. Construction managers must know construction methods and technologies, and must be able to interpret contracts and technical drawings.

Time-management skills. Construction managers must meet deadlines. They ensure that construction phases are completed on time so that the next phase can begin as scheduled. For instance, a building's foundation cannot be constructed until the land is completely excavated.

Writing skills. Construction managers must write proposals, plans, and budgets, as well as document the progress of the work for clients and others involved in the building process.

Pay

The median annual wage for construction managers was $95,260 in May 2019. The median wage is the wage at which half the workers in an occupation earned more than that amount and half earned less. The lowest 10 percent earned

Construction Managers
Median annual wages, May 2019

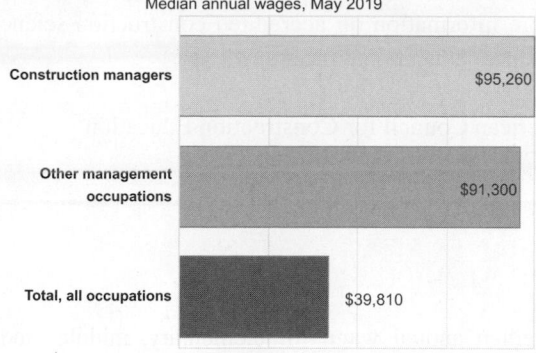

Construction managers — $95,260

Other management occupations — $91,300

Total, all occupations — $39,810

Construction Managers
Percent change in employment, projected 2019-29

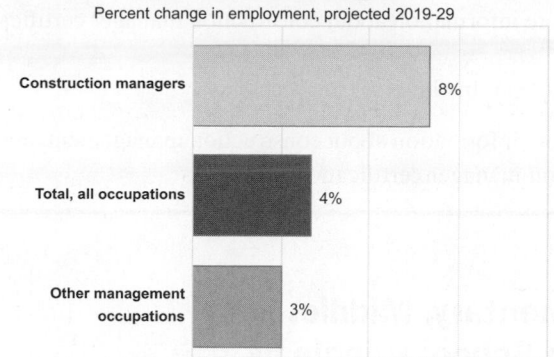

Construction managers — 8%

Total, all occupations — 4%

Other management occupations — 3%

Note: All Occupations includes all occupations in the U.S. Economy.
Source: U.S. Bureau of Labor Statistics, Occupational Employment Statistics.

Note: All Occupations includes all occupations in the U.S. Economy.
Source: U.S. Bureau of Labor Statistics, Employment Projections program.

less than $56,140, and the highest 10 percent earned more than $164,790.

In May 2019, the median annual wages for construction managers in the top industries in which they worked were as follows:

Heavy and civil engineering construction	$98,870
Nonresidential building construction	97,100
Specialty trade contractors	92,710
Residential building construction	85,800

In addition to salary, construction managers may also earn bonuses. Their earnings are highly dependent on the amount of business they generate.

Most construction managers work full time. However, the need to meet deadlines and to respond to delays and emergencies often requires construction managers to work many additional hours. Many construction managers also may be on call 24 hours a day. Some construction managers work more than 40 hours per week.

Job Outlook

Employment of construction managers is projected to grow 8 percent from 2019 to 2029, much faster than the average for all occupations.

Construction managers are expected to be needed as overall construction activity expands. Over the coming decade, population and business growth will result in the construction of new residences, office buildings, retail outlets, hospitals, schools, restaurants, and other structures. Also, the need to improve portions of the national infrastructure may spur employment growth as roads, bridges, and sewer pipe systems are upgraded or replaced.

In addition, a growing emphasis on retrofitting buildings to make them more energy efficient should create jobs for general contractors, who are more likely to manage the renovation and upgrading of buildings than oversee new large-scale construction projects.

To ensure that projects are completed on time and under budget, firms require construction managers to oversee them. Furthermore, construction processes and building technology are becoming more complex, requiring greater oversight and spurring demand for specialized management personnel.

Job Prospects

Job opportunities for construction managers are expected to be good. Specifically, jobseekers with a bachelor's degree in construction science, construction management, or civil engineering, coupled with construction experience, will have the best job prospects.

Employment of construction managers, like that of many other construction workers, is sensitive to fluctuations in the economy. On the one hand, workers in the construction industry may experience periods of unemployment when the overall level of construction falls. On the other hand, peak periods of building activity may produce abundant job opportunities for construction managers.

Employment projections data for construction managers, 2019-29					
Occupational Title	SOC Code	Employment, 2019	Projected Employment, 2029	Change, 2019-29	
				Percent	Numeric
SOURCE: U.S. Bureau of Labor Statistics, Employment Projections program					
Construction managers	11-9021	476,700	517,100	8	40,400

State & Area Data
Occupational Employment Statistics (OES)

The Occupational Employment Statistics (OES) program produces employment and wage estimates annually for over 800 occupations. These estimates are available for the nation as a whole, for individual states, and for metropolitan and nonmetropolitan areas.

Contacts for More Information

For more information about construction manager certification, visit

➤ American Institute of Constructors

For more information about construction management and construction manager certification, visit

➤ Construction Management Association of America

For more information on accredited construction science and management educational programs, visit

➤ ABET
➤ American Council for Construction Education
➤ NCCER

Elementary, Middle, and High School Principals

Summary

Quick Facts: Elementary, Middle, and High School Principals

2019 Median Pay	$96,400 per year
Typical Entry-Level Education	Master's degree
Work Experience in a Related Occupation	5 years or more
On-the-job Training	None
Number of Jobs, 2019	283,200
Job Outlook, 2019-29	4% (As fast as average)
Employment Change, 2019-29	11,100

What Elementary, Middle, and High School Principals Do

Elementary, middle, and high school principals oversee all school operations, including daily school activities.

Work Environment

Principals work in public and private elementary, middle, and high schools. Typically, principals work year round.

How to Become an Elementary, Middle, or High School Principal

Principals typically need a master's degree in education administration or leadership. In addition, they need teaching experience.

Elementary, middle, and high school principals manage the day-to-day operations of schools.

Pay

The median annual wage for elementary, middle, and high school principals was $96,400 in May 2019.

Job Outlook

Employment of elementary, middle, and high school principals is projected to grow 4 percent from 2019 to 2029, about as fast as the average for all occupations. Employment growth will be affected by student enrollment and the number of educational institutions.

State & Area Data

Explore resources for employment and wages by state and area for elementary, middle, and high school principals.

What Elementary, Middle, and High School Principals Do

Elementary, middle, and high school principals oversee all school operations, including daily school activities. They coordinate curriculums, manage staff, and provide a safe and productive learning environment for students.

Duties

Elementary, middle, and high school principals typically do the following:

• Manage school activities and staff, including teachers and support personnel

Principals counsel students.

- Establish and oversee class schedules
- Develop, implement, and maintain curriculum standards
- Counsel and discipline students
- Observe teachers and evaluate their performance
- Meet with parents and teachers to discuss students' progress and behavior
- Assess and prepare reports on test scores and other student achievement data
- Organize professional development programs and workshops for staff
- Manage the school's budget, order school supplies, and schedule maintenance
- Establish and coordinate security procedures for students, staff, and visitors

Elementary, middle, and high school principals direct the overall operation of schools. They set and oversee academic goals and ensure that teachers have the equipment and resources to meet those goals. Principals may establish and supervise additional programs in their school, such as counseling, extracurricular activities, and before- and after-school childcare.

In public schools, principals also implement standards and programs set by the school district, state, and federal regulations. They evaluate and prepare reports based on these standards by assessing student achievement and teacher performance at their school.

Principals serve as the public representative of their school. They listen to, and try to address, the concerns of parents and the community.

The duties of principals vary by the size of the school and district. In large schools and districts, principals may have additional resources and staff to help them achieve goals. For example, large school districts often have instructional coordinators who help with data analysis and with teachers' professional development. Principals also may have staff who help with hiring school personnel. In smaller school districts, principals may need to assume these and other duties themselves.

Many schools have assistant principals who help principals with school administration. Principals typically assign specific duties to their assistant principals. In some school districts, assistant principals handle a subject area, such as literacy or math. Assistants may handle student safety, provide student academic counseling, or enforce disciplinary or attendance rules. They may also coordinate buses or supervise building and grounds maintenance.

Work Environment

Elementary, middle, and high school principals held about 283,200 jobs in 2019. The largest employers of elementary, middle, and high school principals were as follows:

Elementary and secondary schools; local........................77%
Elementary and secondary schools; private...................18

Principals meet with parents and teachers to discuss students' progress.

Elementary, middle, and high school principals may find it rewarding to work with students. However, coordinating and interacting with faculty, parents, students, and community members may be demanding. Principals' work is sometimes stressful because they are accountable for their school meeting state and federal standards for student performance and teacher qualification.

Work Schedules

Principals typically work full time. They may work evenings or weekends to meet with parents and other members of the community and to attend school functions, such as concerts and athletic events.

Typically, principals work year round and do not have summers off, even if students are not in school. During the summer, principals schedule building maintenance, order school supplies, and hire new teachers and other staff in preparation for the upcoming school year.

How to Become an Elementary, Middle, or High School Principal

Most schools require elementary, middle, and high school principals to have a master's degree in education administration or leadership. Principals also need teaching experience.

Education

Principals typically need a master's degree in education leadership or education administration. These master's degree programs teach prospective principals how to manage staff, create budgets, set goals, and work with parents and the community. To enter the master's degree programs, candidates typically need a bachelor's degree in education, school counseling, or a related field.

Work Experience in a Related Occupation

Principals need several years of teaching experience. For more information on how to become a teacher, see the profiles on

Principals must communicate effectively with students, teachers, and parents.

kindergarten and elementary school teachers, middle school teachers, and high school teachers.

Licenses, Certifications, and Registrations

Most states require public school principals to be licensed as school administrators. Licensure requirements vary by state, but most require a master's degree. Some states have alternative programs for candidates who do not have a master's degree in education administration or leadership. Most states also require candidates to pass an exam and a background check.

Principals in private schools are not required to have a state-issued license.

Advancement

An assistant principal can advance to become a principal. Some principals advance to become superintendents or education administrators, which may require additional education. Others become instructional coordinators.

Important Qualities

Communication skills. Principals must communicate effectively with students, teachers, and parents. For example, when dealing with academic issues, they must listen to students and teachers in order to restate their understanding of the problem.

Critical-thinking skills. Principals analyze student test results and testing procedures to determine if improvements are needed. They must assess available options to help students achieve the best results.

Decision-making skills. Because principals are responsible for students, staff, and the overall operation of the school, they consider many factors when making decisions.

Interpersonal skills. Principals work with teachers, parents, and superintendents and must develop positive working relationships with them.

Leadership skills. Principals set educational goals and establish policies and procedures for the school. They need to be able to motivate staff to achieve these goals.

Problem-solving skills. Teachers, students, and other staff report problems to the principal. Principals need to be able to analyze problems and find appropriate solutions.

Pay

The median annual wage for elementary, middle, and high school principals was $96,400 in May 2019. The median wage is the wage at which half the workers in an occupation earned more than that amount and half earned less. The lowest 10 percent earned less than $63,070, and the highest 10 percent earned more than $148,630.

In May 2019, the median annual wages for elementary, middle, and high school principals in the top industries in which they worked were as follows:

Elementary and secondary schools; local............... $97,850

Elementary and secondary schools; private........... 85,930

Principals typically work full time. They may work evenings or weekends to meet with parents and other members of the community and to attend school functions, such as concerts and athletic events.

Typically, principals work year round and do not have summers off, even if students are not in school. During the summer, principals prepare for the upcoming school year, schedule building maintenance, order school supplies, and hire teachers and other staff.

Job Outlook

Employment of elementary, middle, and high school principals is projected to grow 4 percent from 2019 to 2029, about as fast as the average for all occupations. Employment growth will be affected by student enrollment and the number of educational institutions.

There are a limited number of principal positions available per school. If student enrollment increases, more schools will open, which could increase demand. Conversely, stagnant or

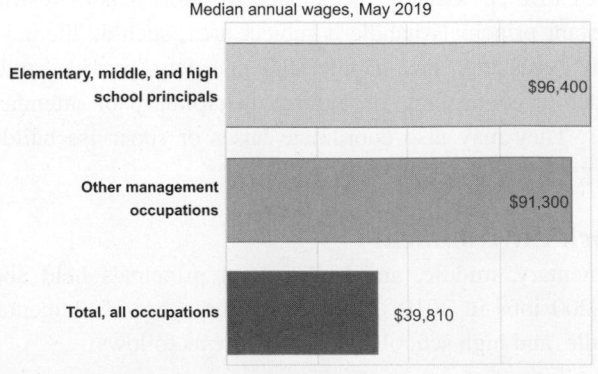

Elementary, Middle, and High School Principals
Median annual wages, May 2019

Elementary, middle, and high school principals	$96,400
Other management occupations	$91,300
Total, all occupations	$39,810

Note: All Occupations includes all occupations in the U.S. Economy.
Source: U.S. Bureau of Labor Statistics, Occupational Employment Statistics.

Elementary, Middle, and High School Principals

Percent change in employment, projected 2019-29

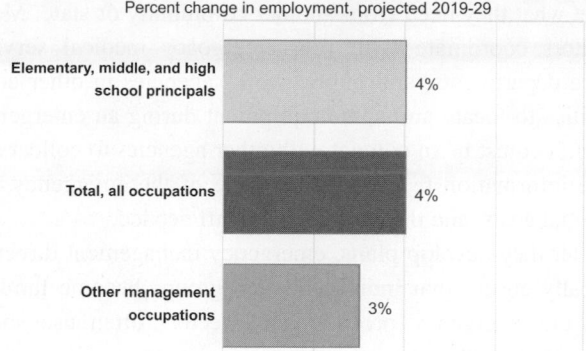

Elementary, middle, and high school principals	4%
Total, all occupations	4%
Other management occupations	3%

Note: All Occupations includes all occupations in the U.S. Economy.
Source: U.S. Bureau of Labor Statistics, Employment Projections program.

decreasing student enrollment may reduce the demand for principals.

Employment growth of school principals will also depend on state and local budgets. Budget constraints may delay the building or opening of new schools. In addition, some school districts may consolidate and close some schools within their districts, thereby limiting employment growth. However, if there is a budget surplus, school districts may open more schools which could lead to an employment growth.

Job Prospects

There may be good opportunities for teachers to advance into principal jobs as large numbers of baby boomers retire.

Employment projections data for elementary, middle, and high school principals, 2019-29					
Occupational Title	SOC Code	Employment, 2019	Projected Employment, 2029	Change, 2019-29	
				Percent	Numeric
SOURCE: U.S. Bureau of Labor Statistics, Employment Projections program					
Education administrators, kindergarten through secondary	11-9032	283,200	294,400	4	11,100

State & Area Data
Occupational Employment Statistics (OES)

The Occupational Employment Statistics (OES) program produces employment and wage estimates annually for over 800 occupations. These estimates are available for the nation as a whole, for individual states, and for metropolitan and nonmetropolitan areas.

Contacts for More Information

For more information on elementary, middle, and high school principals, visit
➤ National Association of Elementary School Principals
➤ National Association of Secondary School Principals

Emergency Management Directors

Summary

Quick Facts: Emergency Management Directors

2019 Median Pay	$74,590 per year $35.86 per hour
Typical Entry-Level Education	Bachelor's degree
Work Experience in a Related Occupation	5 years or more
On-the-job Training	None
Number of Jobs, 2019	10,400
Job Outlook, 2019-29	4% (As fast as average)
Employment Change, 2019-29	500

What Emergency Management Directors Do

Emergency management directors prepare plans and procedures for responding to natural disasters or other emergencies. They also help lead the response during and after emergencies.

Work Environment

Most emergency management directors work for local or state governments. Others work for organizations such as hospitals, colleges and universities, or private companies.

How to Become an Emergency Management Director

Emergency management directors typically need a bachelor's degree and many years of work experience in emergency response, disaster planning, or public administration.

Pay

The median annual wage for emergency management directors was $74,590 in May 2019.

Emergency management directors work with government officials, private companies, and the general public to design emergency response plans.

Job Outlook

Employment of emergency management directors is projected to grow 4 percent from 2019 to 2029, about as fast as the average for all occupations. The importance of preparing for and minimizing the risks from emergencies will help sustain demand and employment for these workers.

State & Area Data

Explore resources for employment and wages by state and area for emergency management directors.

What Emergency Management Directors Do

Emergency management directors prepare plans and procedures for responding to natural disasters and other emergencies. They also help lead the response during and after emergencies, often in coordination with public safety officials, elected officials, nonprofit organizations, and government agencies.

Duties

Emergency management directors typically do the following:

- Assess hazards and prepare plans to respond to emergencies and disasters in order to minimize risk to people and property
- Meet with public safety officials, private companies, and the public regarding emergency response plans
- Organize emergency response training for staff, volunteers, and other responders
- Coordinate the sharing of resources and equipment within and across communities to assist in responding to an emergency
- Analyze and prepare damage assessments following disasters or emergencies
- Review emergency plans of individual organizations, such as medical facilities, to ensure their adequacy
- Apply for federal funding for emergency management planning, responses, and recovery, and report on the use of funds allocated
- Review local emergency operations plans and revise them if necessary
- Maintain facilities used during emergency operations

Emergency management directors are responsible for planning and leading the responses to natural disasters and other emergencies. Directors work with government agencies, nonprofits, private companies, and the public to develop effective plans that minimize damage and disruptions during an emergency.

To develop emergency response plans, directors typically research "best practices" from around the country and from other emergency management agencies. Directors also must prepare plans and procedures that meet local, state, and federal regulations.

Directors must analyze the resources, equipment, and staff available to respond to emergencies. If resources are limited or equipment is lacking, directors must either revise their plans or get what they need from another community or state. Many directors coordinate with fire, emergency medical service, police departments, and public works agencies in other communities to locate and share equipment during an emergency. Directors must be in contact with other agencies to collect and share information regarding the scope of the emergency, the potential costs, and the resources or staff needed.

After they develop plans, emergency management directors typically ensure that individuals and groups become familiar with the emergency procedures. Directors often use social media to disseminate plans and warnings to the public.

Emergency management directors oversee training courses and disaster exercises for staff, volunteers, and local agencies to help ensure an effective and coordinated response to an emergency. Directors also may visit schools, hospitals, or other community groups to provide updates on plans for emergencies.

During an emergency, directors typically maintain a command center at which staff monitor and manage the emergency operations. Directors help lead the response, prioritizing certain actions if necessary. These actions may include ordering evacuations, conducting rescue missions, or opening public shelters for those displaced by the emergency. Emergency management directors also may need to conduct press conferences or other outreach activities to keep the public informed about the emergency.

Following an emergency, directors must assess the damage to their community and coordinate getting any needed assistance and supplies into the community. Directors may need to request state or federal assistance to help execute their emergency response plan and provide support to affected citizens, organizations, and communities. Directors may also revise their plans and procedures to prepare for future emergencies or disasters.

Emergency management directors working for hospitals, universities, or private companies may be called *business continuity managers*. Similar to their counterparts in local and state government, business continuity managers prepare plans and procedures to help businesses maintain operations and minimize losses during and after an emergency.

Work Environment

Emergency management directors held about 10,400 jobs in 2019. The largest employers of emergency management directors were as follows:

Local government, excluding education and hospitals	52%
State government, excluding education and hospitals	15
Hospitals; state, local, and private	8
Colleges, universities, and professional schools; state, local, and private	4
Professional, scientific, and technical services	3

Most emergency management directors must be on call at all times to assist in emergency response.

Although most emergency management directors work in an office, they also typically travel to meet with various government agencies, community groups, and private companies.

During disasters and emergencies, directors often work in stressful situations.

Work Schedules

Most emergency management directors work full time. In addition, most are on call at all times and may need to work overtime to respond to emergencies and to support emergency management operations. Others may work evenings and weekends to meet with various community groups in preparing their emergency response plans.

How to Become an Emergency Management Director

Emergency management directors typically need a bachelor's degree and many years of work experience in emergency response, disaster planning, or public administration.

Education

Emergency management directors typically need a bachelor's degree in a business-related field, emergency management, or public health. Some directors working in the private sector in business continuity management may need a degree in computer science, information systems administration, or another information technology (IT) field.

Small municipalities or local governments may hire applicants whose highest level of educational attainment is a high school diploma. However, these applicants usually must have extensive work experience in emergency management if they are to be hired.

Work Experience in a Related Occupation

Candidates typically need many years of work experience before they can be hired as an emergency management director.

Applicants need years of work experience in law enforcement, fire safety, or an emergency management field.

Their experience usually must be with the military, law enforcement, fire safety, or in another emergency management field. Work experience in these areas enables candidates to make difficult decisions in stressful and time-sensitive situations. Such experience also prepares them to coordinate with various agencies to ensure that proper resources are used to respond to emergencies.

For more information, see the profiles on police and detectives, firefighters, police, fire, and ambulance dispatchers, and EMTs and paramedics.

Licenses, Certifications, and Registrations

Some states require directors to obtain certification within a certain timeframe after being hired in the position.

Many agencies and states offer voluntary certification programs to help emergency management directors obtain additional skills. Some employers may prefer or even require a Certified Emergency Manager (CEM), Certified Business Continuity Professional (CBCP), or equivalent designation. Emergency management directors can attain the CEM designation through the International Association of Emergency Managers (IAEM); the CBCP designation is given by the Disaster Recovery Institute International (DRI).

Certification must be renewed after a specified number of years. Both organizations require candidates to complete certain continuing education courses prior to recertification.

Important Qualities

Communication skills. Emergency management directors must be able to clearly convey their emergency preparedness plans, both orally and in writing, to a variety of audiences.

Critical-thinking skills. Emergency management directors must anticipate hazards and problems that may arise from an emergency in order to respond effectively.

Decision-making skills. Emergency management directors must analyze and choose among options, often in stressful situations. They must identify the strengths and weaknesses, costs and benefits, and other variables of each approach.

Interpersonal skills. Emergency management directors must work with other government agencies, law enforcement and fire officials, and the public to coordinate emergency responses.

Leadership skills. To ensure effective responses to emergencies, emergency management directors need to organize and train a variety of people.

Pay

The median annual wage for emergency management directors was $74,590 in May 2019. The median wage is the wage at which half the workers in an occupation earned more than that amount and half earned less. The lowest 10 percent earned less than $40,430, and the highest 10 percent earned more than $141,230.

In May 2019, the median annual wages for emergency management directors in the top industries in which they worked were as follows:

Professional, scientific, and technical services.....	$106,420
Colleges, universities, and professional schools; state, local, and private...	90,730
Hospitals; state, local, and private	84,330
Local government, excluding education and hospitals...	67,060
State government, excluding education and hospitals...	64,710

Most emergency management directors work full time. In addition, most are on call at all times and may need to work overtime to respond to emergencies and to support emergency management operations. Others may work evenings and weekends to meet with various community groups in preparing their emergency response plans.

Job Outlook

Employment of emergency management directors is projected to grow 4 percent from 2019 to 2029, about as fast as the average for all occupations.

The importance of preparing for and minimizing the risks from emergencies will help sustain demand and employment opportunities for emergency management directors. These workers will be needed to help businesses and organizations continue to provide essential services during and after emergencies.

The outlook for public-sector employment of these managers is often related to budget constraints. Some local and state governments rely on federal financial assistance to fund their emergency management agencies. Counties may not hire full-time, stand-alone emergency management directors, choosing instead to shift the job responsibilities to the fire chief, police chief, or other government employees.

Job Prospects

About 700 openings for emergency management directors are projected each year, on average, over the decade.

Emergency management directors is a relatively small occupation, and modest increases in state and local government budgets mean that openings for new jobs are likely to be limited.

However, openings are expected to result from the need to replace workers who transfer to different occupations or exit the labor force, such as to retire.

Applicants with extensive work experience in an emergency management role are expected to have the best job prospects.

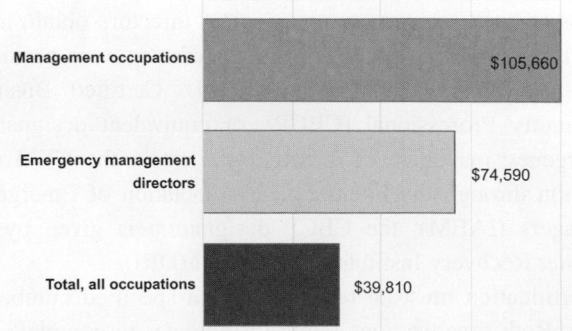

Emergency Management Directors

Median annual wages, May 2019

- Management occupations: $105,660
- Emergency management directors: $74,590
- Total, all occupations: $39,810

Note: All Occupations includes all occupations in the U.S. Economy.
Source: U.S. Bureau of Labor Statistics, Occupational Employment Statistics.

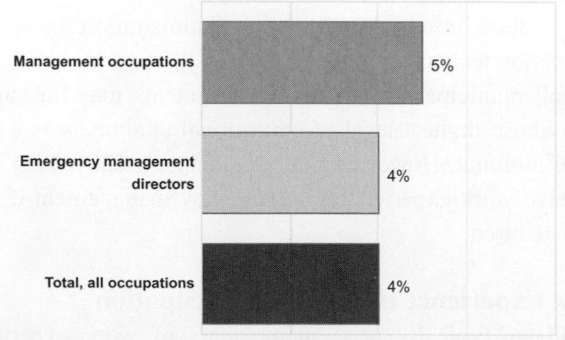

Emergency Management Directors

Percent change in employment, projected 2019-29

- Management occupations: 5%
- Emergency management directors: 4%
- Total, all occupations: 4%

Note: All Occupations includes all occupations in the U.S. Economy.
Source: U.S. Bureau of Labor Statistics, Employment Projections program.

Employment projections data for emergency management directors, 2019-29					
Occupational Title	SOC Code	Employment, 2019	Projected Employment, 2029	Change, 2019-29	
				Percent	Numeric
SOURCE: U.S. Bureau of Labor Statistics, Employment Projections program					
Emergency management directors	11-9161	10,400	10,900	4	500

State & Area Data
Occupational Employment Statistics (OES)
The Occupational Employment Statistics (OES) program produces employment and wage estimates annually for over 800 occupations. These estimates are available for the nation as a whole, for individual states, and for metropolitan and nonmetropolitan areas.

Contacts for More Information
For more information about emergency management directors and their certifications, visit
➤ Disaster Recovery Institute International
➤ National Emergency Management Association
➤ International Association of Emergency Managers

Farmers, Ranchers, and Other Agricultural Managers

Summary

Quick Facts: Farmers, Ranchers, and Other Agricultural Managers

2019 Median Pay	$71,160 per year / $34.21 per hour
Typical Entry-Level Education	High school diploma or equivalent
Work Experience in a Related Occupation	5 years or more
On-the-job Training	None
Number of Jobs, 2019	952,300
Job Outlook, 2019-29	-6% (Decline)
Employment Change, 2019-29	-61,600

What Farmers, Ranchers, and Other Agricultural Managers Do
Farmers, ranchers, and other agricultural managers run establishments that produce crops, livestock, and dairy products.

Farmers, ranchers, and other agricultural managers operate establishments that produce crops, livestock, and dairy products.

Work Environment
Farmers, ranchers, and other agricultural managers typically work outdoors but also may spend time in an office. Their work is often physically demanding.

How to Become a Farmer, Rancher, or Other Agricultural Manager
Farmers, ranchers, and other agricultural managers typically need at least a high school diploma and work experience in a related occupation.

Pay
The median annual wage for farmers, ranchers, and other agricultural managers was $71,160 in May 2019.

Job Outlook
Employment of farmers, ranchers, and other agricultural managers is projected to decline 6 percent from 2019 to 2029. Over the past several decades, increased efficiencies in crop production have led to consolidation and fewer, but larger, farms.

State & Area Data
Explore resources for employment and wages by state and area for farmers, ranchers, and other agricultural managers.

What Farmers, Ranchers, and Other Agricultural Managers Do
Farmers, ranchers, and other agricultural managers run establishments that produce crops, livestock, and dairy products.

Duties
Farmers, ranchers, and other agricultural managers typically do the following:

• Supervise all steps of crop production or ranging, including planting, fertilizing, harvesting, and herding
• Make decisions about crops or livestock by evaluating factors such as market conditions, disease, soil conditions, and the availability of federal programs

Some farmers work primarily with crops and vegetables, whereas other farmers and ranchers handle livestock.

- Choose and buy supplies, such as seed, fertilizer, and farm machinery
- Maintain farming equipment
- Maintain farm facilities, such as water pipes, fences, and animal shelters
- Serve as the sales agent for crops, livestock, and dairy products
- Record financial, tax, production, and employee information

Farmers, ranchers, and other agricultural managers monitor the prices for their products. They use different strategies to protect themselves financially from unpredictable changes in the markets. For example, some farmers carefully plan the combination of crops they grow, so that if the price of one crop drops, they have enough income from another crop to make up for the loss. Farmers and ranchers also track disease and weather conditions, either or both of which may negatively impact crop yields or animal health. By planning ahead, farmers and ranchers may be able to store their crops or keep their livestock in order to take advantage of higher prices later in the year.

Some farmers choose to sell a portion of their goods directly to consumers through farmer's markets or cooperatives to reduce their financial risk and to gain a larger share of the final price of their goods.

Farmers, ranchers, and other agricultural managers negotiate with banks and other credit lenders to get financing, because they must buy seed, livestock, and equipment before they have products to sell.

Farmers and ranchers run farms that are primarily family owned. Those who do not own the land themselves may lease it from a landowner to operate as a working farm.

The size of the farm or range determines which tasks farmers and ranchers handle. Those who run small farms or ranges may do all tasks, including harvesting and inspecting the land, growing crops, and raising animals. In addition, they keep records, service machinery, and maintain buildings.

By contrast, farmers and ranchers who run large farms generally hire others—including agricultural workers—to help with physical work. Some of the workers on large farms are in nonfarm occupations, such as truck drivers, sales representatives, bookkeepers, and information technology specialists.

Farmers and ranchers follow improvements in animal breeding methods and seed science, choosing products that may increase output. Livestock and dairy farmers monitor and attend to the health of their herds, which may include assisting in births.

Agricultural managers take care of the day-to-day operations of one or more farms, ranches, nurseries, timber tracts, greenhouses, and other agricultural establishments for corporations, farmers, and owners who do not live and work on their farm or ranch.

Agricultural managers usually do not participate directly in production activities. Instead, they hire and supervise farm and livestock workers to do most of the daily production tasks.

Managers may determine budgets and decide how to store, transport, and sell crops. They also may oversee the maintenance of equipment and property.

The following are examples of types of farmers, ranchers, and other agricultural managers:

Crop farmers and managers are responsible for all stages of plant growth, including planting, fertilizing, watering, and harvesting crops. These farmers may grow grain, fruits, vegetables, and other crops. After a harvest, they make sure that the crops are properly packaged and stored.

Livestock, dairy, and poultry farmers, ranchers, and managers feed and care for animals, such as cows or chickens, in order to harvest meat, milk, or eggs. They keep livestock and poultry in barns, pens, and other farm buildings. These workers also may oversee animal breeding in order to maintain appropriate herd or flock size.

Nursery and greenhouse managers oversee the production of trees, shrubs, flowers, and plants (including turf) used for landscaping. In addition to applying pesticides and fertilizers to help plants grow, they often are responsible for keeping track of marketing activity and inventory.

Aquaculture farmers and managers raise fish and shellfish in ponds, floating net pens, raceways, and recirculating systems. They stock, feed, and maintain aquatic life used for food and recreational fishing.

Work Environment

Farmers, ranchers, and other agricultural managers held about 952,300 jobs in 2019. The largest employers of farmers, ranchers, and other agricultural managers were as follows:

Self-employed workers..67%

Crop production..19

Animal production and aquaculture............................13

Farmers, ranchers, and other agricultural managers typically work outdoors, but they may spend some time in offices.

Farmers, ranchers, and other agricultural managers typically work outdoors but also may spend time in an office. Their work is often physically demanding.

Some farmers work primarily with crops. Other farmers and ranchers handle livestock.

Injuries and Illnesses

The work environment for farmers, ranchers, and other agricultural managers can be hazardous. Tractors, tools, and other farm machinery and equipment can cause serious injury, and exposure to substances in pesticides and fertilizers may be harmful. These workers must operate equipment and handle chemicals properly to avoid accidents and safeguard themselves and the environment.

Work Schedules

Most farmers, ranchers, and other agricultural managers work full time, and many work more than 40 hours per week. Farm work is often seasonal, and the number of hours worked may change according to the season. Farmers and farm managers on crop farms usually work from sunrise to sunset during the planting and harvesting seasons. During the rest of the year, they plan the next season's crops, market their output, and repair and maintain machinery. Managers of greenhouses, nurseries,

or farms that operate in mild or temperate climates may work year round.

On livestock-producing farms and ranches, work goes on throughout the year. Animals must be fed and cared for every day.

On large farms, farmers and farm managers meet with farm supervisors. Managers who oversee several farms may divide their time between traveling to meet farmers and landowners and working in offices to plan farm operations.

How to Become a Farmer, Rancher, or Other Agricultural Manager

Farmers, ranchers, and other agricultural managers typically need at least a high school diploma and work experience in a related occupation.

Education

Farmers, ranchers, and other agricultural managers typically need at least a high school diploma to enter the occupation. As farm and land management has grown more complex, farmers, ranchers, and other agricultural managers have increasingly needed postsecondary education, such as an associate's degree or a bachelor's degree, in agriculture or a related field.

Most state university systems have at least one land-grant college or university with a school of agriculture. Programs of study include agricultural economics and business, animal science, and plant science.

There are a number of government programs that help farmers connect with farming services. The United States Department of Agriculture (USDA) has service centers across the country that assist new farmers in accessing USDA programs. These service centers connect farmers with programs such as those that provide financing for land and capital, help with creating a business plan, and input on conservation practices.

Work Experience in a Related Occupation

Prospective farmers, ranchers, and agricultural managers typically work as agricultural workers for several years to gain

Farmers and ranchers that care for animals keep livestock in pens, barns, and other farm buildings.

the knowledge and experience needed to run their own farm. Some gain experience while growing up on a family farm. The amount of experience needed varies with the complexity of the work and the size of the farm. Those with postsecondary education in agriculture may not need additional work experience.

Licenses, Certifications, and Registrations

To show competency in farm management, agricultural managers may choose to complete certification programs. The American Society of Farm Managers and Rural Appraisers (ASFMRA) offers the Accredited Farm Manager (AFM) credential. AFM requirements include ASFMRA coursework, a bachelor's degree, experience in farmland management, and passing an exam. A complete list of requirements is available from ASFMRA.

Important Qualities

Analytical skills. Farmers, ranchers, and other agricultural managers monitor and assess the quality of their land or livestock.

Critical-thinking skills. Farmers, ranchers, and other agricultural managers determine how to improve their harvest and livestock while reacting to conditions that may affect their short- or long-term plans.

Initiative. Many farmers, ranchers, and other agricultural managers are self-employed. They must be self-motivated in order to maximize crop or livestock production.

Interpersonal skills. Farmers, ranchers, and other agricultural managers supervise laborers and other workers, so they must be able to communicate and interact with a variety of people.

Mechanical skills. Farmers, ranchers, and other agricultural managers operate complex machinery and occasionally perform routine maintenance.

Physical stamina. Farmers, ranchers, and other agricultural managers—particularly those who work on small farms—must be able to do physically strenuous, repetitive tasks, such as bending, stooping, and lifting.

Pay

The median annual wage for farmers, ranchers, and other agricultural managers was $71,160 in May 2019. The median wage is the wage at which half the workers in an occupation earned more than that amount and half earned less. The lowest 10 percent earned less than $37,530, and the highest 10 percent earned more than $132,760.

Incomes of farmers and ranchers vary from year to year because prices of farm products fluctuate with weather conditions and other factors. In addition to earning income from their farm business, farmers may receive government subsidies or other payments that reduce some of the risks of farming.

Most farmers, ranchers, and other agricultural managers work full time, and many work more than 40 hours per week. Farm work is often seasonal, and the number of hours worked may change according to the season. Farmers and farm managers on crop farms usually work from sunrise to sunset during the planting and harvesting seasons. During the rest of the year, they plan the next season's crops, market their output, and repair and maintain machinery. Managers of greenhouses, nurseries, or farms that operate in mild or temperate climates may work year round.

On livestock-producing farms and ranches, work goes on throughout the year. Animals must be fed and cared for daily.

Job Outlook

Employment of farmers, ranchers, and other agricultural managers is projected to decline 6 percent from 2019 to 2029.

Over the past several decades, increased efficiencies in crop production have led to consolidation and fewer, but larger, farms. This means that fewer farmers are needed to produce the same agricultural output. In addition, as farms become larger they are able to invest more in productivity-enhancing technologies, reinforcing this effect.

Despite steady demand for agricultural products, many small farms operate with slim profit margins and are vulnerable to

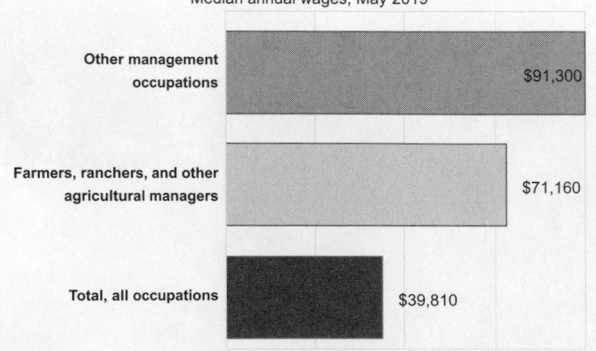

Farmers, Ranchers, and Other Agricultural Managers

Median annual wages, May 2019

Other management occupations	$91,300
Farmers, ranchers, and other agricultural managers	$71,160
Total, all occupations	$39,810

Note: All Occupations includes all occupations in the U.S. Economy.
Source: U.S. Bureau of Labor Statistics, Occupational Employment Statistics.

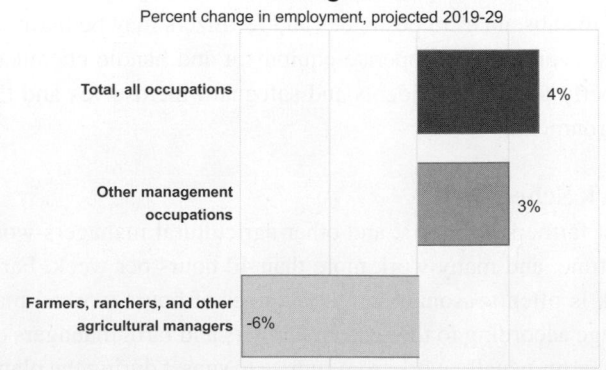

Farmers, Ranchers, and Other Agricultural Managers

Percent change in employment, projected 2019-29

Total, all occupations	4%
Other management occupations	3%
Farmers, ranchers, and other agricultural managers	-6%

Note: All Occupations includes all occupations in the U.S. Economy.
Source: U.S. Bureau of Labor Statistics, Employment Projections program.

poor market conditions. As in the past, operators of smaller farms will likely continue to exit the business over the next decade.

Job Prospects

Despite projected employment declines, about 80,900 openings for farmers, ranchers, and other agricultural managers are projected each year, on average, over the decade.

These openings are expected to result from the need to replace workers who transfer to different occupations or exit the labor force, such as to retire.

Employment projections data for farmers, ranchers, and other agricultural managers, 2019-29					
Occupational Title	SOC Code	Employment, 2019	Projected Employment, 2029	Change, 2019-29 Percent	Numeric
SOURCE: U.S. Bureau of Labor Statistics, Employment Projections program					
Farmers, ranchers, and other agricultural managers	11-9013	952,300	890,600	-6	-61,600

State & Area Data
Occupational Employment Statistics (OES)

The Occupational Employment Statistics (OES) program produces employment and wage estimates annually for over 800 occupations. These estimates are available for the nation as a whole, for individual states, and for metropolitan and nonmetropolitan areas.

Contacts for More Information

For more information about agriculture policy and farm advocacy, visit
➤ Center for Rural Affairs

For more information about federal resources for agriculture, visit the following websites at the U.S. Department of Agriculture:
➤ New Farmers
➤ Farm Service Agency

For more information on farm manager certification, visit
➤ American Society of Farm Managers and Rural Appraisers

Financial Managers

Summary

Quick Facts: Financial Managers

2019 Median Pay	$129,890 per year $62.45 per hour
Typical Entry-Level Education	Bachelor's degree
Work Experience in a Related Occupation	5 years or more
On-the-job Training	None
Number of Jobs, 2019	697,900
Job Outlook, 2019-29	15% (Much faster than average)
Employment Change, 2019-29	108,100

What Financial Managers Do

Financial managers create financial reports, direct investment activities, and develop plans for the long-term financial goals of their organization.

Work Environment

Financial managers work in many industries, including banks, investment firms, and insurance companies. Most financial managers work full time, and some work more than 40 hours per week.

How to Become a Financial Manager

Financial managers typically need a bachelor's degree and 5 years or more of experience in another business or financial occupation, such as accountant, securities sales agent, or financial analyst.

Pay

The median annual wage for financial managers was $129,890 in May 2019.

Job Outlook

Employment of financial managers is projected to grow 15 percent from 2019 to 2029, much faster than the average for all occupations. Several functions of financial managers, including cash management and risk management, are expected to be in high demand over the decade.

State & Area Data

Explore resources for employment and wages by state and area for financial managers.

Financial managers are responsible for the financial health of an organization.

What Financial Managers Do

Financial managers are responsible for the financial health of an organization. They create financial reports, direct investment activities, and develop plans for the long-term financial goals of their organization.

Duties

Financial managers typically do the following:

- Prepare financial statements, business activity reports, and forecasts
- Monitor financial details to ensure that legal requirements are met
- Supervise employees who do financial reporting and budgeting
- Review financial reports and seek ways to reduce costs
- Analyze market trends to maximize profits and find expansion opportunities
- Help management make financial decisions

Financial managers spend much of their time analyzing data and advising senior managers on ways to maximize profits. They often work on teams, acting as advisors to top executives.

Financial managers must have knowledge of the topics, tax laws, and regulations that are specific to their organization or industry. For example, government financial managers must be experts on appropriations and budgeting processes; healthcare financial managers must understand billing, reimbursement, and other business matters related to healthcare.

The following are examples of types of financial managers:

Controllers direct the preparation of financial reports that summarize and forecast an organization's financial position. These reports may include income statements, balance sheets, and analyses of future earnings or expenses. Controllers also are in charge of preparing reports required by governmental agencies that regulate businesses. Often, controllers

oversee the accounting, audit, and budget departments of their organization.

Treasurers and *finance officers* direct an organization's budgets to meet its financial goals. They oversee investments and other plans to raise capital, such as issuing stocks or bonds, to support their organization's growth. They also develop financial plans for mergers (two companies joining together) and acquisitions (one company buying another).

Credit managers oversee an organization's credit business. They set credit-rating standards, determine credit limits, and monitor the collections of past-due accounts.

Cash managers monitor and control the flow of money into and out of an organization to meet business and investment needs. For example, they must project whether the organization will have a shortage or surplus of cash.

Risk managers use strategies to limit or offset an organization's chance of financial loss or exposure to financial uncertainty. Among the risks they try to limit are those arising from currency or commodity price changes.

Insurance managers decide how to limit an organization's losses by protecting against risks, such as for disability payments to an employee who gets hurt on the job or for costs imposed by a lawsuit against the organization.

Work Environment

Financial managers held about 697,900 jobs in 2019. The largest employers of financial managers were as follows:

Finance and insurance	30%
Professional, scientific, and technical services	14
Management of companies and enterprises	11
Government	7
Manufacturing	6

Financial managers perform data analysis and advise senior managers on profit-maximizing ideas.

Financial managers work closely with top managers and with departments that develop the data that financial managers need.

Financial managers work closely with top executives and with departments that develop data needed for analysis.

Work Schedules
Most financial managers work full time, and some work more than 40 hours per week.

How to Become a Financial Manager
Financial managers typically need a bachelor's degree and 5 years or more of experience in another business or financial occupation, such as an accountant, securities sales agent, or financial analyst.

Education
Financial managers typically need at least a bachelor's degree in finance, accounting, economics, or business administration. However, many employers prefer to hire candidates who have a master's degree in those same fields. These disciplines help students learn analytical skills and methods.

Licenses, Certifications, and Registrations
Although it is not required, professional certification indicates competence for financial managers who have it. The CFA Institute confers the Chartered Financial Analyst (CFA) certification to investment professionals who have at least a bachelor's degree or 4 years of work experience, or a combination of experience and education, and who pass three exams. The Association for Financial Professionals confers the Certified Treasury Professional (CTP) credential to those who have at least 2 years of relevant experience or 1 year of experience and a graduate degree in business, finance, or a related field. This association also confers the Certified Corporate Financial Planning Analysis Professional (FP&A) credential to those who have a bachelor's degree or who are currently enrolled

Financial managers usually have experience in another business or financial occupation such as a loan officer, accountant, auditor, securities sales agent, or financial analyst.

in an undergraduate program with a finance-related major and will graduate within 2 years. Both credentials require passing an exam.

Certified public accountants (CPAs) are licensed by their state's board of accountancy and must pass an exam administered by the American Institute of Certified Public Accountants (AICPA).

Work Experience in a Related Occupation
Financial managers usually have experience in another business or financial occupation. For example, they may have worked as a loan officer, accountant, securities sales agent, or financial analyst.

In some cases, companies provide management training to help prepare motivated, skilled financial workers to become managers.

Advancement
Experienced financial managers may advance to become chief financial officers (CFOs). These executives are responsible for the accuracy of an organization's financial reporting.

Important Qualities
Analytical skills. To assist executives in making decisions, financial managers need to evaluate data and information that affects their organization.

Communication skills. Financial managers must be able to explain and justify complex financial transactions.

Detail oriented. In preparing and analyzing reports, such as balance sheets and income statements, financial managers must be precise and attentive to their work in order to avoid errors.

Math skills. Financial managers need strong skills in certain branches of mathematics, including algebra. Ability to understand international finance and complex financial documents also is important.

Organizational skills. Because financial managers deal with a range of information and documents, they must have structures in place to be effective in their work.

Pay
The median annual wage for financial managers was $129,890 in May 2019. The median wage is the wage at which half the workers in an occupation earned more than that amount and half earned less. The lowest 10 percent earned less than $68,370, and the highest 10 percent earned more than $208,000.

In May 2019, the median annual wages for financial managers in the top industries in which they worked were as follows:

Professional, scientific, and technical services	$152,810
Management of companies and enterprises	145,280
Manufacturing	130,900
Finance and insurance	125,600
Government	114,250

Financial Managers
Median annual wages, May 2019

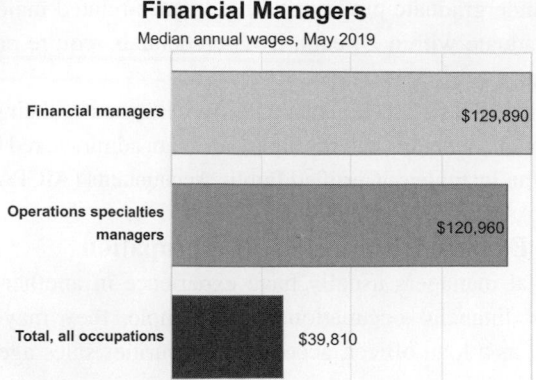

Note: All Occupations includes all occupations in the U.S. Economy.
Source: U.S. Bureau of Labor Statistics, Occupational Employment Statistics.

Most financial managers work full time, and some work more than 40 hours per week.

Job Outlook

Employment of financial managers is projected to grow 15 percent from 2019 to 2029, much faster than the average for all occupations. However, growth will vary by industry.

Services provided by financial managers, such as planning, directing, and coordinating investments, are likely to stay in demand as the economy grows. In addition, several specialties within financial management, particularly cash management and risk management, are expected to be in high demand over the decade.

In recent years, companies have accumulated more cash on their balance sheets, particularly among those with operations in foreign countries. As globalization continues, this trend is likely to persist. This should lead to demand for financial managers, as companies will need expertise in managing cash.

There has been an increased emphasis on risk management within the financial industry, and this trend is expected to continue. Banking institutions are expected to emphasize stability and managing risk over profits. This is expected to lead to employment growth for risk managers.

The credit intermediation and related activities industry (which includes commercial and savings banks) employs a large percentage of financial managers. As bank customers continue to conduct transactions online, the number of bank branches is expected to decline, which should limit employment growth in this sector. However, employment declines are expected to mainly affect clerical occupations, such as tellers, rather than financial managers. From 2019 to 2029, employment of financial managers is projected to grow 17 percent in this industry.

Job Prospects

About 59,600 openings for financial managers are projected each year, on average, over the decade.

Financial Managers
Percent change in employment, projected 2019-29

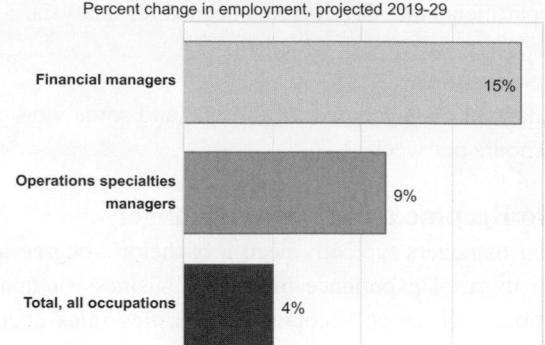

Note: All Occupations includes all occupations in the U.S. Economy.
Source: U.S. Bureau of Labor Statistics, Employment Projections program.

Many of those openings are expected to result from the need to replace workers who transfer to different occupations or exit the labor force, such as to retire.

Candidates with expertise in accounting and finance—particularly those with a master's degree or certification—should have the best job prospects.

Employment projections data for financial managers, 2019-29					
Occupational Title	SOC Code	Employment, 2019	Projected Employment, 2029	Change, 2019-29	
				Percent	Numeric
SOURCE: U.S. Bureau of Labor Statistics, Employment Projections program					
Financial managers	11-3031	697,900	806,000	15	108,100

State & Area Data
Occupational Employment Statistics (OES)

The Occupational Employment Statistics (OES) program produces employment and wage estimates annually for over 800 occupations. These estimates are available for the nation as a whole, for individual states, and for metropolitan and nonmetropolitan areas.

Contacts for More Information

For more information about financial managers, including certification, visit
➤ Global Academy of Finance and Management

For information about the Certified Treasury Professional and the Financial Planning and Analysis Professional designations, visit
➤ Association for Financial Professionals

For information about the Chartered Financial Analyst program, visit
➤ CFA Institute

For more information about the certified public accountant designation, visit
➤ American Institute of Certified Public Accountants (AICPA)

Food Service Managers

Summary

Quick Facts: Food Service Managers

2019 Median Pay	$55,320 per year $26.60 per hour
Typical Entry-Level Education	High school diploma or equivalent
Work Experience in a Related Occupation	Less than 5 years
On-the-job Training	None
Number of Jobs, 2019	352,600
Job Outlook, 2019-29	1% (Slower than average)
Employment Change, 2019-29	2,200

What Food Service Managers Do

Food service managers are responsible for the daily operation of restaurants or other establishments that prepare and serve food and beverages.

Work Environment

Food service managers work in restaurants, hotels, school cafeterias, and other establishments where food is prepared and served. They often work evenings, weekends, and holidays. The work can be hectic, and dealing with dissatisfied customers can be stressful.

How to Become a Food Service Manager

Most applicants qualify with a high school diploma and several years of work experience in the food service industry. However, some may receive additional training at a community college, technical or vocational school, culinary school, or 4-year college.

Pay

The median annual wage for food service managers was $55,320 in May 2019.

Job Outlook

Employment of food service managers is projected to grow 1 percent from 2019 to 2029, slower than the average for all occupations. Those with several years of work experience in food service and a degree in hospitality, restaurant, or food service management will have the best job opportunities.

State & Area Data

Explore resources for employment and wages by state and area for food service managers.

What Food Service Managers Do

Food service managers are responsible for the daily operation of restaurants or other establishments that prepare and serve food and beverages. They direct staff to ensure that customers are satisfied with their dining experience, and they manage the business to ensure that it is profitable.

Duties

Food service managers typically do the following:

- Hire, train, oversee, and sometimes fire employees
- Order food and beverages, equipment, and supplies
- Oversee food preparation, portion sizes, and the overall presentation of food
- Inspect supplies, equipment, and work areas
- Ensure that employees comply with health and food safety standards
- Address complaints regarding food quality or service
- Schedule staff hours and assign duties

Food service managers are responsible for the daily operation of a restaurant.

Food service managers ensure that customers are satisfied with their dining experience.

- Manage budgets and payroll records
- Establish standards for personnel performance and customer service

Managers coordinate activities of the kitchen and dining room staff to ensure that customers are served properly and in a timely manner. They oversee orders in the kitchen, and, if needed, they work with the chef to remedy any delays in service.

Food service managers are responsible for all functions of the business related to employees. For example, most managers interview, hire, train, oversee, appraise, discipline, and sometimes fire employees. Managers also schedule work hours, making sure that enough workers are present to cover each shift. During busy periods, they may expedite service by helping to serve customers, processing payments, or cleaning tables.

Managers also arrange for cleaning and maintenance services for the equipment and facility in order to comply with health and sanitary regulations. For example, they may arrange for trash removal, pest control, and heavy cleaning when the dining room and kitchen are not in use.

Most managers prepare the payroll and manage employee records. They also may review or complete paperwork related to licensing, taxes and wages, and unemployment compensation. Although they sometimes assign these tasks to an assistant manager or a bookkeeper, most managers are responsible for the accuracy of business records.

Some managers add up the cash and charge slips and secure them in a safe place. They also may check that ovens, grills, and other equipment are properly cleaned and secured, and that the establishment is locked at the close of business.

Work Environment

Food service managers held about 352,600 jobs in 2019. The largest employers of food service managers were as follows:

Restaurants and other eating places	49%
Self-employed workers	32
Special food services	4
Accommodation	2

Full-service restaurants (those with table service) may have a management team that includes a general manager, one or more assistant managers, and an executive chef.

Many food service managers work long shifts, and the job is often hectic. Dealing with dissatisfied customers can sometimes be stressful.

Injuries and illnesses

Kitchens are usually crowded and filled with dangerous objects and areas, such as hot ovens and slippery floors. As a result, injuries are a risk for food service managers, who spend some of their time helping in the kitchen. Common hazards include slips, falls, and cuts that are seldom serious. To

Some food service managers oversee multiple locations of a restaurant chain or franchise.

reduce these risks, managers often wear nonslip shoes while in the kitchen.

Work Schedules

Most food service managers work full time. Managers at fine-dining and fast-food restaurants often work long shifts, and some work more than 40 hours per week. Managers of food service facilities or cafeterias in schools, factories, or office buildings usually work traditional business hours. Managers may be called in on short notice, including evenings, weekends, and holidays. Some managers may also manage multiple locations.

How to Become a Food Service Manager

Most applicants qualify with a high school diploma and several years of work experience in the food service industry as a cook, waiter or waitress, or counter attendant. Some applicants have received additional training at a community college, technical or vocational school, culinary school, or 4-year college.

Education

Although a bachelor's degree is not required, some postsecondary education is increasingly preferred for many manager positions, especially at upscale restaurants and hotels. Some food service companies, hotels, and restaurant chains recruit management trainees from college hospitality or food service

Some food service managers start working in industry-related jobs, such as cooks.

management programs. These programs may require the participants to work in internships and to have food-industry–related experiences in order to graduate.

Many colleges and universities offer bachelor's degree programs in restaurant and hospitality management or institutional food service management. In addition, numerous community colleges, technical institutes, and other institutions offer associate's degree programs in the field. Some culinary schools offer programs in restaurant management with courses designed for those who want to start and run their own restaurant.

Most programs provide instruction in nutrition, sanitation, and food preparation, as well as courses in accounting, business law, and management. Some programs combine classroom and practical study with internships.

Work Experience in a Related Occupation

Most food service managers start working in industry-related jobs, such as cooks, waiters and waitresses, or hosts and hostesses. They often spend years working under the direction of an experienced worker, learning the necessary skills before they are promoted to manager positions.

Training

Managers who work for restaurant chains and food service management companies may be required to complete programs that combine classroom instruction and on-the-job training. Topics may include food preparation, sanitation, security, company policies, personnel management, and recordkeeping.

Licenses, Certifications, and Registrations

Although certification is not required, managers may obtain the Food Protection Manager Certification (FPMC) by passing a food safety exam. The American National Standards Institute accredits institutions that offer the FPMC.

In addition, the National Restaurant Association Educational Foundation awards the Foodservice Management Professional (FMP) designation, a voluntary certification to managers who typically meet the following criteria:

- Have supervisory experience in food service
- Have specialized training in food safety
- Pass a multiple-choice exam

The certification attests to professional competence, particularly for managers who learned their skills on the job.

Important Qualities

Business skills. Food service managers, especially those who run their own restaurant, must understand all aspects of the restaurant business. They should know how to budget for supplies, set prices, and manage workers to ensure that the restaurant is profitable.

Communication skills. Food service managers must give clear orders to staff and be able to communicate effectively with employees and customers.

Customer-service skills. Food service managers must be courteous and attentive when dealing with patrons. Satisfying customers' dining needs is critical to business success and ensures customer loyalty.

Detail oriented. Managers deal with many different types of activities. They ensure that there is enough food to serve to customers, they maintain financial records, and they ensure that the food meets health and safety standards.

Leadership skills. Managers must establish good working relationships to maintain a productive work environment. Carrying out this task may involve motivating workers and leading by example.

Organizational skills. Food service managers keep track of many different schedules, budgets, and staff. Their job becomes more complex as the size of the restaurant or food service facility increases.

Physical stamina. Managers, especially those who run their own restaurant, often work long shifts and sometimes spend entire evenings on their feet helping to serve customers.

Problem-solving skills. Managers need to be able to resolve personnel issues and customer-related problems.

Pay

The median annual wage for food service managers was $55,320 in May 2019. The median wage is the wage at which half the workers in an occupation earned more than that amount and half earned less. The lowest 10 percent earned less than $33,210, and the highest 10 percent earned more than $93,040.

In May 2019, the median annual wages for food service managers in the top industries in which they worked were as follows:

Accommodation	$64,620
Special food services	62,240
Restaurants and other eating places	52,770

Food Service Managers
Median annual wages, May 2019

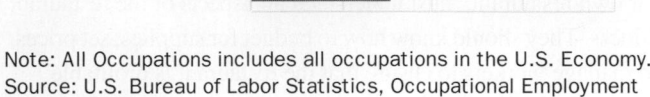

Management occupations — $105,660

Food service managers — $55,320

Total, all occupations — $39,810

Note: All Occupations includes all occupations in the U.S. Economy.
Source: U.S. Bureau of Labor Statistics, Occupational Employment
Statistics.

Food Service Managers
Percent change in employment, projected 2019-29

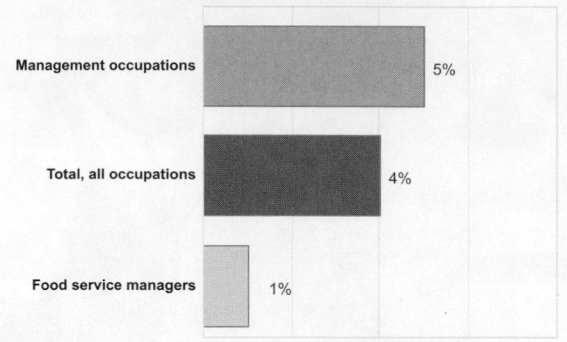

Management occupations — 5%

Total, all occupations — 4%

Food service managers — 1%

Note: All Occupations includes all occupations in the U.S. Economy.
Source: U.S. Bureau of Labor Statistics, Employment Projections
program.

Most food service managers work full time. Managers at fine-dining and fast-food restaurants often work long shifts, and some work more than 40 hours per week. Managers of food service facilities or cafeterias in schools, factories, or office buildings usually work traditional business hours. Managers may be called in on short notice, including evenings, weekends, and holidays. Some managers may also manage multiple locations.

Job Outlook

Employment of food service managers is projected to grow 1 percent from 2019 to 2029, slower than the average for all occupations.

Food service managers will be needed to oversee food preparation and service as people continue to dine out, purchase takeout meals, and have food delivered to their homes or workplaces. However, more dining establishments are expected to rely on chefs and head cooks instead of hiring additional food service managers, which should limit employment growth in this occupation.

Job Prospects

Although job opportunities should be good overall, they should be best for food service managers with several years of work experience in a restaurant or food service establishment. Most job openings will result from the need to replace managers who leave the occupation.

Jobseekers with a combination of work experience in food service and a bachelor's degree in hospitality, restaurant, or food service management should have an edge when competing for jobs at upscale hotels and restaurants.

Employment projections data for food service managers, 2019-29					
Occupational Title	SOC Code	Employment, 2019	Projected Employment, 2029	Change, 2019-29	
				Percent	Numeric
SOURCE: U.S. Bureau of Labor Statistics, Employment Projections program					
Food service managers	11-9051	352,600	354,800	1	2,200

State & Area Data
Occupational Employment Statistics (OES)

The Occupational Employment Statistics (OES) program produces employment and wage estimates annually for over 800 occupations. These estimates are available for the nation as a whole, for individual states, and for metropolitan and nonmetropolitan areas.

Contacts for More Information

For more information about the Food Protection Manager Certification, visit
➤ American National Standards Institute

For more information about food service managers, including a directory of college programs in food service, visit
➤ National Restaurant Association

For more information about food service managers and certification as a Foodservice Management Professional, visit
➤ National Restaurant Association Educational Foundation

For general information about food service managers, visit
➤ Society for Hospitality and Foodservice Management

Human Resources Managers

Summary

Quick Facts: Human Resources Managers

2019 Median Pay	$116,720 per year $56.11 per hour
Typical Entry-Level Education	Bachelor's degree
Work Experience in a Related Occupation	5 years or more
On-the-job Training	None
Number of Jobs, 2019	165,200
Job Outlook, 2019-29	6% (Faster than average)
Employment Change, 2019-29	10,400

What Human Resources Managers Do

Human resources managers plan, coordinate, and direct the administrative functions of an organization.

Work Environment

Human resources managers are employed in nearly every industry. They work in offices, and most work full time during regular business hours. Some travel to attend professional meetings or to recruit employees.

How to Become a Human Resources Manager

Candidates typically need a combination of education and several years of related work experience to become a human resources manager. Although positions typically require a bachelor's degree, some require a master's degree.

Pay

The median annual wage for human resources managers was $116,720 in May 2019.

Job Outlook

Employment of human resources managers is projected to grow 6 percent from 2019 to 2029, faster than the average for all occupations. As new companies form and organizations expand their operations, they will need human resources managers to administer and monitor their programs and to ensure that firms adhere to changing employment laws.

State & Area Data

Explore resources for employment and wages by state and area for human resources managers.

What Human Resources Managers Do

Human resources managers plan, coordinate, and direct the administrative functions of an organization. They oversee the recruiting, interviewing, and hiring of new staff; consult with top executives on strategic planning; and serve as a link between an organization's management and its employees.

Duties

Human resources managers typically do the following:

- Plan and coordinate an organization's workforce to best use employees' talents
- Link an organization's management with its employees
- Plan and oversee employee benefit programs
- Serve as a consultant to advise other managers on human resources issues, such as equal employment opportunity and sexual harassment
- Coordinate and supervise the work of specialists and support staff
- Oversee an organization's recruitment, interview, selection, and hiring processes
- Handle staffing issues, such as mediating disputes and directing disciplinary procedures

Human resources managers oversee an organization's recruitment, interview, selection, and hiring processes.

Human resources managers often coordinate the work of a team of specialists.

Organizations want to attract, motivate, and keep qualified employees and match them to jobs for which they are well-suited. Human resources managers accomplish this aim by directing the administrative functions of human resources departments. Their work involves overseeing employee relations, securing regulatory compliance, and administering employee-related services such as payroll, training, and benefits. They supervise the department's specialists and support staff and make sure that tasks are completed accurately and on time.

Human resources managers also consult with top executives regarding strategic planning and talent management. They identify ways to maximize the value of the organization's employees and ensure that they are used efficiently. For example, they might assess worker productivity and recommend changes to help the organization meet budgetary goals.

Some human resources managers oversee all aspects of an organization's human resources department, including the compensation and benefits program and the training and development program. In many larger organizations, these programs are directed by specialized managers, such as compensation and benefits managers and training and development managers.

The following are examples of types of human resources managers:

Labor relations directors, also called **employee relations managers**, oversee employment policies in union and nonunion settings. They negotiate, draft, and administer labor contracts that cover issues such as wages, benefits, and union and management practices. They also handle labor complaints between employees and management, and they coordinate grievance procedures.

Payroll managers supervise an organization's payroll department. They ensure that all aspects of payroll are processed correctly and on time. They administer payroll procedures, prepare reports for the accounting department, and resolve payroll problems.

Recruiting managers, sometimes called **staffing managers**, oversee the recruiting and hiring responsibilities of the human resources department. They often supervise a team of recruiters, and some take on recruiting duties for filling high-level positions. They must develop a recruiting strategy that helps them meet the staffing needs of their organization and compete effectively to attract the best employees.

Work Environment

Human resources managers held about 165,200 jobs in 2019. The largest employers of human resources managers were as follows:

Professional, scientific, and technical services	14%
Management of companies and enterprises	14
Manufacturing	11
Government	9
Healthcare and social assistance	8

Human resources managers work in offices. Some managers, especially those working for organizations that have offices nationwide, travel to visit other branches, attend professional meetings, or recruit employees.

Work Schedules

Most human resources managers work full time during regular business hours. Some human resources managers work more than 40 hours per week.

How to Become a Human Resources Manager

Candidates typically need a combination of education and several years of related work experience to become a human resources manager. Although most positions require a bachelor's degree, some require a master's degree.

Education

Human resources managers usually need a bachelor's degree. Candidates may earn a bachelor's degree in human resources or in another field, such as business management, education, or information technology. Courses in subjects such as conflict management or psychology may be helpful.

Human resources managers typically need a combination of a bachelor's degree and work experience.

Some jobs may require a master's degree in human resources, labor relations, or business administration (MBA).

Work Experience in a Related Occupation

To demonstrate abilities in organizing, directing, and leading others, human resources managers must have related work experience. Some managers start out as human resources specialists or labor relations specialists.

Management positions typically require an understanding of human resources programs, such as compensation and benefits plans; human resources software; and federal, state, and local employment laws.

Licenses, Certifications, and Registrations

Although certification is voluntary, it shows professional expertise and credibility, and it may enhance job opportunities. Employers may prefer to hire candidates with certification, and some positions may require it. The Society for Human Resource Management (SHRM), HR Certification Institute (HRCI), WorldatWork, and International Foundation of Employee Benefit Plans are among many professional associations that offer certification programs.

Important Qualities

Communication skills. Human resources managers need strong speaking, writing, and listening skills to give presentations and direct their staff.

Decision-making skills. Human resources managers must be able to balance the strengths and weaknesses of different options and decide the best course of action.

Interpersonal skills. Human resources managers regularly interact with people, such as to collaborate on teams, and must develop working relationships with their colleagues.

Leadership skills. Human resources managers must coordinate work activities and ensure that staff complete the duties and responsibilities of their department.

Organizational skills. Human resources managers must be able to prioritize tasks and manage several projects at once.

Pay

The median annual wage for human resources managers was $116,720 in May 2019. The median wage is the wage at which half the workers in an occupation earned more than that amount and half earned less. The lowest 10 percent earned less than $68,300, and the highest 10 percent earned more than $205,720.

In May 2019, the median annual wages for human resources managers in the top industries in which they worked were as follows:

Professional, scientific, and technical services.....	$131,340
Management of companies and enterprises..........	129,510
Manufacturing..	115,000

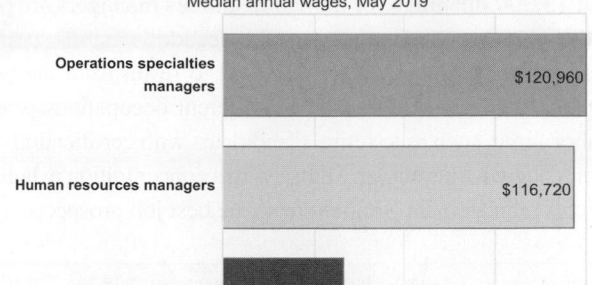

Human Resources Managers
Median annual wages, May 2019

- Operations specialties managers — $120,960
- Human resources managers — $116,720
- Total, all occupations — $39,810

Note: All Occupations includes all occupations in the U.S. Economy.
Source: U.S. Bureau of Labor Statistics, Occupational Employment Statistics.

Government..	102,660
Healthcare and social assistance............................	99,380

Most human resources managers work full time during regular business hours. Some human resources managers work more than 40 hours per week.

Job Outlook

Employment of human resources managers is projected to grow 6 percent from 2019 to 2029, faster than the average for all occupations.

Employment growth depends largely on the performance and growth of individual companies. As new companies form and organizations expand their operations, they will need more human resources managers to administer and monitor their programs.

Human resources managers also will be needed to ensure that firms adhere to changing and complex employment laws regarding topics such as equal employment opportunity, healthcare, and retirement plans.

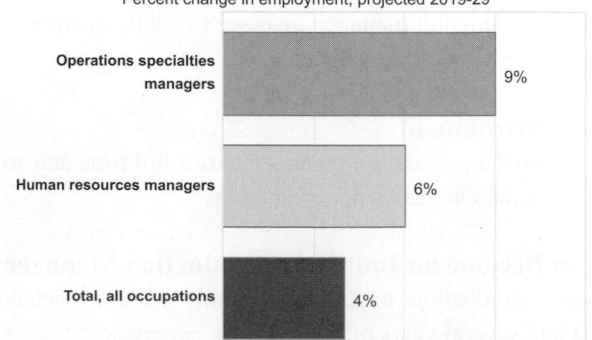

Human Resources Managers
Percent change in employment, projected 2019-29

- Operations specialties managers — 9%
- Human resources managers — 6%
- Total, all occupations — 4%

Note: All Occupations includes all occupations in the U.S. Economy.
Source: U.S. Bureau of Labor Statistics, Employment Projections program.

Job Prospects

About 13,300 openings for human resources managers are projected each year, on average, over the decade.

Many of those openings are expected to result from the need to replace workers who transfer to different occupations or exit the labor force, such as to retire. Candidates with certification or a master's degree—particularly those with a concentration in human resources management—should have the best job prospects.

Employment projections data for human resources managers, 2019-29					
Occupational Title	SOC Code	Employment, 2019	Projected Employment, 2029	Change, 2019-29	
				Percent	Numeric
SOURCE: U.S. Bureau of Labor Statistics, Employment Projections program					
Human resources managers	11-3121	165,200	175,600	6	10,400

State & Area Data

Occupational Employment Statistics (OES)

The Occupational Employment Statistics (OES) program produces employment and wage estimates annually for over 800 occupations. These estimates are available for the nation as a whole, for individual states, and for metropolitan and nonmetropolitan areas.

Contacts for More Information

For more information about human resources managers, including certification, visit
➤ Society for Human Resource Management
➤ HR Certification Institute
➤ International Public Management Association for Human Resources

For information about careers and certification in employee compensation and benefits, visit
➤ International Foundation of Employee Benefit Plans
➤ WorldatWork

For information about careers in employee training and development and certification, visit
➤ Association for Talent Development
➤ International Society for Performance Improvement

Industrial Production Managers

Summary

Quick Facts: Industrial Production Managers

2019 Median Pay	$105,480 per year $50.71 per hour
Typical Entry-Level Education	Bachelor's degree
Work Experience in a Related Occupation	5 years or more
On-the-job Training	None
Number of Jobs, 2019	190,100
Job Outlook, 2019-29	1% (Slower than average)
Employment Change, 2019-29	1,700

What Industrial Production Managers Do

Industrial production managers oversee the daily operations of manufacturing and related plants.

Work Environment

Most industrial production managers work full time and some work more than 40 hours per week.

How to Become an Industrial Production Manager

Industrial production managers typically need a bachelor's degree and several years of related work experience.

Pay

The median annual wage for industrial production managers was $105,480 in May 2019.

Job Outlook

Employment of industrial production managers is projected to grow 1 percent from 2019 to 2029, slower than the average for all occupations. Most of these managers are employed in various manufacturing industries, and may experience growth or decline along with the industries in which they are employed.

State & Area Data

Explore resources for employment and wages by state and area for industrial production managers.

What Industrial Production Managers Do

Industrial production managers oversee the daily operations of manufacturing and related plants. They coordinate, plan, and

Industrial production managers develop the manufacturing plan and establish procedures for manufacturing plants.

Industrial production managers monitor a plant's workers to ensure they meet safety standards.

direct the activities used to create a wide range of goods, such as cars, computer equipment, or paper products.

Duties

Industrial production managers typically do the following:

- Decide how best to use a plant's workers and equipment to meet production goals
- Ensure that production stays on schedule and within budget
- Hire, train, and evaluate workers
- Analyze production data
- Write production reports
- Monitor a plant's workers and programs to ensure they meet performance and safety requirements
- Streamline the production process
- Determine whether new machines are needed or whether overtime work is necessary
- Fix any production problems

Industrial production managers, also called *plant managers*, may oversee an entire manufacturing plant or a specific area of production.

Industrial production managers are responsible for carrying out quality control programs to make sure the finished product meets a specific level of quality. Often called *quality control systems managers*, these managers use programs to help identify defects in products, identify the cause of the defect, and solve the problem creating it. For example, a manager may determine that a defect is being caused by parts from an outside supplier. The manager can then work with the supplier to improve the quality of the parts.

Industrial production managers work closely with managers from other departments as well. For example, the procurement (buying) department orders the supplies that the production department uses. A breakdown in communication between these two departments can cause production slowdowns. Industrial production managers also communicate with other managers and departments, such as sales, warehousing, finance, and research and design.

Work Environment

Industrial production managers held about 190,100 jobs in 2019. The largest employers of industrial production managers were as follows:

Fabricated metal product manufacturing	10%
Transportation equipment manufacturing	9
Chemical manufacturing	8
Machinery manufacturing	8
Food manufacturing	7

Industrial production managers split their time between the production area and a nearby office. When they are working in the production area, they may need to wear protective equipment, such as a helmet or safety goggles.

Work Schedules

Most industrial production managers work full time and some work more than 40 hours per week. In some facilities, managers work night or weekend shifts and must be on call to deal with emergencies at any time.

Industrial production managers work in a variety of manufacturing industries.

Industrial production managers need leadership and interpersonal skills to supervise manufacturing employees.

How to Become an Industrial Production Manager

Industrial production managers typically need a bachelor's degree and several years of related work experience.

Education

Employers prefer that industrial production managers have at least a bachelor's degree. While the degree may be in any field, many industrial production managers have a bachelor's degree in business administration or industrial engineering. Sometimes, production workers with many years of experience take management classes to become production managers. At large plants, where managers have more oversight responsibilities, employers may look for managers who have a Master of Business Administration (MBA) or a graduate degree in industrial management.

Work Experience in a Related Occupation

Many industrial production managers begin as production workers and move up through the ranks. They usually advance to a first-line supervisory position before eventually becoming an industrial production manager. Most earn a college degree in business management or take company-sponsored classes to increase their chances of a promotion.

Alternatively, a worker who joins a firm immediately after graduating from college may work as first-line supervisor before beginning a job as a production manager.

Some begin working as an industrial production manager directly after college or graduate school. They may spend their first few months in training programs, becoming familiar with the production process, company policies, and safety regulations. In large companies, many also spend short periods of time working in other departments, such as purchasing or accounting, to learn more about the company.

Important Qualities

Interpersonal skills. Industrial production managers must have excellent communication skills so they can work well other managers and with staff.

Leadership skills. To keep the production process running smoothly, industrial production managers must motivate and direct the employees they manage.

Problem-solving skills. Production managers must identify problems immediately and solve them. For example, if a product has a defect, the manager determines whether it is a one-time problem or the result of the production process.

Time-management skills. To meet production deadlines, managers must carefully manage their employees' time as well as their own.

Licenses, Certifications, and Registrations

While not required, industrial production managers can earn certifications that show a higher level of competency in quality or management systems. The APICS offers a Certified in Production and Inventory Management (CPIM) credential. The American Society of Quality (ASQ) offers credentials in quality control. Both certifications require specific amounts of work experience before applying for the credential, so they are generally not earned before entering the occupation.

Pay

The median annual wage for industrial production managers was $105,480 in May 2019. The median wage is the wage at which half the workers in an occupation earned more than that amount and half earned less. The lowest 10 percent earned less than $65,050, and the highest 10 percent earned more than $176,070.

In May 2019, the median annual wages for industrial production managers in the top industries in which they worked were as follows:

Chemical manufacturing	$116,110
Transportation equipment manufacturing	111,270
Machinery manufacturing	105,010
Food manufacturing	98,420
Fabricated metal product manufacturing	97,330

Industrial Production Managers
Median annual wages, May 2019

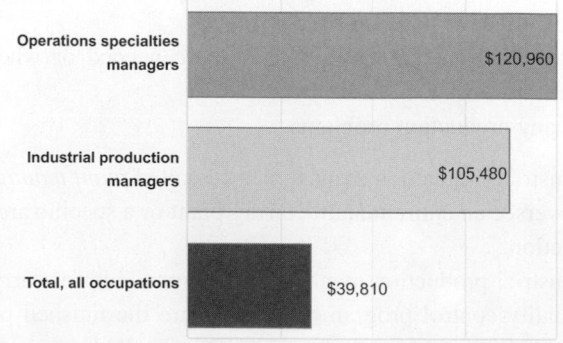

Operations specialties managers	$120,960
Industrial production managers	$105,480
Total, all occupations	$39,810

Note: All Occupations includes all occupations in the U.S. Economy.
Source: U.S. Bureau of Labor Statistics, Occupational Employment Statistics.

Industrial Production Managers

Industrial Production Managers
Percent change in employment, projected 2019-29

Operations specialties managers	9%
Total, all occupations	4%
Industrial production managers	1%

Note: All Occupations includes all occupations in the U.S. Economy.
Source: U.S. Bureau of Labor Statistics, Employment Projections program.

Most industrial production managers work full time and some work more than 40 hours per week.

Job Outlook

Employment of industrial production managers is projected to grow 1 percent from 2019 to 2029, slower than the average for all occupations.

Most of these managers are employed in various manufacturing industries, some of which are expected to have declining employment due to greater productivity. However, because industrial production managers are responsible for coordinating work activities with the goal of increasing productivity, they will continue to be needed in this capacity. Industries projected to add jobs for these workers include motor vehicle parts manufacturing, machine shops, and pharmaceutical and medicine manufacturing.

Job Prospects

Applicants will likely face strong competition for positions, but those who have several years of experience and a bachelor's degree in industrial management or business administration should have the best prospects.

Employment projections data for industrial production managers, 2019-29					
Occupational Title	SOC Code	Employment, 2019	Projected Employment, 2029	Change, 2019-29	
				Percent	Numeric
SOURCE: U.S. Bureau of Labor Statistics, Employment Projections program					
Industrial production managers	11-3051	190,100	191,900	1	1,700

State & Area Data
Occupational Employment Statistics (OES)

The Occupational Employment Statistics (OES) program produces employment and wage estimates annually for over 800 occupations. These estimates are available for the nation as a whole, for individual states, and for metropolitan and nonmetropolitan areas.

Contacts for More Information

For more information about careers in production management and certification, visit
➤ Association for Operations Management (APICS)

For more information about quality management and certification, visit
➤ American Society for Quality

For general information about manufacturing careers, visit
➤ National Association of Manufacturers

Lodging Managers

Summary

Quick Facts: Lodging Managers

2019 Median Pay	$54,430 per year / $26.17 per hour
Typical Entry-Level Education	High school diploma or equivalent
Work Experience in a Related Occupation	Less than 5 years
On-the-job Training	None
Number of Jobs, 2019	57,200
Job Outlook, 2019-29	-12% (Decline)
Employment Change, 2019-29	-6,700

What Lodging Managers Do

Lodging managers ensure that traveling guests have a pleasant experience at their establishment with accommodations. They also ensure that the business is run efficiently and profitably.

Work Environment

Because hotels are open 24 hours a day, evening and weekend work is common. Most lodging managers work full time and are often on call. The work can be pressure filled and stressful.

How to Become a Lodging Manager

Lodging managers usually take one of three education paths: a bachelor's degree in hospitality or hotel management, an associate's degree or a certificate in hotel management, or a high school diploma combined with several years of experience working in a hotel.

Pay

The median annual wage for lodging managers was $54,430 in May 2019.

Job Outlook

Employment of lodging managers is projected to decline 12 percent from 2019 to 2029.

Lodging managers greet and register guests.

State & Area Data

Explore resources for employment and wages by state and area for lodging managers.

What Lodging Managers Do

Lodging managers ensure that guests on vacation or business travel have a pleasant experience at a hotel, motel, or other types of establishments with accommodations. Lodging managers also ensure that the establishment is run efficiently and profitably.

Duties

Lodging managers typically do the following:

- Inspect guest rooms, public areas, and grounds for cleanliness and appearance
- Ensure that company standards for guest services, décor, and housekeeping are met
- Answer questions from guests about hotel policies and services

Lodging managers ensure that company standards for guest services are met.

- Keep track of how much money the hotel or lodging facility is making
- Interview, hire, train, and sometimes fire staff members
- Monitor staff performance to ensure that guests are happy and that the hotel is well run
- Coordinate front-office activities of hotels or motels and resolve problems
- Set room rates and budgets, approve expenditures, and allocate funds to various departments

A comfortable room, good food, and a helpful staff can make being away from home an enjoyable experience for guests on vacation or business travel. Lodging managers occasionally greet and register guests. They also try to make sure that guests have a good experience.

Lodging establishments vary in size, from independently owned bed and breakfasts to motels with just a few rooms or to hotels that can have thousands of guest rooms. Larger hotels with more amenities lead to a greater range of duties for lodging managers, such as granting access to a swimming pool, operating a casino, or hosting conventions.

Many lodging managers use online social media for marketing purposes.

The following are examples of types of lodging managers:

General managers oversee all lodging operations at a property. At large hotels with several departments and multiple layers of management, the general manager and several assistant managers coordinate the activities of separate departments. These departments may include housekeeping, human resources, room operations, marketing and sales, purchasing, security, maintenance, recreational facilities, and other activities. For more information, see the profiles on human resources managers; public relations and fundraising managers; financial managers; advertising, promotions, and marketing managers; and food service managers.

Revenue managers work in financial management, monitoring room sales and reservations, overseeing accounting and cash-flow matters at the hotel, projecting occupancy levels, and deciding which rooms to discount and when to offer special rates.

Front-office managers coordinate reservations and room assignments and train and direct the hotel's front-desk staff. They ensure that guests are treated courteously, that complaints and problems are resolved, and that requests for special services are carried out. Most front-office managers are also responsible for adjusting bills.

Convention service managers coordinate the activities of various departments, to accommodate meetings, conventions, and special events. They meet with representatives of groups to plan the number of conference rooms to be reserved, design the configuration of the meeting space, and determine what other services the groups will need, such as catering or audio-visual requirements. During a meeting or event, they resolve unexpected problems and ensure that hotel operations meet a group's expectations.

Work Environment

Lodging managers held about 57,200 jobs in 2019. The largest employers of lodging managers were as follows:

Traveler accommodation	59%
Self-employed workers	31
RV (recreational vehicle) parks and recreational camps	2

The pressures of coordinating a wide range of activities, turning a profit for investors, and dealing with dissatisfied guests can be stressful.

Work Schedules

Most lodging managers work full time. Because hotels are open around the clock, working evenings, weekends, and holidays is common. Some managers must be on call 24 hours a day, particularly if they reside at the lodging establishment.

How to Become a Lodging Manager

Lodging managers usually take one of three education paths: a bachelor's degree in hospitality or hotel management, an associate's degree or a certificate in hotel management, or a high school diploma combined with several years of experience working in a hotel.

Education

Most full-service hotel chains hire candidates with a bachelor's degree in hospitality or hotel management. Hotel management programs typically include instruction in hotel administration, accounting, marketing and sales, housekeeping, food service management and catering, and hotel maintenance and engineering. Systems training is also an integral part of many degree programs, because hotels use hospitality-specific software

The majority of lodging managers work in traditional hotels and motels.

Most full-service hotel chains prefer candidates with a degree in hospitality or hotel management.

in reservations, billing, and housekeeping management. The Accreditation Commission for Programs in Hospitality Administration accredits about 60 hospitality management programs.

At hotels that provide fewer services, candidates with an associate's degree or a certificate in hotel, restaurant, or hospitality management may qualify for a job as a lodging manager.

Also, many technical institutes and vocational and trade schools offer courses that are recognized by the hospitality industry that may help in getting a job. Currently, some states and the District of Columbia offer high school academic training for prospective lodging managers.

Work Experience in a Related Occupation

Hotel employees who do not have hospitality management training, but who show leadership potential and have several years of related work experience, may qualify for assistant manager positions.

Licenses, Certifications, and Registrations

High school students can enroll in the Hospitality and Tourism Management Program (HTMP) offered by the American Hotel & Lodging Educational Institute (AHLEI). The HTMP is a 2-year program that teaches management principles and leads to professional certification. College students and working professionals can also obtain the Certification in Hotel Industry Analytics (CHIA) through AHLEI.

Advancement

Large hotel chains may offer better opportunities than small, independently owned hotels for advancing from assistant manager to manager or from managing one hotel to being a regional manager. However, these opportunities usually involve relocating to another city or state.

Important Qualities

Business skills. Lodging managers address budget matters and coordinate and supervise workers. Operating a profitable hotel is important—as is the need to motivate and direct the work of employees.

Customer-service skills. Lodging managers must have excellent customer-service skills when dealing with guests. Satisfying guests' needs is critical to a hotel's success and helps to ensure customer loyalty.

Interpersonal skills. Lodging managers need strong interpersonal skills because they interact regularly with many different people. They must be effective communicators and must have positive interactions with guests and hotel staff, even in stressful situations.

Leadership skills. Lodging managers must establish good working relationships to ensure a productive work environment. This objective may involve motivating personnel, resolving conflicts, and listening to complaints or criticism from guests.

Listening skills. Lodging managers should have excellent listening skills. Listening to the needs of guests allows managers to take the appropriate course of action, ensuring guests' satisfaction. Listening to the needs of workers helps managers keep good working relationships with the staff.

Organizational skills. Lodging managers keep track of many different schedules, budgets, and people at once. This task becomes more complex as the size of the hotel increases.

Problem-solving skills. The ability to resolve personnel issues and guest-related dissatisfaction is critical to the work of lodging managers. As a result, they should be creative and practical when confronted with problems.

Pay

The median annual wage for lodging managers was $54,430 in May 2019. The median wage is the wage at which half the workers in an occupation earned more than that amount and half earned less. The lowest 10 percent earned less than $31,380, and the highest 10 percent earned more than $105,720.

In May 2019, the median annual wages for lodging managers in the top industries in which they worked were as follows:

Traveler accommodation $53,690

RV (recreational vehicle) parks and recreational
    camps 49,160

Most lodging managers work full time. Because hotels are open around the clock, working evenings, weekends, and holidays is common. Some managers must be on call 24 hours a day.

Job Outlook

Employment of lodging managers is projected to decline 12 percent from 2019 to 2029.

Stays in traditional lodging establishments have been declining as short-term rentals have risen and offered competition. Both leisure and business traveler bookings at hotels and bed-and-breakfast establishments have declined due to the increase in available options offered by online booking sites, which make it easier for individuals to rent out their space. This is expected to result in decreased demand for lodging managers.

Job Prospects

Those seeking jobs at hotels with the highest level of guest services are expected to face competition, as these positions are highly sought after by people trained in hospitality management or administration.

Applicants with a bachelor's degree in hospitality or hotel management are expected to have the best job opportunities, particularly at upscale and luxury hotels.

Employment projections data for lodging managers, 2019-29					
Occupational Title	SOC Code	Employment, 2019	Projected Employment, 2029	Change, 2019-29	
				Percent	Numeric
SOURCE: U.S. Bureau of Labor Statistics, Employment Projections program					
Lodging managers	11-9081	57,200	50,600	-12	-6,700

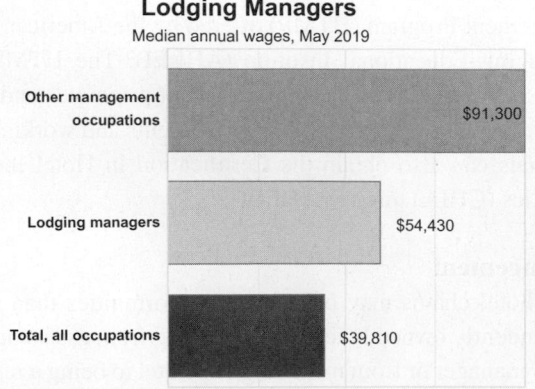

Lodging Managers
Median annual wages, May 2019

Other management occupations — $91,300
Lodging managers — $54,430
Total, all occupations — $39,810

Note: All Occupations includes all occupations in the U.S. Economy.
Source: U.S. Bureau of Labor Statistics, Occupational Employment Statistics.

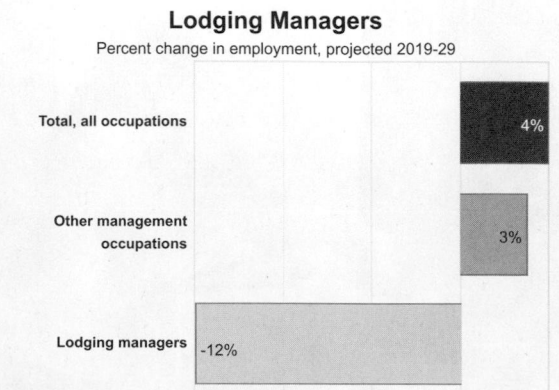

Lodging Managers
Percent change in employment, projected 2019-29

Total, all occupations — 4%
Other management occupations — 3%
Lodging managers — -12%

Note: All Occupations includes all occupations in the U.S. Economy.
Source: U.S. Bureau of Labor Statistics, Employment Projections program.

State & Area Data
Occupational Employment Statistics (OES)
The Occupational Employment Statistics (OES) program produces employment and wage estimates annually for over 800 occupations. These estimates are available for the nation as a whole, for individual states, and for metropolitan and nonmetropolitan areas.

Contacts for More Information
For information about career, professional development, and training programs, visit

➤ American Hotel & Lodging Educational Institute

For information about schools and educational programs in hotel and restaurant management, including correspondence courses, visit
➤ Accreditation Commission for Programs in Hospitality Administration
➤ International Council on Hotel, Restaurant, and Institutional Education

For information about lodging news operations, visit
➤ Hotel News Now

Medical and Health Services Managers

Summary

Quick Facts: Medical and Health Services Managers

2019 Median Pay	$100,980 per year
	$48.55 per hour
Typical Entry-Level Education	Bachelor's degree
Work Experience in a Related Occupation	Less than 5 years
On-the-job Training	None
Number of Jobs, 2019	422,300
Job Outlook, 2019-29	32% (Much faster than average)
Employment Change, 2019-29	133,200

What Medical and Health Services Managers Do
Medical and health services managers plan, direct, and coordinate the business activities of healthcare providers.

Work Environment
Most medical and health services managers work in offices in healthcare facilities, including hospitals and nursing homes, and group medical practices.

How to Become a Medical or Health Services Manager
Most medical and health services managers have at least a bachelor's degree before entering the field; however, master's degrees also are common. Prospective managers typically have some work experience in an administrative or a clinical role in a hospital or other healthcare facility.

Pay
The median annual wage for medical and health services managers was $100,980 in May 2019.

Job Outlook
Employment of medical and health services managers is projected to grow 32 percent from 2019 to 2029, much faster than the average for all occupations. As the large baby-boom population ages and people remain active later in life, there should be increased demand for healthcare services.

State & Area Data
Explore resources for employment and wages by state and area for medical and health services managers.

What Medical and Health Services Managers Do
Medical and health services managers, also called *healthcare executives* or *healthcare administrators*, plan, direct, and coordinate medical and health services. They may manage an entire facility, a specific clinical area or department, or a medical practice for a group of physicians. Medical and health services managers must adapt to changes in healthcare laws, regulations, and technology.

Duties
Medical and health services managers typically do the following:

• Improve efficiency and quality in delivering healthcare services

Medical and health services managers plan, direct, and coordinate the delivery of healthcare.

In group medical practices, medical and health services managers work closely with physicians.

- Develop departmental goals and objectives
- Ensure that the facility in which they work is up to date on and compliant with laws and regulations
- Recruit, train, and supervise staff members
- Manage the finances of the facility, such as patient fees and billing
- Create work schedules
- Prepare and monitor budgets and spending to ensure departments operate within funding limits
- Represent the facility at investor meetings or on governing boards
- Keep and organize records of the facility's services, such as the number of inpatient beds used
- Communicate with members of the medical staff and department heads

Medical and health services managers work closely with physicians and surgeons, registered nurses, medical and clinical laboratory technologists and technicians, and other healthcare workers. Others may interact with patients or insurance agents.

Medical and health services managers' titles depend on the facility or area of expertise in which they work.

The following are examples of types of medical and health services managers:

Nursing home administrators manage staff, admissions, finances, and care of the building, as well as care of the residents in nursing homes. All states require licensure for nursing home administrators; licensing requirements vary by state.

Clinical managers oversee a specific department, such as nursing, surgery, or physical therapy, and have responsibilities based on that specialty. Clinical managers set and carry out policies, goals, and procedures for their departments; evaluate the quality of the staff's work; and develop reports and budgets.

Health information managers are responsible for the maintenance and security of all patient records and data. They must stay up to date with evolving information technology, current or proposed laws about health information systems, and trends in managing large amounts of complex data. Health information managers must ensure that databases are complete, accurate, and accessible only to authorized personnel. They also may supervise the work of medical records and health information technicians.

Work Environment

Medical and health services managers held about 422,300 jobs in 2019. The largest employers of medical and health services managers were as follows:

Hospitals; state, local, and private	33%
Offices of physicians	12
Nursing and residential care facilities	10
Government	8
Outpatient care centers	7

Most medical and health services managers work in offices.

Work Schedules

Most medical and health services managers work full time. Some managers work more than 40 hours per week. Work during evenings or weekends may be required in healthcare

Some medical and health services managers oversee the activities of a number of facilities.

settings that are open at all hours, such as hospitals and nursing homes. Medical and health services managers may need to be on call in case of emergencies.

How to Become a Medical or Health Services Manager

Most medical and health services managers have at least a bachelor's degree before entering the field. However, master's degrees are common and sometimes preferred by employers. Educational requirements vary by facility and specific function.

Education

Medical and health services managers typically need at least a bachelor's degree to enter the occupation. However, master's degrees are common and sometimes preferred by employers. Graduate programs often last between 2 and 3 years and may include up to 1 year of supervised administrative experience in a hospital or healthcare consulting setting.

Prospective medical and health services managers typically have a degree in health administration, health management, nursing, public health administration, or business administration. Degrees that focus on both management and healthcare combine business-related courses with courses in medical terminology, hospital organization, and health information systems. For example, a degree in health administration or health information management often includes courses in health services management, accounting and budgeting, human resources administration, strategic planning, law and ethics, health economics, and health information systems.

Work Experience in a Related Occupation

Many employers require prospective medical and health services managers to have some work experience in either an administrative or a clinical role in a hospital or other healthcare facility. For example, nursing home administrators usually have years of experience working as a registered nurse.

Medical and health services managers must effectively communicate policies and procedures with other health professionals.

Others may begin their careers as medical records and health information technicians, administrative assistants, or financial clerks within a healthcare office.

Important Qualities

Analytical skills. Medical and health services managers must understand and follow current regulations and adapt to new laws.

Communication skills. These managers must effectively communicate policies and procedures to other health professionals and ensure their staff's compliance with new laws and regulations.

Detail oriented. Medical and health services managers must pay attention to detail. They might be required to organize and maintain scheduling and billing information for very large facilities, such as hospitals.

Interpersonal skills. Medical and health services managers discuss staffing problems and patient information with other professionals, such as physicians and health insurance representatives.

Leadership skills. These managers are often responsible for finding creative solutions to staffing or other administrative problems. They must hire, train, motivate, and lead staff.

Technical skills. Medical and health services managers must stay up to date with advances in healthcare technology and data analytics. For example, they may need to use coding and classification software and electronic health record (EHR) systems as their facility adopts these technologies.

Licenses, Certifications, and Registrations

All states require licensure for nursing home administrators; requirements vary by state. In most states, these administrators must have a bachelor's degree, complete a state-approved training program, and pass a national licensing exam. Some states also require applicants to pass a state-specific exam; others may require applicants to have previous work experience in a healthcare facility. Some states also require licensure for administrators in assisted-living facilities. For information on specific state-by-state licensure requirements, visit the National Association of Long Term Care Administrator Boards.

A license is typically not required in other areas of medical and health services management. However, some positions may require applicants to have a registered nurse or social worker license.

Although certification is not required, some managers choose to become certified. Certification is available in many areas of practice. For example, the Professional Association of Health Care Office Management offers certification in medical management, the American Health Information Management Association offers health information management certification, and the American College of Health Care Administrators offers the Certified Nursing Home Administrator and Certified Assisted Living Administrator distinctions.

Advancement

Medical and health services managers advance by moving into higher paying positions with more responsibility. Some health information managers, for example, can advance to become responsible for the entire hospital's information systems. Other managers may advance to top executive positions within the organization. Advancement to top level executive positions usually requires a master's degree.

Pay

The median annual wage for medical and health services managers was $100,980 in May 2019. The median wage is the wage at which half the workers in an occupation earned more than that amount and half earned less. The lowest 10 percent earned less than $58,820, and the highest 10 percent earned more than $189,000.

In May 2019, the median annual wages for medical and health services managers in the top industries in which they worked were as follows:

Government	$111,520
Hospitals; state, local, and private	110,430
Outpatient care centers	95,320
Offices of physicians	91,600
Nursing and residential care facilities	86,820

Most medical and health services managers work full time. Some managers work more than 40 hours per week. Work during evenings or weekends may be required in healthcare settings such as hospitals and nursing homes, which are open at all hours. Medical and health services managers may need to be on call in case of emergencies.

Job Outlook

Employment of medical and health services managers is projected to grow 32 percent from 2019 to 2029, much faster than the average for all occupations. As the large baby-boom population ages and people remain active later in life, there should be increased demand for healthcare services.

This means greater needs for physicians and other healthcare workers, medical procedures, and healthcare facilities, and therefore greater needs for managers who organize and manage medical information and healthcare staff. There should also be increased demand for nursing care facility administrators as the population grows older.

Employment is projected to grow in offices of health practitioners. Many services previously provided in hospitals will shift to these settings, especially as medical technologies improve. Demand in medical group practice management is projected to grow as medical group practices become larger and more complex.

In addition, widespread use of electronic health records (EHRs) will continue to create demand for managers with knowledge of health information technology (IT) and informatics systems. Medical and health services managers will be needed to organize, manage, and integrate these records across areas of the healthcare industry.

Job Prospects

Job prospects for medical and health services managers are likely to be favorable. In addition to rising employment demand, the need to replace managers who retire over the next decade will result in some openings. Candidates with a master's degree in health administration or a related field, as well as knowledge of healthcare IT systems, will likely have the best prospects.

Employment projections data for medical and health services managers, 2019-29					
Occupational Title	SOC Code	Employment, 2019	Projected Employment, 2029	Change, 2019-29	
				Percent	Numeric
SOURCE: U.S. Bureau of Labor Statistics, Employment Projections program					
Medical and health services managers	11-9111	422,300	555,500	32	133,200

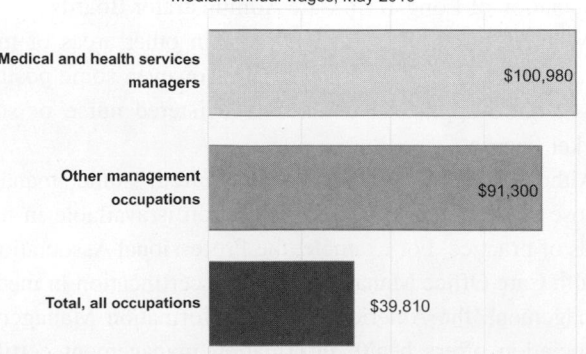

Medical and Health Services Managers
Median annual wages, May 2019

- Medical and health services managers: $100,980
- Other management occupations: $91,300
- Total, all occupations: $39,810

Note: All Occupations includes all occupations in the U.S. Economy.
Source: U.S. Bureau of Labor Statistics, Occupational Employment Statistics.

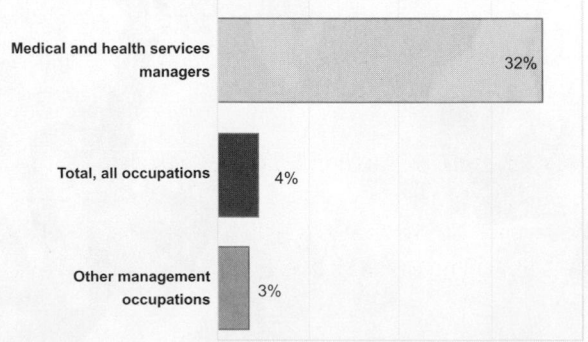

Medical and Health Services Managers
Percent change in employment, projected 2019-29

- Medical and health services managers: 32%
- Total, all occupations: 4%
- Other management occupations: 3%

Note: All Occupations includes all occupations in the U.S. Economy.
Source: U.S. Bureau of Labor Statistics, Employment Projections program.

State & Area Data
Occupational Employment Statistics (OES)
The Occupational Employment Statistics (OES) program produces employment and wage estimates annually for over 800 occupations. These estimates are available for the nation as a whole, for individual states, and for metropolitan and nonmetropolitan areas.

Contacts for More Information
For more information about medical and healthcare management, visit
➤ Professional Association of Health Care Office Management
➤ American Health Information Management Association
➤ American College of Health Care Administrators

For more information about academic programs in this field, visit

➤ Association of University Programs in Health Administration
➤ Commission on Accreditation of Healthcare Management Education

For information about career opportunities in healthcare management, visit
➤ American College of Healthcare Executives

For information about career opportunities in medical group practices and ambulatory care management, visit
➤ Medical Group Management Association

For more information about licensure and training requirements for nursing home and assisted-living facility administrators, visit
➤ National Association of Long Term Care Administrator Boards

Natural Sciences Managers

Summary

Quick Facts: Natural Sciences Managers

2019 Median Pay	$129,100 per year $62.07 per hour
Typical Entry-Level Education	Bachelor's degree
Work Experience in a Related Occupation	5 years or more
On-the-job Training	None
Number of Jobs, 2019	71,400
Job Outlook, 2019-29	5% (Faster than average)
Employment Change, 2019-29	3,400

What Natural Sciences Managers Do
Natural sciences managers supervise the work of scientists, including chemists, physicists, and biologists.

Work Environment
Natural sciences managers spend most of their time in offices, but they also may spend time in laboratories. Most natural sciences managers work full time.

How to Become a Natural Sciences Manager
Natural sciences managers need at least a bachelor's degree in a natural science or a related field. Most natural sciences managers work as scientists before becoming managers.

Pay
The median annual wage for natural sciences managers was $129,100 in May 2019.

Laboratory managers review staff members' methodology and the accuracy of their research results.

Job Outlook
Employment of natural sciences managers is projected to grow 5 percent from 2019 to 2029, faster than the average for all occupations. Employment growth should be affected by many of the same factors that affect employment growth for the scientists whom these managers supervise.

State & Area Data
Explore resources for employment and wages by state and area for natural sciences managers.

What Natural Sciences Managers Do
Natural sciences managers supervise the work of scientists, including chemists, physicists, and biologists. They direct activities related to research and development, and coordinate activities such as testing, quality control, and production.

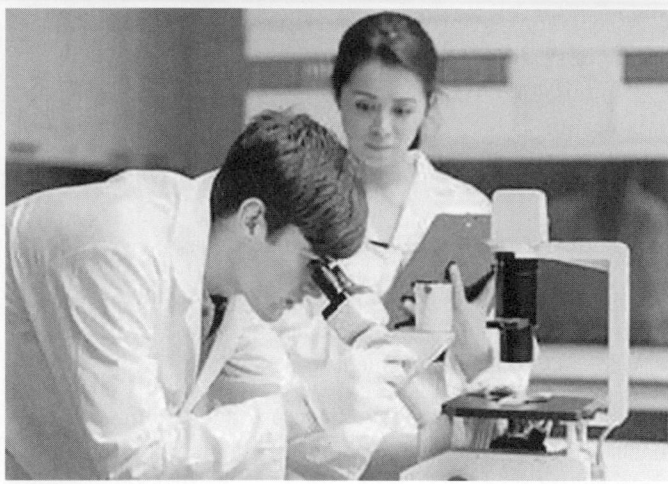

Natural sciences managers direct research and development projects.

Duties

Natural sciences managers typically do the following:

- Work with top executives to develop goals and strategies for researchers and developers
- Budget resources for projects and programs by determining staffing, training, and equipment needs
- Hire, supervise, and evaluate scientists, technicians, and other staff members
- Review staff members' methodology and the accuracy of their research results
- Monitor the progress of projects, review research performed, and draft operational reports
- Ensure that laboratories are stocked with equipment and supplies
- Provide technical assistance to scientists, technicians, and support staff
- Establish and follow administrative procedures, policies, and standards
- Communicate project proposals, research findings, and the status of projects to clients and top management

Natural sciences managers direct scientific research activities and direct and coordinate product development projects and production activities. The duties of natural sciences managers vary with the field of science (such as biology or chemistry) or the industry they work in. Research projects may be aimed at improving manufacturing processes, advancing basic scientific knowledge, or developing new products.

Some natural sciences managers are former scientists and, after becoming managers, may continue to conduct their own research as well as oversee the work of others. These managers are sometimes called *working managers* and usually have smaller staffs, allowing them to do research in addition to carrying out their administrative duties.

Managers who are responsible for larger staffs may not have time to contribute to research and may spend all their time performing administrative duties.

Laboratory managers need to ensure that laboratories are fully supplied so that scientists can run their tests and experiments. Some specialize in the management of laboratory animals.

During all stages of a project, natural sciences managers coordinate the activities of their unit with those of other units or organizations. They work with higher levels of management; with financial, production, and marketing specialists; and with equipment and materials suppliers.

Work Environment

Natural sciences managers held about 71,400 jobs in 2019. The largest employers of natural sciences managers were as follows:

Research and development in the physical, engineering, and life sciences	28%
Manufacturing	17
Federal government, excluding postal service	15
State government, excluding education and hospitals	6
Management, scientific, and technical consulting services	5

Most of the time, they work in offices, but they also may spend time in laboratories. Like managers in other fields, natural sciences managers may spend a large portion of their time using computers and talking to other members of their organization.

Natural sciences managers have different requirements based on the size of their staff. Managers with larger staffs spend their time primarily in offices performing administrative duties and spend little time doing research or working in the field or in laboratories. Working managers who have research responsibilities and smaller staffs may need to work in laboratories or in the field, which may require traveling, sometimes to remote locations.

Natural sciences managers often present their research findings to other managers, top executives, and clients.

Work Schedules

Most natural sciences managers work full time. Some work more than 40 hours per week.

How to Become a Natural Sciences Manager

Natural sciences managers usually advance to management positions after years of employment as scientists. Natural sciences managers typically have a bachelor's degree, master's degree, or Ph.D. in a scientific discipline or a related field, such as engineering. Some managers may find it helpful to have an advanced management degree—for example, a Professional Science Master's (PSM) degree.

Education

Natural sciences managers typically begin their careers as scientists; therefore, most have a bachelor's degree, master's degree, or Ph.D. in a scientific discipline or a closely related field, such as engineering. Scientific and technical knowledge is essential for managers because they must be able to understand the work of their subordinates and provide technical assistance when needed.

Natural sciences managers who are interested in acquiring postsecondary education in management should be able to find master's degree or Ph.D. programs in a natural science that incorporate business management courses. Professional Science Master's (PSM) degree programs blend advanced training in a particular science field, such as biotechnology or environmental science, with business skills, such as communications and program management, and policy. Those interested in acquiring general management skills may pursue a Master of Business Administration (MBA) or a Master of Public Administration (MPA). Some natural sciences managers will have studied psychology or some other management-related field to enter this occupation.

Sciences managers must continually upgrade their knowledge because of the rapid growth of scientific developments.

Work Experience in a Related Occupation

Natural sciences managers usually work several years in the sciences before advancing to management positions. While employed as scientists, they typically are given more responsibility and independence in their work as they gain experience. Eventually, they may lead research teams and have control over the direction and content of projects before being promoted to an managerial position.

Licenses, Certifications, and Registrations

Although certification is not typically required to become a natural sciences manager, many relevant certifications are available. These certifications range from those related to specific scientific areas of study or practice, such as laboratory animal management, to general management topics, such as project management.

Important Qualities

Communication skills. Natural sciences managers must be able to communicate clearly with a variety of audiences, such as scientists, policymakers, and the public. Both written and oral communication are important.

Critical-thinking skills. Natural sciences managers must carefully evaluate the work of others. They must determine if their staff's methods and results are based on sound science.

Interpersonal skills. Natural sciences managers lead research teams and therefore need to work well with others in order to reach common goals. Managers routinely deal with conflict, which they must be able to turn into positive outcomes for their organization.

Leadership skills. Natural sciences managers must be able to organize, direct, and motivate others. They need to identify the strengths and weaknesses of their workers and create an environment in which the workers can succeed.

Problem-solving skills. Natural sciences managers use scientific observation and analysis to find answers to complex technical questions.

Time-management skills. Natural sciences managers must be able to perform multiple administrative, supervisory, and technical tasks while ensuring that projects remain on schedule.

Natural sciences managers typically begin their careers as scientists.

Natural Sciences Managers
Median annual wages, May 2019

Natural sciences managers $129,100

Other management occupations $91,300

Total, all occupations $39,810

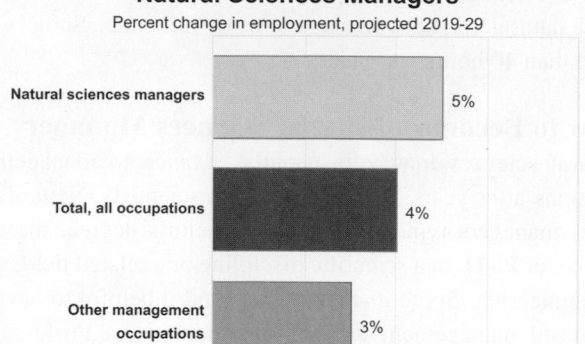

Natural Sciences Managers
Percent change in employment, projected 2019-29

Natural sciences managers 5%

Total, all occupations 4%

Other management occupations 3%

Note: All Occupations includes all occupations in the U.S. Economy.
Source: U.S. Bureau of Labor Statistics, Occupational Employment Statistics.

Note: All Occupations includes all occupations in the U.S. Economy.
Source: U.S. Bureau of Labor Statistics, Employment Projections program.

Pay

The median annual wage for natural sciences managers was $129,100 in May 2019. The median wage is the wage at which half the workers in an occupation earned more than that amount and half earned less. The lowest 10 percent earned less than $66,050, and the highest 10 percent earned more than $208,000.

In May 2019, the median annual wages for natural sciences managers in the top industries in which they worked were as follows:

Research and development in the physical, engineering, and life sciences	$161,930
Manufacturing	145,660
Management, scientific, and technical consulting services	120,470
Federal government, excluding postal service ...	116,850
State government, excluding education and hospitals	83,190

Most natural sciences managers work full time. Some work more than 40 hours per week.

Job Outlook

Employment of natural sciences managers is projected to grow 5 percent from 2019 to 2029, faster than the average for all occupations. Employment growth should be affected by many of the same factors that affect employment growth for the scientists whom these managers supervise. Job growth for managers is projected to increase at roughly the same rate as those for life scientists and physical scientists, but managers tend to be flexible in the number of workers they are able to manage. In addition, research and development activities are increasingly being outsourced to specialized scientific research services firms. This outsourcing will lead to some consolidation of management.

Job Prospects

In addition to job openings resulting from employment growth, openings will arise from the need to replace managers who retire or move into other occupations.

Competition for jobs in this occupation is expected to be strong because of its typically higher salaries, greater control over some types of projects, and better access to resources. Experiences can vary widely with the variety of industries and organizations these managers work in. Private industry, government, and colleges and universities will have different goals. Prospective managers should take these differences into consideration when applying for positions.

Employment projections data for natural sciences managers, 2019-29					
Occupational Title	SOC Code	Employment, 2019	Projected Employment, 2029	Change, 2019-29	
				Percent	Numeric
SOURCE: U.S. Bureau of Labor Statistics, Employment Projections program					
Natural sciences managers	11-9121	71,400	74,800	5	3,400

State & Area Data
Occupational Employment Statistics (OES)

The Occupational Employment Statistics (OES) program produces employment and wage estimates annually for over 800 occupations. These estimates are available for the nation as a whole, for individual states, and for metropolitan and nonmetropolitan areas.

Contacts for More Information

For more information about Professional Science Master's programs, visit
➤ Professional Science Master's

For general information about science careers and news, including articles on natural science management, visit
➤ American Association for the Advancement of Science

To find job openings for natural sciences managers in the federal government, visit
➤ USAJOBS

Postsecondary Education Administrators

Summary

Quick Facts: Postsecondary Education Administrators

2019 Median Pay	$95,410 per year $45.87 per hour
Typical Entry-Level Education	Master's degree
Work Experience in a Related Occupation	Less than 5 years
On-the-job Training	None
Number of Jobs, 2019	190,500
Job Outlook, 2019-29	4% (As fast as average)
Employment Change, 2019-29	7,100

What Postsecondary Education Administrators Do

Postsecondary education administrators oversee student services, academics, and faculty research at colleges and universities.

Work Environment

Postsecondary education administrators work for public and private schools. Most work full time.

How to Become a Postsecondary Education Administrator

Postsecondary education administrators typically need a master's degree. However, there will be some opportunities for those with a bachelor's degree. Employers typically prefer to hire candidates who have experience working in a postsecondary education administrative office, especially for occupations such as registrars and academic deans.

Pay

The median annual wage for postsecondary education administrators was $95,410 in May 2019.

Job Outlook

Employment of postsecondary education administrators is projected to grow 4 percent from 2019 to 2029, about as fast as the average for all occupations. Expected growth may result from increasing student enrollment in colleges and universities.

State & Area Data

Explore resources for employment and wages by state and area for postsecondary education administrators.

What Postsecondary Education Administrators Do

Postsecondary education administrators oversee student services, academics, and faculty research at colleges and universities. Their job duties vary depending on the department in which they work, such as admissions, student affairs, or the registrar's office.

Duties

Education administrators' duties depend on the size of their college or university. Small schools often have small staffs that take on many different responsibilities, but larger schools may have different offices for each of these functions. For example, at a small college, the Office of Student Life may oversee student athletics and other activities, whereas a large university may have an Athletics Department.

Postsecondary education administrators who work in **admissions** decide which applicants should be admitted to the school. They typically do the following:

- Determine how many students to admit to the school
- Meet with prospective students and encourage them to apply
- Review applications to determine which students should be admitted
- Analyze data about applicants and admitted students

Postsecondary education administrators oversee student services, academics, and faculty research at colleges and universities.

Postsecondary education administrators assist students with a variety of tasks, such as registering for classes and completing admissions applications.

Admissions officers also prepare promotional materials about the school. They often are assigned a region of the country to which they travel and speak to high school counselors and students.

Admissions officers who work with the financial aid department offer packages of federal and institutional financial aid to prospective students.

Postsecondary education administrators may be **provosts** or **academic deans**. Provosts, also called *chief academic officers*, help college presidents develop academic policies, participate in making faculty appointments and tenure decisions, and manage budgets. They also oversee faculty research at colleges and universities. Academic deans coordinate the activities of the individual colleges or schools. For example, a large university may have a separate dean for business, law, and medical schools.

Postsecondary education administrators who work in the **registrar's office**, sometimes called *registrars*, maintain student and course records. They typically do the following:

- Schedule course offerings, including space and times for classes
- Oversee student registration for classes
- Ensure that students meet graduation requirements
- Plan commencement ceremonies
- Prepare transcripts and diplomas for students
- Produce data about students and classes
- Maintain the academic records of the institution

Registrars' duties vary throughout the school year. During registration and at the beginning of the academic term, for example, they help students sign up for, drop, and add courses. Registrars need computer skills to create and maintain databases.

Postsecondary education administrators who work in **student affairs** are responsible for a variety of cocurricular school functions. They typically do the following:

- Advise students on topics such as housing, personal problems, or academics
- Communicate with parents or guardians
- Create, support, and assess nonacademic programs for students
- Schedule programs and services, such as athletic events or recreational activities

Postsecondary education administrators in student affairs may specialize in areas such as student activities, housing and residential life, or multicultural affairs. In student activities, they plan events and advise student clubs and organizations. In housing and residential life, they assign students to rooms and match them with roommates, ensure that residential facilities are well maintained, and train residential advisers. In multicultural affairs, they plan events to celebrate different cultures and diverse backgrounds. Sometimes, they manage multicultural centers on campus.

Work Environment

Postsecondary education administrators held about 190,500 jobs in 2019. The largest employers of postsecondary education administrators were as follows:

Colleges, universities, and professional schools; state, local, and private...	79%
Junior colleges; state, local, and private	13

Work Schedules

Postsecondary education administrators generally work full time. Most work year-round, but some administrators may reduce their hours during the summer.

How to Become a Postsecondary Education Administrator

Postsecondary education administrators typically need a master's degree. However, there will be some opportunities for those with a bachelor's degree. Employers typically prefer candidates who have experience working in a postsecondary academic administrative office, particularly for occupations such as registrars and academic deans.

Education

Postsecondary education administrators typically need a master's degree. However, a bachelor's degree may be sufficient for positions at small colleges and universities. Degrees can be in a variety of disciplines, such as social work, accounting, or marketing.

Provosts and deans often must have a Ph.D. Some begin their careers as professors and later move into administration. They have a doctorate in the field in which they taught or in higher education.

Work Experience in a Related Occupation

Employers typically prefer to hire candidates who have several years of experience in a college administrative setting. Some

Postsecondary education administrators work in colleges, universities, community colleges, and technical and trade schools.

Postsecondary education administrators need to build good relationships with colleagues, students, and parents.

postsecondary education administrators work in the registrar's office or as a resident assistant while in college to gain the necessary experience. For other positions, such as those in admissions and student affairs, experience may not be necessary.

Important Qualities

Computer skills. Postsecondary education administrators need to be comfortable working with computers so they can use software to manage student and school records.

Interpersonal skills. Postsecondary education administrators need to build good relationships with colleagues, students, and parents. For example, those in admissions need to be outgoing so they can encourage prospective students to apply to the school.

Organizational skills. Administrators need to be organized so they can manage records, prioritize tasks, and coordinate activities with their staff.

Problem-solving skills. Administrators need to react calmly when a difficult situation arises and develop creative solutions.

Advancement

Education administrators with advanced degrees may be promoted to higher level positions within their department or the college. Some become college presidents, an occupation discussed in the profile on top executives.

Pay

The median annual wage for postsecondary education administrators was $95,410 in May 2019. The median wage is the wage

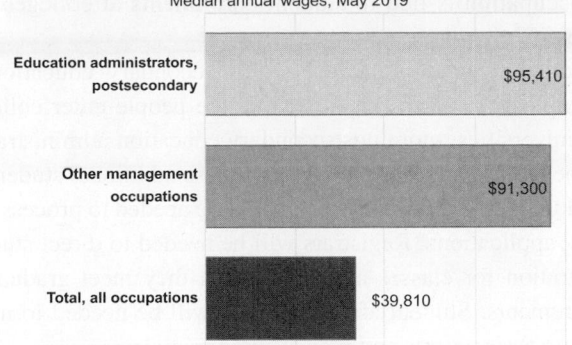

Postsecondary Education Administrators
Median annual wages, May 2019

Education administrators, postsecondary	$95,410
Other management occupations	$91,300
Total, all occupations	$39,810

Note: All Occupations includes all occupations in the U.S. Economy.
Source: U.S. Bureau of Labor Statistics, Occupational Employment Statistics.

at which half the workers in an occupation earned more than that amount and half earned less. The lowest 10 percent earned less than $55,320, and the highest 10 percent earned more than $194,090.

In May 2019, the median annual wages for postsecondary education administrators in the top industries in which they worked were as follows:

Colleges, universities, and professional schools; $97,250
    state, local, and private..
Junior colleges; state, local, and private.................   90,670

As part of their employee benefits plan, many colleges and universities allow full-time employees to attend classes at a discount or for free.

Postsecondary education administrators generally work full time. Most work year-round, but some schools may reduce their hours during the summer.

Job Outlook

Employment of postsecondary education administrators is projected to grow 4 percent from 2019 to 2029, about as fast

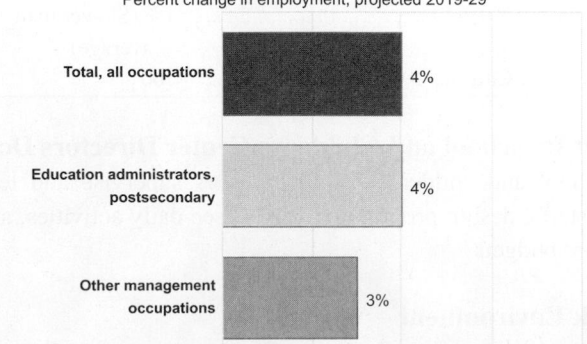

Postsecondary Education Administrators
Percent change in employment, projected 2019-29

Total, all occupations	4%
Education administrators, postsecondary	4%
Other management occupations	3%

Note: All Occupations includes all occupations in the U.S. Economy.
Source: U.S. Bureau of Labor Statistics, Employment Projections program.

as the average for all occupations. Employment growth in the occupation is tied to student enrollments at colleges and universities.

People will continue to seek postsecondary education to accomplish their career goals. As more people enter colleges and universities, more postsecondary education administrators will be needed to serve the needs of these additional students.

Additional admissions officers will be needed to process students' applications. Registrars will be needed to direct student registration for classes and ensure that they meet graduation requirements. Student affairs workers will be needed to make housing assignments and plan events for students.

Provosts and academic dean positions will be limited, since there is typically a set number of these positions per institution.

Despite expected increases in enrollment, employment growth in public colleges and universities will depend on state and local government budgets. If there is a budget deficit, postsecondary institutions may lay off employees, including administrators. If there is a budget surplus, postsecondary institutions may hire more employees.

Job Prospects

Job prospects will be best for candidates who have experience working in higher education.

Employment projections data for postsecondary education administrators, 2019-29					
Occupational Title	SOC Code	Employment, 2019	Projected Employment, 2029	Change, 2019-29	
				Percent	Numeric
SOURCE: U.S. Bureau of Labor Statistics, Employment Projections program					
Education administrators, postsecondary	11-9033	190,500	197,600	4	7,100

State & Area Data
Occupational Employment Statistics (OES)

The Occupational Employment Statistics (OES) program produces employment and wage estimates annually for over 800 occupations. These estimates are available for the nation as a whole, for individual states, and for metropolitan and nonmetropolitan areas.

Contacts for More Information

For more information about registrars or admissions counselors, visit

➤ American Association of Collegiate Registrars and Admissions Officers

For more information about education administrators specializing in student affairs, visit

➤ NASPA - Student Affairs Administrators in Higher Education

Preschool and Childcare Center Directors

Summary

Quick Facts: Preschool and Childcare Center Directors

2019 Median Pay	$48,210 per year $23.18 per hour
Typical Entry-Level Education	Bachelor's degree
Work Experience in a Related Occupation	Less than 5 years
On-the-job Training	None
Number of Jobs, 2019	69,200
Job Outlook, 2019-29	1% (Slower than average)
Employment Change, 2019-29	700

What Preschool and Childcare Center Directors Do

Preschool and childcare center directors supervise and lead their staffs, design program plans, oversee daily activities, and prepare budgets.

Work Environment

Preschool and childcare center directors work primarily in child daycare services. They generally work full time.

How to Become a Preschool or Childcare Center Director

A bachelor's degree and experience in early childhood education are typically required to become a preschool and childcare center director. However, educational requirements vary. Additionally, some employers require these directors to have a nationally recognized credential, such as the Child Development Associate (CDA) credential.

Preschool and childcare center directors lead staff, design program plans, oversee daily activities, and prepare plans and budgets.

Pay

The median annual wage for preschool and childcare center directors was $48,210 in May 2019.

Job Outlook

Employment of preschool and childcare center directors is projected to grow 1 percent from 2019 to 2029, slower than the average for all occupations.

State & Area Data

Explore resources for employment and wages by state and area for preschool and childcare center directors.

What Preschool and Childcare Center Directors Do

Preschool and childcare center directors supervise and lead staffs, design program plans, oversee daily activities, and prepare budgets. They are responsible for all aspects of their center's program.

Duties

Preschool and childcare center directors typically do the following:

- Supervise preschool teachers and childcare workers
- Hire and train new staff members
- Provide professional development opportunities for staff
- Establish policies and communicate them to staff and parents
- Develop educational programs and standards
- Maintain instructional excellence
- Assist staff in communicating with parents and children
- Meet with parents and staff to discuss students' progress
- Prepare budgets and allocate program funds
- Ensure that facilities are maintained and cleaned according to state regulations

Some preschools and childcare centers are independently owned and operated. In these facilities, directors must follow the instructions and guidelines of the owner. Sometimes, the directors are the owners, so they decide how to operate them.

Other preschools and childcare centers are part of a national chain or franchise. The director of a chain or franchise must ensure that the facility meets the parent organization's standards and regulations.

In addition, some preschools and childcare centers, such as Head Start programs, receive state and federal funding. Directors need to follow the requirements set by Department of Health and Human Services for program, staff, and facilities.

Work Environment

Preschool and childcare center directors held about 69,200 jobs in 2019. The largest employers of preschool and childcare center directors were as follows:

Child day care services	65%
Religious, grantmaking, civic, professional, and similar organizations	12
Self-employed workers	9
Elementary and secondary schools; state, local, and private	6

Although preschool and childcare center directors work in schools and childcare centers, they spend most of their day in an office. They also visit classrooms to check on students, speak to preschool teachers or childcare workers, and meet with parents.

Most preschool and childcare center directors work in childcare facilities.

Preschool and childcare center directors assist staff with caring for and teaching children.

Preschool and childcare center directors may find working in an early childhood educational environment rewarding, but they also have significant responsibilities. Coordinating and interacting with staff, parents, and children may be fast paced and stimulating but also stressful.

Work Schedules

Preschool and childcare center directors generally work full time. Some work more than 40 hours per week. They are on the job while the childcare center is open and may work early in the morning or late in the evening. In large facilities, the director and assistant directors may stagger their schedules to ensure that someone is always onsite.

How to Become a Preschool or Childcare Center Director

A bachelor's degree and experience in early childhood education are typically required to become a preschool and childcare center director. However, educational requirements vary. Additionally, some employers require these directors to have a nationally recognized credential, such as the Child Development Associate (CDA) credential.

Education

Most states require preschool and childcare center directors to have at least a bachelor's degree, but educational requirements vary by state. Employers may prefer candidates who have a degree, or at least some postsecondary coursework, in early childhood education. These programs teach child development, provide strategies for instructing young children, and show how to observe and document children's progress.

Work Experience in a Related Occupation

Most positions for preschool and childcare center directors require several years of experience in early childhood education. The length of experience required varies by job.

Preschool and childcare center directors need to be able to interact with children, staff, and parents.

Licenses, Certifications, and Registrations

States may require childcare centers, including those in private homes, to be licensed. To qualify for licensure, staff must pass a background check and meet a minimum training requirement. Some states have more requirements, such as requiring staff to have certifications in cardiopulmonary resuscitation (CPR) and first aid.

Some employers have additional requirements, such as the CDA credential offered by the Council for Professional Recognition. Candidates need to pay a fee, take coursework, obtain experience in the field, and be observed while working with children. This credential needs to be renewed every 3 years.

Important Qualities

Business skills. Preschool and childcare center directors manage childcare centers and need to be able to operate the business effectively.

Communication skills. Directors inform parents and staff about the children's progress. They need good writing and speaking skills to convey this information.

Interpersonal skills. Preschool and childcare center directors must be able to develop relationships with parents, children, and staff.

Leadership skills. Preschool and childcare center directors need leadership skills to supervise staff and inspire diligence. They also must enforce rules and regulations.

Organizational skills. Directors need to maintain clear records about children and staff. In addition, they must be able to multitask when several people or situations require their attention.

Pay

The median annual wage for preschool and childcare center directors was $48,210 in May 2019. The median wage is the wage at which half the workers in an occupation earned more than that amount and half earned less. The lowest 10 percent earned less than $30,850, and the highest 10 percent earned more than $82,590.

In May 2019, the median annual wages for preschool and childcare center directors in the top industries in which they worked were as follows:

Elementary and secondary schools; state, local, and private	$62,120
Religious, grantmaking, civic, professional, and similar organizations	51,990
Child day care services...	46,460

Preschool and childcare center directors generally work full time. Some work more than 40 hours per week. They are on the job while the childcare center is open and may work early in the morning or late in the evening. In large facilities, the director and assistant directors may stagger their schedules to ensure that someone is always onsite.

Preschool and Childcare Center Directors

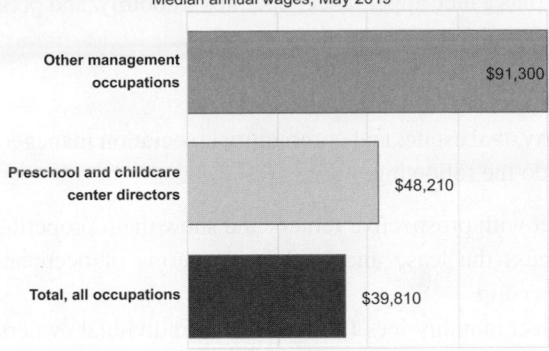

Median annual wages, May 2019

Other management occupations	$91,300
Preschool and childcare center directors	$48,210
Total, all occupations	$39,810

Preschool and Childcare Center Directors

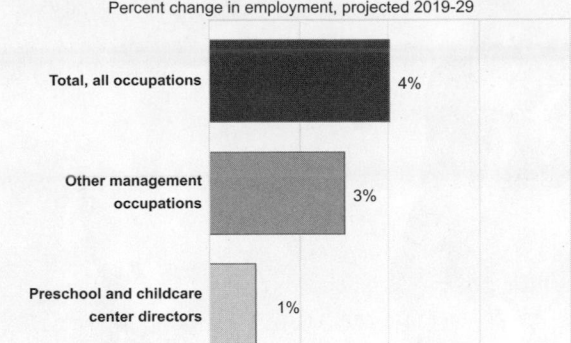

Percent change in employment, projected 2019-29

Total, all occupations	4%
Other management occupations	3%
Preschool and childcare center directors	1%

Note: All Occupations includes all occupations in the U.S. Economy. Source: U.S. Bureau of Labor Statistics, Occupational Employment Statistics.

Note: All Occupations includes all occupations in the U.S. Economy. Source: U.S. Bureau of Labor Statistics, Employment Projections program.

Job Outlook

Employment of preschool and childcare center directors is projected to grow 1 percent from 2019 to 2029, slower than the average for all occupations.

Early childhood education is widely recognized as important for a child's intellectual and emotional development. Working parents are expected to continue to rely on childcare centers and the services they provide; however, the rising cost of childcare and the increasing number of stay-at-home parents are expected to reduce the demand for these workers over the next 10 years.

Employment projections data for preschool and childcare center directors, 2019-29					
Occupational Title	SOC Code	Employment, 2019	Projected Employment, 2029	Change, 2019-29	
				Percent	Numeric
Education and childcare administrators, preschool and daycare	11-9031	69,200	69,900	1	700

State & Area Data
Occupational Employment Statistics (OES)

The Occupational Employment Statistics (OES) program produces employment and wage estimates annually for over 800 occupations. These estimates are available for the nation as a whole, for individual states, and for metropolitan and nonmetropolitan areas.

Contacts for More Information

For more information on childcare centers, visit
➤ Child Care Aware

For information about early childhood education, visit
➤ National Association for the Education of Young Children

For more information about professional credentials, visit
➤ Council for Professional Recognition
➤ National Early Childhood Program Accreditation

Property, Real Estate, and Community Association Managers

Summary

Quick Facts: Property, Real Estate, and Community Association Managers

2019 Median Pay	$58,760 per year $28.25 per hour
Typical Entry-Level Education	High school diploma or equivalent
Work Experience in a Related Occupation	Less than 5 years
On-the-job Training	None
Number of Jobs, 2019	367,900
Job Outlook, 2019-29	0% (Little or no change)
Employment Change, 2019-29	800

What Property, Real Estate, and Community Association Managers Do

Property, real estate, and community association managers take care of the many aspects of residential, commercial, or industrial properties.

Work Environment

Most property, real estate, and community association managers work out of an office. However, many onsite managers spend a large part of their workday doing tasks away from the office, such as showing apartments, inspecting the grounds, or meeting with owners.

How to Become a Property, Real Estate, or Community Association Manager

Although many employers prefer to hire college graduates, a high school diploma combined with several years of related

Licensed real estate managers may show, lease, or sell properties to clients.

work experience is typically required for entry-level positions. Some managers also must have a real estate license.

Pay

The median annual wage for property, real estate, and community association managers was $58,760 in May 2019.

Job Outlook

Employment of property, real estate, and community association managers is projected to show little or no change from 2019 to 2029. Job opportunities should be best for those with a college degree in business administration or real estate and for those who obtain professional credentials.

State & Area Data

Explore resources for employment and wages by state and area for property, real estate, and community association managers.

What Property, Real Estate, and Community Association Managers Do

Property, real estate, and community association managers take care of the many aspects of residential, commercial, or

Onsite managers often show apartments.

industrial properties. They make sure the property is well maintained, has a nice appearance, operates smoothly, and preserves its resale value.

Duties

Property, real estate, and community association managers typically do the following:

- Meet with prospective renters and show them properties
- Discuss the lease and explain the terms of occupancy or ownership
- Collect monthly fees from tenants or individual owners
- Inspect all building facilities, including the grounds and equipment
- Arrange for new equipment or repairs as needed
- Pay bills or delegate bill payment for such expenditures as taxes, insurance, payroll, and maintenance
- Contract for trash removal, maintenance, landscaping, security, and other services
- Investigate and settle complaints, disturbances, and violations
- Keep records of rental activity and owner requests
- Prepare budgets and financial reports
- Comply with anti-discrimination laws when renting or advertising, such as the Americans with Disabilities Act, the Federal Fair Housing Amendment Act, and local fair housing laws

When owners of homes, apartments, office buildings, or retail or industrial properties lack the time or expertise needed for the day-to-day management of their real estate properties, they often hire a property or real estate manager or a community association manager. Managers are employed either directly by the owner or indirectly through a contract with a property management firm.

The following are examples of types of property, real estate, and community association managers:

Property and real estate managers oversee the operation of income-producing commercial or residential properties and ensure that real estate investments achieve their expected revenues. They handle the financial operations of the property, making certain that rent is collected and that mortgages, taxes, insurance premiums, payroll, and maintenance bills are paid on time. They may oversee financial statements, and periodically report to the owners on the status of the property, occupancy rates, expiration dates of leases, and other matters. When vacancies occur, property managers may advertise the property or hire a leasing agent to find a tenant. They may also suggest to the owners what rent to charge.

Community association managers work on behalf of homeowner or community associations to manage the communal property and services of condominiums, cooperatives, and planned communities. Usually hired by a volunteer board of directors of the association, they manage the daily affairs and supervise the maintenance of property and facilities that the homeowners use jointly through the association. Like property managers, community association managers collect monthly fees, prepare financial statements and budgets, negotiate with contractors, and help to resolve complaints. Community association managers also help homeowners and non-owner residents comply with association rules and regulations.

Onsite property managers are responsible for the day-to-day operation of a single property, such as an apartment complex, an office building, or a shopping center. To ensure that the property is well maintained, onsite managers routinely inspect the grounds, facilities, and equipment to determine whether maintenance or repairs are needed. They meet with current tenants to handle requests for repairs or to resolve complaints. They also meet with prospective tenants to show vacant apartments or office space. In addition, onsite managers enforce the terms of rental or lease contracts along with an association's governing rules. They make sure that tenants pay their rent on time, follow restrictions on parking or pets, and follow the correct procedures when the lease is up. Other important duties of onsite managers include keeping accurate, up-to-date records of income and expenditures from property operations and submitting regular expense reports to the senior-level property manager or the owner(s).

Real estate asset managers plan and direct the purchase, sale, and development of real estate properties on behalf of businesses and investors. They focus on long-term strategic financial planning, rather than on the day-to-day operations of the property. In deciding to acquire property, real estate asset managers consider several factors, such as property values, taxes, zoning, population growth, transportation, and traffic volume and patterns. Once a site is selected, they negotiate contracts to buy or lease the property on the most favorable terms. Real estate asset managers review their company's real estate holdings periodically and identify properties that are no longer financially profitable. They then negotiate the sale of the properties or arrange for the end of leases.

Work Environment

Property, real estate, and community association managers held about 367,900 jobs in 2019. The largest employers of property, real estate, and community association managers were as follows:

Real estate	49%
Self-employed workers	38
Civic, social, professional, and similar organizations ...	2

Most property, real estate, and community association managers work out of an office. However, many managers spend much of their time away from their desks. Onsite managers, in particular, may spend a large part of their workday visiting the building engineer, showing apartments, dealing with owners and board members, checking on the janitorial and maintenance

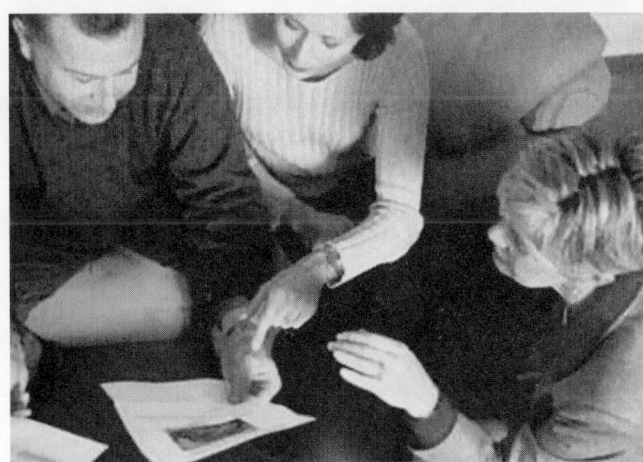

Property, real estate, and community association managers must interact with clients every day.

staff, or investigating problems reported by residents. Real estate asset managers may spend time away from home while traveling to company real estate holdings or searching for properties to buy.

Managing properties or community associations, or selling and leasing real estate, can sometimes be stressful.

Work Schedules

Property, real estate, and community association managers often attend evening meetings with residents, property owners, community association board members, or civic groups. As a result, long workdays are common. Some apartment managers are required to live in the apartment complexes where they work, so that they are available to respond to emergencies even when they are off duty.

Most property, real estate, and community association managers work full time.

How to Become a Property, Real Estate, or Community Association Manager

Although many employers prefer to hire college graduates, a high school diploma combined with several years of related work experience is typically required for entry-level positions. Some managers also must have a real estate license.

Education

A high school diploma or equivalent is typically required for most onsite property management positions. However, many employers prefer to hire college graduates for commercial management positions and offsite positions dealing with a property's finances or contract management. A bachelor's or master's degree in business administration, accounting, finance, real estate, or public administration is preferred for these types of positions.

Work Experience in a Related Occupation

Property, real estate, and community association managers typically have several years of prior work experience. Experience

A high school diploma combined with several years of related work experience is typically required for entry-level positions.

in real estate sales is a good background for onsite managers because real estate salespeople also show commercial properties to prospective tenants or buyers.

Licenses, Certifications, and Registrations

Real estate managers who buy or sell property must have a real estate license in the state in which they practice. In a few states, property and community association managers also must have a real estate license. Managers of public housing subsidized by the federal government must hold certifications.

Property, real estate, and community association managers working in Alaska, Delaware, Florida, Georgia, Hawaii, Illinois, Nevada, Virginia, and the District of Columbia are required to obtain professional credentials or licensure. Requirements vary by state, but many managers working in states without requirements still obtain designations to show competence and professionalism. BOMI International, the Community Associations Institute, the Institute of Real Estate Management, the National Association of Residential Property Managers, and the Community Association Managers International Certification Board all offer various designations, certifications, and professional development courses. Most states require recertification every 2 years.

In addition, employers may require managers to attend formal training programs from various professional and trade real estate associations. Employers send managers to these programs to develop their management skills and expand their knowledge of specialized fields, such as how to operate and maintain mechanical systems in buildings, how to improve property values, insurance and risk management, personnel management, business and real estate law, community association risks and liabilities, tenant relations, communications, accounting and financial concepts, and reserve funding. Managers also participate in these programs to prepare themselves for positions of greater responsibility in property management. With related job experience, completing these programs and receiving a satisfactory score on a written exam can lead to certification or the formal award of a professional designation by the sponsoring association.

Advancement

Many people begin property management careers as assistant managers, working closely with a property manager. In time, many assistants advance to property manager positions.

Some people start as onsite managers of apartment buildings, office complexes, or community associations. As they gain experience, they may advance to positions of greater responsibility. Those who excel as onsite managers often transfer to assistant offsite property manager positions, in which they gain experience handling a broad range of property management responsibilities.

The responsibilities and pay of property, real estate, and community association managers increase as these workers manage more and larger properties. Property managers are often responsible for several properties at a time. Some experienced managers open their own property management firms.

Important Qualities

Communication skills. Property, real estate, and community association managers must understand leasing or rental contracts and must be able to clearly explain the materials and answer questions raised by a resident or group of board members.

Customer-service skills. Property, real estate, and community association managers must provide excellent customer service to keep existing clients and expand their business with new ones.

Interpersonal skills. Because property, real estate, and community association managers interact with people every day, they must have excellent interpersonal skills.

Listening skills. Property, real estate, and community association managers must listen to and understand residents and property owners in order to meet their needs.

Organizational skills. Property, real estate, and community association managers must be able to plan, coordinate, and direct multiple contractors at the same time, often for multiple properties.

Problem-solving skills. Property, real estate, and community association managers must be able to mediate disputes or legal issues between residents, homeowners, or board members.

Pay

The median annual wage for property, real estate, and community association managers was $58,760 in May 2019. The median wage is the wage at which half the workers in an occupation earned more than that amount and half earned less. The lowest 10 percent earned less than $31,030, and the highest 10 percent earned more than $129,160.

In May 2019, the median annual wages for property, real estate, and community association managers in the top industries in which they worked were as follows:

Civic, social, professional, and similar organizations.. $57,580

Real estate... 56,370

Property, real estate, and community association managers often attend evening meetings with residents, property owners, community association board members, or civic groups. As a result, long workdays are common. Some apartment managers are required to live in the apartment complexes where they work, so that they are available to respond to emergencies even when they are off duty.

Most property, real estate, and community association managers work full time.

Job Outlook

Employment of property, real estate, and community association managers is projected to show little or no change from 2019 to 2029.

Employment demand will be driven by the number people living in buildings that property management companies operate, such as apartment buildings, condominiums, cooperatives, planned communities, and senior housing.

Growth in the single-family housing market may have a positive influence on demand, as some new housing developments will require property managers to oversee jointly owned common areas, such as pools, gyms, and business centers and to enforce homeowner association laws. However, the automation of some property management tasks, such as posting vacancies and assigning maintenance requests, may slow employment growth.

Job Prospects

Job opportunities should be best for those with a bachelor's degree in business administration, real estate, or a related field and for those with professional certification.

Because of the projected increase in the elderly population, particularly good job opportunities are expected for those with experience managing retirement centers, age-restricted communities, and healthcare facilities.

Employment projections data for property, real estate, and community association managers, 2019-29					
Occupational Title	SOC Code	Employment, 2019	Projected Employment, 2029	Change, 2019-29	
				Percent	Numeric
SOURCE: U.S. Bureau of Labor Statistics, Employment Projections program					
Property, real estate, and community association managers	11-9141	367,900	368,700	0	800

State & Area Data
Occupational Employment Statistics (OES)

The Occupational Employment Statistics (OES) program produces employment and wage estimates annually for over 800 occupations. These estimates are available for the nation as a whole, for individual states, and for metropolitan and nonmetropolitan areas.

Property, Real Estate, and Community Association Managers

Median annual wages, May 2019

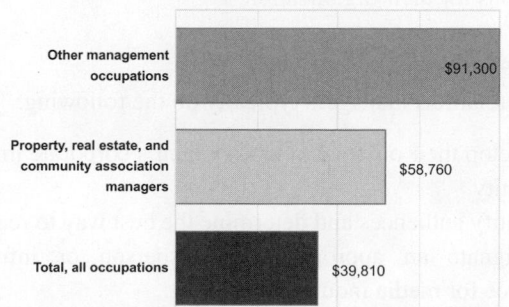

Note: All Occupations includes all occupations in the U.S. Economy.
Source: U.S. Bureau of Labor Statistics, Occupational Employment Statistics.

Property, Real Estate, and Community Association Managers

Percent change in employment, projected 2019-29

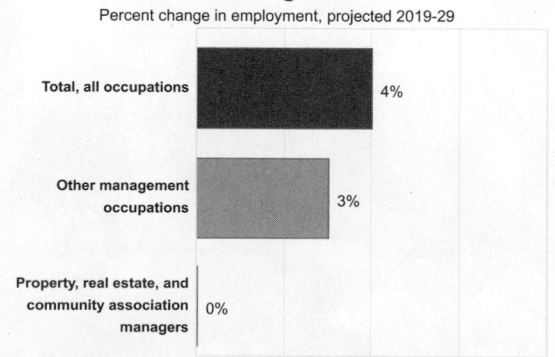

Note: All Occupations includes all occupations in the U.S. Economy.
Source: U.S. Bureau of Labor Statistics, Employment Projections program.

Contacts for More Information

For information about professional designation and certification programs for property, real estate, and community association managers, visit

➤ BOMI International

➤ Community Associations Institute
➤ Community Association Managers International Certification Board
➤ Institute of Real Estate Management
➤ National Association of Residential Property Managers

Public Relations and Fundraising Managers

Summary

Quick Facts: Public Relations and Fundraising Managers

2019 Median Pay	$116,180 per year $55.86 per hour
Typical Entry-Level Education	Bachelor's degree
Work Experience in a Related Occupation	5 years or more
On-the-job Training	None
Number of Jobs, 2019	88,000
Job Outlook, 2019-29	9% (Much faster than average)
Employment Change, 2019-29	8,100

What Public Relations and Fundraising Managers Do

Public relations managers direct the creation of materials that will enhance the public image of their employer or client. Fundraising managers coordinate campaigns that bring in donations for their organization.

Work Environment

Public relations and fundraising managers generally work in offices during regular business hours. However, many of these managers travel to give speeches and to attend meetings and community activities. Some work more than 40 hours per week.

How to Become a Public Relations or Fundraising Manager

Public relations and fundraising managers need at least a bachelor's degree, and some positions may require a master's degree. Many years of related work experience are also necessary.

Pay

The median annual wage for public relations and fundraising managers was $116,180 in May 2019.

Job Outlook

Employment of public relations and fundraising managers is projected to grow 9 percent from 2019 to 2029, much faster than the average for all occupations. Employment of public relations managers will be driven by the need for organizations to maintain their public image, especially with the growth of social media. The need to raise funds for nonprofit organizations will require more fundraising managers.

State & Area Data

Explore resources for employment and wages by state and area for public relations and fundraising managers.

What Public Relations and Fundraising Managers Do

Public relations managers plan and direct the creation of material that will enhance the public image of their employer or client. Fundraising managers coordinate campaigns that bring in donations for their organization.

Duties

Public relations managers typically do the following:

- Develop their organization's or client's corporate image and identity
- Identify audiences and determine the best way to reach them
- Designate an appropriate spokesperson or information source for media inquiries
- Help clients communicate effectively with the public
- Write press releases and prepare information for the media
- Assist and inform an organization's executives and spokespeople

Public relations and fundraising managers plan campaigns to raise donations or improve the public image of their clients.

Public relations and fundraising managers plan an organization's communication with the public, including consumers, investors, and media outlets.

- Devise advertising and promotion programs
- Assign, supervise, and review the activities of staff

Fundraising managers typically do the following:

- Develop and carry out fundraising strategies
- Identify and contact potential donors
- Create and plan different events that can generate donations
- Meet face-to-face with donors
- Apply for grants
- Manage progress toward achieving an organization's fundraising goals
- Assign, supervise, and review the activities of staff

Public relations managers review press releases and sponsor corporate events to help maintain and improve the image of their organization or client.

Public relations managers help clarify their organization's point of view to its main audience through media releases and interviews. They monitor social, economic, and political trends that might affect their organization, and they recommend ways to enhance the firm's image on the basis of those trends. For example, in response to concern about damage to the environment, the public relations manager for an oil company may create a campaign to publicize its efforts to develop cleaner fuels.

In large organizations, public relations managers often supervise a staff of public relations specialists. They also work with advertising, promotions, and marketing managers to ensure that advertising campaigns are compatible with the image the company or client is trying to portray. For example, if a firm decides to emphasize its appeal to a certain group, such as young people, the public relations manager needs to make sure that current advertisements are well received by that group.

In addition, public relations managers may handle internal communications, such as company newsletters, and may help financial managers produce an organization's reports. They may also draft speeches, arrange interviews, and maintain other forms of public contact to help the organization's top executives.

Public relations managers must be able to work well with many types of specialists. In some cases, the information they write has legal consequences. As a result, they must work with the company's or client's lawyers to be sure that the information they release is both legally accurate and clear to the public.

Fundraising managers oversee campaigns and events intended to bring in donations for their organization. Many organizations that hire fundraising workers rely heavily on the donations they gather in order to run their operations.

Fundraising managers usually decide which fundraising techniques are necessary in a certain situation. Common techniques include annual campaigns, capital campaigns, planned giving, and soliciting for major gifts. Social media has created another avenue for fundraising managers to connect with potential donors and to spread their organization's message.

Those who work on annual campaigns focus heavily on contacting donors who have given in the past to request that they give again. Finding new contacts for future donations is also part of a successful annual campaign.

In contrast, fundraising managers who work on capital campaigns generally focus on raising money over a short time period for a specific project, such as the construction of a new building at a university.

Fundraising managers who spend most of their time on planned giving must have specialized training in taxes related to gifts of stocks, bonds, charitable annuities, and real estate bequests in a will. Major gifts are a feature of many fundraising efforts, and fundraising managers generally request these gifts in person, given the large value of the potential donation.

Work Environment

Public relations and fundraising managers held about 88,000 jobs in 2019. The largest employers of public relations and fundraising managers were as follows:

Educational services; state, local, and private	21%
Religious, grantmaking, civic, professional, and similar organizations	21
Professional, scientific, and technical services	15
Management of companies and enterprises	8

Public relations and fundraising managers usually work in offices during regular business hours. However, many must travel to deliver speeches and attend meetings and community activities.

They work in high-stress environments, often managing and organizing several events at the same time.

Public relations managers and specialists work in fairly high-stress environments, often managing and organizing several events at the same time.

Work Schedules

Most public relations and fundraising managers work full time, which often includes long workdays. Some managers work more than 40 hours per week.

How to Become a Public Relations or Fundraising Manager

Public relations and fundraising managers need at least a bachelor's degree, and some positions may require a master's degree. Many years of related work experience are also necessary.

Education

For public relations and fundraising management positions, a bachelor's degree in public relations, communications, English, fundraising, or journalism is generally required. However, some employers prefer to hire candidates who have a master's degree, particularly in public relations, journalism, fundraising, or nonprofit management.

A bachelor's degree and years of work experience are typically needed for public relations or fundraising manager positions.

Courses in advertising, business administration, public affairs, public speaking, and creative and technical writing can be helpful.

Licenses, Certifications, and Registrations

Although not mandatory, public relations managers can become certified through the Public Relations Society of America. Candidates qualify based on a combination of experience and education and must pass an exam to become certified.

The Certified Fund Raising Executive program, offered by CFRE International, is also voluntary, but fundraisers who are awarded certification demonstrate a level of professional competency to prospective employers. To become certified, candidates must meet certain education, professional practice, and professional performance requirements, as well as pass an exam. Fundraisers must apply for renewal every 3 years to keep their certification valid.

The International Association of Business Communicators offers two credentials that allow communications specialists to demonstrate higher levels of knowledge and expertise. Public relations and fundraising managers may apply to take the certification exams when they have 6 to 8 years of experience in the communications field.

Work Experience in a Related Occupation

Public relations and fundraising managers must have several years of experience in a related occupation, such as public relations specialist or fundraiser.

Important Qualities

Interpersonal skills. Public relations and fundraising managers deal with the public regularly; therefore, they must be friendly enough to build a rapport with, and receive support from, their media contacts and donors.

Leadership skills. Managers often lead large teams of specialists or fundraisers and must be able to guide their activities.

Organizational skills. Public relations and fundraising managers are often in charge of running several events at the same time, requiring superior organizational skills.

Problem-solving skills. Managers sometimes must explain how the company or client is handling sensitive issues. They must use good judgment in what they report and how they report it.

Speaking skills. Public relations and fundraising managers regularly speak for their organization. When doing so, they must be able to explain the organization's position clearly.

Writing skills. Managers must be able to write well-organized and clear press releases and speeches. They must be able to succinctly present the key messages they want to get across in order to keep the attention of busy readers or listeners.

Pay

The median annual wage for public relations and fundraising managers was $116,180 in May 2019. The median wage is the wage

Public Relations and Fundraising Managers

Median annual wages, May 2019

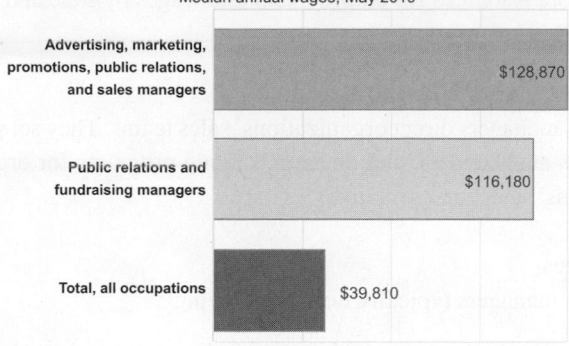

Note: All Occupations includes all occupations in the U.S. Economy.
Source: U.S. Bureau of Labor Statistics, Occupational Employment Statistics.

at which half the workers in an occupation earned more than that amount and half earned less. The lowest 10 percent earned less than $64,790, and the highest 10 percent earned more than $208,000.

In May 2019, the median annual wages for public relations and fundraising managers in the top industries in which they worked were as follows:

Professional, scientific, and technical services.....	$133,480
Management of companies and enterprises..........	131,560
Religious, grantmaking, civic, professional, and similar organizations	117,430
Educational services; state, local, and private	102,530

Most public relations and fundraising managers work full time, which often includes long workdays. Some managers work more than 40 hours per week.

Job Outlook

Employment of public relations and fundraising managers is projected to grow 9 percent from 2019 to 2029, much faster than the average for all occupations.

Organizations continue to emphasize community outreach and customer relations as a way to enhance their reputation and visibility. Public opinion can change quickly, particularly as social media increases the speed at which news travels. Consequently, public relations managers will be needed to coordinate and help respond to news developments to maintain their organization's reputation.

Fundraising managers are expected to become increasingly important for organizations, such as colleges and universities, that depend heavily on donations. More nonprofit organizations are focusing on cultivating an online presence and are increasingly using social media for fundraising activities.

Job Prospects

About 7,600 openings for public relations and fundraising managers are projected each year, on average, over the decade.

Public Relations and Fundraising Managers

Percent change in employment, projected 2019-29

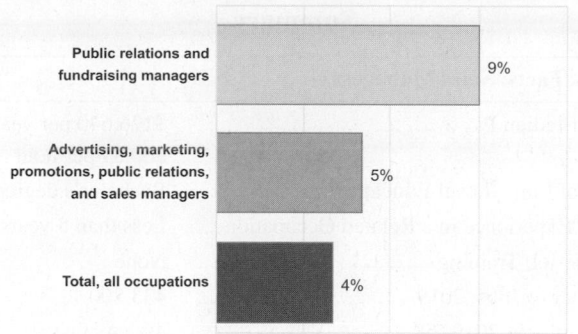

Note: All Occupations includes all occupations in the U.S. Economy.
Source: U.S. Bureau of Labor Statistics, Employment Projections program.

Many of those openings are expected to result from the need to replace workers who transfer to different occupations or exit the labor force, such as to retire.

Prospective public relations managers should face strong competition at businesses that have large media exposure and at prestigious public relations firms.

Job prospects for fundraising managers should be best for those with a master's degree in philanthropic studies or fundraising. These degree programs lead to experience in the industry, giving graduates an advantage over those who do not have such experience.

Employment projections data for public relations and fundraising managers, 2019-29					
Occupational Title	SOC Code	Employment, 2019	Projected Employment, 2029	Change, 2019-29	
				Percent	Numeric
SOURCE: U.S. Bureau of Labor Statistics, Employment Projections program					
Public relations and fundraising managers	11-2030	88,000	96,100	9	8,100

State & Area Data
Occupational Employment Statistics (OES)
The Occupational Employment Statistics (OES) program produces employment and wage estimates annually for over 800 occupations. These estimates are available for the nation as a whole, for individual states, and for metropolitan and nonmetropolitan areas.

Contacts for More Information
For more information about public relations and fundraising managers, including professional certification, visit
➤ CFRE International
➤ International Association of Business Communicators
➤ Public Relations Society of America

Sales Managers

Summary

Quick Facts: Sales Managers

2019 Median Pay	$126,640 per year
	$60.89 per hour
Typical Entry-Level Education	Bachelor's degree
Work Experience in a Related Occupation	Less than 5 years
On-the-job Training	None
Number of Jobs, 2019	433,800
Job Outlook, 2019-29	4% (As fast as average)
Employment Change, 2019-29	15,400

What Sales Managers Do

Sales managers direct organizations' sales teams.

Work Environment

Sales managers often are required to travel. Most sales managers work full time, and they often have to work additional hours on evenings and weekends.

How to Become a Sales Manager

Most sales managers have a bachelor's degree and work experience as a sales representative.

Pay

The median annual wage for sales managers was $126,640 in May 2019.

Job Outlook

Employment of sales managers is projected to grow 4 percent from 2019 to 2029, about as fast as the average for all occupations. Employment growth of these managers will depend primarily on growth or contraction in the industries that employ them.

Sales managers set sales goals, analyze data, and develop training programs for organizations' sales representatives.

State & Area Data

Explore resources for employment and wages by state and area for sales managers.

What Sales Managers Do

Sales managers direct organizations' sales teams. They set sales goals, analyze data, and develop training programs for organizations' sales representatives.

Duties

Sales managers typically do the following:

- Resolve customer complaints regarding sales and service
- Prepare budgets and approve expenditures
- Monitor customer preferences to determine the focus of sales efforts
- Analyze sales statistics
- Project sales and determine the profitability of products and services
- Determine discount rates or special pricing plans
- Develop plans to acquire new customers or clients through direct sales techniques, cold calling, and business-to-business marketing visits
- Assign sales territories and set sales quotas
- Plan and coordinate training programs for sales staff

Sales managers' responsibilities vary with the size of their organizations. However, most sales managers direct the

Sales managers recruit, hire, and train new members of the sales staff.

distribution of goods and services by assigning sales territories, setting sales goals, and establishing training programs for the organization's sales representatives.

Sales managers recruit, hire, and train new members of the sales staff, including retail sales workers and wholesale and manufacturing sales representatives.

Sales managers advise sales representatives on ways to improve their sales performance. In large multiproduct organizations, they oversee regional and local sales managers and their staffs.

Sales managers also stay in contact with dealers and distributors. They analyze sales statistics generated from their staff to determine the sales potential and inventory requirements of products and stores and to monitor customers' preferences.

Sales managers work closely with managers from other departments in the organization. For example, the marketing department identifies new customers that the sales department can target. The relationship between these two departments is critical to helping an organization expand its client base. Sales managers also work closely with research and design departments because they know customers' preferences, and with warehousing departments because they know inventory needs.

Sales managers are increasingly using data on customer shopping habits to identify potential customers more effectively. This allows them more time to facilitate sales through customized sales pitches to individual customers.

The following are examples of types of sales managers:

Business to business (B2B) sales managers oversee sales from one business to another. These managers may work for a manufacturer selling to a wholesaler, or a wholesaler selling to a retailer. Examples of these workers include sales managers overseeing sales of software to business firms, and sales managers overseeing wholesale food sales to grocery stores.

Business to consumer (B2C) sales managers oversee direct sales between businesses and individual consumers. These managers typically work in retail settings. Examples of these workers include sales managers of automobile dealerships and department stores.

Work Environment

Sales managers held about 433,800 jobs in 2019. The largest employers of sales managers were as follows:

Wholesale trade	19%
Retail trade	16
Professional, scientific, and technical services	11
Manufacturing	10
Finance and insurance	9

Sales managers have a lot of responsibility, and the position can be stressful. Many sales managers travel to national, regional, and local offices and to dealers' and distributors' offices.

Sales managers have a lot of responsibility, and the position can be stressful.

Work Schedules

Most sales managers work full time, and they often have to work additional hours on evenings and weekends.

How to Become a Sales Manager

Most sales managers have a bachelor's degree and work experience as a sales representative.

Education

Sales managers are typically required to have a bachelor's degree, although some positions may only require a high school diploma. Courses in business law, management, economics, accounting, finance, mathematics, marketing, and statistics are advantageous.

Work Experience in a Related Occupation

Work experience is typically required for someone to become a sales manager. The preferred duration varies, but employers usually seek candidates who have at least 1 to 5 years of experience in sales.

Sales managers typically enter the occupation from other sales and related occupations, such as retail sales workers, wholesale and manufacturing sales representatives, or purchasing agents. In small organizations, the number of sales manager positions often is limited, so advancement for sales workers

Most sales managers have a bachelor's degree and previous work experience as a sales representative.

usually comes slowly. In large organizations, promotion may occur more quickly.

Important Qualities

Analytical skills. Sales managers must collect and interpret complex data to target the most promising geographic areas and demographic groups, and determine the most effective sales strategies.

Communication skills. Sales managers need to work with colleagues and customers, so they must be able to communicate clearly.

Customer-service skills. When helping to make a sale, sales managers must listen and respond to the customer's needs.

Leadership skills. Sales managers must be able to evaluate how their sales staff performs and must develop strategies for meeting sales goals.

Pay

The median annual wage for sales managers was $126,640 in May 2019. The median wage is the wage at which half the workers in an occupation earned more than that amount and half earned less. The lowest 10 percent earned less than $59,810, and the highest 10 percent earned more than $208,000.

In May 2019, the median annual wages for sales managers in the top industries in which they worked were as follows:

Finance and insurance	$156,060
Professional, scientific, and technical services	150,110
Manufacturing	134,830
Wholesale trade	126,400
Retail trade	86,180

Compensation methods for sales managers vary significantly with the type of organization and the product sold. Most employers use a combination of salary and commissions or salary plus bonuses. Commissions usually are a percentage of the value of sales, whereas bonuses may depend on individual performance, on the performance of all sales workers in the group or district, or on the organization's performance.

Most sales managers work full time, and they often have to work additional hours on evenings and weekends.

Job Outlook

Employment of sales managers is projected to grow 4 percent from 2019 to 2029, about as fast as the average for all occupations. Employment growth of these managers will depend primarily on growth or contraction in the industries that employ them.

An effective sales team remains crucial for profitability. As the economy grows, organizations will focus on generating new sales and will look to their sales strategy as a way to increase competitiveness.

Online shopping is expected to continue to increase, meaning more sales will be completed without a sales worker involved in the transaction. However, "brick and mortar" retail stores also are expected to increase their emphasis on customer service as a way to compete with online sellers. Because sales managers will be

Sales Managers
Median annual wages, May 2019

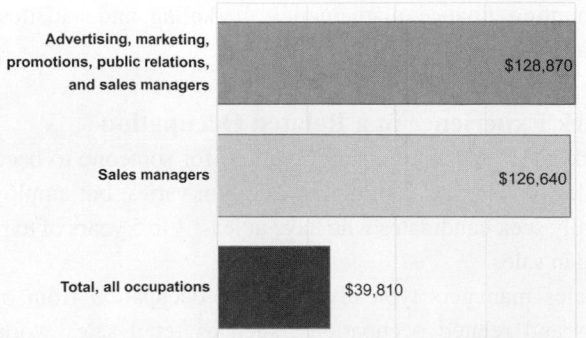

Advertising, marketing, promotions, public relations, and sales managers	$128,870
Sales managers	$126,640
Total, all occupations	$39,810

Note: All Occupations includes all occupations in the U.S. Economy.
Source: U.S. Bureau of Labor Statistics, Occupational Employment Statistics.

Sales Managers
Percent change in employment, projected 2019-29

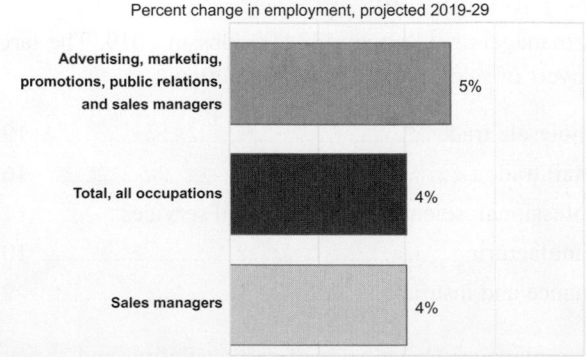

Advertising, marketing, promotions, public relations, and sales managers	5%
Total, all occupations	4%
Sales managers	4%

Note: All Occupations includes all occupations in the U.S. Economy.
Source: U.S. Bureau of Labor Statistics, Employment Projections program.

needed to direct and navigate this mix between online and brick-and-mortar sales, sustained demand is expected for these workers.

Job Prospects

Similar to other managerial positions, competition for these jobs is expected to be strong as there are more applicants than open positions.

Employment projections data for sales managers, 2019-29					
Occupational Title	SOC Code	Employment, 2019	Projected Employment, 2029	Change, 2019-29	
				Percent	Numeric
SOURCE: U.S. Bureau of Labor Statistics, Employment Projections program					
Sales managers	11-2022	433,800	449,200	4	15,400

State & Area Data
Occupational Employment Statistics (OES)

The Occupational Employment Statistics (OES) program produces employment and wage estimates annually for over 800 occupations. These estimates are available for the nation as a whole, for individual states, and for metropolitan and nonmetropolitan areas.

Contacts for More Information

For more information about sales managers, visit
➤ Sales Management Association

Social and Community Service Managers

Summary

Quick Facts: Social and Community Service Managers	
2019 Median Pay	$67,150 per year $32.28 per hour
Typical Entry-Level Education	Bachelor's degree
Work Experience in a Related Occupation	Less than 5 years
On-the-job Training	None
Number of Jobs, 2019	175,500
Job Outlook, 2019-29	17% (Much faster than average)
Employment Change, 2019-29	29,800

What Social and Community Service Managers Do

Social and community service managers coordinate and supervise programs and organizations that support public well-being.

Social and community service managers suggest and implement improvements to programs and services.

Work Environment

Social and community service managers work for nonprofit organizations, for-profit social service companies, and government agencies. Most work full time.

How to Become a Social and Community Service Manager

Social and community service managers typically need at least a bachelor's degree and work experience.

Pay

The median annual wage for social and community service managers was $67,150 in May 2019.

Job Outlook

Employment of social and community service managers is projected to grow 17 percent from 2019 to 2029, much faster than the average for all occupations. Employment growth will be driven by increases in the elderly population and increases in demand for substance abuse treatment and mental health and health-related services.

State & Area Data

Explore resources for employment and wages by state and area for social and community service managers.

What Social and Community Service Managers Do

Social and community service managers coordinate and supervise programs and organizations that support public well-being. They direct workers who provide these services to the public.

Duties

Social and community service managers typically do the following:

- Work with community members and other stakeholders to identify necessary programs and services

Social and community service managers meet with community members and funding providers to discuss their programs.

- Oversee administrative aspects of programs to meet the objectives of the stakeholders
- Analyze data to determine the effectiveness of programs
- Suggest and implement improvements to programs and services
- Plan and manage outreach activities for increased awareness of programs
- Write proposals for social services funding

Social and community service managers work for a variety of organizations. Some of these organizations focus on working with a particular demographic, such as children, people who are homeless, older adults, or veterans. Others focus on helping people with particular challenges, such as substance abuse, mental health needs, and chronic hunger.

A routine part of social and community service managers' job is to show that their programs and services are effective. They collect statistics and other information to evaluate the impact their programs have on the community or their target audience. They are usually required to report this information to administrators or funders. They may also use evaluations to identify opportunities to improve their programs, such as providing mentorship and assessments for their staff.

Although the specific job duties of social and community service managers may vary with the size of the organization, most managers recruit, hire, and train new staff members. They also supervise staff, such as social workers, who provide services directly to clients. Additionally, they may perform some of the services of the workers they oversee.

In large agencies, social and community service managers tend to have specialized duties. They may be responsible for running only one program in an organization and reporting to the agency's upper management. They usually do not design programs but instead supervise and implement programs set up by administrators, elected officials, or other stakeholders.

In small organizations, social and community managers often have many roles. They represent their organization through

public speaking engagements or in communitywide committees; oversee programs and execute their implementations; spend time on administrative tasks, such as managing budgets; and help with raising funds and meeting with potential donors.

Work Environment

Social and community service managers held about 175,500 jobs in 2019. The largest employers of social and community service managers were as follows:

Individual and family services	29%
Religious, grantmaking, civic, professional, and similar organizations	12
Nursing and residential care facilities............................	11
Local government, excluding education and hospitals......	10
Community and vocational rehabilitation services......	9

Social and community service managers work for nonprofit organizations, for-profit social service companies, and government agencies. They also work in a variety of settings, including offices, clinics, hospitals, and shelters.

Work Schedules

Most social and community service managers work full time. Some work more than 40 hours per week.

How to Become a Social and Community Service Manager

Social and community service managers typically need at least a bachelor's degree and work experience. However, some positions also require a master's degree.

Education

Social and community service manager jobs typically require a bachelor's degree in social work, public or business administration, public health, or a related field. However, some positions also require a master's degree.

Social and community service managers work in a variety of settings, including offices, clinics, hospitals, and shelters.

Social and community service managers typically need at least a bachelor's degree and work experience in a related occupation.

Work Experience

Workers usually need experience in order to become a social and community service manager, and it is essential for those with a bachelor's degree. Candidates can get this experience by working as a social worker, substance abuse counselor, or in a similar occupation.

Important Qualities

Analytical skills. Social and community service managers need to understand and evaluate data in order to provide strategic guidance to their organization. They must be able to monitor and assess current programs as well as determine new initiatives.

Communication skills. Social and community service managers must be able to speak and write clearly. Public speaking experience is also helpful because these managers often participate in community outreach.

Managerial skills. Social and community service managers spend much of their time administering budgets and responding to a variety of issues.

Problem-solving skills. Social and community service managers must be able to address client, staff, and agency-related issues.

Time-management skills. Social and community service managers must prioritize and handle numerous tasks, often in a short timeframe.

Pay

The median annual wage for social and community service managers was $67,150 in May 2019. The median wage is the wage at which half the workers in an occupation earned more than that amount and half earned less. The lowest 10 percent earned less than $41,220, and the highest 10 percent earned more than $112,480.

In May 2019, the median annual wages for social and community service managers in the top industries in which they worked were as follows:

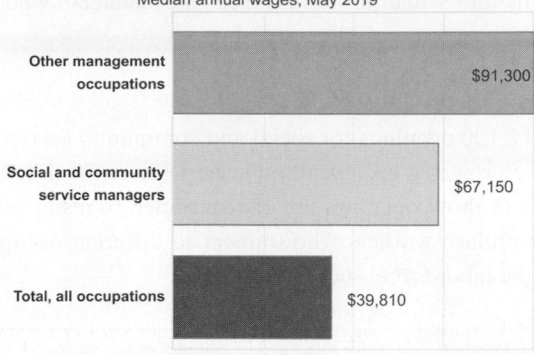

Social and Community Service Managers
Median annual wages, May 2019

Other management occupations	$91,300
Social and community service managers	$67,150
Total, all occupations	$39,810

Note: All Occupations includes all occupations in the U.S. Economy.
Source: U.S. Bureau of Labor Statistics, Occupational Employment Statistics.

Local government, excluding education and hospitals	$85,550
Religious, grantmaking, civic, professional, and similar organizations	70,830
Nursing and residential care facilities	62,020
Individual and family services	61,920
Community and vocational rehabilitation services	60,180

Most social and community service managers work full time. Some work more than 40 hours per week.

Job Outlook

Employment of social and community service managers is projected to grow 17 percent from 2019 to 2029, much faster than the average for all occupations.

Much of the job growth in this occupation is the result of an aging population. An increase in the number of older adults will result in a need for more social services, such as adult daycare, creating demand for social and community service managers. Employment of social and community service managers is expected to increase the most in industries serving older adults.

In addition, employment growth is projected as people continue to seek treatment for their addictions and as people with

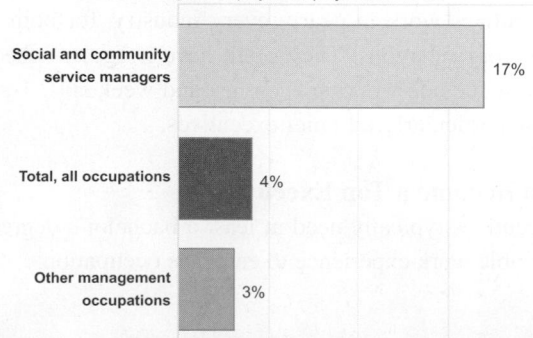

Social and Community Service Managers
Percent change in employment, projected 2019-29

Social and community service managers	17%
Total, all occupations	4%
Other management occupations	3%

Note: All Occupations includes all occupations in the U.S. Economy.
Source: U.S. Bureau of Labor Statistics, Employment Projections program.

substance abuse disorders are increasingly sent to treatment programs rather than to jail. As a result, managers who direct treatment programs will be needed.

Job Prospects

About 17,100 openings for social and community service managers are projected each year, on average, over the decade.

Many of those openings are also expected to result from the need to replace workers who transfer to different occupations or exit the labor force, such as to retire.

Employment projections data for social and community service managers, 2019-29					
Occupational Title	SOC Code	Employment, 2019	Projected Employment, 2029	Change, 2019-29	
				Percent	Numeric
SOURCE: U.S. Bureau of Labor Statistics, Employment Projections program					
Social and community service managers	11-9151	175,500	205,400	17	29,800

State & Area Data

Occupational Employment Statistics (OES)

The Occupational Employment Statistics (OES) program produces employment and wage estimates annually for over 800 occupations. These estimates are available for the nation as a whole, for individual states, and for metropolitan and nonmetropolitan areas.

Contacts for More Information

For more information about social and community service managers, visit

➤ The Network for Social Work Management
➤ Council on Social Work Education
➤ National Association of Social Workers

Top Executives

Summary

Quick Facts: Top Executives

2019 Median Pay	$104,690 per year $50.33 per hour
Typical Entry-Level Education	Bachelor's degree
Work Experience in a Related Occupation	5 years or more
On-the-job Training	None
Number of Jobs, 2019	2,774,300
Job Outlook, 2019-29	4% (As fast as average)
Employment Change, 2019-29	115,000

What Top Executives Do

Top executives plan strategies and policies to ensure that an organization meets its goals.

Work Environment

Top executives work in nearly every industry, for both small and large organizations. They often have irregular schedules, which may include working evenings and weekends. Travel is common, particularly for chief executives.

How to Become a Top Executive

Top executives typically need at least a bachelor's degree and considerable work experience to enter the occupation.

Pay

The median annual wage for chief executives was $184,460 in May 2019.

The median annual wage for general and operations managers was $100,780 in May 2019.

Job Outlook

Overall employment of top executives is projected to grow 4 percent from 2019 to 2029, about as fast as the average for all occupations. Projected employment growth varies by occupation.

State & Area Data

Explore resources for employment and wages by state and area for top executives.

What Top Executives Do

Top executives plan strategies and policies to ensure that an organization meets its goals. They coordinate and direct work activities of companies and organizations.

Top executives are the highest level of management at an organization and often work closely with other executives and managers.

Top executives often report to a board of directors.

Duties

Top executives typically do the following:

- Establish and carry out departmental or organizational goals, policies, and procedures
- Direct and oversee an organization's financial and budgetary activities
- Manage general activities related to making products and providing services
- Consult with other executives, staff, and board members about general operations
- Negotiate or approve contracts and agreements
- Appoint department heads and managers
- Analyze financial statements, sales reports, and other performance indicators
- Identify places to cut costs and to improve performance, policies, and programs

The responsibilities of top executives largely depend on an organization's size. In small organizations, such as an independent retail store, an owner or manager often is responsible for hiring, training, quality control, and day-to-day supervisory duties. In large organizations, chief executives typically focus on formulating policies and planning strategies, while general and operations managers direct day-to-day operations.

The following are examples of types of top executives:

Chief executive officers (CEOs), who are also known by titles such as *executive director*, *managing director*, or *president*, provide overall direction for companies and organizations. CEOs manage company operations, formulate and implement policies, and ensure that goals are met. They collaborate with and direct the work of other top executives and typically report to a board of directors.

There may be other types of chief executives—such as *chief operating officers* (COOs), *chief financial officers* (CFOs), or *chief human resources officers*—who manage a specific part of the organization. The knowledge, skills, and job duties that these executives have differ, depending on which department they oversee.

General and operations managers oversee activities that are too diverse to be classified into one area of management or administration. Responsibilities may include formulating policies, directing daily operations, and planning the use of materials and human resources. These managers make staff schedules, assign work, and ensure that projects are completed. In some organizations, the tasks of chief executive officers may overlap with those of general and operations managers.

Mayors, *city managers*, *county administrators*, and *governors* are chief executive officers of governments. They usually oversee budgets, programs, and the use of resources. Mayors and governors must be elected to office, whereas managers and administrators are typically appointed.

School superintendents and *college* or *university presidents* are chief executive officers of school districts and postsecondary schools. They manage issues such as student achievement, budgets and resources, general operations, and relations with government agencies and other stakeholders.

Work Environment

Chief executives held about 287,900 jobs in 2019. The largest employers of chief executives were as follows:

Self-employed workers	24%
Professional, scientific, and technical services	11
Government	9
Healthcare and social assistance	7
Manufacturing	6

General and operations managers held about 2.5 million jobs in 2019. The largest employers of general and operations managers were as follows:

Retail trade	12%
Professional, scientific, and technical services	11
Wholesale trade	9

Top executives often work many hours, including evenings and weekends.

Top executives work in nearly every industry. They work for both small and large organizations, ranging from businesses in which they are the sole employee to firms with hundreds or thousands of employees.

Because top executives often are held responsible for their organization's success, their work may be stressful.

Top executives frequently travel to attend meetings and conferences or to visit local, regional, national, or international offices of interest.

Top executives often interact with other high-level executives, such as financial managers, human resource managers, or chief technology officers.

Work Schedules

Most top executives work full time, and many work more than 40 hours per week, including evenings and weekends.

How to Become a Top Executive

Top executives typically need at least a bachelor's degree and considerable work experience to enter the occupation.

Education

Many top executives have a bachelor's or master's degree in an area related to their field of work. Top executives in the public sector may have a degree in business administration, public administration, law, or the liberal arts. Top executives of large corporations may have a master's degree in business administration (MBA).

College presidents and school superintendents are typically required to have a master's degree, although a doctorate is often preferred.

Although many mayors, governors, and other public sector executives have at least a bachelor's degree, these positions typically do not have any specific education requirements.

Top executives typically need many years of previous work experience.

Work Experience in a Related Occupation

Many top executives advance within their own organizations, moving up from lower level management occupations or supervisory positions. However, some companies may prefer to hire qualified candidates from outside their organization. Top executives who are promoted from lower level positions may be able to substitute experience for education to move up in the organization.

Chief executives typically need extensive managerial experience, and this experience is expected to be in the organization's area of specialty. Most general and operations managers hired from outside an organization need lower level supervisory or management experience in a related field.

Some general managers move into higher level managerial or executive positions. Executive training programs and development programs often benefit managers or executives.

Licenses, Certifications, and Registrations

Some top executive positions may require the applicant to have a license or certification relevant to their area of management. For example, some employers may require their chief executive officer to be a certified public accountant (CPA).

Important Qualities

Communication skills. Top executives must be able to convey information clearly and persuasively. They must discuss issues and negotiate with others, direct staff, and explain policies and decisions to people within and outside the organization.

Decision-making skills. When setting policies and managing an organization, top executives must be able to assess different options and choose the best course of action.

Leadership skills. Top executives must be able to shape and direct an organization by coordinating policies, people, and resources.

Problem-solving skills. Top executives need to identify and resolve issues within an organization. They must be able to recognize shortcomings and carry out solutions.

Time-management skills. Top executives do many tasks concurrently to ensure that their work gets done and that the organization meets its goals.

Pay

The median annual wage for chief executives was $184,460 in May 2019. The median wage is the wage at which half the workers in an occupation earned more than that amount and half earned less. The lowest 10 percent earned less than $62,290, and the highest 10 percent earned more than $208,000.

The median annual wage for general and operations managers was $100,780 in May 2019. The lowest 10 percent earned less than $45,050, and the highest 10 percent earned more than $208,000.

In May 2019, the median annual wages for chief executives in the top industries in which they worked were as follows:

Top Executives
Median annual wages, May 2019

- Chief executives — $184,460
- Management occupations — $105,660
- Top executives — $103,230
- General and operations managers — $100,780
- Total, all occupations — $39,810

Note: All Occupations includes all occupations in the U.S. Economy.
Source: U.S. Bureau of Labor Statistics, Occupational Employment Statistics.

Manufacturing	$208,000 or more
Professional, scientific, and technical services	208,000 or more
Healthcare and social assistance	166,410
Government	110,230

In May 2019, the median annual wages for general and operations managers in the top industries in which they worked were as follows:

Professional, scientific, and technical services	$140,840
Manufacturing	118,180
Wholesale trade	104,880
Construction	102,270
Retail trade	73,190

Top executives are among the highest paid workers in the United States. However, salary levels vary substantially. For example, a top manager in a large corporation may earn significantly more than the mayor of a small town.

Similarly, earnings for general and operations managers differ across industries because their responsibilities also vary by industry.

In addition to salaries, total compensation for corporate executives often includes stock options and other performance bonuses. These executives also may enjoy benefits such as access to expense allowances, use of company-owned aircraft and cars, and membership to exclusive clubs. Nonprofit and government executives usually receive fewer of these types of benefits.

Top executives often work many hours and have irregular schedules, which may include evenings and weekends.

Job Outlook

Overall employment of top executives is projected to grow 4 percent from 2019 to 2029, about as fast as the average for

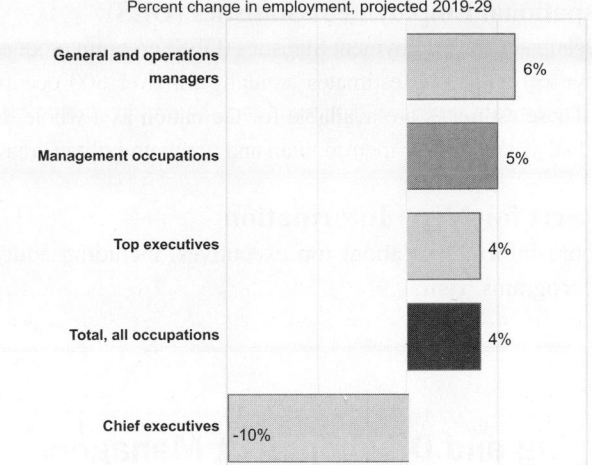

Top Executives
Percent change in employment, projected 2019-29

- General and operations managers — 6%
- Management occupations — 5%
- Top executives — 4%
- Total, all occupations — 4%
- Chief executives — -10%

Note: All Occupations includes all occupations in the U.S. Economy.
Source: U.S. Bureau of Labor Statistics, Occupational Employment Statistics.

all occupations. Projected employment growth varies by occupation.

Employment of general and operations managers is projected to grow 6 percent from 2019 to 2029, faster than the average for all occupations. Organizations will continue to rely on these workers to help them operate successfully.

Employment of chief executives is projected to decline 10 percent from 2019 to 2029. Improving office technology and changing organizational structures have increased these workers' ability to perform tasks previously done by multiple chief executives. In addition, economic activity and employment has become increasingly concentrated in large, established companies, which may lead to fewer new jobs for these workers.

Job Prospects

About 218,300 openings for top executives are projected each year, on average, over the decade.

The high pay and prestige associated with these positions attract many qualified applicants. In addition to those arising from growth, openings are also expected to result from the need to replace workers who transfer to different occupations or exit the labor force, such as to retire.

Those with an advanced degree and extensive managerial experience will have the best job prospects.

Employment projections data for top executives, 2019-29					
Occupational Title	SOC Code	Employment, 2019	Projected Employment, 2029	Change, 2019-29	
				Percent	Numeric
SOURCE: U.S. Bureau of Labor Statistics, Employment Projections program					
Top executives	—	2,774,300	2,889,300	4	115,000
Chief executives	11-1011	287,900	259,100	-10	-28,700
General and operations managers	11-1021	2,486,400	2,630,200	6	143,800

State & Area Data
Occupational Employment Statistics (OES)
The Occupational Employment Statistics (OES) program produces employment and wage estimates annually for over 800 occupations. These estimates are available for the nation as a whole, for individual states, and for metropolitan and nonmetropolitan areas.

Contacts for More Information
For more information about top executives, including educational programs, visit

➤ American Management Association
➤ National Management Association

For more information about executive financial management careers, visit
➤ Financial Executives International
➤ Financial Management Association International

Training and Development Managers

Summary

Quick Facts: Training and Development Managers

2019 Median Pay	$113,350 per year $54.50 per hour
Typical Entry-Level Education	Bachelor's degree
Work Experience in a Related Occupation	5 years or more
On-the-job Training	None
Number of Jobs, 2019	42,300
Job Outlook, 2019-29	7% (Faster than average)
Employment Change, 2019-29	3,100

What Training and Development Managers Do
Training and development managers plan, coordinate, and direct skills- and knowledge-enhancement programs for an organization's staff.

Work Environment
Training and development managers work in nearly every industry. They typically work full time, spending much of their day with people. Some work more than 40 hours per week.

How to Become a Training and Development Manager
Training and development managers typically need a bachelor's or master's degree and related work experience.

Pay
The median annual wage for training and development managers was $113,350 in May 2019.

Job Outlook
Employment of training and development managers is projected to grow 7 percent from 2019 to 2029, faster than the average for all occupations. Job prospects should be favorable due to the continuing need for workplace training and education.

State & Area Data
Explore resources for employment and wages by state and area for training and development managers.

What Training and Development Managers Do
Training and development managers plan, coordinate, and direct skills- and knowledge-enhancement programs for an organization's staff.

Training and development managers work with specialists to design curriculums.

Training and development managers teach training methods to specialists.

Duties

Training and development managers typically do the following:

- Oversee training and development staff
- Assess employees' needs for training
- Align training with the organization's goals
- Create and manage training budgets
- Develop and implement training programs
- Review and select training materials from a variety of vendors
- Update training programs to ensure that they are relevant
- Teach training methods and skills to instructors and supervisors
- Evaluate the effectiveness of training programs and instructors

Training and development managers oversee training programs, staff, and budgets. They are responsible for creating or selecting course content and materials for training programs. Training may be in the form of a video, self-guided instructional manual, or online application and delivered in person or through a computer or other hand-held electronic device. Training also may be collaborative, with employees informally connecting with experts, mentors, and colleagues, often through social media or other online medium. Managers must ensure that training methods, content, software, systems, and equipment are appropriate.

Training and development managers typically supervise a staff of training and development specialists, such as instructional designers, program developers, and instructors. Managers teach training methods to specialists who, in turn, instruct the organization's employees—both new and experienced. Managers direct the daily activities of specialists and evaluate their effectiveness. Although training and development managers primarily oversee specialists and program operations, some also conduct training courses.

Training and development managers often confer with managers of other departments to identify training needs. They may work with top executives and financial managers to identify and match training priorities with overall business goals. They may also prepare training budgets and ensure that expenses stay within budget.

Work Environment

Training and development managers held about 42,300 jobs in 2019. The largest employers of training and development managers were as follows:

Professional, scientific, and technical services	13%
Management of companies and enterprises	13
Educational services; state, local, and private	10
Healthcare and social assistance	10
Finance and insurance	9

Training and development managers may meet with training vendors to choose training materials.

Training and development managers typically work in offices. Some travel between a main office and regional offices or training facilities. They spend much of their time working with people and overseeing training activities.

Work Schedules

Most training and development managers work full time during regular business hours. Some work more than 40 hours per week.

How to Become a Training and Development Manager

Candidates typically need a combination of education and related work experience to become a training and development manager. Although many positions require a bachelor's degree, some jobs require a master's degree.

Education

Many positions require training and development managers to have a bachelor's degree, but some jobs require a master's degree. Although training and development managers come from a variety of educational backgrounds, these workers commonly have a bachelor's degree in business administration, education, or a related field.

Most candidates need a combination of education and related work experience to become a training and development manager.

Some employers prefer or require training and development managers to have a master's degree with a concentration in training and development, human resources management, organizational development, or business administration.

Training and development managers may also benefit from studying instructional design, behavioral psychology, or educational psychology.

Work Experience in a Related Occupation

Related work experience is essential for training and development managers. Many positions require work experience in management, teaching, or training and development or another human resources field. For example, some training and development managers start out as training and development specialists. Some employers also prefer experience in the industry in which the company operates.

Licenses, Certifications, and Registrations

Although it is not required for training and development managers, certification may show professional expertise. Some employers prefer to hire candidates who have certification, and some positions require it.

Many professional associations for human resources professionals offer classes to enhance the skills of their members. Some associations, including the Association for Talent Development and the International Society for Performance Improvement, specialize in training and development and offer certification programs. The Society for Human Resource Management offers general human resources certification.

Important Qualities

Business skills. Training and development managers must understand business operations in order to match training with business goals. They also need to be able to plan and adhere to budgets.

Collaboration skills. Training and development managers need strong interpersonal skills for working with staff, trainees, subject matter experts, and organization leaders. They accomplish much of their work through teams.

Communication skills. Training and development managers must clearly convey information to diverse audiences. They also must be able to effectively instruct their staff.

Critical-thinking skills. Training and development managers use critical-thinking skills when assessing classes, materials, and programs. They must identify the training needs of an organization and make changes and improvements as required.

Decisionmaking skills. Training and development managers must select or create the best training programs to meet the needs of an organization. For example, they must review available training methods and materials and choose those that best fit each program.

Collaboration skills. Training and development managers need strong interpersonal skills because delivering training programs requires working in concert with staff, trainees, subject matter experts, and the organization's leaders. They also accomplish much of their work through teams.

Instructional skills. Training and development managers need to understand the fundamentals of teaching and lesson planning. In addition to developing training, they may lead courses or seminars.

Leadership skills. Managers are often in charge of a staff and programs. They must be able to organize, motivate, and instruct those working for them.

Pay

The median annual wage for training and development managers was $113,350 in May 2019. The median wage is the wage at which half the workers in an occupation earned more than that amount and half earned less. The lowest 10 percent earned less than $64,720, and the highest 10 percent earned more than $196,070.

Training and Development Managers
Median annual wages, May 2019

Operations specialties managers	$120,960
Training and development managers	$113,350
Total, all occupations	$39,810

Note: All Occupations includes all occupations in the U.S. Economy.
Source: U.S. Bureau of Labor Statistics, Occupational Employment Statistics.

In May 2019, the median annual wages for training and development managers in the top industries in which they worked were as follows:

Professional, scientific, and technical services...	$132,590
Management of companies and enterprises........	122,610
Finance and insurance.............................	119,690
Educational services; state, local, and private....	101,790
Healthcare and social assistance..........	98,020

Most training and development managers work full time during regular business hours. Some work more than 40 hours per week.

Job Outlook

Employment of training and development managers is projected to grow 7 percent from 2019 to 2029, faster than the average for all occupations. In many occupations, employees are required to take continuing education and skill development courses throughout their careers, creating demand for workers who develop and provide training materials.

Innovations in training methods and learning technology are expected to continue throughout the decade, particularly for organizations with remote workers. Organizations use social media, visual simulations, mobile learning, and social networks in their training programs. Training and development managers need to continue modifying training programs, allocating budgets, and integrating these features into training programs and curriculums.

In addition, as companies seek to reduce costs, training and development managers may be required to structure programs to enlist available experts, take advantage of existing resources, and facilitate positive relationships among staff. Training and development managers may use informal collaborative learning and social media to engage and train employees in the most cost-effective way.

Job Prospects

About 3,700 openings for training and development managers are projected each year, on average, over the decade.

Many of those openings are expected to result from the need to replace workers who transfer to different occupations or exit the labor force, such as to retire. Overall, job prospects should

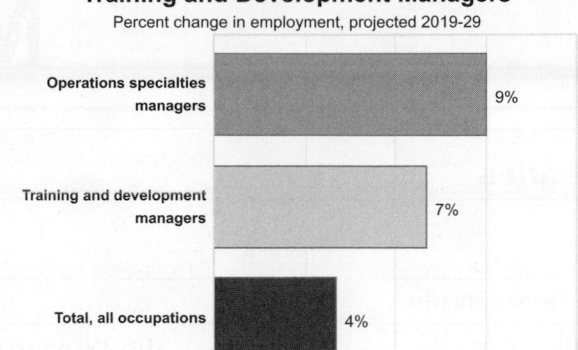

Training and Development Managers
Percent change in employment, projected 2019-29

Operations specialties managers — 9%
Training and development managers — 7%
Total, all occupations — 4%

Note: All Occupations includes all occupations in the U.S. Economy.
Source: U.S. Bureau of Labor Statistics, Employment Projections program.

be favorable due to the continuing need for workplace training and education.

Employment projections data for training and development managers, 2019-29					
Occupational Title	SOC Code	Employment, 2019	Projected Employment, 2029	Change, 2019-29	
				Percent	Numeric
SOURCE: U.S. Bureau of Labor Statistics, Employment Projections program					
Training and development managers	11-3131	42,300	45,400	7	3,100

State & Area Data
Occupational Employment Statistics (OES)

The Occupational Employment Statistics (OES) program produces employment and wage estimates annually for over 800 occupations. These estimates are available for the nation as a whole, for individual states, and for metropolitan and nonmetropolitan areas.

Contacts for More Information

For more information about training and development managers, including certification, visit
➤ Association for Talent Development
➤ International Society for Performance Improvement

For information about human resources management careers and certification, visit
➤ Society for Human Resource Management

Math

Actuaries

Summary

Quick Facts: Actuaries

2019 Median Pay	$108,350 per year $52.09 per hour
Typical Entry-Level Education	Bachelor's degree
Work Experience in a Related Occupation	None
On-the-job Training	Long-term on-the-job training
Number of Jobs, 2019	27,700
Job Outlook, 2019-29	18% (Much faster than average)
Employment Change, 2019-29	4,900

What Actuaries Do

Actuaries use mathematics, statistics, and financial theory to analyze the financial costs of risk and uncertainty.

Work Environment

Most actuaries work for insurance companies. Although most work full time in an office setting, some actuaries who work as consultants may travel to meet with clients.

How to Become an Actuary

Actuaries need a bachelor's degree and must pass a series of exams to become certified professionals. They must have a strong background in mathematics, statistics, and business.

Pay

The median annual wage for actuaries was $108,350 in May 2019.

Job Outlook

Employment of actuaries is projected to grow 18 percent from 2019 to 2029, much faster than the average for all occupations. Actuaries will be needed to develop, price, and evaluate a variety of insurance products and calculate the costs of new, emerging risks.

State & Area Data

Explore resources for employment and wages by state and area for actuaries.

What Actuaries Do

Actuaries analyze the financial costs of risk and uncertainty. They use mathematics, statistics, and financial theory to assess the risk of potential events, and they help businesses and clients develop policies that minimize the cost of that risk. Actuaries' work is essential to the insurance industry.

Duties

Actuaries typically do the following:

- Compile statistical data and other information for further analysis
- Estimate the probability and likely economic cost of an event such as death, sickness, an accident, or a natural disaster
- Design, test, and administer insurance policies, investments, pension plans, and other business strategies to minimize risk and maximize profitability
- Produce charts, tables, and reports that explain calculations and proposals
- Explain their findings and proposals to company executives, government officials, shareholders, and clients

Actuaries use advanced statistics and modeling software to forecast the cost and probability of an event.

Actuaries produce charts, tables, and reports to explain their calculations.

Most actuarial work is done with computers. Actuaries use database software to compile information. They use advanced statistics and modeling software to forecast the probability of an event occurring, the potential costs of the event if it does occur, and whether the insurance company has enough money to pay future claims.

Actuaries typically work on teams that often include managers and professionals in other fields, such as accounting, underwriting, and finance. For example, some actuaries work with accountants and financial analysts to set the price for security offerings or with market research analysts to forecast demand for new products.

Most actuaries work at insurance companies, where they help design policies and determine the premiums that should be charged for each policy. They must ensure that the premiums are profitable yet competitive with other insurance companies.

Actuaries in the insurance industry typically specialize in a specific field of insurance, such as one of the following:

Health insurance actuaries help develop long-term care and health insurance policies by predicting expected costs of providing care under the terms of an insurance contract. Their predictions are based on numerous factors, including family history, geographic location, and occupation.

Life insurance actuaries help develop annuity and life insurance policies for individuals and groups by estimating, on the basis of risk factors such as age, gender, and tobacco use, how long someone is expected to live.

Property and casualty insurance actuaries help develop insurance policies that insure policyholders against property loss and liability resulting from accidents, natural disasters, fires, and other events. They calculate the expected number of claims resulting from automobile accidents, which varies with the insured person's age, sex, driving history, type of car, and other factors.

Some actuaries apply their expertise to financial matters outside of the insurance industry. For example, they develop investment strategies that manage risks and maximize returns for companies or individuals.

Pension and retirement benefits actuaries design, test, and evaluate company pension plans to determine if the expected funds available in the future will be enough to ensure payment of future benefits. They must report the results of their evaluations to the federal government. Pension actuaries also help businesses develop other types of retirement plans, such as 401(k)s and healthcare plans for retirees. In addition, they provide retirement planning advice to individuals.

Enterprise risk actuaries identify any risks, including economic, financial, and geopolitical risks that may affect a company's short-term or long-term objectives. They help top executives determine how much risk the business is willing to take, and they develop strategies to respond to these issues.

Actuaries also work in the public sector. In the federal government, actuaries may evaluate proposed changes to Social Security or Medicare or conduct economic and demographic studies to project future benefit obligations. At the state level, actuaries may examine and regulate the rates charged by insurance companies.

Some actuaries are considered consultants and provide advice to clients on a contract basis. Many consulting actuaries audit the work of internal actuaries at insurance companies or handle actuarial duties for insurance companies that are not large enough to keep their own actuaries on staff.

Work Environment

Actuaries held about 27,700 jobs in 2019. The largest employers of actuaries were as follows:

Finance and insurance	71%
Professional, scientific, and technical services	13
Management of companies and enterprises	6
Self-employed workers	4
Government	3

Actuaries typically work on teams that often include managers and professionals in other fields, such as accounting, underwriting, and finance.

Although actuaries usually work in an office setting, those who work for consulting firms may need to travel to meet with clients.

Work Schedules

Most actuaries work full time and some work more than 40 hours per week.

How to Become an Actuary

Actuaries need a bachelor's degree, typically in mathematics, actuarial science, statistics, or some other analytical field. Students must complete coursework in economics, applied

Actuaries typically work on teams that often include managers and professionals in other fields, such as accounting, underwriting, and finance.

Actuaries need a bachelor's degree and must pass a series of exams to become certified professionals.

statistics, and corporate finance, and must pass a series of exams to become certified professionals.

Education

Actuaries must have a strong background in mathematics, statistics, and business. Typically, an actuary has an undergraduate degree in mathematics, actuarial science, statistics, or some other analytical field.

To become certified professionals, students must complete coursework in economics, statistics, and corporate finance.

Students also should take classes outside of mathematics and business to prepare them for a career as an actuary. Coursework in computer science, especially programming languages, and the ability to use and develop spreadsheets, databases, and statistical analysis tools, are valuable. Classes in writing and public speaking will improve students' ability to communicate in the business world.

Licenses, Certification, and Registrations

Two professional societies—the Casualty Actuarial Society (CAS) and the Society of Actuaries (SOA)—sponsor programs leading to full professional status. The CAS and SOA offer two levels of certification: associate and fellow.

The CAS certifies actuaries who work in the property and casualty field, which includes automobile, homeowners, medical malpractice, and workers' compensation insurance.

The SOA certifies actuaries who work in life insurance, health insurance, retirement benefits, investments, and finance.

Both professional societies require applicants to complete certain educational coursework in economics, finance, and mathematical statistics while in college. Applicants also must pass seven exams for associate-level certification.

Many employers expect students to have passed at least one or two of the initial actuary exams needed for professional certification before graduation.

In addition, both CAS and SOA require that candidates take seminars on professionalism. Both societies have mandatory e-learning courses for candidates.

It typically takes 4 to 7 years for an actuary to earn the associate-level certification, because each exam requires hundreds of hours of study and months of preparation.

After becoming associates, actuaries typically take 2 to 3 more years to earn fellowship status.

The SOA offers fellowship certification in five separate tracks: life and annuities, group and health benefits, retirement benefits, investments, and finance/enterprise risk management. Unlike the SOA, the CAS does not offer specialized study tracks for fellowship certification.

Both the CAS and the SOA have a continuing education requirement. Most actuaries meet this requirement by attending training seminars that are sponsored by their employers or the societies.

Pension actuaries typically must be licensed by the U.S. Department of Labor and U.S. Department of the Treasury's Joint Board for the Enrollment of Actuaries. Applicants must meet certain experience requirements and pass two exams administered through the SOA to qualify for enrollment.

Other Experience

Because there are different types of practice areas, including health, life, pension, and casualty, internships may be helpful for students deciding on which actuarial track to pursue.

Training

Most entry-level actuaries start out as trainees. They are typically on teams with more experienced actuaries who serve as mentors. At first, they perform basic tasks, such as compiling data, but as they gain more experience, they may conduct research and write reports. Beginning actuaries may spend time working in other departments, such as marketing, underwriting, and product development, to learn all aspects of the company's work and how actuarial work applies to each one.

Most employers support their actuaries throughout the certification process. For example, employers typically pay the cost of exams and study materials. Many firms provide paid time to study and encourage their employees to set up study groups.

Employees usually receive raises or bonuses for each exam that they pass.

Advancement

Advancement depends largely on job performance and the number of actuarial exams passed. For example, actuaries who achieve fellowship status often supervise the work of other actuaries and provide advice to senior management. Actuaries with a broad knowledge of risk management and how it applies to business can rise to executive positions in their companies, such as chief risk officer or chief financial officer.

Important Qualities

Analytical skills. Actuaries use analytical skills to identify patterns and trends in complex sets of data to determine the factors that have an effect on certain types of events.

Communication skills. Actuaries must be able to explain complex technical matters to those without an actuarial background. They must also communicate clearly through the reports and memos that describe their work and recommendations.

Computer skills. Actuaries must know programming languages and be able to use and develop spreadsheets, databases, and statistical analysis tools.

Interpersonal skills. Actuaries serve as leaders and members of teams, so they must be able to listen to other people's opinions and suggestions before reaching a conclusion.

Math skills. Actuaries quantify risk by using the principles of calculus, statistics, and probability.

Problem-solving skills. Actuaries identify risks and develop ways for businesses to manage those risks.

Pay

The median annual wage for actuaries was $108,350 in May 2019. The median wage is the wage at which half the workers in an occupation earned more than that amount and half earned less. The lowest 10 percent earned less than $64,860, and the highest 10 percent earned more than $193,600.

In May 2019, the median annual wages for actuaries in the top industries in which they worked were as follows:

Professional, scientific, and technical services..... $110,960
Finance and insurance 110,020
Government.. 101,740
Management of companies and enterprises.......... 98,880

Most actuaries work full time and some work more than 40 hours per week.

Job Outlook

Employment of actuaries is projected to grow 18 percent from 2019 to 2029, much faster than the average for all occupations.

Actuaries will be needed to develop, price, and evaluate a variety of insurance products and calculate the costs of new risks.

More actuaries will also be needed to help companies manage their own risk, a practice known as enterprise risk management. Actuaries will help companies avoid, manage, and respond to any potential financial risks across all areas of their business operations. This analysis helps companies adjust their business or investment strategies to achieve economic returns and respond to new financial regulations and requirements.

Insurance companies will need actuaries to analyze the large amount of information, such as medical or property data, collected from consumers. The increase in available data will allow insurance companies to better develop new products, set competitive prices, predict consumer behavior, and make more accurate projections of future risks and costs.

In addition, health insurance companies will require more actuaries to help evaluate the effects of changing healthcare regulations and guidelines, expand into new insurance markets, and offer products to new customers.

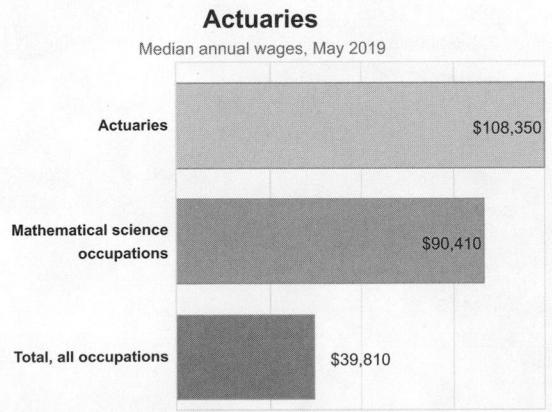

Actuaries
Median annual wages, May 2019

Actuaries	$108,350
Mathematical science occupations	$90,410
Total, all occupations	$39,810

Note: All Occupations includes all occupations in the U.S. Economy.
Source: U.S. Bureau of Labor Statistics, Occupational Employment Statistics.

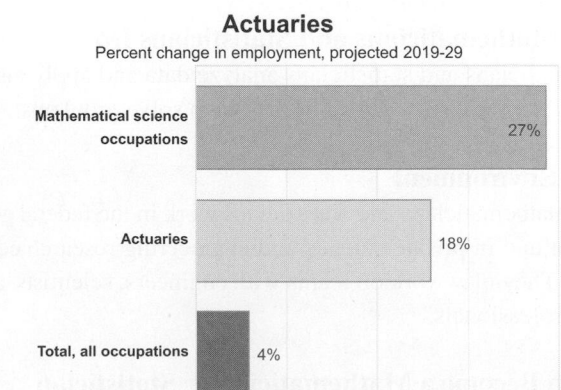

Actuaries
Percent change in employment, projected 2019-29

Mathematical science occupations	27%
Actuaries	18%
Total, all occupations	4%

Note: All Occupations includes all occupations in the U.S. Economy.
Source: U.S. Bureau of Labor Statistics, Employment Projections program.

Job Prospects

Job opportunities should be somewhat competitive for entry-level applicants because the number of students sitting for actuarial exams has increased in the past few years. Students who have passed at least two actuarial exams, have had an internship while in college, and have strong analytical and business skills should have the best job prospects for entry-level positions.

Employment projections data for actuaries, 2019-29					
Occupational Title	SOC Code	Employment, 2019	Projected Employment, 2029	Change, 2019-29	
				Percent	Numeric
SOURCE: U.S. Bureau of Labor Statistics, Employment Projections program					
Actuaries	15-2011	27,700	32,600	18	4,900

State & Area Data
Occupational Employment Statistics (OES)

The Occupational Employment Statistics (OES) program produces employment and wage estimates annually for over 800 occupations. These estimates are available for the nation as a whole, for individual states, and for metropolitan and nonmetropolitan areas.

Contacts for More Information

For more information about actuaries, visit
➤ American Academy of Actuaries

For more information about actuaries in property and casualty insurance, visit
➤ Casualty Actuarial Society

For more information about actuaries in life and health insurance, retirement benefits, investments, and finance/enterprise risk management, visit
➤ Society of Actuaries

For more information about how to become an actuary, visit
➤ Be an Actuary

For more information about pension actuaries and their licensing requirements, visit
➤ American Society of Pension Professionals and Actuaries
➤ U.S. Department of Labor and U.S. Department of the Treasury's Joint Board for the Enrollment of Actuaries

---

Mathematicians and Statisticians

Summary

Quick Facts: Mathematicians and Statisticians

2019 Median Pay	$92,030 per year $44.25 per hour
Typical Entry-Level Education	Master's degree
Work Experience in a Related Occupation	None
On-the-job Training	None
Number of Jobs, 2019	45,700
Job Outlook, 2019-29	33% (Much faster than average)
Employment Change, 2019-29	14,900

What Mathematicians and Statisticians Do

Mathematicians and statisticians analyze data and apply mathematical and statistical techniques to help solve problems.

Work Environment

Many mathematicians and statisticians work in the federal government and in private science and engineering research companies. They may work on teams with engineers, scientists, and other professionals.

How to Become a Mathematician or Statistician

Mathematicians and statisticians typically need at least a master's degree in mathematics or statistics. However, some positions are available to those with a bachelor's degree.

Pay

The median annual wage for mathematicians was $105,030 in May 2019.

The median annual wage for statisticians was $91,160 in May 2019.

Job Outlook

Overall employment of mathematicians and statisticians is projected to grow 33 percent from 2019 to 2029, much faster than the average for all occupations. Businesses will need these workers to analyze the increasing volume of digital and electronic data.

Mathematicians and statisticians solve practical problems in fields such as business, government, engineering, and the sciences.

State & Area Data

Explore resources for employment and wages by state and area for mathematicians and statisticians.

What Mathematicians and Statisticians Do

Mathematicians and statisticians analyze data and apply mathematical and statistical techniques to help solve real-world problems in business, engineering, healthcare, or other fields.

Duties

Mathematicians and statisticians typically do the following:

- Develop new mathematical rules, theories, and concepts in areas such as algebra and geometry
- Decide what data are needed to answer specific questions or problems
- Apply mathematical theories and techniques to solve practical problems in business, engineering, the sciences, and other fields
- Design surveys, experiments, or opinion polls to collect data
- Develop mathematical or statistical models to analyze data
- Interpret data and report conclusions drawn from their analyses
- Use data analysis to support and improve business decisions

Mathematicians and statisticians apply theories and techniques, such as mathematical or statistical modeling, to solve practical problems. Typically, they work with individuals in other occupations to solve these problems. For example, they may work with chemists, materials scientists, and chemical engineers to analyze the effectiveness of new drugs. Others may work with industrial designers to study the aerodynamic characteristics of new automobiles.

To work on these problems, mathematicians and statisticians must first collect data. Statisticians design surveys, questionnaires, experiments, and opinion polls to collect the data they

Mathematicians and statisticians work with formulas and data to help solve problems in industry, academia, and government.

need. Surveys may be mailed, conducted over the phone, collected online, or gathered through some other means.

Some surveys, such as the U.S. census, include data from nearly everyone. For most surveys and opinion polls, however, statisticians use a sampling method to collect data from some people in a particular group. Statisticians determine the type and size of the sample to be surveyed or polled.

After the data are collected, mathematicians and statisticians use specialized statistical software to analyze data. In their analyses, mathematicians and statisticians identify trends and relationships within the data. They also conduct tests to determine the data's validity and to account for high survey non-response rates or sampling error. Some may help create new software to analyze data more accurately and efficiently.

Mathematicians and statisticians present the findings from their analyses and discuss the data's limitations in order to prevent inaccurate conclusions from being drawn. They may present written reports, tables, charts, and graphs to other team members and to clients.

Mathematicians and statisticians work in many fields, such as education, marketing, psychology, sports, or any other field that requires the collection and analysis of data. In particular, government, healthcare, and research and development companies employ many statisticians.

Government. Mathematicians and statisticians working in government develop and analyze surveys that collect a variety of data, including unemployment rates, wages, and other estimates pertaining to jobs and workers. Others help to figure out the average level of pesticides in drinking water, the number of endangered species living in a particular area, or the number of people who have a certain disease.

Healthcare. Statisticians known as biostatisticians or biometricians work in pharmaceutical companies, public health agencies, or hospitals. They may design studies to test whether drugs successfully treat diseases or medical conditions. They may also help identify the sources of outbreaks of illnesses in humans and animals.

Research and development. Mathematicians and statisticians design experiments for product testing and development. For instance, they may help design experiments to see how car engines perform when exposed to extreme weather conditions. Some may analyze consumer data to help develop marketing strategies and prices for consumer goods.

Colleges and universities. Mathematicians and statisticians working in a postsecondary education institution may study theoretical or abstract concepts in mathematics or statistics. They identify, research, and resolve unexplained issues in mathematics and are concerned primarily with exploring new mathematical or statistical theories to increase knowledge and understanding about the field.

However, the mathematician occupation is a relatively small one, and many people with a degree in mathematics or who develop mathematical theories and models may not be formally known as mathematicians. Instead, they work in related fields and professions. In the computer systems design and related services industries, for example, they may be known as computer programmers or systems analysts. In finance, they may be known as *quantitative analysts*. Other industries may refer to them as *data scientists* or *data analysts*.

Computer and information research scientists, physicists and astronomers, economists, actuaries, operations research analysts, engineers, and many other occupations also use mathematics extensively.

Many people with a Ph.D. in mathematics, particularly theoretical mathematics, work as postsecondary teachers in education institutions. They usually have a mix of teaching and research responsibilities. Some may conduct individual research or collaborate with other professors or mathematicians. Collaborators may work together at the same institution or from different locations.

Work Environment

Mathematicians held about 2,900 jobs in 2019. The largest employers of mathematicians were as follows:

Federal government	40%
Colleges, universities, and professional schools; state, local, and private	18
Management, scientific, and technical consulting services	5

Statisticians held about 42,700 jobs in 2019. The largest employers of statisticians were as follows:

Research and development in the physical, engineering, and life sciences	14%
Federal government	11
Healthcare and social assistance	10
Colleges, universities, and professional schools; state, local, and private	7
Insurance carriers and related activities	7

Mathematicians and statisticians may work on teams with engineers and scientists.

Mathematicians and statisticians typically work in offices. They also may work on teams with engineers, scientists, and other professionals.

Work Schedules

Most mathematicians and statisticians work full time. Deadlines and last-minute requests for data or analysis may require overtime. In addition, these workers may travel to attend seminars and conferences.

How to Become a Mathematician or Statistician

Mathematicians and statisticians typically need at least a master's degree in mathematics or statistics. However, some positions are available to those with a bachelor's degree.

Education

In private industry, mathematicians typically need an advanced degree, either a master's degree or a doctorate. For jobs with the federal government, candidates need at least a bachelor's degree in mathematics or significant coursework in mathematics.

Most colleges and universities offer a bachelor's degree in mathematics. Courses usually include calculus, differential equations, and linear and abstract algebra. Many colleges and universities advise or require mathematics students to take

Years of study are required to become a mathematician or statistician.

courses in a related field, such as computer science, engineering, physics, or statistics. Because mathematicians often work with data analysis software, computer programming courses may be particularly beneficial for students.

Many universities offer master's and doctoral degrees in theoretical or applied mathematics. Many students who get a doctoral degree work as professors of mathematics in a college or university.

Statisticians typically need a master's degree but some entry-level positions may accept candidates with a bachelor's degree.

Most statisticians have degrees in mathematics, economics, computer science, or another quantitative field. A degree in statistics typically includes courses in linear algebra, calculus, experimental design, survey methodology, probability, and statistical theory.

Many colleges and universities advise statistics students to take courses in a related field, such as computer science, engineering, or physics. These courses can help prepare students to work in a variety of industries. Coursework in engineering or physical science, for example, may be useful for mathematicians or statisticians working in manufacturing on quality or productivity improvement. A background in biology, chemistry, or health sciences is useful for work testing pharmaceutical or agricultural products.

Because mathematicians and statisticians often work with data analysis software, computer programming courses may be particularly beneficial for students.

Students who are interested in becoming mathematicians or statisticians should take as many math courses as possible in high school.

Important Qualities

Analytical skills. Mathematicians and statisticians use mathematical techniques and models to analyze large amounts of data. They must determine the appropriate software packages and understand computer programming languages to design and develop new techniques and models. They must also be precise and accurate in their analysis.

Communication skills. Mathematicians and statisticians must interact with, and propose solutions to, people who may not have extensive knowledge of mathematics.

Math skills. Mathematicians and statisticians use statistics, calculus, and linear algebra to develop their models and analyses.

Problem-solving skills. Mathematicians and statisticians must devise new solutions to problems encountered by scientists or engineers.

Pay

The median annual wage for mathematicians was $105,030 in May 2019. The median wage is the wage at which half the workers in an occupation earned more than that amount and half earned less. The lowest 10 percent earned less

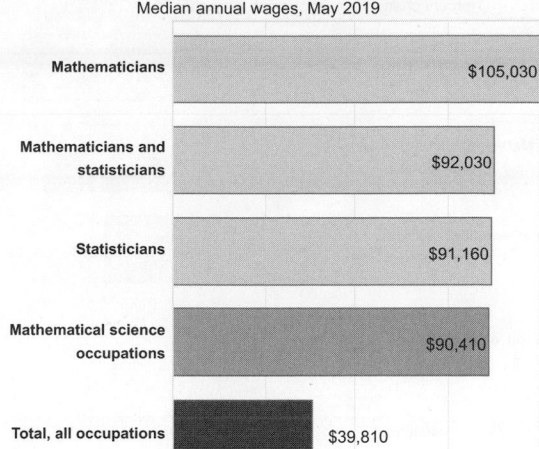

Mathematicians and Statisticians
Median annual wages, May 2019

Mathematicians	$105,030
Mathematicians and statisticians	$92,030
Statisticians	$91,160
Mathematical science occupations	$90,410
Total, all occupations	$39,810

Note: All Occupations includes all occupations in the U.S. Economy.
Source: U.S. Bureau of Labor Statistics, Occupational Employment Statistics.

than $58,100, and the highest 10 percent earned more than $162,060.

The median annual wage for statisticians was $91,160 in May 2019. The lowest 10 percent earned less than $52,690, and the highest 10 percent earned more than $146,770.

In May 2019, the median annual wages for mathematicians in the top industries in which they worked were as follows:

Management, scientific, and technical consulting services	$123,270
Federal government	112,800
Colleges, universities, and professional schools; state, local, and private	62,780

In May 2019, the median annual wages for statisticians in the top industries in which they worked were as follows:

Federal government	$106,670
Research and development in the physical, engineering, and life sciences	102,500
Insurance carriers and related activities	88,040
Healthcare and social assistance	80,920
Colleges, universities, and professional schools; state, local, and private	74,370

Most mathematicians and statisticians work full time. Deadlines and last-minute requests for data or analysis may require overtime. In addition, these workers may travel to attend seminars and conferences.

Job Outlook

Overall employment of mathematicians and statisticians is projected to grow 33 percent from 2019 to 2029, much faster than the average for all occupations. Employment growth will vary by occupation.

Mathematicians and Statisticians

Percent change in employment, projected 2019-29

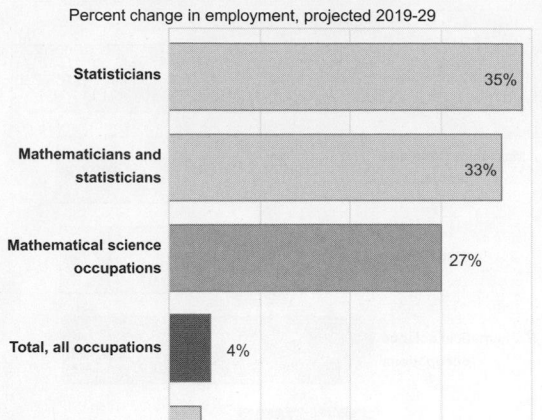

Statisticians	35%
Mathematicians and statisticians	33%
Mathematical science occupations	27%
Total, all occupations	4%
Mathematicians	3%

Note: All Occupations includes all occupations in the U.S. Economy.
Source: U.S. Bureau of Labor Statistics, Employment Projections program.

Employment of statisticians is projected to grow 35 percent from 2019 to 2029, much faster than the average for all occupations. Growth is expected to result from more widespread use of statistical analysis to inform business, healthcare, and policy decisions. The amount of digitally stored data will increase over the next decade as more people and companies conduct business online and use social media, smartphones, and other mobile devices. As a result, businesses will increasingly need statisticians to analyze the large amount of information and data collected. Statistical analyses will help companies improve their business processes, design and develop new products, and advertise products to potential customers.

Many of the new jobs for statisticians are expected to be in research and development, consulting, and computer systems design and related services.

Employment of mathematicians is projected to grow 3 percent from 2019 to 2029, about as fast as the average for all occupations. Much of this growth is expected to be in research-based roles in academia, research and development, and consulting services.

Job Prospects

Job prospects for mathematicians and statisticians are projected to be very good. An increasing number of jobs over the next decade will require high levels of mathematical and statistical knowledge. Job opportunities are expected to be favorable for those with very strong quantitative and data analysis skills. Computer programming skills will remain important to many employers, as will be keeping up with new statistical methods and programming languages.

Many candidates with a background in advanced mathematical techniques and modeling also may find good job opportunities in other, closely related fields.

In addition to technical skills, applicants with strong communication skills and the ability to interpret and present their data and findings will have stronger job prospects.

Employment projections data for mathematicians and statisticians, 2019-29					
Occupational Title	SOC Code	Employment, 2019	Projected Employment, 2029	Change, 2019-29	
				Percent	Numeric
SOURCE: U.S. Bureau of Labor Statistics, Employment Projections program					
Mathematicians and statisticians	—	45,700	60,500	33	14,900
Mathematicians	15-2021	2,900	3,000	3	100
Statisticians	15-2041	42,700	57,500	35	14,800

State & Area Data
Occupational Employment Statistics (OES)

The Occupational Employment Statistics (OES) program produces employment and wage estimates annually for over 800 occupations. These estimates are available for the nation as a whole, for individual states, and for metropolitan and nonmetropolitan areas.

Contacts for More Information

For more information about mathematicians, including training, especially for doctoral-level employment, visit
➤ American Mathematical Society

For more information about statisticians, visit
➤ American Statistical Association
➤ This is Statistics

For specific information on careers in applied mathematics, visit
➤ Society for Industrial and Applied Mathematics

For information on federal government requirements for mathematician positions, visit
➤ U.S. Office of Personnel Management

Operations Research Analysts

Summary

Quick Facts: Operations Research Analysts

2019 Median Pay	$84,810 per year
	$40.78 per hour
Typical Entry-Level Education	Bachelor's degree
Work Experience in a Related Occupation	None
On-the-job Training	None
Number of Jobs, 2019	105,100
Job Outlook, 2019-29	25% (Much faster than average)
Employment Change, 2019-29	26,100

What Operations Research Analysts Do

Operations research analysts use advanced mathematical and analytical methods to help solve complex issues.

Work Environment

Operations research analysts spend most of their time in offices, although some travel may be necessary to meet with clients. Almost all operations research analysts work full time.

How to Become an Operations Research Analyst

Although the typical educational requirement for entry-level positions is a bachelor's degree, some employers may prefer to hire applicants with a master's degree. Analysts typically have a degree in business, operations research, management science, analytics, mathematics, engineering, computer science, or another technical or quantitative field.

Pay

The median annual wage for operations research analysts was $84,810 in May 2019.

Job Outlook

Employment of operations research analysts is projected to grow 25 percent from 2019 to 2029, much faster than the average for all occupations. As technology advances and companies seek efficiency and cost savings, demand for operations research analysis should continue to grow.

State & Area Data

Explore resources for employment and wages by state and area for operations research analysts.

What Operations Research Analysts Do

Operations research analysts use advanced mathematical and analytical methods to help organizations solve problems and make better decisions.

Duties

Operations research analysts typically do the following:

- Identify and solve problems in areas such as business, logistics, healthcare, or other fields
- Collect and organize information from a variety of sources, such as computer databases, sales histories, and customer feedback
- Gather input from workers involved in all aspects of a problem or from others who have specialized knowledge, so that they can help solve the problem
- Examine information to figure out what is relevant to a problem and what methods might be used to analyze it
- Use statistical analysis, simulations, predictive modeling, or other methods to analyze information and develop practical solutions to business problems
- Advise managers and other decisionmakers on the effects of various courses of action to take in order to address a problem
- Write memos, reports, and other documents explaining their findings and recommendations for managers, executives, and other officials

Operations research analysts use statistical analysis and simulations to analyze and solve business problems.

Operations research analysts advise managers and other decision makers on the appropriate course of action to solve a problem.

Operations research analysts are involved in all aspects of an organization. They help managers decide how to allocate resources, develop production schedules, manage the supply chain, and set prices. For example, they may help decide how to organize products in supermarkets or help companies figure out the most effective way to ship and distribute products.

Analysts must first identify and understand the problem to be solved or the processes to be improved. Analysts typically collect relevant data from the field and interview clients or managers involved in the business processes being examined. Analysts show the implications of pursuing different actions and may assist in achieving a consensus on how to proceed.

Operations research analysts use sophisticated computer software, such as databases and statistical packages, to analyze and solve problems. Analysts use statistical software to simulate current and future events and evaluate alternative courses of action. Analysts break down problems into their various parts and analyze the effect that different changes and circumstances would have on each of these parts. For example, to help an airline schedule flights and decide what to charge for tickets, analysts may take into account the cities that have to be connected, the amount of fuel required to fly those routes, the expected number of passengers, pilots' schedules, maintenance costs, and fuel prices.

There is no one way to solve a problem, and analysts must weigh the costs and benefits of alternative solutions or approaches in their recommendations to managers.

Because problems are complex and often require expertise from many disciplines, most analysts work on teams. Once a manager reaches a final decision, these teams may work with others in the organization to ensure that the plan is successful.

Work Environment

Operations research analysts held about 105,100 jobs in 2019. The largest employers of operations research analysts were as follows:

Finance and insurance	28%
Professional, scientific, and technical services	23
Management of companies and enterprises	10
Manufacturing	6
Federal government	6

Some operations research analysts in the federal government work for the Department of Defense, which also employs a large number of analysts through private consulting firms.

Operations research analysts spend most of their time in offices. Some may spend time in the field to gather information and observe business processes directly. Analysts may also travel in order to work with clients and company executives and to attend conferences.

Because problems are complex and often require expertise from many disciplines, most analysts work on teams.

Work Schedules
Almost all operations research analysts work full time.

How to Become an Operations Research Analyst
Although the typical educational requirement for entry-level positions is a bachelor's degree, some employers may prefer to hire applicants with a master's degree. Because few schools offer bachelor's and advanced degree programs in operations research, analysts typically have degrees in other related fields.

Education
Many entry-level positions are available for those with a bachelor's degree. However, some employers may prefer to hire applicants with a master's degree.

Although some schools offer bachelor's and advanced degree programs in operations research, some analysts have degrees in other technical or quantitative fields, such as engineering, computer science, analytics, or mathematics.

Operations research analysts typically work in an office setting.

Analysts typically have a degree in business, operations research, management science, analytics, mathematics, engineering, computer science, or another technical or quantitative field.

Because operations research is based on quantitative analysis, students need extensive coursework in mathematics. Courses include statistics, calculus, and linear algebra. Coursework in computer science is important because analysts rely on advanced statistical and database software to analyze and model data. Courses in other areas, such as engineering, economics, and political science, are useful because operations research is a multidisciplinary field with a wide variety of applications.

Continuing education is important for operations research analysts. Keeping up with advances in technology, software tools, and improved analytical methods is vital.

Other Experience

Some operations research analysts are veterans of the U.S. Armed Forces. Certain positions may require applicants to undergo a background check in order to obtain a security clearance.

Important Qualities

Analytical skills. Operations research analysts use a wide range of methods, such as forecasting, data mining, and statistical analysis, to examine and interpret data. They must determine the appropriate software packages and understand computer programming languages to design and develop new techniques and models.

Communication skills. Operations research analysts often present their data and conclusions to managers and other executives. They also need to communicate technical information to people without a technical background.

Critical-thinking skills. Operations research analysts must be able to figure out what information is relevant to their work. They also must be able to evaluate the costs and benefits of alternative solutions before making a recommendation.

Interpersonal skills. Operations research analysts typically work on teams. They also need to be able to convince managers and top executives to accept their recommendations.

Math skills. The models and methods used by operations research analysts are rooted in statistics, calculus, linear algebra, and other advanced mathematical disciplines.

Problem-solving skills. Operations research analysts need to be able to diagnose problems on the basis of information given to them by others. They then analyze relevant information to solve the problems.

Writing skills. Operations research analysts write memos, reports, and other documents explaining their findings and recommendations.

Pay

The median annual wage for operations research analysts was $84,810 in May 2019. The median wage is the wage at which half the workers in an occupation earned more than that amount

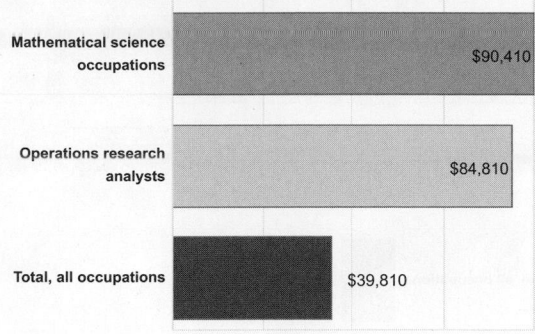

Operations Research Analysts
Median annual wages, May 2019

Mathematical science occupations: $90,410
Operations research analysts: $84,810
Total, all occupations: $39,810

Note: All Occupations includes all occupations in the U.S. Economy.
Source: U.S. Bureau of Labor Statistics, Occupational Employment Statistics.

and half earned less. The lowest 10 percent earned less than $48,670, and the highest 10 percent earned more than $140,790.

In May 2019, the median annual wages for operations research analysts in the top industries in which they worked were as follows:

Federal government	$113,940
Manufacturing	92,320
Management of companies and enterprises	87,220
Professional, scientific, and technical services	86,170
Finance and insurance	85,320

Almost all operations research analysts work full time.

Job Outlook

Employment of operations research analysts is projected to grow 25 percent from 2019 to 2029, much faster than the average for all occupations. As technology advances and companies seek efficiency and cost savings, demand for operations research analysis should continue to grow. In addition, increasing demand should occur for analysts in the field of analytics in order to improve business planning and decisionmaking.

Technological advances have made it faster and easier for organizations to get data. In addition, improvements in analytical software have made operations research more affordable and more applicable to a wider range of areas. More companies are expected to employ operations research analysts to help them turn data into valuable information that managers can use in order to make better decisions in all aspects of their business. Operations research analysts manage and analyze these data to improve business operations, supply chains, pricing models, and marketing. For example, operations research analysts will be needed to help hospitals and physicians improve the delivery of healthcare.

Operations research analysts will continue to be needed in order to provide support for the Armed Forces and assist in the

Operations Research Analysts

Percent change in employment, projected 2019-29

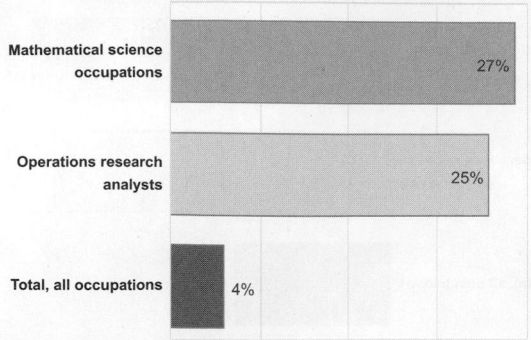

Note: All Occupations includes all occupations in the U.S. Economy.
Source: U.S. Bureau of Labor Statistics, Occupational Employment Statistics.

development and implementation of policies and programs in other areas of government.

Job Prospects

Opportunities should be better for those who have a master's or Ph.D. degree in operations research, management science, or a related field. Applicants with business experience in addition to strong analytical skills will also likely have the best job prospects.

Employment projections data for operations research analysts, 2019-29					
Occupational Title	SOC Code	Employment, 2019	Projected Employment, 2029	Change, 2019-29	
				Percent	Numeric
SOURCE: U.S. Bureau of Labor Statistics, Employment Projections program					
Operations research analysts	15-2031	105,100	131,300	25	26,100

State & Area Data

Occupational Employment Statistics (OES)

The Occupational Employment Statistics (OES) program produces employment and wage estimates annually for over 800 occupations. These estimates are available for the nation as a whole, for individual states, and for metropolitan and nonmetropolitan areas.

Contacts for More Information

For more information about operations research analysts, visit
➤ Institute for Operations Research and the Management Sciences
➤ Military Operations Research Society

Announcers

Summary

Quick Facts: Announcers

2019 Median Pay	$39,790 per year $19.13 per hour
Typical Entry-Level Education	See below
Work Experience in a Related Occupation	None
On-the-job Training	See below
Number of Jobs, 2019	76,000
Job Outlook, 2019-29	1% (Slower than average)
Employment Change, 2019-29	700

What Announcers Do

Announcers present music, news, and sports and may provide commentary or interview guests.

Work Environment

Many announcers work in radio and television studios. Some announcers are self-employed; some work part time.

How to Become an Announcer

Educational requirements for announcers vary. Radio and television announcers typically need a bachelor's degree in journalism, broadcasting, or communications, along with other experience gained from internships or working at their college radio or television station. Public address announcers typically need a high school diploma with some short-term on-the-job training.

Announcers present music, sports, and news to audiences.

Pay

The median annual wage for broadcast announcers and radio disc jockeys was $34,630 in May 2019.

The median annual wage for media and communication workers, all other was $47,580 in May 2019.

Job Outlook

Overall employment of announcers is projected to grow 1 percent from 2019 to 2029, slower than the average for all occupations.

State & Area Data

Explore resources for employment and wages by state and area for announcers.

What Announcers Do

Announcers present music, news, and sports and may provide commentary or interview guests about these other important topics. Some act as masters of ceremonies (emcees) or disc jockeys (*DJs*) at weddings, parties, or clubs.

Duties

Announcers typically do the following:

- Present music, news, sports, the weather, the time, and commercials
- Interview guests and moderate panels or discussions on their shows
- Announce station programming information, such as program schedules, station breaks for commercials, or public service information

Radio and television announcers present news and opinions and take calls from listeners.

- Research topics for comment and discussion during shows
- Read prepared scripts on radio or television shows
- Comment on important news stories
- Provide commentary for the audience during sporting events, at parades, and on other occasions
- Select program content
- Introduce upcoming acts and guide the audience through the entertainment
- Make promotional appearances at public or private events

Radio and television announcers present music or the news and comment on important current events. Announcers are expected to be up to date with current events or a specific field, such as politics or sports, so that they can comment on these issues during their programs. They may research and prepare information on current topics before appearing on air. In addition, announcers schedule guests on their shows and work with producers to develop other creative content.

Radio and television announcers also may be responsible for other aspects of television or radio broadcasting. They may operate studio equipment, sell commercial time to advertisers, or produce advertisements and other recorded material. At many radio stations, announcers do much of the work traditionally done by editors and broadcast technicians, such as broadcasting program schedules, commercials, and public service announcements.

Many radio and television announcers increasingly maintain a presence on social media sites. Establishing a presence allows them to promote their stations and better engage with their audiences, especially through listener feedback, music requests, or program contests. Announcers also make promotional appearances at charity functions or other community events.

Many radio stations now require *DJs* to update station websites with show schedules, interviews, or photos.

The following are examples of types of radio and television announcers:

- *Disc jockeys*, or *DJs*, broadcast music for radio stations. They typically specialize in one kind of music genre and announce selections as they air them. *DJs* comment on the music being broadcast as well as on weather and traffic conditions. They may take requests from listeners, interview guests, or manage listener contests.
- *Podcasters* record shows that can be downloaded for listening through a computer or mobile device. Like traditional talk radio, podcasts typically focus on a specific subject, such as sports, politics, or movies. Podcasters may also interview guests and experts on the specific program topic. However, podcasts are different from traditional radio broadcasts. Podcasts are prerecorded so audiences can download and listen to these shows at any time. Listeners can also subscribe to a podcast to have new episodes automatically downloaded to their computer or mobile devices.
- *Talk show hosts* may work in radio or television and specialize in a certain area of interest, such as politics, personal

finance, sports, or health. They contribute to the preparation of program content, interview guests, and discuss issues with viewers, listeners, or the studio audience.

Public address system announcers entertain audiences to enhance performances or they provide information. They may prepare their own scripts or improvise lines in their speeches.

The specific duties of public address system announcers vary greatly depending on where these announcers work. For example, an announcer for a sports team may have to present starting lineups (official lists of players who will participate in an event), read advertisements, and announce players as they enter and exit a game.

Train announcers are responsible for reading prepared scripts containing details and data related to train schedules and safety procedures. Their job is to provide information rather than entertainment.

The following are examples of types of public address system and other announcers:

- Emcees host planned events. They introduce speakers or performers to the audience. They may tell jokes or provide commentary to transition from one speaker to the next.
- Party DJs are hired to provide music and commentary at an event, such as a wedding, a birthday party, or a corporate party. Many of these *DJs* use digital files or portable media devices.

Work Environment

Broadcast announcers and radio disc jockeys held about 40,800 jobs in 2019. The largest employers of broadcast announcers and radio disc jockeys were as follows:

Radio broadcasting	52%
Self-employed workers	28
Television broadcasting	8
Educational services; state, local, and private	2

Radio and television announcers work with a variety of studio equipment.

Media and communication workers, all other held about 35,200 jobs in 2019. The largest employers of media and communication workers, all other were as follows:

Self-employed workers	25%
Performing arts, spectator sports, and related industries	10
Food services and drinking places	5

Radio and television announcers usually work in well-lit, air-conditioned, soundproof studios. Some radio *DJs* can produce and record their shows while working from home.

The pressure of deadlines and tight work schedules can be stressful.

Work Schedules

Some announcers work part time.

Many radio and television stations are on air 24 hours a day. Some announcers present early morning shows, while others do late-night programs. Some announcers have to work weekends or on holidays.

The shifts, however, are not as varied today as in the past. More stations are recording shows during the day, eliminating the need to have an announcer work overnight hours.

How to Become an Announcer

Educational requirements for announcers vary. Radio and television announcers typically need a bachelor's degree in journalism, broadcasting, or communications, along with other experience gained from internships or working at their college radio or television station. Public address announcers typically need a high school diploma with some short-term on-the-job training.

Education

Public address announcers typically need a high school diploma or equivalent. Radio and television announcers typically need

Many announcers have a bachelor's degree as well as experience working with radio and television equipment.

a bachelor's degree in communications, broadcasting, or journalism, but some jobs require only a high school diploma or equivalent.

College broadcasting programs offer courses, such as voice and diction, to help students improve their vocal qualities. In addition, these programs prepare students to work with the computer and audio equipment and software used at radio and television studios.

Training

Public address system and other announcers typically need short-term on-the-job training upon being hired. This training allows these announcers to become familiar with the equipment they will use during sporting and entertainment events. For sports public address announcers, training also may include basic rules and information for the sports they are covering.

Radio and television announcers whose highest level of education is a high school diploma or equivalent may also need some short-term on-the-job training to learn to operate audio and production equipment.

Other Experience

Some employers expect radio and television announcer applicants to have some announcing experience prior to employment. Applicants typically gain these skills from their college degree program, working on college radio or television stations, or through internships.

Advancement

Because radio and television stations in smaller markets have smaller staff, advancement within the same small-market station is unlikely. Rather, many radio and television announcers advance by relocating to a large-market station.

Announcers typically need a few years at a small-market station to work out the "kinks" of their on-air personalities. During that time, they learn to sound more comfortable and credible as an on-air talent and become more conversational with their cohosts and guests. Therefore, time and experience allow applicants to advance to positions in larger markets, which offer higher pay and more responsibility and challenges.

When making hiring decisions, large-market stations rely on announcers' personalities and past performance. Radio and television announcers need to have proven that they can attract, engage, and keep the attention of a sizeable audience.

Many stations also rely on radio and television announcers to do other tasks, such as creating and updating a social media presence on social networking sites, making promotional appearances on behalf of the station, or even selling commercial time to advertisers. Therefore, an applicant needs to have demonstrated versatility and flexibility at the smaller market station.

Important Qualities

Computer skills. Announcers, especially those seeking careers in radio or television, should have good computer skills and be able to use editing software and other broadcast-related devices.

Interpersonal skills. Radio and television announcers interview guests and answer phone calls on air. Party disc jockeys (*DJs*) and emcees should be comfortable working with clients to plan entertainment options.

Persistence. Entry into this occupation is very competitive, and many auditions may be needed for an opportunity to work on the air. Entry-level announcers must be willing to work for a small station and be flexible to move to a small market to secure their first job.

Research skills. Announcers must research the important topics of the day in order to be knowledgeable enough to comment on them during their program.

Speaking skills. Announcers must have a pleasant and well-controlled voice, good timing, and excellent pronunciation.

Writing skills. Announcers need strong writing skills because they normally write their own material.

Pay

The median annual wage for broadcast announcers and radio disc jockeys was $34,630 in May 2019. The median wage is the wage at which half the workers in an occupation earned more than that amount and half earned less. The lowest 10 percent earned less than $19,330, and the highest 10 percent earned more than $105,180.

The median annual wage for media and communication workers, all other was $47,580 in May 2019. The lowest 10 percent earned less than $22,820, and the highest 10 percent earned more than $92,660.

In May 2019, the median annual wages for broadcast announcers and radio disc jockeys in the top industries in which they worked were as follows:

Television broadcasting	$51,240
Educational services; state, local, and private	45,030
Radio broadcasting	31,670

In May 2019, the median annual wages for media and communication workers, all other in the top industries in which they worked were as follows:

Performing arts, spectator sports, and related industries	$37,690
Food services and drinking places	25,150

In general, announcers working in larger markets earn more than those working in smaller markets.

Some announcers work part time.

Many radio and television stations are on air 24 hours a day. Some announcers present early morning shows, and others do late-night programs. Some announcers have to work weekends or on holidays.

The shifts, however, are not as varied today as in the past. More stations are recording shows during the day, eliminating the need to have an announcer work overnight hours.

Job Outlook

Overall employment of announcers is projected to grow 1 percent from 2019 to 2029, slower than the average for all occupations. Projected employment change varies by occupation.

Employment of broadcast announcers and radio disk jockeys (DJs) is projected to decline 5 percent from 2019 to 2029. Continuing consolidation of radio and television stations will limit employment growth. In addition, over-the-air radio

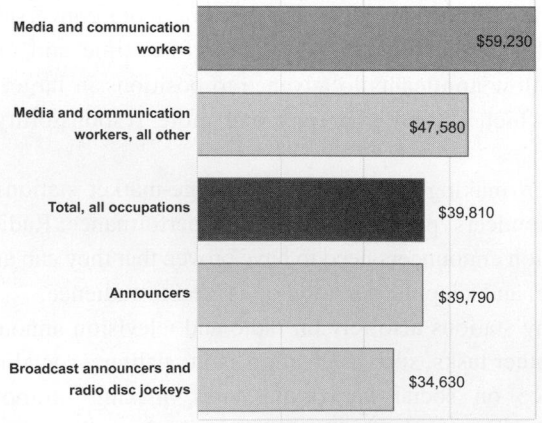

Announcers

Median annual wages, May 2019

- Media and communication workers — $59,230
- Media and communication workers, all other — $47,580
- Total, all occupations — $39,810
- Announcers — $39,790
- Broadcast announcers and radio disc jockeys — $34,630

Note: All Occupations includes all occupations in the U.S. Economy.
Source: U.S. Bureau of Labor Statistics, Occupational Employment Statistics.

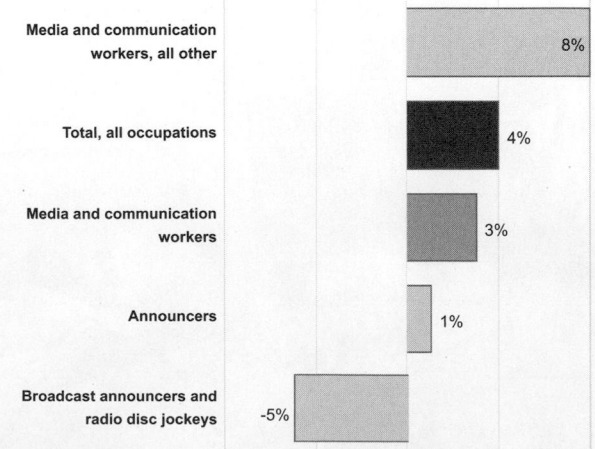

Announcers

Percent change in employment, projected 2019-29

- Media and communication workers, all other — 8%
- Total, all occupations — 4%
- Media and communication workers — 3%
- Announcers — 1%
- Broadcast announcers and radio disc jockeys — -5%

Note: All Occupations includes all occupations in the U.S. Economy.
Source: U.S. Bureau of Labor Statistics, Employment Projections program.

broadcasts will continue to face competition from an increasing number of online and satellite radio stations. More listeners are tuning into these stations, which can be personalized, reducing the number of listeners to traditional radio broadcasts and decreasing the demand for radio DJs.

Employment of media and communication workers, all other is projected to grow 8 percent, much faster than the average for all occupations. However, because it is a small occupation, the fast growth will result in only about 2,800 new jobs over the decade. Demand for additional media and communication workers will increase as the number of Internet-only platforms, such as streaming video and podcasting services, continues to grow, along with the number of shows produced for these platforms.

Job Prospects

Strong competition is expected for people seeking jobs as a radio or television announcer. Many of the openings will be due to people leaving jobs and the need to replace workers who move out of smaller markets or out of the radio or television fields entirely.

Applicants need to be persistent and flexible because many entry-level positions will require moving to a smaller market city. Small radio and television stations are more inclined to hire beginners, but the pay is low.

Those with a formal education in journalism, broadcasting, or mass communications and with hands-on work experience at a radio or television network will have the best job prospects.

In addition, because announcers may be responsible for gathering video or audio for their programs or for updating and maintaining the station's website, multimedia and computer skills are beneficial.

Employment projections data for announcers, 2019-29					
Occupational Title	SOC Code	Employment, 2019	Projected Employment, 2029	Change, 2019-29	
				Percent	Numeric
SOURCE: U.S. Bureau of Labor Statistics, Employment Projections program					
Announcers	—	76,000	76,700	1	700
Broadcast announcers and radio disc jockeys	27-3011	40,800	38,700	-5	-2,100
Media and communication workers, all other	27-3099	35,200	38,000	8	2,800

State & Area Data
Occupational Employment Statistics (OES)

The Occupational Employment Statistics (OES) program produces employment and wage estimates annually for over 800 occupations. These estimates are available for the nation as a whole, for individual states, and for metropolitan and nonmetropolitan areas.

Contacts for More Information

For more information about the broadcasting industry, in which many announcers are employed, visit
➤ National Association of Broadcasters

For more information on sports public address announcers, visit
➤ National Association of Sports Public Address Announcers

Broadcast and Sound Engineering Technicians

Summary

Quick Facts: Broadcast and Sound Engineering Technicians

2019 Median Pay	$45,510 per year $21.88 per hour
Typical Entry-Level Education	See below
Work Experience in a Related Occupation	None
On-the-job Training	Short-term on-the-job training
Number of Jobs, 2019	140,300
Job Outlook, 2019-29	9% (Much faster than average)
Employment Change, 2019-29	13,200

What Broadcast and Sound Engineering Technicians Do

Broadcast and sound engineering technicians set up, operate, and maintain the electrical equipment for media programs.

Work Environment

Broadcast and sound engineering technicians typically work indoors in radio, television, movie, and recording studios. They may also work in hotels, arenas, offices, or schools.

How to Become a Broadcast or Sound Engineering Technician

Broadcast and sound engineering technicians typically need postsecondary education. Depending on the work they do, they may need either a postsecondary nondegree award or an associate's degree.

Pay

The median annual wage for broadcast and sound engineering technicians was $45,510 in May 2019.

Job Outlook

Overall employment of broadcast and sound engineering technicians is projected to grow 9 percent from 2019 to 2029, much faster than the average for all occupations. Growth is expected to stem from businesses, schools, and entertainment industries

Broadcast and sound engineering technicians operate controls to ensure quality audio and video recordings for radio and television broadcasts.

seeking to improve their audio and video capabilities. They will need technicians to set up, operate, and maintain equipment.

State & Area Data
Explore resources for employment and wages by state and area for broadcast and sound engineering technicians.

What Broadcast and Sound Engineering Technicians Do
Broadcast and sound engineering technicians set up, operate, and maintain the electrical equipment for radio programs, television broadcasts, concerts, sound recordings, and movies.

Duties
Broadcast and sound engineering technicians typically do the following:

- Operate, monitor, and adjust audio, video, lighting, and broadcast equipment to ensure consistent quality
- Set up and take down equipment for events and live performances
- Record speech, music, and other sounds on recording equipment or computers, sometimes using complex software
- Synchronize sounds and dialogue with action taking place on television or in movie productions
- Convert video and audio records to digital formats for editing on computers
- Install audio, video, and lighting equipment in hotels, offices, and schools
- Report any problems that arise with complex equipment and make routine repairs
- Keep records of recordings and equipment used

These workers may be called broadcast or sound engineering *technicians*, *operators*, or *engineers*. They set up and operate audio and video equipment, and the kind of equipment they use

Broadcast and sound engineering technicians operate equipment in schools and office buildings.

may depend on the particular type of technician or industry. At smaller radio and television stations, broadcast and sound engineering technicians may have more responsibilities. At larger stations, they may do more specialized work, although their job assignments may vary from day to day.

Broadcast and sound engineering technicians share many responsibilities, but their duties may vary with their specific area of focus. The following are examples of types of broadcast and sound engineering technicians:

Audio and video equipment technicians set up and operate audio and video equipment. They also connect wires and cables and set up and operate sound and mixing boards and related electronic equipment.

Audio and video equipment technicians work with microphones, speakers, video screens, projectors, video monitors, and recording equipment. The equipment they operate is used for meetings, concerts, sports events, conventions, and news conferences. In addition, they may operate equipment at conferences and at presentations for businesses and postsecondary intuitions.

Audio and video equipment technicians also may set up and operate custom lighting systems. They frequently work directly with clients and must provide simple and clear solutions to problems.

Broadcast technicians, also known as *broadcast engineers*, set up, operate, and maintain equipment that regulates the signal strength, clarity, and ranges of sounds and colors for radio or television broadcasts. They operate transmitters, either in studios or on location in the field, to broadcast radio or television programs. Broadcast technicians also use computer programs to edit audio and video recordings.

Sound engineering technicians, also known as *audio engineers* or *sound mixers*, operate computers and equipment that record, synchronize, mix, or reproduce music, voices, or sound effects in recording studios, sporting arenas, theater productions, or movie and video productions. They record audio performances or events and may combine audio tracks that were recorded separately to create a multilayered final product.

Work Environment

Broadcast and sound engineering technicians held about 140,300 jobs in 2019. Employment in the detailed occupations that make up broadcast and sound engineering technicians was distributed as follows:

Audio and video technicians	91,800
Broadcast technicians	32,700
Sound engineering technicians	15,800

Broadcast and sound engineering technicians work with a variety of electronic and recording equipment.

The largest employers of broadcast and sound engineering technicians were as follows:

Radio and television broadcasting	17%
Motion picture and sound recording industries	13
Real estate and rental and leasing	11
Self-employed workers	9
Educational services; state, local, and private	8

Broadcast and sound engineering technicians typically work indoors in radio, television, movie, or recording studios. However, they may work outdoors in all types of weather in order to broadcast news and other programming on location. Audio and video technicians also set up systems in offices, arenas, hotels, schools, hospitals, and homes.

Technicians doing maintenance may climb poles or antenna towers. Those setting up equipment may do heavy lifting.

Work Schedules

Technicians usually work full time. They may occasionally work overtime to meet broadcast deadlines or set up for live events. Evening, weekend, and holiday work is common because most radio and television stations are on the air 24 hours a day.

Technicians who work on motion pictures may be on a tight schedule and may work additional hours to meet contract deadlines with the movie studio.

How to Become a Broadcast or Sound Engineering Technician

Broadcast and sound engineering technicians typically need postsecondary education. Depending on the work they do, they may need either a postsecondary nondegree award or an associate's degree.

Education

Audio and video equipment technicians, as well as sound engineering technicians, typically need a postsecondary nondegree award or certificate. Broadcast technicians typically need an associate's degree. Postsecondary nondegree programs for audio and video equipment technicians and sound engineering technicians may take several months to a year to complete. The programs include hands-on experience with the equipment used in many entry-level positions.

Broadcast technicians typically need an associate's degree. In addition to courses in math and science, coursework for prospective broadcast technicians should emphasize practical skills such as video editing and production management.

Prospective broadcast and sound engineering technicians should complete high school courses in math, physics, and electronics. They must have excellent computer skills to be successful.

Most broadcast and sound engineering technicians have an associate's degree or vocational certification, although some are hired with a high school diploma.

Training

Because technology is constantly improving, technicians often enroll in continuing education courses and receive on-the-job training to become skilled in new equipment and hardware. On-the-job training includes setting up cables or automation systems, testing electrical equipment, learning the codes and standards of the industry, and following safety procedures.

Newly hired workers may be trained in a variety of ways, depending on the types of products and services the employer provides. In addition, new workers' level of education may also dictate how much training they need.

Licenses, Certifications, and Registrations

Although it is not required by most employers, voluntary certification may offer advantages in getting a job as a broadcast or sound engineering technician. Certification tells employers that the technician meets certain industry standards and has kept up to date with new technologies.

The Society of Broadcast Engineers offers operator level, engineering level, broadcast networking, and specialist certifications. Most of these certifications require passing an exam.

The Audiovisual and Integrated Experience Association offers the general Certified Technology Specialist (CTS) credential as well as the design CTS and installation CTS. All three credentials require passing an exam and are valid for 3 years.

Other Experience

Gaining practical experience in a high school or college audiovisual department also helps to prepare for work as an audio and video equipment technician.

Advancement

Although many broadcast and sound engineering technicians work first in small markets or at small stations in big markets, they often transfer to larger, better paying radio or television stations after gaining experience and skills. Few large stations hire someone without previous experience, and they value specialized skills.

Experienced workers with strong technical skills may become supervisory broadcast technicians or chief broadcast engineers. To become chief broadcast engineer at large television stations, technicians typically need a bachelor's degree in engineering or computer science.

Important Qualities

Communication skills. Technicians need to communicate with supervisors and coworkers to ensure that clients' needs are met and that equipment is set up properly before broadcasts, live performances, and presentations.

Computer skills. Technicians use computer systems to program equipment and edit audio and video recordings.

Manual dexterity. Some technicians set up audio and visual equipment and cables, a job that requires a steady hand and good hand-eye coordination. Others adjust small knobs, dials, and sliders during radio and television broadcasts and live performances.

Problem-solving skills. Technicians need to recognize equipment problems and propose possible solutions to them. Employers typically desire applicants with a variety of skills, such as setting up equipment, maintaining the equipment, and troubleshooting and solving any problems that arise.

Pay

The median annual wage for broadcast and sound engineering technicians was $45,510 in May 2019. The median wage is the wage at which half the workers in an occupation earned more than that amount and half earned less. The lowest 10 percent earned less than $24,930, and the highest 10 percent earned more than $86,890.

Median annual wages for broadcast and sound engineering technicians in May 2019 were as follows:

Sound engineering technicians................................ $54,740

Broadcast and Sound Engineering Technicians
Median annual wages, May 2019

Media and communication equipment workers	$48,270
Broadcast and sound engineering technicians	$45,510
Total, all occupations	$39,810

Note: All Occupations includes all occupations in the U.S. Economy.
Source: U.S. Bureau of Labor Statistics, Occupational Employment Statistics.

Audio and video technicians 45,910

Broadcast technicians 40,570

In May 2019, the median annual wages for broadcast and sound engineering technicians in the top industries in which they worked were as follows:

Motion picture and sound recording industries..... $55,220

Educational services; state, local, and private 45,980

Real estate and rental and leasing........................... 42,510

Radio and television broadcasting........................... 38,720

Technicians working in major cities typically earn more than those working in smaller markets.

Technicians usually work full time. They may occasionally work overtime to meet broadcast deadlines or set up for live events. Evening, weekend, and holiday work is common because most radio and television stations are on the air 24 hours a day.

Technicians who work on motion pictures may be on a tight schedule and may work additional hours to meet contract deadlines with the movie studio.

Job Outlook

Overall employment of broadcast and sound engineering technicians is projected to grow 9 percent from 2019 to 2029, much faster than the average for all occupations.

Employment of audio and visual equipment technicians is projected to grow 12 percent from 2019 to 2029, much faster than the average for all occupations. More audio and video technicians should be needed to set up new, technologically advanced equipment or upgrade and maintain old, complex systems for a variety of organizations.

More companies are increasing their audio and video budgets so they can use video conferencing to reduce travel costs and communicate worldwide with other offices and clients. In addition, an increase in the use of digital signs across a wide

variety of industries, such as schools, hospitals, restaurants, hotels, and retail stores should lead to higher demand for audio and video equipment technicians.

Schools and universities are also seeking to improve their audio and video capabilities in order to attract and keep the best students. More audio and visual technicians may be needed to install and maintain interactive whiteboards and wireless projectors so teachers can give multimedia presentations and record lectures.

Employment of broadcast technicians is projected to grow 3 percent from 2019 to 2029, about as fast as the average for all occupation. More consumers may choose free over-the-air television programming instead of cable or satellite services, a practice commonly referred to as "cord-cutting." This may contribute to stronger demand for broadcast television. However, most major networks use a single facility to broadcast to multiple stations, which limits the growth potential for broadcast technicians.

Employment of sound engineering technicians is projected to grow 6 percent from 2019 to 2029, faster than the average for all occupations. The television and motion picture industry will continue to need technicians to improve the sound quality of shows and movies.

Job Prospects

Competition for jobs will be strong. This occupation attracts many applicants who are interested in working with the latest technology and electronic equipment. Many applicants also are attracted to working in the radio and television industry.

Those looking for work in this industry will have the most job opportunities in smaller markets or stations. Those with hands-on experience with complex electronics and software or with work experience at a radio or television station will have the best job prospects. In addition, technicians should be versatile. They should be able to set up, operate, and maintain equipment.

An associate's or bachelor's degree in broadcast technology, broadcast production, computer networking, or a related field also will improve job prospects for applicants.

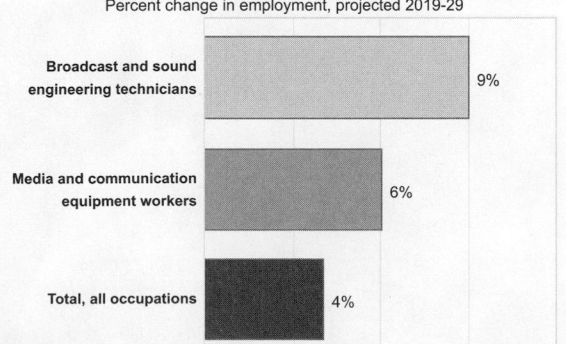

Broadcast and Sound Engineering Technicians

Percent change in employment, projected 2019-29

- Broadcast and sound engineering technicians 9%
- Media and communication equipment workers 6%
- Total, all occupations 4%

Note: All Occupations includes all occupations in the U.S. Economy.
Source: U.S. Bureau of Labor Statistics, Employment Projections program.

Occupational Title	SOC Code	Employment, 2019	Projected Employment, 2029	Change, 2019-29	
				Percent	Numeric
SOURCE: U.S. Bureau of Labor Statistics, Employment Projections program					
Broadcast and sound engineering technicians	—	140,300	153,600	9	13,200
Audio and video technicians	27-4011	91,800	103,100	12	11,300
Broadcast technicians	27-4012	32,700	33,700	3	1,000
Sound engineering technicians	27-4014	15,800	16,700	6	1,000

Employment projections data for broadcast and sound engineering technicians, 2019-29

State & Area Data

Occupational Employment Statistics (OES)

The Occupational Employment Statistics (OES) program produces employment and wage estimates annually for over 800 occupations. These estimates are available for the nation as a whole, for individual states, and for metropolitan and nonmetropolitan areas.

Contacts for More Information

For more career information and links to employment resources, visit

➤ National Association of Broadcasters
➤ Audio Engineering Society

For more information about certification and links to employment information for broadcast technicians, visit
➤ Society of Broadcast Engineers

For more information on certification and career information for audio and video equipment technicians, visit
➤ Audiovisual and Integrated Experience Association

Editors

Summary

Quick Facts: Editors

2019 Median Pay	$61,370 per year $29.50 per hour
Typical Entry-Level Education	Bachelor's degree
Work Experience in a Related Occupation	Less than 5 years
On-the-job Training	None
Number of Jobs, 2019	118,700
Job Outlook, 2019-29	-7% (Decline)
Employment Change, 2019-29	-8,700

What Editors Do

Editors plan, review, and revise content for publication.

Work Environment

Most editors work in offices, whether onsite with their employer or from a remote location. The work can be stressful because editors often have tight deadlines.

How to Become an Editor

Computer proficiency and a bachelor's degree in communications, journalism, or English are typically required to become an editor.

Pay

The median annual wage for editors was $61,370 in May 2019.

Job Outlook

Employment of editors is projected to decline 7 percent from 2019 to 2029. Despite some job growth in online media, declines in traditional print magazines and newspapers will temper employment growth.

State & Area Data

Explore resources for employment and wages by state and area for editors.

What Editors Do

Editors plan, review, and revise content for publication.

Duties

Editors typically do the following:

- Read content and correct spelling, punctuation, and grammatical errors
- Rewrite text to make it easier for readers to understand
- Verify facts cited in material for publication
- Evaluate submissions from writers to decide what to publish
- Work with writers to help their ideas and stories succeed

Editors plan, coordinate, and revise material for publication.

Editors constantly work under pressure to meet deadlines.

- Develop story and content ideas according to the publication's style and editorial policy
- Allocate space for the text, photos, and illustrations that make up a story or content
- Approve final versions submitted by staff

Editors plan, coordinate, and revise material for publication in books, newspapers, or periodicals or on websites. Editors review story ideas and decide what material will appeal most to readers. During the review process, editors offer comments to improve the product and suggest titles and headlines. In smaller organizations, a single editor may do all the editorial duties or share them with only a few other people.

The following are examples of types of editors:

Assistant editors are responsible for a particular subject, such as local news, international news, feature stories, or sports. Most assistant editors work for newspaper publishers, television broadcasters, magazines, book publishers, or advertising and public relations firms.

Copy editors proofread text for errors in grammar, punctuation, and spelling and check for readability, style, and agreement with editorial policy. They suggest revisions, such as changing words and rearranging sentences and paragraphs to improve clarity or accuracy. They also may carry out research, confirm sources, and verify facts, dates, and statistics. In addition, they may arrange page layouts of articles, photographs, and advertising.

Executive editors oversee assistant editors and generally have the final say about which stories are published and how those stories are covered. Executive editors typically hire writers, reporters, and other employees. They also plan budgets and negotiate contracts with freelance writers, who are sometimes called "stringers" in the news industry. Although many executive editors work for newspaper publishers, some work for television broadcasters, magazines, or advertising and public relations firms.

Managing editors typically work for magazines, newspaper publishers, and television broadcasters and are responsible for the daily operations of a news department.

Publication assistants who work for book-publishing houses may read and evaluate manuscripts, proofread uncorrected drafts, and answer questions about published material. Assistants on small newspapers or in smaller media markets may compile articles available from wire services or the Internet, answer phones, and proofread articles.

Work Environment

Editors held about 118,700 jobs in 2019. The largest employers of editors were as follows:

Newspaper, periodical, book, and directory publishers	35%
Self-employed workers	14
Professional, scientific, and technical services	10

Editors usually work full time in offices.

Religious, grantmaking, civic, professional, and similar organizations	9
Other information services	9

Most editors work in offices, whether onsite with their employer or from a remote location. They often use desktop or electronic publishing software, scanners, and other electronic communications equipment.

Jobs are somewhat concentrated in major media and entertainment markets—Boston, Chicago, Los Angeles, New York, and Washington, DC—but improved communications and Internet capabilities are allowing editors to work from a greater variety of locations.

Overseeing and coordinating multiple writing projects simultaneously is common among editors and may lead to stress or fatigue.

Self-employed editors face the added pressures of finding work on an ongoing basis and continually adjusting to new work environments.

Work Schedules

Most editors work full time, and their schedules are generally determined by production deadlines and type of editorial position. Editors typically work in busy offices and have to deal with production deadline pressures and the stresses of ensuring that the information they publish is correct. As a result, editors often work many hours, especially at those times leading up to a publication deadline. These work hours can be even more frequent when an editor is working on digital material for the Internet or for a live broadcast.

How to Become an Editor

A bachelor's degree in communications, journalism, or English, combined with previous writing and proofreading experience, is typically required to be an editor.

Education

Employers generally prefer candidates who have a bachelor's degree in communications, journalism, or English.

Candidates with other backgrounds who can show strong writing skills also may find jobs as editors. Editors who deal with specific subject matter may need related work experience. For example, fashion editors may need expertise in fashion that they gain through formal training or work experience.

Work Experience in a Related Occupation

Many editors start off as editorial assistants, writers, or reporters.

Those who are particularly skilled at identifying good stories, recognizing writing talent, and interacting with writers may be interested in editing jobs.

Other Experience

Editors can gain experience by working on high school and college newspapers and for magazines, radio and television stations, advertising and publishing companies. Magazines and newspapers may have offer student internships. For example, the American Society of Magazine Editors offers a Magazine Internship Program to qualified full-time students in their junior or senior year of college. Interns may write stories, conduct research and interviews, and gain general publishing experience.

A college degree is typically required for someone to be an editor.

Editors need to be proficient in computer use, including electronic publishing, graphics, Web design, social media, and multimedia production.

Advancement

Some editors hold management positions and must make decisions related to running a business. For them, advancement generally means moving up to publications with larger circulation or greater prestige. Copy editors may move into original writing or substantive editing positions or become freelancers.

Important Qualities

Creativity. Editors must be imaginative, curious, and knowledgeable in a broad range of topics. Some editors must regularly come up with interesting content or story ideas and attention-grabbing headlines.

Detail oriented. Editors must be meticulous to ensure that material is error free and matches the style of a publication.

Good judgment. Editors decide whether certain stories are ethical and whether there is enough evidence to publish them.

Interpersonal skills. In working with writers, editors must have tact and the ability to guide and encourage them in their work.

Writing skills. Editors ensure that all written content has correct grammar, punctuation, and syntax. Editors must be able to write clearly and logically.

Pay

The median annual wage for editors was $61,370 in May 2019. The median wage is the wage at which half the workers in an occupation earned more than that amount and half earned less. The lowest 10 percent earned less than $32,620, and the highest 10 percent earned more than $122,280.

In May 2019, the median annual wages for editors in the top industries in which they worked were as follows:

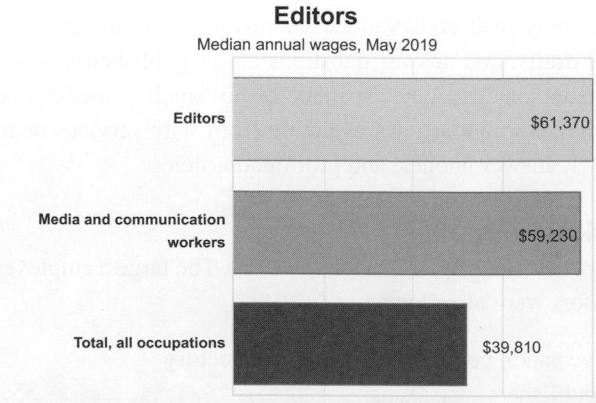

Editors
Median annual wages, May 2019

Editors	$61,370
Media and communication workers	$59,230
Total, all occupations	$39,810

Note: All Occupations includes all occupations in the U.S. Economy.
Source: U.S. Bureau of Labor Statistics, Occupational Employment Statistics.

Editors
Percent change in employment, projected 2019-29

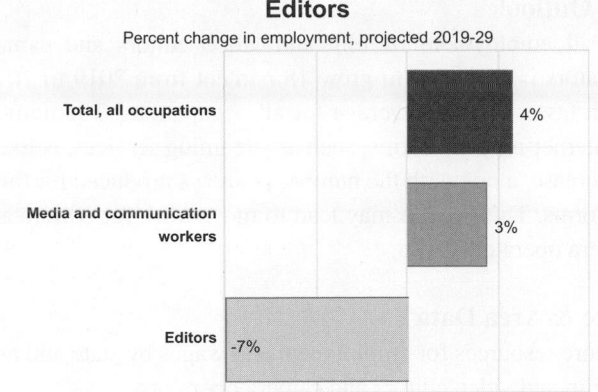

Total, all occupations	4%
Media and communication workers	3%
Editors	-7%

Note: All Occupations includes all occupations in the U.S. Economy.
Source: U.S. Bureau of Labor Statistics, Employment Projections program.

Professional, scientific, and technical services........	$69,270
Religious, grantmaking, civic, professional, and similar organizations	68,530
Other information services	66,530
Newspaper, periodical, book, and directory publishers	57,030

Most editors work full time, and their schedules are generally determined by production deadlines and type of editorial position. Editors typically work in busy offices and have to deal with production deadline pressures and the stresses of ensuring that the information they publish is correct. As a result, editors often work many hours, especially at those times leading up to a publication deadline. These work hours can be even more frequent when an editor is working on digital material for the Internet or for a live broadcast.

Job Outlook

Employment of editors is projected to decline 7 percent from 2019 to 2029. Despite some job growth in online media, decreases in traditional print magazines and newspapers will cause a decline in overall employment of editors.

Job Prospects

Competition for jobs with established newspapers and magazines will be particularly strong because employment in the publishing industry is projected to decline. Editors who have adapted to online media and are comfortable writing for and working with a variety of electronic and digital tools will have the best prospects in finding work. Although the way in which people consume media has changed, editors will continue to add value by reviewing and revising drafts and keeping the style and voice of a publication consistent.

Occupational Title	SOC Code	Employment, 2019	Projected Employment, 2029	Change, 2019-29	
				Percent	Numeric
SOURCE: U.S. Bureau of Labor Statistics, Employment Projections program					
Editors	27-3041	118,700	110,000	-7	-8,700

Employment projections data for editors, 2019-29

State & Area Data
Occupational Employment Statistics (OES)

The Occupational Employment Statistics (OES) program produces employment and wage estimates annually for over 800 occupations. These estimates are available for the nation as a whole, for individual states, and for metropolitan and nonmetropolitan areas.

Contacts for More Information

For more information about editors, visit
➤ American Copy Editors Society
➤ American Society of Magazine Editors
➤ Association of Alternative Newsmedia
➤ Radio Television Digital News Association

Film and Video Editors and Camera Operators

Summary

Quick Facts: Film and Video Editors and Camera Operators

2019 Median Pay	$59,810 per year
	$28.76 per hour
Typical Entry-Level Education	Bachelor's degree
Work Experience in a Related Occupation	None
On-the-job Training	None
Number of Jobs, 2019	67,900
Job Outlook, 2019-29......................................	18% (Much faster than average)
Employment Change, 2019-29	12,400

What Film and Video Editors and Camera Operators Do

Film and video editors and camera operators manipulate moving images that entertain or inform an audience.

Work Environment

Film and video editors and camera operators typically work in studios or in office settings. Camera operators and videographers often shoot raw footage on location.

How to Become a Film and Video Editor or Camera Operator

Film and video editors and camera operators typically need a bachelor's degree in a field related to film or broadcasting.

Pay

The median annual wage for camera operators, television, video, and film was $55,160 in May 2019.

The median annual wage for film and video editors was $63,780 in May 2019.

Job Outlook

Overall employment of film and video editors and camera operators is projected to grow 18 percent from 2019 to 2029, much faster than the average for all occupations. The number of Internet-only platforms, such as streaming services, is likely to increase, along with the number of shows produced for these platforms. This growth may lead to more work for editors and camera operators.

State & Area Data

Explore resources for employment and wages by state and area for film and video editors and camera operators.

What Film and Video Editors and Camera Operators Do

Film and video editors and camera operators manipulate images that entertain or inform an audience. Camera operators capture a wide range of material for TV shows, movies, and other media. Editors arrange footage shot by camera operators and collaborate with producers and directors to create the final content.

Duties

Film and video editors and camera operators typically do the following:

- Shoot and record television programs, motion pictures, music videos, documentaries, or news and sporting events
- Organize digital footage with video-editing software
- Collaborate with a director to determine the overall vision of the production
- Discuss filming and editing techniques with a director to improve a scene
- Select the appropriate equipment, such as the type of lens or lighting
- Shoot or edit a scene based on the director's vision

Film and video editors manipulate images that entertain or inform an audience.

Nearly all video editing work is done on a computer.

Many camera operators supervise one or more assistants. The assistants set up the camera equipment and may be responsible for its storage and care. Assistants also help the operator determine the best shooting angle and make sure that the camera stays in focus.

Likewise, editors often have one or more assistants. The assistants support the editor by keeping track of each shot in a database or loading digital video into an editing bay. Assistants also may do some of the editing tasks.

Most operators prefer using digital cameras because the smaller, more inexpensive instruments give them more flexibility in shooting angles. Digital cameras also have changed the job of some camera assistants: Instead of loading film or choosing lenses, they download digital images or choose a type of software program to use with the camera. In addition, drone cameras give operators an opportunity to film in the air, or in places that are hard to reach.

Nearly all editing work is done on a computer, and editors often are trained in a specific type of editing software.

The following are examples of types of camera operators:

Cinematographers film motion pictures. They usually work with a team of camera operators and assistants. Cinematographers determine the angles and types of equipment that will best capture a shot. They also adjust the lighting in a shot, because that is an important part of how the image looks.

Cinematographers may use stationary cameras that shoot whatever passes in front of them, or they may use a camera mounted on a track and move around the action. Some cinematographers sit on cranes to film an action scene; others carry the camera on their shoulder while they move around the action.

Some cinematographers specialize in filming cartoons or special effects. For information about a career in animation, see multimedia artists and animators.

Studio camera operators work in a broadcast studio and videotape their subjects from a fixed position. There may be one or several cameras in use at a time. Operators normally follow directions that give the order of the shots. They often have time to practice camera movements before shooting begins. If they are shooting a live event, they must be able to make adjustments at a moment's notice and follow the instructions of the show's director. The use of robotic cameras is common among studio camera operators, and one operator may control several cameras at once.

Videographers film or videotape private ceremonies or special events, such as weddings. They also may work with companies and make corporate documentaries on a variety of topics. Most videographers edit their own material.

Many videographers run their own business or do freelance work. They may submit bids, write contracts, and get permission to shoot on locations that may not be open to the public. They also get copyright protection for their work and keep financial records.

Many editors and camera operators, but particularly videographers, put their creative work online. If it becomes popular, they gain more recognition, which can lead to future employment or freelance opportunities.

Work Environment

Camera operators, television, video, and film held about 29,700 jobs in 2019. The largest employers of camera operators, television, video, and film were as follows:

Motion picture and video industries	28%
Self-employed workers	26
Radio and television broadcasting	19
Professional, scientific, and technical services	6
Government	3

Film and video editors held about 38,300 jobs in 2019. The largest employers of film and video editors were as follows:

Motion picture and video industries	49%
Self-employed workers	27
Television broadcasting	6
Professional, scientific, and technical services	5

Camera operators work in a variety of conditions and may have to stand for long periods.

Film and video editors and camera operators typically work in studios or offices. Camera operators and videographers often shoot raw footage on location.

Film and video editors work in editing rooms by themselves, or with producers and directors, for many hours at a time. Cinematographers and operators who shoot movies or TV shows may film on location and be away from home for months at a time. Operators who travel usually must carry heavy equipment to their shooting locations.

Some camera operators work in uncomfortable or even dangerous conditions, such as severe weather, military conflicts, and natural disasters. They may have to stand for long periods waiting for an event to take place. They may carry heavy equipment while on shooting assignment.

Work Schedules

Work hours vary with the type of operator or editor, although most work full time. Those who work in broadcasting may put in additional hours to meet a deadline. Those who work in the motion picture industry may have busy schedules while filming, but they go through a period of looking for work once a film is complete and before they are hired for their next job.

How to Become a Film and Video Editor or Camera Operator

Film and video editors and camera operators typically need a bachelor's degree in a field related to film or broadcasting.

Education

Most editor and camera operator positions require a bachelor's degree in a field related to film or broadcasting, such as communications. Many colleges offer courses in cinematography or video-editing software. Coursework involves a mix of film theory with practical training.

Film and video editors and camera operators must have an understanding of digital cameras and editing software because both are now used on film sets.

Most editor and camera operator positions require a bachelor's degree in a field related to film or broadcasting.

Training

Employers may offer new employees training in the type of specialized editing software those employers use. Most editors eventually specialize in one type of software, but beginners should be familiar with as many types as possible.

Licenses, Certifications, and Registrations

Editors may demonstrate competence in various types of editing software by earning certification, which is generally offered by software vendors. Certification requires passing a comprehensive exam, and candidates can prepare for the exam on their own, through online tutorials, or through classroom instruction.

Advancement

Experienced film and video editors and camera operators with creativity and leadership skills can advance to overseeing their own projects. For more information, see the profile on producers and directors.

Important Qualities

Communication skills. Film and video editors and camera operators must communicate with other members of a production team, including producers and directors, to ensure that the project goes smoothly.

Computer skills. Film and video editors must use sophisticated editing software.

Creativity. Film and video editors and camera operators should be able to imagine what the result of their filming or editing will look like to an audience.

Detail oriented. Editors look at every frame of film and decide what should be kept or cut in order to maintain the best content.

Hand–eye coordination. Camera operators need to be able to move about the action while holding a camera steady.

Physical stamina. Camera operators may need to carry heavy equipment for long periods, particularly when they are filming on location.

Visual skills. Film and video editors and camera operators must see clearly what they are filming or editing in the postproduction process.

Pay

The median annual wage for camera operators, television, video, and film was $55,160 in May 2019. The median wage is the wage at which half the workers in an occupation earned more than that amount and half earned less. The lowest 10 percent earned less than $26,560, and the highest 10 percent earned more than $110,790.

The median annual wage for film and video editors was $63,780 in May 2019. The lowest 10 percent earned less than $32,750, and the highest 10 percent earned more than $168,320.

Film and Video Editors and Camera Operators

Median annual wages, May 2019

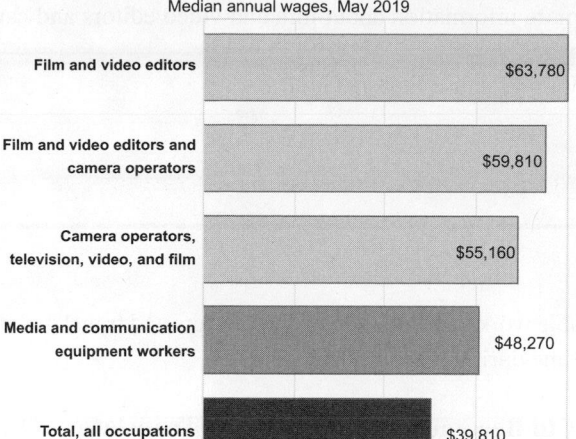

- Film and video editors — $63,780
- Film and video editors and camera operators — $59,810
- Camera operators, television, video, and film — $55,160
- Media and communication equipment workers — $48,270
- Total, all occupations — $39,810

Note: All Occupations includes all occupations in the U.S. Economy.
Source: U.S. Bureau of Labor Statistics, Occupational Employment Statistics.

Film and Video Editors and Camera Operators

Percent change in employment, projected 2019-29

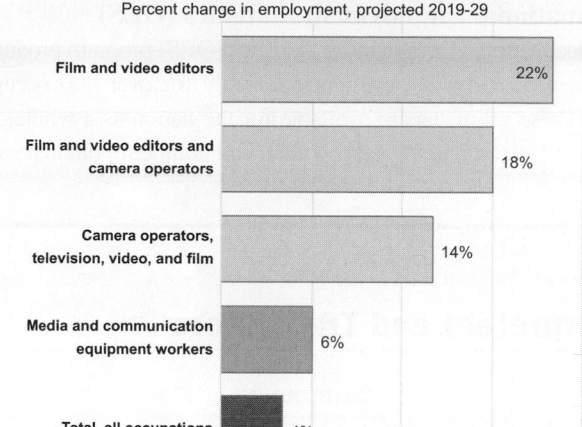

- Film and video editors — 22%
- Film and video editors and camera operators — 18%
- Camera operators, television, video, and film — 14%
- Media and communication equipment workers — 6%
- Total, all occupations — 4%

Note: All Occupations includes all occupations in the U.S. Economy.
Source: U.S. Bureau of Labor Statistics, Employment Projections program.

In May 2019, the median annual wages for camera operators, television, video, and film in the top industries in which they worked were as follows:

Motion picture and video industries	$62,510
Radio and television broadcasting	52,360
Government	52,290
Professional, scientific, and technical services	43,590

In May 2019, the median annual wages for film and video editors in the top industries in which they worked were as follows:

Motion picture and video industries	$69,480
Professional, scientific, and technical services	57,140
Television broadcasting	51,870

Work hours vary with the type of operator or editor, although most work full time. Those who work in broadcasting may put in additional hours to meet a deadline. Those who work in the motion picture industry may have busy schedules while filming, but they go through a period of looking for work once a film is complete and before they are hired for their next job.

Job Outlook

Employment of film and video editors is projected to grow 22 percent from 2019 to 2029, much faster than the average for all occupations.

Employment of camera operators is projected to grow 14 percent from 2019 to 2029, faster than the average for all occupations.

The number of Internet-only platforms, such as streaming services, is likely to increase, along with the number of shows produced for these platforms. This growth may lead to more work for editors and camera operators.

In broadcasting, the consolidation of roles—such as editors who determine the best angles for a shoot, the use of robotic cameras, and the increasing reliance on amateur film footage—may lead to fewer jobs for camera operators. However, more film and video editors are expected to be needed because of an increase in special effects and overall available content.

Job Prospects

Film and video editors and camera operators will face strong competition for jobs. Most job openings are projected to be in entertainment hubs such as New York City and Los Angeles because specialized editing workers are in demand there. Those with experience at a TV station or on a film set should have the best prospects. Video editors may improve their prospects by developing skills with different types of specialized editing software.

Employment projections data for film and video editors and camera operators, 2019-29					
Occupational Title	SOC Code	Employment, 2019	Projected Employment, 2029	Change, 2019-29	
				Percent	Numeric
SOURCE: U.S. Bureau of Labor Statistics, Employment Projections program					
Television, video, and film camera operators and editors	27-4030	67,900	80,400	18	12,400
Camera operators, television, video, and film	27-4031	29,700	33,800	14	4,200
Film and video editors	27-4032	38,300	46,500	22	8,300

State & Area Data
Occupational Employment Statistics (OES)

The Occupational Employment Statistics (OES) program produces employment and wage estimates annually for over 800 occupations. These estimates are available for the nation as a whole, for individual states, and for metropolitan and nonmetropolitan areas.

Contacts for More Information

For more information about film and video editors and camera operators, visit

➤ Motion Picture Editors Guild

Interpreters and Translators

Summary

Quick Facts: Interpreters and Translators

2019 Median Pay	$51,830 per year
	$24.92 per hour
Typical Entry-Level Education	Bachelor's degree
Work Experience in a Related Occupation ...	None
On-the-job Training	None
Number of Jobs, 2019.................................	77,400
Job Outlook, 2019-29..................................	20% (Much faster than average)
Employment Change, 2019-29	15,500

What Interpreters and Translators Do

Interpreters and translators convert information from one language into another language.

Work Environment

Interpreters work in settings such as schools, hospitals, courtrooms, meeting rooms, and conference centers. Some work for translation and interpretation companies, individual organizations, or private clients. Many translators also work remotely. Self-employed interpreters and translators frequently have variable work schedules. Most interpreters and translators work full time during regular business hours.

How to Become an Interpreter or Translator

Although interpreters and translators typically need at least a bachelor's degree, the most important requirement is to have native-level proficiency in English and at least one other language.

Pay

The median annual wage for interpreters and translators was $51,830 in May 2019.

Job Outlook

Employment of interpreters and translators is projected to grow 20 percent from 2019 to 2029, much faster than the average for all occupations. Globalization and large increases in the number of non-English-speaking people in the United States will drive employment growth. Job prospects should be best for those who have professional certification.

State & Area Data

Explore resources for employment and wages by state and area for interpreters and translators.

What Interpreters and Translators Do

Interpreters and translators convert information from one language into another language. Interpreters work in spoken or sign language; translators work in written language.

Duties

Interpreters and translators typically do the following:

- Convert concepts in the source language to equivalent concepts in the target language
- Compile information and technical terms into glossaries and terminology databases to be used in their oral renditions and translations
- Speak, read, and write fluently in at least two languages, one of which is usually English
- Relay the style and tone of the original language
- Render spoken messages accurately, quickly, and clearly
- Apply their cultural knowledge to render an accurate and meaningful interpretation or translation of the original message

Interpreters and translators convert information from one language into another.

Interpreters and translators speak, read, and write in at least two languages fluently.

Interpreters and translators aid communication by converting messages or text from one language into another language. Although some people do both, interpreting and translating are different professions: interpreters work with spoken communication, and translators work with written communication.

Interpreters convert information from one spoken language into another—or, in the case of sign language interpreters, between spoken language and sign language. The goal of an interpreter is to have people hear the interpretation as if it were the original language. Interpreters usually must be fluent speakers or signers of both languages, because they communicate back and forth among people who do not share a common language.

There are three common modes of interpreting: simultaneous, consecutive, and sight translation:

- **Simultaneous interpreters** convey a spoken or signed message into another language at the same time someone is speaking or signing. Simultaneous interpreters must be familiar with the subject matter and maintain a high level of concentration to convey the message accurately and completely. Due to the mental fatigue involved, simultaneous interpreters may work in pairs or small teams if they are interpreting for long periods of time, such as in a court or conference setting.
- **Consecutive interpreters** convey the speaker's or signer's message in another language after they have stopped to allow

for the interpretation. Note taking is generally an essential part of consecutive interpreting.
- **Sight translation interpreters** provide translation of a written document directly into a spoken language, for immediate understanding, but not for the purposes of producing a written translated document.
- *Translators* convert written materials from one language into another language. The goal of a translator is to have people read the translation as if it were the original written material. To do that, the translator must be able to write in a way that maintains or duplicates the structure and style of the original text while keeping the ideas and facts of the original material accurate. Translators must properly transmit any cultural references, including slang, and other expressions that do not translate literally.

Translators must read the original language fluently. They usually translate into their native language.

Nearly all translation work is done on a computer, and translators receive and submit most assignments electronically. Translations often go through several revisions before becoming final.

Translation usually is done with computer-assisted translation (CAT) tools, in which a computer database of previously translated sentences or segments (called a "translation memory") may be used to translate new text. CAT tools allow translators to work more efficiently and consistently. Translators also edit materials translated by computers, or machine translation. This process is called post-editing.

Interpretation and translation services are needed in virtually all subject areas. Although most interpreters and translators specialize in a particular field or industry, many have more than one area of specialization.

The following are examples of types of interpreters and translators:

Community interpreters work in community-based environments, providing vital language interpretation one-on-one or in group settings. Community interpreters often are needed at parent–teacher conferences, community events, business and public meetings, social and government agencies, new-home purchases, and many other work and community settings.

Conference interpreters work at conferences that have non-English-speaking attendees. The work is often in the field of international business or diplomacy, although conference interpreters can interpret for any organization that works with speakers of foreign languages. Employers generally prefer more experienced interpreters who can convert two languages into one native language—for example, the ability to interpret from Spanish and French into English. For some positions, such as those with the United Nations, this qualification is required.

Conference interpreters often do simultaneous interpreting. Attendees at a conference or meeting who do not understand the language of the speaker wear earphones tuned to the interpreter who speaks the language they want to hear.

Health or medical interpreters and translators typically work in healthcare settings and help patients communicate with doctors, nurses, technicians, and other medical staff. Interpreters and translators must have knowledge of medical terminology and of common medical terms in both languages. They may translate research material, regulatory information, pharmaceutical and informational brochures, patient consent documents, website information, and patients' records from one language into another.

Healthcare or medical interpreters must be sensitive to patients' personal circumstances, as well as maintain confidentiality and ethical standards. Interpretation may also be provided remotely, either by video relay or over the phone.

Liaison or escort interpreters accompany either U.S. visitors abroad or foreign visitors in the United States who have limited English proficiency. Interpreting in both formal and informal settings, these specialists ensure that the visitors can communicate during their stay. Frequent travel is common for liaison or escort interpreters.

Legal or judicial interpreters and translators typically work in courts and other legal settings. At hearings, arraignments, depositions, and trials, they help people who have limited English proficiency. Accordingly, they must understand legal terminology. Many court interpreters must sometimes read documents aloud in a language other than that in which they were written, a task known as sight translation. Legal or judiciary interpreters and translators must have a strong understanding of legal terminology.

Literary translators convert journal articles, books, poetry, and short stories from one language into another language. They work to keep the tone, style, and meaning of the author's work. Whenever possible, literary translators work closely with authors to capture the intended meaning, as well as the literary and cultural characteristics, of the original publication.

Localizers adapt text and graphics used in a product or service from one language into another language, a task known as localization. Localization specialists work to make it appear as though the product originated in the country where it will be sold. They must not only know both languages, but also understand the technical information they are working with and the culture of the people who will be using the product or service. Localizers make extensive use of computer and web-based localization tools and generally work in teams.

Localization may include adapting websites, software, marketing materials, user documentation, and various other publications. Usually, these adaptations are related to products and services in information technology, manufacturing and other business sectors.

Sign language interpreters facilitate communication between people who are deaf or hard of hearing and people who can hear. Sign language interpreters must be fluent in English and in American Sign Language (ASL), which combines signing, finger spelling, and specific body language. ASL is a separate language from English and has its own grammar.

Some interpreters specialize in other forms of interpreting for people who are deaf or hard of hearing.

Some people who are deaf or hard of hearing can lip-read English instead of signing in ASL. Interpreters who work with these people do "oral interpretation," mouthing speech silently and very carefully so that their lips can be read easily. They also may use facial expressions and gestures to help the lip-reader understand.

Other modes of interpreting include cued speech, which uses hand shapes placed near the mouth to give lip-readers more information; signing exact English; and tactile signing, which is interpreting for people who are blind as well as deaf by making hand signs into the deaf and blind person's hand.

Trilingual interpreters facilitate communication among an English speaker, a speaker of another language, and an ASL user. They must have the versatility, adaptability, and cultural understanding necessary to interpret in all three languages without changing the fundamental meaning of the message.

Work Environment

Interpreters and translators held about 77,400 jobs in 2019. The largest employers of interpreters and translators were as follows:

Professional, scientific, and technical services	34%
Self-employed workers	21
Educational services; state, local, and private	18
Hospitals; state, local, and private	8
Government	6

Interpreters work in settings such as schools, hospitals, courtrooms, detention facilities, meeting rooms, and conference centers. Judiciary and conference interpreters may travel frequently. Depending on the setting and type of assignment, interpreting may be stressful, as highly technical or sensitive information must be relayed accurately. In some settings,

Legal interpreters must sometimes read documents aloud in a language other than that in which they were written.

interpreters may work as part of a team. With the development of new communication technology, more interpreters are working remotely via video or telephone connections.

Translators who work remotely receive and submit their work electronically, and must sometimes deal with the pressure of deadlines and tight schedules. Some translators are employees at translation companies or individual organizations.

Work Schedules

Self-employed interpreters and translators often have variable work schedules, which may include periods of limited work and periods of long, irregular hours. Most interpreters and translators work full time.

How to Become an Interpreter or Translator

Although interpreters and translators typically need at least a bachelor's degree, the most important requirement is that they be fluent in at least two languages (English and at least one other language).

Education

A bachelor's degree is typically needed to become an interpreter or translator along with proficiency in at least two languages, one of which is usually English.

High school students interested in becoming an interpreter or translator should take a broad range of courses that focus on foreign languages and English writing and comprehension.

Beyond high school, people interested in becoming interpreters or translators have numerous educational options. Those in college typically choose a specific language as their major, such as Spanish or French. Although many jobs require a bachelor's degree, majoring in a language is not always necessary.

Through community organizations, students interested in sign language interpreting may take introductory classes in American Sign Language (ASL) and seek out volunteer opportunities to work with people who are deaf or hard of hearing.

Some interpreters and translators attain a bachelors degree in a specific language or American Sign Language.

Training

Interpreters and translators generally do not need any formal training, as they are expected to be able to interpret and translate before they are hired. However, those working in the community as court or medical interpreters or translators are more likely to complete job-specific training programs or certificates.

Continuing education is a requirement for most state court and medical interpreting certification programs. It is offered by professional interpreter and translator associations such as the American Translators Association and the National Association of Judiciary Interpreters on a regular basis.

Licenses, Certifications, and Registrations

There is currently no universal certification required of interpreters and translators beyond passing the required court interpreting exams offered by most states. However, workers can take a variety of tests that show proficiency. For example, the American Translators Association provides certification in 29 language combinations.

The federal courts offer court interpreter certification for Spanish language interpreters. At the state level, the courts offer certification in at least 20 languages.

The National Association of the Deaf and the Registry of Interpreters for the Deaf jointly offer certification for general sign language interpreters. In addition, the registry offers specialty tests in legal interpreting, speech reading, and deaf-to-deaf interpreting—which includes interpreting among deaf speakers of different native languages and from ASL to tactile signing.

The U.S. Department of State has a three-test series for prospective interpreters—one test in simple consecutive interpreting (for escort work), another in simultaneous interpreting (for court work), and a third in conference-level interpreting (for international conferences)—as well as a test for prospective translators. These tests are not considered a credential, but their completion indicates that a person has significant skill in the occupation. The National Virtual Translation Center and many other organizations also have testing programs.

The Certification Commission for Healthcare Interpreters offers two types of certifications for healthcare interpreters: Associate Healthcare Interpreter, for interpreters of languages other than Spanish, Arabic, and Mandarin; and Certified Healthcare Interpreter, for interpreters of Spanish, Arabic, and Mandarin.

The National Board of Certification for Medical Interpreters offers certification for medical interpreters of Spanish, Cantonese, Mandarin, Russian, Korean, and Vietnamese languages.

Other Experience

Other helpful experience for pursuing this career include spending time in a foreign country, interacting directly with foreign cultures, and studying a variety of subjects in English and at least one other language. Some students study a specialty such as law, engineering, or medicine in order to provide a higher level of interpreting and translation.

A good way for translators to learn firsthand about the occupation is to start working in-house for a translation company. Doing informal or volunteer work is an excellent way for people seeking interpreter or translator jobs to gain experience.

Volunteer opportunities for interpreters are available through community organizations, hospitals, and sporting events, such as marathons, that involve international competitors.

Paid or unpaid internships are other ways that interpreters and translators can gain experience. Escort interpreting may offer an opportunity for inexperienced candidates to work alongside a more experienced interpreter. Interpreters also may find it easier to begin working in industries with particularly high demand for language services, such as court or medical interpreting.

Whatever path of entry new interpreters and translators pursue, they should develop mentoring relationships with experienced workers in the field to build their skills and confidence and to establish and expand a network of contacts. Mentoring may be formal, such as that received through a professional association, or informal, such as that engaged in with a coworker or an acquaintance who has experience as an interpreter or translator. Both the American Translators Association and the Registry of Interpreters for the Deaf offer formal mentoring programs.

Advancement

After interpreters and translators have enough experience, they can move up to more difficult assignments, seek certification, and obtain editorial responsibility. They can also manage or start their own business.

Many self-employed interpreters and translators choose to become self-employed as a means to advance. They may submit resumes and samples to different translation and interpreting companies who will match their skills with various jobs. Many get work on the basis of their reputation or through referrals from clients or colleagues. Some may also start their own companies, where they hire other translators and interpreters to work for them.

Important Qualities

Business skills. Self-employed interpreters and translators need general business skills to manage their finances and careers successfully. They must set prices for their work, bill customers, keep records, and market their services in order to build their client base.

Concentration. Interpreters and translators must be able to concentrate while others are speaking or moving around them.

Cultural sensitivity. Interpreters and translators must be sensitive to cultural differences and expectations among the people whom they are helping to communicate. Successful interpreting and translating is a matter not only of knowing the words in different languages but also of understanding people's cultures.

Dexterity. Sign language interpreters must be able to make quick and coordinated hand, finger, and arm movements when interpreting.

Interpersonal skills. Interpreters and translators, particularly those who are self-employed, must be able to get along with those who hire or use their services in order to retain clients and attract new business.

Listening skills. Interpreters must listen carefully when interpreting for audiences to ensure that they hear and interpret correctly.

Reading skills. Translators must be able to read in all of the languages in which they are working.

Speaking skills. Interpreters and translators must speak clearly in all of the languages in which they are working.

Writing skills. Translators must be able to write clearly and effectively in all of the languages in which they are working.

Pay

The median annual wage for interpreters and translators was $51,830 in May 2019. The median wage is the wage at which half the workers in an occupation earned more than that amount and half earned less. The lowest 10 percent earned less than $28,170, and the highest 10 percent earned more than $94,370.

In May 2019, the median annual wages for interpreters and translators in the top industries in which they worked were as follows:

Professional, scientific, and technical services.......	$57,450
Government...	57,370
Hospitals; state, local, and private...........................	50,980
Educational services; state, local, and private........	50,110

Wages depend on the language, specialty, skill, experience, education, and certification of the interpreter or translator, as well as on the type of employer. Wages of interpreters and translators vary widely. Interpreters and translators who know languages that are in high demand or that relatively few people

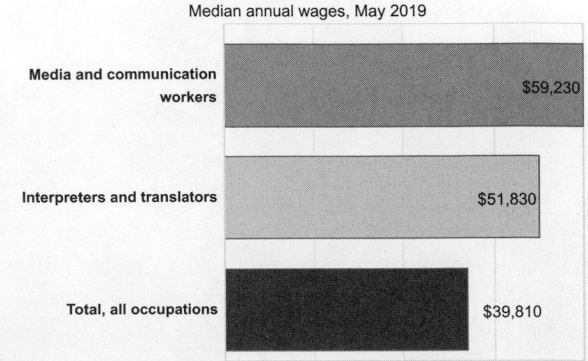

Interpreters and Translators
Median annual wages, May 2019

Media and communication workers — $59,230

Interpreters and translators — $51,830

Total, all occupations — $39,810

Note: All Occupations includes all occupations in the U.S. Economy.
Source: U.S. Bureau of Labor Statistics, Occupational Employment Statistics.

can translate often earn higher wages. Those who perform services requiring a high level of skill, such as conference interpreters, also receive higher pay.

Self-employed interpreters usually charge per hour. Half-day or full-day rates are also common.

Self-employed interpreters and translators often have variable work schedules, which may include periods of limited work and periods of long, irregular hours. Most interpreters and translators work full time.

Job Outlook

Employment of interpreters and translators is projected to grow 20 percent from 2019 to 2029, much faster than the average for all occupations. Employment growth reflects increasing globalization and a more diverse U.S. population, which is expected to require more interpreters and translators.

Demand will likely remain strong for translators of frequently translated languages, such as French, German, Portuguese, Russian, and Spanish. Demand also should be strong for translators of Arabic and other Middle Eastern languages; for the principal Asian languages including Chinese, Japanese, Hindi, and Korean; and for the indigenous languages from Mexico and Central America such as Mixtec, Zapotec, and Mayan languages.

Demand for American Sign Language interpreters is expected to grow due to the increasing use of video relay services, which allow people to conduct online video calls and use a sign language interpreter.

In addition, growing international trade and broadening global ties should require more interpreters and translators, especially in emerging markets such as Asia and Africa. The ongoing need for military and national security interpreters and translators should result in more jobs as well.

Computers have made the work of translators and localization specialists more efficient. However, many of these jobs cannot be entirely automated, because computers cannot yet produce work comparable to the work that human translators do in most cases.

Job Prospects

Job prospects should be best for those who have at least a bachelor's degree and for those who have professional certification. Those with an advanced degree in interpreting and/or translation also should have an advantage.

Job prospects for interpreters and translators should also vary by specialty and language. For example, interpreters and translators of Spanish should have good job prospects because of expected increases in the population of Spanish speakers in the United States. Similarly, job opportunities should be plentiful for interpreters and translators specializing in healthcare and law, because of the critical need for all parties to understand the information communicated in those fields.

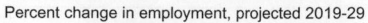

Interpreters and Translators
Percent change in employment, projected 2019-29

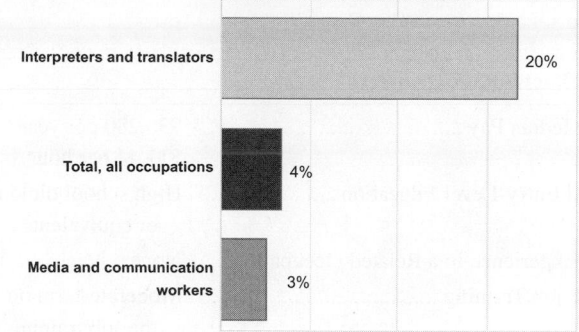

Interpreters and translators — 20%
Total, all occupations — 4%
Media and communication workers — 3%

Note: All Occupations includes all occupations in the U.S. Economy.
Source: U.S. Bureau of Labor Statistics, Employment Projections program.

Interpreters for the deaf will continue to have favorable employment prospects because there are relatively few people with the needed skills.

Employment projections data for interpreters and translators, 2019-29					
Occupational Title	SOC Code	Employment, 2019	Projected Employment, 2029	Change, 2019-29	
				Percent	Numeric
SOURCE: U.S. Bureau of Labor Statistics, Employment Projections program					
Interpreters and translators	27-3091	77,400	92,900	20	15,500

State & Area Data
Occupational Employment Statistics (OES)

The Occupational Employment Statistics (OES) program produces employment and wage estimates annually for over 800 occupations. These estimates are available for the nation as a whole, for individual states, and for metropolitan and nonmetropolitan areas.

Contacts for More Information

For more information about interpreters, visit
➤ Discover Interpreting

For more information about interpreter and literary translator specialties, including professional certification, visit
➤ American Translators Association
➤ Certification Commission for Healthcare Interpreters
➤ International Association of Conference Interpreters
➤ National Association of Judiciary Interpreters and Translators
➤ National Association of the Deaf
➤ National Board of Certification for Medical Interpreters
➤ National Council on Interpreting in Health Care
➤ Registry of Interpreters for the Deaf

For more information about testing to become a federal contract interpreter or translator, visit
➤ U.S. State Department

Photographers

Summary

Quick Facts: Photographers

2019 Median Pay	$36,280 per year
	$17.44 per hour
Typical Entry-Level Education	High school diploma
	or equivalent
Work Experience in a Related Occupation ...	None
On-the-job Training	Moderate-term on-
	the-job training
Number of Jobs, 2019	133,500
Job Outlook, 2019-29	-4% (Decline)
Employment Change, 2019-29	-4,800

What Photographers Do

Photographers use their technical expertise, creativity, and composition skills to produce and preserve images.

Work Environment

Working conditions for photographers vary by specialty. Some photographers travel for photo shoots, working either indoors or outdoors. Others work in studios; still others work in laboratories and use microscopes to photograph subjects.

How to Become a Photographer

Although portrait photographers are not required to have postsecondary education, many take classes because employers usually seek applicants with creativity and a "good eye," as well as a good technical understanding of photography. Photojournalists and industrial and scientific photographers often need a bachelor's degree.

Pay

The median hourly wage for photographers was $17.44 in May 2019.

Job Outlook

Employment of photographers is projected to decline 4 percent from 2019 to 2029.

State & Area Data

Explore resources for employment and wages by state and area for photographers.

What Photographers Do

Photographers use their technical expertise, creativity, and composition skills to produce and preserve images that tell a story or record an event.

Duties

Photographers typically do the following:

- Market or advertise services to attract clients
- Analyze and plan the composition of photographs
- Use various photographic techniques and lighting equipment
- Capture subjects in professional-quality photographs
- Enhance the subject's appearance with natural or artificial light
- Use photo-enhancing software
- Maintain a digital portfolio to demonstrate their work
- Archive and manage imagery

Nowadays, most photographers use digital cameras instead of traditional film cameras, although some photographers use both. Digital cameras capture images electronically, so the photographer can edit the image on a computer. Images can be stored on portable memory devices, such as flash drives. Once the raw image has been transferred to a computer, photographers can use image processing software to crop or modify the image and enhance it through color correction and other specialized effects. Photographers who edit their own pictures use computers, editing software, and high-quality printers.

Some photographers travel for photo shoots, and others work in their own studios.

Photographers capture subjects in commercial-quality photographs.

Some photographers use unmanned aerial vehicles, commonly known as drones, to capture shots. The drones are equipped with an integrated camera to capture 360-degree imagery of buildings, landscapes, scenery, or events.

Photographers who work for commercial clients often present photographs in a digital format to the client. Wedding and portrait photographers, who serve primarily noncommercial clients, also may provide framing services and present the photographs they capture in albums.

Many photographers are self-employed. Photographers who own and operate their own business have additional responsibilities. They must advertise, schedule appointments, set up and adjust equipment, buy supplies, keep records, charge customers, pay bills, and—if they have employees—hire, train, and direct their workers.

In addition, some photographers teach photography classes or conduct workshops in schools or in their own studios.

The following are examples of types of photographers:

Aerial photographers travel in planes or helicopters to capture overhead photographs of buildings and landscapes. They often use cameras with gyrostabilizers to counteract the movement of the aircraft and ensure high-quality images.

Commercial and industrial photographers take pictures of subjects such as buildings, models, merchandise, artifacts, and landscapes. They usually go on location to take pictures for magazine covers, engineering projects, or other purposes.

Drone photographers operate unmanned aerial vehicles with an integrated camera to capture 360-degree imagery of buildings, landscapes, scenery, or events.

Fine arts photographers sell their photographs as artwork. In addition to their knowledge of techniques such as lighting and the use of lenses, fine arts photographers need to have creativity and artistic talent.

News photographers, also called *photojournalists*, photograph people, places, and events for newspapers, journals, magazines, or television. In addition to taking still photos, photojournalists often work with digital video.

Portrait photographers take pictures of individuals or groups of people and may work in studios. Photographers who specialize in weddings, religious ceremonies, or school photographs usually work on location.

Scientific photographers capture scientific or medical data or phenomena. Because they focus on accurately representing subjects visually, these photographers limit the use of software to clarify an image. Scientific photographers who take pictures of objects too small to be seen with the naked eye use microscopes to photograph their subjects.

Work Environment

Photographers held about 133,500 jobs in 2019. The largest employers of photographers were as follows:

Self-employed workers.. 64%

Most photographers stand or walk for long periods while carrying heavy equipment.

Photographic services... 20

Broadcasting (except Internet)....................................... 3

Newspaper, periodical, book, and directory   1
    publishers ....

Working conditions for photographers vary by specialty. Photographers may work indoors or outdoors.

Portrait photographers may work in studios, but they also travel to take photographs at a client's location, such as a school or a home.

News photographers may travel locally or internationally and must be prepared to work in uncomfortable or even dangerous surroundings. For example, a news photographer may be sent to a war zone to capture images. News photographers often work irregular schedules and must be available on short notice.

Aerial photographers work in planes or helicopters to capture a scene, event, or location from an overhead perspective.

Most photographers stand or walk for long periods. They may need to carry heavy equipment.

Work Schedules

Some photographers work part time. Hours often are flexible so that photographers can meet with current and potential clients or visit the sites where they will work. For certain types of photographers, workloads may fluctuate with the season. For example, wedding photographers are typically busiest in the summer and fall.

How to Become a Photographer

Although portrait photographers are not required to have postsecondary education, many take classes because employers usually seek applicants with creativity and a "good eye," as well as a good technical understanding of photography. Photojournalists and industrial and scientific photographers often need a bachelor's degree.

Portrait photographers take pictures of individuals or groups of people and usually work in their own studios.

Education

Postsecondary education is not required for most photographers. However, many photographers take classes or earn a bachelor's degree to improve their skills and employment prospects.

Many universities, community colleges, vocational–technical institutes, and private trade and technical schools offer classes in photography. Basic photography courses cover equipment, processes, and techniques. Art school training in photographic design and composition also may be useful.

Entry-level positions in photojournalism or in industrial or scientific photography generally require a college degree in photography or in a field related to the industry in which the photographer seeks employment. For example, classes in biology, medicine, or chemistry may be important for scientific photographers.

Business, marketing, and accounting classes may be helpful for self-employed photographers.

Training

Photographers' skill or ability for taking good photos is typically cultivated over years of practice. Photographers often start working as an assistant to a professional photographer, learning on the job. This work provides an opportunity to gain experience, build the photographers' portfolios, and gain exposure to prospective clients. In addition, photographers must learn to use photo-editing software.

For many artists, including photographers, developing a portfolio—a collection of their work that demonstrates their styles and abilities—is essential. Art directors, clients, and others often review portfolios when deciding whether to hire a particular photographer.

Licenses, Certifications, and Registrations

Photographers who commercially operate drones, commonly known as unmanned aerial vehicles, must obtain certification from the Federal Aviation Administration (FAA). They must fulfill the following criteria:

- Be at least 16 years old
- Be able to read, speak, write, and understand English (exceptions may be made if the person is unable to meet one of these requirements for a medical reason, such as a hearing impairment)
- Be in good physical and mental condition to operate a small drone safely
- Pass the initial aeronautical knowledge exam at an FAA-approved knowledge testing center

For specific guidelines and information, visit the FAA website's section on unmanned aircraft systems.

Important Qualities

Artistic ability. Photographers capture their subjects in images, and they must evaluate the artistic quality of a photograph. Photographers need a "good eye": the ability to use colors, shadows, shades, light, and distance to compose aesthetically pleasing photographs.

Business skills. Photographers must plan marketing or advertising strategies, reach out to prospective clients, and anticipate seasonal employment.

Computer skills. Most photographers do their own post-production work and must be adept at using photo-editing software. They also use computers to maintain a digital portfolio.

Customer-service skills. Photographers must understand the types of shots their clients want and agree on suitable alternatives for ideas that may be unworkable.

Detail oriented. Photographers must focus on details, especially in postproduction. In addition, photographers accumulate many photographs and must maintain them in an orderly fashion.

Interpersonal skills. Photographers often take pictures of people. They must communicate and be flexible when working with clients in order to achieve the desired composition in a photograph.

Pay

The median hourly wage for photographers was $17.44 in May 2019. The median wage is the wage at which half the workers in an occupation earned more than that amount and half earned less. The lowest 10 percent earned less than $9.92, and the highest 10 percent earned more than $38.19.

In May 2019, the median hourly wages for photographers in the top industries in which they worked were as follows:

Broadcasting (except Internet)	$22.83
Newspaper, periodical, book, and directory publishers	21.74
Photographic services	15.15

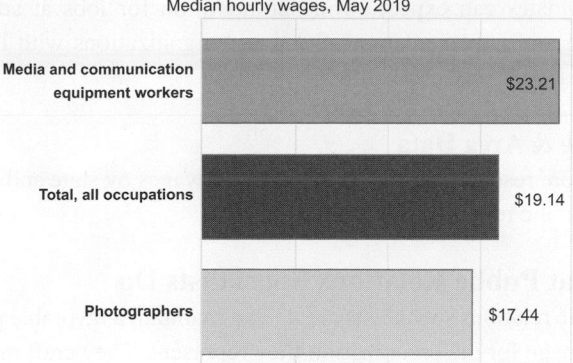

Photographers

Median hourly wages, May 2019

- Media and communication equipment workers: $23.21
- Total, all occupations: $19.14
- Photographers: $17.44

Note: All Occupations includes all occupations in the U.S. Economy.
Source: U.S. Bureau of Labor Statistics, Occupational Employment Statistics.

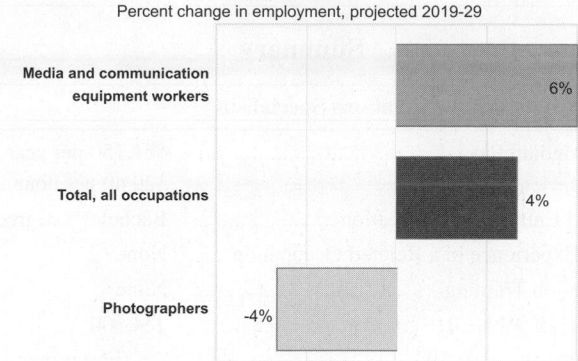

Photographers

Percent change in employment, projected 2019-29

- Media and communication equipment workers: 6%
- Total, all occupations: 4%
- Photographers: -4%

Note: All Occupations includes all occupations in the U.S. Economy.
Source: U.S. Bureau of Labor Statistics, Employment Projections program.

Some photographers work part time. Hours often are flexible so that photographers can meet with current and potential clients or visit the sites where they will work. For certain types of photographers, workloads may fluctuate with the season. For example, wedding photographers are typically busiest in the summer and fall.

Job Outlook

Employment of photographers is projected to decline 4 percent from 2019 to 2029. The decreasing cost of digital cameras and the increasing number of amateur photographers and hobbyists will reduce the need for professional photographers. In addition, stock photographic services available online give individuals and businesses access to stock photographs for a fee or subscription, possibly dampening demand for photographers.

However, the application of newer technologies, such as drone photography, may contribute to increased demand for these workers. For example, drone photography in the commercial sector enables the capturing of images and information for agricultural land, real estate, and new construction projects. In addition, drone photography enables the photographer to create visuals of tall structures, such as cell towers and bridges, that are in need of repair. Drone photography at weddings or special events also captures scenic aerial portraits.

Employment of self-employed photographers is projected to grow. Demand for portrait photographers will remain as people continue to want new portraits. In addition, corporations will continue to require the services of commercial photographers to develop compelling advertisements to sell products.

Job Prospects

Photographers will face strong competition for most jobs. Because of the relative ease with which photographers may enter the occupation, there will be many qualified candidates for relatively few positions.

In addition, salaried jobs may be more difficult to obtain as companies increasingly contract with freelancers rather than hire their own photographers. Job prospects will be best for candidates who have a strong portfolio and related skills, such as in editing photos and capturing digital video.

Employment projections data for photographers, 2019-29					
Occupational Title	SOC Code	Employment, 2019	Projected Employment, 2029	Change, 2019-29	
				Percent	Numeric
SOURCE: U.S. Bureau of Labor Statistics, Employment Projections program					
Photographers	27-4021	133,500	128,700	-4	-4,800

State & Area Data
Occupational Employment Statistics (OES)

The Occupational Employment Statistics (OES) program produces employment and wage estimates annually for over 800 occupations. These estimates are available for the nation as a whole, for individual states, and for metropolitan and nonmetropolitan areas.

Contacts for More Information

For more information about careers in photography, visit
➤ American Society of Media Photographers

For more information about testing and obtaining certification to operate commercial drones or unmanned aerial systems (UASs), visit
➤ Federal Aviation Administration (FAA)

For more information about university photographers, visit
➤ University Photographers' Association of America

Public Relations Specialists

Summary

Quick Facts: Public Relations Specialists

2019 Median Pay	$61,150 per year
	$29.40 per hour
Typical Entry-Level Education	Bachelor's degree
Work Experience in a Related Occupation	None
On-the-job Training	None
Number of Jobs, 2019....................................	274,600
Job Outlook, 2019-29.....................................	7% (Faster than average)
Employment Change, 2019-29	19,700

What Public Relations Specialists Do
Public relations specialists create and maintain a favorable public image for the organization they represent.

Work Environment
Public relations specialists usually work in offices. Some attend community activities or events. Long workdays are common, as is overtime.

How to Become a Public Relations Specialist
Public relations specialists typically need a bachelor's degree in public relations, journalism, communications, English, or business.

Pay
The median annual wage for public relations specialists was $61,150 in May 2019.

Job Outlook
Employment of public relations specialists is projected to grow 7 percent from 2019 to 2029, faster than the average for all occupations. The need for organizations to maintain their public image will continue to drive employment growth. Candidates can expect strong competition for jobs at advertising and public relations firms and organizations with large media exposure.

State & Area Data
Explore resources for employment and wages by state and area for public relations specialists.

What Public Relations Specialists Do
Public relations specialists create and maintain a favorable public image for the organization they represent. They craft media releases and develop social media programs to shape public perception of their organization and increase awareness of its work and goals.

Duties
Public relations specialists typically do the following:

- Write press releases and prepare information for the media
- Respond to information requests from the media
- Help clients communicate effectively with the public
- Help maintain their organization's corporate image and identity
- Draft speeches and arrange interviews for an organization's top executives
- Evaluate advertising and promotion programs to determine whether they are compatible with their organization's public relations efforts
- Evaluate public opinion of clients through social media

Public relations specialists, also called *communications specialists* and *media specialists*, handle an organization's communication with the public, including consumers, investors, reporters, and other media specialists. In government, public relations specialists may be called *press secretaries*. In this setting, workers keep the public informed about the activities of government officials and agencies.

Public relations specialists design media releases to shape public perception of their organization.

Public relations specialists evaluate advertising and promotion programs.

Public relations specialists draft press releases and contact people in the media who might print or broadcast their material. Many radio or television special reports, newspaper stories, and magazine articles start at the desks of public relations specialists. For example, a press release might describe a public issue, such as health, energy, or the environment, and what an organization does concerning that issue.

Press releases are increasingly being sent through the Internet and social media, in addition to publication through traditional media outlets. Public relations specialists are often in charge of monitoring and responding to social media questions and concerns.

Public relations specialists are different from advertisers in that they get their stories covered by media instead of purchasing ad space in publications and on television.

Work Environment

Public relations specialists held about 274,600 jobs in 2019. The largest employers of public relations specialists were as follows:

Educational services; state, local, and private 13%

Advertising, public relations, and related services 13

Government 10

Business, professional, labor, political, and similar
organizations.. 8

Public relations specialists usually work in offices, but they also deliver speeches, attend meetings and community activities, and occasionally travel.

Work Schedules

Most public relations specialists work full time during regular business hours. Long workdays are common, as is overtime.

How to Become a Public Relations Specialist

Public relations specialists typically need a bachelor's degree. Employers prefer candidates who have studied public relations, journalism, communications, English, or business.

Education

Public relations specialists typically need a bachelor's degree in public relations, journalism, communications, English, or business. Through such programs, students produce a portfolio of work that demonstrates their ability to prospective employers.

Other Experience

Internships at public relations firms or in the public relations departments of other businesses can be helpful in getting a job as a public relations specialist.

Some employers prefer candidates who have experience communicating with others through a school newspaper or a leadership position in school or in their community.

Important Qualities

Interpersonal skills. Public relations specialists deal with the public and the media regularly; therefore, they must be open and friendly in order to maintain a favorable image for their organization.

Organizational skills. Public relations specialists are often in charge of managing several events at the same time, requiring superior organizational skills.

Public relations specialists work in many different industries.

Public relations specialists typically need a bachelor's degree.

Public Relations Specialists

Median annual wages, May 2019

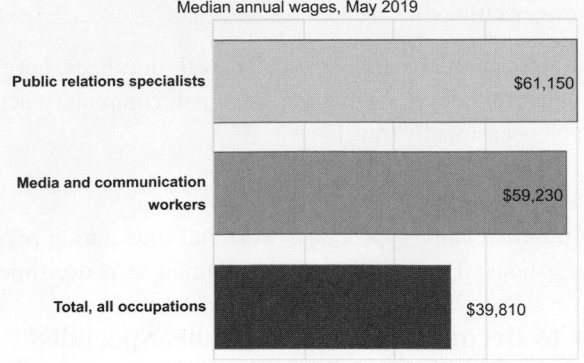

Public relations specialists — $61,150

Media and communication workers — $59,230

Total, all occupations — $39,810

Note: All Occupations includes all occupations in the U.S. Economy.
Source: U.S. Bureau of Labor Statistics, Occupational Employment Statistics.

Public Relations Specialists

Percent change in employment, projected 2019-29

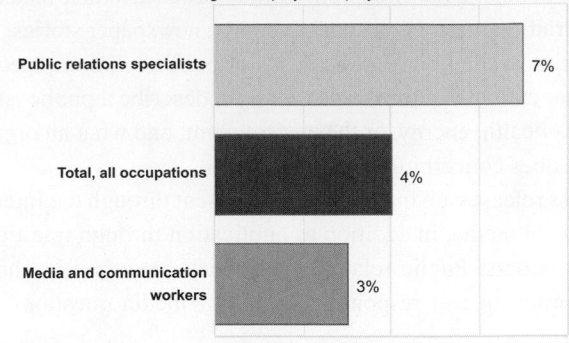

Public relations specialists — 7%

Total, all occupations — 4%

Media and communication workers — 3%

Note: All Occupations includes all occupations in the U.S. Economy.
Source: U.S. Bureau of Labor Statistics, Employment Projections program.

Problem-solving skills. Public relations specialists sometimes must explain how a company or client is handling sensitive issues. They must use good judgment in what they report and how they report it.

Speaking skills. Public relations specialists regularly speak on behalf of their organization. When doing so, they must be able to clearly explain the organization's position.

Writing skills. Public relations specialists must be able to write well-organized and clear press releases and speeches. They must be able to grasp the key messages they want to get across and write them in a short, succinct way, to get the attention of busy readers or listeners.

Pay

The median annual wage for public relations specialists was $61,150 in May 2019. The median wage is the wage at which half the workers in an occupation earned more than that amount and half earned less. The lowest 10 percent earned less than $34,590, and the highest 10 percent earned more than $115,430.

In May 2019, the median annual wages for public relations specialists in the top industries in which they worked were as follows:

Business, professional, labor, political, and similar organizations	$66,340
Government	65,310
Advertising, public relations, and related services	64,230
Educational services; state, local, and private	57,940

Most public relations specialists work full time during regular business hours. Long workdays are common, as is overtime.

Job Outlook

Employment of public relations specialists is projected to grow 7 percent from 2019 to 2029, faster than the average for all occupations.

Organizations will continue to emphasize community outreach and customer relations as a way to maintain and enhance their reputation and visibility. Public opinion can change quickly, particularly because both good and bad news spread rapidly through the Internet. Consequently, public relations specialists will be needed to respond to news developments and maintain their organization's reputation.

The use of social media also is expected to create opportunities for public relations specialists as they try to appeal to consumers and the general public in new ways. Public relations specialists will be needed to help their clients use these new types of social media effectively.

Job Prospects

Because many college graduates apply for a limited amount of public relations positions each year, candidates can expect strong competition for jobs.

Candidates can expect particularly strong competition at advertising firms, organizations with large media exposure, and prestigious public relations firms.

Employment projections data for public relations specialists, 2019-29

Occupational Title	SOC Code	Employment, 2019	Projected Employment, 2029	Change, 2019-29	
				Percent	Numeric
SOURCE: U.S. Bureau of Labor Statistics, Employment Projections program					
Public relations specialists	27-3031	274,600	294,300	7	19,700

State & Area Data

Occupational Employment Statistics (OES)

The Occupational Employment Statistics (OES) program produces employment and wage estimates annually for over 800 occupations. These estimates are available for the nation as a whole, for individual states, and for metropolitan and nonmetropolitan areas.

Contacts for More Information

For more information about public relations managers, including professional certification in public relations, visit

➤ Public Relations Society of America

➤ Public Relations Student Society of America

➤ International Association of Business Communicators

Reporters, Correspondents, and Broadcast News Analysts

Summary

Quick Facts: Reporters, Correspondents, and Broadcast News Analysts

2019 Median Pay	$46,270 per year $22.25 per hour
Typical Entry-Level Education	Bachelor's degree
Work Experience in a Related Occupation	None
On-the-job Training	None
Number of Jobs, 2019	52,000
Job Outlook, 2019-29	-11% (Decline)
Employment Change, 2019-29	-5,800

What Reporters, Correspondents, and Broadcast News Analysts Do

Reporters, correspondents, and broadcast news analysts inform the public about news and events.

Work Environment

Most reporters and correspondents work for newspaper, website, or periodical publishers or in television or radio broadcasting. Broadcast news analysts mainly work in television and radio.

How to Become a Reporter, Correspondent, or Broadcast News Analyst

Employers generally prefer workers who have a bachelor's degree in journalism or communications along with an internship or work experience from a college radio or television station or a newspaper.

Pay

The median annual wage for reporters, correspondents, and broadcast news analysts was $46,270 in May 2019.

Reporters, correspondents, and broadcast news analysts inform the public about news and events happening internationally, nationally, and locally.

Job Outlook

Overall employment of reporters, correspondents, and broadcast news analysts is projected to decline 11 percent from 2019 to 2029. Declining advertising revenue in radio, newspapers, and television will have a negative impact on employment growth for these occupations.

State & Area Data

Explore resources for employment and wages by state and area for reporters, correspondents, and broadcast news analysts.

What Reporters, Correspondents, and Broadcast News Analysts Do

Reporters, correspondents, and broadcast news analysts inform the public about news and events happening internationally, nationally, and locally. They report the news for newspapers, magazines, websites, television, and radio.

Duties

Reporters, correspondents, and broadcast news analysts typically do the following:

- Research topics and stories that an editor or news director has assigned to them
- Investigate new story ideas and pitch ideas to editors
- Interview people who have information, analysis, or opinions about a story or article
- Write articles for newspapers, blogs, or magazines and write scripts to be read on television or radio
- Review articles for accuracy and proper style and grammar
- Develop relationships with experts and contacts who provide tips and leads on stories
- Analyze and interpret information to increase their audiences' understanding of the news
- Update stories as new information becomes available

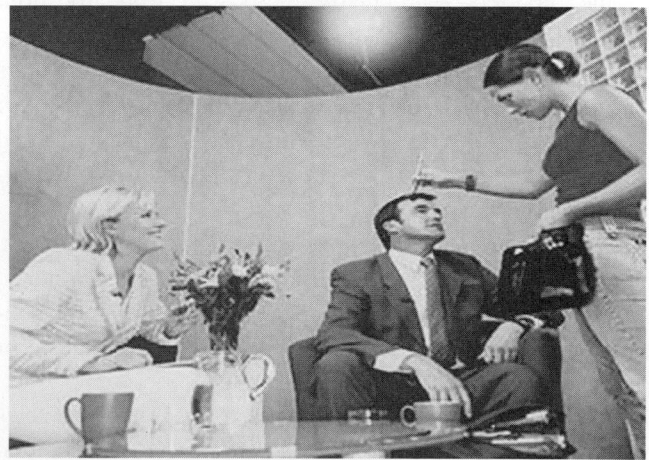

Reporters that work in television set up and conduct interviews, which may be broadcast live or recorded for future broadcasts.

Reporters and correspondents, also called *journalists*, often work for a particular type of media organization, such as a television or radio station, newspaper, or website.

Those who work in television and radio set up and conduct interviews, which can be broadcast live or recorded for future broadcasts. These workers are often responsible for editing interviews and other recordings to create a cohesive story and for writing and recording voiceovers that provide the audience with the facts of the story. They may create multiple versions of the same story for different broadcasts or different media platforms.

Journalists for print media conduct interviews and write articles to be used in newspapers, magazines, and online publications. Because most newspapers and magazines have print and online versions, reporters typically produce content for both versions. This requires that they stay up to date with new developments of a story so that the online editions can be updated with the most current information.

Outlets are increasingly relying on *multimedia journalists* to publish content on a variety of platforms, such as a video content on the website of a daily newspaper. Multimedia journalists typically record, report, write, and edit their own stories. They also gather the audio, video, or graphics that accompany their stories.

Reporters and correspondents may need to maintain a presence on social media networking sites. Many use social media to cover live events, provide additional information for readers and viewers, promote their stations and newscasts, and engage with their audiences.

Some journalists, particularly those in large cities or large news organizations, cover a particular topic, such as sports, medicine, or politics. Journalists who work in small cities, towns, or organizations may need to cover a wider range of subjects.

Reporters who cover international news often live in another country and report news for a specific region of the world.

Some reporters—particularly those who work for print news—are self-employed and take freelance assignments from news organizations. Freelance assignments are given to writers on an as-needed basis. Because freelance reporters are paid for the individual story, they work with many organizations and often spend some of their time marketing their stories and looking for their next assignment.

Reporters also may collaborate with editors, photographers, videographers, and other journalists when working on a story.

Some people with a background as a reporter or correspondent work as postsecondary teachers and teach journalism or communications at colleges and universities.

Broadcast news analysts, also called *anchors*, lead news shows on television or radio. Others are *news commentators*, who analyze and interpret news stories and offer opinions. Some news commentators come from fields outside of journalism and have expertise in a particular subject—for example,

politics, business, or medicine—and are hired on a contract basis to provide their opinion on the subjects being discussed.

Work Environment

Reporters, correspondents, and broadcast news analysts held about 52,000 jobs in 2019. The largest employers of reporters, correspondents, and broadcast news analysts were as follows:

Newspaper, periodical, book, and directory publishers	35%
Radio and television broadcasting	32
Other information services	10

Reporters and correspondents spend a lot of time in the field, conducting interviews and investigating stories. Many reporters spend little to no time in an office. They travel to be on location for events or to meet contacts and file stories remotely.

Injuries and Illnesses

Working on stories about natural disasters or wars can put reporters in dangerous situations. In addition, reporters often face pressure or stress when trying to meet a deadline or cover breaking news.

Work Schedules

Most reporters, correspondents, and broadcast news analysts work full time. Reporters may need to work additional hours or change their schedules in order to follow breaking news. Because news can happen at any time, journalists may need to work nights and weekends. Broadcast news analysts may also work nights and weekends to lead news programs or provide commentary.

How to Become a Reporter, Correspondent, or Broadcast News Analyst

Employers generally prefer to hire reporters, correspondents, and broadcast news analysts who have a bachelor's degree

Reporters and correspondents spend a lot of time in the field conducting interviews and investigating stories.

Journalists need to be persistent in their pursuit of the story as getting the facts of the story can be difficult, especially when those involved refuse to comment.

in journalism or communications along with an internship or work experience from a college radio or television station or a newspaper.

Education

Most employers prefer workers who have a bachelor's degree in journalism or communications. However, some employers may hire applicants who have a degree in a related subject, such as English or political science, and relevant work experience.

Bachelor's degree programs in journalism and communications include classes in journalistic ethics and techniques for researching stories and conducting interviews. Some programs may require students to take liberal arts classes, such as history, economics, and political science, so that students are prepared to cover stories on a wide range of subjects. Students may further specialize in the type of journalism they wish to pursue, such as print, broadcast, or multimedia.

Journalism students may benefit from classes in multimedia design, coding, and programming. Because content is increasingly being delivered on television, websites, and mobile devices, reporters need to know how to develop stories with video, audio, data, and graphics.

Some schools offer graduate programs in journalism and communications. These programs prepare students who have a bachelor's degree in another field to become journalists.

Other Experience

Employers generally require workers to have experience gained through internships or by working on school newspapers, college radio stations, or college TV stations. While attending college, many students seek multiple internships with different news organizations. These internships allow students the opportunities to work on stories and to put together a portfolio of their best writing samples or on-air appearances.

News commentators who come from a field outside of journalism typically have expertise in areas on which they comment.

Work Experience in a Related Occupation

Broadcast news analysts sometimes need work experience as reporters and correspondents. For example, it might take a field reporter at a local news station a few years to become that station's anchor.

Advancement

After gaining more work experience, reporters and correspondents may advance by moving from news organizations in small cities or towns to news organizations in large cities. Larger markets offer job opportunities with higher pay and more responsibility and challenges. Reporters and correspondents also may become editors or news directors.

Important Qualities

Communication skills. Reporters, correspondents, and broadcast news analysts must be able to report the news. Strong writing skills are important for journalists in all kinds of media.

Computer skills. Journalists should be able to use editing equipment and other broadcast-related devices. They should also be able to use multimedia and coding software in order to publish stories on websites and mobile devices.

Interpersonal skills. To develop contacts and conduct interviews, reporters need to build good relationships with many people. They also need to work well with other journalists, editors, and news directors.

Persistence. Sometimes, getting the facts of a story is difficult, particularly when those involved refuse to be interviewed or to provide comment. Journalists need to be persistent in pursuing the story.

Stamina. The work of journalists is often fast paced and exhausting. Reporters must be able to keep up with the additional hours of work.

Pay

The median annual wage for reporters, correspondents, and broadcast news analysts was $46,270 in May 2019. The median wage is the wage at which half the workers in an occupation earned more than that amount and half earned less. The lowest 10 percent earned less than $24,520, and the highest 10 percent earned more than $117,170.

In May 2019, the median annual wages for reporters, correspondents, and broadcast news analysts in the top industries in which they worked were as follows:

Other information services $68,100
Radio and television broadcasting............................. 53,410
Newspaper, periodical, book, and directory
   publishers 36,700

Most reporters, correspondents, and broadcast news analysts work full time. Reporters may need to work additional hours or change their schedules in order to follow breaking news. Because news can happen at any time, journalists may need to

Reporters, Correspondents, and Broadcast News Analysts

Median annual wages, May 2019

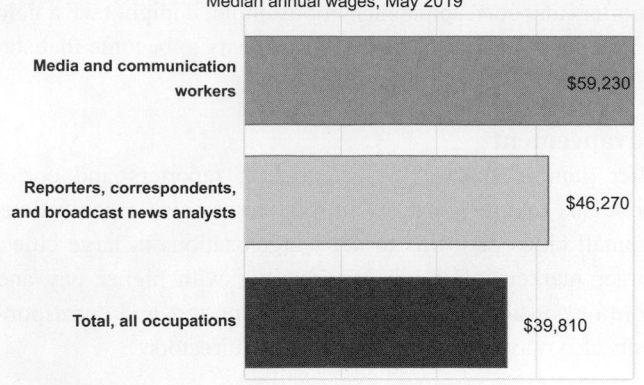

Note: All Occupations includes all occupations in the U.S. Economy.
Source: U.S. Bureau of Labor Statistics, Occupational Employment Statistics.

Reporters, Correspondents, and Broadcast News Analysts

Percent change in employment, projected 2019-29

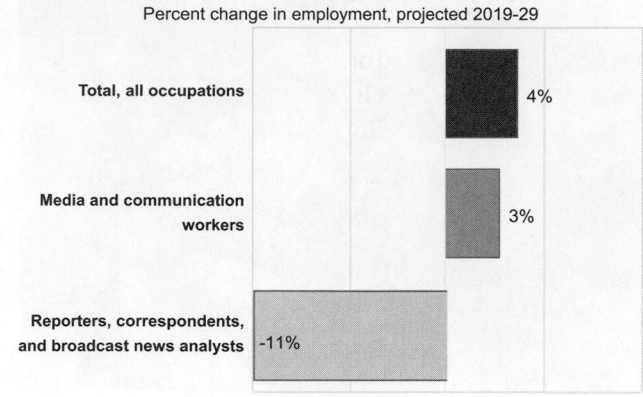

Note: All Occupations includes all occupations in the U.S. Economy.
Source: U.S. Bureau of Labor Statistics, Employment Projections program.

work nights and weekends. Broadcast news analysts may also work nights and weekends to lead news programs or provide commentary.

Job Outlook

Overall employment of reporters, correspondents, and broadcast news analysts is projected to decline 11 percent from 2019 to 2029. Declining advertising revenue in radio, newspapers, and television will negatively affect the employment growth for these occupations.

Readership and circulation of newspapers are expected to continue to decline over the next decade. In addition, television and radio stations are increasingly publishing content online and on mobile devices. As a result, news organizations may have more difficulty selling traditional forms of advertising, which is often their primary source of revenue. Some organizations will likely continue to use new forms of advertising or offer paid subscriptions, but these innovations may not make up for lost print-ad revenues.

Declining revenue will force news organizations to downsize and employ fewer journalists. Increasing demand for online news may offset some of the downsizing. However, because online and mobile ad revenue is typically less than print revenue, the growth in digital advertising may not offset the decline in print advertising, circulation, and readership.

News organizations also continue to consolidate and increasingly are sharing resources, staff, and content with other media outlets. For example, reporters are able to gather and report on news for a media outlet that can be published in multiple newspapers owned by the same parent company. As consolidations, mergers, and news sharing continue, the demand for journalists may decrease. However, in some instances, consolidations

may help limit the loss of jobs. Mergers may allow financially troubled newspapers, radio stations, and television stations to keep staff because of increased funding and resources from the larger organization.

Job Prospects

Reporters, correspondents, and broadcast news analysts are expected to face strong competition for jobs. Those with experience in the field—experience often gained through internships or by working for school newspapers, television stations, or radio stations—should have the best job prospects.

Multimedia journalism experience, including recording and editing video or audio pieces, should also improve job prospects. Because stations and media outlets are increasingly publishing content on multiple media platforms, particularly the web, employers may prefer applicants who have experience in website design and coding.

Employment projections data for reporters, correspondents, and broadcast news analysts, 2019-29					
Occupational Title	SOC Code	Employment, 2019	Projected Employment, 2029	Change, 2019-29	
				Percent	Numeric
SOURCE: U.S. Bureau of Labor Statistics, Employment Projections program					
News analysts, reporters, and journalists	27-3023	52,000	46,200	-11	-5,800

State & Area Data
Occupational Employment Statistics (OES)

The Occupational Employment Statistics (OES) program produces employment and wage estimates annually for over 800 occupations. These estimates are available for the nation as a whole, for individual states, and for metropolitan and nonmetropolitan areas.

Contacts for More Information

For more information about broadcast news analysts, visit
➤ National Association of Broadcasters

➤ Radio Television Digital News Association

For more information about careers in journalism and about internships, visit
➤ Dow Jones News Fund
➤ Society of Professional Journalists

Technical Writers

Summary

Quick Facts: Technical Writers

2019 Median Pay	$72,850 per year
	$35.03 per hour
Typical Entry-Level Education	Bachelor's degree
Work Experience in a Related Occupation	Less than 5 years
On-the-job Training	Short-term on-the-job training
Number of Jobs, 2019	58,400
Job Outlook, 2019-29	7% (Faster than average)
Employment Change, 2019-29	4,300

What Technical Writers Do

Technical writers prepare instruction manuals, how-to guides, journal articles, and other supporting documents to communicate complex and technical information more easily.

Work Environment

Most technical writers work full time. Although technical writers work in a variety of industries, they are concentrated in the computer and management, scientific, and technical industries.

How to Become a Technical Writer

A college degree is usually required for a position as a technical writer. In addition, knowledge of or experience with a technical subject, such as science or engineering, is beneficial.

Pay

The median annual wage for technical writers was $72,850 in May 2019.

Job Outlook

Employment of technical writers is projected to grow 7 percent from 2019 to 2029, faster than the average for all occupations. Employment growth will be driven by the continuing expansion of scientific and technical products. An increase in Web-based product support should also increase demand for technical writers. Job opportunities, especially for applicants with technical skills, are expected to be good.

State & Area Data

Explore resources for employment and wages by state and area for technical writers.

What Technical Writers Do

Technical writers, also called *technical communicators*, prepare instruction manuals, how-to guides, journal articles, and other supporting documents to communicate complex and technical

Technical writers routinely work with other technology experts.

Technical writers often create diagrams to show users how a product works.

information more easily. They also develop, gather, and disseminate technical information through an organization's communications channels.

Duties

Technical writers typically do the following:

- Determine the needs of users of technical documentation
- Study product samples and talk with product designers and developers
- Work with technical staff to make products and instructions easier to use
- Write or revise supporting content for products
- Edit material prepared by other writers or staff
- Incorporate animation, graphs, illustrations, or photographs to increase users' understanding of the material
- Select appropriate medium, such as manuals or videos, for message or audience
- Standardize content across platforms and media
- Collect user feedback to update and improve content

Technical writers create paper-based and digital operating instructions, how-to manuals, assembly instructions, and "frequently asked questions" pages to help technical support staff, consumers, and other users within a company or an industry. After a product is released, technical writers also may work with product liability specialists and customer-service managers to improve the end-user experience through product design changes.

Technical writers often work with computer hardware engineers, computer support specialists, and software developers to manage the flow of information among project workgroups during development and testing. Therefore, technical writers must be able to understand and discuss complex information with people of diverse occupational backgrounds.

Technical writers may serve on teams that conduct usability studies to improve product design. Technical writers may research topics through visits to libraries and websites, discussions with technical specialists, and observation.

Technical writers are also responsible for managing the consistency of technical content and its use across departments including product development, manufacturing, marketing, and customer relations.

Some technical writers help write grant proposals for research scientists and institutions.

Increasingly, technical information is delivered online and through social media. Technical writers use the interactive technologies of the Web and social media to blend text, graphics, multidimensional images, sound, and video.

Work Environment

Technical writers held about 58,400 jobs in 2019. The largest employers of technical writers were as follows:

Technical writers usually work in offices.

Professional, scientific, and technical services............	35%
Manufacturing...	15
Administrative and support services............................	9
Publishing industries (except Internet)........................	6

Most technical writers work full time. They routinely work with engineers and other technology experts to manage the flow of information throughout an organization.

Although most technical writers are employed directly by the companies that use their services, some freelance and are paid per assignment. Freelancers are either self-employed or work for a technical consulting firm and are given short-term or recurring assignments, such as writing about a new product.

Technical writing jobs are usually concentrated in locations with a multitude of information technology or scientific and technical research companies, such as ones in California and Texas.

Work Schedules

Technical writers may be expected to work evenings and weekends to meet deadlines.

How to Become a Technical Writer

A college degree is usually required for a position as a technical writer. In addition, knowledge of or experience with a technical subject, such as science or engineering, is beneficial.

Education

Employers generally prefer candidates who have a bachelor's degree in English or another communications-related subject. Technical writing jobs may require candidates to have both a degree and knowledge of a technical field, such as engineering, computer science, or medicine.

Work Experience in a Related Occupation

Some technical writers begin their careers as specialists or research assistants in a technical field. They eventually develop technical communication skills and assume primary responsibilities for

Some technical writers work on a freelance basis.

technical writing. In small firms, entry-level technical writers may work on projects right away; in large companies, beginning technical writers may shadow experienced writers and interact with specialists before being assigned projects.

Training

Many technical writers need short-term on-the-job training to adapt their narrative style to a descriptive style of writing.

Licenses, Certifications, and Registrations

Some associations, including the Society for Technical Communication, offer certification for technical writers. In addition, the American Medical Writers Association offers extensive continuing education programs and certificates in medical writing. These certificates are available to professionals in the medical and scientific communication fields.

Although not mandatory, these credentials demonstrate competence and professionalism, making candidates more attractive to employers. A professional credential also may increase a technical writer's opportunities for advancement.

Advancement

Prospects for advancement generally include working on projects that are more complex and leading or training junior staff.

Important Qualities

Critical-thinking skills. Technical writers must be able to simplify complex, technical information for colleagues and consumers who have nontechnical backgrounds.

Detail oriented. Technical writers create instructions for others to follow. As a result, they must be precise about every step.

Imagination. Technical writers must think about a procedure or product as if they are someone who does not have technical knowledge.

Teamwork. Technical writers must be able to work well with other writers, designers, editors, illustrators, and the technical workers whose procedure or product they are explaining.

Technical skills. Technical writers must be able to understand complex information. Technical writers may benefit from a background in fields such as engineering or science.

Writing skills. Technical communicators must have excellent writing skills to be able to explain technical information clearly.

Pay

The median annual wage for technical writers was $72,850 in May 2019. The median wage is the wage at which half the workers in an occupation earned more than that amount and half earned less. The lowest 10 percent earned less than $44,320, and the highest 10 percent earned more than $117,250.

In May 2019, the median annual wages for technical writers in the top industries in which they worked were as follows:

Publishing industries (except Internet) $77,120

Professional, scientific, and technical services 73,960

Administrative and support services 73,170

Manufacturing 73,160

Technical writers may be expected to work evenings and weekends to meet deadlines. Most work full time.

Job Outlook

Employment of technical writers is projected to grow 7 percent from 2019 to 2029, faster than the average for all occupations.

The continuing expansion of scientific and technical products and growth in Web-based product support will drive employment demand for technical writers. Growth and change

Technical Writers
Median annual wages, May 2019

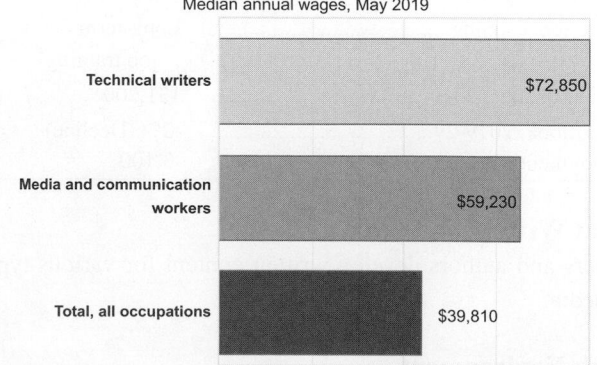

Note: All Occupations includes all occupations in the U.S. Economy.
Source: U.S. Bureau of Labor Statistics, Occupational Employment Statistics.

Technical Writers
Percent change in employment, projected 2019-29

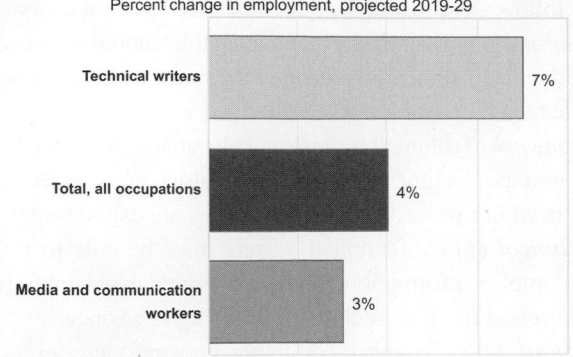

Technical writers — 7%
Total, all occupations — 4%
Media and communication workers — 3%

Note: All Occupations includes all occupations in the U.S. Economy.
Source: U.S. Bureau of Labor Statistics, Employment Projections program.

in the high-technology and electronics industries will result in a greater need for those who can write instruction manuals and communicate information clearly to users.

Employment in professional, scientific, and technical services firms is expected to continue to grow rapidly. These firms should be a good source of new jobs even as the occupation finds acceptance in a broader range of industries.

Job Prospects
Job opportunities, especially for applicants with technical skills, are expected to be good. The growing reliance on technology and the increasing demand for complex medical and scientific information will create job opportunities for technical writers. However, there will be competition among freelance technical writers.

Employment projections data for technical writers, 2019-29					
Occupational Title	SOC Code	Employment, 2019	Projected Employment, 2029	Change, 2019-29	
				Percent	Numeric
SOURCE: U.S. Bureau of Labor Statistics, Employment Projections program					
Technical writers	27-3042	58,400	62,700	7	4,300

State & Area Data
Occupational Employment Statistics (OES)
The Occupational Employment Statistics (OES) program produces employment and wage estimates annually for over 800 occupations. These estimates are available for the nation as a whole, for individual states, and for metropolitan and nonmetropolitan areas.

Contacts for More Information
For more information about technical writers, visit
➤ American Medical Writers Association
➤ National Association of Science Writers
➤ Society for Technical Communication

Writers and Authors

Summary

Quick Facts: Writers and Authors

2019 Median Pay	$63,200 per year $30.39 per hour
Typical Entry-Level Education	Bachelor's degree
Work Experience in a Related Occupation	None
On-the-job Training	Long-term on-the-job training
Number of Jobs, 2019	131,200
Job Outlook, 2019-29	-2% (Decline)
Employment Change, 2019-29	-3,100

What Writers and Authors Do
Writers and authors develop written content for various types of media.

Work Environment
Writers and authors may work anywhere they have access to a computer. Many writers and authors are self-employed.

How to Become a Writer or Author
A college degree in English, communications, or journalism is generally required for a full-time position as a writer or author. Experience gained through internships or any writing that improves skill, such as blogging, is beneficial.

Writers and authors develop written content.

Pay

The median annual wage for writers and authors was $63,200 in May 2019.

Job Outlook

Employment of writers and authors is projected to decline 2 percent from 2019 to 2029.

State & Area Data

Explore resources for employment and wages by state and area for writers and authors.

What Writers and Authors Do

Writers and authors develop content for various types of media, including advertisements; blogs; books; magazines; and movie, play, and television scripts.

Duties

Writers and authors typically do the following:

- Choose subjects that interests readers
- Write fiction or nonfiction scripts, biographies, and other formats
- Conduct research to get factual information and authentic detail

Writers and authors perform research in order to give their stories authentic detail.

- Write advertising copy for newspapers, magazines, broadcasts, and the Internet
- Present drafts to editors and clients for feedback
- Work with editors and clients to shape material for publishing

Writers must establish their credibility with editors and readers through clean prose, strong research, and the use of sources and citations. Writers and authors select the material they want to use and then convey the information to readers. With help from editors, they may revise or rewrite sections, searching for the clearest language and phrasing.

Some writers and authors are self-employed or freelancers. They sell their written content to book and magazine publishers; news organizations; advertising agencies; and movie, theater, and television producers. They may be hired to complete specific short-term or recurring assignments, such as writing a newspaper column, contributing to a series of articles in a magazine, or producing an organization's newsletter.

A number of writers produce material that is published only online, such as for digital news organizations or blogs.

The following are examples of types of writers and authors:

Biographers write a thorough account of a person's life. They gather information from interviews and research about the person to accurately describe important life events.

Bloggers write posts to a Web log (blog) that may pertain to any topic or a specific field, such as fashion, news, or sports.

Content writers write about any topic of interest, unlike writers who usually specialize in a given field.

Copywriters prepare advertisements to promote the sale of a good or service. They often work with a client to produce written content, such as an advertising slogan.

Novelists write books of fiction, creating characters and plots that may be imaginary or based on real events.

Playwrights write scripts for theatrical productions. They come up with a concept, write lines for actors to say, produce stage direction for actors to follow, and suggest ideas for theatrical set design.

Screenwriters create scripts for movies and television. They may produce original stories, characters, and dialogue, or adapt a book into a movie or television script.

Speechwriters compose orations for business leaders, politicians, and others who must speak in front of an audience. Because speeches are often delivered live, speechwriters must think about audience reaction and rhetorical effect.

Work Environment

Writers and authors held about 131,200 jobs in 2019. The largest employers of writers and authors were as follows:

Self-employed workers	63%
Professional, scientific, and technical services	10
Information	10

Writers and authors may work in an office or wherever they have access to a computer.

Writers and authors may have to manage multiple assignments simultaneously.

Writers and authors may work anywhere they have access to a computer.

Jobs are somewhat concentrated in major media and entertainment markets—California, New York, Texas, and Washington, DC—but improved communications and Internet capabilities allow writers and authors to work from almost anywhere. Some writers and authors prefer to work and travel to meet with publishers and clients and to do research or conduct interviews in person.

Work Schedules

Some writers and authors work part time. Most keep regular office hours, either to stay in contact with sources and editors or to set up a writing routine, but many set their own hours. Others may need to work evenings and weekends to produce something acceptable for an editor or client. Self-employed or freelance writers and authors may face the pressures of juggling multiple projects or continually looking for new work.

How to Become a Writer or Author

A college degree in English, communications, or journalism is generally required for a salaried position as a writer or author. Experience gained through internships or any writing that improves skill, such as blogging, is beneficial.

Education

A bachelor's degree is typically needed for a full-time job as a writer. Because writing skills are essential in this occupation, many employers prefer candidates who have a degree in English, communications, or journalism.

Other Work Experience

Writers and authors can get job experience by working for high school and college newspapers, magazines, radio and television stations, advertising and publishing companies, or nonprofit organizations. College theater programs offer playwrights an opportunity to have their work performed. Many magazines and newspapers also have internships for students. Interns may write stories, conduct research and interviews, and gain related experience.

Employers may prefer candidates who are able to create a visual story using tables, charts, infographics, and maps. Knowledge of computer software and editing tools that combine text with graphics, audio, video, and animation may be helpful.

In addition, anyone with Internet access can start a blog and gain writing experience. Some of this writing may lead to paid assignments regardless of education. Writers or authors can come from different backgrounds and experiences.

Training

Writers and authors typically gain writing experience through on-the-job training. They may practice and work with more experienced writers and editors before their writing is ready for publication.

Writers may need formal training or experience related to a particular topic that they want to write about.

Licenses, Certifications, and Registrations

Some associations offer certifications for writers and authors. Certification can show competence and professionalism, making candidates more attractive to employers. For example, the American Grant Writers' Association (AGWA) offers the Certified Grant Writer® credential.

Certification may increase opportunities for advancement.

Advancement

Writers and authors can get a start by putting their name on their work when writing for small businesses, local newspapers, advertising agencies, and nonprofit organizations. However, opportunities for advancement within these organizations may be limited.

Writers and authors may advance their careers by building a reputation, taking on complex writing assignments, and getting published in prestigious markets and publications. Having published work that has been well received and consistently meeting deadlines are important for advancement.

Many editors begin work as writers. Those who are particularly skilled at identifying stories, correcting writing style, and interacting with writers may be interested in editing jobs.

Important Qualities

Adaptability. Writers and authors need to be able to adapt to updates in software platforms and programs, including various *content management systems* (CMS).

Creativity. Writers and authors must be able to develop interesting plots, characters, or ideas for new stories.

Critical-thinking skills. Writers and authors must be adept at understanding new concepts that they convey through writing.

Determination. Writers and authors must have drive and persevere to meet deadlines.

Persuasion. Writers, especially those in advertising, must be able to convince others to feel a certain way about a good or service.

Social perceptiveness. Writers and authors must understand how readers react to ideas to connect with their audience.

Writing skills. Writers and authors must be able to write clearly and effectively to convey feeling and emotion and to communicate with readers.

Pay

The median annual wage for writers and authors was $63,200 in May 2019. The median wage is the wage at which half the workers in an occupation earned more than that amount and half earned less. The lowest 10 percent earned less than $33,660, and the highest 10 percent earned more than $122,450.

In May 2019, the median annual wages for writers and authors in the top industries in which they worked were as follows:

Performing arts, spectator sports, and related industries	$70,990
Religious, grantmaking, civic, professional, and similar organizations	68,560
Professional, scientific, and technical services	63,920
Information	60,440

Some writers and authors work part time. Most keep regular office hours, either to stay in contact with sources and editors or to set up a writing routine, but many set their own hours. Others may need to work evenings and weekends to produce something acceptable for an editor or client. Self-employed or freelance writers and authors may face the pressures of juggling multiple projects or continually looking for new work.

Job Outlook

Employment of writers and authors is projected to decline 2 percent from 2019 to 2029.

Many news outlets, including digital outlets, are downsizing, offering fewer opportunities for writers and authors. Additionally, employment of writers and authors in newspaper, book, periodical, and directory publishers is expected to decline as the industry consolidates and shrinks and as more people access the information they need online.

Job Prospects

Strong competition is expected for most job openings, given that many people are attracted to this occupation. Competition for jobs with newspapers and magazines will be particularly strong because employment in the publishing industry is projected to decline.

Writers and authors who have adapted to online and social media, and who are comfortable writing for and working with a variety of electronic and digital tools, should have an advantage in finding work. The declining costs of self-publishing and the popularity of electronic books will allow many freelance writers to have their work published.

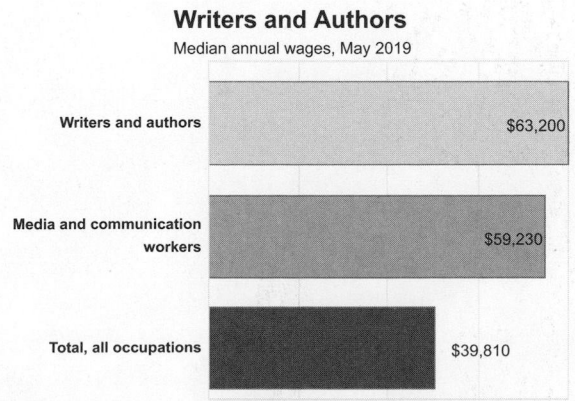

Writers and Authors
Median annual wages, May 2019

- Writers and authors: $63,200
- Media and communication workers: $59,230
- Total, all occupations: $39,810

Note: All Occupations includes all occupations in the U.S. Economy.
Source: U.S. Bureau of Labor Statistics, Occupational Employment Statistics.

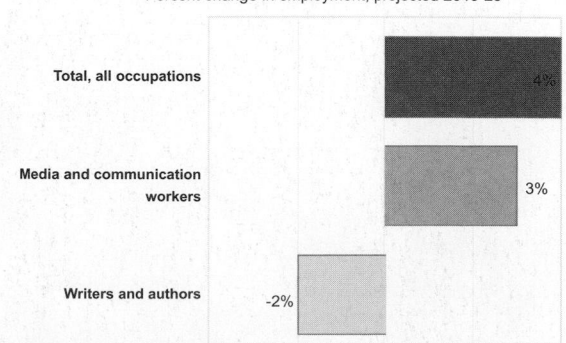

Writers and Authors
Percent change in employment, projected 2019-29

- Total, all occupations: 4%
- Media and communication workers: 3%
- Writers and authors: -2%

Note: All Occupations includes all occupations in the U.S. Economy.
Source: U.S. Bureau of Labor Statistics, Employment Projections program.

Employment projections data for writers and authors, 2019-29					
Occupational Title	SOC Code	Employment, 2019	Projected Employment, 2029	Change, 2019-29	
				Percent	Numeric
SOURCE: U.S. Bureau of Labor Statistics, Employment Projections program					
Writers and authors	27-3043	131,200	128,200	-2	-3,100

State & Area Data
Occupational Employment Statistics (OES)

The Occupational Employment Statistics (OES) program produces employment and wage estimates annually for over 800 occupations. These estimates are available for the nation as a whole, for individual states, and for metropolitan and nonmetropolitan areas.

Contacts for More Information

For more information about writers and authors, visit

➤ American Grant Writers' Association, Inc.
➤ American Society of Journalists and Authors
➤ Association of Writers & Writing Programs
➤ National Association of Science Writers
➤ Society of Professional Journalists
➤ Writers Guild of America East

Military

Military Careers

What They Do
Members of the U.S. military service maintain the U.S. national defense. Although some service members work in occupations specific to the military, such as fighter pilots or infantrymen, many work in occupations that also exist in the civilian workplace, such as nurses, doctors, and lawyers. Members serve in the Army, Navy, Air Force, Marine Corps, or Coast Guard, or in the Reserve components of these branches, and in the Air National Guard and Army National Guard. (The Coast Guard, which is included in this profile, is part of the Department of Homeland Security.)

Duties
The military distinguishes between enlisted and officer careers. Enlisted personnel make up about 82 percent of the Armed Forces and carry out military operations. The remaining 18 percent are officers—military leaders who manage operations and enlisted personnel. About 8 percent of officers are warrant officers, who are technical and tactical experts in a specific area. Army aviators, for example, make up one group of warrant officers.

Enlisted personnel typically do the following:

- Participate in, or support, military operations, such as combat or training operations, or humanitarian or disaster relief
- Operate, maintain, and repair equipment
- Perform technical and support activities
- Supervise junior enlisted personnel

Some members of the military are deployed to other countries or regions to defend U.S. national interests.

Officers typically do the following:

- Plan, organize, and lead troops and activities in military operations
- Manage enlisted personnel
- Operate and command aircraft, ships, or armored vehicles
- Provide medical, legal, engineering, and other services to military personnel

Types of Enlisted Personnel
The following are examples of types of occupations for enlisted personnel:

Administrative personnel maintain information on personnel, equipment, funds, and other military-related activities. They work in support areas, such as finance, accounting, legal affairs, maintenance, supply, and transportation.

Combat specialty personnel train and work in combat units, such as the infantry, artillery, or Special Forces. For example, infantry specialists conduct ground combat operations, armored vehicle specialists operate battle tanks, and seamanship specialists maintain ships. Combat specialty personnel may maneuver against enemy forces and fire artillery, guns, mortars, or missiles to neutralize them. They may also operate various types of combat vehicles, such as amphibious assault vehicles, tanks, or small boats. Members of elite Special Forces teams are trained to perform specialized missions anywhere in the world on a moment's notice.

Construction personnel build or repair buildings, airfields, bridges, and other structures. They also may operate heavy equipment, such as bulldozers or cranes. They work with engineers and other building specialists as part of military construction teams. Some construction personnel specialize in an area such as plumbing, electrical wiring, or water purification.

Electronic and electrical equipment repair personnel maintain and repair electronic equipment used by the military. Repairers specialize in an area such as aircraft electrical systems, computers, optical equipment, communications, or weapons systems. For example, weapons electronic maintenance technicians maintain and repair electronic components and systems that help locate targets and help aim and fire weapons.

Engineering, science, and technical personnel perform a variety of tasks, such as operating technical equipment, solving problems, and collecting and interpreting information. They perform technical tasks in information technology, environmental health and safety, or intelligence:

- Environmental health and safety specialists inspect military facilities and food supplies to ensure that they are safe for use and consumption.

- Information technology specialists manage and maintain computer and network systems.
- Intelligence specialists gather information and prepare reports for military planning and operations.

Healthcare personnel provide medical services to military personnel and their family members. They may work as part of a patient-service team with doctors, nurses, or other healthcare professionals. Some specialize in providing emergency medical treatment in combat or remote areas. Others specialize in laboratory testing of tissue and blood samples; maintaining pharmacy supplies or patients' records; assisting with dental procedures; operating diagnostic tools, such as x-ray and ultrasound machines; or other healthcare tasks.

Human resources development personnel recruit qualified people into the military, place them in suitable occupations, and provide training programs:

- Personnel specialists maintain information about military personnel and their training, job assignments, promotions, and health.
- Recruiting specialists provide information about military careers; explain pay, benefits, and military life; and recruit individuals into the military.
- Training specialists and instructors teach military personnel how to perform their jobs.

Machine operator and repair personnel operate industrial equipment and machinery to make and repair parts for a variety of equipment and structures. They may operate engines, nuclear reactors, or water pumps, usually performing a specific job. Welders and metalworkers, for example, work with various types of metals to repair or form the structural parts of ships, buildings, or equipment. Survival equipment specialists inspect, maintain, and repair survival equipment, such as parachutes and aircraft life-support equipment.

Media and public affairs personnel prepare and present information about military activities to the military and the public. They take photographs, make video programs, present news and music programs, or conduct interviews.

Protective service personnel enforce military laws and regulations and provide emergency responses to disasters:

- Firefighters prevent and extinguish fires in buildings, on aircraft, and aboard ships.
- Military police responsibilities include controlling traffic, preventing crime, and responding to emergencies.
- Other law enforcement and security specialists investigate crimes committed on military property and guard inmates in military correctional facilities.

Support service personnel provide services that support the morale and well-being of military personnel and their families:

- Food service specialists prepare food in dining halls, hospitals, and ships.

- Religious program specialists assist chaplains with religious services, religious education programs, and related administrative duties.

Transportation and material-handling personnel transport military personnel and cargo. Most personnel within this occupational group are classified according to the mode of transportation, such as aircraft, motor vehicle, or ship:

- Aircrew members operate equipment on aircraft.
- Cargo specialists load and unload military supplies, using forklifts and cranes.
- Quartermasters and boat operators navigate and pilot many types of small watercraft, including tugboats, gunboats, and barges.
- Vehicle drivers operate various military vehicles, including fuel or water tank trucks.

Vehicle and machinery mechanical personnel conduct preventive and corrective maintenance on aircraft, automotive and heavy equipment, and powerhouse station equipment. These workers specialize by the type of equipment that they maintain:

- Aircraft mechanics inspect and service various types of aircraft.
- Automotive and heavy-equipment mechanics maintain and repair vehicles, such as Humvees, trucks, tanks, and other combat vehicles. They also repair bulldozers and other construction equipment.
- Heating and cooling mechanics install and repair air-conditioning, refrigeration, and heating equipment.
- Marine engine mechanics repair and maintain engines on ships, boats, and other watercraft.
- Powerhouse mechanics install, maintain, and repair electrical and mechanical equipment in power-generating stations.

Types of Officers

The following are examples of types of officers:

Combat specialty officers plan and direct military operations, oversee combat activities, and serve as combat leaders. They may be in charge of tanks and other armored assault vehicles, artillery systems, special operations, or infantry units. This group also includes naval surface warfare and submarine warfare officers, combat pilots, and aircrews.

Engineering, science, and technical officers' responsibilities depend on their area of expertise. They work in scientific and professional occupations, such as atmospheric scientists, meteorologists, physical scientists, biological scientists, social scientists, attorneys, and other types of scientists or professionals. For example, meteorologists in the military may study the weather to assist in planning flight paths for aircraft.

Executive, administrative, and managerial officers manage administrative functions in the Armed Forces, such as human resources management, training, personnel, information,

Table 1. Active-duty enlisted personnel by broad occupational group and branch of military, and Coast Guard, March 2020

Enlisted	Army	Air Force	Coast Guard	Marine Corps	Navy	Total enlisted personnel in each occupational group
Occupational group						
Administrative...	4,914	14,147	—	10,558	19,598	49,217
Combat Specialty	99,871	947	—	27,641	9,442	137,901
Construction	14,479	4,499	—	5,217	4,063	28,258
Electronic and Electrical Equipment Repair	26,763	29,293	—	11,355	49,215	116,626
Engineering, Science, and Technical	37,426	49,852	—	22,535	44,071	153,884
Healthcare	25,131	14,904	—	—	25,742	65,777
Human Resource Development	16,392	13,423	—	8,523	4,322	42,660
Machine Operator and Production	3,996	6,119	—	2,341	10,756	23,212
Media and Public Affairs	4,752	7,076	—	1,416	3,979	17,223
Protective Service	18,867	34,536	—	8,681	13,125	75,209
Support Service	8,526	5,170	—	1,957	9,145	24,798
Transportation and Material Handling	45,668	28,093	—	21,094	36,914	131,769
Vehicle and Machinery Mechanic	43,884	43,533	—	15,482	47,898	150,797
Non-occupation or unspecified coded personnel	32,353	13,744	—	26,078	1,512	73,687
Total enlisted personnel for each military branch and Coast Guard	383,022	265,336	32,068	162,878	279,782	1,123,086

SOURCE: U.S. Department of Defense, Defense Manpower Data Center

police, or other support services. Officers who oversee military bands are included in this category.

Healthcare officers provide medical services to military personnel in order to maintain or improve their health and physical readiness. Officers such as physicians, physician assistants, nurses, and dentists examine, diagnose, and treat patients. Other healthcare officers provide therapy, rehabilitative treatment, and additional healthcare for patients:

- Dentists treat diseases, disorders, and injuries of the mouth.
- Nurses provide and coordinate patient care in military hospitals and clinics.
- Optometrists treat vision problems and prescribe glasses, contact lenses, or medications.
- Pharmacists purchase, store, and dispense drugs and medicines.
- Physical therapists and occupational therapists plan and administer therapy to help patients adjust to injuries, regain independence, and return to work.
- Physicians, surgeons, and physician assistants examine patients, diagnose injuries and illnesses, and provide treatment to military and their families.
- Psychologists provide mental healthcare and also may conduct research on behavior and emotions.

Human resource development officers manage recruitment, placement, and training programs in the military:

- Personnel managers direct and oversee military personnel functions, such as job assignments, staff promotions, and career counseling.
- Recruiting managers direct and oversee recruiting personnel and recruiting activities.

- Training and education directors identify training needs and develop and manage educational programs.

Media and public affairs officers oversee the development, production, and presentation of information or events for the military and the public. They manage the production of videos and television and radio broadcasts that are used for training, news, and entertainment. Some plan, develop, and direct the activities of military bands. Public affairs officers respond to public inquiries about military activities and prepare news releases.

Protective service officers are responsible for the safety and protection of individuals and property on military bases and vessels. Emergency management officers plan and prepare for all types of disasters. They develop warning, evacuation, and response procedures in preparation for disasters. Law enforcement and security officers enforce all applicable laws on military bases and oversee investigations of crimes.

Support services officers manage military activities in key functional areas, such as logistics, transportation, and supply. They may oversee the transportation and distribution of materials by ground vehicles, aircraft, or ships. They also direct food service facilities and other support activities. Purchasing and contracting managers negotiate and monitor contracts for equipment, supplies, and services that the military buys from the private sector.

Transportation officers manage and perform activities related to the safe transport of military personnel and equipment by air, ground, and water. They operate and command an aircraft or a ship:

- Navigators use radar, radio, and other navigation equipment to determine their position and plan their route of travel.

Table 2. Active-duty officer personnel by broad occupational group and branch of military, and Coast Guard, March 2020

Officer	Army	Air Force	Coast Guard	Marine Corps	Navy	Total officer personnel in each occupational group
Occupational group						
Combat Specialty	19,243	4,212	—	3,636	5,963	33,054
Engineering, Science, and Technical	22,766	14,767	—	4,074	10,406	52,013
Executive, Administrative, and Managerial	11,997	8,019	—	2,389	6,706	29,111
Healthcare	10,127	8,868	—	—	6,870	25,865
Human Resource Development	2,799	2,185	—	775	3,486	9,245
Media and Public Affairs	319	330	—	226	260	1,135
Protective Service	2,954	961	—	354	1,230	5,499
Support Service	1,699	771	—	33	1,042	3,545
Transportation	10,392	16,894	—	4,782	10,476	42,544
Non-occupation or unspecified coded personnel	9,475	6,686	—	5,547	8,418	30,126
Total officer personnel for each military branch and Coast Guard	91,771	63,693	8,588	21,816	54,857	240,725

SOURCE: U.S. Department of Defense, Defense Manpower Data Center

- Pilots in the military fly various types of military airplanes and helicopters to carry troops and equipment.
- Ships' engineers direct engineering departments, including engine operations, maintenance, and power generation, aboard ships.

Work Environment

In March 2020, more than 2.1 million people served in the Armed Forces. More than 1.3 million were on active duty, including the following subtotals:

Army	479,233
Navy	339,048
Air Force	333,167
Marines	184,694

In addition, about 798,046 people served in the Reserves in these branches and in the Air National Guard and Army National Guard. About 41,721 people served in the Coast Guard, which is part of the Department of Homeland Security.

Military members must be physically fit and ready to participate in, or support, combat missions.

The specific work environments and conditions pertaining to military occupations depend on the occupational specialty, unit, branch of service, and other factors. Most active-duty military personnel live and work on or near military bases and facilities throughout the United States and the world. These bases and facilities usually offer housing and amenities, such as stores and recreation centers.

Service members move regularly for training or job assignments, with most rotations lasting 2 to 4 years. Some are deployed internationally to defend U.S. national interests.

Military members must be both physically and mentally fit, and ready to participate in, or support, combat missions that may be difficult and dangerous and involve long periods away from family. Some personnel, however, are rarely deployed near combat areas.

Table 3 shows employment (excluding Coast Guard) for active-duty officers, warrant officers, and enlisted ranks, by grade and branch of service.

Injuries

Members of the military are often placed in dangerous situations with the risk of serious injury or death. Members deployed to combat zones or those who work in dangerous areas, such as the flight deck of an aircraft carrier, face a higher risk of injury or death.

Work Schedules

Military personnel on active duty typically work full time. However, hours vary with the person's occupational specialty, rank, and branch of service, as well as with the needs of the military. Personnel must be prepared to work additional hours to fulfill missions.

How to Become a Member of the Armed Forces

To join the military, applicants must meet age, education, aptitude, physical, and character requirements. These requirements vary by branch of service and for officers and enlisted members.

Table 3. Military rank and employment, excluding Coast Guard, for active-duty personnel, March 2020

Grade	Army	Navy	Air Force	Marine Corps	Coast Guard	Active duty personnel (excluding Coast Guard)
Commissioned Officers:						
O-10	General	Admiral	General	General	Admiral	38
O-9	Lieutenant General	Vice Admiral	Lieutenant General	Lieutenant General	Vice Admiral	140
O-8	Major General	Rear Admiral (Upper Half)	Major General	Major General	Rear Admiral (Upper Half)	286
O-7	Brigadier General	Rear Admiral (Lower Half)	Brigadier General	Brigadier General	Rear Admiral (Lower Half)	410
O-6	Colonel	Captain	Colonel	Colonel	Captain	11,163
O-5	Lieutenant Colonel	Commander	Lieutenant Colonel	Lieutenant Colonel	Commander	27,439
O-4	Major	Lieutenant Commander	Major	Major	Lieutenant Commander	44,018
O-3	Captain	Lieutenant	Captain	Captain	Lieutenant	71,865
O-2	1st Lieutenant	Lieutenant Junior Grade	1st Lieutenant	1st Lieutenant	Lieutenant Junior Grade	32,339
O-1	2nd Lieutenant	Ensign	2nd Lieutenant	2nd Lieutenant	Ensign	26,016
Warrant Officers:						
W-5	Chief Warrant Officer 5	Chief Warrant Officer 5	—	Chief Warrant Officer 5		776
W-4	Chief Warrant Officer 4	Chief Warrant Officer 4	—	Chief Warrant Officer 4	Chief Warrant Officer 4	2,626
W-3	Chief Warrant Officer 3	Chief Warrant Officer 3	—	Chief Warrant Officer 3	Chief Warrant Officer 3	5,151
W-2	Chief Warrant Officer 2	Chief Warrant Officer 2	—	Chief Warrant Officer 2	Chief Warrant Officer 2	6,786
W-1	Warrant Officer 1		—	Warrant Officer 1		3,084
Enlisted Personnel:						
E-9	Sergeant Major	Master Chief Petty Officer	Chief Master Sergeant	Sergeant Major/Master Gunnery Sergeant	Master Chief Petty Officer	10,386
E-8	First Sergeant/Master Sergeant	Senior Chief Petty Officer	Senior Master Sergeant	First Sergeant/Master Sergeant	Senior Chief Petty Officer	27,171
E-7	Sergeant First Class	Chief Petty Officer	Master Sergeant	Gunnery Sergeant	Chief Petty Officer	96,013
E-6	Staff Sergeant	Petty Officer First Class	Technical Sergeant	Staff Sergeant	Petty Officer First Class	164,708
E-5	Sergeant	Petty Officer Second Class	Staff Sergeant	Sergeant	Petty Officer Second Class	227,453
E-4	Corporal/Specialist	Petty Officer Third Class	Senior Airman	Corporal	Petty Officer Third Class	253,860
E-3	Private First Class	Seaman	Airman First Class	Lance Corporal	Seaman	190,083
E-2	Private	Seaman Apprentice	Airman	Private First Class	Seaman Apprentice	76,937
E-1	Private	Seaman Recruit	Airman Basic	Private	Seaman Recruit	47,407

SOURCE: U.S. Department of Defense, Defense Manpower Data Center

After basic training, military members attend additional training at technical schools that prepare them for a particular military occupational specialty.

Although entry requirements for each service vary, certain qualifications for enlistment are common to all branches:

- Minimum of 17 years of age
- U.S. citizenship or permanent resident status
- Have a high school diploma or equivalent
- Never convicted of a felony
- Able to pass a medical exam

Applicants who are 17 years old must have the consent of a parent or legal guardian before entering the military.

Age limits for entering active-duty service are as follows:

- In the Army, the maximum age is 34.
- In the Navy, the maximum age is 34.
- In the Marine Corps, the maximum age is 29.
- In the Air Force, the maximum age is 39.
- In the Coast Guard, the maximum age is 27.

All applicants must meet certain physical requirements for height, weight, vision, and overall health. Officers must be U.S. citizens. Officers and some enlisted members must be able to obtain a security clearance. Candidates interested in becoming officers through training in the federal service academies must be unmarried and without dependents.

Service members are assigned an occupational specialty based on their aptitude, previous training, and the needs of their branch of service. All members must sign a contract and commit to a minimum term of service.

A recruiter can help a prospective service member determine whether he or she qualifies for enlistment or as an officer. A recruiter can also explain the various enlistment options and describe the military occupational specialties.

Women are now eligible to enter all military specialties.

Become an enlisted member

Prospective recruits who wish to enlist must take a placement exam called the Armed Forces Vocational Aptitude Battery (ASVAB), which is used to determine an applicant's suitability for military occupational specialties.

A recruiter can schedule applicants to take the ASVAB without any obligation to join the military. Many high schools offer the exam as a way for students to explore the possibility of a military career. The selection for a certain job specialty is based on ASVAB test results, the physical requirements for the job, and the needs of the service.

Applicants who decide to join the military must pass the physical examination before signing an enlistment contract. The contract involves a number of enlistment options, such as the length of active-duty or reserve-duty time, the length and kind of job training, and the amount of bonuses that may be earned, if any. Most active-duty programs have first-term enlistments of 4 years, although there are some 2-, 3-, and 6-year programs.

All branches of the Armed Services offer a delayed-entry program allowing candidates to postpone entry to active duty for up to one year after enlisting. High school students can enlist during their senior year and enter service after graduation. Others may delay entry because their desired job training is not immediately available or because they need time to arrange their personal affairs.

Become an officer

To become an officer, candidates typically need to have at least a bachelor's degree, be a U.S. citizen, pass a background check, and meet physical and age requirements. Candidates for officer positions do not need to take the ASVAB. Some achieve officer candidacy by completing a degree and training through the federal service academies (Army, Navy, Air Force, Coast Guard, and Merchant Marine) or through the Reserve Officers' Training Corps (ROTC) programs offered at many colleges and universities.

Education

All branches of the Armed Forces require their members to be high school graduates or have equivalent credentials. Officers usually need a bachelor's degree. Some officers entering the service may need to have education beyond a bachelor's degree. For example, officers entering as military lawyers need a law degree.

Those who want to become an officer have several options to meet the education requirements, including the aforementioned federal service academies (Army, Navy, Air Force, Coast Guard, and Merchant Marine), the Reserve Officers' Training Corps (ROTC) programs, Officer Candidate School (OCS), and other programs.

Important Qualities

Leadership skills. Members of the Armed Forces work together to achieve their missions. Those who want to advance ranks need to be able lead others in the completion of assigned duties or missions.

Mental preparedness. Members of the Armed Forces must be mentally fit and able to handle stressful situations that can occur during military operations.

Physical fitness. Members of the Armed Forces must be physically fit to participate in, or support, combat missions that may be difficult or dangerous.

Readiness. Members of the Armed Forces must be ready and able to report for military assignments on short notice.

Training

Training for enlisted personnel. Newly enlisted members of the Armed Forces undergo initial-entry training, better known as *basic training* or *boot camp*. Basic training includes courses in military skills and protocols and lasts 7 to 13 weeks, including a week of orientation and introduction to military life. Basic training also includes weapons training, team building, and rigorous physical exercise designed to improve strength and endurance.

Following basic training, enlisted members attend technical schools for additional training that prepares them for a particular military occupational specialty. This formal training period generally lasts from 10 to 20 weeks. Training for certain occupations—nuclear power plant operator, for example—may take as long as a year. In addition to getting technical instruction, military members receive on-the-job training at their first duty assignment.

Training for warrant officers. All services except the U.S. Air Force have warrant officer programs. Selection to attend Warrant Officer Candidate School is highly competitive and is restricted to those who meet rank and length-of-service requirements. The only exception is the selection process for Army aviator warrant officers, a process that has no requirement of previous military service. Training may last several weeks.

Training for officers. Officer training in the Armed Forces is provided through the federal service academies (Army, Navy, Air Force, Coast Guard, and Merchant Marine), the Reserve Officers' Training Corps (ROTC) program, Officer Candidate School (OCS) or Officer Training School (OTS), the National Guard (State Officer Candidate School programs), and the Uniformed Services University of the Health Sciences.

Training for officers in the federal service academies. The federal service academies provide a Bachelor of Science (B.S.) degree. Midshipmen and cadets receive free room and board, free tuition, free medical and dental care, and a monthly allowance. Graduates receive regular or reserve commissions and typically have a 5-year active-duty obligation, which may be longer for some specialties, such as medicine or aviation. Service academy cadet or midshipman candidates must be nominated by an authorized source, usually a member of Congress. In addition, nominees must submit their academic record, college aptitude test scores, and recommendations from teachers or other school officials. They must also pass a medical examination and have no dependents. Academies make appointments from the list of eligible nominees. Appointments to the Coast Guard Academy, however, are based on merit and do not require a nomination.

Training for officers in ROTC programs. Participants in ROTC programs take regular college courses along with 3 to 5 hours of military instruction per week. After graduation, they may serve as officers on active duty or in the Reserves or National Guard. In the last 2 years of an ROTC program, students receive a monthly allowance while attending school, as well as additional pay for summer training. ROTC scholarships for 2, 3, and 4 years of school are available on a competitive basis.

Training for officers through OCS or OTS. College graduates can earn a commission in the Armed Forces through OCS or OTS training programs in the Army, Navy, Air Force, Marine Corps, Coast Guard, Air National Guard, and Army National Guard. These programs consist of several weeks of academic, physical, and leadership training. Those who complete the programs as officers must usually complete their service obligation on active duty.

Training for officers through the Uniformed Services University of the Health Sciences. Personnel with training in certain health occupations may qualify for direct appointment as officers. For those studying health professions, financial assistance and internship opportunities are available from the military in return for specified periods of military service. Prospective medical students can apply to the Uniformed Services University of the Health Sciences, which offers a salary and free tuition in a program leading to a Doctor of Medicine (M.D.) degree. In return, graduates must serve for at least 7 years in either the military or the U.S. Public Health Service.

Training for officers through direct appointments. Direct appointments are also available for those qualified to serve in other specialty areas, such as the Judge Advocate General's Corps for those in the legal field or the Chaplain Corps for those in religious ministry. All prospective officers who enter the service through a direct appointment attend several weeks of military-related training that typically includes courses in military orientation, academic subjects, and officer leadership and tactics.

Licenses, Certifications, and Registrations

Depending on the occupational specialty, members of the military may need to have and maintain civilian licenses or certifications. For example, officers serving as lawyers, also known as *judge advocates*, may need to have and maintain their state bar licenses to enter and remain in the U.S. military.

Advancement

Each branch of the military has different criteria for determining the promotion of personnel. Criteria for promotion may include time in service and in grade, job performance, a fitness report, and passing scores on written exams. Enlisted personnel can be promoted to higher ranks, which may include serving in a supervisory position and being in charge of junior enlisted members.

Each military service may have other advancement opportunities for its enlisted personnel. For example, enlisted personnel may become warrant officers if they complete a bachelor's degree, have several years of experience in higher enlisted positions, and meet age and physical requirements. The Army offers a direct enlistment option to become a warrant officer aviator.

Officers can also be promoted to higher ranks, which may include the command of a military unit of both enlisted members and officers, or being in charge of an entire military base.

Pay

Basic pay is based on rank and time in service. Pay bands are the same for all branches. Members of the Armed Forces may receive additional pay based on their job assignment or qualifications. For example, they receive additional pay for foreign, hazardous, submarine, or flight duty, or for being medical or dental officers. Retirement pay is generally available after 20 years of service.

Military pay tables and information are available from the U.S. Department of Defense, Defense Finance and Accounting Service.

In addition to receiving basic pay, members of the military are either housed free of charge on base or they receive a housing allowance.

Members who serve for a certain number of years may receive other benefits. These benefits may include educational benefits through the Montgomery GI Bill, which pays for a portion of educational costs at accredited institutions; medical care at military or the U.S. Department of Veterans Affairs hospitals; and guaranteed home loans.

Military personnel on active duty typically work full time. However, hours vary with the person's occupational specialty, rank, and branch of service, as well as with the needs of the military. Personnel must be prepared to work additional hours to fulfill missions.

Job Outlook

BLS employment projections cover the civilian workforce only.

The goal of the Armed Forces is to maintain a force sufficient to deter, fight, and overcome various threats or conflicts in multiple regions at the same time. Emerging conflicts and global events, however, could lead to changes in the size of the military branches. Consequently, the nation is expected to maintain adequate personnel in the Reserve, Army National Guard, and Air National Guard.

Job Prospects

Opportunities should be very good for qualified individuals in all branches of the Armed Forces through 2028. All services have needs to fill entry-level and professional positions as current members of the Armed Forces move up through the ranks, leave the service, or retire.

The military has been an all-volunteer force since the end of the draft in 1973. When the economy is thriving and civilian employment opportunities are generally more favorable, it is more difficult for the military to meet its recruitment quotas. It is also more difficult to meet these goals during times of war, when recruitment goals typically rise. During economic downturns, candidates for military service may face competition.

Similar Occupations

The military employs people in numerous occupational specialties, many of which are similar to civilian occupations. To match military occupations with similar civilian occupations, O*Net OnLine offers the Military Crosswalk Search tool.

Contacts for More Information

Each of the military services publishes handbooks, fact sheets, and pamphlets describing its entrance requirements, its training opportunities, and other aspects of military careers. These publications are available at all recruiting stations; at most state employment service offices; and in high schools, colleges, and public libraries.

For more information on the individual services, visit
➤ U.S. Air Force
➤ Air National Guard
➤ U.S. Army
➤ Army National Guard
➤ U.S. Coast Guard
➤ U.S. Marine Corps
➤ U.S. Navy

In addition, the Defense Manpower Data Center, an agency of the Department of Defense, maintains a website that provides information and resources for parents, educators, and young adults who are curious about joining military service. To see the information, visit
➤ Today's Military

For more information about military testing, visit
➤ ASVAB

Office and Administrative Support

Bill and Account Collectors

Summary

Quick Facts: Bill and Account Collectors

2019 Median Pay	$37,000 per year $17.79 per hour
Typical Entry-Level Education	High school diploma or equivalent
Work Experience in a Related Occupation	None
On-the-job Training	Moderate-term on-the-job training
Number of Jobs, 2019	238,900
Job Outlook, 2019-29	-6% (Decline)
Employment Change, 2019-29	-15,400

What Bill and Account Collectors Do
Bill and account collectors try to recover payment on overdue bills.

Work Environment
Many bill and account collectors work in a call center for a third-party collection agency rather than the original creditor. Most work full time, and some have flexible schedules.

How to Become a Bill and Account Collector
Collectors usually must have a high school diploma. A few months of on-the-job training is common.

Pay
The median annual wage for bill and account collectors was $37,000 in May 2019.

Job Outlook
Employment of bill and account collectors is projected to decline 6 percent from 2019 to 2029. Automation of collections work is expected to continue to reduce employment for these workers.

State & Area Data
Explore resources for employment and wages by state and area for bill and account collectors.

What Bill and Account Collectors Do
Bill and account collectors try to recover payment on overdue bills. They negotiate repayment plans with debtors and help them find solutions to make paying their overdue bills easier.

Duties
Bill and account collectors typically do the following:

- Find consumers and businesses who have overdue bills
- Track down consumers who have an out-of-date address by using the Internet, post office, credit bureaus, or neighbors—a process called "skip tracing"
- Inform debtors that they have an overdue bill and try to negotiate a payment
- Explain the terms of sale or contract with the debtor, when necessary
- Learn the reasons for the overdue bills, which can help with the negotiations
- Offer credit advice or refer a consumer to a debt counselor, when appropriate

Bill and account collectors generally contact debtors by phone, although sometimes they do so by mail. They use

Bill and account collectors try to recover payment on overdue bills.

Collectors look up a person's information on a computer while speaking to them over the phone.

computer systems to update contact information and record past collection attempts with a particular debtor. Keeping these records can help collectors with future negotiations.

The main job of bill and account collectors is finding a solution that is acceptable to the debtor and maximizes payment to the creditor. Listening to the debtor and paying attention to his or her concerns can help the collector negotiate a solution.

After the collector and debtor agree on a repayment plan, the collector regularly checks to ensure that the debtor pays on time. If the debtor does not pay, the collector submits a statement to the creditor, who can take legal action. In extreme cases, this legal action may include taking back goods or disconnecting service.

Collectors must follow federal and state laws that govern debt collection. These laws require that collectors make sure they are talking with the debtor before announcing that the purpose of the call is to collect a debt. A collector also must give a statement, called "mini-Miranda," which informs the account holder that they are speaking with a bill or debt collector.

Collectors usually have goals they are expected to meet. Typically, these include calls per hour and success rates.

Work Environment

Bill and account collectors held about 238,900 jobs in 2019. The largest employers of bill and account collectors were as follows:

Business support services	32%
Credit intermediation and related activities	20
Healthcare and social assistance	9
Professional, scientific, and technical services	7
Management of companies and enterprises	6

Many collectors work in a call center for a third-party collection agency rather than the original creditor. In all industries, they spend most of their time on the phone tracking down or negotiating with debtors. They also use computers and databases to update information and record the results of their calls.

Collectors' work can be stressful because some people become angry and confrontational when pressed about their debts. Collectors often face resistance while trying to do their job duties. Successful collectors must face regular rejection and still be ready to make the next call in a polite and positive voice. Fortunately, some consumers appreciate help in resolving their outstanding debts and can be quite grateful.

Work Schedules

Most bill and account collectors work full time. Some collectors work flexible schedules, often calling people on weekends or during the evenings as they learn the best times to call.

How to Become a Bill and Account Collector

Collectors usually must have a high school diploma. A few months of on-the-job training is common.

Most bill and account collectors work in call centers for third-party collection agencies.

Collectors are trained on the job.

Education

Most bill and account collectors are required to have a high school diploma, although some employers prefer applicants who have taken some college courses. Communications, accounting, and basic computer courses are examples of classes that are helpful for entering this occupation.

Training

Collectors usually receive on-the-job training after being hired. Training includes learning how to use computer software, and instruction on federal debt-collection laws (in the Fair Debt Collection Practices Act) and state debt-collection regulations. Collectors also may be trained in negotiation techniques.

Important Qualities

Listening skills. Collectors must pay attention to what debtors say when trying to negotiate a repayment plan. Learning the particular situation of the debtors and how they fell into debt can help collectors suggest solutions.

Negotiating skills. The main aspects of a collector's job are reconciling the differences between two parties (the debtor and the creditor) and offering a solution that is acceptable to both parties.

Speaking skills. Collectors must be able to speak to debtors to explain their options and ensure that they fully understand what is being said.

Pay

The median annual wage for bill and account collectors was $37,000 in May 2019. The median wage is the wage at which half the workers in an occupation earned more than that amount and half earned less. The lowest 10 percent earned less than $25,800, and the highest 10 percent earned more than $56,860.

In May 2019, the median annual wages for bill and account collectors in the top industries in which they worked were as follows:

Management of companies and enterprises $40,110
Healthcare and social assistance 38,290
Professional, scientific, and technical services 37,960
Credit intermediation and related activities 37,470
Business support services 33,730

Most bill and account collectors work full time. Some collectors work flexible schedules, often calling people on weekends or during the evenings as they learn the best times to call.

Job Outlook

Employment of bill and account collectors is projected to decline 6 percent from 2019 to 2029.

The increasing efficiency of collectors is expected to reduce demand for this occupation. New software and automated calling systems should increase productivity and allow collectors to handle more accounts. This will allow more collections work to be done with fewer employees.

Some collection jobs will likely be sent to other countries where wages are lower, as a way for firms to cut costs. Although this will create some drag on employment of collectors, creditors should continue to hire some collectors in the United States.

Job Prospects

Despite declining employment, about 22,900 openings for bill and account collectors are projected each year, on average, over the decade.

Those openings are expected to result from the need to replace workers who transfer to other occupations or exit the labor force, such as to retire.

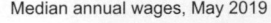

Bill and Account Collectors
Median annual wages, May 2019

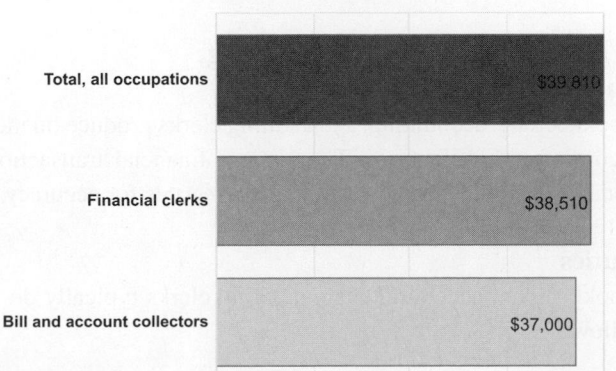

Total, all occupations	$39,810
Financial clerks	$38,510
Bill and account collectors	$37,000

Note: All Occupations includes all occupations in the U.S. Economy.
Source: U.S. Bureau of Labor Statistics, Occupational Employment Statistics.

Bill and Account Collectors
Percent change in employment, projected 2019-29

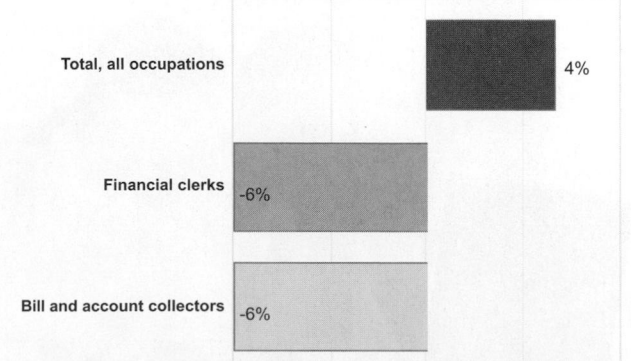

Total, all occupations	4%
Financial clerks	-6%
Bill and account collectors	-6%

Note: All Occupations includes all occupations in the U.S. Economy.
Source: U.S. Bureau of Labor Statistics, Employment Projections program.

Employment projections data for bill and account collectors, 2019-29					
Occupational Title	SOC Code	Employment, 2019	Projected Employment, 2029	Change, 2019-29	
				Percent	Numeric
SOURCE: U.S. Bureau of Labor Statistics, Employment Projections program					
Bill and account collectors	43-3011	238,900	223,500	-6	-15,400

State & Area Data
Occupational Employment Statistics (OES)
The Occupational Employment Statistics (OES) program produces employment and wage estimates annually for over 800 occupations. These estimates are available for the nation as a whole, for individual states, and for metropolitan and nonmetropolitan areas.

Contacts for More Information
For more information about bill and account collectors, visit

➤ ACA International, the Association of Credit and Collections Professionals

---

Bookkeeping, Accounting, and Auditing Clerks

Summary

Quick Facts: Bookkeeping, Accounting, and Auditing Clerks

2019 Median Pay	$41,230 per year $19.82 per hour
Typical Entry-Level Education	Some college, no degree
Work Experience in a Related Occupation	None
On-the-job Training	Moderate-term on-the-job training
Number of Jobs, 2019	1,673,600
Job Outlook, 2019-29	-6% (Decline)
Employment Change, 2019-29	-95,400

What Bookkeeping, Accounting, and Auditing Clerks Do
Bookkeeping, accounting, and auditing clerks produce financial records for organizations and check financial records for accuracy.

Bookkeeping, accounting, and auditing clerks produce financial records for organizations.

Work Environment
Bookkeeping, accounting, and auditing clerks work in offices and may do site visits. Some work part time.

How to Become a Bookkeeping, Accounting, or Auditing Clerk
Most bookkeeping, accounting, and auditing clerks need some postsecondary education and also learn some of their skills on the job. They must have basic math and computer skills, including knowledge of spreadsheets and bookkeeping software.

Pay
The median annual wage for bookkeeping, accounting, and auditing clerks was $41,230 in May 2019.

Job Outlook
Employment of bookkeeping, accounting, and auditing clerks is projected to decline 6 percent from 2019 to 2029. Technological change and automation are expected to reduce demand for these workers.

State & Area Data
Explore resources for employment and wages by state and area for bookkeeping, accounting, and auditing clerks.

What Bookkeeping, Accounting, and Auditing Clerks Do
Bookkeeping, accounting, and auditing clerks produce financial records for organizations. They record financial transactions, update statements, and check financial records for accuracy.

Duties
Bookkeeping, accounting, and auditing clerks typically do the following:

• Use bookkeeping software, spreadsheets, and databases
• Enter (post) financial transactions into the appropriate computer software

As organizations continue to computerize their financial records, many bookkeeping, accounting, and auditing clerks need to use specialized accounting software, spreadsheets, and databases.

- Receive and record cash, checks, and vouchers
- Put costs (debits) and income (credits) into the software, assigning each to an appropriate account
- Produce reports, such as balance sheets (costs compared with income), income statements, and totals by account
- Check for accuracy in figures, postings, and reports
- Reconcile or note and report any differences they find in the records

The records that bookkeeping, accounting, and auditing clerks work with include expenditures (money spent), receipts (money that comes in), accounts payable (bills to be paid), accounts receivable (invoices, or what other people owe the organization), and profit and loss (a report that shows the organization's financial health).

Workers in this occupation engage in a wide range of tasks. Some are full-charge bookkeeping clerks who maintain an entire organization's books. Others are accounting clerks who handle specific tasks.

These clerks use basic mathematics (adding, subtracting) throughout the day.

Bookkeeping, accounting, and auditing clerks use specialized computer accounting software, spreadsheets, and databases to enter information from receipts or bills. They must be comfortable using computers to record and calculate data.

The widespread use of computers also has enabled bookkeeping, accounting, and auditing clerks to take on additional responsibilities, such as payroll, billing, purchasing (buying), and keeping track of overdue bills. Many of these functions require clerks to communicate with clients.

Bookkeeping clerks, also known as *bookkeepers*, often are responsible for some or all of an organization's accounts, known as the general ledger. They record all transactions and post debits (costs) and credits (income).

They also produce financial statements and other reports for supervisors and managers. Bookkeepers prepare bank deposits by compiling data from cashiers, verifying receipts, and sending cash, checks, or other forms of payment to the bank.

In addition, they may handle payroll, make purchases, prepare invoices, and keep track of overdue accounts.

Accounting clerks typically work for larger companies and have more specialized tasks. Their titles, such as accounts payable clerk or accounts receivable clerk, often reflect the type of accounting they do.

The responsibilities of accounting clerks frequently vary by level of experience. Entry-level accounting clerks may post details of transactions (including date, type, and amount), add up accounts, and determine interest charges. They may also monitor loans and accounts to ensure that payments are up to date.

More advanced accounting clerks may add and balance billing vouchers, ensure that account data are complete and accurate, and code documents according to an organization's procedures.

Auditing clerks check figures, postings, and documents to ensure that they are mathematically accurate and properly coded. For smaller errors, such as transcription errors, they may make corrections themselves. In case of major discrepancies, they typically notify senior staff, including accountants and auditors.

Work Environment

Bookkeeping, accounting, and auditing clerks held about 1.7 million jobs in 2019. The largest employers of bookkeeping, accounting, and auditing clerks were as follows:

Professional, scientific, and technical services	13%
Retail trade	8
Wholesale trade	8
Healthcare and social assistance	7
Finance and insurance	6

The professional, scientific, and technical services industry includes the accounting, tax preparation, bookkeeping, and payroll services subindustry.

Bookkeeping, accounting, and auditing clerks work in offices. Bookkeepers who work for multiple firms may visit their clients' places of business. They often work alone, but sometimes they collaborate with accountants, managers, and auditing clerks from other departments.

Work Schedules

Most bookkeeping, accounting, and auditing clerks work full time. They may work longer hours to meet deadlines at the end of the fiscal year, during tax time, or when monthly or yearly accounting audits are performed.

Bookkeeping, accounting, and auditing clerks may work longer hours to meet deadlines at the end of the fiscal year, during tax time, or when monthly or yearly accounting audits are performed.

How to Become a Bookkeeping, Accounting, or Auditing Clerk

Most bookkeeping, accounting, and auditing clerks need some postsecondary education and also learn some of their skills on the job. They must have basic math and computer skills, including knowledge of spreadsheets and bookkeeping software.

Most bookkeeping, accounting, and auditing clerks are required to have some postsecondary education.

Education
Employers generally require bookkeeping, accounting, and auditing clerks to have some postsecondary education, particularly coursework in accounting. However, some candidates can be hired with just a high school diploma.

Training
Bookkeeping, accounting, and auditing clerks usually get on-the-job training. Under the guidance of a supervisor or another experienced employee, new clerks learn how to do their tasks, such as double-entry bookkeeping. In double-entry bookkeeping, each transaction is entered twice, once as a debit (cost) and once as a credit (income), to ensure that all accounts are balanced.

Some formal classroom training also may be necessary, such as training in specialized computer software. This on-the-job training typically takes around 6 months.

Licenses, Certifications, and Registrations
Some bookkeeping, accounting, and auditing clerks become certified. For those who do not have postsecondary education, certification is a particularly useful way to gain expertise in the field. The Certified Bookkeeper (CB) designation, awarded by the American Institute of Professional Bookkeepers, shows that those who have earned it have the skills and knowledge needed to carry out all bookkeeping tasks, including overseeing payroll and balancing accounts, according to accepted accounting procedures.

For certification, candidates must have at least 2 years of full-time bookkeeping experience or equivalent part-time work, pass a four-part exam, and adhere to a code of ethics.

The National Association of Certified Public Bookkeepers offers the Certified Public Bookkeeper (CPB) certification. To obtain the certification, candidates must pass the four-part Uniform Bookkeeper Certification Examination.

Advancement
With appropriate experience and additional education, some bookkeeping, accounting, and auditing clerks may become accountants or auditors.

Important Qualities
Computer skills. Bookkeeping, accounting, and auditing clerks need to be comfortable using computer spreadsheets and bookkeeping software.

Detail oriented. Bookkeeping, accounting, and auditing clerks are responsible for producing accurate financial records. They must pay attention to detail in order to avoid making errors and recognize errors that others have made.

Integrity. Bookkeeping, accounting, and auditing clerks have control of an organization's financial documentation, which they must use properly and keep confidential. It is vital

Bookkeeping, Accounting, and Auditing Clerks

Median annual wages, May 2019

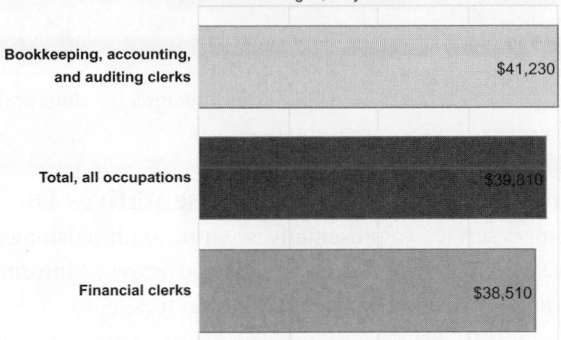

Bookkeeping, accounting, and auditing clerks	$41,230
Total, all occupations	$39,810
Financial clerks	$38,510

Note: All Occupations includes all occupations in the U.S. Economy.
Source: U.S. Bureau of Labor Statistics, Occupational Employment Statistics.

Bookkeeping, Accounting, and Auditing Clerks

Percent change in employment, projected 2019-29

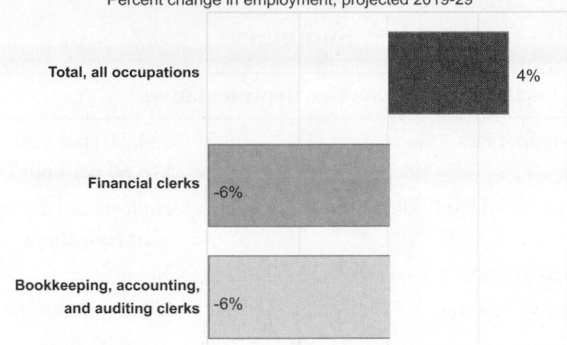

Total, all occupations	4%
Financial clerks	-6%
Bookkeeping, accounting, and auditing clerks	-6%

Note: All Occupations includes all occupations in the U.S. Economy.
Source: U.S. Bureau of Labor Statistics, Employment Projections program.

that they keep records transparent and guard against misusing an organization's funds.

Math skills. Bookkeeping, accounting, and auditing clerks deal with numbers daily and should be comfortable with basic arithmetic.

Pay

The median annual wage for bookkeeping, accounting, and auditing clerks was $41,230 in May 2019. The median wage is the wage at which half the workers in an occupation earned more than that amount and half earned less. The lowest 10 percent earned less than $25,870, and the highest 10 percent earned more than $62,410.

In May 2019, the median annual wages for bookkeeping, accounting, and auditing clerks in the top industries in which they worked were as follows:

Professional, scientific, and technical services	$43,540
Finance and insurance	42,860
Wholesale trade	42,250
Healthcare and social assistance	40,350
Retail trade	36,200

Most bookkeeping, accounting, and auditing clerks work full time. They may work longer hours to meet deadlines at the end of the fiscal year, during tax time, or when monthly or yearly accounting audits are performed.

Job Outlook

Employment of bookkeeping, accounting, and auditing clerks is projected to decline 6 percent from 2019 to 2029.

Technological change is expected to reduce demand for these workers. Software innovations, such as cloud computing, have automated many of the tasks performed by bookkeepers.

As a result, the same amount of bookkeeping work can be done with fewer employees, which is expected to lead to job losses for bookkeepers over the next 10 years.

With more automation of routine tasks, bookkeepers are expected to take on a more analytical and advisory role over the decade. For example, rather than entering data by hand, bookkeepers will focus on analyzing their clients' books and pointing out potential areas for efficiency gains.

Job Prospects

Despite projected declines in employment, opportunities for these workers should be plentiful due to the need to replace workers who leave this large occupation.

Employment projections data for bookkeeping, accounting, and auditing clerks, 2019-29					
Occupational Title	SOC Code	Employment, 2019	Projected Employment, 2029	Change, 2019-29	
				Percent	Numeric
SOURCE: U.S. Bureau of Labor Statistics, Employment Projections program					
Bookkeeping, accounting, and auditing clerks	43-3031	1,673,600	1,578,200	-6	-95,400

State & Area Data
Occupational Employment Statistics (OES)

The Occupational Employment Statistics (OES) program produces employment and wage estimates annually for over 800 occupations. These estimates are available for the nation as a whole, for individual states, and for metropolitan and nonmetropolitan areas.

Contacts for More Information

For more information about bookkeeping, accounting, and auditing clerks, visit
➤ American Institute of Professional Bookkeepers
➤ National Association of Certified Public Bookkeepers

Customer Service Representatives

Summary

Quick Facts: Customer Service Representatives

2019 Median Pay	$34,710 per year $16.69 per hour
Typical Entry-Level Education	High school diploma or equivalent
Work Experience in a Related Occupation	None
On-the-job Training	Short-term on-the-job training
Number of Jobs, 2019	3,018,800
Job Outlook, 2019-29	-2% (Decline)
Employment Change, 2019-29	-59,000

What Customer Service Representatives Do

Customer service representatives interact with customers to handle complaints, process orders, and answer questions.

Work Environment

Customer service representatives are employed in nearly every industry. Most work full time.

How to Become a Customer Service Representative

Customer service representatives typically need a high school diploma and are trained on the job. They should be good at communicating with people and adept at using computers.

Pay

The median hourly wage for customer service representatives was $16.69 in May 2019.

Job Outlook

Employment of customer service representatives is projected to decline 2 percent from 2019 to 2029. There will be less demand for customer service representatives as more of their tasks become automated.

State & Area Data

Explore resources for employment and wages by state and area for customer service representatives.

What Customer Service Representatives Do

Customer service representatives work with customers to resolve complaints, process orders, and provide information about an organization's products and services.

Duties

Customer service representatives typically do the following:

- Listen to customers' questions and concerns and provide answers or responses
- Provide information about products and services
- Take orders, calculate charges, and process billing or payments
- Review customer accounts and make changes, if necessary
- Handle returns or complaints
- Record details of customer contacts and actions taken
- Refer customers to supervisors or more experienced employees

Customer service representatives answer questions or requests from customers or the public. They typically provide services by phone, but some also interact with customers face to face, by email or text, via live chat, and through social media.

The specific duties of customer service representatives vary by industry. For example, representatives who work in banks may answer customers' questions about their accounts. Representatives who work for utility and telecommunications companies may help customers with service problems, such as outages. Those who work in retail stores often handle returns, process refunds, and help customers locate items. Although

Customer service representatives provide information to customers about products and services.

Customer service representatives listen and respond to customers' questions.

selling a product or service is not their main job, representatives may help generate sales while providing information.

Customer service representatives typically use a telephone, computer, and other office equipment. For example, representatives who work in call centers answer the phone and use computers to explore solutions for customers.

Work Environment

Customer service representatives held about 3.0 million jobs in 2019. The largest employers of customer service representatives were as follows:

Retail trade	14%
Insurance carriers and related activities	12
Business support services	11
Wholesale trade	7
Professional, scientific, and technical services	6

Customer service representatives are employed in nearly every industry. Representatives in offices may work in a large room alongside other employees, so the area can be noisy. Working from home is also possible in some companies. Representatives may be under pressure to answer a designated number of calls while supervisors monitor them for quality assurance. In addition, the work may be stressful when representatives must interact with dissatisfied customers

In retail stores, representatives may spend hours on their feet assisting customers in person.

Work Schedules

Although most customer service representatives work full time, some work part time. Customer service representatives often need to work during busy times, which may include evenings, weekends, and holidays.

Jobs in call centers may require representatives to work shifts early in the morning or late at night because some call centers are open 24 hours a day.

How to Become a Customer Service Representative

Customer service representatives typically need a high school diploma or equivalent and receive on-the-job training to learn the specific skills needed for the job. They should be good at communicating and interacting with people and should be adept at using computers.

Education

Customer service representatives typically need a high school diploma or equivalent.

Training

Customer service representatives usually receive short-term on-the-job training, which typically lasts 2 to 4 weeks. Those who work in finance and insurance may need several months of training to learn complicated financial regulations.

General customer-service training may focus on procedures for answering questions, information about a company's products and services, and computer and telephone use. Trainees often receive guidance from an experienced worker for the first few weeks of employment.

In certain industries, such as finance and insurance, customer service representatives must stay current with changing regulations.

Licenses, Certifications, and Registrations

Customer service representatives who provide information about finance and insurance may need a state license. Although licensing requirements vary by state, they usually include passing an exam. Some employers and organizations provide training for these exams.

Advancement

With experience, customer service representatives may advance to supervisory roles.

Many customer service representatives work in call centers.

Customer service representatives should be good at communicating and interacting with people and have some experience using computers.

Important Qualities

Communication skills. Customer service representatives must be able to provide clear information in writing, by phone, or in person.

Computer skills. Customer service representatives must be adept at using computers.

Customer-service skills. Representatives help companies retain customers by professionally answering questions and helping to resolve complaints.

Interpersonal skills. Representatives should be able to create positive interactions with customers.

Listening skills. Representatives must listen carefully to ensure that they understand customers in order to assist them.

Patience. Representatives should be patient and polite, especially when interacting with dissatisfied customers.

Problem-solving skills. Representatives must determine solutions to customers' problems. By doing so, representatives contribute to customer loyalty and retention.

Pay

The median hourly wage for customer service representatives was $16.69 in May 2019. The median wage is the wage at which half the workers in an occupation earned more than that amount and half earned less. The lowest 10 percent earned less than $11.05, and the highest 10 percent earned more than $27.11.

In May 2019, the median hourly wages for customer service representatives in the top industries in which they worked were as follows:

Wholesale trade	$18.94
Insurance carriers and related activities	18.28
Professional, scientific, and technical services	17.86
Business support services	14.19
Retail trade	13.65

Although most customer service representatives work full time, some work part time. Customer service representatives often need to work during busy times, which may include evenings, weekends, and holidays.

Jobs in call centers may require representatives to work shifts early in the morning or late at night because some call centers are open 24 hours a day.

Job Outlook

Employment of customer service representatives is projected to decline 2 percent from 2019 to 2029.

There will be less demand for customer service representatives as more of their tasks become automated. Internet self-service or interactive voice-response systems, social media, and mobile applications are increasingly popular because they enable customers to perform simple tasks without speaking to a representative. Improvements in technology will gradually allow these automated systems to perform even more advanced tasks. Some companies will continue to use in-house service centers to differentiate themselves from competitors, particularly for complex inquiries such as refunding accounts or confirming insurance coverage.

However, jobs for customer service representatives are projected to be added in business support services, which includes telephone call centers. Some businesses will contract out their customer service operations to telephone call centers because the call centers provide consolidated sales and customer service functions.

Job Prospects

Despite the projected decline in employment, job prospects for customer service representatives are expected to be good because of the need to replace workers who leave the occupation.

Customer Service Representatives
Median hourly wages, May 2019

Total, all occupations	$19.14
Customer service representatives	$16.69
Information and record clerks	$16.37

Note: All Occupations includes all occupations in the U.S. Economy.
Source: U.S. Bureau of Labor Statistics, Occupational Employment Statistics.

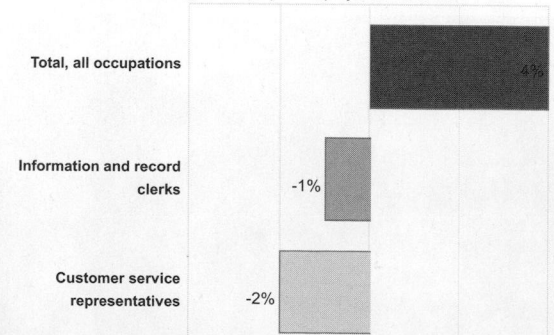

Customer Service Representatives
Percent change in employment, projected 2019-29

Total, all occupations	4%
Information and record clerks	-1%
Customer service representatives	-2%

Note: All Occupations includes all occupations in the U.S. Economy.
Source: U.S. Bureau of Labor Statistics, Employment Projections program.

Employment projections data for customer service representatives, 2019-29					
Occupational Title	SOC Code	Employment, 2019	Projected Employment, 2029	Change, 2019-29	
				Percent	Numeric
SOURCE: U.S. Bureau of Labor Statistics, Employment Projections program					
Customer service representatives	43-4051	3,018,800	2,959,800	-2	-59,000

State & Area Data
Occupational Employment Statistics (OES)

The Occupational Employment Statistics (OES) program produces employment and wage estimates annually for over 800 occupations. These estimates are available for the nation as a whole, for individual states, and for metropolitan and nonmetropolitan areas.

Contacts for More Information

The *Handbook* does not have contacts for more information for this occupation.

Desktop Publishers

Summary

Quick Facts: Desktop Publishers

2019 Median Pay	$45,390 per year $21.82 per hour
Typical Entry-Level Education	Associate's degree
Work Experience in a Related Occupation	None
On-the-job Training	Short-term on-the-job training
Number of Jobs, 2019	10,400
Job Outlook, 2019-29	-19% (Decline)
Employment Change, 2019-29	-2,000

What Desktop Publishers Do

Desktop publishers use computer software to design page layouts for items that are printed or published online.

Work Environment

Many desktop publishers work full time, and they may need to work additional hours to meet publication deadlines.

How to Become a Desktop Publisher

Desktop publishers typically need an associate's degree. They also receive short-term on-the-job training lasting about 1 month.

Pay

The median annual wage for desktop publishers was $45,390 in May 2019.

Job Outlook

Employment of desktop publishers is projected to decline 19 percent from 2019 to 2029. Companies are expected to hire fewer desktop publishers as other types of workers—such as graphic designers, web designers, and editors—increasingly perform desktop-publishing tasks.

State & Area Data

Explore resources for employment and wages by state and area for desktop publishers.

What Desktop Publishers Do

Desktop publishers use computer software to design page layouts for newspapers, books, brochures, and other items that are printed or published online.

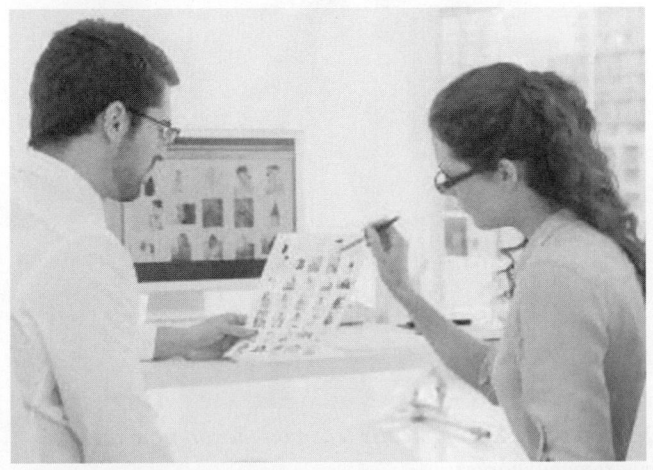

Desktop publishers design layouts for books, newspapers, and other published items.

Desktop publishers edit graphics, such as photographs or illustrations.

Duties

Desktop publishers typically do the following:

- Review text, graphics, or other materials created by writers and designers
- Edit graphics, such as photographs or illustrations
- Import text and graphics into publishing software
- Integrate images and text to create cohesive pages
- Adjust text properties, such as size, column width, and spacing
- Revise layouts and make corrections as necessary
- Submit or upload final files for printing or online publishing

Desktop publishers use publishing software to create page layouts for print or electronic publication. They may edit text by correcting its spelling, punctuation, and grammar.

Desktop publishers often work with other design, media, or marketing workers, including writers, editors, and graphic designers. For example, they work with graphic designers to come up with images that complement the text and fit the available space.

Work Environment

Desktop publishers held about 10,400 jobs in 2019. The largest employers of desktop publishers were as follows:

Newspaper, periodical, book, and directory publishers.....	27%
Self-employed workers......................................	14
Professional, scientific, and technical services.............	11
Printing and related support activities...........................	10

Work Schedules

Many desktop publishers work full time, and they may need to work additional hours to meet publication deadlines.

How to Become a Desktop Publisher

Desktop publishers usually need an associate's degree. They also receive short-term on-the-job training, lasting about 1 month.

Education

Desktop publishers usually need an associate's degree, often in graphic design or graphic communications. Community colleges and technical schools offer desktop-publishing courses, which teach students how to create electronic page layouts and format text and graphics with the use of desktop-publishing software.

Training

Desktop publishers typically receive short-term on-the-job training lasting about 1 month. They learn by working closely with more experienced workers or by taking classes that teach them how to use desktop-publishing software. Workers often need to continue training because publishing software changes over time.

Important Qualities

Artistic ability. Desktop publishers must have a good eye for how graphics and text will look, so that they can create pages that are visually appealing and legible.

Communication skills. Desktop publishers must collaborate with others, such as writers, editors, and graphic designers, and communicate ideas effectively.

Detail oriented. Desktop publishers must pay attention to details such as margins, font sizes, and the overall appearance and accuracy of their work.

Organizational skills. Desktop publishers often work under strict deadlines and must be good at scheduling and prioritizing tasks in order to have documents ready in time for publication.

Many desktop publishers work in the publishing and printing industries.

Desktop publishers typically learn on the job from an experienced worker.

Desktop Publishers
Median annual wages, May 2019

Desktop publishers	$45,390
Total, all occupations	$39,810
Other office and administrative support workers	$34,670

Note: All Occupations includes all occupations in the U.S. Economy.
Source: U.S. Bureau of Labor Statistics, Occupational Employment Statistics.

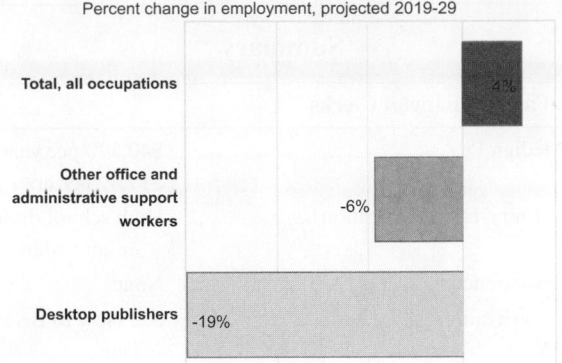

Desktop Publishers
Percent change in employment, projected 2019-29

Total, all occupations	4%
Other office and administrative support workers	-6%
Desktop publishers	-19%

Note: All Occupations includes all occupations in the U.S. Economy.
Source: U.S. Bureau of Labor Statistics, Employment Projections program.

Other Experience

Many employers prefer to hire workers who have experience preparing layouts and using desktop-publishing software. Students may gain experience by working on a publication for a school or other organization.

Pay

The median annual wage for desktop publishers was $45,390 in May 2019. The median wage is the wage at which half the workers in an occupation earned more than that amount and half earned less. The lowest 10 percent earned less than $23,850, and the highest 10 percent earned more than $78,190.

In May 2019, the median annual wages for desktop publishers in the top industries in which they worked were as follows:

Printing and related support activities	$48,720
Professional, scientific, and technical services	46,690
Newspaper, periodical, book, and directory publishers	38,380

Many desktop publishers work full time, and they may need to work additional hours to meet publication deadlines.

Job Outlook

Employment of desktop publishers is projected to decline 19 percent from 2019 to 2029.

Desktop publishing is commonly used to design printed materials, such as advertisements, brochures, newsletters, and forms. Companies are expected to hire fewer desktop publishers, however, as other types of workers—such as graphic designers, web designers, and editors—increasingly perform desktop-publishing tasks.

As organizations increasingly publish their materials electronically instead of printing them, employment of desktop publishers may decline further.

Employment projections data for desktop publishers, 2019-29					
Occupational Title	SOC Code	Employment, 2019	Projected Employment, 2029	Change, 2019-29	
				Percent	Numeric
SOURCE: U.S. Bureau of Labor Statistics, Employment Projections program					
Desktop publishers	43-9031	10,400	8,400	-19	-2,000

State & Area Data
Occupational Employment Statistics (OES)

The Occupational Employment Statistics (OES) program produces employment and wage estimates annually for over 800 occupations. These estimates are available for the nation as a whole, for individual states, and for metropolitan and nonmetropolitan areas.

Contacts for More Information

For more information about the printing industry, visit
➤ Printing Industries of America

Financial Clerks

Summary

Quick Facts: Financial Clerks

2019 Median Pay	$40,540 per year $19.49 per hour
Typical Entry-Level Education	High school diploma or equivalent
Work Experience in a Related Occupation ...	None
On-the-job Training	See How to Become One
Number of Jobs, 2019	1,343,400
Job Outlook, 2019-29	0% (Little or no change)
Employment Change, 2019-29	3,500

What Financial Clerks Do

Financial clerks do administrative work, keep records, help customers, and carry out financial transactions.

Work Environment

Financial clerks usually work in offices, including bank branches, medical practices, and government agencies. Most work full time.

How to Become a Financial Clerk

A high school diploma is typically required for most financial clerk positions. These workers typically learn their job duties through on-the-job training.

Pay

The median annual wage for financial clerks was $40,540 in May 2019.

Job Outlook

Employment of financial clerks is projected to show little or no change from 2019 to 2029.

Financial clerks provide customer service and maintain financial records.

State & Area Data

Explore resources for employment and wages by state and area for financial clerks.

What Financial Clerks Do

Financial clerks do administrative work for many types of organizations. They keep records, help customers, and carry out transactions that involve money.

Duties

Financial clerks typically do the following:

- Keep and update financial records
- Calculate bills and charges
- Offer customer assistance
- Carry out financial transactions

Financial clerks' job duties vary by specialty and by setting. The following are examples of types of financial clerks:

Billing and posting clerks calculate charges and generate bills, which they then prepare to mail to customers. They review documents such as purchase orders, sales tickets, charge slips, and hospital records to calculate fees or charges due. They also contact customers to get or give account information.

Brokerage clerks help with tasks associated with securities such as stocks, bonds, commodities, and other kinds of investments. Their duties include writing orders for stock purchases and sales, calculating transfer taxes, verifying stock transactions, accepting and delivering securities, distributing dividends, and recording daily transactions and holdings.

Credit authorizers, checkers, and clerks review the credit history, and get the information needed to determine the creditworthiness, of individuals or businesses applying for credit. Credit authorizers check customers' credit records and payment histories to decide, based on predetermined standards, whether to approve new credit. Credit checkers contact credit departments of business and service establishments for information about applicants' credit standing.

Financial clerks keep and update financial records.

Gaming cage workers work in casinos and other gaming establishments. The "cage" in which they work is the central depository for money and gaming chips. Gaming cage workers sell gambling chips, tokens, or tickets to patrons. They count funds and reconcile daily summaries of transactions to balance books.

Insurance claims and policy processing clerks process applications for insurance policies. They also handle customers' requests to change or cancel their existing policies. Their duties include interviewing clients and reviewing insurance applications to make sure that all questions have been answered. They also inform insurance agents and accounting departments of policy cancellations or changes.

Loan interviewers, also called *loan processors* or *loan clerks*, interview applicants and others to get and verify personal and financial information needed to complete loan applications. They also prepare the documents that go to the appraiser and are issued at the closing of a loan.

New accounts clerks interview people who want to open accounts in financial institutions. They explain the account services available to prospective customers and help them fill out applications. They also investigate and correct errors in accounts.

Payroll and timekeeping clerks compile and post employee time and payroll data. They verify and record attendance, hours worked, and pay adjustments. They make sure that employees are paid on time and that their paychecks are correct.

Procurement clerks compile requests for materials, prepare purchase orders, keep track of purchases and supplies, and handle questions about orders. They respond to questions from customers and suppliers about the status of orders. Procurement clerks handle requests to change or cancel orders. They make sure that purchases arrive on schedule and that the items meet the buyer's specifications.

Work Environment

Financial clerks held about 1.3 million jobs in 2019. Employment in the detailed occupations that make up financial clerks was distributed as follows:

Billing and posting clerks	484,200
Insurance claims and policy processing clerks	293,900
Loan interviewers and clerks	212,600
Payroll and timekeeping clerks	149,800
Procurement clerks	68,500
Brokerage clerks	48,600
New accounts clerks	44,300
Credit authorizers, checkers, and clerks	26,900
Gambling cage workers	14,600

The majority of financial clerks work full time.

The largest employers of financial clerks were as follows:

Insurance carriers and related activities	21%
Healthcare and social assistance	18
Credit intermediation and related activities	18
Professional, scientific, and technical services	7
Administrative and support services	5

Financial clerks work in a variety of industries, usually in offices.

Work Schedules

Most financial clerks work full time.

How to Become a Financial Clerk

A high school diploma or equivalent is typically required for most financial clerk jobs. These workers typically learn their duties through on-the-job training.

Education

Financial clerks typically need a high school diploma or equivalent to enter the occupation. Employers of brokerage clerks may prefer candidates who have taken some college courses in business or economics and, in some cases, have a 2- or 4-year college degree.

A high school diploma is sufficient for most financial clerk positions.

Training

Most financial clerks learn how to do their job duties through on-the-job training. Some formal technical training also may be necessary; for example, gaming cage workers may need training in specific gaming regulations and procedures.

Advancement

Financial clerks may advance to related occupations in finance. For example, a loan interviewer or clerk may become a loan officer, and a brokerage clerk may become a securities, commodities, and financial services sales agent, after obtaining the required education and license.

Important Qualities

Communication skills. Financial clerks should be able to explain policies and procedures to colleagues and customers.

Math skills. The job duties of financial clerks includes calculating charges and updating financial records.

Organizational skills. Financial clerks must be able to arrange files so they can find them quickly and efficiently.

Pay

The median annual wage for financial clerks was $40,540 in May 2019. The median wage is the wage at which half the workers in an occupation earned more than that amount and half earned less. The lowest 10 percent earned less than $27,730, and the highest 10 percent earned more than $61,160.

Median annual wages for financial clerks in May 2019 were as follows:

Brokerage clerks	$52,750
Payroll and timekeeping clerks	46,180
Procurement clerks	43,310
Insurance claims and policy processing clerks	40,750
Loan interviewers and clerks	40,640
Credit authorizers, checkers, and clerks	40,100

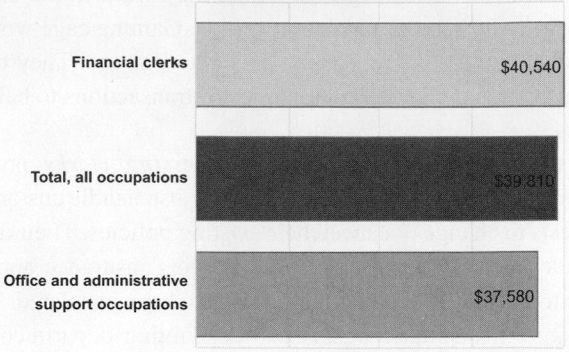

Financial Clerks
Median annual wages, May 2019

Financial clerks	$40,540
Total, all occupations	$39,810
Office and administrative support occupations	$37,580

Note: All Occupations includes all occupations in the U.S. Economy.
Source: U.S. Bureau of Labor Statistics, Occupational Employment Statistics.

Billing and posting clerks	38,740
New accounts clerks	36,550
Gambling cage workers	28,040

In May 2019, the median annual wages for financial clerks in the top industries in which they worked were as follows:

Insurance carriers and related activities	$41,100
Professional, scientific, and technical services	40,680
Credit intermediation and related activities	39,760
Administrative and support services	39,640
Healthcare and social assistance	38,640

Most financial clerks work full time.

Job Outlook

Employment of financial clerks is projected to show little or no change from 2019 to 2029.

The availability of online tools, which allow financial customers to perform many tasks themselves, is expected to reduce demand for occupations such as new accounts clerks,

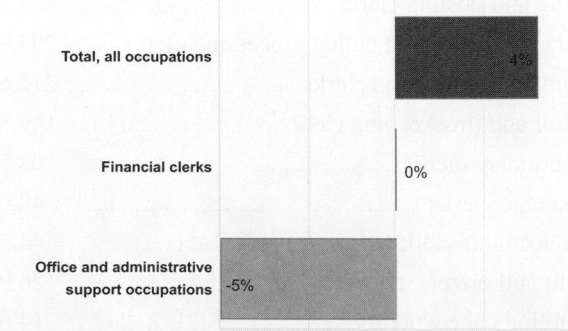

Financial Clerks
Percent change in employment, projected 2019-29

Total, all occupations	4%
Financial clerks	0%
Office and administrative support occupations	-5%

Note: All Occupations includes all occupations in the U.S. Economy.
Source: U.S. Bureau of Labor Statistics, Employment Projections program.

procurement clerks, and credit authorizers, checkers, and clerks. Similarly, productivity-enhancing technology is expected to reduce demand for other clerks, such as payroll and timekeeping clerks and insurance claims and policy processing clerks.

Billing and posting clerks and loan interviewers and clerks do tasks that are less susceptible to automation, namely contacting and interviewing applicants and customers to gather information. Therefore, these clerks are expected to see employment growth in line with the healthcare, banking, and insurance industries, respectively.

Job Prospects

Job prospects for financial clerks are likely to be good, because employers will need to hire new workers to replace those who leave the occupation.

Employment projections data for financial clerks, 2019-29

Occupational Title	SOC Code	Employment, 2019	Projected Employment, 2029	Change, 2019-29 Percent	Change, 2019-29 Numeric
SOURCE: U.S. Bureau of Labor Statistics, Employment Projections program					
Financial clerks	—	1,343,400	1,346,900	0	3,500
Billing and posting clerks	43-3021	484,200	493,500	2	9,300
Gambling cage workers	43-3041	14,600	15,400	6	800
Payroll and timekeeping clerks	43-3051	149,800	143,100	-4	-6,700

Employment projections data for financial clerks, 2019-29

Occupational Title	SOC Code	Employment, 2019	Projected Employment, 2029	Change, 2019-29 Percent	Change, 2019-29 Numeric
Procurement clerks	43-3061	68,500	63,400	-7	-5,100
Brokerage clerks	43-4011	48,600	50,500	4	1,900
Credit authorizers, checkers, and clerks	43-4041	26,900	25,600	-5	-1,300
Loan interviewers and clerks	43-4131	212,600	230,300	8	17,700
New accounts clerks	43-4141	44,300	37,800	-15	-6,500
Insurance claims and policy processing clerks	43-9041	293,900	287,300	-2	-6,600

State & Area Data
Occupational Employment Statistics (OES)

The Occupational Employment Statistics (OES) program produces employment and wage estimates annually for over 800 occupations. These estimates are available for the nation as a whole, for individual states, and for metropolitan and nonmetropolitan areas.

Contacts for More Information

For more information about financial clerks, visit
➤ American Bankers Association
➤ Mortgage Bankers Association

General Office Clerks

Summary

Quick Facts: General Office Clerks

2019 Median Pay	$34,040 per year $16.37 per hour
Typical Entry-Level Education	High school diploma or equivalent
Work Experience in a Related Occupation	None
On-the-job Training	Short-term on-the-job training
Number of Jobs, 2019	3,126,300
Job Outlook, 2019-29	-5% (Decline)
Employment Change, 2019-29	-155,900

What General Office Clerks Do

General office clerks perform a variety of clerical tasks, including answering telephones, typing documents, and filing records.

Work Environment

Although general office clerks are employed in nearly every industry, many work in schools, healthcare facilities, and government offices.

General office clerks perform a variety of administrative tasks, such as copying and scanning documents.

How to Become a General Office Clerk

General office clerks typically need a high school diploma or equivalent. Most learn their skills on the job.

Pay

The median hourly wage for general office clerks was $16.37 in May 2019.

Job Outlook

Employment of general office clerks is projected to decline 5 percent from 2019 to 2029. Nevertheless, overall job opportunities should be good because of the need to replace workers who leave this very large occupation.

State & Area Data

Explore resources for employment and wages by state and area for general office clerks.

What General Office Clerks Do

General office clerks perform a variety of clerical tasks, including answering telephones, typing documents, and filing records.

Duties

General office clerks typically do the following:

- Answer and transfer telephone calls or take messages
- Sort and deliver incoming mail and send outgoing mail
- Schedule appointments and receive customers or visitors
- Provide general information to staff, clients, or the public
- Type, format, or edit routine memos or other reports
- Copy, file, and update paper and electronic documents
- Prepare and process bills and other office documents
- Collect information and perform data entry

Rather than performing a single specialized task, general office clerks have responsibilities that often change daily with the current needs of the employer.

Some clerks file documents or answer phones; others enter data into computers or perform other tasks using software applications. They also frequently use photocopiers, scanners, fax machines, and other office equipment.

The specific duties assigned to clerks will depend on the type of office in which they work. For example, a general office clerk at a college or university may process application materials and answer questions from prospective students, while a clerk at a hospital may file and retrieve medical records.

Work Environment

General office clerks held about 3.1 million jobs in 2019. The largest employers of general office clerks were as follows:

Educational services; state, local, and private	12%
Healthcare and social assistance	12
Government	9
Administrative and support services	8
Professional, scientific, and technical services	8

General office clerks usually work in office settings.

Work Schedules

Most general office clerks work full time.

How to Become a General Office Clerk

General office clerks typically need a high school diploma or equivalent and learn their skills on the job.

Education

General office clerks usually need a high school diploma or equivalent.

Courses in using computer applications, such as word processing and spreadsheet software, may be helpful for those who aren't already familiar with them.

General office clerks type, format, or edit routine memos.

General office clerks work in offices.

General office clerks usually need a high school diploma or equivalent.

Training

General office clerks usually learn their skills while on the job. Their training typically lasts up to one month and may include instructions on office procedures, proper phone etiquette, and the use of office equipment.

Advancement

General office clerks may advance to other administrative positions with more responsibility, such as secretaries and administrative assistants.

Advancement opportunities often depend on work experience.

Important Qualities

Customer-service skills. General office clerks often provide general information to company staff, customers, or the public. They should be courteous and prompt with their responses.

Detail oriented. General office clerks perform many clerical tasks that require attention to detail, such as preparing bills.

Organizational skills. General office clerks file and retrieve records. They need to keep records organized to be able to access them quickly and efficiently.

Pay

The median hourly wage for general office clerks was $16.37 in May 2019. The median wage is the wage at which half the workers in an occupation earned more than that amount and half earned less. The lowest 10 percent earned less than $10.16, and the highest 10 percent earned more than $26.59.

In May 2019, the median hourly wages for general office clerks in the top industries in which they worked were as follows:

Government	$17.90
Professional, scientific, and technical services	16.83
Healthcare and social assistance	16.14

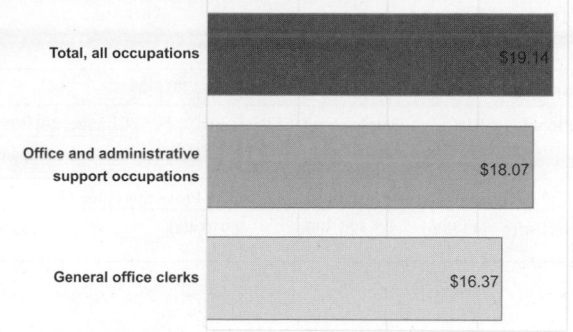

General Office Clerks
Median hourly wages, May 2019

Total, all occupations	$19.14
Office and administrative support occupations	$18.07
General office clerks	$16.37

Note: All Occupations includes all occupations in the U.S. Economy.
Source: U.S. Bureau of Labor Statistics, Occupational Employment Statistics.

Educational services; state, local, and private	15.33
Administrative and support services	15.16

Most general office clerks work full time.

Job Outlook

Employment of general office clerks is projected to decline 5 percent from 2019 to 2029.

Some office clerks will be needed to handle administrative duties in certain industries, such as healthcare and social assistance, but the increasing use of technology that automates document preparation tasks will result in fewer general office clerks needed to perform the work. For example, many organizations maintain electronic documents or use automated phone systems, reducing the need for some general office clerks. In addition, electronic filing systems and file sharing software allow other office workers to do the tasks of general office clerks, further decreasing employment of office clerks.

Job Prospects

Despite declining employment, about 317,500 openings for general office clerks are projected each year, on average, over the decade in this very large occupation.

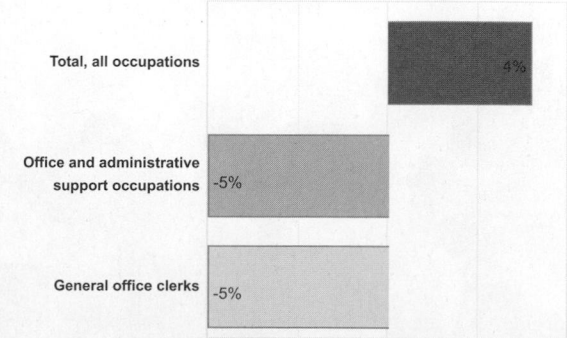

General Office Clerks
Percent change in employment, projected 2019-29

Total, all occupations	4%
Office and administrative support occupations	-5%
General office clerks	-5%

Note: All Occupations includes all occupations in the U.S. Economy.
Source: U.S. Bureau of Labor Statistics, Employment Projections program.

Those openings are expected to result from the need to replace workers who transfer to other occupations or exit the labor force, such as to retire.

Employment projections data for general office clerks, 2019-29					
Occupational Title	SOC Code	Employment, 2019	Projected Employment, 2029	Change, 2019-29	
				Percent	Numeric
SOURCE: U.S. Bureau of Labor Statistics, Employment Projections program					
Office clerks, general	43-9061	3,126,300	2,970,400	-5	-155,900

State & Area Data
Occupational Employment Statistics (OES)
The Occupational Employment Statistics (OES) program produces employment and wage estimates annually for over 800 occupations. These estimates are available for the nation as a whole, for individual states, and for metropolitan and nonmetropolitan areas.

Contacts for More Information
The *Handbook* does not have contacts for more information for this occupation.

Information Clerks

Summary

Quick Facts: Information Clerks

2019 Median Pay	$35,390 per year $17.01 per hour
Typical Entry-Level Education	See below
Work Experience in a Related Occupation	None
On-the-job Training	See below
Number of Jobs, 2019	1,465,800
Job Outlook, 2019-29	-3% (Decline)
Employment Change, 2019-29	-38,000

What Information Clerks Do
Information clerks perform routine clerical duties, maintain records, collect data, and provide information to customers.

Work Environment
Although information clerks are employed in nearly every industry, many work in government agencies, hotels, and healthcare facilities. Most information clerks work full time.

How to Become an Information Clerk
Information clerks typically need a high school diploma and learn their skills on the job. Some employers may prefer to hire candidates with some college education or an associate's degree, depending on the occupation.

Pay
The median annual wage for information clerks was $35,390 in May 2019.

Job Outlook
Employment of information clerks is projected to decline 3 percent from 2019 to 2029.

State & Area Data
Explore resources for employment and wages by state and area for information clerks.

What Information Clerks Do
Information clerks do routine clerical tasks such as maintaining records, collecting data, and providing information to customers.

Information clerks maintain records.

Reservation and transportation ticket agents issue boarding passes to passengers.

Duties

Information clerks typically do the following:

- Prepare routine reports, claims, bills, or orders
- Collect and record data from customers, staff, and the public
- Answer questions from customers and the public about products or services
- File and maintain paper or electronic records

Information clerks do routine clerical tasks in an organization, business, or government. They use telephones, computers, and other office equipment, such as scanners and shredders.

The following are examples of types of information clerks:

Correspondence clerks respond to inquiries from the public or customers. They prepare standard responses to requests for merchandise, damage claims, delinquent accounts, incorrect billings, or complaints about unsatisfactory service. They may also check the organization's records and type response letters for their supervisors to sign.

Court clerks organize and maintain records for courts of law. They prepare the calendar of cases, also known as the docket, and inform attorneys and witnesses about upcoming court appearances. Court clerks also receive, file, and send court documents.

Eligibility interviewers ask questions both in person and over the phone to determine whether applicants qualify for government assistance and benefits. They provide information about programs and may refer applicants to other agencies for assistance.

File clerks maintain electronic or paper records. They enter and retrieve data, organize records, and file documents. In organizations with electronic filing systems, file clerks scan and upload documents.

Hotel, motel, and resort desk clerks, also called *front desk clerks*, provide customer service to guests at the establishment's front desk. They check guests in and out, assign rooms, and process payments. They also keep occupancy records; take, confirm, or change room reservations; and provide information about the hotel's policies and services. In addition, front desk clerks answer phone calls, take and deliver messages for guests, and handle guests' requests and complaints.

Human resources assistants provide administrative support to human resources managers. They maintain personnel records on employees, including their addresses, employment history, and performance evaluations. They may post information about job openings and compile candidates' résumé for review.

Interviewers ask questions over the phone, in person, through mail, or online. They use the information to complete forms, applications, or questionnaires for market research surveys, census forms, and medical histories. Interviewers typically follow set procedures and questionnaires to get specific information.

License clerks process applications for licenses and permits, including administering tests and collecting fees. They determine whether applicants are qualified to receive a particular license or must submit additional documentation. They also maintain records of applications received and licenses issued.

Municipal clerks provide administrative support for town or city governments by maintaining government records. They record, file, and distribute minutes of town or city council meetings to local officials and staff and help prepare for elections. They may also answer information requests from local, state, and federal officials and the public.

Order clerks receive requests from customers and process their payments, which may involve entering the customer address and payment method into the order-entry system. They also answer questions about prices and shipping.

Reservation and transportation ticket agents and travel clerks take and confirm passengers' bookings for hotels and transportation. They also sell and issue tickets and answer questions about itineraries, rates, and tours. Ticket agents who work at airports and railroads also check bags and issue boarding passes to passengers.

Work Environment

Information clerks held about 1.5 million jobs in 2019. Employment in the detailed occupations that make up information clerks was distributed as follows:

Hotel, motel, and resort desk clerks	276,500
Interviewers, except eligibility and loan	201,900
Information and record clerks, all other	166,500
Court, municipal, and license clerks	163,700
Eligibility interviewers, government programs	147,500
Order clerks	146,000
Reservation and transportation ticket agents and travel clerks	126,300
Human resources assistants, except payroll and timekeeping	123,900
File clerks	106,700

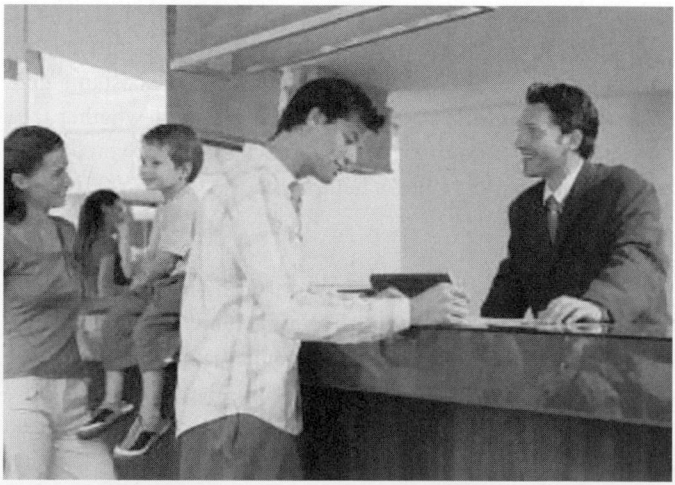

Hotel desk clerks may work evenings, weekends, and holidays.

Correspondence clerks 6,800

The largest employers of information clerks were as follows:

Local government, excluding education and hospitals..	14%
Healthcare and social assistance..................................	12
Transportation and warehousing..................................	7
Federal government...	7
Administrative and support services	6

Information clerks work in nearly every industry. Although most clerks work in offices, interviewers may travel to applicants' locations to meet with them.

The work of information clerks who provide customer service can be stressful, particularly when dealing with dissatisfied customers.

Reservation and transportation ticket agents at airports or shipping counters lift and maneuver heavy luggage or packages, which may weigh up to 100 pounds.

Injuries and Illnesses

Information clerks who work as reservation and transportation ticket agents are sometimes injured on the job. The most common injuries are muscle strains, such as those that may occur from lifting heavy suitcases.

Work Schedules

Most information clerks work full time. However, part-time work is common for hotel clerks and file clerks.

Clerks in lodging and transportation establishments that are open around the clock may work evenings, weekends, and holidays.

How to Become an Information Clerk

Information clerks typically need a high school diploma and learn their skills on the job.

Education

Although candidates for most of these positions usually qualify with a high school diploma, human resources assistants generally need an associate's degree. Regardless of whether they pursue a degree, courses in word processing and spreadsheet applications are particularly helpful.

Training

Most information clerks receive short-term on-the-job training, usually lasting a few weeks. Training typically covers clerical procedures and the use of computer applications. Those employed in government receive training that may last several months and includes learning about government programs and regulations.

Information clerks must be comfortable using computers.

Advancement

Some information clerks may advance to other administrative positions with more responsibilities, such as secretaries and administrative assistants. With completion of a bachelor's degree, some human resources assistants may become human resources specialists.

Important Qualities

Communication skills. Information clerks must be able to explain policies and procedures clearly to customers and the public.

Integrity. Information clerks, particularly human resources assistants, have access to confidential information. They must be trusted to adhere to the applicable confidentiality and privacy rules governing the dissemination of this information.

Interpersonal skills. Information clerks who work with the public and customers must understand and communicate information effectively to establish positive relationships.

Organizational skills. Information clerks must be able to retrieve files and other important information quickly and efficiently.

Pay

The median annual wage for information clerks was $35,390 in May 2019. The median wage is the wage at which half the workers in an occupation earned more than that amount and half earned less. The lowest 10 percent earned less than $22,050, and the highest 10 percent earned more than $58,590.

Information Clerks
Median annual wages, May 2019

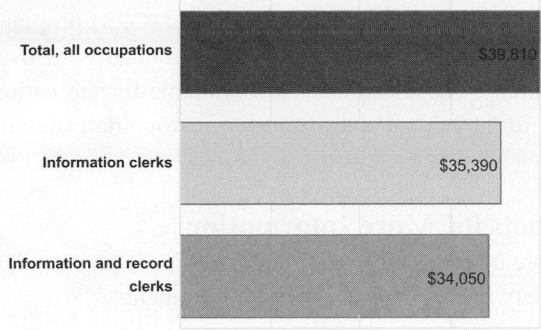

Total, all occupations	$39,810
Information clerks	$35,390
Information and record clerks	$34,050

Note: All Occupations includes all occupations in the U.S. Economy.
Source: U.S. Bureau of Labor Statistics, Occupational Employment Statistics.

Median annual wages for information clerks in May 2019 were as follows:

Eligibility interviewers, government programs	$46,590
Human resources assistants, except payroll and timekeeping	41,430
Information and record clerks, all other	41,360
Court, municipal, and license clerks	39,380
Reservation and transportation ticket agents and travel clerks	38,380
Correspondence clerks	38,140
Interviewers, except eligibility and loan	34,970
Order clerks	34,240
File clerks	32,710
Hotel, motel, and resort desk clerks	24,470

In May 2019, the median annual wages for information clerks in the top industries in which they worked were as follows:

Federal government	$45,980
Local government, excluding education and hospitals	40,000
Transportation and warehousing	39,720
Healthcare and social assistance	35,740
Administrative and support services	34,220

Most information clerks work full time. However, part-time work is common for hotel clerks and file clerks.

Clerks who work in lodging and transportation establishments that are open around the clock may work evenings, weekends, and holidays.

Job Outlook

Employment of information clerks is projected to decline 3 percent from 2019 to 2029. However, demand for information clerks will vary by occupation. (See table below.)

Overall employment of information clerks is expected to decline as organizations and businesses combine their

Information Clerks
Percent change in employment, projected 2019-29

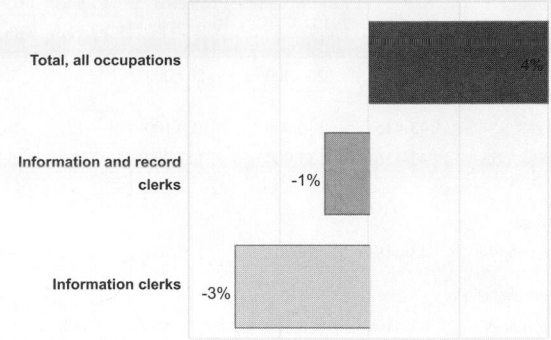

Total, all occupations	4%
Information and record clerks	-1%
Information clerks	-3%

Note: All Occupations includes all occupations in the U.S. Economy.
Source: U.S. Bureau of Labor Statistics, Employment Projections program.

administrative functions. For example, businesses increasingly use online applications for benefits and employment, thereby streamlining the process and requiring fewer workers.

Furthermore, increased use of online ordering and reservations systems and self-service ticketing kiosks will result in the need for fewer clerks to process orders and maintain files. In some businesses, including medical offices, receptionists and other workers do tasks that used to be done by clerks.

However, local governments will continue to need court, municipal, and license clerks for clerical duties in local courts, government agencies, or town councils. Tasks may include preparing dockets of cases to be called, preparing draft agendas or bylaws, keeping financial records, and issuing licenses or permits. There should also continue to be demand from local and state governments for eligibility interviewers to determine whether government assistance, such as unemployment or Social Security benefits, is appropriate for people applying for it.

Job Prospects

Overall job prospects should be good because of the need to replace workers who leave the occupation each year. Workers with clerical or customer service experience and education beyond high school should have the best prospects.

Employment projections data for information clerks, 2019-29					
Occupational Title	SOC Code	Employment, 2019	Projected Employment, 2029	Change, 2019-29	
				Percent	Numeric
SOURCE: U.S. Bureau of Labor Statistics, Employment Projections program					
Information clerks	—	1,465,800	1,427,800	-3	-38,000
Correspondence clerks	43-4021	6,800	6,600	-3	-200
Court, municipal, and license clerks	43-4031	163,700	171,600	5	7,900
Eligibility interviewers, government programs	43-4061	147,500	153,100	4	5,700
File clerks	43-4071	106,700	91,100	-15	-15,600
Hotel, motel, and resort desk clerks	43-4081	276,500	257,400	-7	-19,100

Employment projections data for information clerks, 2019-29

State & Area Data

Occupational Employment Statistics (OES)

The Occupational Employment Statistics (OES) program produces employment and wage estimates annually for over 800 occupations. These estimates are available for the nation as a whole, for individual states, and for metropolitan and nonmetropolitan areas.

Contacts for More Information

For more information about human resources assistants, visit
➤ Society for Human Resource Management

Material Recording Clerks

Summary

Quick Facts: Material Recording Clerks

2019 Median Pay	$30,010 per year $14.43 per hour
Typical Entry-Level Education	High school diploma or equivalent
Work Experience in a Related Occupation	None
On-the-job Training	See below
Number of Jobs, 2019	3,286,000
Job Outlook, 2019-29	-1% (Decline)
Employment Change, 2019-29	-28,100

What Material Recording Clerks Do

Material recording clerks track product information in order to keep businesses and supply chains on schedule.

Material recording clerks ensure proper recordkeeping and inventory control.

Work Environment

Many material recording clerks work full time. Stock clerks and order fillers, the largest occupation within this profile, often work part time

How to Become a Material Recording Clerk

Material recording clerks typically need a high school diploma or equivalent and are trained on the job.

Pay

The median annual wage for material recording clerks was $30,010 in May 2019.

Job Outlook

Overall employment of material recording clerks is projected to decline 1 percent from 2019 to 2029.

State & Area Data

Explore resources for employment and wages by state and area for material recording clerks.

What Material Recording Clerks Do

Material recording clerks track product information in order to keep businesses and supply chains on schedule. They ensure proper scheduling, recordkeeping, and inventory control.

Duties

Material recording clerks typically do the following:

- Keep records of items shipped, received, or transferred to another location
- Compile reports on various aspects of changes in production or inventory
- Find, sort, or move goods between different parts of the business
- Check inventory records for accuracy

Shipping and receiving clerks track outgoing and incoming shipments.

Material recording clerks use computers, tablets, or handheld devices to keep track of inventory. Sensors and tags enable these computers to automatically detect when and where products are moved, allowing clerks to keep updated reports without manually counting items.

The following are examples of types of material recording clerks:

Production, planning, and expediting clerks manage the flow of information, work, and materials within or among offices in a business. They compile reports on the progress of work and on any production problems that arise. These clerks set workers' schedules, estimate costs, keep track of materials, and write special orders for new materials. They perform general office tasks, such as entering data or distributing mail. Expediting clerks maintain contact with vendors to ensure that supplies and equipment are shipped on time.

Shipping, receiving, and traffic clerks keep track of and record outgoing and incoming shipments. Clerks may scan barcodes with handheld devices or use radio frequency identification (RFID) scanners to keep track of inventory. They check to see whether shipment orders were correctly processed in their company's computer system. They also compute freight costs and prepare invoices. Some clerks move goods from the warehouse to the loading dock.

Stock clerks and order fillers receive, unpack, and track merchandise. Stock clerks move products from a warehouse to store shelves. They keep a record of items that enter or leave the stockroom and inspect for damaged goods. These clerks also use handheld RFID scanners to keep track of merchandise. Order fillers retrieve customer orders and prepare them to be shipped.

Material and product inspecting clerks weigh, measure, check, sample, and keep records on materials, supplies, and equipment that enters a warehouse. They verify the quantity and quality of items they are assigned to examine, checking for defects and recording what they find. They use scales, counting devices, and calculators. Some decide what to do about a defective product, such as to scrap it or send it back to the factory to be repaired. Some clerks also prepare reports, such as reports about warehouse inventory levels.

Work Environment

Material recording clerks held about 3.3 million jobs in 2019. Employment in the detailed occupations that make up material recording clerks was distributed as follows:

Stockers and order fillers	2,135,800
Shipping, receiving, and inventory clerks	710,400
Production, planning, and expediting clerks	378,500
Weighers, measurers, checkers, and samplers, recordkeeping	61,300

The largest employers of material recording clerks were as follows:

Food and beverage stores	18%
Manufacturing	13
Wholesale trade	12

Stock clerks and order fillers usually work in retail settings and sometimes help customers. Production, planning, and expediting clerks; shipping, receiving, and traffic clerks; and material and product inspecting clerks usually work in an office inside a warehouse or manufacturing plant.

Although shipping clerks and material inspecting clerks prepare reports in an office, they also spend time in the warehouse, where they sometimes handle packages or automatic equipment such as conveyor systems.

Injuries and Illnesses

Some material recording clerks may need to lift heavy items and bend frequently, which can lead to injury. Using proper lifting techniques can help to reduce the risk of harm.

Many stock clerks work in retail stores.

Work Schedules

Production, planning, and expediting clerks; shipping, receiving, and traffic clerks; and material and product inspecting clerks usually work full time. Some clerks work nights and weekends or holidays when large shipments arrive.

Stock clerks and order fillers, the largest occupation within this profile, usually work part time. Evening and weekend work is common because they work when retail stores are open. They sometimes work overnight shifts when large shipments arrive or when it is time to take inventory.

How to Become a Material Recording Clerk

Material recording clerks typically need a high school diploma or equivalent and are trained on the job.

Education

Material recording clerks typically need a high school diploma or equivalent.

Production, planning, and expediting clerks need to have basic knowledge of computer applications such as spreadsheet software.

Training

Material recording clerks usually learn to do their work on the job. Training for most material recording clerks may last less than a month. Production, planning, and expediting clerks' training can take several months.

Typically, a supervisor or more experienced worker trains new clerks.

Material recording clerks first learn to count stock and mark inventory, and then move onto more difficult tasks, such as recordkeeping. Production clerks need to learn how their company operates before they can write production and work schedules.

Advancement

With additional training or education, material recording clerks may advance to other positions within their firm, such as purchasing agent. Clerks in retail establishments can move into the sales department.

Important Qualities

Communication skills. Production, planning, and expediting clerks are frequently in contact with suppliers, vendors, and production managers and need to communicate the firm's scheduling needs effectively.

Customer-service skills. Stock clerks sometimes interact with customers in retail stores and may have to get the item the customer is looking for from the storeroom.

Detail oriented. Material and product inspecting clerks check items for defects, some of which are small and difficult to spot.

Math skills. Some material recording clerks use math to calculate shipping costs or take measurements.

Pay

The median annual wage for material recording clerks was $30,010 in May 2019. The median wage is the wage at which half the workers in an occupation earned more than that amount and half earned less. The lowest 10 percent earned less than $21,210, and the highest 10 percent earned more than $50,840.

Median annual wages for material recording clerks in May 2019 were as follows:

Production, planning, and expediting clerks	$48,260
Weighers, measurers, checkers, and samplers, recordkeeping	35,040
Shipping, receiving, and inventory clerks	34,190
Stockers and order fillers	27,380

Material recording clerks learn on the job from an experienced worker.

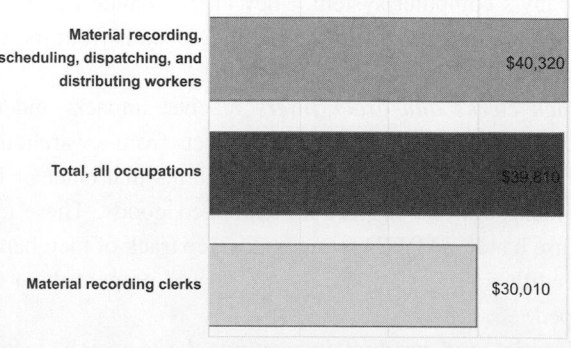

Material Recording Clerks
Median annual wages, May 2019

Material recording, scheduling, dispatching, and distributing workers	$40,320
Total, all occupations	$39,810
Material recording clerks	$30,010

Note: All Occupations includes all occupations in the U.S. Economy.
Source: U.S. Bureau of Labor Statistics, Occupational Employment Statistics.

In May 2019, the median annual wages for material recording clerks in the top industries in which they worked were as follows:

Manufacturing	$37,840
Wholesale trade	33,200
Food and beverage stores	25,730

Production, planning, and expediting clerks; shipping, receiving, and traffic clerks; and material and product inspecting clerks usually work full time. Some clerks work nights and weekends or holidays when large shipments arrive.

Stock clerks and order fillers, the largest occupation within this profile, usually work part time. Evening and weekend work is common because they work when retail stores are open. They sometimes work overnight shifts when large shipments arrive or when it is time to take inventory.

Job Outlook

Overall employment of material recording clerks is projected to decline 1 percent from 2019 to 2029. Employment growth will vary by occupation (see table below).

The increased use of radio frequency identification (RFID) tags should allow these workers to quickly locate an item or count inventory in some retail stores, requiring fewer overall workers to stock shelves and fill orders over the decade.

Both RFID tags and increased use of other technology, such as hand-held devices that read barcodes automatically, allow fewer clerks in warehouses to do the same amount of work. In addition, use of barcodes, electronic and optical readers, and RFID tags is expected to increase accuracy in shipping, thereby reducing the number of times a product needs to be weighed, checked, or measured.

As retail continues to move from traditional brick-and-mortar stores to online commerce, retailers likewise continue to automate warehouse operations. Collaborative robots and other technology help increase efficiency but may reduce the demand for some material recording clerks.

Production, planning, and expediting clerks schedule production and shipment processes, functions that remain difficult to automate.

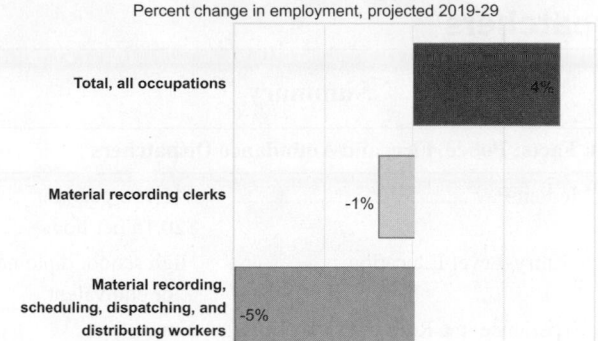

Material Recording Clerks

Percent change in employment, projected 2019-29

- Total, all occupations: 4%
- Material recording clerks: -1%
- Material recording, scheduling, dispatching, and distributing workers: -5%

Note: All Occupations includes all occupations in the U.S. Economy.
Source: U.S. Bureau of Labor Statistics, Employment Projections program.

Employment projections data for material recording clerks, 2019-29

Occupational Title	SOC Code	Employment, 2019	Projected Employment, 2029	Change, 2019-29 Percent	Change, 2019-29 Numeric
SOURCE: U.S. Bureau of Labor Statistics, Employment Projections program					
Material recording clerks	—	3,286,000	3,257,900	-1	-28,100
Production, planning, and expediting clerks	43-5061	378,500	393,300	4	14,800
Shipping, receiving, and inventory clerks	43-5071	710,400	648,800	-9	-61,500
Weighers, measurers, checkers, and samplers, recordkeeping	43-5111	61,300	64,500	5	3,100
Stockers and order fillers	53-7065	2,135,800	2,151,300	1	15,500

State & Area Data
Occupational Employment Statistics (OES)

The Occupational Employment Statistics (OES) program produces employment and wage estimates annually for over 800 occupations. These estimates are available for the nation as a whole, for individual states, and for metropolitan and nonmetropolitan areas.

Contacts for More Information

For more information about material recording clerks, visit
➤ MHI
➤ Warehousing Education and Research Council

Police, Fire, and Ambulance Dispatchers

Summary

Quick Facts: Police, Fire, and Ambulance Dispatchers

2019 Median Pay	$41,910 per year $20.15 per hour
Typical Entry-Level Education	High school diploma or equivalent
Work Experience in a Related Occupation	None
On-the-job Training	Moderate-term on-the-job training
Number of Jobs, 2019	98,300
Job Outlook, 2019-29	6% (Faster than average)
Employment Change, 2019-29	6,100

What Police, Fire, and Ambulance Dispatchers Do

Police, fire, and ambulance dispatchers, also called public safety telecommunicators, answer emergency and nonemergency calls.

Work Environment

Police, fire, and ambulance dispatchers work in emergency communication centers called public safety answering points (PSAPs). Dispatchers must be available around the clock, so they often have to work evenings, weekends, and holidays. Overtime and long shifts—sometimes 12 hours—are common. The pressure to respond quickly and calmly in alarming situations can be stressful.

How to Become a Police, Fire, or Ambulance Dispatcher

Most police, fire, and ambulance dispatchers have a high school diploma. Many states require dispatchers to become certified.

Pay

The median annual wage for police, fire, and ambulance dispatchers was $41,910 in May 2019.

Job Outlook

Employment of police, fire, and ambulance dispatchers is projected to grow 6 percent from 2019 to 2029, faster than the average for all occupations.

State & Area Data

Explore resources for employment and wages by state and area for police, fire, and ambulance dispatchers.

What Police, Fire, and Ambulance Dispatchers Do

Police, fire, and ambulance dispatchers, also called *public safety telecommunicators*, answer emergency and nonemergency calls.

Duties

Police, fire, and ambulance dispatchers typically do the following:

- Answer 9-1-1 emergency telephone and alarm system calls
- Determine the type of emergency and its location and decide the appropriate response on the basis of agency procedures
- Relay information to the appropriate first-responder agency
- Coordinate the dispatch of emergency response personnel to accident scenes
- Give basic over-the-phone medical instructions before emergency personnel arrive
- Monitor and track the status of police, fire, and ambulance units
- Synchronize responses with other area communication centers
- Keep detailed records of calls

Police, fire, and ambulance dispatchers answer emergency and nonemergency calls.

Dispatchers monitor and track the status of police, fire, and ambulance units.

Dispatchers answer calls from people who need help from police, firefighters, emergency services, or a combination of the three. They take emergency, nonemergency, and alarm system calls.

Dispatchers must stay calm while collecting vital information from callers to determine the severity of a situation and the location of those who need help. They then communicate this information to the appropriate first-responder agencies.

Dispatchers keep detailed records of the calls that they answer. They use computers to log important facts, such as the nature of the incident and the caller's name and location. Most computer systems detect the location of cell phones and landline phones automatically.

Dispatchers often must instruct callers on what to do before responders arrive. Many dispatchers are trained to offer medical help over the phone. For example, they might help the caller provide first aid at the scene until emergency medical services arrive. At other times they may advise callers on how to remain safe while waiting for assistance.

Work Environment

Police, fire, and ambulance dispatchers held about 98,300 jobs in 2019. The largest employers of police, fire, and ambulance dispatchers were as follows:

Local government, excluding education and hospitals......	79%
Ambulance services	6
State government, excluding education and hospitals...	6
Colleges, universities, and professional schools; state, local, and private..	3
Hospitals; state, local, and private	2

Dispatchers typically work in communication centers, often called public safety answering points (PSAPs). Some dispatchers work for unified communication centers, where they answer calls for all types of emergency services, while others may work specifically for police or fire departments.

Work as a dispatcher can be stressful. Dispatchers often work long shifts, take many calls, and deal with troubling situations. Some calls require them to assist people who are in life-threatening situations, and the pressure to respond quickly and calmly can be demanding.

Work Schedules

Most dispatchers work 8- to 12-hour shifts, but some agencies require even longer ones. Overtime is common in this occupation.

Because emergencies can happen at any time, dispatchers are required to work some shifts during evenings, weekends, and holidays.

How to Become a Police, Fire, or Ambulance Dispatcher

Most police, fire, and ambulance dispatchers have a high school diploma. Many states and localities require dispatchers to have training and certification.

In addition, candidates must pass a written exam and a typing test. In some instances, applicants may need to pass a background check, lie detector and drug tests, and tests for hearing and vision.

Some jobs require a driver's license, and experience using computers and in customer service can be helpful. The ability to speak Spanish is also desirable in this occupation.

Education

Most dispatchers are required to have a high school diploma.

Training

Training requirements vary by state. The Association of Public-Safety Communications Officials (APCO International) provides a list of states requiring training and certification.

Some states require 40 or more hours of initial training, and some require continuing education every 2 to 3 years. Other states do not mandate any specific training, leaving individual

Dispatchers work in communication centers, often called public safety answering points (PSAPs).

Dispatchers must pass a typing test.

localities and agencies to structure their own requirements and conduct their own courses.

Some agencies have their own programs for certifying dispatchers; others use training from a professional association. The Association of Public-Safety Communications Officials (APCO International), the National Emergency Number Association (NENA), and the International Academies of Emergency Dispatch (IAED) have established a number of recommended standards and best practices that agencies often use as a guideline for their own training programs.

Training is usually conducted in a classroom and on the job, and may be followed by a probationary period of about 1 year. However, the period may vary by agency, as there is no national standard governing training or probation.

Training covers a wide variety of topics, such as local geography, agency protocols, and standard procedures. Dispatchers are also taught how to use specialized equipment, such as two-way radios and computer-aided dispatch software. Computer systems that dispatchers use consist of several monitors that display call information, maps, any relevant criminal history, and video, depending on the location of the incident. Dispatchers often receive specialized training to prepare for high-risk incidents, such as child abductions and suicidal callers.

Licenses, Certifications, and Registrations

Many states require dispatchers to be certified. The Association of Public-Safety Communications Officials (APCO) provides a list of states requiring training and certification. One certification is the Emergency Medical Dispatcher (EMD) certification, which enables dispatchers to give medical assistance over the phone.

Dispatchers may choose to pursue additional certifications, such as the National Emergency Number Association's Emergency Number Professional (ENP) certification or APCO's Registered Public-Safety Leader (RPL) certification, which demonstrate their leadership skills and knowledge of the profession.

Advancement

Training and additional certifications can help dispatchers become senior dispatchers or supervisors. Additional education and related work experience may be helpful in advancing to management-level positions.

Important Qualities

Ability to multitask. Dispatchers must stay calm in order to simultaneously answer calls, collect vital information, coordinate responders, use mapping software and camera feeds, and assist callers.

Communication skills. Dispatchers work with law enforcement, emergency response teams, and civilians. They must be able to communicate the nature of an emergency effectively and coordinate the appropriate response.

Decisionmaking skills. When people call for help, dispatchers must be able to quickly determine the response dictated by procedures.

Empathy. Dispatchers must be willing and able to help callers who have a wide range of needs. They must be calm, polite, and sympathetic, while also collecting relevant information quickly.

Listening skills. Dispatchers must listen carefully to collect relevant details, even though some callers might have trouble speaking because of anxiety or stress.

Typing skills. Dispatchers type the details of calls into computers, and speed and accuracy is of the essence when responding to emergencies.

Pay

The median annual wage for police, fire, and ambulance dispatchers was $41,910 in May 2019. The median wage is the wage at which half the workers in an occupation earned more than that amount and half earned less. The lowest 10 percent earned less than $27,190, and the highest 10 percent earned more than $64,950.

In May 2019, the median annual wages for police, fire, and ambulance dispatchers in the top industries in which they worked were as follows:

State government, excluding education and hospitals	$48,630
Local government, excluding education and hospitals	42,080
Colleges, universities, and professional schools; state, local, and private	39,810
Hospitals; state, local, and private	38,510
Ambulance services	37,430

Most dispatchers work 8- to 12-hour shifts, but some agencies require even longer ones. Overtime is common in this occupation.

Police, Fire, and Ambulance Dispatchers
Median annual wages, May 2019

Public safety telecommunicators	$41,910
Material recording, scheduling, dispatching, and distributing workers	$40,320
Total, all occupations	$39,810

Note: All Occupations includes all occupations in the U.S. Economy.
Source: U.S. Bureau of Labor Statistics, Occupational Employment Statistics.

Police, Fire, and Ambulance Dispatchers

Percent change in employment, projected 2019-29

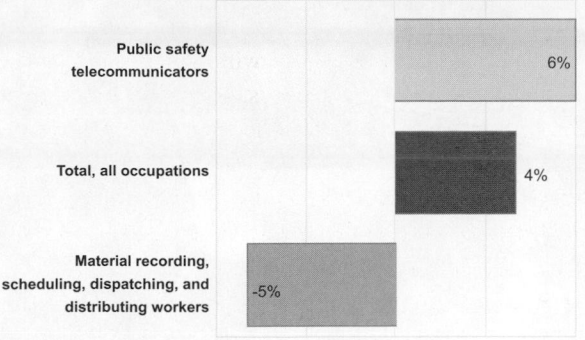

Note: All Occupations includes all occupations in the U.S. Economy.
Source: U.S. Bureau of Labor Statistics, Employment Projections program.

Because emergencies can happen at any time, dispatchers are required to work some shifts during evenings, weekends, and holidays.

Job Outlook

Employment of police, fire, and ambulance dispatchers is projected to grow 6 percent from 2019 to 2029, faster than the average for all occupations.

Although state and local government budget constraints may limit the number of dispatchers hired in the coming decade, population growth and the commensurate increase in 9-1-1 call volume is expected to increase the employment of dispatchers.

Job Prospects

Overall job prospects should be favorable due to employment growth and the need to replace dispatchers who transfer to other occupations or leave the labor force.

Those who can handle demanding schedules and who have strong communication and typing skills should have the best job prospects.

Employment projections data for police, fire, and ambulance dispatchers, 2019-29					
Occupational Title	SOC Code	Employment, 2019	Projected Employment, 2029	Change, 2019-29	
				Percent	Numeric
SOURCE: U.S. Bureau of Labor Statistics, Employment Projections program					
Public safety telecommunicators	43-5031	98,300	104,300	6	6,100

State & Area Data
Occupational Employment Statistics (OES)

The Occupational Employment Statistics (OES) program produces employment and wage estimates annually for over 800 occupations. These estimates are available for the nation as a whole, for individual states, and for metropolitan and nonmetropolitan areas.

Contacts for More Information

For more information about police, fire, and ambulance dispatcher training and certification, visit
➤ Association of Public-Safety Communications Officials
➤ International Academies of Emergency Dispatch
➤ International Municipal Signal Association
➤ National Emergency Number Association

Postal Service Workers

Summary

Quick Facts: Postal Service Workers

2019 Median Pay	$52,060 per year $25.03 per hour
Typical Entry-Level Education	High school diploma or equivalent
Work Experience in a Related Occupation	None
On-the-job Training	Short-term on-the-job training
Number of Jobs, 2019	503,100
Job Outlook, 2019-29	-14% (Decline)
Employment Change, 2019-29	-72,200

What Postal Service Workers Do

Postal service workers sell postal products and collect, sort, and deliver mail.

Work Environment

Postal service clerks and mail sorters, processors, and processing machine operators work indoors, typically in a post office. Mail carriers mostly work outdoors, delivering mail.

How to Become a Postal Service Worker

Most postal service workers have a high school diploma. All applicants for these jobs must pass a written exam.

Pay

The median annual wage for postal service workers was $52,060 in May 2019.

Job Outlook

Overall employment of postal service workers is projected to decline 14 percent from 2019 to 2029. Automated sorting systems, cluster mailboxes, and tight budgets are expected to adversely affect employment. Some job openings will result from the need to replace workers who leave the occupation or

Postal service workers must carefully sort mail.

the labor force, but strong competition should be expected as the number of applicants typically exceeds the number of available positions.

State & Area Data

Explore resources for employment and wages by state and area for postal service workers.

What Postal Service Workers Do

Postal service workers sell postal products and collect, sort, and deliver mail.

Duties

Postal service workers typically do the following:

- Collect letters and parcels
- Sort incoming letters and parcels
- Sell stamps and other postal products
- Get customer signatures for registered, certified, and insured mail
- Operate various types of postal equipment
- Distribute incoming mail from postal trucks

Postal service workers receive and process mail for delivery to homes, businesses, and post office boxes. Workers are classified based on the type of work they perform.

The following are examples of types of postal service workers:

Postal service clerks sell stamps, money orders, postal stationery, mailing envelopes, and boxes in post offices throughout the country. These workers register, certify, and insure mail, calculate and collect postage, and answer questions about other postal matters. They also may help sort mail.

Postal service mail carriers deliver mail to homes and businesses in cities, towns, and rural areas. Most travel established routes, delivering and collecting mail. Mail carriers cover their routes by foot, vehicle, or a combination of both. Some mail carriers collect money for postage due. Others, particularly in

Carriers deliver mail to homes and businesses.

rural areas, sell postal products, such as stamps and money orders. All mail carriers must be able to answer customers' questions about postal regulations and services and, upon request, provide change-of-address cards and other postal forms.

Postal service mail sorters, processors, and processing machine operators prepare incoming and outgoing mail for distribution at post offices and mail processing centers. They load and unload postal trucks and move mail around processing centers. They also operate and adjust mail processing and sorting machinery.

Work Environment

Postal service workers held about 503,100 jobs in 2019. Employment in the detailed occupations that make up postal service workers was distributed as follows:

Postal service mail carriers	326,600
Postal service mail sorters, processors, and processing machine operators	98,500
Postal service clerks	78,100

The largest employers of postal service workers were as follows:

Postal service	100%

Although mail carriers work outdoors, sorters and processors typically work indoors.

Postal service clerks and mail sorters, processors, and processing machine operators work indoors, typically in a post office. Mail carriers mostly work outdoors, delivering mail in all kinds of weather. Although mail carriers face many natural hazards, such as extreme temperatures and wet or icy roads and sidewalks, the work is not especially dangerous. However, repetitive stress injuries from lifting and bending may occur.

Work Schedules

Most postal service workers are employed full time. However, overtime is sometimes required, particularly during the holiday season. Because mail is delivered 6 days a week, many postal service workers must work on Saturdays. Some also work on Sundays.

How to Become a Postal Service Worker

All postal service worker applicants must pass a written exam. The exam covers four areas: address cross comparison, forms completion, memory and coding, and personal characteristics and experience. Jobseekers should contact the post office or

Mail carriers must receive a passing grade on a road test.

mail processing center where they want to work to find out when exams are given.

Postal service mail carriers must be at least 18 years old, or 16 years old with a high school diploma. They must be U.S. citizens or have permanent resident-alien status. Males must have registered with the Selective Service when they reached age 18.

When accepted, applicants must undergo a criminal background check and pass a physical exam and a drug test. Applicants also may be asked to show that they can lift and handle heavy mail sacks. Mail carriers who drive at work must have a safe driving record, and applicants must receive a passing grade on a road test.

Education

Most postal service workers have a high school diploma. All applicants must have a good command of English.

Training

Newly hired postal service workers receive short-term on-the-job training, usually lasting less than 1 month. Those who have a mail route may initially work alongside an experienced carrier.

Important Qualities

Customer-service skills. Postal service workers, particularly clerks, regularly interact with customers. As a result, they must be courteous and tactful and provide good client service.

Physical stamina. Postal service workers, particularly mail carriers, must be able to stand or walk for long periods.

Physical strength. Postal service workers must be able to lift heavy mail bags and parcels without injuring themselves.

Pay

The median annual wage for postal service workers was $52,060 in May 2019. The median wage is the wage at which half the workers in an occupation earned more than that amount

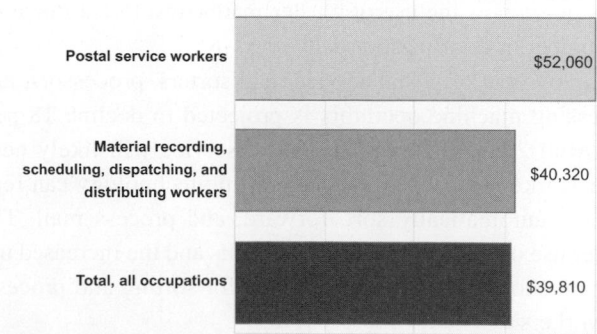

Note: All Occupations includes all occupations in the U.S. Economy.
Source: U.S. Bureau of Labor Statistics, Occupational Employment Statistics.

and half earned less. The lowest 10 percent earned less than $36,990, and the highest 10 percent earned more than $64,420.

Median annual wages for postal service workers in May 2019 were as follows:

Postal service mail sorters, processors, and processing machine operators..	$60,140
Postal service mail carriers	51,310
Postal service clerks...	48,330

In May 2019, the median annual wages for postal service workers in the top industries in which they worked were as follows:

Postal service..	$52,070

Most postal service workers are employed full time. However, overtime is sometimes required, particularly during the holiday season. Because mail is delivered 6 days a week, many postal service workers must work on Saturdays. Some also work on Sundays.

Job Outlook

Overall employment of postal service workers is projected to decline 14 percent from 2019 to 2029. Automated sorting systems, cluster mailboxes, and tight budgets are expected to adversely affect employment. Employment changes, however, will vary by specialty.

Employment of postal service clerks is projected to decline 14 percent from 2019 to 2029. Employment may be adversely affected by the decline in First-Class Mail volume caused by the continued increase in the use of automated and electronic bill pay and email.

Employment of postal service mail carriers is projected to decline 14 percent from 2019 to 2029. The use of automated "delivery point sequencing" systems that sort letter mail directly reduces the amount of time that carriers spend on mail sorting.

The amount of time carriers save on sorting letter mail and flat mail will allow them to increase the size of their routes, which should reduce the need to hire more carriers. In addition, the postal service is moving toward more centralized mail delivery, such as the use of cluster mailboxes, to cut down on the number of door-to-door deliveries.

Employment of postal service mail sorters, processors, and processing machine operators is projected to decline 18 percent from 2019 to 2029. The postal service will likely need fewer workers because new mail sorting technology can read text and automatically sort, forward, and process mail. The greater use of online services to pay bills and the increased use of email should also reduce the need for sorting and processing workers.

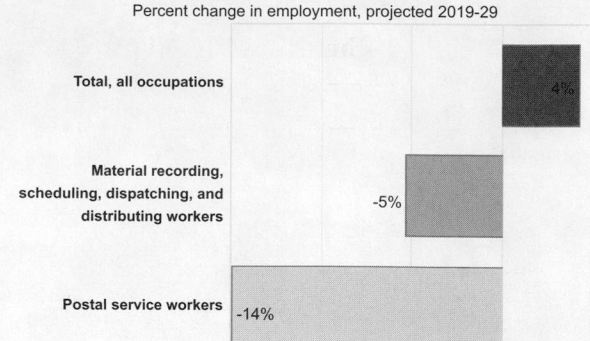

Postal Service Workers
Percent change in employment, projected 2019-29

- Total, all occupations: 4%
- Material recording, scheduling, dispatching, and distributing workers: -5%
- Postal service workers: -14%

Note: All Occupations includes all occupations in the U.S. Economy.
Source: U.S. Bureau of Labor Statistics, Employment Projections program.

Job Prospects

Despite declining employment, some job openings will result from the need to replace workers who leave the occupation or the labor force. However, strong competition can be expected as the number of applicants typically exceeds the number of available positions.

Employment projections data for postal service workers, 2019-29					
Occupational Title	SOC Code	Employment, 2019	Projected Employment, 2029	Change, 2019-29	
				Percent	Numeric
SOURCE: U.S. Bureau of Labor Statistics, Employment Projections program					
Postal service workers	43-5050	503,100	430,900	-14	-72,200
Postal service clerks	43-5051	78,100	67,500	-14	-10,500
Postal service mail carriers	43-5052	326,600	282,500	-14	-44,100
Postal service mail sorters, processors, and processing machine operators	43-5053	98,500	80,900	-18	-17,600

State & Area Data
Occupational Employment Statistics (OES)

The Occupational Employment Statistics (OES) program produces employment and wage estimates annually for over 800 occupations. These estimates are available for the nation as a whole, for individual states, and for metropolitan and nonmetropolitan areas.

Contacts for More Information

For more information about postal service workers, including job requirements, entrance examinations, and employment opportunities, visit
➤ United States Postal Service
➤ National Association of Letter Carriers

Receptionists

Summary

Quick Facts: Receptionists

2019 Median Pay	$30,050 per year $14.45 per hour
Typical Entry-Level Education	High school diploma or equivalent
Work Experience in a Related Occupation...	None
On-the-job Training	Short-term on-the-job training
Number of Jobs, 2019	1,105,300
Job Outlook, 2019-29	4% (As fast as average)
Employment Change, 2019-29	39,500

What Receptionists Do

Receptionists do tasks such as answering phones, receiving visitors, and providing information about their organization to the public.

Work Environment

Receptionists are employed in nearly every industry.

How to Become a Receptionist

Receptionists typically need a high school diploma or equivalent and good communication skills.

Pay

The median hourly wage for receptionists was $14.45 in May 2019.

Job Outlook

Employment of receptionists is projected to grow 4 percent from 2019 to 2029, about as fast as the average for all occupations.

Overall job opportunities should be good, especially in healthcare industries.

State & Area Data

Explore resources for employment and wages by state and area for receptionists.

What Receptionists Do

Receptionists do administrative tasks, such as answering phones, greeting visitors, and providing general information about their organization.

Duties

Receptionists typically do the following:

- Answer the telephone and take messages or forward calls
- Schedule and confirm appointments and maintain calendars
- Greet customers, clients, and other visitors
- Check in visitors and direct or escort them to their destinations
- Inform other employees of visitors' arrivals or cancellations
- Enter customer information into the organization's database
- Copy, file, and maintain paper or electronic documents
- Handle incoming and outgoing correspondence

Receptionists are often the first employee of an organization to have contact with a customer or client. They are responsible for making a good first impression for the organization.

Receptionists' specific responsibilities vary by employer. For example, receptionists in hospitals and doctors' offices may collect patients' personal information and direct patients to the waiting room. Some handle billing and insurance payments.

In large corporations and government offices, receptionists may have a security role. For example, they may control access to the organization by issuing visitor passes and escorting visitors to their destination.

Receptionists use telephones, computers, and other office equipment, such as shredders and printers.

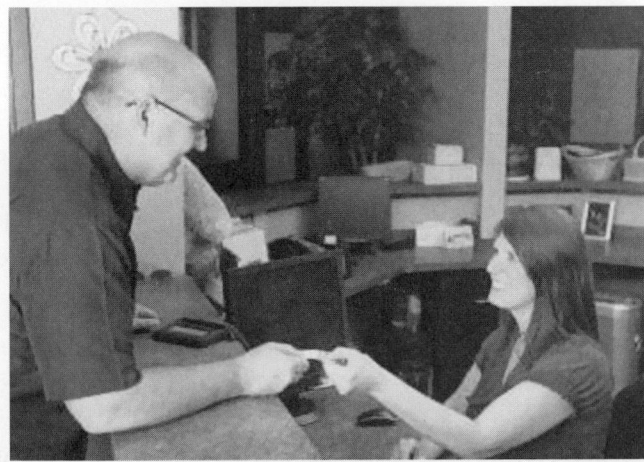

Receptionists provide general information about their organization to visitors.

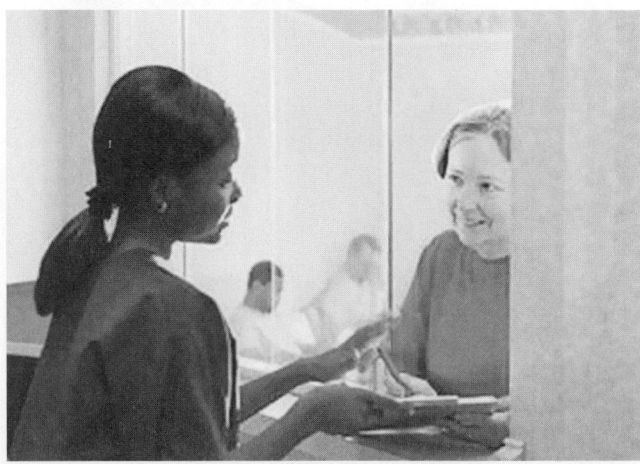

Receptionists greet patients in hospitals and doctors' offices.

Work Environment

Receptionists held about 1.1 million jobs in 2019. The largest employers of receptionists were as follows:

Healthcare and social assistance	46%
Professional, scientific, and technical services	11
Personal care services	6
Administrative and support services	4
Religious, grantmaking, civic, professional, and similar organizations	3

Receptionists are employed in nearly every industry.

Receptionists usually work in areas that are visible and accessible to the public and other employees, such as the front desk of a lobby or waiting room.

Some receptionists face stressful situations. They may have to answer numerous phone calls or deal with difficult visitors.

Work Schedules

Most receptionists work full time. Some receptionists, such as those who work in hospitals and nursing homes, work evenings and weekends.

How to Become a Receptionist

Although hiring requirements vary by industry and employer, receptionists typically need a high school diploma or equivalent and good communication skills.

Education

Receptionists typically need a high school diploma or equivalent, and employers may prefer to hire candidates who have

Receptionists are employed in virtually every industry.

Receptionists need to be good at communicating with people.

experience with certain computer software. Proficiency in word processing and spreadsheet applications may be particularly helpful.

Training

Most receptionists receive short-term on-the-job training, usually lasting a few days up to a month. Training typically covers procedures for greeting visitors, answering the telephone, and using the computer.

Advancement

Receptionists may advance to other administrative occupations with more responsibilities, such as secretaries and administrative assistants.

Important Qualities

Communication skills. Receptionists must speak and write clearly when providing information and corresponding with customers.

Computer skills. Receptionists should be adept at using computers.

Customer-service skills. Receptionists represent the organization, so they should be courteous, professional, and helpful to customers and the public.

Integrity. Receptionists may handle confidential data, especially in medical and legal offices. They must be trustworthy and protect clients' privacy.

Interpersonal skills. Receptionists should be comfortable interacting with people in different types of situations.

Organizational skills. Receptionists take messages, schedule appointments, and maintain employee files. They need good organizational skills to manage their diverse responsibilities.

Pay

The median hourly wage for receptionists was $14.45 in May 2019. The median wage is the wage at which half the workers in an occupation earned more than that amount and half earned less. The lowest 10 percent earned less than $10.16, and the highest 10 percent earned more than $20.86.

Receptionists
Median hourly wages, May 2019

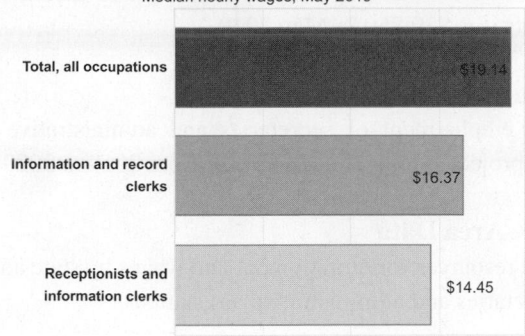

Total, all occupations — $19.14

Information and record clerks — $16.37

Receptionists and information clerks — $14.45

Note: All Occupations includes all occupations in the U.S. Economy.
Source: U.S. Bureau of Labor Statistics, Occupational Employment
Statistics.

In May 2019, the median hourly wages for receptionists in the top industries in which they worked were as follows:

Healthcare and social assistance	$15.08
Professional, scientific, and technical services	14.70
Administrative and support services	14.49
Religious, grantmaking, civic, professional, and similar organizations	13.38
Personal care services	12.13

Most receptionists work full time. Receptionists who work in hospitals and nursing homes may work evenings and weekends.

Job Outlook

Employment of receptionists is projected to grow 4 percent from 2019 to 2029, about as fast as the average for all occupations.

Growing healthcare industries are projected to lead demand for receptionists, particularly in the offices of physicians, dentists, and other healthcare practitioners.

Employment growth of receptionists in other industries is expected to be slower as organizations continue to automate or consolidate administrative functions. For example, many organizations use computer software, websites, mobile applications, or other technology to interact with the public or customers.

Receptionists
Percent change in employment, projected 2019-29

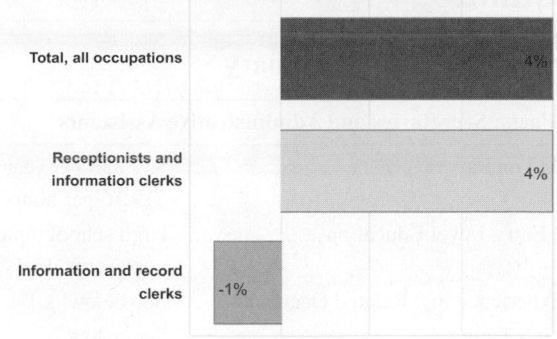

Total, all occupations — 4%

Receptionists and information clerks — 4%

Information and record clerks — -1%

Note: All Occupations includes all occupations in the U.S. Economy.
Source: U.S. Bureau of Labor Statistics, Employment Projections
program.

Job Prospects

Overall job prospects should be good, especially in healthcare industries. Many job openings will stem from the need to replace workers who leave the occupation. Those with related work experience and proficiency using computers should have the best job prospects.

Employment projections data for receptionists, 2019-29					
Occupational Title	SOC Code	Employment, 2019	Projected Employment, 2029	Change, 2019-29	
				Percent	Numeric
SOURCE: U.S. Bureau of Labor Statistics, Employment Projections program					
Receptionists and information clerks	43-4171	1,105,300	1,144,700	4	39,500

State & Area Data
Occupational Employment Statistics (OES)

The Occupational Employment Statistics (OES) program produces employment and wage estimates annually for over 800 occupations. These estimates are available for the nation as a whole, for individual states, and for metropolitan and nonmetropolitan areas.

Contacts for More Information

For more information about training for receptionists and those in other administrative careers, visit
➤ American Society of Administrative Professionals

Secretaries and Administrative Assistants

Summary

Quick Facts: Secretaries and Administrative Assistants

2019 Median Pay	$39,850 per year $19.16 per hour
Typical Entry-Level Education	High school diploma or equivalent
Work Experience in a Related Occupation	See below
On-the-job Training	See below
Number of Jobs, 2019	3,638,800
Job Outlook, 2019-29	-9% (Decline)
Employment Change, 2019-29	-327,400

What Secretaries and Administrative Assistants Do

Secretaries and administrative assistants perform routine clerical and administrative duties.

Work Environment

Although secretaries and administrative assistants work in nearly every industry, many are employed in schools, hospitals, and government, legal, and medical offices. Most work full time.

How to Become a Secretary or Administrative Assistant

High school graduates who have experience using computer software applications usually qualify for entry-level positions. Although most secretaries learn their job in several weeks, many legal and medical secretaries require additional training to learn industry-specific terminology. Executive secretaries usually need several years of related work experience.

Pay

The median annual wage for secretaries and administrative assistants was $39,850 in May 2019.

Job Outlook

Overall employment of secretaries and administrative assistants is projected to decline 9 percent from 2019 to 2029.

State & Area Data

Explore resources for employment and wages by state and area for secretaries and administrative assistants.

What Secretaries and Administrative Assistants Do

Secretaries and administrative assistants perform routine clerical and administrative duties. They organize files, prepare documents, schedule appointments, and support other staff.

Duties

Secretaries and administrative assistants typically do the following:

- Answer telephones and take messages or transfer calls
- Schedule appointments and update event calendars
- Arrange staff meetings
- Handle incoming and outgoing mail and faxes
- Prepare memos, invoices, or other reports
- Edit documents
- Maintain databases and filing systems, whether electronic or paper
- Perform basic bookkeeping

Secretaries and administrative assistants perform a variety of clerical and administrative duties that are necessary to run an organization efficiently. They use computer software to create spreadsheets; manage databases; and prepare presentations,

Secretaries and administrative assistants provide clerical and organizational support.

Secretaries and administrative assistants create and maintain filing systems.

reports, and documents. They also may negotiate with vendors, buy supplies, and manage stockrooms or corporate libraries. Secretaries and administrative assistants also use videoconferencing, fax, and other office equipment. Specific job duties vary by experience, job title, and specialty.

The following are examples of types of secretaries and administrative assistants:

Executive secretaries and executive administrative assistants provide high-level administrative support for an office and for top executives of an organization. They often handle more complex responsibilities, such as reviewing incoming documents, conducting research, and preparing reports. Some also supervise clerical staff.

Legal secretaries perform work requiring knowledge of legal terminology and procedures. They prepare legal documents, such as summonses, complaints, motions, and subpoenas under the supervision of an attorney or a paralegal. They also review legal journals and help with legal research—for example, by verifying quotes and citations in legal briefs.

Medical secretaries transcribe dictation and prepare reports or articles for physicians or medical scientists. They also take simple medical histories of patients, arrange for patients to be hospitalized, or process insurance payments. Medical secretaries need to be familiar with medical terminology and codes, medical records, and hospital or laboratory procedures.

Secretaries and administrative assistants, except legal, medical, and executive form the largest subcategory of secretaries and administrative assistants. They handle an office's administrative activities in almost every sector of the economy, including schools, government, and private corporations. For example, secretaries in schools are often responsible for handling most of the communications among parents, students, the community, teachers, and school administrators. They schedule appointments, receive visitors, and keep track of students' records.

Work Environment

Secretaries and administrative assistants held about 3.6 million jobs in 2019. Employment in the detailed occupations that make up secretaries and administrative assistants was distributed as follows:

Secretaries and administrative assistants, except legal, medical, and executive	2,250,200
Medical secretaries and administrative assistants	623,400
Executive secretaries and executive administrative assistants	593,400
Legal secretaries and administrative assistants	171,800

The largest employers of secretaries and administrative assistants were as follows:

Healthcare and social assistance	23%
Educational services; state, local, and private	15

Secretaries and administrative assistants work in offices.

Professional, scientific, and technical services	12
Government	8
Religious, grantmaking, civic, professional, and similar organizations	6

Secretaries and administrative assistants work in nearly every industry.

Most secretaries and administrative assistants work in an office setting. Some administrative assistants may work out of their own homes as *virtual assistants*.

Work Schedules

Most secretaries and administrative assistants work full time.

How to Become a Secretary or Administrative Assistant

High school graduates who have experience using computer software applications, such as word processing and spreadsheet programs, usually qualify for entry-level positions. Although most secretaries learn their job in several weeks, many legal

Secretaries and administrative assistants may seek training in word processing, spreadsheet, and database software.

and medical secretaries require additional training to learn industry-specific terminology. Executive secretaries usually need several years of related work experience.

Education

High school graduates can take courses in word processing and office procedures at technical schools or community colleges. Some temporary placement agencies also provide training in word processing, spreadsheet, and database software.

Some medical and legal secretaries learn industry-specific terminology and practices by attending courses offered at community colleges or technical schools. For executive secretary positions, employers increasingly prefer to hire those who have taken some college courses or have a bachelor's degree.

Training

Secretaries and administrative assistants typically learn their skills through short-term on-the-job training, usually lasting a few weeks. During this time they learn about administrative procedures, including how to prepare documents. Medical and legal secretaries' training may last several months as they learn industry-specific terminology and practices.

Work Experience in a Related Occupation

Executive secretaries can gain experience by working in administrative positions that have less challenging responsibilities, such as secretaries and general office clerks.

Important Qualities

Decisionmaking skills. Secretaries and administrative assistants often prioritize tasks and make decisions on their employers' behalf, so good judgment is essential.

Interpersonal skills. Secretaries and administrative assistants interact with clients, customers, or staff. They should communicate effectively and be courteous when interacting with others to create a positive work environment and client experience.

Organizational skills. Secretaries and administrative assistants keep files, folders, and schedules in proper order so an office can run efficiently.

Writing skills. Secretaries and administrative assistants write memos and emails when communicating with managers, employees, and customers. Therefore, they must have good grammar, ensure accuracy, and maintain a professional tone.

Pay

The median annual wage for secretaries and administrative assistants was $39,850 in May 2019. The median wage is the wage at which half the workers in an occupation earned more than that amount and half earned less. The lowest 10 percent earned less than $25,720, and the highest 10 percent earned more than $65,510.

Median annual wages for secretaries and administrative assistants in May 2019 were as follows:

Secretaries and Administrative Assistants

Median annual wages, May 2019

Note: All Occupations includes all occupations in the U.S. Economy.
Source: U.S. Bureau of Labor Statistics, Occupational Employment Statistics.

Executive secretaries and executive administrative assistants	$60,890
Legal secretaries and administrative assistants	47,300
Secretaries and administrative assistants, except legal, medical, and executive	37,690
Medical secretaries and administrative assistants	36,580

In May 2019, the median annual wages for secretaries and administrative assistants in the top industries in which they worked were as follows:

Professional, scientific, and technical services	$45,100
Government	43,900
Educational services; state, local, and private	40,450
Religious, grantmaking, civic, professional, and similar organizations	40,300
Healthcare and social assistance	37,240

Most secretaries and administrative assistants work full time.

Job Outlook

Overall employment of secretaries and administrative assistants is projected to decline 9 percent from 2019 to 2029.

Technology enables staff in many organizations to prepare their own documents without the help of secretaries. Additionally, many executive secretaries and executive administrative assistants support more than one manager in an organization, and many managers now do tasks that were previously done by these workers. In legal firms, paralegals and legal assistants use technology that enables them to perform tasks, such as preparing and filing documents, that were previously done by legal secretaries.

Employment growth is projected for medical secretaries, primarily due to the growth of the healthcare industry. For example, baby boomers will require more medical services as they age. Medical secretaries will be needed to handle administrative tasks related to billing and insurance processing of Medicare and other claims.

Secretaries and Administrative Assistants

Percent change in employment, projected 2019-29

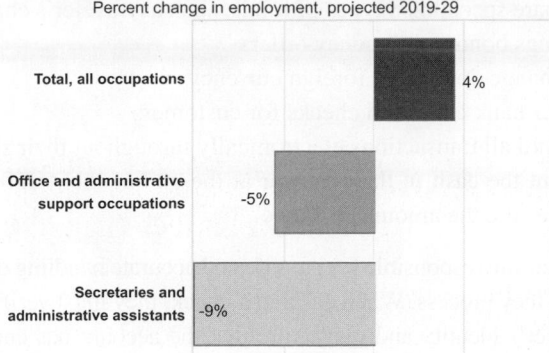

Note: All Occupations includes all occupations in the U.S. Economy.
Source: U.S. Bureau of Labor Statistics, Employment Projections program.

Job Prospects

Most job openings are expected to come from the need to replace secretaries and administrative assistants who leave the occupation.

Occupational Title	SOC Code	Employment, 2019	Projected Employment, 2029	Change, 2019-29	
				Percent	Numeric
SOURCE: U.S. Bureau of Labor Statistics, Employment Projections program					
Secretaries and administrative assistants	43-6000	3,638,800	3,311,400	-9	-327,400
Executive secretaries and executive administrative assistants	43-6011	593,400	472,400	-20	-121,100
Legal secretaries and administrative assistants	43-6012	171,800	133,800	-22	-38,000
Medical secretaries and administrative assistants	43-6013	623,400	682,700	10	59,300

Occupational Title	SOC Code	Employment, 2019	Projected Employment, 2029	Change, 2019-29	
				Percent	Numeric
Secretaries and administrative assistants, except legal, medical, and executive	43-6014	2,250,200	2,022,600	-10	-227,500

Employment projections data for secretaries and administrative assistants, 2019-29

State & Area Data
Occupational Employment Statistics (OES)

The Occupational Employment Statistics (OES) program produces employment and wage estimates annually for over 800 occupations. These estimates are available for the nation as a whole, for individual states, and for metropolitan and nonmetropolitan areas.

- Executive secretaries and executive administrative assistants
- Legal secretaries and administrative assistants
- Medical secretaries and administrative assistants
- Secretaries and administrative assistants, except legal, medical, and executive

Contacts for More Information

For more information about careers in secretarial and administrative work, visit

➤ International Association of Administrative Professionals

For more information about legal secretaries and administrative assistants, visit

➤ NALS

For more information about virtual assistants, visit

➤ International Virtual Assistants Association

Tellers

Summary

Quick Facts: Tellers

2019 Median Pay	$31,230 per year $15.02 per hour
Typical Entry-Level Education	High school diploma or equivalent
Work Experience in a Related Occupation	None
On-the-job Training	Short-term on-the-job training
Number of Jobs, 2019	449,000
Job Outlook, 2019-29	-15% (Decline)
Employment Change, 2019-29	-68,600

What Tellers Do

Tellers are responsible for accurately processing routine transactions at a bank.

Work Environment

Most tellers work in bank branches.

How to Become a Teller

Most tellers have a high school diploma and receive about 1 month of on-the-job training. Some banks do background checks before hiring a new teller.

Pay

The median annual wage for tellers was $31,230 in May 2019.

Tellers process transactions such as cashing checks, depositing money, and collecting loan payments.

Job Outlook

Employment of tellers is projected to decline 15 percent from 2019 to 2029. Online banking and automation technology are expected to continue replacing more job duties that tellers traditionally performed.

State & Area Data

Explore resources for employment and wages by state and area for tellers.

What Tellers Do

Tellers are responsible for accurately processing routine transactions at a bank. These transactions include cashing checks, depositing money, and collecting loan payments.

Duties

Tellers typically do the following:

- Count the cash in their drawer at the start of their shift
- Accept checks, cash, and other forms of payment from customers
- Answer questions from customers about their accounts
- Prepare specialized types of funds, such as traveler's checks, savings bonds, and money orders
- Exchange dollars for foreign currency
- Order bank cards and checks for customers
- Record all transactions electronically throughout their shift
- Count the cash in their drawer at the end of their shift and make sure the amounts balance

Tellers are responsible for the safe and accurate handling of the money they process. When cashing a check, they must verify the customer's identity and make sure that the account has enough money to cover the transaction. When counting cash, tellers must be careful not to make errors. If a customer is interested in financial products or services, such as certificates of deposits (CDs) and loans, tellers explain the products and services offered by the bank and refer the customer to the appropriate personnel.

In most banks, tellers record account changes using computers that give them easy access to the customer's financial information. Tellers also can use this information when recommending a new product or service.

Head tellers manage teller operations. Besides doing the same tasks as those done by other tellers, they perform some managerial duties, such as setting work schedules or helping less experienced tellers. Because of their experience, head tellers may deal with difficult customer problems, such as errors in customer accounts. Head tellers also go to the vault (where larger amounts of money are kept) and ensure that other tellers have enough cash to cover their shift.

Work Environment

Tellers held about 449,000 jobs in 2019. The largest employers of tellers were as follows:

Credit intermediation and related activities 97%
Management of companies and enterprises 1

Tellers verify a customer's identity and financial information before processing a transaction.

Most tellers work in bank branches.

The depository credit intermediation industry includes commercial bank branches, where tellers are primarily employed.

Work Schedules
Most tellers work full time.

How to Become a Teller
Most tellers have a high school diploma and receive about 1 month of on-the-job training. Some banks do background checks before hiring a new teller.

Education
Tellers usually need a high school diploma or equivalent. Some tellers may take some college courses, but a degree is rarely required for a job applicant to be hired.

Training
New tellers usually receive brief on-the-job training, typically lasting about 1 month. Normally, a head teller or another experienced teller trains them. During this training, tellers learn how to balance cash drawers and verify signatures. They also learn the computer software that their bank uses and the financial products and services the bank offers.

Advancement
Experienced tellers can advance within their bank. They can become head tellers or move to other supervisory positions. Some tellers can advance to other occupations, such as loan officer. They can also move to sales positions.

Important Qualities
Customer-service skills. Tellers spend their day interacting with bank customers. They must be friendly, helpful, and patient. They must be able to understand customer needs and explain service options to their customers.

Detail oriented. Tellers must be sure not to make errors when dealing with customers' money.

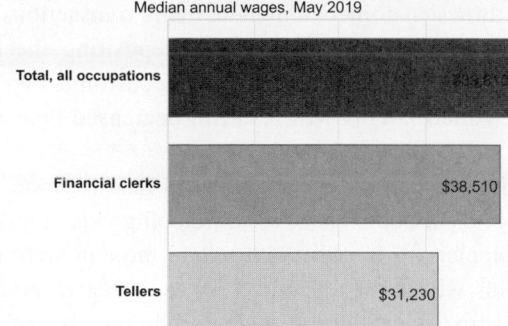

Tellers
Median annual wages, May 2019

Total, all occupations	
Financial clerks	$38,510
Tellers	$31,230

Note: All Occupations includes all occupations in the U.S. Economy.
Source: U.S. Bureau of Labor Statistics, Occupational Employment Statistics.

Math skills. Because they count and handle large amounts of money, tellers must be good at arithmetic.

Pay
The median annual wage for tellers was $31,230 in May 2019. The median wage is the wage at which half the workers in an occupation earned more than that amount and half earned less. The lowest 10 percent earned less than $23,330, and the highest 10 percent earned more than $40,230.

In May 2019, the median annual wages for tellers in the top industries in which they worked were as follows:

Management of companies and enterprises	$32,280
Credit intermediation and related activities	31,190

Most tellers work full time.

Job Outlook
Employment of tellers is projected to decline 15 percent from 2019 to 2029.

Historically, job growth for tellers was driven by the expansion of bank branches, where most tellers work. However, the number of bank branches has been in decline

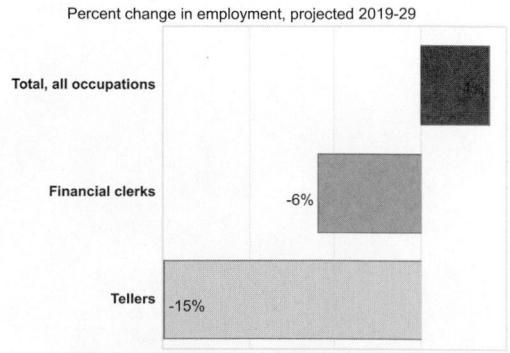

Tellers
Percent change in employment, projected 2019-29

Total, all occupations	
Financial clerks	-6%
Tellers	-15%

Note: All Occupations includes all occupations in the U.S. Economy.
Source: U.S. Bureau of Labor Statistics, Employment Projections program.

Tellers must be friendly, helpful, and patient when interacting with bank customers.

due to technological change. The rise of online and mobile banking allows customers to handle many transactions traditionally performed by tellers, such as depositing checks. As more people use these tools, fewer bank customers will visit the teller window. This will result in decreased demand for tellers.

In addition, automation is expected to lead to fewer tellers per bank branch. Some banks are developing video kiosks that allow customers to interact with tellers through webcams at ATMs. This will allow tellers to service a greater number of customers from one location, reducing the number of tellers needed for each bank.

"Enhanced ATMs" are another emerging form of automation technology. These machines are expected to perform an increasing range of customer service and clerical tasks currently done by tellers, such as issuing debit cards or detecting counterfeit currency. This will allow for far greater productivity for tellers, as they will be left with only the most complex customer service tasks. This also will result in fewer tellers employed per bank branch.

Job Prospects
Despite the projected employment decline, tellers will still find some job openings due to the need to replace workers who leave this large occupation.

Employment projections data for tellers, 2019-29

Occupational Title	SOC Code	Employment, 2019	Projected Employment, 2029	Change, 2019-29 Percent	Numeric
Tellers	43-3071	449,000	380,400	-15	-68,600

SOURCE: U.S. Bureau of Labor Statistics, Employment Projections program

State & Area Data
Occupational Employment Statistics (OES)
The Occupational Employment Statistics (OES) program produces employment and wage estimates annually for over 800 occupations. These estimates are available for the nation as a whole, for individual states, and for metropolitan and nonmetropolitan areas.

Contacts for More Information
For general information about the banking industry, visit
➤ American Bankers Association

Personal Care and Service

Animal Care and Service Workers

Summary

Quick Facts: Animal Care and Service Workers	
2019 Median Pay	$24,990 per year $12.02 per hour
Typical Entry-Level Education	High school diploma or equivalent
Work Experience in a Related Occupation	None
On-the-job Training	See below
Number of Jobs, 2019	350,900
Job Outlook, 2019-29	22% (Much faster than average)
Employment Change, 2019-29	75,500

What Animal Care and Service Workers Do
Animal care and service workers attend to animals.

Work Environment
Animal care and service workers are employed in a variety of settings, including kennels, zoos, stables, animal shelters, pet stores, veterinary clinics, and aquariums. Some parts of the job may be physically or emotionally demanding, and workers risk injury when caring for animals.

How to Become an Animal Care and Service Worker
Animal care and service workers typically have a high school diploma or equivalent and learn the occupation on the job. Many employers prefer to hire candidates who have experience working with animals.

Pay
The median annual wage for animal caretakers was $24,780 in May 2019.

The median annual wage for animal trainers was $30,430 in May 2019.

Job Outlook
Employment of animal care and service workers is projected to grow 22 percent from 2019 to 2029, much faster than the average for all occupations. Employment growth along with high job turnover should result in very good job opportunities.

State & Area Data
Explore resources for employment and wages by state and area for animal care and service workers.

What Animal Care and Service Workers Do
Animal care and service workers attend to animals. They feed, groom, bathe, and exercise pets and other nonfarm animals.

Duties
Animal care and service workers typically do the following:

- Give food and water to animals
- Clean equipment and the living spaces of animals
- Monitor animals and record details of their diet, physical condition, and behavior
- Examine animals for signs of illness or injury
- Exercise animals
- Bathe animals, trim nails, clip hair, and attend to other grooming needs
- Train animals to obey or to behave in a specific manner

Trainers teach animals to respond to commands.

Pet sitters care for pets while the owner is at work or on vacation.

The following are types of animal care and service workers:

Animal trainers teach animals a variety of skills, such as obedience, performance, riding, security, and assisting people with disabilities. They familiarize animals with human voices and contact, and they teach animals to respond to commands. Most animal trainers work with dogs and horses, but some work with marine mammals, such as dolphins. Trainers teach a variety of skills. For example, some train dogs to guide people with disabilities, or they may train animals for a competition.

Groomers specialize in maintaining a pet's appearance. They typically groom dogs and cats, which may include cutting, trimming, shampooing, and styling fur; clipping nails; and cleaning ears. Groomers also schedule appointments, sell products to pet owners, and identify problems that may require veterinary attention.

Groomers may work in or operate a grooming salon, kennel, veterinary clinic, pet supply store, or mobile grooming service, a self-contained business that travels to clients' homes.

Grooms work at stables, caring for horses and maintaining equipment. Responsibilities include feeding, grooming, and exercising horses; cleaning stalls; polishing saddles; and organizing the tack room, which stores harnesses, saddles, and bridles. Experienced grooms sometimes help train horses.

Kennel attendants care for pets, often overnight, in place of owners. They clean cages and dog runs and feed, exercise, and play with animals. Experienced attendants also may provide basic healthcare, bathe animals, and attend to other basic grooming needs.

Nonfarm animal caretakers typically work with cats and dogs in animal shelters or rescue leagues. All caretakers attend to the basic needs of animals and may have administrative duties, such as keeping records, answering questions from the public, educating visitors about pet health, and screening people who want to adopt an animal. Experienced caretakers may have more responsibilities, such as helping to vaccinate or euthanize animals alongside a veterinarian.

Pet sitters look after animals while the pet owner is away. Most pet sitters feed, walk, and play with pets daily. They go to the pet owner's home, allowing the pet to stay in its familiar surroundings and follow its routine. Experienced pet sitters also may bathe, groom, or train pets. Pet sitters typically watch over dogs, but some also take care of cats and other pets.

Zookeepers care for animals in zoos. They plan diets, feed animals, and monitor the animals' eating patterns. They also clean the animals' enclosures and monitor behavior for signs of illness or injury. Depending on the size of the zoo, they may work with one species or multiple species of animals. Zookeepers may help raise young animals, and they often spend time answering questions from the public.

Work Environment

Animal caretakers held about 300,700 jobs in 2019. The largest employers of animal caretakers were as follows:

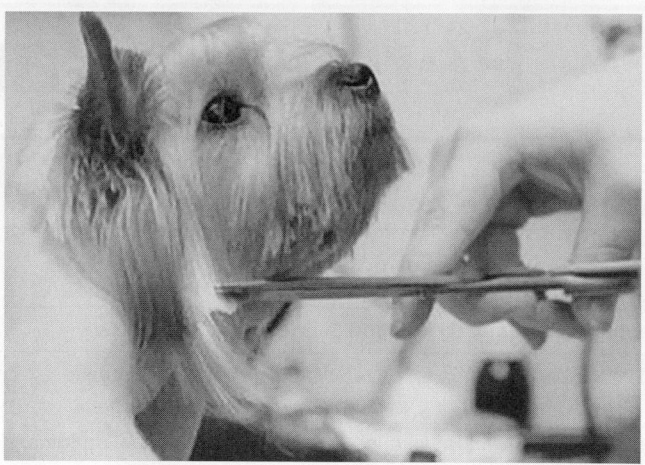

Mobile groomers travel to customers' homes to wash, cut, and brush an animal's coat.

Other personal services	33%
Self-employed workers	26
Professional, scientific, and technical services	12
Retail trade	12
Social advocacy organizations	4

Animal trainers held about 50,200 jobs in 2019. The largest employers of animal trainers were as follows:

Self-employed workers	35%
Support activities for agriculture and forestry	21
Animal production and aquaculture	14
Arts, entertainment, and recreation	7
Retail trade	7

Animal care and service workers are employed in a variety of settings. Many work at kennels; others work at zoos, stables, animal shelters, pet stores, veterinary clinics, and aquariums. Their work may involve travel.

Although animal care and service workers may consider their work enjoyable and rewarding, they face unpleasant and emotionally distressing situations at times. For example, those who work in shelters may observe abused, injured, or sick animals. Some caretakers may have to help veterinarians euthanize injured or unwanted animals.

In addition, a lot the work involves physical tasks, such as moving and cleaning cages, lifting bags of food, and exercising animals.

Injuries and Illnesses

Animal care and service workers may be bitten, scratched, or kicked when working with scared or aggressive animals. Injuries may also happen while the caretaker is holding, cleaning, or restraining an animal.

Work Schedules

Animals may need care around the clock in facilities that operate 24 hours a day, such as kennels, animal shelters, and stables. Caretakers often work irregular schedules, including evenings, weekends, and holidays.

Some nonfarm animal caretakers work part time.

How to Become an Animal Care and Service Worker

Animal care and service workers typically have a high school diploma or equivalent and learn the occupation on the job. Many employers prefer to hire people who have experience with animals.

Education

Animal care and service workers typically need at least a high school diploma or equivalent.

Although pet groomers typically learn by working under the guidance of an experienced groomer, they can also attend grooming schools.

Animal trainers usually need a high school diploma or equivalent, although some positions may require a bachelor's degree. For example, marine mammal trainers usually need a bachelor's degree in marine biology, animal science, biology, or a related field.

Dog trainers and horse trainers may take courses at community colleges or vocational and private training schools.

Most zoos require zookeepers to have a bachelor's degree in biology, animal science, or a related field.

Training

Most animal care and service workers learn through on-the-job training.

Animal trainers may learn their skills from an experienced trainer. Pet groomers often learn their trade under the guidance of an experienced groomer.

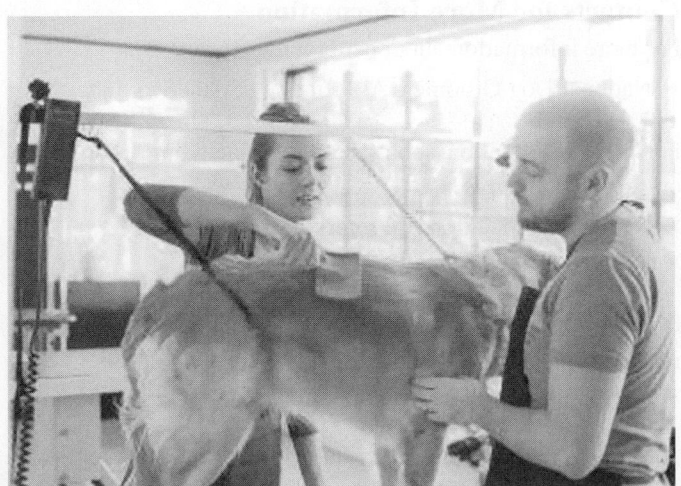

Most animal care and service workers have a high school diploma and learn the occupation on the job.

Licenses, Certifications, and Registrations

Although not required, certifications may help workers establish their credentials and enhance their skills. For example, professional associations and private vocational and state-approved trade schools offer certification for dog trainers.

The National Dog Groomers Association of America offers certification for master status as a groomer. Both the National Association of Professional Pet Sitters and Pet Sitters International offer a home-study certification program for pet sitters. Marine mammal trainers should be certified in scuba diving.

Many states require self-employed animal care and service workers to have a business license.

Other Experience

For many animal care and service workers positions, it helps to have experience working with animals. Volunteering and internships at zoos and aquariums are excellent ways to gain such experience.

Important Qualities

Compassion. Animal care and service workers must be compassionate when dealing with animals and their owners. They should treat animals with kindness.

Customer-service skills. Animal care and service workers should understand pet owners' needs so they can provide excellent customer service. Some workers may need to deal with distraught pet owners. For example, caretakers working in animal shelters may need to reassure owners looking for a lost pet.

Detail oriented. Animal care and service workers are often responsible for maintaining records and monitoring changes in animals' behavior.

Patience. All animal caretakers and animal trainers need to be patient when working with animals.

Physical stamina. Animal care and service workers must be able to kneel, crawl, and lift heavy supplies, such as bags of food.

Problem-solving skills. Animal trainers must be able to assess whether animals are responding to teaching methods and to identify which methods are successful.

Reliability. Animal care and service workers need to care for animals on schedule and in a timely manner.

Pay

The median annual wage for animal caretakers was $24,780 in May 2019. The median wage is the wage at which half the workers in an occupation earned more than that amount and half earned less. The lowest 10 percent earned less than $18,630, and the highest 10 percent earned more than $38,630.

The median annual wage for animal trainers was $30,430 in May 2019. The lowest 10 percent earned less than $20,810, and the highest 10 percent earned more than $59,110.

In May 2019, the median annual wages for animal caretakers in the top industries in which they worked were as follows:

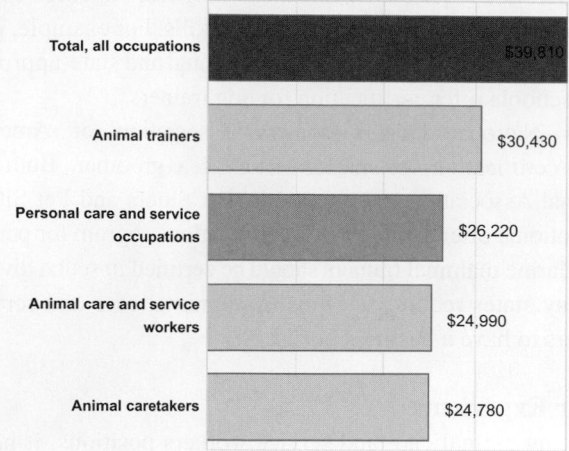

Animal Care and Service Workers
Median annual wages, May 2019

Total, all occupations	$39,810
Animal trainers	$30,430
Personal care and service occupations	$26,220
Animal care and service workers	$24,990
Animal caretakers	$24,780

Note: All Occupations includes all occupations in the U.S. Economy.
Source: U.S. Bureau of Labor Statistics, Occupational Employment
Statistics.

Other personal services	$24,780
Retail trade	24,180
Social advocacy organizations	24,100
Professional, scientific, and technical services	23,670

In May 2019, the median annual wages for animal trainers in
the top industries in which they worked were as follows:

Arts, entertainment, and recreation	$33,910
Retail trade	24,730

Animals may need care around the clock in facilities that
operate 24 hours a day, such as kennels, animal shelters, and
stables. Caretakers often work irregular schedules, including
evenings, weekends, and holidays.

Some nonfarm animal caretakers work part time.

Job Outlook

Overall employment of animal care and service workers is projected to grow 22 percent from 2019 to 2029, much faster than
the average for all occupations.

Many people consider their pets to be a part of their family
and are willing to pay more for pet care than pet owners have in
the past. As more households include companion pets, employment of animal care and service workers in the pet services
industry will continue to grow. Employment of animal care
and service workers in kennels, grooming shops, and pet stores
is projected to increase in order to keep up with the growing
demand for animal care.

Job Prospects

Overall job prospects should be good. Most job openings
will result from the need to replace workers who leave the
occupation.

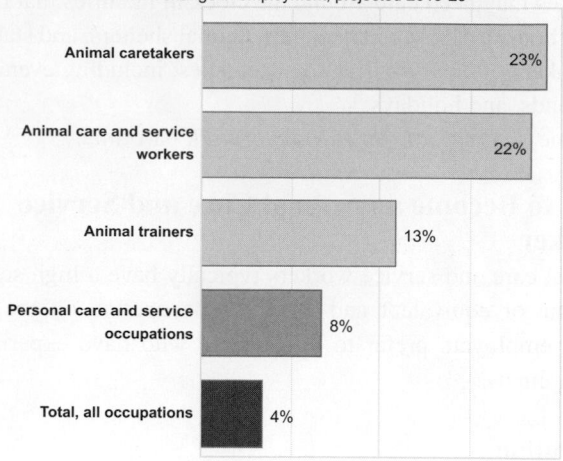

Animal Care and Service Workers
Percent change in employment, projected 2019-29

Animal caretakers	23%
Animal care and service workers	22%
Animal trainers	13%
Personal care and service occupations	8%
Total, all occupations	4%

Note: All Occupations includes all occupations in the U.S. Economy.
Source: U.S. Bureau of Labor Statistics, Employment Projections
program.

Employment projections data for animal care and service workers, 2019-29					
Occupational Title	SOC Code	Employment, 2019	Projected Employment, 2029	Change, 2019-29	
				Percent	Numeric
SOURCE: U.S. Bureau of Labor Statistics, Employment Projections program					
Animal care and service workers	39-2000	350,900	426,400	22	75,500
Animal trainers	39-2011	50,200	56,900	13	6,700
Animal caretakers	39-2021	300,700	369,500	23	68,800

State & Area Data

Occupational Employment Statistics (OES)

The Occupational Employment Statistics (OES) program produces employment and wage estimates annually for over 800
occupations. These estimates are available for the nation as a
whole, for individual states, and for metropolitan and nonmetropolitan areas.

Contacts for More Information

For more information about pet groomers, visit
➤ National Dog Groomers Association of America, Inc.

For more information about pet sitters, including information
on certification, visit
➤ National Association of Professional Pet Sitters
➤ Pet Sitters International

For more information about animal trainers, visit
➤ The Association of Professional Dog Trainers
➤ International Marine Animal Trainers' Association

For more information about keepers, visit
➤ Association of Zoos & Aquariums
➤ American Association of Zoo Keepers

Barbers, Hairstylists, and Cosmetologists

Summary

Quick Facts: Barbers, Hairstylists, and Cosmetologists	
2019 Median Pay	$26,270 per year $12.63 per hour
Typical Entry-Level Education	Postsecondary non-degree award
Work Experience in a Related Occupation	None
On-the-job Training	None
Number of Jobs, 2019	722,600
Job Outlook, 2019-29	-1% (Decline)
Employment Change, 2019-29	-9,200

What Barbers, Hairstylists, and Cosmetologists Do

Barbers, hairstylists, and cosmetologists provide haircutting, hairstyling, and a range of other beauty services.

Work Environment

Barbers, hairstylists, and cosmetologists work mostly in a barbershop or salon. Physical stamina is important, because they are on their feet for most of their shift. Many work full time, but part-time positions are also common.

How to Become a Barber, Hairstylist, or Cosmetologist

All states require barbers, hairstylists, and cosmetologists to be licensed. To qualify for a license, candidates are required to graduate from a state-approved barber or cosmetology program and then pass a state exam for licensure.

Pay

The median hourly wage for barbers was $14.50 in May 2019.

The median hourly wage for hairdressers, hairstylists, and cosmetologists was $12.54 in May 2019.

Job Outlook

Employment of barbers, hairstylists, and cosmetologists is projected to decline 1 percent from 2019 to 2029.

State & Area Data

Explore resources for employment and wages by state and area for barbers, hairstylists, and cosmetologists.

What Barbers, Hairstylists, and Cosmetologists Do

Barbers, hairstylists, and cosmetologists provide haircutting, hairstyling, and a range of other beauty services.

Duties

Barbers, hairstylists, and cosmetologists typically do the following:

- Inspect and analyze hair, skin, and scalp to recommend treatment
- Discuss hairstyle options
- Wash, color, lighten, and condition hair
- Chemically change hair textures
- Cut, dry, and style hair
- Receive payments from clients
- Clean and disinfect all tools and work areas

Barbers, hairstylists, and cosmetologists provide hair and beauty services to enhance clients' appearance. Those who operate their own barbershop or salon have managerial duties that may include hiring, supervising, and firing workers, as well as keeping business and inventory records, ordering supplies, and arranging for advertising.

Barbers cut, trim, shampoo, and style hair, mostly for male clients. They also may fit hairpieces, perform facials, and offer facial shaving. Depending on the state in which they work, some barbers are licensed to color, bleach, and highlight hair

Hairstylists discuss hairstyle options with clients.

Hairstylists provide hair styling and beauty services.

and to offer permanent-wave services. Common tools include combs, scissors, straight razors, and clippers.

Hairstylists offer a wide range of hair services, such as shampooing, cutting, coloring, and styling. They often advise clients, both male and female, on how to care for their hair at home. Hairstylists also keep records of products and services provided to clients, such as hair color, shampoo, conditioner, and hair treatment used. Tools include hairbrushes, scissors, blow dryers, and curling and flat irons.

Cosmetologists provide scalp and facial treatments and makeup analysis. Some also clean and style wigs and hairpieces. In addition, most cosmetologists actively recommend professional hair care products or salon hair care products.

Work Environment

Barbers held about 66,500 jobs in 2019. The largest employers of barbers were as follows:

Self-employed workers	70%
Personal care services	30

Hairdressers, hairstylists, and cosmetologists held about 656,100 jobs in 2019. The largest employers of hairdressers, hairstylists, and cosmetologists were as follows:

Barbers usually work in barbershops and must stand for long periods.

Personal care services	49%
Self-employed workers	41
Retail trade	8

Barbers, hairstylists, and cosmetologists work mostly in a barbershop or salon, although some work in a spa, hotel, or resort. Some lease booth space from a salon owner. Some manage salons or open their own shop after several years of experience.

Barbers, hairstylists, and cosmetologists usually work in pleasant surroundings with good lighting. Physical stamina is important, because they are on their feet for most of their shift. Prolonged exposure to some chemicals may cause skin irritation, so they often wear protective clothing, such as disposable gloves or aprons.

Work Schedules

Many barbers, hairstylists, and cosmetologists work full time; however, part-time positions are also common. Those who run their own barbershop or salon may have long workdays. Work schedules often include evenings and weekends-the times when barbershops and beauty salons are busiest. Those who are self-employed usually determine their own schedules.

How to Become a Barber, Hairstylist, or Cosmetologist

All states require barbers, hairstylists, and cosmetologists to be licensed. To qualify for a license, candidates are required to graduate from a state-approved cosmetology program.

Education

A high school diploma or equivalent is required for some positions. In addition, every state requires that barbers, hairstylists, and cosmetologists complete a program in a state-licensed barber or cosmetology school. These programs are mainly found in postsecondary vocational schools and typically lead to a postsecondary nondegree award or certificate. Most of these workers take advanced courses in hairstyling or in other personal appearance services to keep up with the latest trends. Those who want to open their own business also may take courses in sales and marketing.

Licenses, Certifications, and Registrations

Barbers, hairstylists, and cosmetologists must obtain a license in order to work. Qualifications for a license vary by state, but generally, a person must fulfill the following criteria:

- Reached a minimum age of 16
- Received a high school diploma or equivalent
- Graduated from a state-licensed barber or cosmetology school

After graduating from a state-approved training program, students take a state licensing exam that includes a written test and, in some cases, a practical test of styling skills or an oral exam.

Workers must obtain a license through a state-approved barber, hairstyling, or cosmetology program.

In many states, cosmetology training may be credited toward a barbering license and vice versa, and a few states combine the two licenses. A fee usually is required to apply for a license, and continuing education units (CEUs) may be required with periodic license renewals.

Some states have reciprocity agreements that allow licensed barbers and cosmetologists to get a license in another state without needing additional formal training or state board testing, but such agreements are not common. Consequently, people who want to work in a particular state should review the laws of that state before entering a training program.

Important Qualities

Creativity. Barbers, hairstylists, and cosmetologists must keep up with the latest trends and be ready to try new hairstyles for their clients.

Customer-service skills. Workers must be pleasant, friendly, and able to interact with customers in order to retain clients.

Listening skills. Barbers, hairstylists, and cosmetologists should be good listeners. They must listen carefully to what the client wants in order to make sure that the client is happy with the result.

Physical stamina. Barbers, hairstylists, and cosmetologists must be able to stand on their feet for long periods.

Tidiness. Workers must keep a neat personal appearance and keep their work area clean and sanitary. This requirement is necessary for the health and safety of their clients and for making clients comfortable enough so that they will want to return.

Time-management skills. Barbers, hairstylists, and cosmetologists need to manage their time efficiently when scheduling appointments and providing services. For example, routine haircuts do not require the precise timing of some other services, such as applying neutralizer after a permanent wave. Clients who receive timely hair care are more likely to return.

Pay

The median hourly wage for barbers was $14.50 in May 2019. The median wage is the wage at which half the workers in an occupation earned more than that amount and half earned less. The lowest 10 percent earned less than $9.76, and the highest 10 percent earned more than $27.23.

The median hourly wage for hairdressers, hairstylists, and cosmetologists was $12.54 in May 2019. The lowest 10 percent earned less than $8.86, and the highest 10 percent earned more than $24.94.

In May 2019, the median hourly wages for barbers in the top industries in which they worked were as follows:

Personal care services $14.44

Barbers, Hairstylists, and Cosmetologists
Median hourly wages, May 2019

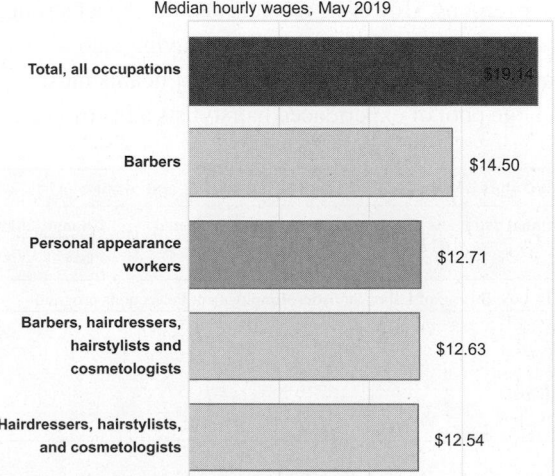

Total, all occupations	$19.14
Barbers	$14.50
Personal appearance workers	$12.71
Barbers, hairdressers, hairstylists and cosmetologists	$12.63
Hairdressers, hairstylists, and cosmetologists	$12.54

Note: All Occupations includes all occupations in the U.S. Economy.
Source: U.S. Bureau of Labor Statistics, Occupational Employment Statistics.

In May 2019, the median hourly wages for hairdressers, hairstylists, and cosmetologists in the top industries in which they worked were as follows:

Personal care services	$13.08
Retail trade	10.37

Barbers, hairstylists, and cosmetologists may receive tips from customers. High quality work and customer service usually contribute to greater tip totals.

Many barbers, hairstylists, and cosmetologists work full time; however, part-time positions are also common. Those who run their own barbershop or salon may have long workdays. Work schedules often include evenings and weekends-the times when beauty salons and barbershops are busiest. Those who are self-employed usually determine their own schedules.

Job Outlook

Employment of barbers, hairstylists, and cosmetologists is projected to decline 1 percent from 2019 to 2029.

The need for barbers will stem primarily from an increasing population, which will lead to greater demand for basic hair care services. In addition, demand for hair coloring, hair straightening, and other advanced hair treatments has risen in recent years, a trend that is expected to continue over the coming decade.

Employment of hairdressers, hairstylists, and cosmetologists in the personal care services industry is expected to decrease. Because of specialization, consumers will continue to choose manicurists and pedicurists and skincare specialists for some services, rather than to visit hairdressers, hairstylists, and cosmetologists for them.

Job Prospects

Overall job opportunities are expected to be good. A large number of job openings will stem from the need to replace workers who transfer to other occupations, retire, or leave the occupation for other reasons. However, workers should expect strong competition for jobs and clients at higher paying salons, of which there are relatively few and for which applicants must compete with a large pool of experienced hairstylists and cosmetologists.

Barbers, Hairstylists, and Cosmetologists
Percent change in employment, projected 2019-29

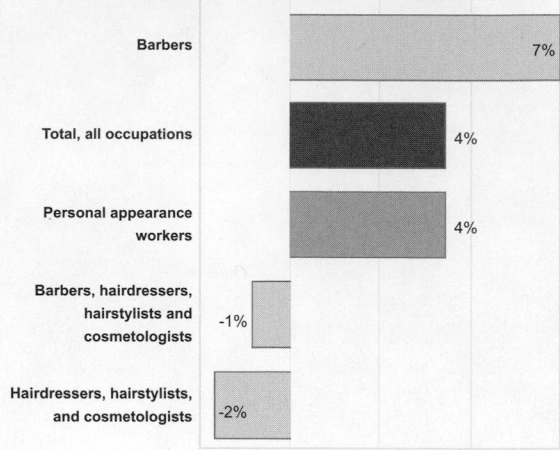

Note: All Occupations includes all occupations in the U.S. Economy.
Source: U.S. Bureau of Labor Statistics, Employment Projections program.

Employment projections data for barbers, hairstylists, and cosmetologists, 2019-29

Occupational Title	SOC Code	Employment, 2019	Projected Employment, 2029	Change, 2019-29	
				Percent	Numeric
Hairdressers, hairstylists, and cosmetologists	39-5012	656,100	641,800	-2	-14,200

State & Area Data
Occupational Employment Statistics (OES)

The Occupational Employment Statistics (OES) program produces employment and wage estimates annually for over 800 occupations. These estimates are available for the nation as a whole, for individual states, and for metropolitan and nonmetropolitan areas.

Contacts for More Information

For more information about barbers, hairstylists, and cosmetologists, including education and training, visit
➤ American Association of Cosmetology Schools
➤ Beauty Schools Directory
➤ National Association of Barber Boards of America

For information about state licensing, practice exams, and other professional links, visit
➤ National-Interstate Council of State Boards of Cosmetology
➤ Professional Beauty Association

Employment projections data for barbers, hairstylists, and cosmetologists, 2019-29

Occupational Title	SOC Code	Employment, 2019	Projected Employment, 2029	Change, 2019-29	
				Percent	Numeric
SOURCE: U.S. Bureau of Labor Statistics, Employment Projections program					
Barbers, hairdressers, hairstylists and cosmetologists	39-5010	722,600	713,300	-1	-9,200
Barbers	39-5011	66,500	71,500	7	5,000

Childcare Workers

Summary

Quick Facts: Childcare Workers

2019 Median Pay	$24,230 per year $11.65 per hour
Typical Entry-Level Education	High school diploma or equivalent
Work Experience in a Related Occupation ..	None
On-the-job Training	Short-term on-the- job training
Number of Jobs, 2019	1,146,400
Job Outlook, 2019-29	2% (Slower than average)
Employment Change, 2019-29	19,500

What Childcare Workers Do

Childcare workers attend to the basic needs of children, such as dressing, feeding, and overseeing play.

Work Environment

Childcare workers typically work in childcare centers, their own home, or private households. Part-time work and irregular hours are common.

How to Become a Childcare Worker

Education and training requirements for childcare workers vary by setting, state, and employer. They range from no formal education to certification in early childhood education.

Pay

The median hourly wage for childcare workers was $11.65 in May 2019.

Job Outlook

Employment of childcare workers is projected to grow 2 percent from 2019 to 2029, slower than the average for all occupations. Most of the openings projected each year are expected to come from the need to replace workers who leave the occupation permanently.

State & Area Data

Explore resources for employment and wages by state and area for childcare workers.

What Childcare Workers Do

Childcare workers attend to the basic needs of children, such as dressing, feeding, and overseeing play. They may help younger children prepare for kindergarten or assist older children with homework.

Duties

Childcare workers typically do the following:

- Supervise and monitor the safety of children
- Prepare and organize mealtimes and snacks for children
- Help children keep good hygiene
- Change the diapers of infants and toddlers
- Organize activities or implement a curriculum that allows children to learn about the world and explore their interests
- Develop schedules and routines to ensure that children have enough physical activity, rest, and playtime
- Watch for signs of emotional or developmental problems in children and bring potential problems to the attention of parents or guardians
- Keep records of children's progress, routines, and interests

Childcare workers read and play with babies and toddlers to introduce basic concepts. For example, they teach them how to share and take turns by playing games with other children.

Childcare workers attend to the basic needs of children, such as dressing, bathing, feeding, and overseeing play.

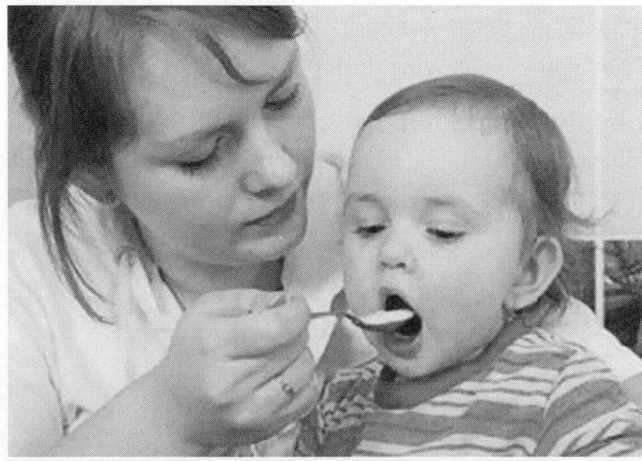

Childcare workers prepare and organize mealtimes and snacks for children.

Childcare workers help preschool-age children prepare for kindergarten. Young children learn from playing, questioning, and experimenting. Childcare workers use play and other instructional techniques to help children's development. For example, they may use storytelling and rhyming games to teach language and vocabulary. They may help improve children's social skills by having them work together to build something in a sandbox. Or they may teach about numbers by having children count when building with blocks. They also involve children in creative activities, such as art, dance, and music.

Childcare workers may also watch school-age children before and after school. They often help these children with their homework and may take them to afterschool activities, such as sports practices and club meetings.

During the summer, when children are out of school, childcare workers may watch older children as well as younger ones while the parents are at work.

The following are examples of types of childcare workers:

Childcare center workers work in facilities that include programs offering Head Start and Early Head Start. They often take a team-based approach and may work with preschool teachers and teacher assistants to teach children through a structured curriculum. They prepare daily and long-term schedules of activities to stimulate and educate the children in their care. They also monitor and keep records of the children's progress.

Family childcare providers run a business out of their own homes to care for children during standard working hours. They need to ensure that their homes and all staff they employ meet the regulations for family childcare providers. They also prepare contracts that set rates of pay, when payment can be expected, and the number of hours children can be in care. Furthermore, they establish policies such as whether sick children can be in their care, who can pick children up, and how behavioral issues will be dealt with. Family childcare providers may market their services to prospective families.

Nannies work in the homes of the families whose children they care for. Most often, they work full time for one family. They may be responsible for driving children to school, appointments, or afterschool activities. Some live in the homes of the families employing them.

Work Environment

Childcare workers held about 1.1 million jobs in 2019. The largest employers of childcare workers were as follows:

Child day care services	27%
Self-employed workers	23
Private households	20
Religious, grantmaking, civic, professional, and similar organizations	8
Elementary and secondary schools; local	8

Family childcare workers care for children in their own homes. They may convert a portion of their living space into a

Childcare workers may spend part of their day outdoors.

dedicated space for the children. Nannies usually work in their employers' homes.

Many states limit the number of children that each staff member is responsible for by regulating the ratio of staff to children. Ratios vary with the age of the children. Childcare workers are responsible for relatively few babies and toddlers. However, workers may be responsible for greater numbers of older children.

Work Schedules

Childcare workers' schedules vary, and part-time work is common.

Childcare centers usually are open year round, with long hours so that parents or guardians can drop off and pick up their children before and after work. Some centers employ full-time and part-time staff with staggered shifts to cover the entire day.

Family childcare providers may work long or irregular hours to fit parents' work schedules. In some cases, these childcare providers offer evening and overnight care to meet the needs of families. After the children go home, family childcare providers often have more responsibilities, such as shopping for food or supplies, keeping records, and cleaning.

Nannies work either full or part time. Full-time nannies may work more than 40 hours a week to cover parents' time commuting to and from work.

How to Become a Childcare Worker

Education and training requirements vary by setting, state, and employer. They range from no formal education to a certification in early childhood education.

Education

Childcare workers' education requirements vary. Some states require these workers to have a high school diploma or equivalent, but others do not have any education requirements for entry-level positions. Employers often prefer to hire workers who have at least a high school diploma. However, workers with postsecondary education or an early childhood education credential may qualify for higher level positions.

Childcare workers in Head Start and Early Head Start programs must meet specific education and certification requirements, which vary by work setting and job title.

States do not regulate educational requirements for nannies. However, some employers may prefer to hire workers with at least some formal instruction in childhood education or a related field, particularly when they will be hired as full-time nannies.

Licenses, Certifications, and Registrations

Many states require childcare centers, including those in private homes, to be licensed. To qualify for licensure, staff often must pass a background check, have a complete record of immunizations, and meet a minimum training requirement. Some states require staff to have certifications in cardiopulmonary resuscitation (CPR) and first aid.

Some states and employers require childcare workers to have a nationally recognized credential. Most often, states require the Child Development Associate (CDA) credential offered by the Council for Professional Recognition. Obtaining the CDA credential requires coursework, experience in the field, and a period during which the applicant is observed while working with children. The CDA credential must be renewed every 3 years.

Childcare workers typically need a high school degree or equivalent.

Other organizations, such as The National Association for Family Child Care (NAFCC) may also offer optional accreditation.

Training

Many states and employers require providers to complete some training before beginning work. Also, many states require staff in childcare centers to complete a minimum number of training hours annually. Training may include information about topics such as safe sleep practices for infants.

Advancement

With a couple of years of experience and a bachelor's degree, childcare workers may advance to become a preschool or childcare center director.

Important Qualities

Communication skills. Childcare workers need good speaking skills to provide direction or information effectively and good listening skills to understand parents' instructions.

Decision-making skills. Good judgment is necessary for childcare workers so they can respond to emergencies or difficult situations.

Interpersonal skills. Childcare workers need to work well with people in order to develop good relationships with parents, children, and colleagues.

Patience. Childcare workers need to be able to respond calmly to overwhelming and difficult situations.

Physical stamina. Working with children can be physically demanding, so childcare workers should have a lot of energy.

Pay

The median hourly wage for childcare workers was $11.65 in May 2019. The median wage is the wage at which half the workers in an occupation earned more than that amount and half earned less. The lowest 10 percent earned less than $8.65, and the highest 10 percent earned more than $17.21.

In May 2019, the median hourly wages for childcare workers in the top industries in which they worked were as follows:

Elementary and secondary schools; local...................	$13.03
Religious, grantmaking, civic, professional, and similar organizations	11.31
Child day care services..	11.12

Pay varies with the worker's education level and work setting. Those in formal childcare settings and those with more education usually earn higher wages. Pay for self-employed workers is based on the number of hours they work and the number and ages of children in their care.

Childcare workers' schedules vary, and part-time work is common.

Childcare Workers
Median hourly wages, May 2019

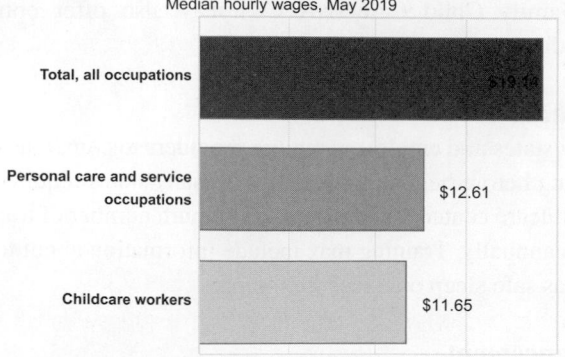

Total, all occupations	$19.14
Personal care and service occupations	$12.61
Childcare workers	$11.65

Note: All Occupations includes all occupations in the U.S. Economy.
Source: U.S. Bureau of Labor Statistics, Occupational Employment Statistics.

Childcare centers usually are open year round, with long hours so that parents or guardians can drop off and pick up their children before and after work. Some centers employ full-time and part-time staff with staggered shifts to cover the entire day.

Family childcare providers may work long or irregular hours to fit parents' work schedules. In some cases, these childcare providers may offer evening and overnight care to meet the needs of families. After the children go home, childcare providers often have more responsibilities, such as shopping for food or supplies, keeping records, and cleaning.

Nannies work either full or part time. Full-time nannies may work more than 40 hours a week to cover parents' commuting time to and from work.

Job Outlook

Employment of childcare workers is projected to grow 2 percent from 2019 to 2029, slower than the average for all occupations.

Parents or guardians who work will continue to need the assistance of childcare workers. In addition, the demand for preschools and childcare facilities, and consequently childcare workers, should remain strong because early childhood education is widely recognized as important for a child's intellectual and emotional development.

However, the increasing cost of childcare may reduce demand for childcare workers.

Job Prospects

Despite limited employment growth, about 160,200 openings for childcare workers are projected each year, on average, over the decade.

Most of those openings are expected to result from the need to replace workers who transfer to different occupations or exit the labor force, such as to retire.

Childcare Workers
Percent change in employment, projected 2019-29

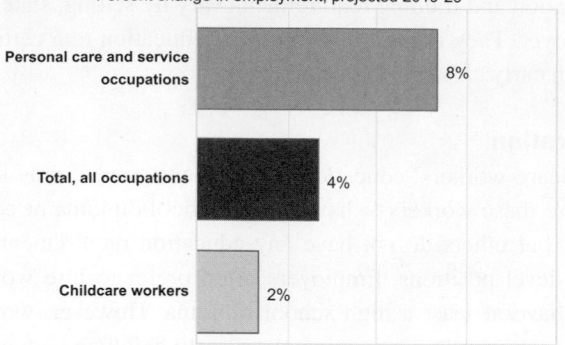

Personal care and service occupations	8%
Total, all occupations	4%
Childcare workers	2%

Note: All Occupations includes all occupations in the U.S. Economy.
Source: U.S. Bureau of Labor Statistics, Employment Projections program.

Workers who attain the Child Development Associate credential should have the best job prospects.

Employment projections data for childcare workers, 2019-29					
Occupational Title	SOC Code	Employment, 2019	Projected Employment, 2029	Change, 2019-29	
				Percent	Numeric
SOURCE: U.S. Bureau of Labor Statistics, Employment Projections program					
Childcare workers	39-9011	1,146,400	1,165,900	2	19,500

State & Area Data
Occupational Employment Statistics (OES)

The Occupational Employment Statistics (OES) program produces employment and wage estimates annually for over 800 occupations. These estimates are available for the nation as a whole, for individual states, and for metropolitan and nonmetropolitan areas.

Contacts for More Information

For more information about becoming a childcare provider, visit
➤ Child Care Aware

For more information about working as a nanny, visit
➤ International Nanny Association

For more information about family childcare providers, visit
➤ National Association for Family Child Care

For more information about early childhood education, visit
➤ National Association for the Education of Young Children

For more information about professional credentials, visit
➤ Council for Professional Recognition

Fitness Trainers and Instructors

Summary

Quick Facts: Fitness Trainers and Instructors

2019 Median Pay	$40,390 per year $19.42 per hour
Typical Entry-Level Education	High school diploma or equivalent
Work Experience in a Related Occupation ...	None
On-the-job Training	Short-term on-the-job training
Number of Jobs, 2019	373,700
Job Outlook, 2019-29..................................	15% (Much faster than average)
Employment Change, 2019-29	57,600

What Fitness Trainers and Instructors Do

Fitness trainers and instructors lead, instruct, and motivate individuals or groups in exercise activities.

Work Environment

Fitness trainers and instructors work in facilities such as health clubs, fitness or recreation centers, gyms, and yoga and Pilates studios. They may work nights, weekends, or holidays.

How to Become a Fitness Trainer or Instructor

The education and training required for fitness trainers and instructors varies by type of specialty, and employers prefer to hire those with certification.

Pay

The median annual wage for fitness trainers and instructors was $40,390 in May 2019.

Job Outlook

Employment of fitness trainers and instructors is projected to grow 15 percent from 2019 to 2029, much faster than the average for all occupations. As businesses, government, and insurance organizations continue to recognize the benefits of health and fitness programs for their employees, incentives to join gyms or other types of health clubs are expected to increase the need for fitness trainers and instructors.

State & Area Data

Explore resources for employment and wages by state and area for fitness trainers and instructors.

What Fitness Trainers and Instructors Do

Fitness trainers and instructors lead, instruct, and motivate individuals or groups in exercise activities, including cardiovascular exercises (exercises for the heart and blood circulation), strength training, and stretching. They work with people of all ages and skill levels.

Duties

Fitness trainers and instructors typically do the following:

- Demonstrate or explain how to perform various exercises and routines to minimize injuries and improve fitness
- Watch clients do exercises to ensure that they are using the correct techniques
- Provide alternative exercises during workouts or classes for different levels of fitness and skill
- Monitor clients' progress and adapt programs as needed
- Explain and enforce safety rules and regulations on sports, recreational activities, and the use of exercise equipment
- Give clients information or resources about nutrition, weight control, and lifestyle issues
- Give emergency first aid if needed

Fitness trainers and instructors lead, instruct, and motivate individuals or groups in exercise activities.

Fitness trainers and instructors work with people of all ages and skill levels.

Both *group fitness instructors* and *specialized fitness instructors* plan or choreograph their own classes. Classes may include cardiovascular exercises, such as aerobics or dance; strength training, such as lifting weights; or both. Instructors choose music that is appropriate for their exercise class and create a routine or a set of moves for participants to follow. Some may teach prechoreographed routines that were originally created by fitness companies or other organizations.

Personal fitness trainers design and carry out workout routines specific to the needs of their clients. They may work with individual clients or teach group classes. In larger facilities, personal trainers often sell their training sessions to gym members. They start by evaluating their clients' current fitness level, personal goals, and skills. Then, they develop personalized training programs for their clients to follow, and they monitor the clients' progress.

Fitness trainers and instructors in smaller facilities often do a variety of tasks in addition to their fitness duties, such as tending the front desk, signing up new members, giving tours of the facility, or supervising the weight-training and cardiovascular equipment areas. Fitness trainers and instructors also may promote their facilities and instruction by various means, such as through social media, by writing newsletters or blog articles, or by creating posters and flyers.

Gyms and other types of health clubs offer many different activities for clients. However, trainers and instructors frequently specialize in only a few areas. The following are examples of types of fitness trainers and instructors:

Personal fitness trainers work with an individual client or a small group. They may train in a gym or in clients' homes. Personal fitness trainers assess the client's level of physical fitness and help them set and reach their fitness goals.

Group fitness instructors organize and lead group exercise classes, which can include aerobic exercises, stretching, or muscle conditioning. Some classes are set to music. In these classes, instructors may select the music and choreograph an exercise sequence. They may lead classes that use specific exercise equipment, such as stationary bicycles.

Specialized fitness instructors teach popular conditioning methods, such as Pilates or yoga. In these classes, instructors show the different moves and positions of the particular method. They also watch students and correct those who are doing the exercises improperly.

Fitness directors oversee the fitness-related aspects of a gym or other type of health club. They often handle administrative duties, such as scheduling personal training sessions for clients and creating workout incentive programs. They may select and order fitness equipment for their facility.

Work Environment

Fitness trainers and instructors held about 373,700 jobs in 2019. The largest employers of fitness trainers and instructors were as follows:

Group instructors may demonstrate how to perform various exercises and routines.

Fitness and recreational sports centers	58%
Self-employed workers	11
Civic and social organizations	10
Educational services; state, local, and private	7
Government	4

Fitness trainers and instructors may work in standalone fitness centers or centers maintained by other types of establishments for their employees or for members of civic and social organizations. Some work in clients' homes.

Work Schedules

Fitness trainers and instructors may work nights, weekends, or holidays. Some travel to different gyms or to clients' homes to teach classes or conduct personal training sessions. Some group fitness instructors and personal fitness trainers hold full-time jobs in other fields and teach fitness classes or conduct personal training sessions during evenings or weekends.

How to Become a Fitness Trainer or Instructor

The education and training required for fitness trainers and instructors varies by type of specialty, and employers prefer to hire those with certification. Personal fitness trainers, group fitness instructors, and specialized fitness instructors each need different preparation. Requirements also vary by facility.

Education

Almost all trainers and instructors have at least a high school diploma before entering the occupation. An increasing number of employers are requiring fitness workers, particularly personal trainers, to have an associate's or bachelor's degree related to a health or fitness field, such as exercise science, kinesiology, or physical education. Programs often include courses in nutrition, exercise techniques, biology, anatomy, and group fitness. Personal trainers also learn how to develop fitness programs for clients of all ages.

Personal trainers may work with individual clients or teach group classes.

Licenses, Certifications, and Registrations

Employers prefer to hire fitness trainers and instructors who are certified. Many personal trainers must be certified before they begin working with clients or with members of a gym or other type of health club. Group fitness instructors can begin work without certification, but employers often encourage or require them to become certified. Most specialized fitness instructors receive certification for their preferred type of training, such as yoga or Pilates.

Many organizations offer certification. The National Commission for Certifying Agencies (NCCA), part of the Institute for Credentialing Excellence, lists certifying organizations that are accredited.

All certification exams have a written part, and some also have a practical part. The exams measure the candidate's knowledge of human physiology, understanding of proper exercise techniques, and ability to assess clients' fitness levels and develop appropriate exercise programs. Many certifying organizations offer study materials to prepare for the exam, including books, webinars, other audio and visual materials, and exam preparation workshops and seminars.

Most trainers or instructors need certification in cardiopulmonary resuscitation (CPR) and automated external defibrillators (AED) before applying for certification in physical fitness.

Training

After becoming a certified personal trainer, new trainers typically work alongside an experienced trainer before they are allowed to train clients alone.

Training for specialized fitness instructors can vary greatly. For example, the duration of programs for yoga instructors can range from a few days to more than 2 years. The Yoga Alliance offers several credentials that require a minimum of between 200 and 500 hours, with a specified number of hours in techniques, teaching methods, anatomy, physiology, philosophy, and other areas.

Important Qualities

Customer-service skills. Many fitness trainers and instructors must sell their services, motivating clients to hire them as personal trainers or to sign up for the classes they lead. Fitness trainers and instructors must therefore be polite, friendly, and encouraging, to maintain relationships with their clients.

Communication skills. Fitness trainers and instructors must clearly explain or demonstrate exercises to clients.

Listening skills. Fitness trainers and instructors must listen carefully to what clients tell them in order to determine the clients' fitness levels and desired fitness goals.

Motivational skills. Getting fit and staying fit takes a lot of work for many clients. To keep clients coming back for more classes or to continue personal training, fitness trainers and instructors must keep their clients motivated.

Physical fitness. Fitness trainers and instructors need to be physically fit because their job requires a considerable amount of exercise. Group instructors often participate in classes, and personal trainers often need to demonstrate exercises to their clients.

Problem-solving skills. Fitness trainers and instructors must evaluate each client's level of fitness and create an appropriate fitness plan to meet the client's individual needs.

Advancement

Fitness trainers and instructors who are interested in management positions should get a bachelor's degree in exercise science, physical education, kinesiology, or a related subject. Experience often is required in order for a trainer or instructor to advance to a management position in a health club or fitness center. Some organizations prefer a master's degree for certain positions.

Personal trainers may eventually advance to a *head trainer* position and become responsible for hiring and overseeing the personal training staff or for bringing in new personal training clients. Head trainers also are responsible for procuring athletic equipment, such as weights or fitness machines. Some fitness trainers and instructors go into business for themselves and open their own fitness centers.

Fitness Trainers and Instructors
Median annual wages, May 2019

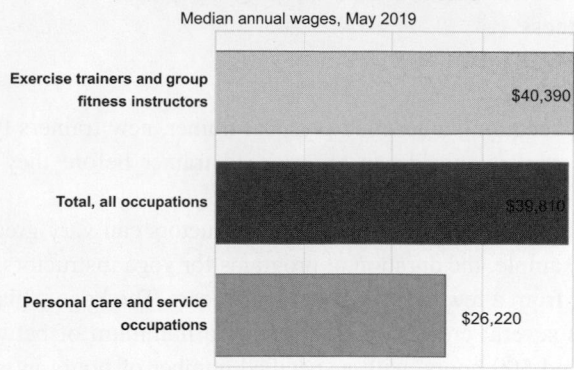

Exercise trainers and group fitness instructors	$40,390
Total, all occupations	$39,810
Personal care and service occupations	$26,220

Fitness Trainers and Instructors
Percent change in employment, projected 2019-29

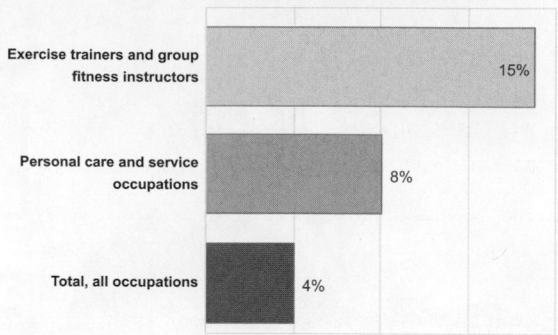

Exercise trainers and group fitness instructors	15%
Personal care and service occupations	8%
Total, all occupations	4%

Note: All Occupations includes all occupations in the U.S. Economy.
Source: U.S. Bureau of Labor Statistics, Occupational Employment Statistics.

Note: All Occupations includes all occupations in the U.S. Economy.
Source: U.S. Bureau of Labor Statistics, Employment Projections program.

Pay

The median annual wage for fitness trainers and instructors was $40,390 in May 2019. The median wage is the wage at which half the workers in an occupation earned more than that amount and half earned less. The lowest 10 percent earned less than $21,110, and the highest 10 percent earned more than $75,400.

In May 2019, the median annual wages for fitness trainers and instructors in the top industries in which they worked were as follows:

Fitness and recreational sports centers	$42,700
Educational services; state, local, and private	38,320
Government	37,440
Civic and social organizations	33,080

Fitness trainers and instructors may work nights, weekends, or holidays. Some travel to different gyms or to clients' homes to teach classes or conduct personal training sessions. Some group fitness instructors and personal fitness trainers work other full-time jobs and teach fitness classes or conduct personal training sessions part time during evenings or weekends.

Job Outlook

Employment of fitness trainers and instructors is projected to grow 15 percent from 2019 to 2029, much faster than the average for all occupations.

As businesses, government, and insurance organizations continue to recognize the benefits of health and fitness programs for their employees, incentives to join gyms or other types of health clubs are expected to increase the need for fitness trainers and instructors. For example, some organizations may open their own exercise facilities onsite to promote employee wellness.

Other employment growth will come from the continuing emphasis on exercise to combat obesity and encourage healthier lifestyles for people of all ages. In particular, the baby-boom

generation should continue to remain active to help prevent injuries and illnesses associated with aging.

Participation in yoga and Pilates is expected to continue to increase, driven partly by older adults who want low-impact forms of exercise and relief from arthritis and other ailments.

Job Prospects

Job prospects should be best for workers with professional certification or increased levels of formal education in health or fitness. Overall opportunities are expected to be good because of the need to replace workers who leave the occupation.

Employment projections data for fitness trainers and instructors, 2019-29					
Occupational Title	SOC Code	Employment, 2019	Projected Employment, 2029	Change, 2019-29	
				Percent	Numeric
SOURCE: U.S. Bureau of Labor Statistics, Employment Projections program					
Exercise trainers and group fitness instructors	39-9031	373,700	431,300	15	57,600

State & Area Data

Occupational Employment Statistics (OES)

The Occupational Employment Statistics (OES) program produces employment and wage estimates annually for over 800 occupations. These estimates are available for the nation as a whole, for individual states, and for metropolitan and nonmetropolitan areas.

Contacts for More Information

For more information about fitness careers and about health and fitness programs in universities and other institutions, visit
➤ American College of Sports Medicine
➤ National Strength and Conditioning Association

For information about certifications for personal trainers and group fitness instructors, visit
➤ American Council on Exercise

- ➤ National Academy of Sports Medicine
- ➤ National Federation of Professional Trainers
- ➤ National Commission for Certifying Agencies (NCCA), part of the Institute for Credentialing Excellence
- ➤ US Registry of Exercise Professionals
- ➤ National Council on Strength and Fitness
- ➤ International Sports Sciences Association

For information about health clubs and sports clubs, visit
- ➤ International Health, Racquet & Sportsclub Association

For information about yoga teacher certification and a list of registered schools, visit
- ➤ Yoga Alliance

Funeral Service Workers

Summary

Quick Facts: Funeral Service Workers

2019 Median Pay	$58,310 per year
	$28.04 per hour
Typical Entry-Level Education	Associate's degree
Work Experience in a Related Occupation	See below
On-the-job Training	See below
Number of Jobs, 2019	55,200
Job Outlook, 2019-29	-4% (Decline)
Employment Change, 2019-29	-2,200

What Funeral Service Workers Do

Funeral service workers organize and manage the details of a funeral.

Work Environment

Funeral service workers are employed in funeral homes and crematories. They are often on call, and long workdays are common, including evenings and weekends. Most work full time.

How to Become a Funeral Service Worker

An associate's degree in funeral service or mortuary science is the typical education requirement for funeral service workers.

Most employers and state licensing laws require applicants to be 21 years old, have 2 years of formal education, have supervised training, and pass a state licensing exam.

Pay

The median annual wage for funeral home managers was $76,350 in May 2019.

The median annual wage for morticians, undertakers, and funeral arrangers was $54,150 in May 2019.

Job Outlook

Overall employment of funeral service workers is projected to decline 4 percent from 2019 to 2029. Those who are licensed as funeral directors and embalmers and who are willing to relocate should have the best job opportunities.

State & Area Data

Explore resources for employment and wages by state and area for funeral service workers.

What Funeral Service Workers Do

Funeral service workers organize and manage the details of a funeral.

Duties

Funeral service workers typically do the following:

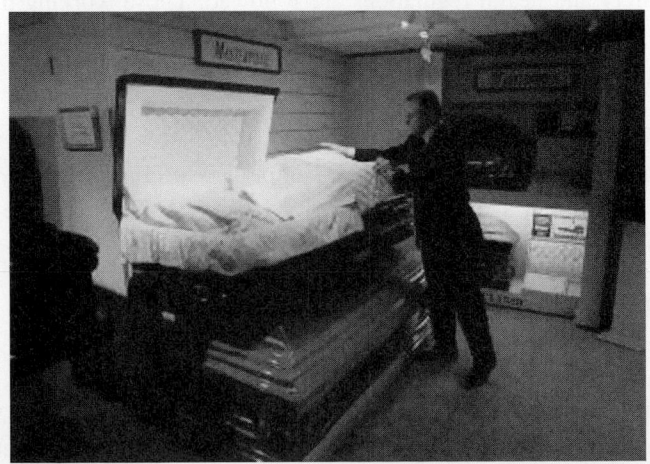

Funeral service workers handle the details of funerals.

Together with the family, funeral directors handle details of the memorial services.

- Offer counsel and comfort to families and friends of the deceased
- Provide information on funeral service options
- Arrange for removal of the deceased's body
- Prepare the remains (the deceased's body) for the funeral
- File death certificates and other legal documents with appropriate authorities

Funeral service workers help to determine the locations, dates, and times of visitations (wakes), funerals or memorial services, burials, and cremations. They handle other details as well, such as helping the family decide whether the body should be buried, entombed, or cremated. This decision is critical because funeral practices vary among cultures and religions.

Most funeral service workers attend to the administrative aspects pertaining to a person's death, including submitting papers to state officials to receive a death certificate. They also may help resolve insurance claims, apply for funeral benefits, or notify the Social Security Administration or the U.S. Department of Veterans Affairs of the death.

Many funeral service workers work with clients who wish to plan their own funerals in advance, to ensure that their needs are met and to ease the planning burden on surviving family members.

Funeral service workers also may provide information and resources, such as support groups, to help grieving friends and family.

The following are examples of types of funeral service workers:

Funeral service managers oversee the general operations of a funeral home business. They perform a wide variety of duties, such as planning and allocating the resources of the funeral home, managing staff, and handling marketing and public relations.

Funeral directors and morticians plan the details of a funeral. They often prepare obituary notices and arrange for pallbearers and clergy services. If a burial is chosen, they schedule the opening and closing of a grave with a representative of the cemetery. If cremation is chosen, they coordinate the process with the crematory. They also prepare the sites of all services and provide transportation for the deceased and mourners. In addition, they arrange the shipment of bodies out of state or out of country for final disposition.

Finally, these workers handle administrative duties. For example, they often apply for the transfer of any pensions, insurance policies, or annuities on behalf of survivors.

Most funeral directors and morticians embalm bodies. Embalming is a cosmetic and temporary preservative process through which the body is prepared for a viewing by family and friends of the deceased.

Work Environment

Funeral home managers held about 28,600 jobs in 2019. The largest employers of funeral home managers were as follows:

Funeral directors often have long workdays.

Self-employed workers	67%
Death care services	33

Morticians, undertakers, and funeral arrangers held about 26,600 jobs in 2019. The largest employers of morticians, undertakers, and funeral arrangers were as follows:

Death care services	94%
Self-employed workers	5

Funeral services traditionally take place in a house of worship, in a funeral home, or at a gravesite or crematory. However, some families prefer holding the service in their home or in a social center.

Funeral service workers typically perform their duties in a funeral home. Workers also may operate a merchandise display room, crematory, or cemetery, which may be on the funeral home premises. The work is often stressful, because workers must arrange the various details of a funeral within 24 to 72 hours of a death. In addition, they may be responsible for managing multiple funerals on the same day.

Although workers may come into contact with bodies that have contagious diseases, the work is not dangerous if proper safety and health regulations are followed. Those working in crematories are exposed to high temperatures and must wear appropriate protective clothing.

Work Schedules

Most funeral service workers are employed full time. They are often on call, and long workdays are common, including evenings and weekends.

How to Become a Funeral Service Worker

An associate's degree in funeral service or mortuary science is the typical education requirement for funeral service workers. Most employers require applicants to be 21 years old, have 2 years of formal education, have supervised training, and pass a state licensing exam.

Becoming a funeral director requires courses in ethics, grief counseling, and business law.

Education

An associate's degree in funeral service or mortuary science is the typical education requirement for all funeral service workers. Courses taken usually include those covering the topics of ethics, grief counseling, funeral service, and business law. All accredited programs also include courses in embalming and restorative techniques.

The American Board of Funeral Service Education (ABFSE) accredits 60 funeral service and mortuary science programs, most of which are 2-year associate's degree programs offered at community colleges. Some programs offer a bachelor's degree.

Although an associate's degree is typically required, some employers prefer applicants to have a bachelor's degree.

High school students can prepare to become a funeral service worker by taking courses in biology, chemistry, and business, and by participating in public speaking.

Part-time or summer jobs in funeral homes also provide valuable experience.

Training

Those studying to be funeral directors and morticians must complete training, usually lasting 1 to 3 years, under the direction of a licensed funeral director or manager. The training, sometimes called an internship or an apprenticeship, may be completed before, during, or after graduating from a 2-year funeral service or mortuary science program and passing a national board exam.

Licenses, Certifications, and Registrations

Most workers must be licensed in Washington, DC and every state in which they work, except Colorado, which offers a voluntary certification program. Although licensing laws and examinations vary by state, most applicants must meet the following criteria:

- Be 21 years old
- Complete an ABFSE accredited funeral service or mortuary science program
- Pass a state and/or national board exam
- Serve an internship lasting 1 to 3 years

Working in multiple states will require multiple licenses. For specific requirements, applicants should contact each applicable state licensing board.

Most states require funeral directors to earn continuing education credits annually to keep their licenses.

The Cremation Association of North America (CANA); International Cemetery, Cremation and Funeral Association (ICCFA); and the National Funeral Directors Association (NFDA) offer crematory certification designations. Many states require certification for those who will perform cremations. For specific requirements, applicants should contact their state board or one of the above organizations.

Work Experience in a Related Occupation

Funeral service managers typically have multiple years of experience working as a funeral director or mortician before becoming managers.

Important Qualities

Business skills. Knowledge of financial statements and the ability to run a funeral home efficiently and profitably are important for funeral directors and managers.

Compassion. Death is a delicate and emotional matter. Funeral service workers must be able to treat clients with care and sympathy in their time of loss.

Interpersonal skills. Funeral service workers should have good interpersonal skills. When speaking with families, for instance, they must be tactful and able to explain and discuss all matters about services provided.

Time-management skills. Funeral service workers must be able to handle numerous tasks for multiple customers, often over a short timeframe.

Pay

The median annual wage for funeral home managers was $76,350 in May 2019. The median wage is the wage at which half the workers in an occupation earned more than that amount and half earned less. The lowest 10 percent earned less than $44,120, and the highest 10 percent earned more than $161,870.

The median annual wage for morticians, undertakers, and funeral arrangers was $54,150 in May 2019. The lowest 10 percent earned less than $29,370, and the highest 10 percent earned more than $89,880.

Funeral Service Workers
Median annual wages, May 2019

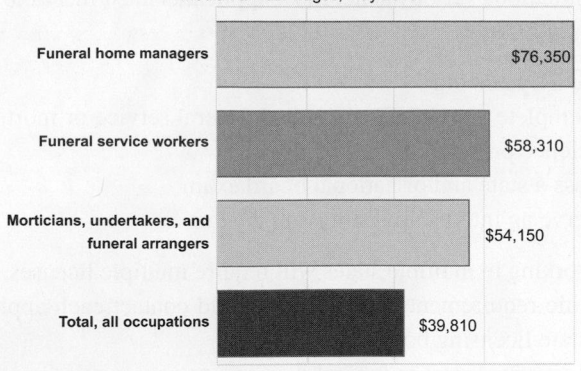

Note: All Occupations includes all occupations in the U.S. Economy.
Source: U.S. Bureau of Labor Statistics, Occupational Employment
Statistics.

In May 2019, the median annual wages for funeral home managers in the top industries in which they worked were as follows:

Death care services.. $76,280

In May 2019, the median annual wages for morticians, undertakers, and funeral arrangers in the top industries in which they worked were as follows:

Death care services.. $53,890

Most funeral service workers are employed full time. They are often on call, and long workdays are common, including evenings and weekends.

Job Outlook

Overall employment of funeral service workers is projected to decline 4 percent from 2019 to 2029.

Demand for funeral service workers is expected to go down over the next decade as consumers increasingly prefer cremation, which costs less and requires fewer workers than traditional funeral arrangements.

Job Prospects

Job prospects for funeral service workers are expected to be good overall. Opportunities should be particularly favorable for those who are licensed as both a funeral director and an embalmer, for those willing to relocate, and for certified crematory operators.

Some job openings should result from the need to replace workers who retire or leave the occupation each year.

Funeral Service Workers
Percent change in employment, projected 2019-29

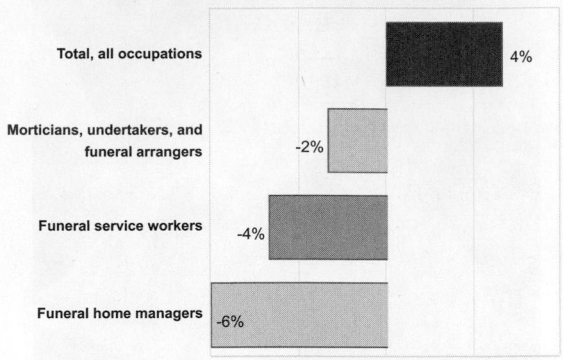

Note: All Occupations includes all occupations in the U.S. Economy.
Source: U.S. Bureau of Labor Statistics, Employment Projections program.

Employment projections data for funeral service workers, 2019-29					
Occupational Title	SOC Code	Employment, 2019	Projected Employment, 2029	Change, 2019-29	
				Percent	Numeric
SOURCE: U.S. Bureau of Labor Statistics, Employment Projections program					
Funeral service workers	—	55,200	53,000	-4	-2,200
Funeral home managers	11-9171	28,600	26,900	-6	-1,600
Morticians, undertakers, and funeral arrangers	39-4031	26,600	26,100	-2	-500

State & Area Data
Occupational Employment Statistics (OES)
The Occupational Employment Statistics (OES) program produces employment and wage estimates annually for over 800 occupations. These estimates are available for the nation as a whole, for individual states, and for metropolitan and nonmetropolitan areas.

Contacts for More Information
For more information about funeral service workers, including accredited mortuary science programs, visit
➤ National Funeral Directors Association

For scholarships and educational programs in funeral service and mortuary science, visit
➤ American Board of Funeral Service Education
➤ National Funeral Directors & Morticians Association, Inc.

For information about crematories, visit
➤ Cremation Association of North America
➤ International Cemetery, Cremation and Funeral Association
➤ Candidates should contact their state board for specific licensing requirements.

Gaming Services Workers

Summary

Quick Facts: Gaming Services Workers

2019 Median Pay	$23,520 per year
	$11.31 per hour
Typical Entry-Level Education	High school diploma or equivalent
Work Experience in a Related Occupation...	See below
On-the-job Training	See below
Number of Jobs, 2019	187,300
Job Outlook, 2019-29.................................	10% (Much faster than average)
Employment Change, 2019-29	19,000

What Gaming Services Workers Do

Gaming services workers serve customers in gambling establishments, such as casinos or racetracks.

Work Environment

Most gaming services workers are employed in the casino hotels, local government or gambling industries. Because most establishments are open 24 hours a day, 7 days a week, employees often must work during nights, weekends, and holidays.

How to Become a Gaming Services Worker

Most gaming jobs require a high school diploma or equivalent. Some casinos may require gaming managers to have a college degree. In addition, all gaming services workers must have excellent customer-service skills.

Pay

The median annual wage for gaming services workers was $23,520 in May 2019.

Many gaming services workers are employed by casinos.

Job Outlook

Employment of gaming services workers is projected to grow 10 percent from 2019 to 2029, much faster than the average for all occupations. Since some states benefit from casinos in the form of tax revenues, additional states currently without commercial gaming establishments may allow new casinos to be built over the next decade.

State & Area Data

Explore resources for employment and wages by state and area for gaming services workers.

What Gaming Services Workers Do

Gaming services workers serve customers in gambling establishments, such as casinos or racetracks. Some workers tend slot machines or deal cards. Others take bets or pay out winnings. Still others supervise or manage gaming workers and operations.

Duties

Gaming services workers typically do the following:

- Interact with customers and ensure that they have a pleasant experience
- Monitor customers for violations of gaming regulations or casino policies

Many gaming dealers specialize in one type of game.

- Inform their supervisor or a security employee of any irregularities they observe
- Enforce safety rules and report hazards
- Explain how to play the games to customers

The following are examples of types of gaming services workers:

Gaming managers and supervisors direct and oversee the gaming operations and personnel in their assigned area. Supervisors circulate among the tables to make sure that everything is running smoothly and that all areas are properly staffed. Gaming managers and supervisors typically do the following:

- Keep an eye on customers and employees to ensure compliance with all gaming and casino rules
- Communicate with other departments if security or customer-service issues arise
- Address customers' complaints about service
- Explain house operating rules, such as betting limits, if customers do not understand them
- Ensure payouts are correct
- Schedule when and where employees in their section will work
- Interview, hire, and train new employees

Slot supervisors oversee the activities of the slot department. The job duties of this occupation have changed significantly, as slot machines have become more automated in recent years. Because most casinos use slot machines that give out tickets instead of cash and thus require very little oversight, workers in this occupation spend most of their time providing customer service to slot players. Slot supervisors typically do the following:

- Watch over the slot section and ensure that players are satisfied with the games
- Refill machines with tickets when they run out
- Oversee payment of large jackpots
- Respond to and resolve customer complaints
- Interview, hire, and train new employees

Gaming dealers operate table games such as craps, blackjack, and roulette. They stand or sit behind tables while serving customers. Dealers control the pace and action of the game. They announce each player's move to the rest of the table and let players know when it is their turn. Most dealers are often required to work at least two games, usually blackjack or craps. Gaming dealers typically do the following:

- Give out cards and provide dice or other equipment to customers
- Determine winners, calculate and pay off winning bets, and collect on losing bets
- Continually inspect cards or dice
- Inform players of the rules of the game

- Keep track of the amount of money that customers have already bet
- Exchange paper money for gaming chips

Gaming and sports book writers and runners handle bets on sporting events and take and record bets for customers. Sports book writers and runners also verify tickets and pay out winning tickets. In addition, they help run games such as bingo and keno. Some gaming runners collect winning tickets from customers in a casino. Gaming and sports book writers and runners typically do the following:

- Scan tickets and calculate winnings
- Operate the equipment that randomly selects bingo or keno numbers
- Announce bingo or keno numbers when they are selected
- Oversee the cash that comes in (on bets) and goes out (on winnings) during their shift

Work Environment

Gaming services workers held about 187,300 jobs in 2019. Employment in the detailed occupations that make up gaming services workers was distributed as follows:

Gambling dealers	102,900
First-line supervisors of gambling services workers	58,000
Gambling service workers, all other	10,900
Gambling and sports book writers and runners	10,400
Gambling managers	5,100

The largest employers of gaming services workers were as follows:

Local government, excluding education and hospitals	25%
Self-employed workers	17
Spectator sports	4

Slot supervisors are in charge of the slot department.

Some gaming services occupations are physically demanding. Gaming dealers spend most of their shift standing behind a table. Although managers and supervisors may spend some limited time working in an office, they must frequently walk up and down the casino floor.

A casino atmosphere also may expose gaming services workers to hazards such as secondhand smoke from cigarettes, cigars, or pipes. Noise from slot machines, gaming tables, and loud customers may be distracting to some, although workers may wear protective headgear in areas where machinery is used to count money.

Work Schedules

Most casinos are open 24 hours a day, 7 days a week. Employees are often scheduled to work nights, weekends, and holidays, which are typically the busiest times for casinos.

How to Become a Gaming Services Worker

Most gaming jobs require a high school diploma or equivalent. Some casinos may require gaming managers to have a college degree. In addition, all gaming services workers must have excellent customer-service skills.

Education

Gaming dealers, gaming supervisors, sports book writers and runners, and slot supervisors typically need a high school diploma or equivalent. Educational requirements for gaming managers, however, differ by casino. Although some casinos may only require a high school diploma or equivalent, others require gaming managers to have a college degree. Those who choose to pursue a degree may study hotel management, hospitality, or accounting in addition to taking formal management classes.

Training

Individual casinos or other gaming establishments have their own training requirements. New gaming dealers may be sent

Dealers should have good customer-service skills.

to gaming school for a few weeks to learn a casino game, such as blackjack or craps. These schools teach the rules and procedures of the game, as well as state and local laws and regulations related to the game.

Although gaming school is primarily for new employees, some experienced dealers have to go to gaming school if they want to be trained in a new casino game.

Completing gaming school before being hired may increase a prospective dealer's chances of being hired, but it does not guarantee a job. Casinos usually audition prospective dealers for open positions to assess their personal qualities.

Gaming and sports book writers and runners usually do not have to go to gaming school. They can be trained by the casino in less than 1 month. The casino teaches them state and local laws and regulations related to the game, as well the particulars of their job, such as keno calling.

Licenses, Certifications, and Registrations

Gaming services workers must be licensed by a state regulatory agency, such as a state casino control board or gaming commission. Licensing requirements for supervisory or managerial positions may differ from those for gaming dealers, gaming and sports book writers and runners, and all other gaming workers. However, all applicants for a license must provide photo identification and pay a fee. They also must typically pass an extensive background check and drug test. Failure to pass the background check may prevent candidates from getting a job or a gaming license.

Age requirements also vary by state. For specific licensing requirements, visit the state's gaming commission website.

Work Experience in a Related Occupation

Gaming and slot supervisors and gaming managers usually have several years of experience working in a casino. Gaming supervisors often have experience as a dealer or in the customer outreach department of the casino. Slot supervisors usually have experience as a slot technician or slot attendant. Some also may have worked in entry-level marketing or customer-service positions.

Advancement

Gaming managers are often promoted from positions as slot or gaming supervisors. They also may be moved from a management job in another part of the resort, such as hospitality, after learning about casino operations through an internship or on-the-job training.

Gaming dealers can advance to gaming supervisors and eventually managers. A slot supervisor can also advance to gaming manager.

Important Qualities

Communication skills. Gaming services workers must explain the rules of the game to customers and answer any questions

Gaming Services Workers
Median annual wages, May 2019

Total, all occupations	$39,810
Gaming services workers	$23,520
Entertainment attendants and related workers	$23,260

Note: All Occupations includes all occupations in the U.S. Economy.
Source: U.S. Bureau of Labor Statistics, Occupational Employment Statistics.

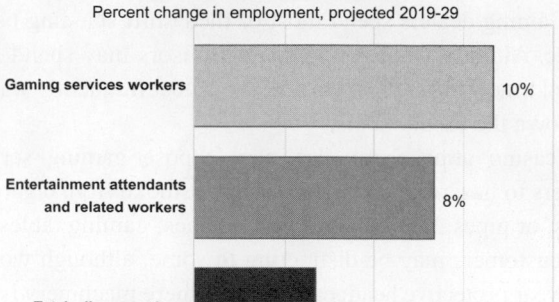

Gaming Services Workers
Percent change in employment, projected 2019-29

Gaming services workers	10%
Entertainment attendants and related workers	8%
Total, all occupations	4%

Note: All Occupations includes all occupations in the U.S. Economy.
Source: U.S. Bureau of Labor Statistics, Employment Projections program.

they have. Simple misunderstandings can cost a customer a lot of money and damage the reputation of the casino.

Customer-service skills. All gaming jobs involve a lot of interaction with customers. The success or failure of a casino depends on how customers view the casino, making customer service important for all gaming services occupations.

Leadership skills. Gaming managers and supervisors oversee other gaming services workers and must guide them in doing their jobs and developing their skills.

Math skills. Because they deal with large amounts of money, many casino workers must be good at math.

Organizational skills. Gaming managers and supervisors must be well organized to handle administrative and other tasks required in overseeing gaming services workers.

Patience. All gaming services workers must keep their composure when they handle a customer who becomes upset or breaks a rule. They also must be patient in dealing with equipment failures or malfunctions.

Pay

The median annual wage for gaming services workers was $23,520 in May 2019. The median wage is the wage at which half the workers in an occupation earned more than that amount and half earned less. The lowest 10 percent earned less than $17,270, and the highest 10 percent earned more than $58,930.

Median annual wages for gaming services workers in May 2019 were as follows:

Gambling managers	$74,970
First-line supervisors of gambling services workers	50,710
Gambling service workers, all other	28,300
Gambling and sports book writers and runners	24,750
Gambling dealers	21,260

In May 2019, the median annual wages for gaming services workers in the top industries in which they worked were as follows:

Spectator sports	$25,050
Local government, excluding education and hospitals	25,000

Most casinos are open 24 hours a day, 7 days a week. Employees are often scheduled to work nights, weekends, and holidays, which are typically the busiest times for casinos.

Job Outlook

Employment of gaming services workers is projected to grow 10 percent from 2019 to 2029, much faster than the average for all occupations. Growth will vary by detailed occupation (see table). Because gambling managers is a small occupation, however, the fast growth will result in only about 500 new jobs over the 10-year period.

Employment will be driven by the increasing popularity of gambling establishments. Additional states currently without commercial gaming establishments may allow new casinos to be built over the next decade in an effort to bring in more tax revenue.

As more states approve expansions in the number of gaming establishments, the competition for customers will increase. Those establishments that fail to keep or attract customers may close, thereby negating some of the jobs created from new casinos.

Job Prospects

Although jobs are expected to open as workers leave the occupation, strong competition is expected for jobs at casinos. Those with work experience in customer service at a hotel or resort should have better job prospects because of the importance of customer service in casinos.

Those already with a gaming license and knowledge and training in different casino games will have the best job prospects.

Occupational Title	SOC Code	Employment, 2019	Projected Employment, 2029	Change, 2019-29	
				Percent	Numeric
SOURCE: U.S. Bureau of Labor Statistics, Employment Projections program					
Gaming services workers	—	187,300	206,300	10	19,000
Gambling managers	11-9071	5,100	5,600	9	500
First-line supervisors of gambling services workers	39-1013	58,000	67,500	16	9,500
Gambling dealers	39-3011	102,900	110,700	8	7,900
Gambling and sports book writers and runners	39-3012	10,400	10,800	4	400
Gambling service workers, all other	39-3019	10,900	11,600	7	700

Employment projections data for gaming services workers, 2019-29

State & Area Data
Occupational Employment Statistics (OES)
The Occupational Employment Statistics (OES) program produces employment and wage estimates annually for over 800 occupations. These estimates are available for the nation as a whole, for individual states, and for metropolitan and nonmetropolitan areas.

Contacts for More Information
For more information about gaming services workers, visit
➤ American Gaming Association
➤ Casino Careers

Manicurists and Pedicurists

Summary

Quick Facts: Manicurists and Pedicurists

2019 Median Pay	$25,770 per year $12.39 per hour
Typical Entry-Level Education	Postsecondary non-degree award
Work Experience in a Related Occupation	None
On-the-job Training	None
Number of Jobs, 2019	155,300
Job Outlook, 2019-29	19% (Much faster than average)
Employment Change, 2019-29	29,900

What Manicurists and Pedicurists Do
Manicurists and pedicurists clean, shape, and beautify fingernails and toenails.

Work Environment
Manicurists and pedicurists usually work in a nail salon, spa, or hair salon. The job involves a lot of sitting. Those who own a mobile grooming company travel to their clients' locations.

How to Become a Manicurist or Pedicurist
Manicurists and pedicurists must complete a state-approved cosmetology or nail technician program and then pass a state exam for licensure, which all states except Connecticut require.

Pay
The median hourly wage for manicurists and pedicurists was $12.39 in May 2019.

Manicurists and pedicurists clean, shape, and beautify fingernails and toenails.

Job Outlook
Employment of manicurists and pedicurists is projected to grow 19 percent from 2019 to 2029, much faster than the average for all occupations. New types of nail services, such as mini-sessions and mobile manicures and pedicures, may drive employment growth.

State & Area Data
Explore resources for employment and wages by state and area for manicurists and pedicurists.

What Manicurists and Pedicurists Do
Manicurists and pedicurists clean, shape, and beautify fingernails and toenails.

Duties
Manicurists and pedicurists typically do the following:

Manicurists and pedicurists polish or buff nails.

- Discuss nail treatments and services available
- Remove nail polish
- Clean, trim, and file nails
- Reduce calluses and rough skin
- Massage and moisturize hands (for a manicure) and feet (for a pedicure)
- Polish or buff nails
- Advise clients about nail and skin care for hands and feet
- Promote and sell nail and skin care products
- Clean and disinfect their work area and tools

Manicurists and pedicurists work exclusively on the hands and feet, providing treatments to groom fingernails and toenails. A typical treatment involves soaking the clients' hands or feet to soften the skin in order to remove dead skin cells. Manicurists and pedicurists apply lotion to the hands and feet to moisturize the skin. They also may shape and apply polish to artificial fingernails.

Manicurists and pedicurists use a variety of tools, including nail clippers, nail files, and specialized cuticle tools. They must be focused while they perform their duties, because most of the tools they use are sharp. Keeping their tools clean and sanitary is important.

Some manicurists and pedicurists operate their own nail salon, which requires performing business tasks such as keeping inventory records and ordering supplies. They also hire and supervise workers and sell nail care products, such as nail polish and hand or foot cream. A small but growing number of workers make house calls. Mobile manicure and pedicure services are popular because clients consider them convenient.

Work Environment

Manicurists and pedicurists held about 155,300 jobs in 2019. The largest employers of manicurists and pedicurists were as follows:

Personal care services	70%
Self-employed workers	27

Manicurists and pedicurists usually work in a nail salon, spa, or hair salon. The job involves a lot of sitting. Manicurists and pedicurists who provide mobile services may travel to their clients' locations.

Manicurists and pedicurists use chemicals when working on fingernails and toenails, so they often wear protective clothing, including protective gloves and masks.

Work Schedules

Although most manicurists and pedicurists work full time, many have variable schedules and work part time. Schedules may vary according to the type of establishment. For example, a full-service salon may require manicurists and pedicurists to work an 8-hour day. However, a boutique hair salon may require fewer work hours on a part-time basis. Longer work days are not unusual for self-employed workers. Weekends and evenings tend to be the busiest times for manicurists and pedicurists.

How to Become a Manicurist or Pedicurist

Manicurists and pedicurists must complete a state-approved cosmetology or nail technician program and then pass a state exam for licensure, which all states except Connecticut require.

Manicurists and pedicurists work in spas or nail salons, and often sit for long periods.

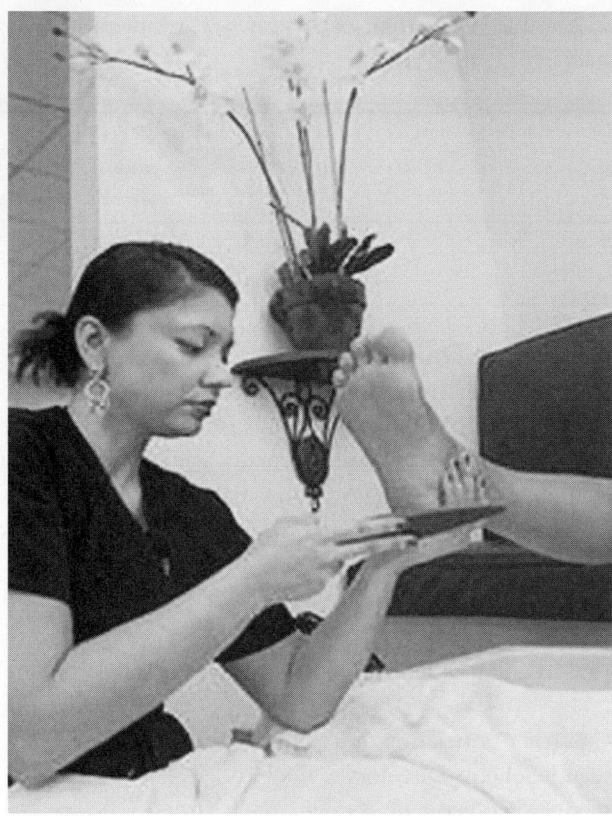

Manicurists and pedicurists must pass a state-approved cosmetology program before licensure.

Education

Manicurists and pedicurists must complete a state-approved cosmetology or nail technician program. Currently, there are hundreds of programs nationwide.

Licenses, Certifications, and Registrations

State licensing requirements vary. However, applicants need to be at least 16 years old and have a high school diploma or the equivalent. After completing a state-approved cosmetology or nail technician program, manicurists and pedicurists must take a written exam and a practical exam to get a license through their state board. Mobile manicure and pedicure services require a separate license.

The National–Interstate Council of State Boards of Cosmetology provides information on state examinations for licensing, with sample questions. The Professional Beauty Association and the American Association of Cosmetology Schools also provide information on state examinations, as well as offering other professional links.

Important Qualities

Business skills. Manicurists and pedicurist who run their own nail salon must understand general business principles. For example, they should be skilled at administrative tasks, such as accounting and personnel management, and be able to manage a salon efficiently and profitably.

Creativity. The ability to neatly finish small, intricate designs is important, as is the ability to suggest nail designs and match them to individual tastes.

Customer-service skills. Good listening and interpersonal skills are important in working with clients. Also, meeting the needs of clients, including interacting with them while doing a manicure or pedicure, encourages repeat business.

Dexterity. A steady hand is essential in achieving a creative and precise nail design. In addition, because manicurists and pedicurists often use sharp tools, they must have good finger dexterity.

Pay

The median hourly wage for manicurists and pedicurists was $12.39 in May 2019. The median wage is the wage at which half the workers in an occupation earned more than that amount and half earned less. The lowest 10 percent earned less than $9.73, and the highest 10 percent earned more than $17.66.

In May 2019, the median hourly wages for manicurists and pedicurists in the top industries in which they worked were as follows:

Personal care services.. $12.40

Although most manicurists and pedicurists work full time, some have variable schedules and work part time. Schedules may vary according to the type of establishment. For example, a full-service salon may require manicurists and pedicurists to work an 8-hour day. However, a boutique hair salon may require fewer work hours on a part-time basis. Longer work days are not unusual for self-employed workers. Weekends and evenings tend to be the busiest times for manicurists and pedicurists.

Job Outlook

Employment of manicurists and pedicurists is projected to grow 19 percent from 2019 to 2029, much faster than the average for all occupations.

Manicurists and Pedicurists
Median hourly wages, May 2019

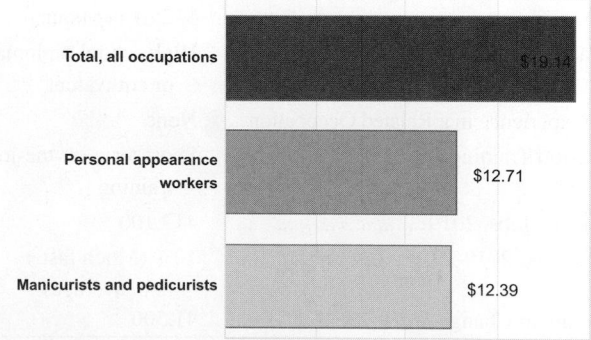

Total, all occupations	$19.14
Personal appearance workers	$12.71
Manicurists and pedicurists	$12.39

Note: All Occupations includes all occupations in the U.S. Economy.
Source: U.S. Bureau of Labor Statistics, Occupational Employment Statistics.

Manicurists and Pedicurists
Percent change in employment, projected 2019-29

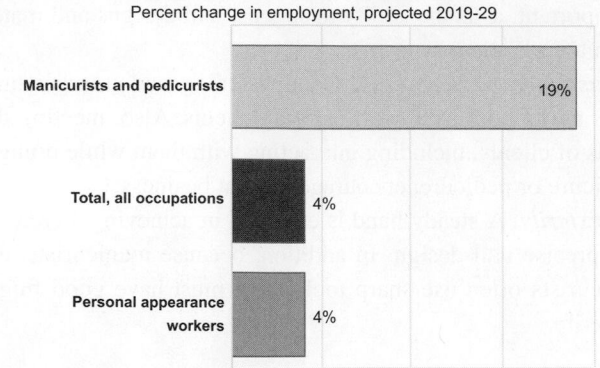

Note: All Occupations includes all occupations in the U.S. Economy.
Source: U.S. Bureau of Labor Statistics, Employment Projections program.

The projected increase in employment reflects demand for new types of nail services, such as mini-sessions (quick manicures at a low cost) and mobile manicures and pedicures (nail services offered outside of the salon).

The desire among many women and a growing number of men to lead a healthier lifestyle through better grooming and wellness also should result in higher employment for manicurists and pedicurists.

Considered a low-cost luxury service, manicures and pedicures will continue to be in demand by individuals at all income levels.

Job Prospects

Job opportunities should be very good overall. The growing number of nail salons and the need to replace workers who leave the occupation each year will result in many job openings.

Employment projections data for manicurists and pedicurists, 2019-29					
Occupational Title	SOC Code	Employment, 2019	Projected Employment, 2029	Change, 2019-29	
				Percent	Numeric
SOURCE: U.S. Bureau of Labor Statistics, Employment Projections program					
Manicurists and pedicurists	39-5092	155,300	185,200	19	29,900

State & Area Data
Occupational Employment Statistics (OES)

The Occupational Employment Statistics (OES) program produces employment and wage estimates annually for over 800 occupations. These estimates are available for the nation as a whole, for individual states, and for metropolitan and nonmetropolitan areas.

Contacts for More Information

For information about training and cosmetology schools, visit
➤ American Association of Cosmetology Schools
➤ Beauty Schools Directory
➤ International Pedicure Association

For information about state licensing, practice exams, and other professional links, visit
➤ National–Interstate Council of State Boards of Cosmetology
➤ Professional Beauty Association

Recreation Workers

Summary

Quick Facts: Recreation Workers

2019 Median Pay	$26,350 per year $12.67 per hour
Typical Entry-Level Education	High school diploma or equivalent
Work Experience in a Related Occupation	None
On-the-job Training	Short-term on-the-job training
Number of Jobs, 2019	417,100
Job Outlook, 2019-29	10% (Much faster than average)
Employment Change, 2019-29	41,500

What Recreation Workers Do

Recreation workers design and lead activities to help people stay active, improve fitness, and have fun.

Work Environment

Recreation workers are employed in a variety of settings, including recreation centers, parks, summer camps, and nursing and

Recreation workers may lead children in nature study activities at a day camp.

residential care facilities. Many workers spend much of their time being physically active in the outdoors.

How to Become a Recreation Worker

Education and training requirements for recreation workers vary with the type of job, but workers typically need at least a high school diploma or the equivalent and a few weeks of on-the-job training.

Pay

The median annual wage for recreation workers was $26,350 in May 2019.

Job Outlook

Employment of recreation workers is projected to grow 10 percent from 2019 to 2029, much faster than the average for all occupations. As more emphasis is placed on the importance of lifelong well-being, more recreation workers will be needed to work with children and adults in a variety of settings.

State & Area Data

Explore resources for employment and wages by state and area for recreation workers.

What Recreation Workers Do

Recreation workers design and lead activities to help people stay active, improve fitness, and have fun. They work with groups in summer camps, fitness and recreational sports centers, nursing care facilities, nature parks, and other settings. They may lead such activities as arts and crafts, sports, music, dramatics, or games.

Duties

Recreation workers typically do the following:

- Plan, organize, and lead activities for groups or recreation centers

- Explain the rules of activities and instruct participants at a variety of skill levels
- Enforce safety rules to prevent injury
- Modify activities to suit the needs of specific groups, such as seniors
- Administer basic first aid if needed
- Organize and set up the equipment that is used in recreational activities

The specific responsibilities of recreation workers vary greatly with their job title, their level of training, and the state they work in.

The following are examples of types of recreation workers:

Activity specialists provide instruction and coaching primarily in one activity, such as dance, swimming, or tennis. These workers may work in camps, aquatic centers, or anywhere else where there is interest in a single activity.

Recreation leaders are responsible for a recreation program's daily operation. They primarily organize and direct participants, schedule the use of facilities, set up and keep records of equipment use, and ensure that recreation facilities and equipment are used and maintained properly. They may lead classes and provide instruction in a recreational activity, such as kayaking or golf.

Camp counselors work directly with youths in residential (overnight) or day camps. They often lead and instruct children and teenagers in a variety of outdoor activities, such as swimming, hiking, horseback riding, or nature study. Counselors also provide guidance and supervise daily living and socialization. Some counselors may specialize in a specific activity, such as archery, boating, music, drama, or gymnastics.

Work Environment

Recreation workers held about 417,100 jobs in 2019. The largest employers of recreation workers were as follows:

Local government, excluding education and hospitals...... 28%

Recreation workers lead groups in activities such as arts and crafts.

Activity specialists who teach dance usually provide instruction indoors.

Many workers spend much of their time outdoors. Others provide instruction indoors, for activities such as dance or karate. Still others typically spend most of their time in an office, planning programs and special events.

Recreation workers may face some injury risk while participating in physical activities.

Work Schedules

Many recreation workers, such as camp counselors or activity specialists, work weekends or part-time or irregular hours, or may be seasonally employed. Seasonal workers may work as few as 90 days or as long as 9 months during a season, depending on where they are employed and the type of activity they lead. For example, in areas of the United States that have warm winters, outdoor swimming pools may employ related recreation workers for a majority of the year. In other areas of the country, they may work only during the summer.

How to Become a Recreation Worker

Education and training requirements for recreation workers vary with the type of job, but workers typically need at least a high school diploma or the equivalent and receive on-the-job training.

Education and Training

Recreation workers typically need at least a high school diploma or the equivalent. Many receive on-the-job training that typically lasts less than a month.

Entry-level educational requirements vary with the type of position. For example, an activity leader position working with the elderly will have different requirements than a position as a summer camp counselor working with children.

Recreation workers maintain order and safety.

Some positions may require a bachelor's degree or college coursework. In 2017, the Council on Accreditation of Parks, Recreation, Tourism, and Related Professions, a branch of the National Recreation and Park Association (NRPA), accredited more than 70 bachelor's degree programs in recreation or leisure studies. A bachelor's degree in other subjects, such as liberal arts or public administration, may also qualify applicants for some positions.

Important Qualities

Communication skills. Recreation workers must be able to communicate well. They often work with large groups of people and need to give clear instructions, motivate participants, and maintain order and safety.

Flexibility. Recreation workers must be flexible when planning activities. They must be able to adapt plans to suit changing environmental conditions and participants' needs.

Leadership skills. Recreation workers should be able to lead both large and small groups. They often lead activities for people of all ages and abilities.

Physical strength. Most recreation workers should be physically fit. Their job may require a considerable amount of movement because they often demonstrate activities while explaining them.

Problem-solving skills. Recreation workers need strong problem-solving skills. They must be able to create and reinvent activities and programs for all types of participants.

For recreation workers who generally work part time, such as camp counselors and activity specialists, certain qualities may be more important than education. These qualities include a worker's experience leading activities, the ability to work well with children or the elderly, and the ability to ensure the safety of participants.

Licenses, Certifications, and Registrations

The NRPA offers four certifications for recreation workers:

- Certified Parks and Recreation Professional (CPRP)
- Certified Parks and Recreation Executive (CPRE)
- Aquatic Facility Operator (AFO)
- Certified Playground Safety Inspector (CPSI)

Applicants may qualify for certification with different combinations of education and work experience. They also must take continuing education classes to maintain their certification.

The American Camp Association offers certificates for various levels of camp staff, including Entry-Level Program Staff Certificate and Camp Director Certificate. Individuals who complete online courses may show their advanced level of knowledge of core competencies.

Some recreation jobs require other kinds of certification. For example, first aid and CPR (cardiopulmonary resuscitation) certifications may be required for leading camp or sports activities. These certifications are available from organizations such as the American Heart Association or the American Red Cross.

Jobs for recreation workers may also require a valid driver's license and the ability to pass a background check.

Specific requirements vary by job and employer.

Advancement

As workers gain experience, they may be promoted to positions with greater responsibilities. Recreation workers with experience and managerial skills may advance to supervisory or managerial positions. Eventually, they may become directors of a recreation department or may start their own recreation company.

Pay

The median annual wage for recreation workers was $26,350 in May 2019. The median wage is the wage at which half the workers in an occupation earned more than that amount and half earned less. The lowest 10 percent earned less than $18,860, and the highest 10 percent earned more than $44,000.

In May 2019, the median annual wages for recreation workers in the top industries in which they worked were as follows:

Nursing and residential care facilities......................... $28,460

Social assistance 27,700

Local government, excluding education and   25,680
   hospitals..

Religious, grantmaking, civic, professional, and   25,440
   similar organizations ....

Many recreation workers, such as camp counselors or activity specialists, work weekends or part-time or irregular hours, or may be seasonally employed. Seasonal workers may work as few as 90 days or as long as 9 months during a season, depending on where they are employed and the type of activity they lead. For example, in areas of the United States that have warm winters, outdoor swimming pools may employ related

Recreation Workers
Median annual wages, May 2019

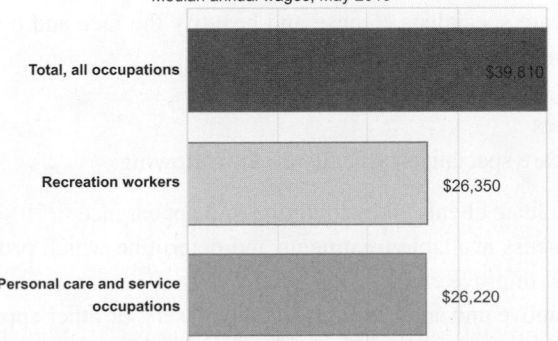

Note: All Occupations includes all occupations in the U.S. Economy.
Source: U.S. Bureau of Labor Statistics, Occupational Employment Statistics.

Recreation Workers
Percent change in employment, projected 2019-29

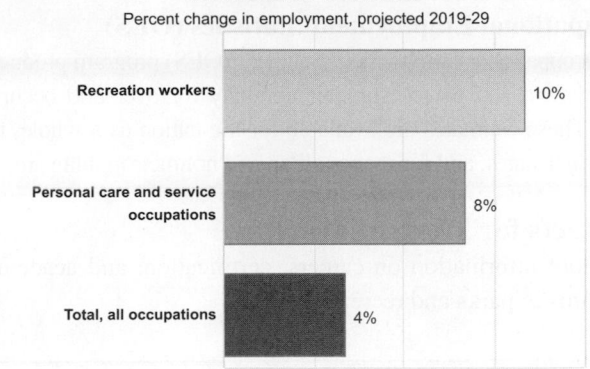

Note: All Occupations includes all occupations in the U.S. Economy.
Source: U.S. Bureau of Labor Statistics, Employment Projections program.

recreation workers for a majority of the year. In other areas of the country, they may work only during the summer.

Job Outlook

Employment of recreation workers is projected to grow 10 percent from 2019 to 2029, much faster than the average for all occupations. As more emphasis is placed on the importance of lifelong well-being, more recreation workers will be needed to work with children and adults in a variety of settings.

Additional recreation workers are expected to be needed to work for fitness and recreational sports centers, youth centers, sports clubs, and other for- and not-for-profit organizations because some parks and recreation departments may seek to cut costs by contracting out the services of activity specialists.

In addition, as the baby-boom generation grows older, there will be more demand for recreation workers to work with older clients, especially in continuing care retirement communities and assisted living facilities for the elderly.

Job Prospects

Job prospects will be best for those seeking part-time, seasonal, or temporary recreation jobs. Because workers in these jobs tend to be students or young people, they must be replaced when they leave for school or jobs in other occupations, thus creating many job openings.

Workers with higher levels of formal education related to recreation should have better prospects at getting year-round full-time positions. Volunteer experience, part-time work during school, and a summer job also are viewed favorably for both full- and part-time positions.

Employment projections data for recreation workers, 2019-29					
Occupational Title	SOC Code	Employment, 2019	Projected Employment, 2029	Change, 2019-29	
				Percent	Numeric
SOURCE: U.S. Bureau of Labor Statistics, Employment Projections program					
Recreation workers	39-9032	417,100	458,700	10	41,500

State & Area Data
Occupational Employment Statistics (OES)
The Occupational Employment Statistics (OES) program produces employment and wage estimates annually for over 800 occupations. These estimates are available for the nation as a whole, for individual states, and for metropolitan and nonmetropolitan areas.

Contacts for More Information
For more information on careers, certification, and academic programs in parks and recreation, visit

➤ National Recreation and Park Association

For more information about a career as a camp counselor, visit
➤ American Camp Association

For more information on first aid and CPR certifications, visit
➤ American Heart Association
➤ American Red Cross

Skincare Specialists

Summary

Quick Facts: Skincare Specialists

2019 Median Pay	$34,090 per year $16.39 per hour
Typical Entry-Level Education	Postsecondary non-degree award
Work Experience in a Related Occupation	None
On-the-job Training	None
Number of Jobs, 2019	78,600
Job Outlook, 2019-29	17% (Much faster than average)
Employment Change, 2019-29	13,100

What Skincare Specialists Do
Skincare specialists cleanse and beautify the face and body to enhance a person's appearance.

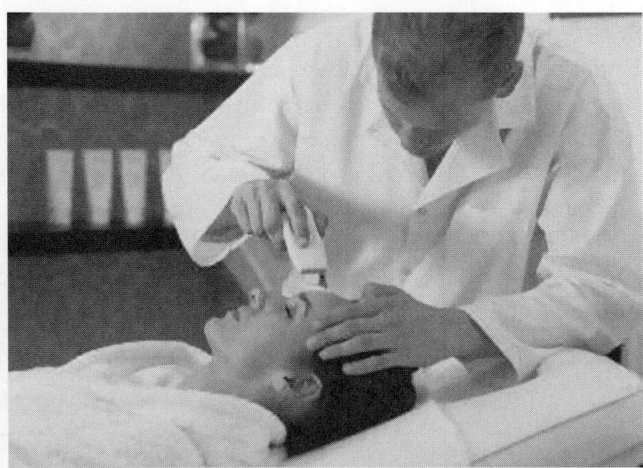

Skincare specialists provide treatments, such as peels, masks, or scrubs, to remove dead or dry skin.

Work Environment
Skincare specialists usually work in salons and beauty and health spas, and some are self-employed. Although most work full time, many work evenings and weekends.

How to Become a Skincare Specialist
Skincare specialists must complete a state-approved cosmetology or esthetician program and then pass a state exam for licensure, which all states except Connecticut require.

Pay
The median hourly wage for skincare specialists was $16.39 in May 2019.

Job Outlook
Employment of skincare specialists is projected to grow 17 percent from 2019 to 2029, much faster than the average for all occupations. The desire among many women and a growing number of men to reduce the effects of aging will result in employment growth. Good job opportunities are expected.

State & Area Data
Explore resources for employment and wages by state and area for skincare specialists.

What Skincare Specialists Do
Skincare specialists cleanse and beautify the face and body to enhance a person's appearance.

Duties
Skincare specialists typically do the following:

- Evaluate clients' skin condition and appearance
- Discuss available treatments and determine which products will improve clients' skin quality
- Remove unwanted hair, using wax, lasers, or other approved treatments

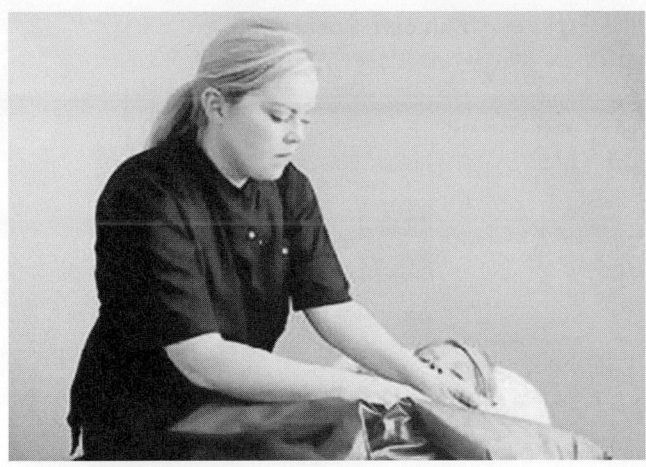

Skincare specialists remove unwanted hair using wax or laser treatment.

- Clean the skin before applying makeup
- Recommend skin care products, such as cleansers, lotions, or creams
- Teach and advise clients on how to apply makeup, and how to take care of their skin
- Refer clients to another skincare specialist, such as a dermatologist, for serious skin problems
- Disinfect equipment and clean work areas

Skincare specialists give facials, full-body treatments, and head and neck massages to improve the health and appearance of the skin. Some may provide other skin care treatments, such as peels, masks, and scrubs, to remove dead or dry skin.

In addition, skincare specialists create daily skincare routines for clients based on skin analysis and help them understand which skincare products will work best for them. A growing number of specialists actively sell skincare products, such as cleansers, lotions, and creams.

Those who operate their own salons have managerial duties that include hiring, firing, and supervising workers, as well as keeping business and inventory records, ordering supplies, and arranging for advertising.

Work Environment

Skincare specialists held about 78,600 jobs in 2019. The largest employers of skincare specialists were as follows:

Personal care services	48%
Self-employed workers	27
Health and personal care stores	8
Offices of physicians	8
Traveler accommodation	3

Skincare specialists usually work in salons and beauty and health spas. Some work in medical offices. Skincare specialists may have to stand for extended periods of time.

Because skincare specialists must evaluate the condition of the skin, good lighting and clean surroundings are important. Protective clothing and good ventilation also may be necessary, because skincare specialists often use chemicals on the face and body.

Work Schedules

Skincare specialists typically work full time, and many work evenings and weekends. Working more than 40 hours a week is common.

How to Become a Skincare Specialist

Skincare specialists must complete a state-approved cosmetology or esthetician program and then pass a state exam for licensure, which all states except Connecticut require.

Education

Skincare specialists typically complete a state-approved cosmetology or esthetician program. Although some high schools offer vocational training, most people receive their training from

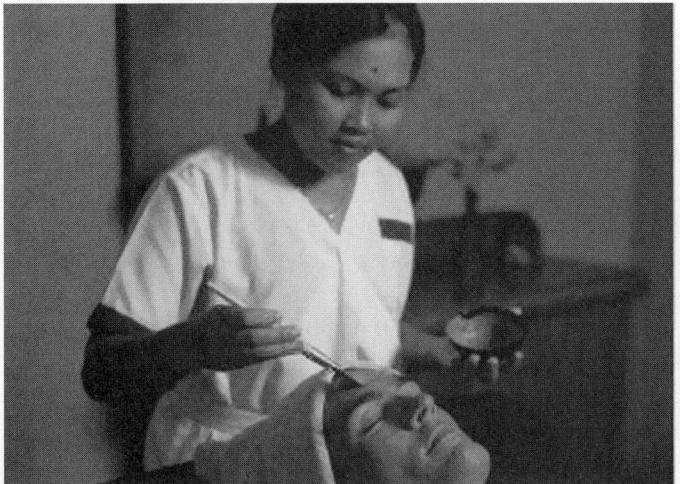

Skincare specialists work in salons, beauty spas, and sometimes in medical offices.

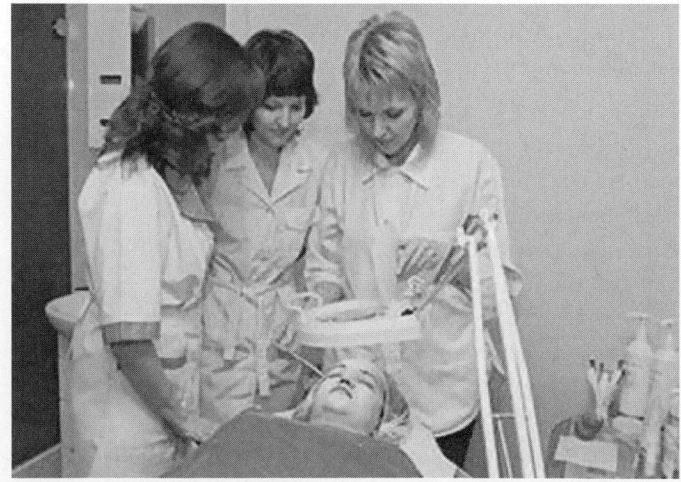

Skincare specialists must pass a state-approved cosmetology program before getting licensed.

Skincare Specialists
Median hourly wages, May 2019

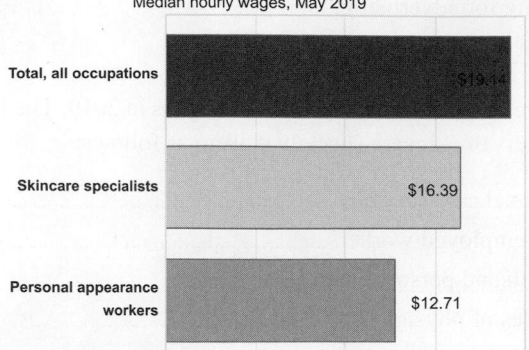

Total, all occupations $19.14

Skincare specialists $16.39

Personal appearance workers $12.71

Note: All Occupations includes all occupations in the U.S. Economy.
Source: U.S. Bureau of Labor Statistics, Occupational Employment
Statistics.

Skincare Specialists
Percent change in employment, projected 2019-29

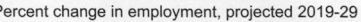
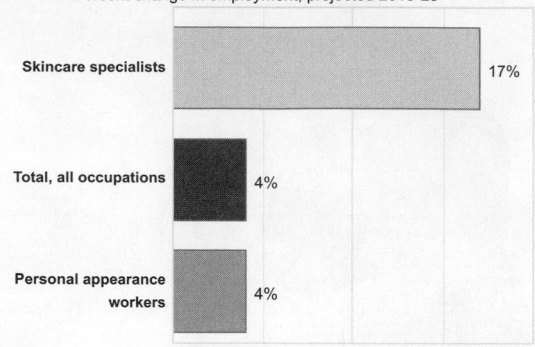

Skincare specialists   17%

Total, all occupations   4%

Personal appearance workers   4%

Note: All Occupations includes all occupations in the U.S. Economy.
Source: U.S. Bureau of Labor Statistics, Employment Projections
program.

a postsecondary vocational school. The Associated Skin Care Professionals organization offers a State Regulation Guide, which includes the number of prerequisite hours required to complete a cosmetology program.

Licenses, Certifications, and Registrations

After completing an approved cosmetology or esthetician program, skincare specialists take a written and practical exam to get a state license. Licensing requirements vary by state, so those interested should contact their state board.

The National-Interstate Council of State Boards of Cosmetology provides contact information on state examinations for licensing, with sample exam questions. The Professional Beauty Association and the American Association of Cosmetology Schools also provide information on state examinations, and offer other professional links.

Many states offer continuing education seminars and programs designed to keep skincare specialists current on new techniques and products. Post-licensing training is also available through manufacturers, associations, and at trade shows.

Important Qualities

Business skills. Skincare specialists who run their own salon must understand general business principles. For example, they should be skilled at administrative tasks, such as accounting and personnel management, and be able to manage a salon efficiently and profitably.

Customer-service skills. Skincare specialists should be friendly and courteous to their clients. Repeat business is important, particularly for self-employed workers.

Initiative. Self-employed skincare specialists generate their own business opportunities and must be proactive in finding new clients.

Physical stamina. Skincare specialists must be able to spend most of their day standing and massaging clients' faces and bodies.

Tidiness. Workers must keep a neat personal appearance and keep their work area clean and sanitary. This requirement is necessary for the health and safety of their clients and increases the likelihood that clients will return.

Time-management skills. Time-management skills are important in scheduling appointments and providing services.

Pay

The median hourly wage for skincare specialists was $16.39 in May 2019. The median wage is the wage at which half the workers in an occupation earned more than that amount and half earned less. The lowest 10 percent earned less than $9.85, and the highest 10 percent earned more than $30.07.

In May 2019, the median hourly wages for skincare specialists in the top industries in which they worked were as follows:

Offices of physicians	$19.80
Personal care services	15.94
Health and personal care stores	15.18
Traveler accommodation	13.67

Skincare specialists typically work full time, and many work evenings and weekends. Working more than 40 hours a week is common.

Job Outlook

Employment of skincare specialists is projected to grow 17 percent from 2019 to 2029, much faster than the average for all occupations.

The projected increase in employment reflects demand for services being offered, such as mini-sessions (quick facials at a lower cost) and mobile facials (making house calls) directly from skincare specialists rather than hairdressers, hairstylists, and cosmetologists. Employment growth also should result from the desire among many women and a growing number of men who seek out skincare services to reduce the effects of aging, to look good on social media platforms, and to lead a healthier lifestyle through better grooming.

Job Prospects

Job opportunities should be good because of the growing number of beauty salons and spas. Those with related work experience should have the best job opportunities.

Occupational Title	SOC Code	Employment, 2019	Projected Employment, 2029	Change, 2019-29	
				Percent	Numeric
Skincare specialists	39-5094	78,600	91,600	17	13,100

Employment projections data for skincare specialists, 2019-29

SOURCE: U.S. Bureau of Labor Statistics, Employment Projections program

State & Area Data
Occupational Employment Statistics (OES)

The Occupational Employment Statistics (OES) program produces employment and wage estimates annually for over 800 occupations. These estimates are available for the nation as a whole, for individual states, and for metropolitan and nonmetropolitan areas.

Contacts for More Information

For information about skincare specialists, visit
➤ Associated Skin Care Professionals

For information about education and cosmetology schools, visit
➤ American Association of Cosmetology Schools
➤ Beauty Schools Directory

For information about the spa industry, visit
➤ International Spa Association

For information about state licensing, practice exams, and other professional links, visit
➤ National-Interstate Council of State Boards of Cosmetology
➤ Professional Beauty Association

Production

Assemblers and Fabricators

Summary

Quick Facts: Assemblers and Fabricators

2019 Median Pay	$33,710 per year $16.21 per hour
Typical Entry-Level Education	High school diploma or equivalent
Work Experience in a Related Occupation	None
On-the-job Training	Moderate-term on-the-job training
Number of Jobs, 2019	1,883,700
Job Outlook, 2019-29	-11% (Decline)
Employment Change, 2019-29	-204,300

What Assemblers and Fabricators Do
Assemblers and fabricators assemble finished products and the parts that go into them.

Work Environment
Most assemblers and fabricators work in manufacturing plants. Some of the work may involve long periods of standing or sitting. Most work full time, and they sometimes work evenings and weekends.

How to Become an Assembler or Fabricator
The education level and qualifications needed to enter these jobs varies with the industry and employer. Although a high school diploma is enough for most jobs, experience and additional training are needed for more advanced assembly work.

Pay
The median annual wage for assemblers and fabricators was $33,710 in May 2019.

Job Outlook
Overall employment of assemblers and fabricators is projected to decline 11 percent from 2019 to 2029. However, many openings are expected each year because of the need to replace workers who leave the occupation.

State & Area Data
Explore resources for employment and wages by state and area for assemblers and fabricators.

What Assemblers and Fabricators Do
Assemblers and fabricators assemble finished products and the parts that go into them. They use tools, machines, and their hands to make engines, computers, aircraft, ships, boats, toys, electronic devices, control panels, and more.

Duties
Assemblers and fabricators typically do the following:

- Read and understand schematics and blueprints
- Position or align components and parts either manually or with hoists
- Use hand tools or machines to assemble parts
- Conduct quality control checks
- Clean and maintain work area, tools, and other equipment

Assemblers and fabricators have an important role in the manufacturing process. They assemble both finished products

Assemblers and fabricators assemble both finished products and the parts that go into them.

Assemblers and fabricators conduct quality checks for faulty components or mistakes in the assembly process.

and the pieces that go into them. The products encompass a full range of manufactured goods, including aircraft, toys, household appliances, automobiles, computers, and electronic devices.

Changes in technology have transformed the manufacturing and assembly process. Modern manufacturing systems use robots, computers, programmable motion-control devices, and various sensing technologies. These technological changes affect the way in which goods are made and the jobs of those who make them. Advanced assemblers must be able to work with these new technologies and use them to manufacture goods.

The job of an assembler or fabricator requires a range of knowledge and skills. Skilled assemblers putting together complex machines, for example, read detailed schematics that show how to assemble the machine. After determining how parts should connect, they use hand or power tools to trim, shim, cut, and make other adjustments to fit components together. Once the parts are properly aligned, they connect them with bolts and screws, or they weld or solder pieces together.

Quality control is important throughout the assembly process, so assemblers look for faulty components and mistakes in the assembly process. They help fix problems before defective products are made.

Manufacturing techniques are moving away from traditional assembly line systems toward lean manufacturing systems, which use teams of workers to produce entire products or components. Lean manufacturing has changed the nature of the assemblers' duties.

It has become more common to involve assemblers and fabricators in product development. Designers and engineers consult manufacturing workers during the design stage to improve product reliability and manufacturing efficiency. Some experienced assemblers work with designers and engineers to build prototypes or test products.

Although most assemblers and fabricators are classified as team assemblers, others specialize in producing one type of product or perform the same or similar tasks throughout the assembly process.

The following are examples of types of assemblers and fabricators:

Aircraft structure, surfaces, rigging, and systems assemblers fit, fasten, and install parts of airplanes, space vehicles, or missiles, such as the wings, fuselage, landing gear, rigging and control equipment, and heating and ventilating systems.

Coil winders, tapers, and finishers wind wire coils of electrical components used in a variety of electric and electronic products, including resistors, transformers, generators, and electric motors.

Electrical and electronic equipment assemblers build products such as electric motors, computers, electronic control devices, and sensing equipment. Automated systems have been put in place because many electronic parts are too small or fragile for human assembly. Much of the work of electrical and electronic assemblers is done by hand during the small-scale production of electronic devices used in all types of aircraft, military systems, and medical equipment. Production by hand requires these workers to use devices such as soldering irons.

Electromechanical equipment assemblers assemble and modify electromechanical devices such as household appliances, computer tomography scanners, or vending machines. The workers use a variety of tools, such as rulers, rivet guns, and soldering irons.

Engine and machine assemblers construct, assemble, and rebuild engines, turbines, and machines used in automobiles, construction and mining equipment, and power generators.

Structural metal fabricators and fitters cut, align, and fit together structural metal parts and may help weld or rivet the parts together.

Fiberglass laminators and fabricators laminate layers of fiberglass on molds to form boat decks and hulls, bodies for golf carts, automobiles, and other products.

Team assemblers work on an assembly line, but they rotate through different tasks, rather than specializing in a single task. The team may decide how the work is assigned and how different tasks are done. Some aspects of lean production, such as rotating tasks and seeking worker input on improving the assembly process, are common to all assembly and fabrication occupations.

Timing device assemblers, adjusters, and calibrators do precision assembling or adjusting of timing devices within very narrow tolerances.

Work Environment

Assemblers and fabricators held about 1.9 million jobs in 2019. Employment in the detailed occupations that make up assemblers and fabricators was distributed as follows:

Miscellaneous assemblers and fabricators 1,389,100

Electrical, electronic, and electromechanical assemblers, except coil winders, tapers, and finishers 291,700

Assemblers and fabricators work in plants and factories.

Structural metal fabricators and fitters	78,500
Engine and other machine assemblers	45,900
Aircraft structure, surfaces, rigging, and systems assemblers	43,900
Fiberglass laminators and fabricators	20,400
Coil winders, tapers, and finishers	13,000
Timing device assemblers and adjusters	1,300

The largest employers of assemblers and fabricators were as follows:

Transportation equipment manufacturing	25%
Temporary help services	12
Machinery manufacturing	10
Computer and electronic product manufacturing	9
Fabricated metal product manufacturing	8

Most assemblers and fabricators work in manufacturing plants, and working conditions vary by plant and by industry. Many physically difficult tasks, such as tightening massive bolts or moving heavy parts into position, have been automated or made easier through the use of power tools. Assembly work, however, may still involve long periods of standing, sitting, or working on ladders, such as in the shipbuilding industry.

Injuries and Illnesses
Some assemblers may come into contact with potentially harmful chemicals or fumes, but ventilation systems normally minimize any harmful effects. Other assemblers may come into contact with oil and grease, and their work areas may be noisy. Fiberglass laminators and fabricators are exposed to fiberglass, which may irritate the skin. Therefore, fiberglass workers must wear gloves and long sleeves and must use respirators for safety.

Miscellaneous assemblers and fabricators have one of the highest rates of injuries and illnesses of all occupations. ("Miscellaneous" titles represent occupations with a wide range of characteristics that do not fit into any of the other detailed occupations.)

Work Schedules
Most assemblers and fabricators are employed full time. Some assemblers and fabricators work in shifts, which may require evening, weekend, and night work.

How to Become an Assembler or Fabricator
The education level and qualifications needed to enter these jobs varies with the industry and employer. Although a high school diploma is enough for most jobs, experience and additional training are needed for more advanced assembly work.

Education
Most employers require a high school diploma or equivalent for assembler and fabricator positions.

Assemblers and fabricators usually receive training in a specialty area.

Training
Workers usually receive several months of on-the-job training, sometimes including employer-sponsored technical instruction.

Some employers may require specialized training or an associate's degree for the most skilled assembly and fabrication jobs. For example, jobs with electrical, electronic, and aircraft and motor vehicle products manufacturers typically require more formal education. Apprenticeship programs are also available.

Licenses, Certifications, and Registrations
The Fabricators & Manufacturers Association, International (FMA) offers certificates and training programs in fabrication, coil processing, and other related topics. Although not required, becoming certified can demonstrate competence and professionalism. It also may help a candidate advance in the profession.

In addition, many employers that hire electrical and electronic assembly workers, especially those employers in the aerospace and defense industries, require certifications in soldering. The Association Connecting Electronics Industries, also known as IPC, offers a number of certification programs related to electronic assembly and soldering.

Important Qualities
Color vision. Assemblers and fabricators who make electrical and electronic products must distinguish different colors, because the wires they often work with are color coded.

Dexterity. Assemblers and fabricators should have a steady hand and good hand–eye coordination, as they must grasp, manipulate, or assemble parts and components that are often very small.

Math skills. Assemblers and fabricators must know basic math and be able to use computers, because the manufacturing process continues to advance technologically.

Mechanical skills. Modern production systems require assemblers and fabricators to use programmable motion-control devices, computers, and robots on the factory floor.

Physical stamina. Assemblers and fabricators must stand for long periods and perform repetitive work.

Physical strength. Assemblers and fabricators must be strong enough to lift heavy components or pieces of machinery. Some assemblers, such as those in the aerospace industry, must frequently bend or climb ladders when assembling parts.

Technical skills. Assemblers and fabricators must understand technical manuals, blueprints, and schematics for a wide range of products and machines in order to manufacture the final product properly.

Pay

The median annual wage for assemblers and fabricators was $33,710 in May 2019. The median wage is the wage at which half the workers in an occupation earned more than that amount and half earned less. The lowest 10 percent earned less than $23,000, and the highest 10 percent earned more than $54,660.

Median annual wages for assemblers and fabricators in May 2019 were as follows:

Aircraft structure, surfaces, rigging, and systems assemblers	$54,210
Engine and other machine assemblers	45,660
Structural metal fabricators and fitters	40,390
Coil winders, tapers, and finishers	36,520
Fiberglass laminators and fabricators	35,480
Timing device assemblers and adjusters	35,080
Electrical, electronic, and electromechanical assemblers, except coil winders, tapers, and finishers	34,810
Miscellaneous assemblers and fabricators	32,350

In May 2019, the median annual wages for assemblers and fabricators in the top industries in which they worked were as follows:

Transportation equipment manufacturing	$38,820
Machinery manufacturing	36,190
Fabricated metal product manufacturing	34,640
Computer and electronic product manufacturing	34,200
Temporary help services	27,390

Wages vary by industry, geographic region, skill, education level, and complexity of the machinery operated.

Most assemblers and fabricators are employed full time and may need to work evenings and weekends.

Job Outlook

Overall employment of assemblers and fabricators is projected to decline 11 percent from 2019 to 2029.

Within the manufacturing sector, employment of assemblers and fabricators will be determined largely by the growth or decline in the production of certain manufactured goods. In general, overall employment of assemblers and fabricators is projected to decline because many manufacturing sectors are expected to become more efficient and able to produce more with fewer workers.

In most manufacturing industries, improved processes, tools, and, in some cases, automation will reduce job growth. Increasingly, new advances in robotics have enabled machinery to perform more complex and delicate tasks previously performed by workers. In addition, assemblers and fabricators are increasingly working alongside robots, also known as "collaborative robotics." These new robots can help workers perform tasks and increase efficiency. However, this increased efficiency may reduce the demand for some assemblers and fabricators.

Cheaper and more advanced robotics, along with the possibility of decreased taxes and regulations, may entice some manufacturers to bring previously offshored production back to the United States. However, the new jobs may be more highly skilled in nature and more dependent upon automated technology.

Advances in three-dimensional printing, also known as additive manufacturing, has the potential to reshape the entire manufacturing sector in the future. Entire parts or even vehicles

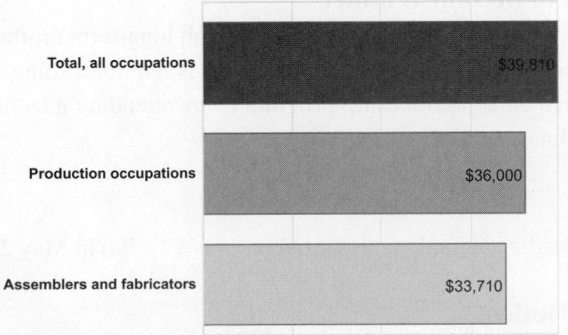

Assemblers and Fabricators

Median annual wages, May 2019

Total, all occupations — $39,810
Production occupations — $36,000
Assemblers and fabricators — $33,710

Note: All Occupations includes all occupations in the U.S. Economy.
Source: U.S. Bureau of Labor Statistics, Occupational Employment Statistics.

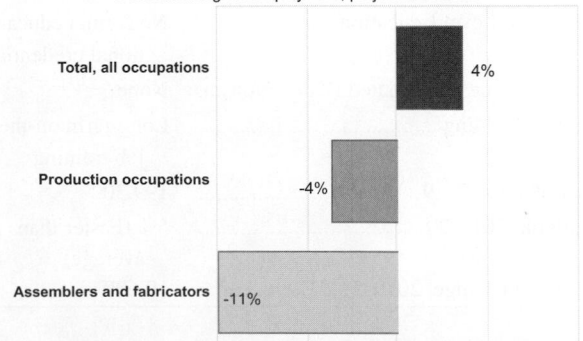

Assemblers and Fabricators

Percent change in employment, projected 2019-29

Total, all occupations — 4%
Production occupations — -4%
Assemblers and fabricators — -11%

Note: All Occupations includes all occupations in the U.S. Economy.
Source: U.S. Bureau of Labor Statistics, Employment Projections program.

might be produced in a single build that would require very little assembly or fabrication by hand. This technology is still emerging though, and may not immediately affect the demand for these workers over the next 10 years.

Job Prospects

Despite declining employment, 156,300 openings for assemblers and fabricators are projected each year, on average, over the decade.

Those openings are expected to result from the need to replace workers who transfer to other occupations or exit the labor force, such as to retire.

Qualified applicants, including those with technical vocational training and certification, are likely to have the best job opportunities.

Employment projections data for assemblers and fabricators, 2019-29					
Occupational Title	SOC Code	Employment, 2019	Projected Employment, 2029	Change, 2019-29	
				Percent	Numeric
SOURCE: U.S. Bureau of Labor Statistics, Employment Projections program					
Assemblers and fabricators	—	1,883,700	1,679,400	-11	-204,300
Aircraft structure, surfaces, rigging, and systems assemblers	51-2011	43,900	36,300	-17	-7,600
Coil winders, tapers, and finishers	51-2021	13,000	10,500	-19	-2,400
Electrical, electronic, and electromechanical assemblers, except coil winders, tapers, and finishers	51-2028	291,700	295,900	1	4,200
Engine and other machine assemblers	51-2031	45,900	39,000	-15	-7,000

Employment projections data for assemblers and fabricators, 2019-29					
Occupational Title	SOC Code	Employment, 2019	Projected Employment, 2029	Change, 2019-29	
				Percent	Numeric
Structural metal fabricators and fitters	51-2041	78,500	66,000	-16	-12,500
Fiberglass laminators and fabricators	51-2051	20,400	19,300	-5	-1,100
Timing device assemblers and adjusters	51-2061	1,300	1,000	-22	-300
Miscellaneous assemblers and fabricators	51-2090	1,389,100	1,211,500	-13	-177,600

State & Area Data

Occupational Employment Statistics (OES)

The Occupational Employment Statistics (OES) program produces employment and wage estimates annually for over 800 occupations. These estimates are available for the nation as a whole, for individual states, and for metropolitan and nonmetropolitan areas.

Contacts for More Information

For more information about assemblers and fabricators, including certification, training, and professional development, visit
➤ Fabricators & Manufacturers Association, International

For information about careers in manufacturing, visit
➤ Nuts, Bolts & Thingamajigs

For information about certifications in electronics soldering, visit:
➤ Association Connecting Electronics Industries

Bakers

Summary

Quick Facts: Bakers

2019 Median Pay	$27,700 per year $13.32 per hour
Typical Entry-Level Education	No formal educational credential
Work Experience in a Related Occupation	None
On-the-job Training	Long-term on-the-job training
Number of Jobs, 2019	199,300
Job Outlook, 2019-29	5% (Faster than average)
Employment Change, 2019-29	10,600

What Bakers Do

Bakers mix ingredients according to recipes in order to make breads, pastries, and other baked goods.

Work Environment

Most bakers work in retail or commercial bakeries (manufacturing facilities), grocery stores or wholesale club stores, and restaurants. Work shifts often include early mornings, late evenings, weekends, and holidays.

How to Become a Baker

Bakers typically learn their skills through long-term on-the-job training. Although no formal education is required, some learn through an apprenticeship program or by attending a technical or culinary school.

Pay

The median annual wage for bakers was $27,700 in May 2019.

Job Outlook

Employment of bakers is projected to grow 5 percent from 2019 to 2029, faster than the average for all occupations. Bakers with years of experience should have the best job opportunities, with

Bakers make a variety of breads and baked goods.

employment driven by the growing demand for specialty baked products.

State & Area Data

Explore resources for employment and wages by state and area for bakers.

What Bakers Do

Bakers mix ingredients according to recipes in order to make breads, pastries, and other baked goods.

Bakers prepare various types of baked goods.

Duties

Bakers typically do the following:

- Check the quality of baking ingredients
- Prepare equipment for baking
- Measure and weigh flour and other ingredients
- Combine measured ingredients in mixers or blenders
- Knead, roll, cut, and shape dough
- Place dough into pans, into molds, or onto baking sheets
- Set oven temperatures and place items into ovens or onto grills

Bakers produce various types and quantities of breads, pastries, and other baked goods sold by grocers, wholesalers, restaurants, and institutional food services.

The following are examples of types of bakers:

Commercial bakers, also called production bakers, work in manufacturing facilities that produce breads, pastries, and other baked products. In these facilities, bakers use high-volume mixing machines, ovens, and other equipment, which may be automated, to mass-produce standardized baked goods. They carefully follow instructions for production schedules and recipes.

Retail bakers work primarily in grocery stores and specialty shops, including bakeries. In these settings, they produce smaller quantities of baked goods for people to eat in the shop or for sale as specialty baked goods. Retail bakers may take orders from customers, prepare baked products to order, and occasionally serve customers. Although the quantities prepared and sold in these stores are often small, they usually come in a wide variety of flavors and sizes. Most retail bakers are also responsible for cleaning their work area and equipment and unloading supplies.

Some retail bakers own bakery shops where they make and sell breads, pastries, pies, and other baked goods. In addition to preparing the baked goods and overseeing the entire baking process, they are also responsible for hiring, training, and supervising their staff. They must budget for and order supplies, set prices, and decide how much to produce each day.

Work Environment

Bakers held about 199,300 jobs in 2019. The largest employers of bakers were as follows:

Bakeries and tortilla manufacturing	30%
Food and beverage stores	26
Restaurants and other eating places	20
Self-employed workers	6

The work can be stressful because bakers follow time-sensitive baking procedures and often work under strict deadlines. For example, bakers must follow daily production schedules to bake products in sufficient quantities while maintaining consistent quality. In manufacturing facilities, they often work with

Bakers stand for extended periods while they prepare dough.

other production workers, such as helpers and maintenance staff, so that equipment is cleaned and ready.

Bakers are exposed to high temperatures when working around hot ovens. They stand for hours at a time while observing the baking process, making the dough, or cleaning the baking equipment.

Injuries and Illnesses

Bakeries, especially large manufacturing facilities, are filled with potential dangers such as hot ovens, mixing machines, and dough cutters. Bakers must take precautions to avoid injury.

Although their work is generally safe, bakers may endure back strains caused by lifting or moving heavy bags of flour or other products. Other common risks include cuts, scrapes, and burns. To reduce these risks, bakers often wear back supports, aprons, and gloves.

Work Schedules

Some bakers work part time.

Grocery stores and restaurants sell freshly baked goods throughout the day. As a result, bakers are often scheduled to work shifts during early mornings, late evenings, weekends, and holidays.

Bakers who work in commercial bakeries that bake continuously may have to work late evenings and weekends.

How to Become a Baker

Long-term on-the-job training is the most common path to gain the skills necessary to become a baker. Some bakers start their careers through an apprenticeship program or by attending a technical or culinary school. No formal education is required.

Education

Although there are no formal education requirements to become a baker, some candidates attend a technical or culinary school. Programs generally last from 1 to 2 years and cover nutrition, food safety, and basic math. To enter these programs, candidates may be required to have a high school diploma or equivalent.

Training

Most bakers learn their skills through long-term on-the-job training, typically lasting 1 to 3 years. Some employers may provide apprenticeship programs for aspiring bakers. Bakers in specialty bakery shops and grocery stores often start as apprentices or trainees and learn the basics of baking, icing, and decorating. They usually study topics such as nutrition, sanitation procedures, and basic baking. Some participate in correspondence study and may work toward a certificate in baking.

Other Experience

Some bakers learn their skills through work experience related to baking. For example, they may start as a baker's assistant and progress into a full-fledged baker as they learn baking techniques.

Licenses, Certifications, and Registrations

Certification is voluntary and shows that a baker has the skills and knowledge to work at a retail baking establishment.

The Retail Bakers of America offers certification in four levels of competence, with a focus on several topics, including baking sanitation, management, retail sales, and staff training.

On-the-job training is the most common method of learning for bakers.

Those who wish to become certified must satisfy a combination of education and experience requirements before taking an exam.

The education and experience requirements vary by the level of certification desired. For example, a Certified Journey Baker requires no education but must have at least 1 year of work experience. A Certified Baker must have 4 years of work experience and 30 hours of sanitation coursework, and a Certified Master Baker must have 8 years of work experience, 30 hours of sanitation coursework, and 30 hours of professional development education.

Important Qualities

Communication skills. Bakers, especially retail bakers, must have good communication skills in order to deal effectively with customers.

Detail oriented. Bakers must closely monitor their products in the oven to keep them from burning. They also should have an eye for detail because many pastries and cakes require intricate decorations.

Math skills. Bakers must possess basic math skills, especially knowledge of fractions, in order to precisely mix recipes, weigh ingredients, or adjust mixes.

Physical stamina. Bakers stand on their feet for extended periods while they prepare dough, monitor baking, or package baked goods.

Physical strength. Bakers should be able to lift and carry heavy bags of flour and other ingredients, which may weigh up to 50 pounds.

Pay

The median annual wage for bakers was $27,700 in May 2019. The median wage is the wage at which half the workers in an occupation earned more than that amount and half earned less. The lowest 10 percent earned less than $20,310, and the highest 10 percent earned more than $41,640.

In May 2019, the median annual wages for bakers in the top industries in which they worked were as follows:

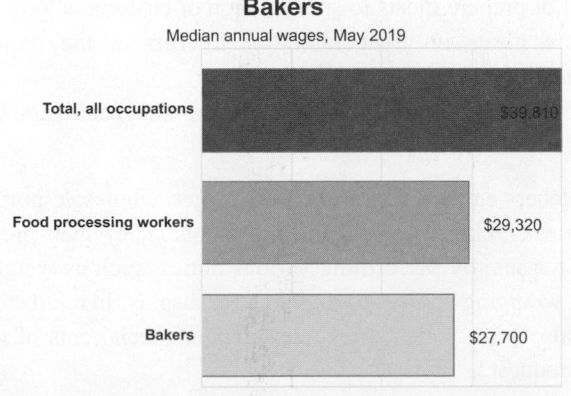

Bakers

Median annual wages, May 2019

- Total, all occupations: $39,810
- Food processing workers: $29,320
- Bakers: $27,700

Note: All Occupations includes all occupations in the U.S. Economy.
Source: U.S. Bureau of Labor Statistics, Occupational Employment Statistics.

Bakers

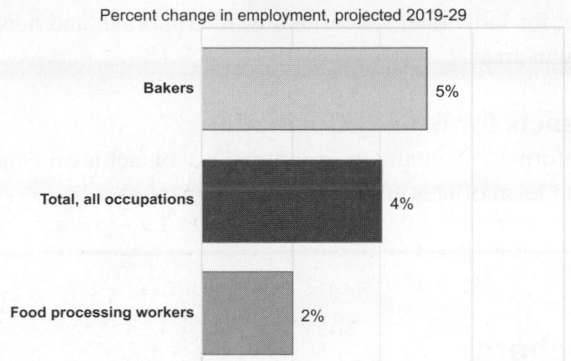

Percent change in employment, projected 2019-29

- Bakers: 5%
- Total, all occupations: 4%
- Food processing workers: 2%

Note: All Occupations includes all occupations in the U.S. Economy.
Source: U.S. Bureau of Labor Statistics, Employment Projections program.

Bakeries and tortilla manufacturing	$28,320
Food and beverage stores	27,940
Restaurants and other eating places	25,940

Some bakers work part time.

Grocery stores and restaurants, sell freshly baked goods throughout the day. As a result, bakers are often scheduled to work shifts during early mornings, late evenings, weekends, and holidays.

Bakers who work in commercial bakeries that bake continuously may have to work late evenings and weekends.

Job Outlook

Employment of bakers is projected to grow 5 percent from 2019 to 2029, faster than the average for all occupations.

Population and income growth are expected to result in greater demand for specialty baked goods, such as cupcakes, pies, and cakes, from grocery stores, retail bakeries, and restaurants.

However, employment of bakers in food manufacturing may be limited as these facilities increasingly use automated machines and equipment to mass-produce baked goods.

Job Prospects

Job opportunities are expected to be good because of the need to replace workers who leave the occupation every year.

Employment projections data for bakers, 2019-29					
Occupational Title	SOC Code	Employment, 2019	Projected Employment, 2029	Change, 2019-29	
				Percent	Numeric
SOURCE: U.S. Bureau of Labor Statistics, Employment Projections program					
Bakers	51-3011	199,300	209,900	5	10,600

State & Area Data

Occupational Employment Statistics (OES)

The Occupational Employment Statistics (OES) program produces employment and wage estimates annually for over 800

occupations. These estimates are available for the nation as a whole, for individual states, and for metropolitan and nonmetropolitan areas.

Contacts for More Information

For information about job opportunities, contact local employers and local offices of the state employment service.

For more information about certification or training programs, visit
➤ AIB International
➤ Retail Bakers of America

Butchers

Summary

Quick Facts: Butchers

2019 Median Pay	$32,500 per year $15.62 per hour
Typical Entry-Level Education	No formal educational credential
Work Experience in a Related Occupation	None
On-the-job Training	Long-term on-the-job training
Number of Jobs, 2019	137,500
Job Outlook, 2019-29	2% (Slower than average)
Employment Change, 2019-29	2,300

What Butchers Do

Butchers cut, trim, and package meat for retail sale.

Work Environment

Most butchers work in grocery stores and specialty meat shops, and some work in animal slaughtering and processing plants. The work can be physically demanding and may include exposure to repetitive motions, dangerous equipment, and cold temperatures.

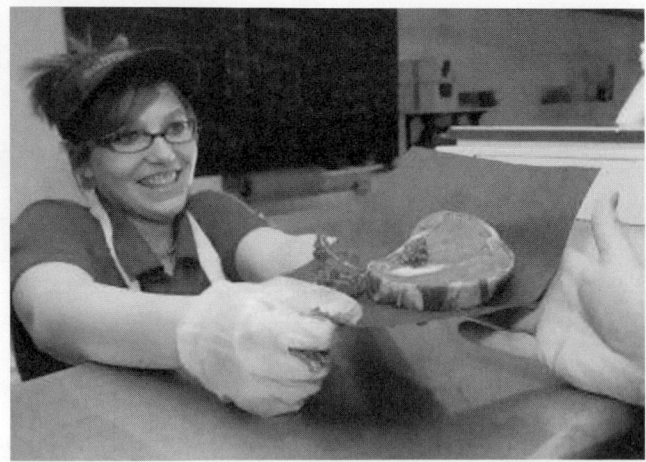

Butchers cut meat to customers' orders.

How to Become a Butcher

Butchers learn their skills on the job. No formal education is required.

Pay

The median annual wage for butchers was $32,500 in May 2019.

Job Outlook

Employment of butchers is projected to grow 2 percent from 2019 to 2029, slower than the average for all occupations. Many job openings will result from the need to replace workers who leave the occupation each year.

State & Area Data

Explore resources for employment and wages by state and area for butchers.

What Butchers Do

Butchers cut, trim, and package meat for retail sale.

Duties

Butchers typically do the following:

- Sharpen and adjust knives and cutting equipment
- Receive, inspect, and store meat upon delivery
- Cut, debone, or grind pieces of meat
- Weigh, wrap, and display meat or meat products
- Cut or prepare meats to specification or customers' orders
- Store meats in refrigerators or freezers at the required temperature
- Clean equipment and work areas to maintain health and sanitation standards

Butchers cut and trim meat from larger, wholesale portions into steaks, chops, roasts, and other cuts. They then prepare meat for sale by performing various duties, such as weighing meat, wrapping it, and putting it out for display. In retail stores, they also wait on customers and prepare special cuts of meat upon request.

Butchers in meat-processing plants are also known as **meatcutters**. They may have a more limited range of duties than those working in a grocery store or specialty meat shop.

Butchers cut meat for display and retail sale.

Because they typically work on an assembly line, those in processing plants usually perform one specific function—a single type of cut—during their shift.

Butchers use knives, grinders, or meat saws. They follow sanitation standards while working and when cleaning equipment, countertops, and working areas in order to prevent meat contamination.

Butchers who run their own retail store also track inventory, order supplies, and perform other recordkeeping duties.

Work Environment

Butchers held about 137,500 jobs in 2019. The largest employers of butchers were as follows:

Food and beverage stores	79%
Animal slaughtering and processing	7
General merchandise stores	6

The work can be physically demanding, particularly for butchers who make repetitive cuts in processing plants. Butchers typically stand while cutting meat and often lift and move heavy carcasses or boxes of meat supplies.

Because meat must be kept at cool temperatures, butchers commonly work in cold rooms—typically around 40 degrees Fahrenheit—for extended periods.

Butchers often lift and move heavy carcasses.

Butchers must keep their hands and working areas clean to prevent contamination, and those working in retail settings must remain presentable for customers.

Injuries and Illnesses

Butchers have one of the highest rates of injuries and illnesses of all occupations. These workers use tools that can be dangerous, such as sharp knives and meat saws, and work in areas with slippery floors and surfaces. To reduce the risk of cuts and falls, workers wear protective clothing, such as cut-resistant gloves, heavy aprons, and nonslip footwear.

Work Schedules

Most butchers work full time. Butchers who work in grocery or retail stores may work early mornings, late evenings, weekends, and holidays. Workers in animal slaughtering and processing facilities may work shifts that start in the early morning or in the afternoon or evening.

How to Become a Butcher

Most butchers learn their skills through on-the-job training lasting more than a year. No formal education is required.

Butchers typically learn their skills on the job.

Education

There are no formal education requirements for becoming a butcher.

Training

Butchers typically learn their skills on the job, and the length of training varies considerably. Training for simple cutting may take only a few weeks. However, more complicated cutting tasks generally require training that may last from several months to more than a year.

Training for entry-level workers often begins by having the worker learn less difficult tasks, such as making simple cuts, removing bones, or dividing wholesale cuts into retail portions. Under the guidance of more experienced workers, trainees learn the proper use and care of tools and equipment. For example, they learn how to sharpen their knives and clean working areas and equipment.

Trainees also may learn how to shape, roll, and tie roasts; prepare sausage; and cure meat. Employees also receive training in food safety to minimize the risk of foodborne pathogens in meats.

Butchers who follow religious dietary guidelines for food preparation may be required to undergo more specialized training and certification before becoming endorsed by a religious organization to prepare meat.

Important Qualities

Customer-service skills. Butchers who work in retail stores should be courteous, be able to answer customers' questions, and fill orders to customers' satisfaction.

Dexterity. Butchers use sharp knives and meatcutting equipment as part of their duties. They must have good hand control in order to make proper cuts of meat that are the right size.

Physical stamina. Butchers spend hours on their feet while cutting, packaging, or storing meat.

Physical strength. Butchers should be strong enough to lift and carry heavy boxes of meat, which may weigh more than 50 pounds.

Pay

The median annual wage for butchers was $32,500 in May 2019. The median wage is the wage at which half the workers in an occupation earned more than that amount and half earned less. The lowest 10 percent earned less than $21,780, and the highest 10 percent earned more than $49,630.

In May 2019, the median annual wages for butchers in the top industries in which they worked were as follows:

General merchandise stores $36,300
Animal slaughtering and processing.................... 32,770
Food and beverage stores..................................... 32,020

Most butchers work full time. Butchers who work in grocery or retail stores may work early mornings, late evenings, weekends, and holidays. Workers in animal slaughtering and processing facilities may work shifts that start in the early morning or in the afternoon or evening.

Job Outlook

Employment of butchers is projected to grow 2 percent from 2019 to 2029, slower than the average for all occupations.

The popularity of various meat products, such as sausages, cured meats, and specialty cuts, is expected to drive employment growth of butchers in retail stores, such as grocery and specialty food stores.

Job Prospects

Many butcher and meatcutter jobs, particularly those in processing plants, are physically demanding. As a result, job opportunities are expected to be good because of the need to replace workers who leave the occupation each year.

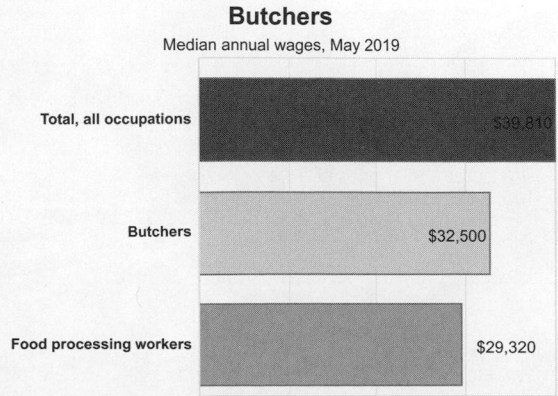

Butchers
Median annual wages, May 2019

Total, all occupations — $39,810
Butchers — $32,500
Food processing workers — $29,320

Note: All Occupations includes all occupations in the U.S. Economy.
Source: U.S. Bureau of Labor Statistics, Occupational Employment Statistics.

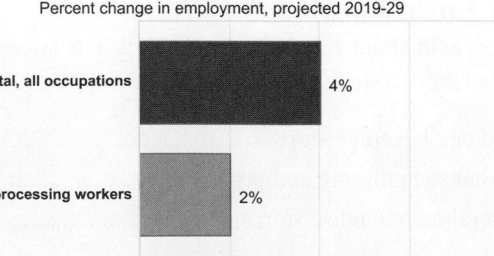

Butchers
Percent change in employment, projected 2019-29

Total, all occupations — 4%
Food processing workers — 2%
Butchers — 2%

Note: All Occupations includes all occupations in the U.S. Economy.
Source: U.S. Bureau of Labor Statistics, Employment Projections program.

Employment projections data for butchers, 2019-29					
Occupational Title	SOC Code	Employment, 2019	Projected Employment, 2029	Change, 2019-29	
				Percent	Numeric
SOURCE: U.S. Bureau of Labor Statistics, Employment Projections program					
Butchers and meat cutters	51-3021	137,500	139,800	2	2,300

State & Area Data
Occupational Employment Statistics (OES)

The Occupational Employment Statistics (OES) program produces employment and wage estimates annually for over 800 occupations. These estimates are available for the nation as a whole, for individual states, and for metropolitan and nonmetropolitan areas.

Contacts for More Information

For information about the meat-processing industry and related trends, visit

➤ North American Meat Institute

Dental and Ophthalmic Laboratory Technicians and Medical Appliance Technicians

Summary

Quick Facts: Dental and Ophthalmic Laboratory Technicians and Medical Appliance Technicians

2019 Median Pay	$37,370 per year $17.96 per hour
Typical Entry-Level Education	High school diploma or equivalent
Work Experience in a Related Occupation	None
On-the-job Training	Moderate-term on-the-job training
Number of Jobs, 2019	81,200
Job Outlook, 2019-29	9% (Much faster than average)
Employment Change, 2019-29	7,400

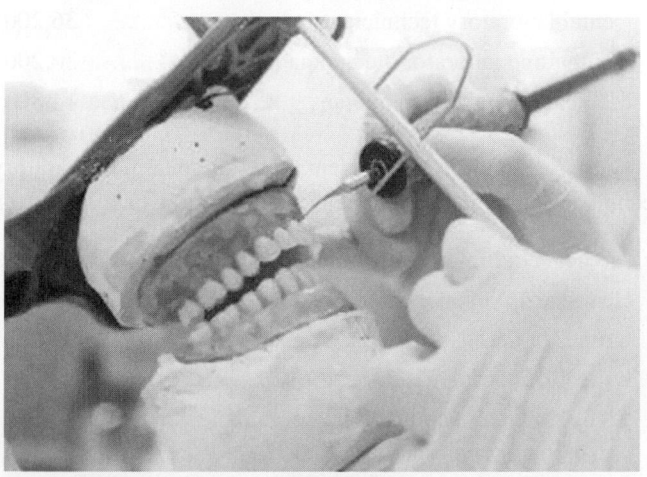

Dental laboratory technicians create crowns, bridges, dentures, and other dental prosthetics.

What Dental and Ophthalmic Laboratory Technicians and Medical Appliance Technicians Do

Dental and ophthalmic laboratory technicians and medical appliance technicians construct, fit, or repair medical appliances and devices.

Work Environment

Dental and ophthalmic laboratory technicians and medical appliance technicians often work in laboratories. Other technicians work in health and personal care stores or in healthcare facilities. Most work full time.

How to Become a Dental or Ophthalmic Laboratory Technician or Medical Appliance Technician

Dental or ophthalmic laboratory technicians or medical appliance technicians typically need a high school diploma or equivalent and receive on-the-job training.

Pay

The median annual wage for dental and ophthalmic laboratory technicians and medical appliance technicians was $37,370 in May 2019.

Job Outlook

Overall employment of dental and ophthalmic laboratory technicians and medical appliance technicians is projected to grow 9 percent from 2019 to 2029, much faster than the average for all occupations. As cosmetic prosthetics, such as veneers and crowns, become less expensive, there should be an increase in demand for these appliances. In addition, as the large baby-boom population grows older, there should be increased demand for orthotic devices, such as braces and orthopedic footwear.

State & Area Data

Explore resources for employment and wages by state and area for dental and ophthalmic laboratory technicians and medical appliance technicians.

What Dental and Ophthalmic Laboratory Technicians and Medical Appliance Technicians Do

Dental and ophthalmic laboratory technicians and medical appliance technicians construct, fit, or repair medical appliances and devices, including dentures, eyeglasses, and prosthetics.

Duties

Dental and ophthalmic laboratory technicians and medical appliance technicians typically do the following:

- Follow detailed work orders and prescriptions
- Determine which materials and tools will be needed
- Bend, form, and shape fabric or material
- Polish and shape appliances and devices, using hand or power tools
- Adjust appliances or devices to allow for a more natural look or to improve function
- Inspect the final product for quality and accuracy
- Repair damaged appliances and devices

In small laboratories and offices, technicians may handle every phase of production. In larger ones, technicians may be responsible for only one phase of production, such as polishing, measuring, or testing.

Dental laboratory technicians use traditional or digital impressions or molds of a patient's teeth to create crowns, bridges, dentures, and other dental appliances. They work closely with dentists, but have limited contact with patients.

Dental laboratory technicians work with small hand tools, such as files and polishers. They work with many different materials, including wax, alloy, ceramic, plastic, and porcelain, to make prosthetic appliances. In some cases, technicians use computer programs or three-dimensional printers to create appliances or to get impressions sent from a dentist's office.

Dental laboratory technicians can specialize in one or more of the following: orthodontic appliances, crowns and bridges,

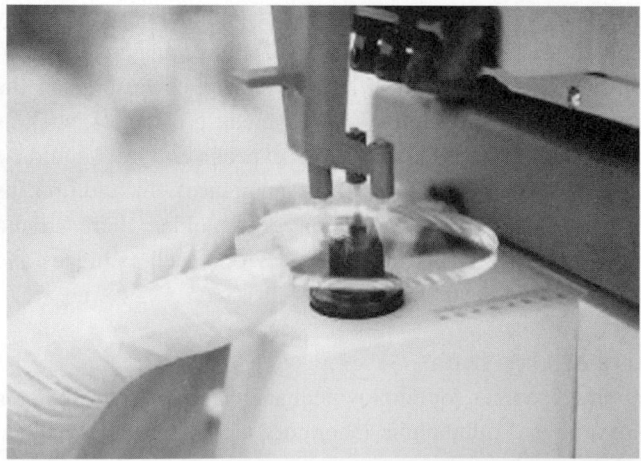

Ophthalmic laboratory technicians often use automated equipment to make lenses.

complete dentures, partial dentures, implants, or ceramics. Technicians may have different job titles, depending on their specialty. For example, technicians who make ceramic restorations such as veneers and bridges, are called *dental ceramists.*

Ophthalmic laboratory technicians make prescription eyeglasses and contact lenses. They are also commonly known as *manufacturing opticians* or *optical mechanics.*

Although they make some lenses by hand, ophthalmic laboratory technicians often use automated equipment. Some technicians manufacture lenses for optical instruments, such as telescopes and binoculars. Ophthalmic laboratory technicians should not be confused with dispensing opticians, who work with customers to select eyewear and may prepare work orders for ophthalmic laboratory technicians.

Medical appliance technicians construct, fit, and repair medical supportive devices, including arch supports, facial parts, and foot and leg braces.

Medical appliance technicians use many different types of materials, such as metal, plastic, and leather, to create a variety of medical devices for patients who need them because of a birth defect, an accident, disease, amputation, or the effects of aging. For example, some medical appliance technicians make hearing aids.

Orthotic and prosthetic technicians, also called *O&P technicians*, are medical appliance technicians who create orthoses (braces, supports, and other devices) and prostheses (replacement limbs and facial parts). These technicians work closely with orthotists or prosthetists.

Work Environment

Dental and ophthalmic laboratory technicians and medical appliance technicians held about 81,200 jobs in 2019. Employment in the detailed occupations that make up dental and ophthalmic laboratory technicians and medical appliance technicians was distributed as follows:

Dental laboratory technicians	36,200
Ophthalmic laboratory technicians	30,200
Medical appliance technicians	14,800

The largest employers of dental and ophthalmic laboratory technicians and medical appliance technicians were as follows:

Medical equipment and supplies manufacturing	58%
Health and personal care stores	12
Offices of dentists	6
Offices of optometrists	5
Professional and commercial equipment and supplies merchant wholesalers	4

Technicians may be exposed to health and safety hazards when they handle certain materials, but there is little risk if they follow proper procedures, such as wearing goggles, gloves, or masks. They may spend a great deal of time standing or bending.

Work Schedules

Most dental and ophthalmic laboratory technicians and medical appliance technicians work full time.

How to Become a Dental or Ophthalmic Laboratory Technician or Medical Appliance Technician

Dental and ophthalmic laboratory technicians and medical appliance technicians typically need at least a high school diploma or equivalent and receive on-the-job training.

Education

Dental and ophthalmic laboratory technicians and medical appliance technicians typically need at least a high school diploma or equivalent. There are some postsecondary programs in dental laboratory technology at community colleges or technical or vocational schools that award an associate's degree or postsecondary certificate. High school students interested in becoming dental or ophthalmic laboratory technicians or medical appliance technicians should take courses in science, human anatomy, math, computer programming, and art.

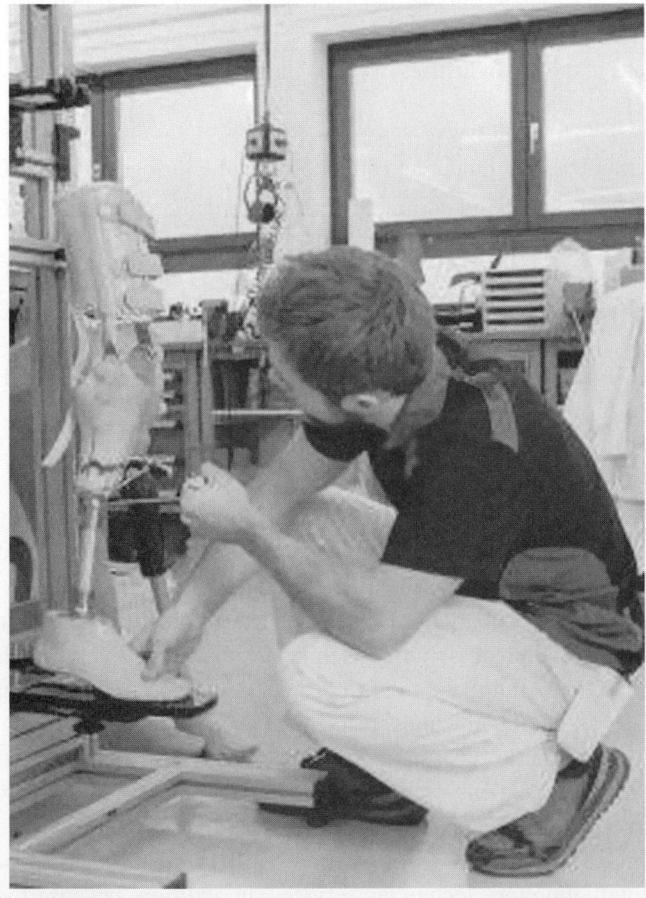

Medical appliance technicians construct, fit, and repair medical supportive devices, including prosthetic limbs.

Training

Most dental and ophthalmic laboratory technicians and medical appliance technicians learn their skills through on-the-job training. They usually begin as helpers in a laboratory and learn more advanced skills as they gain experience. For example, dental laboratory technicians may begin by pouring plaster into an impression to make a model. As they become more experienced, they may progress to more complex tasks, such as designing and fabricating crowns and bridges. Because all laboratories are different, the length of training varies.

Important Qualities

Detail oriented. Dental and ophthalmic laboratory technicians and medical appliance technicians must pay attention to detail. Technicians must follow work orders and prescriptions accurately and precisely. In addition, they need to be able to recognize and correct any imperfections in their work.

Dexterity. Dental and ophthalmic laboratory technicians and medical appliance technicians must work well with their hands because they use precise instruments.

Interpersonal skills. Dental and ophthalmic laboratory technicians and medical appliance technicians need to be able to work effectively with others because they may be part of a team of technicians working on a single project. In addition, they need good communication skills to ensure safety when they work with hazardous materials.

Technical skills. Dental and ophthalmic laboratory technicians and medical appliance technicians need to have an in-depth knowledge of how different tools and materials work. They also must understand how to operate complex machinery. Some procedures are automated, so technicians must know how to operate and change the programs that run the machinery.

Licenses, Certifications, and Registrations

Certification is not required for dental and ophthalmic laboratory technicians or medical appliance technicians. However,

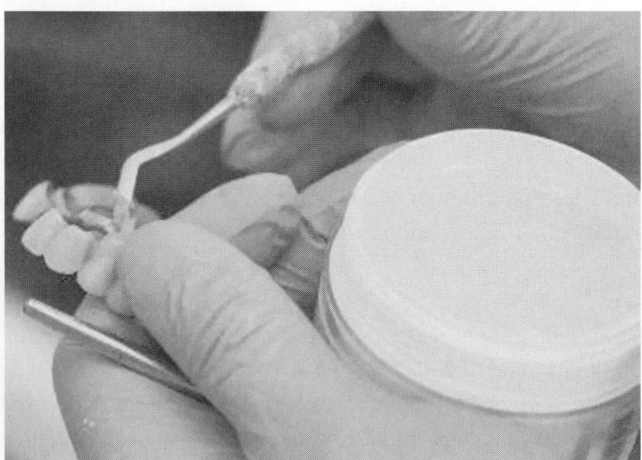

Dental laboratory technicians must work well with their hands because they use precise instruments.

Dental and Ophthalmic Laboratory Technicians and Medical Appliance Technicians

Median annual wages, May 2019

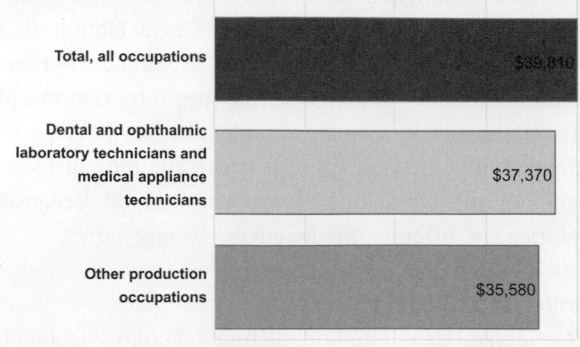

Note: All Occupations includes all occupations in the U.S. Economy.
Source: U.S. Bureau of Labor Statistics, Occupational Employment Statistics.

technicians may choose to earn specialty certifications because they show professional competence in a specialized field.

The National Board for Certification in Dental Laboratory Technology offers certification as a Certified Dental Technician (CDT). Certification is available in six specialty areas: orthodontics, crown and bridge, complete dentures, partial dentures, implants, and ceramics.

To qualify for the CDT, technicians must have at least 5 years of on-the-job training or experience in dental technology or have graduated from an accredited dental laboratory technician program. Candidates also must pass three exams within a period of 4 years.

The American Board for Certification in Orthotics, Prosthetics & Pedorthics offers certification for orthotic and/or prosthetic technicians. Technicians are eligible for the certification exam after completing an accredited program or if they have 2 years of experience as a technician under the direct supervision of a certified orthotist or prosthetist or O&P technician.

Advancement

In large laboratories, dental and ophthalmic laboratory technicians and medical appliance technicians may work their way up to a supervisory level and may train new technicians. Some may go on to own their own laboratory.

Medical appliance technicians can advance to become orthotists or prosthetists after completing additional formal education. These practitioners work with patients who need braces, prostheses, or related devices.

Pay

The median annual wage for dental and ophthalmic laboratory technicians and medical appliance technicians was $37,370 in May 2019. The median wage is the wage at which half the workers in an occupation earned more than that amount and half earned less. The lowest 10 percent earned less than $24,250, and the highest 10 percent earned more than $62,110.

Dental and Ophthalmic Laboratory Technicians and Medical Appliance Technicians

Percent change in employment, projected 2019-29

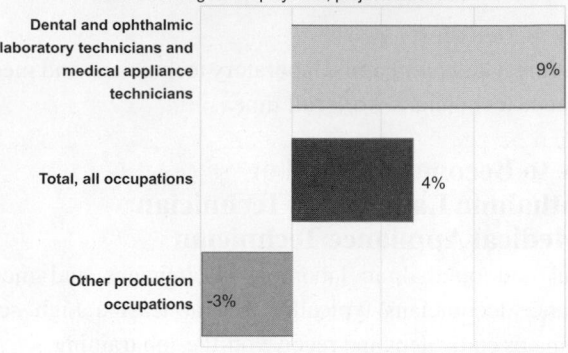

Note: All Occupations includes all occupations in the U.S. Economy.
Source: U.S. Bureau of Labor Statistics, Employment Projections program.

Median annual wages for dental and ophthalmic laboratory technicians and medical appliance technicians in May 2019 were as follows:

Dental laboratory technicians	$41,340
Medical appliance technicians	40,690
Ophthalmic laboratory technicians	32,620

In May 2019, the median annual wages for dental and ophthalmic laboratory technicians and medical appliance technicians in the top industries in which they worked were as follows:

Offices of dentists	$43,900
Medical equipment and supplies manufacturing	38,110
Professional and commercial equipment and supplies merchant wholesalers	33,840
Offices of optometrists	32,240
Health and personal care stores	31,150

Most dental and ophthalmic laboratory technicians and medical appliance technicians work full time.

Job Outlook

Overall employment of dental and ophthalmic laboratory technicians and medical appliance technicians is projected to grow 9 percent from 2019 to 2029, much faster than the average for all occupations. However, because medical appliance and ophthalmic laboratory technicians have relatively small employment numbers, the fast growth will result in only about 1,700 and 2,300 new jobs, respectively, over the decade.

As cosmetic prosthetics, such as veneers and crowns, become less expensive, demand for these appliances will likely increase. Accidents and poor oral health, which can cause damage and loss of teeth, will continue to create a need for dental laboratory technician services. In addition, because the risk of oral cancer increases significantly with age, an aging population will increase demand for dental appliances, given that complications can require both cosmetic and functional dental reconstruction.

There should be increased demand for orthotic devices as the large baby-boom population ages. Diabetes and cardiovascular disease, two leading causes of loss of limbs, are more likely to occur as people age. In addition, advances in technology may spur demand for prostheses that allow for more natural movement.

Moreover, most people need vision correction at some point in their lives. As the population continues to grow and age, more people will need more vision aids, such as glasses and contact lenses, which should increase demand for ophthalmic laboratory technicians.

Job Prospects

Because of demands from an aging population, dental and ophthalmic laboratory technicians and medical appliance technicians should have good job prospects. Technicians who have earned professional certification and who are familiar with high tech skills, such as three-dimensional printing, are likely to have the best job prospects.

Employment projections data for dental and ophthalmic laboratory technicians and medical appliance technicians, 2019-29

Occupational Title	SOC Code	Employment, 2019	Projected Employment, 2029	Change, 2019-29	
				Percent	Numeric
SOURCE: U.S. Bureau of Labor Statistics, Employment Projections program					
Dental and ophthalmic laboratory technicians and medical appliance technicians	51-9080	81,200	88,600	9	7,400
Dental laboratory technicians	51-9081	36,200	39,600	9	3,400

Employment projections data for dental and ophthalmic laboratory technicians and medical appliance technicians, 2019-29

Occupational Title	SOC Code	Employment, 2019	Projected Employment, 2029	Change, 2019-29	
				Percent	Numeric
Medical appliance technicians	51-9082	14,800	16,500	12	1,700
Ophthalmic laboratory technicians	51-9083	30,200	32,500	8	2,300

State & Area Data
Occupational Employment Statistics (OES)

The Occupational Employment Statistics (OES) program produces employment and wage estimates annually for over 800 occupations. These estimates are available for the nation as a whole, for individual states, and for metropolitan and nonmetropolitan areas.

Contacts for More Information

For information about requirements for certification of dental laboratory technicians, visit
➤ National Board for Certification in Dental Laboratory Technology

For information about career opportunities in commercial dental laboratories, visit
➤ National Association of Dental Laboratories

For a list of accredited programs for medical appliance technicians, visit
➤ American Academy of Orthotists & Prosthetists
➤ National Commission on Orthotic and Prosthetic Education

For information on requirements for certification of medical appliance technicians, visit
➤ American Board for Certification in Orthotics, Prosthetics & Pedorthics

Food and Tobacco Processing Workers

Summary

Quick Facts: Food and Tobacco Processing Workers

2019 Median Pay	$30,200 per year / $14.52 per hour
Typical Entry-Level Education	See below
Work Experience in a Related Occupation	None
On-the-job Training	Moderate-term on-the-job training
Number of Jobs, 2019	259,200
Job Outlook, 2019-29	1% (Slower than average)
Employment Change, 2019-29	2,100

What Food and Tobacco Processing Workers Do

Food and tobacco processing workers operate equipment that mixes, cooks, or processes ingredients used in the manufacture of food and tobacco products.

Work Environment

Most food and tobacco processing workers are employed in manufacturing facilities. Because of production schedules, working early morning, evening, or night shifts is common. Most food and tobacco processing workers work full time.

How to Become a Food and Tobacco Processing Worker

There are no formal education requirements for some processing workers. However, food batchmakers and food cooking machine operators typically need a high school diploma.

Food and tobacco processing workers use machines to mix ingredients.

Pay

The median annual wage for food and tobacco processing workers was $30,200 in May 2019.

Job Outlook

Overall employment of food and tobacco processing workers is projected to grow 1 percent from 2019 to 2029, slower than the average for all occupations. The need to replace workers who leave the occupation should result in additional job openings.

State & Area Data

Explore resources for employment and wages by state and area for food and tobacco processing workers.

What Food and Tobacco Processing Workers Do

Food and tobacco processing workers operate equipment that mixes, cooks, or processes ingredients used in the manufacturing of food and tobacco products.

Duties

Food and tobacco processing workers typically do the following:

- Set up, start, or load food or tobacco processing equipment
- Check, weigh, and mix ingredients according to recipes

A food batchmaker stirs curd to make cheese.

- Set and control temperatures, flow rates, and pressures of machinery
- Monitor and adjust ingredient mixes during production processes
- Observe and regulate equipment gauges and controls
- Record batch production data
- Clean workspaces and equipment in accordance with health and safety standards
- Check final products to ensure quality

Food and tobacco processing workers often have different duties depending on the type of machinery they use or goods they process.

Food and tobacco roasting, baking, and drying machine operators and tenders operate machines that produce roasted, baked, or dried food or tobacco products. For example, *dryers of fruits and vegetables* operate machines that produce raisins, prunes, or other dehydrated foods. *Tobacco roasters* tend machines that cure tobacco for wholesale distribution to cigarette manufacturers and other makers of tobacco products. Others, such as *coffee roasters*, follow recipes and tend machines to produce standard or specialty coffees.

Food batchmakers typically work in facilities that produce baked goods, pasta, and tortillas. Workers mix ingredients to make dough, load and unload ovens, operate pasta extruders, and perform tasks specific to large-scale commercial baking. Some workers are identified by the type of food they produce. For example, those who prepare cheese are known as *cheese makers* and those who make candy are known as *candy makers*.

Food cooking machine operators and tenders operate or tend cooking equipment to prepare food products. For example, potato and corn chip manufacturing workers operate baking and frying equipment.

Other workers operate machines that mix spices, mill grains, or extract oil from seeds.

Work Environment

Food and tobacco processing workers held about 259,200 jobs in 2019. Employment in the detailed occupations that make up food and tobacco processing workers was distributed as follows:

Food batchmakers	162,500
Food processing workers, all other	44,200
Food cooking machine operators and tenders	30,400
Food and tobacco roasting, baking, and drying machine operators and tenders	22,100

The largest employers of food and tobacco processing workers were as follows:

Food manufacturing	75%
Employment services	6
Food and beverage stores	5

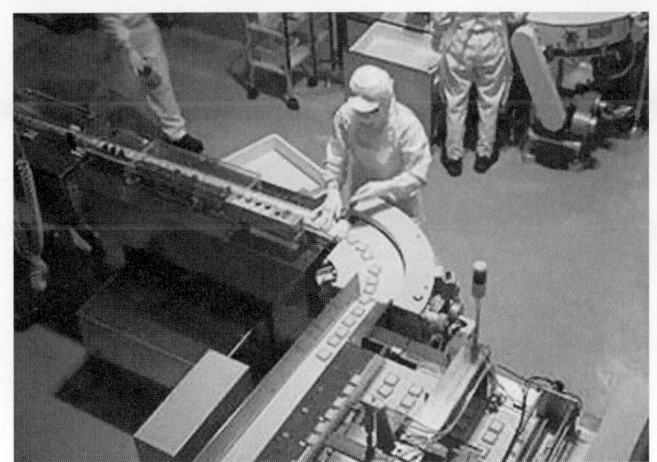

Food processing workers often work on a production line and stand most of the time.

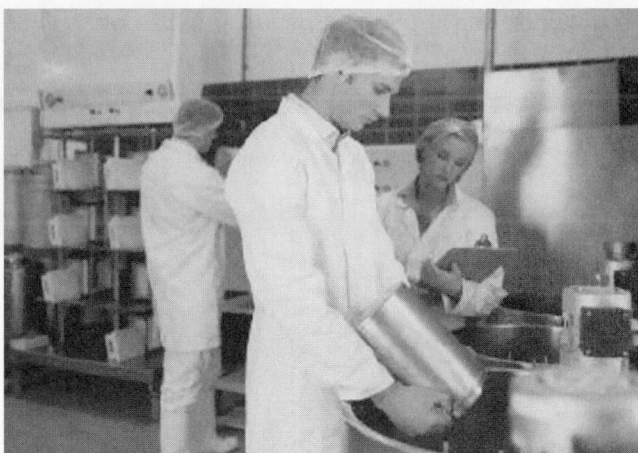

Experienced workers show trainees how to properly use equipment.

Food manufacturing facilities are typically large, open floor areas with loud machinery, requiring workers to wear ear protection to guard against noise. Workers are frequently exposed to high temperatures when working around cooking machinery. Some work in cold environments for long periods with goods that need to be refrigerated or frozen.

Depending on the type of food or tobacco being processed, workers may be required to wear masks, hair nets, or gloves to protect the product from possible contamination.

Workers usually stand for the majority of their shifts while tending machines or observing the production process. Loading, unloading, or cleaning equipment may require lifting, bending, and reaching.

Injuries and Illnesses
Working around hot liquids or machinery that cuts or presses can be dangerous. The most common hazards are slips, falls, and cuts. To reduce the risks of injuries, workers are required to wear protective clothing and nonslip shoes.

Work Schedules
Most food and tobacco processing workers work full time. Because of production schedules, working early morning, evening, or night shifts is common in many manufacturing facilities.

Some food processing positions are seasonal.

How to Become a Food and Tobacco Processing Worker
There are no formal education requirements for some food and tobacco processing workers. However, food batchmakers and food cooking machine operators typically need a high school diploma or equivalent. Food and tobacco processing workers learn their skills through on-the-job training.

Education
Food batchmakers and food cooking machine operators typically need a high school diploma or equivalent.

Because workers often adjust the quantity of ingredients that go into a mix, math and reading skills are considered helpful.

Training
Food and tobacco processing workers learn on the job. Training may last from a few weeks to a few months. During training, workers learn health and safety rules related to the type of food or tobacco that they process. Training also involves learning how to operate specific equipment, following safety procedures, and reporting equipment malfunctions.

Experienced workers typically teach trainees how to properly use and care for equipment.

Important Qualities
Detail oriented. Workers must be able to detect small changes in the quality or quantity of food products. They must also closely follow health and safety standards to avoid food contamination and injury.

Physical stamina. Workers stand on their feet for long periods as they tend machines and monitor the production process.

Physical strength. Food and tobacco processing workers should be strong enough to lift or move heavy boxes of ingredients, which may weigh up to 50 pounds.

Math skills. Workers need to know math skills in order to accurately mix specific quantities of ingredients.

Pay
The median annual wage for food and tobacco processing workers was $30,200 in May 2019. The median wage is the wage at which half the workers in an occupation earned more than that amount and half earned less. The lowest 10 percent earned less than $21,660, and the highest 10 percent earned more than $47,500.

Median annual wages for food and tobacco processing workers in May 2019 were as follows:

Food and tobacco roasting, baking, and drying $31,590
   machine operators and tenders..........................

Food and Tobacco Processing Workers
Median annual wages, May 2019

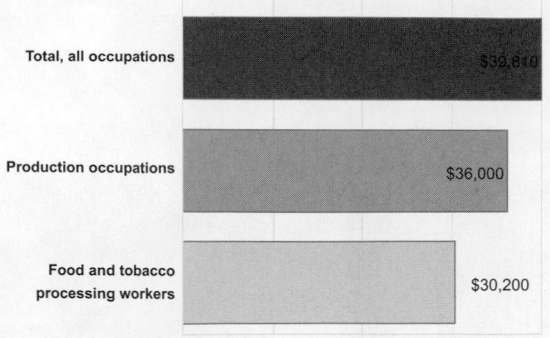

Total, all occupations	$39,810
Production occupations	$36,000
Food and tobacco processing workers	$30,200

Note: All Occupations includes all occupations in the U.S. Economy.
Source: U.S. Bureau of Labor Statistics, Occupational Employment Statistics.

Food cooking machine operators and tenders........ 31,110

Food batchmakers 30,790

Food processing workers, all other 27,550

In May 2019, the median annual wages for food and tobacco processing workers in the top industries in which they worked were as follows:

Food manufacturing $30,990

Food and beverage stores 27,180

Employment services 26,670

Most food and tobacco processing workers work full time. Because of production schedules, working early morning, evening, or night shifts is common in many manufacturing facilities.

Some food processing positions are seasonal.

Job Outlook

Overall employment of food and tobacco processing workers is projected to grow 1 percent from 2019 to 2029, slower than the average for all occupations.

Population growth and continuing consumer preference for convenience foods are expected to drive the demand for food, which will in turn require more food and tobacco processing workers to produce it. However, food manufacturing companies continue to pursue more automation in processing to raise productivity. For example, they use equipment that automatically weighs and mixes ingredients, requiring fewer processing workers. As these companies streamline production processes and implement more automation, they will need fewer workers to operate machines, and this may constrain occupational growth.

Food and Tobacco Processing Workers
Percent change in employment, projected 2019-29

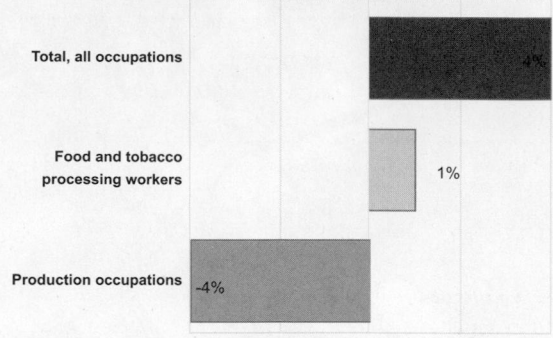

Total, all occupations	4%
Food and tobacco processing workers	1%
Production occupations	-4%

Note: All Occupations includes all occupations in the U.S. Economy.
Source: U.S. Bureau of Labor Statistics, Employment Projections program.

Job Prospects

The need to replace food and tobacco processing workers who leave the occupation should result in additional job openings each year. Those with related work experience in manufacturing will likely have the best job opportunities.

Employment projections data for food and tobacco processing workers, 2019-29					
Occupational Title	SOC Code	Employment, 2019	Projected Employment, 2029	Change, 2019-29	
				Percent	Numeric
SOURCE: U.S. Bureau of Labor Statistics, Employment Projections program					
Food and tobacco processing workers	—	259,200	261,300	1	2,100
Food and tobacco roasting, baking, and drying machine operators and tenders	51-3091	22,100	21,900	-1	-200
Food batchmakers	51-3092	162,500	164,700	1	2,100
Food cooking machine operators and tenders	51-3093	30,400	30,600	1	200
Food processing workers, all other	51-3099	44,200	44,100	0	-100

State & Area Data
Occupational Employment Statistics (OES)

The Occupational Employment Statistics (OES) program produces employment and wage estimates annually for over 800 occupations. These estimates are available for the nation as a whole, for individual states, and for metropolitan and nonmetropolitan areas.

Contacts for More Information

For more information about line workers and food safety, visit
➤ U.S. Department of Agriculture Food Safety and Inspection Service
➤ U.S. Food and Drug Administration

For more information about the food industry, visit
➤ Food Engineering
➤ Grocery Manufacturers Association

Jewelers and Precious Stone and Metal Workers

Summary

Quick Facts: Jewelers and Precious Stone and Metal Workers

2019 Median Pay	$40,870 per year $19.65 per hour
Typical Entry-Level Education	High school diploma or equivalent
Work Experience in a Related Occupation ...	None
On-the-job Training	Long-term on-the- job training
Number of Jobs, 2019	35,100
Job Outlook, 2019-29	-10% (Decline)
Employment Change, 2019-29	-3,500

What Jewelers and Precious Stone and Metal Workers Do

Jewelers and precious stone and metal workers design, construct, adjust, repair, appraise and sell jewelry.

Work Environment

Jewelers and precious stone and metal workers spend much of their time at a workbench or polishing station, using tools and chemicals.

How to Become a Jeweler or Precious Stone and Metal Worker

Jewelers and precious stone and metal workers typically need a high school diploma to enter the occupation, and they learn the skills of the trade through on-the-job training.

Pay

The median annual wage for jewelers and precious stone and metal workers was $40,870 in May 2019.

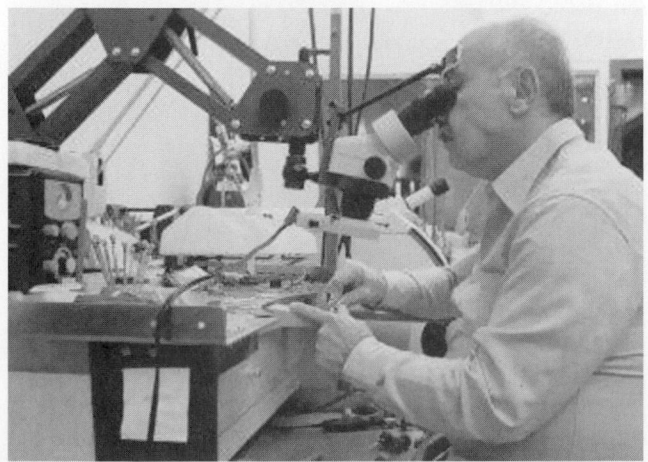

Jewelers and precious stone and metal workers typically work at a jeweler's bench.

Job Outlook

Employment of jewelers and precious stone and metal workers is projected to decline 10 percent from 2019 to 2029. Some job opportunities should be available to replace those who retire or who leave the occupation for other reasons.

State & Area Data

Explore resources for employment and wages by state and area for jewelers and precious stone and metal workers.

What Jewelers and Precious Stone and Metal Workers Do

Jewelers and precious stone and metal workers design, construct, adjust, repair, appraise and sell jewelry.

Duties

Jewelers and precious stone and metal workers typically do the following:

- Design and create jewelry from precious metals and stones
- Examine and grade diamonds and other gems
- Clean and polish jewelry using polishing wheels and chemical baths
- Repair jewelry by replacing broken clasps, altering ring sizes, or resetting stones
- Smooth joints and rough spots and polish smoothed areas
- Compute the costs of labor and material for new pieces and repairs

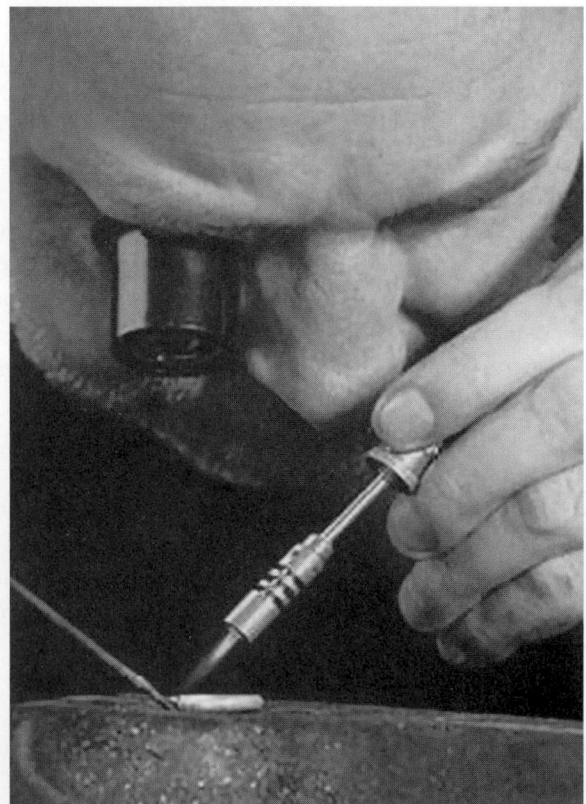

Jeweler's torches are used to resize and repair jewelry.

- Model new pieces with carved wax or computer-aided design, and then cast them in metal
- Shape metal to hold the gems in pieces of jewelry
- Solder pieces together and insert stones

Technology is helping to produce high-quality jewelry at a reduced cost and in less time than traditional methods allow. For example, lasers are often used for cutting and improving the quality of stones, for intricate engraving or design work, and for inscribing personal messages on jewelry. Jewelers also use lasers to weld metals together without seams or blemishes, improving the quality and appearance of jewelry.

Some manufacturing firms use computer-aided design and computer-aided manufacturing (CAD/CAM) to make product design easier and to automate some steps. With CAD, jewelers can create a model of a piece of jewelry on a computer and then view the effect of changing different aspects—for example, the design, the stone, or the setting—before cutting a stone or taking other costly steps. With CAM, they can then create a mold of the piece, which makes producing many copies easy.

Some jewelers also use CAD software to design custom jewelry. They let the customer review the design on a computer and see the effect of changes, so that the customer is satisfied before committing to the expense of a customized piece of jewelry.

The following are examples of types of jewelers and precious stone and metal workers:

Bench jewelers, also known as metalsmiths, silversmiths, goldsmiths, and platinumsmiths, are the most common type of jewelers. They possess a wide array of skills. They usually do tasks ranging from simple jewelry cleaning and repair to making molds and pieces from scratch. Some specialize in particular tasks such as repairs, hand engraving, stringing, wax carving/model making, enameling, stone cutting, soldering, stone setting, and hand building.

Gemologists analyze, describe, and certify the quality and characteristics of gemstones. After using microscopes, computerized tools, and other grading instruments to examine gemstones or finished pieces of jewelry, they write reports certifying that the items are of a particular quality. Most gemologists have completed the Graduate Gemologist program through the Gemological Institute of America.

Jewelry appraisers carefully examine jewelry to determine its value and then write appraisal documents. They determine value by researching the jewelry market and by using reference books, auction catalogs, price lists, and the Internet. They may work for jewelry stores, appraisal firms, auction houses, pawnbrokers, or insurance companies. Many gemologists also become appraisers.

Jewelry designers create design concepts and manage the prototype and model-making process.

Production jewelers fabricate and assemble pieces in a manufacturing setting and typically work on one aspect of the manufacturing process.

Work Environment

Jewelers and precious stone and metal workers held about 35,100 jobs in 2019. The largest employers of jewelers and precious stone and metal workers were as follows:

Self-employed workers	34%
Clothing and clothing accessories stores	29
Jewelry and silverware manufacturing	18

Some jewelers and precious stone and metal workers work from home and sell their products at trade and craft shows. Online sales are also a growing source of sales for jewelers.

Jewelers and precious stone and metal workers spend much of their time sitting at a workbench or standing at a polishing station. Computer-aided design (CAD) is also an important tool in the jewelry industry.

There is exposure to machines, fumes, and toxic or caustic chemicals, and risk of radiation. Many tools, such as jeweler's torches and lasers, must be handled carefully to avoid injury. Polishing processes such as chemical baths also must be performed in a safe manner.

Self-employed workers usually work at home in their workshop or studio. In retail stores, jewelers may talk with customers about repairs, perform custom design work, and sell items to customers. Because many of their materials are valuable, jewelers must follow security procedures, including making use of burglar alarms and, in larger jewelry stores, working in the presence of security guards.

Work Schedules

Most jewelers and precious stone and metal workers work full time.

Many self-employed workers show and sell their products at trade and craft shows during weekends. Retail store workers might also work nonstandard hours because they must be available when customers are not working, such as on holidays and weekends.

Jewelers and precious stone and metal workers use various tools and chemicals.

How to Become a Jeweler or Precious Stone and Metal Worker

Jewelers and precious stone and metal workers typically need a high school diploma to enter the occupation, and they learn the skills of the trade through on-the-job training.

Education

Although most jewelers and precious stone and metal workers have a high school diploma, many trade schools offer courses for workers who seek additional education. Course topics can include introduction to gems and metals, resizing, repair, and computer-aided design (CAD). Programs vary from 3 months to 1 year, and many teach students how to design, cast, set, and polish jewelry and gems, as well as how to use and care for a jeweler's tools and equipment. Graduates of these programs may be more attractive to employers because they require less on-the-job training. Many gemologists graduate from the Gemological Institute of America. Trade programs usually require applicants to have a high school diploma or equivalent.

Training

Many jewelers learn and develop their skills on the job. The length of training required to become proficient depends on the difficulty of the specialty, but often lasts at least a year. Training usually focuses on casting, setting stones, making models, or engraving.

Other Experience

Some workers gain their skills through related work experience. This may include working alongside a bench jeweler or gemologist while performing the duties of a salesperson in a retail jewelry store. Time spent in a store with a bench jeweler or gemologist can provide valuable experience.

Advancement

In manufacturing, some jewelers advance to supervisory jobs, such as master jeweler or head jeweler. Jewelers who work in jewelry stores or repair shops may become managers.

Important Qualities

Artistic ability. Jewelers must have the ability to create designs that are unique and beautiful.

Detail oriented. Jewelers and precious stone and metal workers must pay attention to large and small details on the pieces they make.

Dexterity. Jewelers and precious stone and metal workers must precisely move their fingers and tools in order to grasp, manipulate, and assemble very small objects.

Fashion sense. Jewelry designers must know what is stylish and attractive and presently in demand by consumers.

Interpersonal skills. Jewelers and precious stone and metal workers interact with customers, whether they sell products in stores or at craft shows.

Near vision. Jewelers and precious stone and metal workers need the ability to see details at close range (within a few feet of the observer).

Visualization skills. Jewelers and precious stone and metal workers must imagine how something might look after its shape is altered or when its parts are rearranged.

Pay

The median annual wage for jewelers and precious stone and metal workers was $40,870 in May 2019. The median wage is the wage at which half the workers in an occupation earned more than that amount and half earned less. The lowest 10 percent earned less than $24,520, and the highest 10 percent earned more than $73,420.

In May 2019, the median annual wages for jewelers and precious stone and metal workers in the top industries in which they worked were as follows:

Although most jewelers and precious stone and metal workers have a high school diploma, many trade schools offer courses for workers who seek additional education.

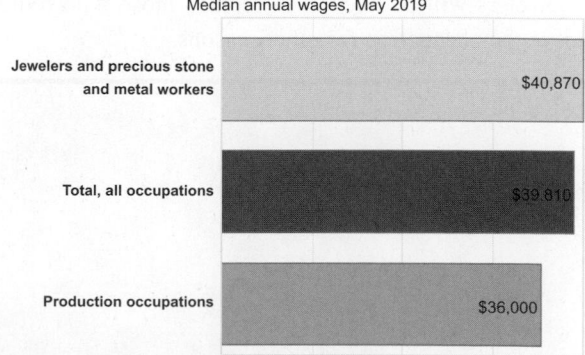

Jewelers and Precious Stone and Metal Workers
Median annual wages, May 2019

Jewelers and precious stone and metal workers	$40,870
Total, all occupations	$39,810
Production occupations	$36,000

Note: All Occupations includes all occupations in the U.S. Economy.
Source: U.S. Bureau of Labor Statistics, Occupational Employment Statistics.

Jewelers and Precious Stone and Metal Workers

Percent change in employment, projected 2019-29

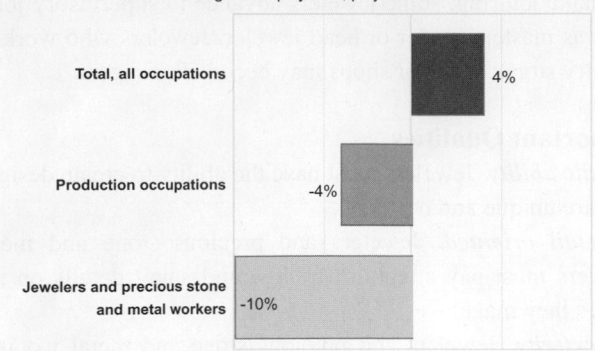

Note: All Occupations includes all occupations in the U.S. Economy.
Source: U.S. Bureau of Labor Statistics, Employment Projections program.

Clothing and clothing accessories stores	$44,670
Jewelry and silverware manufacturing	35,070

Jewelers who work in retail stores may earn commissions for jewelry sold.

Most jewelers and precious stone and metal workers work full time.

Many self-employed workers show and sell their products at trade and craft shows during weekends. Retail store workers might also work nonstandard hours because they must be available when customers are not working, such as on holidays and weekends.

Job Outlook

Employment of jewelers and precious stone and metal workers is projected to decline 10 percent from 2019 to 2029. This is largely because of projected employment declines in jewelry and silverware manufacturing, which are expected due to anticipated increasing imports of jewelry and rising productivity. Additionally, traditional jewelry stores may continue to lose some of their customers to non-traditional sellers, such as department stores and online retailers, and this shift is also likely to result in declining employment levels for jewelers and precious stone and metal workers.

Job Prospects

Some jewelers will be needed to replace those who retire or who leave the occupation for other reasons.

Job opportunities in jewelry stores and repair shops should be best for those who have graduated from a trade school or training program and have related work experience.

Strong competition is expected for mass manufacturing jobs and for jewelry designers who wish to create their own jewelry lines. Although demand for customized and boutique jewelry is strong, it is often difficult for independent designers to establish themselves in the market. Experience with computer-aided design (CAD) makes creating custom pieces of jewelry easier.

During economic downturns, demand for jewelry products and jewelers usually decreases. However, demand for repair workers should remain strong even during economic slowdowns because maintaining and repairing jewelry is cheaper than buying new jewelry.

Employment projections data for jewelers and precious stone and metal workers, 2019-29					
Occupational Title	SOC Code	Employment, 2019	Projected Employment, 2029	Change, 2019-29	
				Percent	Numeric
SOURCE: U.S. Bureau of Labor Statistics, Employment Projections program					
Jewelers and precious stone and metal workers	51-9071	35,100	31,600	-10	-3,500

State & Area Data

Occupational Employment Statistics (OES)

The Occupational Employment Statistics (OES) program produces employment and wage estimates annually for over 800 occupations. These estimates are available for the nation as a whole, for individual states, and for metropolitan and nonmetropolitan areas.

Contacts for More Information

For more information about jewelers, precious stone and metal workers, and gemologists, including job opportunities and training programs, visit

➤ Gemological Institute of America Inc.
➤ Jewelers of America
➤ Manufacturing Jewelers & Suppliers of America

Machinists and Tool and Die Makers

Summary

Quick Facts: Machinists and Tool and Die Makers

2019 Median Pay	$45,750 per year $21.99 per hour
Typical Entry-Level Education	See below
Work Experience in a Related Occupation	None
On-the-job Training	Long-term on-the-job training
Number of Jobs, 2019	460,600
Job Outlook, 2019-29	3% (As fast as average)
Employment Change, 2019-29	12,400

What Machinists and Tool and Die Makers Do

Machinists and tool and die makers set up and operate machine tools to produce precision metal parts, instruments, and tools.

Work Environment

Machinists and tool and die makers work in machine shops, toolrooms, and factories. Although many work full time during regular business hours, overtime may be common, as is evening and weekend work.

How to Become a Machinist or Tool and Die Maker

Machinists and tool and die makers typically are trained on the job. Some learn through training or apprenticeship programs, vocational schools, or community and technical colleges. Although machinists typically need just a high school diploma, tool and die makers may need to complete courses beyond high school.

Pay

The median annual wage for machinists was $44,420 in May 2019.

Machinists and tool and die makers set up and operate many different machines.

The median annual wage for tool and die makers was $53,920 in May 2019.

Job Outlook

Overall employment of machinists and tool and die makers is projected to grow 3 percent from 2019 to 2029, about as fast as the average for all occupations. Many job opportunities are expected to arise from the need to replace workers who leave the occupation each year.

State & Area Data

Explore resources for employment and wages by state and area for machinists and tool and die makers.

What Machinists and Tool and Die Makers Do

Machinists and tool and die makers set up and operate a variety of computer-controlled and mechanically controlled machine tools to produce precision metal parts, instruments, and tools.

Duties

Machinists typically do the following:

- Read blueprints, sketches, or computer-aided design (CAD) and computer-aided manufacturing (CAM) files

Machinists typically use blueprints, sketches, or computer-aided design (CAD) and computer-aided manufacturing (CAM) files.

- Set up, operate, and disassemble manual, automatic, and computer numerically controlled (CNC) machine tools
- Align, secure, and adjust cutting tools and workpieces
- Monitor the feed and speed of machines
- Turn, mill, drill, shape, and grind machine parts to specifications
- Measure, examine, and test completed products for defects
- Smooth the surfaces of parts or products
- Present finished workpieces to customers and make modifications if needed

Tool and die makers typically do the following:

- Read blueprints, sketches, specifications, or CAD and CAM files for making tools and dies
- Compute and verify dimensions, sizes, shapes, and tolerances of workpieces
- Set up, operate, and disassemble conventional, manual, and CNC machine tools
- File, grind, and adjust parts so that they fit together properly
- Test completed tools and dies to ensure that they meet specifications
- Smooth and polish the surfaces of tools and dies

Machinists use machine tools, such as lathes, milling machines, and grinders, to produce precision metal parts. Many machinists must be able to use both manual and CNC machinery. CNC machines control the cutting tool speed and do all necessary cuts to create a part. The machinist determines the cutting path, the speed of the cut, and the feed rate by programming instructions into the CNC machine.

Although workers may produce large quantities of one part, precision machinists often produce small batches or one-of-a-kind items. The parts that machinists make range from simple steel bolts to titanium bone screws for orthopedic implants. Hydraulic parts, antilock brakes, and automobile pistons are other widely known products that machinists make.

Some machinists repair or make new parts for existing machinery. After an industrial machinery mechanic discovers a broken part in a machine, a machinist remanufactures the part. The machinist refers to blueprints and performs the same machining operations that were used to create the original part in order to create the replacement.

Some manufacturing processes use lasers, water jets, and electrified wires to cut the workpiece. As engineers design and build new types of machine tools, machinists must learn new machining properties and techniques.

Tool and die makers construct precision tools or metal forms, called dies, that are used to cut, shape, and form metal and other materials. They produce jigs and fixtures—devices that hold metal while it is bored, stamped, or drilled—and gauges and other measuring devices.

Dies are used to shape metal in stamping and forging operations. They also make metal molds for die casting and for molding plastics, ceramics, and composite materials.

Tool and die makers use CAD to develop products and parts. They enter designs into computer programs that produce blueprints for the required tools and dies. Computer numeric control programmers, described in the metal and plastic machine workers profile, convert CAD designs into CAM programs that contain instructions for a sequence of cutting-tool operations. Once these programs are developed, CNC machines follow the set of instructions contained in the program to produce the part. Machinists normally operate CNC machines, but tool and die makers often are trained to both operate CNC machines and write CNC programs and thus may do either task.

Work Environment

Machinists held about 388,100 jobs in 2019. The largest employers of machinists were as follows:

Machine shops	22%
Machinery manufacturing	19
Transportation equipment manufacturing	12
Employment services	6

Tool and die makers held about 72,500 jobs in 2019. The largest employers of tool and die makers were as follows:

Metalworking machinery manufacturing	20%
Motor vehicle parts manufacturing	16
Aerospace product and parts manufacturing	6
Machine shops; turned product; and screw, nut, and bolt manufacturing	5
Plastics product manufacturing	4

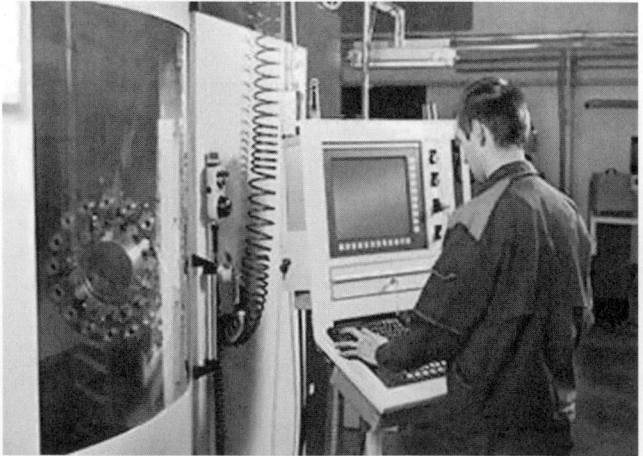

Some machinists and tool and die makers work evenings and weekends because facilities may operate around the clock.

Injuries and Illnesses

Because machinists and tool and die makers work around machine tools that may present hazards, these workers must follow precautions to avoid injuries. For example, workers must wear protective equipment, such as safety glasses, to shield against bits of flying metal, earplugs to dampen the noise produced by machinery, and masks to limit their exposure to fumes.

Work Schedules

Although many machinists and tool and die makers work full time during regular business hours, some work evenings and weekends because facilities may operate around the clock. Some work more than 40 hours a week.

How to Become a Machinist or Tool and Die Maker

Machinists and tool and die makers typically are trained on the job. Some learn through training or apprenticeship programs, vocational schools, or community and technical colleges. Although machinists typically need just a high school diploma, tool and die makers may need to complete courses beyond high school.

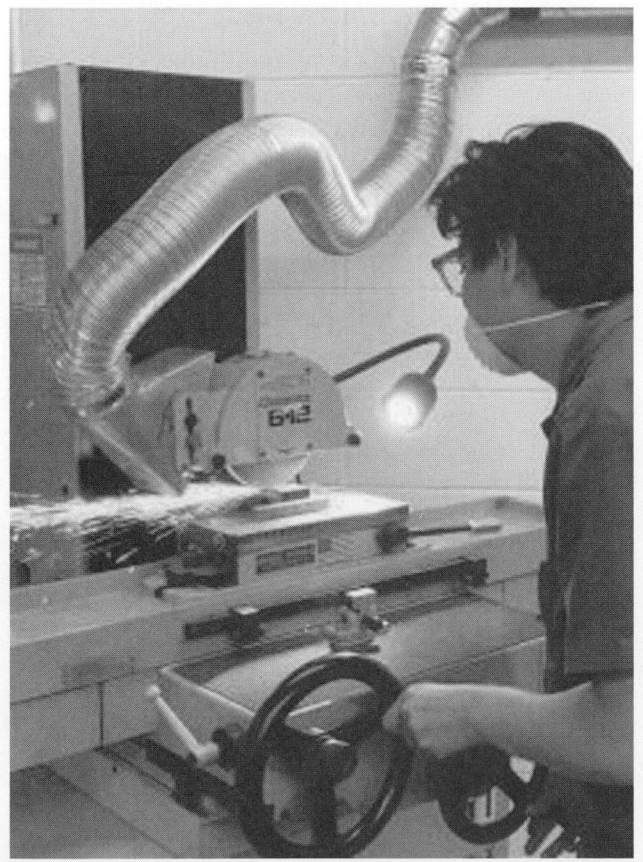

Machinists and tool and die makers typically are trained on the job.

Education

Machinists typically have a high school diploma or equivalent, whereas tool and die makers may need to complete courses beyond high school. High school courses in math, blueprint reading, metalworking, and drafting are considered useful.

Some community colleges and technical schools have 2-year programs that train students to become machinists or tool and die makers. These programs usually teach design and blueprint reading, the use of a variety of welding and cutting tools, and the programming and function of computer numerically controlled (CNC) machines.

Training

There are multiple ways for workers to gain competency in the job as a machinist or tool or die maker. One common way is through long-term on-the-job training, which lasts 1 year or longer.

Trainees usually work 40 hours per week and take additional technical instruction during evenings. Trainees often begin as machine operators and gradually take on more difficult assignments. Machinists and tool and die makers must be experienced in using computers to work with CAD/CAM technology, CNC machine tools, and computerized measuring machines. Some machinists become tool and die makers.

Some new workers may enter apprenticeship programs, which are typically sponsored by a manufacturer. Apprenticeship programs often consist of paid shop training and related technical instruction lasting several years. The technical instruction usually is provided in cooperation with local community colleges and vocational–technical schools. Workers typically enter into apprenticeships with a high school diploma or equivalent.

Licenses, Certifications, and Registrations

A number of organizations and colleges offer certification programs. The Skills Certification System, for example, is an industry-driven program that aims to align education pathways with career pathways. In addition, journey-level certification is available from state apprenticeship boards after the completion of an apprenticeship.

Completing a certification program provides machinists and tool and die makers with better job opportunities and helps employers judge the abilities of new hires.

Important Qualities

Analytical skills. Machinists and tool and die makers must understand technical blueprints, models, and specifications so that they can craft precision tools and metal parts.

Manual dexterity. Machinists' and tool and die makers' work must be accurate. For example, machining parts may demand accuracy to within .0001 of an inch, a level of accuracy that requires workers' concentration and dexterity.

Math skills and computer application experience. Workers must be experienced in using computers to work with CAD/

CAM technology, CNC machine tools, and computerized measuring machines.

Mechanical skills. Machinists and tool and die makers must operate milling machines, lathes, grinders, laser and water cutting machines, wire electrical discharge machines, and other machine tools.

Physical stamina. Machinist and tool and die makers must stand for extended periods and perform repetitive movements.

Technical skills. Machinists and tool and die makers must understand computerized measuring machines and metalworking processes, such as stock removal, chip control, and heat treating and plating.

Pay

The median annual wage for machinists was $44,420 in May 2019. The median wage is the wage at which half the workers in an occupation earned more than that amount and half earned less. The lowest 10 percent earned less than $27,940, and the highest 10 percent earned more than $66,610.

The median annual wage for tool and die makers was $53,920 in May 2019. The lowest 10 percent earned less than $33,820, and the highest 10 percent earned more than $77,940.

In May 2019, the median annual wages for machinists in the top industries in which they worked were as follows:

Transportation equipment manufacturing	$47,470
Machinery manufacturing	44,970
Machine shops	43,300
Employment services	33,550

In May 2019, the median annual wages for tool and die makers in the top industries in which they worked were as follows:

Aerospace product and parts manufacturing	$77,390
Motor vehicle parts manufacturing	57,780
Machine shops; turned product; and screw, nut, and bolt manufacturing	54,210
Metalworking machinery manufacturing	51,360
Plastics product manufacturing	51,350

The pay of apprentices is tied to their skill level. As they reach specific levels of performance and experience, their pay increases.

Although many machinists and tool and die makers work full time during regular business hours, some work evenings and weekends because facilities may operate around the clock. Some work more than 40 hours a week.

Job Outlook

Overall employment of machinists and tool and die makers is projected to grow 3 percent from 2019 to 2029, about as fast as the average for all occupations. Employment growth will vary by specialty.

Employment of machinists is projected to grow 4 percent from 2019 to 2029, about as fast as the average for all occupations. With improvements in technologies, such as computer numerically controlled (CNC) machine tools, autoloaders, high-speed machining, and lights-out manufacturing, machinists will still be required to set up, monitor, and maintain these systems.

Employment of tool and die makers is projected to decline 5 percent from 2019 to 2029. Advances in automation, including CNC machine tools, should reduce demand for tool and die makers to perform tasks, such as programming how parts fit together, that computer software can perform.

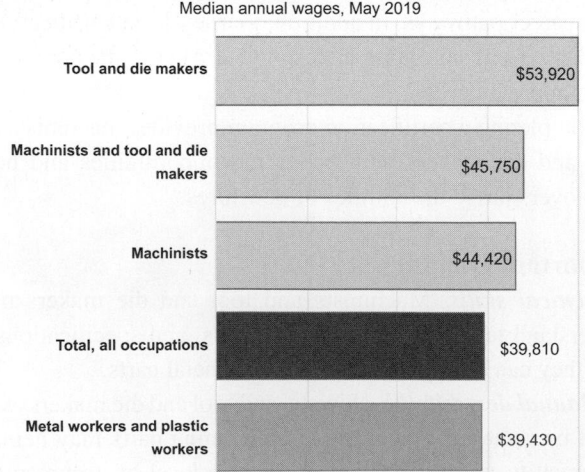

Machinists and Tool and Die Makers
Median annual wages, May 2019

- Tool and die makers: $53,920
- Machinists and tool and die makers: $45,750
- Machinists: $44,420
- Total, all occupations: $39,810
- Metal workers and plastic workers: $39,430

Note: All Occupations includes all occupations in the U.S. Economy.
Source: U.S. Bureau of Labor Statistics, Occupational Employment Statistics.

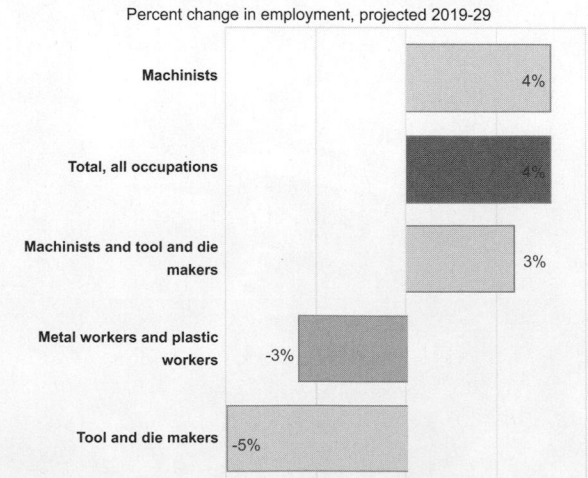

Machinists and Tool and Die Makers
Percent change in employment, projected 2019-29

- Machinists: 4%
- Total, all occupations: 4%
- Machinists and tool and die makers: 3%
- Metal workers and plastic workers: -3%
- Tool and die makers: -5%

Note: All Occupations includes all occupations in the U.S. Economy.
Source: U.S. Bureau of Labor Statistics, Employment Projections program.

Job Prospects

Many job openings for machinists and tool and die makers are expected to arise each year from the need to replace workers who transfer to other occupations or leave the labor force, such as to retire.

Employment projections data for machinists and tool and die makers, 2019-29					
Occupational Title	SOC Code	Employment, 2019	Projected Employment, 2029	Change, 2019-29	
				Percent	Numeric
SOURCE: U.S. Bureau of Labor Statistics, Employment Projections program					
Machinists and tool and die makers	—	460,600	473,000	3	12,400
Machinists	51-4041	388,100	404,400	4	16,300
Tool and die makers	51-4111	72,500	68,600	-5	-3,900

State & Area Data
Occupational Employment Statistics (OES)

The Occupational Employment Statistics (OES) program produces employment and wage estimates annually for over 800 occupations. These estimates are available for the nation as a whole, for individual states, and for metropolitan and nonmetropolitan areas.

Contacts for More Information

For more information about machinists and tool and die makers, including training and certification, visit
➤ Fabricators & Manufacturers Association, International (FMA)
➤ Manufacturing Institute (MI)
➤ National Institute for Metalworking Skills (NIMS)

For information about manufacturing careers, including machinery and tool and die makers, visit
➤ American Mold Builders Association (AMBA)
➤ Association for Manufacturing Technology (AMT)
➤ National Tooling and Machining Association (NTMA)
➤ Precision Machined Products Association (PMPA)
➤ Precision Metalforming Association (PMA)

Metal and Plastic Machine Workers

Summary

Quick Facts: Metal and Plastic Machine Workers

2019 Median Pay	$36,990 per year $17.78 per hour
Typical Entry-Level Education	See below
Work Experience in a Related Occupation	None
On-the-job Training	Moderate-term on-the-job training
Number of Jobs, 2019	1,109,400
Job Outlook, 2019-29	-7% (Decline)
Employment Change, 2019-29	-75,800

What Metal and Plastic Machine Workers Do

Metal and plastic machine workers set up and operate machines that cut, shape, and form metal and plastic materials or pieces.

Work Environment

Metal and plastic machine workers are employed mainly in factories. Workers must adhere to safety standards to protect themselves from workplace hazards. Most work full time, and some work evenings and weekends.

How to Become a Metal or Plastic Machine Worker

Most metal and plastic workers have a high school diploma and learn through on-the-job training typically lasting a year.

Metal and plastic machine workers set up and operate automated and computer-controlled machinery.

Computer numerically controlled (CNC) machine tool programmers, however, typically need to complete courses beyond high school.

Pay

The median annual wage for metal and plastic machine workers was $36,990 in May 2019.

Job Outlook

Employment of metal and plastic machine workers is projected to decline 7 percent from 2019 to 2029. Employment is expected to decline due to advances in technology and foreign competition.

State & Area Data

Explore resources for employment and wages by state and area for metal and plastic machine workers.

What Metal and Plastic Machine Workers Do

Metal and plastic machine workers set up and operate machines that cut, shape, and form metal and plastic materials or pieces.

Duties

Metal and plastic machine workers typically do the following:

- Set up machines according to blueprints
- Monitor machines for unusual sound or vibration
- Insert material into machines, manually or with a hoist
- Operate metal or plastic molding, casting, or coremaking machines
- Adjust machine settings for temperature, cycle times, and speed and feed rates
- Remove finished products and smooth rough edges and imperfections
- Test and compare finished workpieces to specifications
- Remove and replace dull cutting tools
- Document production numbers in a computer database

Consumer products are made with many metal and plastic parts. These parts are produced by machines that are operated by metal and plastic machine workers. In general, these workers are separated into two groups: those who set up machines for operation and those who operate machines during production. Many workers, however, perform both tasks.

Although many workers both set up and operate machines, some may specialize in being a machine setter or a machine operator and tender.

Machine setters, or setup workers, prepare the machines before production, perform test runs, and, if necessary, adjust and make minor repairs to the machinery before and during operation.

Metal and plastic machine workers monitor and adjust machines during operation.

If, for example, the cutting tool inside a machine becomes dull after extended use, it is common for a setter to remove the tool, use a grinder or file to sharpen it, and reinstall it into the machine. New tools are produced by tool and die makers.

After installing the tools into a machine, setup workers often produce the initial batch of goods, inspect the products, and turn the machine over to an operator.

Machine operators and tenders monitor the machinery during operation.

After a setter prepares a machine for production, an operator observes the machine and the products it makes. Operators may have to load the machine with materials for production or adjust the machine's speeds during production. They must periodically inspect the parts a machine produces. If they detect a minor problem, operators may fix it themselves. If the repair is more serious, they may have an industrial machinery mechanic fix it.

Setters, operators, and tenders are usually identified by the type of machine they work with. Job duties generally vary with the size of the manufacturer and the type of machine being operated. Although some workers specialize in one or two types of machinery, many are trained to set up or operate a variety of machines. Machine operators are often able to control multiple machines at the same time because of increased automation.

In addition, production techniques, such as team-oriented "lean" manufacturing, require machine operators to rotate between different machines. Rotating assignments results in more varied work but also requires workers to have a wide range of skills.

The following are examples of types of metal and plastic machine workers:

Computer-controlled machine tool operators operate computer-controlled machines or robots to perform functions on metal or plastic workpieces.

Computer numerically controlled machine tool programmers develop computer programs to control the machining or processing of metal or plastic parts by automatic machine tools, equipment, or systems.

Extruding and drawing machine setters, operators, and tenders set up or operate machines to extrude (pull out) thermoplastic or metal materials in the form of tubes, rods, hoses, wire, bars, or structural shapes.

Forging machine setters, operators, and tenders set up or operate machines that shape or form metal or plastic parts.

Rolling machine setters, operators, and tenders set up or operate machines to roll steel or plastic or to flatten, temper, or reduce the thickness of materials.

Cutting, punching, and press machine setters, operators, and tenders set up or operate machines to saw, cut, shear, notch, bend, or straighten metal or plastic materials.

Drilling and boring machine tool setters, operators, and tenders set up or operate drilling machines to drill, bore, mill, or countersink metal or plastic workpieces.

Grinding, lapping, polishing, and buffing machine tool setters, operators, and tenders set up or operate grinding and related tools that remove excess material from surfaces, sharpen edges or corners, or buff or polish metal or plastic workpieces.

Lathe and turning machine tool setters, operators, and tenders set up or operate lathe and turning machines to turn, bore, thread, or form metal or plastic materials, such as wire or rod.

Milling and planing machine setters, operators, and tenders set up or operate milling or planing machines to shape, groove, or profile metal or plastic workpieces.

Metal-refining furnace operators and tenders operate or tend furnaces, such as gas, oil, coal, electric-arc or electric-induction, open-hearth, and oxygen furnaces. These furnaces may be used to melt and refine metal before casting or to produce specified types of steel.

Pourers and casters operate hand-controlled mechanisms to pour and regulate the flow of molten metal into molds to produce castings or ingots.

Model makers set up and operate machines, such as milling and engraving machines to make working models of metal or plastic objects.

Patternmakers lay out, machine, fit, and assemble castings and parts to metal or plastic foundry patterns and core molds.

Foundry mold and coremakers make or form wax or sand cores or molds used in the production of metal castings in foundries.

Molding, coremaking, and casting machine setters, operators, and tenders set up or operate metal or plastic molding, casting, or coremaking machines to mold or cast metal or thermoplastic parts or products.

Multiple machine tool setters, operators, and tenders set up or operate more than one type of cutting or forming machine tool or robot.

Welding, soldering, and brazing machine setters, operators, and tenders (including workers who operate laser cutters or laser-beam machines) set up or operate welding, soldering, or brazing machines or robots that weld, braze, solder, or heat treat metal products, components, or assemblies.

Heat treating equipment setters, operators, and tenders set up or operate heating equipment, such as heat treating furnaces, flame-hardening machines, induction machines, soaking pits, or vacuum equipment, to temper, harden, anneal, or heat-treat metal or plastic objects.

Plating and coating machine setters, operators, and tenders set up or operate plating or coating machines to coat metal or plastic products with zinc, copper, nickel, or some other metal to protect or decorate surfaces (includes electrolytic processes).

Work Environment

Metal and plastic machine workers held about 1.1 million jobs in 2019. Employment in the detailed occupations that make up metal and plastic machine workers was distributed as follows:

Metal and plastic machine workers usually wear protective equipment, such as safety glasses.

Cutting, punching, and press machine setters, operators, and tenders, metal and plastic	195,700
Molding, coremaking, and casting machine setters, operators, and tenders, metal and plastic	173,400
Computer numerically controlled tool operators	152,400
Multiple machine tool setters, operators, and tenders, metal and plastic	150,500
Extruding and drawing machine setters, operators, and tenders, metal and plastic	77,400
Grinding, lapping, polishing, and buffing machine tool setters, operators, and tenders, metal and plastic	77,100
Plating machine setters, operators, and tenders, metal and plastic	42,100
Welding, soldering, and brazing machine setters, operators, and tenders	37,200
Rolling machine setters, operators, and tenders, metal and plastic	32,600
Lathe and turning machine tool setters, operators, and tenders, metal and plastic	28,200
Computer numerically controlled tool programmers	25,700
Heat treating equipment setters, operators, and tenders, metal and plastic	20,100
Milling and planing machine setters, operators, and tenders, metal and plastic	19,200
Foundry mold and coremakers	17,600
Metal-refining furnace operators and tenders	17,100
Forging machine setters, operators, and tenders, metal and plastic	16,400
Drilling and boring machine tool setters, operators, and tenders, metal and plastic	11,200
Pourers and casters, metal	8,000
Model makers, metal and plastic	4,400
Patternmakers, metal and plastic	3,100

The largest employers of metal and plastic machine workers were as follows:

Fabricated metal product manufacturing........................ 26%

Plastics and rubber products manufacturing................. 16

Transportation equipment manufacturing..................... 14

Primary metal manufacturing... 12

Machinery manufacturing... 10

Injuries and Illnesses

These workers often operate powerful, high-speed machines that can be dangerous, so they must observe safety rules. Operators usually wear protective equipment, such as safety glasses, earplugs, and steel-toed boots to protect them from flying particles of metal or plastic, machine noise, and heavy objects, respectively.

Other required safety equipment varies by work setting and machine. For example, respirators are common for those in the plastics industry who work near materials that emit dangerous fumes or dust.

Welding, soldering, and brazing machine setters, operators, and tenders have one of the highest rates of injuries and illnesses of all occupations.

Work Schedules

Most metal and plastic machine workers are employed full time. Overtime is common, and because many manufacturers run their machinery for extended periods, evening and weekend work is also common.

How to Become a Metal or Plastic Machine Worker

Most metal and plastic workers have a high school diploma and learn through on-the-job training typically lasting a year. Computer numerically controlled (CNC) machine tool programmers, however, typically need to complete courses beyond high school.

Education

Although most metal and plastic machine workers typically have a high school diploma, many computer numerically

Metal and plastic machine workers must be able to stand for long periods and perform repetitive work.

controlled machine tool programmers usually need to complete coursework beyond high school. Some community colleges and other schools offer courses and certificate programs in operating metal and plastics machines including CNC programming.

For most metal and plastic machine workers, high school courses in computer programming, vocational technology, algebra, geometry, trigonometry, and basic statistics are considered useful.

Training

Machine operator trainees usually begin by watching and helping experienced workers on the job. Under supervision, they may start by supplying materials, starting and stopping the machines, or by removing finished products. Then they advance to more difficult tasks that operators perform, such as adjusting feed speeds, changing cutting tools, and inspecting a finished product for defects. Eventually, some develop the skills and experience to set up machines.

The complexity of the equipment usually determines the time required to become an operator. Some operators and tenders are trained on basic machine operations and functions in a few months, but other workers, such as computer-controlled machine tool operators, may need up to a year to become trained.

As the manufacturing process continues to utilize more computerized machinery, training on computer-aided design (CAD), computer-aided manufacturing (CAM), and CNC machines can be helpful.

Licenses, Certifications, and Registrations

Certification can show competence and can be helpful for advancement. The National Institute for Metalworking Skills (NIMS) offers certification in numerous metalworking specializations.

Advancement

Advancement usually includes higher pay and more responsibilities. With experience and expertise, workers can become trainees for more advanced positions. It is common for machine operators to move into setup or machinery maintenance positions. Setup workers may become industrial machinery mechanics and maintenance workers, or machinists or tool and die makers.

Experienced workers with good communication and analytical skills may move into supervisory positions.

Important Qualities

Computer skills. Metal and plastic machine workers often must be able to use programmable devices, computers, and robots on the factory floor.

Dexterity. Metal and plastic machine workers who work in metal and plastic machined goods manufacturing use precise hand movements to make the necessary shapes, cuts, and edges that designs require.

Mechanical skills. Metal and plastic machine workers set up and operate machinery. They must be comfortable working with machines and have a good understanding of how the machines and all their parts work.

Physical stamina. Metal and plastic machine workers must be able to stand for long periods and perform repetitive work.

Physical strength. Metal and plastic machine workers must be strong enough to guide and load heavy and bulky parts and materials into machines.

Pay

The median annual wage for metal and plastic machine workers was $36,990 in May 2019. The median wage is the wage at which half the workers in an occupation earned more than that amount and half earned less. The lowest 10 percent earned less than $25,000, and the highest 10 percent earned more than $58,200.

Median annual wages for metal and plastic machine workers in May 2019 were as follows:

Model makers, metal and plastic	$57,020
Computer numerically controlled tool programmers	56,450
Patternmakers, metal and plastic	46,910
Milling and planing machine setters, operators, and tenders, metal and plastic	43,210
Metal-refining furnace operators and tenders	42,250
Computer numerically controlled tool operators	41,200
Rolling machine setters, operators, and tenders, metal and plastic	40,490
Lathe and turning machine tool setters, operators, and tenders, metal and plastic	40,100
Forging machine setters, operators, and tenders, metal and plastic	39,670
Drilling and boring machine tool setters, operators, and tenders, metal and plastic	38,910
Pourers and casters, metal	38,620
Welding, soldering, and brazing machine setters, operators, and tenders	38,310
Heat treating equipment setters, operators, and tenders, metal and plastic	38,250
Multiple machine tool setters, operators, and tenders, metal and plastic	36,330
Extruding and drawing machine setters, operators, and tenders, metal and plastic	36,320
Grinding, lapping, polishing, and buffing machine tool setters, operators, and tenders, metal and plastic	36,100
Cutting, punching, and press machine setters, operators, and tenders, metal and plastic	35,610
Foundry mold and coremakers	35,590
Plating machine setters, operators, and tenders, metal and plastic	33,500
Molding, coremaking, and casting machine setters, operators, and tenders, metal and plastic	32,130

In May 2019, the median annual wages for metal and plastic machine workers in the top industries in which they worked were as follows:

Machinery manufacturing	$40,120
Primary metal manufacturing	39,280
Transportation equipment manufacturing	38,870
Fabricated metal product manufacturing	37,390
Plastics and rubber products manufacturing	32,370

Most metal and plastic machine workers are employed full time. Overtime is common, and because many manufacturers run their machinery for extended periods, evening and weekend work also is common.

Job Outlook

Employment of metal and plastic machine workers is projected to decline 7 percent from 2019 to 2029. Employment declines are expected to stem from continued advances in technology and foreign competition.

One of the most important factors influencing employment of these occupations is the use of labor-saving machinery. Many

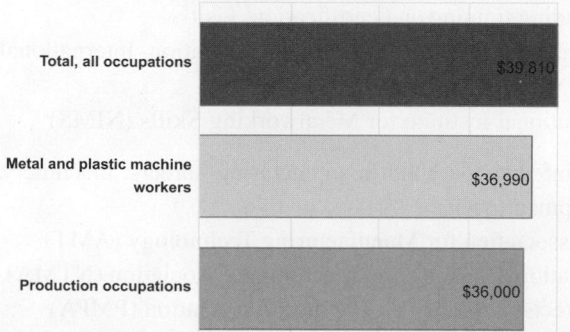

Metal and Plastic Machine Workers

Median annual wages, May 2019

Total, all occupations	$39,810
Metal and plastic machine workers	$36,990
Production occupations	$36,000

Note: All Occupations includes all occupations in the U.S. Economy.
Source: U.S. Bureau of Labor Statistics, Occupational Employment Statistics.

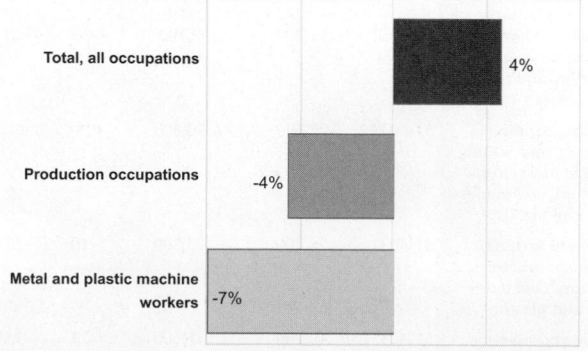

Metal and Plastic Machine Workers

Percent change in employment, projected 2019-29

Total, all occupations	4%
Production occupations	-4%
Metal and plastic machine workers	-7%

Note: All Occupations includes all occupations in the U.S. Economy.
Source: U.S. Bureau of Labor Statistics, Employment Projections program.

firms are adopting technologies such as computer numerically controlled (CNC) machine tools and robots to improve quality and lower production costs. The switch to CNC machinery requires computer programmers instead of machine setters, operators, and tenders. Therefore, demand for manual machine tool operators and tenders is likely to be reduced by these new technologies, and conversely, demand for CNC machine programmers is expected to be strong.

The demand for metal and plastic machine workers is also affected by the demand for the parts they produce. Both the plastic and metal manufacturing industries face foreign competition that limits the orders for parts produced in this country. Some U.S. manufacturers have moved their production to foreign countries, reducing jobs for machine setters and operators. However, some companies are bringing jobs back to the United States from overseas, and this is expected to continue over the coming decade.

Job Prospects

Most job opportunities will result from the need to replace workers who leave these occupations.

Workers who are able to operate CNC machines and have industry certifications should also have best job prospects.

Employment projections data for metal and plastic machine workers, 2019-29					
Occupational Title	SOC Code	Employment, 2019	Projected Employment, 2029	Change, 2019-29	
				Percent	Numeric
SOURCE: U.S. Bureau of Labor Statistics, Employment Projections program					
Metal and plastic machine workers	—	1,109,400	1,033,700	-7	-75,800
Extruding and drawing machine setters, operators, and tenders, metal and plastic	51-4021	77,400	69,200	-11	-8,200
Forging machine setters, operators, and tenders, metal and plastic	51-4022	16,400	13,000	-21	-3,500
Rolling machine setters, operators, and tenders, metal and plastic	51-4023	32,600	28,900	-11	-3,700
Cutting, punching, and press machine setters, operators, and tenders, metal and plastic	51-4031	195,700	179,400	-8	-16,300
Drilling and boring machine tool setters, operators, and tenders, metal and plastic	51-4032	11,200	9,100	-19	-2,100
Grinding, lapping, polishing, and buffing machine tool setters, operators, and tenders, metal and plastic	51-4033	77,100	70,800	-8	-6,300
Lathe and turning machine tool setters, operators, and tenders, metal and plastic	51-4034	28,200	25,300	-10	-2,900
Milling and planing machine setters, operators, and tenders, metal and plastic	51-4035	19,200	15,600	-19	-3,600

Employment projections data for metal and plastic machine workers, 2019-29					
Occupational Title	SOC Code	Employment, 2019	Projected Employment, 2029	Change, 2019-29	
				Percent	Numeric
Metal-refining furnace operators and tenders	51-4051	17,100	17,100	0	0
Pourers and casters, metal	51-4052	8,000	7,300	-9	-700
Model makers, metal and plastic	51-4061	4,400	4,100	-8	-400
Patternmakers, metal and plastic	51-4062	3,100	2,800	-8	-300
Foundry mold and coremakers	51-4071	17,600	16,500	-6	-1,000
Molding, coremaking, and casting machine setters, operators, and tenders, metal and plastic	51-4072	173,400	156,700	-10	-16,700
Multiple machine tool setters, operators, and tenders, metal and plastic	51-4081	150,500	153,600	2	3,100
Welding, soldering, and brazing machine setters, operators, and tenders	51-4122	37,200	34,700	-7	-2,500
Heat treating equipment setters, operators, and tenders, metal and plastic	51-4191	20,100	18,000	-10	-2,100
Plating machine setters, operators, and tenders, metal and plastic	51-4193	42,100	38,400	-9	-3,700
Computer numerically controlled tool operators	51-9161	152,400	141,700	-7	-10,700
Computer numerically controlled tool programmers	51-9162	25,700	31,300	22	5,600

State & Area Data
Occupational Employment Statistics (OES)

The Occupational Employment Statistics (OES) program produces employment and wage estimates annually for over 800 occupations. These estimates are available for the nation as a whole, for individual states, and for metropolitan and nonmetropolitan areas.

Contacts for More Information

For more information about metal and plastic machine workers, including training and certification, visit
➤ Fabricators & Manufacturers Association, International (FMA)
➤ National Institute for Metalworking Skills (NIMS)

For information about manufacturing careers, machinery, and equipment, visit
➤ Association for Manufacturing Technology (AMT)
➤ National Tooling and Machining Association (NTMA)
➤ Precision Machined Products Association (PMPA)
➤ Precision Metalforming Association (PMA)

Painting and Coating Workers

Summary

Quick Facts: Painting and Coating Workers

2019 Median Pay	$37,770 per year $18.16 per hour
Typical Entry-Level Education	See below
Work Experience in a Related Occupation	None
On-the-job Training	Moderate-term on-the-job training
Number of Jobs, 2019	164,200
Job Outlook, 2019-29	2% (Slower than average)
Employment Change, 2019-29	2,500

What Painting and Coating Workers Do

Painting and coating workers paint and coat a wide range of products, often with the use of machines.

Work Environment

Most painting and coating workers are employed full time. They frequently stand for long periods in specially ventilated areas.

How to Become a Painting and Coating Worker

Most painting and coating workers learn on the job after earning a high school diploma or equivalent. Training for new workers usually lasts several months.

Pay

The median annual wage for coating, painting, and spraying machine setters, operators, and tenders was $38,150 in May 2019.

The median annual wage for painting, coating, and decorating workers was $32,950 in May 2019.

Job Outlook

Employment of painting and coating workers is projected to grow 2 percent from 2019 to 2029, slower than the average for all occupations. Employment growth will vary by specialty and industry.

State & Area Data

Explore resources for employment and wages by state and area for painting and coating workers.

What Painting and Coating Workers Do

Painting and coating workers paint and coat a wide range of products, including cars, jewelry, and ceramics, often with the use of machines.

Duties

Painting and coating workers typically do the following:

- Set up and operate machines that paint or coat products
- Select the paint or coating needed for the job
- Clean and prepare products to be painted or coated
- Determine the required flow of paint and the quality of the coating
- Apply paint or coating
- Clean and maintain tools, equipment, and work areas

Painting and coating workers paint items ranging from cars to furniture. They apply paint, varnish, rustproofing, or other types of liquid applications to make a product more attractive and protect it from the elements. The paint finish on an automobile, for example, makes the vehicle more attractive and provides protection from corrosion.

Before workers begin to apply the paint or other coating, they often prepare the surface by sanding or cleaning it carefully to prevent dust from becoming trapped under the paint. Workers also may mask or cover portions of the product with tape and paper before painting the product.

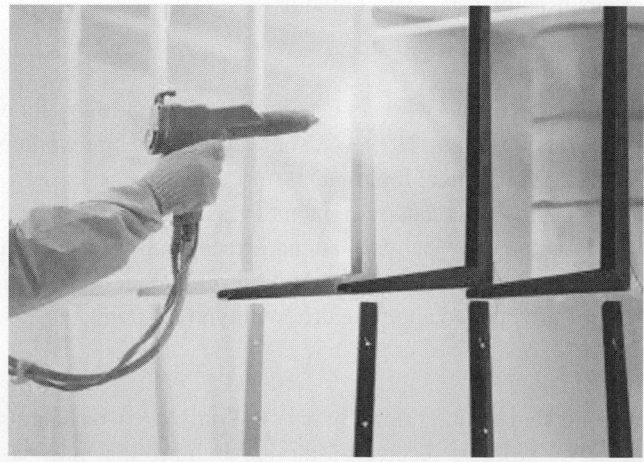

Painting and coating workers paint many different surfaces.

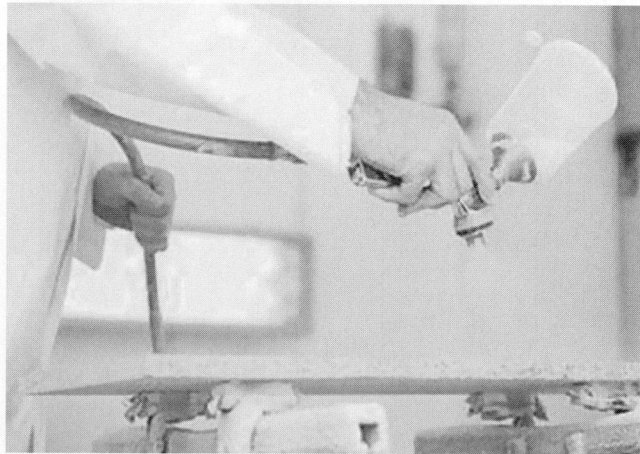

Painters use spray guns to apply paints and coatings in factories.

After the product is prepared, workers may use a number of techniques to apply the paint or coating. A common technique is dipping an item in a large vat of paint or some other coating. Spraying products with paint or another coating is also common. Many factories use automated painting systems.

The following are examples of types of painting and coating workers:

Coating, painting, and spraying machine setters, operators, and tenders position the spray guns, set the nozzles, and synchronize the action of the guns with the speed of the conveyor carrying products through the machine. During the process, these workers program the machine, tend the equipment, watch gauges on the control panel, and check products to ensure that they are being painted evenly. The operator may use a manual spray gun to touch up flaws.

Painting, coating, and decorating workers apply coatings to furniture, glass, pottery, toys, books, and other products. Paper is often coated to give it a gloss. Silver, tin, and copper solutions are frequently sprayed onto glass to make mirrors.

Transportation equipment painters are the best known group of painting and coating workers. They paint various types of transportation equipment, including cars, aircraft, and boats.

Work Environment

Coating, painting, and spraying machine setters, operators, and tenders held about 151,400 jobs in 2019. The largest employers

Workers must wear masks, gloves, and other protective equipment.

of coating, painting, and spraying machine setters, operators, and tenders were as follows:

Fabricated metal product manufacturing	20%
Automotive body, paint, interior, and glass repair	16
Transportation equipment manufacturing	16
Machinery manufacturing	8
Furniture and related product manufacturing	4

Painting, coating, and decorating workers held about 12,800 jobs in 2019. The largest employers of painting, coating, and decorating workers were as follows:

Miscellaneous manufacturing	15%
Furniture and related product manufacturing	9
Nonmetallic mineral product manufacturing	8
Transportation equipment manufacturing	6

Painting and coating is usually done in specially ventilated areas. Nonetheless, workers must wear masks or respirators that cover their nose and mouth.

Painting and coating workers often stand for long periods. They also may have to bend, stoop, or crouch in uncomfortable positions to reach different parts of the products they work on.

Injuries and Illnesses

Painting, coating, and decorating workers have one of the highest rates of injuries and illnesses of all occupations. Hazards include muscle strains and exposure to toxic materials. More sophisticated paint booths and fresh-air ventilation systems are increasingly being installed in factories to provide a safer work environment.

Work Schedules

Most painting and coating workers are employed full time.

How to Become a Painting and Coating Worker

Most painting and coating workers learn on the job after earning a high school diploma or equivalent. Training for new workers usually lasts several months.

Education

Painting and coating workers usually must have a high school diploma or equivalent. However, some employers hire workers who lack a high school diploma.

Taking high school courses in automotive painting can be helpful.

Some automotive painters attend a technical or vocational school where they receive hands-on training and learn the intricacies of mixing and applying different types of paint.

Training

Although some worker training may last only a few days, most entry-level workers receive on-the-job training that may last from 1 month to several months.

Painting and coating workers can usually become proficient in less than 1 year.

Workers who operate computer-controlled equipment may require additional training in computer programming.

Important Qualities

Artistic ability. Some painting and coating workers make elaborate or decorative designs. For example, some automotive painters specialize in making custom designs for vehicles.

Color vision. Workers must be able to blend new paint colors in order to match existing colors on a surface.

Mechanical skills. Workers must be able to operate and maintain sprayers that apply paints and coatings.

Physical stamina. Some workers must stand at their station for extended periods. Continuous standing or activity can be tiring.

Physical strength. Workers may need to lift heavy objects. Some products that are painted or coated may weigh more than 50 pounds.

Pay

The median annual wage for coating, painting, and spraying machine setters, operators, and tenders was $38,150 in May 2019. The median wage is the wage at which half the workers in an occupation earned more than that amount and half earned less. The lowest 10 percent earned less than $25,760, and the highest 10 percent earned more than $61,220.

The median annual wage for painting, coating, and decorating workers was $32,950 in May 2019. The lowest 10 percent

Painting and Coating Workers
Median annual wages, May 2019

Total, all occupations	$39,810
Coating, painting, and spraying machine setters, operators, and tenders	$38,150
Painting and coating workers	$37,770
Production occupations	$36,000
Painting, coating, and decorating workers	$32,950

Note: All Occupations includes all occupations in the U.S. Economy.
Source: U.S. Bureau of Labor Statistics, Occupational Employment Statistics.

earned less than $23,070, and the highest 10 percent earned more than $51,540.

In May 2019, the median annual wages for coating, painting, and spraying machine setters, operators, and tenders in the top industries in which they worked were as follows:

Automotive body, paint, interior, and glass repair	$43,530
Transportation equipment manufacturing	42,410
Machinery manufacturing	37,410
Fabricated metal product manufacturing	34,370
Furniture and related product manufacturing	33,510

In May 2019, the median annual wages for painting, coating, and decorating workers in the top industries in which they worked were as follows:

Transportation equipment manufacturing	$35,510
Miscellaneous manufacturing	34,470
Furniture and related product manufacturing	32,770
Nonmetallic mineral product manufacturing	29,950

Automotive painters in repair shops may receive a bonus or commission in addition to their wages.

Most painting and coating workers are employed full time.

Job Outlook

Overall employment of painting and coating workers is projected to grow 2 percent from 2019 to 2029, slower than the average for all occupations. Employment growth will vary by occupation and industry.

Much of the job growth for painting and coating workers will occur in automotive repair shops, where the irregular nature of the work makes automation difficult.

Although many consumer, commercial, and industrial products require painting or coating and thus will provide job opportunities for these workers, automation in many manufacturing facilities is expected to reduce job opportunities for these workers.

Painting and Coating Workers
Percent change in employment, projected 2019-29

- Total, all occupations
- Painting and coating workers — 2%
- Coating, painting, and spraying machine setters, operators, and tenders — 2%
- Painting, coating, and decorating workers — -1%
- Production occupations — -4%

Note: All Occupations includes all occupations in the U.S. Economy.
Source: U.S. Bureau of Labor Statistics, Employment Projections program.

Job Prospects

In addition to job growth in some industries, many job openings should result from the need to replace workers who leave the occupation.

Employment projections data for painting and coating workers, 2019-29

Occupational Title	SOC Code	Employment, 2019	Projected Employment, 2029	Change, 2019-29 Percent	Numeric
Painting workers	51-9120	164,200	166,700	2	2,500
Painting, coating, and decorating workers	51-9123	12,800	12,700	-1	-100

SOURCE: U.S. Bureau of Labor Statistics, Employment Projections program

Employment projections data for painting and coating workers, 2019-29

Occupational Title	SOC Code	Employment, 2019	Projected Employment, 2029	Change, 2019-29 Percent	Numeric
Coating, painting, and spraying machine setters, operators, and tenders	51-9124	151,400	153,900	2	2,600

State & Area Data
Occupational Employment Statistics (OES)

The Occupational Employment Statistics (OES) program produces employment and wage estimates annually for over 800 occupations. These estimates are available for the nation as a whole, for individual states, and for metropolitan and nonmetropolitan areas.

Contacts for More Information

For more information about job opportunities for painting and coating workers, visit
- Local manufacturers
- Automotive body repair shops
- Motor vehicle dealers
- Vocational schools
- Local unions representing painting and coating workers
- Local offices of state employment services

For a directory of certified automotive painting programs, visit
➤ National Institute for Automotive Service Excellence

Power Plant Operators, Distributors, and Dispatchers

Summary

Quick Facts: Power Plant Operators, Distributors, and Dispatchers

2019 Median Pay	$85,950 per year / $41.32 per hour
Typical Entry-Level Education	High school diploma or equivalent
Work Experience in a Related Occupation	None
On-the-job Training	Long-term on-the-job training
Number of Jobs, 2019	51,700
Job Outlook, 2019-29	-16% (Decline)
Employment Change, 2019-29	-8,100

What Power Plant Operators, Distributors, and Dispatchers Do

Power plant operators, distributors, and dispatchers control the systems that generate and distribute electric power.

Work Environment

Most power plant operators, distributors, and dispatchers work full time. Many work rotating 8- or 12-hour shifts.

How to Become a Power Plant Operator, Distributor, or Dispatcher

Power plant operators, distributors, and dispatchers typically need a high school diploma or equivalent combined with extensive on-the-job training that may include a combination of classroom and hands-on training. Many jobs require a background check and drug and alcohol screenings. Nuclear power reactor operators also need a license.

Pay

The median annual wage for power plant operators, distributors, and dispatchers was $85,950 in May 2019.

Job Outlook

Overall employment of power plant operators, distributors, and dispatchers is projected to decline 16 percent from 2019 to 2029. Although electricity use is expected to grow, technological advances and greater efficiency are expected to reduce employment.

Power plant operators monitor power-generating equipment such as nuclear reactors from control rooms.

State & Area Data

Explore resources for employment and wages by state and area for power plant operators, distributors, and dispatchers.

What Power Plant Operators, Distributors, and Dispatchers Do

Power plant operators, distributors, and dispatchers control the systems that generate and distribute electric power.

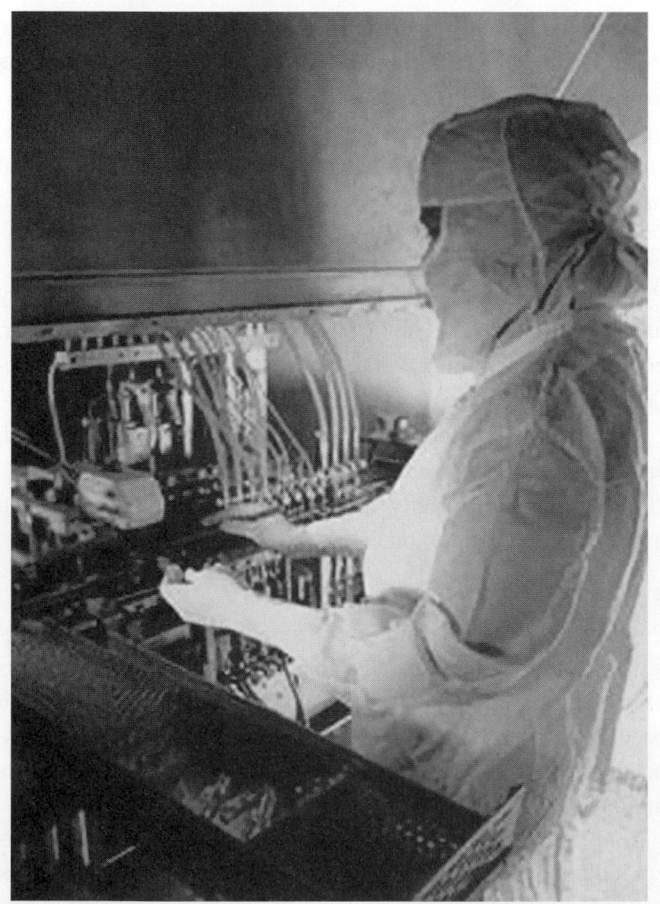

Operators may have to operate or repair complex machinery.

Duties

Power plant operators, distributors, and dispatchers typically do the following:

- Control power-generating equipment, which may use any one type of fuel, such as coal, nuclear power, or natural gas
- Read charts, meters, and gauges to monitor voltage and electricity flows
- Check equipment and indicators to detect evidence of operating problems
- Adjust controls to regulate the flow of power
- Start or stop generators, turbines, and other equipment as necessary

Electricity is one of our nation's most vital resources. Power plant operators, distributors, and dispatchers control power plants and the flow of electricity from plants to substations, which distribute electricity to businesses, homes, and factories. Electricity is generated from many sources, including coal, gas, nuclear energy, hydroelectric energy (from water sources), wind, and solar power.

Nuclear power reactor operators control nuclear reactors. They adjust control rods, which affect how much electricity a reactor generates. They monitor reactors, turbines, generators, and cooling systems, adjusting controls as necessary. Operators start and stop equipment and record the data produced. They also respond to abnormalities, determine the causes, and take corrective action.

Power distributors and dispatchers, also known as *systems operators*, control the flow of electricity as it travels from generating stations to substations and users. In exercising such control, they monitor and operate current converters, voltage transformers, and circuit breakers over a network of transmission and distribution lines. They prepare and issue switching orders to route electrical currents around areas that need maintenance or repair. They detect and respond to emergencies, such as transformer or transmission line failures, which can cause cascading power outages over the network. They may work with plant operators to troubleshoot electricity generation issues.

Power plant operators control, operate, and maintain machinery to generate electricity. They use control boards to distribute power among generators and regulate the output of several generators. They monitor instruments to maintain voltage and electricity flows from the plant to meet fluctuating consumer demand throughout the day.

Work Environment

Power plant operators, distributors, and dispatchers held about 51,700 jobs in 2019. Employment in the detailed occupations that make up power plant operators, distributors, and dispatchers was distributed as follows:

Power plant operators 35,300

Power distributors and dispatchers............................ 11,200

Nuclear power reactor operators................................ 5,300

The largest employers of power plant operators, distributors, and dispatchers were as follows:

Utilities.. 68%

Government 16

Operators, distributors, and dispatchers who work in control rooms generally sit or stand at a control station. The work requires constant attention. Workers also may do rounds, checking equipment and doing other work outside the control room. Transmission stations and substations where distributors and dispatchers work are typically in locations that are separate from the generating station where power plant operators work.

Because power transmission is both vitally important and sensitive to attack, security is a major concern for utility companies. Nuclear power plants and transmission stations have especially high security, and employees work in secure environments.

Work Schedules

Because electricity is provided around the clock, operators, distributors, and dispatchers usually work rotating 8- or 12-hour shifts. Work on rotating shifts can be stressful and tiring because of the constant changes in living and sleeping patterns.

How to Become a Power Plant Operator, Distributor, or Dispatcher

Power plant operators, distributors, and dispatchers typically need a high school diploma or equivalent combined with extensive on-the-job training, which may include a combination of classroom and hands-on training. Many jobs require a background check and screenings for drugs and alcohol.

Nuclear power reactor operators also need a license.

Power plant operators must monitor plant equipment and take action if problems arise.

Most power plant operators work at a control station.

Many companies require prospective workers to take the Power Plant Maintenance and Plant Operator exams from the Edison Electrical Institute to see if they have the right aptitudes for this work. These tests measure reading comprehension, understanding of mechanical concepts, spatial ability, and mathematical ability.

Education

Power plant operators, distributors, and dispatchers typically need at least a high school diploma or equivalent. However, employers may prefer workers who have a college or vocational school degree.

Employers generally look for people with strong math and science backgrounds for these highly technical jobs. Understanding electricity and math, especially algebra and trigonometry, is important.

Training

Power plant operators and dispatchers undergo rigorous, long-term on-the-job training and technical instruction. Several years of onsite training and experience are necessary for a worker to become fully qualified. Even fully qualified operators and dispatchers must take regular training courses to keep their skills up to date.

Nuclear power reactor operators usually start working as equipment operators or auxiliary operators, helping more experienced workers operate and maintain the equipment while learning the basics of how to operate the power plant.

Along with this extensive on-the-job training, nuclear power plant operators typically receive formal technical training to prepare for the license exam from the U.S. Nuclear Regulatory Commission (NRC). Once licensed, operators are authorized to control equipment that affects the power of the reactor in a nuclear power plant. Operators continue frequent onsite training, which familiarizes them with new monitoring systems that provide operators better real-time information regarding the plant.

Licenses, Certifications, and Registrations

Nuclear power reactor operators must be licensed through the NRC. They typically begin working in nuclear power plants as unlicensed operators, where they gain the required knowledge and experience to start the licensing process. To become licensed, operators must meet training and experience requirements, pass a medical exam, and pass the NRC licensing exam. To keep their license, operators must pass a plant-operating exam each year, pass a medical exam every 2 years, and apply for renewal of their license every 6 years. Licenses cannot be transferred between plants, so an operator must get a new license to work in another facility.

Power plant operators who do not work at a nuclear power reactor may be licensed as engineers or firefighters by state licensing boards. Requirements vary by state and depend on the specific job functions that the operator performs.

Power plant operators, distributors, and dispatchers who are in positions which could affect the power grid may need to be certified through the North American Electric Reliability Corporation's System Operator Certification Program.

Advancement

With sufficient education, training and experience, power plant distributors and dispatchers can become shift supervisors, trainers, or consultants.

Licensed nuclear power plant operators can then advance to senior reactor operators, who supervise the operation of all controls in the control room. Senior reactor operators also may become plant managers or licensed operator instructors.

Important Qualities

Concentration skills. Power plant operators, distributors, and dispatchers must be careful, attentive, and persistent. They must be able to concentrate on a task, such as monitoring the temperature of reactors over a certain length of time, without being distracted.

Detail oriented. Power plant operators, distributors, and dispatchers must monitor complex controls and intricate machinery to ensure that everything is operating properly.

Dexterity. Power plant operators, distributors, and dispatchers must use precise and repeated motions when working in a control room.

Mechanical skills. Power plant operators, distributors, and dispatchers must know how to work with machines and use tools. They must be familiar with how to operate, repair, and maintain equipment.

Problem-solving skills. Power plant operators, distributors, and dispatchers must find and quickly solve problems that arise with equipment or controls.

Pay

The median annual wage for power plant operators, distributors, and dispatchers was $85,950 in May 2019. The median wage is the wage at which half the workers in an occupation earned more than that amount and half earned less. The lowest 10 percent earned less than $49,730, and the highest 10 percent earned more than $117,130.

Median annual wages for power plant operators, distributors, and dispatchers in May 2019 were as follows:

Nuclear power reactor operators	$100,530
Power distributors and dispatchers	90,700
Power plant operators	81,990

In May 2019, the median annual wages for power plant operators, distributors, and dispatchers in the top industries in which they worked were as follows:

Utilities	$87,970
Government	83,460

Because electricity is provided around the clock, operators, distributors, and dispatchers usually work rotating 8- or 12-hour shifts. Work on rotating shifts can be stressful and tiring because of the constant changes in living and sleeping patterns.

Job Outlook

Overall employment of power plant operators, distributors, and dispatchers is projected to decline 16 percent from 2019

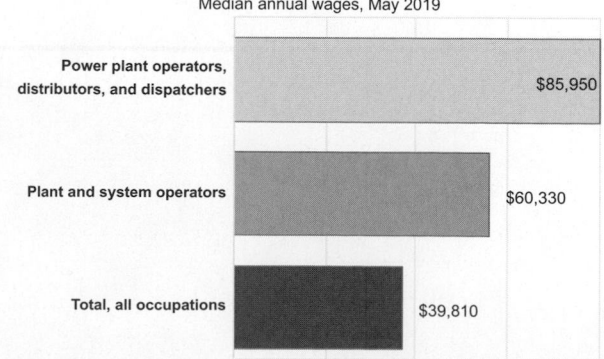

Power Plant Operators, Distributors, and Dispatchers

Median annual wages, May 2019

Power plant operators, distributors, and dispatchers	$85,950
Plant and system operators	$60,330
Total, all occupations	$39,810

Note: All Occupations includes all occupations in the U.S. Economy.
Source: U.S. Bureau of Labor Statistics, Occupational Employment Statistics.

Power Plant Operators, Distributors, and Dispatchers

Percent change in employment, projected 2019-29

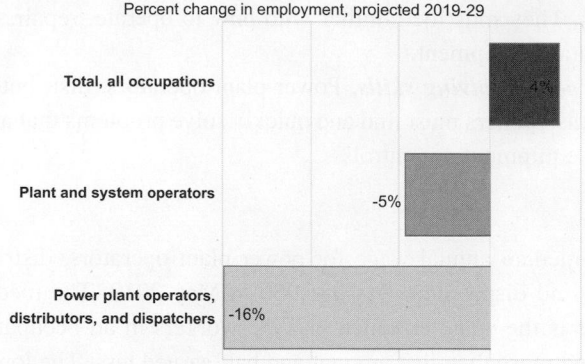

Note: All Occupations includes all occupations in the U.S. Economy.
Source: U.S. Bureau of Labor Statistics, Employment Projections program.

to 2029. Although electricity use is expected to grow, technological advances and greater efficiency are expected to reduce employment.

Power plants are becoming more efficient and, in many cases, have higher electricity-generating capacities. Modernized control rooms in power plants will also provide workers with more information and automate some tasks. As a result, workers are able to work more efficiently, which limits the opportunity for new jobs. Similarly, these efficiency gains are expected to affect employment of nuclear power reactor operators, which is also projected to decline over the decade. No new nuclear plants have opened since the 1990s, and although some are in the application process, opening a new one may take many years.

The projected employment decline for power distributors and dispatchers is due to advances in smart-grid technology. Some tasks that dispatchers perform, such as rerouting power during an outage, can be automated. However, some distributors and dispatchers will still be needed to manage the complex electrical grid.

Job Prospects

Job prospects may be limited as technology advances and these jobs become more automated. Many people will seek these high-paying jobs, so those with strong technical and mechanical skills will have better job prospects.

Employment projections data for power plant operators, distributors, and dispatchers, 2019-29					
Occupational Title	SOC Code	Employment, 2019	Projected Employment, 2029	Change, 2019-29	
				Percent	Numeric
SOURCE: U.S. Bureau of Labor Statistics, Employment Projections program					
Power plant operators, distributors, and dispatchers	51-8010	51,700	43,700	-16	-8,100
Nuclear power reactor operators	51-8011	5,300	3,400	-36	-1,900
Power distributors and dispatchers	51-8012	11,200	10,300	-8	-900
Power plant operators	51-8013	35,300	30,000	-15	-5,300

State & Area Data
Occupational Employment Statistics (OES)

The Occupational Employment Statistics (OES) program produces employment and wage estimates annually for over 800 occupations. These estimates are available for the nation as a whole, for individual states, and for metropolitan and nonmetropolitan areas.

Contacts for More Information

For more information about power plant operators, nuclear power reactor operators, and power plant distributors and dispatchers, visit
➤ American Public Power Association
➤ Center for Energy Workforce Development
➤ International Brotherhood of Electrical Workers

For more information on nuclear power reactor operators, including licensing, visit
➤ U.S. Nuclear Regulatory Commission
➤ Nuclear Energy Institute

For information on certification for power distributors and dispatchers, visit
➤ North American Electric Reliability Corporation

Quality Control Inspectors

Summary

Quick Facts: Quality Control Inspectors

2019 Median Pay	$39,140 per year
	$18.82 per hour
Typical Entry-Level Education	High school diploma or equivalent
Work Experience in a Related Occupation	None
On-the-job Training	Moderate-term on-the-job training
Number of Jobs, 2019	590,100
Job Outlook, 2019-29	-17% (Decline)
Employment Change, 2019-29	-100,400

What Quality Control Inspectors Do

Quality control inspectors examine products and materials for defects or deviations from specifications.

Work Environment

Working conditions vary by industry, establishment size, and specific duty. Most quality control inspectors work full time during regular business hours. Overtime may be required to meet production deadlines.

How to Become a Quality Control Inspector

Most quality control inspectors need a high school diploma and receive on-the-job training that typically lasts as little as 1 month or up to 1 year.

Pay

The median annual wage for quality control inspectors was $39,140 in May 2019.

Job Outlook

Employment of quality control inspectors is projected to decline 17 percent from 2019 to 2029.

State & Area Data

Explore resources for employment and wages by state and area for quality control inspectors.

What Quality Control Inspectors Do

Quality control inspectors examine products and materials for defects or deviations from specifications.

Duties

Quality control inspectors typically do the following:

- Read blueprints and specifications
- Monitor operations to ensure that they meet production standards
- Recommend adjustments to the assembly or production process
- Inspect, test, or measure materials or products being produced
- Measure products with rulers, calipers, gauges, or micrometers
- Operate electronic inspection equipment and software
- Accept or reject finished items
- Remove all products and materials that fail to meet specifications
- Report inspection and test data such as weights, temperatures, grades, moisture content, and quantities inspected

Quality control inspectors monitor quality standards for nearly all manufactured products, including foods, textiles, clothing, glassware, motor vehicles, electronic components, computers, and structural steel. Specific job duties vary across the wide range of industries in which these inspectors work.

Quality control workers rely on many tools to do their jobs. Although some still use hand-held measurement devices, such

Quality control inspectors monitor production operations, ensuring that specifications are met.

Quality control inspectors remove or discard all products and equipment that fail to meet specifications.

as calipers and alignment gauges, workers more commonly operate electronic inspection equipment, such as coordinate-measuring machines (CMMs) and three-dimensional (3D) scanners. Inspectors testing electrical devices may use voltmeters, ammeters, and ohmmeters to test potential difference, current flow, and resistance, respectively.

Quality control workers record the results of their inspections through test reports. When they find defects, inspectors notify supervisors and help to analyze and correct production problems.

In some firms, the inspection process is completely automated, with advanced vision inspection systems installed at one or several points in the production process. Inspectors in these firms monitor the equipment, review output, and conduct random product checks.

The following are examples of types of quality control inspectors:

Inspectors mark, tag, or note problems. They may reject defective items outright, send them for repair, or fix minor problems themselves. If the product is acceptable, the inspector certifies it. Inspectors may further specialize in the following jobs:

- *Materials inspectors* check products by sight, sound, or feel to locate imperfections such as cuts, scratches, missing pieces, or crooked seams.
- *Mechanical inspectors* generally verify that parts fit, move correctly, and are properly lubricated. They may check the pressure of gases and the level of liquids, test the flow of electricity, and conduct test runs to ensure that machines run properly.

Samplers test or inspect a sample for malfunctions or defects during a batch or production run.

Sorters separate goods according to length, size, fabric type, or color.

Testers repeatedly test existing products or prototypes under real-world conditions. Through these tests, manufacturers determine how long a product will last, what parts will break down first, and how to improve durability.

Weighers weigh quantities of materials for use in production.

Work Environment

Quality control inspectors held about 590,100 jobs in 2019. The largest employers of quality control inspectors were as follows:

Manufacturing	63%
Administrative and support services	9
Professional, scientific, and technical services	9
Wholesale trade	5

Work environments vary by industry and establishment size; some inspectors examine similar products for an entire shift, others examine a variety of items.

Quality control inspectors may be required to stand for long periods of time or lift heavy objects.

Inspectors in some industries may be on their feet all day and may have to lift heavy items. In other industries, workers may sit during their shift and read electronic printouts of data.

Workers in heavy-manufacturing plants may be exposed to the noise and grime of machinery. In other plants, inspectors work in clean, air-conditioned environments suitable for testing products.

Injuries and Illnesses

Some quality control inspectors may be exposed to airborne particles, which may irritate the eyes and skin. As a result, workers typically wear protective eyewear, ear plugs, and appropriate clothing.

Work Schedules

Although most quality control inspectors work full time during regular business hours, some inspectors work evenings or weekends. Shift assignments generally are based on seniority. Overtime may be required to meet production deadlines.

How to Become a Quality Control Inspector

Most quality control inspectors need a high school diploma and receive on-the-job training that typically lasts as little as 1 month or up to 1 year.

Education & Training

Education and training requirements vary with the responsibilities of the quality control worker. For inspectors who do simple pass/fail tests of products, a high school diploma and some in-house training are generally enough. Workers usually receive on-the-job training that typically lasts for as little as 1 month or up to 1 year.

Candidates for inspector jobs can improve their chances of finding work by studying industrial trades in high school or in a postsecondary vocational program. Laboratory work in the natural or biological sciences also may improve a person's analytical skills and increase their chances of finding work in

Quality control inspectors usually receive up to one year of on-the-job training.

medical or pharmaceutical labs, where many of these workers are employed.

Training for new inspectors may cover the use of special meters, gauges, computers, and other instruments; quality control techniques such as Six Sigma; blueprint reading; safety; and reporting requirements. Some postsecondary training programs exist, but many employers prefer to train inspectors on the job.

As manufacturers use more automated techniques that require less inspection by hand, workers increasingly must know how to operate and program more sophisticated equipment and utilize software applications. Because these operations require additional skills, higher education may be necessary. To address this need, some colleges are offering associate's degrees in fields such as quality control management.

Licenses, Certifications, and Registrations

The American Society for Quality (ASQ) offers various certifications, including a designation for Certified Quality Inspector (CQI), and numerous sources of information and various levels of Six Sigma certifications. Although certification is not required, it can demonstrate competence and professionalism, making candidates more attractive to employers. It can also increase opportunities for advancement. Requirements for certification generally include a certain number of years of experience in the field and passing an exam.

Important Qualities

Dexterity. Quality control inspectors must quickly remove sample parts or products during the manufacturing process.

Math skills. Knowledge of basic math and computer skills are important because measuring, calibrating, and calculating specifications are major parts of quality control testing.

Mechanical skills. Quality control inspectors use specialized tools and machinery when testing products.

Physical stamina. Quality control inspectors must stand for long periods on the job.

Physical strength. Because workers sometimes lift heavy objects, inspectors should be in good physical condition.

Technical skills. Quality control inspectors must understand blueprints, technical documents, and manuals, which help ensure that products and parts meet quality standards.

Pay

The median annual wage for quality control inspectors was $39,140 in May 2019. The median wage is the wage at which half the workers in an occupation earned more than that amount and half earned less. The lowest 10 percent earned less than $24,660, and the highest 10 percent earned more than $66,260.

In May 2019, the median annual wages for quality control inspectors in the top industries in which they worked were as follows:

Professional, scientific, and technical services	$42,990
Manufacturing	39,690
Wholesale trade	37,810
Administrative and support services	31,060

Although most quality control inspectors work full time during regular business hours, some inspectors work evenings or weekends. Shift assignments generally are based on seniority. Overtime may be required to meet production deadlines.

Job Outlook

Employment of quality control inspectors is projected to decline 17 percent from 2019 to 2029.

Continued improvements in technology allow manufacturers to automate inspection tasks, increasing workers' productivity and reducing the demand for inspectors. Fabrication and assembly workers monitor quality at every stage of production, assuming many of the duties previously done by specialized inspectors. In addition, use of three-dimensional (3D) scanners decreases the amount of time required to inspect parts and finished goods for correct measurement.

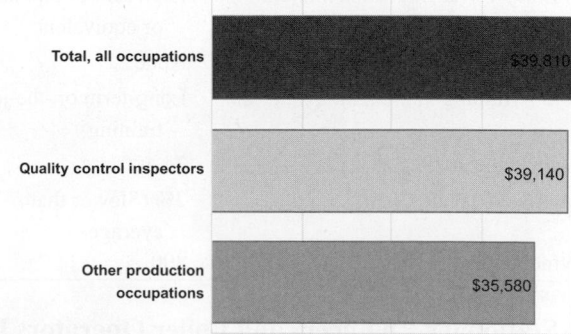

Quality Control Inspectors
Median annual wages, May 2019

Total, all occupations	$39,810
Quality control inspectors	$39,140
Other production occupations	$35,580

Note: All Occupations includes all occupations in the U.S. Economy.
Source: U.S. Bureau of Labor Statistics, Occupational Employment Statistics.

Quality Control Inspectors
Percent change in employment, projected 2019-29

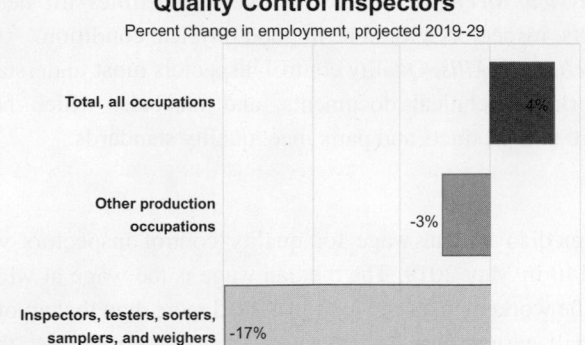

Total, all occupations	4%
Other production occupations	-3%
Inspectors, testers, sorters, samplers, and weighers	-17%

Note: All Occupations includes all occupations in the U.S. Economy.
Source: U.S. Bureau of Labor Statistics, Employment Projections program.

Despite technological advances in quality control in many industries, automation is not appropriate for all inspections. Personal inspections will continue to be needed for products that require testing for taste, smell, texture, appearance, fabric complexity, or performance. Automation will likely become more important for inspecting elements related to size, such as length, width, or thickness.

Job Prospects

Some job opportunities are expected to arise over the coming decade as quality control inspectors retire or leave the occupation for other reasons.

Those with certification and related work experience should have the best job prospects.

Employment projections data for quality control inspectors, 2019-29					
Occupational Title	SOC Code	Employment, 2019	Projected Employment, 2029	Change, 2019-29	
				Percent	Numeric
SOURCE: U.S. Bureau of Labor Statistics, Employment Projections program					
Inspectors, testers, sorters, samplers, and weighers	51-9061	590,100	489,600	-17	-100,400

State & Area Data
Occupational Employment Statistics (OES)

The Occupational Employment Statistics (OES) program produces employment and wage estimates annually for over 800 occupations. These estimates are available for the nation as a whole, for individual states, and for metropolitan and nonmetropolitan areas.

Contacts for More Information

For more information about quality control inspectors, including certification, visit
➤ American Society for Quality (ASQ)

For more information about quality control training, visit
➤ International Society of Automation (ISA)
➤ Quality Assurance Association (QAA)
➤ Society of Quality Assurance (SQA)

Stationary Engineers and Boiler Operators

Summary

Quick Facts: Stationary Engineers and Boiler Operators

2019 Median Pay	$62,150 per year $29.88 per hour
Typical Entry-Level Education	High school diploma or equivalent
Work Experience in a Related Occupation	None
On-the-job Training	Long-term on-the-job training
Number of Jobs, 2019	34,400
Job Outlook, 2019-29	2% (Slower than average)
Employment Change, 2019-29	800

What Stationary Engineers and Boiler Operators Do

Stationary engineers and boiler operators control stationary engines, boilers, or other mechanical equipment.

Work Environment

The majority of stationary engineers and boiler operators work in manufacturing, government, educational services, and hospitals. Those who work in facilities that operate around the clock often work evenings and weekends. Shift work also is common.

How to Become a Stationary Engineer or Boiler Operator

Stationary engineers and boiler operators need at least a high school diploma or equivalent and are trained either on the job or through an apprenticeship program. Many employers require stationary engineers and boiler operators to demonstrate competency through licenses or company-specific exams before they are allowed to operate equipment without supervision.

Pay

The median annual wage for stationary engineers and boiler operators was $62,150 in May 2019.

Stationary engineers and boiler operators manage utility or industrial equipment such as boilers, stationary engines, and generators.

Job Outlook

Employment of stationary engineers and boiler operators is projected to grow 2 percent from 2019 to 2029, slower than the average for all occupations. Those with apprenticeship training should have the best job opportunities.

State & Area Data

Explore resources for employment and wages by state and area for stationary engineers and boiler operators.

What Stationary Engineers and Boiler Operators Do

Stationary engineers and boiler operators control stationary engines, boilers, or other mechanical equipment to provide utilities for buildings or for industrial purposes.

Duties

Stationary engineers and boiler operators typically do the following:

- Operate engines, boilers, and auxiliary equipment
- Read gauges, meters, and charts to track boiler operations
- Monitor boiler water, chemical, and fuel levels
- Activate valves to change the amount of water, air, and fuel in boilers
- Fire coal furnaces or feed boilers, using gas feeds or oil pumps
- Inspect equipment to ensure that it is operating efficiently
- Check safety devices routinely
- Record data and keep logs of operation, maintenance, and safety activity

Most large commercial facilities have extensive heating, ventilation, and air-conditioning systems that maintain comfortable temperatures all year long. Industrial plants often have additional facilities to provide electrical power, steam, or other services. Stationary engineers and boiler operators control and maintain boilers, air-conditioning and refrigeration equipment, turbines, generators, pumps, and compressors.

Stationary engineers and boiler operators start up, regulate, repair, and shut down equipment. They monitor meters, gauges, and computerized controls to ensure that equipment operates safely and within established limits. They use sophisticated electrical and electronic test equipment to service, troubleshoot, repair, and monitor heating, cooling, and ventilation systems.

Stationary engineers and boiler operators also perform routine maintenance. They may completely overhaul or replace defective valves, gaskets, or bearings. In addition, they lubricate moving parts, replace filters, and remove soot and corrosion that can make a boiler less efficient.

Work Environment

Stationary engineers and boiler operators held about 34,400 jobs in 2019. The largest employers of stationary engineers and boiler operators were as follows:

Manufacturing.. 19%

Stationary engineers and boiler operators repair malfunctioning equipment.

Stationary engineers and boiler operators typically work in boiler rooms and mechanical rooms.

In a large building or industrial plant, a senior stationary engineer or boiler operator may be in charge of all mechanical systems in the building and may supervise a team of assistant stationary engineers, assistant boiler tenders, and other operators or mechanics.

In small buildings, there may be only one stationary engineer or boiler operator who operates and maintains all of the systems.

Some stationary engineers and boiler operators are exposed to high temperatures, dust, dirt, and loud noise from the equipment. Maintenance duties may require contact with oil, grease, and smoke.

Workers spend much of their time on their feet. They also may have to crawl inside boilers and work while crouched, or kneel to inspect, clean, or repair equipment.

Injuries and Illnesses

Stationary engineers and boiler operators risk injury on the job. They must follow procedures to guard against burns, electric shock, noise, dangerous moving parts, and exposure to hazardous materials.

Work Schedules

Most stationary engineers and boiler operators work full time during regular business hours. In facilities that operate around the clock, engineers and operators may work either one of three 8-hour shifts or one of two 12-hour shifts on a rotating basis. Because buildings such as hospitals are open 365 days a year and depend on the steam generated by boilers and other machines, many of these workers must work weekends and holidays.

How to Become a Stationary Engineer or Boiler Operator

Stationary engineers and boiler operators typically need a high school diploma or equivalent and are trained either on the job or through an apprenticeship program. Many employers require stationary engineers and boiler operators to demonstrate competency through licenses or company-specific exams before they are allowed to operate equipment without supervision.

Education

Stationary engineers and boiler operators need at least a high school diploma. Students should take courses in math, science, and mechanical and technical subjects.

With the growing complexity of the work, vocational school or college courses may benefit workers trying to advance in the occupation.

Stationary engineers and boiler operators continue training throughout their career.

Training

Stationary engineers and boiler operators typically learn their work through long-term on-the-job training under the supervision of an experienced engineer or operator. Trainees are assigned basic tasks, such as monitoring the temperatures and pressures in the heating and cooling systems and low-pressure boilers. After they demonstrate competence in basic tasks, trainees move on to more complicated tasks, such as the repair of cracks or ruptured tubes for high-pressure boilers.

Some stationary engineers and boiler operators complete apprenticeship programs sponsored by the International Union of Operating Engineers. Apprenticeships usually last 4 years, include 8,000 hours of on-the-job training, and require 600 hours of technical instruction. Apprentices learn about operating and maintaining equipment; using controls and balancing heating, ventilation, and air-conditioning (HVAC) systems; safety; electricity; and air quality. Employers may prefer to hire these workers because they usually require considerably less on-the-job training. However, because of the limited number of apprenticeship programs, employers often have difficulty finding workers who have completed one.

Experienced stationary engineers and boiler operators update their skills regularly through training, especially when new equipment is introduced or when regulations change.

Licenses, Certifications, and Registrations

Some state and local governments require licensure for stationary engineers and boiler operators. These governments typically have several classes of stationary engineer and boiler operator licenses. Each class specifies the type and size of equipment the engineer is permitted to operate without supervision. Many employers require stationary engineers and boiler operators to demonstrate competency through licenses or company-specific exams before they are allowed to operate the equipment without supervision.

A top-level engineer or operator is qualified to run a large facility, supervise others, and operate equipment of all types and capacities. Engineers and operators with licenses below this level are limited in the types or capacities of equipment they may operate without supervision.

Applicants for licensure usually must meet experience requirements and pass a written exam. In some cases, employers may require that workers be licensed before starting the job. A stationary engineer or boiler operator who moves from one state or city to another may have to pass an examination for a new license because of regional differences in licensing requirements.

Advancement

Generally, stationary engineers and boiler operators can advance as they become qualified to operate larger, more powerful, and more varied equipment by obtaining higher class licenses. In jurisdictions where licenses are not required, workers usually advance by taking company-administered exams, ensuring a level of knowledge needed to operate different types of boilers safely.

Important Qualities

Detail oriented. Stationary engineers and boiler operators monitor intricate machinery, gauges, and meters to ensure that everything is operating properly.

Dexterity. Stationary engineers and boiler operators must use precise motions to control or repair machines. They grasp tools and use their hands to perform many tasks.

Mechanical skills. Stationary engineers and boiler operators must know how to use tools and work with machines. They must be able to repair, maintain, and operate equipment.

Problem-solving skills. Stationary engineers and boiler operators must figure out how things work and quickly solve problems that arise with equipment or controls.

Pay

The median annual wage for stationary engineers and boiler operators was $62,150 in May 2019. The median wage is the wage at which half the workers in an occupation earned more than that amount and half earned less. The lowest 10 percent earned less than $39,050, and the highest 10 percent earned more than $100,080.

In May 2019, the median annual wages for stationary engineers and boiler operators in the top industries in which they worked were as follows:

Local government, excluding education and hospitals..	$83,890
Hospitals; state, local, and private............................	65,130
State government, excluding education and hospitals..	63,190
Educational services; state, local, and private.........	58,020
Manufacturing...	57,580

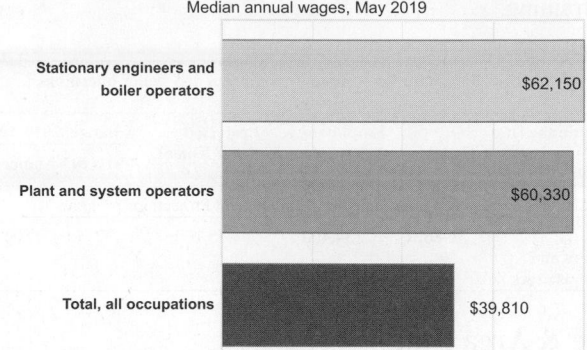

Stationary Engineers and Boiler Operators
Median annual wages, May 2019

Stationary engineers and boiler operators	$62,150
Plant and system operators	$60,330
Total, all occupations	$39,810

Note: All Occupations includes all occupations in the U.S. Economy. Source: U.S. Bureau of Labor Statistics, Occupational Employment Statistics.

Most stationary engineers and boiler operators work full time. In facilities that operate around the clock, engineers and operators may work either one of three 8-hour shifts or one of two 12-hour shifts on a rotating basis. Because buildings such as hospitals are open 365 days a year and depend on the steam generated by boilers and other machines, many of these workers must work weekends and holidays.

Job Outlook

Employment of stationary engineers and boiler operators is projected to grow 2 percent from 2019 to 2029, slower than the average for all occupations.

Steam is an important and cost-effective way to fuel machinery and to provide utilities in large facilities. Workers will be needed for routine maintenance and to ensure that the equipment is working properly.

Job Prospects

Some job openings for stationary engineers and boiler operators are expected to arise from the need to replace workers who leave the occupation or the labor force each year.

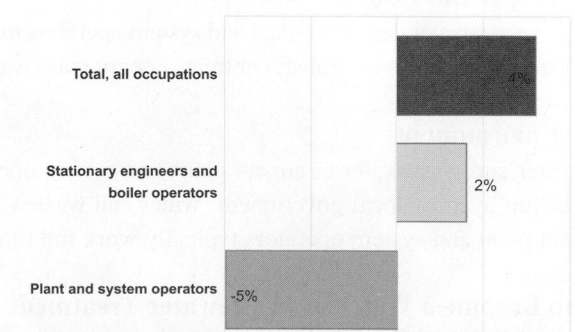

Stationary Engineers and Boiler Operators
Percent change in employment, projected 2019-29

Total, all occupations	4%
Stationary engineers and boiler operators	2%
Plant and system operators	-5%

Note: All Occupations includes all occupations in the U.S. Economy. Source: U.S. Bureau of Labor Statistics, Employment Projections program.

Job opportunities should be best for those with apprenticeship training.

State & Area Data
Occupational Employment Statistics (OES)

The Occupational Employment Statistics (OES) program produces employment and wage estimates annually for over 800 occupations. These estimates are available for the nation as a whole, for individual states, and for metropolitan and nonmetropolitan areas.

Contacts for More Information

For information about apprenticeships, vocational training, and job opportunities, visit

- State employment service offices
- Local chapters of the International Union of Operating Engineers
- Vocational schools
- State and local licensing agencies

Information about apprenticeships is also available from the U.S. Department of Labor's toll-free help line, (877) 872-5627; or the Employment and Training Administration.

For more information about training or becoming a stationary engineer or boiler operator, visit

➤ National Association of Power Engineers, Inc.

Water and Wastewater Treatment Plant and System Operators

Summary

Quick Facts: Water and Wastewater Treatment Plant and System Operators

2019 Median Pay	$47,760 per year $22.96 per hour
Typical Entry-Level Education	High school diploma or equivalent
Work Experience in a Related Occupation	None
On-the-job Training	Long-term on-the-job training
Number of Jobs, 2019	126,400
Job Outlook, 2019-29	-4% (Decline)
Employment Change, 2019-29	-5,400

What Water and Wastewater Treatment Plant and System Operators Do

Water and wastewater treatment plant and system operators manage a system of machines to transfer or treat water or wastewater.

Work Environment

Most water and wastewater treatment plant and system operators are employed by local government. Water and wastewater treatment plant and system operators typically work full time.

How to Become a Water or Wastewater Treatment Plant and System Operator

Water and wastewater treatment plant and system operators typically need at least a high school diploma or equivalent and a license to work. They also complete on-the-job training.

Pay

The median annual wage for water and wastewater treatment plant and system operators was $47,760 in May 2019.

Job Outlook

Employment of water and wastewater treatment plant and system operators is projected to decline 4 percent from 2019 to 2029. As water and wastewater treatment plants become more advanced due to automation, fewer workers may be needed.

State & Area Data

Explore resources for employment and wages by state and area for water and wastewater treatment plant and system operators.

What Water and Wastewater Treatment Plant and System Operators Do

Water and wastewater treatment plant and system operators manage a system of machines, often through the use of control boards, to transfer or treat water or wastewater.

Operators monitor operating conditions, meters, and gauges.

Water and wastewater treatment plant operators collect and test water and sewage samples.

Duties

Water and wastewater treatment plant and system operators typically do the following:

- Add chemicals, such as ammonia or chlorine, to disinfect water or other liquids
- Inspect equipment on a regular basis
- Monitor operating conditions, meters, and gauges
- Collect and test water and sewage samples
- Record meter and gauge readings and operational data
- Document and report test results to regulatory agencies
- Operate equipment to purify and clarify water or to process or dispose of sewage
- Clean and maintain equipment, tanks, filter beds, and other work areas
- Follow U.S. Environmental Protection Agency (EPA) regulations
- Ensure safety standards are met

It takes many steps to get water from natural sources—reservoirs, streams, and groundwater—into people's houses. Similarly, it is a complicated process to convert the wastewater from drains and sewers into a form that is safe to release into the environment.

The specific duties of plant operators depend on the type and size of the plant. In a small plant, one operator may be responsible for maintaining all of the systems. In large plants, multiple operators work the same shifts and are more specialized in their duties, often relying on computerized systems to help them monitor plant processes.

Water and wastewater treatment plant and system operators must be able to manually operate the equipment if there is a plant malfunction due to power outages or electrical issues.

Water treatment plant and system operators work in water treatment plants. Fresh water is pumped from wells, rivers, streams, or reservoirs to water treatment plants, where it is treated and distributed to customers. Water treatment plant and system operators run the equipment, control the processes, and monitor the plants that treat water to make it safe to drink.

Wastewater treatment plant and system operators remove pollutants from domestic and industrial waste. Used water, also known as wastewater, travels through sewer pipes to treatment plants where it is treated and either returned to streams, rivers, and oceans, or used for irrigation.

Work Environment

Water and wastewater treatment plant and system operators held about 126,400 jobs in 2019. The largest employers of water and wastewater treatment plant and system operators were as follows:

Water and wastewater treatment plant and system operators often perform physically demanding tasks.

Local government, excluding education and hospitals..	75%
Utilities..	12
Manufacturing...	4

Water and wastewater treatment plant and system operators work both indoors and outdoors. Their work is physically demanding and usually is performed in locations that are unclean or difficult to access. Operators may be exposed to noise from machinery and are often exposed to unpleasant odors.

Injuries and Illnesses

Water and wastewater treatment plant and system operators sometimes get injured on the job. They must pay close attention to safety procedures because of hazardous conditions, such as slippery walkways, the presence of dangerous gases, and malfunctioning equipment.

Operators are trained in emergency management procedures and use safety equipment to protect their health, as well as that of the public.

Work Schedules

Water and waste treatment plant and system operators typically work full time. Plants operate 24 hours a day, 7 days a week. In small plants, operators are likely to work during the day and be on call nights and weekends. In medium- and large-size plants that require constant monitoring, operators work in shifts to control the plant at all hours.

Occasionally, operators must work during emergencies. For example, they may need to work during weather conditions that cause large amounts of storm water or wastewater to flow into sewers, exceeding a plant's capacity. Emergencies also may be caused by malfunctions within a plant, such as chemical leaks or oxygen deficiencies.

How to Become a Water or Wastewater Treatment Plant and System Operator

Water and wastewater treatment plant and system operators typically need at least a high school diploma or equivalent and a license to work. They also complete on-the-job training.

Education

Water and wastewater treatment plant and system operators typically need a high school diploma or equivalent to become operators. Employers may prefer applicants who have completed a certificate, an associate's, or a bachelor's degree program in a related field such as environmental science or wastewater treatment technology.

Training

Water and wastewater treatment plant and system operators need long-term on-the-job training to become fully qualified. Water and wastewater treatment is a complex process. Trainees

Water and wastewater treatment plant and system operators need long-term on-the-job training to become fully qualified.

learn their skills on the job under the direction of an experienced operator. The trainees learn by observing and doing routine tasks, such as recording meter readings, taking samples of wastewater and sludge, and performing simple maintenance and repair work on plant equipment. They also learn about industrial safety and how to use personal protective equipment.

Larger treatment plants usually combine this on-the-job training with formal classroom or self-paced study programs. As plants get larger and more complicated, operators need more skills before they are allowed to work without supervision.

Licenses, Certifications, and Registrations

Water and wastewater treatment plant and system operators must be licensed by the state in which they work. Requirements and standards vary widely depending on the state.

State licenses typically have multiple levels, which indicate the operator's experience and training. Although some states will honor licenses from other states, operators who move from one state to another may need to take a new set of exams to become licensed in their new state.

Advancement

Most states have multiple levels of licenses for water and wastewater treatment plant and system operators. Each increase in license level allows the operator to perform more complicated processes without supervision.

At the largest plants, operators who have the highest license level work as shift supervisors and may be in charge of large teams of operators.

Important Qualities

Analytical skills. Water and wastewater treatment plant and system operators must conduct tests and inspections on water or wastewater and evaluate the results.

Detail oriented. Water and wastewater treatment plant and system operators must monitor machinery, gauges, dials, and controls to ensure everything is operating properly. Because tap water and wastewater are highly regulated by the U.S. Environmental Protection Agency, operators must be careful and thorough in completing these tasks.

Math skills. Water and wastewater treatment plant and system operators must have the ability to apply data to formulas that determine treatme0nt requirements, flow levels, and concentration levels.

Mechanical skills. Water and wastewater treatment plant and system operators must know how to work with machines and use tools. They must be familiar with how to operate, repair, and maintain equipment.

Pay

The median annual wage for water and wastewater treatment plant and system operators was $47,760 in May 2019. The median wage is the wage at which half the workers in an occupation earned more than that amount and half earned less. The lowest 10 percent earned less than $28,850, and the highest 10 percent earned more than $77,600.

In May 2019, the median annual wages for water and wastewater treatment plant and system operators in the top industries in which they worked were as follows:

Local government, excluding education and
  hospitals.. $47,930
Utilities... 46,400
Manufacturing... 45,840

Water and waste treatment plant and system operators work full time. Plants operate 24 hours a day, 7 days a week. In small plants, operators are likely to work during the day and be on call nights and weekends. In medium- and large-size plants that require constant monitoring, operators work in shifts to control the plant at all hours.

Occasionally, operators must work during emergencies. For example, they may need to work during weather conditions that cause large amounts of storm water or wastewater to flow into

sewers, exceeding a plant's capacity. Emergencies also may be caused by malfunctions within a plant, such as chemical leaks or oxygen deficiencies.

Job Outlook

Employment of water and wastewater treatment plant and system operators is projected to decline 4 percent from 2019 to 2029.

As water and wastewater treatment plants become more advanced with automated systems to manage treatment processes, fewer workers may be needed. Although some work can be automated, plants will still need skilled workers to operate increasingly complex controls and water and wastewater systems.

Job Prospects

Job opportunities are expected to arise from the need to replace workers who leave the occupation permanently over the coming decade. Job prospects will be best for those with training or higher education in water or wastewater systems and good mechanical skills.

Employment projections data for water and wastewater treatment plant and system operators, 2019-29					
Occupational Title	SOC Code	Employment, 2019	Projected Employment, 2029	Change, 2019-29 Percent	Numeric
SOURCE: U.S. Bureau of Labor Statistics, Employment Projections program					
Water and wastewater treatment plant and system operators	51-8031	126,400	121,000	-4	-5,400

State & Area Data
Occupational Employment Statistics (OES)

The Occupational Employment Statistics (OES) program produces employment and wage estimates annually for over 800 occupations. These estimates are available for the nation as a whole, for individual states, and for metropolitan and nonmetropolitan areas.

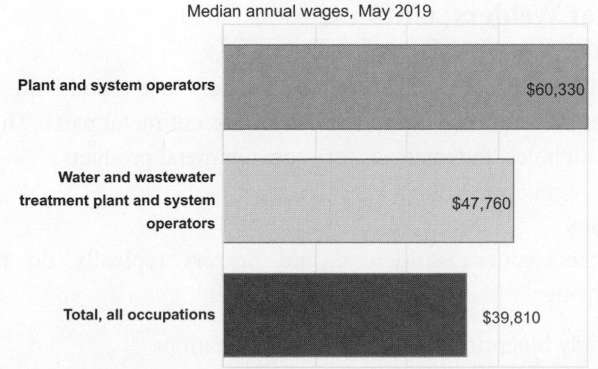

Water and Wastewater Treatment Plant and System Operators
Median annual wages, May 2019

Plant and system operators $60,330
Water and wastewater treatment plant and system operators $47,760
Total, all occupations $39,810

Note: All Occupations includes all occupations in the U.S. Economy.
Source: U.S. Bureau of Labor Statistics, Occupational Employment Statistics.

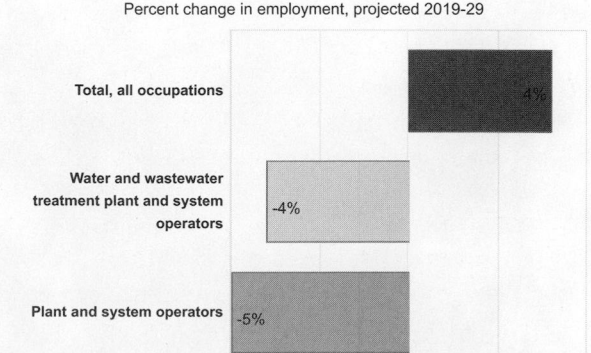

Water and Wastewater Treatment Plant and System Operators
Percent change in employment, projected 2019-29

Total, all occupations 4%
Water and wastewater treatment plant and system operators -4%
Plant and system operators -5%

Note: All Occupations includes all occupations in the U.S. Economy.
Source: U.S. Bureau of Labor Statistics, Employment Projections program.

Contacts for More Information

For information on employment opportunities, contact state or local water pollution control agencies, state water and wastewater operator associations, state environmental training centers, or local offices of the state employment service.

For information related to a career as a water or wastewater treatment plant and system operator, visit
➤ American Water Works Association

➤ The National Rural Water Association
➤ Water Environment Federation
➤ Work for Water

For more information on certification for water or wastewater treatment plant and system operator, visit
➤ Association of Boards of Certification

Welders, Cutters, Solderers, and Brazers

Summary

Quick Facts: Welders, Cutters, Solderers, and Brazers

2019 Median Pay	$42,490 per year $20.43 per hour
Typical Entry-Level Education	High school diploma or equivalent
Work Experience in a Related Occupation	None
On-the-job Training	Moderate-term on-the-job training
Number of Jobs, 2019	438,900
Job Outlook, 2019-29	3% (As fast as average)
Employment Change, 2019-29	13,600

What Welders, Cutters, Solderers, and Brazers Do

Welders, cutters, solderers, and brazers use hand-held or remotely controlled equipment to join, repair, or cut metal parts and products.

Welders, cutters, solderers, and brazers occasionally must work in awkward positions using hand-held welding, flame-cutting, and soldering tools.

Work Environment

Welders, cutters, solderers, and brazers may work outdoors, often in inclement weather, or indoors, sometimes in a confined area. They may work on a scaffold, high off the ground, and they occasionally must lift heavy objects and work in awkward positions. Most work full time and overtime is common.

How to Become a Welder, Cutter, Solderer, or Brazer

A high school diploma or equivalent, combined with technical and on-the-job training, is typically required for anyone to become a welder, cutter, solderer, or brazer.

Pay

The median annual wage for welders, cutters, solderers, and brazers was $42,490 in May 2019.

Job Outlook

Employment of welders, cutters, solderers, and brazers is projected to grow 3 percent from 2019 to 2029, about as fast as the average for all occupations. The nation's aging infrastructure will require the expertise of welders, cutters, solderers, and brazers to help rebuild bridges, highways, and buildings.

State & Area Data

Explore resources for employment and wages by state and area for welders, cutters, solderers, and brazers.

What Welders, Cutters, Solderers, and Brazers Do

Welders, cutters, solderers, and brazers use hand-held or remotely controlled equipment to join or cut metal parts. They also fill holes, indentations, or seams in metal products.

Duties

Welders, cutters, solderers, and brazers typically do the following:

- Study blueprints, sketches, or specifications
- Calculate the dimensions of parts to be welded
- Inspect structures or materials to be welded
- Ignite torches or start power supplies

Welders, cutters, solderers, and brazers use hand-held or remotely controlled equipment to join or cut metal parts.

- Monitor the welding process to avoid overheating
- Maintain equipment and machinery

Welding is the most common way of permanently joining metal parts. In this process, heat is applied to metal pieces, melting and fusing them to form a permanent bond. Because of its strength, welding is used in shipbuilding, automobile manufacturing and repair, aerospace applications, and thousands of other manufacturing activities. Welding also is used to join steel beams in the construction of buildings, bridges, and other structures and to join pipes in pipelines, power plants, and refineries.

Welders work in a wide variety of industries, from car racing to manufacturing. The work that welders do and the equipment they use vary with the industry. Arc welding, the most common type of welding today, uses electrical currents to create heat and bond metals together—but there are more than 100 different processes that a welder can use. The type of weld is usually determined by the types of metals being joined and the conditions under which the welding is to take place.

Cutters use heat to cut and trim metal objects to specific dimensions. Their work is closely related to that of welders. However, instead of joining metals, cutters use the heat from an electric arc, a stream of ionized gas called plasma, or burning gases to cut and trim metal objects to specific dimensions. Cutters also dismantle large objects, such as ships, railroad cars, automobiles, buildings, and aircraft. Some operate and monitor cutting machines similar to those used by welding machine operators.

Solderers and *brazers* also use heat to join two or more metal objects together. Soldering and brazing are similar, except that the temperature used to melt the filler metal is lower in soldering. Soldering uses metals with a melting point below 840 degrees Fahrenheit. Brazing uses metals with a higher melting point.

Soldering and brazing workers use molten metal to join two pieces of metal. However, the metal added during the soldering or brazing process has a melting point lower than that of

the piece, so only the added metal is melted, not the piece. Therefore, these processes normally do not create distortions or weaknesses in the piece, as can occur with welding.

Soldering commonly is used to make electrical and electronic circuit boards, such as computer chips. Soldering workers tend to work with small pieces that must be positioned precisely.

Brazing often is used to connect cast iron and thinner metals that the higher temperatures of welding would warp. Brazing also can be used to apply coatings to parts in order to reduce wear and protect against corrosion.

Work Environment

Welders, cutters, solderers, and brazers held about 438,900 jobs in 2019. The largest employers of welders, cutters, solderers, and brazers were as follows:

Manufacturing	63%
Specialty trade contractors	6
Self-employed workers	5
Repair and maintenance	4

Welders and cutters may work outdoors, often in inclement weather, or indoors, sometimes in a confined area designed to contain sparks and glare. When working outdoors, they may work on a scaffold or platform high off the ground.

Welders, cutters, solderers, and brazers wear protective clothing and goggles for safety.

In addition, they may have to lift heavy objects and work in awkward positions while bending, stooping, or standing to work overhead.

Injuries and Illnesses

Welders, cutters, solderers, and brazers risk injury on the job. They are often exposed to a number of hazards, including very hot materials and the intense light created by the arc. They wear safety shoes, heat-resistant gloves, goggles, masks with protective lenses, and other equipment to prevent burns and eye injuries and to protect them from falling objects.

The Occupational Safety and Health Administration (OSHA) requires that welders work in safely ventilated areas in order to avoid danger from inhaling gases and fine particles that can result from welding processes. However, they can minimize injuries if they follow safety procedures.

Work Schedules

Most welders, cutters, solderers, and brazers work full time, and overtime is common. Many manufacturing firms have two or three 8- to 12-hour shifts each day, allowing the firm to continue production around the clock if needed. As a result, welders, cutters, solderers, and brazers may work evenings and weekends.

How to Become a Welder, Cutter, Solderer, or Brazer

A high school diploma or equivalent, combined with technical and on-the-job training, is typically required for anyone to become a welder, cutter, solderer, or brazer.

Education & Training

A high school diploma or equivalent, combined with technical and on-the-job training, is typically required for anyone to become a welder, cutter, solderer, or brazer. High school technical education courses and postsecondary institutions, such as vocational–technical institutes, community colleges, and private welding, soldering, and brazing schools offer formal technical training. In addition, the various branches of the U.S. Armed Forces operate welding and soldering schools.

Courses in blueprint reading, shop mathematics, mechanical drawing, physics, chemistry, and metallurgy are helpful.

An understanding of electricity also is helpful, and knowledge of computers is gaining importance as welding, soldering, and brazing machine operators become more responsible for programming robots and other computer-controlled machines.

Although numerous employers are willing to hire inexperienced entry-level workers and train them on the job, many prefer to hire workers who have been through training or credentialing programs. Even entry-level workers with formal technical training still receive several months of on-the-job training.

Licenses, Certifications, and Registrations

Courses leading to certification are offered at many welding schools. For example, the American Welding Society offers the Certified Welder designation.

Some welding positions require general certification in welding or certification in specific skills, such as Certified Welding Inspector and Certified Robotic Arc Welding.

The Institute for Printed Circuits offers certification and training in soldering. In industries such as aerospace and defense, which need highly skilled workers, many employers require these certifications. Certification can show mastery of lead-free soldering techniques, which are important to many employers.

Some employers pay the cost of training and testing for employees.

Important Qualities

Detail oriented. Welders, cutters, solderers, and brazers perform precision work, often with straight edges and minimal flaws. The ability to see details and characteristics of the joint and detect changes in molten metal flows requires good eyesight and attention to detail.

Manual dexterity. Welders, cutters, solderers, and brazers must have a steady hand to hold a torch in one place. Workers must also have good hand–eye coordination.

Physical stamina. The ability to endure long periods of standing and repetitive movements is important for welders, cutters, solderers, and brazers.

Physical strength. Welders, cutters, solderers, and brazers must be in good physical condition. They often must lift heavy pieces of metal and move welding or cutting equipment, and they sometimes bend, stoop, or reach while working.

Spatial-orientation skills. Welders, cutters, solderers, and brazers must read, understand, and interpret two- and three-dimensional diagrams in order to fit metal products correctly.

Technical skills. Welders, cutters, solderers, and brazers must operate manual or semiautomatic welding equipment to fuse metal segments.

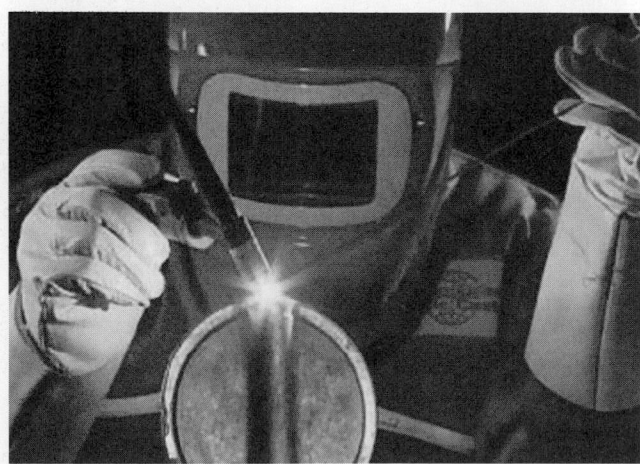

Welders, cutters, solderers, and brazers must have a steady hand to hold a torch in place.

Welders, Cutters, Solderers, and Brazers
Median annual wages, May 2019

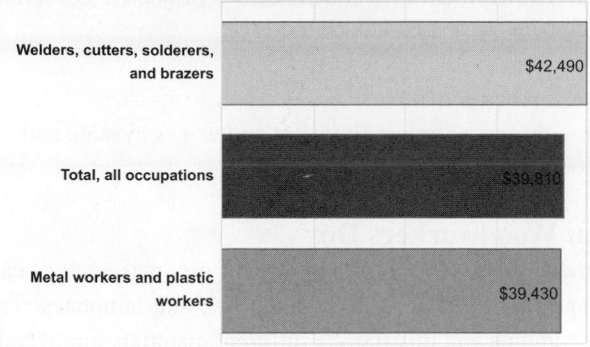

Welders, cutters, solderers, and brazers	$42,490
Total, all occupations	$39,810
Metal workers and plastic workers	$39,430

Note: All Occupations includes all occupations in the U.S. Economy. Source: U.S. Bureau of Labor Statistics, Occupational Employment Statistics.

Pay

The median annual wage for welders, cutters, solderers, and brazers was $42,490 in May 2019. The median wage is the wage at which half the workers in an occupation earned more than that amount and half earned less. The lowest 10 percent earned less than $29,470, and the highest 10 percent earned more than $64,240.

In May 2019, the median annual wages for welders, cutters, solderers, and brazers in the top industries in which they worked were as follows:

Specialty trade contractors	$46,630
Repair and maintenance	42,100
Manufacturing	40,990

Wages for welders, cutters, solderers, and brazers vary with the worker's experience and skill level, the industry, and the size of the company.

Most welders, cutters, solderers, and brazers work full time, and overtime is common. Many manufacturing firms have two or three 8- to 12-hour shifts each day, allowing the firm to continue production around the clock if needed. As a result, welders, cutters, solderers, and brazers may work evenings and weekends.

Job Outlook

Employment of welders, cutters, solderers, and brazers is projected to grow 3 percent from 2019 to 2029, about as fast as the average for all occupations.

The nation's aging infrastructure will require the expertise of welders, cutters, solderers, and brazers to help rebuild bridges, highways, and buildings.

Welders, Cutters, Solderers, and Brazers
Percent change in employment, projected 2019-29

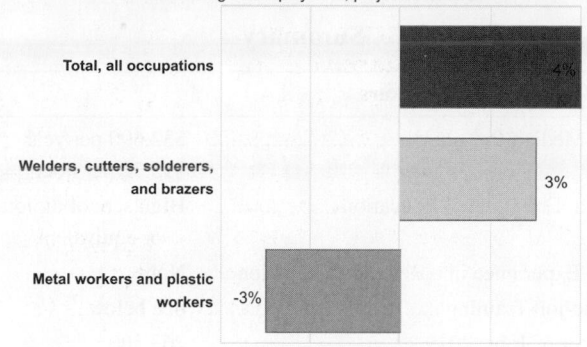

Total, all occupations	4%
Welders, cutters, solderers, and brazers	3%
Metal workers and plastic workers	-3%

Note: All Occupations includes all occupations in the U.S. Economy. Source: U.S. Bureau of Labor Statistics, Employment Projections program.

Job Prospects

Overall job prospects will vary with the worker's skill level. Job prospects should be good for welders trained in the latest technologies. However, welders who do not have up-to-date training may face strong competition for jobs.

For all welders, job prospects should be better for those willing to relocate.

Employment projections data for welders, cutters, solderers, and brazers, 2019-29					
Occupational Title	SOC Code	Employment, 2019	Projected Employment, 2029	Change, 2019-29	
				Percent	Numeric
SOURCE: U.S. Bureau of Labor Statistics, Employment Projections program					
Welders, cutters, solderers, and brazers	51-4121	438,900	452,500	3	13,600

State & Area Data
Occupational Employment Statistics (OES)

The Occupational Employment Statistics (OES) program produces employment and wage estimates annually for over 800 occupations. These estimates are available for the nation as a whole, for individual states, and for metropolitan and nonmetropolitan areas.

Contacts for More Information

For more information about welders, cutters, solderers, and brazers, visit
➤ American Welding Society
➤ Fabricators & Manufacturers Association, International
➤ Institute for Printed Circuits
➤ Precision Machined Products Association

Woodworkers

Summary

Quick Facts: Woodworkers

2019 Median Pay	$32,690 per year $15.72 per hour
Typical Entry-Level Education	High school diploma or equivalent
Work Experience in a Related Occupation	None
On-the-job Training	See below
Number of Jobs, 2019	263,500
Job Outlook, 2019-29	-4% (Decline)
Employment Change, 2019-29	-9,600

What Woodworkers Do

Woodworkers manufacture a variety of products such as cabinets and furniture, using wood, veneers, and laminates.

Work Environment

Most woodworkers work in manufacturing plants. Although working conditions vary, some woodworkers may encounter machinery noise and wood dust.

How to Become a Woodworker

A high school diploma or equivalent is typically required to become a woodworker. Although some entry-level jobs can be learned in less than 1 year, becoming fully proficient generally takes several years of on-the-job training. The ability to use computer-controlled machinery is becoming increasingly important.

Pay

The median annual wage for woodworkers was $32,690 in May 2019.

Workers use automated machinery, such as computerized numerical control (CNC) machines, to do much of the work.

Job Outlook

Overall employment of woodworkers is projected to decline 4 percent from 2019 to 2029.

State & Area Data

Explore resources for employment and wages by state and area for woodworkers.

What Woodworkers Do

Woodworkers manufacture a variety of products such as cabinets and furniture, using wood, veneers, and laminates. They often combine and incorporate different materials into wood.

Duties

Woodworkers typically do the following:

- Understand detailed architectural drawings, schematics, shop drawings, and blueprints
- Prepare and set up machines and tooling for woodwork manufacturing
- Lift wood pieces onto machines, either by hand or with hoists
- Operate woodworking machines, including saws and milling and sanding machines
- Listen for unusual sounds or detect excessive vibration in machinery
- Ensure that products meet industry standards and project specifications, making adjustments as necessary

Woodworkers ensure that products meet industry standards and project specifications.

- Select and adjust the proper cutting, milling, boring, and sanding tools for completing a job
- Use hand tools to trim pieces or assemble products

Despite the abundance of plastics, metals, and other materials, wood products continue to be an important part of our daily lives. Woodworkers make wood products from lumber and synthetic wood materials. Many of these products, including most furniture, kitchen cabinets, and musical instruments, are mass produced. Other products are custom made from architectural designs and drawings.

Although the term "woodworker" may evoke the image of a craftsman who uses hand tools to build ornate furniture, the modern woodworking trade is highly technical and relies on advanced equipment and highly skilled operators. Workers use automated machinery, such as computerized numerical control (CNC) machines, to do much of the work with great accuracy.

Even specialized artisans generally use CNC machines and a variety of power tools in their work. Much of the work is done in a high-production assembly line facility, but there is also some work that is customized and does not lend itself to being performed on an assembly line.

Woodworkers set up, operate, and tend all types of woodworking machines, such as saws, milling machines, drill presses, lathes, shapers, routers, sanders, planers, and wood-fastening machines. Operators set up the equipment, cut and shape wooden parts, and verify dimensions, using a template, caliper, and rule. After the parts are machined, woodworkers add fasteners and adhesives and connect the parts to form an assembled unit. They also install hardware, such as pulls and drawer slides, and fit specialty products for glass, metal trims, electrical components, and stone. Finally, workers sand, stain, and, if necessary, coat the wood product with a sealer or top-coats, such as a lacquer or varnish.

Many of these tasks are handled by different workers with specialized training.

The following are examples of types of woodworkers:

Cabinetmakers and *bench carpenters* cut, shape, assemble, and make parts for wood products. They often design and create sets of cabinets that are customized for particular spaces. In some cases, their duties begin with designing a set of cabinets to specifications and end with installing the cabinets.

Furniture finishers shape, finish, and refinish damaged and worn furniture. They may work with antiques and must judge how to preserve and repair them. They also do the staining, sealing, and top coating at the end of the process of making wooden products.

Wood sawing machine setters, operators, and tenders specialize in operating specific pieces of woodworking machinery. They may operate CNC machines.

Woodworking machine setters, operators, and tenders, except sawing, operate woodworking machines, such as drill presses, lathes, routers, sanders, and planers. They may operate CNC machines.

Work Environment

Woodworkers held about 263,500 jobs in 2019. Employment in the detailed occupations that make up woodworkers was distributed as follows:

Cabinetmakers and bench carpenters	112,200
Woodworking machine setters, operators, and tenders, except sawing	79,300
Sawing machine setters, operators, and tenders, wood	54,500
Furniture finishers	17,400

The largest employers of woodworkers were as follows:

Wood product manufacturing	39%
Furniture and related product manufacturing	38
Self-employed workers	7
Specialty trade contractors	3

Working conditions vary with the specific job duties. At times, workers have to handle heavy, bulky materials and may encounter noise and dust. As a result, they regularly wear hearing protection devices, safety glasses, and respirators or masks.

Injuries and Illnesses

Woodworkers are exposed to hazards such as harmful dust, chemicals, or fumes, and must often wear a respirator or mask.

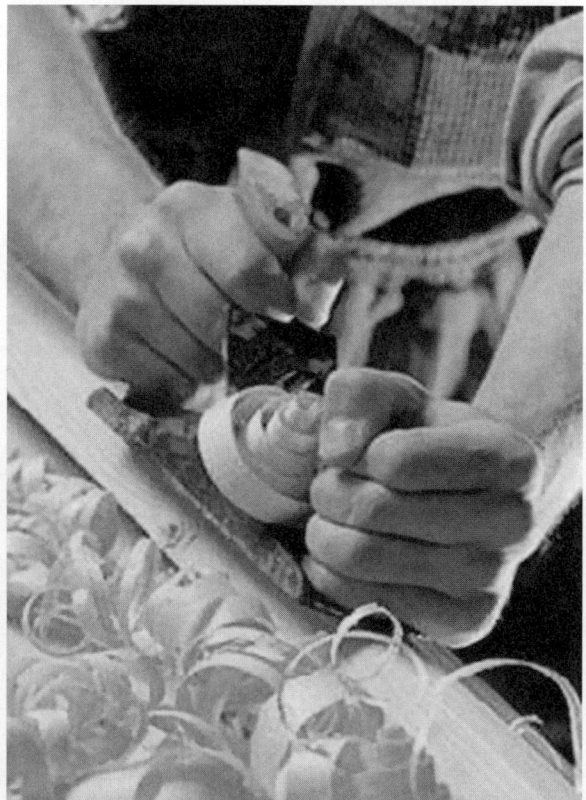

Woodworkers make wood products from lumber and synthetic wood materials.

Others may be exposed to excessive noise and must wear hearing protection devices.

Most injuries involve sprains, back pain, carpal tunnel syndrome, and hernias. These injuries or illnesses come from excessive amounts of awkward bending, reaching, twisting, and overexertion or repetition.

Work Schedules

Most woodworkers work full time during regular business hours.

How to Become a Woodworker

A high school diploma or equivalent is typically required to become a woodworker. Although some entry-level jobs can be learned in less than 1 year, becoming fully proficient generally takes several years of on-the-job training. The ability to use computer-controlled machinery is becoming increasingly important.

Education

Because of the growing sophistication of machinery, many employers are seeking applicants who have a high school diploma or equivalent. People seeking woodworking jobs can enhance their employment prospects by getting training in computer applications and math.

Some woodworkers obtain their skills by taking courses at technical schools or community colleges. Others attend universities that offer training in wood technology, furniture manufacturing, wood engineering, and production management. These programs prepare students for jobs in production, supervision, engineering, and management, and are becoming increasingly important as woodworking technology advances.

Training

Education is helpful, but woodworkers are trained primarily on the job, where they learn skills from experienced workers.

After high school, most woodworkers are trained on the job, learning from more experienced workers.

Beginning workers are given basic tasks, such as placing a piece of wood through a machine and stacking the finished product at the end of the process.

As they gain experience, new woodworkers perform more complex tasks with less supervision. In about 1 month, they learn basic machine operations and job tasks. Becoming a skilled woodworker often takes several months or even years. Skilled workers can read blueprints, set up machines, and plan work sequences.

Licenses, Certifications, and Registrations

Although not required, becoming certified can demonstrate competence and professionalism. It also may help a candidate advance in the profession. The Woodwork Career Alliance of North America offers a national certificate program, with five progressive credentials, which adds a level of credibility to the work of woodworkers.

Important Qualities

Detail oriented. Woodworkers must pay attention to details in order to meet specifications and to keep themselves safe.

Dexterity. Woodworkers must make precise cuts with a variety of hand tools and power tools, so they need a steady hand and good hand-eye coordination.

Math skills. Knowledge of basic math and computer skills are important, particularly for those who work in manufacturing, in which technology continues to advance. Woodworkers need to understand basic geometry in order to visualize how a three-dimensional wooden object, such as a cabinet or piece of furniture, will fit together.

Mechanical skills. The use of hand tools, such as screwdrivers and wrenches, is required to set up, adjust, and calibrate machines. Modern technology systems require woodworkers to be able to use computers and other programmable devices.

Physical stamina. The ability to endure long periods of standing and repetitive movements is crucial for woodworkers, who often stand all day performing many of the same functions.

Physical strength. Woodworkers must be strong enough to lift bulky and heavy pieces of wood.

Technical skills. Woodworkers must understand and interpret design drawings and technical manuals for a range of products and machines.

Pay

The median annual wage for woodworkers was $32,690 in May 2019. The median wage is the wage at which half the workers in an occupation earned more than that amount and half earned less. The lowest 10 percent earned less than $22,310, and the highest 10 percent earned more than $50,070.

Median annual wages for woodworkers in May 2019 were as follows:

Cabinetmakers and bench carpenters......................... $35,790

Woodworkers
Median annual wages, May 2019

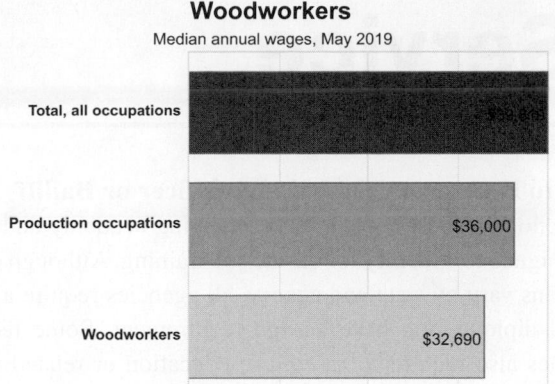

Note: All Occupations includes all occupations in the U.S. Economy.
Source: U.S. Bureau of Labor Statistics, Occupational Employment Statistics.

Furniture finishers	32,480
Woodworking machine setters, operators, and tenders, except sawing	30,990
Sawing machine setters, operators, and tenders, wood	30,410

In May 2019, the median annual wages for woodworkers in the top industries in which they worked were as follows:

Specialty trade contractors	$37,980
Furniture and related product manufacturing	34,290
Wood product manufacturing	30,730

Most woodworkers work full time during regular business hours.

Job Outlook

Overall employment of woodworkers is projected to decline 4 percent from 2019 to 2029.

Some demand for woodworkers is expected in residential and commercial property repairs and renovations. However, automation, especially the use of computerized numerical controlled machines in wood product manufacturing, should reduce the overall need for these workers over the decade.

Job Prospects

Woodworkers who know how to create and carry out custom designs on a computer should have the best job opportunities in manufacturing industries.

Those who can demonstrate leadership, problem-solving, and advanced math skills should also have the best job prospects.

Some job openings will result from the need to replace those who retire or leave the occupation for another job.

Woodworkers
Percent change in employment, projected 2019-29

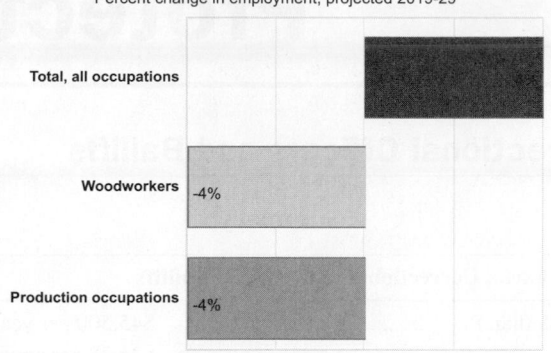

Note: All Occupations includes all occupations in the U.S. Economy.
Source: U.S. Bureau of Labor Statistics, Employment Projections program.

Employment projections data for woodworkers, 2019-29

Occupational Title	SOC Code	Employment, 2019	Projected Employment, 2029	Change, 2019-29 Percent	Numeric
Woodworkers	—	263,500	253,900	-4	-9,600
Cabinetmakers and bench carpenters	51-7011	112,200	108,900	-3	-3,300
Furniture finishers	51-7021	17,400	16,700	-4	-600
Sawing machine setters, operators, and tenders, wood	51-7041	54,500	50,800	-7	-3,800
Woodworking machine setters, operators, and tenders, except sawing	51-7042	79,300	77,400	-2	-1,900

SOURCE: U.S. Bureau of Labor Statistics, Employment Projections program

State & Area Data
Occupational Employment Statistics (OES)

The Occupational Employment Statistics (OES) program produces employment and wage estimates annually for over 800 occupations. These estimates are available for the nation as a whole, for individual states, and for metropolitan and nonmetropolitan areas.

Contacts for More Information

For more information about woodworkers, visit
➤ Architectural Woodwork Institute
➤ Association for Manufacturing Technology
➤ Fabricators & Manufacturers Association, International
➤ National Tooling and Machining Association
➤ Woodwork Career Alliance of North America
➤ Woodworking Machinery Industry Association

Protective Service

Correctional Officers and Bailiffs

Summary

Quick Facts: Correctional Officers and Bailiffs	
2019 Median Pay	$45,300 per year $21.78 per hour
Typical Entry-Level Education	High school diploma or equivalent
Work Experience in a Related Occupation	None
On-the-job Training	Moderate-term on-the-job training
Number of Jobs, 2019	462,300
Job Outlook, 2019-29	-7% (Decline)
Employment Change, 2019-29	-33,100

What Correctional Officers and Bailiffs Do

Correctional officers oversee those who have been arrested and are awaiting trial or who have been sentenced to serve time in jail or prison. Bailiffs are law enforcement officers who maintain safety and order in courtrooms.

Work Environment

Working in a correctional institution can be stressful and dangerous. Correctional officers and jailers have one of the highest rates of injuries and illnesses of all occupations, often resulting from confrontations with inmates. Officers work in shifts that cover all hours of the day and night, including weekends and holidays. Bailiffs' hours are determined by when court is in session.

How to Become a Correctional Officer or Bailiff

Correctional officers go through a training academy and then are assigned to a facility for on-the-job training. Although qualifications vary by state and agency, all agencies require a high school diploma and have an age requirement. Some federal agencies also require some college education or related work experience.

Pay

The median annual wage for bailiffs was $47,830 in May 2019.

The median annual wage for correctional officers and jailers was $45,180 in May 2019.

Job Outlook

Employment of correctional officers and bailiffs is projected to decline 7 percent from 2019 to 2029. State and local budget constraints and prison population levels will determine how many correctional officers are necessary. Bailiffs will continue to be needed to keep order in courtrooms.

State & Area Data

Explore resources for employment and wages by state and area for correctional officers and bailiffs.

What Correctional Officers and Bailiffs Do

Correctional officers are responsible for overseeing individuals who have been arrested and are awaiting trial or who have been sentenced to serve time in jail or prison. Bailiffs, also known as *marshals* or *court officers*, are law enforcement officers who maintain safety and order in courtrooms. Their duties, which vary by court, include enforcing courtroom rules, assisting

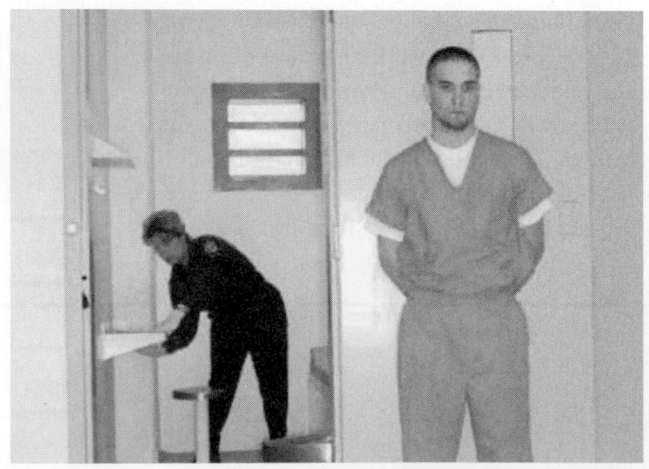

Correctional officers inspect inmates' living quarters.

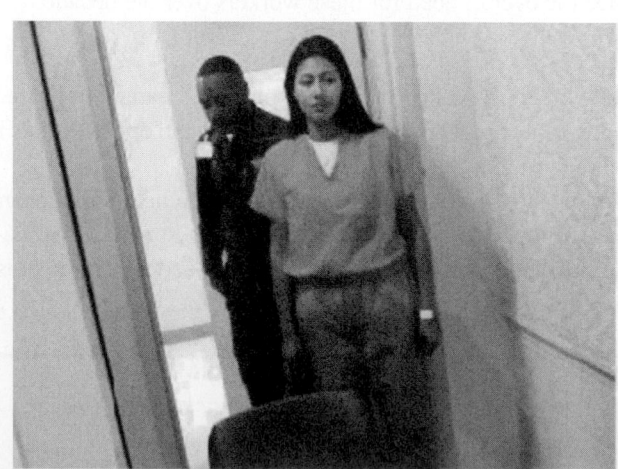

Correctional officers must follow procedures to maintain their personal safety as well as the safety of the inmates they oversee.

judges, guarding juries, delivering court documents, and providing general security for courthouses.

Duties

Correctional officers typically do the following:

- Enforce rules and keep order within jails or prisons
- Supervise activities of inmates
- Inspect facilities to ensure that they meet security and safety standards
- Search inmates for contraband items
- Report on inmate conduct
- Escort and transport inmates

Bailiffs typically do the following:

- Ensure the security of the courtroom
- Enforce courtroom rules
- Follow court procedures
- Escort judges, jurors, witnesses, and prisoners
- Handle evidence and court documents

Inside the prison or jail, correctional officers enforce rules and regulations. They maintain security by preventing disturbances, assaults, and escapes, and by inspecting facilities. They check cells and other areas for unsanitary conditions, contraband, signs of a security breach (such as tampering with window bars and doors), and other rule violations. Officers also inspect mail and visitors for prohibited items. They write reports and fill out daily logs detailing inmate behavior and anything else of note that occurred during their shift.

Correctional officers may have to restrain inmates in handcuffs and leg irons to escort them safely to and from cells and to see authorized visitors. Officers also escort prisoners to courtrooms, medical facilities, and other destinations.

Bailiffs' specific duties vary by court, but their primary duty is to maintain order and security in courts of law. They enforce courtroom procedures that protect the integrity of the legal process. For example, they ensure that attorneys and witnesses do not influence juries outside of the courtroom, and they also may isolate juries from the public in some circumstances. As a neutral party, they may handle evidence during court hearings to ensure that only permitted evidence is displayed.

Work Environment

Bailiffs held about 20,300 jobs in 2019. The largest employers of bailiffs were as follows:

Local government, excluding education and hospitals... 72%

State government, excluding education and hospitals.... 27

Correctional officers and jailers held about 442,000 jobs in 2019. The largest employers of correctional officers and jailers were as follows:

State government, excluding education and hospitals... 53%

Because jail and prison security must be provided 24 hours a day, officers work in shifts that cover all hours of the day and night, including weekends and holidays.

Local government, excluding education and hospitals...   37

Facilities support services   5

Federal government...   4

Correctional officers may work indoors or outdoors, and bailiffs generally work in courtrooms. They both may be required to stand for long periods.

Injuries and Illnesses

Working in a correctional institution can be stressful and dangerous. Correctional officers and jailers may become injured in confrontations with inmates, and they have one of the highest rates of injuries and illnesses of all occupations.

The job demands that officers be alert and ready to react throughout their entire shift.

Work Schedules

Correctional officers usually work full time on rotating shifts. Because jail and prison security must be provided around the clock, officers work all hours of the day and night, including weekends and holidays. Many officers are required to work overtime. Bailiffs' hours are determined by when court is in session.

How to Become a Correctional Officer or Bailiff

Correctional officers and bailiffs typically attend a training academy. Although qualifications vary by state and agency, all agencies require a high school diploma. Federal agencies may also require some college education or previous work experience.

Many agencies establish a minimum age for correctional officers, which is typically between 18 and 21 years of age.

Education

Correctional officers and bailiffs must have at least a high school diploma or equivalent.

Correctional officers typically attend training at an academy before being assigned to a facility.

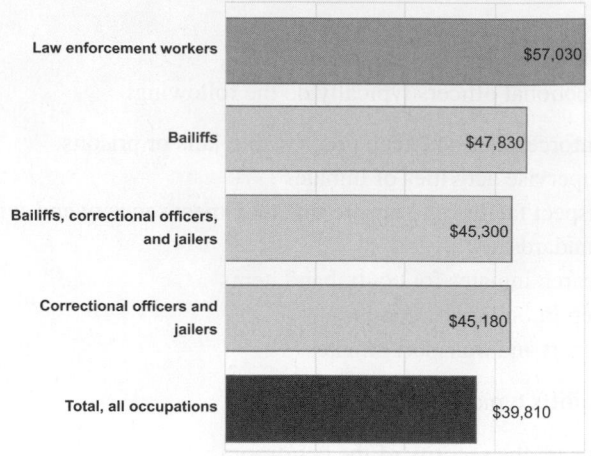

Correctional Officers and Bailiffs
Median annual wages, May 2019

Law enforcement workers	$57,030
Bailiffs	$47,830
Bailiffs, correctional officers, and jailers	$45,300
Correctional officers and jailers	$45,180
Total, all occupations	$39,810

Note: All Occupations includes all occupations in the U.S. Economy. Source: U.S. Bureau of Labor Statistics, Occupational Employment Statistics.

For employment in federal prisons, the Federal Bureau of Prisons requires entry-level correctional officers to have at least a bachelor's degree or 1 to 3 years of full-time experience in a field providing counseling, assistance, or supervision to individuals.

Training

Correctional officers and bailiffs complete training at an academy. Training typically lasts several months, but this varies by state. The International Association of Directors of Law Enforcement Standards and Training maintains links to states' Peace Officer Standards and Training (POST) programs. Academy trainees receive instruction in a number of subjects, including self-defense, institutional policies, regulations, operations, and security procedures.

Important Qualities

Decisionmaking skills. Correctional officers and bailiffs must use both their training and common sense to quickly determine the best course of action and to take the necessary steps to achieve a desired outcome.

Detail oriented. Correctional officers and bailiffs follow and enforce strict procedures in correctional facilities and courts to ensure everyone's safety.

Interpersonal skills. Correctional officers and bailiffs must be able to interact and communicate effectively with inmates and others to maintain order in correctional facilities and courtrooms.

Negotiating skills. Correctional officers must be able to assist others in resolving differences in order to avoid conflict.

Physical strength. Correctional officers and bailiffs must have the strength to physically subdue inmates or others.

Self-discipline. Correctional officers must control their emotions when confronted with hostile situations.

Pay

The median annual wage for bailiffs was $47,830 in May 2019. The median wage is the wage at which half the workers in an

occupation earned more than that amount and half earned less. The lowest 10 percent earned less than $24,620, and the highest 10 percent earned more than $82,900.

The median annual wage for correctional officers and jailers was $45,180 in May 2019. The lowest 10 percent earned less than $31,740, and the highest 10 percent earned more than $78,090.

In May 2019, the median annual wages for bailiffs in the top industries in which they worked were as follows:

State government, excluding education and hospitals	$69,130
Local government, excluding education and hospitals	42,610

In May 2019, the median annual wages for correctional officers and jailers in the top industries in which they worked were as follows:

Federal government	$58,020
Local government, excluding education and hospitals	46,020
State government, excluding education and hospitals	44,090
Facilities support services	39,410

Correctional officers usually work full time on rotating shifts. Because jail and prison security must be provided around the clock, officers work all hours of the day and night, including weekends and holidays. Many officers are required to work overtime. Bailiffs' hours are determined by when court is in session.

Job Outlook

Employment of correctional officers and bailiffs is projected to decline 7 percent from 2019 to 2029. State and local budget

Correctional Officers and Bailiffs
Percent change in employment, projected 2019-29

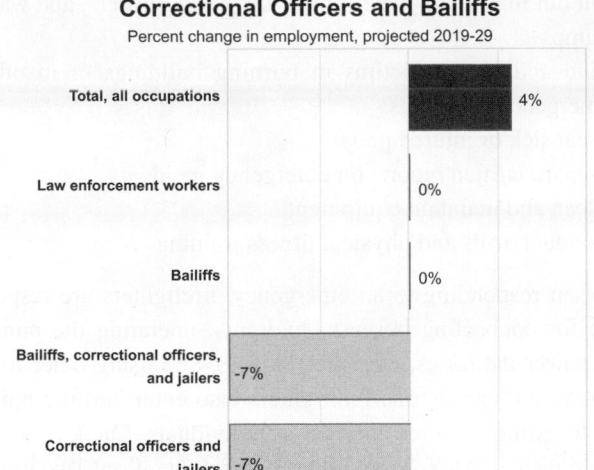

Total, all occupations ▬ 4%

Law enforcement workers 0%

Bailiffs 0%

Bailiffs, correctional officers, and jailers -7%

Correctional officers and jailers -7%

Note: All Occupations includes all occupations in the U.S. Economy.
Source: U.S. Bureau of Labor Statistics, Employment Projections program.

constraints and prison population levels will determine how many correctional officers are necessary.

Although correctional officers will continue to be needed to watch over the U.S. prison population, changes to criminal laws can have a large effect on how many people are arrested and incarcerated each year.

Faced with high costs for keeping people in prison, many state governments have moved toward laws requiring shorter prison terms and alternatives to prison. While keeping the public safe, community-based programs designed to rehabilitate prisoners and limit their risk of repeated offenses may also reduce prisoner counts.

Bailiffs will continue to be needed to keep order in courtrooms.

Firefighters

Summary

Quick Facts: Firefighters

2019 Median Pay	$50,850 per year
	$24.45 per hour
Typical Entry-Level Education	Postsecondary nondegree award
Work Experience in a Related Occupation	None
On-the-job Training	Long-term on-the-job training
Number of Jobs, 2019	335,500
Job Outlook, 2019-29	6% (Faster than average)
Employment Change, 2019-29	20,300

Job Prospects

Despite the projected decline in employment, job prospects should still be good due to the need to replace correctional officers who transfer to other occupations or leave the labor force, such as to retire.

Employment projections data for correctional officers and bailiffs, 2019-29					
Occupational Title	SOC Code	Employment, 2019	Projected Employment, 2029	Change, 2019-29	
				Percent	Numeric
SOURCE: U.S. Bureau of Labor Statistics, Employment Projections program					
Bailiffs, correctional officers, and jailers	33-3010	462,300	429,200	-7	-33,100
Bailiffs	33-3011	20,300	20,300	0	-100
Correctional officers and jailers	33-3012	442,000	408,900	-7	-33,100

State & Area Data
Occupational Employment Statistics (OES)

The Occupational Employment Statistics (OES) program produces employment and wage estimates annually for over 800 occupations. These estimates are available for the nation as a whole, for individual states, and for metropolitan and nonmetropolitan areas.

Contacts for More Information

For more information about Peace Officer Standards and Training (POST), visit
➤ International Association of Directors of Law Enforcement Standards and Training

For more information about career opportunities for correctional officers at the federal level, visit
➤ Federal Bureau of Prisons

For more information about federal government requirements for correctional officers, visit
➤ U.S. Office of Personnel Management

What Firefighters Do

Firefighters control and put out fires and respond to emergencies where life, property, or the environment is at risk.

Work Environment

When on the scenes of fires and other emergencies, the work can be very dangerous. When not on the scene of an emergency, firefighters remain on call at fire stations, where they sleep, eat, and perform other duties during shifts that often last 24 hours. Many work more than 40 hours per week.

How to Become a Firefighter

Firefighters typically need a high school diploma and training in emergency medical services. Most firefighters receive training at a fire academy, must pass written and physical tests, complete a series of interviews, and hold an emergency medical technician (EMT) certification.

Firefighters control fires and respond to other emergencies.

Pay

The median annual wage for firefighters was $50,850 in May 2019.

Job Outlook

Employment of firefighters is projected to grow 6 percent from 2019 to 2029, faster than the average for all occupations. Physically fit applicants with paramedic training will have the best job prospects.

State & Area Data

Explore resources for employment and wages by state and area for firefighters.

What Firefighters Do

Firefighters control and put out fires and respond to emergencies where life, property, or the environment is at risk.

Duties

Firefighters typically do the following:

- Drive firetrucks and other emergency vehicles

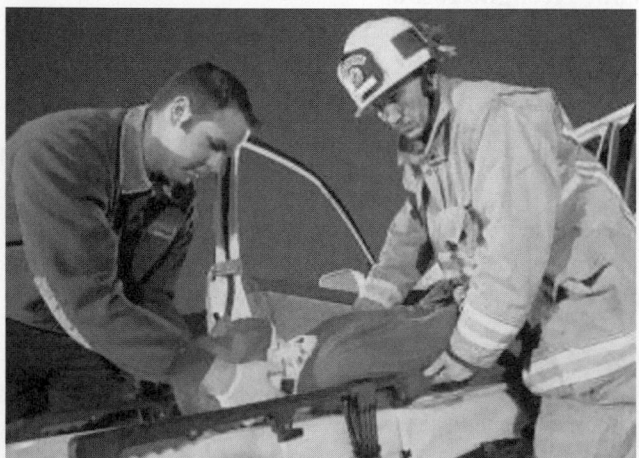
Many firefighters are responsible for providing medical attention.

- Put out fires using water hoses, fire extinguishers, and water pumps
- Find and rescue victims in burning buildings or in other emergency situations
- Treat sick or injured people
- Prepare written reports on emergency incidents
- Clean and maintain equipment
- Conduct drills and physical fitness training

When responding to an emergency, firefighters are responsible for connecting hoses to hydrants, operating the pumps that power the hoses, climbing ladders, and using other tools to break through debris. Firefighters also enter burning buildings to extinguish fires and rescue individuals. Many firefighters are responsible for providing medical attention. Two out of three calls to firefighters are for medical emergencies, not fires, according to the National Fire Protection Association.

When firefighters are not responding to an emergency, they are on call at a fire station. During this time, they regularly inspect equipment and perform practice drills. They also eat and sleep and remain on call, as their shifts usually last 24 hours. Some firefighters may provide public education about fire safety, such as presenting about fire safety at a school.

Some firefighters also work in hazardous materials units and are specially trained to control and clean up hazardous materials, such as oil spills and chemical accidents. They work with hazardous materials removal workers in these cases.

Wildland firefighters are specially trained firefighters. They use heavy equipment and water hoses to control forest fires. Wildland firefighters also frequently create fire lines—a swath of cut-down trees and dug-up grass in the path of a fire—to deprive a fire of fuel. They also use prescribed fires to burn potential fire fuel under controlled conditions. Some wildland firefighters, known as *smoke jumpers*, parachute from airplanes to reach otherwise inaccessible areas.

Work Environment

Firefighters held about 335,500 jobs in 2019. The largest employers of firefighters were as follows:

Local government, excluding education and hospitals...	88%
State government, excluding education and hospitals...	3
Federal government, excluding postal service............	2

These employment numbers exclude volunteer firefighters.

Volunteer firefighters share the same duties as paid firefighters and account for the majority of firefighters in many areas. According to the National Fire Protection Association, about two thirds of firefighters were volunteer firefighters in 2015.

When responding to an emergency, these workers often wear protective gear, which can be very heavy and hot. When not on the scene of an emergency, firefighters work at fire stations, where they sleep, eat, work on equipment, and remain on

Firefighters respond to emergencies such as car accidents.

call. Whenever an alarm sounds, firefighters respond, regardless of the weather or time of day.

Injuries and Illnesses

Firefighters have one of the highest rates of injuries and illnesses of all occupations. They often encounter dangerous situations, including collapsing floors and walls, traffic accidents, and overexposure to flames and smoke. As a result, workers must wear protective gear to help lower these risks.

Work Schedules

Firefighters typically work long periods and varied hours. Overtime is common. Most firefighters work 24-hour shifts on duty and are off the following 48 or 72 hours. Some firefighters may work 10/14 shifts, which means 10 hours working and 14 hours off.

When combating forest and wildland fires, firefighters may work for extended periods. For example, wildland firefighters may have to stay for days or weeks when a wildland fire breaks out.

How to Become a Firefighter

Firefighters typically need a high school diploma and training in emergency medical services. Prospective firefighters must pass written and physical tests, complete a series of interviews, go through training at a fire academy, and hold an emergency medical technician (EMT) certification.

Applicants for firefighter jobs typically must be at least 18 years old and have a valid driver's license. They must also pass a medical exam and drug screening to be hired. After being hired, firefighters may be subject to random drug tests and will also need to complete routine physical fitness assessments.

Education

The entry-level education needed to become a firefighter is a high school diploma or equivalent. However, some classwork beyond high school, such as instruction in assessing patients'

conditions, dealing with trauma, and clearing obstructed airways, is usually needed to obtain the emergency medical technician (EMT) certification. EMT requirements vary by city and state.

Training

Entry-level firefighters receive a few months of training at fire academies run by the fire department or by the state. Through classroom instruction and practical training, recruits study firefighting and fire-prevention techniques, local building codes, and emergency medical procedures. They also learn how to fight fires with standard equipment, including axes, chain saws, fire extinguishers, and ladders. After attending a fire academy, firefighters must usually complete a probationary period.

Those wishing to become wildland firefighters may attend apprenticeship programs that last up to 4 years. These programs combine instruction with on-the-job-training under the supervision of experienced firefighters.

In addition to participating in training programs conducted by local or state fire departments and agencies, some firefighters attend federal training sessions sponsored by the National Fire Academy. These training sessions cover topics including anti-arson techniques, disaster preparedness, hazardous materials control, and public fire safety and education.

Licenses, Certifications, and Registrations

Usually, firefighters must be certified as emergency medical technicians. In addition, some fire departments require firefighters to be certified as a paramedic. The National Registry of Emergency Medical Technicians (NREMT). certifies EMTs and paramedics. Both levels of NREMT certification require completing a training or education program and passing the national exam. The national exam has a computer-based test and a practical part. EMTs and paramedics may work with firefighters at the scenes of accidents.

Firefighters begin their careers by attending fire academy training.

Other Experience

Working as a volunteer firefighter may help in getting a job as a career firefighter.

Advancement

Firefighters can be promoted to engineer, then to lieutenant, captain, battalion chief, assistant chief, deputy chief, and, finally, chief. For promotion to positions beyond battalion chief, many fire departments now require applicants to have a bachelor's degree, preferably in fire science, public administration, or a related field. Some firefighters eventually become fire inspectors or investigators after gaining enough experience.

Important Qualities

Communication skills. Firefighters communicate conditions at an emergency scene to other firefighters and to emergency-response crews.

Compassion. Firefighters, like EMT's and paramedics, need to provide emotional support to those in emergency situations.

Courage. Firefighters' daily job duties involve dangerous situations, such as entering a burning building.

Decisionmaking skills. Firefighters must be able to make quick and difficult decisions in an emergency. The ability to make good decisions under pressure could potentially save someone's life.

Physical stamina. Firefighters may have to stay at disaster scenes for long periods of time to rescue and treat victims. Fighting fires requires prolonged use of strength.

Physical strength. Firefighters must be strong enough to carry heavy equipment and move debris at an emergency site. They also carry victims who are injured or cannot walk.

Pay

The median annual wage for firefighters was $50,850 in May 2019. The median wage is the wage at which half the workers in an occupation earned more than that amount and half earned less. The lowest 10 percent earned less than $25,550, and the highest 10 percent earned more than $92,020.

In May 2019, the median annual wages for firefighters in the top industries in which they worked were as follows:

State government, excluding education and hospitals	$55,030
Federal government, excluding postal service	52,140
Local government, excluding education and hospitals	51,850

Firefighters typically work long periods and varied hours. Overtime is common. Most firefighters work 24-hour shifts on duty and are off the following 48 or 72 hours. Some firefighters may work 10/14 shifts, which means 10 hours working and 14 hours off.

When combating forest and wildland fires, firefighters may work for extended periods. For example, wildland firefighters may have to stay for days or weeks when a wildland fire breaks out.

Job Outlook

Employment of firefighters is projected to grow 6 percent from 2019 to 2029, faster than the average for all occupations.

Although improved building materials and building codes have resulted in a long-term decrease in fires and fire fatalities, firefighters will still be needed to respond to fires. Fires can spread rapidly, so controlling them quickly is very important. Wildland firefighters will still be needed to combat active fires and manage the environment to reduce the impact of fires. Firefighters will also continue to respond to medical emergencies.

Job Prospects

Job prospects for firefighters will be good despite the number of volunteer firefighters that qualify for career firefighter jobs. There will be positions open from those leaving the occupation.

Physically fit applicants with some postsecondary firefighter education and paramedic training should have the best job prospects.

Firefighters

Median annual wages, May 2019

Firefighting and prevention workers	$51,330
Firefighters	$50,850
Total, all occupations	$39,810

Note: All Occupations includes all occupations in the U.S. Economy.
Source: U.S. Bureau of Labor Statistics, Occupational Employment Statistics.

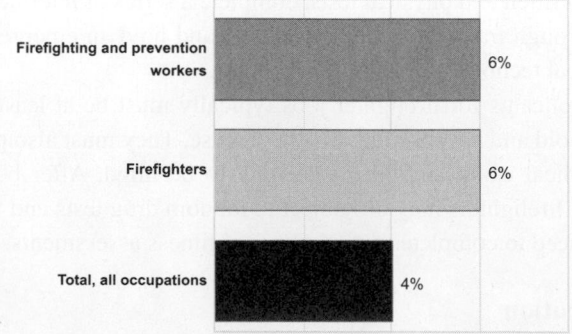

Firefighters

Percent change in employment, projected 2019-29

Firefighting and prevention workers	6%
Firefighters	6%
Total, all occupations	4%

Note: All Occupations includes all occupations in the U.S. Economy.
Source: U.S. Bureau of Labor Statistics, Employment Projections program.

Employment projections data for firefighters, 2019-29					
Occupational Title	SOC Code	Employment, 2019	Projected Employment, 2029	Change, 2019-29	
				Percent	Numeric
SOURCE: U.S. Bureau of Labor Statistics, Employment Projections program					
Firefighters	33-2011	335,500	355,800	6	20,300

State & Area Data

Occupational Employment Statistics (OES)

The Occupational Employment Statistics (OES) program produces employment and wage estimates annually for over 800 occupations. These estimates are available for the nation as a whole, for individual states, and for metropolitan and nonmetropolitan areas.

Contacts for More Information

For information about a career as a firefighter, contact your local fire department or visit

➤ International Association of Fire Fighters
➤ International Association of Women in Fire & Emergency Services
➤ U.S. Fire Administration
➤ National Fire Protection Association

For information about professional qualifications and a list of colleges and universities offering 2- or 4-year degree programs in fire science and fire prevention, visit

➤ National Fire Academy, U.S. Fire Administration

For more information about emergency medical technicians and paramedics, visit

➤ National Registry of Emergency Medical Technicians

Fire Inspectors

Summary

Quick Facts: Fire Inspectors

2019 Median Pay	$60,230 per year $28.96 per hour
Typical Entry-Level Education	See below
Work Experience in a Related Occupation	See below
On-the-job Training	Moderate-term on-the-job training
Number of Jobs, 2019	16,400
Job Outlook, 2019-29	8% (Much faster than average)
Employment Change, 2019-29	1,400

What Fire Inspectors Do

Fire inspectors examine buildings in order to detect fire hazards and ensure that federal, state, and local fire codes are met.

Work Environment

Fire inspectors and investigators work in offices and in the field. They typically work during regular business hours, but investigators may also work evenings, weekends, and holidays because they must be ready to respond when fires occur. Forest fire inspectors and prevention specialists spend much of their time outdoors.

How to Become a Fire Inspector

Fire inspectors and investigators, as well as forest fire inspectors and prevention specialists, typically have previous work experience as a firefighter. These workers need at least a high

Fire investigators work at the scene of a fire to determine its cause.

school diploma or equivalent, and receive on-the-job-training in inspection and investigation.

Pay

The median annual wage for fire inspectors and investigators was $61,660 in May 2019.

The median annual wage for forest fire inspectors and prevention specialists was $45,270 in May 2019.

Job Outlook

Employment of fire inspectors is projected to grow 8 percent from 2019 to 2029, much faster than the average for all occupations. Jobseekers should expect strong competition for the limited number of available positions.

State & Area Data

Explore resources for employment and wages by state and area for fire inspectors.

What Fire Inspectors Do

Fire inspectors examine buildings in order to detect fire hazards and ensure that federal, state, and local fire codes are met. Fire investigators, another type of worker in this field, determine the origin and cause of fires and explosions. Forest fire inspectors and prevention specialists assess outdoor fire hazards in public and residential areas.

Duties

Fire inspectors typically do the following:

- Search for fire hazards
- Ensure that buildings comply with fire codes
- Test fire alarms, sprinklers, and other fire protection equipment
- Inspect fuel storage tanks and air compressors
- Review emergency evacuation plans
- Conduct followup visits to make sure that infractions do not recur
- Review building plans with developers
- Conduct fire and safety education programs
- Maintain fire inspection files
- Administer burn permits and monitor controlled burns

    Fire investigators typically do the following:

- Collect and analyze evidence from scenes of fires and explosions
- Interview witnesses
- Reconstruct the scene of a fire or arson
- Send evidence to laboratories to be tested for fingerprints or accelerants
- Analyze information with chemists, engineers, and attorneys

- Document evidence by taking photographs and creating diagrams
- Determine the origin and cause of a fire
- Keep detailed records and protect evidence for use in a court of law
- Testify in civil and criminal legal proceedings
- Exercise police powers, such as the power of arrest, and carry a weapon

Forest fire inspectors and prevention specialists assess outdoor fire hazards in public and residential areas. They look for fire code infractions and for conditions that pose a wildfire risk. They also recommend ways to reduce fire hazards. During patrols, they enforce fire regulations and report fire conditions to their central command center.

Work Environment

Fire inspectors and investigators held about 14,200 jobs in 2019. The largest employers of fire inspectors and investigators were as follows:

Local government, excluding education and hospitals.....	77%
State government, excluding education and hospitals......	8
Colleges, universities, and professional schools; state, local, and private...	1
Manufacturing..	0

Forest fire inspectors and prevention specialists held about 2,300 jobs in 2019. The largest employers of forest fire inspectors and prevention specialists were as follows:

State government, excluding education and hospitals....	53%
Local government, excluding education and hospitals...	40

Fire inspectors work both in offices and in the field. In the field, inspectors examine buildings such as apartment complexes and offices. They also may visit and inspect other

Fire inspectors inspect building plans to ensure that they meet fire codes.

Fire investigators often work in the field when determining the origin and cause of a fire.

structures, such as arenas and industrial plants. Fire investigators visit the scene of a fire. They may be exposed to poor ventilation, smoke, fumes, and other hazardous agents.

Forest fire inspectors and prevention specialists spend much of their time outdoors, assessing the risks of fires in places such as forests, fields, and other natural or outdoor environments.

Injuries and Illnesses

Working at the scene of a fire can be dangerous. And injuries can occur when workers are patrolling in remote areas with rugged terrain.

Work Schedules

Fire inspectors and investigators typically work during regular business hours, but investigators may also work evenings, weekends, and holidays because they must be ready to respond when fires occur.

How to Become a Fire Inspector

Fire inspectors and investigators, as well as forest fire inspectors and prevention specialists, typically have previous work experience as a firefighter. These workers need at least a high school diploma or equivalent, and receive on-the-job-training in inspection and investigation.

Fire inspectors and investigators usually must pass a background check, which may include a drug test. Most employers also require inspectors and investigators to have a valid driver's license, and investigators usually need to be U.S. citizens because of their police powers.

Education

Because fire inspectors and investigators typically have previous work experience as a firefighter, many have completed a postsecondary educational program for emergency medical technicians (EMTs). Some employers prefer candidates with a 2- or 4-year degree in fire science, engineering, or chemistry. For those candidates interested in becoming forest fire

Many fire inspectors and investigators have a firefighter background.

inspectors and prevention specialists, a high school diploma or equivalent typically is required.

Training

Training requirements vary by state, but programs usually include instruction in a classroom setting in addition to on-the-job training.

Classroom training often takes place at a fire or police academy over the course of several months. A variety of topics are covered, including guidelines for conducting an inspection or investigation, legal codes, courtroom procedures, protocols for handling hazardous and explosive materials, and the proper use of equipment.

In most agencies, after inspectors and investigators have finished their classroom training, they also receive on-the-job training, during which they work with a more experienced officer.

Employers, such as the Bureau of Alcohol, Tobacco, Firearms and Explosives (ATF) and the Federal Bureau of Investigation (FBI), and organizations, such as the National Fire Academy and the International Association of Arson Investigators, offer training programs in fire investigation.

Work Experience in a Related Occupation

Most fire inspectors and investigators are required to have work experience as a firefighter. Forest fire inspectors and prevention specialists typically need firefighting experience before being hired.

Licenses, Certifications, and Registrations

Many states have certification exams that cover standards established by the National Fire Protection Association. Many states require additional training for inspectors and investigators each year in order for them to maintain their certification.

The National Fire Protection Association also offers several certifications, such as Certified Fire Inspector and Certified Fire Protection Specialist, for fire inspectors. Some jobs in the private sector require that job candidates already have these certifications.

In addition, fire investigators may choose to pursue certification from a nationally recognized professional association. Among such certifications and associations are the Certified Fire Investigator (CFI) certification from the International Association of Arson Investigators or the Certified Fire and Explosion Investigator (CFEI) certification from the National Association of Fire Investigators (NAFI). The process of obtaining certification can teach new skills and demonstrate competency.

Important Qualities

Communication skills. Fire inspectors must clearly explain fire code violations to building and property managers. They must carefully interview witnesses as part of their factfinding mission.

Critical-thinking skills. Fire inspectors must be able to recognize code violations and recommend a way to fix the problem. They must be able to analyze evidence from a fire and come to a reasonable conclusion.

Detail oriented. Fire inspectors must notice details when inspecting a site for code violations or investigating the cause of a fire.

Physical strength. Fire investigators may have to move debris at the site of a fire in order to get a more accurate understanding of the scene.

Pay

The median annual wage for fire inspectors and investigators was $61,660 in May 2019. The median wage is the wage at which half the workers in an occupation earned more than that amount and half earned less. The lowest 10 percent earned less than $38,090, and the highest 10 percent earned more than $96,400.

The median annual wage for forest fire inspectors and prevention specialists was $45,270 in May 2019. The lowest 10 percent earned less than $28,090, and the highest 10 percent earned more than $89,710.

In May 2019, the median annual wages for fire inspectors and investigators in the top industries in which they worked were as follows:

Manufacturing	$80,220
Local government, excluding education and hospitals	63,130
Colleges, universities, and professional schools; state, local, and private	60,890
State government, excluding education and hospitals	60,230

In May 2019, the median annual wages for forest fire inspectors and prevention specialists in the top industries in which they worked were as follows:

Local government, excluding education and hospitals	$70,920
State government, excluding education and hospitals	35,390

Fire inspectors and investigators typically work during regular business hours, but investigators may also work evenings, weekends, and holidays because they must be ready to respond when fires occur.

Job Outlook

Overall employment of fire inspectors is projected to grow 8 percent from 2019 to 2029, much faster than the average for all occupations. Employment growth will vary by specialization.

Employment of fire inspectors and investigators is projected to grow 6 percent from 2019 to 2029, faster than the average for all occupations. Fire inspectors will be needed to assess potential fire hazards in newly constructed residential, commercial, public, and other buildings in the coming decade. Fire inspectors will also be needed to ensure that existing buildings meet updated and revised federal, state, and local fire codes each year. Although the number of structural fires occurring across the country has been falling for some time, fire investigators will still be needed to determine the cause of fires and explosions.

Employment of forest fire inspectors and prevention specialists is projected to grow 24 percent from 2019 to 2029, much faster than the average for all occupations. However, because it is a small occupation, the fast growth will result in only about 500 new jobs over the 10-year period. Forest fire inspectors

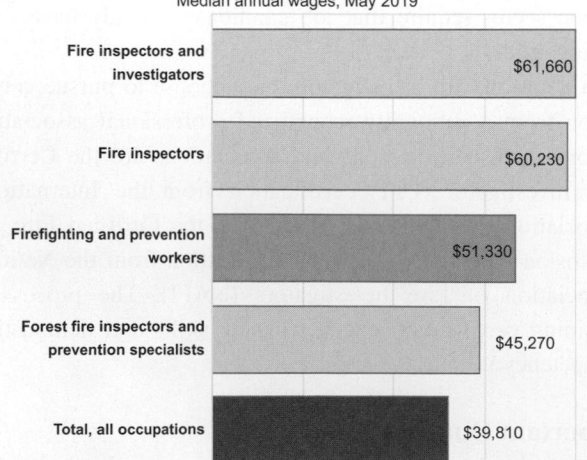

Fire Inspectors
Median annual wages, May 2019

Fire inspectors and investigators — $61,660
Fire inspectors — $60,230
Firefighting and prevention workers — $51,330
Forest fire inspectors and prevention specialists — $45,270
Total, all occupations — $39,810

Note: All Occupations includes all occupations in the U.S. Economy.
Source: U.S. Bureau of Labor Statistics, Occupational Employment Statistics.

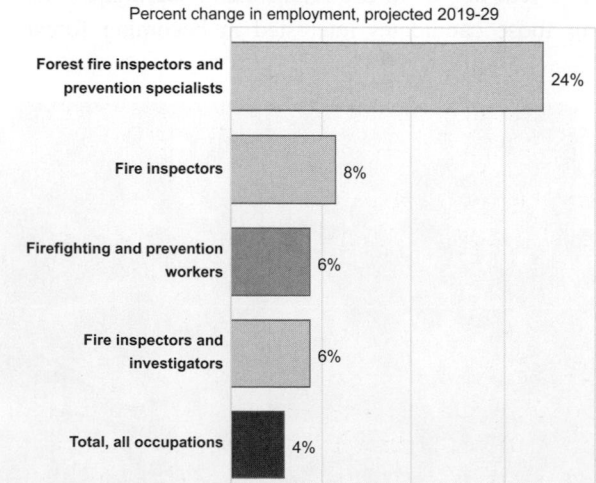

Fire Inspectors
Percent change in employment, projected 2019-29

Forest fire inspectors and prevention specialists — 24%
Fire inspectors — 8%
Firefighting and prevention workers — 6%
Fire inspectors and investigators — 6%
Total, all occupations — 4%

Note: All Occupations includes all occupations in the U.S. Economy.
Source: U.S. Bureau of Labor Statistics, Employment Projections program.

and prevention specialists are expected to be needed to help prevent and control the increasingly destructive wildfires that the United States has been experiencing.

Job Prospects
Jobseekers should expect strong competition for the number of available positions.

Those who have completed some fire science education or who have training related to criminal investigation should have the best job prospects.

Employment projections data for fire inspectors, 2019-29					
Occupational Title	SOC Code	Employment, 2019	Projected Employment, 2029	Change, 2019-29	
				Percent	Numeric
SOURCE: U.S. Bureau of Labor Statistics, Employment Projections program					
Fire inspectors	33-2020	16,400	17,800	8	1,400
Fire inspectors and investigators	33-2021	14,200	15,000	6	800
Forest fire inspectors and prevention specialists	33-2022	2,300	2,800	24	500

State & Area Data
Occupational Employment Statistics (OES)
The Occupational Employment Statistics (OES) program produces employment and wage estimates annually for over 800 occupations. These estimates are available for the nation as a whole, for individual states, and for metropolitan and nonmetropolitan areas.

Contacts for More Information
For more information about federal fire investigator jobs, visit
➤ Bureau of Alcohol, Tobacco, Firearms and Explosives
➤ Federal Bureau of Investigation

For more information about fire inspectors' and investigators' training, visit
➤ National Fire Academy

For information about standards for fire inspectors and investigators, visit
➤ National Fire Protection Association

For information about certifications, visit
➤ International Association of Arson Investigators
➤ National Association of Fire Investigators

Police and Detectives

Summary

Quick Facts: Police and Detectives

2019 Median Pay	$65,170 per year $31.33 per hour
Typical Entry-Level Education	See below
Work Experience in a Related Occupation	See below
On-the-job Training	Moderate-term on-the-job training
Number of Jobs, 2019	813,500
Job Outlook, 2019-29	5% (Faster than average)
Employment Change, 2019-29	40,600

What Police and Detectives Do
Police officers protect lives and property. Detectives and criminal investigators gather facts and collect evidence of possible crimes.

Work Environment
Police and detective work can be physically demanding, stressful, and dangerous. Police and sheriff's patrol officers and transit and railroad police have some of the highest rates of injuries and illnesses of all occupations. Working around the clock in shifts is common.

How to Become a Police Officer or Detective
Education requirements range from a high school diploma to a college degree. Most police and detectives must graduate from their agency's training academy before completing a period of on-the-job training. Candidates must be U.S. citizens, usually at least 21 years old, and able to meet rigorous physical and personal qualifications.

Pay
The median annual wage for police and detectives was $65,170 in May 2019.

Police officers, detectives, and game wardens enforce laws to protect people and their property.

Job Outlook

Employment of police and detectives is projected to grow 5 percent from 2019 to 2029, faster than the average for all occupations. The continued need for public safety is expected to lead to new openings for officers, although demand may vary by location.

State & Area Data

Explore resources for employment and wages by state and area for police and detectives.

What Police and Detectives Do

Police officers protect lives and property. Detectives and criminal investigators, who are sometimes called *agents* or *special agents*, gather facts and collect evidence of possible crimes.

Duties

Police officers, detectives, and criminal investigators typically do the following:

- Respond to emergency and nonemergency calls
- Patrol assigned areas
- Conduct traffic stops and issue citations
- Search for vehicle records and warrants using computers in the field
- Obtain warrants and arrest suspects
- Collect and secure evidence from crime scenes
- Observe the activities of suspects
- Write detailed reports and fill out forms
- Prepare cases and testify in court

Job duties differ by employer and function, but all police and detectives write reports and keep detailed records that will be needed if they testify in court. Most carry law enforcement tools, such as radios, handcuffs, and guns.

The following are examples of types of police and detectives:

Detectives and criminal investigators are uniformed or plainclothes investigators who gather facts and collect evidence

Police officers use computers to check license information.

for criminal cases. They conduct interviews, examine records, observe the activities of suspects, and participate in raids and arrests. Detectives usually specialize in investigating one type of crime, such as homicide or fraud. Detectives are typically assigned cases on a rotating basis and work on them until an arrest and trial are completed or until the case is dropped.

Fish and game wardens enforce fishing, hunting, and boating laws. They patrol fishing and hunting areas, conduct search and rescue operations, investigate complaints and accidents, and educate the public about laws pertaining to the outdoors. Federal fish and game wardens are often referred to as Federal Wildlife Officers.

Police and sheriff's patrol officers are the most common type of police and detectives, and have general law enforcement duties. They wear uniforms that allow the public to easily recognize them as police officers. They have regular patrols and also respond to emergency and nonemergency calls. During patrols, officers look for signs of criminal activity and may conduct searches and arrest suspected criminals.

Some police officers work only on a specific type of crime, such as narcotics. Officers, especially those working in large departments, may work in special units, such as horseback, motorcycle, canine corps, and special weapons and tactics (SWAT). Typically, officers must work as patrol officers for a certain number of years before they may be appointed to a special unit.

Transit and railroad police patrol railroad yards and transit stations. They protect property, employees, and passengers from crimes such as thefts and robberies. They remove trespassers from railroad and transit properties and check IDs of people who try to enter secure areas.

Work Environment

Police and detectives held about 813,500 jobs in 2019. Employment in the detailed occupations that make up police and detectives was distributed as follows:

Police and sheriff's patrol officers	688,400
Detectives and criminal investigators	113,500
Fish and game wardens	7,200
Transit and railroad police	4,500

The largest employers of police and detectives were as follows:

Local government, excluding education and hospitals	77%
State government, excluding education and hospitals	12
Federal government	7

Police and detective work can be physically demanding, stressful, and dangerous. Officers must be alert and ready to react throughout their entire shift. Officers regularly work at crime and accident scenes and encounter suffering and the

Police and detectives regularly work at crime and accident scenes.

Police and detectives must use good judgment and have strong communication skills when gathering facts about a crime.

results of violence. Although a career in law enforcement may be stressful, many officers find it rewarding to help members of their communities.

Some federal agencies, such as the Federal Bureau of Investigation and U.S. Secret Service, require extensive travel, often on short notice. These agents may relocate a number of times over the course of their careers. Some special agents, such as U.S. Border Patrol agents, may work outdoors in rugged terrain and in all kinds of weather.

Injuries and Illnesses
Police and sheriff's patrol officers and transit and railroad police have some of the highest rates of injuries and illnesses of all occupations. They may face physical injuries during conflicts with criminals and other high-risk situations.

Work Schedules
Police and detectives usually work full time. Paid overtime is common, and shift work is necessary because the public must be protected at all times.

How to Become a Police Officer or Detective
Education requirements range from a high school diploma to a college degree. Most police and detectives must graduate from

their agency's training academy before completing a period of on-the-job training. Candidates must be U.S. citizens, usually at least 21 years old, and able to meet rigorous physical and personal qualification standards. A felony conviction or drug use may disqualify a candidate.

Education
Police and detective applicants must have at least a high school diploma or equivalent, although many federal agencies and some police departments require some college coursework or a college degree. Many community colleges, 4-year colleges, and universities offer programs in law enforcement and criminal justice. Knowledge of a foreign language is an asset in many federal agencies and geographical regions.

Fish and game wardens typically need a bachelor's degree; desirable fields of study include wildlife science, biology, or natural resources management.

Federal agencies such as the Federal Bureau of Investigation also typically require prospective detectives and investigators to have a bachelor's degree.

Many applicants for entry-level police jobs have taken some college classes, and a significant number are college graduates.

Training

Candidates for appointment usually attend a training academy before becoming an officer. Training includes classroom instruction in state and local laws and constitutional law, civil rights, and police ethics. Recruits also receive training and supervised experience in areas such as patrol, traffic control, firearm use, self-defense, first aid, and emergency response.

Federal law enforcement agents undergo extensive training, usually at the U.S. Marine Corps base in Quantico, Virginia, or at a Federal Law Enforcement Training Center.

Work Experience in a Related Occupation

Detectives normally begin their careers as police officers before being promoted to detective.

FBI special agent applicants typically must have at least 3 years of professional work experience in areas ranging from computer science to accounting.

Other Experience

Some police departments have cadet programs for people interested in a career in law enforcement who do not yet meet age requirements for becoming an officer. These cadets do clerical work and attend classes until they reach the minimum age requirement and can apply for a position with the regular force. Military or police experience may be considered beneficial for potential cadets.

Cadet candidates must be U.S. citizens, usually be at least 21 years old, have a driver's license, and meet specific physical qualifications. Applicants may have to pass physical exams of vision, hearing, strength, and agility, as well as written exams. Previous work or military experience is often seen as a plus. Candidates typically go through a series of interviews and may be asked to take lie detector and drug tests. A felony conviction may disqualify a candidate.

Advancement

Police officers usually become eligible for promotion after a probationary period. Promotions to corporal, sergeant, lieutenant, and captain usually are made according to scores on a written examination and on-the-job performance. In large departments, promotion may enable an officer to become a detective or to specialize in one type of police work, such as working with juveniles.

Important Qualities

Communication skills. Police and detectives must be able to speak with people when gathering facts about a crime and to express details about a given incident in writing.

Empathy. Police officers need to understand the perspectives of a wide variety of people in their jurisdiction and have a willingness to help the public.

Good judgment. Police and detectives must be able to determine the best way to solve a wide array of problems quickly.

Leadership skills. Police officers must be comfortable with being a highly visible member of their community, as the public looks to them for assistance in emergency situations.

Perceptiveness. Officers, detectives, and fish and game wardens must be able to anticipate a person's reactions and understand why people act a certain way.

Physical stamina. Officers and detectives must be in good physical shape, both to pass required tests for entry into the field, and to keep up with the daily rigors of the job.

Physical strength. Police officers must be strong enough to physically apprehend offenders.

Pay

The median annual wage for police and detectives was $65,170 in May 2019. The median wage is the wage at which half the workers in an occupation earned more than that amount and half earned less. The lowest 10 percent earned less than $37,710, and the highest 10 percent earned more than $109,620.

Median annual wages for police and detectives in May 2019 were as follows:

Detectives and criminal investigators	$83,170
Transit and railroad police	71,820
Police and sheriff's patrol officers	63,150
Fish and game wardens	57,500

In May 2019, the median annual wages for police and detectives in the top industries in which they worked were as follows:

Federal government	$88,060
State government, excluding education and hospitals	68,610
Local government, excluding education and hospitals	63,410

Police and detectives usually work full time. Paid overtime is common, and shift work is necessary because the public must be protected at all times.

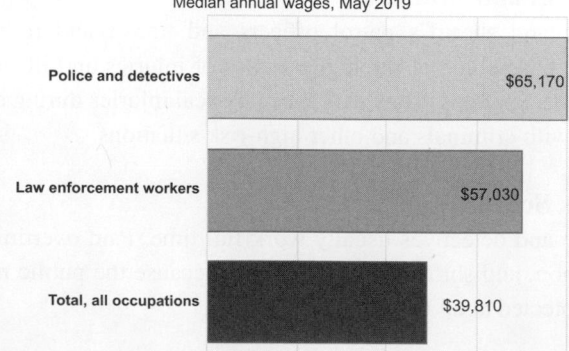

Police and Detectives
Median annual wages, May 2019

- Police and detectives: $65,170
- Law enforcement workers: $57,030
- Total, all occupations: $39,810

Note: All Occupations includes all occupations in the U.S. Economy.
Source: U.S. Bureau of Labor Statistics, Occupational Employment Statistics.

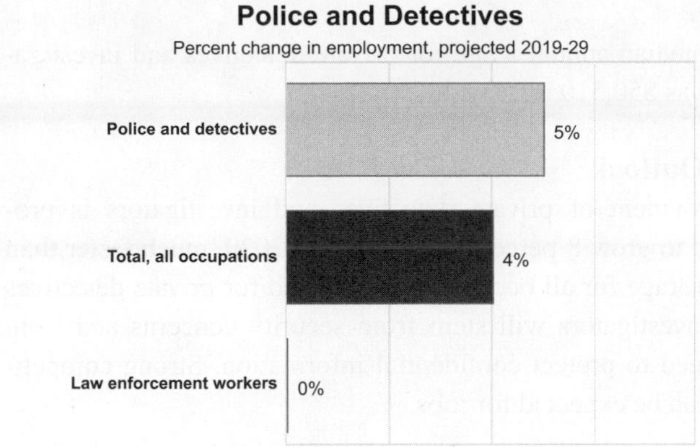

Police and Detectives
Percent change in employment, projected 2019-29

Police and detectives   5%

Total, all occupations   4%

Law enforcement workers   0%

Note: All Occupations includes all occupations in the U.S. Economy.
Source: U.S. Bureau of Labor Statistics, Employment Projections program.

Other Compensation and Benefits

Many agencies provide officers with an allowance for uniforms, as well as extensive benefits and the option to retire at an age that is younger than the typical retirement age. Some police departments offer additional pay for bilingual officers or those with college degrees.

Job Outlook

Employment of police and detectives is projected to grow 5 percent from 2019 to 2029, faster than the average for all occupations.

While a continued desire for public safety is expected to result in a need for more officers, demand for employment is expected to vary depending on location, driven largely by local and state budgets. Even with crime rates falling in recent years, demand for police services to maintain and improve public safety is expected to continue.

Job Prospects

Job applicants may face competition because of relatively low rates of turnover. Applicants with a bachelor's degree and law enforcement or military experience, especially investigative experience, as well as those who speak more than one language, should have the best job opportunities.

Because the level of government spending determines the level of employment for police and detectives, the number of job opportunities can vary from year to year and from place to place.

Employment projections data for police and detectives, 2019-29

Occupational Title	SOC Code	Employment, 2019	Projected Employment, 2029	Change, 2019-29	
				Percent	Numeric
SOURCE: U.S. Bureau of Labor Statistics, Employment Projections program					
Police and detectives	—	813,500	854,200	5	40,600
Detectives and criminal investigators	33-3021	113,500	114,700	1	1,300
Fish and game wardens	33-3031	7,200	7,300	1	100
Police and sheriff's patrol officers	33-3051	688,400	727,400	6	39,100
Transit and railroad police	33-3052	4,500	4,700	4	200

State & Area Data
Occupational Employment Statistics (OES)

The Occupational Employment Statistics (OES) program produces employment and wage estimates annually for over 800 occupations. These estimates are available for the nation as a whole, for individual states, and for metropolitan and nonmetropolitan areas.

Contacts for More Information

For more information about federal law enforcement, visit
➤ Bureau of Alcohol, Tobacco, Firearms and Explosives
➤ Drug Enforcement Administration
➤ Federal Bureau of Investigation
➤ U.S. Customs and Border Protection
➤ U.S. Department of Homeland Security
➤ U.S. Fish & Wildlife Service
➤ U.S. Marshals Service
➤ U.S. Secret Service

Private Detectives and Investigators

Summary

Quick Facts: Private Detectives and Investigators

2019 Median Pay	$50,510 per year $24.28 per hour
Typical Entry-Level Education	High school diploma or equivalent
Work Experience in a Related Occupation ...	Less than 5 years
On-the-job Training	Moderate-term on-the-job training
Number of Jobs, 2019	36,200
Job Outlook, 2019-29	8% (Much faster than average)
Employment Change, 2019-29	3,000

What Private Detectives and Investigators Do

Private detectives and investigators search for information about legal, financial, and personal matters.

Work Environment

Private detectives and investigators work in many places, depending on their assignment or case. Some spend more time in offices, researching cases on computers, while others spend more time in the field, conducting interviews and performing surveillance. Private detectives and investigators often work irregular hours.

How to Become a Private Detective or Investigator

Most private detectives and investigators need several years of work experience and a high school diploma. In addition, the vast majority of states require private detectives and investigators to have a license.

Pay

The median annual wage for private detectives and investigators was $50,510 in May 2019.

Job Outlook

Employment of private detectives and investigators is projected to grow 8 percent from 2019 to 2029, much faster than the average for all occupations. Demand for private detectives and investigators will stem from security concerns and from the need to protect confidential information. Strong competition can be expected for jobs.

State & Area Data

Explore resources for employment and wages by state and area for private detectives and investigators.

What Private Detectives and Investigators Do

Private detectives and investigators search for information about legal, financial, and personal matters. They offer many services, such as verifying people's backgrounds and statements, finding missing persons, and investigating computer crimes.

Duties

Private detectives and investigators typically do the following:

- Interview people to gather information
- Search online, public, and court records to uncover clues
- Conduct surveillance
- Collect evidence for clients
- Check for civil judgments and criminal history

Private detectives and investigators offer many services for individuals, attorneys, and businesses. Examples include performing background checks, investigating employees for

Private detectives and investigators obtain information for clients.

Private detectives and investigators must properly collect and document evidence so that it may be used in a court of law.

possible theft from a company, proving or disproving infidelity in a divorce case, and helping to locate a missing person.

Private detectives and investigators use a variety of tools when researching the facts in a case. Much of their work is done with a computer, allowing them to obtain information such as telephone numbers, details about social networks, descriptions of online activities, and records of a person's prior arrests. They make phone calls to verify facts and interview people when conducting a background investigation.

Detectives also conduct surveillance when investigating a case. They may watch locations, such as a person's home or office, often from a hidden position. Using cameras and binoculars, detectives gather information on people of interest.

Detectives and investigators must be mindful of the law when conducting investigations. Because they lack police authority, their work must be done with the same authority as a private citizen. As a result, detectives and investigators must have a good understanding of federal, state, and local laws, such as privacy laws, and other legal issues affecting their work. Otherwise, evidence they collect may not be useable in court and they could face prosecution.

Skip tracers specialize in locating people whose whereabouts are unknown. For example, debt collectors may employ them to locate people who have unpaid bills.

Work Environment

Private detectives and investigators held about 36,200 jobs in 2019. The largest employers of private detectives and investigators were as follows:

Investigation, guard, and armored car services..........	39%
Finance and insurance...............................	10
Government......................................	8
Self-employed workers	3

Many private detectives and investigators spend time away from their desks while conducting surveillance in the field.

Private detectives and investigators work in many environments, depending on the case. Some spend more time in offices, researching cases on computers and making phone calls. Others spend more time in the field, conducting interviews or performing surveillance. In addition, private detectives and investigators may have to work outdoors or from a vehicle, in all kinds of weather, in order to obtain the information their client needs.

Although investigators often work alone, some work with others while conducting surveillance or carrying out large, complicated assignments.

Work Schedules

Private detectives and investigators often work irregular hours because they conduct surveillance and contact people outside of normal work hours. They may work early mornings, evenings, weekends, and holidays.

How to Become a Private Detective or Investigator

Private detectives and investigators typically need several years of work experience and a high school diploma. In addition, the vast majority of states require private detectives and investigators to have a license.

Although most learn on the job, many private detectives and investigators have a law enforcement background.

Education

Education requirements vary greatly with the job, but most jobs require a high school diploma. Some, though, may require a 2- or 4-year degree in a field such as criminal justice.

Training

Most private detectives and investigators learn through on-the-job training, typically lasting between several months and a year.

Although new investigators must learn how to gather information, additional training depends on the type of firm that hires them. For example, investigators may learn to conduct remote surveillance, reconstruct accident scenes, or investigate insurance fraud. Corporate investigators hired by large companies may receive formal training in business practices, management structure, and various finance-related topics.

Work Experience in a Related Occupation

Private detectives and investigators must typically have previous work experience, usually in law enforcement, the military, or federal intelligence. Those in such jobs, who are frequently able to retire after 20 or 25 years of service, may become private detectives or investigators in a second career.

Other private detectives and investigators may have previously worked as bill and account collectors, claims adjusters, paralegals, or process servers.

Licenses, Certifications, and Registrations

Most states require private detectives and investigators to have a license. Check with your state for more information; Professional Investigator Magazine has links to most states' licensing requirements. Because laws often change, jobseekers should verify the licensing laws related to private investigators with the state and locality in which they want to work.

Candidates may also obtain certification, although it is not required for employment. Still, becoming certified through professional organizations can demonstrate competence and may help candidates advance in their careers.

For investigators who specialize in negligence or criminal defense investigation, the National Association of Legal Investigators offers the Certified Legal Investigator certification. For other investigators, ASIS International offers the Professional Certified Investigator certification.

Important Qualities

Communication skills. Private detectives and investigators must listen carefully and ask appropriate questions when interviewing a person of interest.

Decisionmaking skills. Private detectives and investigators must be able to think on their feet and make quick decisions, based on the limited information that they have at a given time.

Inquisitiveness. Private detectives and investigators must want to ask questions and search for the truth.

Patience. Private detectives and investigators may have to spend long periods conducting surveillance while waiting for an event to occur. Investigations may take a long time, and they may not provide a resolution quickly—or at all.

Resourcefulness. Private detectives and investigators must work persistently with whatever leads they have, no matter how limited, to determine the next step toward their goal. They sometimes need to anticipate what a person of interest will do next.

Pay

The median annual wage for private detectives and investigators was $50,510 in May 2019. The median wage is the wage at which half the workers in an occupation earned more than that amount and half earned less. The lowest 10 percent earned less than $30,390, and the highest 10 percent earned more than $89,760.

In May 2019, the median annual wages for private detectives and investigators in the top industries in which they worked were as follows:

Finance and insurance	$60,300
Government	60,120
Investigation, guard, and armored car services	45,530

Private detectives and investigators often work irregular hours because they conduct surveillance and contact people outside of normal work hours. They may work early mornings, evenings, weekends, and holidays.

Job Outlook

Employment of private detectives and investigators is projected to grow 8 percent from 2019 to 2029, much faster than the average for all occupations. However, because it is a small occupation, the fast growth will result in only about 3,000 new jobs over the 10-year period.

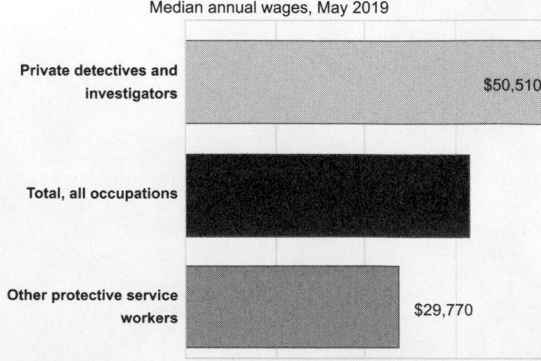

Private Detectives and Investigators
Median annual wages, May 2019

Private detectives and investigators $50,510

Total, all occupations

Other protective service workers $29,770

Note: All Occupations includes all occupations in the U.S. Economy.
Source: U.S. Bureau of Labor Statistics, Occupational Employment Statistics.

Private Detectives and Investigators
Percent change in employment, projected 2019-29

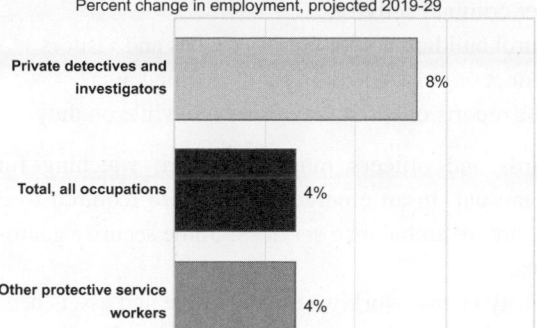

Private detectives and investigators	8%
Total, all occupations	4%
Other protective service workers	4%

Note: All Occupations includes all occupations in the U.S. Economy. Source: U.S. Bureau of Labor Statistics, Employment Projections program.

Continued lawsuits, fraud and other crimes, and interpersonal mistrust create demand for investigative services in industries such as legal services.

Background checks will continue to be a source of work for some investigators, as online investigations are not always sufficient.

Job Prospects

Strong competition for jobs can be expected because private detective and investigator careers attract many qualified people, including relatively young retirees from law enforcement and the military.

Candidates with related work experience, as well as those with strong interviewing skills and familiarity with computers, may find more job opportunities than others.

Employment projections data for private detectives and investigators, 2019-29					
Occupational Title	SOC Code	Employment, 2019	Projected Employment, 2029	Change, 2019-29	
				Percent	Numeric
SOURCE: U.S. Bureau of Labor Statistics, Employment Projections program					
Private detectives and investigators	33-9021	36,200	39,200	8	3,000

State & Area Data
Occupational Employment Statistics (OES)

The Occupational Employment Statistics (OES) program produces employment and wage estimates annually for over 800 occupations. These estimates are available for the nation as a whole, for individual states, and for metropolitan and nonmetropolitan areas.

Contacts for More Information

For more information about private detectives and investigators, including information on certification, visit
➤ National Association of Legal Investigators
➤ ASIS International

For more information about state licensing requirements, visit
➤ Professional Investigator Magazine

Security Guards and Gambling Surveillance Officers

Summary

Quick Facts: Security Guards and Gambling Surveillance Officers

2019 Median Pay	$29,710 per year / $14.29 per hour
Typical Entry-Level Education	High school diploma or equivalent
Work Experience in a Related Occupation	See below
On-the-job Training	See below
Number of Jobs, 2019	1,164,600
Job Outlook, 2019-29	3% (As fast as average)
Employment Change, 2019-29	33,300

What Security Guards and Gambling Surveillance Officers Do

Security guards and gambling surveillance officers protect property from illegal activity.

Work Environment

Security guards work in a variety of places, including industrial settings, retail stores, and office buildings. Gambling surveillance officers work mostly in casinos. Because many buildings and casinos are open 24 hours a day, security guards and officers often must work around the clock.

How to Become a Security Guard or Gambling Surveillance Officer

Security guards and gambling surveillance officers typically need a high school diploma. Gambling surveillance officers may also need experience with security and video surveillance, depending on their work assignment. Most states require guards to be licensed by the state, especially if they carry a firearm.

Pay

The median annual wage for gambling surveillance officers and gambling investigators was $34,190 in May 2019.

The median annual wage for security guards was $29,680 in May 2019.

Job Outlook

Overall employment of security guards and gambling surveillance officers is projected to grow 3 percent from 2019 to 2029,

Security guards conduct security checks over their assigned patrol area.

about as fast as the average for all occupations. Along with openings arising from employment growth, other openings are expected to result from the need to replace workers who leave the occupation.

State & Area Data

Explore resources for employment and wages by state and area for security guards and gambling surveillance officers.

What Security Guards and Gambling Surveillance Officers Do

Security guards and gambling surveillance officers protect property against theft, vandalism, and other illegal activity.

Duties

Security guards and gaming surveillance officers typically do the following:

- Patrol property
- Enforce rules and regulations of an employer's property
- Monitor alarms and video-surveillance systems

Security guards control building access for employees and visitors.

- Respond to emergencies
- Deter criminal activity
- Control building access by employees and visitors
- Conduct security checks over a specified area
- Write reports on what they observed while on duty

Guards and officers must stay alert, watching for anything unusual. In an emergency, they are required to contact police, fire, or ambulance services. Some security guards carry firearms.

Security guards work wherever people and assets need to be protected. Responsibilities vary by employer. In offices and factories, for example, security guards protect workers and equipment and check the credentials of people and vehicles entering and leaving the premises. In retail stores, guards protect people, merchandise, money, and equipment. They may work with undercover store detectives to prevent theft by customers and employees, detain shoplifting suspects until the police arrive, and patrol parking lots.

Gambling surveillance officers work in freestanding casinos and other facilities that have designated areas for gambling, such as hotels, video gaming terminals, and riverboats. They typically work from an observation room within the gaming facility.

Security guards, also called *security officers,* protect property, enforce rules on the property, and deter criminal activity. Some guards are assigned a stationary position from which they monitor alarms or surveillance cameras. Other guards are assigned a patrol area where they conduct security checks.

Gambling surveillance officers and gambling investigators act as security agents for casinos. Using audio and video equipment, they watch casino operations for suspicious activities, such as cheating and theft, and monitor compliance with rules, regulations, and laws. They maintain and organize recordings from security cameras, which are sometimes used as evidence in police investigations.

Work Environment

Gambling surveillance officers and gambling investigators held about 10,500 jobs in 2019. The largest employers of gambling surveillance officers and gambling investigators were as follows:

Local government, excluding education and hospitals	56%
Casino hotels	18
Gambling industries (except casino hotels)	16
State government, excluding education and hospitals	6
Spectator sports	3

Security guards held about 1.2 million jobs in 2019. The largest employers of security guards were as follows:

Some security guards monitor alarms or surveillance cameras from a desk.

Investigation, guard, and armored car services	59%
Educational services; state, local, and private	6
Healthcare and social assistance	6
Accommodation and food services	5
Government	4

Security guards work in a variety of places, including industrial settings, stores, and office buildings. Gambling surveillance officers and investigators are employed in casinos and other gaming facilities only in locations where gambling is legal.

Guards may spend considerable time on their feet patrolling buildings and grounds or may sit for long periods at a single post, such as in a guardhouse at the entrance to a gated facility or community. Others may spend periods of time in a vehicle, patrolling the property and grounds.

Both security guards and gambling surveillance officers may spend much of their shift sitting at a desk or counter in a dark room, observing customers on video surveillance equipment. They may have to monitor activity on multiple screens for long periods of time without distraction.

Work Schedules

Security guards and gambling surveillance officers usually work in shifts of about 8 hours, with rotating schedules. Night shifts are common. Most security guards and gambling surveillance officers work full time. Seasonal work may be available during the holidays and during the warmer summer months in some states.

How to Become a Security Guard or Gambling Surveillance Officer

Security guards and gambling surveillance officers typically require a high school diploma and on-the-job training. Gambling surveillance officers sometimes need experience with security and video surveillance. Most states require security guards to be licensed by the state, especially if they carry a firearm.

Education

Security guards typically need a high school diploma or equivalent, although some jobs may not require formal educational credentials. Gambling surveillance officers also need a high school diploma or equivalent.

Training

Although most employers provide instruction for newly hired security guards and surveillance officers, the amount of training varies. Most security guards learn their job in a few weeks, but gambling surveillance officers and investigators may need several months. Employer-provided training typically covers emergency procedures, crime prevention, and proper communication.

Many states recommend that security guards receive about 8 hours of pre-assignment training, 8 to 16 hours of on-the-job training, and 8 hours of annual training. Instruction may include protection, public relations, report writing, deterring crises, first aid, and other specialized training related to the security guard's assignment.

Training is more rigorous for armed guards because they require weapons training. Armed guards may be tested periodically in the use of firearms.

Most states require that guards be registered with the state in which they work.

Gambling surveillance officers and investigators receive training in topics such as the rules of casino games, gaming regulations, identifying cheating techniques, and the proper use of video and radio equipment.

Drug testing may be required both as a condition of employment and randomly during employment.

Work experience in a related occupation

To enter the occupation, gambling surveillance officers and investigators typically need work experience in casinos or with video monitoring technology. Candidates sometimes gain video monitoring experience by working as a security guard.

Licenses, Certifications, and Registrations

Most states require that security guards be licensed by the state in which they work. Although licensing requirements vary by state, basic qualifications for candidates are as follows:

- Be at least 18 years old
- Pass a background check
- Complete training

Guards who carry weapons usually must be licensed by the appropriate government authority. Positions for armed guards have more stringent background checks and entry requirements than do those for unarmed guards. Most states require rigorous hiring and screening programs, including background, criminal record, and fingerprint checks, for armed guards.

Some states and gaming facilities require a minimum age of 21 to work in a casino.

Some jobs may also require a driver's license.

Important Qualities

Communication skills. Security guards and surveillance officers must communicate effectively with others, even in stressful situations.

Interpersonal skills. Security guards often regularly interact with the public; in addition, they must be able to handle and deescalate confrontational situations.

Observation skills. Security guards and surveillance officers must be alert and aware of their surroundings, and be able to quickly recognize anything out of the ordinary.

Problem-solving skills. Security guards and surveillance officers must be able to quickly determine the best course of action when a dangerous situation arises.

Pay

The median annual wage for gambling surveillance officers and gambling investigators was $34,190 in May 2019. The median wage is the wage at which half the workers in an occupation earned more than that amount and half earned less. The lowest 10 percent earned less than $24,490, and the highest 10 percent earned more than $57,700.

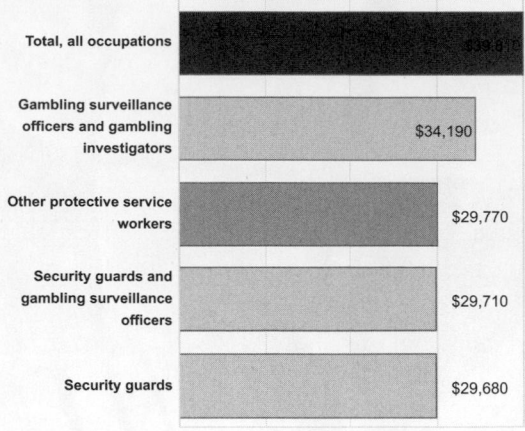

Security Guards and Gambling Surveillance Officers

Median annual wages, May 2019

Total, all occupations	$39,810
Gambling surveillance officers and gambling investigators	$34,190
Other protective service workers	$29,770
Security guards and gambling surveillance officers	$29,710
Security guards	$29,680

Note: All Occupations includes all occupations in the U.S. Economy.
Source: U.S. Bureau of Labor Statistics, Occupational Employment Statistics.

The median annual wage for security guards was $29,680 in May 2019. The lowest 10 percent earned less than $21,150, and the highest 10 percent earned more than $50,310.

In May 2019, the median annual wages for gambling surveillance officers and gambling investigators in the top industries in which they worked were as follows:

State government, excluding education and hospitals	$68,120
Casino hotels	36,930
Gambling industries (except casino hotels)	34,710
Local government, excluding education and hospitals	32,050
Spectator sports	31,500

In May 2019, the median annual wages for security guards in the top industries in which they worked were as follows:

Government	$34,730
Educational services; state, local, and private	34,460
Healthcare and social assistance	34,330
Accommodation and food services	30,260
Investigation, guard, and armored car services	28,470

Security guards and gambling surveillance officers usually work in shifts of about 8 hours, with rotating schedules. Night shifts are common.

Job Outlook

Overall employment of security guards and gambling surveillance officers is projected to grow 3 percent from 2019 to 2029, about as fast as the average for all occupations.

Security Guards and Gambling Surveillance Officers

Percent change in employment, projected 2019-29

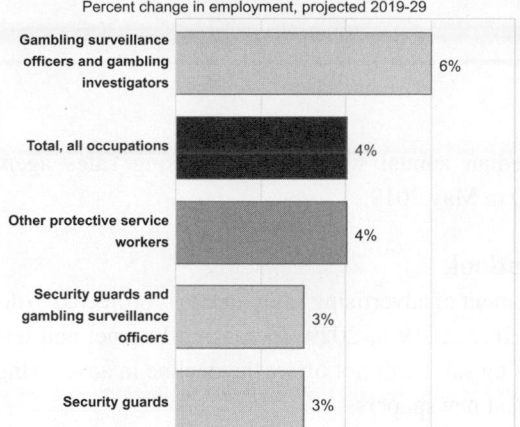

Note: All Occupations includes all occupations in the U.S. Economy.
Source: U.S. Bureau of Labor Statistics, Employment Projections program.

Security guards will continue to be needed to protect both people and property because of concerns about crime and vandalism.

States continue to legalize gambling and casinos continue to grow in number, resulting in the need for gambling surveillance officers and investigators.

Advances in video surveillance and anti-cheating technology may limit the employment of some security guards and gambling surveillance officers and investigators.

Job Prospects

About 144,000 openings for security guards and gambling surveillance officers are projected each year, on average, over the decade.

Many of those openings are expected to result from the need to replace workers who transfer to different occupations or exit the labor force, such as to retire.

Candidates for higher paying positions, which may require extensive training and experience, should face the most competition. Those who have a background in law enforcement may have the best prospects.

Employment projections data for security guards and gambling surveillance officers, 2019-29

Occupational Title	SOC Code	Employment, 2019	Projected Employment, 2029	Change, 2019-29 Percent	Change, 2019-29 Numeric
SOURCE: U.S. Bureau of Labor Statistics, Employment Projections program					
Security guards and gambling surveillance officers	33-9030	1,164,600	1,197,900	3	33,300
Gambling surveillance officers and gambling investigators	33-9031	10,500	11,100	6	600
Security guards	33-9032	1,154,100	1,186,800	3	32,800

State & Area Data

Occupational Employment Statistics (OES)

The Occupational Employment Statistics (OES) program produces employment and wage estimates annually for over 800 occupations. These estimates are available for the nation as a whole, for individual states, and for metropolitan and nonmetropolitan areas.

Contacts for More Information

For more information about security guards, visit
➤ The International Union, Security, Police and Fire Professionals of America

Sales

Advertising Sales Agents

Summary

Quick Facts: Advertising Sales Agents

2019 Median Pay	$53,310 per year $25.63 per hour
Typical Entry-Level Education	High school diploma or equivalent
Work Experience in a Related Occupation	None
On-the-job Training	Moderate-term on- the-job training
Number of Jobs, 2019	139,200
Job Outlook, 2019-29	-6% (Decline)
Employment Change, 2019-29	-9,000

What Advertising Sales Agents Do

Advertising sales agents sell advertising space to businesses and individuals.

Work Environment

Advertising sales agents work under pressure to meet sales quotas. They work in a range of industries, including advertising agencies, radio, television, and Internet publishing.

How to Become an Advertising Sales Agent

Although a high school diploma is typically enough for an entry-level advertising sales position, some employers prefer applicants who have a bachelor's degree. Sales and communication skills are essential.

Pay

The median annual wage for advertising sales agents was $53,310 in May 2019.

Job Outlook

Employment of advertising sales agents is projected to decline 6 percent from 2019 to 2029. Increasing Internet and television advertising sales will not offset the decline in advertising activity in print newspapers.

State & Area Data

Explore resources for employment and wages by state and area for advertising sales agents.

What Advertising Sales Agents Do

Advertising sales agents, also called *advertising sales representatives*, sell advertising space to businesses and individuals. They contact potential clients, make sales presentations, and maintain client accounts.

Duties

Advertising sales agents typically do the following:

- Locate and contact potential clients to offer their firm's advertising services
- Explain to clients how specific types of advertising will help promote their products or services in the most effective way
- Provide clients with estimates of the costs of advertising products or services
- Process all correspondence and paperwork related to accounts

Advertising sales agents contact potential clients, make sales presentations, and maintain customer accounts.

Agents may spend much of their time visiting prospective advertisers and maintaining business with current clients.

- Prepare and deliver sales presentations to new and existing clients
- Inform clients of available options for advertising art, formats, or features and provide samples of previous work for other clients
- Deliver advertising or illustration proofs to clients for approval
- Prepare promotional plans, sales literature, media kits, and sales contracts
- Recommend appropriate sizes and formats for advertising

Advertising sales agents work outside the office occasionally, meeting with clients and prospective clients at their places of business. Some may make telephone sales calls as well—calling prospects, attempting to sell the media firm's advertising space or time, and arranging followup appointments with interested prospects.

A critical part of building relationships with clients is learning about their needs. Before the first meeting with a client, a sales agent gathers background information on the client's products, current clients, prospective clients, and the geographic area of the target market.

The sales agent then meets with the client to explain how specific types of advertising will help promote the client's products or services most effectively. If a client wishes to proceed, the advertising sales agent prepares and presents an advertising proposal to the client. The proposal may include an overview of the advertising medium to be used, sample advertisements, and cost estimates for the project.

Because of consolidation among media industries, agents are increasingly selling several types of ads in one package. For example, agents may sell ads that would be found in print editions, as well as online editions, of a particular publication, such as a newspaper.

In addition to maintaining sales and overseeing their accounts, advertising sales agents analyze sales statistics and prepare reports about clients' accounts. They keep up to date on industry trends by reading about both current and new products, and they monitor the sales, prices, and products of their competitors.

In many firms, the advertising sales agent drafts contracts, which specify the cost and the advertising work to be done. Agents also may continue to help the client, answering questions or addressing problems the client may have with the proposal.

In addition, sales agents may be responsible for developing sales tools, promotional plans, and media kits, all of which they use to help make a sale. In other cases, firms may have a marketing team that sales agents work with to develop these sales tools.

Work Environment

Advertising sales agents held about 139,200 jobs in 2019. The largest employers of advertising sales agents were as follows:

Companies generally set monthly sales quotas and place considerable pressure on advertising sales agents to meet those quotas.

Advertising, public relations, and related services	38%
Newspaper publishers	12
Radio broadcasting	9
Self-employed workers	7
Television broadcasting	6

Selling can be stressful because income and job security depend directly on agents' ability to keep and expand their client base. Companies generally set monthly sales quotas and place considerable pressure on advertising sales agents to meet those quotas.

Getting new accounts is an important part of the job, and agents may spend much of their time traveling to and visiting prospective advertisers and maintaining relationships with current clients. Sales agents also may work in their employer's offices and handle sales for walk-in clients or for those who call or email the firm to ask about advertising.

Work Schedules

Most advertising sales agents work full time. Some advertising sales agents work more than 40 hours a week. Some work irregular hours and on weekends and holidays.

How to Become an Advertising Sales Agent

Although a high school diploma is typically enough education for an entry-level advertising sales position, some employers prefer applicants with a bachelor's degree. Sales and communication skills are essential. Most training for advertising sales agents takes place on the job.

Education

Although a high school diploma is typically the minimum education requirement for an entry-level advertising sales position, some employers prefer applicants with a college degree. Publishing companies with large circulations and broadcasting

Advertising sales agents must actively seek new clients and initiate communication with current clients in order to meet sales quotas.

stations with a large audience typically prefer workers with a college degree. Courses in marketing, communications, business, and advertising are helpful. For those who have a proven record of successfully selling other products, educational requirements are not likely to be strict.

Training

Most training takes place on the job and can be either formal or informal. In the majority of cases, an experienced sales manager instructs a newly hired advertising sales agent who lacks sales experience. In this one-on-one environment, supervisors typically coach new hires and observe them as they make sales calls and contact clients. Supervisors then advise the new hires on ways to improve their interaction with clients. Employers may bring in consultants to lead formal training sessions when agents sell to a specialized market segment, such as automotive dealers or real estate professionals.

Advancement

Agents with proven leadership ability and a strong sales record may advance to supervisory and managerial positions, such as sales manager, account executive, and vice president of sales. Successful advertising sales agents may also advance to positions in other industries, such as corporate sales.

Important Qualities

Communication skills. Advertising sales agents must be persuasive during sales calls. In addition, they should listen to the client's desires and concerns, and recommend an appropriate advertising package.

Initiative. Advertising sales agents must actively seek new clients, keep in touch with current clients, and expand their client base, in order to meet sales quotas.

Organizational skills. Agents work with many clients, each of whom may be at a different stage in the sales process. Agents must be well organized to keep track of their clients and potential clients.

Self-confidence. Advertising sales agents should be confident when calling potential clients (making cold calls). Because potential clients are often unwilling to commit on a first call, agents frequently must continue making sales calls, even if rejected at first.

Pay

The median annual wage for advertising sales agents was $53,310 in May 2019. The median wage is the wage at which half the workers in an occupation earned more than that amount and half earned less. The lowest 10 percent earned less than $25,390, and the highest 10 percent earned more than $118,300.

In May 2019, the median annual wages for advertising sales agents in the top industries in which they worked were as follows:

Advertising, public relations, and related services	$59,080
Television broadcasting	49,760
Radio broadcasting	45,170
Newspaper publishers	39,720

Performance-based pay, including bonuses and commissions, can make up a large portion of an advertising sales agent's earnings. Most employers pay some combination of salaries, commissions, and bonuses. Commissions usually are based on individual sales numbers. Bonuses may depend on individual performance, the performance of all sales workers in a group, or the performance of the entire firm.

Most advertising sales agents work full time. Some advertising sales agents work more than 40 hours a week. Some work irregular hours and on weekends and holidays.

Job Outlook

Employment of advertising sales agents is projected to decline 6 percent from 2019 to 2029.

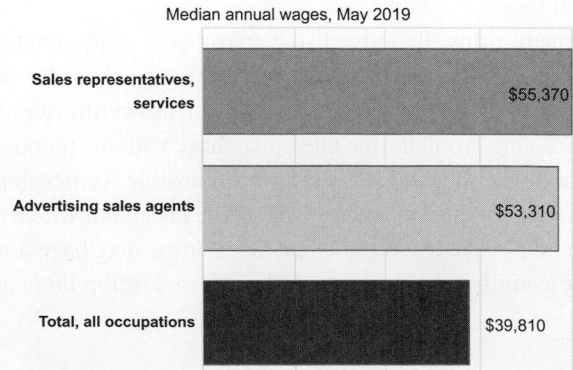

Advertising Sales Agents
Median annual wages, May 2019

Sales representatives, services — $55,370

Advertising sales agents — $53,310

Total, all occupations — $39,810

Note: All Occupations includes all occupations in the U.S. Economy.
Source: U.S. Bureau of Labor Statistics, Occupational Employment Statistics.

Advertising Sales Agents

Percent change in employment, projected 2019-29

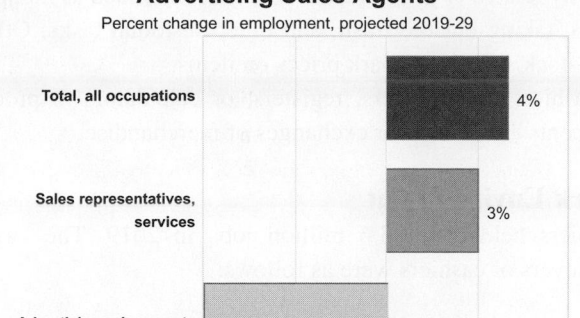

Total, all occupations	4%
Sales representatives, services	3%
Advertising sales agents	-6%

Note: All Occupations includes all occupations in the U.S. Economy. Source: U.S. Bureau of Labor Statistics, Employment Projections program.

Media companies will continue to rely on advertising revenue for profitability. However, employment of advertising sales agents will largely follow broader industry trends, and several of the industries that employ large numbers of these workers are projected to decline. For example, employment in newspaper publishers is expected to decline, although some of this decline may be offset by the sale of digital ads on newspaper websites.

An increasing amount of advertising is expected to be concentrated in digital media, including online video ads, search engine ads, and other digital ads intended for cell phones or tablet-style computers. Digital advertising on the Internet allows companies to directly target potential consumers because websites usually are associated with the types of products that those consumers would like to buy. As a result, employment of advertising sales agents is likely to increase in Internet-focused companies.

Job Prospects

Competition is expected to be strong for jobs as advertising sales agents. Applicants with experience in sales and those with a bachelor's degree and knowledge of digital advertising techniques, such as search engine optimization (SEO), should have the best opportunities.

Employment projections data for advertising sales agents, 2019-29					
Occupational Title	SOC Code	Employment, 2019	Projected Employment, 2029	Change, 2019-29	
				Percent	Numeric
SOURCE: U.S. Bureau of Labor Statistics, Employment Projections program					
Advertising sales agents	41-3011	139,200	130,200	-6	-9,000

State & Area Data

Occupational Employment Statistics (OES)

The Occupational Employment Statistics (OES) program produces employment and wage estimates annually for over 800 occupations. These estimates are available for the nation as a whole, for individual states, and for metropolitan and nonmetropolitan areas.

Contacts for More Information

For information about advertising sales in the newspaper industry, visit
➤ News Media Alliance

For information about the radio advertising industry, visit
➤ Radio Advertising Bureau

Cashiers

Summary

Quick Facts: Cashiers

2019 Median Pay	$23,650 per year $11.37 per hour
Typical Entry-Level Education	No formal educational credential
Work Experience in a Related Occupation	None
On-the-job Training	Short-term on-the-job training
Number of Jobs, 2019	3,600,900
Job Outlook, 2019-29	-7% (Decline)
Employment Change, 2019-29	-265,300

What Cashiers Do

Cashiers process payments from customers purchasing goods and services.

Work Environment

Most cashiers work in retail establishments, such as grocery stores, gasoline stations, and other general merchandise stores.

How to Become a Cashier

Cashiers are trained on the job. There are no formal education requirements to become a cashier.

Pay

The median hourly wage for cashiers was $11.37 in May 2019.

Job Outlook

Employment of cashiers is projected to decline 7 percent from 2019 to 2029. Advances in technology, such as self-service checkout stands in retail stores and increasing online sales, will reduce the need for cashiers.

State & Area Data

Explore resources for employment and wages by state and area for cashiers.

Cashiers process customers' payments.

What Cashiers Do

Cashiers process payments from customers purchasing goods and services.

Duties

Cashiers typically do the following:

- Greet customers
- Scan or register customers' purchases
- Accept payments from customers and give change and receipts
- Bag or wrap customers' purchases
- Process returns and exchanges of merchandise
- Answer customers' questions and provide information about store policies
- Help customers sign up for store rewards programs or credit cards
- Count the money in their register at the beginning and end of each shift

In some establishments, cashiers have to check the age of their customers when selling age-restricted products, such as alcohol and tobacco. Some cashiers may have duties not directly related to sales and customer service, such as mopping floors, taking out the trash, and other custodial tasks. Others may stock shelves or mark prices on items.

Cashiers use scanners, registers, or calculators to process payments and returns or exchanges of merchandise.

Work Environment

Cashiers held about 3.6 million jobs in 2019. The largest employers of cashiers were as follows:

Food and beverage stores	26%
General merchandise stores	21
Gasoline stations	17
Restaurants and other eating places	10
Pharmacies and drug stores	5

The work is often repetitive, and cashiers spend most of their time standing behind counters or checkout stands. Dealing with dissatisfied customers can be stressful.

Work Schedules

Cashiers' work hours vary by employer. Cashiers often work during weekends and holidays. Some cashiers employed in establishments that operate 24 hours a day, such as gasoline stations, work overnight shifts. Part-time work is common.

Employers may restrict the use of time off from Thanksgiving through early January because that is the busiest time of the year for most retailers.

How to Become a Cashier

Cashiers are trained on the job. There are no formal education requirements to become a cashier.

Education

Although most jobs for cashiers have no specific education requirements, some employers prefer applicants with a high school diploma or equivalent. Cashiers should have a basic

Cashiers process returns and exchanges of merchandise.

Cashiers spend most of their time on their feet.

Cashiers need to have good customer service skills.

knowledge of mathematics, because they need to be able to make change and count the money in their registers.

Training

Cashiers receive on-the-job training, which may last a few weeks. An experienced worker typically helps new cashiers learn how to operate equipment such as scanners or registers.

Advancement

Working as a cashier is often a means to advance to other careers in retail. For example, with experience, cashiers may become customer service representatives or retail sales workers.

Important Qualities

Communication skills. Cashiers must pay attention to customers' questions and explain pricing.

Customer-service skills. Cashiers must be courteous and friendly when helping customers.

Dexterity. Cashiers use their hands to operate registers and scan purchases.

Near vision. Cashiers need to see well enough to scan items and process transactions accurately.

Patience. Cashiers must be able to remain calm when interacting with customers.

Physical stamina. Cashiers stand for long periods.

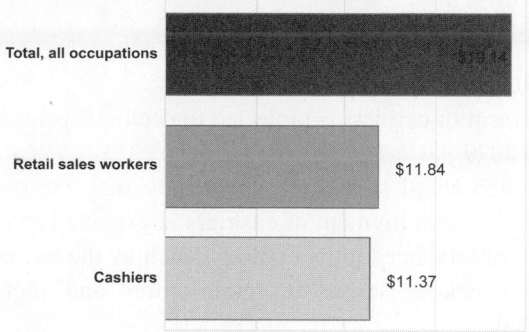

Cashiers
Median hourly wages, May 2019

Total, all occupations	$19.14
Retail sales workers	$11.84
Cashiers	$11.37

Note: All Occupations includes all occupations in the U.S. Economy.
Source: U.S. Bureau of Labor Statistics, Occupational Employment Statistics.

Pay

The median hourly wage for cashiers was $11.37 in May 2019. The median wage is the wage at which half the workers in an occupation earned more than that amount and half earned less. The lowest 10 percent earned less than $8.73, and the highest 10 percent earned more than $15.04.

In May 2019, the median hourly wages for cashiers in the top industries in which they worked were as follows:

Pharmacies and drug stores	$11.94
Food and beverage stores	11.53
General merchandise stores	11.36
Gasoline stations	10.85
Restaurants and other eating places	10.73

Many beginning or inexperienced cashiers earn the federal minimum wage ($7.25 per hour as of July, 24, 2009), but many states set minimum wages higher than the federal minimum.

Cashiers' work hours vary by employer. Cashiers often work during weekends and holidays. Some cashiers employed in establishments that operate 24 hours a day, such as gasoline stations, work overnight shifts. Part-time work is common.

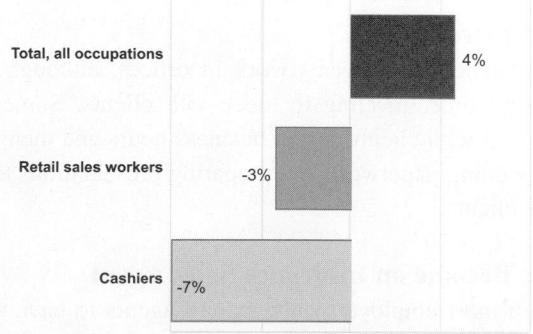

Cashiers
Percent change in employment, projected 2019-29

Total, all occupations	4%
Retail sales workers	-3%
Cashiers	-7%

Note: All Occupations includes all occupations in the U.S. Economy.
Source: U.S. Bureau of Labor Statistics, Employment Projections program.

Employers may restrict the use of time off from Thanksgiving through early January because that is the busiest time of the year for most retailers.

Job Outlook

Employment of cashiers is projected to decline 7 percent from 2019 to 2029.

Although retail sales are expected to increase over the next decade, employment of cashiers is expected to decline because of advances in technology, such as the use of self-service checkout stands in retail stores and increasing online sales.

Job prospects

Job opportunities should be good because of the need to replace the large number of workers who leave the occupation each year.

Employment projections data for cashiers, 2019-29					
Occupational Title	SOC Code	Employment, 2019	Projected Employment, 2029	Change, 2019-29	
				Percent	Numeric
SOURCE: U.S. Bureau of Labor Statistics, Employment Projections program					
Cashiers	41-2011	3,600,900	3,335,500	-7	-265,300

State & Area Data
Occupational Employment Statistics (OES)

The Occupational Employment Statistics (OES) program produces employment and wage estimates annually for over 800 occupations. These estimates are available for the nation as a whole, for individual states, and for metropolitan and nonmetropolitan areas.

Contacts for More Information

The *Handbook* does not have contacts for more information for this occupation.

Insurance Sales Agents

Summary

Quick Facts: Insurance Sales Agents

2019 Median Pay	$50,940 per year $24.49 per hour
Typical Entry-Level Education	High school diploma or equivalent
Work Experience in a Related Occupation	None
On-the-job Training	Moderate-term on-the-job training
Number of Jobs, 2019	501,300
Job Outlook, 2019-29	5% (Faster than average)
Employment Change, 2019-29	27,500

What Insurance Sales Agents Do

Insurance sales agents contact potential customers and sell one or more types of insurance.

Work Environment

Most insurance sales agents work in offices, although some may spend time traveling to meet with clients. Some sales agents meet with clients during business hours and then spend evenings doing paperwork and preparing presentations to prospective clients.

How to Become an Insurance Sales Agent

Although most employers only require agents to have a high school diploma, many agents have a bachelor's degree. Agents must be licensed in the states where they work.

Pay

The median annual wage for insurance sales agents was $50,940 in May 2019.

Job Outlook

Employment of insurance sales agents is projected to grow 5 percent from 2019 to 2029, faster than the average for all occupations. Many clients do their own research and purchase insurance online. However, agents will still be needed to help clients understand their options and choose a policy that is right for them.

State & Area Data

Explore resources for employment and wages by state and area for insurance sales agents.

Insurance sales agents explain various insurance policies and help clients choose plans that suit them.

What Insurance Sales Agents Do

Insurance sales agents contact potential customers and sell one or more types of insurance. Insurance sales agents explain various insurance policies and help clients choose plans that suit them.

Duties

Insurance sales agents typically do the following:

- Call potential clients in order to expand their own customer base
- Interview prospective clients to get information about their financial resources and discuss existing coverage
- Explain the features of various policies
- Analyze clients' current insurance policies and suggest additions or other changes
- Customize insurance programs to suit individual clients
- Handle policy renewals
- Maintain electronic and paper records

Insurance sales agents commonly sell one or more types of insurance, such as property and casualty, life, health, and long-term care insurance.

Property and casualty insurance agents sell policies that protect people and businesses from financial loss resulting from automobile accidents, fire, theft, and other events that can damage property. For businesses, property and casualty insurance also covers workers' compensation claims, product liability claims, or medical malpractice claims.

Life insurance agents specialize in selling policies that pay beneficiaries when a policyholder dies. Life insurance agents also sell annuities that promise a retirement income.

Health and long-term care insurance agents sell policies that cover the costs of medical care and assisted-living services for senior citizens. They also may sell dental insurance and short-term and long-term disability insurance.

Agents may specialize in selling any one of these products or function as generalists providing multiple products.

An increasing number of insurance sales agents offer their clients—especially those approaching retirement—comprehensive financial-planning services, including retirement planning and estate planning. In addition to offering insurance, these agents may become licensed to sell mutual funds, variable annuities, and other securities. This practice is most common with life insurance agents who already sell annuities, but many property and casualty agents also sell financial products.

Many agents spend a lot of time marketing their services and creating their own base of clients. They do this in a variety of ways, including making "cold" sales calls to people who are not current clients.

Potential clients often use comparison shopping tools online to learn about different policies and get information from insurance companies. Clients can either purchase a policy directly from the company's website or contact the company to speak with a sales agent.

Insurance agents also find new clients through referrals by current clients. Keeping clients happy so that they recommend the agent to others is a key to success for insurance sales agents.

Insurance agents may work for a single insurance company or an insurance brokerage.

Captive agents are insurance sales agents who work exclusively for one insurance company. They can only sell policies provided by the company that employs them.

Independent insurance agents work for insurance brokerages, selling the policies of several companies. They match insurance policies for their clients with the company that offers the best rate and coverage.

Work Environment

Insurance sales agents held about 501,300 jobs in 2019. The largest employers of insurance sales agents were as follows:

Insurance agencies and brokerages	61%
Self-employed workers	12
Direct insurance (except life, health, and medical) carriers	9
Direct health and medical insurance carriers	4

Insurance sales agents commonly sell one or more types of insurance, such as property and casualty, life, health, and long-term care.

Most insurance sales agents work in offices, although some may spend much of their time traveling to meet with clients.

Most insurance sales agents work in offices, although some may spend time traveling to meet with clients.

Work Schedules

Some sales agents meet with clients during business hours and then spend evenings doing paperwork and preparing presentations to prospective clients. Most agents work full time and some work more than 40 hours per week.

How to Become an Insurance Sales Agent

Although most employers only require agents to have a high school diploma, many agents have a bachelor's degree. Agents must be licensed in the states where they work.

Education

A high school diploma is the typical requirement for insurance sales agents, although a bachelor's degree can improve one's job prospects. Public-speaking classes can be useful in improving sales techniques, and often agents will have taken courses in business, finance, or economics. Business knowledge is also helpful for sales agents hoping to advance to a managerial position.

Agents must be licensed in the states where they plan to work.

Training

Insurance sales agents learn many of their job duties on the job from other agents. Many employers have new agents shadow an experienced agent. This practice allows the new agent to learn how to conduct the company's business and to understand how the agency interacts with clients.

Because changes in tax laws, government benefits programs, and other state and federal regulations can affect clients' insurance needs and the way in which agents conduct business, employers often expect agents to take continuing professional education courses. Agents can enhance their selling skills and broaden their knowledge of insurance and other financial services by taking courses at colleges and universities or by attending conferences and seminars sponsored by insurance organizations.

Licenses, Certifications, and Registrations

Insurance sales agents must have a license in the states where they work. Separate licenses are required for agents to sell life and health insurance and property and casualty insurance. In most states, licenses are issued only to applicants who complete specified courses and who pass state exams covering insurance fundamentals and state insurance laws. Most state licensing authorities also require agents to take continuing education courses focusing on insurance laws, consumer protection, ethics, and the technical details of various insurance policies.

As the demand for financial-planning services increases, many agents also choose to get licensed and certified to sell securities and other financial products. Licensing and certification requires substantial study time to pass an additional exam—either the Series 6 or Series 7 licensing exam, both of which are administered by the Financial Industry Regulatory Authority (FINRA). The Series 6 exam is for agents who want to sell only mutual funds and variable annuities. The Series 7 exam is the main FINRA series license, which qualifies agents as general securities sales representatives.

A number of organizations offer certifications that show an agent's expertise in insurance specialties. These certifications are not required for employment, but they can give job candidates an advantage over other applicants. Certifications also can be a source of continuing education credit. For details on specific designations, contact The Institutes and The American College of Financial Services.

Important Qualities

Analytical skills. Insurance sales agents must evaluate the needs of each client to determine the appropriate insurance policy.

Communication skills. Insurance sales agents must be able to communicate effectively with customers by listening to their requests and suggesting suitable policies.

Initiative. Insurance sales agents need to actively seek out new customers in order to maintain a flow of commissions.

Self-confidence. Insurance sales agents should be confident when making "cold" calls (calls to prospective customers whom they have not contacted before). They must speak clearly and persuasively and maintain their composure if rejected.

Pay

The median annual wage for insurance sales agents was $50,940 in May 2019. The median wage is the wage at which half the workers in an occupation earned more than that amount and half earned less. The lowest 10 percent earned less than $28,000, and the highest 10 percent earned more than $125,500.

In May 2019, the median annual wages for insurance sales agents in the top industries in which they worked were as follows:

Direct health and medical insurance carriers	$65,180
Direct insurance (except life, health, and medical) carriers	54,110
Insurance agencies and brokerages	49,000

Many independent agents are paid by commission only. Sales workers who are employees of an agency or an insurance carrier may be paid in one of three ways: salary only, salary plus commission, or salary plus bonus.

In general, commissions are the most common form of compensation, especially for experienced agents. The amount of the commission depends on the type and amount of insurance sold and on whether the transaction is a new policy or a renewal. When agents meet their sales goals or when an agency meets its profit goals, agents usually get bonuses. Some agents involved with financial planning receive a fee for their services rather than a commission.

Some sales agents meet with clients during business hours and then spend evenings doing paperwork and preparing presentations to prospective clients. Most agents work full time and some work more than 40 hours per week.

Job Outlook

Employment of insurance sales agents is projected to grow 5 percent from 2019 to 2029, faster than the average for all occupations.

Because the profitability of insurance companies depends on a steady stream of new customers, the demand for insurance sales agents is expected to continue. Employment growth will likely be strongest for independent sales agents as insurance companies rely more on brokerages and less on captive agents as a way to control costs.

Many clients do their own Internet research and purchase insurance online. This practice somewhat reduces demand for insurance sales agents because many purchases can then be made without an agent's services. However, agents will still be needed to interact with clients to help them understand their options and choose a policy that is right for them. Many customers lack the time or expertise to study the different types of insurance to decide what they need and will continue to rely on advice from insurance sales agents.

Agencies are also implementing "marketing automation," a set of software tools that allow agents to maintain contact with their clients more efficiently. Although this is expected to improve insurance sales agents' productivity, it is not expected to substantially reduce employment demand. Agents will still be needed to reach out to new, prospective clients and sell different insurance policies.

Job Prospects

College graduates who have sales ability, excellent customer-service skills, and expertise in a range of insurance and financial services products are likely to have the best prospects. Multilingual agents may have an advantage, because they can serve a wider customer base. In addition, insurance terminology is often technical, so agents who have a firm understanding of the relevant technical and legal terms also should be desirable to employers.

Insurance Sales Agents
Median annual wages, May 2019

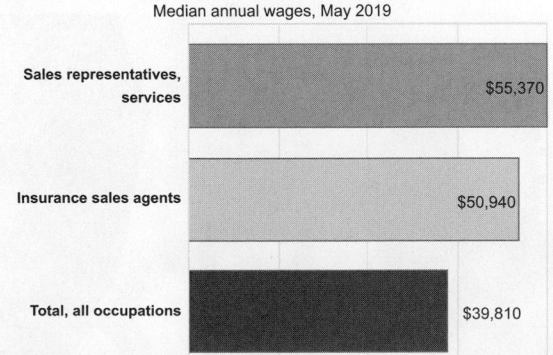

Note: All Occupations includes all occupations in the U.S. Economy.
Source: U.S. Bureau of Labor Statistics, Occupational Employment Statistics.

Insurance Sales Agents
Percent change in employment, projected 2019-29

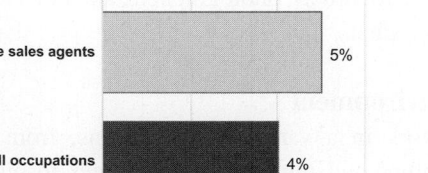
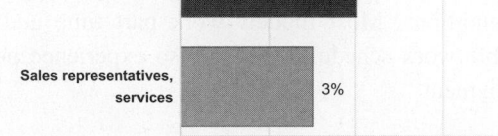

Note: All Occupations includes all occupations in the U.S. Economy.
Source: U.S. Bureau of Labor Statistics, Employment Projections program.

Many beginning agents fail to earn enough from commissions to meet their income goals. These agents may eventually transfer to other careers. Many job openings are likely to result from the need to replace agents who leave the occupation or retire.

Employment projections data for insurance sales agents, 2019-29					
Occupational Title	SOC Code	Employment, 2019	Projected Employment, 2029	Change, 2019-29	
				Percent	Numeric
SOURCE: U.S. Bureau of Labor Statistics, Employment Projections program					
Insurance sales agents	41-3021	501,300	528,800	5	27,500

State & Area Data
Occupational Employment Statistics (OES)
The Occupational Employment Statistics (OES) program produces employment and wage estimates annually for over 800 occupations. These estimates are available for the nation as a whole, for individual states, and for metropolitan and nonmetropolitan areas.

Contacts for More Information
For more information about insurance sales agents, visit
➤ National Association of Professional Insurance Agents
➤ Insurance Information Institute

For more information about insurance sales agents in the healthcare industry, visit
➤ National Association of Health Underwriters

For more information about certifications, visit
➤ The Institutes
➤ The American College of Financial Services

For more information about securities licensure, visit
➤ Financial Industry Regulatory Authority (FINRA)
➤ Information about insurance sales agent licensure is available from state insurance department websites.

Models

Summary

Quick Facts: Models

2019 Median Pay	$28,350 per year $13.63 per hour
Typical Entry-Level Education	No formal educational credential
Work Experience in a Related Occupation	None
On-the-job Training	None
Number of Jobs, 2019...................................	2,700
Job Outlook, 2019-29...................................	1% (Slower than average)
Employment Change, 2019-29	0

What Models Do
Models pose for artists, photographers, and other clients to help advertise products.

Work Environment
Models work in a variety of conditions, from comfortable indoor studios and runway fashion shows to outdoors in all weather conditions. Most models work part time and have unpredictable work schedules. Many also experience periods of unemployment.

How to Become a Model
No formal educational credential is required and training is limited. Specific requirements depend on the client. However, most models must be within certain ranges for height, weight, and clothing size to meet the needs of fashion designers, photographers, and advertisers.

Pay
The median hourly wage for models was $13.63 in May 2019.

Job Outlook
Employment of models is projected to grow 1 percent from 2019 to 2029, slower than the average for all occupations. Companies can now promote their products and brands directly to consumers. This direct promotion will lessen the need for professional models or large-scale advertising campaigns.

State & Area Data
Explore resources for employment and wages by state and area for models.

Models pose for artists and photographers.

What Models Do

Models pose for artists, photographers, or customers to help advertise a variety of products, including clothing, cosmetics, food, and appliances. Models also work as a fit or fitting model, enabling the manufacturer or fashion designer to achieve the best fit for new styles.

Duties

Models typically do the following:

- Display clothing and merchandise in print and online advertisements
- Promote products and services in television commercials
- Wear designers' clothing for runway fashion shows
- Represent companies and brands at conventions, trade shows, and other events
- Pose for photos, paintings, or sculptures
- Work closely with photographers, hair and clothing stylists, makeup artists, and clients to produce a desired look
- Create and maintain a portfolio of their work
- Travel to meet and interview with potential clients
- Conduct research on the product being promoted—for example, the designer or type of clothing fabric
- Answer questions from consumers about the products

Almost all models sign with modeling agencies. Agencies represent and promote a model to clients in return for a portion of the model's earnings. Models typically apply for a position with an agency by submitting their photographs through its website or by attending open casting calls and meeting with agents directly.

Models must research an agency before signing, in order to ensure that the agency has a good reputation in the modeling industry. For information on agencies, models should contact a local consumer affairs organization, such as the Better Business Bureau.

Some freelance models do not sign with agencies. Instead, they market themselves to potential clients and apply for modeling jobs directly. However, because most clients prefer to work with agents, it is difficult for new models to pursue a freelance career.

Models must put together and maintain up-to-date portfolios and composite cards. A portfolio is a collection of a model's previous work. A composite card contains the best photographs from a model's portfolio, along with his or her body measurements. Both portfolios and composite cards are typically taken to all casting calls and client auditions.

Because advertisers often need to target specific segments of the population, models may specialize in a certain area. For example, petite and plus-size fashions are modeled by women whose sizes are respectively smaller and larger than that worn by the typical model. Models who are disabled may be used to model fashions or products for consumers with disabilities. "Parts" models have a body part, such as a hand or foot, particularly well suited to model products such as nail polish or shoes.

Models appear in different types of media to promote a product or service. Models advertise products and merchandise in magazine or newspaper advertisements, department store catalogs, or television commercials. Increasingly, models are appearing in online ads or on retail websites. Models also pose for sketch artists, painters, and sculptors.

Models often participate in photo shoots and pose for photographers to show off the features of clothing and other products. Models change their posture and facial expressions to capture the look the client wants. The photographer usually takes many pictures of the model in different poses and expressions during the photo shoot.

Models also display clothes and merchandise live in different situations. At fashion shows, models stand, turn, and walk to show off clothing to an audience of photographers, journalists, designers, and garment buyers. Other clients may require models to interact directly with customers. In retail establishments and department stores, models display clothing directly to shoppers and describe the features and prices of the merchandise. At trade shows or conventions, models show off a business' products and provide information to consumers. These models may work alongside demonstrators and product promoters to help advertise and sell merchandise.

Models often prepare for photo shoots or fashion shows by having their hair and makeup done by professionals in those industries. The hairstylists and makeup artists may touch up the model's hair and makeup and change the model's look throughout the event. However, models are sometimes responsible for applying their own makeup and bringing their own clothing.

Work Environment

Models held about 2,700 jobs in 2019. The largest employers of models were as follows:

Colleges, universities, and professional schools; state, local, and private 29%

Models make changes to their expressions in order to capture a look desired by the photographer.

Models may work in studios with photographers and stylists.

Junior colleges; state, local, and private 12

Self-employed workers.. 8

Arts, entertainment, and recreation 2

Models work in a variety of conditions, from comfortable photography studios and runway fashion shows to outdoors in all weather conditions.

Models also may need to travel for photo shoots or to meet clients in different cities.

Work Schedules

Models' schedules can be demanding and stressful. Many models work part time and have unpredictable work schedules. They must be ready to work for a show or attend a photo shoot on short notice. The number of hours worked varies with the job. Many models experience periods of unemployment.

How to Become a Model

No formal education credential is required to become a model. Specific requirements depend on the client, with different jobs requiring different physical characteristics. However, most models must be within certain ranges for height, weight, and clothing size.

Education

There are no formal educational credentials required to become a model. Most modeling agencies allow applicants to email photos directly to the agency. The agency will then contact and interview prospective models who show potential. Many agencies also have "open calls," whereby aspiring models can walk into an agency during a specified time and meet directly with agents and clients.

Some aspiring models may attend modeling schools that provide training in posing, walking, applying makeup, and other basic tasks. Although some models are discovered when agents scout for "fresh faces" at modeling schools, attending such schools does not necessarily lead to job opportunities.

Specific requirements depend on the client, but most models must be within certain ranges for height, weight, and clothing size.

Advancement

Models advance by working more regularly and being selected for assignments that offer higher pay. They may appear in magazines, print advertising campaigns, commercials, or runway shows that have higher profiles and provide more widespread exposure.

Because advancement depends on a model's previous work, maintaining a good portfolio of high-quality, up-to-date photographs is important in getting assignments. In addition, actively participating in social media and building a large number of followers increases exposure.

A model's selection of an agency is also important for advancement: the better the reputation and skill of the agency, the more assignments a model is likely to get.

Important Qualities

Specific requirements depend on the client, but most models must be within certain ranges for height, weight, and clothing size. Requirements may change slightly over time as perceptions of physical beauty change.

Discipline. A model's career depends on the person's maintaining his or her physical characteristics. Models must control their diet, exercise regularly, and get enough sleep to stay healthy and photogenic. Haircuts, pedicures, and manicures are necessary work-related expenses.

Interpersonal skills. Models must interact with a large number of people, such as agents, photographers, and customers. It is important to be polite, professional, prompt, and respectful.

Listening skills. Models must take direction from photographers and clients during photo shoots and commercials.

Organizational skills. Models must manage their portfolios and their work and travel schedules.

Persistence. Competition for jobs is strong, and most clients have specific needs for each job, so patience and persistence are essential.

Photogenic. Models spend most of their time being photographed. They must be comfortable in front of a camera in order for photographers to capture the desired look.

Style. Models must have a basic knowledge of hair styling, makeup, and clothing. For photographic and runway work, models must move gracefully and confidently.

Pay

The median hourly wage for models was $13.63 in May 2019. The median wage is the wage at which half the workers in an occupation earned more than that amount and half earned less. The lowest 10 percent earned less than $10.54, and the highest 10 percent earned more than $26.75.

In May 2019, the median hourly wages for models in the top industries in which they worked were as follows:

Colleges, universities, and professional schools; state, local, and private	$18.63
Arts, entertainment, and recreation	17.88
Junior colleges; state, local, and private	16.52

Models' schedules can be demanding and stressful. Many models work part time and have unpredictable work schedules. They must be ready to work for a show or attend a photo shoot on short notice. The number of hours worked varies with the job. Many models experience periods of unemployment.

Job Outlook

Employment of models is projected to grow 1 percent from 2019 to 2029, slower than the average for all occupations.

Rising retail sales, particularly online and e-commerce sales, will encourage businesses to increase their digital advertising and marketing budgets. Demand for models to appear in digital advertisements is expected to lead to increased employment for these workers. However, less expensive digital and social media options are allowing companies to interact and build relationships with customers in new ways. Companies can now promote their products and brands directly to consumers. This direct promotion will lessen the need for professional models or large-scale advertising campaigns, thus moderating their employment demand.

Job Prospects

Many people are drawn to this occupation because of its glamour and potential for fame. Since no education, training, or work experience is required to enter the occupation, many applicants will be competing for very few job openings.

Although more jobs may be available in large cities such as New York and Los Angeles, competition for these jobs is expected to be very strong. Aspiring models may have the best job opportunities in smaller cities, working for smaller modeling agencies and local clients and businesses. Also, participating in social media, and having large numbers of followers may provide increased exposure and job opportunities.

Age, weight, and height requirements are typically less rigid for models appearing in commercials and advertisements than for those looking to become runway or fashion models.

In addition, as the U.S. population becomes increasingly diverse and businesses become more globalized, demand for racially and ethnically diverse models will likely increase.

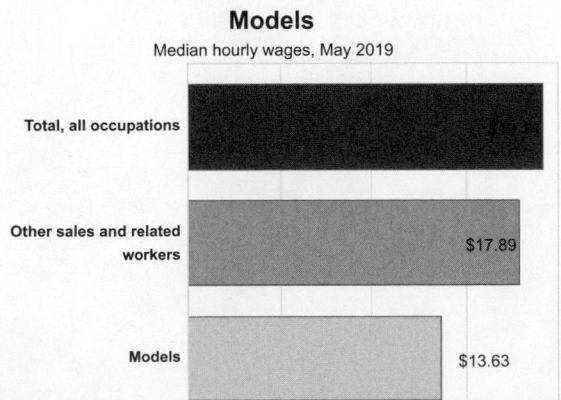

Models
Median hourly wages, May 2019

Other sales and related workers $17.89
Models $13.63

Note: All Occupations includes all occupations in the U.S. Economy. Source: U.S. Bureau of Labor Statistics, Occupational Employment Statistics.

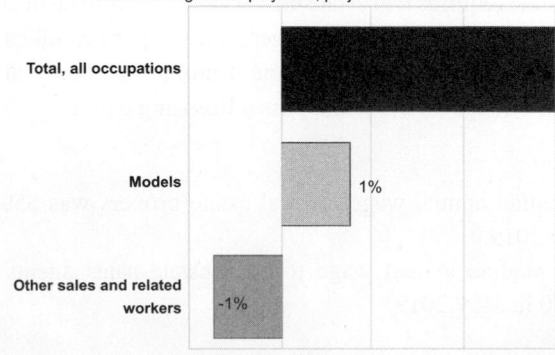

Models
Percent change in employment, projected 2019-29

Models 1%
Other sales and related workers -1%

Note: All Occupations includes all occupations in the U.S. Economy. Source: U.S. Bureau of Labor Statistics, Employment Projections program.

Employment projections data for models, 2019-29					
Occupational Title	SOC Code	Employment, 2019	Projected Employment, 2029	Change, 2019-29	
				Percent	Numeric
SOURCE: U.S. Bureau of Labor Statistics, Employment Projections program					
Models	41-9012	2,700	2,700	1	0

State & Area Data
Occupational Employment Statistics (OES)
The Occupational Employment Statistics (OES) program produces employment and wage estimates annually for over 800 occupations. These estimates are available for the nation as a whole, for individual states, and for metropolitan and nonmetropolitan areas.

Contacts for More Information
For information about modeling schools and agencies in your area, contact a local consumer affairs organization, such as the Better Business Bureau.

Real Estate Brokers and Sales Agents

Summary

Quick Facts: Real Estate Brokers and Sales Agents

2019 Median Pay	$50,730 per year $24.39 per hour
Typical Entry-Level Education	High school diploma or equivalent
Work Experience in a Related Occupation	See below
On-the-job Training	See below
Number of Jobs, 2019	477,200
Job Outlook, 2019-29	2% (Slower than average)
Employment Change, 2019-29	11,300

What Real Estate Brokers and Sales Agents Do
Real estate brokers and sales agents help clients buy, sell, and rent properties.

Work Environment
Most real estate brokers and sales agents are self-employed. Although they often work irregular hours, many are able to set their own schedules.

How to Become a Real Estate Broker or Sales Agent
Every state requires real estate brokers and agents to be licensed. Requirements vary by state but generally require candidates to be at least 18 years old, complete a number of hours of real estate or college courses, and pass a licensing exam.

Pay
The median annual wage for real estate brokers was $59,720 in May 2019.

The median annual wage for real estate sales agents was $48,930 in May 2019.

Job Outlook
Employment of real estate brokers and sales agents is projected to grow 2 percent from 2019 to 2029, slower than the average for all occupations. Demand for these workers will continue, because people turn to real estate brokers and sales agents when looking for a home, such as to buy a larger home or to relocate for a job.

State & Area Data
Explore resources for employment and wages by state and area for real estate brokers and sales agents.

What Real Estate Brokers and Sales Agents Do
Real estate brokers and sales agents help clients buy, sell, and rent properties. Although brokers and agents do similar work, brokers are licensed to manage their own real estate businesses. Sales agents must work with a real estate broker.

Duties
Real estate brokers and sales agents typically do the following:

- Solicit potential clients to buy, sell, and rent properties
- Advise clients on prices, mortgages, market conditions, and related information
- Compare properties to determine a competitive market price

Real estate brokers and sales agents help clients buy or sell real estate.

Real estate brokers and sales agents help clients find a home that meets their needs.

- Generate lists of properties for sale, including details such as location and features
- Promote properties through advertisements, open houses, and listing services
- Take prospective buyers or renters to see properties
- Present purchase offers to sellers for consideration
- Mediate negotiations between buyer and seller
- Ensure that all terms of purchase contracts are met
- Prepare documents, such as loyalty contracts, purchase agreements, and deeds

Because of the complexity of buying or selling a residential or commercial property, people often seek help from real estate brokers and sales agents.

Most real estate brokers and sales agents sell residential property. Others sell commercial property, and a small number sell industrial, agricultural, or other types of real estate.

Brokers and agents can represent either the buyer or the seller in a transaction. Buyers' brokers and agents meet with clients to understand what they are looking for in a property and how much they can afford. Sellers' brokers and agents meet with clients to help them decide how much to ask for and to convince them that the agent or broker can find them a qualified buyer.

Real estate brokers and sales agents must be knowledgeable about the real estate market in their area. To match properties to clients' needs, they should be familiar with local communities, including knowing the crime information and the proximity to schools and shopping. Brokers and agents also must stay current on financing options; government programs; types of available mortgages; and real estate, zoning, and fair housing laws.

The following are examples of types of real estate brokers and sales agents:

Real estate brokers are licensed to manage their own businesses. As independent businesspeople, brokers often sell real estate owned by others. In addition to helping clients buy and sell properties, they may help rent or manage properties for a fee. Many operate a real estate office, handling business details and overseeing the work of sales agents.

Real estate sales agents must work with a broker. Sales agents often work for brokers on a contract basis, earning a portion of the commission from each property they sell.

Work Environment

Real estate brokers held about 100,700 jobs in 2019. The largest employers of real estate brokers were as follows:

Self-employed workers	56%
Real estate and rental and leasing	39

Real estate sales agents held about 376,500 jobs in 2019. The largest employers of real estate sales agents were as follows:

Self-employed workers	56%
Real estate and rental and leasing	35
Construction	3

Workplace size for real estate brokers and sales agents can range from a one-person business to a large firm with numerous branch offices. Many brokers have franchise agreements with national or regional real estate companies. Under this arrangement, the broker pays a fee to be affiliated with a widely known real estate organization.

Some real estate brokers and sales agents work in a typical office environment, while others work out of their homes. In both cases, real estate workers spend much of their time away from their desks, showing properties to customers, traveling to see properties for sale, and meeting with prospective clients.

Work Schedules

Many real estate brokers and sales agents work more than 40 hours per week. They often work evenings and weekends to accommodate clients' schedules. Many brokers and sales agents spend a significant amount of time networking and attending community events to meet potential clients. Although

Real estate brokers and sales agents show properties to prospective buyers.

they frequently work irregular hours, many can set their own schedules.

Some brokers and sales agents work part time and may combine their real estate activities with other careers.

How to Become a Real Estate Broker or Sales Agent

Real estate brokers and sales agents typically must complete a number of real estate courses and pass a licensing exam.

Education

Real estate brokers and sales agents must complete some real estate courses to be eligible for licensure. Although most brokers and agents must take state-accredited prelicensing courses to become licensed, some states may waive this requirement if the candidate has taken college courses in real estate.

As the real estate market becomes more competitive and complex, some employers are preferring to hire candidates with a college degree. Some community colleges, colleges, and universities offer courses in real estate. Some offer associate's and bachelor's degree programs in real estate, and many others offer certificate programs. Courses in finance, business administration, economics, and law also can be useful.

Brokers intending to open their own company often take business courses, such as marketing and accounting.

In addition to offering prelicensing courses, many real estate associations have courses and professional development programs for both beginners and experienced agents. These courses cover a variety of topics, such as real estate fundamentals, real estate law, and mortgage financing.

Licenses, Certifications, and Registrations

All real estate brokers and sales agents must be licensed. Licensing requirements vary by state, but most have similar basic requirements:

Candidates must:

Real estate brokers and sales agents often find new clients through referrals.

- be 18 years old
- complete a number of real estate courses
- pass an exam

Some states have additional requirements, such as passing a background check. Licenses typically are not transferable among states. However, some states have reciprocity agreements in that they will accept some requirements used to get a license in another state (such as course hours).

To obtain a broker's license, individuals generally need 1 to 3 years of experience as a licensed sales agent. They also must take additional formal training courses. In some states, a bachelor's degree may be substituted in place of some experience or training requirements.

State licenses typically must be renewed every 2 to 4 years. In most states, brokers and agents must complete continuing education courses to renew their license. To verify exact licensing requirements, prospective brokers and agents should contact the real estate licensing commission of the state in which they wish to work.

Work Experience in a Related Occupation

To get a broker's license in most states, real estate brokers must have experience working as a licensed real estate sales agent. Requirements vary by state, but most require 1 to 3 years of experience.

Training

Real estate sales agents improve their skills through practice and repetition. Training varies depending on the real estate company. Some provide formal training, while others allow their agents to enter the field immediately after obtaining their license. In some states, agents must be sponsored by a broker while they are working to get their license.

Because of the sales environment and the complexity of real estate deals, new agents may observe and work closely with more senior agents. Larger real estate companies may provide formal classroom training for new agents as a way to gain knowledge and experience, while others provide training to employees studying for their real estate licensing exam.

Advancement

Sales agents who earn their broker's license may open their own offices.

Important Qualities

Business skills. Because most brokers are self-employed, they must manage every aspect of their business. This task includes reaching out to prospective clients, handling their finances, and advertising their services.

Interpersonal skills. Strong interpersonal skills are essential for real estate brokers and sales agents, because they spend much of their time interacting with clients and customers. To attract and keep clients, they must be pleasant, enthusiastic, and trustworthy.

Organizational skills. Real estate brokers and sales agents must be able to work independently, managing their own time and organizing, planning, and prioritizing their work.

Problem-solving skills. Real estate brokers and sales agents need to be able to quickly (sometimes immediately) address concerns clients or potential customers may have with a property. They also mediate negotiations between seller and buyer.

Pay

The median annual wage for real estate brokers was $59,720 in May 2019. The median wage is the wage at which half the workers in an occupation earned more than that amount and half earned less. The lowest 10 percent earned less than $23,600, and the highest 10 percent earned more than $178,720.

The median annual wage for real estate sales agents was $48,930 in May 2019. The lowest 10 percent earned less than $24,930, and the highest 10 percent earned more than $111,800.

In May 2019, the median annual wages for real estate brokers in the top industries in which they worked were as follows:

Real estate and rental and leasing............................ $58,780

In May 2019, the median annual wages for real estate sales agents in the top industries in which they worked were as follows:

Construction... $58,490
Real estate and rental and leasing............................ 45,540

Brokers and sales agents earn most of their income from commissions on sales. The commission varies by the type of property and its value. Commissions often are divided among the buying agent, selling agent, brokers, and firms.

An agent's income often depends on economic conditions, the agent's individual motivation, and the types of property available. Income usually increases as agents become better and more experienced at sales. Earnings can be irregular, especially for beginners, and agents sometimes go weeks or months without a sale. Some agents become active in community organizations and local real estate organizations to broaden their contacts and increase their sales.

Many real estate brokers and sales agents work more than 40 hours per week. They often work evenings and weekends to accommodate clients' schedules. Many brokers and sales agents spend a significant amount of time networking and attending community events to meet potential clients. Although they frequently work irregular hours, many can set their own schedules.

Some brokers and sales agents work part time and may combine their real estate activities with other careers.

Job Outlook

Employment of real estate brokers and sales agents is projected to grow 2 percent from 2019 to 2029, slower than the average for all occupations.

There will be a continued demand for real estate brokers and sales agents, because people turn to these workers when looking for a new home, relocating, or purchasing property for a business, among other reasons. Employment is projected to grow along with the real estate market.

Tighter credit regulations and increasing real estate prices may force some people to continue renting as opposed to entering the housing market.

Moreover, the younger portion of the millennial generation will enter the prime working-age and household-forming age group over the next decade. This generation has delayed home

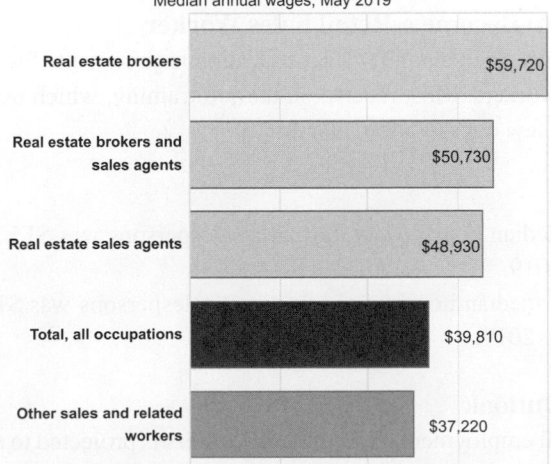

Real Estate Brokers and Sales Agents

Median annual wages, May 2019

Real estate brokers	$59,720
Real estate brokers and sales agents	$50,730
Real estate sales agents	$48,930
Total, all occupations	$39,810
Other sales and related workers	$37,220

Note: All Occupations includes all occupations in the U.S. Economy.
Source: U.S. Bureau of Labor Statistics, Occupational Employment Statistics.

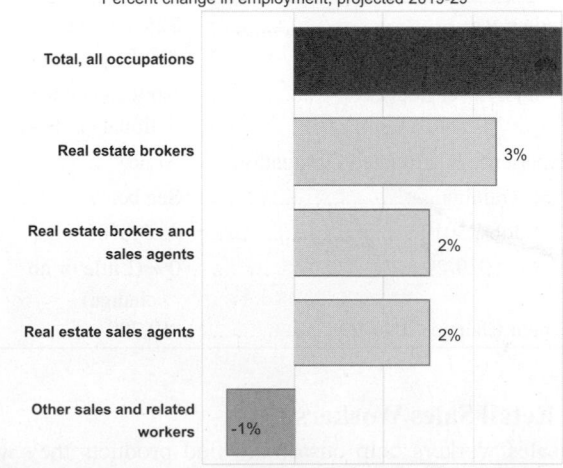

Real Estate Brokers and Sales Agents

Percent change in employment, projected 2019-29

Total, all occupations	
Real estate brokers	3%
Real estate brokers and sales agents	2%
Real estate sales agents	2%
Other sales and related workers	-1%

Note: All Occupations includes all occupations in the U.S. Economy.
Source: U.S. Bureau of Labor Statistics, Employment Projections program.

ownership because of financial and personal considerations. Therefore, their slower entry into the housing market should limit demand for real estate agents and brokers.

The real estate market is highly sensitive to fluctuations in the economy, and employment of real estate brokers and agents will vary accordingly. In periods of economic growth or stability, employment should grow to accommodate people looking to buy homes and businesses looking to expand office or retail space. Alternatively, during periods of declining economic activity or rising interest rates, the amount of work for brokers and agents will slow and employment may decline.

Job Prospects

It is relatively easy to enter the occupation, but getting listings as a broker or an agent depends on the real estate market and overall economic conditions. As the economy expands and more people look to buy homes, job competition may increase as more people obtain their real estate license. In contrast, although the real estate market declines in an economic downturn, there also tend to be fewer active and licensed real estate agents.

New agents will face competition from well-established, more experienced brokers and agents. Because income is dependent on sales, beginners may have trouble sustaining themselves in the occupation during periods of slower activity.

Brokers should fare better because they generally have a large client base from years of experience as sales agents. Those with strong sales ability and extensive social and business connections in their communities should have the best chances for success.

Employment projections data for real estate brokers and sales agents, 2019-29					
Occupational Title	SOC Code	Employment, 2019	Projected Employment, 2029	Change, 2019-29	
				Percent	Numeric
SOURCE: U.S. Bureau of Labor Statistics, Employment Projections program					
Real estate brokers and sales agents	41-9020	477,200	488,500	2	11,300
Real estate brokers	41-9021	100,700	103,300	3	2,700
Real estate sales agents	41-9022	376,500	385,200	2	8,700

State & Area Data
Occupational Employment Statistics (OES)

The Occupational Employment Statistics (OES) program produces employment and wage estimates annually for over 800 occupations. These estimates are available for the nation as a whole, for individual states, and for metropolitan and nonmetropolitan areas.

Contacts for More Information

Information on licensing requirements for real estate brokers and sales agents is available from most local real estate organizations and from the state real estate commission or board.

For more information about opportunities in real estate, visit
➤ National Association of Real Estate Brokers
➤ National Association of Realtors

Retail Sales Workers

Summary

Quick Facts: Retail Sales Workers

2019 Median Pay	$25,440 per year $12.23 per hour
Typical Entry-Level Education	No formal educational credential
Work Experience in a Related Occupation....	None
On-the-job Training	See below
Number of Jobs, 2019.................................	4,633,100
Job Outlook, 2019-29..................................	0% (Little or no change)
Employment Change, 2019-29	-19,700

What Retail Sales Workers Do

Retail sales workers help customers find products they want and process customers' payments.

Work Environment

Most retail sales workers work in clean, well-lit stores. Many sales workers work evenings and weekends. Some retail salespersons work part time.

How to Become a Retail Sales Worker

Typically, there are no formal education requirements for retail sales workers. Most receive on-the-job training, which usually lasts a few days to a few months.

Pay

The median hourly wage for parts salespersons was $15.24 in May 2019.

The median hourly wage for retail salespersons was $12.14 in May 2019.

Job Outlook

Overall employment of retail sales workers is projected to show little or no change from 2019 to 2029. Competition from online

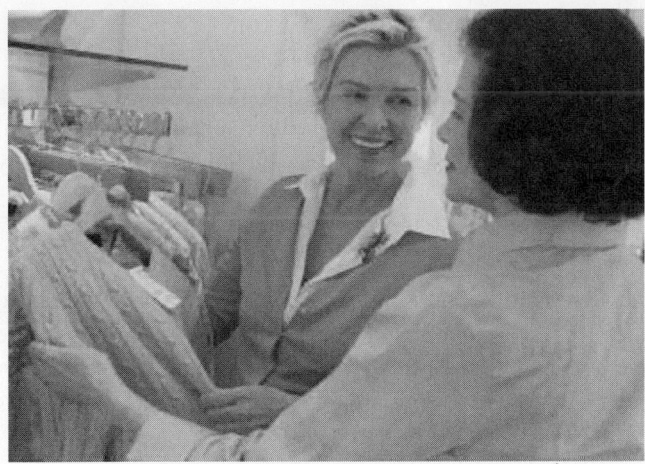

Retail sales workers help customers find the products they want and process customers' payments.

sales will lead to employment declines in brick-and-mortar retail stores.

State & Area Data

Explore resources for employment and wages by state and area for retail sales workers.

What Retail Sales Workers Do

Retail sales workers help customers find products they want and process customers' payments. There are two types of retail sales workers: retail salespersons, who sell retail merchandise, such as clothing, furniture, and automobiles; and parts salespersons, who sell spare and replacement parts and equipment, especially car parts.

Duties

Retail sales workers typically do the following:

• Greet customers and offer them assistance

Retail sales workers maintain knowledge of current sales and promotions.

• Recommend merchandise based on customers' wants and needs
• Explain the use and benefit of merchandise to customers
• Answer customers' questions
• Show how merchandise works, if applicable
• Add up customers' total purchases and accept payment
• Inform customers about current sales, promotions, and policies about payments and exchanges

The following are examples of types of retail sales workers:

Retail salespersons work in stores where they sell goods, such as books, cars, clothing, cosmetics, electronics, furniture, lumber, plants, shoes, and many other types of merchandise.

In addition to helping customers find and select items to buy, many retail salespersons process the payment for the sale, which typically involves operating cash registers.

After taking payment for the purchases, retail salespersons may bag or package the purchases.

Depending on the hours they work, retail salespersons may have to open or close cash registers. This includes counting the money in the register and separating charge slips, coupons, and exchange vouchers. They may also make deposits at a cash office.

For information about other workers who receive and disburse money, see the profile on cashiers.

In addition, retail salespersons may help stock shelves or racks, arrange for mailing or delivery of purchases, mark price tags, take inventory, and prepare displays.

For some retail sales jobs, particularly those involving expensive and complex items, retail sales workers need special knowledge or skills. For example, those who sell cars must be able to explain the features of various models, manufacturers' specifications, different types of options on the car, financing available, and the details of associated warranties.

In addition, retail sales workers must recognize security risks and thefts and understand their organization's procedures for handling thefts, which may include notifying security guards or calling police.

Parts salespersons sell spare and replacement parts and equipment, especially car parts. Most work in either automotive parts stores or automobile dealerships. They take customers' orders, inform customers of part availability and price, and take inventory.

Work Environment

Parts salespersons held about 261,700 jobs in 2019. The largest employers of parts salespersons were as follows:

Automotive parts, accessories, and tire stores	43%
Automobile dealers	22
Wholesale trade	20
Other motor vehicle dealers	4
Repair and maintenance	4

Retail sales workers often stand for long periods and may need supervisory approval to leave the sales floor.

Retail salespersons held about 4.4 million jobs in 2019. The largest employers of retail salespersons were as follows:

Clothing and clothing accessories stores.......................... 20%

Building material and garden equipment and supplies   11
    dealers ....

Sporting goods, hobby, musical instrument, and book   7
    stores ....

Automobile dealers   6

Electronics and appliance stores....................................   4

Most retail sales work is performed in clean, well-lit stores. Retail sales workers spend most of their time interacting with customers, answering questions, and assisting them with purchases.

Workers often stand for long periods and may need permission from a supervisor to leave the sales floor. If they sell items such as cars, plants, or lumberyard materials, they may work outdoors.

Work Schedules

Many sales workers work evenings and weekends, particularly during holidays and other peak sales periods. Because the end-of-year holiday season is often the busiest time for retail stores, many employers limit retail sales workers' use of vacation time between November and the beginning of January.

Some retail salespersons work part time.

How to Become a Retail Sales Worker

Typically, there are no formal education requirements for retail sales workers. Most receive on-the-job training, which usually lasts a few days to a few months.

Education

Although retail or parts sales positions usually have no formal education requirements, some employers prefer applicants who have a high school diploma or equivalent, especially employers who sell technical products or "big-ticket" items, such as electronics or cars.

Training

Most retail sales workers receive on-the-job training, which usually lasts a few days to a few months. In small stores, an experienced employee often trains newly hired workers. In large stores, training programs are more formal and usually conducted over several days.

During training sessions, topics often include customer service, security, the store's policies and procedures, and how to operate the cash register.

A friendly and outgoing personality is important for these workers, as the job requires almost constant interaction with people.

Depending on the type of product they are selling, employees may be given additional specialized training. For example, salespersons working in cosmetics get instruction on the types of products the store offers and for whom the cosmetics would be most beneficial. Likewise, those who sell auto parts may be instructed on the technical functions of various parts, in addition to sales technique.

Because providing exceptional service to customers is a priority for many employers, employees often get periodic training to update and refine their skills.

Advancement

Retail sales workers typically have opportunities to advance to supervisory or managerial positions. Some employers want candidates for managerial positions to have a college degree.

As sales workers gain experience and seniority, they often move into positions that have greater responsibility and may be given their choice of departments in which to work. This opportunity often means moving to positions with higher potential earnings and commissions. The highest earnings potential usually involves selling "big-ticket" items, such as cars, jewelry, furniture, and electronics. These positions often require workers with extensive knowledge of the product and excellent sales skills.

Important Qualities

Customer-service skills. Retail sales workers must be responsive to the wants and needs of customers. They should explain the product options available to customers and make appropriate recommendations.

Interpersonal skills. A friendly and outgoing personality is important for these workers because the job requires almost constant interaction with people.

Math skills. Retail sales workers must have the ability to calculate price totals, discounts, and change owed to customers.

Persistence. A large number of attempted sales may not be successful, so sales workers should not be discouraged easily. They must start each new sales attempt with a positive attitude.

Selling skills. Retail sales workers must be persuasive when interacting with customers. They must clearly and effectively explain the benefits of the merchandise.

Pay

The median hourly wage for parts salespersons was $15.24 in May 2019. The median wage is the wage at which half the workers in an occupation earned more than that amount and half earned less. The lowest 10 percent earned less than $9.89, and the highest 10 percent earned more than $26.97.

The median hourly wage for retail salespersons was $12.14 in May 2019. The lowest 10 percent earned less than $9.09, and the highest 10 percent earned more than $20.57.

In May 2019, the median hourly wages for parts salespersons in the top industries in which they worked were as follows:

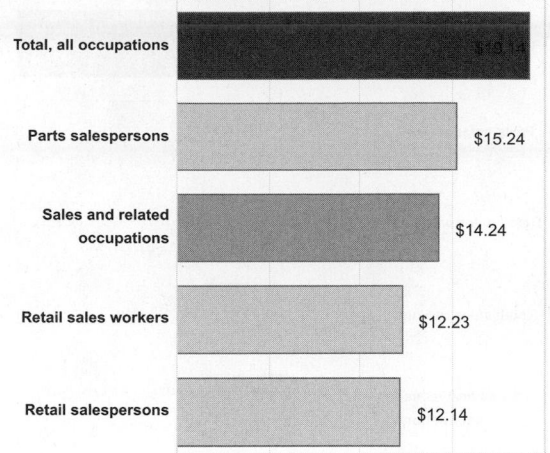

Retail Sales Workers
Median hourly wages, May 2019

Total, all occupations	$19.14
Parts salespersons	$15.24
Sales and related occupations	$14.24
Retail sales workers	$12.23
Retail salespersons	$12.14

Note: All Occupations includes all occupations in the U.S. Economy. Source: U.S. Bureau of Labor Statistics, Occupational Employment Statistics.

Repair and maintenance	$18.99
Wholesale trade	18.66
Automobile dealers	17.11
Other motor vehicle dealers	15.44
Automotive parts, accessories, and tire stores	12.93

In May 2019, the median hourly wages for retail salespersons in the top industries in which they worked were as follows:

Automobile dealers	$16.65
Building material and garden equipment and supplies dealers	13.36
Electronics and appliance stores	12.80
Clothing and clothing accessories stores	11.68
Sporting goods, hobby, musical instrument, and book stores	11.67

Compensation systems vary by type of establishment and merchandise sold. Retail sales workers get hourly wages, commissions, or a combination of the two. Under a commission system, they get a percentage of the sales they make. This system offers sales workers the opportunity to increase their earnings considerably, but they may find that their earnings depend strongly on their ability to sell their product and on the ups and downs of the economy. Commissions are most common for retail sales workers selling "big-ticket" items, such as cars or electronics.

Many retail sales workers work evenings and weekends, particularly during holidays and other peak sales periods. Because the end-of-year holiday season is often the busiest time for retail stores, many employers limit sales workers' use of vacation time between November and the beginning of January.

Some retail salespersons work part time.

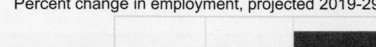

Retail Sales Workers

Percent change in employment, projected 2019-29

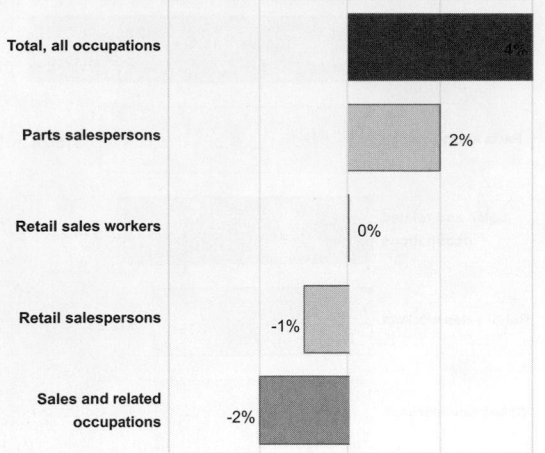

Total, all occupations	4%
Parts salespersons	2%
Retail sales workers	0%
Retail salespersons	-1%
Sales and related occupations	-2%

Note: All Occupations includes all occupations in the U.S. Economy.
Source: U.S. Bureau of Labor Statistics, Employment Projections program.

Job Outlook

Overall employment of retail sales workers is projected to show little or no change from 2019 to 2029.

Competition from online sales will lead to employment declines in brick-and-mortar retail stores.

The increase in online sales is expected to continue over the next decade, limiting growth in the number of physical retail stores and reducing demand for retail sales workers. Online sales also are projected to affect specific segments of the retail industry to varying extents. For example, book and media stores are likely to see the most severe declines due to online competition. However, other retail segments, such as automobile dealers, have experienced much less of an impact.

Although online sales are expected to continue to increase, brick-and-mortar retail stores are also expected to increase their emphasis on customer service as a way to compete with online sellers. In addition, cost pressure may drive retailers to ask their in-store staff to do more. This means they may want workers who can perform a broad range of job duties that include helping customers find items, operating a cash register, and restocking shelves. Because retail sales workers provide this versatile

range of services, they will still be needed in retail stores. In general, although consumers are increasing their online retail shopping, they will continue to do most of their retail shopping in stores. Retail salespersons will be needed in stores to help customers and to complete sales.

People are keeping their cars longer and are buying new cars less often. The need for older cars to be serviced more frequently creates, in turn, more demand for car parts and parts salespersons. Moreover, the growth in demand for ride-hailing services has shifted some public transportation use back to automobiles services, further adding to the need for car parts in upkeep and maintenance. However, employment growth is expected to be slowed by competition from online parts retailers.

Employment projections data for retail sales workers, 2019-29

Occupational Title	SOC Code	Employment, 2019	Projected Employment, 2029	Change, 2019-29	
				Percent	Numeric
SOURCE: U.S. Bureau of Labor Statistics, Employment Projections program					
Retail sales workers	—	4,633,100	4,613,300	0	-19,700
Parts salespersons	41-2022	261,700	267,000	2	5,300
Retail salespersons	41-2031	4,371,400	4,346,300	-1	-25,100

State & Area Data
Occupational Employment Statistics (OES)

The Occupational Employment Statistics (OES) program produces employment and wage estimates annually for over 800 occupations. These estimates are available for the nation as a whole, for individual states, and for metropolitan and nonmetropolitan areas.

Contacts for More Information

For more information about the retail industry, visit
➤ National Retail Federation
➤ Retail Industry Leaders Association

For more information about training for a career in automobile sales, visit
➤ National Automobile Dealers Association

Sales Engineers

Summary

Quick Facts: Sales Engineers

2019 Median Pay	$103,900 per year
	$49.95 per hour
Typical Entry-Level Education	Bachelor's degree
Work Experience in a Related Occupation..	None
On-the-job Training	Moderate-term on-the-job training
Number of Jobs, 2019.................................	64,500
Job Outlook, 2019-29..................................	6% (Faster than average)
Employment Change, 2019-29	4,100

What Sales Engineers Do

Sales engineers sell complex scientific and technological products or services to businesses.

Work Environment

Sales engineers often work under stressful conditions because their income and job security depend on commission from successfully completing sales. Some sales engineers may work additional and irregular hours to meet sales goals and client needs.

How to Become a Sales Engineer

Sales engineers typically need a bachelor's degree in engineering or a related field. Successful sales engineers combine technical knowledge of the products or services they are selling with strong interpersonal skills.

Pay

The median annual wage for sales engineers was $103,900 in May 2019.

Job Outlook

Employment of sales engineers is projected to grow 6 percent from 2019 to 2029, faster than the average for all occupations. As a wider range of technologically sophisticated products comes on the market, sales engineers will be in demand to sell these products and services related to these products.

State & Area Data

Explore resources for employment and wages by state and area for sales engineers.

What Sales Engineers Do

Sales engineers sell complex scientific and technological products or services to businesses. They must have extensive knowledge of the products' parts and functions and must understand the scientific processes that make these products work.

Duties

Sales engineers typically do the following:

- Prepare and deliver technical presentations explaining products or services to existing and prospective customers
- Talk with customers and engineers to assess equipment needs and to determine system requirements
- Collaborate with sales teams to understand customer requirements and provide sales support
- Secure and renew orders and arrange delivery
- Plan and modify products to meet customer needs
- Help clients solve problems with installed equipment
- Recommend improved materials or machinery to customers, showing how changes will lower costs or increase production
- Help in researching and developing new products

Sales engineers specialize in technologically and scientifically advanced products. They use their technical skills to explain the benefits of their products or services to potential customers and to show how their products or services are better than their competitors'. Some sales engineers work for the

Sales engineers sell complex scientific and technological products or services to businesses.

Sales engineers specialize in technologically and scientifically advanced products.

companies that design and build technical products. Others work for independent sales firms.

Many of the duties of sales engineers are similar to those of other salespersons. They must interest the client in buying their products or services, negotiate a price, and complete the sale. To do this, sales engineers give technical presentations during which they explain the technical aspects of the product and how it will solve a specific customer problem.

Some sales engineers team with other salespersons, such as wholesale and manufacturing sales representatives, who concentrate on marketing and selling the product, which lets the sales engineer concentrate on the technical aspects of the job. By working as part of a sales team, each member is able to focus on his or her strengths and expertise.

In addition to giving technical presentations, sales engineers are increasingly doing other tasks related to sales, such as market research. They also may ask for technical requirements from customers and modify and adjust products to meet customers' specific needs. Some sales engineers work with research and development (R&D) departments to help identify and develop new products.

Work Environment

Sales engineers held about 64,500 jobs in 2019. The largest employers of sales engineers were as follows:

Merchant wholesalers, durable goods	27%
Manufacturing	20
Computer systems design and related services	18
Wholesale electronic markets and agents and brokers	6
Telecommunications	5

Some sales engineers have large territories and travel extensively. Because sales regions may cover several states, sales engineers may be away from home for several days or even weeks at a time. Other sales engineers cover a smaller region and spend only a few nights away from home.

Sales engineers may encounter stress because their income and job security often depend directly on their success in sales and customer service.

Work Schedules

Most sales engineers work full time. Some may work additional and irregular hours to meet sales goals and client needs.

How to Become a Sales Engineer

A bachelor's degree is typically required to become a sales engineer. Successful sales engineers combine technical knowledge of the products or services they are selling with strong interpersonal skills.

Education

Sales engineers typically need a bachelor's degree in engineering or a related field. However, a worker without a degree, but with previous sales experience as well as technical experience or training, may become a sales engineer. Workers who have a degree in a science, such as chemistry, or in business with little or no previous sales experience, also may become sales engineers.

University engineering programs generally require 4 years of study. They vary in content, but all programs include courses in math and the physical sciences. In addition, most programs require developing strong computer skills.

Most engineering programs require students to choose an area of specialization. The most common majors are electrical, mechanical, or civil engineering, but some engineering departments offer additional majors, such as chemical, biomedical, or computer hardware engineering. However, some undergraduate programs offer a general engineering curriculum; students then specialize in a particular area either on the job or in graduate school.

Sales engineers often give presentations in which they describe the technical aspects of a product and explain how it will solve a specific customer problem.

Successful sales engineers will have a combination of technical knowledge of the products they are selling and strong interpersonal skills.

Training

New graduates with engineering degrees typically need sales experience and training before they can work independently as sales engineers. Training covers general sales techniques and may involve teaming with a sales mentor who is familiar with the employer's business practices, customers, procedures, and company culture. After the training period, sales engineers may continue to partner with someone who lacks technical skills yet excels in the art of sales.

It is important for sales engineers to continue their engineering and sales education throughout their careers. Much of their value to their employers depends on their knowledge of, and ability to sell, the latest technologies. Sales engineers in high-technology fields, such as information technology and advanced electronics, may find that their technical knowledge rapidly becomes obsolete, requiring frequent retraining.

Advancement

Promotions may include a higher commission rate, a larger sales territory, or elevation to the position of supervisor or sales manager.

Important Qualities

Interpersonal skills. Strong interpersonal skills are a valuable characteristic for sales engineers, both for building relationships with clients and effectively communicating with other members of the sales team.

Problem-solving skills. Sales engineers must be able to listen to the customer's desires and concerns, and then recommend solutions, such as customizing a product for the customer.

Self-confidence. Sales engineers should be confident and persuasive when making sales presentations.

Technological skills. Sales engineers must have extensive knowledge of the technologically sophisticated products they sell in order to explain their advantages and answer questions.

Pay

The median annual wage for sales engineers was $103,900 in May 2019. The median wage is the wage at which half the workers in an occupation earned more than that amount and half earned less. The lowest 10 percent earned less than $59,180, and the highest 10 percent earned more than $174,270.

In May 2019, the median annual wages for sales engineers in the top industries in which they worked were as follows:

Telecommunications	$118,830
Computer systems design and related services	108,320
Wholesale electronic markets and agents and brokers	104,910
Merchant wholesalers, durable goods	103,220
Manufacturing	94,020

How much a sales engineer earns varies considerably by the type of firm and the product sold. Most employers offer a

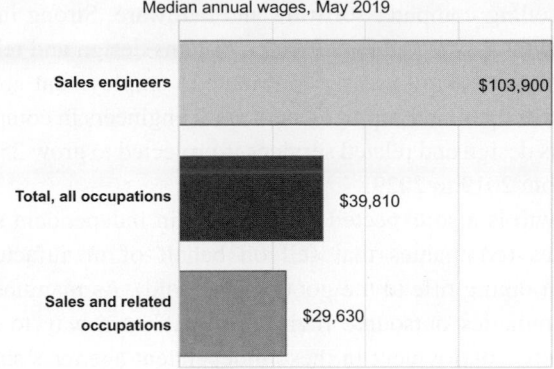

Sales Engineers
Median annual wages, May 2019

Sales engineers — $103,900
Total, all occupations — $39,810
Sales and related occupations — $29,630

Note: All Occupations includes all occupations in the U.S. Economy.
Source: U.S. Bureau of Labor Statistics, Occupational Employment Statistics.

combination of salary and commission payments or salary plus a bonus. Some sales engineers who work for independent sales companies earn only commissions.

Commissions are usually based on the value of sales. Bonuses may depend on individual performance, on the performance of all workers in the group or district, or on the company's performance. Earnings from commissions and bonuses may vary from year to year depending on sales ability, the demand for the company's products or services, and the overall economy.

In addition to their earnings, sales engineers who work for manufacturers are usually reimbursed for expenses such as transportation, meals, hotels, and customer entertainment.

Most sales engineers work full time. Some may work additional and irregular hours to meet sales goals and client needs.

Job Outlook

Employment of sales engineers is projected to grow 6 percent from 2019 to 2029, faster than the average for all occupations. As a wider range of technologically sophisticated products comes on the market, sales engineers will be in demand to help sell products or services related to these products.

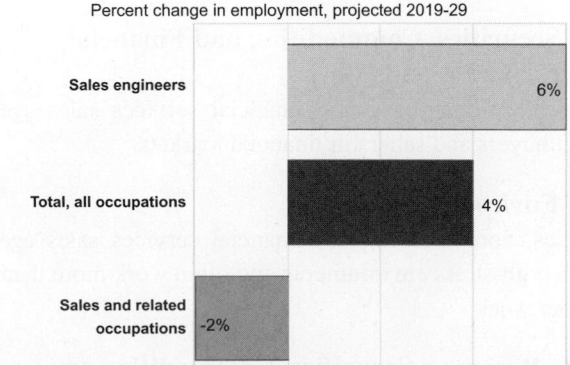

Sales Engineers
Percent change in employment, projected 2019-29

Sales engineers — 6%
Total, all occupations — 4%
Sales and related occupations — -2%

Note: All Occupations includes all occupations in the U.S. Economy.
Source: U.S. Bureau of Labor Statistics, Employment Projections program.

Employment growth is likely to be strong for sales engineers selling computer software and hardware. Strong industry growth is expected in computer systems design and related services, which will greatly contribute to employment growth for the occupation. Employment of sales engineers in computer systems design and related services is projected to grow 25 percent from 2019 to 2029.

Growth is also expected to be strong in independent sales agencies (companies that sell on behalf of manufacturers without taking title to the goods being sold). As manufacturing companies outsource their sales staff as a way to control costs, employment in these independent agencies should increase.

Job Prospects

Job prospects should be good as few candidates possess both the strong technical product knowledge and sales skills this position requires.

Employment projections data for sales engineers, 2019-29

Occupational Title	SOC Code	Employment, 2019	Projected Employment, 2029	Change, 2019-29	
				Percent	Numeric
SOURCE: U.S. Bureau of Labor Statistics, Employment Projections program					
Sales engineers	41-9031	64,500	68,600	6	4,100

State & Area Data
Occupational Employment Statistics (OES)

The Occupational Employment Statistics (OES) program produces employment and wage estimates annually for over 800 occupations. These estimates are available for the nation as a whole, for individual states, and for metropolitan and nonmetropolitan areas.

Contacts for More Information

For more information about careers in sales occupations, visit
➤ Manufacturers' Agents National Association (MANA)
➤ Manufacturers' Representatives Educational Research Foundation (MRERF)

Securities, Commodities, and Financial Services Sales Agents

Summary

Quick Facts: Securities, Commodities, and Financial Services Sales Agents

2019 Median Pay	$62,270 per year $29.94 per hour
Typical Entry-Level Education	Bachelor's degree
Work Experience in a Related Occupation	None
On-the-job Training	Moderate-term on-the-job training
Number of Jobs, 2019	464,200
Job Outlook, 2019-29	4% (As fast as average)
Employment Change, 2019-29	17,400

What Securities, Commodities, and Financial Services Sales Agents Do

Securities, commodities, and financial services sales agents connect buyers and sellers in financial markets.

Work Environment

Securities, commodities, and financial services sales agents work in high-stress environments and often work more than 40 hours per week.

How to Become a Securities, Commodities, or Financial Services Sales Agent

A bachelor's degree is required for entry-level jobs, and a master's degree in business administration (MBA) is useful for advancement.

Pay

The median annual wage for securities, commodities, and financial services sales agents was $62,270 in May 2019.

Job Outlook

Employment of securities, commodities, and financial services sales agents is projected to grow 4 percent from 2019 to 2029, about as fast as the average for all occupations. Demand for investment banking and retirement services are likely to create employment growth.

State & Area Data

Explore resources for employment and wages by state and area for securities, commodities, and financial services sales agents.

Securities, commodities, and financial services sales agents connect buyers and sellers in financial markets.

What Securities, Commodities, and Financial Services Sales Agents Do

Securities, commodities, and financial services sales agents connect buyers and sellers in financial markets. They sell securities to individuals, advise companies in search of investors, and conduct trades.

Duties

Securities, commodities, and financial services sales agents typically do the following:

- Contact prospective clients to present information and explain available services
- Offer advice on the purchase or sale of particular securities
- Buy and sell securities, such as stocks and bonds
- Buy and sell commodities, such as corn, oil, and gold
- Monitor financial markets and the performance of individual securities
- Analyze company finances to provide recommendations for public offerings, mergers, and acquisitions
- Evaluate cost and revenue of agreements

Securities, commodities, and financial services sales agents deal with a wide range of products and clients. Agents spend much of the day interacting with people, whether selling stock to an individual or discussing the status of a merger deal with a company executive. The work is usually stressful because agents deal with large amounts of money and have time constraints.

A security or commodity can be traded in two ways: electronically or in an auction-style setting on the floor of an exchange market. Markets such as the National Association of Securities Dealers Automated Quotation system (NASDAQ) use vast computer networks rather than human traders to match buyers and sellers. Others, such as the New York Stock Exchange (NYSE), rely on floor brokers to complete transactions.

Securities, commodities, and financial services sales agents spend much of the day interacting with people, whether selling stock to an individual or discussing the status of a merger deal with a company executive.

The following are examples of types of securities, commodities, and financial services sales agents:

Brokers sell securities and commodities directly to individual clients. They advise people on appropriate investments based on the client's needs and financial ability. The people they advise may have very different levels of expertise in financial matters.

Finding clients is a large part of a broker's job. They must create their own client base by calling from a list of potential clients. Some agents network by joining social groups, and others may rely on referrals from satisfied clients.

Investment bankers connect businesses that need money to finance their operations or expansion plans with investors who are interested in providing that funding. This process is called underwriting, and it is the main function of investment banks. The banks first sell their advisory services to help companies issue new stocks or bonds, and then the banks sell the issued securities to investors.

Some of the most important services that investment bankers provide are initial public offerings (IPOs), and mergers and acquisitions. An IPO is the process by which a company becomes open for public investment by issuing its first stock. Investment bankers must estimate how much the company is worth and ensure that it meets the legal requirements to become publicly traded.

Investment bankers also connect companies in mergers (when two companies join together) and acquisitions (when one company buys another). Investment bankers provide advice throughout the process to ensure that the transaction goes smoothly.

Investment banking sales agents and traders carry out buy and sell orders for stocks, bonds, and commodities from clients and make trades on behalf of the firm itself. Investment banks primarily employ these workers, although some work for commercial banks, hedge funds, and private equity groups. Because markets fluctuate so much, trading is a split-second decisionmaking process. Slight changes in the price of a trade can greatly affect its profitability, making the trader's decision extremely important.

Floor brokers work directly on the floor—a large room where trading is done—of a securities or commodities exchange. After a trader places an order for a security, floor brokers negotiate the price, make the sale, and forward the purchase price to the trader.

Financial services sales agents consult on a wide variety of banking, securities, insurance, and related services to individuals and businesses, often catering the services to meet the client's financial needs. They contact potential clients to explain their services, which may include the handling of checking accounts, loans, certificates of deposit, individual retirement accounts, credit cards, and estate and retirement planning.

Work Environment

Securities, commodities, and financial services sales agents held about 464,200 jobs in 2019. The largest employers of

Electronic trading is changing the exchange floor environment, with more traders carrying out orders behind a desk and fewer working on the exchange floor.

Brokers and investment bankers must register as representatives of their firm with the Financial Industry Regulatory Authority (FINRA).

securities, commodities, and financial services sales agents were as follows:

Credit intermediation and related activities	48%
Securities, commodity contracts, and other financial investments and related activities..............................	39
Self-employed workers.....................................	4
Management of companies and enterprises..................	3

Most securities, commodities, and financial services sales agents work many hours under stressful conditions. The pace of work is fast, and managers are usually demanding of their workers, because both commissions and advancements are tied to sales.

Investment bankers travel extensively because they frequently work with companies in other countries.

Because computers can conduct trades faster than people can, electronic trading is quickly replacing verbal auction-style trades on exchange floors. The environment of the stock exchange is changing as a result, with more traders carrying out orders behind a desk and fewer working on the exchange floor.

Because most of the major investment banks are in New York City, employment of securities, commodities, and financial services sales agents is concentrated in that metropolitan area.

Work Schedules

Securities, commodities, and financial services sales agents usually work full time and some work more than 40 hours per week. In addition, they may work evenings and weekends because many of their clients work during the day.

How to Become a Securities, Commodities, or Financial Services Sales Agent

A bachelor's degree is required for entry-level jobs, and a master's degree in business administration (MBA) is useful for advancement.

Education

Securities, commodities, and financial services sales agents generally must have a bachelor's degree to get an entry-level job. Courses in business, finance, accounting, or economics are important, especially for larger firms. Many firms hire summer interns before their last year of college, and those who are most successful are offered full-time jobs after they graduate.

Numerous agents eventually get a master's degree in business administration (MBA), which is often a requirement for high-level positions in the securities industry. Because the MBA exposes students to real-world business practices, it can be a major asset for jobseekers. Employers often reward MBA holders with higher level positions, better compensation, and large signing bonuses.

Training

Most employers provide intensive on-the-job training, teaching employees the specifics of the job, such as the products and services offered. Trainees in large firms may receive technical instruction in securities analysis and selling strategies. Firms often rotate their trainees among various departments to give them a broad understanding of the securities business.

Securities, commodities, and financial services sales agents must keep up with new products and services and other developments. They attend conferences and training seminars regularly.

Licenses, Certifications, and Registrations

Brokers and investment bankers must register as representatives of their firm with the Financial Industry Regulatory Authority (FINRA). To obtain the license, potential agents must pass a series of exams.

Many other licenses are available, each of which gives the holder the right to sell different investment products and services. Traders and some other sales representatives also need licenses, although these vary by firm and specialization. Financial services sales agents may need to be licensed, especially if they sell securities or insurance. Most firms offer training to help their employees pass the licensing exams.

Agents who are registered with FINRA must attend continuing education classes to keep their licenses. Courses consist of computer-based training on legal requirements or new financial products or services.

Although not always required, certification enhances professional standing and is recommended by employers. Brokers, investment bankers, and financial services sales agents can earn the Chartered Financial Analyst (CFA) certification, sponsored by the CFA Institute. To qualify for this certification, applicants need a bachelor's degree or 4 years of related work experience and must pass three exams, which require several hundred hours of independent study. Applicants also must have an international passport. Exams cover subjects in accounting, economics, securities analysis, financial markets and instruments, corporate finance, asset valuation, and portfolio management. Applicants can take the exams while they are getting the required work experience.

Advancement

Securities, commodities, and financial services sales agents usually advance to senior positions in a firm by accumulating a greater number of accounts. Although beginners often service the accounts of individual investors, they may eventually service large institutional accounts, such as those of banks and retirement funds. Getting an MBA may also help advancement opportunities.

After taking a series of tests, some brokers become portfolio managers and have greater authority to make investment decisions regarding an account.

Some experienced sales agents become branch office managers and supervise other sales agents while continuing to provide services for their own clients. A few agents advance to top management positions or become partners in their firms.

Many investment banks use an "up or out" policy, in which entry-level investment bankers are either promoted or terminated after 2 or 3 years. Investment banks use this policy to ensure that entry-level positions are not occupied long term, allowing the bank to bring in new workers.

Important Qualities

Analytical skills. To judge the profitability of potential deals, securities, commodities, and financial services sales agents must have strong analytical skills. This includes computer programming skills which they use to analyze financial products.

Customer-service skills. Securities, commodities, and financial services sales agents must be persuasive and make clients feel comfortable with the agent's recommendations.

Decisionmaking skills. Investment banking traders must make split-second decisions, with large sums of money at stake.

Detail oriented. Investment bankers must pay close attention to the details of initial public offerings and mergers and acquisitions because small changes can have large consequences.

Initiative. Securities, commodities, and financial services sales agents must create their own client base by making "cold" sales calls to people to whom they have not been referred and to people not expecting the call.

Math skills. Securities, commodities, and financial services sales agents need to be familiar with mathematical tools, including investment formulas.

Pay

The median annual wage for securities, commodities, and financial services sales agents was $62,270 in May 2019. The median wage is the wage at which half the workers in an occupation earned more than that amount and half earned less. The lowest 10 percent earned less than $35,320, and the highest 10 percent earned more than $204,130.

In May 2019, the median annual wages for securities, commodities, and financial services sales agents in the top industries in which they worked were as follows:

Securities, commodity contracts, and other financial investments and related activities	$86,840
Management of companies and enterprises	78,610
Credit intermediation and related activities	50,060

Many securities and commodities brokers earn a commission based on the monetary value of the products they sell. Most firms pay brokers a minimum salary in addition to commissions.

Trainee brokers usually earn a salary until they develop a client base. The salary gradually decreases in favor of commissions as the broker gains clients.

Investment bankers in corporate finance and mergers and acquisitions generally earn a base salary with the opportunity to earn a substantial bonus. At higher levels, bonuses far exceed base salary.

Securities, Commodities, and Financial Services Sales Agents

Median annual wages, May 2019

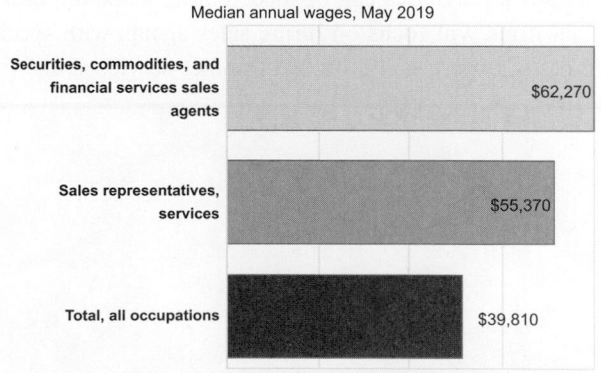

Securities, commodities, and financial services sales agents	$62,270
Sales representatives, services	$55,370
Total, all occupations	$39,810

Note: All Occupations includes all occupations in the U.S. Economy.
Source: U.S. Bureau of Labor Statistics, Occupational Employment Statistics.

Securities, Commodities, and Financial Services Sales Agents

Percent change in employment, projected 2019-29

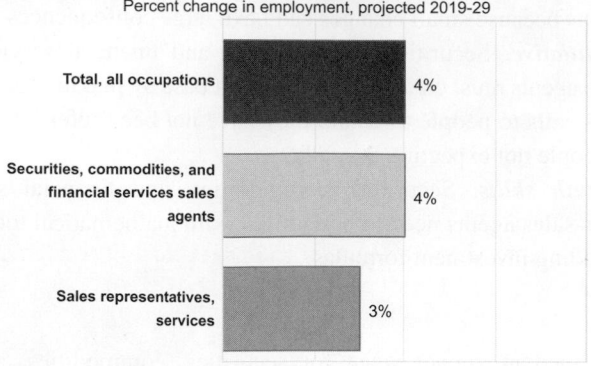

Note: All Occupations includes all occupations in the U.S. Economy.
Source: U.S. Bureau of Labor Statistics, Employment Projections program.

Securities, commodities, and financial services sales agents usually work full time and some work more than 40 hours per week. In addition, they may work evenings and weekends because many of their clients work during the day.

Job Outlook

Employment of securities, commodities, and financial services sales agents is projected to grow 4 percent from 2019 to 2029, about as fast as the average for all occupations.

Services that investment bankers provide, such as helping with initial public offerings and mergers and acquisitions, will continue to be in demand as the economy grows. The United States remains an international financial center, meaning that the economic growth of countries around the world will contribute to employment growth in the American financial industry. An aging population and the decline of traditional pensions may boost demand for these workers, as individuals approaching retirement seek brokers to facilitate securities purchases.

However, continuing consolidation in the financial services industry is projected to slow employment growth for these workers over the next decade. In addition, automated trading systems have reduced demand for securities traders. Because simpler stock purchases can be made online without a broker, financial firms will focus on hiring sales agents with specialized areas of expertise and strong customer-service skills.

Financial regulation, including restrictions on proprietary trading, has shifted employment among traders from investment banks to hedge funds; however, this shift should not affect overall employment growth for the occupation.

Job Prospects

The high pay associated with securities, commodities, and financial services sales agents draws many more applicants than there are openings. Therefore, competition for jobs is intense.

Certification and a graduate degree, such as a Chartered Financial Analyst (CFA) certification and a master's degree in business administration (MBA), can improve an applicant's prospects.

Employment projections data for securities, commodities, and financial services sales agents, 2019-29					
Occupational Title	SOC Code	Employment, 2019	Projected Employment, 2029	Change, 2019-29	
				Percent	Numeric
SOURCE: U.S. Bureau of Labor Statistics, Employment Projections program					
Securities, commodities, and financial services sales agents	41-3031	464,200	481,600	4	17,400

State & Area Data
Occupational Employment Statistics (OES)

The Occupational Employment Statistics (OES) program produces employment and wage estimates annually for over 800 occupations. These estimates are available for the nation as a whole, for individual states, and for metropolitan and nonmetropolitan areas.

Contacts for More Information

For more information about securities, commodities, and financial services sales agents, visit

➤ Securities Industry and Financial Markets Association (SIFMA)

For more information about licensing of securities, commodities, and financial services sales agents, visit

➤ Financial Industry Regulatory Authority (FINRA)

For more information about certification for securities, commodities, and financial services sales agents, visit

➤ CFA Institute

Travel Agents

Summary

Quick Facts: Travel Agents

2019 Median Pay	$40,660 per year $19.55 per hour
Typical Entry-Level Education	High school diploma or equivalent
Work Experience in a Related Occupation	None
On-the-job Training	Moderate-term on- the-job training
Number of Jobs, 2019	82,000
Job Outlook, 2019-29	-26% (Decline)
Employment Change, 2019-29	-21,300

What Travel Agents Do

Travel agents sell transportation, lodging, and entertainment activities to individuals and groups planning trips.

Work Environment

Travel agents typically work in offices, but some work remotely because much of their time is spent on the phone and the computer. Most travel agents work for travel agencies.

How to Become a Travel Agent

A high school diploma typically is required for someone to become a travel agent. However, many employers prefer additional formal training as well. Good communication and computer skills are essential.

Pay

The median annual wage for travel agents was $40,660 in May 2019.

Job Outlook

Employment of travel agents is projected to decline 26 percent from 2019 to 2029. The ability of travelers to use the Internet to research vacations and book their own trips is expected to continue to suppress demand for travel agents. Job prospects should be best for travel agents who specialize in specific destinations or particular types of travelers.

State & Area Data

Explore resources for employment and wages by state and area for travel agents.

What Travel Agents Do

Travel agents sell transportation, lodging, and admission to entertainment activities to individuals and groups planning trips. They offer advice on destinations, plan trip itineraries, and make travel arrangements for clients.

Duties

Travel agents typically do the following:

- Arrange travel for business and vacation customers
- Determine customers' needs and preferences, such as schedules and costs
- Plan and arrange tour packages, excursions, and day trips
- Find fare and schedule information
- Calculate total travel costs
- Book reservations for travel, hotels, rental cars, and special events, such as tours and excursions
- Describe trips to clients and give details on required documents, such as passports and visas
- Give advice about local weather conditions, customs, and attractions
- Make alternative booking arrangements if changes arise before or during the trip

Travel agents sell transportation, lodging, and admission to activities to those planning trips.

Travel agents offer advice on destinations, plan trip itineraries, and make travel arrangements for clients.

Travel agents sort through vast amounts of information to find the best possible trip arrangements for travelers. In addition, resorts and specialty groups use travel agents to promote vacation packages to their clients.

Travel agents also may visit destinations to get firsthand experience so that they can make recommendations to clients or colleagues. They may visit hotels, resorts, and restaurants to evaluate the comfort, cleanliness, and quality of the establishment. However, most of their time is spent talking with clients, promoting tours, and contacting airlines and hotels to make travel accommodations. Travel agents use a reservation system called a Global Distribution System (GDS) to access travel information and make reservations with travel suppliers such as airlines or hotels.

The following are examples of types of travel agents:

Leisure travel agents sell vacation packages to the general public. They are responsible for arranging trip itineraries based on clients' interests and budget. Leisure travel agents increasingly are focusing on a specific type of travel, such as adventure tours. Some may cater to a specific group of people, such as senior citizens or single people.

Corporate travel agents primarily make travel arrangements for businesses. They book travel accommodations for an organization's employees who are traveling to conduct business or attend conferences.

Work Environment

Travel agents held about 82,000 jobs in 2019. The largest employers of travel agents were as follows:

Travel arrangement and reservation services	72%
Self-employed workers	17

They typically work in offices, but some work remotely because much of their time is spent on the phone and the computer. In some cases, busy offices or call centers may be noisy and crowded. Agents may face stress during travel emergencies or unanticipated schedule changes.

Work Schedules

Most travel agents work full time. Some work additional hours during peak travel times or when they must accommodate customers' schedule changes and last-minute needs.

How to Become a Travel Agent

A high school diploma typically is required for someone to become a travel agent. However, many employers prefer additional formal training. Good communication and computer skills are essential.

Education

Employers generally require candidates to have at least a high school diploma, but may prefer those who have a college degree or who have taken classes related to the travel industry. Many community colleges, vocational schools, and industry associations offer technical training or continuing education classes in professional travel planning. Classes usually focus on reservations systems, marketing, and regulations regarding international travel. In addition, some colleges offer degrees in travel and tourism.

Training

Employers in the travel industry always give some on-the-job training on the computer systems that are used in the industry. For example, a travel agent could be trained to work with a reservation system used by several airlines.

Licenses, Certifications, and Registrations

A good way to demonstrate competence for high school graduates with limited experience is to take the Travel Agent Proficiency (TAP) test. The test has no eligibility requirements and is administered by The Travel Institute.

The Travel Institute also provides training and professional certification opportunities for experienced travel agents. Different levels of certification are offered, depending on a travel agent's experience. Travel agents with limited experience can become a Certified Travel Associate (CTA) after completing a series of classes and exams. For those with at least 5 years of experience, the more highly advanced Certified Travel Counselor (CTC) certification can be achieved. Both the CTA and CTC require continuing education each year to maintain certification.

The Cruise Lines International Association (CLIA) offers four levels of certification: Certified (CCC), Accredited (ACC), Master (MCC), and Elite Cruise Counselor (ECC). Each level requires a certain amount of training and product knowledge.

Some states require agents to have a business license to sell travel services. Requirements among states vary greatly. Contact individual state licensing agencies for more information.

Travel agents work in an office environment where they spend much of their time on the phone.

Good communication and computer skills are essential for travel agents.

Other Experience

Some agencies prefer travel agents with firsthand experience visiting a country. These agencies especially prefer travel agents who specialize in specific destinations or particular types of travelers, such as groups with a special interest or corporate travelers.

Important Qualities

Adventurousness. Travel agencies that specialize in exotic destinations or particular types of travel, such as adventure travel or ecotourism, may prefer to hire travel agents who share these interests.

Communication skills. Travel agents must listen to customers, understand their travel needs, and offer appropriate travel advice and information.

Customer-service skills. When customers need to make last-minute changes in their travel arrangements, travel agents must be able to respond to questions and complaints in a friendly and professional manner.

Detail oriented. Travel agents must pay attention to details in order to ensure that the reservations they make match travelers' needs. They must make reservations at the correct dates, times, and locations to meet travelers' schedules.

Organizational skills. Travel agents often work on itineraries for many customers at once. Keeping client information in order and ensuring that bills and receipts are processed in a timely manner is essential.

Sales skills. Travel agents must be able to persuade clients to buy transportation, lodging, or tours. Sometimes they might need to persuade tour operators, airline staff, or others to take care of their clients' special needs. Earnings for many travel agents depend on commissions and service fees.

Pay

The median annual wage for travel agents was $40,660 in May 2019. The median wage is the wage at which half the workers

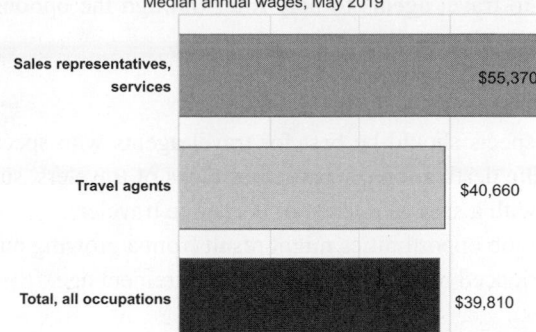

Travel Agents
Median annual wages, May 2019

Sales representatives, services	$55,370
Travel agents	$40,660
Total, all occupations	$39,810

Note: All Occupations includes all occupations in the U.S. Economy.
Source: U.S. Bureau of Labor Statistics, Occupational Employment Statistics.

in an occupation earned more than that amount and half earned less. The lowest 10 percent earned less than $23,660, and the highest 10 percent earned more than $69,420.

In May 2019, the median annual wages for travel agents in the top industries in which they worked were as follows:

Travel arrangement and reservation services.......... $40,260

These wage data include money earned from commissions.

Most travel agents work full time. Some work additional hours during peak travel times or when they must accommodate customers' schedule changes and last-minute needs.

Job Outlook

Employment of travel agents is projected to decline 26 percent from 2019 to 2029.

The ability of travelers to use the Internet to research vacations and book their own trips is expected to continue to suppress demand for travel agents. An increasing amount of travel is also expected to be booked on mobile devices.

However, the sheer number of travel and review websites can make travel planning a frustrating experience for some

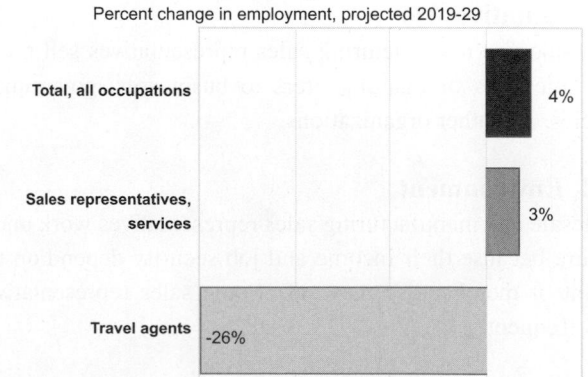

Travel Agents
Percent change in employment, projected 2019-29

Total, all occupations	4%
Sales representatives, services	3%
Travel agents	-26%

Note: All Occupations includes all occupations in the U.S. Economy.
Source: U.S. Bureau of Labor Statistics, Employment Projections program.

consumers. This may lead to an increasing number of people turning to travel agents to help filter through the options and give personal recommendations.

Job Prospects

Job prospects should be best for travel agents who specialize in specific destinations or particular types of travelers, such as groups with a special interest or corporate travelers.

Some job opportunities might result from a growing number of experienced travel agents reaching retirement age.

Occupational Title	SOC Code	Employment, 2019	Projected Employment, 2029	Change, 2019-29	
				Percent	Numeric
Employment projections data for travel agents, 2019-29					
SOURCE: U.S. Bureau of Labor Statistics, Employment Projections program					
Travel agents	41-3041	82,000	60,800	-26	-21,300

Wholesale and Manufacturing Sales Representatives

Summary

Quick Facts: Wholesale and Manufacturing Sales Representatives

2019 Median Pay	$63,000 per year $30.29 per hour
Typical Entry-Level Education	See below
Work Experience in a Related Occupation	None
On-the-job Training	Moderate-term on-the-job training
Number of Jobs, 2019	1,720,700
Job Outlook, 2019-29	2% (Slower than average)
Employment Change, 2019-29	26,200

What Wholesale and Manufacturing Sales Representatives Do

Wholesale and manufacturing sales representatives sell goods for wholesalers or manufacturers to businesses, government agencies, and other organizations.

Work Environment

Wholesale and manufacturing sales representatives work under pressure because their income and job security depend on the amount of merchandise they sell. Some sales representatives travel frequently.

How to Become a Wholesale or Manufacturing Sales Representative

Educational requirements vary for sales representatives and depend on the type of products sold. If the products are not scientific or technical, a high school diploma is generally sufficient for entry into the occupation. If the products are scientific or technical, sales representatives typically need at least a bachelor's degree.

State & Area Data
Occupational Employment Statistics (OES)

The Occupational Employment Statistics (OES) program produces employment and wage estimates annually for over 800 occupations. These estimates are available for the nation as a whole, for individual states, and for metropolitan and nonmetropolitan areas.

Contacts for More Information

For more information about training opportunities, visit
➤ American Society of Travel Agents
➤ Cruise Lines International Association (CLIA)

For more information about voluntary certification opportunities, visit
➤ The Travel Institute

Pay

The median annual wage for sales representatives, wholesale and manufacturing, except technical and scientific products was $59,930 in May 2019.

The median annual wage for sales representatives, wholesale and manufacturing, technical and scientific products was $81,020 in May 2019.

Job Outlook

Overall employment of wholesale and manufacturing sales representatives is projected to grow 2 percent from 2019 to 2029, slower than the average for all occupations. Employment

Wholesale and manufacturing sales representatives sell goods for wholesalers or manufacturers to businesses, government agencies, and other organizations.

growth is expected to be stronger for sales representatives working at independent sales agencies.

State & Area Data

Explore resources for employment and wages by state and area for wholesale and manufacturing sales representatives.

What Wholesale and Manufacturing Sales Representatives Do

Wholesale and manufacturing sales representatives sell goods for wholesalers or manufacturers to businesses, government agencies, and other organizations. They contact customers, explain the features of the products they are selling, negotiate prices, and answer any questions that their customers may have about the products.

Duties

Wholesale and manufacturing sales representatives typically do the following:

- Identify prospective customers by using business directories, following leads from existing clients, and attending trade shows and conferences

Some wholesale and manufacturing sales representatives specialize in technical and scientific products, ranging from agricultural and mechanical equipment to computer and pharmaceutical goods.

- Contact new and existing customers to discuss their needs and explain how specific products and services can meet these needs
- Help customers select products to meet customers' needs, product specifications, and regulations
- Emphasize product features that will meet customers' needs, and exhibit the capabilities and limitations of their products
- Answer customers' questions about the prices, availability, and uses of the products they are selling
- Negotiate prices and terms of sales and service agreements
- Prepare sales contracts and submit orders for processing
- Collaborate with colleagues to exchange information, such as information on selling strategies and marketing information
- Follow up with customers to make sure that they are satisfied with their purchases and to answer any questions or concerns they might have

Wholesale and manufacturing sales representatives—sometimes called *manufacturers' representatives* or *manufacturers' agents*—generally work for manufacturers or wholesalers. Some work for a single organization, while others represent several companies and sell a range of products.

Unlike retail sales workers, who sell goods directly to consumers, wholesale and manufacturing sales representatives deal with businesses, government agencies, and other organizations.

Some wholesale and manufacturing sales representatives work with nonscientific products, such as food, office supplies, and clothing. Other representatives specialize in technical and scientific products, ranging from agricultural and mechanical equipment to computer and pharmaceutical goods.

Wholesale and manufacturing sales representatives who lack expertise about a given product frequently team with a technical expert. In this arrangement, the technical expert—sometimes a sales engineer—attends the sales presentation to explain the product and answer questions or concerns. The sales representative makes the initial contact with customers, introduces the company's product, and obtains final agreement from the potential buyer.

By working with a technical expert, the representative is able to spend more time maintaining and soliciting accounts and less time seeking technical knowledge.

After the sale, representatives may make followup visits to ensure that equipment is functioning properly and may even help train customers' employees to operate and maintain new equipment.

Those selling consumer goods often suggest how and where merchandise should be displayed. When working with retailers, they may help arrange promotional programs, store displays, and advertising.

In addition to selling products, wholesale and manufacturing sales representatives analyze sales statistics, prepare reports, and handle administrative duties such as filing expense accounts, scheduling appointments, and making travel plans.

Staying up to date on new products and the changing needs of customers is important. Sales representatives accomplish this aim in a variety of ways, including attending trade shows at which new products and technologies are showcased. They attend conferences and conventions to meet other sales representatives and clients and to discuss new product developments. They also read about new and existing products and monitor the sales, prices, and products of their competitors.

The following are examples of types of wholesale and manufacturing sales representatives:

Inside sales representatives work mostly in offices while making sales. Frequently, they are responsible for getting new clients by "cold-calling" various organizations, meaning that they call potential customers who are not expecting to be contacted. That way, a representative can establish an initial contact. They also take incoming calls from customers who are interested in their product, and they process paperwork to complete the sale.

Outside sales representatives spend much of their time traveling to and visiting with current clients and prospective buyers. During a sales call, they discuss the client's needs and suggest how they can meet those needs with merchandise or services. They may show samples or catalogs that describe items their company provides, and they may inform customers about the prices and availability of the products they are selling and the ways in which their products can save money and boost productivity.

Work Environment

Sales representatives, wholesale and manufacturing, except technical and scientific products held about 1.4 million jobs in 2019. The largest employers of sales representatives, wholesale and manufacturing, except technical and scientific products were as follows:

Merchant wholesalers, durable goods	32%
Merchant wholesalers, nondurable goods	20
Manufacturing	17
Wholesale electronic markets and agents and brokers	10
Retail trade	5

Sales representatives, wholesale and manufacturing, technical and scientific products held about 321,000 jobs in 2019. The largest employers of sales representatives, wholesale and manufacturing, technical and scientific products were as follows:

Professional and commercial equipment and supplies merchant wholesalers	19%
Manufacturing	17
Merchant wholesalers, nondurable goods	13
Professional, scientific, and technical services	12
Wholesale electronic markets and agents and brokers	7

Some wholesale and manufacturing sales representatives have large territories and travel considerably.

Some wholesale and manufacturing sales representatives have large territories and travel considerably. Because a sales region may cover several states, representatives may be away from home for several days or weeks at a time. Sales representatives who cover a smaller region may not spend much time away from home.

Other wholesale and manufacturing sales representatives spend a lot of their time on the phone, selling goods, taking orders, and resolving problems or complaints about the merchandise. They also use Web technology, including chats, email, and video conferencing, to contact clients.

Workers in this occupation can be under considerable stress because their income and job security often depend directly on the amount of merchandise they sell and their companies usually set goals or quotas that they are expected to meet.

Work Schedules

Most wholesale and manufacturing sales representatives work full time and many work more than 40 hours per week.

How to Become a Wholesale or Manufacturing Sales Representative

Educational requirements vary with the type of product sold. If the products are not scientific or technical, a high school diploma is generally enough for entry into the occupation. If the products are scientific or technical, sales representatives typically need at least a bachelor's degree.

Education

A high school diploma is typically sufficient for many positions, primarily those selling nontechnical or scientific products. However, representatives selling scientific and technical products usually must have a bachelor's degree. Scientific and technical products include pharmaceuticals, medical instruments, and industrial equipment. A degree in a field related to the product sold, such as chemistry, biology, or engineering, is sometimes required.

Many sales representatives attend seminars in sales techniques or take courses in marketing, economics, communication, or even a foreign language to improve their ability to make sales.

Training

Many companies have formal training programs for beginning wholesale and manufacturing sales representatives. These programs may last up to 1 year. In some, trainees rotate among jobs in plants and offices in order to learn all phases of producing, installing, and distributing the product. In others, trainees

Sales representatives of scientific or technical products, such as pharmaceuticals or medical instruments, typically need a degree in a field related to the product sold.

receive formal technical instruction at the plant, followed by on-the-job training under the supervision of a field sales manager.

New employees may be trained by going along with experienced workers on their sales calls. As they gain familiarity with the firm's products and clients, the new workers gain more responsibility until they eventually get their own territory.

Licenses, Certifications, and Registrations

The Certified Professional Manufacturers' Representative (CPMR) certification and the Certified Sales Professional (CSP) certification are both offered by the Manufacturers' Representatives Educational Research Foundation (MRERF). Certification typically involves completing formal technical training and passing an exam. In addition, the CPMR requires 10 hours of continuing education every year in order to maintain certification.

Advancement

Frequently, promotion takes the form of an assignment to a larger account or territory, for which commissions are likely to be greater. Those who have good sales records and leadership ability may advance to higher level positions, such as sales manager, sales supervisor, district manager, or vice president of sales.

Important Qualities

Customer-service skills. Wholesale and manufacturing sales representatives must be able to listen to the customer's needs and concerns before and after the sale.

Interpersonal skills. Wholesale and manufacturing sales representatives must be able to work well with many types of people. They must be able to build good relationships with clients and with other members of the sales team.

Physical stamina. Wholesale and manufacturing sales representatives are often on their feet for a long time and may carry heavy sample products.

Self-confidence. Wholesale and manufacturing sales representatives must be confident and persuasive when making sales presentations. In addition, making a call to a potential customer who is not expecting to be contacted, or "cold-calling," requires confidence and composure.

Pay

The median annual wage for sales representatives, wholesale and manufacturing, except technical and scientific products was $59,930 in May 2019. The median wage is the wage at which half the workers in an occupation earned more than that amount and half earned less. The lowest 10 percent earned less than $30,530, and the highest 10 percent earned more than $125,300.

The median annual wage for sales representatives, wholesale and manufacturing, technical and scientific products was $81,020 in May 2019. The lowest 10 percent earned less than $41,080, and the highest 10 percent earned more than $158,580.

In May 2019, the median annual wages for sales representatives, wholesale and manufacturing, except technical and scientific products in the top industries in which they worked were as follows:

Wholesale electronic markets and agents and brokers	$67,560
Manufacturing..	63,410
Merchant wholesalers, durable goods......................	58,400
Merchant wholesalers, nondurable goods...............	57,590
Retail trade	52,720

In May 2019, the median annual wages for sales representatives, wholesale and manufacturing, technical and scientific products in the top industries in which they worked were as follows:

Wholesale electronic markets and agents and brokers	$91,650
Professional, scientific, and technical services........	88,630
Merchant wholesalers, nondurable goods...............	87,120
Manufacturing..	83,030
Professional and commercial equipment and supplies merchant wholesalers	75,960

Compensation for representatives varies considerably with the type of firm and the product sold. Most employers use a combination of salary and commissions or salary plus bonuses. Commissions usually are based on a percentage of sales. Bonuses may depend on the individual's performance, on the performance of all sales workers in the group or district, or on the company's performance.

Most wholesale and manufacturing sales representatives work full time and many work more than 40 hours per week.

Job Outlook

Overall employment of wholesale and manufacturing sales representatives is projected to grow 2 percent from 2019 to 2029, slower than the average for all occupations.

In addition to a rising total volume of sales, a wider range of products and technologies will lead to increased demand for sales representatives. Although wholesale sales are increasingly being conducted online, these online sales are expected to complement, rather than replace, face-to-face selling. Therefore, online sales are not expected to have a negative effect on employment growth for these workers.

Employment growth is expected to be stronger for sales representatives working at independent sales agencies, because companies often shift their sales activities to independent agencies as a way to cut costs and boost revenue. These independent companies do not buy and hold the products they are selling. Instead, they operate on a fee or commission basis in representing the product manufacturer. Employment of sales representatives in this industry—wholesale electronic markets and agents and brokers—is projected to grow 12 percent from 2019 to 2029.

Job Prospects

Job opportunities should be best for those with previous sales experience. Although the large size of the occupations creates many job openings, the relatively high pay will also likely attract a large number of applicants.

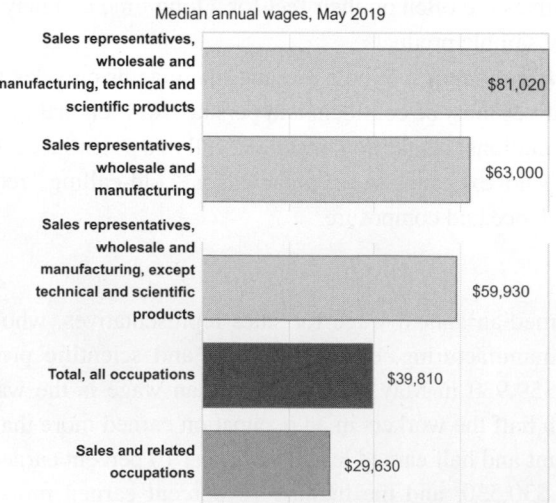

Wholesale and Manufacturing Sales Representatives

Median annual wages, May 2019

Sales representatives, wholesale and manufacturing, technical and scientific products — $81,020

Sales representatives, wholesale and manufacturing — $63,000

Sales representatives, wholesale and manufacturing, except technical and scientific products — $59,930

Total, all occupations — $39,810

Sales and related occupations — $29,630

Note: All Occupations includes all occupations in the U.S. Economy.
Source: U.S. Bureau of Labor Statistics, Occupational Employment Statistics.

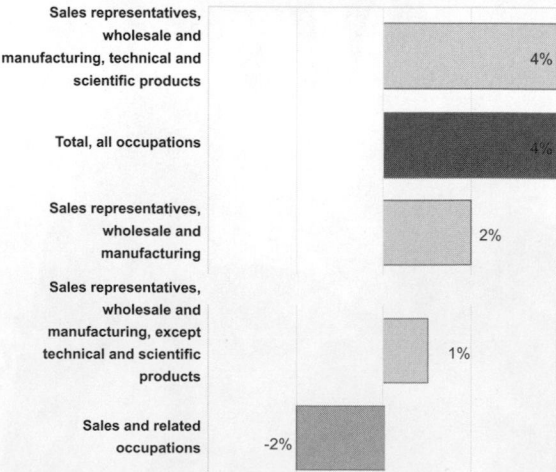

Wholesale and Manufacturing Sales Representatives

Percent change in employment, projected 2019-29

Sales representatives, wholesale and manufacturing, technical and scientific products — 4%

Total, all occupations — 4%

Sales representatives, wholesale and manufacturing — 2%

Sales representatives, wholesale and manufacturing, except technical and scientific products — 1%

Sales and related occupations — -2%

Note: All Occupations includes all occupations in the U.S. Economy.
Source: U.S. Bureau of Labor Statistics, Employment Projections program.

Employment projections data for wholesale and manufacturing sales representatives, 2019-29					
Occupational Title	SOC Code	Employment, 2019	Projected Employment, 2029	Change, 2019-29	
				Percent	Numeric
SOURCE: U.S. Bureau of Labor Statistics, Employment Projections program					
Sales representatives, wholesale and manufacturing	41-4000	1,720,700	1,747,000	2	26,200
Sales representatives, wholesale and manufacturing, technical and scientific products	41-4011	321,000	334,000	4	13,000
Sales representatives, wholesale and manufacturing, except technical and scientific products	41-4012	1,399,700	1,412,900	1	13,200

State & Area Data
Occupational Employment Statistics (OES)

The Occupational Employment Statistics (OES) program produces employment and wage estimates annually for over 800 occupations. These estimates are available for the nation as a whole, for individual states, and for metropolitan and nonmetropolitan areas.

Contacts for More Information

For more information about wholesale sales representatives, visit
➤ Manufacturers' Agents National Association (MANA)

For more information about certification, visit
➤ Manufacturers' Representatives Educational Research Foundation (MRERF)

Transportation and Material Moving

Airline and Commercial Pilots

Summary

Quick Facts: Airline and Commercial Pilots

2019 Median Pay	$121,430 per year
Typical Entry-Level Education	See below
Work Experience in a Related Occupation	See below
On-the-job Training	Moderate-term on-the-job training
Number of Jobs, 2019	127,100
Job Outlook, 2019-29	5% (Faster than average)
Employment Change, 2019-29	6,100

What Airline and Commercial Pilots Do

Airline and commercial pilots fly and navigate airplanes, helicopters, and other aircraft.

Work Environment

Pilots usually have variable work schedules, with overnight layovers that are more common for airline pilots.

How to Become an Airline or Commercial Pilot

Airline pilots typically begin their careers as commercial pilots or flight instructors. Commercial pilots need a high school diploma or equivalent and a commercial pilot's license from the Federal Aviation Administration (FAA). Airline pilots usually need a bachelor's degree and also must have the FAA-issued Airline Transport Pilot (ATP) certificate.

Pay

The median annual wage for airline pilots, copilots, and flight engineers was $147,220 in May 2019.

The median annual wage for commercial pilots was $86,080 in May 2019.

Job Outlook

Overall employment of airline and commercial pilots is projected to grow 5 percent from 2019 to 2029, faster than the average for all occupations. Most job opportunities will arise from the need to replace pilots who leave the occupation permanently over the projection period.

State & Area Data

Explore resources for employment and wages by state and area for airline and commercial pilots.

What Airline and Commercial Pilots Do

Airline and commercial pilots fly and navigate airplanes, helicopters, and other aircraft.

Duties

Pilots typically do the following:

- Check the overall condition of the aircraft before and after every flight

Airline and commercial pilots fly and navigate airplanes, helicopters, and other aircraft.

Commercial pilots are involved in activities such as firefighting and crop dusting.

- Ensure that the aircraft is balanced and below its weight limit
- Verify that the fuel supply is adequate and that weather conditions are acceptable
- Prepare and submit flight plans to air traffic control
- Communicate with air traffic control over the aircraft's radio system
- Operate and control aircraft along planned routes and during takeoffs and landings
- Monitor engines, fuel consumption, and other aircraft systems during flight
- Respond to changing conditions, such as weather events and emergencies (for example, a mechanical malfunction)
- Navigate the aircraft by using cockpit instruments and visual references

Pilots plan their flights by checking that the aircraft is operable and safe, that the cargo has been loaded correctly, and that weather conditions are acceptable. They file flight plans with air traffic control and may modify the plans in flight because of changing weather conditions or other factors.

Takeoff and landing can be the most demanding parts of a flight. They require close coordination among the pilot; copilot; flight engineer, if present; air traffic controllers; and ground personnel. Once in the air, the captain may have the first officer, if present, fly the aircraft, but the captain remains responsible for the aircraft. After landing, pilots fill out records that document their flight and the status of the aircraft.

Some pilots are also instructors using simulators and dual-controlled aircraft to teach students how to fly.

The following are examples of types of pilots:

Airline pilots work primarily for airlines that transport passengers and cargo on a fixed schedule. The captain or pilot in command, usually the most experienced pilot, supervises all other crew members and has primary responsibility for the flight. The copilot, often called the first officer or second in command, shares flight duties with the captain. Some older planes require a third pilot known as a flight engineer, who monitors instruments and operates controls. Technology has automated many of these tasks, and new aircraft do not require flight engineers.

Commercial pilots are involved in unscheduled flight activities, such as aerial application, charter flights, and aerial tours. Commercial pilots may have additional nonflight duties. Some commercial pilots schedule flights, arrange for maintenance of the aircraft, and load luggage themselves. Pilots who transport company executives, also known as corporate pilots, greet their passengers before embarking on the flight.

Agricultural pilots typically handle agricultural chemicals, such as pesticides, and may be involved in other agricultural practices in addition to flying. Pilots, such as helicopter pilots, who fly at low levels must constantly look for trees, bridges, power lines, transmission towers, and other obstacles.

With proper training, airline pilots also may be deputized as federal law enforcement officers and be issued firearms to protect the cockpit.

Work Environment

Airline pilots, copilots, and flight engineers held about 85,500 jobs in 2019. The largest employers of airline pilots, copilots, and flight engineers were as follows:

Scheduled air transportation	86%
Federal government	4
Nonscheduled air transportation	2

Commercial pilots held about 41,600 jobs in 2019. The largest employers of commercial pilots were as follows:

Nonscheduled air transportation	28%
Technical and trade schools; private	12
Support activities for air transportation	10
Ambulance services	10
Manufacturing	3

Pilots assigned to long-distance routes may experience fatigue and jetlag. Weather conditions may result in turbulence, requiring pilots to change the flying altitude. Flights can be long and flight decks are often sealed, so pilots work in small teams for long periods in close proximity to one another.

Pilots have variable work schedules, which may include overnight layovers.

Aerial applicators, also known as crop dusters, may be exposed to toxic chemicals, typically use unimproved landing strips, such as grass, dirt, or gravel surface, and may be at risk of collision with power lines. Helicopter pilots involved in rescue operations may fly at low levels during bad weather or at night, and land in areas surrounded by power lines, highways, and other obstacles. Pilots use hearing protection devices to prevent their exposure to engine noise.

The high level of concentration required to fly an aircraft and the mental stress of being responsible for the safety of passengers can be fatiguing. Pilots must be alert and quick to react if something goes wrong. Federal law requires pilots to retire at age 65.

Most pilots are based near large airports.

Injuries and Illnesses

Although fatalities are uncommon, commercial pilots experience one of the highest rates of occupational fatalities of all occupations.

Work Schedules

Federal regulations set the maximum work hours and minimum requirements for rest between flights for most pilots. Airline pilots fly an average of 75 hours per month and work an additional 150 hours per month performing other duties, such as checking weather conditions and preparing flight plans. Pilots have variable work schedules that may include some days of work followed by some days off. Flight assignments are based on seniority. Seniority enables pilots who have worked at a company for a long time to get preferred routes and schedules.

Airline pilots may spend several nights a week away from home because flight assignments often involve overnight layovers. When pilots are away from home, the airlines typically provide hotel accommodations, transportation to the airport, and an allowance for meals and other expenses.

Commercial pilots also may have irregular schedules. Although most commercial pilots remain near their home overnight, some may still work nonstandard hours.

How to Become an Airline or Commercial Pilot

Airline pilots typically begin their careers as commercial pilots. Commercial pilots usually need a high school diploma or equivalent. Airline pilots need a bachelor's degree. All pilots who are paid to fly must have at least a commercial pilot's license from the Federal Aviation Administration (FAA). In addition, airline pilots must have the FAA-issued Airline Transport Pilot (ATP) certificate.

Interviews for positions with major and regional airlines may reflect the FAA exams for pilot licenses, certificates, and instrument ratings, and can be intense. Airlines frequently conduct their own psychological and aptitude tests to assess the candidates in critical thinking and decisionmaking processes under pressure.

Airline and commercial pilots who are newly hired by airlines or on-demand air services companies must undergo on-the-job training.

Military pilots may transfer to civilian aviation and apply directly to airlines to become airline pilots.

Education

Airline pilots typically need a bachelor's degree in any subject, along with a commercial pilot's license and an ATP certificate from the FAA. Airline pilots typically start their careers flying as commercial pilots. Commercial pilots usually accrue thousands of hours of flight experience in order to get a job with regional or major airlines.

Commercial pilots must have a commercial pilot's license and usually need a high school diploma or equivalent. The most common path to becoming a commercial pilot is to complete flight training with independent FAA-certified flight instructors or at schools that offer flight training. Some flight schools are part of 2- and 4-year colleges and universities.

The FAA certifies hundreds of civilian flight schools, which range from small fixed base operators (FBO) to state universities. Some colleges and universities offer pilot training as part of a 2- or 4-year aviation degree.

Training

Airline and commercial pilots who are newly hired by airlines or on-demand air services companies undergo on-the-job training in accordance with Federal Aviation Regulations (FARs). This training usually includes 6–8 weeks of ground school. Various types of ratings for specific aircraft, such as the Boeing 737 or Cessna Citation, typically are acquired through employer-based training and generally are earned by pilots who have at least a commercial license.

Besides initial training and licensing requirements, all pilots must maintain their experience in performing certain maneuvers. This requirement means that pilots must perform specific maneuvers and procedures a given number of times within a specified amount of time. Pilots also must undergo periodic training and medical examinations, generally every year or every other year.

Work Experience in a Related Occupation

Airline pilots typically begin their careers as commercial pilots. Pilots usually accrue thousands of hours of flight experience as commercial pilots or in the military to get a job with regional or major airlines.

Minimum time requirements to get a certificate or rating may not be enough to get some jobs. To make up the gap between paying for training and flying for the major airlines, many commercial pilots begin their careers as flight instructors and on-demand charter pilots. These positions typically require less experience than airline jobs require. When pilots have built enough flying hours, they can apply to the airlines. Newly hired pilots at regional airlines are typically required to have about 1,500 hours of flight experience. Many commercial piloting jobs have minimum requirements of around 500 hours.

Licenses, Certifications, and Registrations

Those who are seeking a career as a professional pilot typically get their licenses and ratings in the following order:

- Student pilot certificate
- Private pilot license
- Instrument rating
- Commercial pilot license
- Multi-engine rating
- Airline transport pilot certificate

Each certificate and rating requires that pilots pass a written exam on the ground and a practical flying exam, usually called a check ride, in an appropriate aircraft. In addition to earning these licenses, many pilots get a certified flight instructor (CFI) rating after they get their commercial certificate. The CFI rating helps them build flight time and experience quickly and at less personal expense. Current licensing regulations can be found in FARs.

Commercial pilot license. To qualify for a commercial pilot license, applicants must be at least 18 years old and meet certain flight-hour requirements. Student pilots use a logbook and keep detailed records of their flight time. The logbook must be endorsed by the flight instructor in order for the student to be able to take the FAA knowledge and practical exams. For specific requirements, including details on the types and quantities of flight experience and knowledge requirements, see the FARs. Part 61 of Title 14 of the code of federal regulations (14 CFR part 61) covers the basic rules for the certification of pilots. Flight schools can train pilots in accordance with the rules from part 61 or the rules found in 14 CFR part 141.

Applicants must pass the appropriate medical exam, meet all of the detailed flight experience and knowledge requirements, and pass a written exam and a practical flight exam in order to become commercially licensed. The physical exam confirms that the pilot's vision is correctable to 20/20 and that no physical handicaps exist that could impair the pilot's performance.

Commercial pilots must hold an instrument rating if they want to carry passengers for pay more than 50 miles from the point of origin of their flight, or at night.

Instrument rating. Pilots who earn an instrument rating can fly during periods of low visibility, also known as instrument meteorological conditions, or IMC. They may qualify for this rating by having at least 40 hours of instrument flight experience and 50 hours of cross-country flight time as pilot in command, and by meeting other requirements detailed in the FARs.

Airline transport pilot (ATP) certification. All pilot crews of a scheduled commercial airliner must have ATP certificates. To earn the ATP certificate, applicants must be at least 23 years old, have a minimum of 1,500 hours of flight time, and pass written and practical flight exams. Airline pilots usually maintain one or more aircraft-type ratings, which allow them to fly aircraft that require specific training, depending on the requirements of their particular airline. Some exceptions and alternative requirements are detailed in the FARs.

Pilots must pass periodic physical and practical flight examinations to be able to perform the duties granted by their certificate.

Advancement

Commercial pilots may advance to airline pilots after completing a degree, accruing required flight time, and obtaining an ATP license.

Advancement for airline pilots depends on a system of seniority outlined in collective bargaining contracts. Typically, after 1 to 5 years, flight engineers may advance to first officer positions and, after 5 to 15 years, first officers can become captains.

Important Qualities

Communication skills. Pilots must speak clearly when conveying information to air traffic controllers and other crew members. They must also listen carefully for instructions.

Observational skills. Pilots regularly watch over screens, gauges, and dials to make sure that all systems are in working order. They also need to maintain situational awareness by looking for other aircraft or obstacles. Pilots must be able to see clearly, be able to judge the distance between objects, and possess good color vision.

Problem-solving skills. Pilots must be able to identify complex problems and figure out appropriate solutions. When a plane encounters turbulence, for example, pilots assess the weather conditions and request a change in route or altitude from air traffic control.

Quick reaction time. Pilots must respond quickly, and with good judgment, to any impending danger.

Pay

The median annual wage for airline pilots, copilots, and flight engineers was $147,220 in May 2019. The median wage is the wage at which half the workers in an occupation earned more than that amount and half earned less. The lowest 10 percent earned less than $74,100, and the highest 10 percent earned more than $208,000.

The median annual wage for commercial pilots was $86,080 in May 2019. The lowest 10 percent earned less than $45,480, and the highest 10 percent earned more than $179,440.

In May 2019, the median annual wages for airline pilots, copilots, and flight engineers in the top industries in which they worked were as follows:

Scheduled air transportation	$161,110
Nonscheduled air transportation	114,510
Federal government	104,700

In May 2019, the median annual wages for commercial pilots in the top industries in which they worked were as follows:

Manufacturing	$122,150
Nonscheduled air transportation	90,630
Ambulance services	79,830
Support activities for air transportation	77,600
Technical and trade schools; private	76,670

Airline pilots usually begin their careers as first officers and receive wage increases as they accumulate experience and seniority.

In addition, airline pilots receive an expense allowance, or "per diem," for every hour they are away from home, and they may earn extra pay for international flights. Airline pilots and their immediate families usually are entitled to free or reduced-fare flights.

Federal regulations set the maximum work hours and minimum requirements for rest between flights for most pilots. Airline pilots fly an average of 75 hours per month and work an additional 150 hours per month performing other duties, such as checking weather conditions and preparing flight plans. Pilots have variable work schedules that may include several days of work followed by some days off.

Airline pilots may spend several nights a week away from home because flight assignments often involve overnight layovers. When pilots are away from home, the airlines typically provide hotel accommodations, transportation to the airport, and an allowance for meals and other expenses.

Commercial pilots also may have irregular schedules. Although most commercial pilots remain near their home overnight, they may still work nonstandard hours.

Job Outlook

Overall employment of airline and commercial pilots is projected to grow 5 percent from 2019 to 2029, faster than the average for all occupations.

Employment of airline pilots, copilots, and flight engineers is projected to grow 3 percent from 2019 to 2029, about as fast as the average for all occupations. Employment of commercial pilots is projected to grow 9 percent from 2019 to 2029, much faster than the average for all occupations. The number of commercial pilot jobs is projected to increase in various industries, especially in ambulance services, where pilots will be needed to transfer patients to healthcare facilities.

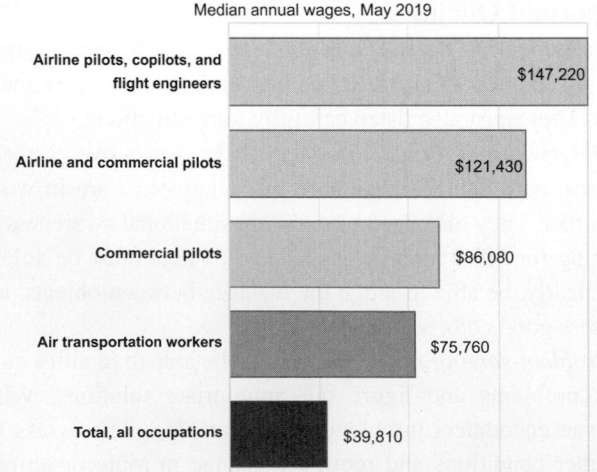

Airline and Commercial Pilots
Median annual wages, May 2019

Airline pilots, copilots, and flight engineers — $147,220
Airline and commercial pilots — $121,430
Commercial pilots — $86,080
Air transportation workers — $75,760
Total, all occupations — $39,810

Note: All Occupations includes all occupations in the U.S. Economy.
Source: U.S. Bureau of Labor Statistics, Occupational Employment Statistics.

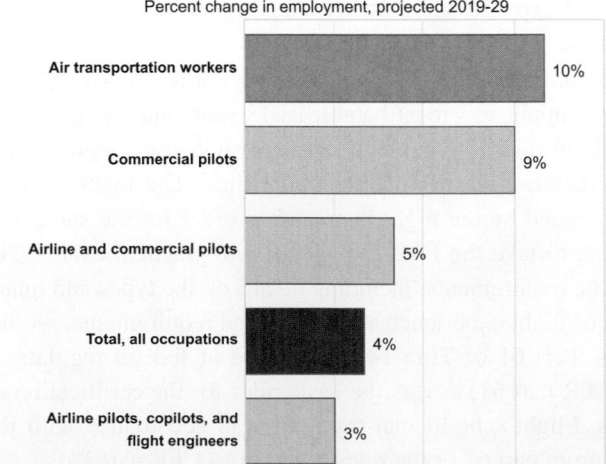

Airline and Commercial Pilots
Percent change in employment, projected 2019-29

Air transportation workers — 10%
Commercial pilots — 9%
Airline and commercial pilots — 5%
Total, all occupations — 4%
Airline pilots, copilots, and flight engineers — 3%

Note: All Occupations includes all occupations in the U.S. Economy.
Source: U.S. Bureau of Labor Statistics, Employment Projections program.

Job Prospects

Most job opportunities will arise from the need to replace pilots who leave the occupation permanently over the projection period.

Job prospects may be best with regional airlines and non-scheduled aviation services because entry-level requirements are lower for regional and commercial jobs. There is typically less competition among applicants in these sectors than there is for major airlines.

Pilots seeking jobs at the major airlines will face strong competition because those firms tend to attract many more applicants than the number of job openings.

Employment projections data for airline and commercial pilots, 2019-29					
Occupational Title	SOC Code	Employment, 2019	Projected Employment, 2029	Change, 2019-29	
				Percent	Numeric
SOURCE: U.S. Bureau of Labor Statistics, Employment Projections program					
Aircraft pilots and flight engineers	53-2010	127,100	133,300	5	6,100
Airline pilots, copilots, and flight engineers	53-2011	85,500	87,900	3	2,400
Commercial pilots	53-2012	41,600	45,400	9	3,800

State & Area Data
Occupational Employment Statistics (OES)

The Occupational Employment Statistics (OES) program produces employment and wage estimates annually for over 800 occupations. These estimates are available for the nation as a whole, for individual states, and for metropolitan and nonmetropolitan areas.

Contacts for More Information

For specific information about licensing requirements and other federal regulations regarding pilots and operators, visit

➤ Regulations concerning the certification of airmen and general flight rules
➤ Regulations concerning air carriers and operators for compensation or hire, and flight schools

For more information about pilots, visit

➤ Aircraft Owners and Pilots Association
➤ Air Line Pilots Association, International
➤ Coalition of Airline Pilots Associations
➤ Federal Aviation Administration
➤ Helicopter Association International
➤ National Agricultural Aviation Association

Air Traffic Controllers

Summary

Quick Facts: Air Traffic Controllers

2019 Median Pay	$122,990 per year / $59.13 per hour
Typical Entry-Level Education	Associate's degree
Work Experience in a Related Occupation	None
On-the-job Training	Long-term on-the-job training
Number of Jobs, 2019	24,300
Job Outlook, 2019-29	1% (Slower than average)
Employment Change, 2019-29	100

What Air Traffic Controllers Do

Air traffic controllers coordinate the movement of aircraft to maintain safe distances between them.

Work Environment

Air traffic controllers work in control towers, approach control facilities, or route centers. Their work can be stressful because maximum concentration is required at all times. Night, weekend, and rotating shifts are common.

How to Become an Air Traffic Controller

There are several paths to becoming an air traffic controller. Candidates typically need an associate's or a bachelor's degree from the Air Traffic Collegiate Training Initiative program. Other applicants must have 3 years of progressively responsible work experience, have completed 4 years of college, or have a combination of both. One must also be a U.S. citizen, submit to medical and background checks, and take exams and courses at the Federal Aviation Administration (FAA) academy.

Air traffic controllers coordinate the movement of air traffic.

Pay

The median annual wage for air traffic controllers was $122,990 in May 2019.

Job Outlook

Employment of air traffic controllers is projected to is projected to grow 1 percent from 2019 to 2029, slower than the average for all occupations. Competition for air traffic controller jobs is expected to be very strong, with many people applying for a relatively small number of jobs.

State & Area Data

Explore resources for employment and wages by state and area for air traffic controllers.

What Air Traffic Controllers Do

Air traffic controllers coordinate the movement of aircraft to maintain safe distances between them.

Duties

Air traffic controllers typically do the following:

- Monitor and direct the movement of aircraft on the ground and in the air
- Control all ground traffic at airport runways and taxiways
- Issue landing and takeoff instructions to pilots
- Transfer control of departing flights to other traffic control centers and accept control of arriving flights
- Inform pilots about weather, runway closures, and other critical information
- Alert airport response staff in the event of an aircraft emergency

Air traffic controllers' primary concern is safety, but they also must direct aircraft efficiently to minimize delays. They manage the flow of aircraft into and out of the airport airspace, guide pilots during takeoff and landing, and monitor aircraft as they travel through the skies. Air traffic controllers use radar, computers, or visual references to monitor and direct the movement of the aircraft in the skies and ground traffic at airports.

Controllers usually manage multiple aircraft at the same time and must make quick decisions to ensure the safety of aircraft. For example, a controller might direct one aircraft on its landing approach while providing another aircraft with weather information.

The following are examples of types of air traffic controllers:

Tower controllers direct the movement of vehicles, including aircraft, on runways and taxiways. They check flight plans, give pilots clearance for takeoff or landing, and direct the movement of aircraft and other traffic on the runways and in other parts of the airport. Most work from control towers, observing the traffic they control. Tower controllers manage traffic from the airport to a radius of 3 to 30 miles out.

Approach and departure controllers ensure that aircraft traveling within an airport's airspace maintain minimum separation for safety. They give clearances to enter controlled airspace and hand off control of aircraft to en route controllers. Approach and departure controllers use radar equipment to monitor flight paths and work in buildings known as Terminal Radar Approach Control Centers (TRACONs). They also inform pilots about weather conditions and other critical notices. Terminal approach controllers assist the aircraft until it reaches the edge of the facility's airspace, usually about 20 to 50 miles from the airport and up to about 17,000 feet in the air.

En route controllers monitor aircraft once they leave an airport's airspace. They work at air route traffic control centers located throughout the country, which typically are not located at airports. Each center is assigned an airspace based on the geography and air traffic in the area in which it is located. As an airplane approaches and flies through a center's airspace, en route controllers guide the airplane along its route. They may adjust the flight path of aircraft to avoid collisions and for safety in general. Route controllers direct the aircraft for the bulk of the flight before handing to terminal approach controllers.

Some air traffic controllers work at the Air Traffic Control Systems Command Center, where they monitor traffic within the entire national airspace. When they identify a bottleneck, they provide instructions to other controllers, helping to prevent traffic jams. Their objective is to keep traffic levels manageable for the airports and for en route controllers.

Work Environment

Air traffic controllers held about 24,300 jobs in 2019. The largest employers of air traffic controllers were as follows:

Federal government	92%
Support activities for air transportation	5
Professional, scientific, and technical services	0

Most controllers work for the Federal Aviation Administration (FAA).

Air traffic controllers authorize flight path changes.

Air traffic controllers often work in semidark rooms.

Air traffic controllers must be able to coordinate the actions of multiple flights.

Air traffic controllers work in control towers, approach control facilities, or en route centers. Many tower and approach/departure controllers work near large airports. En route controllers work in secure office buildings located across the country, which typically are not located at airports.

Approach and departure controllers often work in semidark rooms. The aircraft they control appear as points of light moving across their radar screens, and a well-lit room would make it difficult to see the screens properly.

Air traffic controllers must react quickly and efficiently while maintaining maximum concentration. The mental stress of being responsible for the safety of aircraft and their passengers can be tiring. As a result, controllers retire earlier than most workers. Those with 20 years of experience are eligible to retire at age 50, while those with 25 years of service may retire earlier than that. Controllers are required to retire at age 56.

Work Schedules

Most air traffic controllers work full time, and some work additional hours. The FAA regulates the hours that an air traffic controller may work. Controllers may not work more than 10 straight hours during a shift and must have 9 hours' rest before their next shift.

Controllers may rotate shifts among day, evening, and night, because major control facilities operate continuously. Controllers also work weekend and holiday shifts. Less busy airports may have towers that do not operate on a 24-hour basis. Controllers at these airports may have standard work schedules.

How to Become an Air Traffic Controller

There are several different paths to becoming an air traffic controller. A candidate must have either 3 years of progressively responsible work experience, a bachelor's degree, a combination of postsecondary education and work experience totaling three years, or obtain a degree through an Federal Aviation Administration (FAA)-approved Air Traffic Collegiate Training Initiative (AT-CTI) program.

Additionally, to become an air traffic controller, candidates must

- be a U.S. citizen;
- pass a medical evaluation, including drug screening, and background checks;
- pass the FAA preemployment test, which includes a biographical assessment;
- pass the Air Traffic Controller Specialists Skills Assessment Battery (ATSA); and
- complete a training course at the FAA Academy (and start it before turning 31 years of age).

The biographical assessment, also known as a biodata test, is a behavioral consistency exam that evaluates a candidate's personality fitness to become an air traffic controller. For more information, see the Office of Personnel Management (OPM) page on biodata tests. Applicants who pass both the ATSA and the biographical assessment are eligible to enroll in the FAA Academy.

Controllers also must pass a physical exam each year and a job performance exam twice per year. In addition, they must pass periodic drug screenings.

Some learn their skills and become air traffic controllers while in the military.

Education

Candidates who want to become air traffic controllers typically need an associate's or a bachelor's degree from an AT-CTI program. Other candidates must have 3 years of progressively responsible work experience, have completed 4 years of college, or have a combination of both.

The FAA sets guidelines for schools that offer the AT-CTI program. AT-CTI schools offer 2- or 4-year degrees that are designed to prepare students for a career in air traffic control. The curriculum is not standardized, but courses focus on subjects that are fundamental to aviation. Topics include aviation weather, airspace, clearances, reading charts, federal regulations, and related topics.

Training

Most newly hired air traffic controllers are trained at the FAA Academy, located in Oklahoma City, OK. The length of training varies with the applicant's background. Applicants must be hired by their 31st birthday.

After graduating from the Academy, trainees are assigned to an air traffic control facility as *developmental controllers*, until they complete all requirements for becoming a certified air traffic controller. Developmental controllers begin their careers by supplying pilots with basic flight data and airport information. They then advance to positions within the control room that have more responsibility.

As the developmental controllers master various duties, they earn increases in pay and advance in their training. Those with previous controller experience may take less time to become fully certified.

There are opportunities for a controller to switch from one position to another, provided that additional training is completed. For example, a controller may transfer from an en route position to an airport tower position with additional Academy training. Within both of these positions, controllers can transfer to jobs at different locations or advance to supervisory positions.

Work Experience in a Related Occupation

Applicants may need to have up to 3 years of progressively responsible generalized work experience in any occupation, or a combination of work experience and college education. More work experience is necessary to substitute for less postsecondary education.

Licenses, Certifications, and Registrations

All air traffic controllers must hold an Air Traffic Control Tower Operator Certificate or be appropriately qualified and supervised as stated in Title 14 of the Code of Federal Regulations, Part 65. They must be at least 18 years old, fluent in English, and comply with all knowledge and skill requirements.

Important Qualities

Communication skills. Air traffic controllers must be able to give clear, concise instructions, listen carefully to pilots' requests, and respond by speaking clearly in English.

Concentration skills. Controllers must be able to concentrate in a room where multiple conversations occur at once. For example, in a large airport tower, several controllers may be speaking with several pilots at the same time.

Decisionmaking skills. Controllers must make quick decisions. For example, when a pilot requests a change of altitude to avoid poor weather, the controller must respond quickly so that the plane can operate safely.

Math skills. Controllers must be able to do arithmetic accurately and quickly. They often need to compute speeds, times, and distances, and they recommend heading and altitude changes.

Organizational skills. Controllers must be able to coordinate the actions of multiple flights. Controllers need to be able to prioritize tasks, because they may be required to guide several pilots at the same time.

Problem-solving skills. Controllers must be able to understand complex situations, such as the impact of changing weather patterns on a plane's flight path. Controllers must be able to review important information and provide pilots with appropriate solutions.

Pay

The median annual wage for air traffic controllers was $122,990 in May 2019. The median wage is the wage at which half the workers in an occupation earned more than that amount and half earned less. The lowest 10 percent earned less than $68,330, and the highest 10 percent earned more than $176,320.

In May 2019, the median annual wages for air traffic controllers in the top industries in which they worked were as follows:

Federal government.. $127,810

Professional, scientific, and technical services...   102,520

Support activities for air transportation...............   78,500

The salaries for development controllers increase as they complete successive levels of training. According to the Federal Aviation Administration (FAA), the salaries for more advanced controllers who have completed on-the-job training varies with the location of the facility, the complexity of the flight paths, and other factors. A full explanation of the pay ranges for air traffic controllers can be found on the FAA Aviation Careers Page.

Most air traffic controllers work full time, and some work additional hours. The FAA regulates the hours that an air traffic

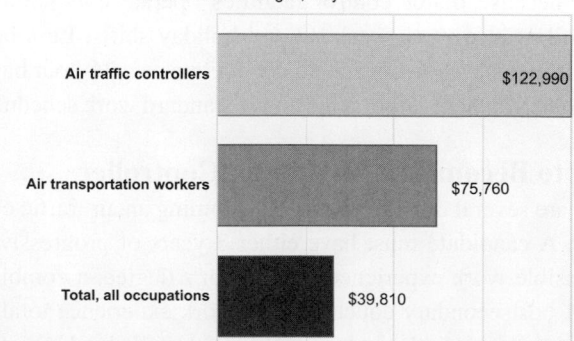

Air Traffic Controllers
Median annual wages, May 2019

Air traffic controllers	$122,990
Air transportation workers	$75,760
Total, all occupations	$39,810

Note: All Occupations includes all occupations in the U.S. Economy.
Source: U.S. Bureau of Labor Statistics, Occupational Employment Statistics.

Air Traffic Controllers

Percent change in employment, projected 2019-29

Air transportation workers   10%

Total, all occupations   4%

Air traffic controllers   1%

Note: All Occupations includes all occupations in the U.S. Economy.
Source: U.S. Bureau of Labor Statistics, Employment Projections program.

controller may work. Controllers may not work more than 10 straight hours during a shift and must have 9 hours' rest before their next shift.

Controllers may rotate shifts among day, evening, and night, because major control facilities operate continuously. Controllers also work weekend and holiday shifts. Less busy airports may have towers that do not operate on a 24-hour basis. Controllers at these airports may have more normal work schedules.

Job Outlook

Employment of air traffic controllers is projected to is projected to grow 1 percent from 2019 to 2029, slower than the average for all occupations.

Although air traffic is projected to increase in the next decade, the satellite-based Next Generation Air Transportation System (NextGen) is expected to allow individual controllers to handle more air traffic. As a result, the demand for additional air traffic controllers should be limited over the next 10 years.

Job Prospects

Competition for air traffic controller jobs is expected to be very strong, with many people applying for a relatively small number of jobs. Those with military experience as an air traffic controller may have an advantage.

Most employment opportunities will result from the need to replace workers who are expected to retire or leave the occupation.

Employment projections data for air traffic controllers, 2019-29					
Occupational Title	SOC Code	Employment, 2019	Projected Employment, 2029	Change, 2019-29	
				Percent	Numeric
SOURCE: U.S. Bureau of Labor Statistics, Employment Projections program					
Air traffic controllers	53-2021	24,300	24,500	1	100

State & Area Data
Occupational Employment Statistics (OES)

The Occupational Employment Statistics (OES) program produces employment and wage estimates annually for over 800 occupations. These estimates are available for the nation as a whole, for individual states, and for metropolitan and nonmetropolitan areas.

Contacts for More Information

For more information about air traffic controllers, visit
➤ Federal Aviation Administration
➤ National Air Traffic Controllers Association
➤ For more information about biodata tests, visit
➤ U.S. Office of Personnel Management

Delivery Truck Drivers and Driver/Sales Workers

Summary

Quick Facts: Delivery Truck Drivers and Driver/Sales Workers

2019 Median Pay	$32,020 per year $15.39 per hour
Typical Entry-Level Education	High school diploma or equivalent
Work Experience in a Related Occupation	None
On-the-job Training	Short-term on-the-job training
Number of Jobs, 2019	1,506,000
Job Outlook, 2019-29	5% (Faster than average)
Employment Change, 2019-29	75,000

What Delivery Truck Drivers and Driver/Sales Workers Do

Delivery truck drivers and driver/sales workers pick up, transport, and drop off packages and small shipments within a local region or urban area.

Work Environment

Delivery truck drivers and driver/sales workers have a physically demanding job. Driving a truck for long periods can be tiring. When loading and unloading cargo, drivers do a lot of lifting, carrying, and walking.

How to Become a Delivery Truck Driver or Driver/Sales Worker

Delivery truck drivers and driver/sales workers typically enter their occupations with a high school diploma or equivalent. However, some opportunities exist for those without a high

Delivery drivers and driver/sales workers transport goods around an urban area or small region.

school diploma. Workers undergo 1 month or less of on-the-job training. They must have a driver's license from the state in which they work and have a clean driving record.

Pay

The median annual wage for driver/sales workers was $25,860 in May 2019.

The median annual wage for light truck drivers was $34,730 in May 2019.

Job Outlook

Overall employment of delivery truck drivers and driver/sales workers is projected to grow 5 percent from 2019 to 2029, faster than the average for all occupations.

State & Area Data

Explore resources for employment and wages by state and area for delivery truck drivers and driver/sales workers.

What Delivery Truck Drivers and Driver/Sales Workers Do

Delivery truck drivers and driver/sales workers pick up, transport, and drop off packages and small shipments within a local region or urban area. They drive trucks having a total weight of 26,000 pounds or less for vehicle, passengers, and cargo. Delivery truck drivers usually transport merchandise from a distribution center to businesses and households.

Duties

Delivery truck drivers and driver/sales workers typically do the following:

* Load and unload their cargo
* Communicate with customers to determine pickup and delivery needs

Delivery drivers drop packages off with customers.

* Report any incidents they encounter on the road to a dispatcher
* Follow all applicable traffic laws
* Report serious mechanical problems to the appropriate personnel
* Keep their truck and associated equipment clean and in good working order
* Accept payments for the shipment
* Handle paperwork, such as receipts or delivery confirmation notices

Most drivers generally receive instructions to go to a delivery location at a particular time, and it is up to them to determine the best route. Other drivers have a regular daily or weekly delivery schedule. All drivers must understand an area's street grid and know which roads allow trucks and which do not.

The following examples are types of delivery truck drivers and driver/sales workers:

Driver/sales workers are delivery drivers who also have sales responsibilities. They recommend new products to businesses and solicit new customers. These drivers may have a regular delivery route and be responsible for adding new clients located along their route. For example, they may make regular deliveries to a hardware store and encourage the store's manager to offer a new product.

Some driver/sales workers use their own vehicles to deliver goods to customers, such as takeout food, and accept payment for those goods. Freelance or independent driver/sales workers may use smartphone apps to find specific delivery jobs.

Light truck drivers, often called *pickup and delivery* or *P&D drivers,* are the most common type of delivery driver. They drive small trucks or vans from distribution centers to delivery locations. Drivers make deliveries based on a set schedule. Some drivers stop at the distribution center once only, in the morning, and make many stops throughout the day. Others make multiple trips between the distribution center and delivery locations. Some drivers make deliveries from a retail location to customers.

Work Environment

Driver/sales workers held about 487,400 jobs in 2019. The largest employers of driver/sales workers were as follows:

Restaurants and other eating places	46%
Wholesale trade	22
Retail trade	9
Self-employed workers	8

Light truck drivers held about 1.0 million jobs in 2019. The largest employers of light truck drivers were as follows:

Couriers and messengers	24%
Retail trade	21
Wholesale trade	17
Self-employed workers	8

Delivery truck drivers and driver/sales workers have physically demanding jobs. When loading and unloading cargo, drivers do a lot of lifting, carrying, and walking. Driving in congested traffic or adhering to strict delivery timelines can also be stressful.

Injuries and Illnesses

Light truck or delivery services drivers have one of the highest rates of injuries and illnesses of all occupations. Injuries can result from workers lifting and moving heavy objects, as well as from automobile accidents.

Work Schedules

Most drivers work full time, and many work additional hours. Those who have regular routes sometimes must begin work very early in the morning or work late at night. For example, a driver who delivers bread to a deli every day must arrive before the deli opens. Drivers often work weekends and holidays.

How to Become a Delivery Truck Driver or Driver/Sales Worker

Delivery truck drivers and driver/sales workers typically enter their occupations with a high school diploma or equivalent. However, some opportunities exist for those without a high school diploma. Workers undergo 1 month or less of on-the-job training. They must have a driver's license from the state in which they work and have a clean driving record.

Education

Delivery truck drivers and driver/sales workers typically enter the occupation with a high school diploma or equivalent.

Training

Companies train new delivery truck drivers and driver/sales workers on the job. This may include training from a driver-mentor who rides along with a new employee to make sure that a new driver is able to operate a truck safely on crowded streets.

New drivers also get training to learn company policies about package dropoffs and returns, taking payment, and what to do with damaged goods.

Driver/sales workers must learn detailed information about the products they offer. Their company also may teach them proper sales techniques, such as how to approach new customers.

Licenses, Certifications, and Registrations

All delivery drivers need a driver's license.

Other Experience

Some delivery drivers begin as package loaders at warehouse facilities, especially if the driver works for a large company. For more information, see the profile on hand laborers and material movers.

Delivery truck drivers load and unload packages.

Drivers need to maintain a clean driving record and be able to navigate city streets.

Important Qualities

Customer-service skills. When completing deliveries, drivers often interact with customers and should make a good impression to ensure repeat business.

Hand–eye coordination. Drivers need to observe their surroundings at all times while operating a vehicle.

Math skills. Because delivery truck drivers and driver/sales workers sometimes take payment, they must be able to count cash and make change quickly and accurately.

Patience. When driving through heavy traffic congestion, delivery drivers must remain calm and composed.

Sales skills. Driver/sales workers are expected to persuade customers to purchase new or different products.

Visual ability. To have a driver's license, delivery truck drivers and driver/sales workers must be able to pass a state vision test.

Pay

The median annual wage for driver/sales workers was $25,860 in May 2019. The median wage is the wage at which half the workers in an occupation earned more than that amount and half earned less. The lowest 10 percent earned less than $18,060, and the highest 10 percent earned more than $48,970.

The median annual wage for light truck drivers was $34,730 in May 2019. The lowest 10 percent earned less than $21,060, and the highest 10 percent earned more than $65,400.

In May 2019, the median annual wages for driver/sales workers in the top industries in which they worked were as follows:

Wholesale trade	$35,640
Retail trade	29,220
Restaurants and other eating places	22,100

In May 2019, the median annual wages for light truck drivers in the top industries in which they worked were as follows:

Couriers and messengers	$49,220
Wholesale trade	33,470
Retail trade	26,340

Some drivers/sales workers, such as pizza delivery workers, receive tips in addition to hourly wages. Sales workers can also receive commissions from the products they sell.

Most drivers work full time, and many work additional hours. Those who have regular routes sometimes must begin work very early in the morning or work late at night. For example, a driver who delivers bread to a deli every day must arrive before the deli opens. Drivers often work weekends and holidays.

Job Outlook

Overall employment of delivery truck drivers and driver/sales workers is projected to grow 5 percent from 2019 to 2029, faster than the average for all occupations. Employment growth will vary by occupation.

Continued growth of e-commerce should increase demand for package delivery services, especially for the large and regional shipping companies. More light truck and delivery drivers will be needed to fulfill the growing number of e-commerce transactions.

Self-employed or independent contractors, who sign up with smartphone-based food delivery companies, may be needed to deliver food from grocery stores and from restaurants that previously provided only takeout services. In addition, robotic driverless vehicles may replace some workers in food delivery.

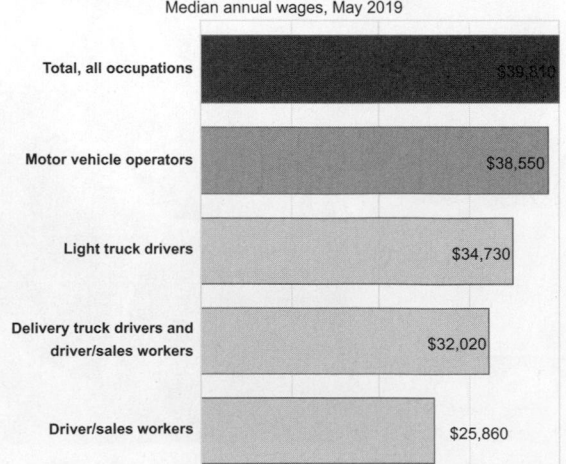

Delivery Truck Drivers and Driver/Sales Workers

Median annual wages, May 2019

Total, all occupations	$39,810
Motor vehicle operators	$38,550
Light truck drivers	$34,730
Delivery truck drivers and driver/sales workers	$32,020
Driver/sales workers	$25,860

Note: All Occupations includes all occupations in the U.S. Economy.
Source: U.S. Bureau of Labor Statistics, Occupational Employment Statistics.

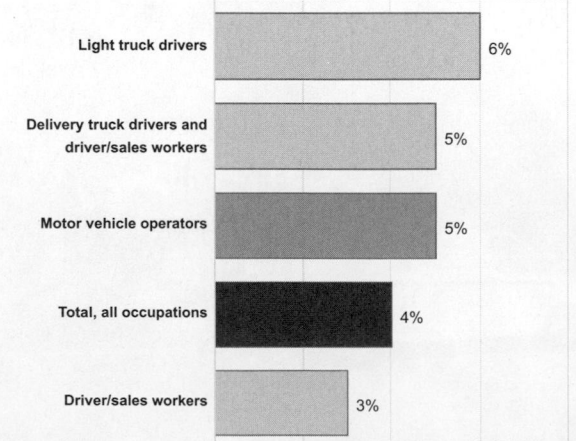

Delivery Truck Drivers and Driver/Sales Workers

Percent change in employment, projected 2019-29

Light truck drivers	6%
Delivery truck drivers and driver/sales workers	5%
Motor vehicle operators	5%
Total, all occupations	4%
Driver/sales workers	3%

Note: All Occupations includes all occupations in the U.S. Economy.
Source: U.S. Bureau of Labor Statistics, Employment Projections program.

Job Prospects

Job opportunities for delivery truck drivers and drivers/sales workers are expected to be good. Job applicants with experience and a clean driving record, or who work for a company in another occupation, should have the best job prospects.

Employment projections data for delivery truck drivers and driver/sales workers, 2019-29					
Occupational Title	SOC Code	Employment, 2019	Projected Employment, 2029	Change, 2019-29	
				Percent	Numeric
SOURCE: U.S. Bureau of Labor Statistics, Employment Projections program					
Delivery truck drivers and driver/sales workers	—	1,506,000	1,581,000	5	75,000
Driver/sales workers	53-3031	487,400	501,900	3	14,500
Light truck drivers	53-3033	1,018,600	1,079,100	6	60,500

State & Area Data
Occupational Employment Statistics (OES)

The Occupational Employment Statistics (OES) program produces employment and wage estimates annually for over 800 occupations. These estimates are available for the nation as a whole, for individual states, and for metropolitan and nonmetropolitan areas.

Contacts for More Information

For more information about truck drivers, including delivery truck drivers and driver/sales workers, visit

➤ American Trucking Associations

Flight Attendants

Summary

Quick Facts: Flight Attendants

2019 Median Pay	$56,640 per year
Typical Entry-Level Education	High school diploma or equivalent
Work Experience in a Related Occupation....	Less than 5 years
On-the-job Training	Moderate-term on-the-job training
Number of Jobs, 2019	121,900
Job Outlook, 2019-29................................	17% (Much faster than average)
Employment Change, 2019-29	21,100

What Flight Attendants Do

Flight attendants provide routine services and respond to emergencies to ensure the safety and comfort of airline passengers.

Work Environment

Flight attendants have variable work schedules, including evenings, weekends, and holidays, because airlines operate every day and some offer overnight flights. Attendants work in an aircraft and may be away from home several nights per week.

How to Become a Flight Attendant

Flight attendants typically receive on-the-job training from their employer and must be certified by the Federal Aviation Administration (FAA).

Pay

The median annual wage for flight attendants was $56,640 in May 2019.

Job Outlook

Employment of flight attendants is projected to grow 17 percent from 2019 to 2029, much faster than the average for all occupations. As airlines continue to replace smaller aircraft with new, larger planes that can accommodate a greater number of passengers, they will require more flight attendants on some routes to attend to passengers.

State & Area Data

Explore resources for employment and wages by state and area for flight attendants.

What Flight Attendants Do

Flight attendants provide routine services and respond to emergencies to ensure the safety and comfort of airline passengers.

Flight attendants provide routine services and respond to emergencies to ensure the safety and comfort of airline passengers.

Flight attendants demonstrate the use of safety equipment and emergency equipment.

Duties

Flight attendants typically do the following:

- Participate in preflight briefings with the pilots, to discuss cabin conditions and flight details
- Conduct preflight inspections of emergency equipment
- Demonstrate the use of safety equipment and emergency equipment
- Ensure that passengers have their seatbelts fastened when required and that all other safety requirements are observed
- Serve and sell beverages, meals, or snacks
- Take care of passengers' needs, particularly those with special needs
- Reassure passengers during the flight, such as when the aircraft hits turbulence
- Administer and coordinate emergency medical care, as needed
- Provide direction to passengers, including how to evacuate the aircraft in an emergency

Airlines are required by law to provide flight attendants for the safety and security of passengers. The primary job of flight attendants is to keep passengers safe, ensuring that everyone follows security regulations and that the flight deck is secure. Flight attendants also try to make flights comfortable and stress free for passengers. At times, they may deal with passengers who display disruptive behavior.

About 1 hour before takeoff, the captain (pilot) may conduct a preflight briefing with flight attendants about relevant flight information, including the number of hours the flight will take, the route the plane will travel, and weather conditions. Flight attendants check that emergency equipment is working, the cabin is clean, and there is an adequate supply of food and beverages on board. Flight attendants greet passengers as they board the aircraft, direct them to their seats, and provide assistance as needed.

Flight attendants demonstrate the proper use of safety equipment to all passengers, either in person or through a video recording before the plane takes off. They also check that seatbelts are fastened, seats are locked in the upright position, and all carry-on items are properly stowed in accordance with federal law and company policy.

A flight attendant's most important responsibility, however, is to help passengers in the event of an emergency. This responsibility ranges from dealing with unruly passengers to performing first aid, fighting fires, protecting the flight deck, and directing evacuations. Flight attendants also answer questions about the flight, attend to passengers with special needs, and generally assist all passengers as needed.

Before the plane lands, flight attendants once again ensure that seatbelts are fastened, seats are locked in the upright position, and all carry-on and galley items are properly stowed.

Before they leave the plane, flight attendants survey the condition of the cabin. They submit reports on any medical, safety, or security issues that may have occurred during the flight.

Work Environment

Flight attendants held about 121,900 jobs in 2019. The largest employers of flight attendants were as follows:

Scheduled air transportation 97%

Flight attendants make sure all overhead luggage is properly stored.

Flight attendants work primarily in the cabin of passenger aircraft. Dealing directly with passengers and standing for long periods can be stressful and tiring. Occasionally, flights encounter air turbulence, which can make providing service more difficult and causes anxiety in some passengers. Handling emergencies and unruly customers also can be difficult and cause stress.

Flight attendants spend many nights away from home and often sleep in hotels or apartments shared by a group of flight attendants.

Injuries and Illnesses

Flight attendants have one of the highest rates of injuries and illnesses of all occupations. To avoid injuries, these workers must follow safety procedures. For example, they must ensure that overhead compartments are closed, especially during turbulence, so that carry-on items don't fall and present a risk to all in the cabin. Attendants also ensure that carts are properly stowed and latched during aircraft emergencies to avoid injuries to passengers and themselves.

Work Schedules

Flight attendants usually have variable schedules. They often work nights, weekends, and holidays because airlines operate every day and have overnight flights. In most cases, a contract between the airline and the flight attendant union determines the total daily and monthly workable hours. A typical on-duty shift is about 12 to 14 hours per day. However, duty time can be increased for international flights. The Federal Aviation Administration (FAA) requires that flight attendants receive at least 9 consecutive hours of rest following any duty period before starting their next duty period.

Attendants usually fly 75 to 100 hours a month and generally spend another 50 hours a month on the ground, preparing flights, writing reports, and waiting for aircraft to arrive. They can spend several nights a week away from home. During this time, employers typically arrange hotel accommodations and a meal allowance. Some flight attendants work part time.

An attendant's assignments of home base and route are based on seniority. New flight attendants must be flexible with their schedule and location. Almost all flight attendants start out working on call, also known as reserve status. Flight attendants on reserve usually live near their home airport, because they may have to report to work on short notice.

As they earn more seniority, attendants may have more control over their schedules. For example, some senior flight attendants may choose to live outside their home base and commute to work. Others may choose to work only on regional flights. On small corporate airlines, flight attendants may work on an as-needed basis.

How to Become a Flight Attendant

Flight attendants receive training from their employer and must be certified by the Federal Aviation Administration (FAA). Flight attendants need a high school diploma or the equivalent and work experience in customer service.

Applicants must be at least 18 years old, be eligible to work in the United States, have a valid passport, and pass a background check and drug test. They must have vision that is correctable to at least 20/40 and often need to conform to height requirements set by the airline. Flight attendants also may have to pass a medical evaluation.

Flight attendants should present a professional appearance and not have visible tattoos, body piercings, or an unusual hairstyle or makeup.

Education

A high school diploma is typically required to become a flight attendant. Some airlines may prefer to hire applicants who have taken some college courses.

Those who work on international flights may have to be fluent in a foreign language. Some enroll in flight attendant academies.

Work Experience in a Related Occupation

Flight attendants typically need 1 or 2 years of work experience in a service occupation before getting their first job as a flight attendant. This experience may include customer service positions in restaurants, hotels, or resorts. Experience in sales or in other positions that require close contact with the public and focus on service to customers also may help develop the skills needed to be a successful flight attendant.

Training

Once a flight attendant is hired, airlines provide their initial training, ranging from 3 to 6 weeks. The training usually takes place at the airline's flight training center and is required for FAA certification.

Flight attendants take care of passenger needs.

Trainees learn emergency procedures such as evacuating aircraft, operating emergency equipment, and administering first aid. They also receive specific instruction on flight regulations, company operations, and job duties.

Toward the end of the training, students go on practice flights. They must complete the training to keep a job with the airline. Once they have passed initial training, new flight attendants receive the FAA Certificate of Demonstrated Proficiency and continue to receive additional on the job training as required by their employer.

Licenses, Certifications, and Registrations

All flight attendants must be certified by the FAA. To become certified, flight attendants must complete their employer's initial training program and pass an exam. Flight attendants are certified for specific types of aircraft and must take new training for each type of aircraft on which they are to work. In addition, attendants receive recurrent training every year to maintain their certification.

Advancement

Career advancement is based on seniority. On international flights, senior attendants frequently oversee the work of other attendants. Senior attendants may be promoted to management positions in which they are responsible for recruiting, instructing, and scheduling.

Important Qualities

Attentiveness. Flight attendants must be aware of any security or safety risks during the flight. They also must be attentive to passengers' needs in order to ensure a pleasant travel experience.

Communication skills. Flight attendants should speak clearly, listen attentively, and interact effectively with passengers and other crewmembers.

Customer-service skills. Flight attendants should have poise, tact, and resourcefulness to handle stressful situations and address passengers' needs.

Decisionmaking skills. Flight attendants must be able to act decisively in emergencies.

Physical stamina. Flight attendants push, pull, and carry service items, open and close overhead buns, and stand and walk for long periods.

Pay

The median annual wage for flight attendants was $56,640 in May 2019. The median wage is the wage at which half the workers in an occupation earned more than that amount and half earned less. The lowest 10 percent earned less than $29,270, and the highest 10 percent earned more than $80,940.

In May 2019, the median annual wages for flight attendants in the top industries in which they worked were as follows:

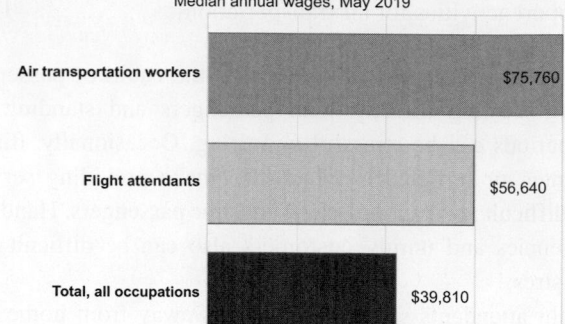

Flight Attendants
Median annual wages, May 2019

Air transportation workers — $75,760
Flight attendants — $56,640
Total, all occupations — $39,810

Note: All Occupations includes all occupations in the U.S. Economy. Source: U.S. Bureau of Labor Statistics, Occupational Employment Statistics.

Scheduled air transportation	$56,830
Nonscheduled air transportation	53,870
Support activities for air transportation	45,200

Flight attendants receive an allowance for meals and accommodations while working away from home. Although attendants are required to purchase an initial set of uniforms and luggage, the airlines usually pay for replacements and upkeep. Flight attendants generally are eligible for discounted airfare or free standby seats through their airline.

Attendants typically fly 75 to 100 hours a month and usually spend another 50 hours a month on the ground, preparing flights, writing reports, and waiting for planes to arrive. They can spend several nights a week away from home. Most work variable schedules. Some flight attendants work part time.

Job Outlook

Employment of flight attendants is projected to grow 17 percent from 2019 to 2029, much faster than the average for all occupations.

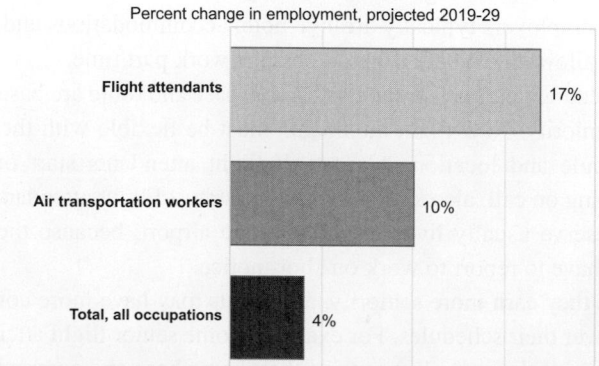

Flight Attendants
Percent change in employment, projected 2019-29

Flight attendants — 17%
Air transportation workers — 10%
Total, all occupations — 4%

Note: All Occupations includes all occupations in the U.S. Economy. Source: U.S. Bureau of Labor Statistics, Employment Projections program.

Many airlines are replacing smaller aircraft with new, larger planes that can accommodate a greater number of passengers. As a result, this change may increase the number of flight attendants needed on some routes.

Job Prospects

Competition for jobs will remain strong because the occupation typically attracts many more applicants than there are job openings. Job prospects should be best for applicants with a college degree.

Many job opportunities will come from the need to replace flight attendants who leave the workforce.

Employment projections data for flight attendants, 2019-29					
Occupational Title	SOC Code	Employment, 2019	Projected Employment, 2029	Change, 2019-29	
				Percent	Numeric
SOURCE: U.S. Bureau of Labor Statistics, Employment Projections program					
Flight attendants	53-2031	121,900	143,000	17	21,100

State & Area Data
Occupational Employment Statistics (OES)

The Occupational Employment Statistics (OES) program produces employment and wage estimates annually for over 800 occupations. These estimates are available for the nation as a whole, for individual states, and for metropolitan and nonmetropolitan areas.

Contacts for More Information

For more information about flight attendants, visit the career webpage of any airline company, contact its personnel department, or visit

➤ Association of Flight Attendants—CWA
➤ Association of Professional Flight Attendants
➤ Federal Aviation Administration

Hand Laborers and Material Movers

Summary

Quick Facts: Hand Laborers and Material Movers

2019 Median Pay	$28,710 per year $13.80 per hour
Typical Entry-Level Education	No formal educational credential
Work Experience in a Related Occupation	None
On-the-job Training	Short-term on-the-job training
Number of Jobs, 2019	4,231,600
Job Outlook, 2019-29	3% (As fast as average)
Employment Change, 2019-29	121,300

What Hand Laborers and Material Movers Do

Hand laborers and material movers manually move freight, stock, or other materials.

Work Environment

Most hand laborers and material movers work full time. Because materials are shipped around the clock, some workers, especially those in warehousing, work overnight shifts.

How to Become a Hand Laborer or Material Mover

There are usually no formal educational requirements for anyone to become a hand laborer or material mover. Employers typically require only that applicants be physically able to perform the work.

Pay

The median annual wage for hand laborers and material movers was $28,710 in May 2019.

Job Outlook

Overall employment of hand laborers and material movers is projected to grow 3 percent from 2019 to 2029, about as fast as the average for all occupations. Job prospects should be good because of the need to replace workers who leave these occupations.

State & Area Data

Explore resources for employment and wages by state and area for hand laborers and material movers.

Many hand laborers pack and transfer materials around a warehouse.

What Hand Laborers and Material Movers Do

Hand laborers and material movers manually move freight, stock, or other materials. Some of these workers feed or remove material to or from machines, clean vehicles, pick up unwanted household goods, and pack materials for moving.

Duties

Hand laborers and material movers typically do the following:

- Manually move material from one place to another
- Pack or wrap products by hand
- Keep a record of the material they move
- Signal machine operators to help move material
- Clean cars, equipment, and workplaces

In warehouses and in wholesale and retail operations, hand laborers and material movers work closely with material moving machine operators and material recording clerks. Some workers are employed in manufacturing industries, loading material onto conveyor belts or other machines.

The following are examples of types of hand laborers and material movers:

Cleaners of vehicles and equipment wash automobiles and other vehicles, as well as storage tanks, pipelines, and related machinery. They use cleaning products, vacuums, hoses, and brushes. Most of these workers clean cars at a carwash, an automobile dealership, or a rental agency. Some clean industrial equipment at manufacturing firms. Some—for example, those who work at a carwash, also known as carwash attendants—interact with customers.

Hand laborers and freight, stock, and material movers move materials to and from storage and production areas, loading docks, delivery trucks, ships, and containers. Although their specific duties may vary, most of these movers, often called *pickers*, work in warehouses. Some workers retrieve products from storage and move them to loading areas. Other workers load and unload cargo from a truck. When moving a package, pickers keep track of the package number, sometimes with a

hand-held scanner, to ensure proper delivery. Sometimes they open containers and sort the material.

Hand packers and packagers package a variety of materials by hand. They may label cartons, inspect items for defects, and keep records of items packed. Some of these workers pack materials for shipment and move them to a loading dock. Hand packers in grocery stores, also known as grocery baggers, bag groceries for customers at checkout.

Machine feeders and offbearers process materials by feeding them into equipment or by removing them from equipment. The equipment is generally operated by other workers, such as material moving machine operators. Machine feeders and offbearers help the operator if the machine becomes jammed or needs minor repairs. Machine feeders also track the amount of material they process during a shift.

Refuse and recyclable material collectors gather garbage and recyclables from homes and businesses to transport to a dump, landfill, or recycling center. Many collectors lift garbage cans by hand and empty them into their truck. Some collectors drive the garbage or recycling truck along a scheduled route and may use a hydraulic lift to empty the contents of a dumpster into the truck.

Work Environment

Hand laborers and material movers held about 4.2 million jobs in 2019. Employment in the detailed occupations that make up hand laborers and material movers was distributed as follows:

Laborers and freight, stock, and material movers, hand	2,986,000
Packers and packagers, hand	640,800
Cleaners of vehicles and equipment	408,400
Refuse and recyclable material collectors	133,600
Machine feeders and offbearers	62,900

The largest employers of hand laborers and material movers were as follows:

Transportation and warehousing	23%
Administrative and support and waste management and remediation services	22
Manufacturing	14
Wholesale trade	13

Hand laborers and material movers lift and carry heavy objects, and their work is usually repetitive and physically demanding. They bend, kneel, crouch, or crawl in awkward positions.

Injuries and Illnesses

Hand laborers and freight, stock, and material movers and refuse and recyclable material collectors have some of the highest rates of injuries and illnesses of all occupations. Moving

Some vehicle and equipment cleaners wash cars.

Refuse and recyclable material collectors lift heavy garbage containers.

Hand laborers and material movers learn on the job.

heavy objects around warehouses or onto trucks, or bending while cleaning a vehicle, may lead to sprains, strains, or overexertion.

Work Schedules

Most hand laborers and freight, stock, and material movers work full time.

Shifts longer than 8 hours are common, and sometimes overtime is available. Because materials are shipped around the clock, some workers, especially those in warehousing, work overnight shifts.

How to Become a Hand Laborer or Material Mover

There are usually no formal educational requirements for anyone to become a hand laborer or material mover. Employers typically require only that applicants be physically able to perform the work.

Education

There are no formal educational requirements for anyone to become a hand laborer or material mover.

Training

Most positions for hand laborers and material movers require less than 1 month of on-the-job training. Some workers need only a few days of training, and most training is done by a supervisor or a more experienced worker who decides when trainees are ready to work on their own.

Workers learn safety rules as part of their training. Many of these rules are standardized through the Occupational Safety and Health Administration (OSHA).

Licenses, Certifications, and Registrations

Refuse and recyclable material collectors who drive trucks that exceed a certain capacity—such as vehicles with the combined weight of the vehicle, passengers, and cargo exceeding 26,000 pounds—must have a commercial driver's license (CDL). Obtaining a CDL requires passing written, skill, and vision tests.

Important Qualities

Customer-service skills. Hand laborers and material movers who work with the public, such as grocery baggers or carwash attendants, must be pleasant and courteous to customers.

Hand–eye coordination. Most hand laborers and material movers use their arms and hands to manipulate objects or move objects into specific positions.

Listening skills. Hand laborers and material movers follow instructions that a supervisor gives them.

Physical stamina. Hand laborers and material movers need the endurance to perform strenuous tasks, such as moving or cleaning objects, throughout the day.

Physical strength. Some hand laborers and material movers must be able to lift and carry heavy objects.

Pay

The median annual wage for hand laborers and material movers was $28,710 in May 2019. The median wage is the wage at which half the workers in an occupation earned more than that amount and half earned less. The lowest 10 percent earned less than $20,800, and the highest 10 percent earned more than $46,050.

Median annual wages for hand laborers and material movers in May 2019 were as follows:

Refuse and recyclable material collectors	$37,840
Machine feeders and offbearers	31,180
Laborers and freight, stock, and material movers, hand	29,510
Packers and packagers, hand	25,910
Cleaners of vehicles and equipment	25,800

In May 2019, the median annual wages for hand laborers and material movers in the top industries in which they worked were as follows:

Wholesale trade	$31,060
Manufacturing	30,610
Transportation and warehousing	30,300
Administrative and support and waste management and remediation services	26,480

Some hand laborers and material movers, such as grocery baggers or carwash attendants, may receive tips.

Most hand laborers and freight, stock, and material movers work full time.

Shifts longer than 8 hours are common, and sometimes overtime is available. Because materials are shipped around the clock, some workers, especially those in warehousing, work overnight shifts.

Job Outlook

Overall employment of hand laborers and material movers is projected to grow 3 percent from 2019 to 2029, about as fast as the average for all occupations. Projected employment change will vary by occupation (see table below).

Some warehouses are installing equipment, such as high-speed conveyors and sorting systems, to increase efficiency. However, laborers and freight, stock, and material movers, hand, will still be needed to move materials in nearly all sectors of the economy.

Grocery stores, which employ many hand packers and packagers, may employ fewer baggers as a growing number of stores have self-checkout stands at which customers or existing cashiers bag groceries themselves. Automation is becoming more viable in warehouses and, if it expands, will reduce the need for workers there.

As the population grows, the amount of trash generated also is expected to increase; consequently, refuse and recyclable material collectors will be needed to remove trash.

Demand for automotive repair and maintenance services, as well as a growing automobile dealers industry, is expected to contribute to employment growth of cleaners of vehicles and equipment.

Many machine feeders and offbearers are employed in manufacturing industries, in which functions are being automated, so employment is expected to remain unchanged.

Job Prospects

Job prospects for hand laborers and material movers are expected to be good. The need to replace workers who leave these occupations should create a large number of job openings.

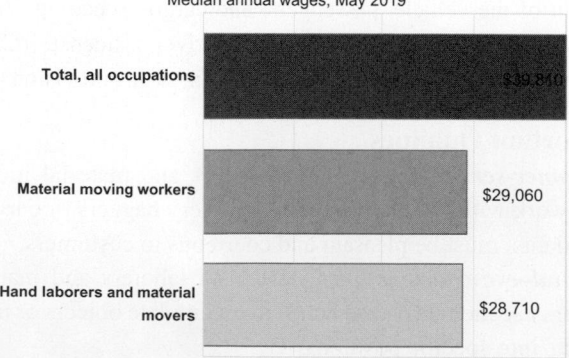

Hand Laborers and Material Movers
Median annual wages, May 2019

Total, all occupations — $39,810
Material moving workers — $29,060
Hand laborers and material movers — $28,710

Note: All Occupations includes all occupations in the U.S. Economy.
Source: U.S. Bureau of Labor Statistics, Occupational Employment Statistics.

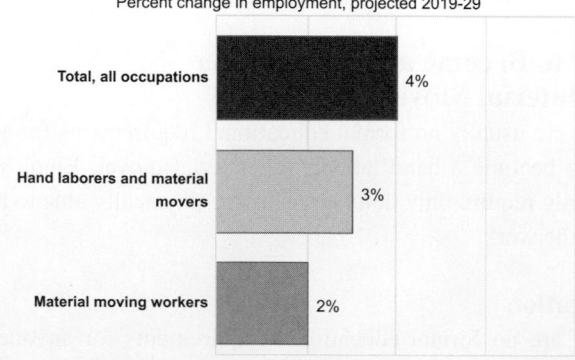

Hand Laborers and Material Movers
Percent change in employment, projected 2019-29

Total, all occupations — 4%
Hand laborers and material movers — 3%
Material moving workers — 2%

Note: All Occupations includes all occupations in the U.S. Economy.
Source: U.S. Bureau of Labor Statistics, Employment Projections program.

Employment projections data for hand laborers and material movers, 2019-29					
Occupational Title	SOC Code	Employment, 2019	Projected Employment, 2029	Change, 2019-29	
				Percent	Numeric
SOURCE: U.S. Bureau of Labor Statistics, Employment Projections program					
Hand laborers and material movers	—	4,231,600	4,353,000	3	121,300
Cleaners of vehicles and equipment	53-7061	408,400	423,100	4	14,700
Laborers and freight, stock, and material movers, hand	53-7062	2,986,000	3,111,700	4	125,700
Machine feeders and offbearers	53-7063	62,900	63,000	0	100
Packers and packagers, hand	53-7064	640,800	609,900	-5	-30,900
Refuse and recyclable material collectors	53-7081	133,600	145,400	9	11,700

State & Area Data
Occupational Employment Statistics (OES)

The Occupational Employment Statistics (OES) program produces employment and wage estimates annually for over 800 occupations. These estimates are available for the nation as a whole, for individual states, and for metropolitan and nonmetropolitan areas.

Contacts for More Information

For more information about hand laborers and material movers, visit
➤ MHI
➤ Warehousing Education and Research Council

Heavy and Tractor-trailer Truck Drivers

Summary

Quick Facts: Heavy and Tractor-trailer Truck Drivers

2019 Median Pay	$45,260 per year $21.76 per hour
Typical Entry-Level Education	Postsecondary non-degree award
Work Experience in a Related Occupation	None
On-the-job Training	Short-term on-the-job training
Number of Jobs, 2019	2,029,900
Job Outlook, 2019-29	2% (Slower than average)
Employment Change, 2019-29	30,600

What Heavy and Tractor-trailer Truck Drivers Do

Heavy and tractor-trailer truck drivers transport goods from one location to another.

Work Environment

Working as a long-haul truck driver is a lifestyle choice because these drivers can be away from home for days or weeks at a time.

How to Become a Heavy or Tractor-trailer Truck Driver

Heavy and tractor-trailer truck drivers usually have a high school diploma and attend a professional truck driving school. They must have a commercial driver's license (CDL).

Pay

The median annual wage for heavy and tractor-trailer truck drivers was $45,260 in May 2019.

Job Outlook

Employment of heavy and tractor-trailer truck drivers is projected to grow 2 percent from 2019 to 2029, slower than the average for all occupations. As the demand for goods increases, more truck drivers will be needed to keep supply chains moving.

State & Area Data

Explore resources for employment and wages by state and area for heavy and tractor-trailer truck drivers.

What Heavy and Tractor-trailer Truck Drivers Do

Heavy and tractor-trailer truck drivers transport goods from one location to another. Most tractor-trailer drivers are long-haul drivers and operate trucks with a total weight exceeding 26,000 pounds for the vehicle, passengers, and cargo. These drivers deliver goods over intercity routes that sometimes span several states.

Truck drivers transport goods around the country.

Some heavy and tractor-trailer truck drivers plan their own routes.

Duties

Heavy and tractor-trailer truck drivers typically do the following:

- Drive long distances
- Report any incidents encountered on the road to a dispatcher
- Follow all applicable traffic laws
- Secure cargo for transport, using ropes, blocks, chains, or covers
- Inspect their trailers before and after the trip and record any defects they find
- Maintain a log of their working hours, following all federal and state regulations
- Report serious mechanical problems to the appropriate people
- Keep their trucks and associated equipment clean and in good working order

Most heavy and tractor-trailer truck drivers' routes are assigned by a dispatcher, but some independent drivers still plan their own routes. When planning routes, drivers must take into account any road restrictions that prohibit large trucks. Drivers also must plan legally required rest periods into their trip.

Some drivers have one or two routes that they drive regularly, and other drivers take many different routes throughout the country. In addition, some drivers have routes that include Mexico or Canada.

Companies sometimes use two drivers, known as teams, on long runs to minimize downtime. On these team runs, one driver sleeps in a berth behind the cab while the other drives.

Certain cargo requires drivers to adhere to additional safety regulations. Some heavy truck drivers who transport hazardous materials, such as chemical waste, must take special precautions when driving and may carry specialized safety equipment in case of an accident. Other drivers, such as those carrying liquids, oversized loads, or cars, must follow rules that apply specifically to them.

Some long-haul truck drivers, also called *owner-operators*, buy or lease trucks and go into business for themselves. In addition to their driving tasks, owner-operators have business tasks, including finding and keeping clients and doing administrative work.

Work Environment

Heavy and tractor-trailer truck drivers held about 2.0 million jobs in 2019. The largest employers of heavy and tractor-trailer truck drivers were as follows:

Truck transportation	44%
Wholesale trade	12
Self-employed workers	8
Manufacturing	7
Construction	6

Working as a long-haul truck driver is a lifestyle choice because these drivers can be away from home for days or weeks at a time. They spend much of this time alone. Driving a truck can be a physically demanding job as well. Driving for many consecutive hours can be tiring, and some drivers must load and unload cargo.

Injuries and Illnesses

Because of the potential for traffic accidents, heavy and tractor-trailer truck drivers have one of the highest rates of injuries and illnesses of all occupations.

Although fatalities are uncommon, heavy and tractor-trailer truck drivers experience one of the highest rates of occupational fatalities of all occupations.

Work Schedules

Most heavy tractor-trailer drivers work full time. The Federal Motor Carrier Safety Administration regulates the hours that a long-haul truck driver may work. Drivers may not work more than 14 hours straight, comprising up to 11 hours driving and the remaining time doing other work, such as unloading cargo.

Some truck drivers travel far from home and can be on the road for long periods at a time.

Between working periods, drivers must have at least 10 hours off duty. Drivers also are limited to driving no more than 60 hours within 7 days or 70 hours within 8 days; then drivers must take 34 hours off before starting another 7- or 8-day run. Drivers must record their hours in a logbook. Truck drivers often work nights, weekends, and holidays.

How to Become a Heavy or Tractor-trailer Truck Driver

Heavy and tractor-trailer truck drivers usually have a high school diploma and attend a professional truck driving school. They must have a commercial driver's license (CDL).

Education

Most companies require their truck drivers to have a high school diploma or equivalent.

Many prospective drivers attend professional truck driving schools, where they take training courses to learn how to maneuver large vehicles on highways or through crowded streets. During these classes, drivers also learn the federal laws and regulations governing interstate truck driving. Students may attend either a private truck-driving school or a program at a community college that lasts between 3 and 6 months.

Drivers learn the federal laws and regulations governing interstate trucking.

Upon finishing their classes, drivers receive a certificate of completion.

Licenses, Certifications, and Registrations

All long-haul truck drivers must have a commercial driver's license (CDL). Qualifications for obtaining a CDL vary by state but generally include passing both a knowledge test and a driving test. States have the right to refuse to issue a CDL to anyone who has had a CDL suspended by another state.

Drivers can get endorsements to their CDL that show their ability to drive a specialized type of vehicle. Truck drivers transporting hazardous materials (HAZMAT) must have a hazardous materials endorsement (H). Getting this endorsement requires passing an additional knowledge test and a background check.

Federal regulations require CDL drivers to maintain a clean driving record and pass a physical exam every two years. They are also subject to random testing for drug or alcohol abuse. Truck drivers can have their CDL suspended if they are convicted of driving under the influence of alcohol or drugs or are convicted of a felony involving the use of a motor vehicle.

Other actions can result in a suspension after multiple violations. The Federal Motor Carrier Safety Administration website has a list of these violations. Additionally, some companies have stricter standards than what federal regulations require.

Training

After completing truck-driving school and being hired by a company, drivers normally receive several weeks of on-the-job training. During this time, they drive a truck accompanied by an experienced mentor-driver in the passenger seat. This period of on-the-job training is given so that the new drivers will learn more about the specific type of truck they will drive and material they will transport.

Important Qualities

Hand-eye coordination. Drivers of heavy trucks and tractor-trailers must be able to coordinate their legs, hands, and eyes simultaneously so that they will react appropriately to the situation around them and drive the vehicle safely.

Hearing ability. Truck drivers need good hearing. Federal regulations require that a driver be able to hear a forced whisper in one ear at 5 feet away (with or without the use of a hearing aid).

Physical health. Federal regulations do not allow people to become truck drivers if they have a medical condition, such as high blood pressure or epilepsy, which may interfere with their ability to operate a truck. The Federal Motor Carrier Safety Administration website has a full list of medical conditions that disqualify someone from driving a long-haul truck.

Visual ability. Truck drivers must be able to pass vision tests. Federal regulations require a driver to have at least 20/40 vision with a 70-degree field of vision in each eye and the ability to distinguish the colors on a traffic light.

Heavy and Tractor-trailer Truck Drivers
Median annual wages, May 2019

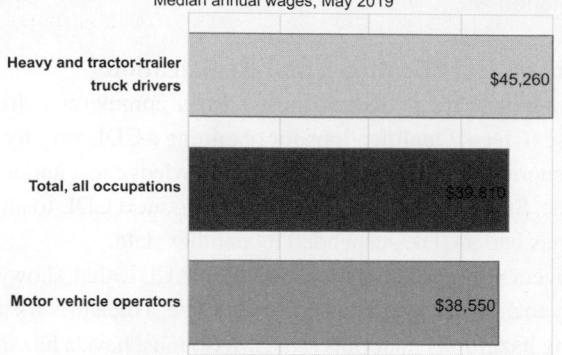

Note: All Occupations includes all occupations in the U.S. Economy.
Source: U.S. Bureau of Labor Statistics, Occupational Employment Statistics.

Pay

The median annual wage for heavy and tractor-trailer truck drivers was $45,260 in May 2019. The median wage is the wage at which half the workers in an occupation earned more than that amount and half earned less. The lowest 10 percent earned less than $29,130, and the highest 10 percent earned more than $66,840.

In May 2019, the median annual wages for heavy and tractor-trailer truck drivers in the top industries in which they worked were as follows:

Truck transportation	$46,370
Wholesale trade	44,610
Construction	43,680
Manufacturing	42,970

Drivers of heavy trucks and tractor-trailers usually are paid by how many miles they have driven, plus bonuses. The per-mile rate varies from employer to employer and may depend on the type of cargo and the experience of the driver. Some long-distance drivers, especially owner-operators, are paid a share of the revenue from shipping.

Most heavy tractor-trailer drivers work full time. The Federal Motor Carrier Safety Administration regulates the hours that a long-haul truck driver may work. Drivers may not work more than 14 hours straight, comprising up to 11 hours driving and the remaining time doing other work, such as unloading cargo. Between working periods, drivers must have at least 10 hours off duty. Drivers also are limited to driving no more than 60 hours within 7 days or 70 hours within 8 days; then drivers must take 34 hours off before starting another 7- or 8-day run. Drivers must record their hours in a logbook. Truck drivers often work nights, weekends, and holidays.

Job Outlook

Employment of heavy and tractor-trailer truck drivers is projected to grow 2 percent from 2019 to 2029, slower than the average for all occupations.

Heavy and Tractor-trailer Truck Drivers
Percent change in employment, projected 2019-29

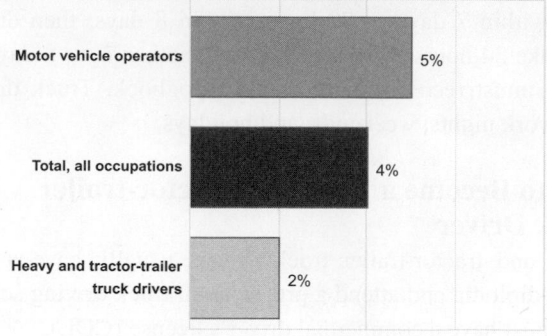

Note: All Occupations includes all occupations in the U.S. Economy.
Source: U.S. Bureau of Labor Statistics, Employment Projections program.

The economy depends on truck drivers to transport freight and keep supply chains moving. As the demand for goods increases, more truck drivers will be needed. Trucks transport most of the freight in the United States, so, as households and businesses increase their spending, the trucking industry should grow.

Technological advancements should result in trucks that are more fuel efficient and easier to drive. For example, automatic transmissions, blindspot monitoring, braking assistance, and variable cruise control are all recently developed features that may become more standard throughout the trucking industries within the next decade. In addition, technological advances may lead to further developments in platooning, which is a method of transport where several trucks form a line and automatically mimic the speed, braking, and steering behaviors of the lead truck. These technologies can help ease driver burden and create a safer driving environment for all vehicles.

Job Prospects

Job prospects are projected to be very good for heavy and tractor-trailer truck drivers with the proper training and a clean driving record. Because of truck drivers' difficult lifestyle and time spent away from home, many companies have trouble finding and retaining qualified long-haul drivers. In addition, many truck drivers are expected to retire in the coming years, creating even more job opportunities.

Employment projections data for heavy and tractor-trailer truck drivers, 2019-29					
Occupational Title	SOC Code	Employment, 2019	Projected Employment, 2029	Change, 2019-29	
				Percent	Numeric
SOURCE: U.S. Bureau of Labor Statistics, Employment Projections program					
Heavy and tractor-trailer truck drivers	53-3032	2,029,900	2,060,500	2	30,600

State & Area Data
Occupational Employment Statistics (OES)

The Occupational Employment Statistics (OES) program produces employment and wage estimates annually for over 800

occupations. These estimates are available for the nation as a whole, for individual states, and for metropolitan and nonmetropolitan areas.

Contacts for More Information
For more information about truck drivers, visit
➤ American Trucking Associations

➤ Federal Motor Carrier Safety Administration

For more information about truck driving schools and programs, visit
➤ Commercial Vehicle Training Association

➤ National Association of Publicly Funded Truck Driving Schools

---

Material Moving Machine Operators

Summary

Quick Facts: Material Moving Machine Operators

2019 Median Pay	$36,770 per year $17.68 per hour
Typical Entry-Level Education	See below
Work Experience in a Related Occupation	See below
On-the-job Training	See below
Number of Jobs, 2019	761,400
Job Outlook, 2019-29	2% (Slower than average)
Employment Change, 2019-29	19,000

What Material Moving Machine Operators Do
Material moving machine operators use machinery to transport various objects.

Work Environment
Most material moving machine operators work full time, and overtime for them is common. Because materials are shipped around the clock, some operators—especially those in warehousing—work overnight shifts.

How to Become a Material Moving Machine Operator
Education and training requirements vary by occupation. Crane operators and excavating machine operators usually have several years of experience in related occupations.

Pay
The median annual wage for material moving machine operators was $36,770 in May 2019.

Job Outlook
Overall employment of material moving machine operators is projected to grow 2 percent from 2019 to 2029, slower than the average for all occupations. Employment growth will vary by occupation.

State & Area Data
Explore resources for employment and wages by state and area for material moving machine operators.

What Material Moving Machine Operators Do
Material moving machine operators use machinery to transport various objects. Some operators move construction materials around building sites or excavate earth from a mine. Others move goods around a warehouse or onto container ships.

Material moving machine operators use machinery to move goods around a warehouse or onto container ships.

Crane and tower operators are commonly employed in construction and water transportation.

Duties

Material moving machine operators typically do the following:

- Set up and inspect material moving equipment
- Control equipment with levers, wheels, or foot pedals
- Move material according to a plan or schedule
- Signal and direct workers to load, unload, and position materials
- Keep a record of the material they move and where they move it to
- Make minor repairs to their equipment

In warehouses, most material moving machine operators use forklifts and conveyor belts. Wireless sensors and tags are increasingly being used to keep track of merchandise, allowing operators to locate them faster. Some operators also check goods for damage. These operators usually work closely with hand laborers and material movers.

Many operators work for underground and surface mining companies. They help to dig or expose the mine, remove the earth and rock, and extract coal, ore, and other mined materials.

In construction, material moving machine operators remove earth to clear space for buildings. Some work on a building site for the entire length of the construction project. For example, certain material moving machine operators help to construct highrise buildings by transporting materials to workers who are far above ground level.

All material moving machine operators are responsible for the safe operation of their equipment or vehicle.

The following are examples of types of material moving machine operators:

Conveyor operators and tenders control conveyor systems that move materials on an automatic belt. They move materials to and from places such as storage areas, vehicles, and building sites. They monitor sensors on the conveyor to regulate the speed with which the conveyor belt moves. Operators also may check the shipping order and determine the route that materials take along a conveyor.

Crane and tower operators use tower and cable equipment to lift and move materials, machinery, or other heavy objects. From a control station, operators can extend and retract horizontal booms, rotate the superstructure, and lower and raise hooks attached to cables at the end of their crane or tower. Operators usually are guided by workers on the ground who use hand signals or who transmit voice signals through a radio. Most crane and tower operators work at construction sites or major ports, where they load and unload cargo. Some operators work in iron and steel mills.

Dredge operators excavate waterways. They operate equipment on the water to remove sand, gravel, or rock from harbors or lakes. Removing these materials helps to prevent erosion and maintain navigable waterways, and allows larger ships to use ports. Dredging also is used to help restore wetlands and maintain beaches.

Excavating and loading machine and dragline operators use machines equipped with scoops or shovels. They dig sand, earth, or other materials and load them onto conveyors or into trucks for transport elsewhere. They may also move material within a confined area, such as a construction site. Operators typically receive instructions from workers on the ground through hand signals or through voice signals transmitted by radio. Most of these operators work in construction or mining industries.

Hoist and winch operators, also called *derrick operators*, control the movement of platforms, cables, and cages that transport workers or materials in industrial operations, such as constructing a highrise building. Many of these operators raise platforms far above the ground. Operators regulate the speed of the equipment on the basis of the needs of the workers. Many work in manufacturing, mining, and quarrying industries.

Industrial truck and tractor operators drive trucks and tractors that move materials around warehouses, storage yards, or worksites. These trucks, often called forklifts, have a lifting mechanism and forks, which make them useful for moving heavy and large objects. Some industrial truck and tractor operators drive tractors that pull trailers loaded with material around factories or storage areas.

Underground mining loading machine operators load coal, ore, and other rocks onto shuttles, mine cars, or conveyors for transport from a mine to the surface. They may use power shovels, hoisting engines equipped with scrapers or scoops, and automatic gathering arms that move materials onto a conveyor. Operators also drive their machines farther into the mine in order to gather more material.

Work Environment

Material moving machine operators held about 761,400 jobs in 2019. Employment in the detailed occupations that make up material moving machine operators was distributed as follows:

Industrial truck and tractor operators	634,700
Excavating and loading machine and dragline operators, surface mining	46,100
Crane and tower operators	45,700
Conveyor operators and tenders	23,900
Hoist and winch operators	4,900
Loading and moving machine operators, underground mining	4,500
Dredge operators	1,600

The largest employers of material moving machine operators were as follows:

Warehousing and storage	25%
Wholesale trade	12
Temporary help services	8

Industrial truck and tractor operators use forklifts in warehousing and storage facilities.

Material moving machine operators work indoors and outdoors in a variety of industries.

Injuries and Illnesses

Some material moving machine operator jobs can be dangerous. For example, crane operators work outdoors at great heights in all types of weather.

Many workers wear personal protective equipment, including gloves, hardhats, harnesses, and respirators to guard against injury.

Work Schedules

Most material moving machine operators work full time, and overtime for them is common. Because materials are shipped around the clock, some operators—especially those in warehousing—work overnight shifts.

How to Become a Material Moving Machine Operator

Education and training requirements vary by occupation. Crane operators and excavating machine operators usually

Material moving machine operators are trained on the job.

have several years of experience in related occupations, such as construction equipment operators or hoist or winch operators.

Education

Although no formal educational credential is usually required, some companies prefer to hire material moving machine operators who have a high school diploma. For crane and tower operators, excavating machine operators, and dredge operators, however, a high school diploma or equivalent typically is required.

Training

Although most material moving machine operators are trained on the job in less than a month, the amount of time spent in training will vary with the type of machine. Some machines, such as cranes and towers, are more complex than others, such as industrial trucks and forklifts. Learning to operate a forklift or an industrial truck in warehouses, for example, may take only a few days; training to operate a crane for port operations may take several months. Most workers are trained by a supervisor or another experienced employee.

During their training, material moving machine operators learn a number of safety rules, many of which are standardized through the Occupational Safety & Health Administration (OSHA) and the Mine Safety and Health Administration (MSHA). Employers must certify that each operator has received the proper training. Operators who work with hazardous materials receive further specialized training.

The International Union of Operating Engineers offers apprenticeship programs for heavy-equipment operators, such as excavating machine operators or crane operators. Apprenticeships combine paid on-the-job training with technical instruction.

Licenses, Certifications, and Registrations

A number of states and several cities require crane operators to be licensed. To get a license, operators typically must complete a skills test in which they show that they can control a crane. They also must pass a written exam that tests their knowledge of safety rules and procedures. Some crane operators and industrial truck and tractor operators may obtain certification, which includes passing a written exam.

Work Experience in a Related Occupation

Crane operators and excavating machine operators usually have several years of experience working as construction equipment operators, hoist and winch operators, or riggers and signalers.

Important Qualities

Alertness. Material moving machine operators must be aware of their surroundings while operating machinery.

Communication skills. Material moving machine operators signal and direct workers to load and unload material. They also receive direction from workers on the ground when moving material.

Coordination. Material moving machine operators should have steady hands and feet to guide and control heavy machinery precisely. They use hand controls to maneuver their machines through tight spaces, around large objects, and on uneven surfaces.

Mechanical skills. Material moving machine operators make minor adjustments to their machines and perform basic maintenance on them.

Visual ability. Material moving machine operators must be able to see clearly where they are driving or what they are moving. They must also watch for nearby workers, who may unknowingly be in their path.

Pay

The median annual wage for material moving machine operators was $36,770 in May 2019. The median wage is the wage at which half the workers in an occupation earned more than that amount and half earned less. The lowest 10 percent earned less than $26,040, and the highest 10 percent earned more than $58,240.

Median annual wages for material moving machine operators in May 2019 were as follows:

Hoist and winch operators	$59,720
Crane and tower operators	56,690
Loading and moving machine operators, underground mining	54,210
Dredge operators	47,040
Excavating and loading machine and dragline operators, surface mining	44,800
Industrial truck and tractor operators	36,200
Conveyor operators and tenders	34,660

In May 2019, the median annual wages for material moving machine operators in the top industries in which they worked were as follows:

Construction	$50,120
Warehousing and storage	36,510
Food manufacturing	35,820
Wholesale trade	35,420
Temporary help services	30,230

Most material moving machine operators work full time, and overtime for them is common. Because materials are shipped around the clock, some operators—especially those in warehousing—work overnight shifts.

Job Outlook

Overall employment of material moving machine operators is projected to grow 2 percent from 2019 to 2029, slower than the average for all occupations. Employment growth will vary by occupation.

Employment of industrial truck and tractor operators is concentrated in warehouses. The demand for warehousing will continue to grow as more consumers choose to purchase products online. However, employment growth for these workers may be tempered

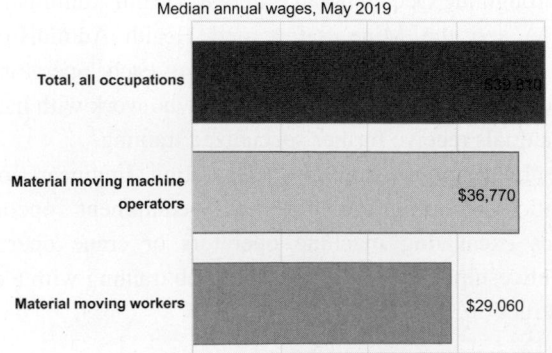

Material Moving Machine Operators
Median annual wages, May 2019

- Total, all occupations: $39,810
- Material moving machine operators: $36,770
- Material moving workers: $29,060

Note: All Occupations includes all occupations in the U.S. Economy.
Source: U.S. Bureau of Labor Statistics, Occupational Employment Statistics.

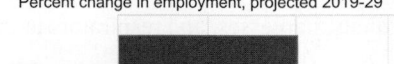
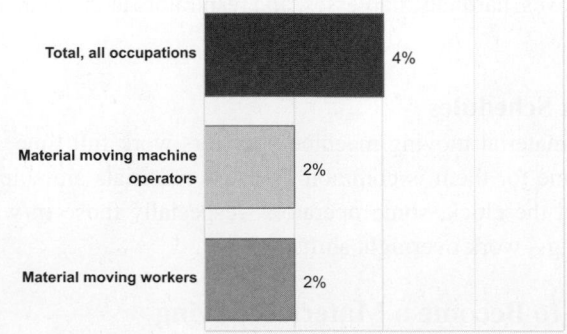

Material Moving Machine Operators
Percent change in employment, projected 2019-29

- Total, all occupations: 4%
- Material moving machine operators: 2%
- Material moving workers: 2%

Note: All Occupations includes all occupations in the U.S. Economy.
Source: U.S. Bureau of Labor Statistics, Employment Projections program.

as more warehouses begin using automated machinery to improve their operations. This equipment increases the efficiency of operators, allowing warehouses to employ fewer of them.

Projected employment growth of conveyor operators and tenders will be limited as equipment such as high-speed conveyors and sorting systems, autonomous vehicles, and robotic pickers increase these workers' productivity.

In addition, employment of underground mining loading and moving machine operators is projected to decline. Most of the decline is in the coal mining industry, as increased use of autonomous vehicles reduces demand for these operators.

Job Prospects

Job prospects are expected to be favorable. Many job openings should be created by the need to replace workers who leave these occupations.

Employment projections data for material moving machine operators, 2019-29					
Occupational Title	SOC Code	Employment, 2019	Projected Employment, 2029	Change, 2019-29	
				Percent	Numeric
SOURCE: U.S. Bureau of Labor Statistics, Employment Projections program					
Material moving machine operators	—	761,400	780,400	2	19,000
Excavating and loading machine and dragline operators, surface mining	47-5022	46,100	47,400	3	1,300
Loading and moving machine operators, underground mining	47-5044	4,500	3,900	-13	-600

Employment projections data for material moving machine operators, 2019-29					
Occupational Title	SOC Code	Employment, 2019	Projected Employment, 2029	Change, 2019-29	
				Percent	Numeric
Conveyor operators and tenders	53-7011	23,900	24,000	0	100
Crane and tower operators	53-7021	45,700	46,500	2	800
Dredge operators	53-7031	1,600	1,700	4	100
Hoist and winch operators	53-7041	4,900	4,600	-5	-200
Industrial truck and tractor operators	53-7051	634,700	652,300	3	17,500

State & Area Data
Occupational Employment Statistics (OES)

The Occupational Employment Statistics (OES) program produces employment and wage estimates annually for over 800 occupations. These estimates are available for the nation as a whole, for individual states, and for metropolitan and nonmetropolitan areas.

Contacts for More Information

For more information about careers as a material moving machine operator, visit

➤ MHI
➤ Warehousing Education and Research Council
➤ International Union of Operating Engineers
➤ National Commission for the Certification of Crane Operators

Passenger Vehicle Drivers

Summary

Quick Facts: Passenger Vehicle Drivers

2019 Median Pay	$33,300 per year $16.01 per hour
Typical Entry-Level Education	See below
Work Experience in a Related Occupation	None
On-the-job Training	See below
Number of Jobs, 2019	1,076,700
Job Outlook, 2019-29	11% (Much faster than average)
Employment Change, 2019-29	115,300

What Passenger Vehicle Drivers Do

Passenger vehicle drivers operate buses, taxis, and other modes of transportation to take people from place to place.

Work Environment

Most passenger vehicle drivers work full time, but part-time work is common. Drivers' schedules may vary, and some work weekends, evenings, or early mornings. School bus drivers work only when schools are in session.

How to Become a Passenger Vehicle Driver

Bus drivers typically need a high school diploma or equivalent; other types of passenger vehicle drivers typically have no

Most bus drivers are school bus drivers.

formal educational requirements. Most passenger vehicle drivers get brief on-the-job training. Additionally, all drivers need a regular driver's license. Some may need a special license, depending on the type of vehicle they drive.

Pay

The median annual wage for bus drivers, transit and intercity was $43,030 in May 2019.

The median annual wage for passenger vehicle drivers, except bus drivers, transit and intercity was $31,340 in May 2019.

Job Outlook

Overall employment of passenger vehicle drivers is projected to grow 11 percent from 2019 to 2029, much faster than the average for all occupations.

State & Area Data

Explore resources for employment and wages by state and area for passenger vehicle drivers.

What Passenger Vehicle Drivers Do

Passenger vehicle drivers transport people, sometimes across state and national borders. Some drive regular routes, while others' destinations vary daily. They operate a range of vehicles, from small cars with limited seating to 60-foot articulated buses (with two connected sections) that can carry more than 100 passengers.

Duties

Passenger vehicle drivers typically do the following:

- Pick up and drop off passengers at designated locations
- Follow a planned route or drive to a requested destination
- Help passengers, including those with disabilities, get into and out of the vehicle
- Obey traffic laws and state and federal transit regulations

Intercity bus drivers transport passengers between cities or towns.

- Follow procedures to ensure passenger safety
- Keep passengers informed of possible delays
- Maintain vehicle by checking tires, lights, and oil
- Keep the vehicle clean and presentable
- Help passengers load and unload belongings

Passenger vehicle drivers must stay alert to ensure their passengers' safety, especially in heavy traffic or bad weather.

The following are examples of types of passenger vehicle drivers:

School bus drivers transport students to and from school and other activities, such as field trips and sporting events, when the academic term is in session. School bus drivers also maintain order on the school bus and report disciplinary problems to the school district or parents.

Shuttle drivers and chauffeurs take passengers on planned trips. Shuttle drivers often drive large vans between airports or train stations and hotels or other destinations. Chauffeurs drive limousines, vans, or private cars and are hired to transport clients either for single trips or on a regular basis. Some chauffeurs do the duties of executive assistants, acting as driver, secretary, and itinerary planner.

Taxi and ride-hailing drivers pick up and drop off passengers, for a fare, on an unplanned basis. Both are summoned, taxi drivers—also called *cabdrivers* or *cabbies*—via a central dispatcher or at a designated pickup location and ride-hailing drivers through a smartphone app. Taxi drivers use a meter to calculate the fare; ride-hailing drivers are paid by a credit card that is linked to the app that passengers use.

Transit and intercity bus drivers usually follow a daily schedule to transport people on regular routes. They ensure that passengers pay the required fare, either by managing the fare box or collecting tickets, and answer questions about schedules and routes. Drivers of local transit buses travel city or suburban streets and may stop frequently. Drivers of intercity buses travel between cities or towns, sometimes crossing state lines. *Motor coachdrivers* transport passengers on chartered trips or sightseeing tours and sometimes act as tour guides.

Work Environment

Bus drivers, transit and intercity held about 223,400 jobs in 2019. The largest employers of bus drivers, transit and intercity were as follows:

Local government, excluding education and hospitals..	38%
Urban transit systems..	15
Charter bus industry..	9
Interurban and rural bus transportation..........................	5

Passenger vehicle drivers, except bus drivers, transit and intercity held about 853,300 jobs in 2019. The largest employers of passenger vehicle drivers, except bus drivers, transit and intercity were as follows:

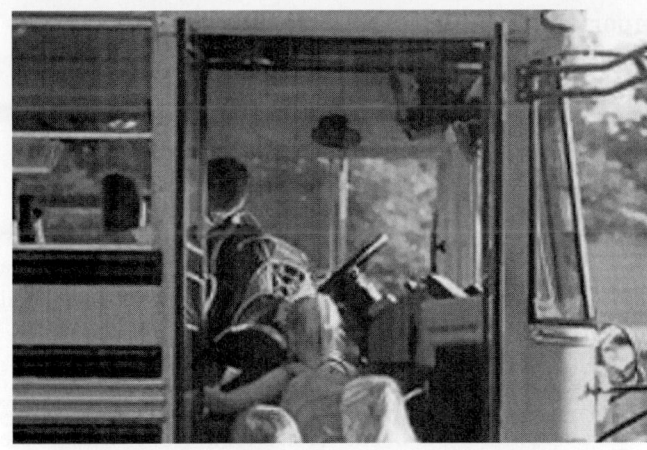

Some school bus drivers make multiple trips if schools in the district open at different times.

Elementary and secondary schools; local...................... 23%

School and employee bus transportation....................... 17

Other transit and ground passenger transportation...... 8

Local government, excluding education and hospitals.... 7

Driving through heavy traffic or bad weather and dealing with unruly passengers can be stressful. Some passenger vehicle drivers may have to pick up heavy luggage and packages, so they must take care to prevent strain or injury.

Some taxi drivers own the cab they drive; others lease it from a dispatch company. Regardless of whether they own or lease their vehicle, taxi drivers may contract with a dispatch company to use its passenger-referral service or facilities for a fee. Ride-hailing drivers typically operate their own vehicles. Taxi drivers and ride-hailing drivers usually pay expenses, such as fuel and maintenance, on their vehicle.

Injuries and Illnesses
Transit and intercity bus drivers have one of the highest rates of injuries and illnesses of all occupations. Other passenger vehicle drivers also sometimes get injured on the job. Most injuries result from traffic accidents.

Work Schedules
Most passenger vehicle drivers work full time, but part-time work is common. Drivers' schedules may vary, and some work weekends, evenings, or early mornings.

School bus drivers work only when school is in session, so their work hours are often limited. Some make multiple runs if schools in their district open and close at different times or if students need transportation to other activities.

Chauffeurs' work hours are based on client needs. Some chauffeurs must be ready to drive their clients at a moment's notice, so they remain on call throughout the day.

Taxi drivers' and ride-hailing drivers' work schedules are often flexible. They can take breaks for a meal or rest whenever they do not have a passenger.

Intercity bus drivers may work all hours of the day, including weekends and holidays. Some spend nights away from home because of long-distance routes. Others make a round trip and go home at the end of each shift.

Bus drivers who cross state lines must follow the Federal Motor Carrier Safety Administration's (FMCSA) hours-of-service regulations. Bus drivers are allowed 10 hours of driving time and 15 hours of total on-duty time before they must rest for 8 consecutive hours. Weekly maximum restrictions also apply but may vary by employer schedule.

How to Become a Passenger Vehicle Driver
Occupational entry requirements vary for different types of passenger vehicle drivers. In addition to education, training, and licensing requirements, some drivers must meet additional standards.

Drivers usually need to have a clean driving record and may be required to pass a background check; they also might need to meet physical, hearing, and vision requirements.

Education
Bus drivers typically need a high school diploma or equivalent. Other types of passenger vehicle drivers typically do not need any formal education; however, many of these drivers have a high school diploma or equivalent.

Training
Bus drivers typically get 1 to 3 months of on-the-job training, but those who already have a commercial driver's license (CDL) may have a shorter training period. For part of the training, drivers may practice various maneuvers with a bus on a driving course. They then begin to drive in light traffic and eventually make practice runs on the type of route that they expect to drive. New drivers make regularly scheduled trips with passengers while accompanied by an experienced driver who gives tips, answers questions, and evaluates the new driver's performance.

All types of bus drivers have to obtain a CDL.

Most taxi and limousine companies provide new drivers with a short period of on-the-job training. This training usually takes from 1 day to 2 weeks, depending on the company and the location. Some cities require the training, which typically covers local traffic laws, driver safety, and street layout. Taxi drivers also get training in operating the taximeter and communications equipment.

Ride-hailing drivers receive little to no training beyond how to work the electronic hailing app so they can pick up customers.

Licenses, Certifications, and Registrations

All bus drivers must have a CDL. Some new bus drivers can earn their CDL during on-the-job training. Qualifications vary by state but generally include passing both knowledge and driving tests. States have the right not to issue a license to someone who has had a CDL suspended in another state.

Drivers can get endorsements for a CDL that reflect their ability to drive a special type of vehicle. All bus drivers must have a passenger (P) endorsement, and school bus drivers must also have a school bus (S) endorsement. Getting the P and S endorsements requires additional knowledge, which is assessed through passing a driving test administered by a certified examiner.

Many states require all bus drivers to be at least 18 years old and those who drive across state lines to be at least 21 years old. Most bus drivers must undergo a background check before they are hired.

Federal regulations require interstate bus drivers to pass a physical exam every 2 years and to submit to random drug or alcohol testing. Most states impose similar regulations. Bus drivers may have their CDL suspended if they are convicted of a felony involving the use of a motor vehicle or of driving under the influence of drugs or alcohol. Actions such as excessive speeding or reckless driving also may result in a suspension.

Other types of passenger vehicle drivers must have a regular automobile driver's license. States and local municipalities set additional requirements; many require taxi drivers and chauffeurs to get a taxi or limousine license. This normally requires passing a background check, testing free of drugs, and passing a written exam about regulations and local geography.

Regulations for ride-hailing drivers vary by state and city. Check with your local area for more information.

The Federal Motor Carrier Safety Administration (FMCSA) requires limousine drivers who transport 16 or more passengers to hold a CDL with a passenger (P) endorsement.

Advancement

Some taxi drivers start their own cab service by purchasing a taxi rather than leasing one through a dispatch company. Chauffeurs may advance with increased responsibilities or experiences, such as driving high-profile clients or different types of cars.

Important Qualities

Customer-service skills. Drivers regularly interact with passengers and must be courteous and helpful.

Dependability. Customers rely on passenger vehicle drivers to pick them up on time and safely transport them to their destination.

Hand-eye coordination. Drivers must watch their surroundings and avoid obstacles and other hazards while operating a vehicle. Federal regulations require bus drivers to have normal use of their arms and legs.

Hearing ability. Passenger vehicle drivers need good hearing. Federal regulations require bus drivers to have the ability to hear a forced whisper in one ear at 5 feet, with or without the use of a hearing aid.

Patience. Drivers must remain calm and composed when driving through heavy traffic and congestion or when dealing with rude passengers.

Physical health. Some medical conditions, such as high blood pressure or epilepsy, may interfere with the safe operation of passenger vehicles.

Visual ability. Passenger vehicle drivers must be able to pass vision tests. Federal regulations require bus drivers to have at least 20/40 vision with a 70-degree field of vision in each eye and the ability to distinguish colors on a traffic light.

Pay

The median annual wage for bus drivers, transit and intercity was $43,030 in May 2019. The median wage is the wage at which half the workers in an occupation earned more than that amount and half earned less. The lowest 10 percent earned less than $26,710, and the highest 10 percent earned more than $70,810.

The median annual wage for passenger vehicle drivers, except bus drivers, transit and intercity was $31,340 in May

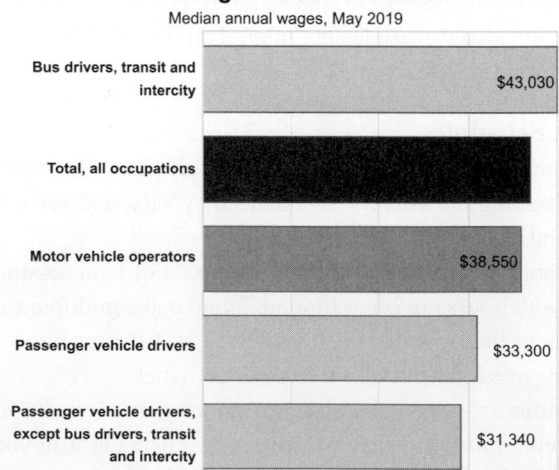

Passenger Vehicle Drivers
Median annual wages, May 2019

Bus drivers, transit and intercity	$43,030
Total, all occupations	
Motor vehicle operators	$38,550
Passenger vehicle drivers	$33,300
Passenger vehicle drivers, except bus drivers, transit and intercity	$31,340

Note: All Occupations includes all occupations in the U.S. Economy.
Source: U.S. Bureau of Labor Statistics, Occupational Employment Statistics.

2019. The lowest 10 percent earned less than $19,320, and the highest 10 percent earned more than $49,500.

In May 2019, the median annual wages for bus drivers, transit and intercity in the top industries in which they worked were as follows:

Local government, excluding education and hospitals..	$53,370
Interurban and rural bus transportation.....................	39,900
Urban transit systems...	39,860
Charter bus industry..	33,340

In May 2019, the median annual wages for passenger vehicle drivers, except bus drivers, transit and intercity in the top industries in which they worked were as follows:

School and employee bus transportation.................	$36,530
Local government, excluding education and hospitals..	34,520
Elementary and secondary schools; local	32,420
Other transit and ground passenger transportation	29,340

Most passenger vehicle drivers work full time, but part-time work is common. Drivers' schedules may vary, and some work weekends, evenings, or early mornings.

School bus drivers work only when school is in session, so their work hours are often limited. Some make multiple runs if schools in their district open and close at different times or if students need transportation to other activities.

Chauffeurs' work hours are based on client needs. Some chauffeurs must be ready to drive their clients at a moment's notice, so they remain on call throughout the day.

Taxi drivers' and ride-hailing drivers' work schedules are often flexible. They can take breaks for a meal or rest whenever they do not have a passenger.

Intercity bus drivers may work all hours of the day, including weekends and holidays. Some spend nights away from home because of long-distance routes. Others make a round trip and go home at the end of each shift.

Some passenger vehicle drivers receive tips. Those who provide good customer service are more likely to receive good tips than those whose customer-service skills are poor.

Job Outlook

Overall employment of passenger vehicle drivers is projected to grow 11 percent from 2019 to 2029, much faster than the average for all occupations.

Employment of passenger vehicle drivers, except bus drivers, transit and intercity is projected to grow 11 percent from 2019 to 2029, much faster than the average for all occupations. Taxi, limousine, and ride-hailing services are concentrated primarily in large metropolitan areas, where people are more likely to

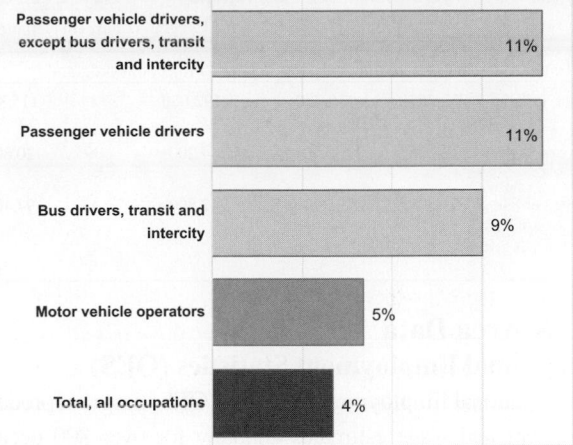

Passenger Vehicle Drivers
Percent change in employment, projected 2019-29

- Passenger vehicle drivers, except bus drivers, transit and intercity — 11%
- Passenger vehicle drivers — 11%
- Bus drivers, transit and intercity — 9%
- Motor vehicle operators — 5%
- Total, all occupations — 4%

Note: All Occupations includes all occupations in the U.S. Economy.
Source: U.S. Bureau of Labor Statistics, Employment Projections program.

use this form of transportation. However, most job growth in this occupation is projected to be from the increasing demand for ride-hailing services, the providers of which are typically independent contractors. Demand is expected to increase due to the conveniences that ride-hailing services offer, such as being able to track the location of the requested driver and to pay for services using a smartphone app. In contrast, demand for taxi and limousine services is projected to decline as consumers opt to use ride-hailing services instead.

Additionally, as more school districts outsource their transportation needs, employment growth for school bus drivers will likely be in companies that districts contract with to provide school bus services.

Demand for special-needs transportation will continue to rise because of an increase in older age groups, which typically are more likely to require these services than are younger groups.

Employment of bus drivers, transit and intercity is projected to grow 9 percent from 2019 to 2029, much faster than the average for all occupations. New Bus Rapid Transit (BRT) systems are expected to open throughout the country, which should create additional employment opportunities. Intercity bus travel that picks up passengers from curbside locations in urban downtowns should continue to grow. This form of travel is expected to remain popular due to the inexpensive fares and passenger amenities, such as Wi-Fi.

Job Prospects

About 132,900 openings for passenger vehicle drivers are projected each year, on average, over the decade.

Many of those openings are expected to result from the need to replace workers who transfer to different occupations or exit the labor force, such as to retire.

Employment projections data for passenger vehicle drivers, 2019-29					
Occupational Title	SOC Code	Employment, 2019	Projected Employment, 2029	Change, 2019-29	
				Percent	Numeric
SOURCE: U.S. Bureau of Labor Statistics, Employment Projections program					
Passenger vehicle drivers	53-3050	1,076,700	1,192,000	11	115,300
Bus drivers, transit and intercity	53-3052	223,400	244,200	9	20,800
Passenger vehicle drivers, except bus drivers, transit and intercity	53-3058	853,300	947,800	11	94,400

State & Area Data
Occupational Employment Statistics (OES)
The Occupational Employment Statistics (OES) program produces employment and wage estimates annually for over 800 occupations. These estimates are available for the nation as a whole, for individual states, and for metropolitan and nonmetropolitan areas.

Contacts for More Information
For more information about school bus drivers, visit
➤ National School Transportation Association

➤ National Association of State Directors of Pupil Transportation Services

For more information about transit bus drivers, visit
➤ American Public Transportation Association

For more information about motor coach drivers, visit
➤ United Motorcoach Association

➤ For more information about taxi drivers and chauffeurs, visit
➤ Taxicab, Limousine, and Paratransit Association

For more information about limousine drivers, visit
➤ National Limousine Association

For more information about ride-hailing drivers, visit
➤ The Ride Share Guy

For more information about commercial licensing, visit
➤ Federal Motor Carrier Safety Administration

Railroad Workers

Summary

Quick Facts: Railroad Workers

2019 Median Pay	$65,020 per year $31.26 per hour
Typical Entry-Level Education	High school diploma or equivalent
Work Experience in a Related Occupation	See below
On-the-job Training	Moderate-term on-the-job training
Number of Jobs, 2019	77,700
Job Outlook, 2019-29	-3% (Decline)
Employment Change, 2019-29	-2,600

What Railroad Workers Do
Workers in railroad occupations ensure that passenger and freight trains safely run on time. They may drive trains, coordinate the activities of the trains, or operate signals and switches in the rail yard.

Work Environment
Nearly all locomotive engineers; conductors and yardmasters; and brake, signal, and switch operators work in the rail transportation industry. Rail yard engineers work in rail transportation and also support activities for rail.

How to Become a Railroad Worker
Railroad workers generally require a high school diploma or equivalent and several months of on-the-job training.

Pay
The median annual wage for railroad workers was $65,020 in May 2019.

Job Outlook
Overall employment of railroad workers is projected to decline 3 percent from 2019 to 2029.

Conductors make sure passengers board safely.

State & Area Data

Explore resources for employment and wages by state and area for railroad workers.

What Railroad Workers Do

Workers in railroad occupations ensure that passenger and freight trains run on time and travel safely. Some workers drive trains, some coordinate the activities of the trains, and others operate signals and switches in the rail yard.

Duties

Railroad workers typically do the following:

- Check the mechanical condition of locomotives and make adjustments when necessary
- Document issues with a train that require further inspection
- Operate locomotive engines within or between stations

Freight trains move billions of tons of goods around the country to ports where they are shipped around the world. Passenger trains transport millions of passengers and commuters to destinations around the country. These railroad workers are essential to keeping freight and passenger trains running properly.

All workers in railroad occupations work together closely. Locomotive engineers travel with conductors and sometimes brake operators. Locomotive engineers and conductors are in constant contact and keep each other informed of any changes in the condition of the train.

Signal and switch operators communicate with both locomotive and rail yard engineers to make sure that trains end up at the correct destination. All occupations are in contact with dispatchers who give them directions on where to go and what to do.

The following are examples of types of railroad workers:

Locomotive engineers drive freight or passenger trains between stations. They drive long-distance trains and commuter trains, but not subway trains. Most locomotive engineers

Locomotive engineers use a variety of controls to operate a train.

drive diesel-electric engines, although some drive locomotives powered by battery or electricity.

Engineers must be aware of the goods their train is carrying because different types of freight require different types of driving, based on the conditions of the rails. For example, a train carrying hazardous material through a snowstorm is driven differently than a train carrying coal through a mountain region.

Locomotive engineers typically do the following:

- Monitor speed, air pressure, battery use, and other instruments to ensure that the locomotive runs smoothly
- Observe track for obstructions, such as fallen tree branches
- Use a variety of controls, such as throttles and airbrakes, to operate the train
- Communicate with dispatchers over radios to get information about delays or changes in the schedule

Conductors travel on both freight and passenger trains. They coordinate activities of the train crew. On passenger trains, they ensure safety and comfort and make announcements to keep passengers informed. On freight trains they are responsible for overseeing the loading and unloading of cargo.

Conductors typically do the following:
- Check passengers' tickets
- Take payments from passengers who did not buy tickets in advance
- Announce stations and give other announcements as needed
- Help passengers to safety when needed
- Ensure safe and orderly passenger conduct
- Oversee loading and unloading of cargo

Yardmasters do work similar to that of conductors, except that they do not travel on trains. They oversee and coordinate the activities of workers in the rail yard. They tell yard engineers where to move cars to fit the planned configuration or to load freight. Yardmasters ensure that trains are carrying the correct material before leaving the yard. Not all rail yards use yardmasters. In rail yards that do not have yardmasters, a conductor performs the duties of a yardmaster.

Yardmasters typically do the following:

- Review schedules, switching orders, and shipping records of freight trains
- Arrange for defective cars to be removed from a train for repairs
- Switch train traffic to a certain section of the line to allow other inbound and outbound trains to get around
- Break up or put together train cars according to a schedule

Rail yard engineers operate train engines within the rail yard. They move locomotives between tracks to keep the trains organized and on schedule. Some operate small locomotives called dinkeys. Sometimes, rail yard engineers are called *hostlers* and drive locomotives to and from maintenance shops or prepare them for the locomotive engineer. Some use remote locomotive technology to move freight cars within the rail yards.

Railroad brake, signal, or switch operators control equipment that keeps the trains running safely.

Brake operators help couple and uncouple train cars. Some travel with the train as part of the crew.

Signal operators install and maintain the signals along tracks and in the rail yard. Signals are important in preventing accidents because they allow increased communication between trains and dispatchers.

Switch operators control the track switches in rail yards. These switches allow trains to move between tracks and ensure trains are heading in the right direction.

Locomotive firers are sometimes part of a train crew and typically monitor tracks and train instruments. They look for equipment that is dragging, obstacles on the tracks, and other potential safety problems.

Few trains still use firers, because their work has been automated or is now done by a locomotive engineer or conductor.

Work Environment

Railroad workers held about 77,700 jobs in 2019. Employment in the detailed occupations that make up railroad workers was distributed as follows:

Railroad conductors and yardmasters	36,000
Locomotive engineers	27,400
Railroad brake, signal, and switch operators and locomotive firers	9,100
Rail yard engineers, dinkey operators, and hostlers	5,200

The largest employers of railroad workers were as follows:

Rail transportation	82%
Local government, excluding education and hospitals	7

Rail yard engineers and brake, signal, and switch operators spend most of their time working outside, regardless of weather conditions.

Conductors on passenger trains generally work in cleaner, more comfortable conditions than conductors on freight trains. However, conductors on passenger trains sometimes must respond to upset or unruly passengers when a train is delayed.

Work Schedules

Because trains are scheduled to operate 24 hours a day, 7 days a week, many railroad workers sometimes work nights, weekends, and holidays. Most rail employees work full time. Federal regulations require a minimum number of rest hours for train operators.

Locomotive engineers and conductors whose trains travel long routes can be away from home for long periods of time. Those who work on passenger trains with short routes generally have more predictable schedules. Workers on some freight trains have irregular schedules.

For engineers and conductors, seniority (the number of years on the job) usually dictates who receives the most desired shifts. Some engineers and conductors, called extra board, are hired on a temporary basis and get an assignment only when a railroad needs an extra or substitute worker on a certain route.

How to Become a Railroad Worker

Workers in railroad occupations generally need a high school diploma or equivalent and several months of on-the-job training.

Education

Rail companies typically require a high school diploma or equivalent, especially for locomotive engineers and conductors.

Training

Locomotive engineers generally receive 2 to 3 months of on-the-job training before they can operate a train on their own. Typically, this training involves riding with an experienced engineer who teaches them the characteristics of that particular train route.

Locomotive engineers who work on long routes are sometimes away from home for long periods at a time.

All train employees need mechanical ability.

During training, an engineer learns the track length, where the switches are, and any unusual features of the track. An experienced engineer who switches to a new route also has to spend a few months in training to learn the route with an engineer who is familiar with it. In addition, railroad companies provide continuing education so that engineers can maintain their skills.

Most railroad companies have 1 to 3 months of on-the-job training for conductors and yardmasters. Amtrak (the passenger train company) and some of the larger freight railroad companies operate their own training programs. Smaller and regional railroads may send conductors to a central training facility or a community college.

Yardmasters may be sent to training programs or may be trained by an experienced yardmaster. They learn how to operate remote locomotive technology and how to manage railcars in the yard.

Conductors and yardmasters working for freight railroads also learn the proper procedures for loading and unloading different types of cargo. Conductors on passenger trains learn ticketing procedures and how to handle passengers.

Rail yard engineers and signal and switch operators also receive on-the-job training, generally through a company training program. This program may last a few weeks to a few months, depending on the company and the complexity of the job. The program may include some time in a classroom and some hands-on experience under the direction of an experienced employee.

Work Experience in a Related Occupation

Most locomotive engineers first work as conductors for several years.

Licenses, Certifications, and Registrations

Locomotive engineers must be certified by the Federal Railroad Administration (FRA). The certification, conducted by the railroad that employs them, involves a written knowledge test, a skills test, and a supervisor determining that the engineer understands all physical aspects of the particular route on which he or she will be operating.

An experienced engineer who changes routes must be recertified for the new route. Even engineers who do not switch routes must be recertified every few years.

At the end of the certification process, the engineer must pass a vision and hearing test.

Conductors who operate on national, regional, or commuter railroads are also required to become certified. To receive certification, new conductors must pass a test that has been designed and administered by the railroad and approved by the FRA.

Advancement

Rail yard engineers, switch operators, and signal operators can advance to become conductors or yardmasters. Some conductors or yardmasters advance to become locomotive engineers.

Important Qualities

Communication skills. All rail employees have to be able to communicate effectively with other crewmembers and passengers to keep the trains on schedule.

Customer-service skills. Conductors on passenger trains ensure customers' comfort, make announcements, and answer any travel questions a passenger has. They must be courteous and patient. They may have to deal with unruly or upset passengers.

Decisionmaking skills. When operating a locomotive, engineers must plan ahead and make decisions minutes or even hours in advance.

Hand-eye coordination. Locomotive engineers have to operate various controls while staying aware of their surroundings.

Hearing ability. To show that they can hear warning signals and communicate with other employees, locomotive engineers have to pass a hearing test conducted by their rail company.

Leadership skills. On some trains, a conductor directs a crew. In rail yards, yardmasters oversee other workers.

Mechanical skills. All rail employees work with complex machines. Most have to be able to adjust equipment when it does not work properly. Some rail yard engineers spend most of their time fixing broken equipment or conducting daily mechanical inspections.

Physical strength. Some rail yard engineers have to lift heavy equipment.

Visual ability. To drive a train, locomotive engineers have to pass a vision test conducted by their rail company. Eyesight, peripheral vision, and color vision may be tested.

In addition, locomotive operators must be at least 21 years of age and pass a background test. They must also pass random drug and alcohol screenings over the course of their employment.

Pay

The median annual wage for railroad workers was $65,020 in May 2019. The median wage is the wage at which half the workers in an occupation earned more than that amount and half earned less. The lowest 10 percent earned less than $43,740, and the highest 10 percent earned more than $98,990.

Median annual wages for railroad workers in May 2019 were as follows:

Locomotive engineers	$67,090
Railroad conductors and yardmasters	65,990
Railroad brake, signal, and switch operators and locomotive firers	60,260
Rail yard engineers, dinkey operators, and hostlers	49,330

In May 2019, the median annual wages for railroad workers in the top industries in which they worked were as follows:

Railroad Workers
Median annual wages, May 2019

Railroad workers	$65,020
Rail transportation workers	$64,890
Total, all occupations	$39,810

Note: All Occupations includes all occupations in the U.S. Economy.
Source: U.S. Bureau of Labor Statistics, Occupational Employment Statistics.

Rail transportation.. $66,360

Local government, excluding education and
  hospitals.. 62,040

Trains are scheduled to operate 24 hours a day, 7 days a week, meaning that many railroad workers sometimes work nights, weekends, and holidays. Most rail employees work full time. Federal regulations require a minimum number of rest hours for train operators.

Locomotive engineers and conductors whose trains travel long routes can be away from home for long periods of time. Those who work on passenger trains with short routes generally have a more predictable schedule. Workers on some freight trains have irregular schedules.

For engineers and conductors, seniority (the number of years on the job) usually dictates who receives the most desired shifts. Some engineers and conductors, called extra board, are hired on a temporary basis and get an assignment only when a railroad needs an extra or substitute worker on a certain route.

Job Outlook

Overall employment of railroad workers is projected to decline 3 percent from 2019 to 2029. Decreasing demand for the transportation of bulk commodities, such as coal and oil, is expected to cause some railroads to reduce employment in an effort to become more efficient.

As more pipelines open in oil- and natural gas-producing areas, the need for rail transportation in these areas may decline. In addition, power plants are increasingly using natural gas instead of coal for electricity production, which should contribute to reduced demand for coal.

However, an increase in intermodal freight—the shipment of goods through multiple transportation modes—may increase demand for some railroad workers.

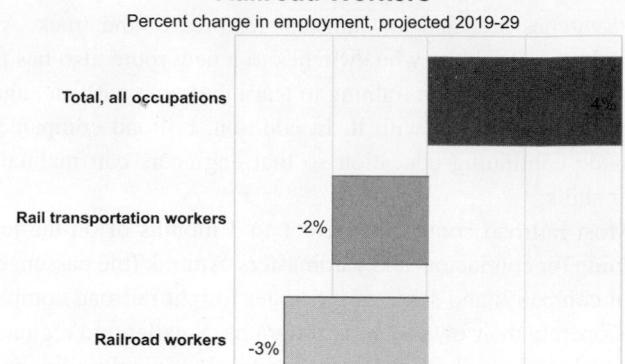

Railroad Workers
Percent change in employment, projected 2019-29

Total, all occupations	4%
Rail transportation workers	-2%
Railroad workers	-3%

Note: All Occupations includes all occupations in the U.S. Economy.
Source: U.S. Bureau of Labor Statistics, Employment Projections program.

Job Prospects

Job opportunities should be competitive for railroad workers. Job openings will primarily stem from the need to replace retiring workers.

Employment projections data for railroad workers, 2019-29					
Occupational Title	SOC Code	Employment, 2019	Projected Employment, 2029	Change, 2019-29	
				Percent	Numeric
SOURCE: U.S. Bureau of Labor Statistics, Employment Projections program					
Railroad workers	—	77,700	75,200	-3	-2,600
Locomotive engineers	53-4011	27,400	26,500	-3	-1,000
Rail yard engineers, dinkey operators, and hostlers	53-4013	5,200	4,900	-7	-400
Railroad brake, signal, and switch operators and locomotive firers	53-4022	9,100	8,600	-6	-500
Railroad conductors and yardmasters	53-4031	36,000	35,200	-2	-800

State & Area Data
Occupational Employment Statistics (OES)

The Occupational Employment Statistics (OES) program produces employment and wage estimates annually for over 800 occupations. These estimates are available for the nation as a whole, for individual states, and for metropolitan and nonmetropolitan areas.

Contacts for More Information

For more information about training programs, certifications, and job opportunities in rail transportation, visit
➤ National Railroad Passenger Corporation (Amtrak)
➤ Association of American Railroads (AAR)
➤ Federal Railroad Administration (FRA)

Water Transportation Workers

Summary

Quick Facts: Water Transportation Workers	
2019 Median Pay	$57,330 per year $27.56 per hour
Typical Entry-Level Education	See below
Work Experience in a Related Occupation	See below
On-the-job Training	See below
Number of Jobs, 2019	81,900
Job Outlook, 2019-29	0% (Little or no change)
Employment Change, 2019-29	200

What Water Transportation Workers Do

Water transportation workers operate and maintain vessels that take cargo and people over water.

Work Environment

Water transportation workers usually work for long periods and can be exposed to all kinds of weather.

How to Become a Water Transportation Worker

Education and training requirements vary with the type of job. There are no educational requirements for entry-level sailors and marine oilers, but other types of water transportation workers typically complete U.S. Coast Guard-approved training programs.

Pay

The median annual wage for water transportation workers was $57,330 in May 2019.

Job Outlook

Overall employment of water transportation workers is projected to show little or no change from 2019 to 2029.

Fluctuations in the demand for bulk commodities is a key factor influencing employment in these occupations.

State & Area Data

Explore resources for employment and wages by state and area for water transportation workers.

What Water Transportation Workers Do

Water transportation workers operate and maintain vessels that take cargo and people over water. The vessels travel to and from foreign ports across the ocean and to domestic ports along the coasts, across the Great Lakes, and along the country's many inland waterways.

Duties

Water transportation workers typically do the following:

- Operate and maintain nonmilitary vessels
- Follow their vessel's strict chain of command
- Ensure the safety of all people and cargo on board

These workers, sometimes called *merchant mariners*, work on a variety of ships.

Some operate large deep-sea container ships to transport manufactured goods and refrigerated cargos around the world.

Others work on bulk carriers that move heavy commodities, such as coal or iron ore, across the oceans and over the Great Lakes.

Still others work on both large and small tankers that carry oil and other liquid products around the country and the world. Others work on supply ships that transport equipment and supplies to offshore oil and gas platforms.

Workers on tugboats help barges and other boats maneuver in small harbors and at sea.

Salvage vessels that offer emergency services also employ merchant mariners.

Cruise ships also employ water transportation workers, and some merchant mariners work on ferries to transport passengers along shorter distances.

Water transportation workers often perform their duties in all types of weather conditions.

Captains and mates supervise other workers.

A typical deep-sea merchant ship, large coastal ship, or Great Lakes merchant ship employs a captain and a chief engineer, along with three mates, three assistant engineers, and a number of sailors and marine oilers. Smaller vessels that operate in harbors or rivers may have a smaller crew. The specific complement of mariners is dependent on U.S. Coast Guard regulations.

Also, there are other workers on ships, such as cooks, electricians, and general maintenance and repair workers.

The following are examples of types of water transportation workers:

Captains, sometimes called *masters*, have overall command of a vessel. They have the final responsibility for the safety of the crew, cargo, and passengers. Captains typically do the following:

- Steer and operate vessels
- Direct crew members
- Ensure that proper safety procedures are followed
- Purchase equipment and supplies and arrange for any necessary maintenance and repair Oversee the loading and unloading of cargo or passengers
- Keep logs and other records that track the ship's movements and activities
- Interact with passengers on cruise ships

Mates, or *deck officers*, direct the operation of a vessel while the captain is off duty. Large ships have three officers, called first, second, and third mates. The first mate has the highest authority and takes command of the ship if the captain is incapacitated. Usually, the first mate is in charge of the cargo and/or passengers, the second mate is in charge of navigation, and the third mate is in charge of safety. On smaller vessels, there may be only one mate who handles all of the responsibilities. Deck officers typically do the following:

- Alternate watches with the captain and other officers
- Supervise and coordinate the activities of the deck crew
- Assist with docking the ship
- Monitor the ship's position, using charts and other navigational aides
- Determine the speed and direction of the vessel
- Inspect the cargo hold during loading, to ensure that the cargo is stowed according to specifications
- Make announcements to passengers when needed

Pilots guide ships in harbors, on rivers, and on other confined waterways. They are not part of a ship's crew but go aboard a ship to guide it through a particular waterway that they are familiar with. They work in places where a high degree of familiarity with local tides, currents, and hazards is needed. Some, called *harbor pilots*, work for ports and help many ships that come into the harbor during the day. When coming into a commercial port, a captain will often have to turn control of the vessel over to a pilot, who can safely guide it into the harbor. Pilots typically do the following:

- Board an unfamiliar ship from a small boat in the open water, often using a ladder
- Confer with a ship's captain about the vessel's destination and any special requirements it has
- Establish a positive working relationship with a vessel's captain and deck officers
- Receive mooring instructions from shore dispatchers

Sailors, or *deckhands*, operate and maintain the vessel and deck equipment. They make up the deck crew and keep all parts of a ship, other than areas related to the engine and motor, in good working order. New deckhands are called *ordinary seamen* and do the least complicated tasks. Experienced deckhands are called *able seamen* and usually make up most of a crew. Some large ships have a *boatswain,* who is the chief of the deck crew. Sailors typically do the following:

- Stand watch, looking for other vessels or obstructions in their ship's path and for navigational aids, such as buoys and lighthouses
- Steer the ship under the guidance of an officer and measure water depth in shallow water
- Do routine maintenance, such as painting the deck and chipping away rust
- Keep the inside of the ship clean
- Handle mooring lines when docking or departing
- Tie barges together when they are being towed
- Load and unload cargo
- Help passengers when needed

Ship engineers operate and maintain a vessel's propulsion system, which includes the engine, boilers, generators, pumps, and other machinery. Large vessels usually carry a *chief engineer*, who has command of the engine room and its crew, and a first, second, and third assistant engineer. The assistant engineer oversees the engine and related machinery when the chief engineer is off duty. Small ships might have only one engineer. Engineers typically do the following:

- Maintain a ships' mechanical and electrical equipment and systems
- Start the engine and regulate the vessel's speed, following the captain's orders
- Record information in an engineering log
- Keep an inventory of mechanical parts and supplies
- Do routine maintenance checks throughout the day
- Calculate refueling requirements

Marine oilers work in the engine room, helping the engineers keep the propulsion system in working order. They are the engine room equivalent of sailors. New oilers usually are called *wipers,* or *pumpmen,* on vessels handling liquid cargo. With experience, a wiper can become a Qualified Member of the Engine Department (QMED). Marine oilers typically do the following:

- Lubricate gears, shafts, bearings, and other parts of the engine or motor
- Read pressure and temperature gauges and record data
- Perform daily and periodic maintenance on engine room machinery
- Help engineers with repairs to machinery
- Connect hoses, operate pumps, and clean tanks
- Assist the deck crew with loading or unloading of cargo, if necessary

Motorboat operators run small, motor-driven boats that carry only a few passengers. They provide a variety of services, such as fishing charters, tours, and harbor patrols. Motorboat operators typically do the following:

- Check and change the oil and other fluids on their boat
- Pick up passengers and help them board the boat
- Act as a tour guide, if necessary

Work Environment

Water transportation workers held about 81,900 jobs in 2019. Employment in the detailed occupations that make up water transportation workers was distributed as follows:

Captains, mates, and pilots of water vessels	38,900
Sailors and marine oilers	31,900
Ship engineers	8,700
Motorboat operators	2,500

The largest employers of water transportation workers were as follows:

Inland water transportation	21%
Deep sea, coastal, and great lakes water transportation	19
Support activities for water transportation	18
Scenic and sightseeing transportation, water	7
Federal government, excluding postal service	6

Water transportation workers usually work for long periods and can be exposed to all kinds of weather. Many people decide that life at sea is not for them because of difficult conditions onboard ships and long periods away from home.

However, companies try to provide pleasant living conditions aboard their vessels. Most vessels are air-conditioned and include comfortable living quarters. Many also include entertainment systems with satellite TV and Internet connections, and meals may be provided.

Work Schedules

Workers on deep-sea ships can spend months at a time away from home.

Workers on supply ships have shorter trips, usually lasting for a few hours or days.

Tugboats and barges travel along the coasts and on inland waterways, and crews are usually away for 2 to 3 weeks at a time.

Those who work on the Great Lakes have longer trips, around 2 months, but often do not work in the winter, when the lakes freeze.

Crews on all vessels often work for long periods, 7 days a week, while aboard.

Ferry workers and motorboat operators usually are away only for a few hours at a time and return home each night. Many ferry and motorboat operators service ships for vacation destinations and have seasonal schedules.

How to Become a Water Transportation Worker

Education and training requirements vary by the type of job. There are no educational requirements for entry-level sailors and marine oilers, but other types of water transportation workers typically complete U.S. Coast Guard-approved training programs. Most water transportation jobs require the Transportation Worker Identification Credential (TWIC) from the Transportation Security Administration and a Merchant Mariner Credential (MMC), plus any related endorsements, from the U.S. Coast Guard.

Education

Sailors and marine oilers usually do not need formal education. Other types of water transportation workers often complete

Long periods away from home are a reality for some workers.

Sailors and marine oilers typically receive training on the job.

U.S. Coast Guard-approved training programs to help them obtain their required credentials.

Employers may prefer to hire workers who have earned a bachelor's degree from a merchant marine academy. The academy programs offer a bachelor's degree and a Merchant Mariner Credential (MMC) with an endorsement as a third mate or third assistant engineer. Graduates of these programs also can choose to receive a commission as an ensign in the U.S. Naval Reserve, Merchant Marine Reserve, or U.S. Coast Guard Reserve.

Training

Ordinary seamen, wipers, and other entry-level mariners get on-the-job training for 6 months to a year. The length of training depends on the size and type of ship and waterway they work on. For example, workers on deep-sea vessels need more complex training than those whose ships travel on a river.

Licenses, Certifications, and Registrations

All mariners working on ships with U.S. flags must have a Transportation Worker Identification Credential (TWIC) from the Transportation Security Administration. This credential states that a person is a U.S. citizen or permanent resident and has passed a security screening. The TWIC must be renewed every 5 years.

Mariners who work on ships traveling on the open ocean require the Standards of Training, Certification, and Watchkeeping (STWC) endorsement. Regional U.S. Coast Guard offices provide this training, and it includes topics such as first aid and lifeboat safety. The STWC training must be completed every 5 years. Mariners who work on inland waterways and the Great Lakes are excluded from the STWC endorsement.

Most mariners also must have a Merchant Mariner Credential (MMC), which they can apply for at a U.S. Coast Guard regional examination center. Entry-level employees, such as ordinary seamen or wipers, do not have to pass a written exam. However, some have to pass physical, hearing, and vision tests, and all must undergo a drug screening, in order to get their MMC. They also have to take a class on shipboard safety. The MMC must also be renewed every 5 years. More information on MMCs and related endorsements is available from the U.S. Coast Guard National Maritime Center.

Pilots are licensed by the state in which they work. The U.S. Coast Guard licenses pilots on the Great Lakes. The requirements for these licenses vary, depending on where a pilot works.

Work Experience in a Related Occupation

Water transportation workers typically progress from lower level positions to higher level ones, making work experience an important requirement for many jobs. A ship engineer, for example, might need experience as a marine oiler, and mates may have previously worked as sailors. In some cases, workers gain the needed hands-on experience as part of their education program.

Advancement

After obtaining their MMC, crewmembers can apply for endorsements that may allow them to move into more advanced positions.

Wipers can get an endorsement to become a Qualified Member of the Engine Department (QMED) after 6 months of experience by passing a written test.

It takes 3 years of experience and the passing of a written test for an ordinary seaman to become an unlimited able seaman. However, several able seaman endorsements below the level of unlimited are available after 6 months to 1 year of experience, depending on the type of ship the seamen work on.

Able seamen can advance to become third mates after at least 3 years of experience in the deck department. This experience must be on a ship similar to the type they hope to serve on as an officer. They also must take several training courses and pass written and onboard exams to receive the third-mate's endorsement on their MMC. The difficulty of these requirements increases with the complexity and size of the vessel. Similarly, QMEDs can receive an endorsement as a third assistant engineer after 3 years of experience in the engine room and upon completion of a number of training and testing requirements. Experience and testing requirements increase with the size and complexity of the ship.

Officers who graduate from a maritime academy receive an MMC with an endorsement of a third mate or third assistant engineer, depending on the department in which they are trained.

To move up each step of the occupation ladder, from third mate/third assistant engineer, to second mate, to first mate, and then to captain or chief engineer, requires 365 days of experience at the previous level. A second mate or second assistant engineer who wants to move to first mate/first assistant engineer also must complete a 12-week training course and pass an exam.

Important Qualities

Customer-service skills. Many motorboat operators interact with passengers and must ensure that the passengers have a pleasant experience.

Hand-eye coordination. Officers and pilots who steer ships have to operate various controls while staying aware of their surroundings.

Hearing ability. Mariners must pass a hearing test to get an MMC.

Manual dexterity. Crewmembers need good balance to maneuver through tight spaces and on wet or uneven surfaces.

Mechanical skills. Members of the engine department keep complex machines working properly.

Physical strength. Sailors on freight ships load and unload cargo. While away at sea, most workers have to do some heavy lifting.

Visual ability. Mariners must pass a vision test to get an MMC.

Pay

The median annual wage for water transportation workers was $57,330 in May 2019. The median wage is the wage at which half the workers in an occupation earned more than that amount and half earned less. The lowest 10 percent earned less than $28,670, and the highest 10 percent earned more than $125,940.

Median annual wages for water transportation workers in May 2019 were as follows:

Ship engineers	$74,610
Captains, mates, and pilots of water vessels	72,340
Motorboat operators	48,260
Sailors and marine oilers	43,480

In May 2019, the median annual wages for water transportation workers in the top industries in which they worked were as follows:

Support activities for water transportation	$65,420
Inland water transportation	57,050
Deep sea, coastal, and great lakes water transportation	55,940
Federal government, excluding postal service	51,940
Scenic and sightseeing transportation, water	40,710

Workers on deep-sea ships can spend months at a time away from home.

Workers on supply ships have shorter trips, usually lasting for a few hours to a month.

Tugboats and barges travel along the coasts and on inland waterways and crews are usually away for 2 to 3 weeks at a time.

Those who work on the Great Lakes have longer trips, around 2 months, but often do not work in the winter, when the lakes freeze.

Crews on all vessels often work long hours, 7 days a week.

Ferry workers and motorboat operators usually are away only for a few hours at a time and return home each night. Many ferry and motorboat operators service ships for vacation destinations and have seasonal schedules.

Job Outlook

Overall employment of water transportation workers is projected to show little or no change from 2019 to 2029.

Fluctuations in the demand for bulk commodities, such as petroleum products, iron ore, and grains, is a key factor

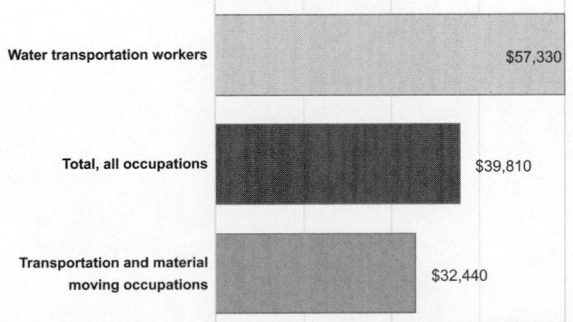

Water Transportation Workers
Median annual wages, May 2019

Water transportation workers $57,330
Total, all occupations $39,810
Transportation and material moving occupations $32,440

Note: All Occupations includes all occupations in the U.S. Economy.
Source: U.S. Bureau of Labor Statistics, Occupational Employment Statistics.

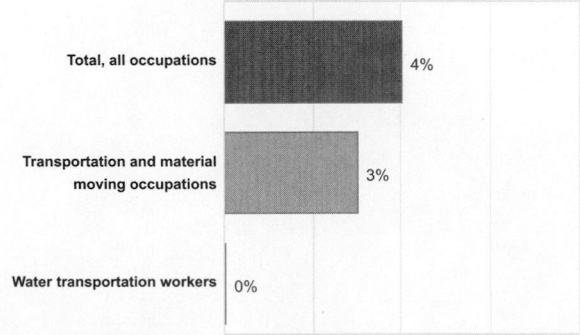

Water Transportation Workers
Percent change in employment, projected 2019-29

Total, all occupations 4%
Transportation and material moving occupations 3%
Water transportation workers 0%

Note: All Occupations includes all occupations in the U.S. Economy.
Source: U.S. Bureau of Labor Statistics, Employment Projections program.

influencing employment in these occupations. When demand for these commodities is high, the need for water transportation workers goes up; when demand slows, so does the need for workers. In addition, larger vessels that can carry more cargo require fewer water transportation workers.

Nevertheless, these workers will continue to be needed as federal laws and subsidies ensure that there always will be a fleet of merchant ships with U.S. flags. Keeping a fleet of merchant ships is considered important for the nation's defense.

Job Prospects

Despite limited employment growth, about 8,100 openings for water transportation workers are projected each year, on average, over the decade.

Most of those openings are expected to result from the need to replace workers who transfer to different occupations or exit the labor force, such as to retire. Some workers—especially sailors and marine oilers—may leave these occupations because they decide that they do not enjoy spending a lot of time away at sea.

High regulatory and security requirements may limit the number of applicants for all types of jobs.

Employment projections data for water transportation workers, 2019-29					
Occupational Title	SOC Code	Employment, 2019	Projected Employment, 2029	Change, 2019-29	
				Percent	Numeric
SOURCE: U.S. Bureau of Labor Statistics, Employment Projections program					
Water transportation workers	53-5000	81,900	82,100	0	200
Sailors and marine oilers	53-5011	31,900	32,200	1	300
Captains, mates, and pilots of water vessels	53-5021	38,900	38,700	0	-100

Employment projections data for water transportation workers, 2019-29					
Occupational Title	SOC Code	Employment, 2019	Projected Employment, 2029	Change, 2019-29	
				Percent	Numeric
Motorboat operators	53-5022	2,500	2,500	0	0
Ship engineers	53-5031	8,700	8,700	1	100

State & Area Data

Occupational Employment Statistics (OES)

The Occupational Employment Statistics (OES) program produces employment and wage estimates annually for over 800 occupations. These estimates are available for the nation as a whole, for individual states, and for metropolitan and nonmetropolitan areas.

Contacts for More Information

For more information about water transportation workers, including employment and training information, visit

➤ Maritime Administration, U.S. Department of Transportation

For more information about licensing requirements and other credentials, visit

➤ National Maritime Center, U.S. Coast Guard
➤ Transportation Security Administration, U.S. Department of Homeland Security

For information about jobs on barges, tugboats, and towboats traveling on inland and coastal waterways, visit

➤ Lake Carriers' Association
➤ Passenger Vessel Association
➤ The American Waterways Operators

Data for Occupations Not Covered in Detail

Although employment for hundreds of occupations is covered in detail in the *Occupational Outlook Handbook*, this page presents summary data on additional occupations for which employment projections are prepared but detailed occupational information is not developed. For each occupation, the Occupational Information Network (O*NET) code, the occupational definition, 2019 employment, the May 2019 median annual wage, the projected employment change and growth rate from 2019 to 2029, and education and training categories are presented

Management Occupations

Legislators
Develop, introduce, or enact laws and statutes at the local, tribal, state, or federal level. Includes only workers in elected positions.
- 2019 employment: **53,700**
- May 2019 median annual wage: **$29,270**
  - Wages come from the Occupational Employment Statistics (OES) program
- Projected employment change, 2019–29:
  - Number of new jobs: **3,300**
  - Growth rate: **6 percent (Faster than average)**
- Education and training:
  - Typical entry-level education: **Bachelor's degree**
  - Work experience in a related occupation: **Less than 5 years**
  - Typical on-the-job training: **None**
- O*NET links:
  - 11-1031.00 - Legislators
- CareerOneStop videos for this occupation:
  - 11-1031.00 - Legislators

Transportation, storage, and distribution managers
Plan, direct, or coordinate transportation, storage, or distribution activities in accordance with organizational policies and applicable government laws or regulations. Includes logistics managers.
- 2019 employment: **139,400**
- May 2019 median annual wage: **$94,560**
  - Wages come from the Occupational Employment Statistics (OES) program
- Projected employment change, 2019–29:
  - Number of new jobs: **4,900**
  - Growth rate: **4 percent (As fast as average)**
- Education and training:
  - Typical entry-level education: **High school diploma or equivalent**
  - Work experience in a related occupation: **5 years or more**
  - Typical on-the-job training: **None**
- O*NET links:
  - 11-3071.00 - Transportation, Storage, and Distribution Managers
  - 11-3071.01 - Transportation Managers
  - 11-3071.02 - Storage and Distribution Managers
  - 11-3071.03 - Logistics Managers
- CareerOneStop videos for this occupation:
  - 11-3071.01 - Transportation Managers
  - 11-3071.03 - Logistics Managers

Education administrators, all other
All education administrators not listed separately.
- 2019 employment: **52,100**
- May 2019 median annual wage: **$85,450**
  - Wages come from the Occupational Employment Statistics (OES) program
- Projected employment change, 2019–29:
  - Number of new jobs: **4,200**
  - Growth rate: **8 percent (Much faster than average)**
- Education and training:
  - Typical entry-level education: **Bachelor's degree**
  - Work experience in a related occupation: **Less than 5 years**
  - Typical on-the-job training: **None**
- O*NET links:
  - 11-9039.00 - Education Administrators, All Other
  - 11-9039.01 - Distance Learning Coordinators
  - 11-9039.02 - Fitness and Wellness Coordinators
- CareerOneStop videos for this occupation:
  - 11-9039.01 - Distance Learning Coordinators
  - 11-9039.02 - Fitness and Wellness Coordinators

Postmasters and mail superintendents
Plan, direct, or coordinate operational, administrative, management, and support services of a U.S. post office; or coordinate activities of workers engaged in postal and related work in assigned post office.
- 2019 employment: **13,400**
- May 2019 median annual wage: **$76,900**
  - Wages come from the Occupational Employment Statistics (OES) program
- Projected employment change, 2019–29:
  - Number of new jobs: **-2,900**
  - Growth rate: **-22 percent (Decline)**
- Education and training:
  - Typical entry-level education: **High school diploma or equivalent**
  - Work experience in a related occupation: **Less than 5 years**
  - Typical on-the-job training: **Moderate-term on-the-job training**
- O*NET links:
  - 11-9131.00 - Postmasters and Mail Superintendents
- CareerOneStop videos for this occupation:
  - 11-9131.00 - Postmasters and Mail Superintendents

Personal service managers, all other; entertainment and recreation managers, except gambling; and managers, all other
This is an OES hybrid
- 2019 employment: **1,189,200**
- May 2019 median annual wage: **$110,630**

○ Wages come from the Occupational Employment Statistics (OES) program
- Projected employment change, 2019–29:
  ○ Number of new jobs: **-21,700**
  ○ Growth rate: **-2 percent (Decline)**
- Education and training:
  ○ Typical entry-level education: **Bachelor's degree**
  ○ Work experience in a related occupation: **Less than 5 years**
  ○ Typical on-the-job training: **None**
- O*NET links:
  ○ 11-9199.00 - Managers, All Other
  ○ 11-9199.01 - Regulatory Affairs Managers
  ○ 11-9199.02 - Compliance Managers
  ○ 11-9199.03 - Investment Fund Managers
  ○ 11-9199.04 - Supply Chain Managers
  ○ 11-9199.07 - Security Managers
  ○ 11-9199.08 - Loss Prevention Managers
  ○ 11-9199.09 - Wind Energy Operations Managers
  ○ 11-9199.10 - Wind Energy Project Managers
  ○ 11-9199.11 - Brownfield Redevelopment Specialists and Site Managers
- CareerOneStop videos for this occupation:
  ○ 11-9199.01 - Regulatory Affairs Managers
  ○ 11-9199.03 - Investment Fund Managers
  ○ 11-9199.04 - Supply Chain Managers
  ○ 11-9199.07 - Security Managers
  ○ 11-9199.08 - Loss Prevention Managers
  ○ 11-9199.09 - Wind Energy Operations Managers
  ○ 11-9199.10 - Wind Energy Project Managers
  ○ 11-9199.11 - Brownfield Redevelopment Specialists and Site Managers

Business and financial operations Occupations

Agents and business managers of artists, performers, and athletes

Represent and promote artists, performers, and athletes in dealings with current or prospective employers. May handle contract negotiation and other business matters for clients.
- 2019 employment: **21,900**
- May 2019 median annual wage: **$73,740**
  ○ Wages come from the Occupational Employment Statistics (OES) program
- Projected employment change, 2019–29:
  ○ Number of new jobs: **2,600**
  ○ Growth rate: **12 percent (Much faster than average)**
- Education and training:
  ○ Typical entry-level education: **Bachelor's degree**
  ○ Work experience in a related occupation: **Less than 5 years**
  ○ Typical on-the-job training: **None**
- O*NET links:
  ○ 13-1011.00 - Agents and Business Managers of Artists, Performers, and Athletes
- CareerOneStop videos for this occupation:
  ○ 13-1011.00 - Agents and Business Managers of Artists, Performers, and Athletes

Compliance officers

Examine, evaluate, and investigate eligibility for or conformity with laws and regulations governing contract compliance of licenses and permits, and perform other compliance and enforcement inspection and analysis activities not classified elsewhere. Excludes "Financial Examiners" (13-2061), "Tax Examiners and Collectors, and Revenue Agents" (13-2081), "Occupational Health and Safety Specialists" (19-5011), "Occupational Health and Safety Technicians" (19-5012), "Transportation Security Screeners" (33-9093), "Agricultural Inspectors" (45-2011), "Construction and Building Inspectors" (47-4011), and "Transportation Inspectors" (53-6051).
- 2019 employment: **337,600**
- May 2019 median annual wage: **$69,050**
  ○ Wages come from the Occupational Employment Statistics (OES) program
- Projected employment change, 2019–29:
  ○ Number of new jobs: **15,600**
  ○ Growth rate: **5 percent (Faster than average)**
- Education and training:
  ○ Typical entry-level education: **Bachelor's degree**
  ○ Work experience in a related occupation: **None**
  ○ Typical on-the-job training: **Moderate-term on-the-job training**
- O*NET links:
  ○ 13-1041.00 - Compliance Officers
  ○ 13-1041.01 - Environmental Compliance Inspectors
  ○ 13-1041.02 - Licensing Examiners and Inspectors
  ○ 13-1041.03 - Equal Opportunity Representatives and Officers
  ○ 13-1041.04 - Government Property Inspectors and Investigators
  ○ 13-1041.06 - Coroners
  ○ 13-1041.07 - Regulatory Affairs Specialists
- CareerOneStop videos for this occupation:
  ○ 13-1041.02 - Licensing Examiners and Inspectors
  ○ 13-1041.03 - Equal Opportunity Representatives and Officers
  ○ 13-1041.06 - Coroners

Farm labor contractors

Recruit and hire seasonal or temporary agricultural laborers. May transport, house, and provide meals for workers.
- 2019 employment: **800**
- May 2019 median annual wage: **$61,910**
  ○ Wages come from the Occupational Employment Statistics (OES) program
- Projected employment change, 2019–29:
  ○ Number of new jobs: **100**
  ○ Growth rate: **10 percent (Much faster than average)**
- Education and training:
  ○ Typical entry-level education: **No formal educational credential**
  ○ Work experience in a related occupation: **Less than 5 years**
  ○ Typical on-the-job training: **Short-term on-the-job training**
- O*NET links:
  ○ 13-1074.00 - Farm Labor Contractors
- CareerOneStop videos for this occupation:
  ○ 13-1074.00 - Farm Labor Contractors

Project management specialists and business operations specialists, all other

This is an OES hybrid
- 2019 employment: **1,361,800**
- May 2019 median annual wage: **$73,570**
  ○ Wages come from the Occupational Employment Statistics (OES) program
- Projected employment change, 2019–29:
  ○ Number of new jobs: **79,800**

○ Growth rate: **6 percent (Faster than average)**
• Education and training:
  ○ Typical entry-level education: **Bachelor's degree**
  ○ Work experience in a related occupation: **None**
  ○ Typical on-the-job training: **None**
• O*NET links:
  ○ 13-1199.00 - Business Operations Specialists, All Other
  ○ 13-1199.01 - Energy Auditors
  ○ 13-1199.02 - Security Management Specialists
  ○ 13-1199.03 - Customs Brokers
  ○ 13-1199.04 - Business Continuity Planners
  ○ 13-1199.05 - Sustainability Specialists
  ○ 13-1199.06 - Online Merchants
• CareerOneStop videos for this occupation:
  ○ 13-1199.01 - Energy Auditors
  ○ 13-1199.06 - Online Merchants

Credit analysts

Analyze credit data and financial statements of individuals or firms to determine the degree of risk involved in extending credit or lending money. Prepare reports with credit information for use in decisionmaking. Excludes "Financial Risk Specialists" (13-2054).
• 2019 employment: **74,900**
• May 2019 median annual wage: **$73,650**
  ○ Wages come from the Occupational Employment Statistics (OES) program
• Projected employment change, 2019–29:
  ○ Number of new jobs: **-3,600**
  ○ Growth rate: **-5 percent (Decline)**
• Education and training:
  ○ Typical entry-level education: **Bachelor's degree**
  ○ Work experience in a related occupation: **None**
  ○ Typical on-the-job training: **None**
• O*NET links:
  ○ 13-2041.00 - Credit Analysts
• CareerOneStop videos for this occupation:
  ○ 13-2041.00 - Credit Analysts

Credit counselors

Advise and educate individuals or organizations on acquiring and managing debt. May provide guidance in determining the best type of loan and explain loan requirements or restrictions. May help develop debt management plans or student financial aid packages. May advise on credit issues, or provide budget, mortgage, bankruptcy, or student financial aid counseling.
• 2019 employment: **35,600**
• May 2019 median annual wage: **$45,950**
  ○ Wages come from the Occupational Employment Statistics (OES) program
• Projected employment change, 2019–29:
  ○ Number of new jobs: **2,700**
  ○ Growth rate: **8 percent (Much faster than average)**
• Education and training:
  ○ Typical entry-level education: **Bachelor's degree**
  ○ Work experience in a related occupation: **None**
  ○ Typical on-the-job training: **Moderate-term on-the-job training**
• O*NET links:
  ○ 13-2071.00 - Credit Counselors
  ○ 13-2071.01 - Loan Counselors
• CareerOneStop videos for this occupation:
  ○ 13-2071.01 - Loan Counselors

Tax preparers

Prepare tax returns for individuals or small businesses. Excludes "Accountants and Auditors" (13-2011).
• 2019 employment: **88,400**
• May 2019 median annual wage: **$43,080**
  ○ Wages come from the Occupational Employment Statistics (OES) program
• Projected employment change, 2019–29:
  ○ Number of new jobs: **-600**
  ○ Growth rate: **-1 percent (Decline)**
• Education and training:
  ○ Typical entry-level education: **High school diploma or equivalent**
  ○ Work experience in a related occupation: **None**
  ○ Typical on-the-job training: **Moderate-term on-the-job training**
• O*NET links:
  ○ 13-2082.00 - Tax Preparers
• CareerOneStop videos for this occupation:
  ○ 13-2082.00 - Tax Preparers

Computer and Mathematical Occupations

Computer occupations, all other

All computer occupations not listed separately. Excludes "Computer and Information Systems Managers" (11-3021), "Computer Hardware Engineers" (17-2061), "Electrical and Electronics Engineers" (17-2070), "Computer Science Teachers, Postsecondary" (25-1021), "Special Effects Artists and Animators" (27-1014), "Graphic Designers" (27-1024), "Health Information Technologists and Medical Registrars" (29-9021), and "Computer, Automated Teller, and Office Machine Repairers" (49-2011).
• 2019 employment: **431,100**
• May 2019 median annual wage: **$88,550**
  ○ Wages come from the Occupational Employment Statistics (OES) program
• Projected employment change, 2019–29:
  ○ Number of new jobs: **24,700**
  ○ Growth rate: **6 percent (Faster than average)**
• Education and training:
  ○ Typical entry-level education: **Bachelor's degree**
  ○ Work experience in a related occupation: **None**
  ○ Typical on-the-job training: **None**
• O*NET links:
  ○ 15-1199.00 - Computer Occupations, All Other
  ○ 15-1199.01 - Software Quality Assurance Engineers and Testers
  ○ 15-1199.02 - Computer Systems Engineers/Architects
  ○ 15-1199.03 - Web Administrators
  ○ 15-1199.04 - Geospatial Information Scientists and Technologists
  ○ 15-1199.05 - Geographic Information Systems Technicians
  ○ 15-1199.06 - Database Architects
  ○ 15-1199.07 - Data Warehousing Specialists
  ○ 15-1199.08 - Business Intelligence Analysts
  ○ 15-1199.09 - Information Technology Project Managers
  ○ 15-1199.10 - Search Marketing Strategists
  ○ 15-1199.11 - Video Game Designers
  ○ 15-1199.12 - Document Management Specialists
  ○ 43-9011.00 - Computer Operators
• CareerOneStop videos for this occupation:
  ○ 15-1199.01 - Software Quality Assurance Engineers and Testers

○ 15-1199.11 - Video Game Designers
○ 43-9011.00 - Computer Operators

Data scientists and mathematical science occupations, all other
This is an OES hybrid
- 2019 employment: **33,200**
- May 2019 median annual wage: **$94,280**
  ○ Wages come from the Occupational Employment Statistics (OES) program
- Projected employment change, 2019–29:
  ○ Number of new jobs: **10,300**
  ○ Growth rate: **31 percent (Much faster than average)**
- Education and training:
  ○ Typical entry-level education: **Bachelor's degree**
  ○ Work experience in a related occupation: **None**
  ○ Typical on-the-job training: **None**
- O*NET links:
  ○ 15-2091.00 - Mathematical Technicians
  ○ 15-2099.00 - Mathematical Science Occupations, All Other

Architecture and Engineering Occupations

Engineers, all other
All engineers not listed separately. Excludes "Sales Engineers" (41-9031), "Locomotive Engineers" (53-4011), and "Ship Engineers" (53-5031).
- 2019 employment: **170,100**
- May 2019 median annual wage: **$99,040**
  ○ Wages come from the Occupational Employment Statistics (OES) program
- Projected employment change, 2019–29:
  ○ Number of new jobs: **2,200**
  ○ Growth rate: **1 percent (Slower than average)**
- Education and training:
  ○ Typical entry-level education: **Bachelor's degree**
  ○ Work experience in a related occupation: **None**
  ○ Typical on-the-job training: **None**
- O*NET links:
  ○ 17-2199.00 - Engineers, All Other
  ○ 17-2199.01 - Biochemical Engineers
  ○ 17-2199.02 - Validation Engineers
  ○ 17-2199.03 - Energy Engineers
  ○ 17-2199.04 - Manufacturing Engineers
  ○ 17-2199.05 - Mechatronics Engineers
  ○ 17-2199.06 - Microsystems Engineers
  ○ 17-2199.07 - Photonics Engineers
  ○ 17-2199.08 - Robotics Engineers
  ○ 17-2199.09 - Nanosystems Engineers
  ○ 17-2199.10 - Wind Energy Engineers
  ○ 17-2199.11 - Solar Energy Systems Engineers

Calibration technologists and technicians and engineering technologists and technicians, except drafters, all other
This is an OES hybrid
- 2019 employment: **91,600**
- May 2019 median annual wage: **$62,990**
  ○ Wages come from the Occupational Employment Statistics (OES) program

- Projected employment change, 2019–29:
  ○ Number of new jobs: **2,000**
  ○ Growth rate: **2 percent (Slower than average)**
- Education and training:
  ○ Typical entry-level education: **Associate's degree**
  ○ Work experience in a related occupation: **None**
  ○ Typical on-the-job training: **None**
- O*NET links:
  ○ 17-3029.00 - Engineering Technicians, Except Drafters, All Other
  ○ 17-3029.01 - Non-Destructive Testing Specialists
  ○ 17-3029.02 - Electrical Engineering Technologists
  ○ 17-3029.03 - Electromechanical Engineering Technologists
  ○ 17-3029.04 - Electronics Engineering Technologists
  ○ 17-3029.05 - Industrial Engineering Technologists
  ○ 17-3029.06 - Manufacturing Engineering Technologists
  ○ 17-3029.07 - Mechanical Engineering Technologists
  ○ 17-3029.08 - Photonics Technicians
  ○ 17-3029.09 - Manufacturing Production Technicians
  ○ 17-3029.10 - Fuel Cell Technicians
  ○ 17-3029.11 - Nanotechnology Engineering Technologists
  ○ 17-3029.12 - Nanotechnology Engineering Technicians

Life, Physical, and Social Science Occupations

Biological scientists, all other
All biological scientists not listed separately.
- 2019 employment: **44,700**
- May 2019 median annual wage: **$82,220**
  ○ Wages come from the Occupational Employment Statistics (OES) program
- Projected employment change, 2019–29:
  ○ Number of new jobs: **1,000**
  ○ Growth rate: **2 percent (Slower than average)**
- Education and training:
  ○ Typical entry-level education: **Bachelor's degree**
  ○ Work experience in a related occupation: **None**
  ○ Typical on-the-job training: **None**
- O*NET links:
  ○ 19-1029.00 - Biological Scientists, All Other
  ○ 19-1029.01 - Bioinformatics Scientists
  ○ 19-1029.02 - Molecular and Cellular Biologists
  ○ 19-1029.03 - Geneticists
- CareerOneStop videos for this occupation:
  ○ 19-1029.03 - Geneticists

Life scientists, all other
All life scientists not listed separately.
- 2019 employment: **7,000**
- May 2019 median annual wage: **$75,910**
  ○ Wages come from the Occupational Employment Statistics (OES) program
- Projected employment change, 2019–29:
  ○ Number of new jobs: **300**
  ○ Growth rate: **5 percent (Faster than average)**
- Education and training:
  ○ Typical entry-level education: **Bachelor's degree**
  ○ Work experience in a related occupation: **None**
  ○ Typical on-the-job training: **None**
- O*NET links:
  ○ 19-1099.00 - Life Scientists, All Other

Physical scientists, all other

All physical scientists not listed separately.

- 2019 employment: **22,800**
- May 2019 median annual wage: **$109,910**
  - Wages come from the Occupational Employment Statistics (OES) program
- Projected employment change, 2019–29:
  - Number of new jobs: **-700**
  - Growth rate: **-3 percent (Decline)**
- Education and training:
  - Typical entry-level education: **Bachelor's degree**
  - Work experience in a related occupation: **None**
  - Typical on-the-job training: **None**
- O*NET links:
  - 19-2099.00 - Physical Scientists, All Other
  - 19-2099.01 - Remote Sensing Scientists and Technologists
- CareerOneStop videos for this occupation:
  - 19-2099.01 - Remote Sensing Scientists and Technologists

Social scientists and related workers, all other

All social scientists and related workers not listed separately.

- 2019 employment: **38,800**
- May 2019 median annual wage: **$83,330**
  - Wages come from the Occupational Employment Statistics (OES) program
- Projected employment change, 2019–29:
  - Number of new jobs: **300**
  - Growth rate: **1 percent (Slower than average)**
- Education and training:
  - Typical entry-level education: **Bachelor's degree**
  - Work experience in a related occupation: **None**
  - Typical on-the-job training: **None**
- O*NET links:
  - 19-3099.00 - Social Scientists and Related Workers, All Other
  - 19-3099.01 - Transportation Planners

Social science research assistants

Assist social scientists in laboratory, survey, and other social science research. May help prepare findings for publication and assist in laboratory analysis, quality control, or data management. Excludes "Teaching Assistants, Postsecondary" (25-9044).

- 2019 employment: **40,100**
- May 2019 median annual wage: **$47,510**
  - Wages come from the Occupational Employment Statistics (OES) program
- Projected employment change, 2019–29:
  - Number of new jobs: **2,300**
  - Growth rate: **6 percent (Faster than average)**
- Education and training:
  - Typical entry-level education: **Bachelor's degree**
  - Work experience in a related occupation: **None**
  - Typical on-the-job training: **None**
- O*NET links:
  - 19-4061.00 - Social Science Research Assistants
  - 19-4061.01 - City and Regional Planning Aides

Forest and conservation technicians

Provide technical assistance regarding the conservation of soil, water, forests, or related natural resources. May compile data pertaining to size, content, condition, and other characteristics of forest tracts under the direction of foresters, or train and lead forest workers in forest propagation and fire prevention and suppression. May assist conserva-

tion scientists in managing, improving, and protecting rangelands and wildlife habitats. Excludes "Conservation Scientists" (19-1031) and "Foresters" (19-1032).

- 2019 employment: **21,200**
- May 2019 median annual wage: **$45,500**
  - Wages come from the Occupational Employment Statistics (OES) program
- Projected employment change, 2019–29:
  - Number of new jobs: **100**
  - Growth rate: **1 percent (Slower than average)**
- Education and training:
  - Typical entry-level education: **Associate's degree**
  - Work experience in a related occupation: **None**
  - Typical on-the-job training: **None**
- O*NET links:
  - 19-4093.00 - Forest and Conservation Technicians

Life, physical, and social science technicians, all other

All life, physical, and social science technicians not listed separately.

- 2019 employment: **71,000**
- May 2019 median annual wage: **$50,550**
  - Wages come from the Occupational Employment Statistics (OES) program
- Projected employment change, 2019–29:
  - Number of new jobs: **3,400**
  - Growth rate: **5 percent (Faster than average)**
- Education and training:
  - Typical entry-level education: **Associate's degree**
  - Work experience in a related occupation: **None**
  - Typical on-the-job training: **None**
- O*NET links:
  - 19-4099.00 - Life, Physical, and Social Science Technicians, All Other
  - 19-4099.01 - Quality Control Analysts
  - 19-4099.02 - Precision Agriculture Technicians
  - 19-4099.03 - Remote Sensing Technicians
- CareerOneStop videos for this occupation:
  - 19-4099.03 - Remote Sensing Technicians

Community and Social Service Occupations

Counselors, all other

All counselors not listed separately.

- 2019 employment: **29,100**
- May 2019 median annual wage: **$42,930**
  - Wages come from the Occupational Employment Statistics (OES) program
- Projected employment change, 2019–29:
  - Number of new jobs: **3,800**
  - Growth rate: **13 percent (Much faster than average)**
- Education and training:
  - Typical entry-level education: **Master's degree**
  - Work experience in a related occupation: **None**
  - Typical on-the-job training: **None**
- O*NET links:
  - 21-1019.00 - Counselors, All Other

Community and social service specialists, all other

All community and social service specialists not listed separately.

- 2019 employment: **105,200**
- May 2019 median annual wage: **$43,790**

○ Wages come from the Occupational Employment Statistics (OES) program
- Projected employment change, 2019–29:
  ○ Number of new jobs: **12,400**
  ○ Growth rate: **12 percent (Much faster than average)**
- Education and training:
  ○ Typical entry-level education: **Bachelor's degree**
  ○ Work experience in a related occupation: **None**
  ○ Typical on-the-job training: **None**
- O*NET links:
  ○ 21-1099.00 - Community and Social Service Specialists, All Other

Clergy
Conduct religious worship and perform other spiritual functions associated with beliefs and practices of religious faith or denomination. Provide spiritual and moral guidance and assistance to members.
- 2019 employment: **243,900**
- May 2019 median annual wage: **$50,400**
  ○ Wages come from the Occupational Employment Statistics (OES) program
- Projected employment change, 2019–29:
  ○ Number of new jobs: **9,700**
  ○ Growth rate: **4 percent (As fast as average)**
- Education and training:
  ○ Typical entry-level education: **Bachelor's degree**
  ○ Work experience in a related occupation: **None**
  ○ Typical on-the-job training: **Moderate-term on-the-job training**
- O*NET links:
  ○ 21-2011.00 - Clergy
- CareerOneStop videos for this occupation:
  ○ 21-2011.00 - Clergy

Directors, religious activities and education
Coordinate or design programs and conduct outreach to promote the religious education or activities of a denominational group. May provide counseling, guidance, and leadership relative to marital, health, financial, and religious problems.
- 2019 employment: **157,500**
- May 2019 median annual wage: **$43,860**
  ○ Wages come from the Occupational Employment Statistics (OES) program
- Projected employment change, 2019–29:
  ○ Number of new jobs: **5,200**
  ○ Growth rate: **3 percent (As fast as average)**
- Education and training:
  ○ Typical entry-level education: **Bachelor's degree**
  ○ Work experience in a related occupation: **Less than 5 years**
  ○ Typical on-the-job training: **None**
- O*NET links:
  ○ 21-2021.00 - Directors, Religious Activities and Education
- CareerOneStop videos for this occupation:
  ○ 21-2021.00 - Directors, Religious Activities and Education

Religious workers, all other
All religious workers not listed separately.
- 2019 employment: **65,000**
- May 2019 median annual wage: **$31,630**
  ○ Wages come from the Occupational Employment Statistics (OES) program
- Projected employment change, 2019–29:

○ Number of new jobs: **2,100**
○ Growth rate: **3 percent (As fast as average)**
- Education and training:
  ○ Typical entry-level education: **Bachelor's degree**
  ○ Work experience in a related occupation: **None**
  ○ Typical on-the-job training: **None**
- O*NET links:
  ○ 21-2099.00 - Religious Workers, All Other

Legal Occupations

Judicial law clerks
Assist judges in court or by conducting research or preparing legal documents. Excludes "Lawyers" (23-1011) and "Paralegals and Legal Assistants" (23-2011).
- 2019 employment: **17,300**
- May 2019 median annual wage: **$54,010**
  ○ Wages come from the Occupational Employment Statistics (OES) program
- Projected employment change, 2019–29:
  ○ Number of new jobs: **600**
  ○ Growth rate: **3 percent (As fast as average)**
- Education and training:
  ○ Typical entry-level education: **Doctoral or professional degree**
  ○ Work experience in a related occupation: **None**
  ○ Typical on-the-job training: **None**
- O*NET links:
  ○ 23-1012.00 - Judicial Law Clerks
- CareerOneStop videos for this occupation:
  ○ 23-1012.00 - Judicial Law Clerks

Title examiners, abstractors, and searchers
Search real estate records, examine titles, or summarize pertinent legal or insurance documents or details for a variety of purposes. May compile lists of mortgages, contracts, and other instruments pertaining to titles by searching public and private records for law firms, real estate agencies, or title insurance companies. Excludes "Loan Officers" (13-2072).
- 2019 employment: **63,600**
- May 2019 median annual wage: **$48,180**
  ○ Wages come from the Occupational Employment Statistics (OES) program
- Projected employment change, 2019–29:
  ○ Number of new jobs: **-1,600**
  ○ Growth rate: **-3 percent (Decline)**
- Education and training:
  ○ Typical entry-level education: **High school diploma or equivalent**
  ○ Work experience in a related occupation: **None**
  ○ Typical on-the-job training: **Moderate-term on-the-job training**
- O*NET links:
  ○ 23-2093.00 - Title Examiners, Abstractors, and Searchers
- CareerOneStop videos for this occupation:
  ○ 23-2093.00 - Title Examiners, Abstractors, and Searchers

Legal support workers, all other
All legal support workers not listed separately.
- 2019 employment: **50,400**
- May 2019 median annual wage: **$58,400**

○ Wages come from the Occupational Employment Statistics (OES) program
- Projected employment change, 2019–29:
  ○ Number of new jobs: **-600**
  ○ Growth rate: **-1 percent (Decline)**
- Education and training:
  ○ Typical entry-level education: **Associate's degree**
  ○ Work experience in a related occupation: **None**
  ○ Typical on-the-job training: **None**
- O*NET links:
  ○ 23-2099.00 - Legal Support Workers, All Other

Educational Instruction and Library Occupations

Family and consumer sciences teachers, postsecondary
Teach courses in childcare, family relations, finance, nutrition, and related subjects pertaining to home management. Includes both teachers primarily engaged in teaching and those who do a combination of teaching and research.
- 2019 employment: **2,500**
- May 2019 median annual wage: **$76,480**
  ○ Wages come from the Occupational Employment Statistics (OES) program
- Projected employment change, 2019–29:
  ○ Number of new jobs: **0**
  ○ Growth rate: **1 percent (Slower than average)**
- Education and training:
  ○ Typical entry-level education: **Master's degree**
  ○ Work experience in a related occupation: **None**
  ○ Typical on-the-job training: **None**
- O*NET links:
  ○ 25-1192.00 - Home Economics Teachers, Postsecondary

Recreation and fitness studies teachers, postsecondary
Teach courses pertaining to recreation, leisure, and fitness studies, including exercise physiology and facilities management. Includes both teachers primarily engaged in teaching and those who do a combination of teaching and research.
- 2019 employment: **19,100**
- May 2019 median annual wage: **$64,380**
  ○ Wages come from the Occupational Employment Statistics (OES) program
- Projected employment change, 2019–29:
  ○ Number of new jobs: **500**
  ○ Growth rate: **3 percent (As fast as average)**
- Education and training:
  ○ Typical entry-level education: **Doctoral or professional degree**
  ○ Work experience in a related occupation: **None**
  ○ Typical on-the-job training: **None**
- O*NET links:
  ○ 25-1193.00 - Recreation and Fitness Studies Teachers, Postsecondary

Postsecondary teachers, all other
All postsecondary teachers not listed separately.
- 2019 employment: **245,900**
- May 2019 median annual wage: **$68,970**
  ○ Wages come from the Occupational Employment Statistics (OES) program
- Projected employment change, 2019–29:

○ Number of new jobs: **4,800**
○ Growth rate: **2 percent (Slower than average)**
- Education and training:
  ○ Typical entry-level education: **Doctoral or professional degree**
  ○ Work experience in a related occupation: **None**
  ○ Typical on-the-job training: **None**
- O*NET links:
  ○ 25-1199.00 - Postsecondary Teachers, All Other

Special education teachers, all other
All special education teachers not listed separately.
- 2019 employment: **36,600**
- May 2019 median annual wage: **$61,190**
  ○ Wages come from the Occupational Employment Statistics (OES) program
- Projected employment change, 2019–29:
  ○ Number of new jobs: **3,100**
  ○ Growth rate: **8 percent (Much faster than average)**
- Education and training:
  ○ Typical entry-level education: **Bachelor's degree**
  ○ Work experience in a related occupation: **None**
  ○ Typical on-the-job training: **None**
- O*NET links:
  ○ 25-2059.00 - Special Education Teachers, All Other
  ○ 25-2059.01 - Adapted Physical Education Specialists

Self-enrichment teachers
Teach or instruct individuals or groups for the primary purpose of self-enrichment or recreation, rather than for an occupational objective, educational attainment, competition, or fitness. Excludes "Coaches and Scouts" (27-2022) and "Exercise Trainers and Group Fitness Instructors" (39-9031). Flight instructors are included with "Aircraft Pilots and Flight Engineers" (53-2010).
- 2019 employment: **386,200**
- May 2019 median annual wage: **$39,190**
  ○ Wages come from the Occupational Employment Statistics (OES) program
- Projected employment change, 2019–29:
  ○ Number of new jobs: **39,800**
  ○ Growth rate: **10 percent (Much faster than average)**
- Education and training:
  ○ Typical entry-level education: **High school diploma or equivalent**
  ○ Work experience in a related occupation: **Less than 5 years**
  ○ Typical on-the-job training: **None**
- O*NET links:
  ○ 25-3021.00 - Self-Enrichment Education Teachers
- CareerOneStop videos for this occupation:
  ○ 25-3021.00 - Self-Enrichment Education Teachers

Substitute teachers, short-term
Teach students on a short-term basis as a temporary replacement for a regular classroom teacher, typically using the regular teacher's lesson plan. Excludes long-term substitute teachers who perform all the duties of a regular teacher; these teachers are coded within the 25-1000 or 25-2000 minor groups.
- 2019 employment: **619,400**
- May 2019 median annual wage: **$28,790**
  ○ Wages come from the Occupational Employment Statistics (OES) program
- Projected employment change, 2019–29:
  ○ Number of new jobs: **15,900**

○ Growth rate: **3 percent (As fast as average)**
• Education and training:
○ Typical entry-level education: **Bachelor's degree**
○ Work experience in a related occupation: **None**
○ Typical on-the-job training: **None**
• O*NET links:
○ 25-3099.00 - Teachers and Instructors, All Other
○ 25-3099.00 - Teachers and Instructors, All Other
○ 25-3099.02 - Tutors
○ 25-3099.02 - Tutors
• CareerOneStop videos for this occupation:
○ 25-3099.02 - Tutors
○ 25-3099.02 - Tutors

Tutors and teachers and instructors, all other

This is an OES hybrid
• 2019 employment: **406,200**
• May 2019 median annual wage: **$39,350**
○ Wages come from the Occupational Employment Statistics (OES) program
• Projected employment change, 2019–29:
○ Number of new jobs: **30,200**
○ Growth rate: **7 percent (Faster than average)**
• Education and training:
○ Typical entry-level education: **Bachelor's degree**
○ Work experience in a related occupation: **None**
○ Typical on-the-job training: **None**
• O*NET links:
○ 25-3099.00 - Teachers and Instructors, All Other
○ 25-3099.02 - Tutors
• CareerOneStop videos for this occupation:
○ 25-3099.02 - Tutors

Farm and home management educators

Instruct and advise individuals and families engaged in agriculture, agricultural-related processes, or home management activities. Demonstrate procedures and apply research findings to advance agricultural and home management activities. May develop educational outreach programs. May instruct on either agricultural issues such as agricultural processes and techniques, pest management, and food safety, or on home management issues such as budgeting, nutrition, and child development. Excludes "Dietitians and Nutritionists" (29-1031).
• 2019 employment: **10,400**
• May 2019 median annual wage: **$49,710**
○ Wages come from the Occupational Employment Statistics (OES) program
• Projected employment change, 2019–29:
○ Number of new jobs: **-400**
○ Growth rate: **-4 percent (Decline)**
• Education and training:
○ Typical entry-level education: **Master's degree**
○ Work experience in a related occupation: **None**
○ Typical on-the-job training: **None**
• O*NET links:
○ 25-9021.00 - Farm and Home Management Advisors
• CareerOneStop videos for this occupation:
○ 25-9021.00 - Farm and Home Management Advisors

Teaching assistants, postsecondary

Assist faculty or other instructional staff in postsecondary institutions by performing instructional support activities, such as developing teaching materials, leading discussion groups, preparing and giving examinations, and grading examinations or papers. Graduate students who teach one or more full courses should be classified in the 25-1000 minor group.
• 2019 employment: **169,600**
• May 2019 median annual wage: **$32,080**
○ Wages come from the Occupational Employment Statistics (OES) program
• Projected employment change, 2019–29:
○ Number of new jobs: **5,800**
○ Growth rate: **3 percent (As fast as average)**
• Education and training:
○ Typical entry-level education: **Bachelor's degree**
○ Work experience in a related occupation: **None**
○ Typical on-the-job training: **None**
• O*NET links:
○ 25-1191.00 - Graduate Teaching Assistants
• CareerOneStop videos for this occupation:
○ 25-1191.00 - Graduate Teaching Assistants

Educational instruction and library workers, all other

All educational instruction and library workers not listed separately.
• 2019 employment: **141,400**
• May 2019 median annual wage: **$40,310**
○ Wages come from the Occupational Employment Statistics (OES) program
• Projected employment change, 2019–29:
○ Number of new jobs: **6,200**
○ Growth rate: **4 percent (As fast as average)**
• Education and training:
○ Typical entry-level education: **Bachelor's degree**
○ Work experience in a related occupation: **None**
○ Typical on-the-job training: **None**
• O*NET links:
○ 25-9099.00 - Education, Training, and Library Workers, All Other

Arts, Design, Entertainment, Sports, and Media Occupations

Merchandise displayers and window trimmers

Plan and erect commercial displays, such as those in windows and interiors of retail stores and at trade exhibitions.
• 2019 employment: **180,400**
• May 2019 median annual wage: **$29,460**
○ Wages come from the Occupational Employment Statistics (OES) program
• Projected employment change, 2019–29:
○ Number of new jobs: **-6,200**
○ Growth rate: **-3 percent (Decline)**
• Education and training:
○ Typical entry-level education: **High school diploma or equivalent**
○ Work experience in a related occupation: **None**
○ Typical on-the-job training: **Short-term on-the-job training**
• O*NET links:
○ 27-1026.00 - Merchandise Displayers and Window Trimmers
• CareerOneStop videos for this occupation:
○ 27-1026.00 - Merchandise Displayers and Window Trimmers

Set and exhibit designers

Design special exhibits and sets for film, video, television, and theater productions. May study scripts, confer with directors, and conduct research to determine appropriate architectural styles.

- 2019 employment: **15,200**
- May 2019 median annual wage: **$54,600**
  - Wages come from the Occupational Employment Statistics (OES) program
- Projected employment change, 2019–29:
  - Number of new jobs: **200**
  - Growth rate: **1 percent (Slower than average)**
- Education and training:
  - Typical entry-level education: **Bachelor's degree**
  - Work experience in a related occupation: **None**
  - Typical on-the-job training: **None**
- O*NET links:
  - 27-1027.00 - Set and Exhibit Designers
- CareerOneStop videos for this occupation:
  - 27-1027.00 - Set and Exhibit Designers

Designers, all other

All designers not listed separately.

- 2019 employment: **13,600**
- May 2019 median annual wage: **$64,620**
  - Wages come from the Occupational Employment Statistics (OES) program
- Projected employment change, 2019–29:
  - Number of new jobs: **-300**
  - Growth rate: **-2 percent (Decline)**
- Education and training:
  - Typical entry-level education: **Bachelor's degree**
  - Work experience in a related occupation: **None**
  - Typical on-the-job training: **None**
- O*NET links:
  - 27-1029.00 - Designers, All Other

Miscellaneous entertainers and performers, sports and related workers

This is an OES hybrid

- 2019 employment: **33,300**
- May 2019 median annual wage: **The annual wage is not available.**
- Projected employment change, 2019–29:
  - Number of new jobs: **1,400**
  - Growth rate: **4 percent (As fast as average)**
- Education and training:
  - Typical entry-level education: **No formal educational credential**
  - Work experience in a related occupation: **None**
  - Typical on-the-job training: **Short-term on-the-job training**
- O*NET links:
  - 27-2099.00 - Entertainers and Performers, Sports and Related Workers, All Other

Lighting technicians and media and communication equipment workers, all other

This is an OES hybrid

- 2019 employment: **26,600**
- May 2019 median annual wage: **$73,460**
  - Wages come from the Occupational Employment Statistics (OES) program
- Projected employment change, 2019–29:

- Number of new jobs: **1,300**
- Growth rate: **5 percent (Faster than average)**
- Education and training:
  - Typical entry-level education: **High school diploma or equivalent**
  - Work experience in a related occupation: **None**
  - Typical on-the-job training: **Short-term on-the-job training**
- O*NET links:
  - 27-4099.00 - Media and Communication Equipment Workers, All Other

---

Healthcare Practitioners and Technical Occupations

Therapists, all other

All therapists not listed separately.

- 2019 employment: **32,600**
- May 2019 median annual wage: **$52,650**
  - Wages come from the Occupational Employment Statistics (OES) program
- Projected employment change, 2019–29:
  - Number of new jobs: **4,800**
  - Growth rate: **15 percent (Much faster than average)**
- Education and training:
  - Typical entry-level education: **Bachelor's degree**
  - Work experience in a related occupation: **None**
  - Typical on-the-job training: **None**
- O*NET links:
  - 29-1129.00 - Therapists, All Other

Acupuncturists and healthcare diagnosing or treating practitioners, all other

This is an OES hybrid

- 2019 employment: **49,600**
- May 2019 median annual wage: **$75,640**
  - Wages come from the Occupational Employment Statistics (OES) program
- Projected employment change, 2019–29:
  - Number of new jobs: **-100**
  - Growth rate: **0 percent (Little or no change)**
- Education and training:
  - Typical entry-level education: **Master's degree**
  - Work experience in a related occupation: **None**
  - Typical on-the-job training: **None**
- O*NET links:
  - 29-1199.00 - Health Diagnosing and Treating Practitioners, All Other
  - 29-1199.01 - Acupuncturists
  - 29-1199.04 - Naturopathic Physicians
  - 29-1199.05 - Orthoptists
- CareerOneStop videos for this occupation:
  - 29-1199.01 - Acupuncturists
  - 29-1199.04 - Naturopathic Physicians

Dietetic technicians

Assist in the provision of food service and nutritional programs, under the supervision of a dietitian. May plan and produce meals based on established guidelines, teach principles of food and nutrition, or counsel individuals.

- 2019 employment: **30,200**
- May 2019 median annual wage: **$28,400**
  - Wages come from the Occupational Employment Statistics (OES) program
- Projected employment change, 2019–29:
  - Number of new jobs: **1,800**
  - Growth rate: **6 percent (Faster than average)**
- Education and training:
  - Typical entry-level education: **Associate's degree**
  - Work experience in a related occupation: **None**
  - Typical on-the-job training: **None**
- O*NET links:
  - 29-2051.00 - Dietetic Technicians
- CareerOneStop videos for this occupation:
  - 29-2051.00 - Dietetic Technicians

Ophthalmic medical technicians

Assist ophthalmologists by performing ophthalmic clinical functions. May administer eye exams, administer eye medications, and instruct the patient in care and use of corrective lenses.

- 2019 employment: **59,500**
- May 2019 median annual wage: **$36,940**
  - Wages come from the Occupational Employment Statistics (OES) program
- Projected employment change, 2019–29:
  - Number of new jobs: **8,500**
  - Growth rate: **14 percent (Much faster than average)**
- Education and training:
  - Typical entry-level education: **Postsecondary nondegree award**
  - Work experience in a related occupation: **None**
  - Typical on-the-job training: **None**
- O*NET links:
  - 29-2057.00 - Ophthalmic Medical Technicians

Hearing aid specialists

Select and fit hearing aids for customers. Administer and interpret tests of hearing. Assess hearing instrument efficacy. Take ear impressions and prepare, design, and modify ear molds. Excludes "Audiologists" (29-1181).

- 2019 employment: **8,100**
- May 2019 median annual wage: **$53,420**
  - Wages come from the Occupational Employment Statistics (OES) program
- Projected employment change, 2019–29:
  - Number of new jobs: **900**
  - Growth rate: **10 percent (Much faster than average)**
- Education and training:
  - Typical entry-level education: **High school diploma or equivalent**
  - Work experience in a related occupation: **None**
  - Typical on-the-job training: **Moderate-term on-the-job training**
- O*NET links:
  - 29-2092.00 - Hearing Aid Specialists
- CareerOneStop videos for this occupation:
  - 29-2092.00 - Hearing Aid Specialists

Health information technologists, medical registrars, surgical assistants, and healthcare practitioners and technical workers, all other

This is an OES hybrid

- 2019 employment: **59,400**
- May 2019 median annual wage: **$49,850**
  - Wages come from the Occupational Employment Statistics (OES) program
- Projected employment change, 2019–29:
  - Number of new jobs: **4,700**
  - Growth rate: **8 percent (Much faster than average)**
- Education and training:
  - Typical entry-level education: **Postsecondary nondegree award**
  - Work experience in a related occupation: **None**
  - Typical on-the-job training: **None**
- O*NET links:
  - 29-9099.00 - Healthcare Practitioners and Technical Workers, All Other
  - 29-9099.01 - Midwives
- CareerOneStop videos for this occupation:
  - 29-9099.01 - Midwives

Healthcare Support Occupations

Medical equipment preparers

Prepare, sterilize, install, or clean laboratory or healthcare equipment. May perform routine laboratory tasks and operate or inspect equipment.

- 2019 employment: **58,700**
- May 2019 median annual wage: **$37,440**
  - Wages come from the Occupational Employment Statistics (OES) program
- Projected employment change, 2019–29:
  - Number of new jobs: **3,400**
  - Growth rate: **6 percent (Faster than average)**
- Education and training:
  - Typical entry-level education: **High school diploma or equivalent**
  - Work experience in a related occupation: **None**
  - Typical on-the-job training: **Moderate-term on-the-job training**
- O*NET links:
  - 31-9093.00 - Medical Equipment Preparers

Pharmacy aides

Record drugs delivered to the pharmacy, store incoming merchandise, and inform the supervisor of stock needs. May operate cash register and accept prescriptions for filling.

- 2019 employment: **37,900**
- May 2019 median annual wage: **$27,850**
  - Wages come from the Occupational Employment Statistics (OES) program
- Projected employment change, 2019–29:
  - Number of new jobs: **-5,900**
  - Growth rate: **-16 percent (Decline)**
- Education and training:
  - Typical entry-level education: **High school diploma or equivalent**
  - Work experience in a related occupation: **None**
  - Typical on-the-job training: **Short-term on-the-job training**
- O*NET links:
  - 31-9095.00 - Pharmacy Aides
- CareerOneStop videos for this occupation:
  - 31-9095.00 - Pharmacy Aides

Healthcare support workers, all other
All healthcare support workers not listed separately.
- 2019 employment: **96,900**
- May 2019 median annual wage: **$38,460**
  - Wages come from the Occupational Employment Statistics (OES) program
- Projected employment change, 2019–29:
  - Number of new jobs: **6,700**
  - Growth rate: **7 percent (Faster than average)**
- Education and training:
  - Typical entry-level education: **High school diploma or equivalent**
  - Work experience in a related occupation: **None**
  - Typical on-the-job training: **None**
- O*NET links:
  - 31-9099.00 - Healthcare Support Workers, All Other
  - 31-9099.01 - Speech-Language Pathology Assistants
  - 31-9099.02 - Endoscopy Technicians

Protective Service Occupations

First-line supervisors of correctional officers
Directly supervise and coordinate activities of correctional officers and jailers.
- 2019 employment: **48,700**
- May 2019 median annual wage: **$63,730**
  - Wages come from the Occupational Employment Statistics (OES) program
- Projected employment change, 2019–29:
  - Number of new jobs: **-3,800**
  - Growth rate: **-8 percent (Decline)**
- Education and training:
  - Typical entry-level education: **High school diploma or equivalent**
  - Work experience in a related occupation: **Less than 5 years**
  - Typical on-the-job training: **None**
- O*NET links:
  - 33-1011.00 - First-Line Supervisors of Correctional Officers

First-line supervisors of police and detectives
Directly supervise and coordinate activities of members of police force.
- 2019 employment: **126,100**
- May 2019 median annual wage: **$91,090**
  - Wages come from the Occupational Employment Statistics (OES) program
- Projected employment change, 2019–29:
  - Number of new jobs: **6,600**
  - Growth rate: **5 percent (Faster than average)**
- Education and training:
  - Typical entry-level education: **High school diploma or equivalent**
  - Work experience in a related occupation: **Less than 5 years**
  - Typical on-the-job training: **Moderate-term on-the-job training**
- O*NET links:
  - 33-1012.00 - First-Line Supervisors of Police and Detectives

First-line supervisors of firefighting and prevention workers
Directly supervise and coordinate activities of workers engaged in firefighting and fire prevention and control.

- 2019 employment: **71,500**
- May 2019 median annual wage: **$77,800**
  - Wages come from the Occupational Employment Statistics (OES) program
- Projected employment change, 2019–29:
  - Number of new jobs: **4,400**
  - Growth rate: **6 percent (Faster than average)**
- Education and training:
  - Typical entry-level education: **Postsecondary nondegree award**
  - Work experience in a related occupation: **Less than 5 years**
  - Typical on-the-job training: **Moderate-term on-the-job training**
- O*NET links:
  - 33-1021.00 - First-Line Supervisors of Fire Fighting and Prevention Workers
  - 33-1021.01 - Municipal Fire Fighting and Prevention Supervisors
  - 33-1021.02 - Forest Fire Fighting and Prevention Supervisors

Miscellaneous first-line supervisors, protective service workers
This is an OES hybrid
- 2019 employment: **85,700**
- May 2019 median annual wage: **$50,490**
  - Wages come from the Occupational Employment Statistics (OES) program
- Projected employment change, 2019–29:
  - Number of new jobs: **1,300**
  - Growth rate: **2 percent (Slower than average)**
- Education and training:
  - Typical entry-level education: **High school diploma or equivalent**
  - Work experience in a related occupation: **Less than 5 years**
  - Typical on-the-job training: **None**
- O*NET links:
  - 33-1099.00 - First-Line Supervisors of Protective Service Workers, All Other

Parking enforcement workers
Patrol assigned area, such as public parking lot or city streets to issue tickets to overtime parking violators and illegally parked vehicles.
- 2019 employment: **8,100**
- May 2019 median annual wage: **$40,920**
  - Wages come from the Occupational Employment Statistics (OES) program
- Projected employment change, 2019–29:
  - Number of new jobs: **-2,900**
  - Growth rate: **-36 percent (Decline)**
- Education and training:
  - Typical entry-level education: **High school diploma or equivalent**
  - Work experience in a related occupation: **None**
  - Typical on-the-job training: **Short-term on-the-job training**
- O*NET links:
  - 33-3041.00 - Parking Enforcement Workers

Animal control workers
Handle animals for the purpose of investigations of mistreatment, or control of abandoned, dangerous, or unattended animals.
- 2019 employment: **13,900**
- May 2019 median annual wage: **$37,590**
  - Wages come from the Occupational Employment Statistics (OES) program

- Projected employment change, 2019–29:
  - Number of new jobs: **900**
  - Growth rate: **7 percent (Faster than average)**
- Education and training:
  - Typical entry-level education: **High school diploma or equivalent**
  - Work experience in a related occupation: **None**
  - Typical on-the-job training: **Moderate-term on-the-job training**
- O*NET links:
  - 33-9011.00 - Animal Control Workers
- CareerOneStop videos for this occupation:
  - 33-9011.00 - Animal Control Workers

Crossing guards and flaggers

Guide or control vehicular or pedestrian traffic at such places as streets, schools, railroad crossings, or construction sites.

- 2019 employment: **86,700**
- May 2019 median annual wage: **$29,760**
  - Wages come from the Occupational Employment Statistics (OES) program
- Projected employment change, 2019–29:
  - Number of new jobs: **5,000**
  - Growth rate: **6 percent (Faster than average)**
- Education and training:
  - Typical entry-level education: **No formal educational credential**
  - Work experience in a related occupation: **None**
  - Typical on-the-job training: **Short-term on-the-job training**
- O*NET links:
  - 33-9091.00 - Crossing Guards

Lifeguards, ski patrol, and other recreational protective service workers

Monitor recreational areas, such as pools, beaches, or ski slopes, to provide assistance and protection to participants.

- 2019 employment: **149,800**
- May 2019 median annual wage: **$23,420**
  - Wages come from the Occupational Employment Statistics (OES) program
- Projected employment change, 2019–29:
  - Number of new jobs: **13,500**
  - Growth rate: **9 percent (Much faster than average)**
- Education and training:
  - Typical entry-level education: **No formal educational credential**
  - Work experience in a related occupation: **None**
  - Typical on-the-job training: **Short-term on-the-job training**
- O*NET links:
  - 33-9092.00 - Lifeguards, Ski Patrol, and Other Recreational Protective Service Workers
- CareerOneStop videos for this occupation:
  - 33-9092.00 - Lifeguards, Ski Patrol, and Other Recreational Protective Service Workers

Transportation security screeners

Conduct screening of passengers, baggage, or cargo to ensure compliance with Transportation Security Administration (TSA) regulations. May operate basic security equipment such as x-ray machines and hand wands at screening checkpoints.

- 2019 employment: **51,400**
- May 2019 median annual wage: **$41,770**
  - Wages come from the Occupational Employment Statistics (OES) program
- Projected employment change, 2019–29:
  - Number of new jobs: **-1,600**
  - Growth rate: **-3 percent (Decline)**
- Education and training:
  - Typical entry-level education: **High school diploma or equivalent**
  - Work experience in a related occupation: **None**
  - Typical on-the-job training: **Short-term on-the-job training**
- O*NET links:
  - 33-9093.00 - Transportation Security Screeners
- CareerOneStop videos for this occupation:
  - 33-9093.00 - Transportation Security Screeners

School bus monitors and protective service workers, all other

This is an OES hybrid

- 2019 employment: **145,600**
- May 2019 median annual wage: **$30,990**
  - Wages come from the Occupational Employment Statistics (OES) program
- Projected employment change, 2019–29:
  - Number of new jobs: **6,200**
  - Growth rate: **4 percent (As fast as average)**
- Education and training:
  - Typical entry-level education: **High school diploma or equivalent**
  - Work experience in a related occupation: **None**
  - Typical on-the-job training: **Short-term on-the-job training**
- O*NET links:
  - 33-9099.00 - Protective Service Workers, All Other
  - 33-9099.02 - Retail Loss Prevention Specialists

Food Preparation and Serving Related Occupations

First-line supervisors of food preparation and serving workers

Directly supervise and coordinate activities of workers engaged in preparing and serving food.

- 2019 employment: **1,039,300**
- May 2019 median annual wage: **$33,400**
  - Wages come from the Occupational Employment Statistics (OES) program
- Projected employment change, 2019–29:
  - Number of new jobs: **60,900**
  - Growth rate: **6 percent (Faster than average)**
- Education and training:
  - Typical entry-level education: **High school diploma or equivalent**
  - Work experience in a related occupation: **Less than 5 years**
  - Typical on-the-job training: **None**
- O*NET links:
  - 35-1012.00 - First-Line Supervisors of Food Preparation and Serving Workers
- CareerOneStop videos for this occupation:

○ 35-1012.00 - First-Line Supervisors of Food Preparation and Serving Workers

Dishwashers
Clean dishes, kitchen, food preparation equipment, or utensils.
- 2019 employment: **522,300**
- May 2019 median annual wage: **$23,970**
  ○ Wages come from the Occupational Employment Statistics (OES) program
- Projected employment change, 2019–29:
  ○ Number of new jobs: **2,400**
  ○ Growth rate: **0 percent (Little or no change)**
- Education and training:
  ○ Typical entry-level education: **No formal educational credential**
  ○ Work experience in a related occupation: **None**
  ○ Typical on-the-job training: **Short-term on-the-job training**
- O*NET links:
  ○ 35-9021.00 - Dishwashers
- CareerOneStop videos for this occupation:
  ○ 35-9021.00 - Dishwashers

Building and Grounds Cleaning and Maintenance Occupations

First-line supervisors of housekeeping and janitorial workers
Directly supervise and coordinate work activities of cleaning personnel in hotels, hospitals, offices, and other establishments.
- 2019 employment: **231,900**
- May 2019 median annual wage: **$40,780**
  ○ Wages come from the Occupational Employment Statistics (OES) program
- Projected employment change, 2019–29:
  ○ Number of new jobs: **19,400**
  ○ Growth rate: **8 percent (Much faster than average)**
- Education and training:
  ○ Typical entry-level education: **High school diploma or equivalent**
  ○ Work experience in a related occupation: **Less than 5 years**
  ○ Typical on-the-job training: **None**
- O*NET links:
  ○ 37-1011.00 - First-Line Supervisors of Housekeeping and Janitorial Workers

First-line supervisors of landscaping, lawn service, and groundskeeping workers
Directly supervise and coordinate activities of workers engaged in landscaping or groundskeeping activities. Work may involve reviewing contracts to ascertain service, machine, and workforce requirements; answering inquiries from potential customers regarding methods, material, and price ranges; and preparing estimates according to labor, material, and machine costs.
- 2019 employment: **170,700**
- May 2019 median annual wage: **$49,370**
  ○ Wages come from the Occupational Employment Statistics (OES) program
- Projected employment change, 2019–29:
  ○ Number of new jobs: **19,400**
  ○ Growth rate: **11 percent (Much faster than average)**

- Education and training:
  ○ Typical entry-level education: **High school diploma or equivalent**
  ○ Work experience in a related occupation: **Less than 5 years**
  ○ Typical on-the-job training: **None**
- O*NET links:
  ○ 37-1012.00 - First-Line Supervisors of Landscaping, Lawn Service, and Groundskeeping Workers

Maids and housekeeping cleaners
Perform any combination of light cleaning duties to maintain private households or commercial establishments, such as hotels and hospitals, in a clean and orderly manner. Duties may include making beds, replenishing linens, cleaning rooms and halls, and vacuuming.
- 2019 employment: **1,474,900**
- May 2019 median annual wage: **$24,850**
  ○ Wages come from the Occupational Employment Statistics (OES) program
- Projected employment change, 2019–29:
  ○ Number of new jobs: **-4,100**
  ○ Growth rate: **0 percent (Little or no change)**
- Education and training:
  ○ Typical entry-level education: **No formal educational credential**
  ○ Work experience in a related occupation: **None**
  ○ Typical on-the-job training: **Short-term on-the-job training**
- O*NET links:
  ○ 37-2012.00 - Maids and Housekeeping Cleaners
- CareerOneStop videos for this occupation:
  ○ 37-2012.00 - Maids and Housekeeping Cleaners

Building cleaning workers, all other
All building cleaning workers not listed separately.
- 2019 employment: **19,400**
- May 2019 median annual wage: **$31,230**
  ○ Wages come from the Occupational Employment Statistics (OES) program
- Projected employment change, 2019–29:
  ○ Number of new jobs: **900**
  ○ Growth rate: **5 percent (Faster than average)**
- Education and training:
  ○ Typical entry-level education: **No formal educational credential**
  ○ Work experience in a related occupation: **None**
  ○ Typical on-the-job training: **Short-term on-the-job training**
- O*NET links:
  ○ 37-2019.00 - Building Cleaning Workers, All Other

Personal Care and Service Occupations

First-line supervisors of personal service and entertainment and recreation workers, except gambling services
This is an OES hybrid
- 2019 employment: **313,100**
- May 2019 median annual wage: **$39,800**
  ○ Wages come from the Occupational Employment Statistics (OES) program
- Projected employment change, 2019–29:
  ○ Number of new jobs: **35,000**

○ Growth rate: **11 percent (Much faster than average)**
• Education and training:
  ○ Typical entry-level education: **High school diploma or equivalent**
  ○ Work experience in a related occupation: **Less than 5 years**
  ○ Typical on-the-job training: **None**
• O*NET links:
  ○ 39-1021.00 - First-Line Supervisors of Personal Service Workers
  ○ 39-1021.01 - Spa Managers

Motion picture projectionists

Set up and operate motion picture projection and related sound reproduction equipment.
• 2019 employment: **4,700**
• May 2019 median annual wage: **$25,150**
  ○ Wages come from the Occupational Employment Statistics (OES) program
• Projected employment change, 2019–29:
  ○ Number of new jobs: **-500**
  ○ Growth rate: **-11 percent (Decline)**
• Education and training:
  ○ Typical entry-level education: **No formal educational credential**
  ○ Work experience in a related occupation: **None**
  ○ Typical on-the-job training: **Short-term on-the-job training**
• O*NET links:
  ○ 39-3021.00 - Motion Picture Projectionists
• CareerOneStop videos for this occupation:
  ○ 39-3021.00 - Motion Picture Projectionists

Ushers, lobby attendants, and ticket takers

Assist patrons at entertainment events by performing duties, such as collecting admission tickets and passes from patrons, assisting in finding seats, searching for lost articles, and helping patrons locate such facilities as restrooms and telephones.
• 2019 employment: **139,000**
• May 2019 median annual wage: **$23,500**
  ○ Wages come from the Occupational Employment Statistics (OES) program
• Projected employment change, 2019–29:
  ○ Number of new jobs: **4,700**
  ○ Growth rate: **3 percent (As fast as average)**
• Education and training:
  ○ Typical entry-level education: **No formal educational credential**
  ○ Work experience in a related occupation: **None**
  ○ Typical on-the-job training: **Short-term on-the-job training**
• O*NET links:
  ○ 39-3031.00 - Ushers, Lobby Attendants, and Ticket Takers

Amusement and recreation attendants

Perform a variety of attending duties at amusement or recreation facility. May schedule use of recreation facilities, maintain and provide equipment to participants of sporting events or recreational pursuits, or operate amusement concessions and rides.
• 2019 employment: **357,700**
• May 2019 median annual wage: **$23,370**
  ○ Wages come from the Occupational Employment Statistics (OES) program
• Projected employment change, 2019–29:
  ○ Number of new jobs: **37,000**
  ○ Growth rate: **10 percent (Much faster than average)**

• Education and training:
  ○ Typical entry-level education: **No formal educational credential**
  ○ Work experience in a related occupation: **None**
  ○ Typical on-the-job training: **Short-term on-the-job training**
• O*NET links:
  ○ 39-3091.00 - Amusement and Recreation Attendants
• CareerOneStop videos for this occupation:
  ○ 39-3091.00 - Amusement and Recreation Attendants

Costume attendants

Select, fit, and take care of costumes for cast members, and aid entertainers. May assist with multiple costume changes during performances.
• 2019 employment: **7,700**
• May 2019 median annual wage: **$41,410**
  ○ Wages come from the Occupational Employment Statistics (OES) program
• Projected employment change, 2019–29:
  ○ Number of new jobs: **400**
  ○ Growth rate: **5 percent (Faster than average)**
• Education and training:
  ○ Typical entry-level education: **High school diploma or equivalent**
  ○ Work experience in a related occupation: **None**
  ○ Typical on-the-job training: **Short-term on-the-job training**
• O*NET links:
  ○ 39-3092.00 - Costume Attendants

Locker room, coatroom, and dressing room attendants

Provide personal items to patrons or customers in locker rooms, dressing rooms, or coatrooms.
• 2019 employment: **16,800**
• May 2019 median annual wage: **$25,110**
  ○ Wages come from the Occupational Employment Statistics (OES) program
• Projected employment change, 2019–29:
  ○ Number of new jobs: **1,400**
  ○ Growth rate: **8 percent (Much faster than average)**
• Education and training:
  ○ Typical entry-level education: **High school diploma or equivalent**
  ○ Work experience in a related occupation: **None**
  ○ Typical on-the-job training: **Short-term on-the-job training**
• O*NET links:
  ○ 39-3093.00 - Locker Room, Coatroom, and Dressing Room Attendants
• CareerOneStop videos for this occupation:
  ○ 39-3093.00 - Locker Room, Coatroom, and Dressing Room Attendants

Entertainment attendants and related workers, all other

All entertainment attendants and related workers not listed separately.
• 2019 employment: **4,800**
• May 2019 median annual wage: **$26,460**
  ○ Wages come from the Occupational Employment Statistics (OES) program
• Projected employment change, 2019–29:
  ○ Number of new jobs: **300**
  ○ Growth rate: **6 percent (Faster than average)**
• Education and training:

- Typical entry-level education: **High school diploma or equivalent**
- Work experience in a related occupation: **None**
- Typical on-the-job training: **Short-term on-the-job training**
- O*NET links:
  - 39-3099.00 - Entertainment Attendants and Related Workers, All Other

Embalmers
Prepare bodies for interment in conformity with legal requirements.
- 2019 employment: **3,900**
- May 2019 median annual wage: **$47,760**
  - Wages come from the Occupational Employment Statistics (OES) program
- Projected employment change, 2019–29:
  - Number of new jobs: **-300**
  - Growth rate: **-8 percent (Decline)**
- Education and training:
  - Typical entry-level education: **Associate's degree**
  - Work experience in a related occupation: **None**
  - Typical on-the-job training: **Long-term on-the-job training**
- O*NET links:
  - 39-4011.00 - Embalmers

Funeral attendants
Perform a variety of tasks during funeral, such as placing casket in parlor or chapel prior to service, arranging floral offerings or lights around casket, directing or escorting mourners, closing casket, and issuing and storing funeral equipment.
- 2019 employment: **34,300**
- May 2019 median annual wage: **$27,930**
  - Wages come from the Occupational Employment Statistics (OES) program
- Projected employment change, 2019–29:
  - Number of new jobs: **-1,000**
  - Growth rate: **-3 percent (Decline)**
- Education and training:
  - Typical entry-level education: **High school diploma or equivalent**
  - Work experience in a related occupation: **None**
  - Typical on-the-job training: **Short-term on-the-job training**
- O*NET links:
  - 39-4021.00 - Funeral Attendants

Makeup artists, theatrical and performance
Apply makeup to performers to reflect period, setting, and situation of their role.
- 2019 employment: **4,700**
- May 2019 median annual wage: **$75,730**
  - Wages come from the Occupational Employment Statistics (OES) program
- Projected employment change, 2019–29:
  - Number of new jobs: **500**
  - Growth rate: **11 percent (Much faster than average)**
- Education and training:
  - Typical entry-level education: **Postsecondary nondegree award**
  - Work experience in a related occupation: **None**
  - Typical on-the-job training: **None**
- O*NET links:
  - 39-5091.00 - Makeup Artists, Theatrical and Performance
- CareerOneStop videos for this occupation:
  - 39-5091.00 - Makeup Artists, Theatrical and Performance

Shampooers
Shampoo and rinse customers' hair.
- 2019 employment: **16,800**
- May 2019 median annual wage: **$22,550**
  - Wages come from the Occupational Employment Statistics (OES) program
- Projected employment change, 2019–29:
  - Number of new jobs: **1,900**
  - Growth rate: **11 percent (Much faster than average)**
- Education and training:
  - Typical entry-level education: **No formal educational credential**
  - Work experience in a related occupation: **None**
  - Typical on-the-job training: **Short-term on-the-job training**
- O*NET links:
  - 39-5093.00 - Shampooers

Baggage porters and bellhops
Handle baggage for travelers at transportation terminals or for guests at hotels or similar establishments.
- 2019 employment: **40,600**
- May 2019 median annual wage: **$25,580**
  - Wages come from the Occupational Employment Statistics (OES) program
- Projected employment change, 2019–29:
  - Number of new jobs: **2,200**
  - Growth rate: **5 percent (Faster than average)**
- Education and training:
  - Typical entry-level education: **High school diploma or equivalent**
  - Work experience in a related occupation: **None**
  - Typical on-the-job training: **Short-term on-the-job training**
- O*NET links:
  - 39-6011.00 - Baggage Porters and Bellhops
- CareerOneStop videos for this occupation:
  - 39-6011.00 - Baggage Porters and Bellhops

Concierges
Assist patrons at hotel, apartment, or office building with personal services. May take messages; arrange or give advice on transportation, business services, or entertainment; or monitor guest requests for housekeeping and maintenance.
- 2019 employment: **42,600**
- May 2019 median annual wage: **$31,390**
  - Wages come from the Occupational Employment Statistics (OES) program
- Projected employment change, 2019–29:
  - Number of new jobs: **2,900**
  - Growth rate: **7 percent (Faster than average)**
- Education and training:
  - Typical entry-level education: **High school diploma or equivalent**
  - Work experience in a related occupation: **None**
  - Typical on-the-job training: **Moderate-term on-the-job training**
- O*NET links:
  - 39-6012.00 - Concierges
- CareerOneStop videos for this occupation:
  - 39-6012.00 - Concierges

Tour and travel guides

This is an OES hybrid

- 2019 employment: **57,300**
- May 2019 median annual wage: **$27,600**
  ○ Wages come from the Occupational Employment Statistics (OES) program
- Projected employment change, 2019–29:
  ○ Number of new jobs: **3,100**
  ○ Growth rate: **5 percent (Faster than average)**
- Education and training:
  ○ Typical entry-level education: **High school diploma or equivalent**
  ○ Work experience in a related occupation: **None**
  ○ Typical on-the-job training: **Moderate-term on-the-job training**
- O*NET links:
  ○ 39-7011.00 - Tour Guides and Escorts
  ○ 39-7011.00 - Tour Guides and Escorts
  ○ 39-7012.00 - Travel Guides
  ○ 39-7012.00 - Travel Guides
- CareerOneStop videos for this occupation:
  ○ 39-7011.00 - Tour Guides and Escorts
  ○ 39-7011.00 - Tour Guides and Escorts
  ○ 39-7012.00 - Travel Guides
  ○ 39-7012.00 - Travel Guides

Residential advisors

Coordinate activities in resident facilities in secondary school and college dormitories, group homes, or similar establishments. Order supplies and determine need for maintenance, repairs, and furnishings. May maintain household records and assign rooms. May assist residents with problem solving or refer them to counseling resources.

- 2019 employment: **115,200**
- May 2019 median annual wage: **$29,450**
  ○ Wages come from the Occupational Employment Statistics (OES) program
- Projected employment change, 2019–29:
  ○ Number of new jobs: **13,600**
  ○ Growth rate: **12 percent (Much faster than average)**
- Education and training:
  ○ Typical entry-level education: **High school diploma or equivalent**
  ○ Work experience in a related occupation: **None**
  ○ Typical on-the-job training: **Short-term on-the-job training**
- O*NET links:
  ○ 39-9041.00 - Residential Advisors
- CareerOneStop videos for this occupation:
  ○ 39-9041.00 - Residential Advisors

Crematory operators and personal care and service workers, all other

This is an OES hybrid

- 2019 employment: **111,300**
- May 2019 median annual wage: **$27,130**
  ○ Wages come from the Occupational Employment Statistics (OES) program
- Projected employment change, 2019–29:
  ○ Number of new jobs: **17,500**
  ○ Growth rate: **16 percent (Much faster than average)**
- Education and training:
  ○ Typical entry-level education: **High school diploma or equivalent**

○ Work experience in a related occupation: **None**
○ Typical on-the-job training: **Short-term on-the-job training**
- O*NET links:
  ○ 39-9099.00 - Personal Care and Service Workers, All Other

Sales and Related Occupations

First-line supervisors of retail sales workers

Directly supervise and coordinate activities of retail sales workers in an establishment or department. Duties may include management functions, such as purchasing, budgeting, accounting, and personnel work, in addition to supervisory duties.

- 2019 employment: **1,476,400**
- May 2019 median annual wage: **$40,350**
  ○ Wages come from the Occupational Employment Statistics (OES) program
- Projected employment change, 2019–29:
  ○ Number of new jobs: **-81,200**
  ○ Growth rate: **-5 percent (Decline)**
- Education and training:
  ○ Typical entry-level education: **High school diploma or equivalent**
  ○ Work experience in a related occupation: **Less than 5 years**
  ○ Typical on-the-job training: **None**
- O*NET links:
  ○ 41-1011.00 - First-Line Supervisors of Retail Sales Workers

First-line supervisors of non-retail sales workers

Directly supervise and coordinate activities of sales workers other than retail sales workers. May perform duties such as budgeting, accounting, and personnel work, in addition to supervisory duties.

- 2019 employment: **409,800**
- May 2019 median annual wage: **$74,760**
  ○ Wages come from the Occupational Employment Statistics (OES) program
- Projected employment change, 2019–29:
  ○ Number of new jobs: **-34,100**
  ○ Growth rate: **-8 percent (Decline)**
- Education and training:
  ○ Typical entry-level education: **High school diploma or equivalent**
  ○ Work experience in a related occupation: **Less than 5 years**
  ○ Typical on-the-job training: **None**
- O*NET links:
  ○ 41-1012.00 - First-Line Supervisors of Non-Retail Sales Workers

Gambling change persons and booth cashiers

Exchange coins, tokens, and chips for patrons' money. May issue payoffs and obtain customer's signature on receipt. May operate a booth in the slot machine area and furnish change persons with money bank at the start of the shift, or count and audit money in drawers. Excludes "Cashiers" (41-2011).

- 2019 employment: **21,700**
- May 2019 median annual wage: **$25,690**
  ○ Wages come from the Occupational Employment Statistics (OES) program
- Projected employment change, 2019–29:
  ○ Number of new jobs: **500**
  ○ Growth rate: **2 percent (Slower than average)**

- Education and training:
  - Typical entry-level education: **No formal educational credential**
  - Work experience in a related occupation: **None**
  - Typical on-the-job training: **Short-term on-the-job training**
- O*NET links:
  - 41-2012.00 - Gaming Change Persons and Booth Cashiers

Counter and rental clerks

Receive orders, generally in person, for repairs, rentals, and services. May describe available options, compute cost, and accept payment. Excludes "Fast Food and Counter Workers" (35-3023), "Hotel, Motel, and Resort Desk Clerks" (43-4081), "Order Clerks" (43-4151), and "Reservation and Transportation Ticket Agents and Travel Clerks" (43-4181).

- 2019 employment: **420,400**
- May 2019 median annual wage: **$28,820**
  - Wages come from the Occupational Employment Statistics (OES) program
- Projected employment change, 2019–29:
  - Number of new jobs: **4,500**
  - Growth rate: **1 percent (Slower than average)**
- Education and training:
  - Typical entry-level education: **No formal educational credential**
  - Work experience in a related occupation: **None**
  - Typical on-the-job training: **Short-term on-the-job training**
- O*NET links:
  - 41-2021.00 - Counter and Rental Clerks

Sales representatives of services, except advertising, insurance, financial services, and travel

Sell services to individuals or businesses. May describe options or resolve client problems. Excludes "Advertising Sales Agents" (41-3011), "Insurance Sales Agents" (41-3021), "Securities, Commodities, and Financial Services Sales Agents" (41-3031), "Travel Agents" (41-3041), "Sales Representatives, Wholesale and Manufacturing" (41-4010), and "Telemarketers" (41-9041).

- 2019 employment: **1,070,500**
- May 2019 median annual wage: **$56,130**
  - Wages come from the Occupational Employment Statistics (OES) program
- Projected employment change, 2019–29:
  - Number of new jobs: **64,200**
  - Growth rate: **6 percent (Faster than average)**
- Education and training:
  - Typical entry-level education: **High school diploma or equivalent**
  - Work experience in a related occupation: **None**
  - Typical on-the-job training: **Moderate-term on-the-job training**
- O*NET links:
  - 41-3099.00 - Sales Representatives, Services, All Other
  - 41-3099.01 - Energy Brokers

Demonstrators and product promoters

Demonstrate merchandise and answer questions for the purpose of creating public interest in buying the product. May sell demonstrated merchandise.

- 2019 employment: **88,100**
- May 2019 median annual wage: **$30,930**

- Wages come from the Occupational Employment Statistics (OES) program
- Projected employment change, 2019–29:
  - Number of new jobs: **2,700**
  - Growth rate: **3 percent (As fast as average)**
- Education and training:
  - Typical entry-level education: **No formal educational credential**
  - Work experience in a related occupation: **None**
  - Typical on-the-job training: **Short-term on-the-job training**
- O*NET links:
  - 41-9011.00 - Demonstrators and Product Promoters

Telemarketers

Solicit donations or orders for goods or services over the telephone.

- 2019 employment: **136,900**
- May 2019 median annual wage: **$26,290**
  - Wages come from the Occupational Employment Statistics (OES) program
- Projected employment change, 2019–29:
  - Number of new jobs: **-19,400**
  - Growth rate: **-14 percent (Decline)**
- Education and training:
  - Typical entry-level education: **No formal educational credential**
  - Work experience in a related occupation: **None**
  - Typical on-the-job training: **Short-term on-the-job training**
- O*NET links:
  - 41-9041.00 - Telemarketers
- CareerOneStop videos for this occupation:
  - 41-9041.00 - Telemarketers

Door-to-door sales workers, news and street vendors, and related workers

Sell goods or services door-to-door or on the street.

- 2019 employment: **72,900**
- May 2019 median annual wage: **$27,420**
  - Wages come from the Occupational Employment Statistics (OES) program
- Projected employment change, 2019–29:
  - Number of new jobs: **-14,600**
  - Growth rate: **-20 percent (Decline)**
- Education and training:
  - Typical entry-level education: **No formal educational credential**
  - Work experience in a related occupation: **None**
  - Typical on-the-job training: **Short-term on-the-job training**
- O*NET links:
  - 41-9091.00 - Door-To-Door Sales Workers, News and Street Vendors, and Related Workers

Sales and related workers, all other

All sales and related workers not listed separately.

- 2019 employment: **142,900**
- May 2019 median annual wage: **$31,820**
  - Wages come from the Occupational Employment Statistics (OES) program
- Projected employment change, 2019–29:
  - Number of new jobs: **2,700**
  - Growth rate: **2 percent (Slower than average)**
- Education and training:

- Typical entry-level education: **High school diploma or equivalent**
- Work experience in a related occupation: **None**
- Typical on-the-job training: **None**
- O*NET links:
  - 41-9099.00 - Sales and Related Workers, All Other

Office and Administrative Support Occupations

First-line supervisors of office and administrative support workers
Directly supervise and coordinate the activities of clerical and administrative support workers.
- 2019 employment: **1,552,400**
- May 2019 median annual wage: **$56,620**
  - Wages come from the Occupational Employment Statistics (OES) program
- Projected employment change, 2019–29:
  - Number of new jobs: **-46,700**
  - Growth rate: **-3 percent (Decline)**
- Education and training:
  - Typical entry-level education: **High school diploma or equivalent**
  - Work experience in a related occupation: **Less than 5 years**
  - Typical on-the-job training: **None**
- O*NET links:
  - 43-1011.00 - First-Line Supervisors of Office and Administrative Support Workers

Switchboard operators, including answering service
Operate telephone business systems equipment or switchboards to relay incoming, outgoing, and interoffice calls. May supply information to callers and record messages.
- 2019 employment: **69,900**
- May 2019 median annual wage: **$30,610**
  - Wages come from the Occupational Employment Statistics (OES) program
- Projected employment change, 2019–29:
  - Number of new jobs: **-15,700**
  - Growth rate: **-23 percent (Decline)**
- Education and training:
  - Typical entry-level education: **High school diploma or equivalent**
  - Work experience in a related occupation: **None**
  - Typical on-the-job training: **Short-term on-the-job training**
- O*NET links:
  - 43-2011.00 - Switchboard Operators, Including Answering Service

Telephone operators
Provide information by accessing alphabetical, geographical, or other directories. Assist customers with special billing requests, such as charges to a third party and credits or refunds for incorrectly dialed numbers or bad connections. May handle emergency calls and assist children or people with physical disabilities to make telephone calls.
- 2019 employment: **5,000**
- May 2019 median annual wage: **$35,750**
  - Wages come from the Occupational Employment Statistics (OES) program
- Projected employment change, 2019–29:

- Number of new jobs: **-1,400**
- Growth rate: **-28 percent (Decline)**
- Education and training:
  - Typical entry-level education: **High school diploma or equivalent**
  - Work experience in a related occupation: **None**
  - Typical on-the-job training: **Short-term on-the-job training**
- O*NET links:
  - 43-2021.00 - Telephone Operators
- CareerOneStop videos for this occupation:
  - 43-2021.00 - Telephone Operators

Communications equipment operators, all other
All communications equipment operators not listed separately.
- 2019 employment: **3,600**
- May 2019 median annual wage: **$42,790**
  - Wages come from the Occupational Employment Statistics (OES) program
- Projected employment change, 2019–29:
  - Number of new jobs: **300**
  - Growth rate: **9 percent (Much faster than average)**
- Education and training:
  - Typical entry-level education: **High school diploma or equivalent**
  - Work experience in a related occupation: **None**
  - Typical on-the-job training: **Short-term on-the-job training**
- O*NET links:
  - 27-4013.00 - Radio Operators

Financial clerks, all other
All financial clerks not listed separately.
- 2019 employment: **32,600**
- May 2019 median annual wage: **$42,420**
  - Wages come from the Occupational Employment Statistics (OES) program
- Projected employment change, 2019–29:
  - Number of new jobs: **2,800**
  - Growth rate: **9 percent (Much faster than average)**
- Education and training:
  - Typical entry-level education: **High school diploma or equivalent**
  - Work experience in a related occupation: **None**
  - Typical on-the-job training: **Short-term on-the-job training**
- O*NET links:
  - 43-3099.00 - Financial Clerks, All Other

Cargo and freight agents
Expedite and route movement of incoming and outgoing cargo and freight shipments in airline, train, and trucking terminals and shipping docks. Take orders from customers and arrange pickup of freight and cargo for delivery to loading platform. Prepare and examine bills of lading to determine shipping charges and tariffs.
- 2019 employment: **97,200**
- May 2019 median annual wage: **$43,740**
  - Wages come from the Occupational Employment Statistics (OES) program
- Projected employment change, 2019–29:
  - Number of new jobs: **5,400**
  - Growth rate: **6 percent (Faster than average)**
- Education and training:
  - Typical entry-level education: **High school diploma or equivalent**
  - Work experience in a related occupation: **None**

○ Typical on-the-job training: **Short-term on-the-job training**
- O*NET links:
  ○ 43-5011.00 - Cargo and Freight Agents
  ○ 43-5011.01 - Freight Forwarders
- CareerOneStop videos for this occupation:
  ○ 43-5011.00 - Cargo and Freight Agents

Couriers and messengers

Pick up and deliver messages, documents, packages, and other items between offices or departments within an establishment or directly to other business concerns, traveling by foot, bicycle, motorcycle, automobile, or public conveyance. Excludes "Light Truck Drivers" (53-3033).
- 2019 employment: **121,800**
- May 2019 median annual wage: **$29,690**
  ○ Wages come from the Occupational Employment Statistics (OES) program
- Projected employment change, 2019–29:
  ○ Number of new jobs: **-2,700**
  ○ Growth rate: **-2 percent (Decline)**
- Education and training:
  ○ Typical entry-level education: **High school diploma or equivalent**
  ○ Work experience in a related occupation: **None**
  ○ Typical on-the-job training: **Short-term on-the-job training**
- O*NET links:
  ○ 43-5021.00 - Couriers and Messengers
- CareerOneStop videos for this occupation:
  ○ 43-5021.00 - Couriers and Messengers

Dispatchers, except police, fire, and ambulance

Schedule and dispatch workers, work crews, equipment, or service vehicles for conveyance of materials, freight, or passengers, or for normal installation, service, or emergency repairs rendered outside the place of business. Duties may include using radio, telephone, or computer to transmit assignments and compiling statistics and reports on work progress.
- 2019 employment: **204,600**
- May 2019 median annual wage: **$40,190**
  ○ Wages come from the Occupational Employment Statistics (OES) program
- Projected employment change, 2019–29:
  ○ Number of new jobs: **-1,900**
  ○ Growth rate: **-1 percent (Decline)**
- Education and training:
  ○ Typical entry-level education: **High school diploma or equivalent**
  ○ Work experience in a related occupation: **None**
  ○ Typical on-the-job training: **Moderate-term on-the-job training**
- O*NET links:
  ○ 43-5032.00 - Dispatchers, Except Police, Fire, and Ambulance

Meter readers, utilities

Read meter and record consumption of electricity, gas, water, or steam.
- 2019 employment: **30,900**
- May 2019 median annual wage: **$42,280**
  ○ Wages come from the Occupational Employment Statistics (OES) program
- Projected employment change, 2019–29:
  ○ Number of new jobs: **-3,600**
  ○ Growth rate: **-12 percent (Decline)**

- Education and training:
  ○ Typical entry-level education: **High school diploma or equivalent**
  ○ Work experience in a related occupation: **None**
  ○ Typical on-the-job training: **Short-term on-the-job training**
- O*NET links:
  ○ 43-5041.00 - Meter Readers, Utilities
- CareerOneStop videos for this occupation:
  ○ 43-5041.00 - Meter Readers, Utilities

Data entry keyers

Operate data entry device, such as keyboard or photo composing perforator. Duties may include verifying data and preparing materials for printing. Excludes "Word Processors and Typists" (43-9022).
- 2019 employment: **172,400**
- May 2019 median annual wage: **$33,490**
  ○ Wages come from the Occupational Employment Statistics (OES) program
- Projected employment change, 2019–29:
  ○ Number of new jobs: **-42,400**
  ○ Growth rate: **-25 percent (Decline)**
- Education and training:
  ○ Typical entry-level education: **High school diploma or equivalent**
  ○ Work experience in a related occupation: **None**
  ○ Typical on-the-job training: **Short-term on-the-job training**
- O*NET links:
  ○ 43-9021.00 - Data Entry Keyers
- CareerOneStop videos for this occupation:
  ○ 43-9021.00 - Data Entry Keyers

Word processors and typists

Use word processor, computer, or typewriter to type letters, reports, forms, or other material from rough draft, corrected copy, or voice recording. May perform other clerical duties as assigned. Excludes "Court Reporters and Simultaneous Captioners" (27-3092), "Medical Transcriptionists" (31-9094), "Secretaries and Administrative Assistants" (43-6010), and "Data Entry Keyers" (43-9021).
- 2019 employment: **52,700**
- May 2019 median annual wage: **$40,340**
  ○ Wages come from the Occupational Employment Statistics (OES) program
- Projected employment change, 2019–29:
  ○ Number of new jobs: **-19,200**
  ○ Growth rate: **-36 percent (Decline)**
- Education and training:
  ○ Typical entry-level education: **High school diploma or equivalent**
  ○ Work experience in a related occupation: **None**
  ○ Typical on-the-job training: **Short-term on-the-job training**
- O*NET links:
  ○ 43-9022.00 - Word Processors and Typists
- CareerOneStop videos for this occupation:
  ○ 43-9022.00 - Word Processors and Typists

Mail clerks and mail machine operators, except postal service

Prepare incoming and outgoing mail for distribution. Time-stamp, open, read, sort, and route incoming mail; and address, seal, stamp, fold, stuff, and affix postage to outgoing mail or packages. Duties may also include keeping necessary records and completed forms.
- 2019 employment: **88,400**

- May 2019 median annual wage: **$30,960**
  - Wages come from the Occupational Employment Statistics (OES) program
- Projected employment change, 2019–29:
  - Number of new jobs: **-6,000**
  - Growth rate: **-7 percent (Decline)**
- Education and training:
  - Typical entry-level education: **High school diploma or equivalent**
  - Work experience in a related occupation: **None**
  - Typical on-the-job training: **Short-term on-the-job training**
- O*NET links:
  - 43-9051.00 - Mail Clerks and Mail Machine Operators, Except Postal Service
- CareerOneStop videos for this occupation:
  - 43-9051.00 - Mail Clerks and Mail Machine Operators, Except Postal Service

Office machine operators, except computer

Operate one or more of a variety of office machines, such as photocopying, photographic, and duplicating machines, or other office machines. Excludes "Billing and Posting Clerks" (43-3021) and "Mail Clerks and Mail Machine Operators, Except Postal Service" (43-9051).

- 2019 employment: **47,300**
- May 2019 median annual wage: **$33,450**
  - Wages come from the Occupational Employment Statistics (OES) program
- Projected employment change, 2019–29:
  - Number of new jobs: **-6,200**
  - Growth rate: **-13 percent (Decline)**
- Education and training:
  - Typical entry-level education: **High school diploma or equivalent**
  - Work experience in a related occupation: **None**
  - Typical on-the-job training: **Short-term on-the-job training**
- O*NET links:
  - 43-9071.00 - Office Machine Operators, Except Computer

Proofreaders and copy markers

Read transcript or proof type setup to detect and mark for correction any grammatical, typographical, or compositional errors. Excludes workers whose primary duty is editing copy. Includes proofreaders of braille.

- 2019 employment: **10,300**
- May 2019 median annual wage: **$40,630**
  - Wages come from the Occupational Employment Statistics (OES) program
- Projected employment change, 2019–29:
  - Number of new jobs: **-300**
  - Growth rate: **-3 percent (Decline)**
- Education and training:
  - Typical entry-level education: **Bachelor's degree**
  - Work experience in a related occupation: **None**
  - Typical on-the-job training: **None**
- O*NET links:
  - 43-9081.00 - Proofreaders and Copy Markers

Statistical assistants

Compile and compute data according to statistical formulas for use in statistical studies. May perform actuarial computations and compile charts and graphs for use by actuaries. Includes actuarial clerks.

- 2019 employment: **10,800**

- May 2019 median annual wage: **$49,870**
  - Wages come from the Occupational Employment Statistics (OES) program
- Projected employment change, 2019–29:
  - Number of new jobs: **700**
  - Growth rate: **6 percent (Faster than average)**
- Education and training:
  - Typical entry-level education: **Bachelor's degree**
  - Work experience in a related occupation: **None**
  - Typical on-the-job training: **None**
- O*NET links:
  - 43-9111.00 - Statistical Assistants
  - 43-9111.01 - Bioinformatics Technicians

Office and administrative support workers, all other

All office and administrative support workers not listed separately.

- 2019 employment: **220,800**
- May 2019 median annual wage: **$35,470**
  - Wages come from the Occupational Employment Statistics (OES) program
- Projected employment change, 2019–29:
  - Number of new jobs: **8,800**
  - Growth rate: **4 percent (As fast as average)**
- Education and training:
  - Typical entry-level education: **High school diploma or equivalent**
  - Work experience in a related occupation: **None**
  - Typical on-the-job training: **Short-term on-the-job training**
- O*NET links:
  - 43-9199.00 - Office and Administrative Support Workers, All Other

---

Farming, Fishing, and Forestry Occupations

First-line supervisors of farming, fishing, and forestry workers

Directly supervise and coordinate the activities of agricultural, forestry, aquacultural, and related workers. Excludes "First-Line Supervisors of Landscaping, Lawn Service, and Groundskeeping Workers" (37-1012).

- 2019 employment: **53,200**
- May 2019 median annual wage: **$48,280**
  - Wages come from the Occupational Employment Statistics (OES) program
- Projected employment change, 2019–29:
  - Number of new jobs: **-600**
  - Growth rate: **-1 percent (Decline)**
- Education and training:
  - Typical entry-level education: **High school diploma or equivalent**
  - Work experience in a related occupation: **Less than 5 years**
  - Typical on-the-job training: **None**
- O*NET links:
  - 45-1011.00 - First-Line Supervisors of Farming, Fishing, and Forestry Workers
  - 45-1011.05 - First-Line Supervisors of Logging Workers
  - 45-1011.06 - First-Line Supervisors of Aquacultural Workers
  - 45-1011.07 - First-Line Supervisors of Agricultural Crop and Horticultural Workers
  - 45-1011.08 - First-Line Supervisors of Animal Husbandry and Animal Care Workers
- CareerOneStop videos for this occupation:

○ 45-1011.00 - First-Line Supervisors of Farming, Fishing, and Forestry Workers
○ 45-1011.05 - First-Line Supervisors of Logging Workers

Agricultural inspectors
Inspect agricultural commodities, processing equipment, and facilities, and fish and logging operations, to ensure compliance with regulations and laws governing health, quality, and safety.
- 2019 employment: **15,200**
- May 2019 median annual wage: **$45,490**
  ○ Wages come from the Occupational Employment Statistics (OES) program
- Projected employment change, 2019–29:
  ○ Number of new jobs: **300**
  ○ Growth rate: **2 percent (Slower than average)**
- Education and training:
  ○ Typical entry-level education: **Bachelor's degree**
  ○ Work experience in a related occupation: **None**
  ○ Typical on-the-job training: **Moderate-term on-the-job training**
- O*NET links:
  ○ 45-2011.00 - Agricultural Inspectors

Graders and sorters, agricultural products
Grade, sort, or classify unprocessed food and other agricultural products by size, weight, color, or condition. Excludes "Agricultural Inspectors" (45-2011).
- 2019 employment: **38,300**
- May 2019 median annual wage: **$25,670**
  ○ Wages come from the Occupational Employment Statistics (OES) program
- Projected employment change, 2019–29:
  ○ Number of new jobs: **0**
  ○ Growth rate: **0 percent (Little or no change)**
- Education and training:
  ○ Typical entry-level education: **No formal educational credential**
  ○ Work experience in a related occupation: **None**
  ○ Typical on-the-job training: **Short-term on-the-job training**
- O*NET links:
  ○ 45-2041.00 - Graders and Sorters, Agricultural Products
- CareerOneStop videos for this occupation:
  ○ 45-2041.00 - Graders and Sorters, Agricultural Products

Construction and Extraction Occupations

First-line supervisors of construction trades and extraction workers
Directly supervise and coordinate activities of construction or extraction workers.
- 2019 employment: **685,000**
- May 2019 median annual wage: **$66,210**
  ○ Wages come from the Occupational Employment Statistics (OES) program
- Projected employment change, 2019–29:
  ○ Number of new jobs: **33,000**
  ○ Growth rate: **5 percent (Faster than average)**
- Education and training:
  ○ Typical entry-level education: **High school diploma or equivalent**
  ○ Work experience in a related occupation: **5 years or more**
  ○ Typical on-the-job training: **None**
- O*NET links:
  ○ 47-1011.00 - First-Line Supervisors of Construction Trades and Extraction Workers
  ○ 47-1011.03 - Solar Energy Installation Managers
- CareerOneStop videos for this occupation:
  ○ 47-1011.00 - First-Line Supervisors of Construction Trades and Extraction Workers

Paperhangers
Cover interior walls or ceilings of rooms with decorative wallpaper or fabric, or attach advertising posters on surfaces such as walls and billboards. May remove old materials or prepare surfaces to be papered.
- 2019 employment: **5,600**
- May 2019 median annual wage: **$40,520**
  ○ Wages come from the Occupational Employment Statistics (OES) program
- Projected employment change, 2019–29:
  ○ Number of new jobs: **0**
  ○ Growth rate: **-1 percent (Decline)**
- Education and training:
  ○ Typical entry-level education: **No formal educational credential**
  ○ Work experience in a related occupation: **None**
  ○ Typical on-the-job training: **Long-term on-the-job training**
- O*NET links:
  ○ 47-2142.00 - Paperhangers

Pipelayers
Lay pipe for storm or sanitation sewers, drains, and water mains. Perform any combination of the following tasks: grade trenches or culverts, position pipe, or seal joints. Excludes "Welders, Cutters, Solderers, and Brazers" (51-4121).
- 2019 employment: **38,900**
- May 2019 median annual wage: **$38,820**
  ○ Wages come from the Occupational Employment Statistics (OES) program
- Projected employment change, 2019–29:
  ○ Number of new jobs: **1,800**
  ○ Growth rate: **5 percent (Faster than average)**
- Education and training:
  ○ Typical entry-level education: **No formal educational credential**
  ○ Work experience in a related occupation: **None**
  ○ Typical on-the-job training: **Short-term on-the-job training**
- O*NET links:
  ○ 47-2151.00 - Pipelayers
- CareerOneStop videos for this occupation:
  ○ 47-2151.00 - Pipelayers

Plasterers and stucco masons
Apply interior or exterior plaster, cement, stucco, or similar materials. May also set ornamental plaster.
- 2019 employment: **27,700**
- May 2019 median annual wage: **$45,440**
  ○ Wages come from the Occupational Employment Statistics (OES) program
- Projected employment change, 2019–29:
  ○ Number of new jobs: **1,100**
  ○ Growth rate: **4 percent (As fast as average)**
- Education and training:
  ○ Typical entry-level education: **No formal educational credential**

○ Work experience in a related occupation: **None**
○ Typical on-the-job training: **Long-term on-the-job training**
• O*NET links:
○ 47-2161.00 - Plasterers and Stucco Masons

Fence erectors
Erect and repair fences and fence gates, using hand and power tools.
• 2019 employment: **34,200**
• May 2019 median annual wage: **$35,800**
○ Wages come from the Occupational Employment Statistics (OES) program
• Projected employment change, 2019–29:
○ Number of new jobs: **800**
○ Growth rate: **2 percent (Slower than average)**
• Education and training:
○ Typical entry-level education: **No formal educational credential**
○ Work experience in a related occupation: **None**
○ Typical on-the-job training: **Moderate-term on-the-job training**
• O*NET links:
○ 47-4031.00 - Fence Erectors

Highway maintenance workers
Maintain highways, municipal and rural roads, airport runways, and rights-of-way. Duties include patching broken or eroded pavement and repairing guard rails, highway markers, and snow fences. May also mow or clear brush from along road, or plow snow from roadway. Excludes "Tree Trimmers and Pruners" (37-3013).
• 2019 employment: **156,100**
• May 2019 median annual wage: **$40,730**
○ Wages come from the Occupational Employment Statistics (OES) program
• Projected employment change, 2019–29:
○ Number of new jobs: **7,800**
○ Growth rate: **5 percent (Faster than average)**
• Education and training:
○ Typical entry-level education: **High school diploma or equivalent**
○ Work experience in a related occupation: **None**
○ Typical on-the-job training: **Moderate-term on-the-job training**
• O*NET links:
○ 47-4051.00 - Highway Maintenance Workers

Rail-track laying and maintenance equipment operators
Lay, repair, and maintain track for standard or narrow-gauge railroad equipment used in regular railroad service or in plant yards, quarries, sand and gravel pits, and mines. Includes ballast cleaning machine operators and railroad bed tamping machine operators.
• 2019 employment: **13,900**
• May 2019 median annual wage: **$56,100**
○ Wages come from the Occupational Employment Statistics (OES) program
• Projected employment change, 2019–29:
○ Number of new jobs: **500**
○ Growth rate: **3 percent (As fast as average)**
• Education and training:
○ Typical entry-level education: **High school diploma or equivalent**
○ Work experience in a related occupation: **None**
○ Typical on-the-job training: **Moderate-term on-the-job training**

• O*NET links:
○ 47-4061.00 - Rail-Track Laying and Maintenance Equipment Operators

Septic tank servicers and sewer pipe cleaners
Clean and repair septic tanks, sewer lines, or drains. May patch walls and partitions of tank, replace damaged drain tile, or repair breaks in underground piping.
• 2019 employment: **30,700**
• May 2019 median annual wage: **$39,870**
○ Wages come from the Occupational Employment Statistics (OES) program
• Projected employment change, 2019–29:
○ Number of new jobs: **3,100**
○ Growth rate: **10 percent (Much faster than average)**
• Education and training:
○ Typical entry-level education: **High school diploma or equivalent**
○ Work experience in a related occupation: **None**
○ Typical on-the-job training: **Moderate-term on-the-job training**
• O*NET links:
○ 47-4071.00 - Septic Tank Servicers and Sewer Pipe Cleaners
• CareerOneStop videos for this occupation:
○ 47-4071.00 - Septic Tank Servicers and Sewer Pipe Cleaners

Miscellaneous construction and related workers
This is an OES hybrid
• 2019 employment: **34,100**
• May 2019 median annual wage: **$39,720**
○ Wages come from the Occupational Employment Statistics (OES) program
• Projected employment change, 2019–29:
○ Number of new jobs: **1,500**
○ Growth rate: **4 percent (As fast as average)**
• Education and training:
○ Typical entry-level education: **High school diploma or equivalent**
○ Work experience in a related occupation: **None**
○ Typical on-the-job training: **Moderate-term on-the-job training**
• O*NET links:
○ 47-4091.00 - Segmental Pavers
○ 47-4091.00 - Segmental Pavers
○ 47-4099.00 - Construction and Related Workers, All Other
○ 47-4099.00 - Construction and Related Workers, All Other
○ 47-4099.02 - Solar Thermal Installers and Technicians
○ 47-4099.02 - Solar Thermal Installers and Technicians
○ 47-4099.03 - Weatherization Installers and Technicians
○ 47-4099.03 - Weatherization Installers and Technicians
• CareerOneStop videos for this occupation:
○ 47-4091.00 - Segmental Pavers
○ 47-4091.00 - Segmental Pavers

Derrick operators, oil and gas
Rig derrick equipment and operate pumps to circulate mud or fluid through drill hole.
• 2019 employment: **12,000**
• May 2019 median annual wage: **$46,990**
○ Wages come from the Occupational Employment Statistics (OES) program
• Projected employment change, 2019–29:
○ Number of new jobs: **3,700**

○ Growth rate: **31 percent (Much faster than average)**
• Education and training:
  ○ Typical entry-level education: **No formal educational credential**
  ○ Work experience in a related occupation: **None**
  ○ Typical on-the-job training: **Short-term on-the-job training**
• O*NET links:
  ○ 47-5011.00 - Derrick Operators, Oil and Gas
• CareerOneStop videos for this occupation:
  ○ 47-5011.00 - Derrick Operators, Oil and Gas

Rotary drill operators, oil and gas

Set up or operate a variety of drills to remove underground oil and gas, or remove core samples for testing during oil and gas exploration. Excludes "Earth Drillers, Except Oil and Gas" (47-5023).
• 2019 employment: **20,900**
• May 2019 median annual wage: **$54,980**
  ○ Wages come from the Occupational Employment Statistics (OES) program
• Projected employment change, 2019–29:
  ○ Number of new jobs: **5,600**
  ○ Growth rate: **27 percent (Much faster than average)**
• Education and training:
  ○ Typical entry-level education: **No formal educational credential**
  ○ Work experience in a related occupation: **None**
  ○ Typical on-the-job training: **Moderate-term on-the-job training**
• O*NET links:
  ○ 47-5012.00 - Rotary Drill Operators, Oil and Gas
• CareerOneStop videos for this occupation:
  ○ 47-5012.00 - Rotary Drill Operators, Oil and Gas

Service unit operators, oil and gas

Operate equipment to increase oil flow from producing wells or to remove stuck pipe, casing, tools, or other obstructions from drilling wells. Includes fishing-tool technicians.
• 2019 employment: **51,700**
• May 2019 median annual wage: **$46,740**
  ○ Wages come from the Occupational Employment Statistics (OES) program
• Projected employment change, 2019–29:
  ○ Number of new jobs: **11,800**
  ○ Growth rate: **23 percent (Much faster than average)**
• Education and training:
  ○ Typical entry-level education: **No formal educational credential**
  ○ Work experience in a related occupation: **None**
  ○ Typical on-the-job training: **Moderate-term on-the-job training**
• O*NET links:
  ○ 47-5013.00 - Service Unit Operators, Oil, Gas, and Mining
• CareerOneStop videos for this occupation:
  ○ 47-5013.00 - Service Unit Operators, Oil, Gas, and Mining

Continuous mining machine operators

Operate self-propelled mining machines that rip coal, metal and non-metal ores, rock, stone, or sand from the mine face and load it onto conveyors, shuttle cars, or trucks in a continuous operation.
• 2019 employment: **15,000**
• May 2019 median annual wage: **$55,280**

○ Wages come from the Occupational Employment Statistics (OES) program
• Projected employment change, 2019–29:
  ○ Number of new jobs: **300**
  ○ Growth rate: **2 percent (Slower than average)**
• Education and training:
  ○ Typical entry-level education: **No formal educational credential**
  ○ Work experience in a related occupation: **None**
  ○ Typical on-the-job training: **Moderate-term on-the-job training**
• O*NET links:
  ○ 47-5041.00 - Continuous Mining Machine Operators
• CareerOneStop videos for this occupation:
  ○ 47-5041.00 - Continuous Mining Machine Operators

Roof bolters, mining

Operate machinery to install roof support bolts in underground mine.
• 2019 employment: **3,300**
• May 2019 median annual wage: **$59,090**
  ○ Wages come from the Occupational Employment Statistics (OES) program
• Projected employment change, 2019–29:
  ○ Number of new jobs: **-500**
  ○ Growth rate: **-16 percent (Decline)**
• Education and training:
  ○ Typical entry-level education: **High school diploma or equivalent**
  ○ Work experience in a related occupation: **None**
  ○ Typical on-the-job training: **Moderate-term on-the-job training**
• O*NET links:
  ○ 47-5061.00 - Roof Bolters, Mining

Rock splitters, quarry

Separate blocks of rough dimension stone from quarry mass using jackhammers, wedges, or chop saws.
• 2019 employment: **5,100**
• May 2019 median annual wage: **$36,070**
  ○ Wages come from the Occupational Employment Statistics (OES) program
• Projected employment change, 2019–29:
  ○ Number of new jobs: **200**
  ○ Growth rate: **4 percent (As fast as average)**
• Education and training:
  ○ Typical entry-level education: **No formal educational credential**
  ○ Work experience in a related occupation: **None**
  ○ Typical on-the-job training: **Short-term on-the-job training**
• O*NET links:
  ○ 47-5051.00 - Rock Splitters, Quarry

Roustabouts, oil and gas

Assemble or repair oil field equipment using hand and power tools. Perform other tasks as needed.
• 2019 employment: **58,500**
• May 2019 median annual wage: **$38,910**
  ○ Wages come from the Occupational Employment Statistics (OES) program
• Projected employment change, 2019–29:
  ○ Number of new jobs: **14,700**
  ○ Growth rate: **25 percent (Much faster than average)**

- Education and training:
  - Typical entry-level education: **No formal educational credential**
  - Work experience in a related occupation: **None**
  - Typical on-the-job training: **Moderate-term on-the-job training**
- O*NET links:
  - 47-5071.00 - Roustabouts, Oil and Gas
- CareerOneStop videos for this occupation:
  - 47-5071.00 - Roustabouts, Oil and Gas

Helpers--extraction workers

Help extraction craft workers, such as earth drillers, blasters and explosives workers, derrick operators, and mining machine operators, by performing duties requiring less skill. Duties include supplying equipment or cleaning work area. Apprentice workers are classified with the appropriate skilled construction trade occupation (47-2011 through 47-2231).

- 2019 employment: **16,900**
- May 2019 median annual wage: **$37,120**
  - Wages come from the Occupational Employment Statistics (OES) program
- Projected employment change, 2019–29:
  - Number of new jobs: **3,400**
  - Growth rate: **20 percent (Much faster than average)**
- Education and training:
  - Typical entry-level education: **High school diploma or equivalent**
  - Work experience in a related occupation: **None**
  - Typical on-the-job training: **Moderate-term on-the-job training**
- O*NET links:
  - 47-5081.00 - Helpers--Extraction Workers

Earth drillers, except oil and gas; and explosives workers, ordnance handling experts, and blasters

This is an OES hybrid

- 2019 employment: **25,300**
- May 2019 median annual wage: **$46,250**
  - Wages come from the Occupational Employment Statistics (OES) program
- Projected employment change, 2019–29:
  - Number of new jobs: **2,000**
  - Growth rate: **8 percent (Much faster than average)**
- Education and training:
  - Typical entry-level education: **High school diploma or equivalent**
  - Work experience in a related occupation: **Less than 5 years**
  - Typical on-the-job training: **Long-term on-the-job training**
- O*NET links:
  - 47-5021.00 - Earth Drillers, Except Oil and Gas
  - 47-5021.00 - Earth Drillers, Except Oil and Gas
  - 47-5031.00 - Explosives Workers, Ordnance Handling Experts, and Blasters
  - 47-5031.00 - Explosives Workers, Ordnance Handling Experts, and Blasters
- CareerOneStop videos for this occupation:
  - 47-5021.00 - Earth Drillers, Except Oil and Gas
  - 47-5021.00 - Earth Drillers, Except Oil and Gas

Underground mining machine operators and extraction workers, all other

This is an OES hybrid

- 2019 employment: **14,100**
- May 2019 median annual wage: **$50,160**
  - Wages come from the Occupational Employment Statistics (OES) program
- Projected employment change, 2019–29:
  - Number of new jobs: **1,300**
  - Growth rate: **9 percent (Much faster than average)**
- Education and training:
  - Typical entry-level education: **High school diploma or equivalent**
  - Work experience in a related occupation: **None**
  - Typical on-the-job training: **Moderate-term on-the-job training**
- O*NET links:
  - 47-5042.00 - Mine Cutting and Channeling Machine Operators
  - 47-5042.00 - Mine Cutting and Channeling Machine Operators
  - 47-5049.00 - Mining Machine Operators, All Other
  - 47-5049.00 - Mining Machine Operators, All Other
  - 47-5099.00 - Extraction Workers, All Other
  - 47-5099.00 - Extraction Workers, All Other
- CareerOneStop videos for this occupation:
  - 47-5042.00 - Mine Cutting and Channeling Machine Operators
  - 47-5042.00 - Mine Cutting and Channeling Machine Operators

Installation, Maintenance, and Repair Occupations

-line supervisors of mechanics, installers, and repairers

Directly supervise and coordinate the activities of mechanics, installers, and repairers. May also advise customers on recommended services. Excludes team or work leaders.

- 2019 employment: **499,100**
- May 2019 median annual wage: **$67,460**
  - Wages come from the Occupational Employment Statistics (OES) program
- Projected employment change, 2019–29:
  - Number of new jobs: **13,300**
  - Growth rate: **3 percent (As fast as average)**
- Education and training:
  - Typical entry-level education: **High school diploma or equivalent**
  - Work experience in a related occupation: **Less than 5 years**
  - Typical on-the-job training: **None**
- O*NET links:
  - 49-1011.00 - First-Line Supervisors of Mechanics, Installers, and Repairers

Computer, automated teller, and office machine repairers

Repair, maintain, or install computers, word processing systems, automated teller machines, and electronic office machines, such as duplicating and fax machines.

- 2019 employment: **112,300**
- May 2019 median annual wage: **$39,530**
  - Wages come from the Occupational Employment Statistics (OES) program

- Projected employment change, 2019–29:
  - Number of new jobs: **-900**
  - Growth rate: **-1 percent (Decline)**
- Education and training:
  - Typical entry-level education: **Some college, no degree**
  - Work experience in a related occupation: **None**
  - Typical on-the-job training: **Short-term on-the-job training**
- O*NET links:
  - 49-2011.00 - Computer, Automated Teller, and Office Machine Repairers

Radio, cellular, and tower equipment installers and repairers

Repair, install, or maintain mobile or stationary radio transmitting, broadcasting, and receiving equipment, and two-way radio communications systems used in cellular telecommunications, mobile broadband, ship-to-shore, aircraft-to-ground communications, and radio equipment in service and emergency vehicles. May test and analyze network coverage.

- 2019 employment: **15,000**
- May 2019 median annual wage: **$55,380**
  - Wages come from the Occupational Employment Statistics (OES) program
- Projected employment change, 2019–29:
  - Number of new jobs: **600**
  - Growth rate: **4 percent (As fast as average)**
- Education and training:
  - Typical entry-level education: **Associate's degree**
  - Work experience in a related occupation: **None**
  - Typical on-the-job training: **Moderate-term on-the-job training**
- O*NET links:
  - 49-2021.00 - Radio, Cellular, and Tower Equipment Installers and Repairers
  - 49-2021.01 - Radio Mechanics

Audiovisual equipment installers and repairers

Install, repair, or adjust audio or television receivers, stereo systems, camcorders, video systems, or other electronic entertainment equipment in homes or other venues. May perform routine maintenance. Excludes "Audio and Video Technicians" (27-4011).

- 2019 employment: **29,700**
- May 2019 median annual wage: **$39,510**
  - Wages come from the Occupational Employment Statistics (OES) program
- Projected employment change, 2019–29:
  - Number of new jobs: **-800**
  - Growth rate: **-3 percent (Decline)**
- Education and training:
  - Typical entry-level education: **Postsecondary nondegree award**
  - Work experience in a related occupation: **None**
  - Typical on-the-job training: **Short-term on-the-job training**
- O*NET links:
  - 49-2097.00 - Electronic Home Entertainment Equipment Installers and Repairers

Security and fire alarm systems installers

Install, program, maintain, and repair security and fire alarm wiring and equipment. Ensure that work is in accordance with relevant codes. Excludes "Electricians" (47-2111) who do a broad range of electrical wiring.

- 2019 employment: **76,300**

- May 2019 median annual wage: **$48,970**
  - Wages come from the Occupational Employment Statistics (OES) program
- Projected employment change, 2019–29:
  - Number of new jobs: **7,800**
  - Growth rate: **10 percent (Much faster than average)**
- Education and training:
  - Typical entry-level education: **High school diploma or equivalent**
  - Work experience in a related occupation: **None**
  - Typical on-the-job training: **Moderate-term on-the-job training**
- O*NET links:
  - 49-2098.00 - Security and Fire Alarm Systems Installers

Bicycle repairers

Repair and service bicycles.

- 2019 employment: **13,200**
- May 2019 median annual wage: **$30,330**
  - Wages come from the Occupational Employment Statistics (OES) program
- Projected employment change, 2019–29:
  - Number of new jobs: **600**
  - Growth rate: **5 percent (Faster than average)**
- Education and training:
  - Typical entry-level education: **High school diploma or equivalent**
  - Work experience in a related occupation: **None**
  - Typical on-the-job training: **Moderate-term on-the-job training**
- O*NET links:
  - 49-3091.00 - Bicycle Repairers
- CareerOneStop videos for this occupation:
  - 49-3091.00 - Bicycle Repairers

Recreational vehicle service technicians

Diagnose, inspect, adjust, repair, or overhaul recreational vehicles including travel trailers. May specialize in maintaining gas, electrical, hydraulic, plumbing, or chassis/towing systems as well as repairing generators, appliances, and interior components. Includes workers who perform customized van conversions. Excludes "Automotive Service Technicians and Mechanics" (49-3023) and "Bus and Truck Mechanics and Diesel Engine Specialists" (49-3031) who also work on recreation vehicles.

- 2019 employment: **15,900**
- May 2019 median annual wage: **$38,570**
  - Wages come from the Occupational Employment Statistics (OES) program
- Projected employment change, 2019–29:
  - Number of new jobs: **800**
  - Growth rate: **5 percent (Faster than average)**
- Education and training:
  - Typical entry-level education: **High school diploma or equivalent**
  - Work experience in a related occupation: **None**
  - Typical on-the-job training: **Long-term on-the-job training**
- O*NET links:
  - 49-3092.00 - Recreational Vehicle Service Technicians

Tire repairers and changers

Repair and replace tires.

- 2019 employment: **113,400**

- May 2019 median annual wage: **$28,640**
  - Wages come from the Occupational Employment Statistics (OES) program
- Projected employment change, 2019–29:
  - Number of new jobs: **2,600**
  - Growth rate: **2 percent (Slower than average)**
- Education and training:
  - Typical entry-level education: **High school diploma or equivalent**
  - Work experience in a related occupation: **None**
  - Typical on-the-job training: **Short-term on-the-job training**
- O*NET links:
  - 49-3093.00 - Tire Repairers and Changers
- CareerOneStop videos for this occupation:
  - 49-3093.00 - Tire Repairers and Changers

Mechanical door repairers
Install, service, or repair automatic door mechanisms and hydraulic doors. Includes garage door mechanics.
- 2019 employment: **23,400**
- May 2019 median annual wage: **$41,570**
  - Wages come from the Occupational Employment Statistics (OES) program
- Projected employment change, 2019–29:
  - Number of new jobs: **800**
  - Growth rate: **4 percent (As fast as average)**
- Education and training:
  - Typical entry-level education: **High school diploma or equivalent**
  - Work experience in a related occupation: **None**
  - Typical on-the-job training: **Moderate-term on-the-job training**
- O*NET links:
  - 49-9011.00 - Mechanical Door Repairers

Control and valve installers and repairers, except mechanical door
Install, repair, and maintain mechanical regulating and controlling devices, such as electric meters, gas regulators, thermostats, safety and flow valves, and other mechanical governors.
- 2019 employment: **53,100**
- May 2019 median annual wage: **$58,100**
  - Wages come from the Occupational Employment Statistics (OES) program
- Projected employment change, 2019–29:
  - Number of new jobs: **100**
  - Growth rate: **0 percent (Little or no change)**
- Education and training:
  - Typical entry-level education: **High school diploma or equivalent**
  - Work experience in a related occupation: **None**
  - Typical on-the-job training: **Moderate-term on-the-job training**
- O*NET links:
  - 49-9012.00 - Control and Valve Installers and Repairers, Except Mechanical Door

Home appliance repairers
Repair, adjust, or install all types of electric or gas household appliances, such as refrigerators, washers, dryers, and ovens.
- 2019 employment: **38,400**
- May 2019 median annual wage: **$40,260**

- Wages come from the Occupational Employment Statistics (OES) program
- Projected employment change, 2019–29:
  - Number of new jobs: **-2,700**
  - Growth rate: **-7 percent (Decline)**
- Education and training:
  - Typical entry-level education: **High school diploma or equivalent**
  - Work experience in a related occupation: **None**
  - Typical on-the-job training: **Moderate-term on-the-job training**
- O*NET links:
  - 49-9031.00 - Home Appliance Repairers

Refractory materials repairers, except brickmasons
Build or repair equipment such as furnaces, kilns, cupolas, boilers, converters, ladles, soaking pits, and ovens, using refractory materials.
- 2019 employment: **800**
- May 2019 median annual wage: **$53,990**
  - Wages come from the Occupational Employment Statistics (OES) program
- Projected employment change, 2019–29:
  - Number of new jobs: **-200**
  - Growth rate: **-19 percent (Decline)**
- Education and training:
  - Typical entry-level education: **High school diploma or equivalent**
  - Work experience in a related occupation: **None**
  - Typical on-the-job training: **Moderate-term on-the-job training**
- O*NET links:
  - 49-9045.00 - Refractory Materials Repairers, Except Brickmasons

Camera and photographic equipment repairers
Repair and adjust cameras and photographic equipment, including commercial video and motion picture camera equipment.
- 2019 employment: **4,200**
- May 2019 median annual wage: **$38,880**
  - Wages come from the Occupational Employment Statistics (OES) program
- Projected employment change, 2019–29:
  - Number of new jobs: **100**
  - Growth rate: **3 percent (As fast as average)**
- Education and training:
  - Typical entry-level education: **High school diploma or equivalent**
  - Work experience in a related occupation: **None**
  - Typical on-the-job training: **Long-term on-the-job training**
- O*NET links:
  - 49-9061.00 - Camera and Photographic Equipment Repairers

Musical instrument repairers and tuners
Repair percussion, stringed, reed, or wind instruments. May specialize in one area, such as piano tuning. Excludes "Audiovisual Equipment Installers and Repairers" (49-2097) who repair electrical and electronic musical instruments.
- 2019 employment: **8,900**
- May 2019 median annual wage: **$36,650**
  - Wages come from the Occupational Employment Statistics (OES) program
- Projected employment change, 2019–29:
  - Number of new jobs: **-600**

○ Growth rate: **-7 percent (Decline)**
- Education and training:
  ○ Typical entry-level education: **High school diploma or equivalent**
  ○ Work experience in a related occupation: **None**
  ○ Typical on-the-job training: **Apprenticeship**
- O*NET links:
  ○ 49-9063.00 - Musical Instrument Repairers and Tuners
- CareerOneStop videos for this occupation:
  ○ 49-9063.00 - Musical Instrument Repairers and Tuners

Watch and clock repairers

Repair, clean, and adjust mechanisms of timing instruments, such as watches and clocks. Includes watchmakers, watch technicians, and mechanical timepiece repairers. Excludes "Timing Device Assemblers and Adjusters" (51-2061).
- 2019 employment: **3,200**
- May 2019 median annual wage: **$42,520**
  ○ Wages come from the Occupational Employment Statistics (OES) program
- Projected employment change, 2019–29:
  ○ Number of new jobs: **-1,000**
  ○ Growth rate: **-32 percent (Decline)**
- Education and training:
  ○ Typical entry-level education: **High school diploma or equivalent**
  ○ Work experience in a related occupation: **None**
  ○ Typical on-the-job training: **Long-term on-the-job training**
- O*NET links:
  ○ 49-9064.00 - Watch Repairers
- CareerOneStop videos for this occupation:
  ○ 49-9064.00 - Watch Repairers

Precision instrument and equipment repairers, all other

All precision instrument and equipment repairers not listed separately.
- 2019 employment: **12,200**
- May 2019 median annual wage: **$58,720**
  ○ Wages come from the Occupational Employment Statistics (OES) program
- Projected employment change, 2019–29:
  ○ Number of new jobs: **400**
  ○ Growth rate: **3 percent (As fast as average)**
- Education and training:
  ○ Typical entry-level education: **High school diploma or equivalent**
  ○ Work experience in a related occupation: **None**
  ○ Typical on-the-job training: **Long-term on-the-job training**
- O*NET links:
  ○ 49-9069.00 - Precision Instrument and Equipment Repairers, All Other

Coin, vending, and amusement machine servicers and repairers

Install, service, adjust, or repair coin, vending, or amusement machines including video games, juke boxes, pinball machines, or slot machines.
- 2019 employment: **37,000**
- May 2019 median annual wage: **$35,420**
  ○ Wages come from the Occupational Employment Statistics (OES) program
- Projected employment change, 2019–29:
  ○ Number of new jobs: **-800**
  ○ Growth rate: **-2 percent (Decline)**
- Education and training:

○ Typical entry-level education: **High school diploma or equivalent**
○ Work experience in a related occupation: **None**
○ Typical on-the-job training: **Short-term on-the-job training**
- O*NET links:
  ○ 49-9091.00 - Coin, Vending, and Amusement Machine Servicers and Repairers

Commercial divers

Work below surface of water, using surface-supplied air or scuba equipment to inspect, repair, remove, or install equipment and structures. May use a variety of power and hand tools, such as drills, sledgehammers, torches, and welding equipment. May conduct tests or experiments, rig explosives, or photograph structures or marine life. Excludes "Athletes and Sports Competitors" (27-2021), "Police and Sheriff's Patrol Officers" (33-3051), and "Fishing and Hunting Workers" (45-3031).
- 2019 employment: **4,000**
- May 2019 median annual wage: **$49,980**
  ○ Wages come from the Occupational Employment Statistics (OES) program
- Projected employment change, 2019–29:
  ○ Number of new jobs: **200**
  ○ Growth rate: **5 percent (Faster than average)**
- Education and training:
  ○ Typical entry-level education: **Postsecondary nondegree award**
  ○ Work experience in a related occupation: **None**
  ○ Typical on-the-job training: **Moderate-term on-the-job training**
- O*NET links:
  ○ 49-9092.00 - Commercial Divers
- CareerOneStop videos for this occupation:
  ○ 49-9092.00 - Commercial Divers

Locksmiths and safe repairers

Repair and open locks, make keys, change locks and safe combinations, and install and repair safes.
- 2019 employment: **21,100**
- May 2019 median annual wage: **$41,940**
  ○ Wages come from the Occupational Employment Statistics (OES) program
- Projected employment change, 2019–29:
  ○ Number of new jobs: **-1,600**
  ○ Growth rate: **-8 percent (Decline)**
- Education and training:
  ○ Typical entry-level education: **High school diploma or equivalent**
  ○ Work experience in a related occupation: **None**
  ○ Typical on-the-job training: **Long-term on-the-job training**
- O*NET links:
  ○ 49-9094.00 - Locksmiths and Safe Repairers
- CareerOneStop videos for this occupation:
  ○ 49-9094.00 - Locksmiths and Safe Repairers

Manufactured building and mobile home installers

Move or install mobile homes or prefabricated buildings.
- 2019 employment: **2,900**
- May 2019 median annual wage: **$33,890**
  ○ Wages come from the Occupational Employment Statistics (OES) program
- Projected employment change, 2019–29:
  ○ Number of new jobs: **-600**
  ○ Growth rate: **-22 percent (Decline)**

- Education and training:
  - Typical entry-level education: **High school diploma or equivalent**
  - Work experience in a related occupation: **None**
  - Typical on-the-job training: **Short-term on-the-job training**
- O*NET links:
  - 49-9095.00 - Manufactured Building and Mobile Home Installers

Riggers

Set up or repair rigging for construction projects, manufacturing plants, logging yards, ships and shipyards, or for the entertainment industry.
- 2019 employment: **23,500**
- May 2019 median annual wage: **$50,860**
  - Wages come from the Occupational Employment Statistics (OES) program
- Projected employment change, 2019–29:
  - Number of new jobs: **1,100**
  - Growth rate: **5 percent (Faster than average)**
- Education and training:
  - Typical entry-level education: **High school diploma or equivalent**
  - Work experience in a related occupation: **None**
  - Typical on-the-job training: **Moderate-term on-the-job training**
- O*NET links:
  - 49-9096.00 - Riggers
- CareerOneStop videos for this occupation:
  - 49-9096.00 - Riggers

Signal and track switch repairers

Install, inspect, test, maintain, or repair electric gate crossings, signals, signal equipment, track switches, section lines, or intercommunications systems within a railroad system.
- 2019 employment: **6,600**
- May 2019 median annual wage: **$73,890**
  - Wages come from the Occupational Employment Statistics (OES) program
- Projected employment change, 2019–29:
  - Number of new jobs: **0**
  - Growth rate: **-1 percent (Decline)**
- Education and training:
  - Typical entry-level education: **High school diploma or equivalent**
  - Work experience in a related occupation: **None**
  - Typical on-the-job training: **Moderate-term on-the-job training**
- O*NET links:
  - 49-9097.00 - Signal and Track Switch Repairers

Helpers--installation, maintenance, and repair workers

Help installation, maintenance, and repair workers in maintenance, parts replacement, and repair of vehicles, industrial machinery, and electrical and electronic equipment. Perform duties such as furnishing tools, materials, and supplies to other workers; cleaning work area, machines, and tools; and holding materials or tools for other workers.
- 2019 employment: **101,100**
- May 2019 median annual wage: **$30,530**
  - Wages come from the Occupational Employment Statistics (OES) program
- Projected employment change, 2019–29:
  - Number of new jobs: **4,400**

- Growth rate: **4 percent (As fast as average)**
- Education and training:
  - Typical entry-level education: **High school diploma or equivalent**
  - Work experience in a related occupation: **None**
  - Typical on-the-job training: **Short-term on-the-job training**
- O*NET links:
  - 49-9098.00 - Helpers--Installation, Maintenance, and Repair Workers

Installation, maintenance, and repair workers, all other

All installation, maintenance, and repair workers not listed separately.
- 2019 employment: **187,700**
- May 2019 median annual wage: **$39,830**
  - Wages come from the Occupational Employment Statistics (OES) program
- Projected employment change, 2019–29:
  - Number of new jobs: **4,700**
  - Growth rate: **2 percent (Slower than average)**
- Education and training:
  - Typical entry-level education: **High school diploma or equivalent**
  - Work experience in a related occupation: **None**
  - Typical on-the-job training: **Moderate-term on-the-job training**
- O*NET links:
  - 49-9093.00 - Fabric Menders, Except Garment

Production Occupations

First-line supervisors of production and operating workers

Directly supervise and coordinate the activities of production and operating workers, such as inspectors, precision workers, machine setters and operators, assemblers, fabricators, and plant and system operators. Excludes team or work leaders.
- 2019 employment: **648,900**
- May 2019 median annual wage: **$61,310**
  - Wages come from the Occupational Employment Statistics (OES) program
- Projected employment change, 2019–29:
  - Number of new jobs: **-2,000**
  - Growth rate: **0 percent (Little or no change)**
- Education and training:
  - Typical entry-level education: **High school diploma or equivalent**
  - Work experience in a related occupation: **Less than 5 years**
  - Typical on-the-job training: **None**
- O*NET links:
  - 51-1011.00 - First-Line Supervisors of Production and Operating Workers
- CareerOneStop videos for this occupation:
  - 51-1011.00 - First-Line Supervisors of Production and Operating Workers

Meat, poultry, and fish cutters and trimmers

Use hands or hand tools to perform routine cutting and trimming of meat, poultry, and seafood.
- 2019 employment: **161,800**
- May 2019 median annual wage: **$28,100**
  - Wages come from the Occupational Employment Statistics (OES) program

- Projected employment change, 2019–29:
  - Number of new jobs: **2,700**
  - Growth rate: **2 percent (Slower than average)**
- Education and training:
  - Typical entry-level education: **No formal educational credential**
  - Work experience in a related occupation: **None**
  - Typical on-the-job training: **Short-term on-the-job training**
- O*NET links:
  - 51-3022.00 - Meat, Poultry, and Fish Cutters and Trimmers
- CareerOneStop videos for this occupation:
  - 51-3022.00 - Meat, Poultry, and Fish Cutters and Trimmers

Slaughterers and meat packers

Perform nonroutine or precision functions involving the preparation of large portions of meat. Work may include specialized slaughtering tasks, cutting standard or premium cuts of meat for marketing, making sausage, or wrapping meats. Work typically occurs in slaughtering, meat packing, or wholesale establishments. Excludes "Meat, Poultry, and Fish Cutters and Trimmers" (51-3022) who perform routine meat cutting.

- 2019 employment: **75,000**
- May 2019 median annual wage: **$29,230**
  - Wages come from the Occupational Employment Statistics (OES) program
- Projected employment change, 2019–29:
  - Number of new jobs: **2,500**
  - Growth rate: **3 percent (As fast as average)**
- Education and training:
  - Typical entry-level education: **No formal educational credential**
  - Work experience in a related occupation: **None**
  - Typical on-the-job training: **Short-term on-the-job training**
- O*NET links:
  - 51-3023.00 - Slaughterers and Meat Packers
- CareerOneStop videos for this occupation:
  - 51-3023.00 - Slaughterers and Meat Packers

Layout workers, metal and plastic

Lay out reference points and dimensions on metal or plastic stock or workpieces, such as sheets, plates, tubes, structural shapes, castings, or machine parts, for further processing. Includes shipfitters.

- 2019 employment: **8,500**
- May 2019 median annual wage: **$49,940**
  - Wages come from the Occupational Employment Statistics (OES) program
- Projected employment change, 2019–29:
  - Number of new jobs: **-900**
  - Growth rate: **-10 percent (Decline)**
- Education and training:
  - Typical entry-level education: **High school diploma or equivalent**
  - Work experience in a related occupation: **None**
  - Typical on-the-job training: **Moderate-term on-the-job training**
- O*NET links:
  - 51-4192.00 - Layout Workers, Metal and Plastic

Tool grinders, filers, and sharpeners

Perform precision smoothing, sharpening, polishing, or grinding of metal objects.

- 2019 employment: **7,100**

- May 2019 median annual wage: **$39,330**
  - Wages come from the Occupational Employment Statistics (OES) program
- Projected employment change, 2019–29:
  - Number of new jobs: **-300**
  - Growth rate: **-5 percent (Decline)**
- Education and training:
  - Typical entry-level education: **High school diploma or equivalent**
  - Work experience in a related occupation: **None**
  - Typical on-the-job training: **Moderate-term on-the-job training**
- O*NET links:
  - 51-4194.00 - Tool Grinders, Filers, and Sharpeners

Metal workers and plastic workers, all other

All metal workers and plastic workers not listed separately.

- 2019 employment: **24,900**
- May 2019 median annual wage: **$34,830**
  - Wages come from the Occupational Employment Statistics (OES) program
- Projected employment change, 2019–29:
  - Number of new jobs: **-2,100**
  - Growth rate: **-9 percent (Decline)**
- Education and training:
  - Typical entry-level education: **High school diploma or equivalent**
  - Work experience in a related occupation: **None**
  - Typical on-the-job training: **Moderate-term on-the-job training**
- O*NET links:
  - 51-4199.00 - Metal Workers and Plastic Workers, All Other

Prepress technicians and workers

Format and proof text and images submitted by designers and clients into finished pages that can be printed. Includes digital and photo type-setting. May produce printing plates.

- 2019 employment: **30,200**
- May 2019 median annual wage: **$40,510**
  - Wages come from the Occupational Employment Statistics (OES) program
- Projected employment change, 2019–29:
  - Number of new jobs: **-6,300**
  - Growth rate: **-21 percent (Decline)**
- Education and training:
  - Typical entry-level education: **Postsecondary nondegree award**
  - Work experience in a related occupation: **None**
  - Typical on-the-job training: **None**
- O*NET links:
  - 51-5111.00 - Prepress Technicians and Workers
- CareerOneStop videos for this occupation:
  - 51-5111.00 - Prepress Technicians and Workers

Printing press operators

Set up and operate digital, letterpress, lithographic, flexographic, gravure, or other printing machines. Includes short-run offset printing presses.

- 2019 employment: **181,400**
- May 2019 median annual wage: **$36,910**
  - Wages come from the Occupational Employment Statistics (OES) program
- Projected employment change, 2019–29:

- Number of new jobs: **-24,200**
- Growth rate: **-13 percent (Decline)**
- Education and training:
  - Typical entry-level education: **High school diploma or equivalent**
  - Work experience in a related occupation: **None**
  - Typical on-the-job training: **Moderate-term on-the-job training**
- O*NET links:
  - 51-5112.00 - Printing Press Operators

Print binding and finishing workers

Bind books and other publications or finish printed products by hand or machine. May set up binding and finishing machines.
- 2019 employment: **45,200**
- May 2019 median annual wage: **$33,040**
  - Wages come from the Occupational Employment Statistics (OES) program
- Projected employment change, 2019–29:
  - Number of new jobs: **-6,700**
  - Growth rate: **-15 percent (Decline)**
- Education and training:
  - Typical entry-level education: **High school diploma or equivalent**
  - Work experience in a related occupation: **None**
  - Typical on-the-job training: **Moderate-term on-the-job training**
- O*NET links:
  - 51-5113.00 - Print Binding and Finishing Workers
- CareerOneStop videos for this occupation:
  - 51-5113.00 - Print Binding and Finishing Workers

Laundry and dry-cleaning workers

Operate or tend washing or dry-cleaning machines to wash or dry-clean industrial or household articles, such as cloth garments, suede, leather, furs, blankets, draperies, linens, rugs, and carpets. Includes spotters and dyers of these articles.
- 2019 employment: **215,200**
- May 2019 median annual wage: **$24,220**
  - Wages come from the Occupational Employment Statistics (OES) program
- Projected employment change, 2019–29:
  - Number of new jobs: **500**
  - Growth rate: **0 percent (Little or no change)**
- Education and training:
  - Typical entry-level education: **No formal educational credential**
  - Work experience in a related occupation: **None**
  - Typical on-the-job training: **Short-term on-the-job training**
- O*NET links:
  - 51-6011.00 - Laundry and Dry-Cleaning Workers
- CareerOneStop videos for this occupation:
  - 51-6011.00 - Laundry and Dry-Cleaning Workers

Pressers, textile, garment, and related materials

Press or shape articles by hand or machine.
- 2019 employment: **38,300**
- May 2019 median annual wage: **$24,190**
  - Wages come from the Occupational Employment Statistics (OES) program
- Projected employment change, 2019–29:
  - Number of new jobs: **-7,200**
  - Growth rate: **-19 percent (Decline)**

- Education and training:
  - Typical entry-level education: **No formal educational credential**
  - Work experience in a related occupation: **None**
  - Typical on-the-job training: **Short-term on-the-job training**
- O*NET links:
  - 51-6021.00 - Pressers, Textile, Garment, and Related Materials

Sewing machine operators

Operate or tend sewing machines to join, reinforce, decorate, or perform related sewing operations in the manufacture of garment or nongarment products.
- 2019 employment: **146,500**
- May 2019 median annual wage: **$26,420**
  - Wages come from the Occupational Employment Statistics (OES) program
- Projected employment change, 2019–29:
  - Number of new jobs: **-13,700**
  - Growth rate: **-9 percent (Decline)**
- Education and training:
  - Typical entry-level education: **No formal educational credential**
  - Work experience in a related occupation: **None**
  - Typical on-the-job training: **Short-term on-the-job training**
- O*NET links:
  - 51-6031.00 - Sewing Machine Operators
- CareerOneStop videos for this occupation:
  - 51-6031.00 - Sewing Machine Operators

Shoe and leather workers and repairers

Construct, decorate, or repair leather and leather-like products, such as luggage, shoes, and saddles. May use hand tools.
- 2019 employment: **10,800**
- May 2019 median annual wage: **$29,560**
  - Wages come from the Occupational Employment Statistics (OES) program
- Projected employment change, 2019–29:
  - Number of new jobs: **-1,100**
  - Growth rate: **-10 percent (Decline)**
- Education and training:
  - Typical entry-level education: **High school diploma or equivalent**
  - Work experience in a related occupation: **None**
  - Typical on-the-job training: **Moderate-term on-the-job training**
- O*NET links:
  - 51-6041.00 - Shoe and Leather Workers and Repairers
- CareerOneStop videos for this occupation:
  - 51-6041.00 - Shoe and Leather Workers and Repairers

Shoe machine operators and tenders

Operate or tend a variety of machines to join, decorate, reinforce, or finish shoes and shoe parts.
- 2019 employment: **5,300**
- May 2019 median annual wage: **$30,570**
  - Wages come from the Occupational Employment Statistics (OES) program
- Projected employment change, 2019–29:
  - Number of new jobs: **-800**
  - Growth rate: **-14 percent (Decline)**
- Education and training:
  - Typical entry-level education: **High school diploma or equivalent**

○ Work experience in a related occupation: **None**
○ Typical on-the-job training: **Short-term on-the-job training**
• O*NET links:
  ○ 51-6042.00 - Shoe Machine Operators and Tenders
• CareerOneStop videos for this occupation:
  ○ 51-6042.00 - Shoe Machine Operators and Tenders

Sewers, hand

Sew, join, reinforce, or finish, usually with needle and thread, a variety of manufactured items. Includes weavers and stitchers.
• 2019 employment: **7,500**
• May 2019 median annual wage: **$29,950**
  ○ Wages come from the Occupational Employment Statistics (OES) program
• Projected employment change, 2019–29:
  ○ Number of new jobs: **-600**
  ○ Growth rate: **-8 percent (Decline)**
• Education and training:
  ○ Typical entry-level education: **No formal educational credential**
  ○ Work experience in a related occupation: **None**
  ○ Typical on-the-job training: **Moderate-term on-the-job training**
• O*NET links:
  ○ 51-6051.00 - Sewers, Hand
• CareerOneStop videos for this occupation:
  ○ 51-6051.00 - Sewers, Hand

Tailors, dressmakers, and custom sewers

Design, make, alter, repair, or fit garments.
• 2019 employment: **37,300**
• May 2019 median annual wage: **$31,520**
  ○ Wages come from the Occupational Employment Statistics (OES) program
• Projected employment change, 2019–29:
  ○ Number of new jobs: **-1,600**
  ○ Growth rate: **-4 percent (Decline)**
• Education and training:
  ○ Typical entry-level education: **No formal educational credential**
  ○ Work experience in a related occupation: **None**
  ○ Typical on-the-job training: **Moderate-term on-the-job training**
• O*NET links:
  ○ 51-6052.00 - Tailors, Dressmakers, and Custom Sewers
• CareerOneStop videos for this occupation:
  ○ 51-6052.00 - Tailors, Dressmakers, and Custom Sewers

Textile bleaching and dyeing machine operators and tenders

Operate or tend machines to bleach, shrink, wash, dye, or finish textiles or synthetic or glass fibers.
• 2019 employment: **9,000**
• May 2019 median annual wage: **$29,460**
  ○ Wages come from the Occupational Employment Statistics (OES) program
• Projected employment change, 2019–29:
  ○ Number of new jobs: **-1,100**
  ○ Growth rate: **-12 percent (Decline)**
• Education and training:
  ○ Typical entry-level education: **High school diploma or equivalent**
  ○ Work experience in a related occupation: **None**

○ Typical on-the-job training: **Short-term on-the-job training**
• O*NET links:
  ○ 51-6061.00 - Textile Bleaching and Dyeing Machine Operators and Tenders
• CareerOneStop videos for this occupation:
  ○ 51-6061.00 - Textile Bleaching and Dyeing Machine Operators and Tenders

Textile cutting machine setters, operators, and tenders

Set up, operate, or tend machines that cut textiles.
• 2019 employment: **13,100**
• May 2019 median annual wage: **$28,730**
  ○ Wages come from the Occupational Employment Statistics (OES) program
• Projected employment change, 2019–29:
  ○ Number of new jobs: **-1,400**
  ○ Growth rate: **-10 percent (Decline)**
• Education and training:
  ○ Typical entry-level education: **High school diploma or equivalent**
  ○ Work experience in a related occupation: **None**
  ○ Typical on-the-job training: **Moderate-term on-the-job training**
• O*NET links:
  ○ 51-6062.00 - Textile Cutting Machine Setters, Operators, and Tenders
• CareerOneStop videos for this occupation:
  ○ 51-6062.00 - Textile Cutting Machine Setters, Operators, and Tenders

Textile knitting and weaving machine setters, operators, and tenders

Set up, operate, or tend machines that knit, loop, weave, or draw in textiles. Excludes "Sewing Machine Operators" (51-6031).
• 2019 employment: **24,800**
• May 2019 median annual wage: **$29,980**
  ○ Wages come from the Occupational Employment Statistics (OES) program
• Projected employment change, 2019–29:
  ○ Number of new jobs: **-3,200**
  ○ Growth rate: **-13 percent (Decline)**
• Education and training:
  ○ Typical entry-level education: **High school diploma or equivalent**
  ○ Work experience in a related occupation: **None**
  ○ Typical on-the-job training: **Short-term on-the-job training**
• O*NET links:
  ○ 51-6063.00 - Textile Knitting and Weaving Machine Setters, Operators, and Tenders
• CareerOneStop videos for this occupation:
  ○ 51-6063.00 - Textile Knitting and Weaving Machine Setters, Operators, and Tenders

Textile winding, twisting, and drawing out machine setters, operators, and tenders

Set up, operate, or tend machines that wind or twist textiles; or draw out and combine sliver, such as wool, hemp, or synthetic fibers. Includes slubber machine and drawing frame operators.
• 2019 employment: **31,000**
• May 2019 median annual wage: **$29,790**
  ○ Wages come from the Occupational Employment Statistics (OES) program

- Projected employment change, 2019–29:
  - Number of new jobs: **-3,000**
  - Growth rate: **-10 percent (Decline)**
- Education and training:
  - Typical entry-level education: **High school diploma or equivalent**
  - Work experience in a related occupation: **None**
  - Typical on-the-job training: **Moderate-term on-the-job training**
- O*NET links:
  - 51-6064.00 - Textile Winding, Twisting, and Drawing Out Machine Setters, Operators, and Tenders
- CareerOneStop videos for this occupation:
  - 51-6064.00 - Textile Winding, Twisting, and Drawing Out Machine Setters, Operators, and Tenders

Extruding and forming machine setters, operators, and tenders, synthetic and glass fibers

Set up, operate, or tend machines that extrude and form continuous filaments from synthetic materials, such as liquid polymer, rayon, and fiberglass.

- 2019 employment: **19,000**
- May 2019 median annual wage: **$36,110**
  - Wages come from the Occupational Employment Statistics (OES) program
- Projected employment change, 2019–29:
  - Number of new jobs: **-1,200**
  - Growth rate: **-6 percent (Decline)**
- Education and training:
  - Typical entry-level education: **High school diploma or equivalent**
  - Work experience in a related occupation: **None**
  - Typical on-the-job training: **Moderate-term on-the-job training**
- O*NET links:
  - 51-6091.00 - Extruding and Forming Machine Setters, Operators, and Tenders, Synthetic and Glass Fibers

Fabric and apparel patternmakers

Draw and construct sets of precision master fabric patterns or layouts. May also mark and cut fabrics and apparel.

- 2019 employment: **6,000**
- May 2019 median annual wage: **$45,070**
  - Wages come from the Occupational Employment Statistics (OES) program
- Projected employment change, 2019–29:
  - Number of new jobs: **-700**
  - Growth rate: **-11 percent (Decline)**
- Education and training:
  - Typical entry-level education: **High school diploma or equivalent**
  - Work experience in a related occupation: **None**
  - Typical on-the-job training: **Moderate-term on-the-job training**
- O*NET links:
  - 51-6092.00 - Fabric and Apparel Patternmakers
- CareerOneStop videos for this occupation:
  - 51-6092.00 - Fabric and Apparel Patternmakers

Upholsterers

Make, repair, or replace upholstery for household furniture or transportation vehicles.

- 2019 employment: **35,200**

- May 2019 median annual wage: **$35,130**
  - Wages come from the Occupational Employment Statistics (OES) program
- Projected employment change, 2019–29:
  - Number of new jobs: **-1,400**
  - Growth rate: **-4 percent (Decline)**
- Education and training:
  - Typical entry-level education: **High school diploma or equivalent**
  - Work experience in a related occupation: **None**
  - Typical on-the-job training: **Moderate-term on-the-job training**
- O*NET links:
  - 51-6093.00 - Upholsterers
- CareerOneStop videos for this occupation:
  - 51-6093.00 - Upholsterers

Textile, apparel, and furnishings workers, all other

All textile, apparel, and furnishings workers not listed separately.

- 2019 employment: **18,700**
- May 2019 median annual wage: **$27,970**
  - Wages come from the Occupational Employment Statistics (OES) program
- Projected employment change, 2019–29:
  - Number of new jobs: **-900**
  - Growth rate: **-5 percent (Decline)**
- Education and training:
  - Typical entry-level education: **High school diploma or equivalent**
  - Work experience in a related occupation: **None**
  - Typical on-the-job training: **Short-term on-the-job training**
- O*NET links:
  - 51-6099.00 - Textile, Apparel, and Furnishings Workers, All Other

Model makers, wood

Construct full-size and scale wooden precision models of products. Includes wood jig builders and loft workers.

- 2019 employment: **1,400**
- May 2019 median annual wage: **$59,260**
  - Wages come from the Occupational Employment Statistics (OES) program
- Projected employment change, 2019–29:
  - Number of new jobs: **0**
  - Growth rate: **0 percent (Little or no change)**
- Education and training:
  - Typical entry-level education: **High school diploma or equivalent**
  - Work experience in a related occupation: **None**
  - Typical on-the-job training: **Moderate-term on-the-job training**
- O*NET links:
  - 51-7031.00 - Model Makers, Wood

Patternmakers, wood

Plan, lay out, and construct wooden unit or sectional patterns used in forming sand molds for castings.

- 2019 employment: **700**
- May 2019 median annual wage: **$64,880**
  - Wages come from the Occupational Employment Statistics (OES) program
- Projected employment change, 2019–29:
  - Number of new jobs: **0**

○ Growth rate: **-5 percent (Decline)**
• Education and training:
  ○ Typical entry-level education: **High school diploma or equivalent**
  ○ Work experience in a related occupation: **None**
  ○ Typical on-the-job training: **Moderate-term on-the-job training**
• O*NET links:
  ○ 51-7032.00 - Patternmakers, Wood

Woodworkers, all other
All woodworkers not listed separately.
• 2019 employment: **11,700**
• May 2019 median annual wage: **$33,110**
  ○ Wages come from the Occupational Employment Statistics (OES) program
• Projected employment change, 2019–29:
  ○ Number of new jobs: **-500**
  ○ Growth rate: **-5 percent (Decline)**
• Education and training:
  ○ Typical entry-level education: **High school diploma or equivalent**
  ○ Work experience in a related occupation: **None**
  ○ Typical on-the-job training: **Moderate-term on-the-job training**
• O*NET links:
  ○ 51-7099.00 - Woodworkers, All Other

Chemical plant and system operators
Control or operate entire chemical processes or system of machines.
• 2019 employment: **29,200**
• May 2019 median annual wage: **$62,550**
  ○ Wages come from the Occupational Employment Statistics (OES) program
• Projected employment change, 2019–29:
  ○ Number of new jobs: **-900**
  ○ Growth rate: **-3 percent (Decline)**
• Education and training:
  ○ Typical entry-level education: **High school diploma or equivalent**
  ○ Work experience in a related occupation: **None**
  ○ Typical on-the-job training: **Moderate-term on-the-job training**
• O*NET links:
  ○ 51-8091.00 - Chemical Plant and System Operators

Gas plant operators
Distribute or process gas for utility companies and others by controlling compressors to maintain specified pressures on main pipelines.
• 2019 employment: **14,700**
• May 2019 median annual wage: **$70,710**
  ○ Wages come from the Occupational Employment Statistics (OES) program
• Projected employment change, 2019–29:
  ○ Number of new jobs: **-800**
  ○ Growth rate: **-6 percent (Decline)**
• Education and training:
  ○ Typical entry-level education: **High school diploma or equivalent**
  ○ Work experience in a related occupation: **None**
  ○ Typical on-the-job training: **Long-term on-the-job training**
• O*NET links:
  ○ 51-8092.00 - Gas Plant Operators

Petroleum pump system operators, refinery operators, and gaugers
Operate or control petroleum refining or processing units. May specialize in controlling manifold and pumping systems, gauging or testing oil in storage tanks, or regulating the flow of oil into pipelines.
• 2019 employment: **41,300**
• May 2019 median annual wage: **$74,180**
  ○ Wages come from the Occupational Employment Statistics (OES) program
• Projected employment change, 2019–29:
  ○ Number of new jobs: **-200**
  ○ Growth rate: **0 percent (Little or no change)**
• Education and training:
  ○ Typical entry-level education: **High school diploma or equivalent**
  ○ Work experience in a related occupation: **None**
  ○ Typical on-the-job training: **Moderate-term on-the-job training**
• O*NET links:
  ○ 51-8093.00 - Petroleum Pump System Operators, Refinery Operators, and Gaugers

Plant and system operators, all other
All plant and system operators not listed separately.
• 2019 employment: **13,200**
• May 2019 median annual wage: **$58,390**
  ○ Wages come from the Occupational Employment Statistics (OES) program
• Projected employment change, 2019–29:
  ○ Number of new jobs: **0**
  ○ Growth rate: **0 percent (Little or no change)**
• Education and training:
  ○ Typical entry-level education: **High school diploma or equivalent**
  ○ Work experience in a related occupation: **None**
  ○ Typical on-the-job training: **Moderate-term on-the-job training**
• O*NET links:
  ○ 51-8099.00 - Plant and System Operators, All Other
  ○ 51-8099.01 - Biofuels Processing Technicians
  ○ 51-8099.02 - Methane/Landfill Gas Generation System Technicians
  ○ 51-8099.03 - Biomass Plant Technicians
  ○ 51-8099.04 - Hydroelectric Plant Technicians
• CareerOneStop videos for this occupation:
  ○ 51-8099.01 - Biofuels Processing Technicians
  ○ 51-8099.02 - Methane/Landfill Gas Generation System Technicians
  ○ 51-8099.03 - Biomass Plant Technicians
  ○ 51-8099.04 - Hydroelectric Plant Technicians

Chemical equipment operators and tenders
Operate or tend equipment to control chemical changes or reactions in the processing of industrial or consumer products. Equipment used includes devulcanizers, steam-jacketed kettles, and reactor vessels. Excludes "Chemical Plant and System Operators" (51-8091).
• 2019 employment: **88,500**
• May 2019 median annual wage: **$49,130**
  ○ Wages come from the Occupational Employment Statistics (OES) program
• Projected employment change, 2019–29:
  ○ Number of new jobs: **1,500**
  ○ Growth rate: **2 percent (Slower than average)**

- Education and training:
  - Typical entry-level education: **High school diploma or equivalent**
  - Work experience in a related occupation: **None**
  - Typical on-the-job training: **Moderate-term on-the-job training**
- O*NET links:
  - 51-9011.00 - Chemical Equipment Operators and Tenders

Separating, filtering, clarifying, precipitating, and still machine setters, operators, and tenders

Set up, operate, or tend continuous flow or vat-type equipment; filter presses; shaker screens; centrifuges; condenser tubes; precipitating, fermenting, or evaporating tanks; scrubbing towers; or batch stills. These machines extract, sort, or separate liquids, gases, or solids from other materials to recover a refined product. Includes dairy processing equipment operators. Excludes "Chemical Equipment Operators and Tenders" (51-9011).

- 2019 employment: **53,100**
- May 2019 median annual wage: **$41,330**
  - Wages come from the Occupational Employment Statistics (OES) program
- Projected employment change, 2019–29:
  - Number of new jobs: **1,900**
  - Growth rate: **4 percent (As fast as average)**
- Education and training:
  - Typical entry-level education: **High school diploma or equivalent**
  - Work experience in a related occupation: **None**
  - Typical on-the-job training: **Moderate-term on-the-job training**
- O*NET links:
  - 51-9012.00 - Separating, Filtering, Clarifying, Precipitating, and Still Machine Setters, Operators, and Tenders

Crushing, grinding, and polishing machine setters, operators, and tenders

Set up, operate, or tend machines to crush, grind, or polish materials, such as coal, glass, grain, stone, food, or rubber.

- 2019 employment: **35,300**
- May 2019 median annual wage: **$37,560**
  - Wages come from the Occupational Employment Statistics (OES) program
- Projected employment change, 2019–29:
  - Number of new jobs: **-2,000**
  - Growth rate: **-6 percent (Decline)**
- Education and training:
  - Typical entry-level education: **High school diploma or equivalent**
  - Work experience in a related occupation: **None**
  - Typical on-the-job training: **Moderate-term on-the-job training**
- O*NET links:
  - 51-9021.00 - Crushing, Grinding, and Polishing Machine Setters, Operators, and Tenders
- CareerOneStop videos for this occupation:
  - 51-9021.00 - Crushing, Grinding, and Polishing Machine Setters, Operators, and Tenders

Grinding and polishing workers, hand

Grind, sand, or polish, using hand tools or hand-held power tools, a variety of metal, wood, stone, clay, plastic, or glass objects. Includes chippers, buffers, and finishers.

- 2019 employment: **29,000**
- May 2019 median annual wage: **$30,600**
  - Wages come from the Occupational Employment Statistics (OES) program
- Projected employment change, 2019–29:
  - Number of new jobs: **-5,600**
  - Growth rate: **-19 percent (Decline)**
- Education and training:
  - Typical entry-level education: **No formal educational credential**
  - Work experience in a related occupation: **None**
  - Typical on-the-job training: **Moderate-term on-the-job training**
- O*NET links:
  - 51-9022.00 - Grinding and Polishing Workers, Hand

Mixing and blending machine setters, operators, and tenders

Set up, operate, or tend machines to mix or blend materials, such as chemicals, tobacco, liquids, color pigments, or explosive ingredients. Excludes "Food Batchmakers" (51-3092).

- 2019 employment: **128,000**
- May 2019 median annual wage: **$37,780**
  - Wages come from the Occupational Employment Statistics (OES) program
- Projected employment change, 2019–29:
  - Number of new jobs: **1,600**
  - Growth rate: **1 percent (Slower than average)**
- Education and training:
  - Typical entry-level education: **High school diploma or equivalent**
  - Work experience in a related occupation: **None**
  - Typical on-the-job training: **Moderate-term on-the-job training**
- O*NET links:
  - 51-9023.00 - Mixing and Blending Machine Setters, Operators, and Tenders
- CareerOneStop videos for this occupation:
  - 51-9023.00 - Mixing and Blending Machine Setters, Operators, and Tenders

Cutters and trimmers, hand

Use hand tools or hand-held power tools to cut and trim a variety of manufactured items, such as carpet, fabric, stone, glass, or rubber.

- 2019 employment: **9,800**
- May 2019 median annual wage: **$30,200**
  - Wages come from the Occupational Employment Statistics (OES) program
- Projected employment change, 2019–29:
  - Number of new jobs: **-2,900**
  - Growth rate: **-30 percent (Decline)**
- Education and training:
  - Typical entry-level education: **No formal educational credential**
  - Work experience in a related occupation: **None**
  - Typical on-the-job training: **Short-term on-the-job training**
- O*NET links:
  - 51-9031.00 - Cutters and Trimmers, Hand

Cutting and slicing machine setters, operators, and tenders

Set up, operate, or tend machines that cut or slice materials, such as glass, stone, cork, rubber, tobacco, food, paper, or insulating material. Excludes "Cutting, Punching, and Press Machine Setters, Operators, and Tenders, Metal and Plastic" (51-4031), "Textile Cutting Machine Setters, Operators, and Tenders" (51-6062), and "Woodworking Machine Setters, Operators, and Tenders" (51-7040).

- 2019 employment: **59,800**
- May 2019 median annual wage: **$35,600**
  - Wages come from the Occupational Employment Statistics (OES) program
- Projected employment change, 2019–29:
  - Number of new jobs: **-2,900**
  - Growth rate: **-5 percent (Decline)**
- Education and training:
  - Typical entry-level education: **High school diploma or equivalent**
  - Work experience in a related occupation: **None**
  - Typical on-the-job training: **Moderate-term on-the-job training**
- O*NET links:
  - 51-9032.00 - Cutting and Slicing Machine Setters, Operators, and Tenders

Extruding, forming, pressing, and compacting machine setters, operators, and tenders

Set up, operate, or tend machines, such as glass-forming machines, plodder machines, and tuber machines, to shape and form products such as glassware, food, rubber, soap, brick, tile, clay, wax, tobacco, or cosmetics. Excludes "Shoe Machine Operators and Tenders" (51-6042) and "Paper Goods Machine Setters, Operators, and Tenders" (51-9196).

- 2019 employment: **72,400**
- May 2019 median annual wage: **$35,480**
  - Wages come from the Occupational Employment Statistics (OES) program
- Projected employment change, 2019–29:
  - Number of new jobs: **-2,300**
  - Growth rate: **-3 percent (Decline)**
- Education and training:
  - Typical entry-level education: **High school diploma or equivalent**
  - Work experience in a related occupation: **None**
  - Typical on-the-job training: **Moderate-term on-the-job training**
- O*NET links:
  - 51-9041.00 - Extruding, Forming, Pressing, and Compacting Machine Setters, Operators, and Tenders
- CareerOneStop videos for this occupation:
  - 51-9041.00 - Extruding, Forming, Pressing, and Compacting Machine Setters, Operators, and Tenders

Furnace, kiln, oven, drier, and kettle operators and tenders

Operate or tend heating equipment other than basic metal, plastic, or food processing equipment. Includes activities such as annealing glass, drying lumber, curing rubber, removing moisture from materials, or boiling soap.

- 2019 employment: **21,600**
- May 2019 median annual wage: **$40,090**
  - Wages come from the Occupational Employment Statistics (OES) program
- Projected employment change, 2019–29:
  - Number of new jobs: **-200**
  - Growth rate: **-1 percent (Decline)**
- Education and training:
  - Typical entry-level education: **High school diploma or equivalent**
  - Work experience in a related occupation: **None**
  - Typical on-the-job training: **Moderate-term on-the-job training**
- O*NET links:
  - 51-9051.00 - Furnace, Kiln, Oven, Drier, and Kettle Operators and Tenders

Packaging and filling machine operators and tenders

Operate or tend machines to prepare industrial or consumer products for storage or shipment. Includes cannery workers who pack food products.

- 2019 employment: **392,100**
- May 2019 median annual wage: **$30,990**
  - Wages come from the Occupational Employment Statistics (OES) program
- Projected employment change, 2019–29:
  - Number of new jobs: **5,500**
  - Growth rate: **1 percent (Slower than average)**
- Education and training:
  - Typical entry-level education: **High school diploma or equivalent**
  - Work experience in a related occupation: **None**
  - Typical on-the-job training: **Moderate-term on-the-job training**
- O*NET links:
  - 51-9111.00 - Packaging and Filling Machine Operators and Tenders

Semiconductor processing technicians

Perform any or all of the following functions in the manufacture of electronic semiconductors: load semiconductor material into furnace; saw formed ingots into segments; load individual segment into crystal growing chamber and monitor controls; locate crystal axis in ingot using x-ray equipment and saw ingots into wafers; and clean, polish, and load wafers into series of special purpose furnaces, chemical baths, and equipment used to form circuitry and change conductive properties.

- 2019 employment: **30,800**
- May 2019 median annual wage: **$38,060**
  - Wages come from the Occupational Employment Statistics (OES) program
- Projected employment change, 2019–29:
  - Number of new jobs: **200**
  - Growth rate: **1 percent (Slower than average)**
- Education and training:
  - Typical entry-level education: **High school diploma or equivalent**
  - Work experience in a related occupation: **None**
  - Typical on-the-job training: **Moderate-term on-the-job training**
- O*NET links:
  - 51-9141.00 - Semiconductor Processors

Photographic process workers and processing machine operators

Perform work involved in developing and processing photographic images from film or digital media. May perform precision tasks such as editing photographic negatives and prints.

- 2019 employment: **12,300**
- May 2019 median annual wage: **$32,280**
  - Wages come from the Occupational Employment Statistics (OES) program
- Projected employment change, 2019–29:

- Number of new jobs: **-2,400**
- Growth rate: **-19 percent (Decline)**
- Education and training:
  - Typical entry-level education: **High school diploma or equivalent**
  - Work experience in a related occupation: **None**
  - Typical on-the-job training: **Short-term on-the-job training**
- O*NET links:
  - 51-9151.00 - Photographic Process Workers and Processing Machine Operators

Adhesive bonding machine operators and tenders

Operate or tend bonding machines that use adhesives to join items for further processing or to form a completed product. Processes include joining veneer sheets into plywood; gluing paper; or joining rubber and rubberized fabric parts, plastic, simulated leather, or other materials. Excludes "Shoe Machine Operators and Tenders" (51-6042).

- 2019 employment: **14,000**
- May 2019 median annual wage: **$34,340**
  - Wages come from the Occupational Employment Statistics (OES) program
- Projected employment change, 2019–29:
  - Number of new jobs: **-200**
  - Growth rate: **-2 percent (Decline)**
- Education and training:
  - Typical entry-level education: **High school diploma or equivalent**
  - Work experience in a related occupation: **None**
  - Typical on-the-job training: **Moderate-term on-the-job training**
- O*NET links:
  - 51-9191.00 - Adhesive Bonding Machine Operators and Tenders

Cleaning, washing, and metal pickling equipment operators and tenders

Operate or tend machines to wash or clean products, such as barrels or kegs, glass items, tin plate, food, pulp, coal, plastic, or rubber, to remove impurities.

- 2019 employment: **16,300**
- May 2019 median annual wage: **$31,850**
  - Wages come from the Occupational Employment Statistics (OES) program
- Projected employment change, 2019–29:
  - Number of new jobs: **200**
  - Growth rate: **1 percent (Slower than average)**
- Education and training:
  - Typical entry-level education: **High school diploma or equivalent**
  - Work experience in a related occupation: **None**
  - Typical on-the-job training: **Moderate-term on-the-job training**
- O*NET links:
  - 51-9192.00 - Cleaning, Washing, and Metal Pickling Equipment Operators and Tenders

Cooling and freezing equipment operators and tenders

Operate or tend equipment such as cooling and freezing units, refrigerators, batch freezers, and freezing tunnels, to cool or freeze products, food, blood plasma, and chemicals.

- 2019 employment: **9,400**
- May 2019 median annual wage: **$35,290**
  - Wages come from the Occupational Employment Statistics (OES) program

- Projected employment change, 2019–29:
  - Number of new jobs: **400**
  - Growth rate: **4 percent (As fast as average)**
- Education and training:
  - Typical entry-level education: **High school diploma or equivalent**
  - Work experience in a related occupation: **None**
  - Typical on-the-job training: **Moderate-term on-the-job training**
- O*NET links:
  - 51-9193.00 - Cooling and Freezing Equipment Operators and Tenders

Etchers and engravers

Engrave or etch metal, wood, rubber, or other materials. Includes such workers as etcher-circuit processors, pantograph engravers, and silk screen etchers. Photoengravers are included in "Prepress Technicians and Workers" (51-5111).

- 2019 employment: **12,900**
- May 2019 median annual wage: **$30,620**
  - Wages come from the Occupational Employment Statistics (OES) program
- Projected employment change, 2019–29:
  - Number of new jobs: **-600**
  - Growth rate: **-5 percent (Decline)**
- Education and training:
  - Typical entry-level education: **High school diploma or equivalent**
  - Work experience in a related occupation: **None**
  - Typical on-the-job training: **Moderate-term on-the-job training**
- O*NET links:
  - 51-9194.00 - Etchers and Engravers
- CareerOneStop videos for this occupation:
  - 51-9194.00 - Etchers and Engravers

Molders, shapers, and casters, except metal and plastic

Mold, shape, form, cast, or carve products such as food products, figurines, tile, pipes, and candles consisting of clay, glass, plaster, concrete, stone, or combinations of materials.

- 2019 employment: **49,400**
- May 2019 median annual wage: **$34,030**
  - Wages come from the Occupational Employment Statistics (OES) program
- Projected employment change, 2019–29:
  - Number of new jobs: **-3,000**
  - Growth rate: **-6 percent (Decline)**
- Education and training:
  - Typical entry-level education: **High school diploma or equivalent**
  - Work experience in a related occupation: **None**
  - Typical on-the-job training: **Long-term on-the-job training**
- O*NET links:
  - 51-9195.00 - Molders, Shapers, and Casters, Except Metal and Plastic
  - 51-9195.03 - Stone Cutters and Carvers, Manufacturing
  - 51-9195.04 - Glass Blowers, Molders, Benders, and Finishers
  - 51-9195.05 - Potters, Manufacturing
  - 51-9195.07 - Molding and Casting Workers
- CareerOneStop videos for this occupation:
  - 51-9195.00 - Molders, Shapers, and Casters, Except Metal and Plastic
  - 51-9195.03 - Stone Cutters and Carvers, Manufacturing

○ 51-9195.04 - Glass Blowers, Molders, Benders, and Finishers
○ 51-9195.05 - Potters, Manufacturing
○ 51-9195.07 - Molding and Casting Workers

Paper goods machine setters, operators, and tenders

Set up, operate, or tend paper goods machines that perform a variety of functions, such as converting, sawing, corrugating, banding, wrapping, boxing, stitching, forming, or sealing paper or paperboard sheets into products.

- 2019 employment: **100,400**
- May 2019 median annual wage: **$39,210**
  ○ Wages come from the Occupational Employment Statistics (OES) program
- Projected employment change, 2019–29:
  ○ Number of new jobs: **-5,700**
  ○ Growth rate: **-6 percent (Decline)**
- Education and training:
  ○ Typical entry-level education: **High school diploma or equivalent**
  ○ Work experience in a related occupation: **None**
  ○ Typical on-the-job training: **Moderate-term on-the-job training**
- O*NET links:
  ○ 51-9196.00 - Paper Goods Machine Setters, Operators, and Tenders

Tire builders

Operate machines to build tires.
- 2019 employment: **21,000**
- May 2019 median annual wage: **$46,010**
  ○ Wages come from the Occupational Employment Statistics (OES) program
- Projected employment change, 2019–29:
  ○ Number of new jobs: **100**
  ○ Growth rate: **0 percent (Little or no change)**
- Education and training:
  ○ Typical entry-level education: **High school diploma or equivalent**
  ○ Work experience in a related occupation: **None**
  ○ Typical on-the-job training: **Moderate-term on-the-job training**
- O*NET links:
  ○ 51-9197.00 - Tire Builders

Helpers--production workers

Help production workers by performing duties requiring less skill. Duties include supplying or holding materials or tools, and cleaning work area and equipment. Apprentice workers are classified in the appropriate production occupations (51-0000).
- 2019 employment: **304,200**
- May 2019 median annual wage: **$29,100**
  ○ Wages come from the Occupational Employment Statistics (OES) program
- Projected employment change, 2019–29:
  ○ Number of new jobs: **20,800**
  ○ Growth rate: **7 percent (Faster than average)**
- Education and training:
  ○ Typical entry-level education: **High school diploma or equivalent**
  ○ Work experience in a related occupation: **None**
  ○ Typical on-the-job training: **Short-term on-the-job training**
- O*NET links:
  ○ 51-9198.00 - Helpers--Production Workers

- CareerOneStop videos for this occupation:
  ○ 51-9198.00 - Helpers--Production Workers

Production workers, all other

All production workers not listed separately. Excludes "Packers and Packagers, Hand" (53-7064).
- 2019 employment: **238,600**
- May 2019 median annual wage: **$29,800**
  ○ Wages come from the Occupational Employment Statistics (OES) program
- Projected employment change, 2019–29:
  ○ Number of new jobs: **5,100**
  ○ Growth rate: **2 percent (Slower than average)**
- Education and training:
  ○ Typical entry-level education: **High school diploma or equivalent**
  ○ Work experience in a related occupation: **None**
  ○ Typical on-the-job training: **Moderate-term on-the-job training**
- O*NET links:
  ○ 51-9199.00 - Production Workers, All Other
  ○ 51-9199.01 - Recycling and Reclamation Workers
- CareerOneStop videos for this occupation:
  ○ 51-9199.01 - Recycling and Reclamation Workers

Transportation and Material Moving ccupations

Aircraft cargo handling supervisors

Supervise and coordinate the activities of ground crew in the loading, unloading, securing, and staging of aircraft cargo or baggage. May determine the quantity and orientation of cargo and compute aircraft center of gravity. May accompany aircraft as member of flight crew and monitor and handle cargo in flight, and assist and brief passengers on safety and emergency procedures. Includes loadmasters.
- 2019 employment: **9,600**
- May 2019 median annual wage: **$53,850**
  ○ Wages come from the Occupational Employment Statistics (OES) program
- Projected employment change, 2019–29:
  ○ Number of new jobs: **500**
  ○ Growth rate: **5 percent (Faster than average)**
- Education and training:
  ○ Typical entry-level education: **High school diploma or equivalent**
  ○ Work experience in a related occupation: **Less than 5 years**
  ○ Typical on-the-job training: **None**
- O*NET links:
  ○ 53-1011.00 - Aircraft Cargo Handling Supervisors

First-line supervisors of transportation and material-moving workers, except aircraft cargo handling supervisors

This is an OES hybrid
- 2019 employment: **456,700**
- May 2019 median annual wage: **$55,060**
  ○ Wages come from the Occupational Employment Statistics (OES) program
- Projected employment change, 2019–29:
  ○ Number of new jobs: **23,500**
  ○ Growth rate: **5 percent (Faster than average)**

- Education and training:
  - Typical entry-level education: **High school diploma or equivalent**
  - Work experience in a related occupation: **Less than 5 years**
  - Typical on-the-job training: **None**
- O*NET links:
  - 53-1021.00 - First-Line Supervisors of Helpers, Laborers, and Material Movers, Hand
  - 53-1021.00 - First-Line Supervisors of Helpers, Laborers, and Material Movers, Hand
  - 53-1021.01 - Recycling Coordinators
  - 53-1021.01 - Recycling Coordinators
  - 53-1031.00 - First-Line Supervisors of Transportation and Material-Moving Machine and Vehicle Operators
  - 53-1031.00 - First-Line Supervisors of Transportation and Material-Moving Machine and Vehicle Operators
- CareerOneStop videos for this occupation:
  - 53-1021.01 - Recycling Coordinators
  - 53-1021.01 - Recycling Coordinators

Airfield operations specialists

Ensure the safe takeoff and landing of commercial and military aircraft. Duties include coordination between air-traffic control and maintenance personnel, dispatching, using airfield landing and navigational aids, implementing airfield safety procedures, monitoring and maintaining flight records, and applying knowledge of weather information.

- 2019 employment: **10,900**
- May 2019 median annual wage: **$52,650**
  - Wages come from the Occupational Employment Statistics (OES) program
- Projected employment change, 2019–29:
  - Number of new jobs: **700**
  - Growth rate: **6 percent (Faster than average)**
- Education and training:
  - Typical entry-level education: **High school diploma or equivalent**
  - Work experience in a related occupation: **None**
  - Typical on-the-job training: **Long-term on-the-job training**
- O*NET links:
  - 53-2022.00 - Airfield Operations Specialists

Ambulance drivers and attendants, except emergency medical technicians

Drive ambulance or assist ambulance driver in transporting sick, injured, or convalescent persons. Assist in lifting patients.

- 2019 employment: **14,900**
- May 2019 median annual wage: **$25,890**
  - Wages come from the Occupational Employment Statistics (OES) program
- Projected employment change, 2019–29:
  - Number of new jobs: **1,400**
  - Growth rate: **9 percent (Much faster than average)**
- Education and training:
  - Typical entry-level education: **High school diploma or equivalent**
  - Work experience in a related occupation: **None**
  - Typical on-the-job training: **Moderate-term on-the-job training**
- O*NET links:
  - 53-3011.00 - Ambulance Drivers and Attendants, Except Emergency Medical Technicians

- CareerOneStop videos for this occupation:
  - 53-3011.00 - Ambulance Drivers and Attendants, Except Emergency Medical Technicians

Motor vehicle operators, all other

All motor vehicle operators not listed separately.

- 2019 employment: **61,700**
- May 2019 median annual wage: **$32,910**
  - Wages come from the Occupational Employment Statistics (OES) program
- Projected employment change, 2019–29:
  - Number of new jobs: **1,900**
  - Growth rate: **3 percent (As fast as average)**
- Education and training:
  - Typical entry-level education: **No formal educational credential**
  - Work experience in a related occupation: **None**
  - Typical on-the-job training: **Short-term on-the-job training**
- O*NET links:
  - 53-3099.00 - Motor Vehicle Operators, All Other

Subway and streetcar operators

Operate subway or elevated suburban trains with no separate locomotive, or electric-powered streetcar, to transport passengers. May handle fares.

- 2019 employment: **10,700**
- May 2019 median annual wage: **$67,880**
  - Wages come from the Occupational Employment Statistics (OES) program
- Projected employment change, 2019–29:
  - Number of new jobs: **600**
  - Growth rate: **5 percent (Faster than average)**
- Education and training:
  - Typical entry-level education: **High school diploma or equivalent**
  - Work experience in a related occupation: **None**
  - Typical on-the-job training: **Moderate-term on-the-job training**
- O*NET links:
  - 53-4041.00 - Subway and Streetcar Operators

Rail transportation workers, all other

All rail transportation workers not listed separately.

- 2019 employment: **2,500**
- May 2019 median annual wage: **$51,600**
  - Wages come from the Occupational Employment Statistics (OES) program
- Projected employment change, 2019–29:
  - Number of new jobs: **-100**
  - Growth rate: **-5 percent (Decline)**
- Education and training:
  - Typical entry-level education: **High school diploma or equivalent**
  - Work experience in a related occupation: **None**
  - Typical on-the-job training: **Moderate-term on-the-job training**
- O*NET links:
  - 53-4099.00 - Rail Transportation Workers, All Other

Bridge and lock tenders

Operate and tend bridges, canal locks, and lighthouses to permit marine passage on inland waterways, near shores, and at danger points

in waterway passages. May supervise such operations. Includes draw-bridge operators, lock operators, and slip bridge operators.
- 2019 employment: **3,300**
- May 2019 median annual wage: **$50,110**
  - Wages come from the Occupational Employment Statistics (OES) program
- Projected employment change, 2019–29:
  - Number of new jobs: **0**
  - Growth rate: **1 percent (Slower than average)**
- Education and training:
  - Typical entry-level education: **High school diploma or equivalent**
  - Work experience in a related occupation: **None**
  - Typical on-the-job training: **Short-term on-the-job training**
- O*NET links:
  - 53-6011.00 - Bridge and Lock Tenders

Parking attendants

Park vehicles or issue tickets for customers in a parking lot or garage. May park or tend vehicles in environments such as a car dealership or rental car facility. May collect fee.
- 2019 employment: **149,800**
- May 2019 median annual wage: **$25,140**
  - Wages come from the Occupational Employment Statistics (OES) program
- Projected employment change, 2019–29:
  - Number of new jobs: **10,900**
  - Growth rate: **7 percent (Faster than average)**
- Education and training:
  - Typical entry-level education: **No formal educational credential**
  - Work experience in a related occupation: **None**
  - Typical on-the-job training: **Short-term on-the-job training**
- O*NET links:
  - 53-6021.00 - Parking Lot Attendants
- CareerOneStop videos for this occupation:
  - 53-6021.00 - Parking Lot Attendants

Automotive and watercraft service attendants

Service automobiles, buses, trucks, boats, and other automotive or marine vehicles with fuel, lubricants, and accessories. Collect payment for services and supplies. May lubricate vehicle, change motor oil, refill antifreeze, or replace lights or other accessories, such as windshield wiper blades or fan belts. May repair or replace tires. Excludes "Cashiers" (41-2011).
- 2019 employment: **118,800**
- May 2019 median annual wage: **$25,200**
  - Wages come from the Occupational Employment Statistics (OES) program
- Projected employment change, 2019–29:
  - Number of new jobs: **2,800**
  - Growth rate: **2 percent (Slower than average)**
- Education and training:
  - Typical entry-level education: **No formal educational credential**
  - Work experience in a related occupation: **None**
  - Typical on-the-job training: **Short-term on-the-job training**
- O*NET links:
  - 53-6031.00 - Automotive and Watercraft Service Attendants

Traffic technicians

Conduct field studies to determine traffic volume, speed, effectiveness of signals, adequacy of lighting, and other factors influencing traffic conditions, under direction of traffic engineer.

- 2019 employment: **7,700**
- May 2019 median annual wage: **$47,480**
  - Wages come from the Occupational Employment Statistics (OES) program
- Projected employment change, 2019–29:
  - Number of new jobs: **500**
  - Growth rate: **6 percent (Faster than average)**
- Education and training:
  - Typical entry-level education: **High school diploma or equivalent**
  - Work experience in a related occupation: **None**
  - Typical on-the-job training: **Moderate-term on-the-job training**
- O*NET links:
  - 53-6041.00 - Traffic Technicians

Transportation inspectors

Inspect equipment or goods in connection with the safe transport of cargo or people. Includes rail transportation inspectors, such as freight inspectors, rail inspectors, and other inspectors of transportation vehicles not elsewhere classified. Excludes "Transportation Security Screeners" (33-9093).
- 2019 employment: **30,200**
- May 2019 median annual wage: **$75,820**
  - Wages come from the Occupational Employment Statistics (OES) program
- Projected employment change, 2019–29:
  - Number of new jobs: **700**
  - Growth rate: **2 percent (Slower than average)**
- Education and training:
  - Typical entry-level education: **High school diploma or equivalent**
  - Work experience in a related occupation: **None**
  - Typical on-the-job training: **Moderate-term on-the-job training**
- O*NET links:
  - 53-6051.00 - Transportation Inspectors
  - 53-6051.01 - Aviation Inspectors
  - 53-6051.07 - Transportation Vehicle, Equipment and Systems Inspectors, Except Aviation
  - 53-6051.08 - Freight and Cargo Inspectors
- CareerOneStop videos for this occupation:
  - 53-6051.07 - Transportation Vehicle, Equipment and Systems Inspectors, Except Aviation

Passenger attendants

Provide services to ensure the safety of passengers aboard ships, buses, trains, or within the station or terminal. Perform duties such as explaining the use of safety equipment, serving meals or beverages, or answering questions related to travel. Excludes "Baggage Porters and Bellhops" (39-6011) and "Flight Attendants" (53-2031).
- 2019 employment: **28,000**
- May 2019 median annual wage: **$26,570**
  - Wages come from the Occupational Employment Statistics (OES) program
- Projected employment change, 2019–29:
  - Number of new jobs: **1,200**
  - Growth rate: **4 percent (As fast as average)**
- Education and training:
  - Typical entry-level education: **High school diploma or equivalent**
  - Work experience in a related occupation: **None**
  - Typical on-the-job training: **Short-term on-the-job training**
- O*NET links:

○ 53-6061.00 - Transportation Attendants, Except Flight Attendants

Aircraft service attendants and transportation workers, all other

This is an OES hybrid
- 2019 employment: **35,800**
- May 2019 median annual wage: **$37,000**
  ○ Wages come from the Occupational Employment Statistics (OES) program
- Projected employment change, 2019–29:
  ○ Number of new jobs: **1,600**
  ○ Growth rate: **4 percent (As fast as average)**
- Education and training:
  ○ Typical entry-level education: **High school diploma or equivalent**
  ○ Work experience in a related occupation: **None**
  ○ Typical on-the-job training: **Short-term on-the-job training**
- O*NET links:
  ○ 53-6099.00 - Transportation Workers, All Other

Gas compressor and gas pumping station operators

Operate steam-, gas-, electric motor-, or internal combustion-engine driven compressors. Transmit, compress, or recover gases, such as butane, nitrogen, hydrogen, and natural gas.
- 2019 employment: **3,700**
- May 2019 median annual wage: **$66,160**
  ○ Wages come from the Occupational Employment Statistics (OES) program
- Projected employment change, 2019–29:
  ○ Number of new jobs: **-100**
  ○ Growth rate: **-2 percent (Decline)**
- Education and training:
  ○ Typical entry-level education: **High school diploma or equivalent**
  ○ Work experience in a related occupation: **None**
  ○ Typical on-the-job training: **Moderate-term on-the-job training**
- O*NET links:
  ○ 53-7071.00 - Gas Compressor and Gas Pumping Station Operators

Pump operators, except wellhead pumpers

Tend, control, or operate power-driven, stationary, or portable pumps and manifold systems to transfer gases, oil, other liquids, slurries, or powdered materials to and from various vessels and processes.
- 2019 employment: **10,500**
- May 2019 median annual wage: **$45,040**
  ○ Wages come from the Occupational Employment Statistics (OES) program
- Projected employment change, 2019–29:
  ○ Number of new jobs: **1,000**
  ○ Growth rate: **10 percent (Much faster than average)**
- Education and training:
  ○ Typical entry-level education: **High school diploma or equivalent**
  ○ Work experience in a related occupation: **None**
  ○ Typical on-the-job training: **Moderate-term on-the-job training**
- O*NET links:
  ○ 53-7072.00 - Pump Operators, Except Wellhead Pumpers

- CareerOneStop videos for this occupation:
  ○ 53-7072.00 - Pump Operators, Except Wellhead Pumpers

Wellhead pumpers

Operate power pumps and auxiliary equipment to produce flow of oil or gas from wells in oil field.
- 2019 employment: **14,100**
- May 2019 median annual wage: **$55,040**
  ○ Wages come from the Occupational Employment Statistics (OES) program
- Projected employment change, 2019–29:
  ○ Number of new jobs: **600**
  ○ Growth rate: **4 percent (As fast as average)**
- Education and training:
  ○ Typical entry-level education: **High school diploma or equivalent**
  ○ Work experience in a related occupation: **Less than 5 years**
  ○ Typical on-the-job training: **Moderate-term on-the-job training**
- O*NET links:
  ○ 53-7073.00 - Wellhead Pumpers
- CareerOneStop videos for this occupation:
  ○ 53-7073.00 - Wellhead Pumpers

Tank car, truck, and ship loaders

Load and unload chemicals and bulk solids, such as coal, sand, and grain, into or from tank cars, trucks, or ships, using material moving equipment. May perform a variety of other tasks relating to shipment of products. May gauge or sample shipping tanks and test them for leaks.
- 2019 employment: **12,200**
- May 2019 median annual wage: **$42,360**
  ○ Wages come from the Occupational Employment Statistics (OES) program
- Projected employment change, 2019–29:
  ○ Number of new jobs: **-200**
  ○ Growth rate: **-2 percent (Decline)**
- Education and training:
  ○ Typical entry-level education: **No formal educational credential**
  ○ Work experience in a related occupation: **None**
  ○ Typical on-the-job training: **Short-term on-the-job training**
- O*NET links:
  ○ 53-7121.00 - Tank Car, Truck, and Ship Loaders

Material moving workers, all other

All material moving workers not listed separately.
- 2019 employment: **29,800**
- May 2019 median annual wage: **$31,770**
  ○ Wages come from the Occupational Employment Statistics (OES) program
- Projected employment change, 2019–29:
  ○ Number of new jobs: **500**
  ○ Growth rate: **2 percent (Slower than average)**
- Education and training:
  ○ Typical entry-level education: **No formal educational credential**
  ○ Work experience in a related occupation: **None**
  ○ Typical on-the-job training: **Short-term on-the-job training**
- O*NET links:
  ○ 53-7199.00 - Material Moving Workers, All Other

Appendix:
Summary of Occupations

Occupation	Job Duties	Entry-Level Education	Median Annual Pay, May 2019
Accountants and Auditors	Accountants and auditors prepare and examine financial records.	Bachelor's degree	$71,550
Actors	Actors express ideas and portray characters in theater, film, television, and other performing arts media.	Some college, no degree	The annual wage is not available.
Actuaries	Actuaries use mathematics, statistics, and financial theory to analyze the financial costs of risk and uncertainty.	Bachelor's degree	$108,350
Administrative Services Managers	Administrative services managers plan, direct, and coordinate activities that help an organization run efficiently.	Bachelor's degree	$96,940
Adult Literacy and High School Equivalency Diploma Teachers	Adult literacy and high school equivalency diploma teachers instruct adults in basic skills, such as reading and speaking English. They also help students earn their high school equivalent diploma.	Bachelor's degree	$54,350
Advertising Sales Agents	Advertising sales agents sell advertising space to businesses and individuals.	High school diploma or equivalent	$53,310
Advertising, Promotions, and Marketing Managers	Advertising, promotions, and marketing managers plan programs to generate interest in products or services.	Bachelor's degree	$135,900
Aerospace Engineering and Operations Technicians	Aerospace engineering and operations technicians operate and maintain equipment used in developing, testing, producing, and sustaining new aircraft and spacecraft.	Associate's degree	$66,020
Aerospace Engineers	Aerospace engineers design primarily aircraft, spacecraft, satellites, and missiles.	Bachelor's degree	$116,500
Agricultural and Food Science Technicians	Agricultural and food science technicians assist agricultural and food scientists.	Associate's degree	$41,230
Agricultural and Food Scientists	Agricultural and food scientists research ways to improve the efficiency and safety of agricultural establishments and products.	Bachelor's degree	$65,160
Agricultural Engineers	Agricultural engineers solve problems concerning power supplies, machine efficiency, the use of structures and facilities, pollution and environmental issues, and the storage and processing of agricultural products.	Bachelor's degree	$80,720
Agricultural Workers	Agricultural workers maintain crops and tend to livestock.		$25,840
Air Traffic Controllers	Air traffic controllers coordinate the movement of aircraft to maintain safe distances between them.	Associate's degree	$122,990
Aircraft and Avionics Equipment Mechanics and Technicians	Aircraft and avionics equipment mechanics and technicians repair and perform scheduled maintenance on aircraft.		$64,310

Occupation	Job Duties	Entry-Level Education	Median Annual Pay, May 2019
Airline and Commercial Pilots	Airline and commercial pilots fly and navigate airplanes, helicopters, and other aircraft.		$121,430
Animal Care and Service Workers	Animal care and service workers attend to animals.	High school diploma or equivalent	$24,990
Announcers	Announcers present music, news, and sports and may provide commentary or interview guests.		$39,790
Anthropologists and Archeologists	Anthropologists and archeologists study the origin, development, and behavior of humans.	Master's degree	$63,670
Appraisers and Assessors of Real Estate	Appraisers and assessors of real estate provide a value estimate on land and buildings.	Bachelor's degree	$57,010
Arbitrators, Mediators, and Conciliators	Arbitrators, mediators, and conciliators facilitate negotiation and dialogue between disputing parties to help resolve conflicts outside of the court system.	Bachelor's degree	$63,930
Architects	Architects plan and design houses, factories, office buildings, and other structures.	Bachelor's degree	$80,750
Architectural and Engineering Managers	Architectural and engineering managers plan, direct, and coordinate activities in architectural and engineering companies.	Bachelor's degree	$144,830
Archivists, Curators, and Museum Workers	Archivists and curators oversee institutions' collections, such as of historical items or of artwork. Museum technicians and conservators prepare and restore items in those collections.		$49,850
Art Directors	Art directors are responsible for the visual style and images in magazines, newspapers, product packaging, and movie and television productions.	Bachelor's degree	$94,220
Assemblers and Fabricators	Assemblers and fabricators assemble finished products and the parts that go into them.	High school diploma or equivalent	$33,710
Athletes and Sports Competitors	Athletes and sports competitors participate in organized, officiated sporting events to entertain spectators.	No formal educational credential	$51,370
Athletic Trainers	Athletic trainers specialize in preventing, diagnosing, and treating muscle and bone injuries and illnesses.	Bachelor's degree	$48,440
Atmospheric Scientists, Including Meteorologists	Atmospheric scientists study the weather and climate.	Bachelor's degree	$95,380
Audiologists	Audiologists diagnose, manage, and treat a patient's hearing, balance, or ear problems.	Doctoral or professional degree	$77,600
Automotive Body and Glass Repairers	Automotive body and glass repairers restore, refinish, and replace vehicle bodies and frames, windshields, and window glass.	High school diploma or equivalent	$42,350
Automotive Service Technicians and Mechanics	Automotive service technicians and mechanics inspect, maintain, and repair cars and light trucks.	Postsecondary nondegree award	$42,090
Bakers	Bakers mix ingredients according to recipes in order to make breads, pastries, and other baked goods.	No formal educational credential	$27,700
Barbers, Hairstylists, and Cosmetologists	Barbers, hairstylists, and cosmetologists provide haircutting, hairstyling, and a range of other beauty services.	Postsecondary nondegree award	$26,270

Occupation	Job Duties	Entry-Level Education	Median Annual Pay, May 2019
Bartenders	Bartenders mix drinks and serve them directly to customers or through wait staff.	No formal educational credential	$23,680
Bill and Account Collectors	Bill and account collectors try to recover payment on overdue bills.	High school diploma or equivalent	$37,000
Biochemists and Biophysicists	Biochemists and biophysicists study the chemical and physical principles of living things and of biological processes.	Doctoral or professional degree	$94,490
Biological Technicians	Biological technicians help biological and medical scientists conduct laboratory tests and experiments.	Bachelor's degree	$45,860
Biomedical Engineers	Biomedical engineers combine engineering principles with medical sciences to design and create equipment, devices, computer systems, and software.	Bachelor's degree	$91,410
Boilermakers	Boilermakers assemble, install, maintain, and repair boilers, closed vats, and other large vessels or containers that hold liquids and gases.	High school diploma or equivalent	$63,100
Bookkeeping, Accounting, and Auditing Clerks	Bookkeeping, accounting, and auditing clerks produce financial records for organizations and check financial records for accuracy.	Some college, no degree	$41,230
Broadcast and Sound Engineering Technicians	Broadcast and sound engineering technicians set up, operate, and maintain the electrical equipment for media programs.		$45,510
Budget Analysts	Budget analysts help public and private institutions organize their finances.	Bachelor's degree	$76,540
Butchers	Butchers cut, trim, and package meat for retail sale.	No formal educational credential	$32,500
Career and Technical Education Teachers	Career and technical education teachers instruct students in various technical and vocational subjects, such as auto repair, healthcare, and culinary arts.	Bachelor's degree	$58,110
Carpenters	Carpenters construct, repair, and install building frameworks and structures made from wood and other materials.	High school diploma or equivalent	$48,330
Cartographers and Photogrammetrists	Cartographers and photogrammetrists collect, measure, and interpret geographic information in order to create and update maps and charts for regional planning, education, and other purposes.	Bachelor's degree	$65,470
Cashiers	Cashiers process payments from customers purchasing goods and services.	No formal educational credential	$23,650
Chefs and Head Cooks	Chefs and head cooks oversee the daily food preparation at restaurants and other places where food is served.	High school diploma or equivalent	$51,530
Chemical Engineers	Chemical engineers apply the principles of chemistry, biology, physics, and math to solve problems that involve the use of fuel, drugs, food, and many other products.	Bachelor's degree	$108,770
Chemical Technicians	Chemical technicians use special instruments and techniques to assist chemists and chemical engineers.	Associate's degree	$49,260
Chemists and Materials Scientists	Chemists and materials scientists study substances at the atomic and molecular levels and analyze the ways in which the substances interact with one another.	Bachelor's degree	$78,790

Occupation	Job Duties	Entry-Level Education	Median Annual Pay, May 2019
Childcare Workers	Childcare workers attend to the basic needs of children, such as dressing, feeding, and overseeing play.	High school diploma or equivalent	$24,230
Chiropractors	Chiropractors treat patients with health problems of the neuromusculoskeletal system, which includes nerves, bones, muscles, ligaments, and tendons.	Doctoral or professional degree	$70,340
Civil Engineering Technicians	Civil engineering technicians help civil engineers to plan, design, and build highways, bridges, and other infrastructure projects for commercial, industrial, residential, and land development projects.	Associate's degree	$53,410
Civil Engineers	Civil engineers design, build, and supervise infrastructure projects and systems.	Bachelor's degree	$87,060
Claims Adjusters, Appraisers, Examiners, and Investigators	Claims adjusters, appraisers, examiners, and investigators evaluate insurance claims.		$66,540
Clinical Laboratory Technologists and Technicians	Clinical laboratory technologists and technicians collect samples and perform tests to analyze body fluids, tissue, and other substances.	Bachelor's degree	$53,120
Coaches and Scouts	Coaches teach amateur or professional athletes the skills they need to succeed at their sport.	Bachelor's degree	$34,840
Compensation and Benefits Managers	Compensation and benefits managers plan, develop, and oversee programs to pay employees.	Bachelor's degree	$122,270
Compensation, Benefits, and Job Analysis Specialists	Compensation, benefits, and job analysis specialists conduct an organization's compensation and benefits programs.	Bachelor's degree	$64,560
Computer and Information Research Scientists	Computer and information research scientists invent and design new approaches to computing technology and find innovative uses for existing technology.	Master's degree	$122,840
Computer and Information Systems Managers	Computer and information systems managers plan, coordinate, and direct computer-related activities in an organization.	Bachelor's degree	$146,360
Computer Hardware Engineers	Computer hardware engineers research, design, develop, and test computer systems and components.	Bachelor's degree	$117,220
Computer Network Architects	Computer network architects design and build data communication networks, including local area networks (LANs), wide area networks (WANs), and Intranets.	Bachelor's degree	$112,690
Computer Programmers	Computer programmers write and test code that allows computer applications and software programs to function properly.	Bachelor's degree	$86,550
Computer Support Specialists	Computer support specialists provide help and advice to computer users and organizations.		$54,760
Computer Systems Analysts	Computer systems analysts study an organization's current computer systems and find a solution that is more efficient and effective.	Bachelor's degree	$90,920
Conservation Scientists and Foresters	Conservation scientists and foresters manage the overall land quality of forests, parks, rangelands, and other natural resources.	Bachelor's degree	$62,410

Occupation	Job Duties	Entry-Level Education	Median Annual Pay, May 2019
Construction and Building Inspectors	Construction and building inspectors ensure that construction meets building codes and ordinances, zoning regulations, and contract specifications.	High school diploma or equivalent	$60,710
Construction Equipment Operators	Construction equipment operators drive, maneuver, or control the heavy machinery used to construct roads, buildings and other structures.	High school diploma or equivalent	$48,160
Construction Laborers and Helpers	Construction laborers and helpers perform many tasks that require physical labor on construction sites.		$36,000
Construction Managers	Construction managers plan, coordinate, budget, and supervise construction projects from start to finish.	Bachelor's degree	$95,260
Cooks	Cooks prepare, season, and cook a wide range of foods.		$26,360
Correctional Officers and Bailiffs	Correctional officers oversee those who have been arrested and are awaiting trial or who have been sentenced to serve time in jail or prison. Bailiffs are law enforcement officers who maintain safety and order in courtrooms.	High school diploma or equivalent	$45,300
Cost Estimators	Cost estimators collect and analyze data in order to estimate the time, money, materials, and labor required to make a product or provide a service.	Bachelor's degree	$65,250
Court Reporters	Court reporters create word-for-word transcriptions at trials, depositions, and other legal proceedings.	Postsecondary nondegree award	$60,130
Craft and Fine Artists	Craft and fine artists use a variety of materials and techniques to create art for sale and exhibition.		$48,760
Customer Service Representatives	Customer service representatives interact with customers to handle complaints, process orders, and answer questions.	High school diploma or equivalent	$34,710
Dancers and Choreographers	Dancers and choreographers use dance performances to express ideas and stories.		The annual wage is not available.
Database Administrators	Database administrators (DBAs) use specialized software to store and organize data.	Bachelor's degree	$93,750
Delivery Truck Drivers and Driver/Sales Workers	Delivery truck drivers and driver/sales workers pick up, transport, and drop off packages and small shipments within a local region or urban area.	High school diploma or equivalent	$32,020
Dental and Ophthalmic Laboratory Technicians and Medical Appliance Technicians	Dental and ophthalmic laboratory technicians and medical appliance technicians construct, fit, or repair medical appliances and devices.	High school diploma or equivalent	$37,370
Dental Assistants	Dental assistants provide patient care, take x rays, keep records, and schedule appointments.	Postsecondary nondegree award	$40,080
Dental Hygienists	Dental hygienists examine patients for signs of oral diseases, such as gingivitis, and provide preventive care, including oral hygiene.	Associate's degree	$76,220
Dentists	Dentists diagnose and treat problems with patients' teeth, gums, and related parts of the mouth.	Doctoral or professional degree	$159,200

Occupation	Job Duties	Entry-Level Education	Median Annual Pay, May 2019
Desktop Publishers	Desktop publishers use computer software to design page layouts for items that are printed or published online.	Associate's degree	$45,390
Diagnostic Medical Sonographers and Cardiovascular Technologists and Technicians, Including Vascular Technologists	Diagnostic medical sonographers and cardiovascular technologists and technicians, including vascular technologists operate special imaging equipment to create images or to conduct tests.	Associate's degree	$68,750
Diesel Service Technicians and Mechanics	Diesel service technicians and mechanics inspect, repair, and overhaul buses, trucks, or any vehicle with a diesel engine.	High school diploma or equivalent	$48,500
Dietitians and Nutritionists	Dietitians and nutritionists advise people on what to eat in order to lead a healthy lifestyle or achieve a specific health-related goal.	Bachelor's degree	$61,270
Drafters	Drafters use software to convert the designs of engineers and architects into technical drawings.	Associate's degree	$56,830
Drywall Installers, Ceiling Tile Installers, and Tapers	Drywall and ceiling tile installers hang wallboard and install ceiling tile inside buildings. Tapers prepare the wallboard for painting, using tape and other materials.	No formal educational credential	$47,360
Economists	Economists collect and analyze data, research trends, and evaluate economic issues for resources, goods, and services.	Master's degree	$105,020
Editors	Editors plan, review, and revise content for publication.	Bachelor's degree	$61,370
Electrical and Electronics Engineering Technicians	Electrical and electronics engineering technicians help engineers design and develop electrical and electronic equipment.	Associate's degree	$65,260
Electrical and Electronics Engineers	Electrical engineers design, develop, test, and supervise the manufacture of electrical equipment.	Bachelor's degree	$101,250
Electrical and Electronics Installers and Repairers	Electrical and electronics installers and repairers install or repair a variety of electrical equipment.		$59,080
Electricians	Electricians install, maintain, and repair electrical power, communications, lighting, and control systems.	High school diploma or equivalent	$56,180
Electro-mechanical Technicians	Electro-mechanical technicians operate, test, and maintain unmanned, automated, robotic, or electromechanical equipment.	Associate's degree	$58,350
Elementary, Middle, and High School Principals	Elementary, middle, and high school principals oversee all school operations, including daily school activities.	Master's degree	$96,400
Elevator Installers and Repairers	Elevator installers and repairers install, maintain, and fix elevators, escalators, moving walkways, and other lifts.	High school diploma or equivalent	$84,990
Emergency Management Directors	Emergency management directors prepare plans and procedures for responding to natural disasters or other emergencies. They also help lead the response during and after emergencies.	Bachelor's degree	$74,590
EMTs and Paramedics	Emergency medical technicians (EMTs) and paramedics respond to emergency calls, performing medical services and transporting patients to medical facilities.	Postsecondary nondegree award	$35,400

Occupation	Job Duties	Entry-Level Education	Median Annual Pay, May 2019
Environmental Engineering Technicians	Environmental engineering technicians carry out the plans that environmental engineers develop.	Associate's degree	$50,620
Environmental Engineers	Environmental engineers use the principles of engineering, soil science, biology, and chemistry to develop solutions to environmental problems.	Bachelor's degree	$88,860
Environmental Science and Protection Technicians	Environmental science and protection technicians monitor the environment and investigate sources of pollution and contamination.	Associate's degree	$46,540
Environmental Scientists and Specialists	Environmental scientists and specialists use their knowledge of the natural sciences to protect the environment and human health.	Bachelor's degree	$71,360
Epidemiologists	Epidemiologists are public health professionals who investigate patterns and causes of disease and injury in humans.	Master's degree	$70,990
Exercise Physiologists	Exercise physiologists develop fitness and exercise programs that help injured or sick patients recover.	Bachelor's degree	$49,170
Farmers, Ranchers, and Other Agricultural Managers	Farmers, ranchers, and other agricultural managers run establishments that produce crops, livestock, and dairy products.	High school diploma or equivalent	$71,160
Fashion Designers	Fashion designers create clothing, accessories, and footwear.	Bachelor's degree	$73,790
Film and Video Editors and Camera Operators	Film and video editors and camera operators manipulate moving images that entertain or inform an audience.	Bachelor's degree	$59,810
Financial Analysts	Financial analysts provide guidance to businesses and individuals making investment decisions.	Bachelor's degree	$81,590
Financial Clerks	Financial clerks do administrative work, keep records, help customers, and carry out financial transactions.	High school diploma or equivalent	$40,540
Financial Examiners	Financial examiners ensure compliance with laws governing financial institutions and transactions.	Bachelor's degree	$81,090
Financial Managers	Financial managers create financial reports, direct investment activities, and develop plans for the long-term financial goals of their organization.	Bachelor's degree	$129,890
Fire Inspectors	Fire inspectors examine buildings in order to detect fire hazards and ensure that federal, state, and local fire codes are met.		$60,230
Firefighters	Firefighters control and put out fires and respond to emergencies where life, property, or the environment is at risk.	Postsecondary nondegree award	$50,850
Fishing and Hunting Workers	Fishing and hunting workers catch and trap various types of animal life.	No formal educational credential	The annual wage is not available.
Fitness Trainers and Instructors	Fitness trainers and instructors lead, instruct, and motivate individuals or groups in exercise activities.	High school diploma or equivalent	$40,390
Flight Attendants	Flight attendants provide routine services and respond to emergencies to ensure the safety and comfort of airline passengers.	High school diploma or equivalent	$56,640

Occupation	Job Duties	Entry-Level Education	Median Annual Pay, May 2019
Flooring Installers and Tile and Marble Setters	Flooring installers and tile and marble setters lay and finish carpet, wood, vinyl, and tile.	No formal educational credential	$42,050
Floral Designers	Floral designers arrange live, dried, and silk flowers and greenery to make decorative displays.	High school diploma or equivalent	$28,040
Food and Beverage Serving and Related Workers	Food and beverage serving and related workers perform a variety of customer service, food preparation, and cleaning duties in eating and drinking establishments.	No formal educational credential	$23,000
Food and Tobacco Processing Workers	Food and tobacco processing workers operate equipment that mixes, cooks, or processes ingredients used in the manufacture of food and tobacco products.		$30,200
Food Preparation Workers	Food preparation workers perform many routine tasks under the direction of cooks, chefs, or food service managers.	No formal educational credential	$24,800
Food Service Managers	Food service managers are responsible for the daily operation of restaurants or other establishments that prepare and serve food and beverages.	High school diploma or equivalent	$55,320
Forensic Science Technicians	Forensic science technicians aid criminal investigations by collecting and analyzing evidence.	Bachelor's degree	$59,150
Forest and Conservation Workers	Forest and conservation workers measure and improve the quality of forests.	High school diploma or equivalent	$31,770
Fundraisers	Fundraisers organize events and campaigns to raise money and other kinds of donations for an organization.	Bachelor's degree	$57,970
Gaming Services Workers	Gaming services workers serve customers in gambling establishments, such as casinos or racetracks.	High school diploma or equivalent	$23,520
General Maintenance and Repair Workers	General maintenance and repair workers fix and maintain machines, mechanical equipment, and buildings.	High school diploma or equivalent	$39,080
General Office Clerks	General office clerks perform a variety of clerical tasks, including answering telephones, typing documents, and filing records.	High school diploma or equivalent	$34,040
Genetic Counselors	Genetic counselors assess individual or family risk for a variety of inherited conditions, such as genetic disorders and birth defects.	Master's degree	$81,880
Geographers	Geographers study the Earth and the distribution of its land, features, and inhabitants.	Bachelor's degree	$81,540
Geological and Petroleum Technicians	Geological and petroleum technicians provide support to scientists and engineers in exploring and extracting natural resources.	Associate's degree	$51,130
Geoscientists	Geoscientists study the physical aspects of the Earth.	Bachelor's degree	$92,040
Glaziers	Glaziers install glass in windows, skylights, and other fixtures in buildings.	High school diploma or equivalent	$44,630
Graphic Designers	Graphic designers create visual concepts, using computer software or by hand, to communicate ideas that inspire, inform, and captivate consumers.	Bachelor's degree	$52,110
Grounds Maintenance Workers	Grounds maintenance workers ensure that the grounds of houses, businesses, and parks are attractive, orderly, and healthy.		$30,890

Occupation	Job Duties	Entry-Level Education	Median Annual Pay, May 2019
Hand Laborers and Material Movers	Hand laborers and material movers manually move freight, stock, or other materials.	No formal educational credential	$28,710
Hazardous Materials Removal Workers	Hazardous materials removal workers identify and dispose of harmful substances such as asbestos, lead, and radioactive waste.	High school diploma or equivalent	$43,900
Health and Safety Engineers	Health and safety engineers combine knowledge of engineering and of health and safety to develop procedures and design systems to protect people from illness and injury and property from damage.	Bachelor's degree	$91,410
Health Educators and Community Health Workers	Health educators teach people about behaviors that promote wellness. Community health workers collect data and discuss health concerns with members of specific populations or communities.		$46,910
Heating, Air Conditioning, and Refrigeration Mechanics and Installers	Heating, air conditioning, and refrigeration mechanics and installers work on heating, ventilation, cooling, and refrigeration systems.	Postsecondary nondegree award	$48,730
Heavy and Tractor-trailer Truck Drivers	Heavy and tractor-trailer truck drivers transport goods from one location to another.	Postsecondary nondegree award	$45,260
Heavy Vehicle and Mobile Equipment Service Technicians	Heavy vehicle and mobile equipment service technicians inspect, maintain, and repair vehicles and machinery used in construction, farming, and other industries.	High school diploma or equivalent	$51,590
High School Teachers	High school teachers teach academic lessons and various skills that students will need to attend college and to enter the job market.	Bachelor's degree	$61,660
Historians	Historians research, analyze, interpret, and write about the past by studying historical documents and sources.	Master's degree	$63,680
Home Health Aides and Personal Care Aides	Home health aides and personal care aides help people with disabilities, chronic illnesses, or cognitive impairment by assisting in their daily living activities.	High school diploma or equivalent	$25,280
Human Resources Managers	Human resources managers plan, coordinate, and direct the administrative functions of an organization.	Bachelor's degree	$116,720
Human Resources Specialists	Human resources specialists recruit, screen, interview, and place workers. They also handle employee relations, compensation and benefits, and training.	Bachelor's degree	$61,920
Hydrologists	Hydrologists study how water moves across and through the Earth's crust.	Bachelor's degree	$81,270
Industrial Designers	Industrial designers combine art, business, and engineering to develop the concepts for manufactured products.	Bachelor's degree	$68,890
Industrial Engineering Technicians	Industrial engineering technicians assist industrial engineers in creating systems that integrate workers, machines, materials, information, and energy to make a product or provide a service.	Associate's degree	$56,550
Industrial Engineers	Industrial engineers devise efficient systems that integrate workers, machines, materials, information, and energy to make a product or provide a service.	Bachelor's degree	$88,020

Occupation	Job Duties	Entry-Level Education	Median Annual Pay, May 2019
Industrial Machinery Mechanics, Machinery Maintenance Workers, and Millwrights	Industrial machinery mechanics, machinery maintenance workers, and millwrights install, maintain, and repair factory equipment and other industrial machinery.	High school diploma or equivalent	$52,860
Industrial Production Managers	Industrial production managers oversee the daily operations of manufacturing and related plants.	Bachelor's degree	$105,480
Information Clerks	Information clerks perform routine clerical duties, maintain records, collect data, and provide information to customers.		$35,390
Information Security Analysts	Information security analysts plan and carry out security measures to protect an organization's computer networks and systems.	Bachelor's degree	$99,730
Instructional Coordinators	Instructional coordinators oversee school curriculums and teaching standards. They develop instructional material, implement it, and assess its effectiveness.	Master's degree	$66,290
Insulation Workers	Insulation workers install and replace the materials used to insulate buildings or mechanical systems.		$44,180
Insurance Sales Agents	Insurance sales agents contact potential customers and sell one or more types of insurance.	High school diploma or equivalent	$50,940
Insurance Underwriters	Insurance underwriters evaluate insurance applications and decide whether to provide insurance, and under what terms.	Bachelor's degree	$70,020
Interior Designers	Interior designers make indoor spaces functional, safe, and beautiful by determining space requirements and selecting essential and decorative items.	Bachelor's degree	$56,040
Interpreters and Translators	Interpreters and translators convert information from one language into another language.	Bachelor's degree	$51,830
Ironworkers	Ironworkers install structural and reinforcing iron and steel to form and support buildings, bridges, and roads.	High school diploma or equivalent	$53,650
Janitors and Building Cleaners	Janitors and building cleaners keep many types of buildings clean, orderly, and in good condition.	No formal educational credential	$27,430
Jewelers and Precious Stone and Metal Workers	Jewelers and precious stone and metal workers design, construct, adjust, repair, appraise and sell jewelry.	High school diploma or equivalent	$40,870
Judges and Hearing Officers	Judges and hearing officers apply the law by overseeing the legal process in courts.	Doctoral or professional degree	$120,090
Kindergarten and Elementary School Teachers	Kindergarten and elementary school teachers instruct young students in basic subjects in order to prepare them for future schooling.	Bachelor's degree	$59,420
Labor Relations Specialists	Labor relations specialists interpret and administer labor contracts.	Bachelor's degree	$69,020
Landscape Architects	Landscape architects design parks and other outdoor spaces.	Bachelor's degree	$69,360
Lawyers	Lawyers advise and represent individuals, businesses, and government agencies on legal issues and disputes.	Doctoral or professional degree	$122,960
Librarians	Librarians help people find information and conduct research for personal and professional use.	Bachelor's degree	$59,500

Occupation	Job Duties	Entry-Level Education	Median Annual Pay, May 2019
Library Technicians and Assistants	Library technicians and assistants help librarians with all aspects of running a library.		$30,560
Licensed Practical and Licensed Vocational Nurses	Licensed practical nurses (LPNs) and licensed vocational nurses (LVNs) provide basic nursing care.	Postsecondary nondegree award	$47,480
Line Installers and Repairers	Line installers and repairers install or repair electrical power systems and telecommunications cables, including fiber optics.	High school diploma or equivalent	$65,700
Loan Officers	Loan officers evaluate, authorize, or recommend approval of loan applications for people and businesses.	Bachelor's degree	$63,270
Lodging Managers	Lodging managers ensure that traveling guests have a pleasant experience at their establishment with accommodations. They also ensure that the business is run efficiently and profitably.	High school diploma or equivalent	$54,430
Logging Workers	Logging workers harvest forests to provide the raw material for many consumer goods and industrial products.	High school diploma or equivalent	$41,230
Logisticians	Logisticians analyze and coordinate an organization's supply chain.	Bachelor's degree	$74,750
Machinists and Tool and Die Makers	Machinists and tool and die makers set up and operate machine tools to produce precision metal parts, instruments, and tools.		$45,750
Management Analysts	Management analysts recommend ways to improve an organization's efficiency.	Bachelor's degree	$85,260
Manicurists and Pedicurists	Manicurists and pedicurists clean, shape, and beautify fingernails and toenails.	Postsecondary nondegree award	$25,770
Market Research Analysts	Market research analysts study market conditions to examine potential sales of a product or service.	Bachelor's degree	$63,790
Marriage and Family Therapists	Marriage and family therapists help people manage and overcome problems with family and other relationships.	Master's degree	$49,610
Masonry Workers	Masonry workers use bricks, concrete and concrete blocks, and natural and manmade stones to build structures.		$46,500
Massage Therapists	Massage therapists treat clients by using touch to manipulate the muscles and other soft tissues of the body.	Postsecondary nondegree award	$42,820
Material Moving Machine Operators	Material moving machine operators use machinery to transport various objects.		$36,770
Material Recording Clerks	Material recording clerks track product information in order to keep businesses and supply chains on schedule.	High school diploma or equivalent	$30,010
Materials Engineers	Materials engineers develop, process, and test materials used to create a wide range of products.	Bachelor's degree	$93,360
Mathematicians and Statisticians	Mathematicians and statisticians analyze data and apply mathematical and statistical techniques to help solve problems.	Master's degree	$92,030
Mechanical Engineering Technicians	Mechanical engineering technicians help mechanical engineers design, develop, test, and manufacture mechanical devices.	Associate's degree	$56,980

Occupation	Job Duties	Entry-Level Education	Median Annual Pay, May 2019
Mechanical Engineers	Mechanical engineers design, develop, build, and test mechanical and thermal sensors and devices.	Bachelor's degree	$88,430
Medical and Health Services Managers	Medical and health services managers plan, direct, and coordinate the business activities of healthcare providers.	Bachelor's degree	$100,980
Medical Assistants	Medical assistants complete administrative and clinical tasks in hospitals, offices of physicians, and other healthcare facilities.	Postsecondary nondegree award	$34,800
Medical Equipment Repairers	Medical equipment repairers install, maintain, and repair patient care equipment.	Associate's degree	$49,280
Medical Records and Health Information Technicians	Medical records and health information technicians organize and manage health information data.	Postsecondary nondegree award	$42,630
Medical Scientists	Medical scientists conduct research aimed at improving overall human health.	Doctoral or professional degree	$88,790
Medical Transcriptionists	Medical transcriptionists listen to voice recordings that physicians and other healthcare workers make and convert them into written reports.	Postsecondary nondegree award	$33,380
Meeting, Convention, and Event Planners	Meeting, convention, and event planners arrange all aspects of events and professional gatherings.	Bachelor's degree	$50,600
Metal and Plastic Machine Workers	Metal and plastic machine workers set up and operate machines that cut, shape, and form metal and plastic materials or pieces.		$36,990
Microbiologists	Microbiologists study microorganisms such as bacteria, viruses, algae, fungi, and some types of parasites.	Bachelor's degree	$75,650
Middle School Teachers	Middle school teachers educate students, typically in sixth through eighth grades.	Bachelor's degree	$59,660
Mining and Geological Engineers	Mining and geological engineers design mines to safely and efficiently remove minerals for use in manufacturing and utilities.	Bachelor's degree	$91,160
Models	Models pose for artists, photographers, and other clients to help advertise products.	No formal educational credential	$28,350
Multimedia Artists and Animators	Multimedia artists and animators create images that appear to move and visual effects for various forms of media and entertainment.	Bachelor's degree	$75,270
Music Directors and Composers	Music directors lead musical groups during performances and recording sessions. Composers write and arrange original music in a variety of musical styles.	Bachelor's degree	$51,670
Musicians and Singers	Musicians and singers play instruments or sing for live audiences and in recording studios.	No formal educational credential	The annual wage is not available.
Natural Sciences Managers	Natural sciences managers supervise the work of scientists, including chemists, physicists, and biologists.	Bachelor's degree	$129,100
Network and Computer Systems Administrators	Network and computer systems administrators are responsible for the day-to-day operation of computer networks.	Bachelor's degree	$83,510

Occupation	Job Duties	Entry-Level Education	Median Annual Pay, May 2019
Nuclear Engineers	Nuclear engineers research and develop the processes, instruments, and systems used to derive benefits from nuclear energy and radiation.	Bachelor's degree	$113,460
Nuclear Medicine Technologists	Nuclear medicine technologists prepare radioactive drugs and administer them to patients for imaging or therapeutic purposes.	Associate's degree	$77,950
Nuclear Technicians	Nuclear technicians assist physicists, engineers, and other professionals in nuclear research and nuclear energy production.	Associate's degree	$82,080
Nurse Anesthetists, Nurse Midwives, and Nurse Practitioners	Nurse anesthetists, nurse midwives, and nurse practitioners coordinate patient care and may provide primary and specialty healthcare.	Master's degree	$115,800
Nursing Assistants and Orderlies	Nursing assistants provide basic care and help patients with activities of daily living. Orderlies transport patients and clean treatment areas.		$29,640
Occupational Health and Safety Specialists and Technicians	Occupational health and safety specialists and technicians collect data on and analyze many types of work environments and work procedures.		$70,480
Occupational Therapists	Occupational therapists treat patients who have injuries, illnesses, or disabilities through the therapeutic use of everyday activities.	Master's degree	$84,950
Occupational Therapy Assistants and Aides	Occupational therapy assistants and aides help patients develop, recover, improve, as well as maintain the skills needed for daily living and working.		$59,200
Operations Research Analysts	Operations research analysts use advanced mathematical and analytical methods to help solve complex issues.	Bachelor's degree	$84,810
Opticians	Opticians help fit eyeglasses and contact lenses, following prescriptions from ophthalmologists and optometrists.	High school diploma or equivalent	$37,840
Optometrists	Optometrists diagnose and treat visual problems and manage diseases, injuries, and other disorders of the eyes.	Doctoral or professional degree	$115,250
Orthotists and Prosthetists	Orthotists and prosthetists design and fabricate medical supportive devices and measure and fit patients for them.	Master's degree	$68,410
Painters, Construction and Maintenance	Painters apply paint, stain, and coatings to walls and ceilings, buildings, large machinery and equipment, and bridges and other structures.	No formal educational credential	$40,280
Painting and Coating Workers	Painting and coating workers paint and coat a wide range of products, often with the use of machines.		$37,770
Paralegals and Legal Assistants	Paralegals and legal assistants perform a variety of tasks to support lawyers.	Associate's degree	$51,740
Passenger Vehicle Drivers	Passenger vehicle drivers operate buses, taxis, and other modes of transportation to take people from place to place.		$33,300
Personal Financial Advisors	Personal financial advisors provide advice to help individuals manage their finances and plan for their financial future.	Bachelor's degree	$87,850
Pest Control Workers	Pest control workers remove unwanted pests that infest buildings and surrounding areas.	High school diploma or equivalent	$37,330

Occupation	Job Duties	Entry-Level Education	Median Annual Pay, May 2019
Petroleum Engineers	Petroleum engineers design and develop methods for extracting oil and gas from deposits below the Earth's surface.	Bachelor's degree	$137,720
Pharmacists	Pharmacists dispense prescription medications to patients and offer expertise in the safe use of prescriptions.	Doctoral or professional degree	$128,090
Pharmacy Technicians	Pharmacy technicians help pharmacists dispense prescription medication to customers or health professionals.	High school diploma or equivalent	$33,950
Phlebotomists	Phlebotomists draw blood for tests, transfusions, research, or blood donations.	Postsecondary nondegree award	$35,510
Photographers	Photographers use their technical expertise, creativity, and composition skills to produce and preserve images.	High school diploma or equivalent	$36,280
Physical Therapist Assistants and Aides	Physical therapist assistants and aides are supervised by physical therapists to help patients regain movement and manage pain after injuries and illnesses.		$48,990
Physical Therapists	Physical therapists help injured or ill people improve movement and manage pain.	Doctoral or professional degree	$89,440
Physician Assistants	Physician assistants practice medicine on teams with physicians, surgeons, and other healthcare workers.	Master's degree	$112,260
Physicians and Surgeons	Physicians and surgeons diagnose and treat injuries or illnesses.	Doctoral or professional degree	This wage is equal to or greater than $208,000 per year.
Physicists and Astronomers	Physicists and astronomers study the ways in which various forms of matter and energy interact.	Doctoral or professional degree	$122,220
Plumbers, Pipefitters, and Steamfitters	Plumbers, pipefitters, and steamfitters install and repair piping fixtures and systems.	High school diploma or equivalent	$55,160
Podiatrists	Podiatrists provide medical and surgical care for people with foot, ankle, and lower leg problems.	Doctoral or professional degree	$126,240
Police and Detectives	Police officers protect lives and property. Detectives and criminal investigators gather facts and collect evidence of possible crimes.		$65,170
Police, Fire, and Ambulance Dispatchers	Police, fire, and ambulance dispatchers, also called public safety telecommunicators, answer emergency and nonemergency calls.	High school diploma or equivalent	$41,910
Political Scientists	Political scientists study the origin, development, and operation of political systems.	Master's degree	$122,220
Postal Service Workers	Postal service workers sell postal products and collect, sort, and deliver mail.	High school diploma or equivalent	$52,060
Postsecondary Education Administrators	Postsecondary education administrators oversee student services, academics, and faculty research at colleges and universities.	Master's degree	$95,410
Postsecondary Teachers	Postsecondary teachers instruct students in a wide variety of academic and technical subjects beyond the high school level.		$79,540

Occupation	Job Duties	Entry-Level Education	Median Annual Pay, May 2019
Power Plant Operators, Distributors, and Dispatchers	Power plant operators, distributors, and dispatchers control the systems that generate and distribute electric power.	High school diploma or equivalent	$85,950
Preschool and Childcare Center Directors	Preschool and childcare center directors supervise and lead their staffs, design program plans, oversee daily activities, and prepare budgets.	Bachelor's degree	$48,210
Preschool Teachers	Preschool teachers educate and care for children younger than age 5 who have not yet entered kindergarten.	Associate's degree	$30,520
Private Detectives and Investigators	Private detectives and investigators search for information about legal, financial, and personal matters.	High school diploma or equivalent	$50,510
Probation Officers and Correctional Treatment Specialists	Probation officers and correctional treatment specialists assist in rehabilitation of law offenders in custody or on probation or parole.	Bachelor's degree	$54,290
Producers and Directors	Producers and directors create motion pictures, television shows, live theater, commercials, and other performing arts productions.	Bachelor's degree	$74,420
Property, Real Estate, and Community Association Managers	Property, real estate, and community association managers take care of the many aspects of residential, commercial, or industrial properties.	High school diploma or equivalent	$58,760
Psychiatric Technicians and Aides	Psychiatric technicians and aides care for people who have mental illness and developmental disabilities.		$32,020
Psychologists	Psychologists study cognitive, emotional, and social processes and behavior by observing, interpreting, and recording how individuals relate to one another and to their environments.		$80,370
Public Relations and Fundraising Managers	Public relations managers direct the creation of materials that will enhance the public image of their employer or client. Fundraising managers coordinate campaigns that bring in donations for their organization.	Bachelor's degree	$116,180
Public Relations Specialists	Public relations specialists create and maintain a favorable public image for the organization they represent.	Bachelor's degree	$61,150
Purchasing Managers, Buyers, and Purchasing Agents	Buyers and purchasing agents buy products and services for organizations. Purchasing managers oversee the work of buyers and purchasing agents.	Bachelor's degree	$69,600
Quality Control Inspectors	Quality control inspectors examine products and materials for defects or deviations from specifications.	High school diploma or equivalent	$39,140
Radiation Therapists	Radiation therapists treat cancer and other diseases in patients by administering radiation treatments.	Associate's degree	$85,560
Radiologic and MRI Technologists	Radiologic technologists perform diagnostic imaging examinations on patients. MRI technologists operate magnetic resonance imaging (MRI) scanners to create diagnostic images.	Associate's degree	$62,280
Railroad Workers	Workers in railroad occupations ensure that passenger and freight trains safely run on time. They may drive trains, coordinate the activities of the trains, or operate signals and switches in the rail yard.	High school diploma or equivalent	$65,020
Real Estate Brokers and Sales Agents	Real estate brokers and sales agents help clients buy, sell, and rent properties.	High school diploma or equivalent	$50,730

Occupation	Job Duties	Entry-Level Education	Median Annual Pay, May 2019
Receptionists	Receptionists do tasks such as answering phones, receiving visitors, and providing information about their organization to the public.	High school diploma or equivalent	$30,050
Recreation Workers	Recreation workers design and lead activities to help people stay active, improve fitness, and have fun.	High school diploma or equivalent	$26,350
Recreational Therapists	Recreational therapists plan, direct, and coordinate recreation-based treatment programs for people with disabilities, injuries, or illnesses.	Bachelor's degree	$48,220
Registered Nurses	Registered nurses (RNs) provide and coordinate patient care and educate patients and the public about various health conditions.	Bachelor's degree	$73,300
Rehabilitation Counselors	Rehabilitation counselors help people with physical, mental, developmental, or emotional disabilities live independently.	Master's degree	$35,950
Reporters, Correspondents, and Broadcast News Analysts	Reporters, correspondents, and broadcast news analysts inform the public about news and events.	Bachelor's degree	$46,270
Respiratory Therapists	Respiratory therapists care for patients who have trouble breathing—for example, from a chronic respiratory disease, such as asthma or emphysema.	Associate's degree	$61,330
Retail Sales Workers	Retail sales workers help customers find products they want and process customers' payments.	No formal educational credential	$25,440
Roofers	Roofers replace, repair, and install the roofs of buildings.	No formal educational credential	$42,100
Sales Engineers	Sales engineers sell complex scientific and technological products or services to businesses.	Bachelor's degree	$103,900
Sales Managers	Sales managers direct organizations' sales teams.	Bachelor's degree	$126,640
School and Career Counselors	School counselors help students develop the academic and social skills needed to succeed. Career counselors help people choose a path to employment.	Master's degree	$57,040
Secretaries and Administrative Assistants	Secretaries and administrative assistants perform routine clerical and administrative duties.	High school diploma or equivalent	$39,850
Securities, Commodities, and Financial Services Sales Agents	Securities, commodities, and financial services sales agents connect buyers and sellers in financial markets.	Bachelor's degree	$62,270
Security Guards and Gaming Surveillance Officers	Security guards and gaming surveillance officers patrol and protect property from illegal activity.	High school diploma or equivalent	$29,710
Sheet Metal Workers	Sheet metal workers fabricate or install products that are made from thin metal sheets.	High school diploma or equivalent	$50,400
Skincare Specialists	Skincare specialists cleanse and beautify the face and body to enhance a person's appearance.	Postsecondary nondegree award	$34,090
Small Engine Mechanics	Small engine mechanics inspect, service, and repair motorized power equipment.		$37,840
Social and Community Service Managers	Social and community service managers coordinate and supervise programs and organizations that support public well-being.	Bachelor's degree	$67,150

Occupation	Job Duties	Entry-Level Education	Median Annual Pay, May 2019
Social and Human Service Assistants	Social and human service assistants provide client services in a variety of fields, such as psychology, rehabilitation, and social work.	High school diploma or equivalent	$35,060
Social Workers	Social workers help people solve and cope with problems in their everyday lives.		$50,470
Sociologists	Sociologists study society and social behavior.	Master's degree	$83,420
Software Developers	Software developers create the applications or systems that run on a computer or another device.	Bachelor's degree	$107,510
Solar Photovoltaic Installers	Solar photovoltaic (PV) installers assemble, set up, and maintain rooftop or other systems that convert sunlight into energy.	High school diploma or equivalent	$44,890
Special Education Teachers	Special education teachers work with students who have a wide range of learning, mental, emotional, and physical disabilities.	Bachelor's degree	$61,030
Speech-Language Pathologists	Speech-language pathologists assess, diagnose, treat, and help to prevent communication and swallowing disorders in children and adults.	Master's degree	$79,120
Stationary Engineers and Boiler Operators	Stationary engineers and boiler operators control stationary engines, boilers, or other mechanical equipment.	High school diploma or equivalent	$62,150
Substance Abuse, Behavioral Disorder, and Mental Health Counselors	Substance abuse, behavioral disorder, and mental health counselors provide treatment and advise people who suffer from alcoholism, drug addiction, or other mental or behavioral problems.	Bachelor's degree	$46,240
Surgical Technologists	Surgical technologists assist in surgical operations.	Postsecondary nondegree award	$48,300
Survey Researchers	Survey researchers design and conduct surveys and analyze data.	Master's degree	$59,170
Surveying and Mapping Technicians	Surveying and mapping technicians collect data and make maps of the Earth's surface.	High school diploma or equivalent	$45,010
Surveyors	Surveyors make precise measurements to determine property boundaries.	Bachelor's degree	$63,420
Tax Examiners and Collectors, and Revenue Agents	Tax examiners and collectors, and revenue agents determine how much is owed in taxes and collect tax from individuals and businesses on behalf of the government.	Bachelor's degree	$54,890
Teacher Assistants	Teacher assistants work with a licensed teacher to give students additional attention and instruction.	Some college, no degree	$27,920
Technical Writers	Technical writers prepare instruction manuals, how-to guides, journal articles, and other supporting documents to communicate complex and technical information more easily.	Bachelor's degree	$72,850
Telecommunications Equipment Installers and Repairers	Telecommunications equipment installers and repairers set up and maintain devices that carry communications signals.	Postsecondary nondegree award	$57,910
Tellers	Tellers are responsible for accurately processing routine transactions at a bank.	High school diploma or equivalent	$31,230
Top Executives	Top executives plan strategies and policies to ensure that an organization meets its goals.	Bachelor's degree	$104,690

Occupation	Job Duties	Entry-Level Education	Median Annual Pay, May 2019
Training and Development Managers	Training and development managers plan, coordinate, and direct skills- and knowledge-enhancement programs for an organization's staff.	Bachelor's degree	$113,350
Training and Development Specialists	Training and development specialists plan and administer programs that improve the skills and knowledge of their employees.	Bachelor's degree	$61,210
Travel Agents	Travel agents sell transportation, lodging, and entertainment activities to individuals and groups planning trips.	High school diploma or equivalent	$40,660
Umpires, Referees, and Other Sports Officials	Umpires, referees, and other sports officials preside over competitive athletic or sporting events to help maintain standards of play.	High school diploma or equivalent	$28,550
Urban and Regional Planners	Urban and regional planners develop land use plans and programs that help create communities, accommodate population growth, and revitalize physical facilities.	Master's degree	$74,350
Veterinarians	Veterinarians care for the health of animals and work to protect public health.	Doctoral or professional degree	$95,460
Veterinary Assistants and Laboratory Animal Caretakers	Veterinary assistants and laboratory animal caretakers handle routine animal care and help scientists, veterinarians, and others with their daily tasks.	High school diploma or equivalent	$28,590
Veterinary Technologists and Technicians	Veterinary technologists and technicians do medical tests that help diagnose animals' injuries and illnesses.	Associate's degree	$35,320
Waiters and Waitresses	Waiters and waitresses take orders and serve food and beverages to customers in dining establishments.	No formal educational credential	$22,890
Water and Wastewater Treatment Plant and System Operators	Water and wastewater treatment plant and system operators manage a system of machines to transfer or treat water or wastewater.	High school diploma or equivalent	$47,760
Water Transportation Workers	Water transportation workers operate and maintain vessels that take cargo and people over water.		$57,330
Web Developers	Web developers design and create websites.	Associate's degree	$73,760
Welders, Cutters, Solderers, and Brazers	Welders, cutters, solderers, and brazers use hand-held or remotely controlled equipment to join, repair, or cut metal parts and products.	High school diploma or equivalent	$42,490
Wholesale and Manufacturing Sales Representatives	Wholesale and manufacturing sales representatives sell goods for wholesalers or manufacturers to businesses, government agencies, and other organizations.		$63,000
Wind Turbine Technicians	Wind turbine service technicians install, maintain, and repair wind turbines.	Postsecondary nondegree award	$52,910
Woodworkers	Woodworkers manufacture a variety of products such as cabinets and furniture, using wood, veneers, and laminates.	High school diploma or equivalent	$32,690
Writers and Authors	Writers and authors develop written content for various types of media.	Bachelor's degree	$63,200
Zoologists and Wildlife Biologists	Zoologists and wildlife biologists study animals and other wildlife and how they interact with their ecosystems.	Bachelor's degree	$63,270

Glossary

A

Annual: recurring, done, or performed every year; yearly

Applicant: a person who formally applies for a job

Apprenticeship: a formal relationship between a worker and a sponsor that consists of a combination of on-the-job training and related occupation-specific instruction in which the worker learns the practical and theoretical aspects of an occupation. Apprenticeship programs are sponsored by individual employers, joint employer–labor groups, and employee associations. Apprenticeship programs usually provide at least 144 hours of occupation-specific technical instruction and 2,000 hours of on-the-job training per year over a 3- to 5-year period. Examples of occupations that utilize apprenticeships include *electricians* and *ironworkers*; see *On-the-job training*

Associate's degree: degree awarded usually for at least 2 years of full-time academic study beyond high school; see *Education*

Average: the quantity calculated by adding together the elements of a set of numbers and dividing the resulting sum by the quantity of numbers summed; see *Mean*

Back to top

B

Baby-boom generation: individuals born between 1946 and 1964, inclusive

Bachelor's degree: degree awarded usually for at least 4 years of full-time academic study beyond high school; see *Education*

Base year: year used as a reference point for comparison with later years. For example, 2019 is the base year for the 2019–29 employment projections. Employment in the base year is actual 2019 data, whereas employment in the target, or projection, year is projected

Business cycle: the periods of growth and decline in an economy. There are four stages in the cycle: expansion, when the economy grows; peak, the high point of an expansion; contraction, when the economy slows down; and trough, the low point of a contraction

Back to top

C

Certification: award for demonstrating competency in a skill or a set of skills, typically through work experience, training, and the passage of an examination, or some combination thereof. Some certification programs may require a certain level of educational achievement for eligibility

Consolidation: the merger of two or more commercial interests or corporations

Current Population Survey (CPS): a national survey that samples 60,000 households on a monthly basis and collects information on labor force characteristics of the U.S. civilian noninstitutional population; the CPS is conducted by the Census Bureau for the Bureau of Labor Statistics

Back to top

D

Demand for workers: total openings, resulting from employment growth and the need to replace workers who leave their occupation

Doctoral or professional degree: degree awarded usually for at least 3 years of full-time academic work beyond a bachelor's degree; for example, some science and other occupations need a doctoral degree, and all *lawyers, physicians, and dentists* need a professional degree for employment; see *Education*

Domestic sourcing: moving jobs to lower cost regions of the United States instead of to other countries

Duties: the major tasks or activities that employees in an occupation usually perform

Back to top

E

Earnings: pay or wages of a worker or a group of workers for services performed during a specific period—for example, hourly, daily, weekly, or annually. Also see *Pay, Wages*

Education: levels of education typically needed for entry into an occupation are classified as follows:

Doctoral or professional degree: degree awarded usually for at least 3 years of full-time academic work beyond a bachelor's degree; for example, *lawyers, physicians and surgeons,* and *dentists*

Master's degree: degree awarded usually for 1 or 2 years of full-time academic study beyond a bachelor's degree

Bachelor's degree: degree awarded usually for at least 4 years of full-time academic study beyond high school

Associate's degree: degree awarded usually for at least 2 years of full-time academic study beyond high school

Postsecondary nondegree award: usually a certificate or other award that is not a degree and is issued by an educational institution. Certifications issued by professional organizations or certifying bodies are not included in this category. Programs may last only a few weeks to 2

years; for example, *nursing assistants, emergency medical technicians (EMTs) and paramedics,* and *hairstylists*

Some college, no degree: a high school diploma or the equivalent, plus the completion of one or more postsecondary courses that did not result in any degree or award

High school diploma or equivalent: the completion of high school or the equivalent, resulting in the award of a high school diploma or the equivalent

No formal educational credential: signifies that a formal credential issued by an educational institution, such as a high school diploma or a postsecondary certificate, is not typically needed for entry into the occupation; for example, *janitors and cleaners, cashiers,* and *agricultural equipment operators*

Employed: the situation of a person who has an agreement with an employer to work full time, part time, or on a contractual basis for that employer

Employment: the number of jobs in an occupation, including full-time jobs, part-time jobs, and self-employment

Employment growth/decline: increase/decrease in the number of jobs

Entry level: the starting level for workers who are new to an occupation; different occupations may require different levels of education, training, or experience upon entry

Back to top

F

Fieldwork: an investigation or search for material, data, etc., such that the work is carried out in the field as opposed to the classroom, the laboratory, or official headquarters—for example, the work *archeologists* perform at a dig site in the desert; the work *historians* or *curators* engage in when they find or collect artifacts for museums; and the work *environmental technicians* do when they collect water samples from a pond, a stream, or an ocean

Five years or more (of work experience in a related occupation): the number of years of experience in a related occupation typically needed for entry into a given occupation; see *Work experience in a related occupation*

Fixed work schedules: schedules of employees who work the same hours on an ongoing basis—for example, 9 a.m.–5 p.m.; see *Work schedules*

Flexible work schedules: schedules of employees who set their own hours within specified guidelines and with a fixed number of total hours; see *Work schedules*

Full time: 35 or more hours per week, according to the Current Population Survey; see *Work schedules*

G

GDP (gross domestic product): the market value of all final goods and services produced within a country in a given period; the most commonly used measure of the size of the overall economy; the Bureau of Economic Analysis (BEA) produces estimates of GDP

Greater than full time: more than 40 hours per week; see *Work schedules*

Growth rate: the percent change in the number of jobs added or lost in a U.S. occupation or industry over a given projections decade; growth rate adjectives used in the OOH are defined by the following percent changes for the 2018–28 employment projections:
* much faster than the average: 8 percent or more
* faster than the average: 5 percent to 7 percent
* as fast as the average: 3 percent to 4 percent
* slower than the average: 1 percent to 2 percent
* little or no change: remain largely unchanged
* decline: decrease 1 percent or more

H

High school diploma or equivalent: award or credential that is equivalent to a high school diploma; see *Education*

Household: all persons who occupy a housing unit such as an apartment or a single-family home

I

Important qualities: characteristics and personality traits that are likely needed for workers to be successful in given occupations

Industry: a group of establishments that produce similar products or provide similar services; see *North American Industry Classification System (NAICS)*

Injury and illness: in general, a *Handbook* profile will discuss injuries and illnesses only if they are particularly high compared with the rate for all other occupations. Whether they meet this criterion is typically determined with the use of injury and illness data from the BLS Survey of Occupational Injuries and Illnesses (SOII) program. The "**Injuries and Illnesses**" section of each profile is used to discuss potential sources of accidents and injuries in the work environment.

Internship: training under supervision in a professional setting. This category does not include internships that are suggested for advancement; see *On-the-job training*

J

Job: a specific instance of employment; a position of employment to be filled at an establishment; *see Employment*

Job outlook: a statement that conveys the projected rate of growth or decline in employment in an occupation over the next 10 years; also compares the projected growth rate with that projected for all other occupations; see *Growth rate*

Job prospects: a qualitative measure of the competition for jobs that takes into consideration factors such as the growth or decline in the number of jobs, the expected number of qualified workers, and/or the expected number of applicants; a comparison of the number of jobs with the number of potential workers and jobseekers

L

Labor force: the sum of all persons 16 years and older in the civilian noninstitutional population who are either employed, or unemployed but available for work and actively looking for work

Less than 5 years (of work experience in a related occupation): the number of years of experience in a related occupation typically needed for entry into a given occupation; see *Work experience in a related occupation*

Licenses: permissions granted by government agencies or other accrediting bodies that allow someone to work in a particular occupation or perform certain duties

Long-term on-the-job training: more than 12 months of on-the-job training, or, alternatively, combined work experience and formal classroom instruction (not including apprenticeships), that is needed for the worker to attain competency in the skills needed in the occupation; see *On-the-job training*

M

Master's degree: degree awarded usually for 1 or 2 years of full-time academic study beyond a bachelor's degree; see *Education*

Mean: the mathematical average of a set of numbers, calculated by adding the numbers together and dividing the result by the number of numbers summed; see *Average*

Median: the middle number in an ordered list consisting of an odd number of numbers; the average of the two middle numbers in an ordered list consisting of an even number of numbers

Moderate-term on-the-job training: more than 1 month, and up to 12 months, of combined on-the-job experience and informal training that is needed for the worker to attain competency in the skills needed in the occupation; see *On-the-job training*

N

New job: an addition of a position to an establishment's payroll, usually as a result of economic expansion

No formal educational credential: signifies that a formal credential issued by an educational institution, such as a high school diploma or a postsecondary certificate, is not typically needed for entry into the occupation; for example, *janitors and cleaners, cashiers,* and *agricultural equipment operators*; see *Education*

None (on-the-job training): no additional occupation-specific training or preparation is typically required for the worker to attain competency in an occupation; see *On-the-job training*

None (work experience in a related occupation): no work experience in a related occupation is typically required for the worker to enter a given occupation; see *Work experience in a related occupation*

Nonfixed work schedules: schedules of employees who work different hours on one job; often used to accommodate particular traits of individual workers or because the work required by the employer varies for each individual; see *Work schedules*

North American Industry Classification System (NAICS): industry classification system used by federal statistical agencies in classifying business establishments for the purpose of collecting, analyzing, and publishing statistical data related to the U.S. economy

Number of jobs: number of actual instances of employment, according to the BLS National Employment Matrix; see https://www.bls.gov/emp/documentation/projections-methods.htm for more information about the matrix

Numeric change in employment: a projected change in the number of jobs in an occupation or industry

O

Occupation: a craft, trade, profession, or other means of earning a living. Also, a set of activities or tasks that employees are paid to perform and that, together, go by a certain name. Employees who are in the same occupation perform essentially the same tasks, whether or not they work in the same industry

Occupational openings: opportunities to enter an occupation; openings occur when occupations grow, creating new jobs, and when workers leave an occupation permanently, resulting in the need to replace them

O*NET: an online research source that provides detailed descriptions of occupations for use by jobseekers, workforce development and human resources professionals, students, and researchers. Created for the U.S. Department of Labor, Employment and Training Administration, by the National Center for O*NET Development

On-the-job training: training or preparation that is typically needed for a worker, once employed in an occupation, to attain competency in the occupation. Training is occupation specific rather than job specific; skills learned can be transferred to another job in the same occupation.

Internship/residency: a formal period of training during which individuals work under the supervision of experienced workers in a professional setting, such as a hospital. Internships and residencies occur after the completion of a formal postsecondary degree program and generally are required for state licensure or certification in fields such as medicine, counseling, and architecture. During an internship or residency, trainees may be restricted from independently performing all of the functions of the occupation. Examples of occupations in the internship or residency category include *physicians and surgeons,* and *marriage and family therapists.* This category does not include internships that are suggested for advancement in one's career, such as a marketing internship, or internships that take place as part of a formal degree program.

Apprenticeship: a formal relationship between a worker and a sponsor that consists of a combination of on-the-job training and related occupation-specific instruction in which the worker learns the practical and theoretical aspects of an occupation. Apprenticeship programs are sponsored by individual employers, joint employer-labor groups, and employee associations. Apprenticeship programs usually provide at least 144 hours of occupation-specific technical instruction and 2,000 hours of on-the-job training per year over a 3- to 5-year period. Examples of occupations that utilize apprenticeships include *electricians* and *ironworkers*.

Long-term on-the-job training: more than 12 months of on-the-job training, or, alternatively, combined work experience and formal classroom instruction, that is needed for workers to develop the skills to attain competency in an occupation. This on-the-job training category also includes employer-sponsored training programs, such as those offered by fire academies and schools for *air traffic controllers*. In other occupations—*nuclear power reactor operators*, for example—trainees take formal courses, often provided at the jobsite, to prepare for the required licensing exams. In addition, the category includes occupations in which workers typically need to possess a natural ability or talent—*musicians and singers*, *athletes*, *dancers*, *photographers*, and *actors*, among others—and that ability or talent must be cultivated over several years, sometimes in a nonwork setting. The category excludes apprenticeships.

Moderate-term on-the-job training: more than 1 month, and up to 12 months, of combined on-the-job experience and informal training that is needed for the worker to develop the skills to attain competency in the occupation; this on-the-job training category also includes employer-sponsored training programs.

Short-term on-the-job training: 1 month or less of combined on-the-job experience and informal training that is needed for the worker to develop the skills to attain competency in the occupation; this on-the-job training category also includes employer-sponsored training programs.

None: no additional occupation-specific training or preparation is typically required for the worker to attain competency in the occupation.

P

Part time: less than 35 hours of work per week, according to the Current Population Survey; see *Work schedules*

Pay: earnings or wages of a worker or a group of workers for services performed during a specific period—for example, hourly, daily, weekly, or annually; also see *Earnings, Wages*

Percent: one part in a hundred. For example, 62 percent (also written "62%") means 62 parts out of 100

Percent change in employment: employment growth rates expressed as percentages

Percentile wage estimate: the value of a wage below which a certain percentage of workers fall

Personal consumption: total goods and services purchased by individuals in the U.S. economy; the amount of goods and services used or purchased by individuals or households in the U.S. economy; a key statistic in measuring or calculating overall GDP

Population: the total number of inhabitants of the United States; also, the total number of observations under consideration in a statistical study

Postsecondary nondegree award: a certificate or other credential that is awarded by an educational institution upon completion of formal postsecondary schooling. (The postsecondary nondegree certificate is different from certifications issued by professional organizations or certifying bodies.) Postsecondary nondegree award programs may last from just a few weeks to 2 years. Examples of those who need postsecondary nondegree awards are *nursing assistants*, *emergency medical technicians (EMTs) and paramedics*, and *hairstylists*; see *Education*

Q

Qualifications: personality traits, education, training, work experience, or other qualities workers need to enter an occupation

Qualities: characteristics and personality traits that are likely needed for workers to be successful in given occupations

R

Related occupations: occupations that have similar job duties; see *Similar occupations*

Residency: training under supervision in a professional setting; see *On-the-job training*

Rotating work schedules: schedules that have a fixed number of hours and time off, but no set weekly hours, over a period of more than 1 week; see *Work schedules*

S

Salary: earnings of a worker or a group of workers for services performed during a specific period—for example, an hourly straight-time wage rate or, for workers not paid on an hourly basis, straight-time earnings divided by hours worked

Seasonal employment: employment that is not expected to last a full year, but that may reoccur; for example, many *retail sales associates* are hired only for the busy holiday season, and forest *firefighters* are more likely to be employed during the summer months, when vegetation is dryer

Self-employed: those who work for profit or fees in their own business, profession, trade, or farm; only the unincorporated self-employed are included in the self-employed category

Short-term on-the-job training: 1 month or less of on-the-job experience and informal training; see *On-the-job training*

Similar occupations: occupations that tend to share common daily tasks or require similar skills, rather than similar wages or education

Some college, no degree: a high school diploma or the equivalent, plus the completion of one or more postsecondary courses that did not result in any degree or award; see *Education*

Standard Occupational Classification (SOC): the coding system used by all federal statistical agencies to classify workers into occupational categories for the purpose of collecting, calculating, or disseminating data

Supply of workers: the number of people in the labor force; for most occupations, the supply of workers is smaller than the total number in the labor force because the supply is limited to those with particular education or training requirements

T

Training: see *On-the-job training*

U

Union membership: the group of workers who join labor unions, hold union memberships, and enjoy benefits of the organized, coordinated efforts of the union to improve the work environment; also, the status of being a member of a union

V

Vocational school: a secondary school that teaches vocational trades, such as construction trades; vocational schools may or may not award degrees

W

Wages: earnings or pay of a worker or a group of workers for services performed during a specific period—for example, hourly, daily, weekly, or annually; also see *Earnings*, *Pay*

Work experience in a related occupation: the level of work experience in an occupation related to a given occupation; the work experience captures work experience that is commonly considered necessary by employers or is a commonly accepted substitute for other, more formal types of training or education

Five years or more: the number of years of experience in a related occupation typically needed for entry into a given occupation is more than 5 years

Less than 5 years: the number of years of experience in a related occupation typically needed for entry into a given occupation is less than 5 years

None: No work experience in a related occupation is typically needed for entry into a given occupation

Work schedules: the number of daily hours, weekly hours, and annual weeks that employees in an occupation are scheduled to, and do, work. Short-term fluctuations and one-time events are not considered, unless the change becomes permanent

Fixed work schedules: schedules under which employees who work those schedules do so on a continual basis, such as 9 a.m. to 5 p.m.

Flexible work schedules: schedules under which employees set their own hours within guidelines and with a fixed number of total hours

Nonfixed work schedules: schedules of employees who work different hours on one job; often utilized to accommodate particular traits of individual workers or because the work required varies by individual

Rotating work schedules: schedules that have a fixed number of hours and time off, but no set weekly hours, over a period of more than 1 week; see *Work schedules*

Full time: between 35 and 40 hours, inclusive, of work per week

Greater than full time: more than 40 hours of work per week

Part time: Less than 35 hours of work per week

X, Y, Z

Index

D

E